Classics Series

Gower

Principles of Modern Company Law

Eleventh Edition

Classics Series

Gower

Principles of Modern Company Law

Eleventh Edition

Paul L. Davies QC (Hon), FBA
Allen & Overy Professor of Corporate Law Emeritus
Senior Research Fellow
Commercial Law Centre
Harris Manchester College
University of Oxford

Sarah Worthington, DBE, QC (Hon), FBA
Downing Professor of the Laws of England
University of Cambridge

Christopher Hare
Travers Smith Associate Professor of Corporate and Commercial Law
University of Oxford
Tutorial Fellow
Somerville College

with a contribution from

Professor Eva Micheler
London School of Economics and Political Science
Ao Universitätsprofessor
Wirtschaftsuniversität Wien

SWEET & MAXWELL THOMSON REUTERS

First Edition 1954
Eleventh Edition 2021

Published in 2021 by Thomson Reuters, trading as Sweet & Maxwell. Thomson Reuters is registered in England & Wales, Company No.1679046. Registered Office and address for service: 5 Canada Square, Canary Wharf, London, E14 5AQ.

For further information on our products and services, visit *http://www.sweetandmaxwell.co.uk*

Typeset by Letterpart Limited, Caterham on the Hill, Surrey, CR3 5XL.

Printed and bound by CPI Group (UK) Ltd, Croydon, CR0 4YY.

No natural forests were destroyed to make this product: only farmed timber was used and replanted.

A CIP catalogue record of this book is available from the British Library.

For orders and enquiries, go to: *http://www.tr.com/uki-legal-contact*; Tel: 0345 600 9355.

ISBN (print): 978-0-414-08811-5

ISBN (proview): 978-0-414-08815-3

ISBN (e-book): 978-0-414-08813-9

ISBN (print and e-book): 978-0-414-08812-2

Acknowledgements

Grateful acknowledgment is made to the Incorporated Council of Law Reporting for England and Wales (ICLR) for permission to quote extracts from the following:

- *Salomon v Salomon & Co Ltd* [1897] A.C. 22
- *Shaw & Sons (Salford) Ltd v Shaw* [1935] 2 K.B. 113
- *Bray v Ford* [1896] A.C. 44
- *Johnson v Gore Wood & Co (No.1)* [2002] 2 A.C. 1
- *Marex Financial Ltd v Sevilleja* [2020] 3 W.L.R. 255
- *Ebrahimi v Westbourne Galleries Ltd* [1973] A.C. 360
- *Alexander Ward & Co Ltd v Samyang Navigation Co Ltd* [1975] 1 W.L.R. 673
- *Smith (Administrator of Cosslett (Contractors) Ltd) v Bridgend CBC* [2002] 1 A.C. 336
- *Agnew v Inland Revenue Commissioner* [2001] 2 A.C. 710

Grateful acknowledgment is made for extracts from the following which have been reproduced by permission of RELX (UK) Limited, trading as LexisNexis:

- *ING Re (UK) Ltd v R&V Versicherung AG* [2007] 1 B.C.L.C. 108
- *EIC Services Ltd v Phipps* [2004] 2 B.C.L.C. 589

From Thomson Reuters, extracts from the following have been reproduced:

- *Commissioner of State Revenue (Vic) v Danvest Pty Ltd* (2017) 107 A.T.R. 12
- *Thorby v Goldberg* (1964) 112 C.L.R. 597
- *Canadian Aero Service v O'Malley* (1973) 40 D.L.R. (3d) 371
- *Re Coroin Ltd* [2014] B.C.C. 14

While every care has been taken to establish and acknowledge copyright, and contact the copyright owners, the publishers tender their apologies for any accidental infringement. They would be pleased to come to a suitable arrangement with the rightful owners in each case.

Preface

> "These concerns about the working of the corporate system were heightened by some unexpected failures of major companies and by criticisms of the lack of effective board accountability for such matters as directors' pay." (Cadbury Committee Report (1992), para.2.2.)

> "However, stakeholder and wider public trust in the credibility of directors' reporting and the statutory audit has been shaken by a succession of sudden and major corporate collapses which have caused serious economic and social damage … The BEIS Committee has taken a close interest in the adequacy of powers to clawback cash or shares paid to directors where a company has failed or underperformed." (BEIS, *Restoring Trust in Audit and Corporate Governance* (2021), Executive Summary and para.5.2.3.)

So, *plus ça change, plus c'est la même chose*? Or, in the post-Brexit vernacular: what goes around comes around. But not entirely. The underlying problems may display a worrying persistency, but the policies favoured by government do change with the times—whether for good or evil. For the Cadbury Committee, when the Great Moderation was already well under way, strengthened board accountability to shareholders was the core element in their policy prescription. For post-Financial Crisis and mid-pandemic BEIS, the interests of creditors, employees and society at large and the duties of shareholders occupy the centre-ground.

Although the BEIS report came too late for detailed analysis in this edition—and anyway contained a set of proposals, some less firm than others—it reflected some more general themes in company legislation which have been strengthening since the last edition of this work in 2016. Thus, the Stewardship Code—much extended in 2020—now emphasises the duties of institutional shareholders more than empowering them à la Cadbury and the latest iteration of the Corporate Governance Code is much less shareholder-centric than its predecessor and, in fact, is in some tension with s.172 of the Act. See Chs 9 and 12. Again, the enhanced reporting requirements for large companies place somewhat more emphasis on employees' interests and considerably more on corporate externalities in the shape of adverse impacts on the environment. See Ch.22. Finally, though not central to this book, the interests of "big" creditors have been downgraded in various ways in favour of management standing as a proxy for the wider social interest in keeping enterprises going. See Chs 29 and 33. In fact, management may well regard "stakeholderism" as a welcome relief from the shackles of strict accountability to shareholders. The dog which has not yet barked—apart from some whining over lost passporting rights in the financial areas—but surely will over the coming years, is Brexit, as the competing pros and cons of equivalence and competition work themselves out in relation to "retained EU law".

The courts proceed according to their own rather different rhythms, and subject to the accidents of litigation. A significant number of interesting and important judgments have been handed down since the last edition. One might mention, as examples, *Children's Investment Fund Foundation (UK) v Attorney General* (2020) on charitable companies, *Singularis Holdings Ltd (In Liquidation) v Daiwa Capital Markets Europe Ltd* (2019) on attribution, *Vedanta Resources Plc v Lungowe* (2019) on holding company liability in corporate groups, *Ciban Management Corp v Citco (BVI) Ltd* (2020) on ostensible authority and the *Duomatic* principle, *Marex Financial Ltd v Sevilleja* (2020) on reflective loss, *Manchester Building Society v Grant Thornton LLP* (2019) and *AssetCo Plc v Grant Thornton UK LLP* (2020) on auditor liability and both *BAT Industries Plc v Sequana SA* (2019) and *Burnden Holdings (UK) Ltd (In Liquidation) v Fielding* (2019) on distributions. Putting the legislative, regulatory and court developments together, one discerns more than enough material to keep students (of whatever age) fully absorbed in trying to analyse this kaleidoscopic subject.

We have reorganised somewhat the running order of the chapters. We hope that this will make the material more accessible to readers, whilst recognising that there is no one right way of presenting corporate law. As a result, the work is now divided into 10 parts (eight previously). The first part is largely the same, but Ch.5 has been moved to Pt 2, which deals with the separate legal entity and corporate actions. There then follow three parts focussed respectively around the board, shareholders and creditors. Part 6 deals with public enforcement. The final four parts are as before: accounts and audit, equity finance, debt finance and winding up etc.

Once again, we wish to record our gratitude to Professor Eva Micheler of the London School of Economics and Political Science for updating Ch.26 on transfers of shares. Sarah Worthington would also like to thank Su-Lynn Kok and Abe Chauhan for their valuable research assistance in updating particular parts of this edition.

We have sought to state the law as at the end of February 2021, although some references to later material have been possible.

PLD, SEW, CH

Ascension Day/Eid ul Fitr 2021

Table of Abbreviations

AADB	Accounting and Actuarial Discipline Board
ADR	American Depositary Receipt
AGM	Annual General Meeting
AIM	Alternative Investment Market
AMP	Accepted Market Practice
APB	Auditing Practices Board
ARC	Accounting Regulatory Committee
ARD	Accounting Reference Date
ARGA	Audit Reporting and Governance Authority
ARP	Accounting Reference Period
ASB	Accounting Standards Board
BEIS	Department for Business, Energy and Industrial Strategy
BERR	Department for Business, Enterprise & Regulatory Reform
BIS	Department for Business Innovation & Skills
BoT	Board of Trade
BR	Business Review
BVI	British Virgin Islands
CA	Companies Act
CARD	Consolidated Admissions Requirements Directive
CDDA	Company Directors Disqualification Act 1986
CEO	Chief Executive Officer
CESR	Committee of European Securities Regulators
CfD	Contract for Differences
CFO	Chief Financial Officer
CGC	UK Corporate Governance Code
CIB	Companies Investigation Branch (of BERR)
CIC	Community Interest Company
CIO	Charitable Incorporated Organisation

CJA	Criminal Justice Act 1993
CLR	Company Law Review
CPR	Civil Procedure Rules
CRR	Capital Redemption Reserve
DB	Defined Benefit (pension scheme)
DC	Defined Contribution (pension scheme)
DEPP	Decision Procedure and Penalties Manual (of FCA)
DTI	Department of Trade and Industry
DTR	Disclosure Guidance and Transparency Rules (of FCA)
DR	Directors' Report
DRR	Directors' Remuneration Report
EBLR	European Business Law Review
EBOR	European Business Organization Law Review
ECJ	European Court of Justice
ECtHR	European Court of Human Rights
EEA	European Economic Area
EEIG	European Economic Interest Grouping
EFRAG	European Financial Reporting Advisory Group
EG	Enforcement Guide (of FCA)
ESMA	European Securities and Markets Authority
ESV	Enlightened Shareholder Value
FCA	Financial Conduct Authority
FRC	Financial Reporting Council
FRRP	Financial Reporting Review Panel
FRS	Financial Reporting Standard
FRSEE	Financial Reporting Standard for Smaller Entities
FSA	Financial Services Authority
FSAP	Financial Services Action Plan (of the EC Commission)
FSMA	Financial Services and Markets Act 2000
GAAP	Generally Accepted Accounting Principles
GEFIM	Gilt-edged and Fixed-Interest Markets
GP	General Principle (of the Code on Takeovers and Mergers)
HKCFAR	Hong Kong Court of Final Appeal Reports
HLG	High Level Group of Company Law Experts
IA	Insolvency Act

IAASB	International Auditing and Assurance Standards Board
IAS	International Accounting Standards
IASB	International Accounting Standards Board
IFRS	International Financial Reporting Standards
IPO	Initial Public Offering
ISA	International Standard on Auditing
JCLS	Journal of Corporate Law Studies
KPI	Key Performance Indicators
LLP	Limited Liability Partnership
LP	Limited Partnership
LR	Listing Rules
LSE	London Stock Exchange
Ltd	Limited
Ltip	Long-term incentive plan
MAD	Market Abuse Directive (Directive 2003/6)
MAR	Market Abuse Regulation (Regulation 596/2014)
MIFID	Directive on Markets in Financial Instruments
MTF	Multilateral Trading Facility
MO	Management Organ (of an SE)
Nasdaq	National Association of Securities Dealers Automated Quotation System (a US stock exchange)
NED	Non-Executive Director
OEIC	Open-ended Investment Company
OFR	Operating and Financial Review
OR	Official Receiver
OSOV	One Share One Vote
OTC	Over the counter
PCP	Permissible Capital Payment
PD	Prospectus Directive (Directive 2003/71)
PIE	Public Interest Entity
PIP	Primary Information Provider
PLC	Public Limited Company
POB	Public Oversight Board
PR	Prospectus Rules (of FCA)
PSC	People with Significant Control
PSM	Professional Securities Market
PUSU	"Put Up or Shut Up"

PIE	Public Interest Entity
RINGA	Relevant Information not Generally Available
RIS	Regulated Information Service
RS	Reporting Standard or Statement
RSB	Recognised Statutory Body
SBEEA 2015	Small Business, Enterprise and Employment Act 2015
SCE	European Cooperative Society
SE	Societas Europaea or European Company
SME	Small or Medium-sized Enterprise
SNB	Special Negotiating Body (of employee representatives)
SO	Supervisory Organ (of an SE)
SPV	Special Purpose Vehicle
SR	Strategic Report
SS	Secretary of State
SSAP	Statement of Standard Accounting Practice
TD	Transparency Directive (Directive 2004/109)
UCITS	Undertakings for Collective Investment in Transferable Securities
UCTA	Unfair Contract Terms Act
USR	Uncertificated Securities Regulations
UKLA	United Kingdom Listing Authority

Documents from the Company Law Review and the Government Response to it

Completing	CLR, *Completing the Structure* (November 2000), URN 00/1335
Developing	CLR, *Developing the Framework* (March 2000), URN 00/656
Final Report	CLR, *Final Report*, 2 vols (July 2001), URN 01/943
Formation	CLR, *Company Formation and Capital Maintenance* (October 1999), URN 99/1145
Maintenance	CLR, *Capital Maintenance: Other Issues* (June 2000), URN 00/880
Modernising	*Modernising Company Law*, 2 vols (July 2002), Cm.5553
Overseas Companies	CLR, *Reforming the Law Concerning Oversea Companies* (October 1999), URN 99/1146
Strategic	CLR, *The Strategic Framework* (February 1999), URN 99/654

TABLE OF CONTENTS

4. FORMATION PROCEDURES

5. CORPORATE MOBILITY

6. THE NATURE AND CLASSIFICATION OF SHARES

PART 2
Separate Legal Personality in Action

7. THE LIMITS OF SEPARATE LEGAL PERSONALITY AND LIMITED LIABILITY

PART 3
Regulating Boards and Individual Directors

9. THE BOARD AND ITS DIRECTORS

10. DIRECTORS' DUTIES

PART 4
Shareholders

11. THE CONSTITUTIONAL ROLE OF SHAREHOLDERS

12. SHAREHOLDER DECISION-MAKING

15. CORPORATE LITIGATION AND THE DERIVATIVE ACTION

PART 5
CREDITORS

16. LEGAL CAPITAL, MINIMUM CAPITAL AND VERIFICATION

17. CAPITAL MAINTENANCE

19. UNDERMINING CREDITORS' CLAIMS

PART 6
Public Enforcement

20. DISQUALIFICATION OF DIRECTORS

21. BREACH OF CORPORATE DUTIES: ADMINISTRATIVE REMEDIES

PART 7
Accounts and Audit

22. ACCOUNTS AND REPORTS

23. AUDITS AND AUDITORS

PART 8
Equity Finance

24. SHARE ISSUES: GENERAL RULES

25. PUBLIC OFFERS OF SHARES

26. TRANSFERS OF SHARES

27. CONTINUING OBLIGATIONS AND DISCLOSURE OF INFORMATION TO THE MARKET

28. TAKEOVERS

29. ARRANGEMENTS, RECONSTRUCTIONS AND MERGERS

30. MARKET ABUSE

PART 9
Debt Finance

31. DEBTS AND DEBT SECURITIES

32. COMPANY CHARGES

PART 10
Winding Up and Its Consequences

33. MANAGING DISTRESSED OR DEFUNCT COMPANIES

TABLE OF CASES

Hill v Spread Trustee Co Ltd; sub nom. Nurkowski, Re [2006] EWCA Civ 542; [2007] Bus. L.R. 1213; [2007] 1 W.L.R. 2404; [2007] 1 All E.R. 1106; [2006] B.C.C. 646; [2007] 1 B.C.L.C. 450; [2006] B.P.I.R. 789; [2006] W.T.L.R. 1009 18–013
Hillman v Crystal Bowl Amusements; Hillman v Ireton Properties; Hillman v Calgary Development Co [1973] 1 W.L.R. 162; [1973] 1 All E.R. 379; (1972) 117 S.J. 69 CA (Civ Div) 12–046
Hindle v John Cotton Ltd (1919) 56 S.L.T. 625 10–021
Hirsche v Sims [1894] A.C. 654 PC 10–021
Hivac Ltd v Park Royal Scientific Instruments Ltd [1946] Ch. 169 CA 10–093
HL Bolton Engineering Co Ltd v TJ Graham & Sons Ltd [1957] 1 Q.B. 159; [1956] 3 W.L.R. 804; [1956] 3 All E.R. 624; [1956] 10 WLUK 28; (1956) 100 S.J. 816 CA 8–043
HLC Environmental Projects Ltd, Re [2013] EWHC 2876 (Ch); [2014] B.C.C. 337 . . . . 10–018, 10–031, 10–106, 10–129, 19–013, 19–019, 19–021
HMS Truculent, The. *See* Admiralty v Owners of the Divina (The HMS Truculent)
Ho Kang Peng v Scintronix Corp Ltd [2014] SGCA 22 8–001
Ho Tung v Man On Insurance Co Ltd [1902] A.C. 232 PC 12–010
Hoare & Co Ltd, Re (1933) 150 L.T. 374 28–075
Hodge v James Howell & Co [1958] C.L.Y. 446 CA 13–017
Hogg v Cramphorn [1967] Ch. 254; [1966] 3 W.L.R. 995; [1966] 3 All E.R. 420; (1966) 110 S.J. 887 Ch D 10–018, 10–022, 10–107, 14–003
Hoicrest Ltd, Re; sub nom. Keene v Martin [2000] 1 W.L.R. 414; [2000] B.C.C. 904; [2000] 1 B.C.L.C. 194; (1999) 96(44) L.S.G. 39; (1999) 143 S.J.L.B. 26 CA (Civ Div) 26–019
Holders Investment Trust, Re [1971] 1 W.L.R. 583; [1971] 2 All E.R. 289; (1970) 115 S.J. 202 Ch D 13–013, 13–014
Holdsworth & Co v Caddies. *See* Harold Holdsworth & Co (Wakefield) Ltd v Caddies
Hollicourt (Contracts) Ltd (In Liquidation) v Bank of Ireland; sub nom. Bank of Ireland v Hollicourt (Contracts) Ltd; Claughton (Liquidator of Hollicourt (Contracts) Ltd) v Bank of Ireland [2001] Ch. 555; [2001] 2 W.L.R. 290; [2001] 1 All E.R. 289; [2001] 1 All E.R. (Comm) 357; [2001] Lloyd's Rep. Bank. 6; [2000] B.C.C. 1210; [2001] 1 B.C.L.C. 233; [2001] B.P.I.R. 47; (2000) 97(45) L.S.G. 41 CA (Civ Div) 33–020
Holmes v Lord Keyes [1959] Ch. 199; [1958] 2 W.L.R. 772; [1958] 2 All E.R. 129; (1958) 102 S.J. 329 CA 12–049
Home & Colonial Insurance Co Ltd, Re [1930] 1 Ch. 102; (1929) 34 Ll. L. Rep. 463 Ch D 33–018
Home & Office Fire Extinguishers Ltd, Re [2012] EWHC 917 (Ch) 14–021
Home Office v Dorset Yacht Co Ltd [1970] A.C. 1004; [1970] 2 W.L.R. 1140; [1970] 2 All E.R. 294; [1970] 1 Lloyd's Rep. 453; [1970] 5 WLUK 19; (1970) 114 S.J. 375 HL 7–014
Home Retail Group Plc, Re [2016] EWHC 2072 (Ch); [2016] 7 WLUK 39; [2017] B.C.C. 39 29–003
Home Treat Ltd, Re [1991] B.C.C. 165; [1991] B.C.L.C. 705 Ch D (Companies Ct) 11–003
Homes of England Ltd v Horsham Holdings Ltd [2019] EWHC 2429 (Ch); [2019] 7 WLUK 578 14–029
Homes of England Ltd v Nick Sellman (Holdings) Ltd [2020] EWHC 936 (Ch); [2020] Bus. L.R. 1163; [2020] 4 WLUK 182; [2020] B.C.C. 607 15–006
Hook v Sumner [2015] EWHC 3820 (Ch); [2015] 11 WLUK 772; [2016] B.C.C. 220 12–006
Hooper v Western Counties and South Wales Telephone Co Ltd (1892) 68 LT 78 31–007
Hopkins v TL Dallas Group Ltd; Hopkins v TL Dallas & Co Ltd [2004] EWHC 1379 (Ch); [2004] 6 WLUK 267; [2005] 1 B.C.L.C. 543 . . . . 8–018, 8–025
Houghton v Saunders [2015] 2 N.Z.L.R. 74 10–136

Oshkosh B'Gosh Inc v Dan Marbel Inc Ltd [1988] 10 WLUK 60; (1988) 4 B.C.C. 795; [1989] B.C.L.C. 507; [1989] P.C.C. 320; [1989] 1 C.M.L.R. 94 CA (Civ Div) 8–036
Ossory Estates Plc, Re (1988) 4 B.C.C. 460; [1988] B.C.L.C. 213 Ch D (Companies Ct) 16–022
Othery Construction, Re [1966] 1 W.L.R. 69; [1966] 1 All E.R. 145; (1966) 110 S.J. 32 Ch D 14–032
Ottercroft Ltd v Scandia Care Ltd; Ottercroft Ltd v Rahimian [2016] EWCA Civ 867; [2016] 7 WLUK 115 7–012
Oval 1742 Ltd (In Creditors Voluntary Liquidation), Re; sub nom. Customs and Excise Commissioners v Royal Bank of Scotland Plc [2007] EWCA Civ 1262; [2008] Bus. L.R. 1213; [2008] B.C.C. 135; [2008] 1 B.C.L.C. 204 32–015
Overnight Ltd (In Liquidation), Re; sub nom. Goldfarb v Higgins [2010] EWHC 613 (Ch); [2010] B.C.C. 796; [2010] 2 B.C.L.C. 186; [2011] Bus. L.R. D30 19–008
Owners of Cargo Laden on Board the Albacruz v Owners of the Albazero (The Albazero; The Albacruz); sub nom. Concord Petroleum Corp v Gosford Marine Panama SA [1977] A.C. 774; [1976] 3 W.L.R. 419; [1976] 3 All E.R. 129; [1976] 2 Lloyd's Rep. 467; (1976) 120 S.J. 570 HL 7–013
Owners of the Borvigilant v Owners of the Romina G; Borvigilant, The; Romina G, The; sub nom. Borkan General Trading Ltd v Monsoon Shipping Ltd [2003] EWCA Civ 935; [2003] 2 All E.R. (Comm) 736; [2003] 2 Lloyd's Rep. 520; [2003] 7 WLUK 186; [2004] 1 C.L.C. 41 8–028
Oxford Benefit Building & Investment Society, Re (1887) L.R. 35 Ch. D. 502 Ch D 10–017
Oxford Fleet Management Ltd (In Liquidation) v Brown [2014] EWHC 3065 (Ch) 12–011
Oxted Motor Co Ltd, Re [1921] 3 K.B. 32 KBD 12–010
P&O Steam Navigation Co v Johnson (1938) 60 C.L.R. 189 High Ct (Aus) 10–142
Pacaya Rubber & Produce Co Ltd (Burns Application), Re [1914] 1 Ch. 542 Ch D 25–038
PAG Management Services Ltd, Re; sub nom. Secretary of State for Business, Innovation and Skills v PAG Management Services Ltd [2015] EWHC 2404 (Ch); [2015] 8 WLUK 106; [2015] B.C.C. 720; [2015] R.A. 519 4–035
Panama New Zealand and Australian Royal Mail Co, Re (1869–70) L.R. 5 Ch. App. 318 CA 32–006
Panel on Takeovers and Mergers v King 2018] CSIH 30; 2018 S.C. 459; 2018 S.L.T. 451; [2018] 2 WLUK 694; [2018] B.C.C. 390; 2018 G.W.D. 14-190 28–009
Panhard et Levassor v Panhard Levassor Motor Co. *See* La SA des Anciens Etablissements Panhard et Levassor v Panhard Levassor Motor Co Ltd
Panorama Developments (Guildford) Ltd v Fidelis Furnishing Fabrics Ltd [1971] 2 Q.B. 711; [1971] 3 W.L.R. 440; [1971] 3 All E.R. 16; [1971] 5 WLUK 114; (1971) 115 S.J. 483 CA (Civ Div) 8–023
Pantmaenog Timber Co Ltd, Re; Official Receiver v Meade-King (A Firm); Official Receiver v Wadge Rapps & Hunt (A Firm); Official Receiver v Grant Thornton (A Firm); sub nom. Official Receiver v Hay; Pantmaenog Timber Co (In Liquidation), Re [2001] EWCA Civ 1227; [2002] Ch. 239; [2002] 2 W.L.R. 20; [2001] 4 All E.R. 588; [2002] B.C.C. 11; [2001] 2 B.C.L.C. 555; (2001) 98(35) L.S.G. 32; (2001) 151 N.L.J. 1212; (2001) 145 S.J.L.B. 210 20–007
Pantone 485 Ltd, Re. *See* Miller v Bain (Director's Breach of Duty)
Paragon Finance Plc v DB Thakerar & Co; Paragon Finance Plc v Thimbleby & Co [1999] 1 All E.R. 400; (1998) 95(35) L.S.G. 36; (1998) 142 S.J.L.B. 243 CA (Civ Div) 10–127, 10–128
Paramount Airways Ltd (No.2), Re; sub nom. Powdrill v Hambros Bank (Jersey) Ltd [1993] Ch. 223; [1992] 3 W.L.R. 690; [1992] 3 All E.R. 1; [1992] B.C.C. 416; [1992] B.C.L.C. 710; (1992) 89(14) L.S.G. 31; (1992) 136 S.J.L.B. 97; [1992] N.P.C. 27 CA (Civ Div) 5–008
Paramount Powders (UK) Ltd, Re; sub nom. Badyal v Badyal [2019] EWCA Civ 1644; [2019] 10 WLUK 81; [2020] B.C.C. 152; [2020] 2 B.C.L.C. 1 . . . . . 14–032, 14–034
Park Business Interiors Ltd v Park, 1991 S.L.T. 818; 1991 S.C.L.R. 486; [1990] B.C.C. 914; [1992] B.C.L.C. 1034 OH 16–017

Railtrack Plc (In Administration) (No.2), Re; sub nom. Winsor v Bloom; Winsor v Special Railway Administrators of Railtrack Plc [2002] EWCA Civ 955; [2002] 1 W.L.R. 3002; [2002] 4 All E.R. 435; [2002] 2 B.C.L.C. 755; [2003] B.P.I.R. 507; [2002] A.C.D. 103; (2002) 99(35) L.S.G. 37; (2002) 146 S.J.L.B. 183 32–043
Rainford v James Keith & Blackman Co Ltd [1905] 2 Ch. 147 CA 26–010
Rainham Chemical Works Ltd (In Liquidation) v Belvedere Fish Guano Co Ltd; Ind Coope & Co v Rainham Chemical Works Ltd; sub nom. Belvedere Fish Guano Co Ltd v Rainham Chemical Works Ltd [1921] 2 A.C. 465 HL 2–007, 7–011, 8–056
Raithatha v Baig [2017] EWHC 2059 (Ch); [2017] 7 WLUK 583; [2018] B.P.I.R. 743 . . . . . 10–041, 10–047
Rakusens Ltd v Baser Ambalaj Plastik Sanayi Ticaret AS; sub nom. Rakussens Ltd v Baser Ambalaj Plastik Sanayi Ticaret AS [2001] EWCA Civ 1820; [2002] 1 B.C.L.C. 104; (2001) 98(42) L.S.G. 37; (2001) 145 S.J.L.B. 237 5–004
Rama Corp Ltd v Proved Tin & General Investments Ltd [1952] 2 Q.B. 147; [1952] 1 All E.R. 554; [1952] 1 T.L.R. 709; [1952] 2 WLUK 12; (1952) 96 S.J. 197 QBD 8–021
Rampgill Mill, Re [1967] Ch. 1138; [1967] 2 W.L.R. 394; [1967] 1 All E.R. 56; [1966] 2 Lloyd's Rep. 527; (1967) 111 S.J. 130 Ch D (Companies Ct) 32–015
Randall and Quilter Investment Holdings Plc, Re [2013] EWHC 4357 (Comm) 26–004
Ransomes Plc, Re; sub nom. Winpar Holdings Ltd v Ransomes Plc; Ransomes Plc v Winpar Holdings Ltd [2000] B.C.C. 455; [1999] 2 B.C.L.C. 591 CA (Civ Div) 17–034
Ratners Group Plc, Re (1988) 4 B.C.C. 293; [1988] B.C.L.C. 685 Ch D (Companies Ct) 17–034
Ravenhart Service (Holdings) Ltd, Re. *See* Reiner v Gershinson
Rawnsley v Weatherall Green & Smith North Ltd [2009] EWHC 2482 (Ch); [2010] B.C.C. 406; [2010] 1 B.C.L.C. 658; [2010] B.P.I.R. 449; [2010] P.N.L.R. 6 19–012
Rayfield v Hands [1960] Ch. 1; [1958] 2 W.L.R. 851; [1958] 2 All E.R. 194; (1958) 102 S.J. 348 Ch D 11–002, 11–003, 14–002
Rayner (Mincing Lane) Ltd v Department of Trade. *See* JH Rayner (Mincing Lane) Ltd v Department of Trade and Industry
Read v Astoria Garage (Streatham) Ltd [1952] Ch. 637; [1952] 2 All E.R. 292; [1952] 2 T.L.R. 130 CA 11–026, 14–002
Real Meat Co Ltd (In Receivership), Re [1996] B.C.C. 254 Ch D 32–008
Recher's Will Trusts, Re; sub nom. National Westminster Bank Ltd v National Anti Vivisection Society [1972] Ch. 526; [1971] 3 W.L.R. 321; [1971] 3 All E.R. 401; [1971] 5 WLUK 15; (1971) 115 S.J. 448 Ch D 3–001, 11–002
Redcard Ltd v Williams; sub nom. Williams v Redcard Ltd [2011] EWCA Civ 466; [2011] 4 All E.R. 444; [2011] Bus. L.R. 1479; [2011] 4 WLUK 572; [2013] B.C.C. 689; [2011] 2 B.C.L.C. 350; [2011] 2 E.G.L.R. 67; [2011] 25 E.G. 106; [2011] 19 E.G. 96 (C.S.); (2011) 161 N.L.J. 635; [2011] 2 P. & C.R. DG11 8–004
Redwood Master Fund Ltd v TD Bank Europe Ltd [2002] EWHC 2703 (Ch); [2002] 12 WLUK 288; [2006] 1 B.C.L.C. 149 . . . . . 13–008, 13–009, 13–011, 31–029, 31–030
Reeves v Commissioner of Police of the Metropolis [2000] 1 A.C. 360; [1999] 3 W.L.R. 363; [1999] 3 All E.R. 897; (2000) 51 B.M.L.R. 155; [1999] Prison L.R. 99; (1999) 96(31) L.S.G. 41; (1999) 143 S.J.L.B. 213 . . . . . 23–039, 23–040
Regal (Hastings) Ltd v Gulliver [1967] 2 A.C. 134; [1942] 1 All E.R. 378 HL 7–007, 10–083, 10–085, 10–086, 10–088, 10–089, 10–098, 10–101, 10–108, 10–109, 10–118, 10–121, 10–133, 15–002, 15–005, 28–028
Regentcrest Plc (In Liquidation) v Cohen [2001] B.C.C. 494; [2001] 2 B.C.L.C. 80 Ch D 10–029, 10–097
Registrar of Companies v Swarbrick [2014] EWHC 1466 (Ch); [2014] Bus. L.R. 625; [2014] 5 WLUK 390; [2014] 2 B.C.L.C. 695 4–023
Reid (Nicholas Landon) v Reid (Michael John); sub nom. John Reid & Sons (Strucsteel) Ltd, Re [2003] EWHC 2329 (Ch); [2003] 3 WLUK 582; [2003] 2 B.C.L.C. 319 14–016
Reid v Explosives Co Ltd (1887) L.R. 19 Q.B.D. 264 CA 32–039

TABLE OF STATUTES

TABLE OF STATUTORY INSTRUMENTS

TABLE OF EUROPEAN MATERIAL

Treaties and Conventions

Directives

Regulations

TABLE OF TAKEOVERS CODE

PART 1

INTRODUCTORY

The company, incorporated under the successive Companies Acts, is a dominant institution in our society, and all the more so with increasing government or public sector retreat from a number of areas in which previously it had been a monopoly or near-monopoly provider of services or, less often, of goods. Yet, the role of a company registered under the Companies Act is not easy to describe with accuracy. Even in the area of profit-making business activity, where it is a major force, it has no exclusive position and faces competition, at least in relation to smaller businesses, from other legal forms, such as the partnership or the sole trader (if the latter is a legal form at all). Moreover, the company is not just a vehicle for making profits: it can be, and is increasingly, used in the not-for-profit sector, i.e. where the aim of the undertaking is either not to make profits or, if it is, not to distribute them to the members of the company. And finally, the registered company is not the only type of company; companies may also be created by Act of Parliament or royal charter, although this happens rather rarely.

The dominance of companies registered under the Companies Act arises largely because this is a highly flexible vehicle for carrying on business, whether for profit or not-for-profit. Of course, the question inevitably arises in a particular case whether the proposed activity should be carried on through a company or another legal form, but none of these other legal forms is used across so many types and scales of activity as is the corporate form. In other words, the company has many competitors in the shape of other legal vehicles for carrying on business, but it is perhaps not much of an exaggeration to say that for all these other vehicles their primary competitor is the company. Companies are used as business vehicles from the smallest, one-person business to the largest, multi-national undertaking. This flexibility, together with a range of significant economic benefits, makes companies registered under the Companies Acts the principal vehicle for business association in the UK.

Of course, business today is often a multi-national activity. British companies may carry on activities in other states, and companies from other jurisdictions may carry on business in the UK. The desire to facilitate such cross-border corporate activity was a fundamental concern for the EU and, as a former Member State, the UK has benefitted to a large degree from the EU's programme of harmonisation for company law. This has left a lasting mark on British company law. Despite the challenges of Brexit, continued globalisation means that the international dimension of British company law is not diminished; rather, that international dimension is likely to be re-focused, so that other influences replace those of the EU as new economic partnerships are forged.

In this part we shall try to analyse the function of the modern company and its structure, discuss its advantages and disadvantages, see how it is created and introduce the international element of British company law.

CHAPTER 1

TYPES AND FUNCTIONS OF COMPANIES

USES TO WHICH THE COMPANY MAY BE PUT

Although company law is a well-recognised subject in the legal curriculum and forms the subject of a voluminous literature, its exact scope is not obvious since, as Buckley LJ has indicated, "the word 'company' has no strictly technical meaning".[1] Explicitly or implicitly, many courses on "company law" solve the subject's definitional problems by concentrating on those companies created by registration under the Companies Acts. This book follows that approach. Since 1–001

[1] *Re Stanley (Henry Morton)* [1906] 1 Ch. 131 Ch D at 134.

there are around 4.7 million such companies in the UK today,[2] in practical and pragmatic terms this is a sensible solution given that the law applicable to such companies is a matter of major concern to many people. However, to state that a book is going to deal, principally, with companies formed under particular legislation does not enhance one's understanding of the role that such companies perform in society.

The term "company" implies an association between a number of people for one or more common objects.[3] The purposes for which persons may wish to associate are multifarious, ranging from those as basic as marriage and car-sharing to those as sophisticated as the objects of the Confederation of British Industry or a political party. However, in common parlance the word "company" is normally reserved for associations pursuing economic purposes, i.e. to carry on a business for gain.[4] There are, however, two reasons why it would be wrong to say that company law is solely concerned with associations used to carry on business for gain. First, companies are not the only legal vehicles that people may use in order to associate for gainful business. Secondly, companies incorporated under the Companies Acts may pursue not-for-profit business or purposes that can only doubtfully be characterised as businesses at all. We will look at each of these matters in turn.

Business vehicles: companies and partnerships (limited and unlimited)

Partnership Act 1890 and Companies Act 2006

1–002 English law provides two main types of organisation for those wishing to associate in order to carry on business for gain: partnerships and companies. Historically, the word "company" was colloquially applied to both,[5] but the modern lawyer regards companies and company law as distinct from partnerships and partnership law. Partnership law, which has long been largely codified in the Partnership Act 1890, is based on the law of agency, with each partner becoming an agent of the others.[6] A partnership, therefore, affords a suitable framework for a small association of persons having trust and confidence in each other.[7] A more complicated form of association, with a large and fluctuating membership, requires a more elaborate organisational structure, which ideally confers corporate personality on the association with the result that the association constitutes a distinct legal person, subject to legal duties and entitled to legal rights separate from those of its members. The modern company can achieve this easily and cheaply by incorporating nowadays under the CA 2006.

[2] Companies House, *Incorporated Companies in the UK January to March 2021* (29 April 2021).

[3] *JH Rayner (Mincing Lane) Ltd v Department of Trade and Industry* (1987) 3 B.C.C. 413 QBD (Comm) at 430.

[4] This is not a universal truth, as one refers still to an infantry company, a livery company and the "glorious company of the Apostles".

[5] It was common for partners to carry on business with the suffix "—& Company" following the partnership name.

[6] Partnership Act 1890 s.5.

[7] *Ebrahimi v Westbourne Galleries Ltd* [1973] A.C. 360 HL at 379.

At first sight, the distinction drawn above might be taken to imply that the critical difference between partnerships and companies lies in the former being used to carry on small businesses and the latter large ones (or, more accurately, that the partnership form is used by a small number of people to carry on a business and the corporate form by a large number). Such a differentiation previously had some currency, since the mid-Victorian legislature was apparently animated by just such an idea.[8] In that earlier era, there was a statutory cap on the number of partners in a partnership, such that incorporation was compulsory when larger numbers of people wished to associate themselves for business purposes. Thus, s.716(1) of the CA 1985 (re-enacting a provision first introduced by the Joint Stock Companies Act 1844, which in fact set the limit slightly higher at 25), provided that, in principle, an association of 20 or more persons formed for the purpose of carrying on a business for gain must be formed as a company[9] (and so not as a partnership); whilst the Limited Liability Act 1855 required companies with limited liability to have at least 25 members.[10] The Joint Stock Companies Act 1856, however, quickly reduced the minimum number of members to seven for companies,[11] and the House of Lords in *Salomon v Salomon & Co Ltd*[12] had, by the end of the nineteenth century, effectively enabled companies to be incorporated with a single member (the other six being bare nominees for the seventh). Almost a century later, the adoption of EC Directive 89/667[13] enabled private companies to be officially formed with a single member. The CA 2006 extended this facility to public companies.[14] As regards the maximum limit on the number of partners in a partnership, this too has been eliminated over the past two decades. Accordingly, the CA 2006 contains no equivalent to s.716 of the CA 1985. **1–003**

This gradual collapse of the Victorian segregation of the two business forms does not, however, mean that they are equally well adapted to different sizes of business. In fact, it is clear that where a large and fluctuating number of members is involved, the company has distinct advantages as an organisational form. This is because inherent to the company form is the distinction between the members of the company (usually shareholders acting in general meeting) and the

[8] The legislature seems, however, to have been influenced in this view more by problems of civil procedure in relation to large partnerships, rather than by the idea that the partnership itself was inappropriate for large numbers of joint venturers: see Law Commission and Scottish Law Commission, *Joint Consultation Paper on Partnership Law* (London, 2000), paras 5.51–5.61.

[9] If it was formed as a partnership it would be automatically dissolved for illegality: see Partnership Act 1890 s.34. Nowadays, a company could be formed as a registered, statutory or chartered entity (see paras 1–031 to 1–033) or indeed as an Open-Ended Investment Company under the Financial Services and Markets Act 2000 s.236 (see para.1–036).

[10] Limited Liability Act 1855 restricted limited liability to relatively substantial companies in other ways, such as requiring that 25 members have subscribed for shares with a nominal value of at least £10, of which 20% had to be paid up.

[11] The Joint Stock Companies Act 1856 also removed the capital requirements of the 1855 Act.

[12] *Salomon v Salomon & Co Ltd* [1897] A.C. 22 HL. See paras 2–001 onwards.

[13] Directive 89/667 on single-member private limited-liability companies [1989] OJ L395/40, subsequently consolidated in Directive 2009/102 in the area of company law on single-member private limited liability companies [2009] OJ L258/20 and then Directive 2013/24 adapting certain directives in the field of company law, by reason of the accession of the Republic of Croatia [2013] OJ L158/365.

[14] CA 2006 s.7(1), which is not confined to private companies.

company's management (vested in a board of directors). Although this division between management and "ownership" can be replicated within a partnership, the partners must explicitly choose this option, as the default rule is the far less practical one of universal participation in management.[15]

Limited Liability Partnerships Act 2000

1–004 On the other hand, where a small number of persons intend to set up a business with everyone involved in its management, company law's division between shareholders and directors often becomes a nuisance, for they are the same (or nearly the same) people. In such cases, the internal machinery and procedures imposed by company law often appear impossibly cumbersome. Despite the legislative scheme in the CA 2006 being amended to meet the needs of small companies,[16] the practical problems have proved troubling. As a result, the Limited Liability Partnerships Act 2000 now provides a useful hybrid means of legal association.[17] To a degree, the title of this legislation is somewhat misleading, however, since the limited liability partnership (LLP), despite being a hybrid, actually has more in common with a company than a partnership. The LLP is usually governed by company law principles, often adapted to its particular needs.[18] In particular, like companies, the LLP has a separate legal personality and the partners have limited liability.[19] The corollary is that partnership law principles do not generally apply to the LLP,[20] except in two crucial respects. First, the members of the LLP are taxed as if they were partners.[21] Secondly, the internal decision-making machinery for companies, which is based on the division between members and directors, is abandoned for the LLP, and the members have the same freedom as in a partnership to decide on their internal decision-making structures.[22] The LLP has proved a reasonably attractive legal form, especially for professional businesses such as solicitors' firms.[23]

---

15 Partnership Act 1890 s.24(5).

16 This issue is the focus of Ch.12, although it is also discussed throughout this work.

17 For more detail, see generally G. Morse et al (eds), *Palmer's Limited Liability Partnership Law*, 3rd edn (London: Sweet & Maxwell, 2017).

18 Limited Liability Partnerships Act 2000 s.1(5). For the application of the CA 2006 to the LLP, see Limited Liability Partnerships (Application of Companies Act 2006) Regulations 2009 (SI 2009/1804), which repeals and replaces much of SI 2001/1090. See also SI 2008/1911, SI 2008/1912, SI 2008/1913, SI 2009/1833, SI 2016/340 and SI 2016/599, which apply different parts of the CA 2006 to LLPs.

19 Limited Liability Partnerships Act 2000 s.1.

20 Limited Liability Partnerships Act 2000 s.15.

21 Limited Liability Partnerships Act 2000 s.10.

22 Limited Liability Partnerships Act 2000 s.5.

23 There were around 51,000 LLPs on the register as at March 2020 (although there were around 4.2 million private companies registered at the same date): see Companies House, *Companies Register Activities: 2019 to 2020* (25 June 2020), Table 1.

Limited Partnership Act 1907

The Limited Liability Partnerships Act 2000 is to be sharply distinguished from the earlier, but confusingly and similarly named, Limited Partnership Act 1907. The limited partnership is a true partnership, which is governed by the Partnership Act 1890 and the common law of partnership, "except so far as they are inconsistent" with the special features of the 1907 Act.[24] Such notable features include the fact that some (but not all) of the partners in a limited partnership have limited liability,[25] but that, in return for such limited liability, those partners are prohibited from taking part in the management of the partnership business and do not have power to bind the partnership as against outsiders.[26] Moreover, certain information about the limited partnership has to be publicly filed (in fact, with the registrar of companies).[27] From 1 October 2009, limited partnerships have had to indicate their nature in their names by the addition of the words "limited partnership" or "LP".[28] In essence, the Limited Partnership Act 1907 provides for the possibility of a "sleeping partner": someone who contributes assets to the partnership and accordingly wishes to become a partner in order to safeguard his or her investment and secure an appropriate return on those funds, but who does not wish to become involved in the business' management. There were more than 53,000 limited partnerships in existence in 2020.[29] Whilst the number of limited partnerships remains modest in comparison to the number of private companies, the former have been increasing in recent years due to the attractiveness of the limited partnership in certain specialised fields of commercial activity.[30] For present purposes, however, there is a gulf between, on the one hand, the registered company and the limited liability partnership (which are both in essence creatures of company law) and, on the other, the partnership and the limited partnership (which are creatures of partnership law). **1–005**

[24] Limited Partnership Act 1907 s.7.

[25] Limited Partnership Act 1907 s.4(2), which requires that there must be at least one general partner who is liable for the debts and obligations of the firm.

[26] Limited Partnership Act 1907 s.6. For the position with respect to "private fund limited partnerships", see Legislative Reform (Private Fund Limited Partnerships) Order 2017 (SI 2017/514), inserting Limited Partnership Act 1907 s.6A.

[27] Limited Partnership Act 1907 s.8.

[28] Legislative Reform (Limited Partnership) Order 2009 (SI 2009/1940), inserting Limited Partnership Act 1907 s.8B.

[29] Companies House, *Companies Register Activities: 2019 to 2020* (25 June 2020), Table 1. It is not, however, clear how many limited partnerships are active, since the 1907 Act requires such entities to register, but provides no mechanism for de-registration.

[30] This is particularly the case for venture capital or private equity investment funds, where the investors can be limited partners distinct from the managers of the fund, who are the general partners. Further, in property investment transactions, tax-exempt investors may wish to be excluded from any management role: see Law Commissions, *Limited Partnerships Act 1907: A Joint Consultation Paper* (2001), Pt I.

Non-business vehicles: charitable, community interest and limited by guarantee companies

Not-for-profit companies

1–006 As already noted above, the statement that company law is the law relating to associations formed with a view to carrying on business for gain is neither a wholly accurate nor complete description. Indeed, there is no requirement at common law, in the CA 2006 or anywhere else that the activities of registered companies should be so limited.[31] In practice, a company may be not-for-profit in the strong sense that a constitutional provision prohibits the distribution of profits to the company's members, either by way of dividend or when distributing surplus assets in a winding up. Alternatively, a company may be not-for-profit in the weaker sense that it is not being run in order to make a profit, albeit that the company may from time to time make such a profit that can then be distributed amongst its members. "Not-for-profit" is not, however, a term of art in British company law, in the way it is in the many state corporate laws in the US.

1–007 Not-for-profit companies may pursue purposes that are charitable in the strict legal sense (in which case the company will have to comply with both the relevant companies and charities legislation, as well as being subject to the supervisory jurisdiction of the Charities Commission).[32] As well as having to comply with two separate statutory frameworks, charitable companies also have one other notable feature: as indicated by the Supreme Court in *Children's Investment Fund Foundation (UK) v Attorney General*,[33] members of a charitable company may owe fiduciary duties in a manner that has never yet been envisaged for ordinary trading companies. Alternatively, a company may be established for purposes that are in the public interest, albeit not falling within the rather narrow legal definition of charity.[34] Yet further, a company's purpose may be to promote a particular private interest, albeit that the pursuit of that private interest does not involve making a profit. A typical example is provided by *Kaye v Oxford House*

---

[31] In this regard, the corporate form contrasts sharply with both the partnership and the LLP, as the intention (if not the actuality) of carrying on the business for profit is part of the actual legal definition for those latter forms of business association: see Partnership Act 1890 s.1(1); Limited Liability Partnerships Act 2000 s.2(1). Indeed, an unincorporated association that satisfies the criterion of carrying on business for profit is characterised as a partnership, without the need for any further formality in that regard.

[32] See, for example, *Charity Commission for England and Wales v Cambridge Islamic College* [2018] UKUT 351 (TCC); *Children's Investment Fund Foundation (UK) v Attorney General* [2020] UKSC 33; [2020] 3 W.L.R. 461. For the current legislation applicable to charities, see Charities Act 2011. Since 2006, it has been possible to register a company with the Charities Commission as a "Charitable Incorporated Organisation". There is no obligation for associations pursuing charitable objects to incorporate, although they increasingly do so in order to obtain the benefits of limited liability, especially as such organisations are increasingly carrying more financial risk.

[33] *Children's Investment Fund Foundation (UK) v Attorney General* [2020] 3 W.L.R. 461.

[34] An adaptation of the corporate form for companies pursuing (non-charitable) public interest goals is the "Community Interest Company" (or CIC), which is considered further in para.1–012.

(Wimbledon) Management Co Ltd,[35] where the leaseholders of each flat in a block of flats held a share in a management company with responsibility for maintaining the building and its common parts. Under such an arrangement, each leaseholder will fund the company's operations, usually through the payment of service charges, to the level needed for the company to discharge its obligations in respect of the building and common parts and the leaseholders would be surprised, even indignant, if the company made a significant profit on its activities.

Company limited by guarantee

The Companies Acts have long provided a particular form of company that may be regarded as particularly well-suited for companies pursuing a not-for-profit activity, namely the company "limited by guarantee". This can be contrasted with the company "limited by shares",[36] which is normally used for profit-making activities and is by far the more common type of company. Although the CA 2006 does not permit the creation of a company in which the members are free from any liability whatsoever, the legislation does permit shareholders, as an alternative to them limiting their personal liability to the amount payable on their shares,[37] to agree that they will subscribe an agreed amount to be paid in the event of the company's liquidation.[38] The guarantee company is widely used by charitable and analogous organisations (such as schools, colleges and the "Friends" of museums and art galleries) since incorporation with limited liability is often more convenient and less risky than placing the assets in a trust structure.[39] Indeed, when a company is limited by guarantee, the division of such an undertaking into shares is arguably unnecessary (since no sharing of profits is contemplated) and undesirable (since those incorporating the company may regard membership divorced from shareholding as a more appropriate expression of the company's public-interest objectives). **1–008**

It might be thought that a company limited by guarantee imposes a lesser financial burden upon its members than one limited by shares, since the members of the former type of company do not have to invest any money in the concern upon incorporation, as would be the norm for investors subscribing for shares. It is certainly true that the members of a guarantee company are under no liability, so long as the company remains a going concern; they are liable, to the extent of their guarantees, only if the company is wound up and the members' **1–009**

---

[35] *Kaye v Oxford House (Wimbledon) Management Co Ltd* [2019] EWHC 2181 (Ch); [2020] B.C.C. 117. See also *Chong v Alexander* [2016] EWHC 735 (Ch); *Puzitskaya v St Paul's Mews (Islington) Ltd* [2017] EWHC 905 (Ch).

[36] CA 2006 s.3(1).

[37] It is no longer possible to create a hybrid form of company (i.e. a company limited by guarantee, but also with a share capital), although this was an option prior to 22 December 1980: see CA 2006 s.5.

[38] CA 2006 s.3(3).

[39] There were around 115,000 guarantee companies in existence in 2020: see Companies House, *Companies Register Activities: 2019 to 2020* (25 June 2020), Table 1. See, for example, *Children's Investment Fund Foundation (UK) v Attorney General* [2020] 3 W.L.R. 461.

contributions are needed to enable the company's debts to be paid.[40] That said, the par value of shares is usually set at a very low level (often as little as one penny per share)[41] and a member of a company limited by shares is only obliged to buy one share. Similarly, the guarantee given by a member is also often set at a nominal level. Accordingly, it is doubtful whether this argument concerning the initial financial burden on shareholders carries much weight when choosing between a company limited by shares or by guarantee and ultimately the financing aspects of not-for-profit companies probably play little role in a person's decision whether or not to become a member of such a company. Given the lack of any real practical difference between the two corporate forms, companies limited by shares can be (and are in fact) used for non-profit purposes. For example, in the case of a service company for a block of flats, each leaseholder will often hold one share in the company.[42]

1–010 A more important advantage of the guarantee company would, however, seem to be that admission to, and resignation from, membership are easier than in a company limited by shares. Upon resignation from a share company, the member's share has to be transferred in some way, whether back to the company or to a new member; and the admission of a new member requires a new share to be created, unless another member is resigning at exactly the same time and is seeking to transfer one or more shares. The issuance, transfer and repurchase of shares are all matters that are (sometimes heavily) regulated by the CA 2006 in the interests of protecting the company's creditors,[43] with the consequence that the transfer of membership in a not-for-profit company limited by shares can be cumbersome. Where membership of such a company is not attached to shares, however, joining and leaving can be as easy as in any club or association: joining is simply a matter of agreement between the company and prospective member and leaving generally involves a member's unilateral decision, albeit sometimes subject to certain conditions relating to notice or discharge of obligations owed to the company.[44]

Company limited by shares

1–011 A company limited by guarantee is, however, unsuitable where the association's primary object is to carry on a business for profit and to divide that profit among the members. Just as a partnership agreement will need to prescribe the partners'

---

40 CA 2006 s.3(3).

41 According to CA 2006 s.542(1), shares must have a "fixed nominal value" in order to be valid, but there is no regulation of the level at which that value should be set. See further para.16–003.

42 See, for example, *Kaye v Oxford House (Wimbledon) Management Co Ltd* [2020] B.C.C. 117. A share-based structure may be particularly convenient if members' obligations differ, such as when the obligation to contribute to the company's costs is related to the size of the flats. In that case, different contribution obligations can be attached to each share, although such differentiation may result in the creation of different classes of share: see CA 2006 s.629.

43 See Chs 16 and 17.

44 Where membership changes are expected to be relatively rare and where a new member will always be available to replace the departing one, as with a service company formed by the leaseholders of a block of flats, this potential disadvantage of the share company is unlikely to manifest itself. Consider *Kaye v Oxford House (Wimbledon) Management Co Ltd* [2020] B.C.C. 117.

shares, so will a company's constitution need to define its members' shares, and it will be convenient for those shares to be expressed in comparatively small denominations to maximise their transferability. When a member subscribes for shares, he or she is obliged to pay their nominal value (and any premium) in money or money's worth.[45] Accordingly, the company is said to be "limited by shares" because a member's liability to contribute towards the company's debts in the event of liquidation is limited to the consideration that the member has promised to pay for the shares in question; and, once payment has been made (so that the shares are "paid up"), the member is under no further liability.[46] A fundamental distinction between companies limited by shares and limited by guarantee, however, is that the law assumes that the working capital of the former type of company will be, to some extent at any rate, contributed by its members; the members' initial financial contributions "float" the company on its launching and are not a mere life-belt to which creditors may cling when the company sinks, which is how the guarantee company might be viewed. That said, as the CA 2006 lays down no minimum capital requirement for private companies,[47] the shareholders' initial contribution to the financing of a company limited by shares may in reality be exiguous.

Community Interest Company (CIC)

Despite companies limited by guarantee having long been available for non-profit purposes, there exists a not-insignificant limitation in terms of such a company's initial financing. Since there are no shares to be sold, the guarantee company must either operate on the basis that it needs no long-term working capital (many clubs can exist simply on their subscription income) or it must borrow that capital from an external lender. It was partly to address this concern that Pt 2 of the Companies (Audit, Investigations and Community Enterprise) Act 2004 introduced a new type of company,[48] namely the "Community Interest Company" (or CIC). Subject to any particular modifications introduced by the 2004 Act, the CA 2006 applies to the CIC.[49] A CIC may be either a company limited by shares or by guarantee; its purposes are limited to the pursuit of community interests[50]; distributions to the company's members and the payment of interest on debentures are subject to a cap; and the company's assets are otherwise "locked in".[51] It follows that investors in a CIC may have less incentive to exercise control over the company because their potential rewards are more limited than in an ordinary company. In terms of regulating the CIC, the Regulator of Community Interest Companies is given potentially extensive powers of **1–012**

[45] CA 2006 s.582(1).

[46] CA 2006 s.3(2). See also IA 1986 s.74(2)(d), discussed further in paras 7–001 to 7–003.

[47] See Ch.16.

[48] Companies (Audit, Investigations and Community Enterprise) Act 2004 s.26(1). A particular company may be formed as a "CIC" or subsequently convert into one. For the detailed procedures applicable to the CIC, see Community Interest Company Regulations 2005 (SI 2005/1788) (as amended).

[49] CA 2006 s.6(2). See also Community Interest Company Regulations 2005 (SI 2005/1788) (as amended).

[50] Companies (Audit, Investigations and Community Enterprise) Act 2004 s.35.

[51] Companies (Audit, Investigations and Community Enterprise) Act 2004 ss.30–31.

intervention in its affairs.[52] As registration as a CIC is not compatible with charitable status,[53] such companies do not attract the tax relief afforded to charities. Accordingly, it is unclear how attractive the CIC would be where the community purposes for which it was established also happened to be charitable (which, however, is not necessarily the case).[54]

The advantages of the modern corporate form

1–013 So far, two negative (and therefore not wholly helpful) propositions have been advanced. First, the corporate form is not limited to the association of large numbers of people carrying on a business, but can also be employed by a small number of investors, even by an individual entrepreneur. Secondly, the use of the company is not confined to those wishing to carry on a profit-making activity. That said, a positive proposition has also emerged from the above discussion: the comparative advantage of the company (as against, for example, the partnership or the trust) does indeed lie in the association of large numbers of people seeking to carry on a large-scale business. This is for two reasons.

The first is more obvious. Company law, by insisting upon the central role of directors in the running of the company, permits a large and fluctuating body of members (the shareholders) to delegate both the general oversight and the day-to-day operation of the company's business to a small and committed group of business experts (the directors). The quid pro quo of this delegation is that shareholders must in turn have a means of overseeing and controlling the directors. Over the years, successive Companies Acts and the common law have developed a set of legal rules and principles for regulating the relationship between shareholders and directors when authority is delegated by the former to the latter.[55]

Secondly, and less obviously, by providing for the creation of separate legal personality, limited liability and transferable shares, company law makes it possible to isolate business risks within the business vehicle (thus insulating the shareholders). This in turn facilitates the raising of risk capital from the public for the financing of corporate ventures. Raising funds by the sale of shares often gives companies greater financial flexibility than when capital is raised through borrowing, and accordingly shielding shareholders from risk is a crucial element in financing all businesses, except those where the risk of failure is very low.[56] Although there are other mechanisms for isolating risk and financing enterprises, none is both as simple and flexible as the company.

1–014 This analysis is borne out by the statistics classifying businesses by their legal type. These show that of those businesses in the private sector of the UK economy in 2020 employing more than 250 employees, 7,740 were organised as

---

[52] Companies (Audit, Investigations and Community Enterprise) Act 2004 ss.41–51, although there is the possibility of an appeal to an Appeal Officer under s.28.

[53] Companies (Audit, Investigations and Community Enterprise) Act 2004 s.26(3).

[54] There were some 18,904 CICs that had been registered by March 2020: see Regulator of Community Interest Companies, *Annual Report* 2019/2020, Foreword.

[55] See Pt 3.

[56] See Pts 5, 8 and 9.

companies and only 40 as partnerships (with 10 as sole traders). On the other hand, of those businesses with fewer than five employees, 1,574,145 were companies (around 78% of all companies), 140,810 were partnerships (around 72% of all partnerships), and 381,635 were sole traders (around 89% of all sole traders).[57] These data reveal not only (as one would expect) that there are many more small businesses than large businesses, but also (and more relevant for present purposes) that among large businesses the corporate form predominates, whilst in small businesses the company as a business vehicle faces a distinct challenge from both the partnership and those who make no formal distinction between their personal and business lives (the sole trader).

Accordingly, on the basis of the above analysis, it could be suggested that there are nowadays three distinct types of company from a functional perspective: **1–015**

(1) Companies formed for purposes other than the profit of their members, namely companies formed for social, charitable or analogous purposes. In such cases, incorporation is merely a more modern and convenient substitute for the trust.
(2) Companies formed to enable a single trader or a small body of partners to carry on a business. In these companies, incorporation is usually a device for personifying the business and divorcing the company's liability from that of its members (and vice versa) despite the fact that the members retain control of the company's operations and share its profits. In such cases, the company is often a tax-efficient substitute for a partnership.
(3) Companies formed in order to enable the investing public to share in the enterprise's profits without taking any part in its management. In this last type of case, which is economically (albeit not numerically) by far the most important category, the company is being used as a device analogous to the trust. In contrast to the first category, the corporate form is designed to facilitate the raising and use of capital by enabling a large number of investors to participate in endeavours that are too large for any of them individually, and to entrust the management of that endeavour to a much smaller number of expert managers.

However, this threefold categorisation needs to be treated with caution. First, there may be hybrid companies, or companies that at a particular moment of their growth cycle straddle the second and third categories above. For example, a company that was previously wholly controlled by the members of a particular family may have begun to bring in one or two outside financiers (sometimes called "business angels") in order to expand the business. These outsiders will naturally want a share in the company's control. At a still later stage in the company's development, the family members may have retired from actively managing the company and may have brought in professional managers to run the company (to whom shares may have been allocated), but the family members may still be the predominant shareholders. **1–016**

[57] Office for National Statistics, *UK Business: Activity, Size and Location 2020* (29 September 2020).

Secondly, even if a company is squarely within the third category and has a large number of shareholders that are distinct from the directors, there may still be significant variations in the extent to which the shareholders' interests are dispersed and can be traded. At one end of this scale is a company listed on the London Stock Exchange[58] with many thousands of shareholders who are readily able to trade their shares with other investors; whilst, at the other end of that scale, is a company that does in fact have several hundred shareholders (many of whom may well be the company's employees), but that has never made a formal offer of its shares to the public, with the result that its shares may not be traded on a public exchange.

DIFFERENT TYPES OF REGISTERED COMPANY

1–017 The above discussion highlights that the range of functions performed by a company formed by registration under the relevant legislation is extremely wide. Nevertheless, whatever their function, the companies are all subject to a single piece of legislation, namely the CA 2006. It might be questioned how sensible this is. Would it be better to have distinct legislation for different types of company, or is it possible to achieve sufficient differentiation between different sorts of company within a single piece of legislation? It is possible to tackle this question by reference to five possible divisions between different categories of company: the first three categories have long been recognised in British law, whilst the fourth category has not been formally recognised (although it is to some extent catered for in practice) and the fifth category has arguably become recognised in recent years.

Public and private companies

1–018 A legal division commonly found in the company laws of many jurisdictions is between public and private companies: the former category includes companies that are permitted to offer their securities (whether shares or marketable debt securities[59]) to the public,[60] even if this does not in fact occur, whilst the latter category includes those companies that are not so permitted. This distinction is embedded in the CA 2006, since it is mandatory that a company's name distinguish private companies ("limited" or "Ltd") from public ("public limited company" or "Plc") ones.[61] The obvious importance of the distinction is that companies not offering their shares to the public need not be concerned with the rules governing the public-issuance process, which are nowadays largely set out

---

58 See Ch.25.

59 See Ch.31.

60 CA 2006 s.755. See also Financial Services and Markets Act 2000 s.74 (and its associated regulations), which prevent a private company from having its securities listed on a trading exchange. See further paras 25–015 to 25–017. The largest Initial Public Offering (IPO) on the London Stock Exchange was completed in May 2011 by Glencore International Plc, which raised $10 billion at admission, albeit that the NYSE listing of Alibaba Holdings Group in 2014 more than doubled that.

61 CA 2006 ss.58–59, although companies registered in Wales may use the Welsh equivalents. See Ch.4.

in the Financial Services and Markets Act 2000 (FSMA 2000) rather than the CA 2006.[62] As well as being important in legal terms, whether a company is public or private also generally indicates the social and economic importance of the company. As a result of the significance of public companies for society in general, these companies tend to be more tightly regulated than private companies in a number of ways that do not directly concern the offering of shares to the public.

However, unlike many continental European countries, there is no separate legislation for public and private companies. The unified approach of the CA 2006 seems to be feasible because, although British public companies are more highly regulated than private companies, the British legislation has always had less ambitious regulatory goals for public companies than our continental counterparts. For example, the German *Aktiengesetz*, which applies to public companies, divides the board of directors into two bodies (the supervisory board and the management board) and deals in some detail with the allocation of functions between them and the method of appointing their members.[63] By contrast, the CA 2006 says very little about what the board is to do or how its members are to be appointed,[64] and the legislation certainly does not require the creation of separate supervisory and management boards.[65] Instead, these matters are left to be decided by each company in its own constitution. Consequently, different sizes and types of company can adjust these matters to suit their own particular situation, whereas in Germany a separate and more flexible statute for private companies (*GmbHGesetz*) has been enacted to relieve private companies of the demands of the *Aktiengesetz*. **1–019**

Whilst separate legislation is the most straightforward way of distinguishing between the different levels of regulation required by public and private companies, this can also be readily achieved in a single piece of legislation. The risk with the latter solution, however, is that too little thought will often be given to the explicit application or disapplication of the relevant rules to different types of company. As a consequence, public companies may become under-regulated or private ones over-regulated. To address precisely this concern, the Company Law Review[66] considered the rules then applicable to private companies to ascertain which ones resulted in over-regulation and should be eliminated entirely or applied only in a modified form. The Review also advocated re-ordering the **1–020**

[62] See Ch.25.

[63] Other legislation requires the mandatory presence of employee representatives on the boards of large German public companies, but this requirement applies also to the boards of large private companies.

[64] Nevertheless, the CA 2006 s.168 contains an important provision enabling an ordinary majority of the shareholders to remove any director at any time. See further paras 11–022 onwards.

[65] In British companies, there is typically only a single board, but there is nothing in the CA 2006 to prevent a company from establishing a separate "management board" below the main board or some other corporate organ (such as a Family Council in family-owned companies). This is sometimes done. On the division within a single board between executive and non-executive directors, see Ch.9.

[66] See para.3–003.

provisions in the companies legislation at that time to make it clearer which ones applied to private companies.[67] The CA 2006 embodies this approach.

1–021 The choice between a public and a private company is one for the incorporators themselves to make or, after incorporation, is a decision for the shareholders.[68] The default legal rule is that a company is private, unless the parties state otherwise.[69] As considered above, an overwhelming proportion of registered companies are private in nature: as of June 2020, only about 6,198 companies on the register in Great Britain were public (down from 9,200 in 2009 and 7,500 in 2015), whilst the total number of private registered companies was around 4.2 million.[70]

This is a significant change from the position that pertained when the notion of the private company was introduced by the Companies (Consolidation) Act 1908. At that time, the view was that, as a private company was exempt from some of the usual publicity requirements in the legislation, access to that status should be significantly restricted. Accordingly, a company could only qualify as private if it (1) limited its membership to 50; (2) restricted the right to transfer its shares; and (3) prohibited any invitation to the public for its shares. Only the third of these requirements has survived as a legal requirement for a company to have private status.[71]

Officially listed and other publicly traded companies

1–022 Although public companies may offer their shares to the public, some choose not to. Even if such a public offer is made, those shares may or may not be subsequently traded on a public share exchange, such as the London Stock Exchange. Accordingly, offering shares to the public and arranging for those shares to be traded on a public market are two separate things, although these two matters are undoubtedly linked: the public's willingness to buy the shares offered is likely to be increased if the shares can subsequently be traded on a public market. This is because a public market makes it much easier for a shareholder to sell shares to another investor, or to purchase more shares in the same company,

---

67 Company Law Review (CLR), *Final Report I*, Ch.2. Particular CLR proposals are noted at appropriate points subsequently, but one illustration of the recommendations was the removal of the prohibition on private companies giving financial assistance for the acquisition of their shares. See further paras 17–041 onwards.

68 A company originally incorporated as private may, subject to certain safeguards, transform itself into a public one, or vice versa: see paras 4–036 onwards.

69 CA 2006 s.4(2)(a).

70 Companies House, *Companies Register Activities: 2019 to 2020* (25 June 2020), Table 1. The total number of companies on the register has been increasing quite rapidly, whilst the number of public companies gently declined over the same period. Now fewer than one in 400 companies is a public one.

71 Whilst private companies are very likely to restrict the transfer of their shares (see Ch.26) and to have fewer than 50 members, these are no longer necessary legal incidents of being a private company.

should that be desired. Consequently, although theoretically distinct, public offerings of shares and the admission of those shares to trading on a public market often go hand-in-hand.[72]

Over the years, the companies legislation has generally drawn very few differentiations according to whether a public company's shares have actually been offered to the public or are in fact publicly traded, and the CA 2006 makes even fewer distinctions than its predecessors. That said, a company taking either of these steps will be required to comply with FSMA 2000 and the rules made pursuant to that legislation by the Financial Conduct Authority (FCA).[73] Naturally, this regulatory framework is mainly concerned with the issues thrown up by public share offers and public trading (as discussed subsequently), but it is important to note at this stage a curiosity of the British approach to capital markets regulation: admission to a public market may create obligations for the company of a recognisably "company law"-type, which could have been included in the CA 2006, but were not. This is particularly true for certain aspects of the "Listing Rules" promulgated by the FCA. A company seeking to have its shares traded on the Main Market (whether a Premium or Standard Listing)[74] of the London Stock Exchange must first have them admitted to the "Official List" of securities, which is a list maintained by the FCA, acting in its capacity as the UK Listing Authority (UKLA).[75] Although a main purpose of this regulatory framework is to secure proper disclosure of information about the company at the time its shares are offered to the public,[76] the UKLA is also empowered to impose on listed companies rules governing their conduct thereafter.[77] Such listing rules relate mainly to the orderly conduct of the public share market, but they also contain rules regulating the internal affairs of companies, which thus supplement both the provisions of the CA 2006 and the common law relating to companies.[78] In particular, the Listing Rules contain provisions for premium-listed companies on related-party transactions[79] and significant transactions,[80] which accordingly **1–023**

[72] For further discussion, see Ch.25.

[73] On 1 April 2013, the former Financial Services Authority was replaced by the Financial Conduct Authority (responsible for policing the City and the banking system), and a new Prudential Regulatory Authority (responsible for carrying out the prudential regulation of financial firms, including retail banks, investment banks, building societies and insurance companies), with all other responsibilities being assumed by the Bank of England and its Financial Policy Committee.

[74] The Listing Regime is divided into two segments, giving UK and overseas issuers the same choice of Listing Regimes. These are either Premium or Standard, with Premium Listing requiring adherence to more stringent standards (including for overseas companies), namely to "comply or explain" against the UK Corporate Governance Code, and the requirement to offer pre-emption rights. Standard Listing requires adherence to the lower minimum standards, originally derived from EU law, requiring companies, amongst other things, to provide a corporate governance statement and to describe their internal control and risk management systems' main features.

[75] FSMA 2000 Pt VI.

[76] See Ch.25.

[77] FSMA 2000 s.96.

[78] Companies whose shares are traded on secondary markets, such as the Alternative Investment Market, may also be subject to exchange rules that perform a similar function, but the rules of secondary markets are less demanding than the Listing Rules, which apply to the Main Market/Official List.

[79] Listing Rules LR 11.

[80] Listing Rules LR 10.

supplement the statutory rules on directors' and controlling shareholders' conflicts of interest, as well as setting limits on the constitutional division of powers within companies,[81] and providing the legal anchor for the UK Corporate Governance Code.

1–024 This last is probably the best-known example of such a "supplementary" Listing Rule. Premium-listed companies must indicate to their shareholders each year how far they have complied with the UK Corporate Governance Code (a Code drafted by the Financial Reporting Council[82] and attached to the Listing Rules) and to explain areas of non-compliance.[83] This Code deals with the composition and functions of the board of directors. In short, the fact of listing leads to the increased regulation of a small group of very important British and overseas companies to which additional company law obligations are attached.[84]

1–025 The identification of publicly traded companies as a separate group for company law purposes has become increasingly important in recent years and it is unlikely that the importance of this category will diminish in the future. It is not immediately obvious, however, that the additional regulation of such companies should be confined to listed companies on the Main Market and not extend to those whose shares are traded on "secondary" markets, such as the Alternative Investment Market (AIM).[85] Nor is it obvious that such additional regulation should be embodied in the Listing Rules rather than the CA 2006.

1–026 As a result of the importance, even in core company law matters, of a company having its securities traded on a public market, an ambiguity has arisen in the term "public company". For the company lawyer, a public company still usually means a company which is public, rather than private, for the purposes of the CA 2006, as discussed above. For the capital markets lawyer, however, satisfying the definition in the CA 2006 is not enough to make a company public: the company must also have offered its shares to the public and/or must have made a public market available for the trading of its shares. This ambiguity can be avoided by using the term "publicly traded" to refer to the latter type of company.

Limited and unlimited companies

1–027 The distinction between members limiting their liability by shares or by guarantee has already been considered.[86] Since limited liability is the principal advantage that reportedly drives entrepreneurs' decisions to incorporate, it is noteworthy that the CA 2006 also provides a category of private company where members' liability is unlimited. Such an unlimited company may have a share capital (in order to provide working capital and to provide a measure for each

---

[81] For further discussion, see paras 10–074, 11–011 to 11–012 and 13–002.

[82] See paras 3–001 to 3–002.

[83] Listing Rules LR 9.8.6 and 9.8.7. See further para.9–020.

[84] There are some 1,500 British listed companies, although most of the Listing Rules apply to all companies with primary listings, no matter where incorporated.

[85] The CLR considered that the Combined Code (the predecessor to the UK Corporate Governance Code), for example, should apply to all quoted companies: see Completing, para.4.44.

[86] See paras 1–008 and 1–009.

member's rights in the company), but that capital no longer functions as a limit on liability.[87] Given the legal and economic benefits for entrepreneurs of limited liability, it is not surprising that few unlimited companies are formed.[88] Whilst there is no reason why such companies would require entirely separate legislation, the CA 2006 nevertheless adopts the position that some statutory requirements applicable to registered companies generally ought not to be applied to unlimited companies. This is true in particular of the obligation to publish the company's accounts[89] (since creditors of unlimited companies can ultimately rely on the credit of the shareholders), and the prohibition on a company acquiring its own shares[90] (since the risk of such transactions only really applies to creditors who are confined to the company's assets to satisfy their claims and who accordingly have no claim against the shareholders). Consequently, the unlimited company may be attractive for those shareholders who are willing to stand behind their company and for whom the advantages of privacy or flexibility of capital structure are important.

Classification according to size: large, medium and micro companies

Classifying companies according to their size does not necessarily lead to differentiation in terms of technical legal categories, although the CA 2006 does recognise the different needs of the various sizes of company. At one end of the scale is the listed company (with a diffuse shareholding structure and external management expertise), whereas, at the other end, is the very small (potentially single-member) company, in which the directors and shareholders are the same and business turnover is comparatively small. According to the Office for National Statistics, 69% of active companies in the UK have a turnover of less than £250,000 and 78% have fewer than five shareholders,[91] whilst the CLR reported research indicating that 70% of registered companies have only two shareholders.[92] Nevertheless, the CLR concluded against having separate legislation for companies whose directors and shareholders were identical and whose businesses were small in size (sometimes called "micro" companies). This conclusion was based on a concern that it would be economically undesirable to create a regulatory barrier that might discourage companies from growing if they suddenly became subject to a different legal regime when their directors and shareholders ceased to be identical.[93] For the same reason, the CLR was opposed to a distinct regime for micro companies even within a single piece of **1–028**

[87] CA 2006 s.3(4). Only a private company can be unlimited, as a public company must be limited by shares or guarantee: s.4(2).

[88] There are currently reported to be 4,263 private unlimited companies registered with Companies House and this has steadily declined from earlier reporting periods: see Companies House, *Company Register Activities: 2019 to 2020* (31 March 2020), Table C1.

[89] CA 2006 s.448, on which see para.22–040. Although there is no requirement for unlimited companies to publish their accounts, these must still be produced for members' internal purposes.

[90] CA 2006 s.658 is restricted by its terms to "limited" companies, on which see para.17–002.

[91] Office for National Statistics, *UK Business: Activity, Size and Location 2020* (29 September 2020), Tables 14 and 15.

[92] Developing, paras 6.8–6.9.

[93] Strategic Framework, Ch.5.2.

legislation.[94] Instead, the CLR applied most of its reforms to private companies across the board, but those reforms were usually crafted as default rules with the intention that they would apply to micro companies in particular, with larger private companies opting out of the default regime where appropriate. The key advantage of adopting a uniformly applicable system of default rules is that the legal regime does not formally cease to be applicable to particularly small companies as they expand, but, as the business grows, the company has the option of "cherry-picking" those aspects of the regime most appropriate to its business at the relevant time. The CA 2006 has adopted this same approach. As considered above, those who require a form of business association that gives still further flexibility than that permitted to a private company, especially in relation to the internal decision-making structure, should opt for a Limited Liability Partnership.[95]

Classification according to activity: for-profit and not-for-profit companies

1–029 Although the term "not-for-profit company" is not formally used in the CA 2006, for the reasons discussed above, associations pursuing such benevolent aims frequently incorporate as companies limited by guarantee, which are not regulated in any fundamentally different way from a company limited by shares.[96] The same can be said of the community interest company (or CIC),[97] which is ordinarily a company limited by shares or by guarantee and is formed under the CA 2006, albeit that the Companies (Audit, Investigations and Community Enterprise) Act 2004 nowadays provides a modified set of legal principles that those forming a CIC can adopt to meet the needs of an entity whose aims are to promote the interests of the community (or a section of it) rather than to make a private profit for its members.[98]

1–030 Those not-for-profit companies that are also charities[99] are presently subject to the burden of double regulation by virtue of the CA 2006 and the Charities Act 2011.[100] Consequently, there is a strong efficiency argument that there should be a special form of charitable company that need only comply with a single regulatory regime. This has now been achieved by the Charities Act 2006 introducing the Charitable Incorporated Organisation (CIO) in England and Wales, although adopting this form is optional.[101] The CIO form of business association is available to companies whose purposes are charitable, and is designed for their particular needs. Unlike a CIC, however, a CIO is not

[94] Developing, Ch.6; Final Report I, para.2.7.

[95] See para.1–004.

[96] See para.1–008.

[97] See para.1–012.

[98] Whilst profitable trading will be a precondition of the company's survival, that profit will be devoted mainly to the promotion of the relevant community objectives.

[99] For the categorisation of not-for-profit companies, see paras 1–006 to 1–007.

[100] See, for example, *Children's Investment Fund Foundation (UK) v Attorney General* [2020] 3 W.L.R. 461. As the regulation of charities is a devolved matter, the Charities and Trustee Investment (Scotland) Act 2005 applies in Scotland.

[101] Developing, paras 9.7–9.40; Completing, paras 9.2–9.7; Final Report I, paras 4.63–4.67.

registered by the Registrar of Companies under the CA 2006, but by the Charity Commissioners under the Charities Act 2011.[102] Despite the CIO being governed primarily by charities law,[103] many of the legal principles applicable to CIOs will be familiar to company lawyers, such as the duties incumbent on CIO trustees and the principles governing third-party contracting.[104] Similarly, the case law under the CA 2006 should be capable of application to the CIO. There are currently just over 21,000 CIOs registered in England and Wales.[105]

UNREGISTERED COMPANIES AND OTHER FORMS OF INCORPORATION

Statutory and chartered companies

Beyond the different types of company registered under the CA 2006, there are alternative forms of incorporation that are available for carrying on business, even large-scale businesses. These include companies formed by special Act of Parliament or by means of a charter granted by the Crown, whether by virtue of the Royal Prerogative or statutory powers conferred upon the Crown to grant charters of incorporation.[106] In 2020, there were 41 companies in existence formed under special Acts of Parliament and 872 incorporated by Royal Charter.[107] **1–031**

In the past, incorporating companies by private Acts of Parliament was comparatively common, since public utility undertakings (such as railway, gas, water and electricity undertakings) required special powers and monopolistic rights that could only be conferred by a special legislative grant. To facilitate this, during the nineteenth century, public general Acts[108] were passed providing standard clauses that would be deemed to be incorporated into the private Acts unless expressly excluded. As a result of post-war nationalisation measures, most of these statutory companies were taken over by public boards or corporations set up by public Acts (but many, if not most, of them have now been "privatised" and become registered companies). These boards and corporations fall outside the scope of this work. Nevertheless, some statutory companies remain in existence

---

[102] See, for example, *Charity Commission for England and Wales v Cambridge Islamic College* [2018] UKUT 351.

[103] Charities Act 2011 Pt 11.

[104] Charities Act 2011 ss.218, 221.

[105] Companies House, *Company Register Activities: 2019 to 2020* (31 March 2020), Table C1.

[106] There are a number of ad hoc statutes under which the Crown has been given power to grant charters in cases falling outside its prerogative powers. Moreover, by the Chartered Companies Acts 1837 and 1884, the Crown's prerogative was expanded to granting charters for a limited period, as well as extending them. Thus, the BBC Charter was initially for 10 years and has thereafter been prolonged from time to time.

[107] Companies House, *Statistical Tables on Companies Registration Activities 2019/20* (31 March 2020), Table B3.

[108] See, for example, Companies Clauses Acts 1845–1889. These Acts, containing the general corporate powers and duties, were supplemented in the case of particular utilities by various other "Clauses Acts", such as the Lands Clauses Consolidation and Railways Clauses Consolidation Acts 1845, the Electric Lighting (Clauses) Act 1899, and numerous Waterworks Clauses Acts, and Gasworks Clauses Acts.

and others may still be formed. The statute under which these companies are formed need not incorporate them, but this is invariably done nowadays.

As for companies chartered by the Crown,[109] the charter normally confers corporate personality, but, as it was regarded as dubious policy for the Crown to confer a full charter of incorporation on an ordinary trading concern, the Crown was empowered by the Trading Companies Act 1834 and the Chartered Companies Act 1837 to confer by letters patent all or any of the privileges of incorporation without actually granting a charter. Nowadays, an ordinary trading concern would not contemplate trying to obtain a Royal Charter, as incorporation under the CA 2006 would be far quicker and cheaper. In practice, therefore, this method of incorporation is used only by organisations formed for charitable objects (or analogous purposes), such as learned and artistic societies, schools and colleges, which might seek the greater prestige that a charter is thought to confer.

1–032 The fact that companies created by statute and "letters patent" are not registered under the CA 2006 has an important regulatory consequence: in the absence of contrary provision, the CA 2006 will not apply to such companies. In policy terms, this may give such "unregistered" companies an unfair competitive advantage as against companies registered under the CA 2006, and may mean that third parties dealing with such companies are inadequately protected. This problem was addressed, but only partially solved, by s.1043 of the CA 2006, which applies some, but not all, of the CA 2006's provisions to unregistered companies, which qualify as "bodies incorporated in and having a principal place of business in the United Kingdom",[110] unless the relevant company is incorporated by or under a general public Act of Parliament.[111] In addition, to fall within the scope of the CA 2006, an unregistered company must have been formed "for the purpose of carrying on a business that has for its object the acquisition of gain".[112] In other words, the problems of unfair competition and inadequate third-party protection are not perceived as arising in relation to not-for-profit companies, which, as discussed, constitute the main type of company created by the Crown.

According to s.1043, only those parts of the CA 2006 specified by regulation will apply to unregistered companies within its scope,[113] and any charter, enactment or other instrument (such as letters patent) constituting the company is

---

[109] For the relevant procedure, see para.4–003.

[110] This is an interesting nod on the part of British law towards the "real seat" theory of incorporation (on which see further paras 5–002 onwards), for this section does not apply to a British unregistered company which does not have a place of business in the UK. By contrast, a company registered under the CA 2006 will be governed by that Act, even if it conducts the whole of its business outside the UK.

[111] CA 2006 s.1043(1)(a). This would include the CA 2006 itself, but also, for example, the Co-operative and Community Benefit Societies Act 2014 (on which see para.1–035).

[112] CA 2006 s.1043(1)(b). Open-ended investment companies are also excluded (s.1043(1)(d)) and protected cell companies registered under Pt 4 of the Risk Transformation Regulations 2017 (SI 2017/1212) (s.1043(1)(e)), as well as other unregistered companies specifically excluded by direction of the Secretary of State (s.1043(1)(c)).

[113] CA 2006 s.1043(2), (3). See also Unregistered Companies Regulations 2009 (SI 2009/2436) reg.3 and Sch.1.

subordinated to those parts of the CA 2006 that are thereby made applicable.[114] The main areas of regulation so applied are those relating to accounts and audit, corporate capacity and directors' authority, company investigations and fraudulent trading.[115] More recently, the regulation of persons with significant control have been extended to unregistered companies.[116] Nevertheless, this omits some large and important parts of the CA 2006, such as those dealing with the removal of directors, fair dealing by directors, distribution of profits and assets, registration of charges, arrangements and reconstructions and takeover offers, and the control of unfairly prejudicial conduct.

An alternative policy embodied in the CA 2006 is aimed at encouraging unregistered companies to register under its provisions and accordingly become subject to their full force. Such a step is facilitated by enabling unregistered companies to register under the CA 2006 without having to take the unnecessary steps of forming a new company and winding up the old one,[117] although these steps may sometimes be taken as part of larger scheme to restructure the association's ownership and management.[118] As far as statutory and letters patent companies are concerned, a basic distinction is drawn between those which are "joint stock companies" (essentially those with a share capital)[119] and those which are not. Only the former may make use of this special registration process for previously unregistered companies and such an entity must register as a company limited by shares and not as an unlimited or guarantee company.[120] The details of the effect of registration, provisions for the automatic vesting of property, savings for existing liabilities and rights and similar matters are contained in regulations.[121] **1–033**

Building societies, friendly societies and co-operatives

Although the Victorian legislature devoted considerable efforts to elaborating the predecessors to the CA 2006 in order to facilitate large-scale business, its efforts were not so confined. Even in the area of commercial activities, the Victorian legislature was aware that the company form, despite its flexibility, would not suit **1–034**

---

[114] CA 2006 s.1043(4).

[115] Unregistered Companies Regulations 2009 (SI 2009/2436) reg.3 and Sch.1.

[116] Information about People with Significant Control (Amendment) Regulations 2017 (SI 2017/693) regs 33 and 36, inserting Sch.1 paras 12A–12C and 20A–20B from 26 June 2017. See also Companies and Limited Liability Partnerships (Filing Requirements) Regulations 2015 (SI 2015/1695) reg.9(2).

[117] CA 2006 s.1040(1)–(2).

[118] CA 2006 s.1040(6).

[119] CA 2006 s.1041.

[120] CA 2006 s.1040(4), qualifying the broader provision in s.1040(3).

[121] CA 2006 s.1042. See the Companies (Companies Authorised to Register) Regulations 2009 (SI 2009/2437), applying the relevant parts of the CA 2006. Part 33 of the CA 2006 also allows for the registration of the few remaining "deed of settlement" companies, a private law form of quasi-incorporation that was invented to avoid the costs of statutory or royal incorporation and that was overtaken by the possibility of formation by registration under a general Act in the middle of the nineteenth century. For details, see pp.29–31 of this book's sixth edition.

all types of business, especially when the organisation's members were intended to have a different relationship with the association than shareholders have with a company.

Some of these other forms of incorporation were confined to specific activities, such as building societies,[122] whose principal purpose is lending secured on residential property. The building society is an incorporated body, very similar to a company—which is why it has been easy for many of them in the recent past to "demutualise" by converting into registered companies—but its members are those who place funds on deposit with the society or borrow from it, rather than those who invest risk capital by purchasing shares.

A less striking example is the friendly societies legislation,[123] which until recently contemplated only the formation of unincorporated bodies, but now permits incorporation of bodies whose purposes include the provision on a mutual basis of insurance against loss of income arising out of sickness, unemployment or retirement. Originally, the friendly society constituted a type of self-help response to the risks of ordinary life before the rise of the welfare state from the beginning of the twentieth century. Even nowadays, friendly societies have a continuing role to play in areas neglected by the welfare system.

1–035 However, probably the most important of the "non-company" incorporated bodies were those created under the old Industrial and Provident Societies Acts, dating from the middle of the nineteenth century. Nowadays, the incorporation of co-operative societies is governed by the Co-operative and Community Benefit Societies Act 2014. Co-operatives can be deployed in a wide range of commercial settings, and membership and financial rights are usually allocated according to the extent to which people have participated in the society's business, whether as customers (as in retail co-operatives), producers (as in, for example, agricultural co-operatives) or as employees (as in worker co-operatives). There were over 10,900 registered societies (including industrial and provident societies) in existence in 2020,[124] and they are of particular importance in some limited areas of commercial activity.[125] Together with trade unions,[126] all these entities are outside the scope of this work.

---

[122] For the current legislation, see Building Societies Acts 1986–1997, although this legislation can trace its origins to an Act of 1874.

[123] See Friendly Societies Act 1992, although its origins can be traced as far back as the Friendly Societies Act 1793.

[124] Companies House, *Statistical Tables on Companies Registration Activities 2019/20* (31 March 2020), Table B3. As the registration function had previously been delegated to the Financial Services Authority, this has now been transferred to the Financial Conduct Authority since the Co-operative and Community Benefit Societies Act 2014 came into force.

[125] For a fascinating comparative attempt to explain the successes and failures of the co-operatives, see H. Hansmann, *The Ownership of Enterprise* (USA: Harvard University Press, 1996).

[126] This is another expression of the Victorian genius for collective self-help, but the legal status of trade unions presented the Victorian legislature with much more difficulty.

Open-ended investment and protected cell companies

The Victorian penchant for devising corporate vehicles for specialised purposes was revived in 1996 with the creation of the Open-Ended Investment Company. It is perhaps an indication of the changes in the nature of the UK economy over the previous 150 years that the specialised purpose for such entities was that of "collective investment". At its simplest level, collective investment means the coming together of a number of investors, often a large number of relatively small investors, who pool their resources for the purpose of achieving overall better returns on their investments. Those investments will typically involve the purchase of corporate securities, although the range of investments is not necessarily so confined. The intention is that the better return will result partly from the greater size of the fund to be invested and partly from the employment of specialised management to discharge the investment task.[127] **1–036**

Both the trust (in the shape of "unit trusts", which can trace their origin back to the 1860s) and the registered company (in the shape of the "investment company") have long been used for the purpose of collective investment. In the case of an investment company, an investor buys shares in a company whose resources are allocated to the purchase of investments. However, as noted already in relation to guarantee companies,[128] a company limited by shares suffers from the disadvantage that the company is not free to repurchase its own shares. Accordingly, an investor who wishes to dispose of his or her shares in the investment company will normally have to sell the shares to another investor, but the market price of those shares (depending on supply and demand) may well be less than the value of the underlying investments held by the investment company. These difficulties can be avoided by the use of the unit trust, in which the trustees are free to make a standing offer to buy back units from investors at a price that fully reflects the value of the underlying assets held in trust. During the 1990s, however, the trust came to be regarded as a peculiarity of English law that might not fare well on an international plane, when competing with continental European and US investment funds, which are organised on a corporate basis.

The UK Government's response was the creation of a corporate vehicle that had the same freedom as the trust to repay its investors with the value of the investments held by the company. Thus, s.262 of FSMA 2000 now permits the Treasury to make regulations for the creation of corporate bodies to be known as open-ended investment companies (OEIC), and an essential ingredient of an OEIC's definition is that investors must have the expectation that they will be able to realise their investment within a reasonable period and at a value calculated mainly by reference to the value of the property held within the scheme by the company.[129] Accordingly, the Open-Ended Investment Company Regulations 2001 require that an OEIC's shareholders be entitled either to have their shares redeemed or repurchased by the OEIC upon request at a price related to the value of the scheme property or to sell their shares on a public exchange at

[127] For the legal definition of a "collective investment scheme", see FSMA 2000 s.235.
[128] See para.1–008.
[129] FSMA 2000 s.236(3).

the same price.[130] In general, the Regulations are a combination of provisions drawn from the CA 1985[131] (but without the crucial general principle found in the CA 2006 preventing a company limited by shares from acquiring its own shares)[132] and FSMA 2000 concerning the authorisation of those wishing to engage in investment business.[133] More recently, collective investment has been further encouraged by the development of protected cell companies, which have an administrative "core" with "cells" that engage in different collective investment activities.[134] The principal advantage of such a company is that it permits the segregation of liabilities between the different "cells" in the company, so that the different parts of the protected cell company's collective investment activities can be ring-fenced one from the other, thereby reducing the risk for investors and facilitating collective investment overall.[135]

European Union Forms of Incorporation

European Economic Interest Grouping and UK Economic Interest Grouping

1–037 During the UK's membership of the EU, the creation of corporate bodies largely remained a matter for national law, rather than EU law. Nevertheless, there were two forms of incorporation provided in the UK by EU law (and this will remain the case for continuing Member States). Both types of corporate form were concerned with promoting cross-border co-operation between companies formed in different Member States; both were consequently rather specialised forms of incorporation; both were implemented by Regulations that were directly applicable in the UK (although in both cases supplementary national legislation was required); but the two forms differed in most other respects. The first of the corporate forms created by EU law is the European Economic Interest Grouping (EEIG), which is based on the model of the French *groupement d'intérêt économique* (GIE) and is designed to enable existing business undertakings in different Member States to form an autonomous body to provide common services ancillary to the primary activities of its members. Any of the EEIG's profits belong to its members, which are jointly and severally responsible for its liabilities. In addition, the members of the EEIG, acting collectively as a body, may take "any decision for the purpose of achieving the objects of the grouping".[136] Although the EEIG's managers also constitute an organ of the Grouping that may bind it as against third parties, Regulation 2137/85 does not insist upon the delegation of management authority from the EEIG's members to

130 Open-Ended Investment Company Regulations 2001 (SI 2001/1228, as amended by SI 2005/923, SI 2009/553, SI 2011/1613 and SI 2011/3049) reg.15(11).

131 Open-Ended Investment Company Regulations 2001 (SI 2001/1228) Pt.III.

132 CA 2006 s.658 onwards.

133 Open-Ended Investment Company Regulations 2001 (SI 2001/1228) Pt.II.

134 The Risk Transformation Regulations 2017 (SI 2017/1212) regs 42–43.

135 The Risk Transformation Regulations 2017 (SI 2017/1212) regs 44–45 and 48–49.

136 Regulation 2137/85 on the European Economic Interest Grouping [1985] OJ L199/1 art.16.

its managers.[137] This factor, when combined with the members' lack of limited liability, means that the EEIG is as much like a partnership as a company.

The basic requirements for the formation of an EEIG are simply the conclusion of a written contract between its members and the EEIG's registration in the Member State where it is to have its principal establishment—which is a choice for the members to make. An EEIG must have at least two members, which must be companies or partnerships "formed in accordance with the law of a Member State" or, in some cases, a natural person, but at least two of the EEIG's members must carry on their principal activities in different Member States.[138] If these requirements are satisfied, Regulation 2137/85 confers upon the EEIG full legal capacity,[139] although the EEIG is only ever intended to be ancillary in nature given that its activities "shall be related to the economic activities of its members and must not be more than ancillary to those activities".[140] This feature of the EEIG is reinforced by such an entity being prohibited from exercising management over its members' activities or those of another undertaking; from holding shares in a member company; from employing more than 500 workers[141]; or from being a member of another EEIG. **1–038**

Although the legal requirements for EEIG were mostly directly applicable in the domestic legal order by means of Regulation 2137/85, these were supplemented in the UK by the European Economic Interest Grouping Regulations 1989, for EEIGs which chose the UK as their state of registration. These conferred corporate personality on EEIGs,[142] nominated the Companies Registrar as the registering authority,[143] and applied parts of the CA 2006 and the IA 1986 to EEIGs.[144] Given that the EEIG was designed only for the provision of ancillary services to its members and that it was forbidden to make profits for itself, it is not surprising that the EEIG did not have a significant take-up in the UK, though the number of EEIGs with their principal establishment in the UK grew steadily from 23 in 1991 to 285 in 2020.[145] **1–039**

Whilst the EEIG obviously continues to exist in other EU Member States by virtue of Regulation 2137/85, the UK's departure from the European Union effectively excluded UK-incorporated companies from them. A UK-based company will not be able to become part of a new EEIG given the requirement in the EU Regulation that a member company be formed under the law of a Member

[137] Regulation 2137/85 on the European Economic Interest Grouping [1985] OJ L199/1.

[138] Regulation 2137/85 on the European Economic Interest Grouping [1985] OJ L199/1 art.4.

[139] Regulation 2137/85 on the European Economic Interest Grouping [1985] OJ L199/1 art.1(2).

[140] Regulation 2137/85 on the European Economic Interest Grouping [1985] OJ L199/1 art.3(1).

[141] This restriction seems to have been motivated in part to prevent the EEIG being used by German companies to avoid domestic legislation mandating worker participation in board activity, once a company has 500 employees.

[142] European Economic Interest Grouping Regulations 1989 (SI 1989/638) reg.3 (as amended by SI 2009/2399), although this provision has been revoked by the European Economic Interest Grouping (Amendment) (EU Exit) Regulations 2018 (SI 2018/1299) reg.4 from 31 December 2020.

[143] European Economic Interest Grouping Regulations 1989 (SI 1989/638) regs 2 and 9.

[144] European Economic Interest Grouping Regulations 1989 (SI 1989/638) regs 18–19 and Sch.4. The Company Directors Disqualification Act 1986 also applies to EEIGs: reg.20.

[145] Companies House, *Statistical Tables on Companies Registration Activities 2019/20* (31 March 2020), Table B3.

State of the EU.[146] By the same token, a UK company became ineligible to continue as a member of an existing EEIG. The impact of this on EEIGs registered outside the UK was beyond the reach of UK law. However, UK law had to deal with the status of EEIGs registered in the UK, whose status was now in doubt. Following the amendments introduced by the European Economic Interest Grouping (Amendment) (EU Exit) Regulations 2018, any existing EEIGs with their official address within the UK automatically converted to a United Kingdom Economic Interest Grouping (UKEIG) on the day of the UK's departure.[147] The Registrar of Companies will have issued a certificate of conversion highlighting the change. Whilst much of the European Economic Interest Grouping Regulations 1989 continues to apply unchanged to UKEIGs, the most significant legal change has been the loss of any separate corporate personality for such entities.[148] It is doubtful that the status of being a UKEIG will be attractive to its members, since it will have lost its EEIG status in other Member States. Many will probably have taken advantage of the provisions in Regulation 2137/85 to transfer their registered address to another Member State before the UK's exit. Those which are mandatorily converted may well take steps to dissolve themselves, perhaps with the EU members forming a new EEIG which does not include a UK member. An existing or future EEIG with a registered address outside the UK, but with an established place of business within the jurisdiction, must continue to register its particulars with the Registrar of Companies within one month of establishing its business in the UK or face criminal penalties.[149] Neither the UKEIG nor the EEIG will receive significant further analysis.

The European Company (societas europaea or SE) and the UK Societas

1–040 In contrast to the EEIG, the European Company[150] is not intended for ancillary corporate activities but rather to facilitate the cross-border merger of companies and their mainstream activities in a manner consistent with the development of the EU's single market. That said, a cross-border merger did not necessarily need a European Company: an English company could have merged with, for example, a French company, so as to produce a resulting company that was either English or French (or indeed registered in some third state). This facility was provided by

[146] Regulation 2137/85 on the European Economic Interest Grouping [1985] OJ L199/1 art.4.

[147] European Economic Interest Grouping (Amendment) (EU Exit) Regulations 2018 (SI 2018/1299) reg.9, inserting new European Economic Interest Grouping Regulations 1989 (SI 1989/638) reg.9.

[148] European Economic Interest Grouping (Amendment) (EU Exit) Regulations 2018 (SI 2018/1299) reg.4.

[149] European Economic Interest Grouping Regulations 1989 (SI 1989/638) reg.12 (as amended by SI 2018/1299).

[150] There is also provision for a European Co-operative Society (SCE) (Regulation 1435/2003 [2003] OJ L207/1) and an accompanying directive on the involvement of employees (Directive 2003/72 [2003] OJ L207/25). These were initially transposed domestically by the European Cooperative Society Regulations 2006 (SI 2006/2078), but these have since been revoked in their entirety by the Financial Services (Miscellaneous) (Amendment) (EU Exit) Regulations 2019 (SI 2019/710) reg.25(a).

the EU's Cross-Border Mergers Directive,[151] which the UK's departure from the EU has rendered inoperable by UK companies. Alternatively, the English or French company could offer to buy the shares of the other company by a process known as a "takeover offer".[152] If the offer is accepted by the shareholders of the offeree company, that company becomes a subsidiary of the offeror company, but the important point for present purposes is that, in a takeover, there is no need for structural changes to the pre-existing companies: the two companies continue as before after the takeover, albeit with different shareholders in the target company (and perhaps also in the bidder). In this way, the English or French company could build up a string of subsidiaries operating in as many EU Member States as desired.

Given that the desired result could be achieved by other means, one might question what the European Company added. From a company law perspective, the advantages are mainly psychological. Where an English (or French) company has built up a group structure operated effectively across the EU through one or more takeovers, the corporate group's parent or lead company will be clearly identified as either English or French, as the case might be. Accordingly, those working for, or dealing with, a cross-border group might find it more acceptable if the group was formed at an EU level by a special form of incorporation, without being identified with any particular Member State.[153] There might even be some saving of transaction costs if all the existing national subsidiaries could be folded into a single SE. Accordingly, when the English and French companies merge, they might choose to do so by folding themselves into a newly formed SE or instead might choose to roll their various national subsidiaries into an SE, regardless of whether the parent company was English, French or itself a newly formed SE. **1–041**

Despite the SE being conceived as long ago as 1959,[154] the vision of a supra-national corporate form had been crucially compromised by the time that Regulation 2157/2001 came into force in October 2004.[155] Essential to the concept of an EU form of incorporation, divorced from the law of the Member States, is the notion that the EU legislation should provide a comprehensive code of company law rules for the SE. Unfortunately, Regulation 2157/2001 not only failed to regulate adjacent legal areas concerning corporate taxation, control of **1–042**

---

[151] Directive 2005/56 on cross-border mergers of limited liability companies [2005] OJ L310/10, repealed by Directive 2017/1132 on certain aspects of company law [2017] OJ L169/46. These were implemented into domestic law by the Companies (Cross-Border Mergers) Regulations 2007 (SI 2007/2974), but these have been revoked by the Companies, Limited Liability Partnerships and Partnerships (Amendment etc) (EU Exit) Regulations 2019 (SI 2019/348) reg.5(a). See further para.29–016.

[152] See Ch.28.

[153] This psychological argument can easily be over-stated, as there is no guarantee that the shareholdings or management of a SE will be spread equally across the Member States in which it operates.

[154] By Professor P. Sanders of the University of Rotterdam, although the French claim co-paternity.

[155] Regulation 2157/2001 on the Statute for a European company (SE) [2001] OJ L294/1. The European Company must use the abbreviation SE as either a prefix or suffix to its name and in the future other types of entity will not be able to avail themselves of this acronym: Regulation 2157/2001 art.11.

anti-competitive behaviour, intellectual property and insolvency,[156] but also relied heavily on the national laws of Member States for core company law concepts.[157] Regulation 2157/2001 only approaches the necessary level of detail for SEs in four areas: formation, transfer of an SE's registered office,[158] board structure and employee involvement.[159] In the latter two instances, the detailed rules vary according to the SE's contractual and constitutional choices, as well as the national origins of the companies forming the SE. Outside these four areas, the SE is governed by the law relating to public companies in its jurisdiction of registration.[160] Accordingly, there are at least as many different SEs as there are EU Member States, which fact is compounded by the absence of an EU registry for the SE and the consequent need for registration in a particular EU Member State. This is no doubt the correct technical position, given that the SE is to be embedded in the domestic law of its state of registration, but this does highlight that, for example, a German-registered SE looks rather different from a French-registered one.[161] The psychological advantages of having a non-national parent company were also significantly reduced.

1–043 Unlike a domestic company, the SE could only be formed by existing companies (or analogous entities), but not by natural persons. Moreover, consistently with the cross-border objectives of Regulation 2157/2001, those existing companies must already have a cross-border presence.[162] In such circumstances, the four methods of formation are: merger, formation of a SE holding company, formation of a SE subsidiary and transformation.[163]

1–044 Despite the fanfare surrounding the development of the SE, this legal form has had a limited impact in this jurisdiction. As at March 2020, there were only 47 SEs registered in the UK and the turnover of such companies appears relatively high, with 22 being formed in the last year and 14 closing over that same time frame.[164] With the UK's departure from the EU at the end of 2020, these figures will not now increase. First, it will no longer be possible to form any new

---

156 Regulation 2157/2001 art.63 and Preamble 20.

157 Regulation 2157/2001 art.15(1). For the necessary changes in the UK to apply the CA 2006 to SEs, see European Public Limited-Liability Company (Amendment) Regulations 2009 (SI 2009/2400).

158 See para.5–010.

159 For the position on employee involvement in board activities, see Directive 2001/86 supplementing the Statute for a European company with regard to the involvement of employees [2001] OJ L294/22, implemented by the European Public Limited-Liability Company (Employee Involvement) (Great Britain) Regulations 2009 (SI 2009/2401 and 2009/2402), as amended by SI 2018/1298.

160 Regulation 2157/2001 arts.9(1)(c)(ii) and 10. This is an automatic consequence of the Regulation's application, without the Member State having to provide for it or to identify the applicable parts of its domestic law. For this reason, Regulation 2157/2001, as adopted, is relatively short at 70 articles (with a further 17 articles in the Directive), whereas the initial proposal in 1975 contained 284 articles.

161 It has been unkindly remarked that the SE proposal started as a "sausage" and ended up as a "sausage skin".

162 Regulation 2157/2001 art.2(2)(b).

163 Regulation 2157/2001 art.2. In addition, an established SE can set up further SEs as subsidiaries: art.3(2).

164 Companies House, *Statistical Tables on Companies Registration Activities 2019/20* (31 March 2020), Table B3.

UK-registered SEs in the future, as it is a fundamental requirement of an SE that its registered office "be located within the Community".[165] Nor will UK-registered companies be able to form new SEs with companies registered in an EU Member State since the various methods of forming an SE are only available to companies "formed under the law of a Member State, with registered offices and head offices within the Community".[166] More complex is the position with respect to existing SEs. As Regulation 2157/2001 remains (for the time being at least) part of the EU law retained post-Brexit,[167] the legal status of existing SEs that are registered in an EU Member State will not change within either the domestic or EU legal orders. In relation to existing SEs registered in the UK, however, there is the difficulty that their registered office is no longer in the EU and so their legal status was in doubt. To address this problem, SEs still registered in the UK at the end of 2020 were automatically re-registered as a UK Societas and the company's designation will be changed from "SE" in its name to "UK Societas".[168] These changes are reflected in the "certificate of conversion" issued to the former SE. Most importantly, this change in status does not impact upon the UK Societas' legal personality, alter its rights or obligations or render defective any legal proceedings to which the entity was party.[169] It is thought that the status of a UK Societas will not be attractive to UK-registered SEs, because they will no longer have the status of an SE under Community law. It was expected therefore that UK-registered SEs would either have changed their country of registration to another EU Member State before the end of 2020 or will convert (as is possible) from a UK Societas to a UK Plc within a relatively short time (though they are not bound to take this step).

CONCLUSION

After a period of stability in the variety of legal forms on offer to those who wish to incorporate their businesses—before 2000, the last significant innovation had been the introduction of the private company at the beginning of the twentieth century—at least five significant new forms of incorporation have been made available in the last couple of decades: the limited liability partnership, the community interest company, the charitable incorporated organisation, the European Company (or *societas europaea*) and now the UK Societas. These innovations reflect different driving forces at the policy level. The LLP was a response to the desire of large partnerships to find a form of incorporation with limited liability in an increasingly litigious world, but that nevertheless provided the tax advantages and internal management flexibility traditionally associated with an ordinary partnership. The CIC reflected the Government's desire to encourage the deployment of entrepreneurial skills towards the solution of social **1–045**

[165] Regulation 2157/2001 art.7.

[166] Regulation 2157/2001 art.2(1).

[167] European Union (Withdrawal) Act 2018 s.3(2)(a).

[168] European Public Limited-Liability Company (Amendment etc.) (EU Exit) Regulations 2018 (SI 2018/1298) reg.8, inserting European Public Limited-Liability Company Regulations 2004 (SI 2004/2326) reg.12A.

[169] European Public Limited-Liability Company (Amendment etc.) (EU Exit) Regulations 2018 (SI 2018/1298) reg.97, inserting Regulation 2157/2001 art.AAA1.

problems; and the CIO a desire to involve private bodies in the delivery of welfare-state objectives. The SE reflected the goal of the European Commission and Union more generally to deepen the single European market by promoting cross-border mergers and the UK Societas is a consequence of the opposite desire on the part of the UK electorate. Of the three, only the SE produced an innovation in the core areas of company law, but, as noted, its impact has been limited.

CHAPTER 2

ADVANTAGES AND DISADVANTAGES OF INCORPORATION

LEGAL ENTITY DISTINCT FROM ITS MEMBERS

As indicated previously,[1] a fundamentally important consequence of incorporation—indeed the one from which all the other consequences flow—is that a company has a separate corporate personality, such that it is a legal entity distinct from its members. Accordingly, a company is capable of enjoying rights and being subject to duties that are not the same as those enjoyed or borne by its members. In other words, it has "legal personality" and is often described as being an *artificial person* in contrast with a human being, a *natural person*.[2] Such corporate personality only became an attribute of the ordinary joint stock company at a comparatively late stage in its development, and it was not until *Salomon v Salomon & Co Ltd*[3] at the end of the nineteenth century that its implications were fully grasped even by the courts. The decision in *Salomon*, which has been described as the "unyielding rock on which company law is constructed",[4] merits further attention. **2–001**

Salomon had carried on a prosperous business as a leather merchant for many years. In 1892, he decided to convert his business into a limited company. To this end, Salomon & Co Ltd was formed with Salomon, his wife and five of his children as members, and Salomon as managing director. The company purchased Salomon's business as a going concern for £39,000—"a sum which **2–002**

[1] See para.1–004.

[2] A company, even if it has only one member, is a "corporation aggregate" as opposed to the somewhat anomalous "corporation sole" in which an office (such as that of a bishop) is personified.

[3] *Salomon v Salomon & Co Ltd* [1897] A.C. 22 HL.

[4] *Prest v Petrodel Resources Ltd* [2013] UKSC 34; [2013] 2 A.C. 415 at [66] per Lord Neuberger.

represented the sanguine expectations of a fond owner rather than anything that can be called a business-like or reasonable estimate of value".[5] The new company paid the purchase-price by issuing £10,000 in debentures, conferring a charge over all the company's assets; issuing £20,000 in fully paid £1 shares; and paying the balance in cash. The result was that Salomon held 20,001 of the 20,007 issued shares, and each of the remaining six shares was held by a member of his family, apparently as Salomon's nominee. The company almost immediately ran into difficulties and only a year later the then holder of the debentures appointed a receiver over the company's assets, following which the company went into liquidation. The company's assets were sufficient to discharge the debentures, but nothing was left for the unsecured creditors.

2–003 In these circumstances, Vaughan Williams J and a strong Court of Appeal held that the whole incorporation transaction was contrary to the true intent of the companies legislation in force at that time, since the company was a mere sham, or an alias, agent, trustee or nominee for Salomon, who remained the real proprietor of the business. Accordingly, Salomon was liable to indemnify the company against its trading debts. The House of Lords, however, unanimously reversed the lower courts' decision. Their Lordships held that the company had been validly formed, since the legislation merely required seven members, each holding at least one share. The legislation said nothing about the shareholders needing to be independent, or that they should take a substantial interest in the undertaking, or that they should have a mind and will of their own, or that there should be anything like a balance of power in the company's constitution. Hence, the business belonged to the company and not to Salomon, and Salomon was *its* agent. In the blunt words of Lord Halsbury LC[6]:

> "Either the limited company was a legal entity or it was not. If it was, the business belonged to it and not to Mr Salomon. If it was not, there was no person and no thing to be an agent at all; and it is impossible to say at the same time that there is a company and there is not."

Alternatively, as Lord Macnaghten put the matter[7]:

> "The company is at law a different person altogether from the subscribers …; and, though it may be that after incorporation the business is precisely the same as it was before, and the same persons are managers, and the same hands receive the profits, the company is not in law the agent of the subscribers or trustee for them. Nor are the subscribers, as members, liable in any shape or form, except to the extent and in the manner provided by the Act."[8]

2–004 The *Salomon* case established that (1) provided the formalities of the relevant companies legislation are satisfied, a company will be validly incorporated, even

---

[5] *Salomon v Salomon & Co Ltd* [1897] A.C. 22 at 49 per Lord Macnaghten.

[6] *Salomon v Salomon & Co Ltd* [1897] A.C. 22 at 31.

[7] *Salomon v Salomon & Co Ltd* [1897] A.C. 22 at 51.

[8] For an early statutory recognition of the same principle, see the House of Commons (Disqualification) Act 1782, which disqualified those holding Government contracts from election to Parliament, but expressly provided (s.3) that the prohibition did not extend to members of incorporated companies holding such contracts.

if it is only a "one person" company[9]; and (2) the courts will be reluctant to treat a shareholder as personally liable for the debts of the company by "piercing the corporate veil".[10] Whereas acceptance of the former argument would have involved denying the separate legal personality of the company, the second could have been upheld without that consequence, though it would have involved undermining the concomitant of the separate legal personality concept, namely limited liability (which is considered further below).

The objection of the unsecured creditors in *Salomon* was based on the overvaluation of the business that was originally sold to the company in exchange for shares and debentures. Nowadays, in the case of a public company, the transferred business would have to be independently valued insofar as it was being used as consideration for shares,[11] whereas, in the case of a private company or even of debentures issued by a public company, the main protection for unsecured creditors lies in disclosure of the company's financial position through its financial reporting obligations.[12] Unlike some countries, English law has not developed any significant doctrine whereby loans to a company by its major shareholders are treated as equity in the company's liquidation. Even today, the unsecured creditor's best hope lies in the invalidation of a floating charge created within two years of a successful petition for the company's winding-up or administration,[13] or in the availability of assets constituting the "prescribed part" that would otherwise be subject to a floating charge.[14] The fundamental objection to the position in *Salomon* was that Salomon was able to give himself protection against the downside risks of his business failing by taking security over the company's assets by means of the debentures, whilst also taking the full benefit of any upside gains through his shareholding when the company was successful.[15] **2–005**

Of course, the *Salomon* decision does not mean that a promoter can with impunity defraud a company that he forms, or swindle his existing creditors. **2–006**

---

[9] The principle in *Salomon* has been taken to its logical conclusion with the recognition of "single-member" companies: see Directive 2009/102 on single-member private limited liability companies [2009] OJ L258/20. See also CA 2006 s.123(1).

[10] *Prest v Petrodel Resources Ltd* [2013] 2 A.C. 415 at [35], [77], [82], [100], [103]. See further Ch.7.

[11] For the valuation procedures applicable to shares issued in a public company in exchange for non-cash consideration, see paras 16–019 to 16–021. Since Salomon was the only beneficial shareholder, however, it made little difference to him whether he was issued with 20,000 or 10 shares in exchange for the business; the value of the shares in aggregate (no matter how many or how few) would have been the same, since they represented the economic value (if any) of the business. An independent valuation might not only protect creditors from being misled about the value of the assets contributed to the company, but might also enable any new shareholders to ensure their relative financial inputs are reflected in the relative size of their shareholdings.

[12] See generally Ch.22.

[13] IA 1986 s.245. See para.32–014.

[14] IA 1986 s.176A.

[15] Consider *Agnew v Inland Revenue Commissioner* [2001] UKPC 28; [2001] 2 A.C. 710 at [10]; *Re Spectrum Plus Ltd (In Liquidation)* [2005] UKHL 41; [2005] 2 A.C. 680 at [97] and [131]–[132]. In *Salomon*, it is possible to view Salomon as a victim, rather than the villain of the piece, as he had mortgaged his debentures in order to raise funds to support the tottering company. That said, the result would have been the same even if Salomon had not taken such steps, and even if he had been the only creditor to receive anything from the business, since this is inherent in the company's separate legal personality.

Indeed, it was argued in *Salomon* that the company was entitled to rescind the sale of the business in view of Salomon's wilful overvaluation, but the House of Lords held that there was no basis for rescission on the facts, since all the company's shareholders were fully conversant with the sale transaction's details and had effectively affirmed that deal. Had Salomon concealed the profit from his fellow shareholders, the position would have been different.[16] Nor was there any fraud on Salomon's pre-incorporation creditors that would have entitled Salomon's creditors or trustee-in-bankruptcy to set aside the sale,[17] since the purchase price received from the company was used by Salomon to pay off his creditors in full.

2–007 The *Salomon* decision opened up new vistas to company lawyers and the world of commerce: the decision finally establish the legality of the "one-person" company long before EC law required this[18]; it highlighted that incorporation was as readily available to the small private partnership and sole trader as to the large public company; and revealed that it was possible for a trader not merely to limit his liability to the money invested in the enterprise, but even to avoid any serious risk to that investment by subscribing for secured debentures rather than shares. At the same time, *Salomon* was considered shocking in permitting entrepreneurs to immunise themselves from ordinary business risks and the decision has subsequently been much criticised on that basis.[19] A partial justification for this position might be that those dealing with a limited company do so at their peril, since the publicity requirements surrounding such companies should mean that third parties know, or should know, what to expect.[20] In particular, a search against the information held by Companies House will reveal a company's filing history, its latest annual accounts and whether there are any charges over its assets.[21] Whilst such an argument might have some force in relation to creditors who are sufficiently sophisticated and deep-pocketed to adjust their positions ahead of time and to absorb the losses, it is much less convincing when creditors are unable to diversify the risks (such as employees) or unable to adjust their positions *ex ante* (such as certain tort victims). Nevertheless, the complete separation of the company and its members has never been doubted since the *Salomon* case and the separate corporate personality doctrine is what underpins much of the company's success as an effective business structure. Accordingly, it

[16] See further paras 10–141 to 10–142.

[17] IA 1986 ss.423–425.

[18] *Persad v Singh* [2017] UKPC 32; [2017] B.C.C. 779 at [20].

[19] See, for example, O. Kahn-Freund, "Some Reflections on Company Law Reform" (1944) 7 M.L.R. 54 (a thought-provoking article still well worth study) in which *Salomon* is described as a "calamitous decision". For a more positive assessment, see D. Goddard, "Corporate Personality—Limited Recourse and its Limits" in R. Grantham and C. Rickett (eds) *Corporate Personality in the Twentieth Century* (Oxford: Hart Publishing, 1998). On the rationales for limited liability, see paras 7–002 to 7–008.

[20] There are undoubtedly many who think that "Ltd" is an indication of size and stability (whilst this may be true of "Plc", it is certainly not the case with "Ltd"), rather than a warning that their claims will be confined to the company's assets (however few), with no access to the shareholders' property.

[21] The House of Lords in *Salomon* displayed no sympathy for those who do not search the public registers. As Lord Watson stated ([1897] A.C. 22 at 40): "A creditor who will not take the trouble to use the means which the statute provides for enabling him to protect himself must bear the consequences of his own negligence".

is unsurprising that the *Salomon* principle has subsequently been confirmed numerous times by the Privy Council,[22] House of Lords[23] and Supreme Court.[24] Indeed, rather than questioning the validity of the *Salomon* principle, recent judicial analysis has focused much more upon whether that principle should be treated as absolute in nature or subject to limited exceptions: in *VTB Capital Plc v Nutritek International Corp*,[25] Lord Neuberger left open the point whether any attempt to sidestep the *Salomon* principle would be "contrary to high authority, inconsistent with principle, and unnecessary to achieve justice". Whilst the importance and inviolability of the *Salomon* principle has now been reinforced in *Prest v Petrodel Resources Ltd*,[26] the Supreme Court has affirmed the possibility of "piercing the corporate veil", albeit in exceptionally limited circumstances.[27] This "piercing" jurisdiction will be considered subsequently.[28]

LIMITED LIABILITY

It follows from the fact that a corporation is a separate person that its members are not as such liable for its debts.[29] Accordingly, the company's members will be completely free from any personal liability for that company's debts, as well as other forms of corporate liability, whether contractual, tortious or equitable. The company alone, and not its members, is liable to discharge the corporate obligations. The significance of this position is that, when a company enters insolvent liquidation, the liquidator (acting on behalf of the company) would likely seek contributions from the company's members so as to bring the **2–008**

[22] *Lee v Lee's Air Farming Ltd* [1961] A.C. 12 PC at 25–27; *Kuwait Asia Bank EC v National Mutual Life Nominees Ltd* [1991] 1 A.C. 187 PC at 196; *La Générale des Carrières et des Mines v FG Hemisphere Associates LLC* [2012] UKPC 27; [2012] 2 Lloyd's Rep. 443 at [22]–[24]; *Persad v Singh* [2017] B.C.C. 779 at [20].

[23] *Woolfson v Strathclyde RC*, 1978 S.L.T. 159 HL at 161; *Daimler Co Ltd v Continental Tyre and Rubber Co (Great Britain) Ltd* [1916] 2 A.C. 307 HL at 338 and 350; *Rainham Chemical Works Ltd (In Liquidation) v Belvedere Fish Guano Co Ltd* [1921] 2 A.C. 465 HL at 475–476; *Dimbleby & Sons Ltd v National Union of Journalists* [1984] 1 W.L.R. 427 HL at 435; *Williams and Humbert Ltd v W&H Trade Marks (Jersey) Ltd* [1986] A.C. 368 HL at 429; *Standard Chartered Bank v Pakistan National Shipping Corp (No.2)* [2002] UKHL 43; [2003] 1 A.C. 959 at [37]; *Stone & Rolls Ltd (In Liquidation) v Moore Stephens (A Firm)* [2009] UKHL 39; [2009] 1 A.C. 1391 HL at [160]–[161] and [220].

[24] *Re Paycheck Services 3 Ltd* [2010] UKSC 51; [2010] 1 W.L.R. 2793 at [42]; *Benedetti v Sawiris* [2013] UKSC 50; [2014] A.C. 938 at [222]; *VTB Capital Plc v Nutritek International Corp* [2013] UKSC 5, [2013] 2 A.C. 337 at [122] and [138]; *Prest v Petrodel Resources Ltd* [2013] 2 A.C. 415 at [8], [66], [90] and [106]; *Bilta (UK) Ltd (In Liquidation) v Nazir* [2015] UKSC 23; [2016] A.C. 1 at [183]–[184]; *Singularis Holdings Ltd (In Liquidation) v Daiwa Capital Markets Europe Ltd* [2019] UKSC 50; [2019] 3 W.L.R. 997 at [27]–[28]; *Marex Financial Ltd v Sevilleja* [2020] UKSC 31; [2020] 3 W.L.R. 255 at [23], [102], [133], [188].

[25] *VTB Capital Plc v Nutritek International Corp* [2013] 2 A.C. 337 at [126] and [130].

[26] *Prest v Petrodel Resources Ltd* [2013] 2 A.C. 415 at [8], [66], [90] and [106].

[27] *Prest v Petrodel Resources Ltd* [2013] 2 A.C. 415 at [34]–[35]. See also *Antonio Gramsci Shipping Corp v Lembergs* [2013] EWCA Civ 730; [2013] I.L.Pr. 36.

[28] See Ch.7.

[29] This sentence was quoted and relied on by Kerr LJ in *JH Rayner (Mincing Lane) Ltd v Department of Trade* [1989] Ch. 72 CA (Civ Div) at 176 as an accurate statement of English law, although (as his Lordship pointed out) it is not accurate in relation to most Civil Law countries—including Scotland, so far as partnerships are concerned—or to international law: ibid. at 176–183.

company's assets up to the level needed to meet its creditors' claims. In the case of companies limited by shares or by guarantee,[30] however, the members' obligation to contribute to the insolvent company's assets is limited (hence, by transfer, the term "limited company") and is not in any sense open-ended. Where a company is limited by shares, each member is liable to contribute (when called upon to do so) the full nominal value of the shares held insofar as this has not already been paid by the shareholder in question or any prior holder of those shares (which will normally be the case).[31] In the case of a guarantee company, each current member (or anyone who was a member in the preceding year[32]) is liable to contribute a specified (normally modest) amount to the company's assets in the event of its being wound up.[33] In effect, without being directly liable to the company's creditors, the member is in both cases a limited guarantor of the company's liabilities, since the company is able to compel a member to contribute to the discharge of its obligations up to the limit of the member's guarantee or up to the amount unpaid on the particular member's shares. In the more usual case where the company's shares are all fully-paid, however, no further liability will arise on the part of the member in the absence of specific statutory provision to the contrary. Such provisions are rare.[34]

2–009 In relation to the issue of limited liability, other forms of association may be usefully contrasted with the position applicable to companies limited by shares or guarantee. First, an unincorporated association, not being a legal person, cannot itself be liable for the debts contracted on its behalf. Accordingly, it is only the association's actual officials (or the association's individual members if those officials have actual or apparent authority to bind them) who will be bound by the obligations purported to be concluded on that association's behalf. Whichever individuals are bound, they will be liable to the full extent of their assets, unless they have expressly or impliedly restricted their responsibility to the extent of the association's funds, as its officials may well do. Accordingly, the extent to which an unincorporated association's member will be liable depends on the membership terms set out in the association's constitution. Indeed, in the case of clubs and presumably most learned and scientific societies, there will generally be an implied term that the members are not personally liable for obligations incurred on the club's behalf. Secondly, each partner in a partnership (which, as discussed previously,[35] is an association carrying on business for gain) acts as an agent for all the other partners, so that acts done by any one partner in "carrying on in the normal way business of the kind carried on by the firm" bind all the partners.[36] Only if the third party dealing with the partnership knows or has notice of the limitation placed on the partner's authority (or "does not know or believe him to be a partner") will the other members escape liability.[37] Moreover,

[30] See paras 1–008 to 1–011.
[31] IA 1986 s.74(2)(d).
[32] IA 1986 s.74(2)(a).
[33] IA 1986 s.74(3).
[34] See Ch.19.
[35] See paras 1–002 to 1–003.
[36] Partnership Act 1890 s.5. As this applies equally to Scotland, it largely negatives the consequence of a Scottish firm being a separate person.
[37] Partnership Act 1890 ss.5 and 8.

any attempt to restrict the partners' liability to partnership funds by inserting such a provision into the partnership agreement will be ineffective, even if known to the creditors[38]; the partners can only restrict their financial liability in respect of authorised acts by concluding an express agreement to that effect with the creditor concerned.[39] This explains the impetus for the limited liability partnership,[40] which is essentially an incorporated legal entity with the internal flexibility of a partnership, but the advantage of limited liability. Thirdly, in the case of an unlimited company,[41] the default position is that its members are obliged to contribute to the assets of the company up to the total amount of liabilities owed by the company to its creditors.[42]

Even in the context of companies limited by shares or guarantee, the doctrine of separate legal personality only operates to shield members (operating in that particular capacity) from personal liability in the event of the company's liquidation to the extent that the member in question has not given some personal written guarantee of the company's liabilities or the company's constitution does not contain express provision to the contrary. Each of these qualifications on limited liability will be considered further. **2–010**

As regards the first qualification, members who become involved in the management of the company's business will not be able to avail themselves of limited liability in relation to their conduct as directors and will not necessarily be protected from personal liability by the notion of the company's separate legal personality. The extent to which directors, in carrying out their activities and duties on behalf of the company, may be personally liable (or make the company liable) to third parties for contractual, tortious or equitable obligations will depend upon the operation of the ordinary principles relating to agency, vicarious liability, voluntary assumption of responsibility, attribution and identification (in criminal law). These are matters discussed further below.[43] **2–011**

As regards the second qualification, it is possible (albeit unusual) that a company's shares were issued to members on the basis that they should be required to contribute to the company's assets in the event of its insolvency. In such circumstances, the company's creditors would be entitled to look to its shareholders for satisfaction. Ordinarily though, the broad effect of the courts recognising the company's separate legal personality (and consequently its members' limited liability) is at first sight a legal regime that is very unfavourable to the company's potential creditors, which is a situation that they will naturally seek to readjust by contract in their favour, so far as this lies in their power. For commercial lenders, such as banks, there are a number of possibilities that can be used separately or cumulatively. Apart from the obvious commercial response of charging a higher interest rate on loans to entities whose members have limited liability, such lenders may seek to sidestep the barrier created by the limited **2–012**

[38] *Re Sea, Fire and Life Assurance Co* (1854) 3 De G.M. & G. 459 Ct of Chancery.

[39] *Hallett v Dowdall* (1852) 21 Q.B. 2 QB.

[40] Limited Liability Partnerships Act 2000, discussed in para.1–004.

[41] See para.1–027.

[42] IA 1986 s.74(1).

[43] See further Ch.8.

liability principle by demanding personal guarantees from the company's managers or shareholders as the price for lending the funds in the first place. In addition, these guarantees may be secured on the guarantor's *personal* assets. Further or alternatively to taking personal security from those standing behind the company, a large lender may seek to improve the priority of its claim by taking security against the *company's* assets. As considered further below, nineteenth-century chancery practitioners were quick to respond to this need by creating a flexible and all-embracing form of security (the floating charge) to supplement the traditional fixed charge that was already available.

2–013 Whilst these self-help remedies may provide a ready solution to the limited liability problem for sophisticated lenders, this may not be practicable for trade creditors or employees.[44] Even in the case of large commercial lenders, there is a real danger that, as the company's financial position deteriorates, the company's controllers will take risks with the company's capital that were not within the parties' contemplation when the loan was arranged. For these reasons, as the legislature has not overturned the *Salomon* principle and as the one-person company is now expressly recognised by domestic law through the influence of EU law,[45] the CA 2006 and IA 1986 are full of provisions that are only really explicable as responses to some of the difficulties created by the concept of limited liability. In particular, the extensive publicity and disclosure obligations placed upon limited liability companies,[46] the wrongful trading provisions,[47] and the expanded provisions on the disqualification of directors, especially on grounds of unfitness,[48] must all be seen in this light.

PROPERTY

2–014 One obvious advantage of the company's separate legal personality is that it enables the company's property to be more clearly distinguished from that of its members. In an unincorporated association, the society's property is usually the joint equitable property of its members, although the members' rights to that property differ from their distinct rights to their own personal property, since members must deal with the former type of property according to the association's rules and no individual member can claim any particular asset.[49]

[44] Whilst employees are protected to some degree by virtue of their statutory preferential treatment in a liquidation (see IA 1986 ss.175, 386 and Sch.6), unsecured creditors are generally considered to have the worst of all worlds. Not only does limited liability normally stop unsecured creditors from suing the shareholders or directors, but the commercial lenders' fixed and floating charges will often soak up all of the company's available assets. The unsecured creditors' position has been improved by virtue of the "prescribed part": see IA 1986 s.176A.

[45] Directive 89/667 on single-member private limited liability companies [1989] OJ L395/40, now codified in Directive 2009/102 on single-member private limited liability companies [2009] OJ L258/20 and implemented by CA 2006 s.123(1).

[46] See Ch.22, although the directors of unlimited liability companies are not normally required to deliver accounts and reports to the Registrar of Companies for general publication: see CA 2006 s.448(1).

[47] IA 1986 ss.214–215, discussed in paras 19–005 to 19–006.

[48] Company Directors Disqualification Act 1986 s.6, discussed in Ch.20.

[49] *Neville Estates Ltd v Madden* [1962] Ch. 832 Ch D.

The holding of property by an unincorporated association is, however, complicated by the fact that the nature of the transaction depends upon the proper interpretation of the transferor's intention, the precise nature of the association and the surrounding circumstances. Similarly, in the case of a trading partnership, some legal complexity surrounds the true nature of the partners' interests in particular property,[50] as well as creditors' claims against that property.[51] In contrast, following incorporation, corporate property belongs to the company alone, and its members have no direct proprietary rights to the corporate property, but merely property in the form of a "share" that confers certain rights against the company as a separate legal entity.[52] Accordingly, a change in the company's membership leaves the company unaffected, whereas this would cause inevitable dislocation in a partnership; whilst the departure of a partner will require some division of the partnership's assets, a company's property will remain untouched by the transfer of a particular member's share and no realisation or division of that property will be necessary.

Identification of the corporate property is not the only advantage of employing a company; the separate corporate personality also enables that property to be segregated (or partitioned) from the members' personal assets. Thus, the claims of the company's creditors will be against the corporate property only and the claims of the members' personal creditors against that particular member's own property. Accordingly, neither set of creditors is in competition with the other; and each only has to monitor dispositions of the assets against which its claims lie.[53] **2–015**

SUING AND BEING SUED

Closely allied to the proprietary question are issues relating to legal actions, since a corporate cause of action is simply a type of intangible property vested in the company's name. Whilst the problems associated with unincorporated associations (such as clubs and learned societies) suing and being sued have long bedevilled the English common law,[54] no statutory provision has yet been introduced to deal with this: sometimes the association's committee (or other agents) may be personally liable or authorised to sue; otherwise, the only alternative course is a "representative action", whereby one or more persons may sue or be sued on behalf of all the interested parties in the association.[55] Resort to **2–016**

---

[50] Partnership Act 1890 ss.20–22. See also *Re Fuller's Contract* [1933] Ch. 652 Ch D.

[51] Partnership Act 1890 s.23. See also Insolvent Partnerships Order 1994 (SI 1994/2421), as amended.

[52] "Shareholders are not, in the eye of the law, part owners of the undertaking. The undertaking is something different from the totality of the shareholdings": see *Short v Treasury Commissioners* [1948] 1 K.B. 116 CA at 122 per Evershed LJ; affirmed [1948] A.C. 534 HL.

[53] R. Kraakman and H. Hansmann, "The Essential Role of Organizational Law" (2000) 110 Yale L.J. 387.

[54] Problems of suit seem to have underlain the former restriction of the number of partners to a maximum of 20: see para.1–003.

[55] For the application of this procedural device in the context of unincorporated associations, see *Artistic Upholstery Ltd v Art Forma (Furniture) Ltd* [1999] F.S.R. 311 Ch D; *Howells v The Dominion Insurance Company Ltd* [2005] EWHC 552 (Admin); *Chandra v Mayor* [2017] 1 W.L.R. 729 Ch D.

this procedure is only available when a number of conditions are satisfied,[56] but these are not only ill-defined and inadequately explored, but they also remain somewhat obscure and difficult. Whilst this creates difficulties for an association wishing to enforce its rights (or, more properly, its members' rights), there is a corresponding advantage for the association seeking to evade its liabilities.[57] Many of these difficulties have now been solved for partnerships by allowing the firm to sue or be sued in the partnership's name. Accordingly, partnerships raise no significant difficulties regarding the pure mechanics of suit, although there may still be complications in enforcing judgments against partnerships.[58]

None of the above difficulties arise when an incorporated company is suing or being sued: as a legal person, a company can take action to enforce its legal rights and can be sued for breach of its legal duties.

PERPETUAL SUCCESSION

2–017 One of the key advantages of an artificial person is that, unlike a natural person, it is not susceptible to "the thousand natural shocks that flesh is heir to"[59]: the vicissitudes of the flesh have no direct effect on the disembodied company,[60] as a company cannot become incapacitated by illness, mental or physical, and it has not (or need not have) an allotted span of life.[61] This is not to say that the death or incapacity of the company's human members or managers might not cause the company considerable difficulties. The death, imprisonment or insanity of all the company's directors might be inconvenient, but will not be calamitous for the company provided that the director is removed promptly; the director may be the company's brains, but lobectomy is a simpler operation on a legal person than a

---

[56] Civil Procedure Rules 1998 r.19.6. The requirements of r.19.6 are strictly interpreted: see *Emerald Supplies Ltd v British Airways Plc* [2010] EWCA Civ 1284; [2011] C.P. Rep. 14.

[57] "An unincorporated association has certain advantages when litigation is desired against them": see *Bloom v National Federation of Discharged Soldiers* (1918) 35 T.L.R. 50 CA at 51 per Scrutton LJ.

[58] Partnership Act 1890 s.23.

[59] W. Shakespeare, *Hamlet* (1603), Act III, Scene 1.

[60] In *Stepney Corp v Osofsky* [1937] 3 All E.R. 289 CA at 291, Greer LJ stated that a corporate body has "no soul to be saved or body to be kicked". This epigram is believed to be of considerable antiquity. G. Williams, *Criminal Law: The General Part*, 2nd edn (London: Steven & Sons), p.856, has traced it back to Lord Thurlow and an earlier variation to Coke, cf. the decree of Pope Innocent IV forbidding the excommunication of corporations because, having neither minds nor souls, they could not sin: see C.T. Carr, *The General Principles of the Law of Corporations* (Cambridge: CUP, 1905), p.73. In *Rolloswin Investments v Chromolit Portugal Cutelarias e Produtos Metalicos SARL* [1970] 1 W.L.R. 912 QBD, it was held that, since a company was incapable of public worship, it was not a "person" within the meaning of the Sunday Observance Act 1677, so that a contract concluded on a Sunday was not void (the court was unaware that the Act had already been repealed by the Statute Law (Repeals) Act 1969). "A company cannot eat or sleep" (see *De Beers Consolidated Mines Ltd v Howe (Surveyor of Taxes)* [1906] A.C. 455 HL at 458) nor can it appear on television as an entertainer (see *Newstead (Inspector of Taxes) v Frost* [1978] 1 W.L.R. 1441 CA (Civ Div) at 1447).

[61] A company's duration may be fixed in its articles (see IA 1986 s.84(1)(a)), but this is rarely done in practice. Where this is done, the company would not automatically terminate upon the expiration of the term, but the expiration of the term does provide a ground on which the members may by ordinary resolution wind the company up voluntarily. It is otherwise with chartered companies.

natural one. Similarly, the death of a member leaves the company unmoved,[62] even if there are too few surviving members to hold a meeting,[63] and it should be irrelevant that a bulk of members have become enemy aliens.[64] Whilst the company's members may come and go, the company can go on forever.

Whilst unincorporated associations do not share this advantage of perpetual succession, the difficulties can be ameliorated by the use of a trust (although this can itself be problematic if the relevant trust is established for a non-charitable purpose). Indeed, it is arguable that the trust never functioned at its simplest until it was able to enlist the aid of its own child, the incorporated company, to act as a trust corporation with perpetual succession. If the association's property is vested in trustees, the death, disability or retirement of an individual member/beneficiary will be unproblematic, although in such circumstances the association's constitution may prevent the member, the deceased member's estate or his representative from taking a share of the assets (which is the usual position with a club or learned society). Similarly, the death or incapacity of the trustees is nothing more than a nuisance and can be solved by appointing replacement trustees.[65] In contrast, upon the retirement or death of a partner in a partnership, the default rule is that the partnership is automatically dissolved, in the absence of agreement to the contrary.[66] In such circumstances, the partner's estate will be entitled to be paid his or her share. Whilst it is possible to avoid the resulting dislocation to the firm's business by inserting special clauses in the articles of partnership that provide a formula for the valuation and deferred payment of the departing partner's share, the difficulties cannot be eradicated altogether. **2–018**

The above problems do not arise with an incorporated company. Whilst the member of a company or his estate is not generally entitled to be paid out by the company,[67] if the member (or a personal representative, trustee in bankruptcy, or receiver) wishes to realise the value of his or her shares, these can be sold, whereupon the purchaser will (on entry in the share register) replace the former holder as member. This is not, however, always as straightforward as it sounds. The original member might not be able to find a purchaser at all, especially one who meets any constitutional restrictions that might be imposed on transfer,[68] or who has sufficient free capital to purchase the shares. Nowadays, the position has been improved by the fact that a company may, subject to stringent conditions, purchase its own shares,[69] as has long been permitted in other jurisdictions. **2–019**

---

[62] During the Second World War, all the members of one private company, while in general meeting, were killed by a bomb, but the company survived (not even a nuclear bomb could have destroyed it!). See also *Re Noel Tedman Holding Pty Ltd* (1967) Qd.R. 561 Qd Sup Ct where the only two members were killed in a road accident.

[63] This is less problematic nowadays in light of CA 2006 s.318(1).

[64] cf. *Daimler Co Ltd v Continental Tyre and Rubber Co* [1916] 2 A.C. 307.

[65] Trustee Act 1925 ss.36 and 41; Trusts of Land and Appointment of Trustees Act 1996 ss.19–20.

[66] Partnership Act 1890 s.33(1).

[67] See Ch.17.

[68] For an unsuccessful attempt to use the unfair prejudice jurisdiction to secure the return to the shareholder's estate of the capital represented by his shares, see *Re Company (No.004475 of 1982)* [1983] Ch. 178 Ch D (discussed in *Re A Company* [1986] B.C.L.C. 382).

[69] See paras 17–011 to 17–022.

2–020 The continuing existence of a company, irrespective of changes in its membership or its management, is also helpful in other ways. When an individual sells an incorporated business to another, difficult questions may arise regarding the purchaser's performance of existing contracts,[70] the possibility of assigning personal rights,[71] and the continuing validity of agreements made with customers who are ignorant of the change of proprietorship.[72] Similar problems may arise when altering a partnership's make-up.[73] In contrast, as the sale of an incorporated business merely involves the transfer of shares, none of these difficulties arises: the company remains the proprietor of the business, remains liable to perform the existing contracts and retains their benefit, as well as being capable of entering into future agreements. Accordingly, no legal difficulties concerning vicarious performance, assignments or mistaken identity arise.

2–021 Although control of a company's business may change by its shareholders transferring their shares to new investors, it does not necessarily follow that the company will always choose this method of effecting a change in control. The company's directors or shareholders could decide instead to sell the company's underlying business to the new investors, who, perhaps, may form their own company to acquire the business. In this type of transaction, the transferring company (rather than its shareholders) will be left holding the consideration received on the sale of its business. Such an asset-based transfer method is likely to be particularly attractive to the transferring company if it is divesting itself of only part of its business (although a transfer of control by sale of shares may still be possible if the relevant part of the business is held in a separate subsidiary company). When a company disposes of the whole or part of its business (as opposed to the shareholders deciding to transfer their shares), similar difficulties arise as mentioned above in relation to an unincorporated association selling its business.[74] Accordingly, whilst a company may choose to transfer its business or assets, a company limited by shares (but not one limited by guarantee) is more likely to see changes of control occurring by way of share-transfer.

---

[70] *Robson v Drummond* (1831) 2 B. & Ad. 303 KB; cf. *British Waggon Co v Lea & Co* (1880) 5 Q.B.D. 149 QBD.

[71] *Griffith v Tower Publishing Co Ltd* [1897] 1 Ch. 21 Ch D (publishing agreement held not assignable); *Kemp v Baerselman* [1906] 2 K.B. 604 CA (agreement non-assignable if one party's obligation depends on the other's "personal requirements"); *Crane Co v Wittenborg A/S* unreported 21 December 1999 CA (Civ Div) at [26]–[32]; cf. *Tolhurst v Associated Portland Cement Manufacturers (1900) Ltd* [1902] 2 K.B. 660 CA.

[72] *Boulton v Jones* (1857) 2 Hurl. & N. 564 Ex Ct (discussed in *Shogun Finance Ltd v Hudson* [2004] 1 A.C. 919 HL at [94]–[97], [103], [126] and [154]).

[73] See *Brace v Calder* [1895] 2 Q.B. 253 CA, where the retirement of two partners was held to operate as the wrongful dismissal of a manager. See further *Briggs v Oates* [1990] I.C.R. 472 Ch D at 478–481; *Rose v Dodd (formerly t/a Reynolds & Dodds Solicitors)* [2005] EWCA Civ 957 at [44]–[46]. For a similar position with respect to guarantees, see Partnership Act 1890 s.18. In practice, such difficulties are often avoided by implying a novation.

[74] See para.2–020.

TRANSFERABLE SHARES

By separating (or partitioning) the underling business and assets (owned by the company) from the shares in the entity (owned by its members), incorporation greatly facilitates the transfer of the members' interests. Approximately the same legal ends could be achieved (without formally incorporating a company) through a trust coupled with an agreement in a deed of settlement for the transfer of interests under the trust. Even after the transfer of the interest under the trust, however, the beneficiary-member will remain liable for the firm's debts incurred whilst he or she was a beneficiary-member (although this assumes that there would be personal liability in the first place, which is not always the case). This ongoing liability (i.e. the absence of limited liability associated with companies) means that opportunities to transfer are, in practice, much restricted. Similarly, a partner in a partnership has a proprietary interest that can be assigned (subject to the partnership deed's terms), but that assignment does not divest the assignor of his or her status or liability as a partner; the assignment merely affords the assignee the right to receive whatever dividends the firm distributes in respect of the assignor's partnership share.[75] An assignee will only replace an assignor as partner if all the other partners agree,[76] and the assignor will not be relieved of any existing partnership liabilities unless the existing partners and the partnership's creditors agree, expressly or impliedly, to the release.[77] 2–022

With an incorporated company, the transfer of a member's interest is usually straightforward in both legal and practical terms. Where a company's liability is limited by shares, these shares constitute items of property that are freely transferable, in the absence of express provision to the contrary. Accordingly, the replacement of one person as member with another is largely a matter between the parties themselves,[78] although there are frequently constitutional provisions in private companies conferring discretion on directors whether or not to register a particular share transfer.[79] 2–023

Besides the directors' discretion to refuse registration to a particular share transfer, the power to transfer shares may also be subject to additional constitutional restrictions. For private companies, some form of restriction on share transfers was formerly essential in order to satisfy the then current statutory definition; although this is no longer a statutory requirement, it may still be desirable if a company is to retain its character as an incorporated private partnership. In practice, these constitutional restrictions are often so stringent as to make transferability largely illusory. Nor does the CA 2006 outlaw restrictions on share transferability in public companies, although such restrictions (except as regards partly paid shares) are unusual, and are prohibited by the Listing Rules if 2–024

[75] Partnership Act 1890 s.31.

[76] Partnership Act 1890 s.24(7).

[77] Partnership Act 1890 ss.17(2)–(3).

[78] CA 2006 s.544. Whilst a member does not generally have any continuing liability post-transfer, a shareholder will continue to be liable for calls if liquidation follows within a year of the transfer and the shares were either not fully paid up or were redeemed or re-purchased out of capital: see IA 1986 ss. 74 and 76. See further para.17–017.

[79] Companies (Model Articles) Regulations 2008 (SI 2008/3229) Sch.1 art.26(5).

the shares are to be marketed and traded on the Stock Exchange.[80] Whilst on their face, these constitutional restrictions appear similar to the constraints upon partners seeking to transfer their partnership interest, there is a fundamental difference: in a partnership, the default position is that the partnership interest is non-transferable unless there is express agreement permitting this and the various legal and practical hurdles are overcome; whereas, in a company, the statutory default position is that shares are freely transferable in the absence of express restriction.[81] This difference is explicable by virtue of the fact that a partnership involved an essentially personal relationship between the partners, whereas this is often absent between the members of a company. Certainly, in a public company, the relationship between members is essentially impersonal and financial with there being little justification for restricting changes in membership. That said, the constitutional ability to restrict share transfers recognises that some private companies are functionally incorporated partnerships, so that a partnership-based approach to transferability can be maintained.[82]

MANAGEMENT UNDER A BOARD STRUCTURE

2–025 A further important feature of the company is that it provides a structure for the pursuit of larger and riskier endeavours by allowing many investors to participate by purchasing shares, whilst separating that investment function from the task of managing the company, which is delegated to a smaller group of expert managers who partly constitute (and are partly supervised by) a board of directors. This separation of (what is conventionally, but controversially, termed) the company's "ownership" (or shareholding) from its "control" (or management) is a feature of large companies and accordingly it is critical that company law should deal with the consequences of such separation. By contrast, as with share transferability, this separation is not a feature of small companies, where "owners" and "managers" are often the same (or substantially the same). As indicated previously,[83] the corporate machinery for separating these roles may be unduly cumbersome for small companies, but it remains crucial to the efficient functioning of large companies.

2–026 The legal implications of separating "ownership" and "control" were first explored in the US by Adolf Berle and Gardiner Means,[84] who highlighted the revolutionary change this division had for our traditional conceptions regarding the nature of property. If a person invests in traditional forms of wealth-generating property (such as a farm or a shop) he or she becomes tied to that property and the business thereon. The modern public company provides a new form of property, in which there is little relationship between the "owner" and the

[80] Listing Rules LR.2.2.4.

[81] CA 2006 s.544(1).

[82] The courts have shown a welcome tendency to recognise the functional equivalence between partnerships and some closely-held companies: see *Ebrahimi v Westbourne Galleries Ltd* [1973] A.C. 360 HL; *O'Neill v Phillips* [1999] 1 W.L.R. 1092 HL at 1099.

[83] See para.1–028. See further Ch.12.

[84] A.A. Berle and G.C. Means, *The Modern Corporation and Private Property* (New York: Macmillan Company, 1933), reprinted in 1968 with a new preface.

relevant business; indeed, the "owner" is no longer tied to the business, but can realise the value of his investment in that business whenever needed by selling shares, and without removing the business assets that the enterprise will require indefinitely. Nowadays, most large businesses, at least in the US and the UK, are run not by individual entrepreneurs, but rather by large public companies, in which many individuals have rights as shareholders (and property rights in the form of shares) arising from their direct or indirect capital contributions. After home ownership, direct or indirect[85] investment in companies probably constitutes the most important single item of property for most people, and yet whether this property proves profitable for its "owners" no longer depends on their own energy and initiative, but rather on that of the management from which they are divorced. The modern shareholder in a public company is no longer a "quasi-partner", but simply a supplier of capital who can "cash out" by selling his or her interest to another investor—"[t]he separation of ownership from management and control in the corporate system has performed this essential step in securing liquidity."[86]

Even when, as is increasingly the case, the shareholding in a large company is concentrated in the hands of one or more institutional shareholders (such as pension funds and insurance companies), shareholder participation in management remains discontinuous or episodic, despite the more significant potential for such intervention than in the case of widely dispersed individual shareholders. Indeed, any such participation is usually precipitated by some crisis in the company's affairs, rather than as a means of managing the company on a day-to-day basis.[87]

Even though the company's board (especially the "managing director" or the "chief executive officer") is the driving force behind a large company's operations, the CA 2006 (unlike its continental counterparts) says comparatively little about the board's structure and functions. There is certainly a statutory requirement that a company have directors, with two directors being required for public companies and a single director being necessary for a private one.[88] Accordingly, whilst much of the CA 2006 imposes administrative burdens on the directors and operates on the assumption that a board of directors exists, the precise composition, structure and functions of the board are largely left for companies themselves to determine in their articles of association[89] or even through mere corporate practice. That said, where the relevant company is listed, **2–027**

---

[85] For most people, their investment is indirect (as shares are increasingly held through intermediaries) and even unconscious (as shares are often an investment class purchased by occupational pension schemes).

[86] A.A. Berle and G.C. Means, *The Modern Corporation and Private Property* (New York: Macmillan Company, 1933) at p.284.

[87] P. Davies, "Institutional Investors in the United Kingdom" in D. Prentice and P. Holland (eds), *Contemporary Issues in Corporate Governance* (Oxford: Oxford University Press, 1993). Whereas previously institutional investors would simply divest themselves of underperforming investments, increasingly greater levels of engagement are expected on the part of institutional investors: see Financial Reporting Council, *The UK Stewardship Code* (2020).

[88] CA 2006 s.154.

[89] See Ch.9.

the possibility of such private ordering has become significantly qualified by the development in recent decades of the UK Corporate Governance Code and its predecessors.[90]

2–028 In light of this "hands off" approach evident in the CA 2006, is it still possible to say that English company law provides the machinery required for the separation of ownership and control to flourish? The answer would appear to be affirmative. The most obvious example of such machinery lies in the duties originally created by the common law, but now reformulated in the CA 2006, that require the directors to exercise their corporate powers competently and loyally in the best interests of the company (which is normally equated with the shareholders' best interests, although these have increasingly to be balanced against a wider set of concerns).[91] Accordingly, one might say that English company law's approach to regulating the separation of "ownership" and "control" is to allow companies the maximum freedom in deciding upon the division of powers between shareholders and board, as well as the board's functions, but then to regulate the manner in which the board discharges those functions. Such an approach assumes, however, that the shareholders have a well-functioning forum in which to challenge the directors' decision-making[92] or that they have effective tools with which to hold the directors to account when they fall short.[93] As will be considered further below, neither proposition represents an absolute truth. It is for this reason that there has increasingly been reliance on mechanisms other than the enforcement of directors' legal duties as a means of control: the soft law standards found in the UK Corporate Governance Code nowadays seek to control the company's directors through alternative oversight mechanisms (whether non-executive directors or independent sub-committees) or by enhancing scrutiny of certain inherently conflicted decisions, such as executive pay.[94]

These issues are, however, for consideration in later chapters. For present purposes, it is important to note the fact that in large companies there are two decision-making bodies (the shareholders in general meeting and the board of directors), and that, in terms of management functions, the board is invariably the more important organ.

Borrowing

2–029 The discussion so far has only focused on the advantages or disadvantages that flow inevitably or naturally from a company's incorporation. There are, however, important incidental benefits in terms of borrowing and taxation.

2–030 At first sight, it might be considered that a sole trader, or partners in a partnership, would find it easier to borrow funds from external lenders due to their being personally liable. In practice, however, this is not necessarily the case, since a company is often able to grant a more effective charge over its assets to secure

[90] See paras 9–016 to 9–020.

[91] CA 2006 s.172(1), discussed in detail in Ch.10.

[92] See Ch.12.

[93] See Chs.14–15.

[94] See paras 9–016 to 9–020.

the proposed borrowing. The ingenuity of equity practitioners in the nineteenth century led to the evolution of an unusual, but highly beneficial, type of security known as the floating charge: in essence, the charge "floats" over a class (or even all) of the company's assets, without preventing the chargor from disposing of those assets in the usual course of business (at least until some event occurs that causes the charge to become crystallised and fixed). This type of charge is particularly useful for companies with no (or few) fixed assets (such as land) that could be included in a normal security, but with a valuable and fluctuating stock-in-trade. Since this stock needs to be used by the company in the ordinary course of its business, a fixed charge would be impracticable, as the chargee's consent would be required every time an item was sold, and a new charge would have to be executed whenever any new stock was purchased. A floating charge obviates these difficulties; the security permits the stock to be used by the company in the course of its business, but (provided the security instrument is sufficiently clearly and widely drafted) it will attach to the proceeds of the stock as well as any new stock acquired.

In theory, there is no principled reason why floating charges could not also be granted by sole traders and ordinary partnerships, as well as incorporated companies (and now, LLPs). Two pieces of legislation, however, effectively precluded that: first, in the previous legislation concerning individual bankruptcy, there was a "reputed ownership" provision,[95] which has never applied to corporate liquidations and was even repealed for individuals in the IA 1986[96]; and, secondly, there was the Bills of Sale Acts 1878 and 1882, which (still today) governs charges over chattels granted by individuals, rather than companies.[97] Where an individual granted a charge that qualified as a bill of sale, it would have to be registered in the Bills of Sale Registry in statutory form,[98] which involves specifying the relevant chattels in detail in a schedule.[99] Accordingly, where the charged chattels belong to an indeterminate and fluctuating class of assets (as is usually the situation with a floating charge),[100] it will obviously be impossible to draw up the schedule with the required degree of specificity. On that basis, a floating charge will generally be incompatible with the Bills of Sale Acts 1878 and 1882.

---

[95] Bankruptcy Act 1914 s.38(1)(c).

[96] Although its repeal was first recommended by the Blagden Committee (see Board of Trade, *Bankruptcy Law Amendment Committee* (1957), Cm.221), this only occurred as a result of the reforms suggested by the Cork Committee (see *Report on Insolvency Law and Practice* (1982), Cm.8558, Ch.23).

[97] Whilst this was always accepted to be the case in relation to mortgages (see Bills of Sale Act 1882 s.17), it was subsequently accepted (after an exhaustive review of the conflicting authorities) that both Acts only applied to individuals: see *Slavenburg's Bank v International Natural Resources* [1980] 1 W.L.R. 1076 QBD; followed in *Online Catering Ltd v Acton* [2010] EWCA Civ 58; [2011] Q.B. 204 at [17]–[21].

[98] Bills of Sale Act 1882 s.9.

[99] The schedule does not extend to future goods, although a limited power of replacement is permitted albeit nothing as fluid or extensive as under a floating charge: see Bills of Sale Act 1882 ss.5 and 6(2).

[100] Given that the touchstone is whether the chargor can use the collateral in the ordinary course of business, it is theoretically possible to have a floating charge over a single, unchanging asset: see *Smith (Administrator of Cosslett (Contractors) Ltd) v Bridgend CBC* [2001] UKHL 58; [2002] 1 A.C. 336.

2–031 Should English law ever (somewhat belatedly) reform its law relating to personal property security interests, as has already occurred in many other common law jurisdictions, the Bills of Sale Acts are likely to be repealed. This will make it practicable for unincorporated businesses to raise finance by granting a floating charge,[101] or some comparable form of security along the lines of art.9 of the US Uniform Commercial Code. In the meantime, the advantages of the floating charge are in practice limited to bodies corporate. Such a security interest is also advantageous from the lender's perspective: the lender can easily obtain an effective security on "all the undertaking and assets of the company both present and future" and may even combine this with a fixed charge over the company's strategic assets (such as its land). Previously, an all-encompassing floating charge gave the secured lender the advantages associated with being able to appoint an administrative receiver, albeit that this benefit has now largely disappeared,[102] but not the additional grounds for invalidating such a charge.[103] Nevertheless, the lender can still place itself in a far stronger position than if it merely relied upon the personal covenants in the loan agreement. Accordingly, given that the floating charge has advantages for both parties, a business frequently incorporates precisely to enable further borrowing upon the strength of a floating charge. More cynically, as in *Salomon v Salomon & Co Ltd*,[104] a trader may secure priority over the company's future creditors by taking a floating charge over the company's assets to secure the purchase price of the business transferred to the company.[105]

TAXATION

2–032 Once a company reaches a certain size, the attraction of limited liability is likely to outweigh any advantages derived from other forms of business association. In particular, investors are unlikely to put their money into a company where their liability is not limited, given that they will have little or no control over the running of the company. In closely-held companies, where investors will have a much stronger say in management and personal guarantees to large lenders may negate the benefits of limited liability, tax considerations will play a significant role in determining whether or not to incorporate a business.[106] A detailed consideration of the different tax benefits that may accrue to companies depending upon their size is beyond the present discussion. In small companies,

---

[101] Individual farmers can already grant a floating charge to a bank over farming stock and agricultural assets, as the former "reputed ownership" provision in the bankruptcy legislation and the Bills of Sale Acts are effectively excluded: see Agricultural Credits Act 1928 ss.5 and 8(1)–(2). This exception might be justified on the basis that farming stock and agricultural assets are more readily distinguishable from a farmer's other assets, unlike, say, the stock of an antique dealer who lives over his shop.

[102] IA 1986 s.72A(1).

[103] IA 1986 s.245. For detailed discussion of the floating charge, see Ch.32.

[104] *Salomon v Salomon & Co Ltd* [1897] A.C. 22.

[105] As well as losing priority to subsequent fixed charges, a floating charge's ability to "scoop the pool" of corporate assets has now been restricted by the Enterprise Act 2002 introducing "a prescribed part" of the assets subject to a floating charge that must be kept available for the unsecured creditors: see IA 1986 s.176A. See further Ch.32.

[106] The governing or regulatory bodies of some professions may still require businesses to adopt the partnership form, although this has become more flexible in recent years.

however, considerations of tax efficiency may determine whether an investor looks to obtain a return on his or her capital through the payment of directors' fees for participating in the company's management or by receiving dividends on his or her shares or both.[107]

FORMALITIES AND EXPENSE

Turning to the disadvantages, incorporation is necessarily attended with a need to comply with formalities, a loss of privacy (as discussed below) and greater expenses than would normally apply to a sole trader or partnership. There is no formality attendant upon becoming a sole trader, as the individual businessperson already exists. Similarly, a partnership arises out of the mere existence of a relationship between the parties that involves them carrying on business in common with a view of profit;[108] an informal arrangement suffices, although it would be commercially prudent to record the partnership agreement in writing. Accordingly, an unincorporated firm can operate its business without any formality and publicity beyond that which may be prescribed by the regulations (if any) for the particular sector. If the sole trader or partnership adopts a trading name that differs from the true name of the sole trader or partners, then it will have to comply with the statutory requirements applicable to business names (as would a company trading under a pseudonym), but these are not onerous.[109] Unless insolvent, in which case there may need to be a more formal bankruptcy process, an unincorporated business can be wound up equally cheaply, privately and informally. **2–033**

In contrast to the above, an incorporated company necessarily involves formalities, publicity and expenses at its birth, throughout its active life, and upon its final dissolution. That said, the costs of forming a private company (which is how most companies begin, even if they subsequently become public companies), are very low. A competent incorporation agent should be able to set up a basic company for less than £200. These costs are kept low by the fact that English law does not require a private company, unlike a public one, to have a minimum share capital.[110] Consequently, the incorporators are entitled to borrow whatever money they need to set the company up, without having to invest their own funds (which they may not have) from the outset of the company's life. The combined effect of there being no minimum capital requirement and the shareholders having limited liability could, however, be an unwelcome invitation to trade at the creditors' expense. Accordingly, whilst English law has no ex ante controls on a private company's initial capitalisation, it has developed significant ex post controls on those who act to the creditors' detriment after the company has been formed.[111] **2–034**

[107] See Ch.14.
[108] Partnership Act 1890 s.1(1).
[109] CA 2006 ss.1200–1206. See further paras 4–020 to 4–021.
[110] See paras 16–009 to 16–011.
[111] See further Chs 17–18.

2–035 Once the company is incorporated, there are also ongoing statutory formality and reporting requirements to meet. These ensure a degree of transparency for companies that is not required of sole traders or partnerships. At the least, the public records held by Companies House must remain accurate (so, for example, changes to the company's directors, and to its constitution, must be filed[112]), and the state of the company's business is, at least to some extent, to be visible to those who might deal with the company in the future. Accordingly, any security granted by the company over its assets should be registered,[113] and annual accounts may need to be filed depending upon the company's size.[114]

2–036 As indicated above, the formal and procedural requirements in the CA 2006, together with the requirement of two separate decision-making organs (namely, the shareholders' general meeting and the board of directors), might arguably be considered over-elaborate and cumbersome for small, closely-held companies. As considered further, however, a number of steps have now been taken to alleviate the formal burden on such companies,[115] without ever going to the extent of permitting small companies to adopt a single decision-making body.

PUBLICITY

The company's affairs

2–037 As indicated earlier, one of the downsides of incorporation is the much greater publicity required of companies when compared to partnerships: in particular, the former, but not the latter, are required to make their annual accounts available publicly through filing at Companies House.[116] One example of convergence between companies and partnerships in this regard is the relaxation for small companies in relation to the production of accounts in what was an over-elaborate format and the requirement to have those accounts audited.[117]

The company's members and directors

2–038 In addition to the publicity requirements surrounding a company's financial affairs, it is probably unsurprising that there should also be public registers of both the company's directors and members given that the company can only act through these individuals. As between the board and the general meeting, more publicity is generally required of the former than the latter (although such disclosure is nowadays increasingly limited by concerns related to privacy and

[112] CA 2006 ss.26 and 167. See further para.11–003.

[113] See paras 32–022 to 32–030.

[114] See Chs 22–23.

[115] See Ch.12.

[116] The public filing of financial information is considered the quid pro quo of limited liability. Accordingly, unlimited companies are not required to file their accounts publicly (see CA 2006 s.441), whereas the limited liability partnership is subject to the same publicity regime as companies: see generally Limited Liability Partnerships (Accounts and Audit) (Application of Companies Act 2006) Regulations 2008 (SI 2008/1911).

[117] See Chs 22–23.

personal safety).[118] With respect to the disclosure of the company's members, such a technique has never been particularly reliable for the simple reason that the CA 2006 prohibits any sort of trust over shares from being entered on the members' register.[119] The consequence of this prohibition is that the shares' "real" owners are not readily discoverable, even though the (disclosed) legal owner must comply absolutely with the beneficiaries' directions with respect to voting and distributions in respect of those shares. This has now been changed as a result of a newly introduced register of persons with significant control of a company.[120] These are considered subsequently together with other controls on shareholder votes.[121]

CONCLUSION

The balance of advantage and disadvantage in relation to incorporation no doubt varies from one business context to another, at least for small firms; as regards larger trading organisations, the arguments in favour of incorporation are normally conclusive. This difference may reflect the firms' respective needs for expert centralised management and significant capital to finance their operations. For large firms, the division between board and shareholders, the transferability of shares and the conferment of limited liability on the shareholders are helpful for raising capital. Where a large firm does not have significant capital requirements (such as large professional firms), these have happily traded as partnerships in the past, as this was often required by the rules of the relevant profession. In some ways, unlimited liability was seen as a badge of professional respectability and trustworthiness. In more recent times, however, the threat of crippling monetary awards for professional negligence has led the accountancy profession in particular to press for an appropriate form of limited liability vehicle to conduct their business. As considered above,[122] this led to the creation of the limited liability partnership, which combines the limited liability of the company with the flat internal hierarchy of the partnership. In circumstances where a large firm needs a significant amount of risk capital, however, the corporate form predominates. **2–039**

The main policy issue, therefore, has been how far small firms should have easy access to the corporate form. Ever since *Salomon v Salomon & Co Ltd*,[123] English law has favoured free access to the corporate form, and the Company Law Review endorsed that approach.[124] The debate essentially centres around whether small businesses should have limited liability, since that can significantly impact third parties who deal with the company; issues surrounding the separate

---

118 CA 2006 Pts 8 Ch.2 (members) and 10 Ch.1 (directors). See further Chs 9 and 13 respectively.

119 CA 2006 s.126.

120 CA 2006 ss.790C and 790M.

121 See Ch.13.

122 See para.1–004.

123 See para.2–001.

124 Developing, paras 9.61–9.71.

legal personality, the company's management under a board structure and the transferability of shares have little impact upon third parties and only really concern those within the company.

CHAPTER 3

SOURCES OF COMPANY LAW

INTRODUCTION

As far as domestic companies are concerned, the most important sources of company law, as well as their hierarchy, are those familiar from other bodies of law, namely primary legislation, secondary legislation, rules made by statutorily recognised bodies to which the legislature has delegated rule-making powers,[1] the common law, and the company's own constitution (in particular, its articles of association). Whilst the last of these may at first appear unfamiliar, contract lawyers are used to the notion that the rules applicable to a particular scenario are as likely to be found in the parties' own agreement as in statutory or common law rules. Similarly, it is familiar conceit that member's rights in a trade union, club, society or other unincorporated association are to be found in the association's rule-book or constitution.[2] **3–001**

In addition to these formal sources of law, there may be examples of "self-regulation" where non-legal pressures persuade corporate actors to abide by rules that have no legislative or common law foundation, but that are nevertheless observed in practice as a result of self-interest in avoiding more stringent and/or mandatory regulatory intervention by the State. Historically, the leading example of "self-regulation" in the company law area was the Panel on Takeovers and Mergers, which administered the City Code on Takeovers and Mergers, but the regulation of takeovers has now been placed on a statutory footing by the CA

[1] These bodies may themselves be agencies created by statute or they may be pre-existing bodies which the legislature recognises for the purposes of rule-making. An example might be the Financial Conduct Authority and Prudential Regulatory Authority created by the Financial Services and Markets Act 2000 (as amended), the former of which produces conduct of business standards in its regulatory handbook.

[2] For the "contract-holding" theory applicable to unincorporated associations, see *Re Recher's Will Trusts* [1972] Ch. 526 Ch D; *Re Lipinski's Will Trusts* [1976] Ch. 235 Ch D.

2006,[3] although its non-statutory methods of working have survived to a considerable extent.[4] Accordingly, "self-regulation" is a less obvious feature of company law than it used to be. Increasingly, however, British company law has examples of so-called "market-controlled" regulation, whereby the State co-opts market actors as regulators. This is increasingly a feature of the corporate governance area, most notably the UK Corporate Governance Code and the UK Stewardship Code developed by the Financial Reporting Council,[5] both of which are considered in more detail subsequently.

3–002 As well as the source of a particular company law principle, there may also be an issue concerning the form that that principle should take. In particular, legal rules may be located at a point along a spectrum running from "hard law" to "soft law". At the "hard" end of that spectrum, the obligation may be imposed on a legal actor without giving any choice as to whether or not they comply with it (in other words, a "mandatory" rule).

Moving further along that spectrum, the rule may permit those to whom it initially applies to modify or remove entirely the obligation that is imposes. Such "default" rules are relatively common in company law. It might, however, be questioned what the function of default rules might be, given that their regulatory objects are apparently free to deprive the rule of its regulatory force. Where the legal obligation can be easily removed, the rule may nevertheless perform the important (and cost-saving) function of relieving parties of having to work out the most suitable rule for themselves. This is because, in formulating the relevant default rule, the legislature will have sought to identify the rule that most parties in the relevant situation would devise for themselves. Only if a particular party wants something different from the generally applicable "norm" will they have to engage in the process of altering the default rule. Indeed, such default rules are particularly efficient in respect of procedural matters and the provisions in the CA 2006 dealing with shareholder meetings are frequently expressed as being "subject to any provision in the company's articles".[6] As it is relatively easy for companies to make alternative arrangements in their articles of association upon their formation or later, statutory provisions that are made subject to the company's constitution may be regarded as a "pure" type of default rule. In other situations, the procedure to be followed for amending default rules may be more demanding and the rule's regulatory objectives may accordingly be more sophisticated. For example, many of the statutory duties imposed on directors may be disapplied by a majority vote of the shareholders either before or after a breach has occurred.[7] The procedure for disapplying a director's duties is more demanding than in the case of the "pure" default rule considered above, since those upon whom the obligation is imposed (the directors) need to obtain the consent of another group of actors within the company (the shareholders) before the applicable rule is modified. The rationale underlying the more demanding

---

[3] CA 2006 ss.942–965, as amended by the Takeovers (Amendment) (EU Exit) Regulations 2019 (SI 2019/217).

[4] See Ch.28.

[5] Financial Reporting Council, *The UK Corporate Governance Code* (July 2018); *The UK Stewardship Code* (2020).

[6] See Ch.12.

[7] CA 2006 s.180. See further Ch.10.

standard for relaxation of the basic rule is that directors are forced to disclose to the shareholders their actual or potential wrongdoing and accordingly are required to bargain with the shareholders as to the consequences of their wrongful conduct. Such a "strong" default rule may be useful where that rule will apply to a broad range of circumstances, so that the rule-maker is unable to predict how any particular case should be dealt with (otherwise the rule would be mandatory). In such a case, it is also important to stipulate the process for disapplication carefully so as to avoid the risk that the directors themselves might attempt to modify the rule (given their conflict of interest). In yet other circumstances, the procedure for amending the default rule may be so demanding that it is little used in practice. Indeed, such a rule may in reality no longer operate as a default rule in substance. For example, although this is not in fact the case, if the rule regarding shareholder modification of directors' duties required there to be a meeting of shareholders to discuss every breach of duty as it arose, then such a procedure would be regarded as so cumbersome and unpredictable in a large company that the default rule would in substance be mandatory.[8] Accordingly, a director would simply have the bare choice between complying with the modification procedure or simply breaching their duty and hoping for the best.

At the "soft" end of the spectrum, there are "rules" that may in reality be little more than recommendations or exhortations. In general, no legal sanction will be attached to the breach of a "soft" rule, so that legal actors can effectively choose how far to comply with the relevant recommendation. One option for giving such "soft" rules some teeth is to adopt them on a "comply or explain basis". In such a situation, the only formal obligation imposed by the rule is for the relevant legal actor to explain publicly how far they have complied with the relevant recommendation and to provide the reasons for any areas of non-compliance. Accordingly, making the necessary disclosures satisfies all the legal actor's formal legal obligations, even if that disclosure demonstrates that the recommendation has not in fact been complied with at all. That said, the publicity resulting from disclosure may generate pressures on the company to comply (or to comply more fully) with the recommendations, whether from within the company (for example, the shareholders) or from without (government or activist groups). The primary example of such a mechanism in company law is the UK Corporate Governance Code,[9] which imposes a "comply or explain" obligation on companies.

Before considering the different sources of company law, it is worth considering how the complex and diverse body of corporate rules remains fit for purpose in providing a framework for business activity. Keeping company law under review is now principally the task of the Department of Business, Energy and Industrial Strategy (BEIS),[10] which is the Government Department currently responsible for company and insolvency law, among many other matters. As for financial **3–003**

[8] For analysis of default rules, see S. Deakin and A. Hughes, "Economic Efficiency and the Proceduralisation of Company Law" (1999) 3 C.F.I.L.R. 169.

[9] See further paras 9–016 to 9–020.

[10] Its predecessors were the Department for Business, Innovation and Skills (BIS), the Department for Business, Enterprise and Regulatory Reform (BERR), and, before that, the Department of Trade and Industry (DTI), which was responsible for the Company Law Review.

services law, including public offerings of securities and their listing, the Treasury is the leading source of policy. Equally, in recent years the Law Commissions (English and Scottish) have also played an important part in company law reform producing significant reports on directors' duties and shareholder remedies.

One of the most significant reform projects in recent times was, however, the Company Law Review, which was carried out by the Department of Trade and Industry. This may be seen as the latest in a series of reviews of company law carried out by the various predecessors of BEIS since the introduction of incorporation by registration in the middle of the nineteenth century. Its method of operation was, however, rather different from that of its predecessors. Those earlier reviews had consisted of small committees of enquiry that took formal evidence, but did not engage in widespread consultation; they also tended to concentrate on particular aspects of the subject in need of reform, rather than upon a comprehensive review. The two most recent Committee reports of this older type that are still important for an understanding of the current law are the Jenkins[11] and Cohen[12] Committee reports (so referred to after the names of their chairmen). In contrast, the Company Law Review proposed comprehensive reform following extensive consultation. In the long term, however, the Company Law Review was unconvinced that ad hoc, periodic, comprehensive reviews of the type it had undertaken were the best way forward, since they depend so heavily upon governmental commitment to devote the necessary resources to the exercise. The Review recommended instead that a standing Company Law and Reporting Commission should have the remit of keeping company law under review and reporting annually to the Secretary of State its views on where, if anywhere, reform was needed. In addition, the Secretary of State would be obliged to consult the Commission on proposed secondary legislation.[13] In this way, company law reform would have become a continuing and expert process, so that less weight would need to be placed on ad hoc, across-the-board reviews. This proposal was, however, rejected by the Government,[14] so the ad hoc approach remains the order of the day.

Primary legislation

3–004 The principal legislative source of company law principles is the CA 2006, which is the latest in a long line of legislation arising out of the periodic reform of the original legislation in the mid-nineteenth century. The drafting of the CA 2006 followed the most comprehensive review of company law ever undertaken, and the resulting legislation is reportedly the longest ever passed by the UK Parliament.

The legislative reform process began in 1998 with the then Secretary of State commissioning an independent review of company law.[15] This Company Law

[11] *Report of the Company Law Committee* (1962), Cmnd.1749.
[12] *Report of the Committee on Company Law Amendment* (1945), Cmnd.6659.
[13] Final Report I, para.5.22.
[14] Modernising I, pp.48–49.
[15] DTI, *Company Law Reform: Modern Company Law for a Competitive Economy* (1998).

Review (CLR) was carried out with the support of DTI civil servants, a Project Director, a permanent Steering Group[16] and Consultative Committee, as well as a series of ad hoc Working Groups.[17] The Steering Group produced a number of consultative documents, some very large, and a two-volume final report. In its Final Report, the CLR declared its aim to have been the production of a company law framework that was "primarily enabling or facilitative" and designed to "strip out regulation that is no longer necessary". Facilitating corporate activity does not necessarily mean that there should be no relevant statutory law, however, since the framework of company law "should provide the necessary safeguards to allow people to deal with and invest in companies with confidence".[18] Whilst the Government's immediate response was enthusiastic, developments were rather slow.[19] In November 2005, a Bill was finally introduced into Parliament and it received the Royal Assent a year later. The CA 2006 was then phased in over a period of time, ending on 1 October 2009. The resulting legislation has some 1,300 sections and 16 Schedules. This may seem an odd result for a legislative process aimed at being facilitative, but two points can be made in defence of its length. First, enabling legislation is not to be confused with the absence of statutory law: often confining law narrowly takes more statutory words than a sweeping prohibition. Secondly, the CA 2006 is drafted in a lengthy manner, paradoxically to make it more user-friendly. Few people read legislation from beginning to end; rather, they need to find quickly the provisions relevant to their problem. Setting out the provisions in a disaggregated form (for example, by separating those provisions dealing with public companies from those applicable to private companies on a particular topic, even if the provisions are similar) is helpful in that regard.

Other legislation besides the CA 2006 is also important. Provisions relating to the insolvency of companies have been hived off into the IA 1986, which also contains provisions aimed at protecting the company's creditors in the twilight period before the company enters a formal insolvency procedure.[20] In the same year, the Financial Services Act 1986 (now replaced by the Financial Services and Markets Act 2000 (FSMA 2000) took over the provisions relating to the public offering and listing of shares. FSMA 2000 has been heavily modified over the years to reflect the burgeoning EU law in this area,[21] although the UK's departure from the EU will certainly halt (and more likely reverse) this trend. That said, the IA 1986 and FSMA 2000 illustrate a perennial difficulty of classification: should the principles relating to corporate insolvency, capital markets or securities law be addressed in a piece of general company law legislation or in more specialist legislation? Whilst there are arguments both **3–005**

---

[16] Two editors of this edition were involved in this process: Paul Davies, as a member of the Steering Group from March 1999, and Sarah Worthington, as a member of one of the Working Groups. Accordingly, discussion of the CLR in subsequent chapters should be read in light of that involvement.

[17] For further details, see Final Report II, Annex E.

[18] Final Report I, para.9.

[19] See generally *Modernising Company Law*, 2 vols (July 2002) Cm.5553, followed by *Company Law Reform* (March 2005), Cm.6456.

[20] See, for example, IA 1986 s.214. See further paras 19–005 to 19–012.

[21] See further Ch.25.

ways, the practical reality is that functionally important parts of the statutory law relating to companies are not actually found in legislation with the word "company" in their title.

In addition to the general company law legislation considered above, companies are subject to two other types of primary legislation. First, like other legal actors, companies are subject to generally applicable civil and criminal legislation.[22] Secondly, companies may also be subject to more specific legislation either dealing with particular corporate law concerns (such as the disqualification of directors)[23] or the operation of particular companies (such as the community interest company).[24]

Secondary legislation

3–006 Given the length of the CA 2006, a major commitment of parliamentary time is required to pass such legislation. Thereafter, government ministers may take the view that company law has had its turn and will accordingly be reluctant to devote additional parliamentary time to proposals for its further reform. This can be problematic for those parts of the CA 2006 dealing with issues where the technical or economic context is changing rapidly, so that frequent statutory updates are required. One possible solution to this difficulty involves using subordinate legislation to amend the CA 2006 given that parliamentary scrutiny of secondary legislation is much reduced and accordingly much less time-consuming.[25] The CA 2006 contains important examples of relying upon subordinate legislation for reform in particular areas, such as companies' accounts[26] and share capital.[27] In the first area, the Government had to be particularly responsive to corporate collapses and financial crises and, in the second area, to developments outside the UK (whether at EU[28] or broader international levels). Whilst the CLR proposed that there should be a general power to use secondary legislation to amend the CA 2006, this was abandoned after opposition in Parliament.[29]

---

22 See, for example, Bribery Act 2010, which is not just applicable to companies. See further paras 8–047 and 10–101.

23 See Company Directors Disqualification Act 1986, on which see further Ch.20.

24 See Companies (Audit, Investigations and Community Enterprise) Act 2004, on which see para.1–012.

25 Whilst primary legislation requires three readings and a committee stage in each House of Parliament over several months, there will only be a single short debate for secondary legislation. Where the "negative resolution" procedure is employed, there will only be a debate if MPs take the necessary steps to initiate one. See generally CA 2006 ss.1288–1292.

26 CA 2006 s.468.

27 CA 2006 s.657.

28 Whilst there was a specific power to enact subordinate legislation to comply with the UK's obligations to implement EU legislation in the company law and other areas (see European Communities Act 1972 Sch.2), this power was repealed on 31 January 2020 (see European Union (Withdrawal) Act 2018 s.1).

29 See Final Report I, paras 5.7 and 5.10; Modernising, I, p.9. For a more general power to reform legislation by statutory instrument when certain criteria are met, see Legislative and Regulatory Reform Act 2006 s.1.

Although quicker to implement than primary legislation, secondary legislation suffers from two defects. First, subordinate legislation is subject to less democratic scrutiny than primary legislation. Accordingly, whilst the Company Law Review advocated greater use of secondary legislation, it also recommended that "the basic principles and architecture of the new framework would be set out in primary legislation".[30] Secondly, despite the conscientious consultation process in which the relevant Government Department is likely to engage before drafting and passing subordinate legislation, there may not be the same level of technical or legal expertise available as when primary legislation is employed. Delegating the law-making powers to an expert body, rather than a Government Department, may ameliorate this problem.

Delegated rule-making

Financial Conduct Authority

Currently, the Financial Conduct Authority (FCA) provides the primary example of rule-making powers delegated to an external body outside central government. Although the FCA is a private company limited by guarantee[31] and is financed by a levy on those who conduct financial services business, it has extensive public functions and is itself subject to the controls appropriate to public bodies. In essence, the FCA has power to issue elaborate sets of rules, without the need for any formal approval by either Parliament or a Governmental Department.[32] The public interest is protected, however, by the FCA's statutory duty to publish a "policy statement" regarding the imposition of sanctions for breaches of its rules.[33] The FCA performs two key functions for present purposes. First, the FCA took over from the Stock Exchange the long-standing (and originally self-regulatory) task of producing the Listing Rules (LR) for companies whose securities have been entered onto the "official list".[34] In exercising this function, the FCA acted as the UK Listing Authority (UKLA)—though the FCA is now phasing out the use of that term to refer to the FCA's primary market functions. In that regard, the LR's primary aim is to further policies relevant to listed companies only and to introduce an additional set of core rules that are applicable to such companies, but not unlisted companies. Secondly, the FCA has also introduced a range of financial services rules in its regulatory handbook that are particularly relevant to company law, such as the "Prospectus Regulation Rules" sourcebook (PRR), the "Disclosure Guidance and Transparency Rules" sourcebook (DTR), the "Market Conduct" sourcebook (MAR)[35] and the Financial Crime Guide (FCG). Indeed, the consequence of giving the FCA extended 3–007

---

30 Final Report I, para.5.4.

31 Financial Services and Markets Act 2000 s.1A. See further para.1–008.

32 Financial Services and Markets Act 2000 s.73A.

33 Financial Services and Markets Act 2000 ss.93–94.

34 For the meaning of "official list", see paras 25–015 to 25–017.

35 See further Ch.30.

rule-making powers is that certain corporate law topics are now found in the FCA's regulatory handbook, rather than in primary legislation dealing with company or financial services law.[36]

Financial Reporting Council

3–008 The second area in which delegated rule-making can currently be found on a significant scale is in relation to corporate governance, accounting standards, the accuracy of accounts, auditing standards and the regulation of auditors and accountants. The functions of the Financial Reporting Council (FRC) and its various subsidiaries in these areas are fundamentally important. Like the FCA, the FRC and its subsidiaries are companies limited by guarantee, but its directors are appointed by the Secretary of State. Accordingly, the FRC, although more expert than a Government Department (and partly financed by those whom it regulates), is tied into the governmental machinery. Following reforms implemented in the UK after the Enron and other corporate scandals in the US,[37] as well as further reforms after the Global Financial Crisis in 2008, the FRC's powers have expanded significantly in recent years. However, after a highly critical governmental review by Sir John Kingman, the FRC is undergoing a set of reforms from which it is likely to emerge as the Audit Reporting and Governance Authority (ARGA), more conventionally structured and with yet wider powers.[38] For present purposes, like the FCA, the FRC's powers are delegated by the Secretary of State (who can therefore re-allocate them).[39]

Common law

3–009 Despite the size of the CA 2006 (and its satellite legislation), the legislation is not a code of English company law. Indeed, the companies legislation has never aspired to lay down all the core company law principles. Accordingly, there are still important common law principles that cover topics as diverse as shareholder decision-making,[40] unlawful shareholder distributions[41] and the separate corporate personality.[42] Nevertheless, the CA 2006 probably travels further down this road than its predecessors. There are two particularly important common law areas that are now on a statutory footing in the CA 2006: the Law Commissions recommended that there should be a statutory statement of directors' common

[36] For the disclosure of directors' and "major" shareholders' interests in shares, see Ch.27.

[37] The main legislative expression of these reforms was the Companies (Audit, Investigation and Community Enterprise) Act 2004, some parts of which have survived in the CA 2006.

[38] Kingman Committee, *Independent Review of the Financial Reporting Council* (December 2018). For acceptance of the recommendations of the Kingman Committee, see Department for Business, Energy and Industrial Strategy, *Restoring Trust in Audit and Corporate Governance* (March 2021). See further para.23–011.

[39] CA 2006 ss.457 and 1217 and Sch.10.

[40] *Re Duomatic Ltd* [1969] 2 Ch. 365 Ch D.

[41] *Progress Property Co Ltd v Moorgarth Group Ltd* [2010] UKSC 55; [2011] B.C.C. 196.

[42] *Salomon v Salomon & Co Ltd* [1897] A.C. 22 HL.

law duties[43] (although not the remedies for breach)[44] and the English Law Commission recommended that the enforcement of those duties by minority shareholders on behalf of the company should be both reformed and stated in legislative form.[45] Both recommendations were broadly endorsed by the Company Law Review and subsequently included in the CA 2006.[46] This represented a significant encroachment by statutory company law into areas that were originally developed by the common law and traditionally its preserve.

Whilst these changes formally altered the balance between statute and common law in the company law field, this shift has had a much less pronounced effect upon the role of judges in developing company law than one might otherwise have expected. As regards directors' duties, whilst there can be little doubt that the statutory duties in the CA 2006 "have effect in place of [the common law and equitable] rules and principles as regards the duties owed to a company by a director",[47] the individual statutory duties are drafted at a rather high level of generality. Nevertheless, pre-existing authorities remain relevant where the particular statutory duty simply repeats, rather than reforms, the equivalent common law duty. Even where this is not the case, the fact that the statutory duties are framed in terms of broad standards, rather than precise rules, means that judges will retain an important role in developing the content of those standards, as well as applying them to specific scenarios.[48] Indeed, the CA 2006 specifically (and somewhat uniquely) requires the courts to seek positive guidance from the common law when considering the statutory directors' duties, given that "[t]he general duties shall be interpreted and applied in the same way as common law rules or equitable principles, and regard shall be had to the corresponding common law rules and equitable principles in interpreting and applying the general duties".[49] Moreover, there continue to exist common law duties that are not reflected in the statutory duties in the CA 2006.[50]

As regards the enforcement of these statutory directors' duties, the CA 2006 confers a judicial discretion whether or not to allow a minority shareholder to being a derivative action on the company's behalf.[51] Whilst it is clear that the common law derivative action is intended to be displaced by the new statutory version,[52] the common law will continue to be relevant when a court is considering the statutory factors,[53] which resemble closely the considerations that

---

[43] *Company Directors: Regulating Conflicts of Interest and Formulating a Statement of Duties* (1999), Cm.4436,.

[44] For the implementation of this suggestion, see CA 2006 s.178.

[45] *Shareholder Remedies* (1997), Cm.3769.

[46] CA 2006 ss.170–181 and 260. See further Chs 10 and 15.

[47] CA 2006 s.170(3).

[48] The English courts have become increasingly accustomed to fleshing out such broad standards as a result of having to develop the parameters of the unfair prejudice jurisdiction in CA 2006 s.994(1): see further Ch.14.

[49] CA 2006 s.170(4).

[50] *Goldtrail Travel Ltd (In Liquidation) v Aydin* [2014] EWHC 1587 (Ch) at [65]; affirmed [2016] EWCA Civ 371; [2016] B.C.C. 707.

[51] CA 2006 s.260(1).

[52] CA 2006 s.260(2).

[53] CA 2006 s.263(3). A particularly clear example of the parallel between the common law (see *Smith v Croft (No.2)* (1987) 3 B.C.C. 207 Ch D) and statutory derivative actions (see CA 2006 s.263(4)) is the relevance of the independent shareholders' views.

used to be relevant at common law. Moreover, as the statutory derivative action does not appear comprehensive in its coverage,[54] there does actually appear to be a continuing role for the common law in relation to "double derivative actions"[55] and overseas companies.[56] Accordingly, even in those areas of company law now governed by statute, common law principles have a continuing and vibrant role.

THE COMPANY'S CONSTITUTION

The significance of the constitution

3–010 A particularly notable feature of English company law is the extent to which the company itself is permitted to regulate its own internal affairs by determining what rules to include in its constitution, in particular its articles of association (which "prescribe regulations for the company").[57] Although the CA 2006 does not explicitly state as much, the generally unstated assumption underlying that legislation is that a company's articles may deal with any matter that is not regulated by any of the other sources considered above. What is particularly significant about the articles of association, however, is the sheer number of substantive matters that they regulate. Indeed, many of these issues are central to the company's operations, such as the division of power between the shareholders and board of directors, as well as the composition, structure and operation of the board of directors.[58] Many jurisdictions (as diverse as Germany[59] and the US)[60] regulate such matters through their primary legislation, rather than the company's constitution.

That said, the Model Business Corporation Act (MBCA) in the US (like its German equivalent) often uses default rules that can be amended by contrary provision in the company's constitution, so that in practice the shareholders can ultimately adopt whatever set of rules they want, as in the UK. For example, the MBCA vests broad management powers in the board of US companies,[61] but nevertheless allows the shareholders to reduce the board's powers and take those powers for themselves by means of provisions in the constitution or shareholder agreement.[62] Accordingly, the practical allocation of power ultimately depends on the ease with which the default rules may be overridden.[63] In contrast, the boards of British companies only have such management powers as are conferred on the board by the company's articles of association (and the default model articles for

[54] *Universal Project Management Services Ltd v Fort Gilkicker Ltd* [2013] EWHC 348 (Ch); [2013] B.C.C. 365.

[55] *Harris v Microfusion 2003-2 LLP* [2016] EWCA Civ 1212; [2017] C.P. Rep. 15.

[56] *Abouraya v Sigmund* [2014] EWHC 277 (Ch); [2015] B.C.C. 503.

[57] CA 2006 s.18(1).

[58] For premium-listed companies, the UK Corporate Governance Code (July 2018) now trespasses upon the company's autonomy, since the Code requires the company to "comply" with defined best practices or "explain" why not. See further paras 9–016 to 9–020.

[59] *Aktiengesetz*, Pt 4, subdivisions 1–2.

[60] Model Business Corporation Act (3rd edn, 2002) Ch.8.

[61] Model Business Corporation Act (3rd edn, 2002) s.8.01(b).

[62] Model Business Corporation Act (3rd edn, 2002) s.7.32(a)(8).

[63] See para.3–002.

all companies contain a provision to that effect).[64] Despite the UK and US adopting different starting points with respect to the division of corporate powers between the directors and shareholders, the ultimate position is probably the same in both jurisdictions. Despite the similarity in practical outcome, there is nevertheless a theoretical difference between the UK and US approaches: on the one hand, the US (and German) approach is based on the principle that the allocation of powers between the company's organs involves a legislative act, even if shareholders may alter the initial legislative allocation; whereas, the English approach is based on the notion that the shareholders constitute the ultimate source of managerial authority within the company and that the shareholders formally delegate those managerial functions to the directors, so that the board becomes the company's central decision-making body for as long as that delegation lasts.[65] Moreover, there may be a practical difference depending upon whether the shareholders decide to override the default rules upon the company's formation or at some later stage: in the former case, the barriers to disapplying the default position may be relatively low; whereas, in the latter case, the position is more complex, as it will be necessary to determine who must pass the resolution necessary to disapply the default rule, who must call the necessary meetings (the directors or a shareholder), and what level of voting support is required to adopt the change (whether a simple majority or some sort of super majority). For example, as will be considered in Chs 13 and 14, s.21 of the CA 2006 provides that the company's constitution may only be altered by a special resolution, which requires a three-quarter majority of shareholders entitled to vote.

Model articles of association

Given the importance of the company's constitution as a source of English company law, there is a statutory requirement that a company must register articles of association,[66] which "must be contained in a single document".[67] The mandatory nature of this requirement is underlined by the CA 2006 authorising the Secretary of State (under a long-standing power[68]) to promulgate "model" articles of association for different types of company.[69] These standard-form articles operate in a default manner,[70] so that no company will be left without a constitution through oversight or as a result of not having the funds or professional advice to develop bespoke articles. Whilst the current model articles 3–011

---

[64] Companies (Model Articles) Regulations 2008 (SI 2008/3229) Sch.1 art.3 (private companies) and Sch.3 art.3 (public companies): "Subject to the articles, the directors are responsible for the management of the company's business, for which purpose they may exercise all the powers of the company".

[65] See further Ch.11.

[66] CA 2006 s.18(1)–(2). The company's articles of association must be registered as a public document with Companies House: see *Monaghan v Gilsenan* [2021] EWHC 47 (Ch) at [30].

[67] CA 2006 s.18(3)(a).

[68] See, for example, Companies (Tables A to F) Regulations 1985 (SI 1985/805).

[69] CA 2006 s.19(1).

[70] CA 2006 s.20(1). See also *Global Corporate Ltd v Hale* [2017] EWHC 2277 (Ch); [2018] B.C.C. 306 at [42].

only apply to companies incorporated after 1 October 2009,[71] the model articles promulgated under the CAs 1948 or 1985 will apply by default to the many companies still in existence that were incorporated before that date.[72] Whereas the same model constitution applied to public and private companies in the past, one innovation introduced by the CA 2006, following a suggestion of the Company Law Review,[73] was to introduce different model articles for private and public companies limited by shares, as well as for companies limited by guarantee.[74] Indeed, given the range of different corporate forms,[75] it is surprising that the same model was for so long considered adequate for all companies limited by shares.[76]

3–012 When a limited company is formed, the default position is that the company will be treated as having adopted the relevant model articles, save to the extent that the incorporators choose to adopt different articles, either in whole or in part.[77] The version of the model articles applicable to any particular company is the version that was in force when the company was incorporated,[78] and the subsequent promulgation of revised model articles will not affect companies that are already registered,[79] but only those registered in the future. Accordingly, if the company's incorporators say nothing about its constitution, the relevant model will apply in full.[80] At the other extreme, by adopting a full set of bespoke articles, the model articles will be disapplied entirely. Companies usually adopt an intermediate position, however, by registering articles that adopt the default model, subject to a list of specific amendments. The provisions of model articles are not only displaced by express contrary provision, but may equally be displaced by implication to the extent that the bespoke articles are inconsistent with the model articles.[81] In such a case, the model articles essentially perform a "gap-filling" role. Whilst this intermediate position is responsive to the company's needs, it creates a practical difficulty in that the full articles of the company can only be established through a fairly laborious process of checking the bespoke articles against the model articles to determine the extent to which the former is inconsistent with the latter. This can hardly have been the intention underlying the CA 2006, which contains a clear requirement that the company's

---

71 See generally Companies (Model Articles) Regulations 2008 (SI 2008/3229).

72 Companies incorporated under the CA 1985 could adopt the model articles of association in Companies (Tables A to F) Regulations 1985 (SI 1985/805), with the default constitution for companies limited by shares being set out in "Table A".

73 Final Report II, Ch.17.

74 See Companies (Model Articles) Regulations 2008 (SI 2008/3229) Schs 1 (for private companies limited by shares), 2 (for companies limited by guarantee) and 3 (for public companies).

75 See further Ch.1.

76 In practice, this may not have created significant difficulties, since company formation agents developed their own standard-form articles for different types of company.

77 CA 2006 s.20(1), which applies to all types of limited company. By contrast, CA 1985 s.8(2) only created a default for companies limited by shares.

78 CA 2006 s.20(2).

79 There are numerous companies incorporated under the CA 1985 with articles of association still based upon Companies (Tables A to F) Regulations 1985 (SI 1985/805).

80 CA 2006 s.20(1)(a). If no model articles is prescribed, the company must still register a set of articles: CA 2006 s.18(2).

81 CA 2006 s.20(1)(b).

articles of association "be contained in a single document".[82] Clearly, the ambition was that shareholders should be able to ascertain their rights immediately by means of a simple check of a single document. Having to piece together the constitution from different sources neither accords with the legislation's aims nor promotes transparency as to the contents of the company's constitution.

Scope of the company's constitution

3–013 Unlike its predecessors, the CA 2006 non-exhaustively defines what falls within the scope of a company's constitution.[83] Whilst the term "constitution" includes the articles of association, that is not the only constitutional document. Also included within the term "constitution" are certain types of resolution or agreement,[84] namely special resolutions of the shareholders (whether passed as such or by virtue of the shareholders' unanimous agreement)[85]; any resolution or agreement that effectively binds all the members of a class of shareholders, even though not agreed by all those members (for example, a resolution varying class rights)[86]; any unanimous resolution or agreement adopted by the members of the company or a particular class, provided that resolution or agreement would not otherwise be binding on them unless passed by a particular majority or in a particular manner[87]; and any other resolution or agreement made part of the constitution by any other enactment.[88] In practice, special resolutions comprise the most significant of these categories. Given its vestigial role under the CA 2006, the memorandum of association is unsurprisingly no longer part of the company's constitution.[89] Unless binding on every member, shareholder agreements are not generally regarded as part of the company's constitution; but that rule has one important exception, noted in passing here.[90]

FOREIGN AND EU LAW

3–014 The law applicable in other jurisdictions has always been an important source of British company law, particularly those jurisdictions sharing a common law origin. Those jurisdictions have often provided a guide as to principles that ought to be adopted in this jurisdiction, such as the recognition of creditor-facing duties

---

[82] CA 2006 s.18(3)(a).

[83] *Keymed (Medical & Industrial Equipment Ltd) v Hillman* [2019] EWHC 485 (Ch) at [85].

[84] CA 2006 s.17. Where a company was created before 1 October 2009, its memorandum of association will also be treated as part of its constitution: see CA 2006 s. 28. See also *National Federation of Occupational Pensioners v Revenue and Customs Commissioners* [2018] UKFTT 26 (TC) at [127]–[128].

[85] CA 2006 s.29(1)(a). See further *Re Duomatic Ltd* [1969] 2 Ch. 365; considered further in paras 12–009 to 12–011.

[86] CA 2006 s.29(1)(d). See further Ch.13.

[87] CA 2006 s.29(1)(b)–(c).

[88] CA 2006 s.29(1)(e).

[89] For the residual function of the memorandum, see para.4–031.

[90] Shareholder agreements generally are included as part of the constitution for the purposes of the CA 2006 s.40.

by directors[91] and the recognition that non-executive directors could be liable for failing to supervise the board.[92] Equally, foreign jurisdictions may indicate steps to avoid to the English courts, such as imposing too readily duties on directors to shareholders[93] or regulating alterations to the articles too closely.[94] Following Brexit, large parts of EU law will have the same status in the UK as the foreign law of any other jurisdiction. That said, even after Brexit, some parts of EU law will continue to have direct effect in the UK through the transitional concept of "retained" EU law, which includes "EU-derived domestic legislation",[95] "direct EU legislation"[96] and accrued rights under the European Communities Act 1972.[97] Of these concepts, the most significant for company law is the notion of "EU-derived domestic legislation", since the CA 2006 has much content that derives from the EU's harmonisation programme. Accordingly, the practical reality is that EU law is not just another foreign law, but it will continue to have a significant impact on the content and operation of English company law for many years to come. Accordingly, it remains important to understand the background and impact of EU harmonisation on domestic company law.

3–015 When the European Economic Community was founded in the middle of the 1950s, a very different approach was taken in the Treaty of Rome. It was expected that, in the Community, companies based in one Member State would penetrate more readily the economies of other Member States, without necessarily establishing subsidiaries in those States. It was decided that this was acceptable only if accompanied by a programme for the mandatory harmonisation by the Community of the company laws of the Member States.[98] In other words, in the minds of the drafters of the original EC Treaty, freedom of establishment for companies and harmonisation of company laws in the EU were closely linked. Consequently, the Treaty on the Functioning of the European Union (TFEU) provided[99] that the Council of Ministers by qualified majority vote, on a proposal from the European Commission and with the consent of the European Parliament,[100] may adopt Directives[101] which aim to protect the interests of members "and others"[102] by "co-ordinating to the necessary extent the safeguards which…are required by Member States of companies and firms …

[91] *Kinsela v Russell Kinsela Pty Ltd* (1986) 4 N.S.W.L.R. 722.

[92] *Daniels v Anderson* (1995) 37 N.S.W.L.R. 438.

[93] *Coleman v Myers* [1977] N.Z.L.R. 225.

[94] *Gambotto v WCP Ltd* (1995) 182 C.L.R. 432.

[95] European Union (Withdrawal) Act 2018 s.2.

[96] European Union (Withdrawal) Act 2018 s.3. This notion includes regulations, but does not generally include directives.

[97] European Union (Withdrawal) Act 2018 s.4.

[98] J. Wouters, "European Company Law: *Quo Vadis?*" (2000) 37 C.M.L.R. 257 at 269; and G. Wolff, "The Commission's Programme for Company Law Harmonisation" in M. Andenas and S. Kenyon-Slade (eds), *EC Financial Market Regulation and Company Law* (London, 1993), p.22. This position was adopted in particular by France.

[99] Article 50(2)(g) TFEU.

[100] Under the "ordinary" legislative procedure of the EU: see art.294 TFEU.

[101] Directives are binding on the Member States as to the principles to be embodied in national legislation, but give the states some flexibility in the transposition of the Directive into national law: see art.288 TFEU. Article 50 does not provide for the adoption of Regulations, which are directly applicable in the Member States.

[102] This includes creditors and, probably, employees.

with a view to making such safeguards equivalent throughout the Union". Thus, reliance on other Member States' company laws was to be accompanied by EU legislation that made those laws "equivalent", at least in certain respects. The proposed programme for extensive mandatory harmonisation, from the top down, of Member States' domestic company laws got off to an impressive start, but by the middle 1990s, if not earlier, it had run out of steam, with only part of the proposed programme of "company law directives" enacted. This may have been because the theory linking freedom of establishment with the need for harmonised company law was never satisfactorily articulated. There was little empirical evidence that "members and others" were suffering in the EU's single market from the lack of a harmonised company law. There was also the criticism that, once a policy had been embodied in EU company law, it was more difficult to change it than in the case of domestic legislation, at least for the majority of Member States. In other words, the EU legislative process was more "sticky" than national ones.

In any event, for harmonisation to be fully successful there must exist a common best rule for all the Members States; the EU Commission, which has a monopoly on the initiation of Community legislation, must be able to identify it; and the participants in the Community's legislative process must accept that common rule. None of these characteristics was ever completely in place. The structure of shareholding (dispersed or concentrated) differs across the Member States, at least in relation to large companies, so that the dominant problem in some jurisdictions is the relationship between management and shareholders as a class and in other jurisdictions that between controlling and non-controlling shareholders. In some Member States, board-level representation of employees is an important part of the domestic industrial relations system, whilst in others it is not. Both features made the identification of a single common rule very difficult in the most sensitive areas of company law. As to the EU Commission, it never had the time or the resources to develop the highly sophisticated comparative law analysis that legislating for an ever-growing bloc of countries requires. Finally, since the adoption of legislation requires a supermajority vote of the Member States, there was plenty of scope for the states to defend national interests, normally by watering down the proposals put forward by the EU Commission. It may be difficult to say whether the resistance of a Member State is driven by the fact that the EU Commission has proposed an inefficient rule for that state or by pressure from incumbent national interests that might lose out if the efficient rule is adopted.

Nevertheless, some parts of the proposed programme of company law directives were enacted by the middle of the 1990s. This period saw the adoption of the First (safeguards for third parties),[103] Second (formation of public companies and the maintenance and alteration of capital),[104] Third (mergers of

[103] Directive 68/151 [1968] OJ L68/151.
[104] Directive 77/91 [1977] OJ L26/1.

public companies),[105] Fourth (accounts),[106] Sixth (division of public companies),[107] Seventh (group accounts),[108] Eighth (audits),[109] Eleventh (branches)[110] and Twelfth (single-member companies) Directives,[111] though they were not adopted in that precise order. Subsequently, there have been significant directives on takeovers, cross-border mergers and shareholders' rights (though, significantly, the twenty-first century directives are no longer allocated a number in an overall proposed programme of directives). However, the Directives were not equally important for the UK. Some of them did not significantly alter the existing national law either because the EU rule reflected existing national law; because Member States were given a range of options in implementing the Directive and could choose to preserve the status quo; or because the subject-matter of the Directive was not important in the UK.[112] As far as the UK is concerned, the most important Directives have been the First (which triggered a review of the common law rules on ultra vires and agency as they applied to companies)[113]; the Second (which led to a tightening of the rules on dividend distributions and legal capital generally)[114]; and the Fourth (which led to a re-thinking of the relationship between the law and accountancy practice).[115] Of lesser impact were the Eighth on audits[116] and the Eleventh on branches.[117] Apart from the Second, which froze the law on legal capital in an unideal position, the impact of the Directives on UK company law has been beneficial overall.

By contrast, some proposals were never adopted by the Community legislature because it proved difficult to obtain the necessary level of Member State support for the more controversial proposed harmonisation measures. This was true, in particular, of the proposed Fifth Directive which dealt with two sensitive topics upon which Member States were pretty equally split: should the board be a one-tier structure (as is the practice in the UK) or a two-tier one, consisting of separate supervisory and management boards, and, even more controversially, should employee representation on the board (whether one-tier or two-tier) be mandatory?[118] The Fifth Directive was never adopted. For many years, the issue of mandatory employee representation also held up agreement on the European

[105] Directive 78/855 [1978] OJ L295/36.
[106] Directive 78/660 [1978] OJ L222/11.
[107] Directive 82/891 [1982] OJ L378/47.
[108] Directive 83/349 [1983] OJ L193/1.
[109] Directive 84/253 [1984] OJ L126/20.
[110] Directive 89/666 [1989] OJ L395/36.
[111] Directive 89/667 [1989] OJ L395/40.
[112] For similar reasons, the overall significance of the EU company law directives has been questioned: see L. Enriques, "EC Company Law Directives and Regulations: How Trivial Are They?" (2006) 27 *University of Pennsylvania Journal of International Economic Law* 1.
[113] See para.8–029.
[114] See further Chs 16–18.
[115] See further Ch.22. The Seventh Directive on group accounts was less important since domestic law already recognised the principle of group accounting.
[116] See further Ch.23, but the Eighth Directive was revised in 2006 (Directive 2006/43 on statutory audits of annual accounts and consolidated accounts [2006] OJ L157/87) and the second version was more significant.
[117] See para.5–004.
[118] See further Ch.9.

Company[119] and on a Directive on cross-border mergers, and the issue was only resolved by abandoning any significant commitment to uniformity, or even equivalence, of rules on employee representation. Equally controversial has been the draft Ninth Directive on corporate groups, where the majority of states deal with group problems through the general mechanisms of company law, whereas Germany has developed a separate regime for addressing issues of minority shareholder and creditor protection in group situations.

Such was the state of uncertainty into which the company law harmonisation programme had fallen by the end of the twentieth century that, at the end of 2001, the Commission appointed a High Level Group of Experts (HLG) with the brief of providing "recommendations for a modern regulatory European company law framework". The HLG's Final Report[120] proposed a "distinct shift" in the approach of the EU to company law. An important implication of this new approach was that the EU should concentrate, as far as new Directives were concerned, on those areas of company law where it had an especial legislative advantage, principally in relation to cross-border corporate issues. The most significant Directives adopted in the company law area since then have fitted this pattern: the Cross-Border Mergers Directive (2005, amended in 2019 so as to embrace the transfers of the jurisdiction of incorporation—but no longer applicable in the UK)[121]; and the Directive on Shareholder Rights (2007 amended in 2017, which continues as part of "retained EU law").[122] However, it should be noted, in relation to the latter, that although the driving concern of the Commission was the difficulties facing a shareholder in Member State A wishing to exercise voting rights in a company incorporated and listed in Member State B, the Directive approaches this issue by conferring minimum rights on all shareholders in companies whose shares are traded on a regulated market. It is the limitation of the Directive to companies with publicly traded shares that really indicates the cross-border impetus of the Directive.

CONCLUSION

Whilst some of the sources of company law cannot be described as unexpected, **3–016**
such as primary and secondary legislation and the common law, other sources are more noteworthy. Although the use of contractual and delegated rule-making mechanisms are not unique to company law, they are maybe slightly more surprising when one considers the size of the CA 2006. Whilst there are certainly mandatory statutory rules, company law relies heavily upon "private ordering" to

[119] See paras 1–040 onwards.

[120] *Final Report of the High Level Group of Company Law Experts on a Modern Regulatory Framework of Company Law in Europe* (Brussels, 4 November 2002).

[121] Directive 2005/56 on cross-border mergers of limited liability companies [2005] OJ L310/1, later consolidated, amended by Directive 2019/2121 amending Directive 2017/1132 as regards cross-border conversions, mergers and divisions [2019] OJ L321/1. See further Ch.29.

[122] Directive 2007/36 on the exercise of certain rights of shareholders in listed companies [2007] OJ L184/17; Directive 2017/282 amending Directive 2007/36 as regards the encouragement of long-term shareholder engagement [2017] OJ L132/1.

make the system work. In terms of EU law, whilst its status has changed in recent times as regards the UK, the EU harmonisation programme is likely to have left an indelible mark on UK company law.

CHAPTER 4

FORMATION PROCEDURES

FORMATION OF DIFFERENT TYPES OF COMPANY

4–001 As considered previously,[1] there are three basic types of domestic incorporated company—statutory, chartered and registered—each with fundamentally different procedures for their formation. The class of "registered" company, includes not only companies registered by the Registrar of Companies under the CA 2006, but also Charitable Incorporated Organisations (CIOs) registered by the Charity Commissioners under the Charities Act 2011.[2] This chapter's focus is companies registered under the CA 2006, for these are overwhelmingly the most common and important type of company. The category of registered company includes both public companies (limited by shares) and private companies (whether limited by shares, by guarantee, or unlimited),[3] as well as more specialist corporate forms, such as the community interest company (CIC), which may be limited by shares or by guarantee,[4] and former European Companies (SEs)[5] that have now automatically converted to the UK Societas form.[6] Only brief reference will be made to these more unusual forms of registered company for comparison purposes.

---

[1] See paras 1–017 to 1–031.

[2] See para.1–030. See also *Charity Commission for England and Wales v Cambridge Islamic College* [2018] UKUT 351 (TCC). Registering under the Charities Act 2011 as a CIO is optional. Alternatively, companies with charitable objects may register under the CA 2006 (with all that entails) but will also be obliged to comply with the Charities Act 2011. Additionally, certain types of association may also require registration under particular legislation: see Building Societies Act 1986–1997, Friendly Societies Act 1992 and Co-operative and Community Benefit Societies Act 2014.

[3] CA 2006 ss.3–5.

[4] CA 2006 s.6. See further para.1–012.

[5] Regulation 2157/2001 on the Statute for a European company [2001] OJ L294/1, with the application of the CA 2006 secured by the European Public Limited-Liability Company (Amendment) Regulations 2009 (SI 2009/2400). The European Company (SE) was introduced in 2004, with Companies House acting as the registration body for UK-based SEs. An SE cannot be formed by natural persons, but only by existing companies (or analogous bodies) operating by way of merger, joint subsidiary, joint holding company or transformation: see Regulation 2157/2001 art.2(1). It will no longer be possible for UK-registered companies to form new SEs, as result of the requirements in Regulation 2157/2001 arts 2(1) and 7. Nevertheless, EU-registered SEs will continue to be recognised in the UK as part of EU retained law: see European Union (Withdrawal) Act 2018 s.3(2)(a). See further paras 1–040 to 1–044. Following Brexit, a UK-registered European Economic Interest Grouping (EEIG) will automatically become a United Kingdom Economic Interest Grouping (UKEIG), whilst EU-based EEIGs with a UK presence must continue to register with the Companies Registrar: see European Economic Interest Grouping (Amendment) (EU Exit) Regulations 2018 (SI 2018/1299), amending European Economic Interest Grouping Regulations 1989 (SI 1989/638). See further para.1–039. Neither the SE nor the EEIG has created a significant splash: see Companies House, *Statistical Tables on Companies Registration Activities 2019/20* (31 March 2020), Table B3.

[6] European Public Limited-Liability Company (Amendment etc.) (EU Exit) Regulations 2018 (SI 2018/1298) reg.8, inserting European Public Limited-Liability Company Regulations 2004 (SI 2004/2326) reg.12A.

Statutory companies

Statutory companies are formed by passing a Private Act of Parliament, usually when the enterprise is required for public purposes or requires special powers (such as compulsory land acquisition for public utilities). The procedure is generally the same as that applicable to Private Bill legislation, but such entities are only governed by the CA 2006 to the extent expressly provided.[7] The number of statutory companies (and specialist practitioners in the area) is dwindling,[8] given the move first to nationalisation and now to privatisation, both of which are achieved under Public Acts of Parliament. **4–002**

Chartered companies

The creation of new chartered trading companies by royal charter is now unlikely, although this is not uncommon in the case of charitable or public bodies. The procedure is for the corporation's promoters to petition the Crown (through the office of the Lord President of the Council) praying for the grant of a charter, which is usually annexed to the petition in draft form. If the petition is granted, the promoters and their successors then become "one body corporate and politic by the name of—and by that name shall and may sue or be sued plead and be impleaded in all courts whether of law or equity…and shall have perpetual succession and a common seal." Sometimes a charter will be granted to the members of an existing company limited by guarantee and registered under the CA 2006, in which case the assets of the existing company will be transferred to the new chartered body before being wound up, unless the Registrar can be persuaded to strike the company off the register in order to avoid the expense of a formal liquidation.[9] **4–003**

Registered companies

The vast majority of companies nowadays are formed by registration under the CA 2006, whatever their objects. Those persons seeking to register the company (termed its "promoters") are often discussed as if they can only be natural persons, but this is not always the case: an existing company frequently forms a new company that will form part of the same corporate group as either a parent, subsidiary or sister company.[10] In terms of the registration process itself, specific statutory functions are allocated to the Registrar of Companies and the Secretary of State, although their statutory powers are typically exercised by employees and **4–004**

---

[7] CA 2006 s.1043. See also Unregistered Companies Regulations 2009 (SI 2009/2436) reg.3 and Sch.1. See further paras 1–031 to 1–033.

[8] Companies House, *Statistical Tables on Companies Registration Activities 2019/20* (31 March 2020), Table B3.

[9] See Ch.33.

[10] A corporate group can be formed other than by creating a new company, since the original company may acquire the shares of an existing company if it intends to expand by acquiring an established business, rather than by establishing a new business from scratch.

authorised delegates.[11] Indeed, most of the powers discussed subsequently are exercised by Companies House, which is an executive agency of the Department for Business, Energy and Industrial Strategy (BEIS).[12] The procedure to be followed is considered next.

FORMING A COMPANY BY REGISTRATION

Registration documents

4–005 Besides the explicit requirement that a company cannot be formed for an unlawful purpose,[13] there are few legal restrictions upon incorporating a company in British company law.[14] In order to register a company under the CA 2006,[15] the promoters must deliver specified documents to the Registrar of Companies and pay a registration fee.[16] The statutory list of documents that need to be filed provide a helpful checklist for promoters in identifying the various decisions that must be taken early on. The documents required for registration are:

(1) A memorandum of association in prescribed form indicating that those subscribing to the memorandum wish to form a company and agree to become its initial members by taking at least one share each.[17]

---

[11] Contracting Out (Functions in Relation to the Registration of Companies) Order 1995 (SI 1995/1013) regs 3 and 5 and Schs 1 and 3 (as amended by SI 2001/3649 and SI 2015/971), enacted pursuant to the Deregulation and Contracting Out Act 1994.

[12] *Sebry v Companies House* [2015] EWHC 115 (QB); [2015] B.C.C. 236 at [49]–[58].

[13] CA 2006 s.7(2). This prohibition has been interpreted as banning both purposes that are criminal and those that might be regarded as contrary to public policy: see *R. v Registrar of Joint Stock Companies, Ex p. More* [1931] 2 K.B. 197 CA; *R. v Registrar of Companies Ex p. Attorney General* [1991] B.C.L.C. 476 DC; *Rossendale BC v Hurstwood Properties (A) Ltd* [2019] EWCA Civ 364; [2019] B.C.C. 774 at [25]. For a similar position with respect to limited partnerships, see *Bank of Beirut SAL v HRH Prince El-Hashemite* [2015] EWHC 1451 (Ch); [2016] Ch. 1 at [92]. The Registrar of Companies is unlikely to be liable to third parties who suffer loss by dealing with a registered company on the basis that the Registrar owed them a common law duty to exercise reasonable care in registering that company or issuing a trading certificate (see *Yuen Kun Yeu v Attorney General of Hong Kong* [1988] A.C. 175 PC; approved in *N v Poole BC* [2019] UKSC 25; [2019] H.L.R. 39 at [41]), but the Registrar can owe such a duty to a company appearing on the register to ensure that its details are correct, and in particular that a winding-up order is not erroneously registered against its name (see *Sebry v Companies House* [2015] B.C.C. 236).

[14] A public company must have a minimum initial share capital: see CA 2006 ss.761 and 765.

[15] For the purposes of the CA 2006, a "company" includes those companies registered under earlier legislation going back to 1856, even though the registration requirements have changed over time: see CA 2006 s.1(1). See further *Credit Suisse International v Stichting Vestia Groep* [2014] EWHC 3103 (Comm) at [255].

[16] See Registrar of Companies (Fees) (Companies, Overseas Companies and Limited Liability Partnerships) Regulations (SI 2012/1907) Sch.1 para.8 (as amended by SI 2016/621), stipulating fees ranging from £10–£30 for electronic registration, and £40–£100 for non-electronic registration. The fee is £20 to register a CIC or unlimited company. To facilitate electronic filing, Companies House currently operates a web-based and software-based incorporation service using designated software.

[17] CA 2006 ss.7(1)(a), 8 and 16(2). For the form of memorandum, see Companies (Registration) Regulations 2008/3014 (hereafter "Registration Regulations") reg.2 and Schs 1–2. In contrast to this very basic document, the memorandum of a company registered before 1 October 2009 (an "old-style memorandum") was a radically different and important constitutional document: see *Guinness v Land Corp of Ireland* (1882) 22 Ch. D. 349 CA at 376–378 and 381; *Welton v Saffery* [1897] A.C. 299 HL

(2) An application for registration, stating[18]:
   (a) The company's proposed name.[19]
   (b) Whether the company's registered office is to be in England and Wales, Wales, Scotland or Northern Ireland,[20] together with that registered office's address.[21]
   (c) Whether the liability of the members is to be limited and, if so, whether by shares or guarantee.[22] In the latter case, the application must include a statement of guarantee,[23] which must indicate the amount which each member of the company agrees to contribute to the company on its winding up.[24] In the case of a company having a share capital,[25] a statement of capital and initial shareholdings must be part of the application.[26] This statement must state the total number of shares to be taken by the subscribers, together with their aggregate nominal value, any amount unpaid on those shares and the details of any class rights.[27] These details must also be broken down for each individual subscriber,[28] together with each person's name and address.[29]
   (d) Whether the company is to be public or private.[30]
   (e) A statement of the company's proposed officers,[31] which indicates the persons who have consented to act as the company's first directors and secretary,[32] including the details that have to be

at 329; *HSBC Bank Middle East v Clarke* [2006] UKPC 31 at [21]–[26]. Such memoranda are nowadays deemed to be part of the company's articles of association: see CA 2006 s.28.

18 CA 2006 s.9(1)–(2).

19 CA 2006 s.9(2)(a). See further paras 4–013 to 4–021.

20 CA 2006 s.9(2)(b). This place of registration will determine the company's domicile, which cannot be abandoned in the same way as an individual: see *Carl Zeiss Siftung v Rayner & Keeler Ltd (Pleadings: Striking Out)* [1970] Ch. 506 Ch D at 544.

21 CA 2006 s.9(5)(a).

22 CA 2006 s.9(2)(c). See further paras 4–010 to 4–011.

23 CA 2006 s.9(4)(b).

24 CA 2006 s.11(2)–(3). The statement must include each subscriber's name and address: see Registration Regulations reg.4.

25 Whilst a company having a share capital will usually be limited, an unlimited company may still have a share capital, although this is not possible in the case of a company limited by guarantee: see CA 2006 s.5(1). See also *Hunters Property Plc v Revenue and Customs Commissioners* [2018] UKFTT 96 (TC) at [39].

26 CA 2006 s.9(4)(a).

27 CA 2006 s.10(2). The company's power to issue different classes of share will be contained in its articles of association. For the exercise of this power, see Ch.24.

28 CA 2006 s.10(4).

29 Registration Regulations reg.3.

30 CA 2006 s.9(2)(d).

31 CA 2006 s.9(4)(c).

32 CA 2006 s.12(1) and (3). Whilst a private company need no longer have a company secretary, a public company must: CA 2006 ss.270–271. Accordingly, in most cases, the statement will simply indicate the company's first directors. See also *Premier Model Management Ltd v Bruce* [2012] EWHC 3509 (QB) at [47].

included in the register of directors (unless an election has been made to record the information centrally).[33]

(f) A statement of initial significant control,[34] namely the particulars of individuals or legal entities who are considered to exercise significant control over the company on incorporation.[35] This includes persons or legal entities holding 25% of the shares or voting rights in the company, those who have the right to appoint or remove a majority of the board of directors, and those who have the right to exercise, or actually exercise, significant influence or control over the company.[36]

(3) A copy of the proposed articles of association, to the extent that the company's internal regulations are not supplied by the default model articles.[37]

(4) A statement of the type of company that the company is intended to be, together with its intended principal business activities.[38] The type of company must be identified by reference to a statutory classification scheme,[39] whereas the company's intended business must be determined according to the Standard Industrial Classification 2007.[40]

(5) A statement of compliance, which the Registrar may accept as sufficient evidence that the requirements of the CA 2006 have been satisfied.[41]

4–006 In addition to the above filing requirements, a CIC must satisfy two further conditions. First, a CIC's articles of association must contain the provisions set out in the appropriate schedule to the Community Interest Company Regulations 2005, which deal with such issues as (in companies with a share capital) distribution of the CIC's assets, the directors' power to refuse registration of shares and the exercise of voting rights.[42] Secondly, the CIC's promoters must provide the Registrar with a "community interest statement", which is a document signed by each of the company's first directors and which declares that the company will carry on its activities for the benefit of the community and indicates how the company's activities will benefit the community.[43] Upon receipt of the necessary documentation, the Registrar will forward it to the

---

[33] CA 2006 s.162. This initial statement is the first expression of an obligation which will continue throughout the company's life to inform the Registrar about these matters periodically, although a company can elect to keep the information centrally: CA 2006 s.167A. See further para.9–007.

[34] CA 2006 s.9(4)(d), inserted by the Small Business, Enterprise and Employment Act 2015 s.93 to improve transparency around who owns and controls UK businesses. See further paras 13–022 to 13–026.

[35] CA 2006 s.12A. For the identification of persons with "significant control", see CA 2006 ss.790C, 790K, 790M and Sch.1A.

[36] CA 2006 Sch.1A. See further para.13–023.

[37] CA 2006 ss.9(5)(b). For the default application of the model articles, see CA 2006 s.20. See further paras 3–011 to 3–012.

[38] CA 2006 s.9(5)(c), inserted by the Small Business, Enterprise and Employment Act 2015 s.93.

[39] CA 2006 ss.9(5A). See also Companies and Limited Liability Partnerships (Filing Requirements) Regulations 2016 (SI 2016/599) reg.6 and Sch.4.

[40] CA 2006 ss.9(5B). See also Companies and Limited Liability Partnerships (Filing Requirements) Regulations 2016 (SI 2016/599) reg.7.

[41] CA 2006 s.13.

[42] Community Interest Company Regulations 2005 (SI 2005/1788) reg.8 and Sch.2.

[43] Community Interest Company Regulations 2005 (SI 2005/1788) regs 2 and 11.

Regulator of Community Interest Companies (the CIC Regulator),[44] who will decide whether the proposed CIC satisfies the "community interest test",[45] in other words whether "a reasonable person might consider that [the CIC's] activities are being carried on for the benefit of the community".[46] Only if the CIC Regulator concludes that the "community interest test" is satisfied will the Registrar register the company as a CIC.[47] If the CIC Regulator reaches the opposite conclusion, then any subscriber to the proposed CIC's memorandum of association can appeal that determination to the CIC Appeal Officer.[48]

Certificate of incorporation

None of the above requirements is particularly demanding, although this is part of a deliberate policy choice to make the benefits of incorporation readily accessible. If Companies House is satisfied that the registration requirements in the CA 2006 have been met, then it must register the company,[49] allocate the company a "registered number",[50] and provide the company with a certificate of incorporation.[51] Such a certificate is conclusive evidence that the requirements of the CA 2006 have been met and that the company is duly registered thereunder.[52] This is so even if the company's registration has been procured by fraud.[53] As considered further below,[54] challenging a certificate of incorporation is difficult. 4–007

The effect of incorporation is that "the subscribers to the memorandum, together with such other persons as may from time to time become members of the company, are a body corporate by the name stated in the certificate of incorporation".[55] Further, the subscribers to the memorandum become the holders of the shares specified in the statement of capital and the directors and secretary (if any) named in the statement of proposed officers are deemed to have been appointed to their offices.[56] 4–008

44 Companies (Audit, Investigations and Community Enterprise) Act 2004 ss.27(1) and 36(3).

45 Companies (Audit, Investigations and Community Enterprise) Act 2004 s.36A(2).

46 Companies (Audit, Investigations and Community Enterprise) Act 2004 s.35(2). For the exclusion of political activities or activities only benefitting members of a particular body or employees of a particular entity, see Community Interest Company Regulations 2005 (SI 2005/1788) regs 3–4.

47 Companies (Audit, Investigations and Community Enterprise) Act 2004 s.36D(2).

48 Companies (Audit, Investigations and Community Enterprise) Act 2004 s.36B(3).

49 CA 2006 s.14.

50 CA 2006 s.1066(1).

51 CA 2006 s.15(1). As well as setting out the company's details, the incorporation certificate must be signed by the registrar and authenticated by his or her official seal: CA 2006 s.15(2)–(3).

52 CA 2006 s.15(4). See also *Rossendale BC v Hurstwood Properties (A) Ltd* [2019] B.C.C. 774 at [25]. The certificate of incorporation is also conclusive that a company is a CIC: see Companies (Audit, Investigations and Community Enterprise) Act 2004 s.36B(2).

53 *Bank of Beirut SAL v Prince El-Hashemite* [2016] Ch. 1 at [84]–[86] and [103]–[106].

54 See paras 4–032 onwards.

55 CA 2006 s.16(2). This makes clear the company's nature as an incorporated association: see *Rossendale BC v Hurstwood Properties (A) Ltd* [2019] B.C.C. 774 at [25].

56 CA 2006 s.16(5)–(6).

Purchase of a shelf-company

4–009 The majority of new companies are formed by specialist company-formation agents.[57] Historically, these agents ran their businesses by registering large numbers of companies, and then holding them ready to sell "off the shelf" to promoters who wanted to incorporate rapidly. The agents themselves (and persons associated with them) were the original subscribers, first members and officers of the company. Accordingly, the company promoter would simply purchase the shares, vote in new officers, change the company's name and registered office, and report all these amendments to Companies House. Given the speed of electronic registration nowadays, company-formation agents can meet promoters' specific requests very quickly and directly without having to employ a shelf company.

CHOICE OF TYPE OF REGISTERED COMPANY

4–010 Arguably, one of the first decisions for a company's promoter is to decide which of the several different types of registered company they wish to form, since this will impact the documents to be filed. First, the promoter must choose between a limited or unlimited company.[58] Both types of company are fully liable to their creditors; the distinction relates to the extent of the members' liability (to their company, rather than directly to their company's creditors[59]) to meet the company's debts. In an unlimited company, the members will ultimately be personally liable (jointly, severally and to an unlimited extent) for the company's debts in the event of its formal liquidation,[60] whereas a shareholder's liability in a limited company is capped at the amount of his or her investment (or guarantee).[61] Accordingly, a promoter is likely to avoid unlimited companies as a corporate form, especially if the company intends to trade actively. In contrast, if the intention is that the company merely holds land or investments, then the absence of limited liability may not matter. Indeed, unlimited companies confer certain advantages as regards returning capital to the members[62] and avoiding the public disclosure of the company's financial position.[63] Indeed, the absence of limited liability may also render the company more acceptable in certain circles (for example, the turf).

Secondly, if the promoter decides upon a limited company, there is then a decision as to whether the company should be limited by shares or by

---

[57] Developing, para.11.32, estimating that 60% of registrations are carried out by such persons.

[58] See para.1–027 above. Formerly, a further (rarely adopted) option was to incorporate a limited company with unlimited liability on the directors' part: see CA 1985 s.306. There is no equivalent in the CA 2006.

[59] *Oakes v Turquand* (1867) L.R. 2 H.L. 325 HL.

[60] IA 1986 s.74(1).

[61] IA 1986 s.74(2)(d) and (3).

[62] The prohibition against a company acquiring its own shares applies only to limited companies: see CA 2006 s.658(1).

[63] An unlimited company is not required to file its annual accounts and reports (and so make them publicly available): see CA 2006 s.448.

guarantee.[64] As considered previously,[65] this choice is largely driven by the purpose for which the company is being formed: a trading company is likely to be limited by shares, with companies limited by guarantee being particularly well-suited to non-profit-making activity.

Thirdly, overlapping (and closely bound up with) the above two distinctions, is the further issue of whether the company should have a share capital or not. If, as is most likely, the proposed company is to be limited by shares, then this further question does not arise. The position is likewise if the company is to be limited by guarantee.[66] If the company is unlimited, it may or may not have its capital divided into shares. That choice is again dependent upon the company's purpose: if the company is intended to make and distribute profits, share capital would be appropriate and useful. **4–011**

Fourthly, if the company is to be limited by shares or by guarantee with a share capital,[67] the promoter will further have to decide whether the company will be public or private. As discussed previously,[68] public and private companies fulfil essentially different economic purposes: the former type of company is used to raise capital from the public to fund the corporate enterprise's business, whereas the latter type is designed to confer separate legal personality on the business of a single trader or partnership. Accordingly, the choice will in practice be clear-cut, and the norm will be to form a private company initially, with the incorporator's ultimate ambition being for the company to "go public". A company will rarely be in a position to become public from the outset. In the unusual circumstances where a company is public from incorporation, that company will nowadays have to be a company limited by shares; its certificate of incorporation will have to state that it is a public company; and it will have to satisfy special requirements concerning its registration,[69] including having the prescribed minimum share capital.[70] Any other type of company will, perforce, be a private company.

Finally, there is the question (which again cuts across the above distinctions) as to whether the company's objects should be exclusively charitable, so as to make it a charitable company.[71] In such circumstances, the promoter might opt to register the charitable company under the CA 2006 or to register a CIO under the Charities Act 2011.[72] Alternatively, if the company's objects are not charitable in **4–012**

[64] CA 2006 s.3(1).

[65] See paras 1–008 to 1–010.

[66] Since the CA 1980, companies limited by guarantee can no longer have a share capital: see CA 2006 s.5.

[67] Given that it is no longer possible to form a company limited by guarantee with a share capital, this possibility only applies to companies incorporated before 1980: see CA 2006 s.5.

[68] See paras 1–018 to 1–021.

[69] CA 2006 s.4(2).

[70] Before a public company starts trading, it must have a nominal allotted share capital that is not less than the statutory "authorised minimum" of £50,000 or its prescribed euro equivalent, denominated in sterling or euros, but not both: see CA 2006 ss.761, 763 and 765. At least one-quarter of the nominal value of the public company's shares must be paid up: see CA 2006 s.586.

[71] See para.1–030. See, for example, *Children's Investment Fund Foundation (UK) v Attorney General* [2020] UKSC 33; [2020] 3 W.L.R. 461.

[72] According to Charities Act 2011 s.220, "each member of a CIO must exercise the powers that the member has in that capacity in a way that the member decides, in good faith, would be most likely to further the purposes of the CIO": see *Re The Ethiopian Orthodox Tewahedo Church St Mary of Debre*

nature, it has been possible since 2004 for a limited company to be formed as a "community interest company" (CIC) under the Companies (Audit, Investigations and Community Enterprise) Act 2004. Although not formally charities, a CIC must nevertheless satisfy the "community interest test", which is satisfied "if a reasonable person might consider that [the company's] activities are being carried on for the benefit of the community".[73] A CIC must comply with additional statutory requirements, such as its articles restricting the payment of dividends and the transfer of corporate assets, other than for full consideration.[74]

In practice, irrespective of the above distinctions, the vast majority of companies incorporated in England and Wales are private companies limited by shares, which are neither charitable nor community interest companies.[75]

CHOICE OF COMPANY NAME

4–013 As well as the various decisions considered above, the incorporators must decide on a suitable corporate name to be included in the application for registration.[76] A company's name is significant, since it identifies the artificial person,[77] describes its status as a limited public or private company,[78] and over time becomes the basis of the company's reputation and goodwill. Given the importance of a company's name, there are legal requirements concerning the choice of corporate name (including its length),[79] its mandatory publicity,[80] its protection from abuse, and its alteration.[81]

Tsion, London [2020] EWHC 1493 (Ch) at [44]–[59]. See further *Charity Commission for England and Wales v Cambridge Islamic College* [2018] UKUT 351.

73 Companies (Audit, Investigations and Community Enterprise) Act 2004 s.35(2).

74 Companies (Audit, Investigations and Community Enterprise) Act 2004. See also Community Interest Company Regulations 2005 (SI 2005/1788) regs 7–11.

75 During 2020, private limited companies accounted for around 93% of all entities on the register at Companies House: see Companies House, *Statistical Tables on Companies Registration Activities 2019/20* (31 March 2020), Table C1.

76 CA 2006 s.9(2)(a).

77 Although the corporate name remains important, its significance has been diminished now that the Registrar has to allot each company a unique registered number (see CA 2006 s.1066), which must be stated on the company's business letters and order forms: CA 2006 s.82(1)(a).

78 CA 2006 ss.58–59. See further para.4–014.

79 Largely for reasons of not overloading the Companies House computer system, a limit has been placed on the number of characters in a company's name (no more than 160) and on the permitted characters and format of the name: see CA 2006 s.57. See also Company, Limited Liability Partnership and Business (Names and Trading Disclosures) Regulations 2015 (SI 2015/17) reg.2. The longest registered name at the time of the DTI consultation was 159 characters: see Department of Trade and Industry, *Implementation of the Companies Act 2006: Consultation Document* (February 2007), para.2.38. Like the famously long Welsh place name, Llanfairpwllgwyngyllgogerychwyrndrobwllllantysiliogogogoch, it is more a description than a name.

80 The Secretary of State has power to require companies to give appropriate publicity to their names at their places of business and on business correspondence and related documentation: see CA 2006 s.82(2)(a). See also Company, Limited Liability Partnership and Business (Names and Trading Disclosures) Regulations 2015 (SI 2015/17) regs 20–29. Where a company has a common seal, its name must appear legibly thereon: see CA 2006 s.45(1)–(2).

81 See further paras 4–022 onwards.

Warning the public about limited liability or other status

If the company is a limited company, its name must end with the prescribed suffix "limited" (or "Ltd") if the company is private, or "public limited company" (or "Plc") if it is public.[82] The purpose of this formal requirement is to warn third parties dealing with the company that its members have limited liability,[83] although whether this warning is very effective is open to question. In addition, the company's actual name must not include (except at the end of its name) the words "public limited company", "community interest company" or "community interest public limited company" or their abbreviations or Welsh equivalents. Similarly, the company may not use "limited" or "unlimited" (or their abbreviations or Welsh equivalents) anywhere in the name, unless the company is in fact a limited or unlimited company.[84] Such a prohibition primarily prevents any blurring or undermining of the warnings implied by the abbreviations, "Ltd" or "Plc".[85] **4–014**

The CA 2006 provides three narrow exemptions to the requirement that a private company should have "limited" at the end of its name.[86] First, charitable companies are exempted from that requirement.[87] Secondly, companies are exempted from that requirement where this is permitted by regulation[88]: accordingly the Company, Limited Liability Partnership and Business (Names and Trading Disclosures) Regulations 2015 exempt a company limited by guarantee that has as its objects "the promotion or regulation of commerce, art, **4–015**

---

[82] CA 2006 ss.58–59. In the case of a Welsh company (namely, a company with its registered office in Wales under the CA 2006 s.88(1)), the Welsh equivalents ("cyfyngedig" (or "cyf") or "cwmni cyfyngedig cyhoeddus" (or "ccc")) may (but need not) be used instead. Similarly, in the case of a "community interest company" that term (or its abbreviation "cic") must be used as the suffix, if it is a private company, and "community interest public limited company" (abbreviated to "community interest plc"), if it is public: see Companies (Audit, Investigations and Community Enterprise) Act 2004 s.33. The Welsh equivalents are "cwmni buddiant cymunedol" ("cbc") and "cwmni buddiant cymunedol cyhoeddus cyfyngedig" ("cwmni buddiant cymunedol ccc"). Moreover, in relation to a societas europaea, the requirement was that the name must begin or end with "SE", and no company or firm formed on or after 8 October 2004 may use that abbreviation otherwise in its name: see Regulation 2157/2001 on the Statute for a European Company [2001] OJ L294/1 art.11. Whilst this continues to apply to SEs registered in EU Member States, former UK-registered SEs have now converted to a new form, the "UK Societas" and accordingly such a company's name must now bear that designation: see European Public Limited Liability Company (Amendment etc.) (EU Exit) Regulations 2018 (SI 2018/1298) reg.8, inserting European Public Limited-Liability Company Regulations 2004 (SI 2004/2326) reg.12A.

[83] *Fairhold Mercury Ltd v HQ (Block 1) Action Management Co Ltd* [2013] UKUT 487; [2014] L. & T.R. 5 at [21].

[84] CA 2006 s.65(1). See also Company, Limited Liability Partnership and Business (Names and Trading Disclosures) Regulations 2015 (SI 2015/17) reg.4. Moreover, a company may not use the terms "open ended investment company", "investment company with variable capital" or "limited liability partnership" (or their abbreviations or Welsh equivalents).

[85] A moneylender would presumably be prevented from incorporating as "Unlimited Loans Ltd" (there being no authorised abbreviation for "unlimited").

[86] CA 2006 s.60.

[87] CA 2006 s.60(1)(a).

[88] CA 2006 s.60(1)(b).

science, education, religion, charity or any profession".[89] This exemption only applies if the company's articles require its income to be devoted to the promotion of those objects, forbid the payment of dividends or any return of capital to members and require the company's assets on a winding-up to be transferred to a body with like objects or a charity.[90] In essence, this exemption covers charitable companies or companies with public interest objectives that cannot be used to make a profit for their members. Thirdly, certain companies are exempted under the "grandfather" provision, which protects companies exempted under earlier rules.[91]

Prohibition on illegal or offensive names

4–016 More important than what a corporate name must contain is what it must not. Certain corporate names are prohibited, if, in the Secretary of State's opinion, use of the name would constitute a criminal offence or be "offensive".[92] An example would be a company that uses a name (such as "bank") suggesting it is authorised to carry out an activity regulated by the Financial Conduct Authority.[93]

Names requiring special approval

4–017 As well as the above outright prohibition on some corporate names, other possible names may only be adopted with the Secretary of State's express approval. This would include names that would be likely to give the impression that the company is connected in any way with central government, a local authority or other specified public authority.[94] Permission is also required to use certain specified "sensitive words or expressions" in a corporate name.[95] Where the necessary permission is sought, the Secretary of State can require the person seeking permission to consult with the government department or other body that has an interest in the matter, so that it can raise any objections and the reasons

[89] Company, Limited Liability Partnership and Business (Names and Trading Disclosures) Regulations 2015 (SI 2015/17) reg.3(2).

[90] Company, Limited Liability Partnership and Business (Names and Trading Disclosures) Regulations 2015 (SI 2015/17) reg.3(3). The Department of Trade and Industry had originally proposed to confine the exemption to statutory regulators established as companies (for example, the (now defunct) Financial Services Authority) on the grounds that the community interest company catered sufficiently for other companies deserving exemption, but the consultation changed this view: see Department for Trade and Industry, *Implementation of the Companies Act 2006: Consultation Document* (February 2007) para.2.47. See also BERR, *Government Response to consultation on Companies Act 2006: Company and Business Names* (URN 07/1244/GR), para.2.8.

[91] CA 2006 ss.60(1)(c), 61–62.

[92] CA 2006 s.53.

[93] Financial Services and Markets Act 2000 s.24. The same principle would apply to non-financial activities requiring the prior authorisation of a regulatory body.

[94] CA 2006 s.54(1). See also Company, Limited Liability Partnership and Business (Names and Trading Disclosures) Regulations 2015/17 reg.9 and Sch.4.

[95] CA 2006 s.55. See also Company, Limited Liability Partnership and Business Names (Sensitive Words and Expressions) Regulations 2014/3140 regs 3–4 and Sch.1, listing around 135 "sensitive" words.

therefor.[96] Whatever body must be consulted,[97] the application for the company's registration must indicate that this has occurred and provide a copy of any response.[98]

Prohibition on using a name already allocated

Even if not prohibited or "sensitive", a corporate name cannot be the same as one already on the Registrar's index of names.[99] This can potentially present a significant obstacle given that there are over two million names on that index, which include companies incorporated under the CA 2006 or earlier legislation, unregistered companies, overseas companies that have registered particulars in the UK, limited liability partnerships, limited partnerships, European Economic Interest Groupings registered in the UK, UK Economic Interest Groupings, open-ended investment companies, protected cell companies, charitable incorporated organisations and societies registered under the Co-operative and Community Benefit Societies Act 2014.[100] Certain differences are to be disregarded when judging whether a name is "the same as another name" and certain expressions are to be treated as the same,[101] thus expanding the scope of the prohibition. Hence, sole traders called Smith, Jones, Brown or Davies may have difficulty in continuing to use their name following incorporation.[102] **4–018**

There is, however, power to permit registration of a name that would otherwise be prohibited, if the company seeking registration is part of the same corporate group as the entity with the same name and that entity agrees to the new company's registration with that name.[103] These requirements seek to safeguard the interests of the existing company and to minimise the risk of confusion on the part of the public, albeit that the risk is not eliminated entirely given that a third party could still confuse a corporate group's well capitalised parent company with its undercapitalised subsidiaries bearing the same name.

---

96 CA 2006 s.56.

97 For the specified bodies, see Company, Limited Liability Partnership and Business Names (Sensitive Words and Expressions) Regulations 2014/3140 regs 3–4 and Sch.2. For example, if the name includes "Charitable" or "Charity", the Charity Commission or Office of the Scottish Charity Regulator must be asked; if "Dental" or "Dentistry", the General Dental Council; and if "Windsor" (because of its royal associations), the Ministry of Justice, the Welsh Assembly Government or the Scottish Executive.

98 CA 2006 s.56(3).

99 CA 2006 s.66.

100 CA 2006 s.1099(2)–(3).

101 CA 2006 s.66(3). See also Company, Limited Liability Partnership and Business (Names and Trading Disclosures) Regulations (SI 2015/17) reg.7 and Schs 2–3. For example, the words "company" and "cwmni" at the end of a company's name are to be disregarded in judging whether two names are the same (so that if this is the only difference, the names will be considered the same) and "@" and "at" are to be treated as the same.

102 Those with less common surnames can often surmount this difficulty by, for example, inserting an appropriate place-name: e.g. Gower (Hampstead) Ltd.

103 CA 2006 s.66(4). See also Company, Limited Liability Partnership and Business (Names and Trading Disclosures) Regulations (SI 2015/17) reg.8. If the existing body's consent is subsequently withdrawn, that will not affect the registration of the new company.

Restrictions on using defunct company names and phoenix companies

4–019 Whilst the above restrictions do not prevent a company from adopting a defunct company's name, a former director or shadow director of a company that went into insolvent liquidation must not act as a director, nor participate in the management, of a company with the same or a similar name for the next five years.[104] Breach of this prohibition attracts both civil and criminal liability.

Use of a business name other than the corporate name

4–020 Both individuals and partnerships may conduct their businesses under their individual names.[105] Similarly, a company may trade under its registered name.[106] Alternatively, individuals, partnerships or companies may adopt a "business name" (or "trading name"), but the choice of such names is now subject to broadly the same restrictions and permissions as apply to the initial choice of a company's registered name.[107] In relation to business names, however, the convenient administrative sanction of refusing its registration is unavailable, since unincorporated businesses do not require registration in order to carry on business. Consequently, the regulation of business names makes contravention a criminal offence.[108] In addition, just as companies are obliged to make disclosure of their registered names during the course of business,[109] so unincorporated businesses must similarly disclose any business name during the course of their activities.[110] Unlike in the case of a company,[111] however, neither the Secretary of State nor an adjudicator is empowered to direct an unincorporated business to change its business name because it is the same as, or too like, the name of an existing business, corporate or unincorporated.

4–021 The above discussion highlights that it may sometimes be difficult to find a name acceptable to the incorporators, the Registrar and the Secretary of State. Without such a name, however, it will be impossible to complete the documents required to register the company and unsafe to order the stationery that the company will need once registered. One solution might be a system enabling a promoter to obtain advance clearance from the Registrar of a chosen corporate name. Unlike some other common law countries, however, there has never been a procedure in the UK whereby a name can be reserved for a prescribed period of time. That said, prior to 1981, it was possible (and usual) to write to the Registrar submitting a name (or two or three alternative names) to ask if it was available. If the reply was affirmative it was usually safe to proceed, so long as one did so promptly.

[104] IA 1986 s.216. See further paras 19–022 onwards.

[105] CA 2006 s.1192(2)–(3).

[106] CA 2006 s.16.

[107] CA 2006 ss.1192–1199, replacing the Business Names Act 1985.

[108] CA 2006 ss.1193(4), 1194(3), 1197(5), 1198(2) and 1207.

[109] CA 2006 s.82.

[110] CA 2006 ss.1200–1204. The same civil sanction is applied as in the case of companies: CA 2006 s.1206.

[111] See further paras 4–022 to 4–023.

Nowadays, the incorporators (or their professional advisers) have to search the index[112] with the attendant risks of getting things wrong.

MANDATORY AND ELECTIVE NAME CHANGES

Even if a company's promoters manage to secure its registration under a particular name, there is no guarantee that they will be able to retain that name. Indeed, the Secretary of State has power to direct a company to change its name in certain circumstances. Alternatively, a change of name may be judicially required following a successful application to the "company names adjudicator" or to the courts (in the context of a passing off action) if the chosen name either exploits or damages the goodwill or reputation of another business. The final option is that a company may, of course, choose to change its own name. **4–022**

Requirements to change a name

The Secretary of State may direct a company to change its name if the company, which was previously exempt from the requirement to include "limited" in its name,[113] ceases to be entitled to that exemption[114]; if the company's name is so misleading as to its activities that it is likely to cause harm to the public[115]; if the company provided misleading information or gave an unfulfilled undertaking in order to be registered by that name[116]; or if the name is **4–023**

> "the same as or, in the opinion of the Secretary of State, too like[117] … a name appearing at the time of registration in the registrar's index of company names … or a name that should have appeared in that index at that time".[118]

---

[112] A search would ideally also encompass the Register of Trade Marks to ensure that the proposed name does not infringe someone's registered trade mark.

[113] CA 2006 s.60.

[114] CA 2006 s.64(1)(a). There is no time limit for giving such a direction.

[115] CA 2006 s.76. There is no time limit for giving such a direction. The company may apply to the court to set aside the direction within three weeks of its being given, but otherwise must comply with the direction (or the court order) within six weeks: s.76(3)–(5). For example, in *Association of Certified Public Accountants of Britain v Secretary of State for Trade and Industry* [1997] B.C.C. 736 Ch D the court confirmed the direction for a name change, stating that the public risked being harmed by paying more for the company's services as a result of the word "Certified" in the company's name misleading them as to the qualifications of the company's members. In general, however, little use is made of this power. Undoubtedly, the names of many companies give totally misleading indications of the nature of their activities but this, on its own, has apparently not been thought "likely to cause harm to the public".

[116] CA 2006 s.75(1). A direction may be given up to five years after registration: CA 2006 s.75(2)(a).

[117] The requirement that names be "too like" does not require any actual deception of third parties: see *Charity Commission for England and Wales v Cambridge Islamic College* [2018] UKUT 351 (TCC) at [35]–[37]. See further *Re Calmex Ltd* (1988) 4 B.C.C. 761 Ch D (Companies Ct), where the corporate names were not thought to be "too like", even though they were sufficiently alike to have caused a petitioning creditor to obtain a winding up order against the wrong company with damaging consequences.

[118] CA 2006 s.67.

In this regard, however, the Secretary of State's power is limited to directing the company to change its name, rather than directing the Registrar to amend the register.[119] If such a direction is given, the company may change its name by special resolution or by any other procedure specified in its articles[120] (or, if the Secretary of State's direction relates to the exemption from using the word "limited", by board resolution).[121] In every case, the company and each of its officers commits an offence if the Secretary of State's direction is not complied with.[122]

The last of these powers enables the Secretary of State to correct any failure to comply with the prohibition on a company being registered with a name that is the same as an existing corporate name on the register[123] (whether because the name had not then been entered on the index or because the similarity between the names had simply escaped detection). More interestingly, the Secretary of State's ability to direct a change of name extends beyond the statutory prohibition on registering a company with the "same" name as an existing company to encompass the situation where a corporate name is "too like" that of an existing company, with the result that the name might cause confusion in the minds of the public.[124] It is not necessary to establish that any existing company (with the same or similar name) is likely to suffer damage to its business goodwill (as for the passing off action, considered later), but the Secretary of State only has 12 months from the registration of the new company to issue a relevant direction.[125] Once that time period has elapsed, the new company is also likely to have acquired goodwill in its name, with the result that it would suffer loss if the Secretary of State could subsequently require the company to change its name. In those circumstances, it is right that (after the 12-month period has elapsed) any complainant should have to satisfy the more stringent tests of a passing off action.

Passing off actions

4–024 The Secretary of State's power to direct a change of name that is the same as another company's name is primarily directed at securing a company's rapid compliance with the statutory requirements relating to corporate names (albeit that there is also the wider ability to direct a change when a name is "too like" another). More usually, however, the corporate name in question satisfies the statutory requirements, but nevertheless may be deceptively similar to the name

119 CA 2006 s. 67(1). See *Halifax Plc v Halifax Repossessions Ltd* [2004] EWCA Civ 331; [2004] B.C.C. 281, where the same constraints appeared to apply to an action for trademark infringement. See also *Registrar of Companies v Swarbrick* [2014] EWHC 1466 (Ch) at [55]; *Shard Financial Media Ltd v Blue Moon Group Ltd* [2018] EWHC 3735 (IPEC) at [7]–[8].

120 CA 2006 s.77(1). See further para.4–030.

121 CA 2006 s.64(3).

122 See, for example, CA 2006 s.68(5).

123 CA 2006 s.66.

124 A risk of confusion is sufficient and there is no need that actual deception have occurred: see *Charity Commission for England and Wales v Cambridge Islamic College* [2018] UKUT 351 (TCC) at [35]–[37]. An interlocutory application in a passing off action may provide speedier relief: see *Glaxo Plc v Glaxowellcome Ltd* [1996] F.S.R. 388.

125 CA 2006 s.68(2)(a).

of an existing company that is carrying on the same type of business (broadly defined).[126] In such cases, the newer company is effectively cashing-in on the reputation of the earlier company and appropriating its goodwill and connections. This type of problem is remedied by the tort of passing off. This gives the earlier company the possibility of obtaining damages or an injunction against the newer company provided the former can demonstrate that the latter's choice of name presents a serious threat to its business. The practical effect of such an injunction is that the offending company must either change its name[127] or dissolve itself.[128] Intention to pass off is irrelevant.[129] A similar claim can be advanced in relation to use of another's registered trade mark.[130]

More recently, the courts have also been alert to pre-emptive strikes, whereby entrepreneurs register companies with the names of existing traders or famous people who may wish to use that corporate name in the future. This practice (termed "cybersquatting") gives the corporate name a ransom value that can be used to extract an inflated sum from those who might also have an interest in using that name. Such conduct has been characterised as an abuse of the registration process,[131] or the creation of a potential instrument of fraud[132] (as the name might be used for passing off, although this is rarely the objective of the initial registrant). In light of this, the Company Law Review, which considered the law on corporate names to be broadly satisfactory, was attracted by the idea that there should be a new statutory basis for ordering a name to be changed when the use of a corporate name constituted an abuse of the registration process.[133] This suggestion effectively sought to put the common law controls of cybersquatting on a statutory footing. **4–025**

---

[126] For the breadth of interests protected, see *Burge v Haycock* [2001] EWCA Civ 900; [2002] R.P.C. 28. Where the passing off relates to internet activity, it will be necessary to show an impact on customers within the jurisdiction: see *Starbucks (HK) Ltd v British Sky Broadcasting Group (No 2)* [2015] 1 W.L.R. 2628.

[127] A court cannot order the Registrar to change the company's name, which must be altered by the company itself: see paras 4 023 to 4–028.

[128] See, for example, *Tussaud v Tussaud* (1890) 44 Ch. D. 678 Ch D (an injunction was ordered preventing a member of the Tussaud family from registering Louis Tussaud Ltd to carry on a waxworks show, although the court would not restrain an individual from trading under his or her own surname); *La SA des Anciens Etablissements Panhard et Levassor v Panhard Levassor Motor Co Ltd* [1901] 2 Ch. 513 Ch D; *Exxon Corp v Exxon Insurance Consultants International Ltd* [1982] Ch. 119 CA (Civ Div).

[129] *British Diabetic Association v Diabetic Society Ltd* [1996] F.S.R. 1 Ch D.

[130] *Baume & Co Ltd v AH Moore Ltd (No.1)* [1958] Ch. 907 CA; *Parker-Knoll Ltd v Knoll International Ltd (No.3)* [1962] R.P.C. 243 CA; *Anglian Windows Ltd v Anglian Roofline Ltd* [2014] EWHC 4204 (IPEC).

[131] *Glaxo Plc v Glaxowellcome Ltd* [1996] F.S.R. 388 Ch D; *Direct Line Group Ltd v Direct Line Estate Agency Ltd* [1997] F.S.R. 374 Ch D.

[132] *British Telecommunications Plc v One in a Million Ltd* [1999] E.T.M.R. 61 CA (Civ Div) (which concerned registration of an internet domain name, not a company name, but the principle is the same). For the application of this principle to corporate names, see *Azumi Ltd v Zuma's Choice Pet Products Ltd* [2017] EWHC 609 (IPEC); [2017] E.T.M.R. 24 at [60]; *Bayerische Motoren Werke AG (BMW) v BMW Telecommunications Ltd* [2019] EWHC 411 (IPEC) at [11]–[17]. See also *Yoyo.Email Ltd v Royal Bank of Scotland Group Plc* [2015] EWHC 3509 (Ch); [2016] F.S.R. 18 at [13]–[16]; *Media Agency Group Ltd v Space Media Agency Ltd* [2019] EWCA Civ 712; [2019] F.S.R. 27 at [28].

[133] Completing, para.8.30.

Company names adjudicators

4–026 Following the Company Law Review, the CA 2006 set up a new procedure whereby a person (including another company) can apply to a "company names adjudicator",[134] apparently at any time, for an order that a company's name must be changed because it is either "the same as a name associated with the applicant in which he has goodwill"[135] or "sufficiently similar to such a name that its use in the UK would be likely to mislead by suggesting a connection between the company and the applicant".[136] Accordingly, this statutory mechanism operates alongside the tort of passing off to protect the applicant from the respondent taking "opportunistic advantage" of the applicant's reputation and goodwill in its name.[137] If either statutory condition is made out, then the applicant will succeed, unless the respondent company can bring itself within one of five statutory defences.[138]

The first defence is that the disputed name was registered by the respondent before the applicant commenced the activities upon which it relies to demonstrate its goodwill.[139] This defence is not necessarily limited to the situation where the respondent company registered its name first in time, but may extend to the situation where the applicant company is registered first but has remained dormant until after the respondent company was registered. The second defence is that the respondent company is operating under the disputed name[140]; has formerly operated under the name, but is now dormant; or is proposing to operate under that name and has incurred substantial start-up costs in preparation for starting business. This is an important defence for the respondent company because it means that operating its business under the disputed name (or even incurring substantial costs in preparing to operate that business) protects the respondent company from having to change its name. The third defence operates to protect companies whose business involves promoting other companies, namely where the respondent company can show that the disputed name was registered in the ordinary course of a company formation business and is consequently available for sale to the applicant on that business' standard

134 "Company names adjudicators" are appointed by the Secretary of State: see CA 2006 s.70(1).

135 For these purposes, "goodwill" includes the company's reputation at large (see CA 2006 s.69(7)), so that (unlike the tort of passing off) the goodwill does not need to be situated in the jurisdiction: see *MB Inspection Ltd v Hi-Rope Ltd* [2010] R.P.C. 18 (Company Names Tribunal) at [41]; *Zurich Insurance Co v Zurich Investments Ltd* [2011] R.P.C. 6 (Company Names Tribunal) at [33]. The names of two companies can still be the "same", even if one has the suffix "Ltd" and the other has the suffix "Plc": see *Zurich Insurance Co v Zurich Investments Ltd* [2011] R.P.C. 6 at [37]. The test for whether two names are the "same" is strict: at [39] (concluding that "Zurich" and "Zurich Investments Ltd" were not the same).

136 CA 2006 s.69(1). Two names would be "similar" when they are capable of misleading third parties by suggesting a connection between the applicant and respondent: see *Zurich Insurance Co v Zurich Investments Ltd* [2011] R.P.C. 6 at [40]. The fact that the two companies operate in the same line of business is a relevant, albeit not determinative, consideration: ibid.

137 *Zurich Insurance Co v Zurich Investments Ltd* [2011] R.P.C. 6 at [55].

138 CA 2006 s.69(4).

139 CA 2006 s.69(4)(a).

140 CA 2006 s.69(4)(b). See further *Barloworld Handling Ltd v Unilift South Wales Ltd* [2009] F.S.R. 21 (Arbitration) at [7] (defence succeeded); *Zurich Insurance Co v Zurich Investments Ltd* [2011] R.P.C. 6 at [44] (defence failed).

terms.[141] Accordingly, the applicant can resolve the issue by the simple expedient of purchasing the respondent company for a modest sum. The fourth defence is that the respondent company adopted the disputed name in good faith,[142] which requires the adjudicator to examine what the respondent company knew and whether its conduct would be considered honest according to normally accepted standards.[143] The fifth defence covers the situation where the applicant's interests "are not adversely affected to any significant extent".[144]

The first three of the defences above do not apply, however, if the applicant company can demonstrate that the respondent's main purpose in registering the disputed name was to obtain money or other benefits from the applicant or to prevent the applicant from registering that name.[145] Accordingly, starting to use the disputed name will not protect the respondent company if it was aiming to extort a large sum of money from the applicant in exchange for abandoning its rights to the name.

If the adjudicator upholds the complaint, an order must be made requiring the respondent to change its name "to one that is not an offending name" and to take all steps within its power to achieve that end, including not forming another company with a similar offending name.[146] The adjudicator's order may be enforced in the same way as an order of the High Court (or decree of the Court of Session)[147] and, if the name is not changed by the respondent within the specified time, the adjudicator can effect the change.[148] In contrast, if the applicant fails before the adjudicator, it retains the option of bringing a passing off claim, since that type of claim is not necessarily defeated by the circumstances covered by the statutory defences available before an adjudicator. For example, a defendant cannot avoid liability for passing off simply by demonstrating that the disputed name is being used (the second statutory defence considered above) or by showing that the name was registered in good faith (the fourth statutory defence considered above). Whatever the adjudicator's decision, however, there is the possibility of an appeal to the courts. **4–027**

[141] CA 2006 s.69(4)(c).
[142] CA 2006 s.69(4)(d).
[143] *Zurich Insurance Co v Zurich Investments Ltd* [2011] R.P.C. 6 at [51].
[144] CA 2006 s.69(4)(e). The level of prejudice must be assessed at the application's filing date: see *MB Inspection Ltd v Hi-Rope Ltd* [2010] R.P.C. 18 at [51]; *Zurich Insurance Co v Zurich Investments Ltd* [2011] R.P.C. 6 at [46].
[145] CA 2006 s.69(5).
[146] CA 2006 s.73(1). Although the company is the primary respondent, the applicant may also join the respondent's directors or members (s.69(3)), which will impact the range of persons caught by the adjudicator's order.
[147] CA 2006 s.73(3). Accordingly, this would include an order for contempt of court.
[148] CA 2006 s.73(4). This avoids the problem in *Halifax Plc v Halifax Repossessions Ltd* [2004] B.C.C. 281, where, after a successful trade mark infringement and passing-off action, the court had no power of its own motion to alter the defendant company's name, but only jurisdiction to order the shareholders to secure such a change.

Company's election to change its name

4–028 As considered above, a company may, in general, change its name by special resolution or by any other procedure specified in its articles.[149] If the name change also reflects a change in the company's status (for example, from private to public), then there are additional requirements that must be satisfied, as considered below.[150]

Effect of a name change

4–029 Whether a company changes its name voluntarily or following a direction from the Secretary of State or a "company names adjudicator",[151] notice must be given to the Registrar who will replace the company's old name with its new one and issue an amended certificate of incorporation.[152] The company's change of name is effective from the date on which that certificate is issued,[153] but that change does not affect any of the company's rights or obligations or render defective any legal proceedings to which it is party,[154] since the basic corporate entity remains unchanged.

CHOICE OF APPROPRIATE ARTICLES

4–030 As well as choosing a suitable corporate name, those incorporating a company must also decide upon the company's constitution. The most significant document is the company's articles of association, which provides most of the rules governing the company's internal operation as these are not provided by the general law. To facilitate the incorporation process, the CA 2006 provides model articles of association,[155] and the company's promoters must determine the extent to which that standard-form constitution should be disapplied or adopted (whether explicitly or by default).[156] Frequently, company formation agents have their own standard forms that formally exclude the model articles altogether, although those templates are themselves typically developed from the statutory model and its predecessors. At the other extreme, a promoter might choose to adopt the model articles wholesale,[157] although this is rarely done as most companies would to some extent wish to tailor their constitution to their own particular needs. For example, the Model Articles for Private Companies Limited by Shares give the directors a discretion to refuse to register share transfers,[158]

[149] CA 2006 s.77(1). See further para.4–022.

[150] See paras 4–036 onwards.

[151] CA 2006 s.77.

[152] CA 2006 s.80.

[153] CA 2006 s.81(1).

[154] CA 2006 s.81(2)–(3). Accordingly, contracts concluded prematurely under the new name will not be pre-incorporation contracts on which the individual who acted will be personally liable: see further para.8–030.

[155] See para.3–011.

[156] See para.3–012.

[157] CA 2006 s.9(5)(b).

[158] The Companies (Model Articles) Regulations 2008 (SI 2008/3229) Sch.1 art.26(5).

but the incorporators are likely to prefer more elaborate provisions that require a departing member to offer their shares first to existing shareholders.

Under previous versions of the CA 2006, the most important constitutional document was the memorandum of association, which contained the key public-facing information about the company and was largely unalterable once the company had been incorporated. One significant change under the CA 2006 was the downgrading of the memorandum of association to a purely vestigial role.[159] Whilst the current legislation still requires the memorandum to be delivered to the Registrar as a necessary step in the formation process,[160] the document simply needs to state that the subscribers to the memorandum (of whom there need only be one)[161] wish to form a company, agree to become members of that company upon its formation and (in the case of a company having a share capital) agree to take at least one share each.[162] The memorandum of association has to be authenticated by each subscriber.[163] In that regard, the Registrar is empowered to specify the method of authentication, but this must not impede the electronic delivery of the memorandum (and the other registration documents) to the Registrar.[164] **4–031**

CHALLENGING THE CERTIFICATE OF INCORPORATION

In deciding whether or not to register a particular company, the Registrar's functions are administrative, rather than judicial. Nevertheless, the Registrar's refusal to register a company can be challenged by judicial review,[165] albeit with scant hope of success.[166] The converse situation (where there is a challenge to the Registrar's decision to register a company) is more problematic. As a general rule, a company's registration cannot be challenged due to the incorporation certificate's conclusive effect.[167] Accordingly, British company law has been virtually immune from the problems associated with defectively incorporated **4–032**

---

[159] The CLR had recommended that the memorandum of association be abolished entirely (see Final Report I, para.9.4), although this was (oddly) thought by some to raise the question of whether this indicated an intention to alter the nature of the company as an incorporated association. The compromise was to give the memorandum a vestigial role.

[160] CA 2006 s.9(1).

[161] CA 2006 s.7(1).

[162] CA 2006 s.8(1). According to CA 2006 s.112(1), the subscribers to the company's memorandum are deemed to have agreed to become members of the company and they do in fact become members upon its registration.

[163] CA 2006 s.8. Bizarrely for such a simple document, the memorandum of association must be in the prescribed form. For the very straightforward forms prescribed for companies with or without share capital, see Registration Regulations Schs 1–2.

[164] CA 2006 s.1068(3) and (5).

[165] *Rossendale BC v Hurstwood Properties (A) Ltd* [2019] B.C.C. 774 at [25].

[166] See, for example, *R. v Registrar of Joint Stock Companies* [1931] 2 K.B. 197, where the Court of Appeal rejected an application for mandamus to order the Registrar to register a company formed for the sale in England of tickets in the Irish Hospital Lottery on the ground that such sales were illegal in England.

[167] CA 2006 s.15(4).

companies that have plagued the US and many continental jurisdictions.[168] Nevertheless, the protection afforced by the incorporation certificate's statutory conclusiveness, whilst strong,[169] is not absolute. In particular, according to the CA 2006 (as with its predecessors), an incorporation certificate does not appear to bind the Crown, so that the Attorney-General can apply for an order of certiorari quashing the registration.[170] Such an application succeeded in *R. v Registrar of Companies Ex p. Attorney General*,[171] where a prostitute had succeeded in incorporating her business under the corporate name of "Lindi St Claire (Personal Services) Ltd" (the Registrar having previously rejected her first preference of "Prostitutes Ltd" or "Hookers Ltd" and having shown no enthusiasm for "Lindi St Claire (French Lessons) Ltd"). With scrupulous frankness, the incorporator had specified the company's primary object in its constitution as being "to carry on the business of prostitution".[172] Upon the Attorney-General's application for certiorari, the court quashed the company's registration on the ground that the company's stated business was contrary to public policy.[173] Such proceedings are unlikely to be commenced by the Attorney-General (or any other Crown servant) unless public policy considerations are involved. Accordingly, this is not an appropriate mechanism for dealing with technical breaches of the incorporation formalities.[174] Nor will the Registrar generally be liable in the tort of negligence to any third party dealing with a company that has been registered in error,[175] although there can unusually be liability to a registered company that suffers loss as a result of its details being recorded incorrectly.[176]

---

168 See R. Drury, "Nullity of Companies in English Law" (1985) 48 M.L.R. 644. The First Company Law Directive contained three provisions dealing with nullity.

169 See, for example, *R. v Registrar of Companies Ex p. Central Bank of India* (1985) 1 B.C.C. 99501 CA (Civ Div), where the Court of Appeal held that the effect of s.98(2) of the CA 1948 (under which a charge's certificate of registration was "conclusive evidence that the requirements as to registration have been satisfied") was to make evidence of non-compliance inadmissible for judicial review proceedings, thus precluding the court from quashing the registration. See further *Bank of Beirut SAL v Prince El-Hashemite* [2016] Ch. 1 at [91]–[103] (strictly dealing with a limited partnership), where Nugee J considered that even a fraudulent registration would not necessarily undermine an incorporation certificate's conclusiveness.

170 See *Bowman v Secular Society Ltd* [1917] A.C. 406 HL, although certiorari was denied as the Society's purposes were not considered unlawful.

171 *R. v Registrar of Companies Ex p. Attorney General* [1991] B.C.L.C. 476; approved in *Rossendale BC v Hurstwood Properties (A) Ltd* [2019] B.C.C. 774 at [25].

172 The incorporation would have potentially succeeded had the incorporator been less frank by stating, for example, that the company's primary object was "to carry on the business of masseuses and to provide related services" (*R. v Registrar of Companies Ex p. Attorney General* [1991] B.C.L.C. 476).

173 This was despite the fact (as the incorporator indignantly protested) she paid income tax on her earnings. Given that prostitution can be carried on without necessarily committing any criminal offence and given that Lindi St Claire continued (without incorporation) her profession (for which she subsequently became a well-known spokeswoman), this case might well be seen as an example of the "unruly horse" of public policy unseating its judicial riders.

174 Judicial review may be available in respect of matters incorrectly recorded on the register that are not covered by the certificate of incorporation: see *Re Calmex Ltd* (1988) 4 B.C.C. 761 at 488.

175 Consider *Yuen Kun Yeu v Attorney-General of Hong Kong* [1988] A.C. 175; approved in *N v Poole BC* [2019] H.L.R. 39 at [41].

176 *Sebry v Companies House* [2015] B.C.C. 236. The Registrar's duty of care is limited to registering the information correctly and does not extend to verifying that information: see *Chief Land Registrar v Caffrey & Co* [2016] EWHC 161 (Ch); [2016] P.N.L.R. 23 at [36].

In the case of trade unions, however, an incorporation certificate may arguably not be conclusive as to the fact and validity of the trade union's incorporation. This suggestion flows from s.10(3) of the Trade Union and Labour Relations (Consolidation) Act 1992 (TULRA) (repeating similar provisions in earlier legislation), which declares that the registration of a trade union under the CA 2006 shall be void. On its face, this provision ought to override the conclusive effect of a company's certificate of incorporation under s.15(4) of the CA 2006. Whilst there is certainly authority suggesting that a party (besides the Crown) might rely on TULRA as a defence to a claim by a registered company whose objects make it a trade union,[177] those decisions concerned earlier (and less comprehensive) predecessors of s.15(4) that only covered ministerial acts leading to registration, but not more substantive matters.[178] Accordingly, those authorities are unlikely to remain relevant to the (more comprehensive) approach to conclusiveness in s.15(4) of the CA 2006. That said, Drury has unearthed a more recent example of a company being removed from the register as a nullity because its objects made it a trade union.[179] The company in question was one formed by junior hospital doctors to represent their interests, but they later realised that its objects made it a trade union within the statutory definition. The Department of Trade took the view that the predecessor of TULRA overrode what is now s.15(4) of the CA 2006 and accordingly the Registrar removed the company from the register for "void registration",[180] without any court order[181] or challenge by the junior doctors. Presumably, the Registrar's action could be regarded as having been taken on behalf of the Crown and as rectifying a mistake that he, or one of his predecessors, had made. On this approach, TULRA would appear to override the CA 2006.[182] **4–033**

In light of the above analysis, it seems probable (albeit not certain) that nobody (other than the Crown) can plead the nullity of a registered company unless and until the company has been removed from the register as a result of action taken by (or on behalf of) the Crown. Removal by the court on the Attorney-General's application would be tantamount to a declaration that the company never existed as a corporate body. Such an outcome is commercially undesirable if the company has been trading for some time in a guise that members, managers and creditors believed to be a valid registered company.[183] Accordingly, it will generally be more appropriate that the company be formally wound up and its **4–034**

177 *Edinburgh & District Water Manufacturers Defence Association v Jenkinson & Co* (1903) 5 F. 1159 IH (2 Div); *British Association of Glass Bottle Manufacturers v Nettlefold* (1911) 27 T.L.R. 527 (where, however, the company was held not to be a trade union).

178 *British Association of Glass Bottle Manufacturers v Nettlefold* (1911) 27 T.L.R. 527 at 529.

179 Drury, "Nullity of Companies in English Law" (1985) 48 M.L.R. 644 at 649–650.

180 See Registrar of Companies, *Companies in 1976*, Table 10.

181 Consider Directive 2017/1132 relating to certain aspects of company law [2017] OJ L169/46 art.11(a), which requires that "[n]ullity must be ordered by a decision of a court of law".

182 Support for this view can be derived from the fact that, unless the company agreed, the Registrar could only take this step if the incorporation was considered void, rather than merely voidable (which would be the case where, for example, registration had been secured by fraudulent misrepresentations).

183 Consider Directive 2017/1132 relating to certain aspects of company law [2017] OJ L169/46 art.12(4), which preserves the validity of any commitments concluded by or with the "company" before its nullity.

assets distributed to creditors,[184] with a declaration that the company has never existed only being used in a narrow window after incorporation.

COMMENCEMENT OF BUSINESS

4–035 From the date of registration mentioned in the certificate of incorporation, a private company becomes "capable of exercising all the functions of an incorporated company".[185] The company may, however, choose not to exercise those functions. Indeed, it is inherent in the notion of a "shelf company" that the company will remain dormant for a time after registration and only begin trading at some later date. In the case of a public company, however, there is a further legal obstacle to its commencing trading, as it requires a further certificate from the Registrar (a "trading certificate") certifying that the amount of its allotted share capital is not less than the required minimum.[186] In the absence of a trading certificate, a public company must not do business or exercise any borrowing powers, unless it has first re-registered as a private company.[187] A trading certificate is "conclusive evidence that the company is entitled to do business and exercise any borrowing powers".[188] By analogy with the certificate of incorporation, as the Crown similarly does not appear bound by the trading certificate's conclusive effect, the Attorney-General could seek certiorari to quash the Registrar's decision to grant the certificate. One important difference, however, is that (unlike quashing the incorporation certificate) quashing the trading certificate does not involve the undesirable consequence of nullifying the company itself. An alternative (more likely) course would be for the Secretary of State, if he has grounds for suspecting that the company's share capital has not been properly allotted, to institute an investigation.[189] If those suspicions prove well-founded, the Secretary of State may petition the court to wind up the company.[190]

---

[184] If such a company were to be wound up, there may be a question as to whether the entity should be treated as a "registered company" (given that it has not been declared a nullity) or an "unregistered company" (given that it might have been so declared): see IA 1986 ss.73(1) and 220.

[185] CA 2006 s.16(3).

[186] CA 2006 s.761(1). See further paras 16–009 to 16–011. In the more usual case where the company was originally registered as a private company, but it subsequently converts to a public one, similar requirements will have to be met, but there is no suspension of business required during the conversion process.

[187] CA 2006 s.97(1).

[188] CA 2006 s.761(4).

[189] See Ch.21.

[190] IA 1986 ss.124 and 124A. For the applicable principles, see *Re PAG Management Service Ltd* [2015] EWHC 2404 (Ch); [2015] B.C.C. 720; *Secretary of State for Business, Energy and Industrial Strategy v PAG Asset Preservation Ltd* [2020] EWCA Civ 1017; [2020] B.C.C. 979.

RE-REGISTRATION OF AN EXISTING COMPANY

At some later stage in a company's life, it may wish to convert to a company of a different type. In most cases, this is achieved without the expense of effecting a complete re-organisation[191] or forming a new company. Whilst the methods for converting from one type of company to another are nowadays collated in Pt 7 of the CA 2006, not every conceivable option is covered so that some conversions may have to be done in two distinct steps. 4–036

(i) Private company becoming public

The most common way of forming a public company is by a private company converting to that status, rather than a public company incorporating as such from the outset. A private company limited by shares can re-register as a public company by passing a special resolution to that effect, by satisfying three statutory conditions and by then making an application to the Registrar for re-registration.[192] Those three conditions all relate to the company's legal share capital, which is subject to more onerous requirements for public than private companies. First, the nominal value of the company's allotted share capital must be not less than the authorised minimum (currently £50,000) and the associated rules regarding the payment for shares in public companies must have been satisfied.[193] Secondly, the company must produce unqualified recent accounts showing (as certified by the auditor) that the company's net assets (its assets less liabilities) are not less than the aggregate of its called-up share capital and undistributable reserves.[194] Whilst there is no precise equivalent of this rule applying to public companies upon their formation, this will be the practical reality for a public company before it begins trading.[195] Thirdly, if the company has allotted shares in the period after the aforementioned accounts were drawn up and before the special resolution is passed, those shares must have complied with the rules applicable to non-cash consideration for shares in public companies, assuming that the relevant shares were issued wholly or partly other than for cash.[196] Furthermore, if a private unlimited company seeks to re-register as a public company, it will also have to become limited, as this constitutes one of the 4–037

[191] See further Ch.29.

[192] CA 2006 s.90(1).

[193] CA 2006 s.91(1). See further Ch.16.

[194] CA 2006 s.92. This requirement does not concern the company's minimum capital, but rather the relationship between the company's net assets and the legal capital raised.

[195] A public company with net assets less than its called-up share capital and undistributable reserves cannot make a distribution to its members: see CA 2006 s.831(1).

[196] CA 2006 s.93. In addition, the rules requiring independent valuation of non-cash assets transferred to a public company in the "initial period" apply to a company re-registered as public, although the company's members are substituted for the subscribers to the memorandum when the issue arises in the re-registration context: see CA 2006 s.603(a). See further paras 16–016 onwards. As these requirements apply after re-registration, compliance is not a pre-condition of re-registration.

essential requirements for a public company.[197] To this end, the company simply needs to add to the special resolution the necessary changes to its articles.[198]

A company will be re-registered as a public company if the Registrar is satisfied from the documents submitted as part of the re-registration application that the statutory conditions have been met.[199] Upon the company's re-registration as a public company, the Registrar will issue an amended certificate of incorporation[200] and any alterations to the company's name and articles will take effect.[201] In essence, the amended certificate is effectively a combined incorporation and trading certificate, both of which would have been required had the company been initially registered as a public company.

(ii) Public company becoming private limited company

4–038 Converting from a public to private company (an operation that must not be confused with ceasing to have securities traded on a public market, which does not necessarily involve any change in the company's status under the CA 2006, or with "privatisation" in the sense of de-nationalisation) is comparatively straightforward, unless there is disagreement between the members. A public company can convert to a private company limited by shares or by guarantee[202] by passing a special resolution making the necessary alterations to its name and articles and by applying (in the prescribed form) to the Registrar.[203] That said, there are special safeguards for those objecting to the change of status, since the loss of public status may have adverse consequences for the company's members, especially their ability to dispose of their shares. Accordingly, members who have not consented to, or voted against, the resolution can, within 28 days of the resolution, apply to the court for its cancellation if there is support from[204]:

(1) holders of not less than 5% in nominal value of the company's share capital or any class thereof; or
(2) if the company is not limited by shares,[205] not less than 5% of the members; or

---

197 CA 2006 s.4(2).

198 CA 2006 s.90(4). This is simpler than adopting the two-stage process of re-registering as limited and then re-registering as a public company.

199 CA 2006 s.94 (including a statement of proposed secretary, if the company does not already have one, since this is not a requirement for a private company: CA 2006 ss.94(1)(b) and 95).

200 CA 2006 s.96(2). As with the original certificate, the new incorporation certificate is conclusive evidence that the re-registration requirements have been met: see CA 2006 s.96(5). See further para.4–032.

201 CA 2006 s.96(4).

202 This simple process does not enable the conversion to an unlimited company: see CA 2006 s.97(1).

203 CA 2006 s.97.

204 CA 2006 s.98(1). See further *Re DNick Holding Plc* [2013] EWHC 68 (Ch); [2014] B.C.C. 1.

205 This second category of objectors is somewhat puzzling since, until the Registrar issues a new certificate, the company remains a public company and yet a public company is required to have a share capital: see CA 2006 s.4(2). Presumably, this second category caters for an "old public company" that has still not re-registered under the transitional provisions: see Companies Act 2006

(3) not less than 50 members.

To give dissenting members the opportunity to make such an application, the Registrar must not issue a new incorporation certificate until 28 days have expired without an application having been made or, if it has been made, until the application has been withdrawn or dismissed and a copy of the court order delivered to the Registrar.[206] Where such an application is made, the court has broad powers to cancel or confirm the resolution. If the resolution is confirmed, the court may impose "such terms and conditions as it thinks fit", which could include providing the dissenting shareholders with an exit right (rather than forcing them to accept the company's change of status) by ordering the company to purchase the relevant members' shares.[207] Following confirmation of the resolution, the Registrar will issue a new incorporation certificate with the usual conclusive effect.[208]

One circumstance in which a public company will have to re-register as a private company is if the court confirms a reduction of its capital that has the effect of reducing the nominal amount of its allotted share capital below "the authorised minimum" (currently £50,000).[209] In such a case, the confirmation order will not be registered (and accordingly not come into effect, unless the court otherwise directs) until the company has re-registered as a private company.[210] In such a case, the court may (and, in practice, will) authorise this registration to be achieved through a special expedited procedure without any need to resort to the procedure discussed above. Instead of the company having to pass a special resolution, the court will specify what alterations must be made to the company's name and articles. The company may then apply in the prescribed form to the Registrar, who will issue a new certificate of incorporation.[211] Unlike when the company chooses to become private, there is no procedure for the dissenting minority to object, since the company has no option but to become private when its capital is reduced below the authorised minimum. **4–039**

(iii) Private or public limited company becoming unlimited

Obviously, the type of conversion that presents the greatest dangers to a company's members is from a limited company to an unlimited one. Nevertheless, such conversions are not completely banned, as members may legitimately conclude that forfeiting the advantages of limited liability makes sound commercial sense, given that this may enable them to operate with the same flexibility (especially as regards capital withdrawals) and financial privacy **4–040**

(Consequential Amendments, Transitional Provisions and Savings) Order 2009 (SI 2009/1941) Sch.3. Given that there will be few such "old public companies" nowadays that have not re-registered, they will not be discussed further.

206 CA 2006 s.97(2).

207 CA 2006 s.98(3)–(6).

208 CA 2006 s.101.

209 CA 2006 s.648. See paras 17–028 onwards.

210 CA 2006 ss.650–651. See further *Re Steris Plc* [2019] EWHC 751 (Ch); [2019] B.C.C. 924.

211 CA 2006 ss.651(3)–(4).

as a partnership whilst still retaining the advantages of separate corporate personality (other than limited liability). Accordingly, the CA 2006 permits a limited company to re-register as an unlimited company, but only if *all* the members agree.[212] As with other types of conversion, an application (in the prescribed form) has to be lodged with the Registrar, together with supporting documents.[213] Those documents must contain a compliance statement by the company's directors indicating that the persons by (or on whose behalf) the application form is authenticated constitute the whole of the company's membership and that, in the case of authentication through an agent, the directors have taken all reasonable steps to satisfy themselves that the agent was authorised to act on behalf of the particular member.[214] The Registrar will then issue a new certificate of incorporation with the usual conclusive effect.[215]

Before such a certificate will be issued, however, there is one further precondition that must be satisfied. This derives from the fact that a company is not permitted repeatedly to chop and change between being limited and unlimited. Accordingly, once a limited company has been re-registered as unlimited, it cannot subsequently re-register as a public company[216] or as a private limited company.[217] Similarly, it is not possible for a company to register as unlimited if the company has previously been re-registered as limited,[218] nor can a public company have previously been re-registered as either limited or unlimited.[219] This restriction avoids third parties dealing with the company becoming confused as to the potential liability of the company's members if that company were permitted to vacillate between corporate forms. That said, there is no ban on companies switching back and forth between private limited company and public limited company forms.

(iv) Unlimited company becoming a private limited company

4–041 The CA 2006 permits an unlimited company to re-register as a private limited company, whether limited by shares or by guarantee, so long as the company has not previously been re-registered as limited.[220] As far as the company's members are concerned, the crucial requirement is the passing of a special resolution indicating the nature of the conversion and making the necessary alterations to the company's name and articles.[221] When such a conversion occurs, however, it is not the members' interests that need safeguarding, but those of the creditors. Somewhat surprisingly, however, the only statutory protection afforded to the company's creditors is the addition of the new suffix, "Ltd", to the company's

212 CA 2006 ss.102(1)(a) (private companies) and 109(1)(a) (public companies).
213 CA 2006 ss.102(1)(c) and s.109(1)(c) (for private and public companies respectively).
214 CA 2006 ss.103(4) and 110(4) (for private and public companies respectively).
215 CA 2006 ss.104 and s.111 (for private and public companies respectively).
216 CA 2006 s.90(2)(e).
217 CA 2006 s.105(2).
218 CA 2006 s.102(2).
219 CA 2006 s.109(2).
220 CA 2006 s.105.
221 CA 2006 s.105(1)(a).

name so as to alert them to the fact that the company has become a limited one.[222] The real protection for the company's creditors lies in the insolvency legislation: anyone who was a member of the company at the time of its re-registration remains potentially liable in respect of the corporate debts and liabilities contracted prior thereto if winding up commences within three years of that re-registration.[223]

(v) Becoming or ceasing to be a community interest company

A limited company (whether limited by shares or guarantee and whether public or private) may convert to a community interest company.[224] This requires a special resolution by the company's members in order to effect the quite extensive necessary changes to the company's constitution,[225] as well as approval from the Regulator of Community Interest Companies, who needs to be convinced that the company satisfies the community interest test.[226] Once formed, a CIC can only change its status by electing either to be dissolved or to convert to a charity or registered society.[227] The justification for this restriction is that a CIC could otherwise readily avoid the constraints on distributions by changing legal form. **4–042**

CONCLUSION

Although the rules surrounding the use of corporate names are sometimes problematic and complex, the process of registering a company in the UK is in general both speedy and cheap. Moreover, the rules governing the conversion from one corporate form to another are not complex either, once one penetrates the detail. Most of the conversion procedures are little used, except for the procedure allowing the conversion of companies from private to public form and vice versa, which is extensively used. **4–043**

---

[222] CA 2006 s.105(4).

[223] IA 1986 s.77(2).

[224] Companies (Audit, Investigations and Community Enterprise) Act 2004 s.37(1). Only a limited company may convert to a community interested company (CIC): see Companies (Audit, Investigations and Community Enterprise) Act 2004 s.26(2). Accordingly, if an unlimited company wishes to become a CIC, it must first convert to a limited company under CA 2006 s.105. The restriction operates in both directions as a CIC cannot re-register as an unlimited company: see Companies (Audit, Investigations and Community Enterprise) Act 2004 s.52(1).

[225] See para.1–012.

[226] Companies (Audit, Investigations and Community Enterprise) Act 2004 s.38(2).

[227] Companies (Audit, Investigations and Community Enterprise) Act 2004 s.53.

CHAPTER 5

CORPORATE MOBILITY

INTRODUCTION

Corporate law scholarship in the UK, as in most jurisdictions, often assumes that the companies operating in the jurisdiction are also incorporated in it. While this is true of the majority of those companies, it is not a universal feature of the corporate population. Companies incorporated elsewhere do operate within the UK. Some are incorporated nearby (Jersey, Guernsey, Ireland, other European countries); some in more distant countries (for example, Hong Kong, Singapore, Malaysia, Russia, China, US, Australia); and some in countries which are not only more distant but, at first sight, rather unlikely candidates for incorporation, such as the British Virgin Islands or the Cayman Islands. One may guess that, in the last group, very little operational activity of the company occurs in the place of incorporation. Assuming that the operation of foreign-incorporated companies in the UK is permitted, as indeed it is, a set of questions arises whether any provisions of domestic company law should be applied to them. As far as general company law is concerned, in the main only some disclosure rules are applied. **5–001**

So, the general principle of UK private international law is that UK law recognises as a legal entity a body validly incorporated under the law of a foreign jurisdiction. Many countries operate on the same basis, though they vary a bit in the extent to which parts of domestic company law are applied to foreign-incorporated companies. Why this laissez-faire attitude? Perhaps because the view is taken that if those who establish a company choose to regulate its "internal" affairs according to a particular set of company laws, there is no ground for interfering with this choice. This approach might be thought to assume that all those affected by the choice of place of incorporation are involved in making that choice or in some way protected from its consequences. Where this assumption is less reliable, then deference to the law of the place of incorporation is sometimes displaced. Thus, we see in Ch.29[1] that, in the interests of creditor protection, UK courts have been willing to accept jurisdiction in relation to schemes of arrangement involving foreign-incorporated companies, provided they have the requisite connection with the UK. And in Ch.25[2] we note that the domestic rules applying to publicly traded companies often apply equally to foreign-incorporated companies. This could be justified on the basis of both investor-protection and requiring all companies which obtain the benefits of public trading in the UK also to bear its burdens.

This, then, is the first aspect of corporate mobility: the freedom to operate in jurisdictions other than that of incorporation. More controversial has been the second aspect, namely, the freedom of a company to change its jurisdiction of incorporation. Contrary to its approach to the recognition of foreign-incorporated companies, UK law provides no straightforward mechanism whereby a company may depart from or arrive in a UK jurisdiction, even if that other jurisdiction is a jurisdiction within the UK. There is no mechanism whereby the company can simply fill in the relevant forms at the current place of incorporation and in the proposed new jurisdiction and see its place of incorporation transferred. This might be put on the basis that such a system cannot work without the cooperation of the authorities in the other jurisdiction, but that hardly explains its absence within the UK. There are work-arounds, of course. The company might set up a new company in the jurisdiction of choice and transfer its business to the new company, though that is likely to be expensive in tax terms. Or the company might use a scheme of arrangement to transfer its shareholders' interests from the shares in the company to equivalent shares in a new holding company set up in the jurisdiction of choice, as we discuss below.[3] So long as the UK was a member of the EU, there were additional mechanisms for the transfer of the jurisdiction of incorporation, whether into or out of the UK. A popular one was the cross-border merger.[4] Less popular was the creation of a European Company through the merger of two or more companies previously incorporated in different Member States. Just as the UK was leaving the EU, the EU was in the process of implementing a mechanism for the transfer of a company's "seat" from one EU jurisdiction to another without a merger.[5] However, the UK has now deprived itself of the use of these mechanisms.

5–002 These two aspects of corporate mobility are the focus of this chapter. It is worth noting at this point, however, that there is one issue which ties the two aspects together. This is the situation where the company is incorporated in jurisdiction A but carries on none of its operational activities there, which are in fact conducted wholly or mainly in jurisdiction B. How does this affect the two aspects of corporate mobility just identified? Under the UK rules, the answer is normally not at all, especially if the company chooses to be incorporated in the UK, but to

[1] At para.29–005. And see a further example of creditor protection in para.5–008.

[2] At para.25–001.

[3] See para.5–011.

[4] See para.29–016.

[5] Directive 2019/2121 amending Directive 2017/1132 as regards cross-border conversions, mergers and divisions [2019] OJ L321/1. Since this Directive was required to be transposed by the Member States by a date after 31 December 2020, it was not transposed in the UK, and it would have been inoperable in any event once the UK left the EU.

operate elsewhere. The UK is what is referred to as an "incorporation theory" state: the validity of a company's incorporation in the UK does not depend on where that company carries on or intends to carry on its operational activities.[6] If the UK did provide some easy mechanism for the transfer in of companies incorporated elsewhere, that mechanism presumably would be constructed on the same principle. Other states are "real seat" states, where the validity of incorporation depends upon the company having its headquarters or central place of management within the state of incorporation. Such a state might not recognise the validity of the UK incorporation of a company which carried on no operational activities in the UK. Assuming that state in principle allowed the transfer in of companies incorporated elsewhere, it would probably not permit a transfer in of a company which did not have the requisite connection with the transferee real seat state. Non-recognition would put in jeopardy the validity of the company's contracts, the ownership of its property and the limited liability of its members—not a risk many companies would be prepared to run. Moreover, the real seat rules of another state might affect the UK's recognition of a company allegedly incorporated there. If the company had no operations in its claimed state of incorporation and so was not validly incorporated there, then the UK courts could not logically recognise its existence either.

Again, so long as the UK was a member of the EU, some of the adverse consequences of the real seat theory were removed by virtue of the provisions in the Treaty on the Functioning of the European Union which guaranteed freedom of establishment within the EU to EU-incorporated companies.[7] Extensive use was made of them by small businesses from other jurisdictions to incorporate in the UK, while carrying on business wholly in the state where the controlling entrepreneurs were located. This was done apparently to avoid demanding minimum capital rules in other EU jurisdiction.[8] But this protection no longer exists, for the good reason that the establishment rights only apply within the EU.

Finally, it should be noted that the issue of foreign incorporation is different from foreign control of groups of companies which contain a British subsidiary. Most foreign multinational groups operating in the UK do so through a British subsidiary which is probably one of a number of subsidiaries in the group headed by the foreign parent. Multinationals may present host governments with many delicate problems—in corporate law mainly in the area of corporate governance—but determining which corporate law rules apply to the company operating in the UK is not normally one of them.

OVERSEAS COMPANIES

British law might have refused to recognise companies not incorporated in one of the UK jurisdictions, thus putting in jeopardy the validity of transactions entered into by non-UK incorporated companies in the UK and in effect requiring companies which wished to carry on business in the UK to do so through a 5–003

6 For the requirements of incorporation, see Ch.4.

7 Articles 49 and 54 TFEU.

8 See M. Becht, C. Mayer and H. Wagner, *Where Do Firms Incorporate? Deregulation and the Costs of Entry* (2008) 14 *Journal of Corporate Finance* 241.

British subsidiary. In fact, British law has never adopted such an approach. As Lord Wright said in 1933: "English courts have long since recognised as juristic persons corporations established by foreign law in virtue of the fact of their creation and continuance under and by that law".[9] Thus, as a general rule,[10] a company incorporated outside the UK need not form a British subsidiary company in order to do business in the UK. It may trade through an agency or branch in this country or, indeed, simply contract with someone in the UK without establishing any form of presence in this country.[11] Of course, when a company incorporated elsewhere intends to carry on a substantial business in the UK, it is likely to form a British subsidiary in order to do so. This might be regarded as a sign of commitment to the British economy, and it also allows the foreign parent company to ring-fence its British operations by putting them in a separate subsidiary with limited liability.[12] The point, however, is that the foreign company is not obliged to take this route; it can do business in the UK in its own right, if it so wishes.

UK law is broadly content to leave the regulation of the internal affairs of companies to the law of the jurisdiction in which they have their registered office, even though those dealing with it may not be aware that this is a non-UK jurisdiction or be aware of the implications of this fact for their rights against it. However, to combat this risk a requirement is imposed on overseas companies with a significant presence in the UK to make public disclosures which match those of required of domestic companies.

The rules on disclosure by foreign companies are to be found in Pt 34 of the Act and regulations made under it.[13] This Part is entitled "overseas companies",[14] a term that might be thought to conjure up a picture of companies formed in some distant and exotic location, as they sometimes are, though in fact it may be only the English Channel or the Irish Sea which separate the country of incorporation from the UK. An overseas company is simply "a company incorporated outside the United Kingdom".[15] The regulatory objectives of this Part are relatively modest. The Act does not attempt to regulate all overseas companies which do business in the UK (for example, over the internet) but only those which have some sort of base in the UK. The rules aim principally to ensure that there is available in the UK some basic information about a company incorporated elsewhere which has established a presence in this country from which it does business. That information is, essentially, the information a British company would have to provide on incorporation[16] or as part of its annual financial

---

[9] *Lazard Bros & Co v Midland Bank Ltd* [1933] A.C. 289 HL at 297.

[10] In particular industries, a company operating in the UK may be required to do so through a British subsidiary, for reasons relating mainly to supervision of their activities.

[11] For example, where the contract is concluded over the telephone or the internet by someone in the UK with a company established in another country.

[12] See Ch.7.

[13] Overseas Companies Regulations 2009 (SI 2009/1801), as amended.

[14] Before 2006 the even more quaint term "oversea" company was used.

[15] CA 2006 s.1044. This means that Channel Island and Isle of Man companies are "overseas" companies as well.

[16] See Ch.4.

returns,[17] plus some information relating to those who represent the overseas company in the UK. However, some provisions go beyond disclosure.

Establishment: branch and place of business

An initial question, clearly, is the sort of base the non-UK company needs to have in order fall within the overseas company disclosure rules. Most of the obligations under the Overseas Companies Regulations 2009 are expressed to apply whenever an overseas company opens or operates an "establishment" in the UK; and "establishment" is defined to mean a branch within the meaning of the Eleventh EU Company Law Directive[18] or a place of business which is not a branch.[19] The terms "branch" and "place of business" obviously overlap to a large extent, but it seems that both at the top and at the bottom of the spectrum a place of business may exist even though a branch does not. To take the bottom end, this situation may arise because, it seems, activities ancillary to a company's business may constitute a place of business but not a branch. It is difficult to be absolutely certain about this, because the Eleventh Directive does not define a "branch" whilst the Regulations do not define a "place of business", but it seems to be the case. It has been said in case law that establishing a place of business, as opposed to merely doing business, in this country requires "a degree of permanence or recognisability as being a location of the company's business".[20] However, it is not fatal to the establishment of a place of business that the activities carried on there are only subsidiary to the company's main business, which is carried on outside the UK, or are not a substantial part of the company's overall business.[21] **5–004**

As to the meaning of a branch some clues may be derivable from the EU legislation referring to bank branches.[22] This does contain a definition of a bank branch, from which some guidance may be obtainable. That definition refers to a place of business through which the bank "conducts directly some or all of the operations inherent in the business".[23] So it may be that purely ancillary activities, such as warehousing or data processing, do not constitute the

[17] See Ch.22.

[18] Directive 89/666 concerning disclosure requirements in respect of branches opened in a Member State by certain types of company governed by the law of another State [1989] OJ L395/36. This is an area of UK company law which continues to be influenced by its (in this case, partial) EU origins.

[19] Overseas Companies Regulations 2009 regs 2, 3, 30 and 68.

[20] *Re Oriel Ltd (In Liquidation)* (1985) 1 B.C.C. 99444 CA (Civ Div) at 99447. See also *Cleveland Museum of Art v Capricorn Art International SA* (1989) 5 B.C.C. 860 QBD (Comm).

[21] *South India Shipping Corp v Export-Import Bank of Korea* (1985) 1 B.C.C. 99350 CA (Civ Div); *Actiesselkabat Dampskibs Hercules v Grand Trunk Pacific Railway* [1912] 1 K.B. 222 CA. Registration in the UK of an establishment in order to carry on business amounts to the creation of a place of business, even if business has not yet commenced at the establishment: *Teekay Tankers Ltd v STX Offshore & Shipping Co* [2014] EWHC 3612 (Comm). However, the business must be the business of the company, not of its agent or subsidiary: *Rakusens Ltd v Baser Ambalaj Plastik Sanayi Ticaret AS* [2001] EWCA Civ 1820; *Matchnet Plc v William Blair & Co LLC* [2002] EWHC 2128 (Ch).

[22] References to EU legislation and CJEU decisions remains legitimate for UK courts seeking to implement "retained" EU law. See para.3–014.

[23] See, for example, Directive 94/19 on deposit guarantee schemes [1994] OJ L135/5 art.1(5).

establishment of a branch though they could amount to a place of business. To like effect is the definition of a branch adopted by the Court of Justice for the purposes of the Brussels Convention: a branch has the appearance of permanency and is physically equipped to negotiate business with third parties directly.[24] At the other end of the spectrum, a company incorporated outside the UK but which has its head office here, clearly has a place of business in the UK, but it might be argued that this is not a branch, since a branch supposes that the head office is elsewhere.

Disclosure obligations

5–005 The Act and the Overseas Companies Regulations impose disclosure requirements on an overseas company having an establishment in the UK in regard to all phases of its life. An overseas company which opens an establishment must file with the Registrar within one month information relating to both itself and the establishment.[25] Subsequent alterations in the registered particulars must also be notified.[26] Failure to do so constitutes a criminal offence on the part of both company and any officer or agent of the company who knowingly and wilfully authorises or permits the default,[27] but, apparently, does not affect the validity of transactions the company may enter into through its unregistered operation. There is no need in a work of this nature to go into the detail of what is required.[28] Overall, the policy can be said to be to put the person dealing with the overseas company through its establishment in a similar information position as would obtain if the company were one incorporated under the Act.

A crucial concern of those who deal with overseas companies is how to serve legal documents on the company. The particulars relating to the establishment must give the name and service address of every person resident in the UK authorised to accept service on behalf of the company or a statement that there is no such person. If there is no such person or if the registered person refuses to accept service, then service can be effected at any place of business in the UK.[29] In addition, the information must state the extent of the powers of the directors of the overseas company to represent the company in dealings and in legal

[24] *Etablissements Somafer SA v Saar-Ferngas AG* (33/78) EU:C:1978:205; [1979] 1 C.M.L.R. 490.

[25] CA 2006 s.1046 and the Overseas Companies Regulations 2009 Pt 2. The information about the company must include a certified copy of its constitution (reg.8(1)). The residential addresses of directors or permanent representatives are subject to the same protective provisions as in the case of UK-incorporate companies: Pt 4. Although the disclosure obligation applies in principle each time the overseas company opens an establishment in the UK (reg.4(2)), the company need not repeat the company-specific information each time, but simply cross-refer to it (reg.5). This applies even though the establishments are in different UK jurisdictions.

[26] Overseas Companies Regulations 2009 Pt 3.

[27] Overseas Companies Regulations 2009 regs 11 and 17.

[28] The former, slightly reduced disclosure requirements for companies incorporated in EEA states no longer obtain.

[29] CA 2006 ss.1056 and 1139(2). In *Teekay Tankers Ltd v STX Offshore & Shipping Co* [2015] 2 B.C.L.C. 210 the judge confirmed the traditional view that, despite the apparently narrower wording of reg.7(1)(e), the service did not have to concern the business of the establishment (as opposed to the business of the company more generally).

proceedings[30] and give a list of those authorised to represent the company as a permanent representative of the company in respect of the branch.[31]

Ongoing disclosure requirements fall into two categories. First, the "trading disclosure" rules which apply to domestic companies are adapted so as to apply to overseas companies "carrying on business in the United Kingdom".[32] These rules are, rightly, not confined to those overseas companies which have an establishment in the UK, though doing business "in" the UK is not defined. The aim of the rules is to provide third parties with certain information at the point at which they deal—or are likely to deal—with overseas companies. Thus, the company must display its name and country of incorporation at every location at which it carries on business[33]; its name on its business letters and a wide range of analogous documents[34]; and, where it has an establishment in the UK, a range of further information on these documents and on its websites.[35] There are penalties for non-compliance,[36] but non-compliance also carries civil consequences on the same basis as that applied to domestic companies.[37] **5–006**

Secondly, annual reporting requirements are applied to overseas companies, but, in this case, only if they have an establishment in the UK.[38] These requirements vary according to whether the overseas company is required by the law of the country in which it is incorporated (its "parent" law) to prepare, have audited and to disclose annual accounts. If it is, the overseas company discharges its disclosure obligations by delivering to the Registrar a copy of the accounting documents prepared in accordance with the parent law.[39] The "accounting documents" include not only the accounts themselves (including the consolidated accounts, if relevant) and auditors' report but also the directors' report.[40] The company has the relatively generous period of three months from the date the documents were first disclosed under the parent law to file them with the Registrar.[41] If it is not so required, the overseas company is subject to a version of

---

[30] Overseas Companies Regulations 2009 reg.6(1)(e).

[31] Overseas Companies Regulations 2009 reg.7(1)(f). Part 4 of the regs applies provisions equivalent to those operating in relation to domestic companies for the protection of directors' residential addresses from public disclosure. See para.9–007.

[32] CA 2006 s.1051 and 2009 Regs Pt 7. And see above paras 4–013 to 4–017.

[33] Overseas Companies Regulations 2009 regs 60–61 (and at the service address of every person authorised to accept service on behalf of the company in respect of the branch).

[34] Overseas Companies Regulations 2009 reg.62.

[35] Overseas Companies Regulations 2009 reg.63.

[36] Overseas Companies Regulations 2009 reg.67.

[37] Overseas Companies Regulations 2009 reg.66. See CA 2006 s.83.

[38] CA 2006 s.1049 and 2009 Regs Pt 5. Unlimited overseas companies are exempted (as domestic ones are) from this obligation, and special rules (not considered here) apply to credit or financial institutions (Pt 6).

[39] The most recent accounting documents have to be included with the initial return to the Registrar (reg.9(1), (2)). Thereafter, Pt 5 applies (reg.32(5)). The accounts delivered to the Registrar must identify the legislation under which the accounts have been prepared, which GAAP has been used, if any; and whether they have been audited and, if so, according to which Generally Accepted Auditing Standards (reg.33).

[40] Overseas Companies Regulations 2009 reg.31(2). The auditors' report is not required if the company is exempted from audit.

[41] Overseas Companies Regulations 2009 reg.34.

the accounting and filing requirements applied to domestic companies.[42] In addition to the option, available to domestic companies, to file accounts in accordance with International Accounting Standards, the overseas company may choose to prepare its accounts in accordance with its parent law.[43] However, the accounts of companies in this second category are not subject to an audit requirement. Despite the absence of an audit requirement, the obligation to produce annual accounts is clearly a burdensome one for overseas companies which are not required by their parent law to do so—though there must now be few countries in the world which do not require their companies to produce annual financial statements—and, indeed, have them audited.

Finally, if an overseas company closes an establishment in the UK, it must give notice to the Registrar.[44] As to the overseas company itself, it must give information to the Registrar if it is wound up or becomes subject to insolvency proceedings.[45]

The Act lays down a general rule that documents delivered to the Registrar must be in English.[46] However, the company's memorandum or articles of association may be delivered in another language, provided they are accompanied by a certified translation into English.[47]

Execution of documents and names

5–007 Although the overseas companies provisions are primarily concerned with disclosure, there are two sets of provisions going beyond this. One set is largely facultative. It applies, with appropriate modifications, the domestic rules about execution of documents and seals to overseas companies, whether or not that company has an establishment in the UK or even whether or not it can be said to do business "in" the UK.[48] The second set applies to company names and is regulatory in intent.[49] An overseas company is required to register, on creation, the name of its establishment in the UK. That name may be its corporate name or

[42] Overseas Companies Regulations 2009 Pt 5 Ch.3. See Ch.21. This is a considerable improvement on the previous law which applied to overseas companies in such cases a modification of an out-dated set of accounting rules based on the 1948 Act.

[43] 2006 Act s.395, as applied to overseas companies by reg.38. This assumes, of course, that the parent law does not *require* preparation, audit and filing of the accounts of the overseas company, in which case it will fall within the first category of companies.

[44] CA 2006 s.1058 and reg.77—transfer of an establishment from one jurisdiction of the UK to another counts as the closure of one establishment and the opening of another.

[45] CA 2006 s.1053(2) and Overseas Companies Regulations 2009 Pt 8.

[46] CA 2006 s.1103(1).

[47] CA 2006 s.1105 and the Registrar of Companies and Applications for Striking Off Regulations 2009 reg.7.

[48] CA 2006 s.1045 and the Overseas Companies (Execution of Documents and Registration of Charges) Regulations 2009 (SI 2009/1917) Pt 2.

[49] The rules on company charges created by overseas companies (s.1052) are also regulatory and are considered in paras 32–022 onwards. They were reduced in scope in 2011.

the name under which it proposes to carry on business in the UK (its alternative name).[50] In principle, the domestic rules on company names[51] are applied to the overseas company's registered name.[52]

Other mandatory provisions

In the final analysis, Pt 34 applies the equivalent of only a small part of the British Act to overseas companies and, as we have seen, where the home state requires the production of public, audited accounts, even Pt 34 relies on the rules of the state of incorporation rather than on the rules of the British Act. Some further protection for third parties, based on British law, may apply as a result of provisions in the IA 1986. Thus, the rules restricting the re-use by successor companies of the name of a company which has gone into insolvent liquidation[53] apply to overseas companies. This is achieved by use of the formula that the relevant sections of the IA 1986 apply also to companies "which may be wound up under Part V of this Act".[54] Part V of the IA 1986 permits the court in certain circumstances compulsorily to wind up an "unregistered" company, the definition of which is broad enough to include overseas companies.[55] To fall within Pt V the overseas company need not have an established place of business in Great Britain nor, indeed, any assets here at the time the application for winding up is made.[56] The courts have also accepted that the jurisdiction to wind up unregistered companies brings into play certain other sections of the IA 1986, even though those sections do not in terms apply to "Part V" companies.[57] These include the important provisions relating to fraudulent and wrongful trading.[58] Important though these provisions may be, they apply only to companies which have been placed in an insolvency procedure in the UK, which in the case of an overseas company may well not happen.[59] Finally, the Company Directors Disqualification **5–008**

[50] CA 2006 ss.1047(1), (2) and 1048—and it may alter its alternative name and toggle between its corporate and alternative names.

[51] See paras 4–013 onwards.

[52] CA 2006 s.1047(4), (5)—and to any alteration of the registered name. The former relaxations for EEA-incorporated companies have been removed.

[53] See para.19–022.

[54] IA 1986 ss.216(8) and 217(6).

[55] IA 1986 s.220 ("any company", except, of course, those incorporated under the British companies legislation). See *Re Paramount Airways Ltd (No.2)* [1992] B.C.C. 416 CA (Civ Div) at 425. Voluntary winding-up of an unregistered company, however, is not permitted: s.221(4).

[56] *Stocznia Gdanska SA v Latreefers Inc* [2001] B.C.C. 174 CA (Civ Div). However, the company must have some connection with Great Britain and there must be some good reason for winding it up here.

[57] See previous footnote.

[58] See *Stocznia Gdanska SA v Latreefers Inc* [2001] B.C.C. 174; and IA 1986 ss.213 and 214. See also Ch.19.

[59] In the case of insolvent companies with the centre of their main interests in another EU Member State, Regulation 2015/848 on insolvency proceedings [2015] OJ L141/19 favours the opening of insolvency proceedings in that other Member State.

Act 1986[60] also applies to a company incorporated outside Great Britain if it is a company capable of being wound up under the IA 1986.[61]

CHOOSING AND CHANGING JURISDICTIONS

5–009 It is implicit in what we have said above that UK law gives companies operating in the UK considerable freedom to choose their jurisdiction of incorporation. Even when they intend to carry on business wholly or mainly in the UK, the company is not obliged to incorporate in a UK jurisdiction. The second aspect of corporate mobility we investigate is the freedom of a company to move its registered office to another legal jurisdiction, without at the same time having to locate its head office or any other aspect of its operations in the new jurisdiction. This is a significant question because, under the British conflicts of law rules and those of most other jurisdictions, the company law applicable to a company is determined by the jurisdictional location of its registered office. If companies are free to choose and subsequently alter their jurisdiction of incorporation and so the law applicable to the company, but do not have to move any of their operations, then the scene is set, potentially, for regulatory competition among states as they seek to offer the law which is most attractive to companies and for regulatory arbitrage by companies as they move to the jurisdiction which offers the law which they favour. Corporate mobility does not in itself ensure regulatory competition by states and regulatory arbitrage by companies. Regulatory competition also requires that states conceive it to be in their interests to attract or retain incorporations and regulatory arbitrage requires that companies perceive that the advantages of choosing the most favourable law outweigh any potential disadvantages. Without corporate mobility, however, regulatory competition will certainly not occur.

Nor does it follow that the result of competition would be that companies (or companies of a particular type) incorporate overwhelmingly in a particular state. This is certainly what has happened in the US where regulatory competition has led a large proportion of publicly traded companies to incorporate in the state of Delaware, even though none of their operations are within that state. It might be, instead, that states all bring their company laws in line with the model which companies prefer (in order not to lose incorporations) so that what competition produces is not migration of companies but convergence of states' company laws. In this perspective, the power to choose and alter the jurisdiction of incorporation puts pressure on those responsible for company law in a particular country to ensure that it remains attractive to businesses. The CLR thought this was the correct approach in principle: "In general, it is desirable that businesses should remain in Great Britain because it is attractive for them to do so, and not because

[60] See Ch.20.

[61] IA 1986 s.22(2). See also *Re Seagull Manufacturing Co Ltd (In Liqudiation) (No.2)* [1993] B.C.C. 833—Act applicable to foreigners outside the jurisdiction and to conduct which occurred outside the jurisdiction, though presumably only in relation to a company falling within the Act. In the case of undischarged bankrupts the connecting factor is instead whether the company has an established place of business in Great Britain.

company law in some sense locks them in".[62] Alternatively, competition might lead not to harmonisation on a single model but to a form of "specialisation" in which different jurisdictions offer somewhat different corporate laws, each adapted to the dominant form of business organisation to be found in their jurisdiction. Whatever the precise result, it would be the operation of competitive pressures rather than legislative fiat which determined the nature and extent of the harmonisation process.[63]

We have seen above that UK law provides considerable freedom to companies to choose a foreign company law whilst operating wholly or mainly in the UK. By reason of being an incorporation theory state, UK law is equally relaxed about a company incorporated in the UK undertaking all or most of its operations outside the UK—though if those operations take place mainly in a real seat state, it may need to look carefully at that state's rules. There is nothing in the UK rules on incorporation which requires the company to commit itself to operating any part of its business in the UK or even to disclose where it intends to operate—though, if it seeks outside investors, it will need to disclose its intentions to them, either by law or in practice. But what about subsequent transfer out by a company incorporated in a UK jurisdiction or transfer in from a non-UK jurisdiction?

Subsequent transfer

If a company incorporated in a foreign jurisdiction, but operating in the UK, wishes to move its registered office to another foreign jurisdiction, that is a matter for the jurisdictions involved. If the foreign jurisdictions allow this to happen, British law will normally recognise the result. However, British law is directly engaged if a company registered in one of the UK jurisdictions wishes to move its registered office to a foreign jurisdiction—or if a company registered in a foreign jurisdiction wishes to move its registered office to the one of the UK jurisdictions. Curiously, in contrast with its liberal stance at the point of incorporation, British law provides no simple mechanism whereby a company may make such a move, even as between the British jurisdictions. When the founders apply to register a company in the UK, they must state in which of the three UK jurisdictions its registered office is to be situated: England and Wales, Scotland or Northern Ireland.[64] There is no simple mechanism provided whereby the registered office can be changed subsequently from the jurisdiction of incorporation to another.[65] Thus, a company which is formed with its registered office in England and Wales cannot decide by a mere resolution of its shareholders to transfer its registered office to Scotland, still less to some foreign 5–010

[62] Completing, para.11.55.

[63] For an extended analysis of the issues discussed in this paragraph see J. Armour, "Who Should Make Corporate Law? EC Legislation versus Regulatory Competition" (2005) 58 *Current Legal Problems* 369.

[64] CA 2006 s.9(2)(b).

[65] The facility for companies whose registered office is in fact in Wales to alter the statement so as to toggle between "Wales" and "England and Wales" does not involve a change of legal jurisdiction. The change has an impact on the availability or otherwise on the use of Welsh in the company's official documents and in communications with Companies House. See s.88.

jurisdiction.[66] Nor, will British company law accept an incoming company on the basis of a resolution of its shareholders to move the registered office to the UK.

5–011 However, as we have noted, it is possible to produce a transfer of registered office (at least out of the UK) in a somewhat more elaborate way. The transferring company might go into (solvent) liquidation in its current jurisdiction and in that process transfer its assets to a company newly incorporated in the jurisdiction of choice, but the tax consequences of winding up often make that course of action unattractive. A similar, but more tax efficient procedure, is to use a scheme of arrangement.[67] Under a scheme, the assets of the existing company are transferred to a new company formed in the jurisdiction of choice or the shareholders in the existing company exchange their shares for shares in the new company, the existing company becoming a subsidiary of the new one. Either way, the physical location of the operating assets does not change, only the jurisdiction in which the owning company or ultimate parent is located. This mechanism will certainly work if the new jurisdiction is within the UK, but it will also work with most non-UK jurisdictions.[68]

The scheme is thus a useful mechanism for companies wishing to exit one of the UK jurisdictions. Crucially, schemes have protections for minority shareholders and creditors, who might be disadvantaged by the shift of jurisdiction of incorporation. These protections are requirements for supermajority shareholder approval and court sanction, at which creditors likely to be adversely affected by the scheme may object.[69] However, it will be a rare case where the scheme procedure can be used by a company wishing to transfer into a UK jurisdiction. A scheme involves an alteration of the rights of the shareholders of the transferring company and a UK court will normally regard that as a matter for the law of the exiting jurisdiction, so that the scheme of arrangement is not available to the transferring company, and the court in the transferring jurisdiction might not recognise the validity of what the exiting company was attempting to do.[70] What is needed to effect a transfer into the UK is a mechanism for coordinating the laws and procedures of the courts (or other authorities) in the exiting and receiving jurisdictions. So long as the UK was part of the EU such a mechanism was available under the Cross-Border Mergers Directive[71] and the implementing UK Regulations[72] (now repealed). The resulting company could be established purely for the purpose of the merger (i.e. it did not have to have any prior operations), so that the cross-border merger could be used simply for the purpose of transferring the company's place of incorporation.

---

[66] Since British law adopts the incorporation theory, a UK company may freely move its headquarters out of the UK without imperilling the validity of its incorporation in the UK in the eyes of British law. This is useful for companies which wish to retain British company law but does not address the issue of companies which wish to change the applicable company law.

[67] On schemes of arrangement see Ch.29.

[68] *Re Man Group Plc* [2019] EWHC 1392 (Ch), discussed at para.29–004.

[69] See Ch.29. Creditors are particularly likely to be affected if the company against which their claims lie is leaving the UK, because their rights against its assets will now be governed by a different law.

[70] See paras 29–005 and 29–016.

[71] Directive 2005/56 on cross-border mergers of limited liability companies [2005] OJ L310/10.

[72] Companies (Cross-Border Merger) Regulations 2007 (SI 2007/2974).

The cross-border merger, although effective, does have some costs for the transferring company. For many years the EU Commission contemplated, but did not bring forward, a Directive dealing explicitly with the transfer of the company's registered office across border but within the EU. Eventually a Directive was adopted in 2019[73] (but with a transposition date after the UK's final exit from the EU). However, it is so hedged with conditions that it is doubtful whether it will make cross-border transfer of the registered offices within the EU any easier.[74]

Reform?

British company law has traditionally adopted a welcoming stance towards companies incorporated elsewhere. This is shown both by the limited extent to which it applies the provisions of the British Act to such companies and its acceptance of incorporation as the connecting factor in its private international law rules. However, it is much less open to transfers by British companies of the registered office to other jurisdictions or the simple transfer in of the registered office by companies already incorporated in other jurisdictions (as opposed to their conduct of business in the UK). While the UK was a Member State of the EU, substantial changes were being made on this second aspect of the UK position, and there was the prospect of further reform. These possibilities have largely disappeared. **5–012**

However, it would be possible for the UK to make changes in its laws unilaterally, certainly in relation to transfers of jurisdiction within the UK and even outside it. This would not be a simple matter, since it would require adequate protections for minority shareholders and existing creditors. However, it is difficult to believe that these could not be provided so as to allow a straightfoward transfer of the registered office. The Company Law Review proposed such a scheme.[75] The CLR proposals envisaged the possibility of transfer of the registered office within the UK but also outside it. The basis of the proposal was that transfer in principle should be permitted (i.e. the opposite of the present law) but subject to adequate safeguards for shareholders and creditors. The main elements of protection for members would be the requirement that the board draw up a detailed proposal about the transfer, that the proposal should require approval by special resolution of the shareholders (thus requiring a three-quarters majority approval) and that dissenting members should have the power to apply to the court which might order such relief as it thought appropriate. Thus, for shareholders, the protective techniques invoked were disclosure, supermajority approval and court control. For the protection of creditors, it was additionally proposed that the directors would have to declare the company to be solvent and able to pay its debts as they fell due for the 12 months after emigration, the creditors would have the right to apply to the court to

[73] Directive 2019/2121 amending Directive 2017/1132 as regards cross-border conversions, mergers and divisions [2019] OJ L321/1.

[74] See European Company Law Experts, "The Commission's 2018 Proposal on Cross-Border Mobility—An Assessment" (2019) 16 *European Company and Financial Law Review* 196.

[75] Completing, paras 11.54–11.70 and Final Report I, Ch.14.

challenge the proposal and the company would have to accept service in the UK even after emigration in respect of claims arising from commitments incurred before emigration.[76]

Transfer would have been permitted, on compliance with these rules, to any EU or EEA Member State, but transfer to a non-EU state would be dependent upon the Secretary of State having approved that state for this purpose, the criteria for approval being related mainly to levels of creditor protection, especially for creditors resident outside the state. Finally, for transfer within the UK a less detailed proposal would need to be developed by the board and the right of dissenting shareholders to apply to the court would be removed. The full range of creditor protections, however, would apply since there are significant differences in security and property law between the three jurisdictions.[77] However, the Government rejected the CLR's proposals for international migration, on grounds of feared loss of tax revenues.[78]

CONCLUSION

5–013 As we have noted, the freedom of companies to choose the applicable company law, separately from the place in which their operations are based, can operate to promote competition among states to attract incorporations. The US has always been the prime example of this process, where Delaware has clearly won the race to attract the incorporation of large companies, even though few of them have significant operations in that state. There has always been a fierce debate between those who have seen Delaware's victory as a result of a race to the bottom (low corporate standards, mainly to the benefit of senior management) and those who view it as a race to the top (a system of rules most likely to promote the operating efficiency of companies). In Europe the race had not emerged when the European Economic Community was set up in the middle of the 1950s and, as we describe in Ch.3,[79] the founding fathers seemed keen to avoid it. The Treaty did not deal effectively with the split between Member States' laws based on the incorporation theory, on the one hand, and the real seat, on the other, which was a major impediment to competition. The development by the Court of Justice of the freedom of establishment provisions so as to provide companies with freedom of choice at the point of formation occurred only at the end of the last century[80] and took many observers by surprise. By contrast, the working through of the application of freedom of establishment to subsequent transfers of seat had reached the final stages of being worked out only at the point when the UK left.

---

[76] If the company, after emigration, maintained a place of business in the UK it would become subject to the information provision rules for overseas companies (above); if not, it would in any event have to file with Companies House contact details relating to its new jurisdiction.

[77] Immigration would also be permitted but there the regulatory burden would fall mainly on the former state of registration. The British requirements would parallel those for a domestic company which re-registers: Final Report I, para.14.12 and paras 4–020 onwards.

[78] Modernising, pp.54–55.

[79] See paras 3–015 onwards.

[80] *Centros Ltd v Erhverus-og Selkabsstyrelsen* (C-212/97) EU:C:1999:126; [1999] B.C.C. 983; *Uberseering BV v Nordic Construction Co Baumanagement GmbH (NCC)* (C-208/00) EU:C:2002:632; [2005] 1 C.M.L.R. 1.

With the UK's exit from the EU, the prospects for easy corporate mobility into and out of the UK have receded, though the UK law maintains its open stance towards the recognition of companies validly incorporated in foreign jurisdictions. This means that the UK company law is open to competition from foreign systems at the point of incorporation, but much less so once a company has become incorporated in the UK and has built up substantial operations. However, this does not necessarily mean that there is no post-incorporation competitive pressures on UK company law. With the UK exit from the EU, there will be almost a "natural experiment" in relation to the bottom up versus top down explanations for the harmonisation of company laws in Europe. The UK will be outside the top down harmonisation system, but it will still wish to provide an effective set of rules for companies incorporated in its jurisdiction, while the EU will keep an eye on UK company law developments. Will this drive UK company law in a different direction from that pursued within the EU, as the two legislators make different policy choices, or will a high level of harmonisation continue to be maintained de facto in order to avoid competitive disadvantages? If it is partly one and partly the other—the more likely outcome—what will be the factors determining the split? **5–014**

CHAPTER 6

THE NATURE AND CLASSIFICATION OF SHARES

LEGAL NATURE OF SHARES

What is the juridical nature of a share? This remains a question more easily asked than answered. In the former deed of settlement company, which was merely an enlarged partnership with the partnership property vested in trustees, a member's "share" clearly entitled them to some form of beneficial interest in the company's assets. That said, the precise nature of that beneficial interest was admittedly not crystal clear, since a member could not, while the firm was a going concern, claim any particular asset or prevent the directors from disposing of those assets. Similarly, there has been difficulty in identifying the precise nature of a partner's interest in a modern partnership's assets. Whilst a partner appears to have a "beneficial interest" in the partnership assets (involving some sort of proprietary nexus between each partner and those assets) this does not necessarily equate with a partner having a vested "equitable interest" in the partnership property.[1] Each partner's interest might be viewed as a proprietary interest that floats over the partnership assets throughout the duration of the firm, albeit that the interest "crystallises" and becomes fixed on the partnership assets upon its dissolution. In *Commissioner of State Revenue (Vic) v Danvest Pty Ltd*, the Victorian Court of Appeal recently described a partner's interest as follows[2]: 6–001

> "[The partners] acquired equitable choses in action embracing (a) a right to approach a court of equity to secure the proper administration of the partnership property by the partners or the manager of the partnership; and (b) a right to a proportion of the surplus *after* dissolution and the realisation of the assets and payment of the debts and liabilities of the partnership. Whilst such a chose in action may be an 'interest' in itself, it does not confer an interest 'in' any property … not does it effect any change in the beneficial ownership of that property. It may be described as an expectancy in so far as that term connotes that it is not until the dissolution of the partnership and the subsequent realisation of assets and the payment of debts and liability that the interest of each partner in the property, being a factional interest in a surplus

[1] *Commissioner of State Revenue (Vic) v Danvest Pty Ltd* (2017) 107 A.T.R. 12.
[2] *Commissioner of State Revenue (Vic) v Danvest Pty Ltd* (2017) 107 A.T.R. 12 at [82]–[83].

of assets over liabilities, can be ascertained finally. Until then, any interest is indefinite and fluctuating and comprises merely a personal right to secure the proper administration of those assets."

At one time, a shareholder was similarly considered to have a proprietary nexus with the assets of the incorporated company in which he held shares, except that the shareholder–company relationship was conceived as involving a trust, since "the legal interest of all the stock is in the company, who are trustees for the several members".[3] This trust conception has, however, long since been rejected. Accordingly, shareholders have ceased to be regarded as having an equitable interest in the company's assets: as Evershed LJ has stated, "shareholders are not, in the eyes of the law, part owners of the undertaking".[4] This means that "no shareholder had any right to any item of property owned by the company, for he has no legal or equitable interest therein".[5] As a result of this conceptual shift, the word "share" has become something of a misnomer, since shareholders no longer share any property in common, albeit that they share certain default rights in respect of dividends, return of capital on a winding up, voting, and the like.

Whilst a share no longer confers any proprietary right to the company's assets, a share is itself a form of property recognised by the law that can be transferred to third parties, whether by selling, mortgaging or bequeathing the share. In fact, shares are particularly suited to the modern commercial era by virtue of their exceptional liquidity. To deny that shares are "owned" would be as unreal as to deny, on the basis of feudal theory, that land is owned—indeed, far more unreal given that the owner of shares in a public company is likely to be considerably less fettered in dealing with his property than a landowner. Nor are shareholders' proprietary rights to their shares nowadays regarded as equitable in nature. The legal ownership of shares is clearly recognised and distinguished from equitable ownership in much the same way as a legal estate in land is distinguished from equitable interests therein.[6] As a form of property, a share has been described as a chose in action.[7] Such a description does little to advance the discussion, however, as "chose in action" is a notoriously vague term that is used to describe a mass of interests having little or nothing in common, except that they confer no right to possession of a physical thing. Choses in action range from purely personal rights under a contract and debts to patents, copyrights and trade marks. Indeed, a share could be equated with rights under a contract, since a share makes its holder privy to a statutory contract between the members inter se and the company on the terms set out in the company's articles of association,[8] which effectively define the members' rights to participate in the association's

---

[3] *Child v Hudson's Bay Co* (1723) 2 P. Wms. 207 Ct of Chancery at 208–209. As in the case of a partnership interest, a share had long been recognised as being personalty (rather than realty), even if the company owned freehold land: see CA 2006 s.541.

[4] *Short v Treasury Commissioners* [1948] 1 K.B. 116 CA at 122. See also *Inland Revenue Commissioners v Laird Group Plc* [2003] UKHL 54; [2003] 1 W.L.R. 2476 at [35]. See further para.2–014.

[5] *Macaura v Northern Assurance Co Ltd* [1925] A.C. 619 HL at 626.

[6] See Ch.26.

[7] *Colonial Bank v Whinney* (1886) 11 App. Cas. 426 HL at 448. See also *Your Response Ltd v Datateam Business Media Ltd* [2014] EWCA Civ 281; [2014] C.P. Rep. 31 at [25]–[26].

[8] CA 2006 s.33(1). See further Ch.11.

decision-making processes by attending and voting at general meetings. A share is, however, something more than a mere contractual right in personam. Some support for this view can be derived from authorities relating to infant shareholders, who are liable for calls on their shares unless they repudiate the allotment during infancy or on attaining majority,[9] and who cannot recover any money paid unless there has been a total failure of consideration.[10] As Parke B stated in *North Western Railway Co v M'Michael*[11]:

> "[Infant shareholders] have been treated, therefore, as persons in a different situation from mere contractors for then they would have been exempt, but in truth they are purchasers who have acquired an interest not in a mere chattel, but in a subject of a permanent nature."

The above discussion highlights the reality that a share cannot readily be placed into a single juridical category, but constitutes a complex amalgam of proprietary and contractual rights. The complexity of defining a share's juridical nature is further increased when a shareholder does not directly hold those shares, but instead holds them through intermediaries acting on his or her behalf. In such circumstances, a shareholder does not directly own the share itself, but simply has the ultimate economic interest in the share.[12] Such intermediated shareholding structures not only impact upon how the shareholder exercises his rights under the company's articles and under the CA 2006,[13] but also affects the manner in which his or her interest is transferred.[14] The following analysis will focus on the nature of shares that are held directly by the shareholder.

In terms of formal legal definition, the CA 2006 defines a "share" as a "share in the company's share capital".[15] As this provides little assistance, the common law has proved more helpful in determining a share's juridical nature. In particular, in *Borland's Trustee v Steel Bros & Co Ltd*, Farwell J provided the following guidance[16]: **6–002**

> "A share is the interest of a shareholder in the company measured by a sum of money, for the purpose of liability in the first place, and of interest in the second, but also consisting of a series of mutual covenants entered into by all the shareholders *inter se* in accordance with

[9] *Cork & Brandon Railway v Cazenove* (1847) 10 Q.B. 935 QB; *North Western Railway Co v M'Michael* (1851) 5 Ex. 114 Ex Ct. It is unclear whether an infant who repudiates the shares during infancy remains liable for calls falling due before repudiation, since the majority in *Cazenove* considered that liability would continue, but Parke B in *M'Michael* (at 125) disagreed.

[10] *Steinberg v Scala (Leeds) Ltd* [1923] 2 Ch. 452 CA at 458–459.

[11] *North Western Railway Co v M'Michael* (1851) 5 Ex. 114 at 123. Parke B also suggested (at 125) that the shareholder had "a vested interest of a permanent character in all the profits arising from the land and other effects of the company", but this cannot be supported in light of subsequent authority.

[12] See generally *Re DNick Holding Plc* [2013] EWHC 68 (Ch); [2014] B.C.C. 1; *Secure Capital SA v Credit Suisse AG* [2017] EWCA Civ 1486; *Deutsche Trustee Co Ltd v Bangkok Land (Cayman Islands) Ltd* [2019] EWHC 657 (Comm); *SL Claimants v Tesco Plc* [2019] EWHC 2858 (Ch).

[13] See paras12–018 to 12–020.

[14] See paras 26–012 to 26–015.

[15] CA 2006 s.540(1).

[16] *Borland's Trustee v Steel Bros & Co Ltd* [1901] 1 Ch. 279 Ch D at 288; approved in *Re Paulin* [1935] 1 K.B. 26 CA; affirmed in *Inland Revenue Commissioners v Crossman* [1937] A.C. 26 HL at 40, 51 and 66. See also *Grays Timber Products Ltd v Revenue and Customs Commissioners* [2010] UKSC 4; 2011 S.L.T. 63 at [27]; *Lomas v Burlington Loan Management Ltd* [2016] EWHC 2417 (Ch) at [137].

> [s.33 of the CA 2006]. The contract contained in the articles of association is one of the original incidents of the share. A share is not a sum of money … but is an interest measured by a sum of money and made up of various rights contained in the contract, including the right to a sum of money of a more or less amount."

Consistently with the suggestion above that a share is an amalgam of contractual and proprietary rights, Farwell J's definition not only lays considerable stress on the shareholder's contractual rights as defined in the company's articles of association,[17] but also the fact that the shareholder obtains some form of interest *in* the company.[18] Given that a shareholder has no direct proprietary interest in the company's assets, the latter suggestion might appear somewhat contradictory. This apparent contradiction stems from the company being (on the one hand) a separate legal person that is the subject of its own rights and duties, but (on the other hand) a "res" that is the object of such rights and duties.[19]

In determining the nature of a shareholder's interest "in" a company, Farwell J mentions that it is "measured by a sum of money". This is a reference to the (arbitrary and illogical) requirement (rejected in certain other common law jurisdictions) that each share must be ascribed a "fixed nominal value" or notional par value.[20] Whilst a share's nominal value is frequently meaningless (and may even be misleading), it does fix a shareholder's minimum liability to contribute to the company's assets in the event of insolvency.[21] Even as a measure of liability, however, a share's nominal value is less significant now that shares are almost invariably issued on terms that they are to be fully paid-up on or shortly after allotment and at a price that frequently exceeds their nominal value. A share's nominal value also determines a shareholder's key rights against the company, namely an entitlement to a proportionate share of the company's profits should a dividend be declared by the board[22]; a proportionate claim to the company's surplus assets if all the creditors are repaid following the company's winding-up[23]; and the relative weight of a shareholder's voting entitlement.[24] In theoretical terms, the fact that a member has rights "in" the company (as well as against it) distinguishes the shareholder as an equity investor from creditors providing debt finance (whether as a commercial lender, supplier of goods and services or bondholder): whilst a creditor similarly has contractual rights against the company, the return on their investment is fixed in advance and is not dependent upon the company's profitability; and, even when the creditor has

[17] CA 2006 s.33(1).

[18] *Marex Financial Ltd v Sevilleja* [2020] UKSC 31; [2020] B.C.C. 783 at [105]: "A share confers rights in a company as well as rights against a company."

[19] "A whole system has been built up on the unconscious assumption that organisations, which from one point of view are considered individuals, from another are storehouses of tangible property": see T. Arnold, *The Folklore of Capitalism* (New Haven, Conn., 1959), p.353. The proprietary analysis of the share (even if it does not extend to the company's assets) sometimes makes courts resistant to their compulsory acquisition, even at a fair price: see *Gambotto v WCP Ltd* (1995) 127 A.L.R. 417 HC (Australia). See further para.13–010.

[20] CA 2006 s.542(1). See further para.16–003.

[21] IA 1986 s.74(2)(d).

[22] Companies (Model Articles) Regulations 2008 (SI 2008/3229) Sch.1 art.30(4) and Sch.3 art.70(4).

[23] IA 1986 s.107.

[24] CA 2006 s.284.

taken security to protect its position, it has a proprietary claim against the company's earmarked assets, but never "in" the company itself.

At first sight, the above analysis might seem rather academic, especially as it is increasingly possible to combine the respective advantages of equity and debt by drafting the rights attached to particular securities in a sufficiently careful manner.[25] Accordingly, in practice, it can be difficult to preserve any hard and fast distinction between the rights of shareholders and creditors. Nevertheless, an analysis of the share's juridical nature is not entirely theoretical, as courts have sometimes had to consider the issue in order to determine the basis on which shares should be valued. The leading example is *Short v Treasury Commissioners*,[26] where the entire shareholding of Short Bros was being acquired by the Treasury under a Defence Regulation providing for payment of the shares' value "as between a willing buyer and a willing seller".[27] On the basis of that formula, the shares were valued by reference to their quoted share price. The company's shareholders argued, however, that stock exchange prices were not a reliable determinant of value when a company's entire shareholding was being acquired. Instead, the shareholders contended that either the whole undertaking should be valued (with the value thus determined being apportioned among the shareholders) or the value should be the price that one buyer would give for the whole bloc of shares (which price would then be similarly apportioned). Whilst the Court of Appeal rejected both these suggestions, it is significant for present purposes that the first argument was rejected on the basis that "[s]hareholders are not, in the eye of the law, part owners of the undertaking", with the consequence that a shareholder has no proprietary interest in the company's assets.[28] 6–003

The principle in *Short* has been applied recently by the Privy Council in *Shanda Games Ltd v Maso Capital Investments Ltd*,[29] which concerned the merger of two companies in the Cayman Islands that triggered the right of dissenting shareholders to have their shares acquired by the company at a "fair value", which, if necessary, was to be determined by the court. Accordingly, the dispute concerned whether "fair value" for a minority shareholding required the shares to be valued on a pro rata basis (as a proportionate share of the value of the company's business and undertaking) or a discounted basis (to reflect the fact that the dissenting shareholders only held a minority interest). Applying *Short*, Lady Arden adopted the second option on the basis that "a share is a share in the capital of a company, not a share in the undertaking and assets"[30] and that "the shareholder is only entitled to be paid for the share with which he is parting,

[25] Consider M. Pickering, "The Problem of the Preference Share" (1963) 26 M.L.R. 499.

[26] *Short v Treasury Commissioners* [1948] 1 K.B. 116 CA; affirmed [1948] A.C. 534 HL. See also *Inland Revenue Commissioners v Laird Group Plc* [2003] 1 W.L.R. 2476 at [35].

[27] This popular formula is much criticised by economists who argue (with some force) that the willingness of the buyer and seller depends on the price and not vice versa.

[28] *Short v Treasury Commissioners* [1948] 1 K.B. 116 at 122. The shareholders' second contention was rejected because the regulation implied that each shareholding was to be separately valued. This illustrates the expropriatory nature of the legislation: had the willing buyer been characterised as a buyer of control, there is no doubt that a premium to the market price would have been payable (even though no individual seller had control) because some sharing of the benefits of control would have been necessary to induce the shareholders to sell. See further Ch.28.

[29] *Shanda Games Ltd v Maso Capital Investments Ltd* [2020] UKPC 2; [2020] B.C.C. 466.

[30] *Shanda Games Ltd v Maso Capital Investments Ltd* [2020] B.C.C. 466 at [46].

namely a minority shareholding, and not for a proportionate part of the controlling stake which the acquirer thereby builds up, still less a pro rata part of the value of the company's net assets or business undertaking".[31] In a different context, the nature of the shareholder's interest identified in *Short* has recently been used by a majority of the Supreme Court to justify the so-called "reflective loss" principle barring shareholders from recovering their personal losses to the extent that these effectively reflect losses suffered by the company.[32]

The Presumption of Equality Between Shareholders

6–004 A company limited by shares must necessarily issue some shares, and the initial legal presumption is that, in respect of those shares, shareholders' rights and liabilities should be equal. The same starting point applies to partnerships in the absence of agreement to the contrary.[33] Indeed, in *Marex Financial Ltd v Sevilleja*,[34] Lord Hodge recently stated that "[i]t is a significant principle of company law that, in the absence of agreement to the contrary such as that expressed in the terms of a share issue, shares confer the same rights and impose the same liabilities". In that regard, the shareholders' rights will ordinarily be threefold, namely a proportionate share of any dividends declared; a proportionate claim to any capital returned (upon a court-authorised or permitted reduction), as well as participation in surplus assets on a winding up; and the right to attend meetings and vote thereat. Unless there is some indication to the contrary (usually in the company's articles of association), each share will confer a like right in each of these three respects.[35]

So far as voting is concerned, this equality of treatment between each share is a comparatively recent development. By analogy with the principle applicable to partnerships, members' voting rights were traditionally divorced from the size of their financial interest in the payment of dividends and capital by the company. Accordingly, the number of votes was determined by the number of shareholders, rather than the number of shares that each held. An intermediate position between these two approaches was reflected in the Companies Clauses Act 1845,[36] which provided that, in the absence of contrary provision in the special statute, every shareholder had one vote for every share they held up to ten, then one further vote for every five additional shares up to 100 and an additional vote for every ten shares held beyond 100. This approach weighted the voting in favour of smaller shareholders. As the size of shareholdings increased, attempts were made to control their voting strength by introducing "voting caps", but these could easily

[31] *Shanda Games Ltd v Maso Capital Investments Ltd* [2020] B.C.C. 466 at [47]. See also *Monaghan v Gilsenan* [2021] EWHC 47 (Ch) at [38]–[45], considering the term "fair value" in a compulsory transfer provision.

[32] *Marex Financial Ltd v Sevilleja* [2020] B.C.C. 783 at [23], [31], [80], [102], [105]. See further paras 14–010 to 14–011.

[33] Partnership Act 1890 s.24(1).

[34] *Marex Financial Ltd v Sevilleja* [2020] B.C.C. 783 at [103].

[35] *Birch v Cropper* (1889) 14 App. Cas. 525 HL. See generally C. Hare, "The Principle of Equal Treatment of Shareholders in English Law" in P. Jung, *Der Gleichbehandlungsgrundsatz im Gesellschaftsrecht* (Mohr Siebeck, 2021), Ch.1.

[36] Companies Clauses Act 1845 s.75.

be evaded by a shareholder splitting up their holdings and vesting parcels in different nominees. Whilst it remains possible to insert "voting caps" into the articles, the more usual course nowadays is to create separate classes of shares, with shares in different classes carrying a different number of votes. As will be considered subsequently,[37] however, the traditional analogy with partnerships still persists nowadays given that the primary voting mechanism for shareholders at common law remains a show of hands, whereby each member present at a meeting is entitled to one vote irrespective of the number of shares held.[38] Whilst such a voting mechanism might be excluded by the constitution, the converse is in fact the case, since the model articles of association for private companies preserve the show of hands as the primary voting mechanism.[39] This can be justified on efficiency grounds, as a show of hands can provide a speedy, if somewhat inaccurate, way of establishing the views of the meeting.[40]

As considered subsequently,[41] the problems associated with a show of hands are tempered by the default articles of association allowing some shareholders, the meeting's chairman or the directors to demand a poll,[42] whereby votes are cast instead according to the principle "one share, one vote".[43] There is certainly a strong argument for applying the equality principle to the voting rights attached to shares that otherwise have the same rights and duties, since a particular shareholder's influence over the corporate affairs would then reflect the size of his or her investment in the company. Accordingly, governance rights and financial risk would then be coterminous. If one is serious about this principle, then the obvious corollary is that it should not be possible to diminish the voting rights attached to shares. Indeed, in 1962, the Jenkins Committee on Company Law considered the adoption of a rule that would have prohibited non- or restricted-voting ordinary shares. The majority view was against this proposition, however, as it would constitute an interference with freedom of contract; but three members of the committee, including the original author of this book, dissented.[44] Accordingly, the equal treatment of shares with respect to voting is not mandatory and companies are free to issue shares with no, restricted or, even, weighted voting rights.[45] Such arrangements are relatively rare in listed companies because institutional shareholders have traditionally been reluctant to

---

[37] See Ch.12.

[38] CA 2006 s.284(2).

[39] Companies (Model Articles) Regulations 2008 (SI 2008/3229) Sch.1 art.42.

[40] For criticism of the show-of-hands mechanism, see paras 12–048 to 12–049.

[41] See Ch.12.

[42] Companies (Model Articles) Regulations 2008 (SI 2008/3229) Sch.1 art.44 and Sch.3 art.36.

[43] CA 2006 s.284(3). See also *Re Sirius Minerals Plc* [2020] EWHC 1447 (Ch) at [19]. For an example of a constitutional provision to the contrary, see *Puzitskaya v St Paul's Mews (Islington) Ltd* [2017] EWHC 905 (Ch). For an unsuccessful attempt by the European Commission to build support for such a principle, see Commission of the European Communities, *Impact Assessment on the Proportionality between Capital and Control in Listed Companies* SEC(2007) 1705.

[44] *Report of the Company Law Committee* (1962), Cm.1749, paras 123–140 and pp.207–210.

[45] See *Bushell v Faith* [1970] A.C. 1099 HL; approved in *Russell v Northern Bank Development Corp Ltd* [1992] B.C.C. 578 HL. However, for premium-listed companies on the London Stock Exchange the Listing Rules at the moment require equality of votes within the same class of shares and proportionality across different classes of equity shares (Listing Rules LR 7.2.1A—Principles 3 and 4), but the admission of "dual class" shares is under discussion.

buy shares whose votes do not reflect the financial risk. Accordingly, the solution to the problem in the UK is driven by the market, rather than determined by regulation.

With respect to the financial rights that arise out of holding shares, the default position is similarly that a shareholder is entitled to be paid a proportionate share of any dividends declared by the board[46] and any authorised return of capital by the company.[47] It is not uncommon, however, for a company to issue preference shares conferring more attractive financial rights (whether regarding dividends or capital) for those holding such shares.[48] That type of share is considered further below.[49]

6–005 A similar presumption of equality operates in relation to shareholders' liabilities, but this too can be altered by the articles. In the case of a company limited by shares, a shareholder's only liability is generally to pay the nominal value of their shares,[50] together with any premium,[51] insofar as payment has not already been made by the shareholder or a previous holder. Whilst the presumption of equality means that each shareholder remains liable to pay the same nominal value on their shares, those shares will not necessarily be issued at the same price (so that a different premium will be payable) and shareholders will not necessarily be treated alike as regards calls for any unpaid part of the purchase price. Indeed, if so authorised by its articles, a company may make different arrangements between shareholders upon the issue of shares regarding "the amounts and times of payments of calls on their shares"; may accept from any member the whole or part of the amount remaining unpaid on any shares, even though no part of the amount payable on the shares has been called up; or pay a dividend in proportion to the amount paid up on each share where a larger amount is paid up on some shares than on others.[52] Subject to such a provision, however, calls must be made pari passu.[53]

CLASSES OF SHARES

6–006 The possibility of having differential rights attached to shares was for many years doubted, unless this was permitted by an express provision in the original constitution. In the absence of such a provision, the continued equality of shares was considered to be so fundamental that it could not be abrogated by the subsequent alteration of the articles, so as to allow the issue of shares that were preferential to those already issued.[54] This notion was, however, finally rejected

---

[46] *Routledge v Skerritt* [2019] EWHC 573 (Ch); [2019] B.C.C. 812 at [48].

[47] *Revenue and Customs Commissioners v McQuillan* [2017] UKUT 344 (TCC) at [23].

[48] A company's articles may also provide that a dividend is payable in proportion to the amount paid up on each share: see CA 2006 s.581(c).

[49] See para.6–007.

[50] CA 2006 s.542(1).

[51] CA 2006 s.610(1).

[52] CA 2006 s.581.

[53] *Galloway v Halle Concerts Society* [1915] 2 Ch. 233 Ch D.

[54] *Hutton v Scarborough Cliff Hotel Co* (1865) 2 Drew. & Sm. 521 Ct of Chancery.

in *Andrews v Gas Meter Co*,[55] where a company (whose original constitution provided for only one class of shares) was permitted to alter its constitution, so as to issue a second class of shares with rights that ranked to some extent ahead of the existing shares. Nowadays, the prima facie equality between shares in relation to voting, dividends and any return of capital can be modified by the articles of association dividing the company's share capital into different "classes" with different rights attached to each class.[56] Indeed, the number of possible classes is only limited by the total number of shares issued by the company, since the different combination of rights attached to shares is almost infinite. That said, the practice of publicly traded companies is not to complicate their capital structures by having numerous different share classes, although it is not uncommon for public and private companies to have two or three different classes (sometimes more). In that regard, the rights attached to each class of share will normally be set out in the company's articles, although (in contrast to other common law countries) that is not compulsory.[57] Given the need for some level of disclosure regarding class rights, however, legislative steps have been taken to ensure that any classes (and their associated rights) can be ascertained from the company's public documents. The necessary publicity is achieved through the "return of allotments" (i.e. the information that a company has to provide to the Registrar of Companies within one month of any share allotment).[58] The return must provide the "prescribed particulars" of the rights attached to the shares in each class.[59] Similarly, if a company assigns a name or other designation to a class of its shares (or changes an existing designation) that fact must also be notified.[60] The same notification requirement applies to any variation of class rights.[61]

Preference shares

Where the difference between a company's class rights concerns its shareholders' financial entitlements (namely rights to dividends and return of capital), the likelihood is that the different classes will be given a particular designation to distinguish between them (often simply "preference" or "ordinary" shares, with the former sometimes being further designated by the label "first" or "second" where there are two classes of preference shares). Most commonly, a preference shareholder receives a fixed dividend and/or a return of capital ahead of (or in "preference to") any payment to the ordinary shareholders. That said, an investor **6–007**

[55] *Andrews v Gas Meter Co* [1897] 1 Ch. 361 CA. See also *Citco Banking Corp NV v Pusser's Ltd* [2007] UKPC 13; [2007] B.C.C. 205 at [12].

[56] CA 2006 s.629(1). See further Ch.13.

[57] This is now true even in relation to redeemable shares, provided the articles or a resolution of the company authorises the directors to determine the terms of redemption: see CA 2006 s.685. See further para.17–010. Where a share certificate is issued, a shareholder's rights may sometimes be set out on the back of that certificate, but a misstatement regarding the shareholder's rights in the certificate will not override any conflicting statement in the company's articles or any offer document: see *Re Hunting Plc* [2004] EWHC 2591 (Ch).

[58] On allotment, see para.24–016.

[59] CA 2006 s.555(4)(c). For the equivalent provision applicable to unlimited companies, see CA 2006 s.556(3). See further Companies (Shares and Share Capital) Order 2009 (SI 2009/388) arts.2–3.

[60] CA 2006 s.636.

[61] CA 2006 s.637. For the variation of class rights, see Ch.13.

looking to acquire preference shares should not expect that their interests will be preferred to those of ordinary shareholders in terms of the company's day-to-day operations. Instead, such an investor should consider the relative advantages and disadvantages of preference shares over ordinary shares in terms of security, levels of risk and control. Indeed, whilst it is common for a preference shareholder to have superior financial rights in comparison to ordinary shareholders, they often exercise weaker levels of control as preference shares frequently have no voting rights. This balance of risk and reward often means that preference shares are difficult to distinguish from certain types of debt instrument, such as bonds or debentures,[62] except that the former afford less assurance of getting one's money back or obtaining a return on investment. It is precisely because preference shares have these debt-like features that they are often classified as "hybrid" investments. On the other hand, if in addition to having "preferential" dividend or capital entitlements, the shares are also "participating" (in that they confer a further right, beyond the preferential entitlements, to share in the company's profits after the ordinary shareholders have received a specified return), then they might more properly be regarded as a form of equity with preferential rights over the ordinary shares (and in consequence should be, and often are, designated as "preferred ordinary" shares). Indeed, the CA 2006 defines "equity share capital" as being all a company's issued share capital except that part of its capital that "neither as respects dividends nor as respects capital, carries any right to participate beyond a specified amount in a distribution".[63] Accordingly, participating preference shares will ordinarily fall within the statutory definition of equity capital, even if the shareholder's right to participation is confined to surplus assets when the company is wound up, whereas their dividend right is limited to a fixed (and perhaps not very generous) amount.

Given their hybrid nature, the reality is that an enormous variety of different rights (whether relating to dividends, return of capital, voting, conversion into ordinary shares,[64] redemption and other matters) may be attached to shares that are conventionally described as "preference" shares.[65] Whether any particular share is more akin to a debenture or other debt instrument, or closer in nature to the ordinary share, will depend upon the proper interpretation of the articles or other instrument creating those shares. Unfortunately, locating a share on the spectrum from pure debt to pure equity investments has proved difficult given

---

[62] *Re Isle of Thanet Electric Supply Co* [1950] Ch. 161 CA; approved in *Lomas v Burlington Loan Management Ltd* [2016] EWHC 2417 (Ch) at [89], fn.14.

[63] CA 2006 s.548. Accordingly, a limitation on either dividends or a return of capital in a winding up will take the share out of the ordinary class.

[64] The apparently simple matter of converting preference shares into ordinary shares can become one of considerable complexity, at least where the preference shares are to be converted into a different number of ordinary shares that may also have a different nominal value, since there is a danger that the conversion transaction may involve either an unauthorised return of capital or the issue of shares at a discount: see further Ch.17. For ways of avoiding these issues, see *Practical Law for Companies* (1995), Vol.VI, No.10.

[65] Consider M. Pickering, "The Problem of the Preference Share" (1963) 26 M.L.R. 499.

that the legal drafting in this regard has often been rather lax.[66] Given this lack of clarity, the courts have developed various "canons of construction" to guide the interpretational exercise, although these canons have themselves fluctuated over time as courts have overruled earlier decisions. This has the unfortunate consequence of defeating the legitimate expectations of investors who purchased preference shares on the basis that a particular construction would be applied to their rights.[67] Previous editions of this book have traced these vacillations in some detail,[68] including the line of virtually irreconcilable decisions relating to the winding-up of the Bridgewater Navigation Company in 1889–1891.[69] Given that a degree of legal stability has now been achieved in that regard, such detailed analysis is no longer required, although in more recent times the English courts have favoured the natural meaning of words in their context,[70] rather than relying upon canons of construction,[71] when interpreting contracts more generally. Subject to that caveat, the present canons of construction will be considered next.

Canons of construction

(1) Prima facie all shares are presumed to rank equally, so that, if some are to have priority over others, provision must be made to that effect in the terms of issue. **6–008**

(2) If, however, the shares are expressly divided into separate classes (which would by definition displace the presumption of equality), the precise nature of the rights attached to each class of shares depends upon the proper interpretation of the language purporting to create those rights.[72]

(3) If in relation to a separate class of shares nothing is expressly stated about the rights conferred upon that class with respect to dividends, the return of capital, attendance at meetings or voting, then the presumption is that the rights of that class in that particular respect are the same as the ordinary shareholders. Accordingly, a share with a preferential right to dividends does not necessarily imply a similar preferential right as to the return of

---

[66] A particularly egregious example would be to provide that the company's share capital is divided into so many "X per cent Preference Shares" and so many "Ordinary Shares" and then to issue the shares without further clarification.

[67] For a classic illustration of this problem in relation to whether additional participation rights might be implied, see *Scottish Insurance Corp Ltd v Wilsons & Clyde Coal Co Ltd*, 1949 S.L.T. 230 HL; overruling *Re William Metcalfe & Sons Ltd* [1933] Ch. 142 CA.

[68] 4th edn (1979), pp.414–421.

[69] Compare *Re Bridgewater Navigation Co* [1891] 2 Ch. 317 CA; and *Birch v Cropper* (1889) 14 App. Cas. 525.

[70] *Wood v Capita Insurance Services Ltd* [2017] UKSC 24; [2017] A.C. 1173.

[71] See *Investors Compensation Scheme Ltd v West Bromwich Building Society (No.1)* [1997] P.N.L.R. 541 HL at 559: "Almost all the old intellectual baggage of 'legal' interpretation has been discarded". For judicial warnings about over-reliance on *contra proferentem* as an interpretational guide, see *K/S Victoria Street v House of Fraser (Stores Management) Ltd* [2011] EWCA Civ 904; [2011] 2 P. & C.R. 15 at [68]; *Transocean Drilling UK Ltd v Providence Resources Plc* [2016] EWCA Civ 372 at [20]–[21]; *Persimmon Homes Ltd v Ove Arup & Partners Ltd* [2017] EWCA Civ 373; [2017] P.N.L.R. 29 at [51]–[52].

[72] *Scottish Insurance v Wilsons & Clyde Coal Co*, 1949 S.L.T. 230; *Re Isle of Thanet Electric Supply Co* [1950] Ch. 161 CA.

capital (or vice versa).[73] Nor will an exclusion from further participation in dividends beyond a fixed preferential rate necessarily imply an exclusion from further participation in capital distributions (or vice versa), although the former may provide some indication of the latter.[74]

(4) Where shares are entitled to participate in surplus capital on a winding-up, the presumption is that such shares participate in all surplus assets and not merely those assets representing undistributed profits that might have been distributed as a dividend to another class.[75]

(5) Any rights expressly attached to shares in respect of dividends, capital or voting are presumed to be exhaustive so far as that particular matter is concerned. Accordingly, if shares have a preferential dividend, they are presumed to be non-participating as regards further dividends[76]; and if shares have a preferential right to a return of capital, they are presumed to be non-participating as regards any surplus assets.[77] The same approach clearly applies to attendance at meetings and voting[78]: if shareholders are given a vote in certain circumstances (such as, for example, if their dividends are in arrears), the implication is that those shareholders were not intended to have a vote in other circumstances. Indeed, preference shareholders commonly have their voting rights expressly restricted to situations where their dividends have not been paid for a period of time; this is because it is only in such circumstances that the preference shareholders will need to assert their voice in the management of the company.[79]

(6) In relation to the presumption of "exhaustive rights" above, the onus on the person seeking to rebut the presumption is not lightly discharged. Accordingly, the fact that there is an express provision making the shares "participating" as regards either dividends or capital is no indication that

---

[73] *Re London India Rubber Co* (1867–68) L.R. 5 Eq. 519 Ct of Chancery; *Re Accrington Corp Steam Tramways Co* [1909] 2 Ch. 40 Ch D.

[74] This is implied in *Scottish Insurance v Wilsons & Clyde Coal*, 1949 S.L.T. 230; *Dimbula Valley (Ceylon) Tea Co Ltd v Laurie* [1961] Ch. 353 Ch D.

[75] See *Dimbula Valley (Ceylon) Tea Co Ltd v Laurie* [1961] Ch. 353; *Re Saltdean Estate Co Ltd* [1968] 1 W.L.R. 1844 Ch D; which "distinguished" *Re Bridgewater Navigation Co* [1891] 2 Ch. 317 (on the basis that the contrary decision of the Court of Appeal depended on the peculiar wording of the company's articles), but it is thought that *Bridgewater* can now be ignored; in *Scottish Insurance v Wilsons & Clyde Coal*, 1949 S.L.T. 230 at 235, Lord Simonds pointed out the absurdity of supposing that "parties intended a bargain which would involve an investigation of an artificial and elaborate character into the nature and origin of surplus assets".

[76] *Will v United Lankat Plantations Co Ltd* [1914] A.C. 11 HL.

[77] *Scottish Insurance v Wilsons & Clyde Coal*, 1949 S.L.T. 230; *Re Isle of Thanet Electric Supply Co* [1950] Ch. 161 CA; *Jones v Garnett (Inspector of Taxes)* [2007] UKHL 35 at [35].

[78] Quaere whether attendance at meetings and voting should not really be treated as two separate rights. It seems, however, that the express exclusion of a right to vote will usually remove the right to be summoned to (or presumably to attend) general meetings: see *Re MacKenzie & Co* [1916] 2 Ch. 450 Ch D. If a shareholder has a right to vote, but the company's constitution does not indicate how many, CA 2006 s.284 indicates that the shareholder will have one vote for every share on a poll or, if their shares have been converted to stock (on which see para.6–011), the shareholder will have one vote for every £10 worth of stock. In a company without a share capital, each member has one vote only.

[79] See, for example, *Re Bradford Investments Plc (No.1)* [1990] B.C.C. 740 Ch D (Companies Ct).

they are also intended to be participating as regards the other. Indeed, this has been taken as evidence to the contrary.[80]

(7) If a share has a preferential right to dividends, that right is presumed to be cumulative (in the sense that, if not paid in one year, it must nevertheless be paid in a later year before any subordinate class of shareholder receives any dividend).[81] This presumption can be rebutted by language indicating an intention that any preferential dividend in one year is only payable out of the profits available in that year for that purpose.[82]

(8) There is a presumption that even preferential dividends are only payable once declared.[83] Accordingly, even cumulative preferential dividends are presumed not to be payable in a winding-up, unless previously declared.[84] This presumption may, however, be rebutted by the slightest indication to the contrary.[85] Accordingly, it may be advantageous to specify that the dividend is automatically payable on certain dates (assuming profits are available), rather than upon a resolution of the directors or shareholders. Furthermore, when dividend arrears are payable, these are presumed to be payable in a winding up, provided surplus assets are available. Those assets need not represent accumulated profits that might have been distributed by way of dividend.[86] Dividend arrears are only payable up to the commencement of the winding-up.[87]

As Evershed MR pointed out in *Re Isle of Thanet Electric Supply Co*,[88] the cumulative effect of applying these canons of construction has been that, over the past 100 years,

---

[80] See *Re National Telephone Co* [1914] 1 Ch. 755 Ch D; *Re Isle of Thanet Electric Supply Co* [1950] Ch. 161 CA; *Re Saltdean Estate Co Ltd* [1968] 1 W.L.R. 1844. This produces strange results. If, as the House of Lords suggested in *Scottish Insurance*, the fact that shares are non-participating as regards dividends is some indication that they are intended to be non-participating as regards capital (on the ground that the surplus profits have been appropriated to the ordinary shareholders), where the surplus profits belong to both classes while the company is a going concern, both should participate in a winding-up in order to preserve the status quo.

[81] *Webb v Earle* (1875) L.R. 20 Eq. 556.

[82] *Staples v Eastman Photographic Materials Co* [1896] 2 Ch. 303 CA.

[83] *Burland v Earle* [1902] A.C. 83 PC; *Re Buenos Ayres Gt Southern Railway* [1947] Ch. 384; *Godfrey Phillips Ltd v Investment Trust Ltd* [1953] 1 W.L.R. 41. Semble, therefore, non-cumulative shares lose their preferential dividend for the year in which liquidation was commenced: see *Re Foster & Son* [1942] 1 All E.R. 314; *Re Catalina's Warehouses & Mole Co Ltd* [1947] 1 All E.R. 51 Ch D. If the share's terms clearly so provide, a prescribed preferential dividend may be payable so long as there are adequate distributable profits (on which see Ch.18): see *Evling v Israel & Oppenheimer Ltd* [1918] 1 Ch. 101 Ch D.

[84] *Re Crichton's Oil Co* [1902] 2 Ch. 86 CA; *Re Roberts & Cooper Ltd* [1929] 2 Ch. 383 Ch D; *Re Wood, Skinner & Co* [1944] Ch. 323 Ch D; *Re F de Jong & Co* [1946] Ch. 211 CA at 216–217. See also *Re Bradford Investments Plc* [1990] B.C.C. 740.

[85] *Re Walter Symons Ltd* [1934] Ch. 308 Ch D; *Re F de Jong & Co Ltd* [1946] Ch. 211; *Re EW Savory Ltd* [1951] 2 All E.R. 1036 Ch D; *Re Wharfedale Brewery Co* [1952] Ch. 913 Ch D.

[86] *Re New Chinese Antimony Co Ltd* [1916] 2 Ch. 115 Ch D; *Re Springbok Agricultural Estates Ltd* [1920] 1 Ch. 563 Ch D; *Re Wharfedale Brewery Co* [1952] Ch. 913; not following *Re WJ Hall & Co* [1909] 1 Ch. 521 Ch D.

[87] *Re EW Savory Ltd* [1951] 2 All E.R. 1036.

[88] *Re Isle of Thanet Electric Supply Co* [1950] Ch. 161 at 175.

> "the view of the courts may have undergone some change in regard to the relative rights of preference and ordinary shareholders and to the disadvantage of the preference shareholders whose position has … become somewhat more approximated to [that] of debenture holders."

There is a good deal of truth in this statement, since, unless preference shareholders are expressly granted additional "participating" rights, they are unlikely to share in any way in the surplus "equity", or to have voting rights except in narrowly prescribed circumstances. At the same time, preference shareholders enjoy none of the advantages of debenture-holders: they only receive a return on their investment if profits are earned[89] (and not necessarily even then); they rank after the company's creditors in a winding-up[90]; and they have significantly fewer effective remedies against the company. Suspended midway between true creditors and true members, preference shareholders risk getting the worst of both worlds, unless the instrument creating the shares is drafted carefully.

Ordinary shares

6–009 Where, as is often the case, the company's shares all belong to a single class, these will necessarily be "ordinary shares". Indeed, if a company has a share capital it must perforce have at least one ordinary share, regardless of whether it also has any preference shares. Ordinary shares (as the name implies) constitute the residuary class whose rights to dividends and capital payments can only be asserted once the rights of preference shareholders, if any, have been satisfied. In essence, ordinary shareholders are entitled to the "equity" in the company, which equates to a share of any dividends declared during the company's solvency and a share of any residual assets following its liquidation. The ordinary shareholders accordingly bear the lion's share of the business risk, since they may take the bulk of the company's profits (after the directors and managers have been remunerated) in good years, but receive nothing in lean ones. This feature unmistakably distinguishes ordinary shares from debentures and other debt instruments, since the latter will be entitled to a fixed return on investment regardless of the company's profits. That said, "ordinary shares" may shade imperceptibly into "preference shares", when the latter type of share has substantial additional participation rights in income or capital, or a fortiori both. In such cases, it is largely a matter of taste whether such shares are designated "preference shares" or "preferred ordinary shares". Moreover, even as between ordinary shares that rank equally as regards financial participation, there may be different classes reflecting unequal voting rights. In such a case, the ordinary shares will commonly be differentiated as "A", "B", "C" (etc.) ordinary shares. Some public companies have issued non-voting "A" ordinary shares; others have issued shares with a high number of votes compared to the other shares. In either

---

[89] CA 2006 s.830(1), providing that "a company shall not make a distribution except out of profit available for the purpose". See para.18–004.

[90] IA 1986 s.107.

case, effective control may be retained by a small number of shareholders leading to a further rift between ownership and control.[91]

Special classes

Whilst most shares fall into one or other of the classic categories of "preference" or "ordinary" share, a company may nevertheless create shares for particular purposes and/or on terms that cut across the usual categories of share. An example is a share issued under an "employee share scheme". Under the statutory definition of such schemes,[92] the scheme's beneficiaries may include not only present and former employees of the company in question, but also employees of any company in the same group. The scheme can also extend to the spouses, civil partners, children or stepchildren under the age of 18 of any such employees. When employees' share schemes were first introduced, the normal practice was to create a special class of share that usually carried restrictions regarding voting and transferability; only share option schemes (designed to incentivise top management) offered ordinary shares with voting rights. As employees' share schemes nowadays offer voting shares,[93] so that they may enjoy the special tax concessions conferred on "approved" schemes, employee shares will rarely lead to the creation of a special class of share. Nevertheless, with respect to shares under an employees' share scheme, the CA 2006 contains special provisions regarding their allotment, financing and re-purchase by the company or the scheme's trustees by disapplying the normal restrictions on companies purchasing their own shares or providing financial assistance in that regard.[94] **6–010**

Conversion of shares into stock

Since the introduction of the CA 2006, shares may no longer be converted into stock,[95] although it is permissible (and sometimes advantageous) to convert debentures into debenture stock.[96] Such a change is of minor, almost undetectable, significance, given that stock nowadays has no advantage over shares. For example, in the case of shares, the size of a person's shareholding is measured by the number of shares held, whereas a person's stockholding is measured by the total par value of their stock, as stock is not divided into separate units. Whilst a stockholder can accordingly transfer very small proportions of their holding, a shareholder can never transfer less than one share, but this confers little advantage, as companies tend to take steps to keep the market value of shares to a manageable size (for example, by issuing bonus shares,[97] if the **6–011**

---

[91] See generally para.6–004.

[92] CA 2006 s.1166.

[93] It is unlikely that employees' share schemes will lead to employees controlling a large public company, as has occurred in the US.

[94] See paras 17–005 and 17–046. For the approach to pre-emptive rights, see para.24–007.

[95] CA 2006 s.540(2), although stock can be reconverted into shares: see CA 2006 ss.617(3)(b) and 620(1).

[96] See para.31–012.

[97] See para.16–024.

market value becomes large). From the company's perspective, there were some administrative savings associated with stock until the CA 1948.[98] The CA 2006 still permits stock to be re-converted to shares by ordinary resolution of the shareholders, but that decision is now irreversible.[99] Ironically, the phrase "stock exchange" has now become even more of a misnomer than it was previously.

[98] The saving arose out of the fact that each share had to have a distinctive number, which created additional administrative costs, whereas stock was not subject to this requirement. This is no longer the case for fully-paid shares that rank pari passu: see CA 2006 s.543.

[99] CA 2006 s.620.

PART 2

SEPARATE LEGAL PERSONALITY IN ACTION

We saw in Pt 1 that the separate legal personality of the company is a necessary feature of the creation of a company, and that limited liability, although optional, is overwhelmingly chosen by those who incorporate a company. Despite this, there is often an unshakeable instinct to treat the company and its members as a single unit, and not as separate persons. This is widespread. Outsiders are most inclined to do this when they have claims against the company that the company is unable to meet: there is then an urge to look behind the company to the deeper pockets of its members and hope that remedies can be found there. *Salomon v Salomon* was just such a case. And, in the other direction, especially in small owner-managed companies, the members themselves may have a tendency to treat the company's assets as their own, to use as they wish. But British company law is firmly committed to the principles of separate legal personality and limited liability, and it is only rarely that the common law will set those principles aside. Statute law has shown a greater willingness to do so in recent years, especially where limited liability has been abused. The first chapter in this Part examines the limits of separate legal personality and the exceptions to limited liability: these instances may be rare, but where they exist they can have a profound impact on the rights and remedies of those inside and outside the company. In this way they provide potentially important additions to all the various rules protecting both insiders and outsiders that are considered in detail in later parts.

Having created an artificial person, the law then has to decide how that artificial person will be legally able to operate in the world, whether it is lawfully entering into its own contracts or transferring its own property, or unlawfully committing torts or crimes. How will the company "act" or "know" or "intend"? This can be done only by attributing the acts and knowledge and intentions of natural persons to the company in appropriate situations. The delineation of those situations has proved to be a taxing exercise, mainly because the rules of attribution need to vary from one area of liability to another. There is no reason to suppose that the rules should be the same in relation to, for example, contractual and criminal liability—and in fact every reason to suppose that they should not be. The second chapter in this Part analyses the rules of attribution.

CHAPTER 7

THE LIMITS OF SEPARATE LEGAL PERSONALITY AND LIMITED LIABILITY

INTRODUCTION

The most fundamental feature of a company is its separate legal personality. Despite this, there is often a powerful instinct to treat the company and its members as indistinguishable, especially when there is a single controlling shareholder, whether an individual or a holding company. This instinct works in two directions. The parties running businesses are often inclined to treat their companies as indistinguishable from themselves.[1] Equally, in the other direction, third parties with claims against under-resourced companies often expect the companies' members to meet the liabilities of the entities they control. This expectation persists even though members of these companies almost invariably have the protection of limited liability.[2] This second instinct is the concern of this chapter. 7–001

[1] As noted by Lord Sumption in *Swynson Ltd v Lowick Rose LLP (In Liquidation) (formerly Hurst Morrison Thomson LLP)* [2017] UKSC 32; [2017] P.N.L.R. 18 at [1]. This particular problem, and its resolution, is dealt with elsewhere: see especially Pts III and IV.

[2] Limited liability is a choice, but one with compelling attractions for members. Section 3 of the CA 2006 gives the incorporators the option of limiting members' liability via provisions in the articles: either to the amount, if any, unpaid on the shares (company limited by shares) or to the (usually nominal) amount the members agree to contribute in a winding up (company limited by guarantee—a much less popular choice). Section 3 is reinforced by the IA 1986 s.74. In the absence of making this election, the liability of the shareholders is unlimited.

All the cases point in one direction: the law is robust in insisting on the separate corporate personality of companies,[3] and in preserving the benefits of members' limited liability. While the company may sue its directors for mismanagement, and sue its shareholders for failing to abide by their contractual commitments, the company cannot simply require these parties to contribute to the company's resources in order to meet the company's liabilities.[4] Moreover, outsiders with claims against the company cannot simply pursue those claims against the company's members (or directors) because those parties have resources and the company does not.[5] Why the law is so protective of members, permitting them to self-assert their own limited liability, is considered in the first part of this chapter.

All is not lost for third party litigants, however. Recall the failed arguments in *Salomon v Salomon*.[6] Those arguments all resorted to the general law, and looked for connections between the company and its members that might provide a basis on which the members could be made personally liable for the company's debts (or, in other contexts, its other obligations). In addition, the members may have breached primary duties owed directly to the litigant, and the litigant can then sue directly on the basis of this separate claim.[7] Nothing in this approach denies the separate legal personality of companies (indeed, it often relies upon it), nor the limited liability of members. In the second part of this chapter we consider the types of statutory and common law grounds which might support such claims.

But that does not cover the field. Disgruntled litigants without such alternative claims may want more. At the end of this chapter we consider whether there are any circumstances where a court may simply "pierce the corporate veil", ignoring the separate legal personality of the company to go behind the company to assert claims directly against its members. We will see that while the Supreme Court has said that such a claim is possible, it appears difficult to conceive of circumstances where such a claim could be made out given the tenor of the judgments in *Prest v Petrodel Resources Ltd*.[8]

THE RATIONALE FOR LIMITED LIABILITY

7–002 The company laws of all economically advanced countries make available corporate vehicles through which businesses can be carried on with the benefit of limited liability for their members. For shareholders this means that their liability for the company's debts is limited to the amount they have paid or have agreed to pay to the company for its shares. For most shareholders this means that, once the shares have been paid for, whether they were acquired directly from the company or from an existing shareholder, the worst fate that can befall them if the

---

[3] For a simple illustration, see, e.g. *Goldtrail Travel Ltd (In Liquidation) v Aydin* [2017] UKSC 57 at [18]: when a company is required to pay a sum into court, the question is whether the *company* can pay, not whether its controlling shareholder can pay.

[4] Again, see the relevant sections of Pts 3 and 4.

[5] *Salomon v Salomon & Co Ltd* [1897] A.C. 22 HL.

[6] *Salomon v Salomon & Co Ltd* [1897] A.C. 22.

[7] Although see the potential constraints imposed in some circumstances by the reflective loss principle: para 14–008 to 14–011.

[8] *Prest v Petrodel Resources Ltd* [2013] UKSC 34; [2013] B.C.C. 571.

company becomes insolvent is that they lose the entire value of their investment. However, their other assets—their homes, pension funds, domestic goods—will be unaffected by the collapse of the company in which they have invested. To put the matter from the creditors' perspective, their claims are limited to the assets of the company and cannot be asserted against the shareholders' assets. This can be regarded as a strong rule because, if the opposite economic development occurs and the company is highly successful, the shareholders are likely to receive all the residual benefit of that success, once the creditors have been satisfied, either through dividends or the capital appreciation of their shares.[9] So, there is an apparent asymmetry in the risks and rewards which are allocated to shareholders: they benefit, through limited liability, from a cap of their down-side risk, whereas the chance of up-side gain is unlimited.

Why does the law treat shareholders in this favourable way? During the battle for legislative acceptance of the principle of limited liability in the middle of the nineteenth century,[10] the argument which seems to have weighed most heavily with the legislator was that limited liability would facilitate the investment by members of the public, who were not professional investors, of their surplus funds in the many large capital projects which companies were being set up to carry out at that time, in particular the construction of a national network of railways. Members of the public, whose primary activity and expertise did not lie with the running of companies, would be much less willing to buy shares in such companies if the full range of their personal assets were at risk. They might be prepared to become lenders of money to such companies, but it was the flexibility of risk capital through shares which those companies sought.[11] The shareholders might earn a big return if the company's project was successful, but equally, at least in the case of ordinary shares, the company would be free to pay them nothing or very little, if the project achieved only modest success, whereas debt holders would normally be entitled to their fixed return by way of interest and repayment of capital, no matter whether the project was successful, provided the company stayed out of insolvency. **7–003**

In addition, as Halpern, Trebilcock and Turnbull[12] have pointed out, limited liability facilitates the operation of public securities markets because it relieves investors of the need to be concerned about the personal wealth of fellow investors. If, by contrast, shareholders were jointly and severally liable for a company's debts, my shares would be more valuable to me if the wealth of my fellow investors increased (because I would be less likely to have to pay more than the proportion of the company's debts which my shares constituted of the company's total share capital), and vice versa if the wealth of my fellow shareholders decreased. So limited liability facilitates the trading of the company's shares at a uniform price on the public exchanges and reduces shareholders' monitoring costs. This adverse effect of unlimited liability could be

[9] IA 1986 s.107.

[10] For an account, see the 6th edition of this book at pp.40–46.

[11] The distinction between equity and debt is discussed further in para.31–002.

[12] "An Economic Analysis of Limited Liability" (1980) 30 University of Toronto L.J. 117.

mitigated, of course, by making the shareholders liable only on a proportionate basis (i.e. liability on the part of each investor only for his or her "share" of the company's debts).[13]

Further, limited liability encourages equity investment by those of modest means by facilitating diversification of investment across a number of companies in different sectors and perhaps countries, thus reducing the investor's company-specific and country-specific risks. Under a regime of unlimited liability, investors would be incentivised to monitor closely the companies in which they were invested and this would push them towards reducing the range of their investments in order to reduce monitoring costs.

7–004 The above arguments in favour of limited liability are stronger in relation to companies which have offered their shares to the public, but less persuasive for companies which have not and do not plan to do so, i.e. for all private companies (which constitute the overwhelming number of companies on the register)[14] and even for some public companies. Yet, as we saw in Ch.2, a great deal of effort was expended on the part of practitioners in the second half of the nineteenth century in securing the extension of limited liability to all companies, including the smallest, a goal achieved when the House of Lords handed down its decision in *Salomon v Salomon*,[15] and the legislature decided not to reverse that decision. That decision has remained controversial,[16] but so entrenched in our law is the principle of limited liability for all companies, large or small, that arguments for the reversal of *Salomon* have made no progress with policy-makers.[17]

7–005 Before proceeding with the other rationales for limited liability, corporate groups deserve special mention. The rationales for limited liability identified above typically assume that shareholders are natural persons. However, most large businesses are run through group structures of holding and subsidiary companies rather than through a single company.[18] Each of the constituent corporate components is a separate legal entity with its own rights and obligations, and the parent or holding company is no more liable for the wrongs of its subsidiary companies than any other controlling shareholder in similar circumstances. This is the inevitable consequence of separate legal personality and limited liability.

Yet in this particular context the legal regime that delivers these ends is often regarded with considerable public opprobrium. The motivation for the group structure is typically assumed to be an unethical desire to avoid legal responsibilities, yet the same presumption is not typically made when start-ups or corner-stores decide to incorporate. Both need to manage or ring-fence risk. If the multinational enterprise is operating in different fields of business or in different jurisdictions, then one obvious means of crystallising risk is to divide its units

[13] Though the current rule of insolvency law, if limited liability does not apply, is joint and several liability: IA 1986 s.74(1).

[14] See Ch.1.

[15] *Salomon v Salomon & Co Ltd* [1897] A.C. 22; para. 2–001.

[16] In O. Kahn-Freund, "Some Reflections on Company Law Reform" (1944) 7 M.L.R. 54, 54, the decision was described as "calamitous".

[17] This case has been put in its most attractive form by A. Hicks, R. Drury and J. Smallcombe, *Alternative Company Structures for the Small Business*, ACCA Research Report 42 (1995).

[18] See further at paras 7–013 and 7–022 to 17–024.

into separate ventures. It is true there are instances of deliberately underfunded multi-national subsidiaries, but equally there are underfunded start-ups and underfunded corner-store businesses. The problem appears so much greater because its scale is so much greater. But if an individual Mr Salomon can incorporate one or more separate shoe-stores and run them as risk-units with the benefit of the upside should they prosper and the protection of limited liability should they falter, then it is hard to see why Salomon Co Ltd cannot do the same. If that is seen as unacceptable, then a statute might make Mr Salomon, or Salomon Co Ltd, liable alongside his companies for particular types of wrongs committed by them (as is done on occasion, especially with health and safety obligations). Indeed, the legislature could adopt this approach with every type of wrong committed by the subsidiaries, but that would undo limited liability and immediately take us full circle to the reasons why the legislature so far has been persuaded that the upside of limited liability for shareholders is worth its costs. Notwithstanding the arguments on both sides, the heated politics of the issue persist. Later in this chapter we will see what other means exist for sheeting liability home to the holding company.

Returning to the rationales for limited liability, those so far identified equate the societal benefit of limited liability with the greater ease with which companies can raise risk capital. From the creditors' point of view, however, limited liability may seem unattractive precisely because it confines creditors' claims to the company's assets. This may seem all the more unattractive since shareholders, with their asymmetrical awards (i.e. downside protection but upside advantage), may fail to constrain management engaged in reckless risk-taking, thus increasing the probability of corporate failure. In response, creditors may monitor management more closely, thus increasing their own costs of providing credit. Those costs might otherwise have been borne by the shareholders if motivated to monitor by their own unlimited liability. From the point of view of corporate finance, it may not matter where those costs are allocated, provided the costs of effective monitoring are roughly the same in the two cases. **7–006**

However, from this a rationale for limited liability has been advanced which takes as its starting point the monitoring incentives of creditors and provides a general justification for limited liability precisely on the grounds that it *reduces* the costs of creditor monitoring (and not only in relation to free-standing, publicly traded companies). This is the "asset partitioning" rationale.[19] What limited liability facilitates, together with the concept of separate legal personality, is the segregation of collections of assets between investors and the company. Just as limited liability prevents creditors of a company from asserting their claims against the shareholders' assets, so the doctrine of the company as a separate legal person prevents the creditors of a *shareholder* from asserting their claims against the company's assets. In other words, a creditor of the company does not have to face competition for corporate resources from the shareholder's own creditors; and a creditor of the shareholder does not have to face competition from the company for the shareholder's resources. Corporate personality and

[19] H. Hansmann and R. Kraakman, "The Essential Role of Organizational Law" (2000) 110 Yale L.J. 387; H. Hansmann, R. Kraakman and R. Squire, "Law and the Rise of the Firm" (2005–6) 119 Harvard L.R. 1335.

limited liability thus enable each set of creditors to be safe in confining their monitoring efforts to the company's or the shareholder's assets, as the case may be, and creditors may be expected to specialise in these different forms of monitoring. Overall, creditors' monitoring costs can be expected to be reduced under a system of asset partitioning.

More generally, this form of asset partitioning is seen as likely to be of overall benefit to society because it protects the integrity of the assets which the company has assembled to conduct its business and the benefits the company then generates, and does so not only for its investors, but also for others by way of employment and tax payments. This rationale of asset partitioning as a justification for limited liability and separate personality is as powerful within corporate groups as it is between the individual company and its shareholders.

Of course, what makes asset partitioning advantageous is that it enables creditors to focus their monitoring on the asset position of the company and ignore the asset position of the shareholders and directors who control the company. Creditors can make provisions in their contracts with the company to ensure they are entitled to the information they need for effective monitoring. That is invariably done with high value contracts or with those dealing frequently with each other, but the rules of company law assist creditors even where it would not be efficient for them to make individual provision.

Company law provides a number of useful disclosure rules. The first is notification of limited liability in the very name of the company through mandatory attachment of the suffix "ltd" or "plc" to the company's name.[20] Creditors are also entitled to see who the company's members are, what shares they hold and who holds the beneficial interests in those shares, if substantial, so that they can know who is in ultimate control of the company. They are also entitled to see who its officers are (so that they know with whom to deal), what its constitution is (so that they know what the company may do and how it may do it), and what its capital is and how it has been obtained (so that they know whether to trust it). And unless it is an unlimited company they are also entitled to see its accounts, or at least a modified version of them—again in order to know whether to trust it. The exemption of the unlimited company from the obligation to file accounts with the Registrar[21] is a particularly strong illustration of the link between publicity and limited liability.

7–007 Perhaps continuing in this vein, an alternative or supplementary way of looking at limited liability emphasises that it is not a mandatory rule. Limited liability is, it might be said, a default rule and those who do not like it can contract out of it. The incorporators themselves may opt out of limited liability across-the-board, by forming an unlimited liability company—though this occurs but rarely.[22] Alternatively, particular creditors may contract with the company and its shareholders on the basis that both will be liable on the obligations undertaken. This is especially common where the rationales for limited liability are most in question, in relation to groups and small companies. Those setting up small

[20] See para. 4–014.

[21] CA 2006 s.448. On the general disclosure requirements see in particular paras 2–037 to 2–038, 4–005, 16–014, 27–007 to 27–010 and Ch.21.

[22] See para.1–027.

companies, into which they are not willing to inject a significant amount of share capital, will usually find that a bank will not lend money to the company unless the shareholders give a personal guarantee of the loan to the company.[23] In this way, the personal assets of the shareholders become available to the bank if there is default on the loan; the bank is not confined to the assets of the company. Equally, those dealing with an undercapitalised subsidiary in a group of companies may obtain a guarantee from the parent company[24] or, less securely, the parent company may issue a "letter of comfort".[25] However, this ability of creditors to protect their own interests, while common in the case of large or frequent creditors, is typically not available to all creditors, and of course is not possible for tort victims.[26] For these creditors, their only resort is to default rules, whether they be company law default rules or general law rules.

Finally, sight should not be lost of the argument that the incentives to take risks, associated with the asymmetric position of the shareholders, has a positive value. The purpose of commercial companies is to embark on risky ventures. A company dominated by risk-averse creditors might not add much to the store of social wealth because they would put pressure on the management to avoid risk. **7–008**

GENERAL LAW ROUTES TO MEMBER LIABILITY TO THIRD PARTIES

There are a number of ways in which litigants with claims against a company may, on occasion, advance alternative claims against the company's members (or directors)[27] without in any way contradicting the principles of limited liability or separate legal personality. This possibility arises because the general law or some particular statute imposes liability not only on the company but also on the company's members or directors in the given circumstances. Since the rules then in operation are simply part of our general law, and not special company law rules, there is no need to treat them in detail here. Nevertheless, a flavour of their scope adds context to the picture just painted of limited liability and separate legal personality; it indicates the natural limits to the consequences of these principles. **7–009**

In considering these illustrations it is important to note that none of them involves denying the separate legal personality of the company; they should not therefore be described as examples of lifting or piercing the corporate veil: they do not. On the other hand, they emphasise that the statutory election of limited liability means only that shareholders are not liable to contribute generally to the

[23] cf. the facts of *Regal (Hastings) Ltd v Gulliver* [1967] 2 A.C. 134 HL, one of the leading cases on directors' fiduciary duties, but where the underlying problem arose out of the third party's request for a personal guarantee which the directors were unwilling to give.

[24] See *Re Polly Peck International Plc (In Administration) (No.4)* [1996] B.C.C. 486 Ch D (involving a single purpose finance vehicle which had no substantial assets of its own).

[25] *Re Augustus Barnett & Son Ltd* (1986) 2 B.C.C. 98904 Ch D (Comm); *Kleinwort Benson Ltd v Malaysia Mining Corp Bhd* (1989) 5 B.C.C. 337 CA (Civ Div) (letter of comfort not intended in this case to create legal relations).

[26] It has been suggested that limited liability should not apply to involuntary creditors: H. Hansmann and R. Kraakman, "Towards Unlimited Shareholder Liability for Corporate Torts" (1991) 100 Yale L.J. 1879.

[27] In this regard, also see paras 8–054 to 8–060.

company's coffers beyond what is initially promised; it does not mean that shareholders are freed of other liabilities that might arise from their own actions or inaction.

Contract, including agency

7–010 Members or directors may readily be made liable, through contract, for the company's obligations.[28] As noted earlier, such an additional personal undertaking is often required by creditors as a condition of lending to an under-resourced company. This type of personal undertaking may be one which accepts joint and several liability with the company for the debt, or which accepts the role of guarantor of the company's liability.

7–011 Claimants may alternatively attempt to rely on agency arguments. Third parties with apparent claims against the company may argue that the company was acting merely as an agent for the shareholders, not as a principal on its own behalf. This was one of the arguments advanced, unsuccessfully, in *Salomon v Salomon.* If accepted, the company's acts as agent would create obligations between the claimant and the shareholders, not between the claimant and the company. Attractive though this argument might appear to claimants seeking resort to the deep pockets of controlling shareholders, such an agency relationship is enormously difficult to establish. There is no presumption of agency from the mere fact that the shareholder or director exercises control over the company's actions and determines what the company will do (any corporate action involves this), and, in the absence of an express agency agreement between the parties,[29] it will be very difficult to establish such a relationship. In *Adams v Cape Industries Plc*,[30] the attempt failed.[31] While it was clear that CPC rendered services to Cape and in some cases acted as its agent in relation to particular transactions, that did not suffice to satisfy the conditions which the Court had held to be necessary if Cape was to be regarded as "present" in the US. This same sort of analysis can be applied to the argument that a company holds its assets on trust for its shareholders. This is not the normal case, even if the shares are held by a single shareholder, although on very particular facts such a trust may be found.[32]

---

[28] See para.7–007.

[29] As in *Southern v Watson* [1940] 3 All E.R. 439 CA, where, on the conversion of a business into a private company, the sale agreement provided that the company should fulfil existing contracts of the business as agents of the sellers; and in *Rainham Chemical Works Ltd (In Liquidation) v Belvedere Fish Guano Co Ltd* [1921] 2 A.C. 465 HL where the agreement provided that the newly formed company should take possession of land as the agent of its vendor promoters.

[30] *Adams v Cape Industries Plc* [1990] B.C.C. 786.

[31] See too *Polly Peck International Plc* [1996] B.C.C. 486.

[32] As in *Prest v Petrodel Resources Ltd* [2013] B.C.C. 571; para.17–017.

Tort

Equally, members or directors may be liable to third party claimants in tort for the harms caused by the company's operations if the circumstances are apt. Indeed, the facts may be such that the individual actor (whether member, director or employee) is the person *primarily* liable for the wrong,[33] and the company is merely vicariously liable[34]: this is often the case where the negligent acts of individuals (such a machinery operators) cause harm to victims. The result is that the tort victim may sue the primary wrongdoer or the company for the harm caused. Alternatively, the facts may render both the company and the individual liable as joint tortfeasors on ordinary principles.[35] 7–012

Alternatively, the claims advanced by the claimant against company and controlling shareholder may be quite different. In *Sevilleja v Marex Financial Ltd*,[36] Sevilleja owned and controlled two companies incorporated in the British Virgin Islands which he used as trading vehicles. The creditor, Marex, obtained judgment against these companies for sums due under contract, but before the judgment was finalised Sevilleja procured the transfer of funds from the companies' bank accounts to accounts under his personal control and did so in order to prevent the judgments from being satisfied. The companies were placed in voluntary liquidation. The creditor successfully brought claims against Sevilleja for the economic tort of inducing or procuring the violation of its rights under the judgments, although only after serious argument about the role of the company law principle of "reflective loss" discussed later in this work.[37]

But in this area the most controversial and attention-grabbing claims are those advanced by tort victims in the context of corporate groups.[38] In the typical scenario, the tort victim has been harmed by the activities of an underfunded 7–013

[33] And note that the individual cannot escape personal liability on the basis that he was merely acting on behalf of the company and not on his own behalf: *Standard Chartered Bank v Pakistan Shipping Corp (No.2)* [2002] UKHL 43; [2002] B.C.C. 846 (director liable for fraud). On the other hand, the fact that the individual was acting on behalf of the company and not on his own behalf may mean that all the elements of the tort cannot be made out against the individual: *Williams v Natural Life Health Foods Ltd* [1998] B.C.C. 428 HL (no assumption of personal responsibility by the director, in a claim for negligent misrepresentation).

[34] See para.8–039.

[35] *Ottercroft Ltd v Scandia Care Ltd* [2016] EWCA Civ 867.

[36] *Sevilleja v Marex Financial Ltd* [2020] UKSC 31; [2020] B.C.C. 783.

[37] Note that this claim in tort does not automatically deliver the same quantum by way of remedy as the claim for payment of the judgment debt: all depends on the harm actually caused to Marex by the economic tort. More importantly, note too the complications that arose in this case because both Marex and the BVI companies each had claims against the respondent, Marex in tort and the BVI companies for breach of fiduciary duty. Marex also had claims against the BVI companies. This network of claims raised the risk of double recovery by Marex and double liability of the respondent. The Supreme Court was asked to decide whether the principle of "reflective loss" should operate to deny at the outset Marex's claim against the respondent. The Court held it did not, but with the majority and minority adopting very different reasons: see the discussion in Ch.14 at para.14–010.

[38] For further discussion on corporate groups, see at paras 7–022 to 7–024. This, alongside the discussion earlier, indicates how committed British company law is to the sanctity of the separate personality of the company and the associated limited liability of its shareholders. Nevertheless, neither of those two principles lies in the way of imposing liability on those within the corporate structure for breaches of any specific duties which it is shown they owe to third parties.

subsidiary, and so claims are made instead against the holding company with far deeper pockets; alternatively, the claimant may simply think it more attractive to litigate in the UK jurisdiction of the parent than in the foreign jurisdiction of the subsidiary. In the early cases, these claims were advanced on the invariably unsuccessful basis that the corporate veil should be pierced (and the separate legal personality of the subsidiary ignored) so as to entitle the tort victims to impose liability directly on the parent company[39]; or alternatively that the corporate structure was a sham, designed to enable the parent company to avoid its legal liabilities by the device of an intermediary subsidiary[40]; or that the corporate group should be regarded as a "single economic unit" and liability imposed accordingly[41]; or finally that the very fact of control of the subsidiary by the parent should visit liability on the parent.[42] None of these arguments met with success.

The approach now is to concede the separate legal personality of the subsidiary, but to argue instead that the parent company owes its own duties directly to the tort victim, and can be made liable for breach of those duties. These claims typically concern employees suffering serious injuries to health after working on mining sites run by the local subsidiaries who are unable to meet the claims of the numerous employees affected. The employees therefore bring claims directly against the parent company. This approach bypasses the issues of separate legal personality and direct attacks on limited liability, and simply advances direct claims under the general law. Where those claims can be established—which is not necessarily easy on usual parent/subsidiary facts—the tort victims will succeed on orthodox tort law principles.[43]

---

[39] *Adams v Cape Industries Plc* [1990] B.C.C. 786.

[40] *Adams v Cape Industries Plc* [1990] B.C.C. 786, where the point was made that there is an important difference between adopting a structure that manages future risks (as Salomon did in *Salomon v Salomon*) and adopting a structure that endeavours to escape from existing legal liabilities. The latter is impermissible, and the courts will ensure the existing liabilities are met, but even that does not require piercing the corporate veil: see the discussion of *Prest v Petrodel Resources Ltd* at paras 7–018 to 7–021.

[41] This is plainly an argument that simply asserts a policy preference for denying group entities separate legal personality. See the response in *Adams v Cape Industries Plc* [1990] B.C.C. 786. It is a different matter if a particular statute makes provision to that effect, indicating that the group (not an individual company) will hold certain rights or be subject to certain liabilities as a group, or that particular components of the group will hold those rights and liabilities, regardless of the rules that would apply in the absence of the statutory provision. See, e.g. the early case of *DHN Food Distributors Ltd v Tower Hamlets LBC* (1976) 32 P. & C.R. 240 CA (Civ Div), where the two arguments (the statutory basis and the "single economic unit" argument) are perhaps inappropriately run together: the case might now be regarded as an aberration. See *The Albazero* [1975] 3 All E.R. 21 CA (Civ Div) at 28; *Adams v Cape Industries Ltd* [1990] B.C.C. 786 at 826.

[42] Denying the argument, see *Salomon v Salomon & Co Ltd* [1897] A.C. 22; *Adams v Cape Industries Plc* [1990] B.C.C. 786; and *Prest v Petrodel Resources Ltd* [2013] B.C.C. 571.

[43] See *Vedanta Resources Plc v Lungowe* [2019] UKSC 20; [2019] B.C.C. 520, especially [44]–[62]; *Okpabi v Royal Dutch Shell Plc* [2021] UKSC 3 (also see J. Goudkamp, "Duties of care and corporate groups" (2017) 133 L.Q.R. 560); *AAA v Unilever Plc* [2018] EWCA Civ 1532; [2018] B.C.C. 959, especially [36]–[37] (application for permission to appeal refused by UKSC); *Chandler v Cape Plc* [2012] EWCA Civ 525; [2012] P.I.Q.R. P17; *Lubbe v Cape Plc* [2001] I.L.Pr. 12 HL (conflict of laws issues); *Connelly v RTZ Corp Plc (No.2)* [1997] I.L.Pr. 805 HL.

Vedanta Resources Plc v Lungowe[44] is illustrative: over 1,000 Zambian villagers sought approval to bring claims in negligence against Vedanta Resources Plc, a UK-incorporated parent company of a Zambian copper-mining subsidiary, claiming that waste discharged from the copper mine had polluted the local waterways, causing personal injury to the local residents, as well as damage to property and loss of income. Although only a permission claim, the Supreme Court judgment sets out the current approach to these claims, making a number of important points.[45] **7–014**

First, the court denied that that it was necessary to discover some special form of the tort of negligence in the parent/subsidiary context:[46] the general tort principles which determine whether A owes a duty of care to C in respect of the harmful activities of B were appropriate and adequate for the task.[47] It thus followed that whether Vedanta itself was liable in negligence to the claimants turned on whether Vedanta had sufficiently intervened in the management of the mine owned by its subsidiary such that it had assumed a duty of care to the claimants. In that context, the court noted that such intervention was not an inherent element of a parent/subsidiary relationship: just because the parent *could* intervene did not mean that it had; it simply meant it had the opportunity. What might count as sufficient intervention to attract a duty of care was necessarily fact dependent, especially given the enormous variability in management models that might be adopted in corporate groups, but it was suggested that typically it might arise (1) where the parent had effectively taken over management of the subsidiary's actions; or (2) where it had given relevant advice to the subsidiary about how it should manage a risk.

By way of comment, and although the first category appears analytically more straightforward, even here it may not be easy to establish the necessary duty of care owed by the parent to the claimant villagers to protect them from harm.[48] The Supreme Court made passing reference to the House of Lords decision in *Dorset Yacht Co Ltd v Home Office*,[49] where the negligent discharge by the Home Office of its responsibility to supervise Borstal boys led to seven of them escaping and causing serious damage to moored yachts in the vicinity, including one owned by the plaintiff. But it may be hard to pin responsibility on the parent for supervising its subsidiary, and the degree of control that the parent might elect to exert may not meet the necessary hurdle. Failing that, a direct duty of care

---

44 *Vedanta Resources Plc v Lungowe* [2019] UKSC 20; [2020] A.C. 1045. This approach was then followed in *Okpabi v Royal Dutch Shell Plc* [2021] UKSC 3.

45 The claimants needed approval to bring their claims in England, against the UK parent, because the alleged tort and the harm occurred in Zambia, where both the claimants and the subsidiary are domiciled. They were successful at every level in the proceedings. *Royal Dutch Shell* was similarly a permission claim. Both cases thus considered the jurisdiction of the court to hear the issues, only setting out the relevant law in that context as a precursor to a trial on the merits where more factual detail may deliver further nuances in statements of principle.

46 So the test for the duty of care set out in *Caparo Industries Plc v Dickman* [1990] 2 A.C. 605 is not the starting point: *Vedanta Resources Plc v Lungowe* [2019] B.C.C. 520 at [49]; *Okpabi v Royal Dutch Shell Plc* [2021] UKSC 3 at [25].

47 *Vedanta* at [2019] B.C.C. 520 [54] and at [50] commending the summary by Sales LJ in *AAA v Unilever Plc* [2018] EWCA Civ 1532 at [36] (another challenge to jurisdiction on similar issues).

48 It may be easier to find such a duty owed to the subsidiary's employees in the context where the parent has taken over control of the subsidiary.

49 *Home Office v Dorset Yacht Co Ltd* [1970] A.C. 1004 HL.

owed by the parent to the villagers to protect them from personal and property damage will need to be found, being one that does not simply ignore all the learning on separate legal personality in the drive to deliver a remedy.[50]

The second category, where the parent gives advice to the subsidiary, raises even more questions. If the advice is incorrect (and harmfully so if implemented), then the normal route would be for the villagers to sue the subsidiary in respect of physical harm, and the subsidiary to sue the parent for the misleading advice which led to that harm. If the advice is correct but not followed, then that might raise claims between parent and subsidiary, but it is difficult to see what it adds by way of facilitating a claim by the villagers against the parent. The fact that the parent *could* enforce compliance by the subsidiary with the advice does not mean that it must, or that the parent breaches a duty to the villagers if it does not enforce it—unless there *is* a duty owed to the villagers to protect them, but that is the very question that these issues of control and advice are seeking to answer.

Whatever the analytical difficulties, these cases certainly highlight the tension between law and policy in relation to corporate groups.[51] There is an instinct to protect the end victim of a wrong perpetrated by a company within a corporate group, but doing that while remaining committed to separate legal personality has proved difficult. One obvious route is statutory: in various countries liability for environmental harm is not only strict, but is imposed on the group, not simply the domestic actor; indeed, sometimes this group liability might extend to liability for the actions of contractors to group companies. But in the common law realm, as in *Vedanta*, it is becoming increasingly difficult to know how to advise companies within groups. Group oversight, the development of considered group-wide policies and best practices, the provision of financial support as well as health, safety and environmental training, would all seem to be desirable best practice. Yet these very features may unravel the crucial asset partitioning and risk management that the law permits through incorporation.

The key point in all of this, however, in the context of this chapter, is that the liability of the parent company for wrongs committed by its subsidiary is not delivered simply by "piercing the corporate veil" and finding the members of the subsidiary (i.e. the parent company) liable for the wrongs of the subsidiary. It has to be shown that the members themselves owe a legal duty to the victims, and that this duty has been breached by the members, so that liability is incurred by them for the loss thereby caused.

Statute

7–015 As well as the general law, particular statutes can provide routes to similar ends. As might be expected given the policy of permitting limited liability, there are no provisions in the CA 2006 specifically deeming shareholders to be liable for a company's debts or other obligations. There are some provisions imposing

[50] Finally, it might, hypothetically, be suggested that the parent should be made vicariously liable for the torts of the subsidiary, or the subsidiary's employees, with all the difficulties of justification that requires: see para.8–039, especially the authorities cited in fnn.134–137. However, this route seems implausible while also holding fast to separate legal personality.

[51] Also see paras 7–022 to 7–024.

liability on directors, but these provisions make the directors liable to the company, not to the company's creditors, so they too do not provide litigants with an alternative to their claims against the company.[52] By contrast, other statutes make it clear that not only is the company to be liable, but that the members or shareholders, or, more usually, the directors of the company are also to be liable. These statutes are interpreted strictly: a statute that renders an individual within the company liable for one specific purpose will not be extrapolated to deliver any wider liability. For example, in *Campbell v Peter Gordon Joiners Ltd*,[53] the claimant was injured at work and the company did not have adequate insurance cover to compensate the injury. The claimant therefore sought instead to sue the company's sole director. The Supreme Court noted that the company's failure to have in place appropriate insurance was a breach of its obligations under s.1(1) of the Employers' Liability (Compulsory Insurance) Act 1969, and in defined circumstances that Act also imposed an equivalent criminal liability on the director or other officer, not on the basis that he was directly responsible, but that he was "deemed to be guilty" of the offence committed by the company. The 3:2 majority held that Act went no further than this: its imposition of criminal liability did not also render the director liable in a civil suit where the company was liable. By contrast, the minority held that, on either a formal approach to the statute or a functional approach, the statute imposed on the director a duty and, impliedly, consequential civil liability, as well as, explicitly, criminal liability. In short, the approach in these cases may be clear, but the resolution in specific contexts is not necessarily straightforward.[54]

These same types of statutory rules can also work in reverse. A statutory obligation imposed on a director in his personal capacity cannot be enforced against the director's company, even a company under the complete control of the director, unless the statute specifically provides for that. This was the issue in *Prest v Petrodel Resources Ltd*.[55] There the Matrimonial Causes Act 1973 entitled a court to order a husband to transfer his property to his wife. The court could thus order the husband to transfer his shares in a wholly owned company to his wife,[56] but it could not, by way of alternative, order the *company* to transfer *its* assets (a London house) to the director's wife. **7–016**

Property

Continuing with *Prest v Petrodel Resources*, another remedial route can be noted. Since the facts in that case were such that the first form of order described in the preceding paragraph could not be enforced in England because the husband's **7–017**

[52] See, e.g. CA 2006 ss.563(2), 767(3), 1173(1) (defining "officer"); CDDA 1986 s.15; IA 1986 ss.214 ("insolvent trading"), 216–17 (improper reuse of a corporate name after insolvency).

[53] *Campbell v Peter Gordon Joiners Ltd* [2016] UKSC 38; 2016 S.L.T. 887.

[54] See too *Mustafa v Environment Agency* [2020] EWCA Crim 597; [2021] Env. L.R. 5, where the company director was convicted for offences under environmental regulations.

[55] *Prest v Petrodel Resources Ltd* [2013] B.C.C. 571.

[56] As in *Hart v Hart* [2018] EWCA Civ 1053. And then once the wife had become the sole shareholder and director of what had been the husband's company, the court could further order that the wife, as director, or her company, could recover corporate documents from the husband that he should not now have in his possession but was refusing to hand over.

shares were held in overseas companies, and the second form of order was not permitted, it seemed the wife would be left without a remedy in her divorce proceedings. But the general law—property law—came to the rescue. The court achieved its ends by the alternative reasoning that, on the particular facts of the case, the company's property was held by the company on trust for the sole shareholder because it had been acquired by the company from that shareholder gratuitously, yet with no proof that a gift was intended.[57] This illustrates a more general point that parties with claims against companies may be able to pursue the benefits of those claims against individual directors or shareholders who hold title to the assets, but on trust for the company; equally, as in *Prest*, parties with claims against individuals (here the husband) may be assisted in pursuing the benefits of those claims if they can show that some third party (here the company) holds assets on trust for the individual.[58]

"PIERCING THE CORPORATE VEIL"

7–018 The preceding sections laid out the possibilities that exist within the general law to enable third parties with claims against a company, especially a company that cannot meet those claims, to advance alternative claims against individuals within the corporate structure who may have deeper pockets. Such claims are certainly possible, and can be enormously beneficial to the claimant. But none of these claims relies solely on the simple generic fact that the corporate insider (typically a controlling shareholder or a director) has some active role within the company; nor do they directly deny shareholders their agreed statutory limited liability; and nor do they deny the company's own separate legal personality.

That leaves one final question for this section: is there any rule of company law which *does* permit the courts to "pierce the corporate veil" and deny the company's separate legal personality, allowing a claimant to go behind the corporate structure and advance claims against the individual actors within the company? This question was the subject of extensive analysis by the Supreme Court in *Prest v Petrodel Resources Ltd*.[59] The unanimous answer was that yes, the courts do have this power, but the strong qualifier was that this possibility was only available in cases where the corporate controller has sought to evade his own existing legal liabilities (see below),[60] and even then it was available only as a last resort.[61] Lord Neuberger could not identify a single instance where the doctrine of piercing the corporate veil had been invoked properly and successfully.[62] Perhaps more significantly, it seems that the majority (and perhaps even the minority), while wishing to retain the power to pierce, could not

[57] Thus meeting the requirements for the presumption of a resulting trust.

[58] These proprietary arguments are used, and useful, in a wide range of circumstances, including in company's claims against its defaulting director: see *Burnden Holdings (UK) Ltd v Fielding* [2018] UKSC 14; [2018] B.C.C. 867, considered at para.10–024.

[59] *Prest v Petrodel Resources Ltd* [2013] B.C.C. 571.

[60] *Prest v Petrodel Resources Ltd* [2013] B.C.C. 571 at [35] (Lord Sumption) and [81] (Lord Neuberger).

[61] *Prest v Petrodel Resources Ltd* [2013] B.C.C. 571 at [35] (Lord Sumption), [62]–[63] (Lord Neuberger), [103] (Lord Clarke).

[62] *Prest v Petrodel Resources Ltd* [2013] B.C.C. 571 at [64] (Lord Neuberger).

envisage circumstances that came within this test which would warrant the piercing of the corporate veil under this special company law rule where the desired outcome would not already have been delivered by alternative orthodox analyses under the general law that exposed the company's controllers to personal liability.[63] As a result, it is difficult to see much future for the rule.[64]

Nevertheless, clearly this Supreme Court decision is now the departure point for any modern discussion of piercing the corporate veil, despite the very many earlier cases addressing the issue. Lord Sumption's analysis is pivotal.[65] His approach was to adopt a new terminology, shifting the emphasis to two distinct principles, "the concealment principle" and "the evasion principle".[66] In doing this he set aside the old approach of challenging the doctrines of separate legal personality and limited liability on the basis of general notions of fraud, or the company being a "sham" or "façade",[67] or even that the "interests of justice" required judicial intervention.

Under Lord Sumption's revised characterisation, concealment cases are those where a company has been used as a device or a façade in an attempt to conceal or avoid the personal liability of the individual controlling the company. These cases were not to be resolved by piercing the corporate veil: the court could simply look at the company and the true facts lying behind it, and then find the relevant parties liable on the application of the various orthodox principles considered earlier in this chapter. To the extent that earlier cases had described this approach as "piercing the veil", they were inaccurate. For example, when a wrongdoer deposits his ill-gotten proceeds in his company's bank account rather than his own, a court may simply decide that the company has received these funds as the agent or the nominee of the wrongdoer, and find its way to appropriate remedies against both the primary wrongdoer and his company on that basis.[68] This does not deny the separate legal personality of the company; rather, its separate personality is essential to the analysis. **7–019**

By contrast, evasion cases are those where a company had been interposed between the individual and the outside world so as to enable the individual to evade or frustrate the enforcement of existing obligations or liabilities to which the individual is subject. In these circumstances, and these circumstances only, the court could "pierce the corporate veil", but only for the sole purpose of depriving the company or its controller of the advantage they would otherwise **7–020**

---

[63] *Prest v Petrodel Resources Ltd* [2013] B.C.C. 571 and see too [100] (Lord Mance) and [103] (Lord Clarke).

[64] See *Antonio Gramsci Shipping Corp v Recoletos Ltd* [2013] EWCA Civ 730; [2013] I.L.Pr. 36 at [66] (Beatson LJ).

[65] Despite being obiter, it has been accepted and applied in subsequent cases: see, e.g. *Gramsci Shipping Corp v Recoletos Ltd* [2013] I.L.Pr. 36 at [44]–[47] and especially [64]–[66]; *Rossendale BC v Hurstwood Properties (A) Ltd* [2019] EWCA Civ 364; [2019] B.C.C. 774.

[66] *Prest v Petrodel Resources Ltd* [2013] B.C.C. 571 at [28].

[67] For example, *Woolfson v Strathclyde RC,* 1978 S.L.T. 159 HL.

[68] See *Prest v Petrodel Resources Ltd* [2013] B.C.C. 571 at [31]–[33]; and the discussion of *Gencor ACP Ltd v Dalby* [2001] W.T.L.R. 825 Ch D; and *Trustor AB v Smallbone (No.2)* [2002] B.C.C. 795 Ch D. Now see *Pennyfeathers Ltd v Pennyfeathers Property Co Ltd* [2013] EWHC 3530 (Ch).

have obtained from the interposing company's separate legal personality.[69] The evasion principle could not be used to undermine the allocation of future liabilities; that is legitimate business planning.[70] It followed that the veil could not be pierced in the *Prest* case because the husband's companies were established long before the husband's legal obligations on divorce came into being.

There are only two cases where the "piercing" argument has been successful in the past. Both were discussed in *Prest*.[71] In the first, *Gilford Motor Co Ltd v Horn*,[72] the former a director of a company sought to avoid a personal post-employment competition restraint by setting up and carrying on the rival business through a company which he controlled, rather than carrying it on directly. In that case the court extended the injunction to the company as well as to Horne himself. Similarly, in *Jones v Lipman*[73] a defendant sought to avoid a decree of specific performance against himself by conveying the land subject to the order to a company he owned. The order was again enforced against the company. In both cases, however, the result could be explained—and indeed Lord Neuberger suggested it would be better explained[74]—without recourse to the doctrine of piercing the veil, simply on the basis of the general law rule that the knowledge of the sole shareholder could be imputed to his company.

7–021 Further, it is clear that the evasion principle is not merely an illustration of the notion that "fraud unravels all". In a case heard shortly before *Prest*, but one that is consistent with it, the Supreme Court in *VTB Capital Plc v Nutritek International Corp*[75] refused to ignore the separate legal personality of the company where the effect would have been to make the controlling shareholders liable to third parties on a contract which the company had entered into with those third parties. It did not matter that the contract may have been induced by fraud, and indeed a fraud perhaps perpetrated by the controlling shareholders. Under orthodox principles, the third parties would have claims against the fraudsters in tort. There was no reason of either principle or policy why those remedies should be dramatically enhanced by rendering the alleged fraudsters liable to expectation damages on the contract when no one had understood them to be a party to it.[76]

The conclusion to this section can be summarised simply: from *Salomon v Salomon* to *Prest v Petrodel Resources Ltd*, the courts have maintained a firm commitment to the separate legal personality of companies and the limited liability of shareholders. There are routes to finding shareholders liable, with their

[69] *Prest v Petrodel Resources Ltd* [2013] B.C.C. 571 at [28], [35] (Lord Sumption), [81] (Lord Neuberger).

[70] i.e. it does not question *Salomon v Salomon and Co Ltd* [1897] A.C. 22. See, e.g. the discussion of what was seen as a legitimate use of special purpose vehicles in *Rossendale BC v Hurstwood Properties (A) Ltd* [2019] B.C.C. 774 at [39]–[54].

[71] *Prest v Petrodel Resources Ltd* [2013] B.C.C. 571 at [29]–[30] (Lord Sumption), [69]–[73] (Lord Neuberger).

[72] *Gilford Motor Co Ltd v Horne* [1933] Ch. 935 CA.

[73] *Jones v Lipman* [1962] 1 W.L.R. 832 Ch D.

[74] *Jones v Lipman* [1962] 1 W.L.R. 832 at [69]–[73].

[75] *VTB Capital Plc v Nutritek International Corp* [2013] UKSC 5; [2013] B.C.C. 514.

[76] *VTB Capital Plc v Nutritek International Corp* [2013] 2 A.C. 337 at [120]–[145] (Lord Neuberger).

companies, but generally these routes rely on the same general legal principles as apply between two non-corporate actors where it is sought to make both liable for the same wrong.

COMPANY GROUPS

Limited liability

The final area for consideration is the operation of the doctrine of limited liability within groups of companies. We have touched on this issue already.[77] Even relatively modest businesses often operate through groups of companies and large businesses invariably do so, and so the issue is one of great practical importance. Where the companies in the group are wholly owned, directly or indirectly, by the parent, only the rationale of asset partitioning[78] provides a reason for the extension of limited liability to intra-group relations, since the raising of equity capital and the trading of shares on public exchanges could occur effectively with limited liability confined to the shareholders of the parent company. Where the subsidiary is only partly owned by the parent, and in particular where the "outside" shares are traded on a public market, the other rationales for limited liability also apply within groups.[79] British law does in fact apply the doctrine of limited liability to intra-group shareholders as much as to extra-group shareholders and the courts will not, as we have seen, "pierce the veil" within a group of companies simply on the grounds that the group constitutes a single economic entity. However, from time to time there have been proposals for statutory provisions to modify the veil within groups, but, so far, without result. **7–022**

How might those with claims against a subsidiary be disadvantaged as a result of the company becoming, or being, a member of a group of companies? In general the answer is because, at least in a group with an integrated business strategy,[80] business decisions may be taken on the basis of maximising the wealth of the group as a whole (which usually means the value of the parent company), rather than of the particular subsidiary of which the claimant is a creditor. This phenomenon may show itself in a variety of ways. Three examples may be given. Most obviously, the parent may instruct the board of the subsidiary to do something which is not in the best interests of the subsidiary, because that decision will maximise the benefits of the group. Secondly, the parent may allocate new business opportunities to the subsidiary which can maximise the benefit for the group, even though another subsidiary could develop the opportunity effectively, if less profitably. Finally, if a subsidiary falls into insolvency, the parent may refrain from rescuing it, even though the group has sufficient funds to do so.

---

[77] See paras 7–013 to 7–014.

[78] The rationales for limited liability are discussed at paras 7–002 to 7–008.

[79] This situation is not usual, but is certainly not unknown, in the UK: "Governance concerns rise after London IPOs", *Financial Times*, 16 June 2011.

[80] This does not include all groups of companies: in conglomerate groups (i.e. groups of diversified businesses) the advantages of common ownership may well reside in something other than the imposition of a single business strategy (for example, access to sources of finance or managerial expertise).

It is far from clear that the actions described above in the second and third examples do, or ought to, involve any illegality on the part of those involved. Unless the business opportunity had been generated by a particular subsidiary,[81] it is not clear that it has, or ought to have, any claim to take all the opportunities arising within the group which it could effectively develop. Nor is it obvious that the descent into insolvency of a properly capitalised subsidiary which has fully disclosed the risks of its business should be allowed to threaten the economic viability of the remainder of the group's operations. In short, the overruling of limited liability within corporate groups is likely to require sophisticated and nuanced regulation if it is to make sense in policy terms.

7–023 The strongest case for intervention is the first: directions to the subsidiary to act in a way which is disadvantageous to it (and its creditors and outside shareholders) in order to benefit the parent (and its creditors and shareholders). Egregious cases of this type are already caught not only by the general law,[82] but also by existing British company law, for example, the application of the rules against fraudulent trading to all those party to it and of wrongful trading to shadow directors, both of which extensions may bring in parent companies, at least in some circumstances. These are examples of the overall domestic approach to group problems, i.e. the extension of general creditor-protection rules to deal with the particular situation of group creditors.[83] An alternative approach would be the development of distinct rules for corporate groups. This alternative approach is to be found in German law dealing with public companies which contains a separate section dealing with the issue of creditor and minority shareholder protection within groups,[84] though even these provisions do not purport to deal comprehensively with group issues but focus predominantly on the first example of disadvantageous behaviour given above. Even within Germany, however, these provisions are not thought to work effectively.[85]

The German statutory regulation of public companies provides two models of regulation, one of which is contractual and thus optional. Under the optional provision, in exchange for undertaking an obligation to indemnify the subsidiary for its annual net losses incurred during the term of the agreement, the parent

[81] On "corporate opportunities" see at paras 10–083 to 10–091.

[82] See paras 7–013 to 7–014.

[83] Creditor-protection rules are considered in Ch.19. In addition, another strategy is the threat of disqualifying directors (see Ch.20). For an example of the use of the latter strategy, see *Re Genosyis Technology Management Ltd* [2006] EWHC 989 (Ch)—directors disqualified for causing debts due to subsidiary to be paid to parent company.

[84] *Aktiengesetz* Book Three.

[85] For a discussion of German "*Konzernrecht*", see K.J. Hopt, "Legal Elements and Policy Decisions in Regulating Groups of Companies" in C.M. Schmitthoff and F. Wooldridge (eds), *Groups of Companies* (London: Sweet & Maxwell, 1991), p.81; H. Wiedemann, "The German Experience with the Law of Affiliated Enterprise" in K.J. Hopt (ed.), *Groups of Companies in European Laws, Legal and Economic Analyses on Multinational Enterprises* (Berlin: Walter de Gruyter, 1982), Vol. II, p.21. For a comparative perspective, see Forum Europaeum Corporate Group Law, "Corporate Group Law for Europe" (2000) 1 *European Business Organization Law Review* 165; and V. Priskich, "Corporate Groups: Current Proposals for Reform in Australia and the United Kingdom and a Comparative Analysis of the Regime in Germany" (2002) 4 I.C.C.L.J. 37; and K.J. Hopt, "Groups of Companies" in J. Gordon and G. Ringe (eds), *Oxford Handbook of Corporate Law and Governance*, online edn (OUP, 2015).

acquires the right to instruct the subsidiary to act in the interests of the group rather than its own best interests. This option has been taken up only by a small number of companies, presumably because the incentive to do so (i.e. protection from the potential liabilities for ignoring the separate legal personality of the subsidiary) is too small. The Company Law Review proposed something similar: in exchange for a guarantee by the parent of the liabilities of its subsidiary, the subsidiary would be freed from the obligation to publish separate accounts, thus reducing the costs of running the group.[86] However, the proposal was not proceeded with, partly because it was again thought that the incentive provided was not large enough to induce a substantial take-up of the option and, partly and conversely, because there were fears about loss of information about subsidiary companies if the option were taken up, especially where the subsidiary was the main British operating company of a foreign parent.[87]

The second strand of the German statutory regime is mandatory and applies to de facto groups. The core provision[88] is that the parent is liable for the damage to the subsidiary if the parent causes the subsidiary to enter into a disadvantageous transaction, unless, within the fiscal year, the parent has compensated the subsidiary for the loss or agreed to do so. The provision has proved less effective than expected seemingly because of difficulties of proof, both in relation to identifying particular disadvantageous transactions (especially where there is a continuous course of dealing between parent and subsidiary) and then in identifying the loss caused by those transactions. The weakness of the mandatory de facto group regime also undermines the optional contractual group rules, since it is escape from the obligatory former rules which could have provided a major incentive for companies to enter into the optional regime.[89]

Nevertheless, the German model, which has been followed within the EU only by Portugal and Croatia, was used by the European Commission in its preliminary consideration of a draft Ninth Company Law Directive on groups in the early 1980s. However, so remote from the traditions of the other Member States was this idea that the draft was never adopted by the full Commission. The *Report of the High Level Group of Company Law Experts*,[90] whilst not proposing a revival of the Ninth Directive, did propose that Member States should be required to introduce into their company laws the principle that the management of the parent company should be entitled to pursue the interests of the group, even if a particular transaction was to the disadvantage of a particular subsidiary, provided **7–024**

[86] Completing, Ch.10. On parent and subsidiary company reporting requirements see immediately below.

[87] Final Report I, paras 8.23–8.28. Nevertheless, a variant of the idea (exemption from audit but not from producing accounts in exchange for a guarantee from the parent) has been implemented in UK law: see para.23–007.

[88] *Aktiengesetz* s.317.

[89] A possible partial solution, which the German courts have used for private companies (GmbH), would be to use the contractual group model under which exercise of influence to disadvantageous ends would make the parent liable for all the subsidiary's losses, whether they could be related to a particular disadvantageous contract or not.

[90] *Report of the High Level Group of Company Law Experts* (Brussels, 4 November 2002), Ch.V. For more detailed consideration of the options, see Forum Europaeum, fn.117. The proposal was made again—this time for an EU Recommendation—in the *Report of the Reflection Group on the Future of EU Company Law* (Brussels, April 2011), Ch.4.

that, over time, there was a fair balance of burdens and advantages for the subsidiary.[91] The modalities of the incorporation of this principle into national law would be for each Member State to decide. The Report thus put as much stress on the need for group management to be able to run a coherent group policy as it did on the protection of creditors and minority shareholders in the subsidiary. In fact, British law has a somewhat similar approach, but applies it to the directors of the subsidiary, not the parent.[92] The directors of a subsidiary ought to consider whether it is in the interests of the subsidiary to follow instructions from the parent—though it is likely that the subsidiary directors, who will often be employees of the parent, do not in fact go through this exercise. It may well be in the interests of the subsidiary to do what the parent requires, for example, where the business of the subsidiary is dependent on inputs from other group companies.

The High Level Group also proposed greater disclosure of information about the group, both of a financial and, more important, of a non-financial kind, relating, in particular, to control relations within the group and the types of dependency created. Although the latter proposal has achieved some legislative result in the Takeovers Directive,[93] proposals for action beyond disclosure have not been taken up at EU level.

Finally, in some jurisdictions, part of the solution to the group problem, especially in the case of the third example given above, is to be found in insolvency law, where the court may be given a discretion in certain circumstances to bring a solvent group company into the insolvency of another group company.[94] The High Level Group also supported this principle.

Ignoring separate legal personality without compromising limited liability

7–025 If it is rare for British law to ignore the principle of limited liability within groups, it would be completely wrong to conclude that the law is not prepared to override the separate legal personality of companies within groups where this does not involve any infringement of the principle of limited liability. There are many instances in which domestic company law takes account of group structures, though these instances tend to be ad hoc, rather than the result of the application of a single general principle.

Perhaps the best-known example is in the area of financial reporting. It has long been recognised that, in relation to financial disclosure, the group phenomenon cannot be ignored if a "true and fair" view of the overall position of the company is to be presented, and that accordingly when one company (the

[91] This is often referred to as the *Rozenblum* doctrine, after the name of the French case (*Bulletin criminel* 1985 No.54) in which the principle was articulated.

[92] See further paras 10–036 to 10–044. The potential liability of the parent company as a shadow director of the subsidiary is largely excluded by s.251(3) of the CA 2006, unless the subsidiary is in the vicinity of insolvency.

[93] See paras 22–011 to 22–015.

[94] On New Zealand law and Australian proposals, see R.P. Austin, "Corporate Groups" in R. Grantham and C. Rickett (eds), *Corporate Personality in the Twentieth Century* (Oxford: Hart Publishing, 1998), especially pp.84–87.

parent or holding company) controls others (the subsidiary and sub-subsidiary companies) the parent company must present group financial statements as well as its own individual statements, thus avoiding the misleading impression which the latter alone might give.[95] The subordinate companies in the group must also produce individual accounts. This is discussed more fully in Ch.22.

The Companies Acts have also long used the concept of the parent-subsidiary relationship in areas other than that of financial disclosure. Clearly if one is to ban or control certain types of transaction between a company and its directors it is essential to ensure that this cannot be easily evaded by effecting the transactions with or through another company in the group. Hence many of the sections in Ch.4 of Pt 10 (Transactions with Directors Requiring Approval of Members) contain such anti-avoidance provisions.[96] Similarly, the prohibition on financial assistance for the purchase of a company's own shares extends to financial assistance by any of its subsidiaries.[97]

Finally, a note on terminology. In non-legal and much legal discourse, the expressions "parent" and "holding" company are used interchangeably. Until the CA 1989, UK company legislation used the latter, but the EU Company Law Directives use the former, which seems preferable, since "holding" suggests that the sole function of the parent is to control the operations of subsidiaries, whereas it too may well be undertaking one or more of the trading activities of the group. Now, in the CA 2006, the two terms have slightly different meanings, the definition of a "parent" company being broader than that of a "holding" company; and the term "parent" company being used in relation to company accounts and that of "holding" company elsewhere where the Act recognises group situations.[98] This came about because, when the Seventh Directive compelled a change in the definition for the purposes of accounts, it was represented that to apply the whole of the extended definition to other cases would introduce an unreasonable degree of uncertainty.[99] Hence it was decided to adopt a narrower definition in the non-accounts area, albeit one based on the EU definition. While it is a pity that it was thought necessary to have different definitions for what is essentially the same concept, there is no doubt that both are considerable improvements on the previous definition[100] since they recognise that what counts is "control" and not majority shareholding which, because of non-voting shares or weighted voting, will not necessarily afford control.

From all of this it might reasonably be concluded that the issue of limited liability **7–026**
within groups has not received the same degree of legislative attention as many

[95] To take a simplified example: if a parent company A has two wholly-owned subsidiaries, B and C, and in a financial year B makes a loss of £100,000 while C makes a distributable profit of £10,000 all of which it pays to A by way of dividend, the individual accounts of A (assuming it has broken even) will show a profit of £10,000 whereas in fact the group has made a loss of £90,000.

[96] See paras 10–066 to 10–080.

[97] See paras 17–041 to 17–052.

[98] "Parent company" is defined in s.1162 and Sch.7 and "holding company" in s.1159 and Sch.6 of CA 2006.

[99] For purposes of consolidation a measure of uncertainty is acceptable because, when in doubt, one can play safe and simply consolidate.

[100] 1948 Act s.154. Under the former s.154(10)(a)(ii) holding more than half in nominal value of a company's equity share capital (voting or non-voting) made it a subsidiary.

other areas of corporate law. Like the judges who are resistant to claims to lift the veil of an undercapitalised subsidiary to impose liability on a parent, the legislature has touched on limited liability within groups only gingerly, whilst showing itself perfectly able to recognise group structures in other areas of company law.

CONCLUSION

7–027 The conclusion to this chapter can be brief. In the long line of cases from *Salomon v Salomon* to *Prest v Petrodel Resources Ltd*, the courts have by and large maintained a firm commitment to the core ideas of the separate legal personality of companies and the limited liability of shareholders: those two bookend cases in particular have been emphatic in their support for these corporate underpinnings.[101] That is not to say that controlling shareholders (including holding companies) are safe hiding behind their fixed financial investment in the purchase of their shares, regardless of what wrongs their companies might commit. They are exposed, like any individual, to claims based on statute, tort, contract, property and unjust enrichment. These claims may rope them into the arena, making them liable in some way for the harm caused to outsiders dealing with their companies.[102] But the arguments to this end need to be made out carefully; liability is not assumed simply by virtue of association or even control: in short, however rich the temptation is to think of companies and their controllers as acting as one, in law they are not.

---

[101] In the US, the veil is lifted more readily: see P. Blumberg, *The Multinational Challenge to Corporate Law* (Oxford: Oxford University Press, 1993), especially Pt II. However, even in the US it seems the courts have never lifted the veil so as to remove limited liability in the case of a public company and will not do so as a matter of routine in private companies: R. Thompson, "Piercing the Corporate Veil: An Empirical Study" (1991) 76 Cornell L.J. 1036. Probably, the most significant addition to the grounds for lifting the veil which US law adds to the categories recognised by British law is that of inadequate capitalisation. As we shall later, British law has approached that problem through the statutory doctrine of wrongful trading rather than through lifting the veil. Indeed, at a more general level, the approach of British law to regulation of the abuse of limited liability is a combination of facilitating self-help and statutory constraints. These mechanisms are examined in Ch.19.

[102] For empirical studies (although all the claims might not now be seen as ones ignoring separate legal personality), see A. Dignam and P.B. Oh, "Disregarding the Salomon principle: an empirical analysis, 1885-2014" (2019) 39 O.J.L.S. 16; C Mitchell, "Lifting the Corporate Veil in the English Courts: an Empirical Study" (1999) 3 C.F.I.L.R. 15.

CHAPTER 8

CORPORATE ACTIONS

GENERAL PRINCIPLES

8–001 One consequence of the abstract nature of a company as a legal person is that all its decisions and its actions must inevitably be taken by natural persons. Its decisions may be taken by either (1) its primary decision-making bodies (the board of directors or the members collectively); or (2) its officers (including individual directors), agents or employees. Its acts will necessarily be delivered by (2). But still we need to know which of these decisions and actions "count" as the decisions and acts of the company and which do not. Similar problems arise where the question is simply whether the company "knew" about a certain fact or situation. Put another way, the question is whether the decision taken, act done or knowledge held by the natural persons can properly be *attributed* to the company. There clearly needs to be some linkage between the natural persons in question and the company for the company's legal position to be regarded as having been altered. Much of this chapter is about identifying the linkages that the law has accepted and those it has rejected. Those connections are clearly easier to identify where the board or shareholders as a body have purported to act as the company, but corporate life would be difficult or inappropriately regulated if the company's legal position could be affected only by actions of the board or the shareholders collectively. On the one hand, a large company would find contracting a cumbersome activity if all contracts, even relatively minor ones, had to be approved by the board or the shareholders collectively. On the other, it would be surprising if a company could escape all tortious or criminal liability where the wrongful act was authorised or committed by a senior manager who was neither a director nor a shareholder.[1]

In this chapter we are concerned with the answers to these questions primarily in two contexts. The first is where the company purports to enter into a contract with an outside third party. If a company could not acquire and enforce contractual rights and subject itself effectively to contractual duties, it would find the carrying on of its business a very difficult matter. This is obviously true of companies with a commercial purpose, but the statement is true of all companies needing to deal with third parties. The company would find it difficult to plan its future in the absence of enforceable contractual rights, and, in the absence of contractual duties enforceable against the company, counterparties would be unwilling to contract with companies or would routinely require guarantees of the company's obligations from individuals within the company. What is required is a simple and straightforward set of rules whereby the company can contract through the actions of individuals, for the benefit of both companies and third parties.[2] The law has developed two principal approaches to providing those

[1] The leading case in this area is *Meridian Global Funds Management Asia Ltd v Securities Commission* [1995] B.C.C. 942 PC (concerning employees), but there has been substantial activity in the senior courts in recent years. See *Bilta (UK) Ltd (In Liquidation) v Nazir* [2015] UKSC 23; [2015] B.C.C. 343; and *Singularis Holdings Ltd (In Liquidation) v Daiwa Capital Markets Europe Ltd* [2019] UKSC 50; [2020] B.C.C. 89 (both concerning directors, and both cases doubting *Stone & Rolls Ltd (In Liquidation) v Moore Stephens (A Firm)* [2009] UKHL 39; [2009] P.N.L.R. 36); and *Julien v Evolving TecKnologies and Enterprise Development Co Ltd* [2018] UKPC 2; [2018] B.C.C. 376 (concerning shareholders). And overseas, see *Ho Kang Peng v Scintronix Corp Ltd* [2014] SGCA 22; *Moulin Global Eyecare Trading Ltd v Commissioner of Inland Revenue* [2014] HKCFA 22; 17 HKCFAR 218; *Christine DeJong Medicine Professional Corp v DBDC Spadina Ltd* [2019] S.C.C. 30.

[2] At least this is the "ex ante" position, i.e. before any contracting has taken place. Ex post, i.e. once a "contract" has been made and has been broken, one or other party may have an interest in arguing that the agreement was never effective as a contract. Ex ante, however, when neither company nor counterparty will know whether it will wish to enforce or avoid the agreement, it is suggested that both will be in favour of rules facilitating contracting.

rules. Where the company contracts through the decision-making bodies established in its articles of association (board of directors, shareholders collectively), the solution is provided by organisational law and is straightforward. The company is bound because its constitutionally established decision-making bodies have committed it to the contract. Where, however, the contract is entered into on the company's behalf other than by these bodies, some further set of rules is required. There was no need to develop a company-specific set of overall rules to achieve this goal. The common law of agency, applying to non-corporate as well as corporate principals and their agents, furnished the bed-rock structure. However, as we shall also see, agency and organisational rules have had to be tweaked in order to deal with some particular features of corporate structure and doctrine.

The second situation is where the individual acting on behalf of the company commits a wrongful act. Is the company liable in this situation? This question arises principally in the criminal law and in tort, though it exists in other areas, such as wrongdoing in equity. The company may seem to have an obvious interest in not being liable for the wrongdoing of those connected with it. However, on a more sophisticated view it is doubtful whether this is true. If companies, some of which are powerful economic actors and all of which contribute to the functioning of the economy, are seen to be free of liability for the wrongful acts of those acting for them, there is then likely to be increased political pressure for rules which reduce the freedom of action of companies.[3] From the point of view of the efficient enforcement of the law, it can be argued, further, that corporate liability gives those in control of the company a strong incentive to constrain wrongful action on the part of those acting on its behalf and so corporate liability contributes to law enforcement—an argument that has appealed to the legislature in recent years. **8–002**

With wrongdoing it is again appropriate to hold the company liable where the constitutional decision-making bodes of the company have committed the wrong. Normally, this means the company is liable because board or shareholders collectively have authorised the wrongdoing, though in the case of a company with only a single shareholder or director, that person might actually commit the wrongful act. Beyond those bodies, general doctrines of the common law again provided a second basis for corporate liability, without the need to establish a company-specific set of rules. In the law of tort, the doctrine of vicarious liability is available to provide a framework for corporate liability and proved to be as capable of dealing with most cases of corporate principals as it was with non-corporate ones. In criminal law and some cases of non-criminal liability, however, vicarious liability has proved controversial, at least in relation to serious crimes, whether the person sought to be made vicariously liable was a company or not. Here, in both tort and criminal arenas, the law developed a third layer of rules for those areas where vicarious liability did not "work" in relation to companies.

---

[3] An analogy is provided by the application in the nineteenth century of the ultra vires doctrine to companies (see para.8–029). In this case the externality which drove the application of this restriction seems to have been fear of the negative impact of limited liability on the position of creditors.

This third layer of rules, like the first, is company-specific, in the sense that it requires consideration of how a particular liability rule relates to the specific processes whereby decisions are taken and implemented within companies. Sometimes these rules were made by the legislature, sometimes by the courts. Thus, from the beginning of the twentieth century the courts developed the notion of corporate "direct" liability, whereby the actions and states of mind of the person connected with the company were attributed to the company so as to make it the primary wrongdoer. Unlike with vicarious liability, where it is only the liability of the connected person which is visited on the company and the company itself is not a wrongdoer, with direct liability the company itself becomes the wrongdoer.[4] As we shall see below, the courts had difficulty in establishing the boundaries of direct liability and it has only lately begun to be developed in a satisfactory way. Legislative interventions to create direct liability have been uncommon. The principal example is the Corporate Manslaughter and Corporate Homicide Act 2007, which imposes criminal liability for this serious crime in circumstances where the common law rules on direct liability proved inadequate.

8–003 Overall, therefore, the broad answer to this fundamental question—how does a company decide, act or know?—is provided through a tripartite hierarchy of rules. At the top are the rules setting up the constitutional structure of the company and its decision-making bodies, i.e. its articles of association; then general doctrines of the common law such as agency and vicarious liability; and at the bottom, where neither of these approaches is available, statutory or common law rules attributing liability specifically to companies in some cases. The top and bottom layers in this tripartite division involve analysis of issues peculiar to companies (or at least corporations). The middle (and, practically, often the most important layer) consists of general common law doctrines, which are not company-specific, though their application to companies raises some difficulties which do not arise where companies are not involved. Following the terminology developed by Lord Hoffmann in *Meridian Global Funds Management Asia Ltd v Securities Commission*[5] the first layer can be referred to as company law's "primary rules of attribution" because of their location in the constitution of the company; the second as its "general rules of attribution"—general because they apply also to principals who are not companies but natural persons; and the third as its "special rules of attribution" because their function is to provide for corporate liability in situations where such liability is thought to be appropriate but neither of the first two approaches to attribution is capable of achieving that result. The residual and ill-defined function of the third approach no doubt explains why definition of its scope has proved so controversial, both in the courts and the legislature. But, generalising, it might be said—as Lord

[4] *Bilta (UK) Ltd v Nazir* [2015] B.C.C. 343 (also known as *Jetivia SA v Bilta (UK) Ltd (In Liquidation)*) at [70] (Lord Sumption), [186] and [203] (Lords Toulson and Hodge). Thus, although Lord Sumption disagreed with the approach of the other judges to the disposition of this case, both accepted this distinction between vicarious and direct liability.

[5] *Meridian Global v Securities Commission* [1995] B.C.C. 942 at 945. For the facts, see below at para.8–044.

Hoffmann did in *Meridian Global*[6]—that each of these layers is directed at the sole issue of establishing whose acts (or decisions or knowledge) legitimately count as the company's acts (or decisions or knowledge) in the particular context.[7]

In the context of examining corporate liability, we also consider, briefly, whether the individual corporate actors—the directors or other agents whose acts count as the company's acts—carry any personal liability for the wrongs the company has committed, or for their own wrongs committed in the course of the company's wrongful actions.[8]

CONTRACTUAL RIGHTS AND LIABILITIES

As noted above, decisions can be taken by or on behalf of a company to enter into a contract or other transaction with a third party in two ways, either by the decision-making bodies established under the Companies Act by the company's articles of association (i.e. its board of directors or the shareholders acting collectively) or by persons (who may include individual directors) acting as its agents. Where the board or the shareholders collectively act, they constitute the company, i.e. they act *as* the company. They are not its agents.[9] For this reason, there will be no question of them being personally liable on any resulting contract, which will exist only between the third party and the company. Where the company contracts through an agent, the law of agency produces a similar result in the standard case–i.e. that the contract exists only between the third party and the company—but the agent is potentially more exposed.[10] Despite the similarity of the results in the two cases, the rules applicable in the two situations are not identical and we need to examine them separately. We begin with corporate contracting through the directors or shareholders collectively[11] and then **8–004**

[6] *Meridian Global Funds Management Asia Ltd v Securities Commission* [1995] B.C.C. 942 at 945.

[7] A conundrum emerges from all of this. Note that Lord Hoffmann's formulation does not capture the distinctly different way in which vicarious liability operates, where it is not apt to say that the individual's wrongful *act* counts as the company's wrongful *act*: rather, the company is simply made *liable* for the individual's wrongful act. As we shall see later, however, it is increasingly common to find direct liability: a company can be found to have fraudulently induced a contract; it is not merely vicariously liable for its director's fraud. Similarly, note that with contracts the persistent analysis is the tripartite agency relationship (principal, agent, third party): the company does not simply enter into a contract directly via a person whose acts in entering into the contract count as the company's acts. Yet when knowledge is important in contracting, or illegality, or intention, we immediately revert to the "whose acts count" direct approach.

[8] See paras 8–054 to 8–060.

[9] In the 19th century the courts did often categorise the board as the agent of the company, but this view seems not to have survived the early twentieth century re-characterisation of the articles as a constitution, dividing the powers of the company between the shareholders collectively and the board. For a discussion of this development whereby the board came to be seen as acting as the company rather than on its behalf, see Lord Walker of Gestingthorpe NPJ in *Moulin Global Eyecare Trading Ltd v Commissioner of Inland Revenue* [2014] 3 HKC 32 HKCFA at [61]–[64].

[10] The agent may have warranted his own authority, and will be liable to the third party if the warranty is false, or he may have contracted in a manner that renders the contract binding between the agent and the third party rather than the principal and the third party.

[11] The directors or shareholders may operate not by making a contractual offer to or accepting an offer made to them by a third party but by approving the agreement in principle and by authorising

move on to contracting through agents. The potential personal liability of directors and agents in this context, limited though it is, is considered later.[12]

Contracting through the board or the shareholders collectively

8–005 Where the articles confer management powers on the board or the shareholders collectively and, in the exercise of those management powers, either of those bodies enters into contracts with third parties, the conclusion that an effective contract results is straightforward. With such a contract, the question of how authority to contract was conferred upon the board or the shareholders collectively is easily answered: it is to be found in the company's constitution, principally its articles. A difficulty only arises if either the board or the shareholders go beyond the powers conferred upon them by the articles. As we saw in Ch.3 (and also see Ch.11), it is rare for the board and the shareholders each to have unrestricted and equivalent management powers—though it seems that the constitutional arrangements of the company could be set up in this way. Normally, the articles of association divide up the management powers of the company between the shareholders and the directors, giving the greater part to the directors, but not all. It is thus possible for a third party to contract with the company via the board in an area where the board cannot act at all or where the board's powers are restricted. The same issue may also arise in contracting through the shareholders collectively. Third parties probably expect the shareholders' powers under the articles to commit the company to contracts to be limited, but, by contrast, they normally expect that the board will have wide management powers. Consequently, they are likely to be surprised if, after apparently contracting with the company through the board, they are met with the argument that the board did not have power to bind the company.[13]

---

someone else to contract on behalf of the company when all the details have been settled. So, board involvement in the contracting process does not necessarily mean that the board contracts as the company; instead an agent may contract on the company's behalf acting within the authority conferred by the board. Where the company contracts directly, its decision needs to be manifested in some way to the counterparty. Until the last quarter of the nineteenth century, the company executed a contract by having its seal attached to a written contract by a person authorised to attach it, and that procedure is still available (CA 2006 s.43). Now the contract may be executed by a company without a seal, normally by the signatures of two directors or of a director and the secretary or of one director whose signature is attested by a witness (CA 2006 s.44) and a company need no longer have a common seal (CA 2006 s.45). If, however, the company wishes to execute the contract as a deed, rather than a simple contract, the rules are somewhat more constraining: CA 2006 ss.44 and 46 (these sections do not apply in Scotland). For benevolent interpretation of CA 2006 s.44 see *Williams v Redcard Ltd* [2011] EWCA Civ 466; [2013] B.C.C. 689.

[12] See below, paras 8–030 to 8–036 and 8–056 to 8–058.

[13] Thus, even in relation to private companies, the model articles confer responsibility for the management of the company on the board "for which purpose they may exercise all the powers of the company" (Companies (Model Articles) Regulations 2008 (SI 2008/3229) Sch.1: Model Articles for Private Companies Limited by Shares art.3, and, similarly, Sch.2: Model Articles for Private Companies Limited by Guarantee art.3). By implication the powers of the shareholders do not extend to management, except to the extent that the articles of a particular company (or, of course, the Act) explicitly confer management powers upon them. Under the model articles a major qualification to art.3 is to be found in art.4 (for both private companies limited by shares or by guarantee) which gives

An immediate question then arises: should the contract fail (i.e. be void) because it is outside the powers conferred upon the contracting organ by the articles of association? Or should the contract stand, so as to meet the expectations of third parties contracting with the company? The first option favours the shareholders, and asserts that the constitutional arrangements of the company should be paramount: either the articles are followed or the company is not contractually committed. The second option favours security of transactions, reduces transaction costs between the company and outsiders, and makes trading with companies more attractive because third parties' reasonable expectations are met. Modern law favours the second option, with statutory and common law rules that protect third parties.[14] However, this was not company law's initial stance: that was to favour rigid constitutional limits on what the company could do. Third parties were expected to familiarise themselves with the company's constitutional documents which were publicly available. The only concession was to allow that where there had been an attempt to comply with the constitutional requirements, third parties could assume that the compliance was full unless they were on notice to the contrary. The remnants of this older approach remain, with its rules on constructive notice and the special "rule in *Turquand's* case",[15] otherwise known as the "indoor management rule". Whether these latter rules are needed, or have much scope for operation within the modern framework, is considered in the context of the general rules, but these older rules are outlined first, as they explain much of the impetus for change.

Constructive notice and the rule in Turquand's case

In the nineteenth century, the answer to whether the company was bound by a transaction which was permitted under the constitution, but which was entered into by the board (or shareholders)[16] outside their powers as laid down in the articles was seen to turn principally on whether the third party knew of this lack of authority. If the third party knew the board had so acted, then the transaction was not binding on the company unless the company chose to ratify it.[17] The view taken was that a third party, knowing of the board's lack of authority, had no legitimate claim to hold the company to the contract against the company's wishes. **8–006**

This potentially defensible position was rendered much less defensible, however, by the harsh application of the doctrine of constructive notice. The rule

---

the shareholders a reserve power of intervention: at any time the shareholders may by special resolution instruct the directors in what action to take or refrain from taking in a specific situation.

[14] This does not turn the allocation of management powers in the articles into a dead letter. The directors may still be liable to the company for acting in breach of the articles (a liability expressly preserved by s.40(5) of the Act and then identified by s.171—see paras 10–016 and 10–024). The directors may thus be liable to make good to the company any loss it suffers as a result of unauthorised contracting and, in the unlikely event the shareholders get wind of proposed unauthorised contracting, they might be able to secure an injunction against the directors to restrain it.

[15] *Royal British Bank v Turquand* (1856) 6 El. & Bl. 327 Ex Chamber.

[16] In the 19th century the question arose really only in relation to the board because the shareholders' powers were then regarded as unlimited (except by the objects clause). See para.9–002.

[17] On ratification, see para.8–028.

as developed by the courts in the nineteenth century was that anyone dealing with a company registered under the companies legislation was deemed to have notice of its "public documents", including its articles filed at Companies House.[18] By treating third parties as knowing what they would have known had they read and understood the articles, the courts substantially enhanced the restrictive impact of provisions in the articles limiting the board's authority, and frequently deprived third parties of plausible claims to reliance losses. The company might choose to ratify the contract but was not bound to do so, so that the third party's contractual rights and duties rested on the company's decision.

8–007 This harsh nineteenth century position was moderated somewhat by the "rule in *Turquand's* case",[19] or the "indoor management rule". In *Turquand*[20] itself security for a loan had been given by a company through its directors, but the articles provided that the directors could borrow only such sums as were authorised by the shareholders in general meeting and the requisite authority had not been given. Jervis CJ said that third parties were bound to read the company's articles, but they were not bound to investigate further: a third party reading the company's articles would discover "not a prohibition on borrowing, but a permission to do so under certain conditions. Finding that the authority might have been made complete by a resolution, he would have a right to infer the fact of a resolution authorising that which on the face of the document appeared to be legitimately done".[21] This was certainly a benign interpretation of the constructive notice doctrine, since the courts might equally have said (and indeed might now say)[22] that the third party was put on notice to enquire whether the shareholders had in fact given the requisite authority.

This rule was developed further into the "indoor management rule" in *Mahoney v East Holyford Mining Co*.[23] As Lord Hatherley put it[24]:

> "where there are persons conducting the affairs of the company in a manner which appears to be perfectly consonant with the articles of association, then those so dealing with them, externally, are not to be affected by any irregularities which may take place in the internal management of the company. They are entitled to presume that that of which only they can have knowledge, namely, the external acts, are rightly done, when those acts purport to be performed in the mode in which they ought to be performed."

Under this rule, if a decision that the company should enter into a contract had purportedly been made by the board of directors, then the company could not, for

[18] *Ernest v Nicholls* (1857) 6 H.L. Cas. 401 PC: "If [third parties] do not choose to acquaint themselves with the powers of the directors, it is their own fault and if they give credit to any unauthorized persons they must be contented to look to them only" (Lord Wensleydale).

[19] *Royal British Bank v Turquand* (1856) 6 El. & Bl. 327.

[20] The account in the text of the facts has been somewhat altered to relate the holding to a modern company.

[21] *Royal British Bank v Turquand* (1856) 6 El. & Bl. 327 at [332].

[22] At least where the third party's own due diligence had revealed the relevant constitutional provision, but the third party then made no further enquires: *East Asia Co Ltd v PT Satria Tirtatama Energindo* [2019] UKPC 30.

[23] *Mahoney v East Holyford Mining Co Ltd* (1874–75) L.R. 7 H.L. 869 HL.

[24] *Mahoney v East Holyford Mining Co Ltd* (1874–75) L.R. 7 H.L. 869 at 894.

example, escape from the obligation by asserting that the directors had not been properly appointed,[25] or that the board meeting was inquorate,[26] or that there was no board meeting at all.[27]

On the other hand, these concessions and their limits are clearly based on estoppel, so they do not apply to third parties who actually know the facts giving rise to the invalidity, or who are put on enquiry and do not then make the enquiries that a reasonable person would have made in all the circumstances.[28]

That raises one further question. Can *insiders*, especially directors, rely on the indoor management rule in their own dealings with their company? Put another way, are these individuals truly third parties, or are they individuals against whom it is perfectly proper to maintain the tougher version of the constructive notice rule, since they should reasonably be taken know and understand the limitations contained in their own company's constitution? In *Morris v Kanssen*[29] the claimant seeking to rely on the *Turquand* rule had assumed the functions of a director of the company at the time of the disputed transaction. The House of Lords held that, as he was thus under a duty to see that the company's articles were complied with, it would be inconsistent to allow him to take the benefit of the rule. However, in *Hely-Hutchinson v Brayhead Ltd*,[30] in the lower court, Roskill J interpreted the exclusion more narrowly, and far more generously: a director was an "insider" only if he had entered into the transaction on behalf of the company or the transaction with the company was so intimately connected with his position as a director as to make it impossible for him not to be treated as knowing of the limitations on the powers of the officers through whom he dealt. However, on appeal the Court of Appeal expressly declined to affirm this approach, finding alternative grounds for reaching their conclusion. **8–008**

The remaining role of these rules in the modern context emerges later.[31]

Statutory protection for third parties dealing with the board

Even with the judicial concessions just described, the resulting state of the law was unattractive. No third party could safely refrain from reading and analysing the company's articles, for fear of finding a ban or restriction on the board's contracting powers which could not be removed by some internal corporate **8–009**

[25] *Mahoney v East Holyford Mining Co Ltd* (1874–75) L.R. 7 H.L. 869. For the equivalent statutory protection provided by s.161, see para.9–010.

[26] *County of Gloucester Bank v Rudry Merthyr Steam & House Coal Colliery Co* [1895] 1 Ch. 629 CA.

[27] *Re Bonelli's Telegraph Co* (1871) L.R. 12 Eq. 246 Ct of Chancery.

[28] See the extended obiter discussion in *East Asia Co Ltd v PT Satria Tirtatama Energindo* [2019] UKPC 30 at [86]–[93]. Noted H. Tjio and D. Ang, "No Magic to the Indoor Management Rule" [2020] L.M.C.L.Q. 217. This approach is the same as that taken with ostensible authority, as this case makes plain: see the relevant discussion below at para.8–025. Also see *B Liggett (Liverpool) Ltd v Barclays Bank Ltd* [1928] 1 K.B. 48 KBD; *Wrexham Associated Football Club Ltd (In Administration) v Crucialmove Ltd* [2006] EWCA Civ 237; [2007] B.C.C. 139.

[29] *Morris v Kanssen* [1946] A.C. 459 HL (see para.8–008). See also *Howard v Patent Ivory Manufacturing Co* (1888) 38 Ch. D. 156 Ch D.

[30] *Hely-Hutchinson v Brayhead Ltd* [1968] 1 Q.B. 549 CA (Civ Div).

[31] See para.8–027.

procedure. In modern times the policy view has been taken that commerce will be promoted by relieving third parties from the need to check the company's constitutional documents before engaging with the company's board. The company is free to limit the authority of the board, but the constitution is no longer seen as an obviously appropriate way to communicate such limitations to third parties. Other more direct methods must be employed. In line with this policy, the legislature enacted statutory provisions which extend the protection afforded to third parties. The reforms were first introduced in 1972,[32] and the current version is s.40 of the 2006 Act.[33]

Subsection (1) of s.40 provides:

> "(1) In favour of a person dealing with a company in good faith, the power of the directors to bind the company, or authorise others to do so, shall be deemed to be free of any limitations under the company's constitution."

This provision overtakes the indoor management rule because it simply removes all limitations on the powers of the board to contract for the company which the articles impose, whether those limitations are removable by shareholder resolution or are absolute. It effectively repeals the constructive notice rule within the scope of application of the section. But the section is subject to some limitations.

(a) *"In favour of a person dealing with a company in good faith"*

8–010 This phrase makes it clear that the section is for the benefit of third parties, not the company. The company cannot rely on it to make the contract binding as against a third party where the agent lacked authority and the third party seeks to escape from the contract. However, this point is not as important as it might seem, since the company can often make such a contract binding on itself and the third party by ratifying it (see para.8–028). More importantly, these words demonstrate that not all third parties are to benefit from the section. Only "good faith" third parties will do so. But later provisions make it clear that "bad faith" will be difficult to establish. Section 40(2) provides a three-tiered set of protections for third parties. First, it provides that a person dealing with the company "is not bound to enquire as to any limitation on the powers of the directors to bind the company or authorise others to do so".[34] This sets aside the "put on enquiry" qualification to the indoor management rule. The fact that circumstances indicated that there might be some limitation on the directors' authority in the articles and the third party failed to follow this up will not now by itself put the third party in the "bad faith" category.

---

[32] The change was required upon the UK's entry into the EU in order to comply with the First Company Law Directive. Without this stimulus it is unclear when this sensible reform would have been introduced.

[33] Section 40 does not apply to a charitable company, except in the cases set out in s.42, principally where T (1) is unaware the company is a charity; or (2) gives full consideration in the transaction and is unaware of the directors' lack of authority. In addition, ratification of an unauthorised act requires the consent of the charity commissioners. For Scotland see s.112 of the CA 1989 which makes similar provisions.

[34] CA 2006 s.40(2)(b)(i).

Secondly, the third party is presumed to have acted in good faith, unless the contrary is proved, so that the burden of proof falls on the company rather than the third party.[35] Thirdly, and most startling, the section provides that the third party is not to be regarded as acting in bad faith "by reason only of his knowing that an act is beyond the powers of the directors under the company's constitution". This appears to contemplate that a person dealing with directors with actual knowledge that they are exceeding their powers will not necessarily be found to be in bad faith. The section does not provide, of course, that actual knowledge cannot be an ingredient in the establishment of bad faith, but it does prohibit the simple equation of knowledge and bad faith.[36] One might think that only a little needs to be added to knowledge of lack of authority to produce bad faith.[37]

(b) "Dealing with a company"

Subsection (2) assists in the interpretation of "dealing". It provides: **8–011**

> "(2) For this purpose—
> (a) a person 'deals with' a company if he is a party to any transaction or other act to which the company is a party."

A person deals with the company so long as he is a party to a transaction (e.g. a contract) or an act (e.g. a payment of money) to which the company is also a party. Despite this, the courts remain reluctant to bring gratuitous transactions with the meaning of the subsection.[38]

(c) Persons

Section 40 seems to apply quite generally to "persons" dealing with the company in good faith. However, again there is an obvious policy question about whether corporate insiders (especially directors) should be permitted to take advantage of the section when they deal with the company.[39] **8–012**

This time the legislature has provided the answer in s.41. Where the company enters into a transaction which exceeds a limitation on the powers of the directors under the company's constitution and the other parties to the transaction include a

[35] CA 2006 s.40(2)(b)(ii).

[36] *Barclays Bank Ltd v TOSG Trust Fund Ltd* [1984] B.C.L.C. 1 at 18.

[37] In *Ford v Polymer Vision Ltd* [2009] EWHC 945 (Ch), the judge was prepared to send to trial the issue of the third party's good faith where the disputed transaction was so one-sided against the company as to raise the question whether the claimant knew or ought to have known the directors were acting in breach of duty in entering into it. Note that the breach of duty was not the directors' failure to observe the articles; to allow bad faith to be established on the basis of breach of that duty would completely undermine the section.

[38] *EIC Services Ltd v Phipps* [2004] EWCA Civ 1069; [2004] B.C.C. 814 at [35], excluding an issue of bonus shares on the grounds that the subsection requires either a bilateral transaction or an act to which both company and third person are parties and which is binding on the company, if s.40 is to apply; and *Re Hampton Capital Ltd* [2015] EWHC 1905 (Ch), excluding a restitutionary claim for money misappropriated from the company. See also *International Sales & Agencies Ltd v Marcus* [1982] 3 All E.R. 551 QBD at 560, but decided on different wording.

[39] See para.8–027 for the response in the context of the indoor management rule.

director of the company or its holding company or a person connected with such a director,[40] the transaction, far from being enforceable against the company, is voidable at the instance of the company.[41] Furthermore, whether or not the transaction is avoided, such parties *and* any director who authorised the transaction on behalf of the company are liable to account to the company for any gains made and to indemnify the company against any loss resulting from the transaction.[42] Thus, the company might seek to stay with the contract (perhaps because it is too late to obtain a substitute performance elsewhere) but sue the director acting outside the articles for damages (for example, where at the time of contracting the substitute consideration was available at a lower price). The transaction ceases to be voidable in any of the four events[43] set out in subs.(4) but this, in principle, does not affect the company's other remedies.[44] The section does not affect the operation of s.40 in relation to any party to the transaction other than a director or a person with whom the director is connected but where that other party is protected by s.40 and the director is not, the court may make such order affirming, severing or setting aside the transaction on such terms as appear to be just.[45]

Despite the presence of s.41, a majority of the Court of Appeal (Robert Walker LJ, as he then was, dissenting on this point) held in *Smith v Henniker-Major*[46] that s.40 was not available to the director, at least on the facts of that case, where the director dealing with the company was also chairman of the company (and therefore under an obligation to see that its constitution was properly applied) and was responsible for the error in the transaction with himself (a rare legal recognition of the importance of the chairman of the board). The point may seem an arcane one, since the director in that case clearly fell within what is now s.41, but it has some importance, because a transaction within s.40, but caught by s.41, is binding unless set aside by the company, whereas, if the transaction is outside s.40 and governed by the common law, it will not be binding on the company unless ratified by it. In other words, s.41 is more favourable to third parties than the common law. It is submitted that the reasons given by Robert Walker LJ are the more convincing, i.e. that, in the light of the fact that the legislature has expressly addressed the issue of corporate insiders in s.41, there is no need for the courts to give the word "person" an unnaturally limited meaning in s.40.[47] In

[40] CA 2006 s.41(2), (7)(b). The meaning of "connected person" is discussed in para.10–070.

[41] CA 2006 s.41(2).

[42] CA 2006 s.41(3). There is a defence for non-director defendants (i.e. connected persons who are not directors) if they can show they did not know the directors were exceeding their powers: s.41(5).

[43] (1) restitutio in integrum is no longer possible; (2) the company has been indemnified; (3) rights of a bona fide purchaser for value (other than a party to the transaction) would be affected; or (4) the transaction is affirmed by the company.

[44] But note that actual indemnification is one of the situations in which the transaction ceases to be voidable: s.41(4)(b).

[45] CA 2006 s.40(6). See *Re Torvale Group Ltd* [2000] B.C.C. 626 Ch D (Companies Ct).

[46] *Smith v Henniker-Major & Co* [2002] EWCA Civ 762; [2002] B.C.C. 768. Also see *Re Sherlock Holmes International Society* [2016] EWHC 1392 (Ch); [2016] P.N.L.R. 31; and *Re Sprout Land Holdings Ltd (In Administration)* [2019] EWHC 807 (Ch); [2019] B.C.C. 893, both concerned with the similar question of whether internal reliance on s.161 is possible.

[47] For the same reason it is submitted that the dicta in *EIC Services v Phipps* [2004] B.C.C. 814 at [37] to the effect that even shareholders are not intended to be protected by s.40, should not be

short, it is submitted that corporate insiders, dealing with the company in good faith, are within s.40 but that the protection they obtain is that laid down in s.41.[48]

(d) The directors

The section expressly removes the effect of any limitations in the company's constitution "on the powers of directors to bind the company" or to authorise others to do so,[49] but it goes no further. Thus, a person who deals with the company through its shareholders in general meeting obtains no benefit from the section. Equally, the section does not cover limitations which are not directed at the powers of the directors, for example a limitation that the company cannot commit to a particular type of contract without the approval of X, who might be a shareholder of the company. In these cases, those dealing with the company will have the validity of their contracts assessed under the common law, including the rules of agency discussed below, and the rules of constructive notice as modified by the indoor management rule considered earlier. **8–013**

Even where the third party deals with the directors, however, all may not be plain sailing. The problems are typically of two types. First, earlier versions of the statutory provision had referred to limitations in the company's constitution "on the powers of the *board* of directors to bind the company", whereas the current version refers only to limitations "on the powers of directors", yet the effect of the change is still not clear. Secondly, if the directors have not been properly appointed, or the board is inquorate, are those types of flaws covered by the section? One would assume so, but what if there had been no attempt at all to appoint directors or hold a board meeting, would the actions of those in fact managing the company be covered nevertheless? It was held at first instance under the previous version of the section (referring to powers of the board) that the third party was not protected if the board was inquorate: if there were not enough members of the board present under its rules to constitute a meeting of the board, the directors could not be said to have done anything.[50] However, s.40, by substituting the word "directors" for the phrase "board of directors", seems designed to settle this point in the third party's favour. If the directors collectively have decided to contract, it does not matter that their decision does not constitute a valid board decision. Nevertheless, the underlying problem remains. It can hardly be the case that third parties, dealing with persons with no connection with the company, can claim the benefit of s.40 on the grounds that the failure of those persons to be elected directors by the company is a "limitation under the

---

followed. Since Parliament dealt with the position of directors in s.41, it is unlikely it would not also have dealt with shareholders if it had wished to qualify the protection conferred on them by s.40.

[48] It is true that s.41(1) preserves "any rule of law by which the transaction may be called in question" but the *Smith* decision proceeded on the basis of an interpretation of s.40, not by application of an independent rule of law.

[49] The significance of the extension of the section to those authorised by the directors is discussed in para.8–026.

[50] *Smith v Henniker-Major & Co* [2002] B.C.C. 544 Ch D; upheld on appeal ([2002] B.C.C. 768), but with only Carnwath LJ fully supporting the judge's reasoning on this point and Robert Walker LJ taking the contrary view. In other words, in the latter's view the quorum requirement is to be treated as one of the limitations in the company's constitution which the section is designed to override. This approach seems preferable.

company's constitution" which third parties are entitled to ignore, provided they are good faith third parties. As has been said, the "irreducible minimum" for s.40 to operate must be "a genuine decision taken by a person or persons who can on substantial grounds claim to be the board of directors acting as such".[51]

(e) *Any limitation under the company's constitution*

8–014 The company's constitution includes its articles of association, which constitute the principal element of the constitution.[52] The definition of the company's constitution in the Act extends further to include special and other supermajority resolutions and their equivalents.[53] But for the purposes of s.40, the constitution also includes in addition ordinary resolutions of the company or a class of shareholders and, notably, agreements among the members of the company or any class of them.[54] In short, the constitution here means any formal rules laid down by the shareholders generally (or any class of them) for the conduct of the company's affairs.

(f) *The internal effects of lack of authority*

8–015 As the opening words of s.40 make clear, the purpose of the section is to protect good faith third parties dealing with the company. Its aim is not to alter the internal effect of directors' actions taken without authority, except insofar as such amendment is needed to protect third parties. Consequently, the Act preserves individual shareholders' powers to bring an action to restrain the directors from doing an act to which would be in excess of their powers.[55] Such relief cannot be granted, however, if it would impede the fulfilment of the company's legal obligations to the third party. The provision thus operates in the narrow window where the directors are proposing to exceed their powers, but have not yet done so, or have exceeded their powers without creating a legally binding obligation on the company (e.g. creating a contractual option in the company's favour). Further, s.40(5) preserves the liability of directors "and any other person" who causes the company to contract in breach of limitations contained in its constitution.[56] Likewise, it seems likely that the section does not affect the liability of a third party to return property or its value to the company as a constructive trustee, where corporate property is received knowing (to the appropriate extent) that its transfer is in breach of directors' duties.[57]

---

[51] *Smith v Henniker-Major & Co* [2002] B.C.C. 768 at [41], per Robert Walker LJ. Note this concerned the earlier version of the provision; under the current law the word "directors" would be substituted for "board of directors" in the quotation cited. Also see fn.46.

[52] CA 2006 s.17(a).

[53] CA 2006 s.29.

[54] CA 2006 s.40(3).

[55] CA 2006 s.40(4).

[56] That liability may arise under s.171, requiring directors "to act in accordance with the company's constitution". See para.10–017. "Constitution" for the purposes of s.171 is defined in s.257. The "other person" might be someone who assists the director in the breach of duty.

[57] *International Sales & Agencies Ltd v Marcus* [1982] 3 All E.R. 551; *Re Hampton Capital Ltd* [2015] EWHC 1905 (Ch). Also see para.10–131.

Contracting through agents

The second situation we need to consider is where the company contracts through an agent acting on its behalf rather than through the organs of its directors or shareholders. As noted above, it would be highly inconvenient for companies and their counterparties if all contracts required board or shareholder approval. A low-cost mechanism is needed whereby individual managers within the scope of their duties can contract with third parties on behalf of the company. In some cases the company may wish to confer contracting authority even on outsiders. That mechanism is provided by the law of agency, which is based on the notion of authority. Under agency law a person, the principal (P), who authorises another, the agent (A), to contract on his or her behalf with a third party (T) will be bound by the contract which results from A's successful negotiations with T. The resulting contract will exist between P and T. A will not be a party to it and will normally owe no duties to T in relation to the contract.[58] Thus, if the company (P) authorises a manager (A) to contract with third parties in a particular area of the company's activities, that manager will be able to bring about contracts between the company and third parties without the need for specific board consent for each contract. **8–016**

The first and obvious question is, how does a corporate P confer authority upon a managerial A? It is conceivable that the articles will confer power upon a particular person to contract on the company's behalf, just as the articles normally confer broad managerial powers on the board. However, such provisions in the articles are rare. The articles are altered only infrequently and through a procedure requiring shareholder consent,[59] whilst the allocation of contracting powers across the company's managerial hierarchy may require frequent adjustment. More commonly, therefore, corporate agents are authorised through a process of delegation and sub-delegation of managerial powers by the board. The board will typically appoint the company's senior managers with wide managerial powers, which will explicitly or implicitly include powers to contract with third parties on the company's behalf. Those managers may appoint more junior managers with authority to contract within the scope of their functions. And so on. The result is a highly flexible system for the distribution of contracting powers across the company. In companies with large businesses, contracting authority can be widely dispersed; in small businesses the articles may allocate all contracting powers to the board or even to the shareholders; equally, all manner of other patterns of contracting authority can be created.

The system works smoothly so long as A in fact has authority to contract. Legal disputes arise when A acts beyond the authority conferred or when A was never given any authority. Then the question arises whether the agreement negotiated by A with T purportedly on behalf of P has resulted in a binding contract between P and T. The underlying policy questions are the same as with board contracting. **8–017**

[58] The classic exception to this statement is where A does not disclose to T the fact of the agency (the "undisclosed principal" case). On discovering the truth, T can choose to continue to hold A to the contract or to treat the contract as one with P. The other exception is when A "warrants" his actual authority to T, and that warranty is not true: T can then recover damages for reliance losses.

[59] See Ch.13.

Is priority to be given to the company's allocation of contracting authority (implying the company is not bound if A has exceeded the authority conferred by P or simply has no authority) or are T's reasonable expectations that A had authority to be protected (implying that *in some cases* T should be able to enforce the agreement against P despite A's lack of authority)? A principal function of the law of agency is to protect the reasonable expectations of T. However, identifying the appropriate balance between T and P is not easy.

There are two significant questions to be answered. *First*, assuming ignorance on the part of T of A's lack of authority, was it reasonable for T to suppose that the unauthorised A did in fact have authority to enter into the contract in question on behalf of the company? *Secondly*, if T knew or could have found out about A's lack of authority, does that deprive T of the protection that a positive answer to the first question would have conferred upon T?

We could say that neither question arises in relation to board contracting—or rather that the answers are very straightforward—because s.40 in effect embodies the proposition that it is reasonable for good faith third parties to assume that the contracting powers of the board are unlimited, and s.40 itself sets out the limits to that assumption. Formally, s.40 removes only those limitations which are contained in the company's constitution. Once these are taken out of the picture, however, it is difficult to see what other restrictions on a board's powers might be set up against T, since the board's managerial powers are derived from the constitution.[60]

However, s.40 provides no similar general basis for making an assumption of unlimited contracting powers in relation to sub-board agents—the constraints on their powers are not generally found in the company's constitution. Such an assumption would deprive the board of all control over the allocation of contracting power within the company. So both questions require answers in relation to sub-board agents. First, assuming T's ignorance of the lack of authority, on what basis is T entitled to treat (sub-board) A as authorised to contract, even though A had no actual authority to enter into the contract in question? And secondly, even if the contract would be binding on P on this basis, should the opposite answer be given if T knew or had the means of finding out about A's lack of authority? The answers to these questions are provided by the common law of agency, though, as we shall see, there is some debate about the relevance of s.40 to sub-board agents.

Agency principles in outline

8–018 Since this is not a book on the law of agency, for our purposes we can concisely state the main features of its rules of attribution in relation to contracts as follows. P is bound by the transactions negotiated on its behalf by A if A acted within either:

---

[60] An example might be thought to be where the shareholders have exercised their art.4 powers (para.9–004) to direct the board by special resolution not to exercise a power that art.3 prima facie confers on the board. However, the definition of the company's constitution (s.17) includes special resolutions (s.29). Of course, the board's managerial powers might be limited by a mandatory rule of company law (as was previously the case with the ultra vires doctrine) but such restrictions are rare.

(1) the actual scope of the authority conferred by P prior to the transaction, or else P subsequently ratified the transaction; or
(2) the ostensible (or apparent) scope of A's authority.

As far as (1) is concerned, this captures the process of delegation and sub-delegation referred to above. All that needs be added is that actual authority may be conferred expressly or impliedly. Authority to perform acts which are reasonably incidental to the proper performance of an agent's duties will be implied unless expressly excluded,[61] so that actual authority to contract may be inferred in appropriate cases from the appointment of A to a particular role, or the allocation to A of particular managerial tasks, where no explicit reference is made to contracting limitations. In addition, where A on previous occasions has been allowed by P (i.e. with P's knowledge and consent) to exceed the actual authority originally conferred, A may thereby have acquired actual authority to continue so to act.

As far as (2) is concerned, this is the crucial concept which agency law uses to hold P liable even in the absence of A's actual authority, in order to protect the legitimate interests of T. Ostensible or apparent authority is the authority which the particular A has been held out to T by P as having. Of course, that holding out may be by way of P indicating to T that A occupies a particular role, with all that implies. For this reason the line between ostensible or apparent authority and implied actual authority may seem blurred, but it is not: the establishment of actual authority focuses exclusively on the relationship between P and A and the authority that P has granted to A, whilst apparent or ostensible authority focuses on the relationship between P and T, and what representations have been made by P to T.[62]

The doctrine of ostensible or apparent authority attempts to hold a balance between the interests of the company and of the third party. On the one hand, a company should not normally be liable for the acts of persons whom it has not authorised to act on its behalf. As a qualification to that starting point, however, it would be reasonable to hold the company to the acts of an unauthorised agent if the company had in some way misled the third party into thinking the person is so authorised. But that act of misleading T has to be a proper act of the company. That means the representation can only be one made by someone who in fact has the authority to assert the extent of A's authority: i.e. typically either the company's primary decision-making body or an agent of the company who could himself have negotiated the contract or else delegated to A the appropriate power **8–019**

---

[61] *Hely-Hutchinson v Brayhead Ltd* [1968] 1 Q.B. 549 CA (Civ Div).

[62] For example, a person may be appointed to a particular role to which certain powers are normally attached, but those powers may be expressly constrained by the appointer. A's actual authority is accordingly limited. However, if P simply presents A as occupying the nominated role, A may well have apparent authority to act accordingly. This argument was advanced in *Hopkins v TL Dallas Group Ltd* [2004] EWHC 1379 (Ch), where the agent was held not to have actual authority to act in breach of his fiduciary duties or for improper purposes (an assertion which merits revisiting, see paras 10–022 and 10–023), but to have ostensible authority to so. However, here T had actual knowledge or was at least on notice of the issue, so could not hold P to the contract, for reasons considered at para.8–025.

necessary to negotiate it.[63] It follows from this that A cannot confer ostensible authority on himself simply by representing to T that he has the necessary authority.[64] On the other hand, if the company has indeed made such representations on which the third party has acted in good faith, the company will be estopped from setting up the truth of the relationship between the company and the agent as a ground of non-liability.[65]

8–020 But this approach raises one further issue. It is certainly the law that an agent cannot "self-authorise"; it is also the law that the company' representation to the third party must bind the company, so it must be made by someone with authority to make the representation. Typically it is made by someone with actual authority in relation to the transaction in question, but could it also be made by someone with only ostensible authority? Logic suggests the answer is yes, since the representor's ostensible authority (if valid) must track back in an unbroken line to someone within the company who has actual authority to make the representation in question. This was the view of Toulson J (as he then was) in *ING Re (UK) Ltd v R&V Versicherung AG*[66]:

> "I accept that the same principle [of ostensible authority] can also apply at one remove where T relies on a representation made by an agent having ostensible (but not actual) authority to make such a representation on behalf of P. Thus, where P represents or causes it to be represented *to T* that A1 has authority to represent *to T* that A2 has authority to act on P's behalf, and T deals with A2 as P's agent on the faith of such representations, P is bound by A2's acts to the same extent as if he had the authority which he was represented as having. The critical requirement is that A2's authority must be able to be traced back to the principal by *a representation or chain of representations upon which T acted* and whose authenticity P is estopped from denying by his representation through words or conduct." [67] (Emphasis added.)

Whether this is a good approach as a matter of policy is less clear: will it alter the delicate balance which ostensible authority holds between the interests of the company and the interests of the third party? So far, the dearth of cases suggests not, and perhaps Toulson's J's indication that each of the representations relied upon must be made to T is sufficient practical safeguard.[68]

---

[63] See para.8–020.

[64] *Armagas Ltd v Mundogas SA (The Ocean Frost)* (1986) 2 B.C.C. 99197 HL; *Hudson Bay Apparel Brands LLC v Umbro International Ltd* [2010] EWCA Civ 949; [2010] E.T.M.R. 62.

[65] Contrary to what was thought at one time, this is so even if the officer or agent has forged what purported to be a document signed or sealed on behalf of the company: *Uxbridge Permanent Benefit Building Society v Pickard* [1939] 2 K.B. 248 CA; explaining dicta in *Ruben v Great Fingall Consolidated* [1906] A.C. 439 HL; *Kreditbank Cassel GmbH v Schenkers Ltd* [1927] 1 K.B. 826 CA; *South London Greyhound Racecourses Ltd v Wake* [1931] 1 Ch. 496 Ch D; *Lovett v Carson Country Homes Ltd* [2009] EWHC 1143 (Ch); [2011] B.C.C. 789.

[66] *ING Re (UK) Ltd v R&V Versicherung AG* [2006] EWHC 1544 (Comm).

[67] *ING Re (UK) Ltd v R&V Versicherung AG* [2006] EWHC 1544 (Comm) at [100], although on the facts in this case the argument was not made out for a good many reasons. See too the earlier dicta in *Egyptian International Foreign Trade Co v Soplex Wholesale Supplies Ltd (The Raffaella)* [1985] 2 Lloyd's Rep. 36 CA (Civ Div) at 43 (Browne-Wilkinson LJ).

[68] The proposition is subjected to extended discussion in *Skandinaviska Enskilda Banken AB (Publ), Singapore Branch v Asia Pacific Breweries (Singapore) Pte Ltd* [2011] SGCA 22 at [38]–[59], with the conclusion, especially at [55]–[59], that the analysis to such ends needs to be especially careful. Also see para.8–024.

Establishing the ostensible authority of corporate agents

The application of these general principles of the law of agency to establish a corporate agent's actual or ostensible authority is a fact-dependent exercise, focusing on the P/A or P/T relationship, as the case may be. Nevertheless, certain broad lines of approach have emerged. Individual non-executive directors have no managerial responsibility unless the board specifically delegates it to them, and the courts have accordingly been restrictive in their approach to the ostensible authority of such directors.[69] Even they, however, may be assumed to have some individual ministerial authority, for example, to authorise the use of the company's seal.[70] By contrast, if the person acting for the company is its chief executive officer or managing director, then, unless there are suspicious circumstances, or the transaction is of such magnitude as to imply the need for board approval, that person may safely be assumed to be authorised. In practice, that person will probably have actual authority[71] but, even if not, he or she will have ostensible authority and his or her acts will bind the company.[72] It is typical to assume that such authority, whether actual or ostensible, in conferred by the board, but it could, equally, and in the right circumstances, be conferred by the shareholders.[73] Moreover, it is not uncommon for the board of directors to allow one of their number to assume the position of managing director even though never formally appointed to that position and in these circumstances the courts may either find the managing director to have been given actual authority by a course of dealing over time,[74] or they may find that he has ostensible authority because the company has held him out to third parties as their managing director.[75] **8–021**

Much the same applies to other executive directors, except that, if the descriptions of their posts suggest particular areas of responsibility ("finance director", "sales director" or the like), they cannot be assumed to have authority outside those areas. Some decisions have even suggested that a non-executive chairman of the board has, as such, individual authority equating with that of a **8–022**

---

[69] *Rama Corp v Proved Tin & General Investments Ltd* [1952] 2 Q.B. 147 QBD.

[70] cf. the Companies (Model Articles) Regulations 2008 (SI 2008/3229) Sch.3: Model Articles for Public Companies art.81. On the seal, see fnn.11 and 65.

[71] *Hely-Hutchinson v Brayhead Ltd* [1968] 1 Q.B. 549.

[72] *Freeman & Lockyer v Buckhurst Park Properties (Mangal) Ltd* [1964] 2 Q.B. 480 CA, especially the judgment of Diplock LJ at 506. It follows that, within a corporate group a senior executive of a subsidiary will not be assumed to have authority to bind the parent, though such authority may be established on the facts of the case: *Hudson Bay Apparel Brands LLC v Umbro International Ltd* [2010] E.T.M.R. 62.

[73] *Ciban Management Corp v Citco (BVI) Ltd* [2020] UKPC 21; [2020] B.C.C. 964. This was an unusual case where the sole beneficial owner of all the shares in a BVI company had been endeavouring to hide his assets from creditors. To that end, not only did he hold his shares beneficially rather than being the registered owner, he also gave all his instructions to the company's directors through an intermediary. The case thus concerned the ostensible authority of the shareholder's agent, not the company's agent, although the general principles are the same.

[74] *Hely-Hutchinson v Brayhead* [1968] 1 Q.B. 549.

[75] See, e.g. *Biggerstaff v Rowatt's Wharf Ltd* [1896] 2 Ch. 93 CA; *Clay Hill Brick Co Ltd v Rawlings* [1938] 4 All E.R. 100 KBD; *Freeman & Lockyer v Buckhurst Park Properties Ltd* [1964] 2 Q.B. 480.

managing director,[76] but the proposition is doubted.[77] This is not to deny that the chair of the board has important corporate governance responsibilities[78] but rather to question whether those responsibilities involve contracting on behalf of the company. Nor is it to deny that a company might appoint someone to a chairman post with executive responsibilities, though the corporate governance rules frown on the cumulation of the positions of chief executive and chair of the board.[79]

8–023 A third party will often deal with an officer or employee below the level of director. For many years, the courts showed a marked reluctance to recognise any ostensible authority even of a manager.[80] But this has now changed and it may be taken that a manager, even if actual authority is lacking, will generally have ostensible authority to undertake everyday transactions relating to the branch of business which he or she is managing (though probably not if they are unusual, or unusually significant, transactions),[81] and the secretary will similarly have such authority in relation to administrative matters.[82] Indeed, almost every employee of a trading company will surely have ostensible authority to bind the company in some transactions, and usually actual authority too, although the extent of that authority may be very limited. For example, people behind the counter in a department store clearly have both actual and ostensible authority to sell the goods on display for cash at the marked prices. Whether their actual or ostensible authority extends beyond that (for example, to take goods back if the customer returns them) we shall probably never know, for it is unlikely to be litigated—at any rate against the customer.[83]

8–024 In all the above cases the question has been whether the agent had actual or ostensible authority to *contract* on behalf of the company. In a small number of

[76] *British Thomson Houston Co Ltd. v Federated European Bank Ltd* [1932] 2 K.B. 176 CA; *Clay Hill Brick Co v Rawlings* [1938] 4 All E.R. 100.

[77] In *Hely-Hutchinson v Brayhead* [1968] 1 Q.B. 549, per Roskill J at first instance at 560D, and per Lord Wilberforce at 586G.

[78] See para.12–054.

[79] See paras 9–016 to 9–020.

[80] *JC Houghton & Co v Nothard, Lowe & Wills Ltd* [1927] 1 K.B. 246 CA; affirmed on other grounds [1928] A.C. 1 HL; *Kreditbank Cassel v Schenkers* [1927] 1 K.B. 826; *South London Greyhound Racecourses v Wake* [1931] 1 Ch. 496 Ch D; see also the observations of Willmer LJ in *Freeman & Lockyer v Buckhurst Park Properties (Mangal) Ltd* [1964] 2 Q.B. 480 CA at 494.

[81] See *Armagas Ltd v Mundogas SA* (1986) 2 B.C.C. 99197. There an employee who bore the title of "Vice-president (Transportation) and Chartering Manager" was held not to have ostensible authority to bind his company to charter back a vessel which it was selling. But there were complicating factors in that case for the employee was colluding with an agent of the other party in a dishonest arrangement and did not purport to have any general authority to bind the company but merely alleged that he had obtained actual authority for that particular transaction. Also see *MCI WorldCom International Inc v Primus Telecommunications Inc* [2003] EWHC 2182 (Comm), where an in-house lawyer negotiating a contract did not have ostensible authority to give undertakings as to the future financial soundness of a parent company; and *East Asia Co Ltd v PT Satria Tirtatama Energindo (Bermuda)* [2019] UKPC 30 at [50] (where it was noted that authority to negotiate does not imply authority to close the deal, especially an unusual or unusually large one).

[82] *Panorama Developments (Guildford) Ltd v Fidelis Furnishing Fabrics Ltd* [1971] 2 Q.B. 711 CA (Civ Div). How far, if at all, the secretary's ostensible authority extends to the commercial side of the company's affairs is still unclear; see, per Salmon LJ at 718.

[83] The issue might arise in litigation between salesperson and employer.

cases, however, the question has been whether the company is bound if the agent has authority (whether actual or ostensible) not to contract but only to make binding representations on behalf of the company about whether another person (with actual authority to contract) has committed the company to the contract. Can the company be bound on the basis of such a representation, even if the representation made is false? In *First Energy (UK) Ltd v Hungarian International Bank Ltd*,[84] a senior branch manager of the bank was held to have ostensible authority to communicate to a third party the head office approval of a loan application, even though he did not have authority to contract on the bank's behalf, as the third party knew, and the head office had not in fact approved the loan. The court held that once the third party had accepted the "offer" communicated by the manager, it could sue the bank on the resulting contract.

This line of authority advances the security of third parties' transactions but, unless confined to particular and unusual facts, is capable of inappropriately extending companies' liability for unauthorised contracts. This is because its effect is not simply to render the company liable for the agent's false (but authorised) representation, but also to render the company liable to make good the truth of that representation; in short, the agent's false assertion that there is a contract means that a binding contract exists, even though no one with authority has agreed to the contract, and even though the agent—to the knowledge of the third party—cannot agree to the contract. In those circumstances why should an agent who cannot agree *to* the contract be able to achieve that end simply by asserting that there *is* a contract?[85]

The relevance of the third party's knowledge

We now turn to the second question identified in para.8–017. Even if A has ostensible authority, it can be argued that T has no legitimate claim to protection if T knows or ought to have known that the agent was not actually authorised. After all, ostensible authority is an estoppel-based doctrine, and T is only protected if his reliance on P's representation was reasonable. Under the agency rules the balance shifts decisively in favour of P if T knew that A did not have actual authority to contract. The law will also deprive T of the benefit of the **8–025**

[84] *First Energy (UK) Ltd v Hungarian International Bank Ltd* [1993] B.C.C. 533 CA (Civ Div). See also *The Raffaella* [1985] 2 Lloyd's Rep. 36 at 43.

[85] See the serious reservations concerning *First Energy* expressed (obiter) by the Singapore Court of Appeal in *Skandinaviska Enskilda Banken AB (Publ), Singapore Branch v Asia Pacific Breweries (Singapore) Pte Ltd* [2011] SGCA 22 at [57]–[61], especially at [59]: "if the agent merely has authority to make general representations about the transaction and does not have any authority (whether actual or ostensible) to enter into the transaction on the principal's behalf, it is not possible for him to give himself such authority by falsely representing that his principal has approved the transaction, which representation carries with it the implication that the principal has given him (the agent) the requisite authority to bind the principal to the transaction"; it would be to the contrary if the agent *had* specific authority to make the representation that the principal was indeed bound. Of course the third party should have remedies flowing from the agent's misrepresentations. See the approach in S. Worthington, "Corporate Attribution and Agency: Back to Basics" (2017) L.Q.R. 118, suggesting that the binding nature of the representation that a deal had been agreed entitles the third party to sue for losses suffered as a result of relying on the false representation; it does not entitle him to claim that the promised facts were indeed true: that is not how misrepresentations are remedied.

doctrine of ostensible authority if T was put on enquiry as to whether A was acting within the scope of authority and did not then make the enquiries that a reasonable person would have made in the circumstances[86]: T cannot then reasonably rely on the representation of authority, and the estoppel again fails. Thus, in one case where T had contracted with a single director rather than with the board as a whole, that director was held not to have created a contract with the company because the contracts were abnormal in relation to the business of the company (implying no ostensible authority) and because the circumstances were such as to raise questions about whether A was acting properly (T put on enquiry).[87]

The long line of authorities confirming that third parties cannot rely on an agent's ostensible authority where they have actual or constructive knowledge to the contrary was challenged in *Akai Holdings Ltd v Kasikornbank Public Co Ltd*,[88] and Lord Neuberger NPJ expressed his preference for a test based on actual or dishonest knowledge rather than constructive knowledge, that being more in line with the expectations of business. Whether that is true might be doubted, and the suggestion was immediately the subject of serious academic criticism. It has now been subjected to careful judicial analysis by the Privy Council in *East Asia Co Ltd v PT Satria Tirtatama Energindo (Bermuda)*, and seems unlikely to be taken up.[89]

In addition to T's actual or constructive knowledge of A's lack of authority, T is also taken to have constructive notice of the constitution, as discussed above in relation to board contracting.[90] It follows that T may be deprived of the benefit of his contract where A has entered into it in breach of a provision in the articles limiting A's authority—even though T has not read the articles. The rule in *Turquand's Case* and the indoor management rule modify the constructive notice doctrine to some extent, as we have seen, but otherwise this doctrine continues to operate at common law. The issue is typically less important in relation to sub-board agents, because the restrictions on their authority are less likely to be found in the company's articles. Yet, it is not impossible to think of cases where the articles might be relevant to sub-board agents' contracting powers, especially in small companies. Take as an illustration a provision in the articles requiring shareholder approval for contracts above a certain value. If this is couched as a prohibition on anyone other than the shareholders contracting, the constructive notice doctrine will defeat T contracting via a sub-board agent. If, however, to vary the situation slightly, sub-board agents are permitted to contract for

[86] What is reasonable depends on all the circumstances.

[87] *Hopkins v TL Dallas Group Ltd* [2004] EWHC 1379 (Ch). Similarly, see *East Asia Co Ltd v PT Satria Tirtatama Energindo (Bermuda)* [2019] UKPC 30.

[88] *Akai Holdings Ltd v Kasikornbank Public Co Ltd* [2010] HKCFA 64; [2011] 1 H.K.C. 357.

[89] See the extended obiter discussion in *East Asia Co Ltd v PT Satria Tirtatama Energindo (Bermuda)* [2019] UKPC 30, setting out the long line of authorities favouring constructive knowledge as the test for reliance on ostensible authority and on the indoor management rule ([75]–[82]), a consideration of *Akai* [2010] HKCFA 64; [2011] 1 H.K.C. 357 ([83]–[85]), and then a robust defence of the status quo ([86]–[93]).

[90] See paras 8–006 to 8–009.

high-value contracts provided they have obtained the prior approval of the shareholders, then the indoor management rule will probably save T unless T has been put on enquiry.

Thus, given the importance of knowledge and constructive notice in the common law of agency, there is some incentive for T dealing with sub-board agents to try and bring themselves within s.40, even though that section applies only to limitations on authority located in the company's constitution. The advantages T may seek from s.40 are, in relation to constitutional limitations, (1) escape from the doctrine of constructive notice; (2) where T has some knowledge, not being put under a duty to enquire; and (3) again where T has some knowledge, benefitting from the wide definition of good faith in the section. There are two situations where this question may arise. First, assume T contracts with a single director (in the case of a company having multiple directors) rather than the board. Can T invoke s.40 in relation to authority limitations in the articles? Before 2006 the answer was clearly in the negative because the section referred to "the power of the board of directors" whilst now it refers to "the power of the directors" to bind the company. We have suggested in para.8–013 a reason why this change was made. That reason suggests the change was intended to extend the section only to cases of the directors acting collectively (but, for some procedural reason, not as a board) rather than to cases of contracts with individual directors, which the wording is not apt to cover. Even if s.40 can be extended, it should be noticed that s.40 does not operate so as to confer ostensible authority on a single director but only to allow T potentially to rely on such ostensible authority as the director has despite T's actual or constructive knowledge. The ostensible authority of the single director has to be established as a prior step in the argument on the basis of the principles discussed in para.8–021. **8–026**

Secondly, the section protects from limitations in the articles not only the power of the directors to bind the company but also their power "to authorise others to do so".[91] Thus, if the articles state that only the shareholders can enter into high-value contracts, a good faith T can rely as against the company on an agreement made either by the board or by someone who has been specifically authorised by the board to enter into high-value contracts. It is not clear whether s.40 goes beyond this base case. First, does it apply only where the board endeavours to give express actual authority to T (despite the prohibition on the constitution) or does it capture situations of implied actual authority as well?[92] In other words, must the board authorisation expressly say that A may enter into high value contracts or is it enough to appoint A to a managerial position incidental to which is entering into high-value contracts? Secondly, must A have been appointed by the directors or is it enough that A was appointed by a senior manager who was appointed by the directors and whose functions include the appointment of junior managers? The underlying question is whether the

[91] CA 2006 s.40(1). It is clear that the section creates no presumption that A has been authorised by the board to contract. Only if A has been so authorised will the exclusion of limitations in the articles on the board's powers to authorise be removed in favour of a good faith T. See *Wrexham Associated Football Club Ltd v Crucialmove Ltd* [2007] B.C.C. 139 at [47]. But see fn.11 on why it might be convenient for the board to act in this way.

[92] For this distinction see para.8–018.

extension in s.40 to "authorising others" was intended to cover only situations where the board approves the contract in principle but delegates the actual contracting decision to a manager or whether the extension is designed to exempt the management hierarchy as a whole from the restrictions in the articles on their contracting power. It seems likely that, if Parliament had intended the broader result, it would have used clearer words. Overall, therefore, it seems that A's authority to bind the company, where A is not the board of directors or an apparent board, will be determined overwhelmingly by the common law of agency coupled with constructive notice of the company's public documents as modified by *Turquand*.[93]

Knowledge of the constitution as an aid to third parties: endeavours to build authority on the "indoor management rule"

8–027 So far, we have considered knowledge (actual or constructive) of the company's constitution as something negative from T's point of view, as something which could deprive T of the security of the transaction with the company. Can T rely on knowledge of the articles as a building block in a claim against the company? Admittedly this would have to be actual knowledge, not constructive,[94] but even here it is now clear that mere knowledge that the board of directors *might* have delegated authority to a particular person does not estop the company from denying that it has done so.[95] If T wanted to rely on his knowledge of the articles to build an argument, he would have to establish that "the conduct of the board, in the light of that knowledge, would be understood by a reasonable man as a representation that the agent had authority to enter into the contract sought to be enforced".[96] That is unlikely. Nor does the indoor management rule assist. That rule, and the assumptions it permits, is a rule of estoppel: although it operates in favour of third parties, those parties first need to establish that the agent in question *has* been given actual authority or held out as having ostensible authority, and this rule then enables the third party to assume that any necessary internal processes required to exercise that authority were properly carried out.[97]

---

[93] The CA 1989 contained a provision (inserted as s.711A into the CA 1985) which would have abolished generally the doctrine of constructive notice arising from the public filing of corporate documents. However, the section was never brought into force and the CA 2006 contains no equivalent provision.

[94] Constructive notice is a negative doctrine curtailing what might otherwise be the apparent scope of the authority, and not a positive doctrine increasing it. Any doubt on this point was finally dispelled by the Court of Appeal in *Freeman & Lockyer v Buckhurst Park Properties Ltd* [1964] 2 Q.B. 480, especially Diplock LJ at 504.

[95] *Mercantile Bank of India v Chartered Bank of India* [1937] 1 All E.R. 231 is sometimes misunderstood in this regard. The headnote is misleading in suggesting that it was the fact that the articles expressly empowered the board to delegate by powers of attorney that brought about the estoppel. It was the actual exercise of that power by the board that did so. The only relevance of the articles (of which third parties were deemed to have notice) was that they did not preclude the grant of such powers of attorney.

[96] *Freeman & Lockyer v Buckhurst Park Properties Ltd* [1964] 2 Q.B. 480 at 508 (Diplock LJ). See also Atkin LJ in *Kreditbank Cassel v Schenkers* [1927] 1 K.B. 826 at 844.

[97] *East Asia Co Ltd v PT Satria Tirtatama Energindo (Bermuda)* [2019] UKPC 30 at [61]–[64]; approving the comments of Dawson J in *Northside Developments Pty Ltd v Registrar General* [1990]

Ratification by the company of unauthorised contracting

We have already noted that the legal effect of lack of actual or ostensible authority on the agent's part is that the transaction is void: it is not binding on the company unless it is ratified by the company. The company thus has an option to take up the transaction or to treat it as not binding on it. Determining who has the power to ratify the transaction is a matter for the company's constitution.[98] There is no requirement in the Act, as there is for breaches of directors' duties, that ratification must be by the shareholders,[99] though it appears the shareholders will usually be able to ratify unauthorised actions of the board or sub-board agents.[100] Normally, it is a matter of finding who, under the company's constitution, has actual authority to enter into the transaction, and then securing their approval of it. In addition, it is not necessary that ratification should take the form of an express decision to approve the transaction. Ratification can be implied from conduct[101] and the conduct may amount to ratification if the company has knowledge of the essentials of what the agent has done, even if it did not know that the agent had acted without authority.[102] If there is ratification, it has retrospective effect, i.e. it renders the transaction with the company binding on it as from the time it was entered into by the agent. It is sometimes difficult to distinguish a subsequent ratification (which is a unilateral act of the company) from the entering into by the company and the third party of a new transaction which replaces the one entered into by the agent without authority.[103] There is also a time limit on the ratification process in the sense that ratification will not be permitted if it would unfairly prejudice a third party.[104] **8–028**

The ultra vires doctrine and the objects clause

Before finishing our consideration of corporate contracting, we need briefly to consider the ultra vires doctrine and its relationship with a particular type of clause, though one now increasingly rarely found in the articles, namely, the objects clause. Although the ultra vires doctrine caused a lot of anxiety to third **8–029**

---

170 C.L.R. 146; [1993] A.L.R. 385 which had been cited with approval by Lord Neuberger NPJ in *Akai* [2010] HKCFA 64; [2011] 1 H.K.C. 357 at [59].

[98] And the parties able to ratify an agent's unauthorised dealing to make it binding on the company are not necessarily the same parties as would be required to give the agent such authority for all future dealings, nor the same as might be required in order to remedy other wrongs; all depends on the company's constitution, and who is give the different powers to exercise: *Irvine v Union Bank of Australia* (1877) 2 App. Cas. 366 PC.

[99] See paras 10–111 to 10–118.

[100] *Grant v United Kingdom Switchback Railway Co* (1888) 40 Ch. D. 135 CA. If ratification would involve a breach of the articles *by the shareholders*, then shareholder approval, it seems, would need to be by a majority equivalent to that for a change in the articles.

[101] *Re Mawcon* [1969] 1 W.L.R. 78 Ch D.

[102] *ING Re (UK) Ltd v R&V Versicherung AG* [2006] EWHC 1544 (Comm).

[103] This was the point upon which the "ratification" failed in *Smith v Henniker-Major & Co* [2002] B.C.C. 768.

[104] See the discussion ibid. and in *The Borvigilant* [2003] EWCA Civ 935.

parties during its history,[105] that is no longer the case because the third party is protected against its effects by s.39 of the Act, whether the third party has acted in good faith or not. The objects clause defines the capacity of the company, i.e. it states what the company is legally capable of doing, whether it acts through its board or via the shareholders collectively or through an agent. A company was required by the early legislation to include a statement of its objects in its memorandum of association and from that the courts deduced that the company did not have legal capacity to act outside its objects. Any such action was in principle void. This was normally referred to as the ultra vires doctrine.[106] It had a major and adverse impact on the security of third parties' transactions with the company. Not even ratification was available in relation to ultra vires acts. So, it is not surprising that the doctrine was the object of reform; what is surprising is that reform took so long.

There is no longer a provision in the Act requiring a company to set out its objects.[107] Unless it chooses otherwise, the company's objects will be unrestricted, i.e. it will have unlimited capacity.[108] Even if a company chooses to adopt restrictions on its capacity (which will appear today necessarily in the articles rather than the memorandum of association),[109] those restrictions will not affect the validity of the acts of the company: s.39(1) provides that "the validity of an act done by a company shall not be called into question on the ground of lack of capacity by reason of anything in the company's constitution". Thus, the ultra vires doctrine, so far as it is based on the company's objects clause,[110] no longer threatens the security of third parties' transactions.[111] A company may also amend or remove its object clause by the same means as it can use for altering its articles,[112] except in the case of charitable companies.[113]

---

[105] For a brief history of the ultra vires doctrine and its reform in 1972 and again in 1989 see the fifth edition of this book (London: Sweet & Maxwell, 1992), pp.166 onwards.

[106] "Ultra vires" is a Latin expression which lawyers and civil servants use to describe acts undertaken beyond (ultra) the legal powers (vires) of those who have purported to undertake them. In this sense its application extends over a far wider area than company law. For example, those advising a minister on proposed subordinate legislation will have to ask themselves whether the enabling primary legislation confers vires to make the desired regulations.

[107] This is based on an interpretation of art.2(b) of the Second Directive (Directive 2012/30 on coordination of safeguards [2012] OJ L315/74) as requiring the company's articles to state its objects (if it has them) but not as requiring the company to have objects.

[108] CA 2006 s.31(1).

[109] See para.4–031.

[110] For the possible deployment of the ultra vires doctrine from other doctrinal bases see para.18–016.

[111] CA 2006 s.39 does not attempt to deal with the internal aspects of the ultra vires doctrine, thus underlining that these are matters to be dealt with according to the ordinary rules on directors' duties or the enforcement of the articles as between shareholder and company. A particularly complex issue of this sort is addressed in s.247, concerning gratuitous payments by directors to employees where a company is closing down or transferring a business. In *Parke v Daily News (No.2)* [1962] Ch. 927 Ch D such payments were held to be ultra vires the company. That issue is no longer relevant and the matter now is largely dealt with in the section as one of directors' duties. However, interestingly the section does mandatorily extend the powers of the directors to make such payments, even if the company's constitution does not confer such powers. However, there are strict controls over the exercise of the power in the interests of the shareholders and other creditors of the company.

[112] This provision applies equally to companies already in existence when this reform was introduced by the CA 2006 and which necessarily had objects clauses in their memorandum of association.

Nevertheless, many existing companies will continue to have objects clauses and some newly created ones may choose to adopt them. The central point is that, whilst the ultra vires doctrine is dead as a restriction on the capacity of the company, objects clauses continue to limit the authority of the board, the shareholders collectively or any of its agents to bind the company, in the same way as any other provision in the articles. The objects clause is part of the company's constitution and the rules discussed above, including s.40 of the Act, apply to it accordingly. Equally, a director may be liable to the company for exceeding the limits set out in the objects clause, as with any other authority limitation in the articles. Indeed, it is precisely because the rules on authority hold the balance between the interests of the company and of third parties in what is now regarded as the appropriate way that it was possible for s.39 to be cast in such blunt terms.

Pre-incorporation and post-dissolution contracts

The final issue to consider in the context of company liability in contract is what happens if parties purport to enter into contracts on behalf of a company before it comes into existence (pre-incorporation) or after it has been dissolved (post-dissolution). Both problems are now relatively rare, but the lessons to be learnt from them are important. The first situation used to be common when the formation of companies was a complicated and costly endeavour, and so, in advance of the eventual incorporation, "promoters"[114] would try to settle the most important undertakings to buy assets, businesses or services from third parties so that the company would be ready to function once launched. Now, however, it is simple and cheap to register a company, so those contemplating doing so can take this step before they need to enter the necessary contractual engagements. The latter problem, by contrast, typically arises by accident: a company has been struck off the register for some reason, and the parties acting on its behalf are not aware of the fact. 8–030

Objects clauses set out in the memoranda of existing companies are to be treated as provisions in the articles, by virtue of s.28(1), and as such will benefit from s.39 and also from the CA 2006 alteration/removal regime.

[113] CA 2006 s.31 preserves the operation of ss.197 and 198 of the Charities Act 2011, applying in England and Wales. The broad effect of that section is that where a charity is a company, no alteration which has the effect of the body ceasing to be a charity will affect the application of any of its existing property unless it bought it for full consideration in money or money's worth. In other words, although the company is not prevented from changing its objects (so long as it obtains the prior written consent of the Charity Commission) in such a way that they cease to be exclusively for charity, its existing property obtained by donations continues to be held for charitable purposes only. In effect, the company will be in an analogous position to an individual trustee of a charitable trust: part of its property will be held for charitable purposes only and part of it not. And, presumably, it will have to segregate the former. Scotland and Northern Ireland have separate legislation on this point.

[114] A "promoter" is a term of business, not law, used to describe the people who conceive of the scheme for the formation of a company for a specific endeavour and then take all the necessary legal and practical steps to launch the company. Promoters owe fiduciary duties to the company to be formed, and generally owe a duty of utmost good faith, so as to not mislead any potential investors, and disclose all material facts about the company's business: *Erlanger v New Sombrero Phosphate Co* (1878) 3 App. Cas. 1218 HL.

Until a company has been incorporated it cannot contract or do any other act. Nor, once incorporated, can it become liable on or entitled under contracts purporting to be made on its behalf prior to incorporation, since ratification is not possible when the ostensible principal did not exist at the time when the contract was originally entered into.[115] Hence, preliminary arrangements will either have to be left to mere "gentlemen's agreements" or the company's promoters will have to undertake personal liability. Which of these courses will be adopted depends largely on the demands of the other party. If our village grocer is converting his business into a private company of which he is to be managing director and majority shareholder he will obviously not be concerned to have a binding agreement with anyone, since all power on both sides of the deal rests with him. If, however, promoters are arranging for the company to take over someone else's business, the seller certainly, and the promoters probably, will wish to have a binding agreement immediately. In this event the sale agreement can only be made between the vendor and the promoters, and it will be provided that the personal liability of the promoters is to cease when the company in process of formation is incorporated and enters into an agreement in similar terms.

8–031 If the law just described is not appreciated, then difficulties can easily arise: promoters may purport to cause the as yet unformed company to enter into transactions with third parties. As already noted, these contracts cannot bind the non-existent entity, and the company, once formed, cannot ratify or adopt the contract.[116] Prior to statutory amendments driven by the UK's entry into the EU, the legal position as between the promoter and the third party seemed to depend on the terminology employed. If the contract was entered into by the promoter and signed "for and on behalf of XY Co Ltd" then, according to the early case of *Kelner v Baxter*,[117] the promoter would be personally liable. But if, as is much more likely, the promoter signed the proposed name of the company, adding his own to authenticate it (e.g. XY Co Ltd, AB Director) then, according to *Newborne v Sensolid (Great Britain) Ltd*,[118] there was no contract at all. This was hardly satisfactory.

8–032 The resulting statutory intervention took a clear if rather dramatic stand. The relevant provision is now CA 2006 s.51, which reads:

---

[115] This is because ratification dates back to the date of the transaction, so it cannot be effective unless, at that time, the person now ratifying both existed and had capacity to enter into the transaction. Contrast the position when a public company enters into transactions after its registration but before the issue of a trading certificate (see para.16–010) or when a company changes its name (see para.4–023).

[116] It must enter into a new contract on the same terms. Of course, in the absence of a new contract the company cannot accept delivery of goods or payment of the price without coming under a restitutionary obligation.

[117] *Kelner v Baxter* (1866–67) L.R. 2 C.P. 174 CCP. See also *Natal Land & Colonization Co Ltd v Pauline Colliery and Development Syndicate Ltd* [1904] A.C. 120 PC.

[118] *Newborne v Sensolid (Great Britain) Ltd* [1954] 1 Q.B. 45 CA. In that case it was the promoter who attempted to enforce the agreement but it appears that the decision would have been the same if the other party had attempted to enforce it, as was so held in *Black v Smallwood* [1966] A.L.R. 744 HC: see also *Hawkes Bay Milk Corp Ltd v Watson* [1974] 1 N.Z.L.R. 218; cf. *Marblestone Industries Ltd v Fairchild* [1975] 1 N.Z.L.R. 529. The promoter should, it seems, be liable for breach of implied warranty of authority: *Royal Bank of Canada v Starr* (1985) 31 B.L.R. 124.

> "(1) A contract that purports to be made by or on behalf of a company at a time when the company has not been formed has effect, subject to any agreement to the contrary, as one made with the person purporting to act for the company or as agent for it, and he is personally liable on the contract accordingly."

The obvious aim of the provision is to increase security of transactions for third parties by avoiding the consequences of the contract with the company being a nullity. The provision imposes contractual liability on the promoter, and applies even if the new company is never formed.[119] To avoid the promoter's personal liability under the statute, the third party must explicitly agree to forego the protection—consent cannot be deduced simply from details of the contract which, interpreted widely, would be inconsistent with the promoter accepting personal liability, such as the promoter signing as agent for the company.[120]

The presence of the statutory provision has had an effect on the courts' perception of the common law in this area. In *Phonogram Ltd v Lane*,[121] Oliver LJ said that the "narrow distinction" drawn in *Kelner v Baxter* and the *Newborne* case did not represent the true common law position, which was simply: **8–033**

> "does the contract purport to be one which is directly between the supposed principal and the other party, or does it purport to be one between the agent himself—albeit acting for a supposed principal—and the other party?"[122]

This question is to be answered by looking at the whole of the contract and not just at the formula used beneath the signature. If after such an examination the latter is found to be the case, the promoter would be personally liable at common law, no matter how he signed the document.

On this analysis the difference between s.51 and the common law is narrowed, but not eliminated. At common law, if the parties intend to contract with the non-existent company, the result will be a nullity and the third party protected only to the extent that the law of restitution provides protection. Under the statute, a contract which purports to be made with the company will trigger the liability of the promoter, unless the third party agrees to give up the protection. In **8–034**

[119] *Phonogram Ltd v Lane* [1982] 3 C.M.L.R. 615 CA (Civ Div). This is subject to the normal contractual rule that if the misrepresentation about the identity of the counterparty induced the contract to the other party's detriment, then rescission at the option of the injured party is possible: *Braymist Ltd v Wise Finance Co Ltd* [2002] EWCA Civ 127; [2002] B.C.C. 514, although in that case the necessary facts were not made out.

[120] *Phonogram Ltd v Lane* [1982] 3 C.M.L.R. 615. See also *Royal Mail Estates Ltd v Maple Teesdale* [2015] EWHC 1890 (Ch); [2015] B.C.C. 647; affirmed [2015] EWHC 3237 (Ch), where the court held that an express agreement that the benefit of the contract was personal to the company did not exclude the effect of the equivalent of s.51 of the CA 2006, such that the agent may still be liable on the pre-incorporation contract. See, however, the decision of the First-tier Tribunal (Tax Chamber), obiter, in *Binap Ltd v Revenue and Customs Commissioners* [2013] UKFTT 455 (TC), where an agreement to the contrary was inferred from conduct of the parties, including the tendering of invoices to the company instead of the promoter. This approach goes against the trend of other cases, and appears doubtful.

[121] *Phonogram Ltd v Lane* [1982] 3 C.M.L.R. 615.

[122] *Phonogram Ltd v Lane* [1982] 3 C.M.L.R. 615 at 621. This approach was applied by the Court of Appeal in *Cotronic (UK) Ltd v Dezonie (t/a Wendaland Builders Ltd)* [1991] B.C.C. 200 CA (Civ Div); and in *Badgerhill Properties Ltd v Cottrell* [1991] B.C.C. 463 CA (Civ Div).

other words, the common law approaches the question of the third party's contractual rights against the promoter as a matter of the parties' intentions, with no presumption either way, whereas the statute creates a presumption in favour of the promoter being contractually liable. The common law is still important in those cases which fall outside the scope of the statute.

8–035 Despite the improvements which the statute has effected, there are still problems with its operation. First, the section does not make it clear whether the promoter acquires a right under the statute to enforce the contract, as well as the risk of being subjected to contractual obligations, but that has now been confirmed to be the case.[123]

Secondly, and more seriously, the reforms have done nothing to make it simpler for companies to "assume" or adopt the rights and obligations of a pre-incorporation transaction. Many common law countries have recognised, either by judge-made law or by statute, that a company when formed can effectively elect to adopt pre-incorporation transactions purporting to be made on its behalf without the need for a formal novation, and that the liability of the promoter ceases when the company adopts it. In 1962, the Jenkins Committee recommended this reform but it still has not happened. At present the only way in which the company can adopt the contract is by entering into a post-incorporation agreement in the same terms. Even if the company does so, that will not relieve the promoters of personal liability (at any rate while the new agreement remains executory)[124] unless they are parties to the new agreement, which expressly relieves them of liability under the pre-incorporation agreement. The need for all this is frequently overlooked. This may not matter much if all those concerned remain able and willing to perform their obligations under the pre-incorporation agreement. But it can be calamitous if one or more of them becomes insolvent or wants to withdraw because changes in market conditions have made the transactions disadvantageous to him or them.

8–036 Finally, we return to the second of the problems mentioned at the start of this section: what is to happen if parties purport to enter into contracts on behalf of a company after it has been dissolved (i.e. post-dissolution contracts)? The common law resolution of this problem is precisely the same as for pre-incorporation contracts, since precisely the same reasoning operates. But, by contrast, no assistance is provided by s.51: that section bites only when the contract purports to be made on behalf of a company "which has not been formed", a description not apt to cover a company that was formed but has now been struck off.[125]

---

[123] *Braymist Ltd v Wise Finance Co Ltd* [2002] B.C.C. 514.

[124] If the new contract has been fully performed by the company, after incorporation, and by the other party, that clearly will end any liability under the pre-incorporation contract.

[125] In *Cotronic (UK) Ltd v Dezonie* [1991] B.C.C. 200. See also *Badgerhill Properties Ltd v Cottrell* [1991] B.C.C. 463. On the other hand, it is submitted that the decision in *Oshkosh B'Gosh Inc v Dan Marbel Inc Ltd* (1988) 4 B.C.C. 795 CA (Civ Div), that s.51 does not apply to a company which trades under its new name before completing the statutory formalities for change of name, is correct, since a change of name does not involve re-incorporation. See para.4–023.

Overview of the rules on corporate contracting

A third party dealing with the company through its board of directors has a higher level of security of transaction than a person dealing with the company otherwise. In the former case, the primary rules of attribution start from the position that the board has power to bind the company—subject to the articles—and s.40 goes on to protect a good faith third party (widely defined) from attack based on limitations contained in the articles. By contrast, where the third party, T, deals with an agent, A's authority to bind the company needs to be established under the standard agency rules and s.40 offers less (probably much less) protection against attacks based on limitations contained in the articles, throwing T in some cases back onto the indoor management rule. This may not be an inappropriate result. The standard division of powers within a company is one which allocates general management powers to the board.[126] So, the third party's expectations as to the security of the transaction will be particularly high when that person deals with the company through the board. The primary rules of attribution and s.40 recognise this. By contrast, where the company contracts through an agent, it has a legitimate claim to be able to limit the scope of its agent's authority, just as a natural person can. Otherwise, the directors would lose a significant method of controlling the conduct of the company's business and boards would either have to run the risk of acquiring contractual obligations through unauthorised means or devote a disproportionate amount of board time to the contracting process. T can have no legitimate expectation that the board would routinely delegate all its powers to any particular person. However, even in this case, the interests of the third party are by no means neglected. The general rules of attribution—agency rules—will protect the third party who has acted reasonably but been misled by the company as to the authority of the corporate agent, just as they do when P is not a company. Looking at the transaction from the company's perspective, where the deal was not authorised, but the engagement is an attractive one, the company can elect to ratify the deal made by its unauthorised agent. Finally, special care has to be taken by third parties to ensure that the company with which they are proposing to deal does indeed exist, and that it has the capacity to enter into the proposed arrangement. 8–037

TORT LIABILITY

We saw earlier that both companies and their potential counterparties benefit from rules which facilitate contracting between them. The rules discussed in the first part of this chapter are designed to effect such facilitation. Since the purpose of these rules is to produce a contract between P and T, it is wholly acceptable that in the normal case those who act as or on behalf of the company do not acquire any liability under the contract. Whether the company contracts directly with the third party via its constitutional bodies or contracts indirectly via an agent, we have seen that this is the result normally achieved. If the company contracts directly, the individuals taking those decisions for the company do not 8–038

126 See para.9–003.

become parties to the contract. If the company acts indirectly through an agent, then, once negotiations are successfully concluded between A and T, A drops out of the picture, becoming neither a party to the contract nor personally liable under it unless A has chosen to accept liability under it (something that may not be entirely easy to determine).[127] The same rule applies even if the contract between P and T fails to come into existence because of A's lack of authority: even then, A will not be liable on the contract where it was clear he was acting as an agent and not personally.[128] However, A may be liable to T for breach of A's "warranty of authority" if A misrepresented the extent of his authority, no matter how innocently.[129]

When it comes to tort, however, the non-liability of the person acting as the company or on behalf of the company cannot be the typical outcome. These are situations of civil wrongdoing, and it would be odd if the addition of corporate liability removed liability from the individual who could be shown also to have committed a personal wrong. If responsibility for wrongdoing is attributed to the company on the basis of vicarious liability, the outcome is in accordance with this postulate. It will necessarily be the case that both agent/employee and company are liable. This happens because, with vicarious liability, the liability of the agent is attributed to the company, even though the wrongful acts of the agent are not. Why the law should adopt this approach is considered later. The agent remains a wrongdoer; indeed, if the agent does not, vicarious liability cannot arise.[130] Where, however, the basis of the principal's liability is not vicarious liability, but direct liability, the question will arise whether the agent is also liable. Sometimes, perhaps often, they will both be liable but sometimes not.

Vicarious liability of the company

8–039 Actions against the company in tort (and for other forms of civil liability) are overwhelmingly based on the vicarious liability of the company for the wrongs of its agents and employees, so that both the employee/agent and the company are liable, jointly, to the tort victim. There can be no finding of vicarious liability unless the employee/agent is shown to have committed a wrong. But that is only the first step. A company is not automatically vicariously liable for all the wrongs of its employees or agents; there must be some connection between the company's activities and the acts of the tortfeasor if the company is also to be held liable. Defining the nature of this link has been the central problem within the doctrine of vicarious liability. Over the years, the test has changed. However, even from an early date the courts were unwilling to confine the scope of the company's (or any principal's) vicarious liability to those actions actually

[127] For a discussion of this issue in the context of pre-incorporation contracts, see paras 8–030 to 8–036, where the default position is that A is liable.

[128] *Lewis v Nicholson* (1852) 18 Q.B. 503 QB.

[129] *Collen v Wright* (1857) 8 E. & B. 647 Ex Chamber.

[130] See *Bilta (UK) Ltd v Nazir* [2015] B.C.C. 343, per Lords Toulson and Hodge at [186]: "Such vicarious liability is indirect liability; it does not involve the attribution of the employee's act to the company. It entails holding that the employee has committed a breach of a tortious duty owed by himself, and that the company as his employer is additionally answerable for the employee's tortious act or omission".

authorised by the company. Thus a company did not escape vicarious liability simply because its agent or employee had done an act which had been prohibited by the company, or had done a deliberate act for his own benefit, even one which had prejudiced the employer.[131] This led to the famous (but unclear) dichotomy between doing an unauthorised act (no vicarious liability) and doing an authorised act in an unauthorised manner (vicarious liability). In more recent decisions on the doctrine, however, the House of Lords and then the Supreme Court moved beyond this distinction to a looser test, and sought to impose vicarious liability whenever there was a "sufficiently close connection" between the wrongful acts of the agent or employee and the activities which those persons were employed to undertake. The move in this direction was initially motivated by cases of sexual abuse, which, under the old test, would have left the victims without claims against companies managing their care. But the tests formulated were designed to apply generally, and the fact that the wrongful acts were clearly unauthorised and not for the employer's benefit did not prevent the imposition of liability, provided this test was satisfied.[132]

At a very general level, the tests for "sufficiently close connection" in tort and ostensible authority in the law of agency might appear to perform a similar role, i.e. the protection of the legitimate interests of third parties coming into contact with businesses. However, they are by no means identical doctrines: ostensible authority turns on a holding out by the principal of the agent to the third party,[133] where the principal's own actions are what attract the imposition of contractual liability; by contrast, vicarious liability does not depend upon any action by the company, nor on what the third party understood to be the agent's connection with the company—the third party may not even know of it at the time the tort was committed—but simply upon an objective assessment of the relationship between the agent's actions and the company's activities. In short, vicarious liability can be seen as a loss distribution device based on social and economic policy[134]: liability is sheeted home to the company not because it has committed a tort but because it has created a risk that a tort would be committed,[135] and so it is considered just and reasonable to hold the company liable.[136] Too vague a test of what constitutes a "sufficiently close connection" leaves it to judges to decide whether it is "fair" that a particular company should be made liable for the harm caused by its employee or agent. That is risky. The rule of law, and the likelihood

---

[131] *Lloyd v Grace, Smith & Co* [1912] A.C. 716 HL (fraud on a client by solicitors' clerk); *Morris v CW Martin & Sons Ltd* [1966] 1 Q.B. 716 CA (theft by employee of customer's coat); *Bellman v Northampton Recruitment Ltd* [2018] EWCA Civ 2214 (assault committed by a managing director after a Christmas party but noting how rare a finding of vicarious liability in these circumstances would be).

[132] *Lister v Hesley Hall Ltd* [2001] UKHL 22 (sexual abuse of children in a care home by the staff employed to look after them); *Dubai Aluminium Co Ltd v Salaam* [2002] UKHL 48 (firm vicariously liable for knowing assistance by a solicitor partner in a breach of trust); *Mohamud v WM Morrison Supermarkets Plc* [2016] UKSC 11; [2016] P.I.Q.R. P11 (assault by employee on a customer for reasons personal to the employee). At the same time, the range of "employee like" relationships which may give rise to vicarious liability has been expanded: *Cox v Ministry of Justice* [2016] UKSC 10; [2016] P.I.Q.R. P8 (vicarious liability for acts of a prisoner).

[133] See para.8–018.

[134] *Dubai Aluminium Co Ltd v Salaam* [2002] UKHL 48 at [107] (Lord Millett).

[135] *Dubai Aluminium Co Ltd v Salaam* [2002] UKHL 48 at [21] (Lord Nicholls).

[136] *Bernard v AG of Jamaica* [2004] UKPC 47 at [18] (Lord Steyn).

of like cases being treated alike, is best served by clear criteria for the imposition of liability, notwithstanding that the policy reasons for choosing to impose liability in the first place are social.[137]

Direct liability of the company

8–040 Although, overwhelmingly, the tortious liability of companies is approached by the courts through the doctrine of vicarious liability, the company can also be liable directly. Initially, as with contract, this was on the grounds that its constitutional bodies (the board or shareholders collectively) had committed a tort: the company's liability is then direct, not vicarious.[138] Of course, if the elements of the tort can also be made out against the individuals who took the corporate decision, then they too will be personally liable for the harm caused by their own wrongs.[139] In that context, there is nothing dividing the practical outcome from what obtains when the company is found to be vicariously liable: both the company and the individual actors will be liable to the tort victim. Moreover, given the width of the doctrine of vicarious liability, it is rarely necessary to consider, in a claim by a third party against the company, whether the company is liable directly or vicariously.

However, sometimes the tort in question cannot be committed by the individual employee or agent (e.g. breach of a statute imposing obligations on companies to act in certain ways, but no equivalent obligations on individuals),[140] or has not in fact been committed by the individual (because all the elements of the tort cannot be shown as against the employee or agent).[141] In those cases, if the company is found liable in tort, then it can only be because the company itself has committed the tort, directly. How might the company commit a tort directly? The analysis in *Meridian Global*, considered at the start of this chapter,[142] indicates how: once again, we ask whose acts (or knowledge or intention if that is relevant to the tort) count as the acts (or knowledge or intention) of the company *for this purpose*? This is not necessarily an easy question, as we saw when the

---

[137] See the extended discussion of this difficult balancing issue in *Skandinaviska Enskilda Banken AB (Publ), Singapore Branch v Asia Pacific Breweries (Singapore) Pte Ltd* [2011] SGCA 22 at [75] onwards. Also see *Ming An Insurance Co (HK) Ltd v Ritz-Carlton Ltd* [2002] 3 HKLRD 844, where the Court of Final Appeal of Hong Kong applied the "close connection" test to impose vicarious liability on an employer for the negligent driving of its employee.

[138] *Bilta (UK) Ltd v Nazir* [2015] B.C.C. 343 at [187]. Also see *Campbell v Paddington Corp* [1911] 1 K.B. 869 KBD (concerning the acts of a borough council, but the principles are the same).

[139] *Standard Chartered Bank v Pakistan National Shipping Corp (No.2)* [2002] UKHL 43; [2002] B.C.C. 846, where the fraudulent representation made by the relevant company agent (not the corporate organ) was attributed to the company: the company was thus directly liable for the fraud. But the agent was also personally liable for the fraud: all the elements of the tort could be made out against him, and he could not escape liability by saying he had only committed the tort as an act of the company and not as his own act.

[140] For example, competition law provisions and other market regulations are often (but not invariably) directed at companies, not individuals. See *Director General of Fair Trading Appellant v Pioneer Concrete (UK) Ltd* [1995] 1 A.C. 456 HL; *Meridian Global v Securities Commission* [1995] B.C.C. 942.

[141] *Williams v Natural Life Health Foods Ltd* [1998] B.C.C. 428 HL; *WB Anderson & Sons Ltd v Rhodes (Liverpool) Ltd* [1967] 2 All E.R. 850 Assizes, both considered below.

[142] See paras 8–001 to 8–003.

same question was considered in the context of corporate contracting. It is harder still when the act being considered is necessarily a wrong. Companies would escape all direct liability if the acts of corporate agents never counted as the acts of the company if they were wrongful (with the reasoning being that surely the company would not clothe its agents with authority to commit wrongs), but liability may be too onerous if every wrongful act by an agent were deemed to be the same wrongful act committed by the company. In locating the correct place for the line to be drawn, it is perhaps predictable that some of the same language used in establishing vicarious liability is again used here—i.e. was the act one that was "within the scope" of the employee's role—but it must be remembered that the purpose of the question is very different in the two contexts.[143] In particular, if the company is being found vicariously liable for the wrong, rather than directly liable, then there is no "wrongdoer" justification for the liability, so the approach taken needs to be carefully consistent with policy reasons for choosing to impose liability, vicariously, in the first place.[144]

Two particular examples are illustrative. The first is *Williams v Natural Life Health Foods*,[145] where the House of Lords held that the controlling director and shareholder of a company who had made negligent misstatements whilst contracting on behalf of a company had not assumed personal responsibility for the truth of those statements; responsibility was assumed (in the usual case) only on behalf of the company. Thus, it was the company that had committed the tort (by making the false statement through its agent, and assuming responsibility for them, also through its agent), and the agent had not (since all the necessary elements of the tort were not present).[146] The reasoning of the court is important: it demonstrates how the company is made directly liable, and also indicates that the individual can be personally liable, but only if all the elements of the particular tort in question can be made out against him.[147] As the court made

---

[143] Contrast the language in *Director General of Fair Trading Appellant v Pioneer Concrete (UK) Ltd* [1995] 1 A.C. 456; with the clearer approach in *Meridian Global v Securities Commission* [1995] B.C.C. 942.

[144] See, again, the extended discussion in *Skandinaviska Enskilda Banken AB (Publ), Singapore Branch v Asia Pacific Breweries (Singapore) Pte Ltd* [2011] SGCA 22 at [75] onwards in the context of assertions that a company was vicariously liable for its agent's fraud.

[145] *Williams v Natural Life Health Foods* [1998] B.C.C. 428.

[146] In this case the claim against the company was not pursued to its conclusion because the company was insolvent and wound up. However, the House of Lords (obiter) set out the basis of the company's liability: false statements had been made on its behalf by its managing director on the company's notepaper.

[147] Thus, the courts appear reluctant to exempt from personal responsibility agents who are professionally qualified. See *Merrett v Babb* [2001] EWCA Civ 214; [2001] P.N.L.R. 29 (surveyor employed by a partnership); *Phelps v Hillingdon LBC* [2001] 2 A.C. 619 HL (educational psychologist employed by the local education authority).

clear, this approach applies not only to negligent misstatements, but also to cases of negligent delivery of services due under a contract,[148] and presumably also to other wrongs.[149]

The second illustration is even sharper. In *WB Anderson and Sons Ltd v Rhodes (Liverpool) Ltd*,[150] Rhodes (the company) was held liable for negligent misrepresentation. The Rhodes employee who made the representation was not negligent, as he could only have known the true facts if other Rhodes employees had told him, and they, negligently, did not. However, those latter employees were not liable for negligent misrepresentation, since they had made no representations. Nevertheless, Rhodes was liable—directly—for the tort.

CRIMINAL LIABILITY AND STATUTORY LIABILITY

8–041 As we have just seen, vicarious liability provides a substantial basis upon which companies are held liable in tort. In criminal law, by contrast, vicarious liability is regarded with suspicion, especially in relation to serious crimes involving mens rea. The reasons are self-evident: the policy basis for vicarious liability is simply not present for many (but not all) crimes.[151] Consequently criminal law has had to place greater reliance on the direct liability of the company. On this approach, the acts and state of mind of certain officers or employees must necessarily be attributed to the company. However, the criminal law has had great difficulty in determining the criteria for this, and thus for direct liability. If the criteria are broadly set, there will be little difference from the company's point of view between vicarious and direct liability; if narrowly set, companies will often escape criminal punishment. Where the offence is set out in legislation, the particular wording of the statute will be crucial.

Regulatory offences imposing strict liability

8–042 But not all crimes require mens rea. In the case of regulatory offences based on strict liability, it will be relatively easy to convince the court that Parliament intended the acts of even very junior persons in the business to be attributed to the

[148] Thus, *Fairline Shipping Corp v Adamson* [1975] Q.B. 180 QBD is now to be seen as a case where the director did personally assume responsibility for the performance of the services which the company had contracted to provide, despite the rather thin evidence of such an assumption. See also para.28–064, for the application of this principle to statements made by target boards in takeover bids.

[149] *Standard Chartered Bank v Pakistan National Shipping Corp (No.2)* [2002] B.C.C. 846, and see fn.143; *Contex Drouzhba Ltd v Wiseman* [2007] EWCA Civ 1201; [2008] B.C.C. 301. Similarly with equitable wrongs based on knowing receipt, where the company receives the relevant assets (not the company's agent or employee) and the question is whether the agent or employee's knowledge can be attributed to the company to render the company directly liable in knowing receipt: *El-Ajou v Dollar Land Holdings Plc (No.1)* [1994] 2 All E.R. 685 CA (Civ Div) (but also see para.8–048). Note that the agent or employee may also be personally liable, not for any receipt based claim (no receipt) but for dishonestly assisting in the wrong: *Royal Brunei Airlines Sdn Bhd v Tan* [1995] B.C.C. 899 PC.

[150] *WB Anderson & Sons Ltd v Rhodes (Liverpool) Ltd* [1967] 2 All E.R. 850.

[151] See para.8–039.

company.[152] This will be so even for statutory offences where the liability can be said to be strict, but subject to defences such as "taking all reasonable steps". In *R. v British Steel Plc*[153]it was not a defence for the company that the senior management had taken all reasonable care to avoid a breach of the statutory duty; it was necessary that those actually in charge of the dangerous operation should have done so. Where liability is imposed in this way, then on usual principles the fact that the employees were acting contrary to their instructions does not mean that their acts cannot be attributed to the company.[154]

Direct liability: "directing mind and will"

Outside the area of strict liability offences, the early approach of the courts was to impose criminal liability for crimes with a mental element only on the basis of an "identification" doctrine. This doctrine had its origins in statutory civil liability and was only later transferred to the criminal law. The classic formulation is found in *Lennard's Carrying Co Ltd v Asiatic Petroleum Co Ltd*,[155] concerning corporate civil liability under the merchant shipping legislation which required a finding of "actual fault or privity" on the part of the company. This formulation was taken to exclude vicarious liability as a technique for holding the company liable. There, Lord Haldane based "identification" on the concept of a person "who is really the directing mind and will of the corporation, the very ego and centre of the personality of the corporation".[156] This was both an anthropomorphic and limited concept of attribution. Lord Haldane would only extend the directing mind and will concept beyond the constitutional organs of the company to include those individuals given the equivalent of board powers by the articles or by the general meeting.[157] **8–043**

In the period immediately after the Second World War the same idea was applied in the criminal law and its use was eventually approved and clarified by the House of Lords in 1972 in the case of *Tesco Supermarkets Ltd v Nattrass*.[158]

[152] *Meridian Global v Securities Commission* [1995] B.C.C. 942. This step was taken at an early stage. See *Mousell Bros Ltd v London & North Western Railway Co* [1917] 2 K.B. 836 KBD, where the tenor of the judgment may suggest reasoning based on vicarious liability (though that term is not used), speaking of actions "within the scope" of the employee's employment, although there was no effort given to finding that the employee was primarily liable (and, given the terms of the statute, that finding could not have been made). The actual analysis adopted in the judgments would now—given *Meridian Global*—lead immediately to a finding of direct liability.

[153] *R. v British Steel Plc* [1995] 1 W.L.R. 1356 CA (Crim Div).

[154] *Re Supply of Ready Mixed Concrete (No.2)* [1995] 1 A.C. 456 HL.

[155] *Lennard's Carrying Co Ltd v Asiatic Petroleum Co Ltd* [1915] A.C. 705 HL. See also *The HMS Truculent* [1952] P. 1 PDAD; *The Lady Gwendolen* [1965] P. 294 CA.

[156] *Lennard's Carrying Co Ltd v Asiatic Petroleum Co Ltd* [1915] A.C. 705 at 713. Lord Haldane's dictum was probably influenced by the clear distinction drawn between agents and organs in German company law, Haldane having studied in Germany in his youth.

[157] In the case itself the defendant company was held liable on the basis of the actions of the managing director of another company which managed the ship on behalf of the defendant company, but this was on the basis that the defendant company had failed to reveal the nature of the manager's relationship with the defendant company.

[158] *Tesco Supermarkets Ltd v Nattrass* [1972] A.C. 153 HL. The earlier cases included *DPP v Kent & Sussex Contractors Co* [1944] K.B. 146 KBD; *R. v ICR Haulage Ltd* (1945) 30 Cr. App. R. 31 CCA; *Moore v I Bresler Ltd* [1944] 2 All E.R. 515 KBD; and *HL Bolton Engineering Co Ltd v TJ Graham*

Their lordships took a similar view of what constituted the directing mind and will as in the earlier case, except that they added persons to whom the board had delegated its functions.[159]

Broader justifications for direct liability: beyond "directing mind and will"

8–044 Of course, this concept of "directing mind and will" is only really needed in circumstances where the formulation of the particular offence is thought to rule out the attribution to the company of the acts and state of mind of persons not falling within the "directing mind and will" concept. But attribution of any sort is always context specific,[160] so it follows naturally—and is now seen to follow naturally—that where the crime is more broadly formulated, the company can be held directly liable on the basis of what more junior employees thought and did, as Tesco itself discovered in a later case.[161] This is simply a specific reminder of the general proposition that once we have decided that a company can act, or know, or intend certain consequences, the real difficulty comes in determining whose act or knowledge[162] or state of mind is to be legally attributed to the company for the particular purpose.[163]

The real breakthrough came in *Meridian Global*,[164] although there had been earlier cases to similar effect. *Meridian Global* was a case involving administrative penalties for breaches of securities legislation. Lord Hoffmann focused on the rule in question. He held that where statutory liability was to be imposed on a company, then the question of who, for the purposes of the rule, was to be treated as the company, was to be determined by the company's own practical internal decision-making structure: the company might as a matter of practice repose the relevant responsibility in the corporate organs, or in particular directors, or in those lower down the employee chain. In *Meridian Global* itself, where the question was whether the company was in breach of the New Zealand laws requiring disclosure of substantial shareholdings knowingly held by an

& Sons Ltd [1957] 1 Q.B. 159 CA—in some of which a very broad interpretation was given to the concept of the directing mind and will. See too *R. v Alstom Network UK Ltd* [2019] EWCA Crim 1318; [2019] 2 Cr. App. R. 34, denying that in a criminal case the "directing mind and will" invariably needed to be present in court for the company to have a fair trial.

[159] Since the individual whose acts were in question was a lowly employee in the case, the judges did not have to explore in detail what board delegation meant: was delegation of board powers enough (as Lord Diplock suggested) or did the board need to delegate in addition its responsibility for a certain area of the company's business (as Lord Reid indicated)?

[160] *Meridian Global v Securities Commission* [1995] B.C.C. 942.

[161] *Tesco Stores Ltd v Brent LBC* [1993] 1 W.L.R. 1037 DC.

[162] See below at para.8–048.

[163] See also Law Commission, *Criminal Liability in Regulatory Contexts*, Consultation Paper 195, 2010, paras 5.45–5.83. Despite the practical uncertainties raised by the approach, the Law Commission, paras 5.103–5.110, commended the *Meridian Global* approach (see below) to the courts in all cases where the statute does not itself deal precisely with the issue of corporate liability. On this approach the identification doctrine, at least in its classic form, would be just one possible result of the exercise of statutory construction: see, e.g. *R v St Regis Paper Co Ltd* [2011] EWCA Crim 2527.

[164] *Meridian Global v Securities Commission* [1995] B.C.C. 942 at 947–948.

investor,[165] the relevant persons for the purpose of determining what knowledge the company had were the two senior investment managers who were in charge of dealing in the markets on behalf of the company as its "controllers"; it did not matter that these individuals were not members of the board, still less that they were not the company's "directing mind and will".[166]

However, that is not to deny that context matters, and different outcomes can be expected in civil and criminal claims because the appropriate rules of attribution can be different in different contexts. It is not hard to conceive that a company would be made liable in a civil claim for the fraud of any number of its junior employees, but less clear that the company itself would be *criminally* liable for each of those frauds. In the former context, the question is whose acts and intentions count as the company's in the dealing with this third party; in the latter context, given that the company can be criminally liable for fraud, it is whose acts or intentions would make that so.[167] It follows that there ought not to be a blanket rule that corporate criminal liability necessitates board knowledge or intention (the directing mind approach), or, slightly more expansively, that the relevant knowledge or intention must be of someone to whom the board has specifically delegated the relevant role; but nor should we be surprised that corporate criminal liability arises far less often than corporate civil liability.

Corporate manslaughter

The *Meridian Global* approach to corporate liability may come to dominate the issue in relation to statutory crimes. However, the Court of Appeal refused to adopt it in respect of the common law crime of manslaughter by gross negligence.[168] The court instead held that for this important common law crime a company could be convicted only if an identifiable human being could be shown to have committed that crime and that individual met the strict test for the identification of that person with the company (i.e. the "directing mind and will" test). As a consequence it became impossible to secure convictions for corporate manslaughter when serious fatalities occurred in the course of a company's business unless the company was a "one man company". This was because the gross negligence required could rarely be located sufficiently high up in the corporate hierarchy. **8–045**

As long ago as 1996, the Law Commission proposed a solution to this difficulty in its recommendation that a company should be criminally liable if management failure was a cause of a person's death, without the need to show

165 For the equivalent British rules see Ch.27.

166 For a careful summary of the law, see *Serious Fraud Office v Barclays Plc* [2018] EWHC 3055 (QB); [2020] Cr. App. R. 28 at [56]–[87]. Also see E. Ferran, "Corporate Attribution and the Directing Mind and Will" (2011) L.Q.R. 239. As an example of an unsuccessful attempt to attribute criminal liability to a company on the basis of the actions of its wrongdoing directors, and thus make the company (rather than its directors) subject to a confiscation order under the Proceeds of Crime Act 2002, see *Faichney v Vantis HR Ltd* [2018] EWHC 565 (Ch), especially [51] onwards.

167 See Lord Reid's judgment especially in *Tesco Supermarkets Ltd v Nattrass* [1972] A.C. 153.

168 *Re Attorney-General's Reference (No.2 of 1999)* [2001] B.C.C. 210 CA (Crim Div).

that any human being was guilty of manslaughter or, indeed, any other crime.[169] On this approach the company could be liable criminally even though none of those whose actions were attributed to it was criminally liable. The focus would be on the quality of the operating systems deployed by the company rather than the guilt of individuals.

After a remarkably tortuous legislative passage extending over a number of years, the Corporate Manslaughter and Corporate Homicide Act 2007[170] eventually reached the statute book. It creates an offence for companies[171] to cause a person's death as a result of the way its activities are organised or managed where that organisation or management amounts to a gross breach of a duty owed by the company to the deceased. The new statutory offence replaces the common law as far as companies are concerned.[172] The requirement for a gross breach of duty owed to the deceased[173] reflects the common law of manslaughter by gross negligence. No individual has to be identified whose acts themselves constitute the offence of manslaughter and whose acts and knowledge can then be attributed to the company. The company can be convicted on its organisational failings alone, irrespective of the guilt of any individual person. However, some rule still has to be provided to identify the persons whose organisational failings are attributed to the company. Here, the notion that the company should be found guilty only for failings at a senior level is retained in the provision that corporate guilt arises "only if the way in which [the company's] activities are managed or organised by its senior management is a substantial element in the breach".[174] If the failings are wholly at subordinate level, the company will not be guilty. However, significant failings at lower levels are bound to raise the question of whether the senior levels of management should have picked up these lower level failings.

8–046 If the company is found guilty under this 2007 Act, it is liable to an unlimited fine.[175] Whether this operates as an effective corporate deterrent has been doubted. The financial penalty falls on the shareholders rather than on the senior management whose failings led to the criminal offence.[176] This may encourage

[169] Law Commission, *Legislating the Criminal Code: Involuntary Manslaughter* (1996), Law Com. No.237, HC Paper No.171.

[170] The offence is corporate manslaughter in England, Wales and Northern Ireland; corporate homicide in Scotland.

[171] And for other corporate bodies, which need not concern us here, though the question of how far public sector bodies should be the brought within the scope of the Act was one of the most contentious in Parliament.

[172] 2007 Act s.20.

[173] The existence of the duty is a question of law for the judge (s.2(5)); whether the breach of the duty is "gross" a question for the jury (s.8). The duty in question must be a duty under the law of negligence falling into one of the categories listed in s.2, though these categories are widely defined.

[174] 2007 Act s.1(3).

[175] 2007 Act s.1(6).

[176] And *Safeway Stores Ltd v Twigger* [2010] EWCA Civ 1472, if correct (see para.8–050), suggests the sums cannot be recovered from those directors. Instead, the fine reduces the value of the shareholders' equity. The share price may fall even further to reflect the reputational harm suffered by the company as a result of the crime. However, not all crimes reduce the willingness of customers to deal with companies nor show that the directors were acting contrary to the interests of the shareholders. Possibly even the reverse can be true. See J. Armour, C. Mayer and A. Polo, "Regulatory Sanctions and Reputational Damage in Financial Markets", Oxford Legal Studies

the shareholders to take action which is adverse to the interests of the directors (e.g. removing them) or put pressure on them to avoid repetitions of the offence. But whether these possibilities will be effective depends on the shareholder/management balance and relations in the company. It is perhaps least likely to operate in this way in large companies for which the 2007 Act was particularly designed. Greater pressure on the shareholders to take action might arise if the consequence of a criminal conviction were the exclusion of the company from a certain area of business, but that raises even more strongly the question of the rationale for imposing a penalty on shareholders for managerial wrongdoing.

A greater deterrent impact may result from the reputational harm the management, not the company, will likely suffer if the company is found guilty of corporate manslaughter whilst they were in charge of it. In this respect, the court's power to order the company to give publicity to the fact of its conviction may be helpful.[177] At one stage it had been mooted that convictions would be required to be reported in the company's annual report: this is not an essential requirement, although such publication could be required as part of a court's publicity order.

The court has a further power—which may operate more directly on the management of the company—to order a convicted company to take steps, not only to remedy the breach and any matter resulting from it which were a cause of the death, but also "any deficiency, as regards health and safety matters, in the organisation's policies, systems or practices of which the relevant breach appears to the court to be an indication". The application for the order may be made only by the prosecution, which must consult the relevant enforcement authority (for example, the Health and Safety Executive) about what should be asked for. The order will set a time limit for the specified steps to be taken and may require the company to provide evidence to the relevant enforcement authority that those steps have been taken.[178] However, the enforcement authority is given no greater monitoring role in relation to the management of the company than this, though it may think it appropriate to use its general inspection powers more vigorously in relation to a company which has been convicted of corporate manslaughter than one which has not.

The Bribery Act 2010

The Corporate Manslaughter and Corporate Homicide Act creates strong incentives for companies to organise their businesses so as not impose risks of serious harm on their employees and outsiders. Similar indirect criminal liability for failure to address risks within the organisation could be imposed on a wider basis. It appears to be becoming attractive to the legislature to impose such liability where the risk in question is the risk of a criminal act being committed **8–047**

Research Paper No.62/2010; ECGI—Finance Working Paper No.300/2010 available at SSRN: *http://ssrn.com/abstract=1678028* [Accessed 16 March 2021].

177 2007 Act s.10. Non-compliance with a publicity order is itself a criminal offence.

178 2007 Act s.9.

within the organisation, presumably on the basis that the senior management of the company are better at discouraging criminal acts within it than are the ordinary law enforcement bodies.

A significant step in this direction was taken in the Bribery Act 2010. This Act not only updates and extends the substantive offence of bribery, but it also imposes (in ss.7 and 8) criminal liability on companies for failing to prevent bribery by a person associated with the company. In addition, s.14 imposes on "senior officers" (not just directors) of the company "consent or connivance" liability in respect of actual bribery (as set out in ss.1, 2 and 6). The associated person could be simply an employee or agent of the company. The liability arises only if the associated person was intending to obtain a business advantage for the company. More important, it is a defence for the company that it has in place adequate procedures designed to prevent bribery by employees and agents. In essence, the threat of criminal liability is used to induce companies to put in place adequate internal controls over bribery.

This incentive rationale for imposing criminal liability for failure to prevent crime could be used extensively in relation to crime committed within the scope of a company's business. In its *UK Anti-Corruption Plan 2017–2022*[179] the government restated its intent to focus on corporate failure to prevent economic crime, and the approach is already adopted in part in the Criminal Finances Act 2017 (see Pt 3).

ATTRIBUTING KNOWLEDGE TO THE COMPANY IN CONTRACT, TORT AND CRIME

8–048 In assessing liability in contract, tort or crime, the knowledge of the defendant—here, the knowledge of the company—can be a key element in establishing the cause of action. *Meridian Global* makes it plain that the knowledge of individuals within a company can be attributed to the company for the purpose of finding the company liable for some wrong where knowledge is a material factor. The principle is clearly of general operation, although it can sometimes be remarkably difficult to identify whose knowledge, and which knowledge, should count as the company's knowledge in certain contexts. As we have already seen, it is certainly true that the knowledge of the "directing mind and will" of a company will generally be attributed to the company (but see below for the specific problems which can arise when the "directing mind" is the *defendant* in a claim by the company).[180] However, will anything less suffice? *Meridian Global* itself indicates that it will. But the difficulty then is what test is to be used to identify the person whose knowledge will count, and which aspects of that person's knowledge will count, as the company's knowledge in a given context? That is a little more difficult. The test is not simply "directing mind and will": that would be too narrow. Nor is it simply "agency": an agent may have actual or ostensible authority to bring the company into a contractual relationship

---

[179] HM Government, "UK anti-corruption strategy 2017 to 2022" (December 2017) available at: *https://www.gov.uk/government/publications/uk-anti-corruption-strategy-2017-to-2022* [Accessed 16 March 2021].

[180] See paras 8–049 to 8–053.

with third parties (that is the purpose of the agency rules), but that does not mean that anything the agent knows will also be "known" by the company; that would be far too wide a test.

In *El Ajou v Dollar Land Holdings Plc*,[181] the knowledge of a chairman who had responsibility for a particular category of transactions on the company's behalf was attributed to the company for the purposes of making the company liable for knowing receipt of the proceeds of a fraud. This finding was reached unanimously on the ground that the director was the "directing mind and will" of a company in relation to those transactions (only), but the court also held, unanimously, that the same conclusion could not have been reached on "agency" arguments. That conclusion has been doubted on the facts,[182] but the alternative "agency" analysis—arguably improperly so described—then looks very carefully at what knowledge should be *imputed* or *attributed* to the company on the basis of the role of the agent (rather like Hoffmann LJ did in *El Ajou*),[183] an approach which is on all fours with Lord Hoffmann's later judgment in *Meridian Global*. In short, the answer is invariably context specific, and perhaps for that reason difficult; it asks not what the agent was authorised or obliged to do, but asks the rather different question, looked at from an external perspective: i.e. given the various delegations within the company, whose knowledge is to count as the company's knowledge *for this purpose*?[184]

ATTRIBUTION ISSUES WHEN THE COMPANY IS THE CLAIMANT

We have been concerned in this chapter with how a company becomes liable in respect of wrongdoing when the wrongful acts and states of mind must necessarily have been those of natural persons. Our core case has been an action by the third party against the company. But the claim may be in the other direction: the company may sue in respect of wrongs done to it. In these circumstances, third party defendants may suggest the company's claim can be blocked on grounds of the company's own consent or illegality or its contributory negligence. In the ordinary course, this presents no special problem of attribution. But the difficult cases are claims by the company against its own wrongdoing directors or against third parties who ought to have discovered the very wrongdoing in issue (e.g. claims by the company against its auditors or bankers).[185] **8–049**

[181] *El-Ajou v Dollar Land Holdings Plc* [1994] 2 All E.R. 685.

[182] Watts, (2000) 116 L.Q.R. at 529. See also *Bilta (UK) Ltd v Nazir* [2015] B.C.C. 343 at [197].

[183] Which is why labelling the approach an "agency" approach is inapt—agency looks to the agreement between the principal and the agent; this does not.

[184] Thus, it is suggested, Lord Briggs was not correct to say that the ordinary basis for attributing the knowledge of directors or agents "is that they owe a duty to the company to report relevant knowledge about its affairs": *Julien v Evolving TecKnologies and Enterprise Development Co Ltd* [2018] UKPC 2 at [54]. Imputation of an agent's knowledge does not turn on the agent's duty to disclose (see *El-Ajou v Dollar Land Holdings Plc* [1994] 2 All E.R. 685 at 703–704) but, "simplified somewhat, on the general principle that principals should not be in a better position by employing agents than acting themselves": see P. Watts, "Attribution and limitation" (2018) 134 L.Q.R. 350, 353.

[185] The basis of these particular corporate claims is important, and considered in Ch.10 (actions against directors) and Ch.23 (auditors). Generally on this issue, see S. Worthington, "Corporate Attribution and Agency: Back to Basics" (2017) 133 L.Q.R. 118.

By way of illustration, consider a company whose managing director has used the company to defraud third parties and has then siphoned off the proceeds for his own benefit in circumstances where the company's auditors or bankers failed to detect the fraud. Third parties will certainly be able to sue the company for fraud: the director's fraud will be attributed to the company. But what should happen when the company sues its directors or its auditors or bankers for the losses caused by their respective breaches: how should attribution work to determine the company's own role in the wrong?

8–050 Consider first the claims against the company's directors. When a company (or its liquidator) is suing its own directors for wrongs they have done to the company, those directors may argue that the company's claim cannot be made out because the company knew of the wrong and thus acquiesced in it, or negligently failed to put stop to it, or is party to the illegality and so cannot sue to recover because of the illegality bar.[186] Logic suggests such arguments would make a mockery of directors duties, so they should be bound to fail when the defendant directors are raising their *own* personal knowledge and wrongdoing as the sole source of the company's attributed knowledge and wrongdoing, and suggesting that they then have a valid defence to the company's claim. The circularity and inappropriateness of this argument was recognised by the Supreme Court in *Bilta (UK) Ltd v Nazir*,[187] but only after a number of earlier false steps.[188]

The fact that the law will not permit attribution in these circumstances seems so sensible as not to merit debate, but the reason why this is so is less clearly articulated than might be hoped. When, if ever, is a director's act, knowledge, or intention to be attributed to a claimant company? In *Bilta (UK) Ltd v Nazir*, Lord Neuberger put it this way[189]:

> "the question is simply an open one: whether or not it is appropriate to attribute an action by, or a state of mind of, a company director or agent to the company or the agent's principal in relation to a particular claim against the company or the principal must depend on the nature and factual context of the claim in question."

In short, context is all, with the particular purpose of the duty in question between the claimant and defendant being the most important aspect of that context. A little more guidance will undoubtedly become necessary as more cases test the boundaries, especially in the face of the contrary findings in *Safeway Stores Ltd v*

[186] The current version of the illegality bar is set out in *Patel v Mirza* [2016] UKSC 42, a decision which has been the subject of a good deal of criticism.

[187] *Bilta (UK) Ltd v Nazir* [2015] B.C.C. 343. In the same vein, see *Singularis Holdings Ltd v Daiwa Capital Markets Europe Ltd* [2020] B.C.C. 89; *Moulin Global Eyecare Trading (In Liquidation) v The Commissioner of Inland Revenue* [2014] HKCFA 22. For similar conclusions in the criminal context, see *Attorney General's Reference (No.2 of 1982)* (1984) 1 B.C.C. 98973 CA (Crim Div); *R. v Phillipou (Christakis)* (1989) 5 B.C.C. 665 CA (Crim Div); *R. v Rozeik (Rifaat Younan)* [1996] B.C.C. 271 CA (Crim Div); *Faichney v Vantis HR Ltd* [2018] EWHC 565 (Ch), especially at [51] onwards (see fn.166).

[188] See *Stone & Rolls Ltd v Moore Stephens* [2009] P.N.L.R. 36; *Re Hampshire Land Co (No.2)* [1896] 2 Ch. 743 Ch D. *Bilta* and *Singularis* have expressed serious doubt about *Stone & Rolls*, but the difficult case of *Safeway Stores Ltd v Twigger* [2010] EWCA Civ 1472 (see fn.176) has not been overruled.

[189] *Bilta (UK) Ltd v Nazir* [2015] B.C.C. 343 at [9], expressly agreeing with Lord Mance's analysis at [37]–[44]. *Singularis* is to the same effect: see [2020] B.C.C. 89 at [30], [34] and [35].

Twigger.[190] For now, however, the attribution rules would seem to suggest that no individual can benefit from claims which rely on *their own* acts or knowledge counting as the company's acts or knowledge so as to give them either a claim or a defence against the company.

A company's claims against its directors are also subject to the limitation defence. The Limitation Act 1980 sets out rules for different types of claims. Some of those time limits are measured from the time the claimant knew of or could reasonably have discovered the wrong committed against it. Companies are clearly subject to the Act. That raises the question of whose knowledge will be attributed to the company for these purposes. Typically it is the company's board that decides whether or not to litigate, and its knowledge would certainly count. But what is to happen when the company is litigating against its directors? If the directors' knowledge of their own wrongdoing is to count as the company's knowledge, then time will run from the date of the wrongdoing even though "the company" (independent of its directors) may have no knowledge or means of knowledge at that stage. But if the directors' knowledge is not to count, then the shareholders' knowledge must count if the company is to be subject to any limitation rule at all in such claims. In *Julien v Evolving TecKnologies and Enterprise Development Co Ltd*,[191] the Privy Council declined to answer the question as to how that might be done, but set out clearly the difficulties facing such endeavours, even when the company had only a single shareholder, as in this case. **8–051**

A different issue, and a still more difficult question, arises where companies are not suing their directors, but suing other third parties, such as their auditors or bankers. In these circumstances the company may resist having the knowledge of its own directors' wrongdoing attributed to them in a manner that would defeat the company's claim entirely (because of causation and/or illegality) or reduce it significantly on the basis of the company's own contributory negligence. The leading case is *Singularis Holdings Ltd (In Liquidation) v Daiwa Capital Markets Europe Ltd*.[192] There, the company's "directing mind" (though not the only director) and sole shareholder fraudulently deprived the company of substantial sums by directing its broker-banker to pay the money away. The court held that the bank was in breach of its *Quincecare* duty: acting carefully, it should have **8–052**

[190] *Safeway Stores Ltd v Twigger* [2010] EWCA Civ 1472 CA (but doubted in *Bilta*, see fn.227). The case looks increasingly difficult to justify. The question the court had to answer, and one it conceded was difficult, was whether, if a company had been fixed with the improper intentions of its company officers and subjected to a regulatory sanction (under the Competition Act), the company could then seek an indemnity from those same defaulting officers. The answer might seem simple: that the breach of duty by the officers had caused the company a loss, for which it could seek compensation. But this possibility was decisively rejected by the Court of Appeal. The policy underpinning the Competition Act 1998 was to impose "personal" sanctions on firms, the court held, and this liability could not then be offloaded onto individuals. To reach this end, the court relied on the illegality defence (i.e. the disqualifying principle of ex turpi causa).

[191] *Julien v Evolving TecKnologies and Enterprise Development Co Ltd* [2018] UKPC 2; [2018] B.C.C. 376.

[192] *Singularis Holdings Ltd v Daiwa Capital Markets Europe Ltd* [2020] B.C.C. 89. *Stone & Rolls Ltd v Moore Stephens* [2009] P.N.L.R. 36, which only applied to "one-man companies", has not been overruled, but its approach has been seriously doubted: see *Bilta (UK) Ltd v Nazir* [2015] B.C.C. 343; and *Singularis* itself.

realised that something suspicious was going on and suspended payment until it had made reasonable enquiries to satisfy itself that the payments were properly to be made. The Supreme Court held that the company should not be denied its claim on the basis that the knowledge of the company's "directing mind" should be attributed to the company, because that would be to "denude the [*Quincecare*] duty of any value in cases where it is most needed".[193] This, the court said, meant that the court did not need to consider the particular defences raised by the bank: attribution was simply not possible in any event, although even if it had been possible, all the defences would have failed.[194]

In other words, once again, attribution is context specific, and the purpose of the duty in issue is what is key in determining context. But whether this generalises the issues too far is worth pause. Banks owe their customers the *Quincecare* duty. Attribution cannot affect the existence of the duty; nor can it affect whether the bank's conduct breaches the duty—that is determined by what the bank does in making the payments requested by its customers. But it can affect whether the bank's breach of duty is considered to have caused the customer's loss, given what the customer may be taken to know. It is here that attribution is important, and it is here that allowing attribution would "denude the [*Quincecare*] duty of any value in cases where it is most needed". But putting the analysis this way also makes it plain that the same argument—that attribution should not be allowed—may not be apt if the bank admits that it has breached its duty and caused loss, but argues that the company is also contributorily negligent, or that the company cannot advance its claim because of the illegality defence.

Take a company's claim against its auditors. The causation question (and the possibility that attribution would denude the auditor's duty of any real value) raises easier questions than contributory negligence and illegality. For example, "denuding the duty of any real value" may be an apt answer as to why a company should still be able to claim against its auditors even though the company's "directing mind" knew of the frauds and indeed tried to keep them from being discovered by the auditor. The short answer is that it is the auditor's job to detect such frauds: this is the "very thing" their duty requires of them.[195] But even so, if the circumstances are apt, should the auditors be able to rely on the alternative defences that the company is contributorily negligent, or that its claim is barred by the illegality defence?

8–053 So far as contributory negligence is concerned, if attribution were barred by a blanket rule, this would provide an incentive for companies not to manage their internal risk systems effectively; on the other hand, allowing the defence would have the opposite effect, reducing the incentive of the auditors to discover

193 *Singularis Holdings Ltd v Daiwa Capital Markets Europe Ltd* [2020] B.C.C. 89 at [35].

194 Nonetheless, the court held the defences to be without merit in any event, those claimed being that any fraudulent conduct on the part of the "directing mind" was to be treated as the misconduct of the company, with the consequences (1) that the company was complicit in the fraudulent activity and could not bring a claim arising from its own illegal activity ("the illegality defence"); (2) that the company's loss was caused by its own fault and not by that of the defendant, so there was no causation in law ("the causation argument"); and (3) that the defendant bank would have an equal and countervailing claim in deceit.

195 And, despite the outcome in *Stone & Rolls*, perhaps *Bilta* and *Singularis* would now lead to this outcome.

wrongdoing within the company when that is "the very thing" their duty requires them to do. Nevertheless, on balance, it would seem the defence of contributory negligence has value. However, its use needs to be careful: in this regard the company's negligence is not automatically built on the actions of subordinate employees; the *company's* contribution to the loss comes from its failure to have in place appropriate management systems, not from the mere fact that those systems did not prevent all fraud, perhaps even including that it did not prevent the fraud of the "directing mind and will".[196]

The illegality defence raises even more problems, partly, but not only, because the defence itself remains uncertain.[197] This defence was in issue in an extreme form in the case of *Stone & Rolls Ltd v Moore Stephens*.[198] The defendant auditors successfully sought to raise the defence of illegality as a complete defence to liability. In this case, the sole beneficial shareholder and controlling shadow director of a company had established the company for the purpose of committing large-scale fraud on banks. The company, in liquidation, sought compensation for the negligent failure of the auditors to discover the fraud. The House of Lords allowed attribution, and denied the company its claim, on the basis that the company was a "one man company" and the illegality defence prevented the wrongdoer from using court processes to profit from his own wrong. It mattered not that the wrongdoing auditors would escape liability (that is often the consequence of the illegality defence), nor, with less justification, that the company's creditors would then recover nothing. The case has been so roundly criticised that it seems nothing can now safely be taken from the judgments.[199] It would now seem—rightly it is suggested—that the illegality defence would not apply where the claims advanced by the company will go to benefit the company's innocent shareholders or creditors. But, unlikely though the scenario is, could the controller of a solvent one man company fraudulently denude the company for his own benefit and then have his company sue the auditors who failed to detect the fraud, thus benefitting, albeit indirectly, yet again? The answer to that, it is suggested, ought to be no.

To summarise, as was said in *Singularis*, "the key to any question of attribution [is] always to be found in considerations of the context and the purpose for which the attribution [is] relevant".[200]

PERSONAL LIABILITY OF DIRECTORS AND OTHER AGENTS

In this final section we turn from examining the liability of companies for their own actions to considering the personal liability of the directors or agents who 8–054
"caused" the company act, and in particular, "caused" the company to breach its contract or commit a tort or crime. Two different claimants may have these

---

[196] See, e.g. *Barings Plc (In Liquidation) v Coopers & Lybrand (No.7)* [2003] EWHC 1319 (Ch); [2003] P.N.L.R. 34.

[197] *Patel v Mirza* [2016] UKSC 42, and see fn.186.

[198] *Stone & Rolls Ltd v Moore Stephens* [2009] P.N.L.R. 36.

[199] See fn.1.

[200] *Singularis* [2020] B.C.C. 89 at [30] and repeated at [34]. To the same ends, see S. Worthington, "Corporate Attribution and Agency: Back to Basics" (2017) L.Q.R. 118.

directors or other agents in their sightlines. First, the company: if the company is found to have committed some wrong, then meeting the resulting liability will drain the company's resources at a cost to the company's shareholders. The company's response may be to pursue the individuals whose actions counted as the company's and thereby caused or contributed to the company's loss. In principle, the legal rules are straightforward: if the company can show that the individual director or agent acted in breach of a duty owed to the company (a duty that might be found in contract or tort or under statute), and that the breach caused loss, then recovery of compensation should follow. We examine in detail the rules which apply in this context when the company's claim is against its own directors: the duties owed by directors to their companies are set out in CA 2006, and the related law is considered in detail in Ch.10.[201]

But the company is not the only potential claimant. Third parties injured by the company's breach of contract, or its tort or crime, may wish to sue the individual actors behind the company, especially if those individuals have deeper pockets than the company. We have already seen that third parties cannot simply "pierce the corporate veil", ignoring the company's existence to pursue its shareholders.[202] But can they pursue the very individuals whose acts delivered the corporate wrongs done to them? The answer is, yes, they can, although—other than in tort cases—only rarely. However, to reach that conclusion requires the third parties to establish a particular duty owed to them by the director or agent and a breach of that duty causing loss to the third party. Neither the duty nor any liability to the third party arises simply because the director or agent was the moving hand in the company's wrongdoing, except of course in cases where the company is vicariously liable for that very wrong. We need to consider the different contexts separately, and begin with vicarious liability.

Liability of corporate agents when the company is vicariously liable

8–055 Where the company is vicariously liable for a tort, it follows automatically, given the nature of vicarious liability, that the victim of the tort can sue either the agent who committed the tort (and is directly liable) or the company (which is vicariously liable). The agent and the company are joint tortfeasors.[203] This means that not only can the victim of the tort sue either the company or the wrongdoing agent; it also means that the company can claim a contribution from the agent towards the damages payable by the company to the third party. Since, in this context, the company is a wholly innocent party, that contribution will usually be a complete one, i.e. an indemnity.[204] Of course, there may be good non-legal reasons for reluctance on the part of the company, as an employer, to seek a contribution from an employee. Equally, where the employee has acted in

[201] We do not consider the various claims a company may make against its employees or other non-director agents, as these raise no special issues of company law. Note, however, the point made at para.8–055.

[202] See Ch.7, especially paras 7–018 to 7–021.

[203] *New Zealand Guardian Trust Co Ltd v Brooks* [1995] B.C.C. 407 PC.

[204] Civil Liability (Contribution) Act 1978 s.1; *Lister v Romford Ice and Cold Storage Co Ltd* [1957] A.C. 555 HL.

a way required by the employer in the discharge of his duties, the employee may have a claim for an indemnity against the employer, so that the employer's contribution claim would be barred for circularity. However, this will not be the case where commission of the act which attracted tortious liability on the company constituted a breach of duty or of the contract of employment on the part of the agent or employee.[205]

Liability of non-involved directors

The question is sometimes raised as to whether a director can be liable in tort to a third party injured by a corporate wrong simply by virtue of his directorship of the company. The justice of the claim is often seen to lie in the failure of the non-involved director to prevent the harm caused by the wrongdoers in the company. Even putting the assertion in that way makes it clear that, in principle, that the answer is in the negative, even if the active tortfeasors are other directors of the company. As long ago as 1878, Fry J said in a case of fraudulent misrepresentation[206] that two classes of person could be responsible to the third party for the fraud (the agent who actually made the fraudulent misrepresentations and the principal on the basis of direct or vicarious liability) but that "one agent is not responsible for the acts of another agent". This principle has been confirmed in a number of subsequent cases.[207] 8–056

On the other hand, all directors are responsible for the management of their company, and so the non-involved directors may well be liable in negligence to their own company, not to the third party, for the losses caused to their company by their own lack of reasonable vigilance, if that can be shown to be the case.[208] But otherwise it is true that involvement in the management of the company does not lead to personal liability unless the director or manager personally commits a wrong.

Liability of directors and agents as accessories or for their own torts

Thus it follows that if the third party wishes to sue an individual within the company, and not (or not merely) the company itself for the harm suffered, then the third party must establish a claim directly against that individual. We have seen this already in Ch.7 in the context of "piercing the corporate veil". There are two broad approaches to such claims: the first is to find that the corporate actor is an accessory to the company's wrongdoing; the second is to find that the corporate actor has committed a separate wrong. As illustrated below, neither approach is established merely by asserting that the corporate agent was the 8–057

[205] As already noted, the duties of directors are discussed in Ch.10. For non-director managers the conduct might be a breach of their contracts of employment. See M.R. Freedland, *The Personal Employment Contract* (Oxford: OUP, 2003), pp.146–147.

[206] *Cargill v Bower No.2* (1878) 10 Ch. D. 502 Ch D at 513–514.

[207] *Rainham Chemical Works Ltd (In Liquidation) v Belvedere Fish Guano Co Ltd* [1921] 2 A.C. 465 HL; *Performing Right Society Ltd v Ciryl Theatrical Syndicate Ltd* [1924] 1 K.B. 1 CA; *British Thomson-Houston Co Ltd v Stirling Accessories Ltd* [1924] 2 Ch. 33 Ch D.

[208] See para.10–047.

"moving hand" in the company's own wrongdoing, whether that wrongdoing is the commission of a tort or the breach of a contract.

Take accessory liability in the context of torts committed by the company. If a director, whilst not committing the tort themselves, authorises or procures the commission of the tortious act by someone else, whether that act constitutes deceit or some other tort, there will be liability on the part of the director as a joint tortfeasor with the person who commits the tort. This liability arises under the normal rules applying to accessory liability in the law of tort, but it is an important extension of tort liability in the company context. Given the managerial role of directors in companies' affairs, they are more likely to procure the commission of tortious acts than to commit those acts themselves. It is not necessary that that the director authorising or procuring the tortious acts should realise their tortious nature or display any other particular mental element in relation to the acts, unless this is a requirement of the tort being so authorised or procured.[209] Accessory liability for equitable wrongs is also possible.[210]

The rules about accessory liability for directors who procure tortious acts, together with the vicarious liability of the company for unauthorised and forbidden acts sufficiently connected with the company's business, provide a strong incentive for directors to acquaint themselves with, and to secure observance by the company's agents of, the tort rules which impinge upon the company's business. Nevertheless, the principle of personal liability is still controversial in some quarters.[211] In many ways the policy issues raised in this context are the mirror images of the difficult doctrinal and policy issues raised in the context of finding the company vicariously liable for the torts of its agents.[212]

8–058 Similarly difficult issues arise where the company is found liable for breach of contract. Here, however, the approach is not quite the same as in tort. The starting point is clear. If the contract is between the company and the third party, then only the company can be sued on the contract[213]: it is not possible to insist, merely from involvement, that the agent negotiating the contract is also a contracting party, nor, equally, that the agent causing the breach by the company

209 *C Evans & Sons Ltd v Spritebrand Ltd* (1985) 1 B.C.C. 99316 CA (Civ Div); *Mancetter Developments v Garmanson and Givertz* (1986) 2 B.C.C. 98924 CA (Civ Div); *MCA Records Inc v Charly Records Ltd (No.5)* [2001] EWCA Civ 1441; [2002] B.C.C. 650; *Koninklijke Philips Electronics NV v Princo Digital Disc GmbH* [2003] EWHC 2588 (Pat); cf. *White Horse Distilleries Ltd v Gregson Associates Ltd* [1984] R.P.C. 61 Ch D.

210 *Royal Brunei Airlines Sdn Bhd v Tan* [1995] B.C.C. 899, and also see fn.149.

211 See the attempt by Nourse J in the *White Horse* case (see fn.209) to restrict the director's personal liability to those situations where he acted "deliberately or recklessly and so as to make [the tortious conduct] his own, as distinct from the act or conduct of the company". This approach seems to have been motivated by a desire to preserve the benefits of limited liability, especially in a one-person company. In other words, Nourse J proposed a general "assumption of responsibility" test (for all torts) in the case of tortious conduct authorised by the directors. See also *MCA Records* (fn.209) where the court drew a distinction between control exercised through the constitutional organs of the company (e.g. voting at board meetings—not attracting tortious liability) and control exercised otherwise (potentially attracting tortious liability). Some of these distinctions—supposedly based on doctrine or principle—might, and should now, be drawn more carefully.

212 In that context, see the discussion at para.8–039 and the authorities noted in fn.137.

213 See para.8–016.

is also personally liable for that breach.[214] But can the agent be held liable for the tort of inducing the breach of contract by the company, or the tort of conspiracy with the company to cause loss by unlawful means? We saw such claims advanced in *Sevilleja v Marex Financial Ltd*,[215] although there the focus of the court's judgment was not on the tort itself, but on issues of reflective loss.

The line of authority is often said to start with the much-debated case of *Said v Butt*.[216] There the plaintiff procured a theatre ticket in another's name, knowing that if his true identity were known he would have been refused admission. When admission was refused, the plaintiff sued the theatre's managing director for causing, or inducing, the breach of contract. McCardie J dismissed the claim on the basis that the non-disclosure rendered the contract void in any event, since the identity of the plaintiff was a material element in its formation. However, obiter, he held that a director would not be liable for inducing a breach of contract by his company if the director was acting bona fide within the scope of his authority. This principle has been extended to cover the tort of conspiring to cause loss by unlawful means where the means is breach of contract (if there is a different between the two claims). Two issues are immediately apparent: why is there such a difference between the typical liability of the agent in tort, and, secondly, how extensive is the protection offered by the rule in *Said v Butt*? Neither question has been well addressed by the courts.

The first might be answered by acknowledging that it is widely recognised that not all contracts can, or will, be performed: in that sense, although performance is expected, what is required by the law is performance or the payment of damages. By contrast, tort law does not operate on the basis that harm can be caused so long as it is paid for: those who commit torts, or cause them to be committed, are personally liable for the harm caused. Further, with contracts, the company is clearly the primary recipient of any benefits from the contract and might thus be regarded as justifiably the primary bearer of its burdens. It might then seem justifiable that the director, or corporate agent, should only be liable to third parties in limited contexts.[217]

But what are those limited contexts? McCardie J suggest the director is not liable if he or she acts within authority and bona fide, but is it bona fide to act in a way which will necessarily cause the company to breach its contract with the third party? This area of the law has now been usefully examined in some detail by Lane J in *Antuzis v DJ Houghton Catching Services Ltd*.[218] The case

[214] Of course, as noted above, the *company* may be able to sue such an agent for the loses his or her actions have caused to the company.

[215] *Sevilleja v Marex Financial Ltd* [2020] UKSC 31; [2020] B.C.C. 783: see the discussion above at para.7–012 and below at para.14–010 on reflective loss.

[216] *Said v Butt* [1920] 3 K.B. 497 KBD. See the detailed analysis of this case by Steven Chong JA in *Arthaputra v St Microelectronics Asia Pacific Pte Ltd* [2018] SGCA 17 at [54] onwards; cited extensively by Lane J in *Antuzis v DJ Houghton Catching Services Ltd* [2019] EWHC 843 (QB) at [113]. In the UK, also see *G Scammell & Nephew Ltd v Hurley* [1929] 1 K.B. 419 CA at 443 and 449; *DC Thomson & Co Ltd v Deakin* [1952] Ch. 646 CA at 680–681; and especially *Ridgeway Maritime Inc v Beulah Wings Ltd (The Leon)* [1991] 2 Lloyd's Rep. 611 QBD (Comm) at 624–25 (Waller J).

[217] Indeed, a different rule would mean that directors or other corporate agents involved in performing contracts would almost invariably be personally liable to third parties for their breach. That is clearly an unworkable conclusion.

[218] *Antuzis v DJ Houghton Catching Services Ltd* [2019] EWHC 843 (QB).

concerned Lithuanians working as chicken catchers in dreadful conditions, on less than the minimum wage, working extremely long hours, with payments withheld as a form of punishment, and without holiday pay. The issue before the court was whether the company's sole shareholder and director, and the company secretary, could be made personally liable for inducing the company to breach the claimants' employment contracts. After an extensive review of the law, some of which is noted above, Lane J concluded that

> "it is the [director's or agent's] conduct and intention in relation *to his duties towards the company—not towards the third party*—that provide the focus of the 'bona fide' enquiry to be undertaken pursuant to the rule in *Said v Butt*"[219] (emphasis added),

and only where that conduct constituted a breach by the agent of his or her duties to the company would the agent be found liable in tort to the third party for inducing the company's breach of contract. He illustrated the rationale as follows[220]:

> "There is, plainly, a world of difference between, on the one hand, a director consciously and deliberately causing a company to breach its contract with a supplier, by not paying the supplier on time because, unusually, the company has encountered cash flow difficulties [where the director would not be personally liable in tort], and, on the other hand, a director of a restaurant company who decides the company should supply customers of the chain with burgers made of horse meat instead of beef, on the basis that horse meat is cheaper [where the director would be liable in tort]."

In *Antuzis*, the director and secretary were clearly acting in breach of several of their duties to the company; in short, they were not acting bona fide vis-à-vis their company. They could thus be found liable to the company's employees for the tort of inducing a breach of the employment contracts, provided only that all the elements of that tort could be made out.[221]

Liability of directors when the company has committed a crime

8–059 We turn next to the context where the company has committed a crime. Is a director exposed to criminal liability where he or she has not committed the criminal act for which the company is liable? In principle, the answer is no, but there are important exceptions. The common law generally treats as guilty of the offence those who counsel or procure the commission of that offence, in this context the commission of the offence by the company.[222] This common law liability will arise even in relation to statutory offences, unless the statute excludes it. Further, many statutes expressly impose a somewhat similar liability expressly upon directors and managers where they "consent to or connive in" the

---

[219] *Antuzis v DJ Houghton Catching Services Ltd* [2019] EWHC 843 (QB) at [114]. Lane J found support for this conclusion in the judgment of *The Leon* [1991] 2 Lloyd's Rep. 611 at 624–625.

[220] *Antuzis v DJ Houghton Catching Services Ltd* [2019] EWHC 843 (QB) at [120].

[221] For a clear exposition of the necessary elements of the tort itself, see *OBG Ltd v Allan* [2007] UKHL 21; [2007] E.M.L.R. 12 at [39]–[44] (Lord Hoffmann).

[222] See para.8–055, for the similar approach in tort.

commission of an offence by the company.[223] Under this rule the director or manager can be criminally liable personally where he or she is fully aware of or approves the corporate criminal offence, even though that awareness or approval do not encourage or assist the commission of the offence by the company. The imposition of criminal liability in this situation puts strong pressure on directors and managers to intervene and prevent wrongdoing within the company when they are aware of it.

Liability for the principal offence may also be imposed under another common statutory formula which goes considerably beyond consent or connivance. Under this second statutory formula, liability is imposed when neglect by a director or manager has contributed to the commission of the offence by the company.[224] Here, a causal link between the neglect by the director and the commission of the offence by the company must be shown (an element not required under the "consent or connivance" formula) but the director or manager is made liable for the principal offence without necessarily being subjectively aware of the wrongdoing within the company. The Law Commission has suggested that it is unfair to impose liability upon the director for the principal offence in this second case, if the offence requires proof of fault or conviction carries a high stigma. However, the Commission did accept that it is appropriate in some circumstances to impose a separate liability for negligently failing to prevent the commission of an offence by the company.[225]

Finally, the director (or manager) might be civilly liable, either to the victim of crime or to the offending company. The first might arise if the statute creating the criminal offence is interpreted as also creating, by inference, a civil duty, owed by the company's directors (not the company) to the potential victims, to ensure compliance with the statute, and liability in damages to the victims if that duty is breached: for reasons that are perhaps self-evident, the argument is rarely successful.[226] Alternatively, and with more obvious justification, the director may be held liable to the *company* for the loss suffered by it as a result of the commission of an offence, on the grounds that permitting or causing the company to commit the offence was a breach of duty or breach of contract by the director as against the company.[227]

The Corporate Manslaughter Act deserves special comment. Since the real **8–060**
deterrent effect of any sanction turns on its impact on the management of the

[223] The standard formulation covers "a director, manager, secretary or similar officer", those who purport to act as such, and the members of the company if its affairs are conducted by the members and the member had a membership function. See, e.g. CA 2006 s.1255 (in respect of Pt 42 on "Statutory Auditors"); Fraud Act 2006 s.12.

[224] An example is s.400 of the Financial Services and Markets Act 2000, which imposes consent or connivance liability as well.

[225] This would avoid the stigma associated with conviction for the principal offence, e.g. where the company has been convicted of an offence involving dishonesty.

[226] For an unsuccessful attempt to run this argument, see *Campbell v Peter Gordon Joiners Ltd* [2016] UKSC 38; 2016 S.L.T. 887, considered above at para.7–015.

[227] But contrast *Safeway Stores Ltd v Twigger* [2010] EWCA Civ 1472 where such a claim fell foul of the illegality defence on the grounds that it would be inconsistent with the purpose of the particular statute imposing liability on the company that the company should recover its loss from the directors. The correctness of this decision has been doubted: *Bilta (UK) Ltd v Nazir* [2015] B.C.C. 343 at [52] (Lord Mance) and [156]–[162] (Lords Toulson and Hodge).

company, one may wonder whether the criminal liability of the company is something of a side-show, unlike in tort law where the compensatory goals of tort law are advanced by corporate liability. One might further wonder whether the crucial issue rather is the personal criminal liability of the directors or other senior managers, as discussed immediately above, rather than the liability of the company. Thus, it is not surprising that, during the passage of the 2007 Act, there was an intensive debate about whether penalties—whether by way of criminal sanctions or by way of disqualification—should be imposed on those members of the senior management of the company who were to blame for the organisational failings. In this debate, the wheel thus came full circle: under the directing mind and will doctrine the crimes of individual managers make the company liable; now the question was how far corporate crime should make individual managers liable. The Government resisted strongly any moves in this direction. The 2007 Act creates corporate offences only and excludes criminal liability even in relation to the counselling and procuring form of the offence, though disqualification is possible.[228]

CONCLUSION

8–061 As we observed at the beginning of this chapter, since the company is a separate but abstract legal person, it can act only through natural legal persons. From this trite proposition a complex body of law has emerged to determine which people in which circumstances can be regarded as having acted as or on behalf of the company. Nevertheless, some lines on the map are clear. In relation to contracting the modern tendency has been to promote the security of third parties' transactions by reducing the impact of restrictions in the company's constitution upon the effectiveness of the contracting process. As far as directors are concerned, the operation of the rules of agency normally means they are not liable or entitled on the resulting contracts, but only the company is. By contrast, in the areas of tort and crime the personal liability of those acting on behalf of the company is the normal rule. However, there is a growing tendency to extend corporate liability in tort and crime in recent years through expansion of direct liability, the downgrading the "directing mind and will" test, and an increasing number of focused statutory interventions.

[228] 2007 Act s.18. Conviction for an indictable offence in connection with the management of the company is a basis for disqualification, as is, even without conviction, unfitness to be involved in the management of a company. See Ch.20.

PART 3

REGULATING BOARDS AND INDIVIDUAL DIRECTORS

Over the past 30 years, corporate governance has been a popular and highly contested topic in company law and has generated an enormous literature.[1] The subject came to prominence in the US with the work leading to the publication of the American Law Institute's *Principles of Corporate Governance* in 1994 and in the UK the topic is associated above all with the Cadbury Committee Report of 1992 and its associated Code of Best Practice,[2] which has provided a focal point for the subsequent spread of corporate governance codes throughout Europe.[3] Board best practice, implemented via such codes is now commonplace, with the codes subject to constant review.

Notwithstanding this modern focus on the topic, the subject matter of corporate governance, whether recognised under that name or not, is as old as the large company. The feature which the corporate governance debate takes as its starting point is the appearance, in large companies, of a group of senior managers who are separate and distinct from the shareholders. Of course, in economically large companies with large groups of shareholders, there are good reasons why the functions of management should be carried out by a smaller, separate, though possibly overlapping, group of people: where the numbers of shareholders are large, taking management decisions through the shareholders

[1] It is too vast to cite but for a representative sample of this work, see K.J. Hopt et al (eds), *Comparative Corporate Governance* (Oxford: Clarendon Press, 1998); K.J. Hopt et al (eds), *Corporate Governance in Context* (Oxford: OUP, 2005); M. Moore and M. Petrin, *Corporate Governance: Law, Regulation and Theory* (London: Red Globe Press, 2017); A. Keay, *Board Accountability in Corporate Governance* (London: Routledge, 2017); and J.N. Gordon and W.-G. Ringe (eds), *The Oxford Handbook of Corporate Law and Governance* (Oxford: OUP, 2020). And placing this endeavour in context, see B.R. Cheffins, "The History of Corporate Governance" in M. Wright et al. (eds), *The Oxford Handbook of Corporate Governance* (Oxford: OUP, 2013), p.46; and "The Rise of Corporate Governance in the U.K.: When and Why" (2015) C.L.P. 387.

[2] *Report of the Committee on the Financial Aspects of Corporate Governance* (1992). See further below, paras 19–016 to 19–021.

[3] Such codes have become a standard feature in continental Europe: see Weil, Gotshal & Manges (on behalf of the European Commission), *Comparative Study of Corporate Governance Codes Relevant to the European Union and its Members* (January 2002). For an index of codes, see *https://ecgi.global/content/codes* [Accessed 9 February 2021].

would be impossibly cumbersome. Further, perhaps especially where the company's capital needs have led to a public offering of its shares, there is no reason to suppose that those who buy the shares have the necessary expertise or commitment to run a large business organisation, and that is likely to be just as true of professional fund managers as it is of individual members of the public. In such a situation, the emergence of a specialist cadre of corporate managers is a natural development, managers who do not simply do as the shareholders say but who develop and implement corporate strategy as their own responsibility. In order for such managers to exercise these functions, it is necessary that a very broad set of discretionary powers be conferred upon them. In some jurisdictions this is done through the companies legislation itself, although in the UK this result is achieved by the practice of including provisions in the company's articles giving the board of directors extensive power to manage the company's business and to exercise the company's powers.

Thus arises the central issue of the corporate governance debate, which is the accountability of the senior management of the company for the extensive powers vested in them. Since the historical development was, or is perceived to have been, one of a movement from a situation in which shareholders were both investors and managers to one in which management became a separate function from that of investment, it is natural to think of the accountability issue as being one of the accountability of the managers to the shareholders. This is the tradition in British company law, tempered only by the qualification, which we note at several points in Pt 3 but which we will see again particularly in Pt 5, that, as the company nears insolvency, accountability to the creditors is as important as, and even replaces, accountability to the shareholders. However, the separation out of management as a distinct function creates the possibility of imposing lines of accountability on management towards other groups who have a long-term interest in the company (usually referred to as "stakeholders"). This accountability can be achieved in various ways. For example, in about half of the Member States of the EU, one particular group of such stakeholders, the employees, has become a notable beneficiary of the accountability rules of corporate law with that outcome achieved mainly through board representation. A similar route was once proposed by an official committee for the UK,[4] but board representation is not an idea which has taken root within British company law, though some traces of it can be found. In its detailed examination of company law, the Company Law Review did not find sufficient support for the stakeholder model to justify a major shift in the accountability rules,[5] and so it concentrated its efforts on promoting a modernised and inclusive version of the tradition of accountability to shareholders.[6] That "enlightened shareholder value" approach found its way into the CA 2006.

Given this particular focus, any desired improvements in the corporate governance of companies are likely to be mediated through a focus on the company's managers, especially on the quality, composition and practices of the

---

[4] *Report of the Committee of Inquiry on Industrial Democracy*, Cmnd.6706 (1975) (the Bullock Report).

[5] Strategic, Ch.5.1; Developing, Ch.2.

[6] Final Report, Ch.3. For what this might entail, see paras 10–026 to 10–039.

board of directors, or alternatively through a focus on the shareholders, and the role they are expected to play in monitoring the company's management. This Part focuses on the former; Pt 4 focuses, in part, on the latter.

Despite the widespread focus on corporate governance issues, some ("managerialists") have gone so far as to argue that elaborate accountability structures are not necessary because management will function so as to adjudicate neutrally and impartially among the competing claims of the various stakeholder groups on the company. This vision, however, ignores the fact that management itself is an important stakeholder group and it is difficult to see why, in the absence of accountability rules, managers would not give in to the temptation to overvalue their own claims on the company and undervalue those of other groups, for example, in the setting of their own remuneration. However, the managerialists make a better point when they argue that the accountability rules will be self-defeating if they operate so as to prevent or discourage managers from discharging effectively the tasks which the institution of centralised management entrusts to them. In other words, the accountability rules, no matter to whom the accountability lies, must not be so restrictive as to stifle the entrepreneurial talents of the managers, which talents constitute the rationale for conferring the wide discretion upon them in the first place.

Since the emergence of specialised management is not a phenomenon limited to the last 30 years—large companies with such managements can be traced back at least as far as the late nineteenth century—it is not surprising that company law has always contained some mechanisms whereby the accountability issue can be addressed. The very requirement that a company appoint directors[7] provides a rudimentary mechanism for accountability. Unlike a partnership, where all the partners are prima facie entitled to participate in the management of the partnership,[8] in a company the requirement for directors presupposes that directors will play an important role, at least in large companies. In short, the default rule in partnerships is management by the partners; in companies, it is management by the directors. However, since British company law, unlike the corporate governance codes, says little or nothing about the structure and composition of the board of directors, the board's position in company law is deeply ambiguous. The board is the point of contact between the shareholders as a group and the senior management of the company, but whether, in any particular company or in companies generally, it acts predominantly as a monitor of the management on behalf of the shareholders or mechanism through which the managers promote their control of the company is a matter for empirical investigation—and the situation may vary from company to company and from time to time. As we shall see in the following chapter, in order to reduce the likelihood of boards acting purely as instruments of management domination, modern corporate governance codes have been concerned to restrict the proportion of board seats held by the managers of the company by requiring the presence of a proportion of "non-executive" directors on the board.

---

[7] CA 2006 s.154 (at least two for public companies and one for private companies).

[8] Partnership Act 1890 s.24(5); LLP Regulations 2001 (SI 2001/1090) reg.7(3). However, the partners are free to create, by agreement, delegation structures akin to those found in companies, and in large partnerships normally do so.

Despite the ambiguous role of the board, it constitutes a convenient focus for the legislature and the courts when developing rules to constrain the exercise by management of the discretion vested in them. Whether the board monitors management or does the managing itself (or does a bit of each), imposition of accountability rules on the board should have an impact, directly or indirectly, on the way the management function is discharged. The underlying aim of the law may be control of the management function, but the subjects of the legal rules are the directors. The issue of how far those controls extend to managers who are not directors is, as we shall see, controversial. By the same token, when the articles delegate a wide discretion from the shareholders, they do so by conferring power, not on the company's managers as such, but on the board of directors. The rules conferring the powers and the rules constraining the exercise of the powers focus on the board rather than on the senior management as a whole. Thus, although the corporate governance debate starts from the functional differentiation between investment and management, company law operates by regulating the actions, not of managers in general, but of the board of directors.

In this Part we look at the rules which the courts, the legislature and business bodies have created to constrain the board collectively and the directors individually in the exercise of the discretion vested in them. The first set of rules focuses on the structure and composition of the board of directors, matters upon which the Companies Acts and the common law have traditionally had little to say, but which are a central focus for the corporate governance codes. These codes typically do not concern themselves with the outcomes that should be delivered by boards—companies are too diverse for such a generalised approach—but by the processes and approaches that should be adopted to deliver these outcomes. Secondly, this time focusing on individual directors, we consider the set of rules which the common law and the legislature have spent much effort in elaborating, from the very beginnings of modern company law in the first half of the nineteenth century. This is the law of "directors' duties" and, as important, the law relating to the enforcement of those duties. These duties operate directly upon the directors so as to control the ways in which they exercise their discretion. When these duties are breached, the decision which the directors have taken may be ineffective or at least capable of being set aside, or the director may have to compensate the company for any harm it has suffered, or account to the company for profits made from the breach of duty, or some other remedy may be available. In considering these two sets of rules, however, we should not lose sight of the fact that there is a third important source of control over directors, and that lies in the hands of those who have the power to elect and remove them. In Ch.11 we consider the extent to which the shareholders have the power to appoint or, more importantly, remove the directors of the company. How easy is it, for example, for the shareholders to remove directors who exercise their powers in a way which elicits the disapproval of the shareholders?

Although the rules discussed in this Part are a central part of company law and the subject of public controversy, it is important to stress that the problem they aim to deal with is premised upon a distinction between those who are shareholders in the company and those who are its directors. In the case of economically small companies—being the majority of companies on the register—this situation does not obtain because the shareholders and the directors are the same people. For such companies, the rules analysed in this Part are of less significance. It would be wrong to say that they are of no significance, since pursing directors for compensation can loom large if these companies become insolvent. In addition, those who are the owner/controllers of a small company may fall out with one another and one faction may be tempted to act in a way which is in breach of their duties as directors, for example, by diverting corporate opportunities away from the jointly-owned company to another controlled wholly by themselves. However, even when there is a falling out among the owner-controllers, the situation is probably better analysed as a conflict between one group of shareholder/directors and another group, rather than a conflict between shareholders on the one hand and directors on the other. We discuss this issue further in Pt 4 of this work.

Finally, even when one is dealing with an economically large company with shareholders who are distinct from the managers, the complexity of the problems thrown up by the shareholder/director relationship depends significantly upon the structure of the company's shareholdings, in particular on whether they are concentrated or dispersed. Where there is concentrated shareholding (for example, one shareholder who holds a block of shares which gives him or her de facto control of the company), there will normally be little difficulty in that shareholder ensuring that the directors do as the shareholder wishes. The more problematic issue is likely to be whether the controlling shareholder takes appropriate account of the interests of the non-controlling shareholders. In this case, again, the potential conflict is one between controlling and non-controlling shareholders rather than between shareholders and directors, although again some aspects of directors' duties, for example, those concerning related-party transactions, may be relevant here. However, block-holder control of economically large companies is relatively uncommon in the UK, where a more dispersed pattern of shareholding still prevails, notwithstanding the increasing power of institutional investors. Consequently, the issue of shareholder and director relationships is a crucial one.

Chapter 9

THE BOARD AND ITS DIRECTORS

The Role of the Board

The board of directors is the most important decision-making body within the company. Every company must have directors,[1] and the CA 2006 sets out certain mandatory responsibilities that fall to them.[2] Otherwise, however, the board's powers and responsibilities are as determined by the company's own constitution. This might suggest that little can be said about the general role of all boards, but that is not quite true. Most companies, large and small, adopt articles that give management power to the board of directors, and we can consider the consequences of that general model.[3] At that generic level, the ambition 9–001

[1] CA 2006 s.250 provides that "'director' includes any person occupying the position of director, by whatever name called". For details on individual directors and how they are appointed, see paras 9–007 to 9–009.

[2] See below, para.9–006.

[3] That is also the default governance model set out in the model articles: see art.3 for both private and public companies: "Subject to the articles, the directors are responsible for the management of the company's business, for which purpose they may exercise all the powers of the company". The qualifier, "subject to the articles", is invariably important, and the articles themselves are subject to any mandatory provisions in CA 2006. Enterprises of different sizes are readily accommodated by the further provision, in art.5 of both models, which gives boards wide powers of delegation in respect of

concerning the role and importance of boards can be seen from the wording of the first Principle (Principle A) of the UK Corporate Governance Code[4]: "A successful company is led by an effective and entrepreneurial board, whose role is to promote the long-term sustainable success of the company, generating value for shareholders and contributing to wider society". The next two Principles (Principles B and C) expand on that:

> "The board should establish the company's purpose, values and strategy, and satisfy itself that these and its culture are aligned. All directors must act with integrity, lead by example and promote the desired culture.
>
> The board should ensure that the necessary resources are in place for the company to meet its objectives and measure performance against them. The board should also establish a framework of prudent and effective controls, which enable risk to be assessed and managed."

And then two further Principles (Principles D and E) indicate the necessary focus of the board on shareholders, stakeholders and the workforce. Even after making allowances for the fact that the UK Corporate Governance Code applies formally only to companies with a Premium Listing of equity shares on the London Stock Exchange,[5] and that in small companies things may appear very differently, this is a formidable specification for the board's role.

By contrast, it would be difficult to glean any similar understanding of the importance of the board from a reading of the Companies Act, which leaves determination of the role of the board very largely to the company's constitution. Leaving the board's role to be determined by individual companies has a number of advantages, a less obvious one being that it greatly facilitates the use of a single Act to regulate all manner and sizes of company. Jurisdictions which make legislative provision for the role of the boards of large companies often need a separate statute for smaller companies, one which gives these members a freedom nearer to that enjoyed by the members of a British company.

A company's articles can be worded quite generally, often simply allocating management power to the board, and allowing the board to delegate at will.[6] In large companies, the detailed rules setting out these delegations are most unlikely to be in the company's constitution: amending them as the company's needs change would be far too cumbersome, and in any event the detail would not be seen as warranted or desirable in a public document. By contrast, small companies often have quite specific limitations and constraints set out in their articles, precisely because amending those details is then more difficult. These constraints typically restrict the way in which decisions are taken on major changes to business direction, admission of new members, and alteration of the articles. This is because members of small companies have typically united to

---

all the powers conferred upon them by the articles: "to such person to such an extent and on such terms and conditions as they think fit". All the directors' powers, including their power to delegate and the obligation which then arises to supervise their delegates, are subject to the duties directors owe their companies: see Ch.10.

[4] Financial Reporting Council, *UK Corporate Governance Code* (July 2018). This Code consists of 18 Principles (A to R) and 41 more detailed Provisions (1 to 41). It is supported by the *Guidance on Board Effectiveness* issued by the FRC at the same time.

[5] For the meaning of "Premium Listing" see below at paras 25–006 and 25–016.

[6] See fn.3 above.

pursue a common purpose, and changes to any of these fundamental elements may be seen to go to the foundations of their endeavour.

The legal effect of the articles

The board and shareholders

In managing companies, one of the key questions that may arise in an internal dispute is who has the upper hand: the shareholders or the directors? Put another way, is the relationship between the shareholders and their elected directors simply one of principal and agent,[7] with the shareholders having ultimate power to order the directors to act as the shareholders wish? Or, alternatively, do the articles effect a constitutional settlement, dividing powers between the shareholders and the directors and restricting each respective corporate organ to its own domain? At one level, this may seem to be simply a matter of choosing the appropriate default rule. But in truth the distinction reflects far more than that. The principal/agent view harks back to the early days of joint settlement companies: these had emerged, effectively, as "large partnerships" permitted by statute to operate as "companies". Building on the partnership model, the members of these companies might appoint delegates to do their bidding (as partners would), but members did not thereby restrict their own powers. By contrast, once the separate legal personality of the company was firmly established, this analysis could not hold water: there was now a new and dominant entity in the mix, and the constitutional settlement model was the only logical resolution. Of course, as noted earlier, the form of the constitutional settlement was at large, and the individuals who decided to incorporate and become members of the company were in control of writing the rules. What it did mean, however, was that later on, when disputes arose, those settled rules prevailed; the members could not simply tear them up and start again.[8] The evolution from one model to another is instructive, and is set out below. 9–002

Until the end of the nineteenth century, it was generally assumed that the general meeting was the supreme organ of the company and the board of directors was merely an agent of the company subject to the control of the company in general meeting. It followed that the shareholders could at any time by ordinary resolution give the directors binding instructions as to how they were to exercise their management powers. Thus, in *Isle of Wight Railway v Tahourdin*,[9] the court refused the directors of a statutory company an injunction to restrain the holding of a general meeting, one purpose of which was to appoint a committee to reorganise the management of the company. 9–003

[7] i.e. in legal terms. It is clear that, in terms of the functional analysis of economists, directors are agents and shareholders principals because the former have the factual power to affect the well-being of the latter. But this does not mean the authority of the directors is conferred upon them in such a way as to make them the legal agents of the shareholders.

[8] Although they could change the rules—i.e. amend the articles—but only in accordance with the processes set out in the articles and CA 2006: see Ch.13.

[9] *Isle of Wight Railway Co v Tahourdin* (1883) 25 Ch. D. 320 CA, especially at 329.

In 1906, however, just a decade after *Salomon v Salomon*,[10] the Court of Appeal in *Automatic Self-Cleansing Filter Syndicate Co v Cuninghame*,[11] made it clear that in registered companies the division of powers between the board and the company in general meeting depended entirely on the construction of the articles of association and that, where powers had been vested in the board, the general meeting could not interfere with their exercise. The articles were held to constitute a contract by which the members had agreed that "the directors and the directors alone shall manage".[12] Hence the directors were entitled to refuse to carry out a sale agreement adopted by ordinary resolution in general meeting where that decision fell within the management powers conferred upon the board. *Tahourdin*'s case was distinguished on the ground that the wording of s.90 of the Companies Clauses Act 1845 was different—though that section does not in fact seem to have been relied on in the earlier case.

The new approach did not secure immediate acceptance,[13] but since *Quin & Axtens v Salmon*[14] it has been generally accepted that where the relevant articles are in the normal form, as exemplified by successive model sets of articles, the general meeting cannot interfere with a decision of the directors unless the directors are acting contrary to the provisions of the Act or the articles.[15]

In *Shaw & Sons (Salford) Ltd v Shaw*,[16] in which a resolution of the general meeting disapproving the commencement of an action by the directors was held to be a nullity, the modern doctrine was expressed by Greer LJ as follows[17]:

> "A company is an entity distinct alike from its shareholders and its directors. Some of its powers may, according to its articles, be exercised by directors, certain other powers may be reserved for the shareholders in general meeting. If powers of management are vested in the directors, they and they alone can exercise these powers. The only way in which the general body of the shareholders can control the exercise of the powers vested by the articles in the directors is by altering their articles, or, if opportunity arises under the articles, by refusing to re-elect the directors of whose actions they disapprove.[18] They cannot themselves usurp the powers which by the articles are vested in the directors any more than the directors can usurp the powers vested by the articles in the general body of shareholders."

---

[10] *Salomon v Salomon & Co Ltd* [1897] A.C. 22 HL. See Ch.2.

[11] *Automatic Self-Cleansing Filter Syndicate Co Ltd v Cuninghame* [1906] 2 Ch. 34 CA.

[12] *Automatic Self-Cleansing Filter Syndicate v Cuninghame* [1906] 2 Ch. 34 at 44 per Cozens-Hardy LJ. Also see *Gramophone & Typewriter Ltd v Stanley* [1908] 2 K.B. 89 CA, especially at 98 per Fletcher Moulton LJ and at 105–106 per Buckley LJ (despite the fact that the then current edition of his book took the opposite view).

[13] *Marshall's Valve Gear Co Ltd v Manning Wardle & Co Ltd* [1909] 1 Ch. 267 Ch D.

[14] *Quin & Axtens Ltd v Salmon* [1909] 1 Ch. 311 CA; affirmed [1909] A.C. 442 HL.

[15] But for contrary views, see G.D. Goldberg, "Article 80 of Table A of the Companies Act 1948" (1970) 33 M.L.R. 177; M.S. Blackman, "Article 59 and the distribution of powers in a company" (1975) 92 S.A.L.J. 286; and G. Sullivan, "The Relationship between the Board of Directors and the General Meeting in Limited Companies" (1977) 93 L.Q.R. 569.

[16] *John Shaw & Sons (Salford) Ltd v Shaw* [1935] 2 K.B. 113 CA. See also *Rose v McGivern* [1998] 2 B.C.L.C. 593 at 604.

[17] *John Shaw & Sons (Salford) Ltd v Shaw* [1935] 2 K.B. 113 at 134.

[18] They can now remove the directors by ordinary resolution: s.168, below at paras 11–022 to 11–030.

And in *Scott v Scott*[19] it was held, on the same grounds, that resolutions of a general meeting, which might be interpreted either as directions to pay an interim dividend or as instructions to make loans, were nullities. In either event the relevant powers had been delegated to the directors, and until those powers were taken away by an amendment of the articles the members in general meeting could not interfere with their exercise. As Lord Clauson[20] rightly said, "the professional view as to the control of the company in general meeting over the actions of directors has, over a period of years, undoubtedly varied".[21] From 1985 onwards the model set of articles sought to make the position clear, for those companies adopting them, on the lines indicated in the above cases.

All this may seem to suggest that all power resides in the board of directors. Much of it does, but the shareholders too have significant powers. First, the company's articles often reserve significant powers to the shareholders. In the current model articles for both private and public companies, the grant of authority to the board is qualified by the phrase "subject to the articles", and there is a specific article dealing with the "members' reserve power".[22] This article makes it clear that the members may by special resolution (i.e. as would be needed to change the articles) instruct the directors "to take, or refrain from taking, specified action". By implication, any instruction given by the shareholders by ordinary majority to the board within the area of authority delegated to the directors is not binding on the directors. Secondly, and regardless of what the articles may say, the CA 2006 reserves to the shareholders certain crucial decisions that the company might wish take.[23] **9–004**

However, despite all these features of the constitutional settlement between directors and shareholders, it might be said that to a considerable extent they have been overtaken by a change made by statute in 1948, when what is now s.168 was introduced, giving the shareholders the ability to remove directors at any time by

---

[19] *Scott v Scott* [1943] 1 All E.R. 582 Ch D. See also *Black White and Grey Cabs Ltd v Fox* [1969] N.Z.L.R. 824 CA, where the cases were reviewed, as they were by Plowman J at first instance in *Bamford v Bamford* [1970] Ch. 212 CA (Civ Div).

[20] *Scott v Scott* [1943] 1 All E.R. 582 at 585D. Lord Clauson was sitting as a judge of the Chancery Division.

[21] This is clearly seen if the judgments in the above cases are compared with that in *Foss v Harbottle* (1843) 2 Hare 461 Ct of Chancery; see below, paras 15–004 to 15–006. The modern view was reiterated at first instance in *Breckland Group Holdings v London and Suffolk Properties* (1988) 4 B.C.C. 542 Ch D, noted in K.W. Wedderburn, "Control of Corporate Actions" (1989) 52 M.L.R. 401, and L.S. Sealy, "Company Law—Power of the General Meeting to Intervene" [1989] C.L.J. 26.

[22] Article 4 in each case. However, the special resolution altering the articles or giving instructions to the directors does not have the effect of invalidating anything done by the directors before the passing of the resolution: art.4(2). If the directors have merely resolved to take course X before the shareholders resolve by special resolution to take contradictory course Y, then presumably the shareholder resolution constitutes a binding instruction to the directors not to implement their prior resolution. However, if in implementation of their prior resolution the directors have contracted on behalf of the company with a third party, that third-party contract would remain binding on the company. If extensive powers of direction are exercised by the shareholders, it is conceivable that they might come to be regarded as de facto or shadow directors of the company, despite the strictness of the tests applied: see paras 10–009 to 10–011.

[23] See Ch.11.

ordinary resolution.[24] Thus, at the very moment when the modern interpretation of the articles as a constitutional settlement became fully accepted, the legislature changed the rules so as to give shareholders a removal power, one exercisable without cause and by ordinary majority. Although a removal power is different in many ways from a power to give instructions, it does enable the shareholders to exert considerable pressure on the board: the disgruntled shareholders can say, in effect, if you choose not to follow our views, we will by ordinary majority seek to remove you from office. That can be a powerful inducement to the directors to follow the line of action preferred by the shareholders.

Collective decision-making and delegation: the board and senior management

9–005 The assumption is that directors will act collectively as a board unless they have the power to delegate and do so. Moreover, strictly speaking their decisions should be taken at a meeting convened in accordance with the company's articles, unless their decision is unanimous.[25] However, as we saw in the previous chapter, procedural informality often has little practical relevance given the indoor management rule and the CA 2006 s.40.[26] And although delegation is the norm,[27] this foundational rule of collective action can be seen in claims by directors asserting their rights to participate in management.[28]

As to delegation, the articles typically permit delegation of "any of the powers which are conferred on [the directors] under the articles ... as they think fit" and "any such delegation may authorise further delegation of the directors' powers by any person to whom they are delegated".[29] In this way, a simple provision in the company's constitution can enable anything from the simple appointment of an agent to the networks of delegations typically seen in multinationals. Moreover, the same article also provides that the directors "may revoke any delegation in whole or part, or alter its terms and conditions". This power, however, has to be exercised carefully: although the alteration or revocation of the mandate may be effective, it may also constitute a breach (perhaps even a de facto termination) of the service contract entered into by the company with the manager, giving rise to claims for compensation on the part of the manager against the company, sometimes of a substantial character.[30]

In practice such delegation is of enormous importance in large companies. In particular, there is normally a very large grant of managerial power to the most senior of the company's managers, who will almost invariably be a member of

[24] See Ch.11, noting the constraints on the shareholders in exercising this power, and the protections in place for directors.

[25] *Re Duomatic Ltd* [1969] 2 Ch. 365 Ch D; *Runciman v Walker Runciman Plc* [1993] B.C.C. 223 QBD.

[26] See paras 8–005 to 8–015.

[27] Model art.5 for both private and public companies.

[28] *Pulbrook v Richmond Consolidated Mining Co* (1878) 9 Ch. D. Ch D 610 at 612 (Jessel MR); *Re Harmer* [1959] 1 W.L.R. 62 CA at 87 (Romer LJ).

[29] Model art.5 for both private and public companies.

[30] See too para.11–026: removal of someone as a director of the company may automatically terminate their service contract, and that termination may (or may not) be a breach of contract by the company; all depends on the wording of the particular terms of the contract.

the board of directors as well. Such a person, traditionally known as the "managing director" but now more often, following US terminology, as the "chief executive officer" (CEO), is the driving force behind the implementation of the company's strategy, and often a significant party in its formulation.[31] Of increasing importance as well is the "chief financial officer" (CFO). As we shall see below, the major motivation behind the development of the UK Corporate Governance Code was the desire to place the CEO within a framework of accountability to the board, a problem created, but not solved, by use of the extensive delegation power contained in the articles.

The mandatory functions of the directors

Scattered throughout the Act are obligations which are imposed specifically on the directors and which therefore may not be delegated to others or assumed by the shareholders.[32] It would be too tedious to list them all. What should be noted, however, is that they relate to two main areas of corporate life: production of the annual accounts and reports and compliance with the formal administrative obligations of the company, in particular its communications with Companies House. Thus, the directors are under a duty to prepare accounts and reports each year; having done that, to approve them and send copies to the Registrar; and, in most cases, to lay them before the shareholders in general meeting.[33] But these statutory provisions do not purport to impose a particular division of decision-making about the company's ordinary business activities as between the shareholders in general meeting, the board and the management.[34] That is left to the company's own constitution. **9–006**

One further point should be noticed about these obligations. In many cases, the obligation is laid not only on the director, but upon any "officer" of the company, and the sanction for non-compliance, normally a minor criminal sanction, is laid on any "officer who is in default". Examples are where the company fails to carry out its final task with respect to the annual accounts, i.e. fails to send a copy to every shareholder,[35] or where the company fails to keep an accurate record of its members.[36] The Act defines "officer"[37] as including "a director, manager or secretary" and "any person who is to be treated as an officer of the company for the purposes of the provision in question". These are thus cases where the Act imposes liabilities on sub-board managers. This is sensible in principle, given that

---

[31] See para.9–018 for the ideal role of the board, led by its chair, who are primarily responsible for strategy, and contrast that with the CEO and executive team, who are primarily responsible for execution. The overlap occurs because the CEO is typically a member of the board, and indeed other senior executives may also be on the board. Hence the distinction between non-executive directors (NEDs) and executive directors.

[32] Similarly, the Act accords certain decisions to the shareholders alone: see Ch.10.

[33] CA 2006 Pt 16, discussed further in Ch.22.

[34] Although certain unusual decisions, especially concerning large transactions between the company and its directors, require the additional approval of the shareholders: see Ch.11.

[35] CA 2006 s.425.

[36] CA 2006 s.113.

[37] CA 2006 s.1121. Where the director or officer is itself a company, there is no liability unless one of the latter's officers is in default, in which case he or she is criminally liable as well as the corporate officer or director: s.1122.

such administrative tasks are likely to be delegated to levels of management below the board.[38] But the net can be cast too wide: the CLR recommended that the definition of manager should normally be restricted to a person who "under the immediate authority of a director or secretary is charged with managerial functions which include the relevant function"[39] but this limitation was not adopted. The CLR also recommended that, for all those covered by the definition of officer, i.e. including directors, default should be taken to have occurred only where the person had authorised, actively participated in, knowingly permitted or knowingly failed to take active steps to prevent the action in question, and this recommendation is reflected in the Act.[40]

APPOINTMENT OF DIRECTORS

9–007 The Act in s.250 provides that "'director' includes any person occupying the position of director, by whatever name called". This is intrinsically circular as a definition, but is intended to capture all those who control the entire range of central management functions within the company, and not those lower down the corporate hierarchy to whom only more limited powers of management are delegated (even if these lower order positions control the operations in an entire region or product sector).[41] When the Act prescribes rules concerning "directors", such rules apply only to those in central management, unless the provision makes explicit its wider ambit. But the law does nothing to control the growing and potentially misleading practice of giving employees the title of director, even though they perform none of the central management functions of a director and are thus not directors under the Act; nor, in the other direction, does the law require all directors under the Act to carry that title, and indeed directors of many large business corporations are "vice presidents" (below the CEO), and the directors of some charities or guarantee companies are still called "governors" or the like.

Section 154 requires all public companies to have two directors (as defined in the Act) and private companies one,[42] but the Act says little about the means of appointing the directors, leaving this to the articles of association. Its main

[38] To some extent the statute is following the lead given by the decision in *Meridian Global Funds Management Asia Ltd v Securities Commission* [1995] B.C.C. 942 PC. The CLR reported that, under the previous law, the uncertainty as to who was a manager meant that prosecution of sub-board managers was rarely attempted: Final Report, Ch.14, fn.296.

[39] Final Report, para.15.54, though for particular offences it would be possible to cast the net wider. It would not be necessary for such a manager to be employed by the company, as where the particular administrative function had been out-sourced to an independent organisation.

[40] CA 2006 s.1121(3).

[41] Of course, such regional directors and product directors might also have a seat on the board, and play a role in running the entire organisation, but that does not always follow. Much can be gleaned from a close reading of cases on de facto and shadow directors: see paras 10–009 to 10–014.

[42] At least one of those directors must be a natural person (s.155)—as opposed to a corporate director—in order to improve the enforceability of directors' obligations. Since 2015 there have been plans to introduce s.156A, requiring all company directors to be natural persons, subject to certain yet-to-be-defined exceptions: see s.87 of the Small Business, Enterprise and Employment Act 2015. CA 2006 also contains a mechanism for dealing with the situation where the company does not comply with ss.154 or 155. The Secretary of State may issue a direction to the company, specifying

concern is to give publicity to those who are appointed. On initial registration, the company must send to the Registrar of Companies particulars of the first directors[43] and a statement that they have consented to act. Thereafter the company must send particulars of any changes, with corresponding statements that any new directors consent to act.[44] The company must also maintain a register giving particulars of its directors.[45] Both registers are open to inspection by members of the public and so the public can obtain information about who the directors are either from Companies House or from the company's registered office. This is a crucial provision, enabling people to know who controls what might otherwise appear to be faceless companies, thus facilitating the enforcement of the obligations to which directors are subject.

However, in the interests of the personal safety of directors,[46] the detail on the public registers has been reduced. The company's public register no longer has to contain the director's residential address, but only a service address (which might be the company's registered address), though the company must continue to maintain a register of the directors' residential addresses which is not open to public inspection. Moreover, the company is prohibited from disclosing, except in limited circumstances, the residential address of a director or former director.[47] Equally, whilst the company must give to the Registrar the information which is contained in both its public and non-public registers, the Registrar must omit this "protected information" from the Registrar's public register and not otherwise disclose it, except in limited circumstances.[48]

As far as the process of appointment is concerned, and contrary to popular belief, the Act requires neither that directors be elected by the shareholders in general meeting nor that they submit themselves periodically to re-election by the shareholders. This may often be the case, though it is far from universal practice, but, if it is, it is a consequence of the provisions of the company's articles, not of **9–008**

the action the company must take and failure to comply with the Secretary of State's direction constitutes a criminal offence on the part of the company and any officer in default, including a shadow director: s.156.

[43] CA 2006 s.12.

[44] CA 2006 s.167.

[45] CA 2006 ss.162 onwards.

[46] Especially safety from threats, or actual infliction, of violence by protestors or harm to the persons or property of the directors of companies carrying on lawful activities to which the protestors objected.

[47] CA 2006 ss.163, 165 and 241. The company, on the application of a member, liquidator or creditor or other person with a sufficient interest, may be ordered by the court to disclose the residential address if there is evidence that service of documents at the service address is ineffective or it is necessary or expedient to do so in connection with the enforcement of a court order: s.244.

[48] CA 2006 ss.240 and 242. The Registrar may use protected information for the purposes of disclosure to a public authority specified in regulations or, again subject to regulations, a credit reference agency, for otherwise the company might not be able to obtain credit: s.243 and the Companies (Disclosure of Address) Regulations 2009 (SI 2009/214). Further, the Registrar may put the director's address on the public record if communications sent to the director by the Registrar remain unanswered or there is evidence that service of documents at the director's service address is ineffective. The director and the company must be consulted before this step is taken. If it is, the company must alter its public record as well: ss.245 and 246.

the Act's requirements.[49] Equally, there is nothing to prevent articles providing that directors can be appointed by a particular class of shareholders rather than the shareholders as a whole, or appointed by debenture holders, or indeed appointed by third parties.[50] If the articles are silent, however, then the right to appoint directors lies with the shareholders, who can appoint by ordinary resolution.[51] The power of the majority of the shareholders to appoint directors (and equally, presumably, the power of any other group) must "be exercised for the benefit of the company as a whole and not to secure some ulterior advantage".[52]

In public companies, the appointment process is typically more formal and structured. The articles of public companies normally provide for retirement of board members by rotation on a three-year cycle and for the filling of the vacancies at each annual general meeting.[53] The Act provides that each appointment in a public company shall be voted on individually[54] unless the meeting agrees unanimously that two or more shall be included in a single resolution. However, there are often provisions in the company's articles (as to notice to be given by shareholders to the company of their proposed candidates, etc.) which make it difficult for shareholders, if they are so minded, to put up candidates against the board's nominees. So, the crucial decisions for the shareholders in public companies are normally whether to accept the board's nominees for election at the annual general meeting and whether subsequently to exercise their removal rights.[55]

9–009 Unless the articles so provide, directors need not be members of the company. At one time it was customary so to provide,[56] but now the possibility of a complete separation of shareholders and directors is recognised and the model articles no longer provide for a share qualification. Of course, it is common for directors of public companies to become shareholders, often in a major way, under a share-option or other incentive scheme (discussed below),[57] but even in these cases being a shareholder is not a formal condition of being a director.

---

[49] The model articles for both private and public companies give the power of appointment to the shareholders and also to the directors: art.17 (private companies) and art.20 (for public companies, although art.21(2) provides that a director appointed by the directors holds office only until the next AGM).

[50] In the case of community interest companies, s.45 of the Companies (Audit, Investigations and Community Enterprise) Act 2004 explicitly empowers the Regulator of CICs to appoint a director of a CIC and for that person not to be removable by the company.

[51] *Woolf v East Nagel Gold Mining Co Ltd* (1905) 21 T.L.R. 660; *Worcester Corsetry Ltd v Witting* [1936] Ch. 640 CA.

[52] *Re Harmer* [1959] 1 W.L.R. 62 at 82. For the detail on restrictions applying to shareholder voting, see Ch.13.

[53] Model public company articles, art.21. The model for private companies makes no such provision. The board also has power to appoint directors (arts 17 (private) and 20 (public))—this is a useful power for filling vacancies arising unexpectedly between annual general meetings—and again, directors of public companies appointed by the board come up for re-election at the next AGM (art.21), with private companies having no equivalent.

[54] CA 2006 s.160. This is designed to prevent the members being faced with the alternative of either accepting or rejecting the whole slate of nominees.

[55] See paras 11–022 to 11–030.

[56] CA 1929 Table A art.66.

[57] See 11–017 to 11–021.

As to age requirements, the law has undergone a complete reversal in recent years. The earlier provisions on maximum age have been discarded, but the CA 2006 introduced a minimum age requirement of 16, apparently because of evidence that appointment of young directors was being used in order to exploit their immunity from prosecution or the unwillingness of public authorities to prosecute young persons.[58] Any such appointment is void, although the person appointed remains subject to the duties of directors under the Act.[59] This may mean that the company will no longer be in compliance with the requirements as to the minimum number of directors and will thus be open to a direction from the Secretary of State as to the action it must take to remedy this situation.[60] However, the Secretary of State has power to make regulations permitting the appointment of classes of person under the age of 16, which regulations may make different provisions for different parts of the UK.[61] Other than this, no positive qualifications are required of directors,[62] although, as we will see in Ch.20, individuals may be disqualified from acting as directors on the ground of misconduct or unfitness.

Sometimes the articles entitle a director to appoint an alternate director to act for him at any board meeting that he is unable to attend. The extent of the alternate's powers and the answer to such questions as whether he is entitled to remuneration from the company or from the director appointing him will then depend on the terms of the relevant article.[63]

Consequences of defective appointments

Given all the rules just mentioned, the process of appointing directors is not always conducted perfectly. Nevertheless, the acts undertaken by those purporting to be the company's directors are generally valid even though the director is not, or is no longer, validly appointed—see the very broad wording of s.161: **9–010**

> "(1) The acts of a person acting as a director are valid notwithstanding that it is afterwards discovered—
> (a) that there was a defect in his appointment;
> (b) that he was disqualified from holding office;
> (c) that he had ceased to hold office;
> (d) that he was not entitled to vote on the matter in question.
>
> (2) This applies even if the resolution for his appointment is void under section 160 (appointment of directors of public company to be voted on individually)."

---

58 CA 2006 s.157.

59 CA 2006 s.157(4),(5). Existing under-age directors ceased to be directors on the section coming into force (s.159(2)).

60 See CA 2006 s.156, and see fn.42.

61 CA 2006 s.158. This particular aspect of the regulation-making power is necessary because, under devolution, the age of criminal responsibility could vary within the UK.

62 Although the general law prevents bankrupts and certain other classes of individuals from acting as directors.

63 See the Companies (Model Articles) Regulations 2008 (SI 2008/3229) Sch.3: Model Articles for Public Companies arts 13 and 25–27, which go far to clarify the alternate's position. The Model Articles for Private Companies make no provision for alternates.

This means that third parties dealing with the company are generally protected (unless they knew of the defect at the time, rather than "afterwards discovered" it), and the company's remedy is to take action, if that is possible, against those responsible for the appointment or those acting improperly as directors. Section 161 thus supplements the general rules discussed in Ch.8.[64]

In *Morris v Kanssen*,[65] the House of Lords held that an earlier statutory provision in narrower terms applied only when there had been a "defective appointment" and not where there had been "no appointment" at all. That case is a reminder that the rule remains estoppel based: the third party cannot rely on the fact that an appointment to a directorship might conceivably have been made, only on the fact that an attempted appointment was made properly, and so if that was the flaw in the dealing, the third party is protected.[66] Section 161(1)(a) would seem to secure that distinction in the current version, although the section also provides relief in other circumstances. Further, being estoppel based, the rule can only be relied upon by third parties acting in good faith; this can be especially limiting if insiders, especially the directors themselves, seek to rely on s.161.[67]

REMUNERATION AND REMOVAL OF DIRECTORS

9–011 As is plain from the foregoing discussion, the management of most companies typically rests with the directors. By contrast, the remuneration and removal of directors lies largely in the hands of the company's shareholders, and is thus a powerful tool in supporting the governance role exercised by shareholders. Those issues are dealt with in detail in Ch.11. But even where the shareholders have the last say, the proposals themselves often emerge from the directors for consideration by the shareholders. To that end, there are good reasons for the best practice controls on remuneration contained in the UK Corporate Governance Code. In companies not subject to the Code—i.e. most companies in the UK—the controls on remuneration can be more of an ad hoc affair, often emerging as issues attracting complaint in unfair prejudice petitions (Ch.14), or in breach of directors' duties claims (Ch.10), or complaints concerning unlawful distributions of capital (Chs 18 and 19). This is despite the notional control exerted by shareholders, and is especially so, of course, where the shareholders and directors are the same people, as is often the case in small companies.

---

[64] See paras 8–006 to 8–009, on s.40 and *Turquand*/the indoor management rule.

[65] *Morris v Kanssen* [1946] A.C. 459 HL.

[66] Also see *British Asbestos Co Ltd v Boyd* [1903] 2 Ch. 439 Ch D at 444–445 (Farwell J).

[67] See *Re Sherlock Holmes International Society* [2016] EWHC 1392 (Ch); [2016] P.N.L.R. 31 at [53]–[62], especially [61], dismissing the extraordinary claim that a sole director might rely on s.161 to validate a transaction he made in breach of his s.171 duty to act within powers; *Re Sprout Land Holdings Ltd (In Administration)* [2019] EWHC 807 (Ch); [2019] B.C.C. 893 at [6], obiter, expressing the view that in the right circumstances an insider could rely on s.161.

STRUCTURE AND COMPOSITION OF THE BOARD

When we looked at the role of the board in the first section of this chapter, we saw that, broadly, the range of responsibilities allocated to the board is left by the law to be determined by the company's articles of association. In this final section we look at the rules on board structure and composition. Here again the law leaves matters to be determined by the company's constitution; here, moreover, generalisations are impossible and we simply make brief comment on issues currently seen as important. By contrast, looking beyond legal rules to "soft law" interventions, this is an area in which the "corporate governance" movement of the past three decades has had a significant impact. Only Premium Listed companies are formally subject to the UK Corporate Governance Code. Nevertheless, some aspects of its best practices have inevitably filtered down, at least to some extent, to small and medium enterprises although probably not to businesses that are effectively small incorporated partnerships. **9–012**

Legal rules on board structure

Before turning to the composition of the board, let us look at its structure. An important difference between legal systems is considered to be whether they require one-tier or two-tier boards. In Germany, for example, a two-tier board is mandatory for public companies (*Aktiengesellschaften*), and so the relevant statute (*Aktiengesetz*), besides requiring both a supervisory and a managing board, stipulates the functions of each and the methods of appointment to each board. In other EU countries, two-tier boards are sometimes mandatory, but not always, and, where adopted, the mandatory division of responsibilities can vary. In broad terms, the task of running the company (in an operational sense) is entrusted to the managing board, while the supervisory board is typically focused on long term strategic planning and it is this board which appoints, guides and monitors the management board. Usually, a person may not be a member of both boards. **9–013**

By contrast, in Britain, the US and Commonwealth countries, the one-tier board is the norm, with the board being responsible for setting the corporate strategy and controlling and managing its effective execution, so that both the managing and supervisory functions are discharged by a single body. Although this is the norm, it is not obvious that the law in Britain requires a single board: the Act does not require the directors to act as a board,[68] and so it hardly needs to address the further question of whether the board is to be a one-tier or a two-tier board.[69] That means the advantages and disadvantages of each approach merit thought. Even 20 years ago, the CLR found some evidence that "the practice of delegating [from 'the board'] day to day management and major operational questions to a 'management board' is becoming increasingly common in this country".[70] This infringes no provision of the statute, and, provided the articles

---

[68] Although see para.9–002 for the early common law assumption.

[69] For the same reason the Act says nothing about the division of function between the board and its committees nor about the role of the chair of the board.

[70] Developing, para.3.139.

permit such further delegation by the board and provided the board monitors effectively the functioning of the "management board", it involves no breach by the directors of their duties or risk of disqualification on grounds of unfitness.[71]

Legal rules on board composition: diversity and inclusion

9–014 The lack of diversity and inclusion on the boards of large UK companies has for some time been a matter attracting frequent criticism. The focus is typically on gender, ethnicity, disability and wider inclusion. In none of these areas have the issues been addressed by setting down quotas in legislation, but, increasingly, by setting targets and then measuring the individual contributions of the largest companies to achieving those targets. It is instructive that greatest progress has been achieved on gender diversity, where public data has been recorded for longer, and the least on disability and inclusion, where such systematic records do not appear to exist. The detail is set out below. But it is worth noting an inherent tension in this area. Everyone seems to agree that better decisions are made if a more diverse group of people comes together to make them. And everyone also seems to agree that corporate success would be enhanced if there were more emphasis on relevant expertise and experience in board appointments. It is not impossible to combine both, but it can be a tricky exercise, especially as companies seek to address new, but common, modern challenges. In particular, if diversity "rules" put pressure on companies to show results along that dimension, they will have a natural tendency to put expertise in second place, and that may be detrimental to company performance.[72] There is also evidence that companies are squaring the circle by increasing the total number of board appointments, and that may reduce the availability of effective talent by spreading it more thinly. These dilemmas and practical difficulties may explain why the government has stopped short of legislative quotas, but that has not removed the public pressure of targets.

Gender diversity was the first issue to be tackled systematically. It was perhaps seen as the area in which progress could most easily be made. In 2010, Lord Davies of Abersoch was commissioned to review gender diversity on boards. His report, published in February 2011,[73] presented a business case for diversity: improving performance; accessing the widest talent pool; being more responsive to the market; and achieving better corporate governance. He rejected the use of "quotas", at least for the time being, but set out recommendations designed to achieve 25% female representation on boards by 2015. The effect was positive and the target achieved,[74] with the threat of mandatory quotas no doubt providing

[71] See below, Chs 10 and 20.

[72] See A. Balogh, "Professional Expertise on Boards, Corporate Lifecycle, and Firm Performance" (30 June 2016), *SSRN* available at SSRN: *https://ssrn.com/abstract=2802417* or *http://dx.doi.org/10.2139/ssrn.2802417* [Accessed 13 February 2021].

[73] The "Davies Report": *Women on Boards* (February 2011) available at: *http://www.bis.gov.uk/assets/biscore/business-law/docs/w/11-745-women-on-boards.pdf* [Accessed 16 March 2021].

[74] Women on FTSE 100 boards number 23.5% as at March 2015, up from 12.5% in 2010: BIS, "Women on boards 2015: fourth annual review" (2015) available at: *https://www.gov.uk/government/publications/women-on-boards-2015-fourth-annual-review* [Accessed 16 March 2021].

its own incentive for action.[75] However, it is notable that most of the increase came from non-executive board appointments, not executive ones, and was in what are anecdotally described as "more junior" roles. Lord Davies then pushed further, recommending a new target of 33% of women on FTSE 350 Boards by 2020.[76] The Hampton-Alexander Review Committee, an independent review body, has now taken up the issue, building on the work of the Davies Review, and aiming to further increase the number of women in senior positions in FTSE 350 companies.[77] Thus the pressure continues in the UK, perhaps enhanced by the EU's decision to launch its own consultation and investigation on gender imbalance as a cross-EU issue.[78] This makes rising targets increasingly likely.

Ethnic diversity has risen to prominence only more recently, and, despite the 2017 Parker Review Committee (chaired by Sir John Parker) adopting a similar approach to that taken with gender, progress has so far been less than hoped for. The first Report was produced in 2017, *The Parker Review: A Report into the Ethnic Diversity of UK Boards*[79]: it made a series of recommendations and set a target for all FTSE 100 boards to have at least one director from an ethnic minority background by 2021—"One by 2021" as the Report put it. In 2017, fewer than 50% of FTSE 100 boards (49 out of 100 companies analysed) had ethnic minority representation on their boards. An update report in 2020 indicated the figure had grown to 63%, but the Committee pointed out that this is still far short of the numbers needed to meet the target of 100% by 2021.[80] **9–015**

In moving from diversity to inclusion, this far looser concept has so far been promoted more by assertion of an aspiration than by targeted action. The one area where there is a history of action, however, even if not in the UK, is the inclusion of employees on boards. If the division between one-tier and two-tier board structures (noted earlier) is an important dividing line in European jurisdictions, an even more crucial one is the requirement for employee representatives on the board. There is an inaccurate view that most continental European company laws require employee representation on the model adopted for large companies in Germany (that is, an equal division between employee and shareholder representatives), whereas that model is unique to Germany. Nevertheless, about

---

[75] The Equality and Human Rights Commission has issued guidance on such appointments: "Appointments to Boards and Equality Law" available at: *http://www.equalityhumanrights.com/en/publication-download/appointments-boards-and-equality-law* [Accessed 16 March 2021].

[76] See *Women on boards: 5 year summary (Davies review)* (2015) available at: *https://www.gov.uk/government/publications/women-on-boards-5-year-summary-davies-review* [Accessed 16 March 2021].

[77] The Hampton-Alexander Reviews: BEIS, *FTSE women leaders: Hampton-Alexander review* (2016) available at: *https://www.gov.uk/government/publications/ftse-women-leaders-hampton-alexander-review* [Accessed 16 March 2021].

[78] See European Council, "Gender balance on corporate boards" available at: *https://www.consilium.europa.eu/en/policies/gender-balance-corporate-boards/#* [Accessed 16 March 2021].

[79] The Parker Reviews: BEIS, *Ethnic diversity of UK boards: the Parker review* (2016) available at: *https://www.gov.uk/government/publications/ethnic-diversity-of-uk-boards-the-parker-review* [Accessed 16 March 2021].

[80] See the Parker Review Update: EY Press Release, "New Parker Review report reveals 'slow progress' on ethnic diversity of FTSE boards" (5 February 2020) available at: *https://www.ey.com/en_uk/news/2020/02/new-parker-review-report-reveals-slow-progress-on-ethnic-diversity-of-ftse-boards* [Accessed 16 March 2021].

half the Member States of the EU require minority employee representation on the boards of private sector companies. The UK, by contrast, does not have mandatory board representation for employees: employees do not have a legal right to a say in strategy and management. Equally, the UK at present lacks the informal public mechanisms used with gender and ethnicity that might address diversity and inclusion on boards through employee engagement. The picture for disability inclusion is the same. That said, employee-engagement is certainly prominent on the radar of policy-makers: the Directors' Report is required to make reference to this issue,[81] and, for companies subject to the UK Corporate Governance Code, it too sets out best practice in this area.[82]

THE UK CORPORATE GOVERNANCE CODE: ALTERNATIVE MEASURES TO IMPROVE CORPORATE GOVERNANCE

History of the UK's corporate governance codes

9–016 If the particular and more recent focus on diverse and inclusive boards has been sluggish in general terms, the UK can be said to have led the western world in putting pressure on the largest companies to improve their standards of corporate governance generally. The focus was on board processes, not board decision outcomes, with the rationale being that better processes of decision-making would be likely to lead inevitably to better decision-outcomes. In addition, the UK pioneered developments in how this was done, using soft law means of "comply or explain" (described below) rather than mandatory rules. The initial focus was simply on the proportion and role of non-executive directors on the board. Before changes were introduced, non-executive directors (NEDs) held a not especially active, prestigious or powerful role; the executive directors were the dominant force within the company, with the CEO embodying managerial authority. Whether these changes, and others like them, have improved the business success of companies is still debated.[83]

The corporate governance movement in the UK began with the 1992 report of the Cadbury Committee.[84] As is often the case with company law reform, this committee was constituted as a result of scandal, in this case the sudden descent into insolvency of major companies which had only recently issued annual financial statements which revealed nothing of the horror to come.[85] The Cadbury Committee concluded, however, that the causes of these problems were not to be

---

[81] See para.22–028 and the Large and Medium-sized Companies and Groups (Accounts and Reports) Regulations 2008 (SI 2008/410) Sch.7 Pt 4. The latter falls far short of a board representation requirement, but is capable of being fulfilled by it.

[82] See below at para.9–018 and CGC Provision 5.

[83] S. Bhagat and B. Black, "The Uncertain Relationship between Board Composition and Firm Performance" (1999) 54 Business Lawyer 921. More recently, see C. Weir et al, "An Empirical Analysis of the Impact of Corporate Governance Mechanisms on the Performance of UK Firms", *SSRN* available at: *http://ssrn.com/abstract=286440* [Accessed 16 March 2021], suggesting—rather depressingly—that neither the independence of the committee membership nor the quality of the committee members had any significant effect on performance.

[84] *Report of the Committee on the Financial Aspects of Corporate Governance* (1992).

[85] *Report of the Committee on the Financial Aspects of Corporate Governance* (1992), Preface.

found in the narrow area of accounts and auditing, though it gave attention to the role of auditors, but reflected more widespread defects in the corporate governance systems of large British companies. In consequence, its proposed reforms (in the "Cadbury Code" of best practice) heralded a general reform of board composition and functioning in large UK companies.

What was the corporate governance problem which Cadbury sought to address? Although the committee identified a number of problems, the central one was in companies that were dominated by a single over-powerful managing director or CEO. Other members of the board often provided only the illusion of constraint on the CEO, given that the other executive directors were the CEO's managerial subordinates and the NEDs may equally owe their board positions to the patronage of the CEO. Whilst making no finding that all or even a majority of large British companies were governed in this way, the Committee's proposals focused on putting in place a board structure which would render such dominance by a single person less likely. This was done through the introduction of various counter-balances to the executive management of the company. From the point of view of top management, therefore, the Cadbury Code might be presented as an attack on their discretion.[86] **9–017**

In that context, the subsequent review by the Hampel Committee,[87] delivered six years later, can be seen as a failed attempt by management to win back some of the ground which it had conceded to the Cadbury Committee. The Preliminary Report of the Hampel Committee[88] struck a distinctly sceptical note, asserting that "there is no hard evidence to link success to good governance", a phrase which was not repeated in the Final Report, and implicitly criticising Cadbury for giving rise to a "box ticking" approach to corporate governance. Past debate on corporate governance, it said, had focused too much on accountability and not enough on the governance contribution to business prosperity, and the Committee wished to "see the balance corrected".[89] Only in the final report could the Hampel Committee bring itself to say that it endorsed the "overwhelming majority"[90] of the recommendations of the Cadbury Committee (and of the Greenbury Committee[91] which had reported in the interim on the particular and still controversial subject of directors' remuneration). Hampel's main contribution was to propose, as indeed happened, that the recommendations of the Cadbury and Greenbury Committees, as refined by Hampel, should be brought together in a "Combined Code".

---

[86] Which, however, can be seen as a general trend in corporate law and regulation and by no means a British peculiarity: G. Hertig, "Western Europe's Corporate Governance Dilemma" in T. Baums, K.J. Hopt and N. Horn (eds), *Corporations, Capital Markets and Business in the Law* (Kluwer Law International, 2000), pp.276–278.

[87] The Hampel Committee was set up, as recommended by the Cadbury Committee, to review the operation of the Cadbury Code of Best Practice which that earlier committee had put in place. Their report is *Final Report of the Committee on Corporate Governance* (London: Gee & Co Ltd, 1998).

[88] Committee on Corporate Governance, *Preliminary Report* (August 1997).

[89] This sentiment does survive to the Final Report: see *Final Report of the Committee on Corporate Governance* (1998), para.1.1.

[90] Final Report, para.1.7.

[91] *Directors' Remuneration, Report of a Study Group* (London: Gee & Co Ltd, 1995). See para.11–030.

Following a further set of corporate failures, this time in the US and forever to be associated with the name of the Enron company, the Government commissioned another review of the Combined Code, which was carried out by Derek Higgs. The Government's overt role in the appointment of Mr Higgs was an innovation, since the earlier bodies had been appointed by private associations, such as the Confederation of British Industry and the accounting bodies, although they were generally observed or even serviced by civil servants. The Higgs report constituted a ringing endorsement of the approach of the Cadbury Committee and contained recommendations for the strengthening of the Combined Code, but along the lines already established by that Committee.[92] For example, it contained proposals, later implemented, for an increase in the proportion of NEDs on the board from one third to one half, at least in the largest listed companies.

Developments did not stop there, but, remuneration apart (which remains under close scrutiny, as discussed in Ch.11), the current principles of corporate governance in the UK are in essence the product of the Cadbury Committee whose recommendations, without much violation of the truth, are often treated as a proxy for all the corporate governance reforms in the UK since the 1990s.[93] The most important requirements of the current UK Corporate Governance Code ("CGC")[94] are described below, and then we consider the special mechanism by which the Code is enforced.

The requirements of the UK Corporate Governance Code

9–018 The CGC is now overseen and regularly reviewed and updated by the Financial Reporting Council. Its principal suggestions are summarised below. Their detail might be tested against the stated objectives of the CGC, which is to set higher standards of corporate governance so as to promote transparency and integrity in business, which will in turn attract investment in the UK for the long term, and thus benefit the economy and wider society. The CGC recommendations are further supported by the more recent UK Stewardship Code, noted below. In the CGC itself:

---

[92] D. Higgs, *Review of the Role and Effectiveness of Non-Executive Directors* (London: The Stationery Office, January 2003). In the preface to his report Mr Higgs stated: "From the work I have done, I am clear that the fundamentals of corporate governance in the UK are sound, thanks to Sir Adrian Cadbury and those who built on his foundations". For a review of the Higgs Report (and of the contemporaneous Report by Sir Robert Smith on the role of the audit committee), see P. Davies, "Enron and Corporate Governance Reform in the UK and the European Community" in J. Armour and J. McCahery (eds), *After Enron* (Oxford: Hart Publishing, 2006).

[93] In addition to the Reports already mentioned, there are also important Reports from Turnbull (1999, updated 2005) on financial reporting available at: *https://www.frc.org.uk* and at *https://www.icaew.com/technical/corporate-governance/codes-and-reports/turnbull-report*); Myners (*Institutional Investment in the United Kingdom: A Review* (2001)) available at: *http://uksif.org/wpcontent/uploads/2012/12/MYERS-P.-2001.-Institutional-Investment-in-the-United-Kingdom-AReview.pdf*); and Davies (*Women on Boards* (2011) available at: *http://www.bis.gov.uk/assets/biscore/business-law/docs/w/11-745-women-on-boards.pdf* [All accessed 16 March 2021]).

[94] See fn.4. See too the *Feedback statement: UK Corporate Governance Code* (2018) available at *https://www.frc.org.uk/news/july-2018/a-uk-corporate-governance-code-that-is-fit-for-the* (as is the CGC itself) [Accessed 16 March 2021].

- There is great emphasis on independence and constructive challenge within the boardroom. At least one half of the board as a whole should be comprised of NEDs, all of whom should be independent.[95] As well, the board "should include an appropriate combination of executive and non-executive directors (and, in particular, independent non-executive directors) such that no one individual or small group of individuals dominates the board's decision taking".[96] The board as a whole sets the company's strategy and supervises its implementation.[97] In the case of the NEDs, however, "supervising" also includes monitoring the performance of the company's executive directors.[98] The CGC provides a definition of independence, which is essentially conceived of as independence from the management. Thus, a person who has been an employee of the company within the previous five years, or has had a material business relationship with it in the previous three years, or holds cross-directorships, or represents a significant shareholder, or has been on the board for more than nine years is not categorised as independent.[99]
- The qualities and qualifications of the individuals appointed to the board are clearly crucial, and the CGC provides that there should be "a formal, rigorous and transparent procedure, and an effective succession plan" for the appointment of new directors to the board, with the search for board candidates being conducted, and appointments made, "based on merit and objective criteria and, within this context, should promote diversity of gender, social and ethnic background, cognitive and personal strengths".[100] To increase accountability and keep the board refreshed, directors should be subject to annual re-election.[101] A measure of the perceived workload of executive directors, NEDs and chairs is evident in the CGC rule that boards "should not agree to a full time executive director taking on more than one non-executive directorship in a FTSE 100 company nor the chairmanship of such a company".[102]
- These individuals on a board can only achieve their potential if the company has good relationships with its shareholders, stakeholders and workforce,[103] and the company has a clear purpose and strategy aligned with a healthy corporate culture.[104] The chair should seek regular engagement with major shareholders[105]; the board should take effective

---

[95] CGC, Provision 11. Also note Principles J and L on diversity.

[96] CGC, Principle G. However, there is some evidence of British boards now going in the same direction as in the US and having only one or two executive directors on them: *Financial Times*, UK edn, 31 December 2007, p.2.

[97] CGC, Principles B and C.

[98] CGC, Principle H and Provision 13.

[99] CGC, Provision 10.

[100] CGC, Principle J. Gender diversity has attracted increasing concern: see the 2011 Davies Report, *Women on boards http://www.bis.gov.uk/assets/biscore/business-law/docs/w/11-745-women-on-boards.pdf* [Accessed 16 March 2021], and amended B.2.4.

[101] CGC, Provision 18.

[102] CGC, Provision 15. More generally, see Principle H.

[103] CGC, Principles D and E.

[104] CGC, Principle B.

[105] CGA, Provision 3.

action when receiving significant shareholder votes against resolutions and should report back to them promptly[106]; and proper workforce engagement should be pursued through one or more of the strategies of having a director appointed from the workforce; a formal workforce advisory panel and a designated non-executive director; or other arrangements which meet the circumstances of the company and the workforce.[107] There should also be processes in place to ensure that the workforce is able to raise concerns and have them dealt with effectively.[108]

- The board should have remuneration[109] and audit[110] committees on which the NEDs should be the only members, and a nomination committee on which they should be the majority of the members.[111] These three committees clearly deal with the three most sensitive governance matters and their workings should be reported in the company's annual report.[112] The whole scheme will fail if the executive directors can control the appointment of the NEDs; remuneration decisions place the executive directors in a position of acute conflict of interest; and assessment by the shareholders of the performance of the management will be impossible in the absence of accurate financial data about the company but, by the same token, this is an area where the management has the greatest incentive to put an unduly optimistic interpretation on the company's position.
- The company's remuneration practices should be proportionate and support the long-term success of the company, with formal and transparent procedures in place, and with NEDs exercising independent judgement and discretion when deciding these matters.[113] Remuneration should take into account workforce remuneration when setting director remuneration, and formulaic calculations of performance-related pay should be rejected.[114]
- The CEO and the chair of the board should not be the same person, and the CEO should not move on to become chair of the board (that would compromise independence).[115] The two roles are seen as quite distinct. The chair of the board, whose role by contrast is unspecified and indeed hardly recognised in statutory company law, "leads the board and is responsible for its overall effectiveness in directing the company".[116] The chair should

---

106 CGA, Provision 4.

107 CGA, Provision 5.

108 CGA, Provision 6.

109 CGC, Provision 32. The chair of the board cannot chair the committee and should only be a member if they were independent on appointment. The committee should consist of independent NEDs, with a minimum membership of three, or in the case of smaller companies, two. Before appointment as chair of the remuneration committee, the appointee should have served on a remuneration committee for at least 12 months. And see Provision 34 on remuneration of these NEDs, which in any event is not to include share options or other performance related elements.

110 CGC, Principle M and Provision 24. The chair of the board should not be a member, and the committee should consist of at least three independent NEDs (two in smaller companies).

111 CGC, Provision 17. The chair of the board should not chair the committee when dealing with the appointment of their successor.

112 CGA, Provisions 23, 26 and 41.

113 CGA, Principles P, Q and R.

114 CGA, Provision 33.

115 CGC, Provision 9, with indications of what should be done if this is proposed.

116 CGC, Principle F.

promote a culture of openness and debate, facilitate the effective contribution of all NEDs, and ensure the directors receive accurate, timely and clear information.[117]

- A senior independent director should be identified and be available as a sounding board for the chair, as an intermediary for the other directors, and as a person for shareholders to contact if they think that contact through the CEO or chair of the board would be inappropriate.[118]
- There should be a clear division of responsibilities between the board and the executive,[119] and a formal, written, publicly available statement of the various responsibilities of the board and its committees.[120]
- There should be a formal and rigorous annual evaluation of the board, its committees, the chair and the individual directors.[121]

There are two points to be made about these provisions. The first is that the stress on the monitoring role of the independent NEDs has the effect of reproducing within the single-tier board the distinction between management and supervision (or monitoring) that is to be found within the two-tier board system. Whether it is better to extend this functional distinction into a structural division between managing and supervisory boards depends on whether one thinks it is preferable to set strategy and also to manage the control of operations in the same single tier, or somehow to separate the various tasks between two tiers.[122] That may also depend on how one views the purpose of having a more inclusive board (e.g. by having mandatory employee representation), and whether such inputs are best delivered by a single tier or a two tier system. **9–019**

Secondly, although independent NEDs may no longer be the cat's-paws of the CEO, which in the past they often were, it is far from clear that the CGC provisions provide the independent NEDs with effective incentives to exercise control over strong-minded CEOs. Since executive management is unlikely easily to accept supervision by the non-executives, the non-executives may well have a battle on their hands to impose their will where there is a divergence of view. Even when explicitly trained, as Higgs recommended, why should the NEDs fight this battle rather than opt for a quiet life? Self-esteem will provide some incentive to this end, no doubt, as does the NEDs' increasingly explicit accountability to the shareholders under the CGC.

But the potentially insoluble shortcomings here are, more recently, being addressed in quite a different way, by making shareholders, especially the institutional shareholders, more accountable for the exercise of their own powers over the governance of their companies.[123] The explicit linking of these two

---

117 CGA, Principle F.

118 CGC, Provision 12.

119 CGA, Principle G.

120 CGC, Provision 14.

121 CGA, Provision 21.

122 See P. Davies, "Board Structure in the United Kingdom and Germany: Convergence or Continuing Divergence" (2000) 2 I.C.C.L.J. 435.

123 See FRC, *The UK Stewardship Code* (2020), which applies on a "comply or explain" basis (see below) to institutional investors. Also see para.12–017.

powerful governance strands was promoted in the 2012 Kay Report,[124] which highlighted the serious problems of short-termism and consequential lack of trust in UK equity markets, with both executive remuneration packages and institutional investor practices coming into focus as needing reform.[125]

Enforcement of the UK Corporate Governance Code

9–020 We referred earlier to the UK Corporate Governance Code as "soft law". This is perhaps misleading. At the centre of the CGC there is a perfectly "hard" obligation. The Listing Rules require both UK-registered and overseas-registered companies with Premium Listing in the UK to disclose in their annual report the extent to which they have complied with the CGC in the previous 12 months and to give reasons for areas of non-compliance (if any).[126] More precisely, the company must explain how it has applied the Principles set out in the CGC (i.e. compliance at the level of principle is obligatory), and must also state whether it has complied with the lower-level Provisions of the CGC. The sanctions which can be applied to both companies and directors for non-compliance with the listing rules are extensive.[127]

The "softness" of the law is a result of the lack of legal consequences if compliance with the disclosure obligation imposed by the LR reveals non-compliance with the CGC. It would be perfectly in compliance with the listing rules for the company to report that it has not complied with the CGC in any respect, provided it also gave reasons for its wholesale rejection. Any further action on the basis of the reported non-compliance is for the shareholders, as the recipients of the annual reports, not for the FCA or any other governmental body. This has been called the principle of "comply or explain". It suggests that, even in relation to the relatively small group of Premium Listed companies, UK regulators still feel hesitant about their ability to devise governance structures which will be suitable for all the companies in the identified population. The possibility of not complying fully with the CGC gives the companies in question flexibility in adapting the provisions of the CGC to their particular circumstances, whilst the need to "explain" gives the CGC a somewhat greater force than a recommendation which companies are free to accept or reject. The freedom to explain rather than comply in full with the CGC has been used in particular by small listed companies.[128] "Comply or explain" clearly puts shareholders in a pivotal position in determining whether the CGC's requirements will bite in

---

[124] *The Kay Review of UK Equity Markets and Long-Term Decision Making: Final Report* July 2012) available at: *https://www.gov.uk/government/uploads/system/uploads/attachment_data/file/253454/bis-12-917-kay-review-of-equity-markets-final-report.pdf* [Accessed 16 March 2021].

[125] See paras 11–016 and 12–017.

[126] LR r.9.8.6(5) and (6), and LR rr.9.8.7 and 9.8.7A. UK-registered and overseas-registered companies with Standard Listing do not have to comply with the CGC, but do have to provide a statement on their corporate governance regime that meets the somewhat lower EU corporate governance standards: LR r.14.3.24.

[127] See para.25–032.

[128] See the FRC, *Annual Reviews of Corporate Governance Reporting* available at *https://www.frc.org.uk/directors/corporate-governance-and-stewardship/developments-in-corporate-governance-and-stewardsh* [Accessed 16 March 2021].

practice, and much of its impact is due to the support which institutional shareholders have given to the CGC.[129] In short, "softness" is not the same as self-regulation, with its risk of being merely self-interested: the compulsory disclosure regime, backed by the statutory right given to shareholders to dismiss directors, gives the CGC far greater bite.

How effective is this regime?[130] There is evidence of some non-compliance with even the "hard" obligation of the LR; and some companies fail to explain areas of non-compliance and rather greater numbers give explanations which can hardly be considered as adequate.[131] The level of enforcement by the FCA is relatively low. Non-compliance with the CGC itself is a more slippery concept, since there is no obligation to abide by it provided non-compliance is adequately explained. But in general companies have chosen to comply; and indeed the move has often been from inadequate explanation of non-compliance to full compliance rather than to adequate explanation.[132] In this sense, the comply or explain mechanism is clearly changing corporate behaviour, although some companies do make proper use of the explanation mechanism to give good reasons why in their particular case one or more provisions of the CGC are inappropriate.[133]

The CGC is subject to both praise and criticism. For example, its application only to Premium Listed companies can be seen as too narrow. Certainly, the Cadbury Committee recommended that its Code of Practice should be observed by all large companies. The restriction to listed companies seems to have arisen because the Listing Rules provided a convenient enforcement mechanism, not because this category aptly defines the companies for whom such rules are most appropriate. Within this limited class, however, the regime surely succeeds in putting pressure on companies to adopt higher standards of best practice, standards which would generally be seen as too onerous to be adopted as mandatory legislative minima (the composition of audit and remunerations committees is an illustration). Moreover, these standards can be regularly and flexibly reviewed in ways not possible with statutory or regulatory rules. The best evidence of these benefits might be seen in the widespread adoption of similar regimes internationally.[134]

---

[129] On the role of institutional shareholders see paras 12–013 to 12–017.

[130] See fn.128. See too the *Feedback Statement: UK Corporate Governance Code* (2018) available at *https://www.frc.org.uk/news/july-2018/a-uk-corporate-governance-code-that-is-fit-for-the* [Accessed 16 March 2021], which describes the outcome of the 2017 review of and consultation on the CGC carried out by the FRC against a background of declining trust in big business.

[131] *Feedback Statement: UK Corporate Governance Code* (2018). Also see S. Arcot and V. Bruno, "In Letter but not in Spirit: An Analysis of Corporate Governance in the UK" available at *http://papers.ssrn.com/sol3/papers.cfm?abstract_id=819784* [Accessed 16 March 2021]).

[132] See previous note.

[133] And it seems such companies do not suffer in market terms from using such an approach and seem in fact to perform well: S. Arcot and V. Bruno, *One Size Does Not Fit All After All: Evidence from Corporate Governance* (available at: *http://ssrn.com/abstract=887947* [Accessed 16 March 2021]).

[134] See FRC, *25th Anniversary of the UK Corporate Governance Code* available at: *https://www.frc.org.uk/directors/corporate-governance-and-stewardship/uk-corporate-governance-code/25th anniversary-of-the-uk-corporate-governance-co* [Accessed 16 March 2021].

THE WATES CORPORATE GOVERNANCE PRINCIPLES FOR LARGE PRIVATE COMPANIES

9–021 The ideas embedded in the UK Corporate Governance Code have not only spread by osmosis to smaller companies, but modified and simplified versions of them are slowly becoming mandatory. The Companies (Miscellaneous Reporting) Regulations 2018 now requires (in reg.26) that all companies of significant size[135] that are not already required to provide a corporate governance statement, to disclose their corporate governance arrangements, including which corporate governance code, if any, the company applied in the financial year, how it was applied, and how and why the company departed from it. This is already labelled an "apply and explain" approach, distinguishing it from the familiar "comply or explain". The manner of reporting is not specified, and that in itself may prove a challenge.

The new rules do not specify which code must be adopted, so the Wates Corporate Governance Principles for Large Private Companies (the Wates Principles), published in December 2018, are likely to be popular. These Principles were prepared at the request of the government by a coalition of partners, chaired by James Wates CBE, with secretariat support from the Financial Reporting Council. They introduce six principles of good corporate governance said to offer "sufficient flexibility for a diverse range of companies to explain the application and relevance of their corporate governance arrangements, without being unduly prescriptive". The Principles, in abbreviated form, address the following issues, providing supporting guidance without prescribing how the Principles ought to be applied:

(1) Purpose and leadership: An effective board develops and promotes the purpose of a company, and ensures that its values, strategy and culture align with that purpose.
(2) Board composition: Effective board composition requires an effective chair and a balance of skills, backgrounds, experience and knowledge.
(3) Director responsibilities: The board and individual directors should have a clear understanding of their accountability and responsibilities.
(4) Opportunity and risk: A board should promote the long-term sustainable success of the company, and establish oversight for the identification and mitigation of risks.
(5) Remuneration: A board should promote executive remuneration structures aligned to the long-term sustainable success of a company.
(6) Stakeholder relationships and engagement: Directors should foster effective stakeholder relationships aligned to the company's purpose.

Given the non-prescriptive approach adopted, it is likely that the Principles will reinforce the practices of companies already operating with good governance, but the harder question is whether it will be enough to change the behaviours of the

[135] Specified as companies with more than 2,000 employees and/or a turnover of more than £200 million and a balance sheet of more than £2 billion. There are estimated to be approximately 1,700 such companies.

others. The incentive of compulsory public reporting, even without regulatory sanction for poor performance, is likely to be a powerful driver. In addition, given the flexibility of the Principles, even smaller companies are likely to find them useful as a framework for assessing the strengths and weaknesses in their own practices.

CONCLUSION

The boards of directors have long been the "black box" of British company law. In large companies, with numerous and dispersed shareholding bodies, the central management of the company's business is necessarily in the hands of the board. Yet company law has traditionally specified very little about how this body should operate. That the board is central to the operation of companies was recognised from the beginning by the development of a wide range of duties which apply to directors who undertake to act on behalf of the company (considered in Ch.10). However, the questions of which functions should be assigned to the board and of how the board should organise itself for the effective discharge of those duties were ones that company law did not seek to answer. All that constituted the "internal management" of the company which it was for the shareholders to design. **9–022**

That still remains largely the case, although the case law on the disqualification of directors (considered in Ch.20), conceived with the interests of creditors in mind, has begun to lead to the formulation of more demanding principles about the proper conduct of directors of all companies. For listed companies, however, things have changed over the past quarter of a century. Now there is not only a small-scale corporate governance industry in existence, but the central tenets of its beliefs have been given regulatory expression in the UK Corporate Governance Code which, with the support of the institutional shareholders, exerts a real, although not completely inflexible, pressure on companies to conform to a particular model of board composition and operation. A company whose business is producing outstanding profits can probably afford to ignore this Code to a large extent, but should its business performance falter, it is likely to find the pressures to conform to that model irresistible.

CHAPTER 10

DIRECTORS' DUTIES

INTRODUCTION

10–001 In Ch.9 we saw that it is common for the articles of large companies to confer extremely broad discretionary powers upon the boards of companies. The arguments in favour of giving the centralised management a broad power to run the company are essentially arguments of efficiency. At the same time, the grant of a broad discretion creates a real risk that the powers will be exercised by the directors other than for the purposes for which they were conferred and, in particular will be exercised more in the interests of the senior management themselves than of anyone else. A central part of company law is thus concerned with providing a framework of rules which, on the one hand, constrains the potential abuse by directors of their powers, whilst on the other hand does not so constrain the directors that the efficiency gains from having a strong centralised management are dissipated. This is an age-old problem for company law and one that is constantly re-visited by successive generations of rule-makers, for no one approach can be shown to have struck the balance in an appropriate manner. It was a major issue in the debates leading up to the passage of the CA 2006.

On the part of the rule-makers, a number of distinct responses to this intractable problem can be identified. In Chs 9 and 11 we examine the extent to which rules relating to the structure and composition of the board itself and to the power of the shareholders to remove members of the board are used to constrain the exercise by the board of its powers and to produce accountability to the members of the company. In Ch.11 we also analyse the opportunities which the shareholders have to intervene directly in the management of the company by securing the passing at general meetings of resolutions binding the company or by subjecting the performance of the management to critical review. The taking of managerial decisions by the shareholders themselves is necessarily an activity of limited potential in large companies, since it flies in the face of the efficiency arguments for centralised management in the first place. Indeed, well-directed criticism of board performance may be more effective, especially if accompanied by an implicit or explicit threat of removal if performance is not improved.

In addition to rules on board structure and the governance rights of the members of the company, there is a third set of rules of great longevity in our law which are intended to operate so as to constrain the board's exercise of its powers. These are the duties which company law lays directly on the individual members of the board as to limits within which they should exercise their powers. These rules for directors were developed by the courts at an early stage, often on the basis of analogy with the rules applying to trustees. The substantial corpus of learning on the nature and scope of these general fiduciary or equitable and common law duties of skill and care has remained until very recently largely within the common law. Now these rules appear as a statutory enactment of high-level principles in the CA 2006 Ch.2 of Pt 10 which is headed: "General Duties of Directors".[1]

THE SCOPE AND GENERAL NATURE OF THE DUTIES OWED: S.170

The main aim behind the initial proposals for a "high level" statutory statement of directors' duties was to promote understanding of the basic principles underlying this area of law, especially among directors themselves. It was thought that this objective would be furthered if there was a relatively brief statutory statement of those principles in place of the previous situation whereby those principles had to be deduced from an elaborate body of case law. The behavioural premises upon which this view was based were never extensively investigated, but the move also had to overcome legal objections to codification. The first objection to codification was that such a reform might "freeze" the law of directors' duties, **10–002**

[1] Both the Law Commission and the CLR made what was then a controversial recommendation favouring this "high level" statutory restatement of the common law principles. The details of the issues in play are set out in more detail in the 10th edn of this book at paras 16-1 to 16-3, as summarised more briefly here.

impeding its further development as circumstances changed. This was thought at the time—and has turned out to be—unlikely, given that such "high-level" statements as are included in CA 2006 give the courts plenty of interpretative scope when applying the principles to the changing circumstances of commercial life. In addition, s.170(4) adds two propositions: first, the statutory general duties "shall be interpreted and applied in the same way as the common law duties or equitable principles", so that the existing case law on the common law duties will remain, in most cases, relevant to the interpretation of the statutory duties; and secondly, "regard shall be had to the corresponding common law rules and equitable principles in interpreting and applying the general principles". This second proposition is most unusual as an instruction on statutory interpretation, but it enables the courts, in developing the statutory duties of directors, to take into account developments in the equivalent common law duties applying to trustees and agents. Self-evidently, there was no desire on the part of the legislature to cut the law of directors' duties off from its historical roots in the duties applying to other persons acting in a fiduciary character.

A second objection to codification was that a high-level statutory statement would cause confusion or uncertainty about the relationship between the statutory statement and existing common law rules. These matters are dealt with explicitly in subss.170(3) and (4). The first subsection establishes the proposition that the general duties replace ("have effect in place of") the common law principles on which they are based. Consequently, any allegation of breach of duty by the director to the company must be identified as a breach of one or more of the general duties set out in the statute, unless the statutory statement expressly preserves the common law duties, as it does in relation to creditors' interests.[2] And s.170(4) indicates, as already noted, how the common law cases are to be used.

On the other hand, the statutory statement is more than simply a restatement of the common law. In some cases it clarifies areas of uncertainty in the common law, for example, in relation to the standard of care expected of directors, whilst in others it adopts a different approach from that of the common law, for example, in relation to the authorisation by independent directors of conflicts of duty. This makes it important to understand when the statute departs from the common law in order to determine the relevance, or not, of analogous common law decisions to the interpretation of the statute.

The seven duties set out in Ch.2 of Pt 10 cover only the substantive content of the directors' duties. Codification of the remedies for breaches of duty was contemplated, but not pursued to its conclusion.[3] The Act simply provides in s.178 that the civil consequences of breaches of the statutory duties are to be those which would apply at common law. The means that any difficulties and uncertainties on the remedial front in the common law—and there are a number—persist in assessing the consequences for directors of a breach of their statutory duties.

[2] See paras 19–013 to 19–019.

[3] The work is summarised in R.C. Nolan, "Enacting Civil Remedies in Company Law" (2001) 1 J.C.L.S. 245.

INTRODUCTION TO THE DIRECTORS' VARIOUS DUTIES

Historical background

We turn now to the substance of the duties which directors assume when they take up office. It is common to divide those duties into duties of loyalty and duties of care, broadly corresponding to the two main types of risk which shareholders run when management of their company is delegated to the board: the board may be active, but not in the direction of promoting the shareholders' interests; or the board may be slack or incompetent. Further, this division also corresponds with the two basic common law sources of the rules on directors' duties in English law: duties of loyalty based on equitable principles, developed initially by courts of equity, and duties of skill and care which now rest, with some particular twists, on the principles of the law of negligence.[4] However, it is notable that the general duties laid out in Ch.2 of Pt 10 are not divided or ordered in quite this way. The duty of care appears as the fourth of seven duties, the other six of which are based on various aspects of the equitable duties of loyalty. Here, for obvious reasons, we will follow the divisions and ordering set out by the statute. 10–003

The various duties of good faith and loyalty which the law requires of directors were developed by the courts by analogy with the duties of trustees, and the analogies remain crucial. It is easy to see, historically, how this came about. Prior to the Joint Stock Companies Act 1844 most joint stock companies were unincorporated and depended for their validity on a deed of settlement vesting the property of the company in trustees. Often the directors were themselves the trustees and even when a distinction was drawn between the passive trustees and the managing board of directors, the latter would quite clearly be regarded as "trustees" in the eyes of a court of equity in so far as they dealt with the trust property. With directors of incorporated companies, the description "trustees" was less apposite because the assets were now held by the company, a separate legal person, rather than being vested in trustees. However, it was not unnatural that the courts should extend such duties to them by analogy. For one thing, the duties of the directors should obviously be the same whether the company was incorporated or not; for another, historically, the courts of equity tended to apply the label "trustee" indiscriminately to anyone in a fiduciary position. Now we would more properly distinguish between "trustees" (who hold trust property) and "fiduciaries" (who do not, but who owe similar duties in the management of property for the benefit of others). The duties of good faith and loyalty which this relationship imposes are in material respects identical with those imposed on trustees. Moreover, when it comes to remedies for breach of duty, the trust analogy provides a strong remedial structure. Directors who dispose of the company's assets in breach of duty, for example, are regarded as committing a breach of fiduciary duty similar to a breach of trust, and those persons (including

[4] Although, historically, in the context of trustees, this duty too was first developed by the courts of equity.

the directors themselves) into whose hands the assets come may find that they are under a duty to restore the value of the misapplied assets to the company.[5]

Given the modern statutory statement of the general duties owed by directors, these analogies and their various limitations are of less substantive importance than they once were. Nevertheless, an eye must be kept on them for two reasons: the statutory duties themselves are subject to interpretation in the light of analogous common law cases (s.170(4)); and the remedial consequences of statutory breaches remain to be determined by the appropriate corresponding common law rules (s.178).

There is one final point to note with these duties: they are owed individually by each of the directors to their company. As we saw in Ch.8, the authority of the directors to bind the company depends on their acting collectively as a board, unless authority has (or can be assumed to have) been further delegated under the company's constitution to an individual director.[6] By contrast, their duties are owed by each director individually. One of several directors may not have power to saddle the company with responsibility for his acts, but he will invariably be a fiduciary of the company, and will also owe all the separate statutory duties to it. To this extent, directors again resemble trustees who must normally act jointly but each of whom severally owes duties of loyalty and care and skill towards the beneficiaries.

Categories of duties

10–004 Turning now to the main elements of the directors' statutory duties, we divide them as below into seven categories, following the scheme of the Act. The first three categories describe distinct duties, all being concerned with the manner in which directors exercise their powers, being that the directors must:

(1) act within the scope of the powers which have been conferred upon them, and for proper purposes;
(2) act in good faith to promote the success of the company; and
(3) exercise independent judgment; and
(4) then comes the duty of care and skill.

The final three categories of duties are all examples of fiduciary duties of loyalty, and in particular the rule against directors putting themselves in a position in which their personal interests (or alternatively their duties to others) conflict with their duty to the company. However, it is useful—and CA 2006 has seen it as useful—to sub-divide this "no conflict" principle further because the specific rules implementing the principle differ according to whether the conflict arises:

[5] See *JJ Harrison (Properties) Ltd v Harrison* [2001] EWCA Civ 1467; [2002] 1 B.C.L.C. 162 at 173 (Chadwick LJ); *Madoff Securities International Ltd (In Liquidation) v Raven* [2013] EWHC 3147 (Comm) at [292] (Popplewell J); and *Fern Advisers Ltd v Burford* [2014] EWHC 762 (QB) at [18] (HH Judge Mackie QC). See further below, at para.10–130. The language has become increasingly precise over time.

[6] See para.8–016.

(5) out of a transaction with the company (self-dealing transactions);
(6) out of the receipt from a third party of a benefit for exercising their directorial functions in a particular way; or
(7) out of the director's personal exploitation of the company's property, information or opportunities.

For the purposes of analysis it is inevitable that the duties are separated out in some way such as that adopted in the CA 2006. However, s.179 specifically provides that, except where a duty is explicitly excluded by something in the statute, "more than one of the general duties may apply in any given case". In practice, here as in other areas of the law, the facts will frequently suggest breach of more than one of the duties [7] and, where this is so, the claimant can choose to pursue all or any of them, subject of course to the usual rules against double recovery or advancing inconsistent claims.[8]

TO WHOM AND BY WHOM ARE THE DUTIES OWED?

To whom are the general duties owed and who can sue for their breach?

The company

Before turning to the individual directors' duties, we need to ask who are their targets, i.e. to whom are these duties owed? The answer in British law is clear: the common law formulation was that the duties of the directors were owed to "the company" and that is repeated in s.170(1) in respect of the statutory duties. The importance of this point arises mainly in relation to the enforcement of those duties. First, it tells us that those duties are not owed to persons other than the company, for example, individual shareholders or employees. Secondly, it tells us that only those who are able to act as or on behalf of the company can enforce the duties.[9] Despite this, that does not prevent individual shareholders and other stakeholders endeavouring to advance personal claims against wrongdoing directors. These are rarely successful, for the reasons considered next. **10–005**

Individual shareholders

Although it is clear that the statutory duties are owed only to the company, that leaves open whether, at common law, fiduciary or other duties are owed by the directors to shareholders individually. Traditionally, the common law has been reluctant to recognise directors' general duties as being owed to shareholders individually. This is hardly surprising. Recognition of duties owed individually **10–006**

[7] Note Charities Act 2011 s.105(9): an order under this section may authorise an act even though it involves a breach of one or more of the general duties just described.

[8] *Tang Man Sit v Capacious Investments Ltd* [1995] UKPC 54.

[9] See Ch.8 (taking actions on behalf of the company) and 9 (decisions by boards for the company) but importantly see Ch.15 (the statutory derivative action, enabling shareholders to bring claims against directors for the benefit of the company).

would undermine the collective nature of the shareholders' association in a company. It would also undermine the rule that the duties are owed to and are enforceable by the company. If the directors owed to individual shareholders a set of duties parallel to those owed by them to the company, the restrictions on the derivative action could easily be side-stepped by means of the individual shareholder suing to enforce, not the company's rights, but his or her own rights.[10]

However, the precept that directors' duties are not owed to individual shareholders applies only to those duties which directors are subject to simply by virtue of their appointment and actions as directors. There may well be, in a particular case, dealings between one or more directors and one or more of the shareholders as a result of which a duty of some sort becomes owed by a director to one or more shareholders. For example, in *Peskin v Anderson*,[11] Mummery LJ distinguished clearly between the fiduciary duties owed by directors to the company which arise out of the relationship between the director and the company, and fiduciary duties owed to shareholders which are dependent upon establishing "a special factual relationship between the directors and the shareholders in the particular case".

The crucial question, therefore, is what sort of dealing needs to take place between director and shareholder in order to trigger a fiduciary or other duty owed to an individual shareholder by the directors. Such a duty will certainly arise where the directors place themselves, as against shareholders individually, in one of the established legal relationships to which fiduciary duties are attached, such as agency. This may arise, for example, where the shareholders authorise the directors to sell their shares on their behalf to a potential takeover bidder.[12] If, in the course of such a relationship, the directors come across information which is pertinent to the shareholders' decision whether or on what terms to sell the shares, they would normally be obliged to disclose it to the shareholders on whose behalf they are acting. On the other hand, in *Percival v Wright*,[13] which is the leading authority for the proposition that the directors' duties as directors are not owed to the shareholders individually, the directors purchased shares from their members without revealing that negotiations were in progress for the sale of the company's undertaking at a favourable price. They were held not to be in breach of duty through their non-disclosure. Here, however, the key feature was that the shareholders approached the directors directly and sought to persuade the directors to purchase their shares themselves; they did not seek to have the directors act as the shareholders' agents to sell the shares to third parties.

10–007 Nevertheless, there is no doubt that the directors of a company are likely to have much more information at their disposal about the company and so are likely to

---

[10] On similar grounds the court rejected an attempt to create a parallel set of duties owed by directors to individual shareholders via implied terms in the articles of association: *Towcester Racecourse Co Ltd v Racecourse Association Ltd* [2002] EWHC 2141 (Ch).

[11] *Peskin v Anderson* [2001] 1 B.C.L.C. 372 CA (Civ Div) at 379. To the same end, see *Sharp v Blank* [2015] EWHC 3220 (Ch); [2015] B.C.C. 187.

[12] *Briess v Woolley* [1954] A.C. 333 HL; *Allen v Hyatt* (1914) 30 T.L.R. 444 PC.

[13] *Percival v Wright* [1902] 2 Ch. 421 Ch D. This applies even if all the shares are owned by a holding company with which the directors have service contracts: *Bell v Lever Brothers Ltd* [1932] A.C. 161 HL.

be at an advantage when dealing with the members. The law of agency, as we have just seen, will cover some, but not all of this ground. Can the doctrine of a "special factual relationship" be extended beyond the law of agency? Commonwealth authority established some time ago that it can. In *Coleman v Myers*[14] the New Zealand Court of Appeal found that a fiduciary duty of disclosure arose, even in the absence of agency, in the case of a small family company where there was a gross disparity of knowledge between the directors and the shareholders and where the shareholders of the company had traditionally relied on the directors for information and advice. When the directors negotiated with the shareholders for the purchase of their shares and, therefore, were clearly not acting on behalf of the shareholders, they were nevertheless held to be subject to a fiduciary duty of full disclosure of relevant facts about the company to the shareholders. The New Zealand decision was approved by the English Court of Appeal in *Peskin v Anderson*,[15] though the English decision also reveals the limits of the rule. In the English case, directors were not obliged to disclose to shareholders their plans for the company, even though the shareholders' decision on the sale of their shares would have been affected by the knowledge, where the directors were not parties to or otherwise involved in the sale of the shares, and the company's interests arguably required the directors' plans to be kept secret until they matured.[16]

This means that, despite the recent significant developments in English law based on a "special relationship" exception to the general proposition that directors do not owe duties directly to the shareholders, the exception is essentially one of significance for family or small companies, and does not substantially reduce, within companies with large shareholder bodies, the significance of the general proposition. The cases already noted affirm that this is true even where advice is given by directors in the course of a takeover bid. In *Re A Company*[17] Hoffmann J held that directors were not obliged to offer their shareholders advice on the bid, but, if they did so, they must do so "with a view to enabling the shareholders to sell, if they so wish, at the best price" and not, for example, in order to favour one bid, which the directors supported, over another, which they did not.[18] This identifies two strands: the directors' advice must be

[14] *Coleman v Myers* [1977] 2 N.Z.L.R. 225 NZCA. In the Supreme Court, Mahon J had held that *Percival v Wright* was wrongly decided but the Court of Appeal distinguished it. See also *Brunningshausen v Glavanics* (1999) 46 N.S.W.L.R. 538 CANSW.

[15] *Peskin v Anderson* [2001] 1 B.C.L.C. 372 at 397, following the decisions of Browne-Wilkinson VC in *Re Chez Nico (Restaurants) Ltd* [1991] B.C.C. 736 Ch D at 750 and, though not cited, of David Mackie QC in *Platt v Platt* [1999] 2 B.C.L.C. 745 Ch D (the Court of Appeal in that case did not deal with the point: [2001] 1 B.C.L.C. 698 CA (Civ Div)).

[16] Similarly, see *Sharp v Blank* [2015] EWHC 3220 (Ch); [2017] B.C.C. 187, with Nugee J denying the directors owed a fiduciary duty to the shareholders in the context of Lloyds Banking Group's acquisition of Halifax Bank of Scotland Plc.

[17] *Re A Company* [1986] B.C.L.C. 382. The case involved an application under s.459 (now CA 2006 s.994, see Ch.14), but the judge's analysis appears to have related to the common law.

[18] See also *Re Charterhouse Capital Ltd* [2014] EWHC 1410 (Ch) at [276] in particular (Asplin J); as affirmed in [2015] EWCA Civ 536; [2015] B.C.C. 574 (in particular at [50]). In addition, takeover bids for public and listed companies will be governed by the City Code on Takeovers and Mergers (see Ch.28), which both requires directors to give advice and attempts to ensure that that advice is given to serve the shareholders' needs. These more demanding provisions of the Code will in practice overtake those of the common law.

careful, and must also be given so as to achieve its (proper) purposes, and not the directors' own (improper) purposes.[19] Neither strand imports a "fiduciary" duty of loyalty to the shareholders.

Other stakeholders

10–008 If British company law has been reluctant to recognise general duties owed by directors to individual shareholders, it perhaps goes without saying that it has not recognised such duties owed to individual employees or creditors[20] or other groups[21] upon whom the successful functioning of the company depends. It is important to distinguish this issue (duties owed directly to stakeholder groups) from the question of how far directors' duties owed to the company require the directors to take into account the interests of stakeholder groups. Explicit duties of this latter kind are embodied in the CA 2006 and are dealt with below in our analysis of the statutory duties.

By whom are the general duties owed?

De facto and shadow directors

10–009 The general statutory duties discussed in this chapter are clearly owed by those who have been properly appointed as directors of the company. From the early days, however, the courts have also applied the common law and statutory duties to persons who act as directors, even though they have not been formally appointed as such—normally referred as "de facto directors". There seems to be no doubt that the general statutory duties apply to de facto directors,[22] whatever the debate over whether a person is indeed a de facto director or is merely performing some lower-level management role.[23] Although there is no single test

[19] On proper purposes requirement, see para.10–018.

[20] *Yukong Line Ltd of Korea v Rendsburg Investments Corp of Liberia (The Rialto)* [1998] B.C.C. 870 QBD (Comm); and see below at paras 19–013 to 19–019.

[21] For example, the beneficiaries of a trust which the company, as trustee, is managing: *Bath v Standard Land Co* [1911] 1 Ch. 618 CA; *Gregson v HAE Trustees Ltd* [2008] EWHC 1006 (Ch); [2008] 2 P. & C.R. DG9, confirming that although the beneficiary could not pursue a claim against the director directly (since the director's duty was owed to the trustee company, not to the beneficiary, although the beneficiary was in turn owed duties by the trustee company), the beneficiary would, in any event, be protected by the liquidator's ability to pursue the insolvent trustee company's claim against its defaulting director.

[22] Indeed, there is statutory support for this in the definition of a director in s.250, with "director" defined as including "any person occupying the position of director, by whatever name called".

[23] The easy cases are those such as *Re Canadian Land Reclaiming & Colonizing Co* (1880) 14 Ch. D. 660 CA concerning a director not properly appointed because of his failure to take up shares in the company which action its articles stipulated to be a condition for appointment as director. For a more detailed discussion in a modern context of what makes a person a de facto director, see *Secretary of State for Trade and Industry v Tjolle* [1998] B.C.C. 282; and *Gemma Ltd (In Liquidation) v Davies* [2008] EWHC 546 (Ch); [2008] B.C.C. 812. This latter case, at [40], shows that the important question is whether the person is factually engaged in the central management of the company on an equal footing with the other directors and performing tasks that can only properly be discharged by directors, regardless of whether the person is held out as a director of the company (although holding out may provide important supporting evidence that the individual is acting as a director). Also see

for de facto directors, the central question which the courts seek to answer is whether the individual was "part of the corporate governing structure"[24] or has "assumed the status and functions of a company director"[25] so as to attract responsibility under the Act as if he or she were a de jure director.

This factual question is often difficult to answer, but the problem is exacerbated where the issue is whether a de jure director of one company can, in the course of acting in that role, become a de facto director of another company. Does the formal role with one company protect against liability to the other company? In answering this question, the Supreme Court in *Commissioners of HM Revenue and Customs v Holland*[26] divided 3:2 over what Lord Collins described as differences over matters of law and principle.[27] The issue was whether an individual who was the only active director of the sole corporate director[28] of the principal companies was, in those circumstances, also a de facto director of the principal companies, held to be part of the corporate governance of them and having fiduciary and other directors' duties imposed on him in relation to them. Those in the majority thought that such a finding would contradict the principle of separate legal personality, and reflect a failure to recognise the distinction between a company and its directors, where, as here (so they held), the individual had done nothing other than discharge his duties a director of the corporate director, and in circumstances where the law condones corporate directorships.[29]

This argument has its attractions. Indeed, it follows, although not explicitly, the approach adopted in determining the individual liability of company directors to third parties in contract and in tort in circumstances where the company, by virtue of the acts of its directors, is also liable to the same parties.[30] In the fiduciary arena it is suggested that the question to ask is not whether the purported director assumed fiduciary responsibilities to the company; the answer to that, at least from the director, is likely to be precisely not (and hence the

---

Revenue and Customs Commissioners v Holland [2010] UKSC 51; [2011] B.C.C. 1, discussed below, declining to identify a single defining test ([26], [39], [93]) but supporting the focus on finding real influence in the central governance of the company (paras [36], [91]). See also *Elsworth Ethanol Co Ltd v Hartley* [2014] EWHC 99 (IPEC) at [54], and, as an illustration of the highly factual nature of the question, [58]–[85] (Judge Hacon); and *Smithton Ltd (formerly Hobart Capital Markets Ltd) v Naggar* [2014] EWCA Civ 939; [2014] B.C.C. 482 at [33]–[44] (Arden LJ). See also generally *Secretary of State for Business, Innovation and Skills v Chohan* [2013] EWHC 680 (Ch); [2015] B.C.C. 755 (Hildyard J); *Vivendi SA v Richards* [2013] EWHC 3006; [2013] B.C.C. 771 (Newey J).

[24] *Secretary of State for Trade and Industry v Tjolle* [1998] B.C.C. 282 at 290 (Jacob J).

[25] *Re Kaytech International Plc* [1999] B.C.C. 390 CA (Civ Div) at 402 (Robert Walker LJ).

[26] *Holland* [2011] B.C.C. 1.

[27] *Holland* [2011] B.C.C. 1 at [53].

[28] This is no longer permitted: every company must now have at least one human director (s.155); and corporate directorships will be fully prohibited (subject to exceptions) if and when the long-proposed ss.156A–156C, introduced by s.87 of the Small Business, Enterprise and Employment Act 2015, are brought into force.

[29] *Holland* [2011] B.C.C. 1 at [25], [28]–[29], [39]–[40], [42]–[43], [94]–[96]. Also see previous note. This follows the trend in other jurisdictions where the legislature has intervened to require that all directors be natural persons: e.g. as under the Corporations Act 2001 s.201B (Australia), the Canada Business Corporations Act 1985 s.105(1)(c), the New York Business Corporation Law s.701, and the Delaware General Corporate Law s.141(b) (see *Holland* at [96], Lord Collins).

[30] See above, paras 8–054 to 8–058. By contrast, see *Holland* [2011] B.C.C. 1 at [117]–[118] (Lord Walker) on the approach in tort cases.

corporate directorship structure). Better to ask, as in negligent misstatement cases,[31] whether, in the circumstances, and looking at what the purported director did, the company is entitled to demand that the individual be subjected to fiduciary obligations. Where the formal structure of a corporate directorship has been transparently erected, the answer is surely no, even though, absent that structure, it would perhaps equally certainly have been yes.

The practical effect in *Holland* was that the principal companies' acknowledged liability to the Inland Revenue was not met by the principals, which were insolvent, nor by the corporate director, which though liable was an undercapitalised intermediary, nor by Holland, since he was not a de facto director of the principal companies.[32] In the circumstances it is difficult not to feel some sympathy for the views of the dissenting minority: Lords Walker and Clarke would have preferred a conclusion that, while a de facto director is not formally invested with office, if what he actually does amounts to taking all the important decisions affecting the relevant company, and seeing that they are carried out, he is acting as a director of that company.[33] Lord Walker even suggested that the majority's contrary characterisation of Holland's activities amounted to "the most arid formalism",[34] adding that if on these facts Holland could not be found to be both the de jure director of the corporate director and, at the same time, the de facto director of the principal companies, then it was difficult to imagine facts which would ever give rise to such a conclusion; the result, Lord Walker thought, would be to make it "easier for risk-averse individuals to use artificial corporate structures in order to insulate themselves against responsibility to an insolvent company's unsecured creditors".[35] This, clearly, is not the goal, although nor too is riding roughshod over legitimate corporate risk allocation structures.

10–010 As well as rules on de jure and de facto directors, the legislature has created a third category of director—the "shadow director". This is a person, not formally appointed as a director, but in accordance with whose directions or instructions the directors of a company are accustomed to act.[36] A number of specific statutory duties which supplement the general duties, and are to be found in Chs 3 and 4 of Pt 10, are expressed to apply also to shadow directors. In relation to the general duties contained in Ch.2, s.170(5) initially unhelpfully provided that they apply to shadow directors "to the extent that the corresponding common law rules

[31] Where, again, the question is often said to be simply whether the adviser "assumed" responsibility for the advice being given, although the court, taking a more objective approach, seems to search for whether the advisee is entitled to insist that the adviser did so do that.

[32] Although perhaps the desired remedy might be achieved in two steps, with the principal companies suing the corporate director, liquidating it, and it (through its liquidators) then suing Holland for the liabilities his management failings had caused to it, with the proceeds of this second claim then passed down the chain to meet the corporate director's primary liability to the principal companies. The issue in *Holland* is that the wrong in the first step was wrongly paying away dividends (a strict liability claim); in the second step it would perhaps have to have been negligently advising that the payments were permissible in the circumstances, and the facts may not have readily supported such a claim (given the legal advice etc obtained by Holland).

[33] *Holland* [2011] B.C.C. 1 at [114]–[115], [129]–[134], [139], [144]–[145].

[34] *Holland* [2011] B.C.C. 1 at [115].

[35] *Holland* [2011] B.C.C. 1 at [101] and [115].

[36] CA 2006 s.251(1).

or equitable principles apply"; this has now been amended to provide that shadow directors will equally be subject to the general duties "where and to the extent that they are capable of so applying".

This legislative change conclusively confirms the slow judicial working towards the same position. In the early case of *Ultraframe (UK) Ltd v Fielding*,[37] Lewison J had taken the view that directors' fiduciary duties did not automatically apply to shadow directors, on the grounds that a shadow director, unlike a de facto or properly appointed director, had not undertaken to act on behalf of the company and so had not put him- or herself in a fiduciary relationship with the company. This decision provided a relatively easy route for the true mover behind the company's strategy to distance him- or herself from liability for the decisions taken, by appointing a compliant board and giving it instructions at crucial points.[38] By contrast, almost a decade later the equally careful analysis of Newey J in *Vivendi SA v Richards*[39] doubted this approach and concluded that, by definition of the role,[40] a shadow director's self-appointed involvement in influencing governance decisions must at law inevitably mean that shadow directors commonly owed fiduciary duties to at least some degree.[41] This judicial and statutory change is welcome. If the purpose of the law of directors' duties is to constrain the exercise of the discretion vested in the board, it would be unfortunate if those rules did not reach all those involved in that exercise.

The early source of this definitional difficulty probably lay in the firm distinction which the courts sought to draw between a de facto and a shadow director. In *Re Hydrodam (Corby) Ltd*[42] Millett J took the view that in nearly all cases the two categories were mutually exclusive: **10–011**

> "A *de facto* director … is one who claims to act and purports to act as a director, although not validly appointed as such. A shadow director, by contrast, does not claim or purport to act as director. On the contrary, he claims not to be a director. He lurks in the shadows, sheltering behind others who, he claims, are the only directors of the company to the exclusion of himself."

[37] *Ultraframe (UK) Ltd v Fielding* [2005] EWHC 1638 (Ch); [2006] F.S.R. 17 at [1279] onwards—the case went on appeal but the CA did not consider this issue. cf. *The Rialto* [1998] B.C.C. 870, in which Toulson J, in a brief and unargued dictum, took the opposite view.

[38] The judge did accept that the shadow director might attract liability under the rules relating to the involvement of third parties in breaches of directors' duties (see para.10–130), but these provisions are relatively restrictive.

[39] *Vivendi SA v Richards* [2013] B.C.C. 771.

[40] *Sukhoruchkin v Van Bekestein* [2014] EWCA Civ 399 at [39]–[41], notes the differences in approach between *Ultraframe* and *Vivendi* without preferring one or other, but also notes that any conclusions are necessarily built on the foundation of the UK statutory definition of a shadow director, and so may not be appropriate in the context of other statutory definitions (as in the instant case).

[41] See *Vivendi SA v Richards* [2013] B.C.C. 771 at [133]–[145], especially [142]. See also *Smithton Ltd v Naggar* [2014] B.C.C. 482 at [33]–[45] (Arden LJ).

[42] *Re Hydrodam (Corby) Ltd (In Liquidation)* [1994] 2 B.C.L.C. 180 Ch D at 183.

This view that the categories are mutually exclusive is increasingly doubted,[43] even though certain statutory provisions apply to both shadow directors and directors whilst others apply only to directors (in which category the courts have long included de facto directors). Despite this, the modern trend, supported by the statutory change in terminology in s.170(5), is that the differences between the two categories of directors should not be the main focus of attention when determining the applicability of the general statutory duties of directors. As Robert Walker LJ pointed out in *Re Kaytech International Plc*,[44] "the two concepts do have at least this much in common, that an individual who was not a *de jure* director is alleged to have exercised real influence in the corporate governance of a company".[45] In principle, the general duties should apply to all these people with "real influence". If there is a difference, it is likely to be practical, in that the general rules should be applied to shadow directors only to the extent that they have exercised control over the board, as the statutory formula implicitly recognises, while they should apply to de jure directors in full[46]: it is not inherent in the definition of a shadow director that he or she should have controlled all the activities of the board[47]; by contrast, most de facto directors assume general directorial responsibilities.

Finally, in the context of shadow directors, two statutory exceptions are provided. First, it is recognised that boards are very likely—indeed are well-advised—to act in accordance with the directions, advice or guidance of their professional advisers or of parties acting under statutory or Ministerial authority. These advisers are not thereby to be regarded as shadow directors (s.251(2)). Secondly, and perhaps more controversially, a company is not to be regarded as the shadow director of its subsidiary for the purpose of the general duties by reason only that the directors of the subsidiary are accustomed to act on the instructions of the parent (s.251(3)).[48] And, although the Act is silent on this, the parent is also unlikely to be classified as a de facto director, rather than a shadow director, if it is not involved in a direct way in the central management of the subsidiary. A parent company can thus impose a common policy on the group of companies which it controls without placing itself in breach of duty to the subsidiary (for example, because the group policy is not in the best interests of the subsidiary). Note, though, that s.251(3) does not answer the separate question

---

[43] As well as the cases which follow, see too *McKillen v Misland (Cyprus) Investments Ltd* [2012] EWHC 521 (Ch), which describes de facto and shadow directors at [19]–[31], concluding at [32]–[34] that there is no sharp dividing line between the two classes (David Richards J); similarly, see *Smithton Ltd v Naggar* [2014] B.C.C. 482 at [33]–[45] (Arden LJ).

[44] *Re Kaytech International Plc* [1999] 2 B.C.L.C. 351 CA (Civ Div) at 424.

[45] Also see *Holland* [2011] B.C.C. 1 at [110], [127]—Lords Walker and Clarke respectively, although both dissenting on the majority's finding that the defendant was not a de facto director.

[46] Supporting this approach, see *Re System Building Services Group Ltd (In Liquidation)* [2020] EWHC 54 (Ch); [2020] B.C.C. 345 at [52]–[65] (Trower J).

[47] *Secretary of State for Trade and Industry v Deverell* [2000] B.C.C. 1057 CA (Civ Div) at [35]. The conclusion to be drawn from all these cases is perhaps that it is often possible to find that the shadow director owes all the general duties of de jure directors in relation to any decisions where he or she directed the outcome, but whether the shadow director is also subject to other duties, e.g. on pursuing corporate opportunities (see para.10–081), needs to be more carefully determined on a case by case basis. See also *Vivendi SA v Richards* [2013] B.C.C. 771 at [133]–[145] (Newey J); and *Smithton Ltd v Naggar* [2014] B.C.C. 482 at [33]–[45] (Arden LJ).

[48] A non-corporate controlling shareholder does not have the same protection.

of whether the directors of the subsidiary can agree to implement the group policy without placing themselves in breach of duty to the subsidiary, which is discussed in para.10–031.

Senior managers

The general statutory duties set out in Ch.2 of Pt 10 clearly do not apply to managers who are not directors of the company.[49] However, it is important to note that, when applying the law relating to directors' duties, the courts do not distinguish between the actions of the director as director and actions as manager, where the director is an executive director of the company. Those duties will apply to both aspects of the director's activities.[50] In consequence, some actions by senior managers of the company, provided they are also directors of the company, will be subject to the controls of the general statutory duties. Although management theory may posit that it is the role of the board in large companies to set the company's strategy and to oversee its execution, rather than to execute it itself, the law of directors' duties does not make this distinction in the case of a director who has both a board position and a non-board executive function. **10–012**

However, it can also be asked whether these general statutory duties (or common law fiduciary duties) apply to the senior managers of the company who are not formally appointed as directors. In *Canadian Aero Services Ltd v O'Malley* the Canadian Supreme Court approved a statement from an earlier edition of this book that directors' common law fiduciary duties (as they then were) apply to those "officials of the company who are authorised to act on its behalf and in particular to those acting in a senior management capacity".[51] That view has not been adopted expressly in any English court. Moreover, it is clear that, in principle, the employment relationship is not a fiduciary relationship, so that it would be inappropriate to apply the full range of fiduciary or directors' duties even to senior employees. However, this proposition is subject to a number of qualifications. First, a senior employee who does in fact discharge the duties of a director may be classed as a de facto director, under the principles discussed above. Secondly, the courts have held that, as a result of the specific terms of an employee's contract and of the particular duties undertaken by him or her, a common law fiduciary relationship may arise between employee and employer, even in the case of employees who are not part of senior management, though the fiduciary duty may be restricted to some part of their overall duties.[52] The view of the Canadian Supreme Court is not inconsistent with these developments, since it

---

[49] Unless the "manager" can be classified as a shadow or de facto director: see para.10–009. Contrast the position in other jurisdictions, such as Australia, where the general statutory duties apply not only to directors but also to "officers".

[50] For an illustration, see *Item Software (UK) Ltd v Fassihi* [2004] EWHC Civ 1244; [2004] B.C.C. 994, where the consequence of this approach was to subject the director to a higher standard of fiduciary duty than would have been applicable had he only been an employee, albeit a senior one.

[51] *Canadian Aero Services Ltd v O'Malley* (1973) 40 D.L.R. (3d) 371 at 381.

[52] *University of Nottingham v Fishel* [2000] I.C.R. 1462 QBD; *Shepherds Investments Ltd v Walters* [2006] EWHC 836 (Ch); [2007] F.S.R. 15; *Helmet Integrated Systems Ltd v Tunnard* [2006] EWCA Civ 1735; [2007] F.S.R. 16; *Ranson v Customer Systems Plc* [2012] EWCA Civ 841. The issues remain controversial: see the disagreement in *Generics (UK) Ltd v Yeda Research & Development Co Ltd* [2012] EWCA Civ 726; [2012] C.P. Rep. 39 at [19]–[36] (Sir Robin Jacob) contrasted with

too was derived from an analysis of the functions of the employees in question as senior management employees, though there will be scope for argument on the facts of each case about how extensive the fiduciary aspects of the employee's duties are. It goes without saying that, should a senior manager place him or herself in an agency relationship with the company, then the normal fiduciary incidents of that relationship would arise. Thirdly, the implied and mutual duty of trust and confidence which is imported into all contracts of employment can in some cases operate in substantially the same way as certain directors' general duties.[53] This is particularly the case in relation to competitive activities on the part of an employee or the non-disclosure by senior managers of the wrongdoing of fellow employees and in some cases their own wrongdoing.[54]

10–013 The exclusion of senior managers as such from the statutory general duties of directors probably depends upon the continuation of the UK practice, as recommended in the UK Corporate Governance Code,[55] that the board should contain a substantial number of executive directors. If British practice were to move in the US direction of reducing the number of executive directors on the board, sometimes to one (the CEO), and there are indications of a move in that direction, then confining the statutory duties to members of the board might become a policy which needed to be re-considered.[56]

Finally, the above discussion has concerned the fiduciary duties of employees and directors. In relation to the statutory duty of care (see below), which equally applies only to directors, the common law duty of care required of employees

[41]–[84] (Etherton LJ), with whom Ward LJ was persuaded to agree ([91]–[121]). Generally, see *Airbus Operations Ltd v Withey* [2014] EWHC 1126 (QB); *Halcyon House Ltd v Baines* [2014] EWHC 2216 (QB).

[53] Note, however, that the employee's duty of "mutual trust and confidence" finds its roots in contract rather than the law of fiduciary obligations, as emphasised by Lewison LJ (with whom Lloyd and Pill LJJ agreed) in *Ranson v Customer Systems Plc* [2012] EWCA Civ 841 CA at [36]–[40]; and the distinction between the contractual duty of fidelity and the duties of a fiduciary are discussed at [41]–[43].

[54] *Shepherds Investments Ltd v Walters* [2007] F.S.R. 15 at [129]–[130]; *Sybron Corp v Rochem Ltd* [1984] Ch. 112 CA (Civ Div); *Tesco Stores Ltd v Pook* [2003] EWHC 823 (Ch). On disclosure of wrongdoing, the main difference between a senior manager and a director concerns the extent to which they are obliged to disclose their own wrongdoing: see *Bell v Lever* [1932] A.C. 161 (suggesting an employee is never under a duty to disclose his own wrongdoing); and *Item Software (UK) Ltd v Fassihi* [2004] B.C.C. 994, taking a narrower view. However, all may depend on the employee's contract: in *Ranson v Customer Systems Plc* [2012] EWCA Civ 841, it was held that an employee can have an obligation to disclose his own wrongdoing, but that this can only arise out of the terms of the contract of employment, not by any analogy with the fiduciary duties owed by company directors (see [44]–[61]). The analysis may matter: *Threlfall v ECD Insight Ltd* [2012] EWHC 3543 (QB) at [111]–[126] (Lang J); *Haysport Properties Ltd v Ackerman* [2016] EWHC 393 (Ch); [2016] B.C.C. 676.

[55] See paras 9–016 to 9–021.

[56] Contrast the Australian Corporations Act 2001, which defines an "officer", in s.9, as a person "(i) who makes, or participates in making, decisions that affect the whole, or a substantial part, of the business of the entity; or (ii) who has the capacity to affect significantly the entity's financial standing", and then makes officers subject to many of the statutory duties applying to directors (see ss.179 onwards). CA 2006 does not take this approach with directors' duties (ss.170 onwards), although elsewhere it does make rules which apply more generally to "officers" (defined inclusively in s.1173), typically in connection with reporting requirements (see, e.g. s.113(7)). Even though corporate directors are to be abolished (see fn.28), it remains possible, it seems, to have "corporate officers" (see s.1122).

seems to come very close to that now required of directors (taking account of the fact that the application of the reasonable care standard will produce different results in different circumstances).[57]

Former directors

At common law the general duties of directors attach from the date when the director's appointment takes effect[58] but do not necessarily cease when the appointment ends. The second part of the common law position is explicitly confirmed by s.170(2) which provides that a person who ceases to be a director continues to be subject to two of the seven general duties, namely those relating to corporate opportunities of which he had become aware whilst still a director and the taking of a benefit from a third party in respect of acts or omissions whilst still a director. However, those two duties are to be applied by the courts to former directors "subject to any necessary adaptations", for example, to take account of the fact that the former director may no longer have up-to-date knowledge of the conduct of the company's affairs. In this way it can be said that liability is imposed in respect of actions which straddle the time before and after the director ceased to hold office.[59] **10–014**

Particularly difficult issues can arise in relation to the analysis of actions by directors, whilst still directors, but after they have given notice of resignation. In such cases the director is not (yet) a former director and the issue is discussed at para.10–087.

Directors of insolvent companies

When a company enters into an insolvency procedure (liquidation, administration or receivership), the situation under British law, unlike that in the US, is that the powers of the directors are substantially curtailed and the direction of the business passes into the hands of the insolvency practitioner appointed to act in one or other of these roles and who acts in the interests of the creditors. This is likely to have a substantial impact on what the law of directors' duties requires of the directors in practice, but does not in principle relieve the directors of their obligations to the company.[60] **10–015**

[57] For employees see *Lister v Romford Ice and Cold Storage Co Ltd* [1957] A.C. 555 HL; and *Janata Bank v Ahmed* [1981] I.C.R. 791 CA (Civ Div) and for the duty of care required of directors, see the following section. For a case where the defendant was sued for breach of his duty of care both as a director and as an employee, see *Simtel Communications Ltd v Rebak* [2006] EWHC 572 (QB).

[58] In *Lindgren v L&P Estates Ltd* [1968] Ch. 572 CA (Civ Div), the Court of Appeal rejected an argument that a "director-elect" is in a fiduciary relationship to the company.

[59] This point is discussed further below in relation to the taking of corporate opportunities, which is where it most often arises.

[60] Directors cannot, for example, be held liable for the failure to exercise powers which they no longer have. In *Ultraframe (UK) Ltd v Fielding* [2006] F.S.R. 17 at [1330] Lewison J suggested the "no conflict" rule would not apply either (though the "no profit" and basic loyalty duties would continue to bite). Also see *Re System Building Services Group Ltd (In Liquidation)* [2020] EWHC 54 (Ch); [2020] B.C.C. 345. And see paras 19–002 to 19–011.

DUTY TO ACT WITHIN POWERS: S.171

10–016 We turn now to a discussion of each of the individual duties in turn. The first is the duty imposed on directors by s.171 requiring the directors to act only within the powers that have been conferred upon them. This is an obvious duty for the law to impose. Indeed, this is not a duty confined to directors, or even to fiduciaries; later on we shall examine similar restrictions as they apply to shareholders.[61] As regards the directors, however, s.171 deals with two manifestations of this principle: the director must "act in accordance with the company's constitution" and must "only exercise powers for the purposes for which they are conferred". These are strict constraints on the directors, and are not excused simply because a director acted in good faith and in the honest belief that what was being done was best for the company.[62] We look at limb each in turn.

Acting in accordance with the constitution

Constitutional limitations

10–017 As we saw in Ch.3,[63] in contrast to many other company law jurisdictions, the main source of the directors' powers is likely to be the company's articles, and the articles, therefore, are likely also to be a source of constraints on the directors' powers. The articles may confer unlimited powers on the directors, but they are likely in fact to set some parameters within which the powers are to be exercised, even if the limits are generous, as they typically will be. So, it is perhaps not surprising that s.171 contains the obligation "to act in accordance with the company's constitution". And it should be noted that the term "constitution" helpfully goes beyond the articles. It includes resolutions and agreements which are required to be notified to the Registrar and annexed to the articles, notably any special resolution of the company.[64] It also embraces any resolution or decision taken in accordance with the constitution and any decision by the members of the company or a class of members which is treated as equivalent to a decision of the company.[65] Thus, the duty includes an obligation to obey decisions properly taken by the shareholders in general meeting, for example, giving instructions to the directors without formally altering the articles.[66]

This duty was recognised in the early years of modern company law and is reflected in a number of nineteenth-century decisions, usually involving the purported exercise by directors of powers which were ultra vires the company[67]

---

[61] See para.13–005 to 13–013.

[62] See *Fairford Water Ski Club Ltd v Cohoon* [2020] EWHC 290 (Comm) at [51]: "Observance of the duty embodied in section 172 will not excuse what is otherwise a breach of section 171."

[63] See para. 3–013.

[64] CA 2006 ss.17, 29–30.

[65] CA 2006 s.257.

[66] As we saw at para.9–004, under the model articles the shareholders by special resolution may give directors instructions as to how they should conduct the management of the company, even in areas where the articles confer managerial powers upon the directors.

[67] *Re Lands Allotment Co* [1894] 1 Ch. 616 CA. On ultra vires see at para.8–029.

or payments of dividends or directors' remuneration contrary to the provisions in the company's articles.[68] The remedies for this type of breach are considered below.[69]

Improper purposes

The rule

The second proposition contained in s.171(b) is that a director must "only exercise powers for the purposes for which they are conferred". Often the improper purpose will be to feather the directors' own nests or to preserve their control of the company in their own interests, in which event it will also be a breach of one or other of the various duties, considered below, to act avoid conflicts and to act in good faith to promote the success of the company. Indeed, the particular wording of the s.172(1) statutory duty to act in good faith to promote the success of the company can be seen as assisting generally in defining proper purposes.[70] But even if no other breach is committed, directors may nevertheless be in breach of this particular duty if they have exercised their powers for a purpose outside those for which the powers were conferred upon them. The improper purposes test, like the requirement to act in accordance with the company's constitution, is an objective test.[71] Or, more precisely, the question of whether a particular purpose is proper or not is a question of law, decided objectively, while the question of which purposes actually motivated the particular director in question is, of course, subjective.[72] Notice the narrow limits to the proper purposes rule: if the directors have acted for purposes which are objectively proper, not improper, then the court will not, in addition, review the **10–018**

[68] *Re Oxford Benefit Building & Investment Society* (1886) 35 Ch. D. 502 Ch D (an early example of a company's accounts recognising profits which had not been earned); *Leeds Estate, Building and Investment Co v Shepherd* (1887) 36 Ch. D. 787 Ch D. It might be said that the requirement upon the directors to repay the dividends was based on the illegality of their payment as a matter of statute or common law, but the directors were also required to repay their remuneration, the payment of which was objectionable only because it was done in breach of the company's articles. (The articles entitled the directors to remuneration only if dividends of a certain size were paid, a rule which, perhaps naturally, encouraged the directors not to be too careful about observing the restrictions on their dividend payment powers.)

[69] See paras 10–022 and 10–023.

[70] See paras 10–026 to 10–029.

[71] See *Howard Smith Ltd v Ampol Petroleum Ltd* [1974] A.C. 821 PC at 834, citing *Fraser v Whalley* (1864) 2 Hem & M. 10 KB; *Punt v Symons & Co Ltd* [1903] 2 Ch. 506 Ch D; *Piercy v S Mills & Co Ltd* [1920] 1 Ch. 77 Ch D; *Ngurli v McCann* (1954) 90 C.L.R. 425 HC (Australia); *Hogg v Cramphorn* [1967] Ch. 254 Ch D at 267. The "improper purpose" test, as a requirement distinct from good faith in the common law test, has been rejected, however, in British Columbia: *Teck Corp Ltd v Millar* (1973) 33 D.L.R. (3d) 288.

[72] But see *Eclairs Group Ltd v JKX Oil & Gas Plc* [2015] UKSC 71; [2016] B.C.C. 79 at [15] (Lord Sumption SCJ), it seems confining himself to the latter point.

decision as also being either reasonable or unreasonable,[73] with the potential for substituting their own view as to the judgements the directors should have reached in managing the company.[74]

The leading authority in this area is the 2015 Supreme Court decision in *Eclairs Group Ltd v JKX Oil & Gas Plc*,[75] but it is helpful to begin discussion with an earlier decision. The statutory formulation of the proper purposes duty reflects the prior common law case law. That case law was reviewed by the Privy Council in *Howard Smith Ltd v Ampol Petroleum Ltd*,[76] which considered the decisions on this subject of courts throughout the Commonwealth. It concerned, as have many of the cases, the power of directors to issue new shares, but the duty is by no means so confined.[77] In this case a majority shareholder (Ampol) in a company called Millers made an offer to acquire the shares in Millers it did not already own. However, the directors of Millers preferred a takeover offer from Howard Smith, which could not succeed so long as Ampol retained a majority holding. Consequently, the directors caused the company to issue sufficient new shares to Howard Smith that Ampol was reduced to a minority position and Howard Smith could launch its offer with some hope of success, since its bid price was higher than Ampol's.

It was argued that the only proper purpose for which a share-issue power could be exercised was to raise new capital when the company needed it.[78] This was rejected as too narrow.[79] There might be a range of purposes for which a company may issue new shares—a view reflected in the statutory reference to proper purposes in the plural. It might be a proper use of the power to issue shares to use that power in order to secure the financial stability of the company[80] or as part of an agreement relating to the exploitation of mineral rights owned by the

[73] Although it may of course review them as being negligent or not: s.174, para.10–045 to 10–050.

[74] The best analysis of this is probably in the trusts case, *Edge v Pensions Ombudsman* [2000] Ch. 602 CA (Civ Div) at 627E–630G; but also see *Equitable Life Assurance Society v Hyman* [2002] 1 A.C. 408 HL at [17]–[21].

[75] *Eclairs Group Ltd v JKX Oil & Gas Plc* [2016] B.C.C. 79, noted S. Worthington, "Directors' Duties and Improper Purposes" [2016] C.L.J. 202. See too the comprehensive overview of the area in *Stobart Group Ltd v Tinkler* [2019] EWHC 258 (Comm) at [426]–[488] (HH Judge Russen QC).

[76] *Howard Smith Ltd v Ampol Petroleum Ltd* [1974] A.C. 821. Also usefully see *Harlowe's Nominees Pty Ltd v Woodside (Lakes Entrance) Oil Co NL* (1968) 121 C.L.R. 483 (HCA).

[77] The principle applies generally. For examples in relation to other powers, see *Stanhope's Case* (1865–66) L.R. 1 Ch. App. 161 Lord Chancellor; *Manisty's Case* (1873) 17 S.J. 745 (forfeiture of shares); *Galloway v Halle Concerts Society* [1915] 2 Ch. 233 Ch D (calls); *Bennett's Case* (1854) 5 De G.M. & G. 284 Ct of Chancery; and *Australian Metropolitan Life Association Co Ltd v Ure* (1923) 33 C.L.R. 199 HC (Australia) (registration of transfers); *Hogg v Cramphorn* [1967] Ch. 254 Ch D (loans); *Lee Panavision Ltd v Lee Lighting Ltd* [1991] B.C.C. 620 CA (Civ Div) (entering into a management agreement); *Equitable Life Assurance Society v Hyman* [2002] 1 A.C. 408 HL; *Criterion Properties Plc v Stratford UK Properties LLC* [2002] EWCA Civ 1883; [2003] B.C.C. 50 (giving joint venture partner an option to be bought out at a favourable price); *Re HLC Environmental Projects Ltd* [2013] EWHC 2876 (Ch); [2014] B.C.C. 337 (payments made when the company was in financial distress); *Stobart Group Ltd v Tinkler* [2019] EWHC 258 (Comm) (issue of shares so as to influence the outcome of the election of the chairman).

[78] This has often been assumed and the directors had apparently been so advised and sought, unsuccessfully, to show that this was their purpose.

[79] *Howard Smith Ltd v Ampol Petroleum Ltd* [1974] A.C. 821 at 8310–836.

[80] *Harlowe's Nominees Pty Ltd v Woodside Oil Co* (1968) 121 C.L.R. 483.

company.[81] Provided the purpose of the issue was a proper one, the mere fact that the incidental (and desired) result was to deprive a shareholder of his voting majority or to defeat a takeover bid would not be sufficient to make the purpose improper. But if, as in the instant case, the purpose of the share issue was to dilute the majority voting power so as to enable an offer to proceed which the existing majority was in a position to block,[82] the exercise of the power would be improper despite the fact that the directors were acting in what they considered to be the best interests of the company, and were not motivated by a desire to obtain some personal advantage.

Which purposes are improper?

Perhaps the greatest puzzle in this area is to know by what criteria the courts judge whether a particular purpose is proper. This is generally stated to be a matter of construction of the articles of association.[83] That is all very well if the articles are prescriptive, but this is rarely the case. In *Howard Smith v Ampol*, for example, the clause giving the directors power to issue shares was drawn in the widest terms. The "purposes" limitation which the Privy Council read into the directors' powers derived not from a narrow analysis of that clause, but from placing the share issue power within the company's constitutional arrangements as a whole, as demonstrated in particular by the terms of its articles of association. In essence, to do what the directors did in that case was regarded as undermining the division of powers between shareholders and the board which the articles had created[84]; and in that context the case comes close to deciding that it is always a breach of the directors' duties to exercise their powers to promote or defeat a takeover offer, which decision should be left to the existing body of shareholders. This is certainly the proposition upon which the City Code on Takeovers and Mergers (the Takeover Code) is based, which provisions will prevail once a bid for a listed company is imminent.[85] In *Criterion Properties Plc* 10–019

---

[81] *Teck Corp Ltd v Miller* (1972) 33 D.L.R. (3d) 288 BC Sup.Ct.

[82] Or, conversely, to block a bid: *Winthrop Investments Ltd v Winns Ltd* [1975] 2 N.S.W.L.R. 666 NSWCA. See too *Stobart Group Ltd v Tinkler* [2019] EWHC 258 with the issue intended to influence the election of the chairman.

[83] *Re Smith and Fawcett* [1942] Ch. 304 CA at 306.

[84] *Howard Smith Ltd v Ampol Petroleum Ltd* [1974] A.C. 821 at 837: "The constitution of a limited company normally provides for directors, with powers of management, and shareholders, with defined voting powers having to appoint the directors, and to take, in general meeting, by majority vote, decisions on matters not reserved for management. Just as it is established that directors, within their management powers, may take decisions against the wishes of majority shareholders, and indeed that the majority of shareholders cannot control them in the exercise of these powers while they remain in office so it must be unconstitutional for directors to use their fiduciary powers over the shares in the company purely for the purpose of destroying an existing majority, or creating a new majority which did not previously exist. To do so is to interfere with that element in the company's constitution which is separate from and set against their powers". This principle was applied by the Court of Appeal in *Lee Panavision Ltd v Lee Lighting Ltd* [1991] B.C.C. 620, where the incumbent directors entered into a long-term management agreement with a third party knowing that the shareholders were proposing to exercise their rights to appoint new directors.

[85] See para.28–020.

v Stratford UK Properties LLC,[86] however, neither Hart J nor the Court of Appeal ruled out the possibility that in some cases it might be a proper purpose of the exercise of directors' powers for them to be used to block or discourage a takeover, but the issue was not presented in a sharp fashion in that case, since both courts were agreed that the "poison pill" adopted by the directors in that case was disproportionate to the threat faced by the company. It follows from this approach, however, that in a different type of company with a different constitution, in which, say, ownership and control were not separated, a broader view might be taken of the directors' powers under the articles.

In other words, the context is all-important. This seems to be the explanation of the expansive approach taken in *Re Smith and Fawcett Ltd*,[87] where the clause in question (regarding the admission of new members to a small company) was widely construed so as to produce the effect equivalent to the partnership rule of strict control by the board over the admission of new members.

But these illustrations indicate the difficulty, and provide little by way of real guidance when the context is novel, as it was in *Eclairs Group Ltd v JKX Oil & Gas Plc*.[88] The opposing judgments as the case made its way up to the Supreme Court are instructive. JKX suspected a hostile takeover bid by Eclairs, one of its shareholders, whom it alleged was seeking to destabilise it and ultimately acquire it at less than its proper value. The directors of JKX had the power[89] to request details of the parties who held interests in Eclairs' shares, and to disenfranchise Eclairs if it failed to respond adequately to the request. This the company did. It was not disputed that the power to disenfranchise had been exercised so as to disentitle these shareholders from voting at JKX's AGM, thus ensuring the passage of certain resolutions, rather than for the purpose of enforcing the company's demand for information. At first instance,[90] Mann J held this to be an improper purpose, so the purported restrictions on voting were held ineffective. The Court of Appeal allowed the appeal (Briggs LJ dissenting),[91] distinguishing

---

[86] *Criterion Properties Plc v Stratford UK Properties LLC* [2002] EWHC 496 (Ch) (Hart J); and [2003] B.C.C. 50. The issue was not analysed by the House of Lords, which focused on the logically prior question of the director's authority (actual or apparent) to enter into the contract on behalf of the company: [2004] UKHL 28; [2004] B.C.C. 570. The "poison pill" arrangement entitled the joint venture partner of the potential target company (Criterion) to require Criterion to buy out its interest in the venture on terms which were very favourable to the partner and thus very damaging economically to Criterion. However, this arrangement was capable of being triggered not only by a takeover but also by any departure of the existing management of Criterion, even in circumstances, which in fact arose, which were wholly unconnected with a takeover.

[87] *Re Smith and Fawcett Ltd* [1942] Ch. 304, where in a quasi-partnership company it was held that the directors, in exercising a power to refuse to register a transfer of shares, could "take account of any matter which they conceive to be in the interests of the company … such matters, for instance, as whether by their passing a particular transfer the transferee would obtain too great a weight in the councils of the company or might even perhaps obtain control" (at 308). Similarly, see *Gaiman v National Association of Mental Health* [1971] Ch. 317 Ch D. In modern law the position would now have to be considered in the light of any "legitimate expectations" enforceable under s.994. See Ch.20.

[88] *Eclairs Group Ltd v JKX Oil & Gas Plc* [2016] B.C.C. 79.

[89] Under Pt 22 of the CA 2006 (see ss.793 onwards) and the company's articles.

[90] *Eclairs Group Ltd v JKX Oil & Gas Plc* [2013] EWHC 2631 (Ch).

[91] *Eclairs Group Ltd v JKX Oil & Gas Plc* [2014] EWCA Civ 640; [2015] B.C.C. 821.

previous cases of improper purposes on three overlapping grounds[92]: that here the purported "victim" was a "victim of his own choice, not a victim of any improper use of a power of the board of directors" since it was his choice how to respond to the questions properly raised[93]; that since no restrictive purposes had been expressed in the statute or the articles, none should be implied unless that was necessary to their efficacy; and, in any event, a restricted proper purpose test would essentially frustrate the purpose or utility of the provisions in question. Although the Court of Appeal did not put it so strongly, their expansive approach could essentially denude the proper purposes doctrine of any substantive role whenever a power was expressed in wide terms—as powers typically are. The Supreme Court disagreed, holding unanimously that the proper purpose doctrine had a central role to play in controlling the exercise of power by directors. But they too provided little guidance as to how these "proper purposes" should be discovered. Lord Sumption SCJ, with whom the other judges agreed, suggested that the relevant improper purposes would "usually [be] obvious from [the] context", and should be inferred from the "mischief" which might follow from exercise of the power.[94]

That is not much to go on, but, taking the cases together, perhaps two broad categories of "improper purpose" can be identified as operating quite generally, even when powers are expressed in the widest possible terms: use of a power for the purpose of "feathering the director's nest" (these are the easy cases) or for influencing the outcome of existing constitutional balances of power in the company (the harder cases) will typically be regarded as improper.[95] Note that it is not the incidental, or even inevitable, delivery of these ends which is outlawed: many perfectly proper actions by directors will deliver such results. Rather, it is this being the motivation for the exercise of the power, where that motivation has been deemed improper. But even this is not the end of the analysis; there is a further question. **10–020**

When is a power exercised for improper purposes?

Directors are rarely actuated by a single purpose. This was true in the *Howard Smith* case, where the company did have a genuine need for fresh capital. If the directors are motivated by a variety of purposes, some proper and some improper, how should the courts determine whether the exercise of power is tainted? Section 171(b) indicates that a director must "only exercise powers for the purposes for which they are conferred". This suggests that *any* improper **10–021**

[92] As summarised by Lord Sumption SCJ in *Eclairs Group Ltd v JKX Oil & Gas Plc* [2016] B.C.C. 79 at [28].

[93] *Eclairs Group Ltd v JKX Oil & Gas Plc* [2015] B.C.C. 821 at [136].

[94] *Eclairs Group Ltd v JKX Oil & Gas Plc* [2016] B.C.C. 79 at [31] and [30] respectively. For earlier academic considerations, see Completing, para.3.14; and R.C. Nolan, "The Proper Purpose Doctrine and Company Directors" in B. Rider (ed.), *The Realm of Company Law* (Kluwer Law International, 1998). Now also see S. Worthington, "Powers" in W. Day and S. Worthington (eds), *Challenging Private Law: Lord Sumption on the Supreme Court* (Hart Publishing, 2020) Ch.16.

[95] In the same vein, it would be improper for a director to act for the purpose of favouring his or her nominator, with the cases again suggesting, if only by inference, that a "but for" test is appropriate: see, e.g. *Kuwait Asia Bank EC v National Mutual Life Nominees Ltd* [1990] B.C.C. 567 PC.

motivating purpose will constitute a flaw. Nevertheless, and perhaps for very pragmatic reasons, that has never been the rule applied in the corporate context except where the exercise of power is motivated by the director's dishonesty or self-interest.[96] Otherwise the courts have typically suggested that a decision will be considered flawed only if the proven improper purpose is the "primary" or dominant purpose for the decision,[97] or if the decision would not have been taken "but for" the improper purpose (even if the improper purpose was not the dominant purpose),[98] or perhaps an either/or version of these two tests[99] if it is thought that they are likely to lead to different answers on the facts. Each alternative poses enormous forensic difficulties, since all require proof of matters peculiarly within the minds of the directors and in relation to which the directors' evidence is "likely to be both artificial and defensive".[100] But in *Eclairs Group Ltd v JKX Oil & Gas Plc*, Lord Sumption SCJ (with whom Lord Hope SCJ agreed) put forward a principled preference for the "but for" test[101]:

> "The fundamental point [in selecting the right test], however, is one of principle. The statutory duty of the directors is to exercise their powers 'only' for the purposes for which they are conferred. … If equity nevertheless allows the decision to stand in some cases, it is not because it condones a minor improper purpose where it would condemn a major one. … The only rational basis for such a distinction is that some improprieties may not have resulted in an injustice to the interests which equity seeks to protect. Here, we are necessarily in the realm of causation. … One has to focus on the improper purpose and ask whether the decision would have been made if the directors had not been moved by it. If the answer is that without the improper purpose(s) the decision impugned would never have been made, then it would be irrational to allow it to stand simply because the directors had other, proper considerations in mind as well, to which perhaps they attached greater importance. … Correspondingly, if there were proper reasons for exercising the power and it would still have been exercised for those reasons even in the absence of improper ones, it is difficult to see why justice should require the decision to be set aside."

However persuasive that might seem, and whatever the practical advantages of a single simple test, the majority of the Supreme Court declined to commit themselves to this as a statement of the law, given that the issues surrounding mixed purposes had not been argued before the Supreme Court.[102] The matter thus remains unsettled.[103] But it is hard to fault the logic that a decision should be held improper only if it would not in fact have been taken the way it was but for

[96] *Eclairs Group Ltd v JKX Oil & Gas Plc* [2016] B.C.C. 79 at [17] (Lords Sumption and Hodge SCJJ), citing *Mills v Mills* (1938) 60 C.L.R. 150 at 1810–186, where Dixon J indicated the difficulties.

[97] *Howard Smith Ltd v Ampol Petroleum Ltd* [1974] A.C. 821 at 832 (Lord Wilberforce).

[98] *Mills v Mills* (1938) 60 C.L.R. 150 at 186; *Whitehouse v Carlton House Pty* (1987) 162 C.L.R. 285 at 294 HC (Australia): although this interpretation, supported in *Eclairs Group Ltd v JKX Oil & Gas Plc* [2016] B.C.C. 79 by Lord Sumption SCJ (with whom Lord Hope SCJ agreed) (at [21]–[22]) was doubted by Lord Mance SCJ (with whom Lord Neuberger PSC agreed) (at [53]). See also *Hirsche v Sims* [1894] A.C. 654 PC; *Hindle v John Cotton Ltd* (1919) 56 S.L.T. 625.

[99] *Eclairs Group Ltd v JKX Oil & Gas Plc* [2016] B.C.C. 79 at [49].

[100] *Eclairs Group Ltd v JKX Oil & Gas Plc* [2016] B.C.C. 79 at [20] (on the "primary" purpose test), and see too [54] (on both).

[101] *Eclairs Group Ltd v JKX Oil & Gas Plc* [2016] B.C.C. 79 at [21], but see generally [21]–[23].

[102] Lord Mance SCJ (with whom Lord Neuberger PSC agreed) set out his doubts at *Eclairs Group Ltd v JKX Oil & Gas Plc* [2016] B.C.C. 79 at [51]–[54].

[103] Accordingly, in *Stobart Group Ltd v Tinkler* [2019] EWHC 258 (Comm) at [437], HH Judge Russen QC concluded that the test in *Howeard Smith v Ampol* remained the correct one to apply.

the improper consideration. If that test is not met, then—as Lord Sumption put it—no injustice has been done, and the decision should stand.

The only troubling element is the hypothetical rider aired by the court. The problem raised was this: assume the directors in fact decided the way they did only because of the presence of an improper purpose, but they might still have decided the same way had that improper purpose not been present. Should their decision then be allowed to stand? The answer, surely, is no, it should not stand. Principle suggests the court's task is simply to determine whether the decision *actually* taken by the directors should stand. It is not to hypothesise about what the directors might have done for exclusively "proper" motivating purposes. The focus of the court's intervention is not on judging the practical outcome reached, but on judging the directors' motivations in reaching it. And in any event, in practice the question would seem impossible to contemplate sensibly on most facts before the court: *JKX* and *Howard Smith* are surely illustrative of that—the directors could insist they would have taken the same decisions if acting only for proper purposes, but their targets and timing make that seem unlikely.

Despite this, in the early stages of the JKX litigation, Mann J raised this question himself, and also held that the facts supported the conclusion that the JKX directors would indeed have taken the same decision if they were acting for exclusively proper purposes, but he declined to let the company take the argument at that late stage in the litigation.[104]

Remedies

The directors necessarily breach the duty in s.171 if they act contrary to its provisions; it is irrelevant that the contravention was in the interests of the company, or that the directors were not subjectively aware of their breach of s.171.[105] In other words, directors are under a duty to acquaint themselves with the terms of the company's constitution and its limits, and to abide by them. If the flawed decision causes loss to the company, the company may seek compensation from its defaulting directors. In addition, it is often said that a breach by the directors of s.171 renders invalid any decision so made, and that in turn may affect third parties relying on the decision. But that outcome depends crucially on the analysis set out in Ch.8, and cannot be assumed to be the case in all (or even most) circumstances.[106] These remedies map the common law and equitable rules (s.178). **10–022**

At common law different legal consequences follow for acts done without power (or "in excess" of power, s.171(a)) and acts done within power but in abuse of it (s.171(b)). At common law, where an act or decision of the directors is beyond their constitutional authority or power as set out in the company's constitution (i.e. in breach of s.171(a)), then the transaction it effects is void, i.e. of no effect, *unless the third party can rely on the directors' ostensible authority*. The qualifier is obviously crucial, and typically operates to protect third

[104] *Eclairs Group Ltd v JKX Oil & Gas Plc* [2016] B.C.C. 79 at [42]–[43].

[105] See the cases cited in fnn.68 and 71.

[106] See S. Worthington, "Powers" in W. Day and S. Worthington (eds) *Challenging Private Law: Lord Sumption on the Supreme Court* (Oxford: Hart Publishing, 2020) Ch.16.

parties.[107] Moreover, this is also one of the situations where the trust analogy is used to strong effect. If the contravention of the constitution has involved the improper distribution of the company's assets, the directors are regarded by analogy as if in breach of trust and are liable to replace the assets, whether or not they were the recipients of them.[108] This gives the directors a strong incentive to remain within the company's constitution.[109]

Where the directors act for an improper purpose (in breach of s.171(b)), however, then at common law their act is voidable by the company (i.e. valid until set aside by the company, and incapable of being set aside if third party rights have intervened),[110] not potentially void (subject to estoppel-based claims of ostensible authority) as in the case where the directors purport to exercise a power they do not have. Thus, bona fide third parties are safe if they act before the shareholders (or liquidator, or other) set aside the directors' decision.[111]

10–023 In both cases, however, the impact of these common law rules on third parties' interests has now been substantially softened by the statutory protections (especially s.40) for those dealing with the company in good faith.[112] In favour of such persons the powers of the directors to bind the company are treated as free of any limitation contained in the company's constitution. Helpful as this is to third parties, it does not help the directors, for s.40(5) makes it clear that liability on the part of the director to the company may be incurred under s.171, even if—perhaps especially if—the third party with whom the directors dealt on behalf of the company is able to enforce the transaction against the company.[113] In fact, to the extent that s.40 protects the position of third parties as against the company

---

107 See Ch.8 generally, especially para.8–021.

108 See the cases cited in fnn.68 and 71. See, e.g. *LRH Services Ltd (In Liquidation) v Trew* [2018] EWHC 600 (Ch) at [196] (remedy in respect of unlawful dividends is directors repay the whole sum, not just damages for losses caused to company). Contrast—instructively—the facts in *Auden McKenzie (Pharma Division) Ltd v Patel* [2019] EWCA Civ 2291; [2020] B.C.C. 316 (noted S. Worthington, "More Disquiet with Equitable Compensation" [2020] C.L.J. 220). The most recent Supreme Court authority on quantification of this form of compensation comes from the non-company case of *AIB Group (UK) Plc v Mark Redler & Co Solicitors* [2014] UKSC 58; [2015] P.N.L.R. 10.

109 They might escape liability, however, where, for example, the provisions of the constitution were not clear; and see also the discussion of s.1157, para.10–129.

110 See the analysis of the cases in *Hunter v Senate Support Services Ltd* [2004] EWHC 1085 (Ch); [2005] 1 B.C.L.C. 175 at [173]–[179]. Note the importance of the absence/excess of authority versus abuse of authority distinction in *Hogg v Cramphorn* [1967] Ch. 254—a decision to attach multiple voting rights to shares issued to the company's pension fund, in breach of the company's articles, was ineffective, whereas the issue itself, for improper purposes, was voidable only; *Guinness v Saunders* [1990] 2 A.C. 663 HL—fixing of directors' remuneration by a board committee, rather than the full board, in breach of the articles, meant that the decision was void and the recipient director had to repay the money; *Smith v Henniker-Major Co* [2002] EWCA Civ 762; [2003] Ch. 182 at [48]—inquorate board meeting; cf. *Hely-Hutchinson v Brayhead Ltd* [1968] 1 Q.B. 549 CA, where the correct body acted but the director was in breach of his obligation under the articles to comply with disclosure provisions: here the decision was voidable but not void.

111 *Bamford v Bamford* [1970] Ch. 212 CA (ratification by shareholders of decision taken for an improper purpose); and *Criterion Properties Plc v Stratford UK Properties LLC* [2004] B.C.C. 570 (on the application of the statutory protection for the benefit of third parties).

112 See above at para.8–009. Unless the third party is a director of the company or a person connected with the director. See s.41 and para.8–012.

113 CA 2006 s.40(1).

it increases in importance the company's potential remedy against the director. Companies that are now restricted in their ability to escape from transactions with third parties on the grounds that the directors have exceeded their powers may be tempted to look to the directors to recover compensation for the loss suffered as a result of entering into them.

It is also worth recalling at this point the related provisions of s.41, which apply where the third party contracting with the company is a director of the company or a person connected with the director. Then the protection afforded by s.40 does not apply and instead s.41 imposes liability both on directors who authorise such transactions (as s.171 does)[114] *and* on the director[115] (or connected person) who enters into the transaction with the company.[116] Both sets of directors are liable to account to the company for any gain made from the transaction and to indemnify the company for any loss which it suffered as a result of the transaction. Section 41 in its specific area of operation thus reinforces the principle underlying s.171 that directors should observe the limitations on their constitutional powers.

The jurisdiction to bring claims is worth further comment. It is clear that both duties stated in s.171 are owed to the company, as are the other statutory duties, and so may be pursued by the company directly, or by shareholders in a derivative claim. But can the defaulting directors be sued by parties other than the company? A failure on the part of the directors to observe the express limits on their powers contained in the company's constitution (i.e. s.171(a) breach) may also put *the company* in breach of the contract with the shareholders created by the articles. As we will see in Ch.14,[117] at least some breaches of the articles by the company can be complained of by a shareholder, who might, for example, obtain an injunction to restrain the company from continuing to act in breach of the articles—in effect restraining the directors from causing the company to act in breach of its articles. Equally, such acts by the directors may form the basis of a claim in unfair prejudice.

Where the breach is of the duty to act for proper purposes (i.e. s.171(b)), however, then allowing a wider class of people to complain has been more poorly defended; no case seems to have turned on standing. In some cases, minority shareholders have been allowed to sue but the question of their standing has often not been argued nor its basis explained.[118] As a matter of logic and of equitable precedent, this duty to act for proper purposes, owed by directors to the company, may also be owed (at common law only, since there is no enacted statutory equivalent) by the directors to a wider class of people, entitling this wider class to

---

[114] Liability under s.171 is preserved by s.41(1) but it would seem more attractive to proceed under s.41 where this is possible.

[115] Including a director of the company's holding company.

[116] The transaction itself is voidable by the company (s.41(2) and (4)), but not void, as it would be at common law. It will cease to be avoidable if (1) restitution of the subject-matter of the contract is not possible; (2) the company has been indemnified for the loss suffered; (3) the rights of bona fide purchasers without notice have intervened; or (4) the shareholders in general meeting have ratified the transaction.

[117] See paras 14–002 to 14–006.

[118] See many of the cases cited earlier, including the leading case of *Howard Smith v Ampol* [1974] A.C. 824 PC. By contrast, in *Eclairs Group Ltd v JKX Oil & Gas Plc* [2016] B.C.C. 79, the shareholders would be expected to have jurisdiction to complain.

seek common law or equitable remedies from the directors for breach.[119] Alternatively, or in addition, and as described above, the directors' wrongs to the company may entitle the shareholders to pursue related or parasitic remedies, such as for breach of the contract in the articles (although note the arguments against),[120] or a claim in unfair prejudice.[121]

Beyond s.171: limitations on directors' powers imposed by the general law

10–024 Besides limitations on the directors' powers suggested by s.171 (i.e. limitations found in the company's constitution or in the general limitation on the exercise of powers for improper purposes), the general law may also limit what directors may do (or what companies may do, which will necessarily control the actions of the board and individual directors), or limitations may be found in the CA or in the common law relating to companies. Often these provisions will suggest that liability is strict, in that the motivations of the director are immaterial. As well, these provisions may set out the consequences of any failure to abide by the relevant rules, and, where this is the case, those rules will prevail. But where no remedies are specified, the law of directors' duties may provide an answer, if not directly then by analogy.

We see an example of this situation in Ch.18 where the directors, in breach of the Act, made a distribution to shareholders otherwise than out of profits. In the absence of statutory specification of the liabilities of the directors to the company in that situation, the courts have had recourse to the notion that if directors, "as quasi-trustees for the company, improperly pay away the assets to the shareholders, they are liable to replace them".[122] Other examples are to be found in Ch.17,[123] where directors are regarded as having acted in breach of trust when they used the company's assets to give financial assistance for the purchase of the company's shares in breach of the statutory prohibition. In this way, directors who apply the company's assets in breach of restrictions contained in the Act are made liable to replace them. It is not thought that these liabilities, derived from the trustee-like duties imposed on directors in the handling of the company's assets, have been overtaken or displaced by the statutory duties set out in Ch.2 of Pt 10 and in s.171 in particular.

---

[119] For the likely limited remedial impact of this, see S. Worthington, "Directors' Duties, Creditors' Rights and Shareholder Intervention" (1991) 18 Melbourne University Law Review 121. Also see *Equitable Life Assurance Society v Hyman* [2002] 1 A.C. 408 HL.

[120] But for the perhaps preferable view that acting for an improper purpose is an abuse of power but not a breach of the articles see *Winthrop Investments Ltd v Winns Ltd* [1975] 2 N.S.W.L.R. 666 NSWCA. Also see *Rolled Steel Products (Holdings) Ltd v British Steel Corp* [1986] Ch. 246 CA (Civ Div).

[121] *Re Sherborne Park Residents Co Ltd* (1986) 2 B.C.C. 528.

[122] Sir George Jessel MR in *Flitcroft's Case* (1882) 21 Ch. D. 519 CA; quoted with approval by the Court of Appeal in *Bairstow v Queen's Moat Houses Plc* [2001] EWCA Civ 712; [2002] B.C.C. 91. See below, para.18–012.

[123] See para.17–052. See also the discussion of *Re Duckwari (No.2)* [1998] 2 B.C.L.C. 315 CA, at fn.292.

However, this approach has been rendered less secure by the judgment of Zacaroli J in *Burnden Holdings (UK) Ltd (in liquidation) v Fielding*.[124] In that case, the claimants contended that the liability of directors involved in making an unlawful distribution[125] was strict; the defendants that it was fault-based. It had been assumed to be strict,[126] but Zacaroli J conducted a detailed forensic examination of the authorities and concluded liability was fault-based, summarising his conclusions at [139] as follows[127]:

> "First, directors, although not trustees, were to be treated as if they were trustees in relation to the company's funds. Second, if they knew the facts which constituted an unlawful dividend, then they would be liable as if for breach of trust irrespective of whether they knew that the dividend was unlawful. Third, however, if they were unaware of the facts which rendered the dividend unlawful then provided they had taken reasonable care to secure the preparation of accounts so as to establish the availability of sufficient profits to render the dividend lawful, they would not be personally liable if it turned out that there were in fact insufficient profits for that purpose. Fourth, they were entitled to rely in this respect upon the opinion of others, in particular auditors, as to the accuracy of statements appearing in the company's accounts."

And continuing at [158]:

> "I consider this to be consistent with first principles, so far as it applies to the payment of unlawful dividends. The question whether there are sufficient distributable profits may turn on fine questions of accounting judgment. Directors are not required to be accountants and the comments of Lord Davey and Lord Halsbury LC in *Dovey's case* [1901] A.C. 477 as to directors being entitled to rely on the judgment of others whom they appoint to carry out specialist financial roles within the company are as pertinent today as when they were made in 1901."

If correct, this introduces some oddities that will need to be addressed carefully. It suggests that directors can rely on accountants and auditors to produce the accounts, but not on lawyers or other professionals to confirm that a distribution based on those accounts is lawful. It also suggests there is a fundamental divide between directors exercising their powers outside the scope of their duties in this context, and exercising them outside scope in every other context, where liability is strict and advice will not provide a defence: a scope limitation sets boundaries the director cannot cross, not boundaries the director must be careful not to cross. If the director is truly to be treated as a trustee of the company's funds, then, by analogy, liability for acting outside scope might have been expected to be strict.[128]

---

124 *Burnden Holdings (UK) Ltd (in liquidation) v Fielding* [2019] EWHC 1566 (Ch).

125 CA 2006 s.830(1): a company may only make distributions out of profits available for that purpose. Thus directors have no authority to make distributions unless there are distributable profits. See Ch.18.

126 Dicta of Lord Hope in *Revenue and Customs Comrs v Holland* [2011] B.C.C. 1 at [47]. Contrast *Dovey v Cory* [1901] A.C. 477 HL; *Bairstow v Queen's Moat Houses Plc* [2002] B.C.C. 91.

127 *Burnden Holdings (UK) Ltd (in liquidation) v Fielding* [2019] EWHC 1566 (Ch) at [139], with the survey of cases from [103]–[157], concluding at [157] that the current law was as set out in [139].

128 See below para.10–106. To the same end, see the strict approach in the BEIS Consultation Paper, *Restoring Trust in Audit and Corporate Governance* (March 2021), CP 382, Chs 2 and 5. Also see paras 18–007 to 18–010 and Ch.22. Also see the analysis in the context of trustees, especially on advice, in *Pitt v Holt* [2013] UKSC 26; [2013] 2 A.C. 108.

10–025 Continuing with a different example, what is even more typical in this area is that different potential routes lead to the same remedial ends. An illustration is found in the decision of the Court of Appeal in *MacPherson v European Strategic Bureau Ltd*.[129] Here the directors of an insolvent company caused it to enter into a number of contracts which, the court found, amounted to an informal winding up of the company. Under the contracts, the directors as creditors were the primary beneficiaries rather than the creditors of the company as a whole, as would have been the case had the company been wound up formally under the provisions of the Act and the insolvency legislation. Chadwick LJ said that it was a breach of the duties which directors owe to the company for them to attempt such a scheme[130]:

> "It is an attempt to circumvent the protection which the 1985 Act aims to provide for those who give credit to a business carried on, with the benefit of limited liability, through the vehicle of a company incorporated under that Act."

In consequence, the contracts were not enforceable by the directors (who were obviously aware of the facts giving rise to the breach of duty) against the company. This case can thus be seen as demonstrating a limitation on the directors' powers derived from the statutory rules on limited liability and payments to shareholders out of capital. It could also be seen as a breach of the directors' core duty of loyalty (discussed immediately below) as it applies in the vicinity of insolvency where the creditors' interests are predominant.

DUTY TO PROMOTE THE SUCCESS OF THE COMPANY: S.172

Settling the statutory formula

10–026 The duty to promote the success of the company is the modern version of the most basic of the duties of good faith or fidelity owed by directors. Its importance is underlined by the duty, in larger companies, to report to the shareholders on its delivery.[131] It is the core duty to which directors are subject, in the sense that it applies to every exercise of judgement which the directors undertake, whether

---

[129] *MacPherson v European Strategic Bureau Ltd* [2000] 2 B.C.L.C. 683 CA (Civ Div).

[130] *MacPherson v European Strategic Bureau Ltd* [2000] 2 B.C.L.C. 683 at 701.

[131] This requirement (applicable for financial years beginning on or after 1 January 2019) is for all companies with at least 1,000 employees to provide a formal s.172 compliance statement in their annual Strategic Report (publication of which is required under s.414A of the CA 2006). See para.22–027. This statement will explain how the company's directors comply with the requirements in s.172 to have regard to employee interests and to fostering relationships with suppliers, customers and others. The government additionally asked the GC100 group of the largest listed companies to prepare new advice and guidance on the practical boardroom interpretation of s.172: see GC100, *Guidance on Directors' Duties: Section 172 and Stakeholder Considerations* (October 2018) available at: *https://uk.practicallaw.thomsonreuters.com/Link/Document/Blob/I59d0a3ddd47f11e8a5b3e3d9e23d7429.pdf?targetType=PLC-multimedia&originationContext=document&transitionType=DocumentImage&uniqueId=bb0dd755-9efa-4efa-a588-9a5e6861fa2e&contextData=%28sc.Default%29&comp=pluk*; see also ICSA/IA, *The Stakeholder Voice in Board Decision Making* (September 2017) available at: *https://www.icsa.org.uk/assets/files/free-guidance-notes/the-stakeholder-voice-in-Board-Decision-Making-09-2017.pdf* [Both accessed 15 December 2020].

they are testing the margins of their powers under the constitution or not and whether or not there is an operative conflict of interest. Together with the non-fiduciary duty to exercise care, skill and diligence, the duty to promote the success of the company expresses the law's view on how directors should discharge their functions on a day-to-day basis. Thus, it is not surprising that its proper formulation has always been controversial, and perhaps never more so than during the deliberations leading to its statutory enactment in CA 2006, since this was an area of directors' duties where it was not proposed that the statute should simply repeat the common law. The common law duty was typically formulated as one which required the directors to act in good faith in what they believed to be "the best interests of the company". This, predictably, follows the equivalent formulation in relation to trustees, who are required to act bona fide in the best interests of their beneficiaries.

That historical common law formulation differs in significant ways from what is now found in s.172(1) of the Act. This section requires the director to act "in the way he considers, in good faith, would be most likely to promote the success of the company for the benefit of its members as a whole"; and then sets out a non-exhaustive list of six matters to which the directors must "have regard" when deciding on the appropriate course of action.

The common law formulation made it clear that the duty was owed to the company, so that only those who could claim to act as, or on behalf of, the company could enforce the duty. Section 170(1) repeats that. But, that aside, the common law formulation that directors must act *in the interests of* "the company" was seen by many a being close to meaningless in providing guidance to directors. Because the company is an artificial legal person, it was seen as impossible to assign interests to it unless one goes further and identifies the company with the interests of one or more groups of human persons. As Nourse LJ remarked, "The interests of a company, as an artificial person, cannot be distinguished from the interests of the persons who are interested in it".[132] In practice, the common law normally identified the interests of the company with those of its shareholders, current and future if that was appropriate,[133] and thus took the further step envisaged by Nourse LJ. In addition, at common law it was seemingly permissible for the directors to take into account stakeholder interests when acting in the interests of the company. The point was made a long time ago, albeit in the context of ultra vires, by Bowen LJ, who famously said: "The law does not say that there are to be no cakes and ale, but there are to be no cakes and ale except such as are required for the benefit of the company".[134] It is in this sense that the view of the Law Society,[135] opposing any statutory reformulation

[132] *Brady v Brady* [1988] B.C.L.C. 20 CA at 40.

[133] *Gaiman v National Association for Mental Health* [1971] Ch. 317 at 330: "both present and future members". Also see below, para.10–035.

[134] *Hutton v West Cork Railway* (1883) 23 Ch. D. 654 CA at 673, the "cakes and ale" being in this case gratuitous benefits for the employees. For this reason directors can normally justify modest, business-related political or charitable donations on the part of their companies, though the broader public policy issues arising out of such donations are recognised in the requirement that such donations be disclosed in the directors' report and in some cases approved by the shareholders: see paras 10–100 and 22–028. Also see para.15–021.

[135] The Law Society, *Company Law Reform White Paper* (June 2005), p.6.

as being unnecessary, can be understood; they urged instead that "the concept of the company as a legal entity separate from its members, and in whose interests the directors must act, is well understood".

10–027 If the old test of "the interests of the company" was too vague, what should a clearer statutory version require? Given the concentration of economic power in large companies, the question of which interests the directors were required to pursue when exercising their powers was of considerable interest and controversy across the political spectrum. Should the directors be required to promote the success of the company by acting primarily for the benefit of the shareholders (the shareholder primacy model), or should they perhaps give equal status to all the company's various stakeholders, including not simply the shareholders but also employees, customers, suppliers, and indeed even the local community and the environment (the pluralist model)? The different interests ranged on either side added heat to the debate. The final outcome was, perhaps predictably, something between these two extremes, although undoubtedly closer to the first and so also to the old common law test. The statutory formulation clearly rejects the "pluralist" approach, at least to the extent that it might have given all stakeholders some sort of equivalent status, allowing all to have the right to enforce directors' duties. But, at the other end of the spectrum, shareholder primacy was refined: the shareholders or members are certainly to be the primary beneficiaries of the directors' efforts in seeking the success of the company, hence the current formulation that the director must act "in the way he considers, in good faith, would be most likely to promote the success of the company for the benefit of its members as a whole"; but the directors are also subject to an obligation (not merely a power), although clearly a subordinate obligation, to "have regard to" the interests of other stakeholders. The subordinate nature of this second duty is made clear by the words "in doing so", i.e. in discharging the central duty. Put another way, the shareholders' position as the object of the directors' efforts in achieving the success of the company is not shared with other groups of persons upon whom the success of the company's business may also be thought to depend, for example, its employees or other stakeholders. To this extent, at least, the rule of shareholder primacy is reiterated in the section.

This strategy of rejecting pluralism but adopting a modernised version of shareholder primacy emerged from the CLR, and was described there as a philosophy of "enlightened shareholder value (ESV)".[136] Thus, in promoting the success of the company for the benefit of its members as a whole, s.172(1) requires that the director:

> "in doing so [must] have regard (amongst other matters) to—
> (a) the likely consequences of any decision in the long term,
> (b) the interests of the company's employees,
> (c) the need to foster the company's business relationships with suppliers, customers and others,
> (d) the impact of the company's operations on the community and the environment,
> (e) the desirability of the company maintaining a reputation for high standards of business conduct, and
> (f) the need to act fairly as between members of the company (s.172(1))".

[136] See Developing, Ch.3 and Completing, Ch.3.

The ESV approach can be said to embody the insight that the success of the company or the interests of the shareholders are not likely to be advanced if the management of the company conducts its business so that its employees are unwilling to work effectively, its suppliers and customers would rather not deal with it, it is at odds with the community in which it operates and its ethical and environmental standards are regarded as lamentable. However, it is crucial to note that the interests of the non-shareholder groups are to be given consideration by the directors only to the extent that it is desirable to do so in order to promote the success of the company for the benefit of its members as a whole. The non-shareholder interests do not have an independent value in the directors' decision-making, as they would have under a pluralist approach. For this reason, it seems wrong in principle to regard the section as requiring the directors to "balance" the interests of the members with those of the stakeholders. The members' interests in and benefits from the company's success are paramount, but the interests of stakeholders are to be taken into account when determining the best way of promoting the company's success to that end.[137]

It may be asked whether the ESV approach amounts to a development or a repetition of the common law. The answer is that it represents a development, but a modest one. What the Act adds to the common law is a *duty* on the part of the directors to take account of stakeholder interests when it is in the interests of the success of the company for the benefit of members to do so (but not a corresponding right in the stakeholders, or the shareholders, to enforce that duty). However, the statutory restatement may nevertheless have had an impact, if only by disabusing those directors and their advisers who might have been inclined to take an unduly narrow interpretation of the duty previously held. **10–028**

If the move from permission to well-described obligation is what lies at the root of the ESV approach, it becomes of great importance to know how the duty is enforced. As set out immediately below, s.172 imposes a (mainly) subjective test,[138] so, as with the predecessor common law duty, litigation is likely to be relatively uncommon and probably even less often successful. This is because it is very difficult to show that the directors have breached this duty of good faith, except in egregious cases or cases where the directors have, obligingly, left a clear record of their thought processes leading up to the challenged decision.[139]

---

137 But note the important distinction drawn in *LRH Services Ltd (In Liquidation) v Trew* [2018] EWHC 600 (Ch) at [29] (HH Judge David Cooke): "It is to be noted that the requirement [in s.172] is to promote *the success of the company* for the benefit of the members, not to promote the interests of the members directly, which may be a different thing. An obvious instance where there may be divergence is in consideration of distributions, which are of immediate benefit to members but may adversely affect the ability of the company to succeed." (Emphasis in the original.)

138 *LNOC Ltd v Watford Association Football Club Ltd* [2013] EWHC 3615 (Comm) at [64] (HH Judge Mackie QC).

139 The classic case where the directors did all too clearly reveal their reasoning is *Dodge v Ford Motor Co* (1919) 170 N.W. 668. Henry Ford openly took the view that the shareholders had been more than amply rewarded on their investment in the company and so proposed to declare no further special dividends but only the regular dividends (of some 60% per annum!) in order to reduce the price of the cars, to expand production and "to employ still more men, to spread the benefits of this industrial system to the greatest possible number, to help them build up their lives and their homes" (at 683). This was held to be "an arbitrary refusal to distribute funds that ought to have been distributed to the stockholders as dividends" (at 685).

Instead, the major role in giving some degree of practical substance to the ESV duty lies with the extended reporting requirements to shareholders imposed on directors, as described in Ch.22.[140]

Finally, and for the avoidance of doubt, the duty of the directors to act in good faith to promote the success of the company for the benefit of its members does not exempt the directors (or the company) from compliance with its other legal obligations, for example, health and safety or discrimination legislation, even if it could be shown that non-compliance would promote the company's overall success.[141]

Interpreting the statutory formula

Defining the company's success

10–029 Several important points arise on the interpretation of the language contained in this section. First, it is to be noted that corporate *success* for the benefit of the members is the word used to identify the touchstone for the exercise of the directors' discretion. Success is a more general word than, for example, "value", which it might have been thought was what the shareholders are interested in. However, the more general word is clearly the appropriate one, because not all companies formed under the Act are aimed at maximising the financial interests of their members. Companies may be charitable; they may have non-profit-making objectives without being charities, as in the case of a company formed by leaseholders to hold the freehold of a block of flats; they may be companies set up within a corporate group simply to hold a particular asset rather than to exploit it, even though the overall purpose of the group is to make profits; or they may be commercially-oriented but without aiming to distribute profits, in which case the company may, but is not obliged to, be incorporated as a CIC. In all these cases, maximising the value of the company is not the primary objective of its members and perhaps not even an objective at all. Section 172(2) makes it clear that:

> "where or to the extent that the purposes of the company consist of or include purposes other than the benefit of its members, subsection (1) has effect as if the reference to promoting the success of the company for the benefit of its members were to achieving those purposes."

The underlying thrust of the section is that it is the members who are to define the purposes of the company against which the directors can give meaning to the requirement to promote its success. The definition of the purpose of the company may be set out in its constitution. This is less likely to be the case now that the company is no longer required to have an objects clause, but certainly in the case of companies with non-commercial or non-profit objectives this fact is likely to appear clearly enough from the company's articles. In other words, the position,

---

[140] See fnn.131 and 134.

[141] For example, *Dymoke v Association for Dance Movement Psychotherapy UK Ltd* [2019] EWHC 94 (QB) (s.172 does not permit a company to ignore the rules of natural justice or the terms of a contract in determining the process used to expel a member simply because expulsion is seen, bona fide, as in the interests of the company).

usually, is that the company is to be regarded as a commercial company unless its constitution indicates otherwise, and in the typical case the directors will define success in commercial terms.

A more important underlying question is the extent to which the section is intended to constrain directors' decisions about precisely how to pursue the success of the company. Should the company aim for expansion through a series of takeovers or by organic growth? Should the company aim for expansion at all or for exploitation of a niche position? It seems clear that the section does not claim to address this sort of issue at all. This is to be left to the directors, who in turn are accountable to the shareholders for their decisions through the company's corporate governance mechanisms rather than through the courts. To this end, the section imposes a subjective test for compliance: the director must act "in the way he considers, in good faith, would be most likely to promote the success of the company". This aspect of the statutory duty is one shared with the previous common law formulation, and that was interpreted by the courts in such a way as to leave business decisions to the directors. As Lord Greene MR put it in *Re Smith & Fawcett Ltd*, directors were required to act "bona fide in what they consider—not what a court may consider—is in the interests of the company".[142] In most cases, it is true, compliance with the rule that directors must act in good faith was tested on common sense principles, the court asking itself whether it was proved that the directors had not done what they believed to be right, and normally accepting that they had unless satisfied that they had not behaved as honest men of business might be expected to act. However, even where the director had not acted as an honest business person might be expected to act, this is not necessarily a demonstration of breach of the duty of good faith. Thus, in one case where the directors' decision had caused substantial harm to the company it was held that this was merely a piece of evidence, perhaps a strong piece, against their contention that they had acted in good faith, rather than proof absolute that they had not.[143] These decisions on the meaning of good faith in the context of the core duty of fidelity at common law seem equally applicable to the statutory duty.

Failure to have regard, or due regard, to relevant matters

The concept of ESV enshrined in the statutory duty imposes an obligation on directors to "have regard" to the list of factors set out in subs.172(1)(a)–(f). Does this give rise to a corresponding power in the courts to scrutinise the decisions of directors to establish whether they have indeed taken account of these factors, or perhaps even whether, on an objective basis, they have taken *appropriate* account **10–030**

[142] "and not for any collateral purpose" [this closing phrase seeing its statutory parallels in s.171(b)]: [1942] Ch. 304 at 306.

[143] *Regentcrest Plc (In Liquidation) v Cohen* [2001] B.C.C. 494 Ch D. See also *Extrasure Travel Insurances Ltd v Scattergood* [2003] 1 B.C.L.C. 598 Ch D at [90]. It is to be noted that in neither the formulation of Lord Greene MR nor in s.172 is there a requirement upon the director to act "honestly" as well as "in good faith", though the word "honestly" is used in a number of court decisions in this area. However, the CLR did not believe that the adverb "honestly" added anything of importance to the requirement of good faith and its use might create uncertainty, and so it did not recommend its use either here or elsewhere in the statutory restatement: Completing, para.3.13.

of these factors? The answers to these questions seem inextricably linked to the "improper purposes" issues discussed earlier (s.171(b)); the older common law rule similarly juxtaposed the two requirements.[144]

On the first question, a proper reading of the section does suggest that a failure by directors to have regard to each item on the list of factors would constitute a breach of duty and render the directors' decision challengeable. This principle was already established at common law, although perhaps in a more limited form: although much was left to the directors' discretion (as described below) in determining what was in the interests of the company, the directors might breach that duty where they failed to direct their minds at all to the question of whether a transaction was in the interests of the company, even though a board which had considered the question might well have acted in the same way. A good illustration of the principle is afforded by *Re W&M Roith Ltd*.[145] There the controlling shareholder and director wished to make provision for his widow. On advice, he entered into a service agreement with the company whereby on his death she was to be entitled to a pension for life. On being satisfied that no thought had been given to the question whether the arrangement was for the benefit of the company and that, indeed, the sole object was to make provision for the widow, the court held that the transaction was not binding on the company.[146]

In this case it might be said that the straightforward financial success of the company was clearly compromised by the decision, since the widow was unlikely to provide the company with any corresponding corporate benefit. In such circumstances, the directors needed to be able to demonstrate that their decision was based on due consideration of the corporate benefit, and this they could not do.[147] However, had they been able to do that, the court would have been unlikely to second-guess their conclusions even if the court itself might not have reached the same decision.

10–031 But this strict approach might be thought impractical. By contrast, in *Charterbridge Corp v Lloyds Bank*,[148] the directors of a company forming part of a corporate group had considered the benefit of the group as a whole, but without giving separate consideration to that of the company alone, when they caused the subsidiary company of which they were directors to give security for a debt owed by the parent company to a bank. It was held, perhaps surprisingly given the accepted common law formulation of the requirement on directors, that "the proper test in the absence of actual separate consideration must be whether an intelligent and honest man in the position of a director of the company concerned could have reasonably believed that the transactions were for the benefit of the company". Here the collapse of the parent company would have been "a disaster"

---

144 *Re Smith and Fawcett Ltd* [1942] Ch. 304 at 306 (Lord Greene MR).

145 *Re W&M Roith Ltd* [1967] 1 W.L.R. 432 Ch D.

146 Following *Re Lee, Behrens & Co Ltd* [1932] 2 Ch. 46 Ch D; but cf. *Lindgren v L&P Estates Ltd* [1968] Ch. 572 CA, where it was held that there had been no failure on the part of the directors to consider the commercial merits.

147 Similarly, see *Scottish Co-operative Wholesale Society Ltd v Meyer* [1959] A.C. 324 HL.

148 *Charterbridge Corp v Lloyds Bank* [1970] Ch. 62 Ch D. A similar approach has been adopted in the area of unfair prejudice. See *Nicholas v Soundcraft Electronics Ltd* [1993] 1 B.C.L.C. 360 CA.

for the subsidiary.[149] The decision perhaps suggests that although directors must act in ways *they* consider would be most likely to promote the interests (or the success) of the company, it is also true that where, objectively, on balance, their decision can be seen to do that, it will not be overturned; the directors will not be held to be in breach of their duty at common law to act in the interests of the company (or, under the statute, their duty to promote the success of the company) *merely* because they did not give explicit thought to the question, at least in the absence of proven detriment.[150]

On the other hand, and despite the *Charterbridge* decision, it must be said that the core duty of good faith does not recognise a duty "to the group" or to other companies in the group. It insists that the main focus of directors must be on the interests of their subsidiary, even if it accepts that the interests of the subsidiary are in many cases intimately related to the continuing existence of the group.[151] Directors in corporate groups must guard against their inevitable inclination to promote the interests of the group as a whole (or some part of it).

These cases all concern the common law duty. Their analysis is in principle equally applicable to breaches of the statutory provisions, and indeed finding a breach of the core statutory duty of good faith on the ground that not all the required interests have been taken into account is perhaps more likely under the ESV approach because the statute is so much clearer about the precise range of matters to which directors must have regard in the discharge of their duty to promote the success of the company for the benefit of its members. To that extent, the retreat from the strict approach in *Re W & M Roith Ltd*[152] is welcome. Moreover, since the statutory list of factors is non-exhaustive, it would follow that a director would be in breach of duty in failing to take account of any matter which he or she considered relevant to the decision in question. However, in truth the statutory formulation largely makes explicit what was already implicit in the earlier common law, so it does not require boards to approach decision-making, or to document their decisions, in a totally novel fashion. Of course, to the extent that boards might previously have ignored potential adverse impacts on **10–032**

[149] cf. *Extrasure Travel Insurances Ltd v Scattergood* [2003] 1 B.C.L.C. 598, accepting the law as stated in the *Charterbridge* case, but coming to a different conclusion on the facts because (a) the directors of the subsidiary never considered whether the survival of the parent was crucial to the subsidiary; and (b) no reasonable director would have concluded that the steps taken by the directors would lead to the survival of the parent.

[150] *Re HLC Environmental Projects Ltd (In Liquidation)* [2014] B.C.C. 337 at [92]–[93] (John Randall QC); *Green v El Tai* [2015] B.P.I.R. 24 Ch D at [110] (Registrar Jones); *Madoff Securities International Ltd v Raven* [2013] EWHC 3147 (Comm) at [194].

[151] See also *Lindgren v L & P Estates Co Ltd* [1968] Ch. 572 at 595, per Harman LJ (no duty owed by director of holding company to subsidiary); and *Bell v Lever* [1932] A.C. 161 at 229, per Lord Atkin (no duty owed by director of subsidiary to the parent company). The statutory qualification to the definition of a "shadow director" in s.251(3) (para.10–011), excluding a company in relation to its subsidiaries, supports this approach. The cases do not distinguish between wholly-owned subsidiaries and those with outside minority shareholders. Only in the latter case does the imposition of a group policy potentially have an adverse effect on the interests of the shareholders, for which the unfair prejudice provisions may now provide a remedy (see Ch.14). It should also be noted that it is apparently legitimate for the company's articles to permit or require the directors to take into account the interests of other companies in the group, because in that way it could be said that the articles have defined what is to be regarded as "success" for the company in question.

[152] *Re W & M Roith Ltd* [1967] 1 W.L.R. 432.

shareholders' interests by failing to analyse the impact of a proposed decision on non-shareholders, the section is likely to have produced a change of practice.

On the second question, of whether the directors have not simply taken account of the listed factors but have taken *appropriate* account of them, the earlier common law cases suggest that the courts will generally resist any request to second-guess the directors' judgement of how best to act in the interests of the company.[153] The only exception is perhaps when, in the court's view, no reasonable director could have considered the chosen course of action to be in the company's interests (by analogy with the public law "*Wednesbury* unreasonableness" test). Such facts as raise this concern are often seen to go to the question of whether the court believes that the director did in fact consider the relevant matter at all (and so is part of the analysis of the first question just considered), but to the extent that the court's determination is not simply evidential, but judgemental, the resulting judicial oversight of directors' management decisions has remained very restrained, and in any event is limited to overturning the impugned decision, not substituting the courts' decision (except to the extent that this is implicit in the courts' unravelling of what has been done). Indeed, it is notable that the architect of the public law *Wednesbury* principle, Lord Greene MR, was also the judge who in *Re Smith & Fawcett* (quoted earlier) was concerned to stress the freedom of directors from control by the courts in the exercise of their good faith judgement, while also adding a "proper purposes" limitation analogous to the public law principle and to the statutory principle now found in s.171(b).

The most authoritative statement of this approach to judicial review is that of Lord Woolf in *Equitable Life Assurance Society v Hyman*,[154] although his approach was not part of the arguments of the other two judges in that case (or in the House of Lords on appeal). The complaint in this case was between groups of corporate creditors each complaining about the effect of the directors' decision; in other cases where the *Wednesbury* principle has been invoked, the disputes have typically been among members of the company about their rights and interests as shareholders rather than disagreements about the setting of the company's business strategy.[155] It might be thought, therefore, that the inclusion in subs.(1)(f) of "the need to act fairly as between the members of the company" as one of the factors of which the directors need to have regard could turn out to be significant, although the shareholders typically have more amenable avenues for complaint than reliance on a duty the directors owe to the company.

On the other hand, it might be better, analytically, to see this type of objective judicial review, where relevant, as situated entirely under s.171(b), with s.172 merely providing an explicit list of proper considerations required to be taken

[153] See para.10–029; and *Edge v Pensions Ombudsman* [2000] Ch. 602 CA at 627E–630G; *Equitable Life Assurance Society v Hyman* [2002] 1 A.C. 408 at [17]–[21].

[154] *Equitable Life Assurance Society v Hyman* [2000] 2 All E.R. 331 CA (Civ Div) at [17]–[21] (per Lord Woolf). In the House of Lords ([2002] 1 A.C. 408) Lord Steyn dealt with the case as a matter of an implied term in a contract, whilst Lord Cooke, dealing with it as a matter of the exercise of a discretion for a proper purpose, did not cite the *Wednesbury* principle but confined himself to mention of the *Howard Smith v Ampol* case (see fn.71). See also *Hunter v Senate Support Services Ltd* [2005] 1 B.C.L.C. 175 at [165]–[232].

[155] See the previous note and the cases referred to therein. However, it should also be noted that *Re Smith & Fawcett Ltd* was itself an intra-member dispute.

into account in directors' decision-making. Such an approach would effectively align s.171(b) "improper purposes" with the mandatory considerations listed in s.172, but would remind complainants of the inherent limitations in the claim being advanced. And, in a different direction, to the extent that unfair treatment of minorities by controlling persons is the chief mischief to be dealt with, a remedy can often be provided under the unfair prejudice provisions discussed in Ch.14.

A duty to disclose wrongdoing

This has become an increasingly troubling area of directors' duties. In what is still a controversial decision, the Court of Appeal in *Item Software (UK) Ltd v Fassihi*[156] held that a director was under a duty to disclose his own breaches of fiduciary duty. This obligation was recognised as novel, but seen as derived from, i.e. being an aspect of, the core duty of good faith and loyalty, not a "separate and independent" self-standing duty.[157] Quite what this means is not clear, since in *Item Software* itself the finding of a distinct duty to disclose was seen as essential to delivering the remedy awarded. The director had pursued a corporate opportunity (the relevant breach of duty is discussed below) by setting up a competing business and attempting to persuade a client of the company to engage with his new business rather than renew its existing contract with the company. The director had also suggested that the company should take a tough stance in negotiations with the client, hoping, it seems, to further encourage the client in his direction. In the end, however, the client renewed the contract with neither the company nor the director's new business. This meant that the company could not sue its director for an account of the profits he had made from stealing the client for his own business, as he had made none. Moreover, the trial judge had found as a fact that the director's endeavours to encourage a tough negotiating stance had made no difference to the company's approach to the client. It followed that the company could not sue the director for the loss caused by his failure to act in good faith for the benefit of the company, at least in respect of this intervention, since that breach had caused no loss. In short, the facts appeared to suggest that there could be no account of profits and no compensation for loss, and yet the director had clearly behaved in an underhand way in breach of his duties of loyalty. In the face of this seemingly unacceptable result, the trial judge also found, as a fact, that, had the company known of the director's activities, it would have modified its negotiating tactics and accepted the client's best offer to renew, the one which it had in fact rejected as too low. Thus, it was said, *if*—but only if—it could be shown that the director had a *duty* to disclose this information about his wrongdoing to the company, then the director would have committed a breach of that duty and the company would have a remedy, the remedy being **10–033**

[156] *Item Software (UK) Ltd v Fassihi* [2004] B.C.C. 994. Also see *GHLM Trading Ltd v Maroo* [2012] EWHC 61 (Ch); *IT Human Resources Plc v Land* [2014] EWHC 3812 (Ch).

[157] *Item Software (UK) Ltd v Fassihi* [2004] B.C.C. 994 at [40]–[41] and [44]. Also see *Stupples v Stupples & Co (High Sycombe) Ltd* [2012] EWHC 1226 (Ch) at [59] (HHJ David Cooke); *First Subsea Ltd v Balltec Ltd* [2014] EWHC 866 (Ch) at [191]: Norris J emphasised that the duty to "self-report" is "not a discrete and free-standing duty. It is one aspect of a bundle of interrelated obligations which together constitute 'good faith' and 'loyalty'." Contrast *Shepherds Investments Ltd v Walters* [2006] EWHC 836 (Ch) at [132] (Etherton J).

recovery of the loss it had suffered because it failed to obtain the benefit of the (admittedly less attractive) contract with the client.

Such a duty to disclose the director's wrongdoing was novel,[158] and indeed there were authorities against such a duty in the context of employees.[159] Whether this was the only route to a remedy is doubted, especially when establishing the requisite novel duty was far from straightforward.[160] Moreover, holding that there is such a duty has consequences that are potentially unattractive.[161] Consider, for example, a director who fails to disclose a wrongdoing for which he might have been dismissed by his company: should the company automatically be able to recover the salary paid in the intervening period? The accepted answer is no[162]: if losses are to be recovered, they must be for proven failings in the period before dismissal.[163]

More importantly, the duty would seem to be surplus to needs. The court should have been able to rely simply on the fact that the core duty of good faith and loyalty requires a director to protect the company from harm, bringing to the attention of the company threats to its business of which the director becomes aware.[164] The twist in this case was that the duty was imposed even though the threat arose out of the director's own wrongdoing, but it would be odd if the director's wrongdoing could relieve him or her from a course of action which

---

[158] *Item Software (UK) Ltd v Fassihi* [2004] B.C.C. 994 at [44].

[159] *Bell v Lever* [1932] A.C. 161, a case which has caused endless difficulties. It is perhaps best seen as a case which (i) confirms that when a company is negotiating a contract (or varying or terminating that contract) with its employee, or indeed with a director, then the employee or director owes no duty to the company to disclose its own wrongdoing: the parties are clearly in an adversarial position, each acting in their own self-interests, and it cannot be said that the company in that context is relying, or entitled to rely, on the employee or director owing the company any duty to look after the company's interests or to assist the company in looking after its own interests; (ii) advances the more questionable and quite general proposition that an employee's duty to act in good faith and in the interests of his employer does not require the employee to disclose his own misconduct when it was committed; and (iii) confirms that a company that has negotiated an agreement with its employee (or, on the same basis, a director) may be able to set that agreement aside on the grounds of mistake, although the general law makes plain that the nature of the mistake is crucial.

[160] As set out in *Item Software (UK) Ltd v Fassihi* [2004] B.C.C. 994, it seemed to require a series of steps that linked two separate directors' duties, directed at different ends, and out of one of them (the conflicts duty) derived a duty to disclose wrongdoing (see [39], even though the function of disclosure had before only been seen as the means whereby the director sought to whitewash/seek approval to pursue the conflict), adding that this duty to disclose assisted in delivering accounting remedies in the conflicts/account of profits context (see [66]), and then simply asserting that this same duty must obviously be seen as an inherent aspect of the good faith duty, and could be used in that different context to deliver compensation for loss (see [40]–[41])—and so was of assistance on the facts in the instant case.

[161] See the extended discussions in *Bell v Lever* [1932] A.C. 161; *Balston Ltd v Headline Filters Ltd* [1990] F.S.R. 385 Ch D; *British Midland Tool Ltd v Midland International Tooling Ltd* [2003] EWHC 466 (Ch), all resisting the conclusion that someone might owe a specific duty to disclose their own wrongdoing.

[162] See *Bell v Lever* [1932] AC 161 at 228, 230–31; cited in *Balston Ltd v Headline Filters Ltd* [1990] F.S.R. 385 at 408; *Item Software (UK) Ltd v Fassihi* [2004] B.C.C. 994 at [51].

[163] See, e.g. *HPOR Servicos de Concultoria Ltda v Dryships Inc* [2018] EWHC 3451 (Comm); *Wey Education Plc v Atkins* [2016] EWHC 1663 (Ch).

[164] *British Midland Tool Ltd v Midland International Tooling Ltd* [2003] EWHC 466 (Ch).

would otherwise need to be taken.[165] Liability thus arises straightforwardly from the failure to act in good faith to protect the company[166]: there was no need for a super-added duty to disclose.[167]

The harder question, then, is whether there are any circumstances where a director would *not* be liable for his failure to disclose that his own activity posed risks of harm to the company. The decision of the House of Lords in *Bell v Lever Brothers Ltd*[168] (although a case concerning employees) suggests an example. The court in *Item Software v Fassihi* was content with the outcome in that case, even as it might apply to directors, but confined the conclusion to situations where directors were negotiating an improvement in the terms of their employment or compensation for the termination of their services with the company, on the grounds that disclosure in such a case would be contrary to the expectations of the parties.[169] More importantly, it would be contrary to the entitlements of the parties. In those circumstances the parties are clearly in an adversarial position, each acting in their own self-interests, and it cannot be said that the company in that context is relying, or is entitled to rely, on the director owing the company any duty to look after the company's interests or to assist the company in looking after its own interests. Because there is no duty to protect the company, there is no liability for failing to protect. But outside that context, directors owe a duty to act in good faith for the benefit of the company—there is a duty to protect—and liability for failing to do so. **10–034**

In *Item Software v Fassihi* this novel duty to disclose was used to justify a finding that the company was entitled to compensation for the loss caused by its director's failure to disclose his own wrongdoing (or, as seems preferable, his failure to act in good faith to protect the company), where, had he done so, the negotiating outcome would have been better for the company. Can the same duty to disclose be employed to advantage when the company seeks an account of the profits made by the director from his wrongdoing, not compensation for loss suffered by the company? In another difficult decision, *Parr v Keystone Healthcare Ltd*,[170] the Court of Appeal suggests this is possible, welding together the good faith duty (with, according to *Item Software*, its associated duty to disclose) with the different duty not to engage in activities which involve a

---

165 See *Shepherds Investments Ltd v Walters* [2006] EWHC 836 (Ch) at [132] (Etherton J) for the preferable approach. The possibility that the duty to act in good faith for the benefit of the company might, in some circumstances (but not as a general rule), require the directors to disclose the wrongdoing of others, or suffer the resulting liability for failing to do so, has long been settled: see *British Midland Tool Ltd v. Midland International Tooling Ltd* [2003] EWHC 466 (Ch), especially at [86] and also [89].

166 As effectively conceded in *Item Software (UK) Ltd v Fassihi* [2004] B.C.C. 994 at [44].

167 See the pithy comment of Lord Aitken in *Bell v Lever* [1932] A.C. 161 at 228: "The servant owes a duty not to steal, but, having stolen, is there superadded a duty to confess that he has stolen? I am satisfied that to imply such a duty would be a departure from the well established usage of mankind and would be to create obligations entirely outside the normal contemplation of the parties concerned."

168 *Bell v Lever* [1932] A.C. 161. See fn.159.

169 *Item Software (UK) Ltd v Fassihi* [2004] B.C.C. 994 at [51]–[58].

170 *Parr v Keystone Healthcare Ltd* [2019] EWCA Civ 1246. See the discussion at para.10–109 especially.

conflict of duty and interest. We look at this case later, but the potential developments surrounding the "duty to disclose" should be noted in the present discussion.

The problem of "short-termism"

10–035 The common law focus on shareholders led to a widespread but, it is submitted, erroneous view that the law required directors acting in the interests of shareholders to prioritise their short-term interests. The better view, it is suggested, is that the directors were not bound to any particular timeframe; on the contrary, they must take into account both the long- and the short-term interests of the shareholders and strike a balance between them.[171] The CLR proposed in its draft statement of directors' duties to specify an obligation on the directors to take into account "the likely consequences (short and long term) of the actions open to the director".[172] As we have seen, s.172 refers merely to "the likely consequences of any decision in the long term". If anything, the omission of the reference to short-term interests in the non-exhaustive list emphasises the importance of long-term consequences. That bias is repeated in the UK Corporate Governance Code.[173]

Corporate groups

10–036 We have already considered the potential problem faced by directors within corporate groups, where their instinct may be to look to the overall success of the group, whereas their duty of good faith and loyalty is owed only to their appointing company.[174]

Employees

10–037 Among the factors to which a director of a company must have regard under s.172(1) are "the interests of the company's employees". This is as one would expect: any comprehensive list of stakeholder interests will necessarily include the employees. But the practical impact of this on employees is limited. Indeed, it was said of the predecessor provision[175] that its real impact was to dilute directors' accountability to shareholders rather than strengthen accountability to employees. This is because employees cannot use the section offensively, whilst

[171] See Counsel's Opinion quoted in the Report by Mr Milner Holland of an investigation under s.165(b) of the CA 1948 into the affairs of the Savoy Hotel Ltd and the Berkeley Hotel Company Ltd, Board of Trade, 1954. This somewhat obscure source has long been regarded as the *locus classicus* on this point. See also *Gaiman v National Association for Mental Health* [1971] Ch. at 330: "both present and future members".

[172] CLR, Final Report I, p.345 (Principle 2, Note (1)).

[173] CGC, Provision 1. See too BIS, *A Long-Term Focus for Corporate Britain: A Call for Evidence* (2010). Responses were published, but then nothing more was done: see ***https://www.gov.uk/government/consultations/a-long-term-focus-for-corporate-britain-a-call-for-evidence*** [Accessed 16 December 2020].

[174] See para.10–036.

[175] CA 1985 s.309, although expressed in different terms to s.172(1)(b).

directors can use it defensively when sued by shareholders, by arguing that a decision apparently unfavourable to the shareholders is unchallengeable because it was taken in the interests of the employees.[176] Writ large, this illustrates the argument against the pluralist approach to this core duty of good faith. So long as the duty is perceived subjectively, increasing the number of equal-status groups whose interests the directors must promote makes proof of breach difficult, almost to the point of impossibility. Correcting that defect by making the duty objective, however, paves the way for excessive judicial intervention in the taking of board-level decisions, thus inducing caution on the part of those who ought to be risk-takers. The best view is probably that any broadly-formulated pluralist provision could not by itself operate so as to alter the decision-making processes of a board unless coupled with further changes in company law, such as board-level representation for the relevant stakeholder groups.

There is, however, one particular and limited derogation from the core duty which is made in favour of employees. This is to be found in s.247, involving the power to make gratuitous payments to employees on the cessation of the company's business.

Creditors

There is one surprising omission from the statutory list of matters to which the directors must have regard, namely, the interests of the creditors, except to the extent it is embraced by subs.172(1)(c). Of course, so long as the company's business is flourishing, the creditors' position is not prejudiced by such an omission. Their contractual rights against the company plus the company's desire to preserve its reputation and thus access to future credit will act so as to protect the creditors. However, once the company's fortunes begin to decline, conflict between the interests of the shareholders and the creditors may emerge in a strong form; the directors have an incentive to take excessive risks to protect their own and the shareholders' position, knowing that, if the company is in the vicinity of insolvency, the downside risk will fall wholly on the creditors, whilst the upside benefit will get the company out of trouble. We will see in Ch.19 how this problem is dealt with, both by statutory insolvency laws operating in the lead up to insolvency, and by common law rules operating still earlier.[177] All these rules are embraced by the simple strategy of providing, expressly, in s.172(3), that the duty imposed under that section "has effect subject to any enactment or rule of law requiring directors, in certain circumstances, to consider or act in the interests of creditors of the company". 10–038

[176] cf. *Re Saul D. Harrison & Sons Plc* [1995] 1 B.C.L.C. 14 CA at 25, where resort was had to the CA 1985 s.309 to undermine the shareholder petitioning under s.459 against the board/majority shareholders of the company.

[177] See especially the discussion at para.19–013. Also see A. Keay, "Financially distressed companies, preferential payments and the director's duty to take account of creditors' interests" (2020) 136 L.Q.R. 52.

Donations

10–039 In the abstract, a decision on the part of the directors to give the company's assets away would appear to be a *clear* example of a decision not taken in good faith to promote the success of the company for the benefit of its members. On the other hand, companies are always being approached to support various causes, and do in fact make donations of various sorts. Company law has sought to distinguish between donations which promote the company's business (legitimate) and those which do not (illegitimate). Traditionally, that distinction was drawn by the law relating to ultra vires, but now the focus is on directors' powers: in the absence of an express provision in the articles or elsewhere conferring upon directors the authority to make donations, is there an implied power to do so in order to further the company's business?[178] And if there is such a power, has it been exercised appropriately?[179] This second question has various strands. Thus, in *Re Lee, Behrens and Co Ltd*,[180] where the company's constitution conferred an express power on the directors to make the gift in question, Eve J identified the relevant tests as follows: "(i.) Is the transaction reasonably incidental to the carrying on of the company's business? (ii.) Is it a bona fide transaction? and (iii.) Is it done for the benefit and to promote the prosperity of the company?".

In practice, the courts have tended not to examine very closely the link between the donation and the company's business when it seemed to them that the donation was in the public interest, so that a substantial donation by a large chemical company to promote scientific tertiary education was upheld even though the gift might not be used to promote the study of chemistry in particular and the company had no greater claim on the graduating students than any of its rivals.[181] It seems unlikely that this approach will change in the future, in the light of pressures on companies to be "good citizens" in their communities and of the recognition that companies may secure "reputational" advantages from supporting activities which seem remote from their businesses, for example, a bank sponsoring an opera production (presumably thus enhancing its reputation among wealthy potential customers).[182] By contrast, donations which shift assets away from shareholders in the direction of other stakeholders in the company have traditionally been treated with suspicion, but that attitude may also be undergoing a change and, in any event, it is normally possible to present such apparent gifts as part of an exchange where the company is a going concern.[183]

[178] The courts are likely to give a positive answer to this question.

[179] Thus, in *Evans v Brunner, Mond & Co Ltd* [1921] 1 Ch. 359 Ch D, where the question was whether a shareholders' resolution expressly conferring power on the directors to make a certain class of donation was ultra vires, Eve J said obiter of the authority conferred by the resolution that it "is certainly impressed with this implied obligation on those to whom it is given, that they shall exercise the discretion vested in them bona fide in the interests of the company whose agents they are".

[180] *Re Lee, Behrens and Co Ltd* [1932] 2 Ch. 46. Also see *MSL Group Holdings Ltd v Clearwell International Ltd* [2012] EWHC 3707 (QB) (Sir Raymond Jack) at [41]–[42], [45].

[181] *Evans v Brunner, Mond & Co Ltd* [1921] 1 Ch. 359.

[182] The donation can then be presented as a contract: a payment in exchange for exposure of the company's name before a valued target audience, in fact a form of advertising, although this will have tax consequences for both sides.

[183] Thus, in *Parke v Daily News Ltd* [1962] Ch. 927 Ch D the payments to the employees failed because it could not be argued that a company about to enter liquidation any longer had a

The upshot of the law in this area is that directors probably have some leeway to steer donations or other similar arrangements (such as sponsorship) in the direction of their favourite charities or pastimes, without serious threat of legal challenge, provided such donations are not of excessive size and provided there is some link with the company's business.

However, in one area, that of corporate political donations, such leeway is arguably constitutionally objectionable. Consequently, in that area, as we shall see, the law has required shareholder approval of donations since reforms made in 2000.[184]

DUTY TO EXERCISE INDEPENDENT JUDGMENT: S.173

At common law, this issue is typically described as a duty not to fetter the exercise of discretion. In s.173, this is put in positive terms, as a duty to exercise independent judgment. At the level of principle the requirement is uncontroversial. However, there are five points relating to the practical working of this principle which need to be considered. **10–040**

Taking advice and delegating authority

First, and perhaps most obviously, the principle does not prevent directors seeking and acting on advice from others. Indeed, the board might well infringe its duty to take reasonable care if it proceeded to a decision without appropriate advice from outsiders (investment bankers, lawyers, valuers). What the board cannot do is treat the advice as an instruction, although in complex technical areas the advice may leave the board with little freedom for manoeuvre, for example, where lawyers advise that the board's preferred course of action would be unlawful. The individual directors on the board must regard themselves as taking responsibility for the decision reached,[185] probing the issues for themselves after taking appropriate advice.[186] **10–041**

Secondly, just as the duty of care does not prevent a board from delegating its functions to non-board employees (provided it has in place appropriate internal controls—see above), so the duty to exercise independent judgment does not prohibit such delegation.[187] However, it seems that s.173 was not intended to

(shareholder) interest in fostering good relations with its employees. The specific decision in that case was reversed, within limits, by what is now s.247, which confers a power on the company, if it would otherwise not have it, to make provisions for the benefit of employees on the cessation or transfer of its business, which power is exercisable "notwithstanding the general duty imposed by s.172 (duty to promote the success of the company)".

[184] See para.10–100. Also see para.15–021.

[185] *Dickinson v NAL Realisations (Staffordshire) Ltd* [2017] EWHC 28 (Ch) at [158]–[159] (wife (who was a director) and second director could not simply leave decisions to the third director—in the absence of a proper delegation and the implementation of appropriate monitoring, the third director's views could not simply be adopted as the final decision); *Madoff Securities International Ltd v Raven* [2013] EWHC 3147 (Comm) at [191]–[192] (Popplewell J).

[186] *Raithatha v Baig* [2017] EWHC 2059 (Ch) at [36].

[187] See *Madoff Securities International Ltd v Raven* [2013] EWHC 3147 (Comm) at [191] (Popplewell J).

overrule the common law rule that *delegatus non potest delegare*, i.e. that a person to whom powers are delegated (as powers are to directors under the articles) cannot further delegate the exercise of those powers, *unless* the instrument of delegation itself authorises further delegation.[188] In practice, wide powers of further delegation are conferred on the directors by the articles, and it is indeed difficult to see how the board of a large company could otherwise effectively exercise its powers of management of the company. However, this rule means that the articles may effectively prevent further delegation beyond the board by simply not providing for this.

Exercise of future discretion

10–042 Thirdly, it was debated at common law whether the non-fettering rule prevented a director from contracting with a third party as to the future exercise of his or her discretion. The answer ultimately arrived at was that this was permissible in appropriate cases. The starting point at common law, despite the paucity of reported cases on the point,[189] seems to be that directors cannot validly contract (either with one another or with third parties) as to how they shall vote at future board meetings or otherwise conduct themselves in the future.[190] This is so even though there is no improper motive or purpose and no personal advantage reaped by the directors under the agreement. This, however, does not mean that if, in the bona fide exercise of their discretion, the directors have entered into a contract on behalf of the company, they cannot in that contract validly agree to take such further action at board meetings or otherwise as is necessary to carry out that contract. As was said in a judgment of the Australian High Court[191]:

> "There are many kinds of transaction in which the proper time for the exercise of the directors' discretion is the time of the negotiation of a contract and not the time at which the contract is to be performed … If at the former time they are bona fide of opinion that it is in the best interests of the company that the transaction should be entered into and carried into effect, I can see no reason in law why they should not bind themselves to do whatever under the transaction is to be done by the board."

[188] *Re Cartmells' Case* (1873–74) L.R. 9 Ch. App. 691 CA of Chancery.

[189] But see *Clark v Workman* [1920] 1 Ir.R. 107; and an unreported decision of Morton J in the *Arderne Cinema* litigation (see paras 13–011 onwards); and the Scottish decision in *Dawson International Plc v Coats Paton Plc*, 1989 S.L.T. 655 (1st Div.) where it was accepted that an agreement by the directors would be subject to an implied term that it did not derogate from their duty to give advice to the shareholders which reflected the situation at the time the advice was given.

[190] Contrast the position of shareholders who may freely enter into such voting agreements: paras 13–029 to 13–032. What if the directors and the members enter into an agreement which fetters the directors' discretion? This was discussed, but not clearly settled, by the Canadian Supreme Court in *Ringuet v Bergeron* [1960] S.C.R. 672, where the majority held the voting agreement valid because, in their view, it related only to voting at general meetings. The minority held that it extended also to directors' meetings and was void, but they conceded that the position might have been different had all the members originally been parties to the agreement: see ibid., at 677. But cf. *Fulham Football Club Ltd v Cabra Estates Plc* [1994] 1 B.C.L.C. 363 CA at 393.

[191] *Thorby v Goldberg* (1964) 112 C.L.R. 597 Aust. HC, per Kitto J at 601–606.

The principle in *Thorby v Goldberg* was applied by the English Court of Appeal in *Cabra Estates Plc v Fulham Football Club*,[192] so as to uphold an elaborate contract which the directors had entered into on behalf of the company for the redevelopment of the football ground and under which, inter alia, the club was entitled to some £11 million and the directors agreed to support any planning application the developers might make during the coming seven years. This is surely correct: if individuals may contract as to their future behaviour in these matters, it is desirable that companies should be able to do so too. The application of the "no fettering" rule would make companies unreliable contracting parties and perhaps deprive them of the opportunity to enter into long-term contracts which would be to their commercial benefit.

Section 173(2)(a) now provides that the duty to exercise independent judgment is not infringed by a director acting "in accordance with an agreement duly entered into by the company that restricts the future exercise of discretion by its directors", including presumably the rider that the agreement must be one entered into by the directors in the bona fide opinion that it is in the best interests of the company to do so (i.e. "duly" entered into). Section 173(2)(b) goes on to state that no breach of the independent judgment rule arises if the director acts "in a way authorised by the company's constitution". Thus, the articles may authorise restrictions on the exercise of independent judgment, which might be a useful facility in private companies.

However, s.173(2)(a) protects the directors only from the argument that they have failed to exercise independent judgment by entering into the agreement which restricts their future freedom of action. Can the subsequent exercise of their powers as the contract demands be said to be a breach of their core duty of loyalty, if at that time they no longer believe it to be in accordance with their core duty to act in accordance with the contract? There are a number of cases in which, where shareholder consent has been required for a disposal of assets or for a takeover, the courts have been reluctant to construe agreements on the part of the directors not to co-operate with rival suitors or to recommend a rival offer to the shareholders as binding the directors, if they come to the view that the later offer is preferable from the shareholders' point of view.[193] This line of cases might be justified on the basis that shareholders are peculiarly dependent upon the advice of their directors and that they might find themselves in a poor position to take the decision which had been put in their hands, if they were given advice by the directors which did not reflect the situation as the directors saw it at the time it fell to the shareholders to take their decision. The continuing validity of the no fettering rule in this context could be reconciled with the provisions of s.173 on the basis that that section deals only with the fiduciary duties owed by the director to the company (see s.170(1)), whereas the situation just mentioned

[192] *Cabra Estates Plc v Fulham Football Club* [1994] 1 B.C.L.C. 363; noted by Griffiths, [1993] J.B.L. 576.

[193] *John Crowther Group Plc v Carpets International* [1990] B.C.L.C. 460; *Rackham v Peek Foods Ltd* [1990] B.C.L.C. 895; *Dawson International Plc v Coats Paton Plc*, 1989 S.L.T. 655. The correctness of these decisions was left open by the Court of Appeal in *Cabra Estates*. Even here it must be accepted that the shareholders may in consequence lose a commercial opportunity which would otherwise be open to them. See the discussion at para.28–035.

triggers the duty owed by directors to the shareholders to give them advice in the shareholders' best interest, if they choose to give them advice at all.[194]

Duties of strenuously dissenting directors

10–043 Fourthly, there are limits to the duty to act independently. In particular, a director cannot rely on this duty as providing an excuse for his efforts to destabilise the company while still remaining as a board member. *Stobart Group Ltd v Tinkler*[195] illustrates the problem. After Tinkler had been dismissed as the company's CEO but remained a director, he sought to mobilise shareholder support to remove the sitting chairman. The Court held that the duty to exercise independent judgment exists only in order to support the *board's* management of the company's business in an efficient and competent manner[196]: it does not entitle an individual director to act outside the boardroom independently of the board. In particular, if there is conflict between board members about specific issues, then the dissenting director should confine himself to raising the matter at board level and ensuring that any continuing opposition is minuted; or, if the issues are serious, raising the matter at a general meeting with the other directors present, not acting solo and not engaging with shareholders individually; or, finally, if neither of those deliver satisfaction, resigning.

Nominee directors

10–044 Finally, the independent judgment principle could cause difficulties for "nominee" directors, i.e. directors not elected by the shareholders generally but appointed by a particular class of security holder or creditor to protect their interests. English law solves such problems by requiring nominee directors to ignore the interests of the nominator,[197] though it may be doubted how far this injunction is obeyed in practice. The Ghana Companies Code 2019 s.190(4)[198] adopted what might be regarded as the more realistic line by permitting nominee directors to "give special, but not exclusive, consideration to the interests" of the nominator, but even this formulation would not permit the "mandating" of directors and thus the creation of a fettering problem.

---

[194] See para.10–006.

[195] *Stobart Group Ltd v William Andrew Tinkler* [2019] EWHC 258 (Comm).

[196] *Stobart Group Ltd v William Andrew Tinkler* [2019] EWHC 258 (Comm) at [414], and more generally see [413]–[415].

[197] *Boulting v ACTT* [1963] 2 Q.B. 606 CA at 626 per Lord Denning MR; *Kuwait Asia Bank EC v National Mutual Life Nominees Ltd* [1991] 1 A.C. 187 PC. The latter case shows that this principle has the advantage of not making the nominator liable for any breaches of duty to the company by the nominee director. Also see *Thompson v The Renwick Group Plc* [2014] EWCA Civ 635, where the Court rejected the view that a parent assumes a duty of care to employees of its subsidiary in health and safety matters by virtue of that parent company having appointed an individual as director of its subsidiary company with responsibility for health and safety matters.

[198] The provision appears in the equivalent of CA 2006 s.172, not s.173.

DIRECTORS' DUTIES OF SKILL, CARE AND DILIGENCE: S.174

Historical development

Before the statutory enactment of directors' duties, the long-debated issue in this area was the appropriate standard of care to be required of directors. Historically, the common law was based upon a very low standard of care, because it was subjectively formulated. The traditional view is to be found in a stream of largely nineteenth-century cases which culminated in the decision in 1925 in *Re City Equitable Fire Insurance Co.*[199] Those cases seem to have framed the directors' duties of skill and care with non-executive rather than executive directors in mind and, moreover, on the basis of a view that the non-executive director had no serious role to play within the company but was simply a piece of window-dressing aimed at promoting the company's image.[200] The result was a conceptualisation of the duty in highly subjective terms. The proposition was famously formulated by Romer J in the *City Equitable* case that "a director need not exhibit in the performance of his duties a greater degree of skill than may reasonably be expected from a person of *his* knowledge and experience".[201] The courts were also influenced by a model of corporate decision-making which gave the shareholders effective control over the choice of directors. If the shareholders chose incompetent directors, that was their fault and the remedy lay in their hands. As we shall see,[202] that is no longer an accurate picture of the degree of control exercised by shareholders in most medium and large companies. Furthermore, the proposition formulated by Romer J was highly inappropriate for executive directors, appointed to their positions and paid large, sometimes very large, sums of money for the expertise which they assert they can bring to the business. The implicit view of the role of the non-executive director also became anachronistic after the development of the corporate governance codes in the 1990s, which allocated a major role to the non-executive directors in the monitoring of the executive directors.[203] 10–045

Even before the enactment of the CA 2006 this was an area of the law that was changing. The courts were influenced by the development of more demanding and objective statutory standards for directors whose companies were facing

---

199 *Re City Equitable Fire Insurance Co* [1925] Ch. 407 CA, a decision of the Court of Appeal but always quoted for the judgment of Romer J at first instance, because the appeal concerned only the liability of the auditors.

200 The most famous example of this is perhaps *Re Cardiff Savings Bank* [1892] 2 Ch. 100 Ch D, where the Marquis of Bute, whose family, despite its Scottish antecedents, owned, and indeed had largely rebuilt, Cardiff Castle, was appointed president of the Bank at the age of six months and attended only one meeting of the board in his whole life. He was held not liable for any negligence in the management of the Bank.

201 *Re City Equitable Fire Insurance Co* [1925] Ch. 407 at 427 (emphasis added). This test also contains *an* objective element, because the director could be held liable for failing to live up to the standard which a person of the director's skill is reasonably capable of reaching, but that leaves the strong subjective element that the director can never be required to achieve a standard higher than he or she is personally capable of reaching.

202 See Ch.11.

203 See para.9–018.

insolvency,[204] and began to develop the common law requirements by analogy with those statutory provisions, and indeed in line with the general laws of negligence which, in their modern guise, post-dated *Re City Equitable Fire Insurance Co*. The beginnings of the modern approach at common law can be found in *Dorchester Finance Co v Stebbing*,[205] but it was a pair of first instance decisions by Hoffmann J[206] in the 1990s which marked a move towards a fully objective approach. He explicitly adopted as an accurate expression of the common law the test contained in s.214(4) of the Insolvency Act in relation to wrongful trading.[207] This inchoate change in the common law now finds explicit expression in s.174 of the CA 2006. This section first requires that "a director of a company must exercise reasonable care, skill and diligence" and then goes on to define what is meant by reasonable care, using a formulation which tracks very closely s.214 of the IA 1986:

> "This means the care, skill and diligence that would be exercised by a reasonably diligent person with (a) the general knowledge, skill and experience that may reasonably be expected of a person carrying out the same functions carried out by the director in relation to the company, and (b) the general knowledge, skill and experience that the director has."

However, it should be noted that in one particular area the statute has exempted directors from liability for negligence. In the case of misstatements in or omissions from the directors' report and the directors' remuneration report liability arises on the part of directors to the company only on the basis of knowledge or recklessness.[208]

The statutory standard

10–046 The crucial difference between the statutory formulation and that of Romer J is that in the latter the director's subjective level of skill sets the standard required of the director, whereas under the CA 2006 the director's subjective level does so only if it improves upon the objective standard of the reasonable director. Limb (a) of the statutory formula sets a standard which all directors must meet and it is not one dependent on the particular director's capabilities; Limb (b) adds a subjective standard which, however, can operate only to increase the level of care

[204] Principally the wrongful trading provisions, to be found in s.214 of the IA 1986, considered at para.19–005 to 19–012.

[205] Decided in 1977 but fully reported only in 1989: [1989] B.C.L.C. 498 Ch D.

[206] *Norman v Theodore Goddard* [1991] B.C.L.C. 1027 (where the judge was "willing to assume" that s.214 of the IA 1986 represented the common law); and *Re D'Jan of London Ltd* [1994] 1 B.C.L.C. 561 Ch D (Companies Ct) where the director was found negligent on the basis of an objective test, though it has to be said that the director could probably have been found liable on the facts on a subjective test of diligence (he signed an insurance proposal form without reading it). See also *Cohen v Selby* [2001] 1 B.C.L.C. 176 CA at 183; and *Brumder v Motornet Service and Repairs Ltd* [2013] 1 W.L.R. 2783 CA at [45]–[47] (Beatson LJ).

[207] See para.19–005.

[208] CA 2006 s.463. See below, para.22–034. It should be noted that this clause exempts the director only in respect of statements in the relevant reports and not in respect of any negligent conduct to which the statements inaccurately refer.

required of the director.[209] Whether the statutory provision is to be regarded as simply endorsing the current common law or, probably better, as effecting a change in the common law which was under consideration but not fully developed by the courts, this is clearly an area where a court applying s.174 should be cautious in its use of the older common law authorities as an aid to interpretation under s.170(4).

What does this all mean for directors? First, although directors, executive and non-executive, are subject to a uniform and objective duty of care, what the discharge of that duty requires in particular cases will not be uniform. As the statutory formulation itself recognises, what is required of the director will depend on the functions carried out by the director,[210] so that there will be variations, not only between executive and non-executive directors[211] but also between different types of executive director (and equally of non-executives) and between different types and sizes of company.

Secondly, the imposition of an objective duty of care does not necessarily require a directorship to be regarded as a profession. The vexed issue of what constitutes a profession does not have to be addressed; all that is required is an assessment of what is reasonably required of a person having, as the statute puts it, the knowledge, skill and experience which a person in the position of the particular director ought to have. Given the enormous range of types and sizes of companies, it would be odd if all directors were to be regarded as professional. On the other hand, as was pointed out by the Court of Appeal of New South Wales, an objective approach does require even non-executive directors, as a minimum, to "take reasonable steps to place themselves in a position to guide and monitor the management of the company".[212] The days of the wholly inactive or passive director would thus seem to be numbered—or, at least, a director who is so runs a high risk of being held negligent.

Thirdly, directors are permitted to engage in substantial delegation of management functions to non-board employees. This is an inevitable reflection of the fact that companies are organisations, sometimes very big organisations, the running of which may require a large staff. In *City Equitable* Romer J put this point in very robust terms. He said that "in respect of all duties that, having regard to the exigencies of business, and the articles of association, may properly be left to some other official, a director is, in the absence of grounds for **10–047**

[209] The section attributes to the director the knowledge, skill and experience of *both* the reasonable person and the particular director in question, so the latter is important only when it *adds* to the attributes of the reasonable person.

[210] One potentially significant omission from s.174 of the CA 2006 in comparison with the IA 1986 is that s.214(5) of the latter explicitly extends the meaning of "carried on" to include functions entrusted to the director as well as those actually carried out, if that should be thought necessary.

[211] Note how in the Australian case of *Daniels v Anderson* (1995) 16 A.C.S.R. 607 the Court of Appeal of NSW, applying an objective test, found that the non-executive directors were not liable for the failure to discover the foreign exchange frauds being committed by an employee, but the chief executive officer was so held.

[212] *Daniels v Anderson* (1995) 16 A.C.S.R. 607 at 664. The language of monitoring fits in well with the views of the Cadbury and Greenbury Committees and their successors on the proper role for the board of directors.

suspicion, justified in trusting to that official to perform such duties honestly".[213] In the more recent cases of *Daniels v Anderson* and *Norman v Theodore Goddard*,[214] where objective tests were applied, at least some of the directors escaped liability as a result of the application of this proposition. However, insofar as this dictum suggests that, once an appropriate delegate has been chosen and the task delegated to that person, the director is under no further duties, it cannot stand with recent developments in the law, as the next point indicates.

Fourthly, an objective standard of care is not inconsistent with extensive delegation nor, however, does it permit the directors to escape from the second requirement of always being in a position to "guide and monitor" the management. These two things are to be reconciled by the directors ensuring that there are in place adequate internal control systems which will throw up problems in the delegated areas whilst there is still time to do something about them. As it has been put, the freedom to delegate "does not absolve a director from the duty to supervise the discharge of the delegated functions".[215] The need for adequate internal control systems was stressed by the Report of the Turnbull Committee,[216] one of the lesser known of the reports which contributed to the Combined Code, and its successor the UK Corporate Governance Code, but arguably the most important for what it has to say about directors' responsibility for sub-board structures of control. Although neither the Turnbull Report nor the UK Corporate Governance Code are legislative instruments binding the courts, it is likely that, in appropriate cases, the courts' view of what an objective standard of care requires will be influenced by these provisions. Indeed, that process is already evident in the area of disqualification of directors on grounds of unfitness. Thus, in *Re Barings Plc (No.5)*[217] directors were disqualified for failing to have such internal controls in place in relation to trading activities in an overseas subsidiary, whose losses eventually caused the demise of the bank.

Fifthly, the principles relating to delegation to sub-board managers apply also to the division of functions among the directors themselves. Inevitably, executive directors will carry a greater load of management responsibility than non-executive directors and, even within the executive directors, there will be specialisation (for example, the chief financial officer will carry particular responsibility in that area). However, all directors "have a continuing duty to

[213] *Re City Equitable Fire Insurance Co* [1925] Ch. 407 at 429. See also *Dovey v Cory* [1901] A.C. 477. But the matter must not be delegated to an obviously inappropriate employee or official, as was the case in *City Equitable* itself.

[214] *Daniels v Anderson* (1995) 16 A.C.S.R. 607; *Norman v Theodore Goddard* [1991] B.C.L.C. 1027.

[215] *Re Barings Plc (No.5)* [2000] 1 B.C.L.C. 433 at 489 (per Jonathan Parker J), approved by the CA at 536. See also *Equitable Life Assurance Society v Bowley* [2004] 1 B.C.L.C. 180 at 188–189; *Brumder v Motornet Service and Repairs Ltd* [2013] 1 W.L.R. 2783 at [55] (Beatson LJ).

[216] Institute of Chartered Accountants in England and Wales, *Internal Control: Guidance for Directors on the Combined Code* (1999). The Report fleshes out the bare principles now contained in the UK Corporate Governance Code (Principles M, N and O and Provisions 24–31) that boards should maintain sound systems of risk management and internal control, should review them annually, and should report to the shareholders that they have done so. See too the Financial Reporting Council's revised *Guidance on Risk Management, Internal Control and Related Financial and Business Reporting* available at: *https://www.frc.org.uk/Our-Work/Publications/Corporate-Governance/Guidance-on-Risk-Management,-Internal-Control-and.pdf* [Accessed 17 December 2020].

[217] *Re Barings Plc (No.5)* [2000] 1 B.C.L.C. 523 CA. See para.20–010.

acquire and maintain a sufficient knowledge and understanding of the company's business to enable them properly to discharge their duties as directors" and certainly no board may permit itself to be dominated by one of their number.[218]

Further, however, it follows from the inevitable acceptance of extensive delegation, at least in large companies, that directors cannot be guarantors that everything is going well within the company. Subordinate employees may be fraudulent or negligent and the directors may not discover this in time, but this does not necessarily mean that the directors have been negligent. That conclusion will depend on the facts of the situation, including the quality of the internal controls.[219]

In addition, note the very different conclusions if the directors are validly *instructed* by the shareholders to act in a particular way. If the directors then act in the manner instructed, they will not be liable to the company in negligence if the decision turns out to have been unwise.[220]

Sixthly, although nearly all decided English cases have arisen out of alleged failures by directors to act or to act effectively, negligence suits can equally arise where the directors have indeed acted, but their actions have delivered disastrous consequences for their company. Here too, however, since companies are in business to take risks, the fact that a business venture does not pay off and even leads the company into financial trouble does not necessarily indicate negligence, though it may encourage the shareholders to replace the directors. In the US, where an objective standard for directors' competence is well-established, the "business judgment" rule generally operates to relieve the directors of liability in such cases (i.e. cases where the directors have acted, not those where they have failed to act). The business judgment rule involves the specification of a set of procedural steps, which, if followed, will give the directors the benefit of a presumption that they were not negligent. The Law Commissions thought such a rule unnecessary in the UK[221]; and there is certainly a risk with the business judgment rule that the courts will come to regard cases where the procedural **10–048**

[218] *Re Barings Plc (No.5)* [2000] 1 B.C.L.C. 523 CA; *Re Westmid Packaging Services Ltd* [1998] 2 B.C.L.C. 646 at 653; *Weavering Capital (UK) Ltd (In Liquidation) v Peterson* [2012] EWHC 1480 (Ch) at [173]–[174] (Proudman J); affirmed in [2013] EWCA Civ 71; *Raithatha v Baig* [2017] EWHC 2059 (Ch) at [35]–[37]. In *Madoff Securities International Ltd v Raven* [2013] EWHC 3147 (Comm), the court held that some directors were entitled to rely, and therefore had not failed to exercise reasonable care and skill by relying, on the expertise and experience of other members on the board. On the other hand, the failure of the directors with the appropriate experience to apply their minds to the question as to whether the transactions were in the interests of the company constituted a breach of the duty to exercise reasonable skill and care (Popplewell J).

[219] See, e.g. *Lexi Holdings Plc v Luqman* [2009] EWCA Civ 117; [2009] 2 B.C.L.C. 1: the managing director of a company was found liable for stealing £59.6 million which had been lent by banks to the company. Overturning the trial judge, the Court of Appeal also held his two sisters jointly liable (with their brother) for the stolen money on the basis that the state of the company's accounts should have aroused their suspicions, given their knowledge of their brother's earlier imprisonment for deception, and they should have acted accordingly; their inactivity was a breach of duty.

[220] *Ciban Management Corp v Citco (BVI) Ltd* [2020] UKPC 21 (see para.8–021); *Multinational Gas & Petrochemical Co v Multinational Gas & Petrochemical Services Ltd* [1983] Ch. 258 CA (Civ Div).

[221] Law Commission and Scottish Law Commission, *Company Directors: Regulating Conflicts of Interest and Formulating a Statement of Duties* (1999), Cm.4436, Pt 5.

standards have not been met as presumptively negligent.[222] The Commissions thought that one could expect the courts to be alive to the probability that they are better at dealing with conflicts of interest than with the assessment of business risks and to the desirability of avoiding the luxury of substituting the courts' hindsight for the directors' foresight.[223]

10–049 Finally, as with auditors,[224] showing breach of a duty of care is one thing; showing that the loss suffered by the company was a consequence of the breach of duty may be quite another. Thus, the true explanation of the finding of no liability in *Re Denham & Co*[225] is only in part that the director was entitled to rely on others. Equally important was the judge's view that, even if the director had made the inquiries he should have made, he would probably not have discovered the fraud.

Overall, it can be said that both the developments at common law and in the Act have brought the standard of care, skill and diligence required of directors into line with that required generally in other areas of social and business life by the law of negligence. However, an inevitable result of the move from a subjective to an objective test will be to give the courts a greater role in defining the functions of the board, no matter how sensitive the courts are to the need to avoid the use of hindsight. For example, the courts' decisions on the rigour with which the board has to supervise the discharge of delegated tasks will help to define the monitoring role of the board, whilst decisions about whether the audit committee of the board has sufficiently scrutinised the tasks carried out by the external auditors will help to define the relationships between audit committee, auditors and management. Thirty years ago one might have predicted that the courts would either be ineffectual in the discharge of these responsibilities (through a desire to avoid reliance on hindsight) or produce undesirable interventions. However, today, as a result of developments associated with the emergence of the UK Corporate Governance Code, discussed in Ch.9, there is a body of best practice available, at least for large companies, on which the courts can draw, although they will not be bound by it. A striking example of the creative use of such material is to be found in the judgment of Austin J in *ASIC v Rich*,[226] where the Australian court had recourse to a wide range of "best practice" material, including corporate governance reports from the UK, in holding that the duties of the chair of the board of a listed company extended beyond responsibility for simply chairing meetings of the board.

---

[222] cf. *Smith v Van Gorkam* (1985) 488 A. 2d 858.

[223] For a critique see C.A. Riley, "The Company Director's Duty of Care and Skill: the Case for an Onerous but Subjective Standard" (1999) 62 M.L.R. 697.

[224] See paras 23–038 to 23–042.

[225] *Re Denham & Co* (1883) 25 Ch. D. 752 Ch D. See also *Cohen v Selby* [2001] B.C.L.C. 176, stressing the need at common law to show that the negligence caused the loss suffered by the company. The classic statement of the problem is that by Learned Hand J in *Barnes v Andrews* (1924) 298 F. 614 at 616–617.

[226] *ASIC v Rich* [2003] NSWSC 85. The judge referred in particular to Annex D of Mr Derek Higg's review of the role of non-executive directors: above, para.9–017.

Remedies

The standard remedy for breach of a director's duty of care is compensation for the harm caused to the company by the director's negligence. Section 178(2), specifying the remedies for breach of the general duties, may suggest that the remedy for this breach of duty (s.174) will be assessed on common law, not equitable, principles, thus laying to rest the debates in that area.[227] In any event, the better view, it is suggested, is that the remedy is not assessed differently merely because the director is a fiduciary. As Millett LJ said in *Bristol and West Building Society v Mothew*,[228] "it is inappropriate to apply the expression [breach of fiduciary duty] to the obligation of a trustee or other fiduciary to use proper skill and care in the discharge of his duties". Nor does it matter that the duty of care to which the director is subject was developed, historically, by the courts of equity before the common law developed its own more widely applicable version. This history led to the use of different terminology ("compensation" in equity; "damages" at common law), and different appropriately contextual explanations of issues of standards of care, rules on causation, remoteness and measure of damages. But even in equity the breach gave access only to compensatory remedies, and the modern tendency has been to assimilate the requirements for liability for breach of the duty of care in equity and at common law.[229] 10–050

Overview of the No-Conflict Rules: ss.175–177

As fiduciaries, directors must not place themselves in a position in which there is a conflict between their duties to the company and their personal interests or duties to others.[230] This fundamental common law principle was perhaps most famously stated by Lord Herschell in *Bray v Ford*[231]: 10–051

[227] See *Henderson v Merrett Syndicates Ltd* [1995] 2 A.C. 145; *Bristol & West Building Society v Mothew* [1998] Ch. 1 CA.

[228] *Bristol and West Building Society v Mothew* [1998] Ch. 1. The case provides a good example of the difference between a compensatory and a restitutionary remedy. A building society had advanced money to a purchaser after receiving negligent information from its solicitor. The purchaser defaulted, and the building society sued the solicitor. A restitutionary claim would have required the solicitor to put the building society back in the position in was in before it made the loan (i.e. to meet the whole of the society's loss), whereas the compensatory claim required him only to compensate the society for the loss caused to it by his negligence. This might have been nil if the solicitor's negligence had not affected the building society's assessment of the ability of the purchaser to keep up the repayments on the loan.

[229] In the *Mothew* case (see previous footnote) Millett LJ referred to the distinction between equitable compensation and common law damages for breach of the duty of care as "a distinction without a difference". But also see para.10–106 for the current terminology.

[230] Overwhelmingly, the conflict is between the director's personal interest and his duty to the company of which he is director, but where the same person is director of two competing companies, he or she may then be subject to competing duties. See *Clark Boyce v Mouat* [1994] 1 A.C. 428 PC; *Bristol and West Building Society v Mothew* [1998] Ch. 1; *Transvaal Lands Co v New Belgium (Transvaal) Land and Development Co* [1914] 2 Ch. 488 CA.

[231] *Bray v Ford* [1896] A.C. 44 HL at 51–52.

> "It is an inflexible rule of a court of equity that a person in a fiduciary position is not, unless otherwise expressly provided,[[232]] entitled to make a profit; he is not allowed to put himself in a position where his interest and duty conflict. It does not appear to me that this rule is founded upon principles of morality. I regard it rather as based on the consideration that, human nature being what it is, there is a danger, in such circumstances, of the person holding a fiduciary position being swayed by interest rather than by duty, and thus prejudicing those he was bound to protect. It has, therefore, been deemed expedient to law down this positive rule."

It can be argued that this common law "no conflict" principle (often separated, as here, into no-conflict and no-profit rules) underlies all three of the remaining general duties of directors set out in the CA 2006: the self-dealing transaction rules discussed immediately below (ss.175(3) and 177, and Pt 10, Chs 3, 4 and 4A, the latter provisions all dealing with specific and invariably substantial types of property transactions with directors); the principle that a director must not make personal use of the company's property, information or opportunities (s.175(1) and (2)); and, finally, the requirement that directors must not receive benefits from third parties in exchange for the exercise of directorial powers (s.176). In the first case (self-dealing), the conflict arises because the director is, in a very practical sense, on both sides of a transaction with the company, and so motivated perhaps by self-interest rather than by duty.[233] In the case of directorial exploitation of corporate property or opportunity, by contrast, the director uses, for his or her own ends, the company's property or opportunities, to the exclusion of the company. Finally, in the case of what the common law calls, generically, "bribes", the risk is that the director exercises his or her powers in the interests of the third party rather than the company because of the personal benefit conferred on the director by that third party.

10–052 Although, at a broad level, it is undoubtedly true that the purpose of all three duties is to discourage directors from putting their personal interests ahead of their duties to the company, it is also true that the more specific rules under each duty have now developed sufficiently separately, especially, as we shall see, in terms of the action required of the director to comply with the duty, that it is sensible to consider them separately, as the CA 2006 does.[234]

These various "no conflict" rules are probably the most important of the directors' various duties of good faith and loyalty. As we have seen, the core good faith rule is overwhelmingly subjective and so difficult to enforce, whilst, given the width of the powers conferred upon directors by the articles, the requirement that they stay within their powers under the constitution, and use those powers for proper purposes, tends to have only a marginally constraining impact upon directors' activities.

---

[232] The rules on who needs to provide such consent differ as between the different statutory categories of conflicts, as discussed below.

[233] Or the danger of "being swayed by interest rather than driven by duty": *Breitenfeld UK Ltd v Harrison* [2015] EWHC 399 (Ch) at [68] (Norris J).

[234] On the importance of distinguishing between self-dealing transactions and personal exploitation of corporate opportunities see *Bell v Lever* [1932] A.C. 161 per Lord Blanesburgh; *Sinclair Investments (UK) Ltd v Versailles Trade Finance Ltd* [2011] EWCA Civ 347 (which has however, on the issue of proprietary remedies, been overruled by the Supreme Court in the next case); *FHR European Ventures LLP v Cedar Capital Partners LLC* [2014] UKSC 45; [2015] A.C. 250.

TRANSACTIONS WITH THE COMPANY (SELF-DEALING): SS.175(3) AND 177

The scope of the relevant provisions

The structure of the CA 2006 is a little more complex than the above might suggest. Section 175 is the apparently general section dealing with, as the side-note says, "the duty to avoid conflicts of interest". However, self-dealing transactions are excluded from s.175 by s.175(3): "this duty does not apply to a conflict of interest arising in relation to a transaction or arrangement with the company", an exclusion which is wider than might appear at first sight.[235] In these circumstances a number of other provisions are instead brought into play. 10–053

If we were to summarise their general effect, the general strategy adopted by the CA 2006 in managing these problematic self-dealing transactions is to put in place a fairly lenient default rule, requiring only that the self-interest of the self-dealing director be disclosed to the board in advance of the transaction being agreed to by the company (regardless of whether that agreement is then by the board or by some delegated manager). But then the Act goes on to identify particular specific categories of self-dealing transactions as being especially vulnerable to inadequate oversight by the board (either simply because of their size, or because of their commonality amongst the directors which might then risk mutual back-scratching[236]), and with these the Act requires not only disclosure to the board but also approval by the general meeting. Perhaps predictably, the protective regime is even stricter with listed companies, with particular ex ante approval rules for related party transactions, and strict ex post disclosure rules demanded by modern accounting standards. All of these various rules are examined in this section, but their significance is far more easily understood if we start with the common law rules from which these variations are derived.

As far as self-dealing transactions are concerned, by the middle of the nineteenth century it had been clearly established that the trustee-like position of directors was liable to vitiate any contract which the board entered into on behalf of the company with one of their number. This principle received its clearest expression in *Aberdeen Railway Co v Blaikie Bros*,[237] in which a contract between the company and a partnership of which one of the directors was a

---

[235] This exclusion is typically thought to refer only to arrangements between the company and the director himself or his nominee/alter ego. But see *Burns v Financial Conduct Authority* [2017] EWCA Civ 2140 at [76], noting that the exclusion was broad enough to cover a conflict of duty and interest arising when the company was contemplating an arrangement with V and the company's director was actively soliciting a remunerative relationship with V for her own personal benefit. The transaction in issue was one with the company (i.e. it fell within s.175(3), and involved a conflict for the director because "she owed an undivided duty of loyalty to [the company] to consider [V's] possible future business relationship with [the company] dispassionately and with her mind unclouded by any potential conflict of interest" such as raised by her own future prospects with V.

[236] Loans to directors and directors' service contracts are the obvious examples.

[237] *Aberdeen Railway Co v Blaikie Bros* (1854) 1 Macq. H.L. 461 HL.

partner was avoided at the instance of the company, notwithstanding that its terms were perfectly fair. Lord Cranworth LC said on that occasion[238]:

> "A corporate body can only act by agents, and it is, of course, the duty of those agents so to act as best to promote the interests of the corporation whose affairs they are conducting. Such agents have duties to discharge of a fiduciary nature towards their principal. And it is a rule of universal application that no one, having such duties to discharge, shall be allowed to enter into engagements in which he has, or can have, a personal interest conflicting, or which possibly may conflict, with the interests of those whom he is bound to protect….So strictly is this principle adhered to that no question is allowed to be raised as to the fairness or unfairness of a contract so entered into."

It is important to note that, provided there is a conflict of interest which is not just fanciful, a director is in breach of this duty whether or not the conflict had an effect upon the terms negotiated between the parties to the transaction and whether or not the terms of the transaction could be regarded as fair in any event. It is therefore a strict liability rule. Strict though this rule is from the director's point of view, it makes the task of the courts somewhat easier. In the British jurisdiction, the courts do not scrutinise self-dealing transactions, as they do in some jurisdictions, to see if they are fair. If there is a conflict of the type covered by the self-dealing rules, there is a breach of duty on the part of the director.

Approval mechanisms

10–054 However, the lesson likely to be drawn from Lord Cranworth's statement that directors should not contract with their company was not necessarily correct or wise, even from the company's point of view. The director may in fact be the best source of a particular asset which the company wishes to acquire, and so an outright ban on self-dealing would cut against the company's interests. An obvious example is a contract between a director and the company for the provision of the full-time services of the director to the company.[239] The crucial issue underlying the rule thus became, even at common law, the identification of the procedure which the director needed to observe in order to rid him- or herself of the taint of conflicted contracting. At common law the rule was that disclosure of the conflict in advance to, and approval of the contract by, the shareholders was the appropriate procedure whereby an interested director could enter into a contract with the company. This was because the shareholders, acting as the company and thus as the beneficiaries of the directors' duty, could waive compliance with it, if they wished.

This search for the appropriate internal decision-maker to approve the self-dealing transaction is shared with the other no-conflict rules, as we shall see. Moreover, this approach had a further consequence. If the shareholders did approve the transaction, it would then be virtually impossible for the company later (via a new board, or a liquidator) to challenge it in court. In other words, shareholder approval (or "whitewash" as it is sometimes called) was a robust technique for protecting the director. Shareholder approval did not, for example,

---

[238] *Aberdeen Railway Co v Blaikie Bros* (1854) 1 Macq. H.L. 461 at 471–472.

[239] See below at paras 10–078 and 11–013.

simply create a presumption of fairness which a court might overturn, as it does in some other systems. The robustness of the "whitewash" provisions is again a feature of the other no-conflict rules, as we shall see, although it is not without some limits.

Nevertheless, directors found shareholder approval an inconvenient rule and one which they regarded as in many cases tantamount to a prohibition on contracting with the company. Just as the normal restraints on trustees can be modified by express provisions in the will or deed under which they were appointed,[240] so (at common law) can the normal fiduciary duties of directors be modified by express provision in the company's articles, which of course bind all the members of the company. Directors therefore sought through provisions in the articles to substitute the more congenial requirement of mere disclosure, rather than disclosure and approval; and disclosure to the board rather than to the shareholders in general meeting. Such provisions became common-form in the articles of registered companies. Indeed, in some cases the articles gave directors permission to engage in self-dealing transactions without any form of disclosure. This practice caused the legislature to step in and require (in a provision which was introduced in 1929 and became s.317 of the CA 1985) that directors disclose conflicts to the board, irrespective of any provisions in the articles. Thus, the board would be aware of the conflict and could decide what to do about it.

Section 177 of the CA 2006 adopts this approach and imposes a rule of disclosure to the board. Thus, the modern rule on self-dealing has become, in principle, and subject to some crucial exceptions,[241] simply a requirement of disclosure to the board. There is no duty to *avoid* such dealings (hence s.175(3)). And approval by others, whether shareholders or fellow directors, is not formally required, although presumably it could be imposed by the articles.[242] **10–055**

Notice, further, that the CA 2006 deals in separate places with disclosure of interests in proposed transactions (s.177, Ch.2 of Pt 10) and disclosure in relation to existing transactions (s.182, Ch.3 of Pt 10). The former is one of the general duties imposed on directors; the latter is not. Beyond doctrinal elegance, however, the division is important in relation to the sanctions for breach of the two disclosure duties, for the categories of directors who are bound by the two duties, and to some extent for the methods of disclosure. Whether there is any merit, in remedies, in this split is questionable.

In what follows, we shall look at each of these two rules in turn, and then at the crucial exceptions noted earlier where the tougher requirement of shareholder approval is made compulsory.

---

240 The most common example is a "charging clause" enabling professional trustees and their firms to charge fees for acting as trustees or executors.

241 See paras 10–066 to 10–079.

242 See para.10–062.

Duty to declare interests in relation to proposed transactions or arrangements: s.177

10–056 A director who is "in any way, directly or indirectly" interested in a proposed transaction or arrangement with the company must declare to the other directors the "nature and extent" of that interest and do so before the company enters into the transaction or arrangement (s.177(1)).[243] If the declaration, once made, becomes or proves to be inaccurate or incomplete, a further declaration must be made (s.177(3)).

Purpose of the disclosure requirement

10–057 The aim of s.177 is to put the other directors on notice of the conflict of interest, so that they may take the necessary steps to safeguard the company's position. What steps the other directors should take, once put on notice, is not dealt with in the section nor, indeed, in precise terms elsewhere in the CA 2006. No doubt, they will be in breach of their duties of care and, perhaps, good faith if they take no or inadequate steps, but such a conclusion would require analysis of the other directors' actions (or inaction) under the principles discussed above. It is not difficult to envisage a board culture in which the steps taken on the basis of the declaration are minimal, especially if all the directors from time to time make such disclosures and trust that their disclosure will be readily accepted if they readily accept disclosures by others.

It is also to be noted that the CA 2006 leaves to the company's articles the task of deciding whether, if the proposed transaction is to be entered into by the board, the interested director is entitled to vote or count towards he quorum at the meeting at which the decision is taken.[244]

Who is subject to this duty?

10–058 Since s.177, dealing with proposed transactions, is one of the general duties of directors, it applies also to shadow directors, although only "where and to the extent that [it is] capable of so applying": s.170(5).[245] By contrast, s.182, in relation to disclosure of interests in existing transactions, applies explicitly to shadow directors: s.187(1). There would seem to be no argument that s.177 is "incapable" of applying to shadow directors, all the more so in the light of the absolute rule in s.187. And the practical arguments for requiring disclosure of interests in relation to proposed transactions are even stronger than those relating

243 For the potential breadth of this provision, see *Burns v Financial Conduct Authority* [2017] EWCA Civ 2140 at [76], noted at fn.235.

244 The model articles for both public and private companies (arts 14 and 16 respectively) exclude the director from both, but subject to important exceptions where the director can both be counted and vote.

245 See paras 10–010 to 10–011.

to existing transactions, since in relation to the former the company has the luxury of being legally free to withdraw from negotiations if the terms seem unfavourable.[246]

The interests to be disclosed

The director must disclose interests in a "transaction or arrangement". This clearly includes contracts, which will be the paradigm example of a transaction or arrangement, but it also embraces non-contractual arrangements,[247] and it matters not whether the transaction or arrangement is entered into by the company through its board or through a subordinate manager.[248] **10–059**

Both direct and indirect interests must be disclosed. The extension of the section to "indirect" interests means that the director need not himself be the other party to the transaction. It is enough, for example, that he is a shareholder in the company which is the other party, or is a member of a contracting partnership. This is not a novel development: the common law had recognised indirect conflicts of interest during the nineteenth century.[249]

The director must disclose not only the nature but also the extent of the relevant interest.[250] It is obviously more informative to be told not simply that X is a shareholder in the contracting party but also whether X is a 1% shareholder or holds a controlling interest.

The section includes a number of restrictive clarifications of the scope of the disclosure principle. The words of Lord Cranworth, quoted above, that the common law embraced personal interests "which possibly may conflict" with the director's duty were thought to be too broad, and in consequence s.177(6)(a) provides that a director does not have to declare an interest "if it cannot

---

246 The argument that disclosure to the board is pointless in the case of a shadow director, because the board by definition does what the shadow director wants, needs to be qualified because (1) the definition of a shadow director requires only that the board be accustomed to do what the shadow director wants, not that it does it on every occasion (see s.251); and (2) because, if the argument is correct, it is not clear why shadow directors are required to disclose interests in relation to existing transactions.

247 cf. *Re Duckwari (No.2)* [1998] 2 B.C.L.C. 315 CA (Civ Div) at 319, interpreting the word "arrangement" in what is now s.190. The predecessor to s.177 was s.317 of the CA 1985, which made this point clear (see s.317(5)—"whether or not constituting a contract"). However, it is not thought that the omission of the words "whether or not constituting a contract" from s.177 indicates an intention to confine the section to contractual transactions or arrangements. See also *Financial Conduct Authority v Capital Alternatives Ltd* [2014] EWHC 144 (Ch) at [51].

248 The arguments in favour of this view, given in the fifth edition of this book at p.577, in relation to CA 1985 s.317 seem equally applicable to s.177. Those arguments were approved by the judge in *Neptune (Vehicle Washing Equipment) Ltd v Fitzgerald* [1996] Ch. 274 Ch D, whose decision was treated as authoritative by the Law Commissions (see fn.1), para.8.38 and was approved on consultation.

249 See, for example, *Aberdeen Railway Co v Blaikie Bros* (1854) 1 Macq. H.L. 461 HL; *Transvaal Lands Co v New Belgian Land Co* [1914] 2 Ch. 485 CA; *Newgate Stud Co v Penfold* [2004] EWHC 2993 (Ch); [2008] 1 B.C.L.C. 46, suggesting the common law rule catches transactions between the company and any person whose relationship with the director is such as to create "a real risk of conflict between duty and personal loyalties".

250 The courts when interpreting provisions in companies' articles have long required disclosure of the extent as well as the nature of interests. See, for example, *Imperial Mercantile Credit Association v Coleman* (1873) L.R. 6 H.L. 189 HL.

reasonably be regarded as likely to give rise to a conflict of interest".[251] This probably does no more than re-state the common law.[252]

Section 177(5) does not require the director to disclose an interest in relation to a transaction unless he or she is aware *or* ought reasonably to be aware of both the interest and the transaction. A director might be excusably unaware of an interest he or she has in a third party who is contracting with the company (for example, where the managers of a unit trust in which the director holds units have recently bought a large stake in the third party) or in the transaction (for example, where it is to be entered into at sub-board level).

Nor need the director disclose interests of which the other directors are or ought reasonably to be aware, on the grounds that such disclosure is or ought to be unnecessary (s.177(6)(b)).

Also excluded is the need for a director to disclose an interest in the terms of his service contract that is being or has been considered by a meeting of the directors or the appropriate committee of the board (s.177(6)(c)). It might be thought that this last exception is covered by the previous one, and in most cases this will be so. However, where the service contract is to be decided on by a committee of the board, for example, its remuneration committee, it is conceivable that directors who are not on that committee will not be aware of the transaction and the director's interest.

Methods of disclosure

10–060 Assuming the duty to disclose does bite, s.177(2) lays down three non-exhaustive methods of making the disclosure.[253] These are (1) at a meeting of the directors; (2) by written notice to the directors (as per s.184); or (3) by a general notice (as per s.185).

The first two options provide methods of giving notice in relation to an identified transaction. Notice given outside a meeting must be sent to each director and the notice is deemed to be part of the proceedings of the next directors' meeting and so must be included in the minutes of that meeting.[254] A general notice, by contrast, is given in the absence of any specific identified transaction, and is notice by which the director declares that he is to be regarded as interested in any transaction or arrangement which is subsequently entered into by the company with a specified company, firm or individual because of the director's interest in or connection with that other person.[255] As usual, the nature and extent of the interest has to be declared. Unlike a specific notice, however, a

[251] A similar provision is to be found in s.175(4)(a) in relation to the statutory duty to avoid conflicts of interest.

[252] cf. *Boardman v Phipps* [1967] 2 A.C. 46 at 124, per Lord Upjohn: "In my view [the phrase] means that the reasonable man looking at the relevant facts and circumstances of the particular case would think that there was real sensible possibility of conflict".

[253] cf. s.177(2) ("may (but need not)"). It thus appears that an oral declaration of interest to other directors outside a directors' meeting, for example, is permissible in respect of proposed transactions.

[254] CA 2006 ss.184 and 248.

[255] CA 2006 s.185. It should not be necessary to say so, but note that it is insufficient to give general notice pursuant to ss.177(2)(b) and 185 where the transaction in question is not one which is entered into with the company (and therefore falls outside the remit of s.175(3)): *Re Coroin Ltd* [2012] EWHC 2343 (Ch) at [582]–[583] (David Richards J).

general notice must either be given at a meeting of the directors or, if given outside a meeting, the director must take reasonable steps to ensure that it is brought up and read out at the next meeting after it is given.[256] Thus, in relation to a general notice, the board must positively be given the opportunity to discuss the notice, though there is no obligation on the board actually to do so. The giver of a general notice is not exempted from the requirement to provide a further declaration if the first notice becomes inaccurate, as it might if the nature or extent of the director's interest in the third party altered, for example, if the director's shareholding in the third party increased significantly. Thus, even a general notice cannot simply be given once and forgotten.

Remedies

Breach of s.177 (failure to declare interest in proposed transactions) is subject to civil sanctions, not criminal ones, but those sanctions are defined only generally. They are "the same as would apply if the corresponding common law rule or equitable principle applied".[257] **10–061**

Those civil sanctions seem to be as follows. Where the self-dealing director acts in breach of the statutory disclosure rule, but subject to what is said next on special provisions in the company's articles, the transaction is voidable at the option of (i.e. not binding on, at the election of) the company, unless third party rights have intervened. On orthodox principles, avoidance (i.e. rescission) is the *only* remedy,[258] unless the director has also infringed some other rule that will deliver an alternative remedy.[259] And if rescission is no longer possible for any reason, then the court will decline to intervene. This may seem odd, especially since self-dealing transactions are illustrations of the "no conflicts" duty, for which directors are typically required to disgorge the profits they have made. But the courts in these self-dealing cases say that the director's profit is "unquantifiable", since that would involve the courts fixing a new contract price for the parties. Given all the other situations in which courts are content to make commercial assessments of value, this seems unduly reticent.

---

256 CA 2006 s.185(4).

257 CA 2006 s.178.

258 This is especially evident in older cases dealing with promoters: *Erlanger v New Sombrero Phosphate Co* (1878) 3 App. Cas. 1218 HL; *Re Cape Breton Co* (1887) 12 App. Cas. 652 HL. But note there are some cases (outside the corporate area) allowing "pecuniary rescission": see *Mahoney v Purnell* [1996] 3 All E.R. 61 QBD (an undue influence case, not self-dealing).

259 And this may well be possible: for example, a misuse of the company's property (and a self-dealing transaction may fall into that category) may involve a conflict of duty and interest (for which rescission is potentially available); *and* a breach of the duty to act bona fide and for proper purposes (for which equitable compensation is recoverable, even if the director has not made a profit from the misuse (*Gwembe Valley Development Co Ltd v Koshy (No.3)* [2003] EWCA Civ 1478; [2004] 1 B.C.L.C. 131)); *and* perhaps also negligence (in that the advice to the company in favour of the self-interested deal may have been poor and caused loss, for which common law damages are available). See *Costa Rica Railway Co Ltd v Forward* [1901] 1 Ch. 746 CA; *Imperial Mercantile Credit Association v Coleman* (1873) L.R. 6 H. L.189; *JJ Harrison (Properties) Ltd v Harrison* [2001] 1 B.C.L.C. 158 Ch D; and [2002] 1 B.C.L.C. 183 CA; *Madoff Securities International Ltd v Raven* [2013] EWHC 3147 (Comm); *Airbus Operations Ltd v Withey* [2014] EWHC 1126 (QB).

A continuing role for the articles in setting tighter constraints

10–062 We know from s.170(3) that the duties laid out in Ch.2 of Pt 10 "have effect in place" of the common law rules and equitable principles on which they are based. Consequently, in a self-dealing transaction, a director must comply with the provisions of s.177 and disclose his or her interests to the board. If the director does this, then s.180(1) provides that "the transaction or arrangement is not liable to be set aside by virtue of any common law rule or equitable principle requiring the consent or approval of the members of the company". Thus, in the standard case, compliance with s.177 disclosure rules will mean that the director is not in breach of the relevant duty of loyalty, and that the transaction is therefore binding on the company.

However, s.180(1) specifically operates without prejudice to any "provision of the company's constitution requiring such consent or approval". Thus, the company's articles may reinstate the common law principle of shareholder approval and, where this is done, a transaction entered into without such approval will not be binding on the company, subject to the protections for third parties contained in s.40 (to the limited extent that these rules may be relevant in a self-dealing transaction).[260] As we have seen already, the impact of restrictions in the articles upon the validity of the transaction will vary according to whether the restriction requires a particular organ or group within the company to take the decision on the self-dealing transaction with the director, or merely to approve it. Breach in the first case renders the transaction void; in the second, voidable only.[261] These provisions cannot, however, oust the disclosure requirements in s.177.

In short, the shareholders remain masters of the rules on self-dealing transactions but now the onus is on those who want to move away from board disclosure and require shareholder approval or some other additional control, whereas under the prior law the burden of action lay on those who wished to introduce into the articles provisions modifying the common law requirement of shareholder approval.

Duty to declare interests in relation to existing transactions or arrangements: s.182

10–063 Section 182 requires the compulsory disclosure to the board of existing self-dealing transactions, unless the interest has already been declared in relation to a proposed transaction.[262] This section catches situations such as the interests of a newly appointed director in the company's existing transactions or interests

[260] See paras 8–009 onwards.

[261] See *Guinness Plc v Saunders* [1990] 2 A.C. 663 HL, where the wrong body under the company's articles (a committee of the board rather than the full board) acted to pay a bonus to the director so that the decision to pay the bonus was void, the committee being without power to act, and the money was therefore repayable by the director; cf. *Hely-Hutchinson v Brayhead Ltd* [1968] 1 Q.B. 549, where the correct body acted, but the director was in breach of his fiduciary obligations unless the right consents and approvals were given: here the decision was voidable but not void.

[262] CA 2006 s.182(1).

in existing contracts which an established director has just acquired, for example, because he or she has become a shareholder in one of the company's suppliers.

But why should a board wish to know about the interests of its directors in concluded transactions? What practical use can it make of the information? An example might be where the company has a power under an existing contract (for example, to terminate it unilaterally) to which knowledge of the director's interest is relevant.

Methods of disclosure

The details on what must be disclosed, and how, are broadly those applicable to proposed transactions (discussed immediately above), with the following amendments and exceptions. First, the disclosure must be made "as soon as is reasonably practicable".[263] Secondly, the statutory methods of giving notice discussed earlier in the non-mandatory context of s.177 are the only ones permitted in relation to existing transactions.[264] It presumably follows that a failure to make a declaration in the prescribed manner will render the declaration either a nullity or incomplete, and a further declaration will be required (s.182(3)).[265] Thirdly, a sole director is required to make a declaration only where the company is required to have more than one director but that is not the case at the time of the disclosure. That declaration must be recorded in writing and is deemed to be part of the proceedings at the next meeting of the directors after it is given.[266] Fourthly, the obligation applies explicitly to shadow directors.[267] However, not surprisingly, the method of giving notice at a meeting of the directors is not available to a shadow director nor is a general notice required to be given or brought up at a meeting of directors. Instead, a general or specific notice is to be given in the case of a shadow director by notice in writing to the directors, though that will then cause the notice to be treated as part of the proceedings of the next directors' meeting and minuted accordingly.[268] **10–064**

Remedies

Finally, only a criminal sanction (a fine) is provided in respect of breaches of this statutory duty to disclose.[269] This duty, being found in Ch.3, is not one of the general duties in Ch.2, and so the various common law remedies imported by **10–065**

[263] CA 2006 s.182(4). The formulation in s.177(4)—before the company enters into the transaction—is clearly not available.

[264] CA 2006 s.182(2).

[265] How this requirement will be reconciled with s.182(6)(b), indicating that the duty does not apply if the other directors are already aware of the interest, or ought to be aware of the interest, is unclear.

[266] CA 2006 s.186. In the case of a proposed transaction the declaration has no point (if a further director is appointed before the transaction is completed, the s.177 obligation will arise at that point) but an interest in an existing transaction will be of continuing relevance and the declaration will be available to the new director immediately when appointed. Indeed, in most cases the sole director will have to make disclosure as soon as the proposed transaction is completed.

[267] CA 2006.187(1).

[268] CA 2006 s.187(2)–(4).

[269] CA 2006 s.183. The disputes in relation to the remedies for breach of the predecessor provision, CA 1985 s.317 (see ninth edition of this book, p.568), have been laid to rest in the current Act.

virtue of s.178 do not also apply here to breaches of s.182. Nevertheless, these demands of compulsory disclosure certainly contribute, like the general duties, to aiding better corporate governance.

TRANSACTIONS BETWEEN THE COMPANY AND DIRECTORS REQUIRING SPECIAL APPROVAL OF MEMBERS: PT 10, CHS 4 AND 4A

10–066 The move over the years from shareholder approval of self-dealing transactions (as required by the common law) to mere board disclosure amounted to a significant dilution of the legal controls over this class of no-conflict cases. The move, which had been substantially achieved by the first quarter of the last century, was later shown to have weaknesses in those areas where the temptation to give way to conflicts of interest was high and scrutiny of the terms of the self-dealing transaction by the other members of board could not be relied upon to be effective. Consequently, not only did the legislature introduce what is now s.177 of the CA 2006, but it also went further and, at various times, introduced statutory provisions which restored the common law principle of shareholder approval in certain specific classes of case. These provisions are now gathered together in Chs 4 and 4A of Pt 10 of the CA 2006. Consequently, a complete understanding of the law relating to self-dealing transactions requires knowledge not only of s.177 and Ch.3 of Pt 10 of the CA 2006 but also of Chs 4 and 4A.

Relationship with the general duties

10–067 Where either Ch.4 or Ch.4A applies, then compliance with the general duties is not enough to put the director in compliance with the requirements of the CA 2006 (s.180(3)). Indeed, without this rule, Chs 4 and 4A would have little point. In the interests of avoiding having to obtain multiple approvals, however, s.180(2) provides that securing shareholder approval under those Chapters will relieve the director from having to comply with ss.175 (the duty to avoid conflicts of duty and interest) and 176 (duty not to accept benefits from a third party).[270] The subsection also applies even if the situation is one which in principle falls within Chs 4 or 4A but no shareholder approval is in fact required under that Chapter, for example, because the transaction is one of small value. In such a case neither Chs 4 or 4A, nor ss.175 and 176 apply. However, since the paradigm transaction falling under Chs 4 and 4A is a transaction *with* the company, it follows that in the usual case ss.175 and 176 would not bite in any event; only s.177 would be applicable. Shareholder approval is to be given by ordinary resolution of the shareholders unless the articles of association require a higher level of approval, which might extend to unanimity (s.281(3)).[271]

However, the other general duties will apply to transactions falling within Chs 4 and 4A (s.180(2)). Thus, the duty of the directors to promote the success of the company and to act within their powers will still apply, and crucially will apply to

[270] Both duties discussed below.

[271] If approval is required under more than one of the sets of statutory provisions discussed below, the requirements of each must be met, but not so as to require separate resolutions for each: s.225.

all the directors, not just the self-dealing one. This is important because transactions within Chs 4 and 4A will typically require both board and shareholder decisions. The board in the exercise of its powers under the articles takes the decision whether to enter into the proposed transaction and the shareholders then decide whether to approve the proposal as required by statute.[272] Thus, it is important that directors taking the decision whether to enter into the proposed transaction should be under the core duty of loyalty and be required to act within their powers. Further, the self-dealing director will remain under the duty to disclose the nature and extent of his or her interest to the board under s.177. This may seem unnecessary because such disclosure will be part of the process of seeking shareholder approval. However, the board decision may well precede the shareholder decision by some time. In any event, the board decision will be the only one in the case of a transaction falling within Chs 4 or 4A but not requiring shareholder approval under its provisions. In either case, disclosure of the conflict to the board in advance of the board decision, as s.177 requires, is obviously desirable.

Chapter 4 of Pt 10 brings within its scope three types of transaction: (1) substantial property transactions; (2) loans and analogous transactions; and (3) two sets of decisions affecting the remuneration of directors, namely, decisions about the length of directors' service contracts and decisions about gratuitous payments to directors upon loss of office. These situations were reviewed by the Law Commission which made various proposals for reform, mainly in matters of detail.[273] A number of these provisions contain financial limits. These are capable of being altered by statutory instrument as the Secretary of State sees fit, subject to negative resolution in Parliament (s.258). Chapter 4A of Pt 10 contains special provisions dealing with the remuneration of directors of quoted companies or unquoted traded companies. Its requirements are considered in Ch.11.[274] In outline, remuneration and loss of office payments are not to be made to directors of such companies unless they are consistent with an approved directors' remuneration policy, or alternatively unless the appropriate amendment to that policy has been approved by the members (ss.226B and 226C). These additional requirements do not negate any necessary Ch.4 requirements, although approval by the members under Ch.4 will satisfy the equivalent need for Ch.4A approval (s.226F).

Unlike the position with the general duties, the statute expressly applies all the provisions of Ch.4 to shadow directors (s.223), though note the qualification that a company is not to be regarded as the shadow director of its subsidiary simply because the directors of the subsidiary are accustomed to act in accordance with its instructions or directions (s.251(3)).[275] **10–068**

---

[272] The shareholders' meeting could in principle both approve the transaction and instruct the board to enter into it, but if the transaction falls within the managerial powers of the directors, such an instruction would have to take the form of a special resolution. See para.9–004.

[273] Law Commissions, fn.1.

[274] See paras 11–013 to 11–021.

[275] The statute leaves it up to the courts to decide how far the general duties apply to shadow directors, but does exclude holding companies in the circumstances set out in s.251, if the shadow director principle applies at all. See para.10–011.

A further and helpful characteristic of Chs 4 and 4A, in comparison with the general duties of Ch.2, is that they stipulate not only the duties to obtain shareholder approval, but also the consequences of failure to obtain it, in terms of both the directors (and others) being in breach of duty and of the validity of the transaction in question.

The provisions of Ch.4 apply only to "UK registered companies".[276] These are defined as companies registered under the CA 2006 or its predecessors, but excluding overseas companies.[277] The exclusion of companies registered in other jurisdictions is not surprising. However, confining the statutory provisions to companies registered under the Companies Acts excludes also companies incorporated in the UK but in some other way than under the Companies Acts, for example, companies formed by royal charter or Act of Parliament.[278] The provisions of Ch.4A extend more broadly, to companies quoted domestically, or officially listed in an EEA state, or on the New York or Nasdaq stock exchange (s.385).

Substantial property transactions

The scope of the requirement for shareholder approval

10–069 Section 190 requires prior shareholder approval of a substantial property transaction between the company and its director. It was said of the predecessor of s.190:

> "The thinking behind that section is that if directors enter into a substantial commercial transaction with one of their number, there is a danger that their judgment may be distorted by conflicts of interest and loyalties, even in cases of no actual dishonesty … It enables members to provide a check … It does make it likely the matter will be more widely ventilated, and a more objective decision reached."[279]

Given the motivations for oversight with this type of self-dealing, it is perhaps not surprising that the definition of the transactions caught is very wide, so wide indeed that the section imposes substantial inroads on the default rule in s.177, where disclosure to the board is all that is required.

10–070 A substantial property transaction is an arrangement (note the vagueness of this term) in which the director acquires[280] from, or has acquired from him or her by,

[276] CA 2006 ss.188(6)(a), 190(4)(b), 197(5)(a), 198(6)(a), 201(6)(a), 203(5)(a), 217(4)(a), 218(4)(a) and 219(6)(a).

[277] CA 2006 ss.1158 and 1.

[278] See para.1–031.

[279] *British Racing Driver's Club Ltd v Hextall Erskine & Co (A Firm)* [1996] 3 All E.R. 667 Ch D at 681–682. The case is a good illustration of the operation of both the dangers and their remedy. Technically, the transaction is not between the directors and one of their number but rather between a director and the company, but of course the decision on behalf of the company is taken by the other directors. See also *Granada Group Ltd v The Law Debenture Pension Trust Corp Plc* [2015] EWHC 1499 (Ch) (affirmed in [2016] EWCA Civ 1289) in which Andrews J provides an extensive discussion of the predecessor to s.190; and *Smithton Ltd v Naggar* [2014] B.C.C. 482.

[280] Defined in s.1163 to include the creation or extinction of an estate or interest in, or right over, any property and the discharge of any person's liability other than for a liquidated sum.

the company a substantial non-cash asset[281] of a value which exceeds either £100,000 or 10% of the company's net assets (provided the latter figure exceeds £5,000) (s.191).[282] The approval must be given either before the director enters into the transaction or the transaction must be conditional upon the approval being given, i.e. everything can be agreed between the parties but the transaction must not become binding on the company until the shareholders give their consent.[283] If this principle is not followed, then the director in question, the contracting party (if different) and the directors who authorised the transaction are all potentially liable to civil sanctions (as set out in s.195). However, the company itself is not subject to any liability by reason of the failure to obtain the necessary approval (s.190(3)), a necessary provision since the purpose of the rules is to protect the company's assets. Although s.190 requires prior approval of the transaction, nevertheless approval by the members of the company within a reasonable period after the transaction has been entered into will mean that the transaction can no longer be avoided by the company, but the other civil consequences of breach of s.190 will follow (s.196). Those civil consequences are dealt with below.

It will be noted that the section does not in its terms preclude the self-dealing director from voting as a member at a general meeting to approve or affirm the transaction, although the common law rules relating to the propriety of this will still apply.[284]

Approval is also required if the contracting party is a director of the company's holding company or a person connected with the director (of the company or the holding company). The extension of the section in this way is in order to pre-empt rather obvious avoidance devices. In the case of the director of a holding company (and a person connected with that director), the section requires the approval of the members of the holding company as well as of the members of the company, unless the company is a wholly-owned subsidiary of the holding company, in which case, for obvious reasons, the authorisation of the subsidiary's members is dispensed with (s.190(2) and (4)(b)).[285] The policy here appears to be that the director of the holding company may be in an institutional position to influence the actions of the subsidiary, so that the risk of unfair dealing with the subsidiary's property arises here as well. On the other hand, such a policy explains why the section is not extended to transactions between the company

[281] Also defined in s.1163 and meaning "any property or interest in property other than cash". See *Re Duckwari Plc (No.1)* [1997] 2 B.C.L.C. 713; and *Ultraframe (UK) Ltd v Fielding* [2006] F.S.R. 17, where the term was held to include a lease, a licence to exploit intellectual property, a supply of assets, and a sale of stock, but not a supply of services.

[282] The value of the net assets is to be determined by the latest accounts or, if none have been laid, by reference to its called-up share capital: s.191(3). Non-cash transactions need to be aggregated to test for their compliance with the statutory thresholds: s.190(5).

[283] Some degree of certainty of entering into the transaction or arrangement is needed despite the fact that a conditional arrangement may otherwise fall within s.190: *Smithton Ltd v Naggar* [2014] B.C.C. 482 at [110] (Arden LJ, with whom Elias and Tomlinson LJJ agreed).

[284] See paras 10–115 to 10–118.

[285] CA 2006 s.190(4)(a) dispenses with the requirement for shareholder approval if the company is not a UK-registered company. So, if the only British company is a wholly-owned subsidiary of a foreign company, the requirements for shareholder approval, if any, will be determined by the system of company law governing the foreign company.

and a director of its subsidiary or of a sister company in the group, because those directors have no institutional position of influence over the company. If, in the particular case, such a situation of influence does exist, then it may be that the director of the subsidiary will fall within the definition of a shadow director in relation to the parent or will be regarded as a connected person in relation to a director of the parent.

The provisions on connected persons deal with a different set of avoidance devices, applicable to free-standing companies as well as companies which are members of groups, whereby the contract is diverted to a person with whom the director is connected, such as the director's spouse. However, to cover all possibilities, the resulting definition of a "connected person" is highly complex. Section 252 puts into that category members of the director's family, as widely defined in s.253. It adds companies (in fact, "bodies corporate")[286] with which the director is "connected", and s.254 defines the necessary connection as being where the director and persons connected with him or her are interested in at least 20% of the equity shares of the company or control at least 20% of the voting power at a general meeting. Section 252 then adds a person who is a trustee of a trust the beneficiaries (including discretionary beneficiaries) of which include the director or a person who is connected with the director under the above provisions and, finally a (business) partner of the director or of a person connected with the director. The detail need not be further examined here, but it will provide many hours of delight for those trying to avoid the provisions of Ch.4 of Pt 10 of the Act.

Exceptions

10–071 Because of the width of the connected person definition, certain transactions have to be taken out of the requirement for shareholder approval, notably certain transfers of property between group companies. Here, no director or indeed any other individual is a party to the transaction, but one of the companies might be a person connected with the director, for example, where a holding company, in which a person has a 20% shareholding, enters into a substantial transaction with a subsidiary company of which that person is a director (s.192(b)). To provide a safe harbour, also excluded from s.190 are transactions between a company and a person in his character as a member of the company (even if that person is also a director of the company), thus protecting substantial distributions *in specie* to its members by the company (s.192(a)). Also excluded are transactions by a company in insolvent winding up or administration (s.193—though not transactions by a company in administrative receivership), presumably because the directors are no longer in control of the company; and certain transactions on a recognised stock exchange effected through an independent broker (s.194), presumably because the broker and the market provide the assurance that the terms of the trade are fair. Finally, s.190 does not apply to anything the director is entitled to under his or her service contract or any payment for loss of office falling under the provisions discussed below (s.190(6)).

286 CA 2006 s.1173(1), so that bodies incorporated outside the UK are included.

Remedies

Section 195 provides an extensive suite of civil remedies for breach of s.190, which operate in addition to any common law remedies,[287] and which at one stage looked likely to provide a template for the remedies to be made available for breach of the general duties.[288] The transaction or arrangement is voidable at the instance of the company unless restitution of the subject-matter of the transaction is no longer possible, third party rights have intervened, an indemnity has been paid (s.195(2)) or the arrangement has been affirmed within a reasonable time by a general meeting (s.196). It should be noted that a third party is one who "is not a party to the arrangement or transaction" entered into in contravention of s.190 (s.195(2)(c)). So, a connected person who is a party to the transaction will not count as a "third party" even if that person did not know of the connection with the director. Consequently, the connected person will not be able to prevent the transaction being avoided by the company by claiming to be a good faith third party without actual knowledge of the contravention—even though such a connected person may be relieved of liability to the company, as we see below. This statutory regime is therefore broader than its common law equivalents. **10–072**

The same is true of the financial liability of those involved in the transaction. As we saw earlier, the orthodox equitable rule in relation to self-dealing transactions is that they are simply voidable.[289] Section 195(3), by contrast, contemplates liability both to account to the company for any gain which has been made by the defendant (directly or indirectly)[290] and (jointly and severally with any others liable under the section) to indemnify the company from any loss resulting from the arrangement or transaction. This has perhaps been interpreted more narrowly in some ways, and more widely in others, than might have been expected from the statutory words themselves. In the normal case, it has been held, a gain will be made by the director where the director acquires an asset from the company, and a loss suffered by the company where the company acquires an asset from the director[291]: regarded this way, the statutory provisions provide a mechanism for effecting notional rescission of the self-dealing transaction, but doing so in money rather than by re-delivery of the assets originally exchanged. This seems sensible.

---

287 CA 2006 s.195(8).

288 See fn.3.

289 Although see fn.259, for possible alternative claims.

290 Thus, the duty to account is confined to the profit made by the person who is so accountable (though indirect profit is taken into account): there appears to be no duty on a director to account, for example, for a profit made solely by a connected person, though the connected person may be liable to account.

291 *NBH Ltd v Hoare* [2006] EWHC 73 (Ch); [2006] 2 B.C.L.C. 649 Ch D at [44]–[49]: when a director (or a connected person) sold an asset to the company at an undervalue (i.e. without loss to the company, here with that fact reinforced by the company's subsequent sale of the asset for a profit), the director was not liable for his own profits on the sale of the asset (and indeed their measurement might be difficult, and certainly could not be assumed to be the difference between the price at which the director acquired the asset, perhaps years ago, and the price for which it was later sold to the company). Also see *Re Duckwari Plc (No.2)* [1999] Ch. 253 at 261 (Nourse LJ). cf. the quite different situation described in fn.292.

So too is the notion that s.195(3) makes the remedy of accounting of profits additional to the right to avoid the transaction. Thus, any profit made by the director, but not captured by the company through avoidance of the transaction, can still be sought by the company; or the company may seek an accounting of profit even though the transaction cannot any longer be avoided. This is wider than the common law, but the advantages are clear.

In the case of losses, actual payment of an indemnity, by any person, removes the power to avoid the transaction. However, if the transaction has been avoided, the company could still sue for an indemnity against any losses not recovered by the reversal of the transaction. Further, and more surprisingly, the Court of Appeal has deduced from the fact that an indemnity deprives the company of its power to avoid the transaction that the indemnity, in relation to assets acquired by the company, must include losses incurred after the completion of the transaction in question, even if those losses were not caused by the absence of shareholder consent, provided the losses result from the acquisition. This means that the director is at risk of having to indemnify the company for losses caused by post-transaction adverse movements in the market.[292] Where a transaction is avoided, the company, by restoring the situation prior to the transaction, protects itself against both transaction losses and post-transaction losses, and it was held that an indemnity must go as far.

Finally, s.195(8) preserves any other remedy the company may have against the director or to avoid the transaction, for example, under the common law or any other provisions of the Act. It might be wondered what common law remedies would not be covered by the comprehensive provisions of s.195. One answer is that the remedies created by s.195 are not proprietary, because the section applies to Scotland which does not recognise proprietary remedies in this situation. However, so far as the common law applying in other parts of the UK confers a proprietary character on the company's remedies against directors,[293] s.195 preserves it.

10–073 A further notable feature of the section is the range of persons made potentially liable. Under s.195(4)(a) and (b) liability is imposed upon the director who entered into the transaction (including the director of the holding company where the transaction is with him or her) and on the connected person if that person was the party to the transaction. This is to be expected. However, s.195(4)(c) extends liability to a director (of the company or the holding company) with whom the party to the arrangement is connected, where the transaction was with the

[292] See *Re Duckwari (No.2)* [1999] Ch. 253; and *Re Duckwari (No.3)* [1999] Ch. 268 CA. In these cases, the company recovered by way of indemnity the loss (with interest) suffered after the acquisition of a piece of land (at a fair price) from a director without shareholder approval when the property market subsequently collapsed, but not the higher rate of interest actually paid by the company on the funds borrowed to effect the purchase. The court in the former case based its decision that the post-acquisition loss was recoverable also on the argument that, if the statute had not made express provision for the company's remedies, the director would have been liable to restore to the company the money paid for the property (less its residual value) on the grounds that the payment amounted to receipt of corporate assets paid to the director in breach of trust on the part of the directors; and there was no suggestion in the statute that Parliament wished to give the company remedies inferior to the common law ones.

[293] See para.10–109.

connected person. In other words, by using a connected person to effect the transaction the director does not escape personal liability to indemnify the company against losses or to account for profits, if the director made a profit thereby—though the subsection is not confined to such instrumental cases. Finally, and this is most important, s.196(4)(d) extends liability to any director of the company who authorised the arrangement, or any transaction in pursuance of it, even if neither that director nor a person connected with him entered into the arrangement. Thus, s.195 creates incentives not only for directors not to breach s.190 but also for directors to monitor compliance with the requirements of that section on the part of their fellow directors and, even more difficult, of persons connected with fellow directors. These liabilities arise whether or not the arrangement has been avoided by the company, and—perhaps oddly—they are not expressly discontinued even if the company confirms the arrangement under s.196.

This is therefore an extremely wide-ranging remedial scheme. First, the potential defendants are not just the director who was in a position of conflict of duty and interest and entered into the transaction, but also the person connected with him or her and the director so connected (where the transaction was with the connected party) and the non-self-dealing directors of the company who authorised the transaction. And secondly, the remedies range exceptionally broadly—rescission, account of profits, compensation for losses. For these reasons, two defences are provided against the liabilities created by s.195(3) and (4).

Where the arrangement is entered into by a connected person, the director with whom the connection exists is not liable if the director shows that he or she took "all reasonable steps to secure the company's compliance" with s.190 (s.195(6)). This defence does nevertheless require the director to be active, by taking "reasonable steps". For example, a director with a controlling holding in another company, which might engage in substantial property transactions with the company, would appear to be required at least to disclose to the company of which he is a director the existence of the connection and to warn of the need for shareholder approval, should a transaction be contemplated. Moreover, the director would seem required to take reasonable steps to monitor developments in both business and personal life which might give rise to "connections" of a statutory kind, so as to be able to disclose them.[294]

A further defence is provided for the connected person and an "authorising" director. They are not liable if they show that they "did not know the relevant circumstances constituting the contravention" (s.195(7)), which, given the width of the connected person definition, is not a fanciful situation. This wording does seem wide enough to cover the situation where the connected person (an estranged step-son, for example) does not know of the step-father's directorship. In this case, the connected person does not appear to be under any legal pressure to monitor the activities of the person with whom he or she is connected so as to ascertain, for example, of which companies the other person has become a

[294] It would not seem a legitimate reading of the section to interpret it so as to require the taking of reasonable steps only in relation to connections of which the director is actually aware, though the more remote the connection, the less the taking of reasonable steps would require.

director. The defence in s.195(7) is one based on simple ignorance. However, if the connected person does know of the connection, it does not appear that he or she escapes liability on the basis that there was a failure to understand that the law requires shareholder approval in such a case.

Additional rules for listed companies

10–074 In the case of companies whose shares are Premium Listed on the London Stock Exchange, there are further requirements for shareholder approval in the Listing Rules[295] drawn up by the Financial Conduct Authority (FCA). Such approval is required for certain "related-party" transactions,[296] such transactions defined to include transactions with a director or shadow director of the listed company or of another company within the same corporate group (not just of the holding company) or a person who has been such a director within the previous 12 months or an associate of such a director, or a person with significant influence.[297] On the other side of the transaction is the listed company or any of its subsidiaries. In addition, the category also includes transactions between the listed company and any person, the purpose and effect of which is to benefit a related party.[298] The requirement for shareholder approval applies to *any* related-party transaction within this ambit (other than a transaction of a revenue nature in the ordinary course of business, small transactions and certain specified types of transaction),[299] so that the FCA rules have a wider range than those contained in Ch.4 of Pt 10 of the CA 2006. The Listing Rules make every effort to ensure that the shareholders are well-advised, including requiring the directors to obtain an independent expert's report to support the directors' statement that the transaction or arrangement is fair and reasonable as far as the security holders are concerned (although the independent report itself does not have to be disclosed) (LR 13.6.1(5)). Crucially, on the approval resolution the related party may not vote and the related party must also take all reasonable steps to ensure any associates do not vote either.[300] The principle of shareholder approval and disinterested voting is thus taken much further in the Listing Rules than in the Act.

Loans, quasi-loans and credit transactions

Arrangements covered

10–075 As in other areas of life—a recent example being the funding of political parties—loans constitute an easy way of avoiding the rules governing the

---

[295] LR 11.1.

[296] Although only where the "related party" is "large", i.e. those at or above the 5% level on the class tests. This significantly restricts the number of shareholder approvals required. At or above the 0.25% level, there is a public disclosure obligation (on the company).

[297] LR 11.1.4.

[298] LR 11.1.5.

[299] LR 11.1.10–6. The specific exemptions are set out in LR 11 Annex 1.

[300] LR 11.1.7.

disposition of assets. A transaction can be presented as a loan when it is in effect a gift, either because the loan is never expected to be re-paid or because the terms of the loan are non-commercial. Given their control over the company's day-to-day activities, the directors are in a good position to effect such transactions for their own benefit, thus indirectly increasing their remuneration; and history has shown that from time to time they give into the temptation to do so. Consequently, loans have long been subject to special regulation by the Companies Acts. In 1945 the Cohen Committee[301] recommended that the legislation move beyond requiring disclosure of the loans to directors to prohibiting them. It said: "We consider it undesirable that directors should borrow from their companies. If the director can offer good security, it is no hardship for him to borrow from other sources. If he cannot offer good security, it is undesirable that he should obtain from the company credit which he would not be able to obtain elsewhere". The 1948 Act thus introduced a prohibition on loans to directors.

Now in the CA 2006 the prohibition has been re-cast in terms of a requirement for prior shareholder approval (s.197).[302] At the same time, the criminal sanctions previously attaching to these provisions were removed so that the sanctions are now purely civil. The result is to produce a much greater degree of parallelism between the provisions on loans and those on substantial property transactions, discussed above. On the other hand, the change arguably downgrades the protection available to creditors. In owner-controlled companies making a loan to the directors can be used as a way of siphoning assets out of the company to the shareholders where the company does not have distributable profits. If the company becomes insolvent, the administrator or liquidator will not be able to sue the directors for the recovery of the loans under the CA 2006, unless either the controllers, acting as shareholders, have forgotten to approve their decision to make the loans, taken as directors (which may happen), or the insolvency practitioner can discharge the greater burden of showing a breach of the directors' core duty of good faith or some other duty, such as the wrongful trading provisions or the common law creditor-regarding duties or can impugn the shareholder approval whitewash.[303]

As with substantial property transactions, a headache for the legislature has been the need to predict and pre-empt avoidance devices on the part of directors. With various exceptions and exemptions, the CA 2006 brings within its compass simple loans (s.197), loans to both the directors of holding companies[304] and persons connected with directors (of both the company and its holding company),[305] and also extends the rules to transactions analogous to loans. Thus,

[301] *Report of the Committee on Company Law Amendment* (1945), Cmnd.6659, para.94. It is interesting to note that one of the corporate governance reforms made in US federal law in the aftermath of the Enron affair was to introduce in the Sarbanes-Oxley Act 2002 a ban on loans by companies to their directors: s.402(a).

[302] This has removed a doubt arising under the old law about whether the company could seek to enforce its rights of civil recovery under the statute, on the grounds that it was seeking to rely on an illegal transaction.

[303] See Ch.19 and paras 10–111 to 10–118.

[304] CA 2006 ss.197(1). See also ss.198(2) and 201(2).

[305] See ss.200 and 201(2).

the provisions extend to what are called "quasi-loans" (s.198), to "credit transactions" (s.201) and to "related arrangements" (s.203). These provisions are hardly simple.

Sections 197 and 203 apply to any company; ss.198 and 201 only apply to a public company or a company, even if private, which is "associated with" a public company. Two companies are associated if one is subsidiary of the other or both are subsidiaries of the same body corporate.[306] It does not matter which is the public and which the private company.

10–076 A loan is a well-known concept. A quasi-loan is not. Essentially, quasi-loans are transactions, to which the company is a party, resulting in a director or a connected person obtaining some financial benefit for which the director is liable to make reimbursement to the company.[307] An example might be the company providing a credit card to the director, the company undertaking the obligation to meet the payments due to the credit card issuer and the director having an obligation to reimburse the company. This is not a loan because no funds are advanced by the company to the director, but the effect is the same as if the director took out the credit card in his or her own name and the company lent the director the money to pay the card issuer. The sections require disclosure to the shareholders of the core elements of the proposed transaction and approval from the members before the company enters into a loan or quasi-loan transaction with a director or director of the holding company or a person connected with such a director. Approval is also required if the company, instead of making the loan or quasi-loan, gives a guarantee or provides security in relation to loan or quasi-loan made by a third party. Thus, if an unconnected bank makes a loan to the director, but the company guarantees the loan, approval will be required.

Section 201 deals with credit transactions. A credit transaction is one in which goods, services or land are supplied to the director but payment for them is left outstanding, including hire-purchase, conditional sale, lease or hire agreements (s.202). Again, such a transaction is not a loan, because no funds are advanced to the director, but the economic effect is the same as if the company had made a loan to the director and the director had then used those funds to obtain the goods, land or services in question. The section applies to both credit transactions entered into by the company with the director (i.e. the company provides the goods, services or land) and transactions entered into by a third party with the director but the company gives a guarantee or security to the third person (s.201(2)).

Finally, s.203(1) requires shareholder approval for a further set of "arrangements" entered into, not by the company, but by a third party with or for the benefit of a relevant director or connected person. In order for such an arrangement to be caught it must be one which (1) would have required shareholder approval if it had been entered into by the company; and (2) the third party acquires a benefit from the company or a body corporate associated with it.

[306] CA 2006 s.256. The reference to "body corporate" brings in companies incorporated outside the UK (s.1173(1)), so two British subsidiaries of a foreign company will be associated. If one is public and the other private, both will be caught by the quasi-loans provisions, even though the rules on quasi-loans do not apply to the holding company (see s.198(6)).

[307] CA 2006 s.199.

Thus, the company cannot induce a third party to do something without shareholder approval which, if done by the company, requires such approval, where the third party obtains a benefit from the company for doing that thing. Section 203(1) also brings within the shareholder approval requirement situations where the company assumes responsibility under an arrangement previously entered into by a third party which, if entered into by the company, would have required the shareholders' approval. Thus, if a bank makes a loan to the director, but later the company assumes the obligation to repay the loan, the assumption of obligation by the company will require shareholder approval. By virtue of s.203 the company cannot avoid shareholder approval by doing indirectly what it cannot do directly.

Method of approval and related disclosures

Shareholder approval is by ordinary resolution, unless the articles impose a higher requirement.[308] Because of the potential complexity of the transactions covered by the provisions, it is not surprising that the Act requires full details of the proposed arrangement to be disclosed to the shareholders in writing in advance of their consideration of the approval resolution. Those details must disclose in particular the value the director will receive under the transaction and the amount of the company's liability.[309] As usual, approval is not required of the members of a wholly-owned subsidiary.[310] **10–077**

Additional disclosure is required in the annual accounts issued at the end of the relevant financial year (s.413). Section 413 applies to "advances and credits" granted by the company to its directors and "guarantees of any kind" entered into by the company on behalf of its directors. The wording does not map easily onto the transactions dealt with in Ch.4 of Pt 10 of the Act and is in fact derived from the Directives on companies' accounts.[311] Given that shareholders will already have approved these arrangements, there is perhaps no need for the accounts provisions to mimic the provisions of the sections discussed above. Indeed, it is possible that nothing specific about disclosure of the above transactions in the accounts would have been required by the Act had the Directives not required otherwise.

Exceptions

Having brought a wide range of transactions within the net of those needing shareholder approval, the statute then proceeds to provide "safe harbours", i.e. to identify certain situations where the member approval requirement is not required because the transaction is thought to be legitimate or to raise only a small risk of abuse. First, the requirement does not apply to anything done by the company to put the director or connected person in funds to meet expenditure incurred for the purpose of the company or to perform properly the duties of an officer of the **10–078**

---

308 CA 2006 s.281(3).

309 CA 2006 ss.197(3)–(4), 198(3), (5), 200(4)–(5), 201(4)–(5), and 203(3)–(4).

310 CA 2006 ss.197(5)(b), 198(6)(b), 200(6)(b) and 203(5)(b).

311 Articles 43(1) and (13) of Directives 78/660 [1978] OJ L222/11 and 83/459.

company or to enable the person to avoid incurring such expenditure. However, a cap of £50,000 is placed on the value of arrangements falling within the exemption (s.204).[312] Thus, if the credit card mentioned above is confined to business expenditures, and has an appropriate credit limit, it will not require shareholder approval.

Secondly, shareholder approval is not required for arrangements designed to put the director of the company or holding company in a position to defend civil or criminal proceedings alleging breach of duty, to apply for relief in relation to such an action,[313] or to defend regulatory proceedings, in relation to the company or any associated company (ss.205–206). However, other than in the case of regulatory proceedings, the arrangement must be reversed (for example, the company repaid a loan) if the defence is not successful.

Thirdly, certain minor value arrangements are exempted (under £10,000 for loans and quasi-loans; under £15,000 for credit transactions) (s.207(1)–(2)). Fourthly, credit transactions entered into by the company in the ordinary course of its business on no more favourable terms than it is "reasonable to expect" the company would offer to an unconnected person are exempted (s.207(3)). Fifthly, loans and quasi-loans by money-lending companies are exempted if made in the ordinary course of the company's business and no more favourable terms[314] than it is "reasonable to expect" the company would offer to an unconnected person (s.209).[315] Finally, arrangements for the benefit of associated companies[316] are permitted, even if they are connected persons, in order to facilitate intra-group transfers (s.208).

Remedies

10–079 The civil remedies provided under s.213 are similar to those under s.195 in relation to substantial property transactions, i.e. avoidance of the transaction,[317] recovery of profits made and an indemnity against loss, the latter two remedies being exercisable against the director receiving the loan, etc. those connected with that director and the directors authorising the loan.[318] The same defences are provided.

---

[312] In practice, this is likely to be a heavily used exception. Transactions have to be aggregated for the purpose of determining whether monetary thresholds have been crossed (s.210) and s.211 gives some guidance on the valuation of different types of arrangement.

[313] See para.10–129.

[314] However, a loan to purchase or improve a main residence for the director may be made by a money-lending company on non-commercial terms if the company has a home-loan scheme for its employees, it regularly makes such loans to its employees and the terms of the loan are the standard ones under the scheme: s.209(3)–(4).

[315] CA 2006 s.209(2). This is a somewhat narrower exception than that for credit transactions because credit transactions are exempted when entered into by any company (provided this is done in the ordinary course of the company's business) whereas the loan exception applies only to money-lending companies, i.e. those whose ordinary business includes the making of such loans. So, if the ordinary course of a company's business requires it to enter into a one-off credit transaction, it may make use of s.207(3), whether or not its ordinary business includes entering into this class of transaction.

[316] CA 2006 s.256.

[317] And s.214 makes the same provision as s.196 in relation to affirmation.

[318] It has been held that it is sufficient to impose liability on the director who authorised the loan (s.213(4)(d)), jointly and severally with the director who received it, that the director was aware from

Directors' service contracts and gratuitous payments to directors

A director contracting with his or her company in relation to the remuneration to be received constitutes a paradigm example of a conflict of interest, which is likely to exist in a very strong form. However, Ch.4 of Pt 10 does not in general require shareholder approval of directors' remuneration. It does so only in two specific areas. Approval is required for directors' service contracts of more than two years' duration (s.188) and of gratuitous payments for loss of office (ss.215 onwards). These provisions are discussed elsewhere in the work, as part of our more general discussion of the control of directors' remuneration and in relation to takeovers.[319] In addition, there are the more demanding requirements of shareholder approval of the remuneration policies of all quoted companies, or, alternatively, specific approval of particular remuneration or loss of office payments.[320] 10–080

CONFLICTS OF INTEREST AND THE USE OF CORPORATE PROPERTY, INFORMATION AND OPPORTUNITY: S.175

The scope and functioning of s.175

Section 175(1) states that "a director must avoid a situation in which he has, or can have, a direct or indirect interest that conflicts, or possibly may conflict, with the interests of the company".[321] Section 175(7) makes it clear that a conflict of interests includes a conflict of duties. Subject to a restriction in relation to charitable companies,[322] s.175(3) excludes from the scope of the section one central type of situation involving conflict of interest, namely, "a conflict of interest arising in relation to a transaction or arrangement with the company". These self-dealing transactions are covered by s.177, as discussed above, rather than by s.175.[323] However, it should be noted that s.175(3) has the effect of 10–081

the annual accounts of the practice of making loans to the recipient director, even if he was unaware of the precise amounts. See *Neville v Krikorian* [2007] 1 B.C.L.C. 1 CA; followed in *Queensway Systems Ltd v Walker* [2006] EWHC 2496 (Ch); [2007] 2 B.C.L.C. 577. In that case the authorising director was also held to be in breach of his general duties to the company by not seeking to recover the loans (which were repayable on demand) as soon as he knew of their existence.

319 See paras 11–013 to 11–021 and paras 28–027 to 28–031.

320 See paras 11–016, 11–018, 11–019, 11–028 and 11–029.

321 Subject to the exception—"not reasonably regarded as likely" to give rise to a conflict—in s.175(4)(a), which parallels the provision in s.177(6)(a). See para.10–059.

322 In the case of charitable companies self-dealing transactions fall within s.175, unless the articles permit the s.175 duty to be disapplied and, even then, the articles may not effect a blanket disapplication but may do so only "in relation to descriptions of transactions or arrangements specified" in the articles (s.181(2)). Thus, for charitable companies, board or shareholder authorisation will be required in many cases for directors' conflicted transactions with the company. The tougher rules for charitable companies are probably based on the premise that monitoring of the directors by the members of a charitable company is generally less effective than in the case of a non-charitable company and that the Charity Commission cannot make up the whole of the monitoring deficit.

323 The provisions are thus described as "mutually exclusive": *Re Coroin Ltd* [2012] EWHC 2343 (Ch) at [583] (David Richards J); affirmed at [2013] EWCA Civ 781, but not mentioning this point.

excluding self-dealing transactions even if s.177 does not apply its normal rule of disclosure to the board of the self-dealing transaction in question, for example, decisions on directors' remuneration (s.177(6)(c)). Having excluded self-dealing transactions, s.175 applies, as is expressly stated in s.175(2), "in particular to the exploitation of any property, information or opportunity" of the company. However, this is simply an inclusive assertion: it is important to note that s.175 imposes a general obligation to avoid conflicts of interest. Any conflict situation not excluded by s.175(3) will fall within its scope, whether or not it involves the exploitation of property, information or opportunity of the company. The example of a person acting as a director of competing companies is discussed below. Deciding whether a situation does indeed involve the necessary conflict is often the most difficult question in this area. If anything, recent developments in the case law seem to have brought an even wider range of situations within the conflicts category.[324]

As with the self-dealing transactions discussed above, the secondary aim of the rules in this area is to identify the appropriate body or bodies to handle the conflict situation on behalf of the company. As with self-dealing transactions, again, the common law rule was shareholder approval.[325] Section 175 introduces, as we shall see, the mechanism of approval by the uninvolved members of the board, as an alternative to shareholder approval. However, unlike s.177 which simply imposes an obligation of disclosure to the board for self-dealing transactions, s.175 requires the board, assuming it wishes to act, to approve the director putting him- or herself in a position of conflict of duty and interest. This difference in the roles of the board is necessary because, unlike self-dealing transactions, situations falling within s.175 will not necessarily generate a transaction to which the company is party. An example would be where a director diverts a corporate opportunity for personal benefit. The decision for the board is thus not whether to enter into the transaction (the typical question in the self-dealing case), but whether to approve what would otherwise be the director's breach of duty. Nevertheless, the statute has clearly made it easier for directors to obtain approval for the exploitation of a conflict personally, by permitting the non-involved members of the board to give approval (subject to safeguards).

There are two crucial questions to be answered in the area of corporate opportunities: first, how does the law identify an opportunity as a "conflicted" one and, secondly, what processes does it specify for the company to give authority for the taking of the corporate opportunity by the director personally? The statute deals with the second issue in part but with the first issue hardly at all, where reliance is placed on the common law. We look at each of these two issues in turn.

---

[324] Notably *Bhullar v Bhullar* [2003] EWCA Civ 424; [2003] B.C.C. 711; and *Allied Business and Financial Consultants Ltd v Shanahan*; sub nom. *O'Donnell v Shanahan* [2009] EWCA Civ 751; [2009] 2 B.C.L.C. 666. Also see *Sharma v Sharma* [2013] EWCA Civ 1287; [2014] B.C.C. 73; and *Pennyfeathers Ltd v Pennyfeathers Property Co Ltd* [2013] EWHC 3530 (Ch).

[325] In *Queensland Mines Ltd v Hudson* [1978] 52 A.L.J.R. 379 the Privy Council appeared to accept a board decision as releasing the corporate interest in an opportunity, but in that case the only members of the company were two other companies, each represented on the board of the company in question.

A strict approach to conflicts of interest

The reason for depriving a director of a profit made from unauthorised exploitation of a corporate opportunity is not an objection to directors making profits as a result of or in connection with or whilst holding their office, but rather that the prospect of a personal profit may make the director careless about promoting the company's interest in taking the opportunity. If taking the opportunity personally does not involve any conflict with the interests of the company, there is no reason to deprive the director of his or her profit. It follows that some of the prior case law on corporate opportunity, to the extent it seemed to be based on a free-standing "no profit" rule, is to be regarded with caution under the new statutory provisions. However, as we shall see below, there is a high degree of overlap between a "no conflict" approach and a "no profit" approach if both are given a rigorous interpretation. **10–082**

That the approach of s.175 to the "no conflict" principle is rigorous is suggested by two features of the section. First, s.175(1), echoing Lord Cranworth LC in *Aberdeen Rly Co v Blaikie Bros*,[326] includes within the principle a personal interest which "possibly may conflict" with that of the company. Secondly, s.175(2), referring to corporate opportunities, etc. says that "it is immaterial whether the company could take advantage of the property, information or opportunity". On the other hand, the primacy of the conflict approach is asserted by s.175(4)(a), which provides that the section is not infringed if "the situation cannot reasonably be regarded as likely to give rise to a conflict of interest". These parts of the section are to some degree in tension with one another. One thing is clear: it is certainly not enough for the director to escape liability under this section that he or she acted in good faith (i.e. had honestly formed the view that the company's interests were not capable of being harmed by what was done), for the question of whether an actual or potential conflict of interest has arisen is one for the court.

In identifying situations as involving a conflict, s.175 applies "in particular" to exploitation by the director of "property, information or opportunity" of the company. Misuse of corporate assets generally presents no particular problem[327]; even the most unsophisticated directors should realise that they must not use the company's property as if it was their own (although even this is frequently overlooked or ignored in a "one-man" company). It is misuse of corporate information or a corporate opportunity—in practice the two are likely to overlap—which gives rise to difficulties. The main difficulty in the law relating to the misuse of corporate information and opportunities (hereafter referred to simply as corporate opportunities) is isolating the criteria for the identification of a *corporate* opportunity as opposed to one the director is free to exploit personally without seeking any authorisation from the company. To put it another way, what sorts of linkages between the opportunity and the company are needed

[326] *Aberdeen Rly Co v Blaikie Bros* (1854) 1 Macq. 461.

[327] Except the problem of knowing when "corporate assets" end and "corporate information" or "corporate opportunity" begin. The present law does not draw a clear distinction between them and the decisions frequently treat the latter as "belonging" to the company, i.e. as being its "property" or "asset". The modern law on remedies tends to encourage this, as precise distinction seems irrelevant for those purposes.

to make the opportunity a "corporate" one, for which exploitation personally the director needs the authorisation of the company? In two relatively recent decisions, the Court of Appeal has taken a broad view of the criteria, but we need to put those decisions in the context of the prior case law.

The limits of "corporate" opportunities

10–083 In a famous decision during the Second World War, *Regal (Hastings) Ltd v Gulliver*,[328] the House of Lords, following the law relating to trustees,[329] held directors liable to account to the company for the profit made from their personal exploitation of a corporate opportunity once it was established[330]:

> "(i) that what the directors did *was so related to the affairs of the company* that it can properly be said to have been done in the course of their management and in utilisation of their opportunities and special knowledge as directors; and (ii) that what they did resulted in a profit to themselves." (Emphasis added.)

Although this case is based on a "no profit" rationale which the Act now expressly rejects, it is not difficult to re-cast it in conflict terms. The facts, briefly, were as follows: company A owned a cinema and the directors decided to acquire two others with a view to selling the whole undertaking as a going concern. For this purpose, they formed company B to take a lease of the other two cinemas. But the lessor insisted on a personal guarantee from the directors unless the paid-up capital of company B was at least £5,000 (which in those days was a large sum). Company A, the directors concluded, was unable to subscribe more than £2,000 and the directors, although initially willing to do so, changed their minds about giving personal guarantees. Accordingly, the original plan was changed; instead of company A subscribing for all the shares in company B, company A took up 2,000 and the remaining 3,000 were taken by the directors and their friends. Three weeks later, all the shares in both companies were sold to new shareholders at the agreed price, a profit of nearly £3 per share being made on each of the shares in company B. The new controllers then caused company A to bring an action against the former directors to recover the profit they had made from subscribing for shares in company B.

Basic issues of scope: when is an "opportunity" a "corporate opportunity"?

10–084 It is not difficult to see a conflict of interest in these facts. The initial plan had indeed been for company A to pursue the opportunity itself. It was then the directors who declined to give personal guarantees, thus creating the opportunity for them to participate personally in the financing of the acquisition and to share in the profits from the re-sale, thereby depriving the company of the ability to take the whole of the profit on the sale of the subsidiary. It was also the directors

328 *Regal (Hastings) Ltd v Gulliver* [1967] 2 A.C. 134 HL.
329 Notably *Keech v Sandford* (1726) Scl. Cas. Ch. 61.
330 Lord Macmillan in *Regal (Hastings) Ltd v Gulliver* [1967] 2 A.C. 134 at 153.

who, with the same result, decided not to obtain additional finance for the company to capitalise the subsidiary at the required level, even though the subsequent sale three weeks later was in contemplation when the additional cinemas were being acquired, so that it is difficult to believe that it would have been impossible for the company to obtain bridging finance for such a short period. These facts were emphasised in the judgment of Lord Russell of Killowen, even though he, like the other judges, based his reasoning on the "no profit" principle noted above.

Thus, it is submitted that a modern court, applying the "no conflict" principle, could come to the same result as the House of Lords in this case, especially as s.175(2) now explicitly provides that "it is immaterial whether the company could take advantage of the property, information or opportunity".[331] This is a crucial qualifier. It may at first sight seem an odd provision: was it not the possibility that the company could have taken up the opportunity itself which in *Regal* provided the basis for the conflict of interest, so that the existence of that possibility can hardly be characterised as "immaterial"? However, the rule can be justified as relieving the court of having to make a judgment it was not well-placed to make, i.e. whether the company was genuinely unable to raise the finance itself. It may also be justified as a prophylactic rule. It is the duty of the director to obtain the opportunity for the company. If the director is to be relieved of this duty and made free to take the opportunity personally where there is only a low chance of the company obtaining the opportunity itself, this will give the director an incentive not to strive as hard as he or she might to promote the company's interests. Section 175(2) removes this incentive.

It will be observed, however, that the claim in *Regal* was in another respect **10–085** wholly unmeritorious. Recovery by the company benefited only the purchasers, who in this way received an undeserved windfall resulting, in effect, in a reduction in the price which they had freely agreed to pay. It also appears that the directors had held a majority of the shares in company A, so that there would have been no difficulty in obtaining authorisation or ratification of their action by the company in general meeting[332]; but acting, as it was conceded they had, in perfect good faith and in full belief in the legality and propriety of their actions, it had not occurred to them to go through this formality. Nor does this account exhaust the anomalies inherent in the decision. The chairman (and, apparently, the dominant member) of the board, instead of agreeing himself to subscribe for shares in company B, had merely agreed to find subscribers for £500. Shares to that value had, accordingly, been taken up by two private companies of which he

---

[331] More difficult to explain in this way might be the trusts case of *Boardman v Phipps* [1967] 2 A.C. 46, where two of their lordships found against liability on the grounds that there was no conflict of interest on the part of the trustees, who made a profit out of confidential information obtained from the trust, which the trust itself was prohibited from acting on, whilst the majority found in favour of liability on the basis of confidential information plus profit. However, Lord Cohen (in the majority) also found that there was a conflict of interest, so that it might be argued that the majority view was that a conflict needed to be found for liability to be established. Lord Upjohn, dissenting, said that for a conflict of interest to arise there must be "a real sensible possibility of conflict" in the eyes of a reasonable person, a dictum which seems to be reflected in s.175(4)(a) of the Act.

[332] See the cogent editorial note in [1942] 1 All E.R. 378 at 379. It was conceded that had this been done, there could have been no recovery: see further on this question, paras 10–115 to 10–116.

was a member and director, and by a personal friend of his. It was accepted that the companies and friend had subscribed beneficially and not as his nominees and, accordingly, neither he nor they were held to be under any liability to account for the profit which they had made.[333]

The company's solicitor also escaped; though he had subscribed for shares and profited personally, he could retain his profit because he had acted with the knowledge and consent of the company exercised through the board of directors. The directors themselves could avoid liability only if a general meeting had approved,[334] but the solicitor, not being a director, could rely on the consent of the board. And this despite the fact that the board had acted throughout on his advice. Hence the two men most responsible for what had been done escaped liability, while those who had followed their lead had to pay up. The law provides adequate justification for why this should be so, but what seems wrong with the application of the conflicts rule in this case is that recovery was, it seems, in favour of quite the wrong people.[335] Had it not been for the change in ownership of company A, it might well have been equitable to order the profiting directors to disgorge their profits to the company, thus, in effect, causing the directors' profits to be "shared" among all the members in the sense that the remedy would enhance the value of their shares. As it was, however, the funds paid to the company benefited the new owners, not the old ones, and these were new owners who had been perfectly happy to pay the agreed price for the acquisition of their shares in the old company. For this reason the case is often seen as one where equitable principles were taken to inequitable conclusions.

10–086 Of the many subsequent decisions that have followed or commented on the *Regal* case, four are of particular interest for what more they say about how the courts determine whether an "opportunity" is a "corporate opportunity", the personal pursuit of which will involve the director in a potential conflict of duty and interest. These are *Industrial Development Consultants v Cooley*,[336] *Canadian Aero Service v O'Malley*[337] (a decision of the Canadian Supreme Court in which the judgment was delivered by Laskin J—later the CJ), *Bhullar v Bhullar*[338] and *Allied Business and Financial Consultants Ltd v Shanahan*; sub nom. *O'Donnell v Shanahan*.[339]

The facts in the first two cases were very similar. In both, the companies concerned had been eager to obtain, and were in negotiation for, highly remunerative work in connection with impending projects. In both, it was unlikely that the companies would have obtained the work, but in each there was

---

[333] The companies and friend had not been sued. Recovery might have been obtained from them if they had fallen within the rules relating to third parties' involvement in breaches of directors' duties. And in that case could the director be made liable for the third party's profits? See para.10–130.

[334] This would continue to be the case even under the Act because there appear to have been no uninvolved directors who could have given authorisation.

[335] Some American jurisdictions, in like circumstances, allow what is there known as "pro rata recovery" by those shareholders who have not profited. We, unfortunately, lack any such procedure.

[336] *Industrial Development Consultants v Cooley* [1972] 1 W.L.R. 443 per Roskill J.

[337] *Canadian Aero Service v O'Malley* [1973] 40 D.L.R. (3d) 371 Can. SC.

[338] *Bhullar v Bhullar* [2003] B.C.C. 711.

[339] *Allied Business and Financial Consultants Ltd v Shanahan* [2009] EWCA Civ 751; [2009] B.C.C. 822.

a director whose expertise the undertaker of the project was anxious to obtain. Accordingly, each of the directors concerned resigned his office and later joined the undertaker of the project, in *Cooley* directly, in *Canadian Aero Service* indirectly through a company formed for the purpose which entered into a consortium with the undertaker. In both the directors were held liable to account for the profits which they made.

In neither case is it difficult to analyse the facts through a conflict-of-interest prism, since both directors were under a duty to obtain the opportunity for the company, unlikely though it was that they would succeed, though the reasoning of the courts involved was not expressed exclusively in this way. In *Cooley*, liability was based on misuse of information[340]: the defendant, while managing director, had obtained information and knowledge that the project was to be revived and had deliberately concealed this from the company and taken steps to turn the information to his personal advantage. It was irrelevant that the approach had been made to him and that his services were being sought as an individual consultant and would be undertaken free from any association with the company.[341] "Information which came to him while he was managing director and which was of concern to the plaintiffs and relevant for the plaintiffs to know, was information which it was his duty to pass on to the plaintiffs." It might seem remarkable that the plaintiffs should receive a benefit which "it is unlikely that they would have got for themselves had the defendant complied with his duty to them" but "if the defendant is not required to account he will have made a large profit as a result of having deliberately put himself into a position in which his duty to the plaintiffs who were employing him and his personal interests conflicted".[342] This is an expression of the policy, as noted above, which now finds expression in s.175(2) of the CA 2006. The quotation also demonstrates that the basis of the decision was not a mere misuse of information but the conflict of interest and duty to which its use gave rise.

In *Canadian Aero Service*, the decision was based firmly on misuse of a corporate opportunity, conceived of as generating a conflict of interest. On this Laskin J said[343]:

> "An examination of the case-law shows the pervasiveness of a strict ethic in this area of the law. In my opinion this ethic disqualifies a director or senior officer[[344]] from usurping for himself or diverting to another person or company with whom or with which he is associated a maturing business opportunity which his company is actively pursuing; he is also precluded from so acting even after his resignation where the resignation may fairly be said to be prompted or influenced by a wish to acquire for himself the opportunity sought by the company, or where it was his position with the company rather than a fresh initiative which led him to the opportunity which he later acquired."

---

340 Roskill J presumably chose this rather than the more obvious loss of opportunity because the chance that the company could have secured the opportunity was minimal: Roskill J assessed it at not more than 10%: [1972] 1 W.L.R. 443 at 454.

341 So that, "in one sense, the benefit did not arise because of the defendant's directorship: indeed, the defendant would not have got this work had he remained a director": [1972] 1 W.L.R. 443 at 451.

342 *Industrial Development Consultants v Cooley* [1972] 1 W.L.R. 443 at 453.

343 *Canadian Aero Service v O'Malley* (1973) 40 D.L.R. (3d) 371 at 382.

344 See para.10–012 on the question of how far English fiduciary principles apply to non-board senior managers.

Effect of director's resignation

10–087 Another feature of the *Cooley* and *O'Malley* cases was that the directors in question resigned before taking up the opportunity, but were nevertheless held liable to account to the company for the profits subsequently made. The issue was considered by Lawrence Collins J in *CMS Dolphin Ltd v Simonet*,[345] who concluded that the answer lay in the proposition that the opportunity is treated as the property of the company, so that a director who resigns after learning about such an opportunity "is just as accountable as a trustee who retires without properly accounting for trust property". As we have seen above,[346] this approach to the issue of resignation has been confirmed in s.170(2)(a) of the CA 2006, and without the need for very dubious characterisation of the opportunity as the property of the company. It follows, of course, that if what the director has learned before his or her resignation does not fall within the category of a corporate opportunity, it is no breach of this aspect of fiduciary duties to exploit the information personally thereafter; the line can be difficult to draw.[347] This means that, beyond the boundaries of these statutory rules, or any contractual[348] or equitable restraints on the director (for example, rules on breach of confidence), he or she is otherwise free to exploit his or her enhanced knowledge, talents and skills after resignation as a director.[349]

Effect of board determinations of the scope of a company's activities

10–088 The last two cases of the four noted earlier are in many ways the more interesting. In *Bhullar v Bhullar*,[350] in contrast to *Cooley* and *Canaero*, the defendants did not

---

[345] *CMS Dolphin Ltd v Simonet* [2001] 2 B.C.L.C. 704 Ch D at 733. Alternatively, it can be said that the conflict of personal interest and duty to the company arises at the moment the opportunity emerges and that subsequent resignation does not operate retrospectively to cure the breach (indeed, it is often an expression of the director's preference for his or her personal interest). It is true that the profit arising out of the breach is made after resignation, but there is no reason why the company should not recover this if the breach occurred before resignation, just as a director who takes a decision adverse to the company in breach of the core duty of loyalty or duty of care does not reduce his or her liability to the company by resigning immediately after taking the decision. cf. *Lindsley v Woodfull* [2004] 2 B.C.L.C. 131 at [28]–[30] CA. See also *FHR European Ventures LLP v Mankarious* [2013] EWCA Civ 17; [2014] Ch. 1 at [56]–[59] (not affected by the appeal at [2014] UKSC 45; [2015] A.C. 250).

[346] See para.10–014.

[347] *Island Export Finance Ltd v Umunna* [1986] B.C.L.C. 460; *Balston Ltd v Headline Filters Ltd* [1990] F.S.R. 385; *Framlington Group Plc v Anderson* [1995] 1 B.C.L.C. 475 Ch D; *Halcyon House Ltd v Baines* [2014] EWHC 2216 (QB); *First Subsea Ltd v Balltec Ltd* [2014] EWHC 866 (Ch) (appealed unsuccessfully on limitation matters [2017] EWCA Civ 186); *Weatherford Global Products Ltd v Hydropath Holdings Ltd* [2014] EWHC 2725 (TCC); [2015] B.L.R. 69. Also see *Imam-Sadeque v Bluebay Asset Management (Services) Ltd* [2012] EWHC 3511 (QB); [2013] I.R.L.R. 344 (in the context of a former employer-employee relationship).

[348] See, e.g. *Dranez Anstalt v Hayek* [2002] EWCA Civ 1729; [2003] 1 B.C.L.C. 278, finding a restraint of trade clause too wide and therefore unenforceable.

[349] See generally *Odyssey Entertainment Ltd v Kamp* [2012] EWHC 2316 (Ch); *Halcyon House Ltd v Baines* [2014] EWHC 2216 (QB); *First Subsea Ltd v Balltec Ltd* [2014] EWHC 886 (Ch) (appealed unsuccessfully on limitation matters [2017] EWCA Civ 186).

[350] *Bhullar v Bhullar* [2003] B.C.C. 711. In the same vein, also see *Towers v Premier Waste Management Ltd* [2011] EWCA Civ 923; [2012] 1 B.C.L.C. 67, requiring the company to be given the option to reject the opportunity.

seek to divert to themselves an opportunity which their company was actively pursuing. On the contrary, this case concerned a falling out between two families who had set up the company to acquire properties. During the resulting disputes about how to untangle their affairs, the family on the claimant side of this litigation informed the family on the defendant side that it did not want the company to acquire any further properties. Subsequently, by chance and without reliance on any information confidential to the company, the defendant directors discovered that a property adjacent to one of the company's properties was for sale and purchased it themselves. The claimants nevertheless succeeded in their argument that the opportunity to purchase the property should have been made available to the company, whose own property would have been much more valuable if joined with the adjacent property, and that the defendants accordingly held the newly acquired property on trust for the company.[351] This is a notable decision on two grounds.

First, it very explicitly moves English law in the direction of the US "line of business test", i.e. if the opportunity falls within the company's existing line of business activities, then the opportunity is a corporate one, even if no property or information of the company was deployed by the director to obtain the opportunity, and even if the company was not at the time actively pursuing the particular opportunity. There was no suggestion in *Bhullar* that the directors had used their position in the company to bring the opportunity to maturity and then diverted it for themselves, as in *Canaero*, and certainly no suggestion that the company was seeking further acquisitions. Nevertheless, this broad test recognises that, for the purpose of the conflict of interest and duty rule, the duties of a director are pervasive; they are not ones arising only when the company itself is actively engaged in pursuing the same opportunity or is an essential contributor to its pursuit. On the other hand, this wider concept of the scope of corporate opportunities cannot be taken to extremes. Companies are now unlikely to be constrained by narrowly circumscribed objects, yet their core business is usually clear: a "corporate opportunity" is necessarily one falling within this core—as per the US "line of business" test—but it cannot, and does not, capture within its embrace every possible interesting opportunity simply because the company *could*, theoretically, pursue it itself.[352]

Secondly, however, the application of this extended understanding of a corporate opportunity to the facts of the case may seem questionable, for the court attached no weight to the fact that, before the opportunity arose, the board decided, albeit informally, at the initiative of the claimants and for reasons which were apparent, not to acquire any more properties.[353] Nevertheless, the claimants were, in effect, able to reverse their decision after the event once a particularly attractive opportunity arose. It is not clear why the claimants should have been permitted to act in such an opportunistic way. In *Regal*, where the claimants' behaviour was also opportunistic, as we have seen, it could be said that it was the defendant directors who decided that the company could not afford the

[351] Thus, they could be obliged to convey it to the company, subject to the company's payment to them of the costs of purchase.
[352] See para.10–089.
[353] The issue is hardly touched upon in the reasoning of the court.

opportunity who were the ones who later took it themselves, and that such behaviour is necessarily suspect. In *Bhullar*, however, it was the claimants, not the defendants, who took the initiative to restrict the scope of company's future activities.[354]

One possible rationale, however, although not one even hinted at in the judgment, is that the company was effectively in the throes of a messy winding up of an incorporated partnership. In these circumstances directors would not normally embark on any further acquisitions (as the claimant had made clear), and directors' duties move instead to maximising the value of the company's assets in preparation for dissolution. To *that* end, the acquisition of a property adjacent to an existing block owned by the company *is* a corporate opportunity, since two adjacent blocks of land would be more valuable to the company than a single block of land plus cash.[355]

10–089 The second point to note is not unrelated to the first. If the courts are, rightly it is submitted, to extend liability beyond the maturing business opportunity so as to embrace opportunities within the company's line of business, a director needs to be able to establish what the company's business actually is. Of course, this may not be simple, and it is probably right that any ambiguity ought to be resolved against the director and in favour of the company, so requiring the director to act with undeviating loyalty in furthering the company's possible wider interests.[356] On the other hand, it would seem undesirable to extend the corporate opportunity doctrine to any business opening which a director comes across and which the company could exploit, even though the company was neither already exploiting that type of opportunity nor seeking to do so.[357] To do so would come close to restoring the "no profit" rule which the section does not adopt, and indeed to do so without the usual limitations inherent in that common law rule.[358] This sort of rule would increase the costs of being a director (the director is at risk of losing

[354] It is possible that the court thought that the purchase of the adjacent property did not fall unambiguously within the decision not to purchase new properties.

[355] In the same vein, see the partnership case of *Chan v Zacharia* (1984) 154 C.L.R. 178 at 199 (Deane J): on a dissolution of the doctors' partnership, one doctor renewed the partnership lease in his own name; the court decided that he held this asset on trust for the partnership because, on dissolution, there was an obligation on the partners to gather in the partnership assets, maximising the value for partnership, and these proceeds should then be split between the partners; one partner could not, in advance of that, simply take the future benefit of one of the assets for himself.

[356] Companies' business models change from time to time, often quite rapidly, and the obvious place for a director to look for a current definition is in the decisions of the board setting its business strategy, but it also seems right that the company's interests might legitimately be seen as extending more widely to encompass at least those broader but related corporate endeavours that any proactive directors ought at least periodically to consider and critically review as possible new corporate endeavours. These too should be included within the compass of the directors' duties of loyalty.

[357] For example, the non-executive director of a company providing business services learns on the golf course from a friend who does not know of his directorship of an opportunity to invest in a restaurant project. Does the director need the authorisation of the company to make the investment, simply because his company is financially able to take it up? It is suggested that the answer is in the negative. For some recognition of the force of this argument see *Wilkinson v West Coast Capital* [2005] EWHC 3009 (Ch); [2007] B.C.C. 717.

[358] That being, as stated in *Regal*, that the opportunity came to the directors "by reason and only by reason of the fact that they were directors of Regal, and in the course of their execution of that office": per Lord Russell at [1967] 2 A.C. 134 at 147.

the opportunity to the company) and in the case of non-executive directors in particular this might seem a high cost as against the potential rewards of the directorship.

In particular, an answer needs to be provided to the question posed in *Regal*: does the equitable principle involve "the proposition that, if the directors bona fide decide not to invest their company's funds in some proposed investment, a director who thereafter embarks his own money therein is accountable for any profits he may derive therefrom?"[359] The reason this question is unresolved, it is suggested, is to be found in the underdeveloped state of the law on the role of the board in the area of corporate opportunities, for the board performs two closely linked but conceptually distinct roles. It may authorise the taking by the director of an opportunity which is a corporate one, as s.175 contemplates, but, through its direction of the company's business strategy, its decisions may, or ought, to have the effect of taking some opportunities out of the category of being corporate, with the consequence that authorisation is not required, because there is no conflict of interest. As s.175(2) says, it may indeed be "immaterial" whether the company could take advantage of the opportunity, but if it is an opportunity outside the range of the company's business activities, present or in contemplation, can the situation "reasonably be regarded as likely to give rise to a conflict of interest", as s.175(4)(a) requires? It is suggested that the line of business test provides a way of reconciling these two provisions of the section, with due regard being accorded to decisions of the board in determining the company's business strategy.

This "scope of business" reasoning has, however, been dealt an unexpected and it is suggested rather unfortunate blow in the final case on our list. In *O'Donnell v Shanahan*,[360] the deputy judge held that there had been no breach of fiduciary obligations because the impugned opportunity (which concerned a property development) arose outside the scope of the business of the principal company (which focussed upon the provision of loans, mortgages and financial advice[361]), and further there had been no use of the company's property or information in acquiring the benefit.[362] The Court of Appeal took the opposite view. The company operated as a quasi-partnership with three members, the petitioner and the two defendants (the latter also ran a property development partnership on the side). Although not part of the company's usual business, the company had, in an ad hoc fashion, agreed to procure finance for and advise one particular investor who was interested in purchasing a development property. In return, the company would earn fees and a commission. Valuation reports were obtained and other **10–090**

[359] per Lord Russell (quoting Greene MR) at [1967] 2 A.C. 152. cf. the answer given in *Peso Silver Mines v Cropper* (1966) 58 D.L.R. 2d 1 and the criticism of that decision by Beck, (1971) 49 Can. B.R. 80.

[360] *Allied Business and Financial Consultants Ltd v Shanahan*; sub nom. *O'Donnell v Shanahan* [2008] EWHC 1973 (Ch); [2009] B.C.C. 517; overturned in [2009] EWCA Civ 751; [2009] 2 B.C.L.C. 666. The case was brought as an unfair prejudice petition under CA 1985 s.459 (now CA 2006 s.994). See Ch.14.

[361] This was as defined in the company's constitution, although there was also the common broader power to carry on any other business considered by the directors to be advantageous.

[362] Any use of the valuation report (see below) was, if anything, in breach of the rights of the first potential buyer, not the company.

work done, but the deal did not proceed. After further negotiations, the two defendants and a third party procured the opportunity for themselves, and did so on the basis that no commission would be paid to the company. The defendants did, nevertheless, pay the petitioner a sum representing her notional share of the lost commission. Later, after the falling out, the petitioner claimed that the investment in the development property was made in breach of the "no conflict" and "no profit" rules, without her consent, and that she was entitled to a share in the profits.

The Court of Appeal agreed, holding that the opportunity had arisen in the course of the directors' activities as company directors and therefore it should have been disclosed to the company which should have been given a chance to decide whether or not it wished to exploit the opportunity itself. It was immaterial that property development was not the focus of the company's activities. The "scope of business" test, described in *Aas v Benham*[363] (and heavily relied upon by the deputy judge), was held inapplicable: it was, the court held, a partnership precedent; its application was limited to partnerships where the partnership activities were clearly defined in restrictive partnership deeds; by contrast, in companies (even, it seems, quasi-partnership companies, as here) and trusts, *Aas v Benham* had no application—directors were simply fiduciaries in whatever activities they engaged. According to Rimer LJ[364]:

> "I would regard it as correct to characterise the nature of a director's fiduciary duties as being so unlimited and as akin to a 'general trusteeship'. In my judgment, the decision in *Aas v Benham* provides no assistance in determining the nature and reach of the 'no profit' rule so far as it applies to trustees and directors. In particular, in the present case, the scope of the company's business was in no manner relevantly circumscribed by its constitution: it was fully open to it to engage in property investment if the directors so chose."

And later, given this, he reached the same conclusions on the "no conflict" rule. It followed that the two directors had breached their fiduciary duties and were required to account for the profits earned on the development project (should the facts establish there were any). This would, in turn, boost the assets of the company, which would in turn increase the share price, and thus improve the return to the petitioner who was seeking to have her shares repurchased as her remedy under the unfair prejudice petition.

Moreover, the court dismissed without discussion as seemingly irrelevant the fact that the petitioner had accepted her share of the notional commission from the defaulting directors, and had at least implicitly acquiesced in the purchase of the development property by the defendants.

Finally, although it is true that unfair prejudice claims can be pursued successfully without proof of matters that would constitute legal wrongs, here the entire focus of the Court of Appeal's reasoning was on the question of whether there had been a breach of the no-conflict fiduciary duties.

10–091 Where does this leave directors? It is easy to explain that it is, and ought to be, irrelevant to the question of fiduciary breach whether the company could, or would, exploit the opportunity in question. Those questions are more relevant

---

[363] *Aas v Benham* [1891] 2 Ch. 244 CA.

[364] *O'Donnell v Shanahan* [2009] EWCA Civ 751; [2009] 2 B.C.L.C. 666 at [68]–[69].

when the alleged breach is of the good faith duty (s.171), or even the care and skill duty (s.174). But the gist of the "no conflict" rule is to compel, so far as possible, unwavering loyalty to the corporate endeavour. Both the duty and its remedies are geared to this end. This, it is suggested, implicitly and inevitably requires the courts to pay some regard to the scope of that endeavour. Instead, the two cases just described (*Bhullar v Bhullar*[365] and *O'Donnell v Shanahan*[366]) favour an approach that is automatically broad, and one that, taken only a little further, would verge on finding that any opportunity that is at all interesting financially will be seen as of interest to the company. Taken to such extremes, this raises the risks for directors, and increases the chances of pure windfall gains to the company and its shareholders: there would be no safe harbour for directors other than to present every entrepreneurial idea to the board before pursuing it individually, notwithstanding the nature of the corporate business or whether there is a real, sensible prospect of a conflict. This effectively gives the company a right of first refusal on opportunities seen by the directors as worth pursuing. Within the company's scope of business, broadly interpreted, this is precisely the goal of the no-conflict rule, but outside that context it is suggested the assumption of a broader rule lacks either analytical rigour or policy justification. It risks raising the fiduciary "no-conflict" rule from pragmatic prophylaxis to something far more draconian.

Since all these cases were determined under the common law, it remains to be seen how far the statutory encapsulation has imposed its own pressure in s.175(4) to deny a breach if "the situation cannot reasonably be regarded as likely to give rise to a conflict of interest". However, recent authorities do not appear to deviate from these common law authorities on the tests for determining the scope of the director's duty.[367]

Competing and multiple directorships

It is common for directors to hold directorships in more than one company, certainly where the companies are part of a group but also where they are independent of one another. In such cases an issue arises in relation to the compatibility of this practice with the no-conflict rule set out in s.175, whether conceived of as a conflict of interest and duty (s.175(1)) or a conflict of duty and duty (s.175(7)). There are two situations which need to be looked at: the first is where directorships are held in companies which are in business competition with one another, or indeed where the director in any other way enters into **10–092**

[365] *Bhullar v Bhullar* [2003] B.C.C. 711.

[366] *Allied Business and Financial Consultants Ltd v Shanahan*; sub nom. *O'Donnell v Shanahan* [2008] EWHC 1973 (Ch); [2009] B.C.C. 517; overturned in [2009] EWCA Civ 751; [2009] 2 B.C.L.C. 666.

[367] See *Towers v Premier Waste Management Ltd* [2011] EWCA Civ 923; [2012] B.C.C. 72 at [51]; *Sharma v Sharma* [2013] EWCA Civ 1287; [2014] B.C.C. 73 at [51]–[52]; *Richmond Pharmacology Ltd v Chester Overseas Ltd* [2014] EWHC 2692 (Ch); [2014] Bus. L.R. 1110 at [69]–[72]. Also see generally *Pennyfeathers Ltd v Pennyfeathers Property Co Ltd* [2013] EWHC 3530 (Ch); and *Invideous Ltd v Thorogood* (judgment reversed on other grounds in [2014] EWCA Civ 1511).

competition with the company; and, secondly and more commonly, where the companies are not competitors but where nevertheless their interests may conflict from time to time.

Competing with the company

10–093 One of the most obvious examples of a situation which might be expected to give rise to a conflict between two sets of a director's duties[368] is where the director carries on or is associated with a business competing with that of the company. Certainly fiduciaries without the consent of their principals are normally precluded from competing with them, and this is specifically stated in the analogous field of partnership law.[369] For a while, and strangely therefore, it was supposed that a similar rule did not apply to directors.[370] However, the one definite, if inadequately reported, decision that a director could not be restrained from acting as a director of a rival company appears to be based on the conclusion that competing directorships were not unconstitutional (i.e. not contrary to the articles or the director's contract) rather than that they were not in breach of the director's fiduciary duty.[371] It has been held that the duty of fidelity flowing from the relationship of employer and worker may preclude the worker from engaging, even in his spare time, in work for a competitor,[372] notwithstanding that the worker's duty of fidelity imposes lesser obligations than the full duty of good faith owed by a director or other fiduciary agent. It seems impossible to suggest, therefore, that a director can compete whereas a subordinate employee cannot.

In the light of the above it was not surprising that in *In Plus Group Ltd v Pyke*[373] the Court of Appeal expressed unease with the state of the law as set out above, but resisted the temptation to engage in a wholesale review of the case law in this area in the situation facing them where the defendant director had been

[368] CA 2006 s.176(7) makes it clear that the section applies to a conflict of duties.

[369] Partnership Act 1890 s.30.

[370] It clearly does not apply to members, even in a private company, for members, as such, are not fiduciaries, though such conduct might give rise to a remedy under the unfair prejudice provisions. See Ch.14.

[371] *London & Mashonaland Exploration Co v New Mashonaland Exploration Co* [1891] W.N. 165; approved by Lord Blanesburgh in *Bell v Lever* [1932] A.C. 161 at 195. By contrast, the dicta in *Item Software (UK) Ltd v Fassihi* [2004] B.C.C. 994 at [63] per Arden LJ, suggests, it seems, that although a finding that directors could not hold multiple directorships would be a "substantive extension" of the duties of directors, there was—as in this case—no suggestion that those multiple directorships would not be subjected to the full panoply of fiduciary restrictions. See also *First Subsea Ltd v Balltec Ltd* [2014] EWHC 866 (Ch), in which the former directors were found to have breached their duties of loyalty even though the setting up of a competing business itself was not a breach (appealed unsuccessfully on limitation matters [2017] EWCA Civ 186).

[372] *Hivac Ltd v Park Royal Scientific Instruments Ltd* [1946] Ch.169 CA. If correct it must apply to an executive director: see *Scottish Co-op Wholesale Society Ltd v Meyer* [1959] A.C. 324 at 367 per Lord Denning. Also see *Allfiled UK Ltd v Eltis* [2015] EWHC 1300 (Ch) (the granting of an interim injunction restraining the use of confidential information and intellectual property in a new company pending trial, but allowing the new company to continue trading in the meantime).

[373] *In Plus Group Ltd v Pyke* [2002] EWCA Civ 370; [2002] 2 B.C.L.C. 201, especially the judgment of Sedley LJ. Also see *Halcyon House Ltd v Baines* [2014] EWHC 2216 (QB) at [220]–[227]; and *First Subsea Ltd v Balltec Ltd* [2014] EWHC 866 (Ch) at [193]–[203] (appealed unsuccessfully on limitation matters [2017] EWCA Civ 186).

wholly, and probably wrongfully, excluded from any influence over the operation of the claimant companies, in which he was also a substantial shareholder. The Court held that in these circumstances the claimant companies could not obtain an account of the profits made by the director as a director of a competing company which he had established. In taking this approach, the court indicated that the logical way forward was simply to examine the rule against competition in the circumstances of each case. The early *Mashonaland* case must then be seen not as one laying down a rule that competition is in principle permitted, but as one where, as in the *Pyke* case, it was inappropriate to apply the no-competition rule.[374]

It can also be argued that s.175 has made it much easier for directors to deal with such conflicts of duty. If both companies consent to the situation, there is no breach of fiduciary duty arising simply from taking up directorships in competing companies, but so long as consent at common law required the approval of the shareholders, directors would regard the process of obtaining consent as a burdensome one. Under s.175, by contrast, the non-conflicted directors of the companies involved will normally be in a position to give their consent (subject to the different default rules for private and public companies noted below). Note, however, that is not the end of the story. Even when a director has consent to act for two principals, his fiduciary duties persist: he must comply with all his duties to each of them, unless he has their consent to do otherwise.[375]

Two difficulties remain, however. First, the section does not contemplate, in the way that s.177 does, a general declaration of interest. The director must seek approval from the non-involved directors for taking up the position as a director of the competing company and, should the nature of that situation change—for example, should the competing company start an additional line of business in competition with the other company—a further consent would apparently be required. However, it may not always be easy to judge when a situation has arisen which requires further consent. Secondly, even if consent is given to the taking up of the directorship, the director is likely to be faced with constant difficulties in avoiding breaches of the core duty of loyalty to the companies concerned as he or she performs the duties of the directorships. The director would be required to treat both companies equally, which might reduce his or her utility to both companies.[376] It has been recognised that one who is a director of two rival concerns is walking a tight-rope and is at risk if he fails to deal fairly with **10–094**

[374] As Brooke LJ pointed out, the *Mashonaland* case was a "startling" one, but the director there had never acted as a director of the claimant company nor attended a board meeting. As for the *In Plus Group* case, Lewison J in *Ultraframe (UK) Ltd v Fielding* [2006] F.S.R. 17 suggested that the "no conflict" principle applied only to the powers a director has, so that a director excluded from exercising powers, even if wrongfully, was no longer subject to the principle—and certainly not at the suit of those who excluded him.

[375] *Bristol and West Building Society v Mothew* [1998] Ch. 1 at 18, where Millett LJ describes what needs to happen. This is why, in most cases, consent to the initial double-engagement is typically only given where the two principals have interests which are aligned.

[376] For example, if the director came across a corporate opportunity, might he not have to offer it at the same time to both companies? Consent to acting as a director of competing companies would not of course involve consent to personal exploitation of any corporate opportunity the director might come across.

both.[377] However, it should be noted that the legal problem here arises not so much from the no-conflict rule as from the fact that, by becoming a director of two companies, the director owes a core duty of loyalty to each.

In practice, it is in fact rare for a director to act for competing companies, except in the very problematic case where the director forms a new company for the purpose of competing with the current company when, as he plans, he ceases to be associated with it. The tension then is to balance the freedom of individuals to exploit their talents after their association with a company ceases, and the obligations of fiduciary loyalty intended to protect the company from misuse of the company's business opportunities or trade secrets. The company cannot, of course, prevent the departing director from applying his acquired general (and non-confidential) knowledge and experience of the company's line of business and its markets for the benefit of his new employer. And, moreover, simply forming an intention to leave the company and compete with it, and indeed taking preparatory steps towards that end but without actually engaging in any competitive activity, has been held not to constitute any breach of the director's duty of loyalty, however much it may seem to be lacking in merit.[378] But actual competitive activity (such as recruiting the company's employees to work in the new business) will not only be a breach of the no-conflict rule, but the director's core duty of good faith and fidelity will require disclosure of this threat to the company's business to its board, even if it involves the director disclosing his or her own wrongdoing.[379] The rigour of the fiduciary principles is, however, somewhat abated in those cases where the resignation of the directors has been forced upon him or her and the director has not actively sought to seduce the company's customers away or to exploit an opportunity belonging to it.[380] Beyond that, the courts seem to have adopted rather pragmatic solutions based on common sense and the merits of the case. This is an area in which context is all. So in *Foster Bryant Surveying Ltd v Bryant*, Rix LJ summarised the existing cases as follows[381]:

---

377 See, per Lord Denning in *Scottish Co-op Wholesale Society v Meyer* [1959] A.C. 324 at 366–368. This concerned an application under what is now the unfair prejudice provisions (on which see Ch.14) but Lord Denning obviously had doubts about whether the *Mashonaland* case was still good law. See also *Bristol and West Building Society v Mothew* [1998] Ch. 1 at 18 (per Millett LJ); and *Global Energy Horizons Corp v Gray* [2012] EWHC 3703 (Ch), generally affirmed on appeal [2020] EWCA Civ 1668.

378 *Balston Ltd v Headline Filters Ltd* [1990] F.S.R. 385 at 412 (Falconer J); *Halcyon House Ltd v Baines* [2014] EWHC 2216 (QB).

379 *British Midland Tool Ltd v Midland International Tooling Ltd* [2003] 2 B.C.L.C. 523 at [77]–[92]; *CMS Dolphin Ltd v Simonet* [2001] 2 B.C.L.C. 704. On the "duty to disclose" see para.10–033. Also see *Allfiled UK Ltd v Eltis* [2015] EWHC 1300 (Ch); *Habro Supplies Ltd v Hampton* [2014] EWHC 1781 (Ch); *First Subsea Ltd v Balltec Ltd* [2014] EWHC 866 (Ch) (appealed unsuccessfully on limitation matters [2017] EWCA Civ 186).

380 *Foster Bryant Surveying Ltd v Bryant* [2007] 2 B.C.L.C. 239 (no breach of duty where a director, forced to resign, agreed during his notice period, and on the initiative of a major customer, to work for it after the notice ran out). The case contains a full discussion of the authorities. Also see *Allfiled UK Ltd v Eltis* [2015] EWHC 1300 (Ch); *Harbo Supplies Ltd v Hampton* [2014] EWHC 1781 (Ch); and *Towers v Premier Waste Management Ltd* [2011] EWCA Civ 923.

381 *Foster Bryant Surveying Ltd v Bryant* [2007] EWCA Civ 200; [2007] 2 B.C.L.C. 239 at [76]–[77].

> "At one extreme (*In Plus Group v Pyke*[382]) the defendant is director in name only. At the other extreme, the director has planned his resignation having in mind the destruction of his company or at least the exploitation of its property in the form of business opportunities in which he is currently involved (*IDC*,[383] *Canaero*,[384] *Simonet*,[385] *British Midland Tool*[386]). In the middle are more nuanced cases which go both ways: in *Shepherds Investments v Walters*[387] the combination of disloyalty, active promotion of the planned business, and exploitation of a business opportunity, all while the directors remained in office, brought liability; in *Umanna*,[388] *Balston*,[389] and *Framlington*,[390] however, where the resignations were unaccompanied by disloyalty, there was no liability." (Citations added.)

After resignation, however, the director will be able to compete freely subject to any contractual restraints, the law relating to trade secrets and the rules relating to conflicts which arose before resignation (see s.170(2)).

Multiple directorships

The law relating to multiple directorships of a non-competing type is basically as set out above, though obviously a directorship of another non-competing company creates a lesser conflict problem. Indeed, in the case of a non-executive director of a company (i.e. one who is not bound to devote all his time and efforts to the company) taking a non-executive directorship in another, non-competing company can be said not to raise a conflict issue at all. However, it is no doubt good practice to obtain the consent of each board to the position, and in the case of an executive director such consent would seem to be necessary. **10–095**

When conflicts of interest arise at a later date, for example, where the director is on the boards of two companies which are on opposite sides of a transaction, it is common for the director simply to withdraw from a role on the board of either company. Provided the articles make provision for this solution, the Act appears to relieve the director of liability in such a case, even liability arising under the core duty of loyalty.[391] In the absence of appropriate provisions in the articles, however, the director's position is precarious. If a person is a director of two non-competing companies but one makes a takeover bid for the other, how can the director discharge the core duty of loyalty to both in such a situation? Withdrawal may ensure equal treatment but can hardly be said to amount to a discharge of the duty to promote the success of the (each) company. In that situation, resignation from one of the involved companies may be the only possible step. However, where the conflict is less pressing, the strategy of withdrawal may seem appropriate.

---

382 *In Plus Group v Pyke* [2002] EWCA Civ 370; [2002] 2 B.C.L.C. 201.

383 *Industrial Development Consultants Ltd v Cooley* [1972] 1 W.L.R. 443.

384 *Canadian Aero Service Ltd v O'Malley* (1973) 40 D.L.R. (3d) 371.

385 *CMS Dolphin Ltd v Simonet* [2001] 2 B.C.L.C. 704.

386 *British Midland Tool Ltd v Midland International Tooling Ltd* [2003] 2 B.C.L.C. 523.

387 *Shepherds Investments v Walters* [2006] EWHC 836 (Ch).

388 *Island Export Finance Ltd v Umunna* [1986] B.C.L.C. 460.

389 *Balston Ltd v Headline Filters Ltd* [1990] F.S.R. 385.

390 *Framlington Group Plc v Anderson* [1995] 1 B.C.L.C. 475.

391 CA 2006 s.180(4)(b): general duties not infringed "where the company's articles contain provisions for dealing with conflicts of interest" and the director acts in accordance with them. Again, it will be interesting to see what types of provision are thought acceptable by the institutional shareholders in respect of listed companies.

Approval by the board

10–096 We now reach discussion of the second of the two principal issues arising under s.175. Assuming the impugned transaction does involve an unacceptable conflict, whose permission must the director obtain for personal exploitation of it? Section 175 introduces the possibility of board approval, supplementing the orthodox common law doctrine of shareholder approval which we discuss below in relation to directors' duties as a whole.[392] Previously the common law had never condoned mere board approval in these circumstances,[393] and its use by the statute in this way is a major innovation.

By virtue of s.175(4)(b), authorisation may be given by the board itself for a conflict of interest on the part of one of their number, so that no breach of duty is committed.[394] The conflicted director him- or herself is excluded in the calculation of the quorum needed for the directors' meeting at which authorisation is given, and the director's vote is disregarded in determining whether board approval has been given (s.175(6)). Any "interested" director is also similarly excluded, but when a director can be said to be interested in another director's authorisation to take a corporate opportunity is left to the courts to decide. Any other director participating in the opportunity would clearly be interested, but how far the concept of interest goes beyond that is not clear. Notably, if there is no authorisation in advance of the taking of the opportunity, subsequent ratification of the director's breach of duty by the company requires a decision of the shareholders.[395]

Nevertheless, it might be asked whether this is a wise innovation. On the one hand, a requirement of shareholder approval is a heavy one, and may deter directors from proceeding with courses of action which, if asked, shareholders would approve, thus imposing unnecessary restrictions on directors' entrepreneurial activities. On the other hand, the risk with board approval is that, although the approving directors may have no interest in the particular case, they may have an underlying interest in a culture of easy conflict approvals ("you scratch my back and I'll scratch yours"). No doubt, such conduct would be a breach of the other duties imposed on directors, discussed above, but such breaches may be difficult to detect and to prove in court.

---

392 See paras 10–111 onwards.

393 See *Benson v Heathorn* (1842) 1 Y. & C.C.C. 326 at 341–342 per Knight-Bruce VC; and *Imperial Mercantile Credit Association v Coleman* (1871) L.R. 6 Ch. App. 558 at 567–568 per Hatherley LC. As a matter of principle, however, it might be asked why the board, acting properly as the company (so with the conflicted directors undoubtedly excluded from voting), could not give such informed consent: see S. Worthington, "Corporate Governance: Remedying and Ratifying Directors' Breaches" (2000) 116 L.Q.R. 638. The statutory rule now adopts precisely this approach.

394 Nor is any transaction or arrangement with the company liable to be set aside on the grounds that the shareholders have not given their approval: s.180(1). This provision applies to conflicts of interest generally under s.175, although the present discussion relates to corporate opportunities.

395 Section 239(2)(a), on which see para.10–112. It is submitted that the standard use of the word "authorise" in company law is to refer to ex ante permission, whilst ratification refers to permission given after the breach. It is clear that the CLR's proposal, on which s.175 is based, contemplated the non-involved members of the board giving permission only in advance. See Final 1, p.346, cl. 6 where the phrase adopted is "the use [of the corporate opportunity] has been proposed to and authorised by the board".

It may be for this sort of reason that the statute allows, or requires, the company's constitution (notably the articles) to have some control over whether uninvolved directors can authorise conflicts of interest. In the case of private companies, the board can act as the authorising body unless something in the company's articles or other parts of its constitution restricts the board from so acting. In the case of public or charitable[396] companies, the company's constitution must positively empower the directors to act in this way, and the articles might (but need not) then regulate in further detail the scope or manner of exercise of the authorisation power. Compliance with the articles would in either case be a pre-condition for the valid exercise of the directors' powers of authorisation (s.178(5)). The more restrictive rule applied to public companies reflects a more protective instinct.[397] However, the statute, surprisingly, does not adopt a proposal of the CLR that board authorisations should be reported to the shareholders in the subsequent directors' report.[398] **10–097**

We shall see below that, in relation to shareholder approval, the common law developed a doctrine that certain breaches of duty are not capable of approval by the company, the case of *Cook v Deeks*[399] being a leading authority in this area. Does such a restriction apply to authorisation given by the independent members of the board? There is no mention of such a restriction in s.176 and, since independent board approval is an invention of the statute, it would seem that this limitation cannot be imported into the board's power of authorisation. Is this surprising? There are two controls over board authorisation which do not exist in relation to shareholder authorisation at common law. First, interested directors are excluded by the statute from voting on a board resolution, whereas at common law interested directors were seen as entitled to vote, both as directors on the board resolution and as shareholders to authorise the taking of a corporate opportunity (the modern statutory rule on shareholder voting is now different[400]). The exclusion of interested directors from voting might be thought to reduce the danger of biased corporate decisions or unfair treatment of minority shareholders, although it does not eliminate it. Secondly, the non-involved voting directors, unlike shareholders, are subject to fiduciary duties when exercising their votes. The core duty of loyalty requires directors to give priority to the promotion of the success of the company when deciding whether to authorise, for example, the taking of a corporate opportunity, though such a breach might be difficult to prove.[401]

Where the board does not have approval power (because it is explicitly removed by the articles in a private company, or not granted in a public or charitable company, or not practically possible because all the directors are

396 CA 2006 s.181(2)(b).

397 Of course, the provision may be inserted in the company's articles upon incorporation, but at least those who become its shareholders then know what they are letting themselves in for. In the case of subsequent amendments to the articles it will be interesting to see what sorts of board approval provisions institutional investors are prepared to accept in the articles of listed companies.

398 CLR, Final Report I, para.3.25.

399 *Cook v Deeks* [1916] 1 A.C. 554 PC.

400 In relation to ratification, s.239(3),(4) now excludes interested directors from voting as shareholders, but it seems they are still entitled to do so on authorisations. On ratification, see para.10–111.

401 cf. the discussion of *Regentcrest Plc v Cohen* [2001] 2 B.C.L.C. 80 in para.10–029.

conflicted), then approval will need to be obtained in accordance with any specific rules set out in the company's articles, or in accordance with the common law default rule which requires the approval of the shareholders in general meeting, as discussed below.

A conceptual issue: is there invariably a duty to report the "opportunity" to the company?

10–098 Section 175 is based on the existence of a conflict of duty and interest (or a conflict of duties).[402] In the area of corporate opportunity, this conflict arises because of the conflict between the interest of the director in personal exploitation of the opportunity and his or her duty to offer the opportunity to the company (or pursue it on behalf of the company). The duty to offer the opportunity to the company arises because it has been characterised as a corporate one: that is why the identification of the criteria for making the opportunity a corporate one is so central to this body of law, and why the uninhibited approach of the most recent cases seems questionable.[403]

However, one can ask, what is the nature of this duty? It is generally accepted that, if the director does not wish to exploit the opportunity personally, no breach of s.175 arises because there is then no personal interest conflicting with the director's duty to the company. In other words, a director who does nothing can never be found liable under s.175. Might the director, however, be liable for breach of some other duty, for example, the duty of care or good faith? In principle, this possibility exists. In the case of the core duty of loyalty the director would have to form the view that the promotion of the success of the company required the opportunity to be communicated to the company, and then fail to do so. The duty of care seems a more promising avenue of approach because it is based on an objective test. However, it would not necessarily be correct to infer from the existence of a duty for the purposes of the no-conflict rule a duty for the purposes of the duty of care. The courts have traditionally developed far more demanding standards of loyalty than of care and that approach may continue under the statute.[404]

---

[402] This notwithstanding that the wording of the section itself pitches the conflict as one between the director's and the company's *interests*, not the duty of one and the interests of the other. This, it is suggested, does not evince an intention to alter the underlying premises of the common law. Rather, the director's duty is seen to be to act in the interests of the company (at common law, or, under s.171, to act to promote the success of the company—see paras 10–026 onwards).

[403] See paras 10–084 to 10–091.

[404] It is difficult to believe that the directors in *Regal*, having concluded that the company could not finance the project, would have been held liable in negligence for not putting additional money of their own into the company so that it could take up the opportunity, whereas in *Cooley* it might be said that failing to follow up for the company an opportunity of the very type the director had been hired to pursue would seem to constitute a plausible case of negligence.

Remedies

The detail of the remedies available to the company for breach by directors of their duties to the company are dealt with later,[405] but it is useful at this stage to note their broad outline in relation to the conflicts cases, as their key characteristic differs fundamentally from the remedies so far encountered. For all breaches of directors' duties, if discovered at the planning stage, it is true that the court may be persuaded to order an injunction to prevent the plan being implemented. But, once the breach is committed, we have seen that by and large the remedy has been compensation to the company for the loss thereby caused, whether that compensation is assessed using common law or equitable rules (the former for the duty of care, it is suggested; the latter otherwise). **10–099**

The only exception so far has been with the self-dealing rule, where the orthodox remedy is rescission of the contract,[406] not compensation for loss or an account of profits.[407] In these cases, as with all the "no-conflict" duties here, the aim of the remedy is to strip the defaulting director of the benefits of his or her disloyal distraction from undeviating focus on the company's interests, but the courts have typically declined to value the contract between the company and the director, and have therefore required the remedy to be solely by way of putting the parties back into their pre-contracting status.

With the conflicts of interests cases just considered, however, this difficult valuation problem does not arise. Where the conflict arises not from any self-dealing, but typically from the director's misuse of the company's property, information or opportunity, then, too, the remedy aims to strip the defaulting fiduciary of the profits of his or her disloyal activities. If the disloyal venture is not profitable, then it follows that the company does not have a remedy under this head; if it is profitable, the director must account for the profit. This seems straightforward. The point to note, however, is that the focus of these no-conflict remedies is profit-stripping; the company is not entitled, under this head, to recover losses: to recover those, the company must, and very often can on the same facts, sue its disloyal fiduciary for some other failure, be it failure to act within powers, or breach of the duty of good faith or care and skill, provided it can prove the elements of those quite different claims.[408]

---

[405] See paras 10–103 to 10–110.

[406] With all the limitations inherent in that option if the company is no longer able to return the property acquired from the director. We noted earlier that the option of "pecuniary rescission", which, while requiring the court to value the assets transferred, might enable better justice to be done between the parties. This is, effectively, what the statute allows in those cases governed by statutory provisions. Indeed, where the statute has intervened, the remedies are both more varied and more extensive. See paras 10–072 and 10–079.

[407] Unless the facts allow reliance on the statutory remedies: see paras 10–072 and 10–079.

[408] For example, if the director has diverted the company's property into a loss-making conflicting opportunity, then there will be no account of profits for breach of the conflict rule (there are no profits), but the director may be compelled to restore the company's property which has been used in an unauthorised fashion, or to compensate the company for its negligent or unfaithful use.

POLITICAL DONATIONS AND EXPENDITURE

10–100 It may be convenient here to deal briefly with a final situation where shareholder approval of directors' acts is required, namely for political donations and expenditure. These provisions are to be found in Pt 14 of the CA 2006, rather than Pt 10, although they can be presented as aiming to control a potential conflict of interest. That conflict is between the personal interests of the directors in promoting a particular political party and the interests of the shareholders as a body in not having corporate assets spent in ways which do not help to promote the success of the company. Of course, the provisions also have a wider constitutional significance, which is not a concern for this book, especially in the light of the long-standing regulation of the use by trade unions of their funds for political purposes.[409] What is required is not shareholder approval of a particular transaction, but shareholder approval of a company policy. The shareholder resolution approving political expenditure "must be expressed in general terms" and in fact "must not purport to authorise particular donations or expenditure".[410] If passed, the resolution has effect for four years, though the articles may impose a shorter period.[411]

The CA 2006 requires an authorising resolution for (1) corporate donations to political parties registered under the relevant legislation, to other political organisations and to independent candidates[412]; and (2) other political expenditure.[413] The latter is expenditure of a promotional type and other corporate activities which are "capable of being reasonably regarded as intended to affect public support for a political party or other political organisation",[414] even though there is no direct donation to a political party. A resolution is required of the shareholders (by ordinary resolution unless the articles impose a higher standard) in the case of a free-standing company; and of the shareholders of the (ultimate) holding company as well if the company is part of a group. However, in a group situation some relief is provided from the need to obtain multiple authorisations in that a resolution is not required of the company itself if it is a wholly-owned subsidiary.[415] There is one exception to this relief: even a wholly-owned subsidiary requires a resolution of its shareholders, if the parent company is not "UK registered", i.e. registered under the Act or any of its predecessors.[416] This is because a holding company which is not UK registered is not required to pass a resolution conferring approval on the political expenditure of its UK subsidiaries,

---

409 See now the Trade Union and Labour Relations (Consolidation) Act 1992 Part I Ch.VI.

410 CA 2006 s.367(5).

411 CA 2006 s.368.

412 CA 2006 s.364. A donation to the political fund of a trade union is included, but not any other type of donation to a union: s.374.

413 CA 2006 s.366. There is an exemption for small donations (no more than £5,000 over any period of 12 months): s.378.

414 CA 2006 s.365. Also included is expenditure on activity designed to influence voters' attitudes in referendums.

415 CA 2006 s.366(3)–(4). Provision is made for a single resolution to be passed in groups of companies, for example, covering donations by a holding company and any of its subsidiaries (even where those subsidiaries change during the period of the validity of the resolution): s.367(1), (2), (4), (7).

416 CA 2006 ss.1158 and 1.

so that, in such a case, the obligation on the wholly-owned subsidiary revives.[417] This may often be a rather pointless formality, but at least it will require the directors of the UK subsidiary to explain to the foreign parent the provisions of the Act on political donations.

The resolution may give authority for political expenditure generally or confine it to one or more of the following: donations to political parties and independent candidates, donations to other political organisations and political expenditure. In any event, the resolution must set a monetary limit for the expenditures during the period to which it applies.[418]

Where a free-standing company makes a political payment or incurs expenditure without the required shareholder approval, the directors of the company making the payment will be jointly and severally liable to restore to the company the expenditure (with interest) and to compensate the company for any loss or damage it has suffered in consequence, though this second head of loss might be difficult to show.[419] The liability provisions of Pt 14 also extend to shadow directors.[420] Where the company in default is a subsidiary, the directors of the ultimate UK holding company will also be liable (to the subsidiary) but only if they failed to take all reasonable steps to prevent the breach by the subsidiary.[421]

There is anecdotal evidence that the effect of these provisions of the Act (introduced in 2000) has been to persuade the directors of many companies not to make political donations from corporate funds, rather than to seek to shareholder approval to do so. Of course, wealthy business figures make large donations to political parties, but do so out of their personal wealth, which may be derived from the activities of businesses they control.

DUTY NOT TO ACCEPT BENEFITS FROM THIRD PARTIES: S.176

The scope of s.176

Section 176 provides that a director "must not accept a benefit from a third party conferred by reason of (a) his being a director, or (b) his doing (or not doing) anything as a director".[422] A "third party" means a person other than the company, an associated body corporate or a person acting on behalf of such companies. The connection of this rule with the no-conflict principle is underlined by the provision that the duty is not infringed if the benefit "cannot reasonably be regarded as likely to give rise to a conflict of interest" 10–101

[417] CA 2006 s.366(4)(b). The CA 1985 had a series of more complex provisions attempting to deal with non-UK holding and subsidiary companies, but these have been abandoned.

[418] CA 2006 s.367(3), (6).

[419] CA 2006 s.369(1), (2), (3). If the donation is repaid by the recipient, presumably the first head of loss falls away. This was made explicit under the previous law.

[420] CA 2006.379(1).

[421] CA 2006 s.369(3)(b), (4).

[422] Benefits from associated companies are excluded as are benefits received by the director from a company which supplies his or her services to the company: s.177(2)–(3).

(s.176(3)).[423] This being so, it may be wondered what the purpose of s.176 is, for could not the situations it deals with be handled under the general no-conflict section (s.175)? The answer, and it is an important one, is that there is no provision in s.176 for authorisation to be given by uninvolved directors for the receipt of third-party benefits. The risk of such benefits distorting the proper performance of a director's duties is so high that it is rightly thought to be proper to require authorisation from the shareholders in general meeting (even though that turns the rule into a near-ban on the receipt of third-party benefits). Although the point is not expressly dealt with in s.176, the availability at common law of shareholder authorisation is preserved by s.180(4)(a).[424] Finally, the fact that s.175 applies to a situation does not prevent s.176 being relied upon as well, i.e. the sections are cumulative rather than mutually exclusive in their operation.[425]

The common law termed such payments "bribes", although that seems a misnomer as it is enough at common law that there has been the payment of money or the conferment of another benefit upon an agent whom the payer knows is acting as an agent for a principal in circumstances where the payment has not been disclosed to the principal.[426] There is no need to show that the payer of the bribe acted with a corrupt motive; that the agent's mind was actually affected by the bribe; that the payer knew or suspected that the agent would conceal the payment from the principal; or that the principal suffered any loss or that the transaction was in some way unfair. None of these matters seem to be requirements of s.176 either. Thus, the term "third party benefits" is more appropriate than the term "bribe".

On the other hand, so far as true bribes are concerned, enormous changes have been introduced by the Bribery Act 2010, as we have seen. This Act was designed to bring the UK in line with international norms on anti-corruption legislation. It makes it a criminal offence to give or receive a bribe, but, most significantly, it also introduces a corporate offence of failing to prevent bribery.[427]

Remedies

10–102 At common law the remedies available in the case of third party benefits were extensive. These common law remedies, so far as they give the company remedies against the defaulting director, continue to apply by virtue of s.178, despite the change of nomenclature in s.176. Although that section imposes a duty only on the director, the common law also imposed obligations on (and

[423] This might be contrasted with the predominant view under the earlier common law rules that the "no profit" rule (which would catch such benefits) did not necessarily involve a conflict of duty and interest, although of course in practice it very often might: see the earlier discussion of *Regal (Hastings) Ltd v Gulliver* at para.10–083.

[424] "The general duties have effect subject to any rule of law enabling the company to give authority for anything to be done by the directors that would otherwise be a breach of duty."

[425] "Except as otherwise provided, more than one of the general duties may apply": s.179.

[426] *Industries and General Mortgage Co Ltd v Lewis* [1949] 2 All E.R. 573 KBD; *Taylor v Walker* [1958] 1 Lloyd's Rep. 490 QBD; *Logicrose Ltd v Southend United FC Ltd* [1988] 1 W.L.R. 1256; *Pullan v Wilson* [2014] EWHC 126 (Ch); [2014] W.T.L.R. 669; *FHR European Ventures LLP v Cedar Capital Partners LLC* [2015] A.C. 250; *Parr v Keystone Healthcare Ltd* [2019] EWCA Civ 1246.

[427] See para.8–047.

provided remedies against) the third party, and these are presumably unaffected. Thus, where such a benefit has been paid to a director, the company may rescind the contract between it and the third party (provided the third party knew the recipient was a director of the company), and it matters not whether the payer is the third party or the third party's agent.[428] In addition, or instead, both the third party and the director are jointly and severally liable in damages in fraud to the company, the amount of the recovery depending upon proof of actual loss.[429] Alternatively, the company may hold both the director and the third party jointly and severally liable to pay the amount of the benefit to the company as money had and received to its use, this liability being naturally not dependent upon proof of loss. Against the director, such a personal liability to account is straightforward: the bribe is akin to a secret profit made out the director's position. Against the third party it is a rather peculiar remedy, though one which seems to be established.[430] However, the company must choose between the remedies of damages and account, the choice no doubt depending on the amount of the provable loss which the company suffered as a result of the bribe, though it need not do so until judgment.[431]

In *Attorney-General for Hong Kong v Reid*,[432] the Privy Council took the further step of recognising a proprietary remedy by way of a constructive trust in favour of the company (or other principal) against the director (or other agent) in respect of the bribe. The significance of this remedy being available, in addition to the personal remedy to account, is that the company may then make further tracing claims to any investment profits made by the defaulting director through the use of the original benefit (whilst falling back on the personal claim if the investment has been unprofitable); the company may also follow the benefit (and its traceable substitutes) into the hands of third parties who are not bona fide purchaser for value; and, importantly, all these proprietary claims will prevail over the claims of the unsecured creditors in the event of the director's (or the third party's) insolvency. After a great deal of academic and judicial debate, the

[428] *Taylor v Walker* [1958] 1 Lloyd's Rep. 490; *Shipway v Broadwood* [1899] 1 Q.B. 369 CA. There is not space here to explore the complications which may arise when the payer is also the director of a company and makes unauthorised use of that company's assets to effect the bribe. See also *Airbus Operations Ltd v Withey* [2014] EWHC 1126 (QB) in relation to the position of employees.

[429] *Mahesan v Malaysia Government Officers' Co-operative Housing Society Ltd* [1979] A.C. 374 pC at 381. The cause of action appears to lie in fraud.

[430] *Mahesan v Malaysia Government Officers' Co-operative Housing Society Ltd* [1979] A.C. 374 at 383.

[431] *Mahesan v Malaysia Government Officers' Co-operative Housing Society Ltd* [1979] A.C. 374; and *United Australia Ltd v Barclays Bank Ltd* [1941] A.C. 1 HL. Where the briber is or acts on behalf of a supplier, the damages are unlikely to be less than the amount of the bribe, but could be more.

[432] *Attorney-General for Hong Kong v Reid* [1994] 1 A.C. 324 PC; declining to follow *Metropolitan Bank v Heiron* (1880) 5 Ex. D. 319 CA; and *Lister & Co v Stubbs* (1890) 45 Ch. D. 1 CA. The decision was controversial among academic writers but was mostly followed by the courts, although see *Sinclair Investments (UK) Ltd v Versailles Trade Finance Ltd (In Administrative Receivership)* [2011] EWCA Civ 347. See the judgment of Lawrence Collins J in *Daraydan International Ltd v Solland International Ltd* [2004] EWHC 622 (Ch); [2005] Ch. 119; *Sinclair Investments* (ibid.); and *FHR European Ventures LLP v Cedar Capital Partners LLC* [2014] Ch. 1; affirmed [2015] A.C. 250 for a review of both the subsequent court decisions and the academic writings. Now see para.10–109.

Privy Council's conclusions in this case were confirmed by the Supreme Court in *FHR European Ventures LLP v Cedar Capital Partners LLC*,[433] as discussed in more detail below.[434]

REMEDIES FOR BREACH OF DUTY

10–103 As we have already noted, although there is a statutory statement of the general duties owed by directors, the remedies for breach of these duties are not similarly stated. Rather, s.178 simply provides that "the consequences of a breach (or threatened breach) of ss.171–177 are the same as would apply if the corresponding common law rule or equitable duty applied"; and that the duties contained in the sections (other than s.174) are "enforceable in the same way as any other fiduciary duty owed to a company by its directors". It should be noted that s.178 applies only to the general duties laid out in ss.171–177, not to the provisions to be found in Ch.3 of Pt 10 dealing with disclosure of interests in existing transactions (for which the statute provides only criminal sanctions)[435]; nor to the provisions contained in Chs 4 or 4A of Pt 10, requiring shareholder approval for certain transactions with directors, for which a self-contained statutory civil code of remedies is provided.[436] It should also be noted that the second proposition in s.178 is not applied to the duty to exercise reasonable care, skill and diligence, in line with the modern view that this is not a fiduciary duty. The remedy for that breach is normally confined to damages.[437]

We have sought to indicate the principal remedies available for each of the duties as we have gone along. Nevertheless, it may be useful to bring them together here, since it is important to appreciate both the areas of overlap and the areas of difference. The principal remedies available are: (a) declaration or injunctions; (b) damages or compensation; (c) restoration of the company's property; (d) rescission of the contract; (e) account of profits; and (f) summary dismissal.

(a) Declaration or injunction

10–104 A declaration is simply an order that a particular state of affairs (i.e. particular rights and obligations) exists, and can be enormously useful as a remedy: e.g. a declaration that X is shadow director, or that Y holds certain assets on constructive trust, or that decision Z was made for improper purposes or beyond powers. Such a declaration can indicate what ought to be done by the parties, and what further orders might be made, either immediately or after a trial of the related issues. Injunctions are primarily employed where the breach is threatened but has not yet occurred.[438] If action can be taken in time, this is obviously the most satisfactory course: an injunction can be ordered to prevent the threatened

433 *FHR European Ventures LLP v Cedar Capital Partners LLC* [2015] A.C. 250.

434 See para.10–109.

435 See para.10–065.

436 See paras 10–072 to 10–073 and 10–079. Also see 11–016 onwards.

437 See para.10–050.

438 *United Pan-Europe Communications NV v Deutsche Bank AG* [2000] 2 B.C.L.C. 461 CA.

breach. However, this is not possible unless those minded to take action are aware of the threat, and in all but the smallest companies that will not often be the case. An injunction may also be appropriate where the breach has already occurred but is likely to continue, or if some of its consequences can thereby be avoided.[439]

(b) Damages or compensation

Damages are the appropriate remedy for breach of a common law duty of care, or non-compliance with the terms of the director's contract or the company's constitution: this remedy seeks to repair the harm suffered by the *company* as a result of the wrong. Equitable compensation is the analogous equitable remedy for breach of the now statutory but originally equitable duty of good faith (acting to promote the success of the company) or acting for improper purposes[440]: this remedy seeks to repair losses to the company's *assets* suffered as a result of the wrong.[441] As discussed next, the means of achieving this has generated heated academic controversy.[442] Both are inevitably personal remedies. All the directors who participate in the breach[443] are jointly and severally liable with the usual rights of contribution inter se.[444] **10–105**

(c) Equitable compensation: "restoration" of property

Although the directors are not trustees of the company's property (which is held by the company itself as a separate legal person), we have noted at a number of points in this chapter that the courts sometimes treat directors as if they were such trustees. In particular, where a director disposes of the company's property in unauthorised ways, and in consequence the company's property comes into his or her own hands, the director will be treated as a constructive trustee of the property for the company.[445] This means that the property, or its proceeds, can be recovered by way of proprietary claim against the director, so far as traceable[446]; **10–106**

439 For example, to enjoin the delivery up of confidential documents improperly taken away by a former director: *Measures Bros v Measures* [1910] 2 Ch. 248 CA; *Cranleigh Precision Engineering Ltd v Bryant* [1965] 1 W.L.R. 1293; *Allfiled UK Ltd v Ellis* [2015] EWHC 1300 (Ch).

440 Although often when actions are for improper purposes, the remedy is a declaration to that effect and an order that the decision be taken again, properly this time, by the appropriate body.

441 See *AIB Group (UK) Plc v Mark Redler & Co Solicitors* [2014] UKSC 58; [2015] A.C. 1503, especially at [47]–[77] (Lord Toulson JSC) and [90]–[138] (Lord Reed JSC); and *Libertarian Investment Ltd v Hall* (2013) 16 HKCFAR 681 Hong Kong Court of Final Appeal at [84]–[96] (Ribeiro PJ) and [166]–[175] (Lord Millett NPJ).

442 See the paragraph immediately following.

443 Either actively or by subsequent acquiescence in it: *Re Lands Allotment Co* [1894] 1 Ch. 616 CA. Merely protesting will not necessarily disprove acquiescence: *Joint Stock Discount Co v Brown* (1869) L.R. 8 Eq. 381 Ct of Chancery.

444 Civil Liability (Contribution) Act 1978. The application of the principle of joint and several liability is discussed more fully at para.23–032 in relation to auditors.

445 *JJ Harrison (Properties) Ltd v Harrison* [2002] 1 B.C.L.C. 162. For an early recognition of the principle see *Re Forest of Dean Coal Co* (1878) 10 Ch. D. 450 Ch D.

446 For discussion on the use of the tracing remedy, see *Relfo Ltd (In Liquidation) v Varsani* [2014] EWCA Civ 360 CA; [2015] 1 B.C.L.C. 14; *FHR European Ventures LLP v Mankarious* [2016] EWHC 359 (Ch).

and that the company's claim against its defaulting director will have priority over any competing claims of the director's unsecured creditors (since the property is the company's property, not the director's). The doctrinal underpinnings of these conclusions are rarely unpicked, but they must surely rely more on analysing the claim as a profitable breach of the conflicts rules (the conflict being obvious),[447] for which proprietary disgorgement of the gains is available,[448] rather than analysing the claim as merely an unauthorised (and therefore potentially void) contract and indeed one where the identity of the counterparty is irrelevant.[449] Where these proprietary disgorgement claims are available against the defaulting directors, they can be enormously valuable to the company.

Alternatively, if the director no longer has the company's assets or their traceable proceeds, or if their use did not generate a profit, or if the company's assets were initially, and without authority, paid away to third parties rather than to the director,[450] then the company may, in the alternative, sue the director for compensation (equitable compensation) for the losses suffered as a result of the director's initial unauthorised disposition of the company's property. One aspect of this is straightforward: the remedy is necessarily personal, and so the company's claim against its defaulting director will rank equally with the claims of the directors' general creditors.

But beyond that, this remedy has proved enormously controversial. It was long argued that the claim in issue was for "restoration of property" (albeit in money), and not for compensation. This had the enormous advantage, so it was said, that the claim was not dependent upon proof of loss on the part of the company, as a damages claim would be.[451] It was further suggested that it then followed that if, for example, £1 million was paid out by the director in the unauthorised purchase of X when it should have been paid out in the authorised purchase of Y,[452] then the appropriate remedy was effectively for the director to restore to the company the misappropriated £1 million.[453] By contrast, if the remedy were simply compensation, then the director would be required to restore to the company what the company *should* have had absent the breach, i.e. Y, if possible, or the

---

447 Whether under s.177 (if the director has contracted with the company) or under s.175 (if not).

448 See para.10–061 (where the self-dealing transaction is voidable); and paras 10–099 and 10–108 to 10–109 (on accounting for gains derived from other unauthorised conflicts).

449 See, e.g. the void remuneration contract in *Guinness v Saunders* [1990] 2 A.C. 662. Although the proprietary nature of the remedy was not in issue (there being no insolvency risk), *Westdeutsche Landesbank Girozentrale v Islington LBC* [1996] A.C. 669, is authority for it being unavailable to reverse a void contract, at least where the defendant is not a fiduciary. The argument is far easier in trusts cases: see *Foskett v McKeown* [2001] 1 A.C. 102 HL, where the proprietary claim to stolen trust funds and their investment proceeds was considered to be "part of our law of property" (Lord Millett), not dependent on either unjust enrichment (the HL holding so explicitly) or on fiduciary disloyalty (implicitly, as the suggestion was not raised).

450 The company may also have claims against the third parties: see para.10–130.

451 The cases typically cited are *Bishopsgate Investment Management Ltd (In Liquidation) v Maxwell (No.1)* [1993] B.C.C. 120 CA (Civ Div) at 140 (Hoffmann LJ); *Bairstow v Queens Moat Houses Plc* [2002] B.C.C. 91 at [49]–[54] (Robert Walker LJ); *Re Loquitur* [2003] S.T.C. 1394 at [135]–[137] (Etherton J); *Revenue and Customs Commissioners v Holland*; sub nom. *Re Paycheck Services 3 Ltd* [2011] B.C.C. 1 at [96]–[98] (Rimer LJ) and at [46], [48], [49] (Lord Hope).

452 Or, alternatively, should have been retained by the company as part of its own assets.

453 Less an allowance for the value of X, being the benefit the company did receive.

monetary value of Y.[454] Moreover, this former claim to a "restoration" remedy was regarded as being available in addition to, and by way of an alternative option to, the usual compensation remedy. The effect was thus to enable a company to claim *either* £1 million (adjusted for what had in fact been received, as noted above) if the authorised investment had crashed, *or* Y (or, more accurately, it or its value, again adjusted) if the proper investment was a winner. This gave the company a "heads I win, tails you lose" remedial menu.

In fact few cases went so far, and we seem now to have reached the preferable and far more defensible position that a choice between "£1 million" or "Y" is only available when the recipient of the £1 million is the defaulting director him- or herself. In these circumstances, the claim to the £1 million is better viewed as *not* for "restoration" as a self-standing option, but as a claim for disgorgement made out under one or other of the various conflicts rules. Otherwise, however, the company's claim is merely one for compensation, and—equitable or otherwise—this compensation is directed solely at reversing loss, not at some sort of free-standing "restoration" where no loss (or some far smaller loss) has been suffered.[455]

This approach also supports the practice of enabling the company to recover dividends and other distributions paid out by directors without authority. In this context, the director is typically held liable for the entire sum paid out without authority.[456] However, in cases where it can be shown that a smaller sum could legitimately have been paid out (e.g. by way of lawful dividend), then the court may be persuaded to exercise its discretion under s.1175 to relieve the director from liability for that permissible sum, but only where that would not leave those funds in the director's hands at the expense of third parties with claims against the company.[457]

---

454 Again with the company giving allowance for what it had in fact received, being the value of X.

455 See the detailed analyses in *Libertarian Investment Ltd v Hall* (2013) 16 HKCFAR 681 Hong Kong Court of Final Appeal at [84]–[96] (Ribeiro PJ) and [166]–[175] (Lord Millett NPJ); and *AIB Group (UK) Plc v Mark Redler & Co Solicitors* [2014] UKSC 58; [2015] A.C. 1503 at [47]–[77] (Lord Toulson JSC) and [90]–[138] (Lord Reed JSC). Also see *HLC Environmental Projects Ltd* [2013] EWHC 2876 (Ch) at [136]–[145]; *Madoff Securities International Ltd v Raven* [2013] EWHC 3147 (Comm) at [292]–[293], [296]–[306]; but also see the more difficult case of *Auden McKenzie (Pharma Division) Ltd v Patel* [2019] EWCA Civ 2291, noted in S. Worthington, "More Disquiet with Equitable Compensation" [2020] C.L.J. 220.

456 This may at first sight seem inconsistent with the "£1 million or Y" discussion in the preceding paragraphs, since here £1 million has been paid out by way of unlawful dividends (for example), and yet the director is held liable repay £1 million to the company, not "Y". But this is because in these circumstances there is no defined "Y": the director is not permitted to distribute unlawful dividends, but there is no *obligation*—no *duty*—to use those funds for some other end (e.g. the purchase of "Y"). This is what makes *Auden McKenzie (Pharma Division) Ltd v Patel* (see previous fn) so difficult. In dismissing a strike out claim, the court was prepared to condone the argument that an unlawful disposition need not be repaid because these funds *might* have been distributed to the same parties lawfully, so there was no loss to the company. The fact that something could have been done legally, but was not, does not excuse the defendant from liability: see (in a disgorgement context) *Murad v Al-Saraj* [2005] EWCA Civ 959 (at para.10–108).

457 As discussed in para.18–012 and illustrated by the outcome in *LRH Services Ltd (In Liquidation) v Trew* [2018] EWHC 600 (Ch) at [195]–[196].

(d) Avoidance of contracts

10–107 An agreement between the director and the company that breaches the no-conflict rules may be avoided, provided that the company has done nothing to indicate an intention to ratify the agreement after finding out about the breach of duty,[458] that restitutio in integrum is possible,[459] and that the rights of bona fide third parties have not supervened.[460] It might now be doubted how strong a bar restitutio in integrum really is, given the wide powers the court has to order financial adjustments when directing rescission.[461]

Equally, a contract entered into by the company in breach of the directors' duties to exercise their powers for a proper purpose is in principle avoidable by the company, but again subject to the considerations noted above and the rights of good faith third parties.[462] Where, however, the directors have simply acted without power or authority, the contract will be void, not voidable, unless the counterparty can rely on the directors having ostensible authority or deemed authority under the provisions of CA 2006.[463]

(e) Accounting for profits: disgorgement of disloyal gains

10–108 This liability arises as a response to profitable contracts or arrangements between the director and a third party which are held to be in breach of the conflict of interest rules[464] or the duty not to accept benefits from third parties.[465] In such

[458] *Lagunas Nitrate Co v Lagunas Syndicate* [1899] 2 Ch. 392 CA, a case concerning promoters' liability, but the operative principles are the same. The right to rescind will be lost if the company elects not to rescind or is too late to do so: *Re Ambrose Lake Tin Co* (1880) 11 Ch. D. 390 CA; *Re Cape Breton Co* (1885) 29 Ch. D. 795 CA (affirmed sub nom. *Cavendish Bentinck v Fenn* (1887) 12 App. Cas. 652 HL); *Ladywell Mining Co v Brookes* (1887) 35 Ch. D. 400 CA; *Gluckstein v Barnes* [1900] A.C. 240 HL; *Re Lady Forrest (Murchison) Gold Mine* [1901] 1 Ch. 582; *Burland v Earle* [1902] A.C. 83 PC; *Jacobus Marler v Marler* (1913) 85 L.J.P.C. 167n; *Hely-Hutchinson v Brayhead Ltd* [1968] 1 Q.B. 549; *Salt v Stratstone Specialist Ltd t/a Stratstone Cadillac Newcastle* [2015] EWCA Civ 745.

[459] *Erlanger v New Sombrero Phosphate Co* (1878) 3 App. Cas. 1218 HL at 1278 (Lord Blackburn); *Bentinck v Fenn* (1887) 12 App. Cas. 652 HL, where rescission was not possible because the company had already re-sold the properties.

[460] *Transvaal Lands Co v New Belgium (Transvaal) Land & Development Co* [1914] 2 Ch. 488 CA.

[461] This is certainly the case when fraud is involved and perhaps even when it is not: *Erlanger v New Sombrero Phosphate Co* (1873) 3 App. Cas. 1218; *Spence v Crawford* [1939] 3 All E.R. 271 HL; *Armstrong v Jackson* [1917] 2 K.B. 822; *O'Sullivan v Management Agency and Music Ltd* [1985] Q.B. 428 CA; *Salt v Stratstone Specialist Ltd t/a Stratstone Cadillac Newcastle* [2015] EWCA Civ 745.

[462] *Hogg v Cramphorn* [1967] Ch. 254; *Bamford v Bamford* [1970] Ch. 212; *Criterion Properties Plc v Stratford UK Properties LLC* [2003] B.C.C. 50.

[463] *Guinness Plc v Saunders* [1990] 2 A.C. 663. A void contract is much more threatening to the position of third parties, though in the case of third parties contracting with companies the provisions of s.40 and ostensible authority may save the day: see Ch.8.

[464] For example, in relation to the use of corporate information or opportunity discussed at paras 10–081 onwards.

[465] See the "bribe" cases at para.10–101, and also the secret/undisclosed commission case of *Imperial Mercantile Credit Association v Coleman* (1873) L.R. 6 H.L. 189, where the defaulting director proposed to the company a contract from the execution of which he stood to derive a secondary undisclosed profit. Also see *Airbus Operations Ltd v Withey* [2014] EWHC 1126 (QB).

cases there can be no question of rescinding the contract at the instance of the company, since the company is not party to it, and an account of profits to strip the defaulting fiduciary of any benefits will be the sole remedy.

As we have seen, recovery of the profit by the company is not conditional on proof of any loss suffered by the company; the profit is recoverable not as damages or compensation but because the company is entitled to call upon the disloyal director to account to it.[466] All the profits made by the director[467] and *attributable*[468] to the breach must be disgorged, but not those attributable to other sources.[469] This is sometimes ameliorated in the case of trustees, but only where their bona fides are not in question; then the courts have sometimes permitted the trustee an "allowance" in the accounting process to provide a reasonable remuneration (including a profit element) for the work carried out in effecting the profitable deal.[470] However, beyond such an allowance (if permitted), the mere fact that the director could have made the same profit without breaching his or her duty[471] or that the company, if asked, would have given its consent to the director's activities,[472] is irrelevant.

---

[466] *Murad v Al-Saraj* [2005] EWCA Civ 959.

[467] In general the director is not jointly liable for profits made by others (e.g. the company with which the director is associated, although such third parties may themselves have secondary liability, see para.10–130): *Regal (Hastings) Ltd v Gulliver* [1967] 2 A.C. 134; *Ultraframe (UK) Ltd v Fielding* [2006] F.S.R. 17 at [1550]–[1576], cf. *CMS Dolphin Ltd v Simonet* [2001] 2 B.C.L.C. 704; *Clegg v Pache (Deceased)* [2017] EWCA Civ 256 (if the director is the 100% owner, then the starting point is that the nominee will have the relevant knowledge and must disgorge 100% of the profits made). By contrast, a director may be jointly liable for the whole of the profits made by his partnership as a result of his breach: *Imperial Mercantile Credit Association v Coleman* (1873) L.R. 6 H.L. 189. Also see *Airbus Operations Ltd v Withey* [2014] EWHC 1126 (QB) at [451]–[465]; and *Northampton Regional Livestock Centre Co Ltd v Cowling* [2015] EWCA Civ 651 CA.

[468] Note that the test is not one of "causation", but whether the profits were generated "within the scope" of the directors' conduct that was in breach of fiduciary duty: *Gray v Global Energy Horizons Corporation* [2020] EWCA Civ 1668 at [126], [128].

[469] This can sometimes raise nice questions: *Murad v Al-Saraj* [2005] EWCA Civ 959; *Warman International Ltd v Dwyer* (1995) 182 C.L.R. 544 Aust. HC (account of profits limited to first two years of operation of diverted business opportunity). Notice, too, the argument that the test may either *be* different, or at least have different outcomes, when applied to a third party "dishonest assistant" rather than a director/fiduciary: *Novoship (UK) Ltd v Mikhaylyuk* [2014] EWCA Civ 908; [2015] Q.B. 499 at [111]–[115].

[470] *Boardman v Phipps* [1967] 2 A.C. 46; *O'Sullivan v Management Agency and Music Ltd* [1985] Q.B. 428. In *Guinness v Saunders* [1990] 2 A.C. 663 at 693–694 their lordships were very reluctant to entertain the possibility of an allowance for work done, for good reasons, but in the event the action was not decided as a breach of the conflict rules, but as a contract not properly authorised according to the terms of the articles, so the defaulting director was required to return the company's property, not account for profits made. See fn.261. The same hard line was taken in *Quarter Master UK Ltd v Pyke* [2004] EWHC 1815 (Ch); [2005] 1 B.C.L.C. 245 at [76]–[77]; and in *Gray v Global Energy Horizons Corporation* [2020] EWCA Civ 1668, noting at [209]–[217] that an allowance would be granted only in exceptional circumstances, although distinguishing at [230] the deduction of expenses actually incurred in generating the profits, which was not discretionary but was an essential step in determining the profits actually made. The relevant law is summarised in *Davies v Ford* [2020] EWHC 686 (Ch) at [394]–[404].

[471] *Murad v Al-Saraj* [2005] EWCA Civ 959 at [67] (Arden LJ).

[472] *Regal (Hastings) Ltd v Gulliver* [1967] 2 A.C. 134 at 150 (Lord Russell); *Murad v Al-Saraj* [2005] EWCA Civ 959 at [71] (Arden LJ).

10–109 Moreover, if the disloyal gain is identifiable in the director's hands, then the director will hold that asset on constructive trust for the company; in short, the disgorgement remedy is proprietary.[473] This conclusion has been confirmed in England only relatively recently,[474] even though it has long been the position in other common law jurisdictions.[475] In those jurisdictions, however, the courts claim to have a discretion as to whether or not to award a constructive trust on the facts before the court: they have what is described as a "remedial constructive trust", while the English courts insist that the constructive trust is "institutional" only, so that if the facts support its existence then there is not discretion in the court to deny it to a successful claimant. This latter approach seems preferable, and indeed the practice in other jurisdictions—despite their asserted flexibility—is overwhelmingly the same. The constructive trust, being proprietary, carries with it significant advantages.[476] There seems little merit in asserting that these follow from the wrong, and then denying the claimant their benefits, usually just when they are most needed.[477]

All of this is now uncontroversial. But a note of controversy has been raised by a recent Court of Appeal decision which marries breach of the "duty to disclose",[478] typically generating compensation remedies, with the disgorgement remedy available for breach of the various duties to avoid conflicts of duty and interest, in a way that tests the foundations of both. In *Parr v Keystone Healthcare Ltd*,[479] P had been a director of K, and in that role had committed various breaches of fiduciary duty for which K had successfully sought remedies. The difficult issue arose over the price P had received for the sale of his shares in K. The company's articles and the shareholder agreement between P and W (the majority shareholders) included a "bad leaver" provision: in the event of certain defaults by P—including those he had committed—either K or W were entitled to purchase P's shares at a 50% discount on a fair valuation. In ignorance of P's breaches (and indeed with P warranting, falsely given the fiduciary breaches, that there was no outstanding liability to K), W purchased P's shares at full market price through a nominee, H. In short, W, through H, had paid double what needed to be paid for the shares. However, instead of W (or H) seeking remedies under

[473] *FHR European Ventures LLP v Cedar Capital Partners LLC* [2015] A.C. 250. Applying this analysis, see *FHR European Ventures LLP v Mankarious* [2016] EWHC 359 (Ch). Note, however, that the "profits" must be "property" before they can be held on constructive trust: see *Gray v Global Energy Horizons Corporation* [2020] EWCA Civ 1668 at [459], noting that a "corporate opportunity" is not property that can be held on constructive trust, although the profits derived from such an opportunity might be so held.

[474] The proprietary approach had been taken in *Attorney General of Hong Kong v Reid* [1994] 1 A.C. 324, the court there declining to follow *Metropolitan Bank v Heiron* (1880) 5 Ex. D. 319 CA; and *Lister & Co v Stubbs* (1890) 45 Ch. D. 1 CA. See the comments at fn.432.

[475] *FHR European Ventures LLP v Cedar Capital Partners LLC* [2015] A.C. 250 at [45] (Lord Neuberger PSC). *Chan v Zacharia* (1984) 154 C.L.R. 178 Aust. HC, is typically cited.

[476] These were noted earlier at para.10–099.

[477] One of the rare examples where the court's jurisdiction to do just this was both asserted and utilised is *Grimaldi v Chameleon Mining NL (No.2)* [2012] FCAFC 6, see especially [583]. But a close reading of the complicated facts of that case suggest an English court might well have reached precisely the same conclusion on orthodox "institutional" constructive trust grounds.

[478] Recall that this duty, if it exists at all as a distinct duty, is seen as part of the duty to act in good faith, breach of which therefore gives rise to claims for compensation. See paras 10–033 to 10–034.

[479] *Parr v Keystone Healthcare Ltd* [2019] EWCA Civ 1246.

the sale contract, backed by the shareholders' agreement, the *company*, K,[480] sought to compel P to disgorge 50% of the purchase price received, alleging these were profits P had made as a result of his breach of fiduciary duty to K. The Court of Appeal allowed the claim, asserting that the defaulting director's concealment of his various breaches of fiduciary duty "was itself a breach of duty [which] led to his receipt of twice as much as he was entitled to ... that is a sufficient connection between the breach and the profit to bring the equitable principle [requiring disgorgement] into play."[481]

It is true that P breached his fiduciary duty to K (for which remedies were successfully obtained in the lower court); and it is also true that P sold his shares for more than the circumstances warranted. But that sale did not breach any fiduciary duties P owed to K, and it involved no non-disclosure to K, only non-disclosure to W.[482] This sale was not "a transaction with the company" (ss.175(3) and 177), nor the taking by P of a corporate opportunity which should have accrued to K,[483] nor the taking of a benefit from a third party in circumstances which related to P being a director and where acceptance of that benefit could reasonably be regarded as likely to give rise to a conflict between P's interests and his duties to K (s.176). This is not a *Regal (Hastings) Ltd v Gulliver* scenario,[484] despite the reliance placed on that case by the Court of Appeal. In that case Lord Russell stressed that the fiduciary rule in issue "insists on those, *who by use of a fiduciary position make a profit*, being liable to account for that profit" (emphasis added).[485] In *Regal*, the company could sue the directors for the profit they had made on the sale of their shares because it was held that the *company*, not the directors should have owned those shares in the first place: ownership of the shares was the corporate opportunity that the directors had appropriated for themselves, disloyally (so it was held) excluding the company from taking the benefit. There are no parallels in the case in hand. In short, although K could point to breaches of fiduciary duty by P, it could not point to breaches of fiduciary duties to K which had generated these profits, and there is no reason to allow K to recover profits generated by breaches to strangers, even strangers who own and control K. The case is a reminder, again, that the fiduciary rules imposed on directors are demanding, but their demands should be strictly applied within the limited scope set by the rules themselves; that is broad enough to deliver the protections the rules seek.

480 Now fully owned by W via the nominee H.

481 *Parr v Keystone Healthcare Ltd* [2019] EWCA Civ 1246 at [23].

482 Although, of course, if the *company*, K, and not W/H, had been the counterparty to the sale contract, then there would have been a breach of P's fiduciary duty to K, and, in addition, the circumstances would have generated both contract and tort remedies as well.

483 It would have been different if the articles *entitled* K to acquire P's shares at a 50% discount in the circumstances which obtained, and P had instead, in breach of that provision, sold the shares to W/H/some independent third party: K would then have been entitled to recover the *full* price received by P.

484 *Regal (Hastings) Ltd v Gulliver* [1967] 2 A.C. 134. See para.10–083.

485 *Regal (Hastings) Ltd v Gulliver* [1967] 2 A.C. 134 at 144–145.

(f) Summary dismissal

10–110 The right which an employer has at common law to dismiss an employee who has been guilty of serious misconduct has no application to the director as such, not being an employee.[486] However, it could be an effective sanction against executive directors and other officers of the company, since it may involve loss of livelihood rather than simply of position and directors' fees. However, it tends to be used only in the clearest cases. Generally, the company prefers the director to "go quietly", which means that his or her entitlements on departure are calculated as if the contract were unimpeachable, even if there is scope for arguing that the company has the unilateral right to remove the director for breach of contract.[487]

SHAREHOLDER APPROVAL OR "WHITEWASH" OF SPECIFIC BREACHES OF DUTY

10–111 It is a normal feature of the law, including the law relating to directors, that those to whom duties are owed may release those who owe the duties from their legal obligations. Thus the company ought in principle to be able to release the directors from their general duties. But in deciding how this might be achieved in practice, a number of difficult issues emerge.

What is being decided?

10–112 The company will normally act by resolution, either of the board of directors or of the general meeting, and it is important to ask precisely what their resolution seeks to achieve. This is the first issue. Decisions to authorise or ratify a breach, where effective, have the result of putting the directors in a position where either they do not commit a breach of duty to the company or are treated as not having been in breach. Where such approval is given in advance of the breach of duty, it is normally referred to as *authorisation* and where it is given afterwards it is referred to as *ratification*.[488] Both these decisions should be distinguished from *affirmation*, where the shareholder resolution has the effect of making binding on the company a transaction which is otherwise voidable by the company because of the director's breach of duty, and from *adoption* where the transaction is one the director had no power at all to enter into, but the shareholders do,[489] and they

---

[486] The right which the shareholders have under s.168 to remove a director at any time by ordinary resolution (see paras 11–023 onwards) could be prayed in aid, and the articles sometimes provide that a director must resign if called upon by a majority of the board to do so.

[487] Hence the importance of regulating the contractual entitlements of the director when the contract is concluded. See paras 11–013 onwards.

[488] This terminology seems to be adopted by the Act. For example, s.263, dealing with derivative actions, distinguishes between whether a breach is likely to be "(i) authorised by the company before it occurs, or (ii) ratified by the company after it occurs": s.263(2)(c) and (3)(c). See para.15–013.

[489] If this is to be effective, the general meeting must have the necessary authority to take the decision.

decide the company should enter into it.[490] Affirmation or adoption does not of itself constitute implicit forgiveness, and the company may (the context is important) nevertheless still enforce its remedies against the director, for example, for compensation. However, a single resolution may be intended to deliver more than one end, for example to both forgive the directors and make the transaction binding on the company, and it is a matter of interpretation whether any particular resolution does this. Finally, ratification must also be distinguished from a mere decision not to sue the director. Such a decision has no effect on the director's legal position as being in breach of duty, and unless the decision not to sue constitutes a binding contract or *waiver*, the company can always change its mind later and sue the director, subject to the statute of limitations.[491]

Ratification is inevitably given in respect of an identified wrong already committed. Authorisation, by contrast, may be given in relation to a specific breach of duty or generally, i.e. where no specific breach of duty is in contemplation or has yet occurred. The obvious mechanism to use to provide general ex ante authorisation of the release from a category of duties is an appropriate provision in the articles of association. It is also obvious that such authorisation in the articles (or elsewhere) may be regarded with more suspicion than a specific release (whether authorisation in advance or ratification after the event) because, provided that full disclosure of the relevant facts is made to the shareholders in advance of their decision,[492] they will, in the latter case, know precisely the nature of the infringement of the company's rights to which they are consenting. By contrast, a general waiver of the benefit of a nominated duty in advance is necessarily a less informed waiver, and shareholders, when voting on a change to the articles, may underestimate the chances of situations arising in the future where they would not want to give approval.[493] In other words, a provision in the articles may be less reliable an indication of shareholder preferences than specific authorisation of a particular breach. In this section we are concerned with the particular cases of what might be called "ad hoc" approval by the company, i.e. approval of a particular actual or proposed breach of duty. In the next section we discuss whether approval can be given in advance for broad categories of future breaches, where no or little detail is available concerning the particular breaches which may occur in the future.

---

[490] For an example of affirmation see ss.196 and 214 (paras 10–072 onwards and para.10–079): shareholders making substantial property transactions and loan transactions binding on the company, but not relieving the directors of their breach of duty.

[491] This can be difficult. Section 239(6)(b) preserves "any power of the directors to agree not to sue, or to settle or release a claim made by them on behalf of the company" but does not tell us anything about the extent of that power. Suppose the directors in good faith enter into a contract with one of their number on behalf of the company not to sue him or her for breach of duty. Can the director obtain an injunction to stop the litigation if the shareholders in general meeting or an individual shareholder in a derivative action later institutes litigation? Since the contract gives the director nearly the whole of what is obtainable by ratification, but ratification requires shareholder approval or may not be available at all (see below), it might be thought odd policy to allow the board to enter into such a contract on behalf of the company, and yet clearly they can. The problem is discussed in H. Hirt, *The Enforcement of Directors' Duties in Britain and Germany* (2004), pp.95–96.

[492] See, for instance, *Sharma v Sharma* [2013] EWCA Civ 1287; [2014] B.C.C. 73; and *Pennyfeathers Ltd v Pennyfeathers Property Co Ltd* [2013] EWHC 3530 (Ch).

[493] A fortiori if the change has already been made and the question for an investor is whether he or she should acquire shares in that company.

Authorisation and ratification are recognised in the CA 2006. Section 180(4)(a), recognising but not seeking to amend the common law rules on authorisation, states that the directors' general duties "have effect subject to any rule of law enabling the company to give authority … for anything to be done (or omitted) by the directors … that would otherwise be a breach of duty".[494] And s.239 recognises the common law doctrine of ratification, but also seeks to regulate and modify it in certain important respects. This regulation is welcome by way of clarification, but one undesirable side-effect is that the rules applying to ratification are no longer in all respects the same as those applying to authorisation, so that it may matter, oddly, if the company gives its approval the day before or the day after the directors breach their duty. And it will be interesting to see if the common law on authorisation develops so as to align more with the revised statutory rules.

Who can take the decision for the company?

10–113 The next concern is which corporate organ should take the decision for the company. If the company were deciding whether or not to pursue its legal claims against third parties, or affirm voidable contracts, or waive breaches of duty committed by third parties dealing with the company, then in the ordinary course it would be the board of directors (or its delegates) who would take these decisions. But where the claims in issue are the company's claims against one or more of its directors, the common law has typically assumed that the decision will be taken by the general meeting (subject to one important qualification, noted below[495]). This appears to track the approach taken in trusts cases, where it is the beneficiaries who decide whether or not to pursue claims against wrongdoing trustees. But of course in these trusts cases the claim in issue *is* the beneficiaries' claim, whereas in the corporate scenario it is the company's. Nevertheless, there are sound and rather obvious reasons for adopting a parallel general rule, and so it has persisted.

But, whatever the advantages of such a default rule, the underlying question is simply which corporate organ should take the decision in issue, and the answer to that is not—and need not be—set in stone. The articles may make different provisions. And we have already seen that the CA 2006 itself ousts the common law default rule in certain circumstances, and hands the relevant decision to the directors. For example, advance authorisation of self-dealing transactions is determined by the board of directors (ss.177, 180(1)(b))—indeed authorisation in this context is a misnomer; mere disclosure to the board is all that is required, and the company will then go ahead with the transaction if it approves, or call it off if it does not. So too in relation to breaches of the conflict of interest rule (ss.175, 180(1)(a)), where the default rule of shareholder authorisation is again replaced by board authorisation (subject to the articles not prohibiting/permitting this for private/public companies respectively). In both these contexts, the risk profile supporting the common law default rule is considered too low to warrant the cost

[494] This does not necessarily mean that the doctrine of authorisation is confined to breaches of the general duties.

[495] See para.10–114.

and inefficiency of its use here. By contrast, there are no statutory alternatives for advance authorisation of proposed breaches of the other general duties (ss.171–174 and 176): there the common law default rules would apply.

Again, by contrast, note that there are no parallel statutory provisions for ratification decisions: if a breach is to be forgiven after the event, then the CA 2006 does not in its terms recognise a reason to relax the protections afforded by the common law default rule, which gives the decision to the general meeting. Indeed, as we will see in the next few paragraphs, the Act rather goes the other way, and stiffens the relevant restrictions.

As a result of these statutory inroads, there is no necessary alignment in the approval mechanisms for prior authorisation and for subsequent ratification, even at the level of which organ is to take the decision in question. The company's own articles might further complicate the picture. This reinforces the need identified at the outset to be clear about what the company is purporting to decide.

There is one important qualification to the preceding analysis. The underlying assumption has been that the shareholders in general meeting constitute the appropriate expression of "the company" for the purpose of approval. However, this is not always true. As we shall see,[496] when the company is in the vicinity of insolvency, the common law takes the view that the creditors are the persons with the primary economic interest in the company. One important consequence of this is that the general meeting in such a situation may no longer approve breaches of the directors' duties: that is a matter for the creditors who, however, have no means of acting until the company goes into an insolvency procedure and an insolvency practitioner is appointed to act on their behalf.[497] 10–114

Disenfranchising particular voters

Settling the appropriate corporate organ to take the company's decision is not the end of the analysis. Whichever organ makes the decision for the company, there is an obvious concern to see that the decision is a good one for the company. If the decision is to be taken by the board of directors, the directors' general duties, especially those in ss.171–174, go a long way to ensuring that their deliberations are appropriately focused on the corporate benefit. Even so, where the decision is one concerning authorisation or ratification of a breach of duty by one of their number, the niceties are obvious. The CA 2006 deals with these head on. In those rare cases where the authorisation decision is given to the board of directors, as it is in the s.175 conflicts cases, then conflicted directors are excluded in the calculation of the quorum, and their votes are disregarded in determining whether 10–115

[496] See para.19–013.

[497] See *West Mercia Safetywear Ltd v Dodd* [1988] B.C.L.C. 250; *Aveling Barford v Perion Ltd* (1989) 5 B.C.C. 677 Ch D; *Re DKG Contractors Ltd* [1990] B.C.C. 903 Ch D; *Official Receiver v Stern* [2002] 1 B.C.L.C. 119 CA (Civ Div) at 129. Also see, more recently, *Madoff Securities International Ltd v Raven* [2013] EWHC 3147 (Comm) at [272]–[288] (Popplewell J); *Goldtrail Travel Ltd (In Liquidation) v Aydin* [2014] EWHC 1587 (Ch) at [113]–[118] (Rose J), where there was the added complication of the potential ratification being by the sole shareholder who was the wrongdoing director (not addressed in the appeal [2016] EWCA Civ 371).

board approval has been given (s.175(6)).[498] This straightforward statutory disenfranchisement effectively eliminates the moral dilemma of "asking turkeys to vote for Christmas".[499]

The CA 2006 does not stop there. A similar approach is taken to ratification decisions, notwithstanding that these are decisions for the general meeting. Section 239(4) indicates that the ratification resolution is to be regarded as passed "only if the necessary majority is obtained disregarding the votes in favour of the resolution by the director … and any member connected with him".[500] This may not capture every member whose motivations might be thought suspect, but it certainly goes some distance towards that.

Given these two very substantial inroads, both directed rather sensibly at disenfranchising the defaulting directors (along with certain associated parties), it is perhaps surprising that the CA 2006 Act did not continue in the same vein and apply the same rule to authorisation decisions taken by the general meeting. The same mischief is equally in issue in both cases. But instead these are left to the common law default rules, with the Act merely acknowledging this approach in s.180(4)(a). This reticence is seemingly repeated in the provisions of Chs 4 and 4A of Pt 10, which, as we have seen, appear to permit interested directors to vote on the resolutions required by those Chapters (subject to any stricter rules applying to listed companies). This difference in approach to authorisation and to ratification is both odd and undesirable, especially since controlling directors will generally be able to choose the timing of the necessary shareholder resolution, and thus whether it is to be a resolution of authorisation or ratification.[501]

10–116 The common law default rules on authorisation (and, prior to the CA 2006, equally applicable to ratification) have long been a source of concern. Starting from the unexceptional position that the appropriate organ for making these decisions was the general meeting, the common law view was that it then followed that directors who were in breach of duty were entitled to cast their votes as shareholders in favour of the forgiveness of their own wrongs to the company.[502] This conclusion was seen as justified because shareholders, unlike

[498] Any "interested" director is also similarly excluded, although when a director can be said to be so interested is left to the courts to decide.

[499] There are other illustrations of a similar approach. For example, where the board is required to decide whether the company should enter into a transaction with one of its directors (i.e. a s.177 transaction), the model articles for both public and private companies (arts 14 and 16 respectively) exclude the self-dealing director from both the quorum and vote head counts, but subject to important exceptions where the director can both be counted and vote.

[500] Section 239(4). An equivalent provision is made for written resolutions in s.239(3). Those "connected with" the director are defined by the sections discussed above in the context of substantial property transactions: see para.10–070, except that here a fellow director can be a connected person if he or she otherwise meets the criteria: s.239(5)(d). Also see *Goldtrail Travel Ltd (In Liquidation) v Aydin* [2014] EWHC 1587 (Ch) at [116]–[118] (Rose J), not affected by the appeal [2016] EWCA Civ 371).

[501] See para.10–112.

[502] *North-West Transportation v Beatty* (1887) 12 App. Cas. 589 PC; *Burland v Earle* [1902] A.C. 83 PC; *Goodfellow v Nelson Line* [1912] 2 Ch. 324 Ch D; *Northern Counties Securities Ltd v Jackson & Steeple Ltd* [1974] 1 W.L.R. 1133 Ch D. The contrary views of Vinelott J in *Prudential Assurance Co Ltd v Newman Industries Ltd (No.2)* [1981] Ch. 257 Ch D, to the effect that interested shareholders may not vote on ratification resolutions, was regarded as heretical by many (see Wedderburn, (1981) 44 M.L.R. 202), but in the light of modern developments might be seen as prescient.

directors, were not subject to fiduciary duties, and indeed their shares, and the rights attached to them, were to be regarded as their property, with all the inherent rights to use that property in their own interests. There is much to be said for the view that the law in this area should—and indeed, properly analysed, does—start from a different point. Property and fiduciary obligation do not come into it. At a most basic level, the shareholders hold, and exercise, a power on behalf of the company. All such powers come with constraints requiring that they be exercised "in good faith and for proper purposes", as it is typically put.[503] However broadly this particular approval power is conceived, it would not seem to cover use by interested members to deliver to themselves forgiveness by the company for their wrongs and relief from their need to provide the company with appropriate remedies.[504]

Voting majorities

10–117 The next issue to consider is the necessary majority for approval decisions. Subject to what is said in the next paragraph, the common law default rule, unaffected by any of the statutory interventions noted earlier, is for company authorisation or ratification to be by an ordinary majority of either the directors or the shareholders (depending on the appropriate organ for the decision in question). The company's articles may, of course, make other provision. The CA 2006 is silent on the matter so far as authorisation is concerned, merely preserving the common law. And so far as ratification is concerned, the Act again preserves the common law, with s.239(2) stipulating that the ratification decision "must be taken by the members" and "may" be taken by ordinary majority, unless the company's articles or some common law or statutory rule requires a higher level of approval.[505]

But that is not necessarily the end of the matter. The majority, especially the majority shareholders, may approve a breach of duty by the directors and, in so doing, act unfairly towards the minority, most obviously where they themselves are the directors in question. This could be seen simply as an example of majority unfairness towards the minority which can be handled through the general mechanisms for dealing with such unfairness, and which we discuss in Pt 4. However, the issue is perhaps better dealt with—despite the precedents to the contrary—by straightforwardly addressing the core problem of the validity of the decision being taken, and to that end disenfranchising the interested directors/shareholders, as discussed earlier.[506] Perhaps because this was not the common law approach, and yet the difficulties in this area were plain to see, an alternative

---

[503] See paras 10–018 onwards (directors), 13–008 onwards (shareholders), and 31–029 onwards (bondholders).

[504] See S. Worthington, "Corporate Governance: Remedying and Ratifying Directors' Breaches" (2000) 116 L.Q.R. 638. Pursuing a similar line, see Completing, paras 5.85 and 5.101. The Bill preceding CA 2006, as originally introduced, also disqualified from voting those "with a personal interest, direct or indirect, in the ratification".

[505] CA 2006 s.239(7). The shareholders may also act informally by unanimous consent: s.239(6)(a).

[506] See para.10–115.

tack was taken: certain breaches of directors' duties were regarded as "unratifiable". This is a difficult approach to explain or defend, and we address it briefly in the next paragraphs.

"Non-ratifiable breaches"?

10–118 As noted in the previous paragraph, a further question which has bedevilled the common law, and which the CA 2006 acknowledges but does not answer,[507] is whether all breaches of duty by a director are capable of being ratified. At common law it has long been held that some breaches of directors' duties are not ratifiable, but it is much less clear how wide that rule is. Moreover, it is assumed that the doctrine of the non-ratifiable breach restricts the scope of authorisation as much as it does that of ratification. Since the Act does not address either aspect of the issue, there is at least the benefit of retained equivalence, so far as non-ratifiability is concerned, between the approval rules applying before and after the breach.[508]

But which breaches are not ratifiable? The most commonly formulated proposition is that a majority of the shareholders may not by resolution expropriate to themselves company property, because the property of the company is something in which all the shareholders of the company have a (pro rata) interest. Consequently, a resolution to ratify directors' breaches of duty which would offend against this principle of equality is ineffective (unless, presumably, all the shareholders of the company agreed to the resolution and any relevant capital maintenance rules were complied with).[509] But this is a principle easier to formulate than to apply. The principle was applied in *Cook v Deeks*,[510] where the directors had diverted to themselves contracts which they should have taken up on behalf of the company. By virtue of their controlling interests they secured the passing of a resolution in general meeting ratifying what they had done. It was held that they must nevertheless be regarded as holding the benefit of the contracts on trust for the company, for "directors holding a majority of votes would not be permitted [by the law] to make a present to themselves".[511] The same may apply when the present is not to themselves but to someone else.

---

[507] CA 2006 s.239(7) says it does not "affect any rule of law as to acts that are incapable of being ratified by the company". Those rules would seem to apply equally to prior authorisation by the shareholders. Section 180(4)(a) does not require otherwise, since it preserves existing powers of authorisation only.

[508] *Franbar Holdings Ltd v Patel* [2008] EWHC 1534 (Ch); [2009] 1 B.C.L.C. 1.

[509] See *Re Halt Garage (1964) Ltd* [1982] 3 All E.R. 1016 Ch D; *Aveling Barford Ltd v Perion Ltd* [1989] B.C.L.C. 626; *Rolled Steel Products (Holdings) Ltd v British Steel Corp* [1986] Ch. 246 at 296; *Madoff Securities International Ltd v Raven* [2013] EWHC 3147 (Comm) at [268]–[269]. Similarly, see s.239(6)(a).

[510] *Cook v Deeks* [1916] 1 A.C. 554 PC. See also *Menier v Hooper's Telegraph Works* (1873–4) L.R. 9 Ch. App. 350 CA in Chancery; cf. *Azevedo v Imcopa Importacao* [2013] EWCA Civ 364; [2015] Q.B. 1 at, in particular, [66] and [71].

[511] *Cook v Deeks* [1916] 1 A.C. 554 at 564. Followed by Templeman J in *Daniels v Daniels* [1978] Ch. 406 Ch D, where he refused to strike out a claim alleging that the majority had sold to themselves property of the company at a gross undervalue. In that case, the majority had not actually sought to ratify their actions, but the question was whether the wrong was ratifiable so as to prevent the

Where, then, is the line to be drawn between those cases where shareholder approval is ineffective, and those in which shareholder approval has been upheld? How, in particular, can one reconcile *Cook v Deeks* with the many cases in which the liability of directors has been held to disappear as a result of ratification in general meeting, notwithstanding that the voting majority has been carried by the interested directors?[512] Why, in *Regal (Hastings) Ltd v Gulliver*,[513] did the House of Lords say that the directors would not have been liable to account for their profits had the transaction been ratified, while, in *Cook v Deeks*, the Privy Council made the directors account notwithstanding such ratification? A satisfactory answer, consistent with common sense and with the decided cases, is difficult (and perhaps impossible) to provide.[514]

Beyond the proposition that ratification is not effective where it would amount to misappropriation, or expropriation, of corporate property, it is difficult to formulate any further limitations which command general consent. But even this general consent might be misplaced. *Every* approval decision amounts to a prospective or retrospective appropriation of corporate property: in every case the company is giving up a valuable claim, typically to compensation for losses or disgorgement of gains from the director. It is not a misappropriation of corporate property for the company to do this; it is an inherent aspect of the company's legal autonomy that it can. In *Cook v Deeks*, it was surely not the nature of the corporate opportunity, or its value, or any other attribute related to the type of breach or the nature of the corporate opportunity, which denied the directors their claim to valid ratification. Had *all* the shareholders approved the ratification deal, it would have stood. What could not be tolerated was the suggestion that the three defaulting directors could *themselves* take this decision in the face of a dissenting minority holding a contrary view. If this is right, then the directors' breaches were not *un*-ratifiable; they were simply not effectively ratified by the wrongdoers themselves. The same conclusion is equally true when the company is on the brink of insolvency, or where the directors' breach consists in acting against the creditors' interests. The directors' breaches in these circumstances are not *un*-ratifiable; but they can only be ratified by the appropriate corporate organ, and, exceptionally, that is not the general meeting—even a general meeting governed by a majority of disinterested shareholders.[515] Despite the pervasiveness of the notion of un-ratifiable breaches, the relevant precedents all arguably incline more to expressing concern with the validity and appropriateness of the vote and the voting organ taking the approval decision rather than to the nature of the breach as being un-ratifiable.

---

minority from suing in a derivative action by virtue of the rule in *Foss v Harbottle* (1843) 2 Hare 461 Ct of Chancery. Today such a transaction might well be caught by s.190 of the Act (see para.10–069).

[512] For example, *NW Transportation Co v Beatty* (1887) 12 App. Cas. 589; *Burland v Earle* [1902] A.C. 83; *Harris v A Harris Ltd*, 1936 S.C. 183 IH (2 Div); *Baird v Baird & Co*, 1949 S.L.T. 368 OH.

[513] *Regal (Hastings) Ltd v Gulliver* [1967] 2 A.C. 134, para.10–085.

[514] It has troubled a number of writers: see, in particular, Wedderburn, [1957] C.L.J. 194; [1958] C.L.J. 93; A.B. Afterman, *Company Directors and Controllers* (Sydney, 1970), pp.149 onwards; Beck in Ziegel (ed.), *Studies in Canadian Company Law* (Toronto, 1973), Vol.II, pp.232–238; Sealy [1967] C.L.J. 83 at 102 onwards; S. Worthington, "Corporate Governance: Remedying and Ratifying Directors' Breaches" (2000) 116 L.Q.R. 638.

[515] See para.10–114.

If this is right, then the issue may largely disappear, since the CA 2006 has in large measure addressed the concern with interested parties voting. Section 239, by depriving the directors in breach of the right to vote, avoids the result which the Privy Council was so desirous of avoiding in *Cook v Deeks*, and does so without the need to resort to the concept of a "non-ratifiable wrong". In other words, the rule against making presents of the corporate assets seems much less strong (provided the creditors' interests are not affected) if the non-involved shareholders approve. This consideration may lead the courts in future to narrow, and maybe even eliminate,[516] the class of non-ratifiable wrongs.[517]

GENERAL RULES EXEMPTING DIRECTORS FROM LIABILITY

Statutory constraints on providing exemptions from liability

10–119 Although directors may secure specific authorisation or ratification of their actions from the shareholders, they are likely to regard that route to legal absolution as uncertain and unduly public. Historically, they have sought to use the articles to obtain general shareholder approval for certain categories of, or even all, breaches of duty. We have seen above that the articles were widely used in this way in respect of self-dealing transactions, and in fact the legislature in the CA 2006 accepted that outcome by re-writing the statutory duty in relation to self-dealing transactions as a duty to disclose to the board rather than as a duty to obtain the approval of the shareholders.

However, in some cases the articles went further, and included provisions exempting the directors from liability for all breaches of duty (unless fraud was involved). Parliament responded in the CA 1929.[518] In the current version of that reform (s.232(1)) the principle is laid down that "any provision that purports to exempt a director[519] of a company (to any extent) from any liability that would otherwise attach to him in connection with any negligence, default, breach of duty or breach of trust in relation to the company is void".

This is a very important statutory provision. Subject to its exceptions, the section turns the directors' duties provisions into mandatory rules. Although the common law may regard those duties as existing for the benefit of the shareholders and thus to be waivable by the shareholders in the articles, the section takes a different view, perhaps reflecting doubt about the reality of the consent expressed in approvals given in advance of the event.

---

[516] A wrong is only truly un-ratifiable if there is no corporate organ with the *capacity* to act. It is difficult, perhaps impossible, to conceive of circumstances where this would be the case.

[517] For further elaboration, see S. Worthington, "Corporate Governance: Remedying and Ratifying Directors' Breaches" (2000) 116 L.Q.R. 638, a focus on proper purposes. Adopting this approach, obiter, see *Wang Pengying v Ng Wing Fai* [2021] HKCA 100.

[518] Responding to the decision in *Re City Equitable Fire Insurance Co Ltd* [1925] Ch. 407, where a provision in the company's articles exempted the directors from liability except in cases of "wilful neglect or default".

[519] The earlier provisions applied also to any auditor or officer of the company. Since the enactment of the CA 2006 the provisions on auditors have developed in a separate direction and are discussed below in Ch.23, whilst officers have now disappeared from the section as well—and have not been replaced, it should be noted, by shadow directors.

Different treatment of conflicts of interest

Despite the general prohibition in s.232, s.232(4) then provides that "nothing in this section prevents a company's articles from making such provision as has previously been lawful for dealing with conflicts of interest". Thus it is clear that *some* inroads are permitted in the articles in relation to the "no conflict" duties. This conclusion is reinforced by the provisions of s.180(4)(b) to the effect that "where the company's articles contain provisions for dealing with conflicts of interest, [the general duties] are not infringed by anything done (or omitted) by the directors, or any of them, in accordance with those provisions".[520] The test for the legality of such provisions which s.232 adopts is whether the provision had "previously been lawful for dealing with conflicts of interest"; and it seems that s.180(4)(b) must be interpreted as subject to a similar restriction. 10–120

What is the meaning of this Delphic phrase? What could the articles previously (i.e. before the CA 2006) do in relation to conflicts of interest? In order to answer this question one needs to know the history of judicial interpretation of the predecessor of s.232, namely, s.310, later s.309A, of the CA 1985. This was a highly debated question, arising previously mainly in relation to self-dealing transactions, because that was where the problem arose in practice. The debated question was whether articles substituting informing the board for shareholder approval were compatible with the predecessors of s.232. That particular question is no longer relevant because s.177 adopts outright the principle of disclosure to the board.[521] However, the answer given to the question under the former law may tell us how to approach under the CA 2006 an article dealing with any other conflict of interest.

The only intellectually respectable answer in that debate was given by Vinelott J in *Movitex Ltd v Bulfield*.[522] His explanation drew a distinction between (1) "the overriding principle of equity" that "if a director places himself in a position in which his duty to the company conflicts with his personal interest or duty to another, the court will set aside the transaction without enquiring whether there was any breach of duty to the company"; and (2) the director's "duty to promote the interests of [the company] and when the interests of [the company] conflicted with his own to prefer the interests of [the company]". While any proposed modification of (2) would infringe s.310 of the CA 1985, the shareholders of the company in formulating the articles could modify the application of (1), "the overriding principle of equity", provided that in doing so they did not exempt the director from, or from the consequences of, a breach of that duty to the company.[523]

But even this is not as clear as it might be. In unravelling the issues, it seems important to recognise that "the overriding principle of equity" in (1) requires, or enables, courts to set aside self-dealing transactions whenever there is a *potential* conflict, without requiring investigation of whether the alleged conflict is real. So it might simply be this evaluative step which the articles can legitimately address, 10–121

[520] See *Bilta (UK) Ltd v Nazir* [2015] UKSC 23; [2016] A.C. 1 at [104].

[521] See paras 10–056 onwards.

[522] *Movitex Ltd v Bulfield* [1988] B.C.L.C. 104 Ch D.

[523] *Movitex Ltd v Bulfield* [1988] B.C.L.C. 104 at 120–121.

although if it turns out that a real conflict exists they cannot go further and exempt the director from the obligation to prefer the company's interests. *Movitex* implicitly, and perhaps explicitly, takes this line. And that evaluative step could legitimately be taken by any appropriately qualified organ of the company. Again, in *Movitex*, it seemed important that the decision, allocated to the board of directors, was conditional on full disclosure and on disenfranchising the interested director from both quorum and voting numbers.[524] But to regard the board's decision as limited to this evaluative function denies reality. Indeed, the limitation seems unnecessary. We have seen that the company can prospectively authorise what *would* otherwise be a breach of the conflicts rules; there is no limitation to a mere evaluation that what is proposed would *not* constitute an actual breach. Although the common law default rule holds that this decision is for the general meeting, it must surely be open to the articles to settle an alternative but appropriately qualified organ of the company for the purposes of making this decision. This, more realistically, was what was done in *Movitex*. It is also what is now done in the current Act in ss.175 and 177. But this approach, recognising the possibility of advance authorisation, then lays bare the question at the outset: given the rigours of s.232, can ss.232(4) and 180(4)(b) legitimately permit the articles to make any inroads into the conflicts rules beyond specifying the appropriate corporate organ for any necessary evaluations, authorisations and ratifications?

Moreover, given that the duty in relation to self-dealing transactions has become, under the CA 2006, a simple duty of disclosure, where will there be an incentive for provisions in the articles to be deployed in future which provide further inroads relating to directors' liability for conflicts of interest? The obvious areas are corporate opportunities and multiple directorships. Translated into corporate opportunity terms, however, the *Movitex* approach indicates that the articles cannot exempt the director from obtaining the company's authorisation (and note the difficulties in determining whether that is appropriately given[525]) before taking personally an opportunity the company was actually pursuing (as in *Cook v Deeks*[526] and *Industrial Development Consultants v Cooley*[527]) or probably one which the company had an interest in considering because it falls within its current line of business (as in *Bhullar v Bhullar*[528]), because in that situation there would be an actual conflict of interest. However, the articles might conceivably exempt the director from taking without authorisation an opportunity which the company (normally the board) had rejected in good faith (as in *Regal*[529]), but the better argument here is that such a decision by the board puts the opportunity outside the scope of conflicts which are caught by the equitable or statutory rule, so nothing more would need to be said in the articles, and indeed if anything were said it would be otiose.[530] Similarly, the *Movitex* case would

---

524 See paras 10–054 onwards, for discussion of the issues.

525 See paras 10–115 onwards.

526 *Cook v Deeks* [1916] 1 A.C. 544.

527 *Industrial Development Consultants v Cooley* [1972] 1 W.L.R. 443.

528 *Bhullar v Bhullar* [2003] B.C.C. 711.

529 *Regal (Hastings) Ltd v Gulliver* [1967] 2 A.C. 134. Although there may be nice questions on disclosure at the board rejection stage.

530 See paras 10–084 to 10–086.

suggest that an article permitting multiple directorships would be upheld by virtue of s.232(4) only if there is no actual conflict of duties for the director in consequence of the taking up of additional directorships. Given this, there would once again seem to be little point to such a provision.

Arrangements providing directors with an indemnity

The ban, contained in s.232, on provisions exempting directors from liability extends (subject to important exceptions) to any provision by which the company provides, directly or indirectly, an indemnity to a director or a director of an associated company in respect of these liabilities (s.232(2)). Under an indemnity arrangement the director remains in principle liable but the company picks up the financial consequences of that liability. The indemnity prohibition applies also to indemnities provided in favour of directors of associated companies, thus preventing evasion of the section in group situations, whereby all the directors have the benefit of indemnity provisions, but in no case is the indemnity provided by the company of which they are a director. The provisions referred to in the section are those "contained in a company's articles or in any contract with the company or otherwise".[531] The indemnity might be provided by means of the company promising to indemnify the director or, indirectly, by the company taking out insurance on the director's behalf, so that the indemnity is to be provided by the insurance company. As we shall see, the legislation is less strict in relation to permitted insurance than in respect of permitted direct indemnities (labelled "third party" indemnities in the Act). **10–122**

Insurance

Since 1989 a company has been free (but of course not obliged) to buy insurance against any of the liabilities mentioned in s.232 for the benefit of its directors (s.233) and it is in fact common practice to do so, at least in large companies. At first sight, this is very odd. Insurance certainly means, assuming the policy limits are large enough, that the company receives compensation for any loss it suffers as a result of the breach of duty. On the other hand, the company pays for the insurance and so, over time at least, the insurance premia will roughly equal the losses inflicted on the company by the directors, so that the company ends up paying for the directors' breaches of duty. This seems to deprive the directors' duties rules of any deterrent effect as against the directors and to mean that the insurance simply operates as a way of smoothing the losses inflicted on the company by the directors. **10–123**

This argument has considerable force, but needs to be assessed subject to the following qualifications. First, the impact of s.233 depends upon the extent of the cover which the insurance market is prepared to make available at any particular

[531] CA 2006 s.232(3). In *Burgoine v Waltham Forest LBC* [1997] B.C.C. 347 Ch D, it was held that the phrase "or otherwise" did not extend the section beyond indemnities, etc. given by the company (as opposed to a third party), though that is now subject to the extension of the indemnity prohibition to the directors of associated companies. Presumably, the force of these words is to ban such provisions in members' or directors' resolutions.

time. It is unlikely that insurance is available against the consequences of a breach of duty involving fraud or wilful default, because of the moral hazard problem for the insurance company in providing such cover.[532] And it may be difficult to obtain cover against the liability to account for profits made as opposed to losses inflicted on the company. In any event, the policy is likely to be subject to monetary limits, so that liability remains to some extent personally with the director in the case of large claims.

Secondly, it is conceivable that insurance companies will adjust their premia according to the claims experience of the company so that a financial incentive is generated for the company to monitor the actions of its directors or refuse to insure those with a bad claims record, or insurance companies may even engage in more general monitoring of the corporate governance arrangements in the company, thus somewhat restoring the deterrent effect of the duties.[533]

Finally, it may be that qualified persons will be unwilling to take on board positions without the benefit of such insurance. This might be true particularly of non-executive directors, whose financial benefits from the company may be modest (at least in comparison with the remuneration of executive directors) and whose knowledge of and control over the company is necessarily limited. They could buy such insurance themselves, for the section does not restrict the taking out of insurance against directors' liabilities by the directors themselves.[534] However, they would no doubt expect the cost of such insurance to be reflected in their fees, and it may be cheaper and more effective for the company to provide that insurance itself.

Third party indemnities

10–124 Despite the term "third party indemnities" the indemnity under discussion here is one provided by the company in favour of the director. It is a "third party" indemnity because it relates to litigation which might be brought by a third party (i.e. someone other than the company) against the director.[535] Under an indemnity provision the company promises that the director will not be out of pocket in relation to the claim made against him or her (whether by way of a judgment against the director, a settlement of the litigation or by the incurring of legal costs), so that, to the extent of the indemnity, the cost of the director's breach of duty is borne directly by the company. As we have seen, it will be rare for breaches of the duties discussed in this chapter to lead to liability other than to the company, but this may not be the case where the liability arises under a foreign

[532] The provisions to be found in such insurance contracts are analysed by C. Baxter, "Demystifying D&O Insurance" (1995) 15 O.J.L.S. 537, now a somewhat dated, but nevertheless useful, article. The insurance may extend, of course, to protection against liabilities beyond those discussed in this chapter.

[533] Evidence from the US suggests that neither form of control by insurance companies is strong, probably because the directors, who control the decision where to place the insurance, would not welcome it. See T. Baker and S. Griffin, "Predicting Governance Risk: Evidence from the Directors' and Officers' Liability Insurance Market" (2007) 74 Chicago L.R. 487; and "The Missing Monitor in Corporate Governance: The Directors' and Officers' Liability Insurer" (2007) 95 Georgetown L.J. 1795. This view is concurred in by Baxter, "Demystifying D&O Insurance" (1995) 15 O.J.L.S. 537.

[534] This seems to be the implication of the *Burgoine* decision, fn.531.

[535] CA 2006 s.234(2).

system of law, notably US law, and s.232 is not in terms confined to liabilities arising under the law of a UK jurisdiction. A director may prefer insurance to a promise of an indemnity by the company, because on insolvency the company's promise may not be worth very much, but an indemnity may be regarded by the director as better than nothing, and the company may prefer, in effect, to self-insure by promising an indemnity.

Note, however, that the company may not promise an indemnity against liability or costs incurred in an action brought by the company. This may be provided for only through the purchase of insurance by the company, as discussed above. Why is this? It may have been thought, on the one hand, that a complete indemnity would come very close to an exemption from liability, thus defeating the purpose of s.232. On the other hand, despite the failings of the insurance market, insurance requires an assessment of the extent of and the costs of the risks involved by another commercial organisation, which will exclude some risks from those it is prepared to underwrite. This provides some external control over the liabilities from which directors can be exempted, for example, where they have acted deliberately in breach of duty. Equally, the need to buy insurance will bring the cost of the protection home to the board which is arranging for it, whilst an indemnity, which carries no immediate costs for the company, might be too easy a provision to slip into the articles.

The Act prohibits provision of certain forms of indemnity (s.234(3), as elaborated in s.234(4)–(6)), in particular in relation to:

- a fine imposed on a director in criminal proceedings;
- the costs of defending criminal proceedings in which the director is convicted;
- a penalty payable to a regulatory authority;
- costs incurred in connection with an application for relief (see below) which is unsuccessful; or
- the costs of defending civil proceedings brought by the company or an associated company in which judgment is given against the director.

The last category of exclusion may seem surprising, given that liability to the company or associated company is not within the definition of a "third party indemnity" (s.234(2)) but it is to be noted that what s.234(3) deals with is not the director's liability to the company or associated company but the director's liability for costs incurred in defending civil proceedings brought by such a company, which liability may be incurred to a third party, i.e. the director's legal team. The exclusion thus completes the policy objective of preventing the indemnity from operating in respect of any aspect of a claim brought by the company or an associated company, but only if the company is successful in the claim. If no judgment is given against the director, either because the director is successful or because the case is settled, a provision requiring the company to indemnify the director against legal costs is permitted. The section achieves the same result in relation to criminal proceedings against the director: only the costs of successfully defending a criminal charge may be the subject of an indemnity provision. However, it appears that the costs of an unsuccessful defence in a regulatory procedure (for example, one brought by the Financial Conduct Authority) may be the subject of an indemnity provision (though not the cost of any penalty imposed by the FCA).

However, the real importance of the section is not revealed by what it says by way of exclusion but what it does not exclude. In the case of a civil action brought by a third party (for example, shareholders in a class action) the indemnity provision may cover both the liability of the director and the costs of defending the action, whether successfully or unsuccessfully.

10–125 An indemnity provision which meets the requirements of s.234 is termed a "qualifying indemnity provision". A qualifying indemnity provision[536] must be disclosed to the shareholders in the directors' annual report (s.236); and must be made available for inspection in the usual way by any shareholder of the company without charge, who may also require a copy of it to be provided upon payment of the prescribed fee (ss.237 and 238).

It should finally be noted that what s.234 creates is a permission for the company, not an obligation, and it is a permission to have a provision (in the company's articles or in a contract with a director, for example) which provides for an indemnity of the relevant type. The section does not deal with ad hoc decisions by boards of directors to pay an indemnity in a particular case, where there is no existing provision dealing with this matter. Such a decision is governed by the directors' duties discussed above and by the general law of the land.[537] It is also possible that a company might wish to lend the director money in advance to defend proceedings brought against him or her, whether criminal, civil or regulatory. We have already seen that a company is exempted from the normal rules on shareholder approval if it decides to make such a loan, or enter into an analogous transaction, for this purpose. However, the loan must be on terms that it is repayable if the director is unsuccessful in the proceedings.[538] A loan on different terms or for a different purpose (for example, to meet a liability in a judgment rather than to defend proceedings) would need shareholder approval.

Pension scheme indemnity

10–126 Where a company runs an occupational pension scheme (a less frequent situation these days than previously), the company may be a trustee of the trust through which the scheme is organised and the director may act on behalf of the company in its capacity as such a trustee.[539] Section 235 permits provisions indemnifying

[536] Whether made by the company or not, so that the directors of an associated company must report it as well; and copies must be available for inspection by the shareholders of both companies.

[537] It has been suggested in a trade union case that, whereas a once-off ex post decision to indemnify an officer against a fine was unobjectionable (if authorised by the union's rules), "continued resolutions authorising the refunding of fines might fairly be said to lead to an expectation that a union would indemnify its members against the consequences of future offences" and that would be against public policy: *Drake v Morgan* [1978] I.C.R. 56 QBD at 61.

[538] See para.10–078.

[539] Of course, the director may be appointed personally by the company to be a trustee of the scheme, but it may have been thought that, in such a case, any liability would not be incurred in the capacity of director but as trustee or appointee, so that any indemnity provision would not fall within s.232.

the director against any liability incurred in connection with the company's activities as trustee of the scheme, subject to the same restrictions as in s.234 in relation to criminal and regulatory proceedings. However, s.235 permits indemnity arrangements in relation to civil suits, whether brought by a third party or by the company, which indemnity may extend to both costs and liability. In other words, as far as the director's activities on behalf of the company as trustee are concerned, a complete indemnity arrangement is permissible in relation to civil liability. The same reporting and copy requirements apply in relation to a qualifying pension scheme indemnity provision as in relation to a third-party indemnity provision.

Limitation of actions

The question of whether directors acting in breach of their fiduciary and other duties have the benefit of the Limitation Acts is another area where the analogy between the director and the trustee is to the fore, the specific provisions of the Limitation Act 1980 dealing with actions by a beneficiary against a trustee being applied to actions by a company against a director.[540] The crucial question is whether there is any limitation period in such cases, for until the late nineteenth century trustees did not have the benefit of a limitation period in actions by beneficiaries.[541] Under s.21 of the 1980 Act a limitation period of six years is applied to such actions (unless some other section of the Act applies a different limitation period), but there are two exceptions where the old rule of no limitation continues to operate. These are s.21(1)(a) where the claim is based upon "any fraud or fraudulent breach of trust to which the trustee was a party or privy"; and s.21(1)(b) where the action is to recover "from the trustee trust property or the proceeds of trust property in the possession of the trustee or previously received by the trustee and converted to his use". In a standard case, therefore, of an action against a director to recover a profit made in breach of his fiduciary duties or for equitable compensation, the limitation period will be six years. Only where the claimant can go further and bring himself within either the (a) or (b) exception will the Act not apply.[542] **10–127**

As to s.21(1)(a), it should be noted that it is a strong rule, since defendants in actions based on fraud are not generally deprived by the Limitation Act of the benefit of a limitation period. To benefit from this exception the claimant has to show not simply that the director acted in breach of duty, but that he or she intended to act either knowing that the action was contrary to the interests of the company or recklessly indifferent as to whether it was.[543]

---

540 *Burnden Holdings (UK) Ltd v Fielding* [2018] UKSC 14 at [11], citing the familiar cases in this area: *Paragon Finance Plc v DB Thakerar & Co* [1999] 1 All E.R. 400 CA (Civ Div); *JJ Harrison (Properties) Ltd v Harrison* [2002] 1 B.C.L.C. 162, especially Chadwick LJ at [25]–[29]; *Williams v Central Bank of Nigeria* [2014] UKSC 10; [2014] A.C. 1189, especially Lord Sumption at [28]; *First Subsea Ltd (formerly BSW Ltd) v Balltec Ltd* [2018] Ch 25, especially Patten LJ at [50]. But note that this assumption is not applicable to claims by third parties against a director, where the normal limitation periods apply.

541 The position was changed by the Trustee Act 1888.

542 *Burnden Holdings (UK) Ltd v Fielding* [2018] UKSC 14.

543 *Gwembe Valley Development Co Ltd v Koshy (No.3)* [2004] 1 B.C.L.C. 131 at [131].

As to s.21(1)(b), it means that there is no limitation period in those cases where a director has misapplied company property which has come into his or her hands and the company is seeking restoration of that property. This rule applies even though the company's property is no longer in the hands of the director,[544] and indeed applies even where the property is delivered into the hands of third parties, but the director has the economic benefit of the transfer.[545] As it was put some hundred years ago, the rule is intended to prevent the director from "coming off with something he ought not to have".[546]

On the other hand, all these cases recognise that s.21(1)(b) only excludes the six-year limitation period for claims seeking recovery of property that was the company's originally. They do not cover claims in respect of corporate opportunities or bribes,[547] although it remains possible to bring such claims within s.21(1)(a) if it is possible to prove the rather strict fraud requirements.[548] This approach may seem odd, especially given that the very foundation of the director's proprietary liability for corporate opportunities and bribes is that these assets "belong" to the company; that might seem especially so, for example, where a maturing business opportunity is captured by defaulting directors,[549] or a bribe taken that might otherwise have gone to enhancing the purchase price received by the company.[550] But this is the law, unless and until amended by the Supreme Court.[551]

10–128 However, in recent years the scope of both s.21(1)(a) and (b) has been debated in relation to third parties who are often called "constructive trustees" by the courts under the doctrines of accessory liability and knowing receipt discussed below, and in other circumstances too. The courts have drawn a distinction between two types of constructive trustee, constructive trustees properly so-called and others in respect of whom the term would better be abandoned.[552] The first case is the case of the person who, though not expressly appointed as a trustee, has assumed the duties of a trustee by a lawful transaction which was independent of and preceded the breach of trust now in issue. Such a person falls within s.21(1)(a) (if the facts fit) and s.21(1)(b). So a director who receives company property in breach of fiduciary duty holds that property on constructive trust, and the limitation defence is not available.

---

544 *JJ Harrison (Properties) Ltd v Harrison* [2002] 1 B.C.L.C. 162; *Re Pantone 485 Ltd* [2002] 1 B.C.L.C. 266.

545 *Burnden Holdings (UK) Ltd v Fielding* [2018] UKSC 14 at [22].

546 *Re Timmis, Nixon v Smith* [1902] 1 Ch. 176 Ch D at 186.

547 *Burnden Holdings (UK) Ltd v Fielding* [2018] UKSC 14 at [22]; *First Subsea Ltd (formerly BSW Ltd) v Balltec Ltd* [2018] Ch 25 at [59], [62]–[63]; *Gwembe Valley Development Co Ltd v Koshy (No 3)* [2004] 1 B.C.L.C. 131 at [119]–[120].

548 *Burnden Holdings (UK) Ltd v Fielding* [2018] UKSC 14 at [11]; preferring *First Subsea Ltd (formerly BSW Ltd) v Balltec Ltd* [2018] Ch 25 (see especially at [59], [62]–[63]) to any further limitations that may have been suggested in *Gwembe Valley Development Co Ltd v Koshy (No 3)* [2004] 1 B.C.L.C.131, especially at [111] and [118].

549 *Cook v Deeks* [1916] 1 A.C. 554.

550 *FHR European Ventures LLP v Cedar Capital Partners LLC* [2015] A.C. 250.

551 *Williams v Central Bank of Nigeria* [2014] A.C. 1189. See S Worthington, "Exposing Third Party Liability in Equity: Lessons from the Limitation Rules" in P.S. Davies and J.E. Penner (eds), *Equity, Trusts and Commerce* (Oxford, Hart Publishing, 2017) Ch.14.

552 *Paragon Finance Plc v D B Thackerar & Co* [1999] 1 All E.R. 400.

The second case is where the trust obligation arises as a direct consequence of the unlawful transaction which the claimant challenges and where the constructive trust is imposed simply to provide an effective proprietary remedy in equity.[553] Such a person does not fall within s.21(1)(a) or (b). The Supreme Court in *Williams v Central Bank of Nigeria*[554] has held, by majority, that third parties who are dishonest assistants or knowing recipients are in this fortunate position (for them), and can therefore rely on the normal limitation periods. The analysis remains controversial, however, with doctrinal and policy considerations pulling in both directions.

Relief granted by the court: s.1175

Whether or not the director is able to secure forgiveness from the company, the director, and any officer of the company (including auditors and liquidators), has the option of appealing to the court to prevent the full application to him or her of the statutory duties included in Pt 10 or indeed any analogous duties arising, for example, at common law. Under s.1157 the court has a discretion to relieve, prospectively or retrospectively, against liability for negligence, default, breach of duty or breach of trust, provided that it appears to the court that the director has acted honestly and reasonably and that, having regard to all the circumstances, he or she ought fairly to be excused. The court may relieve on such terms as it thinks fit. The requirement of reasonableness might suggest that s.1157 is not available in relation to the directors' duties of care, skill and diligence but this appears not to be the case.[555] However, the section is not available in respect of third-party (as opposed to corporate) claims against the director,[556] and, more important for present purposes, will not be applied even to corporate claims where that would be inconsistent with the purposes underlying the rule imposing the liability against which relief is sought.[557] **10–129**

---

[553] These are the definitions set out by Millett LJ in *Paragon Finance Plc v DB Thackerar & Co* [1999] 1 All E.R. 400.

[554] *Williams v Central Bank of Nigeria* [2014] A.C. 1189. But note the strong dissent of Lord Mance. The issues are clearly difficult. The court's conclusions rely heavily on the judgment of Millett LJ in *Paragon Finance Plc v DB Thackerar & Co* [1999] 1 All E.R. 400, although interestingly his analysis is used by both sides, and even Millett LJ, in *Paragon* at 414, had noted that "there is a case for treating a claim against a person who has assisted a trustee in committing a breach of trust as subject to the same limitation regime as the claim against the trustee".

[555] *Equitable Life Assurance Society v Bowley* [2004] 1 B.C.L.C. 180 at [45]; *Re D'Jan of London Ltd* [1994] 1 B.C.L.C. 561 at 564; *Northampton Regional Livestock Centre Co Ltd v Cowling* [2014] EWHC 30 (QB) at [159]–[170] (reversed in part by the Court of Appeal); and *Re HLC Environmental Projects Ltd* [2014] B.C.C. 337 at [108]. And see *Re Powertrain Ltd* [2015] EWHC 3998 (Ch) (concerning liquidators).

[556] *Customs and Excise Commissioners v Hedon Alpha Ltd* [1981] 1 Q.B. 818 CA.

[557] *Re Produce Marketing Consortium Ltd* [1989] 1 W.L.R. 745 Ch D (Companies Ct) (wrongful trading liabilities excluded).

LIABILITY OF THIRD PARTIES

10–130 Despite the wide range of civil remedies which exist to support the substantive law of directors' duties, it is often the case that the directors are not in fact worth suing, at least if they are uninsured. They may once have had property belonging to the company but, by the time the company finds this out, they may no longer have it. They may have made large profits which they should account for to the company, but may well have spent them by the time the writ arrives. Companies are therefore likely to want to identify some more stable third party, often a bank, which is worth powder-and-shot, either instead of or in addition to the directors.[558]

But under what conditions may the company hold a third party liable in connection with a breach of duty by the directors? This is not a matter dealt with in the Act in relation to the general duties of directors. It is left to the common law, which is rather complex, although it is an area which recent decisions of the Privy Council and House of Lords have helped to clarify. Only the briefest sketch of the relevant principles is attempted here.

10–131 It has long been recognised that there are two bases of third-party liability, one resting on receipt by the third party of company property ("knowing receipt" or "unconscionable receipt" claims) and the other resting on complicity on the part of the third party in the director's breach of duty ("dishonest assistance" claims). The main conceptual contribution of the Privy Council in *Royal Brunei Airlines Sdn Bhd v Tan*[559] was to make it clear that the principles supporting the imposition of liability in these two situations are different from one another.

In the case of dishonest assistance claims, which the court helpfully termed "accessory" liability, the liability is a reflection of a general principle of the law of obligations. This imposes personal liability upon third parties who assist in or procure the breach of a duty or obligation owed by another, the liability of the third party being enforceable by the person who is the beneficiary of the duty whose performance has been interfered with. Provided there has been a breach of duty by the director, whether committed knowingly or not, the third party accessory will be liable to the company if the third party has acted dishonestly. After some to-ing and fro-ing, it seems, rightly, to be agreed that the test of dishonesty is objective: the accessory is dishonest if, by ordinary standards, the defendant's mental state would be characterised as dishonest, and it is irrelevant that the defendant him- or herself takes a different view.[560] The third party is

---

[558] See, for example, *Selangor United Rubber Estates v Cradock (No.3)* [1968] 1 W.L.R. 1555.

[559] *Royal Brunei Airlines Sdn Bhd v Tan* [1994] UKPC 4; [1995] 2 A.C. 378, noted by Birks, [1996] L.M.C.L.Q. 1; and Harpum, (1995) 111 L.Q.R. 545. The facts of the case did not raise an issue of directors' duties. In fact, the fiduciary duty in question was owed by the company and the principle of accessory liability was used to make the director liable to the claimant for the *company's* breach of duty. But the principle of the case is clearly of general application.

[560] *Barlow Clowes International Ltd v Eurotrust Ltd* [2005] UKPC 37; [2006] 1 W.L.R. 1476 at [15] (Lord Hoffmann), also excusing, at [15], as "ambiguous" the earlier majority views, including his own, in favour of subjective dishonesty in *Twinsectra Ltd v Yardley* [2002] UKHL 12; [2002] 2 A.C. 164 (Lord Millett dissenting vigorously), which had in turn varied the views of Lord Nicholls in *Royal Brunei Airlines Sdn Bhd v Tan* [1995] 2 A.C. 378, who favoured an objective test. The final position represents a return to orthodoxy, both *Group Seven Ltd v Notable Services LLP* [2019] EWCA Civ

often said to be obliged to account "as a constructive trustee". This label is uninformative, and indeed confusing, and should be discarded, but the cases confirm that the accessory is liable to compensate the principal (the company, here) for losses caused by the director's breach of fiduciary duty and, it seems, for any profits generated personally by the accessory from that breach.[561]

Given the dishonesty element in accessory liability, such claims are unlikely against solvent and respectable third parties.[562] The alternative is the personal claim based on "knowing receipt" of the company's property,[563] at least if the term "knowing" is given a wide enough connotation. The essence of this claim is restitutionary, being the return of the value of the company's property that was received as a result of the director's breach, and regardless of the fact that the third party may no longer have the property or its identifiable proceeds in its hands.[564] A common situation found in the cases is one where the directors have used the company's assets in breach of the statutory prohibition on the provision of financial assistance towards the purchase of its shares, and the assets in question have passed through the hands of a third party.[565] **10–132**

The scope of knowing receipt liability depends heavily upon the degree of knowledge on the part of the third party which is required to trigger it, an issue which has been much discussed in the courts over recent decades. Although the issue remains unsettled, the tendency in recent decisions has been to resist imposing liability on the basis of constructive knowledge in ordinary commercial transactions, on the grounds that the doctrine of constructive knowledge presupposes an underlying system of careful and comprehensive investigation of the surrounding legal context, which is typical of property transactions but atypical of commercial transactions (including the non-property aspects of commercial property transfers).[566] This probably misconceives the notion of constructive notice, which is inherently and deliberately context sensitive, so that in commercial contexts the right question would be, what would a reasonable

614; and *Starglade Properties Ltd v Nash* [2010] EWCA Civ 1314; [2011] 1 P. & C.R. D.G. 17 confirm that the *Barlow Clowes* decision represents the law in England. Also see *Bank of Ireland v Jaffery* [2012] EWHC 1377 (Ch) (in the context of a bank's former senior executive).

561 See *Fyffes Group Ltd v Templeman* [2000] 2 Lloyd's Rep. 643 QBD (Comm); *Ultraframe (UK) Ltd v Fielding* [2006] F.S.R. 17, holding that the accessory's liability was not confined to damages but included a liability to account for profits which the accessory had made (but not profits made by the director); *Charter Plc v City Index Ltd* [2007] EWCA Civ 1382; [2008] Ch. 313; *Novoship (UK) Ltd v Mikhaylyuk* [2015] Q.B. 499; *Williams v Central Bank of Nigeria* [2014] A.C. 1189. Notice in particular the argument that the causal test may either be different, or at least have different outcomes, when applied to a third party "dishonest assistant" rather than a director/fiduciary: *Novoship (UK) Ltd v Mikhaylyuk* [2015] Q.B. 499 at [111]–[115].

562 Which is not to say that the first basis of liability is never available: see *Canada Safeway Ltd v Thompson* [1951] 3 D.L.R. 295.

563 If the third party does still have the property or its identifiable proceeds to hand, then a proprietary constructive trust or tracing claim may be possible, subject only to the bona fide purchaser defence.

564 *El Ajou v Dollar Land Holdings Plc* [1994] 2 All E.R. 685 CA (Civ Div) at 700 per Hoffmann LJ.

565 See para.17–052; and *Belmont Finance Corp v Williams Furniture Ltd (No.2)* [1980] 1 All E.R. 393 CA.

566 See *Eagle Trust Plc v SBC Securities Ltd* [1993] 1 W.L.R. 484 Ch D; *Cowan de Groot Properties Ltd v Eagle Trust Plc* [1992] 4 All E.R. 700 Ch D; *Eagle Trust Plc v SBC Securities Ltd (No.2)* [1995] B.C.C. 231 Ch D.

commercial party know in *this* context (given the usual and reasonable enquiries that such a party would—or would not—have made)?

In any event, in *Bank of Credit and Commerce International (Overseas) Ltd v Akindele*[567] the Court of Appeal struck out on a new tack. Whilst confirming that dishonesty is not a requirement for liability under the "knowing receipt" head, the Court abandoned the search for a single test for knowledge in this area. Instead, the question to ask was whether the recipient's state of knowledge was such as to make it unconscionable for him or her to retain the benefit of the receipt. The Court thought this would enable judges to "give common sense decisions in the commercial context", though it has to be said that the test is so open-ended that it is unlikely to bring about a common approach on the part of the courts.

10–133 Third-party liability may also arise in relation to corporate opportunities. Here, the question again arises of how far a corporate opportunity constitutes an asset of the company. We have seen above[568] that this question is relevant to the question of whether the director's taking of the opportunity can be ratified by a simple majority of the shareholders. It arises again here: does receipt by a third party either of the opportunity itself or of assets arising out of its exploitation fall within the "knowing receipt" principle? What is clear is that merely entering into a contract with the company which remains executory does not put the third party in a position in which he or she can be said to be in receipt of corporate assets.[569] Where the corporate opportunity is regarded as an asset of the company, however, it follows that the company will be able to seek to recover profits made out of exploitation of the opportunity by the third party (provided of course that the important requirement of knowledge is met), even if the defaulting director does not him- or herself make any personal profit.[570]

Whether in such a case the *director* can be held liable, with the third party, for the third party's profits is much debated. In principle this should not be possible unless the director can in some way be made personally liable for the defaults of the third party. This may be possible if the third party is a partnership of which the director is a member, but logic suggests that generally the director's own liability will be restricted to his or her allocated share of the profits. It will also be possible, on orthodox principles, in the narrow circumstance where the third party is a company but the company is a sham, hiding the director.[571] But where the third-party company is not a sham, it might still be disputed whether the director can be liable with the third party for the third party's profits on the grounds that

---

[567] *Bank of Credit and Commerce International (Overseas) Ltd v Akindele* [2001] Ch. 437 CA (Civ Div). See also the use of this test in *Criterion Properties Plc v Stratford UK Properties LLC* [2003] B.C.C. 50.

[568] See para.10–118.

[569] *Criterion Properties Ltd v Stratford UK Properties Ltd* [2004] B.C.C. 570.

[570] As in the case of the chairman in *Regal (Hastings) Ltd v Gulliver* [1967] 2 A.C. 134, although in that case the language of the court was not noticeably proprietary in tone. Also see *Clegg v Pache (Deceased)* [2017] EWCA Civ 256.

[571] For the third-party partnership see *Imperial Mercantile Credit Association v Coleman* (1873) L.R. 6 H.L. 189; and on the sham third-party company see *Trustor AB v Smallbone (No.2)* [2001] 1 W.L.R. 1177 Ch D; *Glencor ACP Ltd v Dalby* [2000] 2 B.C.L.C. 734 Ch D, but note the modern analysis of these latter cases as set out in *Prest v Petrodel Resources Ltd* [2013] UKSC 34; [2013] 2 A.C. 415 and discussed in paras 7–018 onwards.

director and third party are jointly in breach of trust or whether the position is that each is liable only for the profits made personally.[572]

LIABILITY OF PROMOTERS

Extensive though these rules on directors' duties are, they leave a window of time which is potentially unregulated. This is the period during which individuals with good ideas for a new business set to work on creating a company and bringing it into existence ready to do business. This may seem a relatively unimportant time in the scheme of things, especially now that buying a company off the shelf makes the process so quick.[573] But two particular problems are common. The first is the practical problem of how a company not yet in existence can enter into contracts which bind the company once it is formed: this issue was addressed in Ch.8.[574] The second is the intuitive concern with the probity of transactions between the newly formed company buying assets, for example, from the very people who set the company up and determine its first steps. The risk is that these deals overly advantage the originators, or "promoters", at the expense of the company and those persuaded to become its members. This is dealt with here. **10–134**

Meaning of "promoter"

Much of the current law on promoters emerged in the nineteenth century, when there were no restrictions on inviting the public to subscribe for shares in newly formed companies, and the caricature "company promoter" was an individual of dubious repute who made it his profession to form bogus companies and foist them off on a gullible public, to the latter's detriment and his own profit. But even in those days a much more typical example was the village grocer who converted his business into a limited company.[575] The motivations of each might be different, and the grocer less likely than the professional to abuse his position since he can be expected to remain the majority shareholder in his company, whereas the promoter, if a shareholder at all, usually intends to off-load his holdings onto others as soon as possible. But both create, or help to create, the company, and seek to sell it something, whether it be their services or a business. Both are well-placed to take advantage of their position by obtaining a recompense grossly in excess of the true value of what they are selling.[576] For that reason it has long been held that both should be subjected to rather onerous **10–135**

[572] Contrast *CMS Dolphin Ltd v Simonet* [2001] 2 B.C.L.C. 704 at [98] onwards; and *Ultraframe (UK) Ltd v Fielding* [2006] F.S.R. 17 at [1516] onwards. See also *Novoship (UK) Ltd v Mikhaylyuk* [2015] Q.B. 499.

[573] See para.4–009, and here using "off the shelf" to refer to the modern direct electronic registration, including by promoters themselves.

[574] See paras 8–030 to 8–035.

[575] Or a bootmaker: see the discussion of *Salomon v Salomon & Co Ltd* [1897] A.C. 22 HL, at paras 2–001 onwards.

[576] For example, *Re Darby* [1911] 1 K.B. 95.

common law and equitable duties, given the power that they wield over the company. The parallels with the rules applying to directors of companies already in existence will become clear shortly.

10–136 But who should be subject to such tough rules? Both the professional promoter and the village grocer are promoters to the fullest extent, in that each "undertakes to form a company with reference to a given project, and to set it going and takes the necessary steps to accomplish that purpose".[577] But a person who has taken a much less active and dominating role may also be a promoter. Indeed, the potential activities of promoters are so varied that no comprehensive definition has ever been formulated, beyond confining it to activities related to bringing a company into existence.[578] The expression may, for example, cover any individual or company that arranges for someone to become a director, places shares, or negotiates preliminary agreements.[579] Nor need he or she necessarily be associated with the initial formation of the company: one who subsequently helps to arrange the "floating off" of its capital (in the manner explained in Ch.25) will equally be regarded as a promoter.[580] On the other hand, those who act in a purely ministerial capacity, such as solicitors and accountants, will not be classified as promoters merely because they undertake their normal professional duties[581]; although they may if, for example, they have agreed to become directors or to find others who will.[582]

Who constitutes a promoter in any particular case is therefore a question of fact,[583] and the promoter's role continues until the particular functions of promotion come to an end.[584] The expression has never been clearly defined either judicially[585] or legislatively, despite the fact that it is frequently used both in decisions and statutes; this vagueness is apt to be embarrassing when legislation requires promoters to be named or transactions with them to be disclosed.[586]

In many ways the risks of promotion are now lower. In private companies the rules very easily merge with those applying to corporate directors, since in this context the promoter usually becomes, and was always intended to become, a director of the newly formed company. And, as far as public companies are concerned, these days, promoters cannot simply invite the public to subscribe for

---

[577] Cockburn CJ in *Twycross v Grant* (1877) 2 C.P.D. 469 CA at 541.

[578] *Whaley Bridge Calico Printing Co v Green* (1879) 5 Q.B.D. 109 QBD at 111 (Bowen J).

[579] cf. *Bagnall v Carlton* (1877) 6 Ch. D. 371 CA; *Emma Silver Mining Co v Grant* (1879) 11 Ch. D. 918 CA; *Whaley Bridge Calico Printing Co v Green* (1879) 5 Q.B.D. 109; *Lydney & Wigpool Iron Ore Co v Bird* (1886) 33 Ch. D. 85 CA; *Mann v Edinburgh Northern Tramways Co* [1893] A.C. 69 HL; *Jubilee Cotton Mills v Lewis* [1924] A.C. 958 HL; and the cases cited below.

[580] *Lagunas Nitrate Co v Lagunas Syndicate* [1899] 2 Ch. 392 CA at 428.

[581] *Re Great Wheal Polgooth Co* (1883) 53 L.J. Ch. 42; *Houghton v Saunders* [2015] 2 N.Z.L.R. 74.

[582] *Lydney & Wigpool Iron Ore Co v Bird* (1886) 33 Ch. D. 85 CA; *Bagnall v Carlton* (1877) 6 Ch. D. 371 CA.

[583] See J.H. Gross (1970) 86 L.Q.R. 493.

[584] As they will when the directors are appointed and take over the management: Cockburn CJ in *Twycross v Grant* (1877) 2 C.P.D. 469 at 541 CA.

[585] For attempts, in addition to Cockburn CJ's description (above), see those of Lindley J in *Emma Silver Mining Co v Lewis* (1879) 4 C.P.D. 396 at 407; and Bowen J in *Whaley Bridge Calico Printing Co v Green* (1879) 5 Q.B.D. 109 at 111.

[586] e.g. under CA 2006 s.762(1)(c) (in relation to obtaining a trading certificate: see para.4–037).

shares in any proposed new venture: only a public company can invite the public to subscribe for shares, and before a public company is listed on the Main Market of the Stock Exchange or quoted on the Alternative Investment Market, it must be able to show some track record. Consequently, here too the duties of the promoters are often swallowed up in such cases in those of the directors.[587] But corporate promotion continues, even if on a smaller scale, and indeed more recently there has been an increase in public offers of unlisted shares, including shares in new start-up ventures, so the law on promoters may become increasingly important again.[588]

Duties of promoters

The problems which must be dealt with are clear. Promoters are in a particularly advantaged position to sell their own assets or services to the company at an inflated price; to mislead likely investors into buying shares in the new company; and, once that is done, perhaps to induce the company to confirm that all is proper, and any breach might be waived. **10–137**

(a) Statutory rules

There are various statutory rules—although not a great number—which are likely to apply to promoters, but do so in the same way that they apply to other parties in similar circumstances. These include rules relating to untrue statements that appear in listing particulars or prospectuses[589]; rules relating to sales of assets to public companies[590]; and rules relating to exchanging assets for shares, where the concern is that the shares may have been issued at a discount[591]: these are all left for discussion in more general terms in later chapters. **10–138**

(b) Common law and equitable rules

Then there are the rules—the duties imposed on promoters—that have been developed by the courts. Promoters are of course subject to the general law on fraud, misrepresentation, negligence, unjust enrichment, and so on, and in the right context these duties can be important. But their most significant duties are equitable. In a series of cases in the last quarter of the nineteenth century, the courts were alert to the possibilities of abuse inherent in the promoter's position, and thus determined that promoters stand in a fiduciary position towards the company,[592] with all the duties of disclosure and accounting which that implies. **10–139**

---

[587] As pointed out in Ch.25, the handling of public issues is now virtually monopolised by investment bankers whose activities are highly regulated.

[588] See, e.g. the regulatory controls exerted via the restrictions on "financial promotion" in s.21 of FSMA 2000.

[589] See Ch.25.

[590] See Ch.16.

[591] See Ch.16.

[592] *Erlanger v New Sombrero Phosphate Co* (1878) 3 App. Cas. 1218 at 1236 (Lord Cairns). Since the duty is owed to the company, any action against the promoters must be taken by the company, not by its members: *Foss v Harbottle* (1843) 2 Hare 461 at 489.

These fiduciary restrictions profoundly affect three particular contexts: unless promoters obtain the fully informed consent of the company, they cannot enter into any sale or purchase transactions with the company (the conflict between their personal interest in the transaction and their duty to obtain the best price for the company is obvious), or be remunerated, or take commissions from third parties (absent consent, these both constitute secret profits). These fiduciary duties have not been restated in the CA 2006,[593] as directors' fiduciary duties have been, and so they remain regulated by the common law. However, the two sets of rules are likely to continue to influence each other, and the detail of promoters' duties and their application can be gleaned from the analogous cases concerning directors.

(c) *Full disclosure and consent*

10–140 The main difficulty with promoters' fiduciary duties has been deciding how to effect proper disclosure to, and obtain approval from, the company as a separate entity. As we saw earlier, the powers of the company are generally exercised by the board of directors or (where that is not possible or where otherwise agreed) by the shareholders in general meeting.[594] But adopting either option typically raises a very real practical problem: voting may in either case be dominated by the promoter, thus allowing the promoter to be judge in his or her own cause. That does not seem right, and here, as elsewhere, the courts have struggled towards an effective solution to the problem.[595]

The first leading case on the subject, *Erlanger v New Sombrero Phosphate Co*,[596] suggested that it was the promoter's duty to ensure that the company had an independent board of directors and to make full disclosure to it. In that case Lord Cairns said[597] that the promoters of a company:

> "stand undoubtedly in a fiduciary position. They have in their hands the creation and moulding of the company; they have the power of defining how, and when, and in what shape, and under what supervision, it shall start into existence and begin to act as a trading corporation…I do not say that the owner of property may not promote and form a joint stock company and then sell his property to it, but I do say that if he does he is bound to take care that he sells it to the company through the medium of a board of directors who can and do exercise an independent and intelligent judgment on the transaction."

Such a decision would undoubtedly be effective, but will anything less suffice? An entirely independent board would be impossible in the case of most private and many public companies, and since *Salomon v Salomon*[598] it has never been doubted that the fully informed consent of the members would be equally

---

593 This is wise, because promoters can adopt very different roles so their particular duties and liabilities require close examination of the facts: *Lydney and Wigpool Iron Ore Co v Bird* (1886) 33 Ch. D. 85 at 93; *Ladywell Mining Co v Brookes* (1887) 35 Ch. D. 400 at 407 and 411 per Cotton LJ.

594 See paras 9–002 onwards.

595 See paras 10–018 onwards (directors), 13–008 onwards (shareholders) and 31–029 onwards (bondholders).

596 *Erlanger v New Sombrero Phosphate Co* (1878) 3 App. Cas. 1218.

597 *Erlanger v New Sombrero Phosphate Co* (1878) 3 App. Cas. 1218 at 1236.

598 *Salomon v Salomon & Co Ltd* [1897] A.C. 22: see para.2–006. Also see *Lagunas Nitrate Co v Lagunas Syndicate* [1899] 2 Ch. 392 at 426 (Lindley MR).

effective. In that famous case it was held that the liquidator of the company could not complain of the sale to it at an obvious over-valuation of Mr Salomon's business, all the members having acquiesced therein. Note, however, that in this case the shareholders' consent was unanimous, and so it might be thought irrelevant that Salomon himself held the overwhelming majority of the shares: all who could agree on the company's behalf had done so; there was no dissent. But could Salomon have carried such a vote against a unanimously opposed independent minority? Logic suggests not, yet the cases pull both ways.[599] Even the older cases saw the problem. This was evident in the speeches of the House of Lords in the second great landmark case in the development of this branch of the law, *Gluckstein v Barnes*.[600] That case made it clear that a promoter could not escape liability by disclosing to a few cronies who constituted the company's initial members, when it was the intention immediately to float off the company to the public or to induce some other dupes to purchase the shares. "It is too absurd", said Lord Halsbury with his usual bluntness:

> "to suggest that a disclosure to the parties to this transaction is a disclosure to the company. They were there by the terms of the agreement to do the work of the syndicate, that is to say, to cheat the shareholders; and this, forsooth, is to be treated as a disclosure to the company, when they were really there to hoodwink the shareholders."

The modern trend is in the same direction, and would seem to favour denying Salomon—or any other director or promoter—the right to be the person whose own votes determine the outcome of the company's decision when the question in issue is forgiveness or waiver of his own wrongs to the company.[601]

Finally, still on disclosure and consent, a number of older cases have suggested that a promoter cannot effectively contract out of his or her fiduciary duties simply by inserting a clause in the articles whereby the company and the subscribers agree to waive their rights.[602] This is clearly right if the articles purport to exclude fiduciary duties entirely, or even to consent in advance to their general waiver during the period of promotion.[603] On the other hand, if the articles provide full disclosure of the terms of a material transaction with one of the promoters, and new subscribers join the company on the basis that they confirm their consent to that arrangement, then there seems no reason at all, on general principles, why this should not meet the demands of full disclosure and informed, and indeed unanimous, consent.

---

599 Contrast two cases on directors, admittedly in different contexts, but both involving breaches of fiduciary duty: *North-West Transportation v Beatty* (1887) 12 App. Cas. 589; and *Cook v Deeks* [1916] 1 A.C. 554.

600 *Gluckstein v Barnes* [1900] A.C. 240 at 247.

601 See fn.598 and 599. Also see S. Worthington, "Corporate Governance: Remedying and Ratifying Directors' Breaches" (2000) 116 L.Q.R. 638, since the concerns are equally applicable.

602 *Gluckstein v Barnes* [1900] A.C. 240; *Omnium Electric Palaces v Baines* [1914] 1 Ch. 322 CA at 347 per Sargant J. Such "waiver" clauses used to be common, apparently, and, except as regards actual misrepresentations (on which see Misrepresentation Act 1967 s.3), there is still no statutory prohibition of them: s.232 (invalidating exemption clauses) applies only to directors.

603 *Armitage v Nurse* [1998] Ch. 241 CA.

Remedies for breach of promoters' duties

10–141 There are various remedies available against promoters, but the most common are for breach of their fiduciary duties: the company (to whom these duties are owed) brings proceedings for recovery of any secret profits which the promoter has made, or for rescission of contracts it has with the promoter.[604]

A promoter, being a fiduciary, is not entitled to make a secret profit. A promoter's profit is most likely to derive from an over-priced sale of the promoter's property to the newly formed company: this is considered next. But if other profits are made by way of ancillary transactions, there is no doubt that these too may be recovered. The classic illustrations are bribes or secret commissions paid by third parties to the promoters for the benefit of particular privileges in future engagements with the company. But there are more complex cases too, as in *Gluckstein v Barnes*[605] itself. In that case a syndicate had been formed for the purpose of buying and reselling Olympia, then owned by a company in liquidation. The syndicate first bought up at low prices certain charges on the property and then bought the freehold itself for £140,000. They then promoted a company of which they were the directors, and to it they sold the freehold for £180,000, which was raised by a public issue of shares and debentures. In the prospectus the profit of £40,000 was disclosed. But in the meantime the promoters had had the charges on the property repaid by the liquidator out of the £140,000 original sale price, and had thereby made a further profit of £20,000. This was not disclosed in the prospectus, though reference was made there to a contract, close scrutiny of which might have revealed that some profit had been made. Four years later the new company went into liquidation and it was held that the promoters must account to the company for this secret profit of £20,000. Alternatively, the same facts may permit the company to sue the promoter for damages for fraud (deceit), or perhaps for misrepresentation.

By contrast, the remedy in the far more common scenario where the promoter sells his or her property to the company without proper disclosure is that the company may rescind the contract. Rescission must be exercised on normal contractual principles[606]; that is to say, the company must have done nothing to show an intention to ratify the agreement after finding out about the non-disclosure[607] and restitutio in integrum must still be possible.[608] The restitutio requirement means the company must be in a position to return the property,[609] prima facie in its original state (although it is immaterial if it is no

---

[604] Note the critical comments in *Bentinck v Fenn* (1887) L.R. 12 App.Cas. 652 HL, where the unsuccessful action was pursued—inappropriately—by a contributor.

[605] *Gluckstein v Barnes* [1900] A.C. 240. And see *Jubilee Cotton Mills v Lewis* [1924] A.C. 958 HL.

[606] S. Worthington, "The Proprietary Consequences of Rescission" (2002) Restitution Law Review 28–68.

[607] *Lagunas Nitrate Co v Lagunas Syndicate* [1899] 2 Ch. 392. Here again "the company" must mean the members or an independent board; clearly ratification by puppet directors cannot be effective.

[608] *Re Leeds & Hanley Theatre of Varieties* [1902] 2 Ch. 809 CA; *Steedman v Frigidaire Corp* [1933] 1 D.L.R. 161 PC; *Dominion Royalty Corp v Goffatt* [1935] 1 D.L.R. 780 Ont. CA; affirmed [1935] 4 D.L.R. 736 Can. SC.

[609] And, even then, note the dicta in *Smith New Court Securities v Scrimgeour Vickers (Asset Management) Ltd* [1997] A.C. 254 HL at 262 (Lord Browne-Wilkinson) suggesting that if the law denied rescission where shares had been on-sold on the market by the claimant, but an equivalent

longer of the same value[610]) although the courts' wide discretion to order financial adjustments when directing rescission means the rule now operates as much less of an impediment.[611]

If rescission of the contract between company and promoter is no longer possible (because of delay, affirmation or inability to effect restitutio), the alternative remedy of an account of profits, designed to strip the defaulting fiduciary of the profits of the breach, is not generally allowed.[612] In principle, the court could of course assess the market value of the asset at the date of sale and on that basis force the promoter to account, but this, it has been argued, would be to make a new contract for the parties.[613] The only exception, it seems, and a rare one at that,[614] arises where the very specific duties owed by the promoter at the time of the initial purchase make it possible to say that this original purchase by the promoter was, at least in equity, a purchase for the company[615]; then the re-sale by the promoter to the company is nugatory, and the company can accordingly recover the difference between the two prices as a simple secret profit made by the promoter.[616] **10–142**

This restricted view of when an account of profits is available can clearly work an injustice if restitutio in integrum has become impossible, and the company then seems to have no remedy against its defaulting promoter. In practice, the courts have avoided this injustice by upholding other remedies against the promoter, either finding that the promoter was fraudulent, and accordingly liable for damages in a common law action for deceit,[617] or negligent in allowing the

---

parcel could be repurchased for return to the defendant, then the law needed review. However, the orthodox position is, and as yet remains, that rescission is not available if the original asset cannot be returned: *Re Cape Breton Co* (1885) 29 Ch. D. 795 CA, affirmed sub nom. *Cavendish Bentinck v Fenn* (1887) 12 App. Cas. 652 HL; *Ladywell Mining Co v Brookes* (1887) 35 Ch. D. 400 CA.

610 *Armstrong v Jackson* [1917] 2 K.B. 822.

611 *Erlanger v New Sombrero Phosphate Co* (1878) 3 App. Cas. 1218; *Spence v Crawford* [1939] 3 All E.R. 271 HL.

612 *Re Ambrose Lake Tin & Copper Mining Co Ex p. Moss* (1880) 14 Ch. D. 390 CA; *Re Cape Breton Co* (1885) 29 Ch. D. 795 CA; affirmed sub nom. *Cavendish Bentinck v Fenn* (1887) 12 App. Cas. 652 HL; *Ladywell Mining Co v Brookes* (1887) 35 Ch. D. 400 CA; *Lady Forrest (Murchison) Gold Mine* [1901] 1 Ch. 582; *Burland v Earle* [1902] A.C. 83 PC; *Jacobus Marler Estates v Marler* (1913) 85 L.J.P.C. 167n; *Cook v Deeks* [1916] 1 A.C. 554 at 563 at 564; *Robinson v Randfontein Estates* [1921] A.D. 168 S.Afr.S.C.App.Div.; *P&O Steam Nav Co v Johnson* (1938) 60 C.L.R. 189 Aust. HC.

613 *Re Cape Breton Co* (1885) 29 Ch. D. 795.

614 See especially *Omnium Electric Palaces v Baines* [1914] 1 Ch. 332; and also [1914] 1 Ch. 332 at 347 per Sargant J. Also see *Re Ambrose Lake Tin & Copper Mining Co Ex p. Moss* (1880) 14 Ch. D. 390.

615 cf. *Cook v Deeks* [1916] 1 A.C. 554. There seems to be no objection in principle to the establishment of a trust in favour of an unformed company—for there can certainly be a trust in favour of an unborn child. By contrast, there cannot be an agency relationship with an unformed principal, so this approach cannot alleviate the problem of pre-incorporation contracts dealt with earlier at paras 8–030 to 8–036.

616 See Lord Parker's clear explanation in *Jacobus Marler Estates Ltd v Marler* (1913) 85 L.J.P.C. 167n.

617 *Re Olympia Ltd* [1898] 2 Ch. 153, affirmed sub nom. *Gluckstein v Barnes* [1900] A.C. 240 at 247; *Re Leeds and Hanley Theatre of Varieties* [1902] 2 Ch. 809 (and perhaps Vaughan Williams LJ takes an even wider view of when damages are available, at 825).

company to purchase at an excessive price,[618] the damages being the difference between the market value and the contract price. It is not possible to reach these same ends using the Misrepresentation Act 1967,[619] since the court's discretionary jurisdiction to award damages in lieu of rescission for innocent or negligent misrepresentations inducing a contract[620] does not, it seems, exist unless rescission is available at the time the court exercises the discretion.[621]

The company is not, however, the only party able to bring claims against the promoters. As already noted, the promoter may be liable to those who have acquired securities of the company in reliance on misstatements in listing particulars or prospectuses to which the promoter was a party. The remedies available against him are the same as those against the officers of the company or others responsible for the listing particulars or prospectuses and are dealt with in Ch.25. In addition, other participants may have claims at common law.

Remuneration of promoters

10–143 A promoter is not entitled to recover any remuneration for his services from the company unless there is a valid contract to that end between promoter and company. Indeed, older cases have suggested that without such a contract the promoter is not even entitled to recover preliminary expenses or the registration fees,[622] but whether these decisions would survive modern unjust enrichment analysis is perhaps moot. In this respect the promoter is at the mercy of the directors of the company. Until the company is formed it cannot enter into a valid contract[623] and the promoter therefore has to expend the money without any guarantee of repayment. In practice, however, recovery of preliminary expenses and registration fees does not normally present any difficulty. The directors will normally be empowered to pay them and will do so. It may well be, however, that the promoter will not be content merely to recover his expenses; certainly a professional promoter will expect to be handsomely remunerated. Nor is this unreasonable. As Lord Hatherley said,[624] "The services of a promoter are very peculiar; great skill, energy and ingenuity may be employed in constructing a plan and in bringing it out to the best advantages". Hence it is perfectly proper for the promoter to be rewarded, provided, as we have seen, that there is full disclosure to the company of the rewards to be obtained.

---

[618] Note the restrictions described by Lord Parker in *Jacobus Marler Estates v Marler* (1913) 85 L.J.P.C. 167n at 168.

[619] Misrepresentation Act 1967 s.2(1) and s.2(2), allowing damages to be awarded in lieu of rescission.

[620] And the mere non-disclosure of the amount of the promoter's profit is not misrepresentation: *Lady Forrest (Murchison) Gold Mine* [1901] 1 Ch. 582; *Jacobus Marler Estates Ltd v Marler* (1913) 85 L.J.P.C. 167n.

[621] *Salt v Stratstone Specialist Ltd* [2015] EWCA Civ 745.

[622] *Re English and Colonial Produce Co* [1906] 2 Ch. 435 CA; *Re National Motor Mail Coach Co* [1908] 2 Ch. 515 CA.

[623] See below.

[624] In *Touche v Metropolitan Ry Warehousing Co* (1870–71) L.R. 6 Ch. App. 671 Lord Chancellor at 676.

The reward may take many forms. The promoter may purchase an undertaking and then promote a company to repurchase it at a profit, or the undertaking may be sold directly by the former owner to the new company, the promoter receiving a commission from the vendor. A once-popular device was for the company's capital structure to provide for a special class of deferred or founders' shares which would be issued credited as fully paid in consideration of the promoter's services.[625] Such shares would normally provide for the lion's share of the profits available for dividend after the preference and ordinary shares had been paid a dividend of a fixed amount. This had the advantage that the promoter advertised his or her apparent confidence in the business by retaining a stake in it; but all too often the stake (which probably cost the promoter nothing anyway) was merely window-dressing. And if, in fact, the company proved an outstanding success the promoter might do better than all the other shareholders put together. Today, when the trend is towards simplicity of capital structures, founders' shares are out of favour and, in general, those old companies which originally had them have got rid of them on a reconstruction.[626] A more likely alternative is for the promoter to be given warrants or options entitling him or her to subscribe for shares at a particular price (e.g. that at which they were issued to the public) within a specified time. If the shares have meanwhile gone to a premium this will obviously be a valuable right.

CONCLUSION

This is a long chapter, and its detailed rules on directors' duties are an enormously important and frequently used tool in regulating the management of companies by their directors. The most substantial reform in this area in recent times has undoubtedly been the statutory enactment of the general duties in the CA 2006, replacing their earlier common law counterparts. This in itself was reform of a unique sort, with its careful management of the inevitable ongoing interplay between the statutory rules and their common law counterparts (see especially s.170(4)). But what can be said of the consequences? At this relatively short distance down the track, no seismic shifts have occurred, either for good or for ill. This should come as no surprise, since what was done was largely intended to be a restatement of the past, with a few relatively minor added tweaks to improve rules and practices where problems were already well known and aired. **10–144**

[625] The promoter should obtain a contract with the company prior to rendering the services, for past services are not valuable consideration: *Re Eddystone Marine Insurance* [1893] 3 Ch. 9 CA. Hence if the services are rendered before the company was formed the promoter will have to pay for the shares. Moreover, in the case of a public company, an undertaking to perform work or supply services will no longer be valid payment: s.585(1) and see para.16–018. But provided the shares are given a very low nominal value this may not be a serious snag.

[626] There have been many interesting battles between holders of founders' shares and the other members. If the holdings of founders' shares are widely dispersed there is obviously a risk of block being acquired on behalf of the other classes in the hope of outvoting the remaining founders' shareholders at a class meeting to approve a reconstruction. To safeguard their position, in a number of cases the founders' shareholders formed a special company and vested all the founders' shares in it, thus ensuring that they were voted solidly at any meeting.

Section 172, imposing a general duty on directors to promote the success of the company, might be thought of as one exception to that minimal-change approach, especially as it contains an explicit recognition of stakeholder interests for the first time in British company law, which had previously referred only to members and employee interests.[627] However, those stakeholder interests are to be pursued by directors only where such action is needed to promote the success of the company for the benefit of its members. The core duty of loyalty is thus still shareholder-centred. Further, it seems clear that the prior common law permitted directors to take into account stakeholder interests where promoting the interests of the company (shareholders) required it.[628] Consequently, the novelty of the statutory formulation of the core duty of good faith and fidelity may be the added obligation—rather than entitlement—of directors to take stakeholder interests into account where the promotion of the success of the company requires this. This is only a marginal change in legal obligation, however, and there is as yet nothing to suggest that this revised statutory articulation of the need to take into account stakeholder interests in this way has had much impact, even when coupled with larger changes in legal rules and the social and economic context within which companies operate.[629]

The statutory rules are explicitly more constraining than the common law in their provisions on negligence (s.174), the core duty of loyalty (s.172) and the rules on ratification (s.239). The changes to the core duty of loyalty (s.172) have already been noted. So far as the duty of care is concerned, the objective standard of care introduced by s.174 is undoubtedly a strong contrast with the subjective formulation of that duty to be found in the nineteenth-century negligence cases. But common law decisions were already well-advanced in moving the law in an objective direction, and so it might be said that s.174 merely confirmed what was already emerging in the case law.[630] Equally, s.239[631] introduced important changes to the rules on who may vote on a shareholder resolution to ratify a breach of directors' duties by excluding the votes of the directors in question and those connected with them. But this trend too was evident in a trickle of cases, and clearly easily justified on policy grounds. It is undoubtedly an important reform in closely held companies, but its real impact will only be felt, even there (or especially there), if these rules also trigger a parallel change in the common law authorisation rules and their approach to disenfranchising interested voters. This, it is suggested, is a far better approach than tinkering further with the difficult notions of "un-ratifiable wrongs".[632]

Going in the other direction, and tending to relax rather than tighten the constraints on directors, perhaps the most significant statutory changes were those that allowed the independent members of the board to authorise breaches of the directors' duty not to place themselves in a position of conflict of duty and

[627] See paras 10–026 to 10–039 and for the prior statutory law see CA 1985 s.309.

[628] *Hutton v West Cork Ry Co* (1883) 23 Ch. D. 654 per Bowen LJ: "Most businesses require liberal dealings".

[629] For example, changes within company law about narrative reporting (see paras 22–024 onwards) or outside company law the increasing legal and political significance of environmental issues.

[630] See paras 10–045 to 10–050.

[631] See para.10–115.

[632] See paras 10–118.

interest (or of duty and duty).[633] Although the principle of board decision-making was already established under the prior law in relation to self-dealing transactions (at least as a matter of practice, via provisions in the articles), its extension to corporate opportunities and other conflicted situations was a new step. The argument in favour of the extension is that shareholder authorisation, as the sole method of authorisation permitted by the prior law, was in practice too uncertain and too public to be a practical form of permission, so that the prior law operated in fact so as to allow directors to pursue corporate opportunities only at the risk of the company later deciding to take from the director the profit earned from the exploitation of the opportunity. The argument against the extension is that the dynamics of board relationships mean that the uninvolved members of the board may not exercise a genuinely independent judgment on whether to release the corporate interest in the opportunity, even if this is what the law requires of them. This argument may be less strong in companies listed on the main market of the London Stock Exchange and so required to comply with the provisions of the UK Corporate Governance Code as to independent non-executive directors, but that is a very small proportion of the companies incorporated under the Companies Acts. In the result, outside the area of benefits received by directors from third parties,[634] the board is now the guardian of the company's position in situations of conflict, contrary to the wisdom of the common law that only the shareholders could be relied upon for this purpose.

[633] CA 2006 s.175 and see paras 10–096 to 10–097.

[634] See paras 10–101 to 10–102.

PART 4

SHAREHOLDERS

An important determinant of behaviour in a company is the structure of its shareholding along the continuum between highly dispersed and atomised shareholdings to one person holding all the shares. Where there are many shareholders, each with only a very small shareholding, the risk to the shareholders is that the management will be the true controllers of the company and they may not give the shareholders' interests proper consideration. Indeed, the default position for British company law is that the management of the company rests with the board and the shareholders are generally not competent to interfere with those decisions. On one level, this is one of the principal advantages of incorporation: delegation of management functions to experts allows shareholders to spread their investments and diversify their portfolio of holdings. On another level, passive investment means that shareholders have no effective say in corporate affairs. Passivity is not an option in closely held companies and is increasingly seen as undesirable on the part of institutional investors in large companies. Accordingly, there is a renewed interest in the constitutional powers of the shareholders. These have always existed at common law, but there has been a steady growth of statutory mechanisms whereby shareholders can influence corporate direction. That said, shareholder powers tend to focus on the really significant issues in a company's life (such as constitutional change, alterations in form or the company's end-of-life). More recently, shareholders have been given a "say on pay", which they can add to their ability to remove the board. Chapter 11 examines those circumstances when the balance of power in a company shifts back to the shareholders.

There is, however, little point giving the shareholders extensive powers if the procedural mechanisms by which they are exercised are not fit for purpose. The shareholders' traditional means of expressing their collective will is through the general meeting. The statutory rules dealing with the calling and conduct of shareholder meetings has all the feel of a game, where detailed knowledge of procedure is a distinct advantage. Not only are the directors more likely to understand those rules than the shareholders, but in many ways the board acts as the gatekeeper. The ability of the shareholders to use the general meeting to challenge the board can never be as effective when the board has the incentive and the legal tools to influence shareholder decision-making. Recognition of this fact has, however, led to the development of alternative mechanisms, whether increased use of electronic meetings or the development of decision-making processes that do not rely on a formal meeting. Chapter 12 examines the conduct of shareholder meetings and the other forms of decision-making in which they can engage.

Whatever powers are given to shareholders, and no matter how effectively they can be enforced, the fact that the day-to-day management of the company resides with the board means that their decisions may negatively impact the company (and indirectly the shareholders). When such conduct is serious enough to involve a director in a breach of his duties to the company, a difficult issue arises as to how those breaches might be enforced. Whilst this will ordinarily be for the corporate organs (the board or, failing that, the general meeting) to do, the wrongdoing directors may have control over both meetings with the result that they can effectively stymie the claims against them. In those circumstances, the law hunts around for an independent decision-maker.

When faced with such a dysfunctional company, shareholders in both closely held and public companies are left with two options: to exercise their "voice"; or to "exit" the company. In terms of "voice", where the shareholder is a majority or institutional shareholder, their "voice" may be heard through the exercise of the internal corporate levers or the commencement of litigation. The difficulty has been incentivising such shareholders to do so. In relation to minority shareholders, the courts have long had concerns about them by-passing the internal corporate decision-making structures, but this has been allowed in the litigation context albeit subject to stringent safeguards. Whilst the nature of those safeguards has changed over time, the basic question is whether the company's interests would be best served by having the proceedings brought. Where this is the case, a minority can sue on behalf of the company and recover compensation on its behalf. This is considered in Ch.15. The alternative is "exit". Whilst this is not a problem in companies with tradeable shares, it is a real difficulty in closely held companies. Whilst a minority shareholder in such a company has never been given an unrestricted right of exit, his shares might be bought out, if he can establish that the directors (or other controllers) have acted in an unfairly prejudicial manner. The unfair prejudice jurisdiction is considered in Ch.14, along with any other personal claims that such a shareholder might bring.

It is not solely the board, however, that can engage in unfairly prejudicial conduct. Unfair treatment of the minority can equally occur at the hands of the majority shareholders. Indeed, the majority shareholders may use their power to divert to themselves a greater part of the company's earnings than their contribution to the company's share capital justifies. Such "private benefits of control" are probably impossible to eradicate without interventionist rules whose costs would probably outweigh the rewards—and, in any event, some benefits constitute legitimate returns for the majority's monitoring efforts. Nevertheless, if the law is to encourage investors to place their money in companies controlled by a small group of shareholders, then it must deal with the more outrageous examples of majority opportunism. Apart from the unfairness of majority exploitation of the minority, there is a strong efficiency argument in favour of minority protection. If the holders of minority stakes of ordinary shares in companies are not so protected, they will protect themselves, probably by only being prepared to buy such shares at a lower price, thus in effect buying insurance against the majority's unfair treatment of them. This will raise the company's cost of capital, so that the cost of the unfair treatment is ultimately transferred back to the controllers of the company. On this argument, it is as much in the interests of the majority as it is of the minority shareholders that effective legal limits should be placed on the freedom of the majority to act opportunistically towards the minority. These limits are considered in Ch.13.

companies are not so protected, they will protect themselves, probably by only being prepared to buy their shares at a lower price, thus in effect buying insurance against the majority's unfair treatment of them. This will raise the company's cost of capital, so that the cost of the unfair treatment is ultimately transferred back to the controllers of the company. On this argument, it is as much in the interests of the majority as it is of the minority shareholders that effective legal limits should be placed on the freedom of the majority to act opportunistically towards the minority. Those limits are considered in Ch.13.

CHAPTER 11

THE CONSTITUTIONAL ROLE OF SHAREHOLDERS

INTRODUCTION

Not infrequently, one encounters the description of shareholders as being the "owners" of the company. As highlighted already,[1] this is a misnomer in two fundamental respects: first, whilst a shareholder undoubtedly has a bundle of valuable rights in the company, including the right to vote upon resolutions proposed at a general meeting, a shareholder does not have any legal or equitable interest in the company's assets[2]; and, secondly, with the exception of closely-held companies, shareholders generally delegate the company's running to management and the board.[3] Indeed, as considered already, not only do the model articles expressly delegate the management function to the board,[4] but there is a long-standing principle of non-interference by shareholders in the board's sphere of competence.[5] Such a situation naturally raises questions concerning what (if any) functions the shareholders continue to perform in the company (beyond being passive recipients of dividends); and what constitutional role is played by the general meeting, which is the organ through which the shareholders may take collection action. Indeed, one would expect shareholders to have some constitutional role simply by virtue of the fact that one of the key legal incidents of shareholding is having a right to vote at the general meeting. 11–001

[1] See para.6–001.

[2] *Macaura v Northern Assurance Co Ltd* [1925] A.C. 619 HL at 626; *Short v Treasury Commissioners* [1948] 1 K.B. 116 CA at 122; *Shanda Games Ltd v Maso Capital Investments Ltd* [2020] UKPC 2; [2020] B.C.C. 466 at [46]–[47].

[3] See paras 2–025 to 2–028.

[4] Companies (Model Articles) Regulations 2008 (SI 2008/3229) Sch.1 art.3 and Sch.3 art.3.

[5] *Automatic Self-Cleaning Filter Syndicate Co v Cunninghame* [1906] 2 Ch. 34 CA; *John Shaw & Sons (Salford) Ltd v Shaw* [1935] 2 K.B. 113 CA. See also *Stobart Group Ltd v Tinkler* [2019] EWHC 258 (Comm) at [395].

By reference to the general sources of company law considered above,[6] there are three from which shareholders' principally derive their rights and powers: the shareholders' agreement, as reflected in the company's articles of association and any supplementary shareholder agreements; the common law, in terms of residual powers to manage the company and control board activity; and statute, whereby shareholders may have certain matters reserved to their exclusive control, may be given a power to veto certain transactions or may be given an opportunity to input into the decision-making process. Each of these sources of shareholder power will be considered in turn.

SHAREHOLDERS' CONTRACTUAL RIGHTS

The company's constitution

11–002 The common law tends to classify the rule-books and constitutions of clubs, trade unions, friendly societies or other unincorporated associations as being contractual in nature.[7] Partnerships similarly have a contractual foundation.[8] Accordingly, it is unsurprising that the CA 2006 adopts the same contractual analysis for the company's articles of association by providing that "the provisions of the company's constitution bind the company and its members to the same extent as if there were covenants on the part of the company and of each member to observe it".[9] The origins of this provision can be traced back (with variations) to the Joint Stock Companies Act 1844[10] and the CA 1862.[11] As the articles constitute a multi-party contract between the company and each member, it is accordingly enforceable by the shareholders against the company and between the shareholders inter se.[12] Conversely, non-members cannot enforce the articles.[13] The contractual effect of the articles is particularly useful for shareholders when there has been a breach or threatened breach of company's

[6] See Ch.3.

[7] For the "contract-holding" theory applicable to unincorporated associations, see *Re Recher* [1972] Ch. 526 Ch D; *Re Lipinski* [1976] Ch. 235 Ch D.

[8] Partnership Act 1890 ss.1 and 19.

[9] CA 2006 s.33(1).

[10] The current provision explicitly states that the company is also bound by the terms of its articles of association, which is important in giving shareholders rights against the company itself. Nevertheless, practitioners had long treated earlier versions of the articles as binding between members and the company, despite the statutory wording making no reference to the company, although this view was only based on first-instance authority: see *Hickman v Kent or Romney Marsh Sheepbreeders Association* [1915] 1 Ch. 881 Ch D. The treatment of the articles as a deed has also been removed from the current provision, thus removing the consequence that a debt owed by a member to the company was a "specialty" debt, with its special limitation period, rather than an ordinary one: see CA 1985 s.14(2). See also *Re Compania de Electridad de Buenos Aires* [1980] Ch. 146 Ch D at 187. Nowadays, such a debt is viewed as a simple contractual debt: see CA 2006 s.33(2). See also *Zavarco Plc v Nasir* [2020] EWHC 629 (Ch); [2020] Ch. 651 at [33]–[34]; *Re Taunton Logs Ltd* [2020] EWHC 3480 (Ch) at [25].

[11] *Children's Investment Fund Foundation (UK) v Attorney General* [2020] UKSC 33; [2020] 3 W.L.R. 461 at [73].

[12] *Haven Insurance Co Ltd v EUI Ltd* [2018] EWCA Civ 2494 at [3].

[13] *The New Saints FC Ltd v The Football Association of Wales Ltd* [2020] EWHC 1838 (Ch) at [36], fn.15.

articles,[14] such as payment of dividends in the wrong form, a breach of a member's right of pre-emption (or first refusal) when another member wishes to sell his shares,[15] or the refusal by a remaining member or director to comply with a constitutional obligation to buy the shares of a retiring member (a less common provision).[16] Despite the analogy between the articles of association and an ordinary contract underlining the former's enforceability, the company's articles of association nevertheless constitute a rather peculiar form of contract as many contractual principles are in fact inapplicable.

The difficulty with maintaining the analogy between a company's articles of association and an ordinary contract stems from the fact that the former is clearly more than just a private bargain between the company and its members. Indeed, any bespoke articles of association need to be filed with the Registrar of Companies to incorporate the company.[17] As these documents will be formally registered,[18] they become public from the moment of the company's formation. Even when the company relies upon the model articles for its constitution, they will nevertheless be public because these are set out in a statutory instrument[19] or because the company supplies to the registrar for public registration its own articles which amend in part the statutory model.[20] Given that incorporation is essentially a facility provided by the State, it is unsurprising that the company's constitution has always been public.[21] Accordingly, third parties dealing with, or investing in, the company have a legitimate expectation that the registered articles represent an accurate statement of the company's internal regulations. **11–003**

The publicity surrounding the articles of association has resulted in the courts declining to apply many standard contract law principles to articles of association,[22] despite the CA 2006 emphasising its contractual status. In particular, the courts have been reluctant to apply any general contractual principles to the statutory contract that might result in the articles of association having a content that is substantially different from what a reasonably well-informed third party would understand them to mean. There are several instances of this approach. First, the Court of Appeal, in *Scott v Frank F. Scott (London) Ltd*,[23] held that a company's articles of association (unlike an ordinary contract) cannot subsequently be rectified to give effect to what the incorporators actually intended, but failed to embody in the registered document, since a person examining the registered documents could have no way of realising that an error had been made in recording the incorporators' agreement into the articles. Secondly, whilst a term can be implied into an ordinary contract whenever

---

[14] *Marex Financial Ltd v Sevilleja* [2020] UKSC 31; [2020] 3 W.L.R. 255 at [103].

[15] *Borland's Trustee v Steel Bros & Co Ltd* [1901] 1 Ch. 279 Ch D (member seeking declaration that rights of pre-emption in articles were valid); cf. *Lyle & Scott v Scott's Trustees* [1959] A.C. 763 HL.

[16] *Rayfield v Hands* [1960] Ch. 1 Ch D, where Vaisey J was prepared to make an order in effect for specific performance.

[17] CA 2006 s.9(5)(b).

[18] CA 2006 s.14.

[19] Companies (Model Articles) Regulations 2008 (SI 2008/3229) Sch.1 art.3 and Sch.3 art.3.

[20] CA 2006 ss.9(5)(b) and 14.

[21] For the equivalent position in EU Law, see Directive 2017/1132 relating to certain aspects of company law [2017] OJ L169/46 art.14(a).

[22] *Flanagan v Liontrust Investment Partners LLP* [2015] EWHC 2171 (Ch) at [241].

[23] *Scott v Frank F. Scott (London) Ltd* [1940] Ch. 794 CA.

"business necessity" requires,[24] the Court of Appeal, in *Bratton Seymour Service Co Ltd v Oxborough*,[25] refused to imply terms into the statutory contract from extrinsic evidence of surrounding circumstances where that evidence would not be readily discoverable by third parties who would accordingly have no means of anticipating what additions might otherwise be made implicitly to the constitution. That said, Steyn LJ did not rule out a "purely constructional implication", where a term was implied "purely from the language of the document itself".[26] Thirdly, whilst the terms of an ordinary contract may be interpreted in light of the contract's wider context,[27] the interpretation of the articles of association requires "the total exclusion of extrinsic evidence",[28] so that articles of association will be interpreted in more literal fashion than commercial contracts in general. Finally, in *Bratton Seymour*, Steyn LJ expressed the view that the usual grounds upon which an ordinary contract might be vitiated were inapplicable to the articles of association, since the statutory contract "was not defeasible on the grounds of misrepresentation, common law mistake, mistake in equity, undue influence or duress".[29] Indeed, the maxim *ut res magis valeat quam pereat* has always been applied strongly in the context of the company's articles.[30]

The policy behind limiting the application of general contractual principles to the articles makes sense: not only is this consistent with the statutory conclusiveness of the certificate of incorporation,[31] but it is also consistent with the wider policy of protecting third parties' expectations by allowing them to rely on what they find upon searching the public registry. This sensible position is, however, somewhat undermined when the articles are subsequently altered.[32] If

[24] *Marks & Spencer Plc v BNP Paribas Securities Services Trust Co (Jersey) Ltd* [2015] UKSC 72; [2016] A.C. 742 at [16]–[21]; doubting *AG for Belize v Belize Telecom Ltd* [2009] UKPC 10; [2009] B.C.C. 433. See also *Duval v 11-13 Randolph Crescent Ltd* [2020] UKSC 18; [2020] A.C. 845 at [51].

[25] *Bratton Seymour Service Co Ltd v Oxborough* [1992] B.C.L.C. 693 CA; approved in *Chartbrook Ltd v Persimmon Homes Ltd* [2009] UKHL 38; [2009] 1 A.C. 1101 at [40]. In *Bratton*, the majority shareholders were effectively seeking to avoid the prohibition on constitutional alterations that increase a shareholder's financial liability to the company without their consent: see CA 2006 s.25(1). See also *Towcester Racecourse Co Ltd v Racecourse Association Ltd* [2002] EWHC 2141 (Ch); [2003] 1 B.C.L.C. 260, where, in any event, the judge regarded the suggested implied terms as inconsistent with the express terms of the articles. See also *Re Coroin Ltd* [2011] EWHC 3466 (Ch); affirmed [2012] EWCA Civ 179; [2012] B.C.C. 575, where the court was prepared to admit as extrinsic evidence the shareholder agreement pursuant to which the articles were adopted. See also *Cosmetic Warriors Ltd v Gerrie* [2015] EWHC 3718 (Ch) at [27].

[26] *Bratton Seymour Service Co Ltd v Oxborough* [1992] B.C.L.C. 693. See also *AG for Belize v Belize Telecom Ltd* [2009] B.C.C. 433 at [37]; *London Borough of Lambeth v Secretary of State for Communities and Local Government* [2018] EWCA Civ 844 at [64]–[65].

[27] *Wood v Capita Insurance Services Ltd* [2017] UKSC 24; [2017] A.C. 1173 at [11]–[14].

[28] *Cherry Tree Investments Ltd v Landmain Ltd* [2012] EWCA Civ 736; [2013] Ch. 305 at [39]–[45]. See also *Re Euro Accessories Ltd* [2021] EWHC 47 (Ch) at [30]–[34]. A more permissive approach was, however, suggested in *Cosmetic Warriors Ltd v Gerrie* [2015] EWHC 3718 (Ch) at [27].

[29] *Bratton Seymour Service Co Ltd v Oxborough* [1992] B.C.L.C. 693 at 698. On the other hand, investor protection was not inconsistent with the implication of terms based on the construction of the language used in the articles, for here the basis of the implication was available to those who read the company's constitution.

[30] *Rayfield v Hands* [1960] Ch. 1.

[31] CA 2006 s.15(4), considered further in para.4–007.

[32] CA 2006 s.21(1).

this is done by means of a special resolution passed at a general meeting, the CA 2006 contains certain publicity requirements to protect third parties, namely sending the Registrar of Companies a copy of the amended articles,[33] together with a copy of the resolution itself.[34] Failure to inform the registrar is a criminal offence and may attract civil penalties.[35] In *Gunewardena v Conran Holdings Ltd*,[36] however, Mann J has suggested that, in circumstances where the wrong documents are filed, the company's articles will remain those agreed between the shareholders (rather than the documents filed with Companies House) since the status of the articles "does not depend on registration". The position is a fortiori if no documents are filed. The same problem arises in even more acute form when shareholders rely upon the doctrine of informal, unanimous shareholder consent to amend the articles.[37] Whilst the CA 2006 now requires such resolutions to be communicated to the Registrar,[38] the informality alone means that this may not happen, so that the registered articles will no longer reflect the company's actual constitution.[39] Accordingly, third parties cannot always be certain that what they see is what they get.

Putting these concerns aside, the above differences between the statutory contract and an ordinary contract do raise the question of how helpful it is to analogise them, especially as yet other differences exist. First, whereas an ordinary contract's terms can all be enforced (subject to issues of illegality or public policy), there exists authority supporting the view that provisions of the corporate constitution cannot be enforced to the extent that they confer "outsider" rights on members.[40] Secondly, an ordinary multi-lateral contract can only be altered by unanimity, whereas a three-quarter majority suffices for the articles.[41] Thirdly, whilst third parties may now acquire rights to enforce an ordinary contract, this remains impossible under the statutory contract in the articles.[42] Finally, even assuming that damages are now a remedy available to a shareholder for breach of the statutory contract,[43] equitable relief in the form of an injunction or order for specific performance is more likely to be awarded than damages for loss suffered. This contrasts sharply with the remedial position under an ordinary contract. Accordingly, given that it is not even clear how the ordinary principles of contractual formation would apply to the statutory contract, analogising the articles of association with a contract is not only unhelpful, but may be potentially misleading. It would suffice if, as in other jurisdictions,[44] the CA 2006

[33] CA 2006 s.26(1).

[34] CA 2006 ss.29–30.

[35] CA 2006 ss.26–27.

[36] *Gunewardena v Conran Holdings Ltd* [2016] EWHC 2983 (Ch); [2017] B.C.C. 135 at [69]–[71].

[37] *Cane v Jones* [1980] 1 W.L.R. 1451 Ch D; *Re Home Treat Ltd* [1991] B.C.L.C. 705 Ch D (Companies Ct). See further Ch.12.

[38] CA 2006 ss.29–30.

[39] *Cane v Jones* [1980] 1 W.L.R. 1451; *Re Home Treat Ltd* [1991] B.C.L.C. 705.

[40] See paras 14–002 to 14–003.

[41] CA 2006 s.21(1). Of course, the parties may agree that a multilateral contract may be altered in the future through a mechanism which does not involve the consent of each party to it, as is often done in bond contracts. See paras 31–029 to 31–030.

[42] Contracts (Rights of Third Parties) Act 1999 s.6(2).

[43] CA 2006 s.655.

[44] CA 1993 (NZ) s.172.

simply made the articles of association enforceable at the instance of the shareholders without any reference to a contract being necessary.

Shareholder agreements

11–004 As considered previously,[45] shareholders have a significant amount of freedom in fashioning the company's constitution. This facilitates the introduction of a significant element of "private ordering" into the rules governing a company's operations. The articles of association are, however, not the only means by which shareholders can develop their own rules for corporate governance. An alternative mechanism is the shareholders' agreement. This may be concluded between some or all of the company' shareholders, but the company itself may not always be privy to such an agreement.[46] A shareholders' agreement operates separately from (albeit alongside) the company's articles of association. As a general rule, shareholders' agreements are not normally treated as part of the company's constitution, although exceptionally certain types of agreement fall within the definition of the "constitution" depending upon their nature[47] or the particular circumstances.[48]

11–005 Given that the shareholders effectively have a choice between manifesting their agreement in the articles or in a separate shareholder agreement, it is important to consider the differences between these two options.[49] Indeed, as will be shown, a shareholder agreement displays both the advantages and disadvantages associated with private contracting. First, the principal advantage of a shareholder agreement is that it is essentially private and does not require registration at Companies House.[50] Secondly, shareholder agreements derive their binding force from contract law, whereas the articles of association derive their contractual force from the CA 2006.[51] Accordingly, as considered above,[52] the former is subject to ordinary contractual principles, whereas the latter is not always. This may have an impact on the remedies available for breach: whilst breach of the articles of association will usually be enforced by means of an injunction or an order for specific performance, a shareholders' agreement will sound in damages. Thirdly, whilst the articles of association automatically bind new members who join the company, shareholder agreements do not.[53] Although it is possible for a new member to become party to a shareholder agreement, the CA 2006 does not

---

45 See Ch.3.

46 If the agreement seeks to fetter the company's statutory powers under the CA 2006, it will be void to the extent of the company's participation in the agreement: see *Russell v Northern Bank Development Corporation Ltd* [1992] 1 W.L.R. 588 HL.

47 CA 2006 s.29(1).

48 For example, a shareholders' agreement is part of the constitution in relation to issues concerning the directors' powers to bind the company: see CA 2006 s.40(3)(b). See further para.8–014.

49 For the shareholder agreement as a form of minority shareholder protection, see Ch.13.

50 *Re Euro Accessories Ltd* [2021] EWHC 47 (Ch) at [30].

51 Consider *Russell v Northern Bank Development Corporation Ltd* [1992] 1 W.L.R. 588.

52 See para.11–003.

53 The reference to "members" in the CA 2006 s.33(1) is to those who at any one time are the members of the company.

provide any mechanism whereby this may be achieved automatically. Accordingly, at common law, a novation would be required necessitating the unanimous consent of all parties. This may not be easily achieved. One solution might be for the parties to provide a contractual mechanism facilitating the arrival and departure of new members.[54]

CONSTITUTIONAL POWERS OF THE GENERAL MEETING AT COMMON LAW

Despite the fact that the model articles of association ordinarily vest management powers exclusively in the board, the common law has long recognised circumstances where shareholders are given an effective voice. There are three such instances, namely when the board is unable to exercise its powers; when the board's decision exceeds its powers or involves a breach of duty; and when the shareholders act unanimously. Each will be considered in turn. **11–006**

The first and (arguably) most dramatic instance arises when the board cannot exercise the powers vested in it. In such circumstances, the general meeting retains a residual power to manage the company in the absence of an effective board. Accordingly, management by the general meeting has been considered effective when the board can no longer act because it is deadlocked[55]; where there are no directors in place[56]; where it is not possible to obtain an effective quorum for the board meeting[57]; or where the directors are disqualified from voting.[58] Whilst this exception is difficult to reconcile with the strict theory of a division of powers and its exact limits remain unclear, there is no doubt that it represents a pragmatic response to a difficult situation. In order to keep this exception within workable limits, however, there does seem some good sense in the view that the shareholders may only take the substantive decision when the company's articles do not give them some effective way of reconstituting the board, so as to remove any impediment to board decision-making.[59] **11–007**

The second exception arises when the directors have exceeded their powers whether by exercising powers that they do not have or purporting to exercise powers that the company has reserved to the general meeting. In such circumstances, the general meeting may decide to ratify the directors' actions, both in the sense of making binding unauthorised transactions and forgiving the **11–008**

---

[54] Consider the "consent in advance" mechanism for the transfer of participation rights in syndicated loans: see *Habibsons Bank Ltd v Standard Chartered Bank (Hong Kong) Ltd* [2010] EWCA Civ 1335 at [20]–[23].

[55] *Baron v Potter* [1914] 1 Ch. 895 Ch D. See also *Abdelmamoud v The Egyptian Association in Great Britain* [2018] EWCA Civ 879 at [38]. Contrast situations in which a board cannot do what the majority of the directors want because of the opposition of a minority acting within its powers under the articles: see, for example, *Quin & Axtens Ltd v Salmon* [1909] A.C. 442 HL; *Breckland Group Holdings Ltd v London & Suffolk Properties* [1989] B.C.L.C. 100 Ch D.

[56] *Alexander Ward & Co Ltd v Samyang Navigation Co Ltd* [1975] 1 W.L.R. 673 HL at 679, citing the corresponding passage from the 3rd edn of this book.

[57] *Foster v Foster* [1916] 1 Ch. 532 Ch D. See also *Neptune (Vehicle Washing Equipment) Ltd v Fitzgerald* [1996] Ch. 274 Ch D at 282.

[58] *Irvine v Union Bank of Australia* (1877) 2 App. Cas. 366 PC.

[59] *Massey v Wales* (2003) 57 N.S.W.L.R. 718 NSWCA.

directors for exceeding their powers.[60] For the purpose of ratifying past conduct of the board, as opposed to conferring powers on the board for the future, an ordinary, rather than a special, resolution will suffice.[61] Indeed, the board of directors is entitled to refer of its own accord any matter to the general meeting to ratify what the board has done or to enable the general meeting to decide what action should be taken. This is what occurred in *Bamford v Bamford*,[62] where the directors were alleged to have breached their duties to act in good faith and for a proper purpose by allotting shares to frustrate a takeover. As a response to proceedings being commenced by two shareholders, the board summoned a general meeting to consider a resolution ratifying the allotment of shares. According to the Court of Appeal, it was open to the general meeting to ratify the directors' conduct if (and all the conditions are important) the act is within the powers of the company and the general meeting acts with full knowledge and without oppression of the minority. What is potentially less clear is whether the board, without first taking a decision on a matter within its powers, can simply refer the matter to the general meeting for an initial decision. At first instance in *Bamford*,[63] Plowman J considered that the general meeting might act in this way under its residual powers,[64] although this would depend upon the precise terms of the company's articles. Indeed, one might justify the board seeking the general meeting's view as a delegation by the former of its powers on the particular issue (back) to the shareholders. In contrast, the Court of Appeal considered the issue irrelevant on the particular facts and accordingly expressed no view on the point. Given that the general meeting has the ability to ratify the directors' conduct *after* the event, it would seem absurd if the board could not also seek the general meeting's view *before* entering the relevant transaction. Given the uncertainty in *Bamford*, however, the safest course may be for the directors to take action expressly "subject to ratification by the company in general meeting".

11–009 The third (possible) exception arises when the shareholders seek to bind the company by their unanimous agreement or consent.[65] This common law unanimous informal consent principle has been preserved by the CA 2006.[66] Whilst this possibility will be considered in more detail in the context of shareholder decision-making more generally,[67] the rationale for the "unanimous informal consent" principle is to enable shareholders in small companies to exercise their powers without the need to hold a meeting and to observe all the formalities (for example, as to notice) that shareholder meetings entail.[68] This could be achieved by, for example, circulating a resolution, to which each shareholder individually indicates their consent. Whilst this introduces a degree of flexibility into shareholder decision-making, the obvious disadvantage of this

---

60 CA 2006 ss.171(b), 180(1) and 239(1).
61 *Grant v UK Switchback Rys* (1888) 40 Ch. D. 135 CA.
62 *Bamford v Bamford* [1970] Ch. 212 CA (Civ Div).
63 *Bamford v Bamford* [1970] Ch. 212.
64 See para.11–007.
65 *Re Duomatic Ltd* [1969] 2 Ch. 365 Ch D.
66 CA 2006 s. 281(4). See also Modernising, paras 2.31–2.35.
67 See further Ch.12.
68 *Ciban Management Corporation v Cico (BVI) Ltd* [2020] UKPC 21; [2020] 3 W.L.R. 705 at [31]–[32].

mechanism is that it requires unanimity on the part of all the shareholders entitled to vote, not just those who turn up at a meeting.[69] It is largely because of this last requirement that informal unanimous consent has been overtaken by the statutory written resolution procedure, which does not require unanimity, as a way of streamlining shareholder decisions.[70]

There are, however, dicta in the cases suggesting that the shareholders' unanimous consent can bind the company, even on matters that the constitution allocates to the board.[71] Nevertheless, none of the decided cases clearly present the situation of the shareholders unanimously taking a decision that had been allocated by the constitution to the board. The closest that one gets to support for such a view is *Re Express Engineering Works Ltd*,[72] in which the relevant decision concerned the purchase of certain property. This would clearly have fallen within the clause conferring general management powers on the board. Whilst the unanimous informal consent principle was applied, all the directors were disqualified from acting in relation to the purchase. Accordingly, a better explanation of *Express Engineering* is that the shareholders were in reality exercising the default powers discussed above.[73] Indeed, any suggestion that shareholders can unanimously usurp board powers would be inconsistent with the restatement of the principle in *Ciban Management Corporation v Citco (BVI) Ltd*,[74] where Lord Burrows (borrowing words from *Salomon*) stated that "anything the members of a company can do by formal resolution *in a general meeting*, they can also do informally if all of them assent to it". This envisages, consistently with the majority judicial view, that unanimous informal consent is confined to the exercise of those powers conferred upon the general meeting, rather than the board.

---

[69] Given that the term "member" for the purposes of the CA 2006 includes any person whose name appears on the share register, a company's shareholders will not be able to give the requisite unanimous consent when one of the shareholders has died or been dissolved if their name has not been removed: see *Re BW Estates Ltd (No.2)* [2017] EWCA Civ 1201; [2018] Ch. 511 at [80]–[88].

[70] CA 2006 ss.288–300, especially s.296(4). See further Ch.12.

[71] *Multinational Gas & Petrochemical Co Ltd v Multinational Gas and Petrochemical Services Ltd* [1983] Ch. 258 CA (Civ Div) at 268–269 and 289–290; *Meridien Global Funds Management Asia Ltd v Securities Commission* [1995] 2 A.C. 500 PC at 506. Consider *Dunn v AAH Ltd* [2009] EWHC 692 (QB) at [37]–[41]. See also Company Law Review, which suggested that company law should be codified on the basis that "the members of the company may, by unanimous agreement, bind or empower the company, *regardless of any limitation in its constitution*" (emphasis added): see Final Report I, para.7.17. The Report states that this is how the rule is recognised at common law, though this may rather overstate things. A further argument might be that, as the model articles permit the shareholders to give directions to the board by way of special resolution, they should be capable of doing so unanimously: see Companies (Model Articles) Regulations 2008 (SI 2008/3229) Sch.1 art.4.

[72] *Re Express Engineering Works Ltd* [1920] 1 Ch. 466 CA, approved in *Parker & Cooper Ltd v Reading* [1926] Ch. 975 Ch D at 984; *Re BW Estates Ltd (No.2)* [2018] Ch. 511 at [56]. See also *Euro Brokers Holdings Ltd v Monecor (London) Ltd* [2003] 1 B.C.L.C. 506 CA, where the decision in question (under a shareholders' agreement) required a resolution of the board, but unanimous shareholder agreement was treated as a substitute. In *Monecor*, however, the board was disabled from acting, so the case could be seen as one in which the shareholders had a default power to act.

[73] *Baron v Potter* [1914] 1 Ch. 895.

[74] *Ciban Management Corporation v Citco (BVI) Ltd* [2020] 3 W.L.R. 705 at [31], citing *Salomon v Salomon & Co Ltd* [1897] A.C. 22 HL (emphasis added).

11–010 Despite the weight of authority, it is worth pausing on the merits of allowing the shareholders unanimously to depart from the constitution. The requirement of unanimity certainly means that there are no concerns about the protection of minority shareholders; this was one of the factors that weighed heavily with the courts when introducing the doctrine that shareholders could not (by ordinary resolution at least) give directors instructions on matters within their competence. As regards the relationship between the board and the general meeting, allowing unanimous shareholder consent to override the articles, especially within the directors' sphere of competence, would certainly emphasise the primacy of shareholders as against the directors, albeit that they must act unanimously. That said, unlike directors, shareholders are not subject to the same range of fiduciary and non-fiduciary duties, although such duties may exist in charitable companies.[75] Whilst such duties would not be required to protect minority shareholders, they might in particular be required to protect the company's creditors or other stakeholders in the company. As suggested in *Ciban Management Corporation v Citco (BVI) Ltd*,[76] however, the protection of creditors ought not to be a serious concern, given that an established qualification to the unanimous informal consent principle is when the transaction in question jeopardises the company's solvency or causes loss to the creditors. Nevertheless, other stakeholders will not necessarily be protected from adverse corporate decisions in the same way as if they were taken by the board.[77] In practice, however, as shareholders have statutory power to dismiss directors, this issue of potentially conflicting jurisdiction is unlikely to arise frequently.

STATUTORY POWERS OF THE GENERAL MEETING

11–011 Despite the flexibility to divide decision-making powers between shareholders and the board in the company's constitution, there are a number of situations where legislation requires the shareholders to approve the board's decision (and sometimes even permits the shareholders to take or initiate the decision themselves). Such instances usually relate to decisions that will likely impact upon the shareholders' legal, contractual or constitutional rights, even if the practical impact on any single member will be small (as is often the case with changes to the articles). The principal examples of this legislative technique of empowering the shareholders include alterations to the company's articles[78]; alterations to the type of company, for example, switching from public to private or vice versa[79]; decisions to issue shares[80] or to disapply pre-emption rights on

[75] *Children's Investment Fund Foundation (UK) v Attorney General* [2020] 3 W.L.R. 461. For the imposition of such duties on majority shareholders in other jurisdictions, see generally H. Birkmose, *Shareholders' Duties* (Kluwer Law International, 2017); E Lim, *A Case for Shareholders' Fiduciary Duties in Common Law Asia* (Cambridge University Press, 2019).

[76] *Ciban Management Corporation v Citco (BVI) Ltd* [2020] 3 W.L.R. 705 at [40].

[77] CA 2006 s.172(1).

[78] CA 2006 s.21(1). The adoption of the initial constitution is also an act of the shareholders, since the incorporators become members of the company: see para.4–005.

[79] CA 2006 ss.89–111, discussed in Ch.4.

[80] CA 2006 ss.549–551, discussed in Ch.24.

issuance[81]; decisions to reduce share capital, re-purchase shares, redeem or re-purchase shares out of capital in the case of private companies or give financial assistance in the case of private companies[82]; alterations to the class rights attached to shares[83]; adoption of schemes of arrangement[84]; and decisions to wind the company up voluntarily.[85] Each of these scenarios place limits on the extent to which the board may proceed solely on its own initiative by virtue of the articles. The rationale for limiting the board's reach in such circumstances is usually due to the fact that the shareholders' interests are principally involved in such decisions and that the shareholders are probably as well-equipped as the board to take the relevant decisions.

In addition to these examples, there are four further cases where shareholder approval is justified as contributing directly to good corporate governance, namely the appointment of the company's auditors[86]; the approval of certain transactions entered into by directors or their associates with the company[87]; the ratification of corporate opportunities taken by directors[88]; and the control of any defensive measures taken once a takeover offer is imminent, as set out in the City Code on Takeovers and Mergers, with those rules now having statutory force.[89] Whilst the first of these requirements is designed to promote the independence of the company's auditors from its management (although it may be questioned how successful this is), the other three deal with conflicts of interest between directors and the company. **11–012**

Furthermore, the Listing Rules (applicable to premium-listed companies quoted on the London Stock Exchange) also require shareholders to be notified of certain transactions and to have the opportunity to vote on larger proposed transactions.[90] Approval is required for significant transactions (both acquisitions and disposals) that meet the test of being either "Class 1" transactions or "reverse takeovers".[91] In brief, the Class 1 criteria are met if any one of the financial ratios that compare the size of the transaction with the size of the company is 25% or more[92]; whilst an acquisition is a reverse takeover if any of the ratios is 100% or more, or if the transaction would result in a fundamental change in the company's business, board composition or voting control.[93] The financial ratios relate to the company's gross assets, profits, consideration and gross capital. The rationale underlying these shareholder approval requirements seems to be that a large transaction is as much an investment decision as a management decision, so that the shareholders should be involved in the decision, together with management. There is no counterpart to this Listing Rule requirement in the CA 2006.

[81] CA 2006 ss.569 onwards, discussed in Ch.24.
[82] See generally Ch.17.
[83] CA 2006 ss.630 onwards, discussed in Ch.13.
[84] CA 2006 ss.895 onwards, discussed in Ch.29.
[85] IA 1986 s.84.
[86] CA 2006 Pt 16, Ch.2, discussed in Ch.23.
[87] CA 2006 Pt 10, Ch.4, discussed in Ch.10.
[88] CA 2006 ss.180 and 239.
[89] See Ch.28.
[90] Listing Rules LR 10.1.2.
[91] Listing Rules LR 5.6.3 and 10.5.1.
[92] Listing Rules LR 10.2.2.
[93] Listing Rules LR 5.6.4.

Beyond the above situations, there are two issues in particular that interest the shareholders and over which the shareholders will wish to exercise especial control, namely the remuneration and removal of directors.

Remuneration of directors

11–013 The remuneration of directors comes from two principal sources: fees paid to them for acting as directors and, in the case of executive directors, money and other benefits receivable under their service contracts as managers of the company. The latter is by far the greater source of income for executive directors, especially in large companies. Accordingly, executive pay has been, and continues to be, a source of controversy and the object of increasing regulatory and legislative action in recent years.[94] Reflecting the trust origins of the company, a director is not entitled to a fee for acting as such, unless the articles or a resolution of the company makes provision for such payments, as they invariably will. By contrast, a person who provides additional services as a manager to the company, even if also a director, is entitled to reasonable remuneration on a quantum meruit basis for services actually accepted by the company, even in the absence of a contract, although the two situations may not be easy to distinguish.[95] In practice, these difficulties rarely arise, since the company will have express power under its articles to remunerate directors and employ managers and an explicit contract is usually made in both cases.

11–014 In dealing with the company as to fees and remuneration, the director is, however, in a stark position of conflict of interest, and the traditional common law rule in such a case was that the sanction of the shareholders was needed for the agreement between director and company.[96] Directors found this rule inconvenient. Accordingly, for more than a century, it has been common to provide in the articles that the board shall have power to set directors' remuneration as executives, although the director whose remuneration is at issue

---

[94] The High Pay Centre is an independent, non-party think-tank established specifically to monitor pay at the top of the income distribution: see High Pay Commission (now High Pay Centre), *Cheques with Balances: Why tackling high pay is in the national interest* (Final Report, 22 November 2011). For the government consultation on the issue, see BIS Discussion Paper, *Executive Remuneration* (2011), which resulted in a series of reforms through both primary and secondary legislation applicable to quoted companies. See also the review produced by the Hay Group on the current state of play: see Hay Group, *What's your next move? Executive reward: review of the year 2011*. See also the 2015 government report, *2010 to 2015 government policy: Corporate accountability* available at: *https://www.gov.uk/government/publications/2010-to-2015-government-policy-corporate-accountability/2010-to-2015-government-policy-corporate-accountability* [Accessed 16 March 2021].

[95] *Craven-Ellis v Canons Ltd* [1936] 2 K.B. 403 CA; cf. *Re Richmond Gate Property Co Ltd* [1965] 1 W.L.R. 335 Ch D, which is probably based on a misunderstanding of the earlier case. See also *Diamandis v Wills* [2015] EWHC 312. See generally *Benedetti v Sawiris* [2013] UKSC 50; [2014] A.C. 938 on the general interaction between contract and a claim in restitution for quantum meruit. Such a claim will always be difficult where a procedure exists for approving remuneration: see *Ball v Hughes* [2017] EWHC 3228 (Ch); [2018] B.C.C. 196, applying *Guinness Plc v Saunders* [1990] 2 A.C. 663 HL.

[96] See paras 10–063 onwards.

is not usually permitted to vote on the matter.[97] The current model article applies this rule also to directors' fees, even though under previous model articles the default rule was that fees required shareholder approval.[98] Setting remuneration in this way is a classic case where the risk of "mutual back scratching" arises: directors may not scrutinise too closely the remuneration of a fellow director in the expectation of similar treatment in return when their cases are considered. Indeed, the increased levels of executive remuneration have been a matter of considerable public controversy in recent years, not simply because of the growing gap between executive salaries and the average incomes generally, but also because of the unsatisfactory negotiating process through which executive salaries are set under the typical form of articles. If directors, directly or indirectly, sit on both sides of the table when their remuneration is determined, then the results cannot be justified as emerging from a market process. Indeed, at least in the context of companies with large shareholder bodies, this arguably amounts to an example of a market failure justifying regulatory intervention.

This only raises the question, however, as to the form that that regulation should take. The courts have generally been unwilling to scrutinise directors' remuneration decisions on grounds of excess or waste, refusing even to prescribe that pay must be set by reference to market rates. From the courts' perspective, as long as the decision on remuneration is a genuine one and not an attempt, for example, to make distributions to shareholders/directors where there are no distributable profits,[99] the directors' decision will be upheld. This is probably a wise decision on the part of the courts, which might otherwise find themselves saddled with developing a general policy about the remuneration of directors of large companies. Neither has the legislature shown any enthusiasm to grasp the nettle of determining, substantively, what the level, or rate of increase, of directors' pay should be. Given the unwillingness to address levels of executive remuneration head on, attention has focused on the procedure within the company for the setting of directors' remuneration. Several options are available, some now mandatory at least for larger companies.

Remuneration committees

One strategy has been to exclude executive directors from the process of remuneration setting, so that, not only is the individual executive whose remuneration is at issue forbidden from voting on the decision, but executive **11–015**

[97] Companies (Model Articles) Regulations 2008 (SI 2008/3229) Sch.1 arts 14 and 19 (private companies) and Sch.3 arts 13 and 23 (public companies). For the problems that arise if the company seeks to fix the terms of executive remuneration without complying with its articles, see *Guinness v Saunders* [1990] 2 A.C. 663; *UK Safety Group Ltd v Hearne* [1998] 2 B.C.L.C. 208 Ch D; *Ball v Hughes* [2018] B.C.C. 196.

[98] Companies (Tables A to F) Regulations 1985 (SI 1985/805), Table A art.82.

[99] See *Re Halt Garage (1964) Ltd* [1982] 3 All E.R. 1016 Ch D, which involved a decision by shareholders as to the remuneration to be paid to themselves as directors. The same principle would be applied to a directors' decision, except that the directors would also have to meet their core duty of loyalty: see CA 2006 s.172. In the context of unfair prejudice petitions (that is, in cases of disputes between shareholders), the courts have struck out more boldly and have been willing to assess whether the remuneration paid to the controllers as directors was appropriate: see further paras 14–022 to 14–023.

directors more generally are side-lined in the remuneration-setting process. Adopting this strategy, remuneration decisions in premium-listed companies are now allocated principally to a "remuneration committee" of independent non-executive directors.[100] This committee "should have delegated responsibility for determining the policy for executive director remuneration".[101] In exercising its functions, the remuneration "should promote long-term shareholdings by directors" and "should enable the use of discretion to override formulaic outcomes".[102] Moreover, a remuneration committee is required to ensure that there is a proportionate link between pay and performance.[103] The effectiveness of this as a mechanism depends, however, upon how independent non-executive directors really are when it comes to the setting of executive remuneration. This is a particular concern given the possibility of executive and non-executive directors occupying different roles on a number of different boards. Accordingly, resort has increasingly been had to the shareholders as a control on directors' remuneration.

Mandatory shareholder approval of certain aspects of the remuneration package

(i) General

11–016 Given the possible doubts about the effectiveness of remuneration committees, a complementary strategy has been to revive the common law principle of shareholders approving directors' contracts.[104] Indeed, there has been an increasing regulatory and legislative creep back to this earlier position. For example, as well as requiring shareholder approval for certain termination payments, shareholder approval of the company's general remuneration policy (plus an advisory vote on its implementation) is required for all quoted and traded companies.

(ii) Long-term incentive pay schemes

11–017 Under a discounted option arrangement, a director is given the right to subscribe at some time in the future (normally after a period of years) for shares in the company. The "exercise price" will be set at the time that the option is granted. Given his direct personal interest, the theory is that the director will be incentivised to increase the price of the shares over the intervening period for the benefit of the shareholders. In order to meet the obvious objection that the increase in the stock price may have little to do with the efforts of the directors, a

---

[100] Financial Reporting Council, *UK Corporate Governance Code* (July 2018), s.5, para.32. See further paras 9–016 to 9–020.

[101] Financial Reporting Council, *UK Corporate Governance Code* (July 2018), s.5, para.33.

[102] Financial Reporting Council, *UK Corporate Governance Code* (July 2018), s.5, paras 36–37.

[103] Financial Reporting Council, *UK Corporate Governance Code* (July 2018), s.5, para.40.

[104] Though one should note the argument that such approval is more likely to be effective in relation to sudden leaps in executive pay in a particular company than in controlling a steady, general upward drift in pay across all companies: see B. Cheffins and R. Thomas, "Should Shareholders Have a Greater Say over Executive Pay? Learning from US Experience" (2001) 1 J.C.L.S. 277.

long-term incentive plan (LTIP) substitutes some other form of incentive to be provided by the company in place of the shares. Given the concerns about the alignment, or misalignment, of incentives, the payment of performance-related remuneration to executive directors (it is less typically paid to non-executive directors)[105] is now regarded with far more caution than it was only a few years ago. Instead, simpler and more transparent pay structures are now favoured.[106] Indeed, the UK Corporate Governance Code, rather than focusing on specific performance-related structures,[107] considers the link between pay and performance to be a general principle underlying all remuneration decisions. For example, the Code states that "[r]emuneration policies and practices should be designed to support strategy and promote long-term sustainable success. Executive remuneration should be aligned to company purpose and values, and be clearly linked to the successful delivery of the company's long-term strategy".[108] Moreover, in setting out the list of factors that should drive the setting of executive pay, the Code highlights the need for "proportionality", which means "the link between individual awards, the delivery of strategy and the long-term performance of the company should be clear. Outcomes should not reward poor performance".[109] Other factors that should be considered when setting executive pay are clarity, simplicity, risk, predictability and alignment to culture.[110]

Nevertheless, where a premium-listed company enters into a discounted option arrangement or other long-term incentive plan, the Listing Rules require shareholder approval.[111] Originally, shareholder approval might have been justified on the basis that share options could dilute the position of the other shareholders.[112] When that requirement was later extended to other forms of LTIP, it became a convenient mechanism for the shareholders to express concerns about whether, for example, the performance criteria attached to the LTIP are

[105] Financial Reporting Council, *UK Corporate Governance Code* (July 2018), s.5, para.34.

[106] See High Pay Commission (now High Pay Centre), *Cheques with Balances: Why tackling high pay is in the national interest* (Final Report, 22 November 2011). See also High Pay Centre, *No Routine Riches: Reforms to Performance-Related Pay* (13 May 2015); High Pay Centre, *The Metrics Re-Loaded: Examining Executive Remuneration Performance Measures* (10 June 2015). See also Financial Reporting Council, *UK Corporate Governance Code* (July 2018), s.5, para.40, stating "simplicity" as one of the key factors when determining executive pay.

[107] That said, there is support for "long term shareholdings by executive directors that support alignment with long-term shareholder interests": see Financial Reporting Council, *UK Corporate Governance Code* (July 2018), s.5, para.36.

[108] Financial Reporting Council, *UK Corporate Governance Code* (July 2018), Principle P.

[109] Financial Reporting Council, *UK Corporate Governance Code* (July 2018), s.5, para.40.

[110] Financial Reporting Council, *UK Corporate Governance Code* (July 2018), s.5, para.40.

[111] Listing Rules LR 9.4.

[112] It should be noted that the statutory pre-emption rights of shareholders might lead to a similar requirement for shareholder approval, but the statutory rights (1) do not apply to an allotment of securities under an employees' share scheme (see CA 2006 s.566), which might include a scheme for executive directors; and (2) can be disapplied in advance by shareholder vote (CA 2006 ss.569–571), whereas the rights under the Listing Rules may not be. It should also be noted that the Listing Rules do not require shareholder approval for share option schemes or other long-term incentive plans that are open to all or substantially all the company's employees (provided that the employees are not coterminous with the directors), presumably on the grounds that the wide scope of the scheme is protection against directorial self-interest: see Listing LR 9.4.2.

sufficiently "challenging". Given that obtaining shareholder approval is time-consuming and leaves the director in doubt as to what LTIP his or her remuneration package will include, the company is given permission to dispense with shareholder approval where the option scheme or other LTIP is "established specifically to facilitate, in unusual circumstances, the recruitment or retention of the relevant individual".[113] This permission is subject to disclosure in the company's next annual report of the principal terms of the scheme and the reasons why the circumstances in question were viewed as unusual.[114]

(iii) Mandatory and advisory shareholder votes on remuneration and implementation

11–018 The intervention over LTIPs might have been regarded as the tip of the iceberg. Growing public sentiment against escalating remuneration packages and perceived "payments for failure" (whereby poorly performing managers are nevertheless contractually entitled to handsome rewards on their departure) inevitably prompted renewed consideration of whether shareholders should have a binding vote on some or all aspects of general remuneration policy or particular remuneration agreements.[115] The policy tension is evident: regulation of remuneration packages is fraught with difficulties, practical, policy-based and political, but equally rewards for failure are undesirable (although not every failure is attributable to poor management given that corporate ventures are inherently risky). This concern is evident in the increasingly explicit focus on possible "claw-backs". For example, the UK Corporate Governance Code states explicitly that remuneration schemes "should also include provision that would enable the company to recover and/or withhold sums or share awards and specify the circumstances in which it would be appropriate to do so".[116] Given this climate, increased Government intervention was inevitable, although this happened in stages. In 2002, simple disclosure rules were introduced. The current regime was introduced in 2013.

These reforms apply to quoted and traded companies. The definition of a "quoted company" is wider than just companies incorporated in the UK and subject to the Listing Rules. Instead, the definition in the CA 2006 extends to UK-incorporated companies if they have been included in the official list of any Member State of the European Economic Area or if their securities have been admitted to trading on the New York Stock Exchange or Nasdaq.[117] A "traded company" means a company with voting shares that are admitted to a UK or EU-regulated market.[118] The purpose of these broader definitions is to remove any incentive for UK companies to escape the new "say on pay" requirements by

---

[113] Listing Rules LR 9.4.2(2).

[114] Listing Rules LR 9.4.2–3.

[115] See BIS Discussion Paper, *Executive Remuneration* (2011) available at: *http://www.bis.gov.uk/Consultations/executive-remuneration-discussion-paper* [Accessed 16 March 2021], and Discussion Paper, *Summary of Responses* (ibid), indicating the problems with binding votes, although the possibility remains live.

[116] Financial Reporting Council, *UK Corporate Governance Code* (July 2018), s.5, para.37.

[117] CA 2006 s.385.

[118] CA 2006 s.360C.

listing their securities elsewhere than in London. The Secretary of State has the power to extend further the definition of a "quoted company" by regulation, if necessary.[119] Where the statutory "say on pay" requirements apply, the directors cannot lightly escape their obligations. Subject to very limited defences, it is a criminal offence on the part of every officer in default (albeit not on the part of the company) to fail to give the necessary notices of meetings or put the required resolutions to the vote.[120]

For these purposes, the notion of "remuneration" is defined very broadly: it includes any form of payment or other benefit made to or otherwise conferred on a person in return for them holding, agreeing to hold or having held office as a director of the company (or any other role in connection with the management of the affairs of the company or its subsidiaries whilst a director of the company).[121] The restrictions on remuneration payments, therefore, apply to payments such as those that might be made to new directors to buy-out existing remuneration entitlements at their current company. The restrictions on payments for loss of office extend to amounts paid to settle statutory or contractual claims arising in connection with a director's loss of office. In each case, therefore, unless the remuneration policy contemplates such remuneration payments or payments for loss of office, they must be separately approved by the shareholders (although where other legislation or a court requires a payment to be made, the CA 2006 will not prevent the company from paying it).

In terms of the actual procedures that must be followed for the shareholders' "say on pay", these are threefold.

The first requirement is that the directors of quoted or traded companies must produce and disclose an annual directors' remuneration report (DRR),[122] with its contents now prescribed in enormous detail by the Secretary of State in regulations.[123] The regulations divide the remuneration report into two parts: one, which is not subject to audit, relates to the company's remuneration policy, and another, which is subject to audit, concerns payments actually made to directors in the financial year in question.[124] The legislative approach to the disclosure of remuneration policy in the DDR is interesting: it requires the board to justify, rather than simply report, the company's remuneration arrangements.[125] Moreover, it does that in a very detailed way, requiring the company to provide 11–019

---

[119] CA 2006 s.385(4)–(6).

[120] CA 2006 s.440(1).

[121] CA 2006 s.226A.

[122] CA 2006 ss.420 onwards. The disclosure obligations imposed on companies in relation to the remuneration of their directors vary according to whether the company is a "small company" (CA 2006 ss.381–384), an unquoted company, or a "quoted company" (CA 2006 s.385). The Secretary of State has power to make provision by regulations requiring information about directors' remuneration to be given in notes to a company's annual accounts: CA 2006 s.412. See also the Listing Rules LR 9.8.8.

[123] Large and Medium-Sized Companies and Groups (Accounts and Reports) Regulations 2008 (SI 2008/410) Sch.8, as amended by the Large and Medium-Sized Companies and Groups (Accounts and Reports) (Amendment) Regulations 2013 (SI 2013/1981) Sch.1.

[124] Large and Medium-sized Companies and Groups (Accounts and Reports) (Amendment) Regulations 2013 (SI 2013/1981) Sch.1 Pt 5.

[125] Large and Medium-sized Companies and Groups (Accounts and Reports) (Amendment) Regulations 2013 (SI 2013/1981) Pts 4 and 6.

standardised information, often in tabular form, by which the policy might be assessed, including details of specific remuneration components and the objectives sought to be achieved by their inclusion, as well as illustrative workings of the ramifications for current directors over time. In addition, details are required explaining the way in which the company's overall pay policy has been derived, and how the views of shareholders have been accommodated.

The audited part of the DRR concerns payments actually made to persons who have served as directors during the financial year. The ambition is to require companies to provide reports in a standardised way so that shareholders can compare remuneration outcomes in a variety of ways, whether between directors, across different years, and with other companies. To that end, this part of the DRR requires the company to list its directors by name and provide in a tabular display the "single total remuneration figure" for each of them, along with its component parts (as prescribed and defined in the regulations, including the total amount of salary and fees, all taxable benefits, all money or other assets received by way of performance bonus, and all pension benefits). Any sums subject to claw back must be noted, and previous year comparisons of all elements must be provided.[126] All that must be audited. In addition, the implementation report must also provide performance graphs and tables that set out a number of matters, including the percentage change in the remuneration of the chief executive officer over his term in office, compared with the percentage change in employee pay (with provisions for considering corporate groups as a whole)[127]; the total company spend; and the relative spend on remuneration and distributions to shareholders. Other options, such as the mandatory disclosure of top-to-bottom pay differentials, appear now to be seen as uninformative and therefore as potentially counter-productive[128]; and the mandatory capping of executive pay has never attracted serious support. Finally, the report must contain statements of how the directors' remuneration policy will be implemented by the company in the next financial year; the consideration given by directors to the matter of remuneration; and a statement of the detailed result of the voting on any resolutions in respect of the directors' remuneration report or policy at the last general meeting of the company. To further improve transparency, whenever a director now leaves office, companies will need to publish a statement setting out what payments the director has received or may receive in future. This statement must be published as soon as reasonably practicable. All of this provides an enormous amount of detail, not just to shareholders, and it is difficult to say how it will be used, or by whom.

Even unquoted companies cannot remain entirely silent on the subject of directors' remuneration. The matters about which information may be required

[126] Large and Medium-sized Companies and Groups (Accounts and Reports) (Amendment) Regulations 2013 (SI 2013/1981) Sch.1.

[127] This represents an obvious attempt to persuade directors and shareholders to focus on the issue of widening pay dispersal within companies, with the multiples by which executive directors' remuneration exceeds the average remuneration of employees increasing dramatically.

[128] The mooted mandatory disclosure of the ratio between top executive salaries and the mean or median salaries in the company seems generally to be regarded as too dependent on the size of the company, the nature of its business, and its geographical spread to provide helpful data for cross-company comparisons.

include gains on the exercise of share options; benefits receivable under long-term incentive schemes; compensation for loss of office[129]; contributions and benefits receivable with respect to past services; and consideration receivable by third parties for making available the services of a director.[130] The information must also include benefits receivable by a person "connected with" a director, or by a body corporate "controlled by" a director.[131] However, the relevant rules do not require a binding shareholder vote on policy, and there is no equivalent of the detailed implementation report. All that is required is the disclosure of aggregate remuneration only; where the data are further broken down, there is no requirement for recipients to be identified by name.[132] A small company can omit this information from the accounts it files at Companies House.

In an extension of the usual role of the auditor, if the auditor concludes that the information required (of either a quoted or unquoted company) in relation to directors' remuneration has not been provided, then a statement giving the required particulars must be contained in the auditor's report, so far as the auditor is reasonably able to provide it.[133] This is presumably thought to be a more effective remedy than fining the directors for failure to produce proper accounts and reports, though that sanction is available as well.

The second requirement is a triennial[134] binding vote of the shareholders on the company's remuneration policy.[135] The remuneration policy must both describe and justify: it must set out how the company proposes to pay directors, including every element of the remuneration package, and how the chosen approach supports the company's long-term strategy and performance. In addition, the policy must set out the company's approach to recruitment and loss of office payments. Once a remuneration policy has been approved, a company may only make remuneration and loss of office payments as permitted within the limits of that policy, unless the payment has been approved by a separate shareholder resolution. Failure to pass the remuneration policy would effectively block the company's right to pay its directors. Any arrangements made contrary to an approved policy are void[136] and any payments received by the director are held on trust for the company.[137] In addition, any director who authorised such a **11–020**

129 CA 2006 s.215.

130 CA 2006 s.412(2).

131 CA 2006 s.412(4).

132 Large and Medium-Sized Companies and Groups (Accounts and Reports) Regulations 2008 (SI 2008/410) Sch.5 para.1 requires the disclosure of aggregate remuneration (a rule applied to quoted companies as well); para.2, the amount paid to the highest-paid director (but without naming that person) if the aggregate remuneration exceeds £200,000; and paras 3–5, the aggregates paid by way of early retirement benefits, compensation for loss of office and to third parties by way of directors' services.

133 CA 2006 s.498(4). See further Ch.23.

134 Or more frequently if the policy changes, even in a minor way.

135 CA 2006 s.439A.

136 CA 2006 s.226E(1). The very limited transition exception is that legal obligations made before the legislation introducing these reforms was published on 27 June 2012, assuming they have not been amended or renewed since, will not be subject to the restrictions in CA 2006 Ch.4A: see Enterprise and Regulatory Reform Act 2013 s.82.

137 CA 2006 s.226E(2).

payment is jointly and severally liable to indemnify the company for loss, unless the director is shown to have acted honestly and reasonably in the circumstances.[138]

11–021 Shareholders also have an annual advisory vote on the implementation report, which sets out how the approved pay policy has been implemented, including a single figure for the total pay directors received that year (with this designed to allow shareholders to make ready comparisons year-on-year, and between companies).[139] In this case, however, an adverse vote does not affect directors' entitlements,[140] although the failure will trigger the need for the company to put the remuneration policy to shareholders the following year. That said, failure to pass the report would inevitably have significant practical effect because of likely market reaction, so perhaps the real benefit of the annual advisory vote is that it gives the shareholders a further guaranteed opportunity to express their views on the directors' remuneration. Otherwise, this would only occur if the shareholders requisitioned a resolution to be added to the agenda of the accounts meeting or requisitioned an extraordinary meeting of the shareholders, neither of which is necessarily easy to arrange. If, however 20% or more of votes are cast against the board recommendation for a resolution, the company is required to explain, when announcing the results, what actions it intends to take to consult with shareholders to understand the reasons behind the results.[141] The board will also have to report back to the shareholders within six months on any actions that it has taken, and a final summary should be provided in the annual report.

Removal of directors

11–022 The accountability of directors to the shareholders is obviously enhanced if shareholders can influence directly the choice of those who sit on the board. As considered previously,[142] company law does little to enhance shareholders' control over the appointment process, which is predominantly regulated by the company's articles of association. According to the model articles at least, a director may be appointed by a decision of the directors or an ordinary shareholder resolution.[143] Furthermore, there is nothing in the CA 2006 imposing a mandatory requirement that directors, once appointed, should stand for re-election or that the shareholders should select any replacements for directors who have resigned or have been removed. Accordingly, in legislative terms, there is nothing to prevent shareholders being completely written out of the appointment process. In practice, such extreme cases are rare. The reasons have more to do with market expectations, than legal constraints: large companies might find it particularly difficult to sell their shares to institutional investors on the basis of articles excluding shareholders from the board appointment process.

---

[138] CA 2006 s.226E(2) and (5).

[139] CA 2006 s.439A.

[140] CA 2006 s.439(5). The director and company could agree of course that some item of the remuneration package should be so conditional.

[141] Financial Reporting Council, *UK Corporate Governance Code* (July 2018), s.1, para.4.

[142] See Ch.9.

[143] Companies (Model Articles) Regulations 2008 (SI 2008/3229) Sch.1 art.17.

Indeed, these market expectations have been crystallised into the "best practice" in the UK Corporate Governance Code: as well as establishing a nomination committee with a majority of non-executive directors, "all directors should be subject to annual re-election" and the re-election papers must set out "the specific reasons why [the particular director's] contribution is, and continues to be, important to the company's long-term sustainable success".[144]

Shareholders' statutory termination rights

In contrast to the issues of initial appointment and re-election, the legal position on termination has been entirely different for the past half century or so. Until 1948, the shareholders' power to remove directors depended, as with the issue of appointment, upon the articles of association. Nowadays, a director can be removed by an ordinary resolution of the shareholders at any time,[145] although the articles may provide additional grounds for the directors' removal.[146] This statutory right of the shareholders is mandatory, as it applies "notwithstanding anything in any agreement between [the company] and [the director]".[147] Indeed, in *Dinglis v Dinglis*,[148] the power of removal was described as "one of the most important rights given to shareholders". This is particularly true given that the director's term of office is effectively meaningless in terms of preventing his or her removal. Even if the articles provide for a "staggered board", whereby the directors are appointed for three years at a time and their re-election arranged so that no more than one third of the board comes up for election in any one year, such arrangements can be set at naught if the shareholders decide to remove a particular director. Indeed, the shareholders' power of removal may indirectly give them some influence over the appointment process, since there is little point in the board appointing a director to whom the shareholders object when he or she can be so easily removed. Moreover, there is something of a policy tension **11–023**

[144] Financial Reporting Council, *UK Corporate Governance Code* (July 2018), s.3, paras 17–18. Even as late as 1985, the model set of articles provided that "a managing director and a director holding any other executive office shall not be subject to retirement by rotation": see Companies (Tables A to F) Regulations 1985 (SI 1985/805) Table A art.84. The Companies (Model Articles) Regulations 2008 (SI 2008/3229) contain no provision for regular re-election at all, whether for executive or non-executive directors.

[145] CA 2006 s.168(1). For consideration of whether an administrator might be able to apply to court to remove a director and/or curtail the special notice period, see *Re Inspired Asset Management Ltd* [2019] EWHC 3301 (Ch); *Re MBI Hawthorn Care Ltd* [2019] EWHC 2365 (Ch); [2020] B.C.C. 1.

[146] Although Companies (Model Articles) Regulations 2008 (SI 2008/3229) does not contain any such additional provision, examples include *Bersel Manufacturing Co Ltd v Berry* [1968] 2 All E.R. 552 HL (power of life directors to terminate the appointment of ordinary directors); *Lee v Chou Wen Hsien* [1984] 1 W.L.R. 1201 PC (power of majority of directors to require a director to resign).

[147] CA 2006 s.168(1). Whilst the predecessor provision also explicitly overrode anything to the contrary in the articles (see CA 1985 s.303), this was not repeated in the CA 2006. Arguably, this was considered unnecessary as the legislation would simply override anything inconsistent in a company's articles, although the same would apply to a private agreement. In the case of a community interest company, the Regulator may remove a director at any time, although the director does not appear to have a claim for compensation against the company: see Companies (Audit, Investigations and Community Enterprise) Act 2004 s.46(1). A director can instead appeal to the court against the Regulator's decision, apparently with the effect of reinstating the director if the appeal is successful: ibid s.46(10).

[148] *Dinglis v Dinglis* [2019] EWHC 1664 (Ch) at [183].

with the shareholders' inability to direct the board's decisions by ordinary resolution, when nothing more is required to remove the directors. In practice, the latter power must presumably overshadow the former disability: whilst directors may commit no legal wrong by refusing to obey the shareholders' ordinary resolution, they will be aware that disobedience may trigger their removal from office.

11–024 There are, however, three principal qualifications to the shareholders' statutory power to remove directors. First, although it is not possible to remove that statutory power by contract, the courts have nevertheless endorsed provisions in the articles that enable directors to circumvent it, at least in private companies. According to the House of Lords in *Bushell v Faith*,[149] the shareholders' power to remove directors can be frustrated by a provision in the articles attaching increased votes to a director's shares upon a resolution to remove him, thus enabling him always to defeat such a resolution. Whilst problematic in corporate governance terms,[150] *Bushell* can perhaps be justified on the ground that, in a small private company (whether in effect an incorporated partnership or joint-venture company), it is not unreasonable that each shareholder should be entitled to participate in the company's management and to protect himself against removal. Indeed, the removal of a director from the board of a "quasi-partnership"[151] may so undermine the fundamental understanding between the parties that the aggrieved director may seek a remedy on grounds of unfairly prejudicial conduct,[152] or even the compulsory winding-up of the company on the ground that this would be "just and equitable.[153] Despite significant criticism of *Bushell*,[154] the decision has not been reversed in subsequent legislation and has actually been approved at a high judicial level.[155] Indeed, in *Children's Investment Fund Foundation (UK) v Attorney General*,[156] Lady Arden (in reference to *Bushell*) expressed no disquiet over the notion that "the protection

---

[149] *Bushell v Faith* [1970] A.C. 1099 HL. In *Bushell*, the shares in a private company were held equally by three directors and the articles provided that, in the event of a resolution to remove any director, the shares held by that director would carry three times their normal votes, thereby enabling one shareholder to outvote the other two. According to Lord Upjohn (at 1109): "There is no fetter which compels the company to make voting rights or restrictions of general application and—such rights or restrictions can be attached to special circumstances and to particular types of resolution".

[150] For Lord Morris' strong dissenting view, see *Bushell v Faith* [1970] A.C. 1099 at 1106.

[151] See *Re Westbourne Galleries Ltd* [1973] A.C. 360 HL. See further Ch.14.

[152] CA 2006 s.994(1).

[153] IA 1986 s.122(1)(g). See *Re Westbourne Galleries Ltd* [1973] A.C. 360. See further Ch.14. Moreover, a court could enjoin the breach of a binding agreement between members and a director on how they should vote on any resolution to remove a director, effectively using a shareholder agreement to circumvent CA 2006 s.168: see *Russell v Northern Bank Development Corporation Ltd* [1992] 1 W.L.R. 588. See also *Walker v Standard Chartered Bank Plc* [1992] B.C.L.C. 535. Such a shareholders' agreement would not be invalidated, since CA 2006 s.168(1) only applies to agreements between the director and the company.

[154] See D. Prentice, (1969) 32 M.L.R. 693, noting the Court of Appeal's decision. The development of the unfair prejudice jurisdiction further reduces the need for *Bushell*—but it equally reduces its adverse consequences, since the exercise of the legal right to remove a director may nevertheless constitute unfairly prejudicial conduct. See further Ch.14.

[155] See *Russell v Northern Bank Development Corporation Ltd* [1992] 1 W.L.R. 588.

[156] *Children's Investment Fund Foundation (UK) v Attorney General* [2020] 3 W.L.R. 461 at [160]–[162].

given by Parliament is subject to being rendered less effective by the company exercising other powers, such as the right to attach special rights to shares". In effect, the shareholders' statutory power of removal is now simply the default rule for private companies.

Secondly, even where the articles contain no weighted voting provision, the removal of a director requires the shareholders to satisfy some fairly stringent procedural requirements. Special notice has to be given of any resolution to remove a director (and to appoint someone else instead, if that is proposed).[157] This means the shareholders must give 28 days' notice to the company of their intention to propose the resolution.[158] The company must supply a copy of the notice to the director, who is entitled to be heard at the meeting.[159] Further, the director may require the company to circulate any representations that that person wishes to make.[160] In essence, the object of these procedural requirements is to prevent a director from being deprived of his or her office on a snap vote and without having had a full opportunity of stating the contrary case.[161] That said, a court may disapply some of these procedural protections if it "is satisfied that the rights conferred by this section are being abused".[162] Indeed, in *Schofield v Jones*,[163] the court was prepared to use its power to order a meeting (and direct how it should proceed)[164] when the outgoing director simply refused to attend the meeting to remove him and instead threatened unfair prejudice proceedings in response. 11–025

Thirdly, the shareholders' statutory power of removal cannot deprive a director of any claim for compensation or damages payable in respect of his or her 11–026

---

[157] CA 2006 s.168(2). Whilst the requirement for special notice is designed to protect the director, it may be abused by the outgoing directors. The ruse is that, shortly before the meeting, the outgoing directors resign after having appointed new replacement board members. The removal resolution is now unnecessary in relation to the directors who have resigned and will be ineffective in relation to their replacements (even if the resolution states as one of its objectives the removal of the replacements) because special notice will not have been given by the proposers to the company about the removal of the replacements, since the proposers will not have known who the replacements were to be at the time they served notice on the company: see *Monnington v Easier Plc* [2005] EWHC 2578 (Ch); [2006] 2 B.C.L.C. 283.

[158] CA 2006 s.312. The company must then notify the members in the notice convening the meeting or, if that is not practicable, by newspaper advertisement or other mode allowed by the articles, normally not less than 14 days before the meeting: ibid.

[159] CA 2006 s.169(1)–(2). This effectively means that the written resolution procedure is unavailable when directors are being removed.

[160] CA 2006 s.169(3). If those representations are not received in time to be circulated, the director can require them to be read out at the meeting: CA 2006 s.169(4). The same rule applies if the company does not comply with its obligations under s.169(3). A procedural defect does not invalidate the resolution, as this would provide an easy way for the company to avoid the director's removal.

[161] The statutory power of removal does not "derogate from any power to remove a director that may exist apart from this section": see CA 2006 s.168(5)(b). Accordingly, a director can be deprived of his or her statutory procedural protections if the company acts under an express power to remove him or her by ordinary resolution in the company's articles of association, as the statutory protections are expressly limited to removals "under section 168": CA 2006 s.169(1).

[162] CA 2006 s.169(5).

[163] *Schofield v Jones* [2019] EWHC 803 (Ch); [2019] B.C.C. 932.

[164] CA 2006 s.306(1).

termination.[165] This prohibition applies not only to compensation "in respect of the termination of [the director's] appointment as director", but also for "any appointment terminating with that as director". Accordingly, where an executive director's service contract is terminated at the same time as his directorship (as is invariably the case), compensation for both may be recovered. Indeed, as the continuation of a director's service contract is often made conditional on the continuation of his directorship, the service contract usually terminates automatically upon cessation of the directorship. The practical result of this right to compensation is that the shareholders will only be able to sack a director if they are prepared to saddle the company with liability to pay damages, or a sum fixed by the contract as compensation. Whilst a company should be expected to honour its commitments freely undertaken, the risk is that the director may have been present on both sides of the transaction when the provisions regarding payment of compensation were being negotiated. Accordingly, by negotiating service contracts requiring the company to pay substantial sums by way of compensation upon the director's removal, a director can effectively entrench himself in power, although the disclosure and approval regimes for quoted companies work against this.[166] That said, the dismissed director can only claim damages for breach of contract if a binding contract entitles the director either to hold that position or a related executive position for a fixed term, or to be dismissed only after prescribed or reasonable notice (and that notice requirement is not observed by the company). Similarly, a contractual termination payment will only be payable if the relevant contract specifically so provides. Accordingly, the important question is whether the director's dismissal constitutes either a breach of a contract with the director (giving rise to damages) or a termination triggering specified contractual termination payments.

Broadly, there are two contrasting situations. First, if the director's contract (whether as director or as executive manager) simply incorporates the provisions of the company's articles,[167] then—like the articles themselves—the contract terms are regarded as being subject to the CA 2006 (and its statutory right of removal), as well as being subject to variation if the shareholders use their powers to alter the company's underlying articles. In these circumstances, if the shareholders use their statutory power of dismissal or change the articles to effect the dismissal, then neither act will count as a breach of the director's contract; rather, the dismissal will be entirely in accordance with the terms of that contract.[168] This approach cannot, however, be used by the company to escape

---

[165] CA 2006 s.168(5)(a). For a quoted company or unquoted traded company, there are restrictions on compensation payments: CA 2006 ss.226B–C.

[166] See paras 11–018 onwards.

[167] The articles of association do not operate as an enforceable contract between a director and the company: see CA 2006 s.33(1). See also *The New Saints FC Ltd v The Football Association of Wales Ltd* [2020] EWHC 1838 (Ch) at [36], fn.15. Instead, the articles define the terms of the separate contract between director and company: see *Re Peruvian Guano Co*; sub nom. *Kemp, Ex p.* [1894] 3 Ch. 690 Ch D at 701; *Re New British Iron Co Ex p. Beckwith* [1898] 1 Ch. 324 Ch D at 326–327; *Swabey v Port Darwin Gold Mining Co* (1889) 1 Meg. 385 CA at 387; *Base Metal Trading Ltd v Shamurin* [2004] EWCA Civ 1316; [2005] 1 W.L.R. 1157 at [77].

[168] *Swabey v Port Darwin Gold Mining Co* (1889) 1 Meg. 385 CA; *Read v Astoria Garage (Streatham) Ltd* [1952] Ch. 637 CA; *Newtherapeutics Ltd v Katz* [1991] Ch. 226 Ch D.

past liabilities to the director; on ordinary contractual principles, the shareholders' acts cannot have retrospective effect.[169] Secondly, the director will typically have a separate and independent contract with the company, whether formal or informal.[170] If this contract is for a fixed term or has a notice period, or if termination triggers a compensation payment, then such provisions will inevitably be breached or triggered if the shareholders exercise their statutory dismissal powers. A similar result pertains if the shareholders exercise their power to amend the company's articles in a manner that enables the director to be dismissed or prevents the director from continuing as such (at least where that is a condition of the director's independent contract). In those circumstances, although the courts will not enjoin the shareholders from exercising their statutory or constitutional powers, the company will nevertheless become liable to the director either for damages for breach of contract,[171] or for payment of the agreed termination payment. Depending on the terms of the director's contract, these sums can be so prohibitive that dismissal becomes quite impractical for the company. That problem is considered next.

Control of termination payments

The issue of prohibitive termination payments (whether paid as a fixed sum due under the contract or by way of damages) has increasingly occupied the time of policy-makers in recent years, at least in relation to public companies. Whilst part of the concern has related to the chilling effect that high termination payments can have upon the removal of directors, the other issue was that termination payments can be perceived as delivering "rewards for failure" to departing directors. That said, if directors were never entitled to contractual protection on termination, there is a chance that they might take too cautious an approach to risky business ventures. Indeed, in some circumstances (such as where there has been clear wrongdoing by the director), the company may prefer to pay something to the director so that he goes quietly, rather than insist on its contractual rights. Accordingly, the aim is to pitch termination payments at the right level. In that regard, there are a number of contractual devices that directors can employ to enhance the levels of compensation payable upon termination, such as entering into a long fixed-term contract, potentially with a rolling fixed term[172]; including long notice-periods for the lawful termination of the contract **11–027**

[169] *Swabey v Port Darwin Gold Mining Co* (1889) 1 Meg. 385; *Bailey v Medical Defence Union* (1995) 18 A.C.S.R. 521 H Ct Australia.

[170] For the complications of informal arrangements, see *James v Kent* [1951] 1 K.B. 551 CA; *Pocock v ADAC Ltd* [1952] 1 All E.R. 294 (Note) KBD.

[171] *Southern Foundries v Shirlaw* [1940] A.C. 701 HL; *Shindler v Northern Raincoat Co* [1960] 1 W.L.R. 1038 Assizes. In light of *Shirlaw*, a court will not grant an injunction to restrain the alteration of the articles.

[172] Under a rolling fixed-term contract, the fixed term is renewed from day to day, so that the full length of the term always remains to run. Under an ordinary fixed-term contract, a director removed in the last three months of a fixed three-year term, would not receive much benefit from the fixed term; under a "three-year roller", the director would always have the full protection of the three-year term. Moreover, it is possible to structure the contract so that, although the company is bound by the fixed term, the director is permitted to terminate the contract by giving relatively short notice.

by the company[173]; or including express entitlements to compensation if the contract is terminated.[174] None of these provisions would protect a director if the company was entitled to terminate the service contract without notice on grounds of a serious breach of contract by the director. A mere lack of economic success on the company's part, however, is unlikely to amount to a sufficiently fundamental breach of contract, since economic failure by the company does not necessarily betoken lack of effort or commitment on the director's part.

British company law tries to steer a course between these competing considerations by a combination of disclosure and shareholder approval requirements (both advisory and binding) in relation to agreed termination payments and other contractual terms.

Disclosure

11–028 Simple disclosure is a powerful tool. Formerly, the members might have known nothing about the directors' service contracts, especially the potential consequences of any decision to remove them. In this respect at least, the position of shareholders was improved quite some time ago: each director's service contract (or a memorandum of its terms if it is an unwritten contract) must be available for shareholders' inspection at any time.[175] A member has the right to request an inspection and obtain a copy of the service contract.[176] The previous exemptions for service contracts with less than 12 months to run or for directors required to work wholly or mainly outside the UK have been removed. As noted earlier,[177] in relation to quoted and traded companies, the CA 2006 now also requires the directors to produce an annual remuneration report (DRR),[178] which, like the other annual reports, must be provided to the members and the Registrar.[179] There are several crucial features of the DRR. First, the shareholders have a binding vote on the company's remuneration policy,[180] and that policy must provide details, in a prescribed and accessible form, of the company's policy on the

---

[173] In *Runciman v Walter Runciman Plc* [1993] B.C.C. 223 QBD, the directors' service contracts required five years' notice for lawful termination, a provision that had been increased from three years due to a prospective takeover bid. The *UK Corporate Governance Code* (July 2018), s.5, para.38 recommends that "[n]otice or contract periods should be one year or less", or, if higher periods are required to attract someone from outside the company, they should be reduced accordingly after the initial period in office.

[174] This express provision may be a liquidated damages clause, although it might be a penalty if disproportionate to any compensation that would otherwise be payable to him for breach of contract: see *Cavendish Square Holding BV v El Makdessi* [2015] UKSC 67. The *UK Corporate Governance Code* (July 2018), s.5, para.39 provides, however, that "compensation commitments in directors' terms of appointment do not reward poor performance".

[175] CA 2006 s.228(1). This applies also to shadow directors and to service contracts with subsidiary companies: CA 2006 s.230. Section 228 refers to "service contracts", unlike its predecessor (s.318 of the CA 1985) which referred to "contracts of service". It is suggested that this change makes it clear that both contracts of service and contracts for services are covered.

[176] CA 2006 s.229(1)–(2). Failure to comply constitutes a criminal offence on the part of every officer of the company who is in default.

[177] See para.11–019.

[178] CA 2006 s.420(1).

[179] CA 2006 ss.423(1) and 441(1).

[180] CA 2006 s.439A.

duration of directors' contracts, on notice periods, and on termination payments.[181] Secondly, to ensure the policy and practice are aligned, the company must provide an annual implementation report, as part of the DRR, detailing all payments actually made, again broken down into accessible detail.[182]

Shareholder approval

(i) Termination payments

Failure to gain shareholder approval in advance of termination payments made to directors of quoted and traded companies can have significant consequences. Any termination payments that are not in compliance with the company' agreed remuneration policy, or have not been separately agreed by the shareholders, cannot be made.[183] Any obligation to make payment to a director in such circumstances "has no effect".[184] If any payment is actually made, the payment is held by the director on trust for the company and any director who authorised the payments is jointly and severally liable to indemnify the company for any consequential losses.[185] On the other hand, if the payment is in compliance with the remuneration policy, but contained in an implementation report voted down by the shareholders, this will have no effect on the validity of the payment.[186] **11–029**

With respect to other companies, it is unlawful for a company to give a director of the company (or of its holding company) any payment by way of compensation for loss of office or as consideration for or in connection with his retirement from office,[187] without particulars of the proposed payment (including its amount) being disclosed to members of the company and the proposal being approved by them (and the members of the holding company, where appropriate). In other words, the directors cannot increase the cost of a removal without the consent of the shareholders. This prohibition does not apply, however, to payments by way of compensation for breach of contract, to payments to which the director is contractually entitled (unless the contract was concluded in connection with the termination), or to pension payments in respect of past services, apparently whether contractually required or not.[188] Accordingly, the

---

[181] Large and Medium-sized Companies and Groups (Accounts and Reports) (Amendment) Regulations 2013 (SI 2013/1981) Sch.1 Pt 4.

[182] Large and Medium-sized Companies and Groups (Accounts and Reports) (Amendment) Regulations 2013 (SI 2013/1981) Sch.1 Pt 3.

[183] CA 2006 s.226C.

[184] CA 2006 s.226E(1).

[185] CA 2006 s.226E(2).

[186] CA 2006 s.239(5).

[187] CA 2006 s.217. The circumstances in which the section bites are widely defined in s.215. There are specific provisions in ss.218 and 219 dealing with compensation payments made in connection with takeover bids or transfers of the company's assets, which are discussed in paras 28–027 onwards.

[188] CA 2006 s.220. The exclusion of covenanted payments, in the standard case, is in line with the previous law (see *Taupo Totara Timber Co v Rowe* [1978] A.C. 537 PC; *Lander v Premier Pict Petroleum*, 1997 S.L.T. 1361 OH) and was recommended by the Law Commission (*Company Directors: Regulating Conflicts of Interests and Formulating a Statement of Duties*(1999), Cm.4436, para.7.48). Given the requirement for approval of contracts of more than two years' duration, it makes all the more peculiar the exemption from shareholder approval of covenanted termination payments equivalent to more than two years' salary.

shareholders' ability to regulate termination payments is limited. Nevertheless, any unauthorised payment for loss of office to the director is held by the recipient on trust for the company and any director who authorised the payment is jointly and severally liable to indemnify the company for any loss suffered (for example, where the payment is not recoverable from the recipient).[189]

(ii) Terms governing the length of the contract—all companies

11–030 More generally, the legislature has sought to limit excessive termination payments by reducing the possible term for which a director can be appointed, as well as making sure these limits cannot be avoided by a combination of notice periods and fixed or rolling contractual terms.[190] If such a contractual term has the effect that the contract cannot be terminated by the company within a two-year period (referred to as the "guaranteed term"), then prior approval by a resolution of the general meeting is required.[191] In the absence of shareholder approval, the provisions establishing the "guaranteed term" are void and the contract is deemed to contain a term entitling the company to terminate the agreement upon giving reasonable notice.[192] This requirement applies to shadow directors and to service contracts with subsidiaries.[193] It is arguable, however, that for public companies the period of two years is too long. The Greenbury Committee thought there was a strong case for reducing the period to one year.[194] Although the Listing Rules do not adopt the one-year limit, the boards of premium-listed companies are nevertheless required to report to the shareholders annually giving "details of the unexpired term of any director's service contract of a director proposed for election or re-election at the forthcoming annual general meeting, and, if any director proposed for election or re-election does not have a directors' service contract, a statement to that effect".[195] This allows the shareholders to remain apprised of the length of directors' service contracts and the length of time remaining thereon. That said, the UK Corporate Governance Code, which also applies to premium-listed companies does provide such a limit: "[n]otice or contract periods should be one year or less. If it is necessary to offer longer periods to new directors recruited from outside the company, such periods

---

[189] CA 2006 s.222(1), thus at last implementing the report of the Cohen Committee: *Report of the Committee on Company Law Amendment* (1945), Cm.6659, p.52. The recipient will normally be the director, but the legislation covers compensation payments to persons connected with the director or at the direction of the director or a person connected with the director: CA 2006 s.215(3).

[190] Ensuring that the limits cannot be easily circumvented is achieved through the complex definition of "guaranteed period": see CA 2006 s.188(3). Section 188(4) performs the same role for guaranteed terms made up of more than one contract. Under the previous legislation, the relevant period was the very long one of five years, but both the Law Commission and the CLR had recommended a reduction.

[191] CA 2006 s.188.

[192] CA 2006 s.189. That period of reasonable notice might be less than two years. Thus, the director pays a potential penalty for failing to secure shareholder approval, in that the contract may become subject to a notice period shorter than the two years that the contract could have contained without shareholder approval.

[193] CA 2006 ss.188(1) and 223.

[194] *Directors' Remuneration, Report of a Study Group* (Gee, 1995), para.7.13.

[195] Listing Rules LR 9.8.8.

should reduce to one year or less after the initial period".[196] Although this provision is not mandatory, a premium-listed company must "comply or explain" why it has not done so.

CONCLUSION

Given that the company's management powers are invariably vested in the board, it is easy to dismiss the shareholder as a relic of a bygone age in terms of corporate power. Whilst the shareholders have not always been able to secure effective constitutional control through the articles or at common law, it is noticeable that the courts never turned their back on the shareholders as a source of constitutional power. In more recent times, the shareholders have become much more of a force to be reckoned with: not only has the list of shareholders' decisions in the CA 2006 gradually increased, but shareholders nowadays have a significant role in the context of removing directors and having a "say on pay". That said, there is little point having powers if it is not possible to exercise them effectively. The procedures for meetings are considered in the next chapter. **11–031**

[196] Financial Reporting Council, *UK Corporate Governance Code* (July 2018), s.5, para.38.

CHAPTER 12

SHAREHOLDER DECISION-MAKING

THE ROLE OF THE SHAREHOLDERS

As the previous chapter demonstrated, whilst most decisions about the company's business will be taken by the board, shareholders' decision-making still has an important, indeed crucial, role to play in the governance of companies. Quite apart from the specific decisions for which the CA 2006 requires shareholder consent,[1] the traditional model of directorial accountability to the shareholders depends heavily upon the ability of the shareholders to review the performance of the board (notably when the annual report and accounts are presented to them) and to take decisions if they think that performance has not been adequate, for example, by removing the existing directors and installing a new board.[2] **12–001**

Shareholder activism depends on individual motivation, certainly, but is also crucially underpinned by the rights of shareholders at general meetings. Although most intervention by substantial shareholders will take place in private (moving into the public arena of the general meeting only if private pressure is

[1] See further paras 11–011 onwards.

[2] See further paras 11–022 onwards.

unsuccessful) the pressure which such shareholders can bring to bear privately depends in large part upon the prospect of their being able to get their way in the public meeting if the private pressures are unsuccessful. Without doubt, the crucial factor, if it comes to a public fight between the incumbent management and these shareholders, is the ability of an ordinary majority of the shareholders at any time to remove the directors.[3]

Nevertheless, the shareholder meeting has had a bad press in recent years. In small companies, it is argued that the meeting is an unnecessary encumbrance because the shareholder/directors frequently meet together informally; in large companies, shareholders do not show sufficient interest in using the general meeting, often allowing it to be captured by single-issue pressure groups whose primary objective is to advance the policies they stand for, rather than any general interests as shareholders. The CA 2006 has been amended incrementally over recent years to address the first set of concerns. The second, and more intractable, set of problems can only be addressed with "a sharper focus on the shareholder".[4] A "more effective machinery for enabling and encouraging shareholders to exercise effective and responsible control" was one of three core policies of the Company Law Review in the corporate governance area,[5] an approach that increasingly chimes with current government policy initiatives.[6]

12–002 Before considering these problems, it is important to be alert to one preliminary issue, which is the question of who is entitled to vote on shareholder decisions. It should not be supposed that all shareholders, not even all ordinary shareholders, necessarily have the right to vote on shareholder resolutions; or, even if they do, that they have voting rights as extensive as those attached to other shares that apparently carry the same level of risk. As considered above,[7] the rights attached to classes of shares, including the number of votes per share, are matters for the company to determine in its articles of association or in the terms of issue of the shares. The exclusion of preference shareholders from voting rights, except in limited circumstances, is common, and the issuance of non-voting ordinary shares is not unknown, though it is fiercely opposed by institutional shareholders.[8] Thus, "shareholder democracy", which is in any event a democracy of shares rather than of shareholders, is, or may be, an imperfect one. Company law does not require equal voting rights for shares carrying the same risk nor equivalent rights for shares of different classes of risk.[9]

---

[3] CA 2006 s.168. See paras 11–022 onwards.

[4] Final Report I, para.1.56.

[5] Final Report I, para.3.4. The other two were the proposed statement of directors' duties (see Ch.10), and improved disclosure and transparency provisions (see Ch.22).

[6] From a governmental point of view, putting pressure on shareholders to regulate boards of directors reduces the pressure on the Government to regulate substantively in the contested area. For the example of the recent re-regulation of directors' remuneration, see paras 11–013 onwards.

[7] See further Ch.6.

[8] Additional voting rights may be confined to certain types of resolution, for example, the "golden share" held by the Government after some recent privatisations may operate so as to allow the Government to out-vote all other shareholders on certain specified resolutions: see Graham, (1988) 9 Co. Law. 24.

[9] CA 2006 s.284 lays down a rule of "one share, one vote" (for all shares, whether ordinary or preference), except where the vote is taken on a "show of hands" (see paras 12–048 to 12–049), but allows the articles to make alternative provisions, so that the distribution of voting rights (including

In these circumstances, there is a risk, where voting and cash-flow rights are not proportionate, that the controlling shareholder (controlling in terms of votes but not necessarily in terms of capital committed to the company) will take excessive risks with the company's business at the expense of the non-controlling shareholders (who may be the majority contributors to the company's capital), since the controller does not bear a proportionate part of the downside if the strategy is unsuccessful. Disproportionate voting structures may alternatively be used to maintain the company's existing directors in office, because the controllers elect themselves or their nominees to the board and are reluctant to abandon their control.[10] In most cases, however, since the price of the non-controlling shares (at least where these are traded on public markets) adjusts to reflect these risks, regulatory intervention is directed at disclosure rather than prohibition.[11]

SHAREHOLDER DECISION-MAKING WITHOUT SHAREHOLDER MEETINGS

The nature of the problem

In small companies where shareholders and directors are the same people, requiring them to distinguish between the decisions they take as directors and those that they take as shareholders can seem unduly burdensome. They will tend in fact to take all decisions as directors, since the rules about board meetings are largely under their control, whereas the CA 2006 contains some mandatory rules about shareholder meetings, for example, as to the length of notice required.[12] However, this approach generates legal risks because the rules for the two types of meeting are not the same. For example, voting is normally on the basis of "one person, one vote" on the board, but on the basis of "one share, one vote" at a shareholders' meeting. If the shares are not equally divided among the directors, the outcomes in the two situations may not be the same. Normally, this does not matter as long as all is going well, because decisions will in fact be taken unanimously. However, if relations between the entrepreneurs begin to deteriorate, as in small companies they often do,[13] clear decision-making mechanisms are required. **12–003**

One straightforward way of resolving this problem would be to permit companies where shareholders and directors are the same people to operate with

the creation of classes of non-voting ordinary shares) is under the control of the shareholders: see CA 2006 s.284(4). See *Re Savoy Hotel Ltd* [1981] Ch. 351 Ch D, where the company had created A and B shares, ranking pari passu except in relation to voting rights, with the effect that the holders of the B shares, who owned 2.3% of the equity, could exercise 48.55% of the votes. For premium-listed companies, by contrast, there is (at least currently) a one share/one vote rule: see Listing Rules LR 7.2.1A, Principles 4 and 5.

[10] For the "break-through rule" in relation to takeovers, see paras 28–022 onwards.

[11] Contrast the minority report of the Jenkins Committee in 1962, which recommended a ban on non and restricted-voting shares: see *Report of the Committee on Company Law Amendment* (1962), Cm.1749, "Note of Dissent", cf. the main report at paras 123–136. The dissentients were mainly influenced by the inconsistency between the development of a market for corporate control and the issuance of non or restricted-voting shares. But see n.9 on premium-listed companies.

[12] See para.12–038.

[13] See further Ch.14.

only a single decision-making organ, probably the board. This facility is provided by many state laws in the US. When the Company Law Review consulted on this proposal,[14] it did not find enough support for the idea to take it forward in Britain. Instead, the CA 2006 simply makes it easier for small companies to operate, but still with two decision-making bodies. If incorporators wish, formally, to roll the board and the shareholders' meetings into one whilst still retaining limited liability, they will have to operate as a Limited Liability Partnership.[15]

Written resolutions

12–004 By amending earlier statutory rules, the CA 2006 now provides for much simpler decision-taking within private companies. The default obligation on private companies to hold an AGM has been abolished, and resolutions of the members of a private company may now be taken either as a written resolution or by adoption at a meeting of the members.[16] Both ways of making shareholder decisions are of equal validity and (with two limited but important exceptions, which are discussed below) any decision may be taken in either manner. Indeed, the CA 2006 makes clear that the articles may not deprive a company of its right to take statutory decisions (other than the two exceptions just mentioned) by written resolution,[17] although the articles could require a meeting for decisions that are required pursuant to the company's articles. A written resolution needs to be adopted by the same percentage of support as would be needed for a resolution adopted at a meeting.[18] The necessary consequence has been a greater formalisation of the rules governing written resolutions.

This written resolution procedure renders decision-taking in private companies far less cumbersome, although if a member wishes to have a meeting of members and the board is unwilling to convene one,[19] then—now that a formal AGM is not required—a meeting can only be demanded if the general statutory provisions on the calling of meetings by members have been observed. These provisions normally require the requisitionists to hold 5% of the company's voting share capital.[20]

Where written resolutions not available

12–005 There are only two situations where the written resolution procedure is not available to private companies, and where the company must instead proceed by

[14] Developing, paras 7.95f onwards; Completing, paras 2.35–2.36.

[15] See para.1–004.

[16] CA 2006 ss.336 and 336(1A), requiring an AGM, applies only to public companies and to private companies which are "traded companies". "Traded companies" are defined in CA 2006 s.360C as companies with voting shares that are admitted to trading on a UK or EU regulated market with the consent of the company. For discussion of AGMs, see para.12–029. Private companies may take resolutions in either way: CA 2006 s.281(1).

[17] CA 2006 s.300.

[18] CA 2006 s.296(4), discussed at para.12–024.

[19] CA 2006 s.302 makes it clear that the directors may always call a general meeting of the company.

[20] CA 2006 ss.303–306, discussed at para.12–030. The rule for demanding that a written resolution be circulated also requires 5%, or some lower threshold as specified in the articles: see CA 2006 s.292.

means of a meeting of its members. These are decisions for the removal of either a director[21] or an auditor[22] before the expiration of their period of appointment.[23] In the first scenario, if the CA 2006 did not insist on a meeting, it would render nugatory the director's entitlement[24] to be heard at the meeting considering the resolution for his removal. An auditor does not have the same right to be heard, but only to make written representations to the meeting.[25] In this second scenario, the rationale for insistence upon a meeting is to permit shareholders to question face-to-face those who favour the auditor's removal. Presumably, the rationale is that such discussion will lead to more considered outcomes in relation to potentially significant changes of personnel in central parts of the company's corporate governance structure.

The procedure for passing written resolutions

Written resolutions require the same show of approval as would be needed to pass the resolution if it were proposed at a meeting.[26] This means either 50% or 75%, depending upon whether the resolution required is an ordinary or a special resolution.[27] Of course, in the case of a meeting, the percentage figures refer to those who vote, whether in person or by proxy, whereas in the case of a written resolution it refers to those entitled to vote.[28] In practice, therefore, the consent of a higher percentage of the members is normally needed for the passing of a written resolution than for a resolution at a meeting: typically fewer than half the members attend a meeting either in person or by proxy. Nevertheless, the advantages of not having to call a meeting outweigh this potential disadvantage. **12–006**

The CA 2006 requires a copy of the proposed written resolution to be sent at the same time (as far as is reasonably practical) to every member entitled to vote.[29] However, if this can be done without "undue delay", the company may submit the same copy to each member in turn (or different copies to each of a number of members in turn) or employ a combination of simultaneous and consecutive circulation.[30] It is submitted that the courts should take a rather strict view of what constitutes "undue delay". Near-simultaneous circulation is important because it prevents the proposers circulating the resolution first to its likely supporters, or those with no strong view on the matter, thus securing their

[21] CA 2006 s.168. See further paras 11–022 onwards.

[22] CA 2006 s.510. See further para.23–019.

[23] CA 2006 s.288(2).

[24] CA 2006 s.169(2).

[25] CA 2006 s.511(3)–(6).

[26] CA 2006 s.296(4).

[27] See para.12–024. See also *Hook v Sumner* [2015] EWHC 3820 (Ch); [2016] B.C.C. 2020 at [12].

[28] Referred to in s.292(4) as the "eligible" members, but s.289 defines the eligible members as those members who would have been entitled to vote on the date the resolution was circulated. The written resolution provisions do not alter the rules on the distribution of voting rights, discussed at para.12–004.

[29] Although shareholders can be served at different times, "the obligation on the company is so far as possible to give all members the same notice", so that it is not open to the company or directors "to select some members over others in circulation of a proposed resolution": see *Re Sprout Land Holdings Ltd* [2019] EWHC 806 (Ch) at [26].

[30] CA 2006 s.291(3) (for resolutions proposed by directors) and s.293(2) (for resolutions proposed by members). See also *Re Sprout Land Holdings Ltd* [2019] EWHC 806 (Ch) at [26].

support before the opponents have had the opportunity to put their case to the other members. This is important because the written resolution is passed at the point at which it secures the requisite majority of the members. It does not matter whether or not all those members to whom the resolution has been sent have voted at that time, or whether the period for voting has expired or indeed whether all the members have been sent copies of the resolution at that point.[31] Accordingly, if a proposed ordinary resolution is sent to a 51% shareholder and he or she signifies assent before any of the other shareholders have opened their emails, the resolution will be adopted at that point.

A member signifies agreement to a proposed resolution when the company receives from the member or someone acting on the member's behalf a document indicating agreement, the method of signifying agreement having been indicated when the resolution was circulated.[32] Once given, the consent cannot be revoked.[33] This is another consideration in favour of simultaneous circulation. Despite the importance of simultaneous circulation, non-compliance with the statutory requirements (which includes the requirements for informing the members of the method of signifying consent and the final voting date[34]) does not affect the validity of the resolution, if it is passed, though it does constitute a criminal offence on the part of every officer in default.[35]

Written resolutions proposed by members

12–007 Resolutions may be proposed as written resolutions by directors or members.[36] Members holding at least 5% (or some lower percentage, if so fixed by the articles) of the total voting rights exercisable on the resolution in question may request circulation of a resolution,[37] along with a statement of up to 1,000 words in support of the resolution.[38] Once such a request has been made, the company must, within 21 days, initiate the written resolution procedure in the manner described above.[39]

---

[31] CA 2006 s.296(4). The period for voting is 28 days from the date of circulation or whatever other period is fixed in the company's articles: see CA 2006 s.297. If the requisite support is not achieved by that date, the resolution lapses. The circulation date is the first date on which a copy of the resolution is sent or submitted to a member: CA 2006 s.290. A member may signify agreement by a "pre-circulation agreement" that is signed beforehand: see *Re Sprout Land Holdings Ltd* [2019] EWHC 806 (Ch) at [35].

[32] CA 2006 s.293(4)(a). The statement accompanying the proposed resolution must also indicate the final date for voting: CA 2006 s.291(2)(b). Voting may be electronic: CA 2006 ss.296(1)–(2) and 298.

[33] CA 2006 s.291(6)–(7).

[34] CA 2006 s.296(4).

[35] CA 2006 s.296(3).

[36] CA 2006 s.288(3).

[37] CA 2006 s.292(4)–(5). The 5% figure tracks that for requiring a public company to add a resolution to the agenda of its AGM (see paras 12–034 to 12–035), for which the CA 2006 s.292 is the functional substitute, since it is not expected that private companies will typically hold AGMs. However, the original Draft Clauses had proposed that any member might require the company to initiate the written resolution procedure: see *Modernising Company Law—Draft Clauses* (July 2002), Cm. 5553-II, cl.174.

[38] CA 2006 s.292(3).

[39] CA 2006 s.293(1)–(3). As the obligation to circulate the resolution is upon "the company", this must be done "after due consideration by [the company's] directors, and not simply by one director

This requirement is subject to three exceptions:

(1) The requisitionists must tender a sum necessary to cover the costs of the circulation, unless the company has resolved otherwise.[40] These should not be large if electronic circulation is possible.

(2) The resolution must not be ineffective "whether by reason of inconsistency with any enactment or the company's articles or otherwise".[41] There is no point in securing a resolution for the company to do something that the company may not lawfully do; but, in the case of inconsistency with the articles, this may simply affect the level of support the resolution needs (in other words, it must be enough to alter the articles).[42] Nor need the company circulate the resolution if it is defamatory of any person or is frivolous or vexatious.[43]

(3) The company or any other aggrieved person may apply to the court for an order that the company is not obliged to circulate the members' statement on the grounds that the members' circulation rights are being abused.[44]

Wider written resolution provisions under the articles

The CA 1985 explicitly preserved the power of companies to adopt provisions in their articles on the taking of resolutions, and Table A contained a procedure for consenting to written resolutions unanimously without a meeting.[45] Although the CA 2006 does not retain this explicit authorisation,[46] and although the current model sets of articles do not deal with written resolutions, it is difficult to see why the current legislation should be construed as taking this power away from companies. This facility may be useful to those few public companies with small shareholding bodies. For private companies, the incentive to create a special procedure in the articles is now much less, since the procedure under the CA 2006 has dropped the requirement of unanimous consent. **12–008**

who chooses to do so": see *Re Sprout Land Holdings Ltd* [2019] EWHC 806 (Ch) at [24]. Non-compliance is a criminal offence on the part of every officer in default, but again the validity of the resolution, if passed, is not affected by non-compliance: see CA 2006 s.293(6)–(7).

40 CA 2006 s.294.

41 CA 2006 s.292(2)(a).

42 See para.14–007.

43 CA 2006 s.292(2)(b)–(c).

44 CA 2006 s.295. This highlights the need for the directors to apply their minds as to whether the resolution should be circulated: see *Re Sprout Land Holdings Ltd* [2019] EWHC 806 (Ch) at [32]. The requisitionists may have to pay the company's costs (see CA 2006 s.295(2)) and presumably the normal rules as to costs will apply if the application is by a person aggrieved (in other words, the requisitionists will have to pay if they lose). This is a new section, though it mirrors the provision which now appears in relation to meetings: CA 2006 s.317.

45 Companies (Tables A to F) Regulations 1985 (SI 1985/805) Table A art.53.

46 CA 2006 s.300 is, by contrast, concerned with restraining the (private) company's power to exclude a written resolution procedure, rather than its power to have a more generous one than the statutory procedure.

Unanimous consent at common law

12–009 In *Ciban Management Corporation v Citco (BVI) Ltd*,[47] Lord Burrows described the unanimous consent rule as being "the principle that anything the members of a company can do by formal resolution in a general meeting, they can also do informally if all of them assent to it".[48] This rule allows shareholders to decide informally on matters within their sphere of competence, and permits wholly informal methods of giving shareholder consent, provided that consent (being of all those entitled to vote) is unanimous: the level of support that would have been required in a formal meeting or if the written resolution procedure had been followed is thus immaterial. This rule is preserved in the CA 2006,[49] and while the principle applies to both public and private companies, it may be difficult to satisfy in the former case due to the need for unanimity, and may be less significant in the latter case given that the CA 2006 allows for non-unanimous written resolutions. Nevertheless, the case law suggests the rule still has its place. The accepted explanation for the rule is that it would be inequitable to allow the company, or its members, to assert that they are not bound by a decision or an act which all those competent to effect it have decided should be carried out.[50] From this rationale follow the answers to the two questions that have most concerned the courts: what counts as informal consent and how must it be manifested; and which issues lie within the competence of the shareholders to determine in this way.

On the issue of what counts as unanimous consent, Neuberger J (as he then was) summarised the principle in the following terms in *EIC Services Ltd v Phipps*[51]:

> "The essence of the *Duomatic* principle, as I see it, is that [certain specified formalities, here in the company's articles] can be avoided if all members of the group [being the group entitled to determine the matter in issue], being aware of the relevant facts, either give their approval to that course, or so conduct themselves as to make it inequitable for them to deny that they have given their approval. Whether the approval is given in advance or after the event, whether it is characterised as agreement, ratification, waiver, or estoppel, and whether members of the group give their consent in different ways at different times, does not matter."

This statement is supported by earlier authorities, and has been followed subsequently. It highlights a number of important and distinct matters.

---

[47] *Ciban Management Corporation v Citco (BVI) Ltd* [2020] UKPC 21; [2020] 3 W.L.R. 705 at [31]. The unanimous consent rule is often referred to as "the *Duomatic* rule", although that case was not the first to formulate it: see *Re Duomatic Ltd* [1969] 2 Ch. 365 Ch D.

[48] See further para.11–009.

[49] CA 2006 s.281(4)(a), which provides that "[n]othing in this Part affects any enactment or rule of law as to things done otherwise than by passing a resolution". Similarly, the estoppel-based version of the common law rules is similarly preserved by the words, "[n]othing in this Part affects any enactment or rule of law as to cases in which a person is precluded from alleging that a resolution has not been duly passed".

[50] *Baroness Wenlock v River Dee Co* (1883) 36 Ch. D. 675n at 681–2n; *Re Duomatic Ltd* [1969] 2 Ch. 365 at 373; *Re New Cedos Engineering Co Ltd* [1994] 1 B.C.L.C. 797 Ch D at 814; *Wright v Atlas Wright (Europe) Ltd* [1999] 2 B.C.L.C. 301 CA at 314–5; *Euro Brokers Holdings Ltd v Monecor (London) Ltd* [2003] EWCA Civ 105; [2003] 1 B.C.L.C. 506 at [62].

[51] *EIC Services Ltd v Phipps* [2004] EWCA Civ 1069; [2004] B.C.C. 814 at [122], approved in *Ciban Management Corporation v Citco (BVI) Ltd* [2020] 3 W.L.R. 705 at [41].

The first issue concerns who must consent. Buckley J in *Re Duomatic* held that only those entitled to vote on the issue must consent, not all members regardless of that entitlement.[52] This is especially material when, for example, the informal procedure is applied to class meetings.[53] The necessary consents can be inferred even from occasions where the shareholders wear a different hat: for example, in companies where all the shareholders are directors, these individuals can act as directors in a board meeting and simultaneously act as shareholders, thereby informally approving or ratifying unanimously their own unauthorised act as directors, provided, as shareholders, they are competent to do that.[54] In a similar vein, individuals representing corporate shareholders (usually by virtue of being the CEO of the corporate shareholder) can give the necessary consent on behalf of their company, if competent to so act.[55] The consent of an agent with actual or ostensible authority from the shareholder will count for these purposes.[56] Similarly, trustees holding shares on trust can, as the registered holder, validly consent. Agency and trust relationships can, however, generate complications in terms of identifying the relevant consent. If the trustee holds some of the shares personally and some as trustee, his or her consent is only taken as applying to those shares held personally, unless it is expressed to apply to the other shares as well.[57] On the other hand, and in line with the justifications given for the informal consent rule, if the trustee could be compelled to vote in accordance with the wishes of the beneficial owners, then the latter's consents are effective for the purpose of the rule.[58] In *Ciban Management Corporation v Citco (BVI) Ltd*,[59] the **12–010**

[52] *Stubbins Marketing Ltd v Stubbins Food Partnership Ltd* [2020] EWHC 1266 (Ch) at [377]; *Atkinson v Kingsley* [2020] EWHC 2913 (Ch) at [89].

[53] *Re Torvale Group Ltd* [1999] 2 B.C.L.C. 605 Ch D (Companies Ct).

[54] *Re Express Engineering Works Ltd* [1920] 1 Ch. 466 CA; cf. *Shannan v Viavi Solutions UK Ltd* [2018] EWCA Civ 681 at [87], suggesting a "qua shareholder" limitation. The qualification is important: for example, the shareholders cannot consent (whether formally or informally) to the directors making illegal gifts out of capital. This is now taken to be the ratio of *Re George Newman and Co* [1895] 1 Ch. 674 CA. See also paras 10–111 onwards. and 12–011.

[55] *Wright v Atlas Wright (Europe) Ltd* [1999] 2 B.C.L.C. 301 CA; *Multinational Gas Co Ltd v Multinational Gas Services Ltd* [1983] Ch. 258 CA (Civ Div). See also *Madoff Securities International Ltd v Raven* [2013] EWHC 3147 (Ch).

[56] *Ciban Management Corporation v Citco (BVI) Ltd* [2020] 3 WLR 705 at [42], although the shareholder was shown to have "set up a mode of operation" that was designed to mask his identity and to encourage others to rely upon his agent.

[57] *Re Tulsesense Ltd*; sub nom. *Rolfe v Rolfe* [2010] EWHC 244 (Ch); [2010] 2 B.C.L.C. 525 at [40]. By contrast, joint holders of shares are only entitled to one vote per share, and the assent of the "senior" holder is sufficient: see *Re Gee & Co (Woolwich) Ltd* [1975] Ch. 52 Ch D.

[58] *Shahar v Tsitsekkos* [2004] EWHC 2659 (Ch) at [67]. More generally, the Australian case of *Jalmoon Pty Ltd (In Liquidation) v Bow* (1997) 15 A.C.L.C. 230 limits consent to the registered owner. See also *Secretary of State for Business, Innovation and Skills v Hamilton* [2015] CSOH 46 at [59], obiter, simply noting the uncertainty.

[59] *Ciban Management Corporation v Citco (BVI) Ltd* [2020] 3 W.L.R. 705 at [47]. Indeed, Lord Burrows approved the suggestion that "the assent of the beneficial owners of a share can meet *Duomatic* requirements". See also *Dickinson v NAL Realisations (Staffordshire) Ltd* [2020] 1 W.L.R. 1122 at [20]; *Satyam Enterprises Ltd v Burton* [2021] EWCA Civ 287 at [40]–[44]. If there are two or more beneficial owners, then of course all must consent: see *Re Tulsesense Ltd*; sub nom. *Rolfe v Rolfe* [2010] 2 B.C.L.C. 525 at [43]. This may prove problematic in the context of pension funds: see *Dickinson v NAL Realisations (Staffordshire) Ltd* [2020] 1 W.L.R. 1122 at [22]. The unanimous consent of the shareholders in a parent company would satisfy the unanimous informal consent principle in relation to the wholly-owned subsidiary: see *Byers v Chen* [2021] UKPC 4 at [69]–[71].

Privy Council explained that "at least as here where the ultimate beneficial owner and not the registered shareholder is taking all the decisions in the relevant transactions, the *Duomatic* principle applies as regards the consent of (and authority given by) the ultimate beneficial owner".

Secondly, the requirement that the consenting shareholders be aware of the relevant facts simply repeats the orthodox common law requirement that consent counts as such only when it is "fully informed".[60] Often, this will become an enquiry into the nature and extent of the information disclosed.[61] In *Stubbins Marketing Ltd v Stubbins Food Partnership Ltd*,[62] Trower J indicated that the "relevant facts" requiring disclosure were "all the facts which are material to the decision-making process". This would prima facie include any information made mandatory by statute in order for shareholders to take formal decisions on certain matters[63]; there is no reason to suppose that informal decision-making should be successful if less well informed. Put another way, there seems no reason to suppose that the informal procedure specifically endorsed by the CA 2006 would somehow be excluded in those contexts where the legislation has specified information requirements, even if the informal procedure's application needs to be addressed thoughtfully.[64] Nevertheless, it can be strongly argued that such information provisions are inserted solely for the protection of shareholders and can therefore be waived by them (although perhaps only on an informed basis or at least in a conscious fashion).

Thirdly, there is an issue as to what is needed to signify the necessary consent. The above statement by Neuberger J (as he then was) in *EIC Services Ltd v Phipps*,[65] illustrates the breadth of what will count as consent. This breadth is amply supported by the authorities.[66] Despite this breadth, however, the necessary consents must be objectively established,[67] and this necessarily means that they must be expressed in *some* way by each member (even if only by acquiescence[68]): the fact that the person would have consented if asked is not

---

[60] *Stubbins Marketing Ltd v Stubbins Food Partnership Ltd* [2020] EWHC 1266 (Ch) at [365].

[61] *Saatchi v Gajjaar* [2019] EWHC 3472 (Ch) at [47].

[62] *Stubbins Marketing Ltd v Stubbins Food Partnership Ltd* [2020] EWHC 1266 (Ch) at [366]. The "materiality" of the facts might depend upon how they are presented to the shareholders.

[63] See, for example, CA 2006 ss.181(5) (directors' long-term service contracts), 696(5) and 699(6) (on repurchases of company's own shares).

[64] CA 2006 s.281(4). See also *Wright v Atlas Wright (Europe) Ltd* [1999] 2 B.C.L.C. 301 CA. See further para.12–011.

[65] *EIC Services Ltd v Phipps* [2004] B.C.C. 814 at [122], quoted at para.12–009.

[66] See further *Re Oxted Motor Co Ltd* [1921] 3 K.B. 32 KBD; *Parker & Cooper Ltd v Reading* [1926] Ch. 975 Ch D; *Re Pearce Duff & Co Ltd* [1960] 1 W.L.R. 1014 Ch D; *Re Duomatic Ltd* [1969] 2 Ch. 365; *Re Bailey Hay & Co Ltd* [1971] 1 W.L.R. 1357 Ch D; *Re Gee & Co (Woolwich) Ltd* [1975] Ch. 52; *Cane v Jones* [1980] 1 W.L.R. 1451 Ch D; *Re Moorgate Mercantile Holdings Ltd* [1980] 1 W.L.R. 227 Ch D at 242G; *Multinational Gas Co Ltd v Multinational Gas Services Ltd* [1983] 1 Ch. 258 especially at 289.

[67] *Schofield v Schofield* [2011] 2 B.C.L.C. 319 at [32]. The fact that only some shareholders sign the relevant document may be a strong objective indicator that not all have consented: see *Stubbins Marketing Ltd v Stubbins Food Partnership Ltd* [2020] EWHC 1266 (Ch) at [393]–[395]. See further *Dickinson v NAL Realisations (Staffordshire) Ltd* [2020] 1 W.L.R. 1122 at [21]; *Baker v Staines* [2021] EWHC 1006 (Ch) at [141]; *Satyam Enterprises Ltd v Burton* [2021] EWCA Civ 287 at [45].

[68] *Re Bailey Hay & Co Ltd* [1971] 1 W.L.R. 1357 at 1367. See *Kaye v Oxford House (Wimbledon) Co Ltd* [2019] EWHC 2181 (Ch); [2020] B.C.C. 117 at [138]. The fact that a shareholder appoints an

enough,[69] nor is a decision that is merely internal,[70] and of course express objection negates any possibility of inferring consent.[71] A shareholder who has died or been dissolved, yet remains a member, cannot consent.[72] In all of this, however, the cases that rely on something less than assent (albeit informal assent), and instead rely on the interplay of acquiescence, estoppel and laches, are perhaps the most difficult. In *Re Bailey Hay & Co Ltd*,[73] a resolution was passed by two votes in favour and three abstaining at a meeting attended by all the members of the company, but of which the requisite length of notice had not been given (unbeknown to all present, the notice was one day short of the requisite 14 days). That information came to light within the next few months. The court denied a challenge to the validity of the resolution brought over three years later (and, it seems, for technical reasons as a means of defeating a counter-claim), holding that in the circumstances the shareholders should be taken as unanimously assenting to, or acquiescing in, the winding-up[74]; or, alternatively, that their delay (or "laches") in making the claim made it "practically unjust" now to upset the resolution (which had been for the appointment of a liquidator).[75] It might have been preferable to confine the finding of acquiescence to one that the non-voting shareholders could be taken to have acquiesced in the shorter period of notice. That would have produced the same result, and was perhaps better supported by Brightman J's analysis of the facts. Nevertheless, the case is instructive in this difficult area.[76]

The final issue that has troubled the courts is defining which matters may be determined by the unanimous consent rule. The rule, it seems, applies whenever the shareholders are competent to act, although it "cannot be used where there is relevant dishonesty" in the sense of a shareholder perpetrating a fraud on the **12–011**

---

agent or establishes a scheme to hide his involvement is more than mere acquiescence: see *Ciban Management Corporation v Citco (BVI) Ltd* [2020] 3 W.L.R. 705.

[69] *Re D'Jan of London Ltd* [1994] 1 B.C.L.C. 561 Ch D (Companies Ct); it suffices where the only inference that can be drawn is indicative of assent and acceptance: see *Hussain v Wycombe Islamic Mission and Mosque Trust Ltd* [2011] EWHC 971 (Ch) at [37].

[70] *Re Tulsesense Ltd*; sub nom. *Rolfe v Rolfe* [2010] 2 B.C.L.C. 525. See also *Bonham-Carter v Situ Ventures Ltd* [2012] EWHC 230 (Ch); [2012] B.C.C. 717, in which the filing of relevant forms and notices was found to be insufficient to make out a *Duomatic* decision to remove the director (the decision was reversed on appeal in [2013] EWCA Civ 47; [2014] B.C.C. 125, but no permission to appeal had been given on this point).

[71] *Schofield v Schofield* [2011] EWCA Civ 154; [2011] 2 B.C.L.C. 319.

[72] *Re BW Estates (No.2) Ltd* [2018] Ch. 511 at [71]–[72] and [80]–[85].

[73] *Re Bailey Hay & Co Ltd* [1971] 1 W.L.R. 1357. See also *Peña v Dale* [2003] EWHC 1065 (Ch); [2004] 2 B.C.L.C. 508 at [120].

[74] *Re Bailey Hay & Co Ltd* [1971] 1 W.L.R. 1357 at 1366F–1367B.

[75] *Re Bailey Hay & Co Ltd* [1971] 1 W.L.R. 1357 at 1367D–E.

[76] See *Phosphate of Lime Co v Green* (1871–72) L.R. 7 C.P. 43 CCP, where it was held that "acquiescence" by members of a company could be established without proving actual knowledge by each individual member, so long as each could have found out if he had bothered to ask. See also *Ho Tung v Man On Insurance Co* [1902] A.C. 232 PC, where articles of association, which had never been adopted by a resolution, but had been acted on for 19 years and amended from time to time, were held to have been accepted and adopted as valid and operative articles.

company.[77] It follows that the shareholders cannot, even by unanimous agreement, overcome prohibitions on the company's activities imposed by the general law or the CA 2006.[78] They cannot, for example, make illegal gifts out of capital, or distribute the company's assets in ways not authorised by law, or take decisions that are not theirs to take because that right has been given to a named individual or group.[79] Typically, the unanimous informal consent rule is applied when the shareholders have the power to act, but have not followed the necessary formal decision-making requirements, whether these are found in the CA 2006, the company's articles or a shareholders' agreement.[80] Accordingly, unanimous consent can operate to waive formalities required for the protection of shareholders, but not those required for the protection of other parties, notably creditors.[81] Thus, in *Precision Dipping Ltd v Precision Dipping Marketing Ltd*,[82] the requirement for auditor approval of a dividend, where the company's accounts were qualified, could not be waived by unanimous consent of the shareholders because the provision was clearly one aimed at protecting creditors (and possibly shareholders as well). By contrast, in *Wright v Atlas Wright (Europe) Ltd*,[83] the Court of Appeal was prepared to permit unanimous shareholder consent to override the procedural requirements set out above for the approval of a long-service contract.[84] However, it may not always be easy to categorise the function of particular statutory requirements.[85] For example, it seems unlikely that the courts would permit the unanimous consent rule to operate in the two cases excepted from the written resolution procedure (removal of a director or auditor from office before the expiration of their term), since, it

[77] *Ciban Management Corporation v Citco (BVI) Ltd* [2020] 3 W.L.R. 705 at [43], applying *Bowthorpe Holdings Ltd v Hills* [2003] 1 B.C.L.C. 226 at [50]. See also *Auden McKenzie (Pharma Division) Ltd v Patel* [2019] EWHC 1257 (Comm) at [14]–[16]; *Satyam Enterprises Ltd v Burton* [2021] EWCA Civ 287 at [56]–[59].

[78] *Tonstate Group Ltd v Wojakovski* [2019] EWHC 3362 (Ch) at [13]–[17].

[79] *Madoff Securities International Ltd v Raven* [2013] EWHC 3147 at [288]; *Oxford Fleet Management Ltd v Brown* [2014] EWHC 3065 at [102]–[104]. See paras 11–006 onwards on shareholders' residual and confirmation powers.

[80] *Re Torvale Group Ltd* [1999] 2 B.C.L.C. 605; *Euro Brokers Holdings Ltd v Monecor (London) Ltd* [2003] 1 B.C.L.C. 505 at [62]; *Ciban Management Corporation v Citco (BVI) Ltd* [2020] 3 W.L.R. 705 at [39].

[81] In *Ciban Management Corporation v Citco (BVI) Ltd* [2020] 3 W.L.R. 705 at [40], Lord Burrows expressed one recognised qualification as being "that the transaction must not jeopardise the company's insolvency or cause loss to its creditors". See also *Atkinson v Kingsley* [2020] EWHC 2913 (Ch) at [90], indicating that "the principle in *Re Duomatic* only applies if the company was solvent at the time". See further *Re Finch Plc* [2015] EWHC 2430 (Ch) at [28]; *Ball v Hughes* [2017] EWHC 3228 (Ch); [2018] B.C.C. 196 at [148]; *Tonstate Group Ltd v Wojakovski* [2019] EWHC 3362 (Ch) at [10].

[82] *Precision Dipping Ltd v Precision Dipping Marketing Ltd* [1985] B.C.L.C. 385 CA. See also *Atkinson v Kingsley* [2020] EWHC 2913 (Ch) at [93]. See further para.18–007.

[83] *Wright v Atlas Wright (Europe) Ltd* [1999] 2 B.C.L.C. 301.

[84] This was a strong decision because CA 1985 s.319(3) could be read as requiring a resolution in any event in this case, so that the principle of informal unanimous consent had no operation at all. See also *Bonham-Carter v Situ Ventures Ltd* [2012] B.C.C. 717, in which it was held obiter that informal consent of shareholders could not waive the requirements under s.169 as these were, at least in part, for the benefit of director(s) whose removal was sought.

[85] Compare Lindsay J in *Re RW Peak (King's Lynn) Ltd* [1998] 1 B.C.L.C. 183; and Park J in *BDG Roof-Bond Ltd v Douglas* [2000] 1 B.C.L.C. 401 Ch D on the construction of the rules relating to the purchase of own shares. See further *Kinlan v Crimmin* [2006] EWHC 779 (Ch); [2007] B.C.C. 106.

might be said, the purpose of these rules is to protect the director or officer by permitting him or her to make representations against the proposed removal.[86]

In addition, there are certain post-decision formalities that have to be complied with in relation to shareholder resolutions, most importantly the notification of certain resolutions to the Registrar and keeping a record of them in the company's minute book. The obligation to notify the Registrar seems to apply to informal decisions,[87] but the requirement as to recording in the minute book seems not to.[88] Non-compliance involves a criminal sanction, but the decision itself is not invalidated.

IMPROVING SHAREHOLDER PARTICIPATION

Analyses of shareholder participation

Ever since Berle and Means wrote their classic study of patterns of share ownership in large American corporations in the 1930s,[89] it has been common to think that shareholders, at least those in listed companies, are not in general interested in using the rights that the law or the company's articles confer upon them to hold the management of their company to account. This has not always been true. Although the exact historical development is still unclear,[90] there is general agreement that three distinct periods of shareholder structure in such companies can be identified. There was an initial period, beginning with the development of the large company in the nineteenth century, when the shareholdings were held mainly by the founding entrepreneurs and their families. At this time, therefore, the shareholdings were in "concentrated" form and establishing the wishes of the shareholders was relatively easy. However, as the capital needs of such companies grew, some shares were offered to the public, with the outside shareholders being, however, in the minority and with most of them holding only small stakes. By the middle of the last century, family shareholdings had declined and the small outside shareholders, collectively, made up the bulk of the shareholders. This is the second period, so brilliantly analysed by Berle and Means, where the shareholdings in large companies were typically "dispersed", so that the shareholders' ability to act together in a meaningful way was doubtful. 12–012

The thesis advanced by Berle and Means was that, in large companies where shareholdings had become widely dispersed, it was not worthwhile for most shareholders to devote time, effort and resources to seeking to change the policies

[86] See para.12–005 onwards. By contrast, the Company Law Review recommended that the unanimous consent rule should also operate here, since it could be argued that the purpose of these provisions is solely to promote the interests of the members (enabling them to be better informed about the reasons for the proposed removal): see Final Report I, para.7.22.

[87] CA 2006 s.29(1)(b) provides that "any resolution or agreement agreed to by all the members of the company" that would otherwise need to be a special resolution.

[88] CA 2006 s.356(2), referring only to "a resolution".

[89] A.A. Berle and G.C. Means, *The Modern Corporation and Private Property*, revised edn (New York: Transaction Publishers, 1968).

[90] For interesting work on the issue, see B. Cheffins, *Corporate Ownership and Control: British Business Transformed* (Oxford: Oxford University Press, 2008).

of the management that they thought were ineffective. Any return on their relatively small investment from the company's success would be outweighed by the certain costs of seeking to achieve such change in a large company where co-ordination of shareholder action would be intensely difficult. Since these large companies were likely to be listed on a stock exchange, the alternative and cheaper responses of accepting a takeover offer, or simply selling in the market, were likely to prove more attractive. Shareholders in large companies were thus "rationally apathetic" towards their general meeting rights.

Whether this was ever an entirely correct picture is controversial. In any event, that picture had to be modified in the third recognisably distinct historical period. Since the 1960s, there has been a partial re-concentration of shareholdings, not into the hands of entrepreneurial families, but into the hands of "institutional" shareholders, especially pension funds and insurance companies. These different patterns of shareholding have significant implications for the ability, and perhaps the willingness, of shareholders to exercise effectively the governance rights that the law confers upon them.[91] In the early 1990s, when much of the regulatory work on this issue was first conceived, institutional shareholders held about 60% of the equity shares of companies listed on the London Stock Exchange. Although it would be unusual for a single institution to hold more than 5% of the equities of the largest quoted companies, nevertheless the situation is one in which a small group of institutional shareholders could often bring decisive influence to bear on the management of ailing companies. Of course, they may not always wish to do so. Even institutional shareholders will not exercise their rights in general meeting simply for the sake of it. If a takeover offer provides a cheaper remedy for the problem, they may be inclined to accept that, rather than take on the incumbent management of the under-performing company themselves. Nevertheless, "shareholder activism" on the part of the institutions became a bigger part of the corporate scene than it had been, say, 20 years earlier.

However, the make-up of the institutional investors and their associated attitudes towards activism have not remained the same. For reasons that do not need to be explored here, over the past two decades UK institutional shareholders have tended to reduce their exposure to UK equities, whilst foreign institutions and hedge funds have been increasing them.[92] Some of these investors may be expected to be more passive; others, certain types of hedge fund in particular, might be expected to be even more interventionist in relation to their portfolio companies, often identifying specific business decisions that they wish the board to take.[93]

[91] See P. Davies, "Institutional Investors in the United Kingdom" in T. Baums et al. (eds), *Institutional Investors and Corporate Governance* (1994); E. Boros, *Minority Shareholder Remedies* (Oxford, 1995), Ch.3; G.P. Stapledon, *Institutional Shareholders and Corporate Governance* (Oxford, 1996), Ch.2.

[92] B. Cheffins, "The Stewardship Code's Achilles' Heel" (2010) 73 M.L.R. 1004, 1017–18, indicating an increase in foreign investment from 16% to 42%, and a decrease in the holdings of UK pension funds and insurance companies from 52% to 26% between 1993 and 2008.

[93] M. Kahan and E. Rock, "Hedge Funds in Corporate Governance and Corporate Control", ECGI Law Series 76/2006 (suggesting that some hedge funds make investments in order to become activists, rather than in order to protect an investment that has turned out not to perform as expected); W. Bratton, "Hedge Funds and Governance Targets", ECGI Law Series 80/2007. The debate over activist hedge funds has continued unabated since this early work, some arguing that they cause

The role of institutional investors

Given the scale of institutional investment, the role of such investor-shareholders merits attention. Both the Company Law Review (CLR) and the Myners Report,[94] commissioned by the Treasury, as well as the more recent Walker Report[95] and Kay Review,[96] all concluded that the level of institutional intervention in the affairs of their portfolio companies[97] was less than was optimal in the interests of those on whose behalf the institutions invested. This was, the CLR considered, not only a matter of concern to those investors, but also "a matter of corporate governance, impinging on the properly disciplined and competitive management of British business and industry".[98] 12–013

In order to understand the possible reasons for sub-optimal intervention and the reforms that have eventually been adopted, it is instructive to take a specific illustration. Pension funds provide a useful case study, especially as early reform proposals focused in particular upon pension funds, even though, as we shall see, they are not the only significant form of institutional investment. In simplified form,[99] a pension scheme is normally promoted by an employer, who sets up a trust into which both employer and, normally, employees pay regular contributions and out of which pensions are paid.[100] Both the pensioners and the contributing employees may be seen as beneficiaries of the trust. The trustees see to the investment of the contributions, but normally do not discharge that task themselves; instead, they contract that function out to one or more specialist fund managers. The fund managers may be freestanding institutions, but, today, they are likely to be part of larger financial groups (for example, investment banks) that offer other services in addition to fund management. The contract between the pension fund and the fund manager is likely to give the manager the right to vote the shares purchased on behalf of the fund, although the trustees may reserve the right to take voting decisions themselves, either generally or in specific

companies to focus on short-term objectives (to the detriment of society at large), others that they take only small stakes in companies and are dependent on the support of institutional shareholders (whose goals are long-term) for their success. What is clear is that the capacity of activist hedge funds to pressurise management into acceptance of their views is facilitated if shareholders have strong governance rights of the type discussed in this chapter.

[94] *Institutional Investment in the United Kingdom: A Review* (London, 2001).

[95] Sir D. Walker, *A Review of Corporate Governance in UK Banks and Other Financial Industry Entities: Final Recommendations* (26 November 2009) available at: *http://webarchive.nationalarchives.gov.uk/+/http://www.hm-treasury.gov.uk/d/walker_review_261109.pdf* [Accessed 1 January 2021].

[96] J. Kay, *The Kay Review of UK Equity Markets and Long-Term Decision Making* (July 2012) available at: *https://www.gov.uk/government/uploads/system/uploads/attachment_data/file/253454/bis-12-917-kay-review-of-equity-markets-final-report.pdf* [Accessed 1 January 2021].

[97] For example, companies in which the institution has investments.

[98] Final Report I, para.3.54.

[99] *Institutional Investment in the United Kingdom: A Review* (London, 2001), Ch.5.

[100] The fund may promise a certain level of benefits on retirement ("defined benefit" schemes) or only that the pensioner will be entitled to his or her share of the fund at retirement in order to purchase an annuity ("defined contribution" schemes). The distinction, though enormously important for employees in terms of the allocation of investment risk, is not significant for present purposes, although the present trend is firmly away from DB and towards DC. The proposed "activism" obligation, which is considered further below, is the same for both types of scheme.

classes of case. Finally, for reasons of both efficiency and prudence, the fund manager is not likely itself to hold the shares purchased on behalf of the fund, but to have them held by a separate custodian company, which may well be part of a different group of companies from that in which the fund manager sits.

There are three main types of argument that have been advanced to explain the under-use by pension funds or, more often, their fund managers of the corporate governance rights that the law gives them, namely conflicts of interest; a desire for a quiet life; and technical difficulties of voting.

Conflicts of interest and inactivity

12–014 Conflicts of interest arise mainly where the fund manager's group provides other financial services to corporate clients. The management of a portfolio company may be unwilling to buy, or continue buying, these other financial services (for example in connection with public share offerings),[101] if some other part of the same group is using its corporate governance rights on behalf of a pension fund to make life difficult for that management.[102] Indeed, the management of the portfolio company may actively threaten to withdraw its custom from the group if the intervention on behalf of the pension fund continues. In extreme cases, such conduct may amount to the offence of corruption, but that is likely to be very difficult to prove. After floating a number of proposals, the CLR's best suggestion was a requirement that quoted companies be required to disclose in annual reports the identity of their major suppliers of financial services. This would reveal potential conflicts of interest within financial services groups, although it would not eliminate them nor, by itself, guarantee the appropriate handling of the conflicts.[103]

Inactivity on the part of fund managers may, as we have just seen, result from conflicts of interest, but it may also result, as considered by the Myners Report,[104] from a lack of incentives for the fund managers to be active (for example, because the costs of intervention would depress the manager's short-term performance, whilst the benefits of intervention would be reaped only in the medium term; or because the benefits of intervention would accrue to all shareholders, whether they participated in the intervention or not, including rival fund managers). A similar conclusion can be drawn from the Kay Review, where appropriate intervention was seen as compromised by market-driven short-termism, lack of trust, and the easier risk-reducing options of portfolio diversification. The market preference was for "exit", rather than "voice".[105] The CLR's response to Myners' findings was a proposed requirement that managers disclose on demand to trustees their voting record in portfolio companies, as well as a reserve power for the Secretary of State to require the publication of the

---

[101] See further Ch.25.

[102] Even a stand-alone fund manager may suffer from conflicts of interest, for example, where it manages the pension fund of a company in which another pension fund under its management is invested.

[103] In any event, the Government was not minded to pursue this particular recommendation: see Modernising, para.2.47.

[104] *Institutional Investment in the United Kingdom: A Review* (London, 2001), paras 5.83–5.88.

[105] J. Kay, *The Kay Review of UK Equity Markets and Long-Term Decision Making* (July 2012).

voting record, so that the beneficiaries of the pension fund would also be aware.[106] This proposal was controversial, to the point where the clauses were removed from the Bill in the House of Lords against the Government's wishes, but were reinstated in the Commons. These are now found in the CA 2006.[107] In line with the CLR's recommendation, the power is one to make regulations, in relation to which the Government indicated that it was "willing to see how market practice evolves before choosing whether and how to exercise the power".[108] Those regulations may require institutional investors[109] to disclose, either to the public (a particularly controversial point) or specified persons only, information about the exercise or non-exercise of voting rights by the institution or any person acting on its behalf; about the voting instructions given by the institution or person on its behalf; and about the delegation of voting functions[110] in relation to shares that are publicly traded and in which the institution has an interest.[111]

The Myners Report was bolder, proposing a substantive obligation, derived from US law, on the fund manager to monitor and attempt to influence the boards of companies where there was a reasonable expectation that such activity would enhance the value of the portfolio investments.[112] This would include, but not be limited to, the exercise of the right to vote at shareholder meetings. This would not amount to an obligation to vote the shares in portfolio companies on each and every occasion. On the one hand, voting on routine proposals might be neither here nor there in corporate governance terms; on the other, merely voting might be an inadequate form of intervention, if, for example, a private meeting with the management might solve the problem at an earlier stage and avoid an adverse vote. Of course, it is strongly arguable that the fiduciary duties of pension fund trustees already require them to exercise their corporate governance rights actively, if they judge that this will enhance the value of the trust's assets. Those duties would require that a similar obligation be placed upon those to whom they contract out the exercise of their corporate governance rights. It may be very difficult to show, however, that any particular piece of inaction or even a course of inaction over a period of time reduced the value of the trust's assets. **12–015**

The Myners Report did not propose the embodiment of these rules in statutory form, but only in voluntary Statements of Investment Principles, which the fund management industry was to observe on a "comply or explain" basis,[113] with the threat of legal regulation if voluntarism did not work. However, subsequent developments have moved things on. First, there has been the development domestically of the UK Stewardship Code.[114] Secondly, the EU adopted

---

[106] Final Report I, para.6.39.

[107] CA 2006 ss.1277–1280.

[108] HL Debs, Vol.682, col.787 (23 May 2006) (Lord Sainsbury).

[109] CA 2006 s.1278, which contains a broad definition.

[110] CA 2006 s.1280.

[111] CA 2006 s.1279.

[112] *Institutional Investment in the United Kingdom: A Review* (London, 2001), para.5.89.

[113] See para.9–020.

[114] See para.12–030. For the latest version, Financial Reporting Council, *UK Stewardship Code* (2020) available at: *https://www.frc.org.uk/getattachment/5aae591d-d9d3-4cf4-814a-d14e156a1d87/Stewardship-Code_Final2.pdf* [Accessed 1 January 2021].

amendments to the Shareholder Rights Directive in 2017, requiring reporting by institutional shareholders of their "engagement policies" (transposed by the UK before it left the EU).[115] These are discussed further below.

"Fiduciary investors"

12–016 As considered above, the generation of an activism obligation in the case of pension funds starts from the premise that the pension fund's trustees owe fiduciary obligations to the fund's beneficiaries.[116] Outside the trust structure underlying pension funds, however, the relationship between investors and investment managers who invest the money on their behalf is not usually considered a fiduciary one.[117] For example, the relationship between investors and insurance companies, which are as important as pension funds in terms of collective investment activity, is predominantly contractual. Insurance companies also play an important role in the provision of pensions, especially to those who are not part of occupational schemes, although the Myners Report made no recommendations about the activism responsibilities of insurance companies.[118] Accordingly, there are unequal expectations of different types of financial intermediary.

If the value of a particular investment is likely to be increased by the exercise of votes (or other governance rights) by institutional shareholders, it is difficult to understand why the same conduct should not be expected of all intermediaries, irrespective of whether they involve a trust or contractual structure. Indeed, this should be the case for any financial intermediary that acquires funds from investors on the basis that they can be managed more effectively and efficiently on behalf of investors than the investors can do themselves. Indeed, the Kay Review advanced precisely this suggestion by proposing that all intermediaries in the investment chain should be subject to fiduciary obligations in the performance of their functions.[119] When examining this issue, however, the Law Commission came down strongly against any such rule, suggesting that it would add further confusion to fiduciary law, which was difficult to transpose from its traditional context to the very different one of financial services. This conclusion may appear problematic given that the Law Commission recognised the need for enhanced investor protection, but concluded that alternative routes, such as statutory enhancement of the provisions in the Financial Services and Markets

---

[115] Directive 2017/828 [2017] OJ L 132/1, inserting a new art.3g on engagement policy into the original Directive.

[116] The Myners Committee seems to have forgotten this fact, given that it proposed to impose such an obligation on the fund managers only. The mistake was corrected by the Government: see *Institutional Investment in the United Kingdom: A Review* (London, 2001), para.60.

[117] *JP Morgan Bank v Springwell Navigation Corporation* [2008] EWHC 1186 (Comm).

[118] *Institutional Investment in the United Kingdom: A Review* (London, 2001), Ch.9.

[119] J. Kay, *The Kay Review of UK Equity Markets and Long-Term Decision Making* (July 2012), Recommendation 7 available at: *https://www.gov.uk/government/uploads/system/uploads/attachment_data/file/253454/bis-12-917-kay-review-of-equity-markets-final-report.pdf* [Accessed 30 January 2020].

Act 2000[120] to give private investors direct claims against intermediaries, were equally unworkable (as this might create indeterminate liability to an indeterminate class of claimants).[121]

The proposal of the Law Commission for legislation not refliant on fiduciary principles, it turned out, was taken up at EU level. Under the amendments to the Shareholder Rights Directive institutional shareholders (essentially pension funds and insurance companies) and asset managers must disclose their engagement policy in relation to investee companies (or their reasons for not having one) where these are traded on a regulated market. The engagement policy covers a wide range of topics (which do not need to be considered in detail in a book of this kind) but they include "a general description of voting behaviour, an explanation of the most significant votes and the use of the services of proxy advisors. They shall publicly disclose how they have cast votes in the general meetings of companies in which they hold shares. Such disclosure may exclude votes that are insignificant due to the subject matter of the vote or the size of the holding in the company."[122] In the UK, this obligation has been transposed into law by the Financial Conduct Authority in its Handbook.[123] In addition, the UK Stewardship Code, which applies to all institutional investors (whether pension funds or not) and asset managers, has added to the engagement pressures on these financial institutions. That Code is considered next.

The UK Stewardship Code

Given the UK's success with "soft law", it was perhaps inevitable that this would be the outcome. In 2010, the UK Stewardship Code was promulgated by the Financial Reporting Council, applying, like the UK Corporate Governance Code, on a "comply or explain" basis. The latest version of the UK Stewardship Code has moved towards an "apply and explain" approach,[124] which assumes that addressees are in compliance already, but requires them to engage in a deeper level critique as to how compliance has helped achieve the Code's aims. This avoids a tick-box approach to compliance. The Code is addressed in the first instance to fund and asset managers—that is, firms who manage assets on behalf of institutional shareholders such as pension funds, insurance companies, investment trusts and other collective investment vehicles.[125] It sets out good practice on engagement with investee companies, with the goal of helping to **12–017**

[120] Financial Services and Markets Act 2000 s.138D.

[121] Law Commission, *Fiduciary Duties of Investment Intermediaries* (June 2014), Law Com. No.350, paras 11.10–11.33 available at: *https://www.gov.uk/government/uploads/system/uploads/attachment_data/file/325508/41342_HC_368_LC350_accessible.pdf* [Accessed 1 January 2021].

[122] Directive 2017/828 art.3g.1(b).

[123] FCA Handbook, Conduct of Business Sourcebook COBS 2.2B.5; Senior Management Arrangements, Systems and Controls SYSC 3.4.6.

[124] Financial Reporting Council, *UK Stewardship Code* (2020), p.4 available at: *https://www.frc.org.uk/getattachment/5aae591d-d9d3-4cf4-814a-d14e156a1d87/Stewardship-Code_Final2.pdf* [Accessed 1 January 2021]. These principles are similar to those adopted by the Institutional Shareholders' Committee, *The Responsibilities of Institutional Shareholders and Agents—Statement of Principles* (2002).

[125] For the commitment to the UK Stewardship Code, see FCA, Conduct of Business Sourcebook COBS 2.2.3.

improve long-term returns to shareholders and the efficient exercise of governance responsibilities. The responsibility for monitoring company performance does not, however, rest with fund managers alone, and to that end the Code refers to "asset owners" and "asset managers" generally. The Financial Reporting Council expects firms subject to the Code to disclose on their websites how they have applied the Code[126] and strongly encourages all such entities to report how they have complied with each of the principles in the Code. For example, pension fund trustees and other owners can comply directly, or indirectly through the mandates given to fund managers.[127] The Code adopts a similar format to the UK Corporate Governance Code: it sets out 12 Main Principles, each with supporting Guidance elaborating best practice. It indicates that asset managers and owners should:

(1) Ensure that the asset managers' purpose, investment beliefs, strategy and culture enable stewardship that creates long-term value for clients and beneficiaries leading to sustainable benefits for the economy, the environment and society (Principle 1). "Stewardship activities" are widely defined to include "investment decision-making, monitoring assets and service providers, engaging with issuers and holding them to account on material issues, collaborating with others, and exercising rights and responsibilities".[128] Signatories must explain how these factors have improved their stewardship.
(2) Ensure that governance, resources and incentives support stewardship (Principle 2). Signatories need to explain the effectiveness of their chosen governance structures and how they might be improved.
(3) Manage conflicts of interest to put the interests of clients and beneficiaries first (Principle 3), which includes explaining how actual or potential conflicts have been managed. This has echoes of a fiduciary relationship, albeit that the courts are sometimes reluctant to recognise this reality in legal terms.
(4) Identify and respond to market-wide and systemic risks to promote a well-functioning system (Principle 4), as well as reviewing policies, assuring processes and assessing effectiveness of activities (Principle 5).
(5) Take account of client and beneficiary needs and communicate the activities and outcomes of stewardship and investment to them (Principle 6). In essence, this resembles the type of conduct-of-business rule found in the Financial Conduct Authority's Handbook,[129] albeit that it takes the form of a principle in the Code.
(6) Systematically integrate stewardship and investment, including material environmental, social and governance issues, and climate change, to fulfil responsibilities (Principle 7). This requires a contextual approach to the integration process depending on "funds, asset classes and geographies".

[126] Financial Reporting Council, *UK Stewardship Code* (2020), p.6.
[127] For a critical assessment of the likely impact, see B. Cheffins, "The Stewardship Code's Achilles' Heel" (2010) 73 M.L.R. 1004. For its proposed broader 2012 application, see fn.119.
[128] Financial Reporting Council, *UK Stewardship Code* (2020), p.7.
[129] See generally Financial Conduct Authority, Conduct of Business Sourcebook COBS.

(7) Monitor and hold to account managers and/or service providers (Principle 8); engage with issuers to maintain or enhance the value of assets (Principle 9); and, where necessary, participate in collaborative engagement to influence issuers (Principle 10). These principles go to the heart of the Code as there needs to be an explanation as to how engagement has occurred consistently with investment objectives.

(8) Escalate, where necessary, stewardship activities to influence users (Principle 11) and actively exercise rights and responsibilities (Principle 12). This highlights the need to constantly engage and improve upon stewardship activities.

While the ambition is clear, the Financial Reporting Council's own assessment in 2015 was that there was still some way to go in enticing greater participation, encouraging closer adherence to best practice, and ensuring more informative reporting generally.[130] With the introduction of a new Code, the Financial Reporting Council's tone is more positive.[131] It is also worth noting that the Main Principles in the latest iteration of the Code put a new emphasis on the shareholders' role in inducing companies to promote climate change and other ESG (environmental, social and governance) goals, as well as promoting corporate value by ensuring managerial efficiency.[132]

The role of indirect investors

Under the typical arrangement for pension funds, the shares in the portfolio company are held by a custodian company. That custodian company will appear on the portfolio company's share register as the holder of the shares, even though it holds them as a nominee, either for the fund manager or for the pension fund. Clearly, the custodian has no interest in voting the shares in question. Rather, the law is that, if the custodian is a bare nominee for a beneficial owner, the beneficial owner can instruct the nominee how to deal with the shares.[133] In order to bring this about, however, the custodian must confer with the fund manager and, perhaps, through the fund manager with the trustees. The registered holder, however, is not placed under any obligation by company law to engage in this process, which, in any event, may not prove to be possible within the notice period for the meeting,[134] though there may be contractual arrangements in place between the member and others with an interest in the shares that require this consultation. It can be argued that this process would operate more smoothly if **12–018**

[130] Financial Reporting Council, *Developments in Corporate Governance and Stewardship 2015* available at: at *https://www.frc.org.uk/Our-Work/Publications/Corporate-Governance/Developments-in-Corporate-Governance-and-Stewa-%281%29.pdf* [Accessed 1 January 2021].

[131] The latest publication strikes an optimistic tone, but the proof will have to await the next annual report: see Financial Reporting Council, *Review of Corporate Governance Reporting* (November 2020).

[132] See Paul Davies, *The UK Stewardship Code 2010–2020 From Saving the Company to Saving the Planet?* ECGI Law Working Paper 506/2020.

[133] *Kirby v Wilkins* [1929] 2 Ch. 444 Ch D. If the nominee votes the shares without instructions, that right must be exercised in the interests of the beneficiary.

[134] See para.12–038.

the company communicated directly with the beneficial owner or, going further, if the governance rights attached to the shares could be exercised by the beneficial (or "indirect") owner.[135]

The Company Law Review proposed to remove any impediments that existed to the creation of contractual arrangements for giving non-members an input into the exercise of the governance rights attached to the shares, together with a fall-back power for the Government to require such transfers of governance rights if contractual arrangements did not continue to develop on an adequate scale.[136] The Companies Bill followed this formula, but in the debates in Parliament the position of institutional investors was linked to that of many private investors who also hold shares through nominee accounts, partly as a result of the dematerialisation of shares and partly because government tax relief on private investment is often available only in relation to shares held in this way.[137] Thus, the governance rights of indirect investors became politically a much more significant matter than had been initially anticipated. The Government's fall-back proposals were defeated in the Lords.[138] The Government then consulted with those affected on alternative provisions, which contained an element of compulsion, but still with a significant fall-back element. They were introduced at a very late stage in the parliamentary process and received little debate.[139]

Those reforms now contained in the CA 2006 fall into two groups.[140] As recommended by the Company Law Review, some are purely facultative. They help companies to reassign governance rights to indirect shareholders, but do not require it. These provisions apply to all companies. The other group contains the element of compulsion, which at present relates only to shareholders' information rights in companies whose securities are traded on a regulated market, in effect the Main Market of the London Stock Exchange.[141] The Secretary of State, however, has the power by regulation to broaden the scope of this second class of provisions, so as to expand the rights provided or the types of company covered by the CA 2006.[142]

Governance rights—voluntary transfer arrangements for all companies

12–019 The facultative provisions of the CA 2006, which apply to all companies, will be considered first. In this regard, there was a view that two restrictions in particular prevented the transfer of governance rights between the company and the holders of the beneficial interests in shares: first, the CA 2006 provided hat "no notice of any trust shall be entered on the register [of members] or be receivable by the

[135] For the nature of the indirect beneficial owner's interest in shares and the exercise of their rights, see *Eckerle v Wickender Westfalenstahl GmbH* [2013] EWHC 68 (Ch); [2014] Ch. 196. See also *Secure Capital SA v Credit Suisse AG* [2017] EWCA Civ 1486; [2018] 1 B.C.L.C. 325; *SL Claimants v Tesco Plc* [2019] EWHC 2858 (Ch); *Deutsche Trustee Co Ltd v Bangkok Land (Cayman Islands) Ltd* [2019] EWHC 657 (Comm).

[136] Final Report I, paras 7.1–7.4.

[137] See para.26–012.

[138] HL Debs, Vol.681, cols 813 onwards (9 May 2006).

[139] HC Debs, Standing Committee D, Twenty First Sitting, cols 875 onwards (21 July 2006).

[140] CA 2006 Pt 9.

[141] For the meaning of a "regulated market", see para.25–008.

[142] CA 2006 s.151. The regulations are subject to affirmative resolution by Parliament.

registrar";[143] and, secondly, there was a parallel provision in the articles dealing with the position of the company.[144] The Company Law Review proposed that, if this was so, s.126 of the CA 2006[145] should be amended, so as to make clear that it permits the transfer of corporate governance rights to third parties.[146] Such transfers would not be compulsory, but were to be left to contractual arrangements between those holding shares on behalf of others and the persons on whose behalf the shares were held.

The drafters of the CA 2006 clearly took the view that s.126 was not an impediment to the transfer of governance rights, as the legislation did not deal with the issue. Nevertheless, s.145 of the CA 2006 provides that a company in its articles may (and indeed has always been able to) make provision enabling a member to nominate another person to enjoy all or any of the governance rights of a member in relation to the company.[147] That other person need not in fact be the holder of the beneficial interest in the shares, so that, for example, a custodian could nominate a fund manager as entitled to vote the shares, even though the beneficial interest is held by the pension trust. The person to whom the rights are transferred is the "nominated person".[148]

Section 145 of the CA 2006 does not require any such transfer of governance rights to be made. That provision's purpose is rather to ensure that the statutory provisions discussed below in relation to meetings (and, indeed, those discussed above in relation to written resolutions) work properly where contractual governance rights are held by a nominated person. In other words, where rights under the articles are transferred to a nominated person, so are the linked statutory rights. A good example is the right to vote. As considered above,[149] voting rights in a company are not allocated by the CA 2006, but by the company, normally through its articles of association. If the articles permit or require[150] those voting rights to be transferred to a nominated person, and the right to vote is so transferred by a particular member, then the CA 2006 ensures that the statutory right to appoint a proxy to vote at the meeting on behalf of the voter is also transferred to the nominated person.[151] Precisely which additional statutory rights are transferred in this way to a nominated person will depend upon which contractual rights have been transferred to the nominated person under the

143 CA 2006 s.126. This section does not apply in Scotland.

144 See Companies (Model Articles) Regulations 2008 (SI 2008/3229) Sch.3 art.45 (public companies): "Except as required by law, no person shall be recognised by the company as holding any share upon any trust, and except as otherwise required by law or the articles, the company is not in any way to be bound by or recognise any interest in a share other than the holder's absolute ownership of it and all the rights attaching to it".

145 CA 2006 s.126.

146 Completing, paras 5.2–5.12 and Final Report I, paras 7.3–7.4.

147 CA 2006 s.145(1). See also *Eckerle v Wickender Westfalenstahl GmbH* [2014] Ch. 196.

148 An obvious, but perhaps potentially confusing, term to employ, since the nominator will often be a nominee shareholder! Any custodian of relevant shares may use the power, whether in a pension-fund context or otherwise.

149 See para.12–002.

150 Although the section is permissive as to the adoption of "transfer" articles by the company, there seems no reason why the articles should not be mandatory as against the member in appropriate cases.

151 CA 2006 s.145(3)(f). See also *Eckerle v Wickender Westfalenstahl GmbH* [2014] Ch. 196 at [28], citing the 9th edition of this book at [15-36]. On proxies, see paras 12–042 onwards.

articles. The CA 2006 permits the transfer of eight statutory rights,[152] but operates only "so far as necessary to give effect to" a transfer of rights effected under the company's articles.[153] Where the right to vote is transferred, it seems that most of the listed statutory rights will also be transferred. Even so, if the company is a public company, the rights in relation to written resolutions will not be transferred and if the company is a private company, the right to propose a resolution at an AGM will not be transferred, since these rights are specific to private or public companies.[154]

If the linked statutory right is transferred to the nominated person, then anything the member might have done may instead be done by the nominated person and any duty owed by the company to the member is owed instead to the nominated person.[155] Accordingly, there is a genuine transfer of statutory powers and rights to the nominated person. However, no rights enforceable against the company by anyone other than the member are so created by the section *or* by the provisions in the articles creating the transfer system.[156] In fact, the primary sanction for many of the rights covered by the section is a criminal one, to which this provision is irrelevant; but civil rights could arise also, for example, to challenge the validity of a resolution because of an inaccuracy in the circular sent out in support of it.[157] Although s.145 of the CA 2006 is not absolutely crystal clear on the point, presumably its implication is that the right of the member to

---

152 CA 2006 s.145(3). The rights to be sent a proposed written resolution; to require circulation of a written resolution; to require directors to call a general meeting; to require notice of a general meeting; to require circulation of a statement; to appoint a proxy; to require circulation of a resolution for the AGM of a public company; and to be sent the annual report and accounts. In addition, in relation to "traded companies" (defined in CA 2006 s.360C), there are four additional statutory rights subject to transfer, namely the right to ask questions at a meeting; the power to include matters in the business dealt with at the AGM; the right to receive confirmation of an electronic vote; and the right to receive a confirmation of vote after a general meeting.

153 CA 2006 s.145(2). See also *Eckerle v Wickender Westfalenstahl GmbH* [2014] Ch. 196 at [29]–[30].

154 CA 2006 s.145(4)(b) makes it clear that the section does not affect the requirements relating to the transfer of the shares themselves.

155 CA 2006 s.145(2).

156 CA 2006 s.145(4)(a). Accordingly, the articles may not confer enforceable rights on third parties, even if the company wishes to do so, a somewhat strange restriction. This was tested in *Eckerle v Wickender Westfalenstahl GmbH* [2014] Ch. 196, where the claimants, being the ultimate economic owners of certain beneficial interests in the ordinary shares, applied for relief under the CA 2006 s.98 in respect of a special resolution for re-registration as a private company. Norris J held that they were not "holders" of the shares and therefore had no standing to make an application under that provision. Moreover, CA 2006 s.145 could not be read as conferring rights enforceable against the company on anyone other than the registered members: the section does not mean that "if the effective exercise of the transferred right produces a result that is not to the taste of the nominated person then the nominated person can, in order to bring about his desired outcome, himself use any of the provisions of the 2006 Act available to the transferring member": ibid. at [29]. Norris J however recognised that this result would "deprive the claimants as indirect investors of the sort of protection that those who formulated the Companies Act 2006 thought ought to be extended to minority shareholders. That is not a particularly comfortable conclusion at which to arrive: but I consider that I would have to embark upon … an 'impermissible form of judicial legislation' to reach any other conclusion": ibid. at [31]. For a similar approach to "indirect" rights in a different context, see *Secure Capital SA v Credit Suisse AG* [2018] 1 B.C.L.C. 325; *SL Claimants v Tesco Plc* [2019] EWHC 2858 (Ch); *Deutsche Trustee Co Ltd v Bangkok Land (Cayman Islands) Ltd* [2019] EWHC 657 (Comm).

157 See para.12–040.

enforce a right against the company is not affected by the fact that the right has been transferred to a nominated person. To hold otherwise would mean a reduction in the enforceability of members' rights where there was a transfer to a nominated person.

Whether s.145 of the CA 2006 will mean much in practice is going to depend upon three factors: the willingness of companies to adopt articles permitting or requiring the transfer of governance rights; the willingness of nominee shareholding organisations to exercise the power of transfer (if it is permissive); and the willingness of beneficial shareholders to put pressure on nominee shareholders to transfer rights to them and to pay for any associated costs.[158] **12–020**

A further piece of apparent facilitation is to be found in s.152 of the CA 2006. This provision makes clear that a member of a company holding shares on behalf of more than one person (as will typically be the case with nominees, whether they hold on behalf, ultimately, of institutional or private investors) need not exercise all the shareholders' rights (whether given under the contract of issue or provided by statute) in the same way—nor indeed need all of them be exercised on any particular occasion. Accordingly, the holder is enabled to give effect to the different views that the various beneficial owners may hold on the issue in question. It is doubtful whether s.152 changes the previous law, although it can create its own problems.[159] What may be new, therefore, is the further provision that, if the member exercising its rights does not inform the company that not all the rights are being exercised or that some are being exercised in one way and some in another, the company is entitled to assume that all are being exercised and all in the same way.[160] Accordingly, s.152 may be more protective of the company than anything else.

An example of this form of governance contract can be found in some companies using "American Depositary Receipts" (ADRs). A UK company acquiring a US company in a share exchange deal may not wish to issue its shares directly to the US investors, partly in order to avoid some of the complications of US securities laws and partly in order to give the US investors a security denominated in dollars. One way of achieving these consequences is the ADR, the shares being issued to a depositary institution, which in turn issues to the US investors a "depositary receipt"—one for each share—denominated in dollars. The ADR becomes the security that is traded in the US. In some cases, the company's articles may then require the depositary institution to appoint the ADR

[158] For an excellent survey of recent practice and proposals for reform going beyond what the CLR recommended, see R.C. Nolan, "Indirect Investors: A Greater Say in the Company?" (2003) 3 J.C.L.S. 73.

[159] In *Eckerle v Wickender Westfalenstahl GmbH* [2014] Ch. 196, it was noted obiter that the right of a nominee to vote both for and against particular resolutions under the CA 2006 s.152(1) created problems, since then—for the purposes of s.98—the registered holder was "a person who has consented to or voted in favour of the resolution", and so had no standing to complain despite the partial dissenting vote: ibid. at [32].

[160] CA 2006 s.152(2)–(4), which does not specifically require the company's assumption to be a reasonable one, although the assumption only arises when the member does not inform the company otherwise, and presumably the company will need to determine this in a reasonable manner.

holder as its proxy,[161] possibly just for voting purposes but potentially for all governance purposes, including the receipt of communications from the company.[162] In such a case, one sees the company using its contracting power through the articles[163] to overcome the limitations of reliance on mere conferment of information rights (as considered below). There is, however, no legal obligation upon companies to treat the holders of ADRs in this way.

Information rights—mandatory transfer options in traded companies

12–021 A member of a company whose shares are admitted to trading on a regulated market may nominate another person to enjoy those information rights, whether the company has provided in its articles for this to happen or not.[164] This means that the rules on transfer of information rights are mandatory as against listed companies, although of course it is not mandatory for the shareholder to confer this right on someone else. Furthermore, the rights conferred upon the other person do not deprive the nominating shareholder of his or her right to the same information.[165] The fact that the provisions are mandatory as against the company (and increase, at least marginally, the company's costs in relation to the circulation of information) was a strong argument in the Government's eyes against introducing them. Accordingly, the statutory provisions are crafted as far as possible to reduce those costs. Those costs are confined to the largest companies because the provisions, at present, apply only to companies listed on a regulated market.[166] However, there are a number of other ways in which the cost implications of this new rule can be reduced, even for these large companies.

First, the right to nominate a recipient of information rights is restricted to those members who hold shares on behalf of another person and where the recipient is that other person.[167] Secondly, the only rights that may thus be conferred are "information rights" (essentially the right to receive the communications that a company sends to its members, including its annual accounts and reports) or any class of them that includes the nominating shareholder.[168] No other governance rights may be transferred compulsorily as against the company. Thirdly, a company need not accept the conferment of only

161 Such provisions also prevent the depositary institution becoming a significant holder of voting rights at the company's meetings.

162 See R.C. Nolan, "Indirect Investors: A Greater Say in the Company?" (2003) 3 J.C.L.S. 73, who analyses such a set of provisions in the articles of BP.

163 CA 2006 s.145.

164 CA 2006 ss.146(1)–(2).

165 CA 2006 s.150(5)(a).

166 CA 2006 s.146(1). That regulated market may be located in the UK or the EU, but the company must be one subject to the domestic companies legislation. In other words, a company registered in any jurisdiction of the UK will not escape this obligation by listing on a regulated market in, for example, France or Germany, but a company incorporated in Germany and listed on a regulated market in the UK will not be subject to the obligation.

167 CA 2006 s.146(2). The CA 2006 s.145 is not restricted in this way, although the articles are most likely to provide for transfers of rights in such a case.

168 CA 2006 s.146(3)(a) and (4). Rights to require copies of the accounts and reports or to require hard copies of documents are also included within the notion of "information rights": CA 2006 s.146(3)(b).

some of the shareholder's information rights.[169] The company can thus insist on an "all or nothing" conferment of information rights. Fourthly, unless the shareholder, on behalf of the nominated person, requests circulation in hard copy and provides the company with an address, the company may meet its obligation to the nominated person through website publication.[170] Fifthly, all nominations are suspended when there are more nominations in force than the nominator has shares in the company, so that the burden of sorting out the errors is moved away from the company.[171] Sixthly, the company may enquire of a nominated person once every 12 months whether it wishes to retain information rights and the nomination will cease if the company does not receive a positive response within 28 days. Seventhly, to relieve the company of the burden of staying on top of things, if the nomination is terminated or suspended for any reason,[172] the company may continue to abide by that nomination "to such extent or for such period as it thinks fit".[173] Eighthly, the rights conferred upon the nominated person are enforceable only by the member; the rights to be treated for this purpose as if they were conferred by the company's articles.[174]

The right to enjoy information rights is thus, it may be said, rather grudgingly conferred. The main non-restrictive provision is the one that tracks s.145 of the CA 2006 and provides that any enactment or anything in the company's articles relating to communications with members has corresponding effect in relation to communications with nominated persons.[175]

The compulsory information provisions considered above do not in any way touch on the relationship between the nominated person and the member after the information has been received. Accordingly, the nominated person, having received notice of a meeting, for example, has power to instruct the member how to vote, if the member holds the share on a bare trust for the nominated person.[176] That said, there is no legal obligation upon the member, in this case or more generally, to seek the views of the nominated person before voting, in the absence of an instruction (contrary to the position in some other legal systems). Such an obligation may be created by contract, however, either between the nominated person and the member or, conceivably, between the company and the member. This is then a governance issue, as considered previously.

---

[169] CA 2006 s.146(5).

[170] CA 2006 s.147. The right to request hard copy will also give way if the company has adopted electronic communication as its way of communicating with its members generally: CA 2006 s.147(4). See also para.12–057.

[171] CA 2006 s.148(6). CA 2006 s.148(7) deals with the class right variation of this problem.

[172] Besides the two situations just described, the nomination will be terminated at the request of the member or nominated person, and will cease to have effect on the death or bankruptcy of an individual or the dissolution of, or the making of a winding-up order against, a corporate shareholder: CA 2006 s.148(2)–(4).

[173] CA 2006 s.148(8).

[174] CA 2006 s.150(2).

[175] CA 2006 s.150(3)—and even that provision is subject to qualifications in the CA 2006 s.150(4).

[176] *Kirby v Wilkins* [1929] 2 Ch. 444.

THE MECHANICS OF MEETINGS

12–022 When a meeting is to be held, there are procedural requirements to satisfy so that resolutions of the shareholders can be voted upon and decisions effectively made. There is only one method for the adoption of resolutions by public companies,[177] whereas private companies can also use the written resolution method, which it may wish to do where it has a large shareholding body. These issues appear in their sharpest form where a group of shareholders wish to use the shareholders' meeting to challenge some aspect of the management of the incumbent directors. Therefore, this perspective will generally be adopted in the analysis of the procedural requirements, though, of course, those rules may also be relevant in the more usual case where the meeting is called by the board to discuss a matter that the shareholders find relatively uncontentious.

What happens at meetings?

12–023 It is a rare shareholders' meeting that does not end up passing a resolution on some matter or another. As considered above,[178] the CA 2006 requires the shareholders' consent before certain decisions can bind the company, and the articles may add to that list. By assenting to a resolution, the shareholders give the consent that is necessary to make their act the company's act. Once the shareholders have adopted an effective resolution on a particular matter, the board is empowered, and normally obliged, to take the necessary steps to put the resolution into effect. Some decisions are routinely required of shareholders, even especially important ones such as the re-appointment of directors[179] or auditors,[180] or the granting of powers to directors to issue a certain quantity of shares without pre-emption rights.[181] Others occur irregularly. The business of general meetings does not, however, consist entirely of the consideration of proposals for resolutions. For example, the CA 2006 requires the annual reports and accounts to be laid before the company in general meeting,[182] but does not require the meeting to consider any resolution in relation to them. The exercise is not pointless, however, because it gives the shareholders an opportunity to question the board generally on the progress of the company and to express their views on the matter. Often, this item on the agenda provides the opportunity for a wide-ranging debate in a way that would not be possible when voting on specific resolutions. Indeed, there is no reason why an item should not be placed on the agenda simply for the purposes of having a debate, without any resolution being proposed. Nevertheless, apart from the consideration of the annual reports and accounts, it is the consideration of resolutions with which the general meetings largely deal.

---

177 CA 2006 s.281.
178 See paras 11–011 onwards.
179 See para.9–007.
180 See para.23–017.
181 See para.24–009.
182 See para.22–046.

Types of resolution

For decisions required under the CA 2006, the legislation has reduced the types of resolution that the members may take to two: an ordinary resolution and a special resolution.[183] Usually the CA 2006 specifies which type is required, and then determines the principles applicable to that resolution. In contrast, where the legislation is silent about the type of resolution required, then an ordinary resolution is enough, unless the articles specify a higher level of approval, up to and including unanimity.[184] An ordinary resolution is one passed by a simple majority of those voting.[185] A special resolution is one passed by a three-quarters majority,[186] and the notice of the meeting must specify the intention to propose the resolution as a special resolution.[187] For example, special resolutions are required before important constitutional changes can be undertaken. The higher majority required for special resolutions obviously constitutes a form of minority protection, as compared with the simple majority required for an ordinary resolution. It means, for example, that a person with more than 25% of the votes, and indeed in practice often with many fewer votes, can block the adoption of a special resolution.[188] **12–024**

The definition of an ordinary resolution has had the (seemingly unintended) effect,[189] according to the Government,[190] of making void an ordinary resolution passed at a company meeting by use of the casting vote of the chairman. This mechanism was routinely inserted in company articles to save general meeting resolutions from deadlock, and has appeared in all the earlier versions of the Table A model articles, although not in the 2006 model articles.[191] In response to adverse reaction, the Government enacted a saving provision allowing those companies that had such a Table A provision in their articles prior to 1 October 2007 to continue with it, or to re-adopt that provision if they had removed it (assuming it was ineffective).[192] This limited saving means that for all other

---

[183] CA 2006 ss.282 (ordinary resolutions) and 283 (special resolutions).

[184] CA 2006 s.281(3).

[185] CA 2006 s.282.

[186] CA 2006 s.283. Confusingly, this was previously the definition of an extraordinary resolution, a special resolution being one for which a "special" notice period was required. Thus, in effect, the category of special resolution has been abolished and the extraordinary resolution re-named a special resolution.

[187] CA 2006 s.283(6), which must include the text of the proposed special resolution. See also *Re Uniq Plc* [2011] EWHC 749 (Ch) at [27]. In the case of a written resolution, the text of the resolution must state that it is proposed as a special resolution: see CA 2006 s.283(3).

[188] See further Ch.13.

[189] CA 2006 s.282, since early versions of the model articles included provision for the chairman's casting vote.

[190] See *Company and Partnership Law* available at: *http://www.bis.gov.uk/policies/business-law/company-and-partnership-law/company-law/company-law-faqs/resolutions-and-meetings#8* [Accessed 1 January 2021].

[191] This still appears in the model articles in relation to directors' meetings: see Companies (Model Articles) Regulations 2008 (SI 2008/3229) Sch.1 art.13 (private companies) and Sch.3 art.14 (public companies).

[192] Companies Act 2006 (Commencement No.5, Transitional Provisions and Savings) Order 2007 (SI 2007/3495) Sch.5 para.2(1) and (5). This exemption does not apply to traded companies: see Companies Act 2006 (Commencement No.3, Consequential Amendments, Transitional Provisions and Savings) Order 2007 (SI 2007/2194) Sch.3 para.23A(4), inserted by SI 2009/1632 reg.22.

companies the chairman's casting vote in shareholder meetings is abolished. There might be good reasons of shareholder democracy for outlawing this practice, although this instance would surely rank as a minor target. Indeed, it might be wondered whether s.282 of the CA 2006 does render this practice invalid: that provision would clearly embrace as valid a resolution passed as a result of weighted voting rights given in the articles to a director in defined circumstances[193]; there seems little dividing such a case from that of the chairman's casting vote, except possibly an assumption that the chairman is a member, entitled to vote at the shareholders' meeting (an assumption that generally holds true).

12–025 As considered further below, many votes at meetings are taken on a show of hands, and may never proceed further if no one challenges the result. The CA 2006 facilitates the continued use of such votes, though they are controversial, by providing that the majorities are then to be calculated by reference to the individuals entitled to and actually voting, rather than to the votes attached to their shares.[194] By contrast, if a poll is demanded,[195] then the requisite majority on a poll is that of the votes attached to the shares voted by members entitled to vote and actually voting either in person or by proxy, where proxy voting is allowed.[196] In the case of a meeting of a class of shareholders, where the same rules apply, this means the appropriate majority is of the votes of the class in question.[197]

For decisions other than those specified in the CA 2006, the company's articles may make their own specific provision for the required voting entitlements and majorities, requiring higher, lower, weighted or even conditional (for example, conditional on the consent of a nominated person) voting requirements.[198]

Wording and notice of proposed resolutions

12–026 In order for shareholders to decide whether to attend meetings and vote, they will need to receive notice of the meeting and of "the general nature of the business to be dealt with".[199] A resolution is only validly passed if the proper notice has been given and the meeting is conducted according to the rules in the CA 2006 and the company's articles.[200] The CA 2006 adds protections. If special notice of any resolution has to be given (as is sometimes specified in the legislation or the articles), then notice of "it" or "any such resolution" must be given to the

[193] *Bushell v Faith* [1970] A.C. 1099 HL.

[194] CA 2006 ss.282(3) and 283(4). On a show of hands, it is not known how many shares each voter represents.

[195] On a poll, the votes attached to the shares are counted (see para.12–048), so that a single shareholder with 100 shares will outvote 99 shareholders with one vote each.

[196] CA 2006 ss.282(4) and 283(5). On proxy voting, see paras 12–042 onwards.

[197] CA 2006 s.281(1)–(2), which make clear that the same rules apply to voting at class meetings.

[198] For an interesting discussion on the construction of the company's bespoke article on voting entitlement and how this interacts with the corresponding Model Article regulation, see *Sugarman v CJS Investments LLP* [2014] EWCA Civ 1239 at [28]–[40] and [45]–[50].

[199] CA 2006 s.311(2). See further paras 12–037 onwards.

[200] CA 2006 s.301.

company at least 28 days before the meeting.[201] There are even stricter rules for special resolutions, reflecting their more serious nature, requiring that "the resolution is not a special resolution unless the notice of the meeting included the text of the resolution and specified the intention to propose the resolution as a special resolution", and, further, that "if the notice of the meeting so specified, the resolution may only be passed as a special resolution".[202]

All of this is clearly intended to protect those who decide not to attend the meeting, even more so than those who do attend.[203] The question then arises as to whether the meeting can vary in any way the resolution that is proposed to be passed. This, one might have supposed, would be entirely legitimate so long as the amendment was not such as to take the resolution beyond the scope of the business notified to the members in the notice of the meeting. Instead, however, the rules developed by the courts, and now reflected in both the CA 2006 and the Model Articles for Public Companies (those for private companies are silent), are far stricter in relation to special resolutions. The Model Articles for Public Companies allow amendments by ordinary resolution in limited circumstances[204]: an ordinary resolution can be amended if proposed by a member and "the proposed amendment does not, in the reasonable opinion of the chairman of the meeting, materially alter the scope of the resolution"[205]; while a special resolution can only be amended if the chairman so proposes and "the amendment does not go beyond what is necessary to correct a grammatical or other non-substantive error in the resolution".[206]

The potential impact of these provisions is readily illustrated by the decision of Slade J in *Re Moorgate Mercantile Holdings Ltd*,[207] from which the statutory and model-article rules are clearly derived. *Moorgate* suggests that, in relation to special resolutions, no amendment can be made if it in any way alters the substance of the resolution as set out in the notice. Grammatical and clerical errors may be corrected, or words translated into more formal language; and, if the precise text of the resolution was not included in the notice,[208] it may be

[201] CA 2006 s.312. See also *Harding v Edwards* [2014] EWHC 247 (Ch) at [46].

[202] CA 2006 s.283(6). See also *Re Uniq Plc* [2011] EWHC 749 (Ch) at [27], suggesting that a special resolution can "be construed so as to correct the error".

[203] In *Tiessen v Henderson* [1899] 1 Ch. 861 Ch D at 866–7 and 870–1, Kekewich J recognised the purpose of notice rules as being to give "fair warning of what was to be submitted to the meeting".

[204] The Companies (Model Articles) Regulations 2008 (SI 2008/3229) Sch.3: Model Articles for Public Companies art.40.

[205] Companies (Model Articles) Regulations 2008 (SI 2008/3229) Sch.1 art.40(1)(b).

[206] Companies (Model Articles) Regulations 2008 (SI 2008/3229) Sch.1 art.40(2)(b).

[207] *Re Moorgate Mercantile Holdings Ltd* [1980] 1 W.L.R. 227, which concerned the confirmation of a special resolution reducing the company's share premium account, which had been "lost". The notice of the meeting proposed that the whole of it (£1,356,900.48) "be cancelled". Before the meeting was held, it was realised that £327.17 resulting from a recent share issue could not be said yet to have been "lost". Accordingly, at the meeting the resolution was amended and it was resolved that the share premium account be reduced to £327.17. Confirmation was refused on the ground that the resolution had not been validly passed. But in a later case (Unreported, but see (1991) 12 Co. Law. at 64, 65), where the facts were virtually identical, a reduction was confirmed because the "substance" (i.e. the amount of the reduction) remained unchanged.

[208] CA 2006 s.283(6).

converted into a formal resolution, provided always that there is no departure whatever from the substance as stated in the notice.[209]

12–027 Slade J considered this outcome to be desirable on policy grounds,[210] as well as being demanded by the terms of the applicable legislation.[211] He also considered that it would prevent substantial embarrassment to the chairman of the meeting and to any persons holding "two-way" proxies on behalf of absent members.[212] Accordingly, no less strict rule would do. Slade J emphasised that his decision had no relevance to ordinary resolutions and that in relation to them the criteria for permissible amendments might well be wider.[213] This is clearly so if the precise terms of the resolution are not set out in the notice, but come within a statement of "the general nature of the business to be dealt with at the meeting".[214] Even if the terms of an ordinary resolution are set out in the notice, however, it seems that some amendments may be made at the meeting. It might even perhaps be that, if the chairman refuses to allow a permissible amendment to be moved, the resolution will be invalid.[215] It is submitted that an amendment is permissible if, but only if, the amended resolution is such that no member who had made up his mind whether or not to attend and vote (and, if he had decided to do so, how he should vote) could reasonably adopt a different attitude to the amended version.[216] The criticisms of that test by Slade J[217] apply equally to an ordinary resolution, but it is difficult to find any other test short of applying to ordinary resolutions the test applied to special resolutions, namely that no amendment of substance, however trivial, may be made. Does the suggested test really face the chairman and two-way proxy-holders with the substantial embarrassments that Slade J foresaw?[218]

There may, nevertheless, be one type of ordinary resolution to which the stricter rule applies. This is when "special notice" of the ordinary resolution is required. Special notice is defined as notice to be given to the company by the proposers of the resolution (not by the company to the members in general) of at least 28 days before the meeting at which the resolution is to be moved.[219] The statutory wording in the CA 2006 bears a close resemblance to that considered in *Re Moorgate Mercantile Holdings* and makes it arguable that no amendment of

---

[209] *Re Moorgate Mercantile Holdings Ltd* [1980] 1 W.L.R. 227 at 242C.
[210] *Re Moorgate Mercantile Holdings Ltd* [1980] 1 W.L.R. 227 at 242A–243.
[211] The provision was worded in terms similar to CA 2006 s.312, rather than the stricter s.283(6).
[212] *Re Moorgate Mercantile Holdings Ltd* [1980] 1 W.L.R. 227 at 243F.
[213] *Re Moorgate Mercantile Holdings Ltd* [1980] 1 W.L.R. 227 at 242H, citing *Betts & Co Ltd v Macnaghten* [1910] 1 Ch. 430 Ch D.
[214] CA 2006 s.311(2).
[215] *Henderson v Bank of Australasia* (1890) 45 Ch. D. 330 CA, although contrast the explicit provision in the Model Articles for Public Companies: see the Companies (Model Articles) Regulations 2008 (SI 2008/3229) Sch.3 art.40(3).
[216] This was the advice given to the chairman in the *Moorgate* case: see *Re Moorgate Mercantile Holdings Ltd* [1980] 1 W.L.R. 227 at 230A.
[217] *Re Moorgate Mercantile Holdings Ltd* [1980] 1 W.L.R. 227 at 243D–G.
[218] If the articles say (as did Companies (Tables A to F) Regulations 1985 (SI 1985/805) Table A art.82) that directors' fees shall be such as "the company may by ordinary resolution determine" and the directors give notice of an ordinary resolution to increase the fees by £10,000 p.a., surely a member should be entitled to move an amendment to reduce the increase (though the directors clearly should not be permitted to move an amendment to increase it further)?
[219] CA 2006 s.312.

substance, however trivial, can be made to the resolution stated in the special notice. Hence, if, say, special notice has been given of a single resolution to remove all the directors,[220] or both of two joint auditors,[221] an amendment seeking to exclude from the resolution some or one of them may be impermissible. If so, this seems a regrettable emasculation of such powers as members have (and which the relevant sections were intended to enhance) and also seems unfair to the directors or auditors whom the members may wish to retain.[222] Even where an amendment to an ordinary resolution may be proposed on the above principles, the company's articles may aim to restrict the shareholders' freedom, say, by providing that, where the text is fully set out in the notice of the meeting, the chairman has a discretion not to consider amendments of which at least 48 hours' notice in writing has not been given to the company.

Convening a meeting of the shareholders

No discussion of amendments to resolutions can be debated until there is a meeting. Clearly, therefore, the shareholders' meeting is not of much value as a vehicle of shareholder control if the meeting cannot easily be convened. The law distinguishes between annual general meetings (AGMs) and any other meeting of the shareholders.[223] The advantage of the former from our perspective is that, in principle, it must be held on a regular annual basis, whereas the CA 2006 provides procedures for the convening of other meetings, but says nothing about their frequency. Even the AGM is not compulsory if the company is a private one.[224] 12–028

Annual general meetings

The law, rather oddly, whilst requiring the holding of AGMs by public companies and private companies that are traded companies, does not prescribe the business that has to be transacted at the AGM and in particular does not say that the annual directors' report and the accounts must be laid before the AGM,[225] or that the directors due for re-election must be considered then. In fact, it is normal for these matters to be taken at the AGM, and for the shareholders to have an opportunity to question the directors generally on the company's business and financial position. This customary practice has been encouraged by the UK 12–029

[220] CA 2006 s.168. This seems to be permissible—the singular "director" includes the plural—and CA 2006 s.160 relates only to voting on *appointments*, not to *removals*.

[221] CA 2006 s.510.

[222] Nor should proxy-holders have any doubts on how they should vote. If instructed to vote for the resolution they would vote against the amendment but, if that was passed, for the amended resolution. If instructed to vote against, they would vote for the amendment, but against the resolution as amended. If given a discretion, they would exercise it.

[223] The law used to distinguish between AGMs and extraordinary general meetings (EGMs), but the CA 2006 no longer uses the latter term, no doubt because in the case of a private company it is the only type of meeting that can be held.

[224] CA 2006 ss.336–340, concerning AGMs, apply only to public companies.

[225] CA 2006 s.437, which requires public companies to lay before the company, in a general meeting, copies of its reports and accounts.

Corporate Governance Code and its predecessors,[226] which recommends that in premium-listed companies (i.e. those companies subjected to the requirements of the CGC) in order "to meet its responsibilities to shareholders and stakeholders, the board should ensure effective engagement with, and encourage participation from these parties".[227] Such effective engagement is likely to involve the AGM as a mechanism for dialogue.

This is now substantially strengthened by the CA 2006: if there is enough member support,[228] members of traded companies can require the company to add new matters to the agenda for the AGM[229]; and at all general meetings of traded companies, the company must provide answers to any question put by a member attending the meeting on any matter relating to the business being dealt with at the meeting.[230] It follows that there now seems to be no limit on the business that may be transacted at an AGM of a traded company, assuming only that it is business properly to be put before the shareholders.[231]

Following the recommendations of the Company Law Review, the timing of the AGM is tied to the company's annual reporting cycle. The AGM must be held yearly within the six-month period (for public companies) or nine-month period (for private traded companies) following its accounting reference date,[232] which determines the beginning and end of the company's financial year.[233] If a company fails to comply with the requirement to hold an AGM, every officer in default is liable to a fine.[234] This puts pressure on the directors, but the power, previously contained in the legislation,[235] for the Secretary of State, on the application of any member, to call or direct the calling of a meeting where the directors have failed to do so has been removed. Thus, the member has no direct

---

[226] See para.9–018.

[227] Financial Reporting Council, *UK Corporate Governance Code* (July 2018), Main Principle D. For engagement through the *UK Stewardship Code* (2020), see para.12–017.

[228] CA 2006 s.338A(3) requires the company "to include such a matter once it has received requests that it do so from—(a) members representing at least 5 per cent of the total voting rights of all the members who have a right to vote at the meeting, or (b)at least 100 members who have a right to vote at the meeting and hold shares in the company on which there has been paid up an average sum, per member, of at least £100." CA 2006 ss.338A(4)–(5) then set out the required format and timing (six weeks' notice, or if later, the time at which notice is given of the meeting).

[229] CA 2006 s.338A(1). Any matters may properly be added, unless they are defamatory of any person or frivolous or vexatious: see CA 2006 s.338A(2). In *Kaye v Oxford House (Wimbledon) Management Co Ltd* [2020] B.C.C. 117 at [134], it was stated that "'vexatious' may properly be applied to a resolution which has the characteristics of being troublesome, burdensome or is proposed for no proper purpose connected to the company, provided that one interprets troublesome or burdensome from the standpoint of the company".

[230] CA 2006 s.319A(1), with s.319A(2) relaxing the requirement slightly by providing that no such answer need be given: "(a) if to do so would—(i) interfere unduly with the preparation for the meeting, or (ii) involve the disclosure of confidential information; (b) if the answer has already been given on a website in the form of an answer to a question; or (c) if it is undesirable in the interests of the company or the good order of the meeting that the question be answered."

[231] In particular, the fact that a special resolution is required to transact a particular piece of business does not mean that that business cannot be considered at an AGM.

[232] CA 2006 s.336(1)–(1A) respectively.

[233] CA 2006 s.391(1)–(2), dealing with the situation where the company changes, as is permitted, its accounting reference date. See further para.22–010.

[234] CA 2006 s.336(3)–(4).

[235] CA 1985 s.367.

and easy way of securing compliance with the AGM requirement, but must rely on the indirect impact of the criminal sanctions.

Other general meetings

As for the convening of meetings other than the AGM of a public company, such meetings are not required at any specific time. The board may convene a meeting of the members of a private or public company at any time.[236] The CA 2006 provides that the directors must convene a meeting on the requisition of holders of not less than 5% of the paid-up capital carrying voting rights.[237] The request must state the general nature of the business to be dealt with at the meeting. It may include the text of a resolution intended to be moved at the meeting, which facility the members will normally be well advised to take up.[238] The resolution must, however, be one that may be "properly moved" at the meeting and, if it is not, it appears the directors are under no obligation to circulate it.[239] Once the meeting has been called, there is no residual discretion in the directors to cancel or postpone the meeting.[240] Accordingly, if the directors conclude, after calling the meeting, that a resolution cannot be "properly moved", the appropriate course of action is to attend the meeting and explain that fact.[241] If the directors fail to convene a meeting within 21 days of the deposit of the requisition (the meeting to be held within a further 28 days of the notice convening it), the requisitionists, or any of them representing more than half of the total voting rights of all of them, may themselves convene the meeting, and their reasonable expenses must be paid by the company and recovered from fees or remuneration payable to the defaulting directors.[242] 12–030

[236] CA 2006 s.302.

[237] CA 2006 s.303. In the case of a company without shareholders, the threshold is members holding at least one-tenth of the voting rights of the members: see CA 2006 s.303(2)(b).

[238] CA 2006 s.303(4). For the purpose for this scheme, see *Kaye v Oxford House (Wimbledon) Management Ltd* [2020] B.C.C. 117 at [92]. This is because (a) that makes their intentions clearer; and (b) if what is proposed is a special resolution, notice of it has to be given to the shareholders (see para.12–039). The company must then give the notice to the shareholders required for a special resolution: see CA 2006 s.304(4).

[239] The resolution is not "properly moved" if it falls within any of the categories of resolution that the directors may refuse to circulate as a written resolution: see CA 2006 s.303(5). See also para.12–005. For an example of the operation of this principle under the prior legislation, see *Rose v McGivern* [1998] 2 B.C.L.C. 593 Ch D. Here a proposed resolution "to elect a new board of not more than ten members" was held to be ineffective on the grounds that it did not provide for the removal of the existing board and there were otherwise no vacancies to which the ten could be elected (quite apart from the failure to state whether the number was in fact to be ten or some lesser number and to state who the ten were to be). The leaders of the requisition subsequently submitted 25 individual resolutions to the company, removing each of the 16 existing directors and appointing 9 new ones, but the company refused to circulate the individual resolutions on the grounds they were too late. For a definition of "vexatious", see *Kaye v Oxford House (Wimbledon) Management Co Ltd* [2020] B.C.C. 117 at [134].

[240] *Kaye v Oxford House (Wimbledon) Management Ltd* [2020] B.C.C. 117 at [99]–[104].

[241] *Kaye v Oxford House (Wimbledon) Management Ltd* [2020] B.C.C. 117 at [103].

[242] CA 2006 s.305(1), (6)–(7). The effect of this is that, if more than 5% requisitioned the meeting, the percentage needed to call a meeting directly is itself increased. The requisitionists may act not only where the directors fail to act in time but also where they fail to include a proposed resolution in

These provisions for requisitioning a meeting work reasonably well in private companies and also in public companies where, for example, the co-operation of only two or three institutional shareholders is required to get across the 5% threshold.[243] Small individual shareholders in public companies are, however, likely to find it a matter of considerable difficulty and expense to enlist the support of a sufficient number of fellow members to be able to make a valid requisition.

The articles may make further provision for the calling of meetings, but they are unlikely to give the members an extensive right to do so, for the management would like nothing better than to be able to call meetings when it suited them, but to be under no obligation to do so when it did not. In fact, the model set of articles for public companies provides for members to convene meetings only where the number of directors falls below two and the remaining director (if any) is unwilling to appoint a further director so as to restore the board's power to act in this area[244]; and no provision for members to convene meetings is made in the Model Articles for Private Companies Limited by Shares (Sch.1).

Meetings convened by the court

12–031 Finally, the court itself has the power to convene a meeting "if for any reason it is impracticable to call a meeting in any manner in which meetings of that company may be called or to conduct the meeting in manner prescribed by the articles or this Act".[245] This power may be exercised by the court "of its own motion or on the application—(a) of any director of the company or (b) of any member who would be entitled to vote at the meeting".[246] The meeting can be "called, held and conducted in any manner the court thinks fit" and the "court may give such ancillary or consequential directions as it thinks expedient and these may include a direction that one member of the company present in person or by proxy be deemed to constitute a meeting".[247]

Most of the litigation concerning the court's power to call a meeting has revolved around responding to quorum requirements for shareholder meetings. In the absence of the required quorum, no resolution can be effectively passed. In contrast to many other jurisdictions, the quorum requirements set by the CA 2006 are not demanding, except in relation to class meetings[248]: two members only are required for meetings of the shareholders as a whole, unless the company's constitution sets a higher figure,[249] and only one member in the case of a

the notice of the meeting or fail to give notice of the proposed resolution as a special resolution, if such it is: see CA 2006 ss.304(3)–(4) and 305(1)(b).

[243] Activist shareholders seeking to obtain changes in the board's policy have made use of it.

[244] Companies (Model Articles) Regulations 2008 (SI 2008/3229) Sch.3 art.28.

[245] CA 2006 s.306(1). See also *Kaye v Oxford House (Wimbledon) Management Ltd* [2020] B.C.C. 117 at [142]–[143].

[246] CA 2006 s.306(2). The section does not make the addition originally proposed of the personal representative of a deceased member of the company who would have had the right to vote at the meeting.

[247] CA 2006 s.306(2)–(4).

[248] See para.12–056.

[249] CA 2006 s.318(2). See *Re BW Estates Ltd (No.2)* [2018] Ch. 511 for the quorum requirement when a registered member dies or is dissolved.

single-member company.[250] It is not even clear that the CA 2006 requires the quorum to be present throughout the meeting.[251] However, staying away can in principle be an effective way of preventing a meeting from being held in a private company with only two shareholders. If the board consists of the same two persons (or their nominees) and also has a quorum requirement of two, the company may become completely deadlocked. The question the courts have had to address is whether its powers to call a meeting can be invoked to overcome this deadlock.

After much litigation over this issue, the courts appear to have reached a more settled position. In principle, the court can call a meeting to break a deadlock created by quorum requirements, because, where the shareholdings are not held equally, the normal principle of majority rule is being frustrated by the quorum requirement.[252] That said, it may be that the quorum requirements have been deliberately adopted in order to produce deadlock if the parties cannot agree, and in that case the court's power should not be used to overrule the parties' clear agreement. A court is likely to conclude that this is the purpose of the quorum requirement, where it takes the form of a class right attached to the shares of one of the parties.[253] Other than that unusual situation, the question of whether the quorum provision was intended to create deadlock in the case of disagreement is a matter of construction of the articles or shareholders' agreement.[254] In future, the quorum requirement will not be effective in private companies to produce deadlock where the shareholdings of the two contestants are not equal (and, of course, the quorum provision is unnecessary if they are). This is because the majority shareholder will be able to secure the passing of at least an ordinary resolution through the written resolution procedure, discussed above, without the need for a meeting. Some different protection in the articles will accordingly be required, such as a requirement for the consent of all shareholders to some or all resolutions of the company.

On the other hand, where the court takes the view that the provisions of the articles or the CA 2006 are being cynically exploited by a group of shareholders to block an effective meeting,[255] it may exercise its power to call a meeting in the

---

[250] CA 2006 s.318(1) (in this case, the rule overrides anything to the contrary in the articles).

[251] Companies (Tables A to F) Regulations 1985 (SI 1985/805) Table A art.41, which made it clear that this was required. The present model articles revert to ambiguity.

[252] *Re El Sombrero Ltd* [1958] Ch. 900 Ch D, where the applicant shareholder held 900 of the company's 1,000 shares, the remaining 100 being held by the two directors whom the applicant wished to remove in exercise of his statutory powers under what is now CA 2006 s.168 and who refused to attend the meeting. The court directed that one member present in person or by proxy should constitute a quorate meeting. See also *Re Opera Photographic Ltd* [1989] 1 W.L.R. 634 CH D (Companies Ct); *Re Sticky Fingers Restaurant Ltd* [1992] B.C.L.C. 84 Ch D (Companies Ct); *Smith v Butler* [2012] B.C.C. 645 CA at [49]–[55].

[253] *Harman v BML Group Ltd* [1994] 1 W.L.R. 893 CA. On class rights generally, see paras 13–014 onwards.

[254] *Ross v Telford* [1998] 1 B.C.L.C. 82 CA; *Union Music Ltd v Watson* [2003] 1 B.C.L.C. 453 CA; *Re Woven Rugs Ltd* [2002] 1 B.C.L.C. 324 Ch D; *Vectone Entertainment Holding Ltd v South Entertainment Ltd* [2004] EWHC 744 (Ch); [2005] B.C.C. 123. Board deadlock is not a pre-requisite to a court ordering a meeting: see *Schofield v Jones* [2019] EWHC 803 (Ch); [2019] B.C.C. 932 at [41].

[255] The most obvious way is not attending a meeting to make it inquorate: see *Schofield v Jones* [2019] B.C.C. 932 at [24] and [35].

broadest way. Thus, in *Re British Union for the Abolition of Vivisection*,[256] a company whose articles required personal attendance in order to vote had had a general meeting badly disrupted by a minority of members, and the committee feared that other members would in future be deterred from attending. On an application by a majority of the committee the court ordered that a meeting be held to consider a resolution for the abolition of the personal attendance rule, at which meeting the personal attendance rule itself would not apply and personal attendance would be permitted only to the members of the company's committee. Similarly, in *Schofield v Jones*,[257] the court ordered a meeting when a shareholder thwarted the majority shareholder's intention to remove a director by not attending the relevant general meetings.

What is a meeting?

12–032 Thanks to modern technology (hastened by a global pandemic), it is no longer necessary that a meeting should require all those attending to be in the same room. If more turn up than had been foreseen, a valid meeting can still take place if proper arrangements have been made to direct the overflow to other rooms with adequate audio-visual links that enable everyone to participate in the discussion to the same extent as if all had been in the same room.[258] This is now explicitly supported by the CA 2006 and model articles.[259] However, a meeting requires two-way, real-time communication among all the participants. If relaxation of the real-time requirement is sought, it is necessary for the company, if a private one, to take decisions through the use of written resolutions.[260]

Getting items onto the agenda and expressing views on agenda items

12–033 Rather than going through the process of requisitioning a meeting in order to discuss a particular piece of business, the shareholders may wish simply to add an item to the agenda of a meeting that the board has called in any event. This is most likely to be attractive in relation to the AGM, which, as we have seen, a public company is obliged to hold.

256 *Re British Union for the Abolition of Vivisection* [1995] 2 B.C.L.C. 1 Ch D. Contrast *Monnington v Easier Plc* [2005] EWHC 2578 (Ch); [2006] 2 B.C.L.C. 283, where the judge took the view that a meeting to remove a director could be convened and conducted in accordance with the CA 2006, but the result, as a consequence of the drafting of the removal section, would be ineffective. In that case, the court had no jurisdiction to use its power to call a meeting to reform the CA 2006.

257 *Schofield v Jones* [2019] B.C.C. 932 at [24] and [35]. The threat of unfair prejudice proceedings did not alter the court's conclusion: *Schofield v Jones* at [38].

258 *Byng v London Life Association* [1990] Ch. 170 CA. For a suitably relaxed modern approach, see *Re Castle Trust Direct Plc* [2020] EWHC 969 (Ch); [2021] B.C.C. 1 at [42]. The Company Law Review proposed that this be made clear in legislation, if there was any doubt about the principle: see Final Report, para.7.7.

259 CA 2006 s.360A. See also Companies (Model Articles) Regulations 2008 (SI 2008/3229) Sch.1 art.37 and Sch.3 art.29. At an electronic meeting, there must be mechanisms for checking identity and ensuring security: see CA 2006 ss.360A(2)–(3). In the case of a traded company, confirmation of any electronic vote must be sent to the person casting the vote "as soon as reasonably practicable": CA 2006 s.360AA(1).

260 See para.12–004.

Placing an item on the agenda

As we have seen, the AGM is normally convened by the board and, as part of that process, the board will be able to stipulate the items that it wishes to have discussed at the meeting. Members representing not less than one-twentieth of the total voting rights of the members entitled to vote on the proposed resolution,[261] or 100 members holding shares on which there has been paid up an average sum per shareholder of not less than £100, may require the company to give notice of their resolutions that can then be considered at the next AGM. In a company with a large shareholding body, shareholders with small shareholdings may find this second criterion easier to meet than the first; whereas a small number of institutional shareholders (perhaps even one) may be able to meet the first criterion. The second criterion for requiring a resolution to be placed on the agenda has also benefited from the steps that the CA 2006 has taken to protect the interests of "indirect" investors, i.e. those who hold their shares through nominees. Subject to safeguards, the 100 "members" may include those who are not members of the company, but whose interest in the shares arises from the fact that a member of the company holds the shares on their behalf in the course of a business and—a very important limitation—the indirect investor has the right to instruct the member how to exercise the voting rights.[262] **12–034**

However, the company is not bound to give notice of the proposed resolution unless certain conditions are met. First, the standard conditions, discussed above in relation to members' written resolutions, as to the effectiveness of the resolution must be met.[263] Secondly, the requisition, identifying the resolution of which notice is to be given, must be received by the company at least six weeks before the AGM or before the company gives notice to the members of the AGM.[264]

The third condition relates to the costs of circulating the resolution. In principle, those requesting the circulation must pay for it (unless the company resolves otherwise).[265] This was the previous law. However, the Company Law Review proposed that members' resolutions received in time to be circulated with the notice of the AGM should be circulated free of charge.[266] The CA 2006 does not accept that proposal and makes only the limited concession that circulation shall be free if the request is received before the end of the financial year preceding the meeting, which may be up to six or nine months before the meeting

[261] CA 2006 s.338. This provision operates on the basis of the distribution of voting rights in the company. Non-voting shares do not count, and multiple voting shares will make the 5% target easier or more difficult to reach according to whether or not their holders support the requisition.

[262] CA 2006 s.153. The right to instruct the member as to the exercise of voting rights is most likely to arise by way of contract between the registered and beneficial owners. The safeguards are designed to verify that the non-members are indirect investors and that there is no double-counting of shares.

[263] CA 2006 ss.338(2) and 338A(1)–(2). See para.12–007. Besides being effective, the resolution must not be defamatory or frivolous or vexatious: see *Kaye v Oxford House (Wimbledon) Management Co Ltd* [2020] B.C.C. 117 at [134].

[264] CA 2006 ss.338(4) and 338A(4). Thus, the board cannot frustrate the requisitionists by convening a meeting on less than six weeks' notice after the receipt of the request, or by giving very long notice of the AGM.

[265] CA 2006 ss.340(2) and 340B(2).

[266] Completing, paras 5.33–5.35.

is held.[267] The limited nature of this concession can be more fully understood when put in the context of a further reform proposal from the Company Law Review that was rejected entirely.

12–035 One major problem with the members' resolution procedure is that it is all too likely that something in the AGM circulation from the board will trigger the wish to place a shareholders' resolution on the agenda, but, since the minimum period of notice for calling the AGM is 21 days[268] (though the company may in fact give longer notice), there may well not be time for the members to respond to the AGM documentation and get their resolution to the company within the six-week limit. In addition, the company's costs of circulation would be much greater in the case where the AGM documentation has already gone out, for the proposed resolution would have to be circulated separately. The Company Law Review proposed to address the problem, at least in part, by requiring quoted companies to put their annual reports and accounts on their website within 120 days of the end of the financial year, after which there would be a "holding period" of 15 clear days, during which the company would be obliged to accept a members' resolution (having the support presently required) for circulation with the notice of the AGM and at the company's cost.[269] This opportunity for enhanced debate over the annual reports and accounts of large companies proved too much for management interests, who secured that this reform was not adopted.

For meetings other than AGMs there is no statutory procedure whereby members can add an item to the agenda of a meeting called by the board. The members do, however, have a statutory power to convene a meeting at any time (without cost to themselves) and to require circulation of a resolution to be considered at that meeting, though normally shareholders holding 5% of the voting rights are needed to secure the convening of such a meeting.[270] The fact that a statutory procedure is not available for adding an item to the agenda of a meeting, other than an AGM, convened by the board probably reflects the impracticability of so doing, when the minimum notice period for convening such a meeting is only 14 days and such meetings are often held urgently.

Circulation of members' statements

12–036 It is not enough, however, for the shareholders to have their resolution circulated in advance of the AGM. It will have much more effect if it is accompanied by a statement from the proposers setting out its merits. Alternatively, the shareholders

---

[267] CA 2006 ss.340(1), 340B(1), 437 and 442. However, the costs of circulation should not be large if the members' resolution can be circulated along with the general circulation for the AGM. The company is obliged to circulate the resolution with the notice if this is possible: CA 2006 s.339(1).

[268] CA 2006 s.307(2). For listed companies the recommended period is rather longer (20 working days), but still not long enough to obviate the problem under discussion. On notice periods, see para.12–038.

[269] Final Report, paras 8.66 and 8.100–101. One can find only a pale reflection of this idea in the provisions enabling 5% of the shareholders to require the company to place on its website a statement about the audit of the company's accounts or an auditor's ceasing to hold office for discussion at the company's accounts meeting (normally its AGM): see CA 2006 ss.527–531, discussed at para.23–022.

[270] See para.12–030.

may wish to circulate only a statement and not a resolution, for example, where they wish to oppose a resolution from the board rather than to propose one of their own. The directors will undoubtedly make use of their power to circulate statements in support of their resolutions. Even if the directors do not directly control many votes, they are for the moment in control of the company and they can get their say in first and use all the facilities and funds of the company in putting their views across. They will have had all the time in the world in which to prepare a polished and closely reasoned circular and with it they will have been able to dispatch stamped and addressed proxy forms in their own favour. All this, of course, is at the company's expense.[271]

Until the CA 1948, members opposing the board's resolution, or proposing their own resolutions, had none of these advantages and, even now, only timid steps have been taken towards counteracting the immense advantage enjoyed by those in possession of the company's machinery.[272] Such steps as have been taken are included in ss.314–316 of the CA 2006. These sections track the provisions of ss.338–340 dealing with members' requests for the circulation of resolutions and add the right, under similar conditions,[273] to have a statement of up to 1,000 words circulated to the members.

In practice, however, this provision is of limited value, except where the statement is in support of a shareholders' resolution and is dispatched with it. The expense still has to be borne by the members—unless the company otherwise resolves[274]—and no substantial saving will result from the use of the company's facilities. In other cases (for example, when the circulars are designed to oppose proposals already forwarded by the board), little extra cost will be incurred by acting independently of the company and this will have a number of advantages. It will avoid any difficulty in obtaining sufficient requisitionists and will prevent delay, which may be fatal if notices of the meeting have already been dispatched. It will also obviate the need to cut the circular to 1,000 words and will enable the opposition to accompany it with proxies in their own favour.[275] Moreover, and from a tactical point of view this is vital, the board will not obtain advance information about the opposition's case, nor be able to send out at the same time a circular of its own in reply. Moreover, in the case of large companies, the

[271] *Peel v LNW Railway* [1907] 1 Ch. 5 CA. For an excellent description of the relative weakness of the opposition, see *Re Dorman Long & Co* [1934] Ch. 635 Ch D at 657–658.

[272] CA 2006 ss.314–316.

[273] Including the extension of the "100 member" right to indirect investors: see CA 2006 s.153(1)(a). The main differences are that the request for the circulation has to be received only one week before the meeting: (CA 2006 s.314(4)(d)) and the company, or any person aggrieved, can make an application to the court for exemption from the obligation to circulate on grounds of abuse (CA 2006 s.317), as in the case of members' statements in support of written resolutions: see para.12–007.

[274] CA 2006 s.316—subject to the limited concession where the request is received before the end of the financial year preceding the meeting. The company is likely so to resolve if the members' resolution is passed (which is unlikely) and may conceivably do so even if it is lost. In cases where it has not so resolved, there have sometimes been disputes on precisely what are properly to be regarded as "the company's expenses in giving effect" to the requisition—e.g. does it include the costs of a circular opposing the members' resolution? It ought not to.

[275] There is clearly no reason why the members' circular should not invite recipients to cancel any proxies previously given to the board, but it seems that the company could refuse to despatch the members' proxy forms unless, perhaps, the words in them were counted against the 1,000 words allowed.

institutional investors will have mechanisms for communicating with each other that are not dependent upon the company's good offices and the financial press will often report the shareholders' concerns, thus encouraging prior communication among the shareholders and attendance at the meeting.

Notice of meetings and information about the agenda

12–037 In most cases, shareholder meetings are convened by the board. The main protection for the shareholders in such a case lies in the information made available to them in advance of the meeting and the length of notice required. On the basis of this information and during this period, they should be able to form a view whether the matter is sufficiently important for them to vote at the meeting or to attend it, and perhaps even to form an alliance with other shareholders to oppose the board, though, as we have noted, the shareholders start off on the back foot and will not have much time to organise their opposition. Naturally, these rules apply also to meetings convened by the members, for the requsitionists may not represent a majority of the members, who, in such a case, need to be protected against being "rail-roaded" into unwise decisions, whether the proposal emanates from the board or a minority of the members.

Length of notice

12–038 Prior to the CA 1948, the length of notice of meetings, and how and to whom notice should be given, depended primarily on the company's articles. The only statutory regulation, which could not be varied, was that 21 days' notice was required for a meeting at which a special resolution was to be proposed. In other cases, the 1929 Act provided that, unless the articles otherwise directed (which they rarely did) only seven days' notice was needed. This left far too short a time for opposition to be organised.[276] Hence, it is now provided by the CA 2006 that any provision of a company's articles shall be void insofar as it provides for the calling of a meeting by a shorter notice-period than 21 days' notice in the case of an annual general meeting, or 14 days' notice in other cases.[277] The company's articles may provide for longer notice but they cannot validly provide for shorter.[278] Traded private companies require 21 days' notice for all meetings (not just the AGM), unless the company offers the facility of voting by electronic means, in which case the shareholders in general meeting may decide to reduce the period to 14 days for meetings other than the AGM.[279] In practice, neither of these statutory provisions has much significance for the AGMs of listed companies, but they might be significant for other meetings of listed companies.

[276] Particularly as the period might be reduced still further by provisions requiring proxy forms to be lodged in advance of the meeting: see para.12–042.

[277] CA 2006 s.307.

[278] CA 2006 s.307(3). The previous requirement of 21 days' notice in the case of special resolutions has been removed. CA 2006 s.360 makes it clear that in this and related contexts "days" means "clear days", i.e. excluding the day of the meeting and the day on which the notice is given.

[279] CA 2006 s.307A does not apply to meetings of shareholders called to approve defensive measures proposed by management in a takeover. See also CA 2006 s.307(1A)(b).

If a meeting is, however, called on shorter notice than the CA 2006 or the articles prescribe, it is deemed to be duly called if so agreed, in the case of an AGM, by all the members entitled to attend and vote.[280] In other cases, a somewhat lower level of agreement will suffice.[281] This is a majority in number of those having the right to attend and vote[282] who must also hold the "requisite percentage" of the nominal value of the shares giving the right to attend and vote. That percentage is 95% in the case of a public company and 90% in the case of a private company (unless the articles increase the percentage, which they may do but not beyond 95%).[283] The effect of requiring, other than for AGMs where unanimity is the rule, the agreement of both a majority in number of members as well as a high percentage of the voting rights is that, where there is one or a small number of major shareholders and a number of small ones, at least some of the small shareholders will need to concur in the major shareholders' view that short notice is appropriate.

Special notice

In certain circumstances, a type of notice, unimaginatively and unhelpfully designated a "special notice", has to be given, the principal examples being when it is proposed to remove a director or to remove or not to reappoint the auditors.[284] In the light of the above discussion,[285] little more needs to be said here except to emphasise that special notice is a type of notice very different from that discussed hitherto. It is not notice of a meeting given *by* the company, but notice given *to* the company of the intention to move a resolution at the meeting. Where any provision of the CA 2006 requires special notice of a resolution, the resolution is ineffective unless notice of the intention to move it has been given to the company at least 28 days before the meeting.[286] The company must then give notice (in the normal sense) of the resolution, with the notice of the meeting or, if that is not practicable,[287] either by newspaper advertisement or by any other method allowed by the articles, at least 14 days before the meeting.[288] **12–039**

[280] CA 2006 s.337(2).

[281] CA 2006 s.307(4) and (7). See also *Schofield v Schofield* [2011] 2 B.C.L.C. 319 CA, where the court held there was no agreement to a shorter notice period, and so the resolutions (dismissing the minority shareholder as director and appointing the majority shareholder in his place) were not validly passed, in circumstances where the minority shareholder had attended and voted at the meeting on the clearly maintained basis that the meeting had not been validly convened by reason of falling short of the 14-day requirement pursuant to CA 2006 s.307.

[282] CA 2006 s.307(5).

[283] CA 2006 s.307(5)–(6). In the case of companies without share capital, the percentages relate to the total voting rights of all the members at the meeting.

[284] CA 2006 ss.168 and 510. See also *Bonham-Carter v Situ Ventures Ltd* [2012] B.C.C. 717.

[285] See paras 11–011 onwards and 23–018 onwards.

[286] CA 2006 s.312(1). This applies whether the resolution is proposed by the board or by a member. The notice is effective if the meeting is called for a date 28 days or less after special notice has been given, so that the board can, in effect, forgive its own tardiness: see CA 2006 s.312(4).

[287] For example, if notices of the meeting have already been despatched.

[288] CA 2006 s.312(2)–(3). It seems, however, that this notice has to be given only if the resolution is to be put on the agenda and that the mover cannot compel the company to do this, unless he can and does invoke the CA 2006 s.338: see *Pedley v Inland Waterways Ltd* [1971] 1 All E.R. 209.

All this achieves in itself is to ensure that the company and its members have plenty of time to consider the resolution, but in the two principal cases where special notice is required, supplementary provisions enable protective steps to be taken by the directors or auditors concerned.

Under this heading, the company's articles may also require notice of certain types of resolution to be given to the company in advance of the meeting, and this requirement may limit shareholders' freedom of action at the meeting itself. For example, the articles may provide that no person shall be appointed as a director at a meeting of the company unless he or she is a director retiring by rotation, a person recommended by the board or a person of whose proposed appointment the company has been given at least 14 days' (and not more than 35 days') notice, together with the proposed appointee's consent.[289] At the general meeting of such a company, it is thus not open to dissenting shareholders to put forward an alternative candidate for director on the spur of the moment, although it appears that the board could do so.

The contents of the notice of the meeting and circulars

12–040 Having previously left this matter to the articles,[290] the CA 2006 now lays down some basic requirements. The notice of the meeting must give the date, time and place of the meeting; provide a statement of the general nature of the business to be transacted at the meeting; and include any other matters required by the company's constitution.[291] The second of these three requirements is obviously the crucial one, for the member is entitled to be put in receipt of sufficient information about the business of the meeting to determine whether he or she will attend it.[292] This raises the question, however, as to how specific the notice must be. If the meeting is an AGM at which all that is to be undertaken is what former Tables A described as "ordinary business",[293] all that is necessary is to list those matters. If, however, resolutions on other matters are to be proposed, it is customary to set out the resolutions verbatim and to indicate that they are to be proposed as special or ordinary resolutions, as the case may be. In the case of special resolutions, s.283(6) of the CA 2006 requires that the notice of the meeting must contain the text of the resolution and indicate the intention to propose it as a special resolution.[294] The notice may also indicate that the resolution shall not be passed unless passed as a special resolution. This apparently curious provision follows from the further provision that anything that

---

289 Such a provision was included in Companies (Tables A to F) Regulations 1985 (SI 1985/805) Table A art.76, but it no longer appears. Consider the difficulties caused for the requisitionists by such a provision in *Rose v McGivern* [1998] 2 B.C.L.C. 593.

290 See, for example, Companies (Tables A to F) Regulations 1985 (SI 1985/805) Table A art.38.

291 CA 2006 s.311, with additional requirements specified in CA 2006 ss.311(3) and 311A in relation to traded companies where the rights and responsibilities of members at meetings must be further elaborated.

292 Contrast *Choppington Collieries Ltd v Johnson* [1944] 1 All E.R. 762 CA with *Batchellor & Sons v Batchellor* [1945] Ch. 169 Ch D.

293 The distinction between the "ordinary" and "special" business of an AGM disappeared from Companies (Tables A to F) Regulations 1985 (SI 1985/805), Table A.

294 CA 2006 s.283(6). See also *Re Uniq Plc* [2011] EWHC 749 (Ch) at [27].

may be done by ordinary resolution may also be done by special resolution.[295] In effect, this gives the proposers of the resolution an ad hoc method of raising the majority required for the passing of an ordinary resolution to that required for a special resolution.

The Company Law Review proposed that the requirement to set out the text of the resolution should be applied to all resolutions,[296] but this suggestion was not taken up. In all cases, the directors should ensure that, if the effect of the proposed business will be to confer a personal benefit on the directors, that should be made clear either in the notice or in a circular sent with it.

In practice, the notice of a meeting will be of a formal nature but, if anything other than ordinary business is to be transacted, it will be accompanied by a circular explaining the reasons for the proposals and giving the opinion of the board thereon. Indeed, it is arguable that the common law principle that members should be put in a position to determine whether to attend the meeting requires such circulars, except where the nature of the business will be obvious to all the members from what is said in the notice of the meeting. Normally, therefore, the circular will be a reasoned case by the directors in favour of their own proposals or in opposition to proposals put forward by others. In deciding whether the nature of the business has been adequately described, the notice and circular can be read together.[297] The circular must not, however, misrepresent the facts; there have been many cases in which resolutions have been set aside on the ground that they were passed as a result of a "tricky" circular.[298] Misleading circulars may not only influence the vote at the meeting, but also the decisions of the members whether to attend. For this reason, the fault in the circular should not be capable of cure even if the truth emerges at the meeting. For the same reason, it has been suggested that the notion of a "tricky" circular should embrace all misleading documents, whether the misinformation is the result of opportunism on the part of those putting it out or a genuine error on their part; and that the same principles should be applied to communications from shareholders to fellow members seeking their support for the requisition of a meeting of the company.[299]

If there is opposition to the board's proposals, the opposers will doubtless wish to state their case and a battle of circulars will result. It is here, however, that the superiority of the board's position becomes manifest. Even if the directors do not directly control many votes, they are for the moment in control of the company and they can get their say in first and use all the facilities and funds of the company in putting their views across. Even institutional shareholders, who may be able to stand the cost of the circulation, may find themselves on the back foot,

---

[295] CA 2006 ss.283(6)(b) and 282(5).

[296] Developing, para.4.45.

[297] *Tiessen v Henderson* [1899] 1 Ch. 861 at 867; *Re Moorgate Mercantile Holdings Ltd* [1980] 1 W.L.R. 227 at 242F.

[298] *Kaye v Croydon Tramways Co* [1898] 1 Ch. 358; *Tiessen v Henderson* [1899] 1 Ch. 861; *Baillie v Oriental Telephone Co* [1915] 1 Ch. 503 CA. See also *Prudential Assurance v Newman Industries Ltd (No.2)* [1981] Ch. 257; [1982] Ch. 204 CA. The circular must be construed in a commonsense way. In the case of listed companies, there is a further safeguard in the requirement that non-routine circulars have to be approved in advance by the FCA: see Listing Rules LR 13.2, but also the exceptions set out in LR 13.8.

[299] *Rose v McGivern* [1998] 2 B.C.L.C. 593; on the former point following the Australian case of *Bain and Co Nominees Pty Ltd v Grace Bros Holdings Ltd* [1983] 1 A.C.L.C. 816.

whilst smaller shareholders may be unable to respond effectively at all. As we have seen,[300] the statutory provisions permitting 5% of the members to require the company to send a statement of their views to all the members are singularly ineffective in practice.

Communicating notice of the meeting to the members

12–041 Having prescribed the basic content of the notice, the CA 2006 then goes on to specify to whom it should be given, thus giving statutory form to something previously contained in the model articles.[301] Those entitled to receive notice of the meeting are every member of the company (whether entitled to vote or not) and every director.[302] Members include those entitled to a share on the death or bankruptcy of a member, if the company has been notified of their entitlement.[303] However, these statutory provisions are subject to any provision in the company's articles (for example, excluding non-voting members from entitlement to receive notice). This also enables companies that need to, to deal with exceptional cases (such as that where holders of share-warrants to bearer are entitled to attend and vote).[304] The articles may also contain more prosaic matters, such as the rules identifying the address that the company will use to communicate with the members and removing the members' entitlement to be notified if the address so identified proves ineffective.[305] Accidental failure to give notice to one or more members shall not affect the validity of the meeting or resolution, and the company's articles can expand this relaxation, except for meetings or resolutions required by the members.[306]

Attending the meeting

Proxies

12–042 One of the important features of company meetings is that the members do not have to appear at the meeting in person; they may appoint another person (a proxy) to attend and vote on their behalf.[307] At common law, attending and voting

---

[300] See para.12–036.

[301] CA 2006 s.310. For the former model provision, see Companies (Tables A to F) Regulations 1985 (SI 1985/805) Table A art.38.

[302] CA 2006 s.310(1).

[303] CA 2006 s.310(2).

[304] The usual practice is to give notice by a newspaper advertisement. The Listing Rules require this form of communication. On bearer shares, see para.24–020.

[305] See Companies (Model Articles) Regulations 2008 (SI 2008/3229) Sch.3 arts.79–80.

[306] CA 2006 s.313. The "accidental omission" provision, of course, would not cover the deliberate omission to give notice to a troublesome member, nor does it cover a deliberate omission based on a mistaken belief that a member is not entitled to attend the meeting: see *Musselwhite v Musselwhite & Son Ltd* [1962] Ch. 964 Ch D. If the omission is "accidental", it applies even if the meeting is called to pass a special resolution: see *Re West Canadian Collieries Ltd* [1962] Ch. 370 Ch D.

[307] For a discussion of the problems in this area, see Shareholder Voting Working Group, *Discussion Paper on Shareholder Proxy Voting* (July 2015) available at: *http://uk.practicallaw.com/9-616-7485* [Accessed 1 January 2021].

had to be in person,[308] but early on it became the normal practice to allow these duties to be undertaken by an agent or "proxy".[309] It should be noted that the system of proxy voting is not the same as that of postal voting. With postal voting the vote is cast directly by the member who holds the vote and he or she votes without attending a meeting. With proxy voting, the proxy votes on behalf of the member, and votes at a meeting. In practice, there may not be much difference between the two when the proxy is given precise instructions and follows them, for then the member in effect makes up his or her mind as to how the vote is to be cast in advance of the meeting. Since 2009, a company's articles may contain provisions permitting a poll taken at a meeting to include votes cast in advance.[310]

Until the CA 1948, however, the right to vote by proxy at a meeting of a company was dependent upon express authorisation in the articles. In practice, this was almost invariably given; but not infrequently it was limited in some way, generally by providing that the proxy must himself be a member. Where there was such a limitation, the scales were further tilted in favour of the board, for a member wishing to appoint a proxy to oppose the board's proposals might find difficulty in locating a fellow member prepared to attend and vote on his behalf. It was also customary to provide that proxy forms must be lodged in advance of the meeting. While this is a reasonable provision, in as much as it is necessary to check their validity before they are used at the meeting, it too could be used to favour the board if the period allowed for lodging was unreasonably short. Moreover, as already pointed out, it had become the practice for the board to send out proxy forms in their own favour with the notice of the meeting and for these to be stamped and addressed at the company's expense.

For all these reasons, although proxy voting gave an appearance of stockholder democracy, this appearance was deceptive and in reality the practice helped to enhance the dictatorship of the board. In recognition of this, the Stock Exchange required that listed companies should send out "two-way" proxies, i.e. forms that enable members to direct the proxy whether to vote for or against any resolution. The FCA's listing rules currently require "three-way" proxies (i.e. for, against or abstain).[311]

The statutory provisions relating to proxies show a further development in the movement of the proxy provisions from the articles to the CA 2006.[312] The effect is in many cases to make the proxy rules mandatory. Unless the CA 2006 expressly allows derogation from its provisions, the articles cannot reduce the statutory entitlements, though the Act gives the articles a general permission to **12–043**

[308] *Harben v Philips* (1883) 23 Ch. D. 14 CA. See also *Woodford v Smith* [1970] 1 W.L.R. 806 Ch D at 810.

[309] The word "proxy" is used indiscriminately to describe both the agent and the instrument appointing him.

[310] CA 2006 s.322A(1), inserted by Companies (Shareholders' Rights) Regulations 2009 (SI 2009/1632).

[311] Listing Rules LR 9.3.6. Notwithstanding recommendations that this should be a statutory requirement in all cases (for example, by the Jenkins Committee, Cm.1749, para.464) it still is not. An abstention from supporting a management proposal on the part of a larger shareholder is taken as a significant event in the case of listed companies.

[312] CA 2006 ss.324–331.

improve them.[313] Any member is entitled to appoint another person (whether a member of the company or not) as his proxy to attend, speak and vote instead of himself at a meeting of the company.[314] In the case of a company having a share capital the member may appoint more than one proxy, provided each proxy is appointed to exercise rights attached to different shares.[315] Previously, this facility was subject to the articles of the company permitting it. It is now mandatory and is useful in the case of fund managers or nominee custodians[316] who may hold shares on behalf of a number of different beneficial owners who may hold different views on the matters at issue.

The members must be informed of their statutory rights to attend, speak and vote by proxy (and of any more extensive rights provided under the company's articles) in the notice convening the meeting.[317] Moreover, if proxies are solicited at the company's expense the invitation must be sent to all members entitled to attend and vote.[318] Thus, the board cannot invite only those from whom it expects a favourable response. Finally, the articles may not require that proxy forms (or other documents required to validate the proxy) must be lodged more than 48 hours before a meeting or adjourned meeting.[319]

12–044 It cannot be said, however, that these provisions have done much to curtail the tactical advantages possessed by the directors. What has been more important has been the partial re-concentration of shareholdings in the hands of institutional shareholders, discussed above. These sophisticated shareholders are well place to make full use of their proxy rights. In fact, policy debate has now shifted from discussion of how management use the proxy machinery to how institutional investors use it. More particularly, given the pressures on the institutions to vote and the wide range of companies in which they invest, they often outsource at least part of the proxy-voting exercise to proxy advisers, who, because they act

[313] CA 2006 s.331.

[314] CA 2006 s.324(1). The restrictions under the previous law as to (1) the proxy's right to speak at meetings of public companies; (2) the proxy's right to vote on a poll; or (3) the member's right to appoint a proxy at all in a company not having a share capital, have all been swept away. The proxy may also demand a poll (CA 2006 s.329) and may even be elected the chair of the meeting (ibid. s.328).

[315] CA 2006 s.324(2).

[316] See para.12–013.

[317] CA 2006 s.325. Failure to comply does not affect the validity of the meeting or anything done at it, but does constitute a criminal offence on the part of every officer in default: see CA 2006 s.325(2)–(4). This notice is not given to the person nominated under s.146 to receive communications from the company (see para.12–021). That person is told that he or she may have a right to appoint a proxy or to instruct the member how to vote, depending on the agreement between the nominated person and the member (CA 2006 s.149). This is not a very useful notice, but it is the best that can be provided.

[318] CA 2006 s.326(1), unless a proxy form or other information is issued at the request of the member and is available to all members upon request: CA 2006 s.326(2). As with s.325, non-compliance is a criminal offence. Nothing is said about the impact of non-compliance on the validity of what is done at the meeting, presumably because s.326, unlike s.325, does not concern the content of the notice of the meeting.

[319] CA 2006 s.327. Hence proxies may now validly be lodged between the original date of the meeting and any adjournment for more than 48 hours. In the case of votes taken on polls, which are sometimes delayed, the relevant time is the time the poll is demanded or, if the poll is not to be taken within 48 hours of being demanded, 24 hours before the time appointed for the taking of the poll.

for many companies, reduce companies' voting costs. These firms provide voting advice, especially to institutional investors, and may therefore have considerable influence on their voting behaviour. Although taking advice is often sensible, especially given the increasing complexity of the equity markets and the large number of (cross-border) holdings of shares, two shortcomings are typically noted: the advisors may have serious conflicts of interest, given that they often provide other services to issuers; and their methodologies may not be robust.

Perhaps predictably, codes of best practice have been developed, with suggestions that they be adopted on a "comply or explain" basis.[320] Amendments to the EU Shareholder Rights Directive in 2017 made it mandatory for proxy advisers to report which code they apply and how they apply it, as well as a wide range of other information about their methodology and any conflicts of interest.[321]

It is, of course, true that, once opposition is aroused, members may be persuaded to cancel their proxies, for these are merely appointments of agents and the agents' authority can be withdrawn,[322] or to change their instructions, since s.324A requires the proxy to vote in accordance with the member's instructions.[323] But in practice this rarely happens.

The issue of termination of the proxy's authority is now partly addressed in s.330. The aim of the provision is to protect things done by the proxy from being brought into question if the company[324] has not received notification of the termination of the proxy's authority before the meeting. Thus, the proxy's vote will still be valid and the proxy will still count towards the quorum and can still validly join in demanding a poll, unless the company receives notice of termination of the authority before the commencement of the meeting.[325] The company's articles may set an earlier time for the notification of the termination, but not so as to make it earlier than 48 hours before the meeting (excluding non-working days).[326] However, s.330 of the CA 2006 deals only with the termination of the proxy's authority by "notice of termination". Accordingly, the Court of Appeal has held that a member may attend and vote in person and the 12–045

---

320 Following ESMA's report into the role of the proxy advisory industry, a group of six proxy advisers published a set of best practice principles for the industry in March 2014. The three main principles, which are supplemented by additional guidance, are service quality, conflicts of interest, and communications, and they apply on a "comply or explain" basis. Consider European Securities and Markets Association, *Follow-up on the Development of the Best Practice Principles for Providers of Shareholder Voting Research and Analysis* (December 2015).

321 Directive 2017/828 [2017] OJ L 132/1, inserting a new art.3j on engagement policy into the original Directive and implemented in the UK by the Proxy Advisors (Shareholders' Rights) Regulations 2019 (SI 2019/926).

322 Unless it is an "authority coupled with an interest" (for example, when given to a transferee prior to registration of his transfer) or is an irrevocable power of attorney under the Power of Attorney Act 1971 s.4.

323 CA 2006 s.324A.

324 Or someone other than the company if the articles require or permit the notice to be given to someone else: see CA 2006 s.330(4).

325 CA 2006 s.330(2)–(3). In the case of voting on a poll to be held more than 48 hours after it is demanded, the relevant time is the time appointed for the poll (CA 2006 s.330(3)(b)).

326 CA 2006 s.330(5)–(7) (noting that s.330(6)(c) has been repealed from 26 May 2015).

company must then accept his vote instead of the proxy's,[327] i.e. the proxy's authority may be terminated by a personal vote. However, two points should be noted about that case. First, it was based on the construction of the particular articles of the company in question, and so does not purport to lay down a general rule. Secondly, the company was aware the shareholder had voted in person and that the votes held by the proxy were accordingly reduced—indeed the company in that case wished positively to insist on the proxy's votes having been reduced. Thus, outside the matters covered by the section, the terms of the articles and the company's knowledge seem to be the crucial determinants of the ability of the proxy to exercise his or her voting rights as against the company, despite the withdrawal of the member's authority.

As between the member and the proxy, on ordinary agency principles, a revocation is generally effective if notified to the proxy before he has voted.[328] During the term of appointment of the proxy, (surprisingly, only since 2009) the proxy is required to vote in accordance with any instructions given by the appointing member.[329] This would seem to overcome the problem addressed in older cases of whether there was any positive obligation on the proxy at all (or merely a negative one not to vote contrary to the principal's instructions),[330] and whether the answer depended upon the existence of a contract or a fiduciary relationship between member and proxy.[331] Failing any such statement or definite instruction from the principal, however, the proxy will have a discretion, and, if this is exercised in good faith, the proxy will not be liable, whichever way he votes or if he refrains from voting.

Corporations' representatives

12–046 Since a company or other corporation is an artificial person that must act through agents or employees, it might be supposed that, when a member is another company, it could attend and vote at meetings only by proxy. This, however, is not so. A body corporate may, by a resolution of its directors or other governing body,[332] authorise such person or persons as it thinks fit to act as its representative at meetings of companies of which it is a member (or creditor) and that representative may exercise the same powers as could the body corporate if it were an individual.[333] With the expansion of the powers of the proxy, on the one

---

[327] *Cousins v International Brick Co* [1931] 2 Ch. 90 CA.

[328] It is possible for an authority coupled with an interest to be irrevocable.

[329] CA 2006 s.324A.

[330] This was discussed, but not decided, in *Oliver v Dalgleish* [1963] 1 W.L.R. 1274 Ch D, which also left open the question of how far the company is concerned to see whether the proxy is obeying his instructions.

[331] See, for example, *Second Consolidated Trust v Ceylon Amalgamated Estates* [1943] 2 All E.R. 567 Ch D at 570; *Re Dorman Long & Co* [1934] Ch. 635 Ch D (this case contains an admirable discussion of the general problems of proxy voting). In both the cases, the proxy-holders were present at the meeting: quaere whether (in the absence of mandatory instruction now, as per s.324A) they can be compelled to attend: see [1934] Ch. 664 at 665.

[332] This might be the company's liquidator: see *Hillman v Crystal Bowl Amusements Ltd* [1973] 1 W.L.R. 162 CA (Civ Div).

[333] CA 2006 s.323(2). This is really a statutory example of an officer acting as an organ of the company rather than as a mere agent.

hand, and the removal of the previous restriction that a company could appoint only a single corporate representative, on the other, it is unclear whether the proxy or the corporate representative is the more attractive mechanism for the corporate shareholder. The representative may have the slight advantage that, unlike a proxy, he or she can simply turn up at the meeting and is not subject to any requirement for documentation to be lodged with the company in advance of the meeting, as a proxy is. This may be particularly valuable where institutional investors are in discussion with the company's management right until the last minute about the acceptability or otherwise of a resolution to be proposed at a meeting and where, if those discussions break down, it will be too late to appoint a proxy.[334]

Voting and verification of votes

Voting as a governance issue

Traditionally, English company law has proceeded on the basis that the votes exercised by a shareholder at a general meeting are property rights deriving from the shares that they own. Given the fundamental starting point in British law that a person can use his property howsoever he chooses, there are two problems: first, shareholders may choose not to exercise their votes at all; or, secondly, they may exercise their votes at the behest of a non-shareholder. Both situations are capable of undermining the legitimacy of shareholder decisions: in the first case, the result is not necessarily representative of the shareholding body as a whole; and, in the second situation, the decision may instead reflect the interests of non-shareholders. **12–047**

As regards the first problem, it was discussed previously that financial intermediaries (such as pension fund trustees) who owe fiduciary obligations imposed by trusts law may owe a duty to consider whether voting rights attached to shares should be exercised in order to promote the interests of the beneficiaries of pension trusts. Following government pressure, institutional shareholders generally have endorsed the UK Stewardship Code, which embodies rules of best practice for their active engagement with companies in which they are invested (including exercising votes attached to shares). For institutional investors, voting is coming close to being a duty.[335] Such a duty is not yet enshrined in the law, but the sense of "duty" will be driven by the self-interest in avoiding the heavy hand of mandatory legal regulation if problems persist—whilst "self-regulation" is arguably inapt to describe such conduct ("market-controlled" regulation

[334] CA 2006 s.323(3)–(4), which deal with the situation where more than one representative is authorised to act on behalf of the company. It has been suggested that these provisions, as revised by the Companies (Shareholders' Rights) Regulations 2009 (SI 2009/1632), now make it clear that representatives can be assigned voting rights in respect of different parcels of shares held by the corporate shareholder in the way that is explicitly provided for in the case of a proxy. See also CA 2006 s.324(2).

[335] See paras 12–013 onwards. Since December 2010, all UK-authorised firms that manage investments for professional clients who are not natural persons are required under the FCA's Conduct of Business Sourcebook (r.2.2.3) to disclose the nature of its commitment to the Stewardship Code or explain its alternative investment strategy.

potentially being more accurate), the same set of drivers is arguably at play as in self-regulating areas. Nevertheless, the developments in the UK Stewardship Code have to some degree addressed the problem of institutional shareholders not voting. Indeed, voting levels at general meetings of large companies improved from one-half to over 60% in the three years 2004 to 2007,[336] but then levelled out to just over 70% by 2015.[337] In a survey conducted during 2016, 63% of respondents reported investors seeking more engagement with senior management and 68% reported increased engagement with a company's investor relations officer, although there was a lower level of engagement with company chairmen and non-executive directors across the board in FTSE companies.[338]

Votes on a show of hands and polls

12–048 The increased focus on engagement by institutional investors has naturally led to them focusing on the voting principles at general meetings and criticising those rules that make their task of engagement more difficult. Most companies' articles of association (including the standard-form articles[339]) provide for the primary voting mechanism to be a show of hands, upon which each member present has one vote.[340] Proxies may also vote on a show of hands,[341] although this may create a practical difficulty for a proxy who has received instructions from some shareholders who support the resolution and others who do not. Given the potential inaccuracy of voting on a show of hands, its retention as the primary voting mechanism probably requires some explanation, particularly as such a voting system is not common in other jurisdictions and accordingly is often misunderstood by foreign investors.[342] The principal argument in favour of retaining the show-of-hands voting system is its speed and simplicity, thereby enabling the company to take uncontroversial decisions quickly, albeit that, for completely uncontroversial decisions, other techniques (such as taking decisions without a vote, if no person present demands one) would do just as well.

Where the matter in question is controversial, with the result that the voting mechanism is likely to come under the greatest pressure and scrutiny, the show-of-hands mechanism has two principal defects. First, a show of hands may disguise the actual level of opposition to the resolution, even if it produces the same result as a poll would have done. For example, a resolution may be passed on a show of hands by 80 to 20, but if a poll had been taken it might have been

---

336 *Review of the impediments to voting UK shares*, Report by Paul Myners to the Shareholder Voting Working Group (July 2007). On the issue of "empty" voting, see para.12–053.

337 See Financial Reporting Council, *Developments in Corporate Governance and Stewardship 2015* (January 2016), p.16, citing figures from European Voting Results Report; ISS (September 2015).

338 Financial Reporting Council, *Developments in Corporate Governance and Stewardship 2016* (January 2017), p. 21.

339 Companies (Model Articles) Regulations 2008 (SI 2008/3229) Sch.1 art.42.

340 CA 2006 s.284(2), inserted by Companies (Shareholders' Rights) Regulations 2009 (SI 2009/1632) reg.2(3), implementing Directive 2007/36 on the exercise of certain rights of shareholders in listed companies [2007] OJ L184/17 art.14, which permitted the UK to retain the show-of-hands mechanism when it was an EU Member State.

341 CA 2006 s.324(1). Previously this was a matter left to be regulated by the articles.

342 Consider Directive 2007/36 on the exercise of certain rights of shareholders in listed companies [2007] OJ L184/17 art.14.

revealed that 500 votes were in favour of the resolution and 400 against. Moreover, despite being the person appointed to receive the proxies solicited by the company, the chairman of the meeting is likely not to vote on a show of hands, obscuring even further the level of opposition. Indeed, these difficulties discourage institutional shareholders in particular from voting by proxy, as their votes would have such little impact. The particular risk posed to institutional investors in using proxies is reflected by the fact that the UK Stewardship Code[343] requires such investors to disclose the extent to which they have relied upon proxies in carrying out their engagement responsibilities.

Secondly, a more serious defect with a show of hands is that it may actually produce a result different from what would have been achieved if the votes had been cast according to the number of shares held. This problem can be addressed by allowing an alternative voting mechanism in such circumstances. That alternative is the poll by which members and proxies cast the number of votes attached to their shares, although a person is not obliged to vote all his or her shares or even to exercise the votes attached to their different shares all in the same way.[344] On a poll, the default position is "one share, one vote".[345] The voting process usually involves signing slips of paper indicating how many votes are being cast in each direction and the number of abstentions. This is certainly a more cumbersome, if more accurate, voting process than a show of hands. In large meetings, it may not be practical to complete the voting process during the meeting because of the need to check proxy forms and count the number of votes cast, although there is scope for increasing the speed and efficiency of voting through technological means.[346] What is not generally permitted, unless the articles specifically provide otherwise, is voting by postal ballot.[347] This may be thought a strange limitation, given that it might in fact provide an effective means of garnering members' views, but it maintains the fiction that the result of a general meeting is only determined after oral discussion between the shareholders. In the case of public companies, however, the reality is that the result is usually determined by proxies lodged before the meeting.[348] 12–049

---

343 Financial Reporting Council, *The Stewardship Code* (2020), Principle 12.

344 CA 2006 s.322. Accordingly, the chairman of the meeting, under a typical three-way proxy, may hold some votes for and some against the relevant resolution, as well as some instructions to abstain, and he can accordingly give effect to each set of instructions. The same principle applies where a nominee holds shares on behalf of more than one person: ibid. s.152.

345 CA 2006 s.284(3). See also *Re Sirius Minerals Plc* [2020] EWHC 1447 (Ch) at [19]. For an example of a constitutional provision to the contrary, see *Puzitskaya v St Paul's Mews (Islington) Ltd* [2017] EWHC 905 (Ch).

346 If proxies have been gathered only by the company and have been lodged with, for example, the chairman of the meeting, then calculating the vote will be relatively straightforward. The position becomes complex when there have been multiple proxy solicitations, such that the process can extend beyond the meeting itself. In traded companies, a confirmation of electronic votes cast must be sent: see CA 2006 s.360AA.

347 *McMillan v Le Roi Mining Co Ltd* [1906] 1 Ch. 331 Ch D. The articles rarely do so provide, except in the case of clubs or other associations formed as companies limited by guarantee.

348 As was stated in *Berendt v Bethlehem Steel Corp* (1931) 154 A. 321 at 322, statements made to a meeting of proxy-holders fall "upon ears not allowed to hear and minds not permitted to judge: upon automatons whose principals are uninformed of their own injury".

In terms of who may demand a poll, the standard-form articles of association allow members present at the general meeting (who pass a defined numerical or control threshold) to demand that a poll be taken, either before a decision on a show of hands has been taken or once the result of a show of hands is clear.[349] A company's articles invariably direct that a demand by the meeting's chairman shall be effective.[350] Indeed, the chairman has a duty to exercise his right to demand a poll, so that effect can be given to the real sense of the meeting, and he is legally obliged to direct a poll if he realises that such a vote might well produce a different result.[351] The directors are also usually given the right to demand a poll, which again strengthens the position of the directors vis-à-vis the shareholders, as the former does not run any risk of not having their full voting power recognised. The significance of the right to demand a poll is underlined by the fact that the CA 2006 renders void any provision in the articles that excludes the right to demand a poll at a general meeting on any question, other than the election of a chairman or the adjournment of the meeting.[352] Nor may the articles make ineffective a demand by not less than five members having a right to vote on the resolution; or by members representing not less than one-tenth of the total voting rights on the resolution; or by members holding voting shares "on which an aggregate sum has been paid up equal to not less than [one-tenth] of the total sum paid up on all the shares conferring that right".[353] Furthermore, a proxy may demand or join in demanding a poll.[354] Accordingly, these various protections make it difficult for the articles to hamstring a sizeable opposition by depriving them of their opportunity to exercise their full voting strength.

Verifying votes

12–050 The Company Law Review received evidence that the voting results produced on a poll were not always accurate because votes were "lost" somewhere along the chain between a shareholder giving instructions regarding how his votes should

---

349 Companies (Model Articles) Regulations 2008 (SI 2008/3229) Sch.1 art.44(2)(c)–(d) and Sch.3, art.36(2)(c)–(d). It is a question of construction of the company's articles of association whether the poll must be demanded before there has been a vote on a show of hands: see *Carruth v ICI* [1937] A.C. 707 HL at 754–755; *Holmes v Keyes* [1959] Ch. 199 CA. The model set of articles for private and public companies provide for a poll to be demanded in advance of the meeting or at the meeting, but before the show of hands decision has been taken, as well as immediately after the result has been declared of the show of hands vote: see Companies (Model Articles) Regulations 2008 (SI 2008/3229) Sch.1 art.44 and Sch.3 art.36.

350 Companies (Model Articles) Regulations 2008 (SI 2008/3229) Sch.1 art.44 and Sch.3 art.36.

351 *Second Consolidated Trust v Ceylon Amalgamated Estates* [1943] 2 All E.R. 567, in which the chairman held proxies (without which there would have been no quorum) which would have defeated the resolutions passed on a show of hands if exercised on a poll.

352 CA 2006 s.321(1).

353 CA 2006 s.321(2). In the absence of anything in the articles, any member may demand a poll (see *R. v Wimbledon Local Board* (1882) 8 Q.B.D. 459 CA), although the model articles provide that two or more members are required to demand a poll: see Companies (Model Articles) Regulations 2008 (SI 2008/3229) Sch.1, art. 44 and Sch.3, art.36. This is significantly more generous than the statutory control in CA 2006 s.321.

354 CA 2006 s.329(1).

be cast and the recording of those votes at the meeting itself.[355] One solution has been to impose a statutory requirement on companies to provide individual members with confirmation that their votes have been received and as to the manner in which they were cast.[356] An alternative solution involves giving members (who represent not less than 5% of the total voting rights or who are not less than 100 in number)[357] the right to requisition an independent assessor's report (normally from the company's auditors) about any poll at a general meeting of the company (but without any cost to the requisitionists).[358] This right applies only within "quoted companies", i.e. companies incorporated in one of the jurisdictions of the UK and listed on the Main Market of the London Stock Exchange or listed on a regulated market in an EEA State or having their shares traded on the New York Stock Exchange or Nasdaq.[359] The report must give the assessor's opinion, with supporting reasons, on a number of matters, notably whether the procedures adopted in connection with the poll were adequate, whether the votes (including proxy votes) were fairly and accurately recorded and whether the validity of the members' appointment of proxies was fairly assessed.[360] The context in which the right is set strongly suggests that the assessor is required to look only at the company's practices and procedures, so that defects in the passing of voting instructions down the chain before those instructions reach the company will not be picked up.

Certainly, the rights that the assessor is given to support the discharge of its reporting function are all rights against the company and associated persons. The assessor has the right to attend the meeting of the company at which the poll is to be taken or any subsequent proceedings if the poll is not taken at the meeting itself and to be given copies of the documentation sent out by the company in connection with the meeting.[361] The assessor has a right of access to the company's records relating to the meeting and the poll and a right to require directors, officers, employees, members and agents of the company (including the operators of its share register) to provide information and explanation (unless this would involve a breach of legal professional privilege).[362] Non-compliance with the request for information or giving knowingly or recklessly misleading information in response to a request is a criminal offence.[363] The company must put on its website a copy of the report as soon as is reasonably practicable and

[355] Final Report, para.6.25. See also *Review of the impediments to voting UK shares*, Report by Paul Myners to the Shareholder Voting Working Group (July 2007), pp.1–4.

[356] CA 2006 s.360AA, which requires a traded company to provide confirmation of receipt of electronic votes. There is also a right for an individual member to request confirmation that votes in a traded company have been "validly recorded and counted": see CA 2006 s.360BA.

[357] These are the same thresholds as apply to a shareholder putting a resolution on the agenda or demanding an AGM.

[358] CA 2006 s.342. The right extends to class meetings at which it is proposed to vary the rights of any class of member: CA 2006 s.352. On variation of class rights, see para.13–015.

[359] CA 2006 s.385. Section 354 gives the Secretary of State the power by regulations, subject to affirmative resolution in Parliament, to extend the types of company to which the assessor's report requirement applies (but also to limit them).

[360] CA 2006 s.347(1).

[361] CA 2006 s.348.

[362] CA 2006 s.349.

[363] CA 2006 s.350.

keep the information there for two years and, at an earlier stage, must post some information about the appointment of the assessor.[364]

Non-compliance with the requirements for an assessor's report appears to have no impact on the validity of the resolution passed, though it is a criminal offence on the part of every officer in default for the company not to respond within one week of receiving a valid request by appointing an independent assessor to produce the report.[365] The request will normally be made before the meeting at which the poll is likely to be requested or conducted, but a valid request may be made up to one week after the date on which the poll is held.[366] The appointed person must meet the statutory requirements for independence, which, however, are drawn so as not to exclude necessarily the company's auditors,[367] and the assessor must not have any other role in relation to the poll upon which the report is to be made.[368]

Establishing who is entitled to vote

12–051 One final issue which should be mentioned is the fundamental one of establishing who is entitled to vote. There are two potential problems. The first arises when the shares in a company are constantly traded. In this case, establishing who can vote can only sensibly be done by establishing some date prior to, but not too far in advance of, the meeting as the "record date". Those who are members on that date may vote, even if by the date of the meeting they have disposed of their shares, and those who have acquired shares since that date may not (except by instructing the shareholder on record how to vote). This is not an entirely satisfactory situation and in some continental European countries it is dealt with by "share-blocking", namely prohibiting trading between the record date and the date of the meeting. However, the disadvantages of this device, in terms of loss of liquidity, outweigh the advantages, and it has not been used in the UK.[369] The alternative is to set the record date close to the meeting date, so as to minimise the effect of trading post the record date, but to accept that some misallocation of voting rights will inevitably occur. This is the UK approach, where the record date is set at not more than 48 hours before the meeting in the case of traded companies.[370]

The second problem is one that has emerged as a practical issue only recently. Directors of public companies have powers to issue statutory disclosure notices calling for information about the persons interested in its shares.[371] If there is non-compliance with the notice, the company can seek a court order restricting the rights attached to the relevant shares, including barring the right to vote.

---

[364] CA 2006 ss.351 and 353.

[365] CA 2006 s.343.

[366] CA 2006 s.342(4)(d).

[367] CA 2006 s.344(2).

[368] CA 2006 s.343(3)(b).

[369] CA 2006 s.360B(1), which prohibits any requirements in a traded company's articles that shares be deposited before the meeting or that shares not be transferred in the period of 48 hours before a meeting.

[370] CA 2006 s.360B(2).

[371] CA 2006 ss.793–797.

Given the powerful sanction, the company's right to seek the power to bar voting is subject to "proper purposes" constraints.[372]

Publicity for votes and resolutions

Whether or not an independent assessor is requested by the members, a quoted company is required to post on its website the text of any resolution voted on through a poll at a general meeting and give the details of the votes cast in favour of or against it.[373] This will include resolutions that are not passed. Again, failure to do so does not affect the validity of the resolution, but does constitute a criminal offence on the part of every officer in default. The UK Corporate Governance Code contains additional reporting and publicity requirements where 20% of the votes have been cast against the board, as the company "should explain, when announcing voting results, what actions it intends to take to consult shareholders in order to understand the reasons behind the result".[374] There subsequently needs to be an update within six months and then a final summary for the annual report. This limits the possibility of a "shareholder revolt" being swept under the carpet. **12–052**

Apart from this new requirement for quoted companies, the publicity requirements for the results of meetings are of a more traditional kind. Every company must keep records containing the minutes of all proceedings of general meetings and copies of resolutions passed otherwise than at meetings (for example, as written resolutions or by unanimous consent), and to keep those records for 10 years.[375] Those records must be open to inspection by any member of the company (but not by the public) free of charge, who, for a prescribed fee, may request a copy of them.[376] The place of inspection is the company's registered office or some other place permitted under regulations made by the Secretary of State.[377] Some resolutions of the company will, however, be available publicly because they have to be supplied to the Registrar. This is true in particular of special resolutions, including such resolutions passed by unanimous consent.[378]

The minutes of the meetings and the records of the resolutions have some legal significance. A record of a resolution passed other than at a meeting, if signed by a director or the company secretary, is evidence of the passing of the resolution, and the minutes of a meeting, if signed by the chair of that meeting or the following one, are evidence of the proceedings at that meeting. A record of proceedings at a meeting is deemed, unless the contrary is proved, to establish that the meeting was duly held, was conducted as recorded and all appointments

---

372 See *Eclairs Group Ltd v JKX Oil & Gas Plc* [2015] UKSC 71, discussed at paras 10–018 onwards.

373 CA 2006 s.341.

374 Financial Reporting Council, *UK Corporate Governance Code* (July 2018), s.1, para.4.

375 CA 2006 s.355. The provisions apply also to class meetings: see CA 2006 s.359.

376 CA 2006 s.358(3).

377 CA 2006 ss.358(1) and 1136.

378 CA 2006 ss.29–30.

made at it were valid. A record of a written resolution produces the same effect as to the requirements of the CA 2006 for passing written resolutions.[379]

"Empty" voting

12–053 The second problem identified above was that of members voting at the behest of non-members. In some cases, this is entirely legitimate. A nominee shareholder must vote as instructed by the beneficial owner. This is unproblematic because the effect of the rule is to reunite the voting right with the person who has the economic interest in the share.[380] The issue with "empty" voting is that the right to vote is in fact exercised by a person with no or only a limited economic interest in it, to the exclusion of the person with the greater economic interest. There are two principal ways in which such voting by those with no or only a limited economic interest in the shares can come about: contracts for differences (CfDs) and "stock lending".[381] Both are fairly sophisticated market arrangements, which do have a legitimate role, although their impact on the allocation of voting rights has not been fully thought through.

In the first case, a person typically contracts with a counterparty for the difference in the price of a security at two points in time, and the counterparty, at least in a "long" CfD, will purchase the security in question as a hedge against its exposure under the CfD. In practice, though not as a matter of law, the holder of the CfD can often determine the way in which the counterparty exercises the votes attached to the shares acquired as a hedge. In this way a non-owner with a limited economic exposure to the share becomes in practice able to vote it. We discuss CfDs further below when dealing with takeovers, which is the one area where regulation (relating to disclosure of interests in shares) has addressed them.[382]

The second common form of "empty" voting arises out of "stock lending". This is a misnomer. With stock lending the shares are not lent by their holder to someone else, rather, in return for a fee, the entire legal interest in the shares is transferred to the borrower, subject only to an obligation to re-transfer an equivalent number of shares (together with any dividend paid on them in the interim) upon demand by the lender. As the borrower has the entire legal interest in the shares, he similarly has all the associated rights to the shares, including the voting rights. This all looks to be as it should be, until it is appreciated that the borrower's purpose in this entire arrangement is not to take the risks associated with ownership, but simply to deal in the shares for reward, passing the risks of movement in share value either to those with whom he/she deals in the

---

379 CA 2006 s.356.

380 Though perhaps less clear, other rules conferring voting rights on non-members can be justified as giving the vote to the person with the primary economic interest in the share. See, for example, the unpaid vendor of shares (*Musselwhite v CH Musselwhite & Sons Ltd* [1962] Ch. 964; but cf. *Michaels v Harley House (Marylebone) Ltd* [2000] Ch. 104 CA (Civ Div)). Or the law may be indifferent as to the allocation by contract of the voting right as between two people each with an economic interest in the share: see *Puddephatt v Leith* [1916] 1 Ch. 200 Ch D (mortgagor and mortgagee).

381 ADRs (see para.12–020) can also give rise to empty voting unless the depository is required to pass the governance rights onto the holder of the depository receipt.

382 See generally paras 27–016 onwards. and para.28–044.

intervening period, or to the lender when equivalent shares are returned. Thus, in practical terms, the borrower has no economic interest in the shares because, no matter how they perform, the borrower's wealth remains the same. By the same token, the lender remains exposed to the performance of the shares, but has lost the voting rights for the period of the loan. Accordingly, the legal interest (and associated voting rights) in the shares are separated from their ultimate economic interest. Once this disassociation occurs, an "empty" voting problem arises, since the borrower will exercise the votes in pursuit of his/her own agenda, without regard to the longer-term interests of the company or shareholding body. Again, there is no formal regulation of the voting issues arising with stock lending. In a report for the Shareholder Voting Working Group,[383] Paul Myners reiterated his earlier recommendation that in the case of contentious votes "the lender should automatically recall the related stock, unless there are good economic reasons for not doing so. Failure to take such action could be extremely detrimental". The Report noted, however, that, in the case of institutional shareholders, where, often, the shares were held by a custodian under a direct contract with the institution, whilst the right to vote the shares was delegated to a fund manager under a separate contract with the institution, the fund manager might be unaware whether the shares held by the custodian had been "lent" (perhaps under an automatic stock lending programme) and so would not be in a position to ask for the re-transfer of their equivalent.[384]

Miscellaneous matters

Chairman

Every meeting needs a person to preside over it, if it is not to descend into chaos. **12–054**
The CA 2006 lays down the default rule that a member may be elected at the meeting by resolution to be its chair, but states that this procedure is subject to any provisions in the articles as to how that person is to be chosen.[385] The articles invariably do deal with the matter. The Model Articles for Public Companies[386] sensibly take the view that the chairman ought to be a member of the board and accordingly provide that the chairman of the board shall also be the chairman of the meeting, which is what normally happens. However, if the chairman of the board is not present within 10 minutes of the time appointed for the start of the meeting, the directors present must appoint a director or member to preside and, if there are no directors present, then those constituting the meeting do that job.

The position of chairman is an important and onerous one, for he or she will be in charge of the meeting and will be responsible for ensuring that its business

---

[383] *Review of the impediments to voting UK shares*, Report by Paul Myners to the Shareholder Voting Working Group (July 2007), p.20.

[384] This situation could also lead to the fund manager purporting to vote shares the custodian did not hold at the relevant time and to the manager's proxy instructions to the company being rejected by the company on the grounds that they related to more shares than were held.

[385] CA 2006 s.319.

[386] Companies (Model Articles) Regulations 2008 (SI 2008/3229) Sch.1 art.39 (private companies) and Sch.3 art.31 (public companies).

is properly conducted.[387] As chairman, he owes a duty to the meeting, not to the board of directors, even if he is a director.[388] He should see that the business of the meeting is efficiently conducted and that all shades of opinion are given a fair hearing. It is the chairman's role to ensure "that the sense of the meeting is properly ascertained with regard to any question which is properly before the meeting",[389] but there is no power to decide what resolutions on the agenda can or cannot be put to the meeting.[390] The role may entail taking snap decisions on points of order, motions, amendments and questions, often deliberately designed to harass him, and upon the correctness of his ruling the validity of any resolution may depend.[391] He will probably require the company's legal adviser to be at his elbow, and this is one of the occasions when even the most cautious lawyer will have to give advice without an opportunity of referring to the authorities.

Adjournments

12–055 One situation in which it may be necessary to adjourn is when the meeting is inquorate, but this is a rare situation in public companies, because the quorum requirement is so low, namely two persons. What may present problems is the converse case where those attending the meeting are too many rather than too few, and the meeting becomes chaotic. It should be emphasised that an adjournment of a meeting is to be distinguished from an abandonment of it. In the latter case, the meeting ends. If a new meeting is convened, new business, as well as any unfinished at the abandoned meeting, may be undertaken so long as proper notice is given of both. In contrast, if a meeting is adjourned, the adjourned meeting can undertake only the business of the original meeting[392] or such of it as had not been completed at that meeting. Indeed, it was thought necessary specifically to provide that where a resolution is passed at an adjourned meeting

---

[387] *Kaye v Oxford House (Wimbledon) Co Ltd* [2020] B.C.C. 117 at [106].

[388] See *Second Consolidated Trust v Ceylon Amalgamated Estates* [1943] 2 All E.R. 567. Conversely, it seems a director may act as chairman of the meeting even though a resolution to be debated is critical of the board's policy: see *Might SA v Redbus Interhouse Plc* [2003] EWHC 3514 (Ch); [2004] 2 B.C.L.C. 449.

[389] *Kaye v Oxford House (Wimbledon) Co Ltd* [2020] B.C.C. 117 at [106].

[390] *Kaye v Oxford House (Wimbledon) Co Ltd* [2020] B.C.C. 117 at [109], applying *National Dwellings Society v Sykes* [1894] 3 Ch. 159 Ch D at 162. Accordingly, where there was "no practical utility in continuing with the meeting because the views of the meeting could not be obtained without the prior question as to who was entitled to exercise votes", the chairman could exercise his or her power to adjourn: see *Findmyclaims.com Ltd v Howe* [2018] EWHC 1833 at [22].

[391] For the sort of situation with which the chairman may have to cope if the members of a public company turn up in far larger numbers than the board has foreseen, see *Byng v London Life Association Ltd* [1990] Ch. 170, where his well-meaning efforts were in vain and the company had to convene a new meeting.

[392] Companies (Model Articles) Regulations 2008 (SI 2008/3229) Sch.1 art.41(6) and Sch.3 art.33(6). But a meeting can be adjourned despite the fact that it was not a meeting at which any substantive resolution could be passed: see *Byng v London Life Association Ltd* [1990] Ch. 170. This must be right for otherwise an inquorate meeting could not be adjourned, as all Tables A have provided that they can.

it shall "for all purposes be treated as having been passed on the date on which it was in fact passed and is not to be deemed to be passed on any earlier date".[393]

The grounds for adjournment are normally set out in the articles. The Model Articles for Public Companies provide for adjournment if those present agree, either at the chairman's suggestion or by adopting a resolution to that effect of their own motion.[394] Basically, this gives effect to the common law rule under which the chairman has no general right to adjourn a meeting if there are no circumstances preventing its effective continuance.[395] A chairman does have a residual common law power to adjourn the meeting "so as to give all persons entitled a reasonable opportunity of speaking at the meeting and of voting".[396] Similarly, where the meeting had "no practical utility" it can be adjourned.[397] Responding to the difficulties demonstrated in *Byng v London Life Association Ltd*,[398] the model article now further provides that the chairman may unilaterally adjourn a meeting if "it appears to the chairman of the meeting that an adjournment is necessary to protect the safety of any person attending the meeting or ensure that the business of the meeting is conducted in an orderly manner". This part of the model article does no more, however, than reflect the position at common law. Helpfully, in *Byng*,[399] this element of the common law power was held to continue to operate, even though the company's articles, reflecting the earlier model sets of articles, contained an express power to adjourn only with the consent of the meeting. That said, the power and duty must be exercised bona fide for the purpose of facilitating the meeting and not as a ploy to prevent or delay the taking of a decision to which the chairman objects[400]; and the chairman's exercise of the common law power must be a reasonable one.[401]

Finally, under the model articles, no notice has to be given if a meeting is adjourned for less than 14 days; otherwise, seven days' clear notice must be given.[402] Clearly if the adjournment is a temporary one and the meeting is resumed at the same place on the same day, this is fair enough; but, otherwise, it seems unfair to members who may, perhaps through no fault of their own, have found themselves unable to attend the meeting as they had intended. As a result, they may not know that it has been adjourned and may be prevented from exercising their rights to attend the adjourned meeting.

---

393 CA 2006 s.332. Were it otherwise, the company might unavoidably contravene the obligation to deliver to the Registrar a copy of the resolution within 15 days of its passage, as required, in the case of a considerable number of resolutions, under the CA 2006 s.380.

394 Companies (Model Articles) Regulations 2008 (SI 2008/3229) Sch.3 art.33. See also Companies (Model Articles) Regulations 2008 (SI 2008/3229) Sch.1 art.41, for private companies.

395 *National Dwellings Society v Sykes* [1897] 3 Ch. 159; *John v Rees* [1970] Ch. 345 Ch D (which concerned, not a company meeting, but one of a Divisional Labour Party); *Byng v London Life Association Ltd* [1990] Ch. 170; *Kaye v Oxford House (Wimbledon) Co Ltd* [2020] B.C.C. 117 at [106]–[107].

396 *Kaye v Oxford House (Wimbledon) Co Ltd* [2020] B.C.C. 117 at [108].

397 *Findmyclaims.com Ltd v Howe* [2018] EWHC 1833 at [22].

398 *Byng v London Life Association Ltd* [1990] Ch. 170.

399 *Byng v London Life Association Ltd* [1990] Ch. 170.

400 *Kaye v Oxford House (Wimbledon) Co Ltd* [2020] B.C.C. 117 at [123]. If the chairman purports to adjourn for such a reason, the meeting may elect another chairman and continue.

401 *Byng v London Life Association Ltd* [1990] Ch. 170.

402 Companies (Model Articles) Regulations 2008 (SI 2008/3229) Sch.3 art.33.

Class meetings

12–056 In addition to general meetings, it may be necessary to convene separate meetings of classes of members or debenture-holders (for example, to consider variation of rights) or of creditors (for example, in connection with a reconstruction or in a winding up). Again, the rules to be observed will depend on the company's articles construed in the light of the general law relating to meetings. However, the CA 2006 does provide that, for meetings of classes of shareholder, the statutory rules apply as they apply to general meetings, with some modifications.[403] The most important of the shareholder protections that are not applied are the members' power to require the directors to convene a meeting and the power of the court to order a meeting.[404] As will be considered further,[405] the company, if it wishes to take certain steps, may be obliged to seek the consent of a class of shareholders and convene a meeting for that purpose, but the class has no general right on its own to meet to consider issues that concern it. On the other hand, some protections are more extensive at class meetings called to vary the rights of the class members: the two people constituting the quorum must represent at least one-third of the nominal value of the class of shares in question, except at an adjourned class meeting[406]; and any one member may demand a poll.[407]

In practice, very similar arrangements are incorporated in debenture trust deeds to regulate the conduct of meetings of debenture-holders.

At class meetings all members other than those of the class ought to be excluded, but if for convenience a joint meeting is held of the company and all separate classes, followed by separate polls, the court will not interfere if no objection has been taken by anyone present.[408]

Forms of communication by the company

12–057 Much of this chapter has concerned information (about meetings, for example) that is required to be supplied by the company to its members. In the case of AGMs of public companies that material will typically include the company's annual accounts and reports,[409] which are today quite bulky documents. One important issue, therefore, is the form that the communication takes. That may be by traditional hard copy, electronically or by publication on the company's website. The CA 2006 takes some tentative steps towards encouraging the use of the latter two forms of communication, whilst not depriving members of their traditional supply of hard copy, if they wish to have it. Thus, the CA 2006 provides that, where a member has received a communication otherwise than in

---

[403] CA 2006 ss.334 and 352 (and s.335 deals with class meetings of companies without share capital).

[404] CA 2006 ss.334(2) and 335(2). See also paras 12–028 to 12–031.

[405] See further Ch.13.

[406] CA 2006 ss.334(4) and 335(4). At an adjourned meeting one person holding shares of the class or his proxy suffices. This makes sense only if the adjournment is because there was no quorum at the original meeting.

[407] CA 2006 ss.334(6) and 335(5).

[408] *Carruth v ICI* [1937] A.C. 707 HL.

[409] See further Ch.22.

hard copy (i.e. electronically or via a website), that member is entitled to be sent, without charge, a hard copy version of the document upon request within 21 days.[410]

More generally, before a company can validly communicate with a member,[411] otherwise than in hard copy, the consent or deemed consent of that member must be obtained. Electronic communication of documents is permitted only if the member has consented to that form of communication, either generally or for a specific class of documents.[412] As to website communication, that is permitted only if there has been actual agreement by the particular member,[413] as for electronic communication, or there has been deemed agreement. Deemed agreement arises where (1) the company's articles provide for website communication or the members have resolved to permit it; and (2) the particular member has been asked by the company to agree to website communication for all or a particular class of documents and the company has not received a response within 28 days.[414] The deemed agreement may be revoked at any time by the member, but the burden is on the member to take this step.[415] To the extent that the deemed consent provisions apply to website communication only, it can be said that the CA 2006 puts more pressure on members to accept that form of communication than to accept electronic documents.

However, website communication has a number of disadvantages for the member over receiving an electronic document, which the CA 2006 aims to redress. First, unless the member constantly monitors the relevant website, he or she may not be aware of the availability of the document. Thus, the company is required to notify the member of the availability of the document, the address of the website and how to access the document.[416] This communication could be via an electronic document, if the member has consented to that form of communication. (Self-evidently, notification via the website itself will not do!) Secondly, hard copy or electronic communication gives the member their own copy of the document, whereas, unless downloaded, the member will lose access to the document when it is removed from the website. Thus, minimum rules are set for the period during which the document must be available on the website. This is 28 days from the date on which the member was notified, as above, unless

---

[410] CA 2006 s.1145.

[411] "Person" is the term used in the CA 2006 Sch.5 in relation to actual consent, so that its provisions embrace not just members but also those to whom governance rights have been transferred or information rights have been given (see para.12–018). The deemed consent provisions (see below) apply only to "members" but that term is expanded to include the two groups mentioned in the previous sentence: CA 2006 Sch.5 para.10(1).

[412] CA 2006 Sch.5 para.6.

[413] CA 2006 Sch.5 para.9(a).

[414] CA 2006 Sch.5 para.10(2)–(3). The request may be repeated at twelve-monthly intervals if it does not produce acceptance or deemed acceptance. Similar provisions exist for debenture-holders: CA 2006 Sch.5 para.11.

[415] CA 2006 Sch.5 para.9(b).

[416] CA 2006 Sch.5 para.13(1).

a specific section of the CA 2006 sets a different period.[417] There are a number of such specific provisions relating to the passing of resolutions.[418]

Forms of communication to the company

12–058 Where the company is the communicator, it is likely to be anxious to move away from the obligation to supply hard copy. When it is the potential receiver of communications, it may not be as anxious to facilitate the members' task. With members' communications to the company, we are necessarily concerned with their freedom to use electronic communications, rather than website-based communication. The general rule in the CA 2006 is that the company is not obliged to accept electronic communications from other persons, unless it has actually consented to this method of communication or is deemed to have accepted it.[419] Important for our purposes is that the CA 2006 provides, where a company gives an electronic address in a notice calling a meeting or in a document from the company inviting the appointment of proxies, it is deemed to have agreed that any document relating to the meeting or proxy solicitation may be sent to it electronically at that address.[420] In some other cases, the CA 2006 simply imposes a mandatory obligation on the company to accept communication in electronic form, for example, with regard to communication of assent to a written resolution.[421] Of course, a difficulty with electronic communications is authentication. What is the equivalent of a signature on a hard copy? Section 1146 provides that an electronic communication is authenticated if the identity of the sender is confirmed in the manner specified by the company or, in the absence of such specification, the document contains a statement of the identity of the sender and the company has no reason to doubt the truth of that statement.

CONCLUSION

12–059 At the beginning of this chapter, it was pointed out that the Company Law Review recommended reforms to improve the governance rights of shareholders, as part of its policy of making a shareholder-centred system of company law operate properly. The exercise of governance rights by shareholders may not be the only or even the most effective way of providing accountability on the part of management to shareholders—the threat of a takeover bid is probably more potent—but governance rights are certainly an important element of the

[417] CA 2006 Sch.5 para.14. The CA 2006 does often require a longer period, for example, quoted companies being required to maintain website availability of the annual accounts and reports until the next set is available: ibid. s.430. There are also minimum standards set for the quality of the website: CA 2006 Sch.5 para.12.

[418] For example, the CA 2006 s.299 (written resolutions: period is from date of circulation to date resolution lapses); s.309 (general meetings: date of notification to date of conclusion of meeting, which would include any adjournment of it). The latter section is also a little more prescriptive about the detail of the notification to be given when it concerns website documents for a general meeting.

[419] CA 2006 Sch.4 para.6.

[420] CA 2006 s.333.

[421] CA 2006 s.296(2).

accountability structure of company law. Having looked at the detail of the current law, how have the proposals of the CLR fared?

There has certainly been a great deal of tidying up and modernisation, notably the facilitation of electronic communication. Moreover, the amendments at EU level to the Shareholder Rights Directive ("rights" being somewhat of a misnomer in relation to the amendments) have imposed hard law obligations on the institutional shareholders in relation to their interactions with investee companies. Although framed formally as disclosure requirements, they are likely to lead to some behavioural changes. Beyond that, in relation to private companies, the written resolution provisions are now much simpler and likely to be more attractive, especially with the abandonment of the requirement of unanimity. For public companies, a major focus of concern was voting by the institutional shareholders, in terms of both the importance institutions attached to voting and the technical difficulties faced by indirect shareholders in casting their votes. The Company Law Review proposed to rely mainly upon market developments and governmental suasion, rather than mandatory legal rules, to deal with both problems. Thus, there were to be fall-back powers only for the Secretary of State to require disclosure of voting by institutional shareholders[422] or to facilitate voting by indirect shareholders. As a result of pressure in Parliament, the fall-back powers designed to overcome the technical barriers to voting by indirect shareholders were given a slightly harder edge, in relation to information provision by quoted companies, but remain otherwise of a fall-back nature.[423] Meanwhile, policy-makers' understanding of the technical problems of voting has expanded with the development of the idea of "empty voting", a topic hardly touched on by the Company Law Review, but it is not clear, even to the Shareholder Voting Working Party, consisting of those professionally involved in the area, what the correct solution should be.[424]

Finally, the Company Law Review placed great store on the alignment of the AGM cycle with that for company reporting. Formally, that has been achieved, but the Government did not implement the further reform intended to take advantage of the alignment. This was the statutory "pause" of two weeks after circulation of the accounts and reports, during which members would be able to formulate resolutions, to be circulated by the company free of charge, to be debated at the AGM. This was undoubtedly a lost opportunity to turn the AGM into a more significant event.

---

[422] CA 2006 ss.277 onwards. See paras 12–013 onwards.

[423] See para.12–021.

[424] See *Review of the impediments to voting UK shares*, Report by Paul Myners to the Shareholder Voting Working Group (July 2007). See also Shareholder Voting Working Group, *Discussion Paper on Shareholder Proxy Voting* (July 2015) available at: *http://uk.practicallaw.com/9-616-7485* [Accessed 1 January 2021].

CHAPTER 13

CONTROLLING MEMBERS' VOTING

INTRODUCTION

In any company law system, a number of techniques are in principle available to control the unfair exercise of voting power by the majority of shareholders. Perhaps the most obvious technique is that the law could identify certain decisions that the majority is simply not permitted to take. There are one or two examples of this technique. First, a member is not bound by an alteration of the articles after the date upon which he or she became a member if its effect is to require the member to take more shares in the company or to increase in any other way the member's liability to contribute to the company's share capital or otherwise pay money to the company.[1] A shareholder must specifically agree in writing to such an alteration before being so bound.[2] In other words, the size of a shareholder's investment in the company is a matter for individual, not collective, decision. Secondly, there is a (admittedly controversial) common law rule whereby conflicted majority shareholders cannot ratify wrongdoing by a director **13–001**

[1] CA 2006 s.25(1).

[2] CA 2006 s.25(2).

that involves the appropriation by the director of corporate property.[3] That said, it is impossible for the legislature or the judges to identify in advance very many substantive decisions that should be prohibited on the basis that they will be unfair to the dissenting minority or the company itself. Assessments based on what is unfair or not are usually fact-specific and therefore not generally appropriate for ex ante decision-making on the part of the rule-maker.

Given the challenges of identifying such transactions, an obvious response would be to shift the focus from substance to procedure. Indeed, the CA 2006 does make much greater use of rules that determine *how* the shareholders are to make decisions, rather than *what* decision to reach. Whilst management decisions are generally vested in the board, the CA 2006 identifies a number of powers reserved for shareholders.[4] Often those decisions must also be taken by a three-quarter majority of those voting (a "supermajority") rather than a simple majority (an "ordinary majority"). Whilst the statutory categorisation of decisions requiring supermajority voting, rather than ordinary voting, is not entirely consistent in policy terms, decisions affecting the rights of the shareholders under the constitution generally require a supermajority. Supermajority voting does not obviate all issues of unfairness to minority shareholders, but it does reduce the incidence of such problems because only one quarter of the votes is needed to block a resolution.

13–002 An intermediate approach between using substantive and procedural protections is to leave the shareholders largely free to take whatever substantive decision they wish, and to focus controls on those aspects of the decision that are most likely to prejudice the minority shareholders. Such protection often takes the form of rules requiring equal treatment of shareholders or equal sharing of benefits.[5] An example of the first technique arises when a premium-listed company repurchases its shares through market purchases,[6] since the Listing Rules seek to ensure equal shareholder treatment by either controlling the price at which the repurchase is made or requiring the repurchase to be made by way of a tender offer to all shareholders.[7] This goes some way towards preventing insiders from taking undue advantage of the repurchase exercise or shifting the balance of power within the company even further in the majority's favour. An example of the second technique is the common law requirement (now contained in the model articles[8]) that dividends be paid equally to shareholders in proportion to their shareholdings. The common law took the nominal value of the shares as its reference point for equality,[9] although the articles often use the amount paid up on the shares as the relevant touchstone when the nominal value differs from the

[3] See para.10–118.
[4] See paras 11–011 onwards.
[5] For a statement of shareholder equality as general company law principle, see *Marex Financial Ltd v Sevilleja* [2020] UKSC 31; [2020] B.C.C. 783 at [103]. See generally C. Hare, "The Principle of Equal Treatment of Shareholders in English Law" in P Jung, *Der Gleichbehandlungsgrundsatz im Gesellschaftsrecht* (Mohr Siebeck, 2021), Ch.1.
[6] See further para.17–020.
[7] Listing Rules LR 12.4.1–2.
[8] Companies (Model Articles) Regulations 2008 (SI 2008/3229) Sch.1 art.30(4) and Sch.3 art.70(4).
[9] *Birch v Cropper* (1889) 14 App. Cas. 525 HL.

amount paid up.[10] Such a requirement makes it difficult for the majority shareholders to use the mechanism of dividend distribution to allocate a disproportionate share of the company's earnings to themselves.[11] As considered above,[12] equivalent norms of equality generally apply to shareholders' voting and capital entitlements.

In addition to controlling the substance or process of decision-making, five further (more innovative) techniques have been developed. First, the statutory derivative action enables a minority shareholder to commence proceedings in the company's name and thus makes it more difficult for a controlling shareholder/director to stymie corporate claims against wrongdoing directors or related third parties.[13] At a procedural level, the derivative action allows minority shareholders to invoke the court's assistance in side-stepping the majority's control of the board or shareholder decision-making processes in order to initiate litigation. Further, although a derivative action is not available if the shareholders have ratified the wrongdoing in question,[14] the CA 2006 prevents interested directors from voting on a shareholder resolution to ratify the wrongdoing.[15] This minority shareholder protection certainly has a strong procedural element by excluding the votes of those interested in the litigation decision,[16] but the rather novel technique also involves shifting the locus for decision-making from the board to the general meeting and, if that fails, to the minority shareholders acting as an independent corporate organ.[17] 13–003

Secondly, the Listing Rules (applicable to premium-listed companies) employ a disenfranchisement technique (in a similar manner to the ratification decision considered above), whereby controllers are excluded from voting on a particular decision in which they are interested. In particular, the Listing Rules (but not the CA 2006) require shareholder approval of transactions with a "related party"[18] and preclude the related party from voting on the issue, as well as imposing a requirement that the related party "take all reasonable steps to ensure that the related party's associates do not vote on the relevant resolution".[19] Crucially, the term "related party" includes a "substantial shareholder",[20] which is in turn widely defined so as to include a person who can control 10% or more of the voting rights in the company or who can exercise substantial control over the

[10] Companies (Model Articles) Regulations 2008 (SI 2008/3229) Sch.3 art.71. There is no equivalent provision for private companies, as all shares (other than those initially subscribed) must be fully paid as to nominal value and any premium: SI 2008/3229 Sch.1 art.21.

[11] This provides a possible rationale for the exemption of dividends from the rules on financial assistance, especially as creditors are also protected by the rule that dividends are only payable out of distributable profits: see CA 2006 s.681(2).

[12] See further paras 6–004 to 6–005.

[13] For detailed discussion of the derivative action, see further Ch.15.

[14] CA 2006 s.263(2).

[15] CA 2006 s.239(4).

[16] The views of the independent shareholders are given a particularly prominent role in the court's discretion whether or not to allow a derivative claim: see CA 2006 s.263(4).

[17] Consider *Alexander Ward & Co Ltd v Samyang Navigation Co Ltd* [1975] 1 W.L.R. 673 HL.

[18] Listing Rules LR 11.1.7(3).

[19] Listing Rules LR 11.1.7(4).

[20] Listing Rules LR 11.1.4.

company.[21] A related party also includes an "associate" of such a person, which is widely defined in a similar manner to the notion of "connected person" in the CA 2006.[22] Moreover, a "related party transaction" is widely defined, so as to include not only transactions between the company and the related party, but also transactions in which the company and related party together finance a transaction or project or any other similar transaction that benefits the related party.[23]

Thirdly, where a minority shareholder disagrees with particular majority decisions, he or she may be provided with the right to exit the company at a fair price. Such exit rights are termed "appraisal" rights. Crucially, they are not simply rights to exit the company (which a shareholder in a listed company hardly needs), but the right to leave at a fair price. Whilst this is a well-developed minority protection remedy in some company law systems,[24] this technique is little used in this jurisdiction. This is perhaps because, whether the right is to be bought out by the company or by the majority shareholder, the effect of such appraisal rights is to place a potentially substantial financial hurdle in the way of certain corporate decisions. That said, a form of appraisal right can be found in provisions dealing with the reorganisation of companies in liquidation.[25] More importantly, both the CA 2006[26] and the Takeover Code provide for appraisal rights where there has been an acquisition or transfer of a controlling bloc of shares in the company. This second exit right is not tied to the taking of any particular business decision, but rather to a shift in the composition of the shareholding body, on the basis that a change in the identity of the controller of the company may well have an adverse impact upon the minority shareholders.[27] In addition, British company law allows a minority shareholder to be bought out of the company on a much more general basis where the shareholder can establish the existence of unfairly prejudicial conduct.[28]

Fourthly, outside the controls on shareholder voting described below, the traditional position in British company law is that shareholders do not owe fiduciary duties to their company or to other shareholders, but the contrary is the case in certain other jurisdictions, and the issue is attracting academic attention in this jurisdiction.[29] Indeed, in *Children's Investment Fund Foundation (UK) v Attorney General*,[30] the Supreme Court considered that the members of a

---

[21] Listing Rules LR 11.1.4A.

[22] CA 2006 s.252.

[23] Listing Rules LR 11.1.5. The closest that the general law comes to requiring shareholders' approval of transactions with significant shareholders is where that shareholder falls within the category of "shadow director" and thus is subject to the statutory self-dealing rules. See further Ch.10.

[24] See, for example, CA 1993 (NZ) ss.110–115.

[25] IA 1986 ss.110–111.

[26] CA 2006 ss.983–985.

[27] The CA 2006 recognises the exit right only if the new controller holds 90% of the voting rights after a takeover bid, whereas the Takeover Code gives an exit opportunity at the 30% level, no matter how the 30% has been acquired.

[28] CA 2006 s.994(1), discussed in detail in Ch.14.

[29] For the imposition of such duties on majority shareholders in other jurisdictions, see generally H. Birkmose, *Shareholders' Duties* (Kluwer Law International, 2017); E. Lim, *A Case for Shareholders' Fiduciary Duties in Common Law Asia* (Cambridge University Press, 2019).

[30] *Children's Investment Fund Foundation (UK) v Attorney General* [2020] UKSC 33; [2020] 3 W.L.R. 461.

charitable company limited by guarantee owed a fiduciary duty of loyalty to the company's charitable purposes when the company's constitution contained restrictions on members receiving profits from the company. Whilst this decision is clearly limited to the special context of charitable companies, it may nevertheless provide a basis for the more general development of shareholder fiduciary duties in the future. Such a development should, it is suggested, be approached with extreme caution, if at all.

Beyond summarising the above techniques, most of which are considered in more detail in other chapters, this chapter focuses on three further issues concerning minority shareholder protection. The first issue concerns the court's power to review the majority shareholders' decision on the ground that it is in some sense unfair to the minority. As noted above, the CA 2006 makes express provision for such a review in certain instances, but here the issue is whether the common law provides a more generalised right of review. This obviates the difficulty of having to predict in advance those decisions that are acceptable and those that are not, since the majority's decision is subject to ex post judicial scrutiny on a case-by-case basis. The second issue concerns whether groups of shareholders who hold class rights should have some veto right over majority decisions that particularly impact those rights. In some ways, this is the inverse of the policy we noted earlier that excludes interested parties from voting on certain decisions. Here, by contrast, the interested parties (the holders of the class rights) need protecting from the non-holders who might seek to harm them, and this is achieved by specifying that the holders are entitled to vote and the non-holders are not. The third issue concerns whether it is possible to reduce the risk of minority shareholders unwittingly placing themselves in a vulnerable position by ensuring that they are aware of the company's shareholding ownership. This has been addressed by increasing disclosure of those persons with "significant control" of the company. Once each of these legal techniques has been addressed, attention will turn to the self-help options available to minority shareholders. 13–004

REVIEW OF SHAREHOLDERS' DECISIONS: BONA FIDE FOR THE BENEFIT OF THE COMPANY AS A WHOLE

The starting point

Throughout the decisions are scattered statements that members must exercise their votes "bona fide for the benefit of the company as a whole",[31] which, if read casually, might suggest that shareholders are subject at common law to precisely 13–005

[31] The original source of this oft-repeated (but potentially misleading) expression seems to be Lindley MR in *Allen v Gold Reefs of West Africa* [1900] 1 Ch. 656 CA at 671–672: "The power thus conferred on companies to alter their articles is limited only by the provisions contained in the statute and the conditions contained in the company's memorandum of association. Wide, however, as the language of [the Act] is, the power conferred by it must, like all other powers, be exercised subject to those general principles of law and equity which are applicable to all powers conferred on majorities enabling them to bind minorities. It must be exercised, not only in the manner required by law, but also bona fide for the benefit of the company as a whole, and it must not be exceeded. These conditions are always implied, and are seldom, if ever, expressed".

the same basic principle as directors. This would be highly misleading, however, and there is no judicial support for such a parallel.[32] Quite to the contrary, it has repeatedly been stated that votes are proprietary rights, which (like other incidents of shares) the holder may exercise in his or her own selfish interests, even if these are opposed to the company's interest.[33] A shareholder may even enter into a contract to vote or not vote in a particular way, which contract may be enforced by injunction provided that the company is not privy to the agreement.[34] Moreover, directors (even though personally interested) can typically vote freely in their capacity as shareholders at the general meeting,[35] unless the CA 2006, the articles or the Listing Rules specifically deprive them of the right to vote.[36] This even applies to those transactions that the CA 2006 requires the general meeting to approve in advance.[37] Accordingly, as stated by Lady Arden in *Children's Investment Fund Foundation (UK) v Attorney General*,[38] "members of companies are not normally fiduciaries in relation to any of their powers". Unlike directors' powers, shareholders' voting rights are not conferred upon them in order that they be exercised in such a way as to prefer the interests of others over the interests of the voting shareholder, where these conflict (as the fiduciary rule would require). This is so whether those others are seen to be "the company" or the minority shareholders or, indeed, any other group.

To deny the fiduciary character of shareholders' voting rights, and to assert their proprietary nature, does not necessarily mean that the exercise of shareholders' voting powers are, or should be, unconstrained by the law.[39] The controlling shareholders may not generally be required to exercise their votes in the best interests of the company or the non-controlling shareholders, but this does not mean that they may trample over the latter's interests with impunity. Although British law has no general abuse of rights doctrine,[40] there are many situations in the general law (and not just within company law) where the exercise of property rights or personal powers is subject to some sort of judicial

---

[32] This may no longer be the case for charitable companies, see *Children's Investment Fund Foundation (UK) v Attorney General* [2020] 3 W.L.R. 461.

[33] *North-West Transportation Co v Beatty* (1887) 12 App. Cas. 589 PC; *Burland v Earle* [1902] A.C. 83 PC; *Goodfellow v Nelson Line* [1912] 2 Ch. 324 Ch D. See also *Children's Investment Fund Foundation (UK) v Attorney General* [2020] 3 W.L.R. 461 at [88].

[34] *Greenwell v Porter* [1902] 1 Ch. 530 Ch D; *Puddephatt v Leith* [1916] 1 Ch. 200 Ch D (mandatory injunction granted). See also *Russell v Northern Bank Development Corporation Ltd* [1992] 1 W.L.R. 588 HL.

[35] For the exceptional cases, see, for example, *Cook v Deeks* [1916] 1 A.C. 554 PC, and the discussion in para.10–118, but for the generality, see *North West Transportation Co v Beatty* (1887) 12 App. Cas. 589 PC; *Burland v Earle* [1902] A.C. 83 PC at 93; *Harris v A Harris Ltd* (1936) S.C. 183 IH (2 Div); *Baird v Baird & Co*, 1949 S.L.T. 368 OH. See also *Northern Counties Securities Ltd v Jackson & Steeple Ltd* [1974] 1 W.L.R. 1133 Ch D, where it was held that, although to comply with an undertaking given by the company to the court the directors were bound to recommend the shareholders to vote for a resolution, the directors (in their capacity as shareholders) could vote against the resolution, if so minded.

[36] See, for example, CA 2006 s.239, excluding the interested director from voting on a resolution to ratify his or her wrongdoing and the provisions on related-party transactions in Listing Rules LR11.

[37] CA 2006 s.188–226F, considered in Ch.11.

[38] *Children's Investment Fund Foundation (UK) v Attorney General* [2020] 3 W.L.R. 461 at [88].

[39] For recognition of the need for such constraints (at least in relation to charitable companies), see *Children's Investment Fund Foundation (UK) v Attorney General* [2020] 3 W.L.R. 461.

[40] *Allen v Flood* [1898] A.C. 1 HL.

review. Accordingly, the issue that arises is not one of principle, but whether the courts or legislature can develop working criteria for the effective review of majority shareholders' decisions. Whilst this task was addressed at an early stage by the courts, the results of that exercise have not been spectacularly successful. The courts have hovered uncomfortably between an unwillingness to determine how businesses should be run and an equally deeply felt unease that simple majoritarianism would leave the minority exposed to opportunistic behaviour.

This balance that the courts have found so difficult to develop and apply to shareholder decisions was first articulated by the Court of Appeal in *Allen v Gold Reefs of West Africa Ltd*.[41] In the context of a vote to alter the company's articles, the Court of Appeal held that, because the power to alter the articles was a power that enabled the majority to bind the minority, it must therefore be exercised "not only in the manner required by law, but also bona fide for the benefit of the company as a whole, and it must not be exceeded. These conditions are always implied, and are seldom, if ever, expressed". Indeed, the existence of this principle has been confirmed recently by the Supreme Court[42] and the Privy Council.[43] Whilst the statement of principle in *Allen* might be thought to embrace ideas related to the absence of power, good faith, and abuse of power, the judicial focus has been almost exclusively on determining the meaning of the phrase, "bona fide for the benefit of the company as a whole". In attempting this task, it is useful to divide the cases into those where the shareholders' decision clearly concerns and affects the company's rights and those where the resolution does not have that effect, but merely impacts the members' rights as between themselves.[44] In the latter category, it is possible to subdivide the authorities into constitutional alterations involving an expropriation of a member's shares, and those not having that effect, although all these distinctions are becoming less marked more recently. **13–006**

Resolutions where the company's interests are centre stage

Like any legal person, a company can forgive directors for the wrongs they do it. This inevitably comes at a financial cost to the company, since it abandons an otherwise valuable claim. Nevertheless, that decision can be taken by the general meeting for perfectly proper reasons. That said, the reasons are unlikely to be considered "perfectly proper" when the decision is carried by the votes of the wrongdoing directors themselves. This is true even if the range of "perfectly proper" reasons is very much at large; there is something unpalatable about forgiveness driven by the wrongdoers themselves. In the context of directors' wrongdoing, the common law has struggled between holding certain decisions "unratifiable" (i.e. the general meeting simply does not have the power to act) and, alternatively, disenfranchising the interested shareholder-directors (i.e. **13–007**

41 *Allen v Gold Reefs of West Africa Ltd* [1900] 1 Ch. 656 CA, cited at fn.31.

42 *Children's Investment Fund Foundation (UK) v Attorney General* [2020] 3 W.L.R. 461 at [88]–[89]; *Marex Financial Ltd v Sevilleja* [2020] B.C.C. 783 at [127].

43 *Re Stanford International Bank Ltd* [2019] UKPC 45 at [97].

44 Consider Rixon, "Competing Interests and Conflicting Principles: An Examination of the Power of Alteration of Articles of Association" (1986) 49 M.L.R. 446.

focusing on the propriety of their decision-making).[45] The current preference in the CA 2006 is for the latter approach.[46] The same tension is evident in other contexts: for example, the common law has denied shareholders the right to dispose of corporate assets when the company is insolvent;[47] but also occasionally disenfranchised shareholders considered to be hopelessly conflicted.[48]

Resolutions more generally

13–008 However intuitively compelling these approaches, they are rarely defended on the basis of principle. That makes it difficult to settle on the appropriate approach in the more difficult, and more common, cases. These are where the general meeting undoubtedly has the power to take a decision, but the majority's objective is not straightforwardly to advance the interests of the company (although sometimes it can be framed that way), but merely to determine relative rights as between the shareholders. In this context, it is inevitable that the majority's preferences will prevail, even in circumstances where there can be no rational complaint that the decision was somehow inappropriate or improper. Whilst it is clear that these decisions are reviewable on the basis of the statement of principle in *Allen*, the current position (with some understatement) has been described as "somewhat untidy".[49] Indeed, what makes it even more difficult to ascertain the precise limits of the *Allen* principle is that it is increasingly being applied in very different contexts, such as the variation of syndicated loans,[50] bond restructurings[51] and class conflicts in schemes of arrangement.[52]

Resolutions to expropriate members' shares

13–009 In expropriation (or compulsory transfer) cases, the arguments for judicial intervention might seem to be at their strongest, but the law falls far short of prohibiting constitutional changes aimed at introducing such clauses. On the

---

45 *Prudential Assurance Co Ltd v Newman Industries Ltd (No.2)* [1981] Ch. 257 Ch D; *Smith v Croft (No.3)* [1987] B.C.L.C. 365.

46 CA 2006 ss.180 and 239.

47 See *West Mercia Safetywear Ltd v Dodd* [1988] B.C.L.C. 250 CA; *Aveling Barford v Perion Ltd* [1989] B.C.L.C. 626 Ch D; *Re DKG Contractors Ltd* [1990] B.C.C. 903 Ch D; *Official Receiver v Stern* [2001] EWCA Civ 1787; [2002] 1 B.C.L.C. 119 at 129. See also *Madoff Securities International Ltd v Raven* [2013] EWHC 3147 (Comm) at [272]–[288]; *Goldtrail Travel Ltd (In Liquidation) v Aydin* [2014] EWHC 1587 (Ch) at [113]–[118]; *BTI 2014 LLC v Sequana SA* [2019] EWCA Civ 112; [2019] B.C.C. 631.

48 In *Bamford v Bamford* [1970] Ch. 212 CA, the directors had issued shares for improper purposes. When it was sought to ratify that decision, it was conceded that the holders of the newly issued shares could not vote.

49 *Constable v Executive Connections Ltd* [2005] EWHC 3 (Ch); [2005] 2 B.C.L.C. 638, where the judge refused to dispose of an expropriation claim summarily.

50 *Redwood Master Fund Ltd v TD Bank Europe Ltd* [2002] EWHC 2703 (Ch) at [81]–[107].

51 *Assénagon Asset Management SA v Irish Bank Resolution Corporation Ltd* [2012] EWHC 2090 (Ch) at [40]–[49]; *Azevedo v Imcopa Importacao E Industria De Oleos Ltda* [2013] EWCA Civ 364; [2014] 1 B.C.L.C. 72.

52 *Re Dee Valley Group Plc* [2017] EWHC 184 (Ch); [2018] Ch. 55.

contrary, it is clear that compulsory transfer articles may be introduced into the company's constitution. The debate, however, concerns the level of judicial scrutiny to which such amendments will be subject. In *Brown v British Abrasive Wheel Co*,[53] a public company was in urgent need of further capital, which shareholders, holding 98% of the shares, were willing to put up. The shareholders were only willing to do so, however, if they could buy out the 2% minority. Having failed to persuade the minority to sell, the majority proposed a special resolution that would add to the articles a provision requiring any shareholder to transfer his shares upon a request in writing by the holders of 90% of the shares. Whilst such a provision could have been validly inserted into the original articles,[54] and although the good faith of the majority was not challenged, the court held that the addition of a general provision enabling the majority to expropriate the minority could not be for the benefit of the company as a whole, but was solely for the benefit of the majority. Accordingly, an injunction was granted restraining the company from passing the resolution. The decision in *Brown* was, however, almost immediately "distinguished" by the Court of Appeal in *Sidebottom v Kershaw, Leese & Co Ltd*.[55] In *Sidebottom*, a director-controlled private company had a minority shareholder who had an interest in a competing business. Objecting to this, the company passed a special resolution adding to the articles a provision empowering the directors to require any shareholder who competed with the company to sell his or her shares at a fair value to the directors' nominees. This alteration to the articles was upheld on the basis that it was obviously beneficial to the company. In contrast, shortly thereafter, in *Dafen Tinplate Co v Llanelly Steel Co*,[56] it was held at first instance that a resolution inserting a new article empowering the majority to buy out any shareholder as they thought proper, was invalid as being self-evidently wider than was necessary in the company's interests.

All of the above cases accepted that a constitutional amendment enabling the shares of a member to be compulsorily transferred would only be upheld if passed bona fide in the interests of the company. In *Brown* and *Dafen Tinplate*, however, the bona fides of the majority was considered reviewable by the court on a more objective basis of reasonableness, rather than good faith and rationality. This position was rejected in *Shuttleworth v Cox Bros Ltd*,[57] which concerned not the expropriation of shares, but the removal of an unpopular life director. Upholding the validity of a resolution inserting in the articles a provision that any director should vacate office if called upon to do so by the board, the Court of Appeal held that it was for the members, and not the court, to determine whether the resolution was for the benefit of the company, and that the court

[53] *Brown v British Abrasive Wheel Co* [1919] 1 Ch. 290 Ch D. See further B. Hannigan, "Altering the Articles for Compulsory Transfer" [2007] J.B.L. 471.

[54] *Phillips v Manufacturers Securities Ltd* (1917) 116 L.T. 209. In *Borland's Trustees v Steel Bros* [1901] 1 Ch. 279 Ch D, an even wider article was inserted with the agreement of all the members. The majority could probably also safely introduce a compulsory transfer provision that only affected shares acquired in the future: consider *Re Charterhouse Capital Ltd* [2015] EWCA Civ 536 at [89]–[100].

[55] *Sidebottom v Kershaw, Leese & Co Ltd* [1920] 1 Ch. 154 CA.

[56] *Dafen Tinplate Co v Llanelly Steel Co* [1920] 2 Ch. 124 Ch D.

[57] *Shuttleworth v Cox Bros Ltd* [1927] 2 K.B. 9 CA.

would intervene only if satisfied that the members had acted in bad faith or irrationally.[58] The same approach has been applied recently to the expropriation of shares by the Court of Appeal in *Re Charterhouse Capital Ltd*[59] and the Privy Council in *Staray Capital Ltd v Cha*.[60] Assuming this position is correct, it becomes unclear why the CA 2006 contains a provision enabling a takeover bidder, who has acquired 90% or more of the target company's shares, to acquire compulsorily the remainder.[61] Indeed, there would have been no need for that provision if a bidder, having acquired a controlling interest, could then cause the target company to insert in its articles a similar expropriatory power. That might suggest that mere bona fides as to the company's benefit does not quite capture the approach being applied by the court. That said, going any further than this has proved controversial.[62]

13–010 An issue similar to that in *Brown* was considered by the High Court of Australia in *Gambotto v WCP Ltd*,[63] where it was proposed to alter the articles to allow a 90% shareholder to acquire the shares of minority shareholders at an objectively fair price (the majority holder in fact holding 99.7% of the shares). The motivation behind the change was to convert the company into a wholly owned subsidiary, which would bring enormous tax advantages for the company. Nevertheless, the court refused to allow the change, holding explicitly that the majority's decision could only be upheld if it were taken in good faith *and* for proper purposes. In the High Court of Australia's view, the general meeting's power to expropriate shares could legitimately be used to save the company from "significant detriment or harm" (as in the *Sidebottom* decision), but not to advance the commercial interests of the majority (as in *Gambotto*, where the tax advantages to the company would indirectly, but greatly, benefit its controlling shareholders). "English authority" was disapproved on the grounds that "it does not attach sufficient weight to the proprietary nature of a share".[64] On one view, this is similar to the more objective approach implicit in *Brown*, as Astbury J equally rejected the majority's right to use their power to expropriate the minority's shares to their own corresponding advantage.[65] Indeed, some echoes

[58] In *Shuttleworth*, the Court of Appeal conceded that, if the resolution was such that no reasonable man could consider it for the benefit of the company as a whole, that fact might be a ground for finding bad faith: see *Shuttleworth v Cox Bros Ltd* [1927] 2 K.B. 9 at 18, 19, 23, 26 and 27. This might be the case if the majority was seeking to acquire the minority's shares for little or no value. For confirmation of the (orthodox) subjective approach in *Shuttleworth*, see *Re Charterhouse Capital Ltd* [2015] EWCA Civ 536 at [90]; *Staray Capital Ltd v Cha* [2017] UKPC 43 at [34]–[35].

[59] *Re Charterhouse Capital Ltd* [2015] EWCA Civ 536 at [90].

[60] *Staray Capital Ltd v Cha* [2017] UKPC 43 at [34]–[35].

[61] CA 2006 s.979, discussed in Ch.28.

[62] *Redwood Master Fund Ltd v TD Bank Europe Ltd* [2002] EWHC 2703 (Ch) at [81]–[107].

[63] *Gambotto v WCP Ltd* (1995) 182 C.L.R. 432.

[64] *Gambotto v WCP Ltd* (1995) 182 C.L.R. 432 at 444.

[65] In *Brown v British Abrasive Wheel Co* [1919] 1 Ch. 290 at 296, Astbury J stated: "The defendants contend that it is for the benefit of the company as a whole because in default of further capital the company might have to go into liquidation. The plaintiff is willing to risk that. The proposed alteration is not directly concerned with the provision of further capital, nor does it ensure that it will be provided. It is merely for the benefit of the majority. If passed, the majority may acquire all the shares and provide further capital. That would be for the benefit of the company as then constituted. But the proposed alteration is not for the present benefit of this company". The decision in *Brown* could potentially be justified on the basis that the majority did not think about the benefit to the

of this approach can be found in *Assénagon Asset Management SA v Irish Bank Resolution Corporation Ltd*,[66] where Briggs J considered that an "exit consent" procedure in a bond restructuring was an invalid expropriation of the minority's rights because the minority was coerced into accepting the proposed terms.

Given the fact that *Brown* and *Dafen Tinplate* were both subsequently doubted by the Court of Appeal, it is unsurprising that the Privy Council in *Citco Banking Corp NV v Pusser's Ltd*[67] explicitly distanced itself from the objective "proper purposes" approach in *Gambotto*, even in the context of expropriation decisions. More recently, however, the decision of the Court of Appeal in *Re Charterhouse Capital Ltd*[68] perhaps raises doubts about the continuing adherence of the English courts to the more relaxed test in *Shuttleworth* and *Citco*. Whilst Etherton C approved an amendment to the articles permitting expropriation of shares (and affirmed the broadly subjective test in *Shuttleworth*), his Lordship consistently referred to the test as embracing not only bona fides, but also the intended proper purpose of the power.[69] As the amendment in *Charterhouse* was simply part of a tidying-up exercise designed to implement the agreed terms of a shareholder agreement that was expressed to take priority over the articles, it would have been difficult for any minority shareholder to argue that the amendment was either irrational or for improper purposes, or in bad faith. Nor have these doubts about the scope of *Charterhouse* been clarified by the Privy Council in *Staray Capital Ltd v Cha*,[70] where Lord Mance simply set out the test from the earlier decision without any further gloss. Given that the amendment in *Staray* concerned a power to expropriate shares that had been acquired by misrepresentation or that were held by a shareholder who caused loss to the company, the amendment would likely have passed even a more stringent objective test.

Other (non-expropriatory) resolutions

If it is not clear what the law requires in cases of compulsory transfer of shares (where the arguments can typically be framed in terms of corporate benefit, even if there are also substantial benefits to the majority), then the position is likely to be even more uncertain when the dispute simply involves a battle of wills between the majority and minority as to how their relations should be regulated by the articles. In such circumstances, cases like *Shuttleworth* suggest that the *only* test can be good faith, since there is no clear objective standard by which to judge whether an amendment is for the company's benefit (other than shareholder irrationality perhaps, and even that requires some conception of "the interests of the company"). In *Greenhalgh v Arderne Cinemas Ltd*,[71] where the proposed 13–011

company's business at all, but only their own benefit, for example, because financing was available on equivalent terms from those who did not require complete control.

[66] *Assénagon Asset Management SA v Irish Bank Resolution Corporation Ltd* [2012] EWHC 2090 (Ch) at [40]–[49].

[67] *Citco Banking Corp NV v Pusser's Ltd* [2007] UKPC 13; [2007] 2 B.C.L.C. 483.

[68] *Re Charterhouse Capital Ltd* [2015] EWCA Civ 536 at [90], [92], [96]–[108].

[69] *Re Charterhouse Capital Ltd* [2015] EWCA Civ 536, see especially [90].

[70] *Staray Capital Ltd v Cha* [2017] UKPC 43 at [34]–[35].

[71] *Greenhalgh v Arderne Cinemas Ltd* [1951] Ch. 286 CA (where the judgment of Evershed MR is reported more fully).

amendment was to remove a pre-emption clause, so as to facilitate a sale of control to a third party, Sir Raymond Evershed MR tried to preserve the application of the traditional test by saying that in inter-shareholder disputes "the company as a whole" did not mean the company as a corporate entity but "the corporators as a general body". According to his Lordship, it was then necessary to ask whether the constitutional amendment was for the benefit of a hypothetical member in the honest opinion of the majority who voted for the resolution. As the case was before the court precisely because of a division of opinion on the issue, the reference to the "hypothetical member" is hardly illuminating. Indeed, as indicated by the High Court of Australia in *Peter's American Delicacy Co Ltd v Heath*,[72] in inter-shareholder disputes, it is "inappropriate, if not meaningless" to ask whether the shareholders had considered the amendment to be in the interests of the company as a whole. Accordingly, some other test of validity is required in such cases.

Little progress has been made over the intervening 75 years on what that test might be. Accordingly, in *Citco Banking Corp NV v Pusser's Ltd*,[73] the Privy Council upheld a change in the articles that entrenched the existing controller of the company (who before the change controlled 28% of the company's shares) by permitting the conversion of his existing shares (carrying one vote per share) into a new class of share carrying 50 votes per share. Those who supported the alteration argued that the resolution was a bona fide decision in the interests of the company because it enabled the company to raise further finance for expansion, since the financiers required that the existing controller remain in control of the company. The genuineness of the majority's belief was not challenged, and the court found that a reasonable shareholder could have held this view about the proposed alteration. Applying the *Shuttleworth* test and reiterating that the burden of proof is on those who challenge the resolution, the court found the test of bona fide in the interests of the company to have been met. Whilst this may all seem unexceptional, the potential ramifications must give some cause for concern. At face value, the Privy Council appears to suggest that a majority could use its power to obtain different benefits to those of the minority (namely, conversion of a tranche of A shares carrying one vote per share to a tranche of B shares carrying 50 votes per share). If that is acceptable, then it would presumably be equally permissible to reclassify the majority's tranche of ordinary shares so as to give differential dividend rights, or rights to capital on winding up. Even if these amendments do not infringe the *Allen* principle (which is doubtful), they must surely fall afoul of the protections in the CA 2006 for shareholders' class rights and pre-emptive rights. In such circumstances, the minority would effectively be reduced to advancing complaints of unfair prejudice,[74] which

[72] *Peter's American Delicacy Co Ltd v Heath* (1939) 61 C.L.R. 457 at 512. In *Peter's*, the amendment provided that shareholders should thenceforth receive dividends rateably according to the amounts paid up on their shares rather than, as previously, according to the number of shares held (whether fully or partly paid). A fortiori the test is not useful if the group in question is made up of a number of distinct sub-groups: see *Redwood Master Fund Ltd v TD Bank Europe Ltd* [2002] EWHC 2703 (Ch); [2006] 1 B.C.L.C. 149, which was not an expropriation case and involved a "class" of creditors, rather than of shareholders.

[73] *Citco Banking Corp NV v Pusser's Ltd* [2007] 2 B.C.L.C. 483.

[74] CA 2006 s.994(1).

usually results in the minority shares being purchased and accordingly excluded completely from further participation in the company. What is intuitively objectionable about the situation in *Citco* is not that the minority is overpowered (that is inevitable with majority rule), but that the majority can use its power to obtain differential benefits *for itself* to the exclusion of the minority. Whilst Lord Hoffmann in *Citco* refused to disenfranchise the benefitted shareholder, especially as there was no attack on his bona fides, his Lordship did note that, even without that shareholder's votes, the resolution would still have been carried by 78% of the vote. On the particular facts of *Citco*, there seems little cause for complaint by the losing minority, but that does not mean that *Citco* does not raise concerns in different circumstances.[75]

The future

Despite the concerns expressed above, it is possible that the future is finally looking a little more certain. All of the cases applying the *Allen* principle illustrate a set of common concerns, which argues in favour of a common approach to this area; there is little point articulating different tests for different sub-categories of shareholder decision-making as this will simply create uncertainty as to the particular sub-category into which to place a particular case. That said, the nature of the particular power and the surrounding corporate context will obviously be material considerations as to *how* a more unified test is applied.[76] In determining the appropriate tests for judicial review, there seem to be three broad ways forward in this area. The first is to demand little of shareholders in their decision-making, other than rationality and bona fides.[77] Such an approach would be consistent with developing notions of judicial review in other areas of private law.[78] The second is to adopt an intermediate position, permitting an objective element in the test applied by the court, and keeping that test focused on "the interests of the company", whilst not going so far as to allow the court to substitute its own commercial view of what might have been best in the circumstances. This position may be illustrated by *Brown v British Abrasive Wheel Co*,[79] which was criticised on precisely that basis by *Shuttleworth* and (perhaps) *Citco*. Whatever its merits, such an approach seems difficult to justify in principle and impossible to administer with certainty. The third, and certainly the most interventionist approach, is to embrace the twin tests of subjective bona **13–012**

[75] Consider the different approach in *Rights & Issues Investment Trust Ltd v Stylo Shoes Ltd* [1965] Ch. 250 Ch D, which was cited in *Citco*, although not followed in its detail. In *Stylo*, along with a substantial increase in the issued ordinary share capital, the articles were amended to double the number of votes attached to special management shares, so as to maintain the control of the existing management. In upholding the shareholders' resolution, Pennycuick J noted (at 255–256) that the rules on class rights needed to be followed, and that the resolution was effective because the management shares had not voted, and yet 92% of the ordinary shareholders (being those with no personal interest in the matter) had voted in favour.

[76] See also Completing, para.5.98.

[77] For support for such an approach, see *Citco Banking Corp NV v Pusser's Ltd* [2007] 2 B.C.L.C. 483 at [20], where a subjective approach was endorsed even in what resembled an expropriation case.

[78] Consider *BP Shipping Ltd v Braganza* [2015] UKSC 17.

[79] *Brown v British Abrasive Wheel Co* [1919] 1 Ch. 290.

fides and objective proper purposes in *Gambotto*. Despite the criticisms visited on that case, this does increasingly appear to be the modern approach, both with shareholder decision-making and more generally.[80] It has a respectable pedigree: it is evident in the explicit language of *Allen*[81] and *Gambotto*, as well as the recent Court of Appeal decision in *Re Charterhouse Capital Ltd*[82] and Privy Council decision in *Staray Capital Ltd v Cha*.[83] Moreover, although not the language used by the courts, this approach might also provide a better explanation of some of the earlier cases.[84]

The starting point for the proposed approach is the perfectly general one that no grant of power is absolute, at least when its exercise binds dissenting parties. The minimum constraints are that the power must be exercised rationally, in good faith, and for the purposes for which the power is granted. It is this last limitation that typically provides the potential tripwire in authorisation and ratification decisions, in expropriation decisions, and in governance decisions such as *Citco*. In different contexts, the concerns (or "purposes") are different; for example, the relevant "proper purposes" might give free rein to shareholders in their appointment and dismissal of directors.[85] This variability might not make the relevant distinctions much easier to solve when presented in terms of improper purposes (or fraud on the power), rather than in terms of "bona fide in the interests of the company", but at least the principles being pursued are clearer. As evidence of this trend, Sir Terence Etherton C in *Re Charterhouse Capital Ltd,* indicated, obiter, that he preferred the formulation in *Peters' American Delicacy Co Ltd v Heath*,[86] that in the case of an amendment in which the company as an entity has no interest, the test should be whether the amendment amounts to oppression of the minority or is otherwise unjust or is outside the scope of the power. This is the sort of test that also applies more broadly to decision-making by other power-holders.[87]

---

[80] The approach does not depend on the identity of the power-holder, and in particular does not depend on the power-holder being a fiduciary. For illustrations, see *Eclairs Group Ltd v JKX Oil & Gas Plc* [2015] UKSC 71 (directors); *Assénagon Asset Management SA v Irish Bank Resolution Corp Ltd (formerly Anglo Irish Bank Corp Ltd)* [2012] EWHC 2090 (Ch) (creditors); *Burry & Knight Ltd v Knight* [2014] EWCA Civ 604 (shareholders).

[81] *Allen v Gold Reefs of West Africa* [1900] 1 Ch. 671.

[82] See especially the earlier discussion of *Re Charterhouse Capital Ltd* [2015] EWCA Civ 536. See also fn.80.

[83] *Staray Capital Ltd v Cha* [2017] UKPC 43 at [34]–[35].

[84] In particular, the test applied by the courts is not to look at the controlling director-shareholder's *actual* bona fides, nor even to assert that *no* reasonable director-shareholder could have thought the decision to be bona fide in the interests of the company (i.e. either an irrationality test, or an indication that the court was simply not persuaded that bona fides were proven). Rather, the courts seem to apply a more objective test, and to assume an improper motivation, or a use of the power for improper ends.

[85] Although even here there are some constraints, since the potential pay-back for appointment of a board of directors intended to serve as the appointer's puppet is classification of the appointer as a shadow director.

[86] *Peters' American Delicacy Co Ltd v Heath* (1939) 61 C.L.R. 457 at 512.

[87] See, for example, *Redwood Master Fund Ltd v TD Bank Europe Ltd* [2006] 1 B.C.L.C. 149; *Assénagon Asset Management SA v Irish Bank Resolution Corp Ltd* [2012] EWHC 2090 (Ch) (bondholders); *Re Dee Valley Group Plc* [2018] Ch. 55 (scheme of arrangement).

Voting at class meetings

13–013 Although the *Allen* principle was developed in the context of decisions by the general meeting, a version of that principle applies to voting at class meetings of shareholders. Whilst the statutory protections in the class-right context will be considered further below, those voting at the class meeting must exercise their votes bona fides in the interests of the class as a whole. Sometimes this principle has been applied stringently. In *Re Holders Investment Trust*,[88] which concerned a capital reduction scheme requiring the court's confirmation, Megarry J approached the matter on the basis that he had to be satisfied, first, that the resolution of the preference shareholders had been validly passed bona fide in the interests of that class; and then that, in the court's view, the scheme was fair to all classes.[89] The application failed at the first step. By analogy with the cases considered earlier, the law requires members voting in class meetings to use their votes for the purpose of—or in the interests of—the class. Confirmation was refused because the resolution of the class meeting of the preference shareholders had been passed as a result of votes of trustees who held a large block of the preference shares but a still larger block of ordinary shares. In casting their votes, the trustees had deliberately voted in the way best designed to favour the ordinary shareholders, since that was what would best serve the interests of their beneficiaries (as of course their trustee obligations required). The court held that use of their power in this way was not permitted, as it was contrary to the protective purposes underpinning the required class meetings. This approach has been recently confirmed in *Re Dee Valley Group Plc*,[90] where Sir Geoffrey Vos C indicated that, in applying the test in *Holders*, "[t]he key is that the members of the class must vote in the interests of the class as a whole and not in their own specific interests if they are different from the interests of the class". Given that the relevant votes in *Dee Valley* were being exercised as part of a wider vote-manipulation plan that involved splitting up a single shareholding across multiple parties for the purpose of defeating a scheme of arrangement, it is not surprising that the votes were discounted. Nevertheless, the authorities suggest that the courts will be more sensitive to abuse of voting power at class meetings than in the wider general meeting.

CLASS RIGHTS

13–014 Putting aside the principle applied in *Holders* and *Dee Valley*, the question arises as to when a separate meeting of a shareholder class is required and how the class in question should be defined. The separate consent of shareholders particularly affected by a proposed resolution may be required by legislation or by the company's own constitution. Indeed, the principle of separate consent is

[88] *Re Holders Investment Trust* [1971] 1 W.L.R. 583 Ch D.

[89] See further para.17–031.

[90] *Re Dee Valley Group Plc* [2018] Ch. 55, applying *British America Nickel Corporation Ltd v MJ O'Brien Ltd* [1927] A.C. 369 PC at 371. See also *Re Tiso Blackstar Group SE Plc* [2020] EWHC 3534 (Ch) at [12].

well-established in relation to proposed alterations of the articles, where those alterations also affect the "rights" of a class of members.

The procedure for varying class rights

13–015 Where a proposed alteration to the articles involves "the variation of the rights attached to a class of shares", the CA 2006 supplements the general requirement of a special resolution[91] with an additional protective mechanism for members of the affected class.[92] Indeed, the statutory provisions on variation in the CA 2006 are made considerably simpler than their predecessors by laying down a single default rule,[93] with equivalent provision being made for companies without shares.[94] As this is only a default rule, it may be displaced by explicit provision to the contrary in the company's articles, which may set a higher or a lower standard.[95] In essence, variation of the rights attached to a class of shares requires the consent of three-quarters of the votes cast at a separate meeting of that class or a written resolution having the support of holders of three-quarters of the nominal value of the class (excluding treasury shares).[96] Without this important protective technique, the class might be swamped by the votes of other classes of shareholder, who would not necessarily have the same interests to protect. Indeed, the class in question might not otherwise have any say in the matter at all, if, for example, it was a class of non-voting shareholders. Preference shares are often non-voting, at least if their dividends are being paid on time, and classes of non-voting ordinary shares are not unknown. Without the separate class meeting, any alteration to the rights of non-voting shareholders would otherwise be a matter entirely for the voting shareholders. Accordingly, the CA 2006 provides the relevant class with a veto over the proposed change, even if they are otherwise non-voting. Obviously, any alteration of the articles must also be approved in the normal way by special resolution (approval by a three-quarters majority of those shareholders entitled to vote under the company's articles), but that is not normally a problem in the cases considered in this section.

Although the statutory protection of a separate class meeting is relatively straightforward, the complexity, such as it is, derives from its attempt to answer the question of what rules should govern any attempt to amend any procedure in the articles for the variation of class rights. If the variation procedure in the articles could be freely amended in the same way as any other article of the company's constitution, the protection intended to be afforded by the articles to the class could easily be undermined. Accordingly, the CA 2006 provides that any amendment to a variation procedure contained in the company's articles itself

---

[91] CA 2006 s.21(1).

[92] CA 2006 ss.630 (companies with share capital) and 631 (companies without).

[93] CA 2006 s.630.

[94] CA 2006 s.631.

[95] The Companies (Model Articles) Regulations 2008 (SI 2008/3229) contain no model variation procedures.

[96] A failure to comply with the statutory procedures may amount to unfairly prejudicial conduct: see *Re Hut Group Ltd* [2020] EWHC 5 (Ch); [2020] B.C.C. 443.

attracts the provisions protecting class rights.[97] That said, if the articles themselves set out a procedure for varying the variation procedure that should be followed as the CA 2006 only provides the default position.[98] In the same vein, the CA 2006 also treats as a variation of the class rights themselves the introduction of a variation procedure into the articles, for that might set a lower standard than the statutory default rule previously applicable.[99] Finally, the statutory protection mechanism is stated to be without prejudice "to any other restrictions on the variation of rights".[100] This appears to suggest that a company might be able to use the entrenchment mechanism in the CA 2006[101] to set an even higher requirement for amendments to the variation procedure contained in the articles than would otherwise apply. For example, the articles could provide that amendments to the variation procedure require the consent of all the members of the class.

On the basis of the above discussion, therefore, the CA 2006 uses two different protective techniques, at least on a default basis: a separate meeting of the class (the main protection) and a supermajority requirement of a three-quarters majority to obtain an effective decision of the class. In addition, however, the CA 2006 makes use of a third technique to protect minority shareholders, namely judicial review of the majority's decision.[102] This acknowledges the fact that, even within a class meeting, the majority of the class can nevertheless act opportunistically towards the minority, although the requirement that votes must be exercised bona fide in the interests of the class will curb the worst excesses.[103] Accordingly, the CA 2006 affords a dissenting minority of not less than 15% of the issued shares of a class,[104] whose rights have been varied in the permitted manner, to apply to the court to have the variation cancelled. The application must be made within 21 days after the consent was given or the resolution passed, but can be made by such one or more of the dissenting shareholders as they appoint in writing. Once such an application has been made, the variation has no effect unless and until it is confirmed by the court. If, after hearing the applicant "and any other persons who apply to be heard and appear to the court to be 13–016

[97] CA 2006 s.630(5). Both in relation to variation of rights and amendments to variation procedures, variation includes abrogation of the right: CA 2006 s.630(6). Class rights and variation procedures contained in the memorandums of existing companies are treated as being contained in the articles: CA 2006 s.28.

[98] CA 2006 s.630(2).

[99] CA 2006 s.630(5).

[100] CA 2006 s.630(3).

[101] CA 2006 s.22, discussed further in para.13–028.

[102] This court review applies to all variation procedures, whether specified in the legislation or in the company's articles: see CA 2006 s.633(1).

[103] See further para.13–013.

[104] CA 2006 ss.633 (for companies with share capital) and 634 (for companies without). Provided that they have not consented to or voted in favour of the resolution—an unfortunately worded restriction that effectively rules out nominees who have not exercised all their votes in one way.

interested",[105] the court is satisfied that the variation would "unfairly prejudice"[106] the shareholders of the class represented by the applicant, it may disallow the variation but otherwise must confirm it.[107] The CA 2006 expressly provides that "the decision of the court is final",[108] which presumably means that it cannot be taken to appeal.[109] This procedure may be particularly useful where the articles adopt a variation procedure considerably less demanding than the default statutory procedure. That said, the dearth of reported cases involving such challenges suggest that the procedure is rarely, if ever, employed. Nevertheless, the possibility of a challenge by a disgruntled minority is useful in highlighting to the board the need to ensure that variations of class rights treat classes fairly. In practice, however, the bigger risk may be a claim under the unfair prejudice jurisdiction.

Whilst the above procedures deal with the situations where the company seeks to vary class rights, they do not impact on variations of class rights effected by an order of the court[110]: that includes the courts' powers relating to arrangements and reconstructions,[111] unfair prejudice[112] or the cancellation of a resolution by a public company to re-register as private.[113]

What constitutes a "variation"

13–017 Whilst the CA 2006 deals at some length with the procedure for varying class rights, it says very little, if anything, about what constitutes a variation of class rights or, indeed, what qualifies as a class right. Both these matters are defined principally by the common law. As a matter of logic, however, the statutory or constitutional procedure is only relevant once it is clear that there is both a "class right" and a relevant "variation". These will be considered in reverse order.

Prior to legislative intervention in this area, it was commonly assumed that provisions in the articles requiring class consent for an alteration were only triggered if the class rights were being changed in a manner adverse to that class' interests. But the relevant provisions of the CA 2006 dealing with the "variation"

---

105 This clearly includes representatives of other classes affected and of the company.

106 The notion of "unfair prejudice" obviously underlies the court's jurisdiction in the CA 2006 s.994, which would seem to provide a better alternative route not requiring 15% support and strict time limits and with a wider range of orders that the court can make.

107 CA 2006 s.633(5). The company must within 15 days after the making of an order forward a copy to the Registrar: CA 2006 s.635.

108 CA 2006 s.633(5).

109 This was certainly the intention of the Greene Committee on whose recommendation the section was based: Cm.2657, para.23. The need for speedy finality seems no greater than on an application under the general unfair prejudice provisions, where there is no such provision and cases can be taken to the House of Lords. But if the application under s.633 is struck out on the ground that the time-limit was not complied with, that can be taken to appeal: see *Re Suburban Stores Ltd* [1943] Ch. 156 CA. See also *Re Sound City (Films) Ltd* [1947] Ch. 169 Ch D, which seems to be the only officially reported case on the predecessors to s.633. Cases in which it might have been invoked (e.g. *Rights & Issues Investment Trust v Stylo Shoes Ltd* [1965] Ch. 250) have been brought instead under the unfair prejudice sections or earlier versions of those sections.

110 CA 2006 s.632.

111 See further Ch.29.

112 CA 2006 s.994.

113 CA 2006 s.98.

of class rights (even though they specifically include their "abrogation")[114] cannot reasonably be construed as limited to "adverse" variations, and, to avoid any subsequent attack on the validity of the resolution, the formal approval of the class to be benefitted should be obtained, even though it might appear a foregone conclusion.

There is no doubt, however, that shareholders most need these statutory procedures when the class is adversely affected by what is proposed. Nevertheless, by imposing a narrow, technical construction on what constitutes a "variation" of class rights, the courts have delivered an outcome where proposed changes may have a serious practical impact on class rights, yet the change may not meet the test of a "variation" of class rights that is protected by the CA 2006 or the articles. The principle applied by the courts is that, as long as the *formal* rights of the complaining shareholders have not been changed, there is no "variation", even if the change has an adverse effect on the value of the class rights. Accordingly, a subdivision[115] or increase[116] of one class of shares has been held not to vary the rights of another class, notwithstanding that the result was to alter profoundly the voting equilibrium of the classes. Similarly, an issue of further shares ranking pari passu with the existing shares of a class was not regarded as a "variation" of the latter rights.[117] Indeed, where there were preference and ordinary shares, an issue of preferred ordinary shares ranking ahead of the ordinary, but behind the preference shares, was not a "variation" of the rights attached to either existing class.[118] Equally, where preference shares were non-participating as regards dividend, but participating as regards capital on a winding-up or reduction of capital, a capitalisation of undistributed profits in the form of a bonus issue to the ordinary shareholders was not a variation of the preference shareholders' rights, notwithstanding that the effect was to deny them their future participation in those profits on winding up or reduction.[119] In the contrary situation, where the shares were participating as regards dividends but not in relation to the return of capital on a winding-up, a reduction of capital by repayment of irredeemable preference shares in accordance with their rights on a winding-up (i.e. at their nominal value) was not regarded as a variation or abrogation of their rights, even though the shareholders were deprived of valuable dividend rights.[120] Even if the dividend rights of the preference

[114] CA 2006 s.630(6).

[115] *Greenhalgh v Arderne Cinemas* [1946] 1 All E.R. 512, where the result of the subdivision was to deprive the holder of one class of his power to block a special resolution.

[116] *White v Bristol Aeroplane Co* [1953] Ch. 65 CA; *Re John Smith's Tadcaster Brewery Co* [1953] Ch. 308 CA.

[117] Contrast *Re Schweppes Ltd* [1914] 1 Ch. 322 CA, concerning s.45 of the 1908 Act, which forbade "interference" with the "preference or special privileges" of a class.

[118] *Hodge v James Howell & Co* [1958] C.L.Y. 446 CA; *The Times*, 13 December 1958.

[119] *Dimbula Valley (Ceylon) Tea Co Ltd v Laurie* [1961] Ch. 353 Ch D. On the meaning of "participation" in this context see further para.6–007. For discussion of bonus shares, see para.16–024. See also *Re Mackenzie & Co Ltd* [1916] 2 Ch. 450 Ch D, which implies that a rateable reduction of the nominal value of preference and ordinary capital (which participated pari passu on a winding up) did not modify the rights of the preference shareholders, notwithstanding that the effect was to reduce the amount payable to them by way of preference dividend while making no difference at all to the ordinary shareholders.

[120] *Scottish Insurance Corp Ltd v Wilson & Clyde Coal Co Ltd* [1949] A.C. 462 HL; *Prudential Assurance Co v Chatterly Whitfield Collieries* [1949] A.C. 512 HL; *Re Saltdean Estate Co Ltd* [1968]

shareholders were fixed, those rights might be valuable, for example, if interest rates have fallen after the issuance of the preference shares. The obvious unfairness of this overly narrow view of what constitutes a "variation" led to a contractual solution: when public companies issued preference shares that were non-participating in a winding-up, the practice developed that upon any redemption or return of capital, the amount repaid should be tied to the average quoted market price of the shares in the preceding months (the market price reflecting the value of the dividend rights, rather than the nominal value of the shares). This so-called "Spens formula" (named after its inventor) affords reasonable protection in the case of listed companies, but preference shareholders in unquoted companies still remain at risk.

13–018 Just as it is possible for the articles to require a variation procedure that is more demanding than the default procedure in the CA 2006 (such as increasing the level of approval required), so it is possible for the articles to define the notion of "variation" more broadly so that certain types of change trigger the statutory protections. Accordingly, as a result of preference shareholders losing their class rights upon a reduction of capital, it became common to introduce special provisions into a company's articles to protect those shareholders. In *Re Northern Engineering Industries Plc*,[121] the court upheld and enforced a provision in the articles that deemed a reduction of capital to be a "variation" of the preference shareholders' class rights when the company proposed to cancel those shares. Very clear wording will be needed, however, if such a provision is to be construed as affording any greater protection than the norm. For example, in both *White v Bristol Aeroplane Co*,[122] and *Re John Smith's Tadcaster Brewery Co*,[123] the articles of association referred to class rights being "affected, modified, dealt with or abrogated". At first instance in both cases,[124] Danckwerts J held that an issue of bonus shares to the ordinary shareholders could not be made without the consent of the preference shareholders because, although their rights would not be abrogated or varied, they would be "affected" by virtue of their votes being less powerful as a result of the increased voting power of the ordinary shareholders. Reversing this decision, the Court of Appeal concluded that the rights of the preference shareholders would not be "affected", since the rights themselves—to one vote per share in certain circumstances—remained precisely as before. The only consequence of the bonus issue was that the preference shareholders' enjoyment of those rights would be affected.

Accordingly, if a shareholder wishes to be protected against this risk, more explicit wording than in *White* would have to be used, making it clear that the clause in the articles was intended to protect the relevant class rights from

1 W.L.R. 1844 Ch D; *House of Fraser v AGCE Investments Ltd* [1987] A.C. 387 HL; *Re Hunting Plc* [2004] EWHC 2591 (Ch); [2005] 2 B.C.L.C. 211. But contrast *Re Old Silkstone Collieries Ltd* [1954] Ch. 169 CA, where confirmation of the repayment was refused because it would have deprived the preference shareholders of a contingent right to apply for an adjustment of capital under the coal nationalisation legislation.

[121] *Re Northern Engineering Industries Plc* [1994] 2 B.C.L.C. 704 CA.

[122] *White v Bristol Aeroplane Co* [1953] Ch. 65 CA.

[123] *Re John Smith's Tadcaster Brewery Co* [1953] Ch. 308 CA.

[124] *Re John Smith's Tadcaster Brewery Co* [1952] 2 All E.R. 751, although Danckwerts J's decision in *White* is not fully reported.

economic, as well as legal, harm (or, in other words, from being "affected as a matter of business").[125] The model articles do not contain such a clause, and companies are unlikely to insert it unless they consider the rights on offer will not otherwise be acceptable to potential purchasers. In the absence of such a clause in the articles, the statutory protections for class-right holders can largely be set at naught by effective work arounds, so that class rights can be gutted of their substance with impunity. This arguably undermines the very protection the legislature intended.

The definition of class rights

Before it is possible to decide whether a class right has been "varied", it is necessary to define the notion of a "class right". This is a matter upon which there is a surprising degree of doubt. According to the CA 2006,[126] shares are to be regarded as belonging to one class if the rights attached to them "are in all respects uniform", so that merely attaching different names to groups of shares does not turn them into different classes of share if the rights attached to them are the same.[127] This definition of a class of shares applies throughout the CA 2006 and not just in relation to the variation of class rights. 13–019

Beyond that sparse definition, the CA 2006 provides no help and does not even state expressly that class rights can only arise if there is more than one class of share.[128] If this were not the case, however, the provisions in the CA 2006 dealing with the alteration of the articles[129] and variation of class rights[130] would overlap to an unacceptable degree. Assuming that two or more classes of share exist, there still needs to be some way of determining whether this counts as a "class right" for the purposes of the legislation. The choices range from restricting "class rights" to the rights attached to any one of the classes that are unique to it (where the right is not held in common with any of the other classes of share) to expanding the definition to include all the rights attached to any of the classes. An intermediate position adds to the first approach the core rights of shareholders (relating to voting, dividends and return of capital on a winding-up), whether or not those rights are unique to the class in that particular case. There is little authority on the issue. Although decided under the previous legislation, Scott J, in *Cumbrian Newspapers Group Ltd v Cumberland and Westmoreland*

---

[125] See *Greenhalgh v Arderne Cinemas Ltd* [1946] 1 All E.R. 512 at 518.

[126] CA 2006 s.629.

[127] This definition does not solve all the problematic cases. Suppose the only difference between the classes is a difference in par values (considered by the Court of Appeal in *Greenhalgh v Arderne Cinemas Ltd* [1946] 1 All E.R. 512, to be enough to create separate classes); or suppose the par values are the same, but some shares are fully paid-up and others only partly so. The CA 2006 provides that the definition of "class rights" is satisfied even if the rights to dividends of shares in the 12 months after allotment are different from those of other shares with otherwise similar rights—as they might be if additional shares were issued part-way through a financial year.

[128] Compare CA 1985 s.127(1).

[129] CA 2006 s.21(1).

[130] CA 2006 s.630(1).

Newspaper and Printing Co Ltd,[131] seemed to favour the first and narrowest view. That said, the second view might be thought to protect more adequately the expectations of shareholders. On the first and narrowest view, a shareholder seeking protection of dividend, voting and return of capital rights that are not unique to the class would have to ensure that there was a variation of rights clause in the articles and that that clause defined class rights in an appropriately broad way. This seems undesirable and cumbersome. The right to class consent (at least for the variation of core rights) would be precisely what companies and, for example, preference shareholders would expect. The law should give effect to those expectations.

13–020 Whilst this basic issue about the definition of a "class right" continues to be unresolved, a more sophisticated aspect of the same question has been considered judicially and has received a surprisingly liberal response. That more sophisticated question is whether the definition of a "class right" includes the situation where nominally the shares are of the same class, but special rights are conferred on one or more members without attaching those rights to any particular shares held by that member or members. This was precisely the issue facing Scott J in *Cumbrian Newspapers*,[132] in which two companies (both publishing rival provincial weekly newspapers in an area where it had become apparent that only one was viable) concluded an arrangement providing that one of the companies (Company A) would publish that one newspaper on condition that it issue 10% of its ordinary share capital[133] to the other company (Company B). Company B was anxious to ensure that the paper should remain locally owned and controlled. To that end, the articles of Company A were amended in such a way as to confer on Company B pre-emptive rights in the event of any new share issue by Company A or on any disposal by other shareholders of their shares in Company A. These rights were not attached to any particular share, but conferred on Company B by name. Further, another new provision in Company A's articles provided that: "If and so long as [Company B] shall be the holder of not less than one-tenth in nominal value of the issued ordinary share capital of" Company A, Company B "shall be entitled from time to time to nominate one person to be a director of" Company A. Company A's articles contained a variation of rights clause. Eighteen years later, Company A's directors proposed to convene a general meeting to pass a special resolution deleting the relevant articles. Company B thereupon applied to the court for a declaration that Company B's rights were class rights that could not be abrogated without its consent.

Scott J pointed out that special rights contained in the articles could be divided into three categories.[134] First, there are rights annexed to particular shares. The

---

[131] *Cumbrian Newspapers Group Ltd v Cumberland and Westmoreland Newspaper and Printing Co Ltd* [1987] Ch. 1 Ch D at 15, although earlier editions of this book have argued for the second view. For a full discussion, see E. Ferran and L.C. Ho, *Principles of Corporate Finance Law*, 2nd edn (Oxford: OUP, 2014), Ch.6.

[132] *Cumbrian Newspapers Group Ltd v Cumberland and Westmoreland Newspaper and Printing Co Ltd* [1987] Ch. 1 at 15.

[133] Whilst there were also preference shares, nothing turned on that. Clearly any attempt to vary the preference shares would have been subject to the equivalent of CA 2006 s.630.

[134] *Cumbrian Newspapers Group Ltd v Cumberland and Westmoreland Newspaper and Printing Co Ltd* [1987] Ch. 1 at 15A–18A.

classic example of this is where particular shares carry particular rights not enjoyed by others, such as in relation to "dividends and rights to participate in surplus assets on a winding up".[135] These would clearly be "rights attached to [a] class of shares" within the statutory definition of a class right.[136] Scott J also held that this category would include cases where rights were attached to particular shares issued to a named individual, but expressed to determine upon transfer by that individual of his shares.

The second category was where the articles purported to confer rights on individuals not in their capacity as members or shareholders.[137] Rights of this sort would not be class rights, for they would not be attached to any class of shares.[138] On the facts, however, Company B's rights did not fall within this second class, since the constitutional provisions in question were "inextricably connected with the issue to [Company B] and the acceptance by [it] of the ordinary shares in the defendant".[139]

In the third category were "rights that, although not attached to any particular shares were nonetheless conferred upon the beneficiary in the capacity of member or shareholder of the company".[140] According to Scott J, the rights conferred on Company B fell into this category.[141] But did this mean that the rights came within the words of the then-equivalent of s.630(1) as "rights attached to any class of shares"? After an analysis of the various legislative provisions then in force and of the anomalies that would result if the legislation in force at that time did not apply to the third category,[142] Scott J concluded that the legislative intent must have been to deal comprehensively with the variation or abrogation of shareholders' class rights. Accordingly, the legislation extended to categories one and three and Scott J accordingly granted the declaration sought.[143]

The same position should pertain under the CA 2006. Indeed, Scott J might have found it easier to reach his decision under the current legislation. In effect,

---

[135] *Cumbrian Newspapers Group Ltd v Cumberland and Westmoreland Newspaper and Printing Co Ltd* [1987] Ch. 1 at 15.

[136] CA 2006 s.630(1).

[137] Scott J referred to *Eley v Positive Life Assurance Co* (1875) 1 Ex. D. 20 in this regard. See further para.14–002. In this second category, the individual will have no enforceable rights in the absence of an express contract with the company additional to the articles.

[138] *Cumbrian Newspapers Group Ltd v Cumberland and Westmoreland Newspaper and Printing Co Ltd* [1987] Ch. 1 at 16A–E.

[139] *Cumbrian Newspapers Group Ltd v Cumberland and Westmoreland Newspaper and Printing Co Ltd* [1987] Ch. 1 at 16G.

[140] *Cumbrian Newspapers Group Ltd v Cumberland and Westmoreland Newspaper and Printing Co Ltd* [1987] Ch. 1 at 16A–17A.

[141] *Cumbrian Newspapers Group Ltd v Cumberland and Westmoreland Newspaper and Printing Co Ltd* [1987] Ch. 1 at 17. He instanced as other examples, *Bushell v Faith* [1970] A.C. 1099 (see para.11–024); and *Rayfield v Hands* [1960] Ch. 1 Ch D (see para.14–002).

[142] *Cumbrian Newspapers Group Ltd v Cumberland and Westmoreland Newspaper and Printing Co Ltd* [1987] Ch. 1 at 18A–22B.

[143] *Cumbrian Newspapers Group Ltd v Cumberland and Westmoreland Newspaper and Printing Co Ltd* [1987] Ch. 1 at 22F–G. That said, Scott J refrained from granting an injunction on the ground that this would "prevent the company from discharging its statutory duties in respect of the convening of meetings". The result was therefore that Company A could hold the meeting if it wished but, if the resolution was passed, it would nevertheless be ineffective in the light of the declaration, unless Company B consented.

Scott J treated the expressions "the rights of a class of members" and the "rights…attached to a class of shares" as synonymous. Both phrases are currently used in the CA 2006, albeit for different types of company.[144] For the purposes of the current legislation, however, the difference is arguably immaterial. In short, Scott J may have anticipated by several decades the position now contained in the CA 2006.

Other cases

13–021 In addition to the general protection for class rights, there are some additional statutory procedures that explicitly require the separate consent of each class of shares for certain corporate decisions. A prime example involves schemes of arrangement, but the definition of a "class" of shares for those purposes is interpreted functionally rather than literally, in contrast with the variation of rights cases.[145]

"People with significant control"—the PSC Register

13–022 Since 2016, almost all companies have a duty to maintain a public register of "people with significant control" of the company's shares,[146] called the company's "PSC Register".[147] This does not require the company to disclose every beneficial interest in its shareholdings, but it does require disclosure of every person (human or corporate) who is able to exert "significant influence or control" over the company.[148] The UK Government's objectives in implementing these reforms on transparency in corporate control was to ensure that the "UK is,

144 CA 2006 ss.630–631.

145 See further Ch.29.

146 CA 2006 s.790M(1).

147 CA 2006 s.790C(10). To achieve this objective, the Small Business, Enterprise and Employment Act 2015 inserted a substantial new Pt 21A into the CA 2006: see CA 2006 ss.790A–790ZG and Sch.1A. This statutory amendment is in turn supplemented by Regulations and formal statutory Guidance: see Register of People with Significant Control Regulations 2016 (SI 2016/339); Companies Act 2006 (Amendment of Part 21A) Regulations 2016 (SI 2016/136); Information about People with Significant Control (Amendment) Regulations 2017 (SI 2017/693). The PSC Register is required for all UK companies, except those companies whose voting shares have been admitted to trading on a regulated market in the UK, EU, Japan, US, Switzerland or Israel, including the London Stock Exchange main market and the Alternative Investment Market: see CA 2006 ss.790B(1) and 790C(7). This is because these companies are already required to make details of major shareholdings public. The provisions will also apply to an LLP: see Limited Liability Partnerships (Register of People with Significant Control) Regulations 2016 (SI 2016/340). See generally Department for Business Innovations and Skills, *The Register of People with Significant Control: Government Response* (December 2015). For similar measures, see EU Directive 2018/843 on the Prevention of the Use of the Financial System for the Purposes of Money Laundering or Terrorist Financing [2018] OJ L156/43.

148 CA 2006 s.790C(2)–(3) and Sch.1A. See also Register of People with Significant Control Regulations 2016 (SI 2016/339); Department for Business, Energy and Industrial Strategy, *Statutory Guidance on the Meaning of "Significant Influence or Control" over Companies in the Context of the Register of People with Significant Control* (June 2017) available at: *https://www.gov.uk/government/uploads/system/uploads/attachment_data/file/523120/PSC_statutory_guidance_companies.pdf* [Accessed 1 January 2021] (PSC Statutory Guidance).

and is seen to be, an open and trusted place to invest and do business. Knowing who ultimately owns and controls our companies will contribute to that objective"; and, in addition, to "deter and disrupt the misuse of companies, and identify and sanction those responsible when illegal activity does take place".[149] This is important not only for combatting money laundering and terrorist financing, but also to prevent tax evasion and corruption.

To fulfil these aims, a relevant company is under a duty to keep a register of people "with significant control over the company" (or PSCs),[150] with the information not being removed from the PSC Register until 10 years after the person ceases to have such control.[151] An individual is deemed to have "significant control" if they meet at least one of the following five conditions, namely that they directly or indirectly hold more than 25% of the company's nominal share capital; directly or indirectly control more than 25% of the votes at the company's general meetings; directly or indirectly are able to control the appointment or removal of a majority of the company's board; actually exercise, or have the right to exercise, significant influence or control over the company; or actually exercise, or have the right to exercise, significant influence or control over any trust or firm (which is not a legal entity) that has significant control (under one of the four other conditions above) over the company.[152] In interpreting these conditions, both the regulations and the formal statutory guidance provide assistance. These conditions applicable to individual shareholders are extended to corporate shareholders.[153] **13–023**

According to the fourth and fifth of the above conditions, the statutory concept of "significant control" actually encompasses a notion of "significant influence or control", which represents the real breadth of the PSC disclosure rules. According to the PSC statutory guidance, the notions of "influence" and "control" are alternatives, with neither needing actually to be exercised by the PSC with a view to his or her own economic benefit.[154] In defining these notions, "control" indicates that the PSC is able to direct the company's activities, while "influence" indicates that the PSC can ensure (in fact, rather than as a matter of legal right) that the company generally adopts the activities which the PSC desires.[155] Besides the obvious situations where a person possesses decision-making or veto powers in relation to a company,[156] the PSC statutory guidance also suggests that such influence could arise because the PSC owns strategic assets (such as intellectual property) or has key relationships that are important to the running of

[149] Department for Business Innovations and Skills, *The Register of People with Significant Control (PSC Register)* (October 2014), Foreword available at: *https://www.gov.uk/government/uploads/system/uploads/attachment_data/file/395478/bis-14-1145-the-register-of-people-with-significant-control-psc-register-register-final-1.pdf* [Accessed 1 January 2021].

[150] CA 2006 s.790M(1).

[151] CA 2006 s.790U(1).

[152] CA 2006 Sch.1A.

[153] CA 2006 s.790C(5)–(7).

[154] PSC Statutory Guidance, paras 1.21 and 1.24.

[155] PSC Statutory Guidance, paras 1.22–1.23.

[156] PSC Statutory Guidance, paras 2.5–2.8.

the company; was the company's founder; or constitutes a shadow director.[157] If the interests in the relevant shares are held jointly, then the conditions for determining "significant control" must be applied as if each joint holder held the entire interest.[158] Accordingly, the intention is clearly that the net be cast sufficiently widely to identify who exactly is pulling the strings behind the corporate veil,[159] but the definition of "significant control" is arguably so wide that it embraces persons whose control or influence is far from sinister, and who have a legitimate interest in not having their details publicised. To this end, the PSC statutory guidance exempts certain parties who exercise a degree of influence over a company's affairs, such as the company's professional advisers, third party suppliers, liquidators, the company's own managing director, and any non-executive directors with a casting vote.[160] This highlights the tightrope being walked in articulating a satisfactory and workable statutory definition of a PSC.

13–024 Even with a watertight definition of a PSC, a further difficulty faced by the company concerns how it is to collect the information that it is required to register. The company has a duty to gather the necessary information and keep it up to date,[161] and the requested parties have a corresponding duty to supply the information and keep it up to date,[162] with the company and every officer or other party in default being criminally liable.[163] The company's ability to obtain the necessary information is strengthened by having the power (without a court order) to disenfranchise, and impose other restrictions on, any shares held by an individual or legal entity that does not respond to the company's enquiries.[164] The risk of misinformation is not insignificant, and the company is required to confirm all the details before they are registered,[165] although quite how the company can fulfil this obligation is unclear. Moreover, given the possible risks associated with disclosing the personal details of those who might exercise "significant control or influence", certain protections are included.[166]

13–025 Once the company has gathered the relevant information, it must make its own PSC Register open to inspection by the public without charge,[167] or alternatively the company may elect to have the register kept by Companies House for this purpose.[168] Access to a company's PSC Register is not, however, unrestricted: those seeking inspection must provide their name, address and the purpose for which they seek access,[169] it being a criminal offence to knowingly or recklessly

---

[157] PSC Statutory Guidance, paras 3.2–3.3. The notion of "influence" extends the PSC concept beyond that of "shadow director", on which see para.10–010.

[158] CA 2006 Sch.1A paras 11–12.

[159] PSC Statutory Guidance, para.1.15.

[160] PSC Statutory Guidance, paras 4.2–4.10.

[161] CA 2006 ss.790D–E.

[162] CA 2006 ss.790G–H.

[163] CA 2006 ss.790F and 790I.

[164] Register of People with Significant Control Regulations 2016 (SI 2016/339) regs 14–21.

[165] CA 2006 s.790M(3).

[166] CA 2006 s.790ZF and Sch.1A.

[167] CA 2006 s. 790N–O. The information on the PSC Register will also need to be confirmed to Companies House at least every 12 months and will be held on a publicly searchable database.

[168] CA 2006 s.790W(1).

[169] CA 2006 s.790O(4).

provide misleading information, or to disclose information on the PSC Register to third parties.[170] Whilst these restrictions are clearly necessary to prevent abuse, it is difficult to predict which purposes might be regarded as "proper", beyond government agencies searching the PSC Register when investigating illicit activities. To curb improper requests, a company is given a time-limited right to apply to court to seek an order that it need not make the requested disclosure.[171]

Whilst the disclosure of PSCs might at first glance appear unremarkable (or even self-evident), this form of mandatory disclosure represents one of the more radical departures from the tradition of British company law for some time.[172] This reform is certainly part of a recent narrative aimed at combatting money-laundering, terrorist financing and corruption, and at piercing legal structures that might be used to advance these activities. It may even be part of a wider appreciation that, even when corporate activities are beneficial, companies wield such power and influence (over 95% of businesses are run through companies) that it is important to have a clear understanding as to who is really in control. **13–026**

SELF-HELP

Whilst the discussion above has proceeded on the basis that minority shareholders can rely on the common law or legislation for protection, a minority shareholder may also negotiate protections over and above those found in company law generally. The only obvious difficulty with self-help techniques is whether shareholders have sufficient bargaining power to introduce such protections. This may be the case, for example, if the minority shareholder is going to bring much-needed investment into the company. Even more generally, there is a strong incentive for shareholders to arrange for protective substantive or procedural rules that will apply in the event of a dispute. Such protections are warranted, given the limited application of the *Allen* principle (in light of its uncertain scope and high threshold for judicial intervention) and the weaknesses of the statutory protections in the event of a proposed alteration to class rights (in light of the narrow interpretation of the term "variation").[173] Moreover, shareholder self-help provisions can operate more broadly to protect shareholders in any corporate decision, irrespective of whether that decision needs to be taken by the shareholders or board of the company. This next section discusses the two principal means by which this sort of protection is delivered: provisions in the company's constitution or in a shareholder agreement. **13–027**

---

[170] CA 2006 s.790R.

[171] CA 2006 s.790P. For the issue of whether access to other types of register is proper, see paras 26–018 and 28–050.

[172] For other forms of market-based disclosure, see Ch.27.

[173] By establishing only default rules, the statutory protections for class-right holders encourage self-help: see para.13–015.

Provisions in the constitution

13–028 The company's articles of association provide an obvious place in which to locate any agreements reached for the protection of minority shareholders because the articles bind the company and its members as they exist from time to time,[174] so that future members are bound by the articles without further ado. That said, protective provisions in the articles will only be an effective way of safeguarding minority interests if they can be enforced. Often the minority shareholder will want to assert that a decision taken in breach of the protective provisions is not binding on the company and that an injunction should be granted to enjoin the company and its directors from acting on the invalid resolution. In principle, such an action should be available since the articles are enforceable as a contract,[175] although that enforcement is subject to several important (and potentially unexpected) limitations.[176]

Whilst the above issues apply to *all* shareholders, the particular weakness of the articles of association as a self-help mechanism for *minority* shareholders is that they are alterable by a special resolution passed by those entitled to vote on shareholder resolutions.[177] Altering the articles of association may provide a ready means of defeating the expectations of non-voting and minority shareholders, at least as long as no class rights have been created. As considered above,[178] even this is not insurmountable for the majority shareholders. The CA 2006 does, however, suggest one possible solution to the risk of future amendment, namely entrenching minority shareholder powers in the constitution.[179] The possibility of "entrenchment" allows the alteration of a constitutional provision to be subjected to a more onerous procedure than just a special resolution.[180] Indeed, whilst it is not possible to make a constitutional provision absolutely unalterable,[181] a provision's alteration can require unanimous consent of all the shareholders, thereby conferring a veto right on the minority shareholder. Given that an entrenchment provision can have a powerful and adverse effect on those it does not benefit, such a provision may only be included in the company's articles at the point of formation or with the subsequent consent of all the company's members. Accordingly, entrenchment is essentially a small-company facility.

Consequently, if the company is already in existence, it may be easier and more attractive to create a new class of shares carrying the relevant protection, to issue those shares to the shareholder to be protected, and then to include a broad variation of rights clause in the articles, so that, for example, the consent of the protected shareholder becomes necessary for the alteration of the protection.[182] Alternatively, the minority shareholder could be given effective control over

---

[174] CA 2006 s.33(1).
[175] CA 2006 s 33(1), considered further in Ch.11.
[176] See further Ch.14.
[177] CA 2006 s.21.
[178] See para.13–017.
[179] CA 2006 s.22.
[180] CA 2006 s.21(1).
[181] CA 2006 s.22(3).
[182] CA 2006 s.360(1).

shareholder resolutions. An example would be a rule that the quorum for a meeting of the shareholders cannot be constituted unless the minority shareholder is present, either in person or by proxy. Thus, the shareholder would effectively be given a veto over the shareholders' decisions, exercisable by refusing to participate in the meeting.[183] Whilst such a protection might be ineffective when the shareholders decide by written resolution, a solution might be to require the minority shareholder's consent for a written resolution or to provide him with weighted voting rights.[184]

Shareholder agreements

Alternatively, the minority shareholder may prefer to proceed by way of an agreement existing outside and separate from the articles. This has the advantage of privacy because such an agreement, unlike the company's constitution, does not have to be filed at Companies House. An issue arises, however, as to whether the company can effectively be made party to such an agreement, as it would be if the agreement were embodied in the company's articles. In this regard, there are two apparently conflicting principles: first, like any other person, a company cannot with impunity break its contracts; and, secondly, a company cannot contract out of its statutory power to alter its articles by special resolution.[185] In *Russell v Northern Bank Development Corp Ltd*,[186] the House of Lords preferred the second of those propositions. According to their Lordships, "a provision in a company's articles which restricts its statutory power to alter those articles is invalid".[187] The agreement in *Russell* provided that no further share capital should be created or issued in the company without the written consent of all the parties to the agreement. All the shareholders and the company were parties. Whilst the agreement was a valid shareholder agreement between the company's members, it was void as regards the company since it constituted a fetter on the company's statutory powers. Just as a company cannot validly contract not to alter its constitution, *Russell* suggests that a company also cannot contract out of its other statutory powers. As regards contracts not to alter a company's articles, however, there are two significant qualifications that may render the initial proposition ineffective in practice, at least for those who are well advised. 13–029

Prior contracts

The first qualification is that the principle of invalidity in *Russell* does not apply where the company has entered into a previous contract on such terms that the company would breach that contract by acting upon its subsequently altered 13–030

[183] The courts have been unwilling to undermine such arrangements through use of their powers under the CA 2006 s.306: see *Ross v Telford* [1998] 1 B.C.L.C. 82 CA (Civ Div). See further Ch.12.

[184] *Bushell v Faith* [1970] A.C. 1099 HL.

[185] CA 2006 s.21(1).

[186] *Russell v Northern Bank Development Corp Ltd* [1992] 1 W.L.R. 588 HL. See Sealy, [1992] C.L.J. 437; Davenport, (1993) 109 L.Q.R. 553; Riley, (1993) 44 N.I.L.Q. 34; Ferran, [1994] C.L.J. 343.

[187] *Russell v Northern Bank Development Corp Ltd* [1992] 1 W.L.R. 588 at 593.

articles. In this situation, the prior contract is not invalid: the *Russell* principle is not relevant because the term in the earlier contract is not broken when the company *alters* its articles, but only when it *acts upon* them. Whilst the authorities have tended to focus on directors' service contracts, the implications for shareholder agreements are that a company can be a party to an agreement not to act in a particular way in the future, provided that the company does not agree to refrain from amending its articles or exercising some other statutory power. In *Southern Foundries (1926) Ltd v Shirlaw*,[188] the company altered its articles so as to introduce a new method of removing directors from office and then used the new method to dismiss the managing director in breach of his 10-year service contract. The managing director successfully obtained damages for wrongful dismissal. Accordingly, the relevant provision in the service agreement was clearly held by the House of Lords to be valid. In particular, Lord Porter stated: "A company cannot be precluded from altering its articles thereby giving itself power to act upon the provisions of the altered articles—but so to act may nevertheless be a breach of contract if it is contrary to a stipulation in a contract validly made before the alteration".[189] Whilst *Shirlaw* concerned a director, the principle is equally applicable to shareholders.

13–031 The principal unresolved issue in relation to this first qualification is whether a claimant seeking to enforce his or her contractual rights against the company is confined to the remedy of damages or whether and, if so, how far, injunctive relief is available to enforce the earlier contract. In *Baily v British Equitable Insurance Co*,[190] the Court of Appeal granted a declaration that to act on the altered article would be a breach of contract. More surprisingly, in *British Murac Syndicate Ltd v Alperton Rubber Co Ltd*,[191] Sargant J went so far as to grant an injunction restraining an alteration of the articles that would have contravened the plaintiff's contractual rights. Although Sargant J's decision is generally regarded as based upon a misunderstanding of the authorities, some sympathy with this approach was expressed by Scott J in *Cumbrian Newspapers Group Ltd v Cumberland and Westmoreland Newspaper and Printing Co Ltd*,[192] as his Lordship could "see no reason why [the company] should not, in a suitable case, be injuncted from initiating the calling of a general meeting with a view to the alteration of the articles". To the extent that injunctive relief is made available in this way (namely, not simply to restrain acting upon the altered article, but to restrain the operation of the machinery for effecting the alteration itself), the notion that the company cannot validly contract not to alter its articles becomes hollow. Such an extension of injunctive relief would also contradict *Shirlaw*,[193] in which Lord Porter stated: "Nor can an injunction be granted to prevent the

[188] *Southern Foundries (1926) Ltd v Shirlaw* [1940] A.C. 701 HL.

[189] *Southern Foundries (1926) Ltd v Shirlaw* [1940] A.C. 701 at 740–741.

[190] *Baily v British Equitable Insurance Co* [1904] 1 Ch. 373 CA.

[191] *British Murac Syndicate Ltd v Alperton Rubber Co Ltd* [1915] 2 Ch. 186, which concerned the claimant's right, under both the articles and a separate contract, to appoint two directors to the board, so long as he held 5,000 shares in the company. Nowadays, the claimant might be protected as the holder of a class right.

[192] *Cumbrian Newspapers Group Ltd v Cumberland and Westmoreland Newspaper and Printing Co Ltd* [1987] Ch. 1 at 24.

[193] *Southern Foundries (1926) Ltd v Shirlaw* [1940] A.C. 701 HL.

adoption of the new articles". Injunctive relief merely to prevent the company acting upon the new articles would not, however, fall foul of this principle.

Binding only the shareholders

The second qualification is that an agreement among the shareholders alone as to how they will exercise the voting rights attached to their shares is not caught by the principle that a company cannot contract out of its statutory powers to alter its articles. This rule was applied to save the agreement in *Russell*, in which the House of Lords benignly severed the company from the agreement in question. Lord Jauncey said that "shareholders may lawfully agree inter se to exercise their voting rights in a manner which, if it were dictated by the articles, and were thereby binding on the company, would be unlawful".[194] The claimant was granted a declaration as to the validity of the agreement, and it seems that their Lordships would have been happy to grant an injunction had the claimant objected substantively to the course of action proposed by the company.[195] This conclusion in *Russell* flows from the more general proposition that the vote attached to a share is a property right that the shareholder is prima facie entitled to exercise and deal with as he or she thinks fit,[196] although the courts may nowadays seek to control attempts by the majority to confer upon themselves the ability to act dishonestly, capriciously or for some improper purpose.[197] Since the company can act only through its members to alter the articles, an agreement binding all the members is as effective as one to which the company is party as well. In one respect, however, a members' agreement is less secure than one that binds the company as well. On a subsequent transfer of a shareholding covered by the agreement, the new shareholder will not be bound without his or her express adherence to the agreement.[198] Essentially, a novation would be required. Nevertheless, the shareholders' agreement does play an important role in establishing the requirement for minority shareholder consent to important changes in the company's financial or constitutional arrangements in situations such as management buy-outs, venture capital investments and joint ventures.[199] **13–032**

Given some of the issues with shareholder agreements, a device analogous to the voting agreement (albeit more sophisticated) is the voting trust. This is not

---

[194] *Russell v Northern Bank Development Corp Ltd* [1992] 1 W.L.R. 588 at 593.

[195] *Russell v Northern Bank Development Corp Ltd* [1992] 1 W.L.R. 588 at 595.

[196] On the enforcement of shareholder agreements, see *Greenwell v Porter* [1902] 1 Ch. 530. In *Puddephatt v Leith* [1916] 1 Ch. 200, a mandatory injunction was granted to compel a shareholder to vote in accordance with his agreement. Some shareholder agreements may make their adherents "concert parties", thus triggering provisions that impose obligations on a member of the shareholder group because of the size of the group interest.

[197] *Braganza v BP Shipping Ltd* [2015] UKSC 17; [2015] 1 W.L.R. 1661.

[198] cf. *Greenhalgh v Mallard* [1943] 2 All E.R. 234 CA. Of course, the selling shareholder may be contractually bound to secure the adherence of the acquiring shareholder, but even so it is difficult to make the arrangement completely water-tight by purely contractual means, especially at the remedial level.

[199] See, for example, *Growth Management Ltd v Mutafchiev* [2006] EWHC 2774 (Comm); [2007] 1 B.C.L.C. 645. See generally, K. Reece Thomas and C. Ryan, *The Law and Practice of Shareholders' Agreements*, 5th edn (London: LexisNexis, 2020). If the power that it is sought to control is one that is exercisable by the board of directors, it may in addition be necessary to alter the articles so as to shift the power in question to the general meeting or to provide for its exercise by the board only with

uncommon in the US, but is less common in the UK. Under a voting trust, the voting rights are separated from the financial interest in the shares, the former being held and exercisable by trustees while the latter remains with the shareholders. Voting policy then becomes a matter for the trustees, who may use their powers to protect minority shareholders, although the voting trust may be driven by other considerations, such as a desire to make a takeover bid more difficult and thus protect the incumbent management.[200]

CONCLUSION

13–033 The mandatory protections for minority shareholders considered above are rather patchy. They apply only to voting at general meetings and not to majority control exercised via the board and, even then, only to certain types of shareholder decision. In the case of the requirements for shareholder voting, the protection provided manages to be, at once, both limited and uncertain in scope. It is perhaps not surprising that shareholders have resorted to private means, and that the legislature has attempted to make more far-reaching protections available under the unfair prejudice jurisdiction and the derivative action. Both are considered in the following chapters.

the consent of the general meeting or to provide that the shareholders shall take all appropriate action to prevent the company taking the steps to which a shareholder, exercising its rights under the agreement, objects.

[200] An offeror, where a trust is in operation, may acquire the majority of the shares, but still not be able to dismiss the incumbent management. Such trusts are common in the Netherlands. See further Ch.28.

CHAPTER 14

PERSONAL CLAIMS AND UNFAIR PREJUDICE

INTRODUCTION

It is axiomatic that only the person in whom a cause of action is vested may enforce the relevant claim. This straightforward principle impacts significantly on the steps that shareholders, especially minority shareholders, can take to remedy the wrongs they feel they have suffered. In this chapter and the next we deal with the various common law and statutory routes open to shareholders, and the impediments, sometimes unexpected, that lie in the way of each. The first route—the one addressed in the next chapter—is noted here in order to provide a complete picture of the landscape of these claims. If the cause of action is vested in the company, then clearly it ought to be for the company alone to take action. This is the "rule in *Foss v Harbottle*",[1] although even at common law it was conceded necessary to have exceptions to the rule, albeit exceptions of a special nature.[2] The exceptions were regarded as essential because the power to commence litigation in the company's name generally lies with the board, not the shareholders.[3] In those circumstances, a company's claim against its defaulting directors is unlikely to be pursued: compensation will then not be recovered for losses sustained, and the defaulting directors will benefit at the expense of the shareholders. To address this particular problem, the common law and now s.260 of the CA 2006 provide for the possibility of a "derivative action", whereby 14–001

[1] *Foss v Harbottle* (1843) 2 Hare 461 Ct of Chancery.

[2] *Edwards v Halliwell* [1950] 2 All E.R. 1064 CA.

[3] *John Shaw & Sons (Salford) Ltd v Shaw* [1935] 2 K.B. 113 CA. See para.15–002.

minority shareholders[4] can seek the court's permission to litigate a corporate cause of action for the benefit of the company, knowing that ultimately this will benefit the disaffected shareholders.

This chapter, by contrast, deals with the various situations where the cause of action is unquestionably vested in the shareholder personally. It might be supposed that in such circumstances the shareholder simply has to decide whether or not to sue, but the issues are rarely so straightforward. Each of the avenues open to shareholders appears beset by its own particular constraints. We consider, first, the shareholders' personal rights to enforce the terms of the corporate constitution, then their rights to enforce other personal claims against either the company, its directors or other related parties. Secondly, we consider the shareholders' statutory right to seek relief when the shareholders' "interests" (i.e. not merely their "rights") have in some way been unfairly prejudiced by those managing the company.[5] Finally, and very much as a last resort for shareholders, we consider shareholders' rights to seek a winding up of their company on the "just and equitable" ground in s.122(1)(g) of the IA 1986. This drastic remedy is rarely granted, unless there is a complete deadlock or an irretrievable breakdown in relationships within the company and there is no way to resolve the issues other than by dissolving the company, distributing its assets, and leaving each of the parties to go their separate ways.

SHAREHOLDERS' PERSONAL RIGHTS

Enforcement of the company's constitution

Only rights held "as a member"

14–002 As noted earlier,[6] the CA 2006 provides that the company's constitution (principally its articles of association) operates as a contract between the company and its members. It would thus seem to follow automatically that members (typically shareholders) can sue on this contract[7] and non-members cannot, even non-members intimately involved with the company (such as directors holding no shares).[8] Further, it might be assumed that the members can enforce any provision within the articles, regardless of the nature of the rights conferred by that provision. This turns out not to be the case. Even though s.33 of the CA 2006 contains no express limitation on the operation of the statutory contract, the courts have held that provisions in the articles of association can only be enforced by members to the extent that the provision confers rights "qua

[4] Majority shareholders are seen as unlikely to be affected by the problem, since they can dismiss the defaulting directors (see CA 2006 s.168) and appoint those who will pursue the relevant claims for the company's benefit.

[5] CA 2006 s.994(1).

[6] See paras 11–002 onwards and CA 2006 s.33(1). See also *Marex Financial Ltd v Sevilleja* [2020] UKSC 31; [2020] B.C.C. 783 at [103].

[7] CA 2006 s.33(1). See also *Haven Insurance Co Ltd v EUI Ltd* [2018] EWCA Civ 2494 at [3].

[8] *The New Saints FC Ltd v The Football Association of Wales Ltd* [2020] EWHC 1838 (Ch) at [36], fn.15. By virtue of Contracts (Rights of Third Parties) Act 1999 s.6(2), that legislation does not operate to confer a right to enforce the provisions of the articles of association on non-members.

member" (or, in their capacity as a member).[9] In *Hickman v Kent or Romney Marsh Sheepbreeders' Association*,[10] Astbury J stated:

> "An outsider to whom rights purport to be given by the articles in his capacity as such outsider, whether he is or subsequently becomes a member, cannot sue on those articles, treating them as contracts between himself and the company, to enforce those rights."

The same limitation applies to the statutory contract as it operates between the members *inter se*.[11]

Given the wording of the section, it would be difficult to interpret it as creating a contract with anyone other than the company and its members. Furthermore, there is perhaps sense in restricting the ambit of the section to matters concerning the affairs of the company, although the CA 2006 itself is not explicitly worded restrictively. The question is whether it is justified to restrict the statutory wording still further, so that it applies only to matters concerning a member *in his capacity of member*.[12] As a consequence of this interpretation, a promoter would be unable to enforce a constitutional provision that the company would reimburse his expenses, even if he subsequently became a member.[13] Nor would a member be entitled to enforce a provision that he or she should be the company's solicitor.[14] More importantly, *Hickman* would also prevent a member who is a director or other corporate officer from enforcing any rights purporting to be conferred by the articles on directors or officers.[15] Only if he or she has a separate contract, extraneous to the articles, will the director have contractual rights and obligations vis-à-vis the company or fellow members. For this reason, executive directors will be careful to enter into service contracts with their company (into which it is entirely permissible to incorporate provisions from the articles of association)[16] in order to safeguard their remuneration. Non-executive directors would be well advised to do likewise.[17]

In this regard, it is somewhat anomalous to treat directors as "outsiders", since for most purposes company law treats them as one form of paradigm "insider". Moreover, directors will breach their statutory duties if they do not act in

[9] While this restriction on the types of *rights* that can be enforced is well-supported by precedent (even if difficult to explain), it is less clear whether the restriction also limits enforcement to those provisions which impose *obligations on a member* "as a member". This would appear not to be the case: see *Rayfield v Hands* [1960] Ch. 1, where the provision concerned the liabilities of members qua directors. See also *Lion Mutual Marine Insurance v Tucker* (1883) 12 Q.B.D. 176 CA, where the provision concerned the liabilities of members qua insurers.

[10] *Hickman v Kent or Romney Marsh Sheepbreeders' Association* [1915] 1 Ch. 881 Ch D at 897. For support in a different context, see *Soden v British & Commonwealth Holdings Plc* [1998] A.C. 298 HL.

[11] *London Sack & Bag Co v Dixon & Lugton* [1943] 2 All E.R. 763 CA.

[12] The *Hickman* case may reflect the high regard in which the courts then held the doctrine of privity of contract.

[13] *Re English & Colonial Produce Co* [1906] 2 Ch. 435 CA.

[14] *Eley v Positive Life Assurance Co* (1876) 1 Ex. D. 88 CA.

[15] *Read v Astoria Garage (Streatham) Ltd* [1952] Ch. 637 CA at 641.

[16] Relatively little is needed for the court to conclude that the articles have been incorporated into the service contract, but there must be something: see *Globalink Telecommunications Ltd v Wilmbury Ltd* [2002] EWHC 1988 (QB); [2003] 1 B.C.L.C. 145.

[17] For a detailed discussion of directors' service contracts, see further Ch.11.

accordance with the company's constitution.[18] Treating directors as "outsiders" also produces some odd results. In *Hickman*, where the dispute concerned a provision in the articles stating that any dispute between the company and a member should be referred to arbitration, the arbitration clause was enforced. In contrast, in *Beattie v E&F Beattie Ltd*,[19] relying on the dictum in *Hickman*, the Court of Appeal declined to enforce a similarly worded arbitration clause in the articles on the basis that the dispute was between the company and the director qua director (even though he was also a member). Further still, in *Rayfield v Hands*,[20] a private company's articles of association provided that a member intending to transfer his shares should give notice to the directors "who will take the said shares equally between them at a fair value". A member gave notice, but the directors refused to buy the shares. Vaisey J held that, as the constitutional provision was concerned with the relationship between the member and the directors qua members, the directors must purchase the shares.[21]

14–003 There is, however, a compelling academic view that the *Hickman* principle can be side-stepped, in most or all cases, by the identification of an appropriate membership right. Lord Wedderburn has pointed out that,[22] in *Quinn & Axtens Ltd v Salmon*,[23] the Court of Appeal and the House of Lords allowed a managing director, suing as a member, to obtain an injunction restraining the company from completing transactions concluded in breach of the company's articles requiring the consent of the two managing directors in relation to such transactions. According to Wedderburn, the granting of injunctive relief in *Quinn* demonstrated that a member had a membership right to require the company to act in accordance with its articles of association, and that this right could be enforced by the member, even though the indirect result was to protect the shareholder's rights as a director. On Wedderburn's analysis, the supposed *Hickman* principle (to the effect that only membership rights may be enforced) is effectively outflanked. It would seem strange if this was not also the case when the statutory contact is enforced between members inter se.[24] Indeed, one might push Wedderburn's insights even further by suggesting that *Quinn* does not simply

---

[18] CA 2006 s.171(b). See further para.10–017.

[19] *Beattie v E&F Beattie Ltd* [1938] Ch. 708 CA.

[20] *Rayfield v Hands* [1960] Ch. 1 Ch D. See also *The National Federation of Occupational Pensioners v The Commissioners for Her Majesty's Revenue and Customs* [2018] UKFTT 0026 (TC) at [129].

[21] It is unclear what the position would have been if the director had not been a member.

[22] Wedderburn, "Shareholders' Rights and the Rule in *Foss v Harbottle*" [1957] C.L.J. 193 at 210–215. See also Beck, (1974) 22 Can.B.R. 157 at 190–193.

[23] *Quinn & Axtens Ltd v Salmon* [1909] 1 Ch. 311 CA; affirmed [1909] A.C. 442 HL. For subsequent dicta in support of this view see, for example, *Re Harmer Ltd* [1959] 1 W.L.R. 62 CA at 85 and 89; *Re Richmond Gate Property Co Ltd* [1965] 1 W.L.R. 335 Ch D (see (1965) 28 M.L.R. 347 and (1966) 29 M.L.R. 608, 612); *Hogg v Cramphorn* [1967] Ch. 254 Ch D; *Bamford v Bamford* [1970] Ch. 212 CA (Civ Div); *Re Sherborne Park Residents Co Ltd* (1986) 2 B.C.C. 99528 Ch D (Companies Ct); *Breckland Group Holdings Ltd v London & Suffolk Properties Ltd* [1989] B.C.L.C. 100 Ch D (see (1989) 52 M.L.R. 401 at 407–408); *Guinness Plc v Saunders* [1990] 2 A.C. 663 HL; *Wise v USDAW* [1996] I.C.R. 691 Ch D at 702.

[24] For subsequent academic discussion of the principle, see Goldberg, (1972) 33 M.L.R. 362; Prentice, (1980) 1 Co. Law 179; Gregory, (1981) 44 M.L.R. 526; Goldberg (replying), (1985) 48 M.L.R. 121; Drury, [1989] C.L.J. 219; Worthington, (2000) 116 L.Q.R. 638.

sidestep the *Hickman* principle, but actually highlights that the principle ought never to have been introduced in the first place.

Despite these criticisms of the "qua member" limitation, when the Company Law Review consulted on reforming this area of the law, no positive responses were forthcoming.[25] Accordingly, the Review recommended that the law be left as it is.[26] This might indicate that, although the *Hickman* principle may not be wholly desirable, the costs of contracting around it are not high given that practice has accommodated itself to the rule. Accordingly, commercial pragmatism has trumped doctrinal purity. This might also explain why there was no pressure to extend reform of the privity doctrine in s.6(2) of the Contract (Rights of Third Parties) Act 1999 to the statutory contract, so as to permit non-members to enforce rights in the articles.

Only matters which are not "mere internal irregularities"

Whilst the Company Law Review was content to leave the *Hickman* principle alone, the same was not true of another common law limitation imposed by the courts upon a shareholder's right to enforce the articles of association. Even when a member seeks to enforce a right conferred qua member, the claim may nevertheless be defeated if the breach in question constitutes "a mere internal irregularity". Classifying a right as "a mere internal irregularity" is effectively shorthand for the idea that certain breaches of the company's constitution should be enforced by the shareholders collectively, rather than by an individual shareholder. That said, the courts have largely failed to discern a principled basis for identifying those breaches that constitute a "mere internal irregularity" and those that do not. Litigation has generally concerned constitutional provisions dealing with the convening and conduct of shareholder meetings, or the selection of board members.[27] For example, in *MacDougall v Gardiner*,[28] the failure by the chairman of a shareholders' meeting to accede to a shareholder's request for a poll was classified as an internal irregularity. In contrast, in *Pender v Lushington*,[29] a chairman's refusal to recognise the votes attached to shares held by nominee shareholders was held to infringe the particular shareholder's personal rights. As the nature of the breaches in *MacDougall* and *Pender* are almost indistinguishable, the two authorities appear irreconcilable. 14–004

In reality, the tension between *MacDougall* and *Pender* probably exemplifies the conflict between two competing policy concerns. On the one hand, there is a policy of respecting the contractual and proprietary rights attached to a share, which would point against diminishing a shareholder's rights in any way.[30] On the other, there has long been a policy of judicial non-interference in the

---

[25] Formation, paras 2.6–2.8.

[26] Completing, paras 5.66–5.67.

[27] The CA 2006 contains default rules on shareholder meetings, but in practice the articles of association perform a significant role: see further Ch.12.

[28] *MacDougall v Gardiner* (1875) 1 Ch. D. 13 CA.

[29] *Pender v Lushington* (1877) 6 Ch. D. 70 Ch D.

[30] *North-West Transportation Co Ltd v Beatty* (1887) 12 App. Cas. 589 PC; *Burland v Earle* [1902] A.C. 83 PC; *Goodfellow v Nelson Line* [1912] 2 Ch. 324 Ch D. See also *Children's Investment Fund Foundation (UK) v Attorney General* [2020] UKSC 33; [2020] 3 W.L.R. 461 at [88].

company's internal affairs, particularly when the majority shareholders can ratify the matter. The rationale for this non-intervention is that, if every minor breach of the articles gave rise to litigation by individual shareholders, then the company's time and assets would be diverted away from its business activities, especially when the majority shareholders are competent to waive minor breaches, thereby making litigation both futile and expensive.

As Smith has suggested,[31] however, the only satisfactory solution to this type of problem is to commit to one policy over the other. Moreover, it is hardly an example of excessive judicial interference for the courts to hold a company (or any other association) to the procedures that it has freely adopted in its constitution to govern its internal decision-making (until such time as the company decides to change those internal rules according to the procedures set down for that to occur).[32] Indeed, safeguarding the procedural entitlements of members might be considered basic to any satisfactory system of company law.[33]

14–005 Part of the confusion in this area may have arisen because of a failure to appreciate that the same situation may give rise to wrongs committed both by the company and against it, and the individual shareholder's position may vary according to which wrong he seeks to redress. Thus, the chairman of a shareholders' meeting who breaches the relevant provisions of the articles may both put the company in breach of its contract with the members and him or herself be in breach of duty to the company to observe its provisions.[34] An analogy can be found in *Taylor v NUM (Derbyshire Area)*,[35] in which the plaintiff successfully sued his trade union[36] in a personal capacity to obtain an injunction restraining the union's officials from continuing a strike in breach of the union's rule-book (indeed, the act was beyond the union's capacity). On the other hand, the member failed to obtain an order requiring the same officials to restore to the union the funds already expended on the strike, as he did not have standing to bring a derivative action on the union's behalf.[37] This same analysis may also be applied to breaches of the articles.[38] In other words, the company may be regarded as breaching its contract with the member if it seeks to act upon an

[31] R Smith, "Minority Shareholders and Corporate Irregularities" (1978) M.L.R. 147. See also R Cheung, "Shareholders' Personal Rights under the Articles—Clarity and Confusion" [2011] J.B.L. 290.

[32] This argument would lack force only if (as is *not* usually the case for companies or, indeed, most associations) the procedure for amending the rules on how decisions are to be taken was the same as the one for taking substantive decisions.

[33] Such a statement would surely be regarded as uncontroversial if made in relation to trade union law. cf. O. Kahn-Freund, *Kahn-Freund's Labour and the Law*, 3rd edn (Stevens, 1983), pp.286 onwards. The courts do not lack techniques for dealing with members whose complaints are purely "technical", that is to say where it is clear that the same result would have been arrived at even if the proper procedure had been followed: see *Harben v Phillips* [1974] 1 W.L.R. 638 Ch D.

[34] CA 2006 s.171(b).

[35] *Taylor v NUM (Derbyshire Area)* [1985] B.C.L.C. 237. For the application of the distinction between personal and derivative actions to companies in an ultra vires context, see *Moseley v Koffyfontein Mines Ltd* [1911] 1 Ch. 73 CA.

[36] To which this distinction between personal rights and mere internal irregularities also applies.

[37] For consideration of derivative actions in the corporate context, see further Ch.15.

[38] In *Devlin v Slough Estates Ltd* [1983] B.C.L.C. 497, the court refused to recognise that an article relating to the preparation of the company's accounts conferred a right upon individual shareholders (as opposed to "the company").

improper resolution (and accordingly should be restrainable by the member), but the company is the proper claimant for the loss (say the wasted costs of organising the meeting) caused to the company by the meeting's chair not conducting the meeting in accordance with the company's regulations.[39]

An alternative approach to those decisions might be based upon the notion advocated by Wedderburn that shareholders have a personal "general membership right" to have the company's affairs conducted in accordance with the articles.[40] On the basis that this view is supported by *Quinn & Axtens Ltd v Salmon*,[41] Wedderburn's approach would undermine not only the "qua member" limitation considered above, but also the "mere internal irregularity" limitation. After some hesitation, the Company Law Review took a bold approach that was consistent with Wedderburn's stance, at least in relation to the "mere internal irregularity" issue. On this approach, *all* rights conferred upon the shareholders by the constitution should be enforceable by individual shareholders both against the company itself and other shareholders.[42] This would not necessarily mean that every breach of the articles would entitle each shareholder to sue the company for damages.[43] Damages would be an available remedy only if the shareholder personally had suffered loss as a result of the breach.[44] Where there is a procedural breach in the conduct of a meeting, equitable relief (such as an injunction preventing the company from acting on an improperly passed resolution) might be more appropriate. In other cases, no remedy at all might be ordered. If the breach of procedure was purely technical, and the resolution would have been passed even if the correct procedure had been followed, the court will not grant any remedy at all, and may even award costs against the claimant shareholder. The Review's proposal was subject to one qualification, namely that the shareholders could opt to include a provision making some or all of the articles unenforceable. In such a case, the relevant article would no longer be enforceable as a term of the contract.[45] Any departure from the default position of enforceability, however, would need to be clearly indicated. Unfortunately, the CA 2006 did not adopt the Review's proposal. **14–006**

Altering the statutory contract

In addition to the two specific common law restrictions on shareholder enforcement of the company's articles of association just noted, there is a further more general issue faced by shareholders. Reflecting the fact that a company is ultimately an association (like a partnership or unincorporated association), the **14–007**

---

[39] There is some suggestion in the language of *MacDougall v Gardiner* (1875) 1 Ch. D. 1; and *Pender v Lushington* (1877) 6 Ch. D. 70 respectively that the decisions may be explicable on the basis that the two courts simply fastened on different legal aspects of a single situation.

[40] Wedderburn, "Shareholders' Rights and the Rule in *Foss v Harbottle*" [1957] C.L.J. 193 at 210–215.

[41] *Quinn & Axtens Ltd v Salmon* [1909] A.C. 442 HL.

[42] Completing, para.5.73; Final Report I, paras 7.34–7.40.

[43] CA 2006 s.655.

[44] For the crucial distinction between corporate and individual loss, see para.14–001.

[45] Nevertheless, it might be possible to invoke the unfair prejudice jurisdiction, considered further below: see CA 2006 s.994(1). Nowadays, most breaches of the articles are litigated under this rubric.

company's constitution can be amended from time to time by way of special resolution.[46] This possibility is important to the sound functioning of the company, as it must be able to adapt its constitution to its business needs and environment and may need to alter its equity investor's balance of risk and reward. Making alterations to the constitution dependent upon unanimous consent would be unrealistic, as it would not always be possible to obtain that consent and some shareholders may take advantage of their hold-out position to extract corporate benefits. Accordingly, members join the company on the understanding that their contractual rights under the company's constitution may be altered (against their will) by the shareholders acting collectively.[47]

On the other hand, allowing the majority to bind an unwilling minority to a changed constitution can create the potential for opportunistic behaviour by the majority. We have already seen that the common law and equity impose general standards of behaviour on the voting majority to counter that risk.[48] There are also two further statutory techniques in the CA 2006 that seek to protect the dissenting minority from changes to the corporate constitution. First, individual consent is required of the affected member if an alteration requires members to subscribe for further shares in the company or increases their liability to contribute to the company's share capital or pay money to the company.[49] Secondly, whilst the company cannot generally contract out of the power to alter its articles,[50] shareholders can "entrench" provisions of the company's constitution, making them capable of amendment or repeal "only if conditions are met, or procedures complied with, that are more restrictive than those applicable in the case of a special resolution."[51] This power cannot be used to make the articles completely unalterable,[52] but it can make constitutional alterations conditional upon a particular shareholder's consent or some higher consent threshold than a special resolution (including unanimity). Entrenched status can be conferred upon provisions in the articles either upon the formation of the company or subsequently, but the latter case requires unanimous shareholder consent.[53] The registrar must be given notice of the adoption of entrenchment provisions and of

---

[46] CA 2006 s.21(1). Changes in the articles must be notified to the registrar: CA 2006 s.26. In the case of charitable companies, the power to amend the articles is subject to the requirement of the charities legislation operating in the three UK jurisdictions: CA 2006 s.21(2)–(3).

[47] *Shuttleworth v Cox Bros & Co (Maidenhead) Ltd* [1927] 2 K.B. 9 CA at 26; *Malleson v National Insurance & Guarantee Corp* [1894] 1 Ch. 200 Ch D at 205.

[48] See generally Ch.13.

[49] CA 2006 s.25(1).

[50] On the impact of this principle on contracts outside the articles, see paras 13–030 onwards.

[51] CA 2006 s.22, following the Company Law Review's proposal: see Formation, para.2.27. Under the prior law, entrenchment could be achieved by placing the provision in the memorandum of association and subjecting it to restrictive alteration conditions (and the prior law did seem to permit making a provision unalterable in any circumstances, other than a court order): see CA 1985 s.17(2)(b).

[52] CA 2006 s.22(3)(a) expressly provides that entrenchment cannot prevent alteration by agreement of all the members. This position is wise given that, even a member who insists on such a provision may, subsequently change their mind.

[53] CA 2006 s.22(2). On formation all the subscribers in effect agree to the contents of the articles, whereas subsequent members join the company on the basis of what those articles provide at that time.

their removal[54]; and the company must certify compliance with the entrenchment provisions whenever it alters its articles.[55] Accordingly, shareholders with particular interests to protect can use entrenchment provisions to sidestep the risk of their rights being altered by special resolution.[56] On the other hand, most companies would be ill-advised to use such provisions on a significant scale.[57]

Enforcement of shareholders' other personal claims

Types of claims

Beyond the enforcement of the statutory contract in the articles of association,[58] shareholders may have a range of other personal rights. Such rights may arise out of a shareholder agreement that can be enforced against the company or other shareholders.[59] Alternatively, a shareholder may have claims of a contractual, tortious or equitable nature against the company or against third parties associated with the company. In general, these claims are simply governed by general private law. However, company law has one company-specific rule—the rule on "reflective loss"—that may bar the shareholders' claim completely. And of course, the general law may make it difficult for the shareholders to formulate a claim that meets the facts that have generated their loss. **14–008**

The latter problem simply restates the common issue of whether the claim can be made out. For example, shareholders are unlikely to be able to advance claims that the company's directors owe them fiduciary duties. Such duties are owed, by virtue of the directors' role, to their company, but not to the company's shareholders. Nevertheless, as noted earlier,[60] such a claim may sometimes be made out on the particular facts.

Equally, shareholders may seek to argue that the directors owe them duties of care to protect them from economic loss. Again, although directors owe such duties to their companies, they do not automatically owe them to the company's shareholders, but again the facts may be such that the directors can be shown to have assumed responsibility in offering advice to the shareholders, typically in connection with the exercise of the rights attached to their shares, including selling the shares.[61]

---

[54] CA 2006 s.23.

[55] CA 2006 s.24.

[56] For the possibility of protection as a class-right holder, see paras 13–014 onwards.

[57] The entrenchment provisions can be overridden by a court order: see CA 2006 s.22(3)(b) and (4). Consider, for example, CA 2006 ss.899–901, discussed further in Ch.29.

[58] CA 2006 s.33(1).

[59] See paras 11–004 onwards and 13–029 onwards.

[60] See paras 10–006 to 10–007. See also *Peskin v Anderson* [2001] 1 B.C.L.C. 372 CA (Civ Div); following *Coleman v Myers* [1977] 2 N.Z.L.R. 225.

[61] *Customs and Excise Commissioners v Barclays Bank Plc* [2006] UKHL 28; [2007] 1 A.C. 181; *South Australia Asset Management Corporation v York Montague Ltd* [1997] A.C. 191 HL; *Gabriel v Little* [2017] UKSC 21; [2018] A.C. 599.

Reflective loss

14–009 Even where the shareholder has a personal claim that might succeed on the principles considered above, there is a second corporate law hurdle that has frequently doomed such claims to failure. This is the "no reflective loss" principle. This principle operates when both the company and the shareholder have a claim against the same director or other third party in circumstances where the shareholder's loss effectively "reflects" the company's loss, in the sense that recovery by the company would also restore the shareholder's position. In those circumstances, the shareholder's claim is barred. Notice that the rule does not merely prevent potential double recovery by the shareholder; that would be unexceptional. Rather, it prevents the shareholder's *claim*, insisting that in these circumstances the shareholder's rights will be satisfied, if at all, through the company's recoveries. This impacts on many of the claims that might be brought by shareholders, since those claims are typically claims to recover capital losses resulting from a drop in the value of shares or revenue losses resulting from the company having to reduce the dividends paid.

This area of the law has been subjected to substantial revision by the Supreme Court in *Marex Financial Ltd v Sevilleja*,[62] but a brief review of two earlier authorities assists in understanding the Supreme Court's judgment. The first substantial articulation of the "no reflective loss" principle was in *Prudential Assurance Co Ltd v Newman Industries Ltd (No.2)*,[63] and the majority in *Marex* largely subscribed to the legal principle as set out in *Prudential*, even though they considered later cases extending the rule to be wrongly decided. In *Prudential*, the directors breached their duties to the company by selling assets at an undervalue to a third party. The directors then obtained the shareholders' consent to the transaction by issuing a misleading circular convening a meeting of the shareholders. Accordingly, as well as liability to the company for stripping the company of its assets, the directors were also liable to the shareholders in the tort of deceit for their deliberate misstatements.[64] However, the Court of Appeal held that the shareholders' personal claim against the directors could not succeed on the facts: the only relevant loss claimed by the shareholders was the diminution in the value of their shares, and that loss was simply a reflection of the loss suffered by the company when its assets were sold at an undervalue (which loss the company could enforce in its own right, thereby remedying the shareholder's loss). As the Court of Appeal indicated,[65] "[w]hen a shareholder acquires a share he accepts the fact the value of his investment follows the fortunes of the company and that he can only exercise his influence over the fortunes of the

[62] *Marex Financial Ltd v Sevilleja* [2020] B.C.C. 783, considered below. See also *Broadcasting Investment Group Ltd v Smith* [2020] EWHC 2501 (Ch); *Nectrus Ltd v UCP plc* [2021] EWCA Civ 57.

[63] *Prudential Assurance Co Ltd v Newman Industries Ltd (No.2)* [1981] Ch. 257 Ch D; [1982] Ch. 204 CA (Civ Div).

[64] Where it might be thought that the appropriate remedy was simply to hold that the approval vote by the shareholders was flawed (being based on deliberately falsified information), and therefore not binding, thus freeing the company to sue the defaulting directors for their breaches.

[65] *Prudential Assurance Co Ltd v Newman Industries Ltd (No.2)* [1982] Ch. 204 at 224.

company by the exercise of his voting rights in general meeting". Accordingly, a shareholder's only potential recourse lies in the company's internal collective processes.

This principle that a shareholder cannot recover a loss that simply "reflects" the company's loss, even though the shareholder has an independent and personal cause of action, was confirmed by the House of Lords in *Johnson v Gore, Wood & Co*,[66] which concerned a claim brought by a company against its negligent solicitors. After the company's claim was settled, the managing director (who also owned virtually all the shares in the company) commenced proceedings against the solicitors to recover the loss in his shareholding's value and in the value of a pension policy established by the company on his behalf. Striking out both heads of claim as an abuse of process,[67] Lord Bingham stated the "reflective loss principle" in the following terms:

> "Where a company suffers loss caused by a breach of duty owed to it, only the company may sue in respect of that loss. No action lies at the suit of a shareholder suing in that capacity and no other to make good a diminution in the value of the shareholder's shareholding where that merely reflects the loss suffered by the company. A claim will not lie by a shareholder to make good a loss which would be made good if the company's assets were replenished through action against the party responsible for the loss, even if the company acting through its constitutional organs, has declined or failed to make good that loss."

Lord Bingham's statement of principle clearly follows from *Prudential* in limiting the "no reflective loss" principle to losses suffered by shareholders (not other possible claimants), being losses suffered in relation to the value of their shares or distributions (and not other types of loss).[68] That approach was justified by the need to respect the company's autonomy, protect the company's creditors and prevent one party recovering for another's loss.[69] In the same case, however, Lord Millett adopted a much more expansive approach: he held that the "reflective loss" principle was justified by the need to avoid "double recovery [to the claimant] at the expense of the defendant".[70] Given the breadth of that justification, the "no reflective loss" principle subsequently became unhooked from its earlier moorings. Not only was the principle relied upon to bar an ever-expanding variety of losses beyond those originally recognised in *Prudential*,[71] but its reach was expanded to claims brought by shareholders in their capacity as creditors or employees of the company.[72] This led to increasingly anomalous results, since a creditor or employee who was a shareholder was in a much worse position than one who was not, and for no

[66] *Johnson v Gore, Wood & Co* [2002] 2 A.C. 1 HL. For a critique, see Mitchell, (2004) 120 L.Q.R. 457.

[67] *Johnson v Gore, Wood & Co* [2002] 2 A.C. 1 at 35–36.

[68] The loss of the pension contributions in *Johnson* "were a form of distribution of the company's profits to its 99% shareholder: an alternative to the payment of dividends or bonuses": see *Marex Financial Ltd v Sevilleja* [2020] B.C.C. 783 at [65].

[69] *Johnson v Gore, Wood & Co* [2002] 2 A.C. 1 at 35.

[70] *Johnson v Gore, Wood & Co* [2002] 2 A.C. 1 at 62.

[71] For the potential breadth of "reflective" losses, see *Webster v Sandersons Solicitors* [2009] EWCA Civ 830; [2009] 2 B.C.L.C. 542. See also *Waddington Ltd v Chan Chun Hoo Thomas* [2009] 2 B.C.L.C. 82 HKCA.

[72] *Gardner v Parker* [2004] 2 B.C.L.C. 554 CA at [70].

apparent reason. Indeed, concerns were expressed that the principle's expansion threatened "to distort large areas of the ordinary law of obligations".[73] In addition, even on the narrow version of the principle, the cases confirmed that the jurisdiction operated even where the company had not, would not, or could not bring a claim in its own name. To meet some of the perceived unfairness this generated, a number of exceptions built up, none based on easily defended principles, and all now outlawed by *Marex*.[74]

14–010 This expansion of the "reflective loss" jurisdiction was stopped in its tracks by the Supreme Court decision in *Marex Financial Ltd v Sevilleja*.[75] A judgment creditor of two BVI-incorporated companies brought two economic tort claims against the defendant (as ultimate beneficial owner and controller of the two companies) who had stripped out their assets so that they were unable to meet the judgment debts.[76] Because the companies' liquidator might bring a claim against the defendant for recovery of the sums in question, the defendant sought to have the judgment creditor's claim against him dismissed on the basis that it infringed the "reflective loss" principle. Given that the courts had previously applied that principle to creditors who also happened to be shareholders, the defendant contended that it would be a logical extension to apply the principle to those only having the status of unsecured creditor.

The Supreme Court unanimously rejected the suggestion that an unsecured creditor could be barred by the "reflective loss" principle, but their reasons varied. The minority reached this conclusion on the basis that the "reflective loss" principle was not justifiable in terms of principle, policy or precedent and should be abandoned entirely.[77] The majority, by contrast, opted for a narrow redrawing of the principle of reflective loss, which then did not capture claims made by a company's creditors since "[t]here is no correlation between the value of the company's assets or profits and the 'value' of the creditor's debt, analogous to the relationship on which a shareholder bases his claim for a fall in share value"[78]: i.e. losses to the company's assets are not matched by (or, more loosely, reflected in) losses to the value of the creditor's claim in a way that is typically the case with shareholders.[79]

---

[73] A. Tettenborn, "Creditors and Reflective Loss: A Bar too Far?" (2019) 135 L.Q.R. 182.

[74] See *Giles v Rhind* [2003] Ch. 618 CA. The defendant's wrongful act had destroyed the company's business, so that it had no funds for litigation. Contrast *Gardner v Parker* [2004] 2 B.C.L.C. 554, where the directors' allegedly wrongful acts as against the company had put the company into administrative receivership (not by itself enough to prevent the company commencing litigation) and where the compromise of the company's claim against the directors, although on generous terms, was not improper.

[75] *Marex Financial Ltd v Sevilleja* [2020] B.C.C. 783. See S. Laing, [2020] C.L.J. 411.

[76] For a discussion of these claims, see para.8–058.

[77] And therefore should not, of course, be expanded still further to creditors who were not even also shareholders, as was being claimed in this case: see *Marex Financial Ltd v Sevilleja* [2020] B.C.C. 783 at [197]–[198].

[78] *Marex Financial Ltd v Sevilleja* [2020] B.C.C. 783 at [84]. This does not mean that, in shareholder cases, the majority thought there was a simple equivalence between the value of the company's assets and the value of a shareholder's shares, or that loss to one would inflict a perfectly proportionate loss to the other; clearly they did not: *Marex* at [32], [49] and [80]–[81].

[79] Although one of the principal complaints by the minority was that this assumed equivalence does not exist, and a shareholder may have suffered distinct and different losses.

That conclusion was sufficient to dismiss the defendant's assertion, but the issue of real interest is what remains of the "reflective loss" principle in its application to shareholders. The majority relied heavily on *Prudential* and *Johnson* to justify a narrowly drawn "reflective loss" principle, recasting it as a bright-line rule of law that prevents a shareholder claiming damages measured by reference to a fall in the value of his or her shares, or a reduction in a dividend, where the company has a claim against the same defendant arising from the same wrongful actions.[80] This being a rule of law, there are no exceptions, regardless of whether the company pursues its own claim.[81] By contrast, claims by shareholders that do not seek such narrowly defined relief are not affected; nor claims by shareholders where the company has no claim of its own; nor, plainly, claims by creditors. The bright-line nature of the rule was highlighted as having significant practical advantages for litigating claimants and defendants.

The rationale advanced by Lord Reed for this rule of law is that the shareholder does not suffer a loss that is distinct from the company's loss: the harms described by the fall in value of the shares or the inability to pay a dividend are harms to the company, met by the company's claims. Permitting a shareholder to advance them would contravene the principle in *Foss v Harbottle*,[82] namely that only the company can assert claims that belong to the company; if the company decides not to do so, there is nothing an individual shareholder can do about it, unless grounds exist for a derivative action or unfair prejudice proceedings.[83] For Lord Sales, the flaw in this lay in the very first assertion, i.e. that the shareholder does not suffer a loss that is distinct from the company's loss. When that *was* the case, however, and when the shareholder was simply seeking to advance a claim that was in reality the company's claim, Lord Sales too would disallow the shareholder's action.

Thus we have a rule of law setting out a principle of reflective loss whereby courts will deem the loss suffered by a shareholder in relation to the diminution in the value of shares or loss of dividends to be irrecoverable, as a matter of law, in cases where the company has a parallel claim against the defendant. But the justification for the rule remains contested.

Given that the principle appears here to stay, it is worth considering its various possible justifications. None advanced so far have been found entirely compelling, but together they suggest there is something in these shareholder claims that merits the discriminatory response now provided by the reflective loss principle. The first rationale, relied on by Lord Reed, has already been noted. The second, relied on by Lord Millett in *Johnson*, is that the rule prevents double recovery by the claimant.[84] Obviously, this can only be relevant if the loss being remedied in both claims is indeed the same loss, and the minority in *Marex* **14–011**

---

[80] *Marex Financial Ltd v Sevilleja* [2020] B.C.C. 783 at [9], [28]–[39] and [52].

[81] *Marex Financial Ltd v Sevilleja* [2020] B.C.C. 783 at [89], rejecting *Giles v Rhind* [2003] Ch. 618 (defendant's wrongful act had destroyed the company's business, so that it had no funds for litigation); *Perry v Day* [2005] 2 B.C.L.C. 405 (directors' wrongful act (as against both shareholder and company) consisted in accepting a settlement giving up the company's claim against the defendant directors); *Kazakhstan Kagazy plc v Maskat Askaruly Arip* [2014] EWCA Civ 381.

[82] See para.14–001.

[83] These claims are described at para.14–012 onwards and Ch.15.

[84] And, equally, prevents the double liability of the defendant.

doubted that. However, even when it is the same loss, *Marex* has held that double recovery is a general concern in litigation, not specific to these types of case, and so not capable of justifying the limited reflective loss exclusionary rule. Instead, the problem of double recovery, and double liability, needs to be managed through the court's case management powers and by application of the principles of unjust enrichment and subrogation.[85]

Thirdly, beyond Lord Reed's approach and double recovery, the principle has been justified on capital maintenance grounds, given that the courts have always frowned upon disguised returns of capital to shareholders.[86] In effect, a shareholder expropriates a corporate asset when it litigates a claim in place of the company. However, whether the shareholder's claim can, or should, be treated as "a claim in place of the company" is clearly the very issue that is contested. In any event, capital maintenance does not provide a satisfactory explanation when a company has distributable profits, so that creditors would not be prejudiced.

Fourthly, and closely reflecting Lord Reed's view, the principle might be justified as respecting the company's autonomy,[87] thus preserving the balance of power between the board and the shareholders, supporting notions of board control over corporate investment and the centralised management of the company's business, as well as the requirement that equity investment be locked into the company. Again, however, where this approach is tested is in explaining how and why these well-accepted principles should impact so dramatically on the shareholder's separate and independent personal cause of action against the defendant.[88]

Fifthly, the principle has been justified on causation grounds, with it being suggested that the true cause of the shareholder's losses in the value of its shares is the company's failure to recover from the defendant, not the defendant's breach of duty to the shareholder.[89] But this logic only follows if the *cause* of the shareholder's loss is the defendant's wrong to the company, not the defendant's wrong to the shareholder, so that remedying that loss, and repairing the harm to the shareholder, can only be accomplished by the company, not the shareholder, suing the defendant. In the end, therefore, this justification, like all the previous ones (bar the generic concern with double recovery), turns on the truth of Lord Reed's starting proposition that "the shareholder does not suffer a loss that is distinct from the company's loss": it is for this reason that the company, not the shareholder, should run the claim against the defendant.

Finally, it has been suggested that a sixth justification can be built by flipping the focus: instead of barring the shareholder's claim when "the shareholder does not suffer a loss that is distinct from the company's loss", it is suggested that the

---

85 This may well be true, but it no doubt leaves a rather messy practical problem: if all claims are allowed, the practicalities of working out what sums should be recovered by each of the parties might perhaps be readily (although not easily) addressed if all the parties and their various claims were before the court at the same time, but that is far from a given.

86 See further Ch.18. See also *Progress Property Co Ltd v Moorgarth Group Ltd* [2010] UKSC 55.

87 *Marex Financial Ltd v Sevilleja* [2020] B.C.C. 783 at [48].

88 See this justification convincingly explored and explained in P.L. Davies, "Reflecting on 'Sevilleja v Marex Financial'" available at: ***https://www.law.ox.ac.uk/research-subject-groups/commercial-law-centre/blog/2020/10/reflecting-sevilleja-v-marex-financial*** [Accessed 15 February 2021].

89 *Giles v Rhind* [2003] Ch. 618 at [78].

shareholder's claim should only be barred where "the shareholder does not have a *claim* that is distinct from the company's *claim*".[90] This shift in focus highlights the essential commonality in the statements of principle and in all the justifications for it (again, bar double recovery), i.e. that the company and the shareholder cannot both claim against the defendant for its failure to protect against *losses to the company's assets*. Even Lord Sales would agree with that. In both *Prudential* and *Johnson*, that was the essence of the shareholder's claim: there was no attempt to identify a distinct duty owed by the defendant to protect the shareholder from losses to the value of its *shares*, or to the value of its *distribution* by way of pension entitlements. Indeed, on the facts, it would have been impossible in those cases to find such a duty.[91] By contrast, in *Marex*, the creditor's claim (i.e. Marex's claim) was clearly distinct from the company's. As Lord Sales put it[92]:

> "If Marex's debtor had been an individual and [the defendant] had stolen all his assets with a view to preventing him paying the debt due to Marex, it would be possible for Marex to bring an *OBG* claim [an unlawful means claim[93]] against him … Marex would not be required to sue the individual debtor to make him bankrupt and then seek to procure his trustee in bankruptcy to pursue [the defendant] in the hope that a recovery would eventually lead to [Marex] receiving a dividend in the bankruptcy … Marex's rights against [the debtor] would not … be postponed [much less barred]".

But, rather proving the point that is made in these reflective loss cases, if a shareholder is substituted for Marex, and a thief had stolen the company's assets, then the company would have a claim in conversion against the thief, but a shareholder would have no claim *at all*, either against the company or against the thief, even if the thief had acted deliberately to drive down the value of the shares.[94] Indeed, this result would have been reached without a thought given to reflective loss: the analysis would simply be that the company has a claim, but the shareholder does not.

All that said, and however disputed these various justifications might appear to be, there is undoubtedly overwhelming support for the view that the ultimate result in *Marex* itself is sound.

---

[90] S. Worthington, "Reflective Loss after *Sevilleja v Marex*" (Chancery Bar Panel, 17 November 2020), with Simon Johnson and Peter Knox QC.

[91] The courts in those cases, and more so in *Marex*, commented on the limited consideration given in these cases to the nature of the shareholder's *claim* against the defendant; attention is focused entirely on the nature of the shareholder's loss. By way of exception, see *Heron International Ltd v Lord Grade* [1983] B.C.L.C. 244 CA (Civ Div) at 261–263, where, in the context of a proposed takeover, the board preferred the lower bidder to the higher bidder and, unusually, was able to take action to enforce its choice on the shareholders. The Court of Appeal distinguished between the harm inflicted on the company's assets by this decision (because it was unclear that the relevant regulator would allow the lower bidder to operate in the industry in question) and the harm suffered directly by the shareholders individually though their inability to accept a higher takeover offer for their shares (assertable in a personal claim).

[92] *Marex Financial Ltd v Sevilleja* [2020] B.C.C. 783 at [199].

[93] See para.8–058.

[94] The *OBG* analogy would not work: the thief would not have met the test of intending to render the company unable to meet its contractual obligations to the shareholder; those continued to be met, perfectly: see *OBG Ltd v Allan* [2007] UKHL 21.

RELIEF FROM UNFAIR PREJUDICE

14–012 We have seen the different mechanisms open to shareholders to enforce their personal "rights", and the various legal constraints that can limit their claims. By comparison, the statutory unfair prejudice jurisdiction set out in s.994 of the CA 2006 is surprisingly broad, seeking to provide relief when a member's "interests" have been unfairly prejudiced. Moreover, the regime provides a much more comprehensive form of protection for shareholders, especially when compared with the patchwork of contractual, common law and statutory protections considered already.[95] Section 994(1),[96] the first of the six sections which constitute Pt 30 of the CA 2006, provides that any member may petition the court for relief on the ground:

> "(a) that the company's affairs are being or have been conducted in a manner which is unfairly prejudicial to the interests of members generally or some part of its members (including at least himself), or (b) that an actual or proposed act or omission of the company (including any act or omission on its behalf) is or would be so prejudicial."

This provision repeats rather than reforms the provisions previously found in s.459 of the CA 1985, so the older cases remain relevant.

Controlling shareholders are not in terms excluded from using the section, although normally any prejudice they suffer will be remediable through the use of the ordinary powers they possess by virtue of their controlling position, and so the conduct of the minority cannot be said in such a case to be *unfairly* prejudicial to the controllers.[97] Section 994 thus operates primarily as a mechanism for minority protection—or, at least, for the protection of non-controlling shareholders, for petitions are often brought where there is an equal division of shares in the company.

By referring to the conduct of the company's affairs, the section is clearly wide enough to catch the activities of controllers of companies, whether they conduct the business of the company through the exercise of their powers as directors or as shareholders or both. The section can even apply to the conduct of corporate groups. Although the conduct of a shareholder, even a majority shareholder, of its own affairs is excluded from the section,[98] nevertheless, where a parent company has assumed detailed control over the affairs of its subsidiary and treats the financial affairs of the two companies as those of a single

[95] See generally Ch.13.

[96] The procedure for petitions is governed mainly by the Companies (Unfair Prejudice Applications) Proceedings Rules 2009 (SI 2009/2469), but also by the Civil Procedure Rules and the practice of the High Court, where this is not inconsistent with the 2009 Rules. Section 994(1A), somewhat bizarrely, specifically states that the removal of an auditor in certain circumstances falls within s.994(1)(a). The reasons for this provision are dealt with at para.23–018. Such claims should generally be heard in public open court: see *Global Torch Ltd v Apex Global Management Ltd* [2013] EWCA Civ 819.

[97] *Re Legal Costs Negotiators Ltd* [1999] 2 B.C.L.C. 171 CA; *Intermedia Productions Ltd v Patel* [2020] EWHC 473 (Ch); [2020] B.C.C. 582 at [112]; cf. *Parkinson v Eurofinance Group Ltd* [2001] B.C.C. 551 Ch D—the majority shareholder, removed from the board, was not able to use his shareholding to obtain redress in respect of a sale of the company's assets by the directors to a company controlled wholly by them, and so was able to use the unfair prejudice provisions.

[98] *Re Unisoft Group Ltd (No.3)* [1994] B.C.C. 766 Ch D (Companies Ct) at 777; *Odutola v Hart* [2018] EWHC 2259 (Ch); *Re Leeds United Holdings Plc* [1996] 2 B.C.L.C. 545 Ch D.

enterprise, actions taken by the parent in its own interest may be regarded as acts done in the conduct of the affairs of the subsidiary; and in some cases conduct of the subsidiary's business may amount to conduct of the business of the parent.[99] The "outside" shareholders in the subsidiary may thus use the section to protect themselves against exploitation by the majority-shareholding parent company.

Parties able to petition

The right to petition for relief under s.994 is conferred upon the members of the company,[100] but s.994(2) extends this right to non-members to whom shares have been transferred[101] or transmitted by operation of law.[102] As in the case of the derivative action, where a similar extension applies, this provision is useful in small companies where the directors of the company may exercise the power they have under the articles to refuse to register as a member a person to whom shares have been transferred, especially as s.771 now requires directors to give reasons for their refusal. If not within this extension, however, a non-member will not be able to petition under the section.[103] For example, if the registered shareholder is a nominee, the person with the beneficial interest in the shares cannot petition; the nominee will, however, be a legitimate petitioner and the interests the nominee may seek to protect include those of the beneficiary.[104] **14–013**

[99] On conduct of the parent as conduct of the subsidiary, see *Nicholas v Soundcraft Electronics Ltd* [1993] B.C.L.C. 360 CA, expanding upon the approach taken in *Scottish Co-operative Wholesale Society Ltd v Meyer* [1959] A.C. 324 HL, by not confining the principle to companies engaged in the same type of business. See also *Re Dominion International Group (No.2)* [1996] 1 B.C.L.C. 634. On conduct of the subsidiary as conduct of the parent, see *Rackind v Gross* [2004] EWCA Civ 815; [2005] 1 W.L.R. 3505.

[100] This may include dead or dissolved shareholders if their name still appears on the register: see *BW Estates Ltd* [2017] EWCA Civ 1201; [2018] Ch. 511. As the rights are conferred on members, members can agree to waive or vary those rights, or, as in *Fulham Football Club (1987) Ltd v Richards* [2011] EWCA Civ 855; [2012] Ch. 333, have disputes determined by arbitration instead.

[101] An agreement to transfer is not enough; a proper instrument of transfer must have been executed and delivered to the transferee: see *Re A Company (No.003160 of 1986)* [1986] B.C.L.C. 391; *Re Quickdome Ltd* [1988] B.C.L.C. 370 Ch D (Companies Ct). However, the fact that the directors have refused to register the transfer does not deny the transferee standing: see *Re McCarthy Surfacing Ltd* [2006] EWHC 832 (Ch).

[102] See *Re Company (No.007828 of 1985)* [1986] 2 B.C.C. 98951 Ch D at 98954 (Harman J): "In my view, transmission by operation of law means some act in the law by which the legal estate passes even though there be some further act (such as registration) to be done; and in my view the mere allegation that there arises a constructive trust cannot possibly amount to a transmission by operation of law".

[103] Exceptionally, in *Re I Fit Global Ltd* [2013] EWHC 2090 (Ch), the court held that a person whose name was not entered in the company's register as required under s.112 was a shareholder and could bring a petition. This was because during the trading of the company, there had been wholly inadequate formal corporate documentation and records.

[104] *Atlasview Ltd v Brightview Ltd* [2004] EWHC 1056 (Ch); [2004] 2 B.C.L.C. 191. Also, the conduct of which a petitioner may complain embraces conduct occurring before the petitioner became a member, even if that conduct is not continuing (though it must prejudice the petitioner), so that the beneficial holder will be able to petition if the shares are transferred to him by the nominee: see *Lloyd v Casey* [2002] 1 B.C.L.C. 454 Ch D.

Section 995 permits the Secretary of State to petition if, as a result of an investigation carried out into a company,[105] he concludes that the affairs of the company have been carried on in a way that is unfairly prejudicial to the members (or some part of them).

Finally, when an administration order is in force, s.994 is supplemented by para.74 of Sch.B1 to the IA 1986, permitting any creditor or member to apply to the court on the grounds that the administrator has acted in a way that has unfairly harmed the interests of the applicant (or proposes to do so) or on the grounds that the administrator is not performing his or her functions as quickly or as efficiently as is reasonably practical.[106]

As to the defendants to the petition, and apart from a requirement that the petition must be served "on every respondent named in the petition",[107] there is no guidance on who should be named. Normally, the net is cast quite widely to catch those directors or members responsible for the conduct in question. In this regard, it is also possible to join former members.[108] The company is usually made a party on a nominal basis.[109] It is also possible to join remoter parties[110] as respondents to the petition.

Scope of the provisions

14–014 When s.994 of the CA 2006 was first introduced in its modern form in 1980, it posed a considerable challenge to the traditionally non-interventionist attitudes of judges in relation to the internal affairs of companies.[111] The extent to which the modern judges have thrown off that traditional attitude emerges very clearly in the discussion that follows. The statutory remedy is capable of ranging very widely over the conduct of corporate affairs; it can address control of both shareholders' voting powers, examined in the immediately preceding chapter, and directors' powers, examined in Ch.10, as well as more subtle forms of unfairly prejudicial management.

Since the right to petition is drafted in deliberately wide terms, the first problem for the courts has been to define its scope. It is suggested that three main

105 See further Ch.21. A petition under s.995 may be instead of, or in addition to, a petition by the Secretary of State to have the company wound up under s.124A of the IA 1986 (see para.21–013), but it is notable that s.995 does not require the Secretary of State to be of the opinion that the public interest would be furthered by the bringing of an unfair prejudice petition. The Secretary of State's power of petition also applies to any company capable of being wound up under the IA 1986 (including in some cases companies not incorporated in the UK), whilst the general right to petition under s.994 applies only to companies incorporated under the CA 2006 and statutory water companies see CA 2006: s.994(3)–(4).

106 This provision is not considered in any detail in this chapter. For administration in general, see para.33–003. An unfair prejudice challenge may also be made to proposals adopted by way of a company voluntary arrangement (see s.6 of the IA 1986) but the court's powers here are confined to setting aside the proposals adopted at the creditors' meeting and ordering meetings to consider revised proposals.

107 Companies (Unfair Prejudice Applications) Proceedings Rules 2009 (SI 2009/2469) reg.4(2).

108 *Re Company (No.005287 of 1985)* [1986] 1 W.L.R. 281 Ch D (Companies Ct).

109 Companies (Unfair Prejudice Applications) Proceedings Rules 2009 (SI 2009/2469) reg.4(1).

110 *Re Little Olympian Each-Ways Ltd (No.3)* [1995] 1 B.C.L.C. 636 Ch D.

111 See the lament of the Lord President (Cooper) in *Scottish Insurance Corp v Wilsons & Clyde Coal Co*, 1948 S.C. 376.

questions have arisen, all requiring the court to decide whether to give the section (or, more accurately, its predecessors) a wide or narrow operation.

First, should the reference to conduct that is unfairly prejudicial to "the interests of members" be interpreted as referring only to their interests "*as* members", as with the jurisprudence on the statutory contract in the articles?[112] Decisions under very early predecessors to s.994 transposed this restriction with full effect,[113] but modern courts now take a more flexible view. The point is an important one, since one very common form of minority oppression is the expulsion of the minority shareholder from a position on the board. Under a narrow interpretation, this could not give rise to a remedy, since it amounts to oppression qua director, not qua member.[114] Now, however, although the qua member restriction remains as part of the unfair prejudice provisions, it is much more flexibly interpreted, and its practical significance is therefore much reduced. It is now accepted that the interests of a member, at least in a small company, may be affected by his or her expulsion from the board, whether because it was expected that the return on investment would take the form of directors' fees or because a board position, even in a non-executive role, may be necessary to monitor and protect the member's investment.[115] Similarly, prejudice to a shareholder's interests as creditor of the company also suffices.[116] It is difficult now to know what form of prejudice would not.[117] This approach is now settled, and will not be considered further.

Secondly, should the sections be seen simply as aimed at providing a more effective way of remedying harms which, independently of the unfair prejudice provisions, are in any case unlawful, or should the remit be wider? This may be termed the "independent illegality" issue. Once the modern statutory wording had been adopted, the courts opted quite early on for the wider approach,[118] holding that the provisions are not concerned simply with greater access and better remedies but, in addition, are designed to render reviewable some types of conduct that, apart from the sections, are not in any way unlawful. In many ways, this constitutes one of their most important judicial contributions to the development of the unfair prejudice jurisdiction, although the move creates its own problems. Deprived of the familiar landmarks of established illegalities, what criteria should the courts deploy in determining whether conduct is unfairly prejudicial, i.e. "unlawful" at least in s.994 terms? This is the second main issue that has faced the courts and it is the one that has absorbed the greatest amount of judicial thought and effort. It is considered in more detail below. **14–015**

[112] See paras 14–002 onwards.

[113] *Re Company (No.004475 of 1982)* [1983] Ch. 178 Ch D, decided under s.210 of the CA 1948. Section 210 referred to "oppression" rather than "unfair prejudice", and was generally interpreted very narrowly, hence the statutory amendments delivering the form we now have, first in s.459 of the CA 1985, and now s.994 of the CA 2006.

[114] *Re Lundie Bros* [1965] 1 W.L.R. 1051 Ch D; *Ebrahimi v Westbourne Galleries Ltd* [1973] A.C. 360 HL.

[115] *Re A Company* [1986] B.C.L.C. 376; *Re Haden Bill Electrical Ltd* [1995] 2 B.C.L.C. 280 Ch D (Companies Ct).

[116] *Re Haden Bill Electrical Ltd* [1995] 2 B.C.L.C. 280; *Gamlestaden Fastigheter AB v Baltic Partners Ltd* [2007] UKPC 26; [2008] 1 B.C.L.C. 468.

[117] *Re J E Cade Ltd* [1992] B.C.L.C. 213 Ch D (Companies Ct).

[118] See fn.130.

Finally, whether or not the courts had extended the range of unfairly prejudicial conduct beyond acts that are independently unlawful, there remains an important issue of the relationship between the unfair prejudice remedy and the derivative action. When a wrong *has* been committed against the company, may a shareholder leap over the restrictions on bringing a derivative action, formerly contained in the rule in *Foss v Harbottle* and now set out in the CA 2006,[119] by presenting a petition founded upon unfair prejudice and obtaining in this way a remedy for the company? Or is the petitioner under s.994 confined to the recovery of personal losses? In other words, are the unfair prejudice petition and the derivative action aimed at redressing different wrongs and, if so, how does one distinguish between them? This is the third issue that we shall consider in more detail after taking a closer look at the second.

"Prejudice" and "unfairness"

14–016 Given that the unfair prejudice jurisdiction is drafted in deliberately wide terms, the principal difficulty that arises involves defining the constitutive elements of "unfair prejudice". The concept is an objective one.[120] As indicated by Hoffmann LJ in *Re Saul D Harrison & Sons Plc*,[121] the petitioner must establish the separate conditions that it has suffered "prejudice" in a relevant capacity and that the prejudice is "unfair": prejudice or unfairness alone is insufficient. For example, a shareholder who is in need of funds may be prejudiced by the company's failure to adopt a scheme for the return of capital to its shareholders, yet there may be nothing unfair in the company's decision to retain the capital in its business in the absence of some formal or informal understanding between the shareholders that the company's capital would be returned at a certain point in its life.[122] Each requirement will be considered in turn.

The concept of "prejudice" is broad,[123] but a petition can still fail on the basis that there is no prejudice.[124] "Prejudice" does not require the shareholder to point to some identifiable loss that is quantifiable in monetary terms, but simply requires the shareholder to show that there has been some "prejudice or harm to the relevant interest".[125] Nor is it necessary for the applicant to demonstrate that

---

[119] See further Ch.15.

[120] *Re Bovey Hotel Ventures Ltd* [1983] B.C.L.C. 290; *Re Saul D Harrison & Sons Plc* [1995] 1 B.C.L.C. 14 CA (Civ Div) at 17.

[121] *Re Saul D Harrison & Sons Plc* [1995] 1 B.C.L.C. 14.

[122] *Re A Company* [1983] Ch. 178; as explained in *Re A Company* [1986] B.C.L.C. 382 at 387; *Re Guidezone Ltd* [2000] 2 B.C.L.C. 321 Ch D (Companies Ct); *Re J&S Insurance & Financial Consultants* [2014] EWHC 2206 (Ch).

[123] *O'Neill v Phillips* [1999] 1 W.L.R. 1092 HL. See also *Michel v Michel* [2019] EWHC 1378 (Ch).

[124] *Re Blackwood Hodge Plc* [1997] B.C.C. 434 Ch D (Companies Ct) at 458–459; *Reid v Reid* [2003] EWHC 2329 (Ch) at [40]–[44]; *Rock (Nominees) Ltd v RCO Holdings Plc* [2004] EWCA Civ 118; [2004] B.C.C. 466 at [73]–[81]; *Watchstone Group Plc v Quob Park Estate Ltd* [2017] EWHC 2621 (Ch) at [118]–[122]. See also *Guinness Peat Group Plc v British Land Co Plc* [1999] 2 B.C.L.C. 243 CA, which concerned the exclusion of the petitioner from an interest in a company where the shareholder's equity was negative. That said, *Guinness Peat* was mainly concerned with the inappropriateness of making such a determination at the strike-out stage of litigation, when the experts on each side were in sharp disagreement as to the applicable valuation methodology.

[125] *Re Saul D Harrison & Sons Plc* [1995] 1 B.C.L.C. 14.

relief will confer some quantifiable economic benefit on him, but simply that the relief will be "of real, as opposed to merely nominal, value to an applicant".[126] In *Re Coroin Ltd*, the Court of Appeal defined "prejudice" in the following manner[127]:

> "Prejudice will certainly encompass damage to the financial position of a member. The prejudice may be to the value of his shares but may also extend to other financial damage which in the circumstances of the case is bound up with his position as a member. ... The prejudice must be to the petitioner in his capacity as a member but this is not to be strictly confined to damage to the value of his shareholding. Moreover prejudice need not be financial in character. A disregard of the rights of a member as such, without any financial consequences, may amount to prejudice falling within the section".

We have already noted that the CA 2006 requires that the relevant conduct be prejudicial "to the interests of members generally or of some part of its members (including at least himself)", and that this is interpreted broadly,[128] unlike the interpretation adopted when considering the shareholders' rights under the constitution.[129]

The requirement for "unfairness", by contrast, can be more difficult to satisfy. **14–017** The term is clearly of wide scope, yet, given the long tradition of judicial non-interference in companies' internal affairs, the courts' initial approach was to limited the concept to conduct that was "unlawful".[130] Quickly, however, a wider approach prevailed in recognition of the fact that the jurisdiction was clearly concerned with controlling certain types of conduct that were not necessarily unlawful. Such an expanded jurisdiction needed some boundaries, and that created its own problems, as considered further below.

In defining the notion of "unfairness", the starting point is still to enquire whether the conduct in question is "unlawful" or not. In *Re Saul D Harrison Ltd*,[131] Hoffmann LJ was clear that conduct would prima facie be considered "unfair" if it was unlawful in the sense that it involved a breach of the company's constitution or directors' duties.[132] Just as with the enforcement of the

---

126 *Gamlestaden Fastigheter AB v Baltic Partners Ltd* [2008] 1 B.C.L.C. 468.

127 *Re Coroin Ltd* [2013] EWCA Civ 781; [2014] B.C.C. 14 at [630]; affirmed on appeal [2013] EWCA Civ 781.

128 See para.14–014.

129 See paras 14–002 to 14–003.

130 Under s.210 of the CA 1948, the House of Lords had defined "oppression" as conduct which was "burdensome, harsh *and wrongful*" (emphasis added): see *Scottish Co-operative Wholesale Society Ltd v Meyer* [1959] A.C. 324. This was the point that gave rise to the notion that the oppression section was aimed only at providing better remedies for existing wrongs. The Jenkins Committee recommended that the restriction, if it existed, should be removed (Report of the Company Law Committee, Cmnd. 1749 (1962), paras 203–206), and the courts, from an early stage, interpreted the substitution of the words "unfairly prejudicial" for "oppressive" as intended to achieve that result: see Hoffmann J in *Re A Company (No.8699 of 1985)* [1986] B.C.L.C. 382 at 387. The courts had already arrived at this position some years previously in the case of petitions to wind up the company: see *Ebrahimi v Westbourne Galleries Ltd* [1973] A.C. 360. See also paras 14–031 onwards.

131 *Re Saul D Harrison* [1995] 1 B.C.L.C. 14.

132 *Re Edwardian Group Ltd* [2018] EWHC 1715 (Ch). A breach of the terms of a shareholders' agreement may also qualify as unlawful conduct for these purposes: see *Faulkner v Vollin Holdings Ltd* [2021] EWHC 787 (Ch).

constitution,[133] however, Hoffmann LJ recognised that trivial or technical breaches of the constitution would not provide a basis for a petition. Beyond the familiar landmarks of established illegalities, however, it was unclear what criteria should be deployed to determine "unfairness". The solution to that conundrum required the courts to undergo a revolution in judicial attitude by becoming more involved in internal corporate affairs. Adopting this new attitude, Hoffmann LJ recognised that a company was more than just its formal documents. Accordingly, shareholders had not just rights, but expectations. Borrowing from public law, he considered that, even if conduct was lawful, it should nevertheless be viewed as "unfair" if it breached the petitioner's "legitimate expectations".[134] More recently, Lord Hoffmann has amended this label to focus on "equitable considerations",[135] but the substantive concept remains the same. The question in issue is whether it might be unfair to allow a party to exercise their strict legal rights in a way that equity would regard as contrary to good faith.

Nevertheless, whatever the language used, the difficult issue is to distinguish those expectations of the petitioner that are to be classified as "legitimate" (and so deserving of legal recognition and protection) from those expectations that the petitioner may harbour as a matter of fact, but that the courts will not protect. Not every factual expectation is legally relevant. Put in modern terms, the task is to distinguish those equitable considerations that merit a judicial response from those that do not. To date, the courts have succeeded in identifying one clear class of legitimate expectations, or equitable considerations, and have hinted at a range of other relevant situations, but without developing them in a comprehensive way. The clearly established category is considered first.

Informal arrangements between members

14–018 The first category of legitimate expectation or equitable consideration arises out of members' informal arrangements. In *Re Saul D Harrison & Sons Plc*, Hoffmann LJ indicated that equitable considerations would arise "out of a fundamental understanding between the shareholders which formed the basis of their association but was not put into contractual form".[136] This principle recognises that the totality of the agreement or arrangements between the company's members is rarely captured in the articles of association.[137] This may be so for a number of reasons, perhaps predominantly because of a desire to avoid transaction costs when establishing the company or when admitting a new person to the company's membership: it is cheaper to adopt some standard, or only slightly modified, form of articles than to bargain for customised rules

[133] See para.14–004.

[134] *Re Saul D Harrison & Sons Plc* [1995] 1 B.C.L.C. 14 at 19.

[135] *O'Neill v Phillips* [1999] 1 W.L.R. 1092, preferring the phrase "equitable considerations" for fear that the term "legitimate expectations" carried connotations that were too wide.

[136] *Re Saul D Harrison & Sons Plc* [1995] 1 B.C.L.C. 14 at 19.

[137] Whilst the equitable considerations will often arise when the company is formed, they may also arise at a later date, for example, when the petitioner becomes a member: see *Tay Bok Choon v Tahanson Sdn Bhd* [1987] 1 W.L.R. 413 PC; *Strahan v Wilcock* [2006] EWCA Civ 13; [2006] 2 B.C.L.C. 555.

dealing with every aspect of the relationships in issue. These gaps are then likely to be filled by some sort of common understanding, perhaps unspoken but evident from the ways of operating.

This approach is especially likely in small "quasi-partnership" companies,[138] but also in other close-knit groups where the shareholders know each other well and may even have worked out a successful method of operation when trading in unincorporated form.[139] When things eventually go wrong—and small companies emulate marriages in the frequency and bitterness of their breakdown—the precise provisions of the articles may seem almost irrelevant to the petitioner's sense of grievance. The unwritten understandings upon which the members of the company operate will then come to the fore. Adding to the complications, these understandings will also include assumptions that, where powers are exercised, they are exercised within the law—for example, powers conferred upon the board will be exercised in accordance with the fiduciary duties of directors—with the result that breaches of fiduciary and other duties may be tied into the shareholders' arrangements as well.[140]

The range of shareholder expectations that may be protected in this way is open-ended, although undoubtedly the most common is the petitioner's expectation that he or she would be involved in the management of the company through having a seat on the board.[141] **14–019**

Whatever the nature of the shareholder's expectation, the crucial point to grasp is that equitable considerations will only arise if it is possible to establish on the facts that an informal agreement, arrangement or understanding did operate outside the articles as a supplement to them. The "starting point" for the court's analysis will always be the articles of association themselves because "keeping promises and honouring agreements is probably the most important element of commercial fairness".[142] To go beyond that, "something more" will be required to dissuade the court from the view that "it can safely be said that the basis of

[138] This term has acquired a technical meaning in the context of winding up on the "just and equitable" ground, but here the concern is not with that particular form of engagement, and its essential element of trust and confidence: see below at paras 14–031 onwards. Here, however, all that matters is whether the relationship is one that has given rise to "legitimate expectations" or "equitable considerations".

[139] Whilst equitable considerations based on informal agreements among all the members is most often recognised in a "quasi-partnership" company, these may arise in any small company, whether the company is to be operated as an incorporated partnership or not: see *Re Elgindata Ltd* [1991] B.C.L.C. 959 Ch D.

[140] *Re Saul D Harrison & Sons Plc* [1995] 1 B.C.L.C. 14 at 18. This aspect of unfair prejudice is, of course, not peculiar to small companies, but applies across the full range of companies. This overlap gives rise to the difficult question of whether the unfair prejudice jurisdiction only provides personal relief or may also extend to corporate relief: see further paras 14–024 to 14–027.

[141] Accordingly, the unfair prejudice jurisdiction not only qualifies the formal articles, but also the statutory powers to remove the directors: see CA 2006 s.168. In this sense, the jurisdiction reinforces the validity of members providing for weighted voting clauses: see *Bushell v Faith* [1970] A.C. 1099 HL.

[142] *Re Saul D Harrison & Sons Plc* [1995] 1 B.C.L.C. 14 at 18.

association is adequately and exhaustively laid down in the articles".[143] If that "something more" cannot be established, the petitioner's claim will fail.[144]

For example, in *Re Coroin Ltd*,[145] David Richards J refused to recognise the requisite informal arrangements where the company's founding members were a group of highly sophisticated and experienced investors with little by way of prior relationship, investing in a project worth many hundreds of millions of pounds, and governed by lengthy and complex formal documentation. The court concluded that it would be hard "to imagine a case where it would be more inappropriate to overlay on those arrangements equitable considerations of the sort discussed by Lord Wilberforce[[146]] and Lord Hoffmann[[147]]". This confirms that the category of protected expectations is almost wholly confined to companies with small (often very small) numbers of members and probably with relatively unsophisticated governance arrangements. Beyond such companies, it becomes increasingly difficult to demonstrate, first, that there was any relevant informal arrangement; and, secondly, that all the members of the company were parties to it.[148] This means that equitable considerations are most unlikely to arise in public companies.

14–020 The approach just described was subsequently confirmed, and indeed re-emphasised, in *O'Neill v Phillips,*[149] the first decision of the House of Lords on what is now s.994. The founding entrepreneur had built up the business, but was slowly handing over control to the petitioner, a trusted employee, allowing the latter to acquire a quarter of the shares in the company. When the petitioner subsequently became the company's managing director, receiving half its profits, there were talks about his acquiring one-half of the company's share capital. Following an economic downturn, however, the company began to falter. The founder then removed the petitioner from his managing directorship, taking back the reins and paying the petitioner only a salary and the dividends due on his 25 per cent shareholding. After the petitioner resigned, he commenced proceedings alleging unfairly prejudicial conduct. The House of Lords rejected this suggestion because there was no agreement or arrangement between the parties, even at an

---

[143] *Ebrahimi v Westbourne Galleries Ltd* [1973] A.C. 360 at 379.

[144] See *Re Saul D Harrison & Sons Plc* [1995] 1 B.C.L.C. 14. See also *Re Posgate and Denby (Agencies) Ltd* [1987] B.C.L.C. 8 Ch D; *Re A Company* [1987] B.C.L.C. 562; *Re A Company* (1988) 4 B.C.L.C. 80; *Re Ringtower Holdings Plc* (1989) 5 B.C.C. 82 Ch D (Companies Ct); *Currie v Cowdenbeath Football Club Ltd* [1992] B.C.L.C. 1029; *Re JE Cade & Sons Ltd* [1992] B.C.L.C. 213 Ch D (Companies Ct); *Murray's Judicial Factor v Thomas Murray & Sons (Ice Merchants) Ltd* [1993] B.C.L.C. 1437 at 1455; *Khoshkhou v Cooper* [2014] EWHC 1087 (Ch).

[145] *Re Coroin Ltd* [2012] EWHC 2343 (Ch) at [636] (the point was not disturbed on appeal, [2013] EWCA Civ 781; [2013] 2 B.C.L.C. 583). See also *Re Migration Solutions Holdings Ltd* [2016] EWHC 523 (Ch); *Wootliff v Rushton-Turner* [2017] EWHC 3129 (Ch).

[146] *Ebrahimi v Westbourne Galleries Ltd* [1973] A.C. 360 (a winding up case).

[147] *O'Neill v Phillips* [1999] 1 W.L.R. 1092.

[148] If not all the members are party to the arrangement, then the issue does not relate to the conduct of the affairs of the company, and so falls outside s.994. See also *Re Blue Arrow Plc* [1987] B.C.L.C. 585 Ch D (Companies Ct); *Re Tottenham Hotspur Plc* [1994] 1 B.C.L.C. 655; *Re Astec (BSR) Plc* [1998] 2 B.C.L.C. 556 Ch D (Companies Ct). Consider *Waldron v Waldron* [2019] EWHC 115 (Ch); [2019] B.C.C. 682.

[149] *O'Neill v Phillips* [1999] 1 W.L.R. 1092.

informal level, that the petitioner should be entitled to receive half the profits, except for so long as he acted as managing director, or that he should be entitled to increase his shareholding to one-half.

Significantly, Lord Hoffmann, who had had a particular influence upon the development of the unfair prejudice jurisdiction in the lower courts,[150] gave the leading judgment in *O'Neill*. Whilst the House of Lords endorsed the substance of the lower courts' established approach, this was accompanied by a terminological shift from the public law language of "legitimate expectations" to the more traditional private law phraseology of constraining the exercise of legal rights by reference to "equitable considerations". Although not obviously more restrictive than "legitimate expectations", the purpose of the phrase "equitable considerations" was to anchor more firmly the courts' assessment of what might constitute "unfair" conduct given the formal and informal bargain struck between the shareholders. Indeed, their Lordships feared that continuing with the label "legitimate expectations" might be interpreted by lower courts as a licence to "do whatever the individual judge happens to think fair"[151] in the light of the petitioner's expectations. A more structured approach than this was required. According to Lord Hoffmann, the correct approach was to ask whether there were equitable considerations that required the exercise of the majority's undoubted statutory or constitutional powers to be constrained in any way by reference to the informal bargain that the company's members had struck. To ascertain the entirety of that bargain, the court would need to consider any informal, non-legally enforceable understandings between the members, as well the terms of the company's formal constitution.[152]

This more "contractual" approach to the assessment of "unfairness" might enable the drawing of an analogy with breach of contract and other doctrines for the discharge of contracts. For example, where the majority shareholders use their legal powers to keep the association on foot in circumstances in which the original agreement between the parties had become fundamentally changed, there may be an analogy with the doctrine of frustration.[153] In this regard, the House of Lords rejected the Law Commission's view that a contractual definition of unfair prejudice would unduly limit the scope of the unfair prejudice jurisdiction,[154] but seemingly more on the grounds that some limitation was a price worth paying for

---

[150] Lord Hoffmann's most significant contribution to the unfair prejudice jurisdiction before *O'Neill* was in *Re Saul D Harrison & Sons Plc* [1995] 1 B.C.L.C. 14 at 18.

[151] *O'Neill v Phillips* [1999] 2 B.C.L.C. 1 at 7e.

[152] *O'Neill v Phillips* [1999] 2 B.C.L.C. 1 at 10–11. In *Re Guidezone Ltd* [2000] 2 B.C.L.C. 321 at 356, Jonathan Parker J took the equitable analogy a stage further by requiring that non-contractual understandings be relied upon by the minority before they could form the basis of an unfair prejudice petition.

[153] *O'Neill v Phillips* [1999] 2 B.C.L.C. 1 at 11b–d.

[154] Law Commission, *Shareholders' Remedies* (1997), Cm.3769, para.4.11. An example might be the view that mismanagement of the company does not amount to a breach of directors' duties: see *Re Elgindata* [1991] B.C.L.C. 959; cf. *Re Macro (Ipswich) Ltd* [1994] 2 B.C.L.C. 354 Ch D. With the elevated standard of care required of directors under the CA 2006 s.174, this may be a declining problem because such cases will fall within the category of "indirect" wrongs: see further para.14–024.

legal certainty than on the grounds that all deserving cases would in fact fall within the section on the contractual approach.[155]

By drawing this contractual analogy, their Lordships considered that legal certainty would be promoted by expelling from this area "some wholly indefinite notion of fairness".[156] Accordingly, where it is possible to prove informal qualifications and supplements to the written constitution, the "extended" agreement sets the boundaries of the courts' intervention.[157] Such increased certainty regarding the notion of "fairness" would have the happy consequence of reducing the costs of litigation by discouraging lengthy and expensive hearings that range over the full history of the company and the relationship between its members. The Company Law Review endorsed the policy balance struck by the House of Lords in *O'Neill*,[158] and so the CA 2006 repeated, rather than reformed, the unfair prejudice jurisdiction contained in the preceding legislation.

14–021 On the basis of *O'Neill*, the strict legal rights of the majority, deriving from the articles of association or the CA 2006, may be subject to "equitable considerations"[159] that operate to channel and restrict the majority's exercise of its discretion and powers, in circumstances where all the members have demonstrably agreed (whether formally or informally) that those legal rights should not be freely exercisable. Putting the proposition in this way highlights the vigour with which the courts have developed the concept of "unfairness" in this context and its limited nature. As indicated above, once the courts had abandoned unlawfulness or illegality as the touchstone of "unfairness", the challenge for the courts was to articulate clearly what the criteria should be. The "informal arrangement" category of unfair prejudice provides a partial answer to this difficulty, since the courts purport to be judging unfairness in any given case by the criteria that the members (albeit informally) have lain down for themselves. On that basis, any charge of unwarranted intervention by the courts in the companies' internal affairs can be easily rebutted.[160] Moreover, in this way, the courts have largely avoided having to develop freestanding legal criteria. This approach to justifying judicial intervention by reference to the shareholders' internal arrangements repeats the emphasis, in *Ebrahimi v Westbourne Galleries Ltd*[161] (a winding up case), that equitable considerations do not flow simply from the nature of the company as a quasi-partnership, but that "something more" must

155 *O'Neill v Phillips* [1999] 2 B.C.L.C. 1 at 8g–h.

156 *O'Neill v Phillips* [1999] 2 B.C.L.C. 1 at 9a.

157 In *Re JE Cade and Son Ltd* [1992] B.C.L.C. 213, Warner J denied the proposition that "where such equitable considerations arise from agreements or understandings between the shareholders dehors the constitution of the company, the court is free to superimpose on the rights, expectations and obligations springing from those agreements or understandings further rights and obligations arising from its own concept of fairness. There can in my judgment be no such third tier of rights and obligations."

158 Final Report I, para.7.41; Completing, paras 5.77–5.79.

159 *Ebrahimi v Westbourne Galleries Ltd* [1973] A.C. 360.

160 This is not to deny that the degree of proof which the court requires of the informal arrangement may vary according to whether the alleged arrangement is usual or unusual in the type of company in question.

161 *Ebrahimi v Westbourne Galleries Ltd* [1973] A.C. 360 at 379. This was a winding-up case, but similar considerations apply there too and the winding-up case-law has strongly influenced the development of this category of unfair prejudice: see paras 14–031 onwards.

exist (something beyond the nature of the company), such as a clear informal agreement between the members, concerning, for example, the participation by the minority in the management of the company.

Even if the petitioner has established a prima facie case of unfairness, the petitioner's own conduct may mean that he or she will not be granted relief. While there is no requirement that the petitioner come to the court with clean hands, the petitioner's conduct might mean that the harm suffered was not unfair or that the relief granted should be restricted.[162] For example, in *Grace v Biagioli*,[163] the petitioner had been removed from his directorship, contrary to the informal agreement he had with the three other people who had established the company. This would normally be a clear example of unfair prejudice. The petitioner had, however, put himself in a position of conflict by seeking to purchase a competing company. The Court of Appeal held this was sufficient to justify his removal from the board in breach of the parties' agreement. In essence, in deciding whether the majority could exercise its legal rights, or was constrained by equitable considerations, the courts are balancing the parties' relative fault.[164] As a consequence, here the prejudice to the petitioner was not unfair. Similarly, there may be no "unfairness" where the petitioner may have consented to, and even benefited from, the company being run in a way that would normally be regarded as unfairly prejudicial to the petitioner's interests.[165]

The balance between dividends and directors' remuneration

Another common source of perceived unfairness arises where the petitioner has never been, or has ceased to be, a director of the company: then a frequent cause of dispute is the payment of excessive remuneration to the company's directors and the failure to declare dividends payable to all the shareholders.[166] Absent any special arrangement in that regard (whether formal or informal), minority shareholders can have no legitimate expectation that dividends will be declared and paid simply because they are shareholders, even in the context of a "quasi-partnership" company.[167] On the other hand, there may be particular circumstances in which it would be unfairly prejudicial to refuse to pay any dividends, to pay only derisory sums, or to fail to consider properly whether or **14–022**

[162] *Re Stratos Club Ltd* [2020] EWHC 3485 (Ch). See also *Ming Siu Hing v JF Ming Inc* [2021] UKPC 1 at [19], where the petitioner's conduct was described as "a factor of infinitely variable weight" in the exercise of the court's discretion pursuant to the unfair prejudice jurisdiction.

[163] *Grace v Biagioli* [2006] 2 B.C.L.C. 70 CA, following *Re London School of Electronics* [1986] Ch. 211 Ch D. See also *Re Home & Office Fire Extinguishers Ltd* [2012] EWHC 917; *Interactive Technology Corporation Ltd v Ferster* [2016] EWHC 2896 (Ch); *Badyal v Badyal* [2018] EWHC 68 (Ch).

[164] *Interactive Technology Corporation v Ferster* [2016] EWHC 2896 (Ch). See also *Ming Siu Hing v JF Ming Inc* [2021] UKPC 1 at [18]–[19].

[165] *Jesner v Jarrad Properties Ltd* [1993] B.C.L.C. 1032 Inner House, although note the qualifications in *Re J&S Insurance & Financial Consultants* [2014] EWHC 2206 (Ch).

[166] *Re CF Booth Ltd* [2017] EWHC 457 (Ch); *Re AMT Coffee Ltd* [2019] EWHC 46 (Ch). Where the distribution to the majority shareholders is unlawful, this would provide a strong basis for an unfair prejudice claim: see *VB Football Assets v Blackpool Football Club (Properties) Ltd* [2017] EWHC 2767 (Ch).

[167] *Irvine v Irvine (No.1)* [2006] EWHC 406 (Ch); [2007] 1 B.C.L.C. 349 at 421.

not dividends should be declared.[168] This might be the case where there was an arrangement that all the profits of the company should always be distributed in one way or another; that the fiscally efficient way of dealing with the profits would be to pay directors generously; or that the petitioner should not be deprived of a profit-share simply by virtue of not being on the board.[169] The courts have also refused to strike out a petition alleging that the non-payment of dividends produced a disparity between the petitioner and respondents as regards their participation in the company's profits because the respondents obtained their return through the payment of directors' remuneration, whilst the petitioners were excluded from any substantial return.[170]

As regards directors' remuneration (which is often the flip side of the coin to non-payment of dividends), an unfair prejudice petition is likely to succeed if the directors have fixed their remuneration in disregard of the constitutional provisions governing that matter.[171] Where the controllers have executive positions within the company and the petitioner does not, it may well be perfectly fair that the payments to the controllers by way of directors' salaries and perks should exceed the petitioner's dividend payments. Where the proper procedures for fixing the directors' remuneration have not been followed, however, the courts unsurprisingly have not shrunk from embarking on the exercise of determining whether the directors' remuneration package is excessive in order to establish whether the petitioner has suffered unfair prejudice. In determining an appropriate level of remuneration for the directors, the courts will refer to "objective commercial criteria" in order to see whether the remuneration was "within the bracket that executives carrying that sort of responsibility and discharging the sort of duties [the respondent] was would expect to receive".[172]

Note, however, that any view of the alleged breaches of the articles or general law in the context of setting directors' remuneration may need to be modified in the light of the parties' own private informal agreements, as discussed in the previous section in considering the general principles in *O'Neill*.

Other categories of unfair prejudice

14–023 Although the case law is dominated by the "informal arrangement" category of unfair prejudice, the language of s.994 of the CA 2006 in no way permits the courts to confine unfairness to that category. That said, once the courts venture beyond defining "unfairness" by reference to unlawfulness or the parties' own internal arrangements, and the linked question of whether the controllers have committed breaches of their fiduciary duties, the issue of how the courts should

[168] *Re McCarthy Surfacing* [2008] EWHC 2279 (Ch); [2009] B.C.L.C. 622; *Re J&S Insurance & Financial Consultants Ltd* [2014] EWHC 2206 (Ch).

[169] *Irvine v Irvine (No.1)* [2007] 1 B.C.L.C. 349 at 421; *Re McCarthy Surfacing* [2009] B.C.L.C. 622; *Sikorski v Sikorski* [2012] EWHC 1613 (Ch).

[170] *Re Sam Weller & Sons Ltd* [1990] B.C.L.C. 80 Ch D.

[171] *Irvine v Irvine (No.1)* [2007] 1 B.C.L.C. 349; *Re Ravenhart Services (Holdings) Ltd* [2004] 2 B.C.L.C. 375.

[172] *Irvine v Irvine (No.1)* [2007] 1 B.C.L.C. 349 at 420. Guidance can be taken from guidelines on the remuneration of directors in listed companies: see *Re Tobian Properties Ltd* [2012] EWCA Civ 998 at [36].

set bounds to their intervention arises in an acute way.[173] Probably for this reason alone, no further clearly defined categories of unfair prejudice can be found in the authorities, although isolated instances exist. An examination of these cases is likely to be important in identifying the significance of unfair prejudice outside the context of small companies.

One approach to identifying "unfairness" beyond the established categories is to reason by analogy from established standards and circumstances, thereby extending the notion of "unfairness" into cognate areas not previously covered. For example, in *Re A Company*,[174] in determining whether unfair prejudice existed, the court relied upon the City Code on Takeovers and Mergers as a guide to what the directors of a target company should do by way of communication with their shareholders, even though the target was a private company falling outside the formal scope of the Code.[175] Similarly, in *McGuinness v Bremner Plc*,[176] when the judge was deciding whether delay on the part of the directors in convening a meeting requisitioned by the petitioners was unfairly prejudicial, the judge found a useful analogy in the model articles under the CA 1985,[177] even though the company in question had not adopted that version. Such reasoning by analogy plays a useful role in defending the courts against the charge of unwarranted or inexpert interference.

An appropriate analogy will not, however, be available in all cases. In those circumstances, the court may have to develop its own criteria. For example, the company may have adopted a policy of only paying low dividends, even though the company could pay more and the controllers have been paid an income by way of directors' fees. Is that unfairly prejudicial to the interests of the non-director shareholders, even in the absence of any informal understanding as to the level of dividend pay-outs or as to the petitioner's participation in the company's management as a director (thus entitling him to directors' fees)? The courts have shown themselves willing to entertain such claims within the unfair prejudice jurisdiction, but have not yet had to adjudicate on the merits of such cases where there is otherwise no breach of directors' duties or no private

[173] As a general rule, if the petitioner cannot establish the existence of an arrangement between the members, the petition is likely to fail: see *George v McCarthy* [2019] EWHC 2939 (Ch).

[174] *Re A Company* [1986] B.C.L.C. 382. See also *Re St Piran Ltd* [1981] 1 W.L.R. 1300 Ch D; cf. *Re Astec (BSR) Plc* [1998] 2 B.C.L.C. 556 at 579. See also *Re Phoenix Contracts (Leicester) Ltd* [2010] EWHC 2375 (Ch).

[175] Although the Code was used only as a guide, the judge borrowed from the Code the proposition that any advice given by the directors should be given in the interests of the shareholders, but he did not borrow the further proposition that the directors were obliged to give the shareholders their view on the bid: see further Ch.28.

[176] *McGuinness v Bremner Plc* [1988] B.C.L.C. 673. See also *Bermuda Cablevision Ltd v Colica Trust Co Ltd* [1998] A.C. 198 PC (analogy with the criminal law, though the directors were acting, presumably, in breach of fiduciary duty). However, the courts have not in general been prepared to use the unfair prejudice petition as a way of curing defects in the statutory protections conferred upon minorities: see *CAS (Nominees) Ltd v Nottingham Forest FC Plc* [2002] 1 B.C.L.C. 613 Ch D (Companies Ct) (avoidance of minority power to block share issue, on which see para.24–004); *Rock Nominees Ltd v RCO (Holdings) Plc* [2004] 1 B.C.L.C. 439 (avoidance of minority's power to reject a "squeeze out" after a takeover, on which see para.28–070).

[177] Companies (Tables A to F) Regulations 1985 (SI 1985/805) Table A art.37.

arrangements in existence.[178] The courts could approach this issue by working out the appropriate distribution policy for the company (or for companies of that type). This seems unlikely. Alternatively, the courts could make reference to a general legal standard by asking whether the dividend policy in question unfairly discriminated between the director-insiders and the shareholder-outsiders.[179] Of these two approaches, the latter is less interventionist, and accordingly more attractive.

Unfair prejudice and the derivative action

14–024 It may seem odd at first sight that a right of petition vested in the individual member might potentially be used to secure the redress of wrongs done to the company, especially those committed by its directors. When a wrong has been committed against the company, it is the company that must sue.[180] Traditionally, the decision to sue is vested in the board; this can create moral dilemmas for directors deciding to enforce breaches of directors' duties.[181] To deal with this issue, we now have a statutory derivative action (considered in Ch.15), whereby an individual shareholder can leap over the company's internal restrictions and seek permission from the court to commence proceedings in the company's name to enforce the company's claims. By contrast, the unfair prejudice jurisdiction protects the "interests" of the members, not just their strict rights, and clearly a wrong done to the company can affect the members' interests. Accordingly, given the breadth of the unfair prejudice jurisdiction, it is not inconceivable that corporate wrongs might be addressed by this route.[182]

Certainly, the Jenkins Committee, whose report recommended the introduction of the unfair prejudice remedy, envisaged that that jurisdiction would have a role in relation to wrongs done to the company:

> "In addition to these direct wrongs[183] to the minority, there is the type of case in which a wrong is done to the company itself and the control vested in the majority is wrongfully used to prevent action being taken against the wrongdoer. In such a case the minority is indirectly wronged."[184]

---

[178] *Re Sam Weller Ltd* [1990] Ch. 682 Ch D, where the judge refused to strike out the claim. The case was largely concerned with the now irrelevant issue of whether the dividend policy affected all the shareholders equally; cf. *Re A Company Ex p. Glossop* [1988] 1 W.L.R. 1068 Ch D (Companies Ct). Where the decisions on policy are in breach of the general law, see *Re McCarthy Surfacing Ltd* [2009] B.C.L.C. 622.

[179] *Re Company (No.004415 of 1996)* [1997] 1 B.C.L.C. 479 Ch D.

[180] *Foss v Harbottle* (1843) 2 Hare 461.

[181] CA 2006 s.170(1).

[182] Before the introduction of the words "of its members generally" into the CA 1985 s.459 in 1989, there was an argument that a wrong done to the company, which affected all the members equally, fell outside the section: see *Re Carrington Viyella Plc* (1983) 1 B.C.C. 98 951, though the exact scope of the point was never finally settled. This argument is no longer available under the CA 2006 s.994(1).

[183] "Direct wrongs", i.e. where the harm is inflicted directly on the minority and not via a diminution in the value of their stake in the company. On the difficulty of recovering for such losses, see *Marex Financial Ltd v Sevilleja* [2020] B.C.C. 783 at [79].

[184] *Report of the Company Law Committee* (1962), Cm.1749, para.206.

There is, however, an ambiguity in this statement. On the one hand, the Jenkins Committee might simply have meant to indicate that, where a wrong done to the company has also inflicted harm on the shareholder, the member can invoke the unfair prejudice jurisdiction to obtain redress for that personal harm. If so, that seems uncontroversial. Unfair prejudice petitions have regularly been entertained by the courts where the petitioner suffers prejudice as a result of wrongdoers' conduct that consists wholly or partly of wrongs done to the company (such as directors' breaches of duty).[185] Moreover, the courts have refused to accept that the availability of a derivative action should constitute a bar to an unfair prejudice petition.[186] As Hoffmann LJ stated, in *Re Saul D Harrison & Sons Plc*,[187] "[e]nabling the court in an appropriate case to outflank the rule in *Foss v Harbottle* was one of the purposes of the section".

On the other hand, the Committee might have meant that the court could award relief to the *company* in a s.994 claim in order to redress the harm done to it.[188] This approach immediately raises the issue of how the unfair prejudice remedy interacts with the statutory derivative action.[189] In particular, what sort of "outflanking" of the derivative action is envisaged? Whilst it may just possibly be legitimate to view the unfair prejudice remedy as designed to overcome the excessively strict limitations on the derivative action imposed by the common law, it will hardly conduce to a coherent reading of the CA 2006 to allow the unfair prejudice jurisdiction to be interpreted in such a manner as to side-step the new statutory derivative action. Any "outflanking" is immaterial if the unfair prejudice remedy simply provides another route to a court-ordered derivative action seeking a remedy for wrongs done to the company, as this is expressly permitted by the CA 2006.[190] Moreover, in exercising its remedial discretion pursuant to the unfair prejudice jurisdiction,[191] a court may have regard to the factors applicable to the standard statutory derivative action.[192] These factors recognise that it may not always be in the company's best interests to enforce its legal rights, even when enforcement is likely to be successful. In practice, however, a shareholder is unlikely to use the unfair prejudice jurisdiction to bring a derivative action instead of seeking the court's permission directly, given that

---

[185] *Re Stewarts (Brixton) Ltd* [1985] B.C.L.C. 4; *Re London School of Electronics* [1986] Ch. 211; *Re Cumana Ltd* [1986] B.C.L.C. 430 (all involving various forms of diversion of the company's business to rival companies in which the majority were interested); *Re A Company Ex p. Glossop* [1988] 1 W.L.R. 1068; *McCarthy Surfacing Ltd* [2009] B.C.L.C. 622 (both involving exercise of directors' powers for an improper purpose); *Re Saul D Harrison & Sons Plc* [1995] 1 B.C.L.C. 14 (failure of directors to act bona fide in the interests of the company). Not all these cases succeeded, but given that they all involved unlawful or illegal conduct, there can be little doubt that they fell within the scope of the unfair prejudice jurisdiction. See also *Albion Energy Ltd v Energy Investments Global BRL* [2020] EWHC 301 (Comm) at [80].

[186] *Re Company (No.005287 of 1985)* [1986] 1 W.L.R. 281; *Re Stewarts (Brixton) Ltd* [1985] B.C.L.C. 4; *Lowe v Fahey* [1996] 1 B.C.L.C. 262 Ch D.

[187] *Re Saul D Harrison & Sons Plc* [1995] 1 B.C.L.C. 14 at 18.

[188] *Apex Global Management Ltd v FI Call Ltd* [2014] B.C.C. 286 at [125].

[189] CA 2006 s.260(1), considered in Ch.15.

[190] CA 2006 s.996(2)(c). Similarly, the provisions relating to the derivative action make clear that such an action can be brought "in pursuance of an order of the court in proceedings under section 994": CA 2006 s.260(2).

[191] CA 2006 s.996(1).

[192] CA 2006 s.263(2)–(3).

the outcome in the former case will be so much less predictable than the latter; the pre-requisites for success under each route are quite different.

14–025 In *Re Charnley Davies Ltd (No.2)*,[193] Millett J attempted to address this difficult problem by distinguishing between corporate and personal loss. *Charnley Davies* involved a petition under the IA 1986 claiming that an administrator had breached his duty of care to the company by selling its business at an undervalue and ought therefore to compensate the company. Whilst concluding that there had been no breach of duty, Millett J nevertheless went on to consider the relationship between a petition based on unfair prejudice and the derivative action. His Lordship considered that an allegation to the effect that the directors had breached their duties to the company was not sufficient to found a petition; what needed to be shown was that there was also conduct on the part of the directors that was unfairly prejudicial to the minority. Accordingly, if the shareholder wished simply to complain about a breach of duty by the directors, this could not be done by way of petition. Instead, the shareholder must sue on behalf of the company, having satisfied the standing restrictions for the derivative action. This is because in an unfair prejudice petition the "gist" of the action is not the wrong done to the company, but the directors' disregard of the minority's interests. This suggests that whether the unfair prejudice petition is the appropriate vehicle for the petitioner's complaint turns primarily on the nature of the remedy being sought. In *Charnley Davies*, the petition sought compensation for the company. The unfair prejudice petition was accordingly an inappropriate vehicle.[194] If the remedy sought had been a purchase of the petitioners' shares at an appropriate price, then the "gist" of the complaint would have been for relief from the unfair prejudice to the minority.[195]

Accordingly, whilst an unfair prejudice petition might arise out of breaches of duty owed by the directors to the company, only the unfair prejudice to the petitioner can ground the relief granted. This approach might be thought to fit well with the view of the Jenkins Committee[196] that the harm to the shareholders in such cases is "indirect" and that the wrong to them consists not in the wrong done to the company, but in the controllers' use of their position to prevent action being taken to redress the wrong done to the company. On this basis, the remedy should seek to address the indirect wrong to the shareholder, rather than the direct wrong to the company. Admittedly, remedying the wrong to the company might be done very straightforwardly by ordering pursuit of a derivative claim, but the analysis delivering this conclusion does rather suggest that the claimant has selected the wrong starting point, and should have commenced the claim under Pt 11. And this in turn seems to contradict the explicit inclusion in s.996(2)(c) of the remedial option of a derivative claim.

[193] *Re Charnley Davies Ltd (No.2)* [1990] B.C.L.C. 760 Ch D (Companies Ct).

[194] See *Albion Energy Ltd v Energy Investments Global BRL* [2020] EWHC 301 (Comm) at [83], where Foxton J similarly considered the gist of the claim brought under the unfair prejudice jurisdiction to be "misconduct simpliciter".

[195] *Re Hut Group Ltd* [2020] EWHC 5 (Ch); [2020] B.C.C. 443 at [56]–[60]. For the possibility of securing a buy-out order following a successful unfair prejudice petition, see CA 2006 s.996(2)(e).

[196] *Report of the Company Law Committee* (1962), Cm.1749, para.206.

Whilst the above analysis focuses on how the choice should be made between the two procedures, there are also two matters of substance relating to the unfair prejudice jurisdiction. The first substantive issue concerns whether, under that jurisdiction, the court can additionally order a remedy in favour of the company rather than just the petitioner. Given the breadth of the courts' remedial discretion under the unfair prejudice jurisdiction, the answer must surely be yes. Despite initial caution, there have been a number of appellate decisions in which corporate remedies have been granted in an unfair prejudice petition. In *Anderson v Hogg*,[197] the Inner House of the Court of Session (Lord Prosser dissenting) awarded relief to the company where the unfair prejudice was based on an unlawful payment by the respondent director of remuneration to himself. Without detailed consideration of the issue, the director was ordered to return the money to the company. More importantly perhaps, the court came close to rejecting Millett J's proposition in *Charnley Davies* that proof of illegality on the part of the director as against the company is not by itself enough to demonstrate unfair prejudice to the petitioning shareholder. Given that *Anderson* essentially involved a two-person company that was in course of solvent liquidation, the distinction between illegality to the company and unfairness to the shareholder was in that instance very fine. **14–026**

In *Clark v Cutland*,[198] the Court of Appeal considered a petition about a two-person company where the controlling director had made large and unauthorised payments to himself by way of contribution to his pension fund. Although *Clark* principally concerned other issues, the unauthorised payments were ordered to be restored to the company. Moreover, as in a derivative action,[199] the Court of Appeal was prepared to contemplate that the costs of the unfair prejudice petition should be borne by the company.[200] This conclusion may not, however, be quite as dramatic as it seems, since the litigation began as separate derivative and unfair prejudice proceedings, which were subsequently consolidated into the unfair prejudice application.[201] Given that the standing requirements for a derivative action would presumably have been satisfied at an early stage of the proceedings in *Clark*, the granting of corporate relief as part of the unfair prejudice proceedings may not be quite as objectionable as might at first sight appear.

Subsequently, in *Bhullar v Bhullar*,[202] the proceedings concerning a two-person (or, at least, a two-family) company were always in the form of an unfair prejudice petition. Indeed, the petition sought the traditional personal relief that the petitioner's shares should be purchased compulsorily by the respondents at a fair price. In addition, the initial petition sought permission to bring a

[197] *Anderson v Hogg*, 2002 S.L.T. 354 IH (Ex Div).

[198] *Clark v Cutland* [2004] 1 W.L.R. 783 CA (considered by Payne, (2004) 67 M.L.R. 500; [2005] C.L.J. 647). See also *Montgold Capital LLP v Ilska* [2018] EWHC 2982 (Ch); [2019] B.C.C. 309 at [40]: "It is obvious from *Clark v Cutland* that both a derivative action and an unfair prejudice petition may run alongside one another in proceedings".

[199] *Wallersteiner v Moir (No.2)* [1975] Q.B. 373 CA. See further CPR r.19.9.

[200] Despite the views in *Clark*, there remains a general principle that corporate funds should not be spent on disputes between shareholders: see *Gott v Hauge* [2020] EWHC 1152 (Ch); *Re Profile Partners Ltd* [2020] EWHC 1473 (Ch).

[201] *Clark v Cutland* [2004] 1 W.L.R. 783 at [2].

[202] *Bhullar v Bhullar* [2004] 2 B.C.L.C. 241.

derivative action in the company's name. Whilst the trial judge refused the compulsory purchase order, he ordered direct corporate relief by declaring that the property in question be held on trust for the company. The Court of Appeal did not demur from this way of proceeding, but did not consider it necessary to address the issue in detail. One explanation might be that the Court of Appeal considered that a derivative action was justified in terms of both the merits and standing requirements for a derivative action, and that it would simply have been a waste of time and money to have a further action commenced by writ, so corporate relief was granted immediately.

A more extensive analysis of the issues raised in *Clark* can be found in the decision of the Hong Kong Court of Final Appeal in *Kung v Kou*.[203] Although the petition in that case was ill-conceived and there were some differences of emphasis in the judgments of Bokhary PJ and Lord Scott, the issue of whether an unfair prejudice petition could be used to avoid the standing rules in *Foss v Harbottle* was addressed head-on and answered in the negative. This answer did not mean that allegations of breaches of duty by directors are irrelevant in unfair prejudice proceedings, for example, as a basis for making out a claim for relief to be granted to the member. Nor did it mean that the court can never, at the end of an unfair prejudice petition hearing, grant a remedy in the company's favour. However, in order to do that the court would have to hear both the company's claim and the member's claim together. According to Bokhary PJ, this would be appropriate only in "rare and exceptional" circumstances. According to Lord Scott, such a course should only be adopted where, at the pleading stage of the petition, it was clear that "the director's liability at law to the company can conveniently be dealt with in the hearing of the petition". Otherwise, the petitioner should seek an order in the petition to bring a derivative action on behalf of the company or, under the statutory derivative action, make such an application directly to the court, rather than by means of an unfair prejudice petition. In short, bar exceptional pleadings, the unfair prejudice petition is normally confined to relief in respect of harm personal to the minority shareholder.[204]

14–027 The second substantive issue is whether the personal remedies available to the petitioner pursuant to the unfair prejudice jurisdiction should be subject to the "no reflective loss" principle with the result that some types of remedy might be unavailable. The answer ought to be clearer given the Supreme Court decision in *Marex Financial Ltd v Sevilleja*.[205] The majority in that case "restricted the principle of reflective loss barring the shareholder's claims to cases where the shareholder claims in respect of loss … in the form of a diminution in share value

---

[203] *Kung v Kou* (2004) 7 HKCFAR 579. This decision was mentioned by the Privy Council in *Gamlestaden Fastigheter AB v Baltic Partners Ltd* [2007] B.C.C. 272, in which Lord Scott made no mention of the restrictive conditions in *Kung*. Rather, his Lordship appears to treat *Kung* as a general permission to award damages to the company in an unfair prejudice petition. More problematically, as the company was hopelessly insolvent, the benefit to the petitioner of any payment by the directors to the company would be obtained only as lender to the company, whose loans would achieve a higher percentage recovery.

[204] See also *Re Hut Group Ltd* [2020] B.C.C. 443 at [55]–[60].

[205] *Marex Financial Ltd v Sevilleja* [2020] B.C.C. 783. See the discussion above at paras 14–010 to 14–011.

or in distributions, which is the consequence of loss sustained by the company" at the hands of the same wrongdoer and for which the company has its own claim. According, not all claims for compensation by a shareholder will be barred. Whatever the earlier doubts about the impact of the principle on unfair prejudice claims, it seems clear that the *Marex* version of the principle will not touch claims for share buy-outs (the most common remedy in unfair prejudice claims) and many other claims of unfair prejudice will not be fashioned in a way that would be caught by the principle.[206] As a matter of policy, any other conclusion would be undesirable as it would largely denude the unfair prejudice jurisdiction of its utility.[207]

Reducing litigation costs

A major issue that has emerged under the unfair prejudice jurisdiction is the length and thus the cost of trials on these petitions. Although the decision of the House of Lords in *O'Neill v Phillips*[208] has done something to reduce the scope of the issues to be explored, the court may still find itself trawling through a great deal of the history concerning the relations between petitioner and respondent. This will be necessary not only to establish the existence of any informal understandings, but also to determine whether they have subsequently been breached. All this will typically occur in relation to small companies, whose net value may not be large. Both the Law Commission and the Company Law Review investigated a number of ways of reducing the costs of unfair prejudice litigation. All were ultimately rejected as ineffective, either by the Commission or the Review.[209] Two suggestions, however, survived: first, that an arbitration scheme be developed as an alternative to litigation before the High Court[210]; and, secondly, where parties did not arbitrate their dispute, parties could rely on the newly introduced general system of case management in the civil courts.[211] **14–028**

Given these demands, the courts themselves have now developed a technique for encouraging an agreed solution to unfair prejudice claims. Where it is clear, as is normally the case, that the relationship between the petitioner and the remaining members cannot be reconstituted by the court and that the only effective remedy available to the minority is to have their shares purchased at a

206 See *Atlasview Ltd v Brightview Ltd* [2004] 2 B.C.L.C. 191, suggesting that proper quantification of remedies would necessarily be alert to double recovery.

207 Consider *Apex Global Management Ltd v FI Call Ltd* [2014] B.C.C. 286 at [125]: "[a]rtificial limitations should not be introduced to reduce the effective nature of the remedy introduced by [the CA 2006 ss.994 and 996]."

208 *O'Neill v Phillips* [1999] 1 W.L.R. 1092.

209 The suggested solutions were: (1) a new unfair prejudice remedy for those excluded from the management of small companies (rejected by the Law Commission, *Shareholders' Remedies* (1997), Cm.3769, para.3.25, as likely to lead to "duplication and complication of shareholder proceedings"; (2) a presumption of unfairness in certain cases of exclusion from management (recommended by the Law Commission, but rejected by the CLR after the proposal received little support from consultees: see Developing, para.4.104); and (3) the development of a model exit article (recommended by the Law Commission, above, Pt V, but rejected by the CLR, Developing, para.4.103, on the grounds that it was not likely to be used by the well-advised and would be a trap for the ill-advised).

210 Final Report I, para.2.27 (this proposal was not confined to unfair prejudice petitions).

211 *Re Edwardian Group Ltd* [2017] EWHC 3112 (Ch).

fair price, then if a suitable ad hoc offer is made to the petitioner for the purchase of the shares, or there is a suitable mechanism to this effect in the company's articles, but the petitioner nevertheless decides to proceed with the petition rather than accept the offer or use the mechanism, that will constitute an abuse of the court's process. Accordingly, the petition will be struck out. In *O'Neill v Phillips*,[212] Lord Hoffmann was keen to endorse and encourage this procedure. He suggested that a petitioner could not be treated as having been *unfairly* prejudiced by the respondent's conduct if: the offer was to buy the shares at a fair price, which normally would be without a discount for their minority status; there was a mechanism for the determination of the price by a competent expert in the absence of agreement; the expert should not give reasons for the valuation, to encourage agreement; both sides should have equal access to information about the company, as well as equal freedom to make submissions to the expert; and the respondent should be given a reasonable time at the beginning of the proceedings to make the offer and should not be liable for the petitioner's legal costs incurred during that period.

Cases where an offer from the respondent has not blocked a petition have usually involved offers that did not give the petitioner all he or she would get if successful at trial,[213] or have involved a valuation by a non-independent expert.[214] The offer that the court has to evaluate may be an ad hoc one or may result from the application of provisions in the company's articles laying down a mechanism to be used where a shareholder wishes to dispose of his or her holding. Although the courts once took a different view,[215] it does not now appear that an offer arising out of the mechanism contained in the articles is to be treated differently from an ad hoc offer, in terms of its effect in excluding an unfair prejudice petition.[216]

Remedies

14–029 If an unfair prejudice petition is successful, the court has a wide remedial discretion to "make such order as it thinks fit for giving relief in respect of the matters complained of".[217] In addition to this general grant, five specific remedies are highlighted.[218] Whilst a court will endeavour to select the remedy that is most

[212] For application to the winding-up remedy, see *CVC/Opportunity Equity Partners Ltd v Demarco Almeida* [2002] B.C.C. 684 PC.

[213] *North Holdings Ltd v Southern Tropics Ltd* [1999] 2 B.C.L.C. 624 CA; *Harbourne Road Nominees Ltd v Kafvaski* [2011] EWHC 2214 (Ch).

[214] *Re Benfield Greig Group Plc* [2002] 1 B.C.L.C. 65 CA, where the non-independence of the expert constituted the alleged unfair prejudice. See also *Griffin v Wainwright* [2017] EWHC 2122 (Ch).

[215] *Re A Company Ex p. Kremer* [1989] B.C.L.C. 365 Ch (Companies Ct).

[216] *Virdi v Abbey Leisure Ltd* [1990] B.C.L.C. 342 CA (Civ Div); *Re A Company Ex p. Holden* [1991] B.C.L.C. 597 Ch D (Companies Ct); *Re Company (No.000836 of 1995)* [1996] 2 B.C.L.C. 192 Ch D (Companies Ct).

[217] CA 2006 s.996(1). For the possibility of an interim injunction, see *Homes of England Ltd v Horsham Holdings Ltd* [2019] EWHC 2429 (Ch); *Loveridge v Loveridge* [2020] EWCA Civ 1104. For interim payments, see *Re Stratos Club Ltd* [2021] EWHC 1008 (Ch).

[218] CA 2006 s.996(2).

appropriate to the particular circumstances,[219] the most common remedy is an order that the petitioners' shares be purchased by the controllers or the company.[220] The reason for the popularity of this remedy, with both petitioners and courts, is readily explained. Unfair prejudice jurisprudence is most firmly established in relation to quasi-partnership companies. When business and, often, personal relations between quasi-partners have broken down and are incapable of reconstitution by a court, the only effective remedy is the minority's exit. A share purchase order gives the petitioner an opportunity to exit from the company with the fair value of his or her investment. This is a result that is usually impossible in the absence of a court order, since often no potential purchasers of the shares are available, and, even if they were, the purchase price a third party would be willing to pay would reflect, rather than remedy, the harm inflicted on the seller by the unfairly prejudicial conduct.[221]

The crucial question in this buy-out process is how the court is to assess the fairness of the price to be paid for the shares. Two important issues have emerged in the valuation process. The first issue is whether the petitioner's shareholding should be valued pro rata to the total value of the company or whether its value should be discounted on the basis that it is ex hypothesi a minority holding and so does not confer control of the company. In this context, the notion of a "quasi-partnership" company has become important.[222] Although many unfair prejudice proceedings concern such companies, the statutory provisions are not confined to them. In relation to whether a minority shareholding should be discounted, the courts have developed a presumption that it should not in a quasi-partnership company, whereas no such presumption applies for other categories of company.[223] In *Re Bird Precision Bellows Ltd*,[224] it was established

---

[219] *Re TPD Investments Ltd* [2017] EWHC 657 (Ch). In *Ming Siu Hing v JF Ming Inc* [2021] UKPC 1 at [14], Lord Briggs indicated that, in examining the evidence in order to select the appropriate remedy, "nothing is off-limits, subject only to the twin tests of relevance and weight".

[220] CA 2006 s.996(2)(e). In the latter case the company's share capital must be reduced. The statutory power is sufficiently widely drawn to include an order that the minority purchase the majority's shares, which has occasionally been ordered: see *Re Brenfield Squash Racquets Club Ltd* [1996] 2 B.C.L.C. 184 Ch D. A court may also break a deadlocked company by ordering one party to purchase the other's shares: see *Re Watercor Ltd* [2017] EWHC 1814 (Ch). The other specific powers under the CA 2006 are the authorisation of proceedings to be brought in the company's name (CA 2006 s.996(2)(c)); requiring the company to do or refrain from doing an act (CA 2006 s.996(2)(b)); requiring the company not to make alterations to its articles of association without the leave of the court (CA 2006 s.996(2)(d)); and regulating the conduct of the company's affairs in the future (CA 2006 s.996(2)(a)). Whatever remedy is contemplated, the court must choose what is appropriate at the time it is granted: see *Re A Company* [1992] B.C.C. 542. Indeed, the court is not limited to ordering the remedy requested by the petitioner: see *Hawkes v Cuddy (No.2)* [2009] EWCA Civ 291; [2009] 2 B.C.L.C. 427 (although in this case, and as is specified now in the Companies (Unfair Prejudice Applications) Proceedings Rules (SI 2009/2469), the petitioner specifically requested particular remedies or "that such other order may be made as the court thinks fit"). The court has a further specific power in the case where the unfair prejudice consists of a public offer of shares by a private company: see CA 2006 ss.757–758, considered further in para.24–002.

[221] See *Grace v Biagioli* [2006] 2 B.C.L.C. 70 CA, for a good example of the court's preference for a "clean break" via a share purchase, rather than a compensation order (which might have remedied the specific harm suffered by the petitioner, but would have left him exposed in the future).

[222] See paras 14–032 to 14–033.

[223] In deciding whether a quasi-partnership exists, the approach set out in *Ebrahimi* (see para.14–033) is often applied: see *Strahan v Wilcock* [2006] 2 B.C.L.C. 555. What was initially a quasi-partnership

that the default principle required a pro rata valuation where the company could be characterised as a quasi-partnership. This is because, when a true partnership is dissolved, the court orders a sale of the partnership business as a going concern and divides the proceeds among the partners according to their interests in the former partnership.[225] That said, the usual company law principle[226] of discounting a minority shareholding applies if the company is not an incorporated partnership, or the petitioner bought the shareholding at a price that reflected its minority status, or the shares devolved upon the petitioner by operation of law.[227]

The second issue is whether the valuation of the shares should be on the basis that the company will continue as a going concern, or on a liquidation or break-up basis, which would normally yield a lower value for the company. The going concern basis will normally be appropriate, but this will depend to some degree on the facts of the case, as will the precise method to be adopted for valuing the going concern.[228]

14–030 Beyond the basis of valuation, a further issue concerns timing. The value put on shares, whether on a pro rata or a discounted basis, will often depend crucially on when the value of the company is assessed. The courts have given themselves the widest discretion to choose the most appropriate date. The competing dates are usually a date close to when the shares are to be purchased or the date when the petition was presented (or the harm complained of was inflicted). In *Profinance Trust SA v Gladstone*,[229] the Court of Appeal thought that the former had become the presumptive valuation date. That said, there are many circumstances when an earlier date might be chosen, such as where the unfairly prejudicial conduct has deprived the company of its business; where the company has reconstructed its business; or even where there has been a general fall in the market since the presentation of the petition. For example, in *Re KR Hardy Estates Ltd*,[230] the court held that the date of the order was the most appropriate valuation date on the facts, since that date had the advantage of both certainty and fairness; whereas, in *Re Cabot Global Ltd*,[231] the court used the date when the parties

may have ceased to be one by the time the facts supporting the petition take place, thus changing the basis of valuation: see *Re McCarthy Surfacing Ltd* [2009] B.C.L.C. 622.

224 *Re Bird Precision Bellows Ltd* [1984] Ch. 419 Ch D; affirmed [1986] Ch. 658 CA (Civ Div).

225 *CVC/Opportunity Equity Partners Ltd v Demarco Almeida* [2002] 2 B.C.L.C. 108 at [41]–[42]; *Strahan v Wilcock* [2006] 2 B.C.L.C. 555. The court might instead work out what the former partner's interest would be worth upon the hypothesis of a sale, without actually holding one.

226 *Shanda Games Ltd v Maso Capital Investments Ltd* [2020] UKPC 2; [2020] B.C.C. 466; *Re Euro Accessories Ltd* [2021] EWHC 47 (Ch).

227 *Irvine v Irvine (No.2)* [2007] 1 B.C.L.C. 445; *Re Elgindata Ltd* [1991] B.C.L.C. 959 at 1007. See also *Re DR Chemicals* (1989) 5 B.C.C. 37 Ch D (Companies Ct).

228 *CVC/Opportunity Equity Partners Ltd v Demarco Almeida* [2002] 2 B.C.L.C. 108; *Parkinson v Eurofinance Group Ltd* [2001] 1 B.C.L.C. 720; *Guinness Peat Group Plc v British Land Co Plc* [1999] 2 B.C.L.C. 243; *Re Planet Organic Ltd* [2000] 1 B.C.L.C. 366 Ch D. See also *Re Annacott Holdings Ltd* [2013] EWCA Civ 119, where it was held that there is no rule that a going-concern valuation can only be adopted for quasi-partnerships.

229 *Profinance Trust SA v Gladstone* [2001] EWCA Civ 1031; [2002] B.C.C. 356. See also *Re McCarthy Surfacing Ltd* [2009] B.C.L.C. 622, for a valuation taking into account the depreciation due to the wrongs complained of.

230 *Re KR Hardy Estates Ltd* [2014] EWHC 4001 (Ch) at [89]–[93].

231 *Re Cabot Global Ltd* [2016] EWHC 2287 (Ch).

parted ways, rather than the date when the shares were ordered to be sold, as the company was insolvent and had ceased trading by the later date.

WINDING UP ON THE JUST AND EQUITABLE GROUND

Legal protection for minority shareholders is now dominated by the unfair prejudice remedy. Despite the breadth of this jurisdiction, it sometimes seems that the only fair way to resolve disputes between disaffected parties is to wind the company up and distribute the assets between the warring factions, giving neither the advantage of continuing to trade in the existing business. Given the court's reluctance to wind up viable businesses and the inevitable costs in doing so, this is very much a remedy of last resort. Nevertheless, setting out the tension faced by the court indicates the circumstances in which the court might see fit to adopt this approach. **14–031**

First, though, what is the source of the court's jurisdiction to make winding up orders? Given the breadth of the remedial jurisdiction granted to the court in unfair prejudice claims (under s.996), an order to wind the company up would certainly seem open. But in *Apex Global Management v FI Call Ltd*,[232] Hildyard J explained why adopting that course was not, in his view, justified, and why the court should instead confine the winding up remedy to claims brought under the statutory provision especially designed for these ends (i.e. s.122(1)(g) of the IA 1986), being a provision that has its own inbuilt and specially designed party protections. The Law Commission had taken the contrary approach, recommending that this winding-up power should be specifically added to the range of remedies available pursuant to the unfair prejudice jurisdiction,[233] but the Company Law Review rejected this suggestion on the ground that it was open to abuse.[234] That seems correct.

The separate statutory procedure in s.122(1)(g) of the IA 1986 provides that a company may be wound up compulsorily by the court on a petition presented to it by a contributory[235] (a term which includes a disaffected shareholder) if the court **14–032**

[232] *Apex Global Management v FI Call Ltd* [2015] EWHC 3269 at [51], indicating that the court might "[adjust] the proportion of distributions upon a winding-up of the company (as in *Re Phoneer* [2002] 2 B.C.L.C. 241), even though in my opinion, the court should not ordinarily make a winding-up order pursuant to section 996, given the specific provisions for such a remedy and the careful protections relevant to the exercise of such jurisdiction: see *Full Cup International Trading Ltd* [1995] B.C.C. 682 (which went to appeal but which was not doubted on this point); see also, as to the more general proposition that the court should normally discourage a process which is less specific and affords less protection than a specially prescribed one, *Re Trix Ltd* [1970] 1 W.L.R. 1421."

[233] *Shareholders' Remedies* (1997), Cm.3769, paras 4.24–4.49.

[234] Developing, para.4.105.

[235] CA 2006 s.124(1). Petitions may also be brought by creditors, directors or the company itself, though such applications are rare. The Secretary of State may petition under s.124A in the public interest on the basis of information received as a result of an investigation into the company's affairs: see further para.21–013. However, public interest grounds for a winding-up order are not available other than to the Secretary of State: see *Re Millennium Advanced Technology Ltd* [2004] EWHC 711 (Ch); [2004] 2 B.C.L.C. 77. The term "contributory" includes even a fully paid-up shareholder provided he or she has a tangible interest in the winding-up, which is usually demonstrated by showing that the company has a surplus of assets over liabilities, though that will not be required if

is of the opinion that it is "just and equitable" to do so.[236] This provision has a long pedigree and can be traced back to the Joint Stock Companies Winding-up Act 1848. "Just and equitable" winding-up was influenced by the then-uncodified partnership law, and originally was mainly used in cases where the company was deadlocked.[237] During the twentieth century, however, it has been broadened and moulded by the courts into a means of subjecting small private companies to equitable principles derived from partnership law when they were in reality incorporated partnerships.

The House of Lords decision in *Ebrahimi v Westbourne Galleries Ltd*[238] represents the apotheosis of this development. Where a quasi-partnership exists, a court will consider a range of factors in determining whether to wind a company up,[239] including whether there had been a breakdown in mutual trust and confidence between the parties, the good faith of the petitioner, the probity of the company or its controllers[240] and any loss of the company's substratum.[241] A petition would generally be dismissed where the petitioner's conduct had effectively brought the issues on him or herself.[242]

14–033 The jurisdiction was put under the spotlight in the Privy Council decision in *Chu v Lau*,[243] a case concerning two equal shareholders and sole directors of a British Virgin Islands shipping company which, with its subsidiary, was engaged in joint-venture businesses with associates. In allowing the appeal and restoring the trial judge's decision to order a winding up, the Privy Council comprehensively analysed the two related (but distinct) and potentially overlapping situations in which a just and equitable winding-up may be ordered where a company's members have fallen out.

---

the petitioner's complaint is that the controllers failed to provide the financial information from which that assessment could be made: see *Re Rica Gold Washing Co* (1879) 11 Ch. D. 36 CA; *Re Bellador Silk Ltd* [1965] 1 All E.R. 667 Ch D; *Re Othery Construction Ltd* [1966] 1 W.L.R. 69 Ch D; *Re Expanded Plugs Ltd* [1966] 1 W.L.R. 514 Ch D; *Re Chesterfield Catering Ltd* [1977] Ch. 373 Ch D at 380; *Re Land and Property Trust Co Plc* [1991] B.C.C. 446 Ch D (Companies Ct) at 448; *Re Newman & Howard Ltd* [1962] Ch. 257 Ch D; *Re Wessex Computer Stationers Ltd* [1992] B.C.L.C. 366; *Re Company (No.007936 of 1994)* [1995] B.C.C. 705 Ch D (Companies Ct). The Jenkins Committee recommended (para.503(h)) that any member should be entitled to petition, presumably on the grounds that this remedy was aimed primarily at protecting minorities, rather than at winding up companies.

[236] IA 1986 s.122(1)(g).

[237] Deadlock continues to provide a basis upon which to wind a company up because it is "just and equitable" to do so: see *Brand & Harding Ltd* [2014] EWHC 247 (Ch).

[238] *Ebrahimi v Westbourne Galleries Ltd* [1973] A.C. 360. See also *Lau v Chu* [2020] UKPC 24; [2020] 1 W.L.R. 4656 at [18]. More recently, the approach in *Ebrahimi* has been highly influential in mapping the contours of the unfair prejudice jurisdiction, but the two jurisdictions are not co-terminous: see *Apex Global Management Ltd v FI Call Ltd* [2015] EWHC 3269 (Ch).

[239] *Re Paramount Powders (UK) Ltd* [2019] EWCA Civ 1644; [2020] 2 B.C.L.C. 1. See also *Secretary of State for Business Innovation and Skills v New Horizon Energy Ltd* [2015] EWHC 2961 (Ch); [2017] B.C.C. 629, applying the principles in *Revenue and Customs Commissioners v Winnington Newtworks Ltd* [2014] EWHC 1259 (Ch); [2014] B.C.C. 675 to "just and equitable" winding-up.

[240] *Pi Trustee Services 5G Ltd v North West Land Fill Ltd* unreported 8 December 2015 Ch D.

[241] *Re Kitson & Co Ltd* [1946] 1 All E.R. 435 CA; *Hussein v House of Vanity Ltd* [2017] EWHC 2615 (Ch).

[242] *Re Paramount Powders (UK) Ltd* [2020] 2 B.C.L.C. 1.

[243] *Chu v Lau* [2020] 1 W.L.R. 4556.

The first is where the company is in functional deadlock; i.e. where the inability of members to co-operate in the management of the company's affairs leads to an inability of the company to function at board or shareholder level. If there is a complete functional deadlock then, regardless of whether the company is a quasi-partnership, a winding-up may be ordered as "a remedy for paralysis". In assessing this, the court can consider conduct post-dating the petition, or whether the paralysis might not be remedied without a new claim.

The second situation is the breakdown of trust and confidence in a quasi-partnership company. The Privy Council noted with approval the criteria by which Lord Wilberforce in *Ebrahimi* sought to restrict the regime to "partnership equivalents"[244]:

> "The superimposition of equitable considerations [as required to constitute a quasi-partnership] requires something more, which typically may include one, or probably more, of the following elements: (i) an association formed or continued on the basis of a personal relationship, involving mutual confidence – this element will often be found where a pre-existing partnership has been converted into a limited company; (ii) an agreement, or understanding, that all, or some (for there may be 'sleeping' members), of the shareholders shall participate in the conduct of the business; (iii) restriction upon the transfer of the members' interest in the company—so that if confidence is lost, or one member is removed from management, he cannot take out his stake and go elsewhere".

Not all the criteria need be satisfied, but—where the company meets the classification as a quasi-partnership—a winding up order may be made if there is an irretrievable breakdown in trust and confidence between the participating members. In such situation, there is no additional requirement of a complete functional deadlock, although the two often go hand in hand. In assessing this breakdown, the court is free to examine every aspect of the business relationship.

Lady Arden, in a separate opinion, also found that a winding up order might be justified on the basis that Lau had been wrongly excluded from participation in the management of the company and its subsidiaries and affiliates. Whether this will eventually come to be regarded as a separate head is unclear. It is a typical complaint in unfair prejudice claims, where less drastic remedies are ordered, and here it might simply be seen as a powerful part of the evidence indicating the breakdown of the quasi-partnership. In a relationship that lacks the characteristics of a quasi-partnership, however, there would seem to be good reasons to deny a winding up order, keeping viable businesses functioning, and to deal with the management problems by less drastic means.

Finally, whilst acknowledging that a winding-up on the just and equitable ground is a shareholders' remedy of last resort, the Privy Council viewed the mere existence of an alternative remedy as not the real point; what mattered was whether the applicant had unreasonably failed to pursue that alternative remedy, rather than request a winding up.

---

[244] *Ebrahimi v Westbourne Galleries Ltd* [1973] A.C. 360 at 380. As a general rule, the relationship of trust and confidence must exist between all the company's incorporators: see *George v McCarthy* [2019] EWHC 2939 (Ch), where this was not the case. See also *UTB LLC v Sheffield United Ltd* [2019] EWHC 2322 (Ch). There may exist exceptional circumstances where a quasi-partnership can exist, despite some shareholders being strangers to the relationship of trust and confidence: see *Re Dinglis Properties Ltd* [2019] EWHC 1664 (Ch).

14–034 All of this shows an understandable reluctance to allow petitioners to wind companies up on a "just and equitable" basis.[245] Nevertheless, it should not be thought that the push is entirely towards the unfair prejudice remedy: there are instances where the court has denied an unfair prejudice petition because the petitioner's conduct did not merit relief, but has instead granted a winding-up order on the grounds that mutual confidence among the quasi-partners had broken down,[246] or that the substratum had failed.[247]

Despite its remarkable substantive development, petitioning to wind up a company on the "just and equitable" ground always suffered from a weakness at the remedial level: if the company was prospering, presenting a winding-up petition was tantamount to killing the goose that might lay the golden egg (while the threat of liquidation might induce the parties to negotiate alternative solutions to their dispute). Given the existence of the potentially endlessly flexible unfair prejudice remedy, one might argue that the role of the winding-up remedy should be quite restricted.[248] The ability to paralyse, or at least disrupt, the normal running of the company's business adds to the negotiating strength of the petitioner, but it is hardly a legitimate use of the winding-up jurisdiction if an unfair prejudice petition could provide the necessary relief. Consequently, a Practice Direction[249] seeks to discourage the routine joining of winding-up petitions to unfair prejudice claims, unless a winding-up remedy is genuinely what is being sought. The Practice Direction is given statutory assistance by the IA 1986, which provides that the court need not grant a winding-up order if it is of the opinion that some alternative remedy is available to the petitioners and that they have acted unreasonably in not pursuing it.[250]

CONCLUSION

14–035 Part 30 of the CA 2006 does not provide, and on no conceivable interpretation could provide, a unilateral exit right for minority shareholders, i.e. a right for minority shareholders at any time to withdraw their capital from the company. Indeed, it might be thought that such a right would be inconsistent with the nature

[245] See, for example, *Pi Trustee Services 5G Ltd v North West Land Fill Ltd* unreported 8 December 2015; *Hussein v House of Vanity Ltd* [2017] EWHC 2615 (Ch).

[246] *Re RA Noble & Sons (Clothing) Ltd* [1983] B.C.L.C. 273; *Jesner v Jarrad Properties Ltd* [1993] B.C.L.C. 1032; *Loch v John Blackwood Ltd* [1924] A.C. 783 PC; *Re Brand & Harding Ltd* [2014] EWHC 247 (Ch). See also *Re Full Cup International Trading Ltd* [1995] B.C.C. 682, where the judge found himself in the presumably unusual position of being unable to fashion an appropriate remedy under s.996 but of being prepared to wind up the company.

[247] *Re Kitson & Co Ltd* [1946] 1 All E.R. 435 CA.

[248] *Re Paramount Powders (UK) Ltd* [2020] 2 B.C.L.C. 1.

[249] CPR Practice Direction, Applications under the Companies Act and Other Legislation Relating to Companies, para.9(1). See *Re A Company (No.004415 of 1996)* [1997] 1 B.C.L.C. 479, where the judge struck out the alternative petition for winding up on the just and equitable ground on the basis that there was no reasonable prospect that the trial judge would order a winding up rather than a share purchase pursuant to the unfair prejudice jurisdiction.

[250] IA 1986 s.125(2). The alternative remedy need not be a legal one. For example, it may be an offer to purchase the petitioner's shares on the same basis as the court would order on an unfair prejudice petition: see *Virdi v Abbey Leisure Ltd* [1990] B.C.L.C. 342. See also *Maresca v Brookfield Development & Construction Ltd* [2013] EWHC 3151 (Ch), where the alternative remedy was for the shareholder to demand repayment of her interest from the company.

of shareholding in companies. In essence, the shareholder is locked into the investment in the company unless he or she is able to find someone else to purchase the shares.[251] Compulsory purchase is not a right for the minority, but a remedy—and not even a remedy the minority can insist upon, though it is the most common—in respect of unfair prejudice committed by the company's controllers. Thus, in *Re Phoenix Office Supplies Ltd*,[252] the Court of Appeal refused a shareholder's petition to have his shares acquired at a non-discounted value, even though he had been removed from his directorship by the other two incorporators in breach of their common understanding. The reason for the decision was that the respondents' conduct had been in response to the petitioner's unilateral decision to sever his relations with the company, which could be seen as a prior and more fundamental breach of the original understandings between the parties. Of course, members may bargain for rights of unilateral exit to be incorporated in the articles of particular companies; but they are rare, since a general right for minority shareholders to withdraw their capital freely would seem wholly to undermine the financing function of shares.

Finally, there is some evidence that the unfair prejudice remedy, whatever its imperfections, has successfully "crowded out" alternative techniques of controlling the exercise of majority power through board decisions. Thus, the Law Commissions' draft statement of directors' statutory duties[253] included a requirement that directors act fairly as between shareholders; a duty reflected to a degree in the current case law.[254] The Company Law Review's initial draft statement contained the same duty,[255] but fairness between shareholders was later reduced to one of the factors to be taken into account by the directors when discharging their duty to promote the success of the company for the benefit of its members.[256] The explanation given for this development was a desire to "make it clear that fairness is a factor in achieving success for the members as a whole, rather than an independent requirement which could override commercial success".[257] It is difficult to believe that this argument would have been accepted in the absence of unfair prejudice as an overriding instrument of minority protection.

---

[251] Of course, if the company and the shareholder wish expressly to bargain for "redeemable" shares, they are free to do so: see para.17–007.

[252] *Re Phoenix Office Supplies Ltd* [2002] EWCA Civ 1740; [2003] 1 B.C.L.C. 76.

[253] *Company Directors: Regulating Conflicts of Interest and Formulating a Statement of Duties* (1999), Cm.4436, Appendix A.

[254] See especially *Mutual Life Insurance Co of New York v Rank Organisation Ltd* [1985] B.C.L.C. 11.

[255] Developing, para.3.40.

[256] Final Report I, Annex C, Sch.2. On the nature of the general duty, see paras 10–026 onwards.

[257] Final Report I, Annex C, Explanatory Notes, para.18.

CHAPTER 15

CORPORATE LITIGATION AND THE DERIVATIVE ACTION

THE NATURE OF THE PROBLEM AND THE POTENTIAL SOLUTIONS

In the previous chapter,[1] the focus was upon the circumstances in which a shareholder seeks to enforce a right or cause of action held in a personal capacity[2] or seeks relief from conduct that unfairly prejudices his or her interests as a shareholder.[3] The present focus concerns situations where the right or cause of action is vested in the company as a separate legal entity, rather than in the shareholder personally. Whilst such a corporate right might arise out of a contract with a third party or a common law or equitable wrong committed by such a party, the most important example concerns breaches of directors' duties. Although there are rare exceptions, directors' duties are owed to the company alone.[4] In such circumstances, the corporate entity is the body with the legal capacity to enforce its rights following a decision taken by the appropriate organ.[5] Whilst that organ will usually be the board, there is an obvious difficulty in the board making an independent decision whether or not to sue one of its own number. Accordingly, this may be a case where it is more appropriate to identify a different decision-maker, whether the general meeting acting as the company or even a minority shareholder acting on the company's behalf. This may seem like **15–001**

[1] See Ch.14.

[2] CA 2006 s.33(1), which confers on a shareholder the right to enforce the company's constitution. See also *Haven Insurance Co Ltd v EUI Ltd* [2018] EWCA Civ 2494 at [3].

[3] CA 2006 s.994(1).

[4] CA 2006 s.170(1).

[5] *Foss v Harbottle* (1843) 2 Hare 461 Ct of Chancery, approved in *Marex Financial Ltd v Sevilleja* [2020] UKSC 31; [2020] B.C.C. 783 at [81].

mere procedure, but the directors' duties discussed previously[6] are not likely to play a significant role in the governance of British companies if, for one reason or another, they cannot be enforced. Accordingly, clarity on when corporate litigation can be initiated is as critical to the corporate governance debate as the shape of the directors' duties themselves.

Simply because a claim can be brought, however, does not mean that it should be: it is not in every case where a director has arguably infringed his or her duties to the company that corporate litigation should be contemplated, let alone initiated. The basic test should be whether "the interests of the company" require that litigation to be instituted, and that question can be answered only on the facts of a particular case. It is easy to imagine many reasons why litigation would actually leave the company worse off than it was before. There may be doubts about whether a judgment in favour of the company will be obtained, either because of disputes about the law or because of difficulties in proving the events alleged to constitute the breach of duty. Alternatively, the proposed defendants may not be in a position to meet the judgment, even if the litigation is successful; the senior management time spent on the litigation might more profitably be used elsewhere; or, finally, whilst winning the legal arguments and obtaining an enforceable remedy, the company may suffer collateral reputational harm that would outweigh any gain from the litigation.[7] In other words, the decision whether to initiate litigation in respect of an alleged breach of directors' duties will not always be an easy one, and a negative decision is not necessarily a sign that the company is being too lax towards its directors. On the other hand, a decision not to sue a director may indeed be heavily influenced by that director's personal interests, rather than those of the company. Conflicts of interest do not magically disappear as one moves from the question of whether a breach exists to the issue of whether liability should be enforced; if anything, they are more acute. Accordingly, the aim is to distinguish between those litigation decisions (especially decisions not to sue) that are in the company's interests and those that are not. Given that such decisions require a close analysis of the particular circumstances, it is impossible to specify in advance those categories of case in which litigation should always be brought and those categories where it never should be. As such a substantive rule would be almost impossible to devise, the solution lies in proceduralism, namely identifying the person or persons who are most likely to make an independent decision as to whether or not corporate litigation should be initiated in any particular case.[8] There are three options.

The board and litigation

15–002 One possible solution to this question would be to say that the litigation decision is like any other management decision that the company might take and so should be left to the normal decision-making processes of the company. Under the constitutions of most companies, the power to manage the company will be

[6] See generally Ch.10.

[7] *Taylor v National Union of Mineworkers (Derbyshire Area)* [1985] B.C.L.C. 237 at 254–255. See also *Hughes v Burley* [2021] EWHC 104 (Ch) at [49].

[8] See generally J. Armour, "Derivative Actions: a Framework for Decisions" (2019) 135 L.Q.R. 412.

vested in the board of directors and, as a general rule, the shareholders cannot interfere with those decisions by ordinary resolution.[9] Certainly, the model articles envisage precisely that.[10] In *Breckland Group Holdings Ltd v London & Suffolk Properties Ltd*,[11] litigation had been commenced in the corporate name by a majority shareholder without the matter having first been considered by the board. Harman J granted an injunction restraining the action until the board had had the opportunity to meet in order to decide whether to discontinue or ratify the proceedings. His Lordship reached this conclusion on the ground that the company had adopted the model articles of association that vested general management powers in the board.[12] Whilst there was earlier authority suggesting that the general meeting would have the power to ratify unauthorised proceedings,[13] *Breckland Holdings* is more consistent with the traditional division of power between the board and general meeting. Indeed, that decision is consistent with *John Shaw & Sons (Salford) Ltd v Shaw*,[14] where the company's articles had allocated the litigation decision to a sub-committee of permanent directors from which the wrongdoing ordinary directors were excluded. The Court of Appeal held that, as the board had delegated its powers to the sub-committee, the shareholders could not by ordinary majority countermand the decision whether or not to sue. Accordingly, the locus of decision-making power when it comes to litigation generally lies with the company's board exclusively.

Given that legal conclusion, the potential conflict of interest becomes apparent when the decision concerns whether or not to sue a director for breach of his duties to the company. Accordingly, there is a real risk that the board may be unwilling to sue the wrongdoing director, even when it is in the best interests of the company to do so. Indeed, the wrongdoers may constitute a majority of the board or may be able to influence a majority of the board. Accordingly, the same incentives that gave rise to the directors' breaches of duty in the first place may cause them to utilise their board positions so as to suppress litigation against themselves. Whilst deliberately suppressing corporate litigation would probably amount to a breach of the directors' duties, this makes little difference if that breach cannot be enforced either. Of course, the board is not always conflicted. The board may act in an independent-minded way or, perhaps more likely, the directors may have lost the influential positions on the board that they had when they committed the original wrongdoing. Thus, the previous board may have been replaced by a new set of directors as a result of a takeover[15]; or, the company having become insolvent, the board may have been replaced by an insolvency practitioner, acting in one capacity or another on behalf of the

[9] *Automatic Self-Cleaning Filter Syndicate Co Ltd v Cunninghame* [1906] 2 Ch. 34 CA.

[10] Companies (Model Articles) Regulations 2008 (SI 2008/3229) Sch.1 art.3 and Sch.3 art.3.

[11] *Breckland Group Holdings Ltd v London & Suffolk Properties Ltd* (1988) 4 B.C.C. 542 Ch D.

[12] *Breckland Group Holdings Ltd v London & Suffolk Properties Ltd* (1988) 4 B.C.C. 542 at 546–547.

[13] *Danish Mercantile Co Ltd v Beaumont* [1951] Ch. 680 CA at 687.

[14] *John Shaw & Sons (Salford) Ltd v Shaw* [1935] 2 K.B. 113 CA. See also *Children's Investment Fund Foundation (UK) v Attorney General* [2020] UKSC 33; [2020] 3 W.L.R. 461 at [14].

[15] See, for example, *Regal (Hastings) Ltd v Gulliver* [1942] 1 All E.R. 378 HL. See further para.10–083.

creditors.[16] Indeed, the importance of litigation against wrongdoing directors (and other officers of the company) in this situation is recognised by the IA 1986,[17] which gives liquidators (and others) in a winding up the benefit of a summary procedure for the enforcement of the directors' breaches of their fiduciary duties, as well as their duty of care. Whilst the liquidator sues in his or her own name, the claim in substance is being brought on behalf of the company, which will be the recipient of any recovery.[18] Crucially, however, the courts regard the section as purely procedural, so that it does not extend the range of duties to which directors are subject.[19] Given the ease of enforcement by the liquidator, compared to when the same issue arises in a solvent company, directors have yet another incentive to avoid liquidation.[20]

The shareholders collectively and litigation

15–003 Despite the litigation decision against wrongdoing directors being vested in the board, the corporate governance implications of leaving such decisions exclusively with the board are self-evident. In recognition of these concerns, there are some indications at common law that, even if the board does not wish to sue, it may be open to the shareholders collectively by ordinary resolution to decide to do so.[21] There may certainly be some good sense behind this suggestion in policy terms. In constitutional terms, however, the route by which the shareholders collectively acquire the power concurrently with the board to initiate litigation against wrongdoing directors is something of a mystery: the allocation of management power to the board by the articles operates, in the absence of an express reservation, to remove that power from the shareholders. Consequently, in the absence of an express provision in the articles conferring upon the shareholders the power to initiate litigation, a shareholder decision to that effect

---

[16] Indeed, the replacement of the board by an insolvency practitioner was regarded at common law as a good reason for not allowing an individual shareholder to sue on behalf of the company: see *Ferguson v Wallbridge* [1935] 3 D.L.R. 66 PC; *Fargro Ltd v Godfroy* [1986] 1 W.L.R. 1134 Ch D. In *Barrett v Duckett* [1995] 1 B.C.L.C. 243 CA, the principle was even extended to deny to a shareholder, who turned down the opportunity to put the company into liquidation, the possibility of bringing a derivative claim. As Peter Gibson LJ stated (at 255): "As the company does have some money which might be used in litigating the claims, it is in my opinion manifest that it is better that the decision whether or not to use the money should be taken by an independent liquidator rather than by [the shareholder]". The fact that a company is in liquidation should certainly be a strong factor when determining whether permission for a statutory derivative action should be brought under the CA 2006 ss.260–263. That said, the courts have tended to follow the approach at common law: see *Re Core Vct Plc* [2019] EWHC 540 (Ch); [2019] B.C.C. 845 at [113]–[116]; *Fakhry v Pagden* [2020] EWCA Civ 1207; [2021] B.C.C. 46 at [70].

[17] IA 1986 s.212.

[18] The court has a discretion under the IA 1986 s.212 to reduce the amount that the defendant has to pay, but not to excuse liability altogether: see *Revenue and Customs Commissioners v Holland* [2010] UKSC 51; [2011] B.C.C. 1.

[19] *Cohen v Selby* [2001] 1 B.C.L.C. 176 CA (Civ Div) at [20]; *Re Mama Milla Ltd* [2015] EWCA Civ 1140; [2016] B.C.C. 1 at [176]–[185]. Nor does IA 1986 s.212 allow the liquidator to escape from any limitation period to which the claim by the company would be subject: see *Re Lands Allotment Co* [1894] 1 Ch. 616 CA; *Re Eurocruit Europe Ltd* [2007] 2 B.C.L.C. 598.

[20] It is precisely this incentive that wrongful trading liability aims to reverse: see IA 1986 s.214.

[21] *Marshall's Valve Gear Co v Manning, Wardle & Co* [1909] 1 Ch. 267 Ch D.

could only be passed by a special resolution, because that is the equivalent of a resolution to alter the articles. The common law appears, however, to regard an ordinary resolution to initiate litigation as sufficient.[22]

There are three possible ways of responding to the judicial suggestions that the general meeting has the ability to initiate corporate litigation by way of ordinary resolution. First, one could simply dismiss those suggestions as representing an outmoded view of the corporate division of powers and rely upon *Breckland Holdings* for the view that the decision to litigate lies with the board and is not shared concurrently with the general meeting. Whilst such a view would introduce doctrinal consistency across all management powers,[23] it would overlook the practical utility of sometimes delegating the litigation decision to the general meeting. Secondly, one might consider the litigation power to be unlike other management powers, so that there is simply an exception to the usual allocation of responsibility that permits the general meeting to initiate litigation when the board does not. Whilst this might explain the conflicting authorities,[24] conferring concurrent jurisdiction on both corporate organs appears to be a recipe for confusion and an invitation to litigation. Thirdly, one might seek to explain the general meeting's control over litigation as a manifestation of their residual powers of management. As considered previously,[25] the general meeting retains a residual power to manage the company in the absence of an effective board (as opposed to a board that legitimately decides not to act). This might include the situation where the directors are disqualified from voting because of their conflict of interests.[26] Indeed, this is precisely the view endorsed by the House of Lords in *Alexander Ward & Co Ltd v Samyang Navigation Co Ltd*,[27] in which corporate litigation was commenced by the shareholders on behalf of a company with no directors whatsoever. Indicating that the general meeting was competent to act "in the absence of an effective board", Lord Hailsham stated[28]:

> "It seems that if for some reason the board cannot or will not exercise the power vested in them, the general meeting may do so. On this ground, action by the general meeting has been held effective where there was a deadlock on the board, where an effective quorum could not be obtained, where the directors are disqualified from voting, or, more obviously, where the directors have purported to borrow in excess of the amount authorised in the articles. Moreover, although the general meeting cannot restrain the directors from conducting actions

---

22 *Danish Mercantile Co Ltd v Beaumont* [1951] Ch. 680 at 687.

23 Whilst *Breckland Group Holdings Ltd v London and Suffolk Properties Ltd* [1989] B.C.L.C. 100 might appear to support exclusive board control of corporate litigation, there was in that case a shareholders' agreement in effect requiring the only two shareholders (or rather their board nominees) to support a decision to commence "material litigation". Accordingly, it is possible to view *Breckland* as being equally consistent with the notion of concurrent jurisdiction with the general meeting.

24 Indeed, this would be consistent with the rule in *Foss v Harbottle* (1843) 2 Hare 461, which concerned whether an individual shareholder should be allowed to sue on behalf of the company or whether the matter should be left to a simple majority of the shareholders. The decision in *Foss* would make no sense if the general meeting did not have some power over the initiation of corporate litigation. This point might be strengthened in light of the approval of *Foss* in *Marex Financial Ltd v Sevilleja* [2020] B.C.C. 783 at [81].

25 See para.11–007.

26 *Irvine v Union Bank of Australia* (1877) 2 App. Cas. 366 PC.

27 *Alexander Ward & Co Ltd v Samyang Navigation Co Ltd* [1975] 1 W.L.R. 673 HL.

28 *Alexander Ward & Co Ltd v Samyang Navigation Co Ltd* [1975] 1 W.L.R. 673 at 679, quoting with approval a passage from the third edition of this book at pp.136–137.

> in the name of the company, it still seems to be the law … that the general meeting can commence proceeding on behalf of the company if the directors fail to do so."

This approach appears to strike a fair compromise between respecting the board's allocated powers to manage the company and allocating the shareholders a greater role in situations that are more problematic. Unless this or a similar view is accepted, the rule in *Foss v Harbottle*,[29] which is considered further below, is difficult to understand: in many cases it denied locus standi to an individual shareholder to enforce the company's rights on the basis that the matter was one for decision by an ordinary majority of the shareholders. If the shareholders in a particular company require a greater say in litigation decisions than suggested in *Alexander Ward*, then they can either include a provision to that effect in the company's constitution,[30] or "by special resolution, direct the directors to take, or refrain from taking, specified action" as permitted by the model articles.[31] Only the former, however, will enable the shareholders to act by way of ordinary resolution. That should not, however, be the default rule.

Whatever the basis for the exercise of the general meeting's power in relation to corporate litigation, it will still not necessarily be the case that the general meeting will always promote the company's best interests. Not only are the shareholders free of any fiduciary duties in the exercise of their powers,[32] but the wrongdoing directors may control the general meeting through their own shareholdings, whether alone or in combination with those other shareholders whose decisions they can influence. Although the Company Law Review recommended that the votes of interested directors and those under their influence should be discounted in relation to litigation decisions,[33] the CA 2006 applies that approach only to shareholders' ratification decisions.[34] This creates something of a tension: if there is a resolution to ratify the wrongdoing, the relevant director may not vote; but, if there is a resolution to commence litigation against a particular director, that director may use his or her votes to stymie the litigation. Moreover, even if the wrongdoers do not control the general meeting, it is not clear how the shareholders will come to consider whether the company should initiate litigation or not. Presumably, the wrongdoing directors will not take steps to put the matter before the general meeting, unless they think the general meeting will support them, and so the shareholders as a group may simply remain ignorant of the fact that there is even an issue to discuss. Certainly, if one or more of the shareholders know the relevant facts, they may use their statutory powers to have the matter put on the AGM's agenda or to have a meeting called to discuss the issue.[35] In both cases, the support of a substantial number of fellow shareholders will be required to initiative these procedural steps and at least half of the shareholders present and voting would need to support the resolution to commence litigation.

---

29 *Foss v Harbottle* (1843) 2 Hare 461.
30 CA 2006 s.21(1).
31 Companies (Model Articles) Regulations 2008 (SI 2008/3229) Sch.1 art.4 and Sch.3 art.4.
32 See para.13–003.
33 Completing, para.5.101.
34 CA 2006 s.239(4).
35 See further Ch.12.

Derivative claims

Given these difficulties, it is hardly surprising that the issue arose as to whether individual shareholders should have standing to commence litigation in the company's name against the alleged wrongdoing directors. This has always been a controversial proposition, since it effectively bypasses the company's usual majoritarian decision-making structures. On the one hand, relatively free access to the courts for individual shareholders suing on behalf of the company (or "derivatively") increases the levels of litigation against wrongdoing directors. Accordingly, if the levels of such litigation are considered to be sub-optimal as a result of wrongdoers influencing litigation decisions at either board or shareholder level, then such increased litigation should be welcomed. Indeed, such minority shareholder claims plug what would otherwise be a "corporate governance gap". On the other hand, it is difficult to demonstrate that such derivative litigation will invariably be brought in the company's interests, as there is the risk that the proceedings are brought to further an individual agenda, rather than a corporate one (namely, the interests of the shareholders collectively). Indeed, as the recoveries from a derivative action accrue to the company, rather than the individual shareholder who is litigating the claim derivatively, a small shareholder will often have little financial incentive to commence corporate action.[36] As a consequence, a minority shareholder may not bring the claim at all or, if he or she does, there is a real risk that the decision is motivated more by personal concerns, rather than a genuine desire to increase the company's value.[37] Moreover, given that different minority shareholders might seek to pursue varying aims, there is a risk that the company becomes so inundated with minority shareholder litigation that the board's energies and the company's resources are diverted away from its core business purposes. Accordingly, derivative actions should only be permitted with appropriate safeguards. **15–004**

Traditionally, the common law has always been more impressed by the risks associated with derivative claims than their corporate governance benefits. To that end, it erected such stringent and elaborate safeguards that the common law derivative action became virtually extinct. The starting point is the so-called "rule in *Foss v Harbottle*",[38] which effectively operated to block the access of minority shareholders to the court, other than on a very limited basis. In essence, *Foss v Harbottle* was built upon "two pillars", each designed to shepherd minority grievances through the company's internal dispute-resolution mechanisms. The first pillar was the "proper plaintiff" or "proper claimant" principle, which meant that "[t]he proper plaintiff in an action in respect of a wrong alleged to be done to **15–005**

[36] Even if the derivative claim is successful, the most that a minority shareholder can expect is a share of the litigation proceeds by way of dividend, although this will reflect the size of the shareholding in question. The directors may, however, legitimately re-invest the funds, rather than declaring a dividend.

[37] For an example of a derivative claim brought for what appears to be a collateral purpose, see *Konamaneni v Rolls-Royce Industrial Power (India) Ltd* [2003] B.C.C. 790 Ch D. In the US, where derivative claims can be brought more freely, it is sometimes argued that the drivers of the litigation are the law firms who stand to take a handsome percentage of awards obtained under contingent-fee arrangements, if the derivative litigation is successful.

[38] *Foss v Harbottle* (1843) 2 Hare 461.

a corporation is, prima facie, the corporation." Accordingly, minority shareholders were not allowed to enforce a corporate claim, but had to raise their issues within the general meeting. The second pillar is the "majority rule" principle, which means that "[w]here the alleged wrong is a transaction which might be made binding on the corporation and on all its members by a simple majority of the members, no individual member of the corporation is allowed to maintain an action in respect of that matter because, if the majority confirms the transaction, *cadit quaestio*; or, if the majority challenges the transaction, there is no valid reason why the company should not sue." This effectively meant that, unless the minority shareholder could persuade the majority to his or her view, then their grievance could go no further. The upshot was an almost complete absence of derivative claims.

Like any rule, there were exceptional circumstances where a minority might sue,[39] such as when the wrong in question affected the shareholder's personal rights[40]; where an illegal or ultra vires act was committed or threatened[41]; or when a particular decision could only be taken by way of a special majority.[42] In most cases, these "exceptions" involved the enforcement of personal, not corporate, rights and so were not within the rationale of *Foss v Harbottle*.[43] There was, however, one true exception to *Foss v Harbottle*,[44] pursuant to which a minority could litigate derivatively on behalf of a company. The common law derivative action depended on the minority demonstrating that the wrongdoing in question amounted to a "fraud on the minority".[45] This had a number of restrictive bars that the minority shareholder had to overcome before the court would grant permission to bring a derivative action on behalf of the company. First, the wrongdoer's conduct had to involve "fraud". This was something of a misnomer, since the concept had a wider meaning than common law fraud.[46] In particular, the notion encompassed wrongs that the majority shareholders could not ratify, such as dishonest conduct[47] or any misappropriation of corporate assets.[48] Fraud would also encompass "self-serving" negligence, where a significant benefit resulted from the conduct in question, but not "mere" negligence.[49] Secondly, the wrongdoing directors had to be "in control" of the general meeting. Whilst this notion of "control" would clearly encompass the situation where the wrongdoers themselves held a majority of shares,[50] it would also encompass de facto control when the wrongdoers were able to secure a

[39] *Edwards v Halliwell* [1950] 2 All E.R. 1064 CA at 1066–1067, affirmed in *Prudential Assurance Co Ltd v Newman Industries Ltd (No.2)* [1982] Ch. 204 CA (Civ Div).

[40] See further Ch.14.

[41] CA 2006 s.39. For illegal acts, see *Smith v Croft (No 2)* [1987] 3 All E.R. 909 Ch D at 937–960.

[42] *Edwards v Halliwell* [1950] 2 All E.R. 1064.

[43] *Foss v Harbottle* (1843) 2 Hare 461.

[44] *Foss v Harbottle* (1843) 2 Hare 461.

[45] See *Prudential Assurance Co Ltd v Newman Industries Ltd (No.2)* [1982] Ch 204: "There is an exception to the rule [in *Foss v Harbottle*] where what has been done amounts to fraud and the wrongdoers are themselves in control of the company".

[46] *Estmanco (Kilner House) Ltd v Greater London Council* [1982] 1 W.L.R. 2 QBD at 12.

[47] *Atwool v Merryweather* (1867–68) L.R. 5 Eq. 464 (Note) Ct of Chancery.

[48] *Menier v Hooper's Telegraph Works* (1873–74) L.R. 9 Ch. App. 350 CA in Chancery; *Cook v Deeks* [1916] 1 A.C. 554 PC; cf *Regal (Hastings) Ltd v Gulliver* [1967] 2 A.C. 134n.

[49] *Daniels v Daniels* [1978] Ch. 406 Ch D; cf *Pavlides v Jensen* [1956] Ch. 565 Ch D.

[50] *Pavlides v Jensen* [1956] Ch. 565.

majority through the votes of shareholders over whom they exercised influence.[51] Thirdly, a majority of the independent shareholders (namely, those not subject to wrongdoer control) would need to support bringing proceedings against the wrongdoer.[52] In effect, the independent shareholders (like any other decision-making organ) had to operate by way of majority rule. Fourthly, the shareholder had to have "clean hands" in bringing the derivative claim.[53] Finally, the derivative claim had to be brought for a proper corporate purpose, rather than to further some personal collateral agenda.[54] Indeed, all these standing requirements had to be satisfied at a preliminary stage, before a court would give permission to commence the derivative action.[55]

Unfortunately, these standing requirements were so strict that common law derivative claims were a rare beast. Furthermore, the principles governing the derivative action were one-sided in their operation: they were effective in excluding derivative actions, but there was no countervailing mechanism whereby a meeting of shareholders could be summoned to consider the litigation question. Nor was there any mechanism depriving interested directors of their votes.[56] Consequently, the rule in *Foss v Harbottle*[57] did nothing to correct the deficiencies of group decision-making by the shareholders, but simply made it difficult for the individual shareholder to sue instead. As a result, the Law Commission in 1997 made recommendations for taking derivative actions in a new direction by allocating the litigation decision to someone external to the company, namely, the court.[58] These proposals were largely endorsed by the Company Law Review and are now embodied in somewhat different form in the CA 2006. Whilst the legislation provides that a derivative claim, as defined therein, can no longer be brought at common law,[59] the CA 2006 omitted certain types of derivative action and certain types of corporate body. Consequently, the rule in *Foss v Harbottle* remains relevant for "double" derivative actions brought even by companies registered under the CA 2006 (i.e. derivative actions brought by a shareholder in a parent company in relation to wrongdoing by the directors of a subsidiary).[60] It also remains relevant for foreign-registered companies,[61] **15–006**

[51] *Prudential Assurance Co Ltd v Newman Industries Ltd (No. 2)* [1982] Ch. 204.

[52] *Smith v Croft (No.2)* [1987] 3 All E.R. 909.

[53] *Nurcombe v Nurcombe* [1985] 1 W.L.R. 370 CA (Civ Div).

[54] *Barrett v Duckett* [1995] 1 B.C.L.C. 243.

[55] In *Prudential Assurance Co Ltd v Newman Industries Ltd (No 2)* [1982] Ch. 204, the court insisted that the question of standing to bring the derivative claim should be decided in advance of, and separately from, the decision on the merits of the case.

[56] The technique endorsed in *Danish Mercantile Co Ltd v Beaumont* [1951] Ch. 680, of commencing litigation in the name of the company (i.e. not derivatively), but without authority to do so, and the court referring the issue to the shareholders for decision when the authority issue is raised, has not been used in practice (perhaps because the solicitors are personally liable in costs if the shareholders do not ratify the decision to sue). As considered above, *Danish* is consistent with the notion that, in the litigation context, shareholders have concurrent jurisdiction with the board.

[57] *Foss v Harbottle* (1843) 2 Hare 461.

[58] Law Commission, *Shareholder Remedies* (1997), Cm.3769.

[59] CA 2006 s.260(2).

[60] *Universal Project Management Services Ltd v Fort Gilkicker Ltd* [2013] EWHC 348 (Ch); [2013] Ch. 551 at [44]–[49]. See also *Bhullar v Bhullar* [2015] EWHC 1943 (Ch) at [19]; *Wilton UK Ltd v*

limited liability partnerships[62] and charitable companies.[63] Despite languishing unloved for so many years, the common law derivative action has moved back into consideration, making its requirements suddenly important once again. Indeed, it is somewhat perverse that this has happened just when the CA 2006 suggests that it should wither and die.

Other possible solutions

15–007 Before turning to the statutory derivative action, it is worth noting that the three mechanisms discussed above—to have litigation decisions taken by the board, by the shareholders as a whole, or by individual shareholders—do not exhaust the possible mechanisms for handling the litigation decision, even within the company. There are other obvious options, and to some extent the final form of the current statutory derivative action cherry-picks the better aspects of each of them.

One alternative might be to give the litigation decision to a sub-set of the members of the board, such as the uninvolved board members or its independent non-executive directors. Such a solution would certainly chime with the approach of the UK Corporate Governance Code,[64] which tends to delegate sensitive issues (such as directors' remuneration and the oversight of the company's audit) to specialist sub-committees populated by non-executive directors. Although it may not be called upon very often (and accordingly the costs may not justify the rewards), there may be scope for a "litigation committee". There is a similar approach taken by the CA 2006 to the authorisation of conflicts of interest,[65] in contrast to the ratification of breaches of duty, where a shareholder decision is required. Since the decision not to sue defaulting directors is, however, akin to a ratification decision, it seems consistent not to use a sub-set of the board to take the litigation decision either, but the analogy with ratification suggests that the litigation decision should be taken only by "independent" shareholders (as considered next). On the other hand, there are benefits to having director input, especially given the powerful duties owed by directors to their companies. Recognising this, the statutory derivative action makes it mandatory for the *court* itself to have regard to the likely approach of a disinterested director, acting in compliance with its duty to promote the success of the company,[66] to the litigation question.[67] Equally, the ratification model also has its attractions, and, backing both horses, the statutory derivative action also requires the court to

---

Shuttleworth [2017] EWHC 2195 (Ch) at [28]; *Popely v Popely* [2018] EWHC 276 (Ch) at [100]–[108]; *Boston Trust Company Ltd v Szerelmey Ltd* [2020] EWHC 1136 (Ch) at [65]–[67]; *Gill v Thind* [2020] EWHC 2973 (Ch) at [43]–[45].

[61] *Abouraya v Sigmund* [2014] EWHC 277 (Ch); *Novatrust Ltd v Kea Investments Ltd* [2014] EWHC 4061.

[62] *Harris v Microfusion 2003-2 LLP* [2016] EWCA Civ 1212 at [13]; *Homes of England Ltd v Nick Sellman (Holdings) Ltd* [2020] EWHC 936 (Ch); [2020] B.C.C. 607 at [44]–[52].

[63] *Mohamed v Abdelmamoud* [2018] EWCA Civ 879.

[64] See generally Financial Reporting Council, *UK Corporate Governance Code* (July 2018).

[65] See paras 10–096 to 10–097.

[66] CA 2006 s.172(1).

[67] CA 2006 s.263(2)(a).

consider the actual or likely views of the non-involved shareholders (namely, those who could have voted to ratify).[68] These considerations are analysed further below.

A further alternative would be to entrust the litigation decision to some smaller group of shareholders, lying somewhere between the shareholders as a whole and the individual shareholder. The common law has never used this device, although it has been used extensively in German law. Nevertheless, the common law was perhaps right to reject this solution, since fixing the appropriate percentage/number of shareholders has proved difficult. However, the strategy has been introduced into British law by the legislature in one specific context[69]: where the company's claims arise in consequence of unauthorised political donations or expenditures made by the company's directors, then the right to sue in the name of the company is conferred, not on individual shareholders, but on an "authorised group" of members. This "authorised group" requires a minority of a particular size, but at the same time excludes individual shareholders from suing, on the basis presumably that they might be motivated by reasons that did not relate to the company's interests.

A final and more radical approach would be to give the right to commence a derivative action to someone outside the company altogether. This is unlikely to be a sensible approach in the general run of companies, where it is difficult to identify anyone outside the company with a legitimate interest in commencing litigation on its behalf. Some vestiges of this technique might be found in the ability of a liquidator or administrator to bring all manner of claims on behalf of the company.[70] A further example is the Secretary of State's ability to seek compensation orders against directors and other persons who are the subject of disqualification orders or undertakings, where their conduct has caused loss to one or more creditors of their insolvent company.[71] Similarly, the Regulator of Community Interest Companies (CIC Regulator) may bring proceedings (subject to a right of appeal by any director of the CIC to the court, which then has broad powers to confirm, discontinue or set terms for the litigation).[72] Presumably, in CIC companies it was thought that the members would have insufficient incentives to initiate litigation. If the CIC Regulator takes this step, the company must be indemnified by the CIC Regulator against the costs and expenses of the litigation, unless, presumably, the court orders that the costs should be borne by the company. This perhaps highlights a further concern with this approach in the context of viable companies.

---

[68] CA 2006 ss.263(2)(b)–(c) and 263(3)(c)–(d).

[69] See paras 15–021 onwards.

[70] IA 1986 s.212. See further Ch.33.

[71] Company Directors Disqualification Act 1986 ss.15A–15C, inserted by Small Business, Enterprise and Employment Act 2015 s.110 from 1 October 2015. An application for a compensation order must be made within two years of the disqualification order or undertaking (see Company Directors Disqualification Act 1986 s.15A(5)). The compensation will be payable either to the Secretary of State for the benefit of a creditor or creditors specified in the order, or a class or classes of specified creditors; or as a contribution to the assets of the company (ibid. s.15B). See generally Ch.20.

[72] Companies (Audit, Investigations and Community Enterprise) Act 2004 s.44.

THE GENERAL STATUTORY DERIVATIVE CLAIM

The scope of the statutory derivative claim

The court's gatekeeper role

15–008 The novelty of the general statutory derivative claim in the CA 2006 is that it outsources the gatekeeping decision to a body outside the company: the court must decide whether it is in the company's interests for litigation to be commenced in any particular case.[73] Whilst a shareholder must certainly take the initiative by commencing derivative proceedings, once the claim form has been issued, the shareholder must seek the court's permission to take any substantive steps in the litigation (other than, in the normal case, informing the company that the claim has been issued and that the shareholder is applying to the court for permission to continue the claim).[74] Even at common law, the court had a role in the early stages of a derivative claim, but this was to check that the claimant had standing to sue.[75] Under the new general derivative claim the court's role is broader,[76] namely, to exercise a constrained discretion to decide whether it is in the best interests of the company for the litigation to be brought. This new procedure has the advantages, on the one hand, that the individual shareholder can easily obtain a decision on the central question (whether it is in the interests of the company for the litigation to be brought), whilst, on the other hand, the individual shareholder's enthusiasm for derivative litigation is subject to the filter of a judge having to be convinced that this particular litigation on behalf of the company is desirable.

Whilst it is true that many of the policy issues that underlay the common law derivative action reappear under the statutory procedure,[77] they are no longer absolute bars to a derivative claim (as was the case at common law), but rather factors that the court must take into account in deciding whether to allow the litigation to proceed. Nowadays, a shareholder who fails to obtain permission to continue a derivative action will receive a reasoned judgment explaining why a derivative claim in the particular case is not in the company's interests, whereas previously the court's decision said nothing about the desirability of the litigation

---

[73] For the earlier history and purpose of the new statutory derivative action, see *Iesini v Westrip Holdings Ltd* [2009] EWHC 2526 (Ch); [2010] B.C.C. 420 at [73]–[83].

[74] CPR 19.9(4) and 19A(2). It should be noted that the obligation to seek the permission of the court to proceed "applies to a derivative claim (where a company, other body corporate or trade union is alleged to be entitled to claim a remedy, and a claim is made by a member of it for it to be given that remedy), whether under Chapter 1 of Part 11 of the Companies Act 2006 or otherwise" (see CPR 19.9(1)(a)), so that it applies also to derivative claims still governed by the common law and not falling within the statutory procedure. See para.15–006. However, CPR 19.9A, laying down specific rules for derivative claims falling within the CA 2006, does not.

[75] *Prudential Assurance Co Ltd v Newman Industries Ltd (No.2)* [1982] Ch. 204.

[76] Under CPR 19.9, the courts recently began to take a broader look at the value to the company of the proposed derivative claim: see *Portfolios of Distinction Ltd v Laird* [2004] EWHC 2071 (Ch); [2004] 2 B.C.L.C. 741 at [51]–[68]; *Airey v Cordell* [2006] EWHC 2728 (Ch); [2007] B.C.C. 785.

[77] CA 2006 ss.263 and 268. See Keay and Loughrey, "Something Old, Something New, Something Borrowed: an Analysis of the New Derivative Action under the Companies Act 2006" (2008) L.Q.R. 469.

from the company's point of view; the focus was simply on whether the litigation decision was one for the shareholders generally or the individual shareholder.

The types of claims covered by the statutory regime

There are a good number of limitations to the statutory jurisdiction. The CA 2006 applies only to derivative claims or derivative proceedings, i.e. claims brought in respect of a cause of action vested in the company and seeking relief on its behalf.[78] As the company is to be bound by (and the potential beneficiary of) any judgment or order made in the derivative proceedings, the Civil Procedure Rules require the company to be made a defendant in the litigation, even though it is the company's rights that are being enforced.[79] In essence, the company is only being joined as a nominal defendant to the proceedings, with the real defendants being the wrongdoing directors.[80] **15–009**

Most derivative claims can now be brought only under the CA 2006,[81] either as a general statutory derivative action,[82] or as a result of a successful unfair prejudice petition.[83] At the outset, it should be noted that the CA 2006 only contemplates derivative actions "arising from an actual or proposed act or omission involving negligence, default, breach of duty or breach of trust by a director of the company".[84] Where the company has a cause of action arising in some other way (for example, a claim against a non-directorial employee), the policy is that a derivative claim is not available, and the litigation decision should be taken according to the division of powers contained in the company's articles of association (i.e. normally exclusively by the board).[85] It is only when the directors themselves are in breach of duty that the general statutory derivative action is available, as that is when the risk of conflicted decision-making by the board or shareholders is most acute. Although the company's cause of action must arise out of breach of a duty by the directors, the defendants are not

---

78 CA 2006 ss.260–264, dealing with derivative claims in England, Wales and Northern Ireland. For derivative actions in Scotland, see CA 2006 ss.265–269. Despite the procedural differences between the different jurisdictions, the underlying policies are the same.

79 CPR 19.9(3). Accordingly, the claim appears in the form of "Shareholder v Director and Company". The reason for this oddity seems to be that anyone can make another person a defendant to a claim, but making a person a claimant requires that person's consent. This results from the fact that a minority shareholder is not in fact a corporate organ that commits the company to legal proceedings.

80 If the shareholder has a personal claim against the directors, the derivative action has no application, as a derivative action covers "a cause of action vested in the company": see CA 2006 s.260(1). For personal claims, see generally Ch.14. Where proceedings are commenced and permission is not sought, this can be cured through the courts' relief from sanctions jurisdiction: see *Wilton UK Ltd v Shuttleworth* [2017] EWHC 2195 (Ch); [2018] EWHC 911 (Ch).

81 The common law exceptions continue to apply to multiple derivative actions, derivative actions against foreign-registered companies and derivative actions on behalf of limited liability companies: see fnn.60–63.

82 CA 2006 s.260(1).

83 CA 2006 s.996(2)(c). See further Ch.14.

84 CA 2006 ss.260(3) and 265(3).

85 Given the courts' current willingness to invoke the common law derivative action (see *Universal Project Management Services Ltd v Fort Gilkicker Ltd* [2013] Ch. 551 at [44]–[49]), there may yet be scope for further expansion.

necessarily limited to and may not even include the directors themselves.[86] As considered above,[87] third parties may become liable to the company as a result of their involvement in the directors' breaches of duty. Accordingly, claims for knowing receipt, dishonest assistance or for a constructive trust are frequently made against third parties in this context. The derivative action may be used against such a third party, even if no director is sued.

As considered previously,[88] the general duties owed by directors can encompass former or shadow directors. For the purpose of the general statutory derivative action, "directors" include former and shadow directors,[89] but this is less significant than it may seem. This definition does not alter the circumstances in which former or shadow directors owe duties to the company; it merely ensures that, where such duties are owed, the derivative action can be used to enforce them.

Shareholder claimants

15–010 A shareholder may bring a general statutory derivative claim in respect of a cause of action that arose before he or she became a member of the company.[90] On the other hand, only members of the company can bring derivative actions[91]: a former member cannot sue, even in respect of a matter that occurred whilst he was a shareholder.[92] This reflects the legal position of shareholders generally: the shareholder has an interest "in" the company that generates certain expectations regarding profits and capital distributions. That interest's quantum alters as the company's assets and business change through its life. Accordingly, once membership has been relinquished, so is the shareholder's interest "in" the company. Once that has occurred, the shareholder cannot be expected to take advantage of legal mechanisms designed to protect the company; it is now somebody else's issue.

There is, however, one useful statutory extension of the notion of a "member". This term is not confined to those who have been entered on the company's register of members—which is a standard requirement for membership[93]—but is extended to those who have acquired the shares by operation of law, even though the transferee is not entered on the register of members.[94] The usual example of such transmission is on death or bankruptcy. The extension of "membership" to include mere transferees is especially useful in quasi-partnership companies, where the directors normally have power under the articles to refuse to admit new

86 CA 2006 ss.260(3) and 265(4).

87 See paras 10–130 onwards.

88 See paras 10–009 and 10–014.

89 CA 2006 ss.260(5) and 265(7).

90 CA 2006 ss.260(4) and 265(5). A person with a beneficial interest in the shares may in exceptional circumstances have standing to bring a derivative action: see *Boston Trust Co Ltd v Szerelmey Ltd* [2020] EWHC 1136 (Ch) at [67]–[71].

91 Where a shareholder has "inchoate standing" (in the sense that an application for rectification of the share register is pending), a court may give conditional permission to bring a derivative action: see *Boston Trust Co Ltd v Szerelmey Ltd* [2020] EWHC 1352 (Ch) at [99].

92 CA 2006 ss.260(1) and 265(1).

93 CA 2006 s.112. See further para.26–005.

94 CA 2006 ss.260(5)(c) and 265(7)(e).

members and are often prepared to use that power to keep out of the company persons with whom they do not wish to work. Making the derivative claim available may enable would-be members to challenge their exclusion or, at least, to challenge action by the controllers of the company—for example, siphoning assets out of the company to the detriment of the would-be member—designed to induce the would-be member to transfer the shares to other members at a low price. Such action by the controllers carries the risk that the would-be member will bring a derivative action to restore the company's position.[95]

Deciding whether to give permission for the derivative claim

The central issue under the new statutory derivative action is the nature of the discretion vested in the court to approve or not the continuance of the derivative claim. That discretion is broad but not unconstrained. The CA 2006 proceeds in three stages by, first, requiring the claimant to make out a prima facie case; secondly, identifying whether the case falls within one of the three situations in which leave must be denied[96]; and, thirdly, assuming the case does not fall within any of those three situations, laying down a number of factors that the court must take into account when deciding whether to give permission to proceed with the derivative action. 15–011

The prima facie case and judicial management of proceedings

The decision whether to grant permission for the derivative action to proceed will potentially require a wide-ranging enquiry on the part of the court. Although the company is a potential beneficiary of the derivative action, there is a risk that companies might find themselves subjected to overly high levels of proposed derivative claims by shareholders who have a fanciful or even self-interested view of the likely benefits to the company from such litigation. Companies would then be distracted from more important tasks by having to explain in court why such claims should not be allowed to proceed further. In partial recognition of this issue, the CA 2006 contains a procedure whereby the court's initial consideration of the claim is on the basis of the evidence submitted by the member alone. If the court does not at this stage think the applicant has established a prima facie case for permission to be granted, the application will be refused. At this initial stage, the company is not a respondent to the application to the court for permission to continue the claim and so is not required to file evidence or be present at any hearing. Only if the application survives this initial examination will the company be invited to file evidence as to whether permission should be granted or not.[97] 15–012

[95] For an extension in the notion of "member" in the context of the CA 2006 s.994(1), see para.14–013.

[96] CA 2006 ss.263(1) and 268(1).

[97] CA 2006 ss.261(2) and 266(3). In England and Wales, this procedure is fleshed out in CPR 19.9A. In some cases, the court has been inclined to merge the first two stages into one: see *Mission Capital Plc v Sinclair* [2008] EWHC 1339 (Ch); *Franbar Holdings Ltd v Patel* [2008] EWHC 1534 (Ch); *Stimpson v Southern Private Landlords Association* [2009] EWHC 2072 (Ch); *Bridge v Daley* [2015] EWHC 2121 (Ch). This may occur if a hearing between the parties is already listed in another matter: see *Hughes v Burley* [2021] EWHC 104 (Ch) at [43].

Mandatory refusal of permission

15–013 Two of the situations where permission must be denied are obvious: where the actual or proposed breach of duty has been authorised or ratified.[98] In such a case, there is no longer any wrong by the director to the company: just as the company can no longer complain about that wrong, neither can the shareholder suing derivatively. Accordingly, the most important ground for mandatory dismissal is the third one: the court must deny permission to continue the derivative action where a person acting in accordance with the directors' core duty of loyalty (to promote the success of the company for the benefit of its members) "would not" seek to continue the claim.[99] Since the core duty of good faith is the modern version of acting "in the interests of the company", it is sensible to use that as the touchstone for bringing the derivative claim. Indeed, this notion of the honest director is used both at the mandatory dismissal stage and again at the permissive stage. At this mandatory stage, the words have been interpreted as requiring the court to be of the opinion that *no* director, acting in accordance with s.172, would seek to pursue the claim, if it is to refuse permission.[100] If some would and some would not, the "no director" test is not satisfied. In terms of the strength of the legal claim (not the only consideration), the claimant must establish that on the merits there is "more than a prima facie case".[101] This means that the merits must be stronger than a seriously arguable case,[102] but need not necessarily reach the threshold of a "strong case".[103] At the permissive stage, more flexibility is both warranted and inevitable.

Discretionary grant of permission

15–014 If the proposed litigation passes the negative test (namely, will it fail to promote the success of the company?), one might have thought that whether the litigation should be allowed to proceed would depend on whether it can pass that test put positively (namely, will the litigation promote the success of the company?). In other words, for permission to continue and the derivative action to be granted, the claim must pass the positive version of that test. To assist in that regard, the CA 2006 sets out seven factors[104] that the court must take into account in

[98] CA 2006 ss.263(2)(b)–(c) and 268(1)(b)–(c). See paras 10–054, 10–066 onwards, 10–096 and 10–111 onwards.

[99] CA 2006 ss.263(2)(a) and 268(1)(a). On the director's core duty of good faith, see CA 2006 s.172(1). See further paras 10–026 onwards.

[100] *Iesini v Westrip Holdings Ltd* [2010] B.C.C. 420, where the court held that the strength of the claim against the board was so weak that *no* director, acting in accordance with CA 2006 s.172, would seek to continue the claim. See also *Zavahir v Shankleman* [2016] EWHC 2772 (Ch) at [36]; *Montgold Capital LLP v Ilska* [2018] EWHC 2982 (Ch) at [20]–[35]; *Gill v Thind* [2020] EWHC 2973 (Ch) at [86].

[101] *Iesini v Westrip Holdings Ltd* [2010] B.C.C. 420 at [79]; *Shandong Offshore Investment (HK) Co Ltd v Andresen* [2018] EWHC 2874 (Ch) at [9]; *Saatchi v Gajjar* [2019] EWHC 3472 (Ch) at [28]–[32].

[102] *Kleanthous v Paphitis* [2011] EWHC 2287 at [42]; *Abouraya v Sigmund* [2014] EWHC 277 at [53].

[103] *Saatchi v Gajjar* [2019] EWHC 3472 at [29]; *Gill v Thind* [2020] EWHC 2973 (Ch) at [37].

[104] CA 2006 ss.263(5) and 268(4), to which the Secretary of State may add by regulation.

deciding whether to allow the litigation to proceed, once that claim has survived the mandatory grounds for dismissal.[105] The thinking behind the drafting of these statutory factors may have been that the court should not be under pressure to allow the litigation to proceed where its financial contribution to the company is likely to be small and there are other factors pointing against the litigation.[106] Alternatively, it may have been thought desirable to give the court more guidance on the factors to be considered than a single general test would provide.

The list of statutory factors, which are explicitly stated not to be exhaustive of the considerations that the court should take into account,[107] are as follows:

- Whether the shareholder seeking to bring the derivative claim is acting in good faith—or whether, for example, the litigation is motivated by personal interests.
- The importance that a person acting in accordance with s.172 would attach to continuing the proceedings,[108] although it is doubtful whether the focus would be solely on financial considerations in that regard. This is difficult: as Lewison J noted in *Iesini v Westrip Holdings Ltd*,[109] it is "essentially a commercial decision, which the court is ill-equipped to take, except in a clear case." In determining whether a director would bring the proceedings consistently with his duties, the court will often further assess the claim's strengths,[110] the likely quantum of recovery,[111] the importance of the claim[112] and the funding arrangements.[113] In that vein, it should be noted that there is one crucial difference between the court's role when it is hearing an allegation that a director has breached the core duty of loyalty and the role of that requirement in the statutory derivative claim. In the former case, provided the director has properly formed a good faith view as to what promoting the success of the company requires, the court has no power to interfere. Under the general statutory derivative action, however, it does not appear that such deference is to be accorded at the permissive stage to the individual shareholder's decision to initiate derivative

105 CA 2006 ss.263(3)–(4) and 268(2)–(3).

106 Conversely, if the potential financial gain is high, a more uncertain case might be worth pursuing: see *Stainer v Lee* [2010] EWHC 1539 (Ch); [2011] 1 B.C.L.C. 537.

107 CA 2006 ss.263(3) and 268(2), which use the words "in particular".

108 *Iesini v Westrip Holdings Ltd* [2010] B.C.C. 420, which failed this test.

109 *Iesini v Westrip Holdings Ltd* [2010] B.C.C. 420 at [85], noting that the decision required consideration of factors, including "the size of the claim; the strength of the claim; the cost of the proceedings; the company's ability to fund the proceedings; the ability of the potential defendants to satisfy a judgment; the impact on the company if it lost the claim and had to pay not only its own costs but the defendant's as well; any disruption to the company's activities while the claim is pursued; whether the prosecution of the claim would damage the company in other ways (e.g. by losing the services of a valuable employee or alienating a key supplier or customer) and so on". For approval of these factors, see *Hughes v Burley* [2021] EWHC 104 (Ch) at [48].

110 *Hughes v Burley* [2021] EWHC 104 (Ch) at [47].

111 *Saatchi v Gajjar* [2019] EWHC 3472 (Ch) at [75].

112 *Robert Glew and Denton and Co Trustees Ltd v Matossian-Rogers* [2019] EWHC 3183 (Ch) at [52]–[56].

113 *Hughes v Burley* [2021] EWHC 104 (Ch) at [48].

proceedings. Rather, the court will have to formulate its own view about whether the proposed litigation will promote the success of the company.[114]

- Whether the act or omission constituting the breach of duty is likely to be ratified by the company (namely, by the shareholders collectively) or—expressed as a separate test—whether in the case of a proposed breach of duty the act or omission is likely to be authorised or ratified by the company. Authorisation can sometimes be given by the non-involved members of the board.[115] These two tests reflect a factor that was very important under the rule in *Foss v Harbottle*,[116] but with one important difference: whereas at common law the possibility of shareholder approval (normally referred to as ratifiability) of the wrong normally barred access to the derivative claim,[117] under the general statutory derivative action the prospect of either authorisation or ratification[118] is not a bar to the derivative claim, but simply a factor weighing against giving permission. The removal of ratifiability as a bar to the derivative claim is one of the most important changes brought about by the statutory procedure. Under the common law, the derivative claim was largely excluded as a mechanism for the enforcement of ratifiable breaches of duty, and that perhaps goes some way to explaining the rise of the concept of "un-ratifiable breaches".[119]
- Whether the company (either through a decision of the board or of the shareholders) has decided not to pursue the claim. What is at issue here is a board or shareholder resolution that, whilst not seeking to ratify the directors' breach of duty, nevertheless contains a decision not to sue the directors.[120] Such a resolution may constitute an argument against allowing the derivative claim to continue, provided the decision was not influenced by the alleged wrongdoers[121]; but this is now only a factor to be taken into account. This represents another significant change from the common law. Under the common law regime, even a non-ratifiable wrong could not be pursued derivatively unless the alleged wrongdoers were in control of the general meeting. Under the statutory derivative action, permission to continue the litigation can be granted by the court, even if the alleged wrongdoers are not in control of the shareholders' meeting.[122] A decision

---

[114] *Iesini v Westrip Holdings Ltd* [2010] B.C.C. 420, finding that, under the CA 2006 s.263(3)(b), a person acting in accordance with s.172 would attach little weight to continuing the action. See also *Re Seven Holdings* [2011] EWHC 1893; *Kleanthous v Paphitis* [2011] EWHC 2287 (Ch).

[115] See para.10–096.

[116] *Foss v Harbottle* (1843) 2 Hare 461.

[117] *Edwards v Halliwell* [1950] 2 All E.R. 1064.

[118] CA 2006 s.263(3)(c), which specifies that the authorisation or ratification must be "by the company", thus importing the mechanisms and their qualifications discussed at paras 10–111 onwards.

[119] On the common law's distinction between ratifiable and non-ratifiable breaches of duty, see para.10–118.

[120] *Bridge v Daley* [2015] EWHC 2121 (Ch).

[121] A decision by the company not to pursue the claim should be given very little weight where the defendant directors constitute the majority of its directors: see *Cullen Investments v Brown* [2015] EWHC 472 (Ch).

[122] *Bamford v Harvey* [2012] EWHC 2858 (Ch). This is, however, likely to be rare: see *Cinematic Finance Ltd v Ryder* [2010] All E.R. (D) 283.

by the shareholders (uninfluenced by the wrongdoers) not to initiate litigation will no doubt count heavily against the derivative claim.

- Whether the facts give rise to a cause of action that vests in the member personally and that he or she could pursue as such, rather than bringing a derivative claim on behalf of the company. Whilst the existence of an alternative remedy is not a bar to a derivative action, it would usually be preferable to pursue that alternative, rather than for the company to incur the costs of a derivative action.[123] Perhaps the most obvious claim a shareholder might bring is a petition based on unfairly prejudicial conduct by the controllers of the company.[124] In determining the weight to be given to an alternative unfair prejudice petition, a court will examine whether the "gist" of the claim is personal or corporate and whether any unfair prejudice claim would be a "concealed" derivative action.[125] Apart from that, the possibilities for a personal action will be limited, since, normally, directors' duties are owed to the company, not to shareholders individually.[126] The shareholder may prefer a derivative claim because the costs of it will fall on the company. When assessing the weight to be allocated to the existence of an alternative personal claim, a court is likely to examine the extent to which the losses arising out of a personal wrong may or may not be irrecoverable under the "reflective loss" principle,[127] whereby the shareholder's losses in a personal claim are irrecoverable where they essentially "reflect" corporate losses. Following the Supreme Court's re-statement of the "reflective loss" principle,[128] there is now a bright line between irrecoverable losses (namely, claims by shareholders for losses to the value of their shares or loss of distributions) and recoverable losses. Where the alternative claim falls into the former category, no weight can be attached to it. Conversely, due weight can be given to shareholders' personal claims falling outside the "reflective loss" principle.
- Finally, and by way of separate subsection, the court is required to have "particular regard" to any evidence as to the views of the other shareholders who have no personal interest in the matter.[129] This again reflects an important element of the common law derivative action, which, however,

[123] *Gill v Thind* [2020] EWHC 2973 (Ch) at [88].

[124] CA 2006 s.994(1). See also *Franbar Holdings Ltd v Patel* [2008] EWHC 1534 (Ch); [2009] 1 B.C.L.C. 1, where the shareholder's concurrent unfair prejudice claim was seen as delivering almost all the shareholder wanted, so the right to pursue the derivative claim was, to that extent, denied. See also *Kleanthous v Paphitis* [2011] EWHC 2287 (Ch); *Singh v Singh* [2014] EWHC 1060 (Ch). The unfair prejudice alternative is important even where the shareholder does not want to be bought out. See generally Ch.14.

[125] *Re Hut Group Ltd* [2020] EWHC 5 (Ch) at [46]–[60], applying *Re Charnley Davies Ltd (No.2)* [1990] B.C.C. 605 Ch D (Companies Ct). See further paras 14–024 onwards. See also *Saatchi v Gajjar* [2019] EWHC 3472 (Ch) at [80].

[126] See para.10–005. See also *Cullen Investments Ltd v Brown* [2015] EWHC 473 (Ch).

[127] *Cullen Investments Ltd v Brown* [2015] EWHC 473 (Ch), where the "no reflective loss" principle was one of the factors considered by the court in reaching its conclusion that no alternative remedy was available in that case. See also *Hughes v Burley* [2021] EWHC 104 (Ch) at [48]. See further Ch.14.

[128] *Marex Financial Ltd v Sevilleja* [2020] B.C.C. 783 at [81].

[129] CA 2006 ss.263(4) and 268(3). Moreover, unlike the other matters to which the court must have regard, this one cannot be altered by the Secretary of State by regulation: ibid. s.263(5)(b).

appeared to say that the individual shareholder did not have standing to bring a derivative claim if a majority of the independent shareholders were against the litigation.[130] Those independent views are now only a factor, but are likely to be a powerful factor for or against the derivative claim where reliable evidence of those views can be provided to the court.

Varieties of derivative claim

Taking over existing claims

15–015 The analysis so far has assumed a derivative claim being brought where the company itself has failed to initiate litigation. No doubt this is the core case. The CA 2006 also specifically provides for a shareholder to apply to the court for permission to take over litigation that the company has already commenced, so that it can be continued derivatively.[131] The logic is that, without this protection, the directors of a company might stultify potential derivative claims by instituting litigation in the company's name, but then failing to pursue the claim with vigour. Accordingly, the CA 2006 deals with this problem by allowing a shareholder to apply to take over the company's litigation in derivative form. Of course, the company's claim must be one that falls within the scope of the general statutory derivative action and the shareholder's application for permission to take over the corporate claim will be subject to the same criteria as applied to litigation commenced in derivative form.[132] In addition, the shareholder must show why he or she should be allowed to take over the company's claim. The permitted grounds are that the proceedings have been conducted by the company in a way that constitutes an abuse of the court's process; that the company has not prosecuted the litigation diligently; or that, for other reasons, it is "appropriate" for the shareholder to be substituted for the company.[133] If the company has already settled the case against the directors, however, there would appear to be no basis upon which this substitution mechanism could operate.

The CA 2006 even provides a mechanism for a shareholder to apply to the court to take over an existing derivative claim. The justification for this mechanism seems to be preventing the directors from stultifying litigation against themselves by securing a friendly shareholder to commence litigation in derivative form, but then not prosecuting the claim effectively.[134] The grounds for taking over a derivative claim are the same as for taking over a claim begun in the company's name, but of course the tests for giving permission to commence a derivative claim do not have to be applied to the claim to take over an existing derivative claim, since these will have been met at an earlier stage. A claim to take over an existing derivative claim can be made whether the claim was originally commenced in derivative form or was commenced by the company, but

---

[130] *Smith v Croft (No.2)* [1988] Ch. 114, cited with approval in *Franbar Holdings Ltd v Patel* [2009] 1 B.C.L.C. 1.

[131] CA 2006 ss.262 and 267.

[132] CA 2006 ss.262(1)–(3), 263(1), 267(1)–(3) and 268(1).

[133] CA 2006 ss.262(2) and 267(2).

[134] CA 2006 ss.264 and 269.

later taken over derivatively; and whether the shareholder from whom the applicant wishes to take over the litigation is the originator of the litigation, took the litigation over from the company or is someone further down the chain of shareholders who has been pursuing the claim derivatively.[135]

Multiple derivative claims

Contrary to the suggestion of the Company Law Review,[136] the CA 2006 does not appear to cater for the possibility of "double" or "multiple" derivative claims, being claims brought by a member of a corporate member of the wronged company. Whereas an ordinary derivative action involves a shareholder litigating on behalf of the company in which he or she directly holds shares, a "double" derivative action involves the situation where a shareholder in the company's parent wishes to litigate in the name of the subsidiary. Where the corporate layers between the shareholder and the relevant company increase further, then there is a "multiple" derivative action.[137] In *Universal Project Management Services Ltd v Fort Gilkicker Ltd*,[138] Briggs J interpreted the statutory reference to a derivative action being brought by a member of "the" company as excluding shareholders with only an indirect interest in a company from the scope of the statutory derivative action. Accordingly, such "multiple derivative actions" fall to be governed by the common law principles, if they are going to be brought at all.[139] This is unfortunate, as it effectively means that the statutory derivative action is confined to dealing with the most straightforward situations; any degree of complexity appears to render the CA 2006 impotent.[140] Given the restrictiveness of the common law derivative action, as considered above,[141] the effect of *Fort Gilkicker* can only be to doom most multiple derivative actions to failure. There are, however, two solutions to avoiding this undesirable result. First, the courts could develop the common law to soften the edges of its standing requirements, although there are few signs of this at present.[142] Indeed, whilst the elements of the common law derivative action are easy enough to apply to a straightforward case, it is unclear how precisely its requirements of wrongdoer control and independent minority views would apply in the context of a corporate group. Secondly, although *Fort Gilkicker* precludes the general statutory derivative **15–016**

[135] CA 2006 ss.264(1) and 269(1).

[136] Developing, para.4.133.

[137] For ease of reference, the term "multiple derivative action" will be used to encompass all derivative actions involving such indirect interests.

[138] *Universal Project Management Services Ltd v Fort Gilkicker Ltd* [2013] Ch. 551 at [44]–[49]. See also *Bhullar v Bhullar* [2015] EWHC 1943 (Ch) at [19]; *Wilton UK Ltd v Shuttleworth* [2017] EWHC 2195 (Ch) at [28]; *Popely v Popely* [2018] EWHC 276 (Ch) at [100]–[108]; *Boston Trust Company Ltd v Szerelmey Ltd* [2020] EWHC 1136 (Ch) at [65]–[67]; *Gill v Thind* [2020] EWHC 2973 (Ch) at [43]–[45].

[139] For recognition of the "multiple derivative action" at common law, see *Waddington Ltd v Chan Chun Hoo Thomas* [2009] 2 B.C.L.C. 82.

[140] Similarly, the common law governs claims relating to foreign-registered companies: see *Abouraya v Sigmund* [2014] EWHC 277 (Ch); *Novatrust Ltd v Kea Investments Ltd* [2014] EWHC 4061.

[141] See para.15–005.

[142] In *Harris v Microfusion 2003-2 LLP* [2016] EWCA Civ 1212 at [15] and [31], approving *Abouraya v Sigmund* [2014] EWHC 277 (Ch), the Court of Appeal continued to limit the common law derivative action to non-ratifiable wrongs.

action being used for a "multiple" claim, there is no reason why such a claim could not be channelled through the unfair prejudice jurisdiction,[143] as this allows a derivative action to be brought as one of the available forms of relief.[144] Indeed, the unfair prejudice jurisdiction has shown itself capable of dealing with the complexity of minority shareholder claims in corporate groups.[145] This would enable the factors applicable to a statutory derivative action to be applied by analogy to a multiple derivative action, rather than such claims being lost to the common law.

The subsequent conduct of the derivative claim

General issues

15–017 The statutory provisions governing the general derivative claim say nothing about the subsequent conduct of the derivative claim, except that the court is given a general power to give permission for the claim to continue "on such terms as it thinks fit".[146] It is perhaps odd that the subsequent conduct of the general derivative claim is less clearly regulated than that of the special derivative claim for unlawful political donations, considered below.[147] In particular, there is no counterpart in the CA 2006 or the Civil Procedure Rules to the duties of care and loyalty that are imposed on those bringing a derivative claim in respect of an unauthorised political donation.[148] It may be that the courts could develop such provisions on the basis of the agent-like status of a shareholder with permission to continue a derivative action on behalf of the company.

Information rights

15–018 Those bringing the general statutory derivative action also lack the specific information rights conferred by the CA 2006 in favour of those seeking to recover derivatively an unauthorised donation from the directors.[149] It is possible that the court might deal with this matter when setting the conditions for the conduct of a derivative action under the CA 2006. However, another avenue may be to secure the board's co-operation with those responsible for the general derivative claim. By permitting the derivative action, the court has effectively determined that a director acting in accordance with the core duty of loyalty would bring the litigation and that there are no other factors outweighing that conclusion. Accordingly, it would be difficult for the board, consistently with its duties, not to co-operate fully with the shareholder who has charge of the derivative claim. Indeed, it may be wondered whether the board's duties do not require it to give

---

143 CA 2006 s.260(2)(b), which expressly retains the unfair prejudice route.

144 CA 2006 s.996(2)(c).

145 See *Nicholas v Soundcraft Electronics Ltd* [1993] B.C.L.C. 360 CA (Civ Div); *Re Citybranch Group Ltd* [2004] EWCA Civ 815; [2005] B.C.C. 11.

146 CA 2006 ss.261(4)(a), 262(5)(a), 264(5)(a), 266(5)(a), 267(5)(a) and 269(5)(a).

147 See para.15–021.

148 See para.15–021.

149 CA 2006 s.373.

serious consideration to bringing the claim in the company's name, although presumably the court's permission would be needed for the derivative claim to be superseded by a corporate one, and the court might be reluctant to so agree if the board's previous attitude towards the claim had been one of unmitigated hostility.

Costs

In *Wallersteiner v Moir (No.2)*,[150] the Court of Appeal established that a consequence of the derivative claim being used to enforce the company's rights is that, where permission is given, the company should normally be liable for the costs of the claim, even, in fact especially, where the litigation is ultimately unsuccessful. This decision is now reflected in the Civil Procedure Rules, which provide that "the court may order the company … to indemnify the claimant against any liability for costs incurred in the permission application or in the derivative claim or both".[151] This is a key provision because, without its protection, the financial disincentive for a shareholder to bring a derivative claim would be very strong, no matter how relaxed the standing rules. If a shareholder can, however, obtain permission from the court to bring a derivative claim, there should be no financial disincentive to proceed.[152] **15–019**

Restrictions on settlement

The Civil Procedure Rules (CPR) also deal with one further post-permission issue. The derivative action is brought to enforce the company's rights for the company's benefit, but a common perversion of the procedure, known in some quarters as "greenmail", involves the shareholder being primarily interested in obtaining some private benefit from the litigation, normally as part of the terms on which the company's claim against the directors is settled. To discourage such behaviour, the CPR empower the court to order that the claim may not be "discontinued, settled or compromised without the permission of the court", thus giving the court the opportunity to scrutinise the terms of any settlement.[153] **15–020**

[150] *Wallersteiner v Moir (No.2)* [1975] Q.B. 373 CA.

[151] CPR 19.9. A court is not likely, however, to give the claimant a blank cheque, but to review the company's obligation to pay stage-by-stage as the litigation proceeds. See *McDonald v Horn* [1995] 1 All E.R. 961 CA (Civ Div) at 974–975; *Stainer v Lee* [2010] EWHC 1539 (Ch); [2011] 1 B.C.L.C. 537 (capped at £40,000), Moreover, such an order does not give the shareholder priority over the unsecured creditors of the company (see *Qayoumi v Oakhouse Property Holdings Plc* [2002] EWHC 2547 (Ch); [2003] 1 B.C.L.C. 352), so that the shareholder may be unwilling to pursue a derivative claim on behalf of a doubtfully solvent company. The court is also unlikely to allow the company's funds to be used in a derivative claim where the dispute is in essence between the shareholders: see *Tonstate Group v Wojakovski* [2019] EWHC 857 (Ch).

[152] Once the shareholder has been given the relevant permission, they "should in principle be indemnified by those companies in respect of their costs": see *Boston Trust Co Ltd v Szerelmey Ltd* [2020] EWHC 3042 (Ch) at [36]. Indeed, even greater security is given in that, in leave proceedings, the court can make a declaratory conditional order as to the costs of the main litigation, requiring the company to indemnify the member at least to a certain extent: see *Wishart v Castlecroft Securities Ltd* [2009] CSIH 65; [2010] B.C.C. 161. Costs might also cover the application for leave: [2010] CSIH 2. However, the court has to exercise considerable care when deciding whether to order a pre-emptive indemnity: see *Bhullar v Bhullar* [2015] EWHC 1943 (Ch).

[153] CPR r.19.9F.

THE STATUTORY DERIVATIVE CLAIM FOR UNAUTHORISED POLITICAL EXPENDITURE

15–021 As noted earlier, minority group shareholder action on behalf of the company has been introduced into British law by the legislature in one specific area. Under the CA 2006, a company's policy of making political donations and incurring political expenditure is subject to approval by the shareholders in general meeting.[154] If this requirement is contravened, every director (and shadow director) of the company at the relevant time is liable to pay to the company the amount of any donation, or expenditure and damages in respect of any loss or damage suffered by the company in consequence of the unauthorised donation or expenditure.[155] The CA 2006 then provides a specific statutory derivative action in order to enforce the directors' liability.[156] However, this right to sue in the name of the company is conferred, not on individual shareholders, as in the general derivative action, but on an "authorised group" of members. In the case of a company limited by shares, this means the holders of not less than 5% of the nominal value of the company's issued share capital or any class thereof; in the case of a company not limited by shares, not less than 5% of its members; or, in either case, not less than 50 members of the company.[157] It seems that the aim of confining the right to sue to a small group of shareholders was to provide a realistic chance of enforcement action being brought, whilst at the same time excluding individual shareholders from suing, as they might be motivated by reasons unrelated to the company's interests. There is no added role for the court to act as gatekeeper by giving permission to proceed.

Having conferred a statutory right of action in relation to donations upon the approved group of members, the CA 2006 not only facilitates the use of the power by the minority, but also ensures that the power is exercised by the group in the interests of the shareholders as a whole. In particular, the fact that the statutory derivative claim is brought on behalf, and in the interests, of the company is emphasised by a number of features in the CA 2006:

(1) The same duties (of care and loyalty) are owed to the company by the authorised group as would be owed to the company, if the claim had been brought by the directors of the company. An action to enforce these duties against the minority, however, cannot be taken without the leave of the court. This presumably protects the minority from the tactical use of counter-litigation by the alleged wrongdoing directors.[158]

---

[154] See para.10–100.

[155] CA 2006 s.369. In some cases (see para.10–100), the liability may fall upon a director of a holding company and be a liability to the subsidiary. In such a case, the derivative action to enforce the subsidiary's rights may be brought by an authorised group of the shareholders of the holding company, as well as by an authorised group of the shareholders of the subsidiary: see CA 2006 s.370(1)(b). This will be a useful facility where the subsidiary is wholly owned by the parent.

[156] CA 2006 s.370.

[157] CA 2006 s.370(3). This mechanism seems to have been chosen in the original legislation in 2000 on the basis of a somewhat bizarre analogy with the group of shareholders who have the right to complain to the court about a resolution whereby a public company re-registers as a private one: see CA 2006 s.98. The analogy is odd because the claim arising under s.98 is not derivative.

[158] CA 2006 s.371(4).

(2) Proceedings may not be discontinued or settled by the group without the leave of the court and the court may impose terms on any leave that it grants.[159] This provision reduces the risk of "gold digging" or "greenmail" claims, where the purpose of the claim is to extract from the company a private benefit for the group in exchange for the settlement of the claim, rather than to advance the interests of the shareholders as a whole.

(3) The group may apply to the court for an order that the company indemnify the group in respect of the costs of the litigation, and the court may make such order as it thinks fit. The group is not entitled to be paid its costs out of the assets of the company, other than by virtue of an indemnification order or as a result of a costs order made in the litigation in favour of the company.[160] Both these provisions recognise the principle that the company in appropriate circumstances should pay for derivative litigation which is brought for its benefit (as is the case with the general statutory derivative claim).[161] Moreover, this makes it less easy for the group to pursue "gold digging" claims in the guise of generous payments by the company to the group by way of recompense for costs incurred in the litigation.

(4) On the other hand, there is conferred upon the group an express right to all information relating to the subject-matter of the litigation that is in the company's possession, so that the group can better decide in what way to prosecute the litigation. This right extends to information which is reasonably obtainable by the company (for example, from another group company). The court may enforce this right by order.[162]

This is quite a different model from the general derivative claim. Use of the more specific derivative procedure here does not bar access to the general statutory derivative procedure.[163] The general procedure will normally be available because payment of an unauthorised donation, or the incurring of unauthorised political expenditure, by the director will usually constitute a breach of the director's general duties. Whether the specific or the general statutory derivative claim will be more attractive is not clear.

CONCLUSION

Although the new statutory derivative claim is doctrinally very different from the common law one that it replaces, it is still not clear what its impact on the levels of derivative litigation will be. In the early days, the Law Commission was rather downbeat in its assessment. In its Consultation Paper it made the following remarks about the policy that underlay its proposed reforms: "a member should be able to maintain proceedings about wrongs done to the company only in **15–022**

159 CA 2006 s.371(5).
160 CA 2006 s.372.
161 See para.15–019.
162 CA 2006 s.373. The right to information does not, however, arise until proceedings have been instituted, and so the right seems not to aid the minority at the stage when it is considering whether to institute litigation.
163 CA 2006 s.370(5).

exceptional circumstances" and "shareholders should not be able to involve the company in litigation without good cause … Otherwise the company may be 'killed by kindness', or waste money and management time in dealing with unwarranted proceedings".[164] Whilst the latter remark is undoubtedly true, it is unclear whether this should lead to derivative claims being available only in exceptional circumstances, because the ability of wrongdoing directors to block decisions in favour of litigation is a matter of empirical fact that has not been extensively investigated—although the unfair prejudice cases suggest that it is a not uncommon feature of small companies.[165] In its final report, the Law Commission stated that "we do not accept that the proposals will make significant changes to the availability of the action. In some respects, the availability may be slightly wider, in others it may be slightly narrower. But in all cases the new procedure will be subject to tight judicial control".[166]

If the common law led to sub-optimal levels of derivative litigation, one would hope that the statutory changes would have a significant impact, even whilst the judges remain fully alive to the fact that the CA 2006, rightly, creates no entitlement in the shareholder to bring a derivative claim. All depends on how the courts exercise their discretion. The CA 2006 does not suggest that the rule in *Foss v Harbottle* should govern the courts from its grave and in due course the courts may strike out more boldly. There is some indication of this trend; but equally it cannot be said that the courts' approach to giving permission for derivative actions has yet been worked out fully.

---

164 Law Commission, *Shareholders' Remedies* (1996), Consultation Paper No.142, para.4.6.
165 See further Ch.14.
166 Law Commission, *Shareholder Remedies* (1997), Cm.3769, para.6.13.

PART 5

CREDITORS

Company law is principally concerned with relations between directors/senior managers and shareholders/investors or relations among the shareholders (for example, between controlling and non-controlling shareholders). However, a significant, but lesser part, of the law is concerned with the relationship between creditors and the company. It might be wondered why the creditor part is not more significant within the body of company law. A large element in the answer appears to be that many legal techniques developed for regulating creditor/debtor relations apply to all classes of debtor, whether they are companies or not. Examples are the taking of real or personal security or putting clauses in loan contracts which restrict the behaviour of the debtor. Even here, there may be developments which are specific to company law, as we see in Ch.32 in relation to floating charges, but the bulk of the law on security is rightly treated as part of commercial, not company, law.

Once a person takes on debt, there has to be some mechanisms in place to deal with the situation where the debtor become unable to meet its obligations. Essentially, the creditor's claims should be given priority over any other uses to which the debtor might want to put the remaining sources of income and assets. Where the debtor is a company, putting this principle into practice can become quite complex, to the point where in modern law the rules dealing with the insolvency of companies have become specialised and no longer simply the rules that apply to all bankrupts, corporate or personal. So, when the company is insolvent, a distinct set of rules for the creditors of companies does emerge. However, this is not a work about insolvency, even corporate insolvency, but we provide a sketch of how these matters are handled in Pt 10.

Consequently, one might start from the other end and ask why company law addresses creditor issues at all and does not leave the matter entirely to commercial law. Part of the answer is that, in so far as creditors are expected to take care of themselves, for example, through security or contractual provisions, they need to know about the financial position of the company they are dealing with. Since the company is a specialised type of organisation, it has been necessary to develop specialised disclosure rules to provide a "true and fair view" of its financial position as it changes over time and to verify through audit their accuracy. It may be that the original impetus for the mandatory production of accounts was to render more effective the reporting by directors to the current shareholders of the company in relation to the discharge by the former of the managerial functions conferred upon them by the latter in the company's articles. However, once the accounts were required to be publicly available, they acquired a second function, being clearly are of use to investors, whether they intended to invest in the company via debt (as creditors) or equity (as shareholders), and to other types of creditor who may be contemplating entering into a medium- or long-term relationship with the company, for example, a supplier developing a specialised and complex piece of equipment which only the company can make use of.

The accounts are a relatively "low cost" piece of creditor protection: they have to be produced in any event for the current shareholders and little additional cost is involved in making them useful to creditors. Why should company law go beyond this example of creditors "piggybacking" on instrument of shareholder protection? The answer in large part is that these additional provisions respond to a core feature of company law which we identified in Ch.7, namely, limited liability for the shareholders of the company. By confining creditors' claims in the normal case to the assets of the company, the doctrine of limited liability exposes creditors to risks of opportunistic conduct on the part of those in control of the company, which company law takes some steps to combat. In very broad terms, that opportunism may take three forms.

First, and most straightforward, company controllers may move assets out of the corporate "box" and into the hands of its shareholders, through transactions in which the company receives nothing in return or a disproportionately low consideration. Secondly, company controllers may alter the make-up of the company's assets and liabilities through transactions which, considered individually, are on commercial terms but which collectively reduce the probability of the creditors (or some of them) being paid in full. Thirdly, since creditors' claims have priority over those of the shareholders in an insolvency (see Ch.33), but have only fixed claims on the company's revenues while the company is a going concern, the controllers of a company have an incentive to finance the company with too little from the shareholders (equity) and too much from the creditors (debt).

Some of the legal strategies which have been developed to counteract the opportunistic conduct on the part of corporate controllers operate throughout the company's life. This is true of what is perhaps the most well-established set of rules we discuss in this Part. These are the rules on legal capital and their associated constraints on the payment of dividends and other forms of distribution. They are designed to dissuade companies from operating with too little equity, though their efficacy in this regard has been challenged. We consider these rules in Chs 16, 17 and 18. However, the more recent rules we consider in Ch.19, which are aimed at the first and second forms of opportunism identified above, begin to have effect when the company is, in the common phrase, in the vicinity of insolvency but before it actually enters into one of the procedures we discuss in Ch.33. This narrower scope of operation is probably due to the fact that the near-insolvency rules seek to cause a re-orientation of the directors' concerns away from the shareholders and towards the creditors, contrary to the steady-state principle stated in s.172 of the CA 2006 that the directors should promote the success of the company for the benefit of its members. That is thought to be required when the company is near insolvency because the temptation of the corporate controllers to engage in first two types of opportunism is at its highest during that time.

This division is not absolute. For example, s.423 of the IA 1986 (discussed in Ch.18) operates throughout the company's life, even though its target is the first type of opportunism identified above. And the rules on distributions may both discourage thinly capitalised businesses from being operated and constrain the movement of assets out of the company as it nears insolvency. Nevertheless, it is central to an understanding of the scope of the provisions discussed in this Part to identify the point at which they are triggered, if they are not always operating, at least in the background.

As to the creditors whose interests the law aims to protect to the appropriate degree, they come in many shapes and sizes. Banks which lend long-term to companies or investors who buy its bonds (see Ch.31) are not the only corporate creditors. At the other end of the scale, any employee who is paid at the end of the month is a creditor for unpaid wages as is a customer who has paid in advance for goods or services, as customers of failed airlines have recently discovered. In between are suppliers who regularly provide goods or services in advance of being paid for them. All these are usually termed "voluntary" or "adjusting" creditors, but there are also "involuntary" creditors such as tort victims. Certainly, tort victims are creditors once they have obtained a judgement against the company, but they are also potential creditors at an earlier stage when all the elements of their tort claim have been fulfilled, even though they have not initiated litigation and the amount of the claim may still be uncertain. Also sometimes put in the involuntary category are the tax authorities, though of course they have access to legislative powers, which are sometimes draconian, to see that their claims are met.

The distinction between voluntary and involuntary creditors is relevant to the question of whether creditors can protect themselves via self-help, and therefore to the optimal type of legal regulation. Certainly, sophisticated and repeat lenders to companies have some capacity to change their position so as to protect their interests, provided they have good information about the company's financial position, for example, by exercising their contractual rights to veto certain management decisions. For other categories of voluntary creditor, their capacity to adjust may well be limited, and it may not exist at all for tort victims. There is also a distinction to be made between debts which will mature in the short term and those which will mature only in the long term. If it is thought appropriate to put in place a legal mechanism to protect creditors, dealing with short-term debts is relatively easy. Where the entitlement will mature only in the long-term, a decision to be made now about how best to protect the future entitlements may raise some difficult issues. A topical example of the problems raised by long-term liabilities are the claims of future pensioners under a scheme funded by both (corporate) employer and employee contributions. If the scheme is "under-funded", i.e. it is estimated that its future income will be insufficient to meet the claims of future pensioners, corrective steps need to be taken. However, it may be difficult to work out how much additional funding is needed: if too little is put in, the claims of the future pensioners may not be met in full when the time for payment arrives; if too much, the company may be unable to use those resources to carry out current projects of economic value, not only to shareholders but to the economy as a whole.

CHAPTER 16

LEGAL CAPITAL, MINIMUM CAPITAL AND VERIFICATION

MEANING AND FUNCTIONS OF CAPITAL

The traditional protective mechanism of company law for creditors, which is as old as limited liability itself, involves laying down rules about the raising and maintenance of "capital". "Capital" is a word of many meanings,[1] but in company law it is used in a very restricted sense. It connotes the value of the assets contributed to the company by those who subscribe for its shares. Its supposed importance to creditors was underlined by Jessel MR in 1882 in the case of *Re Exchange Banking Co*[2]: **16–001**

> "The creditor, therefore, I may say, gives credit to that capital, gives credit to the company on the faith of the representation that the capital shall be applied only for the purposes of the business, and he has therefore a right to say that the corporation shall keep its capital and not return it to the shareholders ... ."

Although the UK rules on capital were to some degree re-cast in pursuance of the Second EU Company Law Directive (the Second Directive) of 1977,[3] the notion of capital as an important protection for creditors is clearly of long-standing in

[1] cf. Capital punishment, capital letter, capital ship, capital city, capital of a pillar, capital and labour, capital and income, and "capital!"

[2] *Re Exchange Banking Co (Flitcroft's Case)* (1882) 21 Ch. D. 519 CA at 533–534. For similar sentiments see *Trevor v Whitworth* (1887) 12 App. Cas. 409 HL.

[3] Directive 77/91 on coordination of safeguards [1977] OJ L26/1 (now replaced by Directive 2012/30 on coordination of safeguards [2012] OJ L315/74, to which version the references in this chapter relate).

UK company law. It is therefore unclear how far, if at all, the exit of the UK from the EU will be taken as an opportunity to depart from the provisions of that Directive.

By and large, the value of what the company receives from investors in exchange for its shares constitutes its capital.[4] One talks about the value of what is received, rather than the assets themselves, because those assets will change form in the course of the business activities of the company. If the company receives cash in exchange for its shares, the directors will turn that cash into other types of asset in order to promote its business: indeed, if they did not, they would probably be in breach of duty. On the other hand, to make the legal rules work which are based on the notion of capital, some easy way of identifying that value has to be specified. In short, this is done by reference to entries in the company's balance sheet made when the shares are issued. One entry will reflect the "nominal" value of the share and the other anything above that nominal value received by the company in exchange for the shares (the "premium")—see paras 16–003 onwards. Those numbers will remain constant, unless the company issues more shares, buys some back or redeems them or reduces its capital (as discussed in Ch.17). The central point is that those entries on the balance sheet constrain the actions of the company in various ways, principally its freedom to make distributions to its shareholders (see Ch.18).

The value of the assets which the company receives in exchange for its shares (its legal capital) will normally be less than the total value of the company's assets. Even where the company has not yet begun to trade, it may have raised money in ways other than share issues. For example, it may have borrowed money from a bank or a group of banks, which loan contributes to the company's cash assets. The value of such loans does not count towards its legal capital, however. This is because the aim of the capital rules is to protect creditors as a class and only assets contributed by shareholders do this effectively. This is because of the general principle that creditor claims take precedence over those of the shareholders. By contrast, the cash provided by a lender will be exactly counterbalanced by an increase on the liabilities which have priority over the claims of the shareholders. In formal terms, more debt simply leaves the prior creditors where they were.[5]

Once a company has begun trading and if it has done so profitably, it will have assets which represent the profits. These, too, do not count as part of the company's legal capital: they may have been earned, at least in part, by deploying the shareholders' contributions to the business but the profits were not

---

[4] In *Kellar v Williams* [2000] 2 B.C.L.C. 390 PC, the Privy Council accepted that it was possible for an investor to make a capital contribution to a company, other than in exchange for the purchase of shares, in which case the contribution is to be treated in the same way as a share premium (see below, para.16–009). Such a procedure is very unusual, of course, since the contributor is left substantially in the dark as to what he or she is getting in exchange for the contribution. However, one can see that an existing shareholder in a company wholly controlled by him might act in this way. The difficulty is to distinguish between such a capital contribution and a loan to the company.

[5] Of course, a contribution made by a creditor may in fact benefit other creditors, for example, a loan made to a company just before insolvency may mean the creditors as a class obtain a larger percentage pay out than if the loan had not been made. That benefit to the earlier creditors is paid for by the later lender, who is normally astute not to open itself up to this risk. Alternatively, the loan may enable a company in financial difficulty to escape its problems, again to the benefit of the prior creditors.

contributed by the shareholders. Normally, they can be distributed to the shareholders. By contrast, if the company trades unsuccessfully, it may run through any profits made in previous years and begin to eat into the value of the assets contributed by its shareholders. Having no profits, no distribution is permitted to be made and, moreover, the value contributed by the shareholders normally has to be replaced before a distribution is made, as we discuss in Ch.18. In short, the legal capital figure represents an historical fact and the law makes it difficult the change that number, as originally entered into the accounts (see Ch.17). The company's net worth (assets less liabilities), by contrast, fluctuates as the company trades and it may or may not be high enough at any one time to permit a dividend to be paid.

One possible use of the legal capital figure is to identify an amount the shareholders must contribute to the company's assets before it is permitted to begin trading. Such rules are called minimum or initial capital rules. British law has never made much use of this concept. Minimum capital has been required of public companies, since the implementation in the UK of the Second European Company Law Directive of 1977, but private companies are not subject to the rule and, historically, apart from a short period in the early years of modern company law in the middle of the nineteenth century, British law has not attached importance to minimum capital requirements for any class of company. **16–002**

However, and contrary to what is sometimes thought, British law currently does make use of legal capital to constrain to a significant extent distributions to shareholders. On this approach the law leaves companies wholly or substantially free to decide their own level of legal capital, but attaches legal consequences to the amount of legal capital the company in fact chooses to raise. This second policy has been central to British company law since its origins and remains so. From the early days the courts have laid down that, given limited liability, "it is clearly against the intention of the legislature that any portion of the capital should be returned to the shareholders without the statutory conditions being complied with".[6]

There are three main points to note about the way in which the rule against the return of capital to shareholders is elaborated. *First*, the value of the company's legal capital is used as a yardstick to measure the amount of a company's net assets which a public company may not return to the shareholders by way of a dividend or other form of distribution. We consider this aspect of the "no return" policy in Ch.18. *Secondly*, the repurchase or redemption of its shares by the company may occur only through tightly controlled procedures which aim to maintain the value of the company's legal capital. This is what is referred to when it is said that the shareholders are "locked into" the company (though they may sell their shares to another investor, of course, if they can find a purchaser). *Thirdly*, the company may reduce the value of its legal capital in its accounts only through procedures which are designed to protect the interests of the creditors. The second and third manifestations of the "no return" policy are considered in Ch.17, together with the rules prohibiting a company from giving financial assistance to a person in connection with the acquisition by that person of its

---

[6] *Re Exchange Banking Co (Flitcroft's Case)* (1882) 21 Ch. D. 519 per Jessel MR.

shares. The second and third sets of rules are normally lumped together under the heading of "capital maintenance", though it is debatable whether the financial assistance rules are linked to the notion of legal capital.

In this chapter we elaborate some of the basic elements of the concept of legal capital and consider in particular the role of the minimum or initial legal capital rule.

NOMINAL VALUE AND SHARE PREMIUMS

Nominal value

16–003 A company proposing to issue shares determines what it wants by way of consideration from those who invest in them and prospective investors decide whether it seems to be a good deal to part with that consideration in exchange for the shares. By an explicit or implicit bargaining process, the success or otherwise of the share issue is determined. Often what the company asks for in exchange is cash, because cash gives it the greatest flexibility in the deployment of its assets. The process of exchanging cash for shares may involve in a small, private company nothing more than handing over a cheque in exchange for a share certificate. In a large company, the process may involve extensive prior disclosure by the company (via a "prospectus"), the involvement of multiple financial intermediaries and sets of lawyers and the admission of the new shares to a stock market. But the company may ask for non-cash, for example, where it offers shareholders in another company its shares in exchange for the shares in that other company (as in a share-for-share takeover, discussed in Ch.28). All this raises issues of investor protection, which we discuss in Part 6 of this work.

This chapter, by contrast, is concerned with creditor protection. One might think that creditors are largely unconcerned with what the company receives for its shares, subject to that amount being accurately valued and recorded in the company's accounts (see paras 16–013 onwards). No matter how small that amount, creditor priority means that creditors benefit. However, there is one aspect of the share issue rules which, in the past, was of great importance to creditors and today still retains some marginal significance. This is the requirement that shares be assigned a "nominal" value by the company which issues them. A share may not be issued for less than its nominal value but may be issued for more—excess being referred to as the "premium". Therefore, two numbers may have to be entered on the company's balance sheet when a company issues shares. One, always required, will reflect the nominal value of the shares; the other, not necessarily required but often present, any premium received. Probably both corporate managers and investors (but not their lawyers) are blissfully unaware of this distinction in most cases when shares are issued, but it still has some role in the creditor protection rules, though much less than previously.

The Act stipulates that shares in a limited company "must each have a fixed nominal value" and that an allotment of shares not meeting this requirement is void.[7] In other words a monetary value needs to be attached to the company's shares. In consequence, one talks of the company having issued a certain number of "£1 shares" or "10p shares" and so on. The par value is a doubtfully useful concept because it does not normally indicate the price at which the share is likely to be issued to investors; still less the price at which the share is likely to trade in the market after issue. The only linkage between the nominal value of the share and the price the subscriber pays for it is the rule that a share may not be issued at less than its nominal value[8]—often referred to as the "no discount" rule.[9] However, the company, whilst being obliged to attach a nominal value to the share, maintains full control over its level. This freedom, coupled with the "no discount" rule, gives the company a strong incentive to keep the nominal value of the share low. The lower the nominal value, the less likely the company is to find itself in the situation, either now or in the future, where investors will be prepared to buy its shares only at less than their nominal value. Equally, a low nominal value in no way constrains the level at which the company may pitch the market value of its shares—provided of course that level is higher than the nominal value. So, often both entries in the balance sheet will need to be made.

Having issued shares once to investors, a company is quite likely to come back again and offer more shares to investors, for example, because it is a start-up company and is burning through its cash pile as it develops its business or because it wants to engage in a share-for-share takeover. In this situation, the par value is likely to be even less related to the consideration required. Suppose a company has initially issued shares at par, has traded successfully, re-invested the profits and seeks capital for further expansion. The second tranche of shares will naturally be issued at a price higher than par; otherwise, the second set of shareholders would obtain a disproportionately large interest in the company. In effect, they would be obtaining an interest in the profits earned in the past without having contributed any of the capital which was used to earn them. The situation can be rectified by setting the share price on the second issue so that it reflects the total value of the shareholders' interest in the company. In the case of publicly traded companies, this will be what the market price of the share reflects. If the company's trading has been unsuccessful, the second offering may well be at a lower price than the first. Here the company may run afoul of the "'no discount"' rule, if it has set the par value of the shares at an optimistically high level.

It is wholly unclear that the concept of par value adds anything by way of either investor or creditor protection. The CLR contemplated abolishing par value for private companies, as many leading jurisdictions have done,[10] but eventually

---

7 CA 2006 s.542(1)–(2). This implements the requirements of the Second Directive, although the requirement of a nominal value was not introduced into UK law by that Directive.

8 CA 2006 s.580—using the word "issued" for the moment in a non-technical sense.

9 Note, however, the discount here is to the nominal value of the share, not to its market value, which is the issue addressed by the pre-emption rules. See paras 24–006 onwards.

10 Strategic, paras 5.4.26–5.4.33. The *Report of the Committee on Shares of No Par Value* (Gedge Committee) (1954), Cmd.9112, had recommended as long ago as 1954 that no-par equity shares should be introduced and the *Report of the Company Law Committee* (Jenkins Committee) (1962), Cmnd.1749, paras 32–34) recommended this reform in relation to all classes of share. Introduction of no-par shares would require some matters to be expressed differently or regulated differently in the contract of issue. For example, the dividend on a preference share is normally expressed as a percentage of its nominal value (but could as easily be expressed as so many pence per share) and

it resiled from the proposal. The Second Directive was thought to require the retention of par value, or something very much like it, for public companies, and the transitional difficulties likely to arise when a company moved from private to public were thought to militate against this reform.[11] So, this might be an area for review in the light of the UK's exit from the EU, but the failure of the UK to introduce a reform proposed long before the UK joined the EU suggests that reform of this matter does not carry a high priority with Government.[12]

No allotment of shares at a discount

16–004 For investors the nominal value requirement is potentially misleading because it tells them nothing about the market price of the share or its value measured in any other way. Does the rule, which was established by the courts in the nineteenth century,[13] that shares must not be issued at a discount to their nominal par value act as a protection for creditors? The common law rule is now stated in the Act,[14] which specifically provides that, if the shares should be so allotted, the allottee (ie the investor who has entered into a contract to take shares) is liable to pay to the company the amount of the discount with interest.[15] This provision is of some value to creditors, but of only limited value, given the company's control over the setting of the nominal value. The creditor is probably more interested in the actual price at which the share was issued and, thus, in the total value of the consideration received by the company from its share issue. In fact, it could be argued that the rule against discounts to nominal value harms creditors, at least where the company nears insolvency. Suppose that, because of the unsuccessful trading of the company, its shares are in fact trading on the market at less than par. The company needs to raise new capital. No sensible investor will pay more than the market price for the shares and yet the Act seems to prevent the company from recognising the economic reality of its situation in the pricing of any new issue, which may help it back to solvency.[16] Yet, in this situation creditors will benefit if the legal capital of the company is increased, no matter how little the

surplus assets are distributed on a winding in accordance with nominal values, so that a different formula would have to be adopted. See *Birch v Cropper* (1889) 14 App. Cas. 525 HL.

[11] Completing, para.7.3.

[12] See fn.10. The Directive (art.8) refers to "accountable par" as a permitted alternative to "nominal value" (but without defining it). The concept appears to be that one takes the total consideration raised through the issue of shares and divides it by the number of shares in issue at any time. Two consequences follow: the shares do not have a fixed nominal value (because the accountable par would change on a new share issue at a different price) but a par value does exist at all times; and the company has no freedom to set the nominal value: it is simply the result of an arithmetical exercise. See Bank of England, *Practical Issues Arising from the Euro* (Issue 8, June 1998), Ch.6, paras 24–28.

[13] Finally in *Ooregum Gold Mining Co of India Ltd v Roper* [1892] A.C. 125 HL.

[14] CA 2006 s.580(1).

[15] CA 2006 s.580(2). For the purposed of the legal capital rules, "allotment" of the shares is often what is importance; "issuance" occurs only at a second stage when the allottee is registered as a member of the company: see para.24–018.

[16] See the facts of *Ooregum Gold Mining Co v Roper* [1892] A.C. 125 where the "no discount" rule enabled the existing shareholders to act in a wholly opportunistic way towards an investor who was willing to and did inject new money into the company at market value (but below the nominal value) of the shares at a time when the existing shareholders were unwilling to advance further capital on any terms.

company receives for any one of its shares. Any contribution from shareholders increases the amount available to satisfy the claims of the creditors.

In fact, there are a number of ways around this problem, though they all involve some trouble and expense. For example, a new class of share may be created with a par value lower than the current market value but otherwise with rights substantially the same as the existing shares. This new class of share can be issued without infringing the prohibition on issuing shares at a discount. Or the existing shares may be divided by resolution of the shareholders into "shares of smaller nominal amounts", as s.618 provides.[17] However, the availability of these "work arounds" do not reduce to any significant extent the incentive to fix low par values initially and to raise most of the consideration for the shares by way of premium.

It might be argued that the rule is better understood as a protection for the shareholders. The rule, it might be said, was intended to protect existing shareholders from directors who proposed to devalue (or "dilute") the existing shareholders' interest in the company by issuing shares to new shareholders too cheaply. However, dilution arises only if the shares are issued to new investors at a price which is lower than the current market price of the shares, so that the "no shares at a discount" rule is not well adapted to shareholder protection either. It will be under-protective of shareholders where the market price is above nominal value and over-protective where it is below. To the contrary, what is surprising from a shareholders' perspective is that there is no precise statutory obligation laid on the company to issue shares at a premium, where the market will bear one.[18] This is probably because the company may have a number of good reasons to contract on the basis that the share will be issued at less than its full market price.[19] However, the directors' duty to promote the success of the company for the benefit of its members[20] will normally require the directors to issue shares at the best obtainable price; otherwise the company will be overpaying for its capital, just as it would be if it bought raw materials at above market price.[21] **16–005**

[17] This solution appears to be adopted quite often in practice, but it is not perfect, especially if the share split is effected only as part of the same exercise whereby the new investor commits itself to the company, rather than in advance of the new investment. Here it may be necessary to turn the "extra" shares generated by the stock split into a new class of essentially valueless and vote-less "deferred" shares, often involving a change of the articles and so a special resolution of the shareholders. Otherwise, the new investor may not obtain the expected influence in the company or return on the investment.

[18] *Hilder v Dexter* [1902] A.C. 474 HL. The argument was there rejected that failing to obtain the premium amounted to the payment of a commission, contrary to what is now s.552 (see below). The decision was undoubtedly right on its facts, since the right to purchase further shares at par was an explicit part of the contract under which the investor had originally become a shareholder in a corporate rescue.

[19] See the previous note and directors' share option schemes, the essence of which is that the director has the right to subscribe in the future for shares in the company at today's share price.

[20] See paras 10–026 onwards.

[21] "If the share stands at a premium, the directors prima facie owe a duty to the company to obtain for it the full value which they are able to get. It is true that it is within their powers under the Companies Acts to issue it at par, even in such a case, but their duty to the company is not to do so unless for good reason." (Per Lord Wright in *Lowry (Inspector of Taxes) v Consolidated African Selection Trust Ltd* [1940] A.C. 648 HL at 679.) See also *Shearer v Bercain Ltd* [1980] 3 All E.R. 295 Ch D: "Those who have practised in the field of company law for any length of time will have spent many hours

The share premium

16–006 It is clear that the amount received by the company by way of the nominal value of the shares issued constitutes part of its legal capital. The amount (often much more significant) received by way of premium is today treated in much the same way. Prior to 1948, when companies issued shares at a premium, the value of the premium was treated differently from the par value. Legal capital was regarded as determined by the nominal or par value of the shares; if they had been issued at a price above par the excess was not "capital" and, indeed, constituted part of the distributable surplus which the company, if it wished, could return to the shareholders by way of dividend.[22] This was, of course, a ridiculous rule, except on the basis that it might be an indirect way of subverting the capital-based distribution rules. If the price paid for the shares was £100,000, the amount received by the company was also £100,000 (assuming no transaction costs) and, from the point of view of creditor protection, it should make no difference to the analysis whether the £100,000 was obtained by issuing 100,000 £1 shares at par or by issuing 100,000 1p shares at £1 (i.e. at a premium of 99p per share). In either case, the issue price (£1 in both cases) determined the amount raised by the company, whilst the par value, set by the company, is a figure determined in order to give the company maximum flexibility under the Act.[23] This situation was changed, however, by the 1948 Act. The rule, now stated in s.610 of the 2006 Act, is that a sum equal to the aggregate amount or value of the premiums shall be transferred to a "share premium account" which, in general, has to be treated as if it were part of the paid-up share capital. However, the Act does not fully assimilate share capital and the share premium. It is still necessary to refer expressly to both, and for the company, in its annual accounts and reports, to distinguish between the share capital account and the share premium account. What, if it were not for arbitrary par values, would be a single item—capital—has to be treated as two distinct items, albeit for most purposes treated identically.

16–007 However, share capital and share premium are not treated as wholly identical, though the 2006 Act has narrowed some of the differences between them. Section 610 provides two "exceptions" and two "reliefs" for the share premium account which do not apply to the share capital account. The first exception is that a company may apply the share premium account in paying up bonus shares.[24] A bonus share is a share issued to the existing shareholders, without requiring any

convincing directors that it is wholly wrong for them to issue to themselves and their friends shares at par when they command a premium, however great the company's need for capital may be." (Per Walton J.) See also *Re Sunrise Radio Ltd* [2009] EWHC 2893 (Ch); [2010] 1 B.C.L.C. 367.

[22] *Drown v Gaumont-British Picture Corp Ltd* [1937] Ch. 402 Ch D. See C. Napier and C. Noke, "Premiums and Pre-acquisition Profits" (1991) 54 M.L.R. 810.

[23] In some cases, the nominal value of the share has a more substantial significance. The dividend entitlement of a preference share is normally set as a percentage of the nominal value of the share, so that choosing a low nominal value for a preference share might imply a high percentage dividend. To produce the equivalent of a 10% dividend on a £1 share, the dividend entitlement on a 1p share would have to be 1000%! In general with preference shares, given their bond-like characteristics (see para.6–007), the nominal value will be set much closer to the issue price, since the nominal value will also determine what the preference shareholder receives in a reduction of capital or liquidation, at least if the holder has no right to participate in surplus assets.

[24] CA 2006 s.610(3).

payment from them, but is paid for, in this case, by reducing the share premium account.[25] Since the effect of this transaction is to reduce the share premium account but to increase the share capital account by an equivalent amount, it is wholly unobjectionable from the creditors' point of view,[26] and it is hardly an exception to the main rule laid down by s.610. It would, of course, be impossible to apply the share capital account in this way.

The second exception is that the share premium account may be applied in writing off the expenses of or the commissions paid on the issue of the shares which generated the premiums.[27] This is a real exception, but now is a relatively minor contrast with share capital. Within limits, share capital may also be used to pay commission.[28] Although the rule in relation to the share premium account is somewhat more broadly phrased than that relating to the capital account, the share premium rule is now tighter than it was previously.[29]

More important (and more interesting) are the "reliefs". Section 610 (as did its predecessors) expressly applies to issues at a premium "whether for cash or otherwise". The result of this was held to be that if, say, on a merger one Company (A) acquired the shares of another (B) in consideration of an issue of A's own shares and the value of B's shares exceeded the nominal value of those issued by A, a share premium account had to be established in respect of the excess.[30] The result of this was that some significant part of B's undistributed profits formerly available for distribution by way of dividend ceased to be distributable (because of the rules we discuss in detail in Ch.18). This caused something of a furore in commercial circles. However, in 1980 the question was again litigated and the earlier decision fully upheld.[31] In consequence, "merger relief" was introduced in the CA 1981. The general effect of the merger relief provisions[32] is that the premium does not have to be transferred to the share premium account when, pursuant to a merger arrangement, one company has acquired at least 90% of *each*[33] class of equity shares[34] of another in exchange for an allotment of its equity shares at a premium. **16–008**

[25] The bonus issue could also be funded by distributable profits. See para.16–024.

[26] The issuance of a bonus share has little impact on the shareholders either in the normal case. The shareholder now has more shares, but since the value of the company is not increased by this exercise, the market price of each share in the expanded class will fall. Sometimes bonus shares are issued precisely to achieve this result because it is thought that the market value of the share has become so large that it is an obstacle to trading them. See *EIC Services Ltd v Phipps* [2004] EWCA Civ 1069; [2004] B.C.C. 814, where the (botched) bonus issue was aimed at reducing the trading price of the shares. A similar result can be obtained by effecting a "stock split" under s.618, an exercise which is possible no matter whether the company has a share premium account of any size.

[27] CA 2006 s.610(2).

[28] CA 2006 s.553 and see para.16–017.

[29] Under the 1985 Act the share premiums account could be written off against a wider range of share issue expenses which, in particular, did not necessarily have to have been incurred in relation to the shares generating the premiums.

[30] *Head & Co Ltd v Ropner Holdings Ltd* [1952] Ch. 124 Ch D.

[31] *Shearer v Bercain Ltd* [1980] 3 All E.R. 295.

[32] CA 2006 ss.612–613.

[33] CA 2006 s.613(3).

[34] Which will include preference shares if they have a right to participate in either dividends or surplus on a winding up beyond a fixed amount: ss.616(1) and 548.

The Act also modifies (rather than removes) the requirement for a transfer to the share premium account in certain cases of reconstruction within a group of companies.[35] The relief applies in the case of issues at a premium by a wholly-owned subsidiary in consideration of a transfer to it of non-cash assets from another company in the group comprising the holding company and its wholly-owned subsidiaries. In this case the company issuing the shares is permitted to value the assets received, not by reference to their market value, but by reference to the cost of their acquisition by the transferor company or their value in the books of the transferor company. In this way, the value of the assets received in exchange for the shares will often be understated, but, to the extent that this understated value in fact exceeds the nominal value of the shares issued, the excess must still be transferred to the share premium account.[36] If this relief is available on the facts of a particular case, the more extensive merger relief is not.[37]

Finally, the Secretary of State is empowered by s.614 to make regulations providing further relief in relation to premiums other than cash premiums or for modifying the reliefs in the Act (but has not done so).

MINIMUM CAPITAL

16–009 With the above preliminaries, we can turn to an analysis of the minimum capital rule. As we have noted, as a result of the Second Directive,[38] a minimum capital requirement was introduced for public companies. Section 761 requires that the *nominal* value of the company's allotted share capital meet a certain minimum level. That was set at the derisory level (for a public company) of £50,000 (or, currently, €57,100),[39] though that is double the amount required by the Directive.[40] Moreover, that £50,000 does not have to be handed over to the company at the time of issue of the shares. It is enough, as with all share issues by public companies, that one quarter of the nominal value of the shares be paid at the time of allotment.[41] The rest may remain unpaid, though of course subject to being called up by the company at a later date or in its liquidation. Nevertheless, the minimum capital requirement puts a little pressure on public companies not to issue shares at a hefty premium (because the premium does not count towards the required minimum). However, the Act retains its traditional aversion to minimum capital requirements in respect of private companies, where none is imposed.

16–010 In the relatively unusual case of a company being formed directly as a public company, the minimum capital requirement operates, not as a condition of its

[35] CA 2006 s.611.

[36] CA 2006 s.611(2)–(5), defining the "minimum premium value".

[37] CA 2006 s.612(4).

[38] See fn.3 above, Second Directive art.6.

[39] CA 2006 s.763 and the Companies (Authorised Minimum) Regulations 2009 (SI 2009/2425) reg.2.

[40] Second Directive art.6: €25,000.

[41] CA 2006 s.586. The consideration does not have to be in cash: assets of equivalent value will do, subject to the restrictions on using non-cash to meet the minimum capital requirement—see para.16–018.

formation, but as a condition of its commencing business.[42] In order to commence business (or to exercise any borrowing powers—an important addition) it must apply to the Registrar for a "trading certificate"[43] (in addition to the formation certificate which it will already have obtained); and the condition for the issuance of a trading certificate is that the nominal value of the company's allotted share capital must be not less than the required or "authorised" minimum.[44] The company is under some pressure to obtain the trading certificate, because if it does not do so within a year from incorporation, it may be wound up by the court and the Secretary of State may petition for that to happen.[45] A public company which trades or borrows without a certificate is liable to a fine, as is any officer of the company (including therefore its directors) who is in default.[46] However, the interests of third parties are properly protected in this case. Transactions entered into by the company in such a case are valid, and further, if the company fails to comply with its obligations, the directors of the company are jointly and severally liable to indemnify third parties in respect of any loss or damage suffered.[47] Thus, personal liability of the directors, criminal and civil, operates to give them a strong incentive not to trade without a trading certificate.

In the more usual case of a company becoming public upon conversion from private status, the requirement that the company's allotted capital be not less than the authorised minimum operates as a condition for the re-registration of the private company as a public one.[48]

If the nominal value of the company's allotted share capital meets the authorised minimum, on either of the occasions described above, it will normally remain at that level thereafter. This is because the nominal value of the shares does not change, no matter how much the value of the company may decline. However, in relatively rare cases the nominal value of the company's allotted capital might subsequently fall below the authorised minimum. There is no general provision in the Act dealing with this eventuality. Rather, provision is made on an ad hoc basis. Thus, if under the reduction of capital procedure[49] the company's capital is reduced below the authorised minimum, the normal requirement is that the company must re-register as a private company before the reduction of capital 16–011

42 CA 2006 s.761.

43 The form of the application, containing a statement of compliance on the part of the company, is set out in s.762. It is not demanding and the Registrar may accept the company's statement of compliance as sufficient evidence of the matters stated in it, and the Registrar must issue the certificate if satisfied the minimum capital requirements are met: s.765(2). The trading certificate, once issued, is conclusive evidence that the company is entitled to commence business: s.761(4). However, by analogy with the decisions referred to in para.4–032 in relation to the certificate of incorporation, it appears that, as this section is not expressed to bind the Crown, the Registrar's decision could be quashed on judicial review at the instance of the Attorney-General.

44 CA 2006 s.761(2). A company's capital may be stated in euros in which case s.763 deals with the fixing of the equivalent prescribed euro amount. Where a company has some share capital denominated in pounds and some in euros, the company's application for a certificate must be made by reference to the sterling capital or to the euro capital alone and not by reference to a mixture of the two types of capital: s.765.

45 IA 1986 ss.122(1)(b) and 124(4)(a).

46 CA 2006 s.767(1)–(2).

47 CA 2006 s.767(3)–(4).

48 CA 2006 ss.90(1)(b), (2)(b) and 91(1)(a).

49 See Ch.17.

order is finalised.[50] Further, the Secretary of State has power to alter the authorised minimum by regulation (subject to affirmative resolution).[51] Were that alteration to be in an upward direction, the Secretary of State also has the power to require existing public companies to bring their nominal values into line with the new authorised minimum or to re-register as a private company.[52]

Objections to the minimum capital requirement

16–012 There are two objections which can be made to minimum capital rules. First, company laws normally set only one (as in the UK) or a small number of minimum capital rules (for example, one for private and another for public companies), but in fact, to be effective, the minimum capital requirement ought to be related to the riskiness of the business which the company undertakes. One purpose of the minimum capital rule might be said to be to require shareholders to provide sufficient assets to the company to enable it to survive its initial and potentially risky period of trading. With only a thin layer of shareholder capital, the company may find that an initially unsuccessful period of trading will put it in a position of insolvency, at least on a balance sheet basis (more liabilities than assets). The shareholders' contribution, it might be said, should be enough to absorb those probable losses. If that is the rationale for a minimum capital requirement, then the appropriate level of minimum capital should be adjusted for the riskiness of the trading the company is proposing to engage in, if a uniform level of protection is to be provided. Across-the-board minimum capital requirements tend either to be too low effectively to protect creditors (as in the case of the current British requirement) or too high, in which case they reduce competition (by discouraging new entrants into the field) whilst over-protecting creditors. However, adjusting capital requirements to the riskiness of the company's business would be a complex and potentially continuing activity, as is shown by the special regulation necessary to implement such a principle in those industries, for example banking and insurance, where capital adequacy requirements are taken seriously (and also where "capital" means net asset value, not "legal" capital). Thus, it is not surprising that the approach of company laws to minimum capital requirements is relatively crude; and in practice in developed economies it tends towards the "too low" end of the spectrum, thus conferring no substantial protection on creditors for fear of discouraging the incorporation of companies.

If, therefore, the minimum capital requirement has no claim to be a genuine assessment of the amount of risk capital the company needs to survive the initial vicissitudes of its business, could it nevertheless be justified as a "cushion" of assets provided by the shareholders for the protection of the creditors when the company begins to fail at some later stage? This is also a difficult argument to sustain. A minimum capital requirement imposed at the time the company

[50] CA 2006 s.650(2). The court may order otherwise. Section 651 provides an expedited procedure for re-registering as a private company in such cases. See also s.662(2)(b), dealing with the consequences of a forced cancellation by a public company of its own shares.

[51] CA 2006 s.764(1),(4).

[52] CA 2006 s.764(3)—no doubt through an expedited procedure.

commences trading does not guarantee any particular level of assets being available for the creditors at this later date or when the company goes into an insolvency procedure. For example, a minimum capital requirement of, say, £3,000 for a private company, even if paid in cash, could soon be returned quite legitimately to the incorporators by means of salary payments for services rendered to the company.[53] It is wholly wrong to think of the minimum capital requirement as obliging the company to put on one side the assets it receives, not deploying them in its business, in order to produce them "out of a hat" when the company fails. Thus, minimum capital rules are likely to be ineffective beyond a very short initial period unless coupled with rules which require the directors to take action if the net value of the company's actual assets declines below the value of its legal capital.

The Act does in fact contain a rule which requires action on the part of the company if its net asset value falls below a certain proportion of its legal capital. However, this rule is not linked to the minimum capital requirement and would therefore survive even if the authorised minimum were abolished. Nor does the rule specify the substantive action the company should take in this situation. Section 656 requires a public company to convene an extraordinary meeting of the shareholders if the net value of its assets falls below one half of its called-up share capital, which may be, and typically will be, far in excess of the authorised minimum.[54] The section does not require the shareholders or the directors to take any particular action in this situation (for example, cause the company to cease trading or raise further capital from the shareholders).[55] This section seems not to be very important in practice, probably because, before it becomes operative, large lenders will have exercised rights under their loan contracts to replace the failing management or otherwise to redress the situation[56] or the wrongful trading provisions[57] will have required the directors to take corrective action. Consequently, it can be argued that, at the initial stage, the minimum capital requirement is too low to confer substantial protection on creditors and that subsequent adverse developments in the company's trading ability are dealt with through mechanisms other than those which focus on the minimum capital.[58]

DISCLOSURE AND VERIFICATION

Whether or not a legal system imposes a minimum capital requirement, there are obvious arguments in favour of requiring the company to disclose the amount it has raised by way of the issuance of its shares and provide some assurance that the amounts stated in the capital accounts are accurate. This information will **16–013**

[53] As we see at para.18–019, directors' remuneration is not normally caught by the rules controlling distributions by companies.

[54] CA 2006 s.547 makes it clear that called up share capital includes capital payments to be made in the future if those future payment dates are laid out in the company's articles, the terms of allotment of the shares or other arrangements for the payment of the shares. This section implements domestically art.19 of the Second Directive.

[55] As is the case in some continental European jurisdictions.

[56] See paras 31–025 onwards.

[57] See paras 19–005 onwards.

[58] See Chs 19 and 20.

facilitate creditor self-help, i.e. making it easier for creditors to decide whether to lend to the company and on what terms. The extent of the facilitation should not be over-estimated. It will perhaps be useful at the point of issuance of the shares, but the creditor is really interested in the company's overall net asset position at the time credit is extended, about which, as the company trades, its legal capital figure gives decreasing guidance.[59] Thus, the creditor is likely to pay more attention to the verification of the company's assets and liabilities as a whole, not just the amounts raised through share issues; and that assurance is provided, to the extent that it is, through the company's annual financial statements and their audit[60]—or through private information a powerful lender is in a position to extract from a potential borrower. In addition, those who are shareholders at the time the shares are issued will have an interest in knowing and verifying the amounts raised through share issues, in order to be satisfied that new shareholders are not being admitted to the company too cheaply.[61]

UK company law has developed over time a number of rules which address the above policies, and they were substantially added to when the Second Directive was implemented in the UK.

Initial statement and return of allotments

16–014 When a company is formed, assuming it is limited by shares, the application for registration must contain a statement of capital and initial shareholdings. This requires disclosure of information relating to the totality of the shares to be taken by the subscribers and to their individual subscriptions. In particular, the number of shares, their aggregate nominal amount, the amounts, if any, to be left unpaid and the prescribed rights attached to the shares must be disclosed.[62] In practice, the answer will often be one £1 share taken by each of two people, the two people being employees of a company formation business, which has created a shelf private company, and who may or may not actually have handed over the £1. When more serious amounts of shares are issued at a later date, similar information has to be given to the Registrar of companies via a "return of allotments".[63] Thus, data about those to whom shares of various classes have been allotted,[64] the amounts paid for the shares and the main rights and obligations attached to those shares are public information, but this is a disclosure provision, not a provision which regulates the amount or types of shares the company issues. Although it is a criminal offence knowingly or recklessly to

---

[59] See para.16–001.

[60] See Chs 22 and 23.

[61] See para.16–005.

[62] CA 2006 s.10. Prescribed are details of the right to vote, to receive a distribution either by way of dividend or capital, and provisions about redemption: Companies (Shares and Share Capital) Order 2009 (SI 2009/388) art.2.

[63] CA 2006 s.555 and see para.23–006.

[64] As we see in para.27–011, those who take the shares may be nominees for others who have the financial interest in them, but this is perhaps of less moment to the creditors whose main interest is in the amount of shares issued, rather than data about their holders. Since the shareholders' liability is limited, it does not matter to the creditors whether the shareholders are rich or poor, at least once the shares are fully paid up.

deliver a false statement to the Registrar,[65] these provisions do not otherwise provide verification of the information delivered.

Abolition of authorised capital

The 2006 Act did away with the former concept of "authorised capital", as recommended by the CLR.[66] This was a concept which sounded important but which fulfilled no identifiable creditor-protection role. Under the old law, a company with a share capital (unless it was an unlimited company) was required to state in its memorandum "the amount of the share capital with which [it] proposes to be registered and the division of that share capital into shares of a fixed amount".[67] Until the authorised capital was allotted, the authorised capital in no way increased the company's assets. The company's authorised capital might have been 10 million shares of £1 each, but if only two of those shares had been allotted, say at par, then its legal capital was £2. If anything, authorised capital served to confuse the potential investor. **16–015**

In fact, the requirement for authorised capital had more to do with relations between directors and shareholders than with creditor relations. The directors could not issue more than the amount of the company's authorised capital without returning to the shareholders for approval of an increase in the authorised amount.[68] However, if the authorised capital was set at a high level, as it normally was, this was not a significant constraint on the directors. Shareholder control of share issues is now effected by other sections of the Act and shareholders, if they wish, can put stronger controls in the company's constitution, so that authorised capital is not needed for the protection of shareholders either.[69]

Consideration received upon allotment

We next turn to the rules which focus on the quality and even the reality of the consideration received by a company upon the issuance of its shares, whether the shares are issued to satisfy the minimum capital requirement or not and irrespective of whether that consideration is referable to the nominal value of the share or the premium payable. Before 1980 the domestic rules in this area were exiguous, but they were strengthened as a result of the Second Directive, which, however, was somewhat relaxed in 2006.[70] As a result, there is a marked divergence between the rules applying to all companies and to public companies only, which were the subject of the Second Directive. **16–016**

---

65 CA 2006 s.1112.

66 Modernising, para.6.5.

67 1985 Act s.2(5)(a).

68 1985 Act s.121.

69 See paras 24–004 onwards.

70 A set of relaxations to the original version of the Second Directive was made by Directive 2006/68 [2006] OJ L264/32. However, in relation to the issues discussed below the Government took the view that the permitted relaxations were so minor and so hedged about with qualifications that it was not worth taking them up: DTI, *Implementation of the Companies Act 2006: A Consultation Document* (February 2007), para.6.23.

Rules applying to all companies

16–017 We should first note that the law does not require that the consideration promised for the shares be immediately due to the company. There is thus a distinction between paid-up (or called-up) capital and uncalled capital, the former being, for example, the amount paid on allotment and the latter the amount payable when the company calls upon the shareholder for the payment in accordance with the terms of the allotment.[71] Long-term uncalled capital could be a valuable indication of creditworthiness, but it is doubtful whether it is extensively used, perhaps because the solvency of multiple individuals is even more difficult for creditors to monitor than that of companies.[72]

A potentially important creditor protection rule restricts the use of capital to pay commissions, etc. Payment by way of commissions, brokerage or the like to any person in consideration for subscribing or agreeing to subscribe is prohibited,[73] even if the shares are issued at a premium, except to the limited extent to which they are explicitly permitted. Without this rule, the amount actually received by the company from an investor in exchange for its shares might be substantially less than appears. However, the Act permits commission for subscribing for shares (or procuring others to do so) to be paid out of capital provided it is limited to 10% of the issue price and is authorised by the articles (which may set a lower percentage).[74] It would be logical if this restriction on the payment of commission did not apply to payments out of distributable profits, since creditors have no claim to limit what the company does with such funds. This is what s.552 appears to say, since it provides that a company "must not apply any of its shares or capital money" in the payment of commissions, etc.[75] However, the section does not do what drafts of the 2006 Act attempted, i.e. to make clear the consequences of infringing the prohibition. Those drafts provided that, if there were an agreement to pay commission, etc. in breach of the prohibition, the agreement was to be void; if the payment had been made, the amount of the inducement was to be recoverable, either from the person to whom it was paid or any third party who knew of the circumstance constituting the contravention and benefited from it.[76] However, a court could deduce these consequences from the prohibition contained in the current section.

A third potential verification issues arises from the fact, as we have seen, that the consideration for the shares does not have to be cash; it can instead be made

---

[71] CA 2006 s.547 defines called-up capital so as to include that amount represented by calls which have been made, whether or not they have been met, and the amount payable under the articles or the terms of allotment on a specified future date, even though that date has not arrived.

[72] As the CLR proposed, the Act no longer contains provisions which permit a company to determine by special resolution that any part of its capital which has not been called up shall be incapable of being called up except in a winding up.

[73] CA 2006 s.552.

[74] CA 2006 s.553. Section 552(3) also permits the payment of "such brokerage as has previously been lawful"—an obscure and potentially wide permission. On the use of the share premium account to pay commissions etc, see para.16–007.

[75] Of course, for a company to make such a payment, even out of distributable profits, might infringe the prohibition on a company giving financial assistance towards the purchase of its own shares, but the latter rule no longer applies to private companies: see para.17–050.

[76] DTI, *Modernising Company Law—Draft Clauses* (July 2002), Cm.5553-II, cl.28.

in kind[77] and very frequently is in private companies.[78] However, except in relation to public companies (discussed below), it seems that the parties' valuation of the non-cash consideration will be accepted as conclusive[79] unless its inadequacy appears on the face of the transaction[80] or there is evidence of bad faith.[81] Hence on an issue of shares for a non-cash consideration in a private company it is possible to some degree to "water" the shares by agreeing to accept payment in property which is worth less than the value of the shares. This was one of the causes of the problems eventually arising in *Salomon v Salomon & Co Ltd* where, as Lord Macnaghten put it, the business acquired by the company on formation from its promoter "represented the sanguine expectations of a fond owner rather than anything that can be called a businesslike or reasonable estimate of value."[82]

Public companies

Shares allotted by a public company must be paid up (in cash or in kind) at least as to one quarter of their nominal value and the whole of any premium due.[83] If this does not occur, the share is nevertheless to be treated as if this had happened and the allottee is liable to pay the company that amount, with interest. This provision reduces the company's and creditors' exposure to the continuing solvency of its shareholders, although it is now relatively uncommon for companies not to require full payment upon allotment. Where the company does want to stagger the payments for the shares, this rule creates a disincentive to setting the nominal value of the shares well below the issue price,[84] because the whole of the premium must be paid up on allotment. **16–018**

The remaining rules for public companies concern the regulation of non-cash issues, but before turning to them it is important to note the width of the definition of "cash consideration" in s.583(3), for these rules do not apply where the consideration is cash, as defined. The section includes within the definition of "cash consideration" an undertaking to pay cash to the company in the future, thus putting the company at risk of the insolvency of the shareholder, but also the reducing the disincentive mentioned at the end of the previous paragraph.[85] Also

---

77 CA 2006 s.582(1) restates the general rule that "shares allotted by a company may be paid-up in money or money's worth (including goodwill and know-how)" but this is followed by exceptions and qualifications relating to public companies only. Again, bonus shares are specifically allowed.

78 For example, when the proprietor of a business incorporates it by transferring the undertaking to a newly formed company in consideration of an allotment of its shares.

79 *Re Wragg Ltd* [1897] 1 Ch. 796 CA; *Park Business Interiors Ltd v Park* [1992] B.C.L.C. 1034.

80 *Re White Star Line Ltd* [1938] Ch. 458 CA.

81 *Tintin Exploration Syndicate v Sandys* (1947) 177 L.T. 412.

82 *Salomon v Salomon & Co Ltd* [1897] A.C. 22 HL at 49. See para.2–002.

83 CA 2006 s.586.

84 See para.16–003 above.

85 CA 2006 s.583(3)(d). There is no apparent limit on the future date which may be fixed for the actual payment, for the five-year limit in s.587 (see below) applies only to non-cash payments, but the undertaking must be one given to the company in consideration of the allotment of the shares: *System Controls Plc v Munro Corporation Plc* [1990] B.C.C. 386 Ch D. And the "cash" must be given to the company, not a third person: s.583(5).

treated as cash is the release of a liability of the company for a liquidated sum.[86] The latter is a useful provision in facilitating equity for debt swaps whereby the creditors of an insolvent company forgo their claims as debtors against the company in exchange for the issue to them of equity shares. The company is thereby released from an often crippling burden of interest payments and the removal of the debt may even produce by itself a surplus of assets over liabilities. This will be to the immediate benefit of the shareholders and non-converting creditors, though if the company prospers in the future, the original shareholders will naturally find that their equity interest has been extensively diluted. It seems that there is no infringement of the rule forbidding issuing shares at a discount to par where the face value of the debt is taken for the purposes of paying up the new shares, even though the market value of the debt at the time of the swap was less than its face value because of the debtor's insolvency.[87]

A public company may not accept, in payment for its shares or any premium on them, an undertaking by any person that that person or another will do work or perform services for the company or any other person.[88] If it should do so, the holder of the shares[89] at the time they are treated as paid up (wholly or partly) by the services is liable to pay the company an amount equal to the nominal value of the shares plus the premium or such part of that amount as has been treated as paid up by the undertaking.[90] Nor may the company allot shares as fully or partly paid-up if the consideration is *any* sort of undertaking to provide a non-cash consideration which need not be performed until after five years from the date of the allotment.[91] If the undertaking should have been performed within five years but is not, payment in cash then becomes due immediately.[92] And (though this is of minimal importance) shares taken by a subscriber to the memorandum of association in pursuance of his undertaking in the memorandum must be paid for in cash.[93]

Valuation of non-cash consideration

16–019 Finally, the possibility of "share-watering" by placing an inflated value on the non-cash consideration is tackled in the case of public companies by requiring

[86] CA 2006.583(3)(c). So, if the company owes the investor a sum of money, the release by the investor of the company from that obligation in exchange for the shares amounts to the provision of a cash consideration for them: *EIC Services Ltd v Phipps* [2004] B.C.C. 814 at [36]–[52] (Neuberger J).

[87] *Re Mercantile Trading Co*; sub nom. *Schroeder's Case* (1870–71) L.R. 11 Eq. 131 Ct of Chancery; *Pro-Image Studios v Commonwealth Bank of Australia* (1990–1991) 4 A.C.S.R. 586, though it should be noted that in this case both the debt and the consideration for the new shares were immediately payable. Independent valuation of the debt is not required because its release constitutes a cash consideration.

[88] CA 2006 s.585. But this section (nor s.587 below) does not prevent the company from enforcing the undertaking: s.591. If a private company wishes to convert to a Plc such undertakings must first be performed or discharged: s.91(1)(d).

[89] Including the holder of the beneficial interest under a bare trust: s.585(3).

[90] CA 2006 s.585(2).

[91] CA 2006 s.587(1). If contravened the consequences are similar to those for contravention of s.585, except that the liability falls on the allottee: s.587(2). If a contract of allotment does not offend s.587(1) but is later varied so as to produce this consequence, the variation is void: s.587(3).

[92] CA 2006 s.587(4). And see s.91(1)(d) regarding a private company converting to a Plc.

[93] CA 2006 s.584.

that consideration to be independently valued. Under Ch.6 of Pt 17 a public company may not allot shares as fully or partly paid-up (as to their nominal value or any premium) otherwise than in cash unless: (1) the consideration has been valued in accordance with the provisions of the Part; (2) a report is made to the company during the six months immediately preceding the allotment; and (3) a copy is sent to the proposed allottee.[94] To this there are exceptions in relation to bonus issues[95] and in relation to most types of takeovers and mergers.[96] But, in other cases, if the allottee has not received the copy of the valuation report or there is some other contravention of the Part, which he knew, or ought to have known, amounted to a contravention, once again he or she is liable to pay in cash with interest.[97] These provisions clearly protect existing shareholders as well as creditors. However, the valuation requirements, especially on a small issue of shares, are potentially time-consuming and expensive.

However, if the correct valuation steps are taken, there is no statutory prohibition on the company issuing shares in a transaction which puts a higher valuation on the non-cash consideration than has emerged in the valuation process. In that situation the directors might well be in breach of their fiduciary duties[98] and the subscriber would be in a poor position to assert that he or she was unaware of this.

The valuation has to be made by a person "qualified to be appointed, or continue to be, an auditor of the company"[99] and that person must meet statutory tests of independence from the company.[100] The expert has a right, similar to that of an auditor, to require from officers of the company the information and explanations required to produce the valuation.[101] The expert may, however, arrange for and accept a valuation from another person who appears to him to have the requisite experience and knowledge and who is not an employee or officer of any company in the group.[102] In practice, therefore, the report will be by the company's auditor supported by another professional valuation of any real property or other consideration which the auditor does not feel competent to value on his own. The report has to go into considerable detail[103] and must support the conclusion that the aggregate of the cash and non-cash consideration is not less than the nominal value and the premium.[104] **16–020**

---

94 CA 2006 s.593(1).

95 CA 2006 s.593(2).

96 CA 2006 ss.594–595. The rules of the Act, the Takeover Code or the FCA will normally ensure that there has been professional assessment of value in such cases.

97 CA 2006 s.593(3). As is a subsequent holder unless he is or claims through a purchaser for value without notice: s.605(1), (3). See *Re Bradford Investments Plc (No.1)* [1990] B.C.C. 740 Ch D (Companies Ct).

98 See para.16–005.

99 CA 2006 ss.596(1) and 1150. For these qualifications, see para.23–010.

100 CA 2006 ss.1151–1152.

101 CA 2006 s.1153. Knowingly or recklessly making a false statement under the section is a criminal offence: s.1153(2)–(4). Unlike the auditor's right, the independent expert's does not extend to employees of the company. See para.23–030.

102 CA 2006 s.1150(2).

103 CA 2006 s.596(3)–(5).

104 CA 2006 s.586(3)(d).

A private company proposing to convert to a public one cannot evade these valuation requirements by allotting shares for a non-cash consideration shortly before it re-registers as a public one. In such a case, the Registrar cannot entertain the application to re-register unless the consideration has been valued and reported on in accordance with the above provisions.[105]

16–021 This relatively straightforward mandatory valuation procedure, imposed where a public company issues shares for a non-cash consideration, is extended by the Act to a category of cases where the company acquires a non-cash asset in exchange for something other than the issuance of shares.[106] This extension applies only during the period of two years after the company has been issued with a trading certificate[107]; only to agreements on the part of the company to acquire non-cash assets from someone who was a subscriber to the memorandum on the company's formation or a member of it on its conversion to a public company[108]; and only where the consideration to be provided by the company is at least equal to one tenth of its issued share capital. This provision is aimed at a purchase by the company of property from the promoters of the company at an excessive price, though it seems relatively easy to avoid by simply not becoming a member of the company until just after either of the two dates which trigger the mandatory valuation rule. Again, these controls protect both creditors and "outside" shareholders, but a significant feature of the extended rule is that it places greater emphasis on the protection of the shareholders through the imposition of the additional requirement that the shareholders approve of the proposed transaction.[109]

Further provisions as to sanctions

16–022 The above provisions, both those relating to all companies and those applying to public companies alone, impose civil liability on the allottee (normally) towards the company, as we have seen. However, by the time the company comes to enforce that liability, it is not unlikely that the shares will be in the hands of someone else. The general policy of the Act is to impose liability also on the subsequent holder[110] of the shares, jointly and severally with the allottee, but subject to a major defence.[111] Following normal equitable principles, that defence is that the holder is a purchaser for value in good faith (i.e. without actual knowledge of the contravention concerned) of the securities or someone who

---

[105] CA 2006 s.93.

[106] CA 2006 s.598.

[107] CA 2006.598(2)—the "initial period". For the requirement for a public company to obtain a trading certificate see para.16–010.

[108] CA 2006 ss.598(1)(a) and 603.

[109] CA 2006 ss.599(1)(c) and 601.

[110] "Holder" is defined to include not just the registered holder of the share but also a person who has the unconditional right to be included in the company's register of members or to have a transfer of the share executed in his favour: ss.588(3) and 605(4). See Ch.27.

[111] CA 2006 ss.588 and 605.

derives title from such a purchaser.[112] Consequently, if the shares have been traded in the normal way on a public market, the current holder will not be liable. On the other hand, a donee of the shares would be jointly and severally liable with the allottee.

The liability which the above provisions impose on the allottee or the current holder of the shares is potentially substantial, in respect of what might be only a technical breach of the statute, for example, the allottee has not been sent a copy of the valuer's report, though the allottee is in fact aware of its contents. Even where there has been a more than technical breach, the liability imposed may be penal. For example, a failure to have non-cash assets valued makes the allottee liable to pay the whole of the consideration due for the shares in cash with interest,[113] without any account being taken of the actual value of the non-cash assets transferred. Consequently, the court has the power to grant relief against liability to make a payment to the company in most cases,[114] but that power to grant relief is limited.[115] In particular, the court must have regard to two "overriding principles", namely:

(1) that a company which has allotted shares should receive money or money's worth at least equal in value to the aggregate of the nominal value of those shares and the value of the premium or, if the case so requires, so much of that aggregate as is treated as paid-up[116]; and
(2) that when the company would, if the court did not grant exemption, have more than one remedy against a particular person it should be for the company to decide which remedy it should remain entitled to pursue.[117]

Share capital and choice of currency

The Act requires the minimum capital requirement for public companies to be satisfied by shares denominated in either pounds sterling or euros, presumably for some sort of verification reason.[118] However, apart from this, the company has considerable freedom to denominate shares in such currency as it wishes. It has never been doubted that this was possible in relation to the share premium account (and other capital reserves) but the issue was debated in relation to the **16–023**

[112] CA 2006 ss.588(2) and 605(3). The requirement for "actual notice" is favourable to the subsequent holder. On the possible meanings of "actual knowledge", see *Eagle Trust Plc v SBC Securities Ltd* [1993] 1 W.L.R. 484 Ch D.

[113] CA 2006 s.593(3).

[114] There is no relief power in relation to the allottee in the case of issuance of shares at a discount or breach of the paying-up requirements: s.589(1).

[115] CA 2006 ss.589 and 606.

[116] The importance of which is demonstrated in *Re Bradford Investments (No.2)* [1991] B.C.C. 379 Ch D (Companies Ct); cf. *Re Ossory Estates Plc* (1988) 4 B.C.C. 460 Ch D (Companies Ct).

[117] CA 2006 ss.589(5) and 606(4). For other matters which the court should take into account, see ss.589(3)–(4) and 606(2)–(3). When proceedings are brought by one person (e.g. a holder of the shares) against another (e.g. the original allottee) for a contribution in respect of liability the court may adjust the extent (if any) of the contribution having regard to their respective culpability in relation to that liability: ss.589(6) and 606(5). And see s.606(6) for exemption from liability under s.604(3)(b).

[118] CA 2006 s.765(1).

share capital account until it was decided in favour of giving the company this freedom in *Re Scandinavian Bank*.[119] The Act now puts the point beyond doubt.[120] Moreover, the Act adds to this freedom by providing a simple procedure for re-denominating share capital from one currency to another (into or out of sterling or from one non-sterling currency to another), including the re-denomination of the shares used to satisfy the minimum capital requirement when trading began. Formerly, this could be achieved only by the cumbersome and potentially expensive procedure of a reduction of capital and an issue of new shares in the desired currency.[121] Now any limited[122] company, subject to contrary provision in its articles, may re-denominate its shares by ordinary resolution of the members.[123] Such re-denomination does not affect the currency in which dividends are required to be paid by the company or calls on shares met by the shareholder.[124]

Such re-denomination, which must be carried out at prevailing rates of exchange,[125] could produce new nominal values of a rather awkward kind, for example, $2.24. The company may respond in two ways: by capitalising distributable reserves so as to increase the nominal values to a more acceptable level, for which no special statutory permission is needed,[126] or by reducing the nominal values so as to achieve the same result, which the statute permits without the need to follow the full reduction of capital procedure. All that is required is a special resolution of the members, provided the decision is taken within three months of the re-denomination resolution and does not reduce the company's share capital by more than 10%.[127] Further, the amount of the reduction must be carried to a "re-denomination reserve" which is a new undistributable reserve created by the Act.[128] It is also conceivable that the reduction following re-denomination could produce the result that neither the euro nor the sterling requirements for the authorised minimum capital of a public company is met, in which case the company will have to re-register as a private company.[129]

---

[119] *Re Scandinavian Bank Group Plc* (1987) 3 B.C.C. 93 Ch D. Of course, until the rules on share capital were brought into line with those on share premium, the company was not in a position to exercise freedom of choice in relation to currency.

[120] CA 2006 s.542(3): shares "may be denominated in any currency and different classes of shares may be denominated in different currencies" (subject, of course, to s.765, fn.117).

[121] As happened in *Re Scandinavian Bank* (1987) 3 B.C.C. 93. For the reduction of capital procedure see paras 17–028 onwards.

[122] Unlimited companies had the freedom already.

[123] CA 2006 s.622(1). The section requires the actual conversion to take place within 28 days of the adoption of the resolution (s.622(5)–(6)).

[124] CA 2006 s.624(1). Other rights and obligations of members under the constitution or the terms of issue of the shares are also expressly preserved.

[125] CA 2006 s.622(3).

[126] On capitalisation issues see below, para.16–024.

[127] CA 2006 s.626. Thus, in the example in the text, the company would not be able to use this procedure to reduce the nominal value to $2, but it would be able to if the unreduced nominal value were $2.20. There must also be notification to the Registrar: s.627.

[128] CA 2006 s.628. For the significance of this for the payment of dividends see para.18–003.

[129] CA 2006 s.766 and the Companies (Authorised Minimum) Regulations 2008 (SI 2008/729) reg.5. A speedy method of re-registration is provided.

TURNING PROFITS INTO CAPITAL

The net worth of a business will fluctuate from time to time according to whether the company makes profits and ploughs them back or suffers losses. But a company's legal capital, i.e. the issued share capital plus share premium account (if any) does not automatically fluctuate to reflect this. It remains unaltered until increased by a further issue of shares, which must be made in conformity with the rules dealt with above, or reduced in accordance with the rules dealt with in Ch.17. If, however, the company has made profits and not distributed them as dividends, its assets will increase substantially beyond its liabilities. This is not necessarily something company or shareholders or creditors need worry about—in fact, they should welcome the profits—but an accounting device is needed to bring the company's books back into balance. This is to be found by including a (notional) liability on the balance sheet in order to balance the "assets" and "liabilities". This is normally described as a "reserve", an expression which may confuse those unaccustomed to accounting practice since it may suggest (falsely) that the company has set aside an actual earmarked fund to meet some potential or actual liability. The crucial point is that this reserve is a distributable reserve, unlike the capital accounts, i.e. the company can distribute assets to its shareholders up to the value in the reserve, and keep its books in balance by reducing the reserve accordingly. **16–024**

In addition to the increase in the company's net assets, its share price will increase substantially, in anticipation of existing and future profits being distributed. A large share price is sometimes thought of as undesirable on the grounds that it makes trading in the shares more difficult and thus reduces their liquidity.[130] Should a profit-rich company wish to address this issue, it can do so by making a "bonus" or "capitalisation" issue to its shareholders.[131] The former expression is likely to be used by the company when communicating with its shareholders, in the hope that they will think that they are being treated generously by being given something for nothing. In fact, they are not.[132] Capitalisation is the word likely to be used when communicating with the workforce (which might otherwise demand a bonus in the form of increased

---

[130] See fn.25.

[131] The two expressions mean the same thing and, indeed, so does a third ("scrip" issue) which is sometimes used. Technically, there is a two-stage process. First, the undivided profits of the company are capitalised and then there is the appropriation to each member who would have been entitled to a distribution of the profits by way of dividend of the amount needed to pay up as fully paid the shares to be issued. See *Topham v Charles Topham Group Ltd* [2002] EWHC 1096 (Ch); [2003] 1 B.C.L.C. 123, especially at 139–141, where the failure of a parent company to carry out the first step (because its accounts in fact showed no distributable profits, though its subsidiary did have such profits) meant that the issue of the bonus shares was ineffective to create any right in the shareholders to receive the shares. cf. *Re Cleveland Trust Plc* [1991] B.C.C. 33 Ch D (Companies Ct), where the company's accounts erroneously showed a distributable profit (in fact the profit so shown was repayable to a subsidiary) and the issue of the bonus shares was held to have been effective, as far as the statute was concerned, but rendered void by the common law doctrine of common mistake.

[132] See fn.26 above and the example in the following paragraph. It is possible that the exercise will slightly increase the market value of the shares if, as a result, they become easier to trade or, as it is sometimes put, "more liquid".

wages). As to the creditors, since capital is in principle not distributable to the shareholders, creditors should welcome this way of dealing with the company's profits.

We have already noted one form of bonus issue, where the shares are paid up out of the share premium account, which is accordingly reduced to the extent of the nominal value of the bonus shares, whilst the share capital account is correspondingly increased. Here, however, the bonus shares are paid up out of the distributable profits reserve. For example, suppose that before the issue the net asset value (taking book values) of the company was £2 million and the issued capital one million shares of £1 each. The shares, on book values, will be worth £2 each.[133] The company then makes a one-for-one bonus issue paid up out of the distributable profits reserve. The immediate effect on a shareholder is that for each former £1 share worth £2 he or she will now have two £1 shares each worth £1.[134] However, a more significant change has occurred, which may have implications for the future. The formerly distributable profit can no longer be distributed because it has been converted into share capital—at least not without going through a formal reduction procedure. The company is thus signalling a need to have greater permanent risk capital than might previously have been understood to be the case. Further, it is likely to stop short of capitalising undistributed reserves to an extent which would impair its freedom to pursue an appropriate dividend policy in the future. Thus, a bonus share paid up out of distributable reserves is a potentially more significant event than an issue of bonus shares paid up from the share premium account, where the decrease in one undistributable account is balanced by the increase in another.

CONCLUSION

16–025 The requirement that a public company has a minimum allotted capital when it begins trading is of doubtful utility to creditors, given the low level at which it is set. Protections of creditors which take as their base the nominal value of the share (notably the rule against issues at a discount to nominal value) are also of doubtful utility, given the company's freedom to set the nominal value of the share, and may even be harmful to their interests in certain circumstances. The rules designed to ensure that a company receives assets of a value equal to the price at which it has issued the shares are more useful to creditors and also promote equal treatment of different groups of members holding the same class of share. However, such rules do not depend for their effectiveness on a concept of legal capital. Such rules could equally well be formulated and enforced even if there were no legal capital rules. The main claim that the legal capital rules have to remain part of our company law must rest, therefore, on their role in constraining the payment of distributions to the members of the company to which we turn in Ch.18.

---

133 This does not mean that listed shares will be quoted at that price: that will depend on many other factors, including in particular the expected future profits and dividends. And the book values, of fixed assets in particular, may not reflect their present values.

134 The *quoted* price is not likely to fall by a half because it is to be expected that the company will seek to maintain approximately the same level of dividend per share as before the issue.

CHAPTER 17

CAPITAL MAINTENANCE

In the previous chapter we saw that the courts from the early days of modern company law attached importance to legal capital as a technique for protecting creditors. Although the legislature steered clear of imposing minimum capital requirements, the legal capital the company actually chose to raise was regarded as a fundamental protection for creditors, and, to that end, the courts developed the rule that capital should be deployed only for the purposes of the business. In the next chapter we look at the working out of the consequences of this view for corporate distributions to shareholders and, perhaps more important, for the identification of "disguised" distributions. In this chapter we consider the implications of the doctrine of legal capital for formal alterations of the company's capital structure. We consider the acquisition by a company of its own shares, a reduction by the company of the amount standing in its share accounts, and the provision by the company of financial assistance for the purchase of its own shares. In all three cases, the initial stance of the law was highly constraining of what the company was permitted to do in each of these three areas, in the interests of creditors. Over the years, the law in all three areas has become more **17–001** relaxed, to a greater or less degree, partly because effective alternative ways of protecting creditors have been found and partly because the interests of the creditors have been re-assessed.

ACQUISITIONS OF OWN SHARES

The general prohibition

17–002 It was held by the House of Lords in the nineteenth century that a company could not acquire its own shares, even though there was an express power to do so in its memorandum, since this would result in a reduction of capital.[1] Assuming that on acquisition by the company the shares were cancelled and nothing put in their place this would necessarily reduce the capital yardstick represented by issued share capital and it could also be regarded as objectionable as a diversion of the company's assets to the shareholders whose shares were acquired, possibly in circumstances in which an ordinary dividend could not be paid because of the rules discussed in the next chapter. Today, however, acquisitions by companies of shares held by their investors are common—though controversial on other grounds. Acquisitions may occur because the company is able to meet its investment needs from internally generated profit and so has less need of externally provided equity finance, or because it wishes to give investors who no longer rate the company as attractive an opportunity to exit it, whilst retaining those shareholders who think the company's prospects are good. Thus, the story of the law's development is from prohibition of acquisition to specification of circumstances in which acquisition by a company of its own shares is allowed. As we shall see, the CA 2006 now legitimises two forms of acquisition: redemption and re-purchase.

The CA 2006 begins by confirming the common law rule that a limited company "shall not acquire its own shares whether by purchase, subscription or otherwise".[2] The prohibition thus catches not only purchases from existing shareholders but also the probably rare case where the company subscribes to its own shares upon issue, whether as a subscriber to the memorandum or not. If the company infringes the prohibition, it and every officer in default is liable to a fine and the purported acquisition is void.[3] In addition, a public company is prohibited from taking a lien or charge over its own shares (that is also treated as void), except to cover the unpaid liability on a partly paid share.[4] Moreover, this central prohibition is buttressed by two further statutory restrictions.

---

[1] *Trevor v Whitworth* (1887) 12 App. Cas. 409 HL. Since at this stage in the development of UK company law, there was no distinction between public and private companies, the rule necessarily applied to all companies incorporated under the Acts.

[2] CA 2006 s.658(1)—the exemption of unlimited companies from this prohibition shows the connection between the rule and creditor protection.

[3] CA 2006 s.658(2).

[4] CA 2006 s.670. There are also exceptions for companies whose ordinary business includes the lending of money and the charge is part of that business, and for charges taken by a private company before it re-registered as public.

Acquisition through a nominee

The first extension, contained in s.660, applies where the company acquires shares, not directly, but through a nominee, where (1) the nominee subscribes to the memorandum for shares; (2) shares are issued to the nominee by the company; or (3) shares are acquired by the nominee as partly paid shares from a third person. The first two cases are clear: where the company's nominee subscribes to its own shares or takes them upon issuance by the company, this is objectionable on the grounds that the company has not raised the additional funds apparently represented by the issued shares. Where a nominee for the company has acquired the shares from an existing shareholder, however, this objection does not arise (the company has already received the consideration) and the legal capital objection to this transaction is unclear, since the amounts stated company's share capital and share premium accounts do not change. This explains why this leg of the nominee extension applies to acquisitions through a nominee from an existing holder only of partly paid shares: the obligation to meet the calls might fall on the company. In all three cases the shares are treated as held by the nominee on its own account and the company is regarded as having no beneficial interest in them.[5] So, the transaction is not void (though its result is very different from what the parties intended) and the company's capital accounts remain unaffected. **17–003**

Further, if the nominee does not meet the financial obligations attached to the shares, then that liability will fall on the other subscribers to the memorandum (where the nominee is a subscriber) and in the other cases it will fall on the directors of the company at the time the shares were issued to or acquired by the nominee.[6] In both cases it is a joint and several liability. This suggests that the rationale of the nominee rules is to ensure that the company receives the full price of the shares it issues.

Company may not be a member of its holding company

Secondly, the prohibition on acquisition of own shares is supplemented by s.136 which provides that a company cannot be a member of its holding company, either directly or through a nominee,[7] and any allotment or transfer of shares in the holding company from an existing shareholder in the parent to the subsidiary or its nominee is void. Section 136 is aimed at preventing the de facto reduction of capital which would result from a subsidiary company acquiring shares in its holding company. The holding company, through its subsidiary, would be returning assets to the selling shareholder.[8] Nevertheless, s.136 does not apply **17–004**

---

[5] CA 2006 s.660(2). In effect, the nominee arrangement is unwound by the law. On the same logic the section does not apply at all if the nominee arrangement does not give the company a beneficial interest in the shares acquired by the nominee: s.660(3)(b).

[6] CA 2006.661(2), but the court has the power to relieve a director who has acted honestly and reasonably from the whole or part of the liability: s.661(3)–(4).

[7] CA 2006 s.144.

[8] However, if such a transaction were permitted, the parent's legal capital account would not be reduced by the fact that one of its members is a subsidiary—any more than in the case of shares held by a nominee—so that it would not become easier for the parent to make distributions.

where the subsidiary, at the time of acquisition of the shares in the holding company, is not a subsidiary of it, but later becomes so, for example, as a result of a takeover.[9] The upshot of the exception is that the resources of the holding company may be expended in buying (in effect) its own shares (i.e. when it completes the takeover), but it has been held, nevertheless, that this result cannot be prevented by relying on the general prohibition on a company acquiring its own shares (s.658) rather than s.136.[10] Presumably the desire to permit a useful commercial transaction was thought, in this instance, to outweigh the policy behind the prohibition on the acquisition of own shares.

Specific exceptions to the general prohibition

17–005 This apparently comprehensive set of prohibitions is, however, subject to a number of exceptions. Thus, a company may acquire its own shares by way of gift[11] or by way of forfeiture for non-payment of calls.[12] In the latter case, however, a public company must cancel the shares and reduce its capital account accordingly if the shares are not disposed of within three years of the forfeiture.[13] Both these exceptions are of long-standing. In 1983 there was added a further complex set of rules to deal with possible problems faced by public companies in relation to shares acquired by the trustees of a company's employee share scheme or pension scheme.[14] These do not need to be further analysed in a work of this kind. There are also scattered throughout the CA 2006 provisions which permit the court to order that a company acquire shares from a shareholder, as a remedy for some wrong which has been done to that shareholder. The best known example is a compulsory purchase order made by the court under the unfair prejudice provisions, considered in Ch.14.[15] Finally, an acquisition of shares by the company under a reduction of capital carried out under the provisions discussed below is exempted from the prohibition.[16]

Where a public company is permitted to acquire its own shares, whether directly or through a nominee, then so long as it holds those shares (i.e. does not cancel or dispose of them) and decides to show those shares as an asset in its balance sheet, an amount equal to the value of the shares must be transferred out

[9] CA 2006 s.137(1)(b)–(c). The company may not exercise the voting rights attached to the shares, once it becomes a subsidiary (s.137(4)), but this does little to help creditors.

[10] *Acatos & Hutchinson Plc v Watson* [1995] B.C.C. 446 Ch D. Technically, the basis of the decision was that the bidder was acquiring the shares of its new subsidiary, not its own shares.

[11] CA 2006 s.659(1)—"otherwise than for valuable consideration". This was held to be permissible at common law in *Re Castiglione's Will Trust* [1958] Ch. 549 Ch D, where the acquisition was through a nominee, but the Act permits direct acquisition in such a case.

[12] CA 2006 s.659(2)(c).

[13] CA 2006 s.662(1)(a), (2), (3)(a).

[14] These problems were originally tackled by the Companies (Beneficial Interests) Act 1983: see now the CA 2006 ss.671–676. The acquisition of such shares is likely to be financed, at least in part, by the company and the company may have a residuary beneficial interest in them which, under these provisions, may be disregarded.

[15] CA 2006 s.659(2)(b), which also lists three other situations where the court may order the purchase of shares, i.e. under ss.98, 721(6) and 759.

[16] CA 2006 s.659(2)(a).

of profits available for dividend to an undistributable reserve.[17] In effect, the amount available for distribution will be reduced by the value of the purchase. Thus, suppose a public company acquires through a nominee fully paid shares from a third party, providing the nominee with the funds to effect the purchase. The company's net asset value will remain the same, the reduction in cash being offset by the value of the shares acquired. However, by virtue of the requirement to create an undistributable reserve, the value of the shares as assets in the balanced sheet is negated by the reserve, thus protecting creditors.[18] To put the matter another way, the purchase of the shares is treated as a distribution to the shareholder whose shares the nominee acquired.

REDEMPTION AND RE-PURCHASE

Introduction

The "no acquisition" principle set out above, with its limited exceptions, clearly rules out any general practice of companies' redeeming or re-purchasing their own shares. However, the law has now moved in the direction of permitting these steps, provided certain conditions are met. The legislature has taken the view in recent times that these transactions could be structured in such a way as not to endanger the interests of creditors and that the nineteenth century prohibition was over-inclusive in its reach. The "no acquisition" principle is thus subject in modern law to a very major exception. However, if the statutory conditions (discussed more fully below) for the lawful redemption or repurchase of shares are not met, then the underlying prohibition on the company's acquisition of its own shares will remain applicable. 17–006

As we have noted,[19] breach of the prohibition is a criminal offence by the company and its officers and the attempted re-purchase or redemption is rendered void. What are the consequences of these provisions for the directors of the company who authorised the failed transaction or for the shareholders who received money from the company in exchange for their shares? As to the directors, an unlawful redemption or re-purchase will amount to a misapplication of the company's assets and, subject to the court's power to forgive reasonable and honest directors, they will be under a liability to compensate the company for the amounts improperly paid out. This is similar to the directors' liability to compensate the company in respect of sums paid out as unlawful dividends, which we discuss in Ch.18.[20]

As to those whose shares are unlawfully redeemed or re-purchased, there is no explicit statutory basis for the company to claw-back the money received, as there is with unlawful dividends.[21] Nevertheless, there are two (rather different)

[17] CA 2006 s.669.

[18] This result will be achieved as a result of the requirement in s.831 that a public company may make a distribution only to the extent that its net assets exceed its legal capital and undistributable reserves (increased in the example by the value of the share purchase).

[19] See para.17–002.

[20] See para.18–012.

[21] See para.18–011.

common law bases on which the recipients might be required to restore to the company the money received. First, if the recipients have the requisite degree of knowledge of the directors' breach of duty, they could be held liable as constructive trustees for the company of the money following their knowing receipt of it.[22] Secondly, since the transaction is void, the company may be able to claim the money back from the recipients on the grounds that there has been a total failure of consideration: the company has paid the money but has not received the shares. This claim is subject to a possible defence of change of position on the part of the recipients.[23] There is a potential obstacle to the company's claim in that a purported acquisition by a company of its own shares is a criminal act on its part, and so its claim is potentially open to an illegality objection on the part of the recipients. However, modern law is tending towards setting aside the illegality objection, where, as here, the company is no longer purporting to acquire its shares but is seeking to unwind the acquisition transaction.[24] In any event, since the "no acquisition" rule is designed to protect creditors, it would be self-defeating for the company not to be able to recover the payments, at least where it had no distributable profits at the time of the purported acquisition.

Redemption and re-purchase

17–007 Redeemable shares are shares which are issued on the basis that they are to be or may be redeemed (i.e. bought back) at a later date by the company. The terms of issue may be that the shares will be redeemed at a certain point or that they may be, and in the latter case the option to redeem may be allocated to the shareholder or the company or both. The process of redemption is thus different from the process of re-purchase, where the CA 2006, under certain conditions, simply permits the company to perform the otherwise unlawful act of re-purchasing its shares. With re-purchase there is no obligation upon the company to make an offer to re-purchase or, if one is made, upon the shareholder to accept it. The redemption arrangement, by contrast, will always create some rights or duties to redeem or be redeemed.

Redeemable shares thus involve an element of planning of its financial structure by a company, because the terms of the redemption have to be set at the time of issue. As compared with non-redeemable shares, the holder of a right to have the shares redeemed is not locked into the company and able to dispose of the shares only to an investor who is prepared to buy them at the prevailing market prices. An investor may welcome the right to exit the company at a particular period in the future on terms set out in advance. Such an arrangement makes the redeemable share a hybrid between debt and equity, the debt holder also being someone who normally has a repayment right at an identifiable point in the future and on pre-set terms. Equally, the company may wish to issue redeemable shares over which it has a redemption right, perhaps as an alternative

---

[22] See paras 10–130 and 18–011.

[23] Both claims are discussed by the Privy Council in *DD Growth Premium 2X Fund (In Liquidation) v RMF Market Neutral Strategies (Master) Ltd* [2017] UKPC 36; [2018] B.C.C. 152 at [58] onwards.

[24] See *Patel v Mirza* [2016] UKSC 42; [2017] A.C. 467

to standard preference shares which can be squeezed out only through the more elaborate and costly procedure of a reduction of capital.[25]

However, the freedom of the company and the shareholder to agree upon a re-purchase of shares is more useful than the redemption procedure, precisely because it does not involve commitment in advance. It is a mechanism which can be resorted to as occasions arise, whilst the occasions when it is desirable to redeem some of the company's shares may be difficult to identify in advance. It is true that the re-purchase provisions do not create a mechanism whereby the shareholder can be compelled to sell the shares back to the company or whereby the company can be compelled to buy them, but there are many instances where company and shareholder interests are aligned so that the repurchase is likely to go ahead in those cases, if the law permits it, as it now does. The company may wish to return unwanted equity capital to the shareholders, either because it has no need at all for the financing represented by the shares repurchased or because it wishes to replace that financing with an alternative, such as debt. More questionably, the incumbent board may wish to buy out a group of shareholders who are causing trouble for the incumbent management—a process referred to in the US literature as "greenmail", presumably after the colour of the dollar bill. As we shall see, there are features of the re-purchase mechanism aimed at combating such opportunism. As for the shareholders, some may welcome the chance to exit the company at an attractive price, whilst those remaining may hope that the company's earnings per share will increase when some of the shareholders are paid off, if indeed it was the case that the capital returned to them was not earning a high reward or if it can be replaced by a cheaper form of financing.

Some history

Redeemable shares have been permissible since the CA 1929. However, prior to the CA 1981, only preference shares could be issued as redeemable.[26] Now, however, as s.684 provides, a company may issue shares of any class which are to be redeemed or are liable to be redeemed, whether at the option of the company or the shareholder. However, the CA 1929 made the crucial breakthrough because it introduced a method whereby redemption could take place without, it was thought, prejudicing the interests of creditors and this method was adopted again when, also in 1981, companies were empowered to re-purchase their own shares, whether or not they were issued as redeemable.[27] This method has two crucial creditor-protection features, which are discussed further below. First, the shares may be redeemed or re-purchased only out of distributable profits or out of the proceeds of a fresh issue of shares made for the purposes of the redemption or re-purchase (though this latter method is not always available). Insofar as distributable profits (as defined in the next chapter) are used to fund the **17–008**

[25] See paras 17–028 onwards and 13–017.

[26] Perhaps because they were already capable of being squeezed out through the reduction procedure (see para.19–035) and the redemption mechanism allowed the parties to contract about the handling of this process.

[27] The crucial policy document was DTI, *The Purchase by a Company of its own Shares* (1980), Cmnd.7944.

redemptions or re-purchases, the creditors have no cause to complain, since the company could have used them to fund dividends instead.

Secondly, as far as the capital accounts are concerned, the capital created by the fresh issue will replace the capital removed by the redemption or re-purchase and so the level of protection afforded to the creditors through the capital accounts will be the same. In addition, provided it is disclosed that redemption or re-purchase of existing shares is the reason for the fresh issue, creditors will not be misled into thinking that the company is issuing shares in order permanently to raise the amounts stated in its capital accounts. However, the impact of a purchase on the company's capital accounts remains to be dealt with if the redemption or re-purchase is funded out of distributable profits. Once the shares are re-purchased the amount stated in the company's capital accounts will be reduced, thus lowering the level of creditor protection. This problem was met by requiring the company to establish an undistributable reserve of an amount equal to the capital reduction when the redemption or re-purchase is funded out of distributable profits. This is known as the "capital redemption reserve" (CRR).

General restrictions on redeemable shares and on repurchases

17–009 Redeemable shares may not be issued unless the company has also issued shares which are not redeemable.[28] This provision eliminates the risk of the company ending up with no members if and when all the redeemable shares are redeemed.[29] However, the CA 2006 makes no stipulation as to the number or value of the non-redeemable shares which are required to have been issued, and so the main form of equity financing for the company could be via redeemable shares. Having redeemed those shares, the company might be left with little equity capital. Somewhat similarly, a re-purchase cannot be made if the result would be that there were no longer any members of the company holding non-redeemable shares or only treasury shares remained.[30]

In the case of a public company, redeemable shares may not be issued unless the company is authorised in its articles to do so and, in the case of a private company, the articles may exclude or restrict the issue of redeemable shares.[31] Thus, the default rule is in favour of the private company having the power to issue redeemable shares and against it in the case of public companies. This requirement is additional to the provisions discussed in Ch.24 which, in some cases, require the directors to seek the authorisation of the shareholders before they take advantage of the power to issue any type of share. The default rule addresses the logically prior question of whether the company has power to issue redeemable shares at all. Nevertheless, both sets of rules create a requirement for

---

28 CA 2006 s.684(4).

29 Moreover, after issue, the non-redeemable shares cannot be re-purchased so as to produce the result that the company has only redeemable or treasury shares in issue: s.690(2). Nor may a private company reduce its share capital through the solvency statement regime so as to produce the result that it has only redeemable shares in issue: s.641(2). In the case of the court-centred reduction, the court could permit such a reduction but, presumably, would be unlikely to do so.

30 CA 2006 s.690(2). On treasury shares, see para.17–023.

31 CA 2006 s.684. The Companies (Model Articles) Regulations 2008 (SI 2008/3229) Sch.3: Model Articles for Public Companies include this power (art.43(2)).

shareholder consent. The main differences between them appear to be that the power to issue redeemable shares, once given in the articles, remains in force until the articles are altered, while the directors' authority to issue shares (of any type) requires periodical renewal but that authority can be given by ordinary resolution.[32]

A company may purchase its own shares (including redeemable shares)[33] subject to any restriction or prohibition in the company's articles.[34] Thus, the default rule for both public and private companies is that the company does have power to re-purchase its shares. The contrast with the default rule for public companies in relation to redeemable shares (no power to do so) can be explained by the greater protection for shareholders which exists in relation to the actual implementation of the re-purchase, as we shall see below.[35]

Concern about the impact of the redemption on the non-redeemable shareholders also lies behind a long-running debate concerning the setting of the terms of the redemption. Under the CA 1985, in order to protect the shareholders whose shares were not to be redeemed (and indeed the offerees holding redeemable shares), the terms and manner of the redemption were required to be set out in the company's articles, so that all would know the position.[36] However, this was thought to be an inflexible requirement and the rule now embodied in the CA 2006 is somewhat more flexible.[37] Fixing the terms in the articles remains the default rule,[38] but, provided either the articles or an ordinary resolution of the company permit it, the directors may fix the terms and conditions of the redemption.[39] Protection for the shareholders is maintained by the requirement that the directors, if they set the terms, must do so before the shares are allotted and the company's statement of capital provided to the Registrar must include the terms of the redemption.[40] **17–010**

The CA 2006 contains two further relevant provisions, one restrictive, the other facultative. First, redeemable shares may not be redeemed until they are fully paid[41]; and the same rule is applied to re-purchases.[42] This avoids the acquisition wiping out the personal liability of the holders in respect of uncalled capital. Secondly, the terms of redemption may provide that, by agreement

---

[32] CA 2006 s.551 and see para.24–005.

[33] Thus enabling the company to "redeem" them prior to a date fixed in the terms and conditions if it can reach agreement with the holder.

[34] CA 2006 s.690. A purported re-purchase in breach of the articles would be void, because the company would no longer be protected from the operation of s.658(2) (para.13–002); cf. *Hague v Nam Tai Electronics Inc* [2006] UKPC 52; [2007] 2 B.C.L.C. 194.

[35] See paras 17–030 onwards—though that protection was somewhat reduced in 2013.

[36] CA 1985 s.160(3).

[37] Though not as flexible as the CLR's recommendation, which would have given the directors an unconditional power to set the terms of the redemption: Final Report I, para.4.5.

[38] CA 2006 s.685(4).

[39] CA 2006 s.685(1),(2).

[40] CA 2006 s.685(3).

[41] CA 2006 ss.686(1).

[42] CA 2006 s.691(1).

between company and shareholder, the amount due is to be paid on a date later than the redemption date[43]; whereas the requirement that the shares be paid for on re-purchase is unqualified.[44]

Once the acquisition is effected, the Registrar must be informed in the usual way and supplied with details of the transaction.[45]

Creditor protection: all companies

17–011 The core of the nineteenth century objection to redemption and re-purchase of shares was creditor protection. Therefore, the crucial step in permitting these transactions was producing a solution to the creditor protection issue. That solution, as now embedded in the CA 2006, consists of two sets of rules: one applying to all companies and the other containing relaxations which only private companies can take advantage of. We will look first at the rules applying to all companies and then at the private company relaxations.

The general solution to the creditor protection issue consisted, as noted, of providing that shares could be redeemed or re-purchased only out of distributable profits or out of the proceeds of a fresh issue of shares made for the purpose of the redemption or re-purchase.[46] Any premium payable on redemption or re-purchase must be paid out of distributable profits alone, unless the redeemed or re-purchased shares were issued initially at a premium, in which case the redemption premium may be paid out of the proceeds of a new issue, up to the amount of the premium received on issue or the value of the company's current share premium account, whichever is the less.[47] This rather complicated rule ensures that the money received on the new issue of shares is paid out only to the extent that it reflects the reduction in the capital accounts arising out of the redemption or re-purchase. If more is needed to redeem the shares, the excess must be provided out of distributable profits.[48]

---

[43] CA 2006 s.686(2)—otherwise the shares must be paid for on redemption: s.686(3).

[44] CA 2006 s.691(2)—except in relation to a private company purchasing shares pursuant to an employee share scheme. See *Dickinson v NAL Realisations (Staffordshire) Ltd* [2019] EWCA Civ 2146; [2020] B.C.C. 271. The payment appears not to have to be wholly in cash (*BDG Roof-Bond Ltd v Douglas* [2000] B.C.C. 770). For the problems to which this lack of flexibility as to timing can give rise see *Peña v Dale* [2003] EWHC 1065 (Ch); [2004] 2 B.C.L.C. 508; *Kinlan v Crimmin* [2006] EWHC 779 (Ch); [2007] B.C.C. 106 (though in the latter case the judge managed to avoid requiring the shareholder to return to the company the money received by resort to the defence of a good faith change of position).

[45] CA 2006 ss.689 (redemption) and 707 (re-purchase).

[46] CA 2006 ss.687(2) and 692(2). So long as the power to redeem shares was limited to preference shares, the company's existing share premium account could be used for the whole of the premium payable on redemption, but this changed once the power was extended to ordinary shares because of the larger premium associated with such shares. See DTI, *The Purchase by a Company of its own Shares* (1980), para.22; and *DD Growth Premium 2X Fund v RMF Market Neutral Strategies (Master) Ltd* [2018] B.C.C. 152 at [49].

[47] CA 2006 ss.687(3), (4) and 692(2)(b), (3).

[48] To see this, let us suppose that, immediately before the re-purchase, a public company has net assets exactly equivalent to its then legal capital. Thus, it has distributable profits of zero. It raises money by issuing 100 new shares at par at £2 per share. Its share capital account will increase by £200, as will its net assets: i.e. the company will still have distributable profits of zero. If it now proposes to re-purchase 100 of its original £1 shares at a premium of £1, the shares having been

Once the shares have been redeemed, they are treated as cancelled and the amount of the company's issued share capital is diminished by the nominal value of the shares redeemed.[49] The company may also cancel its repurchased shares. In these cases the company must create an (undistributable) Capital Redemption Reserve. The amount of this reserve is equivalent to the amount by which the company's issued share capital is diminished by a redemption or re-purchase wholly out of profits[50] or, where the transactions are financed partly by the proceeds of a new issue and partly by distributable profits, the amount by which the proceeds of the new issue fall short of the amount paid on redemption or re-purchase.[51] However, since 2003 the company has had the option not to cancel shares which have been re-purchased but instead to hold them "in treasury", usually for later re-issue. (Treasury shares are considered further at paras 17–023 onwards.) This is a significant difference between the redemption and re-purchase procedures. Where shares are held in treasury, the creation of a CRR is unnecessary, because the company's capital accounts are not altered.

Private companies: redemption or purchase out of capital

In relation to both redemptions and re-purchases of shares, special concessions are made to private companies. It is thought often to be impossible for a private company to redeem or purchase its own shares unless it could do so out of capital and without having to incur the expense of a formal reduction of capital with the court's consent. There might not be sufficient distributable profits, if, as is common, its policy has been to take all the profits out of the company, in one way or another, in the year in which they were earned. And there might be no available takers for a fresh issue of shares. The whole concept of raising and maintaining capital is, in relation to such companies, of somewhat dubious value. Hence it was decided that, subject to safeguards, they should be empowered to redeem or buy without maintaining the former capital yardstick. In particular, the aim was to permit entrepreneurs to withdraw assets from their company to fund their retirement rather than by selling control to a larger competitor. 17–012

There are in fact now two concessions. The first, introduced in 2013 and applying to repurchases only, simply allows a private company to spend in any financial year up to (the lower of) £15,000 or 5% of the nominal value of its share capital on re-purchases. There are no additional formalities to be met, provided only that the company is authorised by its articles to take this action.[52] This provision is clearly crafted with small-scale but potentially frequent re-purchases in mind, probably linked to employee share schemes, rather than one-shot retirement exercises.

---

originally issued at par, this will require £200 from the company, but will only reduce the share capital account by £100 (the nominal value of the shares). This means that the company can only use £100 of its net assets (being the amount that will no longer required in the capital account) to re-purchase the shares. It must thus invariably finance the any premium on re-purchase out of distributable profits or not pay a redemption premium at all.

49 CA 2006 s.688.

50 CA 2006 s.733(2).

51 CA 2006 s.733(3).

52 CA 2006 s.692(1ZA).

17–013 The second set of provisions, which date back to 1981, are now contained in Ch.5 of Pt 18 of the CA 2006. They have been retained even though private companies now have a cheaper, non-court based method of reducing capital.[53] These rules apply to redemptions as well as repurchases, but, to shorten exposition, the rules are stated here in relation to re-purchases.[54]

Section 709 provides that, subject to what follows, a private company, unless restricted or prohibited by its articles from so doing, may make a payment in respect of the purchase of its shares otherwise than out of its distributable profits or the proceeds of a fresh issue of shares. Such a payment is termed a payment "out of capital".[55] This is a very wide definition and may explain why it was thought there might be some cases where re-purchase "out of capital" would be available, whereas a reduction of capital would not. Suppose a company wishes to acquire shares for a price above their nominal value but has no share premium account or capital redemption reserve. No matter how much the share capital account is reduced, this will not free up a sufficient amount of assets to be distributed so as to meet the redemption premium. Assuming, however, that the company has sufficient cash, it may be able to engage in re-purchase by making a payment "out of capital" under s.709. This section helpfully says that a payment other than out of distributable profits or the proceeds of a fresh issue is a payment out of capital (and so in principle permitted) "whether or not it would be regarded apart from this section as a payment out of capital". Provided the company has the necessary cash and follows the provisions of this part of the CA 2006, that is all it needs to be concerned with.[56]

The extent of any such payment out of capital is restricted, however, to what is described as the "permissible capital payment" (PCP).[57] In brief, the rule is that any distributable profits and any proceeds of fresh issue made for the purpose of the re-purchase must first be used before resort may be had to a payment out of capital. The rules for determining distributable profits are those considered in the next chapter in relation to dividends, but there are certain amendments,[58] perhaps the most important of which is that the accounts by reference to which the profits are calculated must be prepared within a period of three months ending with the date of the statutory declaration which the directors are required to make.[59]

The principal protective techniques used in the Chapter in respect of the PCP are, for both creditors and shareholders, the requirement for a solvency statement from the directors; in the case of shareholders, the requirement for approval of the proposed re-purchase by special resolution; and, in both cases again, the availability of a right of objection to the court.

---

[53] See para.17–041.
[54] CA 2006 s.709(1).
[55] CA 2006 s.709(2).
[56] HL Debs, Grand Committee, Tenth Day, cols 31–32 (20 March 2006).
[57] CA 2006 s.710.
[58] CA 2006 s.711.
[59] CA 2006 s.712(6),(7). The available profits so determined have then to be treated as reduced by any lawful distributions made by the company since the date of the accounts and before the date of the statutory declaration: s.712(3)–(4).

Directors' statement

As far as the solvency statement is concerned, the requirements of the CA 2006 are similar to those applied in the case of a solvency statement upon a reduction of capital out of court by a private company, including the requirement for the directors to take into account contingent and prospective liabilities.[60] However, they are not the same. In particular, the directors are apparently unable to make the required forward-looking statement in the case of a purchase out of capital, if they intend to wind the company up within 12 months of the proposed payment.[61] And the forward-looking statement, applying to the immediately following year, is required to be a little fuller. The form of the required statement is that, having regard to the "the amount and character of the financial resources" which will be available to the company in the directors' view, the directors have formed the opinion that the company will be able to carry on business as a going concern throughout that year (and accordingly will be able to pay its debts as they fall due).[62] The emphasis is thus on an opinion which envisages a continuing business, not just the ability of the company to pay its debts.[63] Perhaps because of these differences the statement required on a purchase is termed a "directors' statement" in the Act, whilst the term "solvency statement" is reserved for the statement required of directors under the out-of-court reduction procedure, though both statements are, substantively, statements about the solvency of the company. 17–014

The CA 2006 applies to the directors' statement the same criminal liability for negligence as is applied to the solvency statement.[64] There is also a limited statutory civil liability in negligence to the company if the company goes into winding up within one year of the payment being made to the shareholder.[65] However, a major contrast with the solvency statement is that the directors' statement needs to be accompanied by a report from the company's auditors stating their opinion that the amount of the PCP has been properly calculated and that they are not aware of any matters, after inquiry into the company's affairs, which renders the directors' statement unreasonable in all the circumstances.[66]

---

60 CA 2006 s.714(4). On these requirements upon a capital reduction see para.17–036.

61 Presumably on the grounds that a re-purchase to enable the founding entrepreneur to retire is in those circumstances unnecessary: the withdrawal can take place as part of the winding up. Section 714(3)(b) requires the statement to say that the directors' opinion is that the company will be able to carry on business as a going concern in the following year "having regard to their intentions with respect to the management of the company during the year", so that they could not honestly make the required statement if they contemplated a winding up.

62 CA 2006 s.714(3)(b).

63 As to the opinion about the current position, that relates to the position "immediately following" the date on which the PCP is proposed to be made (s.714(3)(a)) rather than the date of the statement (cf. s.643(1)(a)), so that it requires a small degree of foresight.

64 CA 2006 s.715, cf. s.643(4) (see para.17–038).

65 IA 1986 s.76. See fn.77.

66 CA 2006 s.714(6). The less demanding "solvency statement" approach is used for payments out of capital for purchases under an employee share scheme (s.720A).

Shareholder resolution

17–015 The solvency statement can be said to protect both the creditors of the company and the shareholders who will remain in the company after the re-purchase. An additional protection for the shareholders is the special resolution which is required to be passed within a week of the directors' statement and on the basis of prior disclosure to the members of the directors' statement and auditors' report.[67] In this case it is explicitly provided that the resolution is ineffective if these requirements are not complied with.[68] Crucially, the resolution will not be effective to authorise the purchase out of capital if the shares to which the resolution relates vote on the resolution and their votes were necessary to secure its adoption.[69]

Appeal to the court

17–016 The final protective device (for both creditors and dissenting members) is court scrutiny. The CA 2006 entitles any member of the company, who has not consented to or voted for the resolution, and any creditor of the company, to apply to the court for the cancellation of the resolution, provided this action is taken within five weeks of the passing of the resolution.[70] The court is given the widest powers. For example, it can cancel the resolution, confirm it, or make such orders as it thinks expedient for the purchase of dissentient members' shares or for the protection of creditors, and may make ancillary orders for the reduction of the company's capital.[71]

Legal capital consequences

17–017 If there is no court objection, the PCP must be made between five and seven weeks after the adoption of the resolution.[72] Upon the re-purchase of the shares, the company's share capital account will be reduced accordingly, but, because this is a permitted payment out of capital, there will be no need to transfer a corresponding amount to the CRR, as would happen in the case of a purchase out of distributable profits.[73] A transfer to CRR will be needed only to the extent that distributable profits have been used in part to fund the purchase of the shares.[74] Where the PCP is greater than the nominal value of the purchased shares (i.e. they

[67] CA 2006 s.718(1)–(2)—the method of disclosure varying according to whether a written resolution or a resolution at a meeting is contemplated.

[68] CA 2006 s.718(3), cf. s.642(4) applying to solvency statements, where the validity of the resolution is expressly preserved (see para.17–038) and reliance is placed instead on criminal sanctions to produce compliance with the disclosure obligation: s.644(7).

[69] CA 2006 s.717, cf. s.695.

[70] CA 2006 s.721(1)–(2). The shareholder should know about the resolution but the creditor may not. Consequently, s.719 requires publicity to be given to the resolution, within one week of its adoption, giving the relevant details, including the amount of the PCP and naming a place where the directors' and auditors' reports may be consulted.

[71] CA 2006 s.721(3)–(7).

[72] CA 2006 s.723.

[73] See para.17–011.

[74] CA 2006 s.734(4).

are being purchased at a premium), the company is given permission to reduce its CRR, share premium account and its revaluation reserve accordingly.[75] In other words, the company's capital yardstick will in all probability be reduced to the extent of the PCP.[76] This is, after all, the object of the exercise. Overall, indeed, the effect of the foregoing provisions is that a private company may be able to make a return to one or more of its members which will exhaust its accumulated profits available for dividend and reduce both its assets and its capital yardstick.

As far as the Companies Act is concerned, this is the end of the procedure. However, the Insolvency Act contains a limited mechanism for unscrambling the acquisition. If the company goes into liquidation within one year of the payment being made to the shareholder, that person and, in some circumstances, the directors who authorised the payment are liable to return to the company the amount of the payment out of capital, to the extent that this is needed to meet any deficiency of the company's assets in relation to its liabilities.[77]

Protection for shareholders

Although not central to this chapter, it is convenient to look briefly at how the law handles intra-shareholder conflicts arising in redemptions and re-purchases generally (i.e. beyond the shareholder resolution required for acquisitions out of capital). This is particularly needed for re-purchases. Redemptions, if not out of capital, tend not to raise issues for shareholders because the terms of the redemption are set out at the time of issue of the shares. By contrast, it is clear that re-purchases have implications for the relations of shareholders among themselves. Controlling shareholders—or shareholders whom the management wish to see exit the company—may be given the opportunity to sell their shares when other shareholders are excluded, or may be given the opportunity to sell on more favourable terms. The CA 2006 contains some provisions aimed at controlling such abuses. These protections vary according to whether the purchase is to be an "off-market" or a "market" purchase. The essential distinction between the two situations is whether the purchase takes place on a "recognised investment exchange", i.e. one authorised by the Financial Conduct Authority.[78] In broad terms this means that it is a market purchase if it takes place on the main market of the London Stock Exchange or on the Alternative Investment Market.[79] Market purchases create fewer risks of abuse since the offer will be a public one and the purchases will be effected at an objectively determined market price. If there is no market, the opportunities for favouritism are much greater. **17–018**

[75] CA 2006 s.734(3). Section 734(4) deals with the complication where the purchase is partly by way of PCP and partly by way of the proceeds of a fresh issue.

[76] But note the example given above in para.17–013 where the PCP is greater than the company's CRR and share premium account.

[77] IA 1986 s.76. The directors of the company who signed the statement are jointly and severally liable with the shareholders unless the director can show reasonable grounds for the opinion set out therein.

[78] CA 2006 s.693(2), (5). See para.25–007.

[79] However, even if the trade takes place on a RIE it will not count as a market purchase if the market authorities have given only restricted permission for trading in the shares: s.693(3)(b).

Off-market purchases

17–019 Under s.694 an off-market purchase can be made only in pursuance of a contract the terms of which have been authorised by a resolution of the shareholders before it is entered into, often by way of an authorisation to the directors to enter into a repurchase.[80] Until 2013 a special resolution was required, but now an ordinary one will suffice.[81] The contract so approved may take the form of a "contingent purchase contract", i.e. one where the company's obligation or entitlement to purchase shares is subject to a contingency which may arise sometime in the future.[82] Contingent purchase contracts may be particularly useful because they enable the company to bind or entitle itself to purchase the shares of a director or employee upon termination of employment, or, as an alternative to the creation of a new class of redeemable shares, to meet the requirements of a potential investor in an unquoted company who wants assurance that he or she will be able to find a purchaser if the investor needs to realise the investment in the future.[83] The authorisation can subsequently be varied, revoked or renewed by a like resolution.[84]

In the case of a public company the authorising resolution must specify a date on which it is to expire and that date must not be later than five years after the passing of the resolution,[85] so that directors may not subsequently act on a "stale" authority, but no such rule applies to private companies.[86] Moreover, on any such resolution, whether of a public or private company, a member, holding shares to which the resolution relates, may not exercise the voting rights of those shares[87] and if the resolution would not have been passed but for those votes the resolution is ineffective.[88] This is an interesting example of the exclusion of interested shareholders from voting on resolutions in which they have a personal

---

[80] The contract may be entered into before approval, but in that case no shares may be purchased in pursuance of it before approval is obtained: s.694(2)(b). Under s.693A the requirements discussed in this section are somewhat modified in connection with purchases under an employee share scheme, but these variations are ignored here.

[81] The Government's reasons for downgrading minority protection were not particularly persuasive: BIS, *Implementation of Nuttall Review—Recommendation V: Government response to consultation* (February 2013), para.25 ("sufficient other safeguards"—but none as effective).

[82] CA 2006 s.694(3).

[83] There is the potential small disadvantage to the contingent purchase contract that the consideration for the contract or any variation of it must be provided out of distributable profits (s.705). However, the actual acquisition of the shares may be funded in accordance with the rules discussed in para.13–011.

[84] CA 2006 s.694(4)—but, presumably, not so as to affect the validity of a contract already concluded under the prior authorisation.

[85] CA 2006 s.694(5). Until 2009 the period was 18 months.

[86] BIS, *Implementation of Nuttall Review—Recommendation V: Government response to consultation* (February 2013), para.22, interprets s.694 as meaning that a private company cannot give advance approval at all but it is far from clear that this is what the section says.

[87] Or, on a written resolution, vote any shares held: s.695(2).

[88] CA 2006 s.695 which also provides (1) that it applies whether the vote is on a poll or by a show of hands; (2) that, notwithstanding any provision in the company's articles, any member may demand a poll; and (3) that a vote and a demand for a poll by a member's proxy is treated as a vote and demand by the member.

financial interest.[89] The resolution is also ineffective unless a copy of the contract or a memorandum of its terms is available for inspection by members, and in the case of a resolution passed at a meeting it must be available at the company's registered office for not less than 15 days before it is held.[90] The same requirements apply on a resolution to approve any variation of the contract[91] or to an agreement whereby the company releases its rights under the contract,[92] since both variation and release provide opportunities for favourable treatment of insiders just as the initial off-market contract does.

Essentially, the shareholder protection technique deployed in the case of an off-market purchase is the requirement for approval by the shareholders in advance of the terms of the re-purchase contract with the potential sellers excluded from voting.

Market purchases

Under s.701 a company (necessarily a public one) cannot make a market purchase of its own shares unless the making of such purchases has first been authorised by ordinary resolution of the company in general meeting.[93] Those whose shares will be purchased are not excluded from voting, for the very good reason that, with a market purchase, their identities will not be known in advance. For the same reason, the shareholders are asked to approve in this case, not a contract (even a contingent one) for the purchase of the shares of specified members, but an authorisation to the company (in practice, its directors) to go into the market in the future and acquire its shares on certain terms. The authorisation may be general or limited to shares of any particular class or description and may be conditional or unconditional[94] but it must specify the maximum number of shares to be acquired, the maximum and minimum prices,[95] and a date on which it is to expire, which must not be later than five years after the passing of the resolution.[96] Thus, the potential for a re-purchase resolution to create uncertainty about the appropriate market price of the share is reduced. Moreover, a copy of the resolution required by the section has to be sent to the Registrar within 15 days,[97] so that the market is formally aware of the company's **17–020**

89 See also s.239 for the exclusion of shareholders from voting on the ratification of their own wrongdoing as directors (para.10–115).

90 CA 2006 s.696. In the case of a written resolution the information is sent to the members at or before the copy of the proposed resolution: s.696(2)(a). In either case the names of members holding shares to which the contract relates must be disclosed. These rights, being for the benefit of the shareholders, may be waived by their unanimous agreement: *Kinlan v Crummin* [2006] EWHC 779 (Ch); [2007] B.C.C. 106.

91 CA 2006 ss.697–699.

92 CA 2006 s.700.

93 As in the case of off-market purchases, the authority may be varied, revoked or renewed by a like resolution: s.701(4).

94 CA 2006 s.701(2).

95 CA 2006 s.701(3). The resolution may specify a particular sum or a non-discretionary formula for calculating the price (for example, by reference to the market price of the shares): s.701(7).

96 CA 2006 s.701(5). Again, 18 months until 2009. But the purchase may be completed after the expiry date if the contract to buy was made before that date and the authorisation permitted the company to make a contract which would or might be executed after that date: s.701(6).

97 CA 2006 s.701(8), applying Ch.3 of Pt 3 of the Act to this ordinary resolution.

intentions or at least its powers, but in fact publicly traded companies today will have to make disclosure to the market much earlier than this under the ad hoc disclosure provision discussed in Ch.27. Thus, the directors are given a re-purchase authority but one which is exercisable only within the specified limits as to price, amount and timing.

Companies with a premium listing

17–021 In the case of a re-purchase effected by a company with a premium listing on the Main Market of the London Stock Exchange, the Listing Rules add a further and significant set of rules relating to the exercise by the company of the authority conferred upon it under the statutory provisions, whether the re-purchase is on- or off-market. In order to provide some degree of equality of treatment of shareholders in relation to substantial market re-purchases, which might affect the balance of power within the company, the Listing Rules require re-purchases of more than 15% of a class of the company's equity shares[98] to be by way of a tender offer to all shareholders of the class (i.e. to be on-market) or, alternatively, that the full terms of the re-purchase have been "specifically" approved by the shareholders.[99] A standard tender offer is an offer open to all the shareholders of the class on the same terms for a period of at least seven days, capable of being accepted by the shareholders pro rata with their existing holdings, and setting a fixed or maximum price for the purchase.[100] Thus, in a fixed price tender a shareholder holding 2% of the class may sell shares to the company up to the amount of 2% of the shares the company acquires through the tender process. Where the tender is at a maximum (but not a fixed) price, the shareholder has to indicate the price at which it is prepared to sell its shares to the company (a price not exceeding the maximum set by the company) and the company will implement the tender by accepting the lowest-priced offers first and continue up the price curve until it has fulfilled its tender. Even where the purchase is of less than 15% of the class, the company must either use the tender offer procedure or limit the price it is offering to not more than 5% above the market price of the shares over the five days preceding the purchase.[101] This limits the possibilities for favoured shareholders to sell their shares to the company at an above-market price.

Listing Rules also require the prior consent of any class of listed securities convertible or exchangeable into equity shares of the class to which the re-purchase proposal relates, unless the terms of issue of the security provided that the company might re-purchase the relevant equity shares.[102] Thus, in principle, the holders of convertible bonds will need to consent (by special resolution in a separate meeting) to a re-purchase of the equity shares into which the bonds are convertible. Further, where an off-market transaction is

[98] This includes preference shares which are participating in either dividend or distributions on a winding up: LR, Glossary Definition, "equity share capital".

[99] LR 12.4.2.

[100] LR, Glossary Definition, "tender offer".

[101] LR 12.4.1. If a higher limit is permitted under the market stabilisation rules (see para.30–037), that will replace the 5% figure.

[102] LR 12.4.7–8.

contemplated, the Listing Rules apply their rules concerning related-party transactions.[103] In that case, the LR exclude from voting on the resolution a wider range of persons than would the statute, because the statute excludes only those whose shares are to be re-purchased, whereas the Listing Rules also exclude their associates.[104] Finally, the FCA's Rules not surprisingly address market issues, such as the need for the market to be informed immediately of all the stages of a share re-purchase, from proposal to results[105]; and the need to avoid insider trading by excluding, subject to exceptions, re-purchases during prohibited trading periods.[106] In addition, the Investment Association guidelines[107] propose that companies should always act by special resolution, for both on-market and off-market purchases, so that listed companies, or at least those with large institutional shareholdings, will tend to follow this path, even if the statute does not formally require it.

Payments otherwise than by way of the price

It is conceivable that a company might pay money to a shareholder, not as the price for the shares purchased, but, for example, by way of consideration for: **17–022**

(1) acquiring any right (for example an option) to purchase under a contingent purchase contract;
(2) the variation of any off-market contract; or
(3) the release of any of the company's obligations under any off-market or market contract.[108]

Although such payments are not strictly part of the purchase price,[109] none of them is normal expenditure in the course of the company's business but rather constitute a distribution to members, and the payment would not have been made but for the fact that the company was minded to agree to purchase its shares. Such payments ought therefore to be treated, so far as practicable, in the same way as the purchase price. It is highly unlikely that a company would contemplate making a new issue of shares for the purpose of financing any such payment.[110] Hence, as a matter of creditor protection, the CA 2006 provides that they must be

[103] LR 12.3.1. The rule will catch on-market transactions as well if there was an understanding at the time of the resolution to repurchase that a particular related party would be able to take up the offer.

[104] LR 11.1.7(4)(b). "Associate" is defined widely in LR, Glossary Definition, "associate".

[105] LR 12.4.4–6. In addition the legislation requires ex post disclosure of the shares purchased in the directors' annual report: the Large and Medium-sized Companies and Groups (Accounts and Reports) Regulations 2008 (SI 2008/410) Sch.7 Pt 2.

[106] LR 12.2.1. The specific protections against liability for market abuse in the course of share buy-backs are dealt with in para.30–041.

[107] Investment Association, *Share Capital Management Guidelines* (2016), s.2.1.1.

[108] These difficulties do not arise in relation to redemptions. Nor does the issue of payment for a variation arise in relation to a market contract since these cannot be varied.

[109] Though, in case (1), the division of the total price between that paid for the option and that paid on its exercise may be arbitrary.

[110] Which, in case (1) and perhaps (2), would be made some time before any actual purchase and which in cases (1) and (3) might never be made at all.

paid for out of distributable profits only. If this is contravened, in cases (1) and (2) above, purchases are not lawful, and in case (3) the release is void.[111]

Treasury shares

17–023 The question of whether a company can itself hold the shares it acquires is another issue that arises only in relation to re-purchases of shares, since a cancellation rule is imposed in the case of redemptions.[112] Holding by the company of re-purchased shares ("treasury" shares) was not permitted under the original reforms of 1981, but the subsequent history has been one of progressive liberalisation. In 1998, the Government began consultation over the proposition that companies should be able to retain re-purchased shares and re-issue them, as required.[113] The main argument in favour of this reform was that it would permit companies to raise capital in small lots but at a full market price by re-selling the re-purchased shares as and when it was thought fit to do so. The argument against was that the freedom to re-sell would give boards of directors opportunities to engage in the manipulation of the company's share price, i.e. an argument based on investor protection rather than creditor protection. In 2001, the Government issued a further consultation document which accepted the idea in principle, but only for companies whose shares were traded on a public market, and consulted on further issues related to its implementation.[114] The manipulation danger was thought to be addressed by the separate provisions, contained in the FSMA 2000, dealing with market abuse,[115] and by the restriction on the amount of the treasury shares to 10% of any class (as then required by the Second Directive.

These proposals were implemented in 2003[116] and Ch.6 of Pt 18 of the CA 2006 re-stated them without substantive change. In 2009, however, following amendments to the Second Directive, the 10% limit was removed.[117] In 2013, the restriction to publicly traded shares was removed from the legislation,[118] so that all shares subject to re-purchase may be held in treasury and all companies may hold treasury shares (the previous approach having necessarily excluded private companies from holding shares in treasury).

The principal restriction today on holding treasury shares is that their re-purchase must have been financed out of distributable profits, even in the case of a private company.[119] This limitation seems to have been imposed because it was thought that there would be little demand for re-purchases out of new issues. This approach also simplifies the legal capital issues. Deployment of distributable

---

[111] CA 2006 s.705.

[112] CA 2006 s.688(a).

[113] See DTI, *Share Buybacks* (1998), URN 98/713.

[114] DTI, *Treasury Shares* (2001), URN 01/500.

[115] See Ch.30. Note also that a company cannot assign its rights under a contract to re-purchase shares (s.704), whether the shares are to be held in treasury or not, and this rule reduces the company's ability to trade in its own shares.

[116] By the Companies (Acquisition of Own Shares) (Treasury Shares) Regulations 2003 (SI 2003/1116) and the No.2 Regulations (SI 2003/3031).

[117] This was achieved through the repeal of s.725.

[118] CA 2006 s.741(1)–(2), as amended.

[119] CA 2006 s.724(1)(b).

profits has no impact on the company's capital accounts. Moreover, no balancing transfer to the capital redemption reserve is required where the re-purchased shares are not cancelled.

Sale of treasury shares

The underlying rationale of the treasury share scheme is achieved by the provision that treasury shares may at any subsequent time be sold by the company for cash.[120] When this happens, there is a sale by the company of existing shares, not an allotment of new shares. Consequently, the rules requiring shareholder authorisation of directors to allot shares do not apply,[121] thus facilitating speedy action by the directors. The same argument could be advanced in relation to pre-emption rights for shareholders on allotment, but the Act artificially extends the statutory concept of allotment so as to make pre-emption rights applicable on sales of ordinary shares held in treasury.[122] Although shareholders can waive pre-emption rights in advance, the fact that treasury shares are in principle subject to these rights is another example of the attachment of institutional shareholders to pre-emption rights.[123] **17–024**

Where the proceeds of the sale are equal to or less than the purchase price paid by the company, the money received by the company is to be treated as a realised profit and so potentially distributable by the company.[124] Since the shares will have been acquired out of distributable profits, which were thereby diminished, there can be no creditor-protection objection to the proceeds of the sale being treated as a realised profit. Any excess of the price received by the company over that paid by it, however, must be transferred to the share premium account.[125] This again seems correct. The increase in the price of the shares presumably represents an increase in the value of the company since the shares were purchased, so that the portion of the price obtained on re-sale which represents that increase in value should be treated as legal capital, just as the premium received by the company on the initial issue of shares would be so treated.[126]

Alternatively, the company may transfer treasury shares to meet the requirements of an employees' share scheme.[127] Or it may do what it could have done when it originally acquired the shares, i.e. cancel them.[128] In this latter case its share capital account must be reduced by the amount of the nominal value of

---

[120] CA 2006 s.727(1)(a). Cash is widely defined in s.727(2). There is one minor restriction: where a company has been the subject of a successful takeover offer (which included the treasury shares) and the bidder is using the statutory squeeze-out procedure, the treasury shares can be sold only to the bidder: s.727(4) and see para.28–073.

[121] See para.24–004.

[122] CA 2006 s.560(3).

[123] See para.24–006

[124] CA 2006 s.731(2).

[125] CA 2006 s.731(3). On the share premium account see paras 16–003 and 16–006.

[126] Of course, what is transferred to the share premium account on issue is the excess above the nominal value of the share (see para.16–006), whereas what is being transferred here is the excess above the purchase price.

[127] CA 2006 s.727(1)(b).

[128] CA 2006 s.729. It may be obliged to cancel them if the shares cease to be "qualifying shares": s.729(2),(3).

the shares cancelled and an equivalent amount transferred to the capital redemption reserve.[129] In the usual way the company has to inform the Registrar when it disposes of the shares (in either of the permitted ways) or cancels them, giving the necessary particulars.[130]

Whilst the shares are in treasury

17–025 Whilst the shares are still held by the company, it may not exercise any of the rights attached to them (notably the right to vote) and any such purported exercise is void,[131] so that the directors cannot strengthen their position in the general meeting of the company through the use of the treasury shares. Nor may a dividend be paid or any other distribution be made on the treasury shares.[132] However, the company may receive (fully paid) bonus shares in respect of the treasury shares, for otherwise the proportion of the equity represented by the treasury shares would decline—an uncovenanted benefit to the non-company shareholders. The bonus shares so allotted are to be treated as treasury shares purchased by the company at the time they were allotted.[133] On a subsequent sale of the bonus shares their purchase price is to be treated as nil, so that the full amount received for them must be transferred to the share premium account.[134] This seems correct, since the purpose of issuing bonus shares is to capitalise profits and so the sale price of the bonus shares needs to be added to the company's capital accounts and not be treated as a realised profit.[135]

Failure by the company to perform

17–026 So far, we have assumed that the company has discharged its obligation to redeem shares under the terms of their issue or to re-purchase shares as a result of a contract entered into with the shareholder.[136] Normally, this will be the case but it is conceivable that the company will not fulfil its obligations. This may occur because the company decides to break the contract or because it cannot lawfully perform it since, for example, the new issue of shares has not raised the proceeds expected and the company has inadequate available profits.[137] What are the remedies of a shareholder if the company does not perform the contract to redeem or purchase his shares? Section 735 provides that the company is not liable in

[129] CA 2006 ss.729(4) and 733(4). The directors may do this without following the reduction of capital procedure: s.729(5).

[130] CA 2006 ss.728 and 730.

[131] CA 2006 s.726(1)–(2).

[132] CA 2006 s.726(3)—including a distribution on a winding up.

[133] CA 2006 s.726(4)(a), (5). On capitalisation issues see para.16–024.

[134] CA 2006.731(4)(b).

[135] By the same token, the value of the treasury shares acquired by purchase will be reduced by the bonus issue, thus reducing the amount of realised profit arising on their re-sale.

[136] In the case of on-market re-purchases the mechanisms of the public market are likely to reduce the incidence of failure, since the exchange itself routinely becomes a central counterparty between buyer and seller, once the sale is agreed.

[137] The company could, presumably, protect itself from being in breach by expressly providing in the contract that the purchase is conditional upon its having the needed proceeds or sufficient profits.

damages in respect of any failure on its part to redeem or purchase.[138] It was thought that damages were not an appropriate remedy; it would result in the seller retaining his shares in, and membership of, the company and yet recovering damages (paid perhaps out of capital) from the company.[139] Any other right of the shareholder to sue the company is expressly preserved, but, even then, it is provided that the court shall not grant an order for specific performance (perhaps a more appropriate discretionary remedy) "if the company shows that it is unable to meet the costs of redeeming or purchasing the shares in question out of distributable profits".[140] "Other rights" would include the right to sue in debt for the price, if the company's breach takes the form of a failure to pay for the shares acquired. There is little doubt that also included is the right to sue for an injunction restraining the company from making a distribution of profits which would have the effect of making it unlawful for the company to perform its contract.

However, the ban on the recovery of damages may be capable of circumvention by using an indirect procedure to this end. In *British & Commonwealth Holdings Plc v Barclays Bank Plc*[141] a consortium of banks had promised to take the shares from the shareholder if the company could not redeem them and the company had promised to indemnify the banks in respect of actions by it which made it impossible for it to redeem. It was held that the section did not prevent the banks suing the company on its promises, even though the aim of the whole scheme was to ensure that the shareholder would be able to redeem even if the company had no distributable reserves. The case strongly suggests, but does not finally decide, that s.735 is concerned only with the range of remedies available to the shareholder rather than with ensuring that a company never in effect redeems shares out of capital.

A second issue which arises is the position if the company goes into liquidation at some point before the redemption re-purchase process has been fully completed. In relation to redemptions (but not re-purchases) one issue that may arise is the failure of the company to pay the money due, even though all the other stages in the redemption process have been completed. The statute expressly provides that, by agreement between the company and the redeeming shareholder (presumably as part of the terms of redemption or ad hoc), the amount payable may be deferred to "a date later than the redemption date", whilst for re-purchases the payment must be contemporaneous with the acquisition.[142] The correct analysis of this provision is that on the redemption date (i.e. when all the procedures for redemption have been completed, other than payment), the redeemed shareholder ceases to be a member of the company in relation to those

---

[138] CA 2006 s.735(2).

[139] In any event, the section does not protect the company against paying damages in all cases as a result of its failure to redeem. See *British & Commonwealth Holdings Plc v Barclays Bank Plc* [1995] B.C.C. 1059 CA (Civ Div).

[140] CA 2006 s.735(2)–(3). This ignores the possibility that it has adequate proceeds of a fresh issue but has nevertheless decided to break the contract. Surely the seller should then be entitled to specific performance?

[141] *British & Commonwealth Holdings Plc v Barclays Bank Plc* [1995] B.C.C. 1059 CA. The case also raises issues about financial assistance which are discussed at para.17–045.

[142] CA 2006 s.686(2) (redemption); s.691(2) (re-purchase)—with the limited exception for private companies in s.691(3).

shares and becomes instead an unsecured creditor of the company for the redemption price.[143] If liquidation of the company intervenes between the redemption date and the payment of the money, the former member will have priority over the other shareholders. In an insolvent liquidation this will probably not improve the former member's position significantly, since s.74(2)(f) of the IA 1986 subordinates debts due to a member "in his character as a member" to all other creditor claims on the company, so that the former member does not obtain priority over any creditors. However, if the liquidation is solvent, i.e. the company can meet all the creditor claims but does not have sufficient assets return capital to the shareholders in full, this limited priority may be valuable.[144]

Assuming there is a contract for redemption or re-purchase which has not been fully executed by the company when liquidation intervenes, the CA 2006 provides that the terms of redemption or purchase may be enforced against the company in winding up,[145] but subject to the restriction on specific performance noted above. Once again, however, the shareholder will gain little or nothing by enforcing the contract if the winding up is an insolvent liquidation since the CA 2006 follows the IA 1986 and makes the member a deferred creditor. Any claim in respect of the purchase price is postponed to the claims of all other creditors—and, indeed, to those of other shareholders whose shares carry rights (whether as to capital or income) which are preferred to the rights as to capital of the shares to be redeemed or purchased.[146] Moreover, even this limited right may not be enforced in liquidation if the terms of redemption or purchase provided for performance to take place at a date later than that of the commencement of the winding-up. The section thus aims at contracts which should have, but did not, lead to the redemption or re-purchase of the shares before liquidation intervened. Even then, the right is removed if during the period beginning with the date when redemption or purchase was to take place and ending with the commencement of the winding-up, the company did not have distributable profits equal in value to the redemption or purchase price.[147] In these cases it appears the member is treated in the winding-up as if there were no obligation on the company to redeem or purchase the shares and as if he or she were still a member of the company.

---

143 *Pearson v Primeo Fund* [2017] UKPC 19; [2017] B.C.C. 552.

144 In the Cayman Islands (from which the *Primeo* case—[2017] B.C.C. 552—originated) redeemable preference shares are used as a technique for making investments in mutual funds. Such mutual funds have limited creditors but extensive obligations to shareholder/investors. In this case the fund was a feeder fund for a fund run in New York by Bernie Madoff, which turned out to be a Ponzi scheme. The Cayman fund ended up with assets more than adequate to meet its creditors' claims but less than adequate to protect the shareholder/investors from the full consequences of the investment in the Madoff fund. An investor, who had redeemed, admittedly on the basis of an inaccurate but binding valuation, before the truth emerged and before the liquidation of the fund but had not been paid, could thus claim the amount due in priority to the claims of other investors. See also *Pearson v Primeo Fund* [2017] B.C.C. 552 for the failure of another proposed mechanism for scaling down the unpaid investors' claims.

145 CA 2006 s.735(4).

146 CA 2006 s.735(6). In a solvent liquidation the shareholder may be worse off than if shares had not been redeemed or purchased, if the share gave a right to participate in surplus assets but the purchase or redemption price did not reflect the value of this right.

147 CA 2006 s.735(5).

Conclusion

Even if one takes the view that legal capital is a central doctrine of company law, the above discussion has shown that it is relatively easy to reconcile it with the acquisition by a company of its own shares, provided certain conditions are met. In particular, acquisitions out of distributable profits, coupled with an appropriate adjustment to the company's capital accounts, present no threat to the integrity of the doctrine of legal capital. We should note, however, that the facility for a private company to purchase shares out of capital, provided the decision is supported by what is, in effect, a solvency statement, is a legislative move towards the adoption of an alternative to legal capital as the primary protection mechanism for creditors. 17–027

Even if redemptions and re-purchases can be structured so as to preserve the company's legal capital, there may be other risks to creditors arising from them. As a company buys back its shares, its gearing (i.e. its ratio of debt to equity) proportionately increases and at the same time its assets decrease by the amount paid for the shares. This increases the riskiness of the company's business, because interest on debt normally has to be paid come what may, while dividends on ordinary shares can be suspended in a crisis. The company will now have fewer assets through which to generate the earnings needed to meet its debt obligations. This potential problem will be magnified if the company funds the redemptions or buy-backs by taking on additional debt, as often happens. However, these issues are not confined to redemptions and re-purchases. They arise equally to dividend payment funded by debt and so the two ways of returning value to shareholders need to be considered together.[148]

REDUCTION OF CAPITAL

Why is reduction of capital allowed?

Acquisition by a company of its shares through redemption or re-purchase is akin to a distribution to shareholders, discussed in the next chapter, to the extent that assets are returned by the company to its shareholders. Unlike a distribution, which is a gratuitous disposition by the company, in a redemption or re-purchase the company receives shares in exchange for the assets. However, if the shares are immediately cancelled, the acquisition has a largely gratuitous character; and the cancellation generates a reduction in the company's legal capital yardstick. Only if the re-purchased shares are held in treasury does the company obtain value for the price paid, to the extent that the re-purchased shares can be sold again to investors. 17–028

A reduction of capital, by contrast, does not necessarily involve a return of assets to shareholders, though it may pave the way for such action, either immediately or in the future. What is reduced in a reduction of capital are the

[148] See para.18–021.

amounts stated in the company's capital accounts.[149] The initial puzzle is why the company should be permitted by the law to take this step at all. Having built a creditor-protecting distribution rule on the numbers in the company's balance sheet and especially those in its capital accounts, why should the law allow the company to reduce those numbers so as to facilitate a distribution to shareholders, either immediately or in the future? More generally, the creditors might conceivably rely on the numbers stated in the capital accounts as an indication of its creditworthiness, that is, as indicating the level of the shareholders' commitment to the company, and so feel misled if those numbers are changed in a downwards direction. However, the law has long recognised that it is legitimate to reduce capital in some circumstances, subject to safeguards to protect creditors and to deal with intra-shareholder conflicts, especially conflicts among different classes of shareholder. The reduction of capital rules thus aim to identify those circumstances and the relevant protections. In recent years, the rules have become more generous to companies wishing to take this step.

17–029 The following are examples of situations where a reduction of the numbers in the capital accounts might be thought to be legitimate. Suppose the company has traded unsuccessfully, so that its net asset value (assets less liabilities) is less than its legal capital. However, the company has found a new investor who is prepared to inject equity into the company so that it can try an alternative business plan. In return, however, the new investor wants to make sure that any profits made in the future are available to be paid out immediately and that he or she obtains the fair share of those profits. Thus, the investor requires that, before the issue of new shares is made, the value of the company's legal capital accounts is reduced to reflect the value of the existing shareholders' equity in the company. In short, the new investor does not want the new investment to fund the past losses of the company nor that existing shareholders should participate in future profits except to the extent that their investments have survived the company's previous trading misfortunes. Both these aims can be achieved if the company's legal capital is reduced to the level of its current shareholders' equity.[150] For example, if the company's net asset value is half its legal capital, the shares having all been issued at par, equilibrium could be achieved by reducing the nominal value of the existing shares by half. The new investor would then obtain twice the number of shares—again assuming issuance at par—when the new money is injected compared to the pre-reduction situation. This ensures fairness as between old and new investors as well as allowing future profits to be distributed immediately they are earned. There is no particular reason for the creditors to object to this procedure: any contribution by the new investor to the assets of the company

---

[149] CA 2006 s.641, introducing the reduction procedures, in terms applies only to the share capital account, but the share premium account and capital redemption reserve are treated as share capital for the purposes of the reduction procedure: ss.610(4) and 733(6).

[150] There are other techniques which could be used to achieve the same result, such as issuance at par of a new class of share to the new investor where the new class has a lower par value than and priority as to dividends over the existing shares, but issuing shares of the same class after a reduction may reduce the risk of intra-shareholder disputes in the future. Or the company may split its existing shares into two classes, with one of the classes rendered valueless though the assignment of very minimal rights to it, while the other class carries whatever value the company truly has. See para.16–004.

improves their position because their claims on the company's assets have priority over those of the shareholders (old and new).

A situation at the opposite end of the spectrum is where the company has more equity capital than it needs and wishes to reduce its capital by repaying the holders of a particular class of share. Here, the reduction of capital is indeed accompanied by a return of assets to the shareholders. One might say that the return of assets to the shareholders is the driving force behind the transaction and the reduction of capital is the consequent adjustment to the balance sheet which is necessary to reflect what has been done. Here, reduction of capital appears as a functional substitute for a redemption or re-purchase of shares, as discussed in the previous section of this chapter. However, there is one significant difference. The outcome of the reduction procedure is a decision which is binding on all the shareholders in question. This may also be the case in a redemption (depending on how the terms of issue were drafted), but it is not the case in a re-purchase where, as we have seen, the statutory procedure simply makes it lawful for company and shareholder to agree to the re-purchase.[151] In this use of the reduction procedure, since assets are being returned to shareholders, the interests of creditors can be said to be engaged, whilst the decision as to which shareholders are to be squeezed out of the company and on what terms may provide fertile ground for intra-shareholder conflicts.

The statutory procedures

For many years successive Companies Acts have provided a procedure through which the reduction can be effected and the claims of shareholders and creditors that the proposed reduction is adverse to their interests can be evaluated and protection provided, if it is due.[152] Before the passage of the CA 2006 there was only one procedure. The general principle was that a company might reduce its capital if the proposal was adopted by a special resolution of the shareholders and confirmed by the court. However, a private company rarely needed to resort to that procedure. The main situation in which a private company may wish to reduce capital is when it needs to buy out a retiring member of the company or to return to the personal representatives a deceased member's share of the capital, but has insufficient profits available for dividend to enable it to do so except out of capital. As we have seen above,[153] when companies were empowered to purchase their own shares, special concessions were made to private companies to enable them to do so out of capital and without the need for a formal reduction. This provided a substitute for capital reduction which met the needs of private **17–030**

[151] See para.17–008.

[152] Reduction of capital is to be distinguished from the situation where the company simply divides its share capital into shares of a smaller nominal value (see fn.150) or consolidates them into shares of a larger nominal value, but where the aggregate nominal value of the shares (and thus the company's share capital) remains the same, though there is a smaller or a larger number of shares representing that aggregate. These steps present no creditor protection issues and the matter is one for the shareholders alone (s.618). However, there are potential issues of intra-shareholder conflict with divisions: see *Greenhalgh v Arderne Cinemas Ltd* [1946] 1 All E.R. 512 CA; and para.13–017.

[153] See para.17–012.

companies in many cases.[154] However, the CA 2006 introduced an alternative procedure for the reduction of capital by private companies, for which court confirmation is not needed, but it left in place the special rules enabling private companies to re-purchase shares out of capital. In the case of public companies, the CA 2006 left the previous law largely unchanged.

Whichever procedure is used, the Act provides that a company may reduce its share capital "in any way"[155] but it then sets out three typical situations, which are important because of their different implications for creditor protection. The three situations are: (1) by reducing or extinguishing the amount of any uncalled liability on its shares[156]; (2) by cancelling any paid-up share capital "which is lost or unrepresented by available assets"[157]; and (3) by paying off any paid-up share capital which is in excess of the company's wants.[158] Situations (2) and (3) are exemplified by the examples discussed in para.17–029. In situation (1), which arises only where the company has issued shares as not fully paid up, a shareholder's liability to the company is terminated and so the interests of the creditors are engaged, as are the interests of the shareholders whose commitments to the company are fully paid up.[159]

Procedure applying to all companies

17–031 Under the procedure applying to all companies a reduction of capital requires a special resolution of the members and confirmation by the court.[160] It is the requirement for court approval which is supposed to provide the necessary protection for creditors (as well as for minority shareholders insofar as the supermajority vote requirement does not achieve that end). Obtaining shareholder consent is most likely to raise tricky issues where there is more than one class of share and the reduction does not affect all the classes rateably. If the rights of a class of shareholders are affected by the reduction proposal, the separate consent of that class will be required under the "class rights" provisions discussed in paras 13–014 onwards.[161] In particular, companies have often wanted to cancel the shares issued to preference shareholders, whose entitlement to a fixed

[154] CA 2006 s.617(5) makes it clear that a repurchase or redemption of shares in accordance with the Act does not fall foul of the prohibition on altering share capital contained in that section.

[155] CA 2006 s.641(3).

[156] CA 2006 s.641(4)(a)—in the unlikely event of its having uncalled capital.

[157] CA 2006 s.641(4)(b)(i). Technically share capital (a notional liability) cannot be "lost" (see paras 16–001 onwards) but may well be "unrepresented by available assets". However, this does not seem to have bothered the courts which have interpreted "lost" to mean that the value of the company's net assets has fallen below the amount of its capital (i.e. its issued share capital, and, if any, its share premium account and capital redemption reserve) and that this "loss" is likely to be permanent.

[158] CA 2006 s.641(4)(b)(ii).

[159] Where there is a reduction of capital by means of extinguishing uncalled capital, it is normal accounting practice to create a reserve to reflect the reduction. Section 654 says the reserve is to be undistributable, but allows the Secretary of State to specify cases where the prohibition does not apply. Making ample use of this power reg.3 of the Companies (Reduction of Share Capital) Order 2008 (SI 2008/1915) says the reserve is to be treated as a realised profit under both procedures, unless the court order, the company's articles or a company resolution specify otherwise.

[160] CA 2006 s.641(1)(b). The previous requirement that the company have power under its articles to reduce its capital has been removed.

[161] The issue of how to identify of the rights of preference shareholders is discussed in para.6–007.

preference dividend has moved out of line with interest rates in the market, so that the contribution of those shareholders can be re-financed more cheaply. The courts have held that mere cancellation of preference shares does not infringe their rights, provided the preference shareholders are treated in accordance with the rights they would have on a winding up of the company.[162] Thus, the question becomes whether the reduction of the preference shares meets this test. Although the court probably has discretion to approve a reduction of shares which infringes class rights and which has not secured the consent of that class, it is highly unlikely to do so.[163] Where there is only one class of share, the minority's protections are less extensive,[164] though they do have the chance to oppose the confirmation of the reduction by the court under the reduction procedure.

Creditor objection

Creditor protection is provided through the mechanism of court confirmation of the reduction proposal.[165] The practical pressure generated by the procedure used to be towards making the company discharge or secure all the creditors' claims outstanding at the time of the reduction before application was made to the court for confirmation, these being the remedies the court could order in favour of an objecting creditor.[166] In order to avoid the difficulty of identifying every one of a fluctuating body of trade creditors, companies often felt obliged to short-circuit the objection procedure and arrange for a sufficient sum to be deposited with or guaranteed by a bank or insurance company to meet the claims of all the unsecured creditors before applying for court confirmation. The Company Law Review (CLR) thought that the interests of creditors were thus often over-protected, because creditors obtained either early repayment of or security for their previously unsecured debts, whether or not their chances of repayment had been adversely affected by the repayment of capital.[167] However, its proposal for reform did not make its way into the CA 2006. Nevertheless, the story did not end there. In 2006 the EU amended the Second Directive's provisions on reduction of capital[168] so as to make them less protective of creditors. The Government's initial reaction was not to take advantage of this new flexibility,[169] **17–032**

[162] The proposition that the preference shareholders are treated in breach of their rights by cancellation of their shares and deprivation of a favourable dividend entitlement was decisively rejected by the Court of Appeal in *Re Chatterly-Whitfield Collieries* [1948] 2 All E.R. 593, so that the issue has become whether the terms of the reduction are in accordance with the rights which they would have on a winding up. The effect of the decision was to make preference shares in effect redeemable by the company, even if not formally issued as redeemable, provided the company could satisfy the requirements of the reduction procedure. It is to be noted that a reduction in order to replace preference shares with a cheaper form of financing does not clearly fall within any of the three categories specified in s.641(4) but it does fall within s.641(3)—reduction "in any way": *Re Hunting Plc* [2004] EWHC 2591 (Ch); [2005] 2 B.C.L.C. 211.

[163] CA 2006 s.645 in terms requires only a resolution of the company, not of the class in question.

[164] These possibilities are also discussed in Ch.13.

[165] CA 2006 s.645(1).

[166] CA 2006 s.648(2).

[167] Strategic, para.5.4.5.

[168] Directive 2006/68 amending art.32 of Directive 77/91 on coordination of safeguards [1977] OJ L26/1 (now art.36 of the 2012 version of that Directive).

[169] DTI, *Implementation of the Companies Act 2006* (February 2007), Ch.6.

but after consultation changed its mind.[170] The reduction of capital provisions of the CA 2006 were then amended by statutory instrument[171] so as to make the procedure less protective of creditors, thus achieving, albeit by slightly different wording, the policy recommended by the CLR.

The crucial change is that it is no longer the case that every creditor is entitled to object to the reduction of capital who, at the relevant date, has a debt or claim which would be admissible in proof were the company being wound up.[172] Under the prior law this was the position where the reduction fell within cases (1) or (3) above[173] or analogous cases, i.e. where the company proposed to return excess capital or amend the liability to meet calls.[174] Now, in order to obtain a right of objection the creditor, upon whom the burden of proof lies, must demonstrate not only the existence of situations (1) or (3) and an admissible debt or claim but, in addition, "a real likelihood that the reduction would result in the company being unable to discharge the debt or claim when it fell due".[175] The list of objecting creditors will, in future, thus consist of those who have demonstrated that their claim is subject to real risk of non-payment if the reduction goes ahead, so that the pressure on the company to settle the claims of all creditors should be lessened significantly.

Confirmation by the court

17–033 In principle, the court is required to settle a list of creditors and to do so as far as possible without requiring an application from a creditor to be included on the list.[176] However, this rarely happens.[177] In the past this was because creditors were repaid or secured before confirmation was sought, as indicated in the previous paragraph. It would be an unwanted side-wind of the introduction of the "real likelihood" test if court consideration of the claims of objecting creditors became routine. In fact, the court has power to order that the creditor objection procedure shall not apply in a particular case.[178] Under the new test companies are likely to rely on evidence about their business prospects over the next few

[170] *The Government response to the consultation on the implementation of amendments to the 2nd Company Law Directive* (28 October 2007).

[171] The Companies (Share Capital and Acquisition by Company of Own Shares) Regulations 2009 (SI 2009/2022) reg.3. The Secretary of State has power under s.657 to amend a number of the elements in Pt 17 of the Act.

[172] Not all claims a creditor might make in the future are provable: see *Re Liberty International Plc* [2010] EWHC 1060 (Ch); [2010] 2 B.C.L.C. 665 (debtor liable only if a third party exercises a discretion so as to impose the liability).

[173] See para.17–030. In case (2) there is no right of objection, unless the court so orders: s.645(4).

[174] See s.645(2). The court has a dispensing power under s.645(4), but this was rarely used against creditors whose claims had not been secured.

[175] CA 2006 s.646(1)(b). That likelihood, "beyond the merely possible, but short of the probable", will be more difficult to demonstrate the further into the future the debt falls due: *Re Liberty International* [2010] 2 B.C.L.C. 665 at [19]–[20].

[176] CA 2006 s.646(2)(3).

[177] In *Re Royal Scottish Assurance Plc, Petitioner* [2011] CSOH 2; 2011 S.L.T. 264, Lord Glennie stated that this had not been done, in either Scotland or England, since 1949.

[178] CA 2006 s.645(2)—this was the formal basis on which the prior practice avoided the creditor objection procedure. Under s.645(3) the court may also order that the procedure shall not apply to particular class or classes of creditor because of "the special circumstances of the case".

years as grounds for dispensing with the objection procedure. This is a form of non-statutory solvency certification. To date the courts have been disposed to accept such evidence as grounds for disapplication, stressing in particular that the test is whether the reduction of capital creates a "real risk" of non-payment for the creditor, so that the creditor's continued exposure to the general risks of the company's business is not as such permissible ground for objection.[179]

Even if there are no objecting creditors or their objections have been dealt with, it appears that the court must still have regard to creditor interests when deciding whether to confirm the reduction "on such terms and conditions as it thinks fit". This is shown by the case law concerning reductions of capital because that capital was not represented by available assets (i.e. case (2) above). Here, there is no right of objection for creditors, unless the court so orders.[180] Nevertheless, the courts might regard the interests of creditors in such a case as requiring protection at the confirmation stage. A standard situation falling within case (2) is where a company is required to write down the value of an asset in its accounts (for example, a loan which the company now thinks is unlikely to be re-paid), thus extinguishing its distributable profits. It then wishes to reduce its share capital (and probably its share premium account) so as to permit the distribution of future profits. However, a variation on this theme is where, on the facts, it is possible (and foreseeable at the time of the write-down) that the asset may recover in value. In that case the court may impose a condition that any amount recovered in the future should be put in an undistributable reserve. However, it seems that this will be required only if needed to protect the creditors existing at the time of the write-down[181] and that future creditors are regarded as sufficiently protected by the publicity requirements for the reduction of capital (below).

The court may make ad hoc publicity requirements part of its order confirming the reduction, including the requirement that, for a specified period, the company include the words "and reduced" in its name.[182] Upon delivery by the company of the court order and a statement of its capital,[183] as now reduced, to the Registrar, that official will register and certify them; the registration must be publicised as the court directs; and the reduction takes effect only upon registration.[184] It is conceivable that the reduction in capital would mean that the company no longer met the minimum capital requirements for a public company, in which case it must re-register as a private company before the Registrar will register the reduction (unless the court orders otherwise).[185] **17–034**

[179] *Re Vodafone Group Plc* [2014] EWHC 1357 (Ch); [2014] B.C.C. 554; *Re Sportech Plc, Petitioner* [2012] CSOH 58; 2012 S.L.T. 895; *Re Royal Scottish Assurance Plc* 2011 S.L.T. 264.

[180] CA 2006 s.645(4).

[181] *Re Grosvenor Press Plc* [1985] B.C.L.C. 286; cf. *Re Jupiter House Investments (Cambridge) Ltd* [1985] B.C.L.C. 222.

[182] CA 2006 s.648(3)(4).

[183] Equivalent to that required on an allotment of shares.

[184] CA 2006 s.649(3).

[185] CA 2006 s.650. An expedited re-registration procedure, which dispenses with shareholder authorisation, may be used if the court authorises it (s.651). The basis for this provision is presumably the shareholder authorisation which was a necessary step in the reduction procedure.

Minority shareholders as well may seek—or the court may provide—protection at the confirmation stage, even if the requirements for shareholder approval have been met before application to the court. The two main requirements for shareholder protection which the court will insist on are that the reduction treat the shareholders equitably and that the reduction proposal be properly explained to the shareholders who approved it. It is established that the court must be satisfied on these matters, even if the petition for confirmation is unopposed, as it often will be.[186] However, before a conclusion of inequitable treatment is reached, a significant risk to those shareholders arising out of the reduction must be identified. Thus, in *Re Ransomes Plc*[187] a substantial reduction in share premium account was permitted over the objections of preference shareholders, in order to permit a distribution to the ordinary shareholders, on the grounds that the preference shareholders' entitlements to dividend and return of capital (non-participating in both cases) were not put at risk by the proposed distribution. Even after the proposed distribution, the company would have assets and projected profits well in excess of what was required to meet the preference shareholders' entitlements. In other words, the protection for both creditors and shareholders now revolves around the same general notion: their objections will be plausible if the reduction is likely significantly to harm their entitlements. The apparently strict procedural requirements of proper explanation have been somewhat qualified by the adoption of a "no difference" rider, i.e. the court may forgive procedural inadequacies if convinced that following the correct procedure would have led to the same result.[188]

Procedure available to private companies only

17–035 The provisions for reduction of capital without court confirmation apply only to private companies. These were introduced in 2006 to mitigate the delay and cost involved in court confirmation. The CLR wished to make this procedure available to public companies as well, but with the rider that creditors entitled to object to the reduction could invoke the court to veto or modify the reduction.[189] In place of court confirmation reliance would be put on a solvency statement made by the directors. For both types of company the procedure with court confirmation (above) would be kept as an alternative, because it allows directors to avoid the potential liabilities arising out of the solvency statement.[190] However, in the event the CA 2006 made the procedure of reduction without court approval available to private companies only (which retain the option of using the court-based

[186] *Re Ransomes Plc* [2000] B.C.C. 455; [1999] 2 B.C.L.C. 591 CA (Civ Div) at 602.

[187] *Re Ransomes Plc* [1999] 1 B.C.L.C. 775 Ch D (Companies Ct) (affirmed on appeal; see previous note). See also *Re Ratners Group Plc* (1988) 4 B.C.C. 293 Ch D (Companies Ct); and *Re Thorn EMI Plc* (1988) 4 B.C.C. 698 Ch D (Companies Ct) (reduction of share premium account to write off goodwill arising out of the same transaction as generated the premium).

[188] See previous note—a hypothetical and sometimes difficult judgment, which the courts should use sparingly.

[189] *Company Formation and Capital Maintenance*, para.3.27. However, in the absence of creditor objection, court involvement would not be necessary.

[190] Completing, para.7.9.

procedure).[191] Where the private company chooses not to use the court-based procedure, there is no right for creditors to invoke the court if they think their interests are threatened by the proposed reduction. They, like minority shareholders, have to rely on the solvency statement required of directors in the out-of-court procedure.

Solvency statement

Under the procedure available to private companies only, a special resolution of the shareholders is still required,[192] as discussed above, with the need to hold separate meetings of each class of shares whose rights are varied by the proposed reduction. However, the resolution of the members is to be supported by a solvency statement from the directors rather than confirmed by the court. The essence of the solvency statement is that to some degree it transfers responsibility for the reduction from the court to the directors of the company. This is a gain for the company in terms of speed and cost, but a potential risk for the directors, in so far as personal liability attaches to their approval of the solvency statement as we see in para.17–038. The solvency statement, which must accompany the resolution, is not an entirely novel device in British company law. It was required as part of the (now repealed) "whitewash" procedure available to private companies wishing to give financial assistance for the purchase of their own shares.[193] Something similar is also to be found in the rules governing share re-purchases by private companies from capital.[194] However, unlike the re-purchase statement, the solvency statement on a reduction of capital is not required to be audited. **17–036**

The solvency statement is a statement by each director of the company, who must each sign it.[195] Each director asserts in it that he or she has formed an opinion on two matters. The first relates to the company's current financial position at the time the statement is made and is to the effect that "there is no ground on which the company could be found unable to pay (or otherwise discharge) its debts".[196] The second relates to the future and covers a period of one year after the date of the statement. The second opinion comes in two

[191] DTI, *Company Law Reform* (March 2005), Cm.6456, para.4.8 rejected the application of the alternative procedure to public companies. It was thought that the possibility of creditor objection and thus court involvement would lead public companies to opt for the court-confirmation route, though it is not clear that this is a strong argument against making the option available to public companies.

[192] CA 2006 s.641(1)(a).

[193] CA 1985 s.155. The financial assistance rules no longer apply to private companies: see para.17–057.

[194] See para.17–050.

[195] CA 2006 s.643(1), (3) and the Companies (Reduction of Share Capital) Order 2008 (SI 2008/1915) reg.2. Although the section does not extend to shadow directors, the term "director" does include de facto directors: see s.250. In *Re In a Flap Envelope Co Ltd* [2003] EWHC 3047 (Ch); [2003] B.C.C. 487, a case arising under the financial assistance whitewash procedure, a director who resigned for part of a day in order that the statement could be signed by his replacement, was held to be a de facto director during this period and thus liable to make the statement required under those provisions.

[196] CA 2006 s.643(1)(a).

alternative forms.[197] If it is intended to commence the winding up of the company within a year,[198] then the required opinion is that the company will be able to pay or otherwise discharge its debts within 12 months of the winding up. In any other case, it is that the company will able to pay (or discharge) its debts as they fall due within the 12 months after the date of the statement. The required opinion relates only to the payment or discharge of debts (i.e. claims on the company to pay a liquidated sum). However, the directors are required to take into account contingent and prospective liabilities when forming their opinions.[199] The obligation to take into account prospective liabilities is hardly surprising, since these are liabilities which will certainly become due in the future (though it may not be clear precisely when). Contingent liabilities are those which may (or may not) arise in the future because of an existing legal obligation or state of affairs. Working out how to take the latter into account is clearly a more demanding exercise.

17–037 In *BTI 2014 LLC v Sequana SA*[200] Rose J (whose judgment was not subject to appeal on this point) held that it was not enough to meet the statutory requirements for the solvency statement that the directors honestly held the opinions required to be set out in it. It was necessary for the court to go further and be satisfied that the directors had applied the tests correctly when coming to the opinions stated and in consequence to examine the facts in relation to each director in order to establish whether this was the case or not. One consequence of this approach was that it generated the possibility that an honestly held solvency declaration which has been acted on might be held at a later date—perhaps a much later one—to have been ineffective, with the result that the legality of subsequent corporate transactions was thrown into doubt. However, in the view of the judge, the validity of the solvency statement did not turn on whether the directors had reasonable grounds for their conclusions, provided they had applied the correct tests. Negligent application of the tests might expose the directors to criminal liability (see below), but did not undermine the validity of the solvency statement, unless their negligence was so gross as to suggest that the opinion was not in fact held.

The main question in this case was the correct method for directors to handle contingent and prospective liabilities when forming a view that at the time of the statement "there is no ground on which the company could be found unable to pay (or otherwise discharge) its debts".[201] The court rejected both the extreme approaches, i.e. assuming the worst case, that all the contingent and prospective liabilities materialise in full, and, on the other hand, not requiring the directors to consider the matter further if proper provision has been made for these liabilities in the company's accounts. The up-shot seems to be that these are matters to which the directors are required to apply their judgement as persons of business

[197] CA 2006 s.643(1)(b).

[198] So that the reduction of capital is a prelude to a winding up, as in *Scottish Insurance Corp Ltd v Wilsons & Clyde Coal Co Ltd* 1949 S.L.T. 230 HL.

[199] CA 2006 s.643(2).

[200] *BTI 2014 LLC v Sequana SA* [2016] EWHC 1686 (Ch); [2017] Bus. L.R. 82 at [311] onwards. Her arguments seem equally applicable to the directors' statement required when a private company re-purchases shares out of capital. See para.17–014.

[201] CA 2006 s.643(1)(a). The facts of the *Sequana* case are given at para.18–014.

experience and what needs to be shown to support the validity of the statement is that they did indeed apply their judgement to the facts of the case. In the end, it appears to be the directors' judgement, for example about the likelihood of liabilities materialising and their magnitude and the likely availability of resources to meet those liabilities at the time they materialise, which is decisive.

A copy of the solvency statement must be provided to the members voting on the reduction resolution so that the resolution can be said to be "supported by" the solvency statement.[202] How the resolution is provided differs according to whether the vote is to be at a meeting or by written resolution.[203] The solvency statement must precede the date on which the resolution is passed by no more than 15 days and, if this is not the case, it appears the resolution cannot be said to be supported by a solvency statement. Thus, if the date for passing the resolution slips for one reason or another, the directors will be required to review and re-issue their solvency statement. After the passing of the resolution, the company has a further 15 days to file the copy of the resolution and the solvency statement and a current statement of the company's capital with the Registrar.[204] It is only with the registration of these documents by the Registrar (thus making them publicly available) that the reduction is effective.[205] Failure to deliver the documents to the Registrar on time does not affect the validity of the resolution but it does constitute an offence on the part of every officer of the company in default.[206]

Remedies

The question of the legal consequences and remedies if the procedures for reducing capital are not fully complied with receives different answers under the court confirmation and out-of-court procedures. Under the court approval procedure, objections, procedural and substantive, are expected to be made to the court before it confirms the reduction proposed. Once the court has confirmed the proposal and the registration process has been completed, legal recourse is very limited. With regard to the validity of the reduction, the Act specifically provides that the registrar's certificate[207] is conclusive evidence that the requirements of the Act with respect to the reduction have been complied with and that the company's capital has been reduced.[208] In other words, the reduction transaction has been validly completed. It is just conceivable that the directors putting forward a reduction proposal which is confirmed by the court could be acting in **17–038**

[202] CA 2006 s.642(1).

[203] CA 2006 s.642(2)–(3). Getting these communication provisions wrong does not render the resolution invalid, provided s.642(1) can still be said to have been complied with (CA 2006 s.642(4)). However, it is an offence on the part of every officer in default to fail to comply with this requirement: s.644(7)–(8), but liability is restricted to a fine.

[204] CA 2006 s.644(1)–(2) and the Companies (Share Capital and Acquisition by Company of Own Shares) Regulations 2009 (SI 2009/2022) reg.10.

[205] CA 2006 s.644(3)–(4).

[206] CA 2006 s.644(6)–(7). Nor does an inadvertent error, even on of considerable size, affect the validity of the reduction: *BTI 2014 LLC v Sequana SA* [2017] Bus. L.R. 82 at [341] onwards.

[207] Of the registration of the court order and the company's new statement of capital: see para.17–034.

[208] CA 2006 s.649(6).

breach of general duties to the company, but they will be protected to a considerable extent in practice by the shareholder resolution and by the subsequent examination of the scheme by the court.

In relation to the out-of-court procedure also, the solvency statement and the new statement of capital have to be delivered to the registrar, without which the resolution and thus the reduction of capital does not take effect.[209] However, in this case the registrar does not issue a certificate of registration, still less one providing conclusive evidence that the requirements of the CA 2006 have been complied with. All the Act provides is that certain minor failures to comply with the required procedures do not affect the validity of the resolution.[210] So, the question arises about the legal consequences of a failure not falling within one of the categories expressly dealt with in the Act, such as the failure of one or more of the directors to sign the solvency statement or the application by the directors of the wrong tests for judging the company's position.[211] As ever, there are two main questions: is the transaction valid and are the directors liable?

The statutory rules on out-of-court reductions contain one strong, but far from comprehensive, provision about the legal consequences of failure to comply with its requirements. It is a criminal offence, punishable with imprisonment, for a director to make a solvency statement without having reasonable grounds for the opinions expressed in it—unless the solvency statement is not delivered to the Registrar, so that the reduction does not take effect.[212] This criminalises purely negligent conduct on the part of the director, an unusual step, for the CA 2006 normally confines serious criminal sanctions to knowing or reckless misstatements. This provision is an indication of the importance attached by the legislature to the accuracy of the solvency statement. Beyond that, the reduction provisions are silent on the consequences of failure to comply with them.

17–039 In some cases, the purported reduction of capital will infringe the principle that a company must not acquire its own shares, for example, where the company purports to repay excess capital to its shareholders in exchange for its shares. A reduction of capital is excluded from the "no acquisition" principle but only where it is "duly made".[213] We noted in para.17–002 that a purported transaction in breach of the principle constitutes a criminal offence on the part of both the company and its directors and the transaction itself is void. The invalidity of the transaction generates potential liability to the company for both the directors who proposed the transaction and the shareholders who receive the company's money. Alternatively, a return of capital to shareholders without complying with the provisions of the Act might constitute a breach of the principle that a company may deal with its assets only in accordance with its constitution and the CA 2006.

More generally, however, it is clear from the structure of the CA 2006 that a company has power to reduce its capital only in the ways specified in it. To the extent that the irregular reduction purports to change the numbers stated in the

[209] CA 2006 s.644(4).

[210] CA 2006 s.644(6).

[211] See para.17–043.

[212] CA 2006 s.643(4). The offence is punishable by imprisonment, whether tried summarily or on indictment: s.643(5).

[213] CA 2006 s.659(2)(a).

accounts, then it would appear that the change is invalid.[214] The same would appear to be true if the purported change is the cancellation of a liability to meet calls on the shares.[215] Where the purported reduction involves a return of assets to the members, then the invalidity of the transaction suggests that the recipients are liable to return those assets to the company, subject only to defences such as change of position (i.e. there is no need to show knowledge of their part of the invalidity of the transaction or the directors' breach of duty). As to the directors, then quite apart from breach of the "no acquisition" principle, liability to the company to make good any loss to the company flowing from the irregular reduction could arise because of the general principle that the directors of the company have power to deal with its assets only in accordance with its constitution and the CA 2006.[216] This in turn could give rise to an alternative claim against the shareholders for a return of the assets received, where they had the relevant level of knowledge of the directors' breach of duty.[217]

Reduction, distributions and re-purchase

Provided a private company observes the requirements of the CA 2006, especially the requirement laid upon the directors to have reasonable grounds for the beliefs stated in the solvency statement, it is provided with an inexpensive and quick method of reducing its capital. It is arguable that, in consequence, the test for the legality of a distribution by such a company is a solvency test. Although the cumulative profits test, discussed in Ch.18, still applies to private companies, the impact of that rule can be mitigated by reducing the company's capital to write off losses, provided the solvency test (and other requirements of the private company procedure) are met. However, it may be that this step does not generate profits for a distribution even after the company's capital has been reduced, even to near vanishing point. Consequently, in this case the net accumulated profits rule will still operate as a binding constraint on distributions, especially if the private company was only thinly capitalised in the first place.[218] **17–040**

The simplified procedure for reduction of capital without court approval also constitutes a functional substitute for a re-purchase or redemption out of capital, as discussed above.[219] Which will prove more popular where both mechanisms are available? Re-purchase out of capital has the virtue of familiarity and may continue to be used quite widely, at least initially, but the procedure for reduction out of court seems simpler and cheaper. No auditors' report is required on the

[214] Thus, in *BTI 2014 LLC v Sequana SA* [2017] Bus. L.R. 82 at [316] it is recorded that the parties agreed that, if the reduction of capital has not been carried out properly, then the consequence was that a later distribution was unlawful because the accounts, which reflected the invalid reduction, were improperly drawn up. On the relationship between lawful dividends and the accounts see para.18–007.

[215] Under s.641(4)(a)—though this is not a common modern use of the reduction procedure.

[216] See para.18–017.

[217] Both heads of claim against the shareholders are discussed in para.17–006.

[218] For a discussion of the general test applying to distributions by private companies see para.18–003.

[219] See para.17–013.

directors' solvency statement, no special accounts have to be prepared[220] and there is no right of objection to the court on the part of creditors or non-approving members.

In the course of providing this simplified reduction procedure for private companies (and, to some extent, within the court-confirmation procedure as well), the formal protections for creditors have been reduced. Whether the solvency statement will prove an adequate functional substitute for the right to object to the court remains to be seen.

FINANCIAL ASSISTANCE

Rationale and history of the rule

17–041 Section 678 prohibits a public company (or its subsidiary, public or private) from giving financial assistance to a person for the acquisition by that person of the public company's shares, whether the assistance is given in advance of or after the acquisition. The history of this rule does not constitute one of the most glorious episodes in British company law. The rationale for its introduction was under-articulated; it has proved capable of rending unlawful what seem from any perspective to be perfectly innocuous transactions; and it has proved resistant to a reformulation which would avoid these problems. The CLR eventually decided that, for private companies, the only way forward was to take them out of the scope of the rule altogether, which reform proposal was implemented in the CA 2006. The CLR also proposed a series of amendments to the rule as it applies to public companies,[221] but most of these were not implemented in the CA 2006. The Government took the view that the Second Directive prevented significant changes to the rule as it applies to public companies.[222] It may be that in due course the government will re-visit the issue in the light of the UK's exit from the EU.

The rule against financial assistance for acquisitions of the company's shares was not developed by the nineteenth century judges as part of the capital maintenance regime. Rather, it was a statutory reform introduced in the CA 1929 as a result of the recommendations of the Greene Committee.[223] Although conventionally dealt with, as in this work, under the heading of legal capital, it is clear that in formal terms financial assistance may have no impact on the company's legal capital. If a company lends £100,000 to someone to purchase its shares from another investor and that person does not act as a nominee for the company but acquires the shares beneficially, the company's share capital, share premium account and capital redemption reserve will not be in any way altered

---

[220] Though the directors can hardly make the required statement unless they have at least up-to-date management accounts.

[221] *Company Formation and Capital Maintenance*, paras 3.42 and 3.43. These proposals were derived in the main from proposals for reform made earlier by the DTI itself.

[222] DTI, *Company Law Reform* (March 2005), Cm.6456, paras 42–43.

[223] *Report of the Company Law Amendment Committee* (Greene Committee) (1926), Cmnd.2657. So, the EU did not foist this rule on the UK. To the contrary the UK used its influence at the time of the negotiation of the Second Directive to foist it on the other Member States of the EU which did not already have it.

by that loan or the subsequent purchase of the shares. The Greene Committee seems to have thought that financial assistance offended against the spirit, if not the letter, of the rule in *Trevor v Whitworth* (company prohibited from acquiring its own shares),[224] but the Jenkins Committee commented that, had the ban "been designed merely to extend that rule, we should have felt some doubt whether it was worth retaining".[225]

Nor does financial assistance necessarily reduce the company's net asset position. If in the above example the borrower is fully able to repay the loan, the company is simply replacing one asset (cash) with another (the rights under the loan) and possibly the latter will earn the company a higher rate of return. For obvious reasons, there is no general principle of creditor protection in company law which prohibits the company from altering the risk characteristics of its assets,[226] and so it is by no means clear that the rule against financial assistance be justified on that ground either. In fact, the financial assistance rule seems too broad to be supported on a simple creditor (or even minority shareholder) rationale. If the above loan were for some purpose other than the purchase of shares, the rule would not bite, yet the borrower might in fact be less able to repay the loan than the borrower for the share purchase—and might even be an associate of the controlling shareholder.

In fact, the Greene Committee seems to have been heavily, perhaps inappropriately, influenced by the use of financial assistance in schemes which it disapproved of for more general reasons. The Committee thought, in particular, that it was abusive to finance a takeover by a loan and immediately repay it by raiding the coffers of the cash-rich company which has been taken over or to use the assets of the new subsidiary as security for the takeover loan.[227] Experience during the recent pandemic showed that highly leverage companies were indeed often in a poor position to ride out external shocks because of their high ratio of debt to equity. However, the financial assistance rules do not deal effectively with this problem either. In particular, those rules have for some time permitted a payment of cash from the new subsidiary to the parent provided it is made by way of lawful dividend.[228] Consequently, if the target company engages in a sale and leaseback of its major assets and distributes the cash raised as a dividend to the new parent company, that manoeuvre will escape the financial assistance prohibition. This suggests that, at least under the current law, the objection is not to the use of the subsidiary's cash balances to repay the loan but rather that the aim is to allow repayment only in a way which protects both creditors (by **17–042**

[224] See fn.1.

[225] *Report of the Company Law Amendment Committee* (Jenkins Committee) (1962), Cmnd.1749, para.173. Of course, if the shares are held by the person to whom the assistance is given, not beneficially, but as a nominee for the company, then the provisions discussed at para.17–003 will apply (so that the financial assistance rules are not necessary to address the nominee situation).

[226] In the vicinity of insolvency, however, the law does restrain directors' freedom of action in this regard. See Ch.19.

[227] On variations on this theme see *Selangor United Rubber Estates Ltd v Cradock (No.3)* [1968] 1 W.L.R. 1555 Ch D; *Karak Rubber Co Ltd v Burden (No.2)* [1972] 1 W.L.R. 602 Ch D; and *Wallersteiner v Moir (No.1)* [1974] 1 W.L.R. 991 CA (Civ Div); (petition dismissed) [1975] 1 W.L.R. 1093 HL.

[228] CA 2006 s.681(2).

requiring the dividend to be paid in accordance with the distribution rules)[229] and minority shareholders, since dividends are paid pro rata to the proportion of the share capital held.[230] Again, if the private equity owners of a company load it up with debt before selling it off on the public markets, paying out the cash to themselves as a dividend, the result may well be a highly leverage company, but no assistance will have been given by the company to the public purchasers—and this would be the case even if dividends were included within the rules.

However, the Greene Committee's recommendations were enacted as s.45 of the CA 1929, which was re-enacted with amendments as s.54 of the CA 1948. Section 45 immediately revealed the difficulties involved in trying to draft a prohibition that was properly targeted on the perceived abuses. That section, despite its relative brevity, became notorious as unintelligible and liable to penalise innocent transactions while failing to deter guilty ones. The Jenkins Committee[231] suggested an alternative approach very similar to that eventually adopted in 1981 in relation to private companies, but at the time no action was taken on that suggestion.

However, in 1980 two reported cases[232] caused considerable alarm in commercial and legal circles, suggesting, as they did, that the scope of the section was even wider, and the risk of wholly unobjectionable transactions being shot down even greater, than had formerly been thought. Hence it was decided that something had to be done about it in the CA 1981 which was then in preparation. Probably more midnight oil was burnt on this subject than on all the rest of that Act, and the resulting elaborate provisions were certainly some improvement on s.54. However, they still did not produce the holy grail of a precisely targeted prohibition and, after the controversy generated by the House of Lords decision in *Brady v Brady*,[233] the Government made proposals for the further relaxation of the provisions.[234] However, before these proposals could be implemented, the CLR was established, with the results described above. In the meantime, the difficulty of producing a targeted formula continued to be demonstrated in litigation, for example, in the decision of the Court of Appeal in *Chaston v SWP Group Ltd*[235] in 2002.

---

[229] See Ch.18.

[230] At least, this is the default rule: the Companies (Model Articles) Regulations 2008 (SI 2008/3229) Sch.3: Model Articles for Public Companies art.71.

[231] Jenkins Committee (1962), Cmnd.1749, paras 170–186.

[232] *Belmont Finance Corp v Williams Furniture Ltd* [1980] 1 All E.R. 393 CA (Civ Div); *Armour Hick Northern Ltd v Whitehouse* [1980] 1 W.L.R. 1520 Ch D.

[233] *Brady v Brady* (1988) 4 B.C.C. 390 HL.

[234] DTI, *Company Law Reform: Proposals for Reform of Sections 151–158 of the Companies Act 1985* (1993); DTI, *Consultation Paper on Financial Assistance* (November 1996).

[235] *Chaston v SWP Group Plc* [2002] EWCA Civ 1999; [2003] B.C.C. 140, helpfully considered by E. Ferran, "Corporate Transactions and Financial Assistance: Shifting Policy Perceptions but Static Law" (2004) 63 C.L.J. 225.

The prohibition

Section 678 distinguishes between assistance given prior to the acquisition and that given afterwards.[236] Its subs.(1) says that, subject to exceptions: **17–043**

> "where a person[237] is acquiring or is proposing to acquire[238] shares in a public company, it is not lawful for that company, or a company that is a subsidiary of that company,[239] to give financial assistance directly or indirectly[240] for the purpose of that acquisition before or at the same time as the acquisition takes place."

Subsection (3) provides that, subject to the same exceptions, when a person has acquired shares in a company and any liability has been incurred (by that or any other person) for that purpose, it is not lawful for the company or any of its subsidiaries to give financial assistance, directly or indirectly, for the purpose of reducing or discharging that liability, if at the time the assistance was given the company in which the shares were acquired was a public company. Thus, if A (probably a bank) lends B (a bidder) £1 million to enable B (an acquisition vehicle) to make a takeover of a target company and C (probably B's parent company) guarantees repayment, it will be unlawful for any financial assistance to be given by the target, when taken over, to B or C towards the discharge of their obligations to A. However, since private companies are now excluded from the rule, it is important to know whether the target whose shares were acquired and which is now giving the financial assistance is a public company at the time the assistance is given by it. Thus, in this example, if the target company were a public company at the time of its acquisition, it could nevertheless give financial assistance after the acquisition, provided it had by then been re-registered as a private company. This step is commonly taken in private equity buy-outs.

Section 683 provides that a reference to a person incurring a liability includes: **17–044**

---

[236] On the other hand, the drafters seem to have thought of financial assistance, whether given before or after the event, as a one-off transaction. For the difficulties involved in calculating the impact of the assistance on the company's net assets where the assistance is continuing, see *Parlett v Guppys (Bridport) Ltd (No.1)* [1996] B.C.C. 299 CA (Civ Div).

[237] The Government's interpretation of the section is that the person must be someone other than the company itself: HC Debs, Standing Committee D, cols 856–857 (20 July 2006) (Vera Baird).

[238] In contrast with s.54 of the 1948 Act, which used the expression "purchase or subscription", this section refers to "acquire" or "acquisition" thus extending the ambit of the section to non-cash subscriptions and exchanges.

[239] The sections do not apply to financial assistance by a holding company for the acquisition of shares in its (public) subsidiary; in such a case there is less likelihood of prejudice to other shareholders or to creditors. The subsidiary giving the assistance must be a "company" within the meaning of the Act (see s.1) so that foreign subsidiaries are not caught by the prohibition. This was the view taken previously: see *Arab Bank Plc v Mercantile Holdings Ltd* [1993] B.C.C. 816 Ch D.

[240] A charge given by a company to secure a loan to the company which both lender and company knew was to be on-lent to the purchaser of a company's shares to finance the purchase constitutes indirect financial assistance: *Re Hill & Tylor Ltd (In Administration)* [2004] EWHC 1261 (Ch); [2004] B.C.C. 732; *Central and Eastern Trust Co v Irving Oil Ltd* (1980) 110 D.L.R. (3d) 257 Sup. Ct. Can.

> "his changing his financial position by making an agreement or arrangement (whether enforceable or unenforceable and whether made on his own account or with any other person)[241] or by any other means".

It adds that reference to a company giving financial assistance to reduce or discharge a liability incurred for the purposes of acquiring shares includes giving assistance for the purpose of wholly or partly restoring the financial position of the person concerned to what it was before the acquisition. This results in an enormous extension of the normal meaning of "liability" and seems to mean that, before a company can give any financial assistance to *any* person (whether or not the acquirer), it must assess his overall financial position before and after the acquisition[242] and if, afterwards, it has deteriorated, must refrain from any form of financial assistance which is not covered by one of the exceptions—at any rate if there is a causal connection between the deterioration and the acquisition.

The scope of the prohibition depends crucially on what is meant by "financial assistance". Section 677 apparently defines financial assistance, but in fact fails to do so. It defines the types of financial assistance falling within the CA 2006, without defining what "financial" assistance is—as opposed to other forms of assistance. Given that limitation, however, the section widely defines the types of financial assistance which are covered. In addition to such obvious assistance as gifts, loans, guarantees, releases, waivers and indemnities,[243] the definition includes any other agreement under which the obligations of the company giving the assistance are to be fulfilled before the obligations of another party to the agreement,[244] and the novation of a loan or of other agreement; or the assignment of rights under it. If the financial assistance is of one or more of these types, it is irrelevant whether or not the net assets of the company providing it are reduced by reason of the assistance.[245]

However, this is not all. The list of types of financial assistance concludes with "any other financial assistance given by a company, the net assets[246] of which are thereby reduced to a material extent, or which has no net assets". The effect of this is that, even if the financial assistance does not fall within the specific types that the drafter was able to foresee, it will nevertheless be unlawful if the company has no net assets or if the consequence of the assistance is to reduce its net assets "to a material extent". Only in this last case does it seem to be a requirement of the definition of financial assistance that the company giving it should suffer a financial detriment. Clearly "materiality" is to be determined to some extent by the relationship between the value of the assistance and the value

[241] The words "or with any other person" are somewhat puzzling; one would have expected "or that of any other person". Can there be an agreement or arrangement which is not made with some other person? And, if there can, would it not be covered by "or by any other means"?

[242] The difficulty of doing this after a takeover is mind-boggling.

[243] CA 2006 s.677(1)(a)–(c)—other than an indemnity given in respect of the indemnifier's own neglect or default.

[244] e.g. where a company which is a diamond merchant sells a diamond to a dealer for £100,000, payment to be 12 months hence, the intention being that the dealer will sell the diamond at a profit or borrow on its security thus putting the dealer in funds to acquire shares in the company.

[245] In some cases (e.g. gifts) they will be; in others (e.g. loans or guarantees) they may or may not.

[246] Defined as "the aggregate of the company's assets, less the aggregate of its liabilities" and "liabilities" includes any provision for anticipated losses or charges: s.677(2).

of the net assets: assistance worth £50 would reduce the net assets materially if they were only £100 but immaterially if they were £1 million. But how far is that to be taken? A company with net assets of £billions might regard a reduction of £1 million as immaterial, but it seems unlikely that judges (most of whom are not accustomed to disposing of £millions) would so regard it. At the other end of the scale, it was held in *Chaston*[247] that an expenditure of £20,000 by a subsidiary, whose net assets were only £100,000, was material, even though the assistance was in relation to the purchase of the shares of the parent at a price of some £2.5 million.[248]

As noted, however, assistance will not be unlawful unless it is "financial". Merely giving information (even financial information) is not financial assistance.[249] Moreover, even if financial, the assistance must fall within the admittedly wide definition if it is to be unlawful. In other words, the definition of the types of financial assistance which fall within the Act seems intended to be exhaustive. Thus, timely repayment of a debt due, even if done in order to assist the creditor in the purchase of the debtor's shares, would not seem to be caught,[250] but it might be if the debt were paid early because it could then be said to have an element of gift in it.[251] **17–045**

Finally, the impugned transaction must actually be capable of assisting the acquirer to obtain the shares. In *British & Commonwealth Holdings Plc v Barclays Bank Plc*,[252] the promises, made by the company to indemnify the banks which could be required to acquire the shares from the shareholder if the company did not redeem them, were regarded as an "inducement" to the shareholder to acquire the redeemable shares in the first place but not as financial assistance to the shareholder to do so. However, in *Chaston*[253] this decision was explained on the basis that the company did not expect to have to meet its obligations at the time the promises were made and it was said that there was no general rule that an inducement could not constitute financial assistance. In *Chaston*, the subsidiary of the target had paid for an accountant's report on the target, which was an inducement to the potential bidder to make the offer, but it

---

[247] See fn.235.

[248] If the assistance had been provided by the parent, as it could well have been, no question of financial assistance would probably have arisen.

[249] But reimbursement of the costs of digesting and assessing the information could be, as in *Chaston*. Nor is assistance financial if it consists of the parent instructing its subsidiary to pay money to the vendor of the shares, where no financial asset leaves the parent and the assistance provided by the (foreign incorporated) subsidiary is lawful: *AMG Global Nominees (Private) Ltd v Africa Resources Ltd* [2008] EWCA Civ 1278; [2009] B.C.C. 767. This is a surprising decision and the CA's reliance on the *Arab Bank* case (fn.239) seems misplaced, since the issue there was the legality of the assistance provided by the subsidiary and not, as in *AMG*, the assistance provided by the parent.

[250] cf. *MT Realisations Ltd (In Liquidation) v Digital Equipment Co Ltd* [2003] EWCA Civ 494; [2003] B.C.C. 415—enforcement of security rights was recovery of a legal entitlement rather than the receipt of financial assistance.

[251] See *Plaut v Steiner* (1989) 5 B.C.C. 352 Ch D, but note also the insistence by the Court of Appeal in *British & Commonwealth Holdings Plc v Barclays Bank Plc* [1995] B.C.C. 1059 that the terms used in the definition must be given their technical meaning (in this case in relation to the meaning of an "indemnity").

[252] See para.17–026.

[253] See fn.235.

was also financial assistance in the sense that it reduced the costs the potential bidder incurred in investigating the worth of the target.

Chaston is another example of the financial assistance prohibition striking down an entirely innocuous transaction. The company (or rather its subsidiary) spent a modest amount of money to further a sale of the company to a purchaser—a sale which was clearly in the shareholders' interests (as the subsequent litigation showed) and which carried no additional risks (probably the opposite) for its creditors. For this exemplary business decision the directors of the company were found to be in breach of their fiduciary duties to the company (by providing the unlawful financial assistance) and held personally liable to restore the amount of the assistance to the company, i.e. to the purchaser, which sued as assignee of the subsidiary's claim.[254]

The exceptions

Specific exceptions

17–046 The CA 2006 provides a number of exceptions to the prohibitions. Some are unconditional, i.e. always available. They include allotment of bonus shares, lawful distributions, anything done in accordance with a court order, reductions of capital or redemptions or purchases of shares under the provisions discussed above, and anything done under the reconstruction provisions discussed in Ch.29.[255] Others are conditional. The conditional exemptions apply only to certain types of financial assistance, which are thought to be harmless, for example, where lending money is part of the ordinary business of the company and the financial assistance is provided within that business or the assistance is provided in connection with an employees' share scheme.[256] Even then, the exemption applies only if the company's net assets are not thereby reduced or, if reduced, the reduction is financed out of distributable profits.[257]

The interesting point about the conditional exceptions is that they do link the financial assistance rules to the underlying policy of creditor protection. If there is no reduction in net assets or, even if there is, the creditors cannot legitimately complain because the reduction is financed out of distributable profits, the conditional exceptions apply. Indeed, one possible reform of a general character to the prohibition on financial assistance would be to permit financial assistance financed out of distributable profits if it involves a reduction of net assets.

---

[254] In *Anglo Petroleum Ltd v TFB (Mortgages) Ltd* [2007] EWCA Civ 456; [2007] B.C.C 407, a differently constituted CA took a more commercially robust line, notably in rejecting the argument that any payment by a company which "smoothed the path to the acquisition" of its shares constituted financial assistance.

[255] CA 2006 s.681. There is no express exemption for the expenses of share issues (for example, commissions—see para.16–017), but there clearly should be.

[256] CA 2006 s.682(2). There is also a conditional exception for financial assistance given in connection with private company acquisitions, but this is of such importance that it is treated separately in para.17–050.

[257] CA 2006 s.682(1). Distributable profits are defined in s.683(1), which essentially tracks the rules governing distributions.

General exceptions

As things stand, however, the main and most debated exception to the prohibition is to be found in s.678 itself. This was intended to allay the fears aroused by two decisions in 1980.[258] The section relates to the purposes for which the financial assistance was given. It is a necessary pre-condition for liability under s.678 that the financial assistance should have been given for the purpose of the acquisition of the shares. In some cases the company will be able to show that, although the financial assistance was given in connection with an acquisition of shares, it was not given for that purpose.[259] However, the exceptions come into play where that cannot be shown, i.e. where the purpose of the financial assistance was to facilitate the acquisition of shares. Under s.678(2) the prohibition on a company from giving financial assistance before or at the time of the acquisition nevertheless does not apply if: **17–047**

(1) the company's principal purpose in giving the assistance is not to give it for the purpose of any such acquisition; or
(2) if the giving of the assistance for that purpose is only an incidental part of some larger purpose of the company; and the assistance is given in good faith in the interests of the company.

Subsection (4) provides similarly that the prohibition does not apply in these circumstances to assistance given subsequently to the acquisition.

On the meaning of these difficult subsections there is an authoritative ruling from the House of Lords in the case of *Brady v Brady*,[260] a case remarkable both because of the extent of the judicial disagreement to which it gave rise and because it was ultimately decided on a ground not argued in the lower courts. It related to prosperous family businesses, principally concerned with haulage and soft drinks. The businesses were run and owned in equal shares by two brothers, Jack and Bob Brady, and their respective families, through a parent company, T. Brady & Co Ltd (Brady's), and a number of subsidiary and associated companies. Unfortunately Jack and Bob fell out, resulting in a complete deadlock. It was clear that unless something could be agreed amicably, Brady's would have to be wound-up—which was the last thing that anyone wanted. It was therefore agreed that the group should be reorganised, sole control of the haulage business being **17–048**

---

[258] *Belmont Finance Corp v Williams Furniture Ltd* [1980] 1 All E.R. 393; *Armour Hick Northern Ltd v Whitehouse* [1980] 1 W.L.R. 1520.

[259] *Dymont v Boyden* [2004] EWCA Civ 1586; [2005] B.C.C. 79.

[260] *Brady v Brady* (1988) 4 B.C.C. 390. This case is an illustration (of which *Charterhouse Investment Trust v Tempest Diesels Ltd* (1985) 1 B.C.C. 99544 Ch D is another) of how, all too often, parties agree in principle to a simple arrangement which on the face of it raises no question of unlawful financial assistance but then refer it to their respective advisers who, in their anxiety to obtain the maximum fiscal and other advantages for their respective clients, introduce complicated refinements which arguably cause it to fall foul of the prohibition on financial assistance. In the *Charterhouse* case, where the former s.54 applied, Hoffmann J, by exercising common sense in interpreting the meaning of "financial assistance", was able to avoid striking down an obviously unobjectionable arrangement. But the elaborate definition of that expression in the present Act leaves less scope for common sense.

taken by Jack and that of the drinks business by Bob. As the respective values of the two businesses were not precisely equal, this involved various intra-group transfers of assets and shareholdings which became increasingly complicated as the negotiations proceeded. It suffices to say that, in the eventual agreement, one of the companies had acquired shares in Brady's and the liability to pay for them thus incurred was to be discharged by a transfer to it of assets of Brady's. Bob, however, contended that further valuation adjustments were needed and refused to proceed further unless they were made. Jack then started proceedings for specific performance which Bob defended on various grounds among which was that the agreement would require Brady's to give unlawful financial assistance.

It was conceded that the transfer of assets would be unlawful financial assistance unless, in the circumstances, the prohibition was disapplied by what is now s.678(4). On the face of it one might have thought that the circumstances afforded a classic illustration of the sort of situation that the above provisions were intended to legitimate. At first instance, that view prevailed. In the Court of Appeal,[261] however, while all three judges thought that the conditions relating to "purpose" were satisfied, the majority thought that those relating to "good faith in the interests of the company" were not. In contrast, in the House of Lords it was held unanimously that the good faith requirements were complied with but that the purpose ones were not. Hence the contemplated transfer would be unlawful financial assistance if carried out in the way proposed.

Lord Oliver, in a speech concurred in by the other Law Lords, subjected the purpose requirements to detailed analysis.[262] He pointed out that "purpose" had to be distinguished from "reason" or "motive" (which would almost always be different and wider) and that the purpose requirements contemplated alternative situations. The first is where the company has a principal and a subsidiary purpose: the question then is whether the principal purpose is to assist or relieve the acquirer or is for some other corporate purpose. The second situation is where the financial assistance is not for any purpose other than to help the acquirer but is merely incidental to some larger corporate purpose.[263] As regards the first alternative, he accepted that an example might be where the principal purpose was to enable the company to obtain from the person assisted a supply of some product which the company needed for its business.[264] As regards the second, he offered no example, merely saying that he had "not found the concept of a "larger purpose" easy to grasp" but that:

> "if the sub-paragraph is to be given any meaning that does not in effect provide a blank cheque for avoiding the effective application of [the prohibition] in every case, the concept must be narrower than that for which the appellants contend."[265]

---

[261] *Brady v Brady* (1988) 4 B.C.C. 390.

[262] *Brady v Brady* (1988) 4 B.C.C. 390 at 407. Agreeing with O'Connor LJ in the Court of Appeal ([1988] B.C.L.C. 20 at 25) he described the paragraph, with commendable restraint, as "not altogether easy to construe".

[263] The layout of s.678(2) and (4) now reflects this analysis more clearly than did the previous legislation.

[264] A situation envisaged by Buckley LJ in his judgment in the *Belmont Finance* case ([1980] 1 All E.R. 393 at 402), as giving rise to doubts under the former s.54 of the CA 1948.

[265] *Brady v Brady* (1988) 4 B.C.C. 390 at 408.

The trial judge, and O'Connor LJ in the Court of Appeal,[266] had thought that the larger purpose was to resolve the deadlock and its inevitable consequences; and Croom-Johnson LJ[267] had found it in the need to reorganise the whole group. But if either could be so regarded, it would follow that, if the board of a company concluded in good faith that the only way that a company could survive was for it to be taken over, it could lawfully provide financial assistance to the bidder—the very "mischief" that the legislation was designed to prevent. The logic is, of course, impeccable. But the result seems to reduce the purpose exceptions to very narrow limits indeed and to make one wonder whether the midnight oil burnt on the drafting of the two subsections had achieved anything worthwhile. 17–049

The transaction was in fact saved by application of the special provisions then applying to private companies (now repealed). However, the (eventually) successful outcome in that particular case did not get rid of the awkward issues raised by it. The DTI[268] floated the ideas of substituting "predominant reason" for "principal purpose" or relying solely on the test of good faith in the interests of the company. The CLR supported the first of these suggestions.[269] However, these suggestions do nothing to address the arguments put forward in the House of Lords in favour of giving the purpose requirements a strict interpretation, if the prohibition is to remain a meaningful restriction. In any event, the CA 2006 retains the established wording.

Exemption for private companies

In the reforms of 1981 a more relaxed regime for private companies was introduced, allowing assistance if this did not involve a reduction of the company's net assets or if the financial assistance was given out of distributable profits.[270] The effect of this provision was to tie the financial assistance rules more clearly to the creditor protection concerns of the rules applying to distributions.[271] The CA 2006 went further and removed the financial assistance prohibition from private companies, as the CLR recommended. Section 678 applies only to financial assistance given to a person who is proposing to acquire shares in a public company or, in relation to an acquisition which has occurred, where the company whose shares have been acquired is *at the time of the assistance* a public company. Consequently, where a public company is taken over and then re-registered as a private company, it may give financial assistance by way of reducing or discharging the liabilities of the (new) parent incurred for the purpose of the acquisition.[272] The limitation in s.678 thus focuses on the private status of the company whose shares are subject to the acquisition. Consequently, if a private subsidiary gives financial assistance for the purchase of 17–050

[266] *Brady v Brady* (1987) 3 B.C.C. 535; [1988] B.C.L.C. 20 CA (Civ Div) at 26.

[267] *Brady v Brady* [1988] B.C.L.C. 20 at 32.

[268] DTI, *Company Law Reform: Proposals for Reform of Sections 151–158 of the Companies Act 1985* (1993).

[269] Completing, para.7.14.

[270] CA 1985 s.155(2).

[271] See Ch.18.

[272] Of course, the directors of the (new) subsidiary will need to comply with their fiduciary duties to their company.

the shares of its public parent, as in the *Chaston* case,[273] that situation will still be caught by the prohibition. Moreover, the prohibition is extended by s.679 to catch financial assistance given by a public company towards the acquisition of shares in its private holding company—an unusual but not impossible situation.[274] In this case the status of the provider of the assistance as a public company subsidiary is enough to trigger the rule.

Civil remedies for breach of the prohibition

17–051 The only sanctions prescribed by the CA 2006 for breaches of the prohibition are fining the company[275] and fining or imprisoning (or both) its officers in default.[276] More important are the consequences in civil law resulting from the fact that the transaction is unlawful. Unfortunately, precisely what these consequences are has vexed the courts both of the UK and of other countries which have adopted comparable provisions and it is a pity that the current Act did not attempt to clarify the position.[277]

What has caused the courts to make heavy weather of this is the somewhat curious wording of the prohibition down the years. Since the object of the section is to protect the company and its members and creditors, one would have expected it to say that it is not lawful for any person who has acquired or is proposing to acquire shares of a company to receive financial assistance from the company or any of its subsidiaries. That would have pointed the courts in the right direction to work out the consequences. But instead it declares that it is unlawful for the company to give the assistance, and follows that by imposing criminal sanctions on the company and (the one thing that makes good sense) on the officers of the company who are in default. This could be taken to imply (and was so taken by Roxburgh J in *Victor Battery Co Ltd v Curry's Ltd*)[278] that the object of the prohibition was not to protect the company but to punish it and its officers by imposing fines. This calamitous decision continued to be accepted in England, and was cited with apparent approval by Cross J (subsequently a Law Lord) 20 years later,[279] though rejected by the Australian Courts whose decisions

---

273 See fn.235.

274 CA 2006 s.679. An example might be where a target public company in a takeover is re-registered as a private company (to avoid the ban on its giving financial assistance to its new parent) but still has subsidiary companies which are public companies. Section 679 prevents the subsidiaries giving financial assistance to their immediate parent (unless an exception applies). At least this is what s.679(3) appears to say.

275 Since the prohibition is intended to protect the company and its members and creditors it is difficult to conceive of a more inappropriate sanction than to reduce the company's net assets (still further than the unlawful financial assistance may have done) by fining the company. The CLR had proposed that the criminal sanction on the company be removed: Formation, para.343(d).

276 CA 2006 s.680.

277 The remedies for an unlawful distribution are specifically not applied to unlawful financial assistance: s.847(4)(a).

278 *Victor Battery Co Ltd v Curry's Ltd* [1946] Ch. 242 Ch D.

279 *Curtis's Furnishing Stores Ltd (In Liquidation) v Freedman* [1966] 1 W.L.R. 1219 Ch D. But he ignored it in *South Western Mineral Water Co Ltd v Ashmore* [1967] 1 W.L.R. 1110 Ch D.

helped those in England eventually to see the light. The decision has now been disapproved or not followed in a series of cases[280] and is accepted to be heretical.

Freed from the fetters of that heresy the courts have since given the section real teeth and it is submitted that the following propositions can now be regarded as reasonably well established: **17–052**

(1) An agreement to provide unlawful financial assistance, being unlawful, is unenforceable by either party to it. This proposition is undoubted and authority for it is the decision of the House of Lords in *Brady v Brady*.[281] However, if the contract could be performed legally (i.e. without giving unlawful financial assistance), but unlawful financial assistance is in fact provided, then the legality of the contract depends on whether the other party to it was party to a common design to act unlawfully.[282]

(2) However, the illegality of the financial assistance given or provided by the company normally does not taint other connected transactions, such as the agreement by the person assisted to acquire the shares. It would be absurd if, for example, a takeover bidder which had been given financial assistance by the target company, or by a subsidiary of the company, could escape from the liability to perform purchase contracts which it had entered into with the shareholders of the target. Clearly, it cannot.

(3) This, however, is subject to a qualification if the obligation to acquire the shares and the obligation to provide financial assistance form part of a single composite transaction. The obvious example of this would be an arrangement in which someone agreed to subscribe for shares in a company (or its holding company) in consideration of which the company agreed to give him some form of financial assistance. In such a case the position apparently depends on whether the terms relating to the acquisition of shares can be severed from those relating to the unlawful financial assistance. If they can, those relating to the acquisition can be enforced. If they cannot, the whole agreement is void. The authorities supporting this proposition are the decisions of Cross J in *South Western Mineral Water Co*

---

[280] *Selangor United Rubber Estate Ltd v Cradock (No.3)* [1968] 1 W.L.R. 1555 Ch D; *Heald v O'Connor* [1971] 1 W.L.R. 497 QBD; and Lord Denning MR in *Wallersteiner v Moir* [1974] 1 W.L.R. 991 at 1014H–1015A. The modern view helped Millett J to conclude in *Arab Bank Plc v Mercantile Holdings Ltd* [1993] B.C.C. 816 that the legislation applies to assistance provided by a subsidiary of an English company only where the subsidiary is not a foreign company, on the grounds that the protection of the shareholders and creditors of a company is a matter for the law of the place of incorporation. By the same token, the giving of assistance by the English subsidiary of a foreign parent ought to be regulated by the Act, though it is by no means clear that it is.

[281] *Brady v Brady* (1988) 4 B.C.C. 390. See also *Re Hill &Tyler Ltd (In administration)* [2004] EWHC 1261 (Ch); [2004] B.C.C. 732.

[282] *Anglo Petroleum Ltd v TFB (Mortgages) Ltd* [2007] B.C.C. 407: a contract to lend money to a company where the contract did not require the sum advanced to be used to provide unlawful financial assistance but where the lender knew the money lent was to be used to repay monies due to the company's former parent from the purchaser of the company's shares from the former parent. The CA thought there was no public policy in forcing the lender to investigate whether the proposed use of the loan would constitute unlawful financial assistance and so held the contract of loan enforceable (though this view was, strictly, obiter).

Ltd v Ashmore[283] and of the Privy Council in *Carney v Herbert*.[284] In essence, the facts of both were that shares of a company were to be acquired and payment of the purchase price was to be secured by a charge on the assets of, in the former case, that company and, in the latter, its subsidiary. The agreed security was, of course, unlawful financial assistance. In the former case, the shares had not been transferred or the charge executed; in the latter, they had. In the former it was held that unless the sellers were prepared to dispense with the charge (which they were not) the whole agreement was void and that the parties must be restored to their positions prior to the agreement. In the latter it was held that the unlawful charge could be severed from the sale of the shares and that the sellers were entitled to sue the purchaser for the price. Despite the different results, the Privy Council judgment, delivered by Lord Brightman, cited with approval the decision of Cross J in the earlier case. In both cases a fair result seems to have been arrived at and certainly one preferable to that for which the assisted purchaser contended in *Carney*, namely that he should be entitled to retain the shares without having to pay for them.[285] It is therefore to be hoped that even in a single composite transaction the courts will permit severance or order restitutio in integrum unless there are strong reasons of public policy[286] why the whole transaction should be treated as unlawful so as to preclude the court from offering any assistance to any party to it.

(4) If the company has actually given the unlawful financial assistance, that transaction will be void. The practical effect of that depends on the nature of the financial assistance. If it is a mortgage, guarantee or indemnity or the like, the party to whom it was given cannot sue the company upon it.[287] It is that party who suffers,[288] and the company, so long as it realises in time that the transaction is void, need do nothing but defend any hopeless action that may be brought against it. If, however, the unlawful assistance was a completed gift or loan, the company will need to take action if it is to recover what it has lost. And a long line of cases has established that, in most circumstances, this it will be able to do.[289] Its claim may be based on misfeasance, when recovery is sought from the directors or other officers of the company, or on restitution, conspiracy, or constructive trust, when the

[283] *South Western Mineral Water Co Ltd v Ashmore* [1967] 1 W.L.R. 1110.

[284] *Carney v Herbert* [1985] A.C. 301 PC, on appeal from the Sup. Ct. of NSW.

[285] Yet Lord Brightman seemed to think that this would be the consequence if severance was not possible: see *Carney v Herbert* [1985] A.C. 301 at 309.

[286] In support of this caveat, see *Carney v Herbert* [1985] A.C. 301 at 313 and 317.

[287] See the cases discussed under (3) and *Heald v O'Connor* [1971] 1 W.L.R. 497, where the unlawful assistance was a mortgage on the property of the company whose shares were being acquired, the purchaser guaranteeing the payment of sums due under the mortgage. The mortgage was unlawful. Hence the purchaser escaped liability on the guarantee (though that was lawful) since no payments were lawfully due under the mortgage. It would have been different had the guarantee been an indemnity.

[288] Since the mortgage is illegal and void (not merely voidable) presumably a bona fide purchaser of it without notice could not enforce it either.

[289] *Steen v Law* [1964] A.C. 287 PC; *Selangor United Rubber Estates v Cradock (No.3)* [1968] 1 W.L.R. 1555; *Karak Rubber Co Ltd v Burden* [1972] 1 W.L.R. 602; *Wallersteiner v Moir* [1974] 1 W.L.R. 991; *Belmont Finance Corp v Williams Furniture Ltd* [1980] 1 All E.R. 393; *Smith v Croft (No.2)* (1987) 3 B.C.C. 207 Ch D; *Agip (Africa) Ltd v Jackson* [1991] Ch. 547 CA.

claim is against them or those to whom the unlawful assistance has passed or who have otherwise actively participated in the unlawful transaction. The most popular basis seems to be constructive trust, the argument being that the directors committed the equivalent of a breach of trust when they caused the company's assets to be used for the unlawful purpose and the recipients became constructive trustees thereof. The constructive trust is discussed further in Ch.10.

(5) In the light of propositions (1)–(4) it would also seem to follow that if the unlawful assistance given by the company is a loan secured by a mortgage or charge on the borrower's property[290] then, so long as the company has rights of recovery from the borrower under proposition (4), it should be able to do so by realising its security. This would certainly be so if the mortgage or charge could be severed from the unlawful loan—which, however, might be regarded as impossible since the consideration given for the mortgage or charge *was* the unlawful loan. But, since the effect of the recent case law is to recognise that the object of the prohibition, despite its wording, is to protect the company, the courts ought not to boggle at the conclusion that the security given to the company can be realised to recover what is due to it by the borrower.

(6) The above points all go to the validity of the financial assistance transaction and transactions associated with it. In addition, the directors who cause the company to give the unlawful finance assistance may be found to have been in breach of their duties to the company and the company is not prevented from enforcing those duties against the directors (normally to recover any loss suffered) by virtue of the fact that the company's act in providing the assistance was unlawful.[291]

It will therefore be seen that we have come a long way from the time when it was believed that the only likely sanctions were derisory fines on the company and its officers in default. These developments have caused the banking community some alarm, for there is no doubt that banks could find themselves caught out—as indeed they have been in the past.[292] The fact that money passing in the relevant transactions is likely to do so through banking channels inevitably exposes banks to risks.[293] The government proposed, in consequence, that

---

[290] Unless the company is a public company and the charge is on shares in it, for then the charge may be void under s.670: see para.13–002.

[291] *Steen v Law* [1964] A.C. 287; *Selangor United Rubber Estates v Cradock (No.3)* [1968] 1 W.L.R. 1555; *Chaston v SWP Group Plc* [2003] B.C.C. 140. The same principle is applied to actions the company may have against third parties who are implicated in the provision of the financial assistance: *Belmont Finance Corp Ltd v Williams Furniture Ltd* [1979] Ch. 250 CA (Civ Div).

[292] See, for example, *Selangor United Rubber Estates v Cradock (No.3)* [1968] 1 W.L.R. 1555; *Karak Rubber Co v Burden* [1972] 1 W.L.R. 602.

[293] But they are afforded special protection since the prohibition does not invalidate a loan "where the lending of money is part of the ordinary business of the company" and the loan is "in the ordinary course of its business": s.682(2)(a). This recognises that it would be absurd if, on a public issue of shares by one of the major High Street banks, its branches had to refuse to honour applicants' cheques if they were customers who had been granted overdrafts.

transactions in breach of the prohibition should no longer be void for that reason alone,[294] but the CA 2006 did not take up this proposal.

CONCLUSION

17–053 Despite the stress placed in the nineteenth century cases on the value of maintaining legal capital, this chapter has shown that in three core areas companies now have extensive freedom to engage in transactions previously thought to be outlawed by the doctrine of capital maintenance. This is very clearly true of private companies which may today re-purchase shares out of capital and reduce their share capital through an out-of-court procedure and the acquisition of whose shares has been largely removed from the prohibition on giving financial assistance. Even in relation to public companies, the constraints of redemptions and re-purchases have been relaxed so that these transactions are permitted so long as distributable profits or the proceeds of a new issue are used to this end, leaving the company's capital accounts untouched.

Inevitably in this process, the rules formerly aimed at protecting creditors have been downgraded. It remains to be seen how well their substitutes, especially the solvency statement, will work out. In principle, the solvency statement is better aligned with the matter the creditors are primarily interested in, namely, how far the re-purchase or reduction of capital will adversely affect the capacity of the company to meet the creditors' claims in the future. From the creditors' perspective, this is a more relevant question than whether the company has maintained the legal capital it raised in the past. On the other hand, the solvency statement depends heavily upon the judgment of the directors about the likely impact of the proposed transaction on the company's cash-flows, which the creditors might view as less reliable than the capital numbers in the company's accounts. One important reason the traditional protections of the legal capital doctrine have been softened over the years is the analysis which suggests that, even if fully applied, legal capital has serious limitations as a creditor protection doctrine. As we see in Ch.19, the legislature and the courts have already responded to this analysis by developing forms of creditor protection which do not turn on the concept of legal capital and it seems likely that these non-capital based mechanisms will continue to grow, so that the weakening of protections based on legal capital is less important than it might seem at first sight.

---

[294] DTI, *Consultation Paper on Financial Assistance* (1996), para.14.

Chapter 18

DISTRIBUTIONS AND TRANSFERS AT AN UNDERVALUE

In this chapter we analyse the legal strategies which have been deployed against that form of corporate opportunism which we characterised in the introduction to Pt 5 as moving assets out of the corporate "box". There are two principal ways in which this can happen.[1] First, the company makes a distribution (often by way of a cash dividend) to all its shareholders or a class of them. Secondly, it enters into a transaction at an undervalue with one or more of its controllers, thus reducing the company's assets to the extent of the undervalue. That controller is often a shareholder, so that majority/minority shareholder issues may be raised as well. We considered these in Ch.14. Here we concentrate on creditor issues. These two types of transaction raise rather different issues. A dividend or other distribution is a regular aspect of corporate life, without which investors would be much less likely to put equity into companies. The law's strategy here is to put a cap on distributions, to protect creditors, not to prohibit them. Any other corporate transaction for no consideration or at a gross undervalue immediately raises suspicions that something untoward is happening, but even here such transactions sometimes fulfil a legitimate corporate purpose. So, the law does not prohibit this type of transaction either but does scrutinise them closely. **18–001**

[1] This is not intended to be an exhaustive taxonomy, since the ingenuity of controllers fearing that their company will fall into the hands of its creditors is, if not boundless, at least remarkably wide. As we saw in para.14–009, one possible rationale for the "no reflective loss" rule is that it keeps assets within the company for the benefit of its creditors.

DISTRIBUTIONS

18–002 A reasonably extensive set of rules on distributions is now set out in Pt 23 of the CA 2006. However, the Act preserves the common law rules on distributions and, as we see in para.18–012, they are important when a remedy is sought against directors, on whose liability the statute is silent.

A distribution is defined as "every description of distribution of a company's assets to its members, whether in cash or otherwise".[2] Although this is a definition which embodies the very term which is to be defined, it does make clear that the statutory rules govern not only the common payment by a company of a cash dividend to its shareholders but also the less frequent distribution of non-cash assets to members.[3] The purpose of the statutory rules is to set an outer limit on the amount the company may distribute to its members. Where, within that limit, the company chooses to locate its distribution policy is a matter for the directors and the shareholders, who may have differing views on the matter, managers perhaps preferring to re-invest surplus cash in the business, the shareholders preferring cash in hand.[4] The rules in the model articles for private and public companies limited by shares appear to put the directors in control of the decision. Those rules require both a recommendation from the board and a shareholder resolution to sanction a dividend on ordinary shares,[5] but the shareholders are not permitted to approve a level of dividend above that recommended by the directors.[6] In practice, however, the governance rights of shareholders[7] or the pressure of the capital markets, for example, through the threat of a takeover,[8] may make the directors' veto power over dividends more

---

[2] CA 2006 s.829(1). Certain transactions are specifically exempted from the term: an issuance of bonus shares (for the reasons given at para.16–024); transactions regulated elsewhere in the Act (reductions of capital and redemption or re-purchase of shares (see the previous chapter)); and distributions on a winding up (regulated by the IA 1986): s.829(2). The exclusion of bonus shares permits companies to capitalise unrealised (and thus undistributable) profits, assuming they have power in the articles so to do.

[3] As, for example, in *Burden Holdings (UK) Ltd v Fielding* [2018] UKSC 14; [2018] B.C.C. 867 where the asset distributed to the single member of the company was a share in a subsidiary of the company (though the legal point in the case concerned limitation).

[4] Theoretically, it is far from clear that there is a real conflict here in a publicly traded company. If management retains earnings to invest in good projects, which the market evaluates appropriately, then the company's share price will rise and a shareholder seeking income can sell part of the (now more valuable) shareholding. So, the issue is simply the form of the income: dividend or capital gain. But investors may not trust managers to make good investment decisions or may have different time-frames from the managers for realisation of their investments. In any event, the argument assumes there is a liquid market for the shares. In private companies, non-payment of dividends may be a way of depriving the minority shareholders of a return on their investment. This issues is addressed through the unfair prejudice provisions. See *Re CF Booth Ltd* [2017] EWHC 457 (Ch); *Routledge v Skerritt* [2019] EWHC 573 (Ch); [2019] B.C.C. 812; and generally Ch.14.

[5] Preference shares may have an entitlement under the articles to an annual dividend, assuming distributable profits are available. See para.6–007.

[6] The Companies (Model Articles) Regulations 2008 (SI 2008/3229) Sch.1: Model Articles for Private Companies Limited by Shares art.30; for Sch.3: Model Articles for Public Companies art.70. But directors may unilaterally declare interim dividends. Dividends must be declared pro rata, which is an important protection for minority shareholders.

[7] See Ch.11.

[8] See Ch.28.

apparent than real. If the articles, unusually, say absolutely nothing about the mechanism for determining dividends, the decision probably rests directors under the general grant of management powers to the board by the articles, but it is arguable that this grant does not include determining the return to the shareholders and that the shareholders have retained the distribution decision.

The basic rules

Turning to creditor protection, there are two fundamental rules on distributions set out in the CA 2006 for the protection of creditors, one applying to all companies and other only to public companies. The inter-relationship between the legal capital rules, discussed in the previous chapter, and the rules on distributions appears most clearly in the rule applicable to public companies only and set out in s.831 of the CA 2006.[9] It applies a balance-sheet test for the legality of a distribution. It is unlawful for a company to make a distribution if its net assets (assets minus liabilities) are (or would be after the distribution) less than its called up share capital and undistributable reserves.[10] Its undistributable reserves include its share premium account.[11] Thus, to take a simple example, a company which has issued as fully paid up 200 £1 shares at an issue price of £1.50 will have a share capital of £200 and a value of £100 in its share premium account. Consequently, for such a company it will not be enough to permit a distribution of, say, 10p per share that it has positive net assets of £20, so that it can pay the dividend and still have assets in balance with its liabilities. Instead, it must have positive net assets of £320 before it pays the dividend. The legal capital rules thus lead to greater conservatism in the payment of dividends than would a "bare" net assets test for the legality of dividend payment. One can also see from this example the significance of the share premium account being classified as an undistributable reserve.[12] If, as before 1948, the share premium account were a distributable reserve, the company would need to have positive net assets of only £220 before it made the dividend payment. And had the company chosen to set the par value at 10p (but still issued the shares at the same price, generating a premium of £1.40 per share), it would have needed positive net assets of only £40 before it made the dividend payment. 18–003

Undistributable reserves include more than the share premium account. Also added is the "capital redemption reserve" which we considered in the previous chapter.[13] That is created when a company re-purchases or redeems its shares, and it simply replaces the reduction in the share capital account which the re-purchase or redemption brings about. In other words, the capital redemption reserve operates so as to hold legal capital constant in this situation but it does not increase it. Further, there is added any other undistributable reserve created by an

[9] The rule is derived from art.15(1)(a) of the Second Directive (Directive 77/91 on coordination of safeguards [1977] OJ L26/1). For further discussion of the nature of the balance sheet and the profit and loss account see para.22–002.

[10] CA 2006 s.831(1)–(2).

[11] CA 2006 s.831(4)(a). On the share premium account see para.16–006.

[12] CA 2006 s.610 and para.16–006.

[13] See para.17–011.

enactment other than Pt 23 of the CA 2006.[14] The company itself may also add restrictions in its articles by creating an undistributable reserve.[15]

There is one final item in the list of undistributable reserves, which is the amount by which the company's unrealised profits exceed its unrealised losses. The idea broadly is that unrealised profits are not to be distributed until they are realised. However, the implications of this rule are best examined after looking at the distribution rule which applies to all companies, which also turns on the distinction between realised and unrealised gains and losses.

18–004 The general rule, applying to companies public or private, is set out in s.830[16] and states that a company may "make a distribution only out of profits available for the purpose". It then defines "profits available for the purpose" as the company's "accumulated realised profits, so far as not previously utilised by distribution or capitalisation, less its accumulated, realised losses, so far as not previously written off in a reduction or reorganisation of capital duly made".[17] This second rule, unlike the first one, focuses on the company's profit and loss account, rather than its balance sheet. The thrust of the rule is on two points. First, the company needs to assess its accumulated profits and losses over the years to determine whether, at the point a dividend is under consideration, there are profits to support it. Thus, what are sometimes called "nimble dividends" are not permitted, i.e. the paying of dividends out of profits earned in a particular year, even though in previous years the company has made losses, which have not been replaced.[18] More fully, the company must subtract from the profits it has made over the years any amounts already paid out by way of dividend or any profits which have been capitalised,[19] but it may also deduct from its losses over the years any amount properly written off through a reduction or reorganisation of capital.[20]

Although this is a rule which focuses on the profit and loss account, the requirement for aggregation supports the robustness of the company's balance sheet and particularly its capital statements. Suppose a company, recently established, has made a series of modest losses over its life-time. It will no longer have assets to represent the liabilities created by its share capital and share premium accounts. The requirement that the accumulated losses be removed by profits before any distribution may be made out of profits under s.831 reinforces the legal capital rules by putting the accumulation of assets to support the company's capital before the distribution of dividends.

---

[14] An example of an undistributable reserve created elsewhere in the Act is the re-denomination reserve created by s.620. See para.16–023. This operates in the same way as the CRR.

[15] Which was the cause of the problems in *Re Cleveland Trust Plc* [1991] B.C.C. 33 Ch D (Companies Ct) where the company's constitution provided that certain realised profits "shall be dealt with as capital surpluses not available for the payment of dividends" (at 36), which provision, however, was overlooked.

[16] Derived from art.15(1)(c) of the Directive.

[17] CA 2006 s.830(2). With one exception, the Act does not distinguish between trading profits and capital profits, such as that made on the ad hoc disposal of the company's head office, and both are distributable. In the case of investment companies, however, only revenue profits are in principle distributable: ss.832–835.

[18] This reverses the common law: *Lee v Neuchatel Asphalte Co* (1889) 41 Ch. D. 1 CA; *Ammonia Soda Co Ltd v Chamberlain* [1918] 1 Ch. 266 CA.

[19] See para.11–024.

[20] See Ch.17.

If, on the other hand, the company's aggregate profits over the years exceed its aggregate losses over the years, it may indeed make a distribution under this rule to the extent of the surplus profit, subject, however, to one further—and crucial—qualification. The second feature of s.830 is that it applies to only "realised" profits and "realised" losses. "Unrealised" profits and losses are left out of account in the calculation required by s.830.[21] "Realised" profits and losses are not defined in the CA 2006 which delegates the solution to accounting practice.[22] In fact, the precise line between the two is a matter of some controversy,[23] but for present purposes it is perhaps enough to give two clear examples, one on each side of the line. Suppose a company has a piece of real property which it acquired some years ago for £1 million. Because of inflation in asset prices, the property is now worth £5 million. If the company sells the property at its current valuation, receiving £5 million in cash in exchange, it will report a profit of £4 million (assuming no taxes or transaction costs) which it may distribute in whole to its shareholders (assuming it has no accumulated realised losses from the past which it must set against the profit). If, however, the company simply re-values the property in its books at £5 million (but does not dispose of it), which is something it might do in order to demonstrate that a takeover bidder was offering too low a price for the company or because it has adopted accounting principles which systematically deal with its assets and liabilities on a "mark to market" basis, it has recorded simply an unrealised profit.[24] Since the property will be reflected in the balance sheet at this higher value, under historic cost accounting a counterbalancing entry is needed, which will probably take the form of a "revaluation reserve".[25] **18–005**

The same principle applies to unrealised losses, but here there is an important contrast between the public company rule and the rule for all companies. Under **18–006**

[21] This again reverses the English common law rule which allowed unrealised profits on fixed assets to be distributed: *Dimbula Valley (Ceylon) Tea Co Ltd v Laurie* [1961] Ch. 353 Ch D. Scots law took a stricter view: *Westburn Sugar Refineries Ltd v Inland Revenue Commissioners*, 1960 S.L.T. 297 IH (1 Div).

[22] CA 2006 s.853(4): they are "such profits or losses of the company as fall to be treated as realised in accordance with principles generally accepted at the time when the accounts are prepared". However, s.841 does lay down that provisions in the accounts (other than revaluation provisions) should be treated as realised losses (for example, depreciation provisions); s.844 requires development costs to be treated as a realised loss, even if stated as an asset in the accounts; and s.843 makes provisions about the realised gains and losses of long-term insurance businesses.

[23] Nor is the net balance of realised profits and losses a figure required to be stated in the accounts. So accounting standards tend to ignore the question. For the current professional guidance see ICAEW, *Guidance on Realised and Distributable Profits under the Companies Act 2006* (2017), Tech 02/17BL.

[24] If, however, the re-valued asset is later distributed *in specie* to its shareholders (a perfectly possible, if not common, course of action, because distributions do not have to be in cash) the amount of the unrealised profit is treated as a realised profit for the purpose of determining the legality of the distribution: s.846. The purpose of this provision is to make it possible for the company to distribute assets at book value, even if the value to be found in the company's accounts represents a revaluation of the assets. See further below at para.18–020. The provision was driven initially by a perceived need to facilitate de-mergers, in which assets or shares held by a company might be distributed to its shareholders.

[25] Which is an undistributable reserve unless it represents realised gains. See, for example, the Large and Medium-sized Companies and Groups (Accounts and Reports) Regulations 2008 (SI 2008/410) Sch.1 Pt 2 para.35.

the test for all companies (s.830), a company with an accumulated positive balance of realised profits and realised losses may lawfully distribute them, even if it is carrying extensive unrealised losses (though it may be a breach of directors' duty or imprudent to do so). Thus, a private company, which holds an important asset which has fallen in value but has not disposed of the asset or otherwise realised the loss, may distribute its aggregate accumulated profits without setting off against them the unrealised loss. However, as we saw in para.18–003, a public company applying the balance sheet test is required to treat unrealised losses reflected in the balance sheet as one of the items against which assets must continue to be held when calculating the permitted amount of a distribution (except to the extent that they are covered by unrealised profits). In this important respect, the rule for public companies is more constraining than the general rule.[26]

The fact that such an important part of the mechanism for determining the legality of a dividend as the distinction between realised and unrealised profits and losses is to be found in professional guidance, apparently without any form of public oversight, has been the subject of criticism.[27]

IDENTIFYING THE AMOUNT AVAILABLE FOR DISTRIBUTION

18–007 It is apparent from the foregoing that, in determining whether distributions can be made in accordance with the statutory rules, what counts in most cases are the figures in the company's accounts. This may seem an obvious way to proceed: companies are normally required by the CA 2006 to produce accounts annually and, except for small companies, to have them audited, thus providing a degree of verification; and the declaration of a dividend is normally one of the decisions for the annual general meeting of the shareholders, at which the accounts will be considered as well. The statute calls the accounts which are to be used for assessing the legality of the distribution the "relevant" accounts. Since dividends are paid by individual, not groups of, companies, it is the individual accounts of the paying company, not the group accounts, which are the relevant ones.[28] Beyond that, the general rule is easy to state: the most recent statutory accounts should be used.[29] When that is so, the distribution is lawful so long as it is justified by reference to those accounts and the accounts have been properly prepared in accordance with the Act, or have been properly prepared subject only to matters not material for determining whether the distribution would be

[26] CA 2006 s.831(4)(c). "This means that, in calculating the amount available for distributions, a public company must reduce the amount of its net realised profits available for distribution by the amount of its net unrealised losses" (ICAEW, *Guidance on Realised and Distributable Profits under the Companies Act 2006* (2017), Tech 02/17BL, para.2.31).

[27] House of Commons, Business, Energy and Industrial Strategy Committee, *The Future of Audit*, HC 1718 (April 2019), Ch.3. The Government proposed in March 2021 to transfer guidance or rule-making powers on this issue to the new accounts regulator, ARGA, on which see Ch.22. See BEIS, *Restoring Trust in Audit and Corporate Governance* (March 2021), para.2.2.8.

[28] CA 2006 s.836(2). For an example of the problems that ignoring this point can cause see *Inn Spirit Ltd v Burns* [2002] EWHC 1731 (Ch); [2002] 2 B.C.L.C. 780.

[29] CA 2006 s.836(2).

lawful.[30] This involves compliance, not only with the accounts rules discussed in Ch.22, but all the rules which govern the numbers stated in the accounts. For example, an unlawful reduction of capital may render a subsequent dividend payment unlawful. These accounts must have been duly audited, if subject to audit, and, if the auditors' report is qualified, the auditors must also state in writing whether the respect in which the report was qualified is material in determining whether the distribution would be lawful. This statement must have been laid before the company in general meeting, or sent to the members where no meeting is held.[31]

The time at which the test for the legality of the distribution is to be applied is when the distribution is made. This is an obvious rule but it does cause difficulties for the apparently common practice in private companies, for tax reasons, of declaring dividends on a monthly basis and then re-characterising some of the distributions as remuneration (and paying the higher tax) if at the end of the financial year it turns out the company does not have sufficient distributable profits to cover all the distributions.[32] While this procedure may keep the tax authorities happy and while it is unlikely the director/shareholders would cause the company to sue them for the return of the unlawful dividends under s.847 (see para.18–011), the controllers of the private company will be at risk if during the financial year the company goes into insolvency and the liquidator, acting on behalf of the creditors, takes a different view of where the company's interests lie.

Interim and initial accounts

Typically, the company relies on the annual accounts which the CA 2006 requires it to produce, as discussed in Ch.22. In two cases, however, special accounts will be needed. The first is where at the time of the distribution the last annual accounts do not in fact support the level of distribution proposed to be made. In that event the company may be able to justify the distribution by reference to additional "interim accounts".[33] The second is where it is proposed to declare a dividend during the company's first accounting period or before any accounts **18–008**

---

[30] CA 2006 s.837(2). For a dividend rendered unlawful by an unlawful reduction of capital see *LRH Services Ltd (In Liquidation) v Trew* [2018] EWHC 600 (Ch) at [186]. For a dividend unlawful because the distributing parent company had received the funds from a subsidiary by way of a distribution in breach of the latter's articles see *Re Cleveland Trust Plc* [1991] B.C.C. 33. If the directors are non-negligently ignorant of the defect, they be able to protect themselves against liability by invoking s.1157 (see para.18–012).

[31] CA 2006 s.837(3)–(4). The auditor's statement may be made whether or not a distribution is proposed at the time when the statement is made and may refer to all or any types of distribution; it will then suffice to validate any distributions of the types covered by the statement: s.837(5). This rule also applies if the directors choose to have an audit, although not obliged to do so. The need for the auditors' statement where the accounts are qualified is frequently overlooked and the resulting distribution will be unlawful: *Precision Dippings Ltd v Precision Dippings Marketing Ltd* (1985) 1 B.C.C. 99539 CA (Civ Div); *BDS Roof Bond Ltd (In Liquidation) v Douglas* [2000] B.C.C. 770 Ch D.

[32] *Global Corporate Ltd v Hale* [2018] EWCA Civ 2618; [2019] B.C.C. 431. In this case there were no "interim" accounts (see para.18–008) to support the in-year distributions.

[33] CA 2006 s.836(2)(a).

have been presented in respect of that period.[34] In that event it will have to prepare "initial accounts". Initial accounts enable the company to make a distribution before its first set of financial statements is produced. Interim accounts allow the company to take advantage of an improvement in its financial position since the previous statutory accounts were produced. This might occur, for example, when a realised profit had been made on the sale of fixed assets after the date of the last annual accounts and the company wanted to distribute part or all of it to its shareholders without waiting for the next annual accounts. It could also occur if the net trading profits in the current year are seen to be running at a rate considerably higher than formerly and the directors wished to give the shareholders early concrete evidence of this by paying an immediate dividend. In both these examples the previous year's accounts might well not justify the payment and would have to be supplemented by interim accounts.[35]

Interim dividends

18–009 The term "interim accounts", although now well established in the CA 2006, is potentially confusing because it might lead one to suppose that such accounts are needed whenever it is proposed to declare interim (which are very common) or special dividends, in addition to the normal dividend for the year. That is not so. So long as the company has duly complied with its obligations under the Act in respect of its annual accounts for the previous year, it can, in the current year, pay interim or other special dividends so long as these dividends are supported by the previous year's accounts.[36] It is only when the last annual accounts would not justify a proposed payment that it is necessary to prepare interim accounts. Normally, however, it will not be necessary to prepare interim accounts merely because the company pays quarterly or half-yearly interim dividends, in anticipation of the final dividend for the year, to be declared by the company when that year's accounts are presented. The previous year's accounts are used to support the interim dividends. Of course, the directors will normally declare interim dividends only if they take the view that the accounts to be produced at the end of the year will show that these were justified. Indeed, they might conceivably be in breach of their general duties if this were not the case. However, they do not rely on those prospective accounts for the legality of the in-year dividends. The articles normally provide for interim dividends to be paid

---

[34] CA 2006 s.836(2)(b).

[35] The requirements for interim and initial accounts are set out in ss.838 and 839. They are onerous for public companies, though interim accounts need not be audited. Listed companies probably meet the statutory requirements routinely since they are subject to the FCA's requirements for regular half-year financial statements. See para.27–003.

[36] CA 2006 s.840. However, it sometimes happens that directors pay dividends out of profits in the current year, which annual accounts for the previous year do not support, without remembering to file interim accounts. When this is discovered, the company suffers the embarrassment of having to propose to its shareholders that they approve deeds of release in respect of the company's resulting claims. This they will normally agree to, since, as we see below, the company may have claims against the shareholders who received the dividends as well as the directors who paid them.

on the authority of the directors alone, there not being any regularly scheduled meeting of the shareholders to which the matter could be put.[37]

Adverse developments subsequent to the accounts

The need for interim accounts arises out of possible improvements in the company's financial position which may have occurred since the last statutory accounts were drawn up. What, however, about the opposite situation, where the company's financial position has deteriorated since the statutory accounts were drawn up? If the directors have discovered that the relevant accounts were so seriously inaccurate that they did not in fact give a true and fair view of the state of the company's affairs and its profits or losses at the time the accounts were signed, they clearly should not recommend a dividend, and should withdraw any recommendation they have made; for the dividend, if paid, would be unlawful on the part of the company.[38] If, however, the relevant accounts truly reflected the position as at their date but there has occurred some financial calamity thereafter, payment of the dividend would not, seemingly, be unlawful under the statute. However, as we have seen, a directors' recommendation or decision (in the case of interim dividends) as to the level of the dividend is an essential part of the dividend-setting process. Consequently, the fiduciary and other duties of directors (discussed in Ch.10) are relevant to this particular decision of the board, as to any other. Payment where the company's trading position has recently deteriorated might constitute a breach of the directors' duties—for example, to promote the success of the company. We discuss the specific creditor-facing duties of directors, both statutory and at common law, in Ch.19. 18–010

In its reform proposals of March 2021,[39] BEIS proposed that directors of at least publicly traded companies, when proposing a dividend, should be required to make a statement confirming that they had satisfied themselves that their proposal complied with the statutory rules and their fiduciary duties and their "reasonable expectation" that the proposed payment would not jeopardise the company's solvency over the next two years. The second part of the statement is a further illustration of the growing use of solvency statements, though BEIS was not clear about the sanctions to be attached to inaccurate statements.[40]

However, it is possible that a failure to take post-accounts events into consideration when making a distribution already would constitute, not simply a breach of duty on the part of the directors, but an unlawful act on the part of the company. This is because, despite the statutory provisions on distributions, the

[37] As do the model articles for both public (Model Articles for Public Companies art.70) and private (Model Articles for Private Companies Limited by Shares art.30) companies. The practice of some companies paying only interim dividends was criticised by the BEIS Committee (fn.27), on the grounds that it reduces shareholder control over them. However, it is likely to be a rare case where the shareholders would reject or reduce an interim dividend the directors are prepared to pay.

[38] *Re Cleveland Trust Plc* [1991] B.C.C. 33. See fn.28. And the accounts should be revised; there are now statutory provisions for this: see para.22–037.

[39] BEIS, *Restoring Trust in Audit and Corporate Governance* (March 2021), para.2.2.21.

[40] Beyond saying that the statement might make it easier subsequently to demonstrate a breach of fiduciary duty.

CA 2006 preserves "any rule of law" restricting dividends.[41] Thus, the common law rule prohibiting the return of capital to shareholders[42] continues in force in relation to distributions. We discuss this principle in more detail in paras 18–016 onwards. All we need note here is that the common law rule applies on the basis of the financial position of the company at the time the distribution is declared and so it would be broken if a company made a distribution on the basis of profits shown in the accounts which had been dissipated by the time the directors came to declare the dividend.[43]

CONSEQUENCES OF UNLAWFUL DISTRIBUTIONS

Recovery from members

18–011 No criminal sanctions are provided in the CA 2006 in respect of distributions which it renders unlawful, but something (but not comprehensively) is said about the civil consequences. It is important for the purposes of this chapter to note that these remedies are vested in the company, not the creditors directly, even if the primary purpose of Pt 23 is to protect creditor interests. Consequently, the remedies are most likely to be invoked after there has been a change of control at board level or the company has gone into an insolvency procedure and control has shifted to an administrator or liquidator.

Recovery from the recipients of the distribution is dealt with by s.847. This provides that, when a distribution[44] is made to a member which the member knows, or has reasonable grounds for believing, is made in contravention (in whole or in part) of the statutory distribution rules, that person is liable to repay it or, if the distribution was otherwise than in cash, its value.[45] Thus, by virtue of this section, the payment, though "unlawful", is neither void nor voidable but can nevertheless be recovered from any recipient of it who knew or ought to have known that it was unlawful.

This provision has been interpreted to mean that there is liability to repay the distribution if the recipient knows it has not been paid out of distributable profits, even if that person is unaware that such distributions are illegal.[46] The section is thus potentially wide-ranging in its impact on shareholders if this proposition is coupled with a broad approach to "knowledge" of the company's affairs. This raises the question of whether "reasonable grounds for believing" means that a shareholder is treated as knowing those facts which would have been discovered through proper enquiries (constructive knowledge) or only those to which the

[41] CA 2006 s.851(1)—unless otherwise expressly provided. An example is discussed in para.18–020.

[42] *Trevor v Whitworth* (1887) 12 App. Cas. 409 HL.

[43] See *Peter Buchanan Ltd v McVey* [1955] A.C. 516 (Note) SC at 521–522, a decision of the High Court of Justice of Eire.

[44] Other than a distribution which constitutes financial assistance for the acquisition of the company's own shares given in breach of the Act (see para.17–041) or any payment made in respect of the redemption or purchase of shares in the company (para.17–006): s.847(4).

[45] CA 2006 s.847(2).

[46] *It's a Wrap (UK) Ltd (In Liquidation) v Gula* [2006] EWCA Civ 544; [2006] B.C.C. 626.

recipient turned a blind eye.[47] On the former approach it might be argued that a shareholder who had received the annual reports should be treated as knowing, for example, that the company had no distributable profits or that the auditor had not included the required statement in the case of a qualified report,[48] even if he or she had not in fact read them.[49]

However, this section does not constitute the only basis on which a claim for repayment of dividend can be made against a shareholder. The company may claim repayment at common law.[50] This might be put on one of two bases. The first is that the payment of an unlawful dividend amounts to a misapplication by the directors of corporate property and where "the transferee of the assets has knowledge of the facts rendering the disposition ultra vires, that party is under a duty to restore those assets to the company because he is deemed to hold them as constructive trustee".[51] The second is that the recipients have been unjustly enriched by the unlawful payment and are under an obligation to return it, subject only to the defence of change of position. The first claim may or may not be broader than the statutory claim in terms of its definition of knowledge,[52] whereas the second claim is based on strict liability (subject to the change of position defence). If this second head of recovery were accepted by the courts, it would operate more broadly than the statutory claim which turns on some degree of knowledge on the part of the recipients.[53]

---

[47] Arden and Chadwick LJJ were divided on this issue in *It's a Wrap (UK) Ltd v Gula* [2006] B.C.C. 626—the point not being relevant to the decision in that case. The former is a more natural reading of the language of the section and conforms to the approach of the common law (see below), whilst the latter is a more natural reading of the language of the Directive (an irregularity of which the recipient "could not in view of the circumstances have been unaware"), which the section implemented in the UK.

[48] See para.18–007; and see *Precision Dippings Ltd v Precison Dippings Marketing Ltd* (1985) 1 B.C.C. 99539 CA (Civ Div).

[49] It seems fanciful to suppose that any court would hold that a small shareholder in a listed company should study the relevant accounts and the documents accompanying them and read them with an understanding of the Act to check that their dividends are lawfully payable, no matter how much that court may be committed to the doctrine that ignorance of the law is no excuse. In relation to an institutional investor, however, or a "business angel" who has invested in a start-up company, the proposition is not so fanciful.

[50] This basis of claim is specifically preserved by s.847(3).

[51] *Rolled Steel Products (Holdings) Ltd v British Steel Corp* [1986] Ch. 246 at 303–304 per Browne-Wilkinson LJ. Not surprisingly, the principle applies equally where the transferee is the director receiving the dividend as shareholder: see *Allied Carpets Plc v Nethercott* [2001] B.C.C. 81 QBD; following the earlier case of *Precision Dippings Ltd v Precison Dippings Marketing Ltd* (1985) 1 B.C.C. 99539. Indeed, a director of the company or of another group company is the person in respect of whom the knowledge requirements can most easily be met.

[52] Constructive knowledge appears to suffice for liability at common law: see *Rolled Steel Products v British Steel* (1984) 1 B.C.C. 99158 at 99194–99195 per Slade LJ.

[53] Section 847—and this might be taken as an indication of a legislative intent to exclude the unjust enrichment claim.

Recovery from directors

18–012 The statute provides for no specific remedy against the directors who authorised the unlawful distribution, but here again the common law provides a remedy.[54] It has been clear since the decision in *Flitcroft*'s case[55] in the nineteenth century that directors who cause the company to pay dividends "out of capital" (i.e. where there are no profits available for distribution) are under an equitable duty to restore to the company the value of the assets wrongfully paid away. This was an application of the more general principle that directors are liable to compensate the company for misapplying company assets. In *Bairstow v Queens Moat Houses Plc*[56] the Court of Appeal applied the principle to hold directors liable where the accounts failed to give a true and fair view[57] of the company's financial situation as a result of accounting irregularities of which the directors were aware. Thus, the requirement to restore value applies whether the distribution is unlawful under the statutory rules (as in *Bairstow*) or by virtue of the common law (as in *Flitcroft's* case).

We examine the scope of the common law rules on unlawful distributions in more detail in paras 18–016 onwards. Here, we concentrate on their remedial impact upon directors who act in breach of the statutory rules. A long-debated issue is whether the directors' liability to restore the value of the distribution is a strict one or is based on fault, requiring dishonesty or at least negligence. In *Re Paycheck Services 3 Ltd*[58] Rimer LJ thought obiter that the liability was strict, but subject to the court's discretion to grant relief under s.1157 of the CA 2006, where the director had acted "honestly and reasonably".[59] On appeal to the Supreme Court this view was endorsed, again obiter, by three of the justices.[60]

The principle that the directors should restore the value of corporate assets unlawfully paid away as distributions is potentially a much harsher one than the claim that a shareholder should return to the company dividends improperly paid to that shareholder. The director might have received no dividends him- or herself and yet be liable, in principle, to restore the whole of the amount wrongfully paid out of the company's assets. However, in *Bairstow* the court showed little interest in confining the scope of the directors' liability. The directors were held liable to pay equitable compensation equal to the full amount paid by way of the unlawful

---

[54] If the director is a recipient shareholder, then, of course, he or she may also be liable in that way.

[55] *Re Exchange Banking Co (Flitcroft's Case)* (1882) 21 Ch. D. 519 CA.

[56] *Bairstow v Queens Moat Houses Plc* [2001] EWCA Civ 712; [2002] B.C.C. 91.

[57] On the meaning of this phrase see para.22–017.

[58] *Re Paycheck Services 3 Ltd* [2009] EWCA Civ 625; [2010] B.C.C. 104 at [81]–[85]. There are two competing lines of authority on the point, as laid out in the judgment in this case.

[59] See para.10–129. If the company's claim is brought, as it often is, by a liquidator acting under s.212 of the IA 1986 the court has a power to order an account of such amount "as the court thinks just". It is unclear whether this discretion adds to what is available to the court under s.1157 of the CA 2006. See the debate among the judges in *Re Paycheck Services 3 Ltd* [2010] B.C.C. 104.

[60] *Re Paycheck Services 3 Ltd* [2010] B.C.C. 104 at [45]–[47] (Lord Hope); [124] (Lord Walker); and [146] (Lord Clarke). However, in *Burnden Holdings (UK) Ltd (In Liquidation) v Fielding* [2019] EWHC 1566 (Ch), Zacaroli J after extensive review of the authorities took the view that directors were not liable if they had taken reasonable care to establish the availability of profits to support the dividend.

dividend.[61] The principle in *Flitcroft*'s case, the court held, was not limited to companies which were insolvent at the time of the claim against the director and when the payment would benefit the creditors as the parties now interested in the value of the company's assets. It applied also to solvent companies, where the shareholders had already benefitted from the unlawful dividend and might not be under an obligation to return it, at least under the statute, because they lacked the relevant knowledge of its illegality (see above).[62] In *Bairstow* itself it appeared that the accounting regularities could have been corrected and a lawful dividend paid. However, the court rejected the argument that the amount payable by way of compensation in respect of the unlawful distributions should be reduced by reference to the hypothetical that, had the dividend not been paid unlawfully, it—or some part of it—would have been distributed lawfully. That issue is still to be resolved: the Court of Appeal in *Auden McKenzie (Pharma Division) Ltd v Patel*[63] refused to strike out the argument for a reduction in compensation on a hypothetical basis, whilst recognising that the argument went beyond the established authorities.

Strict liability for directors coupled with reliance by them on court discretion to grant relief under s.1157 is obviously less attractive to them than a fault requirement for initial liability or a more liberal interpretation of the sum required to be repaid. The only relaxation so far accepted is that, where there is a properly drawn set of accounts in existence which justify a distribution up to a particular level but the company exceeds that level, the requirement to make "a distribution out of the profits available for that purpose" means that the directors act improperly, and are obliged to restore, only to the extent of the excess.[64] It is also worth noting that this area of directors' liability, like directors' liability for breach of their statutory duties, has not been codified in the CA 2006. It continues to be developed at common law and by way of analogy with the rules applying to other fiduciaries who mishandle assets under their control.

Given the potentially serious consequences, for both directors and shareholders, if an unlawful dividend is paid, it is not uncommon for companies to put forward shareholder resolutions to adopt a deed of release in respect of the company's claim against its directors or shareholders for restoration of the money paid out. The circular supporting these resolution does not always make it clear that directors are more at risk than shareholders and presents both as having the

[61] *Bairstow v Queens Moat Houses Plc* [2001] 2 B.C.L.C. 531 at 548–550; distinguishing *Target Holdings Ltd v Redferns* [1996] A.C. 421 HL. See also *Inn Spirit Ltd v Burns* [2002] EWHC 1731 (Ch); [2002] 2 B.C.L.C. 780, where a subsidiary had paid a dividend directly to the shareholders of the parent company and the court refused to entertain the question of whether the same amount of dividend could have reached the shareholders' pockets by way of a distribution to the parent and then a distribution by the parent.

[62] The court did leave open the possibility that the repaying directors could claim an equitable contribution from the shareholders who had received the improper dividend with notice of the facts.

[63] *Auden McKenzie (Pharma Division) Ltd v Patel* [2019] EWCA Civ 2291; [2020] B.C.C. 316. The case did not involve unlawful dividends but the argument was that, had the director not misappropriated corporate assets, those assets would have been distributed lawfully to the company's only two shareholders (of whom the director was one) so that the company did not suffer a loss as a result of the misappropriation.

[64] *Re Marini Ltd* [2003] EWHC 334 (Ch); [2004] B.C.C. 172. In this situation it is most unlikely in any event likely that the court would reach the same result under its s.1157 powers, even if the directors were liable in principle to repay the whole distribution.

same interest in passing the resolutions. The resolution is usually put forward only in relation to "technical" breaches of the dividend rules, i.e. situations where the company (or some other company in the group) had the relevant amount of distributable profits but, for example, failed to file the relevant accounts before the distribution was agreed but did so a few days later or failed to pass the profits to the company which was making the distribution. This is probably just as well. Since the principal purpose of the dividend rules is to protect creditors, it is doubtful whether the courts would regard such resolutions as binding on the company where the company did not have the relevant amount of distributable profits, especially as against a liquidator or administrator.

Finally, there is the possibility of an action by the company against its auditors if it can be shown that their negligence led the directors to approve a defective set of accounts. As Lord Oliver said in *Caparo v Dickman*:

> "It is the auditors' function to ensure, so far as possible, that the financial information as to the company's affairs prepared by the directors accurately reflects the company's position in order, first, to protect the company itself from the consequences of undetected errors or, possibly, wrongdoing (by, for instance, declaring dividends out of capital) …".[65]

TRANSFERS AT AN UNDERVALUE

Statutory rules

18–013 Section 423 of the IA 1986 is headed "transactions defrauding creditors".[66] From the point of view of a creditor, the section has the following merits. First, it applies to all transactions (no matter their type) which a company[67] may enter into at an undervalue. It covers gifts, transactions where the company receives no consideration and those where the consideration from the other party is "significantly less" than that provided by the company.[68] Secondly, it applies whether or not the company was in the vicinity of insolvency at the time of the transaction and whether or not the company subsequently entered into an insolvency procedure, so that its location in the IA 1986 is to some degree anomalous. Thirdly, the court has wide remedial powers[69] to be exercised with the aim of "restoring the position to what it would have been if the transaction had not been entered into, and protecting the interests of persons who are victims

[65] *Caparo Industries Plc v Dickman* [1990] B.C.C. 164 HL at 179. See also *Assetco Plc v Grant Thornton UK LLP* [2019] EWHC 150 (Comm), where, however, the grossly negligent auditors escaped liability in relation to the dividend payments on the basis that, on the facts, the directors' decision to pay the dividends broke the chain of causation between the auditor's negligence and the company's loss. We discuss the liability of auditors in more detail in para.23–035.

[66] The section goes back to the Fraudulent Conveyances Act 1571 of Elizabeth I. It still applies only in England and Wales.

[67] The section applies to "any person" but we confine ourselves to transactions by companies. Some decisions (for example, *Re Taylor Sinclair (Capital) Ltd (In Liquidation)* [2001] 2 B.C.L.C. 176 Ch D (Companies Ct)) have built an element of mutuality into the scope of the statutory description of the transactions to which it applies, but this was doubted by David Richards LJ in *BAT Industries Plc v Sequana SA* [2019] EWCA Civ 112; [2019] B.C.C. 631 at [58]–[60].

[68] IA 1986 s.423(1).

[69] IA 1986 s.425.

of the transaction."[70] This will typically involve an order made against the transferee of the assets. The transferee's knowledge (if it exists) of the unlawful purpose and participation in the wrongdoing will significantly affect the way in which the court exercises its discretion.[71] Fourthly, the section can be triggered not only when the company is in an insolvency procedure by the relevant insolvency practitioner, but also by a "victim" when the company is not in insolvency and, with the leave of the court, even if it is.[72] A "victim" is someone who is prejudiced or capable of being prejudiced by the transaction and the definition thus extends beyond a creditor with a current claim against the company to include, for example, someone whose contract the company had broken but who had not yet suffered any resulting damage.[73] In any event, for going concern companies, the remedy lies directly in the hands of a creditor, in contrast to the remedies for unlawful distributions under Pt 23 of the CA 2006.

The section's principal limitation from a creditor's perspective is that it is contravened only if the company acts for the purpose of putting assets beyond the reach of an actual or potential creditor or of prejudicing the interests of such creditor.[74] The fact that the transaction does in fact reduce the probability of the claim being met is not enough. Proof of purpose may be difficult to show, especially where a going concern company enters into a transaction which has a colourable commercial rationale. In complex transactions, proof of undervalue may also raise difficulties.[75]

The salience of s.423 for company lawyers was increased by the decision of the Court of Appeal in *BAT Industries Plc v Sequana SA*[76] that the section applied to dividend distributions. The company in question, which was a no longer a trading company and existed only to meet environmental clean-up liabilities of uncertain size, had paid a dividend to its parent (Sequana), which was found to be in compliance with the provisions of the CA 2006. Nevertheless, BAT brought a s.423 claim against Sequana, on the grounds that BAT had a right to an indemnity from the company in respect of its (BAT's) share of the clean-up costs, which the **18–014**

70 IA 1986 s.423(2).

71 *4Eng Ltd v Harper* [2009] EWHC 2633 (Ch); [2010] B.C.C. 746. Although the court's powers as to remedy are wide, it appears the court cannot make an order against someone who has not benefitted from the transaction, for example, the authorising directors of the transferring company if they have not benefitted: *Johnson v Arden* [2018] EWHC 1624 (Ch); [2019] 2 B.C.L.C. 215.

72 IA 1986 s.424.

73 IA 1986 s.423(5); *Hill v Spread Trustee Co Ltd* [2006] EWCA Civ 542; [2006] B.C.C. 646 at [101]; *Giles v Rhind* [2007] EWHC 687 (Ch); [2007] 2 B.C.L.C. 531.

74 IA 1986 s.423(3). The statutory purpose does not have to be the sole purpose of the transaction nor even a "substantial" one, but it is not enough if the transfer merely had the statutory effect: *Inland Revenue Commissioners v Hashmi* [2002] EWCA Civ 981; [2002] B.C.C. 943; *JSC BTA Bank v Ablyazov* [2018] EWCA Civ 1176; [2019] B.C.C. 96. In the US, where the statute of Elizabeth I had a larger statutory aftermath than in England itself, the Uniform Fraudulent Conveyance Act catches also transactions which leave the company with "unreasonably small" assets for the conduct of its business even if there was no intention to defraud creditors.

75 IA 1986 s.423 thus has some parallels with the "evasion" principle for piercing the corporate veil (see *Petrodel Resources Ltd v Prest* [2013] UKSC 34; [2013] B.C.C. 571, para 7–018), but in the veil piercing cases the corporate assets are made available to the personal creditors of the corporate controller, whereas s.423 typically operates to restore assets to the company for the benefit of the corporate creditors.

76 *BAT Industries Plc v Sequana SA* [2019] B.C.C. 631.

dividend imperilled. The court ordered payment to BAT (not the company, which by this time was no longer part of the Sequana group) of clean-up costs up to the amount of the dividend. To reach this result the court had to hold as a matter of law that the dividend payment was to be characterised as (1) a transaction; and (2) a transaction for no consideration, and then on the facts that the purpose of the dividend was to put company assets beyond the reach of BAT. Overall, the decision shows how s.423 of the IA 1986 can operate as an overriding control over the payment of dividends which are lawful under the companies legislation, provided the victim can show the requisite purpose. This was relatively easy in this case, given the non-trading nature of the paying company.

18–015 Where the company does in fact enter into administration or liquidation, s.238[77] contains a stronger set of provisions for reversing the effects of transactions entered into by a company at an undervalue in the period immediately before the onset of insolvency.[78] That period is two years, provided that at the time of the transaction the company was unable to pay its debts as they fell due or was put in that position by the transaction.[79] The main difference with s.423 is that there is no need to show that the purpose of the transaction was to put assets beyond the reach of creditors. Rather, the court may make an order unless it is satisfied that the transaction was entered into by the company in good faith and for the purpose of carrying on the company's business and that there were reasonable grounds for thinking that the transaction would benefit the company. This last condition is a recognition that in the vicinity of insolvency the company may legitimately engage in transactions in an attempt to avoid administration or liquidation which it would reject if a going concern, for example, selling its stock at a discount in order to shift it rapidly. Under this section, not surprisingly, only the administrator or liquidator (not an individual creditor) may bring the claim. This standing requirement also has the important consequence that recoveries are not caught by any security interest the company may have given and so benefit the unsecured creditors.

The definition of an undervalue transaction and the court's remedial powers are similar to those under s.423.[80] However, it is worth noting that both ss.423 and 238 analyse the relevant transaction wholly from the point of view of the company. It is therefore possible that the other party to the transaction will have acted in good faith and yet be at risk that the transaction is reversed by the court.[81] Where the company is a going concern, this may not matter too much, since the other party is simply put back in the position it was in before the transaction was entered into—though the other party will lose the benefit of its deal. However, if the company is in liquidation and the transaction is reversed, the other party may be left to prove in the insolvency of the company in

77 Like s.423 this section applies only in England and Wales. There is a rather different provision on gratuitous alienations (s.242) applying in Scotland.

78 Defined in s.240(3).

79 IA 1986 s.240(1)(2). This is rebuttably presumed to be the case if the other party to the transaction is connected with the company.

80 IA 1986 s.238(3)–(4), 241.

81 IA 1986 ss.241(2)(2A) and 425(2) in slightly different ways protect those who receive property (or other benefit) in good faith and for value, but only in the case of property (or benefit) received other than from the company, i.e. these provisions benefit only subsequent transferees.

competition with its other unsecured creditors for the return of payments or other transfers made to the company. The remedial provisions, however, are formulated so as to confer upon the court some discretion to avoid an unjust result.[82]

The statute thus treats undervalue transactions in the period immediately before insolvency with more suspicion than when the company is a going concern, without ruling them out entirely.

COMMON LAW

The statutory rules on transfers at an undervalue are supplemented by common law principles. The core principle is that it is unlawful for a company to make a distribution of its assets to its shareholders except in ways permitted by the CA 2006. We saw in para.18–012 how this principle, which dates back to the early years of modern company law in the nineteenth century, has been used to provide a remedy against directors who make distributions in breach of Pt 23 of the Act. Here, we examine in more detail the substantive scope of the rule, which goes beyond the transactions covered by the Act. **18–016**

In *Aveling Barford Ltd v Perion Ltd*[83] the company in question was struggling financially and, although its balance sheet purported to show positive net assets, it had a large cumulative loss on its profit and loss account and so was in no position to make a distribution under the rules contained in Pt 23. Aveling Barford's controller, who was a director of the company and appears to have held all its shares via a parent company registered in Liberia, caused it to transfer a major piece of real property at a significant undervalue to a company registered in Jersey (Perion), whose shares were in turn held on trust for family settlements of the controller. This was a breach of fiduciary duty by the controller as director of the claimant. Further, since Perion was fully aware through the controller of the circumstances of the transaction, the transferee held the property on a constructive trust for the claimant. Aveling Barford's liquidator sued to enforce the constructive trust, thus aiming to bring about a reversal of the transaction. Perion raised the defence that the transaction had been informally ratified by all the shareholders of the claimant, so that the breach of fiduciary duty by the controller had been cured. Hoffmann J rejected this defence on the grounds that the shareholders could not ratify a breach of a mandatory rule setting limits on the company's powers. More precisely, "a transaction which amounts to an unauthorised return of capital is ultra vires and cannot be validated by shareholder ratification or approval."[84] In this case, therefore, the unauthorised return of capital rule was deployed to invalidate the shareholder approval and to leave fiduciary law to operate so as to bring about a restoration of the position

[82] The governing proposition under both sections is that the court should make "such order as it thinks fit" for restoring the prior position: ss.238(3) and 423(2). For a discussion of this issue under the corresponding Scottish provisions see *MacDonald v Carnbroe Estates Ltd* [2019] UKSC 57; 2019 S.L.T. 1469.

[83] *Aveling Barford Ltd v Perion Ltd* (1989) 5 B.C.C. 677.

[84] *Aveling Barford Ltd v Perion Ltd* (1989) 5 B.C.C. 677 at 682. With the abolition of the ultra vires doctrine associated with the statement of purposes contained in the company's memorandum (see Ch.8), the term ultra vires is to be understood as referring simply to a breach of any rule of law setting limits on the company's powers.

which had obtained before the transaction had been concluded, very much as s423 of the IA 1986 does in its sphere. It is also worth noting that the court was willing to treat the transaction as an unauthorised return of capital to shareholders, even though neither the controller of Aveling Barford nor Perion was a member of the company: the ultimate economic interest of the controller in both companies was, implicitly, treated as sufficient for the operation of the principle. Whether this result could have been reached under Pt 23 is doubtful.

18–017 A number of points are left unclear by this decision. One is whether the common law principle applies only where the company does not have distributable profits, as was the case in *Aveling Barford*. In other words, is the principle one which simply reinforces the statutory prohibition on distributions when the company has no distributable profits by catching transactions which might not fall within it? Or is it a somewhat wider principle which constrains how the company deals with its assets in relation to its members even when it does have distributable profits? The effect of the slightly wider principle is that it would rule out informal distributions of assets to members, even if the company could have made a lawful distribution under the procedures contained in Pt 23. An example of the wider operation of the principle is provided by *Ridge Securities Ltd v IRC*.[85] As part of a tax avoidance scheme, a parent company caused its subsidiaries to borrow from it at what the court characterised as a "grotesque" rate of interest.[86] The court held that the interest payments by the subsidiaries were "invalid" or had "no legal operation". [87] The judge, Pennycuick J, put his decision on the following basis (at 495):

> "A company can only lawfully deal with its assets in furtherance of its objects. The corporators may take assets out of the company by way of dividend, or, with the leave of the court, by way of reduction of capital, or in a winding-up. They may of course acquire them for full consideration. They cannot take assets out of the company by way of voluntary distribution, however described, and if they attempt to do so, the distribution is ultra vires the company."

It is to be noted that this passage makes no reference to the issue of whether the subsidiaries had distributable profits at the time of the impugned transaction nor does there appear to have been evidence before the court on this matter. This passage suggests that the common law rule is broader than the statutory provisions on distributions, for it indicates that any return of corporate assets to

---

[85] *Ridge Securities Ltd v Inland Revenue Commissioners* [1964] 1 W.L.R 479 Ch D. See also *MacPherson v European Strategic Bureau Ltd* [2002] B.C.C. 39 CA (Civ Div) at [48]: "In my view, to enter into an arrangement which seeks to achieve a distribution of assets, as if on a winding up, without making proper provision for creditors is, itself, a breach of the duties which directors owe to the company; alternatively, it is ultra vires the company" (per Chadwick LJ); and *British & Commonwealth Holdings Plc v Barclays Bank Plc* [1995] B.C.C. 1059 (replacement of obligation of an insolvent company to redeem shares by an obligation to pay damages of like amount in respect of the failure to redeem would have been ultra vires if it had not been approved by the court as part of a statutory scheme of arrangement—see Ch.29).

[86] "In every case . . . the company concerned bound itself to pay within a few days after the advance a net sum by way of interest far greater than the amount of the advance." (*Ridge Securities Ltd v IRC* [1964] 1 W.L.R 479 at 493.)

[87] Since the question before the court was whether the Revenue were entitled to disregard the interest payments when computing the tax liabilities of the parent, the court did not have to decide what the precise impact of its decision was as between the subsidiaries and the parent.

the shareholders, which is not justified by a statutory provision or the pursuit of the company's objects, will be unlawful, even if the company has distributable profits.

It is clearly not the case that the company is prohibited from contracting with its members and in fact such contracting is common. Some of those contracts will turn out to have been much better deals for the shareholder than for the company. This raises the second question left open the *Aveling Barford*. What turns a transaction with a shareholder into a disguised distribution, which the common law principle will invalidate? This issue was considered by the Supreme Court in *Progress Property Co Ltd v Moorgarth Group Ltd*,[88] where again the court showed no interest in the question of whether the transacting company had distributable profits. Somewhat simplifying the facts, the claimant company (PP) was owned at the time of the transaction as to 75% by T and as to 25% by another person. T was the 100% holder of the shares in MG, the defendant and the other party to the transaction with PP. PP sold to MG its shares in a subsidiary at what was later discovered to be a gross undervalue, thus shifting value out of the company to the benefit of MG and T (as holder of a 100% interest in MG) and to the disadvantage of the 25% shareholder in PP. This was not a case of fraud or obfuscation, but of mistake (or, at least, it was treated as such). The value of the subsidiary whose shares were being transferred was some £4 million after allowing for creditors' claims. However, PP received only approximately £60,000, because as part of the deal PP was released from large liability under an indemnity it supposedly had given to T.[89] In fact, however, the indemnity had never been concluded. The former minority shareholder in PP, who had now acquired all its shares, caused PP to sue MG for the return of the shares which had been the subject of the sale. The question for the Supreme Court was whether this was a transaction within the common law principle. It held that it was not. **18–018**

Throughout the cases, judges have agreed that the label the parties have attached to the transaction is not determinative. It is for the courts to characterise the transaction. The question for the court is whether the label the parties had attached to the transaction was accurate or was the transaction a disguised distribution to members. Giving the first of the agreed judgments in *Progress Property*, Lord Walker favoured a case-by-case assessment. The fact that there was a gross disparity in value between the considerations given and received, as in the instant case, did not necessarily condemn it; the fact that the parties contracted in good faith, as in this case, did not necessarily save it. The result is a rather indeterminate standard for the guidance of future courts: **18–019**

> "If the conclusion is that it was a genuine arm's length transaction then it will stand, even if it may, with hindsight, appear to have been a bad bargain [for the company]. If it was an improper attempt to extract value by the pretence of an arm's length sale, it will be held

[88] *Progress Property Co Ltd v Moorgarth Group Ltd* [2010] UKSC 55; [2011] B.C.C. 196 at [31]–[33].

[89] It was somewhat odd to deal with indemnity supposedly given by PP to T in a transaction between PP and MG, but it made commercial sense if one ignored the corporate entities and focussed on economic exposures.

> unlawful. But either conclusion will depend on a realistic assessment of all the relevant facts, not simply a retrospective valuation exercise in isolation from all other inquiries."[90]

In extreme cases, the result may be obvious, for example, where the company receives nothing by way of consideration, even where that is the result of good faith decisions.[91] Outside gratuitous transactions, Lord Walker's test suggests the courts are reluctant to be put in a position where they may have to scrutinise routinely the exchange of values in commercial transactions between shareholders and their companies. As Lord Walker put it, the parties should have a "margin of appreciation" in relation to the assessment of the value of what was transferred under the contract, at least where the transaction was entered into in good faith. At the other end of the spectrum, a deal negotiated fully and in good faith which in fact turns out badly for the company will not constitute a disguised distribution. Lord Mance, giving the second agreed judgment, put the instant case in that category. The argument that the sale in this case should be re-characterised as a distribution was, he thought, "particularly artificial and unappealing."[92] In large part, this was because the director who negotiated on behalf of PP believed the indemnity to exist and, even if it could be said that he was negligent in not establishing the truth, this did not turn the transaction from an "understandable commercial transaction"[93] into a disguised distribution.

It may be that a question which it will often be helpful to ask is whether the company would have been willing to enter into the same transaction with a non-shareholder. In *Aveling Barford* the answer was clearly "no", whereas in *Progress Property*, where an honest mistake was made as the existence of a liability between the parties, the answer was "yes" (i.e. the company would not have altered the contractual price if the purchaser had been a non-shareholder, assuming a similar mistake about the liability existed). If the company would not have been willing to enter into the transaction on the same terms with a non-shareholder, it will have difficulty escaping the common law principle if there is a large disparity in the considerations given and received.

A final question left open is the position of the other party to the transaction where that party does not have knowledge, actual or constructive, that the transaction is in breach of the common law principle. If that principle is treated as a limitation solely on the powers of the directors, then it would appear that the other party would not be liable to return the assets if it did not have the relevant degree of knowledge of the directors' wrong-doing and that the company's primary remedy would be against the directors. If, however, the rule is a restriction on the company's powers, analogous to the now-repealed ultra vires doctrine attached to the company's statement of purposes in its memorandum, even an innocent third party might be liable to restore the assets to the company, with only limited, if any, defences (as in the cases on distributions discussed in para.18–011). On the latter analysis, the directors remain liable for causing the

---

[90] *Progress Property v Moorgarth Group* [2011] B.C.C. 196 at [29].

[91] *Re Halt Garage (1964) Ltd* [1982] 3 All E.R. 1016 Ch D—payment of remuneration where no services rendered held to be a disguised return of capital.

[92] *Progress Property v Moorgarth Group* [2011] B.C.C. 196 at [36].

[93] *Progress Property v Moorgarth Group* [2011] B.C.C. 196 at [48].

company to exceed its powers, but the legal position of the innocent third party is different. The doctrine has traditionally been formulated in this latter way.

Intra-group transfers

The decision in *Aveling Barford* (above) that the transfer was unlawful caused considerable alarm in commercial circles about the legality of intra-group transfers of assets, which are, of course, a common occurrence as a result of the carrying on of business through groups of companies.[94] Such transfers are usually effected on the basis of the value of the asset as stated in the transferring company's accounts (its "book" value), which may not reflect the current market price of the asset.[95] Advice was given that the common law rule might strike down a transaction where a company transferred an asset at book value to another group company, if the asset was in fact worth more than its book value, possibly even where the transferring company had distributable reserves (which was not the case in *Aveling Barford* itself). **18–020**

The CA 2006 deals with this concern by laying down rules about distributions in kind which apply to both the statutory restrictions on distributions and any other rule of law restricting distributions.[96] The core new provision[97] applies where the transferring company has profits available for distribution.[98] Where this is not the case, the common law will continue to apply unamended, with the apparent requirement that the asset would have to be transferred at market value to be sure of avoiding the risk of infringing the common law rules on distributions. Given the risk of opportunism on the part of controlling shareholders where the company has no distributable profits, this restriction in the new section is probably wise. Assuming distributable profits, the amount of the distribution is assessed under the section at zero, provided the consideration received for the asset is at least equivalent to its book value, and otherwise is restricted to the amount by which the book value exceeds the consideration.[99] If, by contrast, the consideration received upon the transfer of the asset exceeds its book value, the distributable profits of the transferring company are increased by the amount of the excess.[100] Of course, the rules relating to directors' fiduciary duties[101] are unaffected by these changes.

---

[94] The nature of the reaction to the decision is set out by the CLR in Maintenance, Pt II.

[95] Since accounts are often, even today, constructed on a "historical" basis, an asset is likely to be shown in the company's balance sheet at the price paid for it (or perhaps less, if it has been depreciated), rather than at its current market value, which might be higher.

[96] CA 2006 s.851(2)—thus embracing not only the common law rules but also rules contained in a statute other than the Act (unless that Act overrides the Act explicitly or by necessary implication).

[97] CA 2006 s.846 (fn.23) was also added to the common law rules.

[98] CA 2006 s.845(1)—the amount of the distributable profits needs to be enough to cover any discrepancy between the contract price and the book value but does not need to cover the gap between the contract price and the market value. So, for a transfer at book value, distributable profits of £1 will do.

[99] CA 2006 s.845(2).

[100] CA 2006 s.845(3).

[101] On the duties of directors in self-dealing transactions, see paras 10–053 onwards.

REFORM

18–021 There have been two waves of reform initiatives this century in relation to dividends, neither of which has yet borne fruit, though it now increasingly likely that change will come. In both waves the interrelationship between the statutory dividend rules and accounting standards was central to the debate. This is perhaps not surprising since, as we will see in more detail in Ch.22, the statutory accounts rules in the UK contain relatively little detail and depend heavily on accounting standards, domestic or international, for their effective operation. However, different conclusions were drawn about this relationship in the two debates. In the first, at the beginning of the century, it was feared that the trend in accounting standards (especially in the International Financial Reporting Standards) towards valuing assets at current market rather than historical book value had reduced the capacity of companies to pay dividends even though these could safely be made.[102] The "mark-to-market" change is designed to make the accounts more helpful for shareholders and investors, but can be argued to have distorted the creditor protection function of the accounts. Reported profits have become more volatile, whilst retention of the "realised profits" rule for distributions[103] does not permit the company in principle to take advantage of the upward fluctuations in asset values when considering distributions. In the current debate, by contrast, the fear expressed is that accounting standards permit dividends to be paid too readily.[104]

The first debate led to proposals for a radical recasting of the legal framework for dividends. This was not just a response to recent trends in accounting standards but also to arguments that the framework, even as traditionally conceived, did not effectively protect creditors. Many classes of creditor do not rely on the statutory dividend rules. Sophisticated (i.e. large-scale and repeat) creditors, such as banks, place their trust in the terms of their loan contracts, which deal with many risks other than excessive distributions.[105] Trade creditors use other protective techniques, such as retention-of-title clauses or simply not becoming heavily exposed to a single debtor. Finally, involuntary creditors (notably tort victims) necessarily do not rely on the company's balance sheet and really need a guarantee that their claims will be met, which the legal capital rules do not provide (though they may help) but compulsory insurance would—and does in some cases.[106] In other words, it is not at all easy to identify the beneficiaries of the current rules or, therefore, those who would be harmed if those rules were substantially amended.[107]

---

[102] J. Rickford, "Reforming Capital: Report of the Interdisciplinary Group on Capital Maintenance" [2004] E.B.L.R. 1, especially Chs 3 and 4.

[103] See paras 18–003 to 18–004.

[104] House of Commons, Business, Energy and Industrial Strategy Committee, *The Future of Audit*, HC 1718 (April 2019), Ch.3.

[105] See para.31–023.

[106] The most pressing classes of claim (from road accident victims and employees) are subject to mandatory insurance, which, suggestively, is required to be taken out by all those engaged in the relevant activity, whether they operate with limited liability or not.

[107] See J. Armour, "Share Capital and Creditor Protection: Efficient Rules for a Modern Company Law" (2000) 63 M.L.R. 355; and "Legal Capital: An Outdated Concept" (2006) 7 E.B.O.R. 5; and the slightly more optimistic conclusions of D. Kershaw, "The Decline of Legal Capital: An Exploration of

The result of the first debate, therefore, was a proposal to break the link with the accounts when determining the company's legal freedom to make a distribution. As it happens, there is considerable comparative experience with alternative tests, since the US jurisdictions abandoned legal capital a long time ago and so have had to devise alternative tests, and some Commonwealth countries, notably New Zealand, have taken the same step. The Rickford Report, which gives an account of alternatives, recommended an approach based on a solvency test.[108] This is not an entirely new technique even in domestic law, where it is used in certain limited areas.[109] However, its adoption as the sole test for the legality of distributions would be novel. In essence, the directors would have to form a judgment about what level of dividend the company could appropriately pay, without endangering its solvency. It can be said that the directors already take a similar decision when deciding, within the limits set by the distribution rules, what level of distribution it is appropriate to make to shareholders and how much to keep in the company for investment in future projects and the protection of creditors. Under the reform proposal the role of the directors' judgment would be expanded to occupy the whole of the distribution space.

Since company law is structured so as to require the directors to put the shareholders' interests first, so long as the company is a going concern, the obvious risk with this proposal is that the directors will undervalue the interests of the creditors and overvalue those of the shareholders when exercising this expanded decision. At present, the rule-based distribution test gives directors no discretion about the maximum which is distributable; under the reform proposal that issue would become a matter of the directors' judgment about the impact of the proposed distribution on the company's ability in the future to meet its debts as they fall due. In order to counteract a pro-shareholder bias the directors would be required to certify (through a public "solvency statement") that the proposed distribution would not affect the company's ability to meet its debts, either immediately or for a period after the distribution (probably one year). Sanctions (probably both criminal and civil) would be attached to directors whose statement was made negligently. Of course, the threat such liability might cause directors to be cautious in their dividend decisions, in which case the alleged pro-shareholder bias of the solvency test would be counteracted, but it might (and seemingly did) make directors unenthusiastic about the proposed reform.[110]

The second reform proposals (still under consideration) are more limited. They keep the link to the accounts but aim to provide fixes for some particular **18–022**

the Consequences of Board Solvency-based Capital Reductions" in D. Prentice and A. Reisberg (eds), *Corporate Finance Law in the UK and EU* (Oxford: Oxford University Press, 2011), Ch.2.

[108] J. Rickford, "Reforming Capital: Report of the Interdisciplinary Group on Capital Maintenance" [2004] E.B.L.R. 1, Ch.5.

[109] And as we saw in para.18–010, BEIS has proposed to *add* what is in effect a solvency statement to the current distribution rules.

[110] That there is personal liability for directors even under the current rules is clear (para.18–012) but directors might consider a rule-based system easier to comply with than one based on a standard, and the current sanctions do not entail criminal liability.

problems the reformers have identified.[111] For example, the accounts identify profits, but they do not in terms distinguish between realised and unrealised profits, which, as we have seen above, is crucial for the application of the legal rules. A reform might be for the accounts to identify realised profits as well, though it is already the duty of the auditor to satisfy itself that any dividend proposed by the directors is compatible with the accounts.[112] Even a realised profit need not be represented by cash on the balance sheet, though obviously the company needs cash to pay a cash dividend. Thus, a company may lawfully borrow cash in order to pay a dividend, provided the additional liability does not exceed the distributable profits. Nevertheless, the increased debt burden makes the company less resilient to changes in its business fortunes and there have been examples of companies collapsing under the weight of their debts and liabilities shortly after borrowing money to pay a dividend.[113] So, a further reform would be to treat a realised profit as existing only when it is represented by cash or near-cash on the balance sheet, though in principle the fiduciary duties of directors should already constrain reckless borrowing for distributions. A final example is the payment of large dividends when its pension fund is in substantial deficit. The government's response here lies outside the area of the statutory rules on dividend payments. It proposes to give the Pensions Regulator an enhanced power to review, on a three-yearly basis, companies' dividend policies in relation to the funding position of their pension schemes.[114]

Of course, it would be possible to marry a solvency test with reformed and possibly simplified accounts rules[115] or to use the current debates as a springboard for more fundamental reform.[116]

---

[111] The proposals mentioned below were all floated by BEIS in its consultation paper, *Restoring trust in audit and corporate governance* (March 2021), Ch.2. See also the BEIS Committee, *The Future of Audit*, HC 1718 (April 2019).

[112] See fn.65. BEIS proposes (in *Restoring trust in audit and corporate governance* (March 2021)) that directors should have to make a formal statement about their dividend policy at the time of the distributon.

[113] See *The Collapse of Carillion* (House of Commons Research Briefing, 14 March 2018) available at *https://commonslibrary.parliament.uk/research-briefings/cbp-8206/* [Accessed 22 March 2021].

[114] Department for Work and Pensions, *Government Response to the Consultation on Protecting Defined Benefit Pension Schemes—A Stronger Pensions Regulator* (February 2019), p.10.

[115] As the BEIS proposes to a limited extent (see para.18–010). W. Schön, "Comment: Balance Sheet Tests or Solvency Tests—or Both?" (2006) 7 E.B.O.R. 181 proposed that a solvency test could be coupled with the retention of maximum distribution rules which, however, no longer embodied the concept of legal capital.

[116] Eilís Ferran, *Revisiting Legal Capital* (2019) 20 E.B.O.R. 521.

CHAPTER 19

UNDERMINING CREDITORS' CLAIMS

The general approach of UK company law is that creditors of going concern companies need only limited mandatory protection of their interests. By and large, the view is taken that they can take care of themselves, as we described in the introduction to this Part. Because creditors' claims have priority over shareholders' claims when calculating profits, in going concern companies the structure which induces directors to seek profit for the benefit of shareholders will also benefit creditors. We discussed in the previous chapter what might be regarded as two exceptions to this statement. However, on reflection, one can see that they are not exceptions but rather represent implementation of the basic proposition. The distribution rules aim to ensure that dividends are indeed only paid out of profits and that there is no return of capital to shareholders by illegitimate means. The distribution rules clearly aim to protect creditors by preserving the priority of the creditors in relation to the company's net assets and legal capital. Without some constraint on distributions, the notion that creditors of a going concern company are safe with a rule which focuses on the shareholders' welfare would lack conviction. Even so, as we saw, the claim for repayment or restoration of unlawful dividends is vested in the company, not in creditors, individually or collectively, unless the company goes into administration or liquidation, where the office-holder acts in the interests of the creditors. Section 423 of the IA 1986 does indeed vest claims in individual creditors, but the scope of that section is confined by the need to show that the purpose of the transfer was to put corporate assets beyond the reach of creditors. 19–001

However, when the company is in the vicinity of insolvency, the stance of the law changes, in line with the changed incentives of shareholders and directors beholden to shareholders. As the company's economic fortunes decline, the priority rule for creditors will eventually bring about the situation where the shareholders have no economic interest in the company as currently configured, because the creditors' claims equal or exceed the value of the company. The law provides a number of ways of dealing with this situation in a proper fashion (administration, liquidation, re-structuring) but from the shareholders' point of view they have the disadvantage that control of the company is likely to pass to the creditors and that the shareholders' pay-out will be negligible. The current controllers of the company are thus subject to the temptation to try to deal with the problem by illegitimate means.

One obvious illegitimate response to the company's decline is to move assets out of the company before the creditors can invoke the formal mechanisms for their protection. Here, the rules we discussed in the previous chapter, which continue to apply as the company moves towards insolvency and may in fact become more salient in that situation, will provide protection. For example, *Aveling Barford Ltd v Perion Ltd*[1] is a clear example of a corporate controller aiming to extract a prime asset from the company before it became insolvent. In this chapter, therefore, we concentrate on the additional legal strategies which come into play when the company is in the vicinity of insolvency. Thus, most (though not all) of the statutory rules we consider in this chapter are to be found in the IA 1986, not the CA 2006.

However, it would be wrong to analyse the situation in the vicinity of insolvency as a simple conflict between shareholders and creditors. There may be conflicts among the creditors, with some being treated better than others, even though they have no contractual entitlement to better treatment. In some cases, this may occur in order to keep the company going; in others the preferred creditors may also be directors or shareholders of the company or associated with them, so that the promotion of personal interests is what motivates the company's action. *Aveling Barford* was an example of such a case as well.

FRAUDULENT TRADING

19–002 Having said that in this chapter we focus on rules operating in the vicinity of insolvency, the first provisions we analyse (on fraudulent trading) in fact apply formally throughout a company's life. However, the civil provisions about fraudulent trading can be initiated only by a liquidator (s.213) or an administrator (s.246ZA).[2] If the company's business is conducted fraudulently, but it avoids insolvency, these procedures cannot be used (though fraud provisions contained in the general law are available). Even when an insolvency procedure is triggered, then in the nature of things the acts most commonly subject to civil claims for fraudulent trading will have occurred in the period immediately before the onset of insolvency, though the sections are not in terms so limited. Because of the corrosive impact of fraud on the conduct of business, fraudulent trading is

[1] *Aveling Barford Ltd v Perion Ltd* (1989) 5 B.C.C. 677 Ch D, discussed in para.18–016.

[2] The extension to administrators was made only in 2015.

also a specific criminal offence. Section 993 of the CA 2006 contains the criminal offence of carrying on the business of a company with intent to defraud the creditors[3] of the company or of any other person or for any other fraudulent purpose. It carries a sentence of up to 10 years' imprisonment upon conviction on indictment. Here, the company does not need to be in an insolvency procedure for a prosecution to be initiated and this no doubt explains why the criminal aspect of fraudulent trading continues to be located in the CA 2006. Of course, fraud is likely to involve conduct which also breaches general criminal laws.[4] Every person knowingly party to the carrying on of the business fraudulently commits the criminal offence under the section. So, here the personal scope of the criminal liability is defined by reference to being party to the fraud, not that person's position as a director or shareholder of the company.

The IA 1986 mimics for the purposes of civil liability the criteria laid down in s.993 of the CA 2006 for criminal liability, i.e. that the business of a company was carried on with intent to defraud the creditors of the company or of any other person or for any other fraudulent purpose. Assuming the company is in liquidation or administration, the court, on the application of the office-holder, may declare the persons who were knowingly parties to carrying on[5] the business of the company in this way "liable to make such contributions (if any) to the company's assets as the court thinks proper."[6] This is in effect an indirect way of making the persons in question liable for the company's debts (to at least some degree).[7] As with criminal liability, the persons liable are those party to carrying on the business of the company in the fraudulent way; they need have no other connection with the company, i.e. they do not need to be directors of or shareholders in the company—though they often will be.[8] It is enough to establish liability that only one creditor was defrauded and in a single **19–003**

[3] The section embraces fraud on future, as well as present, creditors: *R. v Smith* [1996] 2 B.C.L.C. 109 CA.

[4] It has been regarded as less confusing for juries to face them with a single charge of fraudulent trading rather than with numerous charges of individual acts of fraud: see *R. v Kemp* [1988] Q.B. 645 CA (petition dismissed [1988] 1 W.L.R. 846 HL). The legislature thought so well of the offence that it enacted in s.9 of the Fraud Act 2006 a similar offence in respect of those businesses carried on by persons falling outside the scope of s.993, including sole traders. This shows that the absence of limited liability is not a guarantee of the absence of fraud.

[5] A business may be regarded as "carried on" notwithstanding that the company has ceased active trading: *Re Sarflax Ltd* [1979] Ch. 592 Ch D.

[6] IA 1986 s.213(2)/246ZA(2). This constitutes another reason for concentrating on the conduct occurring immediately before the entry into insolvency. The longer-lived the fraudulent scheme, the less likely it is the early creditors will have suffered a loss. So, older fraud is likely to be less relevant to the setting of the amount of the contribution.

[7] Unlike the situation before 1985, it is no longer possible to impose liability under ss.213 and 246ZA in respect of particular debts or in favour of particular creditors: cf. *Re Cyona Distributors Ltd* [1967] Ch. 889 CA.

[8] And it is no bar to inclusion within the section that the activities in question occurred abroad: *Jetivia SA v Bilta (UK) Ltd* [2015] 1 B.C.L.C. 443 SC. This is on the basis that the winding up of a company incorporated in the UK has effect, as far as domestic law is concerned, in relation to all the assets of the company, no matter where situated. This reasoning would seem equally applicable to liability for wrongful trading under ss.214/246ZB of the Act.

transaction.[9] However, in the case of a one-off fraud there is a risk that the court will not be able to conclude that the business of the company was carried on for fraudulent purposes, in which case liability will not arise.[10]

19–004 Given the wide personal scope of the sections, banks and parent companies (third parties) have at times felt inhibited from providing finance to ailing companies, fearing that they may thereby fall foul of these provisions as persons knowingly party to the fraud. It is sometimes said that their fears are unfounded so long as they play no active role in running the company with fraudulent intent.[11] However, the extent of the exposure of a third-party company to liability under the sections will depend in part on what rule of attribution is used to determine the extent of the knowledge the third party company possesses of the activities within the fraudulently run company. In *Re Bank of Credit and Commerce International SA (No.15)*[12] the Court of Appeal rejected the proposition that only the knowledge of the board of the third party was to be attributed to it. Here, the court attributed to the defendant company the knowledge of a senior manager who had been given authority by the board to set the terms of transactions with the company whose business was being carried on fraudulently and to which fraud the manager had turned a blind eye. Thus, as was already clear and as this case illustrates, a third party can fall within the sections if it participates, with knowledge,[13] in the fraudulent activity of a company, even though that party could not be said to have taken a controlling role within the company.[14] Overall, therefore, these rules encourage third parties, whose dealings with a company might assist the fraudulent running of that company's business, to have in place

---

[9] *Re Cooper Chemicals Ltd* [1978] Ch. 262 Ch D (only one creditor defrauded). Indeed, for criminal liability to arise it is not clear that it is necessary for any person actually to be defrauded provided that the business of the company was carried on with intent to defraud (*R. v Kemp* [1988] Q.B. 645—only potential creditors defrauded).

[10] *Morphitis v Bernasconi* [2003] 2 B.C.L.C. 53 CA. The defrauded person will have remedies under the general law of fraud.

[11] In *Re Maidstone Building Provisions Ltd* [1971] 1 W.L.R. 1085 Ch D at 1092 an attempt to obtain a declaration against the company's secretary, who was also a partner in its auditors' firm, failed because, although he had given financial advice and had not attempted to prevent the company from trading, he had not taken "positive steps in the carrying on of the company's business in a fraudulent manner". In *Re Augustus Barnett & Son Ltd* [1986] B.C.L.C. 170 an attempt against its parent company (Rumasa) failed on the same ground.

[12] *Re Bank of Credit and Commerce International SA (No.15)* [2005] EWCA Civ 693; [2005] B.C.C. 739, following the lead given in *Meridian Global Funds Management Asia Ltd v Securities Commission* [1995] 2 A.C. 500 PC (para.8–003). This step was facilitated by the separation of the criminal and civil liability for fraudulent trading, so that there is no implication from this decision that the same attribution rule would be applied if criminal liability were in question: at [107] and [129].

[13] The required degree of knowledge is "blind eye" knowledge, i.e. "a decision to avoid obtaining confirmation of facts in whose existence the individual has good reason to believe" (*Re Bank of Credit and Commerce International SA (No.15)* [2005] B.C.C. 739 at [14] quoting Lord Scott in *Manifest Shipping Co Ltd v Uni-Polaris Shipping Co Ltd* [2001] UKHL 1; [2003] 1 A.C. 469 HL at [116]). See also *Re Bank of Credit and Commerce International SA (No.14)* [2003] EWHC 1868 (Ch); [2003] B.C.C. 735.

[14] In *Re Gerald Cooper Chemicals Ltd* [1978] Ch. 262 Ch D it was held that a declaration could be made against a creditor who refrained from pressing for repayment knowing that the business was being carried on in fraud of creditors and who accepted part payment out of money which he knew had been obtained by that fraud. *Gerald Cooper Chemicals* was followed in *Re Bank of Credit and Commerce International SA* [2001] 1 B.C.L.C. 263 Ch D.

internal controls designed to identify at an early stage and to deal with situations where relevant employees of the third party have knowledge of the fraudulent activities. In this way the third party may hope to avoid the risk that it will be liable to contribute under the sections.[15]

As to whether those conducting business are doing so fraudulently, what has to be shown is "actual dishonesty involving, according to current notions of fair trading among commercial men, real moral blame".[16] That may be inferred if "a company continues to carry on business and to incur debts at a time when there is, to the knowledge of the directors, no reasonable prospect of the creditors ever receiving payment of those debts",[17] but it cannot be inferred merely because they ought to have realised there was no prospect of repayment. It was this need to prove moral blame that led the Jenkins Committee in 1962 vainly to recommend the introduction of a remedy for "reckless trading"[18] and the Cork Committee, 20 years later,[19] successfully to promote it under the name of "wrongful trading".

WRONGFUL TRADING

Abuse in the shape of fraud is easy to single out as something the law should address, as the long-standing provisions against fraudulent trading indicate. More significant in practice today are the provisions on wrongful trading, added initially in the 1980s. These seek to address the temptation for directors, when the company is in the vicinity of insolvency, but has not yet entered a formal insolvency procedure, to take excessive risks with the business of the company, in the hope of escaping from its financial troubles, but knowing that, if the gamble is unsuccessful, limited liability will place most or all of the additional losses on the creditors. If such action is taken dishonestly, it will probably fall within the fraudulent trading provisions. The wrongful trading provisions of the IA 1986 give directors, contemplating this strategy—but without fraud or at least provable fraud—an incentive to think through the consequences of their proposed actions **19–005**

[15] In *Re Bank of Credit and Commerce International SA (No.15)* [2005] B.C.C. 739 it was left open whether the third party's liability could not be more simply and widely established on the basis of the third party's vicarious liability for breaches of s.213 by its employees. See *Dubai Aluminium Co Ltd v Salaam* [2003] 2 A.C. 366 HL and para.8–039. This approach would strength the incentives of third parties to control participation by their employees in the fraudulent conduct of the company's business.

[16] *Re Patrick Lyon Ltd* [1933] Ch. 786 Ch D at 790, 791.

[17] *Re William C Leitch Ltd* [1932] 2 Ch. 71 Ch D at 77, per Maugham J. See also *R. v Grantham* [1984] Q.B. 675 CA, where the court upheld a direction to the jury that they might convict of fraudulent trading a person who had taken an active part in running the business if they were satisfied that he had helped to obtain credit knowing that there was no good reason for thinking that funds would become available to pay the debts when they became due or shortly thereafter. That dishonesty may be inferred in these cases does not mean, of course, that it can never be established in other cases: *Aktieselskabet Dansk Skibsfinansiering v Brothers* [2001] 2 B.C.L.C. 324 HKCFA.

[18] *Report of the Company Law Committee* (1962), Cmnd.1749, para.503(b).

[19] *Insolvency Law and Practice* (1982), Cmnd.8558. For the argument that the Cork Committee overestimated the potential role of the wrongful trading provisions, partly because existing Companies and Insolvency Act provisions already cover much of the ground, partly because defendants financially able to meet the liability are likely to be few, see R. Williams, "What can we expect to gain from reforming the insolvent trading remedy?" (2015) 78 M.L.R. 55.

for the company's creditors and, having identified those consequences, to accord greater consideration to the interests of those creditors.

The core of the problem is that creditors are highly exposed to the downside risk of the recovery strategy whilst the benefits of it, if they are achieved, will accrue overwhelmingly to the shareholders.[20] This can be seen most clearly if, at the time the strategy is adopted, the company's assets are just enough to meet its liabilities, but no more, so that, if the company then stopped trading and were wound up, the creditors would be repaid but the shareholders would receive nothing. If the directors continue trading, the shareholders will be no worse off, but have a chance (perhaps a small one) of being much better off, whilst the creditors will be no better off but have a chance (perhaps a large one) of being much worse off. This is sometimes, graphically but exaggeratedly, termed "gambling for resurrection".

Whilst continuing to trade is not necessarily against the interests of the creditors, doing so in a risky way is likely to be, whilst potentially benefitting shareholders. The wrongful trading provisions attempt to re-set the incentives of the directors (and shadow directors) by making them personally liable for the increased liabilities of the company if the gamble fails and the court adjudges the directors to have acted negligently. Here, therefore, the statutory provisions do not apply to all those party to the wrongful trading but only those who are in charge of the company's strategy by virtue of their positions on the board or their de facto influence over the board.

19–006 Sections 214 and 246ZB of the IA 1986 empower the court to make a declaration similar to that under ss.213 and 246ZA where the company has gone into *insolvent* administration or liquidation. An insolvent is distinguished from a solvent procedure on a balance-sheet test, i.e. the question is whether the assets of the company were sufficient to meet its liabilities and the costs of the procedure at the point the company entered into it.[21] The basis for imposing the obligation to contribute is that the director (or shadow director) knew, or ought to have concluded, at some point *before* the administration or winding-up, that there was no reasonable prospect that the company would avoid going into insolvent administration or liquidation.[22] A declaration will then be made unless the court is satisfied that the person concerned thereafter took every step with a view to minimising the potential loss to the company's creditors as he ought to have taken, on the assumption that he knew there was no reasonable prospect of avoiding insolvency.[23] In judging what facts the director ought to have known or

[20] Paul Davies, "Directors' Creditor-Regarding Duties in Respect of Trading Decisions Taken in the Vicinity of Insolvency" (2006) 7 E.B.O.R. 301. This risk is particularly strong if the major shareholders are also directors of the company. Where this is not so, as in many publicly traded companies, the directors may conclude that their reputations (and thus prospects of future directorships) will be best served by an orderly wind-down of the company, perhaps through its sale to a third party. Wrongful trading litigation often concerns small companies.

[21] IA 1986 ss.214(6)/246ZB(6). Section 213 formally applies in any winding up (solvent or insolvent) but in practice it is needed only in insolvent winding up.

[22] IA 1986 s.214(2)/246ZB(2). It appears it is sufficient that the directors should have anticipated, for example, insolvent liquidation but the company ends up in insolvent administration.

[23] IA 1986 ss.214(3)/246ZB(3). The burden of proof on knowledge is on the claimant, on "every step" on the directors: *Brook v Masters* [2015] EWHC 2289 (Ch); [2015] B.C.C. 661.

ascertained, what conclusions the director should have drawn and what steps should have been taken, the director is to be assumed to be a reasonably diligent person having both the general knowledge, skill and experience to be expected of a person carrying out the director's functions in relation to the company[24] and the general knowledge, skill and experience that the particular director in fact has.[25] This formulation heavily influenced the general duty of care now imposed on directors by s.174 of the CA 2006.[26] The wrongful trading provisions, s.174 of the CA 2006 and the director disqualification provisions (discussed in the following chapter) constitute the three main areas where sanctions are imposed on directors for negligent discharge of their duties. In the case of s.214/246ZB, however, the beneficiaries of the duty to take care are the creditors rather than the shareholders, whom s.174 of the CA 2006 protects. Answering the questions posed by s.214 is a highly fact-specific exercise. The answers will depend on the sort of company that was involved, the functions assigned to or discharged by the director in question, and any outside advice that was taken.[27]

Shadow directors

Section 214 applies to shadow directors as well as to directors, i.e. a person, other than a professional adviser, in accordance with whose directions or instructions the directors of a company are accustomed to act.[28] This considerably widens the class of persons against whom a declaration can be made, though not as widely as under s.213 which brings in any person who is party to the fraudulent trading (see above). The shadow director definition catches only the person who influences at least a certain category of board decisions on a continuing basis.[29] We discuss the CA 2006 definition of a shadow director in Ch.10.[30] The IA 1986 definition tracks that of the CA 2006, but with one important extension. The CA 2006 definition excludes a parent company in relation to its subsidiaries, even if it would otherwise meet the tests for being a shadow director, as regards liability for breaches of the general duties of directors and conflicted transactions requiring ex ante shareholder approval.[31] The IA 1986 definition contains no such exclusion, thus extending the definition beyond controller shareholders who are **19–007**

[24] This includes functions entrusted to the director even if the director has not carried them out: s.214(5)/246ZB(5). If the director has failed the objective test he or she cannot be excused by the court, under CA 2006 s.1157, on the ground that the director has acted honestly and reasonably: *Re Produce Marketing Consortium Ltd* [1989] 1 W.L.R. 745 Ch D (Companies Ct).

[25] IA 1986 s.214(4)/246ZB(4).

[26] See para.10–045.

[27] The directors are likely to be treated with a particular lack of sympathy by the court if they have not abided by the statutory requirements for keeping themselves abreast of the company's financial position: *Re Produce Marketing Consortium Ltd (No.2)* [1989] B.C.L.C. 520 Ch D (Companies Ct) at 550, which requirements Knox J referred to as the "minimum standards". See Oditah, [1990] L.M.C.L.O. 205; and Prentice, (1990) 10 O.J.L.S. 265.

[28] IA 1986 s.251.

[29] *Secretary of State for Trade and Industry v Becker* [2003] 1 B.C.L.C. 565; *Secretary of State for Trade and Industry v Deverell* [2000] 2 B.C.L.C. 133 CA.

[30] See para.10–009. The CA definition is set out in s.251 of that Act. It is presumably a coincidence that the relevant section numbers in the two Acts are the same.

[31] CA 2006 s.251(3).

natural persons. This does not mean that a parent company is automatically required to make a contribution to the assets of the insolvent subsidiary. The parent company must meet the conditions for being characterised as a shadow director. However, to take a clear case, where the parent engaged in detailed determination of the subsidiary's strategy in the period before insolvency, the parent will find it difficult to demonstrate that it was not a shadow director of the subsidiary. In this case, when s.214/246ZB are triggered, they will apply to the conduct of the directors of the subsidiary and the conduct of the parent company (acting through its board of directors).

The next question, of course, is whether the directors of the parent company themselves can be regarded as directors, either de facto or shadow, of the subsidiary. De facto directors are not the subject of a special statutory definition, for de facto directors are included within the term "director".[32] In *Re Hydrodan (Corby) Ltd*[33] Millett J rejected both characterisations of the parent's directors. In has now been accepted at the highest level that his decision was correct.[34] The defendants were two of eight directors of an indirect parent company (i.e. there were other companies between the parent and the company of which the defendants were alleged to be de facto or shadow directors). The claimant liquidator did not allege that the defendants gave directions to the directors of the indirect subsidiary and on that ground alone the case failed. However, Millett J went on to say that, even if they had, "as directors of the [parent], acting as the board of [the parent], they did so as agents for [the parent] and the result is to constitute [the parent], but not themselves, shadow directors of the company."[35] It was this proposition which divided the Supreme Court in *Revenue and Customs Commissioners v Holland*,[36] with the majority supporting Lord Millett's view. It appears it will be necessary for the directors of the parent to give their instructions directly to the directors of the subsidiary and not via the constitutional decision-making organs of the parent for them to be classified as de facto or shadow directors of the subsidiary.

A second controversial group of potential shadow directors consists of those who have provided long-term finance to the now-failing company. The company is likely to turn to these financiers to secure that the funding remains in place and perhaps even to enhance it. If the financier, usually a bank, agrees to this, it is likely to impose conditions on how the company conducts itself in the future. If these conditions create the risk for the bank that it will be treated as a shadow director for wrongful trading purposes, its incentives to maintain or increase the financing, perhaps already weak, will be reduced. In an early case[37] it was said

---

[32] For further discussion see para.10–009.

[33] *Re Hydrodan (Corby) Ltd* [1994] 2 B.C.L.C. 180 Ch D.

[34] See the judgements (including the dissentients) in *Revenue and Customs Commissioners v Holland* [2010] UKSC 51.

[35] *Re Hydrodan (Corby) Ltd* [1994] 2 B.C.L.C. 180 at 184e.

[36] *Revenue and Customs Commissioners v Holland* [2010] UKSC 51. For further discussion of this case see para.10–009. The issue at stake in that case was whether the defendant was a de facto director, but, given the now common view that the concepts of de facto and shadow directors overlap, nothing turns on this point. Equally, in these two cases the director of the subsidiary was a corporate body (something not now permitted) but the point about the origins of the instruction to the directors of the subsidiary carries the same force if the subsidiary has sentient directors.

[37] *Re PFTZM Ltd* [1995] B.C.C. 280 Ch D (Companies Ct).

that for a bank to impose conditions to protect its own interests, which the company was free to accept or reject, did not constitute the bank a shadow director of the company even though the company might be thought to have no other practicable alternative. However, the conclusion is obviously highly fact dependent: an onerous set of conditions about the management of the company, attached to the loan at its inception and continuing throughout its life, might be interpreted differently.[38]

The declaration

Section 215 (applied to administrations by s.246ZC) contains certain remedial provisions common to both fraudulent and wrongful trading. Those provisions are to have effect notwithstanding that the person concerned may be criminally liable.[39] The court may direct that the liability of any person against whom the declaration is made shall be a charge on any debt due from the company to that person or on any mortgage or charge in that person's favour on assets of the company. This enables the company to set off what it owes to the director against what the director is declared liable to contribute to the company, which may prove valuable in the bankruptcy of the director.[40] In addition, s.215[41] provides that the court may direct that the whole or any part of a debt, and interest thereon, owed by the company to a person against whom a declaration is made, shall be postponed to all other debts, and interest thereon, owed by the company. It is not uncommon, for example, for controlling shareholders/directors of small, failing companies to advance funds to it by way of loan to meet its immediately pressing needs. Thus, even if, for example, the court makes only a small contribution order, which the director is able to meet, the director may suffer a further financial loss by having his or her debts due from the company subordinated to those of the company's other creditors, a potentially important provision since the company ex hypothesi is insolvent. **19–008**

The central question, however, is the amount of the contribution, a matter with which s.215 does not deal in detail. The fraudulent and wrongful trading provisions simply say that the amount of the contribution shall be "as the court thinks proper".[42] The assessment is to be made against each defendant individually rather than on some basis of collective responsibility.[43] It is now

[38] *Re Company (No.005009 of 1987) Ex p. Copp* (1988) 4 B.C.C. 424 Ch D (Companies Ct).

[39] IA 1986 s.215(5).

[40] Including any assignees from that person (other than a good faith assignee for value without notice): IA 1986 s.215(2)–(3).

[41] IA 1986 s.215(4).

[42] IA 1986 s.213(2)/246ZA(2) and 214(1)/246ZB(1).

[43] See the dicta of Park J in *Re Continental Assurance Co of London Plc (No.4)* [2007] 2 B.C.L.C. 287 Ch D at [382]–[390] (s.214); and *Re Overnight Ltd* [2010] EWHC 613 (Ch); [2010] B.C.C. 796 (s.213). The defendants' liability may, but need not, be put on the basis of joint and several liability.

established that contribution orders in relation to both wrongful and fraudulent trading are intended to be compensatory in relation to the company.[44]

19–009 The focus of the contribution order is thus on the loss caused to the company by the wrongful trading.[45] It might be thought that, since the company by definition is in a position where the directors ought to have concluded that there was no reasonable prospect of the company avoiding insolvent liquidation, carrying on trading after that point will inevitably cause losses to the company. However, this may not always be the case. In *Re Ralls Builders Ltd*[46] the directors did continue to trade beyond the point where insolvent liquidation was inevitable (t_1), but did so during the profitable summer period. Consequently, when the building company entered the unavoidable subsequent liquidation (t_2), its net asset position was no worse, perhaps even a little better, than at t_1. In this situation the judge held that the directors should not be required to make any contribution to the company's assets in the liquidation.

This may seem an unproblematic decision, until one remembers that the contribution is to the assets of the company as a whole, not to particular creditors, and the company's list of creditors would have changed between t_1 and t_2. Some of those who were creditors at the earlier time will have been repaid and, more important, some of those who became creditors after t_1 will not have been repaid by t_2. These "subsequent" creditor have no special claim over the contribution ordered by the court but are treated pro rata with other creditors of the same class who existed at t_1 and are still unpaid at t_2. The subsequent creditors can thus claim to have suffered as a result of the company's decision to continue to trade, for, had the company not continued trading, they would not have become creditors of the company at all. The judge held that he could not take account of these facts when assessing the amount of the contribution due to the company, in this case setting it at nil, since the company had lost nothing through the continued trading.

The judge did hold, however, that in this situation the directors could not claim the benefit of the defence laid down in s.214(3) that they had taken every step with a view to minimising the potential loss to the company's creditors, since the subsequent creditors would be likely not to be paid in full, as the directors should have realised, but this holding did not affect his assessment of the loss to the company. The up-shot appears to be that, once the point of no reasonable prospect of avoiding insolvent liquidation or administration is reached, the section shifts the risk of continued trading onto the directors. If the continued trading reduces (or does not increase) the company's net deficiency, no contribution will be required of them. But in the opposite case they will be exposed.[47] In functional terms, the present rules put maximising the value of the company's estate for the benefit of all creditors above doing exact justice as among those becoming

[44] See *Re Produce Marketing Consortium Ltd* [1989] 1 W.L.R. 745 Ch D (Companies Ct), for wrongful trading; and *Morphitis v Bernasconi* [2003] 2 B.C.L.C. 53 CA, for fraudulent trading, the latter reversing the previous understanding in relation to fraudulent trading where a penal element was thought appropriate in some cases.

[45] *Re Purpoint Ltd* [1991] B.C.C. 121 Ch D (Companies Ct); *Re Continental Assurance of London Plc* [2001] B.P.I.R. 862.

[46] *Re Ralls Builders Ltd* [2016] EWHC 243 (Ch); [2016] B.C.C. 293.

[47] As we see below, this is not so where the directors continue to trade before the point of "no reasonable prospect" is reached, even if the continued trading is unsuccessful.

creditors at different times (though egregious cases of inequality among creditors may be caught by the statutory rules on preferences (para.19–020) or the common law duties to creditors (para.19–013)).[48]

No reasonable prospect of avoiding insolvent liquidation or administration

The central provision in ss.214 and 246ZB is that the duty to minimise the potential loss to creditors arises only when the company is in the position where it has no reasonable prospect of avoiding insolvent liquidation or administration and the directors ought to have realised this. This is emphatically not the same as saying that the duty arises as soon as the company is insolvent, whether on a balance sheet or cash-flow test.[49] An insolvent company may have a reasonable prospect of avoiding liquidation or administration on a number of grounds. Its present parlous state may have been brought about by an event which is unlikely to recur so that it will be able to trade out of its difficulties provided its underlying business model is sound.[50] Or its problems may be due to an inappropriate financial structure and there is a good prospect of changing that structure through an arrangement with its long-term creditors or by acquiring additional equity finance. Nor is the situation in which the company finds itself outside its control. The directors may have steps available to them to redress its position, such as selling a prime asset or reducing costs, not to mention initiating the restructuring just mentioned. On the other hand, the directors of an insolvent or soon-to-be insolvent company may indeed be staring into the abyss. There may be no realistic steps they can take to turn the situation around. In that case, the duty to take steps to minimise loss to creditors will bite at that point and, further, the only available course of action open to the directors may be to cease trading. **19–010**

What to do about a failing company—whether to keep trading or not; what remedial measures to seek to put in place—is a matter for the judgement of the directors. That would be the case, even if these two sections of the IA 1986 did not exist. The purpose of these sections is not to take away that judgement from the directors, but to re-orient their decision-making towards the interests of the creditors. As we indicated in para.19–005, as the company nears insolvency the shareholders' economic interest in the company evaporates and the risks attached to the company's business are now borne wholly by the creditors, a situation the directors may opportunistically exploit for the benefit of themselves and the shareholders. **19–011**

---

[48] Kristin van Zwieten, "Disciplining the Directors of Insolvent Companies" (2020) 33 *Insolvency Intelligence* 2.

[49] *Re Hawkes Hill Publishing Co Ltd* [2007] B.C.C. 937 Ch D.

[50] The likely duration of the "temporary" event is clearly crucial. During the Covid-19 emergency of 2020–2021, courts were instructed to assume, when making contribution orders, that the defendant was not responsible for any worsening of the company's position occurring during the emergency: Corporate Insolvency and Governance Act 2020 s.12. This was done on the basis that society would be better off if companies survived, even if the losses suffered by some creditors increased in the case of companies which did not. The measure was thought likely to benefit short-term creditors, such as employees or suppliers.

The legal strategy deployed in the sections for re-structuring directors' decision-making is review by the courts by reference to a negligence standard of the directors' actions or inaction in relation to two crucial issues. The first thing the court has to identify is the point at which there was no reasonable prospect of avoiding insolvent liquidation or administration and to establish whether the directors were of this view at that time.[51] The second is whether the directors took all the steps necessary to minimise the loss to the creditors after that point in time. In para.19–006 we pointed out that the standard of care is essentially an objective one. The drafters of the wrongful trading provisions were careful not to specify the precise action directors were required to take to meet its requirements, such as ceasing trading, as some jurisdictions require. Management remains the duty of the board, but with the court sitting over the board's shoulders.

As we noted in para.19–009, on the second question the courts, understandably, have taken a strict view of what directors need to do once the point of no reasonable prospect of avoiding insolvent liquidation or administration has been reached. On the first question, however, they have shown themselves sensitive to the point that the sections do not equate factual insolvency with having no reasonable prospect of avoiding a formal insolvency procedure. It is in the interests of creditors (higher recovery of their debts) and of shareholders and other stakeholders (such as employees) that, if the company can be turned around or its business disposed of in some other way, this course should be taken rather than that an immediate cessation of trading by an insolvent company should occur.

Thus, in *Re The Rod Gunner Organisation Ltd*[52] the court refused to find "no reasonable prospect" for a period of six months after the company became unable to meet its debts as they fell due, on the grounds that the directors reasonably thought an outside investor was going to come in with substantial funding (though that analysis no longer held once it became clear that the investor would not live up to the directors' expectations of him). Similarly, in *Re Continental Assurance Co of London Plc (No.4)*,[53] where a substantial insurance company had suffered unexpected losses, the court refused to find "no reasonable prospect" during a period of some six months in which the directors commissioned a report as to the company's solvency and decided to continue trading on the basis of the report received, until it later became clear that the company was in fact insolvent. Park J was very aware of the dangers of judging the directors' conduct on the basis of hindsight, and he remarked pithily in relation to the general issue that "ceasing to trade and liquidating too soon can be stigmatised as the cowards' way out". An important, but not determinative, factor in assessing what the directors should have concluded about the company's future is whether they took and acted

[51] The time points the court has to examine are those put forward by the liquidator. See fn.53.

[52] *Re The Rod Gunner Organisation Ltd* [2004] 1 B.C.L.C 110.

[53] *Re Continental Assurance Co of London Plc (No.4)* [2007] 2 B.C.L.C. 287. See also *Re Sherborne Associates Ltd* [1995] B.C.C. 40 QBD (Merc), in which the judge held that the liquidator had to identify and then stick to a particular date by which it was argued the directors should have realised the company had no reasonable prospect of avoiding insolvent liquidation.

upon outside advice as the company's business began to deteriorate and whether the outside advisor was of the view that there was no reasonable prospect of avoiding an insolvency procedure.[54]

However, this is not to say that courts are likely to have the wool pulled over their eyes about the recovery prospects of factually insolvent companies. There are many cases, especially in relation to situations where the directors were waiting for "guardian angels" to put money into the company, where the courts have found the directors to have had unrealistic views of the chances of this development occurring. The directors' expectations may have been unrealistic from the beginning or, more often, to have been entertained by the directors beyond the point at which they should have realised the injection was not likely to be forthcoming.[55]

Funding litigation

Any analysis of the wrongful trading provisions requires an assessment of the effectiveness of their enforcement. In contrast to litigation under the disqualification provisions discussed in the next chapter, where the public purse pays for the cases and there has been a high level of activity, litigation about wrongful trading seems to have been sparse and certainly there are relatively few reported cases. As we have seen, the Act places the initiation of litigation in the hands of the liquidator or administrator ("office-holders"), who do not have access to any public funds to support any litigation they propose to bring. Assuming the insolvent company does have some realisable assets, the office-holder may contemplate using those to fund the litigation in the hope of swelling the ultimate amount available for distribution to the creditors. However, even if the office-holder can secure solicitors who will take the case on a conditional fee basis—not always possible—the litigation is likely to involve some costs (for example, for the insurance to meet the other side's costs if the litigation is unsuccessful), and so the office-holder is likely to be unwilling to risk the company's already inadequate assets on litigation unless there is a very strong chance of success.[56] The office-holder might conceivably seek funding for the litigation from a floating charge holder, but there is little incentive for such a 19–012

[54] *Re Ralls Builders Ltd* [2016] B.C.C. 293, where the judge rejected the earlier of the liquidators' suggested dates for "no reasonable prospect", on the grounds that an outside recovery specialist's advice had not suggested that this was the situation at that time. Snowden J gives an incisive review of the cases on this issue in his judgment.

[55] *Roberts v Frohlich* [2011] EWHC 257 (Ch); [2012] B.C.C. 407; *Re Ralls Builders Ltd* [2016] B.C.C. 293—in relation to the later date suggested by the liquidators; *Re Kudos Business Solutions Ltd* [2012] B.C.L.C. 65.

[56] The question whether the costs of s.214 litigation counted as costs of the liquidation was determined in favour of the liquidator by an amendment to r.4.218 of the Insolvency Rules 1986/1925, made in 2002. In addition, s.176ZA of the IA 1986, inserted by s.1282 of the CA 2006, gave liquidation expenses priority over both preferential debts and assets secured by a floating charge (subject to exceptions to prevent abuse), overruling the result of *Buchler v Talbot* [2004] 2 A.C. 298 HL. Thus, the disincentive to liquidator litigation arising from the risk of the liquidator being left to bear the litigation costs personally has been considerably reduced, if not eliminated.

creditor to provide funding, for the proceeds of fraudulent and wrongful trading claims go to benefit the unsecured creditors, not the holders of a floating charge.[57]

The obvious step for the office-holder to take, faced with this uncertainty, is either to sell the claim to a third party or to obtain funding for the claim by assigning some part of the fruits of the litigation to a third party. A third party whose business consists of buying or funding such claims is in a position to take a more adventurous view of which claims to litigate, because it spreads its risks across a number of such claims, unlike the office-holder who has only "one shot" on behalf of the unsecured creditors of any particular company. However, until the reforms of 2015 the office-holder could not sell the wrongful trading claim under the general power to dispose of the company's assets, because the right to claim under the section is vested in the office-holder personally, not in the company.[58] The 2015 reforms sensibly cut through this difficulty by giving the office-holder an express statutory right to assign a wrongful or fraudulent trading claim (or the proceeds of such an action).[59] However, the rule that the proceeds of such an action are not the property of the company is retained.[60] This means that the proceeds are not swept up by the holders of any floating charge the company has issued, but rather remain available for the benefit of the unsecured creditors.

THE GENERAL DUTY IN RELATION TO CREDITORS

19–013 The wrongful trading reforms of the mid-1980s, discussed in the previous section, create a statutory duty of care on the part of directors towards creditors at the point when insolvency is unavoidable. Despite this statutory reform, the common law had not entirely neglected the interests of creditors at this point in the company's life-cycle and we analyse that development in this section. The statutory statement of the directors' core duty of loyalty in s.172 of the CA 2006[61] recognises and preserves this common law development. Section 172(3) provides that the duty the section creates "has effect subject to any enactment or rule of law requiring directors, in certain circumstances, to consider or act in the interests of the creditors of the company". This removes any doubt that might otherwise have existed about whether the wrongful trading rules had been in any way qualified or reduced as a result of the enactment of s.172, but this provision also preserves ("or rule of law") the common law developments.[62]

---

57 *Re Yagerphone Ltd* [1935] Ch. 395 Ch D.

58 A liquidator or administer who sought to avoid this rule by assigning the fruits of the litigation rather than the claim itself would find it difficult to give the funder sufficient control of the litigation. See *Grovewood Holdings Plc v James Capel & Co Ltd* [1995] Ch. 80 Ch D; *Re Oasis Merchandising Services Ltd (In Liquidation)* [1998] Ch. 170 CA; *Ruttle Plant Ltd v Secretary of State for the Environment, Food and Rural Affairs (No.3)* [2008] EWHC 238 (TCC); [2008] B.P.I.R. 1395; *Rawnsley v Weatherall Green & Smith North Ltd* [2009] EWHC 2482 (Ch); [2010] B.C.C. 406.

59 IA 1986 s.246ZD.

60 IA 1986 s.176ZB.

61 See para.10–026.

62 The CLR in fact proposed that the wrongful trading duty should be embodied in the statutory statement of directors' duties (CLR, Final 1, p.348 (Principle 9)), but the Government rejected this proposal on the grounds that decoupling the substantive provisions at present in s.214 from the remedies available under the IA 1986 would be "incongruous" (*Modernising Company Law* (July

The up-shot appears to be that the common law creditor-facing duty now operates by modifying the duty contained in s. 172, so that the duty to promote the success of the company for the benefit of its members becomes a duty instead to so act for the benefit of the creditors or, at least, to take creditor interests into account as well as those of the shareholders at some point in the decline in the company's fortunes. The circumstances in which this re-casting of the directors' duty under s.172 occurs are those defined at common law.[63] Even before this tipping point is reached and creditor interests are explicitly built into the s.172 duty, it is worth noting that the duty to promote the success of the company for the benefit of the *members* will confer some indirect legal protection upon creditors. A director who, without regard to the interests of the members, takes steps which place the solvency of a going concern company in jeopardy will find it difficult to demonstrate compliance with s.172 even in its normal formulation when it refers only to members.[64] However, our focus in this section is on the questions of when the tipping point is reached and what consequences follow.

By extension of its operation in relation to s.172, the creditor-facing duty is capable of modifying the other statutory duties of directors (as discussed in Ch.10). Thus a conflict of duty and interest can arise on the basis of the director's personal interests and the creditor duty. See *West Mercia Safetywear v Dodd*,[65] where the directors of a failing subsidiary caused it to make a payment to its equally failing parent, in order to reduce the parent's overdraft with the bank which they had personally guaranteed. Or the directors might be liable for negligence in relation to the protection of the creditors' interests.[66] In this section the duty will be referred to as the directors' general duty to the creditors, no matter which specific statutory duties are extended by it.

One important consequence of this analysis is that the general creditor duty is owed to the company (as s.170(1) of the CA provides), not to individual creditors. The phrase "general duty to the creditors" is to be understood in this way. As Gummow J said in the Australian High Court, "the result is that there is a duty of imperfect obligation owed to creditors, one which the creditors cannot enforce save to the extent that the company acts on its own motion or through a liquidator".[67] Typically, enforcement will be by the liquidator or administrator, as with enforcement of the wrongful trading duty. However, in principle the company or a shareholder suing derivatively could seek to enforce breaches of the duty outside insolvency. This could conceivably occur where the former

2002), Cm.5533-I, para.3.12). Had this step been taken, the statutory duties would have been wrapped up into the statutory statement as well (CLR, Final I, para.3.17).

63 Thus, in *BTI 2014 LLC v Sequana SA* [2019] EWCA Civ 112; [2019] B.C.C. 631, David Richards LJ said at [108]: "[The claimant] submits that this duty arose at common law but, since the relevant part of the Companies Act 2006 came into force, it arises under s 172(3)." The court appears to have accepted this submission. See also *GHLM Trading Ltd v Maroo* [2012] EWHC 61 (Ch); [2012] 2 B.C.L.C. 369 at [168] (Newey J). It follows that the duty may be broken even though the directors did not benefit from its breach. See *Re HLC Environmental Projects Ltd* [2013] EWHC 2876 (Ch); [2014] B.C.C. 337.

64 *LRH Services v Trew* [2018] EWHC 600 (Ch) at [29]–[30] and [151]–[154].

65 *West Mercia Safetywear v Dodd* [1988] B.C.L.C. 250 CA.

66 As in *Re Welfab Engineers Ltd* [1990] B.C.C. 600 Ch D (Companies Ct).

67 *Sycotex Pty Ltd v Baseler* (1994) 122 A.L.R. 531 at 550; *Yukon Line Ltd of Korea v Rendsburg Investments Corpn of Liberia* [1998] 1 W.L.R. 294 QBD (Comm).

creditors of the company have taken control of it via a debt for equity swap as a means of avoiding its liquidation. The main disadvantage (from the point of view of unsecured creditors) of the common law duty being owed to the company, not to individual creditors—and it is a significant one—is that its proceeds are typically caught by any security interests the company has granted. As we have seen, this result is avoided under the wrongful trading provisions.[68] Of course, the unsecured creditors may benefit consequentially from recoveries under the general duty, to the extent that these recoveries increase the chances of something being left over for the unsecured creditors after the secured creditors' claims have been satisfied.

When the duty arises

19–014 Starting in Australia in the 1970s,[69] the notion of a common law duty upon directors to take account of the interests of creditors as insolvency approaches has been widely accepted throughout the common-law world. The principle was adopted by the Court of Appeal in *West Mercia Safetywear v Dodd*.[70] As with most significant common-law developments in their relatively early stages, there was and still remains considerable uncertainty about the conceptual boundaries of this doctrine, leading to uncertainties about when the duty bites, about its content, the remedies available and, to a lesser extent, the mechanisms for enforcing it. On the answer to these questions turns the broader issue of what, if anything, the common law duty adds to the statutory wrongful trading remedy.

Only the most imprecise indications have been given by the courts as to when the duty is triggered. The authorities were reviewed by David Richards LJ, with whom the other members of the court agreed, in *BTI 2014 LLC v Sequana SA*.[71] We have already considered one aspect of this litigation in Ch.18 (at para.18–016). A dividend, lawful under Pt 23 of the CA 2006, had been paid by a subsidiary to its parent. As we saw in Ch.18, a potential creditor (a "victim") nevertheless secured a judgment that the dividend was unlawful under s.423 of the IA 1986, as intended to put assets beyond the reach of that creditor. A second claim was made by the subsidiary, now no longer owned by the parent, that the payment of the dividend, although lawful under the Pt 23, nevertheless constituted a breach of its (former) directors' creditor-facing duties and, though this is not explicitly stated in the judgments, that the defendant parent company, knowing of the breach of duty, was liable to repay the dividend. Both Rose J and the Court of Appeal held that the claim failed.

The case squarely raised the question of when the directors' creditor-facing duty arose. The paying company was not insolvent nor was it "on the verge" of insolvency, the phrase used in many previous cases. It was a non-trading company whose continued existence was explicable only because it was liable to meet future environmental clean-up costs. The company had made provision in its accounts for this liability and had declared the dividend on the basis that this

---

[68] See para.19–012.

[69] *Walker v Wimborne* (1976) 137 C.L.R. 1.

[70] *West Mercia Safetywear v Dodd* [1988] B.C.L.C. 250.

[71] *BTI 2014 LLC v Sequana SA* [2019] B.C.C. 631.

provision was to remain intact. However, it was accepted that the ultimate size of the liability was uncertain. It might be considerably more or considerably less than that allowed for in the provision. The claimant argued that the general duty was triggered in this situation on the basis that the payment of the dividend created "a real and not remote" risk to the creditors, that is, if the liability should turn out to be more than the provision.

The Court of Appeal rejected this test for the trigger, both on the authorities and as a matter of principle. As to the authorities, none of them supported the trigger for which the claimant contended and in fact there was no English authority which required the trigger to be defined as anything other than the company being actually insolvent.[72] While this was enough to dispose of the case, David Richards LJ considered the issue further because a number of experienced judges in previous cases had assumed that something less than actual insolvency would trigger the duty, even if those decisions did not support the trigger proposed by the claimant. The court's preferred formulation (clearly by way of dicta) was that the duty is triggered when the company is insolvent or is likely (meaning probably) to become so. This, the court thought, was a preferable test to any of the other formulations proposed, both on grounds of ease of application and ability to capture the situations where it was appropriate for the directors to focus on the creditors' interests.[73]

A much less discussed question is the impact upon directors' creditor facing duties when the company actually enters into an insolvency procedure. Administration does not necessarily entail that the director demits office, though they often choose to resign or are removed by the administrator and, even if they remain in office, their managerial powers are severely circumscribed and transferred to the insolvency practitioner acting as office-holder. However, it has been held that, so long as they continue as directors, they are subject to the above duty in their dealings with the company.[74]

Relationship to wrongful trading

The rejection of the "real risk" test is probably the correct choice in policy terms, **19–015**
for its adoption might mean that directors averse to the risk of personal liability would become unwilling to engage in economically valuable projects unless the shareholders' equity was large enough to absorb the full loss that would be incurred by the company if the "worst case" prediction for the project materialised. On the other hand, on any of the tests considered by the courts, the general duty is capable of being triggered before the directors become subject to the duty under s.214 of the IA 1986. It might be likely or probable that the company would become insolvent before it could be said that the company had

[72] *BTI 2014 LLC v Sequana SA* [2019] B.C.C. 631 at [195]. Even so, it is often unclear whether the courts were using a balance sheet definition of insolvency (liabilities exceed assets) or a cash-flow approach (company does not have enough cash to pay its debts as they fall due).

[73] *BTI 2014 LLC v Sequana SA* [2019] B.C.C. 631 at [213]– [220].

[74] IA 1986 Sch.B1 paras 61 and 64; *Re System Building Services Group Ltd* [2020] EWHC 54 (Ch); [2020] B.C.C. 345 (purchase by director of property at an undervalue from the company in administration). See further para.10–011.

no reasonable prospect of avoiding insolvent liquidation or administration. Indeed, as we saw in para.19–011, under s.214 the courts have held that an actually insolvent company is not necessarily in this position. In this case, the directors will be subject to the general duty to have regard to creditor interests, but may not be subject to the s. 214 duty. Thus, the general duty extends the temporal scope of directors' creditor-facing duties, and this makes it important to examine its relationship to the wrongful trading remedy analysed above.

19–016 One formal difference is that, as we have seen, the wrongful trading remedy can be pursued only if the company goes into insolvent liquidation or administration, while the general duty is not so limited. In the normal course of events it is more likely than not that an insolvent or near-insolvent company will end up in an insolvency procedure. But this need not be the case: the "guardian angel" (referred to above) may indeed turn up and buy the company without placing it in either administration or liquidation. Having obtained control, the new owner may examine the conduct of the old controllers and discover various ways in which they breached their duty to the company by ignoring the interests of the creditors. It will be impossible to pursue these matters under s.214 but a claim against the former directors for breach of duty may have value to the company—to the benefit, no doubt, of its new controller.

This raises the question of what the general creditor duty requires of directors. On the analysis put forward in para.19–013, the requirement is for the directors to continue to abide by the duties set out in ss.171–177 of the CA 2006 (see Ch.10), but those duties are re-oriented away from the shareholders and towards the creditors. There has been some debate about the extent of that re-orientation, an issue usually put in terms of whether, when the re-orientation takes place, the creditors' interests are "paramount". In *Sequana*[75] David Richards LJ preferred the paramountcy test on grounds it was easier for directors to apply, and used that argument to support the view that the creditor-oriented duties should arise only when the company was in insolvency or likely to be (at not at the earlier point proposed by the claimant). It is certainly true that the exclusion of the shareholders' interests would not be an attractive policy if the re-orientation of the duty could occur when the shareholders still had a significant equity interest in the company. On the other hand, even if the shareholders' interests are replaced by those of the creditors when the creditor duty is triggered, the directors, acting in good faith to promote the success of the company for the benefit of its creditors, appear still to be obliged to take into account the stakeholder interests listed in s.172(1), so that to this extent the paramountcy of the duty is qualified.[76]

19–017 The substantive obligations under s.214 of the IA 1986 and the general duties of directors under the CA 2006 are different. As we have seen in para.19–006, the s.214 duty is a focused, negligence-based, duty to take every step to minimise the

---

[75] *BTI 2014 LLC v Sequana SA* [2019] B.C.C. 631 at [199].

[76] See para.10–037. See also *Re Welfab Engineers Ltd* [1990] B.C.C. 600, where Hoffmann J rejected a misfeasance summons against the directors of a failing company, who attempted to save a company as a going concern for the benefit of its employees (including themselves), rather than put it into immediate administration or liquidation, which course of action would have yielded a somewhat greater surplus for the creditors. Their rescue attempt was unsuccessful and the company did eventually end up in liquidation.

potential loss to creditors, while the duties in the CA are formulated in a higher-level and more general way. Where, therefore, both duties overlap and the office-holder is concerned to swell the assets of the company for the benefit of creditors, that person is likely to find that proof of breach of the s.214 duty is more straightforward than breach of the general creditor duty—and that duty will more directly advance the interests of the unsecured creditors (see para.19–013). Where, however, the general duty applies, but the s.214 duty does not, there will certainly be circumstances in which cases of continuing to trade to the detriment of creditors will be capable of being pursued under the general duty. However, as with wrongful trading, it is not inevitable that continuing to trade will constitute a breach of the general duty, even though the company is in financial difficulties. As Scott VC recognised in *Facia Footwear Ltd v Hinchliffe*,[77] where the claim was based on the general creditor duty, "a continuation of trading might mean a reduction in the dividend eventually payable to creditors but it represented the creditors' only chance of full payment. It is, therefore, not in the least obvious that in continuing to trade the directors were ignoring the interests of the creditors". However, this statement does show that the balance of advantage between continuing and ceasing trading is to be struck in the creditors' interests.

The creditor duty and preferences

Because of the generality of the common law duty, it may also be available to regulate opportunistic conduct which does not take the form of continued trading. As Kristin van Zwieten has pointed out,[78] after a reluctant start, the courts have accepted that directors who cause the company to discharge debts or liabilities on a preferential basis in the vicinity of insolvency may be in breach of the general duty to creditors. Here, the general duty acts as a substitute for or extension of the statutory rules on preferences (discussed below) rather than for the statutory wrongful trading provisions. Indeed, *West Mercia Safetywear v Dodd*[79] itself was such a case. The director of a subsidiary caused it to make a payment to its parent in partial discharge of a debt owed by subsidiary to parent at a time when both companies were insolvent, the effect of which was to benefit the director who had guaranteed the bank's lending to the parent. The Court of Appeal held this put the director in position of conflict of duty and interest, for he had acted "in breach of duty when, for his own purposes, he caused the £4,000 to be transferred in disregard of the interests of the general creditors of this insolvent company." This was so even though, on a balance sheet basis, the subsidiary was no worse off after the payment than before, because the cash payment was balanced by a reduction in the subsidiary's liabilities. A more challenging case would be a preference payment not made to corporate insiders. The remaining creditors would still be prejudiced by the payment, but it would be more difficult to identify the breach of duty by the directors. Clearly, there are cases where **19–018**

[77] *Facia Footwear Ltd v Hinchliffe* [1998] 1 B.C.L.C. 218 Ch D (an application for summary judgment). For a similar approach to wrongful trading see above, para.9–009.

[78] "Director Liability in Insolvency and its Vicinity" (2018) 38 O.J.L.S. 382.

[79] *West Mercia Safetywear v Dodd* [1988] B.C.L.C. 250. See also *GHLM Trading v Maroo* [2012] 2 B.C.L.C. 369 at [168]–[171].

preferring a particular creditor, for example, one in a position to halt the company's trading by cutting off further supplies, promotes the success of the company, in which case the general duty could not be said to have been infringed, but it is not impossible that a preference to a non-corporate insider could constitute a payment for an improper purpose.

Remedies

19–019 Although there is no reason why a preference should not count as a type of wrongful trading under s.214, that section will not provide an effective remedy against it, so long as the courts assess the contribution ordered by reference to the loss suffered by the company (see para.19–009). As just indicated, the payment of a debt, however preferential, does not cause a loss to the company, if the debt is paid at the correct value, for the loss of corporate assets is exactly balanced by a reduction in the company's liabilities.[80] There is a loss to the remaining creditors, of course, because the one paid in full no longer has to accept its "share" of the company's losses, which is thrown onto the remaining creditors. So long as loss to the company is the touchstone for the assessment of the contribution, however, this fact is put on one side.

The question arises whether the same difficulty arises in relation to the general creditor duty, since it too is owed to the company and not to individual creditors. If the company seeks equitable compensation from the directors in relation to the preference, can they resist the claim on the grounds that their action caused no loss to the company? If the preference involves payment in breach of duty to the directors themselves, directly or indirectly, the company will have a proprietary claim against the directors for the return of those assets or their value.[81] It is currently controversial whether the company can claim "restorative" compensation against directors in respect of payments by way of preferential payments to third parties or whether compensation is confined to the redress of corporate losses.[82]

STATUTORY PROVISIONS ON PREFERENCES

19–020 Although the use of the general creditor duty to control preferences is a recent development by the courts, there have long been statutory provisions on this topic, currently s.239 of the IA 1986.[83] The provision operates along the same

[80] Subject possibly to the argument that a change in the *composition* of the company's assets caused it loss. The reduction in cash arising out of the discharge of a debt could hinder the company's continued trading. See *Northampton BC v Cardoza* [2019] EWHC 26 (Ch); [2019] B.C.C. 582 at [208].

[81] See para.18–016 for the application of this principle to disguised distributions.

[82] In *Re HLC Environmental Products Ltd* [2014] B.C.C. 337 the judge acknowledged the point but concluded that compensation was available in respect of a payment to a third party. The decision was rendered before a number of appellate decisions which cast doubt on this conclusion which are discussed in para 10–106. For arguments that a remedy is available in this situation, see A. Keay, "Financially distressed companies, preferential payments and the director's duty to take account of creditors' interests" (2020) 136 L.Q.R. 52.

[83] This operates in England and Wales; Scotland has a somewhat different provision in s.243.

lines as s.238 on transactions at an undervalue in the vicinity of insolvency (which we considered at para.18–015), the two sections share the same remedial provisions (in s.215) and the right of action is vested in the liquidator or administrator. The "prior period" is defined, however, more restrictively. For preferences, it is only six months, unless the person receiving the preference is connected with the company, in which case the two-year period re-appears.[84] Of course ss.238 and 239 are aimed at different mischiefs: an undervalue transaction does not necessarily involve a preference and vice versa. A preference is defined as when the company does something which has the effect of putting a creditor of the company in a better position in the event of the company going into liquidation as compared with the position that would have obtained, had that thing not been done.[85] The same provision is applied to the company's sureties and guarantors.

The core restriction on the section is that the court has power to make on order only if the company "was influenced in deciding to give it by a desire to produce" the better position just described.[86] Some of the sting of this condition is removed by the qualification that the relevant desire is rebuttably presumed to exist in the case of a preference give to someone connected with the company.[87] In *Re MC Bacon*,[88] the company, a bacon importer and wholesaler, went into liquidation sometime after losing its principal customer. The liquidator challenged a debenture granted to the company's bank (so not a connected person) during the period where the company was attempting to stay afloat, and when it was probably insolvent or almost so, and could not have continued without the support of its bank. Millett J declined to strike down the debenture, holding that it was not a voidable preference, since the company had not been motivated by a desire to prefer the bank but merely by a desire to avoid their overdraft being recalled. This outcome, although clearly defended in the judgment, raises starkly the substantial practical shortcomings of these preference provisions. The fact that a preference is only voidable if motivated by the insolvent debtor's desire to prefer creates the rather odd result that if the creditor aggressively demands early repayment under threat of refusing further supplies or services, the payment is unlikely to be caught, to the distinct advantage of the creditor who has now been paid in full and the corresponding disadvantage of the remaining unsecured creditors. By contrast, in both the US and Australia, a disposition is voidable if it has the *effect* of preferring one creditor, whatever the debtor's motivation.

What is the relationship between s.239 and the general duty to creditors? The two doctrines tackle the problem of preferences from the two different ends of the transaction. Section 215 (providing remedies for breaches of s.239) seeks to deprive the recipient of the preference of its benefit by reversing the effects of the **19–021**

[84] IA 1986 s.240(1). A connected person is a director or shadow director of the company (s.249) or an associate of these (widely defined in s.435).

[85] IA 1986 s.239(4).

[86] IA 1986 s.239(5). This restriction is not present in s.243, applying in Scotland, but s.243(2) lists a range of transactions to which the section does not apply, including the payment in cash of a due debt "unless the transaction was collusive with the purpose of prejudicing the general body of creditors" (s.243(2)(b)).

[87] IA 1986 s.239(6). *Re Cosy Seal Insulation Ltd* [2016] EWHC 1255 (Ch); [2016] 2 B.C.L.C. 319.

[88] *Re MC Bacon* [1990] B.C.C. 78 Ch D (Companies Ct).

transaction. The court is to make such order as it sees fit "for restoring the position to what it would have been if the company had not given that preference".[89] The general creditor duty imposes liability on the directors of the company who authorised the preference, something which it appears the court does not have power to do under the statute.[90] Subject to the points made in para.19–019 about the scope of equitable compensation, the company may be able to obtain compensation from the directors who authorised the transaction. Both courses of action will go to swell the assets of the company in insolvency and success in the one action is likely to reduce the strength of the remedy available in the other. Moreover, recoveries under the general duty will fall within any security interest the company may have given, whilst recoveries under ss.238 and 239 benefit unsecured creditors. Nevertheless, the general duty may be valuable in a number of situations: where the recipient of the preference is insolvent and the directors are not (or have insurance), where the preference was given outside the limited "prior period", where it is not possible to prove that the directors had the relevant desire. There is no requirement for any particular desire to be shown under the general duty. For example, the directors might simply fail to consider the interests of the creditors as a whole and thus fall to have their conduct judged by a rationality standard rather than by any subjective test.[91]

On the other hand, for the director to cause the company to make a preferential payment, especially where the relevant desire is established by means of the presumption, is not necessarily a breach of the directors' duties under the CA, even taking into account the shift of those duties toward creditors when insolvency looms.[92] The preference, though unlawful under the IA, might have been given in order to promote the success of the company for the benefit of its creditors, for example because the directors (erroneously) thought that getting rid of one troublesome creditor would enable the company to continue trading and to recover.[93] Thus, s.239 and the general duty to creditors overlap but are not congruent. Where they overlap, as with the overlap between the general duty and wrongful trading (see para.19–017), the IA provision is likely to be more attractive to the liquidator or administrator, because of it is formulated in more precise terms. Where they do not—or it is unclear whether they do—then the general expands the capacity of the office-holder to swell the assets of the company for the benefit of its creditors.

PHOENIX COMPANIES AND PROHIBITED NAMES

19–022 The provisions we have analysed above concerned the decisions of directors when the company was insolvent or nearly so, but had not (yet) entered into administration or liquidation. By contrast, ss.216 and 217 of the IA 1986 focus on

[89] IA 1986 s.239(3). A non-exclusive but lengthy list of the court's powers is set out in s.241.

[90] *Johnson v Arden* [2018] EWHC 1624 (Ch); [2019] 2 B.C.L.C. 215.

[91] *Re HLC Environmental Products Ltd* [2014] B.C.C. 337 at [92].

[92] *Re Brian D Pierson Ltd* [2001] B.C.L.C. 275 at 299; *GHLM Trading Ltd v Maroo* [2012] 2 B.C.L.C. 369 at [168].

[93] Of course, they would not necessarily have a defence in these circumstances to a wrongful trading claim, where their decision to continue trading would be assessed objectively. See para.19–006.

what happens after liquidation. In broad terms, they prohibit the use by a new company which emerges from the liquidation of the corporate or trading name of the old or "liquidating" company. In somewhat more detail, s.216 of the IA 1986 makes it an offence (of strict liability)[94] for anyone, who was a director or shadow director of the liquidating company at any time during the 12 months preceding its going into insolvent liquidation, to be in any way concerned during the next five years in the formation or management of a company, or business, with a name by which the original company was known or one so similar as to suggest an association with that company (known as a "prohibited name").

In addition to the criminal offence, s.217 makes a person acting in breach of s.216 personally liable, jointly and severally with the new company and any other person so liable, for the debts and other liabilities of the new company incurred while he or she was concerned in its management in breach of s.216.[95] In this case, therefore, the defendant is personally liable to creditors in relation to a specific set of debts rather than liable, as under the fraudulent and wrongful trading provisions, to make a general contribution to the assets of the company in order to help meet the claims of all its unsecured creditors. Indeed, the personal liability arises, though will normally not be needed by the creditor, even if the company is not in any particular financial difficulty.[96] Also liable is anyone involved in the second company's management who acts or is willing to act on the instructions given by a person whom he knows, at that time, to be in breach of s.216.[97] As we see in the following chapter (para.20–004), liability to compensate particular groups of creditors is also a possible outcome of the compensation provisions now inserted into the Company Directors Disqualification Act 1986, though only in relation to loss caused to those creditors by the conduct which led to the disqualification.

The "Phoenix" syndrome

The obvious first question is, why was this somewhat *recherché* provision included in the IA? Although not in terms confined to this situation, it is clear that the driving force behind its inclusion was a desire to deal with what has become known as the "Phoenix" syndrome. The phenomenon of an entrepreneur 19–023

[94] *R. v Cole* [1998] 2 B.C.L.C. 234 CA.

[95] IA 1986 s.217. That the liability is restricted to debts incurred by the company in the period during which the person was in breach of s.216 (and did not extend to all the debts incurred whilst that person was a director of the company) was accepted by Arden LJ in *ESS Productions Ltd v Sully* [2005] EWCA Civ 554; [2005] B.C.C. 435 at [75]. See also *Glasgow City Council v Craig* [2008] CSOH 171; 2009 S.L.T. 212: liability confined to the debts of that part of the business which was carried on under the prohibited name.

[96] If the claim is brought by an administrator or liquidator of the new company, in contrast to the former position in relation to wrongful trading, the office-holder has always been free to sell the claim to a third party. See *First Independent Factors and Finance Ltd v Mountford* [2008] EWHC 835 (Ch); [2008] B.C.C. 598—claim brought by debt factor which had acquired the claims from two trade creditors at a discount. cf. fn.58.

[97] Though such a person does not commit a criminal offence. For the purpose of both ss.216 and 217, "company" includes any company which may be wound up under Pt V of the IA 1986 (see s.220), but this term has been held not to include an insolvent partnership even though they are capable of being wound up under Pt V. See *Re Newton Coaches Ltd* [2016] EWHC 3068 (Ch); [2017] B.C.C. 34.

operating through a series of undercapitalised companies which went into liquidation and were then replaced by new companies trading under the same or a similar name was identified by the Cork Committee in 1982, whose recommendations led to the IA 1986.[98] It was described in more detail by the Company Law Review in the following terms:

> "The 'phoenix' problem results from the continuance of a failed company by those responsible for that failure, using the vehicle of a new company. The new company, often trading under the same or similar name, uses the old company's assets, often acquired at an undervalue, and exploits its goodwill and business opportunities. Meanwhile, the creditors of the old company are left to prove their debts against a valueless shell and the management conceal their previous failure from the public."[99]

However, it also went on to point out that the actions just described are not necessarily improper. They will be so where their purpose is to deprive the creditors of the first company of the value of that company's assets by transferring them at an undervalue to the second company; or where the purpose of the actions is to mislead the creditors of the second company by disguising the lack of success of the business when it was carried on by the first company. In other cases, however, such purposes may be lacking. The failure of the first company may be for reasons outside the control of its directors and, further, "the only way to continue an otherwise viable business and their own and their employees' ability to earn their livelihood may be for them to do so in a new vehicle using the assets and trading style of the original company".[100] Thus, the regulation of the Phoenix company is not an easy matter: too light a regulation may permit abuses to continue; too heavy a regulation may lead to the cessation of otherwise viable businesses.

19–024 As will be clear from the Company Law Review's description, the Phoenix problem has two aspects. The first is the sale of the liquidating company's assets at an undervalue to the controllers of the new company and the second is the use by the new company of a prohibited name. Sections 216–217 of the IA 1986 appear to tackle only the second aspect. Even if the assets of the liquidating company are acquired at an undervalue, the sections will not bite if the new company avoids a prohibited name.[101] Equally, use of a prohibited name is caught by the sections in principle even if there is no acquisition of assets at an undervalue from the liquidating company.[102] Why is the use of a prohibited name by itself objectionable? The issue here is misleading the creditors of the second

[98] *Insolvency Law and Practice* (1982), Cmnd.8558.

[99] Final Report I, para.15.55.

[100] Final Report I, para.15.56. The facts giving rise to the application to use a similar name in *Re Lightning Electrical Contractors Ltd* [1996] B.C.C. 950 Ch D might be thought to be an example of this: the administrative receivership of a medium-sized company was brought about by the failure of two large client companies to pay the money due from them; the successor company's use of the similar name was supported by the receivers since it enable them to maximise the value of the first company's assets.

[101] The CLR recommended reforms aimed at the first aspect of the problem, but they were not taken up in the CA 2006: CLR, Final Report I, paras 15.65–15.72. The problem with the existing law is perhaps demonstrated by the background facts of *Secretary of State for Trade and Industry v Becker* [2003] 1 B.C.L.C. 565.

[102] See further para.19–025.

company. The company against which the second group of creditors' claims lie appears to be a more credit-worthy operation than it really is, because it appears at first glance to be the first company, whose demise is concealed or at least obscured.[103]

The prohibited name may be the liquidating company's name or a name under which that company carried on business; and the prohibition applies to both the new company's corporate and trading names.[104] These are important extensions, for otherwise the prohibition could be easily avoided by the new company's registered name being quite dissimilar from the liquidating company's but by the new company's trading name being similar to the liquidating company's registered or trading name. Whether the similarity of names is made out is to be judged by the court by reference to the circumstances in which the companies with the allegedly similar names operate, and so it is a highly fact-specific determination.[105] It is clear that no person needs to have been misled by the prohibited act; it is enough to show that the names had a tendency to mislead.[106]

Exceptions

The clearest indication that the focus of these sections of the IA 1986 is upon protecting the creditors of the new company is the fact that the personal liability of the directors of the new company is in respect of the creditors of the new company, not the of liquidating company. Nor is the successor company itself liable for the debts of the liquidating company. So, the extent of the protection afforded by s.216 to the creditors of the liquidating company is at best indirect. However, when one looks at the exceptions to the use of the prohibited name, concern with the treatment of the assets of the liquidating company emerges as a relevant factor. **19–025**

There are two situations in which an otherwise prohibited name may be used. The first is where the court, on an ad hoc basis, gives leave for the name to be used; the second is where the situation falls within one of the cases defined in the Insolvency Rules.[107] In *Penrose v Official Receiver*[108] Chadwick J considered it

---

[103] If misleading the creditors as to the creditworthiness of the second business is the rationale of the section, it is perhaps understandable that the prohibition extends even to the carrying on of the second business in non-corporate form (i.e. potentially without limited liability): (s.216(3)(c)). However, no personal liability is imposed in this case, presumably on the basis that it is unnecessary: s.217(1). In many cases the defendant will be liable as partner or sole trader, but it is conceivable that a person could "directly or indirectly be concerned or take part in the carrying-on" of a non-corporate business without attracting personal liability as a partner or sole trader, so that the absence of personal liability under s.217 is important.

[104] IA 1986 s.216(6). See *R. (Griffin) v Richmond Magistrates Court* [2008] EWHC 84 (Admin). The CLR found that this was a practice used effectively to avoid the impact of the provisions, even though ostensibly caught by them.

[105] *First Independent Factors and Finance Ltd v Mountford* [2008] 2 B.C.L.C. 297.

[106] *Ricketts v Ad Valorem Factors Ltd* [2004] 1 B.C.L.C. 1 CA; *Revenue and Customs Commissioners v Walsh* [2005] EWHC 1304 (Ch); [2005] 2 B.C.L.C. 455, though in the former case there was a disagreement among the judges as to whether the facts needed only to "suggest" an association or give rise to a probability that members of the public would associate the two companies.

[107] Insolvency (England and Wales) Rules 2016 (SI 2016/1024) Pt 22; and the Insolvency (Scotland) (Receivership and Winding Up) Rules 2018 (SSI 2018/347) Pt 12.

relevant to the exercise of his discretion on this matter that granting leave would pose no risk to the creditors of the *liquidating* company and he identified that one of the purposes of s.216 was to reduce the danger that the business of the liquidating company would be acquired at an undervalue.[109] In that case the directors of the new company in fact had paid "'over the odds'" for the assets of the liquidating company and the new company had voluntarily taken over some of the liabilities of the liquidating company, including its workforce. Through the leave provision, s.216 thus provides an incentive for the directors contemplating continued trading under the same name to act properly in relation to the assets of the liquidating company.

19–026 The same result follows from the first of the three excepted cases defined in the Insolvency Rules,[110] though in this case the protection for the creditors of the liquidating company is to be found in the procedural requirement for the involvement of an office-holder in the sale of the assets of the liquidating company. Where the new company purchases the whole of the insolvent company's business from an insolvency practitioner acting for the liquidating company and gives notice of the name the successor company intends to use to all the creditors of the liquidating company, the prohibited name may be used. The thought is that the involvement of the office-holder, owing duties to the creditors of the liquidating company, will ensure that the business of that company will be sold at a proper price.[111] It has to be said that the directors of the liquidating company will often be the only persons with sufficient faith in the business of the liquidating company to take it on and so they will be in a strong bargaining position. The office-holder may be expected to screen out only egregious examples of opportunistic behaviour by the directors.

Although s.216 is triggered only if the company goes into liquidation, it is not uncommon for the company to be put through another insolvency procedure (notably administration) and only for the rump of the company which emerges from administration to be put into liquidation.[112] The restructuring of the company's business, including its potential sale, then occurs in the administration process. Although not originally well adapted to take account of these facts, the rules were amended in 2007 and now embrace cases where the purchase is arranged with an administrator rather than a liquidator.[113]

---

[108] *Penrose v Official Receiver* [1996] 1 B.C.L.C. 389 Ch D.

[109] *Penrose v Official Receiver* [1996] 1 B.C.L.C. 389 at 397i and 398e. Of course, the judge was also concerned with the risk to the creditors of the new company, which he put in terms of their being misled. It was not a factor to be taken into account that the new company was simply under-capitalised, unless there was evidence before the court that the director's conduct in relation to the liquidating company was such as to merit disqualification (as discussed in the following chapter).

[110] SI 2016/1024 Pt 22 r.22.4.

[111] In *First Independent Factors and Finance Ltd v Churchill* [2006] EWCA Civ 1623; [2007] B.C.C. 45 CA (Civ Div) the Court of Appeal put the function of the notice on the basis that it was there to help creditors of the liquidating company make an informed assessment of the risks of extending credit to the new company, i.e. the focus was on their protection in the capacity as potential creditors of the new company.

[112] On the differences between administration and liquidation see para.33–003.

[113] Thus reversing the impact of the decision in *First Independent Factors and Finance Ltd v Churchill* [2007] B.C.C. 45.

The third case[114] excepts from s.216 the situation where the new company has been known by the prohibited name for the whole of the 12 months ending with the liquidation of the first company.[115] The purpose of this provision is, in particular, to permit the transfer of businesses within an existing group of companies. The risk of the creditors being misled, although it exists, is not in this case the result of action taken after the liquidation of the original company but of decisions taken in advance of the liquidation by a period of at least one year—a period thought to be enough to prevent opportunistic use of this exception.[116] This exception has been given a broad interpretation by the courts: it is not necessary to show that the company was known during the 12-month period by the prohibited name it had at the time the debt arose (provided it was known during that period by one or more prohibited names) or that it used the prohibited name in relation to the whole of its business.[117]

CONCLUSION

The legal provisions considered in this chapter can be said to have moved the duties of directors away from promoting the interests of the shareholders and towards the interests of the creditors when the company is in or near insolvency. It is sometimes said that this is a significant qualification upon the general shareholder orientation of British corporate law. At a superficial level this is obviously true, but it is doubtful whether it is true from a more fundamental perspective. The argument for a shareholder orientation of corporate law turns on the shareholders being residual claimants on the company's revenues and thus having the strongest incentives to run the company efficiently. Whatever the merits and de-merits of this argument, it clearly has much less force in relation to insolvent companies when the shareholders' equity in the company has disappeared or all but gone. As Street CJ put it in *Kinsela v Russell Kinsela Pty Ltd*,[118] in this situation **19–027**

> "it is in a practical sense [the creditors'] assets and not the shareholders' assets that, through the medium of the company, are under the management of the directors pending either liquidation, return to solvency or the imposition of some alternative administration."

Even this statement does not quite get one home. Once the company is actually in an insolvency procedure, an office-holder will be appointed formally to run the company in the interests of the creditors. Short of entry into liquidation or administration, as Street CJ recognised, there is always the possibility of a return

[114] The second case (r.22.6) is ancillary to the provision permitting a person to act in breach of s.216 if the court gives permission. The second case permits a director, who applies for leave within seven days of the first company going into liquidation, to continue to act in breach of s.216 for a period of six weeks or until the court disposes of the application for leave, whichever is the shorter.

[115] Rule 22.7—and has not been a dormant company. Otherwise, a shelf company could be formed purely for the purpose of triggering this exception.

[116] Though cf. *Morphitis v Bernasconi* [2003] 2 B.C.L.C. 53 CA: scheme to avoid s.216 by the directors resigning from the company at least a year before it was liquidated.

[117] *ESS Production Ltd v Sully* [2005] 2 B.C.L.C. 547.

[118] *Kinsela v Russell Kinsela Pty Ltd* (1986) 4 N.S.W.L.R. 722 at 730; approved by Dillon LJ in *West Mercia Safetywear Ltd v Dodd* [1988] B.C.L.C. 250.

to solvency, to the benefit of the shareholders. Consequently, it is not at all clear why the shareholders should be excluded from the considerations of the directors, as some of the rules discussed above appear to do. The better argument is not so much that the shareholders have no interest in a return to solvency, but that when the company is insolvent or near it, but it has not entered a formal insolvency procedure, the shareholders' interest in recovery or salvage of its assets is too strong, so that they are likely to behave opportunistically towards creditors. The aim of the provisions considered in this chapter is to correct those tendencies on the part of shareholders and directors beholden to them.

PART 6

PUBLIC ENFORCEMENT

We have already seen in Pt 4 that, when directors breach their duties, difficult questions of enforcement arise. The earlier discussion was based on the assumption that the enforcer would be located within the company, whether (in descending order) the board, the general meeting or a minority shareholder. Such private enforcers, however, generally rely upon the courts to obtain effective redress. Not only is litigation expensive and slow, but there will be informational asymmetries that make it an uphill struggle to get proceedings out of the blocks, let alone progress them efficiently. Moreover, private enforcement only focuses upon the details of the individual claim and does not purport to provide redress more widely for those harmed by the defendant's conduct. Whilst there can be no doubt that private enforcement has its place, it is often a suboptimal solution.

An alternative is to place the enforcement decision in the hands of somebody outside the company or at least independent of its internal structures. There are clear efficiencies to such public enforcement: collective assets can be deployed by specialist agencies to confer the widest possible range of benefits on those impacted by corporate wrongdoing. The most extreme version is to place enforcement directly in the hands of the State. In that regard, Ch.21 considers company investigations. The effectiveness of such State-based enforcement, however, depends upon the resources that the State is prepared to make available. This differs between jurisdictions, but the history of public enforcement is littered with bodies subsequently criticised for having been asleep on the job or never having taken action when necessary. However, there are also some notable exceptions. Whilst money undoubtedly makes a difference, so does access to information. Where the public enforcer has to carry out the information-gathering exercise itself, this has proven to be a significant barrier to all but the most well-resourced enforcement agency. In contrast, where the information is available in pre-digested form, the public enforcer's task is made immeasurably easier. This may account for why company investigations have hardly proved to be a roaring success, but disqualification proceedings have been so successful in achieving their aims that more streamlined procedures have had to be developed. In the former case, the information-gathering exercise falls to the agency; in the latter case, the task has usually been completed by another (such as a liquidator). Disqualification proceedings are considered in Ch.20.

CHAPTER 20

DISQUALIFICATION OF DIRECTORS

The previous chapter examined those statutory provisions that, at the instigation of those in charge of the company's insolvency, may lead to the imposition of a financial liability on directors and shadow directors who, in the period preceding the insolvency, engaged in conduct exploiting the vulnerabilities of creditors and causing a diminution in the company's assets.[1] When the Cork Committee recommended these reforms in 1982, it actually went further and argued that "proper safeguards for the public" required that wrongful trading be supplemented by legislation designed to ensure that "those whose conduct has shown them to be unfitted to manage the affairs of a company with limited liability shall, for a specified period, be prohibited from doing so".[2] In particular, the Cork Committee considered that the law should "severely penalise those who abuse the privilege of limited liability by operating behind one-man, insufficiently capitalised companies".[3] This recommendation is now embodied in the Company Directors Disqualification Act 1986 (CDDA 1986),[4] as later amended. Like wrongful trading liability, the CDDA 1986's central provisions (disqualification on grounds of "unfitness") apply to shadow directors as well as directors.[5] The CDDA 1986 is fundamentally a deterrence measure, designed for the protection of future corporate creditors as a class, rather than seeking compensation for 20–001

[1] See, for example, IA 1986 s.214.

[2] *Report of the Review Committee on Insolvency Law and Practice* (1982), Cm.8558, para.1808.

[3] *Report of the Review Committee on Insolvency Law and Practice* (1982), Cm.8558, para.1815.

[4] This is still the principal legislation, which will be referred to as "CDDA 1986" in this chapter, unless otherwise indicated.

[5] CDDA 1986 ss.6(3C) and 8(1).

existing creditors. Recently, however, a compensation power has been grafted onto the disqualification provisions,[6] thus holding out some prospect that the provisions will also assist the creditors of the company whose directors have been disqualified.

A further significant feature of the CDDA 1986 is that initiation of disqualification action lies exclusively in the hands of the public authorities in the case of the most commonly used statutory provisions (such as where disqualification is based on "unfitness").[7] Initiation of the disqualification process is assigned to the Secretary of State (who will be the relevant government minister at the time), although the minister may delegate that function, and normally does, to the Insolvency Service, a government agency.[8] The Secretary of State also has exclusive control over the initiation of the new compensation provisions.[9] Outside the area of unfitness, the liquidator or any past member or creditor may apply for a disqualification order.[10] It is unclear, however, that there will be any great incentive to make such an application, as the benefits of disqualification accrue to future creditors. In other words, the forward-looking disqualification process and its initiation by the public authorities are linked features of the CDDA 1986. When compensation was grafted onto the legislation in 2015, the opportunity might have been taken to open up the range of potential initiators, but this did not happen.

The introduction of a compensation mechanism was not the only significant reform after 1986. In particular, reforms in the IA 2000 introduced the notion of an out-of-court "disqualification undertaking" in cases of unfitness.[11] This supplements the existing "disqualification order", which only a court can make.[12] In addition, the Small Business, Enterprise and Employment Act 2015 included reforms aimed at taking into account the cross-border environment in which many companies now operate, but which national prudential rules often ignore.[13] These changes make it possible for the conduct of directors in relation to overseas companies (i.e. companies incorporated outside Great Britain[14]) to be taken into account in appropriate circumstances by the court or Secretary of State when considering disqualification. Statutory powers in that regard already existed in the CA 2006,[15] but they have not been used to date: the Secretary of State may make regulations, so that a person disqualified in a foreign jurisdiction would or could be prohibited from acting in relation to a company incorporated in Great

[6] CDDA 1986 s.15A, inserted by the Small Business, Enterprise and Employment Act 2015. For the principles to be applied in making such a compensation order, see *Re Noble Vintners Ltd* [2019] EWHC 2806 (Ch); [2020] B.C.C. 198.

[7] CDDA 1986 ss.6 and 8.

[8] CDDA 1986 s.7.

[9] CDDA 1986 s.15A(1).

[10] CDDA 1986 s.16.

[11] CDDA 1986 s.1A. See further para.20–002.

[12] CDDA 1986 ss.1. See further para.20–002.

[13] CDDA 1986 s.5A. For the policy behind this reform, see BIS, *Transparency & Trust: Enhancing the Transparency of UK Company Ownership and Increasing Trust in UK Business: Government Response* (April 2014), BIS/14/672, Chs 5–9.

[14] CDDA 1986 s.22(2A). The reference is to "Great Britain" rather than the "United Kingdom" because Northern Ireland has separate disqualification legislation, namely the Company Directors Disqualification (Northern Ireland) Order 2002, although its scope is similar.

[15] CA 2006 s.1184.

Britain. The changes made to the CDDA 1986 in 2015 come close to this approach,[16] but are based on conviction abroad for a serious offence, not disqualification abroad. The attraction of the broader approach clearly depends upon the equivalence of the foreign jurisdiction's disqualification provisions to those in the UK.

In addition to the general disqualification ground of "unfitness" in the CDDA 1986, there are a number of more specific situations in which disqualification can be imposed on an individual. Although these individuals are typically a company's directors or shadow directors, some grounds of disqualification apply more broadly in some cases. The specific instances can best be analysed as falling within the following categories: commission of a serious offence, usually involving dishonesty, in connection with the management of a company; being found liable to make a contribution to the assets of the company on grounds of fraudulent or wrongful trading[17]; and failure to comply with the statutory obligations relating to the filing of documents with the Registrar. Finally, there is a long-standing provision in the companies legislation that disqualifies an undischarged bankrupt from being involved in the management of companies,[18] to which was added in 2002 the notion of "bankruptcy restriction orders".

DISQUALIFICATION ORDERS AND UNDERTAKINGS

The power to disqualify has generated a high level of activity. In the years **20–002**
1997–1998 to 2000–2001 between 1,250 and 1,500 directors were disqualified each year by court order and in 2001–2002 (when disqualification undertakings were introduced) the total number of orders and undertakings was nearly 2,000.[19] Since then, the total number of orders and undertakings has fluctuated within a relatively narrow range, but otherwise remained fairly steady. For example, in 2014–2015 there was a combined total of 1,227 (899 undertakings and 328 court orders),[20] which represented about 4% of the total number of directors of failed companies in that year, whereas in 2019–2020 the combined total was 1,485 (1,136 undertakings and 349 orders).[21] Accordingly, the CDDA 1986 has been the basis of considerable activity on the part of the public authorities. Indeed, the rationale behind the introduction of undertakings in unfitness cases by the IA 2000 was the fact that (even where the public authorities and the director could reach agreement on how the provisions of the CDDA 1986 should apply in the particular case) it was necessary to go to court to obtain an order and it was doubtful whether the court could simply accept, and rubber-stamp, the agreement

[16] CDDA 1986 s.5A. See also *Re Genz Holdings* [2018] EWHC 2091 (Ch); [2018] 2 B.C.L.C. 386. See further para.20–012.

[17] IA 1986 ss.213–214.

[18] CDDA 1986 s.11(1)–(2). For consideration of this strict liability basis of disqualification, see *Re Waterfall Media* [2013] B.P.I.R. 1109 Ch D.

[19] DTI, *Companies in 2001–2002* (2002), Table D1.

[20] Companies House, *Statistical Tables on Companies Registration Activities 2014–2015*, Table D1, with over 80% of the orders and undertakings being made on the grounds of "unfitness".

[21] Companies House, *Management Information 2019–2020*, Table 6, with just over 81% of the orders and undertakings made on the grounds of "unfitness". A notable development since 2016 is the increased number of disqualification orders made under the CDDA 1986 s.8.

between them.[22] The amendments to the CDDA 1986 permit the Secretary of State and the director to reach an agreement out-of-court on a disqualification undertaking, which will restrict the director's future activities in the same way as a disqualification order, but without the need for a court hearing.[23] The director can always trigger a court hearing by refusing to agree terms for an undertaking, though he or she will normally be liable for the Secretary of State's costs, as well as his or her own costs, if the court makes an order. Alternatively, a director who has accepted an undertaking may subsequently apply to the court, apparently at any time, for the period of the disqualification to be reduced or for the undertaking to cease to apply.[24] This is equivalent to the power that a court has under the Insolvency Rules to review, vary or rescind disqualification orders.[25] Although the power is broadly framed, the courts are likely to find it appropriate to alter the undertaking for the future (the court has no power to declare that it ought not to have been made) only in limited circumstances. In particular, it would be likely to undermine the undertaking procedure if directors, having entered into an undertaking, were able freely to invoke the power to vary its terms.[26]

Scope of disqualification orders and undertakings

20–003 The scope of the disqualification order or undertaking is obviously a crucial matter in the design of the CDDA 1986. Orders would be too narrow if they simply prohibited a person from acting only as director of a company, since there are many ways of controlling a company's management without actually being a director of that company. A way forward might have been to extend the prohibition to being a shadow director of a company, but the CDDA 1986 in fact avoids the difficulties associated with the definition of that concept and takes an even broader approach. The prohibition imposed by a disqualification order or undertaking extends to "in any way, directly or indirectly, be[ing] concerned or tak[ing] part in the promotion, formation or management of a company".[27] The

[22] The courts had, however, developed a summary procedure for dealing with non-contested cases: see *Re Carecraft Construction Co Ltd* [1994] 1 W.L.R. 172 Ch D (Companies Ct); *Secretary of State for Trade and Industry v Rogers* [1996] 1 W.L.R. 1569 CA (Civ Div). See further *Practice Direction* [1999] B.C.C. 717 Ch D; *Practice Direction: Directors Disqualification Proceedings* [2015] B.C.C. 224 Ch D, both of which are still in principle available, although the summary procedure has effectively been overtaken by the out-of-court undertaking.

[23] CDDA 1986 ss.1 and 1A.

[24] CDDA 1986 s.8A. A director will have to establish "special circumstances" to justify varying the undertaking, which does not include failing to take legal advice or to appreciate the consequences of the undertaking: see *Taylor v Secretary for Business, Innovation and Skills* [2016] EWHC 1953 (Ch). See also *Ahmed v Secretary of State for Business, Enterprise and Industrial Strategy* [2021] EWHC 523 (Ch). This is separate from the director's power to apply to the court for leave to act notwithstanding the undertaking, a power which applies also to orders: see CDDA 1986 s.17.

[25] The Insolvency (England and Wales) Rules 2016 (SI 2016/1024) r.9.25(1).

[26] *Re INS Realisations Ltd* [2006] EWHC 135 (Ch); [2006] 2 B.C.L.C. 239, stating that a director is not normally able to use the variation power to challenge the facts on which the undertaking was premised, but in the particular circumstances of that case the power was used to cause the undertaking to cease to operate. See also *Re Morija Plc* [2007] EWHC 3055 (Ch); [2008] 2 B.C.L.C. 313.

[27] CDDA 1986 ss.1(1) and 1A(1). If a court makes a disqualification order, it must cover all the activities set out in the CDDA 1986 s.1(1), but the court could give the disqualified director limited

courts have taken a broad approach to what being concerned or taking part in the management of a company may embrace.[28] In addition, the disqualified person is prohibited from acting as an insolvency practitioner.[29] Finally, the disqualified person is denied access to limited liability through some corporate form other than a registered company, such as a limited liability partnership, a building society or an incorporated friendly society.[30]

Adherence to a disqualification order or undertaking is secured by criminal penalties.[31] More importantly, a person who has been involved in the management of a company in breach of a disqualification order or undertaking is personally liable for the debts and other liabilities that the company incurred during the time that he or she was involved in the company's management.[32] This demonstrates that it is essentially misuse of the privilege of limited liability that lies at the heart of disqualification orders. Personal liability is also extended to any other person involved in the management of the company who knowingly acts on the instructions of a disqualified person.[33] Indeed, entrusting the management of a company to someone known to be disqualified might well be a basis for disqualifying the entrusting director on grounds of unfitness.[34]

The temporal scope of the disqualification order is also important in assessing its rigour. The approach of the CDDA 1986 is to set maxima and then to leave the actual disqualification period to be fixed in the order or undertaking. The maxima vary from one disqualification ground to another, the longest being in the case of disqualification on grounds of unfitness, where it is set at 15 years.[35] There is also a minimum period of two years in the case of unfitness in relation to insolvent

---

leave to act despite the order. See, for example, *Re Gower Enterprises (No.2)* [1995] 2 B.C.L.C. 201 Ch D (Companies Ct); *Re Seagull Manufacturing Co Ltd* [1996] 1 B.C.L.C. 51 Ch D. For the jurisdiction to correct a disqualification order, see *Re Canonquest Ltd* [1997] B.C.C. 644 CA (Civ Div).

[28] Management of a company is thought to require involvement in the general management and policy of the company and not just the holding of any post labelled managerial, though in small companies it may not be possible to distinguish between policy-setting and day-to-day management: see *R. v Campbell* (1983) 78 Cr. App. R. 95 CA (acting as a management consultant); *Drew v HM Advocate*, 1996 S.L.T. 1062 HCJ Appeal; *Re Market Wizard Systems (UK) Ltd* [1998] 2 B.C.L.C. 282 Ch D (Companies Ct).

[29] CDDA 1986 ss.1(1)(b) and 1A(1)(b).

[30] CDDA 1986 ss.22A–C and E–F. See also Limited Liability Partnership Regulations 2001 (SI 2001/1090), reg.4(2). See further *Re Bell Pottinger Private Ltd* [2021] EWHC 672 (Ch). The disqualified director is also prohibited from acting as the trustee of a charitable trust, whether that trust is incorporated or not: see Charities Act 2011 ss.178 onwards, though the charity commissioners may give leave to act.

[31] CDDA 1986 ss.13 and 14. The equivalent offence in relation to acting when bankrupt has been held to be one of strict liability (see *R. v Brockley* (1993) 92 Cr. App. R. 385 CA; *Re Waterfall Media* [2013] B.P.I.R. 1109) and the arguments used to support that conclusion would seem equally applicable to the offence of acting when disqualified.

[32] CDDA 1986 s.15(1)(a). The creditors have standing to enforce the personal liability: see *Re Prestige Grinding Ltd* [2005] EWHC 3076 (Ch); [2006] B.C.C. 421.

[33] CDDA 1986 s.15(1)(b). The various people made personally liable are jointly and severally liable with each other and with the company and any others who are for any reason personally liable: see CDDA 1986 s.15(2).

[34] See *Re Moorgate Metals Ltd* [1995] 1 B.C.L.C. 503 Ch D.

[35] CDDA 1986 ss.6(4) and 8(4).

companies.[36] After a lack of judicial clarity for a period of time, the Court of Appeal opted for setting the actual period of disqualification on grounds of unfitness by assessing how far below the conduct expected of a director the respondent has fallen.[37] In *Re Sevenoaks Stationers (Retail) Ltd*,[38] the Court of Appeal divided the 2–15 year period for unfitness disqualification into three brackets, reflecting different levels of seriousness, though it cannot be said that it drew the dividing line between them very clearly.[39]

If a prohibition was invalidly imposed because it was tainted by fraud, the director can apply to set the prohibition aside by demonstrating that the elements of fraudulent misrepresentation have been satisfied.[40] Where the prohibition is valid, the prohibition (except that part of it which relates to acting as an insolvency practitioner) may be relaxed by the court, which may give leave to the disqualified person to act in a particular case. In the case of disqualification on grounds of "unfitness",[41] it is the practice to consider such applications at the same time as the disqualification order is made (in those, now minority, cases in which the disqualification is imposed by the court).[42] The leave granted must not be so wide as to undermine the purposes of the CDDA 1986.[43] Often, the leave will relate to the directors' other companies that are trading successfully and that are dependent for their future success on the continued involvement of the applicant. The leave will usually be made conditional upon other steps being taken to protect the public, such as the appointment of an independent director to

---

[36] CDDA 1986 s.6(4). The minima and maxima that are applicable to orders are equally applicable to undertakings: see CDDA 1986 s.1A(2).

[37] *Re Grayan Building Services Ltd* [1995] Ch. 241 CA. In this case, the Court of Appeal held that the respondent could not reduce the period of disqualification by showing that, despite past shortcomings, he was unlikely to offend again. Such evidence, however, could be taken into account on an application for leave. See also *Re Westmid Packing Services Ltd* [1998] 2 All E.R. 124 CA at 131–132; *Secretary of State for Business, Energy and Industrial Strategy v Steven* [2018] EWHC 1331 (Ch) at [40]; *Re Ixoyc Anesis (2014) Ltd* [2018] EWHC 3190 (Ch); [2019] B.C.C. 404 at [99]; *Competition and Markets Authority v Martin* [2020] EWHC 1751 (Ch) at [14]–[16].

[38] *Re Sevenoaks Stationers (Retail) Ltd* [1991] Ch. 164 CA at 176. The three brackets in *Sevenoaks* have also been applied in the context of the CDDA 1986 s.2: see *Secretary of State for Business, Innovation and Skills v Rahman* [2017] EWHC 2468 (Ch); [2018] B.C.C. 567 at [46]–[47].

[39] The court distinguished between a top bracket of over ten years for "particularly serious" cases; a middle bracket of six to ten years for serious cases "which do not merit the top bracket" (see *Re Focus 15 Trading Ltd* [2020] EWHC 3016 (Ch)); and a minimum bracket for "not very serious" cases (*Re Brand Management Services Ltd* [2016] EWHC 2821 (Ch)). See also *Re Westmid Packing Services Ltd* [1998] 2 All E.R. 124 at 132 (fixing of length of disqualification to be done on the basis of "common sense").

[40] *Georgallides v Secretary of State for Business, Energy and Industrial Strategy* [2020] EWHC 768 (Ch).

[41] CDDA 1986 s.6(1).

[42] *Secretary of State for Trade and Industry v Worth* [1994] 2 B.C.L.C. 113 CA, which indeed puts the applicant under some costs pressure to apply then, if his application is based on circumstances existing at the time of the order. If disqualification is by undertaking, a separate application for leave will, of course, be necessary. Leave cannot be given by the Secretary of State, only by the court.

[43] *Secretary of State for Trade and Industry v Barnett* [1998] 2 B.C.L.C. 64 Ch D (Companies Ct); *Re Britannia Homes Centres Ltd* [2001] 2 B.C.L.C. 63 Ch D (leave refused where director with history of insolvencies wished to incorporate a new and wholly-owned company to carry on trading in same line of business). See also *Haughey v Secretary of State for Business, Energy and Industrial Strategy* [2018] EWHC 3566 (Ch); [2019] B.C.C. 483.

the board.[44] Overall, the court has to engage in a balancing exercise: on the one hand, there is the need to protect the public, especially future creditors, from the type of conduct that rendered the director unfit in the first place[45]; whilst, on the other hand, there is the interest of the director, as well as other persons who are dependent upon the company and accordingly have an interest in the director having access to trading with limited liability.[46]

Compensation

The compensation provisions introduced in 2015 mean that the disqualification process may have significance for present as well as future creditors. The possibility of the court awarding compensation arises in all classes of disqualification order or undertaking,[47] provided that the company has become insolvent, the conduct for which the person was disqualified caused loss to one or more creditors and the disqualified person was at any time a director of the company.[48] This appears to mean that only present or former directors may be subject to compensation orders (not shadow directors, for example), but that the conduct leading to the disqualification need not be conduct as a director (it might be conduct as a shadow director provided that person was at some point a director of the company). The initiation of the compensation procedure lies in the hands of the Secretary of State, by way of application to the court or acceptance of a compensation undertaking.[49] There is a time-limit of two years from the initial disqualification order or undertaking in which to seek to add a compensation order,[50] although the issue may also be dealt with at the same time as the initial prohibition. In effect, the company's creditors piggy-back on the efforts of the public authorities to enforce the disqualification provisions. That said, the creditors have no independent right of action. The utility of the new compensation provisions thus depends on the Secretary of State's willingness to use them. Where there is clear loss to creditors and an available mechanism for distributing the compensation, there is no reason why the Secretary of State (or, 20–004

[44] *Re Cargo Agency Ltd* [1992] B.C.L.C. 686 Ch D (Companies Ct); *Re Chartmore Ltd* [1990] B.C.L.C. 673 Ch D; *Re Clenaware Systems Ltd* [2013] EWHC 2514 (Ch); [2014] 1 B.C.L.C. 447. The practice has been followed in Scotland despite doubts whether the power to give leave confers upon the courts the power to specify conditions: see *Secretary of State for Trade and Industry v Palfreman* [1995] 2 B.C.L.C. 301 OH. If the conditions attached by the court are not strictly complied with, the director is in breach of the disqualification order and so exposed to personal liability: see *Re Brian Sheridan Cars Ltd* [1996] 1 B.C.L.C. 327 Ch D (Companies Ct).

[45] *Rwamba v Secretary of State for Business, Energy and Industrial Strategy* [2020] EWHC 2778 (Ch), indicating that issues of deterrence should also be considered.

[46] *Re Barings Plc (No.3)* [2000] 1 W.L.R. 634 Ch D; *Re Tech Textiles* [1998] 1 B.C.L.C. 259 Ch D (Companies Ct). Setting up a new successful company is a relevant factor in favour of relaxation: see *Haughey v Secretary of State for Business, Energy and Industrial Strategy* [2019] B.C.C. 483.

[47] *Re Noble Vintners Ltd* [2020] B.C.C. 198.

[48] CDDA 1986 s.15A(3)–(4), in which insolvency is defined to include insolvent liquidation, administration and administrative receivership.

[49] CDDA 1986 s.15A(1).

[50] CDDA 1986 s.15A(5).

rather, the Insolvency Service on his behalf) should not use them.[51] In order to encourage the Secretary of State to apply for a compensation order, any fees associated with distributing the compensation can be paid out of the compensation to the Secretary of State.[52] But a pre-condition of use of the compensation power is the existence of a disqualification order or undertaking. The Insolvency Service has power to seek these on grounds of unfitness—the most widely deployed ground—only where it regards this course of action as being "in the public interest".[53] It is unclear whether the Service will regard simple loss to creditors as a ground for seeking disqualification and then compensation. The amount of the compensation is not specified precisely, but is to be fixed (by the court or the Secretary of State) having regard "in particular" to the amount of the loss caused, the nature of the conduct which led to the loss and any recompense already made.[54] This suggests that the loss suffered as a result of the director's conduct sets the outer boundary of the compensation to be awarded and, within that, the seriousness of the conduct will be crucial.[55]

DISQUALIFICATION ON GROUNDS OF UNFITNESS

20–005 There are in fact two mechanisms in the CDDA 1986 for obtaining disqualification on the ground of "unfitness", the initiative in both cases lying with the Secretary of State. First, under s.8 of the CDDA 1986, the Secretary of State may apply to the court or accept an undertaking in relation to the range of people (considered next), whether the company is insolvent or not, if he or she decides it is in the public interest to do so.[56] Secondly, under ss.6 and 7 of the CDDA 1986, the Secretary of State may apply to the court to have a director[57] or shadow director[58] of an insolvent[59] company disqualified where the Secretary of

[51] CDDA 1986 s.15B(2), which provides that the compensation may be ordered in favour of the Secretary of State for distribution among the specified creditors (whoever they may be) or, as with wrongful trading awards, may take the form of a contribution to the assets of the company. It is implicit in the second case that the company is in the hands of an insolvency practitioner. It is likely that the Insolvency Service will favour the latter method of distribution, if only because it avoids the costs of undertaking this task.

[52] Disqualified Directors Compensation Orders (Fees) (England and Wales) Order 2016 (SI 2016/1047) art.3(1)–(2). See also *Re Noble Vintners Ltd* [2020] B.C.C. 198.

[53] CDDA 1986 s.7(1) and (2A).

[54] CDDA 1986 s.15B(3). For the broad approach to the notions of "conduct", "creditor" and "loss" for the purposes of the compensation regime, see *Re Noble Vintners Ltd* [2020] B.C.C. 198.

[55] *Re Noble Vintners Ltd* [2020] B.C.C. 198.

[56] CDDA 1986 s.8(1). Until 2015, the power under the CDDA 1986 s.8 was exercisable only on the basis of information obtained via an official investigation into the company (under a variety of powers). Accordingly, it was rarely used. There is evidence that, since 2016, the use of this power has steadily grown: see Companies House, *Management Information 2019–2020*, Table 6.

[57] The notion of a "director" includes a de facto director (see CDDA 1986 s.22(4)), in other words, a person who acts as a director even though he has not been validly appointed as a director or even though there has been no attempt at all to appoint him as director: see *Re Kaytech International Plc* [1999] 2 B.C.L.C. 351 CA; *Secretary of State for Business, Energy and Industrial Strategy v Rahman* [2020] EWHC 2213 (Ch).

[58] CDDA 1986 s.22(5). On the meaning of "shadow director", see further paras 10–010 and 19–007.

[59] A company is insolvent if it goes into liquidation with insufficient assets to meet its liabilities, if an administration order has been made in relation to the company or if an administrative receiver is

State thinks it is expedient in the public interest to do so.[60] Similarly, the Secretary of State may accept a disqualification undertaking from the director if "it is expedient in the public interest that he should do so".[61] If the elements of this ground of disqualification are satisfied, disqualification is mandatory for a minimum period of two years, if unfitness is found[62]; the maximum period is 15 years under both grounds of disqualification.[63] Thus, although in the wake of the Cork Report, business opposition fought off the idea of automatic disqualification in the case of directors of insolvent companies, the Government managed to avoid leaving the issue entirely to the discretion of the courts.[64]

Once the company has become insolvent, the director is liable to have the whole of his or her conduct as director of that company scrutinised for evidence of unfitness.[65] Unlike liability for wrongful trading,[66] that scrutiny is not confined to the director's conduct in the period immediately before the insolvency, and included within that scrutiny is the director's conduct in other companies where he or she was a director or shadow director.[67] These other companies need not have fallen into insolvency and there need not be any particular business or other link between the "lead" company and the other companies in order for the director's conduct in relation to them to be taken into account.[68] In short, once the unfitness provisions are triggered, the scrutiny is capable of reaching out into the whole of the activities of the directors of that company in their capacity as directors. In an important extension in 2015, the court can have regard to the director's conduct in relation to companies incorporated outside Great Britain, so that geography no longer confines the court's examination, although evidential difficulties may do so.[69]

Despite the fact that the "unfitness" bases of disqualification apply to shadow directors, in 2015 the disqualification provisions were extended to other "influencers" of directors' "unfit" conduct. This means that a disqualification order may be made against, or a disqualification undertaking accepted from, a person in accordance with whose directions or instructions the director has acted.[70] These additional provisions are ancillary in the sense that they may be **20–006**

appointed: see CDDA 1986 s.6(2). Accordingly, the disqualification provisions, unlike the wrongful trading provisions, are not confined to companies that go into insolvent liquidation. The court is specifically given power to look at the director's conduct post-insolvency. There are specialised mechanisms for bank insolvencies and administrations: CDDA 1986 ss.21A–C.

60 CDDA 1986 s.7(1).

61 CDDA 1986 s.7(2A).

62 *Competition and Markets Authority v Martin* [2020] EWHC 1751 (Ch) at [13]–[14] and [110].

63 CDDA 1986 ss.1A(2), 6(1), (4) and 8(4).

64 See A. Hicks, "Disqualification of Directors—Forty Years On" [1988] J.B.L. 27, 35 and 38–40.

65 *Re Ixoyc Anesis (2014) Ltd* [2019] B.C.C. 404 at [55]–[60]. See also *Secretary of State for Business, Energy and Industrial Strategy v Broadstock* [2018] EWHC 2146 (Ch).

66 IA 1986 s.214(1).

67 CDDA 1986 s.6(1).

68 *Secretary of State for Trade and Industry v Ivens* [1997] 2 B.C.L.C. 334 CA. However, it would seem that a director cannot be disqualified on the basis of his conduct of the non-lead companies alone.

69 The court may look at the conduct in relation to "one or more other companies or overseas companies": see CDDA 1986 ss.6(1)(b)–(1A) and 8(2)–(2B).

70 CDDA 1986 ss.8ZA(2) and 8ZD(3).

invoked, in the case of an order against the influencer,[71] only if there is a disqualification order or an undertaking on grounds of unfitness in place against the director. In the case of an undertaking given by the influencer, one or other of those two situations must exist or the Secretary of State must be satisfied that an undertaking could be accepted from the director.[72] In many cases, the influencer will be a shadow director and so can be tackled directly.[73] This extension to other "influencers", however, does not depend (as with a shadow director) on the board as a whole being accustomed to act in accordance with the non-director's directions or instruction. The focus is on the specific relationship between the influencer and the person disqualified. Nor does the person disqualified need to be accustomed to act as the influencer wishes, provided the director's conduct was in fact influenced in the required way. This extension to other "influencers" seems to have been part of a wider policy of making transparent where control of companies lies and bringing responsibility home to the real controllers.[74]

The role of the Insolvency Service

20–007 When recommending the "unfitness" basis of disqualification,[75] the Cork Committee stated that its aim was to "replace by a far more rigorous system the present ineffective provisions".[76] The effectiveness in practice of the "unfitness" ground can be said to depend upon two matters. The first matter is the assiduity of the Insolvency Service, to which the Secretary of State normally delegates disqualification powers, in enforcing the provisions of the CDDA 1986; and the second is the courts' approach to the central concept of "unfitness" and how they set the period of disqualification.

In order to maximise the chances of applications being made, the Cork Committee recommended that applications by liquidators or, with leave, other creditors should be permitted.[77] Accordingly, confining applications to the Secretary of State was regarded at the time of the enactment of the IA 1986 as being a retrograde step. There are two reasons why the Insolvency Service might not prove effective. First, there is a possible lack of information about directors' conduct. This is particularly acute when the company is being wound up voluntarily, as the Official Receiver is not then involved.[78] This is addressed by the imposition of a requirement on liquidators, administrators and receivers to report to the Secretary of State about the conduct of directors and shadow

---

[71] CDDA 1986 ss.8ZA(1) and 8ZD(1).

[72] CDDA 1986 ss.8ZC(1) and 8ZE(1).

[73] CDDA 1986 ss.6–8.

[74] Department for Business, Innovation and Skills, *Transparency & Trust: Enhancing the Transparency of UK Company Ownership and Increasing Trust in UK Business* (April 2014), s.4.

[75] CDDA 1986 s.6(1).

[76] *Report of the Review Committee on Insolvency Law and Practice* (1982), Cm.8558, para.1809.

[77] *Report of the Review Committee on Insolvency Law and Practice* (1982), Cm.8558, para.1818.

[78] In Scotland, where there are no Official Receivers, even compulsory liquidations are handled by insolvency practitioners and the potential scope of the problem is accordingly greater.

directors of companies for whose affairs they are responsible.[79] The quality of the information provided is, however, not always high. In 2015, the obligation was strengthened by requiring a "conduct report" containing relevant information in all cases and not only where the office-holder believed that there was a case of "unfitness".[80] Secondly, there was doubt about the quantity and quality of the resources that the Government would devote to the enforcement of the CDDA 1986. Although the early efforts of the Insolvency Service were criticised,[81] the enforcement effort is now substantial, even though only a small percentage of the directors of failed companies are disqualified. Nevertheless, it is clear that the Service still experiences difficulties in commencing applications within the two-year period originally permitted by the statute[82] and in prosecuting them with sufficient vigour so as to avoid the application being struck out on grounds of delay or infringement of the director's human rights[83] (namely, the right to have one's civil rights and obligations determined within a reasonable time[84]). The response of the legislature in 2015 was to extend the period for commencing proceedings to three years, although this does not help, but rather exacerbates, any concerns about there being a fair trial.

There is an additional risk that the human rights of directors will be threatened by the disparity between the state resources available to the Insolvency Service and those available to the director, who, in the case of a small company, may be virtually bankrupt. In particular, there is a danger that the impoverished director will give a disqualification undertaking because he or she cannot afford the costs of a full-scale court examination of the issues. To date, these issues have been

---

[79] See S. Wheeler, "Directors' Disqualification: Insolvency Practitioners and the Decision-making Process" (1995) 15 L.S. 283. Moreover, the statutory scheme does not bite if the company is simply struck off the register without going through any of these procedures.

[80] CDDA 1986 s.7A and SI 2016/180. The obligation is to provide any information about conduct that may help the Insolvency Service decide whether to implement disqualification proceedings. Previously, this information was to be provided by the insolvency practitioner only if the Service asked for it. The request power now exists in relation to all persons other than the insolvency practitioners (CDDA 1986 s.7(4)).

[81] National Audit Office, *The Insolvency Service Executive Agency: Company Director Disqualification* (1993), HC 907.

[82] CDDA 1986 s.7(2). The court may give leave to commence the application out of time, though the Secretary of State must show a good reason for any extension: see *Re Copecrest Ltd* [1994] 2 B.C.L.C. 284 CA; *Re Instant Access Properties Ltd* [2011] EWHC 3022 (Ch); [2012] 1 B.C.L.C. 710.

[83] For the rejection of an argument that disqualification orders infringe a director's "private life", see *Competition and Markets Authority v Martin* [2020] EWHC 1751 (Ch) at [110]. This was considered to be the case even though the disqualification order was mandatory upon a finding of "unfitness": see *Re Property Group (2010) Ltd* [2020] EWHC 1751 (Ch).

[84] Human Rights Act 1998 Sch.1 art.6. See also *Re Manlon Trading Ltd* [1996] Ch. 136 CA (Civ Div); *Davies v UK* [2006] 2 B.C.L.C. 351 ECHR (a case decided in 2002); *Eastaway v UK* [2006] 2 B.C.L.C. 361 ECHR. In the last of these cases, however, the Court of Appeal refused to set aside the disqualification agreement entered into by the director under the *Carecraft* procedure (see fn.22), even though the European Court of Human Rights had held the proceedings to have taken too long: see *Eastaway v Secretary of State for Trade and Industry* [2007] EWCA Civ 425; [2007] B.C.C. 550. The National Audit Office (*The Insolvency Service Executive Agency: Company Director Disqualification* (1993), HC 907, para.18) found that the Insolvency Service in most cases took nearly the full two-year period permitted to bring an application and that up to a further four years might elapse before a disqualification order was made, during which period the director was free to carry on business with limited liability. For the rejection of a "fair trial" argument in the context of a bankruptcy restriction order, see *Bayliss v Official Receiver* [2017] EWHC 3910 (Ch).

little addressed in the authorities, although an appreciation of the situation may lie behind the courts' unwillingness to impose too high a level of competence on directors under the disqualification provisions.[85] As far as the European Convention on Human Rights (ECHR) is concerned, both the domestic courts and the European Court of Human Rights seem agreed that disqualification proceedings are civil in nature, not criminal, so that a lower (but not negligible) standard of fairness is required in conducting them.[86] In particular, the domestic courts have concluded that the ECHR does not require the automatic exclusion of evidence against the director that was obtained from him or her under statutory powers of compulsion.[87] However, the exclusion of such evidence has been achieved in fact, as a matter of interpretation of the domestic law, in the context of the statutory provisions most likely to be of use to the Insolvency Service: under the IA 1986,[88] a company's liquidator or the Official Receiver are empowered to require answers to questions that they put to directors of companies in insolvent liquidation and to require the production of documents. The Court of Appeal has held, however, that these powers cannot be used for the purpose of supporting disqualification applications.[89]

The role of the court

20–008 In terms of the courts' role, some guidance is given by the CDDA 1986 concerning how the courts (and indeed the Secretary of State) should approach disqualification determinations, although the CDDA 1986 was revised in 2015, so as to set out the relevant matters at a higher level of generality than previously and in order to emphasise the width of the courts' investigation. The applicability of the statutory guidance was also widened, so that it now applies to all disqualification decisions, not just to the determination of "unfitness".[90] In all cases, the court must take into account the extent to which the company was in breach of legislative requirements (not necessarily just the requirements of the companies legislation), the defendant's responsibility for the company[91] becoming insolvent, the loss actually or potentially caused by the defendant's conduct and the frequency with which a director has engaged in relevant conduct.[92] Where the defendant is a director—the standard case—the court must have regard to the director's breach of fiduciary duties or other duties applying specifically to directors.[93]

---

[85] See Lord Hoffmann, Fourth Annual Leonard Sainer Lecture (1997) Company Lawyer 194. See further para.20–010.

[86] *R. v Secretary of State for Trade and Industry Ex p. McCormick* [1998] B.C.C. 379 CA; *DC v United Kingdom* [2000] B.C.C. 710 ECHR.

[87] *Official Receiver v Stern* [2000] 1 W.L.R. 2230 CA; cf *Saunders v United Kingdom* [1998] 1 B.C.L.C. 362 ECHR. See also *Bayliss v Official Receiver* [2017] EWHC 3910 (Ch).

[88] IA 1986 ss.235–236.

[89] *Re Pantmaenog Timber Co Ltd* [2001] 4 All E.R. 588 CA.

[90] CDDA 1986 s.12C (replacing the former s.9).

[91] This includes not just the "lead" company, but all other companies, including overseas ones, brought in under CDDA 1986 s.6(1)(b).

[92] CDDA 1986 Sch.1.

[93] A breach of duty is not a necessary pre-condition for a finding of "unfitness", although this will often be the case: see *Re Brooklands Trustees Ltd* [2020] EWHC 3519 (Ch). Moreover, a single

Breach of commercial morality

It is possible to divide the cases in which the courts have found unfitness into two rough categories, namely probity and competence.[94] The concept of "unfitness" is open-ended, however, so that it cannot be claimed that all potential, or even actual, disqualification applications can be forced into one or other of these categories. Further, in the nature of things, many disqualification cases display aspects from both categories. Nevertheless, it is thought that identifying the two categories is a useful analytical starting point. **20–009**

The first category is breach of commercial morality.[95] This category has as its central idea the notion of conducting a business at the expense of its creditors. One possible example of such conduct might be the "phoenix company" described by the Cork Committee in terms of a person who sets up an undercapitalised company, allows it to become insolvent, forms a new company (often with assets purchased at a discount from the liquidator of the old company), carries on trading much as before, and repeats the process perhaps several times, leaving behind him each time a trail of unpaid creditors.[96] More generally, the courts have been alert to finding "unfitness" where the directors have apparently attempted to trade on the backs of the company's creditors.[97] It was thought at one time that particular obloquy attached to directors who attempted to trade out their difficulties by using, as their working capital, monies owed to the Crown by way of income tax, national insurance contributions or VAT, on the grounds that the Crown was an involuntary creditor.[98] Although that particular view has been rejected by the Court of Appeal, the same court has affirmed that, in relation to any creditor, paying only those creditors who pressed for payment and taking advantage of those creditors who did not, in order to provide the working capital that the company needed, is a clear example of

---

breach of duty does not necessarily amount to "unfitness": see *Secretary of State for Business, Innovation and Skills v Marley* [2018] EWHC 236 (Ch). For the potentially more lenient approach taken to the volunteer directors of charitable companies, see *Re Keeping Kids Co* [2021] EWHC 175 (Ch).

[94] According to Neill LJ in *Re Grayan Building Services Ltd* [1995] Ch. 241 at 258, "[t]hose who trade under the regime of limited liability and who avail themselves of the privileges of that regime must accept the standards of probity and competence to which the law requires company directors to conform".

[95] Of course, simple fraud will be a basis for disqualification: see *Re Focus 15 Trading Ltd* [2020] EWHC 3016 (Ch). As a proposition of substantive law, this is straightforward; the complications are procedural: see *Secretary of State v Doffmann (No.2)* [2010] EWHC 3175 (Ch); [2011] 2 B.C.L.C. 541. A breach of trust would similarly usually entail a finding of "unfitness": see *Secretary of State for Business, Energy and Industrial Strategy v Broadstock* [2018] EWHC 2146 (Ch).

[96] *Report of the Review Committee on Insolvency Law and Practice* (1982), Cm. 8558, para.1813. For the operation of the rule forbidding re-use of corporate names in this situation, see IA 1986 s.216. For examples in the disqualification context, see *Re Travel Mondial (UK) Ltd* [1991] B.C.L.C. 120 Ch D (Companies Ct); *Re Linvale Ltd* [1993] B.C.L.C. 654 Ch D; *Re Swift 736 Ltd* [1993] B.C.L.C. 1 Ch D (Companies Ct).

[97] *Re Keypak Homecare Ltd* [1990] B.C.L.C. 440 Ch D (Companies Ct).

[98] *Secretary of State for Business Innovation and Skills v Khan* [2017] EWHC 288 (Ch); *Secretary of State for Business, Energy and Industrial Strategy v Steven* [2018] EWHC 1331 (Ch); *Re Ixoyc Anesis (2014) Ltd* [2019] B.C.C. 404; *Re St John Law* [2019] EWHC 459 (Ch); [2019] B.C.C. 901.

"unfitness".[99] If the directors of the financially troubled company are at the same time paying themselves salaries that are out of proportion to the company's trading success (or lack of it), or making disguised distributions to themselves of corporate assets, the likelihood of a disqualification order being made is only increased.[100]

Recklessness and incompetence

20–010 The previous category focused on opportunistic behaviour by directors towards the creditors of the company by failing to pay the creditors whilst continuing trading. The present category focuses more generally on the recklessness or incompetence of the directors in conducting the company's business. The directors may pay the creditors the money due to them, as long as the company is able to do so, but the directors may be regarded as responsible for bringing about a situation where the company ultimately has to default on its commitments because of the way the directors have chosen to run it. In many cases, of course, both aspects of "unfitness" can be found.

The early cases put liability on the basis of recklessness,[101] but more recently it has been said that "incompetence or negligence to a very marked degree"[102] would suffice. The danger that the courts must avoid in this area is treating any business venture that collapses as evidence of negligence. To do so would be to discourage the taking of commercial risks, which must be the life-blood of corporate activity. Creating a space for proper risk-taking, however, is no longer thought to require relieving directors of all objective standards of conduct. In *Re Barings Plc (No.5)*,[103] the Court of Appeal gave guidance on what constitutes a high degree of incompetence in the common situation of the directors having properly delegated functions to lower levels of management. Provided the articles of association permit such delegation, as they inevitably will do in large organisations, delegation in itself is not evidence of unfitness. The responsible director may be found to be unfit, however, if there is put in place no system for supervising the discharge of the delegated function or if the director in question is not able to understand the information produced by the supervisory system. In other words, in large organisations, directors must ensure that there are adequate internal systems in place for monitoring risk, and failure to do so may be grounds for disqualification.

---

[99] *Re Sevenoaks Stationers (Retail) Ltd* [1991] Ch. 164 CA; *Secretary of State for Trade and Industry v McTighe (No.2)* [1996] 2 B.C.L.C. 477 CA. See also *Secretary of State for Business, Innovation and Skills v Akbar* [2017] EWHC 2856 (Ch); [2018] B.C.C. 448.

[100] *Re Synthetic Technology Ltd* [1993] B.C.C. 549 Ch D (Companies Ct); *Secretary of State v Van Hengel* [1995] 1 B.C.L.C. 545 Ch D (Companies Ct); *Secretary of State for Business Innovation and Skills v Doffman (No.2)* [2011] 2 B.C.L.C. 541.

[101] *Re Stanford Services Ltd* [1987] B.C.L.C. 607 Ch D (Companies Ct).

[102] *Re Sevenoaks Stationers (Retail) Ltd* [1991] Ch. 164 at 184. See also *Re Brooklands Trustees Ltd* [2020] EWHC 3519 (Ch).

[103] *Re Barings Plc (No.5)* [2000] 1 B.C.L.C. 523. The case involved the insolvency of an old and respected merchant bank brought about by the huge losses generated by the unauthorised trading activities of a junior employee whose activities were neither well understood nor effectively monitored by his superiors.

The proposition that directors "have a continuing duty to acquire and maintain a sufficient knowledge and understanding of the company's business to enable them properly to discharge their duties as directors"[104] applies not just to duties delegated to sub-board level, but also to reliance by directors on their board colleagues to take responsibility for particular functions and duties. Such reliance is again in principle acceptable, so that there can be a division of functions on the board, most obviously between executive and non-executive directors. Nevertheless, all directors must maintain a minimum level of knowledge and understanding about the business, so that important problems can be identified and resolved before they bring the company down. Thus, in *Re Richborough Furniture Ltd*,[105] a director was disqualified for three years, on the basis of "lack of experience, knowledge and understanding. She did not have enough experience or knowledge to know what she should do in the face of the problems of pressing creditors, escalating Crown debts and lack of capital. It seems that she was not sufficiently skilful as regards the accounts functions to see that the records were inadequate." Disqualification of incompetent directors has thus become a crucial tool in the enforcement of directors' standards of competence, perhaps more so than actions for breach of the director's general duty of care,[106] which must be funded by private litigants. The two areas of law will no doubt continue to influence each other.

In this area, particular importance is attached by the courts to failure by directors to file annual returns or, now, confirmation statements, to produce audited accounts or to keep proper accounting records.[107] These are the practical expressions of a more general view that all directors must keep themselves au fait with the financial position of their company and make sure that the company complies with the reporting requirements of the CA 2006; otherwise, the directors cannot know what corrective action, if any, needs to be taken.[108] Although this duty may fall with particular emphasis on those responsible for the financial side of the company, all directors must keep themselves informed about the company's basic financial position.[109] On the other hand, seeking and acting on competent outside advice when financial difficulties arise will be an indication of competence, even if the plan recommended does not pay off and the company **20–011**

---

[104] *Re Barings Plc (No.5)* [2000] 1 B.C.L.C. 523 at 536. See also *Re Westmid Packing Services Ltd* [1998] 2 All E.R. 124; *Re Vintage Hallmark Plc* [2007] 1 B.C.L.C. 788 Ch D (Companies Ct).

[105] *Re Richborough Furniture Ltd* [1996] 1 B.C.L.C. 507 Ch D.

[106] See further paras 10–045 onwards.

[107] *Re Focus 15 Trading Ltd* [2020] EWHC 3016 (Ch); *Re Javazzi Ltd* [2021] EWHC 1239 (Ch). These breaches of filing requirements may be ingredients in a finding of unfitness, even though (as considered in para.20–014) non-compliance with the reporting requirements of the legislation is a separate ground of disqualification, albeit only for up to five years. For further discussion of what is required in this area, see further Ch.22.

[108] *Re Firedart Ltd* [1994] 2 B.C.L.C. 340 Ch D; *Re New Generation Engineers Ltd* [1993] B.C.L.C. 435 Ch D (Companies Ct).

[109] *Re City Investment Centres Ltd* [1992] B.C.L.C. 956; *Secretary of State v Van Hengel* [1995] 1 B.C.L.C. 545; *Re Majestic Recording Studios Ltd* [1989] B.C.L.C. 1 Ch D (Companies Ct); *Re Continental Assurance Co of London Plc* [1997] 1 B.C.L.C. 48 Ch D (Companies Ct); *Re Kaytech International Plc* [1999] 2 B.C.L.C. 351 CA.

eventually collapses.[110] It should also be remembered that, in the disqualification area, the courts have required a "marked degree" of negligence[111] before declaring a director unfit. There is a contrast here with wrongful trading and the standard of care under the directors' general duties,[112] where there is no suggestion that a low standard of care is to be applied to directors.[113] It is suggested that this contrast is explained by the fact that a disqualification order can often have the effect of depriving the director of his livelihood and that, once unfitness is found, a two-year disqualification is mandatory.

DISQUALIFICATION ON GROUNDS OTHER THAN UNFITNESS

Serious offences

20–012 The remaining grounds of disqualification in the CDDA 1986 permit, but do not require, the court to disqualify a director.[114] With one exception, disqualification is based on a court order. Disqualification by means of undertaking is not generally available. These other grounds of disqualification are considered more briefly, partly because they have not generated as much controversy as the "unfitness" ground. Disqualifications following conviction for an indictable offence apparently constitute the second most common source (after "unfitness") of disqualification orders.[115]

In relation to serious offences, there are two routes to a disqualification order, depending upon whether the person concerned has actually been convicted of an offence. If there has been a conviction, a disqualification order may be made against a person, whether a director or not, who has committed an indictable

[110] *Re Douglas Construction Services Ltd* [1988] B.C.L.C. 397 Ch D (Companies Ct). Conversely, ignoring a plan produced by outside accountants is likely to be characterised as "obstinately and unjustifiably backing [the director's] own assessment of the company's business": see *Re GSAR Realisations Ltd* [1993] B.C.L.C. 409 Ch D.

[111] *Re Sevenoaks Stationers (Retail) Ltd* [1991] Ch. 164 at 184. See also *Re Brooklands Trustees Ltd* [2020] EWHC 3519 (Ch); *Re Arise Networks Ltd* [2021] EWHC 852 (Ch).

[112] See further paras 10–045 onwards and 19–005 onwards.

[113] Of course, keeping an insolvent company going can be grounds for disqualification for being unfit, but only in strong cases. See, for example, *Re Living Images Ltd* [1996] 1 B.C.L.C. 348, where the directors were aware of the company's parlous condition and keeping it going was described as "a gamble at long odds" and "the taking of unwarranted risks with creditors' money", so that there was a lack of probity involved and not just negligence. cf. the refusal to make a disqualification order in *Re Dawson Print Group Ltd* [1987] B.C.L.C. 601 Ch D (Companies Ct); *Re Bath Glass Ltd* [1988] B.C.L.C. 329 Ch D (Companies Ct); *Re CU Fittings Ltd* [1989] B.C.L.C. 556 Ch D (Companies Ct); *Secretary of State v Gash* [1997] 1 B.C.L.C. 341 Ch D (Companies Ct).

[114] The three brackets in *Sevenoaks* have also been applied in the context of the CDDA 1986 s.2: see *Secretary of State for Business, Innovation and Skills v Rahman* [2018] B.C.C. 567 at [46]–[47].

[115] A. Hicks, *Disqualification of Directors: No Hiding Place for the Unfit?* (1998), ACCA Research Report 59, p.35, found that in 1996 about one quarter of those at that time disqualified were in that position as a result of disqualification under the CDDA 1986 s.2. The proportion has probably fallen since then, with the rise of unfitness disqualifications, especially using undertakings. The Companies House figures (see fnn.20–21) do not distinguish between disqualifications on any of the grounds laid down in CDDA 1986 ss.2–5, but indicate that, in 2014–2015, 217 out of 1227 disqualifications occurred under these provisions, whilst the figure was 240 out of 1,485 disqualifications for 2019–2020.

offence in connection with the promotion, formation, management, liquidation or striking off of a company or in connection with the receivership or management of its property.[116] Usually, the disqualification will be ordered by the same court that convicted the director, and at the time of his or her conviction. If the convicting court does not consider the issue, however, the Secretary of State or the liquidator (or any past or present creditor or member of the company in relation to which the offence was committed) may apply to any court having jurisdiction to wind up the company to impose the disqualification.[117] The courts have taken a wide view of what "in connection with the management of the company" means in this context.[118] Where a disqualification order has been made on this ground, the court retains its power to grant leave to act, but is likely to use it only in exceptional cases.[119] Where a person has been convicted of an equivalent offence outside Great Britain, the Secretary of State may seek a disqualification order from the High Court or Court of Session or accept an undertaking from that person.[120]

Where there has not been a conviction, but the company is being wound up, the court with jurisdiction to wind up the company may impose a disqualification order[121] if it appears that a person has been guilty of the offence of fraudulent trading[122] or has been guilty as an officer[123] of the company of any fraud in relation to it or any breach of duty as an officer.

Disqualification in connection with civil liability for fraudulent or wrongful trading

In addition to the array of civil orders that a court may make in relation to fraudulent or wrongful trading,[124] the CDDA 1986 adds the power to make a disqualification order.[125] The court may act here on its own motion, regardless of whether or not an application is made by anyone for an order to be made. Since **20–013**

---

[116] CDDA 1986 s.2.

[117] CDDA 1986 s.16(2). If the criminal court does consider the matter and decides not to impose disqualification, it is an abuse of process to pursue the same issue before a civil court: see *Secretary of State v Weston* [2014] EWHC 2933 (Ch); [2014] B.C.C. 581. However, the courts have permitted disqualification orders to be pursued in such cases under other grounds for disqualification contained in the CDDA 1986: see *Secretary of State v Rayna* [2001] 2 B.C.L.C. 48 Ch D; *Re Denis Hilton Ltd* [2002] 1 B.C.L.C. 302 Ch D.

[118] *R. v Goodman* [1994] 1 B.C.L.C. 349 CA (insider dealing by a director in the shares of his company); *R. v Georgiou* (1988) 4 B.C.C. 322 CA (Crim Div); *R. v Ward*, The Times, 10 April 1997 (conspiracy to defraud by creating a false market in shares during a takeover bid); *R. v Creggy* [2008] 1 B.C.L.C. 625 CA (facilitating criminal activity by third parties).

[119] *Re Liberty Holdings Unlimited* [2017] B.C.C. 298 Ch D (Companies Ct).

[120] CDDA 1986 s.5A, inserted by Small Business, Enterprise and Employment Act 2015.

[121] CDDA 1986 s.4, upon application by those listed in s.16(2). It is unclear whether the breach of duty referred to must involve the commission of a criminal offence, but the use of the word "guilty" suggests so.

[122] See paras 19–002 to 19–004.

[123] CDDA 1986 s.4(1)(b)–(2), which includes the usual cast of liquidators, receivers and administrative receivers and also shadow directors.

[124] IA 1986 ss.213–214. See further paras 19–002 onwards.

[125] CDDA 1986 s.10.

there are only low levels of litigation involving claims for contribution orders as a result of fraudulent and wrongful trading, the number of such disqualifications is also low.[126]

Failure to comply with reporting requirements

20–014 Again, there are separate provisions according to whether the person to be disqualified has been convicted or not. If he or she has been convicted of a summary offence in connection with a failure to file a document with (or give notice of a fact to) the Registrar, then the convicting court may disqualify that person if in the previous five years he has had at least three convictions (including the current one) or default orders against him for non-compliance with the reporting requirements of the CA 2006 and IA 1986.[127] If the current conviction is on indictment, then there is no need for a special provision in relation to the reporting requirements, because the court may disqualify on the serious offence ground considered in para.20–012, irrespective of any previous convictions. However, where the current conviction is summary, the fact that the earlier convictions were on indictment does not prevent the convicting summary court from taking them into account.[128]

Where there has been no conviction, the Secretary of State, or other potential claimants,[129] may apply to the court having jurisdiction to wind up the company in question for disqualification orders to be made on the grounds that the respondent has been "persistently in default" in complying with the reporting requirements of the CA 2006 and the IA 1986.[130] The "three convictions or defaults in five years" rule applies here too, but without prejudice to proof of persistent default in any other manner.[131] Since the offences involved in these sections may be only summary ones, the maximum period of disqualification is limited to five, instead of the usual 15, years. Nevertheless, the fact that these bases for disqualification are in the CDDA 1986 at all is a testimony to the importance attached recently to timely filing of accounts and other documents. However, the improvement recorded in this area may be due more to the introduction of late filing penalties than the risk of a disqualification order.

REGISTER OF DISQUALIFICATION ORDERS

20–015 Crucial to the effective operation of the disqualification machinery is that publicity should be given to the names of those who have been disqualified. Thus, the CDDA 1986 requires the Secretary of State to create such a register of

---

[126] No disqualification order was made under s.10 in the period 2010–2020 (see fnn.20–21), although it is possible that disqualification in relation to fraudulent trading was imposed in a few cases under the CDDA 1986 s.4.

[127] CDDA 1986 s.5.

[128] Contrast the wording of the CDDA 1986 ss.5(1) and 5(2).

[129] CDDA 1986 s.16(2).

[130] CDDA 1986 s.3.

[131] CDDA 1986 s.3(2).

orders and undertakings, which register is open to public inspection.[132] The register is also to contain details of any leave given to a disqualified person to act despite the disqualification. Either due to doubts about the accuracy of the register or to relieve the Registrar of the need to check it, the CA 2006 contains a power for the Secretary of State to make regulations about the returns that companies have to make to the Registrar about the appointment of directors and secretaries. The regulations may require the return to contain the statement in relation to a disqualified person that the leave of the court to act has been obtained.[133]

BANKRUPTS

The prohibition on undischarged bankrupts acting as directors or being involved in the management of companies can be traced back to the CA 1928. Although bankruptcy does not necessarily connote any wrongdoing, the policy against permitting those who have been so spectacularly unsuccessful in the management of their own finances taking charge of other people's money is so self-evident that it has not proved controversial. Acting as a director when an undischarged bankrupt is a criminal offence.[134] The main point of interest is that this results in an automatic disqualification, not dependent upon the making of a disqualification order by the court. In 2002, the prohibition was extended to include acting in breach of a bankruptcy restriction order or undertaking, themselves creations of the legislative reforms of that year.[135] Bankruptcy restriction orders and undertakings, clearly modelled to some extent on directors' disqualification orders and undertakings, put restrictions on a former bankrupt's activities after discharge from bankruptcy (in general an earlier event than had previously been the case). **20–016**

The disqualification is not absolute, however, because the bankrupt or previous bankrupt may apply to the court for leave to act in the management of a company, but not as an insolvency practitioner.[136] In other words, the CDDA 1986 really reverses the burden of taking action, by placing it upon the bankrupt to show that he or she may be safely involved in the management of companies, rather than upon the State to demonstrate to a court that the bankrupt ought not to be allowed to act.

---

[132] CDDA 1986 s.18. See also the Companies (Disqualification Orders) Regulations 2009 (SI 2009/2471).

[133] CA 2006 s.1189. At the time of writing no regulations have been made.

[134] CDDA 1986 s.11. Acting in breach of the prohibition also attracts personal liability for the company's debts under the CDDA 1986 s.15, although this may not be of much utility in relation to bankrupts and could, apparently, give rise to the making of a disqualification order under s.2 (see para.20–009): see *R. v Young* [1990] B.C.C. 549 CA.

[135] These changes were affected by the Enterprise Act 2002 Sch.20, introducing a new IA 1986 Sch.4A.

[136] IA1986 ss.11(1) and 390(4)(a).

OTHER CASES

20–017 Disqualification has become a popular legislative technique in recent years. The CDDA 1986 itself applies to those in charge of other corporate bodies as if they were companies formed under the CA 2006, such as building societies, incorporated friendly societies, NHS foundation trusts, registered societies and charitable incorporated organisations.[137] Another extension is to apply disqualification to the directors of companies for breaches of provisions other than company law rules. Thus, CDDA 1986 makes provision for disqualification orders and undertakings in relation to directors (and shadow directors) of companies who have broken competition law, where a court or regulator is of the opinion that the director is in consequence unfit to be involved in the management of a company.[138] Finally, breaches of sector-specific rules, such as in the banking sector, could form the basis for disqualification (for example, on grounds of "unfitness"), but the Government stopped short of giving sectoral regulators disqualification powers under the CDDA 1986: instead, they have to operate through the Insolvency Service. Of course, sector-specific legislation may give sectoral regulators disqualification powers in relation to the areas of economic activity they regulate, as is the case with financial regulators—but such provisions are outside the scope of this chapter.

CONCLUSION

20–018 For many years the disqualification provisions of the successive companies legislation seemed to make little impact. Important in principle as a technique for dealing with corporate wrongdoing of one sort or another, especially on the part of directors, the practical consequences of the provisions were limited. The disqualification has come to the fore through a combination of the substantive reforms recommended by the Cork Committee and the acceptance by Government that the promotion of small, and not-so-small, businesses needed to be accompanied by action to raise the standards of directors' behaviour and to protect the public from the scheming and the incompetent. Further, as considered above,[139] controversy about whether directors whose companies are convicted of the proposed new corporate killing offence should be disqualified from acting in connection with businesses delayed progress on that reform proposal, though in the end the legislation did not make use of the disqualification technique. As to disqualification orders in company law, judged by the level of disqualification orders and undertakings actually made, the provisions now have a substantial impact. An independent survey[140] found a widespread consensus that the

[137] CDDA 1986 ss.22A–C and E–F.

[138] CDDA 1986 ss.9A–9E.

[139] See further paras 8–045 to 8–046.

[140] A. Hicks, *Disqualification of Directors: No Hiding Place for the Unfit?* (1998), ACCA Research Report 59. The report makes a number of interesting and thought-provoking suggestions for reform. For a more sceptical account, see R. Williams, "Disqualifying Directors: a Remedy Worse than the Disease?" (2007) 7 J.C.L.S. 213.

provisions performed a useful role and should be retained, although they were certainly capable of improvement, especially at the level of securing compliance with disqualification orders.[141]

It would be wrong, however, to see disqualification as solely a response to the abuse of limited liability within small companies. There is some evidence that the public authorities use disqualification to inflict reputational harm on directors of failed companies in circumstances giving rise to public condemnation where no other remedy is readily available. For example, the directors of Barings Bank, which collapsed as a result of a failure to identify and prevent large foreign exchange bets being placed by a junior trader, were disqualified.[142] Another example is the disqualification undertakings, offered by the four directors of MG Rover Group Ltd after its well-publicised collapse, and accepted by the Secretary of State: the company had gone into administration in April 2005, owing creditors nearly £1.3 billion, causing many employees to lose their jobs and ending large-scale, British-owned car manufacturing. In this case, the groundwork for the disqualification had been provided through a lengthy and expensive public investigation into the collapse of the company.[143] Although a company investigation is no longer a pre-requisite of a disqualification order,[144] such investigations continue to play an important role in the more serious cases. Company investigations are considered in the next chapter.

---

[141] DTI *Companies in 2005–2006* (31 March 2006) reveals that some 90 prosecutions for breach of disqualification orders or of the prohibition on bankrupts acting as directors were launched in that year, producing 81 convictions. More recent statistics appear not to be available. It is difficult to know whether this relatively modest total indicates a high level of compliance with the disqualifications or a low level of detection of breaches.

[142] *Re Barings Plc (No.5)* [2000] 1 B.C.L.C. 523.

[143] Department of Business Innovation and Skills, Press Release (9 May 2011). See further Ch.21.

[144] CDDA 1986 s.8(1).

CHAPTER 21

BREACH OF CORPORATE DUTIES: ADMINISTRATIVE REMEDIES

INTRODUCTION

A distinctive feature of British company regulation for many years has been the conferment of powers of investigation on the relevant Secretary of State, currently the Secretary of State for the Department for Business, Energy and Industrial Strategy (BEIS).[1] Those provisions are still contained in the CA 1985 (rather than the CA 2006),[2] as amended by the CA 1989 and strengthened by the Companies (Audit, Investigations and Community Enterprise) Act 2004.[3] The CA 1985, as amended, empowers the Secretary of State to launch inquisitorial raids on corporate (and even unincorporated) bodies. To this end, the predecessors of BEIS established a sizeable Companies Investigation Branch (CIB), which was headed by the Inspector of Companies. In 2006, the CIB became part of the Insolvency Service Agency, which falls under the general aegis of BEIS.[4] The Secretary of State's powers are draconian, despite the acknowledged need to ensure that the investigatory and inspection powers comply, in both design and use, with the Human Rights Act 1998, and with the fairness standards of domestic public law. The limited use of those powers likely derives more from the Government's desire not to spend public money on matters 21–001

[1] For its earlier guises, see the Department for Business, Innovation and Skills (BIS), the Department of Business Enterprise and Regulatory Reform (BERR), the Department of Trade and Industry (DTI) and the Board of Trade (BoT). References to "BEIS" include its relevant predecessors.

[2] CA 1985 Pt XIV. Unless indicated otherwise, all references are to the CA 1985.

[3] The relevant provisions were not strengthened to the extent recommended by the Department's own review: see DTI, *Company Investigations: Powers for the Twenty-First Century* (2001).

[4] On 1 January 2017, the BEIS Criminal Enforcement Team transferred to the Insolvency Service. As regards insolvency-related fraud and corporate misconduct, the Insolvency Service Criminal Enforcement Team is the principal criminal enforcement agency.

that should ultimately be the sole concern of the company's members or creditors, than concerns over the fairness of the process.[5]

Originally, the Secretary of State's only form of investigatory power involved the appointment of outside inspectors (usually a QC and a senior accountant). Announcing the appointment of inspectors, however, was itself likely to cause damage to the company. As a result, the Secretary of State was generally reluctant to initiate an inspection unless a strong case for doing so could be made out. Indeed, an informal dialogue would normally be opened with the board of directors before taking such a step. Whilst such informal discussions might well encourage the company's board to take the necessary remedial action, they might equally well forewarn the board sufficiently that it has the opportunity to destroy or fabricate evidence. Accordingly, on the recommendation of the Jenkins Committee,[6] the Secretary of State in 1967 was given the power to require the production of books and papers as a preliminary step to commencing an inspection.[7] As this informational power can be exercised in a less public manner,[8] the Secretary of State can ensure that there is a proper evidential foundation for an inspection before one is launched. Nowadays, this power is by far the one most commonly exercised.[9] This is sometimes referred to as the power of (informal or confidential) investigation, by way of contrast with the far more formal and public powers of inspection (by appointment of inspectors). As this is undoubtedly the primary form of intervention in practice, it shall be considered first.

---

[5] DTI, *Company Investigations: Powers for the Twenty-First Century* (2001), gives details of the costs and length of the then most recent formal inspections under the CA 1985 s.432. For example, the inspection into Mirror Group Newspapers Ltd took nearly nine years and cost £9.5 million. However, nearly half that time was taken up with waiting for criminal trials to be completed or with dealing with challenges in the courts to the inspectors by those sought to be inspected.

[6] Jenkins Committee (1962), Cm.1749, paras 213–219.

[7] CA 1985 s.447. For the application of this power in relation to "foreign companies carrying on or which has carried on business in Great Britain", see *R. (KBR Inc) v Director of the Serious Fraud Office* [2018] EWHC 2368 (Admin); [2019] Q.B. 675 at [67]; [2021] UKSC 2 at [34]. Alternatively, the information may be a precursor to winding-up the company on public interest grounds: see *Re Rigil Kent Acquisitions Ltd* [2017] EWHC 3636 (Ch); [2018] B.C.C. 591.

[8] The Department does not normally announce that it has mounted such an investigation and all information about it is regarded as confidential. This has its disadvantages. If a team of officials is going through the company's books and papers, this cannot be concealed from its employees and will soon become known to the Press. This may put the company under a cloud that may never be dispersed because the ending of the inquiries will not normally be announced, nor will their results ever be published (notwithstanding that the conclusion may be that all is well with the company).

[9] The powers to appoint inspectors are used only very infrequently. The number of informal investigations has remained relatively constant at around 150 investigations per year: see generally *Insolvency Service Annual Report 2019–20* (21 December 2020).

INFORMAL INVESTIGATIONS: DISCLOSURE OF DOCUMENTS AND INFORMATION

The Secretary of State may require, or more likely authorise an investigator from the Insolvency Service to require, a company to produce (at the designated time and place) such documents[10] or information as may be specified in the direction. Authorising an investigator to impose the requirement avoids the risk of the documents being destroyed or doctored, since the appointed officer will arrive without any warning[11] at the company's registered office (or wherever else the documents are believed to be held).[12] Whilst the Secretary of State's direct powers are limited to giving directions to the company,[13] the investigator may be authorised further to impose the same requirements on "any other person".[14] This extended power will be useful where, for example, the relevant documents are in the possession of some person other than the company. The power of an investigator to impose a requirement on "any other person" in relation to the production of "information" as well as documents means that, for example, an officer or employee of the company may be required to provide an explanation of a particular document; if the document was not produced by the person in question, then he or she may be required to state to the best of his or her knowledge where that document is.[15] **21–002**

Failure to comply with a direction for the provision of documents or information may be "certified" by the Secretary of State or the investigator to the court.[16] After hearing any witnesses and the defendant, if the court is satisfied that the defendant did not have a reasonable excuse for failing to comply with the relevant direction,[17] the court may treat that person as being in contempt of

---

[10] CA 1985 s.447(8). "Document" is defined as "information recorded in any form". The requirement to produce documents includes the power, if they are produced, to take copies of them or extracts from them: CA 1985 s.447(7). This has been extended to information held on databases from 1 October 2007: see CA 2006 s.1038(2).

[11] The investigation is an administrative act to which the full rules of natural justice do not apply: see *Norwest Holst Ltd v Secretary of State* [1978] Ch. 201 CA at 224. But "fairness" must be observed and directions to produce documents or information should be clear and not excessive: see *R. v Trade Secretary Ex p. Perestrello* [1981] Q.B. 19 QBD (illustrating the problems that may be encountered if the documents are not held in the UK). See also *R. (on the application of 1st Choice Engines Ltd) v Secretary of State for Business, Innovation and Skills* [2014] EWHC 1765. For protection against self-incrimination, see CA 1985 s.447A.

[12] The officer may be accompanied by a policeman with a search warrant: see CA 1985 s.448.

[13] CA 1985 s.447(2).

[14] CA 1985 s.447(3). But this is without prejudice to any lien that the possessor may have: CA 1985 s.447(6).

[15] For an express statement of this power, see *Re Attorney-General's Reference No.2 of 1998* [2000] QB 412 CA, which was decided under an earlier version of CA 1985 s.447. The current version of the power is not confined to officers and employees, but extends to "any other person".

[16] CA 1985 s.453C(2).

[17] CA 1985 s.453C(3). cf. *Re An Investigation under the Insider Dealing Act* [1988] A.C. 660 HL, dealing with an analogous provision, where the court took a narrow view of "reasonable excuse" in the case of a journalist refusing to answer questions in order to protect his sources. This was because the information was needed for the prevention of crime, which is likely to, but need not, be the case under the CA 1985 s.447. For the rationale underlying such contempt proceedings, see *Secretary of State for Business, Innovation and Skills v Marshall* [2015] EWHC 3874 (Ch) at [11].

court.[18] In addition, providing information known to be false in a material particular, or doing so recklessly, is a criminal offence, punishable by imprisonment or a fine.[19] Criminal sanctions are also imposed on any officer of the company who is privy to the falsification or destruction of a document relating to the company's affairs, unless the officer shows there was no intention to conceal the company's affairs or to defeat the law.[20] Furthermore, it is a criminal offence fraudulently to part with, alter or make an omission in such a document.[21] These various provisions are all aimed at extracting information from those who may be unwilling to provide it without compulsion.[22] A person may wish, however, to volunteer information to an investigator, but feel constrained from so doing because the information has been imparted to him or her in confidence, so that disclosure might trigger an action for breach of confidence by the person who initially provided the confidential information. The CA 1985 now confers a limited protection against such claims.[23] There are several requirements that must be satisfied to use this protection, namely that the information must be of a kind that the person making the disclosure could be compelled to disclose under the CA 1985; the disclosure must be in good faith and in the reasonable belief that the information is capable of assisting the Secretary of State; the disclosure must be no more than is reasonably necessary for this purpose; and the disclosure must not be prohibited by legislation or breach an obligation of confidence arising out of the person's status as solicitor or banker.[24]

21–003 When an investigator is authorised by the Secretary of State to obtain documents or information,[25] there is obviously a risk that entry could be denied to the company's premises. The CA 1985 provides for the investigator to be given compulsory powers of entry and search.[26] These powers come in escalating tiers.

---

[18] One effect of proceeding in this way is that the defendant is deprived of the automatic protection of legal professional privilege, which applies if failure to comply is treated as an offence (see CA 2006 s.1129), though the court might regard legal professional privilege as reasonable grounds for non-compliance.

[19] CA 1985 s.451. Prosecution requires the consent of the Secretary of State or DPP in England and Wales and Northern Ireland: see CA 2006 s.1126(2)–(3).

[20] CA 1985 s.450(1). The same restriction on prosecution applies as under s.451: see CA 2006 s.1126(2)–(3).

[21] CA 1985 s.450(2).

[22] *Secretary of State for Business, Innovation and Skills v Marshall* [2015] EWHC 3874 (Ch) at [11].

[23] CA 1985 s.448A(1).

[24] CA 1985 s.448A(2).

[25] CA 1985 s.447.

[26] CA 1985 s.448(1). These powers apply also to inspectors. In addition, there is a power under the CA 2006 s.1132, whereby (on application of the DPP, the Secretary of State or the police) a High Court judge, if satisfied that there is reasonable cause to believe that any person, while an officer of a company, has committed an offence in its management and that evidence of the commission is to be found in any books or papers of, or under the control of, the company, may make an order authorising any named person to inspect the books and papers or require an officer of the company to produce them: see *Re Company (No.00996 of 1979)* [1980] Ch. 138 CA (Civ Div) (reversed by the House of Lords sub nom. *Re Racal Communications Ltd* [1981] A.C. 374 HL, because, under CA 2006 s.1132(5), there can be no appeal from the judge and it was held that this included cases where he had erred on a point of law—and, having discovered that other judges had taken a different view, had volunteered leave to appeal!)

A Justice of the Peace may issue a warrant if satisfied, on information given on oath by the Secretary of State (or by a person appointed or authorised to exercise his powers), that there are documents on any premises, production of which has been directed and which have not been produced.[27] A search warrant cannot be issued, however, unless there has first been a direction to produce the documents sought. This requirement creates the obvious risk that, once the company has been warned of the need to produce certain documents, the company might destroy those documents before the search happens, even if such an action would be a crime. Accordingly, the CA 1989 Act introduced a further provision under which a warrant may be issued if a Justice of the Peace is satisfied: that there are reasonable grounds for believing that an indictable offence has been committed and that there are on the premises documents relating to whether the offence has been committed; that the applicant has power under the CA 1985 to require the production of the documents; and that there are reasonable grounds for believing that, if production was required, the relevant documents would be removed from the company's premises, hidden, tampered with or destroyed.[28] Though narrowly circumscribed by the need to satisfy a Justice of the Peace that the conditions have been satisfied, this power enables the search for the documents to be undertaken by the police rather than by the (probably self-interested) officers of the company.

Although the search warrant power introduced in 1989 undoubtedly increased the investigators' powers, in many cases the possibility may be unavailable if the statutory conditions are not satisfied. Accordingly, where the investigator is unable to obtain a search warrant, he might still be left standing on the doorstep. Consequently, the Companies (Audit, Investigations and Community Enterprise) Act 2004 introduced a right of entry to a company's premises that was neither dependent on a warrant being issued by a Justice of the Peace nor subject to onerous conditions. Nowadays, provided he is authorised to do so by the Secretary of State, an investigator[29] may require entry to the company's premises at all reasonable times if he thinks that it will materially assist in the exercise of his or her investigatory functions in relation to the company.[30] Once on the company's premises, the investigator may remain there for such time as considered necessary to discharge those functions.[31] The power of entry extends to accompanying persons whom the investigator thinks appropriate.[32] Whilst the investigator does not have statutory search powers, the power of entry will in practical terms give the investigator access to relevant persons from whom the production of documents or information can be demanded. Intentional obstruction of the exercise of this power of entry is an offence, punishable with a fine.[33] Furthermore, a failure to cooperate with the investigator once in the company's

[27] CA 1985 s.448(1).

[28] CA 1985 s.448(2).

[29] The power to enter and remain on premises also extends to inspectors.

[30] CA 1985 s.453A(2)(a). The power of entry can be exercised in relation to any premises that the inspector or investigator "believes are used (wholly or partly) for the purposes of the company's business": CA 1985 s.453A(3).

[31] CA 1985 s.453A(2)(b).

[32] CA 1985 s.453A(4).

[33] CA 1985 s.453A(5)–(5A).

premises or to comply with the investigator's directions may be certified to the court and treated as a contempt of court.[34] The power of entry is subject to some procedural safeguards, notably a requirement that the investigator and accompanying persons provide evidence of their identity and authorisation.[35] Furthermore, the investigator must give a written statement, as soon as practicable after entry to the occupiers of the premises, about the investigator's powers and the rights and obligations of the persons on the premises, as well as comply with other conditions.[36]

21–004 When considered cumulatively, the investigator's information-gathering powers are considerable. The draconian nature of the investigator's power may explain why the Secretary of State will be reluctant to use those powers (or authorise others to do so), unless there is clear wrongdoing and a strong public interest in taking action. Over three-quarters of the investigations initiated have been prompted by allegations of fraudulent trading,[37] which is a criminal offence under s.993 of the CA 2006 on the part of any person knowingly party to the fraudulent trading, whether or not the company is in the course of winding up. What should be emphasised, however, is that an investigation initiated by the Secretary of State is something more than just a preliminary step to the appointment of an inspector. Rather than leading to the appointment of inspectors, there may be a decision to take no further action or to follow-up with the company in some more informal manner or to take the formal steps considered below.[38] The timeline for determining what steps will be taken may vary from a few days to several months and, while the investigation continues, the officials will probe deeply and in a way that may be just as intrusive as a formal inspection.[39]

[34] CA 1985 s.453C(1). In *Secretary of State for Business, Innovation and Skills v Marshall* [2015] EWHC 3874 (Ch) at [11], it was stated that "the primary purpose of proceedings … is not to imprison people for contempt but to enable the Secretary of State to make progress in an investigation that has to be carried out in the public interest". See further para.21–002.

[35] CA 1985 s.453B(3).

[36] CA 1985 s.453B(4)–(10). For the detailed procedures that the investigator must follow, see Companies Act 1985 (Power to Enter and Remain on Premises: Procedural) Regulations 2005 (SI 2005/684).

[37] "Our investigations help to protect the public from rogue company directors who abuse their corporate position through fraud, scams or dishonesty" (Insolvency Service, *Annual Report and Accounts 2019–2020*, p.24. Other cases where an investigator has been appointed include when it is suspected that a disqualified person or an undischarged bankrupt has been involved in the management of the company or when a company has been used to promote an unlawful pyramid selling scheme.

[38] See further para.21–013.

[39] *R. (on the application of Clegg) v Secretary of State for Trade and Industry* [2002] EWCA Civ 519; [2003] B.C.C. 128.

FORMAL INVESTIGATIONS BY INSPECTORS

When inspectors can be appointed

As indicated above,[40] the Secretary of State is empowered[41] to appoint one or more competent inspectors[42] to investigate the affairs of a company.[43] An inspector will subsequently report the result of their investigations to him. Whilst the Secretary of State generally has a discretion whether or not to commence an inspection, there is one situation where this is mandatory, namely when the court orders that the company's affairs should be so investigated.[44] The courts rarely make use of this power. **21–005**

Otherwise, the Secretary of State has a discretion whether or not to appoint an inspector in two situations. First, a company or its members may take the initiative to suggest the appointment, although this power is almost never used.[45] The application can be made by: (1) in the case of a company with a share capital, not less than 200 members or members holding not less than one-tenth of the issued shares; (2) in the case of a company not having a share capital, not less than one-fifth of the persons on the company's register of members; or (3) in any case, the company itself.[46] Before making an appointment on this basis, the Secretary of State may require applicants to give security in an amount not exceeding £5,000 for payment of the costs of the inspection[47] and must verify that there is sufficient evidence demonstrating that the applicant has good reason for requiring the inspection.[48] If those good reasons exist, then the Secretary of State may proceed to appoint an inspector. Secondly, the Secretary of State may appoint an inspector of his or her own motion (as it turns out, rather rarely used)[49] on any one (or more) of four grounds. The first ground is that the company's affairs are being conducted or have been conducted with intent to defraud creditors (or the creditors of any other person), for a fraudulent or unlawful

---

[40] See para.21–001.

[41] CA 1985 ss.431–432.

[42] The usual appointees are a QC and a chartered accountant, but less expensive mortals may be appointed in the rarer case when the Department appoints in relation to a private company.

[43] The notion of the affairs of the company refers to its business, including its control over its subsidiaries, whether they are being managed by the board of directors or an administrator, administrative receiver or a liquidator in a voluntary liquidation: see *R. v Board of Trade Ex p. St Martin Preserving Co* [1965] 1 Q.B. 603 QBD.

[44] CA 1985 s.432(1). This seems to make the Secretary of State's refusal to appoint an inspector reviewable by the court if an application is made by anyone with locus standi, and to enable a court in any proceedings (for example, on an unfair prejudice petition) to make an order declaring that the company's affairs ought to be investigated by inspectors. A copy of the inspectors' report will be sent to the court: CA 1985 s.437(2).

[45] It is believed that there have been no appointments since 1990.

[46] CA 1985 s.431(2).

[47] CA 1985 s.431(4). The £5,000 can be altered by statutory instrument. Under the CA 1948, the sum was only £100 which, even then, would not have kept a competent QC and chartered accountant happy for the time that most inspections take.

[48] CA 1985 s.431(3).

[49] CA 1985 s.432(2). This power may be exercise even if the company is being voluntarily wound up: CA 1985 s.432(3).

purpose or in a manner that is unfairly prejudicial to some part of its members.[50] The second ground is that any actual or proposed act or omission of the company (including an act or omission on its behalf) is or would be unfairly prejudicial, or that the company was formed for any fraudulent or unlawful purpose.[51] Both of these grounds bear some resemblance to the jurisdiction permitting a shareholder to petition for relief from unfairly prejudicial conduct,[52] although they also extend to certain types of fraudulent or illegal conduct. The third ground is when those concerned with the company's formation or the management of its affairs have in that regard been guilty of fraud, misfeasance or other misconduct towards the company or its members.[53] Whilst breaches of directors' duties may potentially trigger an inspection, these would have to be serious and widespread to justify the time and resources of an inspection. The fourth ground is that the company's members have not been given all the information with respect to its affairs that they might reasonably expect.[54]

21–006 Given the availability of the more attractive, cheaper and speedier option of an investigation,[55] appointments of formal inspectors have become far less common, except in major cases where there are circumstances suggesting malpractice (such as companies formed or used in unlawful, dishonest, fraudulent or improper ways) and a strong public interest in having an inspection. Indeed, had the reforms proposed in 2001 been implemented, this would have become the sole basis upon which the Secretary of State could exercise his or her discretion to appoint an inspector.[56]

Conduct of inspections

Extent of the inspectors' powers

21–007 The CA 1985 governs the conduct of inspections. If inspectors appointed to investigate the affairs of a company think it also necessary for the purposes of their inspection to investigate the affairs of another body corporate in the same group, they may do so and report the results of that so far as it is relevant to the

[50] CA 1985 s.432(2)(a). A "member" includes a person to whom shares have been transmitted by operation of law: CA 1985 s.432(4).

[51] CA 1985 s.432(2)(b).

[52] CA 2006 s.994(1), considered further in Ch.14. Although the CA 1985 s.432(2)(a) refers only to "some part of the members", rather than using the wording in the CA 2006 of "members generally or some part of the members", this is unlikely to have the absurd result that the Secretary of State should not appoint inspectors if it is thought that *all* the members are unfairly prejudiced. This is especially so given that the precise grounds for appointment do not have to be stated: see *Norwest Holst v Trade Secretary* [1978] Ch. 201 CA.

[53] CA 1985 s.432(2)(c). It seems that the CA 1985 s.432(2) does not entitle the Secretary of State to appoint merely because the directors or officers of the company appear to have breached their duties of care, skill or diligence: see *SBA Properties Ltd v Cradock* [1967] 1 W.L.R. 716 Ch D (which, however, was concerned with an action by the Secretary of State under the CA 1985 s.438, which was repealed on 6 April 2007).

[54] CA 1985 s.432(2)(d). This wording implies that members may "reasonably expect" more information than that to which the CA 2006 entitles them.

[55] CA 1985 s.447.

[56] DTI, *Company Investigations: Powers for the Twenty-First Century* (2001), para.97.

company.[57] In addition, inspectors have powers similar to those of investigators entitling them to require the production of documents and information.[58] They may also require any past or present officer or agent of the company to attend before them and otherwise to give all assistance that he is "reasonably" able to give.[59] In addition, inspectors may examine any person on oath.[60] If any person fails to comply with their requirements or refuses to answer any question put by the inspectors for the purposes of the investigation, the inspectors may certify that fact in writing to the court, which may punish the offender for contempt of court, subject to the important defence of reasonableness.[61]

Control of the inspectors' powers

There are two aspects to the control of inspectors: control exercised by the Secretary of State and control over the inspectors in the interests of third parties. The former type of control was considerably strengthened by the CA 2006,[62] which inserted new provisions into the CA 1985, although to some extent these reforms reflect what was probably already administrative practice. In any event, the inspectors are now under a statutory obligation to comply with any direction given to them by the Secretary of State as to the subject-matter of the inspection, the steps to be taken in the inspection, and whether to report or not report on a particular matter or in a particular way.[63] Furthermore, the Secretary of State may also terminate an inspection.[64] Perhaps anticipating that the exercise of these powers may lead to dissatisfaction among inspectors, they are given an express statutory right to resign, and the Secretary of State has a corresponding power to revoke an appointment as inspector.[65] Former inspectors are, however, under an obligation to produce to the Secretary of State, or any replacement inspector, the 21–008

[57] CA 1985 s.433. Most major corporate scandals involve the use of a network of holding and subsidiary companies, the extent of which may only become apparent during the course of the inspection. The CA 1985 s.433 avoids the need for a formal extension of the inspectors' appointment each time they unearth another member of the group. The extended power applies to a "body corporate" (in other words, not just registered companies under the CA 2006), but does not extend to unincorporated bodies, although such associations may be subjected to investigation on the grounds that associated unincorporated bodies are part of the affairs of the corporate body with which they are associated.

[58] CA 1985 s.434(1)(a).

[59] CA 1985 s.434(1)(b) and (2). On the use of the "reasonableness" defence to protect a director against oppressive use by the inspectors of their powers, see *Re Mirror Group Newspapers Plc* [1999] 1 B.C.L.C. 690 Ch D (Companies Ct). Agents include auditors, bankers and solicitors: see CA 1985 s.434(4).

[60] CA 1985 s.434(3).

[61] CA 1985 s.436.

[62] CA 2006 Pt 32.

[63] CA 1985 s.446A.

[64] CA 1985 s.446B(1). In the case of inspectors appointed by court order, the Secretary of State may only terminate the investigation if matters have come to light suggesting the commission of a criminal offence and those matters have been referred to the appropriate prosecuting authority: see CA 1985 s.446B(2).

[65] CA 1985 s.446C. The Secretary of State can fill any vacancy: see CA 1985 s.446D.

documents and information obtained or generated in the course of the inspection.[66] The inspector is clearly under the close control of the Secretary of State.

As regards control over inspectors in the interests of those being investigated, a number of matters have become clear. The process of inspection is undoubtedly an inquisitorial one. Since the aim of an inspection is to establish facts rather than to determine legal rights, however, the inspection process has been characterised domestically as administrative rather than judicial, so that the inspectors are obliged to act fairly, but are not subject to the full requirements of natural justice. Indeed, the European Court of Human Rights adopted a similar stance regarding the applicability of the right to a fair trial in the European Convention on Human Rights (ECHR)[67] to inspections.[68] Consequently, it would seem that the use of compulsion in investigations and inspections to secure information from those investigated, including compulsion to answer questions put by inspectors, is not in principle unlawful, under either domestic law or the ECHR. Nevertheless, the ECHR has had a significant impact on what can be done subsequently by prosecuting authorities with compelled testimony obtained by inspectors. Indeed, the CA 1985 was subsequently amended by the Criminal Justice and Police Act 2001 to take account of the jurisprudence of the European Court of Human Rights.

Although the full rules of "natural justice" do not apply, the inspectors must act fairly. This involves letting witnesses know of criticisms or allegations made against them (assuming that the inspectors envisage relying on, or referring to, those criticisms in their inspection report) and giving them adequate opportunity to respond. The inspectors are not, however, bound to circulate to witnesses a draft of those parts of the report referring to them, so long as those witnesses have had a fair opportunity of answering any criticisms of their conduct. Inspectors are free to draw conclusions from the evidence about the conduct of individuals, but they should only do so with restraint.[69]

21–009 Inspectors sit in private (and probably do not have the power to sit in public),[70] but allow witnesses to be accompanied by their lawyers—although the latter's role is limited, since the questioning is undertaken by the inspectors and neither the witness nor his lawyers can cross-examine other witnesses. Although the range of persons whom the inspectors may question is very wide, the CA 1985 provides that such persons cannot be compelled to disclose or produce any information or document in breach of legal professional privilege, except that lawyers may be required to disclose the names and addresses of their clients.[71] A

---

66 CA 1985 s.446E. The inspector is under a duty to comply with this requirement, but no sanction is specified. It can be assumed that *in extremis* the Secretary of State could obtain a court order.

67 Human Rights Act 1998 Sch.1 art.6.

68 *Al-Fayed v United Kingdom* (1994) 18 E.H.R.R. 393 ECHR.

69 *Re Pergamon Press Ltd* [1971] Ch. 388 CA; *Maxwell v DTI* [1974] Q.B. 523 CA; *R. (on the application of Clegg) v Secretary of State* [2003] B.C.C. 128.

70 *Hearts of Oak Assurance Co Ltd v Attorney-General* [1932] A.C. 392 HL.

71 CA 1985 s.452(1) and (5). This applies to Departmental investigations as well as to inspections: CA 1985 s.452(2). On the issue of the privilege against self-incrimination, see *Re London United Investments plc* [1992] Ch. 578 CA (Civ Div); *Bishopsgate Investment Management Ltd v Maxwell* [1993] Ch. 1 CA (Civ Div).

banker's duty of confidentiality is protected more narrowly.[72] In particular, it may be overridden by the Secretary of State.[73]

Reports

The inspectors may, and if so directed by the Secretary of State shall, make interim reports.[74] On the conclusion of the inspection, the inspector must make a final report.[75] If so directed by the Secretary of State, the inspector must inform him or her of the matters coming to their knowledge during their investigation.[76] If appropriate, the Secretary of State may forward a copy of any report to the company's registered office.[77] Furthermore, on request and payment of a prescribed fee, the inspection report may be forwarded to any member of the company or other body corporate that is the subject of the report; any person whose conduct is mentioned in the report; the company's auditors; those persons who applied for the inspection in the first instance[78]; and any other person whose financial interests appear to be affected by matters dealt with in the report.[79] The Secretary of State may (and generally will, though not until after any criminal proceedings have been concluded)[80] cause the report to be printed and published.[81] There is, however, one exception to this: inspectors may be appointed on terms that any report they make is not for publication,[82] in which case the statutory obligations relating to reports cannot apply. Given that a report does not generally have to be published unless the Secretary of State thinks fit, one might have thought that it was unnecessary to have this exception. Such an exception, however, has two advantages: it protects the Secretary of State from pressure to publish, even though advised that that might prejudice possible criminal prosecutions; and, since it is an ex ante rule, it makes it clear to the proposed appointees that they will not be able to bask in the publicity from their efforts.[83] **21–010**

---

[72] CA 1985 s.452(1A)–(1B).

[73] CA 1985 s.452(1A)(c). The bankers' protection is differently worded. It can be overridden by the Secretary of State only when it is thought necessary for the purpose of investigating the affairs of the person carrying on the banking business, or the customer is a person upon whom a s.447 requirement has been imposed: see CA 1985 s.452(4).

[74] CA 1985 s.437(1).

[75] CA 1985 s.437(1).

[76] CA 1985 s.437(1A).

[77] CA 1985 s.437(3)(a).

[78] This provision does not apply when the Secretary of State appoints the inspectors of his or her own motion: see CA 1985 s.432(2).

[79] CA 1985 s.437(3).

[80] For an unsuccessful attempt to force the Secretary of State to publish an inspection report while criminal proceedings were still being considered, see *R. v Secretary of State Ex p. Lonrho* [1989] 1 W.L.R. 525 HL.

[81] CA 1985 s.437(3)(c). Thus making the reports available for purchase from HMSO by any member of the public, so long as the reports remain in print. They often make fascinating reading for anyone interested in "the unacceptable face of capitalism".

[82] CA 1985 s.432(2A).

[83] It may also tend to make the officers of the company more co-operative.

POWER OF INVESTIGATION OF COMPANY OWNERSHIP

21–011 In addition to the appointment of inspectors or investigators to examine the affairs of the company in general (even if in particular cases they may be given a more limited remit), the Secretary of State has a narrower power to appoint inspectors or investigators to investigate the company's ownership.[84] This may be a controversial issue and the facts may not be clear, because, although the name of the shareholder has to be entered on the company's share register, that shareholder may be a nominee rather than the beneficial owner of the share. The position has been improved by the advent of a register for shareholders with "significant control" of the company.[85] This will obviously make it more straightforward to understand the shareholdings in a company. The Secretary of State's investigatory powers are essentially complementary to these disclosure requirements.

In the first instance, if the Secretary of State is persuaded that there may be good reasons for intervening, he or she will probably institute preliminary investigations.[86] In that regard, the Secretary of State can require any person to disclose information about the present and past interests in a company's shares or debentures if there is reasonable cause to believe that that information is held by that person. If this step fails to produce a satisfactory answer, the Secretary of State may then appoint inspectors to investigate and report on the company's membership.[87] The Secretary of State may do so at will and must do so if requisitioned by sufficient members to instigate an appointment of inspectors under the more general powers.[88] A fully-fledged investigation may afford the best chance of getting at the truth, but it is expensive and time-consuming.[89] Hence, the amendments introduced by the CA 1989 provide that the Secretary of State shall not be obliged to appoint inspectors if satisfied that the members' application is vexatious.[90] Further, if an appointment is made, the Secretary of State may exclude any matter if satisfied that it is unreasonable for it to be investigated.[91] If the Secretary of State decides to initiate an investigation, the applicants may be required to give security for costs.[92]

The sanctions for failing to provide the requisite information or to cooperate with the inspectors include the possibility of being held in contempt of court.[93] In

---

[84] CA 1985 s.442(1). There was also a power of investigation into share dealings (see CA 1985 s.446), but this was repealed by the CA 2006 from October 2007, although the Financial Conduct Authority has a like investigatory power and is now regarded as the more appropriate body to exercise this type of power. See further para.30–048.

[85] See paras 13–022 onwards.

[86] CA 1985 s.444.

[87] CA 1985 s.442(1). This power is not merely directed at determining share and debenture ownership, but "the true persons who are or have been primarily interested in the success or failure (real or apparent) of the company or able to control or materially to influence its policy": CA 1985 s.442(1).

[88] CA 1985 s.442(3). See further para.21–002, although under s.442(3) the appointment is mandatory.

[89] It is believed that no appointments have been made since 1992.

[90] CA 1985 s.442(3A).

[91] CA 1985 s.442(3A).

[92] See further para.21–005.

[93] CA 1985 s.443.

addition to the sanctions that would apply to other investigatory powers, the Secretary of State may by order direct that the securities concerned shall, until further notice, be subject to restrictions on their transfer and the exercise of rights attached to them.[94] This puts pressure on those holding shares in the company to be more forthcoming. If such restrictions are likely to unfairly prejudice the rights of third parties in relation to the shares in question, the Secretary of State may provide those parties with an exemption from the restrictions.[95]

LIABILITY FOR COSTS OF INVESTIGATIONS

The expenses of any investigation are to be defrayed in the first instance by the Secretary of State, but may be recoverable from certain specified persons.[96] These expenses include such reasonable sums as the Secretary of State may determine in respect of general staff costs and overheads. The persons from whom costs are recoverable include anyone successfully prosecuted as a result of the investigation[97]; those who applied for the appointment of inspectors to carry out a general investigation or an investigation into share ownership up to an amount determined by the Secretary of State[98]; and any body corporate dealt with in an inspectors' report (when the inspectors were not appointed on the Secretary of State's own motion), unless the body corporate was also the applicant, or except insofar as the Secretary of State otherwise directs.[99] Accordingly, in the context of investigations, the only persons at risk of costs are those subsequently prosecuted and, even where inspectors are appointed, the same is true if the Secretary of State takes the initiative to appoint the inspectors. **21–012**

FOLLOW-UP TO INVESTIGATIONS

Following an investigation, whether by inspectors or otherwise, the Secretary of State has a number of powers. The obvious follow-up involves the mounting of prosecutions against those whose crimes have come to light by either the Secretary of State or the Serious Fraud Office. Further, the Secretary of State may petition for the disqualification of a director or shadow director on grounds of unfitness[100] or petition the court for an appropriate order if unfair prejudice to all **21–013**

---

[94] CA 1985 s.445(1). See further Ch.28.

[95] CA 1985 s.445(1A).

[96] CA 1985 s.439(1). The expenses of an inspection are likely to be heavy. The Atlantic Computers investigation cost £6.5 million and the Consolidated Goldfields one nearly £4 million: see DTI, *Company Investigations: Powers for the Twenty-First Century* (2001), Annex A. The total costs to the companies and their officers were probably as great or greater.

[97] CA 1985 s.439(2).

[98] CA 1985 s.439(5).

[99] CA 1985 s.439(4). Inspectors appointed otherwise than on the Secretary of State's own motion may, and shall if so directed, include in their report a recommendation about costs: CA 1985 s.439(6). The exercise of the Secretary of State's rights regarding costs can give rise to indemnification and contribution issues: CA 1985 s.439(8)–(9).

[100] Company Directors Disqualification Act 1986 s.8(1). For statistics on disqualifications under this provision, see Companies House, *Management Information 2019–2020*, Table 6, indicating that only

or some of the company's members has been revealed.[101] Alternatively, or in addition to these forms of relief, the Secretary of State may petition for the winding-up of the company on the ground that "it is expedient in the public interest that a company should be wound up".[102] A court will grant the petition if it concludes that it would be "just and equitable" for the company to be placed into liquidation.[103] In 2015–2016, 85 companies were wound up on the Secretary of State's petition.[104] What the Secretary of State can no longer do is initiate proceedings in the name and on behalf of the body corporate, indemnifying the company against any costs or expenses incurred in connection with the proceedings. This power was removed by the CA 2006,[105] perhaps on the basis that remedies for the benefit of the company should be a matter for its members.[106] By contrast, taking companies off the register and disqualifying unfit persons from future involvement in the management of companies may well be steps that no member has an interest in taking.

Since the majority of investigations and inspections are driven by allegations of potentially serious wrongdoing on the part of those involved in companies, it is hardly surprising that the Secretary of State does not simply receive the information produced by the investigation machinery, but makes use of the possibilities just described to take remedial steps of one sort or another. To this end, there is a long list of exceptions to the starting proposition that information obtained pursuant to the Secretary of State's powers of investigation is confidential and cannot be disseminated more widely without the consent of the company.[107] These so-called "gateways" permit the information to be provided to those who are best placed to take the consequential action.

21–014 This possibility of subsequent action, however, brings into sharp focus the rules that permit investigators and inspectors to secure information compulsorily. Although the domestic courts had held to the contrary before the enactment of the Human Rights Act 1998,[108] the European Court of Human Rights, in *Saunders v*

---

one disqualification order was made on this ground in the period 2012–2016. This has increased since 2016 because there is no longer a requirement to conduct an investigation before using this basis of disqualification. See further Ch.20.

[101] CA 2006 s.995(1). See para.14–013.

[102] IA 1986 s.124A(1).

[103] IA 1986 s.124A(1).

[104] *Insolvency Service Annual Report 2016–7*, p.18. Over the years the annual reports of the Insolvency Service have become far less useful in providing comprehensive information about what the agency does, now simply delivering generalised descriptions of success coupled with selective examples. The winding-up application cannot be made on the basis of information supplied under the voluntary method of providing information, considered in para.21–002: see IA s.124A(1)(a).

[105] CA 1985 s.438 was repealed by the CA 2006 from April 2007.

[106] For the same reason the Department seems to make little or no use of its power to bring unfair prejudice petitions.

[107] CA 1985 s.449. The gateways are set out in the CA 1985 Schs 15C–15D. The same provisions apply to information provided voluntarily: see para.21–002. Where information and documents obtained under the CA 1985 s.447 are disclosed to a court, s.449 no longer operates as a bar to the documents being used during the hearing and a party "must thereafter rely on the supervision by the court on the issue of the maintenance of confidentiality if it is appropriate for it to continue": see *Carton-Kelly v Edwards* [2020] EWHC 131 (Ch) at [43].

[108] *Re London United Investments Plc* [1992] Ch. 578; *Bishopsgate Investment Management Ltd v Maxwell* [1993] Ch. 1.

United Kingdom,[109] concluded that evidence given to inspectors under threat of compulsion cannot normally be used in subsequent criminal proceedings against those investigated, as this would infringe their privilege against self-incrimination. The CA 1985 now provides that compelled testimony (but not documents produced under compulsion) may not be used in either primary evidence or cross-examination in a subsequent criminal trial of the person.[110]

There are, however, exceptions where the defendant him- or herself has relied upon the compelled testimony, or where the offence in question is giving false evidence to the investigator or certain offences under the legislation relating to perjury.[111] Similarly, there is also an exemption for the subsequent use of testimony in disqualification proceedings.[112] Indeed, an inspectors' report can be evidence as to the opinion of the inspectors in such an application, and the courts have come to the same conclusion in respect of a report by investigators.[113] Both the domestic courts and the European Court of Human Rights seem to agree that disqualification applications are not criminal proceedings.[114] If disqualification applications are not criminal proceedings, nevertheless they are clearly proceedings falling within art.6 of the ECHR because they determine the legal rights of the person against whom the application is brought. Unlike the investigation process itself, which lies outside the scope of art.6 of the ECHR,[115] disqualification proceedings will have to comply with the ECHR standards appropriate for civil proceedings. These standards do not specifically include a privilege against self-incrimination, but they do involve general standards of fairness. Indeed, as disqualification orders involve a penal element, the presumption of innocence might be relevant.[116] Presumably, the same considerations will apply where it is proposed to use compelled testimony in purely civil litigation[117]: there will be no ban in principle, but the court conducting the civil trial will need to have regard to general fairness issues. One such issue, already identified by the English courts in the context of compulsory examination under the IA 1986, is the undesirability of allowing statutory powers to give one party a

---

[109] *Saunders v United Kingdom* [1998] 1 B.C.L.C. 362 ECHR; *IJL v United Kingdom* (2001) 33 E.H.R.R. 11 ECHR. For a sceptical assessment, see P. Davies, "Self-incrimination, Fair Trials and the Pursuit of Corporate and Financial Wrongdoing" in B. Markesinis (ed.), *The Impact of the Human Rights Bill on English Law* (Oxford: OUP, 1998). The House of Lords refused to quash the convictions of those involved despite the breach of the Convention: *R. v Saunders*, Times Law Reports, 15 November 2002.

[110] CA 1985 s.447A(1).

[111] CA 1985 s.447A(3). Nor do the amendments specifically exclude evidence to which the prosecuting authorities were drawn as a result of the compelled testimony, where the answers themselves are not used in the criminal trial.

[112] CA 1985 s.441(1).

[113] *Re Rex Williams Leisure Plc* [1994] Ch. 350 CA.

[114] *R. v Secretary of State for Trade and Industry Ex p. McCormick* [1998] B.C.C. 379 CA; *DC v United Kingdom* [2000] B.C.C. 710 ECHR.

[115] *Al-Fayed v United Kingdom* (1994) 18 E.H.R.R. 393.

[116] *Albert and Le Compte v Belgium* (1983) 5 E.H.R.R. 533 ECHR. The Court of Appeal remains of the view that general fairness does not in principle require the exclusion of compelled testimony: see *Re Westminster Property Management Ltd* [2000] 2 B.C.L.C. 396 CA.

[117] The inspectors' report is also admissible: see CA 1985 s.441.

litigation advantage over another in purely civil litigation that that party would not have were the company not insolvent.[118]

CONCLUSION

21–015 Since the scheme of administrative remedies under the CA 1985 is dominated by the power of investigation, and this power is predominantly used in cases of suspected fraudulent trading or breach of the disqualification provisions, it is far from clear that these remedies constitute an important element in the British system of corporate governance (assuming that is defined as the accountability of the senior management to the shareholders as a whole). In reality, these statutory powers of investigation may have more in common with issues concerning the abuse of limited liability.[119] Whilst this area has echoes of the law relating to breaches of directors' duties[120] and the unfair prejudice jurisdiction,[121] the Secretary of State tends to leave these matters to be pursued by companies or shareholders themselves, perhaps now through the reformed derivative action procedure,[122] unless either there is a strong public interest in favour of intervention by the Secretary of State or the misconduct of the directors has been egregious. Nevertheless, administrative remedies are an important part of corporate law, and shareholders may benefit from them indirectly where an inspectors' report reveals matters that lead to the reform of company law.[123]

---

[118] *Cloverbay Ltd v BCCI SA* [1991] Ch. 90 CA.

[119] See further Ch.7.

[120] See further Ch.10.

[121] See further Ch.14.

[122] See further Ch.15.

[123] Indeed, substantial elements of the statutory duties of directors in the CA 2006 are in response to abuses revealed in inspectors' reports.

PART 7

ACCOUNTS AND AUDIT

It has been accepted since the early days of modern company law that mandatory publicity about the company's affairs was an important regulatory tool. For shareholders in large companies with dispersed shareholdings it operates to reduce the risk of management incompetence or self-seeking. The non-director shareholders of a company will have a difficult task to judge the effectiveness of the management of the company if they do not have access to relevant data about the company's financial performance. For creditors it operates to reduce the risks of dealing with an entity to whose assets alone the creditors can normally look for re-payment. In fact, mandatory disclosure has long been seen as something which could legitimately be asked for in exchange for the freedom to trade with limited liability,[1] though there has been controversy throughout the history of company law about how extensive the disclosure rules should be. Today, therefore, there is a major difference between the disclosure rules applicable to ordinary partnerships (without limited liability) and those applicable to companies, with limited liability partnerships being rightly placed in the company category for these purposes, because they benefit from limited liability.[2] Given this range of interests in disclosure of information by companies, it is not surprising that successive company scandals have provoked demands for ever more far-reaching mandatory disclosure of information, and such demands have often been successful. As of the beginning of 2021, following the collapse of the Carillion company in 2018, the Government was contemplating further proposals to change the law considered in the following two chapters, despite an almost continuous process of reform which has occurred throughout this century.

So far as the companies legislation is concerned, the main instrument for delivering mandatory disclosure has been the annual accounts and reports—which the directors are required to produce, have verified by the company's auditors (except for "small" companies), lay before the members in general meeting (or otherwise distribute to them in the case of private companies) and register in a public registry. This development over the years has produced an

[1] An unlimited liability company is not normally required to make its accounts available to the public: see para.21–036.

[2] See G. Morse et al, *Palmer's Limited Liability Partnership Law*, 2nd edn (London: Sweet & Maxwell, 2012), Ch.3.

elaborate body of rules. The desire of the Company Law Review to use mandatory disclosure to promote an "enlightened shareholder value" approach to company law has led to reforms which require disclosure of information which is not directly financial, but concerns the quality of the company's relationships with those who are capable of making a major contribution to the success of the business or about the impact of the company's operations upon the community in which it operates. This has led to the development of what is sometimes called "narrative" or "non-financial" reporting. Further, at EU level the impact of various corporate scandals in the early years of this century only served to make the rules on financial and non-financial reporting even more elaborate, especially in relation to the verification of the accounts through the process of audit. Those developments remain part of domestic law as "retained EU law". Accounts and audit are the subject of the two chapters in this Part.

However, mandatory disclosure can be seen as an instrument, not only of corporate law (for the benefit of shareholders, creditors and other stakeholders) but of financial services or securities law (for the benefit of investors and the efficient functioning of the capital markets). Consequently, we shall return to the issue of mandatory disclosure in Pt 8, where we analyse the additional disclosure requirements which apply to companies whose securities are traded on a public securities market.

CHAPTER 22

ACCOUNTS AND REPORTS

INTRODUCTION

On the basis that "forewarned is forearmed" the fundamental principle underlying the Companies Acts has always been that of disclosure. If the public and the members were enabled to find out all relevant information about the company, this, thought the founding fathers of our company law, would be a sure shield. The shield may not have proved quite so strong as they had expected and in more recent times it has been supported by offensive weapons. However, disclosure still remains the basic safeguard on which the Companies Acts pin their faith, and every succeeding Act since 1862 has added to the extent of the publicity required, although, not unreasonably, what is required varies according to the type of company concerned. Not only may disclosure by itself promote efficient conduct of the company's business, because the company's controllers (whether directors or large shareholders) may fear the reputational losses associated with the **22–001** revelation of incompetence or self-dealing, but the more interventionist legal strategies, going beyond disclosure, depend upon those who hold the legal rights being well-informed about the company's position. For example, shareholders contemplating the enforcement the company's rights against directors for breach of duty or bringing claims of unfair prejudice[1] or removing directors,[2] will need good information about the company in order to assess whether their claims are well-founded. Finally, effective self-help, such as taking contractual protection or altering the pricing of credit or a trade union negotiating with the management, is facilitated by good knowledge of the company's financial position. Thus, disclosure is the bed-rock of company law.

22–002 There are many occasions upon which companies are obliged to make disclosures, especially if their shares are publicly traded, as we see in Chs 27, 28 and 30, but the core disclosure requirement for all companies is the obligation upon the directors to produce annual accounts and associated reports. This chapter is focused on that central disclosure mechanism. This is often regarded as an area of the law which is both challenging for non-accountants and short on interest for them, but it is a central element in the corporate governance of companies and one whose reach has expanded enormously in recent years.

The word "account" has two, somewhat different, associations. One may give an account *of* a set of events, in this case of the company's progress or lack of it over a period of time. One may also account *for* one's conduct in relation to those events. The word as used in the legislation carries both associations, with the latter having become increasingly dominant over time. Hence the frequent statement that the accounts reveal how the directors have discharged their "stewardship" of the company. In the nineteenth century and for much later accounting requirements were formulated almost wholly in terms of quantitative reporting. The accounts were thus dominated by numbers which aimed to reveal the financial performance of the company over a recent reporting period. For this reason, perhaps, it is more common in international discourse to use the term "financial statements" rather than accounts. The two central elements of these financial statements are the profit-and-loss account and the balance sheet (though other names are sometimes used). In very broad terms, the former shows the company's income and expenditure over a period of time, so as to assess its profitability (or lack of it) during that period[3]; the latter shows its assets and liabilities at a moment in time (normally the end of the reporting period), thus revealing its "net asset value" (assets minus liabilities), which may be positive or negative at that point.

To fully serve the disclosure objective, it is not enough for companies to produce numbers which have been assembled on some defensible basis. It is important for shareholders and others to be able to compare performance across companies and, indeed, across jurisdictions. For example, is a company doing well or badly because of factors idiosyncratic to it or because of general industry- or economy-wide factors? Comparability of accounts requires standardised ways of reporting financial events. The production of accounting standards fell initially

[1] See Ch.14.

[2] See Ch.9.

[3] See further para.22–019.

to the domestic accounting profession, which thus came to dominate the area of corporate reporting. That profession then re-appears in the guise of auditors to verify that the accounts do meet those standards and the applicable legal rules and, in particular, present a "true and fair view" of the company's financial position.[4] However, in recent years the production of accounting (and auditing) standards has become the function of bodies on which the public interest is represented more or less strongly and it has become an international activity, at least in relation to publicly traded companies, as we see in para.22–020.

A very significant development in recent decades has been the addition to backward-looking financial reporting of forward-looking qualitative assessments, usually referred to as "narrative" reporting.[5] Even from the early days, the accounts were accompanied by a narrative report from the directors, usually claiming credit if all had gone well during the reporting period or seeking to deflect blame elsewhere, if it had not. However, modern narrative reporting, as it has developed this century, goes well beyond this limited function. Two goals can be distinguished. First, the backward-looking nature of traditional financial accounts provided only limited help in forming assessments about how the company might do in the future, even though this was a primary concern of investors.[6] As the Company Law Review Steering Group said in 2001, when proposing the introduction to what eventually became the Strategic Report,[7] "But companies are increasingly reliant on qualitative and intangible assets such as the skills and knowledge of their employees, their business relationships and their reputation. Information about future plans, opportunities, risks and strategies is just as important as the historical review of performance which forms the basis for reporting at present."[8] The second goal, which has become increasingly important, is a regulatory one. Government, wishing to nudge companies into adopting certain policies it favours, but uncertain how to embody the policy in firm rules, may opt instead for extensive disclosure by the company of the impact of its activities in the chosen area. Whilst disclosure that the company has not promoted the policy the government favours is not by itself illegal, the expectation is that the company's desire to avoid the reputational harm attached to non-promotion will cause it to adapt its behaviour. It is helpful to government, of course, it such steps can be presented as in the "long-term" interest of shareholders as well. **22–003**

---

[4] See Ch.23.

[5] See paras 22–024 onwards.

[6] This limitation, although real, should not be exaggerated. The present value of assets on the balance sheet represents an estimate of their potential future revenue-generating capacity. See, for example, the newspaper headline "John Lewis to scrap staff bonus and cut value of stores by £470m" (*The Guardian*, 17 September 2020), reflecting the shift of customers to online shopping.

[7] The tortured history of the CLR's proposals from "Operating and Financial Review" to "Strategic Report" is given in the 10th edition of this work at para.21–24.

[8] CLRSG, *Final Report* (2001), Vol.1, para.3.33.

FINANCIAL REPORTING

The classification of companies for the purposes of annual reporting

22–004 The accounting rules have developed a classification of companies which is more sophisticated than the core division deployed in the Act between public and private companies. That distinction turns on whether the company is permitted to offer its shares to the public or not.[9] The accounting classification turns mainly on the economic size of the company. Its purpose is to align levels of disclosure to what are perceived to be different levels of public interest in the activities of companies of various sizes and to make those disclosure obligations proportionate to the economic size of the company. However, the public/private distinction still plays a role because public companies are excluded from the three smallest categories of company (micro, small and medium) for (most) accounts purposes, no matter their economic size.[10] Since the ramifications of the classification run throughout the substantive rules on accounts, it is important to set it out at the beginning. The criteria upon which the classification is based were derived from EU law, where the harmonisation of accounting rules was a major focus.

There are five categories of company for accounts purposes: micro, small,[11] medium-sized, large and "public interest entities" (PIE). The criteria for identifying the first four categories are quantitative indicators of the economic size of the company and are designed to be capable of application in a fairly mechanistic way. The PIE category is a cross-cutting category but, for the general run of companies in the UK, it will form a sub-set of the large company category. The criteria used refer to the company's "balance sheet total", a perhaps not entirely clear phrase which refers to amount of the company's assets (without subtracting liabilities)[12]; its turnover[13]; and the number of persons employed by it on average over the year.[14] In order to classified as micro, small or medium-sized the company has to meet two of the three applicable criteria; the "large" category is a residual one into which companies otherwise fall; and the PIE classification turns on a different approach.

---

[9] See para.1–008.

[10] CA 2006 s.384B(1).

[11] Small Business Enterprise and Employment Act 2015 ss.33 and 34 envisage the use of the micro and small business definitions in subordinate legislation to relieve these categories of regulatory duties beyond the accounting area.

[12] CA 2006 ss.382(5) and 384A(6): "The balance sheet total means the aggregate of the amounts shown as assets in the company's balance sheet".

[13] "'turnover' means the amounts derived from the provision of goods and services after deduction of (a) trade discounts, (b) value added tax and (c) any other taxes based on the amounts so derived." (CA 2006 s.474(1)).

[14] Employed means only those employed under a contract of service: ss.382(6) and 384A(7). So, no Uber workers here.

Micro companies

Micro companies are private companies[15] for which the balance sheet maximum is £316,000; the maximum net turnover £632,000 and the maximum number of employees is 10.[16] However, a micro company will not have access to the reporting relaxations if it is a member of a corporate group which prepares group accounts,[17] presumably because those relaxations might undermine the group accounts. In short, the micro exemptions are available principally to stand alone companies, which reinforces their focus on very small businesses. **22–005**

Companies on the borderline of the criteria might find themselves drifting in and out of qualification as micro companies on a yearly basis. This problem is addressed, as it is with the other categories, by requiring that companies meet the criteria for two years in order to qualify as micro and equally by providing that micro status will not be lost unless the criteria are not met for two consecutive years.[18] As is to be expected, the micro company benefits from the least demanding reporting regime. The category was the result of an EU level initiative in 2012.[19] It operated by giving Member States the option to remove from micro companies requirements that would otherwise apply to them under the regime for small companies. The UK chose to take up most of the options made available in the Directive.[20] Of course, the directors of micro companies may choose to report more fully.

Small companies

The criteria are: £5.1 million for balance sheet; £10.2 million for turnover; and 50 employees.[21] A company which qualifies as small can normally benefit from the "small companies regime" for the accounts and reports, which is less stringent than that for larger companies. Some 3 million of the approximately 3.5 million companies in the UK fall within either the "small" or "micro" categories, so that in numerical terms the relaxations for small and micro companies are very important and the full accounting regime is of concern only to the numerical minority of companies.[22] **22–006**

A company which meets the numerical criteria nevertheless cannot count as a small company if it is a public company or carries on insurance, banking or fund management activities or is a member of a group which contains an "ineligible"

---

[15] CA 2006 s.384(B), other than charities and financial companies which are excluded from the micro regime, even if private: ss.384(1).

[16] CA 2006 s.384A.

[17] CA 2006 s.384B(2). On group accounts see para.22–011.

[18] CA 2006 s.384A(3). For small companies see s.382(2). By way of qualification to this, in its first year of operation the company's status is determined by whether it meets the criteria at the end of that year (s.384A(2)), so that a small start-up does not have to wait for a second year to benefit.

[19] Directive 2012/6/EU [2012] OJ L81/3.

[20] BIS, *Simpler Financial Reporting For Micro-Entities: The UK's Proposal To Implement The "Micros Directive": Government Response* (September 2013), BIS/13/1124.

[21] CA 2006 s.382.

[22] BIS, *UK implementation of the EU Accounting Directive: Chapters 1–9: Impact Assessment* (2014), BIS/14/1055.

member.[23] The thought here appears to be that such companies (or groups of which they are members) are engaged in sufficiently sensitive activities that full disclosure is required, especially for the benefit of the relevant regulators, and, in the case of public companies, the fact that they are free to offer their shares to the public suggests that a full financial record should be available.

Medium-sized companies

22–007 Somewhat misleadingly placed some 80 sections away from the provisions on small companies is to be found, in the "supplementary provisions" to Pt 15, the definition of a medium-sized company. The criteria here are: balance sheet total of not more than £18 million, turnover not more than £36 million and not more than 250 employees.[24] There are similarly-motivated, but not identical, exclusions from this category as we saw in the small category, amongst which, crucially, are public companies.[25] In some ways, however, placing these definitions in the "supplementary provisions" of the Part dealing with accounts is appropriate, for medium-sized companies and groups benefit from rather fewer relaxations from the full accounts requirements, as compared with small companies. The CLR recommended the removal of this category on the grounds that it was neither much used nor valued, but this suggestion was not taken up.[26]

Large companies and public interest entities

22–008 Large companies are simply those which do not meet the quantitative criteria needed to fall within the medium-sized or any smaller category.[27] Public interest entities are companies whose securities are admitted to trading on a regulated market in the UK,[28] which the CA 2006 terms a "traded company".[29] In addition, the category includes any bank or insurance company (whether so traded or not). PIEs are already subject to special audit treatment, as we shall see in the next chapter. As for accounting, the principal impact of the rules is that PIEs, like other publlic companies, should always report as large companies.[30] It is seriously open to doubt whether any PIE would qualify as medium-sized even without this express exclusion. The PIE category is, in fact, of most interest in the context of narrative reporting, where extensive disclosure requirements are placed on traded companies, as we shall see below.

There is a further dimension to financial reporting by companies traded on public markets. Those who introduced the reporting obligation in the nineteenth

---

[23] CA 2006 s.384(1). The definition of ineligibility for groups includes a somewhat wider range of financial companies (s.384(2)).

[24] CA 2006 s.465(3).

[25] CA 2006 s.467(1).

[26] Developing, para.8.35.

[27] Directive art.3.

[28] For the meaning of a "regulated" market see para.25–007. In the UK the principal such market is the Main Market of the London Stock Exchange.

[29] CA 2006 s.474(1). BEIS, *Restoring Trust in Audit and Corporate Governance* (March 2021), proposes to include within the PIE category certain large but not publicly traded companies.

[30] As must any group containing a publicly traded company (s.467(2)(a)).

century thought that annual reporting was sufficiently frequent. Modern equity markets, however, have an insatiable thirst for information, which is not satisfied by the annual reporting obligations discussed in this chapter. As we shall see in Ch.27, publicly traded companies are now subject to extensive disclosure requirements which operate throughout the company's financial year. Such rules include more frequent periodic reporting than the annual requirements of the CA 2006, as well as significant requirements for the episodic or ad hoc reporting of particular events. Even in relation to the annual reports, which remain a very significant reporting occasion, it is the point at which the company makes a preliminary announcement to the market of its financial results for the previous year (the "prelims")[31] which moves the market. Such announcements—and the later full accounts and reports, though they are somewhat stale news by then—are pored over by analysts, whose task it is to generate advice for investors.

Accounting records

The statutory provisions relating to the annual accounts begin by imposing on the company a continuing obligation to maintain accounting records.[32] This is logical enough, because, although these records are not open to inspection by members or the public, unless they are kept it will be impossible for the company to produce accurate annual accounts or for the auditors to verify them. Hence, s.386 provides that every company—no matter how categorised for other accounting purposes—shall keep records sufficient to show and explain the company's transactions, to disclose with reasonable accuracy at any time its financial position and to enable its directors to ensure that any balance sheet and profit and loss account will comply with the relevant accounting standards.[33] **22–009**

A company which has a subsidiary undertaking to which these requirements do not apply[34] must take all reasonable steps to secure that the subsidiary keeps such records as will enable the directors of the parent company to ensure that any accounts required of the parent company comply with the relevant requirements.[35]

Failure to comply with the section renders every officer of the company—a term which includes managers and the company secretary as well as directors—who is in default guilty of an offence[36] unless the officer can shows that he or she acted honestly and that, in the circumstances in which the company's business was carried on, the default was excusable.[37] But the company itself is not liable, which seems correct since the shareholders bear the

---

31 Such a preliminary statement used to be obligatory for listed companies, but ceased to be so in January 2007, in the light of the implementation of the Transparency Directive, though companies continue to make such announcements and the Listing Rules regulate the form they must take, if made. See LR 9.7A.1 and Ch.27.

32 CA 2006 ss.386–389.

33 CA 2006 s.386(2). Subsection (3) adds certain specific requirements the records must meet, but, except for unsophisticated businesses, the general standards are likely to be more important.

34 e.g. because it is a foreign subsidiary or a partnership.

35 CA 2006 s.386(5).

36 Punishable by fine or imprisonment or both: s.387(3).

37 CA 2006 s.387(2).

costs of corporate fines but the requirement for accurate records is imposed for their benefit. More effective in practice is probably the duty laid on the auditor to check whether adequate accounting records have been kept and to reveal failure to do so in the auditor's report.[38]

Section 388 provides that accounting records are at all times to be open for inspection by officers of the company.[39] If any such records are kept outside the UK,[40] there must be sent to the UK (and be available for inspection there by the officers) records which will disclose with reasonable accuracy the position of the business in question at intervals of not more than six months and which will enable the directors to ensure that the company's balance sheet and profit and loss account comply with the statutory requirements.[41] All required records must be preserved for three years if it is a private company or for six years if it is a public one.[42]

The financial year

22–010 The first step in the production of the annual accounts is to fix the company's financial year. Sections 390–392 prescribe how this is to be done. The financial year is not required to be the calendar year and is normally not, given the inconvenience of having a major corporate milestone at the end of December. In principle, it is any period of 12 months, but there is both some flexibility around this principle. What that period actually is depends for any particular company on its "accounting reference period" (ARP), which in turn depends on its "accounting reference date" ("ARD"), which is the date in the calendar year on which the company's ARP ends. For companies incorporated after 1 April 1996, the company's ARD will be the anniversary of the last day of the month in which it was incorporated.[43] However, the company may choose a new ARD for the current and future ARPs and even for its immediately preceding one.[44] This it may well want to do for a variety of reasons; for instance, if the company has been taken over and wishes to bring its ARD into line with that of its new parent.[45] The new ARD may operate either to shorten or to lengthen the ARP

---

[38] CA 2006 s.498(2). Failure to keep adequate accounting records could also form the basis of a disqualification of a director under the general heading of unfitness (*Re Galeforce Pleating Co Ltd* [1999] 2 B.C.L.C. 705).

[39] For this reason, accountants may not exercise a lien for unpaid fees over such documents: *DTC (CNC) Ltd v Gary Sargeant & Co* [1996] 1 B.C.L.C. 529 Ch D. Of course, other persons may also have the right of access to the records, for example, the company's auditors: s.499.

[40] e.g. because the company has a branch outside Great Britain.

[41] CA 2006 s.388(2)–(3). The six-monthly requirement seems remarkably lax in the light of both modern management practice and modern electronic technology.

[42] CA 2006 s.388(4). An officer of the company is liable to imprisonment or a fine or both if s/he fails to take all reasonable steps to secure compliance with the preservation requirement or intentionally causes any default: s.389(4). If there has been villainy, destroying all record of it is all too likely.

[43] CA 2006 s.391(4). For companies in Northern Ireland the relevant date is 22 August 1997. For methods of determining the ARD for earlier incorporations see s.391(2)–(3).

[44] CA 2006 s.392. This section applies no matter when the company was incorporated.

[45] Indeed, in this particular situation, in order to promote the production of group accounts, the directors of the parent company are under a presumptive duty to ensure that the financial years of subsidiaries coincide with that of the parent: s.390(5).

within which the change is made,[46] but in the latter case the company may not normally extend the ARP to more than 18 months[47] and may not normally engage in the process of extending the ARP more than once every five years.[48] These are necessary safeguards against obvious abuses, for constantly changing ARPs make comparisons across the years difficult. The company's financial year then corresponds to its ARP, as fixed according to the above rules, except that the directors have a discretion to make the financial year end at any point up to seven days before or seven days after the end of the ARP.[49]

Individual accounts and group accounts

Subject to a very limited exception, s.394 imposes on the directors of every company the duty to prepare for each financial year a set of accounts of the company (its "individual accounts"). This duty applies even to the directors of small and micro companies, though the requirements as to what the accounts have to contain in those cases are less onerous. Subject to more extensive exceptions, noted below, s.399 imposes a duty on directors of a company which is a parent company additionally to prepare a consolidated balance sheet and profit and loss account ("group accounts"). Those group accounts must deal with the state of affairs of the parent company and its "subsidiary undertakings"—taken together.[50] Given the frequency with which even small businesses are carried on through groups of companies or other entities and the limited relevance in such a case of individual accounts, even of the parent company, this is obviously an important extension of the accounts rules. For example, if all the profits are earned in operating subsidiaries and have not been passed up to the parent at the time when the parent's individual accounts are prepared, those accounts would present a very partial picture of the position of the business. **22–011**

However, the obligation to produce group accounts is qualified by one very significant exception: it does not apply to parents of groups subject to the "small companies regime"—or would be were it not for the fact that the parent is a public company.[51] The inclusion of public companies is a potentially significant extension since public companies are normally excluded from the "small" category.[52] It is obvious that this exemption could undermine the requirement for group accounts, for example, where those in control of the business ensured that the operations of the group were carried on and its employees were employed principally in companies below the parent which itself was a small company. Consequently, access to the small companies regime is restricted in two important ways. First, it does not apply if the group contains (normally but not necessarily

[46] CA 2006 s.392(2).

[47] CA 2006 s.392(5), unless an administration order is in force in relation to the company, presumably because the administrator, who is responsible to the court, can be trusted in a way the directors cannot.

[48] CA 2006 s.392(3), unless an administration order is in force (see previous note) or the step is taken to make the ARD coincide with that of an EEA undertaking which is the company's parent or subsidiary company, or the Secretary of State permits it.

[49] CA 2006 s.390(2)–(3).

[50] CA 2006 s.404(1).

[51] CA 2006 s.399(2A)(a).

[52] See para 22–006.

as the parent) a public company that is a "traded" company.[53] Secondly, in order to benefit from the small company group exemption, the test is not whether the parent is small, but whether the group as a whole meets the relevant criteria.[54] The size tests for a small group are the same as for a stand-alone company except that intra-group transactions may be eliminated when calculating turnover and balance sheet totals; alternatively, the parent company may choose instead to benefit from higher levels (by one fifth) without eliminating intra-group transactions.[55] Overall, the combined effect of these two restrictions is to limit significantly the access of groups containing public companies to the exemption from the obligation to produce group accounts.

There is no special exemption for micro companies in relation to group accounts. Indeed, if a micro company is part of a group, the micro relaxations are not available for its individual accounts.[56] However, since, by definition, a micro company will also be a small company, it will be able to benefit from the small company regime when producing its individual accounts as a member of a group and will benefit from the small company exemption from the requirement to produce group accounts if it is the parent company.

There is a similar approach to that used for a small group in the definition of a medium-sized group.[57] However, a medium-sized group is not exempted from the obligation to produce group accounts, but it may report less fully.

22–012 The obligation to produce group accounts does not relieve the directors of the parent company from the obligation to produce individual accounts for the parent[58] nor, subject to one exception, the directors of the other companies in the group from that obligation in relation to their company.[59] The individual and group accounts of companies within a group should be produced, in principle, using the same financial reporting framework.[60] The principle that the production of group accounts should not normally remove the obligation to render individual accounts is as it should be. Creditors, in particular, may well have claims only against particular companies in the group, unless they have contracted for guarantees from other group members, and so the group picture alone might be misleading. Equally, shareholders of the parent may have an interest knowing more about where the profits of the group are actually generated.[61]

---

[53] CA 2006 s.384(2)(a). For the meaning of this term see para.22–008. Companies operating in various financial businesses are also excluded by s.384(2).

[54] CA 2006 s.383(1).

[55] CA 2006 s.383(4)–(7). The choice is available separately in relation to each of the turnover and balance sheet tests: s.383(6).

[56] CA 2006 s.384B(2).

[57] CA 2006 ss.466–467.

[58] CA 2006 s.399(2)—"as well as producing individual accounts". Section 408 permits certain relaxations for the individual accounts of a company which produces group accounts, notably that the company's individual profit and loss account need not be circulated to the shareholders or filed with the Registrar, if notes to the individual balance sheet, which is circulated and filed, show the profit and loss of the company for the financial year.

[59] CA 2006 s.394—"the directors of every company".

[60] CA 2006 s.407. For the meaning of "financial reporting framework" see para.22–016.

[61] Nevertheless, it is crucial to remember that dividends are paid on the basis of only individual accounts alone. If the profits of a subsidiary are paid directly to the shareholders of the parent, all sorts of legal problems arise. See Ch.18, fn.28.

The exception from the obligation for group companies to produce individual accounts relates to subsidiaries which have been dormant throughout the relevant financial year (unless the subsidiary is a traded company—a rare situation). This exemption is subject to conditions, in particular that all the members of the subsidiary agree (easy enough if the subsidiary is wholly owned), that the company is included in appropriately drawn consolidated accounts and that the parent guarantees the liabilities of the subsidiary as they existed at the end of the year in relation to which the exemption applied (and all this is disclosed).[62] All this may seem rather elaborate for exempting a company from producing individual accounts when, by definition, a dormant company has engaged in no significant accounting transactions during the financial year.[63]

Parent and subsidiary undertakings

The obligation to produce group accounts gives rise to the need to define a subsidiary undertaking. The situation may be clear when Company A holds all the voting shares in Company B, but suppose it holds only 30% of them. What is then the position? The answer is provided by ss.1161 and 1162 and Sch.7. The term "undertaking" is used rather than "company" because consolidation of the accounts is required even if the subsidiary business does not take the form of a company or some other body corporate, but is a partnership or other unincorporated body.[64] Thus, although group accounts are required by the CA 2006 to be compiled only by entities which are companies,[65] the shareholders and creditors of and investors in those companies are to be provided with financial information relating to all the businesses the parent controls, no matter what legal form they may take. **22–013**

But what is control? This issue is addressed in s.1162 of and Sch.7 to the Act. Briefly summarised, these situations are where the parent company:

(1) holds a majority of voting rights in the undertaking[66];
(2) is a member of the other undertaking and has the right to appoint or remove a majority of its board of directors[67];
(3) by virtue of provisions in the constitution of the other undertaking or in a written "control contract", permitted by that constitution, has a right, recognised by the law under which that undertaking is established, to exercise a "dominant influence" over that undertaking (by giving directions to the directors of the undertaking on its operating and financial policies

[62] CA 2006 ss.394A–C. Even so, the usual financial companies cannot take advantage of the exemption. At times the authorities have considered a wider policy of exempting subsidiaries generally from producing individual accounts in exchange for a parent company guarantee. However, the policy has always failed on the basis that it would reduce the amount of information available about the activities of potentially economically important subsidiaries.

[63] CA 2006 s.1169.

[64] CA 2006 s.1161(1).

[65] CA 2006 s.399(2).

[66] CA 2006 s.1162(2)(a).

[67] CA 2006 s.1162(2)(b). Membership includes "indirect" membership, i.e. where a subsidiary of the parent is a member of the undertaking in question: s.1162(3).

which those directors are obliged to comply with whether or not the directions are for the benefit of the undertaking)[68];

(4) has the power to exercise or actually exercises dominant influence or control over the undertaking or the parent and alleged subsidiary are actually managed on a unified basis[69];

(5) is a member of another undertaking and alone controls, pursuant to an agreement with other members, a majority of the voting rights in that undertaking[70];

and sub-subsidiaries are to be treated as subsidiaries of the ultimate parent also.[71]

Having its origin in EU law, not all the cases covered are significant in the UK. The most important case in the UK is (1), unless, which is not likely to be common, the requirements of one of the other cases are satisfied. Thus, the answer to our question is that a holding of 30% by Company A in Company B will not, by itself, make Company B its subsidiary. However, companies are not permitted to remain entirely silent about their significant relationships with companies other than subsidiaries. Companies have to disclose in their individual or group accounts certain information about companies, not being subsidiaries, in which they have nevertheless a significant holding.[72] However, such "affiliated" companies do not have to be consolidated into the group accounts.

Parent companies which are part of a larger group

22–014 A parent/subsidiary relationship will exist under the above definition even where the parent (the "intermediate parent") is itself the subsidiary of another company. In groups of companies this situation often exists. There may be a chain of companies in which all but the bottom company meet the statutory definition for being a parent of the company (or companies) below them in the chain. The resulting proliferation of group accounts of varying scope is not likely to be helpful. Consequently, there are exemptions which apply in such cases. The terms of the exemption vary according to the level of the parent's shareholding in the

[68] CA 2006 s.1162(2)(c) and Sch.7 para.4. Parts of the definition reflect the EU origins of the UK's current accounting rules and thus refer to situations probably rarely, if ever, found in the UK. "Contractual subordination" is an example.

[69] CA 2006 s.1162(4). This is a reference to actual domination and the qualifications needed to establish contractual domination do not apply here: Sch.7 para.4(3).

[70] This brings in shareholder agreements which are an established way of exercising control over companies in some continental European jurisdictions, but note that the effect of the agreement must be to give the alleged parent sole control.

[71] CA 2006 s.1162(5). For this reason it is important that the section refers to parent undertakings, since the immediate parent of the indirect subsidiary might not itself be a company.

[72] See, for example, paras 4–6 of Sch.4 to the Large and Medium-Sized Companies and Groups (Accounts and Reports) Regulations 2008 (SI 2008/410, as amended) requiring a company's individual accounts to give certain information about companies in which the reporting company has a "significant holding"—defined as 20% or more of any class of shares in the other company. Similar rules apply to group accounts (paras 20–22) with more detail being required in the cases where the "significant holding" makes the other company an "associated" undertaking or a joint venture with the reporting company (paras 18–19).

intermediate parent, since the "outside" shareholders in the intermediate parent have an economic interest in that company's subsidiaries and so may wish to have intermediate group accounts.

Subject to certain further conditions, an intermediate parent which is a wholly-owned subsidiary of another company is relieved of the obligation to produce group accounts provided that group accounts are produced by its parent.[73] Where the parent of the intermediate parent holds 90% or more of the subsidiary's shares, the exemption needs the approval of (apparently all) the remaining shareholders of the intermediate parent.[74] Where the parent of the intermediate parent holds more than 50% of the allotted shares[75] (but less than 90%), exemption is the default rule. However, if the holders of at least 5% of the total allotted shares in the intermediate parent serve a notice, within six months of the end of the financial year in question, requiring the production of group accounts by their company, then those group accounts must be produced.[76] The higher level of protection where the "outside" shareholders constitute 10% or less of the shareholders is perhaps explicable by reference to the fact that the governance rights of such shareholders are very limited. For example, they are unable to block a special resolution. None of the above exemptions is available, however, if the intermediate parent is a traded company.[77] This is particularly important in relation to the default exemption. For such companies, there will necessarily be a significant block of the company's shares which are not held by that company's parent but are in the hands of public investors. Their interests dictate that the traded company should produce accounts which cover its position together with the position of the undertakings it controls, for that is the economic entity in which the public have invested.[78]

Even where the exemption is available in principle, certain other conditions have to be met. First, the intermediate parent must actually be included in the accounts of a larger group; those accounts must be drawn up in accordance with the relevant standards, and must be audited.[79] Secondly, the individual accounts of the intermediate parent must disclose that it is exempt from the obligation to produce group accounts and give prescribed information in order to identify the

[73] CA 2006 ss.400(1)(a) and 401(1)(a). The sections deal separately with inclusion within UK group accounts and non-UK group accounts.

[74] CA 2006 ss.400(1)(b) and 401(1)(b).

[75] It does not matter whether the allotted shares carry voting rights or not, but unless the "parent" undertaking controls 50% of the voting rights, it will not be under an obligation to produce consolidated accounts in any event. See below. In effect, the requirement to hold 50% of the allotted share capital means that the parent company, which passes the 50% figure by holding weighted voting rights in the subsidiary, will have access to the exemption only if the parent also holds non-voting shares in sufficient quantities.

[76] CA 2006 ss.400(1)(c) and 401(1)(c).

[77] CA 2006 ss400(4) and 401(4).

[78] Of course, those investors may also be strongly interested in the traded company's relations with its parent, for fear that the parent may seek to take a disproportionate share of the company's earnings. But that is a different issue.

[79] CA 2006 ss.400(2)(a)–(b), 401(2)(a)–(c). The requirement for audit is stated expressly in relation only to non-EEA parent companies, but in the case of EEA companies this requirement follows from the provisions of the Audit Directive (see Ch.22).

parent undertaking that draws up the group accounts.[80] Thirdly, the intermediate parent must deliver the group accounts to the Registrar, translated into English, if necessary.[81]

Companies excluded from consolidation

22–015 In principle, all subsidiary companies must be included when consolidation is required. Nevertheless some subsidiary companies may be omitted from the consolidation. Subsidiaries may be omitted if (1) their inclusion is not material for giving a true and fair view of the group (for example, if they are inactive companies); (2) "severe long-term restrictions" substantially hinder the exercise of the parent's rights over the assets or management of the company (a situation most likely to arise from restrictions in foreign legal systems); (3) "extremely rare circumstances mean" that the necessary information cannot be obtained "without disproportionate expense or undue delay"; and (4) the parent's interest is held exclusively with a view to resale.[82] If all the subsidiaries fall within one or other of these categories, no group accounts need be produced—no doubt a rare situation.[83]

Form and content of annual accounts

Possible approaches

22–016 Broadly, there are two model approaches for the legislature to take to the rules governing the financial analysis of the transactions the company has engaged in during the year and the presentation of the results of that analysis in the company's individual or group accounts. It could lay down one or more very general principles and leave it to the accounting profession (or some other non-legislative body) to develop more specific rules (usually referred to as "accounting standards"), to which, however, legal force might or might not be attached; or the legislature could try to set out a detailed set of rules itself. The British tradition is closer to the former model. However, the continental European tradition, which is closer to the second model, had an impact on British law in the 1980s, because that tradition influenced the Fourth and Seventh EEC Directives on companies' accounts, though not to the extent by any means of a complete shift to the latter approach. However, in a later development, the EU moved towards giving standard-setters a bigger role in the setting of the detailed rules, through the adoption of International Accounting Standards (IAS), though with the rider that standard-setting should no longer be purely a matter for the professions and the public interest should be represented in the standard-setting

---

80 CA 2006 ss.400(2)(c)–(d), 401(2)(d)–(e). This is not necessarily its immediate holding company, since that company, by operation of the same rules, might be exempt from the need to produce consolidated accounts. Thus, where there is a chain of three wholly-owned subsidiaries, only the top company will normally have to produce consolidated accounts.

81 CA 2006 ss.400(2)(e)–(f), 401(2)(f)–(g).

82 CA 2006 s.405.

83 CA 2006 s.402.

exercise. The EU rules continue to influence domestic law even after the UK's exit from the EU, because those rules continue as part of domestic law unless and until altered by the UK legislature.[84]

The result is that the current rules are a mixture of legislative provision and accounting standards, to which different degrees of legal recognition are accorded. Moreover, there are two sets of rules, with different mixtures. Here lies the significance of the term "accounting framework". A company which is under an obligation to produce individual accounts is free to do so either by reference to the rules contained in the Companies Act and regulations made thereunder or by reference to International Accounting Standards (IAS).[85] These accounts are called, helpfully if unimaginatively, "Companies Act individual accounts" and "IAS individual accounts" respectively. The same choice is available to companies under an obligation to produce group accounts, except that traded companies must use IAS for their group accounts.[86] Thus, there are also "Companies Act group accounts" and "IAS group accounts".

The choice of frameworks raises the question of switching between them, which is permitted, subject to limitations. For example, if a company switches to IAS accounts, it may change back to Companies Act accounts provided it has not changed to Companies Act accounts during the five-year period leading up to the most recent year of IAS accounts. This rule is clearly aimed at preventing chopping and changing, which would reduce the comparability of the accounts. If the company wishes to change back to Companies Act accounts within that period, it must show that "there is a relevant change of circumstance".[87] Similar rules apply to a switch from IAS to Companies Act accounts.[88]

We will now look at Companies Act accounts and IAS accounts in turn, but first it is necessary to look at two provisions which apply to both Companies Act and IAS accounts.

True and fair view

The traditional overall standard British law has applied to the accounts has been that they must "give a true and fair view of the assets, liabilities, financial **22–017**

[84] See para.3–014.

[85] CA 2006 s.395. A company which is a charity must provide Companies Act individual and group accounts: ss.395(2) and 403(3). Some way into the standard-setting process for the international standards, the term "International Accounting Standards" was replaced by the term "International Financial Reporting Standards" (IFRS) but only for the later adopted standards. In this chapter, we use the acronym IAS to refer to all of them.

[86] CA 2006 s.403. In fact, IAS accounts are mandatory on a wider basis than the section suggests because the London Stock Exchange requires EEA-incorporated companies traded on the Alternative Investment Market to use them as well: LSE, *Aim Rules for Companies* (2018), r.19. In addition, by virtue of s.407 (see para.22–012) there is some pressure to use IAS for the individual accounts of group companies as well.

[87] CA 2006 ss.395(3)–(4B) and 403(4)–(5B). The changes identified in the Act, and they are apparently exclusive, are becoming a subsidiary of a company which does not prepare IAS accounts and the company or its parent ceasing to have securities traded on a regulated market: ss.395(4) and 403(5). Until 2012 the company always had to show a relevant change of circumstance in order to revert to Company Act accounts.

[88] CA 2006 ss.395(5) and 403(6).

position and profit or loss"[89] of the individual company or the companies included in the consolidation in the case of group accounts. For many years this was virtually all the companies legislation said about the content of the accounts. It remains an overriding principle, no matter which accounting framework is used for the presentation of the accounts. The directors must not approve accounts unless they are satisfied that they provide a true and fair view.[90]

The matter is developed a bit further in relation to Company Act accounts. If compliance with the CA 2006 or provisions made under it would not be sufficient to give a true and fair view, the necessary additional information must be given in the accounts or notes to them.[91] Further, if in "exceptional" or "special" circumstances compliance with the statutory provisions would put the accounts in breach of the "true and fair" requirement, the directors must depart from the statute or subordinate legislation to the extent necessary to give a true and fair view.[92] What this qualification seems not to permit, though standard-setters have sometimes taken a different view, is the issuance of a standard which gives a general dispensation to companies to depart from a provision in or made under the Act, on the grounds that a true and fair view requires this. These provisions of the Act contemplate only ad hoc departures from the statutory requirements in the case of particular companies in particular circumstances.

The prohibition on signing accounts which do not give a true and fair view applies equally to IAS accounts as to Companies Act accounts. However, with IAS accounts, domestic law says nothing about what must or may be done to produce that view if the applicable standards by themselves do not achieve it.[93] Nevertheless, the position is probably the same by virtue of the provisions of the IAS themselves. IAS 1 requires that the accounts "present fairly" the company's or group's financial position, which presumably may be equated with a "true and fair view".[94] The application of IAS is presumed to lead to fair presentation, but IAS 1 recognises that further disclosure may be necessary to achieve this result. Departure from IAS in order to achieve fair presentation is recognised as permissible but only "in extremely rare circumstances".

Going concern evaluation

22–018 Much less obvious in the domestic legislation than the true and fair requirement, but often as important at least for publicly traded companies, is the requirement that directors form a view, when they draw up the accounts, whether the company

[89] CA 2006 s.393(1).

[90] CA 2006 s.393(1). The strength of UK commitment to this principle is demonstrated by the modifications to it which were thought necessary when micro companies were relieved of compliance with many standards. See para.22–020.

[91] CA 2006 ss.396(4) and 404(4) (for individual and group accounts respectively).

[92] CA 2006, ss.396(5) and 404(5).

[93] CA 2006 s.393(1) applies but not ss.396 and 405.

[94] The Financial Reporting Council (FRC) strongly argues that "true and fair" remains fully applicable to IAS accounts: FRC, *True and Fair* (June 2014). Future IAS apply in the UK only to the extent that the relevant standard has been adopted by the UK government. That may not be done only if the Secretary of State is of the view that the standard does not infringe the true and fair principle: International Accounting Standards and European Public Limited-Liability Company (Amendment etc.) (EU Exit) Regulations 2019 (SI 2019/685) para.7.

is capable of continuing as a going concern. This assessment is important because the numbers in the accounts are likely to show a much less promising picture where a company may have to sell assets off on a break-up basis rather than continue to use them in its productive enterprise. Both the national and international accounting standards (discussed below) require that the directors make this assessment when preparing financial statements,[95] and that assessment is subject to audit.[96] In addition, the Listing Rules require the directors of a UK company with a premium listing on the Main Market[97] of the London Stock Exchange to insert in its annual financial report a statement on the appropriateness of adopting a going concern basis for the company's accounts and an assessment of the company's prospects.[98] This may be a difficult enough task when the directors have to take account only of factors pertinent to the relevant company, for example, where it is likely to breach its debt covenants and it is unclear how and whether a financial restructuring will work out. It is even more difficult when the broader economy is in turmoil, as in the financial crisis at the end of the first decade of this century or the economic recession produced by the recent Covid-19 pandemic. The Financial Reporting Council will produce additional guidance in such situations but whether it does (or can) reduce the difficulties to a significant degree is open to question.[99]

Companies Act accounts

At the core of Companies Act accounts are a traditional balance sheet and a profit and loss statement.[100] The balance sheet provides a statement of the company's assets and liabilities, as at a particular point in time, usually the last day of the financial year. If, as is to be hoped, the former are greater than the latter, the difference between the figures is sometimes referred to as the shareholders' equity. It is the theoretical amount which the shareholders would receive if the company's business were then sold as a going concern.[101] If the assets are less than the liabilities, the shareholders have no equity in the company and the people with the strongest interest in its economic performance are its creditors.[102] The profit and loss account indicates the company's performance over the financial **22–019**

[95] See International Accounting Standard 1 and Financial Reporting Standard 18.

[96] International Standard on Auditing (ISA) (UK) 570 (2019).

[97] For the definition of these terms see para.25–006 and 25–009.

[98] LR 9.8.6(3). In making these assessments the listed company is required to include the information required by Provisions 30 and 31 of the UK Corporate Governance Code, which call upon the directors to explain how they have reached their assessment, and to comply with the FCA, *Guidance on Risk Management, Internal Control and Related Financial and Business Reporting* (2014). BEIS, *Restoring Trust in Audit and Corporate Governance* (March 2021) proposes to extend this requirement for PIE (as re-defined) through a new "Resilience Statement".

[99] The guidance mentioned in the previous note was the FRC's considered response to the financial crisis. In the Covid-19 recession it produced *COVID-19—Going concern, risk and viability* (June 2020), which contained the statement (p.3) that: "A company can be a going concern even when one or more material uncertainties exist."

[100] CA 2006 s.396. See the similar s.404(1) for group accounts.

[101] Theoretical because what the shareholders will actually receive is what a buyer of the business is willing to pay for it.

[102] We saw at para.19–005 that this situation may induce directors responsive to shareholder interests to embark on projects with a low chance of a high return and high chance of making a loss.

year: has it generated more value than it has consumed? Profit is different from cash flow. A profitable company may have a negative cash flow over a particular period, for example, where it has used a previously large cash balance to buy a new (and profitable) business. Although the new business may have generated cash during the financial year in which it was bought, it is highly unlikely that this cash income will come anywhere near the amount expended to acquire the business. Conversely, a company which has been unprofitable over the year but has managed to dispose of a large asset during that year may end the year with more cash than at the beginning of it.

What does the CA 2006 say about the format of these two accounts? With the enactment of the Fourth and Seventh Directives, UK law also adopted the Continental practice of dealing with matters of form and content to some extent in the legislation itself, and so the domestic legal provisions dealing with the accounts were expanded. Those provisions are now in the Large and Medium-Sized Companies and Groups (Accounts and Reports) Regulations 2008[103] (hereafter the "Large Accounts Regulations") and the Small Companies and Groups (Accounts and Reports) Regulations 2008[104] (hereafter the "Small Accounts Regulations"), both as subsequently amended, as they have been fairly extensively, but mainly in respect of narrative reporting requirements. This account of the Regulations is necessarily brief and we shall omit entirely the special provisions applying to banking and insurance companies.

Part 1 of Sch.1 to both sets of Regulations[105] provides two alternative formats in which the balance sheet and the profit and loss account may be presented. However, the directors cannot shift from the formats adopted in the previous year "unless in their opinion there are special reasons for a change".[106] The formats govern how the accounting information is grouped and the order in which the information, so grouped, is presented to the reader. More important, therefore, are the provisions of the Schedule which go into issues relating to the proper accounting treatment of transactions carried out by the company or contain rules about the valuation of assets and liabilities. These are contained in Pt 2 of the Schedule under the heading "Accounting Principles and Rules". The Principles are (strong) default rules, for the directors may depart from them only if there are "special reasons" for so doing, provided the nature of the departure, the reasons for it and its effect are stated.[107] There a six general principles,[108] of which the most important probably are that accounting policies must be applied consistently within accounts and from year to year and that the amount of any item must be determined on a prudent basis (which leads to the sub-rule that only realised profits may be included in the balance sheet, whereas all liabilities are to be taken into account, whether realised or not).[109] Furthermore, the Schedule explicitly

---

103 SI 2008/409.

104 SI 2008/410.

105 Schedule 6 makes some additional provisions in relation to group accounts.

106 Regulations Sch.1 para.2.

107 Regulations Sch.1 para.10.

108 Regulations Sch.1 paras 11–15A. One of these "principles" is more like a rule: "The opening balance sheet of each financial year shall correspond to the closing balance sheet of the previous financial year."

109 For the significance of this for distributions see para.18–005 and 18–006.

provides a choice to the directors as to the fundamental accounting approach which will be adopted.[110] No longer is a historical cost approach mandatory (under which, for example, assets are carried in the books at their original acquisition price, less depreciation, even though their current market price is much higher) but rather various forms of "marking to market" are permitted.[111]

Finally, it is clear that the "Accounting Principles and Rules" contained in the Schedule are not sufficient to produce a set of accounts for any particular company, except perhaps one of the simplest character. More detailed accounting standards need to be deployed, which are not to be found in the Regulations but in standards developed by the standard-setters, to which we now turn.

Accounting standards

In the UK the professional accountancy bodies had begun as early as 1942[112] to issue accounting standards. At that time and for a long while thereafter they provided the only authoritative guidance on what the "true and fair" requirement meant in particular situations. Those standards covered ever more topics and became ever more sophisticated over time; and, as we have seen, their centrality to the accounts-producing exercise was not ended by the transposition in the UK of the Fourth and Seventh Directives. Two important developments have accompanied the expansion of the role of accounting standards. These two developments are probably not unconnected with one another, their common feature being a recognition of the quasi-public role played by accounting standards. First, accounting standards have achieved legal backing; secondly, the professional bodies have lost their previously complete control over the standard-setting process. **22–020**

Although the 1942 standards were termed "Recommendations", it became accepted in the accounting profession that compliance with the legal obligation to present a "true and fair" view of the company's financial position required in principle adherence to accounting standards—even if on rare occasions that legal obligation had the contrary effect of requiring directors to override the requirements of a particular standard.[113] Thus, when it was thought desirable to simplify the compilation of the accounts of micro companies by removing the obligation to provide the additional information required by accounting standards, it was argued that directors and auditors would be in danger of not meeting the "true and fair" obligation. Consequently, the Act's formulation of the true and fair obligation was amended specifically to require directors of micro companies to ignore the requirements for additional information.[114]

This process described in the previous paragraph was supported by the courts' acceptance of the professional standards as the best evidence of the standard of care required by the law of negligence in relation to accountants performing their professional duties, especially when acting as auditors, though the courts are not

---

[110] Regulations Sch.1 para.16.

[111] See Sch.1 Pt 2 ss.C and D.

[112] In that year the Institute of Chartered Accountants in England and Wales began to issue Recommendations on Accounting Principles.

[113] See para.22–017.

[114] CA 2006 s.393(1A).

bound by the professionally developed standards.[115] In the case of large companies the resulting position was recognised legislatively in a provision added in 1989. This now provides that "it must be stated whether the accounts have been prepared in accordance with applicable accounting standards and particulars of any material departure from those standards and the reasons for it must be given".[116] This in effect puts accounting standards on a "comply or explain" basis, and it was probably the first example of the use of this technique in company law.[117]

The second development—the injection of a public element into the standard-setting bodies—occurred when the CA 1989 conferred on the Secretary of State the power to determine which body or bodies have authority to issue accounting standards which have statutory recognition.[118] Under the current arrangements the Secretary of State has delegated this power to the Financial Reporting Council Ltd (FRC). The FRC is a private company (limited by guarantee), but the Chair and Deputy Chair of the FRC are appointed by the Secretary of State; the remaining directors, executive and non-executive, are appointed and removed by the board itself. Those who have practised in the accounting profession within the previous five years are excluded, so that the board appears to be weighted towards the users of accountants' services. Some of the work of the FRC in the accounting standards area is delegated to a Codes and Standards Committee. The FRC is funded in its accounting, audit and corporate governance activities by the accountancy profession and the preparers of financial statements, through the "preparers' levy" paid by public traded and large private (i.e. non-publicly traded) companies. After heavy criticism of the efficacy of the FRC in the Kingman Report,[119] the government announced its intention to replace it by a stronger but also more standard governmental agency, probably called the Audit, Reporting and Governance Authority (ARGA).[120]

IAS accounts

22–021 International Accounting Standards (IAS) are a reflection of the desire for comparability across jurisdictions for the financial statements of the largest companies. They are produced by the International Accounting Standards Board

[115] *Lloyd Cheyham & Co v Littlejohn & Co* [1987] B.C.L.C. 303 QBD; but cf. *Bolitho v City and Hackney Health Authority* [1998] A.C. 232 HL (court not bound by professional standards where "in a rare case" it is convinced they are not reasonable or responsible).

[116] Large Accounts Regulations Sch.1 para.45. Medium-sized companies are exempt from this obligation (see reg.4(2A)) and the Small Accounts Regulations 2008 do not contain a impose a similar rule.

[117] For its use in relation to the Corporate Governance Code, which was developed only in the 1990s, see above at paras 9–016 onwards. For the more demanding rule about compliance with accounting standards under tax law see *Ball UK Holdings Ltd v Revenue and Customs Commissioners* [2018] 1 B.C.L.C. 29.

[118] Now s.464 of the CA 2006. The current arrangements are set out in the Statutory Auditors (Amendment of Companies Act 2006 and Delegation of Functions etc) Order 2012 (SI 2012/1741). Previously, the delegation was directly to an Accounting Standards Board which was a subsidiary of the FRC.

[119] *Independent Review of the Financial Reporting Council* (December 2018).

[120] At the time of writing formal proposals to this end had not yet been brought forward.

(IASB), which, as in the UK, was initially a purely professional initiative. In parallel with the domestic evolution, as the IAS became more important in practice, the professions lost sole control over the standard-setting process. The IASB became an independent body in 2001, having been founded in 1973 by the professional accountancy bodies of nine leading countries. However, close ties with a particular government, on the model of the FRC, were hardly feasible for the IASB, which adopted a different path away from professional control. In brief, its members are appointed by the trustees of a foundation,[121] which trustees are a self-perpetuating body (i.e. they appoint their own successors). However, this arrangement was subject to criticism, notably from the European Commission, and was modified by the addition of a Monitoring Board consisting of representatives of the public authorities (mainly regulators, including the European Commission).

The IASB produces standards, but their impact depends upon their adoption within particular jurisdictions by the relevant governmental authorities. It is worth noting that the US has not adopted IAS, so that one incentive for other countries to adopt IAS is to provide a platform from which harmonisation of IAS and US Generally Accepted Accounting Principles (US GAAP) can be taken forward. For the UK a major step in the adoption of IAS was a EU Regulation of 2002, which gave the Commission the power to adopt IAS for application throughout the EU.[122] A significant number of IAS were adopted by the Commission through the procedures laid down in the Regulation and that Regulation made IAS mandatory for the group accounts of companies operating on regulated markets in the EU. However, the Regulation permitted Member States to permit the use of IAS more widely and the UK did so, as we have noted.[123] With the withdrawal of the UK from the EU, those standards already adopted by the Commission remain operative as part of domestic law.[124] The adoption of future IASB standards will be a matter for the Secretary of State.[125] Criteria are set out for the grounds on which this decision is to be taken, in particular that the standard must not infringe the "true and fair" principle, but they are of a fairly general nature. The Secretary of State has power to delegate this task by regulation and plans to do so to the UK Endorsement Board, which sits operationally within the FRC but reports directly to the Secretary of State.

Applying the requirements to different sizes of company

We have seen that the form and content of the accounts result from a complex interaction of rules set out in legislation (which itself may be primary or secondary legislation) and accounting standards (which may be national or international). This is a far cry from the days when legislation confined itself to the requirement of a true and fair view, and the rest was national accounting **22–022**

[121] Currently termed the IFRS Foundation.

[122] Regulation 1606/2002 on the application of International accounting standards [2002] OJ L243/1.

[123] See para.22–016.

[124] European Union (Withdrawal) Act 2018 s.3.

[125] International Accounting Standards and European Public Limited-Liability Company (Amendment etc) (UK Exit) Regulations 2019 (SI 2019/685) Pt 2 Chs3 and 4; (draft) International Accounting Standards (Delegation of Functions) (EU Exit) Regulations 2021.

standards. It does not help that the balance between legislation and standards varies somewhat according to whether national or international standards are used by the company. There is one further cross-cutting set of divisions which we need to notice. This is the varying intensity of the rules and standards across companies of different sizes. We need to consider this point only briefly, since this is not a textbook on accounting. The rules we consider here relate to the different requirements for the production of accounts. As we shall see later, differences in economic size are also relevant a number of other accounting matters: what goes into the notes to the accounts and into narrative reporting or the level of publicity to be given to those accounts once produced (through their filing in a public registry). The full force of the rules and standards applies only to large companies and groups and PIEs which are required to report as large companies, even though they are only medium-sized.[126] Medium-sized companies and groups benefit from a modest set of derogations from the requirements for large companies, but not from the obligation to draw up group accounts.

For small companies the derogations are more substantial. As we have seen above, a small company is not required to produce group accounts, though it may choose to do so. In addition, they may draw up "abridged" accounts where all of the members of the company consent to this course of action.[127] This means that some items normally required to be shown separately may be combined in a single heading. So, the accounts are less granular, but equally cheaper to produce and less helpful to competitors. This set of rules is designed to allow the company to cut costs when all the shareholders are insiders but to allow outside shareholders to protect themselves by withholding consent. There are also relaxations in relation to the publication of the abbreviated accounts.[128] (Shareholders receive the accounts as drawn up and are not reliant on the published ones). Finally, the accounting standards applying to small companies have been simplified, for both accounting frameworks.[129]

The largest set of derogations is reserved for the smallest companies, i.e. free-standing micro companies.[130] Accounting standards are further simplified for micro entities.[131]

Notes to the accounts

22–023 Although the British tradition has been for the legislature not to specify the form and content of the accounts, but to leave that to standard-setters, the rules do require the disclosure of specific pieces of information thought to be necessary for a full understanding of the accounts. [132] These are not required to be part of

[126] See para.22–008.

[127] Small Accounts Regulations Sch.1 Pt 1 para.1A.

[128] See para.22–040.

[129] FRC, *FRS 102 The Financial Reporting Standard applicable in the UK and Republic of Ireland*, Pt 1A and *FRS 101 Reduced Disclosure Framework Disclosure exemptions from EU-adopted IFRS for qualifying entities*.

[130] Small Accounts Regulations Sch.1 Pt 1 para.1(1A).

[131] FRC, *FRS 105 The Financial Reporting Standard applicable to the Micro-entities Regime*.

[132] Much of the information required to be disclosed in notes under Pt 3 of Sch.1 to the Large and Small Accounts Regulations 2008 is of this character.

the accounts proper but are to be given in "notes" to the accounts. The legislative notes requirements apply whether the company has produced Companies Act or IAS accounts, though accounting standards may add to the notes requirements. We have seen above the example of the requirement to give information in the notes about non-subsidiary companies in which the reporting company has a significant holding.[133] Another example is the requirement for companies (other than small ones) to disclose "'off balance-sheet"' transactions, without knowledge of which the balance sheet may be entirely misleading.[134]

However, the information required to be provided in the notes may be used to reinforce the shareholders' governance rights as well as supplying potentially useful financial information. Transactions between companies and those who are in a position to influence the terms of those transactions or their associates (related party transactions) constitute a central regulatory problem for company law in relation to both directors and controlling shareholders. Ex post disclosure in the accounts of related party transactions[135] facilitates enforcement of the rights, conferred elsewhere, which shareholders may have against related parties, though it is probably not as effective as the contemporaneous disclosure requirements applied to publicly traded companies.[136] Shareholders reading the notes are thus in a better position to decide whether to seek to invoke their remedies in this area, for example for breach of the duties of directors or for unfairly prejudicial conduct by company controllers.[137]

NARRATIVE REPORTING

The company's financial statements, naturally, are dominated by numbers. But the annual circulation by the directors to the shareholders now includes a number of predominantly non-numerical documents. These constitute what is conventionally referred to as "narrative reporting". Until about a quarter of a century ago, the only statutorily required narrative report was the directors' report, the content of which was determined largely by the directors themselves. Since then, the mandatory content of narrative reporting has expanded enormously and, as part of that process, further reports have been added to the directors' report. Just as important, the notion of the audience to whom the narrative reports are addressed has expanded. Originally, directors thought of their report as addressed to shareholders and, perhaps, potential investors in the company. Today, it is **22–024**

133 See fn.72.

134 CA 2006 s.410A, introduced in 2008, in the wake of the Enron collapse in the US which was in part brought about by the acquisition of liabilities by Special Purpose Vehicles (SPVs) connected with Enron but not counting as its subsidiaries.

135 Small Companies Regulations Sch.1 para.66; Large Companies Regulations Sch.1 para.72. The requirements are applied more stringently to large than medium or small companies. These provisions apply formally only to companies preparing Companies Act accounts, but those preparing IAS accounts are under a similar obligation because of the provisions in IAS 24 (Related Party Disclosures). The two are further tied together by the adoption in paras 66 and 72 of the same definition of "related party" as in the IAS—though unhelpfully it does not reproduce it. IAS 24.9 defines a related party widely so as to include controlling shareholders as well as directors.

136 For these see Listing Rules Ch.11 and *Aim Rules for Companies*, r.13.

137 See paras 10–053 onwards and Ch.14.

common to say that the narrative reports are addressed to all "stakeholders" in the company—although it is not clear that this is what the CA 2006 says and, in any event, the term "stakeholder" is usually undefined and the action which stakeholders might take in response to the information provided left unspecified.[138]

In consequence, the disclosures required are sometimes only indirectly linked to the financial interests of the shareholders.[139] Indeed, in some cases narrative reporting may be intended to induce changes in corporate behaviour which the shareholders might not wish to induce, if left to themselves. Thus, the recent addition of "extractive industry" reporting requires the directors of large companies and PIEs active in those industries to produce an annual report which discloses payments made to foreign governments. The purpose of this requirement is so that "we can provide citizens [of foreign countries] with the detailed information they need to hold their governments to account".[140] The implication is that such payments are often bribes to local politicians or senior officials. The shareholders' interests are not placed centre-stage in this case, but rather those of the foreign citizens. Indeed, if because of corruption or lack of democratic process in those countries, no such accountability occurs, the reporting companies will find themselves at a competitive disadvantage as against companies from jurisdictions which do not impose (or effectively enforce) this reporting requirement. If, on the other hand, the foreign citizens are successful, the benefits will accrue mainly to them rather than the company's shareholders.[141] Perhaps for this reason, the rules, whilst requiring the payment report to be made public (through filing at Companies House), do not require it to be laid before the shareholders.[142] Narrative disclosure can thus be used to bolster policies whose drivers are located outside company law, as conventionally conceived.

In this section we consider the various items that contribute to narrative reporting to the shareholders, with the exception of the directors' remuneration report, important though that is. This has been dealt with in Ch.11[143] and need not be further considered here.

---

138 A typical statement (in this case from BIS, *The Future of Narrative Reporting: Consultation* (September 2011), BIS/11/945) is: "Narrative reporting provides an important link between companies and their investors and wider stakeholders. It is a key element in the framework that allows investors to hold companies to account, both in terms of achieving sustainable long term returns and on the impact of the business to society and the environment." So, reporting is presented as addressed to stakeholders as well as investors, but only investors are mentioned in relation to accountability.

139 See para.22–031.

140 BIS, *UK Implementation of the EU Accounting Directive, Chapter 10: Consultation* (March 2014), BIS/14/622, p.4.

141 On the assumption that bribes do not increase the overall costs of the company but rather are recovered by a lower formal contractual payment to the foreign government. There may be some general gains to the company from operating in countries which have less corruption.

142 See the Reports on Payments to Government Regulations 2014 (SI 2014/3209) reg.14. Along similar lines are s.54 of the Modern Slavery Act 2015 and Regulations 2015/1833 requiring companies with an annual turnover of not less than £36m (as noted above, this is the relevant figure for medium-sized companies) to place on their websites for each financial year a report a report on the steps (if any) it has taken to ensure that slavery and human trafficking are not taking place within its businesses or, and probably more important, within the supply chains for those businesses.

143 At paras 11–013 onwards.

Directors' report

The directors' report (DR), to accompany both the individual and group accounts, has long been a statutory requirement in the UK.[144] However there is no longer a requirement for micro companies to produce a directors' report[145] and companies subject to the small companies regime are relieved of the obligation to disclose some matters.[146] **22–025**

The statute requires the report to contain some fairly straightforward information, for example, a list of those who were directors of the company at any time during the year.[147] Except for exempt small companies, it must also state the amount the directors recommend to be paid by way of dividend to the shareholders.[148] The exemption for small companies is based, presumably, on the argument that public disclosure of dividend recommendations would reveal the income of easily identifiable individuals, for example, where the directors are the only shareholders. More generally, the DR must state any important events which have affected the company since the end of the financial year and indicate the likely future development of its business.[149]

None of the above is very demanding. However, when one turns from the CA 2006 to Sch.7 to the Large Companies Regulations ("Matters to be dealt with in the Directors' Report"), one finds a long catalogue of matter to be included.[150] Some of these, while possibly related to the financial interests of the shareholders, clearly also aim to nudge the company into supporting policies favoured by the government. Thus Pt 3 requires companies employing more than 250 persons to provide information about the employment, training and promotion of disabled persons.[151] Even the requirement in Pt 1 for separate disclosure of the amounts of political donations is not generally necessary to form a view on the financial position of large companies in view of the minimal amounts needed to trigger the disclosure requirement and the modest amounts normally donated. However, this disclosure clearly facilitates the operation of the controls over political donations laid down in Pt 14 of the CA 2006.[152] One can say the same of the buy-back disclosures required in Pt 2, which reinforce the rules in Pt 18 of the Act.[153] One might even take the same view of Pt 6 of the

---

[144] Now CA 2006 s.415.

[145] CA 2006 s.415(1A).

[146] CA 2006 s.415A, notably the amount of the recommended dividend. The exemption applies also to a company that would be subject to the small companies regime but for being a member of an ineligible group.

[147] CA 2006 s.416(1).

[148] CA 2006 s.416(3).

[149] Large Companies Regulations Sch.7 para.7.

[150] There are nearly 40 paragraphs of often detailed requirements.

[151] This disclosure and disclosure of political donations are required also of small companies: Small Companies Regulations Sch.5. However, many small companies will not meet the minimum employment threshold.

[152] See para.10–100. Until recently the amount of charitable donations had to be stated as well.

[153] See paras 17–006 onwards.

Schedule, implementing for traded companies art.10 of the Takeover Directive on the disclosure of a company's control structures.[154] Such disclosures facilitate takeover bids.

Corporate governance statement

22–026 The DR is also the normal home of the corporate governance statement (CGS). Rules made by the Financial Conduct Authority (FCA) require UK companies admitted to trading on a regulated market, for example, the Main Market of the London Stock Exchange, to make a variety of disclosures about their governance arrangements, the default disclosure mechanism being the DR.[155] In many, but not all, cases what is required by the FCA's rules replicates what is required under Sch.7 to the Large Accounts Regulations for the DR. The point of this apparently needless duplication appears to be as follows. Where the Regulations do not require inclusion of a particular item required by the FCA rules, the company has the option of including the disclosure in a document other than the DR,[156] though it is doubtful that many companies would want to take advantage of this. This is referred to as the "separate" CGS.[157] Secondly, the Regulations apply only to Companies Act companies, whereas some of the FCA's requirements apply to companies incorporated outside the UK.[158]

The most important disclosures required by the FCA's rules are:

- the corporate governance code to which the company is subject (or has voluntarily chosen to follow), explanations for departure from the code and information about its corporate governance practices which exceed national legal requirements[159];
- a description of the composition and operation of the board and its committees[160];
- a description of the main features of the company's internal control and risk management systems in relation to the financial reporting process[161]; and
- a description of the company's diversity policy in relation to the board and its results or an explanation why the company does not have one.[162]

However, in 2019 there was introduced into the Regulations requirements for a more extensive set of corporate governance disclosures in the DR by companies with either more than 2000 employees or a turnover of £200 million and a balance sheet total of £2 billion, which cover more than the matters mentioned in

[154] See para.28–024.
[155] CA 2006 s.472A and DTR 7.2.1.
[156] DTR 7.2.9.
[157] CA 2006 s.472A(3).
[158] DTR 1B.1.5A.
[159] DTR 7.2.2-4. On the UK Corporate Governance Code see paras 9–016 onwards.
[160] DTR 7.2.7-8—much of which information is required in any event under the UK CGC.
[161] DTR 7.2.5 and 7.2.10.
[162] DTR 7.2.8—this requirement does not apply to small or medium-sized companies but there are likely to be few such in the category to which DTR 7 applies.

the first two bullet points above.[163] The effect of this extension was to require additional governance disclosures by large companies, including those which are unquoted, which were also obliged to place their disclosures on their website (already required for quoted companies in respect of all the annual reports and accounts).

Governance arrangements within companies are obviously of central importance to shareholders and investors. That statement can also be made about other disclosures required in the DR, with which we have not yet dealt. In recent years, these disclosure requirements have been developed extensively. However, they are best analysed as part of the discussion of the strategic report now required to be produced by larger companies, since companies are permitted to include DR disclosures which the directors consider to be of strategic significance in the SR.[164] Many publicly traded companies are likely to take advantage of this provision, since it enhances the coherence of reporting on strategic matters.

The strategic report

Rationale

Section 414A requires all companies, other than those benefiting from the small companies regime,[165] to produce an annual strategic report (SR) or, in the case of parent companies, to produce a group strategic report. The requirement for a SR reflects the perception that shareholders and investors need more than historical financial data to understand fully the prospects of the company. In addition, they need to be able to gauge the quality of the company's relationships with those upon whose contributions or cooperation the success of the company depends (sometimes called "stakeholders"). For stakeholders, as well, this information may be useful, even if company law itself gives them no particular platform from which to take action on the basis of the information.[166] As the CLR put it, "companies are increasingly reliant on qualitative and intangible assets such as the skills and knowledge of their employees, their business relationships and their reputation. Information about future plans, opportunities, risks and strategies is just as important as the historical review of performance which forms the basis of reporting at present".[167] **22–027**

The second argument for a broader report by the directors was the need to provide a check on the discharge by directors of their "inclusive" duty[168] to promote the success of the company for the benefit of its members but on the

[163] Large Accounts Regulations Sch.7 Pt 8.

[164] CA 2006 s.414C(11). The FRC, *Guidance on the Strategic Report* (2018), para.7A.85 states that material information "should" be put in the SR rather than the DR.

[165] The requirements are relaxed for medium-sized companies, but not excluded entirely. A small company excluded from the small company regime because a member of an ineligible group may also take advantage of this exemption: s.414B.

[166] Trade unions might use the information in collective bargaining with the company or they and other stakeholders might use it in making representations to government or taking other sorts of political action.

[167] Final Report I, para.3.33.

[168] See paras 10–026 onwards.

basis of taking into account the company's need to foster its relationships with stakeholders, its impact upon communities affected and environmental and reputational concerns. This duty is specifically referred to in s.414C(1) on the contents of the SR (see later). Thus, there is a close link between the statement of directors' duties contain in Pt 10 of the CA 2006 and the disclosure obligations of Pt 15, aimed at providing a mechanism whereby the "enlightened" elements of the inclusive duty mean something significant in practice and are not just self-serving.

Contents of the Strategic Report

22–028 Section 414C states that the purpose of the SR is to "inform members of the company" and to help them assess whether the directors have performed their duty under s.172 of the CA 2006 to promote the success of the company for the benefit of its members. Although placing the emphasis on the members ties in well with the shareholder-centred focus of s.172, the CLR proposed that its version of what became the SR should not be so narrowly targeted.[169] Nevertheless, information about non-shareholders may also be relevant to the shareholders. As the FRC has put it, "The annual report should address issues relevant to these other users where, because of the influence of those issues on the development, performance, position or future prospects of the entity's business, they are also material to shareholders."[170] However, it is arguable that the SR at points now goes beyond what is strictly necessary for assessing the director' performance under s.172, even from a broad shareholder perspective.

In 2019 the link between the ss.172 and 414C was strengthened by the addition of a requirement that the SR to contain a statement on *how* the directors had had regard to stakeholder interests, although medium-sized companies were exempted from this additional element of reporting.[171] This statement must be made available on the company's website, even if the general requirement for website publication of the annual accounts and reports does not apply.[172] This new statement is supplemented by additional detailed requirements for disclosures in the DR or, at the company's choice, in its SR. Under the Large Accounts Regulations a company with 250 UK employees or more must disclose its arrangements in relation to its UK employees for providing information to them, consulting them or their representatives, encouraging employee share schemes or similar arrangements and "achieving a common awareness on the part of all employees of the financial and economic factors affecting the performance of the company", as well as stating how the directors have engaged with the employees and how they have had regard to employee interests.[173] With regard to other stakeholders, there is a less detailed requirement, from which medium-sized companies are excluded, for a statement about how the directors have had regard

---

[169] Completing, para.3.33. Thus, non-shareholders would have been included among the addresses of the SR.

[170] FRC, *Guidance on the Strategic Report* (2018), para.3.4.

[171] CA 2006 s.414CZA.

[172] CA 2006 ss.426B and 430. For website publication of the annual accounts and reports see para.22–043.

[173] Large Accounts Regulations Sch.7 Pt 4.

to the "need to foster the company's business relationships with suppliers, customers and others, and the effect of that regard."[174]

Turning more generally to the CA 2006's requirements for the content of the SR, it has to be said that these are not laid out in a user-friendly manner, at least in the case of publicly traded companies. Section 414C lays down requirements applicable to all companies required to produce a SR. However, those requirements are applied more softly to medium-sized companies[175] and more extensively to "quoted" companies.[176] Additional content requirements also are laid down in s.414CB for "traded" companies[177] (and certain financial companies, whether traded or not) provided they employ more than 500 employees (or that number is employed within the group in the case of a parent company).[178] However, to add to the demands on the reader of these provisions on the content of the SR, a "quoted"[179] company is not defined in the same way as a "traded"[180] company, although the definitions overlap considerably. **22–029**

At the core of both definitions is the notion of the company's shares being traded on a public market. For a traded company, that market may be any "regulated" market that operates in the UK, whilst for a quoted company only the "official list" counts in the UK, but the definition extends geographically to cover official listing in any EEA state and the New York Stock Exchange and Nasdaq in the US.[181] Within the UK, the traded company is the larger set of companies, quoted companies being a sub-set of the traded ones. In most cases s.414CB (traded companies) adds more detail to topics required to be covered by s.414C; but in some cases it adds new topics, for example in relation to the impact of the company's activities on anti-corruption and bribery matters.[182] Nothing in ss.414C or 414CB requires disclosure of impending developments or matters in the course of negotiation if, in the directors' opinion, disclosure would be seriously prejudicial to the interests of the company.[183]

Section 414C(2) begins with a matter clearly related to investors' needs. It requires the SR to contain a fair review of the company's business and a description of the principal risks and uncertainties facing it—or them in the case **22–030**

---

[174] See previous note. It appears that a company which qualified as medium-sized on balance sheet and turnover criteria might nevertheless have to make the employee disclosures if it employed 250 or more employees. This is probably a rare case.

[175] No obligation to use "key performance indicators" in relation to non-financial information: s.414C(6).

[176] CA 2006 s.414(7)(8).

[177] See para.22–008.

[178] CA 2006 s.414CA.

[179] CA 2006 s.385.

[180] CA 2006 s.474(1).

[181] For discussion of regulated markets and official listing see para.25–008.

[182] CA 2006 s.414CB(1)(c)(d). Having overlapping content requirements in ss.414C and 414CB for respectively quoted and traded companies is hardly helpful for companies subject to the sections, especially for companies which are both quoted and traded (for example, companies on the Main Market of the London Stock Exchange). It is a lazy way of implementing an EU initiative, which is what s.414CB reflects. That section follows closely the wording the relevant Directive, but only limited steps were taken to fit the new rules into the existing domestic structure.

[183] CA 2006 ss.414C(14) and 414CB(9).

of group accounts.[184] The review required is "a balanced and comprehensive" analysis of the development and performance of the company's business during the financial year and of its position at the end of the year.[185] To the extent that it is necessary for an understanding of the business the review must make use of "key performance indicators", both financial and non-financial.[186] This is an attempt to inject some quantitative analysis into what might otherwise be a set of generalities. The choice of KPIs, however, is left to the directors.[187]

For quoted companies the SR must deal with further matters. At the most general level, the company is required to describe its strategy and its business model.[188] In addition, the SR must address, again "to the extent necessary for an understanding" of the company's business, certain specific issues, disclosing any policies the company pursues on these issues and information about their effectiveness.[189] The list of additional matters potentially to be commented on is:

(1) "the main trends and factors" likely to affect the future of the company's business;
(2) environmental matters, including the impact of the company's business on the environment;
(3) employees; and
(4) social, community and human rights.

Given the UK's accession in 2016 to the Paris Agreement on Climate Change (2015) and the government's commitment to achieving a net carbon-neutral economy by 2050, the emphasis on environmental reporting by companies has increased, especially reporting on the impact of the company on the environment. Thus, reporting obligations were introduced for quoted companies via the DR (or SR, if the company chooses) in 2013 and much extended in 2019 in relation to greenhouse gas emissions, energy consumption and energy efficiency.[190] Subject to a practicability condition, quoted companies must disclose annually the tonnes of carbon dioxide emitted by their operations and the tonnes of CO_2-equivalent resulting from their use of energy whose consumption does not produce such emissions but whose generation does, such as electricity, and provide an overall figure for these two amounts. The disclosure must distinguish between UK and non-UK emissions. The overall consumption figure must be expressed as a ratio with regard to "a quantifiable factor associated with the company's activities", presumably because the bare emission figures do not reveal whether the company's production techniques are highly productive of CO_2. Finally, the

[184] CA 2006 s.414C(13). The proposed "Resilience Statement" would add to this category of disclosures: BEIS, *Restoring Trust in Audit and Corporate Governance* (March 2021), para.3.1.19–3.1.21.

[185] CA 2006 s.414C(3).

[186] CA 2006 s.414C(4)(5), unless the company qualifies as medium-sized. See n.176.

[187] The FRC Guidance n.164 states: "Where possible, KPIs should reflect the way that the board manages the entity's business." (para.7A.71).

[188] CA 2006 s.414C(8)(a)(b).

[189] CA 2006 s.414C(7).

[190] Now the Large Accounts Regulations Sch.7 Pt 7. These disclosures may be of interest to investors, but whether or not that is so, they are clearly aimed at nudging companies in the Government's preferred direction.

company must disclose the principal steps it has taken, if any, to increase its energy efficiency during the financial year.[191]

In 2019 as well a somewhat simplified version of these emission requirements was extended beyond quoted companies.[192] Companies subject to the small companies regime are excluded by reason of not being within the Large Accounts Regulations for any purposes,[193] but so were, in effect, medium-sized companies and groups, as well as companies which would otherwise be within the rules but are covered by a group disclosure.[194] Nevertheless, this is a significant extension of the environmental disclosure requirements, since, subject to a de minimis threshold,[195] the extended rules apply to companies whose shares are publicly traded but are not on the "Official List", to large public companies whose shares are not publicly traded and to large private companies. Both sets of emission rules contain an exception for information the disclosure of which, in the directors' opinion, would be prejudicial to the interests of the company and the report states the information is not disclosed for that reason.[196]

Going in the opposite direction (i.e. additional requirements for large companies) and in a further example of governmental interest in companies and climate change, the FCA added to the Listing Rules in January 2021[197] an additional set of disclosure rules for "premium-listed" companies. Premium-listed companies may be thought of as a subset of traded companies, listed on the Main Market of the London Stock Exchange, which have chosen "premium" rather than "standard" listing.[198] These are required to disclose, on a comply or explain basis, whether they have made "climate change related financial disclosures"[199] in their annual financial reports as recommended in the *Recommendations of the Task Force on Climate-related Financial Disclosures*—an international body.[200] These provisions are applicable to premium-listed companies, whether incorporated in a UK jurisdiction or not.

Returning to the Companies Act and to another policy heavily promoted by the government in recent years, quoted companies must disclose in the SR the

---

[191] See Sch.7 Pt 7 paras (3)–(3D).

[192] Large Accounts Regulations Sch.7 Pt 7A paras 20D–E. For example, emissions outside the UK may be excluded.

[193] Large Accounts Regulations para.2(4).

[194] Large Accounts Regulations Sch.7 Pt 7A paras 20A–20C.

[195] Of 40,000 kWh of annual energy consumption. The same threshold applies to the quoted companies' disclosure requirements. See Sch.7 Pt 7 para.15(5) and Pt 7A para.20D(7).

[196] See previous note.

[197] LR 9.8.6(8). See FCA, *Proposals to enhance climate-related disclosures by listed issuers and clarification of existing disclosure obligations* (March 2020), CP20/03 and (December 2020), PS20/17. The CP does not consider the relationship between its provisions and those in Sch.7 to the Regulations. However, the LR proposals may be overtaken by the climate change disclosure requirements in the proposed "Resilience Statement" (BEIS, *Restoring Trust in Audit and Corporate Governance* (March 2021), para.3.1.15).

[198] For a discussion of premium listing see para.25–006.

[199] Although the term "financial disclosures" might suggest reporting is confined to the adverse impact of climate change or climate change regulation on the company, it is clear that the Task Force was as concerned with the "opportunities" for companies to contribute to the slowing down of climate change. See the Final Report of the Task Force, next note, Section B.

[200] Set up by the Financial Stability Board and reporting in 2017 (available at; *https://www.fsb-tcfd.org/wp-content/uploads/2017/06/FINAL-2017-TCFD-Report-11052018.pdf* [Accessed 27 March 2021]).

number of persons of each gender who were (1) directors; (2) senior managers; and (3) employees of the company.[201] Here, disclosure is being used to promote the government's diversity policies, this time at senior levels in companies.

22–031 Overall, it is evident that narrative reporting has been used to enhance corporate disclosures in three areas in particular. In the order they were dealt with above, they are employee consultation, environmental reporting and gender diversity. These are areas of interest to shareholders and investors more generally, but they also relate to policies promoted by government. It is likely that the impact of the disclosures will depend upon the adoption by government of other strategies for pursuing these policies, operating outside the purely corporate area, and on the level of public support for these policies. As a guess, one may estimate the environmental disclosures are likely to be most effective, closely followed by gender equality, with employee consultation in third place, probably some distance behind.

Verification of narrative reports

22–032 There is a risk that narrative reporting requirements will produce only self-serving and vacuous descriptions rather than analytical material which is of genuine use to those who read the report. The references in ss.414C and 414CB to the use of "key performance indicators" are clearly driven by a desire to inject an element of objectivity into narrative reporting.[202] Beyond that, there are two traditional ways of dealing with this issue in relation to financial statements: audit and accounting standards. The risk with applying audit to the DR and SR is that it will undermine the desideratum that these reports should reflect the directors' view of the business rather than that of its auditors. Consequently, the CA 2006 formerly restricted the audit requirement for the DR and SR to certification that the reports were consistent with the accounts (which are required to be audited). Under the current version of the Act[203] the auditors must state in addition whether they have identified material misstatements in the SR or DR (and describe their nature) in the light of the knowledge of the company acquired in the course of the audit.

No formal accounting standards have been developed for the SR and DR, although this step was contemplated in the development of the predecessor of the SR, but the FRC has published helpful guidance on the compilation of these documents.[204]

---

[201] CA 2006 s.414C(8)(c)–(10). There is no extension here to traded companies.

[202] CA 2006 ss.414C(4)(5) and 414CB(2)(e)(3).

[203] CA 2006 s.496. However, BEIS has proposed (*Restoring Trust in Audit and Corporate Governance* (March 2021), para.3.2.6) that PIE should be required to publish a policy (to be subject to shareholder advisory vote) on how they obtain "assurance" in relation to the non-audited parts of the annual reports.

[204] See fn.164. In late 2020 the "Big Four" accounting firms produced a set of standards for environment, social and governance reporting which they hope the 130 largest global companies, members of the International Business Council, will adopt ("Big Four accounting firms unveil ESG reporting standards", *Financial Times*, 22 September 2020).

Liability for misstatements in narrative reports

An alternative approach to verification is to impose liability ex post for misstatements in narrative reports. There are two areas of potential negligence liability to be considered. First, there is liability on the part of the directors to the company under what is now s.174 of the Act. Secondly, there is liability on the part of the directors or the company (and conceivably others) to third parties, including investors in the market, under the general law on misstatements, whether negligent or fraudulent. However, the extension of narrative reporting prompted reforms, now to be found in s.463, whose aim is not to strengthen the ex post liability regime but to circumscribe it.[205] **22–033**

The case for providing a "safe harbour" in relation to directors' forward-looking statements is that no one can predict the future with certainty and if directors were to be exposed to litigation, or the threat of it, whenever their forward-looking statements turned out to be untrue, they would be very cautious in the statements they made This caution might undermine the value of narrative reporting to its users.[206] However, s.463 goes well beyond forward-looking statements, apparently on the grounds that it would be difficult to distinguish them from other types of statement. The section applies to the entire content of the four narrative reports: DR, SR, the directors' remuneration report and the corporate governance statement (if separate from the DR).[207] In respect of this content, s.463 excludes directors' liability in negligence to the company entirely. The director is so liable in respect of untrue or misleading statements in the reports or omissions from them only if the director has been fraudulent. For liability the director must know that the statement is untrue or misleading or be reckless (not caring) as to whether this is the case or, in the case of omissions, know that the omission amounts to the dishonest concealment of a material fact.[208] Thus, a genuine belief in the truth of the statement, no matter how unreasonable, will save the director from liability.

If the directors' liability to the company is preserved in the case of fraud, their liability to other persons is excluded entirely, even in the case of fraud.[209] Moreover, the liability which is excluded is the liability of "any person", not just of the directors, provided it is not a liability to the company. Thus, investors (including existing shareholders) cannot impose liability on the company in respect of unsuccessful investment decisions which are based on inaccurate information in the narrative reports. It is in fact very unclear whether, even without the section, liability in negligence towards investors on the part of the **22–034**

---

[205] However, s.463(6) preserves liability for civil penalties (imposed, for example. under FSMA 2000) and crimes.

[206] CLR, Final Report I, para.8.38.

[207] CA 2006 s.463(1). The inclusion of the remuneration report is particularly bizarre, since it requires statements of policies but very little in the way of forward-looking statements. See para.11–019.

[208] CA 2006 s.463(2)–(3). The liability excluded is only the liability to compensate the company, though it will be rare for any other liability to be in issue. This closely follows the common law in *Derry v Peek* (1889) L.R. 14 App. Cas. 337 HL.

[209] CA 2006 s.463(4),(5). The liability here excluded is not confined to liability to compensate but embraces any civil remedy, including self-help remedies.

company or the directors would exist under the general law. The issue has been tested at the highest levels only in respect of auditors, where, as we shall see, the starting point of the courts is one of non-liability.[210] The exclusion of liability towards third parties in the case of fraud in narrative reports is questionable, since the common law does impose liability in principle for fraud and it is unclear why fraud should be condoned. In fact, however, the exclusion of liability to third parties is qualified by the provisions of s.90A of and Sch.10A to FSMA 2000, applying to companies with securities traded on a regulated market, which imposes liability in fraud on the company in relation to certain statements made to the market (which might reflect, but be separate from, statements included in the narrative reports).[211]

Section 463 excludes the third-party liability of "any person", but it is not clear who might be liable beyond the directors and the company in respect of errors in the narrative reports. A number of professionals may be consulted and have a hand in the compilation of the reports but they are not normally identified in those reports as responsible for particular parts of it and thus as having particular statements attributed to them, since the reports are the reports of the directors. However, if this did occur, s.463 would protect these persons (other than in respect of their liability to the company). The auditors are required to report on the narrative reports to some extent, as we have seen, but the auditor's report is a separate document and so is not covered by s.463.

APPROVAL OF THE ACCOUNTS AND REPORTS BY THE DIRECTORS

22–035 That the narrative reports are the reports of the directors is clear.[212] The accounts as well are the product of the directors: the directors must draw them up,[213] although in this case, because of the role played by the auditors in verifying the accounts and, in practice, in drawing them up, they are often misconceived as the auditors' accounts. Approval of the accounts and reports is a matter for the board as a whole, not for just its executive directors or the financial director.[214] The fact that they can be signed on behalf of the board by a single director or even the company secretary does not remove the legal responsibility of the board as a whole. If the directors approve accounts or reports that do not comply with the Act, every director who knows that they do not comply or is reckless as to whether or not they comply and who fails to take reasonable steps to secure compliance or to prevent the accounts being approved is guilty of an offence.[215]

---

210 See paras 23–044 onwards.

211 See para.27–021.

212 See ss.414A, 415 and 420: directors' duties to prepare narrative reports.

213 CA 2006 ss.394 and 399.

214 CA 2006 ss.414(1), 414D(1) and 419(1). Section 419A imposes the same duty in relation to the corporate governance report, if it is a separate document, but lays down no specific penalties for non-compliance.

215 CA 2006 s.414(4)–(5), 414D(2)(3) and 419(3)(4). This re-states the previous law somewhat more simply by dropping the requirement that the director be a party to the approval and presuming the existing directors to be parties.

The Auditor's Report

22–036 The final document that has to accompany the annual accounts is the auditor's report thereon—assuming the company is one which is required to have its accounts audited or has chosen to do so. This has to be addressed to the company's members[216] and to state whether in the auditors' opinion on a number of matters, notably whether the annual accounts have been properly prepared in accordance with the CA 2006 or the IAS Regulation, as appropriate and whether they give a true and fair view of the company's financial position.[217] The rights and duties of the auditor in the preparation of the audit report are considered more fully in the following chapter. The auditors' report must state the names of the auditors and be signed by them.[218] However, those names need not appear on the published copies of the report or on the copy filed with the Registrar (see below) if the company has resolved that the names should not be stated on basis that there are reasonable grounds for thinking that publication would create a serious risk of violence to or intimidation of the auditor or any other person, and has provided that information instead to the Secretary of State.[219]

Revision of Defective Accounts and Reports

22–037 Despite the requirements for director and auditor approval, noted above, it is not inconceivable that accounts and reports will be produced by the company which are later discovered to be incorrect. Until the passing of the CA 1989 there were no statutory provisions for revising incorrect accounts and reports. However, it has never been doubted that, if directors discover such defects, they can, and should, correct them. Section 454 makes it clear that the directors may revise the accounts and narrative reports on a voluntary basis. Where the accounts have not yet been sent to the Registrar or the members (see below), the directors have a pretty free hand as to revisions, but if either of those events has occurred, as is likely, the corrections must be confined to what is necessary to bring the accounts and reports into line with the requirements of the CA 2006.[220] Regulations made under the section provide that the revised accounts or reports become, as nearly as possible, the reports and accounts of the company for the relevant financial year, to which the other provisions of the Act apply. For example, they will be subject to audit.[221]

More significant are the statutory powers to compel revision of defective accounts. The Secretary of State has two relevant powers: (1) to keep under review the accounts of traded companies; and (2) to apply to the court for a declaration that the accounts (of any company) or the DR or SR (but not, it

216 CA 2006 s.495(1).

217 See para.23–003 for more detail.

218 CA 2006 s.503.

219 CA 2006 s.506. The reasons for this measure or secrecy in relation to the auditors are the same as those which led to the suppression of public information about directors' residential addresses: see para.9–007.

220 CA 2006 s.454(2).

221 Companies (Revision of Defective Accounts and Reports) Regulations 2008 (SI 2008/373) (as amended).

seems, the remuneration report) do not comply with the CA 2006 and for an order that they be brought into line, with consequential directions.[222] The court may order the costs of the application and of the production of the revised accounts to be borne by the directors in place at the time of the approval of the accounts or report, unless a director can show that he or she took all reasonable steps to prevent approval, though the court also has power to exclude from liability a director who did not know and ought not to have known of the defects.[223] Notice of the application and of its result must be given to the Registrar.[224]

However, in practice these are not activities the Secretary of State undertakes, because there is power to delegate them. Currently, they are delegated to the Conduct Committee of the FRC.[225] The task of dealing with defective reports is thus discharged by the Conduct Committee, rather than by the Department, except in relation to small companies.[226] The Committee has statutory authority to require the production of documents, information and explanations if it thinks there is a question-mark over the compliance of a company's accounts or reports with the Act.[227] It must keep the information received confidential, except for disclosure to a list of approved recipients (relevant Government Departments and Regulators).[228]

The Financial Reporting Review Panel, predecessor of the Conduct Committee, was criticised for being reactive, i.e. acting only on complaints or media revelations that a particular set of accounts was defective rather than checking or investigating of its own motion. In 2018/19 the Conduct Committee reviewed the reports of some 207 companies, sent letters raising queries to 80, and in 11 cases there was a restatement or correction of the numbers in the accounts.[229]

FILING ACCOUNTS AND REPORTS WITH THE REGISTRAR

22–038 The statutory requirement to produce accounts and reports would be of little use if there were no provisions for the information so generated to reach the hands of those who might make use of it. This is done in two ways under the CA 2006: circulation to the members (discussed below) and delivery of the accounts to the Registrar.[230] By delivery to the Registrar, the accounts and reports become public documents.

---

222 Companies (Audit, Investigation and Community Enterprise) Act 2004 s.14(2); CA 2006 s.456(1)–(3). BEIS (*Restoring Trust in Audit and Corporate Governance* (March 2021), para.4.2) has proposed that the new accounting regulator (ARGA) should be able to exercise this power directly.

223 CA 2006 s.456(5)–(6).

224 CA 2006 s.456(2)–(7).

225 Supervision of Accounts and Reports (Prescribed Body) and Companies (Defective Accounts and Directors' Reports)(Authorised Person) Order 2012 (SI 2012/1439) regs 2–4.

226 Where Companies House takes the lead: CLR, Completing, para.12.48.

227 CA 2006 s.459.

228 CA 2006 ss.460–462.

229 FRC, *Annual Review of Corporate Reporting 2018/9*, pp.8–10. The restatement occurs in the following year's accounts.

230 CA 2006 s.441.

Speed of filing

A source of complaint in the past has been the length of time between the end of the financial year and the latest date laid down for filing the accounts and reports with the Registrar. The CLR thought that modern technology permitted speedier filing than had been required in the past and recommended that the period be reduced from seven to six months for public companies and ten to seven for private companies.[231] Section 442 implements the former reform but only marginally reduces the private company period (to nine months).[232] For public companies whose securities are traded on a regulated market the period for publication of the annual accounts and reports is four months from the end of the financial year,[233] though the core elements in the accounts may have been made available earlier through a preliminary public announcement of the results. **22–039**

A linked source of complaint has been non-compliance with the filing time-limits. The formal sanctions are criminal liabilities on the directors and civil penalties on the company. If the filing requirements are not complied with on time, any person who was a director immediately before the end of the time allowed is liable to a fine and, for continued contravention, to a daily default fine, unless the director can prove that she or he took all reasonable steps for securing that the accounts were delivered in time.[234] Furthermore, if the directors fail to make good the default within 14 days after the service of a notice requiring compliance, the court, on the application of the Registrar or any member or creditor of the company, may make an order directing the directors or any of them to make good the default within such time as may be specified and may order them to pay the costs of and incidental to the application.[235]

To these criminal sanctions against directors, the CA 2006 adds civil penalties against the company.[236] The amount of the penalty, recoverable by the Registrar, varies according to whether the company is private or public and to the length of time that the default continues; the minimum being £150 for a private company and £750 for a public company when the default is for not more than one month, and the maximum £1,500 for a private and £7,500 for a public company when the default exceeds six months.[237] There are obvious attractions in affording the Registrar an additional weapon in the form of a penalty recoverable by civil suit to which there is no defence once it is shown that accounts have not been delivered on time. Presumably, the thought is that civil sanctions on the company

[231] CLR, Final Report I, paras 4.49–4.32 and 8.80 onwards.

[232] CA 2006 s.442 deals with some exceptional cases as well. During the Covid pandemic the filing period was temporarily extended: Corporate Insolvency and Governance Act 2020 s.38.

[233] See FCA, Disclosure and Transparency Rule 4.1.3.

[234] CA 2006 s.451. But, to spike the guns of barrack-room lawyers, it is expressly stated that it is not a defence to prove that the documents required were not in fact prepared in accordance with the Act!

[235] CA 2006 s.452. If they fail to do so, they will be in contempt of court and liable to imprisonment. The subsection does not say who may serve such a notice so presumably anyone can: but in practice it is likely to be the Registrar who does so—though the subsection makes it pretty clear that a member or creditor could.

[236] CA 2006 s.453 and the Companies (Late Filing Penalties) and Limited Liability Partnerships (Filing Periods and Late Filing Penalties) Regulations 2008 (SI 2008/497).

[237] The Scheme withstood judicial review in *R. (POW Trust) v Registrar of Companies* [2002] EWHC 2783 (Admin); [2004] B.C.C. 268.

will put pressure on shareholders to intervene and secure compliance on the part of the directors, but it is not clear how effective this mechanism is. It may be that the shareholders simply lose dividends as well as suffer from a failure on the part of the directors to perform a duty intended to protect them.[238] In 2019/20 the compliance rate was nearly 99% across the UK but nevertheless some 1,900 convictions for failure to file accounts on time were obtained and over 214,000 late filing penalties were imposed (totalling over £94 million), mainly in relation to private companies, but it is not clear how much was collected.[239]

Modifications of the full filing requirements

22–040 Filing with the Registrar is such a sensitive issue precisely because the information in the accounts and reports thus becomes publicly available. The CA 2006 itself makes some concessions to the fear of publicity in the case of small, medium-sized and unlimited companies, by way of derogations from the full filing regime. The full regime requires filing of the annual accounts, the directors' report (and conceivably a separate corporate governance statement), the strategic report and (in the case of a quoted company) the directors' remuneration report, and the auditor's report on those accounts and reports (assuming the company is subject to audit).[240] If the company has been required to produce group accounts, then the full regime applies to both the group and individual accounts.[241] The balance sheet must contain the name of the person who signed it on behalf of the board.[242] As we have noted along the way, some categories of company are not required to produce the full range of these accounts and reports, especially small and micro companies, but also some categories of large companies. Naturally, they are not required to file a document they are not required to produce. The issue here is whether directors are required to give publicity to, i.e. file or file in full, a document they are required to produce for their shareholders.

Unlimited companies (necessarily private companies) are in principle exempt from filing any accounts and reports, provided the unlimited company is not part of a group containing limited companies and is not a banking or insurance company.[243] This is a good example of the link between limited liability and public financial disclosure, i.e. the latter is dispensed with if the former is not present.[244] Of course, the unlimited liability company still has to produce and circulate accounts to the members, who have perhaps an even bigger interest in the proper running of the company if their liability is unlimited.

238 The company could, presumably, sue the directors to recover its loss resulting from their default. But unless the company goes into liquidation, administration or receivership this is unlikely to happen.

239 Companies House, *Management Information 2019/20*, Tables 1, 3 and 5 (available at: *https://www.gov.uk/government/statistical-data-sets/companies-house-management-information-tables-2019-20* [Accessed 27 March 2021]). Thus, the average penalty was less than £450.

240 CA 2006 ss.446 and 447.

241 CA 2006 s.471.

242 See para.22–035.

243 CA 2006 ss.448. There are certain other disqualifications set out in the section.

244 The same distinction can be found between partnerships (accounts need not be made public) and limited liability partnerships (public disclosure required).

Small companies (and thus also micro companies) subject to the small company regime are required to produce only individual accounts and, in addition, they may choose to file only a balance sheet and not the profit and loss account and directors' report, though they may make them publicly available, if they wish.[245] Until recently, there was a further relaxation for small companies in that the filed copy of the balance sheet (and the filed copy of the profit and loss account, if one was filed at all) were permitted to be less detailed than the accounts made available to the members, at least where the company produces Companies Act accounts. These were the so-called "abbreviated" accounts.[246] However, in 2015 changes were made which withdrew this facility.[247] The CLR would have required small companies to file both balance sheet and profit and loss account as prepared for the members. It took the view that the filed accounts of small companies were "not meaningful".[248] The general conclusion that little insight into the financial position of a company subject to the small company regime will normally be obtained from consulting its filed accounts probably remains true, given that the option not to file a profit and loss account is still available.

Other information available from the Registrar

The annual accounts and reports are probably the most important documents filed with the Registrar[249] and thus made public, because they give reasonably current (though by no means completely up-to-date) information about the state of the company's businesses.[250] However, the accounts and reports do not constitute the whole of the information about the company which is publicly available from the Registrar, as we see at various points in this work. The next most important document thus made available is probably the company's constitution, mainly its articles of association.[251] After that is the list of the company's directors, which 22–041

[245] CA 2006 s.444(1). On the exemption from group accounts see para.22–011. Small companies excluded from the small companies regime because a member of an ineligible group may choose not to file a directors' report, but must file a profit and loss account: s.444A.

[246] CA 2006 s.444(3)—as originally enacted.

[247] Companies, Partnerships and Groups (Accounts and Reports) Regulations 2015 (SI 2015/980) reg.8. This step was less radical than it might seem at first sight, since a small company may prepare (and therefore publish) *abridged* accounts if all shareholders agree (see para.22–022) and, even if they do not, the disclosure requirements of the Small Regulations are much less demanding than those of the Large Regulations. These regulations also removed the facility for medium-sized companies to file an abbreviated profit and loss account (previously in s.445(3)(4)).

[248] CLR, Developing, paras 8.32–8.34. Although using the term "abbreviated accounts", the CLR appears to include in it the option not to file a profit and loss account at all. The CLR would have dealt with small company sensitivities through the simplified format rules for the accounts prepared for the members.

[249] Actually, there are three Registrars—one for each of the UK jurisdictions—though their functions are similar: s.1060.

[250] Hence with companies whose securities are traded on a regulated market the obligation on the company (a) to produce reports more often than annually; and (b) to report material changes as they occur. See Ch.27.

[251] See para.3–010.

must be updated as changes occur.[252] Amongst the other information available through the Registrar are the list of those with significant economic interests in the company—an important recent addition,[253] the address of its registered office,[254] the amount of its issued share capital[255] and details of charges on its property.[256]

"Any person" has the right to inspect the register maintained by the Registrar, subject to certain limited limitations imposed in the interests of privacy.[257] There is also a right to obtain a copy of material on the register, subject to a fee,[258] and a copy duly certified by the Registrar is evidence in legal proceedings of equal validity to the original.[259] The applicant has the choice in relation to the most central items of information to make the request for inspection or copy electronically or in hard copy, and to receive the information in either way.[260]

Confirmation statement

22–042 This document used to be called the "annual return" until the current term was substituted by the Small Business, Enterprise and Employment Act 2015. As the former name suggested, the confirmation statement is produced each year by the company. It is delivered to the Registrar by the company, but, unlike the accounts and reports considered above, it is not a document sent to the members, nor is it normally filed with the annual reports and accounts.[261] The Registrar is the principal addressee of the annual return[262] (though, of course, any member may access it under the provisions discussed in the previous paragraph). Nevertheless it is convenient to consider it here. Moreover, it is a document required to be submitted by every company, whatever its obligations as to accounts and reports.

The 2015 Act reduced the significance of the previous annual return, which was already a rather historical document. The annual return collated much information that should have been, and probably had been, delivered to the Registrar when the relevant transactions occurred, so its advantage was that an enquirer should find it unnecessary to search back beyond the latest annual return on the file. The new rules approach the issue from the point of view of the

---

[252] See para.9–007. Also to be disclosed is the identity of the company's secretary, if there is one: s.276.

[253] See para.2–038.

[254] See ss.9(5)(a) and 86–87. This is important because it is there that legal process can be served on it.

[255] See para.16–014. The returns of allotments will show to whom the shares were initially issued but not who now owns them.

[256] See Ch.32. This is likely to be more up-to-date than the filed accounts and so a better indicator of creditworthiness.

[257] See ss.1085 and 1087, the latter excluding access, for example, to directors' residential addresses (see para.9–007).

[258] CA 2006 s.1086.

[259] CA 2006 s.1091(3).

[260] CA 2006 ss.1089 and 1090. The information in relation to which this right exists is set out in s.1078.

[261] CA 2006 s.853A. The return date is normally the anniversary of the company's incorporation, i.e. the end of the company's ARP.

[262] Hence the provisions about the confirmation statement are set out in a separate Part of the Act (Pt 24).

company. No longer is the company required to repeat information already provided to the Registrar. Provided the company is up-to-date with its filings, the rules now simply require the company to confirm that the information held by the Registrar is complete and current. If not, the necessary information must be supplied along with the confirmation statement.[263] The disadvantage of this approach to searchers has probably been eliminated through the introduction of electronic search facilities.

Since we have noted at the appropriate points in the book when information must be supplied by the company to the Registrar, such as the statement of capital or the statement of persons with significant control, we need not rehearse those matters again here. The main function of the confirmation statement is to jog the corporate memory about its filing obligations. Despite the criminal sanctions[264] for non-compliance with the obligation to provide a confirmation statement and provision by the Registrar of electronic means for submitting it, companies are not always prompt in complying with this obligation. Compliance levels for filing confirmation statements were overall about one-and-a-half percentage points lower than for the accounts and some 1,270 convictions were obtained in 2019–2020.[265] In fact, failure to file the confirmation statement often alerts the Registrar to more fundamental issues with the company and may lead to the taking of steps which culminate in the company's removal from the register.

Other forms of publicity for the accounts and reports

Although filing with the Registrar is the only form of publicity for the annual accounts and reports mandated for all companies by the Act, in fact large companies often, and other companies sometimes, make their annual statements available more generally; and quoted and traded companies are now required to provide website publication, where access must be available without charge.[266] Where a company chooses or is required to make its annual statements available in a way which is calculated to invite members of the public generally, or a class of them, to read it, then the Act requires the name of the person who signed the balance sheet or the narrative reports on behalf of the company to be stated.[267] In addition, they must be accompanied by the auditor's report (if there is one) and a company preparing group accounts cannot publish only its individual accounts.[268] In short, a non-traded or quoted company is not required to publish its annual accounts other than via the Registrar, but if it does so, it must do so in full. 22–043

The accounts described above are known as the company's "statutory accounts". A company is not prohibited from publishing other accounts dealing with the relevant financial year, thought this is in fact rare. If the company does so, it must include with them a statement that these accounts are not the statutory

[263] CA 2006 s.853A(1).

[264] CA 2006 s.853L: offence by company, every director, shadow director and secretary, and every other officer who is in default.

[265] Companies House, *Management Information 2019/20*, Tables 2 and 5.

[266] CA 2006 s.430. The extension to traded companies was made in 2019.

[267] CA 2006 ss.433 and 436.

[268] CA 2006 s.434.

accounts and disclose whether the statutory accounts have been filed and whether the auditors have reported on them and, if so, whether the auditors' report was qualified. Nor may an auditors' report on the statutory accounts be published with the non-statutory accounts.[269] If the company is listed on a regulated market, it will be required to produce a set of (less elaborate) accounts and a management report six months into the financial year,[270] as well as annual ones. However, such accounts do not fall into the category of "non-statutory accounts" because they do not cover an entire financial year.

CONSIDERATION OF THE ACCOUNTS AND REPORTS BY THE MEMBERS

Circulation to the members

22–044 Since the accounts and reports are communications from the directors to the members, it is not surprising that the Act requires their circulation to the members.[271] However, not only the members but also the company's debenture-holders (i.e. its long-term lenders holding the company's debt securities)[272] must receive copies, since their chances of being repaid depend upon the financial health of the company. Thirdly, anyone who is entitled to receive notice of general meetings of the company is to be sent the accounts and reports, a category which includes the directors themselves (hardly a necessary requirement) and anyone else entitled to notice under the particular company's articles.[273] The obligation to circulate arises only if the company has a current address for the person in question.[274] Finally, those nominated to enjoy information rights will receive copies of the accounts and reports.[275] Just to make sure, the Act also provides that shareholders and debenture-holders can at any time demand copies of the most recent annual accounts and reports and the company must comply with the request within seven days.[276]

Circulation of the Strategic Report only

22–045 There are two linked problems with the circulation requirements. First, the full accounts and reports may be grist to the mills of the analysts, but lots of individual shareholders find the full set more daunting than useful. Secondly, the

---

[269] CA 2006 s.435.

[270] DTR 4.2. See Ch.27. This obligation has its origin in the Transparency Directive, although companies on the Official List have been required to produce half-yearly reports since a much earlier date.

[271] CA 2006 s.423(1). The phrase "annual accounts and reports" is defined in s.471(2) separately for unquoted and quoted companies.

[272] See Ch.31.

[273] CA 2006 s.307. In the case of companies without share capital only this third category need be circulated: s.423(4).

[274] CA 2006 s.423(2)–(3).

[275] CA 2006 s.146. See para.12–021.

[276] CA 2006 ss.431 (unquoted companies) and 432 (quoted companies). This right is also extended to those nominated to enjoy information rights: s.146(3)(b).

circulation requirement is an expensive one for the company to meet.[277] Both these concerns are addressed by the provisions which allow companies to circulate something less than the full accounts and reports. Initially, that something less was a "summary financial statement", but with the introduction of the strategic report, that document became the substitute.

This facility was previously available only to companies whose securities were traded on certain public markets, but now it is in principle open to all companies.[278] Moreover, the burden is on the recipient to ask to continue to receive the full accounts and report. If, after being sent an appropriate notice from the company, the recipient does not respond with a contrary statement within 28 days, he or she will be deemed to have opted for the SR, though that "choice" can be reversed at any time.[279] The provisions are, however, default rules, in the sense that the company in its constitution or the instrument creating the debentures may deprive itself of this facility. The right to send the SR and not the full set of accounts and reports is also dependent on the company observing the relevant provisions of the CA 2006 relating to the audit, filing and approval of the full accounts and reports.[280] The SR must be accompanied by a warning that it is only part of the annual accounts and reports; informing the reader how to obtain full copies; stating whether any of the required auditor certifications was qualified; and containing one (clearly important) figure from outside the strategic report, i.e. the "single total remuneration" figure from the directors' remuneration report in the case of quoted companies.[281]

An alternative, or additional, way, of addressing circulation costs is to encourage members to receive communications (whether full accounts and reports or only the SR) from the company in electronic form or via the company's website. This has been discussed in Ch.12.[282] It is widely used.

Laying the accounts and reports before the members

Circulating the accounts and reports to the members and others allows them to consider them on an individual basis, but such consideration is not likely to lead to significant action in the case of companies with larger bodies of shareholders, unless there is some facility for collective consideration of the accounts and reports. As far as private companies are concerned, there is no longer any statutory requirement for such collective consideration, no matter how large a 22–046

---

[277] It is reported that in 2006 postmen in the UK were restricted as to the number of sets of the annual accounts and reports of HSBC bank they were permitted to carry at any one time, because of the weight of the document.

[278] CA 2006 s.426.

[279] CA 2006 s.426(2)(3) and Companies (Receipt of Accounts and Reports) Regulations 2013 (SI 2013/1973). The consultation may take place as part of the circulation of the annual accounts and reports (and relate to future years) or be a free-standing consultation. Requesting to continue with the full set must be made easy, depending simply on ticking a box on a form, postage on which has been pre-paid by the company, at least if the recipient has an address in the EEA. Those who enjoy information rights are within this procedure as well: s.426(5).

[280] Receipt Regulations reg.5.

[281] CA 2006 s.426A. On the "single total remuneration" figure see para.11–019.

[282] See para.12–057.

shareholding body that company may have. A private company is required by the statute to circulate its annual accounts and reports at the time it delivers them to the Registrar,[283] and any further action is a matter for the shareholders or the company's articles. The shareholders might seek to convene a meeting[284] or the articles might require annual consideration of the accounts and reports at a meeting, which the directors would be obliged to convene.

As far as public companies are concerned, the traditional obligation "to lay the accounts and reports before a general meeting" still applies.[285] This formulation implies that the shareholders are not required to consider a resolution to approve the accounts and reports (as is the case in many countries), but they must be afforded an opportunity to discuss them. Indeed, this item on the agenda is normally used to allow a wide-ranging discussion of the company's business.[286] The CA 2006 calls the meeting at which the accounts and reports are considered the "accounts meeting"[287] and it is in fact normally the company's annual general meeting, though it does not need to be so. The accounts and reports must be circulated at least 21 days before the accounts meeting and that meeting must be held not later than the end of the period for the filing of the accounts and reports with the Registrar, i.e. six months after the end of the financial year in the case of a public company. As we noted in Ch.12,[288] the Government backed away from the CLR's proposal that, after circulation, there should be a pause of two weeks, during which shareholders could formulate, if they wished, resolutions on the accounts and reports to be considered at the meeting.

CONCLUSION

22–047 Part 15 of the Act, dealing with the annual accounts and reports, constitutes a substantial part of the CA 2006, long though that Act is. Part 15 contains over 100 sections, and this is an indication of the central role played by annual reporting in the structure of the companies legislation. Excessive though the detail of the Act, subordinate legislation and accounting standards is to anyone not an accountant, an understanding of the central principles of the annual reporting process is central to understanding the philosophy of company law.

The developments in this Part of the Act law reflect a broader trend in company law towards greater specialisation in the applicable rules according to the economic importance of different types of company. This classification proceeds broadly by reference to direct indicators of economic size (turnover, balance sheet total and number of employees) or by reference to the divorce between ownership and control (i.e. whether the shares are publicly traded), which is an indirect indicator of economic size. For the largest publicly traded

[283] CA 2006 s.424(2). For delivery to the Registrar, see para.22–038. Of course, the company cannot evade this obligation simply by not filing the accounts and report with the Registrar: s.424(2)(a).

[284] See para.12–030.

[285] CA 2006 ss.437–438.

[286] See para.12–023.

[287] CA 2006 s.437(3).

[288] See para.12–059.

companies, not only is financial reporting increasingly demanding, as International Financial Reporting Standards expand their scope, but so are the demands of narrative reporting. This expansion of reporting requirements is driven substantially by investor demand but also in part by a governmental desire to encourage investors (and in some cases pressure-groups) to engage with the management of their investee companies, even beyond what they might themselves do, if left to their own devices. At the other end of the scale, micro companies have obtained a further relaxation of the already reduced rules which apply to small companies. In between, medium-sized companies benefit from some relaxations whilst large, but not publicly traded, companies are slowly being brought with the regime for publicly traded companies (for example, in relation to greenhouse gas emissions and governance arrangements).

CHAPTER 23

AUDITS AND AUDITORS

INTRODUCTION

23–001 The statutory accounts and reports discussed in the previous chapter are the responsibility of the directors. However, all modern company law systems have long accepted the principle that the reliability of the accounts and reports will be increased if there exists a system of independent third-party verification. The temptation to present the accounts in a light which is unduly favourable to the management is one likely to afflict all boards of directors at one time or another—and the temptation is likely to be at its strongest when the financial condition of the company is at its weakest and shareholders, creditors and investors are most in need of access to the truth. To provide such third-party verification is the traditional role of the audit.

Sources of audit law

23–002 We saw in the last chapter that the global nature of modern large businesses creates a strong pressure for global accounting standards and there have certainly been harmonisation initiatives of this sort in EU Law. This is equally the case with auditing, as an essential complement to accounts. Global auditing standards have been developed and adopted in the UK.[1] Moreover, as one might expect, the UK's membership of the EU has had a significant impact on the development of audit law. That process began with an EU directive on auditors' qualifications,[2] but in the wake of various corporate scandals at the beginning of the century (in the US, as much as in Europe) that directive was replaced by one that additionally regulated the auditing process.[3] After the global financial crisis, the auditing regime was again amended by further EU directives in 2013,[4] with the introduction in 2014 of EU Regulation 537/2014,[5] imposing supplementary rules for the largest companies (namely, companies whose securities are traded on regulated markets termed "public interest entities" (PIEs)).[6] Accordingly, EU legislation was not only significant in terms of the substantive principles relating to auditors, but was also instrumental in changing (and simplifying) the domestic institutional arrangements in this area. Whilst the direct effect of this EU legislation has disappeared following the UK's departure from the EU, many provisions will continue to operate by way of "retained" EU law, which includes

---

[1] See para.23–028.

[2] Directive 84/253 on the approval of persons responsible for carrying out the statutory audits of accounting documents [1984] OJ L126/20.

[3] Directive 2006/43 on statutory audits of annual accounts and consolidated accounts [2006] OJ L157/87.

[4] Directive 2013/34 on the annual financial statements [2013] OJ L182/19; Directive 2014/56 on statutory audits of annual accounts and consolidated accounts [2014] OJ L158/196, implemented by Statutory Auditors and Third Country Auditors Regulations 2016 (SI 2016/649) and 2017 (SI 2017/516).

[5] Regulation 537/2014 on specific requirements regarding statutory audit of public-interest entities [2014] OJ L158/77, which is referred to below as the "Regulation".

[6] Regulation art.1. The "PIE" definition embraces in addition banks and insurance companies, whether their securities are traded on a regulated market or not, but the special rules for financial institutions are ignored in this chapter. For the definition of regulated markets, see para.25–008. In the UK, one can think of the term as referring to the Main Market of the London Stock Exchange.

both "EU-derived domestic legislation" and "direct EU legislation".[7] Accordingly, Regulation 537/2014 will continue to operate (until amended or revoked by subsequent domestic legislation)[8] alongside the CA 2006 and the domestic regulations relating to statutory auditors, both of which had previously implemented the EU directives in this area.[9] These traditional forms of "hard law" are also supplemented by softer law in the form of auditing standards promulgated by the Financial Reporting Council or by the relevant professional bodies.[10] In light of the institutional overhaul recommended by the Kingman Committee,[11] however, the current legal patchwork may ultimately be replaced by a more comprehensive legal framework. Indeed, the Government announced in March 2021 that the Financial Reporting Council is likely to be replaced by a new regulator, the Audit, Reporting and Governance Authority.

The duties of the auditor

To summarise briefly the role of the auditor, it is the production of a report to the members of the company that gives the auditor's opinion on a number of issues. The core opinion is whether: **23–003**

(1) The annual accounts give a true and fair view of the financial position of the company (or the group, in the case of group accounts)[12]; have been properly prepared in accordance with the relevant financial reporting framework[13]; and have been prepared in accordance with the requirements of the CA 2006.[14]

(2) The directors' report for the financial year and any strategic report is consistent with the accounts; has been prepared in accordance with the applicable legal requirements; and whether any material misstatements have been identified[15] (the same or similar duties arising in relation to the separate corporate governance statement, if the company has produced one).[16]

[7] European Union (Withdrawal) Act 2018 ss.2–3.

[8] For amendment to the Regulation to take account of Brexit, see Statutory Auditors and Third Country Auditors (Amendment) (EU Exit) Regulations 2019 (SI 2019/177) regs 75–104.

[9] Statutory Auditors and Third Country Auditors Regulations 2016 (SI 2016/649); Statutory Auditors and Third Country Auditors Regulations 2017 (SI 2017/516).

[10] See para.23–011.

[11] Kingman Committee, *Independent Review of the Financial Reporting Council* (December 2018). For acceptance of the recommendations of the Kingman Committee, see Department for Business, Energy and Industrial Strategy, *Restoring Trust in Audit and Corporate Governance* (March 2021).

[12] For the distinction between individual and group accounts see para.22–011.

[13] For the meaning of this term, see para.22–016.

[14] CA 2006 s.495(3), as amended by International Accounting Standards and European Public Limited-Liability Company (Amendment etc) (EU Exit) Regulations 2019 (SI 2019/685) Sch.1(1)(1) para.23. For micro-company accounts the requirement about accounting standards is qualified by CA 2006 s.495(3A), for the reasons explained in para.22–020.

[15] CA 2006 s.496. If misstatements have been made, there must be an indication of their nature: CA 2006 s.496(1)(c). On the directors' report, see para.22–025.

[16] CA 2006 s.497A. For the directors' strategic report, see para.23–027. For the corporate governance statement, see Financial Conduct Authority, Disclosure Guidance and Transparency Rules Sourcebook DTR7.2. In the latter case, the auditor must report whether the DTR has been satisfied.

(3) The auditable part of the directors' remuneration report (DRR) has been properly prepared in accordance with the CA 2006.[17]

The auditor's report must be either "qualified" or "unqualified".[18] An unqualified report is one where the auditor is able to give the opinions mentioned above; a qualified report (which is a serious thing for the company and its members) is one where one or more of the opinions mentioned above cannot be given.[19] The auditor's report to the members must contain opinions on matters (1)–(3) above. In addition:

(4) In relation to PIEs, there must be a discussion in the report of the assessed risks of fraud or material misstatement in the company's accounts.[20] This falls short of requiring an opinion about whether or not there has been fraud or misstatement, but the report must "explain to what extent the statutory audit was considered capable of detecting irregularities, including fraud".[21]

Depending upon the circumstances, the auditor's report may also have to deal with further items. The most important potential matters that may need discussion are:

(5) Those "that may cast significant doubt about the company's ability to continue to adopt the going concern basis of accounting".[22]

In addition, certain matters may need to be mentioned arising out of the auditor's duty, in preparing the report, to carry out investigations so as to be able to form an opinion as to whether:

(6) Adequate accounting records have been kept by the company.
(7) The company's individual accounts are in agreement with the accounting records.
(8) In the case of a quoted company or unquoted traded company, the auditable part of the DRR is in agreement with the accounting records and returns.[23]

The mandatory report on this statement indicates, among other things, the increased importance attached to internal control and risk management, as does the requirement on the auditors to state whether a separate corporate governance statement has been prepared, if the directors have not chosen to include it in their report: see CA 2006 s.498A.

[17] CA 2006 s.497. The auditable part of the DRR is that set out in the Large and Medium-sized Companies and Groups (Accounts and Reports) Regulations 2008 (SI 2008/410) reg.11(3) and Sch.8 Pt 3. On the directors' remuneration report, see para.11–019.

[18] CA 2006 s.495(4).

[19] The auditor may refer to matters to which attention needs to be drawn without necessarily qualifying the report: see CA 2016 s.495(4)(b).

[20] Regulation art.10(2)(c), as amended by the Statutory Auditors and Third Country Auditors (Amendment) (EU Exit) Regulations 2019 (SI 2019/177).

[21] Regulation art.10(2)(d), as amended by the Statutory Auditors and Third Country Auditors (Amendment) (EU Exit) Regulations 2019 (SI 2019/177).

[22] CA 2006 s.495(4)(c). Whilst this requirement was only formally introduced in 2016, auditing standards previously required such discussion in any event.

[23] CA 2006 s.498(1)–(2).

If all is well in relation to the above three issues, the auditor need say nothing in the report. If it is not, the auditor must state this fact:

(9) In addition, if the auditor has failed to obtain all the information and explanations that he or she believes to be necessary for the purposes of the audit, that fact must be stated in the report.[24]

Finally, there are two specific provisions relating to the small company accounts and the DRR:

(10) Where the directors have taken advantage of the relaxations for small companies when preparing the company's accounts, strategic report or the directors' report, the auditor must state in the report his opinion that they were not entitled to do so, if he forms such an opinion.[25]

(11) If the auditor finds that the statutory provisions on the disclosure of directors' remuneration have not been complied with, there is a duty upon the auditor, so far as he or she is reasonably able, to provide the particulars that should have been given in the directors' report or the DRR.[26] Apart from this, however, the auditor is not under an obligation to revise the accounts and reports, so as to bring them into line with the applicable requirements; that is the task of the directors who produce the reports in question.

In the not-uncommon case where more than one person is appointed auditor, it must be disclosed whether they all agree on the matters contained in the report and the reasons for any disagreement must be given.

Undoubtedly, the most important and time-consuming of the auditor's tasks is that listed at (1) above, because it amounts to a general endorsement of the accuracy of the accounts, though (4) is likely to add considerably to the auditor's burdens (and the company's costs) in the case of a PIE. In some cases, the auditor may also be required to report facts uncovered to third parties, especially regulators, though this development has been controversial.[27]

Overarching issues

There are three main issues of principle about audits and auditors. First, is the benefit of the audit greater than its costs for all companies? If not, is there a case for exempting some classes of company from the requirement[28] to have an audit? Secondly, once an audit is required, the temptation on management to present the accounts in an unduly favourable light can be given effect only if they can persuade the auditors to accept such an unduly favourable presentation. What steps, then, can and should be taken to ensure the independence of the auditors **23–004**

---

[24] CA 2006 s.498(3).

[25] CA 2006 s.498(5). For the definition of a small business, see para.22–004.

[26] CA 2006 s.498(4).

[27] See para.23–021.

[28] For the basic requirement of a mandatory audit of the statutory accounts, see CA 2006 s.475(1).

from the management of the company? Thirdly, even if the auditor is independent, what steps should be taken to ensure that a good job will be done, in particular what role should be played by civil liability sounding in damages on the part of the auditor towards those who have relied on the reports? Each of these key issues will be examined in turn below.

The auditor today, at least in large firms, is not an individual practitioner, but a member of a firm, often of international scale, and the audit is carried out by a team of auditors under the leadership of one or more partners in the firm. Where necessary, the discussion below will refer to these realities. Otherwise, the word "auditor" is used to cover both firms and sole practitioners, individuals and teams of auditors.

AUDIT EXEMPTION

Small companies

23–005 Over time, a very substantial set of audit exemptions has been introduced.[29] Arguably, the most significant is the exemption for "small companies",[30] as the definition of what counts as "small" for this purpose has been progressively enlarged. This exemption represented a fairly significant change of governmental policy, as it had previously been committed to a universal audit requirement.[31] What triggered the reversal seems to have been the additional costs generated by the implementation in the CA 1989 of EU law,[32] as this was alleged to have a disproportionate impact on the audit costs of very small firms. Once begun, the exemption process seems to have acquired a life of its own. Despite the opposition from some users of accounts, notably HM Revenue and Customs and some banks, the deregulatory pressure was successful.

An indication of the expansion of the small company exemption from audit can be gained from looking at how the upper turnover figure for exemption has increased over the years. In 1994, this was set at £90,000[33]; it was raised to £300,000 in 1997[34]; and in 2000 was raised again to £1 million.[35] The Company Law Review recommended a further increase to the level for being a small company for accounts purposes; and that, at the same time, the UK's definition of

[29] In 2011, it was reported that 88% of non-dormant companies were exempt from audit of their annual accounts (both individual and group): see Department for Business, Innovation and Skills, *Consultation on Audit Exemptions and Change of Accounting Framework* (October 2011), URN 11/1193, para.32.

[30] CA 2006 s.477(1).

[31] See Department of Trade and Industry, *Accounting and Audit Requirements for Small Firms: A Consultative Document* (1985); *Consultative Document on Amending the Fourth Company Law Directive on Annual Accounts* (1989). The Fourth Directive, however, permitted Member States to exempt small companies from the audit.

[32] Directive 84/253 on the approval of persons responsible for carrying out the statutory audits of accounting documents [1984] OJ L126/20, repealed and replaced by Directive 2006/43 on statutory audits of annual accounts and consolidated accounts [2006] OJ L157/87 from June 2006.

[33] Companies Act 1985 (Audit Exemption Regulations) 1994 (SI 1994/1935).

[34] Companies Act 1985 (Audit Exemption) (Amendment) Regulations 1997 (SI 1997/936).

[35] Companies Act 1985 (Audit Exemption) (Amendment) Regulations 2000 (SI 2000/1430).

a "small" company should be revised upwards to the level permitted by EU law.[36] This initially raised the turnover figure to £4.8 million and then to the current level of £10.2 million.[37] The exempt company must also meet one or other of the limits relating to a company's balance sheet (£5.1 million) and workforce (50 employees), but these are both still elevated.[38] Thus, there has been a move from a very cautious approach to this audit exemption to an approach where the word "small" becomes something of a misnomer. Accordingly, over a relatively short period, a very substantial process of removing third-party assurance in relation to the accounts of small companies has taken place.[39]

In short, after a period in which access for small companies to the audit exemption was somewhat more restricted than access to the small company accounting regime, the government decided in 2012 to adopt the simple rule that companies that are small for accounts purposes are also entitled to the audit exemption.[40] Even if the company meets this condition, it may nevertheless be excluded from the audit exemption, on grounds that parallel the loss of small company status for accounts purposes.[41] In particular, the company must not be a public company.[42] In addition, if the company is a member of a group, it will qualify for the exemption only if the group qualifies as small and is not an ineligible group.[43] Further, even if a company is exempt from audit on the ground of its size (or the ground of dormancy, as considered further below) members representing at least 10% of the nominal value of the company's issued share capital (or any class of it)[44] may demand an audit for a particular financial year, provided the notice is given after the financial year commences and within one year of its end.[45] Thus, notice must be given on a year-by-year basis and the members cannot make a demand relating to future financial years (when they might not meet the size threshold). **23–006**

Where the small company exemption applies and is used, the directors must confirm in a statement attached to the balance sheet that the company was

---

[36] Final Report I, paras 4.29–4.31 and 4.43–4.45. The definition of "small" company for auditing purposes now dovetails with the definition of the same concept for accounts purposes: see CA 2006 ss.382(3) and 477(4).

[37] CA 2006 s.382(3). See further para.22–006.

[38] CA 2006 s.382(3).

[39] In contrast, all but the smallest charitable companies remain subject to audit under the Charities Act 2011. The reason for these more stringent requirements for charities appears to be that the persons with the strongest financial interest in whether a charitable company uses its money properly are its donors, but they are not typically members of the company and so do not have access to the control rights over the management of the company that members usually have. Thus, there is a stronger case for third-party verification than in the case of the accounts of non-charitable small companies. No doubt for this reason one sees in the charities legislation full use being made of the technique of requiring auditors or reporting accountants to make reports to the regulator, the Charities Commission.

[40] CA 2006 s.477(4). See further para.22–006.

[41] CA 2006 ss.478–479.

[42] CA 2006 ss.478(a)–(b). The exclusion extends to companies in the financial services sector.

[43] CA 2006 s.479(1). For the statutory definition of "small" and "ineligible" groups, see CA 2006 ss.383–384. See further para.22–006.

[44] CA 2006 s.476(2). Alternatively, the request can be made by 10% in number of the members, if there is no share capital.

[45] CA 2006 s.476(1).

entitled to the exemption, that no effective notice has been delivered requiring an audit and that the directors acknowledge their responsibilities for ensuring that the company keeps accounting records and for preparing accounts that give a true and fair view of the state of the company's affairs.[46] None of this means, however, that small companies will never have their accounts audited. If a company sees value in providing such assurance to members, creditors or investors, it may choose to have an audit. More likely, banks or other large creditors may insist on an audit as part of the process of considering whether to make a loan to the company. Where the relevant company qualifies as a "micro" company, however, choosing to have an audit will not actually result in the company revealing any more information if it has chosen to stick to the minimum standards for such companies.[47]

Subsidiaries

23–007 Subsidiary companies, of any size, are exempt from the audit requirement, under reforms introduced in 2012, subject to certain conditions.[48] The central requirement is that the parent company guarantees all the outstanding liabilities of the subsidiary at the end of the financial year until they are satisfied in full, and the guarantee must be enforceable against the parent by any person to whom the subsidiary is liable.[49] Apart from extensive publicity requirements, this exemption is confined in various ways. It is available only where the parent is incorporated in the UK; the subsidiary's securities are not traded on a regulated market (it is rare for them to be so traded in the UK); all the company's members agree to forego the audit in the relevant financial year; and the subsidiary's accounts are included in the parent's consolidated accounts.[50] The underlying policy argument is that the audit of the subsidiary's accounts in such cases adds little by way of value to the audit of the consolidated accounts—though, equally, given the requirement for audit at group level, the savings from omitting the subsidiary audit are probably not enormous.

Dormant companies

23–008 A further and less controversial type of company that is exempt from audit is the so-called "dormant" company.[51] A company is dormant during a period when there is "no significant accounting transaction" undertaken, an accounting transaction being one that needs to be recorded in the company's accounting records.[52] Where the company has been dormant since its formation, no other conditions need be met before the exemption is granted.[53] The most obvious and

[46] CA 2006 s.475(2)–(4). This provision applies to the exemption on grounds of dormancy as well.
[47] CA 2006 s.495(3A). On the accounting standards for micro companies, see para.22–020.
[48] CA 2006 s.479A(1).
[49] CA 2006 ss.479A(2) and 479C(3).
[50] CA 2006 ss.479A(1)–(2) and 479B(a).
[51] CA 2006 s.480(1).
[52] CA 2006 s.1169 (1).
[53] CA 2006 s.480(1)(a).

common example of such a company is a "shelf company"[54] while it remains on the shelf (although there may be legitimate reasons for incorporating a company that is intended to remain dormant indefinitely). If the company becomes dormant after a period of activity, then its audit exemption is more circumscribed. It depends on the company not being a parent company required to produce group accounts and its being entitled to produce its individual accounts under the small companies regime,[55] or being entitled to do so but for the fact that it is a public company or a member of an ineligible group.[56] In practice, the most important extension that the dormant company exemption makes to the exemption for small companies is that a dormant company may be a small public company.[57]

Non-profit public sector companies

The exemption for non-profit public sector companies does not require detailed consideration because the relevant companies, although incorporated under the CA 2006, are part of the public sector and accordingly are subject to public sector audit.[58] A company is non-profit making if it is so for the purpose of art.54 of the Treaty on the Functioning of the European Union, even though that article in fact contains no definition of "non-profit making".[59] Such companies were initially excluded from audit because they are outside the scope of art.50(1) TFEU, under which the various audit directives were made. Whilst the rationale for that definition has largely disappeared with Brexit, the CA 2006 has retained the existing definition of "non-profit making" for the time being. **23–009**

AUDITOR INDEPENDENCE AND COMPETENCE

Whilst the small company exemption from audit has been important over the past two decades, the most important policy issue relating to auditors concerns their independence. This was an issue brought to the fore by the collapse of the Enron Company and others in the US in the early years of this century. These corporate collapses and scandals were thought to reveal weaknesses in the requirements concerning auditor independence.[60] The EU reached a similar view as a result of its experience with the financial crisis during 2007–2009.[61] The essence of the independence issue is that the auditor is appointed and remunerated by the company whose accounts and reports are being audited. Although companies are required to have their accounts audited (unless exempted), they are not required to employ any particular auditor or to pay that auditor any particular level of **23–010**

---

54 See para.4–009.

55 See para.22–006.

56 CA 2006 s.480(2).

57 The dormant company exemption is not available to companies whose securities are traded on a public market, but it is rare for such a company to be dormant: see CA 2006 s.481(za).

58 CA 2006 s.482(1).

59 CA 2006 s.482(3).

60 See J. Coffee Jr, *Gatekeepers* (Oxford: OUP, 2006) Ch.5.

61 European Commission, "Proposal for a Regulation on specific requirements regarding statutory audit of public interest entities", COM(2011) 779 final, p.2.

remuneration. Accordingly, there develops the possibility that auditors will compete for mandates on the basis that they will engage in only a cursory scrutiny of the company's accounts, or that they will act in such a way in return for excessive remuneration (which might be disguised as remuneration for the provision of non-audit services to the company). The traditional response to this argument is that in the long-term (or even the medium-term) such a business model is self-destructive. The auditor will obtain a reputation for laxness, which will, perversely, destroy its business. Whilst the company's management may want a lax audit, it is crucial that those who rely on the audit believe that the appropriate checks have been carried out. A lax audit (by an auditor known to be so) is no good, even for evasive management, because the management will not obtain the benefit it desires from the audit opinion. Whilst the reputation argument may have much force, recent experience suggests that it does not operate at all times and in all circumstances so as to guarantee an appropriate level of audit scrutiny. Individuals within the audit firm may have short-term incentives that are not aligned with the firm's longer-term incentive to do a good job, or the investors may move away from attaching much importance to the audited accounts in periods of market exuberance.

Consequently, there is a case for regulation to reinforce the market incentives supporting auditor independence. Much the same arguments can be made in relation to auditor competence. An audit firm has reputational reasons for providing a good service in general, but in particular cases there may be incentives on individuals to operate inefficiently. Nor should the independence and competence issues be viewed as being completely separate: a non-independent auditor displays dependence on management precisely by carrying out an inadequate audit. The fact that the market cannot guarantee independence and competence, however, does not mean that regulation can (some aspects of the problem might be insoluble), nor that all types of regulation are equally appropriate. Indeed, there are eight legal strategies that have been deployed to address these problems:

(1) laying down specific rules disqualifying persons from acting as the auditor of a particular company on the grounds of conflict of interest;
(2) constraining the provision of non-audit services to audit clients;
(3) requiring the mandatory rotation of auditors;
(4) on the basis that the board is the body within the company that has the greatest interest in a lax audit, increasing the role of the shareholders in relation to audit decisions;
(5) on the basis that the executive directors on the board have the greatest interest in a lax audit and that shareholders have serious collective-action problems, increasing the role of the non-executive directors in relation to auditor decisions, usually by means of an audit committee consisting wholly of independent non-executive directors;
(6) attacking the problem not from the side of the company, but from the side of the auditor by subjecting auditors to greater regulatory control and more effective disciplinary mechanisms;
(7) increasing the powers of the auditors as against the company; and

(8) imposing civil liability on auditors towards those who rely on the audited accounts and reports in circumstances where the auditors have been negligent and/or imposing criminal liability for false statements in audit reports.

Each technique has been deployed with greater vigour in recent years (apart from the imposition of civil liability, where indeed the tendency has been to restrict liability where possible).

Regulatory structure

Before considering those various techniques, however, it is necessary to consider the structure of auditor regulation. When the UK was an EU Member State, the UK was required to appoint a "competent authority" with the function of approving auditors and putting in place a system of "public oversight" of those approved auditors' activities.[62] Pursuant to that obligation, the UK appointed the Financial Reporting Council as its competent authority.[63] This institutional structure has been retained post-Brexit. Whilst the Financial Reporting Council must itself oversee the creation of the standards that auditors are required to meet and the manner of their application in practice,[64] it is permitted to delegate tasks to "recognised supervisory bodies" (RSBs),[65] although this is subject to the condition that the competent authority may reclaim the delegated power on a case-by-case basis.[66] There are, however, limits to what may be delegated in this way. The Financial Reporting Council cannot delegate tasks related to the quality assurance system, the conduct of investigations under that system and the imposition of sanctions pursuant to that system.[67] In brief, the RSBs are the professional accounting bodies that meet the standards set out in the CA 2006 for recognition.[68] An elaborate system of regulation of auditors and auditing is thus envisaged. In terms of the regulatory architecture, some matters are determined by the CA 2006, retained EU law[69] or delegated legislation,[70] whilst other matters are governed by standards developed by the Financial Reporting Council and yet **23–011**

[62] Directive 2013/34 on the annual financial statements [2013] OJ L182/19 art.32.

[63] On the Financial Reporting Council, see para.22–020.

[64] For the functions delegated to the Financial Reporting Council, see Statutory Auditors and Third Country Auditors Regulations 2016 (SI 2016/649) reg.3(1).

[65] Regulation art.24(1), as amended by the Statutory Auditors and Third Country Auditors (Amendment) (EU Exit) Regulations 2019 (SI 2019/177) reg.98(1). For the definition of "recognised supervisory body, see Statutory Auditors and Third Country Auditors Regulations 2016 (SI 2016/649) reg.3. The Financial Conduct Authority "must consider whether and how" other aspects of the public oversight function (for example, quality assurance and discipline) may be delegated: see Statutory Auditors and Third Country Auditors Regulations 2016 (SI 2016/649) reg.3(2).

[66] Regulation art.24(2), as amended by the Statutory Auditors and Third Country Auditors (Amendment) (EU Exit) Regulations 2019 (SI 2019/177).

[67] Regulation art.24(1), as amended by the Statutory Auditors and Third Country Auditors (Amendment) (EU Exit) Regulations 2019 (SI 2019/177) reg.98(1).

[68] CA 2006 s.1217 and Sch.10 Pt 1.

[69] European Union (Withdrawal) Act 2018 s.2.

[70] See, in particular, Statutory Auditors and Third Country Auditors Regulations 2016 (SI 2016/649); Statutory Auditors and Third Country Auditors (Amendment) (EU Exit) Regulations 2019 (SI 2019/177), amending the Regulation.

others are governed by the RSBs. It is still the case, however, that the obligation to comply with the Financial Reporting Council's standards flows from the requirements that a statutory auditor be a member of a RSB[71] and that the RSBs' rules require compliance with standards laid down by the Financial Reporting Council.[72]

The current regulatory architecture has recently been heavily criticised by the Kingman Review, which painted a rather unflattering picture of the Financial Reporting Council as "an institution constructed in a different era—a rather ramshackle house, cobbled together with all sorts of extensions over time. The house is–just–serviceable, up to a point, but it leaks and creaks, sometimes badly. The inhabitants of the house have sought to patch and mend. But in the end, the house is built on weak foundations".[73] Accordingly, the recommendation is that the Financial Reporting Council should be replaced as soon as possible with a new independent regulator, the "Audit, Reporting and Governance Authority" (ARGA). The new regulator should have an overarching duty to promote the interests of those consuming (rather than producing) financial information and should be required to promote competition and innovation. As well as having a more effective governance structure, the ARGA would have increased supervisory and enforcement powers and would be charged with the task of promoting "brevity and comprehensibility" in accounts and annual reports. Moreover, in a warning to the "big four" audit firms, the Kingman Review indicated that "[t]he current self-regulatory model for the largest audit firms should end". In light of the UK's departure from the EU, such an overhaul of the legal and architectural framework of audit law is welcome given the current unsatisfactory patchwork of regulations in this area. In March 2021, the Government indicated its general support for the Kingman Committee's recommendations.[74]

DIRECT REGULATION OF AUDITOR INDEPENDENCE

Non-independent persons

23–012 A person may not act as an auditor if he is an officer or employee of the company to be audited or a partner or employee of such an officer or employee or, in the case of the appointment of a partnership, if any member of the partnership is ineligible on these grounds.[75] Nor may a person act if any of these grounds apply

[71] CA 2006 s.1212(1)(a).

[72] CA 2006 Sch.10 para.9.

[73] Kingman Committee, *Independent Review of the Financial Reporting Council* (December 2018), para.4.

[74] Department for Business, Energy and Industrial Strategy, *Restoring Trust in Audit and Corporate Governance* (March 2021). See also Financial Reporting Council, *Operational Separation of Audit Practices* (February 2021).

[75] CA 2006 s.1214(1)–(3). The CA 2006 s.1214(5) expressly states that, for this purpose, an auditor is not to be regarded as an "officer or employee". This hardly needs saying, for if he were, he would become ineligible immediately upon appointment! The definition of "officer" in the CA 2006 s.1261(1) ("officer—includes a director, manager or secretary or, where the affairs of the company are managed by its members, a member") might seem in any event to exclude auditors. Nevertheless, they have been held to be "officers" in a number of corporate contexts: see *Re London & General Bank*

in relation to any associated undertaking of the company.[76] Such an auditor must immediately resign and give notice to the company of the reason for that resignation.[77] Failure to do so is a criminal offence. Further, the appointment or continuation in office of an auditor who is not independent within the statutory definition triggers the Secretary of State's power to require the company to appoint a proper person to conduct a second audit or to review the first audit; and the company may recover the costs of the additional audit work from the first auditor, provided that person knew he or she was not independent.[78] Clearly, however, an employer-employee relationship with the company being audited is far from being the only type of relationship that might impair the auditor's independence (for example, a debtor-creditor relationship or a substantial shareholding[79] in the company might do so). In order to expand upon the narrow approach to independence in the CA 2006, regulations were promulgated requiring the Financial Reporting Council to make standards aimed at ensuring auditor independence on appointment and during the audit.[80] This mandate is discharged by the Financial Reporting Council through its ethical standards.[81]

Non-audit remuneration of auditors

Apart from remuneration for the audit itself, the most common conflicted relationship between an auditor and its audit client arises from the fact that the auditor is normally a member of a firm of accountants that is capable of providing the client with a wide range of services—well beyond audit or even accountancy services. These non-audit revenues from audit clients have increased substantially in recent years.[82] Regulations now require companies to disclose on a disaggregated basis in notes to the accounts the non-audit remuneration received by their auditors.[83] Accordingly, the auditor's potential sources of remuneration 23–013

(No.1) [1895] 2 Ch. 166 CA; *Re Kingston Cotton Mills (No.1)* [1896] 1 Ch. 6 CA; *Mutual Reinsurance Co Ltd v Peat Marwick Mitchell & Co* [1997] 1 B.C.L.C. 1 CA; cf. *Aquachem Ltd v Delphis Bank Ltd* [2008] UKPC 7; [2008] B.C.C. 648 at [17].

[76] CA 2006 s.1214(6), indicating that an "associated undertaking" means a parent or subsidiary undertaking of the company or a subsidiary undertaking of any parent undertaking of the company.

[77] CA 2006 s.1215(1).

[78] CA 2006 ss.1248–1249. These provisions also apply—and in practice are probably more important—where the auditor is ineligible to be appointed (for example, because not qualified) rather than prohibited from acting on grounds of lack of independence: CA 2006 s.1248(3). The sections appear not to apply to lack of independence solely under the Financial Reporting Council's standards.

[79] That said, there might be an argument that the shareholding might make the auditor a more diligent watchdog over the members' interests—but members are not the only people whose interests he should protect.

[80] Statutory Auditors and Third Country Auditors Regulations 2016 (SI 2016/649) Sch.1 paras 3–6.

[81] Financial Reporting Council, *Revised Ethical Standard* (2019), Pt A.

[82] For a valuable analysis of the issues concerning auditor independence, see D. Kershaw, "Waiting for Enron: The Unstable Equilibrium of Auditor Independence Regulation" (2006) 33 *Journal of Law and Society* 388, 394.

[83] The Companies (Disclosure of Auditor Remuneration and Liability Limitation Agreements) Regulations 2008 (SI 2008/489) (as amended by SI 2011/2198) reg.5(3), which was enacted under the CA 2006 s.494.

are divided into eight categories (including remuneration from the audit itself).[84] There needs to be separate disclosure of remuneration earned from the company (and its subsidiaries) and from associated pension schemes,[85] as well as disclosure of amounts paid to the auditor's "associates" and the auditor.[86] The disclosure obligation imposed on medium-sized[87] companies extends only to the audit fee. Regulation of this issue extends, however, beyond disclosure. For PIEs, a long list of non-audit services is simply prohibited from the beginning of the period subject to audit to the completion of the audit.[88] These are non-audit services where the risk of conflict of interest is thought to be high. Such services may not be provided by the auditor or any member of its network[89] to a PIE or any member of its group, if incorporated in the UK.[90] Even permitted non-audit services are subject to controls. Their provision must be approved by the company's audit committee after it has properly assessed any threats to independence.[91] In addition, the amount that is permitted to be paid for the non-audit services is capped at 70% of the average audit fees paid over the previous three years.[92] For non-PIEs, ethical standards imposed by the Financial Reporting Council require auditors to handle threats to their independence arising out of non-audit remuneration.[93] These make the provision of certain high-risk non-audit services inconsistent with an audit engagement.[94]

---

[84] The Companies (Disclosure of Auditor Remuneration and Liability Limitation Agreements) Regulations 2008 (SI 2008/489) (as amended by SI 2011/2198) Sch.2A.

[85] The Companies (Disclosure of Auditor Remuneration and Liability Limitation Agreements) Regulations 2008 (SI 2008/489) (as amended by SI 2011/2198) reg.5(4).

[86] The Companies (Disclosure of Auditor Remuneration and Liability Limitation Agreements) Regulations 2008 (SI 2008/489) (as amended by SI 2011/2198) reg.5(1)(b)(ii) and Sch.1.

[87] The Companies (Disclosure of Auditor Remuneration and Liability Limitation Agreements) Regulations 2008 (SI 2008/489) (as amended by SI 2011/2198) reg.4. For the definition of "medium-sized" companies, see para.22–007.

[88] Regulation art.5(1), as amended by the Statutory Auditors and Third Country Auditors (Amendment) (EU Exit) Regulations 2019 (SI 2019/177).

[89] The major accounting firms are organised as more or less closely linked partnerships operating under a single brand.

[90] Regulation art.5(1), as amended by the Statutory Auditors and Third Country Auditors (Amendment) (EU Exit) Regulations 2019 (SI 2019/177). Examples include tax services and tax advice.

[91] Regulation art.5(4), as amended by the Statutory Auditors and Third Country Auditors (Amendment) (EU Exit) Regulations 2019 (SI 2019/177).

[92] Regulation art.4(2), as amended by the Statutory Auditors and Third Country Auditors (Amendment) (EU Exit) Regulations 2019 (SI 2019/177). This constraint applies only if the auditor has supplied both types of service over a period of three consecutive years.

[93] The Financial Reporting Council has the power to permit the provision of certain non-audit services provided these have "no direct or have immaterial effect" on the audited accounts, the effect on the audited accounts is comprehensively documented in the additional reports to the audit committee and the principles of independence are satisfied: see Statutory Auditors and Third Country Auditors Regulations 2016 (SI 2016/649) reg.13A.

[94] Financial Reporting Council, *Revised Ethical Standard* (2019), s.5. Consider Recommendation 2002/590 on statutory auditors' independence in the EU [2002] OJ L191/22.

Auditors becoming non-independent

Although the auditor may have no other commercial or financial relationship with its client, over a period of time the auditor relationship itself becomes a threat to independence. The auditor may build up personal relationships with the management of the audited company that may make him or her more reluctant to challenge the management's picture of events. The watchdog may have become a lap dog. For PIEs, the key audit partners are required to rotate every seven years and not take up appointment again for three years,[95] as well as there being a gradual rotation mechanism for the most senior personnel on the audit team. This notion of a key audit partner (or "senior statutory auditor")[96] is the auditor designated by the audit firm as primarily responsible for carrying out the audit (normally referred to in the UK as the "engagement auditor"), but also the auditor who signs the report, if different. In fact, the Financial Reporting Council's rules take up the option to make the rotation requirement more demanding (for both PIEs and listed companies) and impose a five-year rotation and a five-year gap.[97] In addition, there needs to be a phased rotation of all the senior personnel in the audit team.[98] Depending upon when the auditor's appointment commenced, the audit firm itself will usually have to rotate at least every 10 years,[99] although a re-tendering process that satisfies statutory criteria may permit an extension up to 20 years.[100] Similar (albeit sometimes less-demanding) standards apply to non-PIEs.[101] Whilst these standards will go some way to ensuring independence, the argument against mandatory rotation of audit firms is that it means the loss of the expertise of the whole of the existing audit team, which occurrence would be likely to reduce the quality of the audits immediately following a change of firm (unless, of course, the audit team simply changed firms, thus defeating the object of the exercise). 23–014

Firm rotation can be looked at as a competition issue as well as an independence issue. Since a mere four firms dominate the global accounting market, choice for large companies is necessarily limited. In an attempt to address this issue, the Competition and Markets Authority issued an order in 2014 requiring mandatory re-tendering of audit engagements at least every ten years for the largest 350 companies on the Main Market of the London Stock

---

[95] Regulation art.17(7), as amended by the Statutory Auditors and Third Country Auditors (Amendment) (EU Exit) Regulations 2019 (SI 2019/177).

[96] CA 2006 s.504(1).

[97] Financial Reporting Council, *Revised Ethical Standard* (2019), para.3.10.

[98] Financial Reporting Council, *Revised Ethical Standard* (2019), para.3.18.

[99] CA 2006 s.494ZA. See also Regulation art.17(1), as amended by the Statutory Auditors and Third Country Auditors (Amendment) (EU Exit) Regulations 2019 (SI 2019/177). Once the period for an engagement has elapsed, the audit firm cannot audit the same PIE within the following four years: ibid. art.17(3). See also CA 2006 s.489C. See further Financial Reporting Council, *Revised Ethical Standard* (2019), para.3.9.

[100] CA 2006 s.494ZA. For the re-tendering process, see Regulation art.16, as amended by the Statutory Auditors and Third Country Auditors (Amendment) (EU Exit) Regulations 2019 (SI 2019/177).

[101] CA 2006 s.494ZA. See also Financial Reporting Council, *Revised Ethical Standard* (2019), paras 3.5 and 3.8.

Exchange.[102] The aim was to give second-tier audit firms an opportunity to break into the market for the provision of audit services to this top class of company and to make it worthwhile for those firms to gear up to provide the requisite audit services.

Both independence and competition goals might be hindered if there were contractual restrictions in place on the choice of auditor. Any such arrangement is considered to be of "no effect".[103]

Auditors becoming prospectively non-independent

23–015 An auditor may have no current conflict of interest with the client-company (nor may he or she have a long association with the company as auditor), but there may be an understanding, falling short of a contract, that the auditor will resign in due course and take up a role in the management of the company. Since accountancy skills are much prized in some areas of management, movement from professional practice to management is quite common. For PIEs, there is a two-year "cooling off" period between ceasing to be the statutory auditor or key audit partner of a PIE and taking up a "key" management position of that company; whereas, in other cases, the cooling-off period is one year.[104] The same periods are applied if the new post is as a non-executive director of the client company or a member of its audit committee (without being either a key manager or a non-executive director—a rare situation).

THE ROLE OF SHAREHOLDERS AND THE AUDIT AUTHORITIES

23–016 The traditional regulatory strategy deployed by the CA 2006 to reinforce auditor independence has been to enhance the role of the shareholders. In many ways, this is an obvious strategy. The accounts and reports are statements from the directors to the members. Accordingly, giving control over the verification of those statements to the recipients, rather than the originators, of the statements appears to be an appropriate strategy. The auditor's relationship with the shareholders is underlined by his or her right to be sent all notices and other communications relating to general meetings, to attend the meeting and to be heard on any part of the business that affects or concerns the auditor.[105] In the case of a private company that takes its decision by written resolution, this right transmogrifies into a simple right to receive the communications relating to the written resolution, but there is no general right to make representations to the

---

[102] The Statutory Audit Services for Large Companies Market Investigation (Mandatory Use of Competitive Tender Processes and Audit Committee Responsibilities) Order 2014. See also Competition and Markets Authority, *Statutory Audit Services Market Study* (Final Report, 18 April 2019).

[103] Regulation art.16(6), as amended by the Statutory Auditors and Third Country Auditors (Amendment) (EU Exit) Regulations 2019 (SI 2019/177); Statutory Auditors and Third Country Auditors Regulations 2016 (SI 2016/649) reg.12(2).

[104] Statutory Auditors and Third Country Auditors Regulations 2016 (SI 2016/649) Sch.1 para.7. See also Financial Reporting Council, *Revised Ethical Standard* (2019), paras 2.47 onwards.

[105] CA 2006 s.502(2).

shareholders before they decide.[106] This is a relatively ineffective provision, although many private companies will be exempt from audit requirements anyway on account of being "small". However, the shareholders have limited opportunities to exercise control, since they meet so infrequently; and, in larger companies, shareholders may face co-ordination problems regarding the exercise of the powers conferred on them. Perhaps for this reason, the auditor's information obligations to the shareholders are often extended to the audit authorities.

Appointment and remuneration of auditors

The normal rule is that the appointment of the auditors must be done at each accounts meeting, normally the annual general meeting,[107] and the appointment is from the conclusion of that meeting until the conclusion of the next such meeting.[108] There are only exceptional circumstances in which the directors may appoint auditors.[109] However, the proposal to appoint the auditors, to re-appoint them or to appoint others in their place comes normally from the board (though it need not) and the meeting, almost invariably, will agree with the board's proposal. This is an example of a situation where the shareholders' co-ordination problems make it difficult, though not impossible, for them to generate a proposal of their own. They might do so if they had reason to believe that the auditor was in the board's pocket, but they rarely have grounds for so thinking. Accordingly, accepting the board's proposal seems the rational course of action for the shareholders. In the case of PIEs, the audit committee is required to put forward recommendations to the shareholders.[110] This both recognises shareholders' potential co-ordination problems and attempts to shift the de facto nomination role out of the hands of the executive directors of the company. 23–017

Where the auditors are appointed by the members in general meeting, their remuneration shall be fixed by the general meeting or in such manner as the general meeting shall determine.[111] This procedure again underlines the fact that the auditors are the members' watchdogs, rather than the directors' lapdogs. In practice, however, the ability to appoint the auditor serves little purpose since the members normally adopt a resolution proposed by the directors to the effect that the remuneration shall be agreed by the directors—as the CA 2006 permits them to do. Even if the shareholders actually fixed the auditor's remuneration, rather than fixing the method for fixing it, they would invariably act on a recommendation from the board. A more effective protection, however, might be

[106] CA 2006 s.502(1).

[107] CA 2006 s.489(4). See further para.22–046.

[108] CA 2006 s.491(1)(b).

[109] CA 2006 s.489(3), namely to fill a casual vacancy in the office of auditor, after a period in which the company has not been required to have an audit and before its first accounts meeting.

[110] In relation to auditors of PIEs with an audit committee, there must be a recommendation from the company's audit committee concerning the auditor's identity: see CA 2006 s.489A. Where there is no audit committee, then the board must engage in a prescribed selection process: CA 2006 s.489B. See also Regulation art.16(2), as amended by the Statutory Auditors and Third Country Auditors (Amendment) (EU Exit) Regulations 2019 (SI 2019/177).

[111] CA 2006 s.492(1).

that the amount of the remuneration, which includes expenses and benefits in kind (the monetary value of which has to be estimated) has to be shown in a note to the annual accounts, thus enabling the members to criticise the directors if the amount seems to be out of line.[112]

For private companies, shareholder meetings are not required to be held, but (assuming the company is subject to audit) the principle of shareholder appointment and determination of remuneration would still apply. Alternatively, the shareholders may act by written resolution. The shareholders have to appoint the auditor within a particular timeframe, namely the period of 28 days beginning with the day on which the accounts and reports were circulated to the members or, if later, the last day for circulating them.[113] Suppose, however, that no resolution with regard to the auditors is circulated to the shareholders, which is not inconceivable in a private company. The CA 2006 provides that, unless the auditor was appointed by the directors under their exceptional powers,[114] failure to re-appoint or to appoint someone else at the end of the year will mean the auditors in place are deemed to be re-appointed.[115] This process of deemed re-appointment in private companies, which may otherwise continue indefinitely, can be excluded by the company's articles.[116] More important in practice, the auditor in post may be required to undergo re-election as a result of a resolution adopted by the members,[117] or a notice received from members holding at least 5% of the voting rights entitled to be cast on a resolution that the auditor should not be re-appointed.[118] The last of these options is the least demanding method of preventing deemed re-appointment.

Removal and resignation of auditors

Requirement for shareholder resolution

23–018 As in the case of directors,[119] a company may at any time remove an auditor from office by ordinary resolution passed at a meeting.[120] Unlike a director, however, an auditor may not be removed prior to the expiration of their term of office other

[112] CA 2006 s.493. See also the Companies (Disclosure of Auditor Remuneration and Liability Limitation Agreements) Regulations 2008 (SI 2008/489) regs 4 and 5. As a general rule, the shareholders only criticise if the amount seems abnormally high; they should perhaps be more alarmed if it is abnormally low.

[113] CA 2006 ss.485 and 487. This disregards the special rules that apply to private companies classified as PIEs because this category embraces only financial institutions (and probably very few of them).

[114] CA 2006 s.485(3).

[115] CA 2006 s.487(2).

[116] CA 2006 s.487(2)(b).

[117] CA 2006 s.487(2)(d).

[118] CA 2006 ss.487(2)(c) and 488.

[119] See para.11–022.

[120] CA 2006 s.510(1)–(2). A meeting is required, as for the removal of a director, even in the case of a private company: CA 2006 s.288(2)(b).

than by resolution of the shareholders.[121] In this way, the auditor is given some protection against management pressure. If management wish to remove the auditor prematurely, they must do so by means of a proposal to the shareholders. If management goes down that route, then the CA 2006 brings into play additional requirements designed to permit (or even require) the auditor to put the contrary case to the shareholders. Hence, not only has "special notice" of 28 days[122] to be given to the company of a resolution to remove an auditor, but notice of the proposed resolution also has to be given to the auditor.[123] The auditor is entitled to make written representations which (if received in time) have to be sent to the members with the notice of the meeting, and which (if not received in time) have to be read out at the meeting.[124] If the resolution is passed, the auditor still retains the right to attend the general meeting at which the term of office would otherwise have expired, or at which the vacancy created by his removal is to be filled.[125] Nor does removal deprive the auditor of any right to compensation or damages (arising, for example, under the contract between the auditor and company) in respect of the termination of the appointment as auditor or any other appointment terminating at that time.[126] Whilst these statutory limitations protect the auditor to some degree against management pressure, they also give the shareholders a free hand over the auditor's removal. If the shareholders of their own motion wish to remove an auditor (that they, for example, regard as being too friendly with management), they are free to do so, provided that they comply with the requirements for special notice and an auditor statement.

A further issue is whether there needs to be any justification provided for the removal of an auditor. At EU level there exists a requirement that auditors can only be removed on "proper grounds".[127] Whilst such a requirement would clearly give the auditor further protection against management pressure where there has been a falling out, it is less easy for the shareholders to act where they think the auditor has become too cosy with the management. In continental European jurisdictions with controlling shareholders as the predominant form of shareholding (even in large companies), it may have been thought unrealistic to regard the directors and the (majority of the) shareholders as two separate groups. It is not unrealistic, however, in dispersed-shareholding jurisdictions such as the UK. Accordingly, the UK Government was clearly reluctant to implement the EU requirement in the obvious way, namely by building a "proper grounds"

[121] CA 2006 s.510(4). In the case of directors, the articles often provide for directors to be removed by resolution of the board. In the case of PIEs, there is a power vested in the Financial Reporting Council to apply to court for the removal of an auditor: CA 2006 s.511A.

[122] CA 2006 s.511(1).

[123] CA 2006 s.511(2).

[124] CA 2006 s.511(3)–(5). The auditor should ensure that it is received in time, since otherwise members may return proxy forms before they see his representations. The representations need not be read at the meeting if that procedure is being abused "to secure needless publicity for defamatory matter": CA 2006 s.511(6). The auditor also has a general right to attend and speak at shareholder meetings. See further para.23–025.

[125] CA 2006 ss.513 and 502(2).

[126] CA 2006 s.510(3).

[127] Directive 2006/43 on statutory audits of annual accounts and consolidated accounts [2006] OJ L157/87 art.38(1).

qualification into the shareholders' statutory power of removal.[128] Rather this requirement was effectively implemented in two alternative ways. First, through the unfair prejudice jurisdiction,[129] so that removal of an auditor on the ground of divergence of opinion on accounting treatments or audit procedures or "on any other improper grounds" shall be deemed conduct that is unfairly prejudicial to the interests of some part of the members.[130] Whilst this approach has the merit of addressing the policy of unfair treatment of minority shareholders, it may be more questionable whether this represented a proper implement of the relevant directive. Whilst this narrow issue has become irrelevant following Brexit,[131] it still leaves the problem that the auditor's dismissal (even if challengeable under the unfair prejudice provisions by a shareholder) still seems to be effective as far as the auditor is concerned. Moreover, as the unfair prejudice jurisdiction only confers standing on "members",[132] the auditor would not have any direct right of challenge on this basis. Whilst the courts' broad remedial discretion might encompass reinstating the auditor,[133] this is far from assured. Secondly, in the case of PIEs, the CA 2006 provides that 5% of the shareholders or the Financial Reporting Council can bring proceedings before a court for the dismissal of the auditor "on proper grounds".[134] Taken together, these two mechanisms strengthen the hand of minority shareholders when it comes to the removal of the auditor.

A breakdown in relations between the auditor and management is more likely to reveal itself in the resignation of the auditor, rather than in any attempt by the management to persuade the shareholders to remove the auditor. Few auditors will want to retain office if relations with the company's management have become seriously strained. At first glance, the CA 2006 makes resignation an easy matter: the auditor resigns simply by sending a notice to that effect to the company.[135] What is really needed, however, is a procedure that makes it difficult for the auditor to "go quietly", in other words to resign office without ensuring that any relevant problems have been ventilated properly. To this end, the CA 2006 contains not only a requirement that the auditor produce a statement of his or her reasons for resigning, but also a requirement that the regulatory authorities be notified. This requirement should put those bodies on the alert about the company's possible mismanagement. There are also notification requirements operating in the case of dismissal. Accordingly, the notification requirements are considered next.

---

[128] CA 2006 s.510. See also DTI, *Implementation of Directive 2006/43: A Consultation Document* (March 2007), paras 3.34 onwards.
[129] CA 2006 s.994(1). See further Ch.14.
[130] CA 2006 s.994(1A).
[131] In general, directives are only part of "retained" EU law to the extent that they have been implemented into the domestic legal order: see European Union (Withdrawal) Act 2018 s.2(2).
[132] See further para.14–013.
[133] CA 2006 s.996(1).
[134] CA 2006 s.511A.
[135] CA 2006 s.516(1).

Notifications

An auditor of a PIE who leaves office at any time and for any reason must send the company a statement of reasons for this occurrence.[136] In the case of a non-PIE, such a statement may be required depending upon the circumstances. In particular, no such statement will be required where the departure from office occurs in those circumstances that the legislature has determined in advance raise no concerns.[137] Nor will a statement be required from an auditor who leaves office at the end of an accounts meeting.[138] This emphasises that the requirement for an auditor's statement is really aimed at departures during a financial year. For both PIEs and non-PIEs, the statement must include reference to any matters connected with the auditor's departure from office that he or she thinks should be brought to the attention of the company's members or creditors.[139] This is called the "section 519 statement". Having produced the statement, an auditor resigning from a PIE can seek to replicate the situation that would pertain on his dismissal by requiring the directors to convene a meeting of the shareholders to consider the statement,[140] although if "going quietly" was the motivation behind the resignation, the auditor is unlikely to take this step.[141] Whether or not the resigning auditor triggers this right, the company must circulate any section 519 statement received from a departing auditor to those entitled to receive copies of the company's accounts.[142] This too is unlikely to generate action on the part of dispersed shareholders, unless the statement reveals egregious conduct. **23–019**

Of greater significance is the obligation to inform a regulator of the s.519 statement. The auditor must send the statement to the Registrar,[143] so that it gets onto the company's public file at Companies House. The statement must also be sent to the appropriate audit authority.[144] Failure to comply with either obligation attracts criminal sanctions. The appropriate audit authority for a PIE is the

---

136 CA 2006 s.519(1). The statement must be virtually contemporaneous with the departure.

137 For those circumstances, see CA 2006 s.519A(3).

138 CA 2006 s.519(2A)—or its equivalent in the case of a private company.

139 CA 2006 s.519(3A). In the case of a dismissal, this obligation to the company may be overtaken in practice by the auditor's entitlement under CA 2006 s.511(3)–(5) to circulate representations to the meeting at which the dismissal is to be considered (an opportunity that arises before the dismissal, whilst the statement of circumstances is to be made only after dismissal). A statement by a non-PIE auditor must state that there are no matters to be drawn to the attention of shareholders and creditors, if this is the case.

140 CA 2006 s.518(3)(a)—or, without requisitioning a special meeting, the auditor might require the statement to be read out at the next regular accounts meeting: CA 2006 s.518(3)(b).

141 The section might be used by a resigning auditor who does not want to go quietly, but who wishes to avoid the ignominy of being sacked.

142 CA 2006 s.520—unless the company is a non-PIE or the statement says that there are no matters to be drawn to the attention of members or creditors. The company may alternatively apply to the court to be relieved of the circulation obligation if the auditor is using the provision to secure publicity for defamatory matter: CA 2006 s.520(4). The company must then send to members or debenture-holders a statement setting out the effect of the order. There is a risk that a company will use the appeal procedure simply to delay circulation of the auditor's statement, discontinuing the application just before it is due to be heard. Such action places the company at risk of having to pay the auditor's costs on an indemnity basis: see *Jarvis Plc v Pricewaterhouse Coopers* [2001] B.C.C. 670 Ch D (Companies Ct).

143 CA 2006 s.521(1).

144 CA 2006 s.522.

Financial Reporting Council, and for a non-PIE a "recognised supervisory body". Accordingly, the regulator is informed of the dispute, if there is one, and is perhaps more likely to take action than dispersed shareholders, at least where the dispute reveals a public interest element. Overall, the management cannot remove an auditor prematurely, whether by dismissal or forced resignation, without facing a serious risk of a row at the general meeting (and, in the case of a listed company, adverse press publicity) and difficulties with the auditing and accounting authorities.

Failure to re-appoint an auditor

23–020 Finally, a management team that has fallen out with its auditors may simply wait until the end of the term of office and replace them. In the case of a public company this is an annual opportunity, since the term of office of the auditor normally runs from one accounts meeting to the next[145]; and, in the case of a private company, the deemed re-appointment mechanism can be brought to an end by appointing substitute auditors during the annual period for appointing them.[146] Moreover, since it is not an uncommon event to change auditors for valid reasons (especially as this is now encouraged by the authorities), failure to re-appoint may not be suspicious. Alternatively, auditors who have fallen out with the management may simply not seek re-appointment. The CA 2006 does, however, take steps to flush out information about a failure to re-appoint in more questionable circumstances. First, special notice (at least 28 days) must be given to the company of a resolution to appoint someone other than the existing auditors,[147] and the company must make use of the advance notice to inform the outgoing auditor and the proposed replacement of the resolution.[148] Secondly, the outgoing auditor then has the right to have representations circulated in advance of the meeting or read out at the meeting, similar to the rights arising on a resolution to dismiss.[149] If, in the case of a private company, the decision is to be taken by written resolution, the right is to have the representations circulated to the members of the company.[150] In the case of a PIE, the outgoing auditor is obliged (rather than simply given the option) to send to the company a statement of the reasons for ceasing to hold office.[151] The auditor must also supply a copy of the statement to the Registrar and the Financial Reporting Council,[152] and the

---

[145] CA 2006 s.491(1)(b).

[146] CA 2006 s.487(2).

[147] CA 2006 s.312.

[148] CA 2006 s.515(2)–(3). This requirement applies also where the period for re-appointment has passed without an appointment being made and the company later decides to appoint someone other than the outgoing auditors. Otherwise, the requirement could be easily avoided.

[149] CA 2006 s.515(4)–(7).

[150] CA 2006 s.514.

[151] CA 2006 s.519(1), which applies where an auditor ceases to hold office "at any time and for any reason".

[152] CA 2006 ss.521(1) and 522(1).

company must circulate the statement to those entitled to receive the accounts,[153] but the company is not required to supply a statement of its reasons to the Financial Reporting Council.[154]

Whistle blowing

The auditor's relationship with the authorities is strengthened, possibly to the detriment of the quality of its relationship with the company, by whistle-blowing provisions. These lay a duty on the auditor to report to the relevant authorities certain types of information discovered during the course of an audit. In the case of PIEs, there is unsurprisingly a requirement that the auditor report suspected fraud or other irregularities to the company, but if the company does not investigate the suspicions, the auditor must report them to the relevant authorities.[155] This duty is supplemented by a more focused obligation to report directly to the authorities evidence discovered in the course of the audit that may result in "material" breaches of the law or regulations governing the authorisation or activities of PIEs; a material threat or doubt as to the continued functioning of the PIE; or the auditor refusing to issue an audit opinion on the financial statements or issuing a qualified opinion.[156] In the latter two cases, the auditor is not necessarily reporting any wrongdoing to the authorities, but is giving them advanced notice of something that will necessarily become public in due course. Such disclosure does not render the auditor liable for breach of any contractual or legal restriction on the disclosure of information.[157] The relevant authority in the UK will often be the Financial Reporting Council, but might alternatively be a different body in some cases, such as the Serious Fraud Office. **23–021**

Although general whistle-blowing requirements of this kind have not previously existed in UK law, UK auditing standards have for some time required auditors to consider whether the public interest requires such action,[158] and on the basis of this professional guidance it has been held that the auditor's legal duties to the company could embrace, as a last resort, a duty to inform relevant third parties of suspected wrongdoing.[159]

---

153 CA 2006 s.520(2). All this is somewhat pointless if the auditor is ceasing to hold office as the result of a re-tendering exercise.

154 CA 2006 s.523(2B)–(2C), which applies only where the auditor is ceasing to hold office other than at the end of an accounts meeting (or its private company equivalent): CA 2006 s.523(1).

155 Regulation art.7, as amended by the Statutory Auditors and Third Country Auditors (Amendment) (EU Exit) Regulations 2019 (SI 2019/177).

156 Regulation art.12, as amended by the Statutory Auditors and Third Country Auditors (Amendment) (EU Exit) Regulations 2019 (SI 2019/177). These provisions are reflected in Financial Reporting Council, *International Standard on Auditing (UK) 200* (revised June 2016; updated January 2020); Financial Reporting Council, *International Standard on Auditing (UK) 210* (revised June 2016; updated July 2017).

157 Regulation art.12(3), as amended by the Statutory Auditors and Third Country Auditors (Amendment) (EU Exit) Regulations 2019 (SI 2019/177).

158 See Financial Reporting Council, *International Standard on Auditing (UK) 250* (revised November 2019), s.B. In the financial services area, extensive reporting obligations are imposed on auditors in favour of the regulator: see FSMA 2000 Pt XXII.

159 *Sasea Finance Ltd v KPMG* [2000] 1 All E.R. 676 CA, where the court refused to strike out a claim for loss suffered by the company where the auditors discovered fraud on the part of those in

Shareholders and the audit report

23–022 The focus on the shareholder role in relation to the appointment and removal of auditors rather obscures the fact that the audit report is a report to the shareholders, to which they might be expected to react. Until recently, there were no specific statutory channels for these reactions. It was assumed that the shareholders would use their general governance powers (for example, by removing directors) or assert market pressure on the company by selling their shares. As considered previously,[160] the UK Government did not adopt the Company Law Review's general proposal for a "pause" between, on the one hand, the delivery of the annual accounts and reports to the members and, on the other, the holding of the annual general meeting. During the "pause", the shareholders would have had an opportunity, at no cost to themselves, to require the company to circulate resolutions for consideration at the annual general meeting in relation to those documents. That said, a weak form of the Review's proposal was introduced in the CA 2006.[161] Shareholders of a quoted company[162] may require the company to post on its website a shareholder statement about the audit of the company's accounts or about the circumstances in which an auditor has ceased to hold office, so that these matters can be considered at the company's accounts meeting (normally its annual general meeting).[163] The tests for defining the members entitled to require website publication are the same as those for requiring circulation of a resolution to be considered at an annual general meeting,[164] namely members representing at least 5% of the total voting rights of those members entitled to vote at the accounts meeting or 100 voting members holding shares (upon which an average of at least £100 has been paid up).[165] The company is required to post the statement on its website within three working days of its receipt and to keep it there until after the accounts meeting,[166] unless the company persuades a court that the shareholders are abusing their rights.[167] A copy of the statement must be sent to the auditor at the same time as it is posted.[168] The company may not charge the shareholders for the costs of website publication, which is likely to be negligible in any event.[169] Finally, when

control of the company and failed to report it to the relevant authorities. See also *Stone & Rolls Ltd v Moore Stephens* [2009] UKHL 39; [2009] 1 A.C. 1391; *AssetCo Plc v Grant Thornton UK LLP* [2019] EWHC 150 (Comm).

160 See para.12–059.

161 CA 2006 ss.527–531.

162 A "quoted company" is a company listed in the UK or any other EEA state or on the New York Stock Exchange or Nasdaq: see CA 2006 ss.531 and 385.

163 CA 2006 s.527(1).

164 See further para.12–034.

165 CA 2006 s.527(2)–(3). This is one of the situations where those to whom governance rights have been transferred may act: CA 2006 s.153(1)(d). See further para.12–019.

166 CA 2006 s.528(4). Failure to post the statement is a criminal offence on the part of every officer in default: CA 2006 s.530.

167 CA 2006 s.527(5)–(6).

168 CA 2006 s.529(3).

169 CA 2006 s.529(2).

the company gives notice of the accounts meeting, it must draw attention to the existence of this facility and that it is without cost to the members, which may encourage them to take it up.[170]

THE ROLE OF THE AUDIT COMMITTEE OF THE BOARD

Introduction

The principal argument in favour of giving directors a greater role in relation to the audit function is that the board is able to give more continuous attention. Indeed, the shareholders' contribution to the process is naturally episodic: shareholder involvement normally occurs at the annual general meeting when the auditors' report is considered and the auditors are appointed or re-appointed. Arguably, the conflict of interest that the board would naturally have on audit matters can be ameliorated by entrusting this supervisory role to an appropriate committee of the board, rather than the whole board. Audit committees are now common among those UK companies that are traded on public securities markets. With respect to companies trading on a regulated market[171] in the UK, the Financial Conduct Authority's Disclosure Guidance and Transparency Rules Sourcebook (DTR) requires a listed company to have a "body" that discharges the functions of monitoring the statutory audit of the annual and consolidated financial statements.[172] One way in which these functions can be discharged is by compliance with the requirements of the UK Corporate Governance Code (CGC).[173] The CGC recommends that companies establish an audit committee (or explain why they have not done so),[174] alongside the remuneration and appointment committees. Accordingly, the default position is that premium-listed companies should have an audit committee. It is possible, however, that in small companies the functions of the audit committee could be discharged by the board as whole, since the DTR simply requires that there be a "body" without specifying what that should be.[175] That said, any departure from the default position in the CGC would have to be "explained". 23–023

Composition of the audit committee

In terms of its composition, the CGC recommends that: the audit committee be composed of independent non-executive members of the board, with a minimum membership of three, or in the case of smaller companies, two; the chair of the 23–024

170 CA 2006 s.528(3).

171 See para.25–007.

172 Financial Conduct Authority, Disclosure Guidance and Transparency Rules Sourcebook DTR 7.1.1 and 7.1.3.

173 Financial Conduct Authority, Disclosure Guidance and Transparency Rules Sourcebook DTR 7.1.7.

174 See Financial Reporting Council, *UK Corporate Governance Code* (July 2018), s.4, para.24. For the core obligation to "comply or explain" for listed companies, see Listing Rules LR 9.8.6(5)–(6).

175 Financial Conduct Authority, Disclosure Guidance and Transparency Rules Sourcebook DTR 7.1.1 and 7.1.3.

board should not be a member of the audit committee; at least one member of the audit committee should have "recent and relevant financial experience"; and the committee as a whole should have competence relevant to the sector in which the company operates.[176] The task of selecting a complying audit committee falls to the board.[177] Accordingly, despite the aims of the CGC being to improve corporate governance, it does not envisage members of the audit committee being directly appointed by the shareholders. Whilst such a mechanism is used at EU level, this has not been part of the practice in the UK and it is unlikely that this will alter.[178]

Functions of the audit committee

23–025 As the audit committee is the central focus for dealings between the auditor and the PIE, its importance is underlined by the fact that there is a statutory list of functions conferred on the audit committee:

(1) The appointment of the auditor is a process run by the audit committee.[179] That committee makes a recommendation for the appointment of the auditor and, except for the renewal of an existing engagement, that recommendation must contain at least two choices, with a reasoned statement of the committee's preference between the candidates. The list of candidates must have resulted from an open and transparent tendering process organised by the committee.[180] Although the details of the procedure are left up to the committee to determine, the selection is required to be made according to publicised selection criteria and to be capable of justification according to those criteria. The aim appears to be to avoid "sweetheart" deals between auditor and the company. Although the committee's recommendations go to the full board and the full board makes the final recommendations to the shareholders, it is likely that the board will simply follow what the committee recommends. If the full board makes a different proposal, it must justify its departure from the committee's proposals and, in any event, the board's list may not include an auditor who has not participated in the selection process.[181]

---

[176] Financial Reporting Council, *UK Corporate Governance Code* (July 2018), s.4, para.24.

[177] Financial Reporting Council, *UK Corporate Governance Code* (July 2018), s.4, para.24.

[178] Shareholder appointment to the audit committee fits more naturally with systems where the audit committee is a stand-alone committee.

[179] Regulation art.16(2), as amended by the Statutory Auditors and Third Country Auditors (Amendment) (EU Exit) Regulations 2019 (SI 2019/177).

[180] Regulation art.16(3), as amended by the Statutory Auditors and Third Country Auditors (Amendment) (EU Exit) Regulations 2019 (SI 2019/177). Except in the case of PIEs that are small or medium-sized or have a market capitalisation of less than €100 million. "Small or medium-sized" has a special meaning (see para.22–004) that establishes a more expansive set of criteria derived from the prospectus directive, involving meeting two of the following three criteria: an average number of employees during the financial year of fewer than 250, a total balance sheet not exceeding €43 million and an annual net turnover not exceeding €50 million: ibid. art.16(4).

[181] Regulation art.16(5), as amended by the Statutory Auditors and Third Country Auditors (Amendment) (EU Exit) Regulations 2019 (SI 2019/177).

(2) Whilst the appointed auditor ultimately reports to the company's members,[182] the audit committee must receive at the same time or earlier a more detailed report that delves into some sensitive matters.[183] This "transparency report" includes the methodology underlying the audit, the quantitative criteria used to determine materiality,[184] the valuation methods used in the financial statements and the judgements underlying the auditor's "going concern" conclusions.[185] The report to the audit committee must also give details of any significant deficiencies in the financial statements; detail any areas of non-compliance (actual or suspected) with the applicable legal rules or the articles of association; explain the grounds on which companies were included in or excluded from the consolidated accounts; report any significant difficulties arising during the conduct of the audit and, finally, describe the extent of the auditor's interaction with the management of the company.[186] It is clear that this list adds considerably to the auditor's standard reporting duties, but also that the audit committee will require a significant level of expertise to understand and evaluate the transparency report submitted.

(3) The approval of the audit committee is required for the provision to the PIE of permitted non-audit services.[187]

(4) Where the audit fee received from the PIE exceeds 15% of the auditor's total fee income over a period of three years, the audit committee must decide whether the audit engagement should continue (in any case, it may not continue for more than two years) and whether the audit report should be subject to review by another statutory auditor.[188] The danger is perceived to be that the auditor may have become too dependent on a single client and so is less likely to be rigorous in its scrutiny. Given the adverse consequences for the auditor of exceeding the 15% threshold over the three-year period, it is likely that auditors will not allow this situation to arise. Ironically, the risk of exceeding the threshold is greater for small auditors trying to break into the PIE market than it is for the established "big four" global auditing networks.

(5) In addition to the general independence requirements for auditors,[189] a PIE's auditor is required to confirm its independence in writing to the audit

---

[182] See para.23–022.

[183] Regulation art.11(1), as amended by the Statutory Auditors and Third Country Auditors (Amendment) (EU Exit) Regulations 2019 (SI 2019/177).

[184] Many accounting rules require the disclosure of only "material" items.

[185] Regulation art.11(2), as amended by the Statutory Auditors and Third Country Auditors (Amendment) (EU Exit) Regulations 2019 (SI 2019/177).

[186] Regulation art.11(2), as amended by the Statutory Auditors and Third Country Auditors (Amendment) (EU Exit) Regulations 2019 (SI 2019/177).

[187] Regulation art.5(4), as amended by the Statutory Auditors and Third Country Auditors (Amendment) (EU Exit) Regulations 2019 (SI 2019/177). See para.23–013.

[188] Regulation art.4(3), as amended by the Statutory Auditors and Third Country Auditors (Amendment) (EU Exit) Regulations 2019 (SI 2019/177).

[189] See paras 23–012 onwards.

committee on an annual basis and to discuss with the committee any threats to its independence and potential safeguards.[190]

(6) Finally, audit committees are themselves subject to periodic review of their effectiveness by the Financial Reporting Council.[191]

Whilst this statutory list provides a useful reminder of the tasks that a PIE's audit committee should undertake, it is doubtful whether it substantially upgrades what has been expected from audit committees in the UK for some time. Indeed, the CGC already covered much the same ground.[192] In addition, the CGC recommends that a separate section of the annual report to the shareholders should explain how the audit committee has discharged its obligations during the year.[193] In 2002, as a result of the efforts of a committee chaired by Sir Robert Smith, extensive extra-CGC guidance for audit committees was produced. Although this guidance has no formal status, even on a "comply or explain" basis, it strongly indicates the enhanced importance of the audit committee.[194] The Financial Reporting Council has also produced guidance on risk management that stresses the potential role of the audit committee.[195] As the current "soft" standards harden, there may be an increased regulatory and litigation focus on these issues.

AUDITOR COMPETENCE

23–026 Although the focus in recent times has been on auditor independence, competence is important as well. Shareholders, investors and creditors may suffer if the auditor (whilst not beholden to management) fails to do a good enough job and produces accounts that are simply not reliable. Moreover, one indicator that there is a lack of independence is a lax audit that does not meet professional standards. Accordingly, tackling competence is an indirect way of tackling a lack of independence and vice versa. There are a number of legal techniques that might be aimed at increasing competence, including controls on those permitted to carry out audits, regulations as to how audits should be carried out or imposing sanctions on those who have carried out sub-standard audits. The sanctions may be criminal, administrative or civil in nature. Competence may also be enhanced by extending the auditor's powers.

---

190 Regulation art.6(2), as amended by the Statutory Auditors and Third Country Auditors (Amendment) (EU Exit) Regulations 2019 (SI 2019/177).

191 Regulation art.27(1)(c), as amended by the Statutory Auditors and Third Country Auditors (Amendment) (EU Exit) Regulations 2019 (SI 2019/177), although this provision is placed in an article dealing predominantly with the operation of the market for audit services.

192 Financial Reporting Council, *UK Corporate Governance Code* (July 2018), s.4, para.25.

193 Financial Reporting Council, *UK Corporate Governance Code* (July 2018), s.4, para.26.

194 For the present version of that guidance, see Financial Reporting Council, *Guidance on Audit Committees* (April 2016).

195 Financial Reporting Council, *Guidance on Risk Management, Internal Control and Related Financial and Business Reporting* (September 2014).

Qualifications

An early concern of audit law was to require that auditors be appropriately trained and qualified at the start of the engagement and continue to be so throughout. To this end, the rules of the recognised supervisory bodies (in other words, the professional accounting institutes)[196] must provide that appointment as statutory auditor be confined to those who hold appropriate qualifications (or, in the case of the appointment of a firm, that each individual responsible on behalf of the firm is so qualified and that the firm is controlled by such persons).[197] The CA 2006 establishes in some detail the terms on which bodies may award professional qualifications.[198] The discharge by the RSBs of this function is overseen by the Financial Reporting Council.[199] Since a person who acts as an auditor without the appropriate qualifications is ineligible to do so,[200] the Secretary of State has the power to require a second audit and to make the ineligible auditor liable for its costs.[201] The Financial Reporting Council has power to recognise and approve third-country qualifications where it is thought that they are equivalent and where the country in question would provide reciprocal treatment of persons qualified in the UK.[202] Whilst Brexit may make the mutual recognition of future qualifications between the UK and an EU Member State less automatic than previously,[203] qualifications that have already been recognised continue to have that status.[204] The names of statutory auditors must be entered into a public register,[205] including third-country auditors. 23–027

Auditing standards

Auditing standards play a similar role in relation to the function of auditing as accounting standards play in relation to drawing up the accounts. An auditor is necessarily concerned with both sets of standards: the auditor must establish that the accounts have been drawn up properly (including in accordance with the relevant accounting standards) and he or she must carry out the job of checking the financial statements in a proper manner (in accordance with auditing standards). In the case of a negligence claim against the auditor, compliance with both accounting and auditing standards is likely to be a matter to which the courts attach great weight.[206] As with accounting standards, auditing standards are becoming internationalised. A strong driver behind this internationalisation is the 23–028

---

[196] See para.23–011.

[197] CA 2006 Sch.10 para.6.

[198] CA 2006 Sch.11.

[199] Statutory Auditors and Third Country Auditors Regulations 2016 (SI 2016/649) reg.3(1)(f)–(j).

[200] CA 2006 s.1212(1)(b).

[201] CA 2006 ss.1248–1249. See further para.23–012.

[202] CA 2006 s.1221.

[203] Although the CA 2006 s.1240A contains a power to approve third countries as equivalent or transitional third countries, which will smooth the transition for EU-qualified auditors in the future.

[204] CA 2006 Sch.10 para.6.

[205] CA 2006 s.1239. See also Statutory Auditors and Third Country Auditors Regulations 2016 (SI 2016/649) Pt.4.

[206] A court will refer to the standards of professional bodies when determining whether a duty of care has been breached: see *Bolam v Friern Hospital Management Committee* [1957] 1 W.L.R. 582 QBD;

International Auditing and Assurance Standards Board (IAASB), which is an independent body based in New York that sets standards for the international auditing of financial statements, in particular the International Standards on Auditing (ISA). Based on this template, the Financial Reporting Council has issued (and has regularly updated) the International Standard on Auditing (UK) (ISA(UK)),[207] which establish the overall objective of the independent auditor and the standards for the conduct of an audit in accordance with the international consensus. Accordingly, whilst the oversight of auditors is performed at a domestic level, the standards themselves are driven by international developments.

Quality assurance, investigation and discipline

23–029 A central function of the Financial Reporting Council is to oversee the monitoring of audit quality in general and to carry out investigations into allegations of inadequate audit and to secure (subject to appeal) disciplinary sanctions.[208] This oversight has been in place since the substantial reform of auditor regulation in the Companies (Audit, Investigation and Community Enterprise) Act 2004, which effectively did away with professional self-regulation in these areas. In respect of PIEs, these functions are to be carried out by the Financial Reporting Council itself.[209] In other cases, the task may be delegated by the Financial Reporting Council to (or shared with) the RSBs. Quality assurance means the periodic inspection of audits carried out in particular companies accompanied by possible recommendations for improvement. This is a feature of modern auditing practice. In particular, there is a requirement that the Financial Reporting Council establish an effective system of audit quality assurance and carry out quality assurance reviews of firms performing statutory audits.[210] Quality assurance reviews should be carried out every six years, but more frequently (every three years) in the case of PIEs.[211] In order to carry out these reviews, inspectors are appointed and they issue an inspection report.[212] In order to facilitate this work of the Financial Reporting Council, an auditor must provide an "annual transparency report",[213] for example, setting out the PIEs for which the auditor acts, the firm's governance and remuneration structure and the auditor's practices designed to ensure independence.

Bolitho v City and Hackney Health Authority [1996] 4 All E.R. 771; *Montgomery v Lanarkshire Health Board* [2015] UKSC 11. For accounting standards, see para.22–019.

[207] For the latest version, see Financial Reporting Council, *International Standard on Auditing (UK) 200* (revised June 2016; updated January 2020).

[208] Statutory Auditors and Third Country Auditors Regulations 2016 (SI 2016/649) reg.3(1)(l)–(m).

[209] Regulation art.24(1), as amended by the Statutory Auditors and Third Country Auditors (Amendment) (EU Exit) Regulations 2019 (SI 2019/177).

[210] Regulation art.26(2), as amended by the Statutory Auditors and Third Country Auditors (Amendment) (EU Exit) Regulations 2019 (SI 2019/177).

[211] Regulation art.26(2), as amended by the Statutory Auditors and Third Country Auditors (Amendment) (EU Exit) Regulations 2019 (SI 2019/177).

[212] Regulation art.26(8), as amended by the Statutory Auditors and Third Country Auditors (Amendment) (EU Exit) Regulations 2019 (SI 2019/177).

[213] Regulation art.13, as amended by the Statutory Auditors and Third Country Auditors (Amendment) (EU Exit) Regulations 2019 (SI 2019/177).

In the case of suspected inadequate audits, the competent authority has investigatory powers and a range of potential sanctions at its disposal,[214] and there are statutory criteria for determining the severity of the sanction in any particular case. In the case of a PIE, the competent authority has "all the supervisory and investigatory powers that are necessary for the exercise of [its] functions", including enhanced information and access rights.[215] The disciplinary sanctions range from private censure, through public censure to a prohibition on acting as an auditor and the imposition of a financial penalty.[216] In important cases, the disciplinary proceedings are commenced in the UK by the Financial Reporting Council pursuant to its "Audit Enforcement Procedure".[217] The proceedings are initiated before a disciplinary tribunal, which is established by (but independent of) the Financial Reporting Council.[218] The tribunal is chaired by an experienced lawyer, and appeal lies to an appeal tribunal.

Empowering auditors

Even if the statutory and professional rules produce loyal and competent auditors, the auditors may nevertheless fail to detect impropriety in the company if they are not given the co-operation of those who work for the company. If an auditor does not receive the co-operation needed to assess the company's accounts, that fact can be reflected in the ultimate report to the shareholders,[219] but it is obviously more desirable that the auditor should be able to obtain the necessary information. The issue of the auditor's powers as against both the audited company and its management is one to which the legislature has given increasing attention in recent years. **23–030**

Auditors have a right of access at all times to the company's books, accounts and vouchers.[220] They are entitled to require such information and explanations as they think necessary for the performance of their duties. Those persons obliged to provide the information and explanations now go beyond the company's officers and embrace (present or past) employees of the company; persons holding or accountable for the company's accounts (for example, where the company has outsourced this function); subsidiary companies incorporated in the UK; and persons falling within the above categories in relation to the subsidiary

---

[214] Statutory Auditors and Third Country Auditors Regulations 2016 (SI 2016/649) Sch.2. For issues of legal professional privilege in relation to requests for information by the Financial Reporting Council, see *Sports Direct International Plc v Financial Reporting Council* [2020] EWCA Civ 177; [2020] 2 W.L.R. 1256; *A v B* [2020] EWHC 1491 (Ch); [2020] 1 W.L.R. 3989. Auditors may also be required to disclose information to other statutory and regulatory bodies: see *Re Revenue and Customs Commissioners' Application* [2018] UKFTT 541 (TC).

[215] Regulation art.23(3), as amended by the Statutory Auditors and Third Country Auditors (Amendment) (EU Exit) Regulations 2019 (SI 2019/177).

[216] Statutory Auditors and Third Country Auditors Regulations 2016 (SI 2016/649) reg.5(1)–(3).

[217] Financial Reporting Council, *Audit Enforcement Procedure* (1 January 2021).

[218] Financial Reporting Council, *Audit Enforcement Procedure* (1 January 2021), Pt 5. See, for example, *Baker Tilly Audit LLP v Financial Reporting Council* [2017] EWCA Civ 406.

[219] CA 2006 s.498(3).

[220] CA 2006 s.499(1).

and the subsidiary's auditor (if different).[221] More problematic (albeit of great importance) is the position of subsidiaries incorporated outside the UK and the relevant persons connected with those subsidiaries. In such a case, the problem of international comity is addressed by putting an obligation on the parent company, if required by its auditors to do so, to take such steps as are reasonably available to obtain such information and explanations from the subsidiary and the relevant persons.[222] A failure to respond "without delay" to a request for information is a criminal offence, unless compliance was not reasonably practicable.[223] It is also a criminal offence knowingly or recklessly to make a statement to the auditors that conveys or purports to convey any information or explanation that is misleading, false or deceptive in any material particular.[224]

The effective exercise of the auditor's powers depends, however, upon the auditor knowing which questions to ask. Since the auditor is by profession an investigator, it is reasonable to suppose that he or she will often be in a position to ask the right questions. The Company Law Review considered that there was a good argument for requiring directors to "volunteer" information, rather than leaving the auditor to find everything out.[225] As considered above,[226] this reform was implemented by adding to the matters that must be disclosed in the directors' report. Nowadays, that report must contain a statement on the part of each director to the effect that, as far as the director is aware, there is no information needed by the auditor of which the auditor is unaware; and that the director has taken all steps he ought to have taken to make him- or herself aware of such information and to establish that the auditor is aware of it.[227] This may require the director to reveal his or her own wrongdoing or that of fellow directors to the auditor.[228] The full extent of what is required of the director is to be assessed by reference to the director's objective duty of care,[229] but the CA 2006 specifically recognises that making enquiries of fellow directors and the auditor might be enough to discharge the duty (in other words, that the director can rely on satisfactory answers from such sources to appropriate questions).[230] A director is criminally liable if the statement is false, but only if the director knew of the falsity or was reckless as to whether the statement was true or false and if he or she failed to take reasonable steps to prevent the (inaccurate) directors' report

[221] CA 2006 s.499(2). Any statements made by such persons may not be used in subsequent criminal proceedings against the maker (except in respect of offences connected with the making of the statement) and the requirement is subject to an exception for legal professional privilege: see CA 2006 s.499(3)–(4).

[222] CA 2006 s.500(1)–(3).

[223] CA 2006 s.501(3).

[224] CA 2006 s.501(1). It is not a criminal offence for the foreign subsidiary or those connected with it to make an inaccurate statement (CA 2006 s.501(1) applies only to s.499), probably an unavoidable loophole, since otherwise British law would be criminalising conduct committed abroad.

[225] Final Report I, paras 8.119–8.122.

[226] See further para.22–024.

[227] CA 2006 s.418(2). Wilfully suppressing relevant information may be a ground for disqualification—potentially lengthy—of a director: see *Re TransTec Plc (No.2)* [2006] EWHC 2110 (Ch); [2007] B.C.C. 313. See further Ch.20.

[228] This is in fact a result that the director's core duty of loyalty may mandate: see further para.10–033.

[229] CA 2006 s.174. See further paras 10–045 onwards.

[230] CA 2006 s.418(4).

from being approved.[231] As considered further below, failure to make the statutory enquiries may also limit the auditor's civil liability towards the company by virtue of the doctrine of contributory negligence.

LIABILITY FOR NEGLIGENT AUDIT

The nature of the issue

Imposing civil liability on an auditor towards the company in the case of a negligent audit is an obvious way of encouraging diligence on the part of auditors. It is also a type of liability that arose quite naturally out of the law of tort, once negligence liability was extended from acts to misstatements. If an auditor produces an audit report that is misleading and the inaccuracy is caused by a lack of care, skill or diligence on the part of the auditor, then those to whom the auditor owes a duty to take care will be in a position to sue the auditor for damages, provided that the inaccurate report has caused them loss. In the case of a single auditor, the liability will lie with that person; in the more common case of a firm being appointed auditor, then the individuals who were negligent will be liable, but so also will the firm. Any claim against the firm may be based upon the fact that the individual's negligence is treated as the negligence of the firm itself or because the firm is vicariously liable for the negligence of the individual. Nevertheless, the question of how wide that liability should be (both in terms of the range of potential claimants and the quantum of liability) raises difficult policy issues. 23–031

The principles for determining the underlying liability of the auditor rests, even after the CA 2006, with the common law,[232] although legislation has played a role in fashioning the way that common law liability applies to auditors. It is important to distinguish among the potential claimants against the auditor between the audit client and other third parties. That the audit client in principle has a claim against the negligent auditor is well-established; that claim being based either on the contract between the auditor and the company or on the tort of negligence.[233] In relation to claims by persons other than the audit client, however, the question of how widely the duty of care in tort is owed has been fiercely debated in the courts; the upshot of the litigation is a rather restricted duty of care to parties other than the client. Of course, the matter might be

[231] CA 2006 s.418(5)–(6). For the process of approving the directors' report, see further para.22–036.

[232] When a firm is appointed as auditor, the senior statutory auditor must sign the report (see CA 2006 s.503(3)), but the person identified as the senior statutory auditor is not thereby subject to any civil liability to which he or she would not otherwise be subject: CA 2006 s.504(3). The members of the audit team do not appear to be protected from liability by the signature of the senior statutory auditor.

[233] It makes little difference how the claim is put, since the implied term in the contract to provide audit services will be, as in tort, only a duty to take reasonable care. In particular, the defence of contributory negligence is available, whichever way the claim is put: see *Forsikringsaktieselskapet Vesta v Butcher* [1989] A.C. 852 CA at 858–868; *Riva Properties Ltd v Foster & Partners Ltd* [2017] EWHC 2574 (TCC) at [216]; *ARB v IVF Hammersmith* [2018] EWCA Civ 2803; [2020] Q.B. 93 at [285]. Of course, the parties could by contract seek to increase the level of the duty (for example, to a warranty that the audit report was accurate), but their freedom to lower the duty is not necessarily unfettered.

decided by contract even in relation to non-clients, but there is less likely to be an explicit contract between the auditor and the non-client upon which the claimant can rely.[234] The thrust of the court decisions on the tortious liability of auditors, however, is that liability exists in relation to non-clients only where a relationship "akin to a contract" has arisen. This narrow formulation of the duty of care owed by auditors to non-client claimants is but one example of a generally cautious attitude on the part of legislators towards auditors' civil liability. One might have thought that increasing the civil liability of the auditor would be an effective way of providing incentives to auditors to be both independent and competent. Unlike all the statutory strategies considered above (which in one way or another have seen some expansion in recent years), judicial decisions and legislative rules have ensured that there has been no such expansion in relation to civil liability; rather, the tendency in recent years has been to rein in civil liability.

23–032 As regards liability to non-clients, the fact that the accounts and reports and the auditor's report are placed in the public domain has a particular impact upon the scope of civil liability.[235] This particular feature of auditors' reports means that a very large number of people may potentially rely on them as the basis for making a wide range of transactional decisions. Unrestricted liability on the part of auditors to third parties who rely on the accounts thus raises the prospect of "liability in an indeterminate amount for an indeterminate time to an indeterminate class".[236] This particular problem underlies the important decision of the House of Lords in *Caparo Industries Plc v Dickman*.[237] The fear is that, by making auditors the effective guarantors of transactions based on the audited accounts, the audit market might unravel through the withdrawal of financially sound auditors who wish to avoid extensive liability.

Even in relation to actions by audit clients, there are difficult issues about the scope of liability. Indeed, the doctrine of joint and several liability may significantly increase auditors' tortious exposure. Under this doctrine, if two or more tortfeasors are liable in respect of the same loss, the injured party may recover from any one of them for the whole of that loss, leaving the defendant to seek contributions from the other tortfeasors. In the classic case, where the misstatements in the company's accounts result from the fraud or negligence of someone within the company and the auditor fails to discover the wrongdoing, the claimant may recover the whole of the loss from the auditor, leaving the auditor to bear the risk that the original wrongdoers (usually directors or employees of the company) are judgment-proof.[238] Thus, claimants are

---

[234] In circumstances where a contract identifies a third party sufficiently clearly (whether by name, class or description), it may be possible for that third party to enforce the contract: see Contracts (Rights of Third Parties) Act 1999 s.1(1)(b). Consider *Chudley v Clydesdale Bank Plc* [2019] EWCA Civ 344; [2020] Q.B. 284.

[235] See further para.22–038.

[236] *Ultramares Corp v Touche* (1931) 174 N.E. 441 at 441 per Cardozo CJ.

[237] *Caparo Industries Plc v Dickman* [1990] 2 A.C. 605 HL. For a re-analysis of the approach to the duty of care in *Caparo*, albeit in a non-audit context, see *Robinson v Chief Constable of West Yorkshire* [2018] UKSC 4; [2018] 2 W.L.R. 595.

[238] In the case of actions by the company, the auditor's liability is significantly qualified by the defence of contributory negligence (see further para.23–039), but the issues relating to contribution still provide a potential rationale for restricting auditor liability to third parties.

encouraged to pursue the defendants with "deep pockets" to recover their whole loss, even though the auditor may not be the party who is principally at fault.[239] Such extensive liability risks encouraging defensive auditing behaviour with the result that the utility of the auditing function is undermined.

These difficulties are only partially addressed (and may even be exacerbated) by the existence of professional indemnity insurance (or equivalent arrangements that audit firms are obliged to carry).[240] That insurance may be very expensive and so increase the cost of audits. Such insurance may also not be available for the full extent of the claim, so that the liability risk is only partially collectivised through the insurance mechanism. More problematically, the presence of insurance may actually encourage litigation against auditors, since claimants will know that auditors are worth suing and that auditors will have an incentive to settle quietly, rather than litigate, provided that liability can be kept within the relevant insurance limits. There has been the odd attempt to move towards the substitution of "proportionate" liability for joint and several liability in the tort of negligence generally,[241] but these experiments have been short-lived.[242] Despite pressure from the accounting profession, there has been similar resistance to any form of "proportionate" liability for auditors on the ground that it simply shifts the risk of the defendant's insolvency from the auditor to the wholly innocent claimant.[243] As the common law was unable to assist auditors, the CA 2006 provided a solution by permitting a "liability limitation agreement" between auditor and audit client, as discussed further below. According to this reform, it is possible to enter an agreement to restrict the auditor's liability to its proportionate share of the loss, although this only deals with claims by the audit client and not potential third-party claimants.

Providing audit services through bodies with limited liability

Where the auditor is an audit firm taking the form of a traditional partnership, further issues arise. The assets of the firm as a whole become available to satisfy the claimant if the loss is caused by a partner (or employee) acting in the ordinary course of the firm's business.[244] In addition, given the absence of limited liability in the traditional partnership, the personal assets of both the negligent partner and fellow partners may be called on to meet the claim.[245] The prospect of personal liability (uncovered by insurance) might induce such defensive action on the part of auditors that the utility of having an audit is reduced because, for example, 23–033

---

[239] One possibility is for the auditor to enter into a "standstill agreement" with the client, thereby encouraging the client to pursue other parties who may be responsible for the conduct in question: see *Exus Travel Ltd v Baker Tilly* [2016] EWHC 2818 (Ch).

[240] CA 2006 Sch.10 para.17.

[241] *Barker v Corus (UK) Plc* [2006] UKHL 20; [2006] 2 A.C. 572.

[242] Compensation Act 2006 s.3, reversing the House of Lords decision in *Corus*.

[243] DTI, *Feasibility Investigation of Joint and Several Liability by the Common Law Team of the Law Commission* (1996); Final Report I, para.8.138. As to the situation where the claimant is not wholly innocent, see paras 23–039 onwards.

[244] Partnership Act 1890 s.10.

[245] Partnership Act 1890 s.12, indicating that joint and several liability operates between the partners.

auditors begin to give qualified audit opinions based on insignificant grounds.[246] Something has now been done to address the issue of personal liability. Audit services may now be provided to a company by an accounting firm that is not a partnership. The CA 2006 provides that both individuals and firms are eligible to be appointed as auditors,[247] but then defines a "firm" as "any entity, whether or not a legal person, that is not an individual".[248] Accordingly, this undermines the old notion that (as a hallmark of professionalism) audit firms should provide services on the basis of personal liability for their quality. Indeed, some accounting firms have now set up their auditing arms as limited companies, although the corporate form remains unattractive for the internal organisation of professional partnerships. It was for this reason that the accounting firms lobbied for, and ultimately obtained in 2000, a new business vehicle: the limited liability partnership,[249] which has the internal structure of a partnership, but benefits from limited liability in its external dealings. The origins of this new business vehicle are demonstrated by the fact that, when originally proposed, the limited liability partnership was to be confined to professional businesses; in the end, this business form was made generally available.[250]

Conducting the audit through a vehicle with limited liability certainly protects the personal assets of the non-negligent partners. Whether the personal assets of the negligent partner are so protected depends on whether the negligent misstatement in the audit report is analysed as having been made by the member, for whose tort the corporate body is vicariously liable (personal assets of the negligent member not protected), or whether the negligent misstatement is analysed as having been made by the corporate body through the auditor, in which case the personal assets of the negligent member are not at risk. The decision of the House of Lords in *Williams v Natural Life Health Foods*[251] supports the latter analysis (personal assets not at risk). Whilst there were some early doubts as to whether *Williams* might extend to statements by professionals,[252] there are instances of the approach in that case being applied to the professional context, such as surveyors.[253] Accordingly, there is no reason why a similar protection should not be available to auditors.

23–034 Assuming *Williams* operates to protect auditors, the benefits of corporate personality and limited liability are restricted to the personal assets of the members: the business of the corporate body itself could still be destroyed by a

[246] The fear of defensive conduct in response to the imposition of liability has been particularly marked in the context of public authority liability: see, for example, *Michael v Chief Constable of South Wales* [2015] UKSC 2; [2015] A.C. 1732; *N v Poole BC* [2019] UKSC 25; [2020] A.C. 780.

[247] CA 2006 s.1212(1).

[248] CA 2006 s.1173(1).

[249] See further para.1–004.

[250] For the origins of the LLP, see G. Morse et al (eds), *Palmer's Limited Liability Partnership Law*, 3rd edn (London: Sweet & Maxwell, 2017), Ch.1.

[251] *Williams v Natural Life Health Foods Ltd* [1998] 1 W.L.R. 830 HL. See also *Standard Chartered Bank v Pakistan National Shipping (No.2)* [2002] UKHL 43; [2002] 3 W.L.R. 1547. See further para.8–040.

[252] *Merrett v Babb* [2001] Q.B. 1171 CA; *Phelps v Hillingdon LBC* [2001] 2 A.C. 619 HL. For discussion, see Whittaker, [2002] J.B.L. 601.

[253] *Summit Advances Ltd v Bush* [2015] EWHC 665 (QB); [2015] P.N.L.R. 18. See also *Fraser Turner Ltd v Pricewaterhousecoopers LLP* [2019] EWCA Civ 1290; [2019] P.N.L.R. 33 at [70].

large claim that exceeds its insurance cover and pushes the body into insolvency. This is, indeed, the public policy crux. If there were many competing firms of auditors, the occasional insolvency might not matter in public policy terms. Nowadays, there are, however, only four international networks of firms capable of carrying out the audits of the largest multinational firms. Indeed, the collapse of Arthur Andersen, in the aftermath of the Enron scandal in the US, is a reminder of how quickly such international firms can disintegrate.[254] The disappearance of another such firm would further reduce competition in the market for the audit of multinational companies from its already low level. This fear should not, however, push legislators into hasty acceptance of arguments for the reduction of auditors' liability without rigorous scrutiny of the likely impact. For example, it was argued that a cap on auditors' liability would increase competition in the audit market, especially for large-firm audits, because a cap would encourage medium-sized audit firms to move into the "big league". The data does not, however, support this suggestion.[255] A more robust approach might be to seek to open up the audit market, especially the market for the audit of the largest companies, to a wider range of firms. As considered above, rules relating to mandatory re-tendering of audit contracts were driven as much by competition concerns as by concerns for auditor independence.[256]

Accordingly, the following analysis considers how the above concerns have impacted the legal liability of auditors, considering separately claims by the audit client and third parties.

CLAIMS BY THE AUDIT CLIENT

Establishing liability

The auditor's liability in contract to its client will usually turn upon the scope of the auditor's engagement and whether the auditor has provided services of the type and quality required by the contract's express and implied terms.[257] As there can be concurrent liability between claims in contract and the tort of negligence,[258] the audit client should be able to establish the existence of a duty of care owed by the auditor relatively easily. Simply stating that a duty of care exists, however, is not the whole story, as it is also important to determine **23–035**

[254] Arthur Andersen did not collapse because of a large liability claim, but because of a loss of reputation resulting from its being charged with, and convicted of, criminal offences (even though these convictions were overturned on appeal).

[255] OFT, *An Assessment of the Implications for Competition of a Cap on Auditors' Liability* (July 2004), OFT 741.

[256] See further para.23–014. For recent concerns over the continued lack of competition in the audit market, see Department for Business, Energy and Industrial Strategy, *Restoring Trust in Audit and Corporate Governance* (March 2021).

[257] There is a statutory implied term that the auditor will provide its services with reasonable skill and care: see Supply of Goods and Services Act 1982 s.13.

[258] *Henderson v Merrett Syndicates Ltd* [1995] 2 A.C. 145 HL.

whether the scope of that duty is sufficiently wide to cover the loss in question.[259] In this regard, the auditor's duty of care will depend in large part on the scope of the audit engagement. This will determine whether the auditor has undertaken to advise the client on particular transactions or simply to provide the client with relevant information. Accordingly, the scope of the auditor's duty of care would be expected to embrace liability in respect of decisions that companies normally take on the basis of the accounts, such as declaring dividends or paying bonuses, whether to staff or policy-holders.[260] The auditor's liability may, however, extend to wider classes of decision, including strategic corporate decisions, if it is clear that the audit engagement contemplated that the company needed the audit information to make such decisions.[261]

The significance of this question in the audit context was emphasised in *Manchester Building Society v Grant Thornton UK LLP*,[262] in which the claimant building society issued fixed mortgage loans, which it hedged by entering into various interest-rate swaps. As the claimant's swaps had to be given a fair (mark-to-market) value in its accounts, the claimant remained exposed to market volatility. To counter this volatility, the defendant accounting firm advised the client to employ hedge accounting and subsequently, as auditor, gave an unqualified report approving the use of hedge accounting by the client. On this basis, the client entered into further swaps and renewed existing swaps. It was subsequently discovered that, for some time, hedge accounting had not been permissible in the client's particular circumstances. The client accordingly suffered significant losses, which it sought to recover from the defendant auditor. The Court of Appeal concluded that, whilst the auditor had provided information on the availability of hedge accounting in the particular circumstances, it had not advised the client on the merits of entering into any of the various swap transactions.[263] Accordingly, as *Manchester Building Society* was an "information" case (rather than an "advice" case), the defendant auditor was only "responsible for the financial consequence of the advice and/or information being wrong", rather than for all the consequences flowing from entering into the particular transaction.[264] In essence, the losses suffered by the client did not fall within the scope of the auditor's duty of care.

The Court of Appeal revisited this issue in *AssetCo Plc v Grant Thornton UK LLP*,[265] in which the client was a listed company and was the parent of an

---

[259] *South Australia Asset Management Corporation v York Montague Ltd* [1997] A.C. 191 HL; *Gabriel v Little* [2017] UKSC 21; [2018] A.C. 599; *Hughes-Holland v BPE Solicitors* [2017] UKSC 21; [2018] A.C. 599.

[260] *Leeds Estate, Building and Investment Co v Shepherd* (1887) 36 Ch. D. 787 Ch D; *Barings Plc (In Liquidation) v Coopers & Lybrand (No.1)* [2002] 2 B.C.L.C. 364 Ch D; *Equitable Life Assurance Society v Ernst & Young* [2003] EWCA Civ 1114; [2003] 2 B.C.L.C. 603; *BTI 2014 LLC v PricewaterhouseCoopers LLP* [2019] EWHC 3034 (Ch) at [118]–[121]; cf. *MAN Nutzfahrzeuge AG v Freightliner Ltd* [2007] EWCA Civ 910; [2007] B.C.C. 986.

[261] *Equitable Life Assurance Society v Ernst & Young* [2003] 2 B.C.L.C. 603; *Sayers v Clarke-Walker* [2002] 2 B.C.L.C. 16 QBD.

[262] *Manchester Building Society v Grant Thornton UK LLP* [2019] EWCA Civ 40; [2019] 1 W.L.R. 4610.

[263] *Manchester Building Society v Grant Thornton UK LLP* [2019] 1 W.L.R. 4610 at [46]–[55].

[264] *Manchester Building Society v Grant Thornton UK LLP* [2019] 1 W.L.R. 4610 at [54] and [70].

[265] *AssetCo Plc v Grant Thornton UK LLP* [2020] EWCA Civ 1151; [2021] P.N.L.R. 1.

apparently successful corporate group. The client engaged the defendant firm to audit its accounts. Whilst the accounts indicated increased earnings and pre-tax profits, the reality was that the client was hopelessly insolvent, and the client's CEO and CFO had dishonestly prepared the accounts. For the relevant years, the defendant had given an unqualified audit report. Following a change of management, the client pursued the auditor in respect of a series of transactions, including irrecoverable loans to subsidiaries, unauthorised expenditure, related-party transactions and unlawful dividend payments. The Court of Appeal accepted that the "scope of duty" principle in *Manchester Building Society* should be applied to determine whether particular losses come within the scope of the auditor's duty: the purpose of that principle was "to distinguish the negligent audit that is merely the occasion for the loss from the negligent audit that gives rise to a liability to make good the loss".[266] The scope of the auditor's duty of care was also emphasised: the audit report was "not to assist the recipient to decide whether to enter into a particular transaction or pursue a particular course of action", but rather to alert the company to undetected errors and to enable the shareholders to scrutinise management.[267] Accordingly, as the auditor had "failed to detect the dishonest concealment of the substantial losses", the company was deprived "of the opportunity to call the senior management to account and to ensure that errors in management are corrected".[268] On this basis, with one exception, the losses suffered by the client fell within the scope of the auditor's duty of care. Particularly significant was the conclusion that the wrongfully paid dividends fell within the scope of the auditor's duty, as the CA 2006 makes clear that whether or not a company can pay dividends depends upon there being distributable profits showing in the company's accounts.[269]

Assuming that it is possible to establish the existence of a duty of care and that its scope extends to the loss in question, it will then be necessary to consider whether the auditor has in fact breached its duty of care by failing to act as a reasonable auditor would and, if so, whether and how much loss has been caused to the claimant. As far as the standard of care is concerned, it is clear in legal terms (although often not accepted in the commercial world) that the auditor is not a guarantor of the accuracy of the directors' accounts and reports. Indeed, the earlier authorities allowed the auditor a broad discretion to rely on information provided by management, so long as no suspicious circumstances had arisen that ought to have put the auditor on inquiry.[270] This view has now changed. According to Lord Denning, in order to perform his task properly, the auditor "must come to it with an inquiring mind—not suspicious of dishonesty, I **23–036**

[266] *AssetCo Plc v Grant Thornton UK LLP* [2021] P.N.L.R. 1 at [101]–[102].

[267] *AssetCo Plc v Grant Thornton UK LLP* [2021] P.N.L.R. 1 at [96]–[97]. See also *Singularis Holdings Ltd v Daiwa Capital Markets Europe Ltd* [2019] UKSC 50; [2020] A.C. 1189 at [36].

[268] *AssetCo Plc v Grant Thornton UK LLP* [2021] P.N.L.R. 1 at [108]–[110].

[269] CA 2006 s.836. See also *BTI 2014 LLC v PricewaterhouseCoopers LLP* [2019] EWHC 3034 (Ch) at [118]–[121].

[270] *Re Kingston Cotton Mill (No.2)* [1896] 2 Ch. 279 CA, where the auditors relied on certificates as to levels of stock, which were provided by the managing director who for years had grossly overstated the true position. cf. *Re Thomas Gerrard & Son Ltd* [1967] 2 All E.R. 525 Ch D, where it was held that the discovery of altered invoices should have caused the auditors to carry out their own check on the stock.

agree—but suspecting that someone may have made a mistake somewhere and that a check must be made to ensure that there has been none".[271] Auditor scepticism is now firmly established in audit regulation. According to the applicable statutory standards, an auditor must ensure that it "maintains professional scepticism throughout the audit".[272] As to what "scepticism" requires, the existence of accounting and auditing standards helps the courts to concretise the duty of care in any particular situation, even though they are not formally binding on the courts.[273] A court that relies on these external standards can be sure that it is not imposing some unexpected requirement on auditors and that there has been some 'public interest' input into the formulation of those standards. Indeed, given that auditor's responsibilities are so extensively set out in both statutory and regulatory form, some auditors may simply be prepared to accept that they have fallen below the requisite standard, thereby focusing their energies on issues of causation.[274]

As to causation, the auditor's failure to detect error in the company's financial statements deprives the directors (or shareholders) of knowledge that could have afforded them an opportunity to take remedial action or to prevent the company from proceeding with some action on a false basis (for example, by declaring a dividend or making representations and warranties in a contract for the sale of the company's business). That remedial action might take a number of forms, ranging from preventing the continuance of mismanagement or fraud to selling a company whose business model would have been shown by a proper audit to be under serious threat from changing economic circumstances. Accordingly, where it can be shown that the company or its board would have taken the same actions or made the same decisions even if the auditor had discharged its functions properly, then "but for" causation will not have been established. In *AssetCo Plc v Grant Thornton UK LLP*,[275] the auditor's failures were held to have deprived both the general meeting and the non-executive directors of the opportunity to call the senior management to account and to ensure the management errors were corrected. In other words, the company in that case was deprived "of the very information that would have caused it to cease its loss-making activities and to

---

[271] *Formento (Sterling Area) Ltd v Selsdon Fountain Pen Co Ltd* [1958] 1 W.L.R. 45 HL. See also *Re Thomas Gerrard & Son Ltd* [1967] 2 All E.R. 525.

[272] Statutory Auditors and Third Country Auditors Regulations 2016 (SI 2016/649) Sch.1 para.1(2). For these purposes "professional scepticism" means "an attitude that includes a questioning mind, being alert to conditions which may indicate possible misstatement due to error or fraud and a critical assessment of audit evidence". The notion of "professional scepticism" was current in auditing practice, even before being put on a statutory footing: see Auditing Practices Board, *Professional Scepticism* (March 2012).

[273] *Lloyd Cheyham & Co Ltd v Littlejohn & Co* [1987] B.C.L.C. 303 QBD. For the significance of "professional scepticism" in determining liability, see *AssetCo Plc v Grant Thornton UK LLP* [2021] P.N.L.R. 1 at [40]. See also, in a different context, *Bolam v Friern Hospital Management Committee* [1957] 1 W.L.R. 582; *Bolitho v City and Hackney Health Authority* [1996] 4 All E.R. 771; *Montgomery v Lanarkshire Health Board* [2015] UKSC 11. For the current professional standards, see Financial Reporting Council, *International Standard on Auditing (UK) 200* (revised June 2016; updated January 2020).

[274] See, for example, *AssetCo Plc v Grant Thornton UK LLP* [2021] P.N.L.R. 1.

[275] *AssetCo Plc v Grant Thornton UK LLP* [2021] P.N.L.R. 1 at [108]–[110].

take the steps necessary to regain its solvency".[276] Accordingly, the auditor's failures had caused the company's losses.

Even with causation established, it will be necessary to determine the quantum of the losses caused. This is not straightforward, as in many cases (for example, where the remedial action was the possible sale of the company's undertaking) what the company will have lost is really the chance to take a particular step (such as finding a purchaser at an acceptable price who might or might not have been forthcoming). The pecuniary value to be placed on that lost opportunity depends upon the degree of likelihood that action would have been taken and that it would have led to the outcome the company alleges would have been reached.[277] The court will have to assess the value of that chance, awarding the chance no value if the court considers it purely speculative.[278] Even where there was a course of action the directors could have taken that was wholly within their own control, liability will depend on its being shown that the step would in fact have been taken.[279] Often this will be difficult to do, especially in the case of fraud or mismanagement, when those involved include the directors. Then, it would seem, to establish any loss, the claimant would have to show on the balance of probabilities that, had the auditors' report been properly qualified, action would have been taken by the shareholders that would have led to the removal of the directors. Furthermore, to recover any substantial damages, the claimant would have to establish a probability that the ill-consequences of the former directors' negligent or fraudulent reign would have been effectively remedied by the steps that would have been taken. The difficulties of establishing such counterfactuals convincingly when there are multiple other courses of action that the company might have pursued are obvious. 23–037

Limiting liability

Even if the claimant can establish liability and substantial loss, there are two types of argument available to the auditors to reduce their liability for the whole of that loss, one based on general defences (full or partial) to tortious liability and the other on contract. 23–038

General defences

The most obviously available defence is contributory negligence, whereby a claimant, who suffers loss as a result partly of his or her own fault and partly the defendant's fault, will have the damages payable by the latter reduced by such amount as the court thinks just and equitable, having regard to the claimant's share of the responsibility for the damage.[280] Accordingly, where harm has been 23–039

---

276 *AssetCo Plc v Grant Thornton UK LLP* [2021] P.N.L.R. 1 at [109].

277 For the modern approach to assessing damages for "loss of a chance", see *Perry v Raleys Solicitors* [2019] UKSC 5; [2020] A.C. 352, applying *Allied Maples Group Ltd v Simmons & Simmons* [1995] 1 W.L.R. 1602 CA (Civ Div).

278 *Equitable Life Assurance Society v Ernst & Young* [2003] 2 B.C.L.C. 603.

279 *AssetCo Plc v Grant Thornton UK LLP* [2021] P.N.L.R. 1.

280 Law Reform (Contributory Negligence) Act 1945 s.1(1).

inflicted on the company through fraud committed by its employees and the directors have failed to discover this (partly because they had inadequate internal controls in place and partly because of the auditor's failings), the directors' failures are effectively the company's failures which the auditors can accordingly pray in aid to reduce the damages payable. The disclosure statement now required of directors in the directors' report is likely to increase the incidence of this defence being run by the auditors.[281]

In fact, even before the advent of the directors' report, a somewhat similar result seems to have been achieved by auditors through the use of "representation letters", which auditors require companies to sign before the auditors will certify the accounts. In these letters, the company typically promises "to the best of its knowledge and belief" that certain important matters concerning the company's financial situation are in a particular state.[282] If such a representation letter is signed negligently on behalf of the company, the auditors will have the partial defence of contributory negligence if subsequently sued by the company: this will be available if the auditors can show that they would not have certified the accounts, or not certified them without further investigation, had they known the true facts. If the representation letter is signed fraudulently, the auditors will have a complete defence: any damages due from the auditors to the company can be wholly set off against the claim the auditors have against the company for the deceit practised by the company on the auditors.[283]

In the above cases, the situation is one where both the auditors and the directors or senior management of the company failed to discover the fraud or negligence of a subordinate employee and where both are at fault in failing to do so. Reducing the company's recovery seems acceptable in this context for otherwise the existence of auditor liability would provide an incentive for companies not to manage their internal risk systems effectively. What is much less clear is whether the auditors should be permitted to build a defence of contributory negligence directly on the actions of the subordinate employee (in other words, in a situation where the only failure to discover the fraud or negligence is that of the auditors). The argument against allowing contributory negligence on this basis is that it reduces the auditor's incentive to discover wrongdoing within the company—sometimes put as the argument that contributory negligence should not be based on conduct within the company which was "the very thing" (or one of the things) that the auditors were under a duty to discover.[284] In essence, where the duty of care was to protect the other party from harm, allowing reliance on such defences would effectively undermine the reasons for imposing a duty of care in the first place.

---

281 See further para.23–030. Although misleading disclosure is not a civil wrong under the CA 2006, it can still constitute "fault" on the part of the company for the purposes of contributory negligence.

282 The representations may include, for example, that "there have been no irregularities involving management or employees who have a significant role in the system of internal control".

283 See *Barings Plc (In Liquidation) v Coopers & Lybrand (No.2)* [2002] 2 B.C.L.C. 410, where an example of a representation letter can be found.

284 *Reeves v Commissioner of Police of the Metropolis* [2000] 1 A.C. 360 HL. See also *Singularis Holdings Ltd v Daiwa Capital Markets Europe Ltd* [2020] A.C. 1189 at [22]–[23].

In *Barings Plc (In Liquidation) v Coopers & Lybrand*,[285] the judge took account of both management failings and the undiscovered fraud of the employee (which was attributed to the company) in assessing the level of the company's contributory negligence. Applying this approach, the judge assessed the company's contributory negligence at a high level, varying over the time of the fraud, beginning at a 50% contribution and ending at 95%. However, the judge did recognise some force in "the very thing" argument,[286] for it appears that he would otherwise have attributed the employee's fraud to the company so as to allow the auditors to avoid all liability. Indeed, the force of that point in *Barings* has now been accepted in *Singularis Holdings Ltd v Daiwa Capital Markets Europe Ltd*,[287] which involved a claim by a client company against an equity and brokerage business for breaching its duty to the company to ensure that payments were not being made fraudulently from the company's account, despite the fact that it was only acting upon the instructions of the client's sole shareholder. The Court of Appeal refused to allow the fraud perpetrated by the company's own shareholder to bar the company's claim entirely, since "[t]he existence of the fraud was a precondition for [the claim], and it would be a surprising result if [the defendant], having breached that duty, could escape liability by placing reliance on the existence of the fraud that was itself a pre-condition for its liability".[288] Nevertheless, as in *Barings*, the Court of Appeal dealt with the matter by reducing the damages to be awarded by 25% to reflect the contributory negligence on the company's part as a result of its board failing to exercise effective control over the company's sole shareholder. **23–040**

This analysis was subsequently approved by the Supreme Court in *Singularis*.[289] That appeal was, however, solely concerned with the issue of attribution, which has already been considered in Ch.8. That said, the attribution issue raised in the present context differs from the issued considered above: the previous analysis considered attribution in the context of litigation by third parties against the company itself[290]; whereas the present concern is litigation by the company against third parties. It is not obvious that the attribution rules should be the same, at least where the third party is the auditor, precisely because the auditor performs a protective function for the company, which a broad approach to attribution might undermine. Accordingly, the focus will be the development of the attribution principles with particular focus on its application to auditor liability.

Indeed, the intersection between attribution principles and auditor liability presented itself in stark form in *Stone & Rolls Ltd v Moore Stephens*,[291] where the defendant auditors sought to raise the defence of illegality as a complete defence **23–041**

---

[285] *Barings Plc (In Liquidation) v Coopers & Lybrand* [2003] EWHC 1319 (Ch); [2003] Lloyd's Rep. I.R. 566 (the trial of the action whose interlocutory proceedings are cited in fn.282).

[286] Basing himself on *Reeves v Commissioner of Police of the Metropolis* [2000] 1 A.C. 360.

[287] *Singularis Holdings Ltd v Daiwa Capital Markets Europe Ltd* [2018] EWCA Civ 84; [2018] 1 W.L.R. 2777.

[288] *Singularis Holdings Ltd v Daiwa Capital Markets Europe Ltd* [2018] 1 W.L.R. 2777 at [79].

[289] *Singularis Holdings Ltd v Daiwa Capital Markets Europe Ltd* [2020] A.C. 1189 at [18]–[19] and [24]–[25].

[290] See further Ch.8.

[291] *Stone & Rolls Ltd v Moore Stephens* [2009] A.C. 1391.

to liability. In this case, a person who was the sole beneficial shareholder and controlling shadow director of a company had established the company for the purpose of committing large-scale fraud on banks. The company, in liquidation, sought compensation through its liquidator (acting in the economic interests of the creditors) for the allegedly negligent failure of the defendant auditor to discover the fraud. The defendant sought to strike out the claim on the basis of an illegality defence, usually referred to by its Latin name: *ex turpi causa non oritur actio* (roughly translated as, "disgraceful conduct does not give rise to a cause of action"). This principle of public policy states that the court will not allow its processes to be used by a claimant to benefit from its own illegal conduct. In *Stone & Rolls*, the majority (by three to two) allowed the defence on the basis that the fraudster's fraudulent intentions should be attributed to the company, given that the fraudster owned, controlled and managed the company. Accordingly, the auditor was able to bar the company's negligence claim by virtue of the attribution principles.

Subsequently, the Supreme Court, in *Jetivia SA v Bilta (UK) Ltd*,[292] revisited the issue. In relation to the decision in *Rolls*, however, Lord Neuberger considered that "it is very hard to derive much in the way of reliable principle from the decision". Indeed, Lords Toulson and Hodge went so far as to suggest "that *Stone & Rolls* should be regarded as a case which has no majority ratio decidendi".[293] In *Jetivia*, however, all their Lordships seemed to agree on one proposition, namely, that the *ex turpi* defence is available only if there are no "innocent" (i.e. uninvolved in the fraud) shareholders or directors in the company. Accordingly, *Jetivia* limits the number of companies that might be precluded from raising a claim against their auditors. There was disagreement, however, on whether the defence was always available in the absence of innocent shareholders (and, perhaps, directors).[294] This was the most significant dividing line between the judges in *Stone & Rolls* itself. Since the company was in liquidation at the time of the litigation, the persons with an economic interest in the success of the claim were its creditors (i.e. the defrauded banks), who were "innocent". If the presence of innocent shareholders would have been enough to prevent use of the *ex turpi* defence by the auditors, presumably on the grounds that a public policy defence should not be deployed to deprive non-involved persons of the value of their interest in the company, it could be argued that the presence of innocent creditors of a company in liquidation should have the same negative impact on the availability of the defence. This argument does not involve acceptance of the proposition that auditors' duties are owed to the company's creditors (an argument that the courts have only accepted in limited situations). The duty here is still one owed by the auditors to the company; the litigation is brought by the body that has the management of the company—the liquidator in this case; and the basis of the auditor's liability remains restoration of the company's assets to the level they would have enjoyed had the auditors not been negligent. The point rather is that, so long as the company is a going

[292] *Jetivia SA v Bilta (UK) Ltd* [2015] UKSC 23; [2015] 1 B.C.L.C. 443 at [46], which involved attribution in a third context, namely where the company sues a director.

[293] *Jetivia SA v Bilta (UK) Ltd* [2015] 1 B.C.L.C. 443 at [154].

[294] Lords Mance and, less strongly, Neuberger thought the point was still open; Lords Sumption, Toulson and Hodge thought the defence was always available in this situation.

concern, the residual economic interest in the company's assets lies with the shareholders, so that excluding liability where all the shareholders are involved in the fraud can be justified. Once the company is in the vicinity of insolvency, however, the residual economic interest shifts to the creditors, as the law now clearly recognises.[295] If the interests of non-involved shareholders trump the *ex turpi* defence when the company is a going concern, it would be consonant with recent developments in company law that the interests of non-involved creditors should be taken into account in the same way.[296]

More recently, the ground has shifted again following *Singularis Holdings Ltd v Daiwa Capital Markets Europe Ltd*,[297] where the Supreme Court has now addressed the point that divided it in *Jetivia*, namely whether attribution should always occur (most commonly in the *ex turpi* context) when there is a "one-man" company, or, in other words, a company where there are no other innocent parties, whether directors or shareholders. A unanimous Supreme Court stressed that it was necessary to avoid bright-line rules in the context of attribution, but that instead the analysis depended increasingly on the context in which the issues arose and the purpose for which attribution was relevant. Accordingly, Baroness Hale indicated that "there is no principle of law that in any proceedings where the company is suing a third party for breach of a duty owed to it by that third party, the fraudulent conduct of a director is to be attributed to the company if it is a one-man company".[298] On that basis, the Supreme Court considered that *Stone & Rolls* "can finally be laid to rest". Accordingly, adopting a contextual focus, the Supreme Court considered that, as the purpose of the duty in that case was "to protect the company against just the sort of misappropriation of its funds as took place here", the wrongdoing shareholder's knowledge should not be attributed to the claimant company.[299] Accordingly, "the very thing" argument that was accepted in *Barings*[300] is likely to persuade a future court not to bar a company's claim against its auditor (absence unusual circumstances) given that the auditor's duty of care performs the same protective function as the banker's duty considered in *Singularis*.

Limitation by contract

Formerly, it was impossible for auditors to limit their liability to the company by means of a contract or by means of a provision in the company's articles, or to obtain an enforceable promise of an indemnity from the company in respect of **23–042**

---

[295] See further paras 19–013 onwards.

[296] This was essentially the reasoning of Lord Mance in *Stone & Rolls*, except that he attached significance to the fact that the company was insolvent at the time of the negligent audit. It might be that a better test is the presence of innocent creditors or shareholders at the time of the litigation. It would be odd if the presence of an innocent shareholder at the time of the negligence should facilitate an action by the company against the auditors, even though that shareholder had left the company by the time of the litigation; and equally odd if the defence were available despite the fact that the fraudsters had sold out to a new set of shareholders by the time of the litigation.

[297] *Singularis Holdings Ltd v Daiwa Capital Markets Europe Ltd* [2020] A.C. 1189. See also *Hamblin v World First Ltd* [2020] EWHC 2382 (Comm).

[298] *Singularis Holdings Ltd v Daiwa Capital Markets Europe Ltd* [2020] A.C. 1189 at [34].

[299] *Singularis Holdings Ltd v Daiwa Capital Markets Europe Ltd* [2020] A.C. 1189 at [35].

[300] *Barings Plc (In Liquidation) v Coopers & Lybrand* [2003] EWHC 1319 (Ch).

such liability. Whilst the starting point remains that such provisions are void,[301] a significant change in the CA 2006 was to permit such contracts, subject to safeguards.[302] Accordingly, a company is nowadays entitled to indemnify the auditor against a liability incurred in defending proceedings, criminal or civil, in which the auditor is successful,[303] or in making a successful application for relief from liability in circumstances where the auditor has acted honestly and reasonably.[304] This is a limited qualification to the prohibition, which does no more than track the provisions relating to directors.[305] The real innovation in the CA 2006, however, is the ability for the auditor and company to conclude a "liability limitation agreement", which limits the auditor's liability to the company arising out of a breach of duty in the conduct of the audit. Such agreements could also enable the parties to introduce proportionate liability by agreement. This reform was recommended by the Company Law Review, but is subject to reasonably strict safeguards. The principal ones are as follows:

(1) The agreement is effective to limit the auditor's liability only to the amount that is fair and reasonable in the circumstances, having regard, amongst other things, to the auditor's responsibilities under the CA 2006 and the professional standards expected of the auditor.[306] If the agreement goes further than is permitted by this provision, then it only operates to limit liability to the level permitted by the CA 2006 (so that the agreement does not fail altogether).[307] The liability limitation agreement is exempted from the usual control mechanisms in the Unfair Contract Terms Act 1977 (UCTA 1977),[308] which applies a reasonableness standard to contracts limiting liability in other contexts. In short, the auditor limitation clause is subject to ex post court control by reference to a broad standard, just as under UCTA 1977; the significance of the exclusion from UCTA 1977 is, however, that a clause that fails the test under the CA 2006 still operates, but at a lower level of substantive protection.

---

301 CA 2006 s.532(1).

302 CA 2006 ss.533–536. Limitation of liability is also promoted at EU level: see Commission Recommendation concerning the limitation of the civil liability of statutory auditors and audit firms [2008] OJ L162/39. However, in the US, the Securities Exchange Commission (SEC) opposes agreements on limitation, whilst accepting mandatory limits on auditors' liability, thus making safeguards in the CA 2006 unusable by UK-incorporated companies that are cross-listed in the US. The SEC fear apparently is that the need to negotiate a limitation undermines the independence of auditors (rather than giving clients the opportunity to obtain improvements in audit quality). This is somewhat ironic in view of the fact that the liability of auditors is limited by statute to proportionate liability in the US.

303 CA 2006 s.533.

304 CA 2006 s.1157. Essentially, the auditor may rely on a promise by the company to pay the costs of a successful defence.

305 See further paras 10–124 to 10–125.

306 CA 2006 s.537(1). In determining what is "fair and reasonable", a court must ignore matters occurring after the loss or damage has been incurred (an attempt to restrain hindsight) and the possibility of recovering compensation from other persons: CA 2006 s.537(3).

307 CA 2006 s.537(2).

308 CA 2006 s.534(3).

(2) The liability limitation agreement may relate to only a single financial year, so that a new agreement is needed for each set of annual reports and accounts.[309]
(3) The agreement must be approved by the members, though, in the case of a private company, the members, before the company enters into the agreement, may pass a resolution waiving the need for approval.[310]

To provide a check that these requirements have been met, a note to the company's accounts must set out the principal terms of the liability limitation agreement and the date on which it was approved by the members (or approval was waived).[311] In relation to such agreements, the Financial Reporting Council has produced guidance.[312] This contemplates three main types of agreement: proportionate liability, a "fair and reasonable" test and a cap on liability, which could be expressed in a number of ways, but most obviously as a multiple of the audit fee. Institutional shareholders have indicated, however, that they will normally vote in favour only of proportionate liability agreements and, in particular, will be opposed to caps on liability.[313] Moreover, institutional shareholders are likely to expect an improvement in audit quality in exchange for their agreement, in particular, less defensive auditing.

Criminal liability

Whilst permitting auditor liability limitation agreements, the CA 2006 also increased the criminal liability of an auditor who knowingly or recklessly makes a statement in the audit report that is misleading, false or deceptive in a material particular.[314] In other words, the deterrent effect of unlimited liability in damages for negligence has to some extent been replaced by a narrower criminal liability for intentional or reckless misstatements.[315] The liability applies to the statement that the accounts give a true and fair view,[316] as well as to statements in the audit report about the compliance of the company's accounts with its accounting records; about whether the necessary information and explanations were forthcoming from management and others; and about whether the company was entitled to prepare accounts under the small companies regime.[317] Curiously, however, the liability applies only to that part of the auditor's report dealing strictly with the accounts. Accordingly, criminal liability does not attach to the 23–043

[309] CA 2006 s.535(1).

[310] CA 2006 s.536. Approval may be given before or after the company enters into the agreement; in the former case only the "principal terms" of the agreement need to be approved. In the case of public companies, approval is likely to be sought at the AGM, which also functions as the "accounts meeting" for the previous year.

[311] The Companies (Disclosure of Auditor Remuneration and Liability Limitation Agreements) Regulations 2008 (SI 2008/489) reg.8.

[312] Financial Reporting Council, *Guidance on Auditor Liability Limitation Agreements* (June 2008).

[313] Institutional Shareholders' Committee, *Statement on Auditor Liability Limitation Agreements* (June 2008).

[314] CA 2006 s.507(1).

[315] HL Debs, Grand Committee, Eighth Day, col.407 (14 March 2006) (Lord Sainsbury of Turville).

[316] CA 2006 s.507(1), which also extends to the associated matters set out in CA 2005 s.495.

[317] CA 2006 s.507(1)–(3).

auditor's report on the directors' or strategic report, the separate corporate governance statement or the auditable part of the directors' remuneration report. In this respect, the criminal liability of auditors is narrower than that of directors, which extends to knowing or reckless authorisation of publication of non-compliant directors' reports as well as of accounts.[318] There was much pressure in Parliament from the auditing profession to remove the liability for recklessness, but the Government stoutly resisted it.[319]

CLAIMS BY THIRD PARTIES

The duty of care in principle

23–044 The issues discussed above relating to breach of duty and loss arise in relation to third-party claims (namely, claims by anyone other than the audit client) as well, but the prior and most controversial issue has been to define the circumstances in which a duty of care will be owed at all by the auditors to third parties. The general common law principles governing the duty of care in relation to economic loss caused by negligent misstatement apply equally to the auditor context. Until less than 60 years ago, this was not a live issue: until the House of Lords decision in *Hedley Byrne & Co Ltd v Heller & Partners Ltd*,[320] the tort of negligence did not recognise a general duty to take care to avoid misstatements causing economic loss. Before *Hedley Byrne*, liability could be based on the tort of deceit (as it can still be nowadays), but that liability remained subject to two major restrictions. First, liability arises only if the statement-maker knows that the statement is false (or makes it not caring whether it is true or false), so that an honest, even if unreasonable, belief in the truth of the statement protects its maker from liability in deceit.[321] Secondly, the statement-maker must intend the claimant (or a class of persons including the claimant) to rely on the statement.[322] The effect of the first limitation is to restrict the circumstances in which liability in deceit will arise; and the effect of the second is to restrict the range of potential claimants, if it does arise. The impact of *Hedley Byrne* was to side-step both these limitations, which are not part of the tort of negligence. It was not, however, at all clear from *Hedley Byrne* (which was not a case concerning the audit) when the new duty of care to avoid misstatements[323] causing economic loss would be imposed on auditors.

[318] CA 2006 ss.414(4) (accounts), 414D(2) (strategic report), 419(3) (directors' report) and 422(2) (directors' remuneration report).

[319] CA 2006 ss.508–509, which provide for the Secretary of State or, in Scotland, the Lord Advocate to give guidance to the regulatory and prosecuting authorities about how misconduct should be handled if it appears to fall both within the criminal prohibition and the regulatory provisions.

[320] *Hedley Byrne & Co Ltd v Heller & Partners Ltd* [1964] A.C. 465 HL. See also *Customs & Excise Commissioners v Barclays Bank Plc* [2006] UKHL 28; [2007] 1 A.C. 181.

[321] *Derry v Peek* (1889) 14 App. Cas. 337 HL. The terms "deceit" and "fraud" (in the civil sense) seem to be used interchangeably.

[322] *Bradford Equitable BS v Borders* [1941] 2 All E.R. 205 HL.

[323] The auditors' public statement is contained in their report (see para.23–003), but in that they opine about the accuracy of the accounts and reports generally, so that their failure to pick up inaccuracies in those documents is inevitably in issue.

The answer to this question in the context of auditors was provided by the House of Lords in *Caparo Industries Plc v Dickman*,[324] which ultimately gave greater comfort to auditors than to investors. In *Caparo*, there was a purchase of a target company listed on the London Stock Exchange by another such company through a takeover offer preceded by share purchases in the market. The target company had issued a profit-warning in March 1984, which caused its share price to halve. In May 1984, the directors of the target made a preliminary announcement of its annual results for the year to March 1984, which confirmed that profits were well short of expectations. This caused a further, albeit less dramatic, fall in the share price. In June 1984, the annual accounts were issued to the shareholders. Shortly before that date, Caparo, which had previously owned no shares in the target, began acquiring shares in tranches until it reached a shareholding of 29.9%. At that point (after the accounts had been circulated), the purchaser made a general offer for the remaining shares, as the Takeover Code required the purchaser to do if it was to acquire any more of the target's shares.[325] Following the take-over, as the target company's economic prospects were discovered to be less promising than initially thought, the purchaser sought to recover its losses as a result of the misleading information about the company that had been made available. In particular, Caparo asserted that the 1984 accounts, although gloomy, in fact overvalued the company. Accordingly, Caparo alleged that the auditors had been negligent both in not detecting the irregularities or fraud that had led to the overstatements in the accounts and in certifying the accounts as representing a true and fair view of the company's financial position.

The House of Lords considered that an examination of the statutory framework for company accounts and audits established a relationship between those responsible for the accounts (the directors) or for the audit report (the auditors), on the one hand, and some other class or classes of persons, on the other. This relationship imposed a duty of care upon the directors or auditors to persons within the relevant class. As the directors owed fiduciary duties to the company and the auditors owed the company a contractual duty by virtue of its employment as the company's auditors, the company itself fell within the class of persons to whom a tortious duty of care was owed. The statutory framework did not, however, establish such a relationship with everybody who had a right to be furnished with copies of the accounts or audit report. A fortiori, there was no such relationship with everybody who had a right to inspect or obtain copies of the accounts from the Registrar of Companies (in other words, the world at large).[326] If any other relationship (besides that with the company) was going to create a duty of care, this could only be with the company's members (and perhaps debenture-holders). As considered above,[327] however, the scope of the duty of

---

[324] *Caparo Industries Plc v Dickman* [1990] 2 A.C. 605. The litigation concerned the preliminary issue whether, on the facts pleaded, a claim against the auditors could succeed, albeit that the facts were never finally established. For a re-analysis of the approach to the duty of care in *Caparo*, albeit in a non-audit context, see *Robinson v Chief Constable of West Yorkshire Police* [2018] 2 W.L.R. 595. Although *Robinson* impacts the legal test in *Caparo*, it does not affect the result in the latter case.

[325] See further para.28–040.

[326] On the circulation and filing of the company's annual reports and accounts, see paras 22–038 onwards.

[327] See para.23–035.

care to members could only extend to the protection of what might be described as the members' corporate governance powers: to safeguard their interests in the company and to hold the management to account. The scope of that duty of care did not extend to losses suffered by the shareholders as a result of buying further shares in the company, even if a perusal of the annual accounts and reports led the shareholders to make that investment decision.[328]

23–045 To establish a duty of care to members that is greater in scope than recognised in *Caparo*, or to establish any duty of care to other persons, there must be an additional "special" relationship with the person who suffered loss, as a result of relying on the accounts or report. To succeed in establishing that additional relationship, Lord Bridge in *Caparo* indicated that the claimant must show that the auditors (or directors) contemplated that the accounts and report "would be communicated to the plaintiff either as an individual or as a member of an identifiable class, specifically in connection with a particular transaction or transactions of a particular kind (e.g. in a prospectus inviting investment)[329] and that the plaintiff would be very likely to rely on it for the purpose of deciding whether or not to enter upon that transaction or upon a transaction of that kind."[330] Accordingly, in *Caparo*, the House of Lords expressed the firm view that negligent auditors were not liable to potential claimants simply on the basis that it was reasonably foreseeable that they would rely on the audited accounts and suffer loss as a result.[331] The House of Lords, therefore, confined the common law duty of care more narrowly. This policy has much to commend it. However, deducing that policy from the statutory framework set by the CA 2006 for company accounts and their audit is not straightforward.[332] Their Lordships'

---

[328] This was the specific point that had to be determined in *Caparo*. The Court of Appeal had held unanimously that auditors owed no duty of care to members of the public who, in reliance on the accounts and reports, bought shares (in the absence of a special relationship) but, by a majority, that they did owe such a duty to existing shareholders who, in such reliance, bought more shares. The House of Lords thought the distinction between liability for investment decisions made by shareholders and investment decisions made by non-shareholders unsustainable.

[329] See further para.25–033, indicating that statutory liability for prospectuses has gone beyond the common law, which will normally be irrelevant. The principles in *Caparo* remain highly relevant where the legislation does not apply: see *Al-Nakib Investments Ltd v Longcroft* [1990] 1 W.L.R. 1390 Ch D, considered at para.25–039.

[330] *Caparo Industries Plc v Dickman* [1990] 2 A.C. 605 at 621E–F. This was clearly the unanimous view, adopting the dissenting judgment of Denning LJ in *Candler v Crane Christmas & Co* [1951] 2 K.B. 164 CA; and affirming the decision of Millett J in *Al Saudi Banque v Clark Pixley* [1990] Ch. 313 Ch D; but rejecting the wider views expressed in *JEB Fasteners Ltd v Marks Bloom & Co* [1981] 3 All E.R. 289 QBD; and in *Twomax Ltd v Dickson, McFarlane & Robinson*, 1982 S.C. 113 OH; and by the majority of the New Zealand Court of Appeal in *Scott Group Ltd v McFarlane* [1978] N.Z.L.R. 553.

[331] The case concerned only the purchase of shares and the court left open the question of whether sales of shares (for example, where the accounts negligently undervalued the company) were within the scope of the duty, on the grounds that only shareholders could sell shares so that sales were necessarily a shareholder activity. However, the judges showed little enthusiasm for this argument; and a thorough-going governance analysis would seem to exclude sales, as well as purchases, on the grounds that both are investment, not governance, decisions.

[332] For a similar refusal to use the common law to supplement the statutory framework, but within an analysis of the statutory purposes that seems more faithful to the legislative intent (in this case the New Zealand Securities Act 1978), see *Deloitte Haskins & Sells v National Mutual Life Nominees* [1993] A.C. 774 PC.

analysis in *Caparo* of that framework gives very little weight to the purposes that Parliament might have had in mind when steadily requiring ever greater levels of public disclosure of financial reports, rather than just their circulation to members and other current investors in the company.

Assumption of responsibility

Unsurprisingly, the case law after *Caparo* has concentrated on seeking to determine the basis or bases upon which it will be possible for claimants to establish a "special relationship" or, as it is now often called in the light of subsequent general developments in the law of negligence, an "assumption of responsibility" on the part of the auditors towards the claimant. On the one hand, third parties naturally seek to point to facts from which liability could be inferred; on the other hand, auditors seek to include statements in their report disclaiming any liability to third parties. A crucial initial issue is that the special relationship does not require that the auditor should consciously have assumed responsibility. The test is an objective one and the question for the court is whether, in all the circumstances, it is appropriate for the auditors to be treated as having assumed responsibility.[333] **23–046**

In *Barclays Bank Ltd v Grant Thornton UK LLP*,[334] the judge held that a disclaimer in an audit report of liability to third parties was effective to negative[335] liability on the part of the auditor towards a sophisticated third party. The disclaimer was clear,[336] and its inclusion in a short audit report was enough to bring the term to the attention of the sophisticated third party. The main issue was whether the disclaimer satisfied the "reasonableness" requirement in the Unfair Contract Terms Act 1977,[337] from which a disclaimer, unlike a limitation of liability agreement, is not exempted.[338] The judge dismissed, as having no real hope of success, the bank's argument that the clause was unreasonable and accordingly struck out the claim. Not only was Barclays in general terms a sophisticated third party, but it was aware of the practice of auditors disclaiming liability to third parties. Indeed, in other aspects of the same transaction, the bank had expressly contracted with the auditors to accept liability, which the auditors had agreed to do, subject to a cap on their liability. The bank was in effect seeking

---

333 *Electra Private Equity Partners v KPMG Peat Marwick* [2001] 1 B.C.L.C. 589 CA; *Caparo Industries Plc v Dickman* [1990] 2 A.C. 605 at 638. See also *Williams v Natural Life Health Foods Ltd* [1998] 1 W.L.R. 830 at 835.

334 *Barclays Bank Ltd v Grant Thornton UK LLP* [2015] EWHC 320 (Comm); [2015] 2 B.C.L.C. 537.

335 Because the clause operated to negative liability (rather than being an exemption clause) it was not subject to the convention that it should be construed narrowly.

336 "To the fullest extent permitted by law, we do not accept or assume responsibility to anyone other than the company and the company's directors … for our audit work, for this report, or for the opinion we have formed." Although given in the context of an audit of the company's accounts for non-statutory purposes, the clause was a variation of the formula recommended by the Institute of Chartered Accountants in England & Wales for statutory audit reports (with the substitution of "members" for "directors").

337 Unfair Contract Terms Act 1977 ss.2 and 11.

338 See para.23–042.

to be better off for not having contracted (because liability would be uncapped) than it was in the situations where it had expressly contracted with the auditors to accept liability.

A number of different situations have been considered by the courts where no disclaimer has been present, though one may imagine that express disclaimers are becoming routine. First, within groups of companies, the courts have accepted that it is arguable that the auditors of a subsidiary company owe a duty of care to the parent company, since the production of individual accounts is an integral part of the process of producing both the parent's accounts and consolidated accounts.[339] However, the losses for which the auditors are potentially liable in such a case will be restricted by the uses to which it can be contemplated the accounts will be put by the parent. Accordingly, in the standard case, the subsidiary's auditors should contemplate that the parent will use the consolidated or parent's accounts for the purposes to which parent companies normally put them (payment of dividends to shareholders of the parent or bonuses to senior staff), but this will not necessarily lead to the auditors being liable for other types of loss, such as the losses flowing from the parent's decision to continue to fund the subsidiary.[340] It is less obvious that, on the above argument, the auditors of the parent will owe a duty of care to subsidiary companies of which they are not the auditors, but the Court of Appeal has refused to strike out such claim where, because of the way the group was run in practice, the auditors of the various group companies co-operated to a high degree.[341]

23–047 A second established area of tortious duty to "third" parties involves the directors of the company by which the auditors have been engaged. Although the CA 2006 presents the compilation of the accounts by the directors and their audit as consecutive and separate events, in practice the two overlap, with the directors finalising the accounts at the same time as the audit is in progress on the basis of draft accounts. On this basis, it has been held to be arguable that the auditors are under a duty to alert the directors immediately if the auditors form the view that the directors' approach to the accounts is misconceived in some respect. The directors are not obliged to accept the auditors' views, but are entitled to be informed before they commit themselves, with the risk that their approach may lead to the accounts being qualified by the auditors.[342]

The most obvious strategy suggested by the *Caparo* decision for investors (or lenders, or sometimes even the company's regulator) proposing to rely on the company's accounts and audit report is to make the auditors aware of their intentions in advance of the transaction and to secure from the auditors an ad hoc assumption of responsibility for the accounts in relation to the contemplated

[339] *Barings Plc (In Administration) v Coopers & Lybrand* [1997] 1 B.C.L.C. 427 CA.

[340] *Barings Plc (In Liquidation) v Coopers & Lybrand (No.1)* [2002] 2 B.C.L.C. 364; *MAN Nutzfahrzeuge AG v Freightliner Ltd* [2008] 2 B.C.L.C. 22 at [56].

[341] *Bank of Credit & Commerce International (Overseas) Ltd v Price Waterhouse* [1998] B.C.C. 617 CA, where, as is often the case in groups, the group's activities were arranged and continued along lines that cut across the separate companies in the group and their respective auditors.

[342] *Coulthard v Neville Russell* [1988] 1 B.C.L.C. 143 CA. The claimant directors, who were subsequently disqualified, sought compensation from the auditors for the losses caused by the disqualification. The court refused to strike out the claim. If loss as a result of the failure to inform the directors is suffered by the company, then no issue of liability to a third party arises.

transaction. Where such an approach is made explicitly and openly and the auditors accept responsibility, there is little to be said against holding the auditors liable for negligent audit. The auditors have the opportunity not to accept wider responsibility or to do so on explicit terms, in which case the auditor may seek to limit its liability or demand payment for taking on additional liability. The question is whether the auditors can or should be made liable on the basis of anything less than a near-explicit bargain with the lender or investor. It has been held that it is not enough to attract liability to the third party that the auditor repeated its conclusions to that person. The crucial question is whether the terms of the request from the third party ought to have made clear to the auditor that the purpose behind the direct communication or face-to-face meeting was individual reliance on the auditor's skill and judgement.[343] Although this approach falls short of an explicit bargain, it does require that the auditor be made aware of the nature of its commitment before liability in tort is imposed towards a third party.

Although the *Caparo* decision was controversial amongst those interested in the general theory of the law of tort (because of its rejection of the foreseeability test in the area of negligent misstatements),[344] and although the court's reliance on the statutory structure for the accounts seems overblown, the line drawn in that case has been followed by other top-level courts in the common law world, notably Australia and Canada.[345] Its effect, in the core case where no duty arises, is to insulate the audit transaction (and thus the fee charged by auditors to companies for carrying it out) from having to bear the investigation costs of other transactions that third parties may wish to carry out (whether by way of loan or equity purchase) with the company. Since the auditors are in a very poor position to estimate the risks associated with those other transactions, about which they will have little, if any, information, exclusion of liability is probably necessary for the maintenance of the market in audit services. The burden thrown on third parties by this approach is, by contrast, relatively slight. If the state of the company's finances is important to their transaction, as it often will be, investors can either pay someone else to replicate the due diligence that the auditors have carried out or, more likely, seek through the special circumstances exception to persuade the auditors to accept responsibility for their report in the context of the third party's transaction. This gives the auditors the opportunity to assess the risks of the particular transaction and to respond appropriately.[346] In principle, there seems to be no reason why the audit should subsidise investigation activities

---

343 *Andrew v Kounnis Freeman* [1999] 2 B.C.L.C. 641 CA (where the tests were held to have been satisfied); *James McNaughton Papers Group Ltd v Hicks Anderson & Co* [1991] 2 Q.B. 113 CA (where they were not); *Galoo Ltd v Bright, Grahame Murray* [1994] 1 W.L.R. 1360 CA (claims partly struck out and partly allowed to proceed). For the application of this approach to circulars issued in the course of takeover bids, see para.28–064.

344 For a re-analysis of the approach to the duty of care in *Caparo*, albeit in a non-audit context, see *Robinson v Chief Constable of West Yorkshire Police* [2018] 2 W.L.R. 595.

345 *Essanda Finance Corp Ltd v Peat Marwick Hungerford* (1997) 188 C.L.R. 241 HC (Australia); *Hercules Management Ltd v Ernst & Young* (1997) 146 D.L.R. (4th) 577 SC (Canada).

346 This analysis depends, of course, on the courts not expanding the special circumstances exception so as to swallow up the *Caparo* rule. Contrast the sophisticated approach in *Peach Publishing Ltd v Slater & Co* [1998] B.C.C. 139 CA; with the rather easy way in which assumption of responsibility was found in *ADT Ltd v BDO Binder Hamlyn* [1996] B.C.C. 808 QBD.

necessary for transactions between third parties and the company in the absence of near-express agreement by the auditors to accept the potential liability.[347]

Other issues

23–048 Even if a duty is established, the claimant will still have to satisfy the other ingredients for tortious liability, as discussed already in relation to claims by the audit client.[348] Accordingly, in *JEB Fasteners Ltd v Marks Bloom & Co*,[349] which would today be regarded as a "special circumstances" case, Woolf J held that all the conditions necessary for success, other than causation, had been established. Therefore, the claimant failed, since it would have entered into the transaction (a takeover) even if the accounts on which it relied had presented a wholly true and fair view of the company's financial position, the claimant's main object having been to secure the managerial skills of two executive directors.[350]

CONCLUSION

23–049 The audit has been subject to two very different legislative policy influences in recent years: on the one hand, a desire to relieve small companies of the need to have one and, on the other, a desire to make the audit of large, especially listed, companies a more effective check on the financial probity and corporate governance standards of management. The former is easy to effect as a matter of legal technique, although conclusive cost/benefit analysis of the audit of small companies is not available to demonstrate where the line should be drawn, and whether the audit should remain mandatory. The latter policy drive has had a positive consequence, so that the status of company auditors has, in the course of the past century, been transformed from that of somewhat toothless strays given temporary house-room once a year, to that of trained rottweilers, entitled to sniff around at any time and, if need be, to bite the hands that feed them. However, even rottweilers may learn that biting the hand that feeds you is not a policy conducive to happiness for the biter. Accordingly, a substantial structure has been put in place aimed at addressing issues of independence and competence, using a wide range of legal techniques, some more firmly located in company law than others. Whilst in the past, the EU has provided a strong impetus behind developments in the UK, domestic law will have to find its own way in the future.

347 If those costs were imposed on auditors, it is likely companies would end up paying them (by way of higher audit fees), so that, for example, the company would be subsidising the due diligence efforts of a potential acquirer. In some cases, the company might want to do so (see for an example para.17–045), but that can again be done through express contract.

348 See para.23–036.

349 *JEB Fasteners Ltd v Marks Bloom & Co* [1981] 3 All E.R. 289, affirmed on other grounds [1983] 1 All E.R. 583 CA.

350 Who, in fact, resigned!

PART 8

EQUITY FINANCE

In the course of this work we have referred frequently to the rights of shareholders but less often to the function which they perform in the company. In Pts 3 and 4, for example, we discussed the accountability of management to the shareholders, but did not investigate in any detail what the shareholders contribute in return for that ultimate control over the company. In very small companies, the purpose of issuing shares may indeed be simply to give the shareholders control over the company. In a two-person quasi-partnership, for example, the founders of the company may take one low-value share each, and no other shares may be issued by the company. The issue of shares in such a case operates to give the partners complete control over the running of the company, for, in all likelihood, they will use their voting rights as shareholders to appoint themselves as directors of the company. Financing for the company will come from elsewhere, probably in the form of a bank loan secured on the partners' personal assets. The two incorporators may also be the company's only—or at least its principal—employees.

However, in larger companies the purpose of share issues is not simply, or even primarily, to allocate control over the company but also to raise finance for it, and it is on that function of the share issue that we concentrate in this part. Ordinary shares constitute a particularly flexible form of finance for companies, because, so long as the company is a going concern, the shareholders are entitled to no particular level of return by way of dividend and cannot withdraw the contribution made in exchange for their shares without the company's consent, given either at the time of issue of the shares (e.g. where the shares are issued as redeemable at the option of the shareholder) or later (e.g. where the company offers to re-purchase some of its shares). During periods of economic strain the company can hang on to the finance provided by the shareholders but reduce or eliminate dividends, while the shareholders hope that things will turn around eventually and they will be well rewarded for their patience. Even where the company is wound up and the shareholders obtain rights to repayment of their investment, they stand at the end of the queue after the creditors and so may find that their rights are in fact worthless.[1] The economic exposure of the ordinary

[1] IA 1986 ss.107 and 143. See generally Ch.33.

shareholders goes a long way to explain the traditional practice of allocating control rights over the management to those shareholders.

When we consider those companies where management and shareholding do not overlap, where they may be many shareholders who find it difficult to coordinate their actions, then control over the company's strategy shifts to the board (as we saw in Pts 3 and 4) and shareholders face the agency problems inherent in their position when trying to hold the board to account. A core role for company law is to try and reduce those agency costs by providing mechanisms for the exercise of shareholder control, without at the same time removing the advantages of centralising supervision of management in the board.

In this part we analyse the steps to law takes to reduce the agency costs of a group of people akin to the shareholders but who are not (or not yet) shareholders. These are investors who are contemplating making an investment in the company and becoming shareholders in it. Where a company is seeking equity finance privately from a small number of investors, the law does little to help them. They are left largely to their own devices to extract information from the possible investee company and have protection only from the general law remedies for misrepresentation or fraud. See Ch.24. Once the company makes a "public offer", however, all that changes. See Ch.25. Somewhat akin to the annual reports a company produces for its shareholders, a company making a public offer of its shares must disclose (in a "prospectus") a vast amount of information about itself and about the shares it is offering, more in fact than is required for annual reporting. There is, of course, a large information gap between the corporate insiders promoting the share issue and the investors, which the prospectus helps to redress. However, it can be debated how helpful the prospectus is in answering the core question which investors face: is the price asked by the company for the share an attractive one in the light of the risks the company faces in its future operations? A prospectus is also an expensive document to produce and, as we shall see, there is much debate about the extent to which companies should be able to approach investors without having to produce a prospectus at all or at least a full prospectus.

Once an investor has bought shares in the company, whether directly from the company or from an existing shareholder, it will have all the advantages and disadvantages of being a shareholder, among the latter being that it is "locked into" the investment and cannot normally demand that the company exchange the shares back into cash (even at current values). Partial mitigation of the "lock in" of the ordinary shareholder's equity contribution is offered if the investor may easily transfer the share to another investor. The capacity to transfer of shares is important in any company, and we discuss the mechanisms for this in Ch.26, the process being highly digitised in the case of publicly traded companies. In publicly traded companies, in particular, where the investor's relationship with the company is primarily financial, an investor is likely to look more favourably upon shares which can easily be sold to another investor if the holder of them wishes to exit from the shareholding. This may provide an exit from a company whose prospects the shareholder no longer rates or allow the shareholder to obtain cash to meet consumption needs without diminishing the company's assets. Thus, large companies, contemplating a public offer of shares, are likely to ensure that the public offer is accompanied by an introduction of the shares to trading on a public securities market. This will restore liquidity to investors by enabling them to dispose of the shares to another investor at any time through the "stock exchange" (if not necessarily at an attractive price) and enable new investors to come into the company, even though the company is not currently making a public offer.

Once a public market for shares exists, there will be a demand for rules to ensure it functions effectively. In fact, there is much academic debate of the "chicken and egg" variety about whether good regulation generates stock markets or stock markets generate a demand for regulation. It could be a bit of both, of course. At any rate, there is now an extensive body of rules aimed at promoting the efficient operation of secondary trading on public markets (i.e. trading among investors, not with the company). Again, there are demanding continuing disclosure rules for companies (both periodic and episodic) as well as for significant shareholders, in order to ensure that the trading on the market is informed. See Ch.27. There are also provisions discouraging market abuse, a term which encompasses not only market manipulation but also, and less obviously, insider trading (i.e. trading while in possession of non-public but price-sensitive information). See Ch.30.

Trading among investors in the company's shares has created one topic of great controversy—the takeover. A person might buy on the market (unlikely because the initial purchases will quickly inflate the stock price) or make an offer to the existing shareholders at a fixed price (more likely) to acquire their shares, conditional on receiving sufficient acceptances to give the offeror control of the company. This is still an investment decision by the offeror, but clearly an investment decision of much greater magnitude than buying a small holding in the company. It often implies a desire by the new controller to alter in some significant way the manner in which the company operates, with potentially significant and often adverse consequences for the company's current board and senior managers and its employees. Less threateningly, this operation can be carried out with the consent of the current management, sometimes still as a takeover and sometimes formally as a scheme of arrangement, which achieves the same functional end. We discuss this in Chs 28 and 29.

CHAPTER 24

SHARE ISSUES: GENERAL RULES

A company which wishes to raise equity finance will seek to place shares (typically ordinary shares) in the hands of investors willing to buy them. This may be a rather simple process in which the directors decide to issue the shares and hand over a share certificate in exchange for a cheque (or some other form of payment) provided by the investor. Or it may be a highly elaborate process, involving months of preparatory work by investment bankers, lawyers and others and the production of an elaborate set of documents for investors to consider before making a decision whether to buy the shares. The crucial regulatory divide is between offers to the public of the company's shares and offers which are non-public. Where there is no public offer, the relevant rules are still to be found mainly in the CA 2006 and the common law of companies, whereas the rules on public offerings are located mainly in the Financial Services and Markets Act 2000, in rules made under it by the Financial Conduct Authority and in retained EU law. 24–001

In this chapter we deal with the rules that apply to all offers of shares, public or private. The additional requirements applying only to public offers are treated in the following chapter. However, it is worth noting that some of the rules discussed in this chapter, for example, the pre-emption rules, have their greatest impact when the offer is a public one. The domestic law considered in this chapter was substantially influenced by the Second Company Law Directive of the EU,[1] but, in contrast with its provisions on legal capital, its rules on share issuance have generally been welcomed by shareholders as strengthening their position, though, often, not as strongly as they would wish.

[1] Directive 77/91 [1997] OJ L26/1, subsequently amended and re-stated as Directive 2012/30 [2012] OJ L315/74. The references in this chapter are to the re-stated Directive.

PUBLIC AND NON-PUBLIC OFFERS

24–002 Given the importance of the public/non-public divide, it is worth looking at it in a little detail. At first sight, the structure of the law is simple. A private company may not make a public offer of its shares; a public company may do, but is not obliged to. Both types of company, therefore, may make private offers of their shares.

Under the CA 2006 the formal distinction between a "public" and a "private" company is indeed that a private company is prohibited from offering securities[2] to the public, either directly or through an offer for sale via an intermediary,[3] whereas a public company may do so. If a private company does make a public offer, the validity of any agreement to sell or allot securities or of any sale or allotment is not affected by breach of the prohibition, thus protecting innocent third parties who wish to enforce their rights under the contract of issuance of the shares,[4] and the criminal sanctions which previously underlay the prohibition have been removed. Nevertheless, the court has a wide range of powers to deal with the consequences of a breach or potential breach, on application of any member or creditor of the company or the Secretary of State or on its own motion in an unfair prejudice application. The court may enjoin the proposed issue[5]; require the company to re-register as a public company (the statute's preferred ex post remedy)[6]; and, if it decides against re-registration, it may wind the company up or make a remedial order.[7] The purpose of the remedial order is to put the person in whose favour it is made (who may be a subsequent holder of the share) in the position they would have been in had the breach of the prohibition not occurred.[8] The court has a wide discretion as to the contents of the remedial order, including the power to order the company and any others "knowingly concerned" in contravention of the prohibition to offer to purchase the securities at a price determined by the court.[9] For a private company to contemplate breaching the prohibition is, thus, a highly risky business, both for it and its officers and advisers. On the other hand, the requirements for becoming a public company are not onerous, so that a private company contemplating a public offer can avoid the above complications by changing its status. The company can even leave conversion until after the issue has succeeded, provided conversion is part of the terms of issue.[10]

By contrast, a public company may lawfully make a public offering of its securities. Its public status under the CA 2006 does not depend on whether it has actually done so. This gives rise to an ambiguity in the meaning of the term "public" company. For those concerned with financial services a public company

[2] CA 2006 s.755. The prohibition applies to both shares and debentures: s.755(5).

[3] See para.25–012 for a discussion of direct and indirect share offerings.

[4] CA 2006 ss.755(1) and 760.

[5] CA 2006 s.757.

[6] CA 2006 s.758(2)—but not if it is "impracticable or undesirable" to do so.

[7] CA 2006 s.758(3). The remedial order may be make whether or not the company is ordered to be wound up.

[8] CA 2006 s.759(1).

[9] CA 2006 s.759(3) and (5). Those involved could include advisers, such as investment banks. Where the company is ordered to re-purchase, the court may reduce its capital.

[10] CA 2006 s.755(3)(b)(4). On the requirements of converting to a public company see para.4–037.

is one that has in fact made a public offering of its shares and, further, has secured the admission of the offered shares to trading on a public market (such as the London Stock Exchange), so that purchasers of the shares and other investors can trade in them among each other after issue. In this work a company which has taken these steps is referred to as a "publicly traded" company or one which has "gone public". By contrast, for company lawyers a "public company" means one that is public in the CA 2006 sense of the term,[11] and so one which may or may not have made a public offer of its securities.

The complication in this simple dichotomy between private companies forbidden to offer shares to the public and public companies permitted to do so and becoming subject to the additional disclosure rules which apply to public offers, if an offer is made, is that the definitions of a public offer for the purposes of the prohibition (contained in the CA 2006) and in FSMA 2000[12] for disclosure purposes are not identical. At first sight this appears to be an example of a lack of joined-up legislation, but further reflection suggests this is not the case. The purpose of the financial services rules (considered in the next chapter) is to determine whether the benefits of providing the additional disclosure (primarily through a prospectus) outweigh the considerable costs of assembling it. The purpose of the CA 2006 rule is to determine whether the company has sufficient economic importance that it should be required to take on the additional obligations which the CA 2006 imposes on public companies. As is clear throughout this work, those additional obligations embrace a wide range of matters, certainly including disclosure but also going beyond it. So, it may make sense that the definitions for these two different purposes are not identical. **24–003**

The "definition" of what is a public offer for the purpose of the CA 2006 is in its s.756. This section makes it clear that "public" includes a section of the public ("however selected").[13] Apart from that, it operates by identifying certain circumstances in which an offer is not to be regarded as a public one. The section excludes an offer which

> "can properly be regarded, in all the circumstances, as not being calculated to result, directly or indirectly, in the shares or debentures becoming available for subscription or purchase by persons other than those receiving the offer or invitation".[14]

Also excluded are offers which are of "domestic concern" to the company, into which category fall, presumptively, offers to the company's existing members or employees, their families, debenture-holders of the company or a trustee for any of the above.[15]

Contrasting the CA 2006 definition with that applied to disclosures (discussed in the following chapter), it is possible to see that some offers regarded as private

---

[11] See para.4–011.

[12] FSMA 2000 ss.102B and 86.

[13] CA 2006 s.756(2).

[14] CA 2006 s.756(3)(a). If the securities do in fact end up in public hands within six months of their initial allotment or before the company has received the whole of the consideration for the shares, the company is presumed to have allotted them with a view to their being offered to the public: s.755(3).

[15] CA 2006 s.756(3)(b)–(6). Such offers may be renounceable in favour of other persons, provided such persons also fall within the "domestic" category.

under the Act might be public for disclosure purposes and that the opposite is true. Thus, the "offerees only" exemption of the CA 2006 appears to set no limit on the number of people who receive the offer nor to impose any qualification as to their experience or qualifications as investors in order to retain the private nature of the offer, whilst the central exemptions in the financial services rules are based on one or other of these limitations.[16] In other words, a private company might make what is a public offer for the purposes of the prospectus rules without contravening the prohibition in the Act. In such a case, of course, the private company will have to comply with the prospectus rules, and so no real problem arises, provided those concerned realise that it is about to fall within the disclosure rules and are prepared to meet the costs. In most cases, the private company will want to save the costs of producing a prospectus by bringing itself within one of the prospectus exemptions as well.[17]

On the other hand, a private company may be prevented by the CA 2006 from making an offer in respect of which, if it were a public company, it would not need to produce a prospectus, because the offer would fall within one of the prospectus exemptions. An example might be an offer addressed to professional investors as a class (rather than specific, named such investors). The Company Law Review, whilst recommending that some alignment of the definition of "public offer" in the Act with that in the Directive, did not think that the lack of fit was in principle objectionable, because different policies were being pursued by the two sets of rules. The CLR's view was that some of these exemptions from the prospectus requirement were "wholly inappropriate" for a private company, because they might allow the private company to reach "very large economic scale". This should be permitted only if the company were prepared to undertake the burdens of a public company.[18]

Of course, most share issues contemplated by private companies come nowhere near being classified as public for the purposes of either the CA 2006 or the prospectus rules.

DIRECTORS' AUTHORITY TO ALLOT SHARES

24–004 Issuance of shares by a company involves essentially three steps. First, the company must decide to make an offer of shares, public or non-public, and set the terms of the offer. Secondly, some person or persons must agree with the company to take the shares (at which point the shares are said to have been "allotted"). Thirdly, in implementation of that contract, those persons must take the shares and be made members of the company, thus completing the process of issuance. We shall look at each stage in turn.

[16] See paras 25–019 onwards.

[17] It is also worth noting that the private company may well face insuperable obstacles if it wants, not only to make an offer which is public in prospectus terms, but also to introduce those shares onto a public market. For example, a private company is not eligible to have its securities admitted to the official list: FSMA 2000 s.74 and the Financial Services and Markets Act 2000 (Official Listing of Securities) Regulations 2001 (SI 2001/2956) reg.3. On the "official list" see para.25–043.

[18] Completing, paras 2.77–2.82; Final Report I, paras 4.57–4.58. Further examples of exemptions under FSMA which might be thought inappropriate for private companies were offers as part of takeovers and of large denomination shares.

The first question is whether the decision to allot shares[19] is one for the board alone or whether the shareholders' concurrence is required. We have seen that the company's decision to allot shares ranking along with or even ahead of the company's existing shares does not normally amount to a variation of the rights of the existing shareholders, so that their consent will not be required under the variation of class-rights procedure,[20] even though the practical value of those rights may well be affected by such an issue. Even if the new shares are to rank behind the existing shares, the shareholders may still have doubts about the directors' plans for the use of the finance which will be raised. Thus, it is a matter of some importance whether the CA 2006 requires the shareholders' consent to a share issue or whether the matter is left entirely to the company's articles of association. If the Act does not intervene, the situation is likely to be that the board will be given authority to allot shares as part of its general management powers, and the articles may or may not give the shareholders a role in the decision-making process. Thus, the question becomes whether the Act should make shareholder consent mandatory or leave this issue to be determined by the company's articles.

Before the CA 2006 the principle in the Act was that consent of the shareholders was required for the allotment of shares, in both private and public companies. However, the CLR proposed[21] to remove the requirement of shareholder authorisation for the allotment of shares by private companies, except where the company already had, or the directors' proposal would create, more than one class of shares. This would be a default rule, for private companies' articles might restore the requirement of shareholder approval. This reform was implemented in the CA 2006.[22] The requirement for shareholder consent was thought to be an unnecessary formality in private companies, with their greater overlap of directors and members. However, such overlap would not necessarily obtain, and there would be the risk of greater opportunism, if the company had, or was about to create, more than one class of share.

Except in relation to the private company with only one class of share, however, shareholder consent, in one form or another, is still required for the allotment of shares. Not to obtain it is a criminal offence on the part of the directors knowingly involved,[23] although such failure does not affect the validity of the allotment.[24] The requirement is applied not only to the allotment of shares but also to the grant of rights to subscribe for or to convert a security into shares in the company in the future, for example, a convertible bond.[25] Otherwise, the requirement of shareholder consent could be avoided easily, for example, by issuing a debt security convertible at a later stage into shares. In this case, the **24–005**

---

19 The rules discussed in this section, unlike those relating to public offers, do not apply to debt securities which have no equity element.

20 See para.13–017.

21 Developing, paras 7.28–7.33.

22 CA 2006 s.550.

23 CA 2006 s.549(3)–(4).

24 CA 2006 s.549(6). *Blomqvist v Zavarco Plc* [2016] EWHC 1143 (Ch); [2016] B.C.C. 542.

25 CA 2006 s.549(1). This may help to explain in part why the "shareholder rights plan" or "poison pill" against takeovers is uncommon in the UK, for the effectiveness of the plan depends heavily upon the directors being able to issue warrants to subscribe for shares without shareholder approval.

requirement for shareholder approval is imposed at the stage of allotment but is not repeated at the conversion stage.[26] However, if, unusually, a convertible bond is convertible into existing, rather than new, shares of the company, then shareholder consent would not be needed at the allotment stage either.[27]

Shareholder authorisation may take the form of the directors putting before the shareholders a proposal for the allotment of a particular amount of shares to fund a specific project, with full details of how the finance raised will be used. This is authorisation for "a particular use of the power".[28] However, authorisation can be given generally, either in the articles or by (ordinary) resolution, for (renewable) periods of up to five years.[29] With general authorisation, where no specific use of the power may be under contemplation at the time, information about how the funds raised will be used will necessarily be very general and will be phrased so as to give management maximum freedom of action. However, the authority, whether general or particular, must state the maximum number of securities which can be allotted under it and the date at which the authority will expire.[30] Moreover, the authorisation may be made conditional,[31] and it may be revoked or varied at any time by resolution of the company, even if the original authority was contained in the articles.[32] Institutional shareholders attach importance to the general requirement for shareholder authorisation of share issues by the board. Guidance from them indicates that their members will not vote in favour of resolutions giving authority above a certain size. That size used to be one third of the company's existing issued share capital. In 2008 the limit was increased, under the pressures discussed in the next section, to two thirds, provided that the second third could be issued only on a pre-emptive basis and the authorisation for the second third was renewed yearly.[33]

---

26 CA 2006 s.549(3).

27 When the section talks about rights to "convert any security into shares in the company" it means newly created shares, not shares already in existence.

28 CA 2006 s.551(2). The section does not in terms require details of the use to which the funds will be put to be given to the shareholders. However, if the directors are also seeking authority in relation to a specific allotment to remove pre-emption rights, they are obliged to put forward a justification: see s.571(6) and para.24–010. Moreover, the general rules on resolutions at meetings of shareholders may require it. See para.12–040. The resolution need only be an ordinary resolution, even if it amends the company's articles (s.551(8)), but the resolutions must be notified to the Registrar (s.551(9)). Authorisation can be given in the articles, but this is unlikely in the case of "particular" authorisation.

29 CA 2006 s.551(2), (3), (4). Renewals of authority are to be given by resolution, even if the original authority was contained in the articles: s.551(4)(a). As s.551(7) makes clear, the time limit relates to the directors' authorisation of the share offer, not to the allotment of the shares (which might occur after the time limit had expired). A time limit is required even for particular exercises of the power.

30 CA 2006 s.551(3). In relation to allotments of rights to subscribe or to convert, what has to be stated is the maximum number of shares that can be allotted pursuant to the rights: s.551(6).

31 CA 2006 s.551(2).

32 CA 2006 s.551(4)(b). This will be a case of an ordinary resolution amending the articles. See fn.28.

33 See now Investment Association, *Share Capital Management Guidelines* (2016), 1.1 (available at *https://www.ivis.co.uk/media/12250/Share-Capital-Management-Guidelines-July-2016.pdf* [Accessed 25 March 2021]).

PRE-EMPTIVE RIGHTS

Policy issues

Whether or not collective shareholder consent is required for allotment of shares, there is a further issue whether the existing shareholders individually should have a "right of first refusal" over the new shares or, in company law terms, whether the shares should be allotted on a pre-emptive basis. The basic principle underlying the pre-emption rules is that a shareholder should be able to protect his or her proportion of the total equity by having the opportunity to subscribe, in proportion to the existing holding, for any new issue for cash of equity capital or securities having an equity element.[34] There are two main reasons why a shareholder might wish to exercise this right and thus to prevent the "dilution" of his or her holding of equity shares. First, if new voting shares are issued and a shareholder does not acquire that amount of the new issue which is proportionate to the existing holding, that person's influence in the company may be reduced because he or she now has control over a smaller percentage of the votes. In listed companies this is likely to be of concern only to large, often institutional, shareholders, but in small companies the issuance of new shares may well have a significant impact upon the balance of power within the company, and perhaps be motived by a desire to bring this change about. Here, pre-emptive rights operate as a potential limit on the freedom of the directors to effect a shift in the balance of control in the company by issuing new equity shares carrying voting rights to new investors.[35] 24–006

Secondly, further allotments by a publicly traded company of shares already in issue are likely to be priced at a discount to the existing market price, in order to encourage their sale. Once the new shares are issued, all the shares of the relevant class, new and old, will inevitably trade on the market at the same price. This new price will be somewhere between the issue price of the new shares and the previous market price of the existing shares, depending upon the size of the discount and the size of the new issue. In the absence of protective regulation, if an existing shareholder does not acquire the relevant proportion of the new shares, the loss of market value of the existing holding will go uncompensated. The new shareholders, in effect, will have been let into the company at a favourable price, and the cost of the discount will fall on the existing shareholders, both in terms of the current price of the shares and in terms of future dividends which will have to be paid to a larger number of shareholders.[36]

---

[34] Pre-emption in relation to new shares issued by the company should be sharply distinguished from pre-emption on the transfer of shares by a shareholder, common in private companies, but entirely a matter for private contracting through the articles. See para.26–007.

[35] See also para.10–018 on the improper purposes doctrine and Ch.14 on the unfair prejudice remedy, which may provide remedies to the company or the shareholder where a purpose of the issue is to reduce the influence of a particular shareholder.

[36] See the distinction drawn between the loss suffered by the company and that by the shareholders when shares are issued for an inadequate consideration in *Pilmer v Duke Group Ltd* [2001] 2 B.C.L.C. 773 Aus. HC. Of course, if the market is efficient, the discounted present value of the future lower dividends will be reflected in the current market price of the share.

The protection against voting dilution afforded by a bare pre-emptive right is only partial. The shareholder must also be in a position financially to take up the shares on offer.[37] A financially constrained existing shareholder is thus not protected against voting dilution by pre-emption. The same might seem to be true of financial dilution. However, here the addition of a further feature to the basic pre-emption model can help. If the shareholder is able to sell his or her pre-emptive rights in the market, that will provide compensation for the loss suffered. The rights will have a value equal to the difference between the issue price of the new shares and the (higher) price at which the whole class will trade after the issue, which will compensate the shareholder for loss caused by the difference between the pre-issue market price and the (lower) market price after the new issue.[38] However, for the rights to be marketable they must be transferable to third parties. There is an established way of providing this facility. The company issues a "renounceable" letter of allotment, which gives the shareholder the option to subscribe for the new shares or to transfer the right to subscribe to a third party, the overall process being known as a "rights issue".[39] Provided the shareholder transfers the right to acquire the new shares before the time for exercising it expires (i.e. "renounces" it) the third party will pay the company for the new shares at their discounted price, having paid the shareholder for the acquisition of the right to subscribe.[40]

The scope of the statutory right

24–007 The CA 2006 creates a pre-emptive right in favour of existing shareholders, but it does not require companies to add the additional feature of a rights issue.[41] The company may simply make what is usually termed an "open" offer to its existing shareholders: the shareholder either takes the shares at the price asked or passes up the offer altogether. It is, however, common practice in listed companies for pre-emptive offers to be made on a renounceable basis.[42] We will first examine the shareholder's statutory entitlements and then see how institutional pressure has moved practice beyond the statute in many cases.

---

[37] In the case of small companies, the shareholder may be able to challenge the decision to issue new shares under the unfair prejudice procedure. See *Re Company (No.007623 of 1984)* (1986) 2 B.C.C. 99191 Ch D (Companies Ct); and *Re Sam Weller Ltd* [1990] Ch. 682 Ch D.

[38] For a worked example of this analysis see Bank of England, *Guidance on Share Issuing* (1999), Technical Annex, showing that the total value of the rights will always match the loss of value on the holding, no matter the size of the discount or the proportion of the existing shares to be issued on a discounted basis. At the time of the trading of the rights the actual post-issue price is unknown but a "theoretical ex rights price" can be easily calculated.

[39] See para.25–014.

[40] A third course of action is for the shareholder to sell part of the rights and to exercise the other part, so as to maintain the value of his or her shareholding in the company (but not the proportion of the shares held), rather than simply to receive compensation for that drop in value by selling all the rights. This action is called, obscurely, "tail-swallowing". The "discount" referred to in this discussion is, of course, a discount to the prevailing market price of the shares, not to their par value, which is not permitted (see para.16–004).

[41] It recognises, of course, that a rights issue is a permissible way of providing the pre-emptive right. See the reference to renouncement of rights to allotment in s.561(2).

[42] For further discussion see E. Ferran, "Legal Capital Rules and Modern Securities Markets" in K.J. Hopt and E. Wymeersch (eds), *Capital Markets and Company Law* (Oxford: OUP, 2003).

The ambit of the statutory pre-emptive provisions extends only to issues for cash of "equity securities". These are defined as ordinary shares (and rights to subscribe for or convert securities into ordinary shares); and an ordinary share is any share other than one where the holder's right to participate in a distribution (whether by way of dividend or return of capital) is limited by reference to a fixed amount.[43] It does not matter whether the existing shares carry votes or not, and in fact it can be argued that pre-emptive rights are particularly important for the holders of non-voting shares, whose financial interests will not be protected by the rules on shareholder authorisation discussed in the previous section. Certain types of share issue are excluded from the pre-emption rules, even if they arguably involve the issue of equity shares for cash: bonus shares (where the pre-emption problem does not arise)[44] or shares to be held under an employees' share scheme.[45] Nor do the rules apply to shares taken by subscribers on the formation of a company.[46] Nor do the rules apply where a company issues shares under a scheme adopted by a company in financial difficulties, on the grounds, presumably, that saving the company is more important than a full protection of shareholder interests.[47]

The limitation of the pre-emptive rights to cash issues means, for example, that a company wishing to acquire a business in exchange for ordinary shares may proceed without being hampered by these rights. Nevertheless, the restriction of the statutory pre-emptive provisions to cash issues does constitute a severe hole in the principle of protecting shareholders against dilution, especially dilution of their voting position. In relation to financial dilution some alternative protection is provided by Ch.6 of Pt 17 of the CA 2006, requiring an independent valuation report in the case of share issues by public companies for a non-cash consideration,[48] but, even so, that section does not confer individual rights upon shareholders in the way that the pre-emption rules do.

Furthermore, the exclusion of share issues which are wholly or partly other than for cash gives rise to possibilities of manipulation so as to avoid the pre-emption rules. For example, if any part of the consideration, even a minor part, is not cash, **24–008**

[43] CA 2006 s.560(1). There is no upper limit to this amount (and it would be impracticable to set one) with the result that it is possible to fix a dividend limitation so high that the holders would in fact be entitled to the whole or the lion's share of profits without affording existing shareholders pre-emptive rights.

[44] CA 2006 s.564. See para.16–024. Since issuance of a bonus share involves the capitalisation of the company's reserves, no payment by shareholders is involved and the shares must be allotted pro-rata to those entitled to the reserve, were it distributed, or, in the case of an undistributable reserve, those whose contributions constituted the reserve (as in the case of the share premium account).

[45] CA 2006 s.566. The section applies even if scheme members are entitled to renounce or assign their rights. Employees' share schemes would be unworkable if every time a further allotment was to be made pursuant to them all equity shareholders had to be offered pre-emptive rights. If, however, employees hold equity shares allotted under the scheme, they presumably have the same rights to protect their proportion of equity as any other shareholder, unless those rights have been excluded or disapplied (see para.24–009).

[46] CA 2006 s.577. Indeed, it is difficult to see how the rules could be so applied.

[47] CA 2006 s.566A. For such schemes see para.29–012.

[48] See para.16–019. But the chapter does not apply to private companies or to share issues even by public companies in connection with takeover offers or mergers, where there is in fact a considerable risk of financial dilution. Listed company shareholders are better protected, for the rule restricting discounts to 10% (see para.24–011) applies also to a "vendor consideration placing".

then it appears that the pre-emption rules are excluded. This may be of particular interest to private companies. In other cases it may well be possible to restructure the transaction so that the cash is provided otherwise than to the issuer in exchange for its shares. Thus, where Company A wishes to acquire part of the business of Company B, the latter wishing to receive cash, Company A might issue new shares to raise the necessary money, if it does not have sufficient available cash, thus attracting the pre-emption provisions in relation to its shareholders. Instead, however, Company A might issue its shares to Company B, in exchange for the latter's assets and thus without attracting the pre-emption provisions, Company A having previously arranged for an investment bank to offer to buy the shares from Company B at a fixed price and to place them with interested investors. Such a "vendor consideration placing" gives Company B the cash it wanted, whilst relieving Company A of the need to abide by the pre-emption rules. However, for companies with a "premium" listing on the Main Market of the London Stock Exchange, the rights of the existing shareholders are protected by, in effect, transferring their pre-emption right to the sale of the shares by the investment bank.[49]

An alternative and now common mechanism for avoiding pre-emption rights which can be used for general fund-raising is the "cash-box" structure. Here, the (operating) company wishing to raise the money forms a new subsidiary for this purpose (a special purpose vehicle or SPV). The SPV issues redeemable preference shares to the investors and the investors transfer their funds to the SPV.[50] The next step is to get ordinary shares in the operating company into the hands of the investors (which is what they want) and the proceeds of the sale of the preference shares into the hands of the operating company (which is what it wants). The first step is achieved by the operating company issuing new ordinary shares to the holders of the preference shares in exchange for those shares. No pre-emption rights arise since the ordinary shares are not issued for cash. The second step is achieved by the SPV redeeming the preference shares, now held by the operating company, out of the proceeds of the issue which it still holds.[51]

Assuming none of the above limitations applies, the pre-emption obligation requires the company not to allot equity securities to any person unless it has first offered, on the same or more favourable terms, to each person who holds shares covered by the right a proportion of those equity securities which is as nearly as practicable equal to the shareholder's existing proportion in nominal value of the existing shares.[52] Only if the period for the existing shareholders to accept the

[49] LR 9.5.9: "A listed company must ensure that in a vendor consideration placing all vendors have an equal opportunity to participate in the placing." On premium listing see para.25–006.

[50] Any pre-emptive rights of the operating company as a shareholder in the SPV will be waived.

[51] For reasons of transactional security, a bank is normally inserted into this process, which acquires the preference shares in the subsidiary (thus underwriting the offer) and the ordinary shares in the operating company, transferring the latter to the investors in exchange for their cash, thus reimbursing itself. If a share premium arises on the redemption transaction, it can be kept out of the share premium account of the operating company through us of the merger relief. See para.16–008. For this reason the bank will normally hold some shares in the SPV in order to keep the operating company's holding below 90%.

[52] CA 2006 s.561. Treasury shares are excluded from the calculations required by this section: s.561(4). The details of how communication is to be made with the shareholders are set out in s.562.

offer has expired (now at least 14 days)[53] without the offer being accepted (or if it was positively rejected within this period) may an offer be made to outsiders. If the pre-emptive offer is not accepted in full, shares not taken up may be allotted to anyone; accepting existing shareholders do not have further pre-emptive rights in respect of those unaccepted shares.

Waiver

The shareholders collectively may forego their statutory pre-emption rights, which may be excluded or disapplied. Exclusion means the statutory provisions (or some aspect of them) do not operate; disapplication may mean that but it also embraces the situation where the statutory provisions apply "with such modifications as the directors may determine"[54] or such modifications as are specified in the disapplication resolution.[55] Not surprisingly, both exclusion and disapplication are easier for private than for public companies. A private company may exclude the obligation to offer pre-emptive rights (or a provision relating to the method of offering, most likely the time during which the offer must be open) through a provision in its articles—either generally or in relation to allotments of a particular description.[56] As for disapplication, if the private company has only one class of shares, so that the directors do not need shareholder authority to issue new shares, its articles or a special resolution of the shareholders may remove the pre-emptive obligation or give the directors power to modify the statutory scheme.[57] **24–009**

In relation to public companies exclusion is available only where the articles provide a pre-emptive alternative to the statutory scheme. This provision is designed to deal with situations where the company has more than one class of ordinary share.[58] The statutory pre-emptive obligation[59] is drafted in such a way as not to differentiate among different classes of ordinary shares, so that an offer of ordinary shares of one class would have to be made pre-emptively to all classes of ordinary shareholder. Section 568 permits a company to substitute an alternative pre-emption scheme in its articles which operates on a class basis. Non-compliance with the procedure in the articles carries the same consequences as non-compliance with the statutory procedure.[60]

As for disapplication, the provisions applicable to public companies (and private companies with more than one class of share) build on the rules about directors' authority to issue shares, discussed above. Where such authorisation is needed and has been given "generally",[61] the articles or a special resolution may

53 CA 2006 s.562(5). Nor can the offer be withdrawn, once made: s.562(4).

54 CA 2006 ss.569(1), 570(1).

55 CA 2006 s.571(1).

56 CA 2006 s.567. A provision in the memorandum or articles which is inconsistent with ss.561 or 562 has effect as an exclusion of that subsection: s.567(3).

57 CA 2006 s.569. On shareholder authority to issue in private companies see para.24–004.

58 CA 2006 s.568. The problem will probably not arise if the other classes of share are not ordinary but preference shares, because they do not usually benefit from a pre-emption right.

59 CA 2006 s.561.

60 CA 2006 ss.568(4)–(5), on which see below.

61 See para.24–005 for the meaning of "general" authorisation.

disapply the pre-emption rights entirely or give the directors a discretion to apply them with such modifications as they may determine.[62] The disapplication lasts only so long as the general authority and, if the authority is renewed, the disapplication will need renewal as well. In other words, the disapplication can be for a maximum period of five years.

Alternatively, where authorisation is required, and it has been given either generally or specifically, a special resolution may disapply the statutory provisions in relation to a particular issuance of shares or determine that they shall apply only with such modifications as are specified in the resolution.[63] Again, the disapplication lasts only so long as the authorisation to which it relates, though this is a less important provision in relation to specified allotments. Unusually for British company law, a special resolution in relation to a specified allotment may not be proposed unless it has been recommended by the directors, and there is circulated a written statement by the directors of their reasons for making the recommendation, the amount to be paid to the company in respect of the proposed allotment, and the directors' justification of that amount.[64] A person, director or otherwise, who knowingly or recklessly authorises or permits the inclusion in the statement of information which is misleading, false or deceptive commits a criminal offence.[65]

It is relatively common for public companies to make use of the disapplication provisions, even where the directors have every intention of respecting the principle of pre-emption, because greater flexibility can be built into the arrangements. A common desire is to exclude from the offer shareholders in foreign jurisdictions whose securities laws are regarded as excessively burdensome in relation to the number of the company's investors located there.[66] Even if the statutory rules have been disapplied, however, a publicly traded company is likely to be subject to the Listing Rules,[67] but these specifically permit pre-emptive offers to exclude holders whom the company considers "necessary or expedient to exclude from the offer on account of the laws or regulatory requirements of" another country.[68] Finally, there may be disapplication in relation to treasury shares, whether held by a public or a private company.[69] The directors do not require shareholder consent to sell treasury shares (since they are already in issue) but such sales are caught in principle by the statutory pre-emption right.[70] However, the directors may be given power to allot free of

---

62 CA 2006 s.570.

63 CA 2006 ss.571.

64 CA 2006 ss.571(5)–(7).

65 CA 2006 s.572.

66 *A Report to the Chancellor of the Exchequer by the Rights Issue Review Group* (November 2008), 6.5.

67 See para.24–011.

68 LR 9.3.12. This is primarily designed to deal with the situation where a company has shareholders resident in the US. Under the Federal securities legislation it may have to register with the SEC if it extends the offer to such shareholders. Hence the present practice is to exclude such shareholders and to preclude those to whom the offer is made from renouncing in favour of a US resident. This practice was upheld in *Mutual Life Insurance of NY v Rank Organisation* [1985] B.C.L.C. 11, but a fairer arrangement would surely be for the rights of the American shareholders to be sold for their benefit?

69 On which see para.17–023.

70 CA 2006 s.560(2)(b).

that right, either generally (by the articles or by special resolution) or in relation to a specified allotment (by special resolution).[71] One of the arguments for permitting treasury shares was that it gave companies freedom to raise relatively small amounts of capital quickly, which a pre-emption right would hinder, so that it seems correct policy to facilitate the disapplication of the pre-emption right to treasury shares.[72]

Sanctions

24–010 A civil (but not a criminal) sanction is provided by the CA 2006. When there has been a contravention of the pre-emption right (either by not providing it at all or by not providing it in the way required by the Act), the company and every officer of it who knowingly authorised or permitted the contravention are jointly and severally liable to compensate any person to whom an offer should have been made for any loss, damage, costs or expenses.[73] Where under the provisions discussed immediately above, the statutory provisions are applied in a modified way, these sanctions will equally apply to a contravention of the modified provisions.[74] The Act does not invalidate an allotment of shares made in breach of the pre-emptive provisions, no doubt in order to protect the legitimate interests of third parties. However, in *Re Thundercrest Ltd*[75] the judge was prepared to rectify the register[76] as against the directors of a small company, with only three shareholders, where the directors responsible for the breach of the pre-emptive provisions had allotted the shares in dispute to themselves.

Listed companies

24–011 Institutional shareholders (pension funds and insurance companies in particular) have traditionally held a very significant proportion of the shares of publicly traded companies.[77] For a long time they have placed a high value on pre-emptive rights. Consequently, market practice, influenced by the institutional shareholders, goes beyond the statutory rights embodied in the CA 2006. Indeed, pre-emptive rights were a feature of market practice in London before the statutory pre-emption right was introduced into legislation in 1980. There are two channels through which the institutional shareholders have been able to advance their views. First, they have been able to influence effectively the rules made by the FCA relating to the listing[78] of companies. Secondly, they have taken

---

71 CA 2006 s.573.

72 However, existing shareholders in listed companies are protected against dilution by the imposition of a limit of 10% to any discount applied on the sale of the treasury shares: LR 9.5.10.

73 CA 2006 s.562. Proceedings must be commenced within two years of the filing of the relevant return of allotments or, where rights to subscribe or convert are granted, within two years from the grant: s.563(3). As noted, the same applies to contraventions of the substitute right in the company's articles relating to classes of ordinary shares: s.568(4)–(5).

74 CA 2006 ss.569(2), 570(2), 571(2), 573(3), (5).

75 *Re Thundercrest Ltd* [1994] B.C.C. 857 Ch D (Companies Ct).

76 See para.26–019.

77 See para.12–013.

78 On listing see para.25–008.

collective action to draw up rules to govern what action they will or will not support as shareholders in the pre-emption area. We will look first at the Listing Rules (LR).

There are two significant rules in the LR, both applying only to companies with a "premium" listing on the London Stock Exchange.[79] First, a premium listed company, which is not incorporated in the UK and which is not subject to pre-emption rights under its law of incorporation, must provide them for its shareholders through provisions in its articles.[80] Secondly, and more important, the LR limit the discount at which a company may issue shares, other than by way of a rights issue, to 10% of the prevailing market price, unless the shareholders approve a higher discount.[81] This means that, if the company sticks to the bare pre-emptive entitlement set out in the statute, those shareholders who cannot afford to take up their rights face only a limited financial loss, as a result of the cap on the discount. To put the matter from the company's point of view, if the success of the pre-emption offer is thought to require a greater discount than 10%, the directors will need the shareholders' consent to proceed with the issue other than as a rights issue.[82] The rule is thus an important restraint on the directors' powers to proceed with an open offer and pushes them instead in the direction of a rights issue, where the shareholders' financial interests are protected. However, this Listing Rule contains one large exception: it does not apply if the shareholders have disapplied their pre-emptive rights under a general authority given to the directors, whether or not the general authority makes mention of the discount issue.[83] Since general disapplications of the pre-emptive right are common in listed companies, the terms upon which institutional shareholders are prepared to vote in favour of disapplication resolutions become central.

Pre-emption guidelines

24–012 The overall picture which emerges of the above analysis is that existing shareholders' right to pre-emption, which the CA 2006 creates, and to pre-emption on a rights basis, which the Listing Rules indirectly create, may be removed by collective decision of the shareholders. So the impact in practice of both the statute and the Listing Rules turns on the terms on which shareholders are willing to forego their rights. Since institutional shareholders are strongly opposed to dilution of their positions, they have sought to agree guidelines determining the circumstances in which consent to disapplication will be given. Originally, the institutions acted alone in drawing up the guidelines but, given

[79] On premium listing see para 25–006. Premium listing is the most popular choice for companies listed on the Main Market.

[80] LR 6.9.2. There is, of course, no requirement that a company whose shares are traded on the LSE be incorporated in the UK.

[81] LR 9.5.10. This rule catches all premium listed companies, irrespective of their place of incorporation.

[82] Since the requirement is that "the terms of the offer or placing at that discount have been specifically approved by the issuer's shareholders", the shareholder approval cannot be given in practice in advance of the decision to issue.

[83] LR 9.5.10(3)(b).

their importance for the financing of companies and the operation of the capital markets, an element of public interest has been injected by conducting the discussions under the auspices of, first, the Bank of England, then the London Stock Exchange and, now, the Financial Reporting Council.[84] Institutionally, this development has resulted in the creation a Pre-emption Group, which issues the guidelines which determine institutional shareholders' attitudes to disapplication resolutions.[85] The guidelines have no legal status but they articulate a strongly held and practically significant attitude on the part of the institutions about the value of pre-emptive rights and how they will vote in disapplication resolutions. This policy of the institutional investors has turned pre-emption on a rights basis into an example of a "strong" default rule whose alteration creates a significant hurdle for the management of the company. Thus, the statutory provisions and the Listing Rules have much more bite because of the difficulty of securing shareholder consent to their disapplication other than in accordance with the guidelines. On the other hand, if there were no default rules in the statute and Listing Rules, the institutional shareholders would face the more demanding task of securing an amendment to a company's articles of association, introducing a pre-emption right.

The guidelines, currently in the form of a Statement of Principles,[86] distinguish between general and specific disapplication resolutions. The institutional investors will vote in favour of general disapplication resolutions where the authority is limited to no more 5% of the ordinary share capital of the company in any one year (plus a further 5% for an acquisition or capital investment which is identified at the time the resolution is put forward). When acting under the general disapplication resolutions, the company should raise no more than 7.5% of the ordinary share capital in any rolling period of three years (excluding the capital investment addition), without consulting with its shareholders. Discounts should be restricted to a maximum of 5% "other than in exceptional circumstances". Authority should not be sought for more than 15 months or until the next AGM, whichever is the sooner.[87] In addition, the guidelines apply not only to share issues falling within the statutory scheme, but also to "cash-box" issues.[88] In consequence, disapplication resolutions have become a common feature of the AGM agenda.

Controversy has raged over the rules relating to specific, non-routine (often large-scale) disapplication resolutions, where the institutions need to be

[84] On which see para.3 008.

[85] *Disapplying Pre-Emption Rights a Statement of Principles* (2015) available at: *https://www.frc.org.uk/medialibraries/FRC/FRC-Document-Library/Preemption%20Group/Revised-PEG-Statement-of-Principles-2015.pdf* [Accessed 25 March 2021]. The first guidelines were adopted in 1987. The Principles are supported by the Investment Association and Pensions and Lifetime Savings Association.

[86] The latest version dates from 2015 and is available on the website identified in fn.85. The Principles are said to apply formally only to companies listed on the Premium Listing segment of the Main Market of the London Stock Exchange, but standard listing companies and those on the Alternative Investment Market are "encouraged" to apply them.

[87] Principles, Pts 2A and 2B.

[88] Pt 1, para.2. On "cash-box" issues see para.24–008. In respect of vendor placings, the institutions' "expectation" is that there will be a claw-back right if the placing involves more than 10% of the company's ordinary capital or is at a discount of more than 5% (para.3).

persuaded to vote in favour of the disapplication resolution and so need to be presented with the business case for proceeding on a non-rights basis. It used to be thought in some corporate circles that institutions would normally vote against specific disapplication resolutions, unless they fell within the criteria for general disapplications. However, after criticism from a government review,[89] the rules were re-drafted to make it clear this was not the case. The Principles now envisage specific resolutions outside the general criteria in the context of a specific project, where the institutions have been consulted in advance and the need for non-pre-emptive finance can be demonstrated and justified.[90]

Criticism and further market developments

24–013 The pre-emptive right, and the rights issue in particular, have always been unpopular amongst management, just as they have been popular amongst shareholders. Two main criticisms are advanced. First, that it reduces the pool of investors to whom a company may turn for additional equity finance and so it pushes up the cost of equity finance. Secondly, a rights issue takes longer to carry out than either an open offer or a placing (i.e. raising finance from a small number of investors without making a public offer) and so exposes the company to market risk during the offer period. The arguments in principle for and against the rights issue were examined in the Myners Review of 2005.[91] Paul Myners came out in favour of rights issues. He was particularly impressed by the corporate governance argument in favour of pre-emption. This was that pre-emption makes it difficult for a management, which has failed its existing shareholders, to obtain finance from a new group of investors, letting them into the company cheaply (and at the expense of the existing investors) as part of an implicit bargain to back the existing management against the complaints of the first group of investors. By contrast, pre-emption makes management seeking further equity finance sensitive to the views of the existing investors from whom it must be raised or who control the access to new investors.

In 2008, the first full year of the financial crisis, the issue came to fore again as a number of banks had to raise large sums of fresh capital. All succeeded in doing so, but often only after great difficulties.[92] The Rights Issue Review Group[93] was appointed to see if the principle of rights issues could be maintained whilst mitigating the associated fund-raising difficulties. The main issue was perceived to be one of timing. If the length of the rights issue process could be reduced, the

[89] DTI, *Pre-Emption Rights: Final Report* (February 2005), URN 05/679. It was in this re-drafting process that the "Guidelines" became "Principles", perhaps to emphasise this point.

[90] Principles, Pt 3.

[91] See fn.89.

[92] The issue arose again in during the COVID-19 pandemic of 2020–21. In this case, the Pre-emption Group itself responded by raising, on a temporary basis, the level institutions might support on a case-by-case basis from 5% to 20% for a fundraising for general corporate purposes, with an additional 5% for specific projects: Pre-Emption Group, *Pre-Emption Group expectations for issuances in the current circumstances* (1 April 2020).

[93] See fn.66.

issuer's exposure to market risk (possibly even to market manipulation)[94] would also be reduced, an important development in turbulent markets.

An obvious first step, now implemented, was to reduce the period for shareholders to decide whether to take up their rights from 21 to 14 days.[95] However, the main timing problem was seen to flow from the need to both secure shareholders' consent and to provide the (now) 14-day period for shareholders to decide whether to take up their rights, and the inability to have those two activities running concurrently. It may not be clear why shareholder consent should be needed if what is proposed is a rights issue. There are three possible answers. First, the directors may not have in place a large enough authority to issue shares (in any way) without shareholder consent, though the changes recently made to the Investment Association Guidance[96] make that now less likely. Secondly, the directors may wish to make a non-statutory pre-emption offer and so need shareholder consent to disapply the statutory pre-emption provisions.[97] Thirdly, the Pre-emption Group's Principles suggest that institutional shareholders expect shareholder approval for deeply discounted rights issues (above 5%), even though the statute does not specify any cap on the level of discount nor does the Listing Rules cap apply if a rights issue is proposed. **24–014**

Assuming shareholder approval is required, the difficulty about making the offer to the shareholders before that approval is obtained is that trading in the rights (so-called "trading in nil paid form") necessarily begins as soon as the offer is made (since the trading must be completed within 14 days). If, however, shareholder approval for the issue is not ultimately obtained, unscrambling the trading may prove very difficult. Consequently, practice is to obtain approval before making the offer. An open offer does not suffer from this difficulty, since there are no rights to be traded in this case, and so the offer can be launched and shareholder approval sought at the same time, the offer being conditional upon shareholder approval being obtained. However, the open offer gives no protection against dilution to the shareholder who cannot take up the offer. Consequently, market practice developed the "compensatory open offer", under which any shares not take up by the shareholder are sold by the company (or its underwriters) into the market and any premium obtained over the offer price is paid to the shareholder who did not take up the offer.[98] In effect, the burden of trading the rights to the new shares passes from the shareholder under a rights issue to the company under the compensatory open offer, but the economic

[94] On which see Ch.30.

[95] CA 2006 s.562(5). The change was made in 2009. Similar changes were made to LR 9.5.6 to cater for non-statutory rights issues.

[96] See para.24–005.

[97] See para.24–009.

[98] This is now required of open offers characterised by a premium listed company as compensatory (LR 9.5.8A). LR 9.5.4 already imposed this rule in favour of offerees in a rights issue who did not take up the offer, so that those unfamiliar with the rights issue procedure were not disadvantaged.

impact on the shareholder should be very similar.[99] This may be a burden the company is happy to accept in order to speed up the fund raising process.[100]

THE TERMS OF ISSUE

24–015 As noted in Ch.6,[101] the rights attached to the shares to be issued are often set out in the company's articles. Even if they are, what will not be set out there is the price or other consideration to be asked in exchange for the shares. Here the directors have a free hand, subject to the rules on capital raising discussed in Ch.16. Normally, these rules are not constraining.

ALLOTMENT

24–016 Assuming there is no requirement for a rights issue (for example, because this is the first issue of a new class of shares or the rights of the existing shareholders have been waived) or the offerees under the rights procedure do not meet the company's capital needs, the company will have to find new investors or encourage new investors to take up the existing investors' rights. This process is not something about which the law says very much if there is no offer to the public of the company's shares[102]—although, as we shall see in the next chapter, this is in fact now a very heavily regulated area, if there is a public offer. What the CA 2006 does assume is that the process of becoming a shareholder is a two-step one, involving first a contract of allotment and then registration of the member. As Lord Templeman said in 1995:

> "The Act of 1985 preserves the distinction in English law between an enforceable contract for the issue of shares (which contract is constituted by an allotment) and the issue of shares which is completed by registration. Allotment confers a right to be registered. Registration confers [legal] title."[103]

This is consistent with the CA 2006 which defines the point at which shares are allotted as the time when a person acquires the unconditional right to be included in the register of members, but does not require actual entry in the register.[104]

---

[99] However, a shareholder cannot engage in tail swallowing (fn.40) under the compensatory open offer.

[100] Because of these market developments the FSA recommended against some of the more radical suggestions from the RIRG which would allow offer and approval periods to run simultaneously. See FSA, *Report to HM Treasury on the implementation of the recommendations of the Rights Issue Review Group* (April 2010). But the *UK Listing Review* (March 2021) recommended (para.5.2) the re-establishment of RIRG to consider them again.

[101] See para.6–006.

[102] The general common law rules on fraud, misrepresentation and negligence will provide some protection to investors: see paras 25–037 onwards.

[103] *National Westminster Bank Plc v IRC* [1995] 1 A.C. 111 HL at 126. From this, Lord Templeman reasoned that shares were not "issued" (the Companies Act does not define the term) for the purposes of a taxing statute until the applicants for the shares were registered as members of the company.

[104] CA 2006 s.558.

Renounceable allotments

In the case of a private company the processes of agreement and registration will be achieved with little formality and without the issue of allotment letters. If someone wants to become a shareholder and the company wants him to, he will be entered on the register and issued with a share certificate without more ado. However, the advantage of constituting the agreement to become a member in a formal letter of allotment is that it facilitates the process described above in relation to rights issues[105] of "renouncing" the entitlement to be registered as a member in favour of someone else, though the technique is not confined to rights issues. Printed on the back of the letter there will be forms enabling, for a short specified period, the allottee to renounce the right to be registered as a member and the person to whom they are ultimately renounced to confirm that he or she accepts the renunciation and agrees to be entered on the register. Normally the original allottee will not insert the name of the person to whom they are to be renounced and the effect is then to produce something similar to a short-term share-warrant to bearer.[106] The renounceable allotment letter is not a negotiable instrument but once the renunciation is signed by the original allottee, the rights can be assigned by manual delivery of the allotment letter without a formal transfer. Before the stated period ends, however, it will be necessary for the name of the ultimate holder to be inserted, a signature obtained, and the allotment letter lodged with the company or its registrars. **24–017**

Failure of the offer

The CA 2006 lays down a default rule for public companies that no allotment of shares shall be made pursuant to an offer to subscribe[107] for shares (whether the offer is to the public or not) unless the shares on offer are taken up in full.[108] This rule is designed to prevent an investor ending up holding shares in a company which is less fully capitalised than was expected when the offer was accepted. If a full take-up of the shares is not achieved within 40 days of making the offer, the money[109] received from the offerees becomes repayable in full, though without interest,[110] and must actually be repaid within a further eight days. The sanction for this latter requirement is that the directors then become jointly and severally liable to repay the money, with interest.[111] If the company actually proceeds with an allotment in breach of the Act then the allotment is voidable by the offeree **24–018**

[105] See para.24–006. Of course, a private company will often not want to grant this facility, which might be inconsistent with its articles (see para.26–007). The statutory scheme of pre-emption rights does not *require* renouncing to be made available.

[106] See para.24–022.

[107] The section thus does not apply to offers for sale of shares (see para.24–020) and does not need to because the issue has been in effect underwritten.

[108] CA 2006 s.578(1).

[109] The rule applies, mutatis mutandis, where the consideration for the offer is wholly or partly otherwise than in cash: s.578(4)–(5).

[110] CA 2006 s.578(2).

[111] CA 2006 s.578(3). A director can escape liability if it can be shown that the failure was not due to misconduct or negligence on the director's part. If the company promises to keep the monies

within one month of the allotment (even if the company is in course of winding up),[112] and any director who knowingly contravenes or permits the contravention of the prohibition on allotment becomes liable to compensate the allottee and the company for any loss, damages, costs or expenses.[113]

Despite these fearsome sanctions, the rule is not enormously important in practice, for two reasons. First, if the offer in terms says that the allotment will proceed, even if not fully subscribed, or will proceed if conditions falling short of full subscription are met, the prohibition on allotment does not apply.[114] So, the rule is really one which requires only that the investors be told what risk they run in relation to the take-up of the offer. Secondly, and by contrast, in relation to offers to the public, failure to achieve a full take-up of the offer is a serious matter, not only for the investors, but also for the issuer, so that the issuer will take steps to avoid this outcome. Issuing companies will arrange for the offer to be "underwritten" in some way (i.e. normally an investment bank agrees to take up the shares which are not bought by the public).[115]

Once the shares have been allotted, the company must make a return of allotment to the Registrar of companies, as discussed in Ch.16.[116]

REGISTRATION

24–019 As Lord Templeman indicated, allotment does not make a person a member of the company. Entry in the register of members is also needed to give the allottee legal title to the shares. Section 112(2) says that a person "who agrees to become a member of the company and whose name is entered on the register of members is a member of the company", so that both agreement and entry are necessary for membership.[117] The CA 2006 now requires registration "as soon as practicable" and in any event within two months of the date of allotment.[118] Even when registered, the shareholder will find difficulty in selling the shares, if they are to be held in certificated form, until a share certificate is received from the company. The share certificate is also required to be made available within the two-month period after allotment,[119] but it still may be that registration occurs

advanced by a subscriber in a separate bank account and does so, it seems that the monies will be held on trust by the company in favour of the investors: *Re Nanwa Gold Mines Ltd* [1955] 1 W.L.R. 1080 Ch D.

[112] CA 2006 s.579(1),(2). This means the assets contributed by the allottee are taken out of the insolvent company's estate, but only if the allotee acts within the one-month period.

[113] CA 2006 s.579(3), subject to a two-year limitation period: s.579(4).

[114] CA 2006 s.578(1)(b).

[115] See para.25–012.

[116] At para.16–014.

[117] On which, see *Re Nuneaton Football Club* [1989] B.C.L.C. 454 CA, holding that "agreement" requires only assent to become a member. The subscribers to the memorandum of association (para.4–005) are the first members of the company and should be entered on its register of members, but in their case it appears that they become members, whether this is done or not: *Evan's Case* (1866–67) L.R. 2 Ch. App. 427 CA in Chancery; *Baytrust Holdings Ltd v IRC* [1971] 1 W.L.R. 1333 Ch D at 1355–1356.

[118] CA 2006 s.554. Failure to register is a criminal offence on the part of the company and every officer in default.

[119] CA 2006 s.769.

before the share certificate is provided. All this will happen much more quickly if the shares are to be held in uncertificated form,[120] as is typical with public offerings.

Bearer shares

A major exception in principle, though much less so in practice, to the requirement of entry on the register in order to become a member of the company was created by share-warrants to bearer. Section 779 provided that a company, if so authorised by its articles, could issue with respect to any fully paid shares a warrant stating that the bearer of the warrant was entitled to the shares specified in it. If similarly authorised, it could provide, by coupons attached to the warrant or otherwise, for the payment of future dividends.[121] Title to the shares specified then passed by manual delivery of the warrant,[122] which was a negotiable instrument.[123] On the issue of the warrants, the company removed from its register of members the name of the former registered holder and merely stated the fact and date of the issue of the warrant and the number of shares to which it related.[124] The bearer of the warrant from time to time was unquestionably a shareholder but to what extent, if at all, he was a member of the company depended on a provision to that effect in the articles.[125] Hence shareholding and membership were not necessarily coterminous if share warrants were issued. However, again subject to the articles, the bearer of the warrant was entitled, on surrendering it for cancellation, to have his name and shareholding re-entered on the register.[126] **24–020**

In practice this exception was unimportant because bearer securities were never popular with British investors nor British companies and were rarely issued and hardly ever in respect of shares, as opposed to bearer bonds (i.e. debt securities which are sometimes issued to attract continental investors who have a traditional liking for securities in bearer form). It is fortunate that bearer shares were such a rarity for, if they had became common, it would have played havoc with many provisions of the CA 2006. In the end, amendments made by the Small Business, Enterprise and Employment Act 2015 prohibited companies from issuing share warrants in the future and made provision for the mandatory

---

[120] See Ch.26.

[121] CA 2006 s.779(3). Share-warrants to bearer must be distinguished from what is perhaps the more common type of warrant, which gives the holder the right to subscribe for shares in the company at a specific price on a particular date or within a particular period. Such warrants are a form of long-term call option over the company's shares. They may be traded, but their transfer simply gives the transferee the option and does not make him or her a member until the option is exercised.

[122] CA 2006 s.779(2).

[123] *Webb, Hale & Co v Alexandria Water Co* (1905) 21 T.L.R. 572.

[124] CA 2006 s.122(1).

[125] CA 2006 s.122(3).

[126] CA 2006 s.122(4)—now repealed.

conversion of existing warrants back into shares, precisely because they were thought likely to undermine that Act's enhanced provisions on disclosure of share ownership.[127]

CONCLUSION

24–021 Where a company makes a non-public offer of shares, a situation which will necessarily include most share offers by private companies, the rules discussed above are all that the company will need to concern itself with. Where, however, a public offer of shares is to be made, the extensive regulation considered in the next chapter will come into play. Even then, the relevant regulation is additional to the rules considered in this chapter and, though it may supplement, it does not replace them. In fact, rules discussed in this chapter, for example those relating to pre-emptive rights, can be very important in public offers, but the point is that such rules are not confined to public offers but apply to share issues of a non-public type as well. Protection of the position of existing shareholders through pre-emption is as important in a private as in a public company, indeed arguably more so in the absence of a market upon which the shares of a disgruntled shareholder can be disposed of.

[127] CA 2006 s.779(4), as added; 2015 Act s.84 and Sch.4. The prohibition operated from May 2015; the period for mandatory reconversion ended a year later.

CHAPTER 25

PUBLIC OFFERS OF SHARES

INTRODUCTION

This chapter is concerned with a subject that takes us into the area of securities regulation or capital markets law. Nevertheless, it is not a subject which books on company law can ignore; how public companies go about raising their capital from the investing public and securing admission of their securities to trading on a public market, and the legal regulations that have to be complied with when they do, are central to the operations of large companies. An elaborate discussion of this specialised branch of legal practice is inappropriate in a book of this sort but an outline is essential. The rules considered in this chapter generally apply to "securities", i.e. both to shares and debt instruments (for example, bonds). The focus of this chapter will be on share issues. Debt securities are the lesser subject in this chapter, because they are less often offered to the public even by companies which issue shares to the public and because bonds are less frequently traded on public markets (as opposed to "over the counter"). Nevertheless, to an **25–001** extent, this chapter crosses the divide between Pts 6 and 7 of the book. It is also important to note that, in general, the rules discussed below apply to all companies seeking to make public offers or to trade their securities on a public market in the UK, no matter where they are incorporated, though in some cases the rules of the place of incorporation are relied on in place of the domestic rules.

Public offers and introductions to public markets

25–002 There are two distinct, though usually combined, operations which may take place when a large company seeks to raise finance from the investing public. In the first place, it needs to make its case to those people who may be interested in investing in it by purchasing its securities. As we shall see below, the company may choose among a number of different ways of putting itself before investors. The most heavily regulated of these methods is the public offer of securities, simply because the company addresses its publicity to a wide range of persons who may include the ill-informed and the gullible as well as the experienced and well-informed. When a company makes a public offer of its shares for the first time, that is usually termed an "initial public offering" (IPO), and this is often a major event in the life of the company. But it may well make further public offerings at a later stage ("secondary" offers), for example, because it wishes to fund further expansion or because it needs to ride out a crisis, such as that induced by the Covid-19 measures. The document (the "prospectus") through which public offers are made is regulated heavily by the law. From this perspective, the law relating to prospectuses can be viewed as a branch of consumer protection legislation, but concerning a product which is very difficult to evaluate. The value of shares depends heavily upon the future performance of the company and cannot be ascertained by visual inspection or trying the product out before purchase.

It will normally be the case that a company seeking to raise substantial funds from investors will also secure that the securities to be issued will be admitted to trading on a public securities market, such as one of the markets operated by the London Stock Exchange. The reason the company will normally take this extra step is that the willingness of investors to buy its securities will be increased if there is a liquid market upon which those securities can be traded after they have been issued. As we have seen, a shareholder is normally "locked into" the company after the shares have been purchased, in the sense that the investor, short of winding up, cannot require the company to buy back the shares, even at the later prevailing market price, except in the case of some types of redeemable share. Equally, bonds are not normally redeemable at the request of the investor until after some specified period has elapsed and perhaps not before they reach their maturity date. Therefore, a person who wishes to withdraw from an investment will normally be constrained to find another investor willing to purchase the securities. A liquid securities market will facilitate this operation, to the benefit of both investors and the company, which is likely to be able to sell its securities at a higher price if investors have access to the liquidity afforded by a public market.

However, the mere admission of securities to trading on an public market also involves putting those securities before the investing public, even if there is no concomitant public offer, since it is now open to the public to acquire the company's securities, this time not directly from the company but from those who already hold them. Hence, there is a strong argument for having the same information disclosure requirements (subject to some minor variations) upon admission of securities to a public market as when the company offers its securities directly to the public. The argument is even stronger if, as is usual, both events occur at the same time. However, there is no legal requirement that both events should happen as part of a package. A company may offer its securities to the public without securing their admission to public market (for example, where it does not expect or want the securities to be traded to any significant degree and so is content to rely on sellers seeking out potential purchasers privately). Or the driving force[1] behind the admission of the securities to the market may be an existing large shareholder (for example, the Government in a de-nationalisation issue) which wishes to liquidate or reduce its holding, but the company does not intend at that time to raise additional finance.

Our main concern in this chapter is with the financing of the company and the public offer of securities as a form of corporate finance. Consequently, the core transaction which we examine is one in which the company both makes a public offer of its shares and, at the same time, secures the admission of the shares to trading on a public market.

Regulatory goals

We have referred above to the law relating to public offers as consumer law and that is a very strong strand in the thinking of those responsible for the rules in this area. However, it would be wrong to see the regulation as nothing but a form of consumer protection. In fact, scholarship today stresses the function of regulation in this area as a way of promoting "allocative efficiency", that is, of promoting investment on the basis of an accurate understanding of the risk and reward profile of particular projects which the issuance of the shares will finance. This objective furthers the interests not only of investors but of companies and of the economy generally, for effective regulation promotes the allocation of scarce investment resources to the projects with the highest returns. Clearly, disclosure is even more important if the risks the investor worries about include the negative externalities of the company's operations, such as carbon dioxide emissions. (We discuss this issue more fully in the following chapter.) But what sort of regulation will best facilitate the accurate assessment of different projects? 25–003

It is conventional in this branch of law to make a distinction between "merit" regulation and disclosure of information. Under the former approach, a regulator permits an offer to be made to the public only if the securities on offer or the company issuing them ("the issuer") pass certain quality tests, whereas the latter simply puts information in the hands of investors and leaves it up to them to make up their own minds about investing. Although the early regulation of public offers

[1] Securities cannot be admitted to the official list (see below) without the consent of the issuer (FSMA 2000 s.75(2)), but the impetus for the listing may come from the shareholder.

(at state level in the US) adopted the merit regulation approach,[2] the disclosure approach has been the predominant one in all jurisdictions since its adoption by federal US law in the great reforms of 1933 and 1934.[3] However, disclosure has never driven out all elements of merit regulation. Although what is required varies from market to market, disclosure is never all that is required. As a Canadian committee once remarked, with heavy irony, "it would be improbable that a securities commission in a disclosure regime would approve a prospectus that said, truthfully, that the promoters of the company intended to abscond with the proceeds of the public offering, or that the company's business enterprise had no hope of success".[4] Thus, elements of merit regulation, referred to in the UK as "eligibility requirements", survive in even the most disclosure-oriented regime.

The triumph of disclosure as the predominant regulatory philosophy in this area is probably a reflection of the decision the investor has to make. Prospective subscribers to the ordinary shares to be issued by a company normally obtain no legal entitlement to a return on their investment and so they are essentially making a judgment about the company's business prospects in the future and the appropriate price to pay in the light of those prospects. If the company makes good profits, the ordinary shareholders will benefit; if it makes heavy losses, those will fall first on the same people. When assessing those prospects, the potential purchaser of shares has to take a view, at a minimum, about how the industry in which the company is active will evolve, about the merits or otherwise of the company's business model and about the qualities of the company's management.[5] Nobody can be sure about the future. Using merit regulation to exclude certain types of issuer or offer risks excluding a company whose track record is not good but which has a perfectly decent story to tell about its future. Further, heavy merit regulation may carry the implication that those offers that are permitted to proceed benefit from some sort of public guarantee of the company's future success, something the public authorities are unlikely to wish to provide. Merit regulation thus tends to play a limited role. This is not to say that disclosure of information makes the investor's task easy, because the one piece of hard information the investor requires—what will be the issuer's financial results in the future?—is by definition not available. However, information about the company's present and recent activities, its proposals for the future and the terms of the securities on offer can help to guide the investment decision, even if it cannot take all risk out of the process. Indeed, if all risk could be eliminated, there would be no need for equity finance in the first place.

25–004 A further question about the disclosure regime, which has been hotly debated, is whether production of the requisite level of information requires mandatory

---

[2] Often referred to as "blue sky laws" because the dodgy securities on offer were backed, it was said, only by the blue sky. The first significant State law in the US seems to have been that of Kansas in 1911.

[3] The Securities Act 1933 and the Securities Exchange Act 1934.

[4] Toronto Stock Exchange, *Toward Improved Disclosure* (Interim Report of the Committee on Corporate Disclosure, 1995), para.3.9.

[5] For debt issues the investor's concern is whether the debt will be re-paid on time and in full, with interest in the interim. Because debt has priority over equity in an insolvency and because debt has no exposure to the up-side of a company's performance, less disclosure is generally required for bond issues in comparison with share issues.

disclosure rules. It can be argued that, a prospectus being a selling document, those companies with good stories to tell would make full disclosure of information and use private "bonding" mechanisms (such as certification by independent third parties) to convince investors of the truth of what they say. Companies with less good stories would follow suit, for fear that investors would deduce from inadequate disclosure that the prospects for the company were dire. Only companies with truly dire prospects would make inadequate disclosure and investors would draw the correct conclusions from such inadequate prospectuses. Whether this theory works in practice seems never to have been tested satisfactorily, but even if self-interest would generate extensive disclosure, mandatory disclosure rules have certain advantages over leaving it to the issuers to decide for themselves the extent of the disclosure. First, the state sanctions available for breaches of the mandatory rules (criminal, civil and regulatory sanctions) may be more credible to investors than the private bonding mechanisms companies themselves could produce. Secondly, mandatory rules may produce more uniformity in disclosure than disclosure decisions taken by issuers on an individual basis (thus helping investors to compare different public offerings). Thirdly, mandatory rules may overcome forces acting against full disclosure even when, from one point of view, disclosure is in the company's interest. An example is the disclosure of information which, whilst it would make the company attractive to investors, would also help the company's competitors.[6]

In any event, mandatory disclosure is now the rule and, in fact, the detail on public offerings is now staggering. Since, as we have noted, the information available is only indirectly relevant to the future-oriented decision the investor has to make, there comes a point where the marginal gain from more information may outweigh the costs of providing it. This issue has been debated especially in relation to small and medium-sized entities (SMEs) since the financial crisis. SMEs traditionally relied on bank funding, which became difficult to obtain post the crisis. Many advocated greater use by SMEs of the financial markets to raise capital. However, the largely fixed costs of capital raising from the public markets absorb a relatively high proportion of the funds raised in the case of small offerings. So, the question of a relaxed disclosure regime for SMEs moved centre stage, as we discuss below.

Turning to the admission of securities to trading on public markets, a regulatory goal has been to ensure that those who control the operation of public markets exercise their admission and expulsion powers fairly. This might be thought necessary to protect the interests of both issuers which wish to make public offerings and investors who have bought the securities on the basis that they would continue to be publicly traded. In practice, this has turned out to be a less important regulatory need, since global competition among public markets for offerings has itself constrained any impulse to act unfairly. The focus of the extant admissions rules has thus shifted to ensuring that the will be an effective market post admission.

[6] J. Coffee Jr, "Market Failure and the Economic Case for a Mandatory Disclosure System" (1984) 70 Virginia L.R. 717.

Listing

25–005 The ideas of a public offer and of trading on a public market are easy enough to grasp. Somewhat less obvious is the concept of "listing". This is partly because of the varying ways in which the term is used. Sometimes it is used to refer to any security which is traded on a public market (i.e. it is on the "list" of securities traded on that market), in which case it adds nothing to what we have already said. In this book, however, we use the term in a narrower sense: a listed security is one which has been admitted to the "official list". The first point to note is that inclusion in the official list is not a pre-requisite for admission to trading on all public markets. For example, it is possible to make a public offer of "unlisted" securities and to secure the admission of those securities to trading on a public market, such as the Alternative Investment Market (AIM) of the London Stock Exchange (LSE). On the other hand, the Main Market of the LSE is a market for listed securities only. So, the question arises as to why a company should wish its securities to be included in the official list. The answer to that is that admission to the official list constitutes a quality mark, which companies may be anxious to have in order to encourage investors to acquire their securities.[7] For this reason, admission to the official list is an important element in the public offer and admission to trading process.

Inherent in the concept of an official list is the idea that somebody controls admission to it in order to ensure that the standards for admission are met. That task used to be discharged by the LSE itself, but, with the demutualisation of the LSE, the Exchange no longer wished to carry out this regulatory function, which was transferred,[8] in consequence, to what is now the Financial Conduct Authority (FCA),[9] established under the Financial Services and Markets Act 2000 (FSMA 2000),[10] as amended. That Act requires the FCA to maintain the "official list" and to admit to the list only such securities as it considers appropriate, and it gives the FCA the power to make listing rules (LR) for the purpose of governing admission to the official list and the subsequent conduct of listed companies.[11] In relation to AIM, however, the LSE has retained control over the admission of securities to the market.[12]

Premium and standard listing

25–006 Although admission to the official list is a mark of quality, the LSE has moved to a position where a further quality mark is available, but, given competitive pressures, it has not made this further status indicator mandatory. An issuer may

[7] Indeed, some investment institutions may be permitted to acquire only listed securities or may be restricted in the proportion of unlisted securities they may hold in their portfolio.

[8] By the Official Listing of Securities (Change of Competent Authority) Regulations 2000 (SI 2000/968). In other European countries the exchange typically still acts as the competent authority.

[9] Previously the Financial Services Authority.

[10] This is the primary piece of domestic legislation considered in this chapter.

[11] FSMA 2000 ss.73A–75.

[12] LSE, *Aim Rules for Companies* (2018), rr.2–9.

choose between "standard" and "premium" listing for equity shares.[13] Standard listing requires compliance only with the minimum standards originally derived from EU law, whilst "premium" listed companies are subject to additional rules, mainly concerned with their corporate governance after admission (and so discussed elsewhere in this work, where relevant) but also having some impact at the admission stage, for example, the requirement for an applicant to appoint a "sponsor".[14] An applicant needs to balance the cost of compliance with these additional rules against the greater willingness of investors to buy shares in companies with higher standards of corporate governance, thus reducing the applicant's "cost of capital". Most companies choose a premium share listing for reputational reasons or under investor pressure. The premium and standard listings constitute two separate "segments" of the Main Market of the LSE.[15]

Recognised exchanges, regulated markets and multi-lateral trading facilities

Most people, if asked, would probably say that there is one stock market for shares in the UK and that is the London Stock Exchange (LSE). However, this is not the case. The LSE itself runs two separate markets for shares, namely the "Main Market" and the "Alternative Investment Market"[16] for well-established and less well-established companies respectively. In both cases the LSE needs the authorisation of the FCA to run the market, carrying on the business of operating a stock market being, not surprisingly, one of the activities regulated under the FSMA 2000.[17] Persons seeking to operate an "investment exchange" in the UK will normally have to make an application to the FCA under Pt XVIII of the FSMA 2000, for official recognition, thus creating a "recognised investment exchange" (RIE). Recognition is a process concerned to establish, for example, the appropriateness of those persons who will have control of the exchange and the financial resources available to it. However, this chapter is not concerned with the approval and supervision of the exchanges, but it is concerned with the conduct of issuers and investors on the markets run by the operator of a RIE. 25–007

What is more important for this chapter is that the two markets just mentioned, although both RIEs, have a different legal status, originally derived from EU law, via the Directive on Markets in Financial Instruments (MiFID).[18] The Main Market is a "regulated market" whilst AIM is a "multi-lateral trading facility" (MTF)—a much more downbeat term. The distinction continues after the UK's

[13] LR 1.5. This choice, which had previously been available only to foreign-incorporated issuers, was made available to domestic issuers in 2010. The choice may be changed subsequently, but subject to supermajority shareholder approval in the case of transfer from premium to standard listing by a commercial company (LR 5.4A). Bonds will always be listed on the standard basis.

[14] See para.25–028.

[15] The Main Market displays two further segments: "High Growth" and "Specialist Funds", but we largely ignore them in this chapter.

[16] AIM replaced the previous Unlisted Securities Market (USM) in 1995.

[17] Without FCA approval the operators of the exchange will fall foul of the "general prohibition" in s.19 of FSMA 2000 on carrying on regulated financial activities in the UK.

[18] Directive 2014/65 ([2014] OJ L173/349), as amended. This is "MIFID II" which replaced "MIFID I" (Directive 2004/39 [2004] OJ L145/1) as from January 2017.

exit from the EU, unless and until the domestic legislation transposing the Directive is amended. In terms of domestic sources, the rules governing the running of regulated markets are to be found largely in the FCA's Recognised Investment Exchange (RIE) Sourcebook,[19] whilst those for MTFs are in Chapter 5 of its Market Conduct Sourcebook. As with the choice between standard and premium listing for issuers, there is no obligation on an exchange operator to apply for regulated status for all or any of its markets, though commercial reasons provide a strong incentive to provide at least one such market. The LSE sought regulated market status for its Main Market, but AIM operates as a MTF.[20]

From the point of view of this chapter, however, the crucial point of difference is that admission to a regulated market is more heavily regulated than admission to a MTF. In particular, as we see below, the Prospectus Regulation (PReg) applies only to admission to a regulated market.[21] For MTFs admission requirements are a matter for the market operator.

Listing and regulated markets

25–008 Although official listing is a concept which refers to the quality of the securities and the issuer, whilst regulated markets are markets of a particular quality, there is a close link between them, at least in the case of shares. The Listing Rules provide that "equity shares must be admitted to trading on a regulated market for listed securities operated by a RIE".[22] Thus, the listing process is not complete unless the shares have been admitted to trading on a regulated market. On the other side, it is only companies whose shares are in the official list which will be admitted by the LSE to the Premium or Standard segments of its Main Market.[23] Thus, listed shares must be traded on a regulated market and the core segments of the Main Market of the LSE will admit only listed securities. The FCA controls inclusion in the official list and the LSE controls admission of the securities to trading on the Main Market.[24] The company has to satisfy both sets of requirements in order to give its securities the status of being on the official list and its shareholders the facility to trade in those securities on the Main Market.

[19] "The recognition requirements and guidance in REC 2 relate primarily to UK RIEs which are recognised, or applying to be recognised, to operate a regulated market in the United Kingdom." (REC 1.1.1(2)).

[20] This decision was taken in 2004 under the then applicable Directive concerning regulated markets, i.e. Directive 93/22, the Investment Services Directive ([1993] OJ L141/27), which was repealed by MIFID. Some of the bond markets run by the LSE are regulated and some not.

[21] Regulation 2017/1129 [2017] OJ L168/12. Other EU-derived provisions, discussed elsewhere in the book, apply also only to regulated markets, for example, the Shareholder Rights Directive.

[22] LR 2.2.3.

[23] LSE, *Admission and Disclosure Standards* (October 2018), para.1.4.1.

[24] Just to complicate things further, the fact that a listed security has been admitted to a regulated market does not mean that trading has to take place on that market. A regulated market is a facility, not a mandatory piece of machinery. It was reported that less than 50% of the trading in FTSE 100 companies (all listed) had taken place in certain weeks in the middle of 2011 on the Main Market of the LSE, the main competitors being MTFs or private markets organised by large investment banks ("dark pools") (*Financial Times*, 19 September 2011, p.20 (UK edn)).

Competition and cross-listing

The LSE has no monopoly on the operation of public markets in securities, even in the UK, and there exist a number of smaller share markets, which seem constantly to be changing hands and which provide some competition for AIM.[25] However, there is no legal reason why a British registered company should not have its securities traded on a public market in another country. A number of large British companies have primary listings in London and secondary listings elsewhere, usually in continental Europe or the US, and some non-British companies equally have secondary listings in London. More interestingly, a small number of British companies have their primary listings outside the UK and a somewhat larger number of foreign companies have their primary listings in London. Indeed, there has been a certain international competition in recent years among the exchanges to secure such listings, notably from Chinese and Russian companies. **25–009**

The regulatory structure

The document containing the information which must be put before potential investors in a public offering is termed a prospectus. Domestic statutory law regulating prospectuses has a long history: the Directors' Liability Act 1890,[26] imposing liability for negligent misstatements in prospectuses, was an advanced piece of legislation for its time and significantly influenced the US Securities Act 1933. However, over the past 30 years EU law gradually occupied the legislative space in relation to public offers, admission of securities to public markets and listing, as part of a broader strategy to create a single European financial market[27]—though remedies for breaches of the rules remained substantially in the hands of the Member States. The result of EU occupation of the field, together with the additional rules adopted at national level, was a multi-layered regulatory structure, where six distinct layers could be identified: primary community law; secondary community law; primary domestic legislation; secondary domestic legislation; FCA rules; and rules generated by stock exchanges. This structure remains in place after the exit of the UK from the EU, albeit with the first two layers operating now as national law. **25–010**

As far as disclosure of information in prospectuses is concerned the central piece of EU law was originally Directive 2003/71 on prospectuses (the Prospectus Directive or PD) as amended in 2010,[28] whilst admission to listing was regulated by the consolidated admissions requirements Directive (CARD).[29]

---

[25] Thus PLUS Stock Exchange became ICAP Securities and Derivatives Exchange which in turn became became NEX Exchange and is currently Acquis Stock Exchange.

[26] The modern version of that law can be found in FSMA 2000 s.90.

[27] For an excellent general analysis of this process see E. Ferran, *Building an EU Securities Market* (Cambridge: CUP, 2004).

[28] Directive 2003/71 on prospectuses [2003] OJ L345/64, as amended by Directive 2010/73 [2010] OJ L327/1.

[29] Directive 2001/34. This Directive consolidated Directives going back to 1979, when the EU first became interested in regulating the admission of securities to public markets. Substantial parts of the 2001 Directive have now been themselves replaced.

In 2017 the PD was replaced by a Regulation (PReg).[30] This Regulation continues in force in the UK, but now as domestic law. The reason for the change from a Directive (requiring transposition into national law) to a Regulation (applying directly) was the EU's desire to produce a situation in which a prospectus, without changes other than translation, could be used simultaneously in more than one Member State in a cross-border offer.[31]

The second notable feature of the PD and now the PReg are the powers conferred on the European Commission to make what we would call subordinate legislation (through *Commission* Directives or Regulations), without going through the full EU legislative process but after consulting the Member States.[32] At multiple places in the PReg, the Commission was also given power to make binding technical standards, but here the draft standards are drawn up by the European Securities Market Authority (ESMA). These powers have been exercised extensively by the Commission and, to the extent that such delegated legislation came into force before UK exit, they became part of domestic law.[33] The purpose of this shift of legislative power to the Commission was said to be to enable the details of the legislation to be adapted more quickly to changing market practices than would be the case if the full EU legislative process had to be used. Law-making by the Commission thus constituted the second layer of rules in this area, after the adoption of the parent legal instrument by the EU legislature. That rule-making power has shifted to the Treasury for the future.[34]

The third level of law-making was autonomous rule-making by the UK legislature, which itself may take the form of primary or secondary legislation. The most obvious expression of the domestic law-making process is Pt VI of FSMA 2000 which contains three broad types of rules: those transposing the EU Directives, those adding to the EU requirements (where EU law permitted this) and those dealing with matters not subject to EU regulation. However, from the outset of domestic financial services regulation, the policy of embodying all the relevant rules in a statute or even in statutory instruments was rejected in favour of conferring broad rule-making and enforcement powers on a regulator, now the FCA. This is a statutory body[35] but funded by market participants and designed to be more attuned to the needs of the markets than would be a governmental department. It has a very wide remit in the financial services area but for the purposes of this chapter we concentrate on its role in public offerings and listing. Rules made by the FCA or its predecessor thus constitute the fifth level of rule-making. For the purposes of this chapter particularly important are its Prospectus Rules (PRR), though on some matters its Listing Rules (LR) are relevant as well. The PRR necessarily have a lesser scope than before the PReg replaced the PD.

---

[30] Regulation 2017/1129 ([2017] OJ L168/12), the majority of which became effective in July 2019, though some parts became effective earlier.

[31] See para.25–045.

[32] PReg art.44. This consultation takes place through the European Securities and Markets Authority (ESMA).

[33] European Union (Withdrawal) Act 2018 s.3.

[34] The Prospectus (Amendment etc.) (EU Exit) Regulations 2019 (SI 2019/1234) reg.66 (inserting new para.45a into the retained PReg).

[35] Established under FSMA 2000, as amended by the Financial Services Act 2012 Pt IA.

The sixth layer of regulation is that done by the exchanges themselves, as a matter of private contract with the issuers which seek to have their securities traded on a market operated by an exchange. This is particularly important in relation to MTFs.

Types of public offer

The rules discussed in this chapter are concerned with public offers of transferable securities. The whole of this body of regulation can be avoided by offering non-transferable securities to the public.[36] However, the illiquidity embodied in non-transferable securities is likely to make them unattractive to investors.[37] Assuming an issue of transferable securities, the company's choices appear to be as follows. On an initial public offering of shares, a company's choice of method will be restricted. If the issue is large it will have to proceed by way of an offer for sale or subscription coupled with admission to listing (or admission to AIM), whilst smaller amounts may be raised via a placing plus an introduction to a public market. (A placing is an offer to a selected group of investors and so is not a general offer.) In the case of bonds, even large amounts are normally raised by means of a placing, because bonds are traditionally bought by institutional, not retail, investors. In the case of shares, a third way of proceeding may be available. Where the company's shares have somehow become sufficiently widely held (which is unlikely without a public offer but conceivable) it may be possible to raise the new money needed by a rights or open offer to its existing shareholders, but this course of action is normally available only on subsequent offers, not on an IPO. We shall look briefly at each type of offer. 25–011

Offers for sale or subscription

A full-blown public offer will prove to be an expensive and time-consuming operation. The company's finance director (and probably other executives) and representatives of the advising investment bank and their respective solicitors will for weeks or months devote most of their time to working as a planning team. At a later stage the services of a specialist share registrar will generally be needed to handle applications and the preparation and dispatch of allotment letters. The offer will have to be made through a lengthy prospectus which will have to be published. To ensure that the issue is fully subscribed, arrangements will have to be made for it to be underwritten. Today this is normally achieved by the sponsoring investment bank agreeing to subscribe for the whole issue and for it, rather than the company, to make the offer to investors. Thus, large public offers are normally in the form of offers for sale (by the intermediary) not offers 25–012

---

[36] PReg art.2(a); FSMA 2000 s.73A(4).

[37] But see the offering by Caxton*fx* in September 2011 when it offered to the public non-transferable debt securities with a four-year maturity, but paying a high interest rate. The main regulation in such a case lies in FSMA 2000 s.21 ("financial promotion"), which requires the offer document to be approved by a person authorised by the FCA. The authorised person will need to be concerned with the adequacy of the disclosures contained in the invitation document.

for subscription (by the issuer), the investment bank having already subscribed for all the shares on offer.[38] In this case, the issuer will normally still draw up the prospectus (since it is in the best position to do so), but the institution offering the securities for sale to the public is relieved of the obligation to repeat the work.[39] In major offerings, a syndicate of investment banks may be employed. The banks will endeavour to persuade other financial institutions to sub-underwrite. Ultimately the cost of all this, including the commissions payable to underwriters and sub-underwriters,[40] will have to be borne by the company.

The most ticklish decision that will have to be made is the price at which the securities should be issued and, for obvious reasons, this is normally left to the last possible moment.[41] If it proves to have been set too low, so that the issue is heavily over-subscribed, the company will be unhappy, while, if it is set too high so that much of the issue is left with the underwriters, it is they who will be unhappy since their commission rates will have assumed that they will end up with a handsome profit and not be left with securities that, initially, they cannot sell except at a loss. Nor, probably, will the company be best pleased since it is generally believed that an under-subscribed issue will reduce the company's prospects of raising further capital in the future. The nightmare of all concerned is that there will be an unforeseen stock market collapse between the date of publication of the prospectus and the opening of the subscription list.[42] The sweet dream is that the issue will be modestly over-subscribed and that trading will open at a small premium.

If the issue is over-subscribed it will obviously be impossible for all applications to be accepted[43] in full. The issuer decides how to deal with this situation and the prospectus will need to say how it intends to do so. Normally this will be by accepting in full offers for small numbers of shares and scaling down large applications, balloting sometimes being resorted to. The company will probably wish to achieve a balance between private and institutional investors. To succeed in that aim multiple applications by the same person will probably be expressly prohibited.[44] An abuse which also needs to be guarded against is that "stags" will apply but seek to withdraw and stop their cheques if it

[38] In an offer for subscription the underwriters simply take up the shares for which the public have not subscribed. Even if there is no underwriting, large offers are often distributed to the public by financial intermediaries, perhaps over a period of weeks.

[39] PReg art.5, provided the issuer's prospectus meets the standards laid down in the PReg and the issuer consents to its use by those making the offer for sale (which it clearly will).

[40] On the legal capital implications of paying commission see para.16–017.

[41] PReg art.17 contemplates that the final price and amount on offer will not be stated in the prospectus itself, but requires it to state either the maximum price or the methodology for settling the offer price. It also requires issuers to permit the withdrawal of acceptance before these matters are stated, though normally issuers do not accept offers and investors do not make them, until these matters are settled.

[42] Which came true in the case of one of the privatisation issues in the "Crash of 1987". Yet thousands of small investors continued to put in applications notwithstanding that the media were warning them that trading would open at a massive discount.

[43] The so-called "offer" by or on behalf of the issuer is normally not an offer (as understood in the law of contract) which on acceptance becomes binding on the issuer. It may be in the case of a rights issue (see below) but on an offer for sale or subscription it is an invitation to investors to make an offer which may or may not be accepted.

[44] Breaches are difficult but not impossible to detect where applications are made in different names.

seems likely that dealings will not open at a worthwhile premium to the offer price. However, offer documents will require applications to be accompanied by cheques for the full amount of the securities applied for, the cheques being cleared immediately on receipt and any refund sent later. This means that an applicant may not only fail to get all or any of the shares hoped for but may, for a period, lose the interest previously being earned on the money.[45]

The offer price is normally stated as a fixed and pre-determined amount per share. It can however, be determined under a formula stated in the offer, though this is uncommon except in offers addressed to professional investors. Alternatively applicants can be invited to tender on the basis that the shares will be allocated to the highest bidders. This, however, is rarely used in relation to issues of company securities (as opposed to share buy-backs).[46]

Placings

Obviously, the expense of an offer for sale or subscription is prohibitive unless a **25–013** very large sum of money is to be raised. For lesser amounts the placing may be more attractive (and may be used for large amounts in the case of bonds). Under this method the investment bank or other adviser to the issuer obtains firm commitments, mainly from its institutional investor clients (instead of advertising an offer to the general public), coupling this with an introduction to trading. The absence of the need for "road-shows" and the like makes this a much less expensive procedure. On the other hand, it prevents the general public from acquiring shares at the issue price. Another way of proceeding is the "intermediaries offer", whereby financial intermediaries take up the offer for the purpose of allocating the securities to their own clients. This way of proceeding should be only marginally more expensive than a straightforward placing, but has the advantage that it is more likely to result in a wide spread of shareholders and a more active and competitive subsequent market. Although these are not "public" offers as far as the financial community is concerned, unless carefully controlled they may end up being public offers under the prospectus rules (as we see below).

Rights offers

Once a company has made an initial public offering of shares it will have **25–014** additional methods whereby it can raise further capital and, even if it proceeds by an offer for sale, this will be less expensive if the securities issued are of the same class as those already publicly traded. Often, it will make what is called a "rights issue" and, if it is an offering of equity shares for cash, it will generally have to do this, or make an open offer, unless the company in general meeting otherwise agrees. This is because of the pre-emptive provisions discussed in the previous chapter.[47] In one sense a rights issue is considerably less expensive than an offer for sale: circulating the shareholders is cheap in comparison with mounting a

45 This causes bona fide applicants who are unsuccessful understandable resentment.

46 See para.17–021.

47 Discussed at paras 24–006 onwards.

sales pitch to attract the public. However, even a rights issue does not wholly escape the disclosure requirements of the PReg.[48] And in another sense a rights offer may be dearer: if the issue price is deeply discounted the company will have to issue far more shares (on which it will be expected to pay dividends) in order to raise the same amount of money as on an offer.

Other methods of issue, which can be used in appropriate circumstances, include exchanges or conversions of one class of securities into another, issues resulting from the exercise of options or warrants, and issues under employee share-ownership schemes—though not all these raise new money for the company. Nor, of course, will capitalisation issues, dealt with in Ch.16. We do not discuss them further in this chapter.

ADMISSION TO LISTING AND TO TRADING ON A PUBLIC MARKET

25–015 We have already noted that admission to trading on a public market is a normally a concomitant feature of a public offer. Although it might seem logical to look at the rules on disclosure of information in relation to offers before looking at the rules governing admission to trading, because admission comes chronologically after the public offer, there are good reasons for the opposite approach. Principally, eligibility or merit requirements are to be found in the market access rules and those requirements therefore feed back into decisions about the types of public offers than can be put forward. Moreover, the information disclosure requirements for admission to markets overlap very considerably with those for public offers and so that aspect of the admission rules can be considered along with the public offer rule. We consider, first, eligibility requirements for admission to the official list (in effect the Main Market of the LSE) and then look at eligibility requirements for AIM, which take a rather different form.

Eligibility criteria for the official list

25–016 The principal source of admissibility requirements are the Listing Rules made by the FCA, partly transposing into domestic law the EU rules from CARD on admission to the official list and partly adding to those minimum requirements. Chapter II of Title III of CARD laid down certain conditions for the admissibility of shares to the official list, and Ch.III laid down a lesser set of requirements for debt securities.[49] Since securities admitted to the official list must also be admitted to trading on a regulated market,[50] the rules on admission to the official list in effect control admission to trading on a regulated market as well.

The admissibility conditions for official listing may be divided into those related to the issuer and those related to the securities on offer. In relation to both equity and debt securities one of two major policy concerns of the LR is to ensure that there should be a liquid market in the securities in question after listing, so

---

48 See para.25–019.

49 The merit requirements are less for debt securities presumably because the security itself will normally give the investor greater contractual protections than in the case of an equity security.

50 See para.25–008.

that subsequent trading in the securities is not unacceptably volatile.[51] The following requirements promote this goal:

(1) The expected market value of the securities to be admitted must be at least £700,000 for shares and £200,000 for debt securities.[52]
(2) All the securities of the class in question must be admitted to listing.[53]
(3) The securities must be freely transferable.[54] Without this requirement the development of a market in the securities would clearly be inhibited.
(4) Where the application is for admission of shares to the Premium segment of the Main Market, a "sufficient number" of the class of shares in question must be distributed to the public, either in the UK or elsewhere, as opposed to being held by insiders. This requirement is stated to be satisfied when 25% of the shares for which admission is sought are in public hands,[55] but the FCA has the discretion to accept a lower percentage, especially in large share issues, if it considers that the market will nevertheless operate properly.[56] Excluded from the notion of shares being in public hands are shares held by directors of the issuer or its subsidiaries, by persons connected with such directors, persons holding 5% or more of the relevant class of shares and persons acting in concert who exceed that figure.[57]

    The other main driver of the LR and the EU rules is that the issuer should have a certain quality.

(5) The company must produce audited accounts for the prior three-year period.[58] For premium list applicants, that historical financial information must show that "at least 75% of the applicant's business is supported by a historic revenue earning record" for the three years in question.[59] In

[51] Where there is only a thin market in a security, the prices at which those securities can be traded may be volatile.

[52] LR 2.2.7. This rule does not apply if the shares on offer are of a class already listed; and, in any event, the FCA may grant a derogation if satisfied that nevertheless there will be "an adequate market for the securities concerned".

[53] LR 2.2.9. The LR do not avail themselves of the exemption in art.49(2) of CARD for the non-admission to listing for "blocks serving to maintain control of the company".

[54] LR 2.2.4. This creates a problem for partly paid shares whose transfer is subject to a lien or other restriction in favour of the company. Where this is not so, the FCA may allow partly paid shares to be listed, provided investors have been made aware of their partly paid status. In exceptional cases where it is convinced the market in the shares will not be disturbed the FCA may list even fully paid shares whose transfer needs the consent of the issuer (rare in listed companies but found in some denationalised companies in order to subject control transfers to scrutiny).

[55] LR 6.14.2(2). The *UK Listing Review* (March 2021) recommended the reduction of this figure to 15%.

[56] LR 6.14.5. Moreover, since the rule applies on a class basis, an overseas (especially a sovereign) issuer may in fact seek to avoid the spirit of the free float rules entirely by listing only a small proportion of its total equity in a separate class of share. A common way of doing this is to use depository receipts rather than shares. Here, an investment bank typically holds the shares and then issues negotiable instruments representing the shares and it is those depository receipts which are listed and traded.

[57] LR 6.14.3—as well as some less obvious insiders.

[58] Regulation 2019/980 [2019] OJ L166/26, Annex I, s.18.

[59] LR 6.2. This is a clear problem for companies which have grown extensively by acquisition in that period. In that case the applicant may provide the information separately in relation to the acquired entity in relation to the period before its acquisition.

addition, that historical financial information must demonstrate that the company has a revenue-earning track record and enable investors to make a reasonable assessment of its future prospects.[60] It must also show that it will be carrying on an independent business as its main activity and that it will have operational control over that business.[61] This requirement is intended as a protection for investors in companies where there is a controlling or controlling group of investors. The aim of these requirements is to show that the company's business is not contingent on the consent of some person or group of persons, especially the controlling shareholders.[62] As a result of opportunistic behaviour on the part of controllers of certain listed companies, the LR were modified in 2015 so as to require controlling shareholders (30% of more of the voting rights) to enter into a written and legally binding agreement with the company, designed to safeguard its independence, especially in relation to related-party transactions and the election of independent directors, in the absence of which the LR's standard related-party transactions are applied to the issuer with particular rigour.[63]

(6) Again for premium listing, the applicant must show, subject to exceptions, that it will have sufficient working capital to meet its requirements for the 12 months after listing.[64] This is some protection against the company suffering a "cash crunch" in the short-term after listing. Of course, where the admission is coupled with a public offer, the working capital is likely to be raised in that offer. The purpose of this requirement is that the applicant shows it has made a realistic forecast of what needs in the near term.

In addition to these specific requirements in relation to the company and its securities, there is a general power, derived from art.11 of CARD and transposed by FSMA 2000 s.75(5), to reject an application for listing if the FCA considers that granting it "would be detrimental to interests of investors". It is unclear in what circumstances this power might be used, though no doubt it is a useful back-stop to deal with the unexpected.

Exchange admission standards

25–017 Since admission to listing requires admission to a regulated market for listed securities, the admission standards of the exchange operating that regulated market are also potentially relevant to the public offer process. However, the admission standards of the LSE for its Main Market do not add significantly to the rules laid down in the LR.[65] In the case of MTFs the eligibility rules of the

60 LR 6.3. A company basing its prospects on products which it has not yet developed or marketed might thus not meet this test.

61 LR 6.4 and 6.6.

62 LR 6.5.

63 LR 6.5.4. The general LR on related party transactions are discussed in para.10–074.

64 LR 6.7. This is a more effective protection for investors than the minimum capital rule for public companies. See para.16–009.

65 LSE, *Admission and Disclosure Standards* (October 2018), 1.4.1. However, the LSE does lay down additional requirements for those seeking admission to the Specialist Fund or High Growth segments of the Main Market.

exchange to which admission is sought are more important, since the LR have no application. The eligibility requirements for AIM companies, perhaps not surprisingly, are less elaborate than for the Main Market. The issuer must ensure that its securities are freely transferable, that they have been unconditionally allotted and that application is made for all shares in a class to be admitted.[66] Where the applicant's business has not been independent and earning revenue for at least two years, "it must ensure that all related parties and applicable employees as at the date of admission agree not to dispose of any interest in its securities for one year from the admission of its securities."[67] This rule obviously reflects in a muted way the independence requirements of the LR, by requiring those subject to the rule to remain exposed to the issuer's success for at least one year after admission, thus giving them an incentive not to remove their support from the company during that period. An "investing company", i.e. one which does not operate its own businesses but invests in others, must raise at least £6 million in equity at or before admission, disclose its investment policy and make no change in that policy without the shareholders' consent.[68] The Exchange has also reserved to itself the power to subject any applicant for admission to a special condition and to refuse admission "admission may be detrimental to the orderly operation, the reputation and/or integrity of AIM."[69] Finally, there is an overall procedural safeguard arising out of the requirement that an applicant for admission must appoint (and subsequently retain) a "nominated adviser". Responsibility for assessing the suitability of the applicant for AIM is placed by the Exchange on the adviser (usually referred to as the "nomad").[70]

THE PROSPECTUS

We now turn to the disclosure requirements which need to be complied with **25–018**
when a public offer and admission to trading on a regulated market are proposed. The core mechanism by which the law achieves its disclosure objectives is the prospectus. The core regulatory provisions here are the Prospectus Regulation (PReg), made by the EU but continued as part of domestic law,[71] and the Prospectus Rules (PRR) made by the FCA. The PReg excludes a small number of types of security from its coverage, of which the most important is probably offers of units in unit trusts, but otherwise covers the overwhelming majority of equity or debt instruments likely to be issued by companies.

At the outset, it is important to note that there are two triggers for the requirement to produce a prospectus: a public offer and the admission of shares to

[66] LSE, *AIM Rules for Companies* (March 2018), r.1.

[67] LSE, *AIM Rules for Companies* (March 2018), r.7.

[68] LSE, *AIM Rules for Companies* (March 2018), r.8.

[69] LSE, *AIM Rules for Companies* (March 2018), r.9.

[70] The Nomad must a declaration to the exchange when an issuer applies to be admitted which includes, among other things, a statement that "it is satisfied that the applicant and its securities are appropriate to be admitted to AIM, having made due and careful enquiry": LSE, *AIM Rules for Companies* (March 2018), r.5; and *AIM Rules for Nominated Advisers* (2018), Sch.2.

[71] For how much longer is unclear. The *UK Listing Review* (March 2021) recommended a "return to first principles as to the core purpose of the prospectus and the kind of transaction for which it should be required" (Recommendation 7).

trading on a regulated market.[72] Where, as is usual, shares are both offered to the public and at the same time admitted to trading on a regulated market, both triggers will be pulled (only one prospectus needs to be produced, of course), but either will do. We have also noted that AIM is not a regulated market and so simple admission to trading on AIM will not trigger the prospectus requirement. However, the prospectus rules will be triggered if the admission to AIM is accompanied by a public offer. To escape those rules the issuer must both avoid admission to trading on a regulated market and make an offer which falls outside the definition of a public offer. An example might be a placing of shares to be admitted to AIM where the placing is crafted in such a way as not to be a public offer. Although such a step may be effective to avoid the prospectus rules, the issuer may still find itself subject to disclosure requirements, because the operator of the non-regulated market is likely to require some level of disclosure. For example, the LSE's own rules for AIM require an applicant for admission to AIM to produce a publicly available "admission document". This document is a slimmed down version of what is required under a former version of the EU prospectus rules.[73] This is not surprising: investors are not likely to be attracted to deal in shares where little information is available about the issuers.

A somewhat similar, but much more limited, example can be found in relation to the Main Market of the London Stock Exchange. This is a regulated market and so, in principle, applicants for admission to listing must produce a prospectus governed by the PReg. However, as just noted, some types of security are wholly excluded from that Regulation, whilst offers to some classes of investor escape the requirements of the PReg, even if the securities are to be traded on the Main Market.[74] Nevertheless, in those excluded cases and also in the case of "specialist securities" (securities which "are normally bought and traded by a limited number of investors who are particularly knowledgeable in investment matters"), which will often be exempt from the PReg, the Listing Rules of the FCA impose an obligation to produce "listing particulars". Listing particulars are the traditional means by which the LSE required disclosure from companies seeking listing. The current listing particulars are closely modelled on the requirements of the PReg.[75] Given the limited requirement for listing particulars and the prohibition on the FCA from imposing a listing particulars requirement on applicants which are covered by the PReg,[76] we can ignore listing particulars for the most part in this chapter and concentrate of the prospectus requirements. However, when we analyse the FSMA rules relating to liability to pay compensation for misleading statements, we will see that they are still framed in relation to listing particulars, although there is a sub-section buried away which says that the liability rules for listing particulars apply also to prospectuses.[77]

---

[72] PReg art.3; FSMA 2000 s.85(1)–(2). The meaning of a regulated market is discussed at para.25–007.

[73] LSE, *AIM Rules for Companies* (March 2018), r.3, Sch.2 and Glossary, referring to Regulation 2004/809 (now repealed at EU level).

[74] See immediately above in this para.25–018.

[75] LR 4.2.3 onwards.

[76] FSMA 2000 s.79(3A).

[77] FSMA 2000 s.90(11). See para.25–033.

The public offer trigger

Producing an acceptable definition of a public offer has long proved a difficult exercise. A predecessor of the current PReg[78] did not even attempt the exercise, noting rather disarmingly in its preamble that "so far, it has proved impossible to furnish a common definition of the term 'public offer' and all its constituent parts". It was lauded as one of the achievements of the current PReg that it does contain such a definition. That definition is as follows: 25–019

> "'offer of securities to the public' means a communication to persons in any form and by any means, presenting sufficient information on the terms of the offer and the securities to be offered, so as to enable an investor to decide to purchase or subscribe to these securities."[79]

This, it will be observed, is not a great example of the drafter's art, for it is hardly helpful to define the trigger for a disclosure obligation in terms of the information which is in fact disclosed. Does this mean that an offer of securities containing insufficient information cannot be a public offer and thus not subject to the disclosure rules? Thus, as before, one has to proceed by taking an essentially broad and imprecise concept ("communication to persons in any form and by any means") and then seeking to give shape to it by examining the specific provisions in the Regulation which state when something is not a public offer, even though on the general approach it might otherwise be.

Of central importance, therefore, are the reasons for excluding some types of offer from the category of a "public" offer or for applying to them only reduced disclosure obligations. Producing and verifying the information required for a prospectus is a costly and time-consuming business. There is therefore a strong argument for not requiring a prospectus (or a full prospectus) if its recipients do not need (all) the information it contains. This could be for a number of reasons. Even if the information would be of benefit to the recipients, the costs of providing it may outweigh the benefits of having it provided. This is likely to be true of small offers. The provisions of the PReg can be seen to reflect these concerns.

Exemptions and reduced disclosure: public offers

The policies underlying the various exemptions from the requirement to produce a prospectus (or a full prospectus) on a public offer can be roughly categorised as follows. 25–020

First, there are exemptions which seek to identify the investors who can look after themselves and so do not need the mandatory prospectus information:

[78] Directive 89/228.

[79] PReg art.2(d).

(1) Offers addressed to "qualified investors" only.[80] These are defined by reference to MIFID II.[81] Included are legal entities authorised to operate in the financial markets (for example, fund managers or investment banks), institutional investors, large companies and governmental bodies at both national and international level, unless they seek to be excluded from this category. Investment firms are also allowed to include in the category of qualified investors other investors, including individuals, who satisfy two of the following criteria and who ask to be considered as qualified investors, provided the investment firm has carried out its own assessment of the expertise, knowledge and experience of the client. The classification carried out by the investment firm for its general activities may be communicated to the issuer for the purpose of share offers, subject to data protection. The criteria are: having carried out at least ten transactions of significant size per quarter over the previous four quarters; having a securities portfolio of at least half a million euros; working or having worked for a year in the financial sector in a position requiring knowledge of securities investment.[82]

FSMA makes an important clarification that included in the category of qualified investor is the offeree who is not qualified but whose agent is, provided the agent has authority to accept the offer without reference to the client.[83] To avoid a rather obvious way around the prospectus requirements, it is provided that, if there is a subsequent resale of the securities by a qualified investor, the question of whether that resale counts as a public offer is to be tested afresh.[84]

(2) Offers of securities where each investor is to pay at least €100,000 in response to the offer.[85] The idea is that such a large consideration will deter all but investors who can look after themselves.

(3) Offers of securities in denominations of at least €100,000—another way of expressing the same point.[86]

A second category of those who, it can be said, do not need the prospectus information, are those who will receive the relevant information through some other mechanism. The PReg identifies on this basis the target's shareholders in a share-exchange takeover bid[87] and the shareholders of companies involved in a

[80] PReg art.1(4)(a). Even though no prospectus is required, information given to some qualified investors must be given to them all: art.22(5). Bond issues are often directed only at financial institutions which fall within this category. Offers to the public of debt securities are relatively rare, though not unknown.

[81] Directive 2014/65, Annex II. See para.25–007.

[82] Directive 2014/65.

[83] FSMA 2000 s.86(2).

[84] PReg art.5. So, an offer for sale (para.25–012) does not escape the prospectus requirement because the offeror is likely to be an exempted person in its acquisition of the shares from the issuer.

[85] PReg art.1(4)(d). The original figure of €50,000 was increased to €100,000 in July 2012.

[86] PReg art.1(4)(c).

[87] PReg art.1(4)(f), (6a)(a), provided the securities offered are of a class already admitted to trading on a regulated market and the transaction is not a reverse takeover. In addition, although a prospectus is not required, a document "containing information describing the transaction and its impact on the issuer" must be made available. It is likely that the information requirements under the Takeover Code

merger.[88] Controversy has surrounded the question whether rights issues[89] should fall into this category. An offer to existing shareholders may be a public offer as a "communication to persons", unless it falls within one of the specific exemptions. However, it was argued that the continuing disclosure obligations of listed companies, discussed in the following chapter, made a prospectus unnecessary in this case. Initially, the PD made no concessions to this argument but in the PReg a "simplified disclosure regime" applies to secondary issues, including therefore rights issues, subject to conditions.[90] The policy choice here is thus not full exemption, but reduced disclosure. For rights issues the main condition is that the issue should relate to shares which have at least an 18-month track record on the market in question.

The third category where a prospectus is not regarded as useful is where those who receive the offer do so other than as part of a fund-raising exercise by the company. The PReg identifies[91] on this basis those receiving new shares in substitution for their existing shares, if there is no increase in the issued share capital; bonus shares and script dividends[92]; and shares issued under employee or directors' share schemes.

The fourth and most contentious case is where the prospectus information is admittedly useful to potential recipients but the cost of providing it is thought to be out of proportion to the benefits flowing from it. The Regulation as a whole does not apply where the total amount to be raised in the offer is no more than €1 million over a period of 12 months.[93] Member States may raise this figure up to €8m and the UK, when a member, the UK took full advantage of this freedom.[94] A further important example of this policy is the exclusion from the prospectus **25–021**

will meet this requirement. See at para.28–061. Where the offer is wholly in cash, the prospectus question does not arise, because the target's shareholders are not acquiring any securities. When the takeover is friendly, it is often implemented via a scheme of arrangement (see para.29–003) rather than an offer to exchange shares. The FCA's view is that a prospectus is not required in this case either, provided those subject to the scheme are not being given a choice, for example, as between cash and shares (see Recital 22 of the PReg). If there is a choice, a prospectus is required, even though the Takeover Code's disclosure rules apply also in this case: FCA, *When a prospectus is required where securities are issued pursuant to Schemes of Arrangement* (August 2020), Technical Note 606.1.

[88] PReg art.1(1)(g), (6a)(b), subject to the same proviso as in the previous note. See at para.29–006. The exemption for offers for sale and "retail cascades" more generally could be placed in this category as well: see para.25–012.

[89] See para.25–014.

[90] PReg art.14. For the requirements of simplified disclosure see Regulation 2019/980 art.4 and Annex 3.

[91] PReg art.1(4)(e), (h)–(i).

[92] On bonus shares see para.16–024. A scrip dividend usually results from an arrangement whereby the company offers and the shareholder chooses additional shares issued by the company instead of a cash dividend. The cash value of the scrip shares counts as a distribution by the company for the rules discussed in Ch.18 (and as income of the shareholder for personal tax purposes). But no stamp duty is payable.

[93] PReg art.1(3). In fact, Member States are forbidden to demand a prospectus in such cases, though they "may require other disclosure requirements at national level to the extent that such requirements do not constitute a disproportionate or unnecessary burden".

[94] PReg art.3(2); FSMA 2000 s.86(1)(e).

requirement of offers addressed to fewer than 150 persons (natural or legal), a number against which any qualified investor offerees do not count.[95]

A contentious issue has been how far SME offerings fall within the category where a prospectus is "useful but too expensive". On the one hand, the fixed costs of producing a prospectus are large, so that the proceeds of small offerings, which are associated with economically small issuers, are significantly reduced by these costs. On the other, small companies are often less well known to the market and, if of recent origin, based on business models which are more risky because less established. The first argument suggests reduced disclosure, the second does not. Initially, no concession was made to SMEs in the PD, but in 2010 there was a policy shift to reduced disclosure in this case.[96] In the PReg additional criteria for reduced disclosure were made available, based on the market on which the trading occurs and the size of the issue. On the other hand, some take the view that the degree of reduction is not generous.

Under art.15 a reduced "growth prospectus" (as the PReg terms it) may be used by an issuer where it is:

(1) a small or medium-sized[97];
(2) a non-SME whose shares are traded on a "growth market" (of which AIM is an example), provided its capitalisation is less than €500 million[98];
(3) it is a regulated market issuer who make offers of €20 million or less (over any 12-month period) and employ fewer than 500 employees; or
(4) a non-SME carrying out an IPO on a growth market where the issue is less that €200 million.

It seems likely that most issuers on AIM will be able to take advantage of the reduced disclosure requirements, both on an initial and a secondary offering, and so they will be under less pressure to construct the offer so as to bring it within the full public offer exemptions.[99]

Probably the most practically significant of the above exemptions as a whole are those for offers to qualified investors and to small numbers of investors. An offer made by a company to institutional investors and brokers operating discretionary portfolios for clients, followed by admission to trading on AIM, can escape the statutory prospectus requirements entirely, though not the Exchange's own disclosure rules.

---

[95] PReg art.1(4)(b). FSMA 2000 s.86(3) treats as an offer to a single person as an offer made to the trustees of a trust, the members of a partnership as such and two or more persons jointly.

[96] PD art.7(2)(e), implemented by Regulation 486/2012 [2012] OJ L150/1.

[97] The criteria for SME status do not follow precisely those used for the purposes of the accounts (see Ch.22), though they focus on the same factors. In the PReg (art. 2(f)) a SME is an issuer whose latest accounts demonstrate that two of the following criteria are met: > 250 employees, balance sheet total ≥ €43 million, annual net turnover ≥ €250 million. A company also qualifies as an SME if its average market capitalisation is > €200 million.

[98] Most AIM companies will meet this criterion. A growth market is an MTF which is registered with the FCA as such, under a number of criteria, of which the most important is probably that half its issuers must be SMEs (see MAR 5.10).

[99] However, a non-public offer via a placing may still have cost advantages. Since AIM is an MTF, the admission to trading trigger is not relevant in this case.

The admission to trading trigger

The second trigger for the prospectus is a request for admission of securities to a regulated market.[100] Thus, if shares are to be introduced onto the Main Market of the LSE, even though there is no offer to the public by the company, a prospectus will normally be required. There is not the same definitional problem about whether an issuer has requested admission to a regulated market as exists with a public offer. However, similar policy issues arise as to whether a prospectus is necessary all admission cases and whether its costs exceeds its benefits. Consequently, there are exemptions (and reduced disclosure requirements) for the second trigger as well.[101] Some of them repeat the public offer exemptions. Repetition is necessary, since public offers are often coupled with admission of those shares to trading on a regulated market, so that a public offer exemption alone would be incomplete. Others are specific to admission, since admission involves elements missing from a public offer. On the other hand, some of the public offer exemptions are incapable of being applied to admission to trading on a public market, for example, where the exemption turns on the some characteristic of the offeree, such as being a qualified investor or being among a small group of offerees, since trading on a public market cannot be confined to such persons. Overall, if an issuer can bring itself within both the public offer and the admission to trading exemptions, it may avoid the need for a prospectus even though it appears to have pulled both triggers, or it may be able to make reduced disclosures. **25–022**

Concentrating on the exemptions and reductions specific to admissions, one sees similar policies at work in this second context as operate with the public offer exemptions. For example, exempted from the admission trigger are shares representing less than 20% of the number of shares of the same class already admitted to trading on that regulated market (measured over a 12-month period).[102] The policy argument is that, if the class of share is already traded on the market, there will be a lot of information about them and the issuer in the market[103] and a relatively small offering of additional shares will not mark a dramatic change of direction for the company. Combined with the qualified investor exception for public offers, the 20% rule enables companies to raise relatively small amounts of new capital via a carefully structured placing, even if the shares in question are admitted to trading on a regulated market.[104]

---

100 PReg art.3(3).

101 PReg art.1(5).

102 PReg art.1(5)(a). Under the PD the percentage was 10%. The 20% rule is also applied to the exemption for shares resulting from the exercise of conversion rights under an existing security (for example, a convertible bond or preference share), provided the shares are of a class already admitted to trading. Of course, the securities being converted may have been subject to a prospectus requirement on issue; and there may be disclosure obligations arising on conversion from other sources, e.g. LR 13.8.16 ("Reminders of conversion rights").

103 As we have noted above, this argument has now been extended to justify reducing the level of disclosure on a rights issue.

104 The LSE does not normally require an admission document for a further issue of shares of any size on AIM (LSE, *AIM Rules for Companies* (March 2018), r.27) and so in the case of an AIM company the public offer exemption is the central consideration.

In order to encourage a single financial market in the EU, securities already admitted to trading on one regulated market are to be admitted to trading on another without the production of a prospectus.[105] Perhaps surprisingly, though no doubt in the hope of reciprocity, this provision survived the UK exit from the EU with only minor amendments. It is subject to conditions, notably that securities of the same class shall have been traded on the other market for at least 18 months[106] and that the ongoing obligations for trading on that other market have been complied with.

Function of the prospectuses

25–023 Subject to the exemptions and reductions discussed above, a full prospectus must be made available before an offer is made to the public or a request is made for admission of securities to trading on a regulated market. The overriding rule to which the prospectus is subject is that it "shall contain the necessary information which is material to an investor for making an informed assessment of" the financial position of the issuer, the rights attached to the securities offered and the reasons for the offer.[107] The reference to materiality is new and is in line with the renewed concerns of the drafters of the Regulation that the information in it should be accessible and that over-disclosure should not lead to a form of factual non-disclosure by obscuring the important facts. Along the same lines it is stated that materiality will vary according to the nature of the issuer, the securities and the reasons for raising finance, a provision probably also aimed at discouraging boilerplate disclosures. Equally, it is stated that the prospectus "shall be written and presented in an easily analysable, concise and comprehensible form."[108]

Summary

25–024 Perhaps the strongest expression of this drive for clarity and concision is the requirement that, in addition to the prospectus, the issuer must produce a summary of it as a separate document.[109] This aims to provide the "key information" that prospective investors need to understand "the nature and the risks" of the issuer and the securities on offer. Although the requirement for a separate summary is not a novelty introduced by the PReg, that Regulation does subject it to very precise specification which indicates the importance the drafters of the Regulation attached to it. It is designed to operate as an introduction to the prospectus and thus must be consistent with the information contained in the full prospectus. In addition it must be "accurate, fair and clear and shall not be misleading"—something one might have thought that went without saying, but it underlines the importance attached to the summary by the drafters. Beyond these

---

[105] PReg art.1(5)(j).

[106] Reflecting the EU's traditional fear that otherwise there would be a regulatory "race to the bottom" with companies securing admittance to the laxest market and then immediately moving to the market of choice.

[107] PReg art.6(1).

[108] PReg art.6(2).

[109] PReg art.7.

generalities, there is very precise regulation of the length of the summary (not more than seven A4 pages), the language to be used ("clear, non-technical, concise and comprehensible for investors"),[110] and its content. The summary must be divided into four prescribed sections and the information to be contained in each section is defined, together with requirements for risk warnings (which, however, must not exceed 15 in total).[111] In addition, there are binding technical standards, issued by the Commission of the basis of an ESMA draft—a function which has now passed to the FCA. There are some, relatively minor, relaxations of these requirements in the case of a growth prospectus—which is, of course, itself a less complex document than a full prospectus.[112]

There is no doubt that prospectuses have become forbiddingly long and detailed documents, a tendency to which the civil liability rules, discussed below, only contribute. It is doubtful whether many retail investors read it in full or at all before deciding whether to invest. To that extent, an introduction to the prospectus seems a valuable addition. However, it raises fundamental questions. Are retail investors to be encouraged to invest on the basis of the summary alone? If not, then the introduction would be better placed at the beginning of the prospectus proper rather than in a separate document. If so, why is the information in the full prospectus regarded as unimportant for them? One may doubt whether retail investors should take risks which professional investors and analysts would avoid on the basis of an analysis of the full prospectus. Going further, one may wonder whether it is wise policy to encourage retail investors to invest directly at all, rather than collectively (though a mutual fund, for example) or on the basis of the professional advice of someone who is in a position to analyse the full prospectus and has done so.[113]

Composition and content of the prospectus

Turning to the prospectus proper, it is usual to think of it as a single document, **25–025**
because this is UK practice. Under the Regulation, however, the prospectus may consist of two documents, if the issuer so chooses, namely, a registration document and a securities note. "The registration document shall contain the information relating to the issuer. The securities note shall contain the information concerning the securities offered to the public or to be admitted to trading on a regulated market."[114] The notion behind the "two documents" approach is that the registration statement is approved by the regulator, published and up-dated on an annual basis, even though no public offer may be contemplated at that time.[115] When an offering is made, the issuer is obliged only

110 PReg art.7.

111 PReg art.7(4)–(10).

112 Regulation 2019/980 art.28.

113 It may be said that in the privatisation issues of the 1980s many members of the public bought shares without reading the prospectus and were encouraged to do so through advertising campaigns. However, there political considerations ensured that in nearly all cases the securities were priced so as to show an immediate gain when trading started and many retail investors sold out at the point. For the naivety of retail investors in privatisations: see fn.42.

114 PReg art.6(3).

115 PReg art.9. This is sometimes termed "shelf registration".

to issue a securities note (describing the securities on offer) and a summary and to up-date the registration document to the extent necessary (which may be not at all) since its last filing with the regulator.[116] Whether this approach will provide for quicker or less expensive equity offerings remains to be seen.

Whether the prospectus consists of one or two documents, its content is heavily regulated. This was so under the PD and the PReg has not amended this approach. This is an area where the Commission was given law-making powers (now passed to the FCA) and in pursuance of this power produced a Regulation,[117] containing 47 articles (only two fewer than the PReg itself) and some 29 annexes. These annexes, together with the five annexes to the PReg itself, contain the detail about the format and the disclosures required for the prospectus. These detailed rules do not displace the overall disclosure obligation mentioned in para.25–023. The purpose of the "sweeping up" rule is thus to require those drawing up a prospectus, after they have complied with the detailed rules in the Regulations, to ask themselves, as a final check, whether overall it gives the investors all the information they require. In addition to all this, the regulator may require further information disclosures during the approval process.[118]

In a work of this nature the disclosure requirements of the PReg and the Commission Delegated Regulation do not need to be analysed in detail. However, it is worth saying that, despite their formidable size, they are not quite as fearsome as they seem. The annexes contain what are sometimes called "building blocks" to be used in the construction of the prospectus, but only some, often a small number, of those building blocks will be relevant to any one prospectus. The disclosures required vary according to whether debt or equity securities are on offer, the nature of the security if it is not a standard share or bond,[119] and on whether a full prospectus is to be issued or a growth prospectus and whether reduced disclosure is permitted.

Some amelioration for issuers is also provided by the permission to incorporate some types of information into the prospectus by simply referring to its existence elsewhere. Information incorporated by reference must be available electronically, hyperlinks to the material must be incorporated into the prospectus and the incorporated material is limited, broadly, to that contained in documents which have had some level of independent verification, such as the issuer's annual accounts or its articles of association.

Nevertheless, the disclosure requirements are extensive and result is likely to be a complex document. Even so, as we have noted above,[120] the prospectus is likely to omit two crucial matters, the price and the amount of securities offered. These are likely to left to the last possible moment, in order to be able to react to late changes in the market.

---

116 PReg art.10(1).

117 Regulation 2019/980.

118 PReg art.20(4).

119 For example, there are special provisions for asset-backed securities, depository receipts, derivative securities, closed-end collective investment schemes and public authority offerors, some or all of which will be irrelevant in many cases.

120 At para.25–012.

Supplementary prospectus

It is not a rare event that information becomes available after the prospectus has been published which requires the published information to be qualified. The PReg requires "every significant new factor, material mistake or material inaccuracy" relating to the information contained in the prospectus which "arises or is noted" after its approval by the regulator and before the closing of the offer to be the subject of a supplementary prospectus.[121] In the case of an offer to the public investors have a right of withdrawal during the two working days after the supplementary prospectus is published. Any person responsible for the prospectus who becomes aware of any of the above is under a duty to notify it to the company or the applicant for admission, if different.[122] It is unclear whether duty to produce a supplement arises if the issuer is unaware of the event and it cannot be said that it should have been.[123] 25–026

Verifying the prospectuses

As we shall see below, the law provides ex post remedies for those who suffer loss as a result of omissions or inaccuracies in a prospectus or supplementary prospectus. However, it is obviously more desirable if the law or regulation can provide ex ante mechanisms designed to ensure that the information as provided is complete and accurate before it is published. A number of such mechanisms are to be found. 25–027

Reputational intermediaries

A first mechanism, long relied on in the UK, not regulated by the PReg but evidently not regarded as prohibited by it, is the use of a "sponsor" as a reputational intermediary. The sponsor guides the applicant for admission to trading through the applicable rules and certifies that there has been compliance. Certification of compliance with the requirements by the intermediary may be more reliable than that by the company alone because of the intermediary's greater experience in the field and because the intermediary's business model depends on its certifications being accurate, for otherwise future issuers will not have an incentive to use that intermediary, as opposed to one of its competitors, and the intermediary may be removed from the list of sponsors by the regulator. Use of an intermediary in this way involves in effect a partial delegation by the FCA or the Exchange of its supervisory powers to an adviser to the company, who is of course paid for by the company. 25–028

[121] PReg art.23.

[122] FSMA 2000 s.87G.

[123] The phrase "is noted" might suggest knowledge is required but "arises" does not. FSMA 2000 s.81 creates a similar obligation to produce supplementary listing particulars (see para.25–018), but s.81(3) makes it clear that knowledge of the new event is required to trigger the obligation.

A company applying for a premium listing of its equity securities on the Main Market of the LSE must appoint a sponsor[124] whose role is defined in general as being to "(1) provide assurance to the FCA when required that the responsibilities of the listed company or applicant under the listing rules have been met"; (2) to provide the FCA with any requested explanation or confirmation to the same end; and (3) guide the listed company or applicant in "understanding and meeting its responsibilities" under the FCA's rules.[125] It is the sponsor (normally an investment bank) which submits the application for listing to the FCA and accompanies it with a "sponsor's declaration" that it has fulfilled its duties and provides information to the FCA about how the applicant fulfils the eligibility requirements for admission and about the outcome of the offer.[126] The sponsor must not submit such an application "unless it has come to a reasonable opinion, after having made due and careful enquiry" that the applicant has satisfied all the requirements of the Listing and Prospectus Rules.[127] The sponsor thus owes duties to both its client (to use reasonable care in guiding it through the application process) and to the FCA when providing assurance to the regulatory body that those requirements have been met.

Vetting by the FCA

25–029 The sponsor's duties thus go beyond taking reasonable care to ensure that an accurate and complete prospectus has been produced and embrace compliance with the eligibility requirements. Nevertheless, securing an accurate and comprehensive prospectus will be the central task of the issuer and its advisers (legal and financial) and to this central task the regulator also contributes. Before publication, the prospectus must be vetted by the FCA.[128] The FCA must take its decision within 10 business days.[129] The purpose of the vetting is to put the FCA in a position to assure itself that the information is complete, comprehensible and consistent before it is published and, to that end, may request additional disclosures. If these are provided, the time limits are re-set at that point; if they

---

[124] LR 8.2.1. A sponsor is also required or its guidance sought on a list of other occasions (see LR 8.2.1–8.2.3). However, a premium listed company is not required to have a sponsor at all times, unlike a company admitted to AIM where a condition for continued admission of the company is that it has a nomad in place: LSE, *AIM Rules for Companies* (2018), r.1. The nomad has similar responsibilities to the sponsor at admission stage and must give the Exchange the same assurance: LSE, *AIM Rules for Companies* (2018), r.5 and *AIM Rules for Nominated Advisers* (2018), Sch.2.

[125] LR 8.3.1.

[126] LR 8.4.3. On eligibility see para.25–016. Given the importance of sponsors, provisions have to be made for their independence, qualifications and supervision. See, for example, LR 8.6 and 8.7, but those matters do not need to be considered further in this book.

[127] LR 8.4.2 and 8.4.8. And has procedures in place to facilitate compliance with the Transparency and Disclosure Rules discussed in the following chapter.

[128] PReg art.20; FSMA 2000 s.87A. The criteria to be used in evaluating prospectuses are set out in detail in Regulation 2019/980 arts 35–45.

[129] PReg art.20; 20 days if the issuer has no securities traded on a regulated market and has never previously made a public offer. Non-approval within the time period is not treated, however, as approval; 5 days if the issuer has used the "shelf registration" procedure and has become a "frequent issuer" (art.9(11). The information submitted to the FCA must include "in searchable electronic format" the documents which the prospectus incorporates by reference: art.19(3).

are not, the regulator may refuse approval.[130] Inevitably, given the time and resources available, the FCA can concern itself only to a certain extent with the accuracy of the information put forward by the company, for example, it should spot glaring inaccuracies appearing on the face of the document. Nor can the FCA guarantee even completeness, except to the extent of seeing that something is said on all the matters upon which the rules require disclosure and that the information is not obviously inadequate. Consistency is perhaps easier to judge. Nevertheless, the obligation to obtain the prior approval of the FCA is, no doubt, a valuable discipline upon the issuer and its professional advisers. It should also be noted in this regard that the FCA and its officers are protected from liability in damages for acts and omissions in the discharge of the functions conferred upon them, unless bad faith is shown or there has been a breach of the Human Rights Act 1998 s.6 (unlawful for a public authority to act in a way incompatible with a convention right), so that it will be rare for the FCA to be worth suing if the prospectus turns out to be incomplete or inaccurate.[131] A refusal of approval on the part of the FCA must be accompanied by reasons and the applicant may appeal to the Tribunal (see below) against the decision.[132] The regulator is more likely simply to require that additional information be provided as a condition for its approval.[133]

Authorisation to omit material

A particularly important part of the approval role of the FCA is the power given it to authorise omissions from the prospectus of information which would normally be required to be included.[134] Given the range of information required to be included in a prospectus, it is likely that the applicant will regard some disclosure to be commercially harmful, because, for example, it will aid competitors. Apart from omission of information "in the public interest" on a certificate from the Treasury,[135] however, the grounds for omission are limited, in the sense that the interests of prospective investors are given predominant weight in striking the balance between them and the issuer and its current shareholders. Omissions may be authorised only if (1) the disclosure would be "seriously detrimental" to the issuer *and* the omission would be unlikely to mislead the public over matters "essential" for an informed assessment of the offer; or (2) if the information is only of minor importance for the offer and unlikely to influence an informed assessment of the offer.[136] One might summarise the policy underlying these rules **25–030**

[130] PReg art.19(4)(5); FSMA 2000 ss.87A and 87C(7)(8).

[131] PReg art.19(9); FSMA 2000 Sch.1ZA para.25. For the implications of this protection for the FCA's obligation to provide an undertaking as to damages when it seeks a freezing order, see *FSA v Sinaloa Gold Plc* [2011] EWCA Civ 1158.

[132] FSMA 2000 s.87D.

[133] FSMA 2000 s.87J.

[134] PReg art.18.

[135] FSMA 2000 s.87B(2)(3).

[136] PReg art.18(1). The same two exemptions are found for AIM admissions documents (LSE, *AIM Rules for Companies* (2018), r.4) and listing particulars (FSMA 2000 s.82).

as being that, where the information is important to investors, they should be provided with it, despite the harm to the company (unless the public interest intervenes).

Publication of prospectuses and other material

25–031 All the effort involved in drawing up a prospectus and having it approved by the FCA is, of course, simply a prelude to its publication when the securities are offered to the public or admission is sought. The PReg places electronic publication in the forefront, in that the prospectus "shall be deemed to be available to the public" when available on the websites of any of the offeror, the person seeking admission to trading, any financial institution involved in marketing the securities or the website of the regulated market or MTF.[137] In addition, the FCA must maintain a list of all approved prospectuses on its site. However, any potential investor is entitled to a hard copy of the prospectus.[138]

Despite the requirement that the prospectus include a summary, it is likely that an issuer will want to publish documentation in addition to the prospectus, designed to generate interest in the offer. Such "advertisements", as the PReg terms them,[139] run the risk of subverting all the careful regulation of the prospectus, if unsophisticated investors read only the advertisements and those documents are carelessly constructed. Consequently, any advertisement must be clearly recognisable as such; must state that a prospectus is or will be available and how it may be obtained; must not contain inaccurate or misleading information; and the information in it must be consistent with the prospectus.[140] There are provisions designed to ensure that no information is contained in advertisements which is not available to all potential investors, either via the prospectus or otherwise. A Commission Delegated Regulation adds to these requirement, including one that the advertisement should advise readers to read the prospectus.[141] However, unlike previously,[142] advertisements do not need to be submitted to the FCA in advance or to be approved by it. On the other hand, since the FSMA 2000 makes it unlawful to offer securities to the public before publication of the prospectus, any advertisement issued in advance of the offer ("warm-up" material) will have to stop short of actually offering the securities to the public.[143]

137 PReg art.21(2). Apparently, it is open to an offeror to achieve publication via a non-electronic format, but it is unlikely it would seek to do so.

138 PReg art.21(11).

139 Defined as a communication which relates to a specific offer of securities or application for admission and aims to "specifically promote the potential subscription or acquisition of securities" (PReg art.2(k)).

140 PReg art.22.

141 Regulation 2017/1129 art.14.

142 FSMA 2000 s.98, requiring prior approval, was repealed in 2005 when the PD was transposed in the UK. The wide definition of "advertisement" makes such a requirement impractical.

143 FSMA 2000 ss.85 and 102B.

SANCTIONS

The rules examined above aim to put at the disposal of investors a considerable amount of information about companies and their securities when the latter are offered to the public. Although there may be adverse market consequences for companies which issue misleading prospectuses (their future fundraising efforts are likely to be greeted with some scepticism), nevertheless an effective prospectus regime is likely to require legal sanctions as well. There are three categories of sanctions in principle available for breach of the disclosure regime: criminal, civil and administrative (or regulatory). However, the criminal and regulatory sanctions are today effectively in the hands of the FCA and so can be looked at together. We start with an analysis of the civil sanctions. **25–032**

Compensation under FSMA 2000

Civil liability may arise out of a failure to provide a prospectus at all or out of misleading statements or omissions in a prospectus which has been issued. As to the former, the FSMA 2000 provides a civil remedy for a person who has suffered loss as a result of a breach of the prohibition on offering shares to the public or seeking admission to a regulated market without a published prospectus, the contravention being treated as a breach of statutory duty.[144] As for misstatements and omissions in the prospectus, PReg art.11 requires Member States to apply their national liability rules to those responsible, but this article has been removed from the Prospectus Regulation as retained in the UK.[145] This was presumably because, after the UK's exit, this particular provision was redundant, not because there was a policy decision not to provide compensation in this situation. In fact, the UK has long had a compensation regime in place, basing liability on negligence and, indeed, reversing the burden of proof. That regime dates back to the Directors' Liability Act 1890, passed in reaction to the decision of the House of Lords in *Derry v Peek*[146] which, by insisting upon at least recklessness, exposed the inadequacy of the common law tort of deceit as a remedy for investors who suffered loss as a result of misleading prospectuses. The modern version of liability under the 1890 Act is now located in s.90 of FSMA 2000, which imposes a wide-ranging liability in negligence. **25–033**

144 FSMA 2000 s.85(4). There is no equivalent in relation to listing particulars. It is also a criminal offence.

145 The Prospectus (Amendment etc.) (EU Exit) Regulations 2019 (SI 2019/1234) reg.40.

146 *Derry v Peek* (1889) 14 App. Cas.337 HL. At this time, of course, liability in the tort of negligence for purely economic loss caused by misstatements was not accepted either (and that remained in effect the case until the House of Lords' decision in *Hedley Byrne & Co Ltd v Heller & Partners Ltd* [1964] A.C. 465 HL), so that the tort of negligence could not be used to circumvent the restrictions on liability under the tort of deceit.

Liability to compensate

25–034 Subject to the exemptions in (b), below, those responsible for the prospectus (or supplementary prospectus)[147] are liable under s.90 to pay compensation to any person who has acquired any of the securities to which it relates and suffered loss as a result of any untrue or misleading statement in it or of the omission of any matter required to be included under the FSMA 2000.[148] This is a considerable improvement on the former provisions, contained most recently in the CA 1985, which applied only in favour of those who subscribed for shares and therefore excluded from protection those who bought on the market when dealings commenced. Now anyone who has acquired[149] the securities whether for cash or otherwise and whether directly from the company or by purchase on the market and who can show that he or she suffered loss as a result of the misstatement or omission will have a prima facie case for compensation.[150]

The inclusion of non-subscribers may seem at first sight an unreasonable extension of liability from the company's point of view, but in fact the prospectus is normally intended to influence not only applications to the company for shares but also the initial dealings in them in the market (the "after market"), since the company has an interest in the securities not trading at below the offer price after issue.[151] In addition, whereas the former version applied only to misleading "statements", the new provisions specifically include omissions. Furthermore, the provisions do not require the claimant to show that he or she relied on the misstatement in order to establish a cause of action: it is enough that the error affected the market price, even if the claimant never read the prospectus. This is sometimes referred to as the "fraud on the market" theory of liability.[152] Obviously, however, a causal connection between the misstatement or omission and the loss will have to be proven. So, for example, market purchasers who buy after such a lapse of time that the prospectus can no longer be said to have a significant influence on the price of the securities will not be able to satisfy this causal test. Finally, the statute does not require the maker of the statement to have "assumed responsibility" towards the claimant, a requirement that limits the operation of the common law of negligent misstatement.[153] In effect, the statute imposes that responsibility on the available defendants.

On the other hand, as far as public offers are concerned, the statutory provisions under discussion apply only to misstatements in prospectuses. This will now include the summary, which is part of the prospectus, but here liability is restricted to situations where the summary is misleading when read together

---

147 Or in listing particulars. See para.25–018.

148 FSMA 2000 s.90(1). Where the rules require information regarding a particular matter or a statement that there is no such matter, an omission to provide either is to be treated as a statement that there is no such matter: s.90(3).

149 "Acquire" includes contracting to acquire the securities or an interest in them: s.90(7).

150 To be assessed presumably on the tort measure, i.e. to restore the claimant to his or her former position: *Clark v Urquart* [1930] A.C. 28 HL, i.e. normally the difference between the price paid and the value of the securities received.

151 For the difficulties the common law has had with this point, see para.25–039.

152 Following US usage. It is not really apt in this context: "negligence on the market" would be more accurate if less resonant.

153 See para.23–044 onwards in relation to auditors, and para.25–039.

with the rest of the prospectus or where liability is based on the omission from it of key information.[154] However, the section does not apply to advertisements issued in connection with a public offer but separately from the prospectus. Nor, it seems, does the section apply to the Admission Document required for an AIM admission (assuming no public offer triggering the requirement for a prospectus). In such cases compensation might be available at common law or under the Misrepresentation Act but, as the origins of the current legislation suggest, investors in that situation will in all likelihood benefit from a lower level of protection than if they could invoke the civil liability provisions of the FSMA 2000.[155]

Defences

Schedule 10 provides persons responsible for the misstatement or omissions with what the headings in the schedule describe as "exemptions", but which are really defences that may be available if a claim for compensation is made. The main purpose of Sch.10 is to implement the policy of imposing liability on the basis of negligence but with a reversed burden of proof, but it also deals with some causation points. The overall effect[156] of these defences is that defendants escape liability under s.90, if, but only if, they can satisfy the court (1) that they reasonably believed that there were no misstatements or omissions and had done all that could reasonably be expected to ensure that there were not any, and that, if any came to their knowledge, they were corrected in time; or (2) that the claimant acquired the securities with knowledge of the falsity of the statement or of the matter omitted. Defence (1) disproves negligence and defence (2) disproves a causal link between the defendant's conduct and the claimant's loss. Where the statement in question is made by an expert and is stated to be included with the expert's consent, the rules are that a non-expert defendant escapes liability on the basis of a reasonable belief that the expert was competent and had consented to the inclusion of the statement. The expert will be subject to the same test for liability as any other responsible person, but what is "reasonable" is likely to be assessed at a higher standard. **25–035**

[154] FSMA 2000 s.90(12). The term "key information" is heavily used in art.7 of the PReg without definition, but see Regulation 2019/979 Ch.1.

[155] The common law rules are discussed briefly below. It is not entirely unarguable that s.90 applies to an AIM admission document, which is a cut-down version of the PD prospectus. The function of the two types of document is the same. The section does not in terms say that it applies only to prospectuses required by the PReg. Nor is it clear that a "prospectus" (not defined for the purposes of s.90) is confined to the documentation accompanying a public offer of shares.

[156] This sentence merely summarises the very complex drafting of Sch.10.

Persons responsible

25–036 The sensitive question of who are "persons responsible" and thus liable to pay the compensation is dealt with by the PRR.[157] In the case of an offer of equity shares, they are[158]:

(1) the issuer—a further improvement on earlier versions which did not afford a remedy against the company itself;
(2) directors of the issuer, unless the prospectus was published without the director's knowledge or consent;
(3) each person who has authorised himself to be named, and is named in the prospectus, as having agreed to become a director, whether immediately or at a future time;
(4) each person who accepts, and is stated as accepting, responsibility for, or for any part of, the prospectus, but only in relation to the part to which the acceptance relates[159];
(5) each other person who has authorised the contents of the prospectus or any part of it, but again only in relation to the part authorised; and
(6) the offeror of the securities or the company seeking admission and its directors where it is not the issuer.[160]

In the case of offers of other types of security,[161] directors of the issuer or offeror are excluded, unless they fall within one of the other categories (stated as accepting responsibility for the prospectus, for example), whilst the guarantor (if there is one, as there might be for offers of debt securities) is made liable for information relating to the guarantee. However, nothing in the rules is to be construed as making a person responsible by reason only of his giving advice in a professional capacity.[162]

Civil remedies available elsewhere

25–037 The liability created by s.90 is not exclusive. Section 90(6) says that the section "does not affect any liability which any person may incur apart from this section", but s.90(8) limits the disclosure obligations of promoters and other fiduciaries to those required under the statutory regime.[163]

---

[157] PRR 5.3. In the case of listing particulars the persons responsible are set out in FSMA 2000 (Official Listing of Securities) Regulations 2001 (SI 2001/2956) reg.6.

[158] PRR 5.3.2.

[159] For example, the reporting accountant and any other "experts".

[160] This takes account expressly of secondary offers, but the offeror will not be liable if it is making the offer in association with the issuer and the issuer has taken the lead in drawing up the prospectus.

[161] PRR 5.3.5.

[162] PRR 5.3.10. This clearly does not exclude the main functions of sponsor required by the Listing Rules.

[163] No person, by reason of being a promoter or otherwise, is to incur any liability for failing to disclose in a prospectus information which would not have had to be disclosed by a person responsible for the prospectus or which a person responsible would have been entitled to omit by virtue of the Act.

As explained above, the damages remedy available under the FSMA 2000 is superior to that available under the general law. However, there may be cases where the legislation does not apply. The most obvious examples are non-prospectus material issued in connection with public offers or, possibly, where there is no public offer, an Admission Document issued in connection with an application for admission to AIM. This Document does require, as we have seen,[164] significant disclosure by applicants, even if less than under the PReg. Alternatively, the claimant may want a remedy other than damages, such as rescission. Thus, a brief examination of the law relating to misrepresentation as it applies to issue documents is in order, but only a sketch of the relevant principles will be provided.

Damages

The common law provides civil remedies for misrepresentations which have caused loss to those who have relied upon them. A misrepresentation is understood at common law as being a misstatement of fact rather than an expression of opinion or a promise or forecast. There must be a positive misstatement rather than an omission to state a material fact. However, this requirement is heavily qualified by a further rule that an omission which causes a document as a whole to give a misleading impression or falsifies a statement made in it is actionable.[165] **25–038**

Historically, the common law has provided a damages remedy only for fraudulent misstatements through the tort of deceit. This requires the maker of the statement to know that it is false or at least to be reckless as to its truth. An honest, even if wholly unreasonable, belief in the truth of the statement will not amount to deceit. As we have seen, it was the decision of the House of Lords to this effect in *Derry v Peek*[166] which led to the introduction of the predecessor of the statutory provisions relating to misstatements in prospectuses which we discussed above. In addition, the tort of deceit requires reliance by the recipient on the statement and, further, that the maker of the statement should have intended the recipient to rely on it. These are formidable hurdles to liability.

Since then, however, there have been two significant developments. Section 2(1) of the Misrepresentation Act 1967 introduced a general, statutory, damages remedy for negligent misstatement, where a person is induced[167] to enter into a contract by the misrepresentation. It also reverses the burden of proof. The 1967 Act was in effect a generalisation of the principle contained in the statutory provisions relating to prospectus liability, and will therefore be of use where the misstatement was not contained in a prospectus but in some other document issued in connection with the offer. Nor, unlike the action at common law for negligent misstatement, considered below, does in require an assumption of responsibility on the part of the defendant.

---

164 See para.25–018.

165 *R. v Kylsant* [1932] 1 K.B. 442 CCA.

166 *Derry v Peek* (1889) 14 App. Cas. 337 HL.

167 On inducement see *Edgington v Fitzmaurice* (1885) 29 Ch. D. 459 CA (contract for the purchase of shares induced by a fraudulent misrepresentation). The inducement need not be the predominant reason for contracting. The detailed law on what constitutes a misrepresentation is not discussed here.

However, the generalisation in s.2(1) extends only to misstatements made by a party to the subsequent contract[168] and the section gives a cause of action only to the other party to it, so that it would seem impossible to use it to sue directors or other experts or advisers who are involved in public offers of shares by the company. The company itself may be sued—and often will be a more attractive target—certainly in an offer for subscription or a rights issue or an open offer and perhaps even on an offer for sale, if the bank making the offer can be regarded as the agent of the issuer. Where the subsection applies, it makes the misrepresentor liable as if fraudulent. This had led the Court of Appeal to conclude that the measure of damages under s.2(1) is a tortious, rather than a contractual, one, but that the rules of remoteness are those applicable to actions in deceit, so that the person misled can recover for all losses flowing from the misstatement.[169]

25–039 Because of these limitations on the new statutory cause of action, it can be said that the more significant development in recent times has been the acceptance of liability for negligent misstatement at common law following the decision of the House of Lords in *Hedley Byrne & Co Ltd v Heller & Partners Ltd*.[170] This is a general principle of liability, not confined within the precise words of a statutory formulation, and so capable of being used against directors and advisers as well as the company itself in the case of negligent misstatements in prospectuses and other documents associated with public offers. Nevertheless, the burden of proof is not reversed under the common law rule, so that the FSMA provision will be more attractive where it is available; and in the case of individual defendants it will be necessary to show that they accepted personal responsibility for the statements made.[171]

Finally, as with the statutory claim, the claimants will have to show that the inaccuracy or omission caused them loss. That assessment is likely to be based on the impact on the market price of the securities upon disclosure of the true state of affairs. An investor who sells before the truth comes out may well suffer no loss, whilst the purchaser from the initial investor may have difficulty in showing reliance on the prospectus, if the sale does not occur within a short period after the initial acquisition.[172]

There is also uncertainty, which emerged in the nineteenth century fraud cases, about the range of possible claimants, in particular whether there is a firm rule that only subscribers may sue[173] or whether this is only a presumption, perhaps

---

[168] Or his agent, but even then not so as to make the agent liable but only the principal: *The Skopas* [1983] 1 W.L.R. 857 QBD (Comm). In the case of statements in the prospectus, even by experts, it seems that the company will be prima facie liable for them and that it carries a heavy burden to disassociate itself from them. See *Mair v Rio Grande Rubber Estates Ltd* [1913] A.C. 853 HL; *Re Pacaya Rubber Co* [1914] 1 Ch. 542 CA.

[169] *Royscot Trust v Rogerson* [1991] 2 Q.B. 297 CA. However, in *Smith New Court Securities Ltd v Scrimgeour Vickers (Asset Management) Ltd* [1997] A.C. 254 HL, a case of deceit, where the consequences of adopting the fraud measure were particularly onerous for the defendant, the House of Lords refused to commit themselves to acceptance of the proposition laid down in the *Royscot Trust* case.

[170] *Hedley Byrne & Co Ltd v Heller & Partners Ltd* [1964] A.C. 465.

[171] Though the provisions of PRR 5.3 (see para.25–036) will be useful here, if only by analogy.

[172] These issues are discussed further at paras 27–025 onwards.

[173] As suggested by *Peek v Gurney* (1873) L.R. 6 H.L. 377 HL.

not a very strong one, capable of being rebutted on the facts.[174] The issue continues to trouble modern judges. In *Al-Nakib Investments Ltd v Longcroft*[175] it was held that allegedly misleading statements in a prospectus issued in connection with a rights issue could form the basis of a claim by a shareholder who took up his rights in reliance upon the prospectus but not when the (same) shareholder purchased further shares on the market. By contrast, in *Possfund Custodian Trustees Ltd v Diamond*[176] the judge refused to strike out a claim that an additional and intended purpose of a prospectus issued in connection with a placing of securities was to inform and encourage purchasers in the aftermarket, so that such purchaser could sue in respect of misstatements. Drawing a distinction between subscribers and market purchasers in the immediate period after dealings commence is, in commercial terms, highly artificial. Companies have an interest not only in the issue being fully subscribed but also in a healthy aftermarket developing so that subscribers can easily dispose of their shares, if they so wish.[177] The statutory provisions on liability for misstatements recognise the force of this argument. Perhaps the way forward in the common law would be for the courts to take a more inclusive view of the issuer's purposes.

Rescission

The common law has traditionally permitted rescission (i.e. reversal) of contracts entered into as a result of a misrepresentation, whether that misrepresentation be fraudulent, negligent or wholly innocent, In the last case, no damages remedy is available on the bases discussed above, but, even where it is, rescission is a potentially useful supplement. In many cases, all the investor may wish or need to do is to return the securities and recover his or her money; and the investor may still claim damages on one of the above bases if rescission does not provide a complete remedy. However, there are two significant limitations on its use. First, s.2(2) of the Misrepresentation Act 1967 gives the court a discretion in substitute damages for rescission, a provision included largely for the benefit of misrepresentors.[178] This subsection might be invoked, for example, where the **25–040**

[174] As suggested by *Andrews v Mockford* [1892] 2 Q.B. 372 CA, where the jury were held to be entitled to conclude that the false prospectus was only one of a series of false statements made by the defendants, whose purpose was not simply to induce subscriptions but also to encourage purchases in the market when dealings began.

[175] *Al-Nakib Investments Ltd v Longcroft* [1990] 1 W.L.R. 1390 Ch D.

[176] *Possfund Custodian Trustees Ltd v Diamond* [1996] 1 W.L.R. 1351 Ch D. At the time the relevant provisions of the companies legislation conferred a statutory entitlement to compensation only upon subscribers.

[177] "The issue of a prospectus establishes a basis for valuation of the securities and underpins the development of a market in them, irrespective of the precise circumstances of the initial offer": DTI, *Listing Particulars and Public Offer Prospectuses: Consultative Document* (July 1990), para.10.

[178] This provision would benefit misrepresentees if the court's power to award damages under s.2(2) were not limited to situations where the misrepresentee still had the right to rescind, thus opening up the possibility of damages under the statute for non-negligent misstatements. Although much debated in first instance decisions, the answer appears to be that the damages remedy is not so widely available: *Salt v Stratstone Specialist Ltd* [2015] EWCA Civ 745.

court thought that the rescission was motivated by subsequent adverse movements in the stock market as a whole rather than the impact of the misrepresentation as such.

Secondly, and more important, the right to rescind expires in practice much more quickly than the right to damages, which is subject only to a long limitation period. By contrast, the right to rescind is quickly "barred". If, after the truth has been discovered, an investor accepts dividends, attends and votes at meetings or sells or attempts to sell the securities, the contract will be taken to have been affirmed,[179] and even mere delay may defeat the right to rescind. The reason for this strictness is that the company may well have secured loans from third parties who have acted on the basis of the capital apparently raised by the company, which the rescission of the shareholder's contract would undermine. A rescission claim is also defeated by the liquidation of the company (at which point the creditors' rights crystallise), or even perhaps by its becoming insolvent but before winding up commences,[180] so that the shareholder must have issued a writ or actually had his name removed from the register before that event occurs.[181] Finally, inability to make restitutio in integrum will bar rescission, though in the case of shares that principle would seem to be relevant mainly where the shareholder has disposed of the securities before discovering that a misrepresentation has been made.[182]

Breach of contract

25–041 Finally, it not uncommonly occurs that the courts, applying the general law of contract, treat a misrepresentation as having been incorporated into the subsequent contract concluded between the parties. The advantage of establishing this would be that the misrepresentee would have a claim to damages to be assessed on the contractual basis, rather than on a tortious basis as is the position with claims based on the statutory prospectus provisions, the Misrepresentation Act or, of course, the *Hedley Byrne* principle. In particular, the shareholder might be able to claim for the loss of the expected profit on the shares. However, it has to be said that prospectuses normally stop short of making explicit promises about the future value or performance of the company, so that finding an enforceable promise in the prospectus may be difficult—unless it be a generalised promise that the statements in the prospectus are true.

---

179 *Sharpley v Louth and East Coast Railway Co* (1876) 2 Ch. D. 663 CA; *Scholey v Central Railway of Venezuela* (1869–70) L.R. 9 Eq. 266 Lord Chancellor; *Crawley's Case* (1869) L.R. 4 Ch. App. 322.

180 *Tennent v The City of Glasgow Bank* (1879) 4 App. Cas. 615 HL.

181 *Oakes v Turquand* (1867) L.R. 2 H.L. 325 HL; *Re Scottish Petroleum Co* (1883) 23 Ch. D. 413 CA. Whether this would apply in the case of rescission as against a transferor (rather than the company) is less clear, but the liquidator's consent would be needed for the re-transfer: IA 1986 s.88.

182 Even in this context one should note the dictum of Lord Browne-Wilkinson in *Smith New Court Securities Ltd v Scrimgeour Vickers (Asset Management) Ltd* [1996] 4 All E.R. 769 HL at 774: "if the current law in fact provides that there is no right to rescind the contract for the sale of quoted shares once the specific shares purchased have been sold, the law will need to be carefully looked at hereafter. Since in such a case other, identical shares can be purchased on the market, the defrauded purchaser can offer substantial *restitutio in integrum* which is normally sufficient". However, this comment was made in the context of a purchase from a shareholder, not a subscription to shares issued by the company.

Criminal and regulatory sanctions

Criminal sanctions play a rather limited role in the area of public offers, but it is to be noted that the central obligation in this area—not to make a public offer of securities or to request admission of securities to a regulated market unless an approved prospectus has been made publicly available—is supported not only by civil but also by criminal sanctions.[183] The principal non-civil sanctions, however, are regulatory ones in the hands of the FCA, which also has power to invoke the criminal law just mentioned.[184] The FCA's sanctions vary considerably according to whether or not the breach of the rules is discovered before or after the public offer or introduction has been completed. **25–042**

Ex ante controls

The FCA has two veto powers relevant to the public offering process. It must refuse admission to listing where the applicant does not meet the eligibility requirements and in certain other cases.[185] The decision must be taken by the Authority normally within six months of the application and failure to do so may be treated by the applicant as a refusal to admit. If the FCA proposes not to accept an application for listing, it must give the applicant a "warning notice", giving the applicant a reasonable period within which to make representations, and if the proposal is confirmed, a decision notice, on the basis of which the matter may be referred to the Upper Tribunal.[186] Secondly, the FCA must not approve a prospectus or an application for admission if it does not contain the required information or other breaches of the applicable rules are detected.[187] This second power provides the force behind the verification process described above,[188] and they are both potentially significant enforcement powers, though, as suggested above, it is probably easier for the FCA to determine whether the eligibility criteria for listing have been met than to make a comprehensive determination at the vetting stage whether the prospectus contains any misrepresentations or omission. **25–043**

It may happen that a defect in the application for admission or for approval of the prospectus is discovered only after approval has been given by the FCA. If the FCA is then to change its mind, it is crucial that it do so quickly, for once public trading has begun, any withdrawal of approval may leave investors

---

[183] FSMA 2000 s.85(3): on indictment the maximum penalty is a prison term of not more than two years or a fine or both.

[184] FSMA 2000 s.401.

[185] FSMA 2000 s.75(4). See para.25–016. Other cases include issues of securities by private companies (s.75(3) and FSMA 2000 (Official Listing of Securities) Regulations 2001 (SI 2001/2956) reg.3), securities already listed in another state where the issuer is in breach of those listing rules (s.75(6)) and where the issuer does not consent to the application (s.75(2) for example, where there is an application for listing by a shareholder of shares already in issue).

[186] FSMA 2000 s.76. The warning notice procedure is laid down in s.387 of FSMA 2000 and fleshed out in the following provisions of Pt XXVI of the Act. Appeal from the Tribunal lies on a point of law to the Court of Appeal or Court of Session.

[187] FSMA 2000 ss.87A and 75(4). For prospectus refusals a similar notification procedure is required as for admission applications (s.87D).

[188] At para.25–029.

holding an illiquid security. Here we near or even cross the line between ex ante and ex post remedies. There is probably slightly greater scope in the case of a prospectus for withdrawal of approval without this adverse outcome, since approval of a prospectus necessarily precedes the opening of the public offer period and the offer period will expire before (formal) trading in the securities begins. Thus, even after approval of the prospectus, the FCA has power to suspend the offer for a period of up to 10 days, if it has reasonable grounds for suspecting that a provision of Pt VI of FSMA (the relevant Part for most of the sections considered in this chapter), the PRR or the PReg has been infringed. During that period the offeror may also be required not to advertise the securities. Going further, if it finds that such a provision has been infringed or even if it has reasonable grounds for suspecting that such infringement is likely, it may require the offer to be withdrawn.[189] These powers may be exercised with immediate effect or upon notice, giving the offeror the opportunity to make representations to the FCA, but in either case the issuer may appeal the decision to the Upper Tribunal.[190]

Somewhat similar powers exist even in the more difficult case of admission to trading. Where admission has not yet occurred, and the FCA has reasonable grounds for suspecting an infringement, it may require the application for admission to be suspended for up to ten days and advertising to cease.[191] More striking is that the FCA has powers of intervention even after admission to trading, subject to procedural safeguards and appeal to the Tribunal.[192] If it has reasonable grounds for suspecting an infringement, it may instruct the market operator to suspend trading for a period of up to ten days and require the suspension of advertisements for the security during this period.[193] If it finds an infringement, it may require the market operator to prohibit trading.[194] These are draconian powers, likely to be exercised only infrequently. If all else fails, the FCA, on its own initiative and with immediate effect,[195] has a general power to discontinue listing "if it is satisfied that there are special circumstances which preclude normal regular dealings in them".[196] One implication of the above rules is that the admission of a company to trading on the basis of an incomplete or inaccurate prospectus or in breach of the admission requirements does not render

[189] FSMA 2000 ss.87K. In the case of admission to trading, there is no withdrawal power where the FCA concludes only that it is likely a requirement will be infringed. This is presumably because of the adverse impact of ending trading on those who have invested in the company's securities, whereas if an offer is withdrawn, the securities on offer are simply not taken up.

[190] FSMA 2000 s.87O. However, the shareholder has no right of appeal, nor even to be consulted by the Authority before the decision is taken, even though his or her financial position is crucially affected. In *R. v International Stock Exchange Ex p. Else (1982) Ltd* [1993] Q.B. 534 CA it was held that the EU Directives did not require that access to the courts be granted to the shareholders. The Court was influenced by the argument that to decide otherwise would enormously slow down decision-taking by the competent authority.

[191] FSMA 2000 s.87L(2).

[192] FSMA 2000 s.87O.

[193] FSMA 2000 s.87L(3).

[194] FSMA 2000 s.87L(4). Parallel powers exist in relation to MTF: s.87LA.

[195] FSMA 2000 s.78(1). The FCA may also proceed by giving notice to the issuer, which it is likely to do in less urgent cases.

[196] FSMA 2000 s.77(1). A more common use of this power is where the "free float" has fallen below 25% (para.25–016) and is not likely to return to that level in the near future (LR 5.2.2). At this point

the admission or the offer ineffective or void. The burden is on the FCA to take action to remedy the situation or not to do so.

Ex post sanctions

The sanctions discussed in the previous paragraph can be applied effectively only to breaches of the rules which the FCA picks up in advance of or shortly after completion of listing, the public offer or admission to trading. The FCA will obviously be reluctant to use its powers to prohibit trading once admission has been secured, and cannot reverse a public offer which has been carried through to the point of the allotment of securities. Furthermore, it can be said that the regulatory sanctions considered so far impose costs on the issuer (i.e. its shareholders) rather than on the officers of the company who may be those responsible for the non-compliance. It is therefore of some significance that the FCA has the power to impose monetary penalties where there has been a breach of Pt VI of the FSMA 2000 or the prospectus or listing rules.[197] The FCA may impose a penalty of such amount as it considers appropriate on the corporate bodies involved, which does not help the new investors. Significantly, however, this penalty-imposing power extends to any person who was a director of the company where the director was "knowingly concerned" in the contravention.[198] The FCA may engage in public censure in lieu of imposing a penalty.[199] In the case of suspected breaches of Pt VI of the FSMA 2000 or of the PRR or LR the FCA also has formal investigatory powers which may help it to uncover the truth.[200] **25–044**

This penalty-imposing power is naturally surrounded by some safeguards. The FCA is required to develop outside the context of a particular case a policy about the circumstances in which it will exercise its powers and the amount of the penalty it will impose.[201] A proposal to impose a penalty must be communicated to the person in question by means of a "warning notice", giving at least 14 days for representations to be made, and a decision to impose a penalty may be appealed to the Tribunal.[202]

---

we have moved into the more general area of the FCA's powers to suspend or cancel listing for reasons unrelated to non-compliance with the prospectus or admission rules, with which this chapter is not concerned.

197 FSMA 2000 s.91(1) and (1A). Section 91(1) includes breaches of the listing rules other than at the public offer stage, as we shall see in the next chapter. It will be recalled that an FCA penalty is one of the matters against which a company may not agree in advance to indemnify the director: para.10–124.

198 FSMA 2000 s.91(2). Since 2012 sponsors are also subject to FCA disciplinary powers: s.88A.

199 FSMA 2000 s.91(3). See also s.87M.

200 FSMA 2000 s.97 and Pt XI. The investigatory powers are not confined to authorised persons, as they normally are under Pt XI.

201 FSMA 2000 s.93. See FCA, *Decision Procedure and Penalties Manual*, Ch.6.

202 FSMA 2000 s.92 and s.387 on warning notices.

CROSS-BORDER OFFERS AND ADMISSIONS

25–045 The EU's strong drive to remove obstacles to cross-border offers and admissions to regulated markets led to the move from a Directive to a Regulation for prospectuses. The notion was that an issuer should be able to use the same documentation (subject in some cases to translation requirements) when it makes an offer or seeks admission to trading in more than one Member State. This is sometimes referred a "passporting" the prospectus or admission. As the PReg puts it, "the prospectus approved by the home Member State and any supplements thereto shall be valid for the offer to the public or the admission to trading in any number of host Member States."[203] With the UK's exit from the EU, the passport provisions of PReg no longer benefit issuers in or from the UK and indeed the whole of relevant chapter of the PReg (Ch.V) has been removed from the version of the Regulation retained in the UK.

The question remains, however, of how prospectuses approved by the UK regulator can be used in the EU (if at all) and, equally, how prospectus approved by an EU regulator can be used (if at all) in the UK. It is clearly the case than an issuer could draw up a prospectus which meets the requirements of each of the states in which it wishes to make a public offer and obtain approval for the prospectus in each of those states. The purpose of passporting is to reduce those costs by requiring something close to a single approval. Without passporting, is there any other mechanism for reducing the costs of cross-border offers? In fact, the EU prospectus rules have long contained provisions on prospectuses approved by regulators in third countries (Ch.VI), which is what the UK has become. The core rule is that a regulator in an EU state can approve a prospectus drawn up under the third country's laws for use within that state (and thus the EU as a whole), provided (1) the third country's information rules are equivalent to those of the PReg; and (2) cooperation arrangements have been agreed with the supervisory authorities of the third country.[204] The EU regulator in question is the competent authority of the state in which the third country issuer first offers its shares to the public or seeks admission to trading (the "home" state).[205] The retained version of the PReg has been amended so as to mirror this provision in relation to the use prospectuses approved by an EU national regulator in the UK.[206]

This may seem straightforward in the case of the use of UK-approved prospectuses in the EU and vice versa. Since the UK's disclosure rules for prospectuses are, to all intents and purposes, those of the EU, the first condition should be easily satisfied in relation to both outgoing and incoming prospectuses. As to the second, the retained version of art.29 of the PReg gives the FCA power to enter into cooperation agreements with EU regulators, just as EU regulators have power under that article to enter into cooperation agreements with the FCA. However, further analysis of art.29 shows that the decision is not so much the decision of the national regulator as of the Commission. The Commission's

[203] PReg art.24. This article is headed: "Union scope of approvals of prospectuses".

[204] PReg art.29.

[205] PReg art.2(m)(iii)—the rule is slightly different for "heavyweight" debt securities.

[206] The Prospectus (Amendment etc.) (EU Exit) Regulations 2019 (SI 2019/1234) reg.54.

power to adopt equivalence criteria through delegated legislation and to "adopt an implementing decision stating that the information requirements imposed by the national law of a third country are equivalent to the requirements under this Regulation" in effect shifts the decision into the hands of the Commission. The decision at that level is as likely to be political as legal. This leaves a third country issuer only with the possibility of proceeding under art.28, which is basic solution mentioned above, i.e. to obtain approval directly from the home state regulator under the provisions of the PReg as it applies in the EU. The language requirements of the PReg[207] and the practices of EU national regulators are probably flexible enough to minimise the need for translation. So long as the UK prospectus requirements track those of the PReg, this "workaround" may be sustainable, but it will come under strain if the UK and EU requirements begin to diverge.

DE-LISTING

This chapter has focused on the processes by which the securities of a company become publicly held and traded on a public market. Whilst a completed public offering cannot easily be reversed,[208] admission to trading is a reversible process. Companies may seek voluntarily to retire from a market upon which their securities are traded, notably after a successful takeover bid (discussed in Ch.28), as a result of which the majority of its shares are held by the bidder. If the securities of the company are all held by one person as a result of the bid, this is a straightforward exercise. If, however, there are some outside shareholders, they may oppose the proposal to de-list because it will reduce the liquidity of the securities even further. Indeed, the proposal to de-list may be part of an attempt by the controllers of the company to squeeze out the minority in a situation where the statutory squeeze-out provisions (also discussed in Ch.28) would not operate. The requirement previously was that companies simply inform their shareholders of the decision to de-list, but the LR now require requests from companies with a premium listing for the cancellation of a primary listing of equity shares to be approved by a three-quarters majority at a meeting of the class of shareholders in question and, where there is a controlling shareholder, a majority of the non-controlling shares, after the circulation to them of a statement, approved by the FCA, of the reasons for this step.[209] This is a significant increase in minority shareholder protection and should increase the willingness of investors to take minority stakes in companies that are controlled by a single investor or are likely to become so. The AIM rules also require a three-quarters majority for cancellation of a company's admission to that market, but without any special provisions about controlling shareholders.[210] **25–046**

[207] PReg art.27.

[208] See the constraints on companies' acquisition of their own shares discussed in Ch.17.

[209] LR 5.2.5. There are certain exceptions to the requirement for shareholder approval, for example, if the company is in severe financial difficulties or the controller has reached a 75% holding as a result of a takeover bid in which the offer document made clear the offeror's intention to de-list.

[210] See fn.66, r.41.

CONCLUSION

25–047 Despite the valiant efforts of EU law in relation to the summary, it is overwhelmingly likely that professional investors and analysts acting on their behalf are the main consumers of prospectuses. Retail investors benefit from the efforts of the analysts indirectly, for example, because of professional investors' influence on the price which the issuer asks in the offer for its securities, which is in turn based on professional investors' reaction to the prospectus. Indeed, the function of analysts in pricing can be said to justify the substantial subsidy the prospectus rules provide to analysts. The company provides on a plate to analysts information which they might otherwise have to work hard to assemble or might have to pay for. There is no reason why the law should promote the private interests of analysts, but it can be said to be legitimate for the law to do so as a way of improving the allocative efficiency of the securities markets.

CHAPTER 26

TRANSFERS OF SHARES

Once shares have been issued by the company, it is only infrequently that the company will buy them back. Moreover, this cannot happen without the company's consent, either at the time the shares were issued (as with shares which are issued as redeemable at the option fof the shareholder)[1] or at the time of re-acquisition (as in the case of shares redeemable at the option of the company or a re-purchase of shares).[2] In any event, the re-acquisition cannot occur unless the rules on capital maintenance, imposed for the benefit of creditors, are observed.[3] Although companies occasionally use surplus cash to re-purchase shares rather than to pay a dividend, a shareholder who wishes to realise his or her investment in the company will normally have to find, or wait for, another investor who will purchase the shares and take the shareholder's place in the company. This is precisely the reason why a company which secures the admission of its shares to a public market is likely to find it easier to persuade investors to buy the shares in the first place. 26–001

Although the above principle is true of all types of company, there is a major difference between companies with large and fluctuating bodies of shareholders whose shares are traded on a public exchange ("listed" companies) and companies with small bodies of shareholders whose composition is expected to be stable and where the allocation of shares is as much about the allocation of control in the company as it is about its financing ("non-listed" companies). In

---

[1] See para.17–007.

[2] See para.17–007.

[3] See paras 17–011 onwards.

the former case, the law or the rules of the exchange will require the shares to be freely tradable as far as the issuer is concerned,[4] so that except in a few cases the transfer of the shares will be simply a matter between the existing shareholder and the potential investor. Free transferability tends to be taken for granted in listed companies, but it does become controversial when what is proposed is the wholesale transfer of the shares to a single person, in the shape of a takeover bidder, because in that situation, even in an open company, the transfer of the shares has clear implications for the control of the company. We shall examine takeovers in the following Ch.28.

In non-listed companies, by contrast, even the transfer of shares by a single shareholder may have implications for the control of the company and often also for its management, since a shareholding in such a company may be perceived as giving rise to a formal or informal entitlement to membership of the board of directors and participation in the management of the company.[5] In those companies, therefore, it is common for the articles of association to contain some restrictions on the transferability of the shares, perhaps by making transfers subject to the permission of the board or requiring the shares to be offered initially to the other shareholders before they can be sold outside the existing shareholder body. The latter obligation is normally referred to as giving the other shareholders pre-emption rights, but these are pre-emption rights arising on transfer and are to be distinguished from pre-emption rights arising on issuance, which are discussed in Ch.24. The latter bind the company; the former the selling shareholder.

26–002 Share transfers involve a two-step process. In the first step the buyer and the seller conclude a sales contract where they agree on the price which the shares are sold for and on other terms of the transaction. Bankers sometimes refer to this first step as "trading". In the second step the transfer is carried out. At the end of the second step the buyer becomes the owner of the shares that formed part of the sales transaction. This second step is sometimes referred to as "settlement". Settlement is a process which in itself consists of two or more stages depending on whether certificated or uncertificated shares are sold.

When shares in private companies and non-listed public companies are sold the buyer and the seller frequently know each other's identity and are often personally involved in negotiating the terms of the transaction. Sales transactions are completed by way of delivery of certain transfer documents from the seller to the buyer and by way of registering the buyer's name on the shareholder register.

When listed shares are sold, the transaction is frequently more standardised. In most cases, the seller does not go out to find a buyer him- or herself, but enlists the services of a broker who sells the shares for him or her. The broker does this either through the electronic trading system operated by a stock exchange or by making a contract with another financial services provider directly. In both cases buyer and seller rarely know each other's identity. After the contract has been concluded, the buyer's name is also entered on the shareholder register, but this settlement process is carried out electronically through a settlement system known as CREST.

[4] Listing Rules LR 2.2.4 as of January 2021.

[5] In the case of an informal entitlement, it may be protected by the unfair prejudice remedy: Ch.14.

In this chapter we will focus on the second step of the transfer process, the completion of the sales transaction. We shall examine the difference between certificated and uncertificated shares, transfers of certificated and transfers of uncertificated shares as well as the rules governing the shareholder register and transmission of shares by operation of law. We shall first address the difference between uncertificated and certificated shares.

CERTIFICATED AND UNCERTIFICATED SHARES

In the UK, shares are predominantly issued in registered form. Companies issuing registered shares keep a register of the names of their shareholders. Until 1996 all registered shares were issued in what is now called the "certificated form". This means that, in addition to having his or her name noted on the shareholder register, every shareholder receives a paper certificate evidencing his or her shareholding. When shares are transferred the seller completes and signs a transfer form and delivers this together with the share certificate to the buyer. The buyer then lodges the certificate with the company to have his or her name entered on its shareholder register. **26–003**

This paper-based transfer process still applies to non-listed shares. These are shares in private companies and shares in public companies which are not listed on the London Stock Exchange (LSE).

Until 1996 listed shares were also transferred by means of paper documents. The LSE operated a transfer system entitled TALISMAN. Under the TALISMAN regime, the LSE received transfer forms and share certificates from buyers and ensured that the sellers' names would be registered on the shareholder register. There was a gap of two to three weeks between trading and settlement. If shares were sold in the meantime, TALISMAN would keep track of that transaction and arrange for the name of the ultimate buyer to be registered.

In the years leading up to the introduction of CREST in 1996, the UK privatised a large number of previously state-owned enterprises. The number of listed shares and with that the number of share transactions increased significantly. When share prices fell sharply on 19 October 1987, trading volumes soared and substantial delays in settlement occurred. Delays in settlement pose a significant risk to a share market. The longer the delay between trading and settlement the greater the risk that parties suffer loss by transactions not completing successfully. In many cases, the law will provide remedies if the transaction comes to a halt part way through, but the enforcement of those rights will be expensive and in some cases, for example, in the insolvency of an involved party, the rights may not have any value.

In the discussion following the 1987 market crash, it became apparent that the paper-based transfer process was unable to cope with large volumes of share transactions. It was decided that paper transfers should be phased out for listed shares and that a new electronic share transfer system should be introduced. This process of replacing paper with electronic shares transfers is referred to as dematerialisation. Listed shares were dematerialised in the UK in 1996 when the CREST system went live. Since then, all UK shares listed on the LSE must be **26–004** compatible with electronic settlement.[6] CREST operates on the basis of ss.784–790 of the CA 2006 and of the Uncertificated Securities Regulations 2001 (USR 2001).[7] These Regulations have termed electronic shares as uncertificated shares and paper shares as certificated shares.[8]

The introduction of uncertificated shares requires the consent of a number of parties. CRESTCo, as the operator of the electronic system, must agree to admit the securities of the company in question to the system, though it clearly has a strong commercial incentive to do so, if the shares are heavily traded. Moreover, since an operator of an electronic system of share-holding and transfer requires the approval of the Treasury and that approval requires the operator's rules not to distort competition,[9] it will not be in a position to set rules which discriminate improperly among companies.

In addition, the company itself must agree to permit its securities to be held in uncertificated form. Shares or individual classes of shares are in principle admissible to the electronic system only where the holding of shares in uncertificated form and their transfer electronically is permitted by the company's constitution.[10] The standard constitution requires the company to issue shareholders with a certificate of their holding.[11] To facilitate the change-over to uncertificated shares, USR 2001 reg.16 permits such provisions in the articles to be disapplied by resolution of the directors, rather than by the normal route for altering the articles by resolution of the shareholders,[12] provided the shareholders are given prior or subsequent notice of the directors' resolution. The Regulations then provide that the shareholders by ordinary resolution may vote to overturn the directors' resolution, but, unless they do so, the articles will be modified pro tanto without the shareholders' positive approval. Thus, the Regulations encourage uncertificated shares by putting the burden of objection on the shareholders.

Shareholders can opt to have uncertificated shares converted into certificated shares. If a shareholders exercises this option conversion is recorded on the central CREST register, the company is notified, updates the register and issues the shareholders with a share certificate.[13] The EU's Central Securities Depositary Regulation requires that all securities that are transferable on a regulated market be issued in book entry form.[14] This requirement will come into force on 1 January 2023 by which point Member States will have to remove any option to convert shares into certificated form for those shares which are transferable on regulated markets.[15] The Chancellor announced on 23 June 2020 that the UK will not adopt the settlement discipline regime, which came into

[6] Listing Rules LR 6.1.23–6.1.24.

[7] USR 2001 (SI 2001/3755).

[8] Certificated and uncertificated shares do not constitute separate classes of shares (*Re Randall ad Quilter Investment Holdings Plc* [2013] EWHC 4357 (Ch)).

[9] USR 2001 Sch.1.

[10] USR 2001 reg.15.

[11] The Companies (Model Articles) Regulations 2008 (SI 2008/3229) Sch.1 art.24 and Sch.3 art.46.

[12] CA 2006 s.21.

[13] USR 2001 reg.28.

[14] Regulation 909/2014 on improving securities settlement in the EU and on central securities depositaries (CSDs) [2014] OJ L257/1 (CSDR) art.3(1).

[15] CSDR art.76(2).

force in the EU in February 2021, contained in the Regulation.[16] No announcement has been made in relation to other elements of the Regulation.

Having briefly looked at the characteristics of certificated and uncertificated shares in this section, we shall examine transfers of certificated shares in the following section. After that transfers of uncertificated shares will be addressed.

TRANSFERS OF CERTIFICATED SHARES

Legal ownership

To transfer certificated shares, the seller needs to complete a transfer form and deliver that form together with the share certificate to the buyer. The transfer form needs to comply either with the requirements contained in the company's constitution or with the simplified requirements put in place by the Stock Transfer Act.[17] **26–005**

This, however, is not enough to make the transferee a member of the company. Neither the agreement to transfer nor the delivery of the signed transfer form and share certificate will pass legal title to the transferee (though it may pass an equitable interest in the shares to the transferee).[18] The normal rule is that a person becomes a member of a company and the legal owner of the shares when they have agreed to this and their name has been entered into the company's register of members. The company enters the transferee's name on the register of members in place of the transferor's name.[19] It is precisely this requirement which gives a closed company the opportunity to control the process of transfer of shares to new holders.

It also follows from this analysis that a share certificate is not a negotiable instrument. Legal title does not pass by mere delivery of the certificate to the transferee but upon registration of the transferee by the company. In fact, even registration is not conclusive of the transferee's legal title. Section 127 provides that the register of members is only "prima facie evidence" of matters directed or authorised to be inserted in it and s.768 correspondingly says that a share certificate issued by the company (for example, to the transferee) is "prima facie evidence" of the transferee's title to the shares.[20] Where there is a conflict

[16] Written statement by Rishi Sunak on 23 June 2020 available at: *https://questions-statements.parliament.uk/written-statements/detail/2020-06-23/HCWS309* [Accessed 26 March 2021].

[17] CA 2006 s.770(1); Stock Transfer Act 1963.

[18] See para.26–008.

[19] And, it seems, what then occurs is a novation (i.e. the relationship between the company and the transferor is ended and is replaced by a new relationship between the company and the transferee) rather than an assignment of the transferor's rights to the transferee (*Ashby v Blackwell* (1765) 2 Eden 299 at 302–303; 28 E.R. 913 (Ct of Chancery) at 914; *Simm v Anglo-American Telegraph Co* (1879) 5 Q.B.D. 188 CA at 204; E. Micheler, "Legal Title and the Transfer of Shares in a Paperless World—Farewell Quasi-Negotiability" [2002] J.B.L 358). If this is the rule, it is favourable to transferees, for in general on assignment the assignee is in no better position than was the assignor.

[20] Or in Scotland "sufficient evidence unless the contrary is shown". It is not thought that the reference in s.768 to a certificate "under the common seal of the company" requires the use of the common seal, if it instead uses an official seal which is a facsimile of its common seal (see s.50) or has the certificate signed by two directors or one director and the secretary (see s.44). Section 768(2) makes the position clear for Scotland.

between the register and the certificate, the former is stronger prima facie evidence than the latter but neither is decisive. Ownership of the shares depends on who is entitled to be registered. Suppose, say, that A, who is registered and is entitled to be registered, loses his certificate, obtains a duplicate from the company[21] and transfers to B who is registered by the company. Subsequently A finds the original certificate and, either because he has forgotten about the sale to B or because he is a rogue, then purports to sell the shares to C. The company will rightly refuse to register C whose only remedy will be against A (who may by this time be a man-of-straw).

More importantly, suppose D loses the certificate to E, a rogue, who forges D's signature and secures entry on the register in place of D. D will nevertheless be entitled to have the register rectified[22] so as to restore D's name, because D is still the holder of the legal title to the shares and so is entitled to be entered on the register. This appears to be so, even if D's conduct has been such as to provide the opportunity for E to commit the fraud, for example because D had deposited the certificate with E.[23] Furthermore, D will be entitled to insist on rectification if, as is all too likely, E has made a further transfer of the shares to a wholly innocent third party, F, who is registered before D learns of the fraud. D may still rectify the register against F. This system of rules provides a high level of protection of D's legal rights, but is hardly conducive to the free circulation of shares.

Estoppel

26–006 However, the position of people such as F is ameliorated by the doctrine of estoppel by share certificate, which may give F a right to an indemnity against the company, if D insists on rectification of the register. In other words, the risk of fraud (or other unauthorised transfer) falls on the company, which is perhaps defensible on the grounds that it is the company which benefits from legal rules which encourage the free circulation of shares.[24] The doctrine of estoppel by share certificate produces what has been termed "quasi-negotiability".[25]

A share certificate contains two statements on which the company knows that reliance may be placed. The first is the extent to which the shares to which it relates are paid up. The second is that the person named in it was registered as the

[21] Companies do this readily enough so long as the registered holder makes a statutory declaration regarding the loss and supplies the company with a bank indemnity against any liability it may incur.
[22] On rectification, see para.26–019.
[23] *Welch v Bank of England* [1955] Ch. 508 Ch D; *Simm v Anglo-American Telegraph Co* (1879) 5 Q.B.D. 188.
[24] The company may in turn be entitled to an indemnity from the person who asked it to register the transfer which led to the issuance by the company of the misleading certificate. An indemnity against the fraudster is likely to be worthless, but the entitlement embraces also the broker who acted on behalf of the fraudster, who may well be worth suing. See *Royal Bank of Scotland Plc v Sandstone Properties Plc* [1998] 2 B.C.L.C. 429 QBD, where the earlier cases are reviewed. Presumably, the rationale for the company's entitlement is that the broker is in a better position to detect unauthorised transfers than is the company. No liability arises, however, if the broker who instructed the issuer to amend the register did so in reliance on genuine but inaccurate share certificates issued by the issuer or its registrar (*Cadbury Schweppes Plc v Halifax Share Dealing Ltd* [2007] 1 B.C.L.C 497 Ch D).
[25] E. Micheler, "Farewell to Quasi-negotiability? Legal Title and Transfer of Shares in a Paperless World" [2002] J.B.L. 358.

holder of the stated number of shares. The company may be estopped from denying either statement if someone in reliance upon it has changed his position to his detriment. This may afford a transferee who, in reliance on the transferor's share certificate, has bought what he believed, wrongly, to be fully paid shares a defence if the company makes a call upon him.[26] The company will also be estopped if the transferee has relied on a false statement in his transferor's certificate that the transferor was the registered holder of the shares on the date stated in the certificate.[27] Thus, F, the transferee from the rogue, will be entitled to an indemnity from the company if the company rectifies the register in favour of D, the legal owner, because F will have relied upon the certificate issued by the company to the rogue.

However, this argument will rarely[28] benefit an original recipient of the incorrect certificate because receipt of the certificate normally marks the conclusion of the transaction and is not something which was relied on in deciding to enter into it. In the example above, E, the rogue, is the original recipient of the incorrect certificate and we need have no regrets about the weakness of E's legal position. However, suppose E, instead of transferring the shares fraudulently into his own name and then disposing of them to F, in fact, as is all too likely, short-circuited this procedure by transferring them directly to F, and the company then issued a new certificate to F. F could not claim to have relied on the new certificate when entering into the transaction which pre-dated its issue. F did rely on the certificate issued to D but E's fraud did not turn on a denial of D's ownership of the shares but rather upon E pretending to be D. In this situation, only a transferee from F would be able to rely on the doctrine of estoppel by share certificate. Perhaps this result may be justified on the basis that D is in a better position to detect E's fraud than is the company.

Restrictions on transferability

The directors of non-listed companies are frequently empowered by the articles to refuse to register transfers or there will be provisions affording the other members or the company[29] rights of pre-emption, first refusal or even compulsory **26–007**

[26] *Burkinshaw v Nicholls* (1878) 3 App. Cas. 1004 HL; *Bloomenthal v Ford* [1897] A.C. 156 HL. If the reason why the shares were not fully paid up is a contravention of the provisions regarding payment in ss.553 onwards of the Act (see Ch.16 at para.16–022) a bona fide purchaser and those securing title from him will be exempted from liability to pay calls by virtue of ss.588(2) and 605(3) and will not have to rely on estoppel.

[27] *Cadbury Schweppes Plc v Halifax Share Dealing Ltd* [2007] 1 B.C.L.C 497; *Dixon v Kennaway & Co* [1900] 1 Ch. 833 Ch D; *Re Bahia and San Francisco Railway Co* (1867–68) L.R. 3 Q.B. 584 QB. This, in contrast with resisting a call, may seem to be committing the heresy of using estoppel as a sword rather than a shield. The justification is that a purchaser who has bought from the registered owner has a prima facie right to be registered in his place and that the company is estopped from denying that the transferor was the registered owner.

[28] But in exceptional circumstances it may do so: *Balkis Consolidated Co v Tomlinson* [1893] A.C. 396 HL; *Alipour v UOC Corp* [2002] 2 B.C.L.C. 770 (where the holder was even held entitled to be registered as a member, since no innocent party was thereby prejudiced).

[29] Acquisition by the company itself will, of course, be lawful only if it is able to comply with the conditions enabling a company to buy its own shares: see at para.17–008. Less usually, the provision may impose an obligation on other members to buy.

acquisition. This does not apply to listed shares because the Listing Rules require there to be no restrictions of the transfer of shares.[30]

Provisions restricting share transfers require the most careful drafting if they are to achieve their purpose; and have not always received it, thereby facing the courts with difficult questions of interpretation. The following propositions can, it is thought, be extracted from the voluminous case law:

(1) The extent of the restriction is solely a matter of construction of the company's constitution. But, since shareholders have a prima facie right to transfer to whomsoever they please, this right is not to be cut down by uncertain language or doubtful implications.[31] If, therefore, it is not clear whether a restriction applies to any transfer or only to a transfer to, say, a non-member,[32] or to any type of disposition or only to a sale[33] the narrower construction will be adopted.

(2) However, this does not help the courts much when faced with a common provision in the articles that a shareholder "desirous" or "intending" or "proposing" to transfer his or her shares to another must give notice to the company to trigger pre-emption procedures. On the one hand, the provision would be unworkable if the courts had held that as soon as a shareholder formed the relevant intention, the provision in the articles was triggered, especially as the shareholder is normally permitted to withdraw the notice, if he or she does not wish to sell to the person who comes forward to buy the shares. There must be something in addition to the required intention. On the other hand, a shareholder who enters into an agreement with an outsider to sell the shares to that person or to give that person an option to buy them will fall within the provision in the articles, even if the outsider has not completed the agreement (and so has only an equitable interest in the shares) or has not taken up the option to purchase.[34] Drafters have spent much ingenuity on producing agreements which do not fall within the second category and have been rewarded. The courts have held that agreements do not trigger the notice provision if they transfer only the beneficial interest in the shares and entitle the transferee to be registered as the legal owner of the shares only once the pre-emption right has been removed from the articles.[35] The execution of a transfer form and its

[30] Except for any restrictions imposed for failure to comply with a notice under CA 2006 s.793 (notice by company requiring information about interests in its shares): Listing Rules LR 2.2.4.

[31] Greene MR in *Re Smith & Fawcett Ltd* [1942] Ch. 304 CA at 306. See also *Re New Cedos Engineering Co Ltd* [1994] 1 B.C.L.C. 797 Ch D (a case decided in 1975); *Stothers v William Steward (Holdings) Ltd* [1994] 2 B.C.L.C. 266.

[32] *Greenhalgh v Mallard* [1943] 2 All E.R. 234 CA; *Roberts v Letter "T" Estates Ltd* [1961] A.C. 795 PC; see also *Rose v Lynx Express Ltd* [2004] 1 B.C.L.C. 455 CA (Civ Div).

[33] *Moodie v Shepherd (Bookbinders) Ltd* [1949] 2 All E.R. 1044 HL.

[34] *Lyle & Scott Ltd v Scott's Trustees* [1959] A.C. 763 HL; distinguished in *Re Coroin Ltd McKillen v Misland (Cyprus) Investment Ltd* [2013] EWCA Civ 781; [2014] B.C.C. 14.

[35] *Re Sedgefield Steeplechase Co (1927) Ltd, Scotto v Petch* [2000] All E.R. (D) 2442 CA (Lord Hoffmann sat as an additional judge of the Chancery Division, where the previous cases are reviewed); *Theakston v London Trust Plc* (1984) 1 B.C.C. 99095 Ch D; see also *Safeguard Industrial Investments Ltd v National and Westminster Bank Ltd* [1981] 1 W.L.R. 286 Ch D.

deposit with the company's auditor, however, can amount to a transfer which triggers pre-emption rights contained in the company's constitution.[36]

(3) Where the regulations confer a discretion on directors with regard to the acceptance of transfers, this discretion, like all the directors' powers, is a fiduciary one[37] to be exercised bona fide in what they consider—not what the court considers—to be in the interest of the company, and not for any collateral purpose. But the court will presume that they have acted bona fide, and the onus of proof of the contrary is on those alleging it and is not easily discharged.[38]

(4) Prior to the CA 2006 it was possible for the articles of association to stipulate that the directors shall not be bound to state their reasons for not registering a transfer.[39] The CA 2006 now states in s.771 that the company must provide the transferee with such further information about the reasons for the refusal as the transferee may reasonable request. This, however, does not include minutes of the meetings of directors. The CLR hoped that this would make it possible to apply the fiduciary tests and s.994 on unfair prejudice in a transparent way to such refusals.[40]

(5) If, on the true construction of the articles, the directors are entitled to reject only on certain prescribed grounds and it is proven that they have rejected on others, the court will intervene.[41] If the directors state their reasons (as they are now obliged to do) the court will investigate them to the extent of seeing whether they have acted on the right principles and would overrule their decision if they have acted on considerations which should not have weighed with them, but not merely because the court would have come to a different conclusion.[42] If the regulations are so framed as to give the directors an unfettered discretion the court will interfere with it only on proof of bad faith.[43]

---

[36] *Hurst v Crampton Bros (Coopers) Ltd* [2002] EWHC 1375 (Ch); [2003] B.C.C. 190 Ch D; *Re Claygreen Ltd* [2005] EWHC 2032 (Ch); [2006] B.C.C. 440.

[37] For the application of the fiduciary principle to the transfer of shares in the context of takeover bids, see paras 28–032 to 28–035.

[38] In *Re Smith & Fawcett Ltd* [1942] Ch. 304 CA, the directors refused to register but agreed that they would register a transfer of part of the shareholding if the transferor agreed to sell the balance to one of the directors at a stated price. It was held that this was insufficient evidence of bad faith but it might today be "unfairly prejudicial" under s.994; see Ch.14. See also *Village Cay Marina Ltd v Acland* [1998] 2 B.C.L.C. 327 PC.

[39] *Berry & Stewart v Tottenham Hotspur Football Co* [1935] Ch. 718 Ch D; see also *Sutherland v British Dominions Corp* [1926] Ch. 746 Ch D.

[40] Final Report I, paras 7.42–7.45.

[41] *Re Bede Steam Shipping Co* [1917] 1 Ch. 123 Ch D; see also *Village Cay Marina Ltd v Acland (Barclays Bank Plc third party)* [1998] 2 B.C.L.C 327 PC; and *Sutherland v British Dominions Corp* [1926] Ch. 746 CA.

[42] *Re Bede Steam Shipping Co* [1917] 1 Ch. 123; *Re Smith & Fawcett Ltd* [1942] Ch. 304 CA. Indeed, if there are rights of pre-emption at a fair price to be determined by the auditors the court can investigate the adequacy of this price only if the auditors give a "speaking valuation" stating their reasons: *Dean v Prince* [1954] Ch. 409 CA; *Burgess v Purchase & Sons Ltd* [1983] Ch. 216 Ch D.

[43] *Re Smith & Fawcett Ltd* [1942] Ch. 304; *Charles Forte Investments Ltd v Amanda* [1964] Ch. 240 CA; *Village Cay Marina Ltd v Acland (Barclays Bank Plc third party)* [1998] 2 B.C.L.C 327 PC.

(6) If, as is normal, the regulations merely give the directors power to refuse to register, as opposed to making their passing of transfers a condition precedent to registration,[44] the transferee is entitled to be registered unless the directors resolve as a board to reject. Hence in *Moodie v Shepherd (Bookbinders) Ltd*[45] where the two directors disagreed and neither had a casting vote, the House of Lords held that registration must proceed. The directors have a reasonable time in which to come to a decision,[46] but since s.771(1) imposes an obligation on them to give to the transferee notice of rejection within two months of the lodging of the transfer, the maximum reasonable period is two months.[47]

The positions of transferor and transferee prior to registration

26–008 It may be of importance to determine the precise legal position of the transferor and transferee pending registration of the transfer which, if there are restrictions on transferability, may never occur. As we have seen, only if and when the transfer is registered will the transferor cease to be a member and shareholder and the transferee will become a member and shareholder. However, notwithstanding that registration has not occurred, the beneficial interest in the shares may have passed from the transferor to the transferee. In the case of a sale of certificated shares the transaction will normally go through three stages: (1) an agreement (which, particularly if a block of shares conferring de facto or de jure control is being sold, may be a complicated one); (2) delivery of the signed transfer form and the certificate by the seller and payment of the price by the buyer; and (3) registration of the buyer's name on the shareholder register.

Notwithstanding that the transfer is not lodged for registration or registration is refused, the beneficial interest in the shares will, it seems, pass from the seller to the buyer at the latest at stage (2) and, indeed will do so at stage (1) if the agreement is one which the courts would order to be specifically enforced.[48] The seller then becomes a trustee for the buyer and must account to him for any dividends he receives and vote in accordance with his instructions (or appoint

[44] It is common to state that transfers have to be passed by the directors but under normal articles that is not so (the Companies (Model Articles) Regulation 2008 Sch.1 art.26) and in the light of s.771 it is doubtful if the articles could make the directors' approval a condition precedent.

[45] *Moodie v Shepherd (Bookbinders) Ltd* [1949] 2 All E.R. 1044.

[46] *Shepherd's case* (1866–67) L.R. 2 Ch. App. 16 CA in Chancery.

[47] *Re Swaledale Cleaners Ltd* [1968] 1 W.L.R. 1710 CA; *Tett v Phoenix Property and Investment Co Ltd* [1986] B.C.L.C. 149; *Re Inverdeck Ltd* [1998] B.C.C. 256 Ch D. And normally it seems that they will not be treated as acting unreasonably if they take the full two months: *Re Zinotty Properties Ltd* [1984] 1 W.L.R. 1249 Ch D at 1260.

[48] See most recently *Patel v Iqbal* [2020] EWHC 1174 (Ch); the fact that the agreement is subject to fulfilment of a condition beyond the control of the parties will not prevent it from being specifically enforceable, notwithstanding that the condition has not been fulfilled, if the party for whose benefit the condition was inserted is prepared to waive it. In *Wood Preservation Ltd v Prior* [1969] 1 W.L.R. 1077 CA, where the condition was for the benefit of the buyer, the court was prepared to hold that the seller ceased to be "the beneficial owner" on the date of the contract notwithstanding that the buyer did not become the beneficial owner until he later waived the condition. In the interim, beneficial ownership was, apparently, in limbo! See also *Michaels v Harley House (Marylebone)* [1997] 1 W.L.R. 967 Ch D; *Philip Morris Products Inc v Rothmans International Enterprises Ltd* [2001] All E.R. (D) 48 (Jul); *Unidare Plc v Cohen* [2005] EWHC 1410 (Ch); [2006] Ch. 489.

him as his proxy).[49] This, however, begs several questions. The first arises because at stage (2) delivery of the documents may not necessarily be matched by payment of the full price; the agreement may have provided for payment by instalments[50] and the seller will then retain a lien on the shares as an unpaid seller. This will not prevent an equitable interest passing to the buyer but the court will not grant specific performance unless the seller's lien can be fully protected,[51] and until paid in full he is entitled to vote the shares as he thinks will best protect his interest.[52] Instead of being a bare trustee his position is analogous to that of a trustee of a settlement of which he is one of the beneficiaries.

The second begged question is whether the foregoing can apply when the articles provide for rights of pre-emption or first refusal when a shareholder wishes to dispose of his shares. In such a case the transferor (perhaps with the full knowledge of the transferee)[53] has breached the deemed contract under CA 2006 s.33 between him and the company and his fellow shareholders. There are observations of the House of Lords in *Hunter v Hunter*[54] to the effect that accordingly the transfer is wholly void, even as between the transferor and transferee.

However, in later cases[55] courts have refused to follow this and, it must surely be right (at any rate if the price has been paid) that the buyer obtains such rights as the transferor had. This will not benefit the buyer if all the shares are taken up when the transferor is compelled to make a pre-emptive offer, but it does not follow that all of them will be taken up and, if not, the transferee has a better claim to those shares not taken up than has the transferor.

When the transaction is not a sale but a gift, there need be no agreement. Even if there is, it will not be legally enforceable under English law because there will be no valuable consideration and because, under the so-called rule in *Milroy v Lord*,[56] "there is no equity to perfect an imperfect gift". One might have supposed, therefore, that if the donor has chosen to make the gift by handing to the donee a signed transfer and the share certificate, rather than by a formal declaration of trust in favour of the donee, the gift would not be effective unless 26–009

[49] *Hardoon v Belilios* [1901] A.C. 118 PC; distinguished in *Wise v Perpetual Trustee Co* [1903] A.C. 139 PC.

[50] The normal practice then is to provide that the transfer and share certificate shall be held by a stakeholder and not lodged for registration until released to the buyer on payment of the final instalment.

[51] *Langen & Wind Ltd v Bell* [1972] Ch. 685 Ch D; *Prince v Strange* (1978) 36 P. & C.R. 59 CA (Civ Div).

[52] *Musselwhite v Musselwhite & Son Ltd* [1962] Ch. 964 Ch D; *JRRT (Investments) Ltd v Haycraft* [1993] B.C.L.C. 401 Ch D; *Michaels v Harley House (Marylebone)* [1997] 1 W.L.R. 967; *Stablewood v Virdi* [2010] EWCA Civ 865.

[53] As in *Lyle & Scott Ltd v Scott's Trustees* [1959] A.C. 763 HL.

[54] *Hunter v Hunter* [1936] A.C. 222 HL.

[55] *Hawks v McArthur* [1951] 1 All E.R. 22 Ch D; *Tett v Phoenix Property Co* [1986] B.C.L.C. 149, where the Court of Appeal was not required to rule on this point because the appellants did not argue that the decision on it at first instance was wrong. *Re Walls Properties Ltd v PJ Walls Holdings Ltd* [2008] 1 I.R. 732; *Cottrell v King* [2004] EWHC 397 (Ch); [2004] B.C.C. 307; but see *Re Claygreen Ltd*; sub nom. *Romer-Ormiston v Claygreen Ltd* [2006] B.C.C. 440.

[56] *Milroy v Lord* (1862) 4 De G.F. & J. 264 QB.

and until the transfer was registered. In modern cases,[57] however, it has been held that so long as the donor has done all he needs to do, or there has been detrimental reliance by the donee, the beneficial interest passes from him to the donee.[58]

Priorities between competing transferees

26–010 Questions may also arise in determining the priority of purported transfers of the same shares to different people. In answering these questions the courts[59] have relied on two traditional principles of English property law: i.e. (1) that as between two competing holders of equitable interests, if their equities are equal the first in time prevails; and (2) that a bona fide purchaser for value of a legal interest takes free of earlier equitable interests of which he has no notice at the time of purchase.

In applying these principles to competing share transfers, a transferee prior to registration is treated as having an equitable interest only but registration converts his interest into a legal one.[60] Hence if a registered shareholder, A, first executes a transfer to a purchaser, B, and later to another, C, while both remain unregistered B will have priority over C. If, however, C succeeds in obtaining registration before B, he will have priority over B so long as he had no notice, at the time of purchase, of the transfer to B. If C did have notice, although he has been registered, his prima facie title will not prevail over that of B, who will be entitled to have the register rectified (assuming that there are no grounds on which the company could refuse to register B) and in the meantime C's legal interest will be subject to the equitable interest of B.[61] If both transfers were gifts, the position would presumably be different; the gift to B[62] would leave A without any beneficial interest that he could give to C and, not being a "purchaser", C could not obtain priority by registration; his legal interest, on his becoming the registered holder, would be subject to the prior equity of B.

---

[57] *Re Rose* [1949] Ch. 78 Ch D; *Re Rose* [1952] Ch. 499 CA; *Pennington v Waine* [2002] 2 B.C.L.C. 448 CA; *Kaye v Zeital* [2010] 2 B.C.L.C. 1 CA (Civ Div); *Curtis v Pulbrook* [2011] EWHC 167 (Ch); [2011] 1 B.C.L.C. 638; *Nosnehpetsj Ltd v Waltersheds Capital Partners Ltd* [2020] EWHC 739 (Ch) at [16] and [19e]; and [2020] EWHC 1938 (Ch) at [34]–[46].

[58] Thus, until the transfer is registered, placing the donee in the same position as if the donor had instead made a declaration of trust.

[59] The leading cases are *Shropshire Union Railway v R.* (1874–75) L.R. 7 H.L. 496 HL; *Société Générale v Walker* (1885) 11 App. Cas. 20 HL; *Colonial Bank v Cady* (1890) 15 App. Cas. 267 HL. For more recent decisions, see *Hawks v McArthur* [1951] 1 All E.R. 22; *Champagne Perrier-Jouet v Finch & Co* [1982] 1 W.L.R. 1359 Ch D; *Macmillan Inc v Bishopsgate Investment Trust Plc (No.3)* [1995] 1 W.L.R. 978 Ch D.

[60] Notwithstanding a suggestion by Lord Selbourne (in *Société Générale v Walker* (1885) 11 App. Cas. 20) that "a present absolute right to have the transfer registered" might suffice, it seems that nothing less than actual registration will do. In *Ireland v Hart* [1902] 1 Ch. 522 Ch D the transfer had been lodged for registration and the directors had no power to refuse but it was held that the legal interest had not passed.

[61] *France v Clark* (1884) 26 Ch. D. 257 CA; *Earl of Sheffield v London Joint Stock Bank* (1888) 13 App. Cas. 332 HL; *Rainford v James Keith & Blackman* [1905] 2 Ch. 147 CA.

[62] So long as it has been "perfected"—as interpreted in the cases following *Re Rose* [1949] Ch. 78; and *Re Rose* [1952] Ch. 499.

It should perhaps be pointed out once again that even registration affords only prima facie evidence of title. If the registered transferor, A, was not entitled to the shares, what will pass when he transfers to B or C is not, strictly speaking, either a legal or equitable interest but only his imperfect title to it, which will not prevail against the true owner. If, for example, the transfer to A was a forgery the true owner will be entitled to be restored to the register.[63] Hence a transferee can never be certain of obtaining an absolute title in the case of an off-market transaction. But his risk is slight so long as he promptly obtains registration of the transfer. And this he can do unless there are restrictions on the transferability of the shares or unless there are good reasons for failing to apply for registration.

The principal example for the latter occurs when the shareholder wants to borrow on the security of his shares. This can be done by a legal mortgage, under which the shareholder transfers the shares to the lender (who registers the transfer) subject to an agreement to retransfer them when the loan is repaid. Generally, however, this suits neither party; the lender normally has no wish to become a member and shareholder of the company and the borrower does not want to cease to be one. Hence a more usual arrangement is one whereby the shareholder deposits with the lender his share certificate and, often, a signed blank transfer, this usually being accompanied by a written memorandum setting out the terms of the loan. The result is to confer an equitable charge which the lender can enforce by selling the shares if he needs to realise his security. Custody of the share certificate is regarded as the essential protection of the lender.[64] In the case of shares, dealt with through CREST,[65] its rules provided for uncertificated shares to be held in "escrow" balances, which provision appears to give the bank an equivalent security.[66]

The company's lien

As we have seen,[67] a public company is not permitted to have a charge or lien on its shares except (1) when the shares are not fully paid and the charge or lien is for the amount payable on the shares; or (2) the ordinary business of the company includes the lending of money or consists of the provision of hire-purchase **26–011**

---

[63] The transferee will have no remedy against the company based on estoppel by share certificate: it made no false statement: see para.26–006. The Forged Transfers Acts 1891 and 1892 enabled companies to adopt fee-financed arrangements for compensating innocent victims of forged transfers but this is purely voluntary and seems to have been virtually a dead-letter since its inception.

[64] Banks usually grant their clients overdrafts on the security of an equitable charge by a deposit of share certificates without requiring signed blank transfers.

[65] Shares not listed or dealt with on the AIM are rarely accepted as security for loans because of their illiquidity and, usually, restrictions on their transferability. Banks will instead want a charge on the undertaking and assets of the company itself plus, probably, personal guarantees of the members or directors.

[66] See Evans, (1996) 11 J.I.B.F.L. 259; see also in relation to the Financial Collateral Directive and its implementation in the UK: L.C. Ho, "The Financial Collateral Directive's practice in England" (2011]) 26 J.I.B.L.R. 151; and *Cukurova Financial International Ltd v Alfa Telecom Turkey Ltd* [2009] 3 All E. R. 849; *Mills v Sportsdirect.com* [2010] EWHC 1072 (Ch); [2010] 2 P. & C.R. DG19.

[67] See para.17–002.

finance and the charge arises in the course of a transaction in the ordinary course of its business.[68] Neither exception is of much importance in the present context.

Hence it is only in respect of private companies that problems are still likely to arise when their articles provide, as they frequently do, that "the company shall have a first and paramount lien on shares, whether or not fully-paid, registered in the name of a person indebted or under any liability to the company". Since the decision of the House of Lords in *Bradford Banking Co v Briggs*[69] it appears to be accepted that the effect of such a provision is that:

(1) once a shareholder has incurred a debt or liability to the company, it has an equitable charge on the shares of that shareholder to secure payment which ranks in priority to later equitable interests and, it seems, to earlier ones of which the company had no notice when its lien became effective; and
(2) in determining whether the company had notice,[70] s.126 has no application; if the company knows of the earlier equitable interest (because, for example, a transfer of the shares has been lodged for registration even if that is refused) it cannot improve its own position to the detriment of the holder of that known equitable interest.

An interesting modern illustration is afforded by *Champagne Perrier-Jouet v Finch & Co.*[71] There the company's articles provided for a lien in the above terms. One of its shareholders[72] had been allowed to run up substantial debts to the company resulting from trading between him and the company and it had been agreed that he could repay by instalments. Another creditor of the shareholder subsequently obtained judgment against him and a charging order on the shares by way of equitable execution. It was held that the company's lien had become effective when the debts to it were incurred (even though they were not then due for repayment) and as this occurred before the company had notice of the charging order,[73] the company's lien had priority.[74]

As this case shows, an equitable charge on shares in a private company with articles conferring a lien on the company is likely to be an even more undesirable form of security than shares in private companies always are. It may, however, be the only security obtainable, for an attempt to obtain a legal charge will almost certainly be frustrated by the refusal of the directors to register the transfer. If,

---

68 CA 2006 s.670; for listed companies see also Listing Rules LR 2.2.4.

69 *Bradford Banking Co v Briggs, Son and Co* (1886) 12 App. Cas. 29 HL.

70 It is not altogether clear why notice should be relevant. Since the company's lien is merely an equitable interest, its priority over another equitable interest should depend on the respective dates of their creation. But the decisions seem to assume that the company's lien will have priority over an equitable interest if the company has not received notice of the latter.

71 *Champagne Perrier-Jouet v Finch & Co* [1982] 1 W.L.R. 1359.

72 He had also been a director and it was argued that the debt he incurred to the company was a loan unlawful under what is now s.197 so that the company could not have a valid lien. It was held that it was not a loan; it would, however, today be "a quasi-loan" as defined in s.198 and as such unlawful if the company was a "relevant company" (e.g. a subsidiary of a public company) as defined in s.198.

73 It also ante-dated the charging order but the court seems to have regarded the date of notice as decisive: see at s.1367B–E.

74 It was also held that if the company enforced its lien by selling the shares it would have to comply with provisions in the articles conferring pre-emptive rights on the other members of the company.

faute de mieux, it has to be accepted, notice should immediately be given to the company, making it clear that this is a notice which it cannot disregard in relation to any lien it may claim, and an attempt should be made to obtain information about the amount, if any, then owed to the company.

TRANSFERS OF UNCERTIFICATED SHARES

We have seen in the previous section that certificated shares are transferred by way of delivery of certain transfer documents to the company. The company being so notified of a transfer then registers the transferee's name on the shareholder register. When uncertificated shares are sold, the register is updated through electronic instructions. **26–012**

For a transfer of uncertificated shares to be possible, both the seller and the buyer need to have access to the CREST system. There are three ways in which investors can access CREST. They can hold an account with CREST themselves and acquire the hard- and software necessary to establish a safe connection with CREST. The cost involved in doing this makes this option unappealing to small scale private investors. An investor can also have his or her account with CREST operated by a broker who accesses the system or his or her behalf. This option is referred to as personal membership in the CREST documentation. With both options, the account is operated in the name of the investor who holds legal title to the shares. The third option for an investor is not to hold an account with CREST but to instruct a broker to act as a nominee on his or her behalf. In that case, the investor's name does not appear on the company's register. The nominee rather than the investor has an account with CREST and holds legal title to the shares. This form of holding shares has recently come under scrutiny.[75]

When uncertificated shares are transferred, both the selling and the buying account holder need to instruct the system to carry out the transfer. When shares are sold through the Stock Exchange's electronic trading system, the sales information is transferred into the CREST system automatically and the selling and the buying account holder have an opportunity to verify the data before the transfer is effected.

Upon receiving transfer instructions, CREST verifies them, matches them and carries them out on the day specified by the parties. On that day CREST transfers the shares from the seller to the buyer and causes the purchase price to be paid over to the seller. The buyer becomes the legal owner of the shares when they are credited to his or her account. This is because, since 2001, CREST not only operates an electronic transfer system, but also keeps the shareholder register for all UK uncertificated shares.[76] Having updated the register, CREST needs to immediately inform the issuing company which keeps a record of all transfers relating to uncertificated shares.

---

[75] Law Commission, *Intermediated securities: who owns your shares? A Scoping Paper* (11 November 2020); see also BIS Research Paper 261, *Exploring the Intermediated Shareholding Model* (January 2016).

[76] USR 2001 reg.27(1) obliges the Operator upon settlement of the transfer to amend the operator register (unless the shares thereafter are to be held in certificated form). The Operator must also, immediately after making the change, notify the company: reg.27(7).

26–013 In order to preserve the integrity of the shareholder register, the USR 2001 stipulates that the Operator must not amend the shareholder register in relation to uncertificated units, unless ordered to do so by a court[77] or unless shares have been transferred by operation of law.[78] Equally, there are only limited circumstances in which the Operator may or must refuse to alter the operator register if it has received appropriate instructions from system members. Of course, the Regulations recognise that, in rare cases, events outside the system may impinge on the Operator's freedom of action in relation to the Operator register, just as they do on the issuer register kept by the company (for the uncertificated shares) or the share register, also kept by the company, for companies which have not entered the electronic transfer system. Thus, unless it is impracticable to stop it, CREST must not make a change in the Operator register which it actually knows is prohibited by an order of a court or by or under an enactment or involves a transfer to a deceased person.[79] There are further cases where CREST may refuse to make a change, for example, where the transfer is not to a legal or natural person or is to a minor.[80] Section 771(1)[81] applies in cases where CREST refuses to register a transfer,[82] but a two-month limit for notifying transferees of a failure to register hardly seems an appropriate one for an electronic system.

Title to uncertificated shares and the protection of transferees

26–014 The CREST system has reduced the time that lapses between trade and settlement. It has also caused transfers of uncertificated shares to be carried out almost simultaneously with payment of the purchase price. This has significantly reduced the transactional risk investors in shares are exposed to. The risk involved in shares transaction has, however, not been eliminated completely. In particular, the USR 2001 do not introduce a rule to the effect that entry on the Operator register confers title to the shares on the person registered. On the contrary, reg.24(1) provides, in the same way as the CA 2006,[83] that "a register of members" is simply prima facie evidence of the matters directed or authorised to be stated in it, and "register of members" is defined to include both the issuer and Operator register of members.[84] In principle, therefore, a legal owner of shares may seek rectification of the Operator register if CREST removes his or her name from it without cause, and a court order restoring the legal owner to the register would be, as we have seen, something to which the Operator is obliged to

[77] USR 2001 reg.27(5)—for example, upon rectification of the register. Or unless it receives an issuer instruction to the effect that the shares have been converted into uncertificated form or there has been a compulsory acquisition of shares after a takeover (see para.28–070): reg.27(1).
[78] USR 2001 reg.27(6). On transfer by operation of law, see para.26–021.
[79] USR 2001 reg.27(2) and (3).
[80] USR 2001 reg.27(4).
[81] See para.14–013.
[82] USR 2001 reg.27(8)–(9).
[83] CA 2006 s.127; para.26–016. Naturally, s.768 (certificate to be evidence of title) has no application to uncertificated shares, though the section seems still to apply to certificated shares of participating companies.
[84] USR 2001 reg.3(1).

respond.[85] In fact, it is doubtful whether the statutory provision under which the Regulations were made is wide enough to effect a general change in the rules as to the status of the register.

This is not to say, however, that the protection of transferees is provided in the same way or to the same extent under the USR 2001 in relation to certificated shares as it is in relation to uncertificated shares. As we have seen, that protection in relation to the latter class of shares depends heavily upon the doctrine of estoppel by share certificate. Since, by definition, there is no share certificate in relation to uncertificated shares, the immediate position seems to be that the third party cannot be protected by this doctrine. Is this in principle a problem for the transferee of shares? The answer is that, if the matter were not dealt with in the Regulations, it would be. There are obvious risks that either an unauthorised person obtains access to the system or a person with authorised access uses the system in an unauthorised way, in both cases sending an instruction to transfer shares not belonging to him or her to an innocent third party. Can the former holder of the shares secure the restoration of his or her name to the Operator register to the detriment of the third party?

One technique for protecting the third party might be to transfer the doctrine of estoppel by share certificate to the entry on the register, but it is no accident that, in relation to certificated shares, the doctrine is based on the certificate, not on the register entry, even though both are available. This is because it is rare for a transferee to rely on the register entry before committing him- or herself to the transaction. This is true of both the Operator register and the issuer register, and so estoppel does not seem an effective protective device as against either the company or CREST.

In fact, the USR 2001 take an entirely different approach to the protection of transferees. If the unauthorised instruction in the situations above is sent in accordance with the rules of the Operator, the recipient of the instruction is entitled, subject to very few exceptions, to act on it and the person by whom or on whose behalf it was purportedly sent may not deny that it was sent with proper authority and contained accurate information.[86] Unlike at common law, where even careless conduct does not prevent the legal owner from asserting his or her title to the shares,[87] even a legal owner who was in no way to blame for the fraud may find that title to the shares has been lost. The transferor may have a remedy in such a case against the system participant whose equipment was used to send the unauthorised instructions.[88] There may also be a liability of the Operator in such a case, but only if the instruction was not sent from a system computer or the system computer it purported to be sent from. Thus, purely unauthorised activity by a broker's employee is not caught.[89] In any event, the liability is capped at **26–015**

[85] USR 2001 reg.27(5).

[86] USR 2001 reg.35.

[87] See para.26–005.

[88] The Regulations do not create such a liability but do preserve it if it exists under the general law (USR reg.35(7)), for example, as between the transferor and his or her broker.

[89] See the definition of "forged dematerialised instruction" in USR reg.36(1). In effect, the Operator is liable for security defects in its system but not for unauthorised use of the system.

£50,000 in respect of each instruction[90] and falls away entirely if the Operator identifies the person responsible, even if the transferor is not able to recover any compensation from that person.[91]

Thus, it seems right to conclude that transferees are somewhat better protected under the USR 2001 than under the common law doctrine of estoppel, since even first transferees from the rogue are protected. However, that protection is provided at the expense of the transferor, rather than of the company, as at common law, and it is certainly arguable that company liability is the better principle because of the benefit companies obtain from effective markets.[92]

Because the transfer of legal ownership is so closely linked to payment, the rules on beneficial ownership have less practical relevance in relation to transfers of uncertificated shares.[93] When uncertificated securities are used as collateral, however, equity continues to play an important role. Moreover, the Financial Collerateral Directive,[94] which aims at reducing the formalities required to create a security interest over securities, has had significant impact on English law.[95]

THE REGISTER

26–016 We have already seen that companies issuing registered shares must keep a register containing the names of their members.[96] We shall now examine the rules governing the shareholder register more closely. The registers of companies which issue only certificated shares are subject to the CA 2006. Companies which issue only uncertificated shares or both certificated and uncertificated shares are subject to the USR 2001.[97]

Under both regimes, the register contains the name and address of each member and the date on which each person was registered as a member and the date on which any person ceased to be a member.[98] It also states the number and

---

[90] USR reg.36(6).

[91] USR reg.36(4), unless the Operator has been guilty of fraud, wilful neglect or negligence (USR reg.36(9)).

[92] E. Micheler, "Farewell to Quasi-negotiability? Legal Title and Transfer of Shares in a Paperless World" [2002] J.B.L. 358.

[93] Equitable ownership arises, however, when uncertificated securities are transferred to a person who opts to have them converted in to certificated securities (USR 2001 reg.31(2)).

[94] Directive 2002/47 on financial collateral arrangements [2002] OJ L168/43 implemented in the UK by the Financial Collateral Arrangements (No.2) Regulations 2003 (SI 2003/3226).

[95] Look Chan Ho, "The Financial Collateral Directive's practice in England" (2011) 26 J.I.B.L.R. 151; *Mills v Sportsdirect.com* [2010] 2 P. & C.R. DG19; see also *Cukurova Financial International Ltd v Alfa Telecom Turkey Ltd* [2009] 3 All E.R. 849.

[96] CA 2006 s.113; the Small Business, Enterprise and Employment Act 2015 amended the CA 2006, introducing a new Ch.2A to Pt 8 which gives private companies the option of keeping the register of members on the register kept by the registrar instead of keeping it on their own register.

[97] The USR 2001 (SI 2001/3755) was introduced to bring forward the point in time at which an investor acquires legal title to uncertificated shares from the moment at which the company amends the shareholder register to the moment at which the Operator of the uncertificated transfer system credits the shares to the buyer's securities account (HM Treasury, *Modernising Securities Settlement* (2001); Bank of England, *Securities Settlement Priorities Review* (September 1998 and March 1998)). This was done by entrusting the Operator of the uncertificated transfer system with the maintenance of the shareholder register for uncertificated shares.

[98] CA 2006 s.113; USR 2001 Sch.4 paras 2(1)–(2) and 4(1).

class[99] of shares held by each member and the amount paid up on each share.[100] In the case of a private company there must also be noted on the register the fact and the date of the company becoming, or ceasing to be a single member company.[101]

The register of members of both certificated and uncertificated shares constitutes prima facie evidence of any matters which are by the respective regulatory regime directed or authorised to be inserted in it.[102]

In order to become a member or shareholder of a company an investor has to have his or her name entered on that shareholder register. An investor who holds shares indirectly through a nominee is unable to enforce shareholder rights against the company.[103] A buyer normally acquires legal title to shares at the point in time at which his or her name is entered on the shareholder register.[104] This rule applies irrespective of whether shares are held in the certificated or in the uncertificated form.

Certificated and uncertificated shares differ in terms of who maintains the shareholder register. The register for certificated shares is maintained by the company itself or by a registrar on behalf of the company. The register for uncertificated shares is maintained by the Operator of the uncertificated transfer system, CREST. The register of companies which issue certificated shares and uncertificated shares consists of two parts. Entries relating to certificated shares are maintained by the company. They are referred to as the "issuer register of members". Entries relating to uncertificated shares are maintained by the Operator of the uncertificated transfer system, and are referred to as "Operator register of members". The company maintains a "record" relating to uncertificated shares. This record does not constitute a shareholder register. It must be regularly reconciled with the Operator register of members.[105] In relation to uncertificated shares, the Operator register prevails over the record kept by the company.[106] The record does not provide for prima facie evidence. It enables the company to inform those inspecting the register about entries that have been made on the register maintained by CREST. **26–017**

[99] In the case of a company without a share capital but with different classes of membership the register has to state the class to which each member belongs (s.113(3); USR 2001 Sch.4 para.2(2)). This fills the lacuna revealed in *Re Performing Right Society Ltd* [1978] 1 W.L.R. 1197 CA (Civ Div).

[100] CA 2006 s.113(3); USR 2001 Sch.4 paras 2(2), (3), 4(1) and 5(1). In the case of the amount paid up, this appears only on the issuer's record.

[101] CA 2006 s.123(2); USR 2001 Sch.4 para.3. It is rather unlikely that a company issuing uncertificated shares would fall into the state of having only one member, but it might do if it became part of a group of companies.

[102] CA 2006 s.127; USR 2001 reg.24(1).

[103] *Eckerle v Wickeder Westfalenstahl GmbH* [2013] EWHC 68 (Ch); [2014] Ch 196; see also *Re Sirius Minerals Plc* [2020] EWHC 1447 (Ch); and *Secure Capital SA v Credit Suisse AG* [2017] EWCA Civ 1486; [2017] 2 Lloyd's Rep. 599; indirect investors may be able to claim under the Financial Services Act see *SL Claimants v Tesco Plc* [2019] EWHC 2858 (Ch); [2020] Bus. L.R. 250.

[104] CA 2006 s.112; *J Sainsbury Plc v O'Connor (Inspector of Taxes)* [1991] 1 W.L.R. 963 CA at 977; *Re Rose* [1952] Ch. 499 at 518–519; *Kaye v Zeital* [2010] 2 B.C.L.C. 1 at [40].

[105] USR 2001 reg.23 and Sch.4 para.5(2).

[106] USR 2001 reg.24(2).

The issuer register may be kept at the company's registered office or at a place specified in regulations under s.1136.[107] If kept otherwise than at the company's registered office, notice must be given to Companies House (and thus to the public) of the place where it is kept and of any change of that place.[108]

If a company has more than 50 members then, unless the register is kept in such a form as to constitute an index of names of members, such an index must be kept at the same place as the register.[109]

26–018 The shareholder register and the index are available for public inspection. Any member of the company may inspect the register free of charge.[110] Any other person may inspect the register on payment of such fee as may be prescribed.[111] In the case of uncertificated shares, the inspection right is granted against the record held by the company rather than against the Operator register itself.[112] This exposes the searcher to the risk that the company's record will not accurately reflect the Operator register. Provided the company regularly reconciles its record with the Operator register, except insofar as matters outside its control prevent such reconciliation, the company is not liable for discrepancies between the record and the register.[113]

The right to inspect the register is a legitimate help to a takeover bidder and makes it possible for members to communicate with each other. It also has, in the past, been abused by traders who advertised their wares by unsolicited mail or telephone calls and who were able to obtain more cheaply than in any other way a list of potential victims by buying a copy of the shareholder register of, say, British Telecom or British Gas. With a view to putting an end to this illegitimate use of the shareholder register, the CA 2006 revised the right to inspect the register. The right to inspect the register may now be denied by the Court if it is satisfied that the request was not sought for a proper purpose.[114]

Under s.358 of the CA 1985 a company had the power to close the shareholder register for any time or times not exceeding in total 30 days in any year. The provision enabled companies to draw up a list of those who are entitled to attend the annual general meeting or to receive dividends. The CA 2006 does not contain a power to that effect. Instead, the company can set a date by reference to

---

[107] Companies (Company Records) Regulations 2008 (SI 2008/3006).

[108] CA 2006 s.114(2); USR 2001 Sch.4 para.6(3)–(4). The place must be in England or Wales if the company is registered in England and Wales or in Scotland if it is registered in Scotland. But if the company carries on business in one of the countries specified in s.129(2) it may cause keep an "overseas branch register" in that country (s.129(2)). This, in effect, is a register of shareholders resident in that country, a duplicate of which will also be maintained with the principal register (s.132). This provision is not affected by the USR 2001 Sch.4 paras 2(7) and 4(4).

[109] CA 2006 s.115.

[110] CA 2006 s.116.

[111] CA 2006 s.116.

[112] USR 2001 Sch.4 para.9.

[113] USR 2001 Sch.4 para.5(3).

[114] CA 2006 s.117; For examples of this see: *Burry & Knight Ltd v Knight* [2014] EWCA Civ 604; [2014] 1 W.L.R. 4046 where it was held that the communication with fellow shareholders about the manner in which company shares are proposed to be valued was a proper purpose, but the communication to fellow shareholders of unsubstantiated allegations about directors' remuneration was not. See also *Burberry Group Plc v Fox-Davies* [2015] EWHC 222 (Ch) where an application of a tracing agent attempting to find "lost" shareholders was refused because the real motive was to extract a fee from these shareholders and that was not a proper purpose.

which the payment of dividends is to be made to the then registered shareholders and then leave it up to shareholders no longer on the register at the time of payment to regularise the position with the purchaser. This has the advantage of not undermining trading in the shares in the company, which was a possible defect in the closure power.

Under the USR 2001, companies participating in CREST are entitled to specify a time not more than 48 hours before a general meeting by which a person must have been entered on the register in order to have the right to attend and vote at the meeting and may similarly choose a day not more than 21 days before notices of a meeting are sent out for the purposes of determining who is entitled to receive the notice.[115] This way of proceeding enables transfers to continue in the period before the meeting (thus reducing the risk to transferees) without landing the company in the position of having to deal with a constantly changing body of shareholders.

Rectification

The register is "prima facie evidence of any matters which are by this Act directed or authorised to be inserted in it".[116] It is not, however, conclusive evidence for, as we have seen, membership is dependent both on agreement to become a member and entry in the register, and it may be that other requirements in the company's articles have to be met. If they are not, it seems that the registered person does not become a member.[117] In any event, if the entry does not truly reflect the agreement or other requirements, the register ought to be rectified. Hence s.125 provides a summary remedy whereby: **26–019**

> "(a) the name of any person is without sufficient cause entered in or omitted from a company's register of members, or
>
> (b) default is made or unnecessary delay takes place in entering on the register the fact of any person having ceased to be a member, the person aggrieved or any member of the company, or the company may apply to the court for rectification of the register."[118]

This wording is defective because it ignores the fact that the register is not just a register of members but also a register of shareholdings and that a likely error is in the amount of a member's shareholding. However, common sense has prevailed and in *Re Transatlantic Life Assurance*[119] Slade J felt able to hold that "the wording is wide enough in its terms to empower the court to order the

---

[115] USR 2001 reg.40.

[116] CA 2006 s.127; USR 2001 reg.24. In case of conflict between the issuer and Operator registers, the latter prevails (USR 2001 reg.24(2)). The rule applies to the Operator register provided the transfer has occurred in accordance with the Regulations.

[117] *POW Services Ltd v Clare* [1995] 2 B.C.L.C. 435 Ch D; *Domoney v Godinho* [2004] EWHC 328 (Ch); [2004] 2 B.C.L.C. 15. The issue of restrictions in the articles is not one which arises in relation to listed companies or companies whose shares are held in uncertificated form, since the Listing Rules and the rules of CREST require such shares to be freely transferable.

[118] CA 2006 s.125(1). This power operates equally in relation to shares held in uncertificated form (USR 2001 reg.25(2)(b)).

[119] *Re Transatlantic Life Assurance* [1980] 1 W.L.R. 79 Ch D. The case arose because the allotment of some shares was void because Exchange Control permission had not been obtained as at that time was necessary. See also *Re Cleveland Trust Plc* [1991] B.C.L.C. 424 Ch D (Companies Ct).

deletion of some only of a registered shareholder's shares".[120] It must follow that it is similarly empowered to order an addition to the registered holding.

On an application the court may decide any question relating to the title of any person who is a party to the application whether the question arises between members or alleged members,[121] or between members or alleged members on the one hand and the company on the other hand,[122] and may decide "any question necessary or expedient to be decided for rectification…".[123] A rectification may also be carried out with retrospective effect.[124] Moreover, the court may order payment by the company of "damages sustained by any party aggrieved".[125]

26–020 There is some uncertainty as to the extent to which the company can rectify the register without an application to the court. But in practice here again common sense prevails. Sections 113, 115 and 122 envisage, and indeed demand, alterations without which the register could not be kept up-to-date and fulfil its purpose, and although there is no express provision for alterations of members' addresses that takes place all the time. Indeed it would be quite absurd if companies could not correct any mistake if all interested parties agree.

The USR 2001 also contemplate that a company may rectify the issuer register other than by order of a court, but, in order to preserve the integrity of the electronic transfer system, require the company in such a case to have the consent of the Operator of the system if the change would involve rectification of the Operator register. Equally, the Operator may rectify the Operator register, but must inform the issuer and the system-members concerned immediately when the change is made.[126]

It must be emphasised, however, that although the register provides prima facie evidence of who its members are and what their shareholdings are, it provides no evidence at all, either to the company or anyone else, of who the beneficial owners of the shares are.[127]

---

120 *Re Transatlantic Life Assurance* [1980] 1 W.L.R. 79 at 84F–G.

121 For example, when A and B are disputing which of them should be the registered holder.

122 For example, when there is a dispute between the company and A or B on whether either should be.

123 CA 2006 s.125(3). Despite this wide wording, it has been held the summary procedure of CA 1985 s.359 should not be used where there was an unresolved and substantial dispute as to the entitlement to shares (*Nilon Ltd v Royal Westminster Investment SA* [2015] UKPC 2 rejecting the view expressed by the Court of Appeal in *Re Hoicrest Ltd* [2000] 1 B.C.L.C. 194 CA).

124 *R I Fit Global Ltd* [2013] EWHC 2090 (Ch); [2014] 2 B.C.L.C. 116.

125 CA 2006 s.125(2). "Compensation" would be a better word than "damages" and "party aggrieved" is an expression which courts have constantly criticised, but apparently without convincing Parliamentary Counsel responsible for drafting Government Bills.

126 USR 2001 reg.25.

127 For the rules dealing with the disclosure of beneficial interests, see paras 27–011 to 27–019.

TRANSMISSION OF SHARES BY OPERATION OF LAW

The CA 2006[128] recognises that shares may be transmitted by operation of law and that, when this occurs, the prohibition on registering unless a proper instrument of transfer has been delivered does not apply.[129] The principal examples of this are when a registered shareholder dies or becomes bankrupt. As regards the death of a shareholder, the Act further provides that a transfer by the deceased's personal representative, even if he is not a member of the company, is as valid as if he had been.[130] The company is bound to accept probate or letters of administration granted in any part of the UK as sufficient evidence of the personal representative's entitlement.[131] However, he or she does not become a member unless he or she elects to apply to be registered and is registered as a member. In the meantime, the effect is that he has the "same rights as the holder had"[132]: **26–021**

> "But transmittees do not have the right to attend or vote at a general meeting, or agree to a proposed written resolution, in respect of shares to which they are entitled by reason of the holder's death or bankruptcy or otherwise unless they become the holders of those shares."[133]

If the shares are those of a listed company, this anomalous position can be ended rapidly because, unless the shares are not fully paid, there will not be any restrictions on transferability and the personal representative will either obtain registration of him- or herself or execute a transfer to a purchaser or to the beneficiaries. In relation to a private company, however, it may continue indefinitely and prove detrimental to the personal representative, the deceased's estate and, sometimes, the company. The personal representative may suffer because it may not be possible for him fully to wind up the estate and to obtain a discharge from his fiduciary responsibilities. The estate may suffer because it may be impossible for the personal representative to sell the shares at their true value, especially if any attempt to dispose of them would trigger rights of pre-emption or first refusal.[134] The company may suffer because, as we have seen,[135] unless such rights have been most carefully drafted, they will not come into operation so long as no action regarding registration is taken by the personal

---

[128] And see the Companies (Model Articles) Regulations 2008 Sch.1 art.27.

[129] CA 2006 s.773; for uncertificated shares see USR reg.27(6).

[130] CA 2006 s.773.

[131] CA 2006 s.774. If it does so without such production of the grant it may become liable for any tax payable as a result of the transmission (*NY Breweries Co v Attorney-General* [1899] A.C. 62 HL) but in the case of small estates, companies may be prepared to dispense with production of a grant if the Revenue confirms that nothing is payable. If the deceased was one of a number of jointly registered members, the company, on production of a death certificate, will have to recognise that he has ceased to be a member and shareholder and that the others remain such. But the whole beneficial interest in the shares will not pass to them unless they and the deceased were beneficial owners entitled jointly rather than in common.

[132] The Companies (Model Articles) Regulations 2008 Sch.1 art.27(2).

[133] The Companies (Model Articles) Regulations 2008 Sch.1 art.27(3).

[134] If there are any restrictions on transfers all the articles relating to restriction on transfers apply both to a notice that the personal representative wishes to be registered and to a transfer from him (The Companies (Model Articles) Regulations 2008 Sch.1 art.28(3)).

[135] See para.26–007.

representative. In order to assist personal representatives, the statute has extended the remedies afforded to members so that they can be invoked by personal representatives of members.[136] It is also now obligatory for the company to give reasons explaining the refusal to register a transferee.[137]

The position on bankruptcy of an individual shareholder[138] is broadly similar. His or her rights to the shares automatically vest in the trustee in bankruptcy as part of his estate.[139] But, as in the case of a personal representative, until the trustee elects to become registered and is so registered, the trustee will not become a member of the company entitled to attend meetings and to vote. In contrast, however, with the position on the death of a member, the bankrupt will remain a member and be entitled to attend and vote—though under a duty to do so in accordance with the directions of the trustee. As in the case of personal representatives, the company's articles will probably provide that any restrictions on transferability apply on any application to be registered and to any transfer by the trustee[140] and these restrictions may handicap the trustee in obtaining the best price on a sale of the shares, particularly if the articles confer pre-emption rights.[141] If a personal representative or trustee in bankruptcy elects to be registered, and is, that becomes personally liable for any amounts unpaid on the shares and not merely representationally liable to the extent of the estate. Trustees in bankruptcy, but not personal representatives, may disclaim onerous property,[142] which the shares might be if they were partly paid or subject to an effective company lien.

---

[136] See, in particular, s.994(2) which makes it possible for personal representatives to invoke the "unfairly prejudicial" remedy which might well be effective if it could be shown that the directors were exercising their powers to refuse transfers in order to enable themselves or the company to acquire the shares of deceased members at an unfair price: see Ch.14.

[137] CA 2006 s.771.

[138] On winding up of a corporate shareholder there is no transmission of the company's property; it remains vested in the company but most of the directors' powers to manage it pass to the liquidator.

[139] IA 1986 ss.283(1) and 306. But not if the shareholder held his shares as a trustee for another person: IA 1986 s.283(3)(a).

[140] The Companies (Model Articles) Regulations 2008 Sch.1 art.28.

[141] In *Borland's Trustee v Steel Bros* [1901] 1 Ch. 279 Ch D, a provision in the articles that in the event of a shareholder's bankruptcy (or death) his shares should be offered to a named person at a particular price was held to be effective and not obnoxious to the bankruptcy laws; for this see most recently *Belmont Park Investment Pty Ltd v BNY Corporate Trustee Services and Lehman Brothers Special Financing Inc* [2011] UKSC 38; [2011] B.C.C. 734.

[142] IA 1986 s.315. Disclaimer puts an end to the interest of the bankrupt and his estate and discharges the trustee from any liability: IA 1986 s.315(3).

CHAPTER 27

CONTINUING OBLIGATIONS AND DISCLOSURE OF INFORMATION TO THE MARKET

INTRODUCTION

Even after a company has been admitted to a public market, in accordance with the rules discussed in the previous chapter, the law imposes "continuing obligations" in relation to disclosure *by* publicly traded companies. These obligations are discussed in the first part of this chapter. In addition, however, the law requires those associated with the company, as directors or major shareholders, to make certain disclosures *to* the company and, through the company, to the market. We turn to them in the second part. These continuing disclosures by the company supplement the annual accounts and reports discussed in Ch.22 and required of all companies. As we saw in that chapter, the rules on annual reporting are applied in an increasingly rigorous way to traded companies; and the continuing disclosure rules are a further expression of the notion that such companies need to meet exacting standards of transparency. **27–001**

The continuing obligations laid on the company partly reflect the disclosure philosophy which dominates the rules on public offerings and admission to trading,[1] but that theory is applied now to the post-admission period so as to inform trading among investors in the securities of the company. Investor protection and allocative efficiency are most obviously advanced by continuing disclosure at the point when a traded company returns to the market to raise

[1] See para.25–003.

further capital, especially in cases where it may do so without issuing a new prospectus.[2] More generally, however, investors' willingness to purchase securities in publicly traded companies (whether on a public offering or from existing shareholders) is likely to be enhanced if they think that market prices reflect the "true state" of the company's business.[3] In addition, the prompt disclosure of significant information by the company will reduce the opportunities for insiders to trade in the securities before the market is aware of new developments. Further, disclosure rules may benefit shareholders, whether or not they contemplate trading in the company's securities. The market price of the stock may indicate to shareholders (or independent directors acting on their behalf) whether all is well with the company's business and whether the exercise of their governance rights would be appropriate—though it might be unwise for shareholders to react to short-term movements in share prices. Continuing disclosure by the company thus has both market and corporate governance implications, which we will explore in this chapter.[4]

Insider trading may also be discouraged by requiring those closely associated with the company's central management (notably its directors) to make disclosures *to* the company and to the market about their trading in the company's securities, since directors are structurally well placed to acquire inside information. Finally, within the shareholder body disclosure of beneficial ownership of shares may also reveal who is really in a position to influence decisions in shareholder meetings or otherwise and so to determine the future course of the company (for example, through the selection of directors). So, the rules about disclosure to the company and the market have market "cleanliness" and corporate governance objectives, just as the rules on disclosure by the company.

27–002 As with the disclosure rules operating at the time of admission to the market, the structure of domestic law has been heavily influence by EU law, notably the Transparency Directive (TD)[5] and the Market Abuse Regulation (MAR)[6]—though those instruments in turn had been influenced by the domestic UK rules in place prior to the emergence of EU law. Despite the UK's exit from the EU, both these instruments constitute "retained" EU law.[7] This means that the domestic rules transposing the TD remain part of the law of the UK but may be amended unilaterally by the UK legislator or regulators in the future. The operative rules

[2] See para.25–020.

[3] The "semi-strong" version of the efficient capital market hypothesis states that all publicly available information about the company is immediately incorporated into market prices. The ongoing mandatory disclosure rules are a crucial mechanism whereby corporate information becomes public. See R. Gilson and R. Kraakman, "The Mechanisms of Market Efficiency" (1984) 70 Virginia L.R. 549, and see later by the same authors on the same topic: (2003) 28 Journal of Corporation Law 215 and (2014) 100 Virginia L.R. 313.

[4] But we shall not deal in any detail with companies incorporated outside the UK whose securities are traded on a regulated market in the UK or with UK-incorporated companies whose sole or primary listing is outside the UK.

[5] Directive 2004/109 ([2004] OJ L390/38), as amended, notably by Directive 2013/50 ([2013] OJ L294/13).

[6] Regulation 596/2014 ([2014] OJ L173/1), as amended. The non-disclosure aspects of this Regulation are discussed in Ch.30.

[7] On which see para.3–014.

are the Transparency Rules (TR) made by the Financial Conduct Authority.[8] Market abuse was initially dealt with at EU level through directives. However, in the reforms enacted in the aftermath of the financial crisis of 2007–2009, the EU moved to the use of a Regulation, which did not require transposition into domestic law but operated directly as part of UK law. It remains in force but now by virtue of its status as domestic law,[9] but amended so as to make it work in the UK in the post-exit situation.[10] In relation to the directly applicable disclosure requirements of MAR, the FCA publishes "guidance" rather than rules, the transparency rules and disclosure guidance being brought together in the Disclosure Guidance and Transparency Rules Sourcebook (DTR) of the FCA.[11]

A further difference between the TD and MAR is that the former applies only to regulated markets.[12] Stock exchanges may choose between regulated and non-regulated status, giving up the advantages of the former for not taking on its disadvantages. The important point for this chapter is that the Main Market of the London Stock Exchange is a regulated market, whilst its Alternative Investment Market for smaller and newer companies is not. The Market Abuse Directive had a similar scope, but, with the move to a Regulation, came the extension of its scope to Multilateral Trading Facilities as well as regulated markets. AIM does count as an MTF, and so the provisions of MAR discussed in this chapter will apply to companies traded on it, but the TD provisions will not. However, the importance of this distinction is reduced by the fact that the LSE's own rules apply the central TD disclosure requirements to issuers traded on it.[13]

PERIODIC REPORTING OBLIGATIONS

The DTR supplement the periodic reporting requirements of the Companies Act in a number of important ways. In relation to the annual accounts, they require speedier publication than the CA 2006 requires (four, rather than six, months from the end of the financial year).[14] Further, the DTR require a somewhat more explicit "responsibility statement" than is to be found in the Act.[15] However, the principal impact of the DTR is to require additional half-yearly reporting. **27–003**

[8] Under powers conferred by s.89A of FSMA 2000, which were originally limited to the implementation of the TD, but are now expressed to cover "disclosure of periodic or ongoing information" generally.

[9] European Union (Withdrawal) Act 2018 s.3 (as amended).

[10] By the Market Abuse (Amendment) (EU Exit) Regulations 2019/310.

[11] In the DTR the term "disclosure *requirements*" refers to MAR arts 17–19. See FCA Handbook, *Glossary*.

[12] TD art.1; cf. MAR art.2.

[13] LSE, *AIM Rules for Companies* (2018), r.17 (significant shareholders) and r.18 (half-yearly reports).

[14] DTR 4.1.3.

[15] DTR 4.1.12 (cf. para.22–035) which require the names of all those responsible within the issuer for the accounts and reports to be stated and the responsibility statement must certify that, to the best of their knowledge, the accounts have been prepared in accordance with the relevant standards and give a true and fair view of the company's financial position, and the management report includes a fair review of the company's business.

For a long time companies with securities[16] traded on the Main Market of the London Stock Exchange have been subject to more frequent reporting requirements, for the market's appetite is not satisfied by yearly reporting. This obligation is currently stated in the DTR, which apply to all regulated markets.[17] The half-yearly reports are required to be less detailed than the annual ones and are not required to be audited (though if they are audited or reviewed, the audit report or review must be published).[18] The accounts required to be produced are a condensed set of financial statements, the directors' report is an "interim review" and the responsibility statement is adjusted accordingly.[19]

27–004 The issue of quarterly reporting has been contentious. Some argue that it adds to the efficiency of securities markets; others than it encourages management to focus on the short-term. The original TD required, not a set of quarterly accounts, but only a quarterly "interim management statement", giving an explanation of material events and transactions which had taken place and their impact on the issuer and a general description of the company's financial position and performance.[20] However, in the 2013 amendments the short-termism argument won out and the quarterly reporting requirement was removed.[21]

As we have noted in Ch.22, the power to review the accounts and reports of companies for compliance with the relevant requirements is one which has been delegated by the Government to the Financial Reporting Council; and that body's powers extend to all the periodic reports required to be produced by traded companies, whether annual or otherwise.[22]

EPISODIC OR AD HOC REPORTING REQUIREMENTS

27–005 In addition to the requirement to make reports every six months, publicly quoted companies are required to report events as they occur. There are two main arguments behind this requirement. First, it can be seen as a way of keeping shareholders and investors up-to-date about developments in the business of the company or about other factors which affect its business. The information should be disclosed because it is relevant to investors and shareholders. The second argument is that the information should be disclosed publicly in order that it shall no longer be known only to a small group of persons who may be tempted to

---

[16] The provisions discussed in this section normally apply whether the traded securities are equity or debt instruments.

[17] For the meaning of a "regulated market" see para.25–008. In the case of shares, the term can be equated, with some degree of inaccuracy, with the Main Market of the LSE. The Alternative Investment Market (AIM) is not a regulated market, but the LSE's own rules for that market require half-yearly statements: LSE, *AIM Rules for Companies* (2018), r.18.

[18] DTR 4.2.9. The FRC has produced guidance on the review of interim statements.

[19] DTR 4.2.3 – 4.2.11.

[20] Original art.6.

[21] The UK might have chosen to retain the requirement as a domestic rule but in fact opted not to do so. In 2020 an EU report commissioned by DG Justice and Consumers went so far as to float the idea of prohibiting quarterly reporting and earnings guidance by listed companies: Publications Office of the EU, *Study on directors' duties and sustainable corporate governance*, p.viii.

[22] Supervision of Accounts and Reports (Prescribed Body) and Companies (Defective Accounts and Directors' Reports) (Authorised Person) Order 2012 (SI 2012/1439) reg.3. See para.22–037.

trade on the basis of the information to their profit precisely because it is not known to the market in general. On this rationale disclosure is a way of reducing opportunities of "insider trading", i.e. trading in securities on the basis of price-sensitive information which is not generally available. On both arguments, the purpose of the rules is to have the information disclosed to the market, but, in the first argument because market participants and shareholders need the information to inform action they might take and, on the second argument, because disclosure is the way of depriving the information of its "inside" character. (Insider trading is discussed in more detail in Ch.30).

The current version of these disclosure requirements is to be found in art.17 of MAR. Article 17(1) states: "An issuer shall inform the public as soon as possible of inside information which directly concerns that issuer." A cursory examination of the statements put out by publicly traded companies shows that this rule generates extensive disclosures. In the design of any rules relating to the disclosure of events "as soon as possible", there are two problems which have to be faced. One is to define the point at which the event has crystallised and so triggers the disclosure obligation. If impending developments or matters under negotiation are disclosed too soon, their completion may be jeopardised and the market possibly be given information whose value is difficult to assess because it relates to inchoate events. The injunction to act "as soon as possible" gives the issuer some leeway, for example, where it receives unexpected information whose ambit is not clear and which it needs to clarify. Beyond that, MAR permits issuers "on their own responsibility" to delay disclosure to protect their "legitimate interests", but subject to the riders that the non-disclosure must not be likely to mislead the public and that the company can ensure the confidentiality of the information on the part of those who are privy to it prior to disclosure.[23] "Own responsibility" means the issuer cannot require the regulatory authority to give advance clearance of non-disclosure, though the FCA must be informed of the decision not to disclose and it may require a written explanation of how the conditions for delay were met. This permission is particularly important since art.7(3) states that, in principle, "an intermediate step in a protracted process shall be deemed to be inside information if, by itself, it satisfies the criteria of inside information as referred to in this Article".[24]

MAR provided for the European Securities Markets Authority (ESMA) to produce guidelines on the tricky issues of what constitutes a legitimate interest and action likely to mislead, though some examples of legitimate interest are given in Recital 50 to the Regulation. For the future, that power has passed to the FCA, but ESMA's existing guidelines[25] remain in force to the extent that they have not been overtaken by the FCA's exercise of its powers. The Guidelines identify six situations in which delay in disclosure could be legitimate, including the negotiation or implementation of transactions which are likely to be prejudiced if they are revealed, for example, negotiations for a major contract or negotiations to sell a major holding in the company, and situations where the

---

[23] MAR art.17(4). Where confidentiality has been breached, see art.17(7).

[24] Following the prior CJEU decision in *Geltl v Daimler AG* (C-19/11) EU:C:2012:397; [2012] 3 C.M.L.R. 32.

[25] ESMA, "Delay in the disclosure of inside information" (ESMA 2016/1478). See also Regulation 2016/1055 [2016] OJ L173/47, Ch III.

company's financial viability is in question and disclosure could prejudice negotiations aimed at the company's recovery. However, even where the issuer has a legitimate interest in non-disclosure, it may refrain from disclosing only if non-disclosure is not likely to be misleading to the market. Here the Guidelines suggest that non-disclosure will be misleading if (1) the information is inconsistent with some prior public statement by the issuer to the market; (2) casts doubt on the issuer's prospects of meeting its financial objectives where these have been the subject of prior public guidance from the company; or (3) the information goes against the market's current expectations where these have been set by signals from the issuer. As is to be expected, investors' interests appear to receive more weight than issuers' commercial concerns.[26]

27–006 The second problem is that public disclosure of adverse developments may make it more difficult for the issuer to handle them. In principle, this situation is also covered by the above rules, but in one case the balance is re-weighted in favour of the issuer. Where the issuer is a financial institution and disclosure of the information would threaten the financial viability of the issuer *and* of the financial system, disclosure can be delayed, subject to the confidentiality test and a public interest test and the consent of the competent financial regulator, whether or not the market is likely to be misled by the non-disclosure.[27] The reason for downgrading investors' interests in this case is that instability in the financial system is likely to be more costly to society as a whole than the costs to investors of non-disclosure. This provision reflects experience in the financial crisis where, at least in the UK, the regulators interpreted the prior EU law strictly so as to require immediate disclosure of the existence of banks' liquidity problems whilst permitting non-disclosure only of the state of the negotiations to solve them—arguably the worst of both worlds.[28]

Where information is required to be disclosed the Regulation requires that to be done in a way which "enables fast access and complete, correct and timely assessment of the information by the public".[29] It also requires the information to be displayed on the company's website for an appropriate period, but this is not in fact a very good way of disclosing information simultaneously to all market participants. In practice, dissemination occurs in the UK via a "Primary Information Provider" ("PIP"), i.e. one approved by the FCA, which carries news about all companies in the market and so does not favour those who happened to be logged onto a particular company's website at the time the information was posted.

[26] The third category is the most controversial since inside information, if it is to move the market, will necessarily alter the market's expectations, so much depends on what is understood by "signals from the issuer".

[27] MAR art.17(5)(6).

[28] The strongest case in point was the run on the Northern Rock Building Society in 2007, when it appeared that the immediate cause of the run was the required disclosure by Northern Rock that it had approached the Bank of England for liquidity support, after it was no longer able to fund itself in the inter-bank market. The provision of Bank support increased the Rock's stability of course, but it was not initially clear to depositors how supportive the Bank would be. See HM Treasury, *Financial Stability and Depositor Protection* (January 2008), Cm.7308, paras 3.41 and 3.43. Article 17(5) does not in terms appear limited to liquidity problems, though that is the only example of a threat to financial stability which it gives.

[29] MAR art.17(1).

Somewhat bureaucratically, art.18 of MAR[30] requires issuers to draw up and keep updated, lists of those working for them (whether as employees or self-employed persons) who have access to inside information; and to send the lists to the FCA, if so requested. Each list must be kept for five years. Those acting on behalf of the issuer (for example, an investment bank or law firm) must also draw up such a list. The list must give the reason why a particular person is on the list. All those on the list must be acknowledge in writing their duties under the insider dealing rules and of their awareness of the sanctions for breaking them.

DISCLOSURE OF DIRECTORS' INTERESTS

In the previous sections we have examined the disclosure obligations imposed on publicly traded companies. We now turn to the obligations imposed on those associated with the company as either directors or major shareholders. **27–007**

Since shortly after the Second World War the Companies Act required directors to disclose to their companies their interests in the securities of the companies of which they were directors, an obligation which was later extended so as to impose upon the director the duty to disclose the interests of spouses, civil partners and children. In the case of a company with securities listed on a recognised investment exchange[31] the company was then under an obligation to notify the exchange, which was permitted to publish the information to the market. Following the implementation of the Market Abuse Directive[32] in the UK, these disclosure obligations were transferred wholly to rules made by the FCA[33] and confined to companies whose securities were admitted to trading on a regulated market (or where an application for admission to such market had been made). With the adoption of MAR to replace the Directive the controlling obligation is now to be found in art.19 of that instrument and, as we have noted, MAR applies to multilateral trading facilities as well as to regulated markets.[34]

The principal, though not the exclusive, rationale behind this disclosure requirement is to combat insider trading. Although directors are not the only people under a temptation to engage in insider dealing, they are particularly at risk because their relationship with the company will routinely generate inside information, i.e. information which, at least for a short while, is known to them but not outside the company. The original provisions requiring disclosure of directors' securities dealings were introduced following a recommendation from the Cohen Committee (1945), which identified the insider dealing rationale for requiring the disclosure:

[30] SMEs whose securities are traded on a SME growth market need draw up a list only if requested by the regulator to do so (art.18(6)). The Financial Services Act 2021 will remove an ambiguity as to whether both issuers and those acting on their behalf have to produce their own lists. They do.

[31] For the meaning of this term see para.25–007.

[32] Directive 2003/6 ([2003] OJ L96/16).

[33] Or rather the FSA, as it then was.

[34] See para.27–002.

> "The best safeguard against improper transactions by directors and against unfounded suspicions of such transactions is to ensure that disclosure is made of all their transactions in the shares or debentures of their companies."[35]

Insider dealing is now a prohibited activity,[36] but the disclosure provisions still operate to supplement the operation of the prohibition, by making detection of improper transactions easier. However, these disclosure rules should not be regarded as aimed solely at insider trading. As the Law Commissions put it:

> "the interests which a director has in his company and his acquisitions and disposals of such interests convey information about the financial incentives that a director has to improve his company's performance and accordingly these provisions form part of the system put in place…to enable shareholders to monitor the directors' stewardship of the company".[37]

So, there are two rationales for director disclosure, insider dealing and corporate governance.

Who has to disclose?

27–008 Article 19(1) imposes the disclosure obligation on any "person discharging managerial responsibilities" (PDMR) and those "closely associated" with them. PDMRs are defined so as to go somewhat wider than just directors so as to include senior (but non-director) executives who (1) have regular access to inside information relating to the issuer; and (2) have power to make managerial decisions affecting the future development and business prospects of the issuer.[38] This is a welcome recognition of the importance of senior executives, though condition (2) will bring only a small number of non-director executives within the definition. To this extent MAR goes beyond the scope of the former companies legislation. On the other hand, the prior law applied the disclosure obligation to shadow directors,[39] who would not seem to fall within the definition of a PDMR, since they will not typically be executives of the company. For example, a large shareholder will not fall within this definition, though its transactions may be caught by the less demanding rules on "vote holder" disclosure, discussed below.

"Closely associated" persons are, in relation to natural persons, spouses and partners, dependent children and any relative who has shared the same household for at least twelve months at date of the transaction. A complex definition of connected artificial persons adds any legal person, trust or partnership, which is managed by a PDMR or a connected natural person or which is directly or indirectly controlled by the PDMR or connected person or which is set up for that

[35] Board of Trade, *Report of the Committee on Company Law Amendment* (June 1945), Cmd.6659, para.87.

[36] See Ch.30.

[37] Law Commission and Scottish Law Commission, *Company Directors: Regulating Conflicts of Interest and Formulating a Statement of Duties: A Joint Consultation Paper* (1998), para.5.2.

[38] MAR art.3(1)(25).

[39] CA 1985 s.324(6). However, a de facto director is probably within the definition.

person's benefit.[40] The notification obligation is imposed on the person who engages in a relevant transaction (see below); a director who does not transact is not obliged to disclose the information relating to connected person's transactions. However, the PDMR must inform connected persons of their obligations under the Regulation, which means the PDMR must identify them, but the connected person's disclosure obligation is not expressly conditioned upon such notification. Equally, the issuer must notify the PDMRs of their obligations, which again involves identifying them, a useful exercise in relation to non-board PDMRs in particular.[41]

What has to be disclosed, to whom and when?

MAR 19(1)(a) requires those subject to it to disclose "transactions on their own account relating to the shares or debt instruments of that issuer or to derivatives or other financial instruments linked thereto." This is narrower in one respect than the former domestic rules. Those required disclosure of interests in the securities of other companies in the same corporate group by a person who was a director of any one group company.[42] The Commission was (and the UK Treasury now is) empowered[43] to produce "delegated acts" specifying the types of transaction which are subject to disclosure, although art.19(7) already includes pledging or lending of securities and the execution of transactions by a third party where that third party acts on behalf of the PDMR or connected person. Article 10 of the Commission's Delegated Regulation 2016/522 ([2016] OJ L88/1) adds a long list of disclosable transactions, including short sales, stock options, call and put options, equity swaps, contracts for differences, and gifts. The transactional scope of the disclosure obligation is thus very wide. However, the Regulation contains one limitation not previously present in UK law. If the value of the transactions in a calendar year does not exceed €5,000, then no disclosure is required and, once that threshold is reached, only transactions above it are disclosable.[44] **27–009**

ESMA's advice,[45] which preceded the adoption of the Delegated Regulation, devoted a lot of attention to the situation where the director or connected person buys or sells units or otherwise invests in a fund which itself has invested in securities of the issuer. In response to this concern, the Regulation itself was amended.[46] The disclosure obligation is removed where the fund's exposure to the issuer's securities is less than 20% of the fund's total assets. Even if the exposure is above this level, no disclosable event occurs if the PDMR did not

---

[40] MAR art.3(1)(26); or, the definition Delphically adds, "the economic interests of which are substantially equivalent to those of such a person".

[41] Regulation art.19(5).

[42] CA 1985 s.324(1). A director of a parent company may well be able to influence what a subsidiary does, even though s/he is not an executive of the subsidiary. However, unless the subsidiary's shares are publicly traded, the point is not important.

[43] MAR art.19(14).

[44] MAR art.19(8). The FCA may raise the threshold to €20,000, but has not chosen to do so.

[45] ESMA, *Technical advice on possible delegated acts concerning the Market Abuse Regulation: Final Report* (2015), 5.2.

[46] By Regulation 2016/1011 [2016] OJ L171/1, introducing a new para.1a into art.19 MAR.

know of and had no reason to suspect a higher exposure level. This means that most retail fund investments are excluded from disclosure, because such funds are not normally allowed such a high degree of investment concentration. Even many non-retail collective investments will fall outside the disclosure obligation. Moreover, the test is applied at the point of investment or disinvestment by the PDMR. If the test is not met on acquisition, for example, the PDMR will not have to disclose if the fund manager later buys securities which take the fund over the threshold, even if the PDMR knows of it, assuming the PDMR has not control over the manager's decision.

27–010 MAR requires information about the transaction to be disclosed to the company (issuer) and to the FCA within three working days of the relevant transaction.[47] MAR also required that the information be released to the market within the same time frame.[48] This caused obvious difficulties for the issuer if notification to it occurred right at the end of the permitted period. Under an amendment to the retained law made in 2021,[49] the issuer was given two working days from the receipt of the information to inform the market. The information to be given to the issuer includes "the price and volume of the transaction" (so that the PDMR cannot simply say that he or she has bought some shares in the company).[50] Given the complexity of the connected persons definition the information is wisely required to specify "the reason for the notification", which both requires the notifying person to work out how the definition applies to them and enables the company to check the reasoning. The financial instrument and the nature of the transaction must also be described.

Disclosure of Major Voting Shareholdings

Rationale and history

27–011 This is a further area where British law has long required disclosure but where EU legislation (via the TD) became dominant, leading to a transfer of a substantial part of the disclosure requirements from the Companies Acts to the FSMA 2000. There is an initial puzzle about why these provisions are necessary at all. It was rare for companies in the UK to issue "bearer" shares and their issuance is now prohibited.[51] Consequently, shares are issued in the name of a person (natural or corporate) and are referred to as "registered" shares. The names of the holders of such shares are publicly available.[52] It may be wondered

---

[47] MAR art.19(1)(2).

[48] MAR art.19(3)—and the information must be stored in a central storage mechanism, as required by FSMA 2000 s.89W.

[49] By the Financial Services Act 2021.

[50] MAR art.19(6)(g). See Regulation 2016/523 ([2016] OJ L88/19) for the reporting templates.

[51] CA 2006 s.779(4). Schedule 4 to the Small Business and Enterprise Act 2015 made provision for the conversion and cancellation of existing bearer shares. See para.24–020.

[52] Either because they are contained in a public register held by the company and reported to the Registrar in the confirmation statement (see para.22–042) or because, in the case of a private company, the company has chosen to have the register held by the Registrar. See CA 2006 Pt 8 and s.853F.

why further provision is required. However, the requirement that the shareholder's name be registered in the company's share register does not mean that the name of the beneficial owner needs to be registered. The use of nominee names has long been popular among big investors and now the dematerialisation of shares[53] has put some pressure upon even small investors to use nominees. Thus, inspection of the share register will not necessarily, perhaps not even typically, reveal who has the beneficial interest in the share.[54]

Granted this, it is still necessary to establish why holders of significant interests in shares should be required to reveal the extent of those interests publicly. In part, but only in small part, these provisions aim to deter insider dealing, as with those discussed in the previous section. However, the main purpose of these provisions is better put as follows:

> "A company, its members and the public at large should be entitled to be informed promptly of the acquisition of a significant holding in its voting shares in order that existing members and those dealing with the company may protect their interests and that the conduct of the affairs of the company is not prejudiced by uncertainty over those who may be in a position to influence or control the company."[55]

This statement explains the concentration in the successive legal regimes on disclosure of holdings of voting shares, because it is disclosure of actual or potential control of the company that is aimed at, rather than interests in its securities in general. As we have seen in para 13–022, a requirement has now been applied to all companies for disclosure of significant control (PSC) interests, largely on law enforcement grounds, but companies traded on regulated markets are exempt from this CA requirement because the rules applicable to them, discussed below, are more demanding.[56]

However, the statement just quoted might be thought to run together two different rationales for the disclosure provisions. One is protection of the management of the company and its members, by making them aware of who is building up a stake in the company. Disclosure here operates as an early-warning device about potential takeover bids in particular. But the statement refers also to the protection of "the public". Public disclosure may be said to be promoting the conceptually separate goal of "market transparency". The argument here is that disclosure of the identity of those with important share stakes in the company is (or could be) an important element in the market's assessment of the value of the company. Obviously, a single set of disclosure rules might aim to promote both policies.

The current law in fact contains two different types of disclosure rule, which **27–012**
illustrate the two rationales. One requires the disclosure of interests in voting shares by the holder of the interest once a certain size threshold has been crossed. This is an obligation generated automatically by the law once the appropriate

---

53 See Ch.26.

54 We have discussed in Ch.12, the problems which this causes in relation to shareholders' governance rights.

55 Department of Trade, *Disclosure of Interests in Shares* (1980), p.2.

56 CA 2006 s.790B(1). In very broad terms the general rules apply to holdings at the 25% level; the rules below at the 3% level.

threshold has been reached. The second, still contained in the Companies Act, is triggered by the company asking any person to reveal the extent of their interest in the company's voting shares. This latter set of disclosure rules we discuss not in this chapter but in Ch.28 dealing with takeovers, because their main impact is as an early warning device for incumbent management in that context.

The principle of automatic disclosure of major shareholdings was introduced as a result, again, of the recommendations of the Cohen Committee[57] in 1945 that the beneficial ownership of shares be publicly disclosed. Over time, the triggering threshold has been lowered, the speed of the required disclosure increased and the range of interests to be disclosed made more sophisticated. EU law also showed an interest in this topic at an early stage[58] and the current EU principles are laid down in the TD, as later amended.[59] The main impact of the TD in the UK was, once again, to spark off a fundamental review of the purposes of these disclosure rules. In particular, the emphasis in the Directive upon disclosure as an instrument to improve the functioning of the securities markets[60] led the DTI to propose[61] that the "market transparency" rationale be given pre-eminence over the others. This policy was implemented by the removal of the automatic disclosure requirements from the companies legislation whilst at the same time the CA 2006 amended FSMA 2000 so as to permit the area to be regulated by FCA's DTR rules, thus giving rise to the current regulatory structure.[62] The result, as with directors' disclosures, was an overall narrowing of the range of companies covered by the regime.

The scope of the disclosure obligation

Which companies are subject to the regime?

27–013 The CA 1985 regime applied to all public companies (in the company law sense of that term—Plcs).[63] The Directive applies only to companies (issuers) whose securities are admitted to trading on a regulated market.[64] The domestic regime implementing the Directive applies a little more widely, in that the FCA is empowered to make vote-holding disclosure rules relating to any share market (not just regulated markets).[65] The DTR in fact apply to any share market operated by a Recognised Investment Exchange ("prescribed markets"), whether

[57] Report of the Committee on Company Law Amendment, Cmd. 6659 (1945), pp.39–45. It is to be noted that the domestic legislation has still not been lowered to the 1% threshold recommended by that Committee.

[58] Its first Directive on disclosure of major shareholdings was Directive 88/627 [1988] OJ L348/62 (17 December 1988).

[59] By Directive 2013/50 [2013] OJ L294/13.

[60] See especially the preamble to the TD.

[61] DTI, *Proposals for Reform of Part VI of the Companies Act 1985* (April 1995).

[62] CA 2006 s.1266, introducing new FSMA 2000 s.89A–G.

[63] CA 1985 s.198.

[64] TD art.2(1)(d).

[65] FSMA 2000 s.89A(1), (3)(a).

regulated or not.[66] Thus, both the Main Market of the LSE and AIM are covered by the current domestic disclosure obligation.[67]

When does the disclosure obligation arise?

The rules are concerned with disclosure of the percentage of voting rights held in a company, as certain thresholds are passed, rather than just holdings of shares. For that reason DTR 5 is entitled "Vote Holder Notification". Holdings of non-voting shares do not have to be disclosed, because they do not contribute to the ability to exercise control over the company. Nor do holdings of shares which are entitled to vote only in particular circumstances have to be disclosed, for example, non-voting preference shares whose shareholders can nevertheless vote when class rights are being varied under the statutory procedure[68] or which are entitled to vote if their preference dividend has not been paid, provided, of course, that an event has not occurred which gives the class of shares general voting rights.[69] By contrast, PDMR do have to disclose holdings of non-voting shares under the rules discussed in the previous section, because opportunities to engage in insider dealing can easily arise in relation to such shares, and holdings of non-voting equity shares may provide economic incentives for directors to act in particular ways, despite the absence of a vote. **27–014**

The disclosure thresholds are 3% of the total voting rights in the company and every 1% increase thereafter. Decreases must also be notified on the same scale.[70] These disclosure triggers are more demanding than those in the TD,[71] but reflect the prior domestic law. Almost as important as the definition of the threshold is the question of how soon after the threshold has been crossed does the notification obligation have to be discharged. A notification obligation which was triggered only, for example, a month after the threshold had been crossed would be of very little use to the company, its shareholders or the market in general. In fact, the current regime, following the 1985 Act, imposes a "two-day" rule, i.e. disclosure as soon as possible but in any event by the end of the second trading day following the day on which the obligation to disclose arose.[72]

In the simple case, the event giving rise to the obligation to disclose will be the purchase or sale of the voting shares of the issuer by an investor who is then obliged to make the notification. However, if the disclosure rule did not extend beyond this, it would be inadequate. For example, Company A, holding 2% of the voting shares of Company X, acquires control of Company B, which also holds 2% of the shares. Neither company had a notifiable interest in Company X beforehand, but after the acquisition Company A should have a notifiable interest.

---

[66] DTR 5.1.1(3); Glossary, *Prescribed Market*. For the definition of a recognised investment exchange see para.25–007.

[67] However, the exemption from PSC disclosures does not apply to prescribed markets, so that AIM companies are subject to both sets of rules. This is apparently the result of the drafting of the EU money laundering rules.

[68] See para.13–014.

[69] DTR 5.1.1(3).

[70] DTR 5.1.2.

[71] TD art.9(1), which has triggers only at 5, 10, 15, 20, 25, 30, 50 and 75%.

[72] DTR 5.8.3.

The notification obligation in relation to X's shares would be triggered by the acquisition of B's shares by A, not the acquisition of X's shares by A or B, which could have occurred much earlier.

The obligation to disclose might even arise as a result of events with which the person upon whom it falls is wholly unconnected. For example, a company engages in a share buy-back programme in relation a class of voting shares. The shareholder does not participate in the buy-back, but as a result of other shareholders' decisions the shareholder finds that his or her holding now exceeds one of the notification thresholds. The opposite development could occur if the company issued new voting shares other than to the existing shareholders. The scheme of the FCA rules on this point is that the company is required at the end of the month in which there has been an increase or decrease in the number of its voting shares to make public details of the resulting voting structure; and that is the event which causes the disclosure obligation to arise.[73]

Indirect holdings of voting rights

27–015 In order to bring in situations other than the simple acquisition or disposal the rules contain two sets of provisions extending its scope. The first is indirect holdings of shares,[74] of which the following are important examples:

(1) Voting rights held by an undertaking controlled by a person are to be treated as voting rights of that person. The rules use of the definition of parent and subsidiary in the CA 2006 to identify a controlled undertaking, with the extension that the controller can include a natural person and not be confined to a controlling company.[75] The controlled undertaking would also have to notify its holding, if one of the triggering events applied.
(2) Voting rights attached to shares held by a nominee on behalf of another will constitute an indirect holding of voting rights by that other person. The nominee will be a direct holder of the voting rights and so have to make disclosure unless, as will often be the case, the nominee may exercise those rights only on the instructions of the beneficial owner.[76]
(3) Voting rights attached to shares deposited with someone are to be treated as voting rights of the depositee, if the depositee has the right to exercise the votes at its discretion in the absence of instructions from the shareholder. In the same way, a person engaged in investment management is to be treated as the holder of voting rights if it can effectively determine the manner in which voting rights attached to shares under its control are exercised, in the absence of specific instructions from the shareholders. One or other of provisions (2) and (3) is likely to be applicable in the common situation in the UK where an institutional shareholder has outsourced the management

[73] DTR 5.6.1. However, where the change occurs as a result of an issuer transaction, for example, a fund raising, DTR 5.6.1A requires the issuer to make an announcement by the end of the business day following the increase of decrease.
[74] DTR 5.2.1.
[75] FSA, *Handbook*, Glossary: "Parent Undertaking"; FSMA 2000 s.420 referring to CA 2006 s.1162. This catches the situation discussed in para.27–014.
[76] DTR 5.1.3(2).

of its investment portfolio to a fund manager, though the shares themselves may be vested in a custodian.[77] The fund manager will be an indirect holder of voting shares, assuming, as will usually be the case, the relevant discretion. The custodian will not have to disclose if, as is usual, it can vote only upon instruction (see (2) above).

A further issue arises where, as is common, the investment management company is part of a larger financial conglomerate. The rules on controlled undertakings ((1) above) would suggest the parent of the group must aggregate the fund-management subsidiary's indirect holdings with its own. However, the DTR provide an exemption from this further aggregation, subject to certain conditions, notably that the fund management subsidiary exercises its voting rights independently of the parent.[78] This seems correct in principle, since the fund manager will be required to exercise the voting rights attached to the shares it controls in the interests of the beneficial owner (the institutional shareholder) and not those of its parent.

(4) Where there is an agreement between two or more people under which they are obliged to implement "a lasting common policy" towards a company through a concerted exercise of voting rights, then each of the parties to the agreement will have the voting rights of the other parties attributed to it.[79] Such "concert parties" are a common feature of the long-term governance of companies in some continental European jurisdictions, but less popular in the UK.

(5) A person will be regarded as an indirect holder of voting rights if he or she has concluded an agreement (for consideration) with the shareholder for the temporary transfer of voting rights. A linked question concerns disclosure obligations in relation to stock lending,[80] which does not fall conceptually within this category (because the shares are transferred as well as votes), but which serves a similar function. The borrower will be treated as acquiring voting rights if such are attached to the stock borrowed. However, will the lender of the stock be regarded as disposing of voting rights, thus potentially triggering a disclosure obligation? It is conceivable that that the lender's right to call for the re-delivery of the stock, which is an acquisition of voting rights, can be netted off against the loss of voting rights arising out of the stock-lending agreement, thus producing no overall change in its position. However, the DTR no longer contain an express exemption for this case, apparently in deference to the views of ESMA.[81]

---

[77] See para.12–013.

[78] DTR 5.4.

[79] The requirement for a "lasting common policy" means that this disclosure rule will not apply to temporary coalitions of shareholders designed to bring about specific changes in the running of the company. If the temporary coalition aims to install a completely new board, it may run foul of the Takeover Panel's rules on concert parties. See para.28–043.

[80] See above at para.12–053.

[81] DTR 5.3.2A. See ESMA, *Indicative list of financial instruments that are subject to notification requirements according to Article 13(1b) of the revised Transparency Directive* (December 2015).

Financial instruments

27–016 The second extension relates to interests in the voting shares of the issuer acquired via holdings of other types of financial instrument which are linked to the issuer's securities. The operation of some of these linked instruments is easy to grasp because they generate rights to acquire or dispose of the issuer's voting shares. Thus an option to buy from or sell the issuer's voting shares to a third party must be disclosed at the time the option is acquired, even though it has not been exercised (and my never be).[82] However, whilst financial instruments generating "the unconditional right to acquire … shares to which voting rights are attached" are clear cases, more recent debate has focussed on instruments which do not give such a right but have a similar economic effect because they are "referenced" to voting shares.[83] In this case, the holder of the financial instrument does not have the right to acquire (dispose of) ownership of the underlying voting shares, but does have the economic exposure of an owner.

The classic example of such financial instruments are "contracts for differences" (CfDs). In these contracts, as more fully explained in Ch.28,[84] the subject-matter of the contract is the difference in the price of a security at two points in time, rather than the actual security itself. As such, it would seem to give rise to no disclosable issue at all, since the holder of the CfD does not acquire a share and, in particular, its voting rights but only an economic interest in how it performs. However, in relation to "long"[85] CfDs the counterparty to the contract (usually an investment bank) will often hedge its position under the contract by buying the underlying security. In some cases this will enable the other person entering into the CfD contract to influence the way the votes attached to those shares are exercised by the bank whilst the contract is on foot or to acquire the shares from the bank when the CfD is settled. If that person has a contractual right to either of these things under the CfD, then there is no doubt that there is a disclosable interest, assuming the CfD relates to voting shares. The debate concerned the much more common situation where no such contractual right exists, but in practice the CfD holder can either acquire the shares or influence the exercise of voting rights.

27–017 The UK decided to include CfDs in its disclosure rules before this step was taken by the EU. Consulting on the issue the FSA, noting that some 30% of equity trades were by way of CfDs, usually in order to increase leverage or to avoid stamp duty, was of the view that investment banks normally require the CfDs to be "closed out" with cash (rather than the delivery of the underlying shares) and are resistant to CfD holders seeking to influence voting rights attached to the shares bought as a hedge. Nevertheless:

---

[82] DTR 5.3.1(1)(a).

[83] DTR 5.3.1(1)(b).

[84] At para.28–044.

[85] If the investment bank has to pay the CfD holder any increase in the value of the share, the holder can be said to have a "long" position and the bank can protect itself by buying the underlying share; if the bank has to pay the holder the decrease in the value of the share, the holder can be said to have a "short" position, but purchasing the underlying share does not protect the bank in that case. It must hedge its exposure in some other way.

> "There are some instances of CfDs being used in ways which the intention of the current regulatory regime is designed to catch...Specifically, we conclude that CfDs are sometimes being used, firstly, to seek to influence votes and other corporate governance matters on an undisclosed basis and, secondly, to build up stakes in companies, again without disclosure. We have therefore decided that we should take action now to address these failures."[86]

After some havering about how to implement this policy, the FSA changed the rules so as the require disclosure of all "long" positions under CfDs.[87] The amended TD followed suit. The contrary argument is that, since most CfDs are settled for cash and the bank's voting behaviour is usually not influenced by the CfD holder, requiring disclosure of all CfDs potentially gives the market a great deal of useless information. However, no one has been able to find a reliable method of distinguishing between those CfDs which do and those which do not give the holder influence over the issuer.

Exemptions

Given the range of notifiable interests, some exemptions needed to be provided, in the interests of both disclosers and recipients of disclosures. We have already noted the one relating to custodians.[88] Another is the acquisition of shares for the purposes of clearing and settlement, i.e. of completing a bargain to buy and sell shares.[89] Probably the most significant is that relating to "market makers", i.e. those who hold shares or financial instruments (usually in a particular range of companies) on their own account in order to be able to offer continuous trading opportunities to those who want to buy or sell those shares.[90] Market makers enhance the liquidity of public securities markets but they do not provide this service for altruistic reasons but in the hope of making a profit overall out of the difference between the prices at which they acquire and dispose of the securities. If they were obliged to disclose the details of their purchases and sales, their ability to make this profit and so their willingness to offer their services as market makers would be reduced. Even this exemption is limited: it does not apply when the market maker's holding in a particular company reaches 10% and it is conditional upon the market maker not intervening in the management of the company or exerting any influence over the company to acquire its shares. There is a similar exemption for financial instruments held in the trading books of banks and related institutions, but in this case the disclosure obligation bites at the 5% level.[91] Finally, there is an exemption for acquisitions during the price stabilisation process after a new issue.[92] **27–018**

---

[86] FSA, *Disclosure of Contracts for Difference* (November 2007), CP 07/20, para.1.24.

[87] DTR 5.3.3(2). For its earlier preference see previous note at paras 1.28 and 5.32–5.34.

[88] See para.27–015.

[89] DTR 5.1.3(1). This is a limited exemption since it applies only to acquisitions made for the sole purpose of settlement and is limited to acquisitions made during the three trading days following the striking of the bargain to which it relates.

[90] DTR 5.1.3(3) and 5.1.4.

[91] DTR 5.1.3(4). This exemption will normally permit the bank party to the CfD (see para.27–016) which buys the underlying shares as a hedge not to disclose its holding of the shares.

[92] DTR 5.1.3(7). On stabilisation see para.30–042.

The disclosure process

27–019 Given the complexity of the situations which might generate an obligation to disclose, the obligation and its associated time limit are not triggered by the occurrence of the disclosable event itself, but when a person "learns of the acquisition or disposal or the possibility of exercising voting rights" or "having regard to the circumstances, should have learned of it".[93]

Assuming a disclosure obligation has arisen, the person upon whom it falls must give the required information. In the case of a direct acquisition or disposal of voting shares the required information is straightforward: simply the "resulting situation in terms of voting rights",[94] i.e. the percentage of shares now held and the date upon which the threshold was crossed. Unlike in the case of disclosure by PDMR there is no obligation to disclose information about the terms upon which the shares were acquired or disposed of. In the case of indirect holdings of shares, some further information is required. For holdings via controlled companies the chain of control must be identified, partly, no doubt, to encourage disclosers to give their mind to this issue. The identity of the shareholder must be given (even if that shareholder has no notification obligation, for example a custodian voting only under instructions) and that of the person entitled to exercise the voting rights, if not the shareholder.[95] For voting rights exercisable through financial instruments, some basic information about those instruments must also be given, notably, the name of the underlying issuer and details about the exercise period (if any) and the date of maturity or expiry of the instrument.[96]

This information must be given to the company. However, the purposes of the disclosure rules can be met only if the information given to the issuer is publicised further. The DTR require issuers on a regulated market to make public the information received as soon as possible and, in any event, by the end of the following trading day, as is now the rule for directors' notifications. In the case of issuers whose securities are traded on a prescribed (but not a regulated) market the maximum period for the further disclosure is the end of the third trading day following.[97] There is a single national storage point for the information.[98]

Overall, it can be said that the rather simple objective of achieving disclosure of vote-holdings at and above the 3% level has generated a fearsomely complex set of rules.

SANCTIONS

27–020 Broadly, sanctions for failure to meet the above disclosure requirements may be private or public. Private remedies are sought by persons who have suffered loss as a result of the breaches of the disclosure obligations (and so are usually aimed

---

93 DTR 5.8.3, following art.12(2) of the TD.

94 DTR 5.8.1.

95 DTR 5.8.1.

96 DTR 5.8.2. For some types of CfDs calculating the number of shares the counterparty would buy for hedging purposes may not be straightforward and may involve an excursion into option pricing.

97 DTR 5.8.12. For the meaning of a "prescribed" market see text attached to fn.62 above.

98 FSMA 2000 s.89W.

at compensation). Public sanctions are initiated by the public authorities, notably the FCA, normally seeking to punish infringers.[99] Those sanctions may be administrative or criminal.

Compensation for misleading statements to the market

The most obvious basis for a private claim for compensation is where an issuer is required to make a disclosure to the market but fails to disclose at all, delays disclosure in circumstances where it is not legitimate to do so or makes a misleading disclosure, and the action or inaction has consequences for the price of the shares. Assuming full disclosure would have moved the price of the security, those who bought or sold shares[100] during the period before the emergence of the truth might have a claim for the difference between the actual price paid and the price the securities would have had if the disclosure obligations had been complied with.[101] The EU instruments actually say rather little about private actions for compensation. The TD stated, but only in relation to its periodic reporting requirements, that Member States "shall ensure that their laws, regulations and administrative provisions on liability apply to the issuers, the administrative, management or supervisory bodies of the issuer or the persons responsible within the issuers".[102] The reference to the "laws" of the Member States means that they had to enable private litigants to sue on the basis of their domestic civil liability rules, but the TD did not require any particular alteration to the domestic liability regime. Moreover, the TD gave the Member States a choice in relation to the defendants against whom the liability could be asserted. Furthermore, this provision on civil liability in the TD did not apply to the disclosure of major shareholdings under that Directive. Nor is there any equivalent to it in MAR, i.e. in relation to episodic disclosures and disclosure of interests by directors and others. Member States are thus had considerable freedom in fashioning civil liability rules. **27–021**

After extensive policy debate, the UK introduced an explicit liability regime (in Sch.10A to FSMA 2000) but imposing liability on issuers only and then only for intentional or reckless statements. The statutory liability applies to information notified or communicated to the market by issuers through a PIP[103] or other recognised communication service.[104] It thus embraces communications to the market by issuers of information communicated to them by PDMR or major vote holders and to the market-moving episodic disclosures required by MAR as well as to the issuer disclosures required by the TD. However, the issuer

---

[99] There is, however, some overlap. See para.27–024.

[100] Whether buyers or sellers would sue would depend on the direction of the price movement had the information been disclosed.

[101] There are also issues of causation here. If I buy at an artificially high price (because the issuer has concealed adverse information) but sell before the truth emerges, I have suffered no loss. If I sell at an artificially low price (because the issuer has concealed positive information), it can be argued that I have suffered a loss only if the price was the main motivation for my sale (rather than some personal financial emergency).

[102] TD art.7.

[103] Above para.27–006 and FSMA 2000 s.89P.

[104] CA 2006 Sch.10A para.2.

is unlikely to attract liability if it accurately passes on the information communicated to it, unless it is aware of the inaccuracy of the information it received. The main focus of the debate was in relation to communications where the issuer is both the generator and communicator of the information, i.e. in relation to periodic and episodic disclosures by the issuer.

27–022 It is a controversial issue whether compensation should be available to investors in relation to misleading periodic or episodic statements put out by companies. Until 2006, FSMA 2000 made no specific provision for compensation to be available directly to investors as a result of misleading statements or non-disclosure to the market—except the extensive and long-standing statutory liabilities for misstatements in prospectuses.[105] It was possible to bring an action in the common law of deceit, but the requirements for that head of tortious liability are particularly demanding, notably the requirements for knowledge of the falsity of the statement or recklessness as to its truth on the part of the maker of the statement, for reliance on the statement by the claimant and that the defendant should have intended the claimant to rely on the statement. An action in common law negligence for purely economic loss reduces the first and third requirements, but brings with it an additional high hurdle for liability, namely, that the defendant should have assumed responsibility to the claimant for taking care in relation to the truth of the statement.[106] Thus, actions for compensation by investors who had taken investment decisions on the basis of false statements to the market were extremely rare.[107]

By and large, government was content with this situation, and it moved to legislate only in the light of art.7 of the TD, which was thought capable of undermining the "assumption of responsibility" requirement in the domestic law of negligence. After enacting a stop-gap measure in 2006, a more considered solution was put in place as from October 2010.[108] The purpose of the new regime was slightly to relax the requirements for liability in fraud (for fear that the domestic remedies would not otherwise meet the EU requirement for "effectiveness"), whilst confirming the virtual absence of a role for negligence liability in this area.[109] The new statutory scheme applies to statements made on multilateral trading facilities as well as regulated markets.[110] The aim was to put in place a comprehensive statutory regime for misstatements to the market.

The potential claimants are those who acquire, dispose of or continue to hold securities in reliance on the published information and the acquisition or disposal

---

[105] See paras 25–034 onwards; and, at least at first instance, the courts refused to find liability for breach of statutory duty on the basis of FSMA 2000's disclosure rules: *Hall v Cable and Wireless Plc* [2009] EWHC 1793 (Comm); [2010] 1 B.C.L.C. 95.

[106] *Caparo Industries Plc v Dickman* [1990] 2 A.C. 605 HL. See para.23–044.

[107] The pre-2006 position is described in HM Treasury, *Davies Review of Issuer Liability: Discussion Paper* (March 2007).

[108] CA 2006 s.90A and Sch.10A.

[109] See HM Treasury, *Davies Review of Issuer Liability: Final Report* (June 2007).

[110] CA 2006 Sch.10A paras 1 and 2.

of securities includes those acts in relation to interests in securities.[111] As far as liability on the part of the company for knowing or reckless misstatements is concerned, it is enough under the statutory scheme that the claimant's reliance on the statement was reasonable.[112] It does not matter whether the company intended to induce reliance. Furthermore, the scheme imposes liability for dishonest delay in making a required announcement, even though at common law failure to speak would not normally trigger liability.[113] The other requirements for the common law of deceit are, however, maintained under the statutory scheme.[114] In principle, the issuer is liable for misleading statements to the market only under the special statutory regime, whilst any other person (e.g. a PDMR who was responsible within the company for the statement) is relieved of all responsibility, except to the company.[115] However, certain other liabilities are preserved.[116] Liability for negligent misstatement is maintained provided there has been an assumption of responsibility on the part of the issuer or PDMR for the truth of the statement (thus preserving the common law of tort). Liability will also arise where the issuer (or, much less likely, the PDMR) has contractually promised the truth of its statement to the claimant, where the requirements of liability under the Misrepresentation Act 1967[117] are satisfied, or where the statement falls within the prospectus liability provisions and in certain other limited cases.[118] In short, the idea is that the issuer and a PDMR should not be liable in negligence to an investor unless they have promised, formally or informally, to that investor to take care in making statements.

The principal argument for excluding liability on the part of the issuer for misstatements to the market is that shifting the loss from claimant to issuer (i.e. its shareholders) has very little social utility. A generous liability rule in effect shifts the loss from a sub-set of the shareholders to the shareholders as a whole, i.e. from the investors who bought shares on the basis of a false statement to the market and were still holding the shares when the truth emerged to the shareholders as a whole.[119] A regular investor in the market is as likely, over the long term, to find itself a shareholder in the company who did not buy shares in the company whilst the misstatement was operative in the market as among those **27–023**

[111] In *Manning & Napier Fund Inc v Tesco Plc* [2019] EWHC 2858 (Ch) Hildyard J managed to construe the language of the schedule so as to bring within it those whose interest in the securities was located at the end of a chain of intermediaries which started with the issuer in question. This litigation was settled subsequently.

[112] CA 2006 Sch.10A para.3(4)(b). See the decision in *Sharp v Blank* [2019] EWHC 3096 (Ch) (para.28–064) finding the claimants' reliance on the market statement unreasonable.

[113] Unless the failure to speak rendered a previous statement misleading. The statutory provision is in para.5. It was a controversial decision to impose liability for delay, but, since liability is confined to dishonest delay, defined narrowly (para.6), it is unlikely to be widespread.

[114] For the purpose of the issuer's liability the attribution rule used is whether "a person discharging managerial responsibilities" within the company knew of the falsehood, was reckless as to its truth or was dishonest as to the concealment (paras 3(2) and 8(5)).

[115] CA 2006 Sch.10A para.7(1)(2).

[116] CA 2006 Sch.10A para.7(3).

[117] See para.25–038.

[118] CA 2006 Sch.10A paras 7(1) and (3).

[119] If the investor disposes of the shares before the truth emerges, then of course no loss is suffered by that investor. See *Hall v Cable and Wireless Plc* [2010] 1 B.C.L.C. 95 at [43]–[46]. This argument assumes the typical situation, i.e. that the company's statement was falsely optimistic.

who did. That investor would rationally favour a rule which leaves the loss where it lies rather than transfers it, at considerable transaction costs (the costs of litigation), from one group of shareholders to the shareholders as a whole. This argument might be thought to apply as much to liability in fraud as to liability in negligence, and yet the statutory scheme shifts the loss in the case of fraud. One response might be that the TD did not permit Member States to remove liability completely; a more principled response might be that fraud has a corrosive effect on markets and the deterrent impact of imposing liability for fraud is useful addition to the law's armoury against fraud.

A striking feature of the new statutory scheme is that, whilst it makes the company liable in fraud to investors, it removes liability to third parties entirely, including for fraud, from PDMR who were involved in making the false statement or were responsible for the dishonest delay.[120] At first sight this seems odd, for the argument against transferring loss does not apply if the loss is transferred from investors to PDMR, rather from investors to shareholders as a whole. Why not make the PDMR liable for both fraudulent and negligent misstatements to the market so as to encourage them to provide accurate statements on behalf of the company? There are two arguments against negligence liability to investors on the part of PDMR in respect of misstatements to the market. First, liability might encourage the PDMR to be excessively cautious in what they say to the market and thus deprive investors of useful information.[121] Secondly, given the prevalence of insurance bought by companies to protect their directors against negligence claims,[122] liability for PDMR would again shift the loss to the shareholders as a whole, through the cost of the insurance premiums payable over the years. There is probably a stronger case for maintaining individual liability to investors in the case of fraud. The statutory scheme does impose that liability, but it lies only to the company.[123] Deterrence of misleading statements is thus to be achieved, not under the statutory compensation scheme, but, if at all, as a result of penalties imposed by the FCA, as discussed below.

Compensation via FCA action

27–024 An alternative route to compensation for investors is via FCA action on their behalf to obtain a compensation order for the benefit of investors. Under ss.382 of FSMA 2000 the FCA has the power to apply to the court for a compensation order against a person who has contravened its rules and any other person knowingly concerned in the contravention. Under ss.383 and 384, applying to the market manipulation prohibition to be found in art.15 of MAR, the FCA can either apply to the court or make an order itself against a contravener. These latter

[120] CA 2006 Sch.10A para.7(2). Of course, individuals will be liable if they have assumed responsibility to the claimant for the truth of their statement or contractually bound themselves in that respect.

[121] See the similar argument developed in para.22–033.

[122] See para.10–123.

[123] For these arguments in greater detail see P. Davies, "Liability for Misstatements to the Market: Some Reflections" (2009) 9 J.C.L.S. 295; and for comment Ferran, ibid, 315.

sections seem at first sight irrelevant to the MAR disclosure rules discussed in this chapter which stem from MAR arts 17–19. However, as we see below, the FCA has been prepared to treat misleading disclosure as falling within one part of the definition of market manipulation contained in art.12 of MAR (discussed more fully in Ch.30), thus opening up the use of ss.383 and 384. This is "disseminating information…which gives, or is likely to give, false or misleading signals as to the…price of a financial instrument".[124]

The Act makes these powers available where profits have accrued to the person in breach or loss or other adverse consequences were suffered by other persons as a result of the contravention. The compensation order may require the person in breach to pay such amount as is thought just, having regard to the profits made or loss suffered. That amount is to be paid out to such persons as the court (or regulator under s.384) may direct who fall within the categories of those who have suffered loss or are the persons to whom the profit is "attributable".[125] These provisions are potentially important. They constitutes a form of class action for investors, with the costs paid by the FCA. However, the FCA's Enforcement Guide[126] suggests that it will not use its powers to seek restitution whenever they are available but only when it regards their use as more effective than alternative courses of action, open to the FCA or to the potential beneficiaries of FCA action.

The sections pose difficult questions of quantum for the court or regulator. Depriving the issuer of the profit through the breach made may be uncontroversial, but losses may have been suffered on a wide scale in the market which go far beyond the profit made, which may be non-existent. For example, where a company makes an inaccurate statement to the market which moves the market price upwards, but the price later falls when the truth emerges, losses may well have been suffered by all those who bought shares in the market after the statement and still held them at its correction, whilst the issuer itself is unlikely to have made any profit at all, if it was not at the time in the process of issuing shares. On the other hand, making the company or individuals provide compensation for all those losses might be disproportionate to the wrong involved.

Nevertheless, in the Tesco case in 2017 the FCA adopted the latter approach.[127] In **27–025**
August 2014 the company made an expected profits statement which was misleading and when the truth was announced a month later the price of its shares fell. The FCA found that the company "knew or could reasonably be expect to know" that the statement was misleading. The knowledge attributed to the company by the FCA was not the knowledge of the board, which did not have it, but "knowledge at a sufficiently high level but below the level of the Tesco plc Board."[128] On this basis the FCA found that the misleading statement constituted

---

[124] MAR art.12(1)(c).

[125] FSMA 2000 ss.382(3),(8), 383(5),(10), 384(5)(6).

[126] EG 11.2.

[127] FCA, *Tesco Plc, Final Notice* (March 2017).

[128] FCA, *Tesco Plc, Final Notice* (March 2017), para.2.3. The individuals in question were dismissed by Tesco and later prosecuted for fraud by the Serious Fraud Office but the judge found the

market abuse on the part of the company.[129] The compensation order, which the company seems not to have opposed, did indeed take as the basis for the compensation order the loss suffered by each investor in the market as a result of the misstatement. That loss was calculated as the drop in the price of Tesco's shares when the correction was published to the market, after allowing for industry and market-wide movements occurring at the same time. This was calculated at 24.5p per share and was required to be paid to investors in respect of shares purchased during the period when the misstatement was operative less those sold before the correction was published.[130] The total amount payable by Tesco was estimated by the FCA to be £85m, plus interest.[131]

The above powers to seek a restitution order from the court extend to the situation where the defendant has committed the criminal offence of making an intentionally or recklessly misleading statement considered below.[132] If such conduct leads to an actual conviction, a further avenue to compensation may be opened up, namely compensation orders made under the general criminal law provisions.[133]

The FSMA 2000 also gives the FCA power to seek injunctions from the courts in respect of apprehended or repeated violation of its requirements.[134]

Administrative penalties for breaches

27–026 The rules and procedures governing the imposition of penalties and the FCA's investigatory powers[135] have been described in a previous chapter in relation to breaches of LR and PR.[136] In this chapter we note only those provisions which are particularly relevant to misstatements or non-disclosure to the market.

A person who contravenes the FCA's transparency rules is liable to the imposition of penalties or to public censure by the FCA.[137] The term "transparency rules" is defined so as to include both the rules relating to periodic or ongoing disclosure of information about issuers and the rules about major vote-holding disclosure.[138] Even where the breach is the issuer's alone, directors

prosecution case so weak as not to require an answer and the defendants were acquitted (*Financial Times*, 23 January 2019). The FCA seems not to have explored, at least publicly, the implications of this development for the compensation order.

[129] Contrary to FSMA 2000 s.118(7). See para.30-037.

[130] FCA, *Tesco Plc, Final Notice* (March 2017), Annex 2, paras 36–37 and the definition of "Net Relevant Share Purchases". Certain transactions equivalent to disposals were also factored in.

[131] FCA, *Tesco to pay redress for market abuse* (Press Release, 28 March 2017). Even this figure was dwarfed by the £129m penalty Tesco paid to Serious Fraud Office under a deferred prosecution agreement to avoid a criminal conviction. This agreement as well might be thought to have been undermined by the failure of the subsequent prosecutions against the individual employees, but it apparently was not revised: see fn.128.

[132] FSMA 2000 s.382(9)(a)(iv). See para.27–032.

[133] See *R. v Rigby (Carl)* [2006] EWCA Crim 1653; [2007] 1 Cr. App. R. (S.) 73 (though the FSA's attempted use of general confiscation powers was unsuccessful). Some £200,000 was paid to Morley Fund Management and £120,000 to Standard Life.

[134] FSMA 2000 ss.380 and 381.

[135] Under s.97.

[136] See para.25–042.

[137] FSMA 2000 s.91(1B),(3).

[138] FSMA 2000 ss.89A(1),(5), 89B.

and officers may be penalised where they were knowingly concerned in the contravention by the issuer.[139] The FCA also has penalty imposing and censuring powers where a person contravenes arts 17–19 of MAR (the "disclosure rules") or is knowingly concerned in the contravention.[140] This provision gives enforcement backing to the rules relating to the disclosure of inside information and the disclosure of PDMR interests.[141]

Thus, directors and PDMR are more exposed to liability under the administrative regime than they are under the rules on compensation.[142] So also is the issuer. Whereas "intention or recklessness" is the standard for issuer liability under Sch.10A, the DTR impose a "reasonable care" standard for issuer liability to administrative penalties in relation to market statements required by the transparency rules.[143] As to the disclosure rules, neither MAR nor FSMA 2000 explicitly address the standard of culpability required for the imposition of penalties. However, FSMA 2000 requires the FSA to develop and publish a statement of its policy about the imposition of administrative penalties in respect of breaches of MAR.[144] That states that, among a long list of matters the FCA will take into account, is "whether the breach was deliberate or reckless." However, this is far from saying that intention or recklessness are pre-conditions for the imposition of a penalty. For example, the policy also states that the FCA will take into account "whether the breach reveals serious or systemic weaknesses of the management systems or internal controls relating to all or part of a person's business", which is suggestive of a negligence standard.[145] Breach of the rules might involve the company not disclosing on time or disclosing on time but inaccurately or incompletely (or, of course, both).

The FCA initially made relatively light use of its penalty-imposing powers.[146] However, it did use them to pick up egregious cases of misleading statements to the market[147] or of failure to disclose market-moving information.[148] The FCA increased its enforcement activity after the financial crisis and adopted a much stronger approach to the size of penalties.[149] As we saw in para.27–025, the FCA characterised misleading disclosures to the market as market abuse on the part of

[139] FSMA 2000 s.91(2A)(2B).

[140] FSMA 2000 s.123(1)(b) and DTR 1.5.3.

[141] FSMA 2000 s.123 and DTR 1.5.3.

[142] The civil penalty liability is expressly preserved in Sch.10A para.10(3)(b).

[143] DTR 1A.3.2. It is possible that a complete failure to disclose is a matter of strict liability.

[144] FSMA 2000 s.124.

[145] FCA, *Decision Procedure and Penalties Manual* (DEPP), 6.2.1.

[146] See HM Treasury, *Davies Review of Issuer Liability: Discussion Paper* (March 2007), Table 1: nine cases over four years, including the cases on breach of s.397, discussed below.

[147] For example, FSA, *Cattles Ltd, Final Notice* (March 2012) for misleading statements in the annual report, penalties imposed on directors but not on the company because of its parlous financial state.

[148] For example, FSA, *Entertainment Rights Plc* (January 2009), delay of 78 days, fine of £224,000 on the company; FSA, *Photo-Me International Plc, Final Notice* (June 2010), delay of 44 days, fine of £500,000.

[149] DEPP Pt 6.

Tesco and would have imposed a substantial penalty on the company had it not already agreed to pay a very large penalty to the SFO as part of a deferred prosecution agreement.[150]

In relation to breaches of the major vote-holding disclosure obligation, the 2013 amendments to the TD introduced an additional sanction not previously available to the FCA. This is the sanction of suspension of the voting rights attached to the shares whose beneficial ownership has not been revealed.[151] As we shall see in Ch.28, a similar, in fact somewhat broader, power exists under domestic law in relation to non-disclosure under the company-triggered provisions there discussed. In relation to major vote-holding disclosure, the FCA now has power to apply to the court (High Court or Court of Session) for a suspension of voting rights, which the court may impose in the case of a "serious" breach of the disclosure provisions.[152]

Criminal sanctions

27–027 In extreme cases non-disclosure or inaccurate disclosure might also constitute the offence now contained in s.89 of the Financial Services Act 2012. Breaches may be prosecuted by the FCA.[153] This offence can be traced back to s.12 of the Prevention of Fraud (Investments) Act 1939 and consists of making a statement knowing it to be false or misleading or reckless whether it is so, or dishonestly concealing material facts. The statement or concealment must be for the purpose, among others, of inducing someone[154] (or reckless whether it may induce someone) to deal in securities (whether as principal or agent).[155] This criminal offence is not limited to dealing on any particular market. The section is a useful weapon in the prosecutor's armoury since only recklessness (not intent) needs to be established.[156] However, the misleading disclosure must be made for the required purpose: the fact that a recipient of the statement makes an investment decision on the basis of a statement which its maker knows to be false would not be enough to secure a conviction. Conviction on indictment may lead to a sentence of imprisonment of up to seven years.[157] All the ingredients for criminal

---

150 For earlier examples see the fine of £17 million imposed by the then FSA on Shell in August 2004 in relation to misstatements made to the market over a number of years about the extent of its oil and gas reserves: FSA, *The "Shell" Transport and Trading Company Plc and The Royal Dutch Petroleum Company NV, Final Notice* (24 August 2004).

151 TD art.28b(2). This is most likely to happen where an intermediary states that it is holding the shares on behalf of another person but refuses to reveal the identity of that other person, possibly because the laws of the jurisdiction in which the intermediary is situated prohibit disclosure without the consent of the other person.

152 FSMA 2000 s.89NA. The criteria for assessing seriousness are set out in subs.(4).

153 FSMA 2000 s.401 (except in Scotland).

154 The person thus persuaded to act need not be the same person as the one to whom the statement is made: s.89(2).

155 FSA 2012 s.89(2) and the Financial Services Act 2012 (Misleading Statements and Impressions) Order 2013/637 art.2.

156 Where the statement is true, but designed to create a false or misleading impression, it may fall within s.90 of FSA 2012. This section is discussed in Ch.30.

157 FSA 2012 s.92.

liability were found in *R. v Bailey*,[158] where the chief executive and chief financial officers of a company were convicted of issuing a misleading trading statement[159] which caused its share price to rise and investors to purchase its shares when the contracts on which the trading statement had been based had not been concluded and in fact never were. The basis of the conviction was recklessness, both as to the truth of the statement and as to whether investors would rely on it. When the truth emerged the share price fell to one-fifth and then one-tenth of its pre-correction level.

CONCLUSION

There is more than one way in which the efficient functioning of the market is promoted by the requirements discussed in this chapter. The reduction of insider trading opportunities is promoted by rules requiring price-sensitive information about the company to be made public or revealing directors' trading in the shares of their companies. However, continuous disclosure of information about companies also helps the accuracy of the price-formation process in securities markets, whilst information about directors' holdings helps shareholders assess the financial incentives to which the management is subject—and perhaps reveals information about the company's prospects. Thus, both market efficiency and corporate governance objectives are promoted by the disclosure requirements. The vote-holder disclosure rules address a different need of investors: to know who is in a position to control the company or, perhaps more importantly, who may be building up a stake in the company as a prelude to effecting a change in the current control position. As so often in company law, the substance of the legal requirement may be the modest one of disclosure, but the underlying objectives, which the disclosure requirements are aimed to promote—it is unclear how effectively—are fundamental. **27–028**

[158] *R. v Bailey (Gareth Scott)* [2005] EWCA Crim 3487; [2006] 2 Cr. App. R. (S.) 36. Although custodial sentences were upheld, the CA reduced them from three-and-a-half years to 18 months and from two-and-a-half years to nine months. The case was decided on an earlier version of the prohibition.

[159] A statement updating the market on the company's trading performance.

Chapter 28

TAKEOVERS

Introduction

28–001 A takeover bid consists of an offer from A (an acquirer—usually another company) made generally to the shareholders of T Co (the "target" company) to acquire the shares not already held by A for a consideration which may be cash or securities of the offeror or a mixture of both. The legal mechanism at the heart of the bid is thus a contractual transfer of shares, but the rules on transfers of shares, discussed in the previous chapter, although relevant, do not capture the significance of the takeover bid. A takeover offer has the aim not simply of a transfer of shares but a shift in the control of T Co—or at least a consolidation of control. Previously, T Co may have been under the control of its board (for example, where its shareholdings were widely dispersed) or of one or a few shareholders with a controlling block of shares. After a successful bid (i.e. one where all or most of the T Co's shareholders accept A's offer) T Co will be controlled by A—or its control will have strengthened as where an offer is made to existing minority shareholders. Depending upon who previously had control of the company, that change of control will therefore be a matter of some moment to the board of T Co (who will have lost control) or the minority shareholders[1] of T Co (who will be faced with a new controller, unless they themselves have accepted a cash offer). The change of control may also affect other stakeholders in the company (for example, employees) because bidders do not normally expend large resources to obtain control of companies simply to run them in the same way as previously. The change of control of T Co may thus have wide ramifications for those who have interests in the businesses run by T Co.

This little description reveals the two main issues which takeover regulation has to address. First, should it seek to prevent the management of T from taking any steps to discourage a potential bidder from putting an offer to its shareholders or from discouraging those shareholders from accepting it? In other words, is the takeover bid to be analysed as a transaction purely between A and T shareholders or as one in the outcome of which the management of the T also has a legitimate self-interest which it may take steps to defend? As we shall see, the rules in the UK have traditionally been based on the former view (no frustration of the bid by the target management). This rule is expressed in a strong form once a bid is imminent, and somewhat less strongly and more diffusely in relation to defensive action taken by target management in advance of any specific offer. This policy gives A a free run at T shareholders and prevents the board from using its management powers so as to frustrate the bid. It is a policy which can be justified on the grounds that it supports the principle of free transferability of the shares of listed companies and, more importantly, on the grounds that it is a significant element in the British system for disciplining management and reducing the agency costs of dispersed shareholders. A board, it is argued, which is at risk of an unwelcome takeover bid will be sure to promote the interests of its shareholders, in order to decrease the chances of a bid being made (because the share price will be high) and to increase the chances that those shareholders will reject an offer if one is made (because they think they will be at least as well off with the current management). In this way, the accountability of the board to the shareholders is promoted by the threat of takeovers, especially "hostile" ones, i.e. offers not recommended by the target board to its shareholders but rather made over the heads of the incumbent management to the shareholders.[2]

The second major issue for takeover regulation concerns the steps to be taken to protect non-controlling shareholders if a bid is launched. Obviously, the transfer of shares could be left, like any other commercial transaction, to be regulated by the ordinary law of contract. In the case of controlling shareholders, who are well-placed to take care of themselves, this is probably sensible policy. However, in the typical case in the UK, where the shareholdings in the target are dispersed, the shareholders may lack information needed to evaluate the offer which has been made to them (especially information about the likely benefits of

[1] Where T Co was previously controlled by one or more large shareholders, they too will have lost control to A, but that is the result of a voluntary transaction between them and A. In so far as issues arise on this aspect of the takeover they can probably be resolved by the law of contract.

[2] This is a crucial and highly controversial argument. For a balanced assessment see J. Coffee Jr, "Regulating the Market for Corporate Control" (1984) 84 *Columbia Law Review* 1145. See also P. Davies, K.J. Hopt and G. Ringe "Control Transactions" in R. Kraakman et al. (eds), *The Anatomy of Corporate Law*, 3rd edn (Oxford: OUP, 2016).

the takeover to the acquirer). Moreover, if left to its own devices, A may be able to put pressure in various ways on T shareholders to accept the bid, often by proposing to treat some groups of target shareholders more favourably than others. To counter these risks we shall see that takeover regulation puts considerable emphasis on two policies: disclosure of information (by both bidder and target) to T shareholders, and equality of treatment of T shareholders. Equality means that some shareholders of the target cannot be offered a better deal than is available generally. As we shall see below,[3] this second policy is taken even to the point of requiring a bid to be launched where a person has acquired in the market or by private treaty a sufficient shareholding in the target to give it control. The "mandatory bid" permits non-controlling shareholders to exit the company at a fair price upon a change of control, even though the bidder would prefer not to acquire any further shares.

Thus, the two central tenets of the British regulation of takeovers are that T shareholders alone decide on the fate of the offer (and must be given information and time to make a judgment) and equality of treatment of T shareholders. The regulation is both orthodox and rigorous in putting the target shareholders centre stage, and in this respect it differs from takeover regulation in both the US and some, though not all, continental European countries (for example, Germany). However, these are not the only objectives of takeover regulation. A takeover offer is disruptive of the normal running of the target company's business and it is therefore politic that this period of disruption should be minimised by the setting of a firm timetable for the bid—provided the shareholders are allocated enough time to evaluate it. Thus, a bidder which has indicated it might make a bid is required to do so or to withdraw within a relatively short period ("put up or shut up"); the offer, if made, remains open only for fixed period; and a bidder whose offer fails is not permitted immediately to come back with another bid. Thus, the bid is a relatively quick and self-contained event and is not capable of immediate renewal. **28–002**

We shall look at these and other aspects of the substantive rules for the regulation of takeover bids below, but we begin by examining the rather special machinery which exists in the UK for the creation and application of those rules.

THE TAKEOVER CODE AND PANEL

Since the takeover does not require a corporate decision on the part of the T Co,[4] there is no obvious act of the target upon which company law can fasten for the purposes of regulating the transaction.[5] For this reason, most European countries treat takeover regulation as part of their securities laws, i.e. they rightly take the transfer of the shares as the central act. The UK follows this pattern, but it **28–003**

[3] See para.28–040.

[4] Sometimes the approval of the A's shareholders is required under the Listing Rules if the proposed transaction is a very large one. See *Sharp v Blank* [2019] EWHC 3096 (Ch) discussed at para.28–064. However, the relationship between acquirer and its shareholders is not dealt with by takeover regulation in the UK, but is left to the general rules concerning shareholder approval of transactions.

[5] As we shall see below, where the takeover is effected by means of a scheme of arrangement (Ch.29), a corporate decision of the target, which company law can regulate, is required, but the

developed takeover regulation long before statutory regulation of the securities markets was established, and so the regulation of takeovers took initially a self-regulatory approach. In the 1950s and 1960s, bidders took full advantage of the absence of regulation.[6] Alarmed by what was happening,[7] a City working party published in 1959 a modest set of "Queensberry Rules" entitled *Notes on Amalgamation of British Businesses*, which was followed in 1968 by a more elaborate *City Code on Takeovers and Mergers* and the establishment of a Panel on Takeovers and Mergers to administer and enforce it. It is this Code, in its various editions, which has since constituted the main body of rules relating to takeovers, with the CA 2006 and the FSMA 2000, and rules and regulations made thereunder, performing an accessory role. However, the element of self-regulation in this arrangement could easily be overestimated. Although the Panel had no statutory authority, its success as a regulator depended largely on the recognition on the part of those routinely involved in advising on takeovers (mainly investment banks and large law firms) that to flout its authority would probably induce Parliament to replace the Code and Panel with something they liked even less.

The Panel and its methods of operation

The status and composition of the Panel

28–004 In any event, discussion of the self-regulatory status of the Panel is now rather beside the point. After a very long gestation period the EU eventually adopted Directive 2004/25/EC on takeover bids (hereafter the "takeover directive"). One of the requirements of the Directive was that Member States should "designate the authority or authorities competent to supervise bids" (art.4(1)), so that the UK was required to place the takeover rules on some sort of a statutory footing. In fact, the proposed change in the legal status of the Panel was the basis for the UK Government's initial opposition to the Directive, despite the fact that the Directive's substantive content was heavily influenced by the City Code.[8] During the EU legislative process changes were made in the draft Directive so as to allay, as far as possible, the Government's fears that the Panel's flexible way of working would be undermined by the statutory basis required by the Directive. With the functional exit of the UK from the EU at the end of 2020, Parliament could return the Panel to its former self-regulatory status. However, this seems an unlikely development. Legal status conferred some useful back-up legal sanctions

scheme is in practice available only where acquirer and target board are in agreement on the desirability of the takeover, so that at least the first main issue in takeover regulation (see para.28–001) will not be present.

[6] A. Johnston, *The City Take-over Code* (Oxford: OUP, 1980), Chs 1–4.

[7] Which, in some cases, was horrendous, with rival bidders badgering each of the target's shareholders by night and day telephone calls offering him a special price because, so it was falsely alleged, only his holding was needed to bring that bidder's acceptances to over 50%. In one case the result was that the bidder who eventually succeeded paid prices ranging from £2 to £15 per share.

[8] Reflecting the fact that a very high proportion of the EU's total of takeover bids (especially "hostile" ones) takes place in the UK.

on the Panel,[9] whilst the Government implemented the Directive in the UK in such a way that the Panel's day-to-day operations carried on much as before, even though now with some of its powers derived from statute.[10]

Article 4 of the Directive made it clear, which might otherwise be in doubt, that the designated authorities may be "private bodies recognised by national law".[11] Thus, s.942 of the CA 2006 simply confers certain statutory powers upon the Panel but does not seek to regulate the constitution of the Panel, in contrast to the way in which, for example, the constitution of the FCA is regulated by FSMA 2000. The legislation recognises the existence of the Panel but does not constitute it. The composition of the Panel is to be found, not in legislation, but in the Code itself. It consists of a Chairman and up to three Deputy Chairmen appointed by the Panel itself and up to a further 20 members appointed by the Panel.[12] In addition, there are individuals appointed by representative bodies of those involved in or affected by takeovers, such as the Association of British Insurers, the Investment Association, the Pension and Lifetime Savings Association, UK Finance and the Confederation of British Industry. The Panel appointees come from similar backgrounds as those of the representative appointees, but include some former senior partners in major law firms and a former General Secretary of the Trades Union Congress.

Internal appeals

A central concern of the Panel (and of the Government when later implementing the Directive) has always been to preserve the Panel's freedom to give flexible and speedy binding rulings in the course of the bid, which could not be easily challenged in litigation before the ordinary courts. A particular concern is to discourage "tactical litigation", i.e. litigation designed to disrupt the bid timetable or to delay the operation of a decision of the Panel which was against the interests **28–005**

---

[9] See para.28–009.

[10] See also Panel on Takeovers and Mergers, *Implementation of the Takeover Directive, Consultation Paper* (November 2005), PCP 2005/5 (hereafter "Panel Consultation Document"), para.2.4: "Overall, the Panel remains confident that while its status and the status of the Code will be different under the new statutory regime, there will be little material substantive change either to its procedures or to the Rules of the Code".

[11] The competent authority may be, of course, a public body of a more traditional kind. The Government did toy, probably not very seriously, with the idea of giving takeover regulation to the FCA, or alternatively keeping the Panel on a non-statutory basis but treating breaches of the Code as breaches of the FCA's rules, but rejected both ideas. See DTI, *Company Law Implementation of the European Directive on Takeover Bids: A Consultation Document* (January 2005), URN 05/11, paras 2.7 and 2.17—hereafter "DTI Consultation Document". That idea does demonstrate, however, that the Government was not obliged to give these functions to the Panel nor is it obliged to leave them there, should the Panel act in a way the Government finds unacceptable.

[12] See *The Takeover Code*, 12th edn (2016, with later amendments), "Introduction", A8 (hereafter the "Code"). The Panel is thus a self-perpetuating body. Under earlier editions of the Code the chair and two deputies of the Panel were appointed by the Governor of the Bank of England, which reflects the historical reality of how the self-regulatory process was initiated, but that person no longer has a formal role in the Panel's composition. The current membership is available at *http://www.thetakeoverpanel.org.uk/structure/panel-membership* [Accessed 6 April 2021]. Sections 957–959 deal with the Panel's present funding arrangements. It is not supported out of taxation, but by fees for its services and a levy on share transactions, but of course a statutory body could be funded in a similar manner, as the FCA is.

of a particular party, but at the same time providing a method of appeal for those with a genuine grievance. From the early days of the Panel this result was achieved through a system of speedy appeal within the Panel itself, coupled with the courts' adoption of a limited and after-the-event approach to judicial review of the Panel's decisions. The latter is clearly something not within the control of the Panel itself. Article 4(6) of the Directive was drafted in such a way as to facilitate the continuation of this arrangement and so the government, when transposing the Directive, decided to maintain the Panel's appeal system rather than seek to devise a new system.[13]

The Panel Executive (i.e. its full-time employees, some of whom are seconded from investment banks, law firms, accountancy firms and similar bodies) gives rulings on the Code in the course of a bid, either on its own initiative or at the request of one or more parties to the bid.[14] The first stage of appeal is to the Hearings Committee, consisting of up to eight members appointed by the Panel from among its "further" Panel-appointed members.[15] Rulings of the Executive may be referred to the Hearing Committee by a party to the takeover or some other person affected by the Executive's ruling (or the Executive may refer a matter to the Hearing Committee itself). The Executive may require any appeal to the Hearing Committee to be lodged within a specific period, possibly a period as short as a few hours. The Hearing Committee normally sits in private and operates informally, but does issue public statements of its rulings.

A party to the hearing before the Hearing Committee may appeal to the Takeover Appeal Board, normally within two business days of receipt in writing of the ruling of the Hearing Committee. The Board was formerly known as the "Appeal Committee" and the change of name indicates that the Board is now an organisation independent of the Panel.[16] This is a rather wider right of appeal than existed previously when many appeals required leave of the appeal body. The Appeal Board is an independent body, whose chairman and deputy chairman, appointed by the Master of the Rolls, will usually have held high judicial office[17] and whose other members (normally four) are experienced in takeovers. The Appeal Board operates in a similar way to the Hearing Committee, including the publication of its decision. It may confirm, vary, set aside or replace the ruling of the Hearing Committee. This was, broadly, the system in operation before Pt 28 of the CA 2006 came into force and s.951 requires that system to be maintained. The section requires, as was the previous practice, that a Panel member who is or has been a member of its Code Committee (responsible for drawing up the Code) may not be a member of the Hearing Committee or Appeal Board. The separation

---

[13] DTI Consultation Document, paras 2.35–36. The system is set out in the Code, "Introduction", ss.6–8.

[14] Delegation by the Panel of functions to officers or members of staff is specifically provided for by s.942(3)(b). In practice, the Panel's efficiency depends upon the parties or their advisers bringing issues to the Panel at an early stage and disclosing full information. The obligation to do so is laid down in the "Introduction" to the Code, paras 6(b) and 9(a). See Panel Statement 2015/15, *Asia Resource Minerals Plc (Formerly Bumi Plc)*.

[15] The rules of procedure of the Hearings Committee are set out in App.9 of the Code.

[16] With its own website available at: *http://www.thetakeoverappealboard.org.uk/* [Accessed 6 April 2021]. For an instructive example of its operating methods see Takeover Appeal Board, *Principle Investment Capital Trust Plc*, Decision 2010/1.

[17] Currently Lord Collins of Mapesbury as chairman and Sir John Mummery as deputy chairman.

of the Code Committee from the committees involved in administering the Code and the organisational separation of the Appeal Board were responses to the Human Rights Act 1998.[18]

Judicial review

The second limb of the system for dealing with tactical litigation consists of self-restraint by the courts in exercising their powers of judicial review. The CA 2006 does not seek explicitly to regulate the process of judicial review of the Panel by the courts, probably wisely, and so the matter is left to the courts themselves. It was perhaps surprising that the pre-Directive Panel, as a body which, as it was put in *R. v Panel on Take-overs and Mergers, Ex p. Datafin Ltd*,[19] performed its functions "without visible means of legal support", was made subject to judicial review at all. However, that was the step taken in the *Datafin* case on the grounds that the Panel, although then a private body, was performing a public function. Its susceptibility to judicial review is now beyond doubt. Having taken that decision of principle, the then Master of the Rolls set out his "expectations" as to how judicial review of the Panel would operate, emphasising its limitations. **28–006**

The first expectation was that the Panel would require immediate obedience to its rulings and the parties would abide by them, even if one of them had signalled it was intending to seek judicial review. Secondly, the grounds for review would be limited: an argument that the Panel had propounded rules which were ultra vires was "a somewhat unlikely eventuality"; the Panel in its interpretation of its rules must be given "considerable latitude"; attacks on the Panel's dispensing powers would be successful only in "wholly exceptional circumstances"; and the Panel's exercise of its disciplinary powers would not be open to attack "in the absence of any credible allegation of lack of bona fides". Thirdly, and most importantly, the expectation was that the courts would only intervene after the bid was concluded ("the relationship between the panel and the court [would] be historic rather than contemporaneous"), perhaps to relieve individuals of disciplinary sanctions, perhaps to deliver a declaratory judgment to guide the Panel in the future. Thus, a party involved in a bid (most obviously the board of the target company) was given little incentive to seek judicial review during the offer in order to secure a tactical advantage (most obviously delay, during which the target's defences could be better organised), but the Panel was not given an entirely free hand in interpreting the Code or its own jurisdiction.

It seems likely that this attitude of deference on the part of the courts to the Panel (and especially the Takeover Appeal Board) will continue, despite the statutory framework within which the Panel is now placed. The statute does one or two things to encourage the courts in that direction. The Panel is given power to "do anything that it considers necessary or expedient for the purpose of, or in connection with, its functions", thus protecting the Panel's vires in its new

[18] The Takeover Panel, *Report on the Year Ended March 31, 2001*, pp.8–9.

[19] *R. v Panel on Take-overs and Mergers, Ex p. Datafin Ltd* [1987] Q.B. 815 CA. See Cane, "Self Regulation and Judicial Review" [1987] C.J.Q. 324. See also *R. v Takeover Panel, Ex p. Guinness Plc* [1990] 1 Q.B. 146 CA.

statutory guise; it is given a wide rule-making power; it is explicitly given a dispensing power; and it is explicitly given the power to make rulings and give directions.[20]

Nevertheless, the fact of putting the Panel on a statutory footing potentially opened up avenues of civil litigation not previously available. The CA 2006 seeks to block off these paths to the courts. Thus, no action for breach of statutory duty lies in respect of contravention of a requirement imposed by or under the Panel's rules or a requirement imposed by the Panel to produce information or documents.[21] Contravention of a rule-based requirement does not render the transaction in which it occurs void or unenforceable or affect the validity "of any other thing" (unless the rules so provide).[22] However, civil litigation between the parties is not entirely excluded by these provisions. A claim based on fraudulent or negligent misstatement, for example, arising out of the documentation put out by bidder or target, is not excluded, but, as we shall see below, such claims were in any event possible before the Directive, and they are constrained by the requirements of the general law of misstatement.

Finally, the Panel itself is not liable in damages in connection with the discharge of its functions, unless it was acting in bad faith or there is a claim against it for breach of s.6(1) of the Human Rights Act 1998 (which in the circumstances laid down in s.8 of that Act could lead a court to award damages for breach by a public authority of the rights guaranteed by the European Convention on Human Rights).[23] This protection extends to members, officers and employees of the Panel and any person authorised by the Panel to act under its information disclosure powers. Thus, the risk of tactical litigation is minimised, but cannot be entirely eliminated.

Powers of the Panel

28–007 This and the following section deal with the areas where there has been the biggest formal change in the Panel's position as a result of its being put on a statutory basis. At least the basic elements of the Panel's powers and the sanctions to support them are now set out in, or provided for by, the legislation. Again, however, the aim of the legislation was to reflect, rather than substantially to alter, the Panel's existing methods of working. The main statutory powers of the Panel are as follows.

First, the Panel is given both an obligation and a power to make rules to govern the conduct of bids.[24] Thus, the legislation does not purport to discharge that rule-making function itself but requires or empowers the Panel to do so. The Panel was required to make rules in those areas where the Directive required

---

[20] See ss.942(2), 943, 944(1) and 945.

[21] CA 2006 s.956(1). The definitions of "rule-based requirement" and "disclosure requirement" are given in s.955(4), the latter referring to the Panel's disclosure powers in s.947, which are discussed below.

[22] CA 2006 s.956(2).

[23] CA 2006 s.961. The provisions of the Convention most likely to affect that Panel are those of a procedural nature, for example, art.6 relating to the fair trials in civil disputes. The liability of the Panel under the Human Rights Act 1998 is not new.

[24] CA 2006 s.943.

Member States to introduce rules and that arrangement is carried forward post-exit by transferring the required areas to new Sch.1C of the CA 2006.[25] However, the Panel is empowered to make rules more generally, a power which is very widely formulated.[26] In consequence, the whole of the Panel's rule-making activity is placed on a statutory basis. The Panel is permitted to arrange for its rule-making power (and, indeed, any of its functions) to be discharged by a committee of the Panel, so that there can be a further stage of delegation before the power to make rules is actually exercised.[27] This reflects the fact that, since the enactment of the Human Rights Act 1998, responsibility for the rules has been assigned to a Code Committee of the Panel and that membership of the Hearing Committee (see above) and of the Code Committee does not overlap. Thus, the "legislative" and "judicial" functions of the Panel have been separated.

Secondly, the Panel "may give rulings on the interpretation, application or effect of rules", in the way described above, such rulings having binding effect "to the extent and in the circumstances specified in the rules".[28] This is the Panel's "judicial" function. Giving the Panel's rulings binding effect was, of course, new, and the sanctions available to support this provision are discussed below. Further, the Panel is authorised to make rules which are "subject to exceptions or exemptions" in the rules themselves and "to dispense with or modify the application of rules in particular cases and by reference to any circumstances", subject to the requirement to give reasons.[29] This reflects the Panel's traditional practice to use its dispensing power where a rule "would operate unduly harshly or in an unnecessarily restrictive or burdensome, or otherwise inappropriate, manner".[30]

The rules may, and do, also confer upon the Panel the power to give directions to secure compliance with the rules.[31] In practice, this is a very important power for the Panel. Having identified a breach of the rules, its focus in practice is on requiring remedial action which will enable the bid to continue in the normal way. This is the great virtue of having a regulator which can give rulings during the course of a bid, as contrasted with a body which comes to the matter only after the bid has succeeded or failed and so no longer has the possibility of getting the transaction back on track.

Thirdly, the Panel may require a person by notice in writing to produce to it **28–008** specified documents or to provide specified information, where such disclosure is "reasonably required in connection with the exercise by the Panel of its functions".[32] This again was a new legal power for the Panel, which in the past

[25] CA 2006 s 943(1), as amended.

[26] CA 2006 s.943(2)–(3). Section 944(1) permits the Panel to make rules in a flexible form.

[27] CA 2006 s.942(3)(a).

[28] CA 2006 s.945.

[29] CA 2006 s.944.

[30] City Code, "Introduction", s.2(c).

[31] CA 2006 s.946 and City Code, "Introduction", s.10.

[32] CA 2006 s.947(1)–(3). The Code itself requires those dealing with it to disclose any known and relevant information (Code, "Introduction", s.9(a)) and the Panel expects this to be the power it normally relies on rather than the statutory one. Those firms subject to the jurisdiction of the FCA are required under its rules to provide information and documents to the Panel and to provide such other assistance which the Panel requests in the performance of its functions and the firm is reasonably able

had been able to survive without it. There is the usual protection for legal professional privilege (or confidentiality of communications in Scotland).[33] There is also the usual requirement that the Panel keep confidential information disclosed to it (whether under the compulsory disclosure power or not) which relates to the private affairs of an individual or to any particular business. A person who breaches this requirement is guilty of a criminal offence unless that person had no reason to suspect that the information had been provided to the Panel in connection with its functions or that the person took all reasonable steps and exercised all due diligence to avoid disclosure in breach of the statute. However, this confidentiality provision is subject to the usual long list of permitted "gateways" for disclosure of the information to other official bodies, and to disclosure by the Panel itself for the purpose of facilitating the carrying out of any of its functions (so that some such information may be found in the public rulings of the Hearing Committee or Takeover Appeal Board).[34]

Sanctions

28–009 Thus, the CA 2006 confers upon the Panel three core powers: to make rules for takeover bids, to interpret those rules and to give directions to implement the rulings, and to require the disclosure of information. None of these functions is new for the Panel: all were previously carried on, though without legislative support. Having put those powers in place, the statute inevitably had to go on and provide sanctions for non-compliance with them on the part of bid participants. As a self-regulatory body and, in particular, as a body with not even a contractual relationship with all those involved in takeovers, whether as participants or advisers, the Panel's formal sanctions were previously extremely limited. The Panel itself could administer only a private reprimand or public censure if there was non-compliance with the Code. For more pressing measures it was dependent on the action of other regulatory authorities, such as the Department of Trade and Industry (now BEIS), the FCA or the Stock Exchange. However, these bodies, even if willing to act, might not have appropriate sanctions at their disposal.[35] In the early days of the Panel such problems threatened the Panel's credibility and even its future, but gradually the Panel gained acceptance for its rulings, partly because of a realisation among advisers in particular that an ineffective Panel was likely to lead to the transfer of its functions to a statutory

---

to provide: see MAR 4.3.5 and fn.44. This disclosure obligation is also subject to an exemption relating to legal professional privilege: see s.413 of FSMA 2000.

[33] CA 2006 s.947(10).

[34] CA 2006 ss.948 and 949 and Sch.2. The permitted recipients include regulatory bodies outside the UK.

[35] In one notorious case, concerning St Piran Ltd, such action by the Exchange proved singularly ineffective, despite belated undertakings by the guilty party to behave in future. See the Annual Reports of the Panel for 1981 and 1984. See also *Re St Piran Ltd* [1981] 1 W.L.R. 1300 CA, where intervention by the Secretary of State was saved from futility only because a shareholder in the company was prepared to bring a petition for the winding-up of the company on the just and equitable ground.

regulator.[36] Further, the Panel's relationship with the FSA in particular was placed on a more explicit footing when FSMA was enacted in 2000.[37]

Perhaps the strongest expression of the new policy of giving the Panel statutory sanctions is to be found in s.955 which confers upon the Panel a power to apply to the court (High Court or Court of Session) where a person has contravened or is likely to contravene a requirement imposed by or under a Code rule or has failed to comply with a disclosure requirement under the statutory provisions just discussed. The court may then make such order as it thinks fit to secure compliance with the requirement, which order will be backed by the sanctions for contempt of court. The Panel, no doubt, expects not to have to make significant use of this new power, just as it has operated effectively in the past without it.

One important question which arises is whether this section will provide an avenue whereby a party can obtain judicial scrutiny of the Panel's or Appeal Board's rulings during the course of the bid. Of course, the decision to apply to the court for an enforcement order is in the hands of the Panel, so that a party cannot trigger the procedure.[38] However, if the Panel does so apply, the question will be whether the courts in this new context will maintain the after-the-event approach which has been adopted for judicial review and simply enforce the Panel's ruling without scrutinising its legality or without scrutinising it rigorously. This may be a more difficult line for the court to take where the court's order is backed by the sanctions for contempt of court than when the Panel's rulings lacked extensive formal sanctions. However, in the first case which raised these issues the Inner House adopted a deferential approach to the Panel in the enforcement context as well.[39] The court held that the purpose of the enforcement provisions was just that: they were not intended to provide a back-door method for the review of the substance of the Panel's decisions. Review was to be handled within the Panel structure, as described above. In addition, the facts found by the Hearing Committee and the Appeal Board were binding on the courts (in the absence of an error on the face of the record).

The statute places at the disposal of the Panel two other important sanctions, **28–010**
relating to compensation and discipline, but they both require adoption by Panel rules in order to be brought into force. Section 954 provides that the rules may confer power on the Panel to order a person to pay such compensation as it thinks just and reasonable if that person is in breach of a rule "the effect of which is to require the payment of money". This power thus falls short of a general remit to require compensation for breaches of the rules, but it covers the situations where

[36] Thus, in *R. v Takeover Panel, Ex p. Guinness Plc* [1990] 1 Q.B. 146, the bidder agreed to pay £85 million to the shareholders of the target company in order to comply with a ruling of the Panel.

[37] See in particular ss.138 and 143 of FSMA 2000. The current provisions are discussed further below.

[38] CA 2006 s.955(2) makes it clear that only the Panel can so apply and not, for example, a party which expects to benefit from the Panel's ruling.

[39] *Panel on Takeovers and Mergers v King* [2018] CSIH 30. See A. Christie and J. Liptrap, "Goldilocks (Control) and the Three Bears" (2020) 21 E.B.O.R. 591.

in the past the Panel has required monetary payments.[40] The Code now applies this section to those rules which determine the price at which an offer has to be made or the form of the consideration (for example, where cash or a cash alternative is required).[41]

As to discipline, there is a general provision in s.952 that the rules may give the Panel the power to impose sanctions on a person who has acted in breach of the rules or of a direction given by the Panel to secure compliance with the rules (see above). This is the section on which the Panel now bases its disciplinary powers, which are exercised, except in case of agreement with the offender, by the Hearings Committee (with appeal to the Takeover Appeal Board). The Code sets out the Panel's disciplinary powers and they are the established ones of private or public censure, reporting the offender's conduct to another body for that body to take action against the offender if thought appropriate, and triggering the "cold shouldering" of the offender.[42] It is clear that s.952 permits the rules to adopt a wider range of penalties, notably financial penalties of the type available to the FCA. However, where the Panel adopts a sanction of a kind not previously provided for by the Code, it must produce, again following the FCA model, a policy statement with respect to the imposition of that sanction and, in the case of a financial penalty, the amount of the penalty.[43] So far, the Panel has not ventured into this territory.

The "cold shoulder"

28–011 The "cold shoulder" is the modern version of reliance by the Panel on sanctions imposed by third parties, but it operates by creating a "'gate-keeper"' to control access to the financial markets for takeover purposes. Under the standard model, where the Panel reports conduct to a third party, it is up to that regulator (domestic or overseas) or a professional body to decide whether it is appropriate to take further action against the person who has broken the rules of the Code. The most likely recipient of such a report from the Panel is the FCA. The FCA might conclude that a person who has broken the Takeover Code is also in breach of its obligations under the FCA's rules and impose sanctions upon that person. The persons most obviously within the FCA's scope are those who need its authorisation to carry on their professional activities within the financial services sector. This will cover the principal advisers to bidders and target companies (notably investment banks) but, crucially, not bidder and target companies themselves or their directors.

While advisers, who are repeat players in the takeover market, are unlikely to want to get on the wrong side of the Panel, clients acting only occasionally and more invested in the outcome of the transaction, may be less respectful of the Code. FCA-required "cold shouldering" is a way of using advisers to discipline

[40] See fn.36, where the company had been in breach of a Code rule requiring the bidder to increase the price offered to the target shareholders because shares had been purchased in the market at that higher price. For the current version of that requirement, see para.28–038.

[41] Code, "Introduction", s.10(c).

[42] Code, "Introduction", s.11(b). The Panel may also withdraw or qualify any special status or exemption it has granted the offender, for example, as an "exempt principal trader".

[43] CA 2006 s.952(2)–(8).

such clients. It was introduced in FSMA 2000 and has been retained even though the Panel now has its own sanctions. Cold shouldering involves advisers within the scope of the FCA's powers being required not to deal with those who have not observed or are not likely to observe the Code. In this situation, there is no suggestion that the adviser is in breach of the Code. Indeed, the "cold shoulder" operates prospectively and covers all those who might act for persons likely not to observe the Code, whether they have acted for that person in the past or not. In this way, the range of the FCA's sanctions is extended to companies and their directors: if they have acted, or are likely to act, in breach of the Code, they may find that they are denied the facilities of the City of London in relation to takeover bids. In a little more detail, the FCA's rules, as contained in its Code of Market Conduct, require firms not to act in connection with transactions to which the Takeover Code applies if they have reasonable grounds to believe that the person in question is not likely to act in accordance with the Takeover Code.[44] The Hearing Committee has the power, as a disciplinary sanction under the Code, to make a public statement that a person is, in its view, not likely to comply with the Code. In such a case the FCA "expects" that the above rule will require firms not to act for the person in question. Even so, a "'one-shot"' bidder from outside the elite of publicly traded companies circles may not be bothered by the threat of a cold shoulder.

Criminal sanctions

Apart from the sanctions which the CA 2006 places in the hands of the Panel, the legislation creates a criminal offence in addition to the one we have already discussed in relation to the disclosure of confidential information. This concerns non-compliance with the Code's rules on bid documentation. As we shall see below, much of the Code is concerned with specifying the information a bidder or target must provide, and failure to comply with these rules will clearly fall within the powers and sanctions of the Panel, discussed above. It is also the case that there might be civil litigation between those involved in the bid in the case of misstatements in the bid documentation. Despite this, when transposing the Directive, the Government feared that inadequacies in the bid documentation might emerge only after the bid had been completed (and when the Panel might be reluctant to involve itself again) so that the Panel's sanctions could not be relied upon, whilst the possibilities of civil litigation were uncertain. Consequently, s.953 creates a narrow criminal offence. It applies only to offers for companies whose voting securities are quoted on a regulated market (which is the scope of the Directive) and it imposes liability on a person only if he knew the offer documentation did not comply with the Code's requirements (or was reckless as to that) and failed to take all reasonable steps to secure compliance. In the case of a response document, the liability falls on any director or officer of the **28–012**

[44] The FCA rules discussed in this paragraph are set out in its Code of Market Conduct 4.3, made under what is now FSMA 2000 s.137A. The range of prohibited services in connection with a bid is widely defined (Code of Market Conduct 4.3.3–4), though it does not extend to the giving of legal advice. Section 143, dealing with formal endorsement of the City Code by the FSA, was repealed in the light of the statutory sanctions given to the Panel.

target company; in the case of an offer, any director, officer or member of the body who caused the document to be published is liable.[45]

THE SCOPE OF THE CITY CODE

28–013 The scope of application of the City Code (i.e. the types of companies and types of transactions to which it applies) was a matter of some complexity so long as the UK was a member of the EU, partly because the scope of the Code was wider than that of the Directive in terms of transactions and companies within its scope, but mainly because in some cases the Directive required the Panel to share jurisdiction with another EU regulator. These complications have now disappeared though it is debatable whether the resulting rules are more functional.

Transactions in scope

28–014 The Code applies not only to takeover bids as defined in para.28–001 but also transfers of control effected via a scheme of arrangement. It is, in fact, not uncommon for non-hostile takeovers to be implemented in the UK via a scheme of arrangement, to which the Code in principle applies.[46] The scheme of arrangement, which is not confined to control-shift transactions, is discussed in Ch.29, but the essence of the scheme, when used as a substitute for a takeover offer, is that the company, through a decision of its shareholders in general meeting, adopts a proposal the end result of which is the same as that achieved by the contractual offer (the shares in the target company end up with the bidder and the shareholders receive a consideration in exchange). The scheme has certain advantages in the case of a non-hostile offer (notably that all the shareholders are bound once the scheme is adopted and approved by the court), so that the squeeze-out mechanism referred to later in this chapter does not have to be used. However, technically the offer is implemented not through each individual shareholder's decision to accept a contractual offer made for the transfer of their shares but by the shareholders collectively, acting as the company, voting to adopt a scheme of arrangement. In this case, a mechanism of corporate law is used to effect the takeover.

The Code also applies to offers by a parent company to acquire the outside shares in a subsidiary as well to other mechanisms which have "as their objective or potential effect (directly or indirectly) obtaining or consolidating control". This

[45] CA 2006 s.953(2), (4). In the parliamentary debates the Solicitor-General gave an assurance that the provision was not intended to reach investment banks when they make offers as agents of bidders—though it must be said that it would be a pretty poor investment bank which knew of the defect in the documentation and did not take reasonable steps to correct it. See HC Debs, Standing Committee D, Nineteenth Sitting, cols 804–806 (18 July 2006).

[46] The Code's provisions, discussed in this and the following paragraph, are set out in its "Introduction", s.3(b). Although a control shift by means of a scheme of arrangement has long fallen within the Panel's jurisdiction, only in 2008 was the Code amended to indicate more fully how it applies to schemes (because of the "significant increase in recent years in the use of schemes of arrangement in order to implement transactions which are regulated by the Code"). See Panel Consultation Paper, PCP 2007/1, *Schemes of Arrangement*, and App.7 to the current Code. For a more detailed analysis see J. Payne, *Schemes of Arrangement* (2014), Ch.3.

formulation covers a wide range of possible methods, not involving a general offer to acquire securities, such as the issue of new shares and share capital reorganisations, which, if structured appropriately, could shift control of the company into new hands. Although not much invoked in practice, the inclusion of these analogous control-shift mechanisms removes any temptation for the parties to seek to avoid the Code's provisions by adopting one or other of them.

Companies in scope

The range of companies within scope of the Code is defined by focusing on the status of the target company. The Code divides such companies into two categories.[47] The first category consists of those companies incorporated in the UK (i.e. they have their registered offices in the UK) whose shares are publicly traded on a regulated market or multilateral trading facility (such as AIM) in the UK.[48] The second category consists of companies registered in the UK, which do not have their securities traded on a public market in the UK but, in the view of the Panel, do have their place of central management and control within the UK. Whereas the first category is necessarily confined to companies which are public in the Companies Act sense of the term, the second category is capable of embracing private companies. However, private companies are brought within the Code only where in the previous decade their securities have been traded in a public or semi-public way or a prospectus has been issued in relation to them. In quantitative terms, the second category is likely to contain few members, but their inclusion at least means the Code's provisions cannot be evaded by first de-listing the target company from a public market. **28–015**

As a result of the removal of the EU shared jurisdiction rules, under the UK rules either the Panel has full jurisdiction or it has none. However, a foreign system might regard itself as having jurisdiction over all or some part of a bid falling within the Panel's jurisdiction. This situation could arise, for example, where the UK target's shares are publicly traded both within the UK and elsewhere. For this reason, no doubt, s.950 requires the Panel to co-operate with any foreign regulator that appears to exercise functions similar to those of the Panel.

The more pressing issue might be thought to be the cases falling outside Panel's jurisdiction. A company incorporated outside the UK but with its shares traded on a UK market (and perhaps not traded elsewhere) will be outside the scope of the Code, even though it may have a substantial number of UK investors. Also outside is a company incorporated in the UK but not having its central place of management in the UK and with its shares publicly traded only outside the UK,[49] though in this case investors are likely to have picked up the possibility that the Code might not be applicable.

47 City Code, "Introduction", ss.3(a)(i)–(ii).

48 For these terms see para.25–007. References to the UK include the Channel Islands and the Isle of Man. We do not further refer to this extension.

49 The absence of public trading in the UK will exclude the company from the first category of target companies within the Panel's jurisdiction and the absence of central management from the UK will take it out of the second one.

THE STRUCTURE OF THE CODE

28–016 The Code currently consists and always has consisted, of a small number of General Principles and a larger number of Rules. Currently, there are six General Principles (GPs) and 38 rules. Before the amendments made in 2006 to accommodate the Directive, there were 10 GPs and the same number of rules as currently. The current six GPs are a slightly elaborated version of the general principles laid down in art.3 of the Directive.[50] The original notion behind the GPs was that they constituted high-level standards, compliance with which was required even though no specific rule of the Code had been broken. This was thought to be a desirable regulatory technique because, as it was put in the seventh edition of the Code, "it is impracticable to devise rules in sufficient detail to cover all the circumstances which can arise in offers".[51] However, the reduction in the number of GPs in the current Code has somewhat reduced the force of this regulatory argument, not simply because the current GPs cover less ground than those previously in place and cover it less rigorously, but also because the Rules have been amended to take account of the loss of coverage at GP level.[52] This movement of material between GPs and Rules casts some doubt on the significance of the distinction between those two types of norm.

In any event, it is also the case that, over successive editions of the Code, the Rules had become more detailed and elaborate, so that the gap-filling rationale given for the GPs had become less convincing. The Rules acquired sub-rules and both acquired "notes", some of which are prescriptive and not just explanatory. And in 2004 the Panel began issuing "Practice Statements", which supplement but are not part of the Code. It is perhaps not surprising that the view just quoted about the role of GPs is not repeated in the current version of the Code. The best view is probably now that the GPs are there because the Directive required them to be and that they serve to highlight some, but not all, of the fundamental principles underlying the Code. It seems likely in the future that the Rules will continue to grow in importance in comparison with the GPs. Both Rules and GPs are interpreted by the Panel purposively,[53] so that no penalty in terms of rigidity of interpretation is paid by dealing with a matter in the Rules. However, after the UK's exit from the EU the inter-relationship between the GPs and the Rules could be re-visited, though there is probably no pressing need to do so.

The current GPs lay down the following desiderata:

(1) Equivalent treatment of shareholders of the same class and the protection of security holders when a person obtains control of the company.
(2) Giving holders of securities in the offeree company sufficient time and information to enable them to reach a properly informed decision on the bid. Providing them with information about the impact of the bid on matters likely to be of particular concern to employees. The first is clearly central to

[50] They are repeated in Pt I of Sch.1C to the CA 2006, in order to continue after exit the effect of references in the Act to the Directive's GP.
[51] City Code, 7th edn (2002), s.B1.
[52] Panel Consultation Document, para.2.1.
[53] City Code, "Introduction", s.2(b).

any takeover regulation; the second constitutes a relatively minor protection of the interests of the employees.

(3) The target board must act in the interests of the company as a whole and must not deny the holders of securities the opportunity to decide on the merits of the bid. The phrase "the company as a whole" is, as ever, ambiguous as to whether it means only the shareholders as a whole or includes stakeholder interests.[54] The answer to that question may not be very significant since the second part of the principle puts the decision on the bid in the hands of the shareholders, to whom the "company as a whole" duty does not apply.

(4) False markets should not be created during the bid, whether in the securities of the offeror, offeree or any other company concerned in the bid, presumably for fear of distorting shareholders' decisions whether to accept the offer.

(5) An offeror may announce a bid only if it has ensured that it can meet in full any cash consideration payable and after taking "all reasonable steps" to secure the implementation of any other type of consideration. Thus, offers may be opportunistic in some ways (for example, a bid for a target which is suffering from a temporary set-back) but not in terms of financing.

(6) The offeree company should not be hindered in the conduct of its affairs by the bid for longer than is reasonable. The point is that a bid is likely to cause the senior management of the target to divert their attention wholly to the bid from the moment it is imminent to the point where it succeeds or fails, so that there is a strong argument that this distraction from the other aspects of company's activities should be subject to limits.

ALLOCATION OF THE ACCEPTANCE DECISION

As already indicated at the beginning of this chapter, a, perhaps the, crucial question for takeover regulation is whether the decision on the bid should be that of the shareholders alone or one to which both shareholders and the target board must consent. Allocating the decision to the shareholders alone facilitates the creation of a market in the control of companies, which acts as a powerful incentive for the managements of companies, at all times and not just when a bid is imminent, to act in the interests of the shareholders. A shareholders-decide rule encourages bidders to make "hostile" takeover offers, i.e. offers which the board of the target opposes but which it is not able to prevent being put to the shareholders. The market in corporate control is probably a much more powerful mechanism for the promotion of the interests of shareholders than all the corporate governance techniques discussed in Pt 3 of this work, including the law of directors' duties. On the other hand, some have argued that the threat of a takeover makes management too responsive to shareholder needs, in particular by inducing management to take a short-term view of the company's success, which may be detrimental to the longer term development of its business and thus to the long-term interests of the shareholders themselves. Those taking this latter view **28–017**

[54] See para.10–026.

would wish to permit management to have some say in whether the bid is successful and would not allocate the decision wholly to the shareholders. Those concerned about the impact of takeovers on non-shareholder groups, notably employees, tend to support this managerialist stance, as being the best protection they can secure in the absence of a stakeholder input into the acceptance decision.[55]

Since the standard takeover transaction is necessarily one between the bidder and the shareholders of the target company (there is no corporate decision), it might be thought that the board of the target company is excluded structurally from any input into the decision on the offer. Despite not being party to the share transfer, the board nevertheless has many possibilities to exercise its general powers of management so as to discourage an offeror from making or continuing with a bid. Thus, the core question becomes whether, in the particular context of a takeover bid, the board should be permitted to exercise its normal management powers, for example by issuing new shares to a friendly investor or by disposing of assets the bidder is anxious to acquire. This is usually referred to as the question of whether takeover regulation should adopt a "no frustration" rule, i.e. whether the board of a target is to be prohibited from taking action which constrains the freedom of the shareholders as a whole to accept an offer, even though such action would normally be within the scope of the board's powers of management.

This issue needs to be addressed at two different points of time: when a bid is imminent and when no bid is in prospect. The reason for this distinction is that the imposition of a strict no frustration rule is feasible once a bid is imminent, because it will operate only so long as the bid is current (which, as noted, is a time-limited event). The imposition of a strict "no frustration" rule where no bid is imminent (i.e. at all times) would limit the board's powers of management in a way which is undesirable even from the shareholders' point of view (because it reduce the benefits shareholders obtain from centralised management), while the risk of self-serving decisions by management is less severe when a bid is not imminent. Thus, even those in favour of the "no frustration" principle would not necessarily want the same rules to apply both pre- and post-bid. In the UK this distinction in point of time is reinforced by a division in terms of regulatory responsibility, for the Takeover Code applies only once a bid is imminent and pre-bid defences are a matter for general company law.

Post-bid defensive measures

28–018 The Code has always adopted a strong "no frustration" rule, thus helping to make the UK a very active takeover market. Rule 21.1 of the Code states that after a bona fide offer has been communicated to the board of the target or the board has reason to believe that such an offer is imminent, no action may be taken by the board without the approval of the shareholders in general meeting which could result in the offer being frustrated or to shareholders being denied an opportunity

[55] For an analysis of the competing views, see R. Kraakman et al (eds), *The Anatomy of Corporate Law*, 3rd edn (Oxford: OUP, 2016), Ch.8.

to decide on its merits.[56] This rule makes it difficult for the existing controllers to erect defences against being ousted from control by an unwelcome takeover unless they have succeeded in doing so in advance. Even then, the pre-bid defence must be one that does not require board action post-bid, for the post-bid action will be caught by r.21.[57] It is a particularly strict rule. Unlike the common law relating to improper purposes,[58] r.21 requires shareholder approval for any action proposed by the directors of the target company which could have the result of preventing the shareholders of the target company from deciding on the merits of the bid. Whether the directors of the target had this purpose in mind or whether it was their predominant purpose in proposing the action in question is beside the point under the rule. The rule looks to consequences, not to purposes. Equally important, the rule requires shareholder approval to be given for the specific defensive measure proposed by the target board and thus to be given in the context of the bid; it cannot be given in general and in advance of the bid.

Rule 21.1(a) spells out some common specific situations where the approval of the shareholders will be required, for example, in relation to share issues; acquisition or, more likely, disposals of target company assets of a "material amount"[59]; entering into contracts other than in the ordinary course of business (which may include the declaration and payment of interim dividends); and the redemption or purchase of shares.[60] But r.21.1(a) covers any frustrating action, whether specifically mentioned in the rules or not, and it has been held by the Panel to cover even the initiation of litigation on behalf of the target once an offer is imminent.[61] The overall effect of the rule is to reduce the defensive tactics available to the management of the target company to three general categories: convincing the shareholders that their future is better assured with the incumbent management than with the bidder; persuading the authorities that the bid ought to be referred to them on public interest grounds; and encouraging another bidder to come forward as a "white knight" and make an alternative offer to the shareholders. In all three situations the directors of the target are thrown back on their powers of persuasion: in all three cases the final decision on the success of these defensive moves rests with others.

However, it is important to understand that the board of the target company is not required as a general rule to co-operate with the bidder and to smooth its path. 28–019

[56] This statement used to appear in the GP, which now contain only a paler reflection of it. It was too strong a statement to be acceptable to all the Member States of the EU.

[57] Thus, a power conferred by shareholders pre-bid upon the board to issue shares or warrants post-bid would not escape r.21, because that rule would catch the post-bid decision by the board to make the issue.

[58] See paras 10–018 onwards.

[59] On which see Note 2 to r.21.1.

[60] Of course, the management of the target company may, and often do, promise as part of their defence to the bid to carry out one or more of these actions after their shareholders have rejected the offer, for example, the payment of a substantial dividend, perhaps after disposing of one of the company's businesses. Rule 21.1(c)(i) specifically states the Panel will normally permit defensive action taken post bid which is conditional on the acquisition not happening.

[61] See Panel Statement 1989/7, *Consolidated Gold Fields* and Panel Statement 1989/20, *BAT Industries*, which explore the complications which arise when the litigation is initiated in a foreign jurisdiction by a partially owned subsidiary or when the "litigation" takes the form of enthusiastic participation in regulatory hearings.

Rule 21 is framed by way of stipulations about what the board must not do, not about what it should do pro-actively. Thus, the board may find itself in a stronger negotiating position than r.21 might suggest if either (1) a recommendation in favour of the offer from the target board is, for one reason or another, important to the bidder; or (2) the bidder needs the target board's cooperation to launch the bid. We discuss such situations below under "bid procedure".

On the other hand, it is to be noted that the no-frustration rule applies to the target board even if the board of the bidder would not be subject to such a restriction if the acquirer were the target of a bid. The "reciprocity" exception to the no-frustration rule is an option for the Member States under art.9 of the Directive, and some Member States have made use of it. UK rules have never contained this qualification, on the grounds that the benefits to the UK of an open market for corporate control are maximised even if foreign bidders, not themselves subject to a "no frustration" rule, have the same freedom as domestic bidders. So far, the forces of economic nationalism have not challenged this rule.

Finally, it is significant that r.21 is a mandatory rule out of which companies may not opt. It is arguable that a strictly mandatory "no frustration" rule does not fit well with policies to encourage shareholder engagement, as discussed in paras 12–016 onwards. There may be a case for permitting the shareholders of the company, by an appropriate majority, to opt out of the "no frustration" rule for a period of time. This might enable the management of a company to embark on the implementation of a strategy which might not benefit the share price in the short-term, secure in the knowledge that they would be free from the risk of an opportunistic takeover offer, at least where the shareholders also conferred upon the board the power to put in place an effective takeover defence.

Defensive measures in advance of the bid

28–020 This is an area where the Code does not operate. Rule 21 applies only once the board "has reason to believe that a bona fide offer might be imminent". Before that point regulation is left to general company law,[62] which, however, has not developed a single rule to deal with pre-bid defensive tactics. Rather, a number of rules may be relevant, depending upon the precise action the directors of a potential target company wish to take. The most general of these company law rules is s.171 of the CA 2006 requiring the directors to exercise their powers for a proper purpose or to obtain shareholder approval of action not proposed for a proper purpose. As we have noted in relation to pre-bid defences, however, because that section focuses on the directors' purpose, rather than on the effects of their acts, the section is a weaker control than r.21. Provided there is a commercial justification which the directors can plausibly put forward as the predominant or motivating purpose of their action, it will be difficult for a shareholder to challenge it on the grounds that a consequence of the decision will

[62] These rules apply to post-bid defensive tactics as well, but there their impact is normally hidden beneath that of r.21 of the Code. They might be important, even post-bid, in the exceptional case where the Code did not apply to the target company, for example, where it was a private company or a public company whose securities were not publicly traded in the UK and whose central management was outside the UK. See para.28–015.

be to make the company less attractive to a bidder or less easy to acquire. In the absence of a current bid, there is also less incentive for a shareholder to seek to challenge the directors' action through a derivative action.

An example of a board decision, having the effect of making the company less easy to take over but having also a plausible commercial justification, might be the creation of a joint venture with another company, to which each commits part of its existing assets, on terms that a change of control in either partner permits the other partner to buy the first partner out.[63] Alternatively, the board of a company might seek to make it less attractive to a bidder by gearing up its balance sheet (i.e. altering the ratio of debt to equity in the company's financial structure) and distributing the immediate gains of that exercise to the shareholders, on the basis that the opportunity of carrying out this exercise is what makes the company attractive to a private equity bidder. It is not surprising that s.171 is less stringent than r.21, since it applies to the directors at all times. If it were re-formulated as an effects rule like r.21, it would subvert the delegation in the articles of managerial powers to the board whenever a decision might have the effect of making the company a less attractive bid target.[64]

Other rules can be pointed to which require shareholder consent in specific circumstances for pre-bid defences. Thus, s.551 requires shareholder authorisation for decisions by the directors of public companies to issue shares or to grant rights to subscribe for or convert any security into shares.[65] This section, together with the improper purposes doctrine, makes it much more difficult for a British company to adopt a US-style "poison pill" or "shareholder rights plan". In the US the efficacy of that device depends crucially on the board being able to adopt the plan without the consent of the shareholders and upon the courts not regarding the adoption of such a plan as a breach of fiduciary duty on the part of the directors. Section 551 lays down the principle of shareholder consent for the conferment of such rights, and a poison pill might well be regarded by British courts as falling foul of the proper purposes doctrine, since the pill has no commercial rationale except in the context of the bid and its role then is simply to make it very unattractive for a bidder to put an offer to the shareholders of which the target board does not approve.[66] However, s.551 is again a less rigorous provision than r.21 of the Code, because it allows shareholders to approve the issuance of shares by directors up to five years in advance, though institutional shareholders are in fact reluctant to give a blank cheque to the directors for such a long period. Asking shareholders to approve share issues in advance, for which permission there may well be good commercial reasons, does not focus shareholders' attention as sharply on the potential costs to them as where **28–021**

[63] For an example of the legal pitfalls which can be created if the drafters of the joint venture agreement are overly ambitious see *Criterion Properties Plc v Stratford UK Properties LLC* [2004] UKHL 28; [2004] B.C.C. 570.

[64] On the division of powers between shareholders and the board see para.11–006.

[65] See para.24–004.

[66] The shareholder rights plan, which comes in many varieties, in its core version gives target shareholders other than the bidder the right to subscribe for shares in the target company at a very attractive price. Given the discrimination between the bidder and non-bidder shareholders a rights plan would also cause difficulties for the target board under s.172(1)(f).

approval is required under r.21 in the course of a bid, when the shareholders know the terms of the offer they will be rejecting if they adopt the defensive measures.[67]

However, it should be noted that pre-bid and post-bid defensive measures do not fall into fully separate categories. For example, a pre-bid defensive tactic (obtaining authority to issue shares to defeat a bidder) which requires action by the directors post-bid (actually to issuing the shares) will be caught by r.21 at the point of exercise of the share-issue power. Thus, r.21 has some chilling effect on pre-bid defensive measures despite its post-bid operation.

The break-through rule

28–022 Another form of pre-bid defensive measure is the creation by companies of capital structures in which the voting rights attached to equity shares are not proportionate to the economic interests held by the equity shareholders, or where there were restrictions on the transferability of the shares. Such capital structures may be adopted with the general aim of keeping control of the company in the hands of a limited group of shareholders, for example, the founders of the company when it makes an initial public offering of its shares. Nevertheless, both arrangements make future bids less likely to succeed, in the former case because the voting shares may be concentrated in the hands of those who oppose a change of control in principle; and in the latter because it may simply not be possible for shareholders to accept the bidder's offer without the permission of the controllers. A disjunction between voting and economic rights can be achieved in a number of different ways, of which the most obvious are the creation of a class of non-voting equity shares or a class of shares with multiple voting rights. In either case, by ensuring that the voting or multiple voting shares are in "friendly" hands, no bid will succeed, even if a majority of the equity shareholders (by capital contributed) would wish it to.

It would seem at first sight that this strategy creates a major problem for the Code, because the rationale for putting the takeover decision in the hands of the shareholders assumes that the shareholders' input into the takeover decision will be proportionate to their economic interest in the company. One might expect that the Code or, more likely, the CA 2006 would show an interest in applying the principle of "'one share, one vote"' (OSOV) to takeover decisions, for example, when shareholders are asked whether they approve defensive measures or, even more relevant, to ensure that a bidder who has acquired acceptances from a majority of the shareholders (voting and non-voting) can also cast a majority of the votes at general meetings, at least those held immediately after the takeover.

28–023 However, this problem has never loomed large in British policy-making. As we have seen in Ch.6 there is nothing in British law that prohibits or regulates such capital structures. Nevertheless, they are uncommon, mainly because of the opposition of institutional shareholders to acquiring non- or limited-voting equity shares. This is not to say that such capital structures do not exist in British companies, but that, broadly, where they continue, institutional shareholders have

[67] Pre-emption rights, which might also stand in the way of rights plans, suffer from the same weakness of disapplication in advance. See s.570 and at para.24–006.

been convinced that there is a good reason for that situation. In other words, the solution to the problem in the UK has traditionally been market-led rather than to be found in the law. However, pressure from institutional shareholders led in 2018 to amendments to formal rules in favour of OSOV. The Principles contained in the Listing Rules and applicable to premium-listed[68] companies now require all shares of the same class of equity shares to have the same number of votes and, more important, where there is more than one class of share, "the aggregate voting rights of the securities in each class should be broadly proportionate to the relative interests of those classes in the equity of the listed company."[69] This is a significant development in UK regulation of "'dual-class"' shares, but because it is a general rule, it removed the need for specific rules to address the problem in the takeover context.

Nevertheless, the EU Directive contained by way of an option for Member States a specific legal device for providing OSOV and for removing restrictions on transfers of shares in the context of a takeover. This was the so-called "'break-through"' rule. It is not surprising that the UK did not take up this option. However, the Directive required the UK to give companies the option of adopting a break-through rule. As far as the editors are aware, no UK company has adopted it. A number of reasons could be put forward for this lack of take up of the break-through rule by individual companies. As already indicated, disproportionate voting rights are not a major issue in the UK. A company which has them has presumably managed to convince its shareholders (at least when it raised new capital) that it is useful to retain them. If the shareholders cease to be convinced, they are likely to press the board to remove them entirely and not just in the context of a takeover. The eighth edition of this book dealt with the break-through rule in some detail[70] and there is no need to repeat that analysis here. Chapter 2 of Pt 28 of the CA 2006 must be a prime candidate for early removal from the statute book.

Disclosure of control structures

A further provision of the Takeover Directive relevant to pre-bid defensive measures was the requirement on companies traded on a regulated market[71] to disclose annually their defensive structures and mechanisms and to provide a report on them. In the UK the mechanism used for this disclosure is the directors' report.[72] The domestic rules, following the Directive, require a wide range of **28–024**

[68] On premium listing see para.25–006.

[69] LR 7.2.1A. "The Listing Principles and Premium Listing Principles should be interpreted together with relevant rules and guidance which underpin the Listing Principles and the Premium Listing Principles." (LR 7.1.3). However, no other provision of the LR appears to refer to this issue. The future of this Principle has been thrown into some doubt by the *UK Listing Review* (March 2021), which proposes accepting dual class shares, subject to conditions.

[70] At paras 28–019 to 28–026.

[71] On which term see para.27–011.

[72] The Large and Medium-sized Companies and Groups (Accounts and Reports) Regulations 2008 (SI 2008/410) Sch.7 Pt 6. The information may alternatively be set out in the strategic report: s.414C(11).

information to be given, though some of it will either not be relevant to British companies or is already required to be disclosed. The main items to be covered are:

(1) the structure of the company's capital, notably the rights and obligations of each class of share, whether all those classes of capital are traded on a regulated market or not;
(2) restrictions on the transfer of securities (i.e. both shares and debentures);
(3) the identity of persons with significant direct or indirect holdings of securities in the company and the size and nature of that holding, so far as known to the company[73];
(4) similar information about a person with "special rights" with regard to the control of the company;
(5) how control rights are exercised under employee share schemes, where the rights are not exercisable by the employees directly;
(6) restrictions on voting rights, notably voting caps (restricting the percentage of total votes a shareholder has, no matter that the shareholding exceeds that percentage) or arrangements for splitting the financial and control rights of securities and placing them in different hands, where the company cooperates in making these arrangements;
(7) agreements between holders of securities, if known to the company, which contain restrictions on transfer or the exercise of voting rights[74];
(8) powers of the board to issue or buy back shares in the company[75];
(9) significant agreements to which the company is party which will operate differently if there is a change of control (such as loans containing repayment covenants upon a change of control—sometimes referred to as "poisoned debt"), but subject to the exception that disclosure is not required if that would be "seriously prejudicial" to the company; and
(10) agreements between the company and its directors or employees for compensation payments to be made upon a change of control.[76]

TARGET MANAGEMENT PROMOTION OF AN OFFER

28–025 In the previous section we have proceeded on the assumption that the target board's conflict of interest in relation to a bid leads them to seek to maintain the independence of the target company and thus of their positions within it, and hence the "no frustration" rule. This does indeed constitute the most obvious

[73] In the case of "vote-holding" such disclosure by the vote-holder to the company and then by the company is required by the Transparency Directive (see para.27–011), but this disclosure obligation goes wider to embrace not just voting shares, though it is not accompanied by any obligation of disclosure on the security-holder.

[74] Shareholder pacts are particularly important in some continental European countries in giving groups of investors holding a substantial, but nevertheless minority, stake in the company complete control of it. See *Financial Times*, UK edn, 28 March 2007, p.15 (discussing Italy).

[75] These are likely to be the subject of annual shareholder resolutions in any event: see paras 17–020 and 24–011 onwards.

[76] Which in the UK will often be required as part of the directors' remuneration report: see para.11–019.

expression of the target board's conflict with the interests of the shareholders, but it is not the only one. The board might perceive its future interests as being best served by the company coming under a new controller, especially, for example, where the bidder is a private equity group which wishes to retain the existing senior management of the target and give them a much larger financial stake in the company than they had when it was in public ownership and traded on a stock market.[77] It is thus incorrect to think that the conflict of interest of the target board will always take the form of resisting the bid, to the detriment of the interests of the shareholders. The board may promote the bid—or, if there are competing bids, one of the bids—to the shareholders, again possibly to their detriment. The Code and the general law use a number of different techniques for addressing the problem of conflicted promotion of a bid by target management.

Disclosure and independent advice

One technique is to inject an element of independence into the advice which the board is required to give to the shareholders on any offer made to the shareholders by a bidder. Under r.3.1 the board is required to obtain competent independent advice[78] on any offer and the substance of that advice must be made known to the shareholders.[79] Of course, independent advice is valuable to the shareholders (and is required) where target management are opposed to the bid and therefore likely to decry its benefits, but in that case, unlike with a recommended offer, the bidder will put the contrary case. Independent advice is even more valuable on a management buyout or an offer by a controlling shareholder to buy the shares not already held by it.[80] In addition, r.25 requires the board to circulate its own opinion on the offer to the shareholders (that is, they cannot simply hide behind the independent advice). If there is a divergence of views within the board or between the board and the independent adviser, this must be disclosed and the arguments for and against acceptance given.[81] **28–026**

Where directors have a conflict of interest, they should not normally join with the other members of the board in expressing a view on the offer. In the case of a management buy-out, the director will normally be regarded as having a conflict of interest if he or she is to have a continuing role in either offeror or offeree

---

[77] It does not necessarily follow that a private equity group will want to keep the existing management of the target in place. Conversely, a public bidder may be happy to keep the existing management, where it is buying the target for synergy reasons rather than because it thinks the target badly run.

[78] Normally from an investment bank not disqualified under r.3.3. A similar obligation applies to the board of the offeror when the offer is made in a "reverse takeover" (i.e. one in which the offeror may need to increase its issued voting equity share capital by more than 100%: see note 2 to r.3.2) or when the directors are faced with a conflict of interests: r.3.2.

[79] In its 2010 review of the Code following the politically controversial takeover of Cadbury Plc by Kraft, the Panel considered the suggestion that independent advice should be required to be given to the shareholders directly, but this was not thought to add significantly to the existing r.3 requirements. See Code Committee of the Takeover Panel, *Review of Certain Aspects of the Regulation of Takeover Bids* (2010/22), paras 6.10–6.12.

[80] Note 1 to r.3.1.

[81] Note 2 to r.25.2.

company.[82] Thus, where the whole of the executive director team of the target is to be taken on by the bidder, the conduct of the target company's response falls on the non-executive directors and if, as happened in a one case, the non-executives are conflicted because they are involved with the bidder as well, the chair of the board may become largely responsible for the target board's response to the bid. Some help is provided to the independent directors by r.21.4, which requires the offeror to provide to the independent directors, on request, all the information which the offeror has furnished to the potential external providers of finance in relation to the buy-out. This does something to equalise the information available to the independent directors and the executive directors who are part of the bidding team. Overall, the distinction between executive and independent non-executive directors, which has become formalised in the Corporate Governance Code, is used by the Takeover Code to handle the most pressing examples of conflict of interest which might lead the board to promote a bid, though at the cost of the non-executive directors suddenly finding themselves more heavily involved in the affairs of the company than they probably contemplated when taking on that role.

Looking at these matters from the bidder's point of view, r.24.6 requires the bidder to disclose in its offer document "any agreement, arrangement or understanding" between it (or any person acting in concert with it) and any of the target's directors or recent directors which are connected with or dependent on the offer, giving full particulars of them. This would clearly include the details of any proposed arrangement concerning employment of the directors of the target in either the target or the offeror after the bid. Rule 16 requires Panel consent for special deals offered by the bidder to some shareholders where that deal is not being extended to all shareholders. This rule creates a potential problem for management buy-outs, where, as will be usual, the target management holds shares in the target company but is also connected with the bidding entity and is being offered the special deal that it will continue to be involved in the running of the target if the bid is successful. In addition, it may be that only the management shareholders in the target company are being offered shares in the acquirer (the other shareholders being offered cash).[83] In practice, the Panel will give its consent so as to facilitate management buy-outs where the management of the target can be regarded as a joint bidder with the other bodies which are financing the bid. For this reason "joint offerors may make arrangements between themselves regarding the future membership, control and management of the business being acquired".[84]

Compensation for loss of office

28–027 A much cruder form of conflict of interest, which may generate managerial promotion of a bid, arises where the director expects to receive compensation if the bid is successful and he or she is removed from office. The anticipation of a

[82] Notes 4 and 5 to r.25.2.

[83] The Panel will normally permit this subject to disclosure to the shareholders as a whole and a fairness opinion from the independent adviser: Note 2 to r.16.2.

[84] Panel Statement 2003/25, *Canary Wharf Ltd*, para.12.

large windfall may shape the directors' response to the bid, consciously or unconsciously. Moreover, in this case a part of the consideration which the bidder is willing to pay for the target may be diverted to the directors. In those jurisdictions which allocate to the target board a major role in the determination of the fate of an offer, such monetary incentives to accept the bid may well be viewed with favour, as aligning the shareholders' and directors' interests. However, in the UK, where the decision on the fate of the bid is allocated primarily to the shareholders, such financial incentives for target directors have been viewed as distorting the allocation of the consideration the bidder is willing to pay and the incentives of the target management to advise the target shareholders dispassionately.

The CA 2006 contains provisions which require shareholder approval for payments in respect of loss of office, which pre-date the creation of the City Code and Panel.[85] These clearly catch "gratuitous" payments for loss of office (i.e. payments to which the director has no contractual entitlement) where the risks of distortion are significant. In the past, contractual entitlements to loss of office compensation were excluded from the member approval requirement, but the Act has now taken modest steps to include some of these within the principle as well.

Gratuitous payments

The provisions on gratuitous payments apply to takeovers of both public and private companies. Two features of the shareholder approval requirement show that the offeree shareholders are the persons the CA 2006 aims to protect. First, approval is required from the holders of the shares to which the offer relates ("relevant" shareholders), and the bidder and associates are excluded from voting in respect of any shares they hold.[86] Obtaining such consent may be problematic or, in the case of payments made under an arrangement entered into after the transfer by the accepting shareholders of their shares to the bidder, even impossible. In such cases the requirement for shareholder consent may operate in practice as a prohibition on such payments.[87] Even in the course of the bid the bidder and target management may regard holding a meeting to obtain shareholder approval as a very unwelcome distraction, although it is possible for the approval to be sought by way of a written resolution where the target company is a private company. Information about the proposed payment, notably its amount, must be made available to the shareholders in advance of the vote.[88] 28–028

Secondly, if approval is not obtained but a payment is nevertheless made, it is treated as held on trust by the recipient for those who have sold their shares as a

[85] Now set out in Ch 4 of Pt 10 of the Act. The requirement for shareholder approval of such payments stems from the *Report of the Committee on Company Law Amendment* (1945), Cmd.6659.

[86] CA 2006 s.219(1)(2)(4). Non-bidder holders of shares of the class may vote, even if their shares are not subject to the offer—a rare situation given the Code's equality rules.

[87] The Act does not require shareholder approval before the transfer of shares to the bidder under the offer but only before the payment is made. However, failure to achieve a quorum at two successive meetings triggers the rule that the payment is deemed to have been approved: s.219(5).

[88] CA 2006 s.219(3). The director is no longer under a statutory obligation, as was the case with the CA 1985, to take all reasonable steps to secure that details of the proposed payment are included in the offer document.

result of the offer and the expenses of making the distribution to those entitled to it are to be borne by the recipient.[89] Here, therefore, the legislation has avoided the absurdity illustrated in *Regal (Hastings) Ltd v Gulliver*.[90] Restitution here is to those truly damnified, rather than to the company when, in effect, that would result in an undeserved reduction of the price that the successful offeror has paid.

28–029 These provisions apply also to payments made in connection with a takeover bid by third party for the shares of a subsidiary of the company whose director is to receive the compensation. This extension might be important where there are outside minority shareholders in the subsidiary.[91] "Takeover bid" is not defined for the purpose of this section, and so it is unclear whether the section embraces a takeover effected by means of a scheme of arrangement. The requirements ought to apply, since the risks are the same, and they are easier to comply with in a takeover by way of a scheme since a shareholder meeting is an essential part of the scheme procedure, as we see in the following chapter. However, "payment for loss of office" is defined. Among other things, s.215(1) includes payments for loss of any other office or employment held in conjunction with the directorship which involves the management of the company or its subsidiaries. This is a very important provision, since compensation payments are often made to executive directors in connection with the loss of their management positions in the corporate group, rather than in connection with the loss of the directorship itself. For this reason, it is also sensible to bring shadow directors within the scope of s.219. Although loss of the status of shadow director itself is not within the section, compensation payments for the loss of other offices or employment within the company held by the shadow director will be caught.[92]

28–030 Although the payer is typically the target company after the takeover has succeeded, the requirement for shareholder approval applies to payments for loss of office made by "any person".[93] This will clearly include payments by a parent company (i.e. the successful bidder) or a subsidiary of the target. Payments to a director include payments to a person connected with a director and payments to any person at the direction or on behalf of the director or connected person.[94] Payments are rebuttably presumed to be payments for loss of office if made in pursuance of an arrangement (not necessarily a contract) made within the period extending from one year before to two years after the transfer of the shares and either bidder or target is privy to the arrangement.[95] So, the provisions cannot be avoided simply by waiting for the transaction to be concluded. If the price paid to

---

[89] CA 2006 s.222(3).

[90] See para.10–083.

[91] CA 2006 s.219(6) makes it clear that approval is not required where compensation is paid in relation to the takeover of a wholly-owned subsidiary. The requirement for shareholder approval also applies only to payments by UK-registered companies.

[92] CA 2006 s.223. This might seem to mean that a company could escape the statutory controls by paying a shadow director compensation for loss of the shadow directorship. However, since the shadow directorship is not a formal position, payment for loss of it is likely to be a misapplication of corporate funds and thus a breach of duty on the part of the authorising directors and recoverable from the shadow director who has received it, knowing of the facts which make its payment improper.

[93] CA 2006 s.219(1).

[94] CA 2006 s.215(3). The definition of a connected person is given in s.252.

[95] CA 2006 s.219(7).

the director for his or her shares is in excess of that available to other shareholders or if, in connection with the transfer of the shares, any valuable consideration is given to the director by any person, the excess is irrebuttably treated as a payment for loss of office.[96] Finally, compensation is treated as including benefits otherwise than in cash, though cash is in fact the typical form of compensation provided.[97] On the other hand, there is a de minimis exception for payments by the company or its subsidiaries where the amount or value of the payment does not exceed £200, a very small amount.[98]

Contractual compensation

A major loophole in the above provisions used to be that they did not apply to loss-of-office payments to which the director was contractually entitled. However, the position has been ameliorated in recent years by two developments: first, a cautious extension of the rules on gratuitous payments to certain contractual ones and, second, an extension of shareholder influence over directors' remuneration payments in general, at least in publicly traded companies. **28–031**

The extension of s.219 (previously confined to gratuitous payments) is aimed at express contractual entitlements for a director to receive a sum of money (or some other form of consideration) upon the occurrence of particular event. These are sometimes referred to as "covenanted payments".[99] Whilst payments "in discharge of an existing legal obligation" are normally excluded from the approval requirements of s.219, this is now so only if the obligation "was not entered into for the purpose of, in connection with or in consequence of" the takeover.[100] Thus, covenants entered into in the face of a bid (even, in appropriate circumstances, before the bid is formally announced) or afterwards (for example, to reward conduct during the bid) will need shareholder approval under the provisions discussed above and payments made without approval will be dealt with accordingly. The CA 2006 accurately assesses the risks to the offeree shareholders in this case to be substantially the same as with a gratuitous payment.

Secondly, contractual payments to directors may become due without any express contractual entitlement to a loss-of-office payment, because the loss of office causes a breach of some other provision in a contract with the director. A common example is where the immediate removal of a target director after a successful takeover breaches a term in that person's service contract. This is a significant situation, since large sums may be payable to an executive director by way of breach of a long fixed-term or long notice contract of service, even if it

---

96 CA 2006 s.216.

97 CA 2006 s.215(2).

98 CA 2006 s.221. The Secretary of State has power to raise the figure: s.258.

99 For the previous position see *Taupo Totara Timber Co v Rowe* [1978] A.C. 537 PC; *Lander v Premier Pict Petroleum*, 1997 S.L.T. 1361 OH. In the former case the director's service contract provided that, if the company were taken over, he could within 12 months resign from the company and become entitled to a lump-sum payment of five times his annual salary.

100 CA 2006 s.220(1) and (3). It does not matter whether the payment is by way of remuneration due, damages for breach of contract or the settlement of a claim.

contains no "covenanted payments".[101] Alternatively, the removal may trigger the "'retirement"' of the director, but payments "by way of pension in respect of past services" are exempted from the need for shareholder approval under s.219,[102] apparently even if they are gratuitous. Directors towards the end of their careers may positively welcome compensation payments which take the form of a pension.

However, under the provisions of Ch.4A of the CA 2006, introduced in 2013[103] and applying only to "quoted companies",[104] payments for loss of office must either be "consistent with" the company's remuneration policy, as approved by the shareholders,[105] or receive specific shareholder approval.[106] Thus, if the director's contractual notice period or contractual term exceeds that stated in the remuneration policy, payment of damages for breach of them will need shareholder approval, at least in relation to the "excess" period, as will the payment of a pension beyond what the policy contemplates. The new rule applies in principle to all payments for loss of office, but it is made clear that, if the payment falls within s.219 (as extended), Ch.4A does not apply.[107] Section 219 is the stronger rule since it requires shareholder approval in the face of a particular proposed loss-of-office payment, while Ch.4A permits approval in advance and for termination payment approval to be bundled up with approval for the directors' remuneration package as a whole. The detailed provisions of Ch.4A largely track those relating to gratuitous payments. In particular, the recipient of an inconsistent and unauthorised payment holds it on trust for those who sold their shares into the offer.[108]

Competing bids

28–032 One post-bid defensive measure which the Code does permit is the search by the target board for an alternative bidder. Such action is not held to breach the no-frustration rule, because the decision on the bids still rests with the shareholders of the target company, whose choices have in fact been widened by the presence of the so-called "white knight". The Code does not explicitly exempt from r.21 the search for a white knight, but the Code is full of provisions which take account of the possibility of a competing bidder emerging and Note 1 to

[101] Such payments escape s.219 only if made "in good faith" (s.220(1)) and so the parties to the payment run a legal risk if they use a damages claim to inflate the compensation payable to the director beyond his or her contractual or statutory entitlements. But the contract or notice period may be designed deliberately to provide a handsome "golden goodbye" if the director is removed from office.

[102] CA 2006 s.220(1)(d). Again the payment must be made "in good faith", which may constrain egregious use of this provision. For an unsuccessful attempt to use instead what is now s.190 of the CA 2006 (see para.10–069) to impose a requirement for shareholder approval in relation to pensions, see *Granada Group Ltd v Law Debenture Pension Trust Corp Plc* [2016] EWCA Civ 1289; [2017] B.C.C. 57.

[103] By the Enterprise and Regulatory Reform Act 2013.

[104] i.e. companies with equity quoted on a top-tier public market: s.385.

[105] See para.11–016.

[106] CA 2006 s.226C.

[107] CA 2006 s.226F.

[108] CA 2006 s.226E(4).

r.21.2 explicitly contemplates the target agreeing an inducement fee with a potential competing bidder. The point is perhaps too obvious for the Code to make it.

However, conflicts of interest on the part of the target board may arise here also, either because the board wishes to discourage a competitor because its interests will be better served by the initial bidder or, vice versa, where the target board seeks a competitor because it does not favour the initial bidder. Of course, in either case the board's decisions may be driven by a desire to promote the interests of the shareholders of the target, rather than the directors' interests, and so the Code and other rules need to focus on this problem with some degree of sophistication. Another troublesome question is whether it is, in principle, in the interests of the shareholders to encourage competing bids. In the context of a particular offer, that is clearly so, since the competitor drives up the price and may even trigger an auction. However, the initial bidder often loses out in the auction, thus throwing away the costs it has incurred in identifying a target and mounting a bid. Knowing of this risk, companies may be less willing to bid initially than if they could be sure that there would be no competitor, thus reducing the incidence of bids, arguably to the detriment of shareholders. It is thus conceivable that the encouragement of competing bids means fewer bids overall. However, on the principle the Code clearly comes out in favour of permitting, even to some extent protecting, competing bidders.

A duty to auction or a duty to be even-handed?

A conceivable policy would be to require the target board to seek out any available competing offers. In bid situations there will often be pressure from shareholders on the board of the target to do this. However, the Code itself contains no such obligation, only a permission for the target board to take this step. In the case law on fiduciary duties the question has sometimes arisen, but the upshot of that limited case law seems be no more than the proposition that, if a competing bid does in fact emerge, the directors may not obstruct the shareholders from accepting the bid the latter prefer, but the directors are not obliged to further that offer by, for example, assenting their own shares to it. In *Heron International Ltd v Lord Grade*[109] there were two competing bids for a company whose directors held over 50% of the shares and where, unusually for a public company, the consent of the directors was required for the transfer of shares. The directors had given irrevocable undertakings to accept what turned out to be the lower bid and stood by those undertakings, so that the higher bidder was defeated. The Court of Appeal declared that: **28–033**

> "Where directors have decided that it is in the best interests of a company that the company should be taken over and there are two or more bidders the only duty of the directors, who have powers such as those in [the company's articles], is to obtain the best price. The directors should not commit themselves to transfer their own voting shares to a bidder unless they are satisfied that he is offering the best price reasonably available."[110]

[109] *Heron International Ltd v Lord Grade* [1983] B.C.L.C. 244 CA.
[110] *Heron International Ltd v Lord Grade* [1983] B.C.L.C. 244 at 265.

This dictum clearly suggests that the directors' freedom to assent their own shares to the bidder favoured by them is restricted by their duty as directors to the company. However, in *Re A Company*,[111] where a similar issue arose in the context of unfair prejudice petition but involving this time a small private company, Hoffmann J refused to accept "the proposition that the board must inevitably be under a positive duty to recommend and take all steps within their power to facilitate whichever is the highest offer", especially where that alleged duty restricted the directors' freedom of action in relation to their own shares. Their duty went no further than requiring them not to exercise their powers under the articles so as to prevent those other shareholders, who wished to do so, from accepting the higher offer, and requiring them, if they gave advice to the shareholders, to do so in the interests of those shareholders and not in order to further the bid preferred by the directors. This view seems more in accord with generally accepted principles of fiduciary law and with the Code which, as we have seen above, requires the directors to give advice to the shareholders in order to promote the interests of the latter, but stops short of requiring directors to take decisions in relation to their shares other than in their own interests.

More generally in relation to the exercise of directorial discretion, the Code can be said to adopt the policy of requiring the directors to be even-handed as between competing bids: they are not required to seek out alternative offers but, if such emerge, the choice between them should be one for the shareholders. This can be seen as an application of the "no frustration" principle in the context of competing bids. The central provision here is r.21.3 which requires the target board to provide information to an offeror or potential offeror which it has made available to another offeror or potential offeror "even if that other offeror is less welcome". This is an important provision, because, as we shall see below, the target board is not normally under an obligation to provide information to a potential bidder to help it decide whether to make an offer or on what terms. However, if the board decides to do so for one offeror or potential offeror, it cannot refuse this facility to a competitor. This principle is applied not only to the information itself but also to the terms on which it is made available (for example, confidentiality requirements). However, the rule does not permit the competitor to ask simply for all the information given to the initial offeror: the competitor has to specify the questions to which it wants answers, and the target company must answer them if it has done so for the other bidder.[112] There is an obvious difficulty in applying this rule in relation to a management buy-out, because the existing management element of the bidder will have comprehensive knowledge of the target company. Note 3 to r.21.3 defines the disclosure obligation in such a case by reference to the information provided to the external providers of finance for the buy-out bid.

28–034 Quite apart from regulation of the conduct of the target board towards competing bidders, the question can be asked whether the design of the takeover Code facilitates the emergence of competitors. In many ways it does, though mainly as a side-wind of the implementation of policies designed to further other goals. Thus, as we shall see below, the timetable for the offer (the required lapse of time

[111] *Re A Company* [1986] B.C.L.C. 382.
[112] Note 1 to r.21.3.

between the initial approach and the formal offer, the need for the formal offer to be open for a minimum period of time) does create a space in which competing bidders have the opportunity to put together an alternative offer. The offeror may seek to dilute this risk by acquiring shares in the target (or commitments to accept the offer) in advance of the public announcement of the approach or offer. As we see below, however, regulation constrains extensive use of this strategy.[113] Moreover, market purchases on any scale are likely to cause the price of the shares to shift upwards significantly, quite apart from the regulation. Overall, the Code does expose a bidder to a significant risk that a rival bid will emerge. Finally, in a recent rule change, an accepting shareholder may withdraw an acceptance of a conditional offer (for example, so as to accept a competing offer) at any time before the offer becomes unconditional as to acceptances or the "unconditional date" is reached.[114]

Binding the target board by contract

Given the risks just alluded to, the initial bidder may well seek, by contract, to enlist the directors of the target on its side in dealing with any future competitor. There are two main contractual techniques which have been used to this end, though obviously they are potentially available only where the target board approves of the proposed bid. First, the initial bidder may wish to secure from the directors of the target company a legally binding undertaking to recommend the bid to the shareholders of the target in any event and not to seek, encourage or co-operate with any "white knight". Such an agreement with the directors is not necessarily against the interests of the target's shareholders, for the initial bidder may not be willing to make a bid at all for the target unless such undertakings are forthcoming. The courts, however, have been unwilling to give full effect to such agreements, especially the commitment always to recommend the initial offer, even if a better one emerges. They have subjected the contractual undertaking to recommend the bid to an implied limitation, which in fact deprives the undertaking of most of its utility to the offeror. The limitation is that the directors should be free to recommend the competing bid if they come to the conclusion that it would be in the best interests of the shareholders that later bid be accepted.[115] There is in fact a lot to be said for this approach, for to hold otherwise would be to undermine both the basic allocation of decision-making power on the fate of the bid to the shareholders. GP 2 states that the shareholders must be given the information necessary to enable them to reach a properly **28–035**

---

[113] See paras 28–038 and 28–040.

[114] Normally, Day 60. See r.34.1. Previously, withdrawal could not occur within the first 21 days, so that an early acceptor was stuck with an acceptance which became unconditional during that period.

[115] *Dawson International Plc v Coats Paton Plc* [1991] B.C.C. 276 OH; *Rackham v Peek Foods Ltd* [1990] B.C.L.C. 895; *John Crowther Group Ltd v Carpets International Plc* [1990] B.C.L.C. 460. See also the decision of the Inner House in the interlocutory proceedings in the *Dawson* case: (1989) 5 B.C.C. 405 IH (1 Div). This is sometimes called the "fiduciary out", though it is to some degree unclear in these cases whether the result was arrived at as a matter of interpretation of the contract in question or of the application of a mandatory rule of fiduciary law. A commitment not to seek a competitor appears to be valid, but difficult to police.

informed decision on the bid and an unbiased recommendation from the directors is an important source of information for them.

Given the uncertainties surrounding agreements which seek to control the target board's actions in relation to competing bidders, it is not surprising that alternative contractual arrangements were developed, focusing on providing a financial incentive to proceed with the deal. A common form of agreement was the "break fee" or "inducement fee", i.e. an agreement between the target company (through its directors) and the initial bidder that, if the bidder's offer is not accepted for one of a number of reasons, which might include the shareholders' acceptance of an alternative offer, the target company becomes liable to pay a sum of money to the disappointed bidder. In this way, the initial bidder seeks to protect itself against the financial costs of its failed bid. However, the effect of a large break fee may be to discourage a competing bidder, since it effectively reduces the value of the target in the hands of the competitor, but not in the hands of the bidder which has negotiated the break fee. The break-fee arrangement might be reciprocal, giving the bidder as well a financial incentive to complete the deal, but, as we see in para.28–058, the Code itself constrains the bidder's freedom to make its offer conditional or to invoke conditions properly attached, so that a financial inducement to proceed is less important in relation to the bidder. An example of its potential use is where the takeover is for some reason dependent upon the consent of the bidder's shareholders (for example, where it constitutes in relation to the bidder a Class I transaction under the Listing Rules) or where regulatory approval is needed for takeover.

The break fee was always regarded with some suspicion by the Code, which imposed a cap on the level of the fee (or similar inducement) at 1% of the offer price. However, in the course of the Panel's 2010 review of the Code it was concluded that break fees and other "deal protection measures", including "no cooperation" agreements, should be prohibited, except in very limited cases. The Code Committee was sceptical about the benefits to target shareholders of inducement fees and other deal protection devices, which it regarded as often imposed by the acquirer for its benefit.[116] Rule 21.2 now prohibits most "offer-related arrangements" between the target and an offeror or person acting in concert with either party—though apparently a major shareholder in the target acting independently could offer an inducement. "Offer-related arrangements" include not only inducement fees but also "other arrangements having a similar or comparable financial or economic effect".[117] However, the potentially adverse impact upon shareholder choice of prohibiting inducement fess is recognised in two situations in notes to r.21.2. Subject to the 1% cap and disclosure, the target company will normally be permitted to agree an inducement fee with a competing offeror where an initial, but not recommended, bid has been launched (so that a competitor can be encouraged). Further, where the board of the target had initiated a formal sale of the company before any firm offer for the target was announced, and sought bidders in that context, it will normally be permitted to

---

[116] See fn.79 at para.5.15.

[117] Code r.21.2(b) contains a list of arrangements which are permitted because they do not infringe substantially the principle of shareholder choice. This new approach also renders less important, but does not remove, the difficult question of whether a break fee constitutes unlawful financial assistance under the statute (para.17–041): *Par OS Plc v Wordlink Group Plc* [2012] EWHC 394 (Comm).

agree an inducement fee (and perhaps other arrangements) with a bidder who participated in that process in order to encourage it to make a formal bid.[118] Here, the formal sale process operates as the assurance that all serious offers have been flushed out.

EQUALITY OF TREATMENT OF TARGET SHAREHOLDERS

Since the UK Code places the decision on the offer firmly in the hands of the target shareholders, it follows that there is a strong regulatory interest in protecting the target shareholders from being manipulated by the offeror into accepting an offer they think is sub-optimal. If the bid decision required the consent of the target management as well, the board could operate so as to filter out manipulative offers, but the no-frustration rule has rendered that strategy largely unavailable in the UK. The possibility of manipulation arises, on the one hand, from the bidder's freedom under the law of contract to formulate the offer as it wishes (in the absence of regulation) and, on the other, from the dispersed nature of the shareholders in a typical UK target company, so that coordination amongst them to reject "coercive" offers may be difficult to organise effectively. Although "the Code is not concerned with the financial or commercial advantages or disadvantages of a takeover",[119] it does contain a wide range of rules designed to preserve the integrity of the target shareholders' decision-making and these rules do shape the substantive content of the offer. The most obvious (but not the only) technique the bidder might deploy to manipulate the target shareholders' decision-making is unequal treatment of the offerees. For example, a bidder might make an attractive offer for target shares, but only for enough of them to give the bidder working control of the target, with the offer being open only for a short-time. Once this offer was satisfied, the bidder might make a lower offer to the remaining shareholders or no offer at all. Although the shareholders collectively would be better off if they all refused the offer and forced the acquirer to bid for all the target shares on the same terms, any individual shareholder will maximise returns by accepting the partial offer. Or the inequality strategy may be implemented the other way around. The acquirer makes a low-level bid for all the shares. Having picked up the unsophisticated shareholders in this way, it makes a higher offer to those who hold out. **28–036**

From the beginning the Code has addressed these "divide and rule" issues though the requirement for equal treatment of target shareholders, a notion which has now been developed to a considerable degree of sophistication. GP 1 of the Code stipulates that "all holders of the securities of an offeree company of the same class must be afforded equivalent treatment" but the Rules in fact go beyond this. In some jurisdictions, equal treatment of shareholders is a fundamental principle underlying all its company law. UK legislation and case law has never articulated it in this way, though the notion surfaces from time to time. In the Takeover Code, however, the equality principle is absolutely central. In all its manifestations, it is a clear demonstration that, whilst the Code facilitates takeovers, it does not have as its goal maximisation of the number of

[118] Notes 1 and 2 to r.21.2.

[119] City Code, "Introduction", s.2(a).

takeovers, for otherwise it would permit differential offers. However, the equality policy is not without its costs. Some of the bids which are discouraged by the equality rules might come from financially constrained bidders who nevertheless would run the company more efficiently than the current controllers.

Partial bids

28–037 Perhaps the most obvious way of implementing the equality principle is to prohibit partial bids, i.e. offers for only some of the outstanding shares in the target. Through a partial bid the offeror acquires sufficient shares to obtain control of the company, but not all the shares are offered for. If the offer is made on a "first come, first served" basis, offerees may rush to accept it, either because it is pitched at an attractive level or, even though it is not, offerees wish to exit the company because of doubts about how well the acquirer will run it in the future. As we shall see in para.28–058, a floor is put under the partial bid strategy by the requirement that the bidder must end up with at least 50% of the voting rights in the target, including the voting rights attached to shares held prior to the offer. If this condition is not met within the bid time-table, the offer lapses and all the shares which have been assented to the offer will remain with their current holders. However, the Code goes much further: by r.36 the Panel's consent is needed for partial offers. To be sure, consent will normally be given if the offer could not result in the offeror being interested in shares carrying 30% or more of the voting rights of the target company, since at this level the acquirer is not regarded as having control.[120] If the partial offer could result in the offeror holding more than 30% but less than 100%, consent will not normally be granted if the offeror or its concert party has acquired, selectively or in significant numbers, interests in shares in the target company during the previous 12 months or if any shares were acquired after the partial offer was reasonably in contemplation.[121] Nor, without consent, may any member of the concert party purchase any further interests in shares within 12 months after a successful partial bid.[122] Both rules promote equality of treatment, since the sellers outside the offer may have been able to dispose of the entirety of their shareholdings and at a better price.

If the Panel does give its consent to a partial offer, some restrictive conditions apply to it in order to promote equality, given the partial nature of the bid. First, all the accepting shareholders must be able to dispose of the same proportion of their holdings.[123] Secondly, where the partial offer could result in the offeror being interested in more than 50% of the votes, shareholders are asked to vote on two questions. The first is, as ever, whether to accept the offer for their shares; and the second is whether they approve of the offer, irrespective of their decision

[120] Code r.36.1. The phrase "interested in shares" is used to include not only legal and beneficial ownership of shares but also having a purely economic interest in them in certain circumstances. See the Definitions section of the Code. In fact, where the other shares are very dispersed, less than 30% could in fact give control. However, the Code is constructed on the basis of equating a 30% holding with control. See the discussion of the mandatory bid below.

[121] Code r.36.2.

[122] Code r.36.3.

[123] Code r.36.7.

to sell their shares. Given the "same proportion" rule, the existing shareholders will remain members of the target company, at least as to part of their shareholdings, even if the bid is successful. They may well regard this as unsatisfactory: hence the requirement that shareholders should have a double opportunity to vote. The partial bid will be successful only if the acquirer obtains at least 50% approval for the bid as well at least the number of acceptances specified in the offer.[124] This rule allows each shareholder effectively to rank his or her preferences without knowing the views of the other shareholders. A shareholder in favour of the offer votes positively on both questions; a shareholder who thinks the offer unattractive but wants to make a partial exit from the company if the majority of the shareholders accept it votes against the bid but in favour of accepting the offer for his or her shares; and a shareholder against the bid and who wants to remain in the company in any event votes negatively on both questions.

Finally, to induce shareholders to exercise both voting opportunities, an offer which could result in the offeror holding shares carrying over 50% of the votes must contain a prominent warning that, if the offer succeeds, the offeror will be free, subject to the 12-month post bid prohibition, to acquire further shares without incurring an obligation to make a mandatory offer.[125]

These Rules of the Code display an obvious antipathy to partial offers. In consequence, partial bids are infrequent, though not unknown.

Level and type of consideration

In pursuit of the equality principle the Code contains rules which determine the minimum level of consideration which is required to be offered for the shares, even when the offer is made to all target shareholders. The purpose of these equality rules is to prevent the offeror from distorting the decision of the target's shareholders by offering an attractive price to some shareholders to gain control whilst offering an inadequate price to the remainder, who then have the choice of accepting the low offer or being locked into the company under a new controller. The first and most obvious expression of the equality principle is to be found in the requirement that, if the offer is revised upwards after an initial offer at a lower price, the original acceptors are entitled to the higher consideration.[126] This rule probably does more to protect inexperienced shareholders (who accept early) than to prevent opportunistic behaviour on the part of offeror companies.[127] The rule on offer increases is supported by r.16.1, under which, except with the consent of the Panel, the offeror may not make any special arrangements, either 28–038

[124] Code r.36.5. The Rule requirement that the specified number of acceptances be met appears to mean that the offeror cannot waive this requirement, something which is possible in a full bid (subject to the 50% rule). This requirement eliminates the possibility that the resulting partial bid is different from the on authorised by the Panel.

[125] Code r.36.6.

[126] Code r.32.3.

[127] The pressures in favour of thoughtless acceptance are further mitigated by the procedural rules requiring the initial offer to be open for acceptance for at least 21 days (r.31.1) and revised offers to be open for at least 14 days (r.32.1).

during an offer or when one is reasonably in contemplation, whereby favourable conditions are offered to some shareholders which are not extended to all of them.[128]

A more significant expression of the equality principle is between those who accept the offer and those who sell their shares to the offeror outside the offer, either before the offer is made or during the offer period. Again, r.6 of the Code seeks to prevent private and favourable deals being done with a few shareholders. An offeror (or person acting in concert) which acquires shares of a class in the three months before the offer period begins or during the offer but before an announcement of a firm offer[129] must set any subsequent general offer for that class at least at the highest level paid outside it.[130] The same rule applies as a result of acquisitions outside the offer but after the firm offer announcement, except that it also requires the offer to be in cash.[131] To a limited extent, r.6 permits inequality because the acquisitions made before the firm offer announcement may have been for cash but the offer is permitted to be on a share-exchange basis (but of a value equal to the highest consideration paid outside the offer). The offerees are subject to the risk of a downward movement in the price of the securities offered, whose value is assessed only around the date of the firm offer announcement.[132]

28–039 However, even in respect of acquisitions made before the offer period, the subsequent offer will have to be in cash (or accompanied by an alternative cash offer, probably provided by the offeror's investment bank rather than the offeror itself), if the conditions of r.11.1 are met. The requirement for cash is applied when the offeror and persons acting in concert acquire "for cash" shares (or interests in them) in the target company which carry at least 10% of the voting rights of the class in question. The danger period (from the bidder's point of view) commences 12 months prior to the offer period and extends until the offer succeeds or lapses. The level of the offer is set by the highest level of the prices paid outside the offer.[133] In this rule "cash" has an extended meaning in its application to acquisitions "for cash", though it bears its ordinary meaning in relation to the requirement that the offer be "in cash". In relation to acquisitions the phrase includes acquisitions by the offeror company in exchange for securities, unless the exiting shareholder is not free to dispose of the securities

[128] Note 1 makes it clear that this bans the not-unknown practice of buying a shareholding coupled with an undertaking to make good to the seller any difference between the sale price and the higher price of any successful subsequent bid. It also covers (Note 3) cases where a shareholder of the target company is to be remunerated for the part he has played in promoting the offer ("a finder's fee").

[129] Code r.6.1 or even earlier if the Panel thinks this is necessary to give effect to General Principle 1: r.6.1(c). For the firm offer announcement see para.28–055.

[130] The Panel has a discretion to relax the highest price rule, though it will do so only rarely: see notes 1 and 4.

[131] Code r.6.2 and Note 3. Cash is required where the acquisitions occur after the firm offer announcement presumably because of the risk that the bidder will purchase shares outside the offer from sophisticated shareholders who will appreciate the risks of accepting shares.

[132] Note 3 to r.6.

[133] The Panel has a discretion to apply the cash rule even if fewer than 10% of the voting rights have been acquired (see r.11.1(c)), something Note 4 to r.11.1 suggests it might do, and at a considerably lower level than 10%, if the vendors were directors of the target.

until the offerees in the general bid receive their consideration (or the offer lapses).[134] The thinking is that, since securities are saleable, they are the equivalent of cash.

The overall effect of r.11.1 is that the offer must be in cash or accompanied by a cash alternative because the sellers prior to the bid or within it have received cash (or its equivalent). The rule is triggered only at the 10% level and so it can be argued that r.11.1 is not a full implementation of the equality principle. Beneath the 10% threshold, r.6.1 applies, not requiring a cash offer as a result of pre-announcement acquisitions and applying only in the three-month period before the bid. The argument against reforming this position is that a stronger rule would discourage bids because bidders would either have to forgo significant pre-bid acquisitions or always launch cash bids where they had made previous acquisitions for cash. Building up a pre-bid stake is a way of obtaining some degree of protection against a competing offer, either because the stake will deter a competitor or because, if the initial bidder fails, it can recoup some of its costs by selling its stake at a profit to the successful bidder.

Rule 11.1 does not deal with the converse case, i.e. where the prior acquisitions were in exchange for securities but the bid is in cash and the target shareholders claim they should be offered the securities provided in the prior acquisitions. This is less often a matter of complaint than the one where the general offerees are excluded from cash, because cash is in general more attractive than securities, but there might be exceptional circumstances where the securities were attractive but not readily available on the market. In the light of this, a new rule was introduced in 2002, similar, but not identical, to r.11.1, but requiring securities to be offered in the general bid. Under r.11.2, if, during the three months prior to the commencement of the offer and during the offer period, the offeror has acquired shares of a class in the target which carry 10% of the voting rights of the class in exchange for securities, then the general bid must offer the same number[135] of securities to the target shareholders. Rule 11.2 does not displace the obligation to offer cash or a cash alternative under r.11.1,[136] so that the offerees may benefit from the operation of both rules. However, r.11.2 is less far-reaching than r.11.1 because it reaches back only to the three months before the bid. In addition, the idiosyncratic definition of "for cash" in r.11.1 will lump together both cash (in the normal sense of the term) acquisitions and many acquisitions in exchange for securities. Rule 11.2 appears to be triggered only when acquisitions in exchange for securities, considered separately, reach the 10% level.[137]

---

[134] See Note 5 to r.11.1.

[135] Which may not now have the same value as when offered prior to the offer: see Note 1 to r.11.2.

[136] Or under the mandatory bid rule, see below.

[137] But the Panel is to be consulted if shares at the 10% level are acquired in the 12 months prior to the offer period or during it for a mixture of cash and shares: Note 5 to r.11.2.

Mandatory offers

28–040 Rules 6 and 11, considered above, all determine, in one way or another, the level and type of consideration an acquirer must offer, should it decide to proceed with a bid. The strongest expression of the equality principle, however, is to be found in the mandatory bid rule. Here, a bidder is obliged to make an offer in a situation where it has obtained without a general offer what the Code regards as effective control of the company and might not therefore wish to make a general offer to the remaining shareholders of a company it already controls. However, because the sellers to the new controller were able to exit the company upon a change of control, the Code requires the remaining shareholders to be given the same opportunity.

Under r.9.1 a mandatory bid is required when:

(1) Any person acquires an interest in shares which (together with any interests held or acquired by any persons acting in concert) carry 30% or more of the voting rights of a company. This rule applies whether the shares taking the acquirer over the threshold were acquired in one go or in a series of transactions and, if the latter, no matter how long the period over which the transactions took place.

(2) Any person who, with persons acting in concert, already holds interests in shares carrying not less than 30% but not more than 50% of the voting rights and who, alone or with persons acting in concert, acquires an interest in additional shares.

In those cases, unless the Panel otherwise consents, such a person must extend offers to the holders of any class of equity share capital, whether voting or non-voting, and also to the holders of any other class of transferable securities carrying voting rights. Offers for the different classes of equity share capital must be comparable and the Panel should be consulted in advance on this.

The effect of this Rule is that, once acquirers have secured "control" (circumstance (1)) or acquisitions have been made to consolidate control[138] (circumstance (2)), a general offer must be made, thus giving all equity shareholders an opportunity of quitting the company and sharing in the price paid for the control or its consolidation. However, the force of the requirement lies not in the obligation to make an offer by itself, but in the supplementary rules which determine the level and nature of the offer which has to be made. After all, an obligation to make an offer which none of the offerees would find attractive

---

[138] In the case of consolidation, the holder will necessarily have been able to cross the 30% threshold without triggering the mandatory bid, notably where it falls into one of the exceptions discussed below. The Code used to allow consolidation of control at the rate of 1% a year without imposing a mandatory bid requirement. However, this facility was removed, seemingly in response to the decision in *Re Astec (BSR) Plc* [1998] 2 B.C.L.C. 556 Ch D (Companies Ct), in which the court took a narrow view of the application of the unfair prejudice remedy in relation to future actions of a shareholder which had obtained "creeping control" of a company under this facility. In this case the acquirer was non-resident in the UK, and so not subject to the Code when it initially acquired 45% of the target. Today, the company's initial purchase would be subject to the Code since the company was incorporated in the UK and its shares were traded on the Main Market of the LSE, and the fact that its headquarters were in Hong Kong would not put it outside the Code. See para.28–015.

would be a futile gesture on the part of the rule-maker. Crucial here are the requirements that a mandatory offer must be a cash offer, or with a cash alternative, and be pitched at the highest price paid by the offeror or a member of its concert party within the 12 months prior to the commencement of the offer.[139] As we have seen, in a voluntary offer this level of consideration is required only if shares carrying 10% or more of the voting rights of that class were acquired in the previous 12 months and the price requirement is relevant only if acquirer chooses to make a general offer. By contrast an acquirer cannot escape the requirement for a mandatory bid by waiting a year before acquiring the shares which carry it over the 30% threshold, though, as with a voluntary offeror, it may be able to influence by waiting the price it has to offer. In addition, a mandatory bid must not contain any conditions other than that it is dependent on acceptances being such as to result in the bidder holding 50% of the voting rights[140]; on a voluntary offer, there may well be further conditions.[141]

Furthermore, where directors of the target company (or their close relatives and family trusts) sell shares to a purchaser as a result of which the purchaser is required by r.9 to make a mandatory offer, the directors must ensure that, as a condition of the sale, the purchaser undertakes to fulfil its obligations under the rule and, except with the consent of the Panel, the directors must not resign from the board until the closing date of the offer or the date when it becomes wholly unconditional, whichever is the later. Further, whether the directors have been involved on the sell side of the acquisition or not, a nominee of the new controller may not be appointed to the board of the target company nor may it exercise the votes attached to any shares it holds in the target company until the formal offer document has been posted.[142] **28–041**

Sometimes, though rather rarely in the UK, given the structure of the shareholdings in publicly traded companies, acquiring control of company A may trigger a mandatory bid in relation to company B, its subsidiary or affiliate, because A already holds 30% or more block of shares in B or because the new controller of A together with A itself will hold such a control block. The Panel may require an offer to be made to the outside shareholders in B, but only if the new controller and those in concert hold 50% of the voting rights in A and either (1) A's holding in B is significant for A; or (2) securing control of B "might reasonably be considered to be a significant purpose" in the acquisition of A.[143]

The mandatory bid requirement of the Code is one of its outstanding features, even if, paradoxically, relatively few mandatory bids are made. Being aware of

---

[139] Code r.9.5. Unless the Panel agrees to an adjusted price in a particular case: see Note 3 to r.9.5 for the factors the Panel will take into account in considering whether to grant a dispensation from the highest price rule. For a strong example of the application of the "highest price" rule, even in the face of a serious market decline triggered by the terrorist bombings in New York, see Panel Statement 2001/15 (WPP Group Plc).

[140] Code r.9.3. The offeror thus takes on the risk that regulatory clearance is not obtained and the offeror has to dispose of the shares acquired. This increases the incentive for a bidder contemplating going over the 30% threshold to cease market or private acquisitions just below that level and make a general voluntary offer which may be made subject to conditions.

[141] For example, on a share for share offer that it is conditional on the passing of a resolution by members of the offeror to increase its issued capital.

[142] Code rr.9.6 and 9.7.

[143] Note 8 to r.9.1. This issue is much more important in jurisdictions with pyramid share structures.

the rule, acquirers normally sit just below the 30% threshold and then make a voluntary bid when they want to go further. This is because, as we have just seen, the acquirer has more flexibility with the formulation of a voluntary bid, so that it is normally desirable to avoid triggering a mandatory one. Even so, a bid made in these circumstances is not truly "voluntary": the acquirer might really have wanted to go to 40% and then rest satisfied that it had enough votes to control the company, but that option is not open to it. The effect of the mandatory bid rule is, usually, to require a person who wishes to obtain control of a company to do so by offering to acquire all or most of the equity share capital of the company. This discourages acquirers who aim to extract benefits from the company personally ("private benefits of control") rather than increase the value of the company for the benefit of all shareholders. Shareholders who understand the acquirer's strategy will accept the offer and, as they exit, the value of the strategy to the acquirer decreases since there will be fewer "'outside'" shareholders to be exploited. On the other hand, the mandatory bid rule discourages acquisitions by those who would increase the value of the company for the benefit of all shareholders but who are wealth constrained and so cannot raise the finance needed to bid for all the outstanding shares. Non-controlling shareholders might be better off if the latter sort of partial bid were allowed to proceed.

Exemptions and relaxations

28–042 Given the major financial consequences for a person who triggers a mandatory bid, one can expect acquirers of shares to take great pains to avoid its consequences, unless they do seek full control of the company. In some cases this may discourage activities which are valuable to the company. In this situation, a great deal of attention comes to be focused on the Panel's discretion to exempt acquirers, wholly or partly, from the mandatory bid obligation. The notes to r.9 indicate it is prepared to do so in certain circumstances, sometimes on its own decision and sometimes only if a majority of the shareholders of the potential target company agree. In these cases, the notes indicate what has to be done to avoid the mandatory bid rule, so that shareholders and companies which anticipate the difficulties likely to arise can navigate their way around it. For example, if a shareholder envisages that a particular financial operation, such as a share issue via a placing,[144] will take it over the 30% limit, it may escape the obligation to bid if it adopts in advance a firm arrangement to off-load the shares to non-connected parties within a very short period after their acquisition.[145] Otherwise, the company's capital raising abilities might be reduced. Again, a redemption or repurchase by a company of its shares may take a shareholder over the 30% mark without the shareholder having taken any action at all. This situation is given a rule of its own (r.37), in which the Panel states that it will normally[146] waive the bid obligation, provided the Panel is consulted in advance

[144] See para.25–013.

[145] Note 7 to r.9.1. Further Notes deal with a number of other cases where dispensation may be granted, for example, convertible securities, further acquisitions after a reduction of the holding below 30%; share lending arrangements.

[146] But not if the person seeking the waiver bought shares in the target company after the point at which it had reason to believe that a redemption or repurchase would take place: Note 2 to r.37.1.

and the independent shareholders of the target agree and the stringent "whitewash" procedure (set out in App.1 to the Code) is followed.

Finally, a Note on Dispensations from r.9, appended to the Rules, lists six situations where a mandatory bid is not normally required, either because the policy behind the rule has not in truth been infringed or because it is subordinated to other policies regarded as of greater value to the company and its shareholders than the equality policy. Into the first category fall (1) inadvertent mistakes, provided the holding is brought below the threshold within a limited period; and (2) situations where, in addition to the person who would otherwise be required to launch a mandatory bid, another single person holds 50% of the voting rights (so that the acquisition of the 30% or more does not in fact confer control on the acquirer).[147]

Into the second category fall situations where the 30% threshold is breached as a result of (3) a rescue operation of a company in a serious financial position, even if the independent shareholders of the target have not approved the acquisitions, since insolvency is a more serious threat to shareholder wellbeing than a new controller; (4) where a lender enforces its rights and acquires shares given as security, provided the excess is disposed of to unconnected persons within a limited period (for otherwise the utility of shares as collateral would be undermined); (5) where a holding of more than 30% of the voting rights results from an enfranchisement of previously non-voting shares, unless the shares were acquired when enfranchisement was in prospect (showing that enfranchisement is to be encouraged); and (6) where a company issues new shares either for cash or in exchange for an acquisition, provided a majority of the independent shareholders agree to removal of the bid obligation, through what is known as the "whitewash" procedure.[148] This last covers a variety of situations, including that where an offeror company makes a share exchange offer as a result of which a large shareholder in the target, who is perhaps already a significant shareholder in the offeror, ends up with more than 30% of the combined entity.[149] Thus, the mandatory bid rule, although strictly formulated in r.9, is applied with some flexibility by the Panel.

Acting in concert

Although the definition of "acting in concert" is relevant to the percentage tests used in all the rules which implement the equality principle, the significant consequences attached to the mandatory bid rule focus particular attention on the concept in this context. Indeed, in its introduction to the notes on r.9.1 the Code states that "the majority of questions which arise in the context of r.9 relate to **28–043**

[147] Dispensation Notes 4 and 5. Note 5 also waives the bid where the holders of 50% of the voting rights indicate they would not accept the bid, no matter by how many people those rights are held.

[148] Dispensation Notes 3, 2, 6 and 1 respectively. In the case of (4) the security must not have been taken at a time when the lender had reason to believe that enforcement was likely, and of (5) the shares must not have been purchased at a time when the purchaser had reason to believe that enfranchisement was likely. The "whitewash" procedure is set out in App.1 of the Code, which involves tight Panel control over the procedure. It is often used for placings by AIM companies.

[149] In the case of entities of equal size, this could occur if a person held 15% of the voting rights of both offeror and target companies.

persons acting in concert", and the notes then provide five pages of guidance on the concept in the context of r.9, in addition to what is said in the "Definitions" section of the Code about the concept in general. When a group of persons act in concert to acquire control of a company, r.9.2 and the note thereto impose the obligation to make a general offer on the person whose acquisition takes the group's holding over the relevant threshold, but also extend the obligation to each of the "principal members" of the group. It appears that the offer need not be made to the other members of the concert party, but only to the outside shareholders.

The "Definitions" section lays down the following general principle:

> "Persons acting in concert comprise persons who, pursuant to an agreement or understanding (whether formal or informal) co-operate to obtain or consolidate control of a company or to frustrate the successful outcome of an offer for a company."

The "Definitions" section then goes on to provide that as many as nine categories of persons are presumed to be acting in concert unless the contrary is proved.[150] These multiple specifications of suspect relationships are a reflection the difficulties of making the Code work effectively given the wide variety of human interactions.

However, as with the core mandatory bid rule itself, so with the definition of a concert party, there are cases where a broad definition may seem to conflict with other valuable policies. A troublesome question has been the relationship between shareholder engagement, which the Government encourages,[151] and acting in concert and the mandatory bid obligation. Shareholders are likely to be deterred from coming together to influence the board if they fear that they will be required by the Code to make a general offer for the company's shares. In principle r.9 does apply to shareholders who obtain control of a company by pooling their existing shares. However, there is one limitation on the pooling rule. Note 1 makes it clear that shareholders are not caught by the mandatory bid obligation at the moment they come together in order to obtain control of a company, even if at that point their prior and independently acquired shareholdings together exceed the 30% threshold. What will trigger the mandatory bid is their subsequent acquisition of further interests in shares. However, even this may not be enough to facilitate engagement, for the rule implies that the price of cooperation to exercise governance rights is the inability to acquire further shares in the company. Since successful engagement will increase the share price, an important method for the activists to gain some reward for their engagement is to invest in

[150] The presumed categories of acting in concert are: (1) a company with any others in the group and associated companies (widely defined, so as to make a company an associated company if another company controls 20% of its equity share capital); (2) a company with any of its directors and their close relatives and related trusts; (3) a company with any of its pension funds or the pension funds of other group or associated companies; (4) a fund manager with any of its discretionary managed clients; (5) a person, that person's close relatives and related trust funds, all with each other; (6) a close relative a founder of the company and related trusts; (7) a connected adviser with its client; (8) the directors of the target company; (9) shareholders in a private company who become, in specified circumstances, become shareholders in a company to which the Code applies.

[151] See paras 12–013 onwards. It may be less happy about intervention by activist hedge funds than it is about engagement by traditional institutional investors.

the company in advance of their intervention but after they have decided to intervene. If they are prohibited from making such acquisitions, a greater part of the benefits of intervention will simply go to the non-intervening shareholders who free ride on the interveners' actions.

The relationship between shareholder engagement and the mandatory bid rule has received explicit attention from the Code Committee[152] and the results of its deliberations are now reflected in Note 2 to r.9.1 and in Practice Statement 26. The Panel was clearly under some pressure not to place obstacles in the way of an important government policy. The Panel through the Note and Practice Statement makes the crucial clarification that Rule 9 applies only to "board control seeking" resolutions. This does not mean that all resolutions to alter the composition of the board are control-seeking. Where there is "no significant relationship" between the requisitionists and the proposed appointees or, if there is, only a single director is proposed for replacement, even if that person is chief executive, r.9 will not normally be triggered. Where it is triggered by inadvertent acquisitions by one of the concert parties, the Panel might require disposal of the interest rather than a mandatory bid. Overall, the Panel's view is that board control seeking resolutions are "rare" and it states that it has never imposed a mandatory bid in this context.[153] Nevertheless, it is clear that a group of shareholders cannot put their nominees on the board with the goal of determining the company's strategy on a continuing basis without be at risk of have to make an offer for the outstanding shares at some point in this process.

Interests in shares

A second notable feature of the percentage tests to be found in the equality rules of the Code is that they apply, not just to the acquisition of shares, but to the acquisition of "interests in shares". A definition of "interests in shares" was introduced as part of a major reform of the Code in 2005. The "Definitions" section of the Code sets out a list of situations which will be regarded as involving the acquisition of an interest in a share. Some of them are quite obvious, such as the acquisition of the right to control the exercise of voting rights attached to shares, without actually owning them, as where a shareholder agrees, as is permissible, to vote in the way the other party to a contract directs.[154] However, the main impetus for the 2005 changes was to deal with the issue of derivatives, and, in particular, with the form of derivative known as a "contract for differences" (CfD), the only form of derivative which will be discussed here. The essence of the CfD is that it is a contract which, on its face, gives a party only an economic interest in the movement of the market price of the security over a period of time and not an entitlement to exercise any of the rights attached to the share. On this basis, a CfD is irrelevant to control of a company. In practice, however, a party to a CfD is often able to control the exercise of voting rights attached to the shares in question and sometimes even to acquire them at the end 28–044

[152] *Shareholder Activism and Acting in Concert* (2002), Consultation Paper 10, issued by the Code Committee of the Panel.

[153] Practice Statement 26, para 1.6-7.

[154] *Puddephat v Leith* [1916] 1 Ch. 200 Ch D.

of the contract. In brief, a party to a "long" CfD contracts to receive from the counterparty any upward difference between the market prices of the security at two points in time (usually the market price at the date of the contract and some later date). The counterparty, usually an investment bank or securities house, will normally hedge its position, but is not obliged to do so, by acquiring a corresponding number of underlying securities at around the "start" price of the CfD. It is this action on the part of the counterparty, usually found but not legally required, that generates issues for the Code. The counterparty holds the shares only for hedging, and will normally be prepared to exercise its voting rights as the other party to the CfD requires (if only to obtain repeat CfD business) and at the end of the contract may well be happy to close out its position by transferring the shares to the other party, if requested.[155]

Thus, a person seeking to exercise control over a company, but being aware of the restrictions in the Code, might have sought to circumvent its restrictions by exercising control rights via CfDs. The changes made prevent that step. The definition of "interests in securities" now provides, generally, that "a person who has long economic exposure, whether absolute or conditional, to changes in the price of securities will be treated as interested in those securities", and, in particular, that a person will be regarded as having an interest in securities if "he is party to any derivative: (1) whose value is determined by reference to their price; and (2) which results, or may result, in his having a long position in them". It should be noted that the Panel's rules contain no "safe harbour" for a person who does have a purely economic interests in shares arising out of CfDs, for example, where the counterparty has not bought the shares in question as a hedge. A person might trigger the mandatory bid rule purely on the basis of economic interests, and would be reliant on the consent of the Panel to escape the consequences of that rule.

Conclusion

28–045 The mandatory bid rule is a very strong expression of the Code's principle that all shareholders in the target company must be treated equally upon a change of control. Without it, those to whom the offeror makes approaches when building the controlling block might be under pressure to sell for fear that no comparable later general offer will be forthcoming. From a corporate governance point of view the mandatory bid rule might be seen as a form of minority shareholder protection. The prospects of minority equity shareholders in a company depend crucially upon how the controllers of the company exercise their powers and the provisions of company law proper, even after the enactment of the new "unfair prejudice" provisions of the CA 2006 (discussed in Ch.14), could be seen as incapable of providing comprehensive protection of minority shareholders against unfair treatment by the new controller. Nevertheless, provision of an

[155] Panel Consultation Papers 2005/1–3, *Dealings in Derivatives and Options*, set out the nature of the problem (see in particular PCP 2005/1, s.A) and the Panel's proposals for reform of the Code. Why should anyone enter into such a contract? Originally, the purpose of the CfD was to allow a person to speculate in relation to the price of the underlying shares without having to spend the money to acquire them. The fee paid to the investment bank under the contract is a form of recompense to the bank for making the acquisition instead of the derivative holder (a sort of interest payment).

opportunity to leave the company and on favourable terms is something of a novelty, for UK company law rarely provides "appraisal" rights to shareholders.[156]

It should be noted that there are two aspects of the policy underlying r.9. The first is the opportunity for all shareholders to exit the company upon a change of control by selling their shares to the new controller, and the second is the opportunity to do so on the most favourable terms that have been obtained by those who sold to the new controller. Of these two aspects it is the second which is the more controversial. In particular, the latter aspect of the Rule makes it impossible for the holder of an existing controlling block of shares to obtain any premium for control upon the sale of the shares. Since the purchaser of the block will know that the Code requires it to offer the same price to all shareholders, the purchaser is forced to divide the consideration for the company's securities rateably among all the shareholders. In the UK, where shareholdings in listed companies are widely dispersed, this is probably not an important issue, but in countries where family shareholdings in even listed companies are of significant size, the Rule might operate as a disincentive to transfers of control.

To whom must an offer be made?

A final form of equality is as between voting and non-voting shares in both voluntary and mandatory bids. Where the target company has more than one class of equity share capital, r.14 requires a "comparable" offer[157] to be made for each class, including non-voting classes, if the acquirer decides to offer for at least one of the classes. Thus, an offeror company may not bid only for equity shares carrying voting rights but must bid for all classes of equity share. This reflects the policy that a change of control in a company is a significant event for all equity shareholders (whose returns depend on the policies and success of the controllers) and so all such shareholders should be given the opportunity to exit the company on fair terms when a change of control is in prospect. The rule is a protection of non-voting shareholders; though it probably does little to reduce the incentives for company controllers to create non-voting or weighted-voting share structures, since their aim is to forestall bids. **28–046**

Separate offers must be made for each class of equity share. The offer for the non-voting equity must not be made conditional upon any particular level of acceptances by that class, unless the offer for the voting shares is also conditional upon the offer for the non-voting shares reaching its acceptance condition. Thus, the non-voting equity shareholders may not be left locked into the target if the

[156] For one of these rare cases see paras 29–017 onwards. Of course, 30% is only a rough approximation of the point at which a change of de facto control of a company occurs. In the early versions of the Code the figure was set at 40%, but it was reduced to 30% in 1974. However, a precise percentage makes the Rule easier to operate than would a case-by-case examination of whether a particular shareholder had acquired sufficient shares in a particular company to enable it to control that company.

[157] Notes to r.14 make it clear that comparable is not the same as identical and that normally the difference between the offers should reflect the differences in market prices over the previous six months. "Equity share capital" seems to be as defined in CA 2006 s.548. See para.6–007.

offeror company obtains control through acceptance from the voting shareholders. However, the offeror can protect itself against ending up with a majority of the non-voting equity but too little of the voting equity by inserting identical conditions, relating to the voting equity, into both offers.

In a voluntary bid, classes of non-equity shares need not be the subject of an offer, even if they carry voting rights.[158] In a mandatory bid the offer must encompass all securities with voting rights, presumably because they count towards the 30% threshold.[159] Of course, a voluntary offeror company may wish to make an offer for non-equity shares carrying voting rights, but an offer is not required, presumably on the theory that the non-equity shareholders are normally protected by their contractual entitlements.[160] Finally, r.15 requires that, on an offer for voting equity share capital, an appropriate offer or proposal must be made to holders of securities convertible into equity shares (who clearly are potentially affected by the change of control).

Wait and see

28–047 It is possible to create pressure on shareholders to accept an offer, even though the same offer is made to all the shareholders. From the point of view of an offeror, there are only two possible outcomes: the offer is accepted by the majority (as defined by the bidder) of the shareholders or it is not. From the point of view of an individual shareholder, considering whether to accept an offer and unable to predict the actions of fellow shareholders, there are three possible outcomes. First, the bid may not be accepted by the relevant majority, in which case it does not matter how the individual votes. Secondly, it may be accepted by the majority and the individual is among the accepting majority. Thirdly, the bid is accepted by the majority and the individual is among the non-accepting minority. Where the bid is not particularly attractive in the eyes of the individual but that shareholder has misgivings about how the bidder will run the company if it obtains control, the individual's preferences may be ranked in the same order as the outcomes just listed. But since that shareholder has only one decision (accept/not accept) he or she cannot rank those preferences fully. In order to avoid the worst outcome (three), he or she may vote for the second outcome, even though the first outcome is the preferred one. If many shareholders considering the offer have the same set of preferences and reason in the same way, the offer may be accepted, even though their first choice is rejection.

There is in fact a simple procedural solution to this problem, which the Code adopts. Rule 31.2(b) requires the bidder to keep the offer open for at least a further 14 days after it has become unconditional (including therefore achieving the level of acceptances the bidder requires). During that period those who had previously not accepted the bid can change their minds. Since the offeree shareholders now have two decisions, they can rank the three preferences fully. Initially, a shareholder who favours the bid will accept it in the usual way; a

---

[158] The implication from Note 3 to r.14.1 is that equity share capital is defined in the same was as in the CA 2006 s.548, but that shares with very limited equity rights are excluded.

[159] Rule 9.1.

[160] See para.6–007.

shareholder who opposes it will not. If and when it becomes clear the majority are in favour of the bid, a non-accepting shareholder who does not want to be locked in under the new controller will now accept the offer. However, the extension rule does not apply in the rare case where the offer is not subject to an acceptance decision, for example, where the offeror already holds 50% or more of the voting rights in the target. Nevertheless, this qualification may generate pressure to accept the offer: a minority shareholder may take a different view of the desirability of remaining invested if the controller, instead of holding only 50% of the shares pre-bid, may move post-bid to, for example, 85%, and so can pass special resolutions without hindrance.

THE PROCEDURE FOR MAKING A BID

In a work of this kind there is no need to deal in detail with the procedure for making a bid. However, we examine it briefly for the light it throws on four further policies relating to the regulation of take-over offers. These are: 28–048

(1) the provision of information to shareholders and time to consider it so that they can take the decision allocated to them by the Code (and to a limited extent the provision of information to non-shareholders);
(2) protecting the company from being "in play" for extended periods of time through threatened or actual takeover offers;
(3) facilitating the move to 100% ownership where the overwhelming majority of the shareholders have accepted the offer (whether at the initiative of the bidder or non-accepting shareholders); and
(4) protecting the public market in the shares of both bidder and target from distortion. It is to be noted that, unlike in some jurisdictions, the shares of neither company are removed from trading during the bid.

We divide the bid process into four periods: before any public announcement of an offer is made; the announcement of a firm intention to make an offer; the period during which the offer is open for acceptance; after the bid is declared unconditional.

Before any public announcement of a bid

There are two linked issues in this period. First, there may develop a "'cat and mouse"' game in which the bidder seeks to acquire as many shares in the target company as it can without its intentions leaking into the market, whilst a potential target, if it suspects a bid may be in the offing, seeks to establish who is acquiring beneficial interests in its shares. Secondly, there is the risk of distortion of the public market through insider dealing in the shares of both bidder and target. 28–049

A potential acquirer, although not yet committed to making a bid, will want to increase the chances of the bid ultimately succeeding by building up as large a stake in the company as possible before making any public announcement about its intentions. Pre-announcement acquisitions are valuable to the potential bidder, not only for this reasons and their relatively low ("undisturbed") price, but also because, if the bidder is defeated in the event by a "white knight" competitor, the defeated bidder can assent these shares into the competitor's bid and make a profit, which may help to off-set some of the costs of its failed bid.[161] As we have seen, the mandatory bid rule puts a cap of 30% on this strategy, but, in fact, long before that stage is reached, the potential bidder's stake in the company will have become public knowledge in the market and the share price will have responded appropriately. Beneficial holdings at the 3% level and above are required to be disclosed under the vote-holding disclosure rules discussed in Ch.27,[162] so that the bidder cannot avoid this disclosure requirement by using nominees or acquiring interests in shares. In effect, a cap of 3% is set on the shares an acquirer can obtain as a launch-pad for the bid or as protection against a competitor. To be sure, future acquirers often do build up stakes in the later target above the 3% level but below 30%, but what is happening has to be disclosed to the market and the future target company.

An alternative approach, which avoids the disclosure requirement[163] but is more risky (because knowledge of the bidder's activities is more likely to seep out into the market), is to contact significant shareholders seeking from them an "irrevocable commitment" to accept the offer, if one is made. In practice, sophisticated shareholders will make such a commitment only subject to qualifications which release the promisor if a rival bid emerges at a higher price. But unsophisticated shareholders may not take this step and may even give the commitment without fully understanding the offer. In consequence, r.4.3 provides that any person proposing to contact a private individual or small corporate shareholder with a view to seeking an irrevocable commitment must consult the Panel in advance. In addition, a Note states that the Panel will need to be satisfied that the proposed arrangements for the contacts will provide adequate information as to the nature of the commitment sought and a realistic opportunity to consider whether or not it should be given and with time to take independent advice.

At the same time as the potential acquirer is buying shares in the market, the board of a potential target company, if aware that it is a potential target, will want to keep a close eye on its share register, both in order to see if a potential bidder is building up a stake in the company and to see if shareholders are appearing who are likely to be susceptible to an offer, if one is made (for example, certain types of hedge fund). Surprisingly, perhaps, Pt 22 of the CA 2006 provides a mechanism by which the target board can investigate the composition of its

[161] On the disincentives of potential bidders to bid because of the wasted costs point, see para.28–032. By contrast, the shares the bidder "acquires" through acceptance of its offer cannot be used in this way, because, if the competitor wins, the initial offer will lapse and so the shareholders who accepted it, rather than the initial bidder, will be able to take the competing bid. Nor may the bidder, after its offer has lapsed, buy more shares in the market at above lapsed offer price (and so cannot acquire more shares at this point to assent to the competitor's offer): r.35.4.

[162] See paras 27–011 onwards.

[163] The Code makes it clear that irrevocable commitments do not count as an interest in securities for its purposes (Definitions, Interests in Securities, Note 9(b)). They would appear to escape the DTR 5 rules on disclosure on the basis that an irrevocable commitment is not a financial instrument. The formal offer document, however, must disclose at that point the irrevocable offers secured: r.24.3(d)(x).

shareholder body. The mechanism was introduced in the CA 1976, apparently to increase the efficiency of the then rather ineffective rules on the mandatory disclosure of beneficial interests in shares, rather than as a warning mechanism for target management.

Company-triggered disclosures

Part 22 of the CA 2006 enables the directors of a public company to serve a notice upon any person suspected of being interested in its voting shares seeking information about that interest and permitting the company to apply to the court for restrictions on rights to vote or transfer the shares if that information is not forthcoming. This is an important power since the name on the share register is often a nominee and not the beneficial owner of the share.[164] So the appearance of a new name on the register does not necessarily reveal much useful information. The statutory provisions are often supplemented by provisions in the company's articles which expand the board's powers, for example, by permitting the directors to impose the restrictions without application to the court and to impose them in a wider range of situations.[165] **28–050**

Section 793 provides that a public company (whether its shares are traded on a public market or not) may serve notice on a person whom it knows to be, or has reasonable cause to believe to be, or to have been at any time during the three years immediately preceding the date of the notice, interested in voting shares of the company, requiring that person to reveal information about the nature of the interest. This includes information about concert party arrangements and about the identity of any transferee of the shares. The notice must require a response to be given in writing within such reasonable time as may be specified in the notice.[166]

The initial notice will normally be sent to the person named on the shareholder register and, if that person is the sole beneficial owner of the shares, this will normally be revealed (at any rate once the likely consequences of refusing to respond have been explained). But in other cases the notice may merely be the beginning of a long and often abortive series of enquiries. If the recipient of the notice is a nominee it may well decline to say more than that, claiming that a duty of confidentiality forbids disclosure or, if the nominee is, say, a foreign bank, that the foreign law makes it unlawful to disclose the name of the person on whose behalf the nominee holds the shares. In principle, this is a breach of the duty under s.793 (since the nominee is bound to give details of the "other interests" known to it, i.e. that of the person upon whose behalf the nominee holds the

---

164 As we have seen in para.27–011.

165 Where the directors impose the restrictions, their freedom of action is limited by the "proper purpose" doctrine applying generally to the exercise by directors of their powers under the articles (see para.10–018). In particular, the purpose of the power to impose restrictions is to further the objective underlying the statutory provisions (revelation of beneficial interests in shares). Failure to disclose does not give the directors a general power to impose restrictions, for example, for the purpose of defeating a resolution to remove the directors: *Eclairs Group Ltd v JKX Oil & Gas Plc* [2015] UKSC 71.

166 If the time allowed is unreasonably short, the notice will be invalid: *Re Lonrho Plc (No.2)* [1989] B.C.L.C. 309 Ch D (Companies Ct).

shares). Alternatively, the nominee may disclose the nominator's identity, but the latter, if resident abroad, may refuse to provide any further information. Ultimately, as a result of the possibility of the freezing and disenfranchisement of the shares (see below), the true ownership may be disclosed—but not always.[167] The information disclosed as a result of the notice (or a succession of notices) must be entered on a public register, with the information being entered against the name of the present holder of the shares.[168] The rules applying to this register, including court control of public access for a non-proper purpose, are the same as those applying to the company's register of members, and most companies will use the share register for this purpose as well.[169]

28–051 This mechanism may also be triggered by the shareholders (perhaps because they suspect directors may have failed to notify their dealings under the rules discussed in Ch.27). However, there is a high threshold for shareholder initiation. The holders of not less than one-tenth of the paid-up voting capital may require the company exercise its powers under s.793, specifying the manner in which those powers are to be exercised[170] and giving reasonable grounds for requiring the powers to be exercised in the manner specified.[171] It is then the company's duty to comply.[172] If it does not, every officer of the company who is in default is liable to a fine.[173] On the conclusion of a shareholder-initiated investigation, the company has to prepare a report of the information received, which report is publicly available.[174]

28–052 There are criminal sanctions for a person who fails to comply with a s.793 notice or who makes false or misleading statements in response. Those sanctions include imprisonment, unless the defendant shows the requirement was frivolous or vexatious.[175] What, however, makes the foregoing sections more effective than they would otherwise be is that, if a person fails to give any information required by the notice, the company may apply to the court for an order directing that the shares in question be subject to restrictions.[176] However, it should be noted that the information a company may require under the notice is, perhaps not surprisingly, limited by what the person actually knows.[177] The restrictions are that:

(1) any transfer of the shares is void;

[167] In some cases the information sought has never been obtained and the shares have remained frozen.

[168] CA 2006 s.808. Assuming there is a present holder and assuming the holder's identity is known. If not, the information must be entered against the name of the holder of the interest.

[169] CA 2006 ss.808–819. For discussion of the share register, see paras 2–038 onwards.

[170] In particular, of course, in respect of which persons they require notices to be served.

[171] CA 2006 s.803.

[172] CA 2006 s.804.

[173] CA 2006 s.804(2).

[174] CA 2006 s.805.

[175] CA 2006 s.795, but see the exemption possibility in s.796.

[176] CA 2006 s.794. Or the company may impose restrictions itself if it has appropriate articles: see fn.165.

[177] Though the articles may entitle the board to impose restrictions in a wider range of circumstances, including where the person asked does not have the information.

(2) no voting rights are exercisable in respect of them;
(3) no further shares may be issued in right of them or in pursuance of an offer made to their holder; and
(4) except in a liquidation, no payment by the company, whether as a return of capital or a dividend, may be made in respect of them.[178]

Thus, although the company may never track down the ultimate beneficial owner of the shares, it can take them out of consideration with regard to a takeover bid through the restrictions imposed by the court or under the articles. Nevertheless, the restrictions constitute a draconian penalty,[179] which may be detrimental to wholly innocent parties, for example bona fide purchasers, or lenders on the security, of the shares. Although the court has a discretion whether to make the order imposing the restrictions, an order should normally be made if the requested information has not been obtained, since "the clear purpose [of Pt 22 of the Act] is to give public companies, and ultimately the public at large, a prima facie unqualified right to know who are the real owners of its voting shares".[180] If an order is made, it has to impose all four restrictions without any qualifications designed to protect innocent parties.[181] However, an application can be made to the court by the company or any aggrieved person for the restrictions to be relaxed on the grounds that they "unfairly affect" the rights of third parties, and the court is given a broad power to do so.[182] The court also has the power to remove the restrictions altogether,[183] but this normally will be done only if the court is "satisfied that the relevant facts about the shares have been disclosed to the company and no unfair advantage has accrued to any person as a result of the earlier failure to make that disclosure".[184] Transfer of the shares offers a possible way out of the potential impasse. If the shares are to be transferred for valuable consideration and the court approves the transfer, an order can be made that the shares should cease to be subject to some or all of the restrictions.[185] Further, the court, on application by the company, may order the shares to be sold,[186] subject to the court's approval as to the terms of the sale and with the proceeds paid into court, and it might (though need not) also direct that the shares should cease to be subject to the restrictions.[187]

As is usual in the disclosure area, what has to be disclosed is not just ownership of shares but "interests in shares". However, the legislation does not use the **28–053**

---

178 CA 2006 s.797(1).

179 Made the more so since any attempt to evade the restrictions may lead to a heavy fine: s.798.

180 *Re FH Lloyd Holdings Plc* [1985] B.C.L.C. 293 at 300; *Re Greers Gross Plc* [1987] 1 W.L.R. 1649 CA.

181 *Re Lonrho Plc (No.2)* [1990] Ch. 695 Ch D (Companies Ct).

182 CA 2006 s.799.

183 CA 2006 s.800: on the application by the company or any person aggrieved.

184 CA 2006 s.800(3)(a).

185 CA 2006 s.800(3)(b)(4).

186 CA 2006 s.801. The only transaction that can be *ordered* is a sale. The word is used in conscious contradistinction to "transferred for valuable consideration" in s.800(3), which would include a share exchange takeover offer: cf. *Re Westminster Group Plc* [1985] 1 W.L.R. 676 CA.

187 CA 2006 s.801(1). The persons who are beneficially interested in the shares may apply to the court for the payment out of their proportionate entitlement: s.802. If they wish to continue with non-disclosure, they will have to forego the proceeds, at least for the time being.

Code's definition of "interests in shares" but has its own, set out in ss.820–823. It is widely formulated so as to include an interest in shares "of any kind whatsoever", but it is not so wide as to include interests in shares of a purely economic character, such as CfDs.[188] Part 22 also contains a "concert party" provision, again not that of the Code, but set out in ss.824 and 825, under which the interests of one concert party can be attributed to all members. The agreement or arrangement must relate to the acquisition of interests in shares and indeed it is not caught by the section until an interest in securities is in fact acquired by one of the parties in pursuance of it.[189] Thus, the section does not apply to a simple voting agreement between existing shareholders. Further, the agreement or arrangement must include provisions imposing restrictions on dealings in the interests so acquired[190]: an agreement to acquire shares which the acquirer is then free immediately to dispose of is not caught by the section. The agreement or arrangement need not be an enforceable contract, but the section does not apply to one which is not legally binding "unless it involves mutuality in the undertakings, expectations or understandings of the parties to it".[191] Each member of the concert party is taken for the purposes of the disclosure notice to be interested in all shares in which any member of the concert party has an interest, whether or not those interests were acquired in pursuance of the agreement.[192] Any notification which a person makes must state whether that person is a party to a concert party agreement, must include the names and (so far as known) the addresses of the other parties and must state whether or not any of the shares to which the notification relates are shares in which the person is interested by virtue of the concert party provision and, if so, how many of them.[193]

Insider trading

28–054 The period before a public announcement of a takeover bid is notorious for abnormal movements in the price of the bidder's and target's shares, suggesting that insider traders have been at work. This activity is controlled, in so far as it is, by the regulations discussed in Ch.30. That regulation exempts trading on behalf of the acquirer on the basis of its knowledge that it will or may make a public offer, but persons other than the acquirer are bound by the normal rules.[194] Since

[188] CA 2006 s.820(1). For a discussion of CfDs, see para.28–044.

[189] CA 2006 s.824(2)(b).

[190] CA 2006 s.824(2)(a).

[191] CA 2006 s.824(5)(6). Of course, the presence of mutuality will normally make the agreement legally binding, but the subsection forestalls avoidance via the doctrine of intention to create legal relations, which the parties might use to declare an agreement not binding at law. The subsection also excludes an underwriting or sub-underwriting agreement provided that that "is confined to that purpose and any matters incidental to it".

[192] CA 2006 s.825(1)–(3).

[193] CA 2006 s.825(4).

[194] See para.30–028. Even those acting on behalf of the bidder may find themselves caught by the insider trading prohibition, if as a result of being granted access to the target's books, they obtain, as is likely, price-sensitive but non-public information. This is because the exemption in Sch.1 to the CJA 1993 is confined to "market information" which is information about the acquisition or disposal of securities. Thus, to take an extreme example, if the bidder's due diligence reveals the company has

the preparation of a bid for a publicly traded company requires an army of financial and legal advisers, a rather large circle of people may come to learn about the potential bid.

As far as the Code is concerned, it follows a twin-track approach: it requires secrecy before a public announcement about the bid and, if that is not forthcoming, it accelerates the public announcement. On the first, the Code insists on the "vital importance of absolute secrecy before an announcement of a bid" (r.2.1). How much this adds to the rules discussed in Ch.30 is unclear. As to the probably more effective public announcement, the bidder is required to make one where the target is subject to "rumour and speculation" or there is "untoward movement" in the target's share price and, in either case, these developments were likely to have resulted from the acquirer's activities.[195] This obligation on the potential bidder arises even if it has not yet approached the board of the target, which the Code normally requires before a public announcement is made. As to the nature of the announcement, it may well be that the potential acquirer is not yet in a position to commit itself to making an offer. If it is, it must say so; otherwise, it announces a possible offer. This may do no more that identify the possible target and state that there is no certainty an offer will in fact be forthcoming. It is likely to say little about any conditions to which the "firm intention" announcement is subject, because the Panel is likely to hold the bidder to its statements.[196] If the acquirer has been able to notify the target board of its interest before an announcement was required, then the obligation to make an announcement in the circumstances mentioned falls on the board of the target.[197] Finally, as a prophylactic, a public announcement is required where the bidder is about to take its discussions about a possible bid beyond "a very restricted number of people" (outside the bidder and target and their immediate advisers).[198]

The firm intention to offer

Rule 1(a) of the Code prohibits an offeror from simply putting its offer directly to the shareholders of the target: it must "notify a firm intention to make an offer in the first instance to the board of the offeree company or its advisers". This is to enable the board of the target to form a view on the merits of the offer and to advise the shareholders accordingly. As we have seen above, the Code requires the board to give such advice to the shareholders and, indeed, to obtain independent advice on the bid and make it known to the shareholders. Rule 1 facilitates this process: without it, the board of the target might be left scrambling **28–055**

just made a potentially very lucrative discovery, the fact that the bidder is now prepared to pay more for the target's shares is market information, but the fact of the discovery would appear not to be.

195 Code rr.2.2(d) and 2.3. Note that the rule does not require the announcement of possible offers, if secrecy is maintained, although some shareholders think it should be.

196 Code r.2.5.

197 Code r.2.2(c) and 2.3(c).

198 Code r.2.2(e).

around trying to fulfil its duties under r.3.To complete the picture, the board of the target must publicly announce at this point the existence of the firm intention on the acquirer's part.[199]

However, as we have just seen, the first public announcement about an offer is not likely to be of a firm intention to make an offer but of a possible offer. The maker of a possible offer statement is not committed to moving to a firm offer. Indeed, the purpose of the possible offer statement may be to "put the company in play" so that the potential bidder can assess the level of support from investors for a formal offer. In effect, this strategy extends the period the company subject to a potential takeover because the obligation to send out the formal offer documents to target shareholders is set only once a firm intention to bid has been announced. Before that point the potential bidder keeps its options open, whilst, no doubt, disparaging the incumbent management of the target to its heart's content—although it does run the risk of making it more likely a competing bidder will emerge.

However, the possible offer announcement does have legitimate functions. First, the offeror may wish to obtain the target board's recommendation of the offer and so wishes to indicate that there is some flexibility in the terms of its offer and that it is prepared to negotiate with the board for its support. Secondly, the offeror may genuinely be in doubt about the value of the target and may wish to secure access to the target's books in order to be able to formulate a precise offer to be put to the shareholders. Especially in the case of highly leveraged bids, it is crucial for the offeror not to find any unpleasant surprises after it has obtained control which would jeopardise its ability to pay the interest on or repay the often very large loans it has taken out to finance the bid. Offers by private equity bidders are often of this character.

Nevertheless, opportunistic use of the possible bid strategy caused the Panel some concern in its 2010 review, on the grounds that it created a "virtual bid" period of uncertain duration, to the detriment of the target. Where a possible offer approach has been made, senior management of the potential target will concentrate on little else until the acquirer walks away or a firm offer is made and is either accepted or rejected. The Panel's response was to strengthen the Code rules which are aptly, if inelegantly, referred to as its "put up or shut up" provisions.

Put up or shut up

28–056 As between potential bidder and target, the impact of the possible offer announcement is asymmetric. For the bidder, the time limit for posting the offer documents to the target shareholders is not triggered until it announces a firm intention to offer. On the other hand, the possible offer announcement triggers the Code's definition of the "offer period", at which point the ban on defensive action by the target board without shareholder approval comes into force.[200] So, the target board is stymied, but the acquirer used to be under no obligation to push on

[199] Code r.2.2(a).

[200] The "Definitions" section of the Code makes it clear that the offer period is triggered by an announcement of a possible offer.

with its offer—subject to the market risk of a competing offer. To meet this concern, the Code for some time had contained a "put up or shut up" (PUSU) provision, enabling the potential target to request the Panel to set a time limit within which the bidder had either to make an announcement of a firm intention to make an offer or to state that it did not intend to make a bid, and in the latter case the bidder (and a person acting in concert) would not normally be able to bid until six months had passed. Such applications to the Panel by potential targets were not infrequent, but in its 2010 review the Code Committee concluded that boards were often reluctant to make such applications, presumably for fear of shareholder ire, even though the company's management was "destabilised" by the possible offer announcement. Consequently, it recommended shifting the burden of action under the PUSU rule.[201] Except with the consent of the Panel, an offeror must now make a further announcement one way or the other within four weeks of the possible bid announcement.[202] However, the Panel will normally extend the deadline for the further announcement if the target board requests this. This amendment clearly promotes the policy underlying GP 6 that "an offeree company must not be hindered in the conduct of its affairs for longer than is reasonable by a bid for its securities".

Faced with the PUSU requirement, a potential bidder might move on to make an announcement of a firm intention to make an offer, but hedge that offer about with conditions, so that it can react appropriately to any negative information about the target which emerges before the formal offer documentation is sent out (which has to happen within 28 days of the firm intention announcement). Where a bidder seeks to make an actual offer subject to conditions, its freedom to do so is severely constrained by the provisions of r.13, but originally that rule did not apply to announcements of a firm intention to make an offer, where, in consequence, the bidder had a freer hand. However, in 2004 the Panel decided to apply the provisions of r.13 (discussed below) to "firm intention" statements as well.[203] This Rule promotes certainty, for both the shareholders and the board of the target company. Thus, the PUSU rule forces the potential bidder to clarify its intentions since a heavily conditional firm intention statement will not meet the Code's requirements. **28–057**

Once a "firm intention" announcement is made, whether because of the operation of the PUSU rule or not, the offeror becomes obliged in the normal case to proceed with its bid and to post the formal offer document to the shareholders within 28 days of the announcement.[204] As important, a firm intention announcement requires the central elements of the offer to be revealed.[205] In consequence, there is also a required delay before the formal offer document may be sent out—not earlier than 14 days after the firm intention statement, unless the

---

[201] See fn.79, paras 3.1 and 5.7.

[202] Code rr.2.6 and 2.8. The deadline is set much later if a competing offeror announces a firm bid for the company before the deadline expires. And the rule will not normally apply to participants in a formal sale process which the company is conducting, presumably because any destabilising effect has been precipitated by the company's management itself.

[203] PCP 2004/4, *Conditions and Pre-Conditions*, especially s.7. The "pre-conditions" to an offer are the conditions attached in the "firm intention" statement. See now r.2.7.

[204] Code r.24.1.

[205] Code r.2.7.

target board consents[206]—so that the target board has time to prepare its response before the shareholders are put in a position to accept the offer.

Evaluation of the offer

Conditions

28–058 Once a company posts its formal offer documents to the shareholders of the target, the bid is open to acceptance by the shareholders to whom it is addressed. One aim of the Code in this situation is that the shareholders should have a clear proposition to accept or reject. As we have noted already, r.13 of the Code imposes restrictions on the conditions which the bidder can attach to its offer. An offer must not be subject to conditions which depend solely on subjective judgments by the directors of the offeror or the fulfilment of which is in their hands. Otherwise, offerors would be free to decide at any time to withdraw an offer, whereas one purpose of the Code is to ensure that only serious offers are put forward for consideration. As r.13.4 makes clear, this means that normally the bidder cannot make its offer subject to satisfactory financing being available for the offer: the bidder must not make an offer, or even announce a firm intention to make an offer, if the financing is not already in place.[207] This implements GP 5. The main exception to this principle arises where the bidder intends to raise the cash for the bid through a new issue of shares and its shareholders' approval is required for the share issue, either by the CA 2006 or under the rules applicable to the market on which the shares are traded. In this case, the offer must be made conditional on the necessary consent and the condition is not waivable by the bidder.[208] Even if the inclusion of the condition does not fall foul of the above restriction, the condition must not actually be invoked by the bidder unless the circumstances which have arisen are of "material significance" to the offeror in the context of the bid.[209]

However, some conditions are common in offers, and are even required by the Code. The offeror is required by rr.9.3 and 10 to make its offer (voluntary or mandatory) for voting securities conditional on acceptances of a sufficient level to give it, together with securities already held, 50% of the voting rights in the offeree company. Thus, the bidder must either end up with legal control of the

[206] Code r.24.1.

[207] In the case of pre-conditions the Code shows a little more flexibility, notably where a regulatory condition must be satisfied for the bid to proceed and that is likely to take a long time, and it would thus not be "reasonable" for the potential offeror to have to maintain, and pay for, committed financing throughout this period.

[208] In fact, this concession may enable the company to escape having to proceed with the bid. The shareholders (including the directors in their capacity as shareholders) will not be obliged to approve the share issue (especially if they think conditions have changed since the offer was first announced): *Northern Counties Securities Ltd v Jackson & Steeple Ltd* [1974] 1 W.L.R. 1133 Ch D. And it is not even clear that the Code can require the directors to recommend approval to the shareholders if the directors think it would be a breach of their core fiduciary duty to do so: see para.28–035. (In the *Jackson & Steeple* case the contrary was held, but on the basis that the directors had already given an undertaking to the court to recommend positively.) Perhaps for this reason, the Code attempts to prevent a mandatory bid obligation arising if its discharge would require shareholder consent: r.9.3(b).

[209] Code r.13.5 and Practice Statement 5, and see the WPP case, above, fn.139.

target company or the bid must lapse and the bidder acquires none of the shares which have been assented to the offer. This is regarded by the Panel as a very important provision, as the extensive notes to r.10 make clear, dealing with the operation of the Rule in a variety of circumstances likely to arise in practice. The offeror may choose to, and often does, make a voluntary offer conditional upon a higher level of acceptances, though it will normally also reserve to itself the right to waive the higher condition during the bid. The offer may be conditional upon the offeror achieving 75% of the voting rights, so as to be able to pass a special resolution; or even on achieving 90% of the shares bid for (so as to be able to avail itself of the statutory squeeze-out procedure discussed below). Hence, an important stage in the progress of a bid is when the acceptance condition is satisfied.

A particular problem for the drafters of the Code is that regulatory approval may be required for the bid to proceed. Regulatory review of bids on competition grounds is of long-standing, but the National Security and Investment Act 2021 extends review to embrace strategic and national interests. The Code was revised in 2021 to address thie resulting uncertainty, but the new provisions are better dealt with in the following paragraph.[210]

Timetable

We have already seen that r.24.1 imposes a 28-day-limit for the posting of the offer document after a firm intention to bid has been announced. That is a maximum limit in order not to leave the target board and shareholders in a state of uncertainty. Once the offer is posted, the Code is still concerned with the overall length of the process, and r.31 makes detailed provisions in this area. It should be noted, however, that these rules do not apply where a takeover is effected via a scheme of arrangement (as discussed in Ch.29) because there the timetable is set by the court through its order for a shareholder meeting and its hearing to sanction the scheme approved by the shareholders. For takeovers made via contractual offers, the starting point is that by 60 days after the posting of the firm offer, the conditions to which the offer is subject must be satisfied or waived by the offeror or the offer will lapse. There are some exceptions, in particular that the "60th day" is set by reference to the competing bidder's timetable if there is a competing offer or can be adjusted where the board of the target company agrees to a longer period. In addition, the Panel will suspend the offer timetable if a regulatory approval has not been given by Day 37 of the offer period, if both offeror and offeree so request or on the request of the offeror alone if the approval is "material". **28–059**

This last provision creates the risk that, if regulatory approvals are slow in coming, as where offeror and offeree have global operations, the offeree company might remain subject to a bid for a very lengthy period of time. To deal with this risk, new r.12 (introduced in 2021) requires offerors to set a "long-stop date" in the offer document. This is the date by which the acceptance condition set by the offeror has to be satisfied and any regulatory clearances (for example, from

[210] Normally a lapsed bid cannot be revived within 12 months: see r.35 below. For the mandatory bid, see note on r.9.4.

competition authorities) have to be obtained, irrespective of any suspension. In a recommended bid the long-stop date is set by agreement between offeror and offeree; in a unilateral offer it is set by the offeror, after consultation with the Panel, and must not be set earlier than the date on which the offeror believes the last regulatory clearance is likely to be obtained. If that date is reached and the acceptance condition is still outstanding, the bid will lapse (unless the offeree agrees to an extension); if the acceptance condition has been met but a regulatory clearance remains outstanding, the offer will lapse if the Panel judges the regulatory clearance to be of "material significance" to the offeror and that it cannot take practical steps to obtain clearance.

However, within the offer period, the Code is also concerned with setting minimum time periods, in order that the shareholders have an opportunity to properly consider the offer and are not pushed into a "snap" decision on it. An offer must remain open for 21 days, even if it is unconditional, and, if conditional, until the offer becomes or is declared unconditional or lapses.[211] The force of the rule is to prevent offerors formulating unconditional offers which put time-pressure on offerees to accept. Any revised offer must be kept open for 14 days.[212] To protect the inexperienced, who accepted the initial offer, they are entitled to the revised consideration, despite their earlier acceptance, and new conditions must not be introduced except to the extent necessary to implement an increased or improved offer and with the prior consent of the Panel.

Revised formal offers are particularly likely to be found if there is a contested takeover. In such circumstances each rival bidder, having already incurred considerable expense, is likely to go on raising its bid and trying to get its new one recommended by the board of the target. Even if it loses the battle, the defeated bidder will at least be able to recover part of the expenses out of the profit it will make by accepting the winner's bid in respect of its own holdings.[213] Moreover, even if there is no contest, an offeror may be forced to increase its bid if proves unattractive to the target shareholders or if the bidder or its associates or members of its concert party acquire shares outside the offer at above the price of its offer, as we have seen above.

28–060 Rule 33.1 makes clear, the foregoing rules apply equally to alternative offers in which the target's shareholders are given the choice between different types of consideration (e.g. shares or cash). In other words, the shareholders retain their options so long as the offer remains open. The previous power of the offeror in a voluntary offer, subject to conditions, to "shut off" one of the alternatives during the offer period has been removed in the 2021 revisions. This is a valuable change because it reduces the pressure on the shareholder to accept the offer before it is clear whether the majority will accept either version of the offer.

[211] See r.31.2.

[212] Rule 32.1(c). It follows that normally no revisions are allowed after day 46, in order to keep within the 60-day time-table and material new information should not be announced by the target company after day 39 (r.31.8) in order to meet the 21 day rule for assessing the offer.

[213] By contrast, the successful bidder may suffer from the "winner's curse" of having overpaid for the target.

Bid documentation

The offer document will be a longer and more detailed document than the announcement of the firm intention to make a bid. After a general statement in r.23 that shareholders must be given sufficient information and advice to enable them to reach a properly informed decision as to the merits or demerits of an offer and early enough to decide in good time, r.24.3 (divided into mutiple sub-rules) states what financial and other information the offer document must contain and r.25 in equal detail what information must be contained in circulars from the target company's board. The information required is extensive and relevant but need not be considered in detail here. It is worth noting that the documentation issued by a bidder on a share-exchange offer need no longer comply with the FCA's rules, since it does not constitute a prospectus.[214] **28–061**

Employees' interests

Following the 2010 review of the Code, the interests of employees received slightly more explicit consideration than before, mainly at the level of information provision. Rule 24.2 requires the bidder to state in its offer document "its intentions with regard to the future business of the offeree company and explain the commercial justification for the offer" as well as its intentions with regard to continued employment of the employees and management of the offeree company, material changes in working conditions, strategic plans for the offeree company and their likely impact on employment, and the redeployment of the fixed assets of the company. It must also state its intentions on these matters in relation to the business of the offeror company. So, much more is required to be stated about intentions vis-à-vis employees than previously. Rule 25.2 requires the board of the target, when giving its opinion on the offer, to include its views, and the reasons for those views, on the implications of the bid for the employees and its views on the offeror's strategic plans. These documents, and any revised offer and a target board opinion thereon, must be made available to the representatives of the employees or, in their absence, to the employees themselves[215]; and the offeree board must attach the opinion of the employee representatives to its response circular or publish it on its website.[216] None of this gives the employees any formal say in the bid decision, though it may give them information upon which to organise political or social pressure in relation to the offer. For a more formal input to the bid decision, the employees or their representatives must look elsewhere. Thus, where a statutory information and consultation arrangement is in place, both bidder and target may need to consult employee representatives on the employment consequences of the bid or of defensive measures.[217] **28–062**

[214] PR 1.2.2(2) and 1.2.3(3).

[215] Code rr.23.2. The same obligation is imposed in relation to bid announcements: r.2.12.

[216] Code r.25.9. Rule 32.6 makes the same provision in relation to the offeree's circular on any revised offer.

[217] Information and Consultation of Employees Regulations 2004 (SI 2004/3426) reg.20. The FCA's rules indicate that disclosure to employee representatives or trade unions will normally be characterised as disclosure "in the proper course of the exercise of [the discloser's] employment,

In the takeover of Cadbury by Kraft in 2009 the bidder unwisely committed itself not to close a factory in the UK which the target management had decided to shut down. Having obtained control, the bidder discovered there were good reasons for the previous management's decision and reneged on its commitment. This caused a political storm, as a result of which r.19 was amended to deal with "post offer" statements and undertakings, i.e. statements made during an offer about how a party (typically the bidder) intends to act after the end of the offer period. The amendments apply generally to post-offer statements and undertakings, but these will often be given in relation to employment matters in order to defuse employee or public opposition to the bid. The amendments first require the party to be clear whether it is making a statement of intention (r.19.6) or giving an undertaking (r.19.5) about its post-offer conduct. The requirements on intention statements are less demanding than those on undertakings. For intention statements the statement must accurately reflect the party's intentions at the time it is made and be made on reasonable grounds. For 12 months after the offer has closed (or such other period given in the statement), a party intending to depart from its statement must consult the Panel and, having done so, it must publicly announce its change of heart and explain the reasons for it. The intention statement rules recognise that intentions may genuinely change but they impose a form of "comply or explain" rule, first in relation to the Panel and then in relation to the market and public opinion, in an attempt to control opportunistic changes of mind.

The rules on undertakings are, not surprisingly, more robust. The Panel must be consulted in advance of the undertaking being given and the undertaking must be precisely formulated. In particular, qualifications or conditions attached to the undertaking must be capable of objective assessment (i.e. not be dependent on the subjective judgement of those giving the undertaking). Even if these conditions are met, a person seeking to invoke a condition or qualification post-bid must obtain the Panel's consent. The giver of the undertaking must report periodically to the Panel on progress, or lack of it, towards its implementation, which reports the Panel may publish. If the Panel has doubts about the quality of these reports, it may appoint an independent supervisor to monitor compliance and to report to the Panel. The regulation of intention statements and undertakings was not an easy issue for the Panel, because it requires regulation of post-offer behaviour. Once the offer period is over the Panel's role has traditionally been limited, as discussed below, to enforcing its rules on when a failed bidder may bid again. It is notable that in extending its regulatory reach the Panel did not put in the forefront the use of its new legal powers,[218] but relied instead on the domestic remedies of Panel consultation and approval and disclosure.

Curiously, however, the strongest mechanism for the protection of employee interests may be found in the pensions legislation. The Pensions Regulator does not have the power to block a takeover (though the government once proposed it should have this power), but it does have the power to require companies to make

profession or duties": MAR 1.4.5(2)(e). The same is likely to be true under s.52 of CJA 1993. However, trading by the representative will not be protected nor necessarily further disclosure of the information. See *Criminal Proceedings against Grøngaard* (C-384/02) EU:C:2005:708; [2006] 1 C.M.L.R. 30.

[218] See para.28–09.

payments into a pension scheme or otherwise to provide financial support for it. A bidder worried that, after the takeover, these powers might be used against it (for example, where the bid was leveraged and thus increased the riskiness of the company's financing arrangements) can approach the Regulator on a voluntary basis to discover whether it is prepared to give clearance on its use of these powers or, if not, what changes to the proposed takeover would secure clearance. These powers of the Regulator puts the pension scheme trustees in a position to negotiate with the bidder as to the terms upon which they will regard it proper not to seek the Regulator's intervention.[219]

Profit forecasts and valuations

In the case of an agreed recommended takeover with no rival bidders, no more may need stating than the Code requires. But, in the case of a hostile bid or where there are two or more rival bids, each of the companies involved will probably want to make optimistic profit forecasts about itself[220] and to rubbish those of the others. All profit forecasts are unreliable and those made in a takeover battle more unreliable than usual. Hence, r.28 (with eight sub-rules) lays down stringent conditions about them. They apply also to "quantified financial benefit" statements, whether they purport to forecast the benefits flowing from a successful takeover or those from actions promised by target management conditional upon rejection of the offer. While it is obvious to require that the forecast "must be compiled with due care and consideration" by the directors of the issuing company whose responsibility it is,[221] the Rule requires various additional steps to make it more likely that this will be the case. There must be a report from financial advisers opining that the directors have met this standard and another from reporting accountants that the forecast has been properly complied on the basis underlying it.[222] Those assumptions and "bases for belief" must themselves be disclosed in the document and be specific and precise.[223] Where a party puts forecasts from investment analysts on its website, there are detailed rules to ensure that this information is presented fairly.[224] All this is wholly admirable but the evidence does not suggest that it has made such forecasts significantly more reliable. **28–063**

Somewhat similar requirements apply when a valuation of assets is given during an offer or in the 12 months prior to the offer.[225] The basic requirements are that the valuer should be regarded as independent by the Panel (not just by the

[219] Pensions Act 2004 ss.38–51. Thus, in the takeover of GKN by Melrose in 2018 the trustees of the GKN schemes secured additional pension contributions from the new owner of up to £1 billion over a period of time: Pensions Regulator, *Regulatory Intervention Report Issued in relation to the GKN PLC Pension Schemes* (2019).

[220] The offeror will not need to do so on a pure cash offer for all the shares; but the target will. Indeed, r.28 does not apply to cash offerors.

[221] Code r.28.3.

[222] Code r.28.1(a)—though these requirements are not applied to profit forecasts made within an existing regulatory framework, such that for preliminary statements of annual results (see para.22–008).

[223] Code r.28.4 and 6.

[224] Code r.28.7.

[225] Code r.29.1.

company) and be qualified to carry out the valuation.[226] The scope and content of the report are specified, requiring notably disclosure of the valuation standards used and the basis of the valuation.[227]

Liability for misstatements

28–064 Rule 19.1 lays down a general principle that all documents, announcements and statements made during the course of an offer "must be prepared with the highest standards of care and accuracy" and the information given must be "adequately and fairly presented". However, this is an area where the remedies for inaccurate statements do not fall wholly in the hands of the Panel. In particular, where an investor claims to have been misled by a statement put out by company involved in a bid (or one of its advisers) and to have suffered a loss thereby, any claim for compensation is likely to be fought out in the ordinary courts on the basis of the general law about misstatements causing economic loss.[228] Although the House of Lords in *Caparo Industries Plc v Dickman*[229] limited the circumstances in which those who are not the addressees of misleading documents may found a claim on them for compensation for economic loss, this does not much dilute the importance of the law of negligent misstatement in the takeover context. Many bidder and target statements made in the course of an offer are intended to persuade the shareholders of the target company for or against a particular course of action and some statements are addressed to the offeror's shareholders as well or instead.[230] Indeed, in the post-*Caparo* case of *Morgan Crucible & Co v Hill Samuel & Co*[231] the Court of Appeal refused to strike out a claim by the bidding company itself against the directors of the target based on inaccurate statements made by the target company in the course of a bid allegedly intended to cause the bidder to raise its bid, which it had done to its detriment.

The requirements for making a misstatement claim in a takeover context were examined in detail in *Sharp v Blank*.[232] The litigation arose out of the acquisition of the Bank of Scotland (HBOS) by Lloyds Bank during the financial crisis at the

---

[226] Code r.29.3.

[227] Code r.29.4.

[228] The Panel now has the power to award compensation but this is not one of the areas in which it has sought to implement the power, nor will compensation under FSMA normally be available. See para.28–009.

[229] *Caparo Industries Plc v Dickman* [1990] 2 A.C. 605 HL. See paras 23–035 onwards.

[230] In addition to the liabilities discussed in the text, the bidder might also be liable in damages under s.2(1) of the Misrepresentation Act 1967 (unless it could disprove negligence) or to have its contract with the accepting shareholders rescinded in equity, though in both cases this could apply only between the bidder and the target company shareholders and where the shareholders had accepted the bidder's offer.

[231] *Morgan Crucible & Co v Hill Samuel & Co* [1991] Ch. 295 CA. However, this decision has to be read in the light of subsequent developments on assumption of responsibility. See *Partco Group Ltd v Wragg* [2002] 2 B.C.L.C. 323 CA, where a successful bidder sued the directors of the target on the basis of statements made to the bidder in the course of due diligence carried out by the bidder prior to making a recommended offer. The CA refused to strike out the claim but were clearly sceptical as to whether it would ultimately succeed, because the directors could be said to have assumed responsibility for the accuracy of the statements only on behalf of the target (now owned by the bidder) and not personally.

[232] *Sharp v Blank* [2019] EWHC 3096 (Ch).

end of the first decade of this century.[233] Although the acquisition had long been in the sights of Lloyds and proved good for the bank's business in the medium term, it turned out disastrously for those who held its shares at the time. They were heavily diluted by the emergency fund-raisings which a combination of the crisis and the acquisition rendered necessary. Some of these shareholders sued under a group litigation order the principal executive directors of the Lloyds and its chairman claiming they were in breach of duties owed to the shareholders not to mislead them and that the bank was vicariously liable for the directors' breaches of duty. The misstatements and omissions were said to be found in two principal documents: first, the announcement made to the market by Lloyds and HBOS jointly at the beginning of the process and, secondly, in the circular sent by Lloyds to its shareholders later on seeking their approval for the offer. The statement to the market was required under both the Listing Rules (because of the size of the proposed transaction) and the Takeover Code because Lloyds had formed a firm intention to bid for HBOS.[234] The later approval by the shareholders of the bidder was required under the Listing Rules (and for the same reason) and probably also, though this is unclear from the judgement, because of the statutory rules on share issues discussed in Ch.24.

In a very detailed opinion, the judge acquitted the directors of any negligence towards the company in the way they had prepared for and carried through the acquisition, but this finding by itself did not wholly dispose of the shareholders' personal claims, which were based on misstatements to them by the directors. On the first claim (the announcement) the court held that the directors owed no duty to the shareholders; on the second, the court held that there was a duty and that it had been broken in two ways, but that these breaches caused no loss to the claimants. The denial in principle of a duty arising out of the announcement was based on two principal arguments. An announcement to the market was just that: it was directed at the market as a whole and so not to any particular sub-group of the market, such as the current holders of Lloyds' shares; and it was an announcement, not a recommendation to Lloyds' shareholders to take any particular action in respect of their shares. On the contrary, the express advice in the announcement was for shareholders to wait for the general meeting circular before taking action. Consequently, the defendant directors could not be taken to have assumed responsibility to the then Lloyds shareholders for the accuracy of the announcement so as to make them subject to a tortious duty to take care towards those shareholders.[235] This holding is an important decision on the rules relating to misstatements to the market, which are discussed further in Ch.27.

On the circular, the defendants accepted that they were under a duty to the shareholders to take care to produce an accurate document which contained all the information shareholders might reasonably expect in order to form a judgement on whether to proceed with the bid. The court found that there had been two breaches of this duty, by way of omission to give information about two non-standard forms of funding of which HBOS was in receipt and of which

[233] The acquisition was in fact a reverse takeover effected through a scheme of arrangement (see Ch.29) promoted by HBOS in the Scottish courts, but nothing turned on that in the instant case.

[234] See para.28–055.

[235] See *Williams v Natural Life Health Foods* [1998] 1 W.L.R. 830 HL and para.23–046.

Lloyds was aware but investors were not. The implication of this information was that the financial position of HBOS was somewhat worse than the market expected. However, the judge found that these omissions caused no loss to the shareholders. His assessment on the facts was that, in the light of the generally negative market sentiment towards HBOS and the likely medium-term benefits to Lloyds from the takeover, it could not be said on the balance of probabilities that revealing the information would have led to market pressure on the board to withdraw its recommendation or to the shareholders not approving the acquisition. The case demonstrates that in complex situations where breaches of duty relate to only minor elements in the transaction, proof of causation can be a major obstacle.[236] Nevertheless, acceptance in litigation of a duty to care owed directly to shareholders by those who produce bid documentation is an important development.

Dealings in shares

28–065 GP 4 states that "false markets must not be created in the securities" of the offeror or offeree company. Such a market may give a misleading impression of the value of the offer. The Code has always sought, however, to permit dealings in the securities of companies involved in a bid to continue during the bid period. Apart from the insider dealing laws, already discussed, the main restrictions are these. Once the "offer period" starts (triggered by the first public announcement about the bid, even if it is only about a possible offer) and has not ended (with the offer becoming or being declared unconditional or its lapsing or being withdrawn),[237] the offeror and persons acting in concert with it must not sell any securities in the target company without the consent of the Panel.[238] Moreover, during that period requirements for disclosure of dealings, additional to and stricter than that required by the CA 2006, come into operation.[239]

Solicitation

28–066 The Code does not require bidder and target communication with shareholders and the public generally to be solely via the offer and response documents. This would be undesirable especially in an offer which is publicly contentious.

[236] See further para.23–048.

[237] See Code, "Definitions".

[238] Code r.4.2. Such action is likely to cause great confusion in the market. If the Panel does consent, it will require 24 hours' notice to be given to the market and will require the sale to be at above the offer price. Not abiding by the Code's provisions on sales might well be a criminal offence under Pt 7 of the Financial Services Act 2012, if the object was to rig the market by causing a fall in the quoted price of the target's shares, thus making the offer more attractive; or under the insider dealing legislation if information available to the offeror suggested that its offer would not succeed and it wanted to "make a profit or avoid a loss" by selling before the quoted market price fell back when the offer lapsed. See Ch.30.

[239] In brief, "Opening Disclosures" must be made by any person at the 1% level (instead of 3%) and full disclosure by the parties to the bid or their "associates" (as defined in "Definitions") and "Dealing Disclosures" must be made daily by those parties. Dealings in derivatives must also be disclosed. See rr.8.1–8.3 and notes. However, in the case of cash offers, dealings in the shares of the offeror do not have to be disclosed.

Nevertheless, there is an obvious temptation for both bidder and target to engage in high-pressure salesmanship in the case of a hostile or, especially, a contested takeover; and firms exist which specialise in the art of persuading reluctant shareholders. There are clear risks arising out of communications outside the formal documentation. The Code addresses itself to two principal risks: misstatements and inequality of information.

On the former r.19 requires the same standard of care and accuracy for statements made outside the formal offer and response documents as apply to them and imposes on the directors of bidder and target companies responsibility for the information contained in them. Rule 20 comes close to ruling out the use of social media to promote or resist a bid, confines to a rather small scope the range of advertisements which parties may publish during a bid (without the Panel's consent) and constrains what may be said and by whom in telephone campaigns conducted by bid parties, where the risk of unauthorised and misleading statements is high.[240]

As to equality of information, r.20.1 which lays down the general principle that "information about companies involved in an offer must be made equally available to all offeree company shareholders as nearly as possible at the same time and in the same manner".[241] Despite this, meetings with institutional shareholders, individually or through their professional bodies, are likely to be held, as, often, are meetings with financial journalists and investment analysts and advisers. Rule 20.2 permits this, provided that "no material new information or significant new opinions" are provided. If that really is strictly observed, one wonders why anybody bothers to attend such meetings.[242] But many do, and when a representative of the financial adviser or corporate broker of the party convening the meeting is present (as must be the case unless the Panel otherwise consents), the representative generally seems able to confirm in writing to the Panel (as the Rule requires) that this provision was observed. If such confirmation is not given, a circular to shareholders (and, in the later stages, a newspaper advertisement also) must be published giving the new information or opinions supported by a directors' responsibility statement. 28–067

The post-offer period

We have noted above that under the Code the offer period begins with first announcement about the bid (whether of a possible offer or a firm intention). It ends when either all the offers made have been withdrawn or have lapsed (typically because a time limit has run out without the offer securing the level of acceptances the bidder wished for or the Code required) or an offer has become or has been declared unconditional (or a scheme of arrangement has become 28–068

[240] Code rr.20.4–20.6.

[241] Subject to exceptions. See, for example, employee representatives discussed in para.28–062.

[242] The risk of new information being given out on a partial basis in such cases materialised in the Kvaerner bid for AMEC, where a financial public relations company employed by the target made statements in closed meetings about the target's future profits which had not been contained in the defence document: Panel statement 1995/9. The PR company was censured by the Panel and dismissed by the target.

effective).[243] An offer may become unconditional as to acceptances where either the level of acceptances set in the offer has been reached or it has not, but the bidder has decided to accept the level actually reached (provided it gives it in total more than 50% of the voting rights).[244] Depending on the outcome of the offers, two main issues arise after the offer period.

Bidding again

28–069 If the offer fails, the Code's policy is that the target should be given some respite before the acquirer makes a second offer. Rule 35.1 provides that, except with the consent of the Panel, in those circumstances[245] neither the offeror nor any person who has acted or now is acting in concert with it may within the next 12 months: (1) make or announce another offer for the target company; (2) acquire any shares of the target company which would require a mandatory bid on the part of the acquirer; (3) be a member of a concert party which acquires 30% or more of the voting rights in the offeree company[246]; (4) make any statement which raises the possibility that an offer might be made for the offeree company; and (5) take any preliminary steps in connection with an offer (to be made after the end of the 12 months) which might become known outside the immediate circle of the company's top management and its advisers. Similar restrictions apply following a partial offer, if one is permitted. Interestingly, the restrictions apply to a partial bid for between 30 and 50% of the target, even if that bid is successful. In other words, having had one bite at the cherry, the bidder cannot come back for a second within 12 months: if the bidder wants to obtain a legally controlling interest through a partial bid, it must try for this the first time around.[247] Overall, these provisions prevent the offeror from continuously harassing the target and, while the maximum waiting period is only 12 months, that may be long enough to enable the target's board to strengthen its defences against further hostile bids by the offeror.

Even if the bid is successful, a shorter delay period will be imposed before a further bid is permitted. If a person or concert party following a takeover offer holds 50% or more of the voting rights it must not, within six months of the closure of the offer, make a second offer, or acquire any shares from the shareholders, on better terms than those under the previous offer.[248] This rule, however, is better seen as another expression of the equality principle rather than a protection of the target (now a subsidiary of the bidder) against disruption.

---

[243] Code, Definitions, Offer Period.

[244] The 50% condition is set by the Code (see para.28–058). Other than that the bidder can set the level it wishes to achieve and reserve the freedom to accept a lower level, provided it makes this clear in the offer document.

[245] Or even if no offer has been made but a firm announcement of an intention to bid has been made. A bidder is not normally free simply to withdraw a bid, but may do in some limited circumstances.

[246] As we have seen above (para.28–042), the obligation to bid might not fall to the particular member of the concert party who is the former bidder.

[247] Code r.35.2.

[248] Code r.35.3.

The bidder's right to squeeze out the minority

If the offer has achieved its acceptance level (whether as initially set or as later adjusted), it is very likely that there will still be shareholders in the target company who have not accepted the offer. The question arises whether the acquirer can squeeze out the non-accepting minority or the latter require the bidder to acquire their shares. Both questions are theoretically important and sometimes important in practice as well. However, normally these issues are handled other than through the formal squeeze out/sell out rules, which are to be found in the CA 2006 rather than the Code, since they involve the compulsory acquisition of shares. **28–070**

It is virtually unknown for even a well-supported offer to achieve 100% acceptance. However, where it is important to the bidder to obtain complete control of the target (for example, where it wishes to conduct its business in a way which will not necessarily be in the interests of the minority shareholders of the target), it will seek to get to a position where it can squeeze out any dissenting (or simply non-responsive) minority shareholders. This may be particularly true of private equity bidders, which will want to use the target's assets to secure the loans made to the bidder to finance the bid. Moreover, the existence of the squeeze-out removes to some degree the incentive for target shareholders not to accept an offer from a bidder who they think will run the target well, so that a target shareholder will be better off not accepting the bid (provided the majority do so).

Since 1929, the Companies Act has contained a provision enabling the bidder to squeeze out a minority after a successful bid. The report of the Company Law Review led to some reforms of the procedure in the CA 2006.[249] Despite the number of statutory provisions devoted to the squeeze-out, its practical importance is less extensive as it constitutes only one way of ejecting an unwanted minority. One attraction of the scheme of arrangement mechanism (discussed in the following chapter) for effecting a takeover is that, once the scheme has been approved by a resolution of the shareholders and approved by the court, all the shareholders will be bound to transfer their shares—though a scheme is not attractive in a competitive situation.[250] Moreover, the majority required for a scheme is less demanding than for a squeeze-out: 75% of those voting on the resolution, rather than 90% of those to whom the offer is addressed required for a post-bid squeeze-out (see below). Not only is a higher percentage required for the squeeze-out, but under that mechanism apathy always counts against the bidder. A de-listing of the company from the public equity markets will also act as a strong incentive for the minority to throw in the towel. Again, this step requires only a 75% vote in favour and, indeed, no vote at all if the

249 Final Report I, pp.282–300. However, that report rejected the argument that a squeeze-out right should be extended so as to operate whether the 90% holding results from a takeover or not, largely on the grounds that valuation in such a case would be difficult. Nevertheless, the functional arguments for the squeeze-out from the 90% holder's point of view are just as strong in such a case.

250 See para.29–003.

intention to de-list has been stated in the offer document and the offeror reaches the 75% figure as a result of the offer.[251]

28–071 The current rules on squeeze-outs are set out in Ch.3 of Pt 28 of the Act. The basic principle is quite straightforward, though its implementation gives rise to some complicated provisions. Assuming a single class of shares has been bid for, the offeror is entitled to acquire compulsorily the shares of the non-acceptors if the offer has been accepted by at least 90% in value of the shares "to which the offer relates" and, if the shares are voting shares, those shares represent at least 90% of the voting rights carried by those shares.[252] Note that the 90% figure relates to the shares bid for, not to the total number of shares of the class, some of which may be held by the offeror before the bid is launched. These shares are to be excluded from both the numerator and the denominator when working out whether the appropriate fraction of the shares has been acquired as a result of the bid. Where there is more than one class of shares bid for, the 90% test is applied to each class separately, so that a bidder could end up in a position to squeeze out the minority of one class but not that of another.[253]

In contrast to the Code, Ch.3 applies to takeovers of any type of company within the meaning of the CA 2006 whether it is public or private.[254] The offeror need not be a company and joint bids are provided for.[255] The definition of "takeover offer" is one to acquire (1) all[256] the shares of the company (or all the shares of a class) which on the date of the offer the offeror does not already hold[257]; and (2) to do so on the same terms for all the shares (or all the shares of a particular class).[258]

28–072 All the apparently simple terms used above are capable of raising questions of interpretation, most, though not all, of which are expressly addressed now in the legislation. What, for example, is an "offer"? In *Re Chez Nico (Restaurants) Ltd*,[259] Browne-Wilkinson VC held that this definition had to be construed strictly, since the provisions enabled a bidder who had acquired 90% of the shares

---

[251] See para.25–046. This is a situation where non-acceptors are likely to change their minds once the acceptance level is known. See para.28–059. In companies with a small number of shareholders there are sometimes contractual provisions (in the articles or a shareholder agreement) requiring the minority to accept on the same terms an offer which the majority have accepted ("drag along" provisions). See *Re Charterhouse Capital Ltd* [2015] EWCA Civ 536; [2015] B.C.C. 574.

[252] CA 2006 s.979(2). If, as is usual, the voting rights are on a one vote per share basis, the two requirements amount to the same thing.

[253] CA 2006 s.979(4). In the case of a company with voting shares or debentures admitted to trading on a regulated market, debentures carrying voting rights are treated as shares of the company: s.990. Voting debentures are uncommon in the UK.

[254] CA 2006 s.974(1); and see *Fiske Nominees Ltd v Dwyka Diamond Ltd* [2002] EWHC 770 (Ch); [2002] B.C.C. 707.

[255] See s.987 on joint offers, which deals with the problem identified in *Blue Metal Industries v Dilley* [1970] A.C. 827 PC, that the legislation at the time of that case was not well-adapted to deal with joint offers.

[256] Hence it does not apply to "partial offers": but, where the Code applies, the Panel would not be likely to allow a partial offer which might lead to the acquisition of 90%.

[257] "Shares" here means shares allotted at the date of the offer and excludes treasury shares (s.974(4)) but see below for the handling of these shares.

[258] CA 2006 s.974(2)–(3). "Shares" here means shares allotted at the date of the offer but the offer may include shares to be allotted before a specified date: s.428(2).

[259] *Re Chez Nico (Restaurants) Ltd* [1991] B.C.C. 736 Ch D.

to expropriate the remaining shares, and that accordingly they operated only if the bidder had made an "offer" in the contractual sense of the word. In the instant case two directors of the company who were its major shareholders had circulated the other shareholders inviting them to offer to sell their shares to them and indicating the price that those directors would be prepared to pay if they accepted the offers. As a result, the directors succeeded in acquiring over 90% and then sought to acquire the remainder. On an application by one of the remaining shareholders, the court declared that the directors were not entitled to do so, since they had not made any "offer" but instead had invited the shareholders offer to them. While this produced the right result in the instant case,[260] the importation into company law of the subtle distinctions drawn by the law of contract seems regrettable; in company law many transactions are described as "offers" or "offerings" when strictly they are invitations to make offers.[261] Moreover, the decision has adverse consequences for a minority shareholder who, instead of wanting to remain a shareholder in the taken-over company, wishes to exercise the right to be bought out (see below); the effect of the decision is that the shareholder will not be entitled to do so if the bidder has proceeded as the directors did in this case.

The requirement that the offer be on the same terms is relaxed in two minor respects by s.976. If the difference simply reflects differences in the dividend entitlements (for example, because later allotted shares carry a lower dividend entitlement in that particular financial year as contrasted with shares allotted earlier), the offer is nevertheless on the same terms. This is deemed to be the case also where an offer is made of "substantially equivalent" consideration to those outside the UK whose law either prohibits or subjects to unduly onerous conditions the consideration offered to the main body of the shareholders.[262]

A similar problem to this second one arises with the requirement that the offer be made to all the shareholders (of the relevant class) where the target has a few shareholders resident in countries with elaborate securities laws and where the inclusion within the offer of such shareholders is likely to trigger the need to comply with those laws. An established technique for dealing with this situation is to make the offer capable of acceptance by the foreign shareholders but to take elaborate steps to ensure that the formal offer documentation is not addressed to them. When challenged in court, this practice was upheld with some unease by

[260] Since the directors had failed to make proper disclosure to the other shareholders.

[261] Browne-Wilkinson VC emphasised that his decision was only on the meaning of "takeover offer" for the purposes of the squeeze-out and sell-out provisions and that he had no doubt that what had occurred would be a takeover offer for the purposes of many statutory or non-statutory provisions. This is certainly true of the non-statutory Code. Indeed, the Panel had treated the *Chez Nico* takeover as subject to the Code (the company had been a Plc at the time of the circularisation and remained subject to the Code after its conversion to a private company since, while a public company, it had made a public offering) but the only penalty that the Panel had imposed was to criticise the two directors for their ignorance of, and failure to observe, the Code: see at p.200.

[262] For example, local securities laws might make a share-exchange offer in a particular jurisdiction "unduly onerous". The requirement for "equivalent consideration" is a better solution than that adopted by the directors in *Mutual Life Insurance Co of New York v The Rank Organisation Ltd* [1985] B.C.L.C. 11, in order to avoid US securities laws, which was simply to exclude the US shareholders from any pre-emption entitlements in a public offering.

the Court of Appeal on the specific facts of the case.[263] Section 978 now gives specific statutory cover to this technique, where the offer was not communicated in order to avoid contravention of local law. In order to deal with the difficulty that the foreign resident might never know of the offer until it receives the compulsory acquisition notice from the offeror, the offer is normally placed on a website and the website address given in the *Gazette*. Section 978(2) also saves from failure under the squeeze-out provisions an offer which is communicated but whose acceptance is made impossible or difficult as a result of local law. Finally, s.978(3) makes it clear the courts should not deduce from the section that, in all other cases, a failure to communicate the offer to each holder or an offer which it is impossible or more difficult for some shareholders to accept fails to be a "takeover offer" within the meaning of the Act: the courts will decide on a case-by-case basis.

28–073 Further, there is the question of which are the shares "already held by the offeror" at the date of the offer and which are the shares "to which the offer relates".[264] In general, the larger the stake held by the offeror before the bid, the more difficult it is for it to achieve the 90%, since the smaller becomes the proportion of the class as a whole which is needed to stop it reaching the threshold.[265] Two types of "'acquisition'" are likely to be important in practice. Section 975(2) excludes shares subject to irrevocable commitments to accept the offer when made from the category of shares "'already held'", provided the undertaking is given for no significant consideration beyond, if this is the case, a promise to make the offer.[266] Secondly, shares acquired during the bid period but outside the offer are treated as "'shares to which the offer relates"', provided the price paid does not at that time exceed the value of the consideration specified in the offer or the offer is subsequently revised so that it no longer does so.[267] Both these provisions are helpful to the bidder.

There are also potentially tricky issues about shares which are allotted after the bid is made (for example, as a result of a conversion of another security into shares of the class in question) and about treasury shares, which may be held in treasury throughout the bid or become or cease to be treasury shares during the bid period. The statute handles this point by giving the bidder a choice whether it includes in the category to which the offer relates after-allotted shares or treasury

---

263 *Re Joseph Holt Plc* [2001] EWCA Civ 770; [2001] 2 B.C.L.C. 604.

264 CA 2006 ss.974(2) and 979(1).

265 This is not compensated for by the fact that the number of shares which the bidder has to acquire to reach 90% acceptances is also reduced. Thus, if there are 200 allotted shares and the bidder holds none of them at the outset, it takes a holding of 21 shares to block the squeeze-out, but if the bidder holds 100 at the outset, 11 objectors are enough to block it, i.e. the blocking percentage falls from just over 10% of the class to just over 5% of the total shares in issue. This would not matter if the bidder could rely on having acquired shares pre-bid rateably from acceptors and non-acceptors, but, in the nature of things, the non-acceptors are likely to be underrepresented among those who have sold out voluntarily to the bidder.

266 For irrevocable commitments see para.28–049. The reason for insisting on no significant consideration is to maintain the rule that the offer must be on the same terms to all the shareholders. In general, shares conditionally acquired ahead of the bid do count as shares already held: s.975(1).

267 CA 2006 ss.977, 979(8)–(10). This rule is also applied to acquisitions by associates.

shares.[268] If the offeror chooses not to make an offer for after-allotted or treasury shares, then, naturally, the compulsory transfer provisions will not apply to them.

Challenging the squeeze-out

Given the demanding nature of the 90% threshold, the above detailed provisions may well be of practical importance in particular cases in establishing whether the threshold has been exceeded. Assuming it has, the successful bidder triggers the compulsory acquisition process by giving notice to the non-accepting shareholders, with a copy to the target company, accompanied by a statutory declaration of its entitlement to serve the notice.[269] That notice must normally be given within three months of the last day on which the offer could be accepted.[270] The effect of the notice is, under s.981(2), that the offeror becomes entitled and bound to acquire the shares on the final terms of the offer. If the offer gave shareholders alternative choices of consideration (e.g. shares or a cash alternative), the notice must offer a similar choice, state that the shareholder may, within six weeks from the date of the notice, indicate the choice by a written communication to the offeror and state which consideration will apply in default of a choice. This applies whether or not any time limit or other conditions relating to choice contained in the offer itself can still be complied with and even if the consideration was to have been provided by a third party who is no longer bound or able to provide it.[271] The remainder of ss.981 and 982 prescribes in detail the procedures that have to be adopted to ensure that the shares which the offeror is bound to acquire are transferred to it and that the consideration that it is bound to pay reaches the shareholders concerned.[272] **28–074**

[268] CA 2006 s.974(4)–(7). A decision to exclude all or any such shares from the offer does not cause it to fail to meet the requirement that the offer be for all the shares or all the shares of a class: s.974(4), which excludes such shares from the universal obligation. Convertible securities, so long as they remain unconverted into shares, are treated as shares of the company but as a class of shares separate from the class into which they can be converted: s.989. Rule 15 of the Code normally requires the bidder to bid for convertible shares. For the problems caused by convertible shares before the introduction of these statutory reforms see *Re Simo Securities Trust* [1971] 1 W.L.R. 1455 Ch D. Rule 4.5 prohibits an offeree company from accepting an offer in respect of shares still held in treasury until after the offer is unconditional as to acceptances. On treasury shares, see above at para.17–023.

[269] CA 2006 ss.979(2), 980. This requirement is buttressed by criminal sanctions for failing to send a notice to the company or for intentionally or negligently making a false statement in the declaration. Section 986(9)–(10) provide a limited exemption from the 90% threshold: if the failure to reach it is due entirely to the non-response of untraceable shareholders, the court may permit the bidder to serve a compulsory acquisition notice, provided it is satisfied (1) the consideration is fair and reasonable; and (2) it is just and equitable to do so (taking into account in particular the number of untraceable shareholders).

[270] Where the offer is not governed by the Code, so that there is no fixed closing date for the offer, the period is six months from the date of the offer.

[271] CA 2006 s.981(4)–(5). Normally the alternative which was to have been provided by a third party will have been cash, in which case the bidder may now have to supply it. If the consideration which cannot now be provided, whether by bidder or third party, was a non-cash one, a requirement for equivalent cash applies. This adopts and codifies the effect of the decision of Brightman J in *Re Carlton Holdings Ltd* [1971] 1 W.L.R. 918 Ch D.

[272] The main problem that has had to be solved is that many of the non-acceptors of the offer will probably be untraceable. The solution adopted causes the offeror little trouble (see ss.982(4)

The dissenting shareholder does not have to take the notice lying down. He or she can appeal to the court under s.986(1) for an order either (1) that the offeror shall not be entitled to acquire the shares; or (2) that the terms of the acquisition shall be amended "as the court thinks fit".[273] The shareholder must act within six weeks of the date on which the acquisition notice was given by the bidder, but the application has the effect of suspending the bidder's rights until the appeal is disposed of. Section 986(4) provides that, where the petitioner seeks relief of type (2), the court may not increase the level of consideration to be provided by the bidder beyond that available in the offer, unless "the holder of the shares shows that the offer value would be unfair" (but it cannot in any event impose a reduction). Thus, the burden of showing unfairness is on the challenger.

28–075 What are the petitioner's chances of success? They will be excellent if the petitioner can show that the statutory requirements for a "takeover offer" have not been met or that the 90% threshold has not been reached, under the provisions discussed above, because then the court will have no jurisdiction to make an order for the compulsory acquisition of the shares.[274] However, it should not be thought that the merits are always on the side of the non-accepting minority. They may simply be interested in exploiting to the full the hold-up power which the bidder's desire for complete control has given them. If the court cannot order a compulsory acquisition because the statutory requirements have not been met, the bidder may think of other devices to achieve the same result.

In *Rock Nominees Ltd v RCO (Holdings) Plc*[275] the bidder, faced with highly opportunistic conduct on the part of a shareholder which narrowly blocked achievement of the 90% threshold, caused the newly acquired subsidiary to sell its business to another company in the same group (at a fair price) and then put the seller into voluntary liquidation, for which only a special resolution is required, distributing the price received on the sale to the shareholders (including the minority) and thus achieving the same result as a compulsory acquisition. The Court of Appeal refused to hold that this was unfairly prejudicial conduct on the part of the majority.[276]

Where the court has jurisdiction, the petitioner will have an uphill struggle in discharging the burden of showing the offer was unfair. If 90% of the shareholders have accepted the offer, that is normally strong evidence that it is a fair one.[277] Consequently, the petitioner may have a better chance of success if he

onwards), but the target company, now a subsidiary of the offeror, may have to maintain trust accounts for 12 years or earlier winding-up and then pay into court.

[273] It seems that the offeror cannot deprive the court of its jurisdiction to amend the terms of the squeeze-out by accepting the petitioner's right not to be squeezed out, at least where the petitioner has not indicated he or she seeks only the right not to be compulsorily acquired: *Re Greythorn* [2002] 1 B.C.L.C. 437 Ch D. In this case the petitioner had reasons for thinking that the closely-held target company had been taken over at a gross undervalue, and the bidder evidently preferred to allow the petitioner to remain in the company than to have that issue examined in court.

[274] Formally, this will not help a petitioners who want a higher price, but they may be able to negotiate one if the bidder cannot squeeze them out at the offer price.

[275] *Rock Nominees Ltd v RCO (Holdings) Plc* [2004] EWCA Civ 118; [2004] 1 B.C.L.C. 439.

[276] This way of proceeding was undoubtedly more expensive for the bidder than a compulsory acquisition. On unfair prejudice, see Ch.14, and on voluntary winding up, para.33–011.

[277] For the courts' traditional reluctance to fix a price (as opposed to simply ratifying or not the bid price) see *Re Grierson, Oldham & Adams Ltd* [1967] 1 W.L.R. 385 Ch D.

or she simply seeks an order that there should be no compulsory acquisition, for there the requirement to show that the offer value is unfair does not apply. Even in relation to simple denial of the compulsory purchase request, however, the British courts have traditionally relied on the high level of acceptances achieved to conclude that they should exercise their discretion in favour of the compulsory acquisition.[278] However, in more recent times the courts have been prepared to refuse compulsory acquisition where, unusually, the acceptances are an unreliable indicator of fairness, without requiring the petitioner to establish what the correct level of consideration should have been. Two such indicators of unreliability have emerged in particular in the cases. If the acceptors of the offer are not independent of the bidder or if the acceptors were not given adequate information upon which to take their decision, the court will not necessarily draw the conclusion that a 90% acceptance indicates a fair offer.[279] In practice, this means the petitioner's chances of success are much greater if the bid was not governed by the Code than if it was, for the Code is likely to be taken as guaranteeing the provision of adequate information. A shareholder who resists the squeeze-out may appear to be left locked into a vulnerable position, but may be confident of its ability to negotiate an attractive private deal with the acquirer, if the acquirer really does need 100% control.

The sell-out right of non-accepting shareholders

The squeeze-out provisions introduced in 1929 were not originally accompanied by a right on the part of the non-accepting minority to have their shares bought by the bidder. This right was added only in 1948. Although formally reciprocal, in fact the two rights perform very different functions. The sell-out right permits the shareholder, who does not wish to accept the bid, but who, if the majority do accept, would rather leave the company as well, to give effect to that set of preferences. He or she can refuse to accept the offer, but then change his or her mind, once the results of the other shareholders' decisions have become clear. However, as we have noted, the Code already provides a more effective mechanism for giving the shareholder that facility, for it requires the offeror to keep the offer open for a further 14 days after it has become unconditional as to acceptances.[280] Since the Code rule is not dependent upon the 90% threshold and it operates without a court order, it is a much more attractive mechanism for those who are quick enough to use it. This perhaps explains why there has been little litigation on the sell-out right provided by the statute. **28–076**

The sell-out right, like the squeeze-out right, depends upon there having been a takeover offer which relates to all the shares in the company, as those terms are defined for a squeeze-out.[281] However, the 90% threshold is calculated in relation to a different set of shares. The question is whether the shares acquired through the offer *together with* other shares which the offeror (or an associate of the

[278] *Re Hoare & Co Ltd* (1933) 150 L.T. 374; *Re Press Caps Ltd* [1949] Ch. 434.

[279] *Re Bugle Press Ltd* [1961] Ch. 270 CA; *Re Chez Nico (Restaurants) Ltd* [1991] B.C.C. 736; *Re Lifecare International Plc* [1990] B.C.L.C. 222 Ch D (Companies Ct); *Fiske Nominees Ltd v Dwyka Diamond Ltd* [2002] B.C.C. 707.

[280] See para.28–047. This obligation is subject to the shut-off of cash alternatives: see para.28–060.

[281] CA 2006 s.983(1).

offeror) held before the offer or acquired during the offer but outside it constitute 90% of the shares in the company (and, where relevant, 90% of the votes). If there is more than one class of share, this rule is applied class by class.[282] In other words, unlike in the squeeze-out, the question is not whether there has been a 90% level of acceptance of the offer, but rather whether the bid has left the offeror holding 90% of the shares. This seems the correct test: the mischief which is sought to be remedied is the minority position into which the bid has put the applicant shareholder and the precise degree of enthusiasm displayed by the other shareholders for the offer is of secondary importance.[283] It is probably rather easier for the sell-out threshold to be attained than the squeeze-out threshold, because, in a sell-out, a lower level of acceptances might be compensated for by a higher level of pre-bid holdings on the part of the bidder or its associates.

28–077 The offeror must give each of the non-accepting shareholders notice of their entitlement to be bought out within one month of the end of the offer period. The shareholder wishing to take up this right must give notice to the offeror, either within three months of the end of the offer period or, if later, as it usually will be, of the notice given by the offeror.[284] Provisions apply as to the consideration to be provided which are equivalent to those for a squeeze-out.[285] It is in this case, rather than in relation to a squeeze-out, that the need to provide a choice of all the original alternatives (including a cash underwritten alternative) is so unpopular with offerors and their advisers. And it is not altogether easy to reconcile with the provisions of the Code. As we have seen, under the Code an offer has to remain open for at least 14 days after it becomes unconditional as to acceptances. However, an offeror is not obliged to keep most types of cash underwritten alternatives open if it has given notice to shareholders that it reserves the right to close them on a stated date being not less than 14 days after the date on which the written notice is given.[286] The effect of the Act is virtually to keep the offer open for considerably longer than is required under the Code in cases where the result is that offeror holds 90% of the shares. And clearly the parties cannot contract out of the statutory provisions. Nor can the Panel or the Code waive them. The CLR endorsed this position.[287]

However, it is sometimes argued that the obligation to keep the full terms of the offer open does not apply if the cash alternative is described in the offeror's offer document as a separate offer by the underwriting investment bank. In the light of the section that argument seems unsustainable. The fact is that, as the section and the Code clearly recognise, the offeror's "offer" may and probably will contain a number of separate offers and that some of those offers may be

[282] CA 2006 s.983(2)–(4), (8). "Associate" is broadly defined in s.988. If conditionally acquired shares are not in fact ultimately acquired and that would mean the threshold would not be met if they were excluded, there is a standstill procedure which may result in the shareholder losing the right to be bought out: s.983(6)–(7).

[283] As with the squeeze-out right, however, this is not a general right for a minority to be bought out, if the final step in the process whereby the majority acquires 90% of the shares is not a takeover bid.

[284] CA 2006 s.984(1)–(4). The offeror's obligation is supported by criminal sanctions on the bidder and any officer in default: s.984(5)–(7).

[285] CA 2006 s.985.

[286] See para.28–060.

[287] Final Report I, para.13.61.

made by third parties. All fall within the phrase "the terms of the offer". The only way, it is submitted, in which offerors and their investment banks might be able to achieve their aim is by making no mention at all of a cash underwritten alternative hoping that an independent investment bank, not acting on behalf of, or paid for its services by, the offeror will come forward and make an offer on its own account to the target's shareholders to buy the shares of the offeror received on the takeover. That is a somewhat unlikely scenario.

Under s.986(3), when a shareholder exercises the sell-out right by notice to the offeror, an application to court may be made either by the shareholder or the offeror and the court may order that the terms on which the offeror shall acquire the shares shall be such as the court thinks fit. The parties may be in disagreement about whether there is an obligation on the offeror to acquire the shares at all or they may be in disagreement about the terms. The same provisions about raising or lowering the consideration in relation to the bid value apply as in a squeeze-out[288]; and the shareholder will be in the same difficulty when arguing that the sell-out should be at a higher level than was provided for in the bid. Assuming the court has jurisdiction, it cannot simply refuse to order the sell-out, for this by definition is what the shareholder is entitled to.

CONCLUSION

UK takeover regulation is committed to the principle that the decision on the offer should lie in the hands of the shareholders rather than the management of the target company (assuming no regulatory concerns). Especially important in this regard are the restrictions imposed by the Code on the defensive steps which are open to the management of the target company and its insistence that the shareholders of the target should not be denied the opportunity to decide on the merits of the bid. In other countries, it is easier for the incumbent management to take steps to defend itself against unwelcome bids, though not necessarily to the point of preventing them entirely. The argument in favour of the regime adopted by the Code is that it provides a cheap and effective method of keeping management on their toes and protects shareholders from management slackness or self-dealing—or, in any event, provides a method for the shareholders to exit the company on acceptable terms if such managerial misbehaviour produces a takeover bid. Further, this rule makes it less easy for target management to resist offers driven by the potential benefits of combining the businesses of offeror and target companies, where target management are nevertheless likely to lose their jobs in the process. The potential disadvantages of this stance are that it deprives the board of the target of full-scale role in either negotiating on behalf of the shareholders or protecting them from coercive bids. The latter concern is addressed by other provisions of the Takeover Code regulating the format in which offers may be put, in particular, the requirements for equal treatment and the Panel's reluctance to sanction partial bids. The board's negotiating role is not entirely removed by the "no frustration" rule but the board cannot in the end **28–078**

[288] CA 2006 s.986(4).

insist that its valuation of the company is correct and the shareholders' mistaken, if the target shareholders take a different view.

The Code's orientation seems to reflect the dominance of the institutional shareholders in the UK which naturally favour a set of rules which maximise their gains from bids but which also reduce their managerial agency costs. Thus, the institutions have also set their faces against the adoption in pre-bid situations, where the Code does not apply, of defensive devices by the management of potential takeover targets. However, it is perhaps easy to overestimate the beneficial effect upon management performance of the threat of the takeover bid, which is not to say that the takeover bid has no role to play in the British system of corporate governance. The core decision to side-line target management in the decision on the takeover offer also makes it difficult to build any protection for non-shareholders, notably employees, into the Takeover Code—though in this respect the Code simply imitates the general orientation of British company law.[289]

[289] For a general review of these issues see P. Davies, "Control Shifts via Contracting with Shareholders" in G. Ringe and J. Gordon (eds), *The Oxford Handbook of Corporate Law and Governance* (Oxford: OUP, 2018).

CHAPTER 29

ARRANGEMENTS, RECONSTRUCTIONS AND MERGERS

THE FUNCTION OF SCHEMES OF ARRANGEMENT

Part 26 of the CA 2006 provides a mechanism to agree and implement "a compromise or arrangement … proposed between a company and its creditors or any class of them or its members or any class of them" (s.895). Proposals made under this Part are normally referred to as "schemes of arrangement". Schemes are frequently used to re-shape the company's structure or businesses, especially in the case of public and publicly-traded companies and so they are very important in practice. Yet, the language of the statute is so widely drawn that it is not apparent what the most common uses of the mechanism may be. In fact, the scheme provisions can be used to carry through a number of different types of transaction which, in other jurisdictions, are often made the subject of separate statutory procedures. It is therefore useful to begin by identifying the principal types of activity for which schemes are or could be used. 29–001

Mergers

In most countries' companies legislation there is to be found a section headed "Mergers" which will contain language somewhat along the following lines: 29–002

> "Any two or more corporations existing under the laws of this State may merge into a single corporation, which may be any one of the constituent corporations, or may consolidate into a

> new corporation formed by the consolidation, pursuant to an agreement of merger or consolidation, as the case may be, complying and approved in accordance with this section."[1]

Thus, the assets of two or more merging companies end up in a single "resulting company" (which may be a new company formed for the purpose of the merger or one of the merging companies). As to the shareholders of the merging companies, traditionally they too end up as shareholders of the resulting company, each of the previously separate bodies of shareholders holding, more or less, the proportion of shares in the resulting company which reflects the respective valuations of the companies which came together to form that company. In liberal jurisdictions, such as the UK, cash may be permitted as merger consideration. In that case, some or all of the shareholders of a merging company exit the company rather than transfer to the combined enterprise. If, in addition, one merging company is already holds a controlling interest in the second merging company and only cash is offered to the non-controlling shareholders of the second company, then the merger constitutes a method of squeezing out the minority shareholders in the second company.

Although it is perhaps not obvious that s.895 contemplates the use of a scheme of arrangement to effect a merger, later sections make it clear that this is the case. Section 900 deals specifically with compromises or arrangements under s.895 "proposed for the purpose of or in connection with a scheme for the amalgamation of two or more companies" and involving the transfer of the undertaking or property of one company involved in the scheme to another.[2] Section 900 gives the court the power to make "ancillary orders" so as to transfer the undertaking from transferor to transferee company (without the parties having make arrangement to do this themselves by contract) and to dissolve the transferor company without winding it up.[3] Equally, the scheme can be used for a "de-merger" or division of a company, whereby part of its undertaking is transferred to another company, again either one formed for the purpose of the de-merger or an existing company.[4] In certain merger and de-merger cases, the transaction will have to comply in addition with the provisions of Pt 27 of the CA 2006, which implemented in the UK the Third and Sixth Company Law Directives of the EU and which remains in force even after the UK's exit from the EU.[5]

In addition to the scheme of arrangement under the CA 2006, it is possible to effect a merger under provisions of the IA 1986. Sections 110 and 111 of that Act are precisely targeted at the transfer of a company's undertaking to another company, in exchange for shares "or other like interests" in the transferee

[1] Delaware General Corporation Law s.251.

[2] CA 2006 s.900(1). The section also applies to the "reconstruction" of a company by way of the transfer of its undertaking or property to another company.

[3] CA 2006 s.900(2)(a), (d).

[4] That a de-merger is a valid scheme is clear, but the courts' ancillary powers under s.900 apply only to "amalgamations" or "reconstructions" (fn.2). The courts have reasoned that a reconstruction requires that the shareholding structure of the transferee company must substantially reflect that of the transferor company (but liabilities may be left with the transferor): *Re South African Supply and Cold Storage Co* [1904] 2 Ch. 268 Ch D, 281–282; *Re MyTravel Group Plc* [2004] EWCA Civ 1734; [2005] 2 B.C.L.C. 123 (Mann J). This may limit the way in which a de-merger is carried out.

[5] See para.29–013.

company, which are distributed to the transferor's shareholders. However, the transferor must be in voluntary winding up to take advantage of this procedure.[6]

Takeovers

As we shall see,[7] it is in fact relatively uncommon for the scheme to be used to effect a merger. More often, what is produced is the scheme equivalent of a takeover, as discussed in the previous chapter. A simple example is the "transfer scheme" whereby the shares in the target not already held by the bidder are transferred to it in exchange for a consideration in cash or shares, provided by the bidder to the target shareholders.[8] A scheme can be used in this way to replicate all of the outcomes of a successful takeover bid.[9] The resulting position is, formally, different from a merger. The target company ends up as a subsidiary of the bidder rather than a single "resulting" company emerging, as in a true merger. If desired, even this result (a single legal entity) can be achieved through a second-step merger of the parent and its new subsidiary. This will be easy to achieve if the new parent holds all the shares in the new subsidiary, but may be more difficult if the subsidiary still has outside shareholders.[10] As we saw in Ch.28, effecting an agreed takeover through a scheme is an increasingly popular move, so that the Takeover Panel, which has always applied its rules to takeovers through schemes (to the extent that its rules are not displaced by statutory rules specific to schemes), has now set out on a systematic basis how its rules apply to schemes.[11] 29–003

---

[6] See para.29–017.

[7] See para.29–013.

[8] This way of proceeding under what is now Pt 26 was sanctioned a century ago in *Re Guardian Assurance Co* [1917] 1 Ch. 431 CA, despite the fact that the element of "arrangement" between the target company and *its* shareholders is vanishingly small, consisting of no more than the company facilitating the transfer of their shares to the bidder. See also *Re Jelf Group Plc* [2015] EWHC 3857 (Ch); [2016] B.C.C. 289.

[9] Popular in the past, because it avoided the payment of stamp duty on the transfer of the shares from target shareholders to the "bidder", was the "reduction" scheme, under which the shareholders of the target agreed to the cancellation of their shares in the target company; the reserve so created in the target was used by the target to pay up new shares which were issued to the offeror; and the shareholders of the target received in exchange for their cancelled shares cash or shares in the offeror company. The company's role in a reduction scheme is thus more significant. However, the Treasury, anxious to remove the stamp duty advantage, promoted amendments to the Act in 2015 which now prohibit the first step (cancellation of the shares) when this is part of scheme to allow the bidder to obtain all the shares in the target company. The prohibition in s.641(2A) is subject to an exception in s.641(2B). The exception applies where the scheme involves a new parent company, where all or substantially all of the members of the company are to become members of the new parent and where their equity interests are to be the same or substantially the same as in the scheme company. In such a case there is no change of control and company reconstructions are facilitated by the exception. The exception was liberally construed in *Re Home Retail Group Plc* [2016] EWHC 2072 (Ch); [2017] B.C.C. 39, where there was a change of control of part of the company's business. See *Re Man Group Plc* [2019] EWHC 1392 (Ch); [2019] 2 B.C.L.C. 495; and *Re STERIS Plc* [2019] EWHC 751 (Ch); [2019] B.C.C. 924 for a standard application of the exemption (transfer of the company's place of incorporation to another jurisdiction—to avoid the adverse consequences of Brexit).

[10] See para 29–008.

[11] See at para.28–014. On the complications which can arise when competing bids are put through the scheme mechanism see *Re Allied Domecq Plc* [2000] B.C.C. 582; and *Re Expro International Group*

An advantage of the scheme is that it becomes binding on all the shareholders in question if approved by three-quarters of the shares (and a majority in number of them),[12] whereas, as we have seen,[13] a takeover offer becomes binding on all shareholders only if accepted by 90% of the shares offered for (which allows the company compulsorily to acquire the shares of the non-accepting shareholders). For this reason, it was argued at one time that, if the scheme procedure was used where a takeover offer could be made, the court should insist on 90% approval of the scheme by the shareholders. However, the argument was rejected on the grounds that in the scheme procedure the shareholders have the protection of the requirement of prior court approval of the scheme, an element not present in the contractual takeover offer.[14] A crucial step in this reasoning is that the court must form its own judgment on the scheme when it comes to consider its approval and not grant approval simply because the appropriate proportion of the members have approved it. The extent to which this is in fact the case we consider below.

In the case of a hostile offer, the disadvantages of the scheme normally outweigh its advantages as against the takeover offer. The main disadvantage is that the shareholders are not bound until they have voted in favour of the scheme or, even, until the court has sanctioned it, and the necessary delays involved in calling a shareholder meeting give rival bidders the time to organise a competing bid. By contrast, in a takeover offer the bidder can start soliciting "irrevocable commitments"[15] even before the formal offer is made, and may then quickly launch the formal offer and aim to build up an unstoppable momentum behind it.[16] It is also easier to make use of the scheme procedure if the cooperation of the target board is forthcoming, since the scheme normally has to be promoted by the target company, either by its board or the shareholders in general meeting,[17] whereas one of the advantages of the contractual offer is that the legal transaction is solely between acquirer and target shareholders individually. Therefore, a scheme is likely to prove attractive only where the takeover is agreed with the board of the target and is not likely to precipitate a rival offer and the offeror is keen to achieve complete ownership of the target.

Plc [2008] EWHC 1543 (Ch); [2010] 2 B.C.L.C. 514. For this reason acquirers proceeding by way of a scheme often reserve the right to revert to a contractual offer if a competing bidder emerges.

[12] CA 2006 s.899(1).

[13] See at paras 28–070 onwards.

[14] *Re National Bank Ltd* [1966] 1 W.L.R. 819 Ch D; *Re BTR Plc (Leave to Appeal)* [2000] 1 B.C.L.C. 740 CA (Civ Div). However, it seems that a scheme cannot be used to override the requirement for individual shareholder consent to a transactions where individual consent is part of a statutory scheme governing that transaction, as in an offer to buy back shares: *Puma Brandenburg Ltd v Aralon Resources and Investment Co Ltd* (Judgment 27/2017) 18 May 2017 CA (Guernsey).

[15] See para.28–049.

[16] Of course, savvy institutional investors will probably not fall for this trick and instead hang on to the last moment before accepting.

[17] See para.29–007.

Other cases

Although a merger (potentially) and a take-over (actually) constitute important uses of the scheme of arrangement, the width of the statutory language means that many other uses are possible. The scheme may be particularly convenient where UK company law does not appear to offer a customised procedure for carrying out the transaction in question. Besides the merger, another example is use of the scheme to shift the jurisdiction of incorporation of the company or of the parent of a corporate group—usually termed "redomiciling" the company.[18] As we have noted, British company law does not provide a simple mechanism for transferring jurisdictions, not even between the jurisdictions which constitute the UK. Forming a new company in the preferred jurisdiction which acquires the assets of the existing company at a market price is likely to prove expensive in tax terms. However, a transfer scheme whereby the court uses its powers to transfer the assets of the existing company makes this transaction fiscally feasible.[19] It should be noted that the scheme provisions do not require that the transferee company be incorporated in the same jurisdiction as the transferor or in a UK jurisdiction at all. **29–004**

Overall, whether the scheme involves just a single company or more than one company, the courts have construed "arrangement" as a word of very wide import and as not to be read down by its association with the word "compromise" in the section, so that an arrangement involving members need not, and usually does not, involve an element of compromise.[20] The term covers almost every type of legal transaction, and, as the takeover example shows, in substance the transaction may be between the shareholders and a third party, though a scheme will only be available if the company is formally a party to the transaction. Only the case of unvarnished expropriation of the shareholders has so far been excluded by the courts from the scope of the term.[21]

[18] See *Re Man Group Plc* [2019] 2 B.C.L.C. 495 and para.5–010. If all that is required is to change the jurisdiction of the parent company in a group, without dissolving the existing parent, it will be enough for the shareholders in the existing UK parent to exchange their shares for shares in a new parent, incorporated elsewhere, and this can still be done through a "reduction" scheme (see fn.9).

[19] In this case the problems mentioned in fn.4, relating to the use of courts' ancillary powers, are unlikely to arise.

[20] *Re National Bank Ltd* [1966] 1 W.L.R. 819 at 829; *Re Calgary and Edmonton Land Co Ltd (In Liquidation)* [1975] 1 W.L.R. 355 Ch D at 363; *Re Savoy Hotel Ltd* [1981] Ch. 351 Ch D at 359D–F; *Re T&N Ltd* [2006] EWHC 1447 (Ch); [2007] Bus. L.R. 1411 at [46]–[50].

[21] *Re National Farmers Union Development Trusts* [1972] 1 W.L.R. 1548 Ch D: held that the court had no jurisdiction to sanction a scheme whereby all the members were required to relinquish their financial rights without any quid pro quo. However, the decision in *Re MyTravel Group Plc* [2005] 2 B.C.L.C. 123, makes it less easy for companies to use the scheme to effect a debt-for-equity swap, which is not an amalgamation and so has to count as a reconstruction if the court is to use its ancillary powers (see fn.4 above). The lack of congruence between the transferor and transferee companies' shareholding structures was brought about in that case by the fact that, as is common in debt/equity swaps, the existing shareholders were to be heavily diluted and most of the shares in the transferee were to be held by the former creditors of the transferor. However, the scheme did in fact proceed in that case but without the exercise of the court's ancillary powers (see the decision of the CA in that case). It is unclear why the ancillary powers are not made available for all schemes which get through the statutory procedure.

Creditors' schemes

29–005 The arrangement may not involve the company's members but wholly concern its creditors. In fact, when the scheme provisions were introduced by the Joint Stock Companies Arrangement Act 1870, they applied only to arrangements with creditors (and indeed only to arrangements proposed by companies in the course of being wound up). The members were added in 1900 but not until the Companies (Consolidation) Act 1908 was the winding-up requirement dropped and the forerunner of the modern provisions emerged. In practice, a very common use of the provisions today is to secure compromises with creditors of a company in financial trouble—and perhaps at the same time with its shareholders.[22] In some cases the getting in and distribution of the company's assets can be effected more quickly and expeditiously through a scheme than a winding-up, in which case the scheme will operate alongside the winding-up, but in effect be determinative of most of the substantive issues; or the company may be able to reconstruct itself as a viable going concern under a scheme without entering formal insolvency.[23] This last goal of creditor schemes was enhanced by the introduction of a new Pt 26A into the CA 2006 by the Corporate Insolvency and Governance Act 2020, which is headed "Arrangements and Reconstructions of Companies in Financial Difficulty". We do not consider creditors schemes in any detail in this work, since they are better located in works on insolvency. However, it is not uncommon for a company in financial difficulty to propose amendments to shareholders' as well as creditors' rights. Thus in Pt 26A it is provided that "'arrangement' includes a reorganisation of the company's share capital"[24] as well as adjustments to creditors' rights. Consequently, we analyse Pt 26A briefly after looking at Pt 26, whose contours the new Part closely follows.

It is worth noting, however, that where the company is in financial difficulty the English courts have been willing to accept jurisdiction over schemes proposed by companies which are not incorporated in the UK and even have no assets here, for example, where the creditors' rights are governed by English law. However, such reasoning has no application to solvent companies where the scheme concerns wholly or primarily the members' rights.[25] Nevertheless, even in members' cases, creditors' rights may possibly be affected and, if so, their consent will be needed.

THE MECHANICS OF THE SCHEME OF ARRANGEMENT

29–006 Given the significance of the scheme for the company's future development, it is not surprising that the scheme procedure is designed with the aim of ensuring that the shareholders of the company or companies involved in the scheme are content

[22] See the debt-for-equity swap discussed in the previous note.

[23] For a modern example see *Re T&N Ltd* [2007] Bus. L.R. 1411.

[24] CA 2006 s.901A(4).

[25] *Re Drax Holdings Ltd* [2003] EWHC 2743 (Ch); [2004] B.C.C. 334, where Lawrence Collins J (as he then was) said obiter at [29]: "It is almost impossible to envisage circumstances in which the English court could properly exercise jurisdiction in relation to a scheme of arrangement between a foreign company and its members, which would essentially be a matter for the courts of the place of incorporation".

with it. Special resolution approval of the scheme is required, to be given separately by each class of affected shareholders. But since even a supermajority approval requirement may not protect minority shareholders, court approval of the scheme is also required—though the effectiveness of this piece of minority protection depends on the rigour of the court's scrutiny of the scheme. Thus, there are three main steps in a scheme of arrangement:

(1) a compromise or arrangement must be proposed between the company and its members[26];
(2) meetings of the members must be held to seek approval of the scheme by the appropriate majorities. These meetings are convened by the court on application to it[27]; and
(3) the scheme is sanctioned (or not) by the court.[28]

Proposing a scheme

This first stage, which is often overlooked, is important because, in practice, it is difficult to use the scheme procedure in a takeover unless the scheme is approved by the board, which then proposes it on behalf of the company. Formally, it would seem that the general meeting could propose a scheme on behalf of the company,[29] but the shareholders' co-ordination problems make this course of action often difficult. The point is illustrated by the decision in *Re Savoy Hotel Ltd*,[30] which is instructive in a number of ways. The company, which had survived a hostile takeover bid in the early 1950s,[31] introduced a dual-class share structure, consisting, at the time of the litigation, of some 28 million A shares and some 1.3 million B shares, with identical financial entitlements, but with the B shares having (in effect) 20 times the number of votes attached to the A shares. The board held directly or indirectly some two-thirds of the B shares. Such a degree of voting leverage may have been thought to have rendered the company impregnable to a takeover. However, this distribution did mean that the A shareholders held just over half the votes in the company. This did not create the risk of an ordinary takeover offer succeeding, because it was reasonable to assume that enough holders of the A shares would oppose a bid to prevent the bidder obtaining 50% of the total votes, as required by the Takeover Code,[32] given that the B shareholders would be solidly against an offer. 29–007

Instead, the bidder (THF) sought to put forward a scheme for the transfer to it of the A and B shares in exchange for cash, the scheme providing that if one class of shareholders did not approve of it (the B shareholders), the scheme could proceed in favour of the other class alone (the A shareholders). It was reasonable to suppose that three-quarters in value and a majority in number of the A class

26 CA 2006 s.895(1).

27 CA 2006 ss.896–899(1).

28 CA 2006 s.896.

29 The possibility of shareholder proposal was recognised in *Re Savoy Hotel Ltd* [1981] Ch. 351.

30 See previous note.

31 See para.10–037 at fn.171.

32 See para.28–058.

shareholders[33] might approve the scheme. The dissentient A class shareholders would then be bound by it (subject to court sanction) and the bidder would end up with just over half the voting shares in the company, even if the scheme were rejected by all the B class shareholders. THF, which held a few A class shares, applied to the court as a member[34] under step (2) above for an order for separate meetings of the A and B shareholders to be held to consider the scheme. Nourse J held that he had power to order such meetings but declined to do so, on the grounds that they would be futile. This was because the scheme had not been proposed by the company but by a shareholder (THF). Thus, step (1) was not satisfied and so the court would not have jurisdiction to sanction it at stage (3).[35]

Convening and conducting meetings

29–008 When the proposed scheme has been formulated, the first step is an application (normally ex parte) to the court by or on behalf of the company (or companies) to which the compromise or arrangement relates for the court to order meetings of the members or classes of members to be summoned.[36] This the court will generally do and will give directions about the length of notice, the method of giving it and the forms of proxy. In the case of shareholders—unlike with creditors where the question has generated endless difficulty—this is a relatively easy task, since the practice of splitting shares into different classes in the articles is a general feature of company law. However, the fact that the members in question have the same rights as against the company does not necessarily mean that they are part of the same class for scheme purposes, because the scheme may propose to treat sub-groups of a single class of members differently. Equally, the fact that shareholders are in different classes under the articles does not necessarily mean they should not be put together for the purposes of voting on the scheme.

The general test for determining whether the members should meet as a whole or in one or more separate classes is whether the rights of those concerned "are not so dissimilar as to make it impossible for them to consult together with a view to their common interest".[37] However, it is easier to state this test than to apply it. In general, it can be said that, the greater the number of classes, the greater the chances the scheme will fail to obtain the consent of one or more of those classes.[38] Further, the tests for determining classes should be reasonably simple

[33] The required level of approval of a scheme. See below.

[34] CA 2006 s.896(2) contemplates applications under step (2) by a creditor or member as well as by the company or its liquidator or administrator.

[35] THF would not be able to get around this problem by seeking to convene a general meeting to propose the scheme, because at a general meeting both A and B shareholders would vote together and the reasons given in the text for why a bid would fail would apply also to a shareholder resolution to propose a scheme.

[36] CA 2006 s.896(1). Sensibly, the courts will recognise that a meeting can occur even if the company has only one shareholder, for otherwise schemes would be less freely available within groups (*Re RMCA Reinsurance Ltd* [1994] B.C.C. 378 Ch D (Companies Ct), but no meeting can be said to have occurred when in a multi-member class only one member in fact attends: *Re Altitude Scaffolding Ltd* [2006] EWHC 1401 (Ch); [2006] B.C.C. 904.

[37] *Sovereign Life Assurance Co (In Liquidation) v Dodd* [1892] 2 Q.B. 573 CA at 583, per Bowen LJ.

[38] *Re Equitable Life Assurance Society (No.2)* [2002] EWHC 140 (Ch); [2002] B.C.C. 319.

and capable of application by the company and the court without extensive investigation into the position of particular members. For this reason, the courts have used the rights of shareholders (as against the company or under the scheme) as the touchstone for determining the class issue, rather than their interests.[39] Interests, it is said, can be taken into account by the court at the third stage when it decides whether to sanction the scheme. Thus, in *Re BTR Plc*,[40] a case of a takeover being effected through a scheme, the judge sanctioned the scheme which had been approved overwhelmingly in a single meeting of the target's shareholders and rejected the argument that those shareholders of the target company who already held shares in the bidder should have been put in a separate class. The judge distinguished the earlier case of *Re Hellenic and General Trust*,[41] where the judge had refused sanction because the ordinary shares in the target already held by a subsidiary of the bidder had been voted in favour of the scheme at a meeting of the target shareholders. The better explanation of *Re Hellenic* was that the subsidiary's shares had to be excluded because the scheme did not concern them: in effect, they were already held by the bidder.

It is certainly the case that the question of whether the approval of members of a particular class or a subset them is required in any case is to be answered by determining with whom the company proposes to effect a compromise or arrangement. If members (or creditors) are not included within the scheme, their consent is not required, and the proposing company appears to have a wide discretion as to the scope of the scheme, provided at least that there is a commercial rationale for its decision.[42] However, neither is the excluded group bound by the scheme so that the company runs the risk that its implementation may later be held to infringe the rights of those left out of it.[43]

In both *Re BTR* and *Re Hellenic* it was the opponents of the scheme who wished to put into a separate class shareholders who, they thought, would be biased in favour of the scheme. In *Re SABMiller Plc*,[44] by contrast, supporters of the schemes sought to include in a meeting two large shareholders who were clearly in favour of the scheme, but whom the company wished to exclude. The principal reason for the company's proposal seems to have been that the exclusion of the large shareholders was thought likely to reduce the risk of the court not giving its sanction: the non-significant shareholders would be able to take a view free of the votes of the large shareholders. There are two odd features

39 *Re UDL Holdings Ltd* [2002] 1 HKC 172 at 179, Hong Kong Court of Final Appeal, per Lord Millett; *Re Noble Group Ltd (No.1)* [2019] B.C.L.C. 505.

40 *Re BTR Plc* [1999] 2 B.C.L.C. 675 Ch D (Companies Ct). The decision and reasoning were upheld on appeal: [2000] 1 B.C.L.C. 740. See also *Re Industrial Equity (Pacific) Ltd* [1991] 2 H.K.L.R. 614.

41 *Re Hellenic & General Trust* [1976] 1 W.L.R. 123 Ch D. On the view of this case adopted in *Re BTR* it was not fatal to the scheme that the subsidiary's shares were voted at the class meeting, but they were to be discounted at the third stage when deciding whether to approve the scheme.

42 *Sea Assets Ltd v Perusahaan Perseroan (Persero) PT Perusahaan Penerbangan Garuda Indonesia* [2001] EWCA Civ 1696, a creditors' scheme, where the company included only its finance creditors and not its trade or procurement creditors, whose non-inclusion was central to the company's continued ability to trade.

43 *Re MyTravel Group Plc* [2005] 2 B.C.L.C. 123; *Re Bluebrook Ltd* [2009] EWHC 2114 (Ch); [2010] B.C.C. 209.

44 *Re SABMiller Plc* [2016] EWHC 2153 (Ch); [2017] B.C.C. 655.

of the case. On the one hand, even if they objectors had succeeded, the now-included large shareholders could not have been compelled to attend and vote at the meeting. On the other, the company's proposal was not that there should be a separate meeting of the two large shareholders. This argument could have been advanced on the grounds that those shareholders had rights under a relationship agreement with the company which put them in a different class from the other shareholders. However, what was proposed (and upheld by the court) was that the two large shareholders should simply bind themselves to accept whatever the remaining shareholders decided. Given the large shareholders' declared support for the scheme, a separate meeting for them would have been an unnecessary expense, though probably not a large one. The court's view might well have been different, at least at the sanction stage, had the large shareholders been doubtful about the scheme but had agreed to be excluded from the class meeting, thus increasing the chances of the scheme going through, it exchange for some private benefit provided to them by the proposing company.[45]

29–009 The issue of how classes should be composed for scheme purposes was rendered particularly acute by the former practice of the courts of leaving the decision about class meetings at stage (2) almost wholly to the company (i.e. of simply accepting what the company proposed) and taking a view whether that decision was correct only at stage (3). By stage (3) it was too late to do anything about the composition of the meetings and the court could only refuse to sanction the scheme on the grounds it had no jurisdiction to do so, since the proper meetings had not been held. This approach was roundly criticised by Chadwick LJ in *Re Hawk Insurance Co Ltd*.[46] A Practice Direction now seeks to ensure that "issues concerning the jurisdiction of the court to sanction the scheme, the composition of classes of creditors and/or members and the convening of meetings to be identified and if appropriate resolved early in the proceedings"—though it still leaves the responsibility of determining the composition of the meetings on the applicant company. Although objections may still be raised at stage (3), if the procedure is followed the court "will expect [objectors] to show good reason why they did not raise a creditor issue at an earlier stage".[47] The CLR proposed that the court should have the discretion to determine the appropriate classes at stage (2), when asked to do so by the company, and that, if it exercised its discretion at this stage, it should be bound by it when it came to consider sanctioning the scheme after member or creditor approval (stage (3)).[48] It further proposed that the court should have a discretion to sanction the scheme even if the appropriate

[45] See para.29–011 below. Such an arrangement would probably have infringed the Takeover Code as well. See para.28–026.

[46] *Re Hawk Insurance Co Ltd* [2001] EWCA Civ 241; [2002] B.C.C. 300. He thought it particularly unfortunate that the court should feel obliged to raise the issue of its own motion at stage (3), even though no member or creditor sought to argue that different class meetings should have been held.

[47] *Practice Statement (Companies: Schemes of Arrangement under Part 26 and Part 26A of the Companies Act 2006)* [2020] B.C.C. 691 Ch D at [1], [2] and [10]. For an account of modern practice, see *Re T&N Ltd* [2007] Bus. L.R. 1411 at [18]–[20]; *Re Apcoa Parking (UK) Ltd* [2014] EWHC 997 (Ch); [2014] B.C.C. 538 at [12]–[16].

[48] The court does already decide at stage (2) other issues relating to the jurisdiction of the court to sanction a scheme at stage (3), though not issues going to the fairness of the scheme: *Re Savoy Hotel* [1981] Ch. 351; *Re Telewest Communications Plc (No.1)* [2004] EWCA Civ 728; [2005] B.C.C. 29 at [14]–[15]; *Re MyTravel Group Plc* [2005] 2 B.C.L.C. 123.

class meetings had not been held, provided the court was satisfied that the incorrect composition of the meetings had not had any substantive effect on the outcome, i.e. it would no longer be a matter going to the jurisdiction of the court.[49] However, these proposed reforms were not taken up in the Act, but the Practice Direction comes close to this result.

Section 897 requires any notice sent out summoning the meetings to be accompanied by a statement explaining the effect of the compromise or arrangement and in particular stating any material interests of the directors (whether in their capacity of directors or otherwise) and the effect on those interests of the scheme in so far as that differs from the effect on the interests of others.[50] The provisions of the Takeover Code are likely to add substantially to the statutory disclosure requirements when the scheme is being used to implement a takeover.[51] Where the scheme affects the rights of debenture-holders, the statement must give the like statement regarding the interests of any trustees for the debenture-holders.[52] If the notice is given by advertisement,[53] the advertisement must include the foregoing statements or a notification of where and how copies of the circular can be obtained, and on making application a member or creditor is entitled to be furnished with a copy free of charge.[54] In an extreme case the court may refuse to order meetings where it has serious concerns that significant relevant information will not be forthcoming before the shareholders have to take a decision.[55] **29–010**

The level of approval required at the meeting is not just the standard special resolution requirement of a three-fourths of the shares in question,[56] for there must also be a (simple) majority in number of the shareholders in favour.[57] The CLR recommended the removal of the number requirement, which does indeed appear anomalous in the context of the Companies Act approach to shareholder approval.[58] However, the number requirement does constitute an additional element of minority protection where 75% of the shares are concentrated in the

[49] Final Report I, paras 13.6–13.7. This would not otherwise affect the tasks to be performed by the court at the sanctioning stage, on which see later.

[50] CA 2006 s.897(1)–(2).

[51] See paras 28–61 onwards.

[52] CA 2006 s.897(3). If the interests of the directors or the trustees change before the meetings are held, the court will not sanction the scheme unless satisfied that no reasonable shareholder or debenture-holder would have altered his decision on how to vote if the changed position had been disclosed: *Re Jessel Trust Ltd* [1985] B.C.L.C. 119; *Re Minster Assets Plc* (1985) 1 B.C.C. 99299.

[53] Which will be the only way of notifying holders of bearer bonds. It may also be necessary to advertise in this way to creditors.

[54] CA 2006 s.897(1)(b), (4). A default in complying with any requirement of the section renders the company and every officer, liquidator, administrator, or trustee for debenture-holders liable to a fine unless he shows that the default was due to the refusal of another director or trustee for debenture-holders to supply the necessary particulars of his interest: s.897(5)–(8). In that case the criminal offence is committed by that director or trustee: s.898.

[55] *Re Indah Kiat International Finance Co BV* [2016] EWHC 246 (Ch); [2016] B.C.C 418.

[56] If creditor consent is required, further difficulties may arise in valuing their claims and thus determining whether the majority does represent three-fourths in value. This is a problem met whenever this formula is employed in respect of creditors—as it is throughout the IA 1986.

[57] CA 2006 s.899(1).

[58] Final Report I, para.13.10—the requirement seems to have been imposed when the scheme provisions concerned only creditors.

hands of one or a few persons. By the same token, in this situation the number requirement puts a potential hold-up power in the hands of those holding a minority by value of the shares. In *Re Dee Valley Group Plc*[59] a shareholder sought to exploit this possibility through the simple expedient of buying 434 shares in the company and then giving one each to the same number of like-minded persons who proposed to vote against the scheme at the court-ordered meeting. Had they done so, then a numerical majority in favour of the scheme would not have been obtained. However, the chairman of the meeting disallowed the votes. The court held he was right to do so, on the grounds that the "share-splitting" scheme was a manipulation strategy. On the facts as known the chairman at the date of the meeting, he was correct to conclude that the shares had been obtained by the donees with the pre-conceived notion of voting down the scheme and not, as the law required, to vote for the purpose of benefitting the class as a whole. In consequence, the chairman was "entitled to protect the integrity" of the court-ordered meeting by disallowing the votes. It is to be noted that this would have been a very effective hold-up strategy, because, if the meeting had not approved the scheme, the scheme could not be taken to the third stage (court sanction) where the court forms its own view of the scheme (see below).

However, it is far from clear that this decision solves the minority hold-up problem entirely. In this case it seems that the objectors opposed the scheme on employment and environmental grounds, of which the chairman was unaware at the time. The judge was of the opinion that such views were not in principle excluded by the requirement to vote in the interests of the class as a whole.[60] If, for example, the shareholders in this case had purchased beneficially and held for a period their individual shares and used the opportunity of the court-ordered meeting to express those views through opposition to the scheme, it appears that their votes would have been valid, even though those votes deprived the majority by value of a financially attractive offer for their shares. Any attempt by the majority in value to engage in counter share-splitting would be at risk of being characterised in turn as manipulative,[61] though the bidder could proceed of course by way of a simple takeover offer where the number requirement does not apply.

The sanction of the court

29–011 The application for the court's approval is made by petition of the applicants and may be opposed by members and creditors who object to the scheme, including a member or creditor excluded from the scheme.[62] Apart from establishing that the

[59] *Re Dee Valley Group Plc* [2017] EWHC 184 (Ch); [2018] B.C.C. 486.

[60] *Re Dee Valley Group Plc* [2018] B.C.C. 486 at [55]. "But it could not, I think, be said that a shareholder acting in the interests of the class might not properly think that the interests of employees of the company, customers or the environment might not outweigh the financial interests of the class and favour rejection of even a good financial offer." (per Sir Geoffrey Vos C).

[61] *Re PCCW Ltd* [2009] HKCA 178. Of course, share splitting by the majority (in value) simply moves the scheme onto the third stage of court sanction. It does not mean that the scheme is approved and thus is not the converse of share splitting by the minority (in value), which stops the scheme it its tracks.

[62] CA 2006 s.899(2)(b)—"any member or creditor".

necessary resolutions were "passed by the statutory majority in value and number…at a meeting or meetings duly convened and held",[63] the court will carry out a limited review of the decisions taken at the meetings. That review aims to establish four principal points (which to some degree overlap)[64]:

(1) that the class was fairly represented by those who attended the meeting;
(2) that the majority acted bona fide and not in order to promote interests adverse to those of the class concerned;
(3) that a member of the class concerned might reasonably approve the scheme; and
(4) that there was no "blot" on the scheme.

The first ground of review enables the court at the sanction stage to take into account whether the passing of the resolutions was secured only by "share splitting" or some other opportunistic allocation of voting rights.[65] However, fair representation does not appear to require that a majority of the outstanding shares (or indeed any other specific percentage) should be present and vote at the meetings convened by the court.[66] This test might be failed if some of the shareholders had a special interest not shared by other members of the class, but then only if there was a "strong and direct" link between that interest and their support for the scheme.[67] The second is analogous to the "bona fides" test applied to majority decisions to change the articles.[68] The third is relatively weak, since it comes close to a rationality rather than a reasonableness test. The question is not whether, for example, most investors in the shareholders' position would have approved the scheme but whether there was any basis on which a shareholder might reasonaly do so. "The scheme proposed need not be the only fair scheme or even, in the court's view, the best scheme."[69]

As to the fourth requirement, "blot" is a word rarely found in companies legislation and cases and its meaning in this context is obscure. It has been said that the word refers "to some technical or legal defect in the scheme, for example that it does not work according to its own terms or that it would infringe some mandatory provision of law."[70] However, it can act as a useful catch-all for matters possibly not included under the previous three heads. Thus, the Guernsey Court of Appeal held that a scheme designed to squeeze out a minority fell within

[63] In *Re Dorman Long & Co Ltd* [1934] Ch. 635 Ch D at 655 and 657.

[64] *Re National Bank Ltd* [1966] 1 W.L.R. 819; *Re Telewest Communications Plc (No.2)* [2004] EWHC 1466 (Ch); [2005] B.C.C. 36; *Re TDG Plc* [2008] EWHC 2334 (Ch); [2009] 1 B.C.L.C. 445.

[65] See fn.61.

[66] *Re TDG Plc* [2009] 1 B.C.L.C. 445, where the number of members voting was 21% of the total, representing 46% of the total value of the class. The judge confirmed the scheme, saying these percentages provided "no basis for saying the representation was not fair" (at [37]).

[67] *Re Lehman Brothers International (Europe) (In Administration) Ltd* [2018] EWHC 1980 (Ch); [2019] B.C.C. 115 at [103]–[105].

[68] See para.13–007.

[69] *Re Telewest Communications Plc (No.2)* [2005] B.C.C. 36 at [20]–[22]. See also Lindley LJ in *Re English, Scottish and Australian Chartered Bank* [1893] 3 Ch. 385 CA; *Re Alabama, New Orleans, Texas and Pacific Junction Railway Co* [1891] 1 Ch. 213 CA per Fry LJ; *Re Apcoa Parking Holdings GmbH* [2014] EWHC 3849 (Ch); [2015] B.C.C. 142. These were all creditors' cases but the same principle applies to members' schemes.

[70] *Re Noble Group Ltd* [2018] EWHC 3092 (Ch); [2019] B.C.C. 349 at [77].

this heading on the grounds, among others, that the shareholders had been pressurised to accept the scheme under threat from the majority (who, naturally, were outside the scheme) that the company would not pay dividends in the future.[71] Even allowing for all four of these heads of review, it is clear that the courts are no more interested than the Takeover Panel in becoming involved in the assessment of the commercial and financial merits of the transaction embodied in the scheme. It is certainly the case that the court rarely refuses sanction to a scheme which has met the requirements for the first two stages of the procedure. To this extent, one may doubt whether court review does act as a substitute for the 90% acceptance level required for a squeeze-out after a takeover.

The scheme becomes binding on the company and all members (or all members of the class concerned) and, if the company is in liquidation, on the liquidator, once it is sanctioned by the court and a copy of the court's order is delivered to the Registrar (so that knowledge of the scheme is publicly available).[72] Indeed, the binding effect of schemes on minorities is one of its attractions over a takeover bid.[73] A particular risk with complicated schemes is that at some point in the proposed arrangements financial assistance for the purchase of a company's own shares will be given. However, the Act removes the risk from anything done to implement a scheme sanctioned by the court.[74]

Companies in financial difficulty

29–012 Schedule 9 to the Corporate Insolvency and Governance Act 2020 introduced a somewhat modified scheme procedure for companies in financial difficulties as a new Pt 26A in the CA 2006. Those financial difficulties, at a minimum, must be such as may affect the company's ability to carry on business as a going concern and the purpose of the compromise or arrangement proposed, again as a minimum, must be to mitigate those difficulties.[75] The proposal is most likely to be of concern to creditors (who are not the main focus of this chapter) but it is also provided that the arrangement proposed may include the reorganisation of the company's capital "by the consolidation of shares of different classes or by the division of shares into shares of different classes" or both,[76] so that shareholders' rights may be altered under the arrangement. For example, as part of a restructuring a company in financial difficulties may wish to bring about

[71] *Puma Brandenburg Ltd v Aralon Resources and Investment Co Ltd* (Judgment 27/2017) 18 May 2017 CA (Guernsey). Contrast *Re Inmarsat Plc* [2019] EWHC 3470 (Ch).

[72] CA 2006 s.899.

[73] The courts have rejected arguments that a scheme which satisfies the requirements of the Act might nevertheless amount to deprivation of possessions contrary to art.1 of the First Protocol of the European Convention on Human Rights: *Re Equitable Life Assurance Society* [2002] B.C.C. 319; *Re Waste Recycling Group Plc* [2003] EWHC 2065 (Ch); [2004] B.C.C. 328.

[74] CA 2006 s.681(2). The same exemption exists for reorganisations under the IA 1986 (discussed in para.29–017 onwards). See *British & Commonwealth Holdings Plc v Barclays Bank Plc* [1995] B.C.C. 1059 CA (Civ Div); *Re Uniq Plc* [2011] EWHC 749 (Ch); [2012] 1 B.C.L.C. 783—though it is unlikely that the courts will sanction schemes which require wholesale exemptions from the financial assistance rules. Financial assistance is discussed at paras 17–047 onwards.

[75] CA 2006 s.901A. For the going concern test see para.22–018.

[76] CA 2006 s.901A(4).

what is effect a reduction of its capital to facilitate the introduction of new investors into the company or to induce creditors to accept a debt-for-equity swap.[77]

The procedure under Pt 26A closely follows that of Pt 26, with shareholder meetings ordered by the court, a vote on the proposal and court sanction of it. However, Pt 26A contains certain relaxations from the full scheme procedure, aimed at increasing the chances of its approval. First, it is specifically provided that an application to the court for meetings to be ordered may be made by any member (or creditor) as well as by the company (or its liquidator or administrator). This solves the issue discussed in para.29–007 in relation to Pt 26 schemes. Secondly, all the members (and creditors) of the company must be included in the meeting(s) but the court on application may exclude a class where none of the members of the class has "a genuine economic interest" in the company.[78] Thus, a class of shareholders need not be summoned where the company is so heavily indebted that their shares are completely "under water", i.e. do not have any current value and will not have any value even if the arrangement is approved and put into effect. This rule thus addresses the issue which was discussed in para.29–008 in relation to Pt 26 schemes. The statement to be circulated to the meeting follows the lines of the one required under a Pt 26 scheme.[79]

The principal relaxation for a Pt 26A proposal—and the one that seems likely to guarantee it will be preferred over a Pt 26 scheme when it is available—relates to the voting requirements at the meeting and the court's power (subject to conditions) to ignore dissenting class votes. As to the first, the approval required is that of "a number representing 75% in value of the … members or class of members."[80] This is, of course, the standard provision for a special resolution of the members, but it omits the additional requirement for a "majority in number" which applies to Pt 26 schemes.[81] More radically, the court may ignore the fact that a particular class of creditors or members did not approve the proposal even on this relaxed basis and sanction it, but the court is not obliged to take this step.[82] In relation to creditors this is often referred to as a "cram down". However, the court's discretion to take this step is subject to two conditions. First, the court must be satisfied that the dissentients will be no worse off under the proposal than they would be under whatever situation the court thinks most likely to occur if the compromise or arrangement is not approved.[83] The second condition, which must be satisfied as well, is that the proposal has been approved by 75% of those members who do have a genuine economic stake in the alternative which would occur if the proposal were not sanctioned.[84] In other words, the dissentients are not to be overruled by those who have no incentive to compare the proposal and the alternative because the alternative is of no value to them.

[77] See paras 16–018 and 17–033.
[78] CA 2006 s.901C(4).
[79] CA 2006 ss.901D–E.
[80] CA 2006 s.901F(1).
[81] See para.29–010.
[82] CA 2006 s.901G.
[83] CA 2006 s.901G(3)–(4).
[84] CA 2006 s.901G(5).

Additional requirements for mergers and divisions of public companies

29–013 Under British practice, amalgamations of domestic companies are rarely carried out by means of transfers of undertakings (as opposed to shares) using a scheme of arrangement. For this, there are said to be two reasons. First, there are limitations on what the courts can achieve under their powers to facilitate a reconstruction or amalgamation.[85] It was held in *Nokes v Doncaster Amalgamated Collieries*[86] that the section does not operate to transfer compulsorily contracts of employment and that principle has been applied to any rights which as a matter of general law are not transferable. However, the Transfer of Undertakings (Protection of Employment) Regulations[87] largely solve the employment issue. Although they do not make transfer mandatory for the employee (only for the employer), they create a strong incentive for the employee to transfer with the business by conferring only very limited compensation rights on the employee as against the employer if the employee chooses not to transfer.

Even if the (non-employment) contract is in principle transferable, the counterparty may have negotiated a right to terminate the contract or to insist on different terms of business if the transferor is replaced by the transferee as the contracting party. Any court order transferring property will not override these third-party rights and so transferor and transferee will have to negotiate an acceptable set of arrangements with the third party. However, it should be noted that contractual restrictions can easily be drafted so as to apply where control of the company changes without there being any transfer of assets (as in a takeover, whether effected by a scheme or not), so that in this respect a merger may put the company in no worse a position. Finally, whether or not the third party has negotiated contractual protection, the statutory provisions[88] give the court power to require protection for any creditor (or, indeed, member) who dissents from the transfer. This issue will not arise in the case of a takeover, since the court is not involved in approving it.

A second part of the explanation may be that a merger effected by a scheme is very likely to trigger Pt 27 of the Act, which imposes extra requirements and costs on the implementation of schemes for reconstruction[89] or amalgamation involving a public company, in order to meet the requirements of the Third Company Law Directive on mergers of public companies.[90] Part 27 continues in force as part of domestic law even after the UK's exit from the EU. However, Pt 27 does not apply where a scheme is used to effect a takeover, because bidder and target remain separate companies after the scheme has been implemented. There

[85] CA 2006 ss.900 and (now) 901J. See para.29–002.

[86] *Nokes v Doncaster Amalgamated Collieries Ltd* [1940] A.C. 1014 HL; *Re TSB Nuclear Energy Investment UK Ltd* [2014] EWHC 1272 (Ch); [2014] B.C.C. 531.

[87] (SI 2006/246).

[88] CA 2006 ss.900(2)(e) and 901J(2)(e).

[89] See fn.4. Part 27 applies to both Pts 26 and 26A schemes (s.903).

[90] Directive 78/855 (now Directive 2011/35 concerning mergers of public limited liability companies ([2011] OJ L110/1)). Directive 82/891 [1982] OJ L378/47 (the "Sixth" Directive) deals with the division of public limited companies.

are three major additional requirements imposed in relation to true mergers,[91] of which the most important is the third. This is the device, not otherwise found in the domestic rules on schemes of arrangement, of an independent expert's report. However, although no formal independent expert's report may be required of the bidder in the case of a proposed takeover by means of a scheme, the Takeover Code lays down extensive rules on the provision of information to the "target" shareholders, including an independent expert's opinion on the fairness of the offer and the Code's rules will apply to takeovers by way of a scheme.[92] Thus, Pt 27 may not add much in substance to the bidder's costs. Perhaps the truth is that tax rules make asset amalgamations through schemes unattractive or that British practitioners have become so familiar with the takeover via share acquisitions that alternative means of amalgamation are not seriously explored. In any event, the scheme-based domestic merger seems to be rare.

The additional requirements of Pt 27 are: **29–014**

(1) Normally, a draft scheme has to be drawn up by the boards of all[93] the companies concerned and publicised via the *Gazette* or, more likely, the company's website. All this must be done at least one month before the meetings are held.[94]
(2) What has to be stated in the board's circulars is considerably amplified as compared with the rules for a standard scheme, but perhaps not as compared with the Takeover Code rules.[95]
(3) In addition, generally[96] separate written reports on the scheme have to be provided to the members of each company by an independent expert appointed by that company or, if the court approves, a single joint report to all companies by an independent expert appointed by all of them.[97]

However, Pt 27, although widely framed, does not apply to all forms of merger. Hence, there is some considerable scope for framing a merger scheme which avoids the additional requirements. In particular, Pt 27 applies only where the consideration for the transfer is or includes shares in the transferee, so that a

[91] The details differ somewhat according to the "Case" (see below) within which the scheme falls, the main differences being between those within Case 1 or 2 (mergers) and Case 3 (divisions).
[92] See para.28–026.
[93] This includes the transferee company, whose consent is not required under a scheme governed purely by Pt 26, unless the rights of the shareholders or creditors of the transferee are proposed to be changed. However, it is enough that the members of the transferee are given the option to call a meeting (on the basis of a 5% threshold: ss.918 and 932) so that the burden of action falls on the shareholders rather than the company in such a case. Of course, if the transferee is a UK listed company, the large transaction provisions of the Listing Rules might require it to obtain shareholder approval. See para.1–024.
[94] CA 2006 ss.905–6A, 920–921A.
[95] CA 2006 ss.908, 910, 923, 925.
[96] The requirement for an independent report can be dispensed with if all the shareholders agree. See s.918A.
[97] CA 2006 ss.909, 924 and 935–937. The matters to be dealt with in the report are specified in some detail. In some respects, it resembles the report required (also as a result of an EU Directive) when a public company makes an issue of shares paid-up otherwise than in cash: see paras 16–019 onwards.

merger for a purely cash consideration is excluded.[98] Secondly, in the case of a merger "by absorption" (see below), where the transferee company already holds all, or in some cases 90%, of the securities carrying voting rights in the transferor, the requirements mentioned above are substantially reduced.[99] This facilitates mergers within corporate groups and, in particular, a merger of parent and new subsidiary following a successful takeover bid. Thirdly, Pt 27 does not apply if the transferor company is being wound up,[100] rather than being dissolved without winding-up after the merger. Thus, the requirements of Pt 27 can be avoided by incurring the expense of putting the transferor into liquidation—probably not an attractive course of action.

29–015 Finally, to fall with Pt 27 the merger must fall within one of two "Cases". The two "Cases" are:

(1) Where the undertaking, property and liabilities of the public company are to be transferred to another public company, other than one formed for the purpose of, or in connection with, the scheme ("merger by absorption").[101]
(2) Where the undertakings, property and liabilities of each of two or more public companies, including the one in respect of which the arrangement is proposed, are to be transferred to a new company, whether or not a public company, formed for the purpose of, or in connection with, the scheme ("merger by formation of new company").[102] Thus, a transfer to a new company, public or private, by a single public company escapes from both 1 and 2, and equally a reconstruction of a single company can be carried out purely under Pt 26.[103]

Broadly similar rules apply to divisions, except that the relevant Case arises where, under the scheme, the undertaking, property and liabilities of the public company are to be divided among, or transferred to, two or more companies each of which is either a public company or a company formed for the purposes of, or in connection with, the scheme ("division by acquisition" or "division by formation of new company").[104]

Despite the discouraging history of the use of schemes to effect true mergers, the CLR consulted on the issue of whether there should be introduced into the Act a statutory merger procedure, as in many other jurisdictions.[105] For the CLR the crucial element of a statutory merger procedure was that the merger should not require approval by the court, though in appropriate cases those adversely affected by the proposal should have a right of appeal to the court. Its goal of providing a "court free" merger procedure was thus in line with what it

---

98 CA 2006 s.902(1)(c).
99 CA 2006 ss.915 and 915A. In these cases, as well, the requirement for a meeting of members is relaxed: ss.916–917 and 931.
100 CA 2006 s.902(3).
101 CA 2006 ss.904(1)(a) and 902(2)(b).
102 CA 2006 ss.904(1)(b) and 902(2)(a).
103 See the scheme proposed in *Re MyTravel Group Plc* [2005] 2 B.C.L.C. 123.
104 CA 2006 ss.919 and 902(2). The Sixth Directive applies to divisions. See fn.90.
105 Completing, paras 11.40–11.53.

recommended in the case of reductions of capital.[106] However, it also took the view that, where the Third Directive applied, it would be impractical to implement a proposal except under the supervision of the court.[107] The result of the restrictions in effect imposed by the Directives was that the statutory merger procedure seemed to the CLR to be feasible only in two cases.[108] However, neither of these proposals was taken up in the Act and it remains to be seen whether, and on what terms, this area is re-visited post-Brexit.

CROSS-BORDER MERGERS

Despite the limited utilisation of the scheme of arrangement to produce true mergers between domestic companies, cross-border mergers involving UK companies with companies incorporated within the EEA became quite common after the transposition of the EU Cross-Border Mergers Directive[109] by means of the Companies (Cross-Border Merger) Regulations 2007.[110] The Regulations provided for cross-border mergers a customised merger procedure, i.e. one not tied to the scheme of arrangement. However, with the UK's exit from the EU, those rather useful Regulations were revoked. Unlike Pt 27 of the Act which can continue in effect even after the UK's exit because it concerns the powers of the UK courts alone, the Cross-Border Mergers Directive imposed reciprocal obligations on the courts of EEA member states, which simply ceased to operate in respect of the UK upon exit, so that the UK Regulations became inoperable. **29–016**

It is true that the domestic scheme procedure is formally available to companies liable to be wound up in the UK under the insolvency legislation[111] and that definition includes foreign incorporated companies with a sufficiently close connection with the UK.[112] However, as we have already noted, the courts are unlikely to be prepared to exercise the domestic jurisdiction in respect of foreign companies when what is proposed is a members' (rather than a creditors') scheme. Even if the UK court did accept jurisdiction, it is far from clear that other EEA courts would recognise the result in the absence of a supporting scaffold of EU law. Of course, it will remain possible to amalgamate two companies across borders by means of an acquisition of shares, since, subject to mandatory national interest legislation in the foreign country, this is simply a contractual transaction between two private parties.

It is also worth noting that it is possible to produce a cross-border merger through a "dual-listed structure". In this arrangement the companies remain

---

106 See paras 17–035 onwards.

107 Completing, para.11.46.

108 Completing, para.11.50; Final Report I, paras 13.14–13.15. These were the merger of wholly-owned subsidiaries of a parent company and where a company formed a new wholly-owned subsidiary, into which the assets and liabilities of an existing company were transferred, the transferor being dissolved.

109 Directive 2005/56 on cross-border mergers of limited liability companies [2005] OJ L310/10.

110 (SI 2007/2974), as amended, a self-standing set of regulations made under the European Communities Act 1972 and constituting a major piece of corporate law which is not located in the CA 2006 at all.

111 CA 2006 s.895(2)(b).

112 See fn.25.

formally independent (i.e. they do not merge) nor does the one become a subsidiary of the other, as in a takeover. Instead, by contract, including provisions in their respective constitutions, the companies produce a unified management (i.e. the same people sitting on the boards of directors of the two companies or, normally, top companies of the two groups of companies which are coming together). The shareholder bodies remain separate but each body is given voting rights in the meetings of the other, so as to produce a single decision from the two votes; and the profits of the two companies are equalised. Such structures are complex to create (and to understand) but may have advantages over a merger, for example, where national susceptibilities are involved. There are not many such companies but a number of well-known multinational companies take this form (Unilever, BHP Billiton, Reed Elsevier) and others did so for a substantial period of time before moving to a more conventional single company (or group) structure (Shell, ABB).

REORGANISATION UNDER SS.110 AND 111 OF THE IA 1986

29–017 Under this type of reorganisation the company concerned resolves first to go into voluntary liquidation[113] and secondly to authorise by a special resolution the liquidator to transfer the whole or any part of the company's business or property to another company[114] or a limited liability partnership (LLP) in consideration of shares or like interests in that company (or membership in the LLP) for distribution among the members of the liquidating company. This procedure affords a relatively simple method of reconstructing a single company or of effecting a merger of its undertaking into that of another. It is often used as a tax-efficient way of effecting a demerger or division of a business.

Use of this method has the advantage, over a scheme, that confirmation by the court is not required,[115] and the advantage over a takeover that all the shareholders of the company are bound by the decision. But what it can achieve is somewhat limited. Creditors of the transferor will be entitled to prove in its liquidation and the liquidator must ensure that their proved claims are met and cannot rely upon an indemnity given by the acquiring company.[116] A high level of member agreement on the use of the sections is also desirable. This is because s.111 provides that, in the case of a members' voluntary winding-up, any member of the company who did not vote in favour of the special resolution may, within

[113] Under former versions of these provisions it had to be a *members'* voluntary liquidation, i.e. one in which the directors have made a "declaration of solvency" declaring that all the company's debts will be paid in full within 12 months. It can now be employed also in a creditors' voluntary liquidation so long as it is sanctioned by the court or the liquidation committee (IA 1986 s.110(3)) but that sanction is unlikely to be given unless all creditors are paid in full. On the two types of voluntary liquidation see paras 33–013 onwards.

[114] Whether or not the latter is a company within the meaning of the CA 2006 (IA s.110(1)) so that it could be a company registered in another jurisdiction.

[115] Though the court's sanction may be needed if the company is to be wound up in a creditors' winding-up.

[116] *Pulsford v Devenish* [1903] 2 Ch. 625 Ch D. On the other hand, the creditors will not be able to follow the assets transferred to the transferee company: *Re City & County Investment Co* (1879) 13 Ch. D. 475 CA.

seven days of its passing, serve a notice on the liquidator requiring the liquidator either to refrain from carrying the resolution into effect or to purchase the member's shares at a price to be determined either by agreement or by arbitration.[117] It is normally essential if advantage is to be taken of stamp duty concessions that the membership of the old company and the new should be very largely the same. If a number of the members elect to be bought out, there is a grave risk that the reorganisation will have to be abandoned as prohibitively expensive.

The CLR found the IA 1986 procedure to be a popular method for reconstructing private or family-controlled companies or groups and also for reconstructing investment trust companies.[118] It therefore recommended its retention with, however, the modernisation of the arbitration procedure which operates when a member exercises the appraisal right and a valuation of the member's interest cannot be agreed. The procedure under the current law is antiquated, invoking as it does the arbitration provisions of the Companies Clauses Consolidation Act 1845 or its Scottish equivalent,[119] doubtfully in compliance with the Human Rights Act and unclear about the basis upon which the member's interest should be valued. The CLR proposed that the valuation should be based on the dissentient's proportionate share of the consideration offered by the transferee for the transferor's business.[120] However, these provisions being in the IA 1986, they were not touched by the CA 2006. **29–018**

CONCLUSION

We remarked at the beginning of this chapter that the CA 2006 does not contain a statutory merger procedure of the type typically found in other jurisdictions. For purely domestic mergers, however, the scheme of arrangement is available for this purpose, but that procedure is available also to achieve a number of other objectives which have nothing to do with mergers of two or more companies. Indeed, since the scheme procedure, although available, is rarely used to achieve a true merger, it would be odd to use the term statutory merger procedure to refer to the scheme of arrangement. Just to confuse things further, the alternative to the merger—the takeover bid—can be, and increasingly is, carried out by means of a scheme. The scheme of arrangement is thus an immensely flexible instrument. However, because it is as much an instrument of insolvency law as of corporate law and because it elides what is regarded in other jurisdictions as the fundamental difference between a takeover bid and a merger, the scheme of arrangement has a rather uncertain image. There can be almost as many types of schemes of arrangement as there are inventive corporate and insolvency lawyers, **29–019**

[117] This is an example, rare under UK law (but more widely used in some other common law jurisdictions), of protecting dissenting members by granting them "appraisal rights". The courts will not permit the company to deprive members of their appraisal rights under the section by purporting to act under powers in its articles to sell its undertaking in exchange for securities of another company to be distributed *in specie*: *Bisgood v Henderson's Transvaal Estates* [1908] 1 Ch. 743 CA.

[118] Completing, para.11.13.

[119] Clauses Consolidation Act 1845 s.111(4).

[120] Final Report I, para.13.13.

which indicates both the significance of the scheme procedure and the impossibility of identifying such a thing as a typical scheme of arrangement.

CHAPTER 30

MARKET ABUSE

INTRODUCTION

With these topics we reach the margins of company law. Market abuse can occur in all markets and the relevant rules apply equally widely. We are concerned in this work, however, only with abuse in the markets for company securities (shares and bonds) and their derivatives. Our analysis will be so confined. 30–001

Market abuse is conventionally regarded, at least within the EU, as covering two rather different activities: insider dealing and market manipulation. Insider dealing (or trading)[1] occurs when a person in possession of price-sensitive but non-public information about a company buys or sells securities in that company and so obtains better terms in the transaction than would have been the case had the counterparty been aware of the information in question. In that way, the insider can either make a profit or avoid a loss, depending on whether the information, once public, will drive the price of the security up or down.[2] The issue is at the margins of company law because the insider dealer does not have to be an insider of the company, for example a director, though he or she very often

[1] The Criminal Justice Act 1993 Pt V and the Market Abuse Regulation (Regulation 596/2014 [2014] OJ L173/1) (MAR) use the word "dealing".

[2] Clearly, the insider buys in the former case and sells in the latter.

is. A governmental official may know that the agency for which he or she works is about to issue an adverse report on a particular company which will affect the price of its shares and then trade in the company's shares before the report is published. Nor is it a requirement of UK law, as it is in some jurisdictions, that the insider trading should constitute a breach of a fiduciary duty owed to the company.

Market manipulation involves conduct which moves the price of the securities to a position which is different from that which the market would have set in the absence of the conduct. By contrast, insider dealing may have no discernible impact on the price of the security, if it takes place in volumes which are very small in comparison with the overall levels of trading in the security. Indeed, the dealer will want to avoid such an impact, if possible, since it will deprive the trader of part of the expected gain and may even give the game away to the enforcement authorities. Penalising market manipulation involves drawing a distinction between legitimate and illegitimate behaviour within markets. If a company announces a bid for another company at a price above the prevailing market price for the shares, that announcement will move the price in an upward direction, but such behaviour is not only regarded as legitimate, it may also be required by takeover rules (as we saw in Ch.28). On the other hand, if I move the market price by making statements which I know to be false, that will be regarded as illegitimate behaviour. In a very early example of market manipulation, from the beginning of the nineteenth century, the fraudsters pretended to be soldiers returning from France with news of the defeat of Napoleon (before this event actually came to pass some time later). The false rumours which they spread caused the price of British government bonds to rise, thus enabling the accused to dispose of their holdings of those bonds at a profit.[3] However, as we shall see below, distinguishing legitimate from illegitimate behaviour in more marginal cases is not easy.

In the case of manipulation it is clear that market participants may suffer loss as a result of the behaviour. They will have acquired or disposed of shares on the basis of an artificial price and their loss will be revealed or incurred when the truth emerges.[4] Equally, the allocative efficiency of the market may suffer. Investors use market prices to determine how to target their resources and so manipulated prices may produce a misallocation of those resources. In the case of insider dealing the harm to the market and its participants is less clear. The insider dealing may not move the share price very much, if at all, and, in so far is it does, it moves the price towards, not away from, its "true" value (i.e. towards the value it will have when the full information is eventually publicly disclosed). Since insider dealing can be avoided by not trading and in public markets many of the other market participants would have traded, whether or not the insider traded,

---

[3] *R. v De Berenger* (1814) 3 M. & S. 67 KB. This was long before there was specific legislation on market manipulation but the defendants were convicted of the common law offence of fraud. The case was also an example of manipulation in the government bond, rather than the corporate securities, market.

[4] Depending on whether they were sellers or buyers. Those who buy at an artificially high price and sell before the truth emerges may suffer no loss but the loss is transferred to those holding the securities at the moment of truth.

the individual harm caused by the dealing is difficult to identify.[5] For this reason, rules prohibiting insider dealing as such are supplemented by rules requiring inside information to be disclosed to the market, as we saw in Ch.27.[6] Such disclosure rules aid allocative efficiency by putting more information into the market, as well as reducing the opportunities for insider trading. Non-disclosure may cause loss to market participants, as we also saw in Ch.27.[7] Since insider trading inevitably involves non-disclosure of the information traded on, it may seem possible to identify the harm caused by insider trading on this basis. However, it is often the case that the duty to disclose is not carried by the trader, but is allocated elsewhere (for example, to the issuer), so that the problem of identifying the harm caused by the dealing remains.

When formulating insider dealing rules, it is crucial to distinguish between information which the insider cannot use privately and information which can be used privately. This is not an easy task. It cannot be said, though it often is, that the aim of the insider dealing rules is to put all market participants in possession of the same information. If equality of information did prevail, there would be no incentive for analysts (and others) to seek out information about companies which is not known to the market in general. Analysts fulfil an important function in keeping the market informationally efficient because they provide information to the market after, or as, they trade on the information for their profit.[8] If they had to disclose the information before trading, their incentive to acquire it in the first place would disappear. As with market manipulation, it can be argued that the key objective is to distinguish legitimate from illegitimate means of acquiring information which is not generally known to the market. Only information acquired by illegitimate means should count as "inside" information. So, for example, an analyst who carefully pieces together public but not easily accessible information to arrive at new facts about the company should not be classified as a holder of inside information. On the other hand, a director, who routinely acquires information about the company before the market does because of his or her position in the company, has no socially valuable claim to be allowed to trade on the basis of that information. 30–002

The above arguments provide reasons why securities market authorities would wish to control market abuse of both types. But they do not tie the regulation very closely to the objectives of corporate law. It is possible to make this connection by focusing on the interests of the company (the issuer) in having effective regulation in place. If insider dealing is rife in the market, the non-insider will know that the market prices will systematically fail to reflect all the available information about the company and will do so in a way which is unfavourable to the outsiders. In the absence of regulation, this will be an inherent risk of holding shares in companies and outsiders will build this risk into their investment decisions, by lowering the price they are prepared to pay for companies' shares. This in turn will increase companies' cost of capital because they will be able to 30–003

[5] The analysis might be different in face-to-face transactions but in fact the market abuse rules apply only to securities which are publicly traded.

[6] See para.27–005.

[7] See paras 27–25 onwards.

[8] The very act of trading will reveal some information to the market about the analysts' position.

issues shares on less favourable terms than if investors could be assured that there was no or little insider trading in the market. Thus, companies have an interest in effective insider dealing legislation or regulation.[9]

The same general argument can be made in relation to market manipulation. If extensive, such behaviour will systematically produce prices which are unfavourable to outsiders, thus again causing them to re-assess the riskiness of corporate securities as a class.

30–004 The law on market abuse has developed rapidly over the past 40 years. The first sanctions against insider dealing were criminal and were introduced by the CA 1980. Those sanctions are now in Pt V of the Criminal Justice Act 1993. Market manipulation was criminalised (beyond the common law) a little later in the Financial Services Act 1986. The present provisions are in Pt 7 of the Financial Services Act 2012. The Financial Services and Markets Act 2000 added administrative sanctions against market abuse (of both types) and widened the definitions of the behaviour which was open to sanction. Enforcement of both the administrative penalties and the criminal law lies in the hands of the Financial Conduct Authority ("FCA"), previously the Financial Services Authority (FSA).

Market manipulation is an area where EU law has played an important role, except in relation to the criminal law rules on market manipulation. Initially, the EU operated via Directives which required transposition into domestic law by the domestic legislator. After the financial crisis, in the name of greater uniformity, the EU adopted a Market Abuse Regulation (MAR),[10] most of whose provisions did not require transposition.[11] Despite the UK's exit from the EU, MAR remains in force as retained EU law, as is the delegated legislation made by the Commission under powers conferred by MAR.[12] However, in the case of the UK, the EU rules tended to lag behind the reforms made at domestic level, so that their impact on the rules applicable to the UK markets was also limited. Even the extensions contained in the MAR related primarily to markets other than the markets in corporate securities.

We analyse first the rules on insider dealing and then those on market manipulation.

[9] See H. Schmidt, "Insider Dealing and Economic Theory" in K.J. Hopt and E. Wymeersch (eds), *European Insider Dealing* (Butterworths, 1991).

[10] See fn.1. MAR came into force, for the most part, as from July 2016.

[11] The area of enforcement and sanctions is the most important one where Member State transformation is required, because there the Regulation is formulated as a direction to the Member States to introduce specified powers.

[12] As amended by the Market Abuse (Amendment) (EU Exit) Regulations 2019 (SI 2019/310), which do not embody fundamental policy changes. The Financial Services Act 2021 makes some minor changes to MAR. For the future the Commission's law-making powers are transferred to the relevant UK authorities.

APPROACHES TO REGULATING INSIDER DEALING

Disclosure

A number of approaches to the regulation of insider dealing are to be found in the current law. Mandatory disclosure has long been used, but disclosure may be used to control insider dealing in a number of different ways. For example, as we saw in Ch.27, directors, as potential insider dealers, may be required to disclose dealings in their company's securities on the theory that, if they know that their dealings will be public knowledge, they will be less likely to trade on the basis of inside information.[13] Indeed, this is the oldest anti-insider dealing technique, having been introduced upon the recommendation of the Cohen Committee of 1945.[14] **30–005**

Alternatively, or in addition, the disclosure rules may aim at those who have the inside information and require them to disclose it, whether or not they are likely to trade on the basis of it. The point here is that putting the information into the public domain reduces the opportunities of others to engage in insider dealing. This, too, we have discussed above in the shape of the obligation laid upon issuers to disclose inside information promptly to the market.[15] Even the obligation to disclose the beneficial ownership of shares at the 3% level and above[16] may constitute a disclosure obligation of this type, for it shows who is accumulating a stake in a company, perhaps preparatory to a bid.[17]

Prohibiting trading

At the other end of the spectrum, the law could ban trading by potential insiders, irrespective of whether they are in possession of inside information or not. This is a blunt instrument, since it deprives those without inside information of trading opportunities. However, this approach is used in a targeted way in relation to particular "high risk" groups. The clearest example of this strategy was the requirement of the *Model Code* that directors, subject to exceptions, should not deal in securities of the company during the "closed period", i.e. within a period of two months preceding the preliminary announcement of the company's annual results and similar limitations were imposed in relation to the announcement of the half-yearly and quarterly[18] reports. In addition, clearance to deal at any time had to be obtained in advance from the chairman of the board, the CEO or the company secretary, as appropriate.[19] Compliance with the Code was not required **30–006**

---

[13] See paras 27–007 onwards.

[14] *Report of the Company Law Committee* (1945), Cmnd.6659, paras 86–87.

[15] See paras 27–005 onwards.

[16] See paras 27–013 onwards.

[17] Though note that for the prospective bidder itself to buy shares on the basis of its knowledge that it is going to launch a bid is not regarded as insider trading (see para.30–028), but it would be for a person in the know to do so for his or her own account.

[18] Which are, of course, no longer mandatory. See para.27–003.

[19] Nor might the company or any other company in the group trade in its securities at a time when the director was prohibited from trading, unless this was done in the ordinary course of securities dealing or at the behest of a third party: LR 9.2.7.

by legislation but was one of the continuing obligations imposed upon companies with a premium listing by the Listing Rules.[20] Such companies were required to ensure that those discharging managerial responsibilities complied with the Code or such stronger requirements as the company might impose.

The notion of a prohibition on trading during a closed period preceding the company's required regular reports was taken up in MAR, though with a lesser closed period of 30 days,[21] and the Model Code provisions were removed from the Listing Rules. The MAR prohibition now applies to all companies traded on the Main Market, whether with a premium listing or not, and to companies traded on AIM.[22] MAR covers "persons discharging managerial responsibilities" (PDMRs) as well as directors[23]; extends to trading on the account of a third party as well as to own account trading; and brings in trading in derivatives and other financial instruments as well as directly in the company's securities.[24] The issuer may allow trading in this period in "exceptional circumstances, such as severe financial difficulty" and certain other limited cases.[25] A Commission Regulation[26] adds some flesh to the bare bones of the MAR exception. The exceptional circumstances must be "extremely urgent, unforeseen and compelling" and outside the control of the PDMR, the manager must be able to explain why the transaction cannot be carried out at a later time and the PDMR must obtain the permission of the issuer, which will review the request against the above criteria, with some guidance being given as to the indicators the issuer should look for when assessing urgency.

The removal of the Model Code left two areas where the Model Code applied more widely than MAR. First, it applied to preliminary announcements of annual results, which are not required, and so fall outside MAR, but are market practice in the UK and are in effect the market moving event rather than the later full publication. Secondly, outside the "exceptional circumstances" MAR has no equivalent to the clearance rules which applied whenever a director proposed to deal (not just during the closed period). Of course, it is possible for a premium listed company to adopt such procedures as an internal matter, provided they do not conflict with, but rather go beyond, the requirements of MAR.

---

20 LR 9.2.8. The code itself was appended to Ch.9. On listing and premium listing see para.25–006.

21 MAR art.19(11).

22 MAR art.2(1).

23 See para.27–008 for the meaning of this term. Unlike the disclosure requirement, the prohibition does not extend to persons "closely associated" with PDMR.

24 MAR art.19(4).

25 MAR art.19(5).

26 Regulation 2016/522 as regards an exemption for certain third countries public bodies and central banks, the indicators of market manipulation, the disclosure thresholds, the competent authority for notifications of delays, the permission for trading during closed periods and types of notifiable managers' transactions [2016] OJ L88/1 arts 7–9. This Regulation continues in force as retained EU law but the power to make regulations in the future is transferred to the Treasury. Apart from "exceptional circumstances" the other cases relate to employee share schemes and certain other situations where the PDMR either does not have control of the trading or the trading is formal only (e.g. moving assets from one account to another without a price change).

Relying on the general law

A third approach is to not to legislate specifically for insider dealing but to rely instead on established doctrines of the common law to deal with it. Company law offers its fiduciary duties for this purpose, and more general doctrines of the common law may also have a role. For one reason or another, however, these doctrines fail to capture the problem of insider dealing comprehensively. Yet they need to be borne in mind because they offer civil remedies under the control of private parties, whereas, as we shall see, the specific insider dealing rules rely wholly on criminal or regulatory sanctions which are, in effect, under the control of the FCA. **30–007**

Directors' fiduciary duties

As pointed out in Ch.10,[27] if directors make use of information acquired as director for their personal advantage they may breach their fiduciary duties to the company and be liable to account to it for any profits they have made. A great advantage of the civil suit brought by the company for breach of fiduciary duty is that it does not have to show that it has suffered loss as a result of the insider dealing, simply that the insider fiduciaries have made a profit in breach of the rules on conflicts of interest.[28] In practice, however, it is unlikely that the company will call directors to account unless and until there is a change of control. If only one director has committed the breach, the others may cause the company to take action against him but most public companies are likely to avoid damaging publicity by persuading the errant director to resign "for personal reasons" and to go quietly. **30–008**

It is also possible that, for example, in relation to a takeover of a small company,[29] the directors may place themselves in the position of acting as agents negotiating on behalf of the individual shareholders and thereby, despite *Percival v Wright*,[30] owe fiduciary duties to the shareholders. If so, they would breach those duties if they persuaded any shareholder to sell at a price which they knew (and the shareholders did not) was materially lower than their likely value on the basis of full disclosure of the information the directors hold about the company. It is, however, highly unlikely that the directors of a listed company would create such a relationship. If they did engage in insider dealing, it would be by dealing impersonally on a stock exchange so that no fiduciary relationship was created.

Hence, the general equitable principle is, on its own, rarely an effective deterrent. Moreover, the law relating to directors' fiduciary duties is simply incapable of applying to the full range of insiders and, except in the rare case where the decision in *Percival v Wright* can be overcome, it has the demerit of

---

[27] See paras 10–081 onwards.

[28] The leading case is the decision of the New York Court of Appeals in *Diamond v Oreamuno* (1969) 248 N.E. 2d 910. The precise situation has not yet arisen in an English court.

[29] For an early example of the directors constituting themselves agents in this way, see *Allen v Hyatt* (1914) 30 T.L.R. 444 PC. Or the court may find a fiduciary relationship in a small company even in the absence of agency: see para.10–006.

[30] *Percival v Wright* [1902] 2 Ch. 421 Ch D: see para.10–006.

concentrating on the relationship between the director and the company rather than on the relationship between the director and other traders in the market.

Breach of confidence

30–009 Somewhat similar criticisms can be made of the second source of equitable obligation which is relevant here, namely that imposed by the receipt of information from another person where the recipient knows or ought to have known that the information was imparted in confidence. However, the range of persons potentially covered by this obligation is much wider that those covered by the fiduciary duties applying to directors of companies. It will extend to the professional advisers of companies who, say, are involved in preparing a takeover bid which the company is contemplating, and to the employees of such advisers, since no contractual link between the confider and the confidant is necessary to support this fiduciary obligation. Indeed, the obligation extends to anyone who receives information knowing that they are receiving it in breach of a duty of confidentiality imposed upon the person communicating the information.[31]

If the duty attaches, the holder of the information may not use it (for example, by trading in securities) or disclose it (for example, to another person so that that person may trade)[32] without the permission of the confider. Breach of the duty gives rise to a liability to account for the profits made, potentially the most useful civil sanction in the case of insider dealing on securities markets. The confidant may have to pay damages to the confider but it is far from clear that the confider actually suffers any loss if the confidant uses the information for the purposes of insider dealing and does not, in so doing, communicate the information to other persons. Moreover, the cause of action again lies in the hands of the person to whom the fiduciary obligation is owed (i.e. the confider), not in the hands of the person with whom the confidant has dealt in the securities transaction or other participants in the market at the time. This might not matter if in fact the duty of confidence was routinely used to deprive insiders of their profits,[33] but, although much inside information must also be received in confidence and although the law in this area has achieved much greater prominence in recent years than it had previously, it does not seem to be so used. This may be because the difficulties of detection and proof, which abound in this area, operate so as to deprive confiders of the incentive to use their private law rights to secure the transfer of insider dealing profits from the insiders to themselves.

Misrepresentation

30–010 When in 1989 the Government was considering its response to the EU's first Directive on insider dealing, it decided to continue its policy of not providing

[31] For both these propositions see *Schering Chemicals Ltd v Falkman Ltd* [1982] Q.B. 1 CA (Civ Div).

[32] And by virtue of the *Schering Chemicals* case (see previous note) the recipient of the information (the "tippee") would also be in breach of duty by using or disclosing the information if aware that it had been communicated in breach of the duty of confidence imposed on the tipper.

[33] That is, one might be more concerned with depriving the insiders of their profits than with working out who precisely are the best persons to receive them.

civil sanctions under the insider dealing legislation partly on the grounds that these worked satisfactorily only in face-to-face transactions and that the general law already provided remedies in that situation.[34] Apart from the insider's liability to the company, discussed above, the Government referred to liability for fraudulent misrepresentation. The suggestion that misrepresentation-based liability, whether for fraudulent, negligent or innocent misrepresentation, does not work in transactions over public markets is undoubtedly correct, since traders simply accept or reject the price the market presents. Even in face-to-face transactions, however, misrepresentation liability faces a formidable obstacle as a solution to insider trading. This is the need to demonstrate either that a false statement has been made or that there was a duty to disclose the inside information to the other party to the transaction. As to the former, the insider can avoid liability by not making any statements to the other party relating to the area of knowledge in which he holds the inside information. Liability might arise if the other party to the transaction has the good luck or the right instinct to extract a false statement from the insider by probing questions, but liability on this basis is unlikely to be widespread.

As to non-disclosure, the current legislation does not adopt the technique contained in some earlier proposals for insider dealing legislation: requiring insiders in face-to-face transactions to disclose the information before dealing.[35] Consequently, the potential plaintiff has to fall back on the common law, which imposes a duty of disclosure in only limited circumstances. The most relevant situation would be where the insider was in a fiduciary or other special relationship with the other party, but, as we have seen above, even as between directors and shareholders, the current law recognises such a relationship only exceptionally, whilst many insiders and their counterparties are simply not in the relationship of director and shareholder at all.[36] There is also little evidence at present of a willingness on the part of the courts to expand the categories of fiduciary or other special relationships in this area[37] or to bring securities contracts within the category of contracts uberrimae fidei.

Prohibiting insider dealing

The above analysis leaves only the approach of prohibiting dealing by those who actually possess inside information. This can be said to constitute the core of the current law. However, the prohibition can take two forms. The first involves the criminalisation of insider dealing and certain associated acts. The original criminal legislation was contained in Pt V of the CA 1980 and was later consolidated in the Company Securities (Insider Dealing) Act 1985. As a result of the adoption by the European Community of the Insider Dealing Directive in **30–011**

[34] DTI, *The Law on Insider Dealing: A Consultative Document* (1989), paras 2.11–2.12.

[35] Companies Bill, H.C. Bill 2 (Session 1978/79), cl.59. As we saw in Ch.27 those with management responsibilities in companies traded on regulated markets are obliged to disclose inside information, but this requirement is likely to pick up few face-to-face transactions.

[36] For example, where the director is selling shares in the company to a person who is not presently a shareholder or where the insider is not a corporate fiduciary at all.

[37] See *Chase Manhattan Equities Ltd v Goodman* [1991] B.C.C. 308 Ch D, where the judge passed up the opportunity to use the FCA's *Model Code* as the basis of an extended duty of disclosure.

1989,[38] some amendment of the British law became necessary, and the Department of Trade and Industry also took the opportunity to simplify the 1985 Act in some respects. However, Pt V of the Criminal Justice Act 1993, the current law, is still recognisably in the mould established by the CA 1980, though it contains some interesting new features and has abandoned some old obfuscations.[39] Experience showed, however, that it was difficult to secure convictions for this offence, partly because of difficulties of detection but partly also because of the standards of evidence and proof required in criminal trials. The legislature responded in the market abuse provisions of the FSMA 2000, which allow the FCA to impose administrative penalties upon those who engage in this activity, which is defined so as to include insider dealing. Thus, the second main form of the prohibition on trading is the deployment of regulatory sanctions against insider dealing, which is the area where EU law has been most influential.

THE CRIMINAL JUSTICE ACT 1993 PT V

30–012 Section 52(1) of the CJA 1993 defines the central offence which it creates in the following terms: "An individual who has information as an insider is guilty of insider dealing if, in the circumstances mentioned in subs.(3), he deals in securities that are price-affected securities in relation to the information". This definition, however, conceals as much as it reveals, for it is much elaborated and qualified in the remaining sections of the Part. The following sections elucidate the central elements of the offences created and of the defences available.

Regulating markets

30–013 Pursuing the reference to s.52(3), contained in the above definition, reveals at once that the CJA 1993 does not aim to control all dealings in shares where one of the parties has price-sensitive, non-public information in his or her possession. On the contrary, it is only when the dealing takes place "on a regulated market" and in certain analogous situations does the Act bite. If, say, the transaction occurs face-to-face between private persons, then the situation is outside the control of this particular legislation. The Act leaves regulated markets to be identified by statutory instrument and that instrument includes any market established under the rules of the London Stock Exchange (thus including AIM).[40]

---

[38] Directive 89/592 coordinating regulations on insider dealing [1989] OJ L334/30. This Directive was replaced by Directive 2003/6 on insider dealing and market manipulation (market abuse) [2003] OJ L96/16 (the Market Abuse Directive) in 2003, but the Government took the view that the criminal law provisions of domestic law did not require amendment as a result, though the 2006 Directive had a substantial impact on the administrative sanction regime. The 2006 Directive was repealed by MAR.

[39] For an analysis of the changes see Davies, (1991) 11 O.J.L.S. 92.

[40] Insider Dealing (Securities and Regulated Markets) Order 1994 (SI 1994/187) art.10, as amended. Confusingly, the term "regulated market" in the CJA 1993 does not have the meaning attached to the term in the EU instruments: see para.25–008. In particular, trading on AIM does fall within the CJA (AIM being a market established under the rules of the LSE), even though AIM is not a regulated market for EU law purposes but a multi-lateral trading facility.

However, the legislation has always applied to certain deals not on regulated markets; these are the analogous situations. They are defined as those where the person with the inside information, when dealing, "relies on a professional intermediary or is himself acting as a professional intermediary".[41] Section 59 makes it clear that the profession in question must be that of acquiring or disposing of securities (for example, as a market maker)[42] or acting as an intermediary between persons who wish to deal (for example, as a broker),[43] and that a person does not fall within the definition if the activities of this type are merely incidental to some other activity or are merely occasional.

Despite this extension, which was in any event required by the 1989 Directive,[44] the main thrust of the legislation is the regulation of dealings on established markets, and the extension was designed to prevent the evasion of such regulation, which might occur if trading were driven off established markets into less efficient, informal arrangements. The concentration of the prohibition on regulated markets also makes it much easier to justify the restriction of the sanctions for breaches of the Act to the criminal law. In addition to the other difficulties which surround the creation of a coherent civil remedy in this area, the fact that the trading has occurred on a public exchange means that the identity of the counterparty to the transaction with the insider is a matter of chance. In any liquid stock many thousands of persons may be trading in the market in the same security and at the same time as the insider. To give a civil remedy to the person who happened to end up with the insider's shares and not to the others who dealt in the market at the same time in the security in question would be arbitrary, whilst to give a civil remedy to all relevant market participants might well be oppressive of the insider.[45] By confining the sanction to the criminal law, Parliament avoided the need to address these difficulties. Moreover, if the main argument against insider trading is that it undermines public confidence in the securities markets, the criminal law is capable of expressing the community's view of that public interest, provided it can be effectively enforced.[46] 30–014

Finally, in this section on the definition of markets a few words should be said about the international dimension of insider dealing. It is now extremely easy, technically, for a person in one country to deal in the shares of a company which are listed or otherwise open to trading in another country; or for a person to deal in shares of a company quoted on an exchange in his or her own country via instructions placed with a foreign intermediary. For the domestic legislator not to deal with this situation runs the risk that the domestic legislation will be circumvented wholesale. To apply the domestic sanctions irrespective of the

[41] CJA 1993 s.52(3).

[42] A firm which has undertaken to make a continuous two-way market in certain securities, so that, in relation to those securities, it will always be possible to buy from or sell to the market maker, though, of course, at a price established by the market maker.

[43] Following the "Big Bang" on the Stock Exchange in 1986 it is no longer required that market makers and brokers be entirely distinct functions, though equally it is not required that brokers make a continuous two-way market in any particular securities. Some broking firms act as market makers as well; others are only intermediaries.

[44] 1989 Directive art.2(3).

[45] In some cases it might not even be possible to identify the counterparty.

[46] See further para.30–030.

foreign element, on the other hand, is to run the risk of creating criminal law with an unacceptable extra-territorial reach. The latter risk is enlarged by the 1989 Directive's requirement that the Member States must prohibit insider dealing in transferable securities "admitted to a market of a Member State"[47] and not just those admitted to its own markets. In line with this requirement, the 1994 Order extends the application of the CJA 1993 to securities which are officially listed in or are admitted to dealing under the rules of any regulated market established within the European Economic Area.[48]

This clearly should not mean, however, that a French citizen dealing on the basis of inside information on the Paris *Bourse* or even on the Milan Exchange in the shares of a British company (or a company of any other nationality) is guilty of an offence under UK law. Consequently, s.62(1)[49] of the CJA 1993 lays down the requirement of a territorial connection with the UK before a criminal offence can be said to have been committed in the UK. This requires the dealer or the professional intermediary to have been within the UK at the time any act was done which forms part of the offence or the dealing to have taken place on a regulated market situated in the UK.[50] Consequently, our French citizen will commit a criminal offence in the UK only if the deal is transacted on a regulated market located in the UK,[51] unless the trader or the professional intermediary through whom the deal is transacted is in the UK at the time of the dealing.[52] This approach does not eliminate all potential of the insider dealing legislation for extra-territorial effect, but it does limit it to situations where there is some substantial connection between the offence and the UK.

Regulating individuals

30–015 A striking feature of the CJA 1993 is that it regulates insider dealing only by individuals. The Act does not use the more usual term "person" to express the scope of its prohibition, so that bodies corporate are not liable to prosecution under the Act. Corporate bodies were excluded, not because it was thought undesirable to make them criminally liable but because of the difficulties it was

[47] 1989 Directive art.5.

[48] See fn.40, arts 4 and 9 and Schedule.

[49] CJA 1993 s.62(2) provides that in the case of the offences of encouraging dealing or disclosing inside information (see para.30–025) either the encourager or discloser must be in the UK when he did the relevant act or the recipient of the encouragement or information must be.

[50] See para.30–013.

[51] If French law adopts the same territorial rules as the UK, the citizen would also commit a criminal offence under French law if he gave the instructions to deal from France. His liability in the UK would not depend, of course, upon the nationality of the company in whose shares on a UK regulated market the trading occurred.

[52] If the French citizen is in the UK at the relevant time, he will commit a criminal offence in the UK even if the trading occurs on a regulated market outside the UK but within the EEA. However, if the market is outside the EEA (say, New York or Tokyo) and involves no professional intermediary who is within the UK it would seem that the offence of dealing is not committed in the UK even if the instruction to deal is given by a person in the UK. This is because the dealing will not have taken place on a regulated market within s.52(3) and the 1994 Order and will not have involved a professional intermediary who is within the scope of s.62. However, the offence of encouraging dealing may have been committed, the encourager being in the UK even if the person encouraged is not. See fn.49.

thought would be faced by investment banks when one department of the bank had unpublished price-sensitive information about the securities of a client company and the dealing department had successfully been kept in ignorance of that information by a "Chinese Wall"[53] or otherwise. If someone in the dealing department entered into a trade, it was thought to be arguable that the bank as a single corporate body would have committed an offence, had the Act applied to corporate bodies, the act of one employee and the knowledge of the other being attributed to the bank. However, it should be noted that these arguments were not regarded as decisive by those who drafted the various versions of the administrative sanction regime. Their policy was to bring insider dealing, even by corporate bodies, within the scope of the regulatory prohibitions but then to deal expressly with the problem of attributed knowledge.[54]

In any event, it should be noted that an individual can be liable under the CJA 1993 even if the dealing in question is done by a company. Companies can act only through human agents, and, as we shall see below,[55] the Act's prohibition on dealing extends to procuring or encouraging dealing in securities. Thus, if the individuals who move the company to deal do so on the basis of unpublished price-sensitive information, they may well have committed the criminal offence of procuring or encouraging the company to deal, even if the company itself commits no offence in dealing. These extensions embrace encouraging and procuring "persons" to deal—though, of course, the encourager or procurer must be an individual.

Inside information

The definition of inside information is a core feature of the CJA 1993 and has always been controversial. The general principle stated in the preamble to the 1989 Directive was: investor confidence in security markets depends inter alia on "the assurance afforded to investors that they are placed on an equal footing and that they will be protected against the improper use of inside information". However, it is much easier to state this general principle than to cast it into precise legal restrictions. As we have noted, placing investors "on an equal footing" cannot mean that all those who deal on a market should have the same information.[56] The aim of the legislation is not to eliminate all informational advantages, but to proscribe those advantages whose use would be improper, often because their acquisition is not the result of skill or effort but of the mere fact of holding a particular position. This general issue will be seen to recur in relation to all four of the limbs of the statutory definition of "inside information". **30–016**

Section 56 defines inside information as information which:

[53] An arrangement designed to prevent information in one part of a firm from being available to individuals working elsewhere in the firm.

[54] See para.30–035.

[55] See para.30–025. Otherwise a person could avoid the prohibition on insider dealing simply by setting up a company to do the trading.

[56] See para.30–002.

(1) relates to particular securities or to a particular issuer of securities and not to securities generally or to issues of securities generally;
(2) is specific or precise;
(3) has not been made public; and
(4) if it were made public would be likely to have a significant effect on the price of any securities.

Particular securities or issuers

30–017 The first limb of the definition is the subject of a crucial clarification in s.60(4) that information shall be treated as relating to an issuer of securities "not only where it is about the company but also where it may affect the company's business prospects". This makes it clear that the definition of inside information includes information coming from outside the company, for example, that the Government intends to liberalise the industry in which the company previously had a monopoly, as well as information coming from within the company, for example, that the company is about to declare a substantially increased or decreased dividend or has won or lost a significant contract. This casts the net very wide, but it is difficult to see that any narrower formulation would have been appropriate.

Whatever the source of the information, it must relate to particular securities or a particular issuer[57] or particular issuers of securities and not to securities or issuers generally. So information relating to a particular company or sector of the economy is covered, but not information which applies in an undifferentiated way to the economy in general. This is not an entirely easy distinction; nor is its policy rationale self-evident. It would seem to mean that knowledge that the Government is, unexpectedly, to increase or decrease interest rates would fall within the definition in relation to bank shares (because interest rates are central to the bank's business of borrowing and lending money) but not in relation to the shares in all companies (where the implication of the rate rise is simply a less rapid future growth of the economy).

Specific or precise

30–018 The second limb of the definition restricts the scope of inside information further: the information must also be specific or precise.[58] The 1989 Directive required simply that the information be "precise",[59] but this was thought by Parliament to be possibly too restrictive, so the alternative of "specific" was added. The example was given of knowledge that a takeover bid was going to be made for a company, which would be specific information, but might not be regarded as precise if there was no knowledge of the price to be offered or the exact date on

[57] The Act uses the term "issuer" rather than "company" because the Act applies not only to securities issued by companies but also to government securities or even, though this is unlikely, securities issued by an individual: s.60(2).
[58] CJA 1993 s.56(1)(b).
[59] 1989 Directive art.1.

which the announcement of the bid would be made.[60] However, the crucial effect of this restriction is that it apparently relieves directors and senior managers of the company and analysts who have made a special study of the company from falling foul of the legislation simply because they have generalised informational advantages over other investors. Having a better sense of how well or badly the company is likely to respond to a particular publicly known development does not amount to the possession of precise or specific information.

Made public

The tension between the policy of encouraging communication between companies and the investment community and of stimulating analysts and other professionals to play an appropriate role in that process, on the one hand, and that of preventing selective disclosure of significant information to the detriment of investors who are not close to the market, on the other, is further revealed in s.58 of the CJA 1993, which deals with the issue of when information can be said to have been "made public". The Government initially proposed to leave the problem to be solved by the courts on a case-by-case basis, but came under pressure in Parliament to deal with the issue expressly. The pressure probably reflected the accurate perception that, with the broadening of the definition of "insider",[61] more weight would fall on the definition of "inside information" and especially this limb of the definition. Section 58 is not, however, a comprehensive attempt to deal with the issue. It stipulates four situations where the information shall be regarded as having been made public and five situations where the court may so regard it; otherwise, the court is free to arrive at its own judgment.[62] **30–019**

The most helpful statement in s.58 from the point of view of analysts is that "information is public if it is derived from information which has been made public".[63] It is clear that this provision was intended to protect analysts who derive insights into a company's prospects which are not shared by the market generally (so that the analyst is able to out-guess competitors) where those insights are derived from the intensive and intelligent study of information which has been made public. An analyst in this position can deal on the basis of the insights so derived without first disclosing to the market the process of reasoning which has led to the conclusions, even where the disclosure of the reasoning would have a significant impact on the price of the securities dealt in. This seems to be the case even where the analyst intends to and does publish the recommendations after the dealing, i.e. there is what is called "front running" of the research.[64]

---

[60] HC Debs,Standing Committee B (Session 1992–93), col.174 (10 June 1993). It seems that, on this argument, precise information will always be specific.

[61] See para.30–022.

[62] In the permissive cases the situation is, presumably, that the facts described in the subsections do not prevent the court from holding the information to have been made public, but whether the court in a particular prosecution will so hold will depend on the circumstances of the case as a whole.

[63] CJA 1993 s.58(2)(d).

[64] Query whether front-running a recommendation, not based upon any research but where its publication will have an impact on the price of the securities because of the reputation of the recommender, would be protected by s.58(2)(d). cf. *US v Carpenter* 91 F.2d 1024 (2d Cir. 1986). The

30–020 The utility of this subsection to the analyst and others is enhanced by the other provisions of s.58(2). Section 58(2)(c) comes close to providing an overarching test for whether information is "made public" by stating that this is so if the information "can readily be acquired" by those likely to deal in the relevant securities. In other words, the public here is not the public in general but the dealing public in relation to the securities concerned (which is obviously sensible) and, more controversially, the issue is not whether the information is known to that public but whether it is readily available to them. This is a more relaxed test than that applied under the previous legislation, which required knowledge of the information on the part of the public.[65] The former test in effect required those close to the market to wait until the information had been assimilated by the investment community before trading. Now it appears that trading is permitted as soon as the information can be readily acquired by investors, even though it has not in fact been acquired. In other words, a person who has advance knowledge of the information can react as soon as it can be "readily acquired" and reap a benefit in the period before the information is in fact fully absorbed by the market—though this is likely to be a very short period in an efficient market. This consequence of s.58(2)(c) is strengthened by the express provisions that publication in accordance with the rules of a regulated market or publication in records which by statute are available for public inspection mean that the information has been made public.[66]

However, the extent of the move away from actual public knowledge in the current legislation should not be exaggerated. The test laid down in s.58(2)(c) is not that information is public if it is available to the relevant segment of investors but whether it "can readily be acquired" by them. That information could be acquired by investors, if they took certain steps, is surely not enough in every case to meet the test of ready availability. One can foresee much dispute over what in addition is required to make information readily available. Section 58(3) helps with this issue to the extent of stating that certain features of the information do not necessarily prevent it from being brought within the category of information which "can be readily acquired". Thus, information is not to be excluded solely because it is published outside the UK, is communicated only on payment of a fee, can be acquired only by observation or the exercise of diligence or expertise, or is communicated only to a section of the public. However, in the context of particular cases, information falling within these categories may be excluded from the scope of "public information", for instance because the information is supplied for a (high) fee or is supplied to a very restricted number of persons. To this extent, the legislation has necessarily ended up adopting the Government's initial standpoint that much would have to depend upon case-by-case evaluation by the courts in the context of particular prosecutions.

---

trader might have a defence under para.2(1) of Sch.1 to the Act, but that would depend upon his having acted "reasonably": see para.30–028. Such conduct might in extreme cases even be a breach of Pt 7 of the FSA 2012. See para.30–029.

[65] Company Securities (Insider Dealing) Act 1985 s.10(b).

[66] CJA 1993 s.58(2)(a) and (b) respectively. The former would cover publication on a Regulatory News Service and the latter documents field at Companies House or the Patents Registry.

Impact on price

The final limb of the definition is the requirement that the information should be likely to have "a significant effect" on the price of the securities, if it were made public.[67] The law has chosen not to pursue those who will reap only trivial advantages from trading on inside information. At first sight, the test would seem to present the court (or jury) with an impossibly hypothetical test to apply. In fact, in most cases, by the time any prosecution is brought, the information in question will have become public,[68] and so the question will probably be answered by looking at what impact the information did in fact have on the market when it was published. However, it would seem permissible for an insider to argue in an appropriate case that the likely effect of the information being made public at the time of the trading was not significant, even if its actual disclosure had a bigger effect, because the surrounding circumstances had changed in the meantime. **30–021**

Insiders

We have already noted[69] the important restriction in the legislation that insiders must be individuals. Beyond that, it might be thought that nothing more needs to be said other than that an insider is an individual in possession of inside information. In other words, the definitional burden should fall on deciding what is inside information and the definition of insider should follow as a secondary consequence of this primary definition. The Government's consultative document on the proposed legislation[70] rejected this approach as likely to cause "damaging uncertainty in the markets, as individuals attempted to identify whether or not they were covered". This is not convincing. Either the definition of inside information is adequate or it ought to be reformed. If it is adequate, so that it can be applied effectively to those who are insiders under the CJA 1993, then it is not clear why it cannot be applied to all individuals, whether they meet the separate criteria for being insiders or not. If the definition of inside information is not adequate, it is not proper to apply it even to those who clearly are insiders under the legislation and it should be changed. In fact, the proposal that insiders should be defined as those in possession of inside information would to some extent reduce uncertainty, because the only question which would have to be asked is whether the individual was in possession of inside information and the additional question of whether the individual met the separate criteria for being classed as an insider would be irrelevant. **30–022**

However, the Government stuck to its guns whilst simplifying the criteria which had been used in the earlier legislation and, following the Directive, expanding the category of insiders quite considerably.[71] By virtue of s.57(2)(a)

---

67 CJA 1993 s.56(1)(d).

68 Insiders have little incentive to trade on the basis of inside information which will never become public or will do so only far into the future.

69 See para.30–015.

70 DTI, *The Law on Insider Dealing* (1989), para.2.24.

71 In particular, the requirement of "being connected with the company" was removed. See the Company Securities (Insider Dealing) Act 1985 s.9.

two categories of insider are defined. The first are those who obtain inside information "through being" a director, employee or shareholder of an issuer of securities.[72] Although it is not entirely clear, it seems that the "through being" test is simply a "but for" test. If a junior employee happens to see inside information in the non-public part of the employer's premises, he or she would be within the category of insider, even if the duties of the employment do not involve acquisition of that information. On the other hand, coming across such information in a social context would not make the junior employee an insider, even though the information related to the worker's employer. In other words, there must be a causal link between the employment and the acquisition of the information, but not in the sense that the information must be acquired in the course of the employee's employment (though the latter remains a possible interpretation of the subsection). It may be thought that shareholders, who were excluded from the definition of insider in the previous legislation, are unlikely to obtain access to inside information "though being" shareholders, but this is in fact a likely situation in relation to large institutional or controlling shareholders, which may, either as a general practice or in specific circumstances, keep in close touch with at least the management of the companies in which they are invested.

The second category of insider identified by s.57(2)(a) is the individual with inside information "through having access to the information by virtue of his employment, office or profession", whether or not the employment, etc. relationship is with an issuer. Thus, an insider in this second category may be, or be employed by, a professional adviser to the company[73]; an investment analyst, who has no business link with an issuer; a civil servant or an employee of a regulatory body; or a journalist or other employee of a media or printing company.[74] Again, the question arises about the exact meaning of the phrase "by virtue of": is it again a simple "but for" test or does it mean "in the course of" (perhaps a slightly stronger suggestion in this second situation)? Even if the latter interpretation is ultimately adopted, this second category would be wide enough to embrace partners and employees of an investment bank or solicitors' firm retained to advise an issuer on a particular matter, employees of regulatory bodies who are concerned with the issuer's affairs, journalists researching an issuer for a story and even employees of a printing firm involved in the production of documents for a planned but unannounced takeover bid.[75] If the broader "but for" test is adopted, then employees of these organisations, not employed on the tasks mentioned, but who serendipitously come across the information in the workplace, would be covered too.[76]

---

72 The relationship does not have to exist with the issuer of the securities which are dealt in. So a director of Company A who is privy to his or her company's plans to launch a bid for Company B is an insider in relation to the securities of Company B (as well as those of A).

73 In the course of their professional duties such individuals may well obtain inside information in relation to a company other than the instructing company. Thus, employees of an investment bank preparing a takeover bid would become insiders in relation to both the proposed bidder (i.e. the bank's client) and in relation to the target company.

74 Of course, the journalist's employer may be a listed company, in which case he would seem to fall within the first category as well.

75 cf. *Chiarella v US* 445 U.S. 222 (1980).

76 An even more restrictive test would be in the course of an employment which is likely to provide access to inside information. Such a test would exclude the famous, if unlikely, example of the cleaner

Recipients from insiders

In practice, the need to define the exact scope of the second category of insider is reduced by the third category, created by s.57(2)(b). In the US persons in this third category are distinguished from primary insiders by the use of the graphic expression "tippee",[77] but the British legislation lumps them in with primary insiders. This third category consists of those who have inside information "the direct or indirect source of" which is a person falling within either of the first two categories. Thus, subject to the point about mens rea made in the next paragraph, the employee of an investment bank who overhears a colleague talking about a takeover bid on which the latter is engaged would be in all probability an insider in the third category if he or she does not fall within the second category. This example also makes it clear that the more striking American terminology might be somewhat misleading. It does not matter whether the primary insider has consciously communicated the information to the secondary insider (i.e. "tipped the latter off"). Provided the latter has acquired the information from an inside source, even indirectly, he or she will fall within the scope of the CJA 1993; indeed, as in the example, the "tipper" may be entirely unaware that inside information has been communicated to anyone else.[78] Furthermore, a certain type of tipping will not in fact make the tippee liable for dealing. If the insider within the first two categories encourages another person to deal without communicating to that other person any inside information, the latter can deal without being exposed to liability under the Act—though the tipper would be liable for encouraging the dealing.[79] **30–023**

Mental element

Finally, the requirement of having information "as an insider" in s.57 was used by the drafters to put a crucial limitation on the scope of the offence created by the CJA 1993. This is the required mental element, a not surprising precondition for criminal liability, but nevertheless one which has made enforcement of the legislation often difficult.[80] The requirement in this regard is a two-fold one: the accused must be proved to have known that the information in question was inside information and that the information came from "an inside source", i.e. accused knew the information was obtained in one of the three ways discussed above. The requirement of knowledge is likely to be difficult to meet, especially **30–024**

---

who finds inside information in a waste-paper basket. However, there seems to be no warrant in the Act or the Directive for such a restrictive test, which would come close to reinstating the clearly discarded test of s.9(b) of the 1985 Act.

[77] The guru of securities regulation, Professor Louis Loss of Harvard Law School, first used this expression and the *Oxford English Dictionary* has credited him with this fact.

[78] Moreover, since it is enough that the individual in the third category "has" the information from a source falling within the first or second categories, it does not matter either whether the "tippee" has solicited the information. Inadvertent acquisition of inside information is covered. This was a point of controversy under the previous legislation until cleared up by the House of Lords, in favour of liability. See *Attorney-General's Reference (No.1 of 1988)* (1989) 5 B.C.C. 625 HL.

[79] See para.30–025.

[80] See para.30–030.

in the case of recipients of information from insiders via a chain of communications. Proving that a "sub-tippee" or even a "sub-sub-tippee" knew that the ultimate source of the information was a primary insider could be fraught with problems.

Prohibited acts

30–025 What is an individual with inside information and who is an insider and meets the required mental element prohibited from doing? There are four prohibitions and, before describing them, it should be pointed out that it is not necessary that the accused should still be an insider at the time he or she does the prohibited act. Once inside information has been acquired by an insider, the prohibitions apply even though the accused resigns the directorship or employment through which he obtained the information.[81] On the other hand, if by the time of the dealing the information enters the public domain, the prohibitions of the Act will cease to apply. It should also be noted that the prohibitions apply not only to the company's securities but also to futures contracts[82] and contracts for differences,[83] where the reference security is a security issued by the company.[84]

First, and most obviously, there must be no *dealing* in the relevant securities.[85] The relevant securities are those which are "price-affected", i.e. those upon the price of which the inside information would be likely to have a significant effect, if made public.[86] Dealing is defined as acquiring or disposing of securities.[87] Thus, a person who refrains from dealing or cancels a deal on the basis of inside information is not covered by the legislation.[88] In principle, it is difficult to defend this exclusion since the loss of public confidence in the market will be as strong as in a case of dealing, if news of the non-dealing emerges. The exclusion was presumably a pragmatic decision based on the severe evidential problems which would face the prosecution in such a case. The dealing prohibition is broken quite simply by dealing; the CJA 1993 does not require the prosecution to go further and prove that the dealing was motivated by the inside information,

[81] This is the significance of prohibiting acts by a person who has information "as an insider", which s.57 makes clear refers to the situation at the time of the acquisition of the information, rather than the simpler formulation of prohibiting acts *by* an insider, which might well refer to the accused's status at the time of the prohibited acts.

[82] A contract of the sale or purchase of securities at a future date.

[83] A contract not involving an agreement to transfer an interest in the underlying securities but simply to pay the difference between the price of the securities on a particular date and their price on a future date. For discussion of the problems which CfDs have created in relation to disclosure obligations, see paras 27–016 and 28–044.

[84] Certain types of security are omitted, perhaps most notably the purchase or sale of units in unit trusts, though shares in companies which operate investment trusts are within the scope of the Act. Presumably, the former were excluded on the pragmatic grounds that it was unlikely that a person would have inside information which would significantly affect the price of the units, which normally reflect widely diversified underlying investments, though query whether this is always the case with more focused unit trusts. See para.27–013. In any event, the Treasury has power to amend the list of securities contained in Sch.2 (see s.54(2)).

[85] CJA 1993 s.52(1).

[86] See s.56(2) and para.30–021.

[87] CJA 1993 s.55.

[88] Ditto an individual who discovers good news and decides not to dispose of its shares.

though the accused may be able to put forward the defence that he would have done what he did even if he had not had the information.[89] The Act covers dealing as an agent (not only as a principal) even if the profit from the dealing is thereby made by someone else, for one can never be sure that the profit made by the third party will not filter back to the trader in some form or other. And it covers agreeing to acquire or dispose of securities as well as their actual acquisition or disposal, and entering into or ending a contract which creates the security[90] as well as contracting to acquire or dispose of a pre-existing security.

Secondly, the insider is prohibited from *procuring*, directly or indirectly, the acquisition or disposal of securities by any other person. Technically, this result is achieved by bringing procuring within the definition of dealing.[91] Procurement will have taken place if the acquisition is done by the insider's agent or nominee or a person acting at his or her direction, but this does not exhaust the range of situations in which procurement can be found.[92] Since the person procured to deal may well not be in possession of any inside information and the procurer has not in fact dealt, without this extension of the statutory meaning of "dealing" there would be a gap in the law.

Thirdly, there is a prohibition on the individual *encouraging* another person to deal in price-affected securities, knowing or having reasonable cause to believe that dealing would take place on a regulated market or through a professional intermediary.[93] Again, it does not matter, for the purposes of the liability of the person who does the encouraging, that the person encouraged commits no offence, because, say, no inside information is imparted by the accused. Indeed, it does not matter for these purposes that no dealing at all in the end takes place, though the accused must at least have reasonable cause to believe that it would. The existence of this offence is likely to discourage over-enthusiastic presentations by company representatives to meetings of large shareholders or analysts.

Finally, the individual must not *disclose* the information "otherwise than in the proper performance of the functions of his employment, office or profession to another person".[94] Unlike in the previous two cases, the communication of inside information is a necessary ingredient of this offence, but no response on the part of the person to whom the information is communicated need occur nor be expected by the accused. However, in effect, this element is built into the liability, for the accused has a defence that "he did not at the time expect any person, because of the disclosure, to deal in securities" on a regulated market or through a professional intermediary.[95] So, even if it occurs outside the proper performance of duties, disclosure which is not expected to lead to dealing will not result in liability, but the burden of proving the absence of the expectation falls on

[89] See para.30–027.
[90] As is the case with derivatives.
[91] CJA 1993 s.55(1)(b).
[92] CJA 1993 s.55(4)–(5).
[93] CJA 1993 s.52(2)(a).
[94] CJA 1993 s.52(2)(b).
[95] CJA 1993 s.53(3)(a).

the accused. This prohibition helps to put the issuer in the position of being the sole source of the disclosure of internally generated inside information to the market.[96]

It should also be noted that, even if none of the statutorily defined acts occurs, a crime under the general criminal law relating to inchoate offences may still be found. Thus, in *Patel v Mirza*[97]—a leading authority on illegality in contracts—the claimant had entered into a contract with the defendant and paid a large sum money to him, so that the claimant could speculate in securities on the basis of inside information which the defendant expected to acquire. In fact, no inside information was obtained and no dealing occurred, but the Supreme Court had no difficulty in accepting that these events constituted a conspiracy to commit an offence under s.52 of the CJA 1993. Another example might be an attempted contravention of the CJA which does not in fact succeed.

Defences

30–026 The CJA 1993 provides a wide range of defences,[98] which fall within two broad categories. First, there are two general defences which carry further the task of defining the mischief at which the Act is aimed.[99] Secondly, there are the special defences, set out mainly but not entirely, in Sch.1 to the Act, which frankly accept that in certain circumstances the policy of prohibiting insider trading should be overborne by the values underlying the exempted practices. These special defences, which were foreshadowed in the recitals to the 1989 Directive, will be dealt with only briefly here.[100]

General defences

30–027 The more important of the general defences is that the accused "would have done what he did even if he had not had the information".[101] This defence benefits liquidators, receivers, trustees, trustees in bankruptcy and personal representatives who may find themselves in the course of their offices advised to trade when in fact themselves in possession of inside information.[102] Thus, a trustee, who is advised by an investment adviser to deal for the trust in a security in relation to which the trustee has inside information, will be able to do so, relying on this defence. But the defence applies more generally than that and would

[96] See paras 27–005 onwards.

[97] *Patel v Mirza* [2016] UKSC 42; [2017] A.C. 467.

[98] We have already dealt, in the previous paragraph, with one of the defences relevant to the disclosure offence.

[99] Though s.53 makes it clear that the burden of proof falls on the accused, thus obviating a possible ambiguity which was found by some in the previous legislation. See *R. v Cross (John Morris)* [1990] B.C.C. 237 CA (Crim Div).

[100] Schedule 1 may be amended by the Treasury by order (s.53(5)), presumably so that it may be kept current with developments in financing techniques.

[101] CJA 1993 s.53(1)(c) and (2)(c). This defence does not apply to the disclosure offence, though it is an essential ingredient of that offence that the disclosure should not have occurred in the proper performance of the accused's functions.

[102] Previously they were covered by more targeted provisions: 1985 Act ss.3(1)(b) and 7.

embrace, for example, an insider who dealt when he did in order to meet a pressing financial need or legal obligation. However, the accused will carry the burden of showing that his or her decision to deal at that particular time in that particular security was not influenced by the possibility of exploiting the inside information which was held.

The other general defence is that the accused did not expect the dealing to result in a profit attributable to the inside information.[103] Although the defence is general in the sense that it is not confined to particular business or financial transactions, the range of situations falling within it is probably quite narrow. The Government's attempts in the parliamentary debates to produce examples of situations for which this defence was needed and which were at all realistic were not entirely convincing.[104]

Special defences

The CJA 1993 provides six special defences, two in the body of the Act and four in Sch.1. One of those provided in the body of the Act appears to be a general defence and is to the effect that dealing is not unlawful if the individual "believed on reasonable grounds that the information had been disclosed widely enough to ensure that none of those taking part in the dealing would be prejudiced by not having the information".[105] In fact, however, this defence is aimed particularly at underwriting arrangements,[106] where those involved in the underwriting may trade amongst themselves on the basis of shared knowledge about the underwriting proposal but that information is not known to the market generally. The other defence provided in the body of the Act[107] concerns things done "on behalf of a public sector body in pursuit of monetary policies or policies with respect to exchange rates or the management of public debt or foreign exchange reserves". So reasons of state, relating to financial policy, trump market integrity.[108] **30–028**

The four special defences provided in the Schedule do not extend to the disclosure of inside information. Where these defences apply, those concerned may trade or encourage others to do so but may not enlarge the pool of persons

---

[103] CJA 1993 s.53(1)(a). The same defence is provided, mutatis mutandis, in relation to the other offences by s.53(2)(a) and (3)(b). Making a profit is defined so as to include avoiding a loss: s.53(6). This is considerably narrower than the defence in the 1985 Act s.3(1)(a), which applied when the individual traded "otherwise than with a view to the making of a profit".

[104] HC Debs (Session 1992–93), Standing Committee B (10 June 1993). A suggestion was where the insider sold at a price which took into account the impact the (bad) information would have on the market when released.

[105] CJA 1993 s.53(1)(b), (2)(b) provide a similar defence in relation to the encouraging offence. For an unmeritorious use of this defence see *Ipourgos Ikonomikon v Georgakis* (C-391/04) EU:C:2007:272; [2007] 3 C.M.L.R. 4 where a group of controlling shareholders and directors engaged in market manipulation of the price a company's shares by trading them amongst themselves. However, since the inside information that they were engaging in this activity was known to all of them, no insider dealing had occurred under the then applicable EU law. Later the EU adopted rules directly aimed at market manipulation.

[106] On underwriting, see para.25–012.

[107] CJA 1993 s.63, applying to all offences under the Act. Technically, s.63 does not provide a defence but rather describes a situation where the Act "does not apply".

[108] As art.2(4) of the Directive permits.

privy to the inside information. In all four cases, what are judged to be valuable market activities would be impossible without the relaxation of the insider dealing prohibition. Thus, market makers[109] may often be in possession of inside information but would not be able to discharge their undertaking to maintain a continuous two-way market in particular securities if they were always subject to the Act. So para.1 of Sch.1 exempts acts done by a market maker in good faith in the course of the market-making business. More controversially, para.5 does the same thing in relation to price stabilisation of new issues.[110]

The final two special defences relate to trading whilst in possession of "market information", which is, in essence, information about transactions in securities being contemplated or no longer contemplated or having or not having taken place. First, an individual may act in connection with the acquisition or disposal of securities and with a view to facilitating their acquisition or disposal where the information held is market information arising directly out of the individual's involvement in the acquisition or disposal.[111] An example is where the employees of an investment bank advising a bidder on a proposed takeover procure the acquisition of the target's shares on behalf of the bidder but before the bid is publicly announced, in order to give the bidder a good platform from which to launch the bid. This defence would not permit the employees to purchase shares for their own account, because they would not then be acting to facilitate the proposed transaction out of which the inside information arose. Even so, permitting a bidder to act in this way is somewhat controversial for those who procure the purchase of the shares know that a bid at a price in excess of the current market price is about to be launched and those who sell out to the bidder just before the public announcement may feel that they have been badly treated.[112] Another situation covered by the provision is that of a fund manager who decides to take a large stake in a particular company. The manager can go into the market on behalf of the funds under management and acquire the stake at the best prices possible, without announcing in advance the intention to build up a large stake, which would immediately drive up the price of the chosen company's shares—though the market may quickly realise what is going on and adjust accordingly.

Under the second and more general "market information" defence the individual may act if "it was reasonable for an individual in his position to have acted as he did" despite having the market information.[113] This is so broadly phrased that it would seem wide enough to cover the situations discussed in the previous paragraph. The more specific provisions were included as well presumably in order to give comfort to those who would otherwise have had to

---

[109] See fn.42.

[110] This is discussed further at para.30–042.

[111] See para.3.

[112] Nevertheless, the Code on Takeovers and Mergers adopts the same approach as the Act. See r.4.1. However the potential bidder would have to comply with the statutory provisions on the disclosure of shareholdings. See paras 27–011 onwards; and P. Davies, "The Takeover Bidder Exemption and the Policy of Disclosure" in K.J. Hopt and E. Wymeersch (eds), *European Insider Dealing* (London, 1991). Even so, the bid facilitation argument ought not to be employed to justify the purchase of derivatives where the aim of the purchase is simply to give the bidder a cash benefit rather than to take a step towards the acquisition of voting control.

[113] See para.2(1). Some guidance on what is reasonable is given in para.2(2).

rely on the general reasonableness provision and who might have wondered whether the courts would interpret it in their favour.

CRIMINAL PROHIBITIONS ON MARKET MANIPULATION

The criminal prohibitions on market manipulation are now to be found in Pt 7 of the Financial Services Act 2012. Section 89 creates an offence in relation to misleading statements made in order to induce trading in securities. It can clearly be used to catch egregious cases of market manipulation[114] and has been discussed in Ch.27.[115] The second offence is more interesting and was introduced by s.47(2) of the Financial Services Act 1986 (now repealed). As reformulated by s.90 of the FSA 2012, this criminalises an act or course of conduct[116] which creates a false or misleading impression as to the market in or price or value of any investment (as widely defined), if done for one or other (or both) of two purposes. The first is where the defendant intends by creating the impression to induce a person to acquire or dispose of investments or to refrain from doing so or to exercise or not to exercise rights attached to investments.[117] It is to be noted that the offence is complete whether or not the accused knew that, or was reckless whether, the impression created was misleading: all that has to be shown is that he acted for the purpose of creating an impression which was in fact misleading. However, a defence is provided where the accused can show that he reasonably believed that the impression was not misleading.[118] In effect, negligence as to the misleading nature of the impression is made a crime and the burden of disproving negligence is placed upon the maker of the impression. **30–029**

The second purpose does depend upon the creator of the impression knowing that it is false or misleading or being reckless as to whether this is the case. If the defendant intends through the impression to make a gain for himself or another or cause loss (or the risk of loss) to another, that person commits an offence, as will also be the case where the defendant is aware that these consequences are likely to result.[119] Thus, if in the *De Berenger* case,[120] the fraudsters had acted somewhat more subtly and refrained from openly stating that Napoleon had been killed but had allowed that impression to arise (for example, through their joyous behaviour as if by soldiers released from a successful army), they would be caught by this version of the second offence.

Some basic forms of manipulative behaviour are offences at common law,[121] but the statute extends and makes clearer the reach of the criminal law in this area. This offence is rarely prosecuted,[122] but the following examples of

---

[114] As in *R. v De Berenger* (1814) 3 M. & S. 67.

[115] See para.27–028.

[116] FSA 2012 s.90(1). The act or course of conduct must occur in the UK or the misleading impression must be created in the UK: s.90(10).

[117] FSA 2012 s.90(2).

[118] FSA 2012 s.90(9)(a).

[119] FSA 2012 s.90(3)(4).

[120] *R. v De Berenger* (1814) 3 M. & S. 67 (see para.30–001).

[121] *Scott v Brown Doering McNab & Co* [1892] 2 Q.B. 724 CA.

[122] Though there has been recent interest in relation to the manipulation of interest-rate or foreign exchange benchmarks, topics outside the scope of this chapter.

contraventions can be given. The promoters of a company fund the underwriters of a share issue to buy shares in the market when dealings begin in order to give the impression that there is a greater market interest in the shares than is in fact the case[123]; or the directors of a company, believing the market price of its shares not to reflect the net tangible asset value of the company, persuade its brokers to buy shares in the market at some four times the previous market price, in order to move the market price closer to what the directors believe to be the "true" value of the shares.[124]

REGULATORY CONTROL OF MARKET ABUSE

Background

30–030 So far, we have looked at the criminal prohibitions on insider dealing and market manipulation. We now turn to the practically more important form of control of market abuse, namely, that administered by regulators, which does not require resort to the criminal law and the criminal courts. In fact, with the enactment of the FSMA 2000, the main thrust of the legal rules controlling market abuse, in which term is to be included both insider dealing and market manipulation, shifted from the criminal law to administrative sanctions which have been placed in the hands of the FCA. At this point, the main source of the rules was Pt VIII of FSMA which was used later to transpose the first EU Directive on market abuse,[125] but in significant ways went beyond that Directive. From the beginning the regulatory sanctions were applied to companies as well as to individuals. Moreover, they applied to all those whose actions had an effect on the market, whether they were persons authorised to carry on financial activities or not. They thus applied as much to industrial companies and their directors, for example, as to investment banks and their directors and employees. These statements are true also of the MAR, now in its retained form the central legal instrument on administrative control.

Part of the reason for the emphasis on administrative penalties from 2000 onwards was that successful deployment of the criminal law on a wide scale against insider dealing and market manipulation proved difficult. Only after the financial crisis of 2007–2008 did the FSA/FCA put substantial resources into the enforcement of the relevant criminal laws. Even so, between 2009 and mid-2015 there were only 27 successful prosecutions for insider dealing (about four a year), of which 23 resulted in custodial sentences (in no case for more than four years).[126] The move towards a regime based on administrative penalties was driven by the desire to address two of the obstacles raised by the criminal offences, namely the need to show intention, at least in relation to insider

[123] As in *Scott v Brown Doering* [1892] 2 Q.B. 724. There is a defence in s.90(9)(b) for such behaviour carried out in accordance with the price stabilisation rules. See para.30–042.

[124] *North v Marra Developments* (1981) C.L.R. 42 HCA. Both this and the case mentioned in the previous note were civil actions in which the criminal nature of the activity was used to defeat a contractual claim on grounds of the illegality of the contract.

[125] Directive 2003/6 on insider dealing and market manipulation (market abuse) [2003] OJ L96/16.

[126] Treasury, Bank of England, FCA, *Fair and Effective Markets Review: Final Report* (June 2015), Chart 11. In general those convicted were not sophisticated criminals. In its *Annual Report* for

dealing,[127] and the high evidential requirements of the criminal law. Even so, in the 12 years to March 2015 the FSA/FCA issued only 85 "Final Notices" in relation to market abuse, i.e. about seven a year.[128]

However, the proposals which were eventually embodied in the FSMA 2000 proved highly controversial during the parliamentary debates on the Bill, those opposing them claiming that they would infringe rights conferred by art.6 of the European Convention on Human Rights (right to a fair trial).[129] The central claim of the opponents was that the penalty regime proposed by the Government, although clearly not part of the domestic criminal law, would be classified as criminal by the European Court of Human Rights, whose classification criteria are independent of those used domestically. Without ever conceding the correctness of this claim, the Government nevertheless did make substantial amendments to its proposals in order to promote the fairness of the new regime, the regime being subject in any event to a general fairness test under the European Convention, even if regarded as civil rather than criminal in nature. These amendments involved in particular the elaboration by the then FSA of a Code on Market Abuse in order to give guidance, some of it binding, on the scope of the prohibitions, and the creation of rights of appeal to an independent tribunal (now the Upper Tribunal) to be granted to persons penalised by the FCA.[130]

In the aftermath of the financial crisis, the debate turned on its head. Now, it was argued that the market abuse provisions were inadequate. This was an argument advanced at EU level as well as at domestic level. It led to the replacement of the EU Directive by a Regulation on market abuse (MAR). MAR both expanded the scope of the substantive EU laws on market abuse, but also removed the need for domestic transposition of those laws. In particular, the guidance by the FCA in its Code was subordinated to the provisions of MAR.[131] Whether there will be a re-balancing of rules in the future as between MAR, as retained, and the FCA's Code on Market Abuse remains to be seen.

2019–2020 the FCA commented: "Criminal cases can take significantly longer to resolve than regulatory cases. No criminal cases were closed in the 2019/20 period." (Enforcement Data, comment on Table 4).

[127] As we have seen, in relation to misleading impressions, mens rea is required only in an attenuated form under the FSA 2012.

[128] FCA, *Fair and Effective Markets Review: Final Report* (June 2015), p.85. In the calendar year 2020 only one Final Notices in relation to market abuse was published.

[129] See Joint Committee on Financial Services and Markets, *Draft Financial Services and Markets Bill: First Report*, Vol. I (Session 1998/99), HL 50-I/HC 328-I, pp.61–67 and Annexes C and D; Second Report, HL 66/HC 465, pp.5–10 and Minutes of Evidence, pp.1–27.

[130] The Financial Services and Markets Tribunal, the predecessor to the Upper Tribunal, tended to view the penalty proceedings as being criminal in nature for the purposes of the Convention. However, the standard of proof required by the Convention is not necessarily that of "beyond reasonable doubt". The standard will depend, as is the case with the civil burden in domestic law, on the seriousness of the allegation which has to be proved. See *Davidson & Tatham v FSA* FSM Case No. 31; *Parker v FSA* [2006] UKFSM FSM037; *Mohammed v FSA* [2005] UKFSM FSM012.

[131] FSMA 2000 s.139A(4).

Insider dealing

30–031 The definition of insider dealing in art.8(1) of MAR is somewhat more simply phrased than under the CJA 1993:

> "For the purposes of this Regulation, insider dealing arises where a person possesses inside information and uses that information by acquiring or disposing of, for its own account or for the account of a third party, directly or indirectly, financial instruments to which that information relates."[132]

As to inside information, as far as trading in corporate securities is concerned, this is:

> "information of a precise nature, which has not been made public, relating, directly or indirectly, to one or more issuers or to one or more financial instruments, and which, if it were made public, would be likely to have a significant effect on the prices of those financial instruments or on the price of related derivative financial instruments"[133]

Since these definitions, not surprisingly, are substantially similar to those to be found in the CJA 1993, it is proposed only to highlight the main features of the regulatory prohibition.

Dealing

30–032 First, the crucial difference between the MAR approach to insider dealing and that of the CJA 1993 is that there is no requirement for a mental element, i.e. no equivalent to the requirement in s.57(1) of the CJA 1993 that the person know the information is inside information and know that he or she has it through being an insider.[134] This was the case also under FSMA 2000. Article 14 of MAR simply says that "a person shall not engage in insider dealing" and the definition of insider dealing (above) contains no requirement as to a mental element. The lack of mental element was further emphasised by the CJEU when it held that a person who "possesses" inside information and trades is presumed to "use" it, i.e. to trade on the basis of the information—though that presumption is rebuttable.[135]

Secondly and new in the UK as far as non-criminal sanctions are concerned, art.14 prohibits attempts to engage in insider dealing, so that even if no dealing occurs, there is exposure to penalties if the person attempted to deal (for example, placed an order with a broker which, for some reason, the broker failed to implement).

Thirdly, again new in the UK, MAR catches a limited number of decisions not to trade or to trade differently, i.e. where the person cancels or amends an order

---

[132] MAR art.8(1).

[133] MAR art.7(1).

[134] See para.30–024. However, knowledge or negligence might to relevant to the size of the penalty imposed: art.31.

[135] *Spector Photo Group NV v Commissie voor het Bank-, Financie- en Assurantiewezen (CBFA)* (C-45/08) EU:C:2009:806; [2011] B.C.C. 827. Rebuttable presumably involves showing that the insider would have traded whether he had the inside information or not. A specific defence of this sort is provided in art.9(3)—trading carried out under an obligation which had come into effect before the inside information was acquired.

for trading already given after receiving the inside information. A simple addition to a trading order would seem to be caught in any event by the prohibition on trading but an alteration of the price at which a person is prepared to trade might not be and is picked up by the provision on amending an existing order. However, a person who is contemplating an order but has not placed one before receiving the inside information is still outside the prohibition.

Fourthly, the definition of insider dealing in art.8(1), unlike the CJA 1993,[136] does not contain a requirement that the possessor of the inside information be, in addition, an insider. However, art.8(4) says that the prohibition applies only to those who acquire the information "as a result of" being a director or shareholder of the company, having access to the information "through the exercise of an employment, profession or duties" or through criminal activities. So, art.8, like the CJA 1993, in fact builds in a requirement of being an insider into its prohibition—though the extension of the insider concept to criminals is novel. In addition to the above categories, art.8(4) applies to any person "who possesses inside information under circumstances … where that person knows or ought to know that it is inside information"—even though that person is not otherwise within art.8(1). In this final case, therefore, a mental element is required to bring the person within the category of insider: either knowledge or negligence as to the inside quality of the information. How the person acquired the information appears not to be relevant to the substantive law but might carry evidential weight when the court assesses whether its possessor knew or ought to have known of its inside character. **30–033**

Fifthly, like the CJA 1993, the prohibition extends beyond dealing. It extends to the situation where the person with inside information "recommends" or "induces" another person to trade (or cancel or amend an order), irrespective of whether the inside information was communicated to the person who trades or, in the case of a recommendation, irrespective of whether trading occurs.[137] If the third party actually responds by trading, etc. that person will also be liable provided that he knows or ought to know that the recommendation or inducement is based on inside information.[138] Mere disclosure of inside information, unaccompanied by any recommendation or inducement, is also prohibited, unless this occurs "in the normal exercise of an employment, a profession or duties".[139] The onward transmission by its recipient of a recommendation or inducement also falls within this prohibition where the recipient knows or ought to know that the recommendation or inducement was based on inside information.[140] This prohibition does not seem confined to the first recipient of the recommendation or inducement.

---

136 See para.30–022.

137 MAR art.8(2).

138 MAR art.8(3). MAR inelegantly talks about the third party "using" the recommendation or inducement.

139 MAR art.10(1). The CJEU has indicated that this exception is to be construed narrowly: Case *Criminal Proceedings against Grongaard* (C-384/02) EU:C:2005:708; [2006] 1 C.M.L.R. 30.

140 MAR art.10(3). Unless the transmitter knows the information underlying the recommendation or inducement, that person would not otherwise fall within the prohibition because not in possession of inside information.

Inside information

30–034 Sixthly, the definition of inside information is slightly broader than its CJA 1993 equivalent in that the information does not have to relate to particular securities or particular issuers of securities, so that information which has an impact on the securities markets generally could be inside information for the purposes of MAR. As with the prior domestic law (under FSMA 2000), the likely impact of the information on the market is tested by reference to what "a reasonable investor" would regard as relevant information.[141] The CJEU has held that the "market impact" test can be satisfied even if the direction of the impact (upwards or downwards) cannot be predicted at the time of trading.[142] Whilst this seems odd at first sight, in situations of market volatility a particular piece of information might predictably move the market without the direction of the movement being clear in advance. A person holding the information could then profit from it by acquiring appropriate financial instruments one of which will pay off in either event, for example, both call and put options over the issuer's securities, only one of which would be exercised depending on the direction of the market impact.[143]

The headline definition of inside information requires that it be "precise" but, unlike the CJA 1993,[144] does not say that it is enough that it is specific, even if not precise. However, art.7(2) says that information about events or circumstances "shall be deemed to be of a precise nature … where it is specific enough to enable a conclusion to be drawn as to the possible effect of that set of circumstances or event on the prices of the financial instruments". This does not in terms say that specific but not precise information may always be inside information, but comes close to it.

As with disclosure of information,[145] knowing when information about a developing situation becomes inside information raises difficult issues. The CJEU held under the prior EU law that the information might cross that threshold before the situation was fully developed and MAR reflects that view.[146] Article 7(2) states that "an intermediate step in a protracted process shall be deemed to be inside information if, by itself, it satisfies the criteria of inside information as referred to in this Article". More generally, art.7(2) treats information as inside information where it relates to circumstances or events which "which may reasonably be expected" to occur as well as circumstances which already exist or have occurred. That same CJEU decision equated a reasonable expectation with a realistic prospect, not a high probability, of occurrence.

[141] MAR art.7(4).

[142] *Lafonta v Autorité des marchés financiers* (C-628/13) EU:C:2015:162; [2015] 3 C.M.L.R. 11. This was in fact a disclosure case, but its rationale seems equally applicable to trading. The Upper Tribunal had taken a different view: *Hannam v Financial Conduct Authority* [2014] UKUT 233 (TCC); [2014] Lloyd's Rep. F.C. 704.

[143] In this respect it is important to note that the definition of insider trading quoted above embraces "financial instruments" and not just the securities issued by the company.

[144] See para.30–018.

[145] See para.27–006.

[146] *Geltl v Daimler AG* (C-19/11) EU:C:2012:397; [2012] 3 C.M.L.R. 32, also a disclosure case.

MAR does not contain one extension beyond inside information which was part of the prior domestic regime. This covered "information which is not generally available" (RINGA) and not just to "inside information",[147] provided a "regular user of the market" would regard the information as relevant to the transaction in question. The effect was to extend the prohibition to information which would not meet the definition of inside information, because it was not specific or precise, but which market users would regard as an illegitimate basis for trading. Domestically, this was a controversial extension, which was kept going from year-to-year until the end of 2014, when it was allowed to expire under the latest version of its "sunset" provision.[148] The Commission proposed a more rigid version of RINGA in its initial proposals for MAR, but in the end the uncertainties thought to be generated by the concept led to its exclusion from MAR.[149] In any event, the matter is now governed by the provisions of MAR and the FSMA 2000 provisions have been repealed.

Persons covered and exemptions

Seventhly, like the prior FCA rules but unlike the CJA 1993, MAR imposes liability on the company as well as on natural persons, but makes it clear that corporate liability does not remove the liability of the persons who traded on behalf of the company.[150] The problem of over-extensive attribution is addressed by removing liability from the company if it has effectively instituted a "Chinese wall" between those within the company who traded and those who held the inside information.[151] **30–035**

Eighthly, inevitably a range of exemptions from the prohibition is provided in order to deal with situations where the otherwise prohibited activity is thought to have a higher value than reducing the incidence of insider trading. Besides the usual exemptions from liability for market makers and brokers acting in the normal course of their business, MAR pay a lot of attention to insider trading in the course of takeovers and mergers. Article 9(5) provides that a person's knowledge that it has decided to acquire or dispose of securities, where that fact is not known to the market, does not "of itself" constitute the use of inside information when that person implements its decision. This provision applies generally (for example, fund managers who have decided to take a major position in a company). Whether it would permit a bidder to build up a stake in the potential target before announcing a bid, at least to the point where the rules on

---

147 FSMA 2000 s.118(4).

148 FSMA 2000 s.118(9).

149 The FCA's Code of Market Conduct gave the following example of RINGA: "An employee of B Plc is aware of contractual negotiations between B Plc and a customer. Transactions with that customer have generated over 10 per cent of B Plc's turnover in each of the last five financial years. The employee knows that the customer has threatened to take its business elsewhere, and that the negotiations, while ongoing, are not proceeding well. The employee, whilst being under no obligation to do so, sells his shares in B Plc based on his assessment that it is reasonably likely that the customer will take his business elsewhere". Query whether this situation would fall within art.7(2) of MAR (above).

150 MAR art.8(5).

151 MAR art.9(1).

disclosure of major shareholding are triggered,[152] is less clear. If a distinction is made between a decision to acquire securities and a decision to make a public offer for securities, then stake-building will not fall within this exemption.

By contrast, art.9(4) applies specifically to inside information obtained "in the conduct of" a merger or public takeover. A person holding such information is not "deemed" from the mere fact of its possession to have used it when proceeding with the merger or takeover, provided the inside information has ceased to be such by the time the shareholders accept the takeover offer or approve the merger, i.e. after the offer has been made. The purpose of this provision might be to deal with the situation where a bidder or potential merger partner obtains information in private discussions with the target company before making an offer or putting forward a merger proposal. Making the offer and taking (conditional) acceptances under it would thus not constitute insider dealing. However, this provision expressly excludes "stake-building" from its protection, although that in turn is qualified because the definition of stake-building excludes acquisitions which trigger an obligation to make an announcement of a takeover.[153] The up-shot is that art.9 is less friendly to stake-building than, one may guess, is generally recognised. The strongest protection of prospective bidders from the risk of insider dealing liability under MAR is probably the difficulty an outsider will have in fixing the precise point at which the bidder actually decided to offer for the target, coupled with the disclosure obligations (discussed in Ch.17) which make it difficult to keep stake-building a secret from the market in any event.

An exemption from the obligation not to disclose inside information is provided, subject to extensive safeguards, in relation to "market soundings", i.e. discussion with selected market participants about a possible course of action in order to establish the market's likely reaction to it. The most common situation is where those acting on behalf of an issuer wish to establish whether the market would absorb a public offering of shares within a price range the issuer would find acceptable. However, market soundings also embrace talks by a potential bidder with large shareholders in the target in order to establish the likelihood of their accepting an offer, if one were made.[154] The information in question here is clearly likely to constitute inside information of the utmost salience. Indeed, unusual trading in advance of a bid announcement is a common feature of securities markets. MAR seeks to address this risk by requiring the discloser to assess whether it will be disclosing inside information during the market soundings (and to keep a written record of its assessment and of the inside information disclosed, if any). If so, the consent of potential recipients of the information to receive it must be obtained (a process sometimes called "[Chinese] wall crossing") and the implications for the recipients of being put in possession of inside information must be explained. The recipients must themselves assess whether they are in possession of inside information.[155] Finally, the Commission has adopted two pieces of subordinate legislation on this topic and ESMA

[152] See para.26–011.

[153] MAR art.3.1(31). This would be the case where the acquisitions triggered a mandatory bid, but an announcement obligation might arise before that (see para.28–049). Those who sell to an undisclosed bidder may well feel aggrieved but will often be without redress.

[154] MAR art.9(1)(2).

[155] MAR art.9(5)(7).

guidelines for market soundings—a flurry of activity which shows the importance of soundings for the operation of the financial markets.[156]

Market manipulation

Transactions and orders to trade

Market manipulation is defined very broadly in art.12 of MAR, as it was under the previous regime. Many of its manifestations have little relevance to the public markets in securities, with which we are primarily concerned. We concentrate on the forms of manipulation which are relevant to such markets. The first two aspects of the definition both arise out of effecting transactions or orders to trade (for example, in securities). The first covers trades which give or are likely to give a false impression as to the market supply or demand or price of a financial instrument or secure the price of the financial instrument at an abnormal or artificial level.[157] As we have seen above, such behaviour constitutes a criminal offence if done for the purpose of inducing investment decisions,[158] but MAR applies on the basis simply of engaging in the proscribed behaviour (subject to the defences discussed below).[159] Indeed, as with insider dealing, attempting to engage in the behaviour is also prohibited. The second covers transactions or orders which employ some form of deception.[160] Annex 1 to MAR gives a non-exhaustive list of the matters regulators should take into account when applying these two aspects of the prohibition. **30–036**

The market itself has developed graphic terms to refer to some of the forms of behaviour falling within these prohibitions. Examples falling within the first type of behaviour are "wash trades" (where a person trades with himself or two persons acting together trade between themselves, but so that there is no real transfer of beneficial ownership or market risk) and "painting the tape" (entering into a series of transactions that are publicly reported for the purpose of suggesting a level of activity or price movement which do not genuinely exist).

Dissemination of information

Given the reliance of markets on information, it is not surprising that a common form of market manipulation consists of supplying misleadingly good or bad information to the market. Colourful examples are "pump and dump" (taking a long position in an investment, disseminating misleading positive information about it, and then selling out) and its opposite, "trash and cash" (taking a short **30–037**

[156] Regulation 2016/960 with regard to regulatory technical standards for the appropriate arrangements, systems and procedures for disclosing market participants conducting market soundings [2016] OJ L160/29; Regulation 2016/959 laying down implementing technical standards for market soundings with regard to the systems and notification templates to be used by disclosing market participants [2016] OJ L160/23; ESMA, *MAR Guidelines: Persons receiving market soundings* (2016).

[157] MAR art.12(1)(a).

[158] FSA 2012 s.90. See para.30–029.

[159] MAR art.15.

[160] MAR art.12(1)(b).

position in a security and disseminating misleading negative information before closing out the short position) fall within this type of market manipulation.[161] The third aspect of prohibited manipulation thus consists of disseminating information which gives or is likely to give a false or misleading impression as to the demand for, supply of or the price of a financial instrument where the disseminator knew or ought to have known that the information was false or misleading.[162] In this case, a negligence standard is built into the definition of the prohibited conduct.[163] In effect, a person who makes a negligent misstatement to the market about a financial instrument is exposed to the FCA's penalties, but without it being a requirement for liability that the maker of the statement should have intended or expected that any particular person or class of person should rely on it, still less that any such reliance should have occurred.[164] As we have seen,[165] there is liability in the FSMA 2000 to the FCA's penalties on the part of an issuer (and its directors) which negligently make a misleading disclosure required by the Transparency Rules. However, liability under the market abuse provisions is a useful supplement because MAR, unlike the TD, is not confined to regulated markets, and market abuse sounds more reprehensible that inaccurate disclosure.[166]

Misleading behaviour and market distortion

30–038 The final forms of market manipulation identified in MAR target various forms of behaviour which may mislead the market but which are not central to the manipulation of securities markets. An example is securing a dominant position in the market for a financial instrument ("cornering" it) so as to establish unfair trading conditions.[167] This can happen in securities markets but is very difficult and very expensive in a deep and liquid market. More common perhaps is trying to influence the opening or closing prices of certain financial instruments, in order to influence the settlement terms of derivatives linked to those prices[168] or

---

[161] FCA, Code of Market Conduct 1.7.2.

[162] MAR art.12(1)(c). See also art.12(2)(d) dealing with statements (not required to be false or misleading) about a financial instrument where the maker of the statement already has a position in the instrument but has not disclosed it.

[163] Though the defences discussed below are still available.

[164] The breadth of the prohibition was thought to put financial journalists at particular risk and so art.21 provides that the liability of journalists is to be assessed on a basis which takes into account the codes of conduct governing that profession, provided the journalist derives no direct or indirect benefit from the dissemination of the information and did not intend to mislead the market.

[165] See Ch.27 at para.27–026.

[166] In fact, inaccurate disclosures to the markets based on misstatements in the company's accounts appear to be a favourite target of the FCA's use of the market abuse provisions in relation to issuers. See FSA, "Final Notice: The "Shell" Transport and Trading Company Plc and The Royal Dutch Petroleum Company NV" (24 August 2004); FCA, "Final Notice: Tesco Plc" (March 2017); FCA, "Final Notice: Redcentric Plc (June 2020).

[167] MAR art.12(2)(a).

[168] MAR art.12(2)(b). This was the conduct at the heart of the "LIBOR" scandal of a decade ago, but it was the conduct of traders that was at issue rather than by non-financial issuers and their senior managers. See House of Commons, Treasury Committee, *Fixing LIBOR: some preliminary findings:*

placing artificial orders which make it difficult for market participants to identify genuine orders or for the market to establish the price of the financial instrument.[169]

Accepted market practices

The principal difficulty with prohibitions on market manipulation is that any effective definition is likely also to catch some behaviour which market participants regard as legitimate. MAR recognises this by exempting from the prohibition on manipulation acts which are done "for legitimate reasons, and conform with [sic] an accepted market practice".[170] A further issue here is that accepted market practices (AMP) are specific to particular markets and so need to be defined at that level. This created a particular problem for the drafters of MAR, whose objective was uniformity of regulation across the EU. Having accepted therefore the principle that AMP are to be established by the relevant market regulators (for the future by the FCA in the UK),[171] MAR constrains the decisions of those regulators to a considerable extent. Seven criteria are laid out which the FCA has to take into account when establishing an AMP (none of which is surprising) and those criteria are supplemented by regulatory technical standards adopted by the Commission (by the FCA in future).[172] **30–039**

Safe harbours

MAR provides safe harbours, for two types of activity, in relation to both the insider trading and market manipulation manifestations of the prohibition on market abuse. These activities are share buy-backs and stabilisation occurring in the period after a public offer of securities. The UK chose to extend the protection to the criminal provisions[173] on misleading statements. In both cases, the exemptions are tightly drawn and were subject to delegated regulation by the Commission. The Regulation[174] existing at the time of UK exit from the EU became UK retained law in the usual way—but is subject to change by the UK Parliament in the future. However, it is not possible for UK law simply to ignore EU law beyond its retained status, because the issuer engaging in the buy-back or issuing new shares may have its shares traded on public markets in both the UK and the EU and so be subject to rules of both types. Consequently, the relevant regulatory standards become (1) where the trading takes place on a UK market, **30–040**

Second Report (Session 2012-13), HC 481. It led to the Financial Services Act 2012. Thirteen traders were charged by the SFO with conspiracy to defraud of whom five were found guilty at trial or pleaded guilty and the remainder acquitted.

[169] MAR art.12(2)(c). There is considerable debate about the extent to which high frequency or algorithmic trading can or bring about such distortions.

[170] MAR art.13(1).

[171] MAR art13(2).

[172] MAR art.13(7) and ESMA, *Report to the Commission on accepted market practices* (December 2018).

[173] FSA 2012 ss.89(3), 90(9).

[174] Regulation 2016/1052 with regard to regulatory technical standards for the conditions applicable to buy-back programmes and stabilisation measures [2016] OJ L173/34.

the retained EU law, as amended domestically, and any further standards adopted after 2020 by the FCA; and (2) where the trading takes place on an EU market, the Commission Regulation as initially adopted plus any additional or amended regulations made by the Commission in the future.[175] Thus, in this case UK law requires compliance with EU law on the part of those listed on UK markets where there is a cross-border element.

Share buy-backs

30–041 The creditor and shareholder protection aspects of share buy-backs have been considered in Ch.17.[176] It is by no means impossible for a company to effect a buy-back programme for its shares without falling foul of the market abuse prohibition, especially as issuers in any event must disclose inside information to the market "as soon as possible"[177] and so should not be holding it when effecting the buy-back. However, it seems to have been thought that buy-backs were an important corporate tool, so that companies should be given a "safe harbour" for their implementation.

The conditions laid down for access to the safe harbour are not particularly novel in the UK, where the Listing Rules have contained similar provisions for permissible buy-backs some time.[178] Putting together the provisions of MAR and the Commission Regulation, the following main points emerge:

(1) The purpose of the buy-back programme must be to reduce the company's capital or to meet its obligations under a debt instrument convertible into equity or an employee share scheme. This appears to mean that the shares bought back will be required to be either cancelled or re-issued for the permitted purposes (rather than held in treasury subject to the board's discretion). And the safe harbour applies only to behaviour directly related to the purpose of the buy-back programme.

(2) Apart from meeting the requirements for shareholder approval and so on,[179] details of the buy-back programme must be disclosed to the market in advance of any purchases and the issuer must report purchases actually made to the competent authority within seven working days, giving amounts acquired and prices. Thus, the acquisitions cannot occur clandestinely and the market will know what may happen and what has happened.

(3) The acquisitions must not be at a price higher than the prevailing market price (even if the authorisation from the shareholders permits a higher price) and, normally, not more than one quarter of the average daily volume of the shares may be bought in any one day. This rule reduces the impact of the acquisitions on the trading price of the share.

---

175 MAR art 5(6), as amended by the Exit Regulations Pt 6.

176 At paras 17–008 onwards.

177 See para.27–006.

178 See, for example, FSA, *The Listing Rules* (May 2000 edn), Ch.15.

179 See para.17–018.

(4) The issuer may not sell its own shares (presumably those held in treasury) during the programme, thus removing an incentive to pay an above-market price. Nor may it effect acquisitions under its programme at a time when it is making use of the permission not to disclose otherwise disclosable inside information. Finally, it may not make purchases under the programme during a "closed period".[180] However, the issuer can avoid all three restrictions by either adopting a programme under which the amounts and times of the acquisitions are set out in the public disclosure required above (a "time-scheduled" programme) or by outsourcing the programme to an investment bank which makes the trading decisions independently of the issuer.

Price stabilisation

Share or price stabilisation is, as its name suggests, a somewhat more questionable procedure from the point of view of market abuse than share repurchases, since the very purpose of the behaviour is to set the market price of the security at a different level from that which would otherwise prevail. However, it is permitted in connection with new shares issues, for reasons which have been put as follows: **30–042**

> "Because new securities are usually issued at irregular intervals, they may result in a temporary oversupply of those securities leading to an artificially low market price during and immediately after issue. Such short-term price fluctuations may be to the detriment of both issuers and investors. Price stabilising activity involves the lead managers of a new issue of securities supporting the price of those securities for a limited period, thereby reducing the risk of price falls."[181]

Putting together the provisions of MAR and the Commission Regulation, the main conditions to be met for the price stabilisation safe harbour are, briefly, as follows:

(1) The stabilisation may be carried out only within a limited period of time, for example, in the case of shares, within 30 calendar days of the date on which shares offered in an initial offer commence trading.[182]

(2) The market must be informed before the shares are offered to the public that stabilisation may be undertaken (but that there is no guarantee that it will or that it will be at any particular level) and of the period during which it may be undertaken and who will be undertaking it.[183] Stabilisation activity must be reported to the FCA within seven working days of its taking place, and within one week of the end of the stabilisation period the market must be informed of what stabilisation activity occurred, including the dates and prices.[184]

---

180 See para.30–006.

181 FSA, *The Price Stabilising Rules* (January 2000), CP 40.

182 Regulation 2016/1052 art.5.

183 Regulation 2016/1052 art.6(1).

184 Regulation 2016/1052 art.6(3).

(3) The price at which the stabilisation activity took place must not be above the offer price.[185]

In the above cases, the underwriters support the price of the shares because there is an over-supply which drives the price down. It could be that there is a higher than expected demand for the shares and the issuer wishes to take advantage of that possibility by selling more shares than had previously been announced. An "overallotment facility" (permitting the underwriters to do this, as written into their agreement with the issuer) is allowed subject to the ex ante and ex post disclosure requirements mentioned above. Overallotment may occur only during the subscription period and may result in no underwriter holding more than 5% of the shares on offer. However, this time limitation may be extended so as to embrace the stabilisation period and the percentage limit raised to 15% if there is an express "greenshoe" clause in the underwriting agreement in favour of some or all of the underwriters. The disclosure rules still apply.[186]

ENFORCEMENT AND SANCTIONS

30–043 Although the substantive rules on market abuse were set at EU level, enforcement and sanctions were always in the hands of national competent authorities. However, this does not mean that MAR ignores these topics. Rather, it proceeded by requiring Member States to confer on their national authorities at least the investigatory and sanctioning powers specified in Chs 4 and 5 of MAR. Although the range of powers and sanctions contained in these chapters is wide, by and large they are not new powers for the FCA. The prior investigation and penalty powers of the FCA in relation to market abuse were set out in Pts VIII and XI of FSMA 2000 but needed some amendment to deal with the provisions of MAR.[187]

Investigation into market abuse

30–044 MAR requires competent authorities to have 13 powers so that they may police and enforce the prohibition on market abuse effectively.[188] Among the more notable ones, are access to data in any form from issuers and others, the right to summon persons and demand answers to questions, to carry out on-site inspections (other than residences), to enter premises and seize documents (subject to judicial control if the Member State requires it), to require recordings of telephone conversations and copies of emails from financial institutions, to require traffic data from telecom operators (if national law permits this) and, crossing the border into remedies, to impose various interlocutory remedies and

185 Regulation 2016/1052 art.7.

186 Regulation 2016/1052 art.8. Together these two mechanisms for dealing with excess demand are termed "ancillary stabilisation" in the Regulation. The term "greenshoe option" seems to have arisen because the first offering in which it was used (in 1919) was by the Green Shoe Manufacturing Company in the US.

187 Effected by the Financial Services and Markets Act 2000 (Market Abuse Regulations) 2016 (SI 2016/680), introducing a number of new sections into Pt VIII.

188 MAR art.23(2).

to require the correction of misstatements to the market. Information obtained must be subject to confidentiality requirements and be governed by national data protection laws.[189]

In order to maximise the chances of potential infringements of MAR coming to light, the FSMA 2000 creates a category of "protected disclosures", more commonly known as "whistle blowing".[190] These disclosures are not to be treated as an infringement of any restriction on disclosure of information "however imposed". This provision takes the discloser out of the prohibitions on disclosure of information discussed above, but also operates more widely, including, presumably, any restrictions to be found in the discloser's contract of employment. The conditions for the protection are that the discloser has at least reasonable grounds for suspecting that another person has engaged in market abuse, that the information came to the discloser in the course of the discloser's employment or profession and that the disclosure is made to a person nominated by the employer to receive such disclosures. This provision obviously applies only where the employer has set up some form of procedure for handling whistle-blowing. This is required for firms providing financial services, but not generally for non-financial companies, though some may have established them voluntarily.[191]

Since market manipulation is often a cross-border activity, MAR requires national competent authorities to cooperate both with ESMA (mainly in the communication of information)[192] and with other national authorities and ESMA for the purposes of investigation, supervision and enforcement.[193] The aim of these provisions was to make it more likely that effective cooperation among national regulators would actually take place. However, with the UK's exit from the EU, these provisions have simply been removed from the retained version of MAR.[194] **30–045**

Since financial activity is often a global matter, however, cooperation among EU regulators in the market abuse area, although highly desirable, is unlikely to be enough. MAR therefore envisages cooperation agreements with the supervisory authorities of third countries on the part of national regulators. The retained version of MAR retains the power for the FCA to enter into such arrangements, including now with EU Member States. On the EU side the process is heavily regulation by the Commission via Implementing Technical Standards, even though the matter is formally one for national regulators.[195] MAR envisages a Commission "template" for such agreements, which national competent authorities are to use "where possible".[196]

---

[189] MAR arts 27–28.

[190] FSMA 2000 s.131A and FCA Handbook, *Senior Management Arrangements, Systems and Controls*, Ch.18, covering disclosure both to the employer and the competent authority.

[191] FSMA 2000 s.131AA.

[192] MAR art.24.

[193] MAR art.25(1).

[194] Exit Regulations reg.13(4)(5).

[195] See ESMA, *Final Report: Draft Regulatory Technical Standards on cooperation arrangements under Regulation (EU) No 596/2014 on market abuse* (October 2019).

[196] MAR art.26.

As regards non-EU third countries, under the pre-MAR rules the UK signed Memoranda of Understanding relating to co-operation with regulators from other leading countries in the financial services field, such as the US, Japan, Hong Kong, Switzerland and Australia. These international agreements are underpinned by s.169 of FSMA 2000, which authorises the FCA to appoint investigators at the behest of a non-British regulator to investigate "any matter". The FCA may permit a representative of the overseas regulator to be present and ask questions, provided the information obtained is subject to the same confidentiality requirements in the hands of the overseas regulator as it would be under the FSMA 2000.[197] The overseas regulator may be required to contribute to the costs of the investigation and the FCA is to consider, before granting the request, whether similar assistance would be forthcoming from the overseas regulator if it were requested by a British regulator, whether the breach of the law to be investigated has no close parallel in the UK, whether the matter is of importance to people in the UK and whether the public interest requires that the assistance be given.[198] In the case of insider dealing, it seems likely that these criteria could easily be satisfied, so that assistance should normally be given, subject to the matter of cost. The Court of Appeal has interpreted the section liberally, notably by not requiring the FCA investigate the genuineness or validity of the foreign regulator's request and by permitting the investigators to require the production of any documents which are relevant to their investigation.[199]

Sanctions for market abuse

30–046 MAR required a wide range of administrative sanctions to be available for breach of the prohibitions on market abuse.[200] In relation to companies and individuals other than investment firms and their managers and employees, the principal sanctions available are:

- injunctions requiring the conduct constituting the market abuse to cease[201];
- disgorgement of profits made or losses avoided through the market abuse[202];
- public warnings[203]; and

[197] FSMA 2000 s.169(7)–(8).

[198] FSMA 2000 s.169(4).

[199] *R. (on the application of Amro International SA) v Financial Services Authority* [2010] EWCA Civ 123; [2010] Bus. L.R. 1541 CA (Civ Div).

[200] MAR art.30. This article was deleted from the retained version of MAR, but it had been implemented in FSMA 2000 before UK exit and those provisions remain in force (with limited changes). In many cases the sanctions were available to the FCA before the adoption of MAR.

[201] FSMA 2000 s.381.

[202] FSMA 2000 s.383. On the potential difficulties with this remedy see para.27–024.

[203] FSMA 2000 s.123(3) and FCA, *Decision Procedure and Penalties Manual* 6.4.

- financial (administrative) penalties which may be some multiple of the profit made or loss avoided under the second head or a free-standing penalty related in the case of companies to their annual turnover.[204]

In the case of investment firms and those employed within them there are additional sanctions consisting of temporary or permanent (1) withdrawal of the authorisation of the firm to carry on financial business; and (2) bans on the individual from discharging managerial responsibilities within such a firm or dealing on their own account.[205]

Administrative penalties

Section 123 of the FSMA 2000 gives the FCA power to impose a penalty of "such amount as the FCA considers appropriate" where there it is satisfied that market abuse has occurred. The penalty provisions were another of the human rights battle grounds in the parliamentary debates preceding the passing of FSMA 2000 and a number of restrictions on the FCA's powers are the result. First, although there is no statutory restriction on the size of penalty the FCA may impose, the FCA is required to produce a statement of policy on the factors which will determine its approach to penalties.[206] That policy now appears in the *Decision Procedure and Penalties Manual* (DEPP) which contains a list of the factors the FCA considers relevant to the decisions whether to seek a financial penalty, whether to substitute public censure for a monetary penalty and to determining the level of penalty. The FCA's views on the appropriate level of penalties were significantly strengthened as from March 2010, under the impact of the financial crisis. **30–047**

Secondly, the FCA may not impose a penalty upon a person without sending first a "warning notice" stating the level of penalty proposed or the terms of the proposed public statement.[207] Thirdly, if the FSA does impose a penalty or make a public statement, it must issue the person concerned with a decision notice to that effect,[208] which triggers the person's right to appeal to the Upper Tribunal.[209] That right must normally be exercised within 28 days.[210] The Tribunal, consisting of a legally qualified chair and one or more experienced lay persons, operates by way of a re-hearing of the case, and so can consider evidence not brought before the FCA, whether it was available at that time or not,[211] and must arrive at its own

[204] FSMA 2000 s.123 gives the FCA power to impose a penalty of "such amount as the FCA considers appropriate". For its policy on this matter (required to be set out by s.124) see FCA, *Decision Procedure and Penalties Manual* 6.5-6.5D.

[205] FSMA 2000 ss.123A-B.

[206] FSMA 2000 ss.124–125.

[207] FSMA 2000 s.126. Sections 392 and 393 extend the warning notice procedure to third parties, but only if the third party is identified in the FCA's decision notice: *Watts v Financial Services Authority* [2005] UKFSM FSM022.

[208] FSMA 2000 s.127. MAR art.34 requires decisions to impose sanctions normally to be published.

[209] FSMA 2000 s.126.

[210] FSMA 2000 s.133(1).

[211] FSMA 2000 s.133(4). Although the hearing function was transferred to the Upper Tribunal in 2010, the statutory provisions in FSMA 2000, as amended, governing the appeal hearing continue to apply.

determination of the appropriate action to be taken in the case,[212] which, presumably, could be a tougher penalty than the one the FCA had proposed. There is a legal assistance scheme in operation for proceedings before the Tribunal, funded by the FCA, which recoups the cost from a levy on authorised persons.[213] Appeals lie on a point of law from the Tribunal to the Court of Appeal or Court of Session.[214]

Fourthly, a prohibition on the use of compelled testimony applies not only to subsequent criminal charges but also to proceedings for the imposition of a penalty, whether before the FCA or the Tribunal.[215]

Injunctions

30–048 The FCA may apply to the court under FSMA s.381 for an injunction to restrain future market abuse, whether such abuse has taken place already or not, and the court may grant an injunction where there is a "reasonable likelihood" that the abuse will occur or be repeated.[216] The court has two further and independent powers under s.381. If, on the application of the Authority, the court is satisfied that a person may be, or may have been, engaged in market abuse, it may order a freeze on all or any of that person's assets. This helps to ensure that any later restitution order has something to bite on. Secondly, if the court is satisfied that the person is or has been engaged in market abuse, it may, on the application of the Authority, order the person to take such steps to remedy the situation as the court may direct (i.e. grant a mandatory injunction).

It is a striking feature of the FSMA 2000 that it also provides in s.129 that, on an injunction (or restitution–see below) application by the FCA, the court may impose a penalty of such amount as it considers appropriate on the person to whom the application relates. In *FCA v Da Vinci Invest Ltd*[217] Snowden J held that this penalty-imposing power was separate from the power set out in s.123 (see para.30–047). Thus, it is not subject to the warning and decision notice procedures which surround the FCA's use of its own penalty powers nor is s.129 covered by the assistance provisions applying to s.123. Even more striking is the fact that s.129 does not in terms confine the court's penalty imposing powers to proof of market abuse. However, given that the power arises only on application to the court in a market abuse case, the judge easily concluded that the drafters of the Act contemplated a financial penalty being imposed only when the court was satisfied that market abuse had occurred. This did not mean, however, that the court could impose a penalty only where it had granted an injunction or made a

---

[212] FSMA 2000 s.133(5). The action must be one the FCA could have taken: s.133A.

[213] FSMA 2000 ss.134–136, even though, in the case of market abuse appeals, the appellant may not be an authorised person. The details of the assistance scheme are set out in Financial Services and Markets Tribunal (Legal Assistance) Regulations 2001 (SI 2001/3632) and the Financial Services and Markets Tribunal (Legal Assistance—Costs) Regulations 2001 (SI 2001/3633).

[214] Now by virtue of the general provisions applying to appeals from the Upper Tribunal.

[215] FSMA 2000 s.174(2).

[216] FSMA 2000 s.381(1).

[217] *Financial Conduct Authority v Da Vinci Invest Ltd* [2015] EWHC 2401 (Ch); [2016] Bus. L.R. 274.

restitution order under Pt 25, but a genuine application by the FCA for such an order was a pre-condition for the court's exercise of its penalty powers.

Restitution orders

Under s.383 of the FSMA 2000 the court has power on an application by the FCA to make a restitution order, where a person has made a gain from a breach of the market abuse provisions of MAR or avoided a loss. Under s.384 the FCA may make a restitution order, but only against persons authorised by it to engage in the provision of financial services. The amount required under the order is to be paid out to such persons as the court (or regulator) may direct who fall within the categories of those who have suffered loss or are the persons to whom the profit is "attributable".[218] We have discussed the difficulties that may arise in applying these provisions in Ch.27 (dealing with disclosures to the market).[219] In the case of market abuse it is possible that the identification of profits made or losses avoided made will be easier than with mere non-disclosure, though difficulties about how that profit should be distributed may still be severe. **30–049**

In addition there is a power for the court, on the application of the FCA or the Secretary of State, to impose a restitution order or an injunction where a breach has occurred or is threatened of Pt 7 of FSA 2012.[220] In practice, it is unlikely this adds anything significant to the courts' and FCA's powers to seek restitution or impose an injunction on grounds of market abuse, since the criminal law is narrower than the civil penalty regime.

Criminal sanctions

The CJA 1993 places exclusive reliance upon criminal sanctions for its enforcement. Section 63(2) states that no contract shall be "void or unenforceable" by reason only of an offence committed under the Act, a provision which was redrafted in 1993, it would seem, in order to close the loophole, as the Government saw it, identified in *Chase Manhattan Equities v Goodman*.[221] Although the Act does not deal expressly with the question of whether a civil action for breach of statutory duty could be built on its provisions, it seems unlikely that the Act would be held to fall within either of the categories identified for this purpose in the case law.[222] **30–050**

The criminal sanctions imposed by the CJA 1993 are, on summary conviction, a fine not exceeding the statutory maximum and/or a term of imprisonment not exceeding six months, and on conviction on indictment an unlimited fine and/or imprisonment for not more than ten years.[223] The power of the judge on

[218] FSMA 2000 ss.383(5), (10), 384(5)(6).

[219] See para.27–024.

[220] FSMA 2000 ss.382(9) and 380(6).

[221] *Chase Manhattan Equities Ltd v Goodman* [1991] B.C.C. 308; [1991] B.C.L.C. 897 Ch D at 930–935, where the judge held that the previous legislative formulation did not prevent the court from holding a contract unenforceable when it had been concluded in breach of the CA 1985's provisions.

[222] See especially *Lonrho Ltd v Shell Petroleum Co Ltd (No.2)* [1982] A.C. 173 HL.

[223] CJA 1993 s.61—the maximum sentence on indictment was increased from seven to ten years by the Financial Services Act 2021.

conviction on indictment to impose an unlimited fine means that, in theory at least, the court could ensure that the insider made no profit out of the dealing.[224] Prosecutions in England and Wales may be brought only by or with the consent of the Secretary of State or the Director of Public Prosecutions. In England and Wales prosecutions may be brought by the FCA as well as by the usual prosecution bodies, the Crown Prosecution Service, the Serious Fraud Office and the relevant government department.[225] Indeed, the FCA has the prime responsibility for bringing criminal prosecutions for breach of the criminal laws in the area of market abuse. As we have noted above, the number of criminal prosecutions brought by the FCA is small, but increasing.[226]

The FCA is also the lead prosecutor under Pt 7 of FSA 2012. This section is less used than the CJA provisions, but will be invoked in what the FCA regards as serious cases.[227]

Disqualification

30–051 In addition to the traditional criminal penalties which may be visited upon those engaging in market abuse, the disqualification sanction is available against them in some cases, the effect of which is to disable the person disqualified from being involved in the running of companies in the future.[228] In *R. v Goodman*[229] the Court of Appeal upheld the Crown Court's decision to disqualify, for a period of 10 years, a managing director convicted of insider dealing. The Crown Court had invoked s.2 of the Company Directors Disqualification Act 1986 which enables a court to disqualify a person who has been convicted of an indictable offence in connection with the management of a company. The Court of Appeal took a liberal view of what could be said to be "in connection with the management of the company", so as to bring within the phrase the managing director's disposal of his shares in the company in advance of publication of bad news about its prospects. It would seem, too, that a disqualification order could be made on grounds of unfitness under s.8 of the 1986 Act upon an application by the Secretary of State in the public interest. In that case, conviction by a court of an indictable offence would not be a pre-condition to a disqualification order, but the court would have to be satisfied that the person's conduct in relation to the company made him unfit to be concerned in the management of a company and this section, unlike s.2, is capable of applying to market abuse only by directors and shadow directors.

---

[224] The Crown Court has power under the Criminal Justice Act 1988, as amended by the Proceeds of Crime Act 1995, to make an order confiscating the proceeds of crime, which could also be used to this end.

[225] FSMA 2000 s.402(1)(a). This implies that some cases which might previously have been dealt with through regulatory sanctions will now be subject to criminal prosecution, but the courts have refused to treat this change of policy as a ground for special leniency when sentencing offenders: *R. v McQuoid (Christopher)* [2009] EWCA Crim 1301; [2010] 1 Cr. App. R. (S.) 43.

[226] See para.30–030.

[227] See para.27–027.

[228] See Ch.20. These powers are in addition to the (probably more important) powers of the FCA to disqualify persons from operating within the financial services industry (FSMA 2000 ss.123A and B), but they extend to persons who do not need authorisation from the FCA.

[229] *R. v Goodman (Ivor Michael)* [1992] B.C.C. 625 CA (Crim Div).

CONCLUSION

Regulation of market abuse has been an area of enormously rapid growth in recent years, to which the adoption of MAR has most recently added. Before 1980 insider dealing was tackled mainly through statutory disclosure requirements, whilst broader forms of market abuse received at best a shadowy control in the common law of crimes. Today, both insider dealing in particular and market abuse in general are the subject of detailed criminal and regulatory rules. Why should this have happened? It may well reflect a deterioration in standards of market conduct as a result of powerful financial incentives to "do the business". Probably, it also an example of the growth of shareholder (or, in this case, investor) power as financial markets have come to play a more important role in national and international business.[230] In general, the regulation discussed in this chapter aims to protect investors, individual and collective, against opportunistic behaviour by corporate and market insiders and thus make securities markets more attractive places in which to participate. **30–052**

Of course, it is another question whether the law is as effective in practice as it could be. Research published by the FSA on "market cleanliness", which refers essentially to the level of insider dealing, suggests that there has been a reduction in recent years in insider dealing ahead of takeover announcements. Looking at trading activity as a whole, it appears that market abuse is a contained, but not insignificant, element of trading on the London market.[231] Until recently, whilst the FCA's budget was not out of line with that of its US equivalent, the Securities Exchange Commission, when adjusted for market capitalisation, it seemed to devote a lower proportion of its budget to enforcement and to impose lower penalties when it did take action.[232] The FCA up-graded the resources it devotes to enforcement and changed its view about the appropriate level of penalties after the financial crisis, and this may explain some part of the statistical trends.

---

[230] cf. the increased importance of shareholder interests in corporate governance, above, Pt 3.

[231] FCA, *Why has the FCAs market cleanliness statistic for takeover announcements decreased since 2009?* (2014), Occasional Paper No.4; FCA, *Market Cleanliness Statistics* (September 2020) (available at *https://www.fca.org.uk/data/market-cleanliness-statistics* [Accessed 31 March 2021]).

[232] J. Coffee Jr, "Law and the Market: The Impact of Enforcement" (2007) 156 University of Pennsylvania L.R. 229.

PART 9

DEBT FINANCE

At various points in this work we have referred to the comparative advantages of equity and debt finance for companies. Even more so than with the rights of shareholders, the rights of lenders to the company depend heavily on the terms upon which they contract with the company. Nevertheless, one can say that, in general, debt is both cheaper and more flexible, but is also more demanding as a form of finance for companies than equity shares. It is cheaper because insolvency priority[1] and contractual flexibility may reduce the risk to lenders, who can therefore be persuaded to lend on more advantageous terms; but it is more demanding because those terms create an entitlement (usually to payment of a fixed or narrowly fluctuating rate of interest, plus repayment of principal), whether the company is doing well or badly, whereas the declaration of a dividend on ordinary shares is usually a matter for the discretion of the directors and is in any event impossible unless the company has distributable profits (itself a term with a restricted legal meaning). Clearly, the rate of interest a company has to pay for its debt depends to some considerable extent on the financial standing of the company and, if that is not enough, on whether it can offer a lender personal or proprietary security for its loan, and the quality of the security offered. Much of the law applicable here is the general law relating to lenders and borrowers, and does not have to be analysed in a book on company law. However, three aspects of the relevant law do deserve discussion in a company law text.

First, as part of its debt-raising activities, a company may issue debt securities and those securities may be traded on a public market, in the same way as equity securities are.[2] Indeed, the line between the two forms of investment in a company can be quite blurred, and—whether the debt securities are traded on the public market or not—debt-holders can play a significant role in the indirect governance of companies. We thus need to say something about the nature of a company's debt obligations. Secondly, although the issue of granting valid security is a general problem in the law of secured lending, Companies Acts have long included their own rules governing the registration of charges granted by

[1] On insolvency, a company's creditors are repaid before the shareholders: see Ch.33.

[2] Thus, some reference to such securities has already been made in Ch.25 (public offers).

companies. These rules have been the subject of attention within various review groups, including the Law Commission, and are examined here. Thirdly, in the creation of one form of security, company lawyers took the lead in the nineteenth century. This was with the floating charge, still a controversial mechanism because of the way it can operate to crowd out the interests of unsecured creditors, in terms both of the scope of the charge and the mechanisms for enforcing it. Thus the floating charge is the third topic we need to look at in some detail. The general issues of debt and debt securities are considered in Ch.31, and the specific issues of the registration of charges and the nature and enforcement of floating charges in Ch.32.

CHAPTER 31

DEBTS AND DEBT SECURITIES

INTRODUCTION

A company will inevitably finance itself not only through issuing shares (of various classes) but also by taking loans or, alternatively, by making use of credit. Given that the majority of UK registered companies are small, typically with an issued share capital of £100 or less, the need for this sort of alternative funding is clear.[1] Of these options, taking loans, i.e. debt financing, including its more sophisticated variants, is the main source of non-equity finance for companies, 31–001

[1] Even companies such as Apple may choose to use loans to maximise returns rather than relying on its substantial operating profits (which grew so much because it also had, until 2012, a policy of not paying dividends on shares).

and is the focus of this chapter. Nevertheless, most companies (small and large) will also make use of various forms of credit, including quite sophisticated forms of asset-based financing.[2]

One basic divide in all debt financing is between simple debts (not always so simple in their documentation, and including large syndicated loans) and marketable "debt securities"[3] (with their obvious parallels with equity securities, i.e. shares).[4] As with shares, debt securities may be issued and traded privately or on public markets, with the latter being more tightly regulated. With the terminology, context is important: the terms "debt" and "debt financing" can be used perfectly generally to embrace all the options open to a company; only as the terms become more specific, and "debt" and "debt securities" are contrasted, do they reveal anything of the nature of the underlying debt instrument.

Some elements of debt financing turn out to be especially important in the corporate context. We focus on these, especially the regulated use of marketable corporate debt contracts (i.e. debt securities), including the transfer of these interests; the protective creditor-imposed governance constraints common in all debt financing; and—at various points—the similarities and differences between debt and equity financing. But some introductory points are necessary before we can address that detail. We start with the basic differences between debt and equity, and the various structural choices in debt financing.

Difference between debt (loans), equity (shares) and hybrid instruments

31–002 Often the expected sharp differences between debt and equity are blurred or non-existent. Take the financing decision itself. The choice is for the directors, and is subject to all their general duties. At first blush the constraints on directors, and the controls given to members, seem greater with share issues than with debt: recall the decisions on "proper purposes" in share issues, and the statutory rules on pre-emption rights.[5] There are no direct general law parallels when the decision concerns debt, but in practice many lenders will impose even greater constraints in their own loan agreements, insisting on contractual terms prohibiting further corporate borrowing, or at least further secured borrowing (i.e. negative pledge clauses), unless the consent of the lender is first obtained.

---

[2] These forms of financing are not discussed here, but include, e.g. the familiar mechanisms of hire-purchase, retention of title, conditional sales, sale and leaseback, finance leases, supply-chain financing, debt/receivables factoring and "repos" (sale on terms providing for repurchase). These are all well-covered in specialist texts such as L. Gullifer and J. Payne, *Corporate Finance Law: Principles and Policy*, 3rd edn (Oxford: Hart Publishing, 2020). With all of these, proper characterisation can be problematic, raising the risk that the courts will instead characterise the arrangement as a charge, which may be void for want of registration: see below, paras 32–022 to 32–030.

[3] With these further subdivided into "bonds" and "stock", although with the use of global notes and intermediation, the modern differences between these have become rather slender.

[4] Or—looking at the transaction from the other end of the telescope—we might speak not of debts and debt securities, but "loans" and "marketable loans". The latter perhaps gives a clearer sense of the similarities and distinctions in issue.

[5] See paras 10–018 to 10–021 and 24–006 to 24–014 respectively.

The same blurring is true of the contrast between members and creditors: in law a member of the company has rights in it, while a creditor has rights against it. In reality, however, the difference between the debt-holder and the share-holder may not be anything like as clear-cut, for the debt instrument may give the holder contractual rights akin to those of a shareholder, e.g. to appoint a director; to receive a share of profits (whether or not available for dividend)[6]; to repayment at a premium; to attend and vote at general meetings.[7] Covenants in the loan instrument may also, as we shall see, give debt holders considerable influence over the way in which the company is managed.[8] Moreover, where the debt instrument is secured by a floating charge on all the assets and undertaking of the company, the holder will have personal and proprietary interests in the company's business, albeit of a different kind from that of its shareholders.

The line between the holder of a debt instrument and a share is particularly narrow if the contrast is made with a preference shareholder, who is a member of the company, but a member whose share rights may limit the shareholder's dividend to a fixed percentage of the nominal value of the share and give that shareholder no right to participate in surplus assets in a winding-up, and perhaps only limited voting rights.[9] The main difference between the two in such a case may then be that the dividend on a preference share is not payable unless profits are available for distribution,[10] whereas the debt holder's interest entitlement is not subject to this constraint; and that the debt holder will rank before the preference holder in a winding-up. Thus, the legal rules operate with a binary divide between debt and equity, but the accounting rules and general practice leads to the creation of securities whose classification in accordance with this divide is problematic.

These difficulties of classification are magnified in relation to securities which are "hybrid" in character, in that the terms of the issue provide for conversion, whether from a preference share convertible into debt, or a debt convertible into equity[11] at a later date and on fixed terms. A simple way of looking at such securities is to say that they are simply one form until conversion, at which point they become the other. However, where the bond is required to be converted into equity at a certain future date, for example, it may be possible to classify it as **31–003**

[6] *Lemon v Austin Friars Investment Trust Ltd* [1926] Ch. 1 CA (instrument not prevented from being a debenture because interest payable only out of profit, which might or might not be earned in any particular year).

[7] But the debt holder's vote should not be counted if the Act requires the resolution to be passed by "members".

[8] See para.31–025.

[9] On whether they should be treated as debt or equity, see W. Bratton and M. Wachter, "A Theory of Preferred Stock" (2013) 161 University of Pennsylvania L.R. 1815. The classification may be different for different purposes, e.g. accounting purposes, or tax purposes.

[10] See para.6–007. Whether the preference shareholder is entitled by contract to the dividend, even if the company cannot lawfully pay it, is a separate question, and a potentially important one, because non-payment of the contractually due dividend may trigger voting rights for the preference shareholders or affect the amount due to the preference shareholders when the company returns to profit or is wound up: *Re Bradford Investments Plc (No.1)* [1990] B.C.C. 740 Ch D (Companies Ct).

[11] An alternative to conversion is to issue debt securities with attached warrants which give the lender the option to subscribe for shares. The debt is then not swapped—it continues—but the lender has the added benefit of an equity interest in the company.

equity in the company's accounts from the beginning, whilst nevertheless treating the interest payable on the debt before conversion as deductible for tax purposes, so that the same security is equity for one purpose and debt for another.[12]

Notably, these hybrid securities do not provide a mechanism for avoiding the statutory rules regulating shares. They do not, for example, provide a way around the prohibition on issuing shares at a discount to their nominal value.[13] And in takeover situations, debts that are convertible to shares, or debts that have voting rights, are treated as if they were shares for the purposes of the squeeze-out and sell-out provisions in the CA 2006.[14]

Should a company use debt or equity in its financing?

31–004 How does a company decide what mix of debt and equity is appropriate for its operations? Clearly its aim is to access the necessary funds at the least cost to the company. The options available will depend on the size of the company, the funding purpose, and the riskiness of the endeavour. The choice can be difficult, since the similarities between corporate debts and shares are often strong, and can be made even stronger in "hybrid" securities, as we have seen. With both debts and shares, the investor has limited liability (limited to the sum invested by way of loan or share price); with both, the rate of return likely to be demanded is reduced if the security is highly liquid; and with both, the desire for some form of governance control is present, and increases with the risk of the investment. True, the return to the debt-holder is a binding and quantified commitment made in advance, and if not met according to its terms the company risks insolvency.

Despite this, financial economists have suggested that the cost of capital is unaffected by the debt to equity ratio: this is based on the Modigliani-Miller propositions that no combination of debt and equity is better than any other, and that a company's total market value is independent of its capital structure.[15] This, as with many economic theories, is based on an "ideal" market. When real market frictions are included, it seems that companies may add some debt without reducing the return to shareholders (thus increasing corporate value) because the interest payable on debt is tax deductible for the company, whereas dividends payable to shareholders are not. But there is a tipping point: too much debt raises the risk of corporate default, and continuing default on debt obligations will, in the end, lead to corporate insolvency, whereas for shareholders it would simply

---

[12] See generally P. Pope and A. Puxty, "What is Equity? New Financial Instruments in the Interstices between Law, Accounting and Economics" (1991) 54 M.L.R. 889.

[13] To issue at a discount debt instruments which can be immediately converted into shares of the full par value would be a colourable device to evade the prohibition on issuing shares at a discount (*Mosely v Koffyfontein Mines* [1904] 2 Ch. 108 CA) but appears to be unobjectionable if the instrument is convertible only when the debentures are due for repayment at par since the shares will then be paid up in cash "through the release of a liability of the company for a liquidated sum": s.583(3)(c). See also at para.16–018 on debt/equity swaps.

[14] See ss.989, 990 (but see ss.983(2)(b) and (3)(b) ignoring such debentures in calculating the 90% threshold for the exercise of the sell-out right).

[15] F. Modigliani and M.H. Miller, "The Cost of Capital, Corporation Finance and the Theory of Investment" (1958) 48 American Economic Review 433; and also see Miller, "The Modigliani-Miller Propositions After Thirty Years" (1988) 2 Journal of Economic Perspectives 99.

lead to no payment of dividends. As well as the negative financial pressures of the debt-equity mix, there are however also advantageous pressures the mix puts on directors in their management of the company: managers can be over-inclined to prefer the interests of either themselves or their shareholders, and debt provides a disciplining effect because it requires directors to find the funds to make principal and interest repayments.

DIFFERENT STRUCTURES IN DEBT FINANCING

Terminology

31–005 The literature on debt financing quickly makes it plain that a wide variety of terms are used to describe different debt financing arrangements, although none constitute terms of art. Perhaps because the debt instrument is simply a creature of contract, and the relationship between debt-holder and company creates no particular conceptual puzzles—the relationship is simply the contractual relationship of debtor and creditor, coupled, if the debt is secured on some or all of the company's assets, with that of mortgagor and mortgagee or chargor and chargee—different terms have come to be used in commercial practice as a matter of fashion, and changing fashion at that. Many of the terms now in popular current usage emerge in the discussions which follow.

Defining a "debenture"

31–006 By contrast, instead of any of the modern terms in use in the market, the rather old-fashioned term "debenture" is the only one used in the CA 2006. And even there it is not defined: s.738 merely says that the term "includes debenture stock, bonds and any other securities of a company,[16] whether or not constituting a charge on the assets of the company".[17] This is helpful in indicating that a debenture need not be secured on the company's assets, but not for much else; and indeed commercial practice rather contradicts this, typically using the word "debenture" to refer precisely to the proprietary security agreement which secures the debt owed by the company to its lender.[18]

This lack of clear definition is despite the fact that the CA 2006 contains a (short) Pt 19, headed "Debentures", as well as frequent references throughout the Act to debentures and debenture holders.[19] The question this raises is whether the term "debenture", as defined in s.738, is wide enough to include all debts (i.e. all loan agreements), or whether it is implicitly limited to "issues" of debt which

[16] And, with unhelpful circularity, "securities" are then defined to "mean shares or debentures" (s.755(5)).

[17] See para.31–012, for more detail on debenture stock and bonds, neither of which are defined in the CA 2006.

[18] See below, Ch.32. And unsecured loans are sometimes referred to as "loan stock", in contradistinction to "debenture stock".

[19] The courts have not done much better: *Levy v Abercorris Slate & Slab Co* (1887) 37 Ch. D. 260 Ch D at 264; *British India Steam Navigation Co v IRC* (1881) 7 Q.B.D. 165 QBD at 172; *Lemon v Austin Friars Trust* [1926] Ch. 1 at 17; *Knightsbridge Estates Co v Byrne* [1940] A.C. 613 HL.

have parallels of some sort with issues of shares, noting of course that the latter embraces private issues as well as issues to the public.[20] The answer matters because of the particular statutory rules which then apply to "debentures".

Outside the statutory context, the term is certainly wide enough to include simple loans. In *Fons HK (In Liquidation) v Corporal Ltd, Pillar Securitisation Sàrl*,[21] the Court of Appeal had to decide whether an unsecured debt was a debenture, thus sweeping it into the assets subjected to a charge. The court reviewed and accepted earlier authorities which had held that simple loan agreements could be considered as debentures, and then held that, in the absence of other contractual terms or circumstances limiting the definition of debentures in the contract before them, the term simply meant an acknowledgement of debt recorded in a written document, whether or not secured. In doing so, the court rejected the approach of the lower court which had adopted a criterion of business common sense in contractual interpretation, and had held that, since an ordinary businessman would be surprised to hear a simple loan agreement described as a debenture, the contractual term did not cover unsecured debts.[22]

Although this case raised uncertainties in the market about similar breadth being assumed in the statutory definition, that seems misplaced. The case itself makes it clear that the necessary interpretation of agreements (and, by analogy, statutes) is contextual, and in the statutory context the term "debenture" is most often used in contexts where the analogy is with other issued securities.[23]

31–007 This is especially true of the statutory provisions requiring registration of "an allotment of debentures" (s.741), the keeping of a register of "debenture holders" (ss.743 onwards), and the prohibition on private companies offering "securities" to the public, with "securities" meaning shares or debentures (s.755(5)).[24] These provisions are quite inapt for general application to all loan contracts.

The issue is perhaps less clear in two further contexts, where the statute overrides equity's traditional rules. First, s.740 provides that contracts to take up and pay for debentures may be specifically enforceable, thus overriding the normal contractual rule that the lender is liable only in damages.[25] The arguments for enforcing subscriptions and underwriting obligations when an "issue" of debt securities is made may be strong, but they do not seem to apply to a single creditor who, in breach of contract, fails to make an advance. Then, damages would seem a perfectly adequate remedy. The issue does not seem to have troubled modern courts,[26] but giving s.740 a more limited remit could be achieved either by defining "debentures" more narrowly, especially since s.740 refers to a contract to "take up and pay for" debentures (terminology which seems

[20] See above, Chs 24 and 25.

[21] *Fons HK (In Liquidation) v Corporal Ltd, Pillar Securitisation Sàrl* [2014] EWCA Civ 304.

[22] *Fons HF (In Liquidation) v Corporal Ltd* [2013] EWHC 1801 (Ch).

[23] See Tijo, (2014) 73 C.L.J. 503; Roberts, [2014] J.I.B.F.L. 431.

[24] Where the difficult issue, if there is one, is usually whether there has been an offer to the public, rather than whether what is offered falls within the exceptionally wide and inclusive definition of a debenture.

[25] Thus overcoming the decision in *South African Territories Ltd v Wallington* [1898] A.C. 309 HL.

[26] Perhaps because the claim would in any event be regarded as one in debt, not damages; or perhaps that damages, assessed in context, would in any event give the company full recovery.

inapt for general loan agreements); or by relying on the use of "may" in s.740, and interpreting it as merely conferring a discretion on the court.

Secondly, s.739 specifically excludes irredeemable and long term debentures from the protective equitable doctrine prohibiting such "clogs on the equity". This, too, seems more appropriately applied to "issues" of debentures, but the statutory predecessor to s.739 was applied very generally, in 1940, in *Knightsbridge Estates Ltd v Byrne*.[27] The House of Lords held that an ordinary mortgage granted by a company was a debenture,[28] and so subject to the statutory provision disentitling the mortgagor from insisting on its equitable right to make early repayment. However, even a narrow application of the statutory provision, holding it inapplicable in this context, might not have prevented the same outcome on these facts: we might now simply say that a mortgagor has no right to early repayment unless the contract provides for it, and that a long but properly agreed maturity term is not itself sufficient to attract equitable relief.[29]

Despite these concerns, the absence of a precise statutory definition of "debenture" has given rise to surprisingly few problems, and to even fewer reported cases. In addition, modern financial markets regulation is typically directed at the product being issued rather than at the issuer or the investors, and it then defines its focus more clearly than by use of the broad term "debenture". Nevertheless, in what follows we have tried to avoid the use of the term "debenture" in favour of either more specific descriptions of the contracts in issue or, by contrast, when breadth is intended, the more generic term, "debt".

Small and large scale loans

Small and medium size companies tend to rely on loans from banks and, especially in very small companies, loans from directors and shareholders.[30] *Salomon*[31] is an old and typical illustration. Invariably the loan terms will be individually negotiated to reflect the risk, and, as we shall see, can be quite demanding in terms of the ongoing obligations imposed on the borrower, the potential consequences of any "event of default", and the various forms of security (proprietary and personal) required to support the company's primary obligation to repay the debt. 31–008

Large-scale debt financing for bigger companies is more varied. It comes in two main forms: from banks (perhaps by way of "indirect financing", so called

[27] *Knightsbridge Estates Ltd v Byrne* [1940] A.C. 613.

[28] Whilst also accepting that the mortgage would not be a "debenture" for the purposes of some of the other sections of the Act: Viscount Maugham at 624. Clearly such a mortgage does not have to be registered in the company's register of debenture holders under s.743 in addition to registration of the mortgage under Pt 25.

[29] See *Hooper v Western Counties and South Wales Telephone Co Ltd* (1892) 68 L.T. 78; *Hyde Management Services (Pty) Ltd v FAI Insurances* (1979–80) 144 C.L.R. 541 Aust. HC. And in the *Knightsbridge Estates* case, Viscount Maugham suggested as much, at least between competent and well-advised contracting parties: at 626.

[30] Care must be taken with these transactions. Often, it is true; the insiders provide loans on very favourable terms. But sometimes the terms are exploitative, and the risk is that they may then be held to amount to an unlawful return of capital: *Ridge Securities Ltd v IRC* [1964] 1 W.L.R. 479 Ch D; *Progress Property Co Ltd v Moore* [2010] UKSC 55; [2011] 1 W.L.R. 1.

[31] *Salomon v Salomon & Co Ltd* [1897] A.C. 22 HL. See para.2–001.

because the banks in turn need to seek investment funds from third parties) and from the capital markets ("direct financing", because the relationship is directly with the lender). Here, too, the terms of the debt security are individually negotiated, even if against industry models. Sizeable transactions may involve both types of debt. The initial debt finance for a major acquisition may, for example, be provided wholly by banks, often under a syndicated loan agreement[32] involving several banks and providing for a variety of types of senior and junior (or "mezzanine") debt, the terms "senior" and "junior" referring to the order in which the debt falls to be repaid (the ranking of their claims on the assets of the debtor). The banks may, subsequently, offload that debt (in a wide variety of ways) to third parties so as to realise the value of the asset earlier than the debt's maturity date (i.e. capitalise the debt) or so as to shed some of the risk. On the company's side, sometimes this form of bank debt is too short-term and is provided on such financially unattractive terms that the company itself has a strong incentive to finance differently or to re-finance the bank loan as soon as possible.

Debts and "debt securities"

31–009 So far the distinction has been between small and large-scale loans, and single and multiple lenders. But lenders are likely to be persuaded to accept a lower rate of return if their loans are highly liquid. This is not to say that traditional loans cannot be transferred, as we shall see, but there is no organised secondary market for their transfer. Thus, as with shares, the company has an incentive to arrange for its debts, as "debt securities", to be traded on a secondary public market, so enabling a lender to liquidate its investment easily by selling it to a third party.[33] It follows that a company might make an offer of "debt securities" (analogous in many ways to "equity securities") on the public (retail or wholesale) markets, much like a company might offer a new issue of its equity securities (shares) so as to raise funds. It might also make similar issues privately. As with shares, public offers are strictly regulated; private offers less so. This is considered below, along with the different and rather more complicated structures used for different debt security issues, although otherwise many of the applicable rules are those which have already been dealt with in relation to shares.[34]

---

[32] With the various banks using either agency or trust structures to manage their relationship with each other: see paras 31–011 onwards.

[33] So, as with shares, the Stock Exchange can provide a primary market for the issuance of debt securities and a secondary market for trading in them.

[34] See Chs 24 and 25 and paras 31–015 onwards.

SINGLE AND MULTIPLE LENDERS

Single lenders

In the simplest of cases, the company borrows from a single lender. The loan contract between the parties will define their rights and obligations. As we will see later, their contract will undoubtedly include covenants restricting the company's power to act completely autonomously,[35] and may include terms providing for the debt to be secured against the company's assets, or for "equity-like" features (such as voting rights for the lender), or for conversion from debt to equity in defined circumstances. **31–010**

The company may repeat this borrowing process as it grows, entering into sequential loans agreements with different lenders, with the general law then governing any competition between the lenders seeking to have their secured or unsecured loans repaid. The general law outcome is often varied by agreement between the lenders (a "subordination agreement"), although the limitations inherent in these subordination agreements should be noted: the borrower cannot agree with lenders that the general insolvency law rules will not apply to the distribution of its own assets, but that some other distribution will be effected; the lenders, by contrast, can agree amongst themselves to share their different insolvency entitlements in any way they wish. Thus a lender who might otherwise have had priority may agree with other lenders to be deferred; or a secured or unsecured lender may agree to take nothing until other lenders have been paid in full.[36] It may be wondered why lenders would agree to this, but it is relatively common for insiders (whether the company's directors or other members of the same corporate group) to agree to be subordinated so as to enable the company to attract further external financing, or at least to attract it on commercially acceptable terms.

This all works well for smaller scale financing needs, but if the company has more substantial needs, then it is likely to need to access a number of different lenders simultaneously. This can be achieved either by means of a syndicated loan or by the issue of marketable debt securities. The underlying contracts for such loans come in as many varieties as individual loans, with covenants and security interests as agreed by contract, but each must also of necessity be overlaid by some sort of organisational structure which enables the different lenders to co-ordinate their information and decision needs in relation to the borrower and, importantly, to control hold-out or independent-mover problems within the group. These problems are not unlike the various co-ordination problems which exist between shareholders.[37] As well, it will be in the interests of the lenders themselves that their chosen structure does not inhibit their rights to transfer their interests, although only debt securities are deliberately designed

[35] See paras 31–023 onwards.

[36] See para.32–012.

[37] See Ch.13.

as marketable securities. We discuss these transfer and governance features later, but first say a little more about the structures themselves.[38]

Syndicated loans

31–011 Syndicated loans are typically embodied in a single contract, signed by all parties, although usually put together by a lead bank or underwriter of the loan, known as the "arranger", "agent", or "lead lender".[39] This lender may put up a proportionally bigger share of the loan, or perform duties like dispersing cash flows amongst the other syndicate members, and other administrative tasks. But the syndicated lenders are explicitly not partners, and their interests are deliberately several, not joint, although, as perhaps one mark of the joint endeavour, their agreement is likely to provide for "no-action clauses" and for pari passu recovery should the borrower become insolvent,[40] thus denying any one lender a first-mover advantage if the debt looks risky.[41] As with all agreements involving multiple lenders, the lenders' own internal governance arrangements are often subject to decision by majority rule (as with shareholders), and to various exclusions of liability by the arranger: these are considered below.[42]

It can be seen even from this brief outline that syndicated loans are essentially scaled up versions of single bank loans (or loans from non-bank entities), and are likely to contain similar sorts of detailed protective covenants, although with the advantage that one lender is not required to carry the entire risk. As with single bank loans, it is also generally true that these transactions are not motivated by the lenders' desire to acquire marketable securities[43]; the lenders' interests may be transferable under general law provisions, and there is a good private market in such interests, but these lenders are quite likely to remain engaged in the deal for its full term.

Debt securities: distinguishing "bonds" and "stocks"

31–012 By contrast, where marketability of the underlying debt is a material consideration, the company usually attracts loans from multiple lenders, again typically financial institutions and specialist investors, by issuing either "bonds" (or "notes" or "commercial paper")[44] or "loan stock" (often labelled "debenture stock" if the loan is secured on a pool of assets, although neither term is a term of

---

[38] See L. Gullifer and J. Payne, *Corporate Finance Law: Principles and Policy*, 3rd edn (Oxford: Hart Publishing, 2020), Ch.8.

[39] On the related duties, see 31–027 to 31–028.

[40] Assuming there is no pragmatic reason for some alternative explicit subordination agreement.

[41] See P. Rawlings, "The Management of Loan Syndicates and the Rights of Individual Lenders" (2009) 24 J.I.B.L.R. 179.

[42] See paras 31–027 to 31–030.

[43] And thus typically are not rated by credit rating agencies.

[44] The difference between the two used to be that bonds had longer maturities than notes or commercial paper, although it was never clear precisely where the dividing line was drawn. Both terms are now used far more indiscriminately.

art, and both are often used more broadly).[45] Such issues are often tradeable on a public secondary market,[46] although this is not essential.[47] There was, historically, a fundamental structural difference between bonds and stock, although in modern practice both the structure and co-ordination problems turn out to be rather similar.

Bonds (or notes) are, in theory, individual debt obligations owed by the company to each of the bondholders, whether they are registered holders or holders of bearer bonds,[48] with the latter being far more common. Historically, each individual lender (bondholder) purchased a number of bonds from the company, denominated in appropriate amounts, much as shareholders purchase equity interests by buying different numbers of issued shares. In the same way, too, each bondholder became the legal owner of its own bonds.[49] Co-ordination problems between the bondholders were, and are still, typically resolved by appointing an appropriately authorised agent, or, more commonly, a trustee for the bondholders,[50] and also requiring, in certain circumstances, majority votes of the bondholders themselves.[51] However, any sense of a clear divide between bonds, as individual debt obligations, and loan or debenture stock (as described below) has become far less distinct given modern practices. As with shares, bonds are now typically held via an intermediary, whether or not they are traded on public markets. So a "global note" is issued by the company to the intermediary (representing the debt due from the company to the intermediary), and the intermediary, as legal owner (of either a registered or a bearer bond, again with the latter being more common, except when intended for the US market) holds its interest on trust for a number—often a large number—of account holders.[52] The intermediary can then perform a number of important services for the account holders, including holding any security for the bond, and, at least from a functional perspective, the resulting organisational structure ends up being similar to that operating with loan stock.[53]

---

45 As already noted, the definition of "debenture" in s.738 includes both "bonds" and "debenture stock".

46 In the future, all traded securities will be obliged to be either dematerialised, or immobilised and held through intermediaries, in order to improve the efficiency and integrity of the market: Regulation 909/2014 on improving securities settlement in the EU and on central securities depositories [2014] OJ L257/1 and Central Securities Depositories (Amendment) (EU Exit) Regulations 2018 (SI 2018/1320).

47 Some would have the necessary characteristics, but nevertheless be traded "over the counter" (OTC).

48 See Ch.24, for the equivalent terminology in relation to shares.

49 This was essential if the bond was a bearer bond, and thus intended to be a negotiable instrument.

50 Although then there is the nice question of what, precisely, is the subject-matter of the trust: see L. Gullifer and J. Payne, *Corporate Finance Law: Principles and Policy*, 3rd edn (Oxford: Hart Publishing, 2020), pp.394 onwards.

51 See para.31–029.

52 For details of the transfer of intermediated securities, see Ch.26.

53 See para.31–014.

With loan or debenture stock, a single debt obligation is issued by the company and typically held by a trustee on behalf of the various stockholders.[54] If the loan is secured, the trustee will also hold the security on trust. The stockholders therefore have only an equitable interest in the debt (secured or not), held as tenants in common in proportion to the amount of the debt they own (with no limit on how the fractions are denominated, in contrast to bonds). Even as beneficiaries under the trust, however, the stockholders are nevertheless entered on the company's register of debenture holders (in contrast to equitable owners of shares, who are not recognised in the company's register of shareholders).[55] These debenture holders receive a certificate (if the stock is certificated); if it is dematerialised, a similar register is kept in the CREST system.[56] It follows that, unlike the largely meaningless distinction between "shares" and "stock",[57] the similar distinction between "debentures" and "debenture stock" is far from meaningless and debenture stock has considerable practical advantages. Thus, in this structure, the stockholders have all the advantages of a protective trustee structure, but with the (relatively few) disadvantages of only having equitable interests in the underlying asset.[58]

31–013 One clear (but now increasingly irrelevant) difference between bonds (and notes) and stock is that the former, in its simplest guise, gives its holder legal title to a debt of a particular amount owed by the company to the bondholder. That debt can be transferred only as a complete unit, since, even with statutory assistance, the transfer of part of debt is not possible.[59] By contrast, stock gives each stockholder a fractional equitable interest in a larger debt. That fractional interest can in turn be transferred in any fraction of that amount. This is an attribute of the flexibility of interests held under a trust structure, and their assignability in equity. It follows that where bonds are issued to an intermediary who holds the debt on trust for a number of account holders, as is now commonplace, the account holders are in a similar position to the stockholders when it comes to transferring their interests. All this is subject to one important qualification: any form of debt security will be issued on its own negotiated terms, and those terms may heavily influence the rights of parties to deal with their individually held interests in the larger security. We consider the transfer of debt securities later in this chapter.

---

[54] Alternatively, the company can create loan stock by deed poll, i.e. by unilaterally executing a deed which promises to pay those registered as stockholders, which is enforceable by anyone who is a stockholder. This structure is less common, usually confined to larger issues with few holders and no active market.

[55] CA 2006 s.126.

[56] See para.26–012.

[57] See para.6–011 where it is noted that conversion of shares into stock is no longer permitted.

[58] Made especially few because the competing interests are also typically equitable, e.g. sale of stock by a stockholder is sale of an equitable interest, so does not raise the spectre of competition with a bona fide purchaser for value. But also see *Re Dunderland Iron Ore Co* [1909] 1 Ch. 446 Ch D at 452, and noted at fn.62.

[59] Law of Property Act 1925 s.136.

Debt securities: trustees for the bondholders or stockholders

As we have already noted, it is now almost invariable practice for an issue of marketable loans to interpose a trustee, normally a trust corporation,[60] between the company and the bondholders or stockholders. The loan contract is then between the company and the trustee, and any security over the company's assets can be made out in favour of the trustees, who hold it on trust for the benefit of the debt security holders. Such an arrangement has many advantages. **31–014**

First, it greatly simplifies the security arrangements.[61] A legal mortgage can be vested in the trustees, on trust for the debt security holders, and the trustees retain custody of the title deeds; a charge can be granted in favour of the trustees, and the rights under the charge document exercised by the trustees for the benefit of the debt security holders. This is difficult, sometimes impossible, with multiple parties.

Secondly, the primary enforcement of the loan (and any security) will be between the company and the trustees, being the parties to the loan agreement.[62] A practical side-effect of this is to impose equality amongst the debt security holders, although their own governance arrangements generally reinforce that.[63]

Finally, it will provide a single trustee corporation or a small body of persons charged with the duty of monitoring the debt security holders' interests and of intervening if they are in jeopardy. This is obviously far more satisfactory than leaving it to a widely dispersed class of investors, each of whom may lack the skill, interest and financial resources required to take action alone.[64] It will also be possible, in the trust deed, to impose on the trustee company or its directors additional obligations, regarding the submission of information and the like, which might not otherwise be practicable.[65] Similarly, the trustees can be empowered to convene meetings of the holders in order to acquaint them with the position and to obtain their instructions. Do not let this create a false sense of security, however: as we note later, trustees are not always motivated to behave proactively.[66]

---

[60] Formerly it was common for banks to undertake this work but they have tended to fight shy of it since *Re Dorman Long & Co* [1934] Ch. 635 drew attention to the conflict of interest and duty which might arise when the bank was both a creditor in its own right and a trustee. Today, therefore, the duties are generally undertaken by other professional trust corporations.

[61] Such securities are, nevertheless, subject to all the rules considered in Ch.32. Note that it is uncommon for major publicly traded companies today to give security over their assets in public issues of debentures.

[62] *Re Uruguay Central and Hygueritas Railway Co of Monte Video* (1879) 11 Ch. D. 372 Ch D; *Re Dunderland Iron Ore Co Ltd* [1909] 1 Ch. 446. Theoretically, although there are trustees, an individual security-holder could take steps to enforce the security (using the *Vandepitte* procedure: *Vandepitte v Preferred Accident Insurance Corp of New York* [1933] A.C. 70 PC), but trust deeds typically contain a "no action" clause. And, in other respects, the security-holder will not be regarded as a creditor of the borrowing company, so, for example, cannot petition for its winding up if there is default: *Re Dunderland Iron Ore Co* [1909] 1 Ch. 446 at 452.

[63] See para.31–029.

[64] Although the governance arrangements typically prohibit this in any event: see para.31–029.

[65] See the facts which gave rise to the litigation in *New Zealand Guardian Trust Co Ltd v Brooks* [1995] 1 W.L.R. 96 PC.

[66] See *Concord Trust v Law Debenture Trust Corp Plc* [2006] 1 B.C.L.C. 616 HL and the discussion at para.31–028.

ISSUE OF DEBT SECURITIES

Private issues

31–015 The act of issuing debt securities (assuming no public offer) is not much regulated by the CA 2006. The one significant provision is to the effect that a contract with a company to "take up and pay for debentures" is specifically enforceable, as noted earlier.[67] Otherwise, in the absence of a public offer, the Act is notable for the absence of regulation of the issuing process, assuming instead that debenture holders will themselves make appropriate provision for their own protection.[68]

In addition, and unlike the rule applying to shares,[69] there is no rule in the CA 2006, even for public companies, requiring the authorisation of either the shareholders or the existing debt security holders for a new issue of debt, although this matter may well be one of the matters regulated in the trust deed of the existing debt securities.[70] In some ways this is surprising, since a large increase in the company's debt could have a significant impact—positive or negative depending on whether the venture in which the new funds are embarked is successful—on the prospects of the shareholders and debt holders.[71] Nor does the Act create pre-emption rights[72] on an issue of debt, probably because the rights of the existing debt holders are not affected by a new issue, although their value might be, since a company seen to be overburdening itself with debt would cause the market value of its existing debt instruments to fall. Again, however, this matter can be dealt with in the trust deed governing the existing debt.

Finally, since debt does not count as legal capital, the rules relating to issue at a discount and to the quality of the consideration received, which apply to shares,[73] are not extended to debt generally or debt securities in particular.[74] For the same reason, the distribution and capital maintenance rules[75] do not apply to loans, so that interest may (normally must) be paid on loans even though no profits have been earned, and debts may be freely repurchased by the company (subject to the loan terms themselves), assuming in both cases it has the cash to do so. The only specific statutory provision in this area in fact facilitates repurchases of debt by providing that redeemed debt securities may be reissued

---

[67] 2006 Act s.740. See above, para.31–007.

[68] See paras 31–027 onwards.

[69] See para.24–004.

[70] See at para.31–025.

[71] Even the "Class 1 transaction" rule of the Listing Rules, requiring shareholder consent, does not apply to an issue of securities, unless the transaction involves the acquisition or disposal of a fixed asset of the company or a subsidiary: LR 10.1.3.

[72] On pre-emption rights for shareholders see para.24–006.

[73] See Ch.16.

[74] *Re Anglo-Danubian Steam Navigation and Colliery Co* (1875) L.R. 20 Eq. 339 Ct of Chancery.

[75] See Chs 17 and 18.

with their original priority, rather than cancelled, unless the company's articles contain provisions to the contrary or the company in some other way resolved to cancel them.[76]

Of course, the general duties of directors will still apply to their decisions relating to the issue of debt securities, even, perhaps especially, in the absence of specific statutory regulation in the area. **31–016**

Although all this is left unregulated, the CA 2006 does contain a number of largely administrative provisions relating to the issue of debt securities. Section 741 requires companies to register an allotment of debentures with the Registrar of companies, as is required for shares, so that the existence of the debentures is public knowledge (unless the debentures are issued as bearer debentures). A company is not obliged itself to keep a register of debenture holders, but, if it does, it must locate it and make it available for inspection by debenture holders and members of the public in the same way as the register of shareholders.[77] This includes the power, applicable also to the share register, to apply to the court for an order not to comply with the request for inspection.[78] Probably more important in practice is the provision which entitles a debenture-holder to be provided at any time (on payment of the appropriate fee) with a copy of the trust deed on which the debentures are secured, if, as is normal, there is such a trust.[79] This provision is perhaps the functional equivalent of the public availability of the articles in the case of shareholders.

Finally, as we shall see in Ch.32, where debentures are secured against the company's assets, it is often necessary to register those security instruments at Companies House, on pain of invalidity against the liquidator on the company's insolvency.

Public issues of debt securities

Matters change radically, however, if there is a public offer of debt securities. In that case, much of the law discussed in Ch.25 will be applicable, and will not be dealt with here. As with shares, these rules are designed to ensure that those buying debt securities on the primary or secondary markets have the appropriate information necessary to assess the risks. One difference, though, is that it might be thought that the risks are inherently smaller with debt securities, since the holder of a debt has the ultimate right to sue for the sum due under the debt, and is also commonly protected by powerful contractual and perhaps proprietary provisions to assist on that front, whereas the holder of the share has a mere expectation of benefit and therefore perhaps requires a wider range of information upon which assess the relevant risks. This is perhaps the explanation **31–017**

---

[76] CA 2006 s.752. On treasury shares, see para.17–023. Note also s.753 which is designed to remove the technical difficulties revealed in *Re Russian Petroleum Co* [1907] 2 Ch. 540 CA when a company secures its overdraft on current account by depositing with the bank a debenture for a fixed amount.

[77] CA 2006 ss.743–748. Less detail is required in the register of debentures, if there is one, than in the share register. On the share register, see para.24–019.

[78] CA 2006 Act s.745.

[79] CA 2006 Act s.749. Non-compliance is a criminal offence on the part of any officer of the company in default.

for the hierarchy of information requirements,[80] which puts equity securities ahead of debt securities issued to the retail market, and then debt securities issued to the wholesale market, and leaves the private syndicated loan market completely unregulated by the CA 2006.

The prohibition on private companies offering their shares to the public extends to a public offer of any securities, including debt securities.[81] If public companies do offer their debt securities to the public, the required disclosure varies depending upon whether the offer is general, or is, on the other hand, either explicitly directed only to sophisticated ("qualified") investors or is of such large denomination (i.e. at least €100,000) that it can be assumed to be addressed only to such a sophisticated ("wholesale") market.[82] And if the issued securities are then to be traded on a secondary market, as would be typical for reasons already discussed,[83] the continuing disclosure rules again depend upon the sophistication of the market participants.[84]

It might be thought that if companies already have listed shares, then they would automatically opt for the more onerous regime, since it opens the debt issue to wider markets and the companies are already subject to onerous disclosure regimes in respect of their equity securities. However, the specific disclosure required for a new issue is substantial, and debt security issues are typically put together in quick order, so companies will make use of whatever exemptions are possible, while still ensuring they have access to the most fruitful markets.

31–018 Although many of the rules on public issues of shares also apply equally to public issues of debt securities, and for similar reasons, one notable difference is that there is no limitation on the payment of underwriting commissions, and an allotment may be made no matter how small a response there is to the offer.[85] This is no doubt because the rights of the debenture-holder are comprehensively specified in the debt contract, whereas with shares, the expected returns may depend very materially on these two features.

Finally, note that an issue may begin as a private issue to an underwriter or other financial institution, and those institutions may then themselves provide the necessary disclosure to enable the securities to be traded on either wholesale or retail markets.

---

[80] See Regulation 2019/980 [2019] OJ L166/26 Annexes 1, 6 and 7.

[81] CA 2006 Act s.755. See para.24–002. For a detailed outline of these rules, see L. Gullifer and J. Payne, *Corporate Finance Law: Principles and Policy*, 3rd edn (Oxford: Hart Publishing, 2020), pp.670–689.

[82] FSMA 2000 ss.102B, 86(1).

[83] Often bonds are traded over the counter (OTC), even though the bonds are listed. Many institutional investors are not permitted to invest in unlisted securities, so listing sometimes simply provides a necessary quality kitemark (as backed by the requirements of the LSE for listing).

[84] See para.25–018.

[85] i.e. for marketable loans, there is no equivalent of CA 2006 ss.552 and 578.

Special rules

A further means of regulation that might be adopted is one that is not focused broadly on all public offers, but more narrowly on specifically defined types of transactions. We see this in evidence in the regulatory regime which has been put in place relating to financial collateral,[86] and to the credit derivatives market.[87] Similarly, specific regulation has been implemented related to covered bonds, in the form of the Regulated Covered Bonds Regulations 2008.[88] Taken as a relatively simple illustration, this serves to indicate the issues that might be thought worth regulating. A "covered" bond (sometimes called a "structured covered bond") is a particular form of bond which is payable by the issuer (typically a bank or building society),[89], but is also backed by a specific pool of high quality assets, in the UK held by a special purpose vehicle (SPV), so that the assets are ring-fenced with the result that, if the issuer becomes insolvent, the repayments on the bond can continue to be made by recourse to the those assets, and in priority to the issuer's general creditors. **31–019**

The regulations are designed to ensure that the asset pool is high quality[90]; that its value is maintained throughout the life of the bond at a high enough figure to ensure that the bond is 8% "over-collateralised",[91] thus guaranteeing sufficient resources to cover realisation costs and bondholder repayment in full; that there is regulated oversight of the collateral by the issuer and the "Asset Pool Monitor" (analogous to an external auditor)[92]; and that there is consistent and frequent reporting to investors. These additional reporting and oversight requirements aside, a covered bond differs from a normal securitisation principally in that the issuer of a covered bond remains liable to the bondholder, whereas a securitisation is typically non-recourse; and the pool of assets associated with a covered bond is regulated so that the issue is compulsorily "over-collateralised".

What has this structure achieved? From the company's point of view, it has turned (illiquid) mortgages into cash which it can use to expand its business. And, conversely, from the investors' point of view, they have made a loan to the company but of a highly secure type. Provided the SPV has been set up in such a way that the assets purchased by the SPV cannot be clawed back by the issuer in the latter's liquidation and provided the issuer is obliged to maintain the quality and value of the mortgages held by the SPV, the note-holders can remain unconcerned about such an event because their security will remain intact. This is

---

[86] For an informative and accessible description, see L. Gullifer, "What Should We Do About Financial Collateral?" (2012) C.L.P. 1.

[87] See *Firth: Derivatives Law and Practice* (London, Sweet & Maxwell); A. Hudson, *The Law on Financial Derivatives*, 6th edn (London, Sweet & Maxwell, 2017).

[88] SI 2008/346, as amended. Also see *Review of the UK's Regulatory Framework for Covered Bonds* (April 2011), FSA and HM Treasury Consultation Paper (Consultation Paper); and the *Regulated Covered Bonds FCA Handbook*.

[89] There were, in 2020, only 14 UK issuers registered to issue covered bonds.

[90] Public sector or residential or commercial mortgages, with the register indicating the class or the mixture, which cannot then be changed over the life of the bond. In order to maintain investor confidence, securitisations do not constitute eligible collateral.

[91] With the FCA having the right to impose over-collateralisation requirements on a case-by-case basis.

[92] 2008 Regulations reg.17A.

why the bond is "covered".[93] Overall, the issuer is incurring debt through the covered bond in order to further the business of itself making secured loans to others, its business model turning on its ability to borrow money through the bond at a lower rate of interest than it itself charges when lending to others.

It will be apparent that the above structure can be created by contract, and so it may be wondered how the need for the Regulations arises. Just like debts and debt securities, such bonds were not brought into existence by the Regulations, even though they are a relatively recent and still little used development in the UK. In fact, the purpose of the Regulations was simply to create a more attractive and ready market for covered bonds, rather than to bring them into existence. That specialised market need not be considered here: the point being made is simply to illustrate the issues that market regulators have in their sight lines.

TRANSFER OF DEBTS AND DEBT SECURITIES

Transfer of simple debts

31–020 Although the rules on legal capital do not stand in the way of re-purchase by a company of its debts, unlike its shares,[94] it may well be financially extremely inconvenient for the company to do so (or indeed it may be prohibited by the lender).[95] However, it is normally possible for the lender to find liquidity in other ways. There may be a private market in the loans, and indeed many banks lending to private equity funds aim to have only a small, if any, proportion of the loans made on their books six months after the transaction completes.[96] These loans can be transferred by outright sales, such as invoice discounting to a financier (of distressed debt if the rating of the debt security is poor), or by securitisation transactions (real or synthetic),[97] or in other ways.

---

[93] The structure would be even simpler if the notes were issued by the SPV and the investors' money paid directly to it. However, investors may have good reasons for preferring the loans to be made to the issuer, so that the investors have the benefit of both the issuer's promise to repay and the claim on the asset pool held by the SPV. Where the note or bond is issued by the SPV itself, the arrangement is referred to as an "asset-backed" or "mortgage-backed" security, but is non-recourse and does not count as a covered bond. Equally, in the UK, if the issuer merely secures the bond against a ring-fenced pool of its own assets, without transferring them to a SPV, the arrangement is certainly a secured bond (assuming the security is properly registered), but it cannot be a covered bond in the UK (although other European jurisdictions have more relaxed rules in this regard, adopting what is called an "integrated model" covered bond), but the UK rules are designed to be as protective as possible to attract the greatest number of market participants.

[94] See paras 17–002 to 17–005. This is because debt is not legal capital.

[95] *Knightsbridge Estates Ltd v Byrne* [1940] A.C. 613.

[96] Also see L. Gullifer and J. Payne, *Corporate Finance Law: Principles and Policy*, 3rd edn (Oxford: Hart Publishing, 2020), Ch.9.

[97] The detail is not examined in this work, but the basic structure is that the bank sells the securities to a SPV, so that the bank obtains immediate cash (inevitably discounted) in return for the debts which were due for repayment in the future, and the sale also ensures that those debts are no longer on the bank's balance sheet. The SPV then in turn issues debt securities to third parties on the basis that their repayment is to come exclusively from the original assets (the debts) now held by the SPV (with the securities repayable on the basis of this non-recourse liability being, more positively, described as "asset-backed securities" (ABS)). This basic structure has been developed in various ways. One of these is "synthetic securitisation", where the debts are not sold to the SPV, but the SPV instead makes

The ability to transfer debt in this way helps persuade lenders to agree to provide finance, but, on the other side, it may also tempt lenders to worry less about the repayment risks, knowing that they can shift those risks to third parties. The financial crisis in 2008 presents clear evidence of this. Where debt securities are traded on public markets, the compulsory disclosure rules are designed to minimise those risks for secondary purchasers, although their effectiveness in this regard might be questioned; otherwise, as elsewhere, the rule is, "buyer beware".

Transfer of debt securities

Turning from transfers of debt generally to transfers of debt securities, these can be absolute (whether at law or in equity) or by way of security interest (see Ch.32). We do not say a great deal about the legal rules here,[98] since the legislation clearly assumes that debt securities will be transferred in much the same way as shares, and so reference can simply be made to the discussion in Ch.26. Hence, initial allotments and subsequent transfers of registered debt securities must be registered (s.741, as s.554 for shares; and s.771 for transfers of both), and the register must be open for inspection with the right to obtain copies of it (ss.743, 744); as with shares, the bond documentation or certificates of debenture stock must be issued by the company to the holder within two months, unless the issue is to a clearing house or its nominee (ss.769, 776, 778, although for debt securities there is no equivalent of s.768 providing for the certificate to be evidence of title); and, as with shares, the transfer, unless by operation of law or by CREST, must be in writing using an appropriate instrument of transfer (s.770). Equally, the Uncertificated Securities Regulations 2001 (SI 2001/3755) (as amended) uses the word "securities", and so permits the transfer of title to debt securities held in uncertificated form.[99] And in relation to these debt securities held in uncertificated form, the Operator is now required to maintain in the UK a register of the names and addresses of those holding debt securities in this way, together with a statement of the size of the individual holdings.[100] **31–021**

Transferees could also be faced with problems, similar to those in relation to shares, regarding equitable and legal ownership of debt securities and the priority

a loan to the bank, secured on the pool of debts, and then the SPV, as before, issues securities to fund that loan. It is crucial to the success of this synthetic structure that the SPV can easily enforce its security against the pooled assets, and to that end the IA 1986 s.72B enables such floating charge security holders to continue to be able to appoint an administrative receiver provided the debt is over £50 million, and despite the abolition of administrative receivers generally. The credit rating of these bonds then depends upon the quality of the secured assets, not the overall credit rating of the company.

[98] Although there are some difficult conceptual problems, especially with transfer of intermediated securities: see L. Gullifer and J. Payne, *Corporate Finance Law: Principles and Policy*, 3rd edn (Oxford: Hart Publishing, 2020), Ch.9. As a result, the trust deeds of debenture stock issues or the documentation associated with bond issues typically provide explicitly that the holder takes free of all equities affecting the current and previous holders (including the account holder for bond issues). The effectiveness of these provisions is not guaranteed, and clear wording is essential: see *Re Kaupthing Singer & Friedlander Ltd*; sub nom. *Newcastle Building Society v Mill* [2009] EWHC 740 (Ch).

[99] Regulation 19 and the definition of "security" in reg.3(1). (Unaffected by the Uncertificated Securities (Amendment and EU Exit) Regulations 2019 (SI 2019/679).) See generally Ch.26.

[100] Uncertificated Securities Regulations 2001 reg.22(3). Also see reg.22(1) and (2).

of competing transferees. On general principles relating to assignments of choses in action, a transfer of legal title to a debt security would be thought to operate as an equitable assignment until it becomes a legal assignment when the company receives notice of it. However, as with shares, given that registration is compulsory under the CA 2006, the rule is that legal title passes from transferor to transferee only at the date of registration. But this is further complicated with debt securities as we also have to consider exactly what is being transferred. It is now usually only the trustee of the debt for the security holders who has legal title to the debt. Then the question of any assignment by the security holders can involve nice questions of law, since the transferor's interest is only ever equitable, as with debenture stock (notwithstanding that the holders must be registered) and also with other intermediated securities, following the common practice with most marketable debt securities.[101]

Other differences flow from the fact that, whereas the rights of shareholders depend mainly on the provisions of the company's articles, which will have been drafted in the interests of the company, those of debt holders depend upon the terms of a contract between lender and borrower and its terms will have to be acceptable to the lender as well as the borrower. Some debt securities will, like shares, include non-assignability clauses, or clauses restricting assignment subject to conditions.[102] This might seem an odd clause to include in a debt, but it will protect the corporate debtor from losing potentially valuable post-assignment rights of set-off against the creditor, or protect against possible transfer of the debt to a third party who may not be quite so generous in deciding when and how to enforce the agreed debt covenants. The question then arises, precisely as with shares, whether a purported assignment in breach of the anti-assignment clause is effective to give the assignee any rights at all. The answer, as with shares, depends upon the precise terms of the clause, but the analysis can be difficult.[103]

31–022 With marketable debt securities, by contrast, there will be no problems arising from restrictions on transferability or from a company's lien; debt securities will invariably provide that the money expressed to be secured will be paid, and that the debt securities are transferable, free from any equities or claims between the company and the original or any intermediate holder.[104] It is possible that the terms of issue of the debt securities will be inconsistent with their being held in

---

[101] The difficult issues of analysis are well described in L. Gullifer and J. Payne, *Corporate Finance Law: Principles and Policy*, 3rd edn (Oxford: Hart Publishing, 2020), Ch.9. Also see above, fn.98.

[102] In *Barbados Trust Co Ltd v Bank of Zambia* [2007] EWCA Civ 148, where consent of the debtor was required, such consent not to be unreasonably withheld.

[103] See *Barbados Trust Co Ltd v Bank of Zambia* [2007] EWCA Civ 148; *Linden Gardens Trust Ltd v Lenesta Sludge Disposal Ltd* [1994] 1 A.C. 85 HL; *Morris v Royal Bank of Scotland Plc* No.HC-2014-001910 unreported 3 July 2015 Norris J; R. Goode, "Inalienable Rights?" (1979) 42 M.L.R. 553; M. Bridge, "The Nature of Assignment and Non-Assignment Clauses" (2016) 132 L.Q.R. 47; L. Gullifer and J. Payne, *Corporate Finance Law: Principles and Policy*, 3rd edn (Oxford: Hart Publishing, 2020), para.9.2.2.6.

[104] Without this, debenture holders and their transferees would be in grave danger, for a debenture, unless in bearer form and thus a negotiable instrument (*Bechuanaland Exploration Co v London Trading Bank Ltd* [1898] 2 Q.B. 658 QBD (Comm)), would, as a chose in action, be transferable only subject to the state of the account between the company and the transferor. As stressed in Ch.26, neither shares (unless in the form of share warrants to bearer) nor debentures (unless bearer bonds) are negotiable instruments like bills of exchange. Although CARD (paras 25–010 and 25–016) requires

uncertificated form, in which case they will need to be altered if the company wishes to make this form of holding debt securities available.[105] The Regulations do not provide a simple shortcut to the necessary amendments, as they do in the case of shares, but they do something to encourage trustees to agree to such amendments without holding a meeting of the debt security holders. A trustee for debt security holders is not to be chargeable with breach of trust by reason only of his assenting to changes in the trust deed necessary to enable the debt security holders to hold the debt securities in uncertificated form or to transfer them or exercise any rights attached to them electronically.[106]

The great contrast, however, between debt and equity securities is that debt securities secured by charges on the company's property throw up problems regarding the priority between conflicting charges. These problems are dealt with in the next chapter.

PROTECTIVE GOVERNANCE REGIMES IN DEBTS

General

The terms on which debt financing is agreed will depend upon the risk-reward calculations between the lender and borrower. Higher interest rates and greater restrictions on the debtor's autonomy, as well as proprietary security, are typical if the risk is high. As well, where there are multiple lenders, the lending parties need to put in place co-ordination rules. These aspects are considered briefly; they are not peculiar to companies. **31–023**

Defining repayment terms

A debt security issued by a company (or indeed any debt) is primarily a matter of contract between lender and company. The legislature does not specify one, or even a number, of forms that the debt security must take, any more than it does with shares. Nor, however, does it even provide any equivalent of the model articles. It is thus difficult to describe a "typical" debt security. However, the security will normally have, unlike a share, an end-date, i.e. a point at which the amount still outstanding has to be repaid (its "maturity date")—though it is possible to make the loan totally irredeemable (s.739). That maturity date can be set as the parties wish, but may be quite long, for example, 40 years. The instrument also typically requires the amount lent to be repaid in regular instalments over the life of the loan (in which case it is called "amortising" debt), although it is also possible for the parties to provide that nothing needs to be repaid either until maturity (which is unlikely in the case of long maturities, unless the loan is backed by very high quality assets) or only after a considerable **31–024**

listed shares and debt securities to be "freely negotiable" (arts 46 and 60) this is interpreted as "freely transferable" and not as prescribing that they must be "negotiable instruments" in full sense.

105 See Ch.26.

106 2008 Regulations reg.40(2), provided notice is given to the holders at least 30 days before the changes become effective.

period of time has passed (say, eight to ten years), at which point the amount becomes repayable which would have been paid over this period through a normal amortisation arrangement. Such debt is sometimes called "bullet" debt, perhaps because of its likely impact on the borrower.[107]

The instrument will normally provide for the periodic payment of a fixed rate of interest at fixed points in time, but there is no reason why the interest rate so specified should not vary (provided there is a clear mechanism for working out what it is at any one time) nor, as we have seen, why interest should not be "rolled up" and be payable at a later date (sometimes on the maturity of the loan). In such a case the lender earns a return by buying the security at a discount to its face (or nominal or principal) value (i.e. the amount the company promises to repay) and takes the return as a capital gain rather than income, but only at maturity or, if the price of security in the market rises, upon sale to a third party.

The lender may have the right to recall or the borrower to repay the loan ahead of the repayment schedule,[108] or they may be specifically prohibited from so doing. Section 739 recognises that the security may be made irredeemable by the borrower, or redeemable only in certain circumstances, "any rule of equity to the contrary notwithstanding". This removes any doubt about the validity of such a restriction.[109]

Protecting the debt holder against the borrower's possible default

31–025 None of the above clauses provide the lender with ongoing reassurance that the borrower remains able to repay the debt. Accordingly, it is common to insert a variety of covenants in the loan documentation with this objective in mind. Through such covenants, lenders become part of the corporate governance structure of the company, and may have a far more significant impact on management than the shareholders if the company is near to breaching its loan covenants.

Of course, the extent to which lenders are able to insert such covenants in their loans depends upon the level of competition in the market for such loans. For a period in the early 2000s up until the middle of 2007, competition among banks for the opportunity to fund private equity buy-outs was so great that "covenant-lite" loans became common, i.e. bank loans with little by way of restrictive covenants inserted. In more normal circumstances, however, substantial loans are typically issued subject to important constraints on management.[110]

The best protection is proprietary security. That is discussed in the next chapter. If the lender does not have the bargaining power to insist on security, or if the company has no further assets over which security might be granted, then

[107] Where such debt is part of a private equity transaction, it is a strong candidate for early re-financing.

[108] And, for example, bank overdrafts are typically repayable on demand and regardless of breach (unless the facility agreement provides otherwise), with the bank not required to refrain from making a demand simply because it will tip the company into insolvency: *Williams & Glyn's Bank Ltd v Barnes* [1981] Com. L.R. 205 HC.

[109] See para.31–007.

[110] Bratton, "Bond Covenants and Creditor Protection" (2006) 7 E.B.O.R. 39.

alternative contractual protections become increasingly important. They are, however, typically included even when security is taken.

Loan covenants typically require the borrowing company to provide the lender with periodic accounting information, perhaps including credit ratings, to conduct its operations so as to maintain pre-determined financial ratios between assets and liabilities, and to refrain from certain defined acts or activities, or at least refrain from them without the prior consent of the lender. The list of prohibitions typically includes disposing of substantial assets, changing the primary business activities of the company, taking on additional loans, granting further security, distributing dividends above a nominated level of return, or changing the management or ownership structure.[111] The list of possibilities does not end there, but their objective is clear. In addition, the debenture may provide for the lender to be part of the management of the company by giving it the right to appoint a director.[112] **31–026**

If any of these covenants is breached, the debenture usually defines this as "an event of default" upon which the lender is given various rights, usually including the right to accelerate repayment, to take new security, to enforce existing security, to impose repayment penalties (drafted, of course, to avoid invalidity as a "penalty clause"),[113] and such like. From this list, the lender can elect the most appropriate course of action. It is not usual to make the consequences of default automatic, as undoing their automatic effect can be very difficult if the breach is, for example, merely technical and one which the lender is inclined to ignore.

It might be asked what consequences would follow if the company decided unilaterally to exercise its powers, either at board level or in general meeting, to subvert these covenants—for example by the general meeting dismissing the debenture holder's nominee director,[114] or effecting other significant changes to the articles. But this is hardly a live issue: the breach would invariably constitute an event of default, normally entitling the debenture-holder to require the debt to be repaid immediately and, if it was secured by a charge on the company's property, to enforce the security. This is a far more effective remedy—and disincentive—than a claim for damages for the breach. Thus, while the value of the lender's rights may depend on the continued prosperity of the company, particularly if the loan is unsecured, lenders (including debt security holders) are not normally subject, as is a shareholder, to any serious possibility that the agreed rights will be varied by the company by corporate action without the lender's consent.

---

[111] However, since these are contractual restrictions, they will not bind third parties (in whose favour, for example, assets have been pledged in breach of covenant), unless equity will intervene (see para.10–130), or the ingredients of the tort of inducing breach of contract have been established, notably knowledge on the part of the third party of the contractual restrictions: *Swiss Bank Corp v Lloyds Bank Ltd* [1979] Ch. 548 Ch D.

[112] Of course, such nominee directors owe their duties to the company, not the nominee: see the discussion at para.10–044.

[113] *Lordsvale Finance Plc v Bank of Zambia* [1996] Q.B. 752 QBD; although now see *Cavendish Square Holding BV v Talal El Makdessi*; sub nom. *ParkingEye Ltd v Beavis* [2015] UKSC 67.

[114] See para.11–023. It seems clear that an injunction could not be granted to restrain the general meeting from removing a nominated director under s.168.

Protecting multiple lenders from their lead intermediary

31–027 With both syndicated loans and debt securities, there is a "leader" in the collaboration between the multiple lenders, with the leader typically being the person to whom the corporate debtor is to make the necessary loan repayments, and who can enforce the debt, or implement acceleration provisions, or agree to modifications of the terms of the debenture. Thus, by contract, the parties provide for collective enforcement of their debt.[115]

But when things go wrong and the debt is not repaid according to its terms, or negotiations seem to go awry, these leaders are especially likely to come in for criticism. Different obligations are owed depending on the selected debt structure and the terms of the contractual engagement, but a brief outline gives the general features.

In syndicated loan agreements, the arranger, in putting the deal together, will clearly owe a duty of care to the other participants, although this duty can be expressly excluded in large measure,[116] especially in relation to misrepresentations as to the features of the loan and the standing of the debtor.[117] Whether, during the term of the loan, the arranger also owes the other lenders general fiduciary duties seems unlikely, unless the particular facts are such as to call into play such a relationship,[118] but otherwise the general rules of contract and tort apply, with no special statutory overlay.

31–028 By contrast, there is less flexibility with debt securities using trustees as intermediaries,[119] as is now the practice. The debt security holders are dependent on the trustees for the proper protection of their interests, and their remedies are primarily against the trustees, rather than the company. This is made all the more attractive since these trustees are likely to have deep pockets, although note that in modern structures with account holders and a string of sub-trusts, the beneficiary's only claim is against the immediate trustee—there is a "no look through" rule preventing access to trustees higher up the chain. The trustees are subject to all the general common law, equitable and statutory duties imposed on trustees, and the extent to which these can be relaxed by the trust deed is limited, not only by the common law,[120] but more importantly by what is now CA 2006

---

[115] *Elektrim SA v Vivendi Holdings 1 Corp* [2008] EWCA Civ 1178.

[116] *IFE Fund SA v Goldman Sachs International* [2007] EWCA Civ 811 at [28]; *Raiffeisen Zentralbank Osterreich AG v Royal Bank of Scotland Plc* [2010] EWHC 1392 at [65].

[117] *Peekay Intermark v ANZ Banking Group* [2006] EWCA Civ 386.

[118] Although see the dicta in *UBAF Ltd v European American Banking Corp* [1984] Q.B. 713 CA (Civ Div) at 728.

[119] It is possible, although now less common, for the company to issue bonds directly to the bondholders, and for the bondholders then to appoint an agent to act as their point of contact. Such an appointed agent will have whatever powers are expressly agreed by the parties, and these may well be fewer than those typically enjoyed by a trustee for the bondholders in a structure where the trustee holds the global note and any associated security on trust for the bondholders. But such an agent is nevertheless subject to common law and equitable duties, providing the bondholders with fairly extensive protection.

[120] *Armitage v Nurse* [1998] 1 Ch. 241. Although see the pro-trustee approach to restrictive clauses in *Citibank NA v MBIA Assurance SA* [2006] EWHC 3215. Also see M. Bryan, "Contractual Modification of the Duties of a Trustee" in S. Worthington (ed.), *Commercial Law and Commercial Practice* (Oxford, Hart Publishing, 2003), p.513.

s.750, which invalidates provisions in trust deeds (or elsewhere) which purport to exempt a trustee from, or to indemnify him against, "liability for breach of trust where he fails to show the degree of care and diligence required of him as a trustee having regard to the provisions of the trust deed conferring on him any powers, authorities or discretions".[121] As a result, the powers and obligations of trustees are likely to be set out fairly fully in the trust deed, and to be supplemented, typically, by arrangements for debt holder voting on difficult issues, so as to protect the trustee against internal complaints and potential litigation concerning the exercise of its powers.[122]

Even so, trustees can be excessively cautious in fulfilling their obligations. In *Concord Trust v Law Debenture Trust Corp Plc*,[123] the House of Lords found that the debtor company had "terrified the trustee" into declining to implement a valid instruction given to it by the requisite majority of the bondholders unless the trustee was given an indemnity by the bondholders against what the court thought was a fanciful liability to the company on the part of the trustee should the trustee's action of declaring a default and accelerating the bond (i.e. requiring it to be repaid) turn out to be ill-founded.

Protecting multiple lenders from each other

As well as settling the boundaries for the relationship between the multiple lenders and their leader, the lenders need some protection from each other. Typical trust deeds therefore include "no action" and "pari passu" provisions, expressly prohibiting individual debt holders from seeking to enforce any rights against the debtor company, or to recover any more individually than would be recovered under collective action. In addition, in syndicated loans, there can be complicated subordination agreements between the different parties. All these, added to the formal collective action structure, are designed to prevent any one party gaining "first mover advantage".[124] **31–029**

But these days the more difficult governance issue concerns the possible judicial review of voting at meetings of debt security holders. There has to be a

[121] But note the exceptions and qualifications in subss.(2)–(4) permitting 75% in value of the debenture holders present and voting to give a release from liability to the trustee in respect of prior specific acts or omissions of the trustee (or on the latter's death or ceasing to act). In addition, reg.40(2) of the Uncertificated Securities Regulations 2001 as amended (Ch.26) exempts the trustees from liability simply for assenting to amendments of the trust deed to enable title to debentures to be held and transferred under the electronic system and for rights attached to debentures to be exercised in that way.

[122] Especially if the trustee's opinion differs: see *Citibank NA v MBIA Assurance SA* [2006] EWHC 3215 (Ch); [2007] EWCA Civ 11 (see "Issue 2" in the Court of Appeal); and *Law Debenture Trust Corp Plc v Concord Trust* [2007] EWHC 1380.

[123] *Concord Trust v Law Debenture Trust Corp Plc* [2006] 1 B.C.L.C. 616. The event of default was a failure to maintain on the board of the borrowing company a nominee of the lenders, who had been placed there to protect the bond-holders' interests. Having accelerated the bond, as a consequence of the HL judgment, and secured substantial payments from the company, the trustee then took an overly cautious line about how much of the monies recovered it could distribute to the bond-holders: *Law Debenture Trust Corp Plc v Concord Trust* [2007] EWHC 1380 (Ch).

[124] The aim is to achieve, by contract between the multiple lenders alone, at least the level of protection that the IA 1986 attempts to deliver between all unsecured creditors, despite the fact that they are often strangers to each other. See Ch.33. See paras 31–023 onwards.

decision-making process, but it must be such that it does not oppress minorities. The trust deed typically provides for the security holders to give directions, often by majority vote (perhaps a simple majority or some special majority, in number or in value or both, depending on the issue under review, or perhaps some other agreed regime that seems, at the time of the agreement, to afford the participants the necessary protection of their personal interests). This decision is commonly required to be reached at a meeting of the security holders, called in an agreed way, with specified notice, and typically allowing representation by proxies. The parallels between this contractually agreed regime for debt securities and the combined statutory and contractual regime for equity securities is obvious, and so too the legal issues in its resolution.[125]

In these circumstances the debt holders do not have the protection of the unfair prejudice provisions which apply only to "members".[126] The issues are left to the common law. The first requirement is that any decision must be fully informed. It is usually left to the trustee to ensure that proposals are fully and fairly explained in the circulars seeking the needed consents.[127] Further, the courts have applied to decisions of a majority of the debenture holders binding on the minority the same common law doctrine applied to decisions by shareholders to alter the articles,[128] i.e. the decision must be made bona fide[129] in the interests of the debenture holders,[130] and for the purposes for which the power is granted.[131] Taking each of these requirements in turn (although in older cases they are often regarded as comprehending a single test), the limits of the controls become readily apparent. It is usually impossible to prove absence of bona fides. Further, as we saw with shareholders, it is often equally difficult to prove that a decision is not "in the interests of the debenture holders", especially if—as with shareholders—this is taken to mean that the decision is one which the debenture holders themselves subjectively view as in their interests, subject only to a rationality test. Indeed, proof that a decision is not in their interests is generally even more difficult than with shareholders, since the voting requirement is often designed precisely to resolve issues where the different debtholders' interests may be in conflict. Faced with these facts, it is necessarily the final strand in the test—the proper purposes aspect—which is to the fore in determining whether the majority decision should stand.

---

[125] See Ch.13.

[126] See para.14–013. Nor, of course, will the class rights provisions afford protection as they too apply only to members. See para.13–019.

[127] The Listing Rules require that any circular must include an explanation of the effect of proposed amendments: LR 17.3.10.

[128] See the detailed discussion at paras 13–005 to 13–013, much of which is equally relevant here.

[129] *Goodfellow v Nelson Line (Liverpool) Ltd* [1912] 2 Ch. 324 Ch D at 333.

[130] *British America Nickel Corp Ltd v MJ O'Brien* [1927] A.C. 369 PC at 371; *Redwood Master Fund Ltd v TD Bank Europe Ltd* [2002] EWHC 2703; [2006] 1 B.C.L.C. 149 at [84], a case concerning syndicated lenders, relying on the shareholder case of *Greenhalgh v Ardene Cinemas Ltd* [1951] Ch. 286 CA at 291; and *Law Debenture Trust Corp Plc v Concord Trust* [2007] EWHC 1380 at [123]; *Assénagon Asset Management SA v Irish Bank Resolution Corp Ltd* [2012] EWHC 2090 (Ch).

[131] *Redwood Master Fund Ltd v TD Bank Europe Ltd* [2006] 1 B.C.L.C. 149 at [101]–[105]; *Assénagon Asset Management SA v Irish Bank Resolution Corp Ltd* [2012] EWHC 2090 (Ch) at [85]–[86].

However, even a "proper purposes" test does not give the courts much leverage to intervene, especially where the various interests of the debenture holders are in conflict, and the vote is designed (i.e. its purpose is) to resolve the outcome in favour of one or other side, and there is nothing in the facts which suggests more than a predictable difference of opinion.[132] **31–030**

On the other hand, there are a small number of cases which show that the rule has some teeth.[133] Thus, in *British America Nickel Corp Ltd v O'Brien*[134] a decision of the majority of the bondholders, modifying their rights, was invalidated on the grounds that one of the bondholders, whose support was necessary for the passing of the resolution, was to receive under the scheme a block of ordinary shares, with that opportunity not available to the other bond-holders.[135] In the *O'Brien* case, Viscount Haldane said that the power of alteration "must be exercised for the purpose of benefiting the class as a whole", and the courts have often been quick to conclude that the purpose is self-interest, not class interest, where there are particular and exclusively personal benefits hanging on the voting outcome (beyond those, of course, which are inherently and necessarily delivered by the vote itself).

This same approach was adopted by Briggs J in *Assénagon Asset Management SA v Irish Bank Resolution Corp Ltd*,[136] with more modern, and more explicit, reference to the equitable requirement of proper purposes in the exercise of power, and the need to ensure powers were not used to oppress minorities. This case involved a more complicated inducement from the debtor company to the debt holder to vote in a particular way,[137] adopting an apparently common technique of requesting "exit consents", which offered the debt holder a lower denomination bond in exchange for a commitment to vote in a way which would, effectively, destroy or extinguish the existing bond. Of course, the bondholders who did not accept this inducement before the pre-meeting deadline (thinking it priced their bonds too conservatively) ran the risk—the prisoner's dilemma—of the vote going against them, and being left with an old bond rendered almost worthless. Gamesmanship was clearly an essential part of the debtor company's strategy,[138] and its effectiveness was ensured because the timing went against effective co-ordination by the bondholders. By contrast, in *Azevedo v*

[132] See the detailed analysis in *Redwood Master Fund Ltd v TD Bank Europe Ltd* [2006] 1 B.C.L.C. 149. Also see *Re The Co-Operative Bank Plc* [2017] EWHC 2269 (Ch) at [45]-[47]; *Re Lehman Brothers International (Europe) (In Administration)* [2018] EWHC 1980 (Ch) at [94]–[106].

[133] R. Peel, "Assessing the Legality of Coercive Restructuring Tactics in UK Exchange Offers" (2015) 4 UCL Journal of Law and Jurisprudence 162.

[134] *British America Nickel Corp Ltd v O'Brien* [1927] A.C. 369 PC.

[135] There appears to be no problem if the opportunity to benefit by voting in a particular way is fully disclosed and available to all members of the class: *Azevedo v IMCOPA—Importacao, Exportaacao e Industria de Oleos Ltda* [2013] EWCA Civ 364.

[136] *Assénagon Asset Management SA v Irish Bank Resolution Corp Ltd* [2012] EWHC 2090 (Ch). Briggs J also held, as an alternative, that the vote belonged beneficially to, and was exercised by, the debtor company, in contravention of the trust deed, so the decision of the majority could not stand because the majority had no power to exercise, i.e. on these facts, the same result could be delivered by an analysis based on absence of power, or, alternatively (as discussed here), on abuse of power.

[137] As in *Azevedo v IMCOPA—Importacao, Exportaacao e Industria de Oleos Ltda* [2013] EWCA Civ 364.

[138] Otherwise the same outcome might have been achieved by a straightforward vote to devalue the old bond to the value of the offered inducement.

IMCOPA—Importacao, Exportaacao e Industria de Oleos Ltda,[139] the Court of Appeal held that it was perfectly permissible for an issuer of loan notes to solicit votes in favour of a resolution for financial restructuring by offering a cash payment to all noteholders of a particular class who voted in favour of the resolution: the note was not a "bribe" if it was openly made to every member of the class; and if a vote was cast in the way in which the issuing company encouraged noteholders to think would be in their best interests as well as in those of the company, that was not the "sale" of a vote, even if the company offered an incentive to fortify the encouragement.[140] But in legal terms, the real question is what distinguishes *Assénagon* from *Azevedo*. In both cases there was an inducement offered to all bondholders, but accepted only by some; in both the vote reduced the value of the old bonds. The legal difference cannot, it seems, lie merely in the size of the inducement or the magnitude of the devaluation. But quite where it lies is not clear. These cases reinforce the conclusion that although this protection is important to debt security holders, and although the principles in play may be readily stated, they are anything but easy to apply with confidence.

Where there is some doubt as to the legitimacy of a decision taken in this way, the parties may feel more secure seeking the sanction of the court via a scheme of arrangement if the company is solvent,[141] or a company voluntary arrangement if the company is insolvent.[142]

CONCLUSION

31–031 From the above analysis it will be clear that the terms and structure of debt which companies take on are left very much to be bargained out between lenders and borrowers. Consequently, most of the law in this area consists of the principles of the law of contract and the law of property, with relatively little in the way of special company law regulation, except where the company wishes to issue its debt securities to the public, or enable those securities to be traded on a secondary market (where the rules are similar to those applying to equity securities), or where the company agrees to give a charge over its property to secure the loan, which is the topic for the following chapter.

[139] See fnn.130 and 135.

[140] ibid. at paras [63], [69]–[71].

[141] CA 2006 s.895; see paras 29–001 onwards. But note *Re Lehman Brothers International (Europe) (In Administration)* [2009] EWCA Civ 1161, indicating that beneficial owners (as opposed to creditors, even those with security) cannot avail themselves of these provisions.

[142] CA 2006 s.899; see para.29–017.

CHAPTER 32

COMPANY CHARGES

INTRODUCTION

Borrowers are often obliged to provide security for the repayment of their debts. In this respect a company is no different from any other borrower. However, there are sufficiently unique features associated with the granting of security by a company to justify it being treated here as a separate topic. In particular, one type of security (the floating charge) is practicable only if created by a body corporate,[1] there is a separate system for the registration of company charges,[2] there are distinct statutory procedures for the enforcement of the floating charge,[3] and certain provisions of the IA 1986 affecting company charges apply on corporate insolvency. Coupled with these, the granting of security by a company is subject to the law relating to corporate capacity and directors' duties,[4] although compliance in that regard is assumed in what follows. **32–001**

---

[1] See para.2–030.

[2] See paras 32–022 onwards.

[3] See paras 32–032 onwards.

[4] See Chs 8 and 10.

SECURITY INTERESTS

The legal nature of security interests

32–002 Some knowledge of this general topic is essential in order to understand the particular nature of the rights conferred on a secured charge holder, the priorities of charges, and the system for the registration of company charges.[5] Some understanding is also needed of nomenclature. Various forms of security are possible, as described below, but the most common form granted by a company is a charge. "Charge" has a restricted technical meaning in equity, although this technical distinction is not always maintained in the literature or in the Act,[6] and, unless the context indicates otherwise, the terms "charge", "security" or "security interest" are often used interchangeably.

Browne-Wilkinson VC, without claiming that it was comprehensive, accepted the following as a description of a security interest[7]:

> "Security is created where a person ('the creditor') to whom an obligation is owed by another ('the debtor') by statute or contract, in addition to the personal promise of the debtor to discharge the obligation, obtains rights exercisable against some property in which the debtor has an interest in order to enforce the discharge of the debtor's obligation to the creditor."

A decade later in *Smith (Administrator of Cosslett (Contractors) Ltd) v Bridgend CBC*, Lord Scott remarked that[8]:

> "a contractual right enabling a creditor to sell his debtor's goods and apply the proceeds in or towards satisfaction of the debt is a right of a security character. [It is important to note that] the conclusion does not depend on the parties' intention to create a security. Their intention, objectively ascertained, is relevant to the construction of their contract. But once contractual rights have, by the process of construction, been ascertained, the question whether they constitute security rights is a question of law that is not dependent on their intentions."

These two statements highlight the essential features of a security interest. First, the classification of security interests is a matter of law, and depends upon the rights agreed between the parties, not on their intention to create one form of security rather than another, nor on the economic effect of their agreement.

---

[5] For more detail, see H.G. Beale, M. Bridge, L. Gullifer and E. Lomnicka, *The Law of Security and Title-Based Financing*, 3rd edn (Oxford: OUP, 2018); L. Gullifer, *Goode and Gullifer on Legal Problems of Credit and Security*, 6th edn (London: Sweet & Maxwell, 2017); E. McKendrick, *Goode and McKendrick on Commercial Law*, 6th edn (London: LexisNexis, 2020), Pt 4, especially Ch.25; and M. Bridge, L. Gullifer, G. McMeel and K.F.K. Low, *The Law of Personal Property*, 2nd edn (London, Sweet & Maxwell, 2019), Ch.15D.

[6] See s.859A(7), defining "charge" to include mortgage, and any other form of security.

[7] *Bristol Airport Plc v Powdrill* [1990] Ch. 744 CA (Civ Div) at 760. Note that the property of a third party can also be made available by way of security, without any associated personal promise by the third party to meet the secured obligation: *Re Bank of Credit and Commerce International SA (In Liquidation) (No.8)* [1997] B.C.C. 965 HL. See also *Curtain Dream Plc v Churchill Merchandising Ltd* [1990] B.C.L.C. 925 Ch D at 935–937; *Welsh Development Agency v Export Finance Co Ltd* [1992] B.C.C. 270 CA (Civ Div); IA 1986 s.248. A charge can be created not only to secure the payment of a monetary obligation but also to secure other types of obligations: *Re Cosslett (Contractors) Ltd* [1998] Ch. 495 CA (Civ Div).

[8] *Smith (Administrator of Cosslett (Contractors) Ltd) v Bridgend CBC* [2001] UKHL 58; [2001] B.C.C. 740 at [53].

Secondly, every security interest ultimately gives the holder of the security a proprietary claim over assets, normally the debtor's, to secure payment of the debt. The position of a secured creditor is to be contrasted with that of an unsecured creditor who merely has a personal claim to sue for the payment of his debt and to invoke the available legal processes for the enforcement of any judgment that he may obtain.

Security interests can be divided broadly into consensual and non-consensual securities. We are interested in the former—i.e. securities agreed by companies to be granted in favour of their creditors. English law recognises only four types of security interest (mortgages, charges, pledges and common law liens),[9] although these can be used in a wide variety of ways to give sophisticated protection to lenders.

It is not possible in a text of this nature to describe security interests in any great detail, but a number of questions typically arise with respect to the creation of such interests by a company: 32–003

(1) First, is the interest created by the security equitable or legal?[10] This has a bearing on priorities: example, in principle the interests of an equitable charge holder can be defeated by a bona fide purchaser for value without notice of the equitable interest, although that rule will have limited impact given the registration required of company charges.[11]
(2) Secondly, is the security interest possessory or not? Put another way, is possession, either actual or constructive, of the property subject to the security is necessary in order to confer a security interest on the security holder? Obviously, if all security interests had to be possessory it would make secured borrowing virtually impossible since the debtor would be unable to use the secured assets in the course of business. For example, the classic example of a possessory security is the pledge, which involves the pledgee (the security holder) taking possession of the goods of the debtor (the pledgor) until the debt is paid or the pledgee takes steps to enforce the pledge. The common law lien is also possessory. This giving up of possession is not practical in many business circumstances, so thankfully English law has long recognised non-possessory security interests, by way of charges. These enable the borrower to retain its assets and use them in its

[9] *Re Cosslett (Contractors) Ltd* [1998] Ch. 495 at 508 (Millett LJ). Note that a *common law lien* arises when possession of goods is given to a creditor otherwise than for security—for example, so that the goods can be stored, repaired or transported—and the creditor is given, by custom, statute or contract, a right to retain the goods (and only that right, unless the parties expand upon it by contract) if the debt is not satisfied.

[10] Most securities created by companies are charges (using that term in its technical sense). A *legal mortgage* is created if the borrower transfers legal title to the property to the lender on the condition that it will be given back when the obligation is met. An *equitable mortgage* is created in the same way, but where the transfer is of equitable title rather than legal title; an equitable mortgage is also created by a specifically enforceable contract to create a legal mortgage. Note that a legal mortgage of land is no longer possible: these arrangements are now deemed by statute to create a *legal charge* (LPA 1925 ss.85(1) and 86(1)). All other charges, using "charge" in its technical sense, are *equitable charges*. These arise where, by contract, a specific item of property is appropriated to, or made answerable for, meeting the debtor's obligation.

[11] See paras 32–022 onwards.

business, while also granting a security over them to a lender, thus supporting the provision of necessary finance for its operations. Such charges can be granted over all forms of property, whether tangible or intangible.

(3) Thirdly, what type of "proprietary" interest is vested in the lender by the security? This has a direct bearing on remedies. The specific remedies of charge holders will be dealt with in some detail later. But brief comment is warranted here on the remedies available to the holders of other types of security interests. First to be contrasted are the mortgage and the charge. Although the words are often used interchangeably, there is technically an essential difference between them: "a mortgage involves a conveyance of property subject to a right of redemption, whereas a charge conveys nothing and merely gives the chargee certain rights over the property as security for the loan".[12] This essential difference has an impact on remedies: unless the charge document expressly provides otherwise (which it now invariably does[13]), the remedy of a chargee is to apply to the court for an order for sale or for the appointment of a receiver; this is because a charge, unlike the mortgage, does not involve conveyance of title to the asset, so a chargee cannot automatically foreclose or take possession. Continuing with other forms of security, the principal remedy of a pledgee is sale of the pledged goods; they can also be sub-pledged, with restrictions,[14] even before the right to sell arises. By contrast, a common law lien holder merely has the right to detain the goods subject to the lien until the debt has been paid.[15]

In determining precisely the form of security that has been granted, or indeed if any security at all has been granted, the parties' own labelling is not determinative. For example, one of the more misleading terms in corporate finance is "stock lending": from its label, it might be imagined that the underlying stock, or security collateral, is merely "on loan" from A to B. If this were the arrangement, and B became insolvent, the collateral would still belong to A, not B, and would not be available to B's creditors. But "stock lending" typically describes an arrangement whereby B "borrows" A's stock for the purpose of shorting stocks on the market.[16] These arrangements necessarily grant the "borrower" the right to deal

[12] *Re Bond Worth Ltd* [1980] Ch. 228 Ch D at 250. These rights are, however, proprietary, and protected as such.

[13] The usual provision is that, in the event of specified types of default by the chargor, the chargee is entitled to appoint a receiver to act as the agent of the chargor to sell the charged assets and use the proceeds to repay the outstanding debt to the chargee, after first paying those with statutory priorities, as discussed later.

[14] To ensure that the pledgee does not breach obligations to the pledgor.

[15] Although the right to sell is often expressly granted by contract. Subsequent security holders of course take subject to the lien: *George Barker (Transport) Ltd v Eynon* [1974] 1 W.L.R. 462 CA (Civ Div).

[16] Shorting, or short-selling, is when an investor (B) "borrows" shares and immediately sells them, hoping to flood the market, drive down the price, then buy back equivalent shares on the market at a lower price and return those shares to the "lender", pocketing the difference. The borrower typically charges a fee for this, so both parties make money on the transaction. The practice is common but controversial.

freely with the underlying securities, and oblige the lender, when the time comes, not to return the precise securities borrowed, but simply equivalent securities plus a fee for their use.[17] This is not "lending" as traditionally understood, and the courts have held, perhaps unsurprisingly, that in these cases it is the borrower who has title to the collateral securities, not the lender, with all the insolvency consequences that attracts.[18]

(4) Fourthly, is the security interest one that is created by the act of the parties or is it one created by operation of law? This is of critical importance with respect to the registration of company charges, since charges created by a company over its assets are registrable, whereas charges (or, more correctly, equitable liens) arising by operation of law are, of course, not.

(5) Fifthly, if the charge has been created by the company, has it been registered as required by the Act? Registration is dealt with later.

(6) Finally, is the charge created by the company fixed or floating? This will have a significant impact on the rights and remedies available to the chargee, and to other third parties associated with the failing company. It too is dealt with later.

To complicate the picture further, there are a number of other devices which do not constitute legal security (because they do not involve the debtor granting an interest in *its* property to the secured creditor), but which nevertheless function in a similarly protective fashion, and so are referred to as quasi-security devices. Negative pledge clauses in unsecured lending, and retention of title by sellers of goods, are two common illustrations. The first involves an agreement by the debtor company and its unsecured creditor that the company will not create any securities which have priority to the creditor's claim. Although this does not vest a security interest in the creditor, it "behaves" like a security interest in that it precludes the debtor from using its assets freely and thus, as with a security interest, it provides the creditor with a measure of protection. In retention of title arrangements, the seller of goods simply retains title to the goods until the buyer has paid for them (or until some later time defined by the contract).[19] Some of the problems raised by this type of security are considered later in the discussion on registration.[20]

[17] "Repos", or sale and repurchase agreements, may equally be subjected to this analysis: on the surface they appear to be much like mortgages, but if the lender has the right to deal with the underlying securities and return only their equivalent, then the agreement is a true sale (plus an agreement the other way to sell equivalent securities), not a mortgage: *Re Lehman Brothers International (Europe) (In Administration)* [2011] EWCA Civ 1544.

[18] *Beconwood Securities Pty Ltd v ANZ Banking Group Ltd* [2008] FCA 594 Aust. Fed. Ct; *Lehman Brothers International (Europe)* [2011] EWCA Civ 1544.

[19] Functionally, but not legally, these arrangements operate much like a chattel mortgage (*Welsh Development Agency v Export Finance Co Ltd* [1991] B.C.L.C. 936 Ch D at 950; [1992] B.C.C. 270), and as a result, there have been several attempts to align their treatment at law with the treatment of other security interests, but so far unsuccessfully. See para.32–031.

[20] See paras 32–024 onwards.

The benefits of taking security

32–004 There are a number of compelling reasons for a creditor to take security rather than rely solely on its personal claims against the debtor company. First, in the event of the debtor company's insolvency, a secured creditor will have priority over unsecured creditors (at least to the extent that the secured assets are of sufficient value to fund repayment of the secured debt), and may also, depending on the seniority of its claim, have priority over less senior security holders. This is a direct consequence of the fact that a security interest confers some type of proprietary interest on its holder. Priority on insolvency is one of the principal reasons for taking security.

Secondly, the secured creditor has the right to trace. If the debtor company wrongfully disposes of the charged property, the creditor is entitled to enforce its security against any identifiable proceeds of the disposition.[21]

Thirdly, a security interest gives its holder particular rights of enforcement depending on the nature of the security interest. Charge become enforceable in circumstances determined by the agreement itself, and the chargee may then take steps to enforce the charge. English law has traditionally placed few impediments in the way of enforcement of a charge: liberal rights are given by statute[22] and can be enhanced by contract. These rights allow the chargee to remain largely outside any concurrent insolvency proceedings and to enforce the charge independently of such proceedings,[23] although, as discussed later, this principle is substantially modified in the case of floating charges. Then various statutory rules give priority to preferential debts and to liquidation expenses,[24] and provide for a defined proportion of the floating charge realisations to be ring-fenced for the unsecured creditors.[25] Further rules operate in relation to the administration procedure (and its accompanying moratorium).[26]

Lastly, a charge often affords a chargee a measure of control over the business of the debtor company. The terms of the security agreement may require the debtor company to report regularly to the chargee and, if the company gets into financial difficulties, the chargee may be made privy to management decisions.[27] In addition, the charge may be so all-embracing that there is no scope for the debtor company to obtain further secured credit. In any event, a charge will obviously deter a second financier from providing funds where its charge would rank after a charge that the company has already created over its assets. Finally,

---

[21] The secured creditor is, alternatively, also able to follow the original secured property into the hands of third parties, and assert its property rights against them, unless the property is acquired by a bona fide purchaser for value without notice of the earlier equitable interest.

[22] IA 1986 s.42(1) and Sch.1, for example.

[23] *Sowman v Samuel (David) Trust Ltd (In Liquidation)* (1978) 36 P. & C.R. 123 Ch D; *Re Potters Oils Ltd (No.2)* (1985) 1 B.C.C. 99593 Ch D (Companies Ct).

[24] See paras 32–015 and 32–017.

[25] See para.32–016.

[26] See para.32–018.

[27] Although the chargee has to be careful not to become a shadow director and thus, e.g., potentially liable under the IA 1986 s.214. The chances of this are, on the whole, minimal: see *Re Hydrodan (Corby) Ltd (In Liquidation)* [1994] B.C.C. 161 Ch D.

unsecured creditors may see little advantage in seeking a winding-up where it appears that the secured creditors are entitled to all the company's assets.[28]

THE FLOATING CHARGE

The practical differences between fixed and floating charges

Subject to the issue of registration, discussed in the next section, the creation of a charge by a company is no different from the creation of a charge by any other debtor. And the creation of a floating charge, although devised for companies and still confined to them and to analogous vehicles, is no more difficult than the creation of a fixed charge. **32–005**

A charge is an equitable proprietary security interest. It is created whenever parties agree that certain property belonging to the debtor (or some third-party guarantor) will be appropriated to the discharge of the debt or other obligation (e.g. the machinery in a factory may be charged in favour of repayment of the loan that funded its purchase, or, alternatively, a loan granted for an entirely separate purpose). The agreement is by contract, without any transfer of title. The proprietary interest created in this way is less than an ownership interest (either legal or equitable), but it allows the secured property to be appropriated and sold, with the proceeds of sale dedicated to the repayment of the outstanding secured obligation.[29] On the debtor's insolvency, this arrangement removes the secured property from any insolvency proceedings,[30] and so the secured creditor is more likely to be repaid in full when compared with the unsecured creditors who have to share pari passu in the proceeds derived from sale of the remaining unsecured assets.

All charges created in this way are either fixed or floating. A fixed (or "specific") charge expressly or impliedly restricts the debtor's power to dispose of, or otherwise deal with, the property without the creditor's consent. By contrast, a floating charge leaves the chargor free to deal with the charged property in the ordinary course of business without reference to the chargee. A floating charge thus has the very practical advantage that it allows a company to give security over assets which are continually turned over or used up and replaced as a matter of routine trading; a business can thus raise money on secured loans without removing any of its property from routine business activities.[31] The charge remains floating and the company is free to use the assets subject to the charge until the charge is converted into a fixed charge. This is

[28] Although see paras 32–015 to 32–017, for the rules on preferred creditors and on the prescribed fund to be dedicated to unsecured creditors from floating charge realisations.

[29] And if the proceeds are more than sufficient to repay all the secured debts (and other claims on the secured assets—see paras 32–015 to 32–017 (preferred creditors etc)), then the excess is returned to the debtor/chargor.

[30] Although see para.32–013, for particular rules relating to floating charges.

[31] See paras 2–014 and 2–030. For valuable analyses of the floating charge see J. Getzler and J. Payne (eds), *Company Charges: Spectrum and Beyond* (Oxford: OUP, 2006). Floating charges and receivers in Scotland are dealt with by CA 2006 Pt 25 Ch.2, and IA 1986 Pt III Ch.II.

referred to as "crystallisation" of the charge. The normal crystallising event is the taking of steps to enforce the charge, but there are others and these are dealt with later.[32]

32–006 No particular form of words is necessary to create a floating charge. From the earliest cases, it was recognised as sufficient if (1) the intention is shown to impose a charge on assets both present and future; (2) the assets are of such a nature that they would be changing in the ordinary course of the company's business; and (3) the company is free to continue to deal with the assets for its own benefit in the ordinary course of its business.[33] Recent authorities make it clear that only the last of these three attributes is crucial.[34]

Interestingly, at the same time that courts in the UK were confirming the legitimacy of floating charges, courts in the US were moving in the opposite direction. According to US courts, allowing such freedom to the debtor/chargor was incompatible with the creation of a genuine security interest and was a fraud on the creditors; if the creditor did not exercise reasonable dominion over the secured asset, then the security was illusory and void,[35] and any rights created could only be contractual, not proprietary.[36]

Despite this early judicial acceptance in the UK, the floating charge has always been treated by the legislature with something approaching suspicion, and successive Companies Acts and Insolvency Acts have adopted a variety of rules designed to restrict its full impact, which is potentially to sweep up *all* the company's resources (by securing "the undertaking" or "all the assets and undertaking" of the company) and dedicate them to securing the debt of *one* of the company's creditors,[37] leaving all the other creditors unprotected, able only to share pari passu in whatever remains of the proceeds from the secured assets (if anything) after the secured creditor has been paid in full.

32–007 Because of these various statutory incursions, floating charges (i.e. all charges *created* as floating charges)[38] are now subjected to more. and more onerous, invalidating provisions (including specific invalidity rules), and are also subjected to prior payment of administrator's and liquidator's costs and expenses, and then prior payment of claims to preferential creditors, and then compulsory distribution of a prescribed part to unsecured creditors. This differential treatment

---

[32] See paras 32–008 onwards.

[33] *Re Yorkshire Woolcombers Association Ltd* [1903] 2 Ch. 284 CA at 295 (Romer LJ); *Illingworth v Houldsworth* [1904] A.C. 355 HL. In practice, it is usual to state specifically that the charge is "by way of floating charge" but it suffices if it is expressed to be on the "undertaking" or the like: *Re Panama New Zealand and Australian Royal Mail Co* (1869–70) L.R. 5 Ch. App. 318 CA in Chancery; *Re Florence Land and Public Works Co Ex p. Moor* (1879) 10 Ch. D. 530 CA; *Re Colonial Trusts Corp* (1879) 15 Ch. D. 465 Ch D.

[34] *Re Spectrum Plus Ltd (In Liquidation)* [2005] UKHL 41; [2005] B.C.C. 694.

[35] *Geilfuss v Corrigan* 95 Wis. 651; 70 N.W. 306 (1897); *Benedict v Ratner* 268 U.S. 354; 45 S.Ct. 566; 69 L.Ed. 991 (1925).

[36] The commercial inconvenience of this judicial approach probably contributed to the early adoption of an alternative mechanism to achieve similar ends by way of the Uniform Commercial Code art.9.

[37] *Re Panama, New Zealand and Australian Royal Mail Co* (1869–70) 5 Ch. App. 318, provided early confirmation that this is possible.

[38] IA 1986 s.251 provides that "floating charge" means "a charge which, *as created*, was a floating charge". See para.32–014.

of floating charges, discussed in more detail below,[39] gives creditors an incentive to ensure their charges are classified as fixed, not floating.[40]

Given the vulnerability of floating charges, the question arises as to why a creditor should bother to obtain one. While obviously the fixed charge accords superior protection, there are sound reasons for taking a floating charge. First, where a subsequent holder of a registrable charge is deemed to have notice of the negative pledge clause which typically accompanies a floating charge,[41] then this accords priority to the floating charge holder. Secondly, the charge provides security against unsecured creditors. Thirdly, the floating charge holder will be able to take steps to enforce the charge and, as will be seen, this accords him considerable control over the company's affairs. Fourthly, the holder of a floating charge will have some measure of control over the company, even without taking any steps to enforce its security.[42] Lastly, the holder of a floating charge may be able to block the appointment of an administrator, although now only in a limited range of cases.[43]

Crystallisation

As indicated above, a floating charge (unlike a fixed charge) leaves the debtor company free to use the secured assets in the ordinary course of its business until some point at which the charge is converted into a fixed charge. "Crystallisation" is the term used to describe this transition point.[44] Crystallisation is an important event, since it enables definition of the pool of assets available to the chargee as security for the obligation: a crystallised charge bites on all the assets that are presently in, or in the future come into, the hands of the chargor and are properly within the description of the charged assets.[45] **32–008**

[39] See paras 32–013 onwards.

[40] See paras 32–019 to 32–021 for the way the courts classify charges as fixed or floating.

[41] And this can be a fraught question given the current registration requirements. See para.32–011.

[42] See para.32–004.

[43] See para.32–032.

[44] The language is often muddled: crystallisation is described as operating as an equitable assignment (by way of charge): *George Barker (Transport) Ltd v Eynon* [1974] 1 W.L.R. 462 at 467, 471, 475; or as conversion to a specific (fixed) charge: *Re Griffin Hotel Co Ltd* [1941] Ch. 129 Ch D. And see the impossible assertion that the company has an equity of redemption: *Ultraframe (UK) Ltd v Fielding* [2005] EWHC 1638 (Ch); [2006] F.S.R. 17 at [1401].

[45] A floating charge agreement does not usually provide for crystallisation over part only of the assets to which it relates. There is no doctrinal reason for this. Partial crystallisation could, theoretically, be provided for by agreement, so long as the class of assets to be affected could be specified with certainty so as to define those with which the chargor can and cannot deal. This practicality creates the problem. It is submitted that *Robson v Smith* [1895] 2 Ch. 118 Ch D is not authority against partial crystallisation since the floating charge in that case did not confer any such right. In any event, such a provision is unlikely to be attractive in practice: it confers no significant benefit on the chargor, since the essence of security is that it only secures the outstanding debt, and any surplus (in cash or kind) is returned to the chargor; and it reduces the rights of the chargee in ways that may turn out to be unnecessarily detrimental when the event occurs.

The effect of crystallisation is to deprive the company of the autonomy to deal with the assets subject to the charge in the normal course of business.[46] The events of crystallisation, on which there is general agreement, are: (1) the making of a winding-up order[47]; (2) the appointment of an administrative receiver[48]; (3) the company's ceasing to carry on business[49]; (4) the taking of possession by the debenture-holder[50]; and (5) the happening of an event expressly provided for in the debenture, often referred to as "automatic crystallisation". Events (1)–(3) are implied as crystallising events in every floating charge agreement unless explicitly excluded.

Automatic crystallisation

32–009 Automatic crystallisation is not a term of art. It covers at least two situations which at first blush appear dissimilar. One is where the charge is made to crystallise on the happening of an event provided for in the charge agreement without there being any need for a further act by the chargee,[51] and the other is where the charge is made to crystallise on the serving of a notice of crystallisation on the company. However, these events have one important common feature, in that they will normally not be known to a person dealing with the company and therefore it seems appropriate to treat them together.

Initially there was some doubt about both the validity and the desirability of automatic crystallisation provisions. On validity, the matter is now settled beyond dispute, following acceptance of the judgment of Hoffmann J in *Re Brightlife Ltd*[52] upholding the validity of a provision enabling the floating charge holder to serve a notice of crystallisation on the company. Hoffmann J saw crystallisation as being a matter of agreement between the parties. On this reasoning there can be no objection to a charge being made to crystallise on the happening of a specified event.

On the other hand, the impact of these clauses can be profound, and there may be policy reasons to restrict their operation.[53] The first incidence of this is seen in

---

[46] At the time the event of crystallisation occurs, there must be: (1) an outstanding obligation which the charge secures; (2) a valid and subsisting charge agreement; (3) identifiable charged assets in which the chargor has an interest or rights.

[47] *Wallace v Universal Automatic Machines Co* [1894] 2 Ch. 547 CA; *Re Victoria Steamboats Ltd* [1897] 1 Ch. 158 Ch D. Even if the winding-up is for purposes of reconstruction: *Re Crompton & Co Ltd* [1914] 1 Ch. 954 Ch D. It is the making of the order and not, for example, the presentation of the petition since there is always the chance that the court will decline to make the winding-up order.

[48] *Evans v Rival Granite Quarries Ltd* [1910] 2 K.B. 979 CA. The same applies to the appointment of a receiver by the court. See para.32–035 on administrative receivership.

[49] This occurs because the cessation removes the raison d'être of the floating charge, which is to permit the company to carry on business in the ordinary way insofar as the class of assets charged is concerned. *Re Woodroffes (Musical Instruments) Ltd* [1986] Ch. 366 Ch D (it is the cessation of business and not ceasing to be a going concern assuming the latter is different). Express provisions for crystallisation will only exclude this implied provision for crystallisation if they expressly do so: *Re Real Meat Co Ltd (In Receivership)* [1996] B.C.C. 254 Ch D.

[50] *Evans v Rival Granite Quarries Ltd* [1910] K.B. 979 at 997.

[51] The crystallising event could, for example, be the failure by the debtor to pay any monies due or to insure the charged property.

[52] *Re Brightlife Ltd* (1986) 2 B.C.C. 99359 Ch D (Companies Ct).

[53] Also see para.33–021.

IA 1986 s.A52, which declares to be void any provision in a floating charge agreement which provides that the charge will crystallise, or that further restrictions on the chargor will become operative, where the trigger for those events is related in any way to the company's actions to obtain a moratorium under IA 1986 Pt A1.[54]

On the desirability of automatic crystallisation clauses, their acceptance as a matter of law indicates at least tacit approval that the benefits outweigh the detriments. The earlier arguments against such clauses focused on the disadvantages suffered by third parties. For example, insofar as insolvency law is committed to the principle that property within the apparent ownership of the company should be treated as the company's in the event of its insolvent liquidation, permitting party autonomy to effect automatic crystallisation clearly undermines this policy, but then English insolvency law is littered with similar exceptions.[55] Similarly, it has been argued that automatic crystallisation may prejudice subsequent purchasers and chargees who do not know, and indeed who may have no way of knowing, that the charge has crystallised.[56] Whether this is indeed the case is not clear cut. The matter is usually resolved as one of priorities, and subsequent purchasers or chargees will not necessarily be defeated by the earlier equitable charge.[57] In addition, Professor Goode has pointed out that the fact that the charge has crystallised will affect the relationship between the chargee and the company, but it does not necessarily affect a third party since, if the company is left free to deal with the assets in the normal course of its business, then the chargee (under the prior, now crystallised, floating charge) should be estopped from denying the company's authority to do so.[58]

The events implied as crystallising events in every floating charge agreement have already been mentioned. For the avoidance of doubt, there are no further implied terms defining events that cause crystallisation. In particular, default in the payment of interest or capital are not implied crystallising events,[59] nor (more controversially) is the crystallisation of another floating charge, whether created earlier or later than the charge in question.[60] Of course, given the validity of automatic crystallisation clauses, these events could be nominated as crystallising events.

---

[54] For details on the moratorium, see para.33–002.

[55] English insolvency law achieves this policy to some extent by requiring registration of non-possessory securities. It does not, however, require registration of title retention clauses or trusts, and any assets in the possession (and apparent ownership) of the company but which are subject to these arrangements do not form part of the company's assets in a winding-up.

[56] It is common when taking a fixed charge or purchasing a substantial asset of the company to serve on it inquiries as to whether any floating charge has crystallised. This provides limited protection since the company can lie or, more likely, it may not appreciate that the charge has crystallised.

[57] The interests that lose out to the crystallised floating charge are the subsequent equitable charge (provided the equities are equal), the common law lien over chattels and the interests of execution creditors: see W.J. Gough, "The Floating Charge: Traditional Themes and New Directions" in P.D. Finn (ed.), *Equity and Commercial Relationships* (Sydney: Law Book Co, 1977), p.262.

[58] E. McKendrick, *Goode and McKendrick on Commercial Law*, 6th edn (London: Penguin, 2020), Ch.25, Pt 6; a similar point is made by W.J. Gough, *Company Charges*, 2nd edn (London: LexisNexis, 1996), pp.255–256.

[59] *Government Stock and Other Securities Investment Co Ltd v Manila Railway Co Ltd* [1897] A.C. 81 HL.

[60] *Re Woodroffes (Musical Instruments) Ltd* [1986] Ch. 366.

Note that even where default does not result in crystallisation, the company will be in breach of contract and the chargee will have appropriate contractual remedies. For example, the holder of an uncrystallised charge may apply for an injunction to prevent the company dealing with its assets otherwise than in the ordinary course of its business.[61]

Priority accorded to floating charges

32–010 Since a floating charge gives the debtor company management autonomy over the secured assets, the most serious risk facing the charge holder is that the assets will be dissipated, without replacement, leaving no security to support the outstanding obligation. Subject to any specific restrictions in the charge agreement, the debtor company is free to deal with the charged assets in the ordinary course of business. Of course this means that the chargor may sell the assets in the ordinary course of business, and purchasers take free of the security.

In addition, the company may grant subsequent security interests, and the earlier floating charge will be deferred to any subsequent fixed legal or equitable charge created by the company over its assets,[62] or any subsequent floating charges provided they are not over precisely the same assets,[63] but are over only part of the pool of assets[64] where the first charge contemplates the creation of the later charge.[65]

Similarly, if debts due to the company are subject to a floating charge, the interest of the floating charge holder will be subject to any lien or set off that the company creates with respect to the charged assets prior to crystallisation,[66] since a floating charge is subject to dealings in the ordinary course of business up until crystallisation.[67] In the same vein, if a creditor has levied and completed

[61] *Re Woodroffes (Musical Instruments) Ltd* [1986] Ch. 366 at 378: "it is a mistake to think that the chargee has no remedy while the charge is still floating. He can always intervene and obtain an injunction to prevent the company from dealing with its assets otherwise than in the ordinary course of its business. That no doubt is one reason why it is preferable to describe the charge as 'hovering', a word which can bear an undertone of menace, rather than as 'dormant'".

[62] *Wheatley v Silkstone & Haigh Moor Coal Co* (1885) 29 Ch. D. 715 Ch D; *Robson v Smith* [1895] 2 Ch. 118 at 124 (any dealing with the property subject to a floating charge "will be binding on the debenture holders, provided that the dealing be completed before the debentures cease to be merely a floating security"); *Re Castell & Brown Ltd* [1898] 1 Ch. 315 Ch D. Although note that if B has *actual* notice that A's charge prohibits the creation of a later charge having priority, then A's charge will prevail: *Siebe Gorman & Co Ltd v Barclays Bank Ltd* [1979] 2 Lloyd's Rep. 142 Ch D (overruled by *Re Spectrum Plus Ltd* [2005] B.C.C. 694, but not on this point): see para.32–011, on negative pledges.

[63] If the subsequent floating charge is over the same assets, then, the equities being equal, the first in time prevails: *Re Benjamin Cope & Sons Ltd* [1914] 1 Ch. 800 Ch D.

[64] *Re Automatic Bottle Makers Ltd* [1926] Ch. 412 CA.

[65] *Re Automatic Bottle Makers Ltd* [1926] Ch. 412, implies that this depends on the wording of the charge and of the express provision, if any, relating to the creation of further charges.

[66] Even though, if *George Barker (Transport) Ltd v Eynon* [1974] 1 W.L.R. 462 is rightly decided, the lien or set off has not actually accrued.

[67] See *Cretanor Maritime Co Ltd v Irish Marine Management Ltd (The Cretan Harmony)* [1978] 1 W.L.R. 966 CA (Civ Div), where the company's assets were subject to an injunction against their removal from the jurisdiction, obtained by an unsecured creditor. On the application of the holder of the debenture whose charge had crystallised, the court discharged the injunction. See also *Capital Cameras Ltd v Harold Lines Ltd* [1991] B.C.C. 228 Ch D (successful application of a receiver to

execution,[68] the debenture-holders cannot compel him to restore the money, nor, unless the charge has crystallised, can he be restrained from levying execution.[69] Put another way, the floating charge holder will take the company's property subject to the rights of anyone claiming by paramount title, and if the incursions into the secured asset arise in the ordinary course of business, then it matters not that they occur after the charge was created but before the charge crystallises.

However, once the floating charge crystallises,[70] this ability to deal with the charged assets in the ordinary course of business ceases, and the usual priority rules apply to determine whether the (now fixed) equitable charge has priority over any subsequently created legal or equitable interests.[71]

Negative pledge clauses

In an effort to enhance the security offered by a floating charge as against subsequent security interests that would otherwise have priority, floating charge agreements almost invariably contain a provision that restricts the right of the company to create charges that have priority to or rank equally with the floating charge (called a negative pledge clause). Such restrictions are strictly construed,[72] but because they limit the company's actual authority to deal with its assets in the ordinary course of business, they remove the basis described above on which floating charges are automatically postponed to later charges. Instead, orthodox priority rules must be applied (e.g. an earlier equitable (floating charge) interest is deferred to a subsequent legal interest provided it was obtained bona fide and without notice of the earlier interest). **32–011**

Notice (actual or constructive) of the terms of the floating charge and any negative pledge, is thus crucial in determining priority disputes.[73] Actual notice is easy enough. But constructive notice raises two problems: which matters are deemed to be noted, and who has such notice? The Act does not answer either question. On the first, the cases indicate that registration provides constructive notice only of those particulars which are required to be included on the register.[74] Since those particulars now include whether or not there is a negative pledge, it would seem that parties will be taken to have constructive notice of such clauses, thus doing away with a great deal of earlier uncertainty when the registration requirements were more limited.[75] But uncertainty remains over

dismiss a *Mareva* injunction). See too *Biggerstaff v Rowatt's Wharf Ltd* [1896] 2 Ch. 93 CA; *Rother Iron Works Ltd v Canterbury Precision Engineers Ltd* [1974] Q.B. 1 CA (Civ Div); *George Barker (Transport) Ltd v Eynon* [1974] 1 W.L.R. 462.

[68] Seizure alone does not suffice: *Norton v Yates* [1906] 1 K.B. 112 KBD.

[69] *Evans v Rival Granite Quarries* [1910] 2 K.B. 979.

[70] On crystallisation, see paras 32–008 onwards.

[71] *Re ELS (formerly English Lifestyle)* [1994] B.C.C. 449 Ch D (Companies Ct).

[72] *Brunton v Electrical Engineering Corp* [1892] 1 Ch. 434 Ch D; *Robson v Smith* [1895] 2 Ch. 118.

[73] *Re Portbase Clothing Ltd* [1993] Ch. 388 Ch D (Companies Ct) at 401. Contrast *Griffiths v Yorkshire Bank Plc* [1994] 1 W.L.R. 1427 Ch D, which must be doubted.

[74] *English & Scottish Mercantile Investment Co Ltd v Brunton* [1892] 2 Q.B. 700 CA; *Wilson v Kelland* [1910] 2 Ch. 306 Ch D.

[75] See, e.g. *English & Scottish Mercantile Investment v Brunton* [1892] 2 Q.B. 700; *Re Castell & Brown Ltd* [1898] 1 Ch. 315; *Re Valletort Sanitary Steam Laundry Co Ltd* [1903] 2 Ch. 654 Ch D.

whether there will also be constructive notice of matters beyond the registered particulars, or what will happen if the particulars do not accurately reflect the terms of the registered charge.

On the second question, as to who will have such constructive notice, there is even less clarity. Registration might be taken to be notice to all the world, but the better view, consistent with the role of constructive notice elsewhere in the law, seems to be that registration is notice only to those who could reasonably be expected to search the register. The boundaries of that rule are not certain, but it should include most lenders, especially secured lenders.

Finally, and despite the foregoing, subsequent interests that can be classed as purchase money security interests may have priority over an earlier floating charge which appears to cover the same assets, although that priority will only extend to the newly purchased assets. This follows, since the company's later purchase, secured by a mortgage or a charge, means that all that the *company* acquires from the purchase is an asset subject to the prior security, which will then take priority, even if there is actual notice of the negative pledge.[76]

Subordination agreements

32–012 Finally, in *Cheah v Equiticorp Finance Group Ltd*,[77] Lord Browne-Wilkinson made it clear that where there were two charges over the same property, the chargees could agree between themselves to alter the priority of their security interests without the consent of the debtor. These types of subordination agreements do not affect the interests, even on insolvency, of either the debtor company or its other creditors; they merely redistribute what would otherwise be allocated to the chargees.[78]

Statutory limitations on the floating charge

32–013 Certain statutory provisions add further to the vulnerability of the floating charge. These provisions relate to (1) defective floating charges—affecting the validity of the charge; (2) preferential creditors—affecting the priority of the charge; (3) compulsory sharing of the security proceeds with other creditors—diminishing the assets available for the floating charge holders; (4) costs of the liquidation—again diminishing the assets available for the floating charge holders; and (5) the right of an administrator to override a floating charge—affecting the enforcement rights of the chargee. These matters are dealt with in turn.

[76] *Re Connolly Bros Ltd (No.2)* [1912] 2 Ch. 25 CA; *Abbey National Building Society v Cann* (1990) 22 H.L.R. 360 HL. This of course presumes that the second security is properly registered, and thus enforceable on insolvency: see *Tatung (UK) Ltd v Galex Telesure Ltd* (1989) 5 B.C.C. 325 QBD (Comm) at 327; *Stroud Architectural Systems Ltd v John Laing Constructions Ltd* [1994] B.C.C. 18 QBD (OR).

[77] *Cheah Theam Swee v Equiticorp Finance Group Ltd* [1992] B.C.C. 98 PC.

[78] See para.31–010.

(i) Defective floating charges

An unsecured creditor with advance notice that insolvent liquidation is imminent may well be tempted to seek security to cover the outstanding obligation, thereby obtaining priority over the other unsecured creditors. Directors, perhaps more than most, are likely to have early warning of such danger in repayment of their own unsecured loans.[79] And the only security likely to be available when the company is distressed is a floating charge security—the company's fixed assets will usually have been secured much earlier. **32–014**

To prevent this, s.245 of the IA 1986[80] provides that a floating charge created in favour of an unconnected person within 12 months of the commencement of the winding-up or the making of an administration order[81] shall be invalid, except to a prescribed extent, unless it is proved that the company was solvent immediately after the creation of the charge.[82] If these conditions are not satisfied, the charge is valid only to the extent of any new value in the form of cash, goods or services supplied to the company,[83] or the discharge of any liability of the company, where these take place "at the same time as, or after, the creation of the charge".[84] It has been held that the phrase in quotations requires the new value to be provided contemporaneously with the creation of the charge.[85] Any delay, no matter how short, in the execution of the debenture after the advance has been made will result in the new value falling outside s.245.[86] Hence those who take a floating charge from a company which cannot be proven to be solvent,[87] and which does not survive for a further year, cannot thereby obtain protection in respect of their debts except to the extent that they provided the company with new value[88] and thus potentially increased the assets available for other creditors.

---

[79] In some cases the company has been deliberately floated with the intention of defrauding creditors by granting floating charges to the promoters and then winding the company up, with the charge attaching to goods which the company has purchased on credit: see Cohen Report, *Report of the Committee on Company Law Amendment* (1945), Cmnd.6659, para.148.

[80] This applies to Scotland: IA 1986 s.245(1).

[81] IA 1986 s.245(3)(b) and (5).

[82] The test of solvency is that laid down in s.123 of the 1986 Act: IA 1986 s.245(4).

[83] The value of the goods or services is their market value: IA 1986 s.245(6). Illustrating the exercise, see *Re Peak Hotels and Resorts Ltd (In Liquidation)* [2019] EWCA Civ 345; [2019] B.C.C. 796 describing the approach, and [2019] EWHC 3558 (Ch); [2020] Costs L.R. 101 implementing the process.

[84] IA 1986 s.245(2)(a)–(b).

[85] *Power v Sharpe Investments Ltd* [1993] B.C.C. 609 CA (Civ Div).

[86] *Power v Sharpe Investments Ltd* [1994] 1 B.C.L.C. 111 at 123a–b. If the delay is de minimis, for example, a coffee-break, it can be ignored: ibid. The inconvenience of this can be avoided by the parties creating a present equitable right to security rather than a promise to create security in the future: see *Re Jackson & Bassford Ltd* [1906] 2 Ch. 467 Ch D.

[87] There is nothing in the section to displace the normal rule that he who asserts must prove, and thus the burden of proof would be on the liquidator or administrator. This should cause no great hardship as they will normally have sufficient information to found their action.

[88] For interesting illustrations of the way in which the rule in *Clayton*'s case ((1816) 1 Mer. 572) may protect a bank when the charge secures a current account, see *Re Thomas Mortimer Ltd* (1925) now reported at [1965] Ch. 186 (Note) Ch D; *Re Yeovil Glove Co Ltd* [1965] Ch. 148 CA. The Cork Committee (*Report on Insolvency Law and Practice* (1982), Cmnd.8558) recommended that *Re Yeovil*

Where the floating charge is in favour of a "connected person", the rules are even more restrictive: the charge is vulnerable for two years after its creation,[89] and there is no need to show that at the time the charge was created the company was insolvent. The definition of connected person is complex, but includes a director, the director's relatives, and companies within a group.[90] Further, not all value is "new value" for the purpose of s.245, as the latter is confined to money, goods or services and excluded are, for example, intellectual property rights and rights under a contract.

These rules apply to floating charges and not to fixed charges. The policy justification for this is questionable. The Cork Committee considered that these rules should not be extended to fixed charges since fixed charges were confined to the company's existing assets, whereas floating charges could capture future assets.[91] This distinction is not in fact true,[92] but why it should make a critical difference in any event is far from clear. It would seem to reflect a preferential treatment given to fixed charges. A fixed charge may of course be attacked as a preference where it is given to secure past value,[93] although not as a transaction at an undervalue since the assets of the company are not diminished by the creation of the charge.[94]

(ii) *Preferential creditors*

32–015 The general rule on insolvency is that pre-insolvency rights are respected, and the company's unsecured creditors share the losses pari passu. However, this general rule has been varied by statute, giving certain classes of creditors added protection by according them a statutory preference over some or all of the company's other creditors.[95] Typically this priority is over the other unsecured creditors, not the secured creditors (who are entitled to realise the secured assets outside this insolvency regime). Perhaps surprisingly, the enforcement of a

---

Glove Co Ltd be reversed by statute (paras 1561–1562) but why this should be so is far from clear since the bank by permitting the company to continue to draw on its overdrawn account is providing it with new value: see Goode, (1983) 4 Co.L. 81.

[89] IA 1986 s.245(3)(a).

[90] See ss.249 and 435 of the IA 1986.

[91] Cork Committee, *Report on Insolvency Law and Practice* (1982), Cmnd.8558, paras 1494 and 1553. The other reason given was that the extension of IA 1986 s.245 to fixed charges would compel creditors to seek repayment if fixed security could not be granted. This argument could also be applied to obtaining a floating charge.

[92] A company can create a fixed charge of accounts receivables, or a mortgage of future property, for example. The critical distinction between a fixed and a floating charge is that assets can be removed from the latter, and not from the former, without the specific consent of the chargee. Whether assets can be added (or not) is immaterial to the characterisation of the charge, and possible with both forms of charge: see paras 32–019 onwards.

[93] One important difference between the rules relating to preferences and to defective floating charges is that the time within which a preference in favour of an unconnected person can be challenged is six months (not 12 months). Also note that a preference will involve a diminution in the company's assets (giving one creditor a preference in repayment), whereas a floating charge constitutes a preferential claim on them.

[94] *Re MC Bacon Ltd (No.1)* [1990] B.C.C. 78 Ch D (Companies Ct).

[95] The same policy decisions have to be made with respect to bankruptcy: see, e.g. IA 1986 s.336 dealing with the matrimonial home.

floating charge is to some extent treated as an insolvency proceeding whether or not the company is in the course of being wound up,[96] and these preferential creditors are given a similar priority out of the pool of floating charge assets (although only to the extent that the general assets of the company are insufficient to meet their claims).[97] To this extent, floating charge holders are treated a little like unsecured creditors (whose repayments are deferred in this way on the company's insolvency) rather than like other secured creditors with mortgages or fixed charges.

There are various reasons supporting the adoption of this policy. It had been a strong criticism by the Cork Committee that banks, through a combination of fixed and floating charges, could scoop the entire asset pool and, in many cases, leave unsecured creditors with nothing in an insolvency. Some unsecured creditors were regarded as more vulnerable than other, especially creditors who could not protect themselves. In addition, as already pointed out, some debt-financing arrangements are structured so that debenture-holders (with floating charge security) closely resemble shareholders, forming a class that is interested in the company rather than merely one with claims against it. In those circumstances especially it was thought unjust that these creditors should obtain priority over employees (one of the categories of preferential creditor) who have priority over the shareholders in the event of the company's liquidation.[98]

The preferential debts of the employees are set out in Sch.6 to IA 1986 and include four months' wages per employee up to a maximum prescribed by the Secretary of State and accrued holiday remuneration.[99] In the case of a floating charge, the relevant date for quantifying the preferential debts is the date of the appointment of the receiver by the debenture-holders.[100] Further protection of employees comes from the rule that anyone who advances money to the company specifically for the payment of the employee debts which would have been preferential is then subrogated to the rights of the employee.[101] It is important to

[96] e.g. the enforcement of the floating charge is dealt with in Pt III of IA 1986; administrative receivers have to be qualified insolvency practitioners (s.230(2)); and s.247(1) defines insolvency as including the appointment of an administrative receiver. IA 1986 ss.40, 175, 386–387 and Sch.6, and CA 2006 s.754 are the most relevant for the subordination of the floating charge. For the ability of these provisions to reach through earlier contractual engagements, see *Re Oval 1742 Ltd (In Creditors Voluntary Liquidation)* [2007] EWCA Civ 1262; [2008] B.C.C. 135. Of course, if realisation of the security and application of the priority rules leaves the chargee carrying a loss, the floating chargee then ranks with the other unsecured creditors to the extent of any outstanding debts.

[97] IA 1986 s.175(2)(b). See para.33–024.

[98] Another argument made in favour of employees is that they have no way of obtaining security for the payment of their salary which is normally made after the provision of the services. This is not strictly correct since money to pay employees could be placed in a trust account to be paid on the appropriate date. But this would be cumbersome and as a matter of practice does not happen.

[99] See IA 1986 Sch.6 paras 9–10. Paragraph 8 brings in contributions to occupational pension schemes. Employees also have other protections. Where the company becomes insolvent, an alternative and speedier route for the employee to recover monies due is by way of application to the Secretary of State: see Pt XII of the Employment Rights Act 1996.

[100] IA 1986 s.387(4)(a). For the date of the appointment see IA 1986 s.33.

[101] IA 1986 Sch.6 para.11. This enables the company to be kept going where it is in financial difficulties but there is some chance that it can trade out of its difficulties. For case law on the previous statutory provisions see *Re Primrose (Builders) Ltd* [1950] Ch. 561 Ch D; *Re James R Rutherford & Sons* [1964] 1 W.L.R. 1211 Ch D; *Re Rampgill Mill* [1967] Ch. 1138 Ch D (Companies Ct).

note that the preferential creditors are given priority where a receiver is appointed with respect to a charge "which, as created, was a floating charge"[102]; thus the fact that the charge has crystallised at the time a receiver is appointed does not result in preferential debts being denied their statutory priority.[103]

There are other preferential debts listed in Sch.6, including a number of categories of debts owed to the government or to government bodies. This list is kept under review, changing as the approach of the government moves between making the merits-based assessments required to identify and list the more deserving creditors in order or priority, as against the simpler, but potentially harsh, route of demanding that all, or almost all, creditors share pro rata in the company's losses.

(iii) Sharing with unsecured creditors—the "prescribed part"

32–016 Employees are not the only preferential creditors to eat into the assets available to the floating chargee, however. There is also now limited preferential treatment for general unsecured creditors. IA 1986 s.176A requires that when the assets of a company subject to a floating charge are realised, a certain proportion (the "prescribed part") must be set aside for the unsecured creditors.[104] The percentage is defined as follows[105]: (1) 50% of the first £10,000; plus (2) 20% of the remainder; up to a maximum of £600,000.[106] The rule does not apply where (1) the company's net property is less than £10,000[107]; or (2) the costs of distribution to unsecured creditors would be disproportionate and the court makes an order accordingly.[108]

This segregation of the prescribed part is made at the outset, and if what remains for the floating charge holder is insufficient to meet the debt due, the chargee is nevertheless not entitled to share in the prescribed part, notwithstanding that the outstanding debt is now unsecured: s.176A(2)(b).[109] This provision is interpreted as confining the prescribed part to the unsecured creditors until they are paid in full, and only returning any excess for the benefit of the floating chargeholder once that has happened, even though the debt secured by the floating charge may remain only partly paid.

These rules may affect companies other than those registered under the IA 1986 if, but only if, they are being wound up under it.[110]

---

[102] IA 1986 s.40(1).

[103] Under the old law the crystallisation of the charge prior to the appointment of a receiver resulted in the preferential creditors being denied their priority: see *Re Brightlife Ltd* (1986) 2 B.C.C. 99359.

[104] Which category does not include the charge holder in relation to that part of the debt which has not been satisfied by the security, unless the unsecured debts have been fully met: IA 1986 s.176A(2).

[105] Insolvency (Prescribed Part) Order 2003 (SI 2003/2097).

[106] It is possible to vary this rule by means of a voluntary arrangement: IA 1986 s.176A(4).

[107] IA 1986 s.176A(3)(a); SI 2003/2097 art.2.

[108] IA 1986 s.176A(3)(b) and (5).

[109] *Re Permacell Finesse Ltd (In Liquidation)* [2007] EWHC 3233 (Ch); [2008] B.C.C. 208; *Re Airbase (UK) Ltd* [2008] EWHC 124 (Ch); [2008] B.C.C.213.

[110] i.e. a floating chargee who appoints a receiver of a statutory or chartered company will not be subject to the claims of preferential creditors unless the company goes into compulsory liquidation under Pt V of the IA 1986.

(iv) *Costs of a moratorium and liquidation*

None of these statutory incursions alters the fact that the very first payments to come out of the floating charge realisations are the costs and expenses of any moratorium[111] and of liquidation (if the company goes into liquidation),[112] in priority even to the receivership expenses.[113] This can be a substantial drain on the funds eventually available to the floating chargee. Then come the costs and expenses of receivership,[114] and only then the preferential creditors, finally leaving a pool (if the parties are lucky) that is split between the floating chargee and the unsecured creditors according to the formula outlined above. **32–017**

The position of fixed charge holders is very different. Their asset pool is not subjected to claims from liquidators to fund liquidation expenses, nor from preferential or unsecured creditors. Any change to these rules would obviously affect both the terms of credit and the amount of credit available to chargors, but it is not clear that this adequately or rationally justifies the present vastly different positions of fixed and floating chargees.

This can have some odd consequences. As noted, the current position, determined by statute, is that assets subject to a floating charge (i.e. assets subject to a charge that was created as a floating charge, even though it will have crystallised on liquidation) are available for payment of liquidation expenses. Where several charges have been granted over the same asset, this rule can lead to nice questions about the priority as between the various charges: if the charge with first priority is a floating charge, then the proceeds are subject to claims for liquidation expenses, but if the first charge (or equal ranking charge) is a fixed charge, the fixed chargee can realise the charged assets without making any such provision (either for the liquidation expenses or for the preferential creditors). This outcome advantages those many creditors who typically take a "fixed and floating charge" over all the company's assets: to the extent that a fixed charge is possible, it ranks equally with the floating charge and is protected from these

---

[111] The Corporate Insolvency and Governance Act 2020 adds an entirely new Pt A1 to IA 1986. This is considered at para.33–002. In brief, however, the Act provides for a free standing moratorium for distressed but viable companies. The moratorium affords companies some breathing space from creditor action to pursue a turnaround plan without adding significant costs; it is focused on the recovery of the *company* rather than the realisation of assets so is a marked shift to a debtor-focused process. The Act also amends IA1986 s.115 and adds s.174A in respect of priorities in payments of expenses, making it clear that fees and expenses of the official receiver acting in any capacity come first, then moratorium debts and priority pre-moratorium debts (defined in s.174A(3)), and only then do the liquidation expenses kick in, followed by the usual order of priorities as outlined above.

[112] IA 1986 s.176ZA. See too *Re Premier Motor Auctions Leeds Ltd* [2015] EWHC 3568 (Ch); [2016] B.C.C. 463 in which the effects of s.176ZA were briefly discussed. Also see para.33–024.

[113] And to the extent that the floating chargee is unable to recoup the outstanding debt from the floating charge proceeds, that shortfall becomes an unsecured debt, repayable pari passu with all the other unsecured debts owed by the company.

[114] Justifying the super-priority of receivership costs (but subject to what follows on the statutory priority, even over these, of liquidation costs), see *Batten v Wedgwood Coal & Iron Co (No.1)* (1884) 28 Ch. D. 317 Ch D. But a receiver has a duty not to incur expenses if to do so would lessen the amount otherwise available to pay the preferential creditors: *Woods v Winskill* [1913] 2 Ch. 303 Ch D; *Westminster Corp v Haste* [1950] Ch. 442 Ch D, both cases concerning the expenses in carrying on the company's business.

expenses.[115] On the other hand, if the charge with priority is a floating charge, even if priority was gained by crystallisation, then the assets are subject to these rules relating to liquidation expenses and preferential debts.[116] These costs, combined with the claims of the preferential creditors, entail a substantial erosion of the entitlement of the floating charge holder.[117]

(v) *Powers of the administrator*

32–018 The final statutory limitation on the right of a floating charge holder is para.70 of Sch.B1 to the IA 1986 which empowers an administrator to sell property subject to a charge which as created was a floating charge without the need to obtain a court order.[118] As protection, the floating charge holder is given the same priority with respect to any property representing directly or indirectly the property disposed of as he would have had with respect to the property subject to the floating charge.[119]

Distinguishing between fixed and floating charges

32–019 The previous sections (on priority, preference and invalidity rules) demonstrate why chargees prefer to have fixed rather than floating security over the assets of a corporate debtor. Prior to 1986, it was possible to achieve this status simply by showing that the charge had crystallised (and thereby become a *fixed* charge) before the commencement of the liquidation or other relevant statutory date.[120] This loophole was eliminated by IA 1986 s.251, which provides that "floating charge" means "a charge which, *as created*, was a floating charge". This means that lenders must now ensure that their security, as created, is categorised as a fixed charge, not a floating charge, if they are to avoid the disadvantages outlined earlier.

Given the consequences that follow the categorisation of a charge as fixed or floating, the courts do not simply accept the labels attached by the parties. The

---

[115] *Re Lewis Merthyr Consolidated Collieries Ltd (No.1)* [1929] 1 Ch. 498 CA; *Re GL Saunders Ltd (In Liquidation)* [1986] 1 W.L.R. 215 Ch D.

[116] *Re Portbase Clothing Ltd* [1993] Ch. 388 at 407–409. A more difficult problem arises where the two successive charges are floating charges, the second one crystallises first and so has priority over the first, but the receiver is not appointed under the second charge but under the first one. *Griffiths v Yorkshire Bank Plc* [1994] 1 W.L.R. 1427 may be technically correct in deciding that since no receiver is appointed under the second charge, the assets are not subject to the claims of preferential creditors. But this leaves the way open for floating chargees to avoid the operation of these provisions, and so the more strained analysis in *Re H&K (Medway) Ltd* [1997] B.C.C. 853, which concluded that the preferential debts had priority over both charges, may be preferable.

[117] The *Portbase* decision operates within strict boundaries. In *Re MC Bacon Ltd (No.2)* [1990] B.C.C. 430 Ch D (Companies Ct) the court held that the costs of the liquidator in bringing an action under s.214 of the 1986 Act and to challenge a transaction as a preference were not costs of realising the company's assets and thus did not enjoy the priority accorded to such expenses in a winding-up.

[118] IA 1986 s.15(1) and (3).

[119] Where the charge has crystallised, the priority will be that of a fixed equitable charge.

[120] This was the case in *Re Brightlife Ltd* (1986) 2 B.C.C. 99359, where the debenture-holder had given the company a notice converting the floating charge into a fixed charge a week before a resolution for voluntary winding up was passed. The court held that the preferential creditors no longer had any right to be paid in priority to the charge.

fact that a charge is called a "fixed" charge by the parties does not necessarily make it so. As Lord Millett indicated in the Privy Council decision, *Agnew v Commissioner for Inland Revenue* (also known as *Re Brumark*)[121]:

> "in deciding whether a charge is a fixed charge or a floating charge, the court is engaged in a two-stage process. At the first stage it must construe the instrument of charge and seek to gather the intentions of the parties from the language they have used … . The object of this stage of the process … is to ascertain the nature of the rights and obligations which the parties intended to grant to each other in respect of the charged assets. Once these have been ascertained, the court can then embark on the second stage of the process, which is one of categorization, [which] is a matter of law."

In *Re Spectrum Plus Ltd*,[122] the House of Lords approved this approach and held that in characterising a charge as fixed or floating, the crucial element is the freedom of the company to use the assets in the ordinary course of its business, not the nature of the assets charged.[123] The House of Lords had to consider a charge over book debts expressed in the same terms as that in *Siebe Gorman*[124] (which had been accepted as a fixed charge: see below). In a decision that overruled *Siebe Gorman* and reversed the Court of Appeal below, the House of Lords held that the charge was floating. This was so, despite the fact that the debenture prohibited the chargor from charging or assigning the debts, and required it to pay the proceeds of collection of the debts into an account with the lending bank (i.e. despite following the recipe prescribed in *Siebe Gorman*), because the debenture did not go on to specify any restrictions on the chargor's operation of the account. This very restrictive definition of a fixed charge removes the element of judgement permitted by earlier cases: a charge is fixed if and only if the chargor is legally obliged to preserve the charged assets, or their permitted substitutes, for the benefit of the chargee. In all other cases, the charge is floating and therefore subject to the disadvantageous statutory regime already described.[125]

The change effected by this approach can be seen most clearly by comparing earlier decisions.[126] The easy cases remain easy. Suppose the charge holder is a bank with a charge over a company's book debts: if use of the proceeds of the book debts is not controlled at all, then the charge is floating[127]; and if use of the **32–020**

[121] *Agnew v Inland Revenue Commissioner* [2001] UKPC 28; [2001] B.C.C. 259 at [32].

[122] *Re Spectrum Plus Ltd* [2005] B.C.C. 694. Also see *Re Armagh Shoes Ltd* [1984] B.C.L.C. 405 Ch D (NI).

[123] Thus clarifying the relevance of the description of a floating charge advanced by Romer LJ in *Re Yorkshire Woolcombers Association Ltd* [1903] 2 Ch. 284 at 295 (see para.32–006).

[124] *Siebe Gorman v Barclays Bank* [1979] 2 Lloyd's Rep.142.

[125] S. Worthington, "An 'Unsatisfactory Area of the Law'—Fixed and Floating Charges Yet Again" (2004) 1 *International Corporate Rescue* 175–184 (adopted by the House of Lords in *Spectrum*); and S. Worthington, "Floating Charges: Use and Abuse of Doctrinal Analysis" in *Company Charges: Spectrum and Beyond* (2006), p.28.

[126] Although also see *Gray v G-T-P Group Ltd* [2010] EWHC 1772 (Ch); [2011] B.C.C. 869, where the charge was held void as an unregistered floating charge, since the agreement between the parties entitled the chargor to draw on the relevant bank account proceeds effectively at will.

[127] *Re Brightlife Ltd* (1986) 2 B.C.C. 99359, although in this case the chargee was not itself a bank.

proceeds is completely restricted, then the charge is fixed.[128] But if neither the freedom nor the control is absolute, then a judgement used to be required. In *Siebe Gorman & Co Ltd v Barclays Bank Ltd*,[129] Slade J (as he then was) held that a debenture over the borrower's book debts and its proceeds was correctly classified by the parties as a fixed charge. The charge agreement provided that the company could not assign or charge the secured book debts, and that the proceeds of the debts had to be paid into a designated bank account with the lending bank, although the chargor was then free to use the funds in the account.[130] On the basis of Slade J's decision, this form of debenture became a precedent and was widely used by most banks. The mere fact that the assets sought to be charged were a fluctuating class of present and future assets was not by itself a fatal objection to the creation of a fixed charge.[131] This decision has now been overruled by *Spectrum*.

In *Re New Bullas Trading Ltd*,[132] the agreement provided for a fixed charge over the book debts while they remained uncollected, but, when collected and paid into a designated account (unless written instructions to the contrary were given by the chargee), the monies so received were released from the fixed charge and became subject to a floating charge. No directions were ever given. The Court of Appeal, reversing Knox J, held that the parties were contractually able to reach such an agreement, and the arrangement constituted a fixed charge over the (uncollected) book debts, and a floating charge over their (collected) proceeds in the bank account. This case, too, was overruled by the House of Lords in *Spectrum* on the basis that, since the chargor was free to deal with the charged assets (the book debts), for its own benefit and without the consent or interference of the chargee, by collecting the debts and using their proceeds at will, the charge over the book debts was floating.

32–021 The restriction on the chargor's ability to deal with the assets must be legally binding. In *Royal Trust Bank v National Westminster Bank Plc*,[133] an instrument creating a charge over book debts gave the chargee bank the right to demand that the company should open a dedicated account and pay all monies received on the collection of the debts into that account, but the bank never exercised this right, and in practice monies collected went into the company's ordinary trading account. The charge was held by Millett LJ to be floating.[134] Similarly, in *Re Double S Printers Ltd*,[135] the chargee, as a director of the company, had de facto control over the proceeds of the charged book debts since he had actual control of

---

[128] *Re Keenan Bros Ltd* [1986] B.C.L.C. 242, where the chargee bank stipulated that the account could not be drawn against without the counter-signature of one of its officers.

[129] *Siebe Gorman v Barclays Bank* [1979] 2 Lloyd's Rep.142.

[130] On this last point, Slade J may have interpreted the arrangement otherwise, assuming the bank was required to give permission for each release of funds; on that basis the decision was accepted in *Agnew*, but, on the contrary interpretation, was overruled in *Spectrum*.

[131] Of course, in many cases, the fluctuating nature of the assets, especially of physical assets, means that managerial control of them can be given to the company only in a way which is inconsistent with a fixed charge: *Smith v Bridgend CBC* [2001] B.C.C. 740.

[132] *Re New Bullas Trading Ltd* [1994] B.C.C. 36 CA (Civ Div).

[133] *Royal Trust Bank v National Westminster Bank Plc* [1996] B.C.C. 613 CA (Civ Div).

[134] All three members of the court concurred in the result; Nourse LJ on other grounds, and Swinford Thomas LJ without giving reasons.

[135] *Re Double S Printers Ltd (In Liquidation* [1999] B.C.C. 303 DR.

the bank account, but this was not backed by any contractual restraint on their disposal in the instrument itself. As in the *Royal Trust Bank* case, it was held that the company's freedom to deal (at least in law) led to the conclusion that the charge was floating. And a legally binding arrangement to create a fixed charge that is in fact ignored by the parties, who operate as if the charge is floating, will be treated by the courts as a sham.[136]

The *Spectrum* decision has substantially affected the rights of companies to grant fixed charge securities over what must remain, for good commercial reasons, their circulating assets, whether these are physical assets used or manufactured by the company or the company's book debts.[137] It remains to be seen what techniques enterprising commercial parties will find to set up effective substitute security that attracts fewer of the disadvantages associated with floating charges.

REGISTRATION OF CHARGES

The purpose of a registration system

Part 25 of the CA 2006 contains provisions relating to the registration of particular details in relation to certain charges with the Registrar of Companies. Following major reform in 2013, the registration system has now changed from a mandatory one (backed by criminal sanctions) to one which is optional with registration at the discretion of the company.[138] The 2013 changes came about following multiple rounds of failed attempts to reform the system. To understand how we have reached the present position, it is worth considering the possible purposes of a registration requirement. **32–022**

First, and most obvious, the aim might be to give potential lenders to the company more accurate information about the company's real vs. apparent wealth by revealing the true extent of any earlier secured lending that may rank ahead of their own contemplated advances.[139] Such information may also be of interest to credit analysts, insolvency practitioners appointed upon the company's insolvency, shareholders and investors. Secondly (and for reasons aligned with the first objective), registration might be treated as an essential part of the process whereby a person obtains a security interest against the company. Without registration, the security interest would be void, and could not be relied upon as against the unsecured creditors of the company in the latter's insolvency.[140] The

136 *Agnew v CIR* [2001] B.C.C. 259.

137 Although see *Russell Cooke Trust Co Ltd v Elliott* [2007] EWHC 1443 (Ch), where a charge described as floating was held to be fixed.

138 CA 2006 s.859A.

139 Registration for this purpose is confined to registration of non-possessory securities. An obligation secured by a possessory security necessarily entails transfer of the secured asset into the possession of the security-holder, so that it does not remain on site as part of the "apparent wealth" of the borrowing company.

140 This rule does not avoid the underlying obligation, and if the loan fell for repayment whilst the company was a going concern, for example, then it could simply be repaid by the company without any question of enforcement of a security arising. The problem arises on insolvency, when the protection of a security interest is most needed.

usual terminology is that registration is necessary for the "perfection" of the security. Thirdly, registration might determine priority among secured creditors. For example, priorities among secured creditors could be determined simply by the date of the registration of the security (and not, for example, by reference to the date of creation of the security, or by whether the later taker of a security knew of the earlier one): such a system is generally referred to as a system of "notice filing".

32–023 As the law stood before the 2013 changes, not one of these objectives was delivered. The first failed, since not all security interests needed to be registered, only those listed in the now-repealed s.860(7). The second failed for the same reason of limited application, although within that limited range any charges that ought to have been registered, but were not, were void as against the liquidator, administrator and any creditor.[141] And the third failed, as it was simply not part of the rules of the system: instead, if the security was valid (including properly registered, if it needed to be), then priority was judged according to the usual common law rules, generally based on the time of creation, the type of interest created, and the notice to subsequent security holders.

What is remarkable about this area of law is that proposals for radical change have been made by highly respected official bodies for over 50 years, but no change of either a radical or a tinkering kind was put in place until 2013 (and even that might be described as merely tinkering).[142] Radical change was proposed by the Crowther Committee in 1971,[143] endorsed by the Cork Committee in 1983,[144] and re-proposed by Professor Diamond in 1989.[145] The CLR began in tinkering mood,[146] partly because consultation on the previous radical proposals had not produced an enthusiastic response, but concluded by advocating radical reform.[147] In this positive spirit, the issue was handed over to the Law Commission,[148] which produced a consultation paper and a "consultative report", both favouring radical change, proposing a comprehensive scheme of notice-filing and associated priority rules that would extend to all securities and quasi-securities, whether granted by companies, unincorporated businesses or individuals.[149] Despite the early support, further consultation on this detailed proposal produced a more cautious response, and the Law Commission's final Report on Company Security Interests in 2005 recommended a less radical

---

[141] CA 2006 s.874, and see the discussion at para.32–024.

[142] Some tinkering reform was included in the CA 1989, but never brought into force.

[143] *Report of the Committee on Consumer Credit* (1971), Cmnd.5427.

[144] *Insolvency Law and Practice* (1982), Cmnd.8558.

[145] *A Review of Security Interests in Property* (HMSO, 1989).

[146] CLR, *Registration of Company Charges* (October 2000), URN 00/1213.

[147] Final Report I, Ch.12.

[148] Reference was also made to the Scottish Law Commission, but in narrower terms: now see *Report on Registration of Rights in Security by Companies* (2004), Scot Law Com. No.197.

[149] Law Commission, *Registration of Security Interests: Company Charges and Property other than Land* (2002), Consultation Paper 164; *Company Security Interests: A Consultative Report* (August 2004), Law Com. Consultation Paper No.176.

scheme, preserving its recommended notice-filing and priority rules for charges and outright sales of receivables, but not including quasi-securities nor, at least to start with, unincorporated debtors.[150]

In July 2005, the Department of Trade and Industry (the predecessor to the Department for Business, Energy and Industrial Strategy) considered these various recommendations and published a consultation document.[151] The results of all this effort can only be seen as disappointing. CA 2006 has now been amended, repealing the original Chs 1 and 2 of Pt 25 and replacing them with Ch.A1, but all to rather minimal effect.

The reformed registration system

What has to be registered

As already mentioned, there is no longer any requirement to register security interests. Any charge created by the company[152] *may* be registered, save for four exceptions,[153] and s.859A(2) compels the registrar to register the charge if a statement pursuant to s.859D is submitted within the stipulated time period. In keeping with this general change of direction, the criminal sanction for non-registration is removed, although it remains the case that failure to register a registrable charge will render it void against the administrator, liquidator or any creditor of the company.[154] There is thus a very powerful practical sanction for non-registration. **32–024**

It might be thought that the move away from a prescribed list of charges which were required to be registered (under the now repealed s.860(7)) would eliminate much of the argument about whether or not the charge was one that required registration. But given the invalidity consequences just noted, and in any event as was very largely the case under the previous rules, all the debate will simply be about whether the creditor's interest is a charge at all,[155] not whether it falls within or outside some prescribed list of charges.

150 Law Commission, *Company Security Interests* (August 2005), Law Com No.296, Cm.6654, especially paras 1.31, 1.46–1.57 and 1.60–1.66.

151 DTI, *The Registration of Companies' Security Interests (Company Charges): The Economic Impact of the Law Commissions' Proposals* (Consultative Document, July 2005).

152 Defined in s.859A(7).

153 CA 2006 ss.859A(1) and (6).

154 CA 2006 s.859H. It is the security which is void, not the underlying obligation (s.859(3) and (4)), and so for this purpose, creditor means secured creditor: *Re Teleomatic Ltd* [1994] 1 B.C.L.C. 90 Ch D (Companies Ct) at 95. Of course, if the company goes into liquidation or administration and the charge is unenforceable, this pro tanto protects the interests of the unsecured creditors: see *R. v Registrar of Companies Ex p. Central Bank of India* [1986] Q.B. 1114 at 1161–1162. The previous provision, in similar terms, but applying only to the listed charges which required registration, was CA 2006 s.874 (now repealed).

155 Or is, instead, e.g. a retention of title agreement or some other quasi-security. See, e.g. *Re Cosslett (Contractors) Ltd* [1996] B.C.C. 515 Ch D; and [1997] B.C.C. 724 CA (Civ Div); and the failed retention of title cases, *Re Bond Worth Ltd* [1980] Ch. 228 Ch D; and *Borden (UK) Ltd v Scottish Timber Products Ltd* [1981] Ch. 25 CA (Civ Div). The one exception to this is that, previously, not all fixed charges required registration, although all floating charges did, and so that particular characterisation could be especially important for validity (see paras 32–019 to 32–021 on the distinction), as well as for all the reasons discussed at para.32–031.

The mechanics of registration

32–025 Registration may be effected by the company itself or by any person interested in the charge. The chargee is the person most motivated to register, so as to protect its security.

The period allowed for registration is 21 days beginning with the day after the date of creation of the charge (s.859A(4)), unless an order granting an extension can be obtained from the court, having regard to the restrictive requirements laid down in s.859F.[156] Section 859E defines the "date of creation of the charge", with ss.(1) stipulating the date of creation, in respect of three different types of charge, depending on whether it is a "standard security" and whether or not it is "created or evidenced by an instrument".

Where the debt is satisfied or the charged property or undertaking has been fully or partially released, a statement to that effect,[157] together with the relevant particulars,[158] should be submitted to the registrar. Upon receipt of such statement and particulars, the registrar must include in the register a statement of satisfaction or a statement recording the release of the charge.[159]

The register is accessible to the public. Reflecting concerns for confidentiality and privacy, certain personal information is not required to be included in the certified copy of the instrument delivered to the registrar.[160]

In addition to this registration at Companies House, the company is no longer required to keep a register of charges on its undertaking and property.[161] However, companies are still required to keep copies of instruments creating and amending charges available for inspection.[162]

Geographical reach of the registration provisions

32–026 The reformed system provides a single scheme for registration irrespective of the place of incorporation of the company within the UK (the previous scheme had one system for England, Wales and Northern Ireland, and a separate one for Scotland). The wide scope of s.859A means that a charge is registrable whether or not it is created in the UK, and whether or not the property being charged is located in the UK, with no special provisions or exceptions for these types of security.

Despite this, if the secured property is located outside the UK, then the effectiveness of any security is likely to depend upon the property law rules applying within that jurisdiction, and not simply on whether the charge should have been registered in the UK.

---

[156] See para.32–028.
[157] CA 2006 s.859L(1)–(3).
[158] CA 2006 s.859L(4).
[159] CA 2006 s.859L(5).
[160] CA 2006 s.859G.
[161] CA 2006 s.876(1)(b) (repealed).
[162] CA 2006 ss.859P and 859Q.

The effect of failure to register

32–027 As already noted, failure to register is no longer a criminal offence, although any registrable but unregistered charge created by the company will be void against the administrator, liquidator or any creditor of the company.[163] The person disadvantaged is the chargee, not the company; hence the rule allowing any person with an interest in the charge to register it. If the charge is not registered, the chargee effectively loses its security. To reduce this hardship, the 2006 Act provides that if the charge is void to any extent for non-registration, then the whole of the sum thereby secured becomes immediately repayable on demand.[164] This, of course, also provides the company with an incentive to register. In addition, the unregistered charge is not void against the company (if still solvent), and there is nothing to prevent the chargee enforcing it (although often to little advantage if the company is solvent).[165] An unsecured creditor has no standing to prevent the holder of an unregistered but registrable charge from enforcing it.[166]

Late registration

32–028 Section 859F enables the company or a person interested in a charge that has not been registered within 21 days of its creation to apply to the court for an order extending the time for registration. This can be done if the court is satisfied that the failure to register was accidental or inadvertent and not likely to prejudice creditors or shareholders, or it is satisfied on other grounds that such relief is just and equitable.[167] This repeats earlier provisions, so older cases remain useful. The jurisdiction of the court is very wide,[168] but the court will not normally make an order once a winding-up has commenced.[169] This is because winding up is a procedure for the benefit of unsecured creditors, and registering a charge after the commencement of winding up would defeat their interests. The court may also refuse to exercise its discretion if the company is insolvent,[170] or if the company is in administration and it is inevitable that this will proceed to insolvent liquidation.[171]

If the court does exercise its discretion, the charge is normally registered on terms that do not prejudice the secured rights acquired by third parties prior to the

---

[163] CA 2006 s.859H. See fn.154.

[164] CA 2006 s.859H(4).

[165] If the chargee does so then the charge is spent and a liquidator or administrator cannot retrospectively challenge the enforcement of the charge.

[166] *Re Ehrmann Bros Ltd* [1906] 2 Ch. 697 CA.

[167] CA 2006 s.859F(2).

[168] CA 2006 s.859F(3). Once a failure to register is discovered, the chargee must act expeditiously: the court will not exercise its discretion favourably where the chargee hangs back to see which way the wind blows: *Re Telomatic Ltd* [1993] B.C.C. 404 Ch D (Companies Ct).

[169] *Re S Abrahams & Sons* [1902] 1 Ch. 695 Ch D. In exceptional circumstances, however, the court may make such an order: *Re RM Arnold & Co Ltd* [1984] B.C.L.C. 535. See *Barclays Bank Plc v Stuart London Ltd* [2001] EWCA Civ 140; [2002] B.C.C. 917, for conditions imposed where liquidation was imminent.

[170] See *Re Ashpurton Estates Ltd* [1983] Ch. 110 CA (Civ Div).

[171] *Re Barrow Borough Transport Ltd* (1989) 5 B.C.C. 646 Ch D (Companies Ct).

actual date of registration.[172] Since a charge does not become ineffective until the normal time limit has expired, this standard proviso only protects third parties acting between the date when the charge ought to have been registered and its actual registration.[173] Unsecured creditors are not protected by such a proviso, and are not part of the court's considerations.[174]

Defective registration

32–029 Section 859M allows applications for rectification of omissions or misstatements in the registered particulars. The jurisdiction is defined in the same way as s.859F (see above). The particulars may, for example, fail to state accurately the property subject to the charge or the amount secured by the charge.[175] Note that the court's power is limited to correcting omissions or misstatements within an entry. The court cannot order the removal of an entry,[176] nor can it order the removal of information that the company would prefer not to be there,[177] and nor does the court's jurisdiction extend to particulars which are not required to be registered.[178]

Effect of registration

32–030 Where a charge is registered, the Registrar has to issue a certificate of registration and this is made conclusive evidence that the requirements of CA 2006 Pt 25 Ch.A1 have been complied with.[179] This provides assurance to any transferees of the security that the validity of its registration cannot be challenged. The conclusiveness of the certificate means that the charge will be treated as validly registered even if it was not, but was registered by mistake[180]; and even if the registered particulars are inaccurate.[181] Note, however, that where there is such inaccuracy, registration validates the charge, but the operative terms are those agreed between the parties notwithstanding that third parties may have been

---

[172] *Re IC Johnson & Co Ltd* [1902] 2 Ch. 101 CA. The proviso will also preserve any agreements about priorities already made by the late-registering chargee with other creditors: ibid.

[173] *Watson v Duff, Morgan & Vermont (Holdings)* [1974] 1 W.L.R. 450 Ch D.

[174] *Re MIG Trust* [1933] Ch. 542 CA at 569–572 (Romer LJ).

[175] See generally, D. Prentice, "Defectively Registered Charges" (1970) 34 Conv. (N.S.) 410. The company's registered number is a detail required to be supplied but not a particular of the charge, so that an error in that regard cannot invalidate the charge: *Grove v Advantage Healthcare (TIO) Ltd* [2000] 1 B.C.L.C. 611.

[176] *Exeter Trust Ltd v Screenways Ltd* [1991] B.C.C. 477 CA (Civ Div).

[177] *Igroup Ltd v Ocwen* [2003] EWHC 2431 (Ch); [2003] B.C.C. 993.

[178] *Igroup Ltd v Ocwen* [2003] B.C.C. 993.

[179] CA 2006 s.859I.

[180] *Ali v Top Marques Car Rental Ltd* [2006] EWHC 109 (Ch); (2006) 150 S.J.L.B. 264.

[181] *National Provincial & Union Bank of England v Charnley* [1924] 1 K.B. 431 CA (where the property charged was incorrectly stated); *Re Mechanisations (Eaglescliffe) Ltd* [1966] Ch. 20 Ch D (amount secured misstated); *Re Eric Holmes (Property) Ltd (In Liquidation)* [1965] Ch. 1052 Ch D; *Re CL Nye Ltd* [1971] Ch. 442 CA (Civ Div) (date of creation misstated).

misled[182] by incorrect particulars.[183] Because the certificate is conclusive evidence of registration, there can be no judicial review of the Registrar's decision to register.[184]

On the other hand, registration does not cure any flaw in the charge itself as between the parties, so the validity of the charge remains challengeable by the company.[185] In addition, registration does not determine priority as between competing security interests (although failure to register renders the charge void, and therefore registration is a necessary, although not sufficient, condition to obtaining priority). Priority is determined by the usual common law and equitable rules of property. Indeed, the register does not necessarily provide accurate information to chargees about earlier charges that may rank ahead of any charge currently being negotiated. This is because of the "21 day invisibility problem", whereby if A registers a charge on 21 January, for example, there is no guarantee that the company has not created a charge shortly prior to this which may be registered within 21 days[186] and thus have priority. In applying the normal priority rules as between competing interests, any person taking a registrable charge over the company's property (and perhaps other persons[187]) will have constructive notice of any matter that requires registration and has been disclosed. To take an example, a person taking a contractual lien is probably not affected by constructive notice of the register, but a person taking a floating charge would be.

Reform proposals and registration systems elsewhere

The fate of recent and not so recent proposals for reform of the UK registration system has already been described.[188] Although some commentators doubt the need for a registration system at all,[189] most developed countries have one. Indeed, the major reform proposals most recently rejected in England and Wales had strong parallels with the systems already operating in the US (Uniform Commercial Code art.9), Canada, New Zealand and Australia, and under 32–031

---

[182] Given this feature, then, on those rare occasions where the mistake is that of the Registrar, it seems unlikely the Registrar would be liable to anyone suffering damages, despite *Ministry of Housing and Local Government v Sharp* (1970) 21 P. & C.R. 166 CA (Civ Div): see *Davis v Radcliffe* [1990] B.C.C. 472 PC and the cases cited therein; *Banque Keyser Ullmann SA v Skandia (UK) Insurance Co* [1990] 1 Q.B. 665 CA (Civ Div) at 796–798 (on appeal [1991] 2 A.C. 249 HL). But (in a quite different context) see *Serby v Companies House* [2015] EWHC 115 (QB); [2015] B.C.C. 236.

[183] See the illustrative cases cited at fn.181.

[184] *R. v Registrar of Companies Ex p. Central Bank of India* [1986] Q.B. 1114; followed in *Re Forthouse Development Ltd (In Administration)* [2013] NICh 6.

[185] Most usually on the grounds of capacity or authority, especially in dealings between the company and its directors.

[186] CA 2006 s.859A(4).

[187] See para.32–011.

[188] See paras 32–022 to 32–023.

[189] U. Drobnig, "Present and Future of Real and Personal Property" (2003) *European Review of Private Law* 623, 660: "If all the information it [the register] offers is a notice that there may exist a security interest, so that intending creditors are put on notice but have to turn to the debtor in order to verify the true state of affairs is not nearly the same effect achieved in countries without a registration system where the courts proceed from a general presumption that business people must know that any major piece of equipment is bought on credit?"

consideration elsewhere. The most disappointing feature of the current position in England and Wales is not simply that the UK has been left with an outdated regime, but that it missed an opportunity to provide the first draft for a model European scheme. The work being done by the EBRD, UNCITRAL and UNIDROIT indicates the demand for sophisticated input on this front.[190] Older editions of this book provided some detail on the Law Commission's various 2002–2005 proposals, assuming that they had not quite been laid to rest,[191] but that detail is not repeated here.[192]

ENFORCEMENT OF FLOATING CHARGES

Receivers and administrators

32–032 The methods of enforcing a security interest depend upon the nature of the rights which it confers, and are often in no way peculiar to company law. However, company law has traditionally provided a distinct proceeding for the enforcement of a floating charge by the appointment of a receiver—termed, since the insolvency reforms of the 1980s, an "administrative receiver".[193] In this section, therefore, we return to our preoccupation with the floating charge. A major reform brought about by the Enterprise Act 2002 was substantially to restrict the use of receivership and to channel the enforcement of floating charges into the administration procedure, which is a general procedure for the handling of insolvent companies and thus not specific to the enforcement of the floating charge.

The main driver behind this reform was the desire to produce an enforcement mechanism for the floating charge in which the relevant insolvency practitioner owed duties to all the creditors of the company and not primarily to the floating charge holder.[194] Consistently with the case law origins of the floating charge in the nineteenth century, the receiver is a person appointed out of court by the charge holder under the provisions of the instrument creating the charge, and who takes management control of the company in order to realise sufficient assets to repay the appointor (the charge holder) and then hands the company back to its directors or to a liquidator,[195] depending on the financial state of the company at the end of the receivership.

---

[190] Fundamental changes for UK in the longer term are being considered by the Secured Transactions Law Reform Project: see *http://securedtransactionslawreformproject.org/* [Accessed 20 December 2020].

[191] Also see paras 32–022 to 32–023.

[192] See the 9th edn of this book, paras 32–53 to 32–56.

[193] The distinction is typically made between a person who has control of all, or substantially all, the assets of a company (an administrative receiver: IA 1986 s.29(2)) and a person who simply has control of a single asset or limited class of secured assets (a receiver). The former is in a position to manage the company as a going concern; the latter is not. Both hold their positions in order to realise the rights of the secured creditor (and other creditors, if the charge is floating—see paras 32–015 to 32–018).

[194] Insolvency Service, White Paper, *Productivity and Enterprise: Insolvency—A Second Chance* (July 2001), Cm.5234, para.2.2.

[195] On winding up and liquidation, see Ch.33.

Compared with receivership, administration is a much more recent mechanism, introduced as a result of the recommendations of the Cork Committee.[196] Perhaps predictably, the statutory administration procedure is based on common law receivership principles. Although the Cork Committee had criticisms to make of receivership, it appreciated its one immeasurable advantage over winding up: receivership was structured on the basis that the receiver would normally continue to run the company and in the process save the viable parts of its business (though often by selling them off to others). Such a "rescue culture" was thought to be more protective of the interests of all stakeholders in the business than a winding-up, and so the Committee recommended that the benefits of receivership be made available where there was no floating charge, so that the rescue culture could be extended to such cases.

Of course, the receivership rules could not simply be applied in total to a situation where there was no floating charge. In the absence of a charge holder to appoint the insolvency practitioner, that task was given to the court, on application by the company or its creditors. Further, the opportunity was taken to give the statutory administrator the benefit of an institution which the receiver, as a product essentially of private law, had not had, namely, a moratorium during the administration on the enforcement of creditors' rights against the company.[197] Finally, and in line with the notion of the administration as an extension of the receivership, the floating charge holder, if such had been created, was initially given, in effect, a veto over the appointment of an administrator.[198] This last feature was subsequently removed by the Enterprise Act 2002 and, going in the opposite direction, is supplanted by a prohibition in the normal case on the appointment by the floating charge holder of an administrative receiver.[199] Thus under the Enterprise Act 2002, it is not possible to appoint an administrative receiver under a floating charge created on or after 15 September 2003, except as in the cases specified in IA 1986 ss.72B–72H. Instead, the chargee is given the right to appoint an administrator: see IA 1986 Sch.B1 para.14(1). Chargees of charges created prior to this date may appoint an administrator, but retain the right to appoint an administrative receiver. The aim, stated in the White Paper preceding the Enterprise Act 2002, was that "administrative receivership should cease to be a major insolvency procedure".[200] The administrative receiver would instead be replaced by an administrator, who is an officer of the court, and must "perform his functions in the interests of the company's creditors as a whole".[201] **32–033**

Note that a chargee whose charge does not cover the whole or substantially the whole of the assets of the company can still appoint a receiver (who will not be an administrative receiver), and cannot appoint an administrator.

---

[196] See Ch.19 fn.111. In the end the Committee's proposals were not implemented precisely in the way the Committee had envisaged.

[197] Now see the new form of moratorium, aimed at rescuing the company: see text at fn.54 and para.33–002.

[198] IA 1986 s.9(2)–(3), repealed by the Enterprise Act 2002.

[199] IA 1986 s.72A. The prohibition does not apply to appointments under floating charges in existence before the date on which the new rules were brought into operation: s.72A(4).

[200] See Insolvency Service, White Paper, *Productivity and Enterprise: Insolvency—A Second Chance* (July 2001), Cm.5234, para.2.5.

[201] IA 1986 Sch.B1 para.3(2).

32–034 This policy of statutory patricide was subject, however, to two qualifications which concern us. First, the White Paper recognised that the procedure for appointing a receiver had the advantages for the floating charge holder of being quick, cheap and entirely under the charge holder's control. It was further recognised that the earlier administration procedure would need to be reformed so as to reproduce those advantages, as far as possible, within the new structure. "Secured creditors," said the White Paper, "should not feel at any risk from our proposals".[202] Accordingly, the current administration procedure is not simply one that applies more generally, but is itself reformed, a new Pt II being inserted into the IA 1986 by the Enterprise Act 2002.[203]

Secondly, the common law administrative receivership system is retained in certain exceptional cases.[204] Most of these do not need to be discussed in a work of this nature, but one is of crucial importance. Under the new IA 1986 s.72B, as interpreted in the new Sch.2A,[205] a receiver may still be appointed where a company issues secured debentures[206] and where (1) the security is held by trustees on behalf of the debenture-holders[207]; (2) the amount to be raised is at least £50 million[208]; and (3) the debentures are to be listed or traded on a regulated market.[209] In terms of enforcement, therefore, an important distinction is drawn between two common forms of corporate finance. Where the debt is raised from the public by way of a large-scale offering of securities, the administrative receivership procedure will continue to be available. Where the debt is raised from a bank (or syndicate of banks), administration will be the enforcement procedure, unless one of the other exceptions contained in IA 1986 ss.72C–72G applies.[210] For this reason it is necessary to discuss briefly both the receivership and administration methods of enforcing the floating charge.[211] We begin with the older procedure.

Receivership

Appointment of an administrative receiver

32–035 Where an appointment of an administrative receiver remains possible, because the casc falls within one of the exceptions noted above and the necessary power is contained in an existing debenture, almost invariably the first step in the

[202] See Insolvency Service, White Paper, *Productivity and Enterprise: Insolvency—A Second Chance* (July 2001), Cm.5234, para.2.6.

[203] Enterprise Act 2002 s.248. The operative provisions are contained mainly in a new Sch.B1 to the IA 1986, set out in Sch.16 to the 2002 Act.

[204] IA 1986 ss.72A–H.

[205] Set out in Sch.18 to the 2002 Act.

[206] IA 1986 s.72B(1)(b) and Sch.2A para.2(1)(a)—which makes a further reference to art.77 of the FSMA 2000 (Regulated Activities) Order 2001 (SI 2001/544), where the inclusion of debentures and debenture stock can be found.

[207] IA 1986 s.72B(1) and Sch.2A para.1(1)(a).

[208] IA 1986 s.72B(1)(a).

[209] IA 1986 Sch.2A para.2.

[210] Note *Feetum v Levy* [2005] EWCA Civ 1601; [2006] B.C.C. 340: a right to appoint an administrative receiver does not amount to step-in rights.

[211] The use of administration generally is not discussed in this work.

enforcement of a charge is for the debenture-holders or their trustee to obtain the appointment of a receiver.[212] This appointment will normally be made by the debenture-holder under an express or implied[213] power in the debenture, or by the court. Where the appointment is pursuant to a provision in the debenture then it must be clear that the conditions justifying the appointment have arisen, otherwise the receiver will be a trespasser and also liable for conversion.[214]

Once the conditions for the enforcement of a charge have arisen, English law places few constraints on the rights of the security holder to enforce the charge, and in this respect the regime is pro-security holder. For example, if the chargee is entitled to payment on demand, it is only necessary to give the company reasonable time to put into effect the mechanics of payment, not reasonable time in which to raise the funds to make payment.[215] Indeed, if the debtor makes it clear that funds are not available, this constitutes a sufficient act of default and there is no need to allow the debtor any time before treating it as being in default.[216] In addition, the chargee is not under any duty to the debtor company to refrain from exercising its rights merely because by doing so it could prevent loss to the company,[217] nor to exercise its rights promptly because the security is declining in value.[218]

If the security is not yet enforceable, but the debenture-holder's position is in jeopardy, the court may exercise its inherent discretion to appoint a receiver.[219] This is now very rare, but can be done by a debenture-holder's action, taken by

[212] If the state of the company is so parlous that it is doubtful whether there will be enough to cover the receiver's remuneration it may be necessary for the trustees to take possession. If the "debenture" is just an ordinary mortgage of particular property, the debenture-holder may, of course, exercise its power of sale without the preliminary step of appointing a receiver.

[213] i.e. under Law of Property Act (LPA) 1925 s.101 when applicable.

[214] Where the appointment is defective, the court can order the person making the appointment to indemnify the receiver: IA 1986 s.34. See also IA 1986 s.232, which deals with the validity of acts of a defectively appointed administrative receiver, and IA 1986 s.234 dealing with the seizure or disposal by an administrative receiver of property that does not belong to the company, and generally see *Re London Iron & Steel Co Ltd* [1990] B.C.C. 159 Ch D (Companies Ct); *Welsh Development Agency v Export Finance Co Ltd* [1992] B.C.C. 270 CA (Civ Div). Also see *Business Mortgage Finance 6 Plc v Roundstone Technologies Ltd* [2019] EWHC 2917 (Ch) concerning the consequences of a sale effected by an invalidly appointed receiver acting without ostensible authority.

[215] *Bank of Baroda v Panessar* [1987] Ch. 335 Ch D; *Quah v Goldman Sachs International* [2015] EWHC 759 (Comm); this is normally a matter of hours during normal banking hours. In addition, the company may be estopped by its conduct from challenging the validity of the appointment of a receiver, and the appointment of a receiver on invalid grounds may be subsequently cured if grounds justifying the appointment are subsequently discovered: *Bank of Baroda* [1987] Ch. 335 at 352–353 and *Byblos Bank SAL v Khudairy* (1986) 2 B.C.C. 99509 CA (Civ Div) respectively. There is no need for the debenture-holder to specify the exact sum due in any demand: see *NRG Vision Ltd v Churchfield Leasing Ltd* (1988) 4 B.C.C. 56 Ch D.

[216] *Sheppard & Cooper Ltd v TSB Bank Plc* [1996] B.C.C. 965 Ch D; *Quah v Goldman Sachs International* [2015] EWHC 759 (Comm).

[217] *Re Potters Oils (No.2)* (1985) 1 B.C.C. 99593 Ch D (Companies Ct); *Standard Chartered Bank Ltd v Walker* [1982] 1 W.L.R. 1410 CA (Civ Div). Also see *Alpstream AG v PK Airfinance Sarl* [2015] EWCA Civ 1318; [2016] 2 P. & C.R. 2.

[218] *China and South Sea Bank Ltd v Tan* [1990] 1 A.C. 536 PC; of course it will always be in the commercial interests of the chargee to exercise his rights if the security is declining in value. On other aspects of the receiver's duties to the company and others, see paras 32–036 to 32–037.

[219] But the court will not normally have any power to appoint a receiver unless the debentures are secured by a charge: *Harris v Beauchamp Bros* [1894] 1 Q.B. 801 CA; *Re Swallow Footwear* Times,

one of the debenture-holders, on behalf of himself and all other holders. "Jeopardy" is established when, for example, execution is about to be levied against the company,[220] or when the company proposes to distribute to its members its one remaining asset.[221]

Despite this option, appointment out of court is certainly preferable. The procedure in a debenture-holders' action is lamentably expensive and dilatory, since the receiver, as an officer of the court, will have to work under its closest supervision and constant applications will have to be made in chambers throughout the duration of the receivership, which may last years if a complicated realisation is involved. Since the 1986 Act allows a receiver, even though appointed out of court, to obtain the court's directions,[222] it is difficult to envisage circumstances in which an application to the court can be justified if the cheaper alternative is available. In the discussion which follows, it will be assumed that what is being referred to is a receiver appointed out of court.

Function and status of the receiver and administrative receiver

32–036 The IA 1986 views the appointment of an administrative receiver as being in some respects similar to insolvency proceedings and regulates it accordingly.[223] Thus administrative receivers must be qualified to act as insolvency practitioners[224] and can only be removed from office by the court.[225] Also, like the liquidator, the administrative receiver can compel those involved in the affairs of the company to provide him or her with information relating to the company's affairs.[226] The effect of the appointment of a receiver upon the company directors is that they no longer have any authority to deal with the relevant company property. They do however officially remain in office and continue to be liable for the submission of documents to Companies House, and may still institute proceedings in the company's name.[227] In other ways, too, the appointment of a receiver must not be equated with that of a liquidator: (1) where a receiver is appointed, the company need not go into liquidation,[228] and if it does, the same person who acted as receiver will normally not be appointed liquidator; (2) liquidation is a class action designed to protect the interests of the unsecured creditors, whereas, as we shall see, receivership is designed to protect the

---

23 October 1956 CA. Also the court will not imply a term into a debenture empowering a chargee, rather than the court, to appoint a receiver where his security is in jeopardy: see *Cryne v Barclays Bank* [1987] B.C.L.C. 548 CA (Civ Div).

220 *McMahon v North Kent Ironworks Co* [1891] 2 Ch. 148 Ch D; *Edwards v Standard Rolling Stock Syndicate* [1893] 1 Ch. 574 Ch D; and see *Re Victoria Steamboats Ltd* [1897] 1 Ch. 158 Ch D.

221 *Re Tilt Cove Copper Co Ltd* [1913] 2 Ch. 588 Ch D.

222 IA 1986 s.35.

223 See IA 1986 s.247(1) for the definition of "insolvency".

224 IA 1986 s.388(1). A body corporate, an undischarged bankrupt, or a person disqualified to act as a director may not act as an insolvency practitioner: see IA 1986 s.390(1) and (4).

225 IA 1986 s.45(1); they can resign, ibid.

226 IA 1986 ss.47 and 236; *Re Aveling Barford Ltd* (1988) 4 B.C.C. 548 Ch D (Companeis Ct); *Cloverbay Ltd (Joint Administrators) v Bank of Credit and Commerce International SA* [1990] B.C.C. 414 CA (Civ Div).

227 See fn.251 and the further discussion in para.32–037.

228 See IA 1986 s.247(2). Although generally a receiver should not be seen as a doctor but rather as an undertaker.

interests of the security holders who appointed the receiver and it is for this reason that a receiver can be appointed even where the company is in liquidation[229]; (3) liquidation terminates the trading power of the company,[230] whereas this is not the case with receivership; (4) a liquidator has power to disclaim onerous property,[231] something not possible in the case of receivership; (5) a liquidator in a compulsory winding-up is an officer of the court,[232] whereas this is not the case with a receiver unless appointed by the court[233]; and (6) lastly, it is easier to obtain recognition of liquidation as opposed to receivership in proceedings in foreign courts. These are the most important differences but there are others, particularly with respect to liability on contracts.[234]

An administrative receiver might be assumed to be the agent of those who appointed him but this is not the case; IA 1986 s.44 makes him the agent of the company.[235] The reason for this is to avoid those who appointed the administrative receiver being treated as mortgagees in possession or being held liable for the receiver's acts, which would be the case were the receiver to be treated as their agent.[236] As many have pointed out, the receiver's agency is a peculiar form of agency. This is because the primary responsibility of the receiver is to protect the interests of the security holders and to realise the charged assets for their benefit.[237] Nevertheless, the way the receiver carries out these responsibilities will profoundly affect parties other than the chargee. If the secured assets are not realised for their full value and there is a shortfall in paying the secured debt, the shortfall may become payable by a guarantor who might feel aggrieved to be called upon if the shortfall seemed unnecessary. Equally, the company—and, if it is insolvent, its creditors—will feel aggrieved if the value of secured asset has been in some way wasted on meeting only the secured creditor's claims when a more careful exercise might have generated a surplus for the benefit of the company. For these reasons, there are a number of parties interested in the various duties the receiver owes in the exercise of his or her role.

---

[229] *Re Potters Oils Ltd (No.2)* (1985) 1 B.C.C. 99593.

[230] Also without the leave of the court legal proceedings cannot be brought against the company: see IA 1986 s.130.

[231] See IA 1986 s.178.

[232] *Parsons v Sovereign Bank of Canada* [1913] A.C. 160 PC.

[233] It is contempt of court to interfere with the exercise of power by a court-appointed receiver without the leave of the court.

[234] See para.33–018.

[235] Also the debenture will invariably provide that irrespective of the type of receiver appointed by the charge holder he is to be the agent of the company. A receiver appointed by the court is not an agent of anyone but an officer of the court: see *Moss Steamship Co Ltd v Whinney* [1912] A.C. 254 HL.

[236] If the chargee interferes with the receiver's discharge of his duties this could, provided the interference is sufficiently pervasive, result in the receiver being treated as the agent of the chargee: see *American Express International Banking Corp v Hurley* (1986) 2 B.C.C. 98993 QBD.

[237] The receiver would not, for example, be considered to be participating in the management of the company since he is not managing the company but the assets of the company: *Re B Johnson & Co (Builders) Ltd* [1955] Ch. 634 CA; *Re North Development Pty Ltd* (1990) 8 A.C.L.C. 1004. But this "control" over the subsidiary's assets may have tax consequences for a holding company in a group structure: see *Farnborough Airport Properties Co v Revenue and Customs Commissioners* [2019] EWCA Civ 118; [2019] 1 W.L.R. 4077.

This has been a fraught question. The powers of administrative receivers are extensive and they will have complete control over the assets subject to the charge under which the appointment was made.[238] In addition they may apply to the court for an order empowering them to dispose of property subject to a prior charge.[239] In the exercise of these extensive powers, the courts struggled with the standards that ought to be imposed. The low water mark was probably the decision of the Privy Council in *Downsview Nominees Ltd v First City Corp*,[240] of course much welcomed by insolvency practitioners. Lord Templeman in that case held that the receiver owed no general common law duty of care to interested parties; his duties lay exclusively in equity, which required him merely to act in good faith, although if he did decide to sell the property (as he invariably would), then he was required to take reasonable care to obtain a proper price. Nevertheless, and predictably, the receiver's role could not withstand the onslaught in the development of common law principles of the duty of care. The position now is that receivers are under a duty to the debtor company to take reasonable care to obtain the best price reasonably possible at the time of sale[241]; this duty is also owed to a guarantor of the company's debts.[242] However, as the receiver in exercising a power of sale is in a position analogous to that of a mortgagee, receivers are not obliged to postpone sale in order to obtain a better price or to adopt a piecemeal method of sale.[243] If they delay the sale, they are also under a duty, while they manage the property, to manage it with reasonable care and due diligence.[244]

32–037 The basis of the receiver's duty set out above was initially considered to involve a controversial extension of the common law of negligence to supplement equity,[245] but the courts now tend to treat it as something which flows directly

---

[238] IA 1986 s.42 confers on an administrative receiver the powers set out in Sch.1 to the Act in so far as they are not inconsistent with the terms of the debenture. There are 23 powers enumerated and they are very wide; for example, No.14 confers on an administrative receiver "Power to carry on the business of the company".

[239] IA 1986 s.43. The rights of the security holder are protected in the same way as they are in the case of administration: see para.32–045.

[240] *Downsview Nominees Ltd v First City Corp Ltd* [1993] B.C.C. 46 PC.

[241] *Cuckmere Brick Co Ltd v Mutual Finance* (1971) 22 P. & C.R. 624 CA (Civ Div); *Bishop v Bonham*(1988) 4 B.C.C. 347 CA (Civ Div); *AIB Group (UK) Plc v Personal Representative of James Aiken (Deceased)* [2012] NIQB 51. Also see *Ahmad v Bank of Scotland* [2016] EWCA Civ 602, which at [38] sets out a summary of the duties of receivers.

[242] *Standard Chartered Bank Ltd v Walker* [1982] 1 W.L.R. 1410; *American Express International Banking Corp v Hurley* (1986) 2 B.C.C. 98993; *AIB Group (UK) Plc v Personal Representative of James Aiken (Deceased)* [2012] NIQB 51.

[243] *Cuckmere Brick Co Ltd v Mutual Finance Ltd* (1971) 22 P. & C.R. 624; *Alpstream AG v PK Airfinance Sarl* [2016] 2 P. & C.R. 2. And if the receiver does wait, he is not liable if the market declines: *Tse Kwong Lam v Wong Chit Sen* [1983] 1 W.L.R. 1349 PC. Note, too, that there is no duty imposed on receivers only to sell as much of the charged property as necessary to discharge the mortgage: *Centenary Homes Ltd v Liddell* [2020] EWHC 1080 (QB) at [69].

[244] *Medforth v Blake* [1999] B.C.C. 771 CA (Civ Div).

[245] See G. Lightman and G. Moss, *The Law of Administrators and Receivers of Companies*, 6th edn (London: Sweet & Maxwell, 2017), Ch.7.

from the special nature of the relationship between the chargee and chargor.[246] The result is that the receiver must act in good faith, and not for improper purposes, and must have regard to the chargor's interests while at the same time allowing that the chargee's interests are paramount. The most recent significant English authority, *Medforth v Blake*,[247] treats the standard of care required in equity as the same as that required at common law, and in that case held the receivers, who negligently conducted the business of which they had taken control, to be liable to the mortgagor, who suffered loss when (after the secured debt had been discharged) the business was handed back to him in a less good state than if it had been properly run by the receivers. Although this decision goes some way towards protecting debtor companies, and, by extension, their unsecured creditors, from the incompetence of receivers, the Court of Appeal made it clear that it was not purporting to overturn the principle that the primary duty of the receiver is to bring about the repayment of the debt owed to the secured creditor. In this particular case, there was no conflict of interest between the mortgagor and mortgagee, since both potentially suffered harm as a result of the receivers' incompetence.[248] The case, thus, is not authority for the proposition that it is negligent for the receivers to give primacy to the appointor's interests as against those of the mortgagor (or the company and its unsecured creditors).

A person dealing with an administrative receiver in good faith and for value is not bound to enquire if the receiver is acting within his or her powers.[249] Unlike a winding-up, the board of directors is not discharged on the appointment of a receiver, but the directors' powers are substantially superseded since they cannot act so as to interfere with the discharge by the receiver of his or her responsibilities: their powers are suspended "so far as is requisite to enable a receiver to discharge his functions".[250] Given the extent of the powers of the administrative receiver, the directors will have a tiny margin within which they are free to exercise their powers. In one case, in rather particular circumstances, it was held that they could bring proceedings in the company's name.[251] This authority has been doubted, however, because of the conflict that would arise were the receiver and the directors to have different views on whether an action

[246] *Parker-Tweedale v Dunbar Bank Plc (No.1)* (1990) 60 P. & C.R. 83 CA (Civ Div) (mortgagee owes no duty to beneficiary of mortgaged property); *Downsview Nominees Ltd v First City Corp* [1993] B.C.C. 46 PC; *Cukurova Finance International Ltd v Alfa Telecom Turkey Ltd* [2013] UKPC 2; [2016] A.C. 923.

[247] *Medforth v Blake* [1999] B.C.C. 771, thus somewhat back-tracking on the decision of the Privy Council in *Downsview Nominees v First City Corp* (1990) 60 P. & C.R. 83. See also *Knight v Lawrence* [1991] B.C.C. 411 Ch D; *Purewal v Countrywide Residential Lettings Ltd* [2015] EWCA Civ 1122; [2016] H.L.R. 4; and *Devon Commercial Property Ltd v Barnett* [2019] EWHC 700 (Ch) especially at [26]–[28] and [180]–[195].

[248] On the facts, the appointor suffered no loss because the business, even in its damaged state, generated enough profit to satisfy the appointor's claims.

[249] IA 1986 s.42(3).

[250] *Re Emmadart Ltd* [1979] Ch. 540 Ch D at 544; see also *Gomba Holdings (UK) Ltd v Homan* (1986) 2 B.C.C. 99102 Ch D.

[251] *Newhart Developments Ltd v Co-operative Commercial Bank Ltd* [1978] Q.B. 814 CA (Civ Div) (it is important to note that in that case the company was indemnified for any costs that it might incur and the receiver had decided not to bring any action against his appointor).

should be brought, or on the handling of any counterclaim.[252] On the other hand, the directors can certainly take proceedings to challenge the validity of the receiver's appointment,[253] or sue the receiver for breach of duty,[254] or oppose a petition to wind up the company.[255]

Finally, as the directors remain in office, the receiver is under an obligation to provide the directors with the information that they request to enable them to comply with their reporting obligations under the CA 2006.[256] The receiver is also obliged at the end of his receivership to hand over to the company any documents belonging to the company other than those brought into existence for the discharge of his own professional duties or his duties to the chargee.[257]

The receiver's liability with respect to contracts

32–038 An administrative receiver taking over the management of a company will need to manage the company's existing (partly performed) contracts, and will need to enter into new contracts on behalf of the company. These raise separate issues.

Consider first the contracts already in existence when the receiver is appointed. As an administrative receiver is the agent of the company, the appointment does not of itself affect existing contracts. If, in the interests of the chargee, the receiver causes the company to repudiate these contracts, the injured parties will be left to their normal contractual remedies in damages, but with the company unlikely to be left with the funds to pay such claims.[258] Since, in doing this, the receiver acts as an agent of the company, he cannot be liable for the tort of inducing a breach of contract.[259] The only exceptions to this general rule are the normal exceptions applying with contracts that are specifically enforceable[260] or subject to injunctions: the appointment of an administrative receiver makes no difference to the court's response in these cases. On the other hand, if the receiver does not repudiate the contract, he is said to "adopt" it.[261] This is rather misleading terminology: the contract is not a new contract at all; it remains the

---

[252] *Tudor Grange Holdings Ltd v Citibank NA* [1992] Ch. 53 Ch D. As Browne-Wilkinson VC pointed out in that case, it would be more appropriate for receivers or their appointor to use IA 1986 s.35. *Tudor Grange* has itself come in for criticism: see *Re Geneva Finance Ltd* (1992) 7 A.C.S.L.R. 415 at 426–432.

[253] *Hawkesbury Development Co Ltd v Landmark Finance Pty Ltd* (1969) 92 WN (NSW) 199.

[254] *Watts v Midland Bank Plc* [1986] B.C.L.C. 15.

[255] *Re Reprographic Exports (Euromat) Ltd* (1978) 122 S.J. 400.

[256] *Gomba Holdings v Homan* [1986] 1 W.L.R. 1301; see also at 1305–1306 where Hoffmann J pointed out that equity may impose on a receiver a duty to account which is wider than his statutory obligations.

[257] *Gomba Holdings (UK) Ltd v Minories Finance Ltd (formerly Johnson Matthey Bankers Ltd) (No.1)* (1989) 5 B.C.C. 27 CA (Civ Div). Once a receiver has sufficient funds to pay off the debt and his own expenses, he should cease managing the company's assets: *Rottenberg v Monjack* [1992] B.C.C. 688 Ch D.

[258] *Airline Airspares v Handley Page* [1970] Ch. 193 Ch D.

[259] *Said v Butt* [1920] 3 K.B. 497 KBD; *Welsh Development Agency v Export Finance Co Ltd* [1992] B.C.C. 270; *Belcher v Heaney* [2013] EWHC 4353 (Ch).

[260] *Freevale Ltd v Metrostore (Holdings) Ltd* (1984) 47 P. & C.R. 481 Ch D; *AMEC Properties v Planning Research & Systems* [1992] B.C.L.C. 1149 CA (Civ Div); and cf. *Ash & Newman Ltd v Creative Devices Research* [1991] B.C.L.C. 403.

[261] *Powdrill v Watson* [1995] 2 A.C. 394.

contract entered into by the company on the terms agreed by the company. Indeed, this itself can cause problems for receivers where adoption brings into play contractual liens[262] or set-offs.[263]

As a matter of policy, it seems desirable to impose a limited duty on the receiver to continue to trade or otherwise act positively where this would not jeopardise the chargee's interests and a failure to do so would impose gratuitous damage on the company.[264] Not to extend his duty in this way would stretch the pro-creditor bias of receivership to ridiculous lengths. But, as described below, this obligation is limited: the primary purpose of receivership is to realise the assets for the benefit of the secured creditor.

Special mention should be made of contracts of employment. These contracts are not automatically terminated by the receiver's appointment unless the receiver does something which is inconsistent with the continuation of the contract,[265] for example by selling the company's business.[266] If the receiver sees no hope of selling the business as a going concern, then he is likely to dismiss the employees forthwith. Such dismissal will likely be because of redundancy, and will almost certainly not be unfair dismissal (provided there is no unfair selection of the persons to be dismissed). The receiver may take some time to decide what to do. Nothing that is done or omitted to be done in the first 14 days of the receiver's appointment is taken as showing that the receiver has adopted a contract of employment.[267] After that, if nothing is done, the receiver will be taken to have impliedly adopted these contracts.[268] Once adopted, the administrative receiver is, by statute, personally liable for the company's liability for wages or salary, contributions to an occupational pension scheme, holiday and sick pay, and deductions for income tax and national insurance,[269] from the date of adoption of the contract.[270] The administrative receiver cannot contract out of this liability for adopted employment contracts,[271] but is entitled to an indemnity out of the assets of the company.[272] **32–039**

262 *George Barker (Transport) Ltd v Eynon* [1974] 1 W.L.R. 462.

263 *Rother Iron Works Ltd v Canterbury Precision Engineers Ltd* [1974] Q.B. 1.

264 *Knight v Lawrence* [1991] B.C.C. 411; *Medforth v Blake* [1999] B.C.C. 771. See para.32–045. Contrast the two obiter comments that a receiver does (*R. v Board of Trade Ex p. St Martins Preserving Co Ltd* [1965] 1 Q.B. 603 QBD) and does not (*Re B Johnson & Co (Builders) Ltd* [1955] Ch. 364) have a duty to preserve the goodwill of the company. Also see *Purewal v Countrywide Residential Lettings Ltd* [2016] H.L.R. 4.

265 *Griffiths v Secretary of State for Social Services* [1974] Q.B. 468 QBD. The appointment of the receiver by the court does terminate contracts of service: *Reid v Explosives Co Ltd* (1887) 19 Q.B.D. 264 CA; cf. *Sipad Holding v Popovic* (1995) 19 A.C.S.R. 108.

266 *Re Foster Clark's Indenture Trust* [1966] 1 W.L.R. 125 Ch D.

267 IA 1986 s.44(2). In the context of administrators, with the same issue in play, see *Re Debenhams Retail Ltd (In Administration)* [2020] EWCA Civ 600; [2020] B.C.C. 548, where the court considered whether administrators had adopted the employment contracts of employees who had been furloughed due to the coronavirus pandemic. It concluded that they had done so. Also see similar issues in *Re Carluccio's Ltd (In Administration)* [2020] EWHC 886 (Ch); [2020] B.C.C. 523. Both cases are noted in Davis (2020) 35 J.I.B.F.L. 482.

268 *Powdrill v Watson* [1995] 2 A.C. 394.

269 *Re FJL Realisations Ltd* [2001] B.C.C. 663 CA (Civ Div).

270 IA 1986 s.44.

271 But contrast newly negotiated contracts.

272 IA 1986 s.44(1)(c).

Where the receiver enters into new contracts, this is done as agent for the company, and the contracts will therefore be binding on the company. More importantly, however, the receiver is also personally liable by statute on any contract entered into on behalf of the company unless the contract provides otherwise.[273] Exclusion of liability may be express or implied. Administrative receivers will invariably try to contract out of liability. They will in any event have a statutory indemnity out of the company's assets[274] and will usually also have an indemnity from the chargee.

Publicity of appointment and reports

32–040 Where a receiver or manager is appointed then this must be stated in various business documents relating to the company.[275] All receivers also have to make prescribed returns to the Registrar,[276] and the administrative receiver has to report to creditors, including unsecured creditors, but will not have to report to those who have opted out of receiving notices.[277] A receiver who fails to comply with his reporting obligations can be ordered to do so[278] and, more importantly, can be disqualified from acting as a receiver or manager.[279] There is no similar obligation to report where a debenture-holder enters into possession and it has been recommended that this omission be corrected.[280]

Administration[281]

Function

32–041 An outline of the origins and purposes of administration is set out in Ch.33,[282] and serves as an introduction to the detail set out here where our focus is not especially on the general rules of administration, but on the special rules applying when the process is used by the holder of a floating charge. The distinct "rescue" goals of the administration procedure are clearly displayed in the statutory definition of the objectives of administration, set out in Sch.B1 to the IA 1986. Three objectives are listed but are put into a clear hierarchy. Priority is given to "rescuing the company as a going concern",[283] which is the objective which the

---

[273] IA 1986 s.44(1)(b) as amended by the Insolvency Act 1994 s.2. He is entitled to indemnification out of the assets of the company (s.44(1)(c)), and can also contract for indemnification by those who appointed him (s.44(3)).

[274] IA 1986 s.44(1)(c).

[275] IA 1986 s.39.

[276] IA 1986 s.38 (receivers) and s.48 (administrative receivers).

[277] IA 1986 s.48.

[278] IA 1986 s.41. Also of relevance are the Insolvency Rules 1986 Pt 3.

[279] Company Directors Disqualification Act 1986 ss.1(1)(a), 3 and 22(7); see *Re Artic Engineering (No.2)* (1985) 1 B.C.C. 99563 Ch D.

[280] Jenkins Committee, para.306(k).

[281] This discussion will concentrate on the appointment of an administrator where the company has granted a floating charge, though, as we have seen (para.32–032) administration is not confined to such situations.

[282] See para.33–003.

[283] IA 1986 Sch.B1 para.3(1)(a).

administrator must pursue unless he or she thinks it is not practicable to achieve it or that the second objective would better serve the creditors' needs.[284] That second objective is "achieving a better result for the company's creditors as a whole than would be likely if the company were wound up".[285] Thus, preservation of the company as a going concern, to the benefit, for example, of employees, is not essential if the creditors would be worse off as a result. The third objective is "realising property in order to make a distribution to one or more secured or preferential creditors".[286] The administrator may pursue this objective only if it is not reasonably practicable to achieve the other two objectives, and it must be pursued in such a way that it will "not unnecessarily harm the interests of the other creditors of the company as a whole".[287] Subject to the qualification implied where the administrator legitimately pursues the third objective, the administrator must act "in the interests of the company's creditors as a whole".[288]

Although on an application to the court, the purpose of the proposed administration has to be stated, that purpose does not have to be confined to a single goal. It is more likely, therefore, that the statutory purposes will simply control the way in which the administrator, after appointment, exercises his or her powers.[289] The floating charge holder may read these provisions with some gloom, for the priority given to the second objective over the third appears to mean that if the creditors as a whole would be better off than in a winding-up, the administrator should pursue that course of action, even if the charge holder will be worse off.[290]

Appointment

As is now generally required in the insolvency area, only a qualified insolvency practitioner may be appointed as an administrator.[291] An administrator may be appointed by the court, on application by the company, its directors or one or more creditors,[292] where the company is or is likely to become unable to pay its debts[293] and the appointment is "reasonably likely" to achieve one of the **32–042**

[284] IA 1986 Sch.B1 para.3(3).
[285] IA 1986 Sch.B1 para.3(1)(b).
[286] IA 1986 Sch.B1 para.3(1)(c).
[287] IA 1986 Sch.B1 para.3(4).
[288] IA 1986 Sch.B1 para.3(2).
[289] And in *Re Lehman Brothers (International) Europe (In Administration)* [2020] EWHC 1932 (Ch); [2020] Bus. L.R. 1875 the court held that there need not be a causal connection between every exercise of the administrators' functions and the achievement of the rescue objective. IA 1986 Sch.B1 para.3 had to be construed in the context of the legislation as a whole; the Act placed multifarious demands on an administrator and there had to be an element of pragmatism. Here, in a solvent but incomplete administration (because some of the creditors' claims had not yet been met), it was open to the administrators to accede to the directors' request to be allowed to return some funds to the shareholders (which the administrators could not do themselves).
[290] This is subject to the "unfair harm" protection discussed below.
[291] IA 1986 Sch.B1 para.5.
[292] IA 1986 Sch.B1 para.12 (or by the chief executive of a magistrates court in the case of fines imposed on companies).
[293] In one context (see IA 1986 Sch.B1 para.35) this is not a requirement: this is where the application is made to the court by a floating charge holder who has the power to make an appointment out of

specified purposes.[294] This seems to put into statutory form the position at which the courts had arrived under the old law, which used a different form of wording, namely, that there must be a "real prospect" that the purpose or purposes will be achieved.[295] The change is important, for a higher hurdle materially increases the costs (as well as decreasing the chances) of securing an administration order, especially by encouraging applicants to commission an extensive report by an independent person in support of the application.

An administrator may also be appointed out of court, and this now is the preferred route in the interest of saving costs. The ability to do this[296] was one of the important changes introduced by the Enterprise Act 2002, to reduce opposition to the reform proposals from banks.[297] The holder of a "qualifying floating charge",[298] being a charge or charges which relate to the whole or substantially the whole of the company's property, may appoint an administrator out of court where the instrument creating the charge gives the holder the power to do so.[299] Such an administrator will still be an officer of the court,[300] and what has been said above about the objectives of the administration still applies. Notice and other documents have to be filed with the court after the appointment.[301] If it turns out that the appointment was invalid (for example, because the appointor did not hold a valid floating charge),[302] the court may order the appointor to indemnify the person appointed against liability arising (for example, to the company in trespass or conversion).[303]

The company or the directors may also appoint an administrator out of court,[304] but not if a receiver is in office,[305] and five days' notice of the intention to appoint has to be given to any floating charge holder, whose consent to the

---

court (see below). As we have seen (para.31–025), the terms of debentures may give charge holders the power to appoint even though the company is able to pay its debts.

[294] IA 1986 Sch.B1 para.11.

[295] *Re Harris Simons Construction Ltd* (1989) 5 B.C.C. 11 Ch D (Companies Ct); *Re Primlaks (UK) Ltd* [1989] B.C.L.C. 734 Ch D; cf. *Re Consumer & Industrial Press Ltd (No.1)* (1988) 4 B.C.C. 68 Ch D (Companies Ct).

[296] Though, as we have seen (para.32–032), the floating charge holder is not excluded from applying to the court for an appointment.

[297] Banks feared not only the cost of court applications, but, more so, the delay involved, during which desperate directors might spirit assets out of the company, once they knew of the petition.

[298] A floating charge over a company's property is a qualifying floating charge if it alone, or in conjunction with other floating or fixed charges, covers the whole, or substantially the whole of the company's property and the contract creating the floating charge states that the chargee may so appoint an administrator (IA 1986 s.72A and Sch.B1 para.14).

[299] IA 1986 Sch.B1 para.15. He or she must give two days' notice of the intention to appoint to the holder of any prior floating charge (so that that person may take action, if desired), but the intention does not have to be advertised generally, which would defeat one of the objectives of this power. In Northern Ireland (under similar provisions) an unregistered chargee could nevertheless appoint under this section: *Dolliver v O'Callaghan* [2017] NICh 27.

[300] IA 1986 Sch.B1 para.5.

[301] IA 1986 Sch.B1 para.46.

[302] i.e. the charge must be enforceable at the time the notice of appointment is filed under para.18: *Fliptex Ltd v Hogg* [2004] EWHC 1280 (Ch); [2004] B.C.C. 870.

[303] IA 1986 Sch.B1 para.21.

[304] IA 1986 Sch.B1 para.22.

[305] IA 1986 Sch.B1 para.25(c).

appointment is required.[306] This has two consequences. First, it gives the floating charge holder the opportunity to act first and appoint an administrator of its own choosing.[307] Secondly, in those cases where the charge holder still has the right to appoint an administrative receiver,[308] such an appointment may be made instead. Alternatively, the floating charge holder could simply block the appointment proposed by the company or its directors by not giving consent. In such a case the company or its directors would presumably apply to the court for an appointment. Indeed, it appears that the court can appoint an administrator even though a receiver has already been appointed,[309] but the situations in which the court may exercise this power are limited.[310] Thus, where the appointment of an administrative receiver is still allowed under the new regime, it is logically given priority over the appointment of an administrator.

Powers and duties

The first task of the administrator is to produce a set of proposals for the future of the company's business, and these are put before the creditors for their approval. This must be done within eight weeks of appointment, and sooner if possible.[311] The time limit may be extended by the court on application by the administrator.[312] Notice of the proposals has to be given to members as well as creditors who have not opted out of receiving notice,[313] since in some cases the members may have a financial interest in the success of the rescue. A wide range of outcomes is possible in the case of an administration. They do not need to be examined in detail here. The plans may be accepted by the creditors, e.g. proposals for a restructuring of their rights under a scheme of arrangement[314] that enables the company to come out of administration and be returned to its previous management, perhaps with the former creditors now owning a majority of the shares. Alternatively, the plans may be rejected, and the company put into liquidation. And there are many variations in between. Whatever the decision reached, the administrator must report the outcome to the court and to the Registrar. Failure to do so attracts a fine.[315] It is worth noting that amendments brought about by the Small Business, Enterprise and Employment Act 2015 has **32–043**

---

306 IA 1986 Sch.B1 paras 26 and 28. On para.26 notice, see *Re Tokenhouse VB Ltd (formerly Vat Bridge 7 Ltd)* [2020] EWHC 3171 (Ch); [2021] B.C.C. 107; *Re Seabrook Road Ltd* [2021] EWHC 436 (Ch).

307 In addition, on an application to the court by a non-floating charge holder, the charge holder has a presumptive right to have its nominee for administrator appointed in place of the applicant's: para.36.

308 See above, para.32–034.

309 IA 1986 Sch.B1 para.12(1)(a) clearly contemplates that a receiver may be in place when the application to the court for an administrator is made, as does para.41, which provides for an administrative receiver to vacate office when an administrator is appointed.

310 IA 1986 Sch.B1 para.39—essentially where the charge holder consents or the charge is thought to be subject to challenge, for example under s.245 (para.32–014).

311 IA 1986 Sch.B1 para.49(5).

312 IA 1986 Sch.B1 paras 49(8) and 107.

313 IA 1986 Sch.B1 para.49(4).

314 See Ch.29.

315 IA 1986 Sch.B1 para.53(2) and (3).

simplified the insolvency procedure by removing the need for creditors' meetings as the default means of decision making.

Between appointment and approval of the proposals, the administrator may exercise all the powers conferred by IA 1986 Sch.B1 para.59 and Sch.1, and this includes the power to dispose of the company's property if an attractive offer is made.[316]

During the administration process, the company benefits from a moratorium on both winding up[317] and legal proceedings for the enforcement of claims against it, unless, in the latter case, the creditor has the consent of the administrator or the court.[318] A somewhat more limited moratorium also applies from the moment any formal step is taken to seek an administration order.[319] The administrator has general authority to manage the company's business, acting as its agent,[320] as well as the powers specified in Sch.1 to the IA 1986[321]; may appoint and remove directors[322]; and, as we have noted,[323] may dispose of property subject to the floating charge[324] and, with the consent of the court, even property subject to a fixed charge.[325] However, the court may so order only if the court thinks the disposal would be likely to promote the purposes of the administration and the net proceeds of the disposal and any additional amount needed to bring that amount up to the market value of the asset is applied to discharging the security. Since the moratorium will prevent the charge holders (fixed or floating) from enforcing their security, the position may be that charge holders not only cannot repossess their property but that the administrator has disposed of it. However, the floating charge holder will have his or her security transferred to the proceeds of the sale,[326] whilst the conditions attached to the court's power to sanction a sale over property in relation to which a fixed charge obtains mean the only detriment to the fixed charge holder is that he cannot control the timing of the realisation of his security, which will be undertaken by the administrator, probably as part of a larger disposal, instead of by the security holder as a single transaction.

---

[316] *Re Transbus International Ltd* [2004] EWHC 932 (Ch); [2004] B.C.C. 401 at [12]–[14].

[317] But not winding up under IA 1986 s.124A on public interest grounds (see para.21–013): see IA 1986 Sch.B1 para.42(4)(a).

[318] IA 1986 Sch.B1 paras 42 and 43. Paragraph 43(4) includes the landlord's right of forfeiture by peaceable re-entry, which had been an issue disputed in the pre-2002 case law. However, intervention by regulators appears to remain outside the moratorium. See *Air Ecosse Ltd v Civil Aviation Authority* (1987) 3 B.C.C. 492 IH (2 Div); *Re Railtrack Plc (In Administration) (No.2)* [2002] EWCA Civ 955; [2002] A.C.D. 103.

[319] IA 1986 Sch.B1 para.44.

[320] IA 1986 Sch.B1 para.69, so that the company, not the appointor, is liable for unlawful acts of the administrator.

[321] IA 1986 Sch.B1 para.59.

[322] IA 1986 Sch.B1 para.61. Note the potential breadth of this power in *Re Inspired Asset Management Ltd* [2019] EWHC 3301 (Ch), allowing the administrator, given the urgency of the situation, to have the same sole director of the company's 8 subsidiaries removed.

[323] See para.32–018.

[324] IA 1986 Sch.B1 para.70.

[325] IA 1986 Sch.B1 para.71.

[326] IA 1986 Sch.B1 para.70(2).

Overall, the administrator has all the powers normally vested in the board of directors,[327] now supplemented by some of those given to liquidators, specifically the power to bring actions against directors claiming compensation on behalf of the company for fraudulent or wrongful trading.[328] In contrast with an administrative receiver,[329] he or she is not personally liable on contracts entered into on the company's behalf. However, the IA 1986 contains an alternative mechanism for ensuring that the administrator secures the discharge of the obligations he or she causes the company to incur. When the administrator relinquishes office, undischarged liabilities are charged on the company's assets and rank ahead of any floating charge or the administrator's own remuneration.[330] **32–044**

The moratorium, which, as we have noted, was not available to the administrative receiver, may prove attractive in reconciling banks to the use of administration. The key focus is on the moratorium on third parties preventing them taking legal proceedings for the enforcement of their claims against the company. Although this prevents the banks themselves from enforcing their security, it also keeps unsecured creditors at bay and may promote the sale of the company's business at a higher price, from which those with security will be the first to benefit financially. However, this form of moratorium is subject to the administrator or the court allowing an individual creditor to proceed with its claim. It follows that the impact of the moratorium depends in part on how willing the courts are to grant leave to creditors. Some guidance on this was given by the Court of Appeal in *Re Atlantic Computer Systems (No.1)*[331]: since the prohibitions in s.11 are intended to assist the administrator to achieve the purpose of the administration, it is for the creditor seeking leave of the court (or the consent of the administrator) to make out a case for it being granted; if leave is unlikely to impede the achievement of the administrator's purpose, then leave should normally be given; in other cases it is necessary to carry out a balancing exercise, weighing the legitimate interests of the creditor applicant against those of the other creditors of the company. Further, the administration should not be conducted at the expense of those who have proprietary rights which they are seeking to exercise, so it will normally be a sufficient ground for granting leave if significant loss would otherwise be suffered by the creditor applicant, unless the loss to other creditors of the company would be significantly greater. In assessing the respective losses, all the circumstances relating to the administration should be taken into account and regard paid to how probable they are likely to be. The conduct of the respective parties may sometimes also be relevant. Similar considerations apply to decisions regarding imposing terms.

---

[327] The directors, although still in place, may not exercise management power without the consent of the administrator: IA 1986 Sch.B1 para.64.

[328] IA 1986 ss.246ZA–246ZC, added by SBEEA 2015. See the discussion of the parallel provisions for liquidators, in IA 1986 ss.213–215, at paras 9–005 to 19–012.

[329] Who, despite the fact that he too acts as an agent is personally liable on contracts he enters into unless they provide to the contrary. See para.32–038.

[330] IA 1986 Sch.B1 para.99(4). For the application of this rule in relation to adopted employment contracts, see *Powdrill v Watson* [1995] 2 A.C. 394; partially reversed by the Insolvency Act 1994; and Pollard, (1995) 24 I.L.J. 141.

[331] *Re Atlantic Computer Systems Plc* [1990] B.C.C. 859 CA (Civ Div). See also *Bristol Airport Plc v Powdrill* [1990] Ch. 744.

Of course, an unpaid creditor of a company in administration does not have an obligation to continue with supplies or to make further advances unless contractually or statutorily required to do so.[332] Thus, the moratorium may protect the company in administration from pressure from its existing creditors, but it falls far short of guaranteeing that the administrator will be able to carry on the business effectively during the administration. That is likely to require fresh funding and the availability (or not) of such funding is one of the matters the court needs to consider when deciding whether to appoint an administrator.

Protections for creditors and members as against the administrator

32–045 It is clear that an administration may give rise to many of the same agency problems which we have examined in previous chapters in relation to companies that are going concerns. There may be conflicts between majority and minority creditors, and administrators may exercise their wide powers unfairly or incompetently. The Schedule provides some remedies aimed at such conduct. First, administrator proposals to the creditors may not involve downgrading the rights of secured or preferential creditors without their consent or use of a scheme of arrangement or a company voluntary arrangement (which contain mechanisms for the protection of minorities).[333] Thus, although the secured creditor is put into a collective insolvency procedure, it is given specific protection that the administrator may not propose action which "affects the right of a secured creditor to enforce his security".[334] Secondly, and more generally, protection against unfair prejudice[335] is extended to actions of the administrator, so that any member or creditor of the company can apply to the court for relief[336] on the grounds that the administrator is acting, has acted or proposes to act in a way which is "unfairly harms" the interests of the applicant.[337] It is not clear whether the substitution of the phrase "unfairly harms" for the phrase "unfairly prejudicial", which is used in the equivalent CA provision[338] and was used in the original version of the IA 1986[339] is intended to produce a substantive change. Thirdly, an application can also be made on the grounds that the administrator "is not performing his functions as quickly or efficiently as is reasonably

[332] *Leyland DAF Ltd v Automotive Products Plc* [1993] B.C.C. 389 CA (Civ Div).

[333] IA 1986 Sch.B1 para.73. Thus, in creditor meetings to approve a scheme secured and unsecured creditors would be put in separate classes: paras 29–008 to 29–010.

[334] It is important not to overestimate the extent of this specific protection. It applies only to the right to enforce the security; it would not apply to action which fails to maximise the value of the assets to which the security attaches.

[335] See Ch.14.

[336] The court has broad relief powers (para.74(3) and (4)), but there is no specific mention of a power to order litigation in the name of the company (though presumably the court could do so under its general authority to "grant relief") or the compulsory purchase of shares (hardly likely to be an appropriate order in an administration).

[337] IA 1986 Sch.B1 para.74. This applies whilst the company is "in administration". If it is not, the creditor may no longer petition; if it is, this paragraph effectively replaces CA 2006 s.994 as far as members are concerned, for the administrator's or court's consent would be needed under the moratorium provisions for a s.994 petition to be launched.

[338] Now CA 2006 s.994.

[339] IA 1986 s.27, now repealed.

practicable",[340] thus giving members and creditors an uncomplicated route to complain about negligence on the part of the administrator.[341] Fourthly, the misfeasance provisions from IA 1986 s.212[342] are elaborated in their application to administrators.[343] Together, these last three provisions lay down standards by which the creditors and members can challenge conduct of the administrator which either falls below the standard of competence they are entitled to expect or which does not give appropriate weight to their interests.[344]

Publication of appointment

A newly appointed administrator must notify the company, the Registrar, and the company's creditors of the appointment.[345] While the company is in administration, every business document must state that fact and name the administrator.[346] **32–046**

Administration expenses

Debts or liabilities arising out of contracts entered into by the administrator have priority (often called "super-priority") over the administrator's own remuneration and expenses.[347] This can amount to a hefty liability. The expenses of administration, including the administrator's remuneration, then have priority over a debt secured by a floating charge.[348] After this, the normal priority rules apply.[349] **32–047**

End of administration

Under IA 1986 s.76, the appointment of an administrator ceases to have effect at the end of the period of one year beginning with the date on which the **32–048**

---

340 IA 1986 Sch.B1 para.74(2).

341 cf. the uncertainties surrounding the use of CA 2006 s.994 (previously CA 1985 s.459) against negligence, paras 14–024 to 14–027.

342 See Ch.19.

343 IA 1986 Sch.B1 para.75. Also see *Davey v Money* [2018] EWHC 766 (Ch); [2018] Bus. L.R. 1903 (noted Polli, (2019) 34 J.I.B.F.L. 512).

344 The risk that these provisions will be used by particular creditors or members opportunistically to block a resolution of the company's difficulties is somewhat reduced by para.74(6) which says that no order by way of relief may be made by the court if it would "impede or prevent the implementation of a scheme agreed under the CA or a company voluntary arrangement agreed under Pt I of the IA or administrator proposals approved by creditors, unless, in the last case, the application is made within 28 days. However, a fixed charge holder can use this procedure even when the court has authorised the administrator to dispose of the property (see para.74(5)(b)), presumably lest the administrator carry out the disposal in an unfair or negligent way".

345 IA 1986 Sch.B1 para.46.

346 IA 1986 Sch.B1 para.45.

347 IA 1986 Sch.B1 para.99. But the provisions are strictly construed, and damages for wrongful dismissal or other payments in lieu are not entitled to super-priority: *Re Leeds United Association Football Club Ltd* [2007] EWHC 1761 (Ch); [2008] B.C.C. 11.

348 IA 1986 Sch.B1 para.99.

349 See paras 32–015 onwards.

appointment took effect, unless the term of office is extended by the court or with the consent of the creditors. The term may be extended by consent only once[350] and by no more than one year.[351]

Alternatively, on the application of the administrator, the court may provide for the appointment of the administrator to cease to have effect, if the purpose of the administration has been sufficiently achieved in relation to the company.[352] Administrators are often keen for these provisions to be interpreted pragmatically in order to enable them to escape accruing business liabilities; the courts have generally complied,[353] including by agreeing to end the administration and put the company straight into a winding up if appropriate.[354] The administrator may now also be obliged to make such an application if the company's creditors decide that he must do so.[355]

CONCLUSION

32–049 A company must be able to raise debt finance, and so it must be able to grant effective security to lenders. It is possible to conceive of a legal regime in which the position of companies giving security is in essence no different from that of any other borrower. There would inevitably be some company law aspects to security transactions—for example, are the directors authorised to enter into the particular transaction contemplated?—but those company law aspects would not be unique to security transactions. As we saw in Ch.8, the issue of directors' authority can easily arise in relation to transactions that do not involve a grant of security.

In fact, however, as this chapter has shown, the current law on the granting of security does have two features that are specific to the corporate nature of the debtor. These are the availability of the floating charge and the system of registration of charges granted by companies. We have also seen, however, that the modern tendency is to whittle away these uniquely corporate features. Thus, the unique enforcement mechanism for the floating charge by means of the appointment of an administrative receiver has been substantially replaced by the general insolvency mechanism of the appointment of an administrator, as introduced by the Enterprise Act 2002. Going further, the Law Commission has queried the justification for retaining the provisions in the Bills of Sales Acts which prevent non-corporate businesses granting floating charges (as have other

[350] IA 1986 Sch.B1 para.78(4).

[351] IA 1986 Sch.B1 para.76(2)(b), as amended by s.127 of the Small Business, Enterprise and Employment Act 2015.

[352] IA 1986 Sch.B1 para.79(3)(b).

[353] *Re TM Kingdom Ltd (In Administration)* [2007] EWHC 3272 (Ch); [2007] B.C.C. 480; *Re GHE Realisations Ltd (formerly Gatehouse Estates Ltd)* [2005] EWHC 2400 (Ch); [2006] B.C.C. 139.

[354] *Re Graico Property Co Ltd (In Administration)* [2016] EWHC 2827 (Ch); [2017] B.C.C. 15, the court holding that, under IA 1986 Sch.B1 para.79(4)(d), it had the power to make any additional order that it thought appropriate provided the order had some relationship to the discharge of the administrators and the termination of the administration. Here the court was prepared to use that power to order the compulsory winding-up of the company, notwithstanding that no petition for that relief had been presented (*Lancefield v Lancefield* [2002] B.P.I.R. 1108 Ch D indicating the jurisdiction to do so existed).

[355] IA 1986 Sch.B1 para.79(2)(c).

bodies before them).[356] Equally, in its proposals for radical reform of the companies charges system, the Law Commission clearly regards the optimal solution as being a registration system applying to charges (and quasi-securities) granted by all debtors,[357] although its proposals were not adopted. Could it be that, like corporate insolvency and public offers of corporate securities before them, security interests granted by companies is a topic which is on its way out of core company law, in order to join up with the rules that apply where a company is not involved?

---

[356] See Law Commission, *Registration of Security Interests: Company Charges and Property other than Land* (2002), CP 164, Pt IX. In one limited area, that of farmers, the problem was addressed as long ago as 1928 in the Agricultural Credits Act of that year.

[357] See Law Commission, *Registration of Security Interests: Company Charges and Property other than Land* (2002), CP 164; *Company Security Interests: A Consultative Report* (August 2004), Law Com. Consultation Paper No.176; Law Commission, *Company Security Interests* (August 2005), Law Com No.296, Cm.6654.

PART 10

WINDING UP AND ITS CONSEQUENCES

This final Part, in a single chapter, surveys the means by which the lives of companies are deliberately brought to an end, against their natural characteristic of perpetual succession, and how, if necessary, they might be resurrected again.

It is commonly assumed that companies will only be wound up (or liquidated or dissolved–the terms are often used as practical equivalents), and their lives brought to an end, when they are insolvent and cannot pay their debts. True, this is the primary reason for liquidating a company, but it is not the only reason. The shareholders may simply decide that their company has served its purpose, and, rather than sell their shares to new owners, they may decide to sell off the company's assets, pay off the company's creditors, and distribute the remaining funds amongst themselves pro rata according to their shareholding, or, if there are different classes of shares, according to the entitlements of each class. Typically, they will not do all this themselves. Having taken the decision, they will appoint an expert, a liquidator, to do the job for them. If the company is solvent and the creditors are all paid off in full, this route to exiting their shareholding would seem to be a matter of choice entirely for the shareholders themselves, and that is largely what we see in the relatively simple rules governing a (necessarily solvent) members' winding up of their company.

The situation is far more complicated if the company is insolvent, as is more commonly the case. When the company's liabilities exceed its assets, innocent creditors will inevitably face losses, whatever efforts are made to protect them. The legal regime that has been put in place—and the one that is the focus of much of the next chapter—is to minimise these inevitable losses by maximising the assets available for distribution to the creditors. In broad terms, two approaches can be taken to this problem, and both are now in use in British company law. The first approach, and the more recently adopted one, emerges from a realisation that the company is more valuable as a "going concern" than as one whose assets are sold off in a fire sale. Thus we now have rules that enable the company's directors to claim a time-limited moratorium—i.e. a pause, or breathing space—from the claims of the company's creditors, while they see if they can get the company back on its feet again. If successful, then the creditors will be paid in full, even if a little later than they had hoped. Alternatively, in more serious cases these similar ends may be sought by putting the company's management into more professional hands, allowing an administrator to take over the company's management from the directors. Again, the goal is to return the company, or at least part of its operations, to the status of a going concern.

If this does not work, however, then the company will need to be wound up by a liquidator. This brings into play the second set of rules, which both enable and require the liquidator to maximise the assets available for distribution, and then govern how those assets will be distributed amongst the creditors, determining which creditors, if any, will have priority over others. In maximising the assets available for distribution, the liquidator will look not only to the profitable sale of the company's obvious assets, but also to the claims the company (or the liquidator personally) may have against the company's directors, or against third parties who have inappropriately received some part of the company's assets prior to the winding up. We saw some of the rules the liquidator will rely on in earlier chapters: see especially Ch.10 on directors' duties, and Ch.19 on the claims available in respect of transactions which undermine the creditors' claims.

In circumstances where there will inevitably be losses, perhaps the best the law can do is minimise these losses to the extent that is can, eliminate any obvious unfairness, and ensure the rules, even if not perfect, are at least certain and effective. Given the ingenuity of commercial parties in seeking to protect themselves against the risks of the company's insolvency, and the sophisticated mix of statute, contract and property law rules at their disposal (see, e.g. Pt 9), this is a challenge, but one against which the current regime might be judged to be doing tolerably well.

CHAPTER 33

MANAGING DISTRESSED OR DEFUNCT COMPANIES

INTRODUCTION

Where a company no longer has the funds to function, or its members no longer wish it to function, the first thought is that there needs to be a process for bringing the existence of the legal entity to an end. If the death of the company is the desired objective, this is achieved by winding up the company, or liquidating it (the two terms can be used interchangeably).[1] The process of winding up, or liquidation, is designed to ensure that, before the company ceases to exist, all its outstanding obligations are met (so far as they can be) and any surplus assets (if there are any) are distributed to the members according to their agreed entitlement.[2] For reasons which might be obvious, especially given the competing interests which may need to be balanced, this process is not undertaken by the company's own directors, but by independent appointees who are qualified insolvency practitioners and who act professionally as company liquidators **33–001**

[1] And, more rarely, simply by striking the company off the register: see paras 33–028 to 33–030.
[2] See Ch.6.

(alternatively, in some circumstances, the process is carried out by the Official Receiver). When this process is completed, the company is removed from the register: it is "dissolved".

Clearly this is a dramatic step, and, as we have seen already, there are less terminal alternatives which may provide avenues for the successful rescue of failing companies: recall the use of administration, administrative receivership and company voluntary arrangements and reconstructions, often also making use of professional outsiders.[3] And as of 2020 there is a new debtor-focused (company-focused) procedure for obtaining a moratorium—a breathing space—giving the company a period during which it is protected from claims by creditors while it seeks to manage itself out of its difficulties.

The provisions relating to all these processes are now to be found almost exclusively[4] in the IA 1986 and the Insolvency (England and Wales) Rules,[5] and not in the Companies Act. This is obviously right when the company is insolvent, and that is typically the case, or close to the case, when the concern is to obtain a moratorium or put the company into administration. But insolvency is far from the only reason for a winding up, although it is the most common reason. Even then, however, putting these rules too in the IA 1986 has the pragmatic advantage of avoiding duplication of the many provisions that apply whether or not the company is insolvent. More importantly, it recognises that, once a company goes into liquidation, solvent or insolvent, the distinction between shareholders and creditors becomes more than usually difficult to draw: the members' interests will, in effect, have become fixed financial interests deferred to those of the creditors. We look at each of these options in turn, recognising that company voluntary arrangements and reconstructions, administrative receivership and large parts of the rules relating to administration have already been explored in earlier chapters.[6]

OBTAINING A MORATORIUM

33–002 In 2020 the government introduced, in IA 1986 Pt A1, a novel free-standing moratorium for distressed but viable companies. The new provisions are intended to support the rescue of a company as a going concern, as opposed merely to the rescue of only the company's business, which is what administration is designed to do. The aim is to afford companies some breathing space from creditor action so as to enable them to pursue a turnaround plan without adding significant fire-fighting costs as they do it. It is focused on the recovery of the company rather than the realisation of its assets, so it demonstrates a marked shift from the creditor-focused administration and insolvency processes to a new debtor-focused process.

The initial period for the moratorium, granted by court order, is only 20 business days but this is capable of being extended or terminated early. The first 20 business day extension is available without consent, so many moratoria are

---

[3] See Chs 32 and 29.

[4] But see Pt 31 of CA 2006, noted at paras 33–028 to 33–030.

[5] Insolvency (England and Wales) Rules 2016 (SI 2016/1024).

[6] See Chs 29 and 32.

likely to last 40 business days. Further extensions are available with the consent of creditors or the permission of the court. During the moratorium period (1) the day to day running of the company's business remains with the directors (again, unlike administration or insolvency) but under the supervision of a monitor (an insolvency practitioner) and with the monitor's consent required before the directors can undertake certain transactions; (2) creditors and lenders will not be able to take enforcement action against the debtor company (including enforcement of security); and (3) landlords cannot exercise rights of forfeiture. In short, it is the UK's first "debtor in possession" process under which the directors of a company are left in control to implement a rescue or restructuring plan, with the benefit of a moratorium, akin to Ch.11 in the US.

On the other hand, all is not weighted in favour of the company. The company must continue to pay certain of its debts during the moratorium. These include amounts due for all new supplies received during the moratorium, rent in respect of a period during the moratorium, wages and salary, and amounts due under financial contracts, including loan agreements. If these are not paid, then the moratorium will cease. This of course will give lenders a large measure of control over the moratorium, but with the benefits to them that if the business can be turned around, then their loans are less likely to fail.

The Government Guidance on the draft legislation states that the new moratorium procedure is aimed at ensuring that companies can maximise their chances of survival during the COVID-19 crisis. It is intended to be a seamless procedure that keeps administrative burdens to a minimum, allows for a speedy entry process and does not add disproportionate costs to already struggling businesses. As might be expected, not all companies are eligible. A new Sch.ZA1 to the IA 1986 lists the companies which are ineligible such as insurance companies, banks, or companies which are party to a capital markets arrangement in an amount of over £10 million. In addition, no application can be made if the company has entered into a moratorium in the previous 12 months without an order of the court, and, finally, the company must be, or likely to become, unable to pay its debts.

As we will see below, if the rescue plan fails and the company goes into insolvency within 12 weeks of the end of the moratorium, then the debts incurred during the moratorium will be given super-priority status in the insolvency process, ranking ahead of even the liquidator's own costs and expenses.[7]

ADMINISTRATION

Administration was dealt with in some detail in Ch.32, since it has become a typical enforcement mechanism adopted by floating charge holders.[8] Nevertheless, its more general outlines are set out here to give a complete picture in this chapter of the options for dealing with distressed companies. Administration is a process that was introduced several decades ago in the hope that it would encourage the rescue of productive businesses, even if that was achieved by disposing of them or their assets to more effective management teams. The only **33–003**

[7] See para.33–024.

[8] See paras 32–041 to 32–048.

process available at the time was insolvency, and that seemed too often to destroy the productive assets of the business in the fire-sale that often ensued in attempting to realise the assets for the unpaid creditors. To achieve better outcomes, a different process was thought necessary. Nevertheless, administration is clearly an insolvency process, or at least a pre-insolvency process, in the sense that it is rarely expected that the current management will be restored to their previous roles after the company has been put back on its feet.

An administrator is a person appointed by the court to manage the company's affairs, business and property in response to a request from the company itself, or from the holder of a qualifying floating charge (i.e. relating to the whole or substantially the whole of the company's property), or from the company's directors or a creditor. The administrator is then asked to formulate a possible plan for dealing with the company otherwise than by putting it into liquidation. The administrator's proposals must within eight weeks of his or her appointment be submitted for the approval of the company's unsecured creditors.

Although administration is a statutory insolvency procedure found in the IA 1986, and can only be invoked in relation to a company that is or is likely to become insolvent, it is also a process that is only available if one of three purposes can be met by the administrator: (1) rescuing the company as a going concern; and, if that is not possible, then (2) achieving a better result for the company's creditors as a whole than would be likely if the company were wound up (without first being in administration)—this is usually achieved by the sale of the business and assets of the company as a going concern; and, finally, if that cannot be achieved, and only then (3) realising property in order to make a distribution to one or more secured or preferential creditors. The third objective may be pursued only if the administrator believes it is not reasonably practicable to achieve either of the other two objectives and the interests of the creditors of the company as a whole will not be harmed unnecessarily. In practice it is rare that the first part of the purpose is achieved and that the company is rescued. It is far more common that the second or third parts of the purpose are achieved and that only part of the business continues as a going concern post sale.

We have already considered administration in the context of an administrator appointed by the holder of a qualifying floating charge over the company's property, and in that context a good number of the relevant details concerning administration have already been covered albeit in a particular context.[9] A number of other more general constraints might be noted here, but only by way of illustration of the conditions under which the administrator must operate.

While a company is in administration there is a moratorium preventing creditors, unless they have the consent of the administrator or the permission of the court, from enforcing their security, putting in execution, or taking control of the company's goods; also no steps may be taken to repossess goods in the company's possession whether under any hire-purchase agreement, conditional sale agreement, chattel leasing agreement or retention of title agreement, except with the consent or permission of the administrator or the court. On the other hand, the administrator's proposals must not affect the rights of secured creditors

[9] See paras 32–041 onwards.

or the priority of preferential creditors unless those parties consent or the proposal is part of a proposed compromise or arrangement.[10]

In carrying out the agreed plans, the administrator has exceptionally wide powers of management, and in exercising those powers is deemed to be acting as an agent of the company: a person dealing with the administrator in good faith and for value is entitled to assume that the administrator is acting within his or her powers.

Administration automatically ends after one year unless the administrator's term of office is extended by consent of the creditors or order of the court. There can only be one extension by consent which cannot be for more than one year, although the court may make any number of extensions for periods it thinks fit.

Recall that the expenses of an administration have priority over a debt secured by a floating charge debts, and the liabilities arising out of contracts entered into by the administrator have priority even over the administrator's remuneration and expenses.[11] This means that it can be important to know which contracts have been entered into by the administrator. To that end some special rules have emerged, including, for example, that nothing done or omitted to be done in the first 14 days after an administrator's appointment is taken as showing that the administrator has adopted any contract of employment, and after the 14 days there must be some conduct by the administrator which amounts to an election to adopt or treat as continuing such contracts of employment before they are considered to give rise to a separate liability in the administration.[12] However, the fact that a contract of employment was not terminated during the 14-day period may readily lead to the conclusion that it has been adopted, although not where the administrator was unaware that the contract existed.[13]

TYPES OF WINDING UP

By contrast, if the decision is that the company's life should be brought to an end, **33–004**
then the appropriate process is to wind up (i.e. liquidate) the company.[14] The basic distinction is between voluntary winding up and compulsory winding up by the court.[15] As their names imply, an essential difference between compulsory winding up by the court and voluntary winding up is that the former does not necessarily involve action taken by any organ of the company itself, whereas voluntary winding up does. But voluntary winding up is subdivided into two

[10] As to which, see para.29–005.

[11] See para 32–047.

[12] *Powdrill v Watson* [1995] 2 A.C. 394 HL at 449.

[13] *Re Antal International Ltd* [2003] EWHC 1339 Ch; [2003] 2 B.C.L.C. 406.

[14] In the typical case the company's assets will be sold and others may use them to conduct a similar business. But this is not the same as selling the company's *business* by transferring its shares to new owners (even new corporate owners, as occurs when small companies are swallowed up by larger competitors).

[15] In relation to the winding up of "unregistered companies" (on which see paras 1–031 to 1–033) winding up by the court is the only method allowed: see IA 1986 Pt V. A company incorporated outside Great Britain which has been carrying on business in Britain may be wound up as an unregistered company notwithstanding that it has ceased to exist under the law of the country of incorporation: IA 1986 s.225.

types—members' voluntary winding up and creditors' voluntary winding up. The essential difference between members' and creditors' winding up is that the former is possible only if the company is solvent, in which event the company's members appoint the liquidator, whereas, if it is not, its creditors have the whip hand in deciding who the liquidator shall be. In all three cases, the winding up process is obviously directed towards realising the assets and distributing the net proceeds to the creditors and, if anything is left, to the members, according to their respective priorities; but it also enables an examination of the conduct of the company's management to be undertaken. This may result in civil and criminal proceedings being taken against those who have engaged in any malpractices thus revealed[16] and in the adjustment or avoidance of various transactions.[17]

Winding up by the court

Grounds for winding up

33–005 Under s.122 of the IA 1986, a company may be wound up by the court on one or more of eight specified grounds. Of these grounds, by far the most important is ground (f), that the company is unable to pay its debts, and the next most important is ground (g), that the court is of the opinion that it is just and equitable that the company should be wound up. The latter has been dealt with in Ch.14 (where we saw that it may be used as a remedy in cases where members are being unfairly prejudiced or there is a deadlocked management, and where it might seem the presence of this minority protection remedy in the IA 1986 is something of an anomaly) and in Ch.21 (where we saw that it may be invoked by the Secretary of State following the exercise of his or her investigatory powers).

Who may petition for a court ordered winding up?

33–006 The company itself can opt for winding up by the court, since ground (a) is that the company has by special resolution resolved that the company be so wound up. But normally that is the last thing that those controlling the company will want: winding up by the court is the most expensive type of winding up and the one in which their conduct is likely to be investigated most thoroughly.[18] Alternatively, s.124 makes it clear that a wide range of people may, in different and limited circumstances, petition for the winding up of a company by the court; the list

---

16 See IA 1986 Pt IV Ch.X.
17 See IA 1986 Pt VI ss.238–246.
18 But it might be used if the court is already involved because the liquidation of the company is part of a scheme requiring its sanction in accordance with the provisions discussed in Ch.29.

includes the company's directors, its members,[19] its creditors (including prospective and contingent creditors), and various parties with official public status.[20]

Proof that a company is unable to pay its debts

Creditors are among those who may petition for a winding up,[21] usually once it becomes widely known that the company is in financial difficulties.[22] This is a remedy of last resort, but nevertheless accounts for about 95% of petitions for court ordered winding ups. And although the company itself or its directors[23] or members[24] may petition, the court will be reluctant to grant it on ground (f) if it is opposed by a majority of the creditors. **33–007**

The IS 1986 s.123 affords creditors owed more than £750 a simple means of establishing ground (f), that the company is unable to pay its debts, by serving a "statutory demand".[25] Because of the presumption of insolvency inherent in this, the courts are astute to prevent creditors relying on the sub-section if the debt itself is disputed,[26] or if the sum is disputed so that £750 may not be owed,[27] or if the statutory demand has not been properly put together or properly served.[28] If the statutory demand procedure is not used, it is usually necessary for the creditor to prove "to the satisfaction of the court that the company is unable to pay its debts as they fall due".[29]

---

[19] Notwithstanding anything to the contrary in the articles: *Re Pervil Gold Mines Ltd* [1898] 1 Ch. 122 CA.

[20] And, as we have noted earlier, the Secretary of State (also see ss.124A, 124B), the FCA (also see s.124C), the Regulator of Community Interest Companies, the Official Receiver of the court, and designated officers of the magistrates court, each in specified circumstances.

[21] IA 1986 s.124.

[22] Until then each may try to obtain judgment and levy execution, thus getting ahead of the pack.

[23] Prior to the 1985/86 statutory reforms, it was held, somewhat surprisingly, that directors could not apply: *Re Emmerdart Ltd* [1979] Ch. 540 Ch D. Now they can. For the interpretation of "the directors" see *Re Equiticorp International Plc* [1989] 1 W.L.R. 1010 Ch D.

[24] But unless the membership has been reduced below two, a member cannot apply unless his (or her) shares were originally allotted to him or have been held and registered in his name for at least 6 months during the 18 months prior to the commencement of the winding up (on which see below) or have devolved on him through the death of a former holder: IA 1986 s.124(2). This is designed to prevent a disgruntled person (e.g. an ex-employee) from buying a share and then bringing a winding up petition (or threatening to do so).

[25] In accordance with IA 1986 s.123(1)(a).

[26] Indeed, a creditor whose debt is bona fide disputed cannot petition at all: *Stonegate Securities Ltd v Gregory* [1980] Ch. 576 CA; *Re Selectmove Ltd* [1995] 1 W.L.R. 474 CA (Civ Div).

[27] *Re Company (No.003729 of 1982)* [1984] 1 W.L.R. 1090 Ch D.

[28] *Re Company (No.008790 of 1990)* [1991] B.C.L.C. 561 Ch D; *Stylo Shoes Ltd v Prices Tailors Ltd* [1960] Ch. 396 Ch D.

[29] IA 1986 s.123(1)(e). See *BNY Corporate Trustee Services Ltd v Eurosail-UK 2007-3BL Plc* [2013] UKSC 28; [2013] 1 W.L.R. 1408. While discrediting the "point of no return" test, the Supreme Court affirmed the decision of the Court of Appeal that the ability of a company to meet its liabilities, both prospective and contingent, was to be determined on the balance of probabilities with the burden of proof on the party asserting "balance-sheet insolvency".

The court's discretion

33–008 The court has a statutory discretion to refuse to order a winding up on a members' petition made on the "just and equitable" ground if some other remedy is available and it seems that the petitioners are acting unreasonably in seeking this rather drastic option rather than some other remedy (typically the unfair prejudice alternative).[30] In addition, the court has an inherent jurisdiction to refuse to make the order if it considers the petition to have been brought for improper or extraneous purposes,[31] and may simply strike out as an abuse of process any petition which is bound to fail.[32]

Liquidators, provisional liquidators and official receivers

33–009 If a winding up order is made, the first step needing to be taken will be to appoint a liquidator to whom, as in all types of winding up, the administration of the company's affairs and property will pass. In contrast with an individual's trustee in bankruptcy, the company's property does not vest in the liquidator[33]; but the control and management of it and of the company's affairs do, and the board of directors, in effect, becomes functus officio.[34] A provisional liquidator may, indeed, be appointed before a final order for winding up is made, and then it is normally the official receiver attached to the court.[35]

The important role played by official receivers in compulsory liquidations in England and Wales is perhaps the major difference between compulsory and voluntary liquidations.[36] Official receivers (ORs) are officers of the Insolvency Service, an Executive Agency of BEIS, attached to courts having bankruptcy jurisdiction.[37] Not only will an OR normally be the provisional liquidator (if one is appointed) but he or she will generally be the initial liquidator and often will remain the liquidator throughout a court ordered winding up. On the making of a winding up order[38] the OR automatically becomes liquidator by virtue of his or her office and will remain so unless and until another liquidator is appointed.[39] The OR may succeed in getting rid of the office by seeking nominations from the

---

[30] IA 1986 s.125(2).

[31] *Re Surrey Garden Village Trust Ltd* [1965] 1 W.L.R. 974 Ch D; *Re JE Cade & Sons Ltd* [1992] B.C.L.C. 213 Ch D (Companies Ct). On the other hand, if the purpose of the petition is legitimate, it does not matter if the petitioner's motive is malicious: *Bryanston Finance Ltd v De Vries (No.2)* [1976] Ch. 63 CA.

[32] *Charles Forte Investments Ltd v Amanda* [1964] Ch. 240 CA.

[33] Unless the court so orders, as it may: IA 1986 s.145(1).

[34] By common law, even though not made explicit in the IA 1986 for compulsory winding ups: *Re Farrow's Bank Ltd* [1921] 2 Ch. 164 CA (contrast the statutory provision in voluntary winding up (s.90(2)).

[35] IA 1986 s.135.

[36] In the latter, their role is principally in relation to disqualification of directors under the Directors Disqualification Act (on which see Ch.20).

[37] Official receivers have the unique distinction of being entitled to act as liquidators notwithstanding that they are not licensed insolvency practitioners under Pt XIII of the IA 1986: ss.388(5) and 389(2).

[38] Except when it is made immediately upon the discharge of an administration order or when there is a supervisor of a voluntary arrangement under Pt I of the Act, when the former administrator or the supervisor of the arrangement may be appointed by the court as liquidator: IA 1986 s.140.

[39] IA s.136(1)–(2).

creditors and members, according to the relevant rules.[40] And if that does not succeed,[41] the OR may decide to refer the need to appoint another liquidator to the Secretary of State who may appoint.[42] But, whenever any vacancy occurs, the OR again becomes the liquidator until another is appointed.[43] The liquidator, provisional liquidator and official receiver are all officers of the court, required to behave as such, if they have been appointed by the court to execute a court ordered compulsory liquidation.

Whether or not the official receiver becomes the liquidator, the OR has important investigatory powers and duties. When the court has made a winding up order, the OR may require officers, employees and those who have taken part in the formation of the company to submit a statement as to the affairs of the company verified by statutory declaration.[44] It is the duty of the OR to investigate the causes of the failure, and to make such report, if any, to the court as he or she thinks fit.[45] The OR may apply to the court for the public examination of anyone who is or has been an officer, liquidator, administrator, receiver or manager of the company, or anyone else who has taken part in its promotion, formation or management, and must do so, unless the court otherwise orders, if requested by one-half in value of the creditors or three-quarters in value of the members.[46] And if the OR is not the liquidator, the person who is must give the OR all the information and assistance reasonably required for the exercise of these functions.[47]

Once a liquidator is appointed, the process of the winding up proceeds very much as it would in the case of a voluntary liquidation since the objective is identical and the liquidator's functions are the same as those in voluntary windings up, namely "to secure that the assets of the company are got in, realised, and distributed to the company's creditors[48] and, if there is a surplus, to the persons entitled to it".[49] The main difference is that, in a winding up by the court, the liquidator in the exercise of powers given under Sch.4 to the IA 1986 will more often be required to obtain the sanction of the court before entering into transactions, and that throughout the liquidation process the liquidator will be subject to the surveillance of the OR, acting, in effect, as an officer of the court.

[40] See IA 1986 s.136(4) and (5). The nominee of the creditors prevails unless, on application to the court, it otherwise orders (s.139) which it is unlikely to do if the company is insolvent.

[41] Which it may not since both creditors and members may be happy to leave the liquidation to the official receiver since that may prove less expensive.

[42] IA 1986 s.137.

[43] IA 1986 s.136(3).

[44] IA 1986 s.131. See also ss.235 and 236. See *Re Chesterfield United Inc* [2012] EWHC 244 (Ch); [2013] 1 B.C.L.C. 709; *Re Comet Group Ltd* [2014] EWHC 3477 (Ch); *Re Corporate Jet Realisations Ltd* [2015] EWHC 221 (Ch).

[45] IA 1986 s.132.

[46] IA 1986 ss.133 and 134. It is this public examination that is the most dreaded ordeal, particularly if the company is sufficiently well known to attract the attention of the general public and the Press.

[47] IA 1986 s.143.

[48] Giving priority, of course, to preferred creditors as set out in Sch.6 to IA 1986.

[49] IA 1986 s.143(1). Normally the members (except in the case of non-profit-making or charitable companies) in accordance with their class rights on a winding up.

In a court-ordered winding up where the liquidator is not the OR, the creditors may appoint a "liquidation committee", so that they have some formal voice in the liquidation proceedings.[50]

Timing of commencement of winding up

33–010 Once the winding up order is made, the winding up is deemed to have commenced as from the date of the presentation of the petition (or, indeed, if the order is made in respect of a company already in voluntary winding up, as from the date of the resolution to wind up voluntarily).[51] This dating back is important since, unless the court orders otherwise, it has the effect of invalidating property dispositions[52] and executions of judgments[53] lawfully undertaken during the period between the presentation of the petition and the order,[54] and of course it will affect the duration of the periods prior to "the onset of insolvency" in which, if certain transactions are undertaken, they are liable to adjustment or avoidance in the event of winding up or administration.[55] The rule is seen as necessary in order to ensure an orderly and fair distribution of the company's assets. At the point when it is recognised that the company needs to go into liquidation, it is inevitable that the company's creditors will have to shoulder losses, but it is also seen as fair that all the company's then existing assets should be devoted to that end. In particular, parties "in the know" should not be able to steal a march, either extracting assets from the company at the potential expense of existing creditors or, more seriously, removing themselves from the class of existing creditors by having their claims met in full in advance of the liquidation. To that end, transactions are invalidates unless the court orders otherwise, which it will do if the risk in the sightlines is not a concern.

Voluntary winding up—general

Instigation of winding up

33–011 In contrast with winding up by the court, voluntary winding up always starts with a resolution of the company. In the unlikely event of the articles fixing a period for the duration of the company[56] or specifying an event on the occurrence of which it is to be dissolved,[57] all that is required is an ordinary resolution in general meeting.[58] Otherwise, what is required is a special resolution that the

---

[50] See para.33–017.
[51] IA 1986 s.129.
[52] IA 1986 s.127. See para.33–020.
[53] IA 1986 s.128.
[54] Which may be considerable if hearings are adjourned, as is not infrequent.
[55] See IA 1986 ss.238–245. See the detailed discussions of these types of dispositions in Ch.19.
[56] This is rare but charters of incorporation of limited duration are not uncommon.
[57] It is possible to conceive of circumstances in which this might be done: e.g. when a partnership converts to an incorporated company because its solicitors and accountants advise that this would be advantageous tax-wise, the partners might wish to ensure that it could be dissolved by a simple majority if they were later advised that it would be better to revert to a partnership.
[58] IA 1986 s.84(1)(a).

company be wound up voluntarily.[59] In either case the resolution is subject to the requirement that a copy of it has to be sent to the Registrar within 15 days[60] and the company must give notice of the resolution by advertisement in the *Gazette* within 14 days of its passing.[61]

Timing of commencement of winding up

A voluntary winding up is deemed to commence on the passing of the resolution[62]; there is no "relating back" as there is in the case of winding up by the court. As from the commencement of the winding up, the company must cease to carry on its business, except so far as may be required for its beneficial winding up,[63] and any transfer of shares, unless made with the sanction of the liquidator, is void, as is any alteration in the status of the members.[64] **33–012**

Members' voluntary winding up

Declaration of solvency

The most important question which the directors of the company will have had to consider prior to the passing of the resolution is whether they can, in good conscience and without dire consequences to themselves, allow the voluntary winding up to proceed as a members', as opposed to a creditors', winding up. In order for that to occur they, or if there are more than two of them, the majority of them, must, in accordance with IA 1986 s.89, make at a directors' meeting[65] a statutory declaration (the "declaration of solvency") to the effect that they have made a full inquiry into the company's affairs and that, having done so, they have formed the opinion that the company will be able to pay its debts in full, together with interest at the "official rate",[66] within such period, not exceeding 12 months from the commencement of the winding up, as may be specified in the **33–013**

[59] IA 1986 s.84(1)(b).
[60] IA 1986 s.84(3).
[61] IA 1986 s.85(1).
[62] IA 1986 s.86. And CA 2006 s.332, which provides that a resolution passed at an adjourned meeting is treated as passed on the day it was in fact passed, prevents companies backdating the commencement of winding up.
[63] IA 1986 s.87(1).
[64] IA 1986 s.88. Contrast the wording of the comparable IA 1986 s.127, in relation to winding up by the court: that avoids also any disposition of the company's property (unless the court otherwise orders) which IA 1986 s.88 does not.
[65] This use of a board meeting as a venue for the making of statutory declarations ensures that all the directors know what is going on.
[66] i.e. whichever is the greater of the interest payable on judgment debts or that applicable to the particular debt apart from the winding up: IA 1986 ss.189(4) and 251.

declaration.[67] This was the origin of the declaration of solvency now used in the out-of-court procedure for a reduction of capital[68] and in respect of an acquisition of shares out of capital.[69]

The declaration is ineffective unless:

(1) it is made within five weeks preceding the date of the passing of the resolution; and
(2) it embodies a statement of the company's assets and liabilities as at the latest practicable date before the making of the declaration.[70]

If a director makes the declaration without having reasonable grounds for believing that the company will be able to pay its debts with interest within the period specified in the declaration, he or she is liable to a fine and imprisonment,[71] and if the debts are not so paid it is presumed, unless the contrary is shown, that the director did not have reasonable grounds for that opinion.[72] It therefore behoves the directors to take the utmost care and to seek professional advice before they make the declaration. Especially is this so because, even if the winding up is a members' one, a licensed insolvency practitioner will have to be appointed as liquidator and the liquidator is likely to detect whether the declaration was over-optimistic long before the expiration of the 12 months. Formerly, small private companies could, and often did, appoint as liquidator one of the directors and, in effect, continued to proceed much as they would have when a partnership was being dissolved. This is no longer possible.[73]

If the professional liquidator, appointed as described below, forms the opinion that the company will not be able to pay its debts within the stated period, he or she must summon a meeting of the creditors and supply them with full information in accordance with IA 1986 s.95 and, as from the date when the meeting is held, the winding up is converted under s.96 from a (solvent) members' to a (insolvent) creditors' voluntary winding up.[74] So long, however, as the liquidator shares the view of the directors (and if they are wise they will have consulted him, as their proposed nominee, before they made the declaration) all should proceed smoothly as a members' winding up.

---

[67] IA 1986 s.89(1). In practice the declaration will play safe and not specify a shorter period than 12 months even if the directors expect that it will be shorter.

[68] See paras 17–035 to 17–040.

[69] See para.17–002 onwards.

[70] IA 1986 s.89(2). The declaration must be delivered to the Registrar within 15 days immediately following the passing of the resolution: IA 1986 s.89(3) and (4).

[71] IA 1986 s.89(4).

[72] IA 1986 s.89(5).

[73] But see para.33–029 for the possible resort to s.1003 of the Companies Act.

[74] Indeed, it may become a winding up by the court, for a winding up order may be made notwithstanding that the company is already in voluntary winding up and an official receiver, as well as the other persons entitled under IA 1986 s.124, may present a petition: IA 1986 s.124(5). But unless the court, on proof of fraud or mistake, directs otherwise, all proceedings already taken in the voluntary winding up are deemed to have been validly taken: IA 1986 s.129(1).

Appointment and obligations of liquidator

The company in general meeting will appoint one or more liquidators for the purpose of winding up the company's affairs and distributing its assets[75] whereupon "all the powers of the directors cease except so far as a general meeting or the liquidator sanctions their continuance".[76] If a vacancy in the office of liquidator "occurs by death, resignation or otherwise" the company in general meeting may fill the vacancy,[77] subject to any arrangement with the creditors.[78] **33–014**

When the company's affairs are fully wound up the liquidator must draw up an account of the winding up, showing how it has been conducted and the company's property disposed of.[79] The liquidator must send a copy of the account to the members of the company first, and then to the Registrar, both within 14 days off the production of the account.[80]

Creditors' voluntary winding up

Instigation of winding up

Here, in contrast with members' winding up, the company is assumed to be insolvent and it is the creditors in whose interests the winding up is undertaken and they who have the whip hand. A members' voluntary winding up can be converted to a creditors' voluntary winding up.[81] Otherwise, if no declaration of solvency has been made by the directors after the members' resolution to wind the company up, the directors must within 7 days of the members' resolution lay a statement of the company's affairs before the creditors, showing the company's financial position.[82] **33–015**

Appointment of liquidator

The company may nominate a person to be the liquidator at the company meeting which passed the resolution for a voluntary winding up, but the directors must also in accordance with the rules seek a nomination from the creditors. If the creditors do so their nominee becomes the liquidator, unless, on application to the court by a director, creditor or member, the court directs that the company's nominee shall be liquidator instead of, or jointly with, the creditors' nominee, or it appoints some other person instead of the creditors' nominee.[83] Provisions, **33–016**

---

75 IA 1986 s.91(1).

76 IA 1986 s.91(2).

77 IA 1986 s.92(1). The meeting to do so may be convened by any continuing liquidators if there was more than one or by a member: IA 1986 s.92(2).

78 This reference to "creditors" is presumably to cover the case where the members' voluntary winding up forms part of a reorganisation of one of the types dealt with in Ch.29, in which creditors are involved.

79 IA 1986 s.94(1).

80 IA 1986 s.94(2)–(3).

81 IA 1986 s.96.

82 IA 1986 s.99.

83 IA 1986 s.100.

similar in effect, apply when a members' winding up is converted to a creditors' winding up because the liquidator concludes that the company's debts will not be paid in full within the 12 months.[84]

"Liquidation committee"

33–017 In a creditors' voluntary winding up, or in a winding up by the court, the creditors may decide in accordance with the rules to establish a "liquidation committee" of, in the former case, not more than five persons.[85] If they do this, the company in general meeting may also appoint members not exceeding five in number.[86] However, if the creditors resolve that all or any of those appointed by the general meeting ought not to be members of the committee, the persons concerned will not be qualified to act unless the court otherwise directs.[87]

The functions of a liquidation committee are to be found in both the Insolvency Act and the Insolvency (England and Wales) Rules, and for present purposes can be summarised by saying that they assist in the work of the liquidator, and in particular they have substantial powers to agree to matters on behalf of the creditors or the company.[88] They also provide additional means whereby the creditors and members can keep an eye on the liquidator. In the latter respect, liquidation committees are likely to be more valuable in creditors' voluntary windings-up than in windings-up by the court owing to the lesser role played by official receivers.

It may be thought somewhat anomalous that, when the company is insolvent, the members should have equal (or any) representation on the liquidation committee. But the Cork Committee rejected the argument that they should not, because "it is rarely possible to assess the interest of shareholders at the outset of proceedings".[89] This is certainly true. What at the commencement of the winding up would seem to be a clear case of the company's liabilities greatly exceeding its assets (so that the shareholders have no prospective stake in the outcome of the winding up) may turn out otherwise if the winding up is prolonged.

In other respects a creditors' winding up proceeds in much the same way as in a members' winding up.

If the required procedures have not been followed, the court can give directions. This was done in *Re WeSellCNC.Com Ltd*,[90] where it was discovered by the appointed liquidator that no declaration of solvency had been made; this was therefore necessarily a "creditors' voluntary winding up" pursuant to IA 1986 s.89, but no creditors' meeting had been summoned (that is not now necessary in any event) and no statement of affairs prepared. Accepting that the company was in fact well and truly solvent with a considerable surplus, and with all creditors

---

84 IA 1986 ss.95 and 96.

85 IA 1986 s.101(1) for a creditors' winding up. The rules are different and more restrictive for a winding-up by the court: IA 1986 s.141.

86 IA 1986 s.101(2).

87 IA 1986 s.101(3).

88 See, e.g. IA 1986 ss.103, 110, 165 and the Insolvency (England and Wales) Rules 2016 rr.6.7(5), 12.42(2), 14.13, 17.23, 17.25, 18.20.

89 Cmnd. 8558, para.939.

90 *Re WeSellCNC.Com Ltd* [2013] EWHC 4577 (Ch).

having been paid and distributions made to shareholders, the judge declared that the liquidation was indeed a creditors' voluntary winding up, but dispensed with the requirement of a creditors' meeting and the laying before it of a statement of affairs.

POWERS AND DUTIES OF THE LIQUIDATOR

In order to make possible the orderly winding up the company, the IA 1986 confers a wide range of powers on the liquidator (ss.165 onwards), and Sch.4 sets out an extensive list of specific powers, including the power to carry on the company's business, to borrow and grant security over the company's property, and to bring and defend proceedings. Importantly, ss.178 onwards empower the liquidator to "disclaim any onerous property", meaning that the liquidator can terminate the company's obligations under any unprofitable contracts, and the contracting counterparty is then left to claim damages as a creditor in the company's insolvency. This power is typically used to terminate the company's leases of premises and other property, on the basis that otherwise the company's available assets would be disproportionately appropriated to the creditor holding the onerous right.[91] **33–018**

In exercising these powers, the liquidator typically acts in the company's name[92] (the company retains its separate legal personality until the winding up is completed and the company is dissolved).[93]

The liquidator's duties are owed to the company,[94] not to individual creditors or members, and the liquidator may therefore be sued in misfeasance proceedings under IA 1986 s.212 and held personally liable for misapplication of the company's assets,[95] negligence[96] or breach of fiduciary duties (conflicts and profits rules) owed to the company.

---

[91] *Re Celtic Extraction Ltd* [1999] 2 B.C.L.C. 555 CA at 568.

[92] With the exception of the exercise of certain statutory powers given specifically to the liquidator: e.g. IA 1986 ss.212, 213 and 214.

[93] But the liquidator may nevertheless sometimes incur personal liability if costs exceed the company's assets: *Re Wilson Lovatt & Sons Ltd* [1977] 1 All E.R. 274 Ch D.

[94] *Knowles v Scott* [1891] 1 Ch. 717 Ch D.

[95] *Re Home and Colonial Insurance Co Ltd* [1930] 1 Ch. 102 Ch D; *Pulsford v Devenish* [1903] 2 Ch. 625 Ch D.

[96] *Re Windsor Steam Coal Co (1901) Ltd* [1928] Ch. 609 Ch D.

COLLECTION, REALISATION AND DISTRIBUTION OF THE COMPANY'S ASSETS

Maximising the assets available for distribution

33–019 The task of the liquidator in winding up the company is to finalise the company's affairs, and to get in the company's assets so as to maximise the return to those entitled to the assets on a winding up.[97] In getting in the assets, the liquidator will take control of all the assets owned beneficially[98] by the company and, crucially, will seek to "claw back" assets which the company should not have disposed of (or should not have disposed of on the terms actually agreed) and will also pursue claims against any officers or third parties who may be liable to the company for breach of their duties or for other wrongs.[99] In this way, the asset pool available for distribution will be maximised, to the benefit of those entitled to share in it.

In all of this, a word ought to be said about the position of secured creditors in order to draw attention to the difference between their position and that of general creditors on a winding up, and also the difference between their position on a winding up compared with that during an administration. As we saw, so far as the latter is concerned, unless the secured creditors have taken steps to enforce their security prior to the administration, they may be in difficulties in doing so while it lasts.[100] In contrast, on a winding up, a secured creditor is in the enviable position of having the choice of realising its security and, if this does not raise sufficient to pay what is due in full, to prove for the balance, or to surrender its security for the benefit of the general body of creditors and prove for the whole debt.[101] Normally, of course, the former option will be adopted.

---

[97] This will be the creditors, and perhaps not even all of them, if the company is insolvent; and both creditors and members if the company is solvent. Special rules govern the order of distribution, as described below.

[98] Thus excluding assets in the company's possession but, e.g. held on hire purchase, or subject to retention of title agreements; or assets which the company does own, but which are held on trust for the benefit of third parties or are subject to valid security interests in favour of third party creditors.

[99] Both options have largely been examined already in earlier chapters: see Ch.19 on fraudulent and wrongful trading, and on preferences, and Ch.10 on directors' duties and claims against associated third parties, since these people are the most likely targets. Note that breaches of directors' duties can occur while the company is in administration or liquidation, as directors remain directors and continue to owe their general duties. In *Re System Building Services Group Ltd (In Liquidation)* [2020] EWHC 54 (Ch), the company, via its liquidator, sued the director for various breaches, including purchase of the company's property at an undervalue from the administrator.

[100] See paras 32–043 to 32–044.

[101] If the winding up follows an administration in which the administrator has exercised his or her powers under Sch.B1, paras 70 and 71 (paras 32–043 to 32–044) it would seem that the effect of paras 70(2) and 71(3) will be to preserve the security holder's rights by treating the sums mentioned in those subsections as the security in the winding up.

Statutory "claw back" and avoidance provisions

In addition to the recoveries already mentioned,[102] it is also the case that, starting from the date of commencement of the winding up,[103] all transfers of shares are avoided,[104] and, for compulsory liquidations, all dispositions of the property by the company (unless the court otherwise orders)[105] and attachments, distress and execution which have not been completed[106] are void. These seemingly straightforward provisions can raise nice legal questions. In *Akers v Samba Financial Group*,[107] an insolvent company was the beneficial owner of shares worth $300 million. The legal owner (and trustee) discharged his own personal obligations by transferring these shares to a third party, who it was assumed took the shares as a bona fide purchaser for value, thus destroying the company's interest in them. The transaction occurred after the commencement of the company's winding up. The circumstances may look suspicious, but the Supreme Court held that the transaction could not be declared void as a "disposition of property" after the commencement of winding up. The conclusion seems unassailable: this was not a disposition by anyone of the company's property; it was simply a circumstance in which the company's property lost its value.[108] The lesson, if there is one, is in the vulnerability of equitable interests in property. **33–020**

In addition, these rules can prove awkward unless the court is minded to approve what has happened. For example, in *Re Gray's Inn Construction Co Ltd*,[109] the company continued to trade unprofitably after the date the winding up petition had been presented; counsel conceded that both sums credited and debited to the company's bank account were "dispositions" which, in the exercise of its discretion, the court mostly declined to validate in the interests of preserving rateable distributions to all creditors rather than enabling some to be paid in full. The banking community has, however, since been reassured that its potential exposure to restitutionary liability of this sort is rather less, with the important Court of Appeal decision in *Hollicourt (Contracts) Ltd v Bank of Ireland*[110] to the effect that where a bank meets a cheque drawn by the company as its customer (whether the account is in credit or overdrawn), it does so merely as the company's agent; as a result, while there is clearly a disposition in favour of the payee, there is no disposition to the bank itself. On the other hand, if the company pays sums into its bank account when the account is overdrawn, then

[102] See fnn.98 and 99.

[103] i.e. presentation of the petition (compulsory winding up, s.129) or passing of the resolution (voluntary winding up, s.86).

[104] IA 1986 ss.88, 127.

[105] IA 1986 s.127, but with specific exemptions for anything done by an administrator while a winding up petition is suspended under para.40 of Sch.B1, or in respect of anything done in a moratorium granted under Pt A1.

[106] IA 1986 s.128, and see ss.183–184 for all winding ups.

[107] *Akers v Samba Financial Group* [2017] UKSC 6. Noted Nolan, (2017) 133 L.Q.R. 353.

[108] Of course, the company has a valid claim against its trustee for breach of trust, but whether the trustee could meet those liabilities is another question.

[109] *Re Gray's Inn Construction Co Ltd* [1980] 1 W.L.R. 711 CA. See also *Express Electrical Distributors Ltd v Beavis* [2016] EWCA Civ 765.

[110] *Hollicourt (Contracts) Ltd v Bank of Ireland* [2001] Ch. 555 CA.

the payment is a disposition to the bank[111]; whereas if the account is in credit then it has been held that the payment is not a disposition,[112] since the transaction simply converts the company's cash receipts into an equivalent claim against the bank.

Far more significantly, however, the liquidator is also given the right to look backwards, and unwind transactions entered into within prescribed periods before the commencement of an insolvent winding up. We have seen this already in relation to avoiding floating charges created within 12 months (or, in the case of connected persons, two years) of that date.[113] Similar rules enable the liquidator to unwind transactions entered into at an undervalue (s.238) within two years of the onset of insolvency, at a time where the company was already insolvent[114] or became so as a result of the transaction.[115] The court has wide powers in framing its orders to effect restitution of the company's estate.[116] Another provision with the same timing restrictions avoids transactions motivated by the desire to prefer one creditor over other (s.239). All these have already been considered in Ch.19.

The common law "anti-deprivation principle"

33–021 The IA 1986 is not the only source of rules enabling recoveries by the liquidator. When a company is insolvent, the widely accepted objective of regulated insolvency distribution, and the clear goal of the statutory rules just considered, is to ensure that the company's assets are preserved for distribution, and that the distribution, when effected, is for the collective benefit of the company's creditors. Put another way, although it is accepted that some businesses will inevitably fail even when run without fault,[117] and that innocent parties will then have to bear the resulting losses, the general consensus is that the losses should then be borne rateably.[118]

This then raises the question of whether there is common law support for this endeavour, or whether the task falls entirely to statute. A number of old cases and one House of Lords authority suggest the common law has a role. In *British Eagle International Airlines Ltd v Cie Nationale Air France*,[119] the House of Lords, by a 3:2 majority, overruled both the Court of Appeal and the trial judge to hold that a contractual netting-out agreement between international airline companies could not operate on Air France's insolvency so as to prevent Air

---

[111] On this point it seems *Re Gray's Inn Construction Co Ltd* [1980] 1 W.L.R. 711, is still good authority.

[112] *Re Barn Crown Ltd* [1995] 1 W.L.R. 147 Ch D (Companies Ct).

[113] IA 1986 s.245, and see para.32–014.

[114] On the s.123 test.

[115] IA 1986 s.240(2). There is a rebuttable presumption that this is the case if the transaction is with a connected person.

[116] IA 1986 s.241.

[117] But where there is fault, the defaulters should contribute to the insolvent company's assets, as we have already seen.

[118] With some minor exceptions for identified vulnerable creditors (see para.33–024), and of course the major exception accorded to secured creditors who often escape the burden of shared loses entirely, and in doing so disproportionately reduce the assets available for those who are unsecured (see Ch.32).

[119] *British Eagle International Airlines Ltd v Cie Nationale Air France* [1975] 1 W.L.R. 758 HL.

France from collecting in full the sums owed to it by certain airlines, even though sums which it owed to different airlines would obviously not be met in full.[120]

Perhaps predictably, the 2008 financial crisis generated litigation which tested the breadth of this common law restriction. The difficult case of *Belmont Park Investments Pty Ltd v BNY Corporate Trustee Services Ltd and Lehman Brothers Special Financing Inc*[121] is the only case to reach the Supreme Court to date. The clause under review was not a *British Eagle* "contracting out" provision (operating against the pari passu rule),[122] but a clause which allegedly effected an insolvency-triggered deprivation to the pool of assets available for distribution. This sort of clause had been outlawed for well over a century, as illustrated by *Ex p. Jay*.[123] In that case, a builder agreed with the owner of the land on which he was to build that, should the builder become bankrupt, all the builder's materials on the owner's land would be immediately forfeited to the owner. The Court of Appeal held the clause to be void. As James LJ put it:

> "a simple stipulation that, upon a man's becoming bankrupt, that which was his property up to the date of the bankruptcy should go over to some one else and be taken away from his creditors, is void as being a violation of the policy of the bankrupt law."

The clause before the Supreme Court in *Belmont* was far more complex, and embedded in a derivatives contract, but it was argued, unsuccessfully, that it operated in the same way and ought to be declared void. The offending provision was one whereby Creditor A, with a security interest in certain assets owned by X, would lose that security interest if the creditor became insolvent, and the security would "flip" (hence the label "flip clause") to Creditor B, who also had claims against X. Since both A's and B's claims were "non-recourse" claims, limited to the assets held by X, the result was that A, who might have expected to be paid in full, was, on its insolvency, unable to recover anything from X. It argued that its "asset"—the security interest supporting the loan—had been taken away by the insolvency-triggered clause. The Supreme Court disagreed, declining to follow the analysis in *Ex p. Jay*. Instead, it gave powerful backing to freedom of contract, and unanimously upheld the "flip clause", denying that it offended the common law anti-deprivation principle and holding instead that the clause defined the asset itself: the security was itself a "flawed asset" with express embedded depletion provisions.

The derivatives markets, and perhaps financial markets more generally, applauded the outcome and the freedom it provides to parties to organise their affairs at will, although the result stands in stark contrast to the strict approach

---

[120] By contrast, had the issue been mutual debits and credits been between Air France and a single third party airline, insolvency set off would have allowed offsetting.

[121] *Belmont Park Investments Pty Ltd v BNY Corporate Trustee Services Ltd and Lehman Brothers Special Financing Inc* [2011] UKSC 38. Commented on in S. Worthington, "Good faith, flawed assets and the emasculation of the UK anti-deprivation rule" (2012) 75 M.L.R. 112.

[122] Where the Supreme Court supported the *British Eagle* approach.

[123] *Re Harrison Ex p. Jay* (1879) 14 Ch. D. 19 CA. Also see *Re Jeavons Ex p. Mackay* (1872–73) L.R. 8 Ch. App. 643 CA in Chancery (concerning royalties).

still favoured in *British Eagle* type arrangements, and also to the broader approach to protecting creditors against flawed asset provisions that is favoured in US bankruptcy legislation.[124]

Benefit of the statutory claw backs and wrongdoer contributions

33–022 Money that is ordered to be paid under most of the sections just noted (ss.238, 239, 213 and 214, but not s.212) typically goes into the general assets of the company in the hands of the liquidator, not to individual victims of the wrongs, and not, importantly, into the clutches of floating charge holders. This is because the right to sue belongs exclusively to the liquidator, not the company. Receipts from s.212 actions, by contrast, are regarded as the products of a chose in action which belonged to the company before liquidation, and so will be caught by an appropriately worded floating charge.[125]

Proof of debts and mandatory insolvency set off

33–023 The liquidator will only pay those debts which are provable in the insolvency, and proved. The rules specifying which debts these are and how they are proved are contained in the Insolvency (England and Wales) Rules 2016/1024. All claims by creditors are provable, whether the debts are present or future, certain or contingent, ascertained or sounding only in damages, provided the company was, on that basis, subject to the claim at the time the winding up commenced. Where there are liabilities in both directions between the company and a creditor, use is made of mandatory insolvency set off rules. It is not necessary for a book such as this to deal with all the detailed legal issues which arise in conducting this exercise, as the difficulties are not specifically matters of company law, but their practical importance in reducing the potential losses that might otherwise be suffered by the creditor should be noted. Further, as already noted, secured creditors often elect to stand outside this process.

Distribution of the company's assets

33–024 Once the liquidator has gathered in the company's assets, they must be distributed in an orderly fashion to those entitled to them. The basic rules are clear.[126] The funds are devoted first, to paying the moratorium debts, if any; then the expenses of liquidation; then the preferred creditors; then the general unsecured creditors; then the deferred creditors; and, finally, if there is anything left, the members, according to the entitlements associated with their class rights. If the funds are

[124] See now the outlawing of "moratorium triggers" in automatic crystallisation clauses in floating charges: IA 1986 s.A52. The typical "insolvency triggers" in such clauses are of course already addressed by specific provisions in the Act which render floating charges, as created, much less attractive than fixed charges. See paras 32–013 onwards.

[125] *Re Anglo-Austrian Printing & Publishing Union* [1895] 2 Ch. 891 Ch D. Also see *Re Oasis Merchandising Services Ltd* [1998] Ch. 170 CA (Civ Div).

[126] See IA 1986 ss. 107, 115, 174A, 175, 386, 387 and Sch.6 and the relevant Insolvency (England and Wales) Rules 2016.

not sufficient to pay all of a particular class in this hierarchy in full, then they share pro rata. It then follows, necessarily, that the classes below that class will receive nothing. It is common knowledge that the unsecured creditors often obtain almost nothing in an insolvent liquidation; the banks take the lion's share, as secured creditors, and the preferential creditors take most of what little then remains.

In examining in more detail the order of distribution of the company's assets, recall, first, that the pool of assets includes only assets owned beneficially by the company.[127] Moreover, the claims of secured creditors to the assets specifically secured rank ahead of any claim in the winding up, including even the costs of liquidation,[128] but with the significant exception noted in Ch.32 in relation to floating charge holders, who must cede priority to quite an astonishing number of preferred claims.[129]

Since the first calls for payment from the company's assets are the debts arising from any moratorium, and then the expenses of liquidation, there is already with the latter and can be expected with the former a lot of debate about precisely which debts, costs and expenses are included. But all this detail, compelling though it is, does not raise issues that are specific to company law. It is, accordingly, left to specialist insolvency law texts.

It is tolerably clear that the objective behind these distribution rules, so far as they apply on insolvency, is for the company's creditors and members to share the inevitable losses roughly according to pari passu rules, whilst marginally adjusting those rules to specially favour those who have contractually pre-agreed security rights[130] or who are non-adjusting creditors with little wherewithal to negotiate for their own priority (e.g. employees), and, by contrast, to disfavour those with debts that are truly of second order importance (e.g. interest only on all provable debts) or with debts that reflect the claims of members to the company's capital (at least as the position appears on insolvency), which claims should, in the natural order of things, be deferred to the claims of the company's creditors.

DISSOLUTION

A company ceases to exist only when it is no longer on the register at Companies House. It follows that all the mechanisms for dissolution (or death) of a company are mechanisms for removing the company from the register. But before we consider what those are, consider the ramifications of removal of the company from the register: this ends the company's separate legal personality; it dissolves the relationship between the company and its members and directors; the company ceases to be a party to any legal relationships—even those that might not have been terminated properly before dissolution; and, finally, any property 33–025

[127] See para.33–018.

[128] But if the security is more than adequate to enable full repayment of the outstanding secured debt, then the extra is added to the insolvency pool to be distributed in the same way as the rest.

[129] See paras 32–015 to 32–017.

[130] The justifications for this are various, not all equally compelling, but the gist is that assets that are owned and worked produce more wealth, which is good for all, and the availability of credit provides liquidity, enabling capital to be used profitably.

that the company is still holding at the time of dissolution is deemed to be bona vacantia and passes to the Crown.[131] Two things are obvious from this list. First, it confirms why all the various mechanisms for winding up a company are so focused on ensuring that *all* the assets of the company are distributed properly. Secondly, life being what it is, it is also obvious that mistakes will happen, and so there is likely to be a need to have some mechanism for restoration of companies to the register (and, further, a provision deeming that they had never ceased to be so registered): this will be especially important when there are assets which could be distributed, or could be used to fund third party claims against the company. We have already seen the careful, structured rules relating to the insolvency process and all the checks and balances that are inherent in the exercise. And we will see later that there is indeed provision for "resurrection" of the company, in the right circumstances.[132]

But returning to dissolution. How is a company removed from the register? There are three different categories of provisions: first, the managed death, where dissolution is the final step taken in the winding up process; secondly, where dissolution is the result of neglect or inaction; and thirdly, orders made by the court in appropriate circumstances. We will not spell out all the administrative steps in each of these arenas, but they must be followed closely if the exercise is to be effective.

Dissolutions following winding up

33–026 In the first category, where the dissolution is a planned final step, the mechanisms vary slightly depending on the form of the winding up (whether voluntary or court ordered, and whether conducted by a liquidator or the official receiver). Such dissolutions are also possible at the end of an administration.[133] But in each case the mechanisms involve a series of administrative steps requiring reports to be sent to various parties, including, of course, the Registrar at Companies House; there then follows a short period of time during which interested notified parties might object; and, if no one does, then the Registrar will strike the company off the register.[134]

33–027 However, there is also a sensible procedure set out in IA 1986 s.202 whereby the OR may bring about an early dissolution if it appears that the realisable assets are insufficient to cover the costs of the winding up[135] and that the affairs of the company do not require any further investigation.[136] Before doing so, the OR must give at least 28 days' notice of the proposal to the company's creditors and

[131] CA 2006 s.1012, and see ss.1013–1014. This includes property held on trust for the company. Of course, if the company had been holding property on trust for third parties, than that trust will not fail for want of a trustee—a new trustee will be appointed to take over from the dissolved company.

[132] See paras 33–031 to 33–033.

[133] See IA 1986 Sch.B1, para.84.

[134] Voluntary liquidations: see IA 1986 ss.94 and 106 (the required reports for the Registrar), then s.201 for the process. Court ordered liquidations (whether by a liquidator or the OR): ss.146, 174(4), 172 and then s.205 for the process.

[135] In Scotland (lacking official receivers) there is a procedure for early dissolution on this ground alone but it involves an application to the court: IA 1986 s.204.

[136] IA 1986 s.202(1)–(2).

members and to an administrative receiver if there is one, and, with the giving of that notice, the OR ceases to be required to undertake any duties other than to apply to the Registrar for the early dissolution of the company. On the registration of that application, the company becomes dissolved at the end of three months unless the Secretary of State, on the application of the official receiver or any creditor, member or administrative receiver,[137] gives directions to the contrary before the end of that period.

There are no similar provisions for early dissolution on a voluntary winding up: once the company has resolved on voluntary winding up it is expected to go through with it. But if there is a vacancy in the liquidatorship and no one can be found who is willing to accept the office because there is clearly not enough left to pay the expenses of continuing it (no insolvency practitioner will accept office in such circumstances unless someone is prepared to pay the costs), it is difficult to see how the Registrar could do other than to strike the company off the register as a defunct company (see below)—as, indeed, that section specifically recognises.

Striking off of defunct companies

Clearly these formal processes involving reports to the Registrar are not suitable for all purposes. What if the company has insufficient assets to make it worthwhile going through that process, or the company is small and simply dies a slow death but never thinks to take this final formal step? In those circumstances the Registrar can initiate the process rather than the company. This method of striking off of defunct companies affords a method whereby a small company can, in practice, often be inexpensively dissolved without the expense of any formal winding up. **33–028**

Under CA 2006 s.1000,[138] the process is remarkably simple. If the Registrar has reasonable cause to believe that a company is not carrying on business or is not in operation, the Registrar may put the company on notice[139] that if it does not respond within a given time it will be struck off. At the expiry of the notice period, and unless cause to the contrary is shown, the Registrar may simply strike the company off the register and publish notice of this in the *Gazette*, whereupon the company is dissolved. This section is most commonly used when the evidence that the company is not carrying on business or in operation is the fact that it is in arrears with the lodging of its annual returns and accounts.[140] The process is thus both a method of inducing compliance in those companies that are operating in breach of their filing obligations, and a method of clearing the register of companies which are indeed defunct.

---

137 There is an apparent inconsistency between IA 1986 s.202(5) which says that the application can be made by the official receiver "or any other person who appears to the Secretary of State to be interested" and IA 1986 s.203(1) which says that it must be by one of the persons mentioned in the text above. Presumably the Secretary of State will not regard any other person as "interested".

138 Although these rules are contained in Pt 31 of CA 2006, rather than IA 1986, they are an integral part of the machinery by which companies cease to exist.

139 In practice writing to the directors at their home addresses as well as, formally, to the company at its registered address.

140 See Ch.22.

This same procedure can also be used when winding up proceedings have been started but insufficient resources are available to complete them. If the Registrar has reasonable cause to believe either that no liquidator is acting or that the affairs of the company are fully wound up and, in either case, that the returns required to be made by the liquidator have not been made for a period of six consecutive months, the Registrar shall publish in the *Gazette* and send to the company or the liquidator (if any) a like notice which causes the company to be dissolved.[141]

33–029 If the Registrar can initiate the striking off of defunct company without the formality of an insolvency process, then it might be asked why the company itself cannot initiate such a step, effectively inviting the Registrar to strike it off. Of course, creditors and members will need protection from directors who might be using this process for their own ends. Nevertheless, the logic of the question means that what was once an informal process, accepted by the Registrar, has now become a formal process enabling a company to do just this. CA 2006 s.1003 sets out the various pre-conditions which must be met by the company (e.g. it must not have traded for three months, and must notify various relevant parties), and then further notice and other obligations are imposed on the Registrar, but, if in the end there are no objections, the company will be struck off.

The one important protective element in these rules allowing the Registrar to strike off companies is that they each contain a provision that dissolution under the procedure does not inhibit the enforcement of any liability of the erstwhile company's directors, managing officers or members, so that these people cannot escape their common law or statutory duties by causing their company to be dissolved.[142] Moreover, a company dissolved under this procedure, like companies dissolved in other ways, may be restored to the register in certain circumstances, as we shall see.

Court ordered dissolutions

33–030 Finally, the court must surely have a role in some cases. We see an example of this when the court orders the dissolution of a company as part of a compromise or arrangement sanctioned by the court under CA 2006 s.899.[143]

Resurrection of Dissolved Companies

33–031 As noted earlier, there will be occasions when a company has been struck off and, in retrospect, that seems to have been unwise or unwarranted or unfortunate. CA 2006 provides for two methods of resurrection of dissolved companies: a limited form of administrative restoration to the register; and court restoration.

---

141 CA 2006 s.1001.

142 CA 2006 ss.1000(7)(a) and 1003(6)(a).

143 CA 2006 s.900(2)(d).

Administrative restoration

Administrative restoration applies only where the company was dissolved by the Registrar under the provisions relating to defunct companies,[144] and even then is confined to situations where the company was in fact carrying on business or in operation at the time it was struck off.[145] Thus, the main purpose of administrative restoration is to deal more cheaply with reversing a striking off which, ideally, should not have occurred in the first place. For probably the same reason, the application for restoration may be made only by a former director or former member of the company, but no application for restoration may be made more than six years after its dissolution. If any of the company's property is vested in the Crown as bona vacantia,[146] the Crown's representative must consent and the applicant must offer to pay any costs of the Crown in relation to the application and, more importantly, dealing with the property during the period of dissolution. Finally, the applicant must deliver to the Registrar such documents as are necessary to bring the company's public records up-to-date and to pay any penalties outstanding at the time the company was dissolved. **33–032**

If these conditions are met, the Registrar is under a duty to restore the company to the register,[147] although it seems the inherent practicalities provide their own limits to the scope of the jurisdiction.[148] If all is well, however, then notice of the decision must be given to the applicant and the restoration takes effect when that notice is sent.[149] Public notice must be given of the restoration.[150] The effect of restoration is that the company is deemed to have continued in existence as if it had not been struck off.[151] However, any consequential directions, if necessary, for placing the company and all other persons in the position (as nearly as possible) as they would have been in had the company not been struck off, are to be given, not by the Registrar, but by a court, to which application may be made within three years of the restoration.[152]

---

[144] CA 2006 ss.1024 and 1025, setting out the elements noted in the text.

[145] See *Re Priceland Ltd* [1997] B.C.C. 207 Ch D (Companies Ct).

[146] See para.33–025.

[147] CA 2006 s.1025(1). There is no formal right of appeal if the Registrar refuses to restore, but (a) presumably judicial review is available; and (b) the disappointed applicant could re-apply under the court-based procedure (see below) and is given 28 days to do so, even if the six-year time limit for that procedure has expired; s.1030(5).

[148] See the discussion in *Bridgehouse (Bradford No.2) Ltd v BAE Systems Plc* [2019] EWHC 1768 (Comm).

[149] CA 2006 s.1027(2).

[150] CA 2006 s.1027(3),(4).

[151] CA 2006 s.1028(1)—but not so as to make the company liable for failing to file reports and accounts during the period of dissolution (s.1028(2))! Section 1033 deals with the situation where the company cannot be restored under its former name without a breach of s.66 because another company now has that name. See Ch.4.

[152] CA 2006 s.1028(3)–(4). The statute appears not to undermine the distinction drawn by the courts between dissolution after winding up and administrative striking off (of either type) in terms of the impact of restoration on action purportedly taken by the company in litigation during the period of dissolution. In the latter case subsequent restoration automatically validates action during the period of dissolution: *Top Creative Ltd v St Albans DC* [2000] 2 B.C.L.C. 379 CA.

Restoration by the court

33–033 The court-based procedure applies to all forms of dissolution[153] and a much wider range of persons may apply for restoration. These include not just former directors or members, but any creditor of the company at the time of its dissolution, anyone who but for the dissolution would have been in a contractual relationship with it, any person with a potential legal claim against the company, any manager or trustee of an employee pension fund, any person interested in land in which the company had an interest, and the Secretary of State.[154] This caters for a much wider range of reasons for wanting to have the company restored to the register, a common one being in order to sue or assert a right against the company. Normally, such persons must act within six years of the date of dissolution,[155] but a claim for restoration in order to bring a claim for damages for personal injury against the company may be made at any time.[156]

The court has power to order restoration if (1) in the case of striking off of a defunct company, it was carrying on business or in operation at the time; (2) in the case of voluntary striking off, the conditions for such a striking off were not complied with; and (3) in any other case the court thinks it just to do so.[157] Restoration, if ordered, takes effect from the time the court's order is delivered to the Registrar and the Registrar must give publicity to the order in the usual way.[158] The effect of restoration by the court is the same as with administrative restoration,[159] and the court may give the necessary directions to effect the principle that the company should be treated as if never dissolved.[160]

---

[153] CA 2006 s.1029(1).

[154] CA 2006 s.1029(2).

[155] CA 2006 s.1030(4). Under the 1985 Act the limitation period for s.651 claims was two years and for s.653 claims 20 years. Six years is the period in England and Wales after which many claims against the company will be time-barred.

[156] CA 2006 s.1030(1)—though if the claim against the company appears to the court to be time-barred, it may not order the restoration of the company: s.1030(2), (3). However, the court may order under s.1032(3) that the period of dissolution should not count for limitation purposes in respect of the personal injury claim. See *Smith v White Knight Laundry Ltd* [2002] 1 W.L.R. 616 CA.

[157] CA 2006 s.1031(1). The wording of the section suggests that the third ground applies as well to a defunct company and voluntary striking off where the particular ground set out in (a) or (b) is not available. On the exercise of the court's discretion see *Re Priceland Ltd* [1997] B.C.C. 207; *Re Blenheim Leisure (Restaurants) Ltd (No.2)* [2000] B.C.C. 821 Ch D; *Re Blue Note Enterprises Ltd* [2001] 2 B.C.L.C. 427 Ch D (Companies Ct).

[158] CA 2006 s.1031(2),(3).

[159] CA 2006 s.1032(1)–(2).

[160] CA 2006 s.1032(3). See *Joddrell v Peaktone Ltd* [2012] EWCA Civ 1035; [2013] 1 W.L.R. 784 at [40]–[49] (Munby LJ) for a description of the retrospective effect of s.1032. Note, too, *County Leasing Asset Management Ltd v Hawkes* [2015] EWCA Civ 1251, where a limitation direction preventing time running was granted in favour of a restored company. Also see *Davies v Ford* [2020] EWHC 686 (Ch) at [375]–[387] and [391]–[393], holding that "treating company as if never dissolved" did not extend so far as treating the old directors as always having been in office for the entire period. On the other hand, given that duties may be owed by directors even when they are no longer in office, especially in relation to assets they hold on trust for their company, this finding did not deliver the limitations it might seem to carry.

CONCLUSION

This final chapter has considered the means by which the lives of companies are deliberately brought to an end, against their natural characteristic of perpetual succession. The overview has been brief, especially given the great complexities and doctrinal and policy difficulties in the current structure. The source of those difficulties is, at root, the result of a simple problem: mostly when companies are wound up, they are insolvent; their liabilities exceed their assets. In such circumstances, innocent parties will inevitably face losses, whatever efforts are made to protect them (and we have seen the lengths to which the winding up regime goes in that regard). Perhaps then the best the law can do is try to minimise obvious unfairness and ensure the rules, even if not perfect, are at least certain. Given the entrepreneurial imagination of commercial parties and our flexible and sophisticated mix of statute, contract and property law rules, this is a challenge, but one against which the current winding up regime might be judged to be doing tolerably well. **33–034**

INDEX

This index has been prepared using Sweet & Maxwell's Legal Taxonomy. Main index entries conform to keywords provided by the Legal Taxonomy except where references to specific documents or non-standard terms (denoted by quotation marks) have been included. These keywords provide a means of identifying similar concepts in other Sweet & Maxwell publications and online services to which keywords from the Legal Taxonomy have been applied. Readers may find some minor differences between terms used in the text and those which appear in the index. Suggestions to *sweetandmaxwell.taxonomy@tr.com*.

All references are to paragraph number